D1266100

KETTRIDGE'S
COMMERCIAL & FINANCIAL TERMS, PHRASES, & PRACTICE

TERMES, LOCUTIONS & PRATIQUE DE COMMERCE & DE FINANCE

PAR

KETTRIDGE

ISBN 0 7100 1671 9

PRINTED IN GREAT BRITAIN
BY UNWIN BROTHERS LIMITED
THE GRESHAM PRESS, OLD WOKING, SURREY, ENGLAND
A MEMBER OF THE STAPLES PRINTING GROUP

French-English and English-French

DICTIONARY

OF

COMMERCIAL & FINANCIAL TERMS, PHRASES, & PRACTICE

COMPRISING

MERCANTILE BUSINESS, EXPORTING AND IMPORTING, PRODUCE EXCHANGE TRANSACTIONS, TRANSPORT AND TRAVEL BY WATER, LAND AND AIR, CUSTOMS, MARINE INSURANCE, FINANCE, BANKING, CURRENCY, FOREIGN EXCHANGE AND STOCK EXCHANGE TRANSACTIONS, COMPANY WORK, ACCOUNTANCY, INCOME TAX, SECRETARIAL AND OFFICE WORK, POSTAL, TELEGRAPHIC AND TELEPHONIC SERVICES, AND ALLIED SUBJECTS

ALSO

ABBREVIATIONS IN COMMON USE, CONVENTIONAL SIGNS, WEIGHTS AND MEASURES

BY

J. O. KETTRIDGE

OFFICIER D'ACADÉMIE, F.S.S.A., A.C.I.S.
INCORPORATED ACCOUNTANT AND AUDITOR,
AND CHARTERED SECRETARY

containing

The Translations of Fifty Thousand Words, Terms, and Phrases
Illustrated by numerous instructive examples, explanations, and commentaries
The whole arranged in progressive alphabetical order
in the readiest form for rapid reference

When nature calls thee to be gone,
What acceptable audit canst thou leave?
—SHAKESPEARE, *Sonnets*, iv.

ROUTLEDGE & KEGAN PAUL
LONDON AND HENLEY
1978

DICTIONNAIRE

français-anglais, anglais-français

DE

TERMES, LOCUTIONS & PRATIQUE DE COMMERCE ET DE FINANCE

COMPRENANT

OPÉRATIONS MERCANTILES, EXPORTATIONS ET IMPORTATIONS, OPÉRATIONS DE BOURSE DE MARCHANDISES, TRANSPORTS ET VOYAGES PAR VOIE D'EAU, PAR VOIE DE TERRE ET PAR VOIE D'AIR, DOUANES, ASSURANCE MARITIME, FINANCE, OPÉRATIONS DE BANQUE, SUR MONNAIES, DE CHANGE ET DE BOURSE DE VALEURS, AFFAIRES DE SOCIÉTÉS COMMERCIALES, COMPTABILITÉ, IMPÔTS CÉDULAIRES, TRAVAUX DE SECRÉTAIRE ET DE BUREAU, POSTES, TÉLÉGRAPHES ET TÉLÉPHONES, ET SUJETS CONNEXES

AINSI QUE

ABRÉVIATIONS EN USAGE ORDINAIRE, SIGNES CONVENTIONNELS, POIDS ET MESURES

PAR

J. O. KETTRIDGE

OFFICIER D'ACADÉMIE, F.S.S.A., A.C.I.S.
INCORPORATED ACCOUNTANT AND AUDITOR,
AND CHARTERED SECRETARY

contenant
Les Traductions de Cinquante Mille Mots, Termes, et Locutions
Illustrés par de nombreux exemples, explications, et commentaires instructifs
Le tout disposé sur des plans originaux
par ordre alphabétique progressif
dans la meilleure forme pour consultation rapide

ROUTLEDGE & KEGAN PAUL
LONDON AND HENLEY
1978

PREFACE

THIS volume is the outcome of a lifelong loving study of the English and French languages, fortified by fifty years experience in the City of London. It is not the product of the labour of a number of collaborators, but the work of one man. It is not a compilation from existing French-English dictionaries, but a new and original production from radical and authentic sources. It is not a random glossary of lifeless words, but a cohesive record of living speech.

The author has endeavoured to produce works which may be regarded as authorities in their several spheres. He has also striven to create the ideal dictionary—comprehensive, relevant, accurate, precise, clear, explanative, illustrative, interesting, original, modern, well arranged, and well displayed.

Illustrative examples and phrases

A wealth of examples and phrases is given. Examples not only fix the use and illustrate the meaning of the vocabulary word, but attest the correctness of the translations ; they show also how the word is used in connection with other words, thus teaching how to read and write the language. Moreover it will be found that many examples impart some useful or interesting piece of knowledge or information.

Explanatory notes

It is often impossible to give trustworthy translations of foreign terms without some explanation of inherent differences of meaning or application ; and it is often impossible to give a succinct technical equivalent of a foreign term at all, inasmuch as the method or system to which the term relates has no application in the other country. In such cases there will be found a note setting out these differences, or explaining the system in use, which will enable the reader to grasp the precise signification of the term, and to make correct use of the translations.

Definitional matter

Whenever a vocabulary word has several distinct meanings, or whenever reasonable doubt may exist as to its meaning or application, each meaning forms the subject of a separate vocabulary entry, the word being defined in its own language, or some other clear indication given to establish its identity, before proceeding to its translation.

Grammatical indications

Grammatical indications are given in full in every case, and peculiarities of grammatical construction that may occur are either explained in notes, or are thrown into relief in examples of use specially chosen for the purpose.

Inversion

The English-French section of this dictionary is the inverted counter-part of the French-English section, the genius of both languages being respected with reverent regard.

Arrangement

The new method of vocabulary arrangement devised by the author and introduced in his previous Dictionaries has been followed in the present volume. It is explained in the following pages. It is claimed that great speed and absolute certainty of reference are attained by this method. It is a logical solution of the hitherto unsolved problem of arranging continuous words, hyphened compound words, unhyphened pairs or groups of words, apostrophic contractions, and phrases of any length or kind, in one alpha-betical and consistent order throughout.

Publishers note: In this (1968) edition additional entries have been included in the form of an Addendum to each section.

CONTENTS

ARRANGEMENT OF WORK

The vocabulary is arranged in natural progressive order : **bearer shares** will be found under **bearer** ; **telephone number** under **telephone** ; **to call the exchange** under **call** ; **what number are you calling ?** under **what**.

In the English language, ideas are expressed by proceeding from the particular to the general, whereas in French the reverse is the case ; thus, **bearer shares** becomes in French **actions au porteur**. It results that although in the English section of the dictionary the different kinds of shares, for instance, are distributed in the vocabulary, owing to the variations in the initial word, in the French section they all come together, forming therein a subject index.

****

Continuous words are arranged in strictly alphabetical succession.

Hyphened compound words, unhyphened pairs or groups of words, apostrophic contractions, and phrases, are not arranged as though the whole assemblage were one word regardless of breaks of continuity, but are grouped progressively under the common factor ; thus,

contre	sea	compte
contre-balancer	sea and land carriage	compte à découvert
contre-caution	sea damage	compte à demi
contre-dater	sea-damaged	compte courant
contre-expertise	sea insurance	compte créditeur
contre-mandat	sea mile	compte d'épargne
contre-ordre	sea peril	compte d'espèces
contre-partie	sea risk	compte d'ordre
contre-passer	sea trade	compte de banque
contre-poser	seagoing	compte de caisse
contre-proposition	seal	compte de réserve
contre-valeur	seaman	compte de vente
contre-visite	seaport	compte débiteur
contrebande	search	compte des profits et pertes
contrefaire	seashore	compte désapprovisionné
contremander	season ticket	compte du grand livre
contresigner	seat	compte gestionnaire
contresurestaries	seaworthy	compte-joint

faire de bonnes affaires	on approval
faire de l'argent	on-carrier
faire déduction des sommes payées d'avance	on 'change
faire défaut	on-cost charges
faire l'acquit de sa charge	on hand, refused
faire l'impossible	on the berth
faire la balance des affaires de l'année	one
faire la contre-partie	one class liner
faire un report	one for one
faire un versement sur des titres non libérés	one man market
faire une application	one way traffic
faire une déclaration en douane	onerous

Where, by reason of their continuity, compound words are thrown forward in the vocabulary, reference thereto is made in the places which the words would have occupied if discontinuous ; thus,

contre	sea
contre-balancer	sea and land carriage
contrebande See below	sea damage
contre-caution	sea-damaged
contre-dater	seagoing V. ci-après
contre-expertise	sea insurance
contrefaire See below	seaman V ci-après
contre-mandat	sea mile
contremander See below	sea peril
contre-ordre	seaport V. ci-après
contre-partie	sea risk
contre-passer	seashore V. ci-après
contre-poser	sea trade
contre-proposition	seaworthy V. ci-après
contresigner See below	seagoing
contresurestaries See below	seal
contre-valeur	seaman
contre-visite	seaport
contrebande	search
contrefaire	seashore
contremander	season ticket
contresigner	seat
contresurestaries	seaworthy

****

When various parts of speech are spelt the same way, they are placed in the following order :— adjective, adverb, noun, preposition, verb transitive, verb intransitive, verb reflexive ; thus,

ferme (*adj.*)	average (*adj.*)
ferme (*adv.*)	average (*n.*)
ferme (*n.m.*)	average (*v.t.*)
fermer (*v.t.*)	average (*v.i.*)
fermer (*v.i.*)	

****

The gender and number given at the end of a French phrase refer to the first noun ; thus, in the phrase **effets à l'escompte, à l'encaissement** (*m.pl.*), the letters *m.pl.* indicate that the noun **effets** is masculine in gender and plural in number.

****

A., B., X., X.Y.Z., or other letters of the alphabet, represent an imaginary name ; as, Mr A., Messrs B. & Co., The X. Company, steamer X., X.Y.Z. shares.
0, 00, 000, 0,000 represent an imaginary number, a certain quantity, so many, so much ; thus, **as consideration for the transfer there has been allotted to the vendors 0,000 shares of 0 each.**

****

Synonyms following one another, whether in the translations or in the vocabulary, are placed in order of generality of use, commencing with the commonest.

****

Where more than one spelling is given, the first is to be preferred.

PLAN DE L'OUVRAGE

Le vocabulaire est rangé par ordre progressif naturel : **bearer shares** se trouvera sous **bearer** ; **telephone number** sous **telephone** ; **to call the exchange** sous **call** ; **what number are you calling ?** sous **what**.

Dans la langue anglaise, les idées s'expriment en procédant du particulier au général, tandis qu'en français le contraire est le cas ; ainsi, **bearer shares** devient en français **actions au porteur**. Il en résulte que quoique dans la section anglaise du dictionnaire les diverses sortes d'actions, par exemple, soient réparties dans le vocabulaire à cause des variations du mot initial, dans la section française elles se trouvent toutes ensemble, formant ainsi un répertoire idéologique.

****

Les mots continus sont rangés strictement par ordre alphabétique.

Les mots composés séparés par des traits d'union, les paires ou groupes de mots non séparés par des traits d'union, les contractions apostrophiques, et les phrases, ne sont pas disposés comme si tout l'assemblage était un seul mot sans égard aux solutions de continuité, mais sont groupés progressivement sous le facteur commun ; ainsi,

contre	sea	compte
contre-balancer	sea and land carriage	compte à découvert
contre-caution	sea damage	compte à demi
contre-dater	sea-damaged	compte courant
contre-expertise	sea insurance	compte créditeur
contre-mandat	sea mile	compte d'épargne
contre-ordre	sea peril	compte d'espèces
contre-partie	sea risk	compte d'ordre
contre-passer	sea trade	compte de banque
contre-poser	seagoing	compte de caisse
contre-proposition	seal	compte de réserve
contre-valeur	seaman	compte de vente
contre-visite	seaport	compte débiteur
contrebande	search	compte des profits et pertes
contrefaire	seashore	compte désapprovisionné
contremander	season ticket	compte du grand livre
contresigner	seat	compte gestionnaire
contresurestaries	seaworthy	compte-joint

faire de bonnes affaires	on approval
faire de l'argent	on-carrier
faire déduction des sommes payées d'avance	on 'change
faire défaut	on-cost charges
faire l'acquit de sa charge	on hand, refused
faire l'impossible	on the berth
faire la balance des affaires de l'année	one
faire la contre-partie	one class liner
faire un report	one for one
faire un versement sur des titres non libérés	one man market
faire une application	one way traffic
faire une déclaration en douane	onerous

Où, en conséquence de leur continuité, les mots composés sont reportés dans le vocabulaire, référence y est faite aux endroits que les mots auraient occupés s'ils avaient été discontinus ; ainsi,

contre	sea
contre-balancer	sea and land carriage
contrebande See below	sea damage
contre-caution	sea-damaged
contre-dater	seagoing V. ci-après
contre-expertise	sea insurance
contrefaire See below	seaman V. ci-après
contre-mandat	sea mile
contremander See below	sea peril
contre-order	seaport V. ci-après
contre-partie	sea risk
contre-passer	seashore V. ci-après
contre-poser	sea trade
contre-proposition	seaworthy V. ci-après
contresigner See below	seagoing
contresurestaries See below	seal
contre-valeur	seaman
contre-visite	seaport
contrebande	search
contrefaire	seashore
contremander	season ticket
contresigner	seat
contresurestaries	seaworthy

****

Lorsque les diverses parties du discours ont la même orthographe, elles sont placées dans l'ordre suivant :—adjectif, adverbe, nom, préposition, verbe transitif, verbe intransitif, verbe réfléchi ; ainsi,

ferme (*adj.*)	average (*adj.*)
ferme (*adv.*)	average (*n.*)
ferme (*n.m.*)	average (*v.t.*)
fermer (*v.t.*)	average (*v.i.*)
fermer (*v.i.*)	

****

Le genre et le nombre donnés à la fin d'une phrase en français se rapportent au premier nom ; ainsi, dans la phrase **effets à l'escompte, à l'encaissement** (*m.pl.*), les lettres *m.pl.* indiquent que le nom **effets** est du genre masculin et au pluriel.

****

A., B., X., X.Y.Z., ou autres lettres de l'alphabet, signifient un nom imaginaire ; ainsi, M. A., MM. B. & Cⁱᵉ, La Société X., steamer X., actions X.Y.Z.

0, 00, 000, 0 000 signifient un nombre imaginaire, une certaine quantité, tant ; ainsi, en rémunération des apports il a été attribué aux apporteurs 0 000 actions de 0 chacune.

****

Les synonymes se suivant, soit dans les traductions ou dans le vocabulaire, sont placés dans l'ordre de la généralité d'emploi, en commençant par les plus ordinaires.

****

Où on donne plus d'une orthographe, on doit préférer la première.

ABBREVIATIONS
USED IN THIS DICTIONARY

Abbrev.	Abbreviation.
adj.	*adjective.*
adv.	*adverb.*
Ant.	Antonym.
Arith.	Arithmetic.
Bkkpg	Bookkeeping.
Cf.	Compare (*confer*).
Com.	Commerce.
e.g.	for example (*exempli gratia*).
f.	*feminine.*
f.pl.	*feminine plural.*
fig.	*figuratively.*
Fin.	Finance.
Geog.	Geography.
i.e.	that is (*id est*).
Insce	Insurance.
interj.	*interjection.*
Internat. Law	International Law.
invar.	*invariable.*
lit.	*literally.*
m.	*masculine.*
m.pl.	*masculine plural.*
Mar. Insce	Marine Insurance.
Mar. Law	Maritime Law.
n.	*noun.*
n.f.	*noun feminine.*
n.f.pl.	*noun feminine plural.*
n.m.	*noun masculine.*
n.m.pl.	*noun masculine plural.*
Naut.	Nautical.
Navig.	Navigation.
opp. to	opposed to.
p.p.	*participle past.*
p.pr.	*participle present.*
pers.	person.
pl.	*plural.*
Polit. Econ.	Political Economy.
prep.	*préposition.*
Produce Exch.	Produce Exchange.
q.v.	which see (*quod vide*).
Radioteleg.	Radiotelegraphy.
Rly.	Railways.
sing.	*singular.*
Stock Exch.	Stock Exchange.
Syn.	Synonym.
Teleg.	Telegraphy.
Teleph.	Telephony.
U.S.A.	United States of America.
v.	*verb.*
v.i.	*verb intransitive* (or *neuter*).
v.t.	*verb transitive* (or *active*).
viz.	namely (*videlicet*).

The sign ' before an initial h denotes that the h is aspirate.

ABRÉVIATIONS
EMPLOYÉES DANS CE DICTIONNAIRE

Abrév.	Abréviation.
adj.	*adjectif.*
adv.	*adverbe.*
Ant.	Antonyme.
Arith.	Arithmétique.
Assce	Assurance.
Assce mar.	Assurance maritime.
Banq.	Banque.
c.-à-d.	c'est-à-dire.
Cf.	Conférer.
Ch. de f.	Chemins de fer.
Com.	Commerce.
Comptab.	Comptabilité.
Dr.	Droit (*Law*).
Dr. internat.	Droit international.
Dr. mar.	Droit maritime.
e.g.	par exemple (*exempli gratia*).
Écon.	Économie.
Écon. polit.	Économie politique.
f.	*féminin.*
f.pl.	*féminin pluriel.*
fig.	*au figuré.*
Fin.	Finance.
Géogr.	Géographie.
interj.	*interjection.*
invar.	*invariable.*
lit.	*littéralement.*
m.	*masculin.*
m.pl.	*masculin pluriel.*
Mar.	Marine.
n.	*nom.*
n.f.	*nom féminin.*
n.f.pl.	*nom féminin pluriel.*
n.m.	*nom masculin.*
n.m.pl.	*nom masculin pluriel.*
Navig.	Navigation.
opp. à	par opposition à.
p.p.	*participe passé.*
p.pr.	*participe présent.*
pers.	personne.
pl.	*pluriel.*
prép.	*préposition.*
Radiotélégr.	Radiotélégraphie.
sing.	*singulier.*
Syn.	Synonyme.
Télégr.	Télégraphie.
Téléph.	Téléphonie.
V. ou *V.*	Voir.
v.	*verbe.*
v.i.	*verbe intransitif* (ou *neutre*).
v.r.	*verbe réfléchi* (ou *pronominal*).
v.t.	*verbe transitif* (ou *actif*).

Le signe ' placé devant un h initial indique que l'h est aspiré.

Tables of
ABBREVIATIONS IN COMMON USE
will be found on pages 641–644 and 319–322.

Les Tables des
ABRÉVIATIONS EN USAGE ORDINAIRE
se trouvent aux pages 319–322 et 641–644.

FRENCH - ENGLISH DICTIONARY

A

à (abréviation de *doit à*) (écritures de journal) (Comptab.) (*prép.*), To; Dr To (abbreviation of *Debtor To*):
lors du dépôt de titres, l'article à passer est: Dépôts à Déposants, when securities are deposited, the entry to be passed is: Deposits To Depositors (*or* Deposits Dr To Depositors).
Divers à Divers *ou* Les suivants aux suivants, Sundries Dr To Sundries; Sundries To Sundries.

à (reports du grand livre) (Comptab.) (*prép.*) (opp. à *par*), To:
à Caisse, To Cash.

à-bon-compte [à-bon-compte *pl.*] (*n.m.*), advance; payment in advance (*or* on account); something on account.

à bord, à flot, à terre, à l'acquitté, à la machine, etc. See under **bord, flot, terre, acquitté, machine,** etc.

à la vapeur ou à la voile (Navig.), under steam or sail.

à moins d'exception formelle stipulée dans la présente police, unless expressly otherwise provided in this policy.

à moins de convention contraire, unless otherwise agreed (*or* provided).

à tout événement, in any event; under any circumstances:
fret acquis à tout événement (*m.*), freight not repayable under any circumstances.

A travers les Marchés (rubrique de journal), Round the Markets; Round the House; Market News.

à-valoir [à-valoir *pl.*] (*n.m.*), advance; payment in advance (*or* on account); something on account.

abaissement (*n.m.*), lowering; fall; reduction:
abaissement du titre des monnaies, lowering the fineness of the coinage.
la concurrence produit l'abaissement des prix, competition causes a lowering of prices; competition brings about a fall in prices.

abaisser (*v.t.*), to lower; to reduce; to bring down:
abaisser le taux officiel d'escompte, to lower, to reduce, the bank rate.

s'abaisser (*v.r.*), to be lowered; to fall; to go down:
le prix de l'argent s'est abaissé, the price of silver has fallen (*or* has gone down).

abandon *ou* **abandonnement** (*n.m.*), abandonment; renunciation; relinquishment; surrender:

abandon d'un voyage, du navire et de la cargaison en mer, abandonment of a voyage, of the ship and cargo at sea.
abandon aux créanciers du navire et du fret, abandonment to creditors of the ship and freight. Cf. **fortune de mer.**
abandon des marchandises en douane, abandonment of goods in customs.
abandon d'une prime (Bourse), abandonment of an option.

abandon (délaissement) (Assce mar.) (*n.m.*), abandonment:
abandon d'un navire, de facultés assurées, abandonment of a ship, of insured goods. See also examples under syn. **délaissement.**

abandonner (*v.t.*), to abandon; to renounce; to relinquish; to surrender; to lose:
abandonner une entreprise, un navire à son sort, to abandon an undertaking, a ship to her fate.
abandonner ses droits, to abandon, to renounce, to relinquish, to surrender, one's rights.
abandonner une option (Fin.), to abandon an option.
abandonner une prime (Bourse), to abandon an option.
l'action X. abandonne une fraction (Bourse), X. shares lost a fraction.
ab. (primes) (Bourse) (*abrév.*), abandonné, -e.

abattement (Impôt sur le revenu) (*n.m.*), abatement:
abattement dégrevant la tranche inférieure du revenu, abatement relieving the lower portion of the income.

abdication (*n.f.*), renunciation; surrender; waiving; waiver:
abdication de droits, renunciation, surrender, waiving, of rights.

abdiquer (*v.t.*), to renounce; to surrender; to waive; to give up:
abdiquer ses biens, to surrender, to give up, one's property.

abolir (*v.t.*), to abolish; to do away with:
abolir un droit de douane, to abolish, to do away with, a customs duty.

abondance (*n.f.*) (Ant.: *rareté*), abundance; plentifulness; plenty.

abondant, -e (*adj.*), abundant; plentiful:
l'argent est abondant (*m.*), money is plentiful.

abonné, -e (pers.) (*n.*), subscriber:
abonné au téléphone, telephone subscriber.
abonné demandé (Téléph.), called subscriber; distant subscriber.

abonné demandeur *ou* abonné appelant (Téléph.), calling subscriber; caller.

abonnement (*n.m.*), subscription:
abonnement à un journal, au téléphone, subscription to a newspaper, to the telephone.
abonnement à conversations taxées (Téléph.), subscription with calls charged for.
abonnement au timbre, composition for stamp duty.

abonnement (carte d'abonnement) (*n.m.*), season; season ticket.

abonner (*v.t.*), to subscribe for:
abonnez-moi à ce journal, subscribe for me to this paper.

s'abonner (*v.r.*), to subscribe:
s'abonner à un journal, to subscribe to a newspaper.
s'abonner au timbre, to compound for stamp duty.

abordage (collision) (Navig.) (*n.m.*), collision; fouling; running foul;
abordage à un autre bâtiment, collision with another ship.
abordage douteux *ou* abordage mixte, doubtful collision; collision due to inevitable accident.
abordage fautif, negligent collision:
l'abordage fautif embrasse l'abordage causé par la faute de l'un des navires et celui dû à la faute des deux navires, negligent collision embraces collision caused by the fault of one of the ships and that due to the fault of both ships.
abordage fortuit, accidental collision; collision due to inscrutable accident.

abordé (navire abordé) (*n.m.*), ship collided with. See example under **abordeur**.

aborder (se rendre à bord) (*v.t.*), to board:
agents des douanes qui abordent un navire (*m.pl.*), customs officials who board a ship.

aborder (faire collision avec) (*v.t.*), to collide with; to come into collision with; to foul; to run foul of; to run into.
aborder et couler un autre navire, to run down another ship.

s'aborder (*v.r.*), to collide; to come into collision; to foul; to run foul of (*or* run into) each other.

aborder (arriver au bord, au rivage; prendre terre) (*v.i.*), to land; to touch:
aborder dans un port étranger, to land in a foreign port.
au premier port où le navire aborde, at the first port where the ship touches.

abordeur (navire abordeur) (*n.m.*), colliding ship:
le dommage causé par l'abordeur à l'abordé, the damage caused by the colliding ship to the ship collided with.

abouchement (*n.m.*), conference; interview.

aboucher (*v.t.*), to bring together; to arrange an interview between:
aboucher les intéressés, to bring the interested parties together.

s'aboucher (*v.r.*), to have an interview; to have a talk; to confer.

abus (*n.m.*), abuse; breach:

abus de confiance, abuse of confidence; breach of trust.

accaparement (*n.m.*), cornering; corner:
l'accaparement du marché, de produits de première nécessité, cornering the market, products of prime necessity.

accaparer (*v.t.*), to corner:
accaparer la majeure partie des titres se trouvant sur le marché, to corner the major part of the stocks to be found on the market.

accapareur (pers.) (*n.m.*), cornerer; corner man.

acceptabilité (*n.f.*), acceptability; acceptableness:
acceptabilité d'une proposition, acceptableness of a proposal.

acceptable (*adj.*), acceptable:
offre acceptable (*f.*), acceptable offer.

acceptation (*n.f.*) (Abrév.: **acc.**), acceptance:
acceptation de certaines conditions, acceptance of certain conditions.
présenter un effet à l'acceptation, to present a bill for acceptance.
acceptation conditionnelle, conditional acceptance.
acceptation contre documents, acceptance against documents.
acceptation de complaisance, accommodation acceptance.
acceptation de délaissement (Assce mar.), acceptance of abandonment.
acceptation de transfert. *See under* feuille **de** transfert.
acceptation en blanc, blank acceptance.
acceptation par intervention *ou* acceptation par honneur *ou* acceptation sous protêt, acceptance for honour; acceptance supra (*or* suprà) protest.
acceptation partielle *or* acceptation restreinte, partial acceptance.
acceptation sans réserves, general acceptance; clean acceptance.
acceptation sous réserves, qualified acceptance.
la lettre de change acceptée s'appelle une acceptation: on trouve aussi dans les bilans des banques, le mot acceptations, an accepted bill of exchange is called an acceptance: also the word acceptances occurs in bank balance sheets.
acceptations pour compte de clients (Banq.), acceptances on account of (*or* acceptances for) customers.

accepté (formule dont on se sert pour l'acceptation des lettres de change) (*p.p. invar.*), accepted:
l'acceptation est exprimée par le mot accepté (*f.*), acceptance is expressed by the word accepted.

accepter (*v.t.*), to accept:
accepter soit la totalité, soit une partie du risque à couvrir, to accept either the whole, or a part of the risk to be covered.
un contrat d'assurance est censé conclu lorsque la proposition de l'assuré est acceptée par l'assureur, an insurance contract is deemed to be concluded when the proposal of the insured is accepted by the insurer.
accepter une lettre de change, to accept a bill of exchange.

ne pas accepter un effet, to dishonour a bill;
to dishonour a bill by non acceptance; not
to accept a bill:
effets qui ne sont pas acceptés (*m.pl.*), bills
which are dishonoured (*or* which are dishonoured by non acceptance) (*or* which are
not accepted). *Cf.* ne pas payer un effet,
under **payer.**

accèptez mes civilités, mes respects, accept
my compliments, my respects.

accepter (se charger de) (*v.t.*), to undertake:
la banque n'accepte aucune opération (de
bourse) à découvert, the bank does not
undertake any (stock exchange) transaction
without cover.

.ccepteur (pers.) (*n.m.*), acceptor:
accepteur d'une lettre, acceptor of a bill.

accessoires (d'un navire) (*n.m.pl.*), furniture (of
a ship):
corps, agrès, apparaux, accessoires, etc., hull,
tackle, apparel, furniture, etc.

accident (*n.m.*), accident:
accident de chemin de fer, railway accident.
accident de mer, accident of the sea; sea
accident.
accident de navigation, accident of navigation.
accident mortel, fatal accident.

accommodement (*n.m.*), settlement; arrangement:
accommodement d'un différend, settlement of
a difference.

accommoder (*v.t.*), to settle; to arrange:
accommoder une affaire à l'amiable, to settle,
to arrange, a matter amicably.

accompagnateur (Bourse) (pers.) (*n.m.*), punter;
scalper.

accompagner (*v.t.*), to accompany:
lettre de voiture accompagnant la marchandise
(*f.*), consignment note accompanying the
goods.

accomplir (*v.t.*), to accomplish; to perform; to
fulfil; to comply with:
l'un des connaissements étant accompli, les
autres restent sans valeur, one of the bills
of lading being accomplished, the others to
stand void.
accomplir un devoir, to perform a duty.
accomplir une formalité, to comply with a
formality.

accomplissement (*n.m.*), accomplishment; performance; fulfilment; compliance:
accomplissement d'un contrat, fulfilment of a
contract.

acconage (*n.m.*), stevedoring.

acconier (pers.) (*n.m.*), stevedore.

accord (*n.m.*), accord; agreement; reconciliation; understanding; consent:
les quasi-contrats diffèrent des contrats en ce
qu'il n'y a pas un accord de volonté entre
les parties (*m.pl.*), quasi contracts differ
from contracts in that there is no accord of
will between the parties.
accord du journal et du grand livre, agreement,
reconciliation, between the journal and the
ledger.
accord occulte, secret agreement.

les livres sont en accord (*ou* sont d'accord)
(*m.pl.*), the books are in agreement; the
books agree.
tomber d'accord, to come to an agreement.
n'être pas d'accord, to disagree.

accord (concession) (*n.m.*), grant:
accord d'un brevet, grant of a patent.

accordable (*adj.*), grantable; allowable.

accorder (*v.t.*), to accord; to grant; to allow;
to give:
accorder un découvert, to grant an overdraft.
accorder un délai à son débiteur, to give one's
debtor time to pay; to allow one's debtor
time; to grant an extension of time to one's
debtor.
accorder une forte remise, un escompte de
5 p. 100, to allow a big discount, a discount
of 5%.

accorder (s') (*v.r.*), to agree:
s'accorder sur le prix d'une chose, to agree on
the price of a thing; to come to terms.

accostage (*n.m.*), coming alongside.

accoster (*v.t.*) *ou* **accoster à**, to come alongside:
chaland qui accoste un navire, un quai (*m.*),
barge which comes alongside a ship, a
wharf.
navire qui accoste à quai ou aux appontements
(*m.*), ship which comes alongside the quay
or the wharves.

accourir en foule aux guichets d'une banque
(descendre sur une banque), to run on a
bank. *Cf.* **course en foule.**

accrédité, -e (*adj.*), accredited:
banquier accrédité (*m.*), accredited banker.

accrédité, -e (pers.) (*n.*), accredited party; party
or person named (in a letter of credit, or the
like); payee *or* beneficiary (of a letter of
credit, or the like):
pour permettre au correspondant de reconnaître
l'identité de l'accrédité, to enable the correspondent to identify the accredited party (*or*
the party, *or* the person, named).
les lettres de crédit portent les indications
suivantes: date de création, nom de
l'accrédité, etc. (*f.pl.*), letters of credit bear
the following particulars: date of creation,
name of the accredited party (*or* of the payee
or beneficiary), etc.

accréditer (Banq., etc.) (*v.t.*), to open a credit for:
accréditer un voyageur, to open a credit for a
traveller.

accréditeur (pers.) (*n.m.*), guarantor; surety;
guarantee; security.

accréditif (*n.m.*), credit: (*Cf.* **crédit.**)
accréditifs ouverts par correspondance, sur la
demande des bénéficiaires, et utilisés par
ceux-ci, sous constatation de leur identité,
credits opened by correspondence, at the
request of the beneficiaries, and utilized by
them, on proof of their identity.
accréditif documentaire, documentary credit.
accréditif non confirmé *ou* accréditif simple,
unconfirmed credit; simple credit.

accroché (-e) (être), to be caught:
spéculateur en bourse qui est accroché (*m.*),
speculator on 'change who is caught.

accroissement (*n.m.*), increase ; growth :
accroissement de la richesse d'une nation, increase in the wealth of a nation.

accroître (*v.t.*), to increase :
accroître sa fortune, to increase one's fortune.

accroître (*v.i.*), to increase ; to grow.

s'accroître (*v.r.*), to increase ; to grow.

accroître (s'acquérir ; courir) (*v.i.*), to accrue :
intérêts accrus (*m.pl.*), accrued interest.

s'accroître (*v.r.*), to accrue.

accueil (*n.m.*), reception ; honour.

accueillir (*v.t.*), to receive ; to honour ; to meet :
accueillir favorablement une proposition, to receive a proposal favourably ; to entertain a proposal.
accueillir une traite, une disposition, une lettre de change, to honour, to meet, a draft, a bill of exchange.

accumulation (*n.f.*), accumulation ; amassing :
éviter l'accumulation d'une paperasse inutile, fléau de toutes les administrations, to avoid the accumulation of useless old papers, the bane of every office.

accumuler (*v.t.*), to accumulate ; to amass :
accumuler des richesses, to accumulate, to amass, wealth.
les ordres accumulés durant la fin de la semaine (*m.pl.*), the orders accumulated over the week end.

s'accumuler (*v.r.*), to accumulate.

accusé de réception [**accusés de réception** *pl.*] (*m.*), acknowledgment ; letter of acknowledgment.

accusé de réception (télégrammes) (*m.*), notice of delivery. *See* télégramme avec accusé de réception.

accuser (faire ressortir) (*v.t.*), to show ; to shew :
compte qui accuse une perte (*m.*), account which shows a loss.
le solde accusé par le livre de caisse, the balance shown by the cash book.

accuser réception, to acknowledge receipt :
accuser réception d'une lettre, to acknowledge receipt of a letter.

achat (*n.m.*) (Ant.: *vente*), purchase ; purchasing ; buying :
achat de valeurs, purchase of stocks ; buying securities.
l'acte de commerce est essentiellement l'achat pour revendre (*m.*), the act of commerce is essentially buying to sell again.
achat et vente de monnaies étrangères, foreign monies bought and sold.
achat à découvert (Bourse), bull purchase.
achat à terme *ou* achat à crédit (Com.) (opp. à *achat au comptant*), credit purchase.
achat à terme (Bourse de valeurs), purchase for the settlement ; buying for the account.
achat à terme ferme (Bourse de marchandises), purchase for future delivery during specified periods.
achat au comptant *ou* achat comptant, cash purchase ; buying for money.
achat d'une prime (Bourse), giving for an option ; buying an option.

achat dont *ou* achat à prime directe (Bourse), giving for the call ; buying a call.
achat par échelons de baisse (Bourse), averaging purchases.
achats professionnels (Bourse), professional purchases ; shop buying.

acheminement (*n.m.*), forwarding ; dispatch ; despatch ; routing :
acheminement des télégrammes par la poste, forwarding telegrams by post.
prescription d'acheminement figurant sur la lettre de voiture (*f.*), direction for routing appearing on the consignment note.
acheminement par fil (Télégr.) (*Abrév.:* Fil), routing by wire.
acheminement par sans fil (Télégr.) (*Abrév.:* Anten.), routing by wireless.

acheminer (*v.t.*), to forward ; to dispatch ; to despatch ; to route :
lettres acheminées par des courriers hebdomadaires (*f.pl.*), letters forwarded (*or* dispatched) by weekly mails.

achetable (*adj.*), purchasable ; buyable.

acheter (*v.t.*) (Ant.: *vendre*), to buy ; to purchase :
acheter une maison, to buy, to purchase, a house.
navires achetés à des armateurs étrangers (*m.pl.*), ships bought from foreign owners.
acheter à bon compte, to buy cheap.
acheter à crédit *ou* acheter à terme (Com.), to buy on (*or* upon) credit.
acheter à découvert (Bourse), to buy a bull ; to bull ; to bull the market :
spéculer sur la bourse, c'est-à-dire acheter ou vendre à découvert, to speculate on the stock exchange, that is to say, to buy a bull or sell a bear (*or* to bull or to bear) (*or* to bull or bear the market).
acheter à la baisse (Bourse), to buy on a fall.
acheter à la commission, to buy on commission.
acheter à la hausse (Bourse), to buy for a rise.
acheter à terme (Bourse de valeurs), to buy for the settlement (*or* for the account).
acheter au comptant *ou* acheter comptant, to buy for cash (*or* for money).
acheter chat en poche, to buy a pig in a poke.
acheter cher *ou* acheter chèrement, to buy at a high price.
acheter dont (Bourse), to give for the call ; to buy a call option :
acheter 25 Rio dont 40 francs, to give 40 francs for the call of 25 Rios. *See also* example *under* acheteur d'un dont, *and* explanations *under* dont *and* prime.
acheter en gros, en demi-gros, en détail, to buy direct, wholesale, retail. (See note under **gros** *ou* **gros commerce.**)
acheter par échelons de baisse (Bourse), to average purchases.
A. *ou* A/. (ordres de bourse) (*abrév.*), achetez ; acheter ; acheté ; achat.

acheteur, -euse (pers.) (*n.*), buyer ; purchaser :
un proverbe oriental dit : « Il faut cent yeux à l'acheteur, un seul au vendeur,» an Oriental proverb says : " The buyer needs a hundred eyes, the seller only one."

acheteur d'un dont (*ou* d'une prime directe),
giver for a call; buyer of a call option:
spéculateur qui est acheteur de 100 actions
X.Y.Z. à 403 dont 3 (*m.*), speculator who is
giver of 3 francs (per share) for the call of
100 X.Y.Z. shares at 400. See explanation
of option dealing under **prime.**
acheteur d'un ou *ou* acheteur d'une prime
indirecte, taker for a put; seller of a put
option.
Note :—The French envisage the purchase of
the shares from the putter. The English
envisage the taker of the rate for the option
to have the shares put, or, and which is the
same thing, the seller of the option to have
the shares put. Hence *acheteur* has to be
translated by *taker* or *seller* in this case. *Cf.*
vendeur d'un ou.
acheteur de bonne foi, bona fide purchaser;
purchaser in good faith.
acheteur de mauvaise foi, mala fide purchaser;
purchaser in bad faith.
cours demandés (acheteurs) (Bourse) (*m.pl.*)
(*Abrév.:* A.), prices bid (buyers).
orges: parcelles Azoff mer noire, mars-avril,
17/6d. payé et acheteur (*ou en abrégé* 17/6
P. & A. *ou* P. et ach.), barley: parcels
Azoff/Black Sea, March-April, 17/6d. paid
and buyers.
quand la place est acheteur, when the market
is a buyer.
acompte (*n.m.*) (Abrév.: **ac.**), amount on
account; instalment; installment; payment on account:
acompte versé *ou* acompte payé, amount paid
on account; instalment paid:
déduire l'acompte versé du total à payer, to
deduct the amount paid on account (*or*
the instalment paid) from the total to be
paid.
prêt remboursable par acomptes (*m.*), loan
repayable by (*or* in) instalments.
acompte sur le capital, payment on account of
capital.
acompte de dividende *ou* acompte sur dividende
ou acompte sur le dividende (opp. à *solde de
dividende*), interim dividend:
déclarer un acompte de dividende, to declare
an interim dividend.
les dividendes sont payables le 1er janvier
(acompte) et le 1er juillet (solde) (*m.pl.*),
dividends are payable 1st January (interim)
and 1st July (final).
acompte de préférence (sur un immeuble),
option money (on a property).
d'acompte, on account:
payer tant d'acompte, to pay so much on
account.
acompte (couverture; provision; marge) (Fin.,
Banq. et Bourse) (*n.m.*), cover; margin:
agent de change qui exige un acompte de 25 0/0
en espèces (*m.*), stockbroker who requires a
cover (*or* a margin) of 25% in cash.
aconage (*n.m.*), stevedoring.
aconier (pers.) (*n.m.*), stevedore.
acquéreur, -euse (*adj.*), purchasing; buying:

l'agent de change acquéreur (*m.*), the purchasing
stockbroker.
acquéreur, -eure *ou* **-euse** (pers.) (*n.*), purchaser;
buyer:
acquéreur de bonne foi, bona fide purchaser;
purchaser in good faith.
acquéreur de mauvaise foi, mala fide purchaser;
purchaser in bad faith.
la privilégiée X. trouve acquéreur à 2 400 fr.
(Bourse), X. preference found buyers at 2,400
francs.
acquérir (*v.t.*), to acquire; to get; to purchase;
to buy; to earn:
acquérir une terre, to acquire a piece of land.
acquérir (s') (s'accroître; courir) (*v.r.*), to accrue:
arrérages qui s'acquièrent jour par jour (*m.pl.*),
interest which accrues day by day.
acquis, -e (*adj.* & *p.p.*), earned; not repayable;
not returnable; non returnable:
le bénéfice acquis sur une vente, the profit
earned on a sale.
le fret, qu'il ait été payé d'avance ou soit
payable à destination, est toujours censé
acquis ou dû, que le navire ou la marchandise
arrive à bon port ou se perde pendant le
voyage, the freight, whether paid in advance
or payable at destination, is always deemed
earned or due, whether the ship or the goods
arrive safely or are lost on the voyage.
fret acquis à tout événement (*m.*), freight not
repayable under any circumstances.
prime d'assurance qui est acquise s'il a commencé à courir les risques (*f.*), insurance
premium which is earned (*or* which is not
returnable) if the risk has attached.
acquisition (*n.f.*), acquisition; purchase; purchasing; buying; earning:
acquisition d'immeubles, purchase of premises.
acquisition du fret, earning of freight.
acquit (quittance) (*n.m.*), receipt; discharge;
acquittance; quittance: (See also **quittance,
récépissé,** and **reçu.**)
acquit de paiement, receipt for payment.
donner acquit, to give a receipt (*or* a discharge).
acquit d'un chèque. Unlike in England, where
a cheque on payment by a banker has simply
to be endorsed by the payee by writing his
name on the back, in France, a cheque has
to be receipted on the back, with the words
" Pour acquit," the date, signature, and often
the address of the payee is added. No receipt
stamp is required.
pour acquit *ou simplement* **acquit,** received.
à l'acquit de, on behalf of; on account of:
verser des fonds, négocier des effets, à l'acquit
d'un tiers, to pay money, to negotiate bills,
on behalf of (*or* on account of) a third party.
acquit à caution [**acquits à caution** *pl.*] *ou* **acquit-à-
caution** [**acquits-à-caution** *pl.*] (Douanes)
(*n.m.*), bond note; transhipment bond.
acquitté, -e (Douanes) (*adj.*), duty-paid:
marchandises acquittées (*f.pl.*), duty-paid goods.
à l'acquitté (Abrév.: A/ *ou* à l'A.) (opp. à *à
l'entrepôt*), duty paid; ex bond:
marchandises vendues à l'acquitté (*f.pl.*),
goods sold duty paid; goods sold ex bond.

vente à l'acquitté *ou* vente à l'A. (*f.*), duty-paid sale; sale ex bond.

triple de la valeur à l'acquitté (amende de douane) (*m.*), treble the duty-paid value.

acquittement (*n.m.*), acquittance; quittance; discharge; release; payment; paying off:

ce n'est qu'après l'acquittement de la police qu'elle entre en vigueur, it is only after acquittance of the policy that it comes into force.

acquittement préalable, prepayment.

acquitter (payer ce qu'on doit) (*v.t.*), to discharge; to pay; to pay off:

acquitter une dette, le passif, to discharge, to pay, to pay off, a debt, the liabilities.

s'acquitter (*v.r.*), to settle, to discharge, one's account.

acquitter (constater le paiement, l'accomplissement, de) (*v.t.*), to receipt:

acquitter une facture, un connaissement, to receipt an invoice, a bill of lading.

acquitter (rendre quitte de) (*v.t.*), to acquit; to discharge; to release:

acquitter quelqu'un d'une obligation, to acquit someone of, to discharge (*or* to release) someone from, an obligation.

acte (action; manifestation de la volonté) (*n.m.*), act:

sacrifice émanant d'un acte volontaire du capitaine (*m.*), sacrifice emanating from a voluntary act of the master.

acte d'avarie commune (Assce mar.), general average act.

acte de Dieu, act of God.

acte (pièce légale qui constate un fait) (Dr.) (*n.m.*), deed; indenture; instrument; muniment; document; agreement; contract; letter; certificate; bond:

acte à l'écrit, instrument in writing; agreement in writing; written contract.

acte authentique, instrument executed in the presence of a *notaire*, or the like, and authenticated by him: opposed to *acte sous seing privé* (*deed under private seal*), an instrument executed by the parties to it without the interposition of such an officer.

acte d'hypothèque, mortgage deed.

acte de caution *ou* acte de cautionnement, letter of indemnity; indemnity; indemnity bond; bond.

acte de compromis (compromis d'avaries), average bond.

acte de francisation, certificate of registry; ship's register (in France, of a ship of French nationality):

l'acte de francisation est la pièce officielle qui sert à prouver la nationalité française d'un navire, the *acte de francisation* is the official document which serves to prove the French nationality of a ship.

acte de nantissement, letter of hypothecation; hypothecation certificate.

acte de propriété, muniment (*or* document) of title; proof of ownership.

acte de transmission *ou* acte de cession *ou* acte de mutation *ou* acte translatif de pro-

priété, conveyance; deed of transfer; transfer deed; instrument of transfer; transfer.

acte de vente, agreement for sale; sale contract.

acte provisoire (acte de francisation), provisional certificate.

acte syndical, underwriting letter.

légaliser un acte, to legalize a document.

actif, -ive (*adj.*), active:

marché actif (*m.*), active market.

transactions actives en valeurs (*f.pl.*), active dealings in stocks.

actif (*n.m.*) (opp. à *passif*), assets; asset:

l'excédent de l'actif sur le passif (*m.*), the excess of assets over liabilities.

Note:—In French balance sheets, the assets appear on the left hand side and the liabilities on the right. This is the reverse of English practice.

actif défectible, wasting assets.

actif disponible *ou* actif liquide, available (*or* liquid) assets.

actif engagé (débiteurs divers, par exemple), trading assets.

actif éventuel [actif éventuel *ou* actifs éventuels *pl.*], contingent asset [contingent assets *pl.*].

actif fictif, fictitious assets.

actif immobilisé, fixed assets; permanent assets; capital assets.

actif net, net assets.

actif réalisable, realizable assets.

action (Dr.) (*n.f.*), action:

intenter une action contre quelqu'un, to bring an action against someone.

action civile, civil action.

action en dommages-intérêts, action for damages.

action en justice, action at law:

protestation suivie d'une action en justice dans le délai de tant de jours (*f.*), protestation followed by an action at law within so many days.

action (part dans une entreprise financière ou commerciale) (*n.f.*) (Abrév.: **act.** *ou* **a/.** *ou* **a.**), share [*in the plural* **actions** (Abrév.: **act.** *ou* **a/.** *ou* **a.**), shares, stock *or* stocks]: (See also **valeur** *ou* **valeurs**, and **titre.**)

actions de chemins de fer, railway shares; railway stock; railway stocks; rails.

actions à l'introduction, shop shares. Cf. **introduction** and **introducteurs.**

actions à la souche, unissued shares.

Note:—In France, the capital of a company limited by shares has to be subscribed in full, consequently there can be no unissued shares, i.e., unsubscribed shares. The Belgian law permits of unissued shares and these are called *actions à la souche.* In France, *actions à la souche* are vendors' or promoters' shares (also founders' shares) undelivered to their owners. According to French law, such shares must remain in the company's custody undetached from the counterfoils (hence *à la souche*) for 2 years following the definite formation of the company (*see note under* assemblée constitutive), or their creation, during which time, although transferable according to civil law, they are not dealable on the stock exchange. There are no such legal restrictions in England, and vendors' shares are good delivery on the London Stock Exchange on and after the date fixed for the special settlement in the shares or securities of the same class subscribed for by the public.

actions à ordre, registered shares transferable by endorsement of the certificate.

actions à vote plural *ou* **actions à vote multiple** *ou* **actions de contrôle,** shares to which plural voting rights are attached. This is often the case with *actions A* (A shares). In contradistinction, shares to which no plural voting rights are attached are called *actions à vote simple.*

actions au porteur, bearer shares; bearer stock; bearer stocks.

actions d'apport *ou* **actions de fondation,** vendors' shares; shares issued as fully paid up otherwise than in cash. *See* actions à la souche *and cf.* actions mixtes.

actions de capital (*Abrév.:* cap.). *Lit.* capital shares, *or* shares forming part of the capital of the company, virtually equivalent to the English term ordinary shares, whether cash shares and/or vendors' shares. There is no occasion for the term capital shares in English because all shares form part of the capital of a company, whereas in France they do not, as for instance, *actions de jouissance, parts de fondateurs,* etc. In French, *actions de capital* is the opposing term to *actions de jouissance,* or the like.

In market news, the expression *actions de capital* is often shortened to *la capital* (*action de* being understood), thus, aux valeurs de cinéma, l'action de jouissance X. est en reprise à 280 contre 265, ainsi que la capital qui s'avance de 325 à 338, among cinema shares, X. jouissance shares recovered to 280 against 265 francs, as did *actions de capital* (*or* ordinary shares, if that was the class that had been repaid and replaced by the *actions de jouissance*), which advanced from 325 to 338 francs.

actions de dividende (*Abrév.:* div.), (in France) participating shares; shares entitled to a dividend only, and not to any fixed interest. It is common with French companies for the articles to provide that a fixed interest of 5% (called *intérêt statutaire* or *intérêt intercalaire*) shall be paid on all shares without distinction, the surplus profits being appropriated as surplus dividend (*superdividende*), etc. This practice of paying interest on shares does not obtain in England. *Actions de dividende* form part of the company's capital, differing in that respect from *actions de jouissance* which have no right in the capital, inasmuch as the capital has been repaid. In case of liquidation *actions de dividende* share in any distribution of assets.

Note:—actions de dividende are often referred to in market news as *la dividende.* *Cf. explanation under* actions de capital.

actions de garantie *ou* **actions déposées en garantie,** qualification shares. (In France and Belgium qualification shares must be lodged in the custody of the company, hence *déposées.* They are held by the company as security for the directors' acts of management, hence *de garantie.*)

actions de jouissance (*Abrév.:* jouiss.) *ou* **actions bénéficiaires,** jouissance shares (in France, shares in respect of which the capital has been repaid pursuant to drawings by lot, but which still participate in profits, and in case of liquidation, in a distribution of reserve assets. Such shares do not exist in England).

actions de numéraire *ou* **actions en numéraire** *ou* **actions financières,** cash shares; shares issued for cash.

actions de numéraire de surplus, surplus cash shares.

actions de primes, promotion shares.

actions de priorité (*Abrév.:* prior.) *ou* **actions privilégiées** *ou* **actions de préférence,** preference shares; preference stock; preference stocks; preferred shares; preferred stock; preferred stocks:

actions de priorité de premier rang, de deuxième rang, first, second, preference shares.

actions de priorité cumulatives, cumulative preference shares.

actions de priorité 7 0/0 non cumulatives, non cumulative 7% preference shares.

la privilégiée X. s'améliore (Bourse), X. preference (*or* X. prefs) were better.

actions de surplus, surplus shares.

actions de travail, staff shares.

actions différées, deferred shares; deferred stock; deferred stocks.

actions estampillées, stamped shares; marked shares (i.e., certificates marked with notice that rights have been exercised, or the like).

actions gratuites, bonus shares:

les actionnaires toucheront une action gratuite pour cinq anciennes (*m.pl.*), the shareholders will receive one bonus share for five old shares.

actions industrielles, (in France) shares allotted in consideration for services (*industrie*), technical advice, commercial credit, etc. They are analogous to *parts de fondateur* (*q.v.*): they should properly be called *parts industrielles,* inasmuch as they do not form part of the registered capital and have no nominal value.

actions libérées *ou* **actions entièrement** (*ou* complètement) (*ou* intégralement) libérées, fully paid shares.

actions mixtes, shares issued as partly paid up otherwise than in cash. *Cf.* actions d'apport.

actions nominatives, registered shares; registered stock; registered stocks.

actions non estampillées, unstamped shares; unmarked shares. *Cf.* actions estampillées.

actions non libérées *ou* actions non entièrement (*ou* non complètement) (*ou* non intégralement) libérées, partly paid shares. **Warning :** — The methods of quoting partly paid shares in France and England are different. - In England the actual price is quoted; in France the nominal value, plus the premium, or minus the discount, is quoted. Thus, in England, a 5s. share, 2s. 6d. paid, being dealt in at 1s. premium, would be quoted 3s. 6d. In France, a 500 franc share, 300 francs paid, being dealt in at 100 francs premium, would be quoted 600 francs, but the actual price would of course be 400 francs, viz.:—fr. 600 (quoted price) less fr. 200 (uncalled) = fr. 400.

In France, as in England, if a share is only partly paid, the amount paid up is stated against the share in the quotation list.

actions ordinaires (*Abrév.* : ord.) *ou simplement* actions, ordinary shares; ordinary stock; shares; stock.

Note :—In naming shares in French without using the word *action* (which is feminine) they must always be spoken of as masculine; thus, **une action Chartered** *or* **un Chartered,** a Chartered share *or* one Chartered; **vendre du Chartered à découvert,** to sell a bear of Chartered.

In the case of stocks or shares referred to collectively under their names, as in market news, the gender is either—

(1) As indicated by the noun itself:—

la Rente italienne est résistante, Italian Rentes are strong.

le Consolidé est faible *ou* les Consolidés sont faibles, Consols are weak.

la Banque de France est ferme, Bank of France stock is firm.

le Nord, Nords (North of France Railway stocks).

le P.-L.-M., P.L.M's.

le Rio *ou* le Rio-Tinto, Rios *or* Rio Tintos.

le Gaz de Paris, Paris Gas.

les pétroles roumains (*m.pl.*) *ou* les pétrolifères roumaines (*f.pl.*), Roumanian oils.

les Forces Motrices du Rhône (*f.pl.*), Forces Motrices du Rhône.

les caoutchoucs (*m.pl.*) *ou* les caoutchoutières (*f.pl.*), rubbers.

(2) Where no gender is indicated as in proper names and foreign shares, they are referred to in the feminine singular, as,

la Van Ryn Deep, Van Ryn Deeps *or* Van Ryn Deep.

la Crown Mines, Crown Mines.

la Meyer and Charlton, Meyer and Charlton *or* Meyer and Charltons.

la Mexican Eagle, Mexican Eagles *or* Mexican Eagle.

la Shell Transport, Shell Transports *or* Shell Transport.

la Linggi, Linggis *or* Linggi.

la Tanganika *ou en abrév.* la Tanga, Tanganikas *or* Tanganika *or abbreviated* Tanks.

l'Anglo-French, Anglo-French.

Such expressions in market news concerning ruling prices as **Smith** *or* **Smiths** (*singular or plural in English*) **rose** (*past tense in English*), **Jones shares** (*plural in English*) **fell,** are rendered in French as follows : — **la Smith** (*singular in French*) **monte** (*generally present tense in French*), **l'action Jones** *or* **les actions Jones** (*generally singular but sometimes plural in French*) **tombe** (*sing.*), **tombent** (*pl.*).

Note further :—**Robinson founders** (' shares *understood*) **rallied, la** (part de *understood*) **fondateur Robinson est en reprise,** and see also **la capital** *under* actions de capital.

par actions (en parlant des sociétés), joint stock :

société par actions (*f.*) *ou* compagnie par actions (*f.*), joint stock company.

banque par actions (*f.*), joint stock bank.

actionnable (Dr.) (*adj.*), actionable.

actionnaire (pers.) (*n.m.* ou *f.*), shareholder; stockholder :

actionnaire de priorité, preference shareholder; preference stockholder.

actionnaire ordinaire, ordinary shareholder; ordinary stockholder.

actionner (Dr.) (*v.t.*), to bring an action against; to sue :

actionner un débiteur, to sue a debtor.

activement (*adv.*), actively :

valeurs activement traitées (*f.pl.*), securities actively dealt in.

activité (*n.f.*), activity.

actuaire (pers.) (*n.m.*), actuary.

actuarial, -e, -aux (*adj.*), actuarial :

science actuariale (*f.*), actuarial science.

actuarialement (*adv.*), actuarially.

addition (action d'ajouter) (*n.f.*), addition.

addition (ce qu'on ajoute) (*n.f.*), addition :

une addition à un mémoire, an addition to a bill.

addition (opération de réunir plusieurs nombres) (Arith.) (*n.f.*), addition; casting; casting up; totting up; totting together; totting; footing up; footing.

addition (total de plusieurs nombres) (Arith.) (*n.f.*), addition; cast.

additionnable (*adj.*), addible; addable :

sommes additionnables (*f.pl.*), addible sums.

additionnel, -elle (*adj.*), additional.

additionnellement (*adv.*), additionally.

additionner (Arith.) (*v.t.*), to add; to add up; to cast; to cast up; to tot up; to tot together; to tot; to foot up; to foot :

additionner une colonne de chiffres, to add up, to cast, to cast up, to tot up, to foot up, a column of figures.

additionneur, -euse (pers.) (*n.*), adder; caster.

additionneuse (*n.f.*), adding machine; adder.

adhérent (pers.) (*n.m.*), adherent; member :

les adhérents d'un syndicat, the members of a syndicate. *Cf.* nombre des adhérents.

adhésion (*n.f.*), adhesion; membership:
les conditions d'adhésion à une association (*f.pl.*), the conditions of membership of an association. *Cf.* nombre des adhésions *and* lettre d'adhésion.

adiré, -e (*p.p.*), lost:
bon adiré (*m.*), lost bond.

adirement (*n.m.*), loss.

adirer (*v.t.*), to lose:
adirer un titre, un chèque, une traite, to lose a certificate, a cheque, a draft.

adjoint, -e (*adj.*), assistant:
secrétaire adjoint (*m.*), assistant secretary.
membre adjoint à un comité (*m.*), assistant member of a committee.

adjoint, -e (pers.) (*n.*), assistant.

adjuger (*v.t.*), to award:
somme adjugée par arbitrage (*f.*), amount awarded by arbitration.

admettre (recevoir; agréer) (*v.t.*), to admit; to allow; to make good:
admettre en avarie commune le dommage causé à un navire ou à sa cargaison, to admit, to make good, as general average the damage done to a ship or her cargo.
admettre un recours, to admit, to allow, a claim.

admettre (comporter) (*v.t.*), to admit of:
cette affaire n'admet aucun retard, this affair admits of no delay.

administrateur, -trice (d'une société) (pers.) (*n.*), director (of a company):
administrateur alternatif, alternate director.
administrateur délégué *ou* administrateur directeur *ou* administrateur gérant, managing director. See example under **déléguer.**
administrateur sous-délégué, assistant managing director.
administrateur sortant, retiring director.
administrateur unique, sole director.

administratif, -ive (*adj.*), administrative:
pouvoir administratif (*m.*), administrative power.

administration (action) (*n.f.*), administration; management; direction; directorate; directorship:
l'administration des postes en France, the administration of the post office in France.
administration d'un navire, management of a ship.

administration (corps d'administrateurs) (*n.f.*) (Abrév.: **adm.** *ou* **admin.**), board; directorate; authorities:
administration des postes, postal authorities.

administrativement (*adv.*), administratively.

administrer (*v.t.*), to administer; to manage; to direct:
administrer les affaires d'une compagnie, to administer the affairs of a company.

admissibilité (*n.f.*), admissibility.

admissible (*adj.*), admissible.

admission (*n.f.*), admission:
admission à la cote (Bourse), admission to quotation.

admission en franchise (Douanes), free admission.
admission temporaire (Douanes), temporary admission.

adopté (se dit d'une proposition) (*invar.*), carried:
adopté à l'unanimité, carried unanimously.

adopter (*v.t.*), to adopt; to carry; to pass; to confirm:
adopter une proposition, to adopt, to carry, to pass, a resolution.
cette résolution est adoptée à l'unanimité, à l'exception de M. X., apporteur, qui s'est abstenu de voter, the resolution was carried unanimously, with the exception of Mr X., vendor, who did not vote.
le procès-verbal de la dernière séance est lu et adopté, the minutes of the last meeting were read and confirmed.

adoption (*n.f.*), adoption; carrying; passing; confirmation.

adresse (*n.f.*), address:
adresse sur une lettre, address on a letter.
prendre le nom et l'adresse (*ou* les nom et adresse) de quelqu'un, to take someone's name and address.
ce côté est exclusivement réservé à l'adresse *ou* côté réservé à l'adresse (carte postale), the address only to be written on this side.
adresse abrégée enregistrée (Télégr.), registered abbreviated address.
adresse complète, full address.
adresse convenue (Télégr.), code address.
adresse de convention *ou* adresse conventionnelle (Télégr.), arbitrary address.
adresse insuffisante, insufficient address.
adresse non enregistrée (Télégr.), unregistered address.
adresse télégraphique, telegraphic address.

adresse (consignation d'un navire, d'une cargaison) (*n.f.*), address.

adresser (*v.t.*), to address; to send:
adresser une lettre à quelqu'un, to address a letter to someone.

s'adresser (*v.r.*), to apply:
les noms de deux maisons auxquelles la banque peut s'adresser pour obtenir des renseignements (*m.pl.*), the names of two firms to which the bank can apply for information.
pour frets et autres renseignements s'adresser aux agents, for freights and further particulars apply to the agents.

adultération des monnaies (*f.*), adulteration, debasement, of the coinage.

adultérer les monnaies, to adulterate, to debase, the coinage.

aérien, -enne (*adj.*), aerial; air (*used as adj.*):
navigation aérienne (*f.*), aerial navigation; air navigation; aviation.

aérodrome (*n.m.*), aerodrome.

aérogare (*n.f.*), air station:
l'aérogare du Bourget, de Croydon, Le Bourget, Croydon, air station.

aéronaute (pers.) (*n.m.*), aeronaut; aviator; airman.

aéronautique (*adj.*), aeronautic; aeronautical.

aéronautique (*n.f.*), aeronautics.
aéronef (*n.m.*), aircraft.
aéroplane (*n.m.*), aeroplane; airplane.
aéroport (*n.m.*), air port:
l'aéroport de Paris, de Londres, the air port of Paris, of London.
aéroport d'embarquement, air port of lading.
aéroport de débarquement, air port of delivery.
affaire (ce qui est l'objet d'une occupation) (*n.f.*), affair; matter; thing; proposition; business; concern:
affaires courantes, current matters.
une affaire de cuivre, a copper proposition.
l'affaire va mal, the thing is going badly.
une affaire commerciale ou industrielle, a commercial or industrial concern (*or* business).
affaire roulante, going concern.
affaire (transaction commerciale) (*n.f.*), piece of business; business; transaction; deal; dealing; bargain; affair:
affaire d'or *ou* affaire magnifique, fine piece of business; lucrative transaction; capital deal; splendid bargain.
prendre une participation dans l'affaire, to take a share in the deal (*or* in the business).
affaires à primes (Bourse), option dealing; option dealings; dealing in options.
affaires d'arbitrage *ou* affaires de couverture, hedging transactions; hedging; covering transactions.
affaires liées (Bourse), combined deal, i.e., selling a stock cum rights and simultaneous buying of the same stock ex rights.
affaires (*n.f.pl.*), business:
faire des affaires avec quelqu'un, to do business with someone.
être dans les affaires, to be in business.
les affaires vont mal, business is bad.
affaire (Dr.) (*n.f.*), action; proceedings:
affaire civile, civil action; civil proceedings.
affectable (*adj.*), chargeable:
terres affectables (*f.pl.*), chargeable lands.
affectation (*n.f.*), charging; charge; application; appropriation; setting aside; setting apart; earmarking:
affectation d'une somme à une telle dépense, charging an amount to a certain expense.
affectation hypothécaire, mortgage charge.
la valeur d'un bâtiment indépendante de son affectation industrielle, the worth of a building independent of its industrial application.
affectation du bénéfice net, conformément aux prescriptions statutaires ou aux décisions de l'assemblée des actionnaires, appropriation of the net profits in accordance with the provisions of the articles or the resolutions of the shareholders' meeting.
affecter (*v.t.*), to charge; to apply; to appropriate; to set aside; to set apart; to earmark:
immeuble affecté à la garantie d'une créance (*m.*), property charged as security for a debt.
affecter un paiement à compte à une certaine dette, to charge, to apply, an instalment to a particular debt.

somme affectée à l'amortissement, à la réserve (*f.*), amount set aside for (*or* amount appropriated to) redemption, reserve.
affecter une certaine somme au paiement de l'intérêt du capital, to set aside, to earmark, a certain amount for payment of the interest on the capital.
affermage (*n.m.*), leasing.
affermer (*v.t.*), to lease:
affermer une ligne de chemin de fer à une autre compagnie, to lease a railway line to another company.
si les propriétés sont affermées, leur revenu brut est constitué par le montant des fermages perçus, if the properties are leased, their gross income is constituted by the amount of the rents collected. (See also example under **fermage**.)
affiche (Publicité) (*n.f.*), poster; sign:
affiche lumineuse, illuminated sign.
afficher (*v.t.*), to post:
avis affiché en Bourse (*m.*), notice posted in the House.
affidavit [**affidavit** *ou* **affidavits** *pl.*] (*n.m.*), affidavit.
affiliation (*n.f.*), affiliation.
affilié, -e (*adj.*), affiliated:
sociétés affiliées (*f.pl.*), affiliated societies.
affilié, -e (*n.*), affiliate; affiliated member.
affilier (*v.t.*), to affiliate:
affilier plusieurs sociétés à une société centrale to affiliate several societies to a central society.
s'affilier (*v.r.*), to affiliate; to become affiliated:
s'affilier à une certaine société, to affiliate with, to become affiliated to (*or* with) a certain company.
affirmatif, -ive (*adj.*), affirmative:
réponse affirmative (*f.*), affirmative reply.
affirmativement (*adv.*), affirmatively; in the affirmative.
affluent (Ch. de f.) (*n.m.*), feeder:
lignes d'intérêt local destinées à servir d'affluents aux grandes lignes (*f.pl.*), local lines intended to serve as feeders to the main lines.
afflux (*n.m.*), afflux; inflow; influx:
afflux d'or apporté par les visiteurs étrangers, inflow (*or* influx) of gold brought by foreign visitors.
affranchi, -e (port payé) (*adj.*), prepaid; post paid; carriage paid:
lettre affranchie (*f.*), prepaid letter; post paid letter.
colis affranchi (*m.*), prepaid parcel; carriage paid parcel.
affranchir (exempter d'une charge) (*v.t.*), to free; to discharge; to release; to relieve; to exempt; to exonerate:
les assureurs sont affranchis des risques suivants, les assureurs sont expressément affranchis de toutes réclamations pour les causes suivantes (Assce mar.), warranted free of; warranted free from any claim in respect of.
affranchir quelqu'un d'une responsabilité, to relieve, to release, someone from a liability.

en France, si les épaves sont réclamées par leurs propriétaires, elles sont affranchies de tous droits de douane lorsqu'elles sont d'origine française, in France, if wreck is claimed by its owners, it is exempted from all customs duties when it is of French origin.

affranchir (payer d'avance) (*v.t.*), to prepay : affranchir le fret, to prepay the freight.

affranchir (payer d'avance le port d'une lettre, d'un envoi) (*v.t.*), to prepay ; to prepay the postage (*or* the carriage) on ; to stamp : affranchir une lettre, to prepay the postage on, to stamp, a letter.

objets non ou insuffisamment affranchis.— taxe double du montant de l'affranchissement manquant ou de l'insuffisance d'affranchissement (*m.pl.*), packets posted unpaid or underpaid.—if posted unpaid, charged with double postage, if posted underpaid, with double the amount short paid.

les colis postaux doivent être obligatoirement affranchis au départ (*m.pl.*), postage on parcels must be prepaid.

affranchissement (exemption d'une charge) (*n.m.*), discharge ; release ; relief ; exemption ; exoneration.

affranchissement (acquittement préalable) (*n.m.*), prepayment ; prepayment of postage (*or* carriage) ; stamping ; payment by sender : affranchissement préalable des frais de douane (Poste), payment by sender of customs charges ; prepayment of customs charges. affranchissement des colis postaux, prepayment of postage on parcels.

affranchissement (prix du port) (*n.m.*), postage ; carriage.

affrètement (*n.m.*), affreightment ; chartering ; charterage ; charter ; freighting :

Note :—The French distinguish specifically **affrètement-location** which is *affreightment by charter* or *chartering* proper, and **affrètement-transport** which is *affreightment by bill of lading.*

l'exploitation commerciale du navire sous la forme d'affrètement revêt plusieurs formes (*f.*), the commercial exploitation of the ship in the form of affreightment assumes several forms.

contrat d'affrètement (*m.*), contract of affreightment.

affrètement d'un navire pour un plein et entier chargement, chartering a ship for a full and entire cargo.

affrètement à cueillette, berth freighting ; liner freighting ; loading on the berth.

affrètement à forfait, freighting by contract.

affrètement à la pièce, freighting by the case.

affrètement à la tête (bétail), freighting per head (cattle).

affrètement à temps *ou* affrètement à terme *ou* affrètement pour un temps déterminé *ou* affrètement en « time charter, » time charter.

affrètement ad valorem, freighting ad valorem.

affrètement au poids, freighting on weight.

affrètement au tonneau *ou* affrètement à la tonne, freighting per ton.

affrètement au volume, freighting on measurement.

affrètement au voyage *ou* affrètement pour un voyage entier, voyage charter.

affrètement coque nue, bare boat charter ; net charter ; net form charter.

affrètement en lourd, dead-weight charter.

affrètement partiel, part cargo charter.

affrètement pour une série de voyages, charter for a series of voyages.

affrètement total, whole cargo charter.

affréter (*v.t.*), to charter ; to freight ; to affreight : affréter un navire, en tout ou en partie, pour le transport de marchandises, pour charger de la marchandise dans un port d'ordres, to charter a ship, wholly or partly, for the carriage of goods, to load cargo in a port of call for orders.

s'affréter (*v.r.*), to be chartered ; to be freighted ; to be affreighted : les tramps s'affrètent pratiquement, soit au voyage, soit au temps (*m.pl.*), in practice, tramps are chartered, either by the voyage, or by time.

affréteur (pers.) (*n.m.*), charterer ; freighter ; affreighter : l'obligation essentielle de l'affréteur, quel que soit le genre d'affrètement, est le paiement du fret (*f.*), the essential obligation of the freighter, whatever may be the kind of freighting, is the payment of the freight.

âge (*n.m.*), age : âge d'un navire, age of a ship.

agence (emploi, charge d'agent ; sa durée) (*n.f.*), agency : obtenir l'agence d'une compagnie, to obtain the agency of a company. durant son agence, during his agency.

agence (bureau) (*n.f.*), agency ; bureau : agence d'information, press agency. agence de placement, employment agency ; employment bureau. agence de publicité, advertising agency ; publicity bureau. agence de recouvrements, debt collecting agency ; debt recovery agency. agence de renseignements, mercantile agency ; enquiry agency. agence de voyages, travel agency. agence en douane, customs agency. agence maritime *ou* agence d'affrètement, shipping agency.

agencement (d'un bureau, ou local analogue) (*n.m.*), fitting ; fitting up.

agencement (*n.m.*) *ou* **agencements** (*n.m.pl.*) (objets mobiliers que l'on ne pourrait déplacer sans les rendre à peu près inutilisables ou sans commettre des détériorations importantes [casiers, rayons, installations de gaz, etc.]), fittings ; fixtures ; fixtures and fittings : mobilier et agencement, furniture and fittings ; furniture, fixtures and fittings.

agencer (pourvoir d'agencements) (*v.t.*), to fit up ; to fit : agencer un bureau, un local, to fit up an office, premises.

agenda [agendas *pl.*] (*n.m.*), diary :
 faire une note sur un agenda, to make a note in
  a diary.
agent (pers.) (*n.m.*), agent ; broker ; officer :
 agent exclusif pour la France et ses Colonies,
  sole agent for France and Colonies.
 l'agent de la compagnie à Marseille, the
  company's agent at Marseilles.
 agent comptable, accountant.
 agent comptable des transferts, registrar of
  transfers.
 agent consulaire, consular agent.
 agent d'assurances, insurance agent.
 agent d'émigration, emigration agent.
 agent de change *ou simplement* agent, stockbroker ; broker. (*Note :*—These French and
  English terms do not correspond exactly,
  the French Bourse system differing materially
  from English Stock Exchange practice. *See
  explanation of Paris markets under* marché des
  valeurs.)
 agent de douane, customs officer ; officer of
  custom.
 agent de police des côtes à terre, coastguard.
 agent de recouvrements, debt collector.
 agent de transport *ou* agent metteur à bord
  [agents metteurs à bord *pl.*], forwarding
  agent ; transport agent.
 agent des contributions directes, officer of
  taxes.
 agents du fisc, Revenue authorities.
 agent du Lloyd, Lloyd's agent.
 agent du service sanitaire, medical officer of
  health ; officer of health ; health officer.
 agent en douane (à ne pas confondre avec
  l'agent de douane), customs agent ; custom
  house broker :
 l'agent en douane remplit, pour les expéditeurs ou les destinataires, les formalités
  de dédouanement des marchandises, the
  customs agent (*or* custom house broker)
  fulfils, for shippers or consignees, the
  formalities of clearing the goods through
  the customs.
 agent gérant, managing agent.
 agent maritime, shipping agent.
 agent taxateur (de bureau télégraphique),
  accepting officer.
 agent terrestre, land agent (agent ashore).
 agent transitaire, transit agent.
 agents s'abstenir (mention dans une petite
  annonce), no agents.
aggravation (*n.f.*), aggravation ; increase :
 aggravation du risque nécessitant un avenant
  à l'assurance, increase, aggravation, of the
  risk necessitating an indorsement to the
  insurance.
aggraver (*v.t.*), to aggravate ; to increase :
 aggraver les impôts, to increase the taxes.
agio (différence entre le pair intrinsèque et le
  cours actuel) (Banq.) (*n.m.*), premium ;
  exchange premium ; premium on exchange ;
  exchange ; agio.
agio (frais d'escompte) (Banq.) (*n.m.*), discount
  charges. *Note :*—Most of the French banks
  make three distinct charges on bills dis-

counted : (1) *escompte* (discount [the only
  charge made in England]), (2) *commission*,
  and (3) *changes* ou *pertes de place* (costs of
  collection *or* bank charges).
agiotage *ou* **agio** (spéculation aléatoire) (*n.m.*),
  gambling (in stocks and shares, foreign
  exchanges, or the like) ; gambling on the
  stock exchange ; agiotage.
agiotage *ou* **agio** (tripotage de bourse) (*n.m.*),
  jobbery ; market jobbery ; rigging the
  market.
agiotage (trafic sur le cours du change) (*n.m.*),
  exchange business ; agiotage.
agioter (spéculer) (*v.i.*), to gamble.
agioteur, -euse (spéculateur) (pers.) (*n.*), gambler.
agir (*v.i.*), to act :
 agir selon le cas, to act according to circumstances.
 agent qui est autorisé à agir pour la compagnie
  (*m.*), agent who is authorized to act for the
  company.
 agissant pour le compte de qui il appartiendra
  ou agissant pour compte de qui il peut
  appartenir, acting for account of whom it
  may concern.
agrafage (*n.m.*), stapling ; fastening.
agrafe (de bureau) (*n.f.*), staple.
agrafer (*v.t.*), to staple ; to fasten :
 agrafer plusieurs feuilles de papier, to staple,
  to fasten, several sheets of paper.
agrafeuse (de bureau) (*n.f.*), staple press :
 agrafeuse coup de poing, single stroke staple
  press.
agréage (*n.m.*) *ou* **agrégation** (*n.f.*), acceptance :
 agréage (*ou* agrégation) de la marchandise en
  gare de départ, acceptance of the goods at
  departure station.
agréé (pers.) (*n.m.*), an attorney or solicitor who
  represents the parties before a *tribunal de
  commerce*.
agréer (*v.t.*), to accept ; to approve ; to approve
  of ; to agree ; to receive favourably :
 agréer une proposition, to accept a proposition ; to approve a proposal ; to receive a
  proposal favourably.
 valeurs agréées par la banque (*f.pl.*), securities
  approved by the bank.
 valeur agréée de l'objet d'une assurance, agreed
  value of the subject matter of an insurance.
 agréez mes civilités, mes respects, accept my
  compliments, my respects.
 Agréez, Monsieur (Messieurs), mes (nos)
  meilleures salutations (*ou* salutations empressées) (formule de politesse précédant
  signature), Yours faithfully ; Yours truly.
s'agréer (*v.r.*), to be acceptable ; to prove
  acceptable :
 propositions qui peuvent s'agréer (*f.pl.*), proposals which may be (*or* which may prove)
  acceptable.
agrément (*n.m.*), consent ; approbation ; approval :
 obtenir l'agrément de quelqu'un à (*ou* pour)
  faire une chose, to obtain someone's consent
  to do a thing.
 solliciter l'agrément de quelqu'un, to ask for
  someone's approbation.

il faut l'agrément du conseil pour devenir action-naire de certaines sociétés, the approval of the board is required in order to become a shareholder in certain companies.

agrès (d'un navire) (*n.m.pl.*), tackle (of a ship).

agroupement (*n.m.*), grouping :
agroupement méthodique de faits, methodical grouping of facts.

agrouper (*v.t.*), to group :
agrouper des chiffres, to group figures.

aide (*n.f.*), aid ; help ; assistance :
aide financière, financial aid.
venir en aide à quelqu'un, to come to someone's assistance.

aide (pers.) (*n.m. ou f.*), assistant.

aide-comptable [**aides-comptables** *pl.*] (*n.m. ou f.*), assistant accountant.

aider (*v.t.*), to aid ; to help ; to assist.

air (*n.m.*), air :
voie d'air (*f.*), airway.

aisance (*n.f.*), easiness ; ease :
l'approche de la fin du mois n'exerçait aucune influence restrictive sur l'aisance monétaire du marché de Paris (*f.*), the approach of the end of the month exerted no restraining influence on the monetary easiness of the Paris market.

ajournable (*adj.*), adjournable ; postponable.

ajournement (*n.m.*), adjournment ; postpone-ment ; putting off :
ajournement d'une assemblée, adjournment of a meeting.

ajourner (*v.t.*), to adjourn ; to postpone ; to put off :
ajourner les délibérations, une cause à huitaine, to adjourn the proceedings, a case for a week.
ajourner le règlement d'une dette, to postpone, to put off, settlement of a debt.

s'ajourner (*v.r.*), to adjourn ; to be adjourned ; to be postponed ; to be put off :
les membres se sont ajournés sine die (*m.pl.*), the members have adjourned sine die.

ajouté (addition à un écrit) (*n.m.*), rider.

ajouter (*v.t.*), to add :
ajouter l'intérêt au capital, le fret à la valeur des marchandises, to add the interest to the capital, the freight to the value of the goods.

s'ajouter (*v.r.*), to be added :
le courtage s'ajoute aux achats ou se retranche des ventes, brokerage is added to purchases or deducted from sales.

ajouter (Impôts cédulaires) (*v.t.*), to add back :
contrôleur qui ajoute les appointements d'un associé au bénéfice accusé par l'entreprise (*m.*), inspector who adds back a partner's salary to the profit shown by the business.

ajustement (*n.m.*), adjustment.

ajuster (*v.t.*), to adjust :
ajuster un différend, un compte, to adjust a difference, an account.

album [**albums** *pl.*] (*n.m.*), guard book :
découper une annonce et la coller dans un album, to cut out an advertisement and stick it in a guard book.

album-tarif [**albums-tarifs** *pl.*] (*n.m.*), illustrated price list.

aléa (*n.m.*), chance ; risk :
les aléas d'une entreprise, the risks of an under-taking ; the chances of a venture.

aléatoire (Dr.) (*adj.*), aleatory :
l'assurance est un contrat aléatoire (*f.*), in-surance is an aleatory contract.

aléatoire (qui est soumis aux chances du hasard) (*adj.*), uncertain ; chance ; contingent ; risky :
résultat aléatoire (*m.*), uncertain result.
gain aléatoire (*m.*), chance gain ; contingent profit.
spéculation aléatoire (*f.*), risky speculation.

aléatoire (*n.m.*), uncertainty ; contingency.

aléatoirement (*adv.*), contingently.

aliment (Assce) (*n.m.*), interest ; risk ; value :
la déclaration d'aliment doit être faite à l'assureur dans le délai fixé au contrat (police d'abonnement), the declaration of interest (*or* of risk) (*or* of value) should be made to the underwriter within the time specified in the contract.
chaque aliment fera l'objet d'une police distincte, each interest (*or* risk) to form the subject of a separate policy.
le navire dans lequel l'aliment est embarqué, ou destiné à l'être, the vessel by which the interest is, or is intended to be, shipped.
la compagnie accepte de faire assurer les marchandises en aliment à une police flottante spécialement contractée à cet effet, the company agrees to insure the goods as interest attaching to a floating policy specially taken out for this purpose.

aliment (Transport maritime) (*n.m.*), inducement :
ces vapeurs feront escale à X. en cas d'aliment suffisant pour ce port, these steamers will call at X. if sufficient inducement for this port.

alimentation (*n.f.*), feeding ; maintenance :
retenus sur les salaires pour l'alimentation des caisses de secours ou de prévoyance (*m.pl.*), stoppages on wages for the maintenance of relief or provident funds.

alimenter (*v.t.*), to feed ; to maintain ; to supply :
réserve alimentée par l'excédent de recettes (*f.*), reserve maintained by the excess of receipts.
nos carnets de commandes sont bien alimentés, our order books are well supplied.

alimenter (Assce mar.) (*v.t.*), to declare, to report, as attaching interest :
l'assuré s'engage à alimenter la présente police d'abonnement par toutes les exportations et/ou importations pour lesquelles elle a été conclue (*m.*), the insured undertakes to declare (*or* to report) as interest attaching to the present floating policy all the exports and/or imports for which it has been concluded.

allant, -e (*adj.*), active :
les valeurs mexicaines sont très allantes (*f.pl.*), Mexican shares are very active.

allant (*n.m.*), activity.

alléchant, -e (*adj.*), alluring :
proposition alléchante (*f.*), alluring proposition.

allège (*n.f.*), lighter ; barge ; craft :

les allèges sont des embarcations servant au chargement et au déchargement de la marchandise, lighters are craft used for loading and unloading cargo.

allège de mer, seagoing barge.

allégement *ou* **allègement** (*n.m.*), lightening.

alléger (*v.t.*), to lighten :

cargaison qui est déchargée dans des embarcations pour alléger un navire échoué (*f.*), cargo which is discharged into craft to lighten a stranded ship.

il est convenu que le navire remontant à Nantes doit alléger à Saint-Nazaire et que les frais d'allègement sont à la charge du réceptionnaire de la marchandise, it is agreed that the ship going up to Nantes shall lighten at Saint-Nazaire and that the expense of lightening shall be paid by the receiver of the goods.

aller (voyage d'aller) (*n.m.*), outward (*or* outbound) voyage (*or* journey) (*or* passage) :

aller et retour, journey there and back ; there and back ; outward and homeward voyages (*or* passages) ; round voyage :

la traversée aller et retour de Calais à Douvres, the crossing there and back from Calais to Dover.

navire frété pour l'aller et le retour (*m.*), ship freighted for the outward and homeward voyages (*or* for the round voyage).

aller (*v.i.*), to go :

aller à bord d'un navire, to go on board a ship.

aller au delà de sa charge, to go beyond one's instructions ; to exceed one's duty.

aller au secours d'un navire en péril, to go to the help of a ship in peril.

alliage (*n.m.*), alloy.

allô ! (Téléph.) (*interj.*), are you there ? ; there ? ; hello ! ; hullo !

allocation (*n.f.*), allocation ; allowance ; remuneration :

allocation d'une part des bénéfices, allocation of a share of the profits.

allocation d'une dépense portée dans un compte, allowance of an expense appearing in an account.

une allocation mensuelle de tant, a monthly allowance of so much.

fixer l'allocation des commissaires, to fix the remuneration of the auditors.

allocution (discours) (*n.f.*), speech ; address :

allocution du président, chairman's speech.

allonge (sur une lettre de change) (*n.f.*), allonge ; rider.

allouable (*adj.*), allowable ; grantable :

dépense allouable (*f.*), allowable expense.

allouance (*n.f.*), allowance ; grant :

une allouance mensuelle de tant, a monthly allowance of so much.

allouer (*v.t.*), to allow ; to grant :

l'intérêt alloué aux dépôts (*m.*), the interest allowed on deposits.

allouer une dépense portée dans un compte, to allow an expense appearing in an account.

allouer une indemnité, to grant compensation.

almanach (*n.m.*), almanac.

alourdir (s') (en parlant des cours de bourse) (*v.r.*), to become heavy.

alourdissement (d'un marché) (*n.m.*), heaviness (of a market).

alphabétique (*adj.*), alphabetical :

répertoire alphabétique (*m.*), alphabetical index.

altération des monnaies (*f.*), debasement, adulteration, of the coinage.

altérer les monnaies, to debase, to adulterate, the coinage.

alternatif, -ive (qui a lieu tour à tour) (*adj.*), alternative :

offre alternative (*f.*), alternative offer.

alternatif, -ive (qui est exercé, qui entre en fonction, tour à tour) (*adj.*), alternate :

administrateur alternatif (*m.*), alternate director.

alternatif (pers.) (*n.m.*), alternate.

alternative (*n.f.*), alternative.

alternativement (*adv.*), alternatively :

compte alternativement débiteur et créditeur (*m.*), account alternatively debtor and creditor.

amarrage (*n.m.*), making fast ; mooring ; berthing.

amarrer (*v.t.*), to make fast ; to moor ; to berth.

s'amarrer (*v.r.*), to make fast ; to moor ; to berth.

amas (*n.m.*), heap ; pile :

amas d'argent, heap, pile, of money.

amasser (*v.t.*), to amass ; to heap up ; to heap ; to pile up :

amasser une fortune, to amass, to pile up, a fortune.

ambassade (*n.f.*), embassy.

ambassadeur (pers.) (*n.m.*), ambassador.

ambitieux, -euse (*adj.*), ambitious :

projet ambitieux (*m.*), ambitious scheme.

ambition (*n.f.*), ambition.

amélioration (*n.f.*) (Ant. : *dépréciation*), appreciation ; improvement ; bettering ; betterment :

amélioration des cours, appreciation, improvement, of (*or* in) prices.

amélioration du sort du personnel, betterment of the lot of the staff.

preneur qui a fait des améliorations (*m.*), lessee who has made improvements.

améliorer (*v.t.*), to appreciate ; to improve ; to better :

améliorer la situation financière d'une banque, to better, to improve, the financial position of a bank.

s'améliorer (*v.r.*), to appreciate ; to improve ; to be better ; to go better :

avec le temps, certaines valeurs s'améliorent, d'autres se déprécient, in time, certain stocks appreciate (*or* go better), others depreciate (*or* go worse).

quelques titres s'améliorent faiblement (*m.pl.*), some stocks appreciated (*or* improved) somewhat (*or* were slightly better).

aménagement (d'un navire) (*n.m.*), fitting ; accommodation ; appointments :

ce steamer a de splendides aménagements pour passagers, this steamer has splendid accommodation for passengers.

navire qui a des aménagements pour 800 passagers (*m.*), ship which has accommodation for 800 passengers.

l'aménagement du port en vue du trafic touristique, the accommodation of the port with a view to tourist traffic.

l'aménagement du navire est luxueux, the appointments of the ship are magnificent.

aménager (*v.t.*), to fit ; to accommodate :

aménager un navire pour le transport de passagers d'entrepont comme navire à émigrants, to fit, to accommodate, a ship for the carriage of steerage passengers as an emigrant ship.

amende (*n.f.*), fine :

toute infraction aux règlements douaniers se traduit par une amende, every breach of the customs regulations results in a fine.

amende de tant de francs au maximum, fine not exceeding so many francs.

amende de principe (Douanes), nominal fine.

amendement (*n.m.*), amendment :

proposer un amendement, to move an amendment.

amender (*v.t.*), to amend :

amender une proposition, to amend a resolution.

amenuisement (des monnaies) (*n.m.*), debasement (of the coinage).

amenuiser (*v.t.*), to debase :

amenuiser la monnaie, to debase the coinage.

amiable *ou* **amical, -e, -aux** (*adj.*), amicable ; friendly :

partage amiable (*m.*), amicable division.

accueil amical (*ou* amiable) (*m.*), friendly reception.

amiable compositeur (*m.*) *ou* arbitre amiable compositeur (*m.*), friendly arbitrator.

amoindrir (*v.t.*), to lessen ; to decrease ; to diminish.

amoindrir (*v.i.*), to lessen ; to decrease ; to diminish.

s'amoindrir (*v.r.*), to lessen ; to decrease ; to diminish.

amoindrissement (*n.m.*), lessening ; decrease ; diminution :

amoindrissement des recettes, de prix, decrease in the receipts, of price.

amonceler (*v.t.*), to heap up ; to heap ; to pile up ; to accumulate :

amonceler des capitaux, to accumulate capital.

s'amonceler (*v.r.*), to heap up ; to pile up ; to accumulate.

amoncellement (*n.m.*), heaping up ; piling up ; accumulation :

amoncellement des capitaux dans les mêmes mains, accumulation of capital in the same hands.

amortir (*v.t.*), to redeem ; to amortize ; to sink ; to pay off ; to write off ; to depreciate :

amortir une annuité, to redeem an annuity.

amortir une dette, to amortize, to pay off, a debt.

amortir une créance, le montant d'un détournement, to write off a debt, the amount of an embezzlement.

amortir le mobilier de 10 0/0 par an, to write 10% per annum off the furniture ; to depreciate the furniture by 10% per annum.

amortissable (*adj.*), (Abrév. : **am.** *ou* **amort.**), redeemable ; amortizable :

obligations amortissables (*f.pl.*), redeemable bonds.

amortissant, -e (*adj.*), redemptional.

amortissement (*n.m.*) (Abrév. : **am.** *ou* **amort.**), redemption ; amortization ; amortizement ; sinking ; paying off ; writing off ; amount written off ; provision for redemption ; reserve ; depreciation ; reserve for depreciation :

amortissement d'un emprunt, de la dette publique, redemption, amortization, sinking, paying off, of a loan, of the national debt.

amortissement d'une créance, writing off a debt.

amortissement des créances douteuses, reserve for doubtful debts ; bad debts reserve.

amortissement sur immeuble (*ou* sur immeubles), provision for redemption of premises ; amount written off premises ; depreciation on premises ; reserve for depreciation of premises.

les amortissements figurent en rouge, the amounts written off are shown in red.

amortissement dégressif, depreciation on diminishing values.

amortissement fixe, fixed depreciation.

ampleur (d'un marché) (*n.f.*), freeness (of a market). Cf. **large.**

an (*n.m.*), year ; annum (*only in the phrase* per annum) :

une fois l'an, once a year.

l'an 19—, the year 19—.

5 pour cent l'an (*ou* par an), 5 per cent. per annum.

analysable (*adj.*), analyzable ; analysable.

analyse (*n.f.*), analysis :

analyse des articles de dépenses, analysis of expense items.

analyser (*v.t.*), to analyze ; to analyse :

analyser une opération, une situation, to analyze a transaction, a position.

analytique (*adj.*), analytic ; analytical :

table analytique (*f.*), analytical table.

analytiquement (*adv.*), analytically.

anatocisme (*n.m.*), capitalization of interest.

ancien, -enne (*adj.*) (Abrév. : **anc.**), old :

actions anciennes (*f.pl.*), old shares.

une action nouvelle contre deux anciennes de la Société X., one new share for two old ones in the X. Company.

ancienneté de nomination (*f.*). See example :

le renouvellement a lieu par ancienneté de nomination (statuts), the directors to retire shall be those who have been longest in office since their last election.

ancre (*n.f.*), anchor.

angarie (Dr. mar.) (*n.f.*), angaria.

angle (*n.m.*), angle ; corner :

angle droit inférieur, bottom right hand corner.

angle droit supérieur, top right hand corner :

les timbres d'affranchissement doivent, autant que possible, être apposés à l'angle droit supérieur du recto (*m.pl.*), stamps in prepayment of postage should, as far as possible, be affixed in the top right hand corner of the address side.

angle gauche inférieur, bottom left hand corner.

angle gauche supérieur, top left hand corner.

animal (*n.m.*), animal :

animaux vivants, live animals ; live stock.

animateur (pers.) (*n.m*), moving spirit :

notre président, M. X., l'animateur de l'établissement, our chairman, Mr X., the moving spirit of the establishment.

Cf. syndicat-animateur.

animation (*n.f.*), animation ; liveliness :

le marché des valeurs continue à faire preuve d'une grande animation, the stock market continues to show a good deal of liveliness.

animé, -e (*adj.*), lively :

bourse animée (*f.*), market lively.

année (*n.f.*), year ; twelvemonth :

année bissextile, leap year ; bissextile year.

année civile, calendar year ; civil year ; legal year :

période de douze mois qui ne coïncide pas avec l'année civile (*f.*), period of twelve months which does not coincide with the calendar year.

année commerciale, year of 360 days, used in all continental interest calculations. See example under **calcul**.

année d'exercice *ou simplement* année, year of office.

année d'imposition, year of assessment :

le revenu de l'année immédiatement antérieure à l'année d'imposition, the income of the year preceding the year of assessment.

année financière, financial year :

le paiement des impôts à la fin de l'année financière, the payment of taxes at the end of the financial year.

année sociale (d'une société par actions), company's year (i.e., financial year) :

l'année sociale commence le 1ᵉʳ janvier et finit le 31 décembre, the company's year begins on 1st January and ends on 31st December.

les résultats des périodes correspondantes de l'année précédente (*ou* antérieure) sont placés en regard de ceux de l'année en cours, afin de faciliter les comparaisons (*m.pl.*), the results of the corresponding periods of the previous year are placed opposite those of the present (*or* current) year, in order to facilitate comparisons.

année (revenu, somme qu'on doit recevoir ou payer par an) (*n.f.*), yearly (*or* annual) income, payment, or the like ; income.

annexe (*n.f.*), schedule ; enclosure :

annexes d'un bilan, schedules to a balance sheet :

société tenue de publier en annexe du bilan annuel le détail de son portefeuille (*f.*), company bound to publish as a schedule to the annual balance sheet details of its investments.

toute annexe doit être épinglée à la lettre, any enclosure should be pinned to the letter.

annexer (*v.t.*), to annex ; to attach :

les documents annexés à la traite (*m.pl.*), the documents attached to the draft.

annonce (*n.f.*), announcement ; advertisement :

annonce d'une vente, announcement, advertisement, of a sale.

annonce à clef, keyed advertisement.

annonce-article [annonces-articles *pl.*] (*n.f.*), puff paragraph.

annonce classée *ou* petite annonce, classified advertisement ; small advertisement.

annonce de fantaisie *ou* annonce courante, display advertisement.

annonce de journal, newspaper advertisement.

annonce illustrée, illustrated advertisement.

annonce judiciaire, advertisement required by law.

annoncer (*v.t.*), to announce ; to advertise :

annoncer le paiement d'un coupon, to announce, to advertise, the payment of a coupon.

annoncier (pers.) (*n.m.*), advertiser.

annuaire (recueil annuel) (*n.m.*), annual ; year book :

annuaire des agents de change, stock exchange year book.

annuaire des valeurs cotées à la bourse de Paris, *the Paris equivalent of the* London stock exchange official intelligence.

annuaire (almanach indiquant l'état et le mouvement du personnel de certaines professions) (*n.m.*), directory :

annuaire des abonnés au téléphone, telephone directory.

annuel, -elle (*adj.*), annual ; yearly :

revenu annuel (*m.*), annual revenue ; yearly income.

annuellement (*adv.*), annually ; yearly.

annuitaire (*adj.*), repayable by annual (*or* by yearly) instalments :

dette annuitaire (*f.*), debt repayable by annual instalments.

annuité (*n.f.*), annuity :

annuité à vie, life annuity.

annuité contingente, contingent annuity.

annuité différée, deferred annuity.

annuité réversible, reversionary annuity.

annuité terminable, terminable annuity.

annulabilité (*n.f.*), voidableness.

annulable (*adj.*), annullable ; cancellable ; cancelable ; voidable ; avoidable ; rescindable.

annulation (*n.f.*), annulment ; cancellation ; cancelation ; avoidance ; rescission.

annulation (Comptab.) (*n.f.*), contraing ; cancellation ; reversal ; reversing.

annuler (*v.t.*), to annul ; to cancel ; to rescind ; to void ; to avoid :

annuler un contrat, to annul, to cancel, to rescind, to void, to avoid, a contract.

annuler un timbre sur un effet, to cancel a stamp on a bill.

annuler (Comptab.) (*v.t.*), to contra ; to cancel ; to reverse :

annuler une écriture par un article inverse, to contra an item by a reverse entry ; to cancel (*or* to reverse) an entry by a contra entry.

annuler une écriture d'ordre, to reverse a suspense entry.

s'annuler (Comptab.) (*v.r.*), to contra each other ; to cancel each other.

antérieur, -e (*adj.*), prior; previous; preceding:
contrat antérieur (*m.*), prior contract.
année antérieure (*f.*), previous (*or* preceding)
year. See examples under **année.**
antériorité (*n.f.*), priority:
antériorité de date d'hypothèque, priority of
date of mortgage.
anticipatif, -ive *ou* **anticipé, -e** (*adj.*), in advance;
anticipated:
versement anticipatif (*m.*), payment in advance.
fret anticipé (*m.*), anticipated freight.
anticipation (*n.f.*), anticipation; advance:
paiement par anticipation (*m.*), payment in
anticipation; payment in advance; prepayment.
anticipation (Com. et Fin.) (*n.f.*), advance:
anticipation sur consignation de marchandises,
advance on consignment of goods.
anticiper (*v.t.*), to anticipate:
anticiper un paiement de huit jours, to
anticipate a payment by a week; to make a
payment a week in advance.
anticiper (*v.i.*), to encroach:
anticiper sur ses revenus, to encroach on one's
income.
antidate (*n.f.*) (Ant.: *postdate*), antedate; antedating:
l'antidate d'un connaissement engage la
responsabilité du capitaine, the antedating
of a bill of lading pledges the responsibility
of the master.
antidater (*v.t.*), to antedate; to date back:
antidater un contrat, to antedate a contract;
to date a contract back.
antidumping (*n.m.*), antidumping.
antiprotectionniste (pers.) (*n.m.* ou *f.*), free trader;
free tradist.
antistatutaire (*adj.*), ultra vires; extra vires:
les commissaires peuvent être déclarés responsables solidairement avec les administrateurs des opérations antistatutaires qu'ils
auraient approuvés et qui auraient amené
la ruine de la société (*m.pl.*), the auditors
may be made liable jointly and severally
with the directors for acts done ultra vires
(*or* extra vires) which they may have
approved and which may have brought about
the company's ruin.
aperçu (d'une dépense) (*n.m.*), rough estimate
(of an expense).
apériteur (Assce mar.) (pers.) (*n.m.*), leading
underwriter.
aplanir des difficultés, to smooth away difficulties.
apostille (en bas d'un écrit) (*n.f.*), postscript;
footnote.
apostille (en marge d'un écrit) (*n.f.*), marginal
note; sidenote.
apostiller (en bas) (*v.t.*), to add a postscript to;
to add a footnote to:
apostiller une lettre, to add a postscript to
(*or* a footnote to) a letter.
apostiller (en marge) (*v.t.*), to make a marginal
note on; to make a sidenote on:
apostiller un acte, to make a marginal note on
a deed.

apparaître (*v.i.*), to appear; to show; to be
shown:
article qui apparaît au débit d'un compte (*m.*),
item which appears in (*or* to) the debit of
an account.
apparaux (d'un navire) (*n.m.pl.*), apparel (of
a ship).
appareil d'écoute *ou simplement* **appareil** (*n.m.*)
(Téléph.), receiver:
décrocher, raccrocher, l'appareil, to remove,
to replace, the receiver.
apparent, -e (*adj.*), apparent:
marchandises en bon état et conditionnement
apparents (*f.pl.*), goods in apparent good
order and condition.
appel (sollicitation) (*n.m.*), call; appeal; invitation:
appel de secours d'un navire en détresse, call
for help of a ship in distress.
appel de marge (Fin.), call of margin.
appel au public pour la souscription d'une
émission, d'un emprunt, invitation to the
public to subscribe to an issue, to a loan.
Cf. faire appel.
appel (*n.m.*) *ou* **appel de fonds** (Fin.), call; calling;
calling up:
faire un appel de fonds, un appel de capitaux,
to make a call, a call of capital.
versement d'appels de fonds (*m.*), payment of
calls.
appel du dernier versement d'un titre non
libéré, calling up the final instalment on a
partly paid share.
appel (Dr.) (*n.m.*), appeal:
cour d'appel (*f.*), court of appeal; appeal
court. *Cf.* faire appel.
appel téléphonique *ou simplement* **appel** (*n.m.*),
telephone call; telephonic call; call;
calling:
répondez sans retard aux appels du bureau
central, reply without delay to calls from the
exchange.
à l'appel: « Ici A. B., » on calling: " A. B.
speaking."
appelable (*adj.*), appealable.
appelant, -e (*adj.*), appellant.
appelant, -e (pers.) (*n.*), appellant.
appeler (*v.t.*), to call:
appeler l'attention sur une erreur, to' call
attention to a mistake.
appeler le bureau, l'opératrice (Téléph.), to
call the exchange, the operator.
appeler (Fin.) (*v.t.*), to call; to call up:
appeler un versement sur des titres non libérés,
to call up, to call, an instalment on partly
paid shares.
appeler (Dr.) (*v.i.*), to appeal:
appeler d'un jugement, to appeal from a
judgment.
appeler les actionnaires, to call the shareholders
together.
applicable (*adj.*), applicable; chargeable:
pertes applicables à l'année (*f.pl.*), losses
applicable to (*or* chargeable against *or* to)
the year.

application (*n.f.*), application; charging; declaration :
applications à une police d'abonnement, applications to, declarations on, a floating policy.

application (ordres de bourse) (*n.f.*), crossing; matching; marrying :
un banquier reçoit ordre de vendre 10 actions X. pour le compte d'Y. et d'en acheter 8 pour le compte de Z. : le banquier fait vendre 2 actions par son agent de change et fait l'application des 8 autres, a banker receives an order to sell 10 X. shares for Y's account and to buy 8 of them for Z's account : the banker sells 2 shares through his stockbroker and crosses (*or* matches) (*or* marries) the 8 others.

application (syndicat de garantie) (*n.f.*), calling upon the underwriters; calling on the underwriters to take up shares : (*Cf.* faire une application *and* syndicat parisien.)
l'application est le plus grand risque que comporte la prise d'une part syndicale, being called upon to take up the shares is the chief risk run in taking a share of the underwriting.
en cas de non placement du montant pris ferme par le syndicat de garantie, c'est-à-dire en cas d'application, il est attribué à chaque syndicataire une fraction du nombre de titres non placés proportionnelle au montant de son engagement syndical, if the amount taken firm by the underwriting syndicate is not placed, that is to say, if the underwriters are called on, each underwriter is allotted a fraction of the number of shares unplaced proportional to the amount of his underwriting commitment.

appliquer (*v.t.*), to apply; to charge :
appliquer à la fabrication le quantum de frais généraux qui lui incombe, to charge against the cost of manufacture the percentage of overhead expenses properly applicable thereto.
s'appliquer aux affaires, to apply oneself, to take, to business.

appoint (*n.m.*), small coin; minor coin; change; small change; odd money :
or, argent, appoint (bordereau de versement), gold, silver, small (*or* minor) coin.
pays dans lequel le pouvoir libératoire du nickel est limité à l'appoint de tant (*m.*), country in which the legal tender of nickel is limited to change for so much.
les monnaies de bronze et de nickel ne servent qu'à faire les appoints, c'est-à-dire qu'on les frappe pour de petites divisions de l'unité monétaire, qu'il était impossible de frapper en métal précieux : elles jouent le rôle de simples jetons, copper and nickel moneys are only used for making up amounts with small coin (*or* with minor coin) (*or* with small change), that is to say, they are struck for small divisions of the monetary unit which it was impossible to strike in precious metal : they are merely tokens.

appointements (*n.m.pl.*), salary :
toucher des appointements, to draw a salary.
appointements du personnel, salaries of staff; staff salaries.
il n'est aux appointements que depuis six mois, he has received a salary for the last six months only.

appointer (*v.t.*), to pay, to give, a salary to :
appointer un employé, to pay, to give, a salary to an employee.

appointement (*n.m.*), wharf.

apport (cession) (Dr.) (*n.m.*), transfer; assignment (of assets by a vendor) :
Note :—In English law, making over of tangible assets is usually referred to as a *transfer*, of intangible assets as an *assignment*, of both together as a *transfer*.
apport d'une usine, de mobilier de bureau, transfer of a works, of office furniture.
apport d'un brevet, d'une concession de mines, assignment of a patent, of a mining licence.
apport-fusion (*n.m.*), transfer and amalgamation.
apport-vente (*n.m.*), transfer and sale.
actions d'apport (*f.pl.*), vendors' shares.
capital-apports (opp. à *capital espèces*) (*n.m.*), capital issued as fully paid up otherwise than in cash (opp. to *cash capital*).

apport (biens apportés) (*n.m.*), capital or other assets brought into a business; assets transferred; assets taken over from vendor :
retirer, perdre, son apport, to withdraw, to lose, one's capital.
plus-value des apports (*f.*), appreciation of assets brought into a business.
apport en société fait à titre onéreux, assets transferred to company for a valuable consideration.
apports en nature ou en numéraire, assets in kind or money brought in (*or* taken over) (*or* transferred).

apport à la gare (Ch. de f.) (*m.*), collection (taking a parcel to the station, by the railway company) :
taxe supplémentaire pour apport à la gare (*f.*), additional charge for collection.

apporter (céder; fournir) (*v.t.*), to transfer; to assign; to bring in; to bring into (a business) :
société en liquidation qui apporte son actif à une société nouvelle (*f.*), company in liquidation which transfers its assets to a new company.
MM. A. et B. apportent conjointement (*ou* font conjointement apport) à la Société X. des biens mobiliers et immobiliers dont la désignation suit, Messrs. A. and B. transfer jointly to the X. Company the real and personal property hereinafter described.
M. X. apporte (*ou* fait apport) à la société des brevets pris ou demandés à son nom, Mr X. assigns to the company the patents taken out or applied for in his name.
le tantième de chaque associé dans les bénéfices est proportionnel à ce qu'il apporte, the interest (*or* share) of each partner in the profits is proportional to what he brings in.

apporteur, -euse (*adj.*), vendor (*used as adj.*):
société apporteuse (*f.*), vendor company.

apporteur (pers.) (*n.m.*), vendor:
actions attribuées aux apporteurs comme prix d'apport (*ou* en rémunération d'apports) (*f.pl.*), shares allotted to the vendors as purchase consideration (*or* as consideration for transfers).

apposer (*v.t.*), to affix; to put; to append; to set; to insert:
apposer un sceau, to affix a seal.
apposer un timbre sur un reçu, to affix a stamp to, to put a stamp on, a receipt.
apposer son parafe à, to put one's initials to; to initial.
endosseur qui appose sa signature sur un effet (*m.*), endorser who appends (*or* puts) (*or* sets) his signature to a bill.
apposer une clause à un contrat, to put, to insert, a clause in a contract.

apposition (*n.f.*), affixing; putting: appending; setting; insertion:
apposition d'un sceau, d'un timbre mobile, affixing a seal, an adhesive stamp.

appréciable (*adj.*), appreciable:
changements peu appréciables (*m.pl.*), hardly appreciable changes.

appréciation (évaluation) (*n.f.*), valuation; estimating the value *or* amount; estimate:
faire l'appréciation de marchandises, to make a valuation of goods.
détails influant sur l'appréciation du risque (Assce) (*m.pl.*), details influencing the valuation (*or* the estimate) of the risk.
appréciation réservée, conservative estimate.
ordre à appréciation (Bourse) (*m.*), discretionary order.

apprécier (*v.t.*), to value; to estimate the value of; to estimate:
apprécier des marchandises, to value goods.

approbation (*n.f.*), approval; approbation; confirmation:
approbation des rapports et des comptes par les actionnaires, approval of the report and accounts by the shareholders.

approuver (*v.t.*), to approve; to approve of; to confirm:
approuver un plan, une convention, to approve a plan, an agreement.
le procès-verbal de la dernière séance est lu et approuvé, the minutes of the last meeting were read and confirmed.

approvisionnement (action) (*n.m.*), supplying; storing; provisioning; stocking.

approvisionnement (provisions, choses rassemblées) (*n.m.*), supply; store; stock; provision:
approvisionnements de bord, ship's stores.

approvisionner (*v.t.*), to supply; to store; to provision; to stock:
approvisionner un navire, to supply, to provision, a ship.
approvisionner un marché en rapport avec ses besoins, to stock a market in keeping with its needs.

approximatif, -ive (*adj.*), approximate; rough:

calcul approximatif (*m.*), approximate calculation; rough reckoning.

approximation (*n.f.*), approximation; rough guess.

approximativement (*adv.*), approximately; roughly.

appui (*n.m.*), support:
pièces à l'appui d'un compte (*f.pl.*), vouchers in support of an account.

appuyer (*v.t.*), to support; to second:
appuyer un compte par des pièces justificatives, to support an account by vouchers.
appuyer une proposition, to support a proposal; to second a resolution.

après-bourse, after hours; street (*used as adj.*):
l'action X. reste après-bourse à 3 560 demandé, X. shares remained after hours (*or* in the street) at 3,560 francs bid.
cours d'après-bourse (*m.*), street price; price after hours.

après-guerre (d'), post-war:
réduire notre écrasante dette d'après-guerre, to reduce our crushing post-war debt.

apte (*adj.*), fit; capable:
navire qui n'est pas apte à faire le voyage convenu (*m.*), ship which is not fit to make (*or* capable of making) the agreed voyage.
les mineurs ne sont pas aptes à contracter (*m.pl.*), minors are not capable of contracting.

apurement (*n.m.*), agreeing; reconciliation; wiping off; getting discharge:
apurement des manifestes (Douanes), agreeing manifests.
en cas de cession, le dépôt de garantie est remboursé au cédant après apurement du compte, in case of transfer, the deposit will be repaid to the transferor after agreeing the account.

apurer (*v.t.*), to agree; to reconcile; to wipe off; to get discharged; to get cancelled:
apurer un compte, to agree, to reconcile, an account.
apurer un solde déficitaire, une dette, to wipe off a debit balance, a debt.
apurer un acquit-à-caution, to get a bond note discharged (*or* cancelled).

arbitrage (jugement amiable) (*n.m.*), arbitration:
arbitrage en cas de grèves, pour le règlement des contestations qui peuvent s'élever au sujet de l'interprétation et de l'application desdits arrangements, arbitration in case of strikes, for settlement of disputes which may arise on the subject of the interpretation or application of the said arrangements.
arbitrage de qualité, de conditionnement (Bourse de marchandises), arbitration for quality, for condition.
somme adjugée par arbitrage (*f.*), amount awarded by arbitration.

arbitrage (sentence arbitrale) (*n.m.*), award; arbitration award.

arbitrage (*n.m.*) *ou* **arbitrage de banque,** arbitrage; arbitraging; arbitration:
arbitrage sur les lettres de change, sur les matières d'or et d'argent, arbitrage (*or* arbitraging) in bills (*or* in exchange), in bullion.
arbitrage de change, arbitration (*or* arbitrage) of exchange.

arbitrage simple, simple arbitration (*or* arbitrage).

arbitrage composé, compound arbitration (*or* arbitrage).

arbitrage (*n.m.*) *ou* **arbitrage de place à place** (entre son propre pays et une ville à l'étranger) (Bourse), arbitrage ; arbitraging :

arbitrage sur des valeurs, arbitrage, arbitraging, in stocks ; stock arbitrage.

les arbitrages ont pour effet de niveler les cours sur tous les marchés du monde, arbitrage (*or* arbitraging) has as effect the levelling of prices on all the markets of the world.

arbitrage (*n.m.*) *ou* **arbitrage de place à place** (entre deux villes dans le même pays) (Bourse), shunting :

arbitrage de valeurs, shunting stocks.

arbitrage (*n.m.*) *ou* **arbitrage de portefeuille** (Bourse), hedging ; hedge ; change ; change of investments :

arbitrage à terme, arbitrages entre le comptant et le terme, hedging for the settlement, hedging between cash and settlement.

faire un arbitrage de portefeuille, de valeurs, to make a change of investments, of stocks.

arbitrage en reports (Bourse) (*m.*), jobbing in contangoes.

arbitrager *ou* **arbitrer** (Bourse) (*v.t.*), to hedge ; to change :

arbitrager (*ou* arbitrer) une valeur contre une autre, si la première est plus chère que la seconde, c'est-à-dire si à leurs cours actuels elle rapporte moins que l'autre, to hedge one stock against another (*or* to change one stock for another), if the first is dearer than the second, that is to say, if at their present prices, it yields less than the other.

arbitragiste (*adj.*), arbitrage (*used as adj.*) :

syndicat arbitragiste (*m.*), arbitrage syndicate.

arbitragiste (pers.) (*n.m.*), arbitrager ; arbitrageur ; arbitragist : arbitrage dealer.

arbitraire (*adj.*), arbitrary :

prix arbitraire (*m.*), arbitrary price.

arbitre (pers.) (*n.m.*), arbitrator ; arbiter :

toute contestation entre parties sera tranchée par des arbitres statuant en dernier ressort (*f.*), any dispute between parties to be settled by arbitrators, whose award shall be final.

arbitre amiable compositeur, friendly arbitrator.

arbitre unique, sole arbitrator.

tiers arbitre, third arbitrator ; umpire.

arbitrer (*v.t.*), to arbitrate. *Cf.* prime à arbitrer.

s'arbitrer (*v.r.*), to be arbitrated upon ; to be fixed by arbitration :

ces dommages peuvent s'arbitrer (*m.pl.*), these damages can be fixed by arbitration.

archives (*n.f.pl.*), archives :

documents conservés dans les archives (*m.pl.*), documents kept in the archives.

argent (*n.m.*) *ou* **argent métal** *ou* **métal argent** (*m.*), silver : *Note :*—The word *argent* alone meaning *money* or *cash*, besides meaning *silver*, the expression *argent métal* or *métal argent* is used when it is not clear from the context that *silver* is meant.

argent en barres, bar silver.

argent métal sans changement hier à Londres, silver without change yesterday in London.

les revenus du gouvernement des Indes sont encaissés en roupies, c'est-à-dire en métal argent : cet argent doit être converti en or, the revenues of the government of India are collected in rupees, that is to say, in silver : this silver has to be converted into gold.

argent (opp. aux monnaies d'or et aux monnaies de cuivre) (*n.m.*), silver ; silver money :

voulez-vous être payé en or, ou en argent? would you like to be paid in gold, or in silver ?

argent (toute sorte de monnaie) (*n.m.*), money ; cash ; loans :

argent ancien (opp. à *argent frais*), old money.

argent au jour le jour (Marché monétaire), day to day money (*or* loans) ; daily money ; daily loans.

argent au mois (Marché monétaire), monthly money (*or* loans) (*or* fixtures).

argent comptant *ou* argent clair *ou* argent sur table, ready money ; prompt cash ; spot cash ; cash down.

argent courant, current money.

argent de poche, pocket money.

argent frais, fresh money :

la société qui, ayant besoin d'argent frais, ne veut pas augmenter son capital, peut recourir à l'émission d'obligations, the company which, having need of fresh money, does not wish to increase its capital, can have recourse to the issue of debentures.

argent liquide *ou* argent sec *ou* argent liquide et sec, hard cash ; hard money ; dry money.

argent mort *ou* argent qui dort, dead money ; money lying idle.

argent remboursable sur demande *ou* argent à vue (Marché monétaire), money on (*or* at) call ; call money ; loans at call.

Argent (cours Argent) (cote) (Abrév. : **A.**) (opp. à *Papier*), price(s) bid (buyers).

arithméticien, -enne (pers.) (*n.*), arithmetician.

arithmétique (*adj.*), arithmetical ; arithmetic.

arithmétique (*n.f.*), arithmetic :

arithmétique mentale, mental arithmetic.

arithmétiquement (*adv.*), arithmetically.

armateur (pers.) (*n.m.*), owner ; shipowner :

Note :—The reasons for translation of the French words *propriétaire*, *armateur*, and *fréteur*, by the single English word *owner* (or *shipowner*) are the following :—

In French law and practice the person concerned with the ship is considered in three qualities, viz. :

(1) As the actual proprietor of the ship. In this case he is known as the *propriétaire*.

(2) As the person who mans, equips, and supplies the ship, when he is known as the *armateur*, or if he owns her as well, as the **armateur-propriétaire**.

(3) As the person letting out a contract of affreightment (charter or bill of lading), when he is still known as the *armateur*, or less commonly, as the *fréteur*.

The uniformity of expression in English, viz., *owner*, is due to the fact that in English law and practice the person presented in any of these three qualities is considered for the time being as the owner, and the possession of the ship is considered for the time as being vested in him.

In England the position and duties of the *armateur* are usually discharged by the ship's *managers*, so that, according to circumstances or context the word *armateur* may have to be translated as *owner or his manager or agent*, as for instance in the translation of an Act of Parliament, or the like, or by one or both of the words *manager or/and agent*, as for instance in the translation of the sentence *le propriétaire du navire ou son armateur loue au chargeur, the shipowner or his manager (or/and agent) lets to the shipper*.

In the large majority of cases, however, *owner* will be found to be the correct and sufficient translation of *armateur*.

l'obligation pour l'armateur de fournir un navire en bon état de navigabilité et approprié au transport de la cargaison (*f.*), the obligation of the owner (*or* shipowner) to provide a seaworthy vessel fit to carry the cargo.

un contrat d'affrètement unit un armateur et un chargeur, a contract of affreightment conjoins an owner and a shipper.

l'armateur est souvent propriétaire du navire ; mais son rôle essentiel est d'armer le navire, qu'il en soit propriétaire ou locataire, the *armateur* is often the owner (*or* proprietor) of the ship ; but his essential function is to man, equip, and supply the ship, be he proprietor or hirer.

Cf. examples under **propriétaire**.

armateur-affréteur [armateurs-affréteurs *pl.*] (*n.m.*), owner-charterer.

armateur-gérant [armateurs-gérants *pl.*] *ou* armateur-titulaire [armateurs-titulaires *pl.*] (*n.m.*), managing owner.

armateur-individu *ou* armateur individuel, individual shipowner (as distinguished from a shipping company).

armement (mise en exploitation d'un navire) (*n.m.*), manning, equipping, and supplying ; manning and supplying ; fitting out ; manning. See examples under **armer** (*v.t.*).

armement (commerce des armateurs ; l'industrie maritime dans son ensemble) (*n.m.*), shipping business (*or* trade) (*or* industry) ; shipowning business ; shipping :

mesures prises pour encourager l'armement national (*f.pl.*), steps taken to encourage the national shipping business (*or* to encourage national shipping).

étudier ce qui peut être fait pour parer à la crise de l'armement, to consider what can be done to meet the crisis in the shipping trade (*or* to meet the shipping crisis).

armement (les armateurs, la masse des armateurs ; la maison de commerce qui arme un navire) (*n.m.*), owners ; shipowners :

les difficultés que rencontrent l'armement (*f.pl.*), the difficulties encountered by owners (*or* by shipowners).

l'affréteur est une personne qui contracte avec l'armement, a charterer is a person who contracts with the owners (*or* the shipowners).

l'armement est tenu de remettre le connaissement au titulaire du reçu provisoire, the owners (*or* the shipowners) are bound to hand the bill of lading to the holder of the mate's receipt.

armement (équipement) (*n.m.*), equipment :
cote donnant les qualités de la coque et de l'armement (*f.*), character giving the qualities of the hull and of the equipment.

armement (appareil de guerre) (*n.m.*), ordnance.

armer (*v.t.*), to man, equip, and supply ; to man and supply ; to equip ; to fit out ; to man :
armer un navire *ou* armer et équiper un navire, to man, equip, and supply a ship.
Note :—The word *équiper* is really not necessary in the French phrase, but is often used.
l'armateur arme le navire, c'est-à-dire le met en état d'entreprendre un voyage, en le munissant de tout ce qui est nécessaire : capitaine, équipage, provisions de bouche, combustibles, the owner mans and supplies the ship, that is to say, puts her in a state to set out on a voyage, by providing her with all that is necessary : master, crew, victuals, fuel.
bateaux armés au cabotage, armés pour la pêche (*m.pl.*), boats equipped for the coasting trade, equipped for fishing.
construire et armer un navire, to build and fit out a ship.
armer un canot, to man a boat.

arracher de l'argent à quelqu'un, to extract, to extort, money from someone ; to get, to squeeze, some money out of someone.

arracher une feuille d'un livre, to tear a leaf out of a book.

arraisonnement (Douanes) (*n.m.*), visiting ; visit.

arraisonner (*v.t.*), to visit :
agents des douanes qui arraisonnent un navire dans la rade (*m.pl.*), customs officers who visit a ship in the roads.

arrangement (*n.m.*), arrangement ; settlement :
faire un arrangement avec quelqu'un, to make an arrangement with someone.
arrangement d'un différend, settlement of a difference (*or* a dispute).

arranger (*v.t.*), to arrange ; to settle :
arranger ses papiers, to arrange one's papers.
arranger une affaire, to arrange, to settle, a matter.

arrérager (*v.i.*), to get into arrears ; to fall into arrear.

arrérages (*n.m.pl.*), interest :
Note :—*arrérages* is usually said of rentes, Government stocks, Treasury bonds, or the like. Cf. **intérêt** and see **jouissance**.
les arrérages de la dette nationale, the interest on the national debt.

les rentes au porteur ont un coupon d'arrérages joint au titre, qui est détaché chaque fois que les arrérages sont payés (*f.pl.*), bearer rentes have an interest coupon attached to the certificate, which is cut off each time interest is paid.

arrêt (cessation) (*n.m.*), stoppage; stopping; stop; suspension; break; standstill; hitch:
arrêt des affaires, stoppage of business.
un point d'arrêt pour les paquebots, a stopping point for passenger ships.
les arrêts d'un train aux stations, the stops of a train at stations.
arrêt en cours de route (Ch. de f., etc.), break of journey.

arrêt (Dr.) (*n.m.*), judgment; decree: (Cf. **jugement.**)
arrêt de la cour d'appel, de la Cour de cassation, judgment of the court of appeal, of the Court of Cassation.

arrêt (Dr. internat.) (*n.m.*), arrest:
arrêts de princes, de gouvernants, d'une puissance étrangère, arrests of princes, of rulers, of a foreign power.

arrêté (Comptab.) (*n.m.*), making up; closing; ruling off; rest:
arrêté de la caisse, making up the cash (balancing up).
la date de l'arrêté de la balance de vérification, the date of the making up of the trial balance.
la date de l'arrêté du compte courant, the date of the rest (*or* of the making up) of the current account.
arrêtés semestriels, half yearly rests.

arrêté (*n.m.*) *ou* **arrêté d'assurance** *ou* **arrêté provisoire** (Assce mar.), cover note; covering note; cover; memorandum of insurance; insurance note; provisional note.

arrêté de compte (*m.*), account settled; account stated.

arrêter (*v.t.*). See examples:
arrêter le paiement d'un chèque, to stop payment of a cheque.
arrêter les affaires, to stop business.
arrêter les services de quelqu'un, to retain someone's services.
arrêter un compte au 30 juin, ses comptes une fois l'an, tous les six mois, to close, to make up, to rule off, an account at the 30th June, one's accounts once a year, every six months.
les comptes sont arrêtés le 30 juin et le 31 décembre de chaque année (*m.pl.*), the accounts are made up at (*or* on) the 30th June and 31st December in (*or* of) each year.
arrêter un marché, to close (*or* to conclude) a bargain.
arrêter un prix, to agree upon a price.
arrêter une filière (Bourse de marchandises), to end a string.
navire qui est arrêté en voyage par ordre d'une puissance étrangère (*m.*), ship which is arrested on the voyage by order of a foreign power.

arrêteur (*n.m.*) *ou* **arrêteur de la filière** (pers.) (Bourse de marchandises), last buyer; receiver.

arrhement (*n.m.*), payment of a deposit; leaving a deposit; giving an earnest.

arrher (*v.t.*), to pay a deposit on *or* to; to leave a deposit on *or* with; to give an earnest for *or* to:
arrher des marchandises, to pay a deposit on, to leave a deposit on, to give an earnest for, goods.
arrher son propriétaire, to pay a deposit to, to leave a deposit with, to give an earnest to, one's landlord.

arrhes (*n.f.pl.*), deposit; earnest; earnest money:
promesse de vendre faite avec des arrhes (*f.*), promise of sale made with deposit (*or* with earnest) (*or* with earnest money).

arrière (**en**), in arrear; in arrears; behindhand:
être en arrière pour ses loyers, to be in arrear, to be behindhand, with one's rent.

arriéré, -e (*adj.*), overdue; outstanding; owing; back; in arrear; in arrears; behindhand:
paiement arriéré (*m.*), overdue payment; outstanding payment.
loyer arriéré (*m.*), back rent; rent in arrear; rent owing.

arriéré (*n.m.*), arrears:
arriéré de loyer, de travail, arrears of rent, of work.

arriérer (*v.t.*), to put off; to defer; to hold over:
arriérer un paiement, to put off, to defer, to hold over, a payment.

s'arriérer (*v.r.*), to get into arrears.

arrimage (*n.m.*), stowing; stowage; trimming; stevedoring:
avec les marchandises légères la perte à l'arrimage est considérable, with measurement goods the loss of stowage (room) is considerable.

arrimer (*v.t.*), to stow; to trim:
arrimer les marchandises à bord, c'est-à-dire les disposer méthodiquement dans la cale, to stow the goods on board, that is to say, to arrange them methodically in the hold.
les fûts doivent être arrimés en longueur (*m.pl.*), casks should be stowed lengthwise.
on ne doit pas arrimer les fûts bouge sur bouge; ce serait un vice d'arrimage, casks should not be stowed bilge on bilge (*or* bulge on bulge); that would be bad stowage.
arrimer le charbon dans les soutes, to trim the coal in the bunkers.

arrimeur (pers.) (*n.m.*), stower; stevedore.

arrivage (*n.m.*), arrival:
arrivage de marchandises, d'un stock d'or australien, arrival of goods, of a stock of Australian gold.
arrivages et départs (de navires), arrivals and sailings.

arrivée (*n.f.*), arrival:
arrivée de la nouvelle récolte, arrival of the new crop.
arrivée d'un train, du navire avec sa cargaison au port de destination, arrival of a train, of the ship with her cargo at the port of destination.
arrivées et départs (de navires), arrivals and sailings.

à l'arrivée *ou* **d'arrivée** (opp. à *au départ* ou
de départ), incoming :
courrier à l'arrivée (*m.*), incoming mail.
communication d'arrivée (Téléph.) (*f.*), incoming call.

arriver (*v.i.*), to arrive :
marchandises arrivant par mer de l'étranger
(*f.pl.*), goods arriving by sea from abroad.
arriver à bon port, to arrive safely :
que le navire arrive à bon port ou se perde
pendant le voyage, whether the ship arrives
safely or is lost on the voyage.
(*steamer*) X. arrivé à Marseille le 31 (*date*), de
Batavia (Mouvement des Navires), (*steamer*)
X., from Batavia, arrived (*or* arrd) (*or* a.)
Marseilles 31 (*date*) (Shipping News).

arriver à un concordat avec ses créanciers, to
compound with one's creditors.

arrondir (*v.t.*), to round up :
taxe arrondie au décime supérieur (*f.*), charge
rounded up to the next higher *décime ;*
fractions of a penny charged as a penny.

article (objet de commerce) (*n.m.*), article ;
requisite ; commodity :
article de marchandise, de bagage, article of
merchandise, of luggage (*or* of baggage).
articles de papeterie, articles of stationery.
articles de voyage, travel requisites.
reprise des cours de l'article (café, par exemple)
(*f.*), recovery in the prices of the commodity
(coffee, for example).
articles de messagerie, parcels ; parcels and
other merchandise by passenger train,
passenger boat, or aeroplane :
articles de messagerie et marchandises,
parcels and goods.

article (division) (*n.m.*) (Abrév. : **art.**), article ;
clause ; section :
articles d'une convention, d'un traité, articles,
clauses, of an agreement, of a treaty.
articles d'un connaissement, d'une police
d'assurance, des statuts d'une société,
clauses of a bill of lading, of an insurance
policy, of the articles of association of a
company.
articles d'une loi, sections of an act :
en vertu des articles — et — de la loi sur
les sociétés, in pursuance of sections —
and — of the companies act.
un article de journal, un article de fond, un
article financier, a newspaper article, a
leading article, a financial article.

article (Comptab.) (*n.m.*), item ; entry : (See
also **écriture.**)
les articles inscrits sur le journal, the items
entered in the journal ; the entries made in
the journal.
un article de dépense dans un compte, an item
of expense in an account.
article borgne, blind entry.
article collectif *ou* article récapitulatif *ou*
article composé (article de journal), combined
entry ; compound entry.
article d'inventaire, closing entry.
article d'ouverture, opening entry ; starting
entry.

article de caisse, cash item.
article de journal, journal entry.
article de redressement *ou* article rectificatif,
correcting entry.
article de virement *ou* article de contre-passement, transfer entry.
article inverse *ou* article de contre-passement,
reverse entry ; reversing entry ; contra
entry.

artillerie (*n.f.*), artillery.

assainir un bilan, to clean up a balance sheet
(to eliminate bad debts, or the like).

assemblée (*n.f.*) (Abrév. : **ass.**), meeting ;
assembly :
assemblée d'actionnaires, meeting of shareholders ; shareholders' meeting.
assemblée de créanciers, meeting of creditors ;
creditors' meeting.
assemblée générale ordinaire, ordinary general
meeting.
assemblée générale ordinaire annuelle, annual
ordinary general meeting.
assemblée générale extraordinaire, extraordinary general meeting.
assemblée constitutive, in France, an *assemblée
constitutive* (a general meeting of shareholders akin to the statutory meeting in
England) must be held to receive and adopt
the *déclaration notariée de souscription et de
versement* (notaire's attestation that the
capital has been subscribed and amount
required by law paid up), to appoint directors
and auditors, and to approve the articles
of association. If assets in kind have been
taken over from vendors, a *deuxième
assemblée constitutive* has to be held. In this
case the first meeting receives the *déclaration
notariée* above referred to and nominates
commissaires aux apports (auditors appointed
to verify the vendors' transfers), and the
second meeting receives the *rapport du
commissaire aux apports*, appoints directors
and auditors, and approves the articles.
The company is not definitely formed
(*constituée*), nor can it commence business
until one or both of these meetings have
been held. Until such time it is described
as a *société en formation.*

assembler (convoquer ; réunir) (*v.t.*), to call
together ; to summon ; to assemble :
assembler les actionnaires, to call the shareholders together.

s'assembler (*v.r.*), to meet ; to assemble :
s'assembler à des jours certains, to meet on
certain days.

asseoir (*v.t.*), to base ; to fix ; to establish :
asseoir l'impôt sur le revenu, to base taxation
on income.
la taxe est assise sur le capital de la créance,
the tax is based on the capital of the debt.
le gouvernement a assis l'impôt sur le revenu à
tant pour cent, the government has fixed
the income tax at so many shillings in the
pound.
asseoir le crédit public, to establish public
credit.

situation financière bien assise (*f.*), strong financial position.

être assis(-e) sur (être gagé sur), to be secured on : hypothèque qui est assise sur des biens (*f.*), mortgage which is secured on property.

assermenté, -e (*adj.*), sworn : traducteur assermenté (*m.*), sworn translator.

assermenter (*v.t.*), to swear ; to swear in : assermenter un témoin, to swear a witness.

assesseur (pers.) (*n.m.*), assessor.

assiette (*n.f.*), basis : assiette d'une hypothèque, de l'impôt, de la contribution foncière, basis of a mortgage, of assessment (*or* of taxation), of contribution (*to taxation*) by landed property.

banque qui a une assiette solide (*f.*), bank which has a firm basis.

assignation sur ses biens présents et à venir (*f.*), charge on one's property present and future.

assis, -e (*p.p. & adj.*). See **asseoir**.

assistance (aide) (*n.f.*), assistance ; aid ; help : l'assistance en mer est le secours prêté par un navire à un autre navire en cas de danger ; le danger est une condition essentielle de l'assistance ; en l'absence de danger, il y a non pas assistance, mais remorquage, assistance at sea is the help given by one ship to another ship in case of danger ; danger is an essential condition of assistance ; in the absence of danger, it is not assistance, but towage.

assistance (réunion de personnes) (*n.f.*), attendance : il y avait une nombreuse assistance à l'assemblée générale, there was a good attendance at the general meeting.

assistants (les) (personnes assemblées dans un même lieu) (*n.m.pl.*), those present : les assistants à l'assemblée générale, those present at the general meeting.

assister (*v.t.*), to assist ; to aid ; to help : assister un navire en détresse, to assist a ship in distress.

assister à, to be present at ; to attend : assister à une assemblée d'actionnaires, à un conseil des administrateurs, to be present at, to attend, a shareholders' meeting, a board meeting.

association (*n.f.*), association ; society ; partnership : (*Note :*—In France, the word *association* in the legal sense now means an *association not for profit*, and is opposed to *société*, a company for the acquisition of gain.)

association d'obligataires, debenture holders' association.

association de cautionnement mutuel, mutual guarantee society.

association des voyageurs de commerce, commercial travellers' association (*or* society).

association commerciale en participation *ou simplement* association en participation, particular partnership ; special partnership. (Strictly, *association* in this case is wrong, but the word still persists : *société en participation* is the correct term.)

associé, -e (pers.) (*n.*), partner ; member ; member of the firm (*or* of the company) : associé (-e) en nom collectif *ou simplement* associé, -e (d'une société en nom collectif), partner (in a partnership or firm).

associé d'une maison de banque, partner in a bank.

associé commanditaire, sleeping partner ; dormant partner ; silent partner ; secret partner. See note under **commanditaire**.

associé commandité, (in France) an active and responsible partner in a **commandite**. See this word in vocabulary.

l'actionnaire est un associé, l'obligataire est un créancier prêteur de la société (*m.*), a shareholder is a member of the company, a debenture holder is a lending creditor of the company.

commissaire qui est aussi associé (*m.*), auditor who is also a member of the company.

assujéti (-e) à (être) *ou* **assujetti (-e) à (être)**, to be subject to ; to be liable to (*or* for) : les lettres de change sont assujetties au droit de timbre (*f.pl.*), bills of exchange are subject to (*or* are liable to) stamp duty.

personne assujettie à l'impôt (*f.*), person liable for tax.

assurable (*adj.*), insurable ; assurable : théoriquement tout risque est assurable, theoretically every risk is insurable.

assurance (*n.f.*), insurance ; assurance : (*Note :*— The words *assurance, assure,* etc., are the older forms of *insurance, insure,* etc., and are now used only, but not exclusively, for life and marine insurance.)

l'assurance d'un chargement est faite sur le fondement du connaissement qui le constate, the insurance of a cargo is made on the foundation of the bill of lading which evidences it.

assurance de la prime, insurance of premium.

assurance à prime *ou* assurance à prime fixe (opp. à *assurance mutuelle*), proprietary insurance (*or* assurance).

assurance à prime liée (*ou* à primes liées) *ou* assurance pour l'aller et le retour, round voyage insurance.

assurance à temps *ou* assurance à terme, time insurance.

assurance accidents aux tiers, third party accident insurance.

assurance au voyage, voyage insurance.

assurance contre l'incendie *ou* assurance contre le feu, fire insurance.

assurance contre la maladie, sickness insurance.

assurance contre le bris de glaces, plate glass insurance.

assurance contre le chômage, unemployment insurance.

assurance contre le risque professionnel, professional risks indemnity insurance.

assurance contre le vol, burglary insurance.

assurance contre les accidents (*ou* contre les accidents corporels), accident insurance ; personal accident insurance.

assurance contre les accidents du travail, workmen's compensation insurance; employers' liability insurance; employers' indemnity insurance.

assurance contre les risques de remboursement au pair, insurance against risks of redemption at par.

assurance cumulative *ou* double assurance, double insurance:
assuré qui est surassuré par assurances cumulatives (*m.*), assured who is over-insured by double insurance.

assurance d'abonnement *ou* assurance flottante (Assce mar.), floating policy insurance.

assurance de cautionnement *ou* assurance de garantie, guarantee insurance.

assurance de crédit, credit insurance.

assurance de responsabilité civile, public liability insurance; third party insurance.

assurance des véhicules automobiles, motor car insurance; motor insurance.

assurance distincte, separate insurance. See example under **distinct, -e.**

assurance en cas de décès *ou* assurance pour la vie entière, whole life insurance.

assurance en cas de vie *ou* assurance à capital différé *ou* assurance à rente différée, endowment insurance.

assurance in quovis *ou* assurance in quo vis *ou* assurance par navire à désigner *ou* assurance sur navire indéterminé, insurance, steamer or steamers to be declared (floating policy insurance).

assurance industrielle *ou* assurance ouvrière, industrial insurance.

assurance maritime, marine insurance (*or* assurance); maritime insurance (*or* assurance); sea insurance (*or* assurance).

assurance mutuelle, mutual insurance; mutual assurance.

assurance pour le compte de qui il appartiendra *ou* assurance pour compte de tiers *ou* assurance pour compte, insurance for account of whom it may concern.

assurance provisoire, provisional insurance.

assurance supplémentaire, additional insurance.

assurance sur bonne arrivée (Assce mar.), insurance subject to safe arrival.

assurance sur corps *ou* assurance sur (*ou* du) navire, hull insurance; insurance on hull; insurance on (*or* of) ship.

assurance sur facultés *ou* assurance sur (*ou* des) marchandises, cargo insurance; insurance on cargo; insurance on (*or* of) goods (*or* merchandise).

assurance sur fret *ou* assurance du fret, freight insurance; insurance of (*or* on) freight.

assurance sur la fidélité du personnel, fidelity insurance.

assurance sur la vie, life insurance; life assurance.

assurance terrestre (opp. à *assurance maritime*), non marine insurance.

Note :—Any of the above expressions containing the words *contre* or *sur* or *sur la* can be shortened by omitting these words

and substituting a hyphen; thus, **assurance-incendie [assurances-incendie** *pl.*]; **assurance-facultées [assurances-facultés** *pl.*], **assurance-vie [assurances-vie** *pl.*], and so on.

assuré, -e (pers.) (*n.*), insured; assured; insurεe:
la prime est la rémunération due par l'assuré à l'assureur, the premium is the remuneration due by the insured to the insurer.

assurer (rendre sûr) (*v.t.*), to insure; to ensure:
assurer l'exécution d'un marché, le salut d'une expédition maritime, to insure, to ensure, the carrying out of a bargain, the safety of a marine adventure.

assurer (garantir) (*v.t.*), to guarantee:
assurer une créance, to guarantee a debt.

assurer (Assce) (*v.t.*), to insure; to assure; to make insurance of:
assurer son mobilier, la cargaison d'un navire, to insure one's furniture, a ship's cargo.
compagnie qui assure une maison contre le risque d'incendie (*f.*), company which insures a house against the risk of fire.

s'assurer (*v.r.*) (Assce), to insure; to assure; to be insured *or* assured:
s'assurer contre l'incendie, contre les risques dont on est responsable, contre le recours des tiers, to insure against fire, against the risks for which one is liable, against a third party claim.
ces titres ne s'assurent pas puisqu'ils sont nominatifs (*m.pl.*), these certificates are not insured because they are registered.

assureur (pers.) (*n.m.*), insurer; assurer; underwriter: (*Note :*—*underwriter* is the more specific and professional term, *insurer* the looser and wider term, but they both mean the same.)
en cas d'assurance partielle, l'assuré est réputé être son propre assureur pour l'excédent, in case of partial insurance, the insured is deemed to be his own insurer for the excess. (*Note :*—Here, for instance, it would be inadvisable to use the word *underwriter*.)
les assureurs du Lloyd, Lloyd's underwriters. (*Note :*—Here, and in the remaining examples, it would be inadvisable to use the word *insurer*.)
assureur contre l'incendie, fire underwriter.
assureur maritime, marine underwriter.
assureur sur corps, hull underwriter.
assureur sur facultés, cargo underwriter.
assureur terrestre, non marine underwriter.

atermoyer (*v.t.*), to defer, to postpone, to put off, payment of:
payer le capital et atermoyer les intérêts, to pay off the capital and defer payment of the interest.

s'atermoyer (*v.r.*), to come to an arrangement with one's creditors; to obtain an extension of time for payment.

atonie (d'un marché, des affaires) (*n.f.*), dulness, dullness, stagnation (of a market, of business).

attache (de bureau) (*n.f.*), paper fastener; paper clip.

attaché (pers.) (*n.m.*), attaché:
attaché commercial, commercial attaché.

attaché (être) (en parlant d'un navire), to belong :
tout navire doit être attaché à un port, appelé le port d'attache (*ou* port d'immatriculation), every ship must belong to a port, called the port of registry.

attaque du découvert *ou* **attaque de** (*ou* **des) baissiers** (Bourse) (*f.*), bear raid :
une vive attaque des baissiers sur X., provoquée par la nouvelle que cette entreprise avait réduit sa production, fait fléchir cette valeur, entraînant l'ensemble de la cote, a hot bear raid on X., aroused by the news that this concern had reduced its output, caused this stock to give way, carrying with it the whole of the list.

attaquer (arguer d'erreur, de fausseté) (*v.t.*), to attack ; to assail ; to impugn :
attaquer un contrat, to attack, to impugn, a contract.

attaquer quelqu'un en justice, to bring an action against someone.

atteindre (*v.t.*), to reach ; to attain :
atteindre un prix élevé, le but de son voyage, to reach a high price, the end of one's journey.

attendre (*v.t.*), to wait for ; to expect :
attendre le train, le facteur, le moment favorable, to wait for the train, the postman, the favourable moment.
navires attendus à Anvers (*m.pl.*), ships expected at Antwerp.

atténuer une perte, to minimize a loss.

atterrir (*v.i.*), to land.

atterrissage (*n.m.*), landing :
port d'atterrissage d'un navire (*m.*), port of landing of a ship.
atterrissage forcé d'un aéroplane, forced landing of an aeroplane.

attester (*v.t.*), to attest :
attester un fait, to attest a fact.

attirer (*v.t.*), to attract ; to draw :
être attiré (-e) par de gros bénéfices, to be attracted by big profits.
attirer l'attention, to attract attention.
attirer l'attention sur un fait, to draw attention to a fact.
attirer les capitaux, to attract capital.

attitré, -e (*adj.*), certified ; accredited ; official ; recognized :
courtier attitré (*m.*), certified broker ; accredited broker ; official broker.
commerçant attitré (*m.*), recognized merchant.

attribuable (*adj.*), allottable.

attribuer (*v.t.*), to appropriate ; to allot :
attribuer des actions à un souscripteur, to allot shares to an applicant.
attribuer intégralement les actions, to allot the shares in full.
nous avons l'honneur de vous informer que sur votre souscription à tant d'actions de la Compagnie X., pour laquelle vous avez versé tant, il vous a été attribué tant d'actions qui, à raison de tant pour le montant des versements de souscription et de répartition, exigent un versement de tant, soit une différence de tant, que vous voudrez bien

verser à . . ., in response to your application, you have been allotted so many shares of the X. Company. The amount payable on application and allotment is so much, you have already paid so much, making amount due from you on allotment so much. Payment of the amount due from you should be made to . . .
le quart des bénéfices excédant 4 0/0 sur le capital de la banque, est attribué a l'État, a quarter of the profits in excess of 4% on the bank's capital, is allotted to the State.

attributaire (pers.) (*n.m.* ou *f.*), allottee.

attribution (*n.f.*), appropriation ; allotment :
attribution des bénéfices à la réserve, appropriation of profits to reserve.
attribution aux fondateurs de tant d'actions entièrement libérées, allotment to the founders of so many fully paid shares.

au-dessous de, below :
au-dessous de la moyenne, below the average.

au-dessus de, above :
au-dessus du pair, above par.

au fur et à mesure des besoins, as required ; as and when required :
conseil d'administration autorisé à emprunter une somme de 10 millions, au fur et à mesure des besoins (*m.*), board authorized to borrow a sum of 10 million francs as required (*or* as and when required).

Au Parquet. See *note under* marché des valeurs.

au port et en mer, in port and at sea.

aubaine (*n.f.*), windfall.

audition (*n.f.*), hearing :
audition d'un appel, hearing of an appeal.

augmentation (*n.f.*), increase ; augmentation ; rise ; advance ; enhancement :
augmentation de prix *ou simplement* augmentation, increase in price ; advance in price ; rise in price ; enhancement of price.
augmentation de capital, increase of capital.
augmentation de valeur, increase of (*or* in) value.
augmentation de poids résultant d'avaries de mer, increase in weight resulting from sea damage.

augmentation (élévation d'un salaire, d'un traitement) (*n.f.*), rise ; increase.

augmenter (*v.t.*), to increase ; to augment ; to raise ; to advance ; to enhance :
augmenter le prix, to increase, to raise, to advance, to enhance, the price.

augmenter (ajouter au traitement) (*v.t.*), to raise the salary of ; to give a rise to ; to increase the wages of :
augmenter un commis, to raise a clerk's salary ; to give a rise to a clerk.

augmenter (*v.i.*), to increase ; to augment ; to rise ; to advance ; to enhance :
augmenter de prix, to increase, to rise, to advance, to enhance, in price.

s'augmenter (*v.r.*), to increase ; to augment ; to rise ; to advance ; to enhance.

aussi près qu'il pourra en atteindre en sécurité, toujours à flot *ou* **aussi près qu'il pourra s'en approcher en sûreté (***ou* **s'en approcher sans**

danger) **étant toujours en flot** ou **aussi près de là qu'il pourra approcher en sécurité, le navire restant à flot** (charte-partie), so near thereunto as she can safely get, always afloat.

aussi vite que le vapeur pourra délivrer d'après les usages de place, as fast as steamer can deliver according to the custom of the port.

authentiquer (v.t.), to authenticate; to certify; to legalize:
authentiquer un acte, to authenticate, to legalize, a document.
Cf. acte authentique, *under* **acte**.

autobus (n.m.), motor bus; motor omnibus.

autocar (n.m.), charabanc.

automobile (n.m. ou f.) ou par abrév. **auto** (n.m. ou f.), motor car; motor; car; automobile.

automobiles (n.f.pl.) ou **valeurs d'automobiles** (f.pl.), motors; motor shares.

automobilisme (n.m.), motoring.

automobiliste (pers.) (n.m. ou f.), motorist.

autorisation (n.f.), authorization; leave:
autorisation de s'absenter, leave of absence.

autorisation de remboursement (Caisse d'épargne) (f.), withdrawal warrant.

autorisé, -e (adj.), authorized:
la circulation autorisée des billets d'une banque, the authorized note circulation of a bank.

autoriser (v.t.), to authorize.

autorité (puissance légitime) (n.f.), authority:
l'autorité des lois, d'un directeur, the authority of the laws, of a manager.

autorité (représentant de la puissance publique) (n.f.), authority:
autorité sanitaire du port, port sanitary authority.

aux pleines conditions (Assce mar.) (opp. à *franc d'avarie particulière*), with particular average; with average.

aux soins de, care of; c/o.:
M. A., aux soins de M. B., Mr A., care of (or, and usually, c/o.) Mr B.

auxiliaire (Comptab.) (adj.), subsidiary:
livres auxiliaires (m.pl.), subsidiary books.

aval [**avals** pl.] (n.m.), guarantee; guaranty; backing (bills of exchange).

bon pour aval ou **pour aval.** See under **bon pour.**

aval de change (m.), exchange contract.

avaler un bouillon, to make a bad spec.

avaliser ou **avaler** (v.t.), to guarantee; to back:
donneur de caution qui s'engage à avaliser (ou à avaler) un effet (m.), surety who undertakes to guarantee (or to back) a bill.

avaliste (pers.) (n.m.), guarantor; surety; guarantee; backer.

avance (n.f.), advance; loan:
avance d'argent ou avance de fonds, advance, loan, of money.
avances à découvert ou avances sur notoriété, unsecured advances; loans without security.
avance à découvert (Banq.), overdraft.
avances à l'équipage sur gages, advances to crew on wages.
avance de fret, advance of freight.
avance en compte courant, advance on current account.

avances garanties ou avances contre garanties, secured advances; loans against security.
avances sur documents, advances on documents.
avances sur un contrat, sur consignation de marchandises, advances on a contract, on consignment of goods.
avances sur valeurs ou avances sur titres, advances on securities; loans on stocks.
vive avance de l'action X. (Bourse), sharp advance of X. shares.

en avance ou **d'avance** ou **à l'avance** ou **par avance,** in advance:
payer d'avance ou payer par avance, to pay in advance; to prepay.
loyer payé d'avance ou *simplement* loyer d'avance (m.), rent paid in advance; rent in advance; rent prepaid.

avancer (v.t.), to advance:
avancer de l'argent à des employés, to advance money to employees.

s'avancer (v.r.), to advance:
l'action X. s'avance de 2 075 à 2 095, X. shares advanced from 2,075 to 2,095 francs.

avant-bourse, before hours. Cf. **après-bourse.**

avant-guerre (d'), pre-war:
chiffres d'avant-guerre (m.pl.), pre-war figures.

avant-port [**avant-ports** pl.] (n.m.), outer port; outer harbour.

avant-veille [**avant-veilles** pl.] (n.f.), two days before.

avantage (n.m.), advantage; benefit.

avarie (n.f.) ou **avaries** (n.f.pl.) (détérioration; dégât), damage; injury:
répondre des avaries occasionnées par la pluie, par les rats, par eau de mer, to be liable for damage caused by rain, by rats, by sea water.
avaries apparentes, apparent damage (to the contents of a parcel).
avaries de mer (*Abrév.*: A7), sea damage.
avaries de route, damage in transit.
avaries occultes, hidden damage (to the contents of a package).

avarie (n.f.) ou **avaries** (n.f.pl.) (Dr. mar.), average:
ne sont pas admis en avarie les loyers et la nourriture de l'équipage, wages and maintenance of the crew not admissible in average.
les avaries seront remboursables sur chaque évaluation, qu'il s'agisse d'avaries particulières ou d'avaries communes, average payable on each valuation, whether the average be particular or general.
navire en état d'avarie (m.), ship under average.
avarie commune ou avaries communes (*Abrév.*: a.c.) ou avarie grosse ou avaries grosses ou grosses avaries, general average; gross average.
avarie-dommage (n.f.) ou avaries matérielles (opp. à *avarie-frais*), average damage.
avarie-frais (n.f.) ou avaries en frais, average expenses.
avarie particulière ou avaries particulières (*Abrév.*: a.p.) ou avarie simple ou avaries simples, particular average; common average; ordinary average.

avarie (*n.f.*) *ou* **avaries** (*n.f.pl.*) (contribution accessoire aux frais de navigation), average :
avaries et chapeau, primage and average.
avarié, -e (*adj.*), damaged ; injured :
marchandises avariées (*f.pl.*), damaged goods.
avarier (*v.t.*), to damage ; to injure :
contenu d'une caisse légèrement avarié d'eau de mer (*m.*), contents of a case slightly damaged by sea water.
supposons qu'au lieu d'être perdues, les marchandises soient simplement avariées, suppose that instead of being lost, the goods are simply damaged.
avec avarie particulière (Assce mar.) (opp. à *franc d'avarie particulière*), with particular average ; with average.
avec droit (Abrév. : **av.-dt**) (opp. à *ex-droit*), with rights ; cum rights ; cum new :
titres avec droit (*m.pl.*), shares with rights ; stocks cum rights (*or* cum new).
avenant (Assce) (*n.m.*), endorsement :
les changements survenus dans le risque font obligatoirement l'objet d'avenants, ou de nouvelles polices, faute de quoi l'assuré peut être déchu de ses droits, changes occurring in the risk necessarily form the subject of endorsements or of new policies, failing which the insured may forfeit his rights.
avenant d'aliment (Assce d'abonnement), endorsement of interest declared.
avenant d'application *ou* avenant de déclaration (Assce in quovis), endorsement of interest declared.
aventure (*n.f.*), adventure ; venture ; risk :
aventure maritime licite, lawful marine adventure.
danger commun menaçant de perte l'aventure (*m.*), common danger threatening the adventure with loss.
aventurer (*v.t.*), to adventure ; to venture ; to risk :
aventurer sa fortune dans une entreprise, to risk one's fortune in an enterprise.
avertir (*v.t.*), to notify ; to warn.
avertissement (*n.m.*), notice ; notification ; warning.
avertissement (Impôts cédulaires) (*n.m.*), notice of assessment.
aviateur (pers.) (*n.m.*), aviator ; airman ; aeronaut.
aviation (*n.f.*), aviation ; aerial navigation ; air navigation ; flying.
avilir (*v.t.*), to depreciate.
s'avilir (*v.r.*), to depreciate :
les marchandises périssables s'avilissent rapidement (*f.pl.*), perishable goods depreciate quickly.
avilissement (*n.m.*), depreciation :
la surproduction amène l'avilissement des prix, overproduction brings about a depreciation in price.
avion (*n.m.*), aeroplane ; airplane :
avion de ligne régulière, air liner.
par avion (inscription sur une lettre, un paquet, etc., transporté par voie aérienne), by air mail.

avis (avertissement) (*n.m.*), advice ; notice ; notification :
avis d'arrivée, advice of arrival.
avis d'attribution *ou* avis de répartition, allotment letter ; letter of allotment ; letter of acceptance. See **attribuer.**
avis d'expédition *ou* avis d'embarquement, advice of shipment ; advice of dispatch.
avis d'opéré *ou* avis d'opération (Bourse), advice of deal.
avis de convocation, notice of meeting :
un exemplaire du journal contenant l'avis de convocation, a copy of the newspaper containing the notice of meeting. See **convoquer & délibérer.**
avis de convocation à l'assemblée générale, notice of general meeting.
avis de délaissement (Assce mar.), notice of abandonment.
avis de non livraison *ou* avis de souffrance, advice of non delivery.
avis de paiement de mandats-poste, advice of payment of money orders.
avis de réception, advice, notice, of receipt.
avis de réception (Poste) (*Abrév. :* AR.), advice of delivery ; acknowledgment of delivery :
avis de réception d'objets chargés, advice of delivery of insured articles.
avis de retour de souscription, letter of regret.
avis de traite, advice of draft.
défaut d'avis, no advice ; no orders ; want of advice.
donner avis un jour d'avance, to give notice a day beforehand.
avis (*n.m.*) *ou* **avis** (*n.m.pl.*) (conseil), advice ; opinion :
donner un bon avis, to give good advice.
il aime à donner des avis, he is fond of giving advice.
aviser (*v.t.*), to advise ; to notify :
aviser son correspondant d'une expédition de marchandises, to advise one's correspondent of a shipment of goods.
aviso [avisos *pl.*] (*n.m.*), dispatch boat ; dispatch vessel ; advice boat.
avitaillement (*n.m.*), victualling.
avitailler (*v.t.*), to victual ; to provision.
avocat (pers.) (*n.m.*), counsel ; barrister ; barrister at law ; attorney ; public attorney ; attorney at law : (*Note :*—In England the words *counsel* or *barrister* are used. In U.S.A. *counsel* or *attorney*.)
les avocats ont le droit de donner des consultations, counsel have the right to give opinions.
avocat-conseil [avocats-conseil *pl.*] (*n.m.*), counsel.
avocat consultant, chamber counsel.
avoir (ce qu'on possède de bien) (*n.m.*), possessions ; property ; holding ; holdings ; fortune :
son avoir en terres, one's possessions in land ; one's holdings of land.
avoirs déposés en banque, property lodged with a bank.
tout son avoir, one's all ; the whole of one's fortune :

les joueurs obstinés perdent tout leur avoir
(*m.pl.*), obstinate gamblers lose their all.

avoir *ou* **Avoir** (Abrév.: **Av.** *ou* **A.**) (Comptab.)
(*n.m.*), credit; creditor; Cr; credit side;
creditor side (of an account):

doit et avoir *ou* Doit et Avoir, debit and
credit; debtor and creditor; Dr and Cr:

diviser la page en Doit et Avoir, to divide
the page into Dr and Cr.

inscrire une somme à l'avoir d'un compte, to
enter an amount to the credit of an account.

déduire du relevé les divers avoirs accordés,
to deduct from the statement the various
credits allowed.

avoirs en banque et chez les correspondants,
credits at the bank and with correspon-
dents.

Avoir (formule sur une facture d'avoir), Credited;
Credit; Cr:

A. B. (*vendeur*) Avoir à Monsieur C. D. (*acheteur*),
Mr C. D. (*buyer*) Credited by (*or* Credit by)
(*or* Cr. by) A. B. (*seller*); A. B. (*seller*)
Credited to Mr C. D. (*buyer*).

avoir (*v.t.*). See examples:

avoir bon caractère, to have a good character.

avoir charge de vendre une propriété, to be
entrusted with the selling of a property.

avoir compte à la banque *ou* avoir compte en
banque, to have an account at the bank.

avoir crédit à la banque *ou* avoir crédit en
banque, to be in credit, to have a balance,
at the bank.

avoir d'autres cordes à son arc, to have other
strings to one's bow.

avoir de boni, to make; to make a profit
of:

avoir mille francs de boni dans une affaire,
to make a thousand francs on a deal.

avoir de la monnaie (être riche), to have money;
to be well off.

avoir de nombreuses disponibilités, to have
plenty of available funds.

avoir débit à la banque *ou* avoir débit en banque,
to be overdrawn at the bank.

avoir des moyens, to have means.

avoir en partage *ou* avoir part, to share:

avoir un bureau en partage, to share an
office.

avoir part à un bénéfice au prorata de sa
mise de fonds, to share in a profit in
proportion to one's holding.

avoir hypothèque sur un bien, to have a
mortgage on a property.

avoir la bourse, to hold the purse.

avoir ses comptes à jour, to have one's accounts
up to date.

avoir seul le droit, to have the sole right; to
have the exclusive right:

les agents de change ont seuls le droit de
constater les cours des valeurs cotées
(*m.pl.*), the brokers (on the Paris Bourse)
have the exclusive right of fixing the prices
of quoted securities.

avoir son plein. See under **plein.**

avoir suffisamment d'argent, to have sufficient
money; to have enough money.

avoir un compte ouvert chez quelqu'un, to
have an account open with someone.

en avoir pour son argent, to get value for one's
money; to get one's money's worth:

il en a pour son argent, he got value for his
money; he got his money's worth.

avoué (pers.) (*n.m.*), attorney; solicitor; lawyer.
In France, an attorney representing parties
before the *cours d'appel* and the *tribunaux
civils.*

ayant cause [**ayants cause** *pl.*] (Dr.) (pers.) (*m.*),
assign.

ayant compte [**ayants compte** *pl.*] (pers.) (*m.*),
customer:

les ayants compte en ville d'un banquier, a
banker's town customers.

ayants compte d'acceptations (bilan de banque),
liability (*or* liabilities) of customers for
acceptance (*or* acceptances).

ayant droit [**ayants droit** *pl.*] (pers.) (*m.*), party
entitled; party; assign:

les intérêts des obligations et les dividendes des
actions sont payés aux ayants droit contre
remise des coupons, the interest on the
debentures and the dividends on the shares
are paid to the parties entitled against
surrender of the coupons.

obtenir le consentement de tous les ayants droit,
to secure the consent of all parties.

connaissement à ordre ou aux ayants droit
(*m.*), bill of lading to order or assigns.

B

bâbord (Naut.) (opp. à *tribord*) (*n.m.*), port.

bac transbordeur (*m.*), ferry boat.

bâchage (*n.m.*), sheeting (covering railway
wagons with sheets).

bâche (*n.f.*), sheet (tarpaulin, or the like, for
covering railway wagons):

bâche appartenant à l'expéditeur *ou* bâche
particulière, owner's sheet; trader's sheet.

bâche appartenant au chemin de fer *ou* bâche
du chemin de fer, company's sheet.

bâcher (*v.t.*), to sheet:

bâcher un wagon de chemin de fer, to sheet
a railway wagon.

bagage (*n.m.*) *ou* **bagages** (*n.m.pl.*), article of
luggage (*or* of baggage); luggage; baggage:
(*Note :—luggage* and *baggage* are synonymous

words. *luggage* is the English word; *baggage* is the American word, but it is largely used in England.)

déclaration du contenu d'un bagage (*f.*), declaration of the contents of an article of luggage.

bagages à main *ou* bagages à la main, hand luggage (*or* baggage).

bagages accompagnés, accompanied luggage.

bagages de cabine, cabin luggage.

bagages de cale, hold luggage.

bagages des voyageurs (*ou* des passagers), passengers' luggage.

bagages en franchise, free luggage (no excess charges to pay).

bagages enregistrés, registered luggage.

bagages non accompagnés, unaccompanied luggage.

bagages non enregistrés (*m.pl.*), unregistered luggage.

bail [**baux** *pl.*] (*n.m.*), lease:
prendre une maison à bail, to take a house on lease.

bailleur, -eresse (pers.) (*n.*), lessor:
le bailleur et le preneur, the lessor and the lessee.

bailleur de fonds (à un particulier) (*m.*), money lender.

bailleur de fonds (à une société en commandite) (*m.*), sleeping partner; dormant partner; silent partner; secret partner.

baisse (diminution de prix) (*n.f.*), fall; decline; drop; falling off:
baisse des blés, des fonds étrangers, du taux de l'intérêt, fall, decline, drop, in wheat, in foreign stocks, in the rate of interest.

la hausse ou la baisse des titres de bourse, des frets, the rise or the fall of stocks and shares, of freights.

une baisse sensible de valeur, a marked falling off in value.

opération à la baisse (Bourse) (*f.*), dealing for a fall; bear transaction.

acheter à la baisse (Bourse), to buy on a fall.

tendance à la baisse (dans les cours) (*f.*), downward tendency (in prices).

mouvement de baisse des valeurs (*m.*), downward movement of stocks.

être en baisse *ou* **être à la baisse,** to be falling; to be a falling market; to be down; to be off:
les valeurs de chemins de fer sont en baisse (*ou* sont à la baisse) (*f.pl.*), railway shares are falling (*or* a falling market *or* down).

vendre en hausse et acheter en baisse, to sell on a rising market and to buy on a falling market.

cuivre en baisse de 1/4 à £69 15 sh. (*ou* £69 3/4), copper down 5s. at £69 15s.; copper 5s. off at £69 15s.

être à la baisse (en parlant des personnes), to go for a fall:
spéculateur qui est à la baisse (*m.*), speculator who is going for a fall.

baisser (*v.t.*), to lower:
baisser un prix, to lower a price.

baisser (*v.i.*), to fall; to decline; to drop; to go down:
l'action X. baisse de 1 375 à 1 331, X. shares fell (*or* dropped) from 1,375 to 1,331 francs.

baissier (Bourse) (pers.) (*n.m.*) (opp. à *haussier*), bear; short:
les baissiers vendent à terme des valeurs qu'ils espèrent racheter à un cours plus faible, bears sell for the settlement stocks which they hope to repurchase at a lower price.

baissier à découvert, uncovered bear.

balance (équilibre entre le débit et le crédit) (*n.f.*), balance: (See also **solde.**)
la balance d'un compte, the balance of an account.

balance de caisse, cash balance.

balance des comptes *ou* balance économique (Écon. polit.), balance of indebtedness:
le simple troc des marchandises exportées contre les marchandises importées ne constitue pas le seul élément de la balance économique d'un pays, the simple exchange of exported goods for imported goods does not constitute the only element of the balance of indebtedness of a country.

balance du commerce *ou* balance commerciale (Écon. polit.), balance of trade; trade balance:
balance commerciale défavorable (*ou* déficitaire), unfavourable (*or* adverse) trade balance:
balance commerciale favorable, favourable trade balance:
la balance est favorable à un pays lorsque le montant de ses exportations dépasse celui de ses importations; sinon elle lui est défavorable, the balance is favourable to (*or* in favour of) a country when the amount of its exports exceeds that of its imports; if not it is unfavourable (*or* adverse) to it.

balance à nouveau, balance carried forward to next account; balance to next account.

balance reportée de l'exercice précédent *ou* balance de l'exercice précédent, balance brought forward from last account; balance from last (*or* from previous) account.

balance de bureau (*f.*), office scales.

balance de vérification *ou* **balance d'ordre** *ou* simplement **balance** (*n.f.*) (Comptab.), trial balance; balance:
balance préparatoire *ou* balance préparatoire d'inventaire *ou* balance de vérification avant inventaire (opp. à *balance d'inventaire*), trial balance before closing; first trial balance; full trial balance.

balance d'inventaire, trial balance after closing; second trial balance; short trial balance.

balance auxiliaire, trial balance of a subsidiary ledger.

balance générale, general trial balance; trial balance of general ledger.

balance mensuelle, monthly balance.

balance par soldes, trial balance showing differences (*or* balances) of the postings.

balance cumulée, trial balance showing total postings. *Note :*—The trial balance showing total ledger postings is not used in English practice, but both the *balance cumulée* and the *balance par soldes* are commonly used in France. The raison d'être of the *balance cumulée* in France is that all transactions are journalized in the journal proper, either in detail or in total, and therefore the totals of the *balance cumulée* have to agree with the totals of the journal. In France, a record of all transactions in the journal proper is required by law : this is not the case in England, where the journal proper is used only for opening and closing entries and for such intermediate entries as have no subsidiary book specially provided to receive them. It is even not uncommon in England for no journal proper to be kept at all.

balancer (*v.t.*), to balance ; to balance up :
balancer un compte, to balance an account.
balancer les livres pour l'année, to balance, to balance up, the books for the year.
dans la balance de vérification, l'ensemble des soldes débiteurs doit balancer celui des soldes créditeurs, in the trial balance, the total of the debit balances should balance that of the credit balances.
inconvénient balancé par des avantages (*m.*), drawback balanced by advantages.
se balancer (*v.r.*), to balance ; to balance each other ; to show a balance :
colonnes qui se balancent (*f.pl.*), columns which balance.
deux articles qui se balancent (*m.pl.*), two items which balance each other.
compte qui se balance par tant de francs au crédit (*m.*), account which shows a balance of so many francs to the credit.
compte courant qui se balance par un solde débiteur (*m.*), current account which shows a debit balance.
balayures (provenant des marchandises entre-posées) (*n.f.pl.*), sweepings (from warehoused goods).
balise (*n.f.*), beacon.
balle (ballot) (*n.f.*) (Abrév. : **B.**), bale.
ballon d'essai (*fig.*) (*m.*), feeler :
lancer un ballon d'essai, to put out a feeler.
ballot (*n.m.*) (Abrév. : **bot**), bale.
bancable (*adj.*), bankable ; bank (*used as adj.*) :
effets bancables (*m.pl.*), bankable bills.
place bancable (*f.*), bank place.
Note :—In France, *papier bancable* is restricted to the meaning *paper bankable at the Banque de France* (i.e., bills complying with the conditions laid down by that bank before being capable of being received by it for discount), and in Belgium to *paper bankable at the Banque Nationale de Belgique.* The question whether the paper is *bankable* or *unbankable* (*non bancable* ou *déclassé*) is of first importance, inasmuch as it is the common practice for French and Belgian banks to rediscount their bills at the Banque de France or at the Banque Nationale respectively.

place bancable means, in France, a bank place of the Bank of France (i.e., one of the numerous places or towns where the Banque de France has a branch or an office), and in Belgium a bank place of the National Bank of Belgium. Bills on localities where these banks have no place of business are called *effets déplacés* or *papier déplacé :* such bills are subject to higher costs of collection.
bancaire (*adj.*), banking ; bank (*used as adj.*) :
établissement bancaire (*m.*), banking establishment.
commission bancaire (*f.*), bank commission.
banco (*adj. invar.*), banco :
deux cents florins banco, two hundred florins banco.
bande (télégraphe enregistreur) (*n.f.*), tape.
bande de journal [bandes de journaux *pl.*] (*f.*), newspaper wrapper :
mettre un journal sous bande, to put a newspaper in a wrapper.
bande en caoutchouc (*f.*), elastic band ; india-rubber band ; rubber ring.
bande gommée en papier transparent (*f.*), adhesive transparent paper tape.
banquable (*adj.*). Same as **bancable.**
banque (opération) (*n.f.*), banking ; banking business :
la banque est le commerce de l'argent (*ou* des capitaux), banking is trade in money.
banque et finances, banking and finance.
faire la banque, to do banking business.
la banque sous toutes ses formes, banking in all its forms.
banque (établissement) (*n.f.*), bank :
banque coloniale, colonial bank.
banque commerciale *ou* banque de commerce, commercial bank ; bank of commerce ; trade bank.
banque d'émission *ou* banque de circulation, bank of issue ; bank of circulation.
banque d'escompte, discount bank ; bank of discount.
banque d'État, government bank ; Government bank ; State bank.
banque de compensation, clearing bank.
banque de dépôt, deposit bank ; bank of deposit.
banque de placement *ou* banque de placement et de spéculation *ou* banque de spéculation et de placement, issuing house.
banque de province *ou* banque provinciale, country bank ; provincial bank.
banque de tout repos, reliable bank.
banque locale, local bank.
banque par actions, joint stock bank :
en France, les grandes banques par actions sont connues sous le nom de sociétés de crédit, in France, the big joint stock banks are known under the name of *sociétés de crédit.*
banque privée *ou* banque particulière, private bank.
banque publique *ou* banque nationale, national bank.
banque régionale, district bank.

banque territoriale *ou* banque agraire *ou* banque hypothécaire, land bank.

banqueroute (*n.f.*), bankruptcy. (*Note :*—In France, *banqueroute* is the failure of a trader occasioned by his own fault and is a punishable offence. Failure brought about by misfortune is called *faillite*.)

banqueroutier, -ère (*adj.*), bankrupt : commerçant banqueroutier (*m.*), bankrupt merchant.

banqueroutier, -ère (pers.) (*n.*), bankrupt.

banquier, -ère (*adj.*), banking : coutumes banquières (*f.pl.*), banking customs.

banquier, -ère (Banq.) (pers.) (*n.*), banker : banquier de l'État, Government banker. banquier payeur, paying banker.

banquier (Bourse) (*n.m.*), broker : banquier en valeurs *ou simplement* banquier, stockbroker ; broker. *See explanation of Paris markets under* marché des valeurs. banquier marron, outside broker. banquier de placement et de spéculation, stockjobber ; jobber ; dealer. *Note :*—These French and English terms do not correspond, as *jobbers* or *dealers* do not exist in France as an integral part of the Bourse system. *See explanation of Paris Bourse under* marché des valeurs.

banquier-coulissier (pers.) (*n.m.*), a title or trade description assumed by certain French bucket shops.

Note :—The designation *banquier* is often grossly misused in France : all sorts of financiers and financial pirates, company promoters, share pushers, runners, and " somethings in the City," style themselves *banquiers :* there are lots of *banquiers* in Paris who are not worth a £5 note.

baraterie (*n.f.*), barratry : baraterie de patron *ou* baraterie du patron et de l'équipage, barratry of the master and mariners.

Note :—The French distinguish between **baraterie criminelle** which is *barratry* in the English sense, and **baraterie civile** (*or* **baraterie simple**) which is a *fault* or *wrongful act* for which the master is legally responsible. le mot *baraterie* en français, comprend toutes les fautes du capitaine, de quelque nature qu'elles soient ; le mot anglais *barratry* ne comprend que les seuls actes intentionnellement frauduleux ou criminels, et ne s'entend pas aux fautes de négligence, incapacité, ou autres semblables, the word *baraterie* in French, includes all the wrongful acts of the master, of whatever nature they may be ; the English word *barratry* includes only intentionally fraudulent or criminal acts, and does not apply to faults of negligence, incapacity, or the like.

barème *ou* **barrème** (livre contenant des calculs tout faits) (*n.m.*), ready reckoner.

barème *ou* **barrème** (Tarification) (*n.m.*), scale : tarification représentée par un barème qui donne les prix (*f.*), tariffication represented by a scale which gives the rates.

barème des prix de transport, scale of charges for carriage.

barge (*n.f.*), barge.

baricaut (*n.m.*), keg.

baril (*n.m.*), barrel ; cask ; keg.

barillet (*n.m.*), keg.

barque (*n.f.*), bark ; barque.

barre (à l'embouchure d'un fleuve) (*n.f.*), bar (at the mouth of a river).

barre d'espacement (machine à écrire) (*f.*), space bar.

barre de fraction (*f.*), bar of division (between the numerator and the denominator of a fraction).

barrement (d'un chèque) (*n.m.*), crossing (of a cheque) : barrement général, general crossing : barrement spécial, special crossing : le barrement est général s'il ne porte entre les deux barres aucune désignation, ou seulement la mention « & Cⁱᵉ ; » il est spécial si le nom d'un banquier est inscrit entre les deux barres. Le barrement général peut être transformé en barrement spécial par le tireur · ou par un porteur, the crossing is general if it bears no wording between the two lines, or only the words " & Co. ; " it is special if the name of a banker is written between the two lines. A general crossing can be converted into a special crossing by the drawer or a holder. *Note :*—Same practice in France as in England. Cf. **chèque.**

barrer (effacer ; rayer ; biffer) (*v.t.*), to strike out ; to cross out : barrer une clause dans une convention, to strike out, to cross out, a clause in an agreement.

barrer (un chèque) (*v.t.*), to cross (a cheque) : la personne qui émet le chèque, ou un porteur, peut le barrer, the person who issues the cheque, or a holder, can cross it.

barrière (*n.f.*), barrier ; wall : pays fermé par des barrières de douanes (*m.*), country closed by customs barriers (*or* walls).

barriquaut (*n.m.*), keg.

barrique (*n.f.*) (Abrév.: bque), cask ; barrel.

bas, basse (*adj.*), low : bas prix (*m.*), low price. les bas emplois d'une administration (*m.pl.*), the low grades of service in an administration. le taux du change est bas, the rate of exchange is low.

bas (partie inférieure) (*n.m.*) (Ant.: haut), bottom ; foot : bas d'une page, bottom, foot, of a page.

base (*n.f.*), base ; basis : base d'un contrat, du crédit, basis of a contract, of credit. base d'imposition *ou* base de cotisation (Impôts cédulaires), basis of assessment. base de la prime (Bourse), option price ; price of option. base de liquidation (Bourse de marchandises). On certain French and Belgian corn exchanges the *base de liquidation*, or settlement price, is a spot price fixed by the Government as a basis of quotation. Any variation in this price representing a rise or fall in the actual market price is quoted as an addition to, or deduction from, this basis. An addition is called a *report* (i.e., over spot), a deduction is called a *déport* (i.e., under spot). Thus, if the actual market price on a certain day was say 126.50 francs, and the *base de liquidation* had been fixed say at 120.00, the price would be quoted *base de liquidation* 120, *report* 6.50.

base du change, basis of exchange.

la base d'évaluation des marchandises déclarées est, aux fins de la présente assurance, fixée par accord mutuel à . . ., the basis of the valuation of the merchandise declared is, for the purpose of this insurance, agreed to be at . . .

baser (*v.t.*), to base :
baser ses calculs sur les prix actuels, to base one's calculations on present prices.

bassin (Navig.) (*n.m.*) (Abrév.: **Bⁱⁿ**),   dock ; basin :
bassin à flot, wet dock.
bassin à sec *ou* bassin sec *ou* bassin de radoub, dry dock ; graving dock.
bassin aux bois *ou* bassin à bois, timber dock.
bassin aux (*ou* à) bois de flottage,   pond.
bassin aux charbons *ou* bassin à charbon *ou* bassin charbonnier, coal dock.
bassin aux pétroles *ou* bassin à pétrole *ou* bassin pétrolier, oil dock.
bassin de batellerie, basin for small craft.
bassin de marée *ou* bassin d'échouage,   tidal basin.
bassin flottant, floating dock.

bateau (*n.m.*), boat ; ship ; vessel : (See also **bâtiment, bord, canot, embarcation, navire, paquebot, steamer, & vapeur.**)
bateau à roues, paddle boat.
bateau à vapeur, steamboat.
bateau à voiles, sailing ship ;   sailing vessel ; sailer.
bateau caboteur,   coasting vessel ;   coasting ship ;   coaster ;   home-trade ship.
bateau charbonnier, coal ship ; collier.
bateau charbonnier à voiles, sailing collier.
bateau-citerne [bateaux-citernes *pl.*] (*n.m.*), tank ship ;   tank vessel ;   tanker.
bateau-citerne à moteur, motor tanker.
bateau-citerne à vapeur,   tank steamer.
bateau de charge, canal boat.
bateau de commerce, trading vessel ; merchant vessel ; merchantman.
bateau de plaisance, pleasure boat.
bateau de sauvetage, lifeboat.
bateau-feu [bateaux-feux *pl.*] *ou* bateau-phare [bateaux-phares *pl.*] (*n.m.*),   lightship ; light vessel.
bateau fluvial *ou* bateau de rivière, river boat.
bateau lent *ou* bateau omnibus,   slow boat.
bateau-magasin [bateaux-magasins *pl.*] (*n.m.*), store ship.
bateau pétrolier, oil ship ; oiler.
bateau-pilote [bateaux-pilotes *pl.*] (*n.m.*), pilot boat.
bateau rapide *ou* bateau express [bateaux express *pl.*],   fast boat.

bateau remorqueur, tug ; tug boat.
bateau sauveteur, salvage boat.

batelage (*n.m.*), lighterage.

batelier (pers.) (*n.m.*), `lighterman.

batellerie (ensemble des bateaux qui font le transport des marchandises sur les fleuves, rivières, et canaux) (*n.f.*), small craft ; river boats ;   canal boats ;   river and/or canal boats.

batellerie (*n.f.*) *ou* **batellerie fluviale**,   inland navigation ;   inside navigation ;   internal navigation :
les prix de revient des transports par chemins de fer sont plus élevés que ceux de la batellerie (*m.pl.*),   the costs of railway carriage are higher than those of inland navigation.

bâtiment (construction en maçonnerie) (*n.m.*), building.
bâtiment des messageries (Ch. de f.),   parcels office ; parcel office.

bâtiment (de mer) (*n.m.*), vessel ;   ship ;   boat : (See also **bateau, bord, navire, paquebot, steamer, & vapeur.**)
bâtiment à vapeur, steamship ;   steamer.
bâtiment à voiles *ou* bâtiment voilier,   sailing ship ;   sailing vessel ;   sailer.
bâtiment au long cours *ou* bâtiment long-courrier [bâtiments long-courriers *pl.*], foreign-going ship ;   ocean-going vessel.
bâtiment de charge,   cargo boat.
bâtiment de commerce *ou* bâtiment marchand, trading vessel ; merchant vessel ; merchantman.
bâtiment de mer, seagoing vessel :
navires et autres bâtiments de mer (*m.pl.*), ships and other seagoing vessels.
bâtiment de plaisance, pleasure vessel.
bâtiment de rivière, river boat.

bâtir sa fortune, to build up one's fortune.

bâton (de cire à cacheter) (*n.m.*), stick (of sealing wax).

battre (pavillon) (*v.t.*), to fly :
navire battant pavillon belge (*m.*), ship flying the Belgian flag.

battre monnaie (*au propre*),   to coin, to mint, money :
« je dois être le maître dans tout ce dont je me mêle, et surtout dans ce qui regarde la Banque [de France], qui est bien plus à l'empereur qu'aux actionnaires, puisqu'elle bat monnaie. » NAPOLÉON 1ᵉʳ dans la séance du 2 avril 1806 du Conseil d'État, " I intend to be the master in everything in which I am concerned, and above all in that which concerns the Bank [of France], which is much more to the emperor than to the shareholders, because it coins money." NAPOLEON I at the sitting of 2nd April 1806 of the Council of State.

battre monnaie (*au figuré*), to raise money ; to find money ; to raise the dust (*slang*) ;   to raise the wind (*slang*) :
battre monnaie en vendant ses titres, en empruntant, to raise money by selling one's stocks, by borrowing.

battre un record, to beat, to break, a record :

activité économique qui a battu les records de l'année antérieure (*f.*), economic activity which has beaten the records of the previous year.

beau (**bel** devant une voyelle ou un *h* muet), **belle** (*adj.*), fine ; handsome :
beau papier (*m.*), fine bills.
réaliser de beaux bénéfices, to realize handsome profits.
à beaux deniers comptants. See under **comptant.**

bec (d'une plume) (*n.m.*), point, nib (of a pen).

belga (*n.m.*), belga. *Note :*—The belga, which is nominally equivalent to 5 Belgian francs, is only a money of exchange. The franc retains its place in the national economy and continues to be used and to circulate in Belgium.

belliqueux, -euse (*adj.*), warlike :
hostilités ou opérations belliqueuses (*f.pl.*), hostilities or warlike operations.

bénéfice (gain ; profit) (*n.m.*) (*s'emploie souvent au pl.*), profit :
bénéfice sur l'opération, sur une vente, profit on the deal, on a sale.
bénéfice d'affrètement, profit on charter.
bénéfice d'exploitation, trading profit.
bénéfice du portefeuille, profit on investments.
bénéfice espéré, anticipated profit :
assurance qui couvre aussi des frais et un bénéfice espéré (*f.*), insurance which also covers expenses and an anticipated profit.
bénéfice brut *ou* bénéfices bruts, gross profit ; gross profits.
bénéfice net *ou* bénéfices nets, net profit ; net profits.
bénéfice net pour balance (compte pertes et profits), balance being net profit.
bénéfices d'écritures (opp. à *bénéfices réalisés*), book profits (opp. to *realized profits*).

bénéfice (avantage ; privilège) (*n.m.*), benefit ; advantage :
bénéfice de sauvetage, de l'admission temporaire, benefit of salvage, of temporary admission.

bénéfice (déport) (Négociations de change à terme) (*n.m.*) (Abrév. : **B.** *ou* **b.** *ou* **D.**) (opp. à *report*), premium ; under spot. See examples under **report.**

bénéficiaire (*adj.*) (opp. à *déficitaire*), profit (*used as adj.*) ; of profit ; showing a profit :
solde bénéficiaire (*m.*), profit balance ; balance of profit.
bilan bénéficiaire (*m.*), balance sheet showing a profit.
suivant que le résultat de l'exercice est bénéficiaire ou déficitaire, according as the result of the trading shows (*or* is) a profit or a loss.

bénéficiaire (pers.) (*n.m.* ou *f.*), beneficiary ; payee :
bénéficiaire d'une police d'assurance, beneficiary of an insurance policy.
bénéficiaire d'une lettre de crédit, beneficiary, payee, of a letter of credit.
bénéficiaire d'un mandat de poste, d'un chèque, d'un effet de commerce (*ou* d'une lettre de

change), d'un billet à ordre, payee of a money order, of a cheque, of a bill of exchange, of a promissory note :
le nom du bénéficiaire à l'ordre duquel le billet est souscrit, the name of the payee to whose order the bill is drawn.

bénéficiel, -elle (*adj.*), profitable.

bénéficier (bonifier ; accorder) (*v.t.*), to allow :
bénéficier quelqu'un d'un escompte, to allow someone a discount.

bénéficier (*v.i.*), to make a profit ; to profit ; to benefit :
bénéficier sur une marchandise vendue, to make a profit on a line of goods sold ; to profit by goods sold.
bénéficier de la plus-value du change, to benefit, to profit, by the appreciation of the exchange.

berge (d'un fleuve) (*n.f.*), bank (of a river).

besoin (*n.m.*), need ; requirement :
besoins actuels, present needs (*or* requirements).
les besoins du marché en capitaux, the market's requirements of money.

besoin (mention sur une lettre de change) (*n.m.*), case of need :
le besoin est la mention par laquelle le tireur, ou l'un des endosseurs, indique que dans le cas de non paiement de la lettre de change par le tiré, l'effet devra être présenté à une tierce personne qui est chargée d'en acquitter le montant : cette mention s'appelle un besoin et la personne qui doit intervenir est désignée sous le nom de recommandataire, a case of need is a notice by which the drawer, or one of the endorsers, indicates that in case of dishonour of the bill of exchange by the drawee, the bill should be presented to a third person who is instructed to pay the amount of it : this notice is called a case of need and the person who it is intended should intervene is designated under the name of referee in case of need.

au besoin *ou* **et au besoin** (lettres de change), in case of need :
au besoin chez M. X. *ou* et au besoin à M. X., in case of need apply to Mr X.

besoin (lettres de change) (pers.) (*n.m.*), case of need ; referee in case of need :
le besoin ou recommandataire est un payeur éventuel que le tireur ou un endosseur indique sur la lettre de change comme pouvant payer en cas de besoin, c'est-à-dire en cas de non acceptation ou de non paiement de la lettre, a case of need or referee in case of need is a contingent payer that the drawer or an endorser names on the bill of exchange to whom the holder may resort in case of need, that is to say, in case the bill is dishonoured by non acceptance or non payment.
porteur d'une lettre qui n'est pas obligé de faire le protêt à tous les besoins indiqué (*m.*), holder of a bill who is not bound t note protest to all the cases of need indicated

biblorhapte (*n.m.*), binder ; file (for papers).

bien (en temps utile) (*adv.*), duly :

nous avons bien reçu votre lettre, we have duly received your letter.

bien (*n.m.*) *ou* **biens** (*n.m.pl.*) (propriété), property; estate:

biens en rentes, funded property.

biens immeubles *ou* biens immobiliers, real property; real estate; realty; immovable property; fixed property.

biens meubles *ou* biens mobiliers *ou* biens personnels, personal property; personal estate; personalty; personals; chattels personal; movable property; movables.

biens présents et à venir, property present and future.

bien venant, -e, coming in regularly:

six mille livres de rente bien venantes, an income of six thousand pounds coming in regularly.

bienfaisance (*n.f.*), charitable donations; donations; charity; charities.

biens-fonds (*n.m.pl.*) *ou* **bien-fonds** (*n.m.sing.*), landed property; land; house property; houses; land and house property:

placer son argent en biens-fonds, to invest one's money in landed and house property; to put one's money in land and houses.

biffage (*n.m.*) *ou* **biffement** (*n.m.*) *ou* **biffure** (*n.f.*), striking out; crossing out; ruling out; deletion.

biffer (*v.t.*), to strike out; to cross out; to delete; to rule out:

biffer une clause dans un contrat, to strike out, to cross out, to delete, a clause in a contract.

biffez la mention inutile, delete, strike out, words not applicable; delete as required.

biffer à l'encre rouge la somme ou le nom du compte erroné, to rule out in red ink the wrong amount or name of account.

bifteck (argot financier) (*n.m.*), (in French financial slang) secret commission or bribe sometimes demanded by a dishonest stock exchange clerk as remuneration for a wrongful service to be rendered, such as falsely marking a price.

bilan (*n.m.*) *ou* **bilan d'exploitation** (compte de l'actif et du passif d'un négociant), balance sheet; statement of affairs: (*Note:—bilan d'exploitation* is the opposing term to *bilan de liquidation*. The full expression is used only when it is necessary to distinguish the one *bilan* from the other.)

bilan au (*ou* arrêté au) 31 décembre 19—, balance sheet at (or as at) (or on) (or made up to) 31st December 19—.

bilan d'entrée, opening balance sheet; balance sheet (or statement of affairs) at commencement of business.

bilan général *ou* bilan d'ensemble, general balance sheet.

Note:—In French balance sheets, the assets appear on the left hand side and the liabilities on the right. This is the reverse of English practice.

See note under **inventaire comptable.**

bilan (*n.m.*) *ou* **bilan de liquidation** (état de situation d'un commerçant en faillite), statement of affairs:

déposer son bilan, to submit a statement of one's affairs (act of bankruptcy); to file one's petition.

billet (Fin.) (*n.m.*), note; bill:

billet à domicile, domiciled bill.

billet à ordre (*Abrév.:* B/), promissory note; note of hand.

billet au porteur, bill payable to bearer.

billet de banque *ou simplement* billet, bank note; note; bill.

billet de complaisance, accommodation bill; accommodation note.

billet de crédit circulaire, circular note; traveller's cheque; cheque for travellers.

billet de fonds. In France, a bill of exchange given for the sale on credit of the goodwill of a business. These bills are distinguished from ordinary bills only by their length and remoteness of due date, which may run into several years.

billet de loterie, lottery ticket.

billet simple, bill payable to the order of a specified person (and not to him or his order). In France this is not an *effet de commerce*, but an *engagement civil non transmissible*: in England such a bill would nevertheless be payable to him or his order at his option.

billet (carte de parcours) (*n.m.*), ticket:

billet à plein tarif *ou* billet à place entière, full fare ticket; ticket at full fare (*or* at full rate).

billet à prix réduit, ticket at reduced rate; reduced rate ticket; cheap ticket.

billet aérien *ou* billet d'avion, air ticket; aeroplane ticket.

billet aller et retour *ou* billet d'aller et retour *ou* billet de retour, return ticket; return.

billet circulaire, circular ticket.

billet collectif, party ticket.

billet combiné, combined ticket.

billet d'adulte [billets d'adultes *pl.*], adult's ticket.

billet d'excursion, excursion ticket.

billet de chemin de fer *ou* billet de place, railway ticket:

l'enregistrement des bagages est effectué sur la présentation du billet de place du voyageur (*m.*), the registration of luggage is effected on production of the passenger's railway ticket.

billet de demi-place (*ou* de demi-tarif) pour les enfants, child's half-fare ticket.

billet de famille, family ticket.

billet de passage *ou* billet de voyage, passage ticket.

billet de première, de seconde, de troisième classe *ou* billet de 1re, de 2e, de 3e classe, first, second, third class ticket; 1st, 2nd, 3rd class ticket.

billet de voyage, travel ticket.

billet de voyageur, passenger ticket.

billet direct, through ticket.

billet garde-place *ou* billet de location de place, reserved seat ticket.

billet global, through ticket (sea-land-sea).

billet-livret [billets-livrets *pl.*] (*n.m.*), book ticket (ticket in book form, as a tour ticket).

billet non utilisé, unused ticket.

billet perdu, lost ticket.

billet périmé, ticket out of date.

billet simple, single ticket; single.

billet de bord *ou* **billet d'embarquement** (*m.*), mate's receipt.

billon (*n.m.*), copper; copper coin; copper or nickel coin.

bimétallique (*adj.*), bimetallic:

système bimétallique (*m.*), bimetallic system.

bimétallisme (*n.m.*), bimetalism; bimetallism.

bimétalliste (*adj.*), bimetallistic:

suivant qu'un État adope un étalon unique ou un étalon double il est dit monométalliste ou bimétalliste, according as a State adopts a single standard or a double standard it is said to be monometallic or bimetallistic.

bimétalliste (pers.) (*n.m.*), bimetalist; bimetallist.

biplan (*n.m.*), biplane.

blanc, -che (où il n'y a rien d'écrit) (*adj.*), blank: papier blanc (*m.*), blank paper.

blanc, -che (*adj.*) *ou* **en blanc** (sans profit ni perte), blank:

opération blanche (*f.*) *ou* affaire en blanc (*f.*), blank transaction; blank deal.

blanc (espace) (*n.m.*), blank:

laisser un blanc dans une lettre, to leave a blank in a letter.

en blanc (sans écrit), in blank; blank:

chèque signé en blanc (*m.*), cheque signed in blank.

endossement en blanc (*m.*), blank indorsement; endorsement in blank.

en blanc (sans garantie), blank; unsecured:

crédit en blanc (*m.*), blank credit.

découvert en blanc (*m.*), unsecured overdraft.

blanc-seing [**blancs-seings** *pl.*] (Dr.) (*n.m.*), blank signature.

bloc (**en**). See under **en**.

bloc-notes [**blocs-notes** *pl.*] *ou* **block-notes** [**blocks-notes** *pl.*] (*n.m.*), pad; memorandum pad.

bloc-sténo [**blocs-sténos** *pl.*] (*n.m.*), shorthand notebook; reporter's notebook; notebook.

blocage *ou* **bloquage** (*n.m.*), tie up; lockup; lumping.

blocus (*n.m.*), blockade.

bloquer (immobiliser) (*v.t.*), to tie up; to lock up:

bloquer une tranche d'actions, to tie up a block of shares.

syndicat qui bloque un certain nombre de titres pour ne pas inonder le marché (*m.*), syndicate which ties up a certain number of shares in order not to flood the market.

on peut admettre que le prix de revient des installations doit être grossi de l'intérêt des capitaux qu'elles ont bloqués pendant leur établissement, it may be admitted that the cost of the plant should be increased by the interest on the capital which it has locked up during its construction.

bloquer (réunir) (*v.t.*), to lump:

articles qui sont bloqués dans le chapitre portefeuille (*m.pl.*), items which are lumped under the heading investments.

bloquer (faire le blocus d'une place, d'une ville) (*v.t.*), to blockade; to block:

port bloqué par l'ennemi (*m.*), port blockaded (or blocked) by the enemy.

bluff (*n.m.*), bluff.

bluffer (*v.t.*), to bluff:

bluffer quelqu'un, to bluff someone.

bluffer (*v.i.*), to bluff.

bluffeur, -euse (pers.) (*n.*), bluffer.

boire un bouillon (faire une fausse spéculation), to make a bad spec.

boîte (*n.f.*), box; case:

une boîte de plumes, a box of nibs.

boîte aux lettres, letter box; posting box.

boîte aux lettres particulière, private letter box; private posting box.

boîte aux lettres réservée aux levées exceptionnelles, late fee letter box.

boîte avec (*ou* de) valeur déclarée *ou* boîte chargée (*Abrév.:* boîte VD. *ou* BVD.) (Poste), insured box.

boîte de transfert (fourniture de bureau), transfer case.

boîte postale *ou* boîte de commerce, post office box.

bomerie (Dr. mar.) (*n.f.*), bottomry.

bon, bonne (*adj.*), good:

une bonne maison a toujours de bons employés, a good house always has good clerks.

titres qui sont de bonne livraison (Bourse) (*m.pl.*), shares which are (or stock which is) good delivery.

bon papier (effets de commerce) (*m.*), good paper; good bills.

bonne créance (*f.*), good debt.

c'est une bonne affaire, it is good business.

nous avons eu une bonne année, we have had a good year.

c'était une bonne occasion, it was a good opportunity.

fournir une bonne caution, to find a good security.

bonne arrivée (d'un navire à destination) (*f.*), safe arrival (of a ship at destination).

bonne fin (*f.*), meeting; protection:

se porter caution pour quelqu'un, c'est garantir la bonne fin des engagements pris par lui envers un tiers, to become surety for someone is to guarantee the meeting of the engagements contracted by him with a third party.

les endosseurs sont solidairement responsables de la bonne fin des effets sur lesquels ils ont apposé leur signature (*m.pl.*), the endorsers are jointly and severally liable for meeting (or to protect) the bills to which they have appended their signature.

il est important pour le tireur d'assurer la bonne fin de l'effet, it is important for the drawer to ensure the protection of the bill; it is essential that the drawer should make sure the bill will be met.

sauf bonne fin (Banq.) (*Abrév.:* s.b.f.), under reserve; under usual reserves:

le montant du chèque est porté à votre crédit sauf bonne fin, the amount of the cheque is passed to your credit under reserve.

bonne qualité moyenne (*f.*), good average quality.

bonnes marques (métaux) (*f.pl.*), good brands.

sur bonnes ou mauvaises nouvelles (Assce mar.). See under **sur.**

bon compte (à) (en déduction de ce qui est dû), on account :
prendre cent francs à bon compte, to take a hundred francs on account.

bon compte (à) (sans grande peine), easily :
s'enrichir à bon compte, to get rich easily.

bon état de navigabilité (*m.*) (opp. à *mauvais état de navigabilité*), seaworthiness.

bon état de navigabilité (en), seaworthy :
un navire est réputé en bon état de navigabilité quand il est à tous égards raisonnablement en état d'affronter les périls ordinaires des mers où a lieu l'aventure assurée, a ship is deemed to be seaworthy when she is reasonably fit in all respects to encounter the ordinary perils of the seas of the adventure insured.

bon marché (*n.m.*), cheapness ; lowness :
le bon marché des capitaux, du crédit, the cheapness of money, of credit.
client qui se laisse tenter par le bon marché (*m.*), customer who allows himself to be tempted by cheapness.
le bon marché des reports, the lowness of contangoes. See example under **cherté.**

bon marché (*invar.*) *ou* **bon marché (à)** *ou* **bon compte (à)** (*adj.*), cheap ; low ; light :
l'argent est bon marché *ou* l'argent est à bon marché (*m.*), money is cheap.
les reports sont bon marché, contangoes are low (*or* are light). See example under **tendre (se).**

bon marché (à) *ou* **bon compte (à)** (*adv.*), cheap ; cheaply :
vendre à bon marché (*ou* à bon compte), to sell cheap (*or* cheaply).

bon marin (en), in a seamanlike manner :
conduire un navire en bon marin, to manage a ship in a seamanlike manner.

bon port (à), safely ; safely into port (*or* harbour) :
que le navire arrive à bon port ou se perde pendant le voyage, whether the ship arrives safely or is lost on the voyage.
amener un navire innavigable à bon port, to bring an unseaworthy ship safely into port (*or* harbour).

bon (bonne) pour, good for :
être bon (bonne) pour en répondre, to be good for the amount.
être bon (bonne) pour payer, to be good for :
être bon pour payer une certaine somme, to be good for a certain sum.
Note :—The formula **bon pour** (or as an abbreviation **B.P.**), often used in French, frequently has no expressed equivalent in English. Thus the guarantor of a bill in France prefaces his signature with **bon pour aval** (*lit.* good for guarantee) or **pour**

aval, whereas in England the guarantor would simply sign his name on the back of the bill.
French bills have **B.P.F.** or **Bon Pour Fr.** in front of the amount in figures on the top of the bill. In England the £ sign only precedes the amount, in the case of an inland bill, and **Exchange for £,** in the case of a foreign bill.
Again, the transferor of a stock in France will write the words **bon pour transfert** before his signature, and the transferee **bon pour acceptation de transfert,** and so on.

bon (*n.m.*), order ; note ; licence ; receipt ; voucher ; bond ; draft :

bon à échantillonner, sampling order.

bon à échéance *ou* bon à échéance fixe *ou* bon de caisse (Banq.), fixed deposit receipt.
Note :—In France, *bons à échéance* can be made payable to bearer, to depositor's order or to the order of a third party. If the deposit is for several years, the **bon de capital** is accompanied by **bons d'intérêts** (interest coupons).
In England, banks do not give receipts for deposits, unless they are asked for. Nor do they issue deposit pass books, unless asked for. The usual practice of the customer being to transfer money to deposit account from current account, the transaction is shown in the current account pass book. In England, a deposit receipt is not a negotiable instrument.

bon à embarquer, receiving note.

bon à lots, prize bond ; lottery bond.

bon à vue, sight draft.

un bon sur la Banque de France, a draft on the Bank of France.

bon au porteur, bearer bond.

bon d'importation, importation licence.

bon d'ouverture (Douanes), inspection order ; inspecting order.

bon de bord *ou* bon de chargement, mate's receipt.

bon de caisse (Banq.), deposit receipt.

bon de caisse (pour la délivrance d'une somme d'argent), cash voucher.

bon de caisse (émis par une société, remboursable à échéance fixe), note.

bon de commande, order form ; order (the written and/or printed instrument).

bon de commission, commission order form ; commission order (the written and/or printed instrument).

bon de la Défense nationale, War bond.

bon de livraison *ou* bon d'enlèvement *ou* bon à enlever *ou* bon à délivrer, delivery order.
Note :—bon de livraison à valoir sur connaissement *is preferable in French when delivery order is a split of a bill of lading.*

bon de livraison du magasin d'approvisionnement, stores delivery note.

bon de paye, pay bill ; pay voucher.

bon de poste, postal order. (*Note :*—postal orders have been abolished in France following the creation of the *chèque postal* and the simplification of the use of low value money orders. *See note under* compte courant postal, *last paragraph*.)

bon de quai, wharfinger's receipt.

bon de réception (d'une marchandise), receiving order.

bon de réquisition du magasin d'approvisionnement, stores requisition note.

bons de souscription, (on the Paris Bourse) scrip certificates printed and issued by the *Chambre Syndicale des Agents de change* (Stock Exchange Committee), representing application rights : these rights certificates are issued to facilitate dealings and are exchangeable in due course for stock certificates or coupons in the companies concerned.

bon de virement. See **virement** (Banq.).

bon du Trésor, Treasury bond ; Exchequer bond.

bon (script ; vale) (*n.m.*), scrip ; deferred interest certificate.

bona fide, bona fide : in good faith :

agir bona fide, to act bona fide ; to act in good faith.

bond (*n.m.*), spurt ; jump :

l'action X. fait un nouveau bond de 805 à 1 020, atteignant ainsi son plus haut cours de cette année, contre 600 au plus bas, X. shares made a fresh spurt (*or* jump) from 805 to 1,020 francs, thus reaching their top price this year, against 600 bottom.

bondir (*v.i.*), to spurt ; to jump.

boni [**bonis** *pl.*] (revenant-bon) (*n.m.*) (Ant. : *mali*), surplus ; over ; unexpended balance.

boni (remise) (*n.m.*), rebate ; allowance.

boni (bénéfice) (*n.m.*), profit ; bonus :

avoir cent francs de boni dans une affaire, to make a hundred francs profit out of a deal.

bonification (*n.f.*), allowance ; rebate ; bonus :

bonification pour écart de qualité, allowance for difference of quality.

l'expression net indique qu'il n'y a pas de bonification d'escompte (*f.*), the expression net indicates that there is no allowance of discount.

jouir d'une bonification d'escompte sur des versements par anticipation, to receive a rebate on calls paid in advance.

bonification (déport) (Bourse) (*n.f.*) (Abrév. : **B.** *ou* **b.** *ou* **D.**), backwardation ; backwardization ; back :

vendeur à découvert qui paie une bonification (*m.*), bear seller who pays a backwardation (*or* a backwardization) (*or* a back).

bonifier (*v.t.*), to allow ; to credit ; to admit ; to make good ; to make up :

bonifier quelqu'un d'une remise, to allow someone a discount ; to credit someone with a discount.

l'intérêt bonifié aux déposants, aux versements anticipatifs (*m.*), the interest allowed (*or* credited) to depositors, on payments in advance.

bonifier une perte, to make good a loss.

bonifier en avarie commune le dommage causé à un navire ou à sa cargaison, to make good,

to admit, as general average the damage done to a ship or her cargo.

bonifier un déficit de poids, to make up a shortage in weight.

bonus [**bonus** *pl.*] (*n.m.*), bonus :

bonus en actions, share bonus.

répartir un bonus en actions nouvelles, to distribute a bonus in new shares.

bonus en espèces, cash bonus.

boom (*n.m.*), boom :

mais après ce boom, c'est la débâcle, but after this boom, there was a slump.

booming (*adj.*), booming :

le marché est booming (Bourse), the market is booming.

bord (*n.m.*) *ou* **bord de la mer** (*s'emploie surtout au pluriel*), shore ; coast ; seashore ; seacoast :

les bords de la mer Baltique, the shores of the Baltic ; the Baltic coast.

bord (d'un fleuve) (*n.m.*), bank (of a river).

bord (navire) (*n.m.*), ship :

le capitaine ne doit quitter son bord que le dernier *ou* le capitaine doit rester le dernier à son bord, the captain should be the last to leave his ship.

marchandises sacrifiées pour les nécessités du bord (*f.pl.*), cargo sacrificed for the necessities of the ship.

les embarcations du bord (*f.pl.*), the ship's boats.

bord (à) *ou* **bord de (à)**, on board ; aboard :

chargement de la marchandise à bord le navire (*ou* à bord du navire) (*m.*), loading the goods on board (*or* aboard) the ship.

frais jusqu'à bord du navire (*m.pl.*), expenses until on board the vessel.

bord à bord, free on board (*or* f.o.b.) to ex ship's sling :

fret payé bord à bord (*m.*), freight paid f.o.b. to ex ship's sling.

bord à quai, free on board (*or* f.o.b.) to landing on quay.

bordereau (*n.m.*), list ; schedule ; statement ; report ; slip ; note ; contract note ; contract ; bordereau :

bordereau d'agent de change *ou* bordereau de bourse, broker's contract note ; stockbroker's contract.

bordereau d'achat, purchase contract ; bought contract.

bordereau de vente, sale contract ; sold contract.

bordereau d'encaissement *ou* bordereau d'effets à l'encaissement (Banq.), list of bills for collection.

bordereau d'escompte *ou* bordereau d'effets à l'escompte (Banq.), list of bills for discount.

bordereau d'expédition *ou* bordereau de chargement, consignment note.

bordereau de caisse, cash statement :

le caissier devrait, chaque jour, établir un bordereau de caisse, pour justifier son encaisse, the cashier should, each day, draw up a cash statement, to prove his cash in hand.

bordereau de change, exchange contract.
bordereau de compte, statement of account.
bordereau de courtage, broker's note.
bordereau de débarquement, outturn report.
bordereau de factage, delivery sheet; carman's delivery sheet.
bordereau de pièces, list, schedule, of documents.
bordereau de portefeuille, list, schedule, of investments :
société qui publie un bordereau de son portefeuille (f.), company which publishes a list of its investments.
bordereau de versement (Banq.), paying in slip; credit slip; deposit slip.
bordereau des litiges (déchargement d'un navire), discrepancy report.
bordereau (valeurs énumérées sur un bordereau) (*n.m.*), bills (or the like) listed on a form (i.e., on a *discount form*, or *bills for collection form*) :
escompter, négocier, un bordereau, to discount, to negotiate, the bills listed on the form.
bornage (Navig.) (*n.m.*), limited coasting trade.
bouche (d'un fleuve) (*n.f.*), mouth (of a river).
bouée (*n.f.*), buoy.
bouger (*v.i.*), to budge; to move :
le cours ne bouge pas, the price does not budge (*or* move).
la privilégiée X. bouge peu aux environs de 1 510 fr., X. preference moved slightly round about 1,510 francs.
bourse (petit sac à argent) (*n.f.*), purse.
sans bourse délier, without putting one's hand in one's pocket; without any outlay.
bourse (lieu; édifice; marché) (*n.f.*), exchange; market; change; 'change; bourse :
bourse de commerce. According to French law, *bourse de commerce* means either a *bourse de marchandises* or a *bourse de valeurs*, but in common usage *bourse de commerce* means a *bourse de marchandises*.
bourse de (*ou* des) marchandises *ou* bourse de commerce, produce exchange; commercial sale rooms. *See note under* marché commercial.
bourse de (*ou* des) valeurs *ou* bourse d'effets publics *ou simplement* bourse, stock exchange; house; bourse :
Note :—The common French expression for *stock exchange* is simply *bourse*. *Bourse de valeurs* or *bourse d'effets publics* is only used to distinguish from some other exchange, such as a *bourse de marchandises*, or when doubt may exist as to what kind of exchange is meant.
la Bourse de Londres, the London Stock Exchange.
la Bourse de Paris, the Paris Bourse. *For information concerning the Paris Bourse, see under* marché des valeurs.
Note :—The full designation of the Paris Bourse building is *Palais de la Bourse*.
bourse maritime *ou* bourse des frets, shipping exchange.
sur la bourse *ou* **à la bourse** *ou* **en bourse,** on the

stock exchange; on the market; in the house; on 'change :
avis affiché en Bourse (*m.*), notice posted in the House.
Ce qui se dit en Bourse *ou* Ce qu'on dit en Bourse *ou simplement* En Bourse (rubrique de journal), Round the House; Round the Markets; Market News.
bourse (cours de la bourse) (*n.f.*), market :
la bourse est en hausse, bourse calme, bourse animée, the market has risen, market quiet, market lively.
bourse (jour de bourse; temps qui dure le marché) (*n.f.*), day; business day; working day; session; market; change; 'change :
deux opérations effectuées dans la même bourse, two deals done the same day (*or* during the same session *or* change).
les titres doivent être livrés dans les dix bourses qui suivent la vente (*ou* livrés avant la dixième bourse qui suit celle de la vente) (*m.pl.*), the stock must be delivered within ten business days of the sale.
cinq bourses pleines avant la date fixée pour le tirage, five clear business days (*or* working days) before the date fixed for the drawing.
actions vendues à la bourse de ce jour (*f.pl.*), shares sold at to-day's market.
boursicoter (*v.i.*), to dabble on the stock exchange.
boursicoteur, -euse *ou* **boursicotier, -ère** (pers.) (*n.*), dabbler on the stock exchange.
boursier, -ère (*adj.*), stock exchange; market (*used as adjs*) :
règlements boursiers (*m.pl.*), stock exchange regulations; market regulations.
transactions boursières (*f.pl.*), stock exchange transactions; market transactions.
boursier, -ère (pers.) (*n.*), operator :
nombre de boursiers préfèrent opérer au jour le jour à l'aide des primes pour le lendemain (*m.*), many operators prefer to deal from day to day by means of one day options.
boussole marine *ou* *simplement* **boussole** (*n.f.*), marine compass; compass.
bout de l'année (*m.*), end, close, of the year.
boutique (*n.f.*), shop; stable :
société véreuse émanant d'une boutique de moralité douteuse (*f.*), shady company emanating from a stable of doubtful morality.
boycottage (*n.m.*), boycott; boycotting.
boycotter (*v.t.*), to boycott.
bracelet en caoutchouc (*m.*), elastic band; india-rubber band; rubber ring.
branche (*n.f.*), branch :
branche de l'industrie, du commerce, branch of industry, of commerce (*or* of trade).
brasseur d'affaires (pers.) (*m.*), shady financier.
brevet (*n.m.*), certificate; licence :
brevet d'expert-comptable reconnu par l'État. In France, certificate granted by the Government to a qualified and registered professional accountant. A State registered accountant is entitled to style himself « Titulaire du Brevet d'Expert-comptable reconnu par l'État » or « Diplômé par le Gouvernement » (D.P.L.G.).

brevet de francisation (d'un navire), certificate of registry (of a ship); ship's register. *See* acte de francisation *the more usual term.*

brevet de pilote, pilot licence.

breveter un pilote, to license a pilot.

brigand (pers.) (*n.m.*), thief.

bris (casse) (*n.m.*), breakage:
bris des objets fragiles, breakage of fragile articles.

bris (d'un navire) (*n.m.*), break up; wreck; break; breaking.
Note :—French law, in the matter of maritime insurance, distinguishes.—
(1) **bris absolu** (absolute break up or total wreck), i.e., total loss of the ship, giving cause for abandonment.
(2) **bris partiel** (partial break), e.g., leak owing to collision, or the like, generally an average loss only.
(3) **échouement avec bris** (stranding with break), giving the option of abandonment.
(4) **échouement sans bris** (stranding without break), ship not broken up but cannot be refloated, giving rise to abandonment. (See note under **échouement.**)

bris (fragment d'un navire brisé) (*n.m.*), wreck; wreckage.

briser (*v.t.*), to break; to break up:
briser un cachet, to break a seal.
navire qui est brisé (*m.*), ship which is broken up (wrecked).

broche (*n.f.*) *ou* **broches** (*n.f.pl.*) (Banq.), small bills; bills of exchange of small amount, viz., bills under 50, 100, 200, 300, 500, or 1,000 francs, according to local acceptation of the term. Cf. **quatre chiffres.**

brochure (*n.f.*), pamphlet; booklet.

bronze (*n.m.*), copper; copper coin.

brouillard (*n.m.*) *ou* **brouillon** (main courante) (*n.m.*), rough book; waste book; day book; book; blotter:
brouillard de caisse (Banq.), counter cash book; teller's cash book.
brouillard de recettes *ou* brouillard d'entrée (Banq.), received cash book; received counter cash book.
brouillard de dépenses *ou* brouillard de sortie (Banq.), paid cash book; paying cashier's counter cash book.

brouillon (premier travail manuscrit) (*n.m.*), draft; rough draft; first draft:
brouillon de lettre, draft of a letter; draft letter.

bruit (nouvelle) (*n.m.*), news; report; rumour; rumor:
les bruits de fusion avec d'autres établissements sont dénués de fondement, the rumours (*or* reports) of amalgamation with other establishments are unfounded (*or* are without foundation).
le bruit court que ——, it is reported (*or* it is rumoured) that ——.

brûlant, -e (en parlant des effets, du papier de commerce, des valeurs) (*adj.*), hot; maturing in a few days; that have (*or* has) only a few days to run:

effets brûlants (*m.pl.*) *ou* papier brûlant (*m.*) *ou* valeurs brûlantes (*f.pl.*), hot bills; bills maturing in a few days; bills that have only a few days to run.

brut, -e (*adj.*) (Ant. : *net*), gross:
bénéfice brut (*m.*) *ou* bénéfices bruts (*m.pl.*), gross profit; gross profits.
recette brute (*f.*), gross receipts.
le montant brut d'une facture est son total sans escompte, the gross amount of an invoice is its total without discount.

brut (*n.m.*), gross; gross amount, proceeds, weight, or the like:
marchandises imposées au brut (*f.pl.*), goods charged with duty on the gross (*or* on the gross weight).

bruyant, -e (*adj.*), noisy:
réunion bruyante (*f.*), noisy meeting.

budget (*n.m.*), budget:
le budget de cet État se solde en équilibre, the budget of this State balances.

budgétaire (*adj.*), budgetary:
recettes budgétaires (*f.pl.*), budgetary receipts.

budgéter (*v.t.*), to budget for:
budgéter des dépenses, to budget for expenses.

buée de cale (*f.*), fumes from hold.

bulletin (*n.m.*), note; bulletin; notice; letter; ticket; voucher; list; form:
bulletin d'admission, admission ticket.
bulletin d'aliment (Assce d'abonnement), notice of interest declared.
bulletin d'application (Assce in quovis), notice of interest declared.
bulletin d'enregistrement des bagages *ou simplement* bulletin de bagages, luggage registration ticket (*or* voucher); luggage ticket; baggage voucher.
bulletin d'envoi, dispatch note.
bulletin d'épargne (Caisse d'épargne postale), coupon book.
bulletin d'expédition *ou* bulletin postal (Service des colis postaux), dispatch note.
bulletin de chargement *ou* bulletin de remise (Ch. de f.), consignment note.
bulletin de chargement (reçu de bord), mate's receipt.
bulletin de commande, order form; order (the written and/or printed instrument).
bulletin de consigne, cloak room ticket.
bulletin de cours, list of prices (*or* of quotations).
bulletin de la bourse (article dans un journal), stock exchange intelligence; money market intelligence; money market.
bulletin de la cote (Bourse), stock exchange daily official list.
bulletin de naissance, birth certificate.
bulletin de pesage, weight note.
bulletin de remboursement, trade charge letter; cash on delivery letter.
bulletin de renseignements, enquiry form.
bulletin de souscription, application form; form of application; letter of application.
bulletin de vente, bill (such as may be given to customers in a shop or store).

bureau (endroit où s'expédient les affaires) (*n.m.*), office ; counting house ; agency ; bureau :
bureau à service permanent *ou* bureau ouvert en permanence, office open always.
bureau d'adresses *ou* bureau d'écritures, addressing office ; envelope addressing agency.
bureau d'affaires, business agency.
bureau d'armement, shipping office.
bureau d'émission (mandats-poste, etc.), issuing office ; office of issue.
bureau d'enregistrement *ou* bureau d'immatricule, registry ; registration office.
bureau d'origine (Poste), office of origin.
bureau de change (bureau du changeur), bureau de change ; exchange office ; exchange.
bureau de change (enseigne d'un bureau de change), bureau de change ; foreign exchange ; foreign monies exchanged ; foreign exchange (*or* moneys) bought and sold ; exchange.
bureau de chèques. *See under* compte courant postal.
bureau de dactylographie, typewriting office.
bureau de départ (Poste), dispatching office.
bureau de dépôt (Poste), office of posting.
bureau de destination *ou* bureau destinataire (Poste), office of destination.
bureau de distribution *ou* bureau distributeur (Poste), delivering office ; delivery office.
bureau de (*ou* de la) douane, custom house.
bureau de l'inscription maritime, marine registry office.
bureau de la régie, excise office.
bureau de messageries, parcels office ; parcel office.
bureau de placement, employment agency ; employment bureau.
bureau de poste, post office.
bureau de poste ambulant, travelling post office.
bureau de publicité, advertising agency ; publicity bureau.
bureau de réception *ou* bureau récepteur *ou* bureau réceptionnaire (des télégrammes), receiving office.
bureau de renseignements, enquiry office.
bureau de tourisme, tourist office.
bureau de tri (Poste), sorting office.
bureau de ville *ou* bureau de réception, receiving office :
les marchandises reçues dans les bureaux de ville des compagnies de chemins de fer (*f.pl.*), the goods received in the receiving offices of the railway companies.
bureau de voyage, travel agency.
bureau des hypothèques, mortgage registry.
bureau des rebuts *ou* bureau du rebut (Poste), returned letter office ; dead letter office.
bureau des transferts, transfer office.
bureau du contentieux, solicitor's office (the office of the law department of an administration).
bureau du fret (d'une compagnie de navigation), freight office (of a shipping company). '
bureau du secrétaire, secretary's office.
bureau du timbre, stamp office.

bureau-gare [bureaux-gares *pl.*] (Poste) (*n.m.*), railway station office.
Bureau international du travail, International Labour Office.
bureau municipal de placement gratuit, labour exchange.
bureau payeur (mandats-poste, etc.), paying office ; office of payment.
bureau principal (Poste) (opp. à *bureau succursale*), head office.
bureau régional, district office.
bureau succursale [bureaux succursales *pl.*], branch office ; suboffice.
bureau télégraphique *ou* bureau du télégraphe, telegraph office.
Bureau Veritas *ou simplement* Veritas (*n.m.*) (société de classification de navires), Bureau Veritas ; Veritas :
le registre du Bureau Veritas est appelé le *Registre Veritas* du nom de l'emblème Vérité adopté par la Société, the register of the Bureau Veritas is called the *Veritas Register* from the emblem Truth adopted by the Society.
bureau (*n.m.*) *ou* **bureau central téléphonique** *ou* **bureau téléphonique,** exchange ; telephone exchange :
appeler le bureau, to call the exchange.
bureau central automatique *ou* bureau automatique, automatic exchange.
bureau central manuel *ou* bureau manuel, manual exchange.
bureau central interurbain *ou* bureau interurbain, trunk exchange.
bureau central régional *ou* bureau régional, toll exchange.
bureau d'attache, home exchange.
bureau local, local exchange.
bureau (meuble) (*n.m.*), table ; desk :
déposer sur le bureau (à une assemblée), to lay on the table :
bilan déposé sur le bureau, balance sheet laid on the table.
bureau américain, roll top desk.
bureau pour dactylographe, typewriter's table.
bureau (d'une assemblée) (*n.m.*). In France, the persons officiating at a shareholders' meeting, or other public meeting. The *bureau*, which generally consists of the chairman, the secretary, and two scrutineers have, for instance, to certify the correctness of the list of shareholders present.
bureau ouvert (à), on demand ; on presentation :
l'échange à bureau ouvert des billets contre espèces (*m.*), the exchange on demand (*or* on presentation) of notes for coin.
bureau restant (mots inscrits sur une lettre, un paquet), to be called for ; poste restante.
but (d'une société) (*n.m.*), objects (of a company) :
la société a pour but : l'achat, la vente, la prise à bail, etc. (statuts), the objects for which the company is established are : to purchase, to sell, to take on lease, etc. (memorandum of association).

buvard (*adj. m.*), blotting :
papier buvard (blanc, rose) (*m.*), blotting paper (white, pink).

buvard (*n.m.*), blotting pad ; blotting case ; blotter.
buvard (tampon) (*n.m.*), blotting dabber.

C

cabine (d'un navire) (*n.f.*), cabin (of a ship) :
cabine de pont, deck cabin.
cabine particulière, private cabin.
cabine téléphonique (*f.*), telephone call office ; telephone box ; telephone kiosk :
cabine téléphonique publique à encaissement automatique *ou* cabine taxiphone publique, prepayment call office.
cabinet (bureau) (*n.m.*), office ; chambers ; agency :
cabinet du directeur, manager's office.
cabinet d'un avocat, chambers or a barrister.
cabinet d'affaires, business agency.
câble (télégraphe sous-marin) (*n.m.*), cable :
câble transatlantique, transatlantic cable.
câble (câblogramme) (*n.m.*), cable :
envoyer un câble, to send a cable.
câble transfert *ou simplement* câble (Opérations de change), cable transfer ; cable ; telegraphic transfer ; telegraph transfer :
au marché des changes, le câble sur Londres se traite à . . ., on the foreign exchange market, London cables were (*or* the London cable *or* the cable on London was) dealt in at . . .
câbler (*v.t.*), to cable :
le directeur a câblé que . . ., the manager has cabled that . . .
câbler (*v.i.*), to cable :
câbler à quelqu'un, to cable to someone.
câblogramme (*n.m.*), cablegram ; cable :
envoyer un câblogramme, to send a cablegram ; to dispatch a cable.
cabotage (*n.m.*) (opp. à *long cours*), coasting ; coasting trade ; coastwise trade ; home trade :
cabotage d'un port français à un autre port français, entre ports français, entre ports de la métropole, coasting from one French port to another French port, between French ports, between home ports.
Note :—In France, *cabotage* is subdivided into **petit cabotage** (between ports of the same sea, i.e., not passing Gibraltar), **grand cabotage** (between ports of two different seas, i.e., passing Gibraltar), and **bornage** (limited coasting trade). **cabotage international** is navigation between a French port and any of the following—a foreign European port, a foreign Mediterranean port, a Moroccan port, an Icelandic port.
Cf. note under **long cours.**
The English term for navigation intermediate between deep-sea navigation and coasting navigation is *short-sea trading*, and a boat engaging in this navigation is called a *short-sea trader*.
caboter (*v.i.*), to coast.
caboteur *ou* **cabotier** (*adj.m.*), coasting.·
caboteur *ou* **cabotier** (*n.m.*), coaster ; coasting vessel (*or* ship) ; home-trade ship.
caboteur *ou* **cabotier** (pers.) (*n.m.*), coaster.
cachet (*n.m.*), seal :
cachet à la cire *ou* cachet de cire, wax seal.
cachet de douane, customs seal.
cachet social, corporate seal.
cachetage (*n.m.*), sealing.
cacheter (*v.t.*), to seal ; to seal up ; to do up :
cacheter une lettre, to seal, to seal up, to do up, a letter.
cadence (*n.f.*), tune :
production qui continue à la cadence de tant de tonnes par jour (*f.*), production which continues to the tune of so many tons a day.
cadre (compartiment d'une page réglée) (*n.m.*), frame ; space :
cadre réservé aux mentions de service, frame, space, for service instructions.
caduc, -uque (*adj.*), lapsed ; statute barred :
si l'assurance est caduque, if the insurance has lapsed.
dette caduque (*f.*), statute barred debt.
cahier de certificats (*m.*), certificate book ; book of certificates.
caisse (coffre de bois) (*n.f.*) (Abrév. : **c.**), case ; box :
une caisse de marchandises, a case of goods.
caisse à claire-voie, crate.
caisses d'origine, original cases. See example under **emballage.**
caisse doublée de fer-blanc, tin-lined case.
caisse doublée de zinc, zinc-lined case. ·
caisse pleine (opp. à *caisse à claire-voie*), close case.
caisse (fonds en caisse ou à la disposition du caissier) (*n.f.*), cash ; cash in hand :
l'employé chargé de l'important service de la caisse est appelé caissier (*m.*), the employee entrusted with the important department of the cash is called cashier.
caisse et Banque de France, cash in hand and at the Bank of France.
caisse (coffre à argent ; bureau ; guichet ; service) (*n.f.*), cash box ; till ; coffer ; register ; office ; cashier's office ; ·cashier's desk ; cash desk ; counter ; cash department :
espèces dans la caisse de la banque (*f.pl.*), cash in the bank's till.

les existences de la (*ou* dans la) caisse (Banq.) (*f.pl.*), the stocks in the till.

titres déposés dans les caisses de la banque (*m.pl.*), securities deposited in the bank's coffers.

généralement les titres au porteur doivent être déposés dans la caisse sociale avant l'assemblée, generally bearer shares must be lodged in the company's office before the meeting.

nous avons pris la liberté de fournir sur votre caisse, we have taken the liberty of drawing on you (*or* on your office).

le spécimen que vous avez déposé à notre caisse, the specimen you have lodged with us (*or* with, *or* in, our office).

caisse des paiements (d'une banque), paying counter.

caisse enregistreuse *ou* caisse contrôleuse, cash register.

en caisse, in hand; on hand; in the till :

vérifier le solde en caisse (*ou* le restant en caisse), les espèces ou billets en caisse, to check the balance in hand, the cash or notes in hand (*or* in the till).

fonds en caisse et en banque (*m.pl.*) *ou* espèces en caisse et à la banque (*f.pl.*) *ou* *simplement* caisse(s) et banque(s), cash in (*or* on) hand and at (*or* in) bank; cash at bankers and in (*or* on) hand.

caisse (livre de caisse) (*n.f.*), cash book.

caisse (établissement financier ou administratif qui reçoit des fonds en dépôt et les administre ou les fait valoir) (*n.f.*), bank; treasury; fund; association :

caisse d'amortissement, sinking fund.

caisse d'épargne, savings bank.

caisse de garantie (Bourse de marchandises), guarantee association.

caisse de liquidation (Bourse de marchandises), clearing house.

Note :—caisses de liquidation et de garantie or simply *caisses de liquidation* exist on certain French *marchés réglementés des bourses de commerce*. They are private institutions; the one at Paris is called « Caisse de liquidation des affaires en marchandises à Paris. » The object of the association is to guarantee the due execution of transactions registered with it by substituting itself, in case of need, for the defaulter, so that, if at the due date of a contract, one of the parties fails to carry out his bargain, the association assumes the liability, ensuring, as the case may be, payment to the seller or delivery to the buyer. The contractants must be members of the association. The association connects up and guarantees only the transactions registered with it. A transaction registered with the association is called a **marché par caisse.** One not registered with it is called a **marché hors caisse.** In Paris, *marchés hors caisse* are connected up by a certain bank, which fulfils the office of clearing house.

In order to cover itself, the association requires from each of the contractants a deposit called **original deposit** or simply **deposit** (called so in French, and sometimes written **deposit,** without an accent on the *e*, or sometimes the French word **dépôt** is used).

Moreover, any or each variation in price gives rise to a call of margin (*appel de marge*) from the loser.

In case of default, the association closes the transaction, officially purchasing against or selling against the defaulter, and summons the defaulter to pay.

Theoretically, the deposits, margins, profits, losses, commissions, and expenses, should occasion so many payments and withdrawals of cash, but in practice, the contractants have a current account with the association, which is debited or credited. Instead of cash, the contractant's current account can be secured by lodging securities, warrants, goods, bonds, or other sureties. The association may accept a purchase as guarantee of a sale, or vice versa. This is called a **jumelage** (contra account).

caisse de prévoyance, provident fund :

caisse de prévoyance du personnel, staff provident fund.

caisse de retraites *ou* caisse des retraites, pension fund.

caisse des retraites pour la vieillesse, old age pension fund.

caisse de secours, relief fund.

caisse hypothécaire, mortgage loan office.

caisse nationale d'épargne *ou* caisse d'épargne postale *ou* caisse nationale d'épargne postale (*Abrév. :* C.N.E.), post office savings bank; postal savings bank.

caisse publique, national treasury.

caissier (pers.) (*n.m.*), cashier.

caissier-comptable [caissiers-comptables *pl.*] (*n.m.*), cashier and bookkeeper.

caissier des titres, securities clerk.

caissière (pers.) (*n.f.*), cashier; lady cashier.

caissier (guichetier) (d'une banque) (*n.m.*), cashier; teller :

caissier des recettes, receiving cashier; receiver.

caissier payeur *ou* caissier des paiements, paying cashier; payer.

caissier principal, chief cashier.

calcul (*n.m.*), calculation; reckoning; computation :

pour simplifier le calcul des intérêts, on a adopté partout, sauf en Angleterre, l'année de 360 jours, parce que ce chiffre de 360, qui appartient au système duodécimal, a un très grand nombre de diviseurs et qu'il fournit, par conséquent, de nombreuses parties aliquotes pour tous les taux d'intérêts, in order to simplify the calculation of interest, the year of 360 days has been adopted everywhere, except in England, because this figure of 360, which belongs to the duodecimal system, has a very large number of divisors and consequently furnishes numerous aliquot parts for all rates of interest.

calcul (combinaisons) (*n.m.*), calculation; calculations :
le résultat a trompé notre calcul, the result has upset our calculations.

calculable (*adj.*), calculable.

calculant, -e *ou* **calculateur, -trice** (*adj.*), calculating; reckoning; computing.

calculateur, -trice (pers.) (*n.*), calculator; reckoner.

calculer (*v.t.*), to calculate; to reckon; to compute :
calculer le prix d'une chose, to calculate the price of a thing.
calculer ses dépenses d'après ses revenus, to regulate one's expenses according to one's income.

se calculer (*v.r.*), to be calculated; to be reckoned; to be computed :
la taxe se calcule sur le montant des capitaux, the tax is calculated on the amount of the capital.

cale (d'un navire) (*n.f.*), hold (of a ship) :
les marchandises sont arrimées dans la cale (*f.pl.*), cargo is stowed in the hold.
Note :—A *bonded shed*, in French, is called a *magasin-cale*, a bonded place being reputed by the Customs as a *cale* or hold of a ship.

cale (rampe d'embarcadère) (*n.f.*), slip; way.

cale d'échouage (*f.*), graving beach.

cale de halage (*f.*), slipway.

cale flottante (*f.*), floating dock.

cale sèche *ou* **cale de radoub** (*f.*), dry dock; graving dock.

calendrier (*n.m.*), calendar.

calepin (*n.m.*), notebook; memorandum book.

calier (pers.) (*n.m.*), holder (one employed in the hold of a vessel).

calme (*adj.*), quiet :
bourse calme (*f.*), market quiet.

cambial, -e, -aux (*adj.*), of or relating to exchange; exchange (*used as adj.*) :
droit cambial (*m.*), law of exchange; law relating to exchange; exchange law.

cambisme (*n.m.*), foreign exchange; foreign exchange transactions (*or dealings*).

cambiste (pers.) (*n.m.*), exchange broker; foreign exchange broker; exchange dealer; cambist.

camion (*n.m.*), lorry :
camion à vapeur, steam lorry.
camion automobile, motor lorry.

camionnage (transport) (*n.m.*), cartage; carting; carriage; carrying : (*Note :—camionnage* is cartage (i.e., collection or delivery) of goods sent or received by goods train, in distinction to *factage*, q.v.)
camionnage au vapeur, de la gare à quai, cartage to the steamer, from the station to the quay.

camionnage (prix du transport) (*n.m.*), cartage; carriage.

camionner (*v.t.*), to cart; to carry.

camionneur (pers.) (*n.m.*), carter; carrier; carman.

campagne (*n.f.*), campaign :
campagne de baisse (Bourse), bear campaign.
campagne de hausse (Bourse), bull campaign.

campagne de presse, press campaign.
campagne de publicité, advertising campaign.
campagne actuelle *ou* campagne en cours (Marché aux grains), present campaign.
campagne future (Marché aux grains), coming campaign.

canal (*n.m.*) *ou* **canal de navigation**, canal; navigation :
le canal de Suez, le canal de Panama, the Suez canal, the Panama canal.
canal éclusé, locked canal.
canal maritime, ship canal :
le canal maritime de Manchester, the Manchester ship canal.
canal maritime en eau profonde, deep-water ship canal.

candidat (pers.) (*n.m.*), candidate :
examen de candidats (*m.*), examination of candidates.

canif (*n.m.*), penknife.

canot (*n.m.*), boat : (See also **bateau** and **embarcation**.)
canot à vapeur, steamboat.
canot de sauvetage, lifeboat.

caoutchouc (bande en caoutchouc) (*n.m.*), elastic band; rubber ring; indiarubber band.

caoutchoucs (*n.m.pl.*) *ou* **caoutchoutières** (*n.f.pl.*) *ou* **valeurs de caoutchouc** (*f.pl.*), rubbers; rubber shares.

caoutchoutier, -ère (*adj.*), rubber (*used as adj.*) :
groupe caoutchoutier (Bourse) (*m.*), rubber group.

capable (*adj.*), capable.

capacité (*n.f.*), capacity :
évaluer la capacité d'achat d'un pays, to estimate the purchasing capacity of a country.
manquer de capacité pour les affaires, to lack capacity for business.
capacité de charge (d'un chaland), carrying capacity (of a barge).

capitaine (pers.) (*n.m.*) (Abrév. : **Cap.** *ou* **Capit.** *ou* **C.**), captain; master; skipper (*colloquial*) :
le capitaine et l'équipage, the master and the crew.
capitaine de navire, ship's captain; shipmaster.
capitaine au cabotage, master of coasting vessel.
capitaine au long cours, deep-sea captain; captain (*or master*) of foreign-going vessel.
capitaine d'armement, marine superintendent.
capitaine de port, harbour master.

capital (somme dont le placement doit rapporter des intérêts) (*en ce sens s'emploie souvent au pluriel*) (*n.m.*), principal; capital; capital sum; money :
capital et intérêt *ou* capitaux et intérêts, principal and interest :
les intérêts s'ajoutent aux capitaux, the interest is added to the principal.
capital d'une lettre de change, principal of a bill of exchange.
capital investi, capital (*or money*) invested.
capitaux de placement, investment capital.

date à partir de laquelle le capital, un capital, commence à porter intérêt (*f.*), date from which the principal (*or* the capital), a capital sum, begins to bear interest.

les intérêts ne courent qu'à partir des dates d'entrée en valeur des capitaux (*m.pl.*), interest only runs from the value dates of the capital sums.

pour se livrer à ce genre d'opérations, il faut disposer d'un certain capital, in order to engage in this kind of transaction, it is necessary to have a certain capital at command.

les capitaux nécessaires à la construction de la ligne, the capital (*or* the money) required to construct the line.

capital reporteur *ou* capitaux reporteurs (Bourse), money lent (on stock taken in).

les capitaux sont rares, money is scarce.

capital (*n.m.*) *ou* **capitaux** (*n.m.pl.*) (biens que l'on possède), capital; assets:

capital de roulement, working capital:
le capital de roulement nécessaire aux besoins de l'exploitation, the working capital necessary to the needs of the undertaking.

capital disponible, available capital.

capital engagé, trading capital.

capitaux fixes *ou* capital fixe *ou* capital immobilisé, fixed capital; fixed assets; permanent assets; capital assets:
les immobilisations représentent tous les capitaux correspondant au capital fixe, et par opposition au capital circulant, capital expenditure represents all capital (*or* assets) corresponding to fixed capital (*or* assets), and as opposed to floating capital (*or* circulating assets).

capitaux mobiles *ou* capitaux mobiliers *ou* capitaux circulants *ou* capitaux roulants *ou* capitaux flottants, floating capital; floating assets; circulating capital; circulating assets; revenue assets.

capital (fonds monnayés ou monnayables d'une société d'exploitation) (*n.m.*) (Abrév.: **cap.**), capital:

capital-actions (*n.m.*), share capital:
société avec un capital-actions de tant (*f.*), company with a share capital of so much.

capital-actions versé, share capital paid up; paid up share capital.

capital appelé, called up capital; capital called up.

capital-apports (opp. à *capital-espèces*), capital issued as fully paid up otherwise than in cash.

capital d'emprunt, loan capital.

capital effectif, paid up capital; capital paid up.

capital entièrement (*ou* complètement) (*ou* intégralement) versé, fully paid capital; capital fully paid up.

capital-espèces (*n.m.*) *ou* capital-numéraire (*n.m.*) *ou* capital de numéraire *ou* capital en numéraire, cash capital.

capital initial *ou* capital d'apport *ou* capital d'établissement, initial capital; opening capital.

capital non appelé, uncalled capital.

capital non entièrement versé *ou* capital non libéré, partly paid capital; capital partly paid up.

capital-obligations (*n.m.*), debenture capital.

capital réel, paid up capital; capital paid up.

capital social (d'une société en nom collectif), capital of a firm; firm's capital; partnership capital. See note under **social.**

capital social (d'une société par actions), capital of a company; capital of the company; company's capital:
le capital social est fixé à . . . francs et divisé en . . . actions de . . . francs chacune (statuts), the capital of the company is . . . francs divided into . . . shares of . . . francs each (memorandum of association).

capital social *ou* capital nominal (opp. à *capital versé*), authorized capital; nominal capital; registered capital:
le capital social d'une compagnie *ou* le capital nominal d'une société, the authorized (*or* the nominal) (*or* the registered) capital of a company.

société au capital nominal de tant (*f.*), company with an authorized (*or* a nominal) (*or* a registered) capital of so much.

capital versé, paid up capital; capital paid up.

capital (**la**) (Abrév.: **cap.**). In French market news *actions de capital* are often referred to as *la capital*. See *explanation and example under* actions de capital.

capitalisable (*adj.*), capitalizable:
intérêts capitalisables (*m.pl.*), capitalizable interest.

capitalisation (*n.f.*), capitalization:
capitalisation des intérêts, des valeurs, du revenu moyen des deux années précédentes, capitalization of interest, of stocks, of the average income for the previous two years.

la capitalisation boursière d'une entreprise s'obtient en multipliant le prix de l'action par le nombre de titres, the market capitalization of a concern is obtained by multiplying the price of the share by the number of shares.

capitaliser (*v.t.*), to capitalize:
capitaliser des intérêts, une rente, to capitalize interest, an income.

capitaliser à 5 0/0 la moyenne des dividendes des quatre dernières années, to capitalize at 5% the average of the last four years' dividends.

l'action capitalise à 4 1/2 0/0 environ son dernier dividende de 125 francs (*f.*), the share capitalizes at about $4\frac{1}{2}\%$ its last dividend of 125 francs.

se capitaliser (*v.r.*), to be capitalized; to capitalize at:
l'intérêt se capitalise en fin d'année, à chaque arrêté (*m.*), the interest is capitalized at the end of the year, at each rest.

actions qui se capitalisent à 4 0/0 (*f.pl.*), shares which capitalize at 4%. *Cf.* taux de capitalisation.

capitalisme (*n.m.*), capitalism.

capitaliste (*adj.*), capitalistic.
capitaliste (*n.m.* ou *f.*), capitalist.
capteur (pers.) (*n.m.*), captor.
capture (*n.f.*), capture ; taking.
caractère (figure) (*n.m.*), character :
les caractères employés pour la classification des navires, the characters used for the classification of ships.
caractère (nature de l'âme) (*n.m.*), character :
avoir bon caractère, to have a good character.
caractéristique (*n.f.*), characteristic ; feature :
la caractéristique du bilan est l'importance du poste obligations, the feature of the balance sheet is the amount of the item debentures.
carbone (papier carbone pour machines à écrire) (*n.m.*), carbon.
carénage (*n.m.*), careenage.
carène (d'un navire) (*n.f.*), bottom (of a ship) :
examen de la carène après échouement (*m.*), sighting the bottom after stranding.
caréner (*v.t.*), to careen.
caréner (*v.i.*), to careen.
cargaison (*n.f.*), cargo ; freight ; lading :
une cargaison de bois, de pétrole, a wood cargo, an oil cargo ; a cargo of timber, of oil.
navire qui débarque la totalité ou une partie de sa cargaison (*m.*), ship which lands the whole or part of her cargo (or freight).
cargaison complète *ou* cargaison entière, full cargo.
cargaison mixte, mixed cargo.
cargo-boat [**cargo-boats** *pl.*] *ou simplement* **cargo** (*n.m.*) (opp. à *paquebot*), cargo boat ; cargo vessel ; freighter.
cargo-citerne [**cargos-citernes** *pl.*] (*n.m.*), tank ship ; tank vessel ; tanker.
cargo-liner [**cargo-liners** *pl.*] (*n.m.*), cargo liner.
cargo mixte (*m.*), cargo and passenger steamer (*or* vessel).
carnet (*n.m.*), book ; notebook ; memorandum book : (See also **livre**.)
carnet à souche *ou* carnet à souches, counterfoil book ; stub book.
carnet d'agent de change *ou* carnet à marchés *ou simplement* carnet, bargain book ; book ; stockbroker's bargain book.
carnet d'échéance *ou* carnet d'échéances, diary (a book for recording in order of due date payments to be made or amounts to be collected) ; bill diary.
carnet de chèques, cheque book.
carnet de commandes (*ou* d'ordres), order book.
ordres en carnet (*m.pl.*) *ou* commandes en carnet (*f.pl.*), orders in hand ; unfilled orders.
carnet de compte *ou* carnet de banque, pass book ; bank pass book.
carnet de formules, book of forms.
carnet de livraison (colis), delivery book.
carnet de passages en douane (automobiles), pass book.
carnet de petite caisse, petty cash book.
carnet de poche, pocketbook ; notebook.
carnet de poche à feuillets mobiles, loose leaf pocketbook.
carnet de recettes, receipts book.

carnet de timbres (Poste), book of stamps.
carnet de voyage circulaire, circular tour ticket.
carnet genre manifold, manifold book.
carotte (en bourse) (*n.f.*), fraudulent overcharge by a stockbroker putting through a bargain to his client at a price other than the real market price : a client thus overcharged is said to be **carotté**.
carrière (profession) (*n.f.*), career :
embrasser une carrière, to take up a career.
cartable (buvard) (*n.m.*), blotter ; blotting pad.
carte (*n.f.*), card :
carte d'abonnement, season ticket ; season :
carte d'abonnement d'élève, scholars' season ticket.
carte d'abonnement de travail, workman's season ticket.
carte d'abonnement ordinaire, ordinary season ticket.
carte d'abonnement pour associés ou gérants d'entreprises commerciales et industrielles, trader's season ticket.
carte d'adresse, address card ; business card.
carte d'assuré, insurance card.
carte d'identité, identity card.
carte d'identité (accompagnant une lettre de crédit, ou analogue), letter of indication.
carte de départs, shipping card.
carte de Noël, Christmas card.
carte du Nouvel An, New year card.
carte-fiche [cartes-fiches *pl.*] (*n.f.*), loose card ; index card ; card.
carte-guide [cartes-guides *pl.*] (répertoire sur fiches) (*n.f.*), guide card.
carte-lettre [cartes-lettres *pl.*] (Poste) (*n.f.*), letter card.
carte marine *ou simplement* carte, chart.
carte pneumatique *ou* carte-télégramme [cartes-télégrammes *pl.*] (*n.f.*), a postcard, which, in certain large towns in France, is transmitted by pneumatic tubes.
carte postale, postcard :
carte postale avec réponse payée (*Abrév.* carte postale avec R.P.), reply paid postcard.
carte postale illustrée, picture postcard.
carte postale-réponse [cartes postales-réponse *pl.*], reply half of reply paid postcard.
carte routière, route map ; road map.
cartel (*n.m.*), cartel :
cartel de banques, cartel of banks.
cartel de l'acier, steel cartel.
carton (*n.m.*), cardboard box ; drawer (of a document cabinet).
carton buvard (*m.*), blotter ; blotting case.
carton ondulé (*m.*), corrugated cardboard.
cartonnier (*n.m.*), document cabinet.
cartothèque (répertoire sur fiches) (*n.f.*), card index.
cartothèque (meuble-fichier) (*n.f.*), card index ; card index cabinet.
cas fortuit (*m.*), fortuitous event.
case (compartiment d'une page réglée) (*n.f.*), frame ; space :
case réservée aux mentions de service, frame, space, for service instructions.

caser des papiers, to put papers away.

casse (*n.f.*), breakage :
casse des objets fragiles, breakage of fragile articles.

casser les cours, to bang the market. See example under **travailler.**

cassette (*n.f.*), cash box.

catalogue (*n.m.*), catalogue ; list :
catalogues illustrés et prix sur demande, illustrated catalogues (*or* lists) and prices on application.

cataloguement (*n.m.*), cataloguing ; cataloging ; listing.

cataloguer (*v.t.*), to catalogue ; to list :
un objet catalogué à tant, an article catalogued (*or* listed) at so much.

cause (ce qui fait que la chose est) (*n.f.*), cause :
cause immédiate (d'un accident de mer), immediate cause ; proximate cause ; final cause ; causa proxima.
cause première *ou* cause primitive (d'un accident de mer), remote cause ; causa remota.

cause (Dr.) (*n.f.*), cause ; case ; action ; proceeding :
cause civile, civil action.
cause sommaire, summary proceeding.

cause (d'un effet de commerce, d'une lettre de change, d'un contrat) (*n.f.*), consideration :
effet de commerce qui énonce la cause de sa création, c'est-à-dire si la valeur en a été fournie en espèces, en marchandises, ou en compte (*m.*), bill of exchange which states the consideration for its creation, that is to say, if value for it has been given in cash, in goods, or in account.
les valeurs de complaisance n'ont pour cause aucune opération commerciale (*f.pl.*), accommodation bills have no commercial transaction as consideration.
la cause dans le contrat d'affrètement, the consideration in the contract of affreightment.
la cause de l'assurance doit être licite, the consideration for the insurance must be legal.
dans une vente, la cause de la vente est le paiement du prix par l'acquéreur, in a sale, the consideration for the sale is the payment of the price by the purchaser.
Cf. **provision.**

causer (*v.t.*), to state the consideration :
billet qui a été causé en valeur reçue comptant (*m.*), bill which states that the consideration received was cash.

caution (pers.) (*n.f.*), surety ; security ; guarantor ; guarantee :
être caution de quelqu'un, to be surety for someone ; to be somebody's guarantor.
soumission cautionnée aux termes de laquelle le déclarant et une ou deux cautions s'engagent de payer le montant des droits de douane, bond under which the declarant and one or two sureties undertake to pay the amount of the customs duties.

caution (garantie) (*n.f.*), surety ; security ; guarantee ; guaranty ; indemnity ; caution money ; letter of indemnity :
caution de banque, bank guarantee.

demander une caution, to ask for security (*or* a guarantee) (*or* an indemnity). See also examples under **fournir.**
obtenir un duplicata d'un certificat perdu en donnant caution, to obtain a duplicate of a lost certificate by giving a letter of indemnity (*or* by giving an indemnity).
caution judicatum solvi (Dr.), security for costs.

cautionné, -e (pers.) (*n.*), guarantee (person guaranteed).

cautionnement (action) (*n.m.*), securing ; guaranteeing ; giving security for.

cautionnement (valeur ou somme déposée) (*n.m.*), security ; indemnity ; caution money ; deposit :
cautionnement déposé par un employé, security given by an employee.
cautionnements exigés pour la délivrance de duplicata des titres perdus, indemnities required for the delivery of duplicates of lost scrip.
cautionnement au gaz, deposit with gas company.
une chose ne se restitue jamais tant que l'affaire n'est pas liquidée : c'est le cautionnement, one thing is never returned so long as the business is not closed : that is the security.

cautionnement (contrat de garantie) (*n.m.*), bond ; surety bond ; indemnity bond ; indemnity ; letter of indemnity :
s'engager par cautionnement, to pledge oneself by an indemnity bond.
cautionnement d'une association de cautionnement pour assurer la fidélité d'une personne sur le point d'être nommée à un poste, bond of a guarantee society to insure the fidelity of a person about to be appointed to a post.

cautionnement (actions affectées à la garantie des actes de gestion) (*n.m.*), qualification :
cautionnement en actions, share qualification ; qualification in shares :
les administrateurs doivent avoir un cautionnement en actions de la société (*m.pl.*), the directors must have a qualification in shares of the company.
les administrateurs doivent être propriétaires, pendant toute la durée de leur mandat, de chacun —— action(s) au moins (statuts d'une société par actions), the qualification of a director shall be the holding of at least —— share(s) in the company (regulations for management of a company limited by shares [Table A]).
Cf. actions de garantie.

cautionner (*v.t.*), to become surety for ; to guarantee ; to secure ; to give security for ; to answer for :
cautionner un caissier, to become surety for, to guarantee, to secure, a cashier.
cautionner des droits de douane, to give security for customs duties.
cautionner la probité de quelqu'un, to answer for someone's honesty.

cavalerie (traites en l'air) (*n.f.*), kites ; windmills.

cave (*n.f.*), cellar ; room :

le stock d'or dans les caves de la banque, the stock of gold in the bank's cellars.

cave forte, strong room.

ce jour (c.-à-d. cours de ce jour) (rubrique de bulletin de la cote), to-day.

Ce qui se dit en Bourse *ou* **Ce qu'on dit en Bourse** (rubrique de journal), Round the House; Round the Markets; Market News.

cédant, -e (pers.) (*n.*), transferor; assignor; grantor :
cédant d'une action, d'un effet de commerce, transferor of a share, of a bill of exchange.

céder (abandonner) (*v.t.*), to cede; to yield; to give up; to surrender; to part with; to dispose of :
céder un droit, to surrender, to cede, a right.
céder une propriété, to give up, to part with, to dispose of, a property.

céder (transférer) (*v.t.*), to transfer; to assign :
céder des actions, un effet, to transfer shares, a bill.
les billets de passage sont personnels et ne peuvent être cédés (*m.pl.*), passage tickets are personal and cannot be transferred.

se céder (*v.r.*), to be transferred.

céder (en parlant des valeurs de bourse) (*v.t.*), to yield; to shed; to lose :
action qui cède quelques fractions (*f.*), share which yields (*or* sheds) (*or* loses) a few fractions.

cédule (Fin.) (*n.f.*), cedula.

cédule (Impôts cédulaires) (*n.f.*), schedule :
si on est imposé aux diverses cédules des impôts sur les revenus, if one is assessed under various income tax schedules.
bénéfice qui est taxée dans une autre cédule (*m.*), profit which is taxed under another schedule.

censé, -e (*adj.*), deemed :
chaque embarcation, radeau, ou allège, sera censé l'objet d'une assurance distincte, each craft, raft, or lighter, to be deemed the subject of a separate insurance.

censeur (préposé du gouvernement) (*n.m.*), censor.

censeur (commissaire des comptes) (pers.) (*n.m.*), auditor.

censure (*n.f.*), censorship :
tous les télégrammes échangés avec ce pays-là sont soumis à la censure, all telegrams exchanged with that country are liable to censorship.

censurer (*v.t.*), to censor.

cent (monnaie) (*n.m.*) (Abrév.: **c.** *ou* **ct** [**cts** *pl.*]), cent.

centime (monnaie) (*n.m.*) (Abrév.: **c.**), centime.

central téléphonique (*m.*), telephone exchange. (See **bureau central**, the more usual expression, for varieties.)

centre (*n.m.*), centre :
centre de tourisme, tourist centre.
centre des affaires, centre of business; business centre :
le cœur de Londres est la City, centre des affaires, the heart of London is the City, the business centre.

cerf-volant [**cerfs-volants** *pl.*] (traite en l'air) (*n.m.*), kite; windmill.

certain (Changes) (*n.m.*), fixed exchange (i.e., rate of exchange); certain exchange; direct exchange. *See* donner le certain *for example.*

certificat (*n.m.*), certificate; scrip: (See also **titre.**)
certificat à passagers, passenger certificate.
certificat d'actions *ou* certificat d'action (*s'il s'agit d'une action seulement*), share certificate.
certificat d'action(s) de priorité, preference share certificate.
certificat d'action(s) ordinaire(s), ordinary share certificate.
certificat d'arrivée (Douanes), certificate of clearing inwards.
certificat d'assurance, insurance certificate; certificate of insurance :
le certificat d'assurance remplace souvent la police d'assurance, ou en est le complément indispensable, au cours d'opérations commerciales, the insurance certificate often replaces the insurance policy, or is its indispensable complement, in the course of commercial transactions.
certificat d'avarie *ou* certificat d'avaries (avaries communes ou particulières), certificate of damage; damage report.
certificat d'embarquement, certificate of shipment.
certificat d'inscription hypothécaire, certificate of registration of mortgage.
certificat d'obligation(s), debenture certificate.
certificat d'origine, certificate of origin.
certificat de bon arrimage, report of stowage.
certificat de chargement, mate's receipt.
certificat de classification *ou* certificat de cote (navires), classification certificate.
certificat de constructeur (de navires), builder's certificate.
certificat de jauge *ou* certificat de jaugeage (navires), certificate of measurement.
certificat de médecin *ou* certificat médical, doctor's certificate; medical certificate.
certificat de navigabilité (d'un navire), certificate of seaworthiness.
certificat de navigabilité (d'un aéroplane), certificate of airworthiness.
certificat de radiation (d'une hypothèque), certificate of satisfaction (*or* reduction), copy of memorandum of satisfaction (of a mortgage).
certificat de sortie (congé maritime), clearance; certificate of clearing outwards.
certificat de visite, inspection certificate; survey certificate.
certificat fiduciaire, trustee's certificate.
certificat hypothécaire, certificate of mortgage; certificate of the existence (*or* non existence) of mortgages. *Note*:—(*or* In France, the **certificat** or **état** is said to be **positif** if mortgages exist, and **négatif** if none exist.
certificat international de route, international travelling pass.
certificat mixte, registered certificate with coupons attached.
certificat nominatif, registered certificate; registered scrip.

certificat nominatif d'action(s), registered share certificate.

certificat-or [certificats-or   pl.] (États-Unis) (n.m.), gold certificate.

certificat provisoire, scrip; scrip certificate; provisional certificate; interim certificate.

certificateur, -trice (adj.), certifying:
notaire certificateur (m.), certifying notary.

certificateur de caution (pers.) (m.), counter surety.

certificatif, -ive (adj.), certificatory; in support:
pièce certificative (f.), voucher; document in support.

certification (n.f.), certification; witnessing:
certification de signatures (Bourse), certification (or witnessing) of signatures (by a broker or notary on transfer of stock).

certifier (v.t.), to certify; to witness:
copie des procès-verbaux certifiée par les administrateurs (f.), copy of the minutes certified by the directors.
copie certifiée conforme à l'original (f.), certified a true copy.

cessation (n.f.), cessation; discontinuance; interruption; suspension; stoppage:
cessation de paiements, suspension, stoppage, of payment (or of payments).
cessation d'entreprise, discontinuance of business.

cesser (v.t.), to cease; to discontinue; to suspend; to stop:
cesser le paiement (ou les payements), to suspend, to stop, payment (or payments).

cesser (v.i.), to cease; to stop; to come to an end:
cesser de vendre, to stop selling.

cessibilité (n.f.), transferability:
cessibilité d'une action, transferability of a share.

cessible (adj.), transferable:
le trait caractéristique de l'action est qu'elle est librement cessible, the characteristic feature of the share is that it is freely transferable.

cession (n.f.), transfer; assignment; cession:
cession d'actions, transfer of shares.
cession de créances, assignment of debts.
cession de biens, assignment, cession, of property (to creditors).

cession-transport [cessions-transports pl.] (n.f.), assignment (of debts or other incorporeal property).

cessionnaire (pers.) (n.m. ou f.) (opp. à cédant), transferee; assignee; grantee:
cessionnaire d'une action, d'un effet de commerce, transferee of a share, of a bill of exchange.
cessionnaire d'une créance, assignee of a debt.

chaise (n.f.), chair:
chaise de pont, deck chair.
chaise tournante, revolving chair.

chaland ou **chalan** (n.m.), barge; lighter:
chaland de mer, seagoing barge.

chalandage (n.m.), lighterage.

chaloupe (n.f.), launch.

chalutier (n.m.), trawler.

chambre (n.f.), chamber; room; house; committee:

chambre de commerce, chamber of commerce.
Chambre de commerce internationale, International Chamber of Commerce.
chambre de compensation, clearing house.
chambre de compensation des banquiers, bankers' clearing house.
chambre de discipline, disciplinary committee.
chambre des valeurs (dans un navire), strong room.
chambre syndicale des agents de change, stock exchange committee.

chambre (cabine d'un navire) (n.f.), cabin.

champ (n.m.), field:
champ d'opérations, d'activité, field of operations, of activity.

chance (n.f.), chance; luck; risk:
les chances sont en sa faveur, the chances are in his favour.
bonne chance, mauvaise chance, porter chance, avoir de la chance, good luck, bad luck, to bring luck, to have luck (or to be lucky).

chancelant, -e (adj.), unsteady:
cours chancelants (m.pl.), unsteady prices.

chanceux, -euse (qui a une chance heureuse) (adj.), lucky; fortunate:
homme chanceux (m.), lucky man.

chanceux, -euse (hasardeux) (adj.), risky:
affaire chanceuse (f.), risky business.

change (troc d'une chose contre une autre) (n.m.), exchange; barter:
monnaie de change (f.), money of exchange.

change (commerce des monnaies et des titres qui les représentent) (n.m.), exchange:
le change des monnaies, des billets de banque, the exchange of moneys, of bank notes.
spéculer sur les changes, to speculate in exchanges.
l'encaissement des traites sur l'étranger soulève des questions de change (m.), the collection of foreign bills raises questions of exchange.
change commercial ou change tiré, commercial exchange; bill exchange.
change direct, direct exchange.
change extérieur ou change étranger ou simplement change, foreign exchange; external exchange; exchange.
change indirect, indirect exchange.
change intérieur, · internal exchange.
change maritime, marine interest; maritime interest.
change nominal, nominal exchange.
change réel ou change manuel ou change menu ou change local, real exchange; money exchange.

change (instrument de transfert; lettre(s) de change) (n.m.), exchange:
acheter du change, to buy exchange.

change (cours du change) (n.m.), exchange; rate of exchange:
le change de Paris sur Londres est le prix en francs, à Paris, des titres payables à Londres en livres sterling, the exchange (or the rate of exchange) of Paris on London is the price in francs, in Paris, of securities payable in London in pounds sterling.
remise en monnaie étrangère convertie en

francs au change du jour (*f.*), remittance in foreign money converted into francs at the exchange of the day.

change à la parité *ou* change à parité, exchange at parity. See **parité** for example.

change au pair, exchange at par. See **pair**.

change défavorable *ou* change contraire, unfavourable exchange; exchange against us:
le change (*ou* le taux du change) est défavorable (*ou* contraire) à notre place, the exchange (*or* the rate of exchange) is against us (*or* unfavourable to [*or* for] our market).

change favorable, favourable exchange; exchange for us.

change fixe (opp. à *change du jour*) (*Abrév.:* ch. f. *ou* ch. fixe), fixed exchange.

change (compte du grand livre) (Comptab.), exchange.

change (*n.m.*) *ou* **bureau de change** (*m.*) (bureau du changeur), bureau de change; exchange office; exchange.

change (*n.m.*) *ou* **bureau de change** (*m.*) (enseigne d'un bureau de change), bureau de change; foreign exchange; foreign exchange bought and sold; foreign monies exchanged; exchange.

change (commission du changeur) (*n.m.*), exchange:
change de place *ou* changes de place *ou* simplement change *ou* changes (Banq.), cost (*or* costs) of collection (of bills of exchange); bank charges (on bills).
Note:—Most of the French banks make three distinct charges for discounting bills: (1) *escompte* (discount [the only charge made in England]), (2) *commission*, and (3) *changes*.

change (menue monnaie) (*n.m.*), change:
demander le change d'une pièce d'argent, to ask for change for a silver coin.

changement (*n.m.*), change; alteration; amendment:
changement d'adresse, de résidence, de siège, du taux officiel, change of address, of residence, of offices, in (*or* of) the bank rate.
changement de classe ou de train, change of class or of train.
changement de route (d'un navire), change of route; deviation:
changement de voyage, de vaisseau, change of voyage, of vessel:
changement de route ou de voyage forcé ou volontaire, forced or voluntary change of route or of voyage.
changements aux déclarations (Douanes), amendments to entries.

changement (des monnaies) (*n.m.*), debasement (of the coinage).

changer (modifier) (*v.t.*), to change; to alter; to amend:
changer ses projets, to change, to alter, one's plans.

changer (troquer une chose pour une autre) (*v.t.*), to exchange; to change:
changer de la monnaie française contre la monnaie anglaise, to exchange, to change, French for English money.

l'action X. change de mains à 1 020, X. shares changed hands (*or* exchanged) at 1,020 francs.

changer (troquer une monnaie pour une valeur de monnaie divisionnaire) (*v.t.*), to change:
changer un billet de banque, to change a bank note.

changeur, -euse (pers.) (*n.*) *ou* **changeur de monnaie**, money changer; changer; money dealer; money jobber:
les changeurs ont été les ancêtres des banquiers modernes, money changers were the ancestors of modern bankers.

chantier (*n.m.*), yard:
chantier à charbon, coal yard.
chantier de construction navale *ou* chantier naval *ou* chantier de construction maritime *ou* chantier de construction de navires, shipyard; shipbuilding yard.
chantier pétrolier, oil yard.

chapeau du capitaine *ou simplement* **chapeau** (*n.m.*), primage:
le chapeau du capitaine est un supplément de fret calculé à raison de tant pour cent sur le fret principal, primage is an additional freight calculated at a rate of so much per cent on the principal freight.

chapitre (rubrique; poste) (*n.m.*), heading; head; item:
articles qui sont bloqués dans le chapitre portefeuille (*m.pl.*), items which are lumped under the heading investments.
explications sur un chapitre du bilan (*f.pl.*), explanations on an item in the balance sheet.

chaque (*adj.*), each:
pilons de —— kilos chaque, stamps of —— kilos each.

charbon (*n.m.*), coal:
charbon de soute, bunker coal; bunkers.

charbonnage (*n.m.*), coaling; bunkering:
la rapidité du charbonnage est limitée par l'arrimage dans les soutes, the speed of coaling (*or* bunkering) is limited by the trimming in the bunkers.

charbonner (faire du charbon) (*v.i.*), to coal; to bunker; to take in coal:
charbonner en route est fort cher, to coal (*or* to bunker) en route is very expensive.
faire relâche pour charbonner, to call to bunker (*or* for bunkering).

charbonnier (*n.m.*), collier; coal ship.

charge (mise à bord) (*n.f.*), loading; lading; shipping; shipment:
le lieu et le temps convenus pour la charge et pour la décharge, the place and time agreed upon for loading and unloading.

à charge (opp. à *à vide*), loaded; when loaded:
parcours à charge (d'un wagon de ch. de f.) (*m.*), journey loaded; loaded journey; journey when loaded.

en charge (en parlant d'un navire), loading; now loading; on the berth; now on the berth:
s/s. X., en charge pour le Havre, partant le 31 janvier, sauf imprévu, s/s. X., now loading (*or* now on the berth) for Havre, sailing 31 January, circumstances permitting.

en charge (opp. à *lège*), load (used as *adj.*) ; laden :
tirant d'eau en charge (*m.*), load draught ; laden draught.

sous charge *ou* **sous vapeur** (en parlant des cours de bourse de marchandises), loading ; loading, loaded, or about to be loaded :
cours : disponible *tant* ; flottant *tant* ; sous charge *tant*, prices : spot *so much* ; afloat *so much* ; loading *so much*.

charge utile (opp. à *poids mort*), live weight :
wagon de chemin de fer qui peut transporter une charge utile de 10 000 kilogrammes (*m.*), railway truck which can carry a live weight of 10,000 kilogrammes.

charge (cargaison) (*n.f.*), cargo ; freight ; lading ; load :
la quantité de marchandises qui constitue la charge d'un navire, the quantity of goods which constitutes the cargo (*or* freight) (*or* lading) (*or* load) of a ship.
charge à la cueillette, general cargo.
charge complète de wagon *ou simplement* charge complète (Ch. de f.), truck load ; full truck load :
expéditions à charge complète (*f.pl.*), truck load consignments.
tarif des charges complètes (*m.*), truck load rates.
charge incomplète de wagon *ou simplement* charge incomplète (Ch. de f.), part truck load.

charge (obligation onéreuse ; dépense) (*n.f.*), charge ; encumbrance ; burden ; onus ; expense :
valeurs grevées d'une charge (*f.pl.*), assets encumbered with a charge.
les intérêts du capital constituent une charge de la production (*m.pl.*), interest on capital constitutes a charge on (*or* an expense of) production.
charges d'exploitation *ou* charges de l'exploitation, working expenses ; expenses of carrying on the business.
charge de la preuve, burden of proof (*or* of proving) ; onus of proof (*or* of proving) :
charge de la preuve qui incombe à l'assureur, burden (*or* onus) of proof which falls on the insurer.
charges du capital, capital charges.
les charges des obligations, the debenture charges.
charges financières, financing expenses.
charges fixes, fixed charges.
charges terminales (Transport), terminal charges.

être à la charge de, to be at the expense of ; to be chargeable to (*or* against) ; to be payable by ; to be on (*or* upon) ; to lie on (*or* upon) ; to devolve on (*or* upon) ; to be borne by ; to be dependent on (*or* upon) :
le droit est à la charge du vendeur, the duty is payable by (*or* chargeable to) the seller.
pertes à la charge de l'année (*f.pl.*), losses chargeable against (*or* to) the year.
les risques laissés à la charge de l'expéditeur par le connaissement (*m.pl.*), the risks left upon the shipper by the bill of lading.

la preuve du paiement est toujours à la charge de celui qui prétend avoir payé, the proof of payment is always upon him who claims to have paid.
tous les frais sont à la charge du destinataire, all charges shall be borne by the consignee.
être à la charge de quelqu'un, to be dependent on (*or* upon) someone.
personnes à la charge du contribuable (Impôt sur le revenu) (*f.pl.*), persons dependent on the taxpayer.
personne à charge (*f.*), dependent person.
Cf. mettre à la charge.

charge (mission ; fonctions ; mandat ; office) (*n.f.*), trust ; duty ; office ; membership ; seat ; instructions :
faire l'acquit de sa charge, to fulfil one's trust.
aller au delà de sa charge, to go beyond one's instructions ; to exceed one's duty.
charge alternative, alternate duty.
en vertu de sa charge, in virtue of his office.
agent de change qui achète la charge à son prédécesseur (*m.*), stockbroker who buys membership (*or* the seat) from his predecessor.

chargé (chargement) (*n.m.*), shipment ; cargo :
preuve de chargé (*f.*), evidence of shipment.
chargé sur le pont, deck cargo ; deck shipment.

chargebot (*n.m.*), cargo boat ; cargo vessel ; freighter.

chargement (mise à bord) (*n.m.*), loading ; lading ; shipping ; shipment :
procéder au chargement des marchandises et à leur arrimage, to proceed with the loading (*or* lading) of the goods and their stowage.
chargement sur le pont *ou* chargement sur le tillac *ou* chargement en pontée, shipment on deck ; deck shipment.
chargement sur premier vapeur, sur navire suivant, shipment on first steamer, on following ship.

chargement (cargaison) (*n.m.*), cargo ; freight ; lading ; load ; shipment ; consignment :
un chargement de bois, de pétrole, a wood cargo, an oil cargo ; a cargo of timber, of oil.
navire qui débarque la totalité ou une partie de son chargement (*m.*), ship which lands the whole or a part of her cargo (*or* freight).
le nom du navire et la valeur du chargement, the name of the ship and the value of the shipment (*or* consignment).
colis faisant partie du chargement (*m.*), package forming part of the shipment (*or* consignment).
chargement complet, full cargo.
chargement du pont, deck cargo ; deck load.
chargement en cueillette, general cargo.

chargement (charge d'une voiture) (*n.m.*), load :
chargement de wagon (Ch. de f.), truck load.

chargement (de la prime) (Assce) (*n.m.*), loading (of the premium) :
les primes versées par les assurés sont des primes brutes, c'est-à-dire des primes nettes majorées d'un pourcentage appelé chargement, servant à couvrir les frais d'administra-

tion, à laisser un bénéfice à l'assureur, à constituer un fonds de réserve pour le cas où les sinistres dépassent les probabilités, etc., the premiums paid by the insured are gross premiums, that is to say, net premiums increased by a percentage called loading, serving to cover administration expenses, to leave a profit to the underwriter, to form a reserve fund in case losses exceed probabilities, etc.

chargement (Poste) (*n.m.*), insurance :
la recommandation ou le chargement est un traitement spécial appliqué aux objets de correspondance dont les expéditeurs veulent assurer la remise, contre reçu, aux destinataires, ou garantir le contenu desdits objets, registration or insurance is a special treatment applied to postal packets of which the senders wish to ensure delivery, against receipt, to the addressees, or to protect the contents of the said packets.

charger (*v.t.*). See examples :
charger la prime (Assce), to load the premium. See example under **chargement**.
charger quelqu'un de répondre à une lettre, to instruct, to direct, someone to reply to a letter.
charger un avoué, to instruct a solicitor.
charger un compte, to inflate, to swell, an account.
charger un compte de tous les frais (Comptab.), to charge an account with all the expenses.
charger un wagon de chemin de fer, to load a railway truck.
charger une lettre (Poste), to insure a letter.
la place (*ou* la position de place) est chargée (Bourse) (opp. à *la place est dégagée* ou *soulagée*), the market is all bulls (*or* is all givers) ; buyers over.

se charger (*v.r.*). See examples :
la banque se charge du recouvrement d'effets qui lui sont remis, the bank undertakes the collection of bills remitted to it.
la nouvelle société se charge de l'actif et du passif, the new company takes over the assets and liabilities.

charger (mettre à bord) (*v.t.*), to load ; to lade ; to ship :
charger des grains en vrac, to ship, to load, to lade, grain in bulk.
navire qui commence à charger sa cargaison (*m.*), ship which begins to load her cargo.
armateur qui a le droit de charger les marchandises sur le navire suivant (*m.*), owner who has the right to ship the goods on the following vessel.
charger un navire en (*ou* à) cueillette, to load a ship with general cargo. *Cf.* affrètement à cueillette.
charger sur le pont *ou* charger sur le tillac *ou* charger en pontée, to ship on deck :
marchandises chargées sur le pont (*ou* sur le tillac) (*ou* en pontée) (*f.pl.*), goods shipped on deck.
navire chargé ou sur lest (*m.*), ship laden or in ballast.

chargé (*ou* ont été chargées) en bon état et conditionnement apparents . . . les marchandises marquées et numérotées comme ci-après (connaissement), shipped in apparent good order and condition . . . the goods marked and numbered as follows.

chargeur (pers.) (*n.m.*), shipper :
les chargeurs sont des commerçants se livrant au commerce d'importation et au commerce d'exportation, shippers are merchants engaging in import trade and export trade.

chariot (*n.m.*), car ; truck ; wagon ; waggon.
chariot (d'une machine à écrire, d'une machine à calculer) (*n.m.*), carriage (of a typewriter, of a calculating machine).
charretée (*n.f.*), cartload.
charretier (pers.) (*n.m.*), carter ; carman.
charrette (*n.f.*), cart.
charriage (*n.m.*), carting ; cartage ; conveyance ; conveying ; carriage ; carrying ; transport ; transportation.
charriage (prix du transport) (*n.m.*), carriage ; cartage.
charrier (*v.t.*), to cart ; to carry ; to convey ; to transport.
charroi (*n.m.*), cartage ; carting ; carriage ; carrying.
charroi (prix du transport) (*n.m.*), cartage ; carriage.
charroyer (*v.t.*), to cart ; to carry.
charroyeur (pers.) (*n.m.*), carter ; carrier ; carman.
charte-partie [chartes-parties *pl.*] (*n.f.*), charter party ; charterparty ; charter :
la charte-partie est le contrat de louage d'un navire. Elle tire son nom de ce qu'autrefois, les contrats d'affrètements étaient écrits sur une pièce (charte) qu'on déchirait ensuite en deux, chacun des contractants conservant une des parties, the charter party (*literally translated* divided charter) is the contract of hiring a ship. It derives its name from the fact that formerly, contracts of affreightment were written on a single sheet (charter) which was afterwards torn in two, each of the contractants keeping one of the parts.
la charte-partie est un écrit dressé pour constater le contrat d'affrètement, a charter party is a written agreement drawn to prove a contract of affreightment.
charte-partie de grain, grain charter.
charte-partie de minerai, ore charter.
chasse au découvert (Bourse) (*f.*), bear squeeze.
chasser le découvert (Bourse), to squeeze the bears.
chaudière (*n.f.*), boiler.
chauds (Bourse de marchandises) (*n.m.pl.*). See under **quatre mois**.
chauffage des locaux (*m.*), heating the premises.
chauffeur (d'un automobile) (pers.) (*n.m.*), chauffeur, driver (of a motor car).
chauffeur (d'un navire) (pers.) (*n.m.*), fireman (of a ship).
chavirement (*n.m.*), capsizing.
chavirer (*v.i.*), to capsize :
navire qui, après un abordage, chavire (*m.*), ship which, after a collision, capsizes.

chef (article capital) (*n.m.*), head; heading:
classer les articles en autant de chefs qu'il y a
de comptes, to classify the items under as
many heads as there are accounts.

chef (pers.) (*n.m.*), head; chief; manager; master:
les chefs d'entreprises industrielles et commerciales, the heads of industrial and commercial undertakings.

chef de bureau, chief clerk; head clerk;
managing clerk; head of counting house.

chef de comptabilité *ou* chef comptable, chief
accountant; head accountant.

chef de file, leader:
banques qui tendent plus ou moins à se
rapprocher de leur chef de file (*f.pl.*), banks
who tend more or less to draw closer to their
leader.

chef de gare *ou* chef de station, station master.

chef de service, head, manager, of department.

chemin de fer *ou* *simplement* **chemin** (*n.m.*)
(Abrév.: **ch. de f.**), railway; railroad; rail:
chemin de fer de l'État, State railway.

chemin de fer souterrain, underground railway.

chemin de fer subséquent, succeeding railway.

chemins de fer (*m.pl.*) *ou* **valeurs** (*ou* **actions**) **de
chemins de fer** (*f.pl.*) *ou simplement* **chemins**
(*n.m.pl.*), railways; railway stocks; railway
shares; rails:
chemins argentins, Argentine rails.

cheminot (pers.) (*n.m.*), railwayman.

chemise (*n.f.*), folder.

chèque (*n.m.*) (Abrév.: **ch.**), cheque:
chèque à barrement général, cheque crossed
generally.

chèque à barrement spécial, cheque crossed
specially.

chèque à ordre, order cheque; cheque to order.

chèque au porteur, bearer cheque; cheque to
bearer.

chèque barré *ou* chèque croisé (opp. à *chèque
ouvert* ou *non barré*), crossed cheque:
le chèque barré ne peut être présenté au
paiement que par un banquier, a crossed
cheque can only be presented for payment
by a banker. (Cf. **barrement**.)

chèque barré « non négociable, » cheque
crossed " not negotiable ":
le chèque revêtu de la mention « non
négociable » ne cesse pas d'être transmissible par endossement comme un chèque
ordinaire, mais le cessionnaire de bonne
foi n'a pas plus de droits que son cédant,
a cheque bearing the words "not
negotiable" does not cease to be transferable by endorsement like an ordinary
cheque, but the transferee in good faith
has no better title to it than his transferor.
(N.B.—Same practice in France as in
England.)

chèque-contribution [chèques-contributions *pl.*]
(*n.m.*). In France, a special cheque for the
payment of taxes.

chèque D.S.V. (déplacé sans visa). A kind of
traveller's cheque, issued by the Banque de
France and payable at any of its branches.
These cheques are issued for fixed sums, in
books of ten. The drawer on delivery of the
book signs all the cheques in the bottom
left hand corner. When he draws a cheque
he signs it a second time in the bottom right
hand corner. The second signature affords
identification of the first. (*Cf.* chèque direct,
chèque indirect.)

chèque de banque *ou* chèque bancaire, bank
cheque.

chèque de place à place, country cheque.

chèque de voyage, traveller's cheque; cheque
for travellers; circular note.

chèque direct, chèque indirect. In France,
banks which have branches or agencies make
a distinction between *chèques directs* and
chèques indirects. The *chèque direct* is payable
only at the place where the drawer has an
account. The *chèque indirect* is payable at a
branch other than that where the drawer has
an account. It has to be certified (*visé*) for
payment by the agency where the account is
open before dispatch to the payee. (*Cf.*
chèque D.S.V.)

chèque-dividende [chèques-dividendes *pl.*](*n.m.*),
dividend warrant.

chèque impayé, unpaid cheque; dishonoured
cheque.

chèque omnibus. In France, a cheque form
other than one extracted from the personal
cheque book of the drawer; a loose cheque
form.

chèque ouvert *ou* chèque non barré, open cheque.

chèque postal, chèque nominatif, chèque d'assignation, chèque au porteur, chèque de
virement. *See under* compte courant postal.

chèque-récépissé [chèques-récépissés *pl.*] (*n.m.*),
cheque with receipt form attached.

chèque sans provision, worthless cheque;
stumer cheque (*slang*); dud cheque (*slang*):
le chèque sans provision est celui dont le
montant dépasse le solde disponible au
compte du tireur, a worthless cheque is
one whose amount exceeds the balance
available in the account of the drawer.
See note under worthless cheque, *in English-
French section.*

chèque sur place, town cheque.

le chèque sur Londres (Opérations de change),
London cheques; cheques on London; the
London cheque:
le chèque sur Londres a fluctué entre —— et
——, London cheques (*or* cheques on
London) (*or* the London cheque) fluctuated
between —— and ——.

chèque visé, marked cheque; certified cheque.

chéquier (*n.m.*), cheque book.

cher, -ère (d'un prix élevé) (*adj.*), dear; expensive;
costly; high priced; high; heavy:
l'argent est cher (*m.*), money is dear.

chère année (*f.*), dear year.

les reports sont chers (*m.pl.*), contangoes are
high (*or* heavy). See examples under **tendre
(se)** and **cherté**.

cher (à un prix élevé) (*adv.*), dear; dearly; at a
high price:
acheter cher, to buy at a high price.

chercher à se procurer de l'argent, to try to get money.

chercher de l'emploi, to look for a place ; to seek employment.

chèrement (*adv.*), dearly ; dear ; expensively ; at a high price :
vendre chèrement, to sell at a high price.

cherté (*n.f.*), dearness ; high price ; highness :
la cherté des capitaux, du crédit, the dearness of money, of credit.
cherté des loyers, des vivres, de la vie, dearness, high price, of rents, of provisions, of living.
cherté des reports (Bourse), highness of contangoes :
le taux des reports est variable et sa cherté ou son bon marché sont subordonnés à la plus ou moins grande abondance de capitaux disponibles comme aussi à la plus ou moins grande quantité de titres à faire reporter, the contango rate is variable and its highness or lowness is dependent on the greater or less plentifulness of available capital as also on the greater or less plentifulness of stock to be given on.

cheval (**opération à**). See under **opération.**

chiffrable (*adj.*), calculable.

chiffrage (*n.m.*), figuring out ; working out ; ciphering ; cyphering.

chiffre (caractère servant à indiquer les nombres) (*n.m.*), figure ; number ; numeral :
énoncer une somme en chiffres, to express an amount in figures.
chiffres arabes, Arabic numerals ; Arabic figures.
chiffres romains, Roman numerals ; Roman figures.
mettre le chiffre au haut d'une page, to put the number at the top of a page.

chiffre (montant) (*n.m.*), figure ; number ; amount :
en chiffres ronds, in round figures ; in round numbers.
chiffre total des actions, total number of shares.
chiffre du capital, amount of the capital.
chiffre d'affaires, turnover :
un chiffre d'affaires de plus de 10 millions, a turnover of over 10 millions.
chiffre-indice [chiffres-indices *pl.*] (*n.m.*), index number.

chiffre (caractère de convention) (*n.m.*), cipher ; cypher :
écrire en chiffres, to write in cipher.

chiffre-taxe [**chiffres-taxes** *pl.*] (*n.m.*), postage due stamp.

chiffré (langage chiffré) (Télégr.) (*n.m.*), cipher ; cypher :
mot en chiffré (*m.*), word in cipher.

chiffrer (évaluer par des calculs) (*v.t.*), to figure out ; to work out :
chiffrer les intérêts, un compte courant, to work out the interest, a current account.

chiffrer (Télégr.) (*v.t.*), to cipher ; to cypher :
chiffrer un télégramme, to cipher a telegram.

chiffrer (numéroter) (*v.t.*), to number ; to page ; to paginate :
chiffrer un registre, to number a register ; to page, to paginate, a book.

chiffrer (calculer au moyen de chiffres) (*v.i.*), to reckon ; to calculate ; to cipher ; to cypher :
chiffrer rapidement, to be good at arithmetic.

se chiffrer (*v.r.*), to figure out ; to work out ; to amount :
opérations qui se chiffrent par plusieurs millions de francs, transactions which amount to several million francs.

chiffrer (figurer) (*v.i.*), to figure ; to appear :
la valeur chiffrée sur les livres, the value figuring (*or* appearing) in the books.

chiffreur, -euse (pers.) (*n.*), calculator ; reckoner.

chiffrier (*n.m.*), rough book ; waste book ; blotter.
chiffrier de caisse (Banq.), counter cash book ; teller's cash book.
chiffrier de recettes *ou* chiffrier d'entrée (Banq.), received cash book ; received (counter) cash book.
chiffrier de dépenses *ou* chiffrier de sortie (Banq.), paid cash book ; paying cashier's counter cash book.

chirographaire (en parlant des dettes, des créances, des créanciers) (*adj.*) (opp. à *garanti* ou *nanti*), unsecured :
créancier chirographaire (*m.*), unsecured creditor. See example under **créancier.**

chirographaire (en parlant des obligations) (*adj.*) (opp. à *hypothécaire*), simple ; naked :
obligation chirographaire (*f.*), simple debenture ; naked debenture.

choix (**de**), choice :
papier de choix (effets de commerce) (*m.*), choice paper.

chômage (*n.m.*), unemployment ; closing ; stoppage :
assurance contre le chômage (*f.*), unemployment insurance.
chômage du dimanche, Sunday closing.
chômage boursier.—A l'occasion de . . ., la bourse sera fermée lundi et mardi prochains, stock exchange closing.—Upon the occasion of . . ., the stock exchange will be closed on Monday and Tuesday next.

chômage (souffrance, détention d'un wagon de ch. de f.) (*n.m.*), demurrage :
chômage de matériel roulant, demurrage of rolling stock.

chômage (d'un navire) (*n.m.*), laying up (of a ship) :
chômage causé par un abordage, laying up caused by a collision.
la période de chômage (police sur corps), the laying up period (hull policy).

chômage (Assce mar.) (*n.m.*), laid up return.

chômer d'ouvrage *ou* simplement **chômer** (*v.i.*), to be out of work ; to be unemployed :
10 000 gens de mer chôment, 10,000 seamen are out of work (*or* are unemployed).

chômeur, -euse (pers.) (*n.*), unemployed person. *Collective pl.* **chômeurs,** unemployed :
les millions versés aux chômeurs (*m.pl.*), the millions paid to the unemployed.

chose (*n.f.*), thing ; property :
marchandises, fret, ou autres choses, ou intérêts, goods, freight, or other things, or interests.

la valeur de la chose assurée, the value of the thing (*or* property) insured. See also example under **objet**.

chronotimbre (*n.m.*), time stamp.

chute (*n.f.*), fall; falling; drop:
chute de colis à (*ou* dans) l'eau au cours des opérations d'embarquement ou de débarquement, fall of packages into the water in the course of shipping or unshipping operations.

chute (des cours) (Bourse) (*n.f.*), collapse, slide, heavy fall (of prices).

chute (débâcle financière) (*n.f.*), smash; crash:
la chute d'une banque, a bank smash (*or* crash).

ci (*adv.*), say:
total: ci 000 000, total: say, 000,000.

ci-contre. See **porté(-e) ci-contre.**

circonscription de remise (*ou* **de distribution**) **gratuite** (*f.*), free delivery area.

circulaire (*adj.*), circular:
lettre circulaire (*f.*), circular letter.

circulaire (*n.f.*), circular:
circulaire convocatrice des actionnaires, circular calling the shareholders together.
la circulaire s'entend de toute communication rédigée en forme de lettre et dont le texte, reproduit à un certain nombre d'exemplaires par un moyen d'impression mécanique, s'adresse indifféremment à toutes les personnes auxquelles la circulaire est envoyée, a circular is understood to mean any communication drawn in letter form and of which the text, reproduced in a certain number of copies by a means of mechanical impression, is addressed indifferently to all the persons to whom the circular is sent.

circulant, -e (*adj.*), circulating; floating:
capitaux circulants (*m.pl.*), circulating capital; circulating assets; floating capital (*or* assets); revenue assets.

circulation (mouvement; trafic) (*n.f.*), circulation; traffic:
circulation à sens unique, one way traffic.

circulation (des trains) (Ch. de f.) (*n.f.*), running, traffic (of trains).

circulation (*n.f.*) (Fin.), circulation; currency:
retirer des pièces de la circulation, to withdraw coins from circulation.
le nombre de billets de banque en circulation, the number of bank notes in circulation.
circulation de l'argent, circulation, currency, of money.
circulation à découvert, uncovered circulation (i.e., uncovered by gold).
circulation fiduciaire *ou* circulation de papier, fiduciary circulation; paper circulation; paper currency.
la circulation autorisée des billets d'une banque, the authorized note currency of a bank.
circulation croisée (effets de commerce), cross firing.

circulation (mouvement; ventes) (Bourse de marchandises) (*n.f.*), turnover; sales:
circulation: 000 tonnes, turnover (or sales): 000 tons.

circulatoire (*adj.*), circulatory:
le pouvoir circulatoire du billet de banque, the circulatory power of the bank note.

circuler (*v.i.*), to circulate; to run:
tout capital qui ne circule pas ne rapporte pas, capital which does not circulate yields nothing.
train qui ne circule pas le dimanche (*m.*), train which does not run on Sunday.

cire (*n.f.*), wax:
cire à cacheter *ou* cire d'Espagne, sealing wax.
cire fine à cacheter, letter sealing wax.
cachet à la cire *ou* cachet de cire (*m.*), wax seal.

clair, -e (*adj.*), clear:
une comptabilité claire, a clear system of accounts.
« Tout ce qui n'est pas clair n'est pas français » (RIVAROL), "What is not clear is not French."

clair (langage clair) (Télégr.) (*n.m.*), plain language:
mot in clair (*m.*), word in plain language.

clandestin, -e (*adj.*), clandestine:
commerce prohibé ou clandestin (*m.*), prohibited or clandestine trade.

clarté (*n.f.*), clearness:
clarté d'un compte, clearness of an account.

classe (*n.f.*), class:
billet de première classe (*m.*), first class ticket.
la classe d'un navire au Registre du Lloyd, the class of a ship in Lloyd's Register.

classé, -e (en parlant des valeurs de bourse) (*adj.*) (Ant.: **déclassé, -e**), placed (i.e., held by the public as investment):
valeurs bien classées (*f.pl.*), well placed shares.

classement (Bourse) (*n.m.*), placing.

classement (*n.m.*) *ou* **classification** (*n.f.*), classing; classification:
classification des comptes, classification of accounts.
classification ferroviaire générale des marchandises, general railway classification of goods.
société de classification de navires (*f.*), ships' classification society.
le Bureau Veritas est une société française de classification, the Bureau Veritas is a French classification society.

classement (de lettres, de documents) (*n.m.*), filing:
classement vertical, vertical filing.

classer *ou* **classifier** (*v.t.*), to class; to classify:
classer les articles en autant de chefs qu'il y en a de comptes, to classify the items under as many heads as there are accounts.
vapeur classé 100 A1 au Lloyd, 3/3 1.1. au Veritas, steamer classed 100 A1 at Lloyd's, 3/3 1.1. at Veritas.

classer (des lettres, des papiers, etc.) (*v.t.*), to file (letters, papers, etc.):
lettres classées par ordre alphabétique (*ou* dans l'ordre alphabétique), par ordre (*ou* dans l'ordre) chronologique, par ordre (*ou* dans l'ordre) idéologique (*f.pl.*), letters filed in alphabetical order, in order of date, under subjects.

classeur (*n.m.*), file ; filing cabinet :
classeur de lettres, letter file.
classeur de bureau, stationery rack.
classeur vertical, vertical filing cabinet.
classier, -ère (pers.) (*n.*), filing clerk.
clause (*n.f.*), clause ; term ; provision ; stipulation :
clauses d'un contrat, clauses, terms, of a contract.
les clauses d'un connaissement, d'une police d'assurance, des statuts d'une société, the clauses of a bill of lading, of an insurance policy, of the articles of association of a company.
clause attributive de juridiction (*ou* de compétence) *ou* clause de compétence, domiciliary clause ; jurisdiction clause.
clause avarie commune, general average clause.
clause collision *ou* clause d'abordage, collision clause ; running down clause.
clause commissoire, commissoria lex.
clause compromissoire *ou* clause d'arbitrage *ou* clause arbitrale, arbitration clause :
une clause compromissoire permettant de soumettre à des arbitres les contestations éventuelles, an arbitration clause authorizing the submission to arbitrators of eventual disputes.
clause contraire (d'un contrat), provision to the contrary ; stipulation to the contrary :
nonobstant toute clause contraire, notwithstanding any provision to the contrary.
clause conventionnelle, agreement clause.
clause d'adresse (charte-partie), address clause.
clauses d'assurances maritimes, marine insurance clauses.
clause d'échelle (navire faisant escale), calling clause.
clause d'exonération *ou* clause exonératoire, relieving clause ; exoneration clause ; exemption clause.
clause de classification (navires), classification clause.
clause de connaissement, bill of lading clause.
clause de garantie, warranty clause.
clause de grève, strike clause.
clause de guerre, war clause.
clause de la nation la plus favorisée, most favoured nation clause.
clause de négligence *ou* clause négligence, negligence clause.
clause de non garantie, non warranty clause.
clause de non responsabilité *ou* clause d'irresponsabilité, non liability clause.
clause de parité, fall clause ; benefit of a fall (in price) clause.
clause de sauvegarde, saving clause.
clause de transbordement, transhipment clause.
clause « depuis le moment où les facultés quittent les magasins de l'expéditeur jusqu'à celui de leur entrée dans les magasins des réceptionnaires » *ou* clause magasin à magasin (Assce mar.), warehouse to warehouse clause.
clause déviation, deviation clause.

clause franc d'avaries communes *ou* clause de franchise d'avaries communes, free of general average clause.
clause franc d'avaries particulières, free of particular average clause.
clause imprimée, printed clause.
clause manuscrite, written clause.
clause « no cure no pay » *ou* clause « pas de résultat, pas de paiement » *ou* clause « aucune rémunération n'est due, si le secours prêté reste sans résultat utile » (Sauvetage), no cure no pay clause.
clause pénale (d'un contrat), penalty clause.
clause que dit être, said to contain clause.
clause résolutoire, determination clause ; avoidance clause.
clause risques de guerre, war risk clause.
clause subrogatoire, subrogation clause.
clause valeur agréée *ou* clause vaille que vaille *ou* clause vaille plus, vaille moins, agreed valuation clause.
clavier (d'une machine à écrire, d'une machine à calculer, d'une caisse enregistreuse) (*n.m.*), keyboard (of a typewriter, of a calculating machine, of a cash register).
clearing-house [**clearing-houses** *pl.*] (chambre de compensation) (*n.m.*), clearing house.
clef de la douane (*f.*), customs lock.
clerc (pers.) (*n.m.*), clerk (in a lawyer's office) :
clerc de notaire, notaire's clerk.
cliché (*n.m.*), stencil.
cliché d'imprimerie (*m.*), printer's block.
client, -e (pers.) (*n.*), client ; customer :
les clients d'un notaire, the clients of a notary ; a notary's clients.
les clients d'une maison de commerce, the customers of a business house ; a firm's customers.
clientèle (ensemble de clients) (*n.f.*), clientele ; clients ; customers ; public ; connection ; custom :
marché en réaction, faute d'ordres de la clientèle (*m.*), market down, for want of orders from the public.
clientèle (fonds de commerce) (*n.f.*), goodwill ; custom.
cloison (de bureau) (*n.f.*), partition :
cloison de verre, glass partition.
cloison étanche (d'un navire) (*f.*), bulkhead.
clore (*v.t.*), to close ; to conclude :
clore un compte (Comptab.), to close an account.
clore un marché, to close, to conclude, a bargain.
clore une séance, to close a meeting.
clos, -e (*adj. & p.p.*), closed ; ended :
l'exercice clos le 31 décembre (*m.*), the year ended 31st December.
clôture (action de terminer) (*n.f.*), closing ; close ; finish :
clôture d'un compte, d'une liquidation, closing an account, a liquidation.
clôture de la navigation, closing, close, of navigation.
clôture de la souscription, closing of the application list.

clôture de la veille (bulletin de cours), yesterday's closing.
clôture précédente (bulletin de cours) (*Abrév.* :
clôt. préc. *ou* clôt. pr.), previous closing ;
previous close.
l'action X. faiblit en clôture (Bourse), X. shares
weakened at the close (*or* at the finish).
clôture (fin d'une discussion suivie du vote) (*n.f.*),
closure.
clôturer (*v.t.*), to close ; to closure :
· clôturer les livres d'une ancienne société, ses
comptes une fois l'an, tous les six mois,
to close the books of an old company,
one's accounts once a year, every six
months.
clôturer les débats, to close, to closure, the
debate.
clôturer (*v.i.*), to close ; to end :
l'action X. clôture à 128 sans grand changement
sur son cours d'il y a huit jours, X. shares
closed at 128 francs without much change in
their price of a week ago.
l'exercice clôturé le 31 décembre (*m.*), the year
ended 31st December.
club d'indemnité (Assce mar.) (*m.*), protection
and indemnity club.
co-intéressé, -e (dans une aventure maritime, par
exemple) (pers.) (*n.*), coadventurer.
coacquéreur, -euse *ou* **-esse** (pers.) (*n.*), joint
purchaser.
coadministrateur, -trice (pers.) (*n.*), codirector.
coalition (Com.) (*n.f.*), combine :
coalition de grands producteurs, combine of
big producers.
coassocié, -e (pers.) (*n.*), copartner ; joint partner.
coassurance (*n.f.*), coinsurance.
coassuré, -e (pers.) (*n.*), coinsured.
cocaution (pers.) (*n.f.*), cosurety ; joint surety ;
joint security ; joint guarantor.
cocontractant, -e (*adj.*), cocontracting.
cocontractant, -e (pers.) (*n.*), cocontractant.
cocréancier, -ère (pers.) (*n.*), joint creditor ;
cocreditor.
code (Dr.) (*n.m.*), code :
code civil (*Abrév.* : C. civ.), civil code. *See note
under* sociétés civiles.
code de commerce (*Abrév.* : C. Co. *ou* C. com.
ou C. de com.), commercial code. *See note
under* sociétés commerciales.
code des douanes, customs code.
code (Télégr.) (*n.m.*), code :
code télégraphique, telegraphic code.
les codes employés pour la rédaction des
télégrammes en langage convenu, the codes
used for the preparation of telegrams in code
language ; the codes used for the coding of
telegrams.
code chiffré, cipher code.
code privé, private code.
codébiteur, -trice (pers.) (*n.*), joint debtor ;
codebtor.
codétenteur, -trice (pers.) (*n.*), joint holder.
codification (Télégr.) (*n.f.*), coding ; putting into
code.
codifier *ou* **coder** (Télégr.) (*v.t.*), to code ; to put
into code :

codifier (*ou* coder) un télégramme, to code a
telegram ; to put a telegram into code.
codirecteur (pers.) (*n.m.*), joint manager.
codirectrice (pers.) (*n.f.*), joint manageress.
codirection (*n.f.*), joint management.
coefficient (*n.m.*), coefficient ; ratio :
coefficient d'exploitation, working coefficient :
on entend par coefficient d'exploitation le
rapport de la dépense à la recette, by working coefficient is understood the ratio of
expenses to receipts.
coefficient de liquidité, ratio of liquid assets to
current liabilities.
coffre (*n.m.*), box ; coffer :
coffres de l'État, coffers of the State.
coffre-fort [**coffres-forts** *pl.*] *ou simplement* **coffre**
(*n.m.*), safe ; strong box.
cofondateur, -trice (pers.) (*n.*), joint founder.
cogérance (*n.f.*), joint management.
cogérant (pers.) (*n.m.*), joint manager.
cogérante (pers.) (*n.f.*), joint manageress.
coin (compartiment) (Bourses belges) (*n.m.*),
section.
co-intéressé, -e. See above.
coliquidateur (pers.) (*n.m.*), joint liquidator.
colis (*n.m.*), parcel ; package :
colis à la main, hand package.
colis à livrer par exprès (Poste), express parcel.
colis avec valeur déclarée *ou* colis chargé,
insured parcel.
colis-avion [colis-avion *pl.*] (*n.m.*), air parcel.
colis contre remboursement *ou* colis grevé de
remboursement, cash on delivery parcel ;
parcel on which a trade charge is to be
collected.
colis finances et valeurs, value parcel.
colis messageries à grande vitesse (Ch. de f.),
express parcel.
colis postal (*Abrév.* : C.P.), postal parcel ;
parcel :
colis postal du régime intérieur, inland parcel.
colis postaux en souffrance *ou* colis postaux
tombés en rebut (*ou* en souffrance), undeliverable postal parcels.
colis sans valeur déclarée *ou* colis non chargé,
uninsured parcel.
colis taré (Douanes), tarer :
le nombre de colis tarés, the number of tarers.
collage (*n.m.*), sticking ; sticking down :
collage des enveloppes, sticking down envelopes.
collationnement (*n.m.*), repetition ; collation ;
comparing ; reading over :
collationnement du télégramme de bureau à
bureau, repetition, collation, of the telegram
from office to office.
collationner (*v.t.*), to repeat ; to compare ; to read
over :
collationner intégralement l'adresse (Télégr.,
etc.), to repeat the address in full.
collationner le numéro (Téléph.), to repeat the
number.
collationner une copie sur l'original, to compare,
to read over, a copy with the original.
colle (*n.f.*) *ou* **colle de pâte**, paste :
colle de bureau, office paste.

collectif, -ive (*adj.*), collective:
responsabilité collective des chemins de fer (*f.*),
collective liability of railways.
collègue (pers.) (*n.m.*), colleague.
coller (*v.t.*), to stick; to stick down:
coller un timbre sur une lettre, to stick a stamp
on a letter.
collision (*n.f.*), collision; fouling; running
foul:
navire qui entre en collision avec un autre
navire (*m.*), ship which comes into collision
with another ship.
collusion (*n.f.*), collusion:
fraude ou collusion, fraud or collusion.
collusoire (*adj.*), collusive; collusory.
collusoirement (*adv.*), collusively.
colocataire (pers.) (*n.m. ou f.*), joint tenant;
cotenant.
colonial, -e, -aux (*adj.*), colonial:
banque coloniale (*f.*), colonial bank.
colonie (*n.f.*), colony.
colonne (*n.f.*), column:
les colonnes d'un registre, d'un journal, une
colonne à part, une colonne de chiffres, une
colonne intérieure, une colonne extérieure, une
colonne de caisse (*ou* une colonne caisse), une
double colonne de caisse, une colonne francs
et centimes, une colonne livres, schellings,
et pence, colonne débitrice, colonne créditrice,
colonne des folios, colonne de détail, colonne
du libellé, colonne pour les observations (*ou*
colonne remarques), colonne de dépouillement (*ou* colonne de ventilation), colonne des
sommes, colonne pour les sommes partielles,
colonne divers, colonne des capitaux, colonne
des intérêts (*ou* colonne d'intérêts), the
columns of a register, of a newspaper, a
separate column, a column of figures, an
inner column, an outer column, a cash
column, a double cash column, a francs and
centimes column, a pounds, shillings, and
pence column, debit column, credit column,
folio column, detail column, particulars
column (*or* description column), remarks
column, analysis column, amount column,
shorts column, sundries column, principal
column, interest column.
à colonnes, columnar:
livre de caisse à colonnes (*m.*), columnar cash
book.
colportage (*n.m.*), hawking:
colportage de titres, share hawking.
colporter (*v.t.*), to hawk.
comandataire (pers.) (*n.m. ou f.*), joint attorney.
combinaison (*n.f.*), combination:
combinaisons financières, financial combinations.
combiner un plan, to devise a plan.
combler (*v.t.*), to fill; to fill up; to make up;
to make good:
combler une vacance accidentelle, to fill, to
fill up, a casual vacancy.
combler un déficit (*ou* un découvert), to make
up a shortage (*or* a deficit).
combler les pertes des mauvais exercices, to
make good the losses of bad years.

combustion spontanée (cause d'incendie) (*f.*),
spontaneous combustion.
comité (*n.m.*), committee:
comité d'assureurs, underwriters' committee.
comité de censure, audit committee.
comité de direction *ou* comité directeur, managing committee.
comité de finance *ou* comité financier, finance
committee.
comité de grève, strike committee.
comité de liquidation (Bourse de valeurs),
settlement department.
comité de réglementation, committee for
general purposes.
comité de surveillance, inspection committee.
command (pers.) (*n.m.*), purchaser; principal
(the real purchaser or principal at a sale, as
distinguished from his agent).
commandant (d'un navire) (pers.) (*n.m.*), commander (of a ship).
commande (*n.f.*) (Abrév.: **c^de**), order:
faire une forte commande de marchandises, to
give a large order for goods.
commandes en carnet (*ou* en portefeuille),
orders in hand; unfilled orders.
commander (avoir l'autorité sur) (*v.t.*), to
command:
vapeur commandé par le capitaine un tel (*m.*),
steamer commanded by captain So-and-so.
commander (Com.) (*v.t.*), to order:
commander des marchandises, to order goods.
se commander (*v.r.*), to order for oneself.
commanditaire (pers.) (*n.m. ou f.*), sleeping
partner; dormant partner; silent partner;
secret partner. In France, a person who
furnishes capital to a *société en commandite
simple*, or one who subscribes for shares in a
société en commandite par actions; a limited
partner. Cf. **commandité, -e.**
commandite (société) (*n.f.*). In France, a partnership or company in which some of the
members furnish the necessary funds without
taking part in the management; limited
partnership.
commandite (fonds versé) (*n.f.*), finance; interest:
la commandite accordée au commerce et à
l'industrie par les banques, the finance
granted to trade and industry by the banks.
sa commandite est de cent mille francs, his
interest is one hundred thousand francs.
commandité, -e (pers.) (*n.*), acting partner. In
France, an active and responsible partner in
a *commandite.*
commanditer (*v.t.*), to finance; to take an
interest in; to advance funds to; to provide
capital for; to financier:
le banquier doit il commanditer des entreprises
commerciales et industrielles ? should the
banker finance commercial and industrial
undertakings ?
se commanditer (*v.r.*), to finance; to find
finance; to financier:
un banqueroutier ne saurait se commanditer, a
bankrupt cannot finance.
commencement (*n.m.*), commencement; beginning:

commencement de l'année, commencement, beginning, of the year.

commencement et fin d'un risque, commencement and end of a risk.

commencer (*v.t.*), to commence; to begin:
commencer les affaires (*ou* les opérations sociales), to commence business.

commencer à courir, to attach:
le risque couvert par la présente police commence à courir dès le moment du chargement à bord du navire d'exportation, the risk under this policy attaches from the time of loading on board the export vessel.

commentaire (*n.m.*), commentary; comment:
commentaires de la presse, press comments.

commenter (*v.t.*), to comment on:
commenter une décision, to comment on a decision.

commerçable (*adj.*), negotiable; dealable:
papier commerçable (*m.*), negotiable paper.

commerçant, -e (*adj.*), commercial; mercantile; trading; business (*used as adj.*); engaged in business:
quartier commerçant (*m.*), business quarter.
femme mariée commerçante (*f.*), married woman engaged in business; feme sole trader (*or* merchant).

commerçant, -e (pers.) (*n.*), trader; merchant:
le crédit personnel est basé sur la réputation du commerçant, personal credit is based on the reputation of the trader.
les chargeurs sont des commerçants se livrant au commerce d'importation et au commerce d'exportation (*m.pl.*), shippers are merchants engaging in import trade and export trade.

commerce (*n.m.*), commerce; trade; trading; business; traders:
le commerce enrichit une nation, commerce enriches a nation.
le commerce va mal, trade (*or* business) is bad.
commerce d'exportation, export trade.
commerce d'importation, import trade.
commerce de banque, banking business; business of banking.
commerce de cabotage *ou* commerce caboteur, coasting trade; coastwise trade.
commerce de demi-gros, wholesale trade; wholesale commerce. See note under **gros** *ou* **gros commerce**.
commerce de détail *ou* petit commerce, retail trade.
commerce de gros *ou* commerce en gros *ou* gros commerce, direct trade; direct commerce. See note under **gros** *ou* **gros commerce**.
commerce de luxe, luxury trade.
commerce de mer *ou* commerce par mer *ou* commerce maritime, sea trade; maritime commerce.
commerce de représentation, agency trade.
commerce de transit, transit trade.
commerce des grains, grain trade.
commerce extérieur *ou* commerce international, foreign trade.
commerce intérieur *ou* commerce métropolitain, home trade; domestic trade.

commerce intermédiaire *ou* commerce de réexportation, reexport trade.

contestations entre la douane et le commerce (*f.pl.*), disputes between the customs and traders.

papier de haut commerce, fine trade bills; prime trade bills; white paper.

commercer (*v.i.*), to trade; to deal:
commercer en France, avec d'autres pays, to trade in France, with other countries.
commercer de tout, to deal in everything.

commercial, -e, -aux (*adj.*), commercial; trading; trade (*used as adj.*); mercantile; business (*used as adj.*):
entreprise commerciale (*f.*), commercial undertaking; trading concern; business enterprise.
papier commercial *ou* papier de commerce (*m.*), commercial paper; mercantile paper.

commercialement (*adv.*), commercially.

commercialiser (*v.t.*), to commercialize.

commercialité (*n.f.*), negotiability; transferability:
commercialité d'un effet, negotiability of a bill.
commercialité d'une dette, transferability of a debt.

commettant (pers.) (*n.m.*), principal. See example under **commissionnaire**.

commettre (*v.t.*), to commit:
commettre des irrégularités, une fraude, to commit irregularities, a fraud.

commis (*n.m.*) *ou* **commis de bureau** *ou* **commis sédentaire** (pers.), clerk; assistant:
commis d'agent de change, stockbroker's clerk.
commis de banque, bank clerk.
commis de magasin, shop assistant.
commis expéditionnaire, copying clerk.
commis principal *ou* commis chef, chief clerk; head clerk.
commis principal (teneur de carnet) (Bourse), authorized clerk. *Note:*—In the *marché du comptant* in the Paris Bourse an *authorized clerk* is called a **commis au comptant** *or* **commis du comptant**.
commis succursaliste, (ship)owner's agent, but exclusive servant of owner.
commis voyageur, commercial traveller.

commise (pers.) (*n.f.*), clerk; lady clerk; assistant:
commise de magasin, shop assistant.

commissaire d'avarie *ou* **commissaire d'avaries** (pers.) (*m.*), average surveyor.

commissaire d'émigration (*m.*), emigration officer.

commissaire de la marine marchande *ou* *simplement* **commissaire** (pers.) (*n.m.*), purser:
le commissaire d'un paquebot, the purser of a liner.

commissaire des comptes *ou* **commissaire aux comptes** *ou* **commissaire-vérificateur** [commissaires-vérificateurs *pl.*] *ou* **commissaire vérificateur des comptes** *ou* **commissaire-censeur** [commissaires-censeurs *pl.*] *ou* **commissaire de surveillance** *ou* *simplement* **commissaire** (pers.) (*n.m.*), auditor:
commissaire aux apports. *See note under* assemblée constitutive.

commissaire maritime (pers.) (*m.*), shipping master.
commissaire-priseur [**commissaires-priseurs** *pl.*] (pers.) (*n.m.*), auctioneer ; appraiser.
commissaire répartiteur (de contributions) (pers.) (*m.*), assessor (of taxes) ; district commissioner.
commissariat de comptes (*m.*), auditorship.
commission (charge ; achat, placement pour autrui) (*n.f.*), commission :
exécuter une commission pour le compte de son commettant, to execute a commission for the account of one's principal.
commission (remise) (*n.f.*) (Abrév. : **com.** *ou* **com** *ou* **con** *ou* **commis.** *ou* **cion**), commission :
commission d'achat, buying commission.
commission d'adresse (charte-partie), address commission.
commission d'encaissement, commission for collection (of bills).
commission d'escompte, discount (bank charge on bills discounted).
commission de banque *ou* commission bancaire, bank commission.
commission de compte *ou* commission de caisse (Banq.), commission (*charged*) for keeping an account ; bank charges (for keeping current account, on overdraft, or the like).
commission de garantie *ou* commission syndicale, underwriting commission.
commission de placement, brokerage (commission paid to stockbrokers or others for introducing applicants for shares).
commissions des voyageurs, travellers' commissions.
commission ducroire, del credere commission.
commissions sur ventes *ou* commissions de vente, commissions on sales ; selling commissions.
commission syndicale additionnelle, overriding commission.
commissionnaire (pers.) (*n.m.*) (Abrév. : **Caire** ou **Cre**), agent ; commission agent ; commission merchant ; factor :
le commissionnaire reçoit de son commettant une rétribution appelée commission, the commission agent (*or* the agent) receives from his principal a retribution called commission.
commissionnaire-chargeur [commissionnaires-chargeurs *pl.*] *ou* commissionnaire-expéditeur [commissionnaires-expéditeurs *pl.*] (*n.m.*), shipping agent.
commissionnaire de transit *ou* commissionnaire-transitaire [commissionnaires-transitaires *pl.*] (*n.m.*), transit agent.
commissionnaire de transport (*ou* de transports) *ou* commissionnaire-messager [commissionnaires-messagers *pl.*] (*n.m.*), forwarding agent ; transport agent.
commissionnaire ducroire, del credere agent.
commissionnaire en douane, customs agent ; custom house broker.
commissionnaire-exportateur [commissionnaires-exportateurs *pl.*] (*n.m.*), export commission agent ; export agent.

commissionnaire-exportateur ducroire [commissionnaires-exportateurs ducroire *pl.*], del credere export agent.
commissionner (*v.t.*), to commission.
commun, -e (*adj.*), common ; average ; mean : un fonds commun, a common fund.
échéance commune (*f.*), average due date ; mean due date.
communauté (*n.f.*), community : communauté d'intérêts, community of interest.
communes (Bourse) (*n.f.pl.*), averaging : les communes se pratiquent pour défendre une mauvaise position, averaging is done to protect a bad position.
communication (*n.f.*), communication : communication à grande distance (Radiotélégr.), long distance communication.
communication (Téléph.) (*n.f.*), call ; communication :
communication interurbaine, trunk call.
communication interurbaine à heure fixe, fixed time trunk call.
communication interurbaine de jour, de nuit, day, night, trunk call.
communication locale, local call.
communication régionale, toll call.
communication (Dr.) (*n.f.*), discovery ; production ; access :
communication de pièces, discovery of documents.
commissaire qui exige communication des titres de propriété (*m.*), auditor who calls for production of the titles to property.
les commissaires ont droit, toutes les fois qu'ils le jugent convenable, de prendre communication des livres de la société (*m.pl.*), the auditors have a right of access at all times to the books of the company.
communiquer (*v.t.*), to communicate ; to produce :
communiquer aux assureurs tous renseignements relatifs à l'expédition, to communicate to the insurers all information concerning the adventure.
communiquer (*v.i.*), to communicate : communiquer par le téléphone, to communicate by telephone.
compagnie (*n.f.*) (Abrév. : **Cie** *ou* **Cie**), company : (See also **société**.)
Note :—In France, concerns such as railways, mines, water, gas or electric light companies, and insurance companies, are usually, though not necessarily, called *compagnies*. Ordinary commercial, industrial, or financial concerns are usually called *sociétés*. Legally, there is no difference between *compagnie* and *société*.
compagnie d'assurance *ou* compagnie d'assurances, insurance company ; assurance company ; office.
compagnie d'assurance (*ou* d'assurances) contre l'incendie, fire insurance company ; fire office.
compagnie d'assurance maritime (*ou* d'assurances maritimes), marine insurance company.
compagnie d'assurance (*ou* d'assurances) sur la vie, life assurance company ; life insurance company ; life office.

compagnie d'assurances à primes (opp. à *compagnie d'assurances mutuelles*), proprietary insurance (*or* assurance) company; proprietary office.

compagnie d'assurances mutuelles, mutual insurance (*or* assurance) company; mutual office.

compagnie d'utilité publique, public utility company.

compagnie de câbles, cable company.

compagnie de chemins de fer, railway company.

compagnie de financement, financing company.

compagnie de lignes régulières (Navig.), liner company.

compagnie de navigation *ou* compagnie d'armement *ou* compagnie de transports maritimes, shipping company; navigation company.

compagnie de navigation à vapeur, steam navigation company.

compagnie de transports, transport company.

compagnie des docks, dock company.

compagnie mère, parent company.

compagnie par actions, joint stock company.

compagnie privée *ou* compagnie particulière, private company: (*Note :—private* or *privée* or *particulière* in this phrase must not be construed as having any legal signification [*cf.* société à responsabilité limitée], but only as having an ordinary meaning, as in the following example.)

construction d'un chemin de fer par l'État avec concession de l'exploitation à des compagnies privées (*f.*), construction of a railway by the State with working concession to private companies.

compagnie sœur, sister company.

et compagnie (*généralement en abrégé* & Cie) (barrement d'un chèque), and company (*usually abbreviated* & Co.). See example under **barrement.**

comparaison (*n.f.*), comparison.

comparaître devant un tribunal, to appear before a court.

comparatif, -ive (*adj.*), comparative:
tableau comparatif (*m.*), comparative table.

comparer (*v.t.*), to compare:
comparer la traduction à l'original, les frais d'une année à l'autre, les cours de lundi avec ceux de la semaine dernière, to compare the translation with the original, one year's expenses with the other's, Monday's prices with those of last week.

compartiment (*n.m.*), compartment:
compartiment d'une voiture à voyageurs (Ch. de f.), compartment of a passenger carriage.

compartiment étanche (d'un navire), watertight compartment (of a ship).

compartiment (Bourse) (*n.m.*), section:
le compartiment minier, the mining section.

compas (boussole marine) (*n.m.*), compass.

compensation (dédommagement) (*n.f.*), compensation: set off; offset:
les actions nouvelles seront libérées par compensation avec le montant des obligations converties (*f.pl.*), the new shares will be paid up by set off (*or* by offset) against the amount of the debentures converted.

compensation (Bourse de valeurs) (Abrév.: comp.) (*n.f.*), making up; make up.

compensation (Bourse de marchandises) (*n.f.*), cutting out; cut out:
liquider une affaire par compensation, to close a transaction by cutting out (*or* by cut out).

compensation (Banq.) (*n.f.*), clearing:
chèques présentés à la compensation (*m.pl.*), cheques presented for clearing.

compenser (*v.t.*), to compensate; to set off; to offset; to make up for:
bénéfices qui compensent ses pertes (*m.pl.*), profits which compensate (*or* which make up for) (*or* which offset) one's losses.

compenser la réparation due avec le solde du fret restant à payer, to set off the reparation due against the balance of freight remaining to be paid.

lors du remboursement d'une perte ou d'une avarie, toutes primes échues dues par l'assuré sont compensées avec l'indemnité due par les assureurs, on payment of a loss or damage, all outstanding premiums due by the insured are set off against the loss due by the underwriters.

compenser une dette, to set off a debt.

réduction accordée pour compenser les erreurs possibles (*f.*), reduction allowed to compensate possible errors.

se compenser (*v.r.*), to be compensated (*or* set off) (*or* offset); to compensate each other:
différences qui se compensent (*f.pl.*), differences which are compensated (*or* which compensate each other).

compenser (Bourse de valeurs) (*v.t.*), to make up:
donner l'ordre à l'agent A. de compenser avec l'agent B., to give the order to the broker A. to make up with the broker B.

les titres doivent être levés ou livrés en liquidation, à moins que l'opération ne soit compensée (*m.pl.*), the stock must be taken up or delivered at the settlement, unless the transaction is made up.

l'action X., qui a été compensée à la dernière liquidation à 80, s'inscrit à 98, X. shares, which were made up at the last settlement at 80, were quoted at 98 francs.

se compenser (*v.r.*), to be made up:
deux opérations qui se compensent l'une par l'autre (*f.pl.*), two deals which are made up the one by the other.

compenser (Bourse de marchandises) (*v.t.*), to cut out.

compenser (Banq.) (*v.t.*), to clear; to pass through the clearing house:
compenser un chèque, to clear a cheque; to pass a cheque through the clearing house.

compenser les dépens (Dr.), to order each party to pay its own costs.

compétition (*n.f.*), competition.

complètement libéré, -e *ou* **complètement versé, -e,** fully paid; fully paid up:

actions complètement libérées (*f.pl.*), fully paid shares.

capital complètement versé (*m.*), fully paid capital ; capital fully paid up.

complètement nanti, -e, fully secured :
créancier complètement nanti (*m.*), fully secured creditor.

compléter la couverture fournie antérieurement (Bourse et Banq.), to margin up :
donneur d'ordre qui est tenu de compléter, s'il y a lieu, la couverture par lui fournie antérieurement (*m.*), principal who is bound to margin up, if necessary. *Cf.* fournir une couverture.

composé, -e (*adj.*), compound :
intérêt composé (*m.*) *ou* intérêts composés (*m.pl.*), compound interest.

composer (*v.t.*) *ou* **composer sur son disque d'appel** (Téléph. automatique), to dial :
l'abonné compose d'abord sur son disque d'appel les trois premières lettres du nom du bureau demandé, indiquées en caractères majuscules ; il compose à la suite les quatre chiffres du numéro demandé (*m.*), the subscriber, in the first place, dials the first three letters of the exchange name wanted, printed in heavy type ; he then dials the four numerals of the number required.

composteur (*n.m.*), office printing outfit (interchangeable rubber-faced type).

comprendre (renfermer en soi) (*v.t.*), to comprise ; to include ; to embrace ; to contain :
si le bénéfice espéré est compris dans l'assurance, if the anticipated profit is comprised (*or* included) in the insurance.

compromettre (*v.t.*), to compromise.

compromettre (*v.i.*), to compromise :
clause compromissoire pour laquelle les parties s'obligent à compromettre, c'est-à-dire à soumettre à l'arbitrage les contestations pouvant naître du contrat (*f.*), arbitration clause under which the parties bind themselves to compromise, that is to say, to submit to arbitration disputes which may arise on the contract.

compromis (contrat par lequel deux personnes conviennent de se soumettre à l'arbitrage d'un tiers) (*n.m.*), bond :
compromis d'arbitrage, arbitration bond.

compromis d'avaries, average bond :
un compromis d'avaries par lequel les intéressés s'obligent à contribuer pour le montant qui sera établi par les dispacheurs, an average bond by which the interested parties bind themselves to contribute to the amount to be fixed by the average adjusters.

compromis d'avaries grosses, general average bond.

compromis (accommodement) (*n.m.*), compromise :
préférer un compromis à un procès, to prefer a compromise to a lawsuit.

comptabiliaire (*adj.*), of or relating to bookkeeping or accountancy :
erreur comptabiliaire (*f.*), error in bookkeeping ; bookkeeping error.

comptabiliairement (*adv.*), in relation to bookkeeping or accountancy :
comptabiliairement parlant, speaking from the accountancy point of view.

comptabilisation (*n.f.*), bookkeeping ; recording (*or* entering) in books :
comptabilisation en partie double, double entry bookkeeping.
comptabilisation en partie simple, single entry bookkeeping.

comptabiliser (*v.t.*), to record ; to enter :
les opérations comptabilisées sur le journal (*f.pl.*), the transactions recorded in the journal ; the operations entered in the journal.
le journal est l'organe classificateur par dates des faits à comptabiliser, the journal is the medium by which facts are recorded in order of date.

comptabilité (*n.f.*), bookkeeping ; accounting ; accountancy ; accounts ; books ; system of bookkeeping ; system of accounts ; accounting system :
comptabilité commerciale, commercial bookkeeping.
comptabilité de banque, bank bookkeeping.
comptabilité de prix de revient, cost accounting.
comptabilité de (*ou* des) sociétés, company bookkeeping.
comptabilité en partie double, double entry bookkeeping.
comptabilité en partie simple, single entry bookkeeping.
comptabilité-espèces (*n.f.*), cash accounting ; cash bookkeeping.
comptabilité industrielle, industrial bookkeeping.
comptabilité-matière *ou* comptabilité-matières (*n.f.*), store accounting ; store bookkeeping ; stock accounting (*or* bookkeeping).
tenir la comptabilité d'une maison, to keep a firm's books (*or* accounts).
une comptabilité rationnelle doit comprendre les livres suivants, a rational system of bookkeeping (*or* of accountancy) should comprise the following books.
depuis longtemps déjà l'art de la tenue de livres a fait place à la science de la comptabilité, for a long time past the art of bookkeeping has made way for the science of accountancy.

comptabilité (service de la comptabilité) (*n.f.*), accounts department.

comptable (responsable) (*adj.*), accountable ; responsible ; answerable :
être comptable d'une somme d'argent, to be accountable for a sum of money.
quittance comptable (*f.*), accountable receipt.

comptable (Comptab.) (*adj.*), of or relating to bookkeeping or accounts :
difficultés comptables (*f.pl.*), bookkeeping difficulties ; difficulties of (*or* in) bookkeeping.
chercher une place comptable, to look for a place as bookkeeper.
faciliter le travail comptable, to facilitate the work of bookkeeping.

une saine organisation comptable, a sound system of accounts.

valeur comptable (*f.*), book value.

comptable (pers.) (*n.m.*), accountant; book-keeper:

comptable professionnel *ou* comptable de profession, professional accountant.

alors que le comptable organise, conseille, et dirige, le teneur de livres exécute, sur les indications du premier, whereas the accountant organizes, advises, and directs, the bookkeeper performs the work, under the former's directions.

comptable gardien de valeurs, cashier, securities clerk, storekeeper, etc. (a clerk responsible for the custody of cash, securities, goods, or other effects).

comptage (*n.m.*), counting; reckoning; calculation:

le comptage et le pesage des caisses, des quantités délivrées, the counting and weighing of the cases, of the quantities delivered.

résultats obtenus par des comptages plus ou moins approximatifs (*m.pl.*), results obtained by more or less approximate calculations.

comptant (*adj. m.*) (Abrév.: **compt.** *ou* **cpt.**), ready; prompt; spot:

argent comptant (*m.*), ready money; prompt cash; spot cash.

à beaux deniers comptants, in cash; in ready money:

payer à beaux deniers comptants, to pay in cash (*or* in ready money).

comptant (*adv.*) *ou* **au comptant,** in cash; for cash; cash (*used as adj.*); in ready money; for money:

la prime est payable comptant au moment de la livraison de la police, the premium is payable in cash on delivery of the policy.

achat réglé au comptant fin de mois (*m.*), purchase paid for in cash at the end of the month.

acheter comptant, to buy for cash.

le changeur n'achète ni ne vend du crédit, toutes ses opérations sont au comptant, the money changer neither buys nor sells credit, all his transactions are for cash.

paiements comptant *ou* paiements au comptant (*m.pl.*), cash payments; payments in cash.

marché au comptant (*m.*), cash bargain; dealing for money.

comptant (*n.m.*), cash; prompt cash; spot cash; ready money:

comptant avec escompte, cash less discount; prompt cash less discount.

comptant contre documents, cash against documents; prompt cash against documents.

comptant d'usage *ou* comptant simple, cash on the usual terms.

comptant net, net cash; net prompt cash:

paiement: comptant net sans escompte à présentation des documents, payment: net prompt cash without discount on presentation of the documents.

comptant à livrer *ou* **comptant-compté** *ou*

comptant contre remboursement *ou* **comptant sur balle,** on or before delivery; cash on or before delivery; cash with order; cash down.

payer comptant-compté, to pay on or before delivery; to pay cash down.

comptant spécial, compte courant, comptant différé, comptant en compte, comptant à règlement différé, etc., names given by French bucket shops to dealings called *opérations au comptant en compte courant, opérations au comptant différé,* etc., the usual plan being to offer the client the facility of buying a certain number of shares but only paying for a few of them. These dealings usually end in the client losing his money.

comptant (Marché des métaux) (*n.m.*) (opp. à 3 *mois*), cash.

compte (calcul; nombre) (*n.m.*), counting; reckoning; calculation; figures; numbers; money:

compte des mots (Télégr.), counting of words.

compte rond, round figures; round numbers; even money:

cent cinquante mille deux cents francs, c'est cent cinquante mille francs, compte rond, one hundred and fifty thousand two hundred francs, is a hundred and fifty thousand francs, even money.

compte (profit; avantage) (*n.m.*), account; benefit; advantage:

agissant pour le compte de qui il appartiendra *ou* agissant pour compte de qui il peut appartenir, acting for account of whom it may concern.

compte (état; tableau; énumération; facture; mémoire) (*n.m.*) (Abrév.: **cᵖᵗᵉ** *ou* **cᵗᵉ** *ou* **C.** *ou* **c.**), account; reckoning:

avoir un compte à la banque, ses comptes à jour, to have an account at the bank, one's accounts up to date.

les comptes présentés par les administrateurs, the accounts presented by the directors.

compte à découvert (Banq.), overdrawn account.

compte à demi *ou* compte à 1/2, joint venture (*or* adventure) account; joint account; joint account, half shares.

compte à 1/3, à 1/4, joint venture (*or* adventure) account $\frac{1}{3}$, $\frac{1}{4}$, shares; joint account, $\frac{1}{3}$, $\frac{1}{4}$, shares.

compte agence, agency account.

comptes annuels, annual accounts; yearly accounts.

compte capital, capital account.

compte collectif (Comptab.), adjustment account; reconciliation account; balance account; total account.

compte conjoint, joint account (an account, as of shares in a share register, pertaining to two or more persons).

compte contre-partie, contra account.

compte courant (*Abrév.:* **cᵖᵗᵉ cᵗ** *ou* **cᵗᵉ cᵗ** *ou* **cᵗᵉ c.** *ou* **C.Cᵗ** *ou* **C/C.** *ou* **c.c.** *ou* **c/c.** *ou* **c/c/**), current account; account current; running account; open account:

avance en compte courant (*f.*), advance on current account.

compte courant et d'intérêts, current account (*or* account current) with interest.

compte courant (Bourse). See **comptant spécial.**

compte courant postal (*Abrév.:* c/c. postal). In France, a post office current account, that is to say, a current account kept with the Government post office acting as bankers, and corresponding to an ordinary current or drawing account with a joint stock or private bank.

Following are some of the more important and interesting particulars and peculiarities of the system :—

The system was inaugurated on 1st July 1918.

Practically any person, association, company, firm, bank, or other body corporate, can hold an account, provided their application is approved. Two or more accounts can be held by one person in the same *bureau* or in different *bureaux.* An account can be transferred from one *bureau* to another.

Application to open an account can be made to any post office. The application form can even be handed to a postman on his round.

The accounts are kept at district offices (17 towns in all), viz.:—Paris, Bordeaux, Clermont-Ferrand, Dijon, Lille, Limoges, Lyons, Marseilles, Montpellier, Nancy, Nantes, Orléans, Rennes, Rouen, Strasbourg, Toulouse, Algiers. These district offices (*bureaux régionaux*) are called **bureaux de chèques** (*cheque offices*).

Every account has a number.

The cheques have printed on them the name of the *bureau*, the number of the account at the *bureau*, and the name and address of the holder of the account. These particulars are printed on the cheque forms by the *bureau* before issue, at the holder's expense.

The holder of the account, or any one else knowing his *bureau* and the number of his account, can pay into the account at any post office, at a *bureau de chèques*, and at certain other places. Payments in are made on paying in slips called **mandats de versement.** 5 francs must be paid in on notification of acceptance of the application to open an account, and the amount to the credit of the account must never fall below 5 francs.

The holders of accounts are urged to, and they generally do, print on their letter headings, invoices, catalogues, etc., the name of their *bureau*, and the number of their account with it, so that other people can pay into it. This is done in the following form, for instance, **Chèques postaux: Paris 0000.** Lists of holders of accounts are kept at post offices and can be consulted by the public, if required.

As regards withdrawals, there are four kinds of cheques, viz.:—

(1) **chèque nominatif,** used when the holder of the account draws out money for his own benefit—a "pay self" cheque.

(2) **chèque d'assignation,** when the holder of the account pays a named third party—a "pay Mr So-and-so or order" cheque.

(3) **chèque au porteur**—an ordinary "bearer" cheque.

(4) **chèque de virement,** a cheque used, and exclusively so, for the transfer of funds from one *c/c. postal* to another *c/c. postal*—a "transfer" cheque (unknown in English banking, an ordinary cheque being used for such purpose).

The three kinds of cheques (1), (2), and (3) are known as **chèques de paiement,** as distinguished from No. (4) viz., **chèques de virement.** Cheques (1) and (2) are transformed by the *bureaux* into **mandats de paiement** (orders to pay), which usually take the form of money orders, and the money is usually paid over by a postman to the beneficiary at his residence, or in the case of amounts over 5,000 francs, at the post office.

The *c/c. postal* can be used for the payment of telegraph and telephone rentals or charges, savings bank deposits, taxes, subscriptions, etc.

Holders of *c/c. postaux* can, if they wish, open a **compte particulier** at their local post office. The *compte particulier* is supplied with funds drawn from the *c/c. postal principal* (i.e., the account at the *bureau de chèques*). The holder of the *compte particulier* can draw on the account on demand, or he can have debited to the account any amounts which he would ordinarily have to pay to the post office in cash.

Letters of credit are issued, called **mandats-lettres de crédit,** payable at post offices, and certain other places.

Comptes courants postaux bear no interest.

Unlike ordinary French bank cheques, *chèques postaux* cannot be transferred by endorsement, are subject to a different stamp duty, and time of validity is not the same.

Every time the account is operated on, a statement showing the transactions and the final state of the account is sent to the holder.

Small charges are made on payments in, on drawings out, and on transfers. These charges are debited to the account.

All correspondence with the *bureau* is free of postage.

The *c/c. postal*, which is enormously used in France, has popularized the use of the cheque, especially the use of the *chèque de virement.* *Virements* have represented as much as 81 per cent of the total transactions on the *c/c. postal.* This was the chief object of the *c/c. postal*, viz., to popularize *virements* and so repress payments in cash in various forms, so prevalent before, thus reducing the national currency requirements. In England this object is achieved by the wide-spread use of ordinary bank cheques, cleared at the Clearing House, which is equivalent to *virements*, in that it avoids movements of cash.

Furthermore, the introduction of *chèques postaux*, together with the simplification of money order transactions (for instance, a French money order under 20 francs may be issued without name of payee, but the holder can insert the name and paying office, if he likes), has resulted in the suppression of postal orders in France.

compte créditeur, credit account; creditor account; account in credit.

compte d'achat (Com.) (opp. à *compte de vente*), account of goods purchased; invoice of goods bought.

compte d'achats (Comptab.), purchases account.

comptes d'apport (Comptab.), capital accounts, reserve accounts, debenture accounts, and the like. (In English bookkeeping, these accounts are included under the denomination *nominal*, or *proprietary*, *accounts*.)

compte d'avances, loan account.

compte d'effets à payer, bills payable account.

compte d'effets à recevoir, bills receivable account.

compte d'épargne, savings account.

compte d'espèces, cash account (account settled promptly in ready money, as opposed to a *credit account*).

compte d'exploitation, trading account; working account.

compte d'immobilisations *ou* compte immobilisations *ou* compte d'établissement, capital expenditure account.

compte d'intérêts *ou* compte d'intérêt, interest account.

compte d'ordre, suspense account.

compte de banque *ou* compte en banque, banking account; bank account.

compte de caisse (Comptab.), cash account.

compte de capital, capital account.

comptes de choses [compte de chose *sing.*] (Comptab.) (opp. à *comptes de personnes*), impersonal accounts; nominal accounts (real or property accounts). *Cf.* comptes de résultats.

compte de consignation, consignment account.

compte de dépôt *ou* compte de dépôts *ou* compte de dépôts à vue *ou* compte de dépôts à vue ou avec préavis *ou* compte de chèques *ou* compte-chèque [comptes-chèques *pl.*] (*n.m.*) *ou* compte d'espèces *ou* compte de dépôt d'espèces (Banq.), current account; drawing account: (See notes under **dépôt.**)

il n'est disposé sur les comptes de dépôt que par des chèques, current accounts can only be drawn on by cheques.

compte de dépôts à terme ou à préavis *ou* compte de dépôts à terme ou avec préavis (Banq.), deposit account:

compte de dépôts à terme, fixed deposit account.

compte de dépôts à préavis (*ou* avec préavis) *ou* compte de dépôts à délai de préavis, deposit account at notice:

compte de dépôts à 7 jours de préavis, deposit account at 7 days' notice.

compte de divers, sundries account.

compte de fret, freight account.

compte de liquidation (Bourse), broker's account; brokers' account; settlement account.

compte de marchandises (Comptab.), goods account.

compte de méthode, suspense account.

compte de (*ou* en) participation, joint venture account; joint adventure account; joint account (in a commercial or financial transaction).

comptes de personnes [compte de personne *sing.*] *ou* comptes des particuliers [compte de particuliar *sing.*] (Comptab.), personal accounts.

compte de prélèvements *ou* compte de levées, drawings account; drawing account (account of amounts drawn out of the business by the trader).

compte de réserve *ou* compte de prévision, reserve account.

comptes de (*ou* des) résultats (Comptab.), nominal accounts; proprietary accounts; fictitious accounts; impersonal accounts (recording gains and losses). *Cf.* comptes de choses, comptes d'apport, *and* résultats de l'exercice.

compte de retour, banker's ticket; notarial ticket; notarial charges (on dishonoured bill). *Cf.* **sans compte de retour**, under **sans.**

compte de revient, cost account.

comptes de valeurs *ou* comptes du gérant *ou* comptes de l'exploitation (Comptab.), real accounts; property accounts; asset accounts.

compte de vente (Com.), account sales.

compte de ventes (Comptab.), sales account.

compte débiteur, debit account; debtor account; account in debit.

compte des (*ou* de) profits et pertes *ou* compte pertes et profits, profit and loss account.

compte désapprovisionné (Banq.), overdrawn account.

compte du grand livre, ledger account.

comptes faits, ready reckoner.

compte gestionnaire, management account.

compte-joint [comptes-joints *pl.*] (*n.m.*), joint account (an account pertaining to two or more persons).

compte loro, loro account.

compte nostro, nostro account.

compte ouvert (*Abrév.:* C.O.), open account.

compte particulier, private account.

comptes personnels *ou* comptes particuliers (opp. à *comptes de choses*), personal accounts.

compte plat *ou* compte non productif d'intérêts, non interest bearing account.

compte prélèvements, drawings account.

compte rendu, report; report of proceedings; account of proceedings:
les comptes rendus annuels présentés aux actionnaires d'une société, the annual reports presented to the shareholders of a company.
compte siège, head office account.
compte succursale, branch account.
compte vostro, vostro account.
à compte ou **à bon compte** (en déduction), on account:
prendre tant de francs à compte (ou à bon compte), to take so many francs on account.
à compte (à crédit), on account; on (or upon) credit:
prendre des marchandises à compte, to take goods on account (or on [or upon] credit).
pour le compte de, on account of; on behalf of:
verser des fonds pour le compte d'un tiers, to pay money on account of (or on behalf of) a third party.
pour le compte d'autrui, on clients' account; for customers.
pour son compte ou pour son propre compte, for one's own account:
en France un agent de change ne peut faire d'opérations pour son propre compte, in France, an *agent de change* (stockbroker) is not allowed to operate for his own account.
en compte, in account; on account:
valeur en compte (f.), value in account.
espèces en compte (f.pl.) (opp. à *espèces pour solde*), cash on account (opp. to *cash to balance*).
compter (v.t.) (nombrer; calculer), to count; to count up; to reckon; to reckon up; to calculate:
compter de l'argent, to count, to count up, money.
compter les jours de l'ouverture jusqu'à la fermeture du compte, to reckon, to calculate, the days from the opening to the closing of the account.
compter la recette et la dépense, to reckon up the receipts and the expenses.
compter (payer; donner) (v.t.), to pay; to pay out; to give:
compter tant de francs à quelqu'un, to pay, to pay out, to give, so many francs to someone.
compter (v.i.), to count; to reckon; to calculate:
dans les télégrammes, un signe de ponctuation compte pour un mot, in telegrams, a sign of punctuation counts as one word.
se compter (v.r.), to be counted; to be reckoned; to be calculated:
en dehors des frontières du pays qui l'a émise, la monnaie ne se compte pas, elle se pèse, outside the frontiers of the country which has issued it, money is not counted, it is weighed.
compter en trop, to overcharge:
marchandises comptées en trop sur notre facture (f.pl.), goods overcharged in our invoice.
compter sur quelqu'un, to count on (or upon), to rely on (or upon), someone.
comptes faits (m.pl.), ready reckoner.

compteur, -euse (pers.) (n.), counter; reckoner:
le caissier n'est pas seulement un compteur d'argent, the cashier is not only a counter of money.
comptoir (succursale d'une banque) (n.m.), branch:
la Banque de France a des comptoirs dans les principales villes, the Bank of France has branches in the principal towns.
comptoir (établissement de commerce, de banque, etc., dans les pays d'outre-mer) (n.m.), agency.
comptoir de liquidation (Bourse de valeurs) (m.), clearing house; clearing.
comptoir de vente (d'un cartel) (m.), selling office.
compulser (v.t.), to examine; to inspect; to look through; to go through:
compulser un livre, to examine, to inspect, to look through, to go through, a book.
concéder (v.t.), to concede; to grant:
concéder un privilège, to concede a privilege; to grant a right.
concéder un monopole, to grant a monopoly.
concessible (adj.), concessible; grantable:
terrains concessibles (m.pl.), concessible lands.
concession (n.f.), concession; grant:
concession de terrain, concession, grant, of land.
concession de chemin de fer, railway concession.
concessionnaire (adj.), concessionary:
société concessionnaire (f.), concessionary company.
concessionnaire (n.m. ou f.), concessionaire; concessioner; concessionary; grantee.
conclure (v.t.), to conclude:
conclure un contrat d'assurance, to conclude a contract of insurance.
concordance (n.f.), agreement; reconciliation:
concordance du journal et du grand livre, des espèces en caisse avec le solde accusé par le livre de caisse, agreement, reconciliation, between the journal and the ledger, of the cash in hand with the balance shown by the cash book.
concordat (convention) (n.m.), scheme of composition; arrangement with creditors.
concordat (décharge) (n.m.), composition:
concordat de 25 0/0, composition of 5s. in the £.
concorder (être d'accord) (v.i.), to agree:
la somme en lettres concorde avec la somme en chiffres, the amount in words agrees with the amount in figures.
concorder (arriver à un concordat) (v.i.), to compound:
concorder avec ses créanciers, to compound with one's creditors.
concourir (pour ou à) (v.i.), to compete (for):
concourir à une émission de titres, to compete for an issue of stock.
concourir (v.i.) ou **venir en concurrence** ou **venir en concours** (prendre le même rang), to rank equally; to rank concurrently; to rank pari passu:
les porteurs d'obligations chirographaires concourent avec les créanciers ordinaires (m.pl.), the holders of naked debentures rank equally (or concurrently) with the ordinary creditors.

créanciers qui par la date de leurs créances viennent en concurrence (*ou* viennent en concours) (*m.pl.*), creditors who rank equally (*or* concurrently) by reason of the dates of their respective debts.

concours (*n.m.*) *ou* **concurrence** (*n.f.*), equality ; equality of rank :
concours de privilèges, equality of rights.
concours entre créanciers, equality (*or* equality of rank) between creditors.

concours agricole (*m.*), agricultural show.

concurrence (rivalité) (*n.f.*), competition :
la concurrence de l'automobile et du chemin de fer, the competition of the motor and the railway.
acheter ou vendre en concurrence avec quelqu'un, to buy or sell in competition with someone.
à concurrence de, amounting to ; to the amount of :
il existe des réserves à concurrence de 1 000 000 fr., there are reserves amounting to 1,000,000 francs.
jusqu'à concurrence de, à concurrence d'un maximum de. See under **jusqu'à.**

concurrencer (*v.t.*), to compete with :
empêcher l'importation étrangère de concurrencer la production nationale, to prevent foreign importation from competing with national production.

concurrent, -e *ou* **concurrentiel, -elle** (*adj.*), competing ; competitive :
industries concurrentes (*f.pl.*), competing industries.
compagnies concurrentielles (*f.pl.*), competitive companies.
produits concurrents d'origine étrangère (*m.pl.*), competitive products of foreign origin.

condamné (-e) aux dépens (être) *ou* **condamné (-e) aux frais (être)** (Dr.), to be ordered to pay the costs.

condition (*n.f.*), condition :
conditions d'un contrat, conditions of a contract.
à condition *ou* **sous condition** (Com.), on approval ; on appro. ; on sale or return ; on sale :
marchandises remises à condition (*f.pl.*) *ou* *simplement* condition (*n.f.*), goods sent on sale or return ; goods on sale.

conditionnel, -elle (*adj.*), conditional :
acceptation conditionnelle (*f.*), conditional acceptance.

conditionnellement (*adv.*), conditionally.

conditionnement (*n.m.*), making up ; make up ; condition :
conditionnement des envois (Poste), make up of packets.
marchandises en bon état et conditionnement apparents (*f.pl.*), goods in apparent good order and condition.

conditionner (*v.t.*), to make up :
les imprimés et papiers de commerce doivent être conditionnés de telle sorte qu'ils puissent être (*ou* de manière à pouvoir être) facilement vérifiés (*m.pl.*), printed papers and com-

mercial papers must be made up in such a way that they can be easily examined.

conducteur (d'un train) (pers.) (*n.m.*), guard (of a train).

conducteur (Transport des animaux par ch. de f.) (pers.) (*n.m.*), attendant :
chevaux de course accompagnés d'un conducteur (*m.pl.*), race horses accompanied by an attendant.

conducteur (d'un omnibus) (pers.) (*n.m.*), conductor (of an omnibus).

conducteur (d'une voiture automobile) (pers.) (*n.m.*), driver, chauffeur (of a motor vehicle).

conduire (*v.t.*). See examples :
conduire ses affaires, to conduct one's business.
le capitaine conduit le navire pour le compte de l'armateur, the master manages the ship on behalf of the owner.
conduire un navire dans un port, à destination, to take, to bring, a ship into a port, to destination.
conduire les marchandises au lieu de leur destination, le voyageur sain et sauf à destination, to carry, to convey, the goods to the place of their destination, the passenger safe and sound to destination.

conduite (direction) (*n.f.*), conduct ; management :
conduite des affaires, conduct of affairs.
tout capitaine chargé de la conduite d'un navire est garant de ses fautes dans l'exercice de ses fonctions, every master entrusted with the management of a ship is responsible for his wrongful acts in the exercise of his functions.
le capitaine n'est pas seulement préposé de la conduite technique du navire et au commandement de l'équipage, the captain is not only entrusted with the technical management of the ship and with the commandership of the crew.

confection (*n.f.*) *ou* **confectionnement** (*n.m.*), making up ; make up :
confection des statistiques, d'un bilan, des lettres pour la poste, making up statistics, a balance sheet, letters for the post.

confectionner (*v.t.*), to make up :
les imprimés et papiers de commerce doivent être confectionnés de telle sorte qu'ils puissent être (*ou* de manière à pouvoir être) facilement vérifiés (*m.pl.*), printed papers and commercial papers must be made up in such a way that they can be easily examined.

conférence (*n.f.*), conference ; meeting :
conférence des avocats, conference of counsel.
conférence des chefs de service, meeting of heads (*or* managers) of departments.
conférence maritime, shipping conference (ring).

conférer (*v.i.*), to confer :
conférer avec son avocat, to confer with one's counsel.

confiance (*n.f.*), confidence ; reliance ; trust :
toute la valeur d'une banque réside dans la confiance qu'elle inspire, the whole worth of a bank lies in the confidence which it inspires.
abus de confiance (*m.*), breach of trust.

confidence (*n.f.*), confidence; secret.
confidentiel, -elle (*adj.*), confidential:
　rapport confidentiel (*m.*), confidential report.
confidentiellement (*adv.*), confidentially.
confier (*v.t.*), to confide; to entrust; to intrust;
　to invest:
　confier à quelqu'un le maniement de sommes
　　importantes, to entrust (*or* to intrust) the
　　handling of large sums of money to
　　someone.
　confier ses intérêts à quelqu'un, sa marchandise
　　à un commissionnaire de transports, to
　　entrust (*or* to intrust) one's interests to some-
　　one, one's goods to a transport agent.
　confier la direction d'une banque à un
　　gouverneur, to invest the management of a
　　bank in a governor.
se confier (*v.r.*), to confide; to rely; to trust:
　se confier en ses amis, to rely on (*or* upon) one's
　　friends; to trust one's friends.
confirmation (*n.f.*), confirmation:
　confirmation de crédit, d'une nouvelle, con-
　　firmation of credit, of a piece of news.
confirmer (*v.t.*) (Ant.: *infirmer*), to confirm:
　confirmer une lettre, to confirm a letter.
　confirmer par lettre le contenu d'un télégramme,
　　par écrit les ordres passés verbalement, to
　　confirm by letter the contents of a telegram,
　　in writing orders given verbally.
confiscation (*n.f.*), confiscation:
　confiscation de marchandise de contrebande, de
　　marchandise faussement déclarée, pour con-
　　travention aux lois, confiscation of smuggled
　　goods, of falsely entered goods, for breach of
　　the laws.
confisquer (*v.t.*), to confiscate.
conformer (se) (*v.r.*), to conform; to comply:
　se conformer aux clauses dans un contrat, à
　　des règlements de quarantaine ou autres, à
　　tous les règlements consulaires en vigueur,
　　aux formalités imposées par la loi, aux
　　conditions exigées par les statuts, aux
　　exigences des assureurs, to comply with the
　　clauses in an agreement, with quarantine or
　　other regulations, with all the consular
　　regulations in force, with the legal require-
　　ments, with the conditions required by the
　　articles of association, with the underwriters'
　　requirements.
congé *ou* **congédiement** (*n.m.*) (renvoi d'une
　personne à gages), dismissal; discharge.
congé (acte qui assigne un terme à une location)
　(*n.m.*), notice; notice to quit:
　locataire qui a donné congé (*m.*), tenant who
　　has given notice.
　le congé donné par l'employeur, par l'employé,
　　the notice given by the employer, by the
　　employee.
congé (exemption de travail ou de service;
　autorisation de s'absenter) (*n.m.*), leave;
　leave of absence; holiday:
　trois mois de congé, three months' leave.
congé (*n.m.*) *ou* **congé maritime** *ou* **congé de
　navigation,** clearance:
　Note :—French ships leaving a French
　　port have to be provided with a **congé.** It

states that the master has complied with the
necessary formalities to have the right to
sail under the French flag. It is available
for one year or for the duration of a voyage
occupying more than a year.
　Foreign ships leaving a French port have
to be provided with a **passeport.** The *passeport* is for foreign ships what the *congé* is for
French ships.
　aucun bâtiment ne peut sortir du port sans
　　congé, no vessel may leave port without
　　clearance.
congé (laisser-passer) (Douanes) (*n.m.*), cart note.
congédier (*v.t.*), to dismiss; to discharge; to
　sack (*slang*):
　congédier un employé, tout le personnel, to
　　dismiss, to discharge, to sack, an employee, all
　　the staff.
conjoint, -e (*adj.*), joint:
　obligation conjointe (*f.*), joint liability; joint
　　obligation.
conjoint (-e) et solidaire, joint and several:
　garantie conjointe et solidaire (*f.*), joint and
　　several guarantee.
conjointement (*adv.*), jointly:
　seul ou conjointement avec des autres, alone
　　or jointly with others.
conjointement et solidairement, jointly and
　severally:
　associés qui sont conjointement et solidaire-
　　ment responsables de tous les actes sociaux
　　(*m.pl.*), partners who are jointly and
　　severally liable for all the firm's acts.
connaissement (*n.m.*), bill of lading; bill:
　connaissement à ordre, bill of lading to (*or*
　　unto) order.
　connaissement à ordres, calling for orders bill
　　of lading.
　connaissement à personne dénommée *ou* con-
　　naissement nominatif, bill of lading to a
　　named (*or* specified) person.
　connaissement au porteur, bill of lading to
　　bearer.
　connaissement avec réserves *ou* connaissement
　　portant des réserves, foul bill of lading;
　　dirty bill of lading.
　connaissement-chef [connaissements-chefs *pl.*]
　　(*n.m.*), original stamped bill of lading.
　Note :—In French practice the *connaissement-
　　chef* or *timbre-chef* (this being the bill of
　　lading which is impressed with the stamp
　　duty paid, the other copies bearing a denoting
　　stamp) is given to the captain, and this is the
　　copy which accompanies the goods, i.e., the
　　captain's copy. The captain presents this
　　connaissement-chef to the consignee on arrival,
　　who endorses his receipt on the back to
　　accomplish it. The consignee can however,
　　if he wishes, give to the captain, duly
　　endorsed, the copy he has received from the
　　shipper. This latter is the English method;
　　the *captain's copy* (exemplaire [ou copie] *du
　　capitaine*) being marked *not negotiable.*
　connaissement collectif, general bill of lading.
　connaissement d'entrée, inward bill of lading;
　　homeward bill of lading.

connaissement de l'État, government bill of lading.

connaissement de sortie, outward bill of lading.

connaissement direct *ou* connaissement à forfait, through bill of lading.

connaissement embarqué, shipped bill of lading.

connaissement fluvial, river bill of lading.

connaissement net *ou* connaissement sans réserve, clean bill of lading.

connaissement reçu pour embarquement *ou* connaissement reçu pour être embarqué *ou* connaissement reçu pour charger, received for shipment bill of lading.

connaissement rouge, red bill of lading.

connu, -e (*adj.*), known :
risque connu (*m.*), known risk.

consacrer (*v.t.*), to devote ; to employ ; to appropriate ; to set apart ; to sanction ; to design to contain :
les trente années qu'il a consacrées à son commerce, the thirty years he has devoted to his business.

le gérant doit consacrer tout son temps aux affaires sociales, the manager must devote his whole time to the company's business.

bâtiments (de mer) consacrés au commerce (*m.pl.*), vessels employed in trade.

usage consacré par la pratique (*m.*), custom sanctioned by practice.

consacrer des fonds au rachat d'une annuité, to appropriate funds to, to set apart sums of money for, the redemption of an annuity.

page du grand livre divisée en colonnes verticales consacrées chacune à un sous-compte (*f.*), page of the ledger divided into vertical columns each designed to contain a subsidiary account.

consciencieusement (*adv.*), conscientiously.
consciencieux, -euse (*adj.*), conscientious.
conseil (avis) (*n.m.*) (*s'emploie souvent au pluriel*), advice ; counsel :
prendre conseil, to take advice.
demander des conseils, to ask for advice.

conseil (réunion de personnes qui délibèrent) (*n.m.*), consultation ; meeting :
assister à un conseil des administrateurs, to be present at a meeting of the directors ; to attend a board meeting.

conseil (assemblée de personnes) (*n.m.*), board ; council ; court :
conseil d'administration, board of directors ; board ; directors :
la société est administrée par le conseil d'administration élu par les actionnaires. Le conseil d'administration choisit le directeur, a company is administered by a board of directors elected by shareholders. The board chooses (*or* the directors choose) a manager.

Le Conseil d'administration (souscription à un avis de convocation, ou analogue), By order of the Board, So-and-So, Secretary.

conseil d'administration des douanes, board of customs.

conseil d'arbitrage, arbitration board.
conseil d'enquête, court of inquiry.
conseil de discipline, disciplinary board.
conseil de gérance, board of management.
conseil de la Société des Nations, council of the League of Nations.
conseil des prises (Dr. mar.), prize court.

conseil *ou* **avocat-conseil** (pers.) (*n.m.*), counsel.
conseillable (*adj.*), advisable ; recommendable : démarche conseillable (*f.*), advisable step.
conseiller (*v.t.*), to advise ; to recommend ; to counsel.

consentement (*n.m.*), consent ; assent :
consentement des parties, consent of the parties.

consentement par écrit, consent (*or* assent) in writing ; written consent :
consentement par écrit des assureurs, written consent of the underwriters.

consentement verbal, verbal consent ; verbal assent.

consentir (*v.t.*), to consent to ; to agree to ; to grant :
consentir une vente, to consent to, to agree to, a sale.

consentir un prêt, un découvert, to grant a loan, an overdraft.

consentir (*v.i.*), to consent ; to agree :
consentir à quelque chose, to consent, to agree, to something.

conservateur des hypothèques (pers.) (*m.*), registrar of mortgages.

conservation (*n.f.*), preservation ; preserving ; keeping ; care :
conservation des objets assurés, preservation of, preserving, care of, the property insured.

conserver (*v.t.*), to preserve ; to keep ; to take care of :
conserver certains registres et documents pendant 5, 10, ans, to keep certain books and documents for 5, 10, years (i.e., not to destroy them).

considérable (*adj.*), considerable ; large ; big :
somme considérable (*f.*), considerable sum ; large amount ; big sum.

considération (*n.f.*), consideration ; considering :
cela mérite considération, that is worth considering (*or* merits consideration).

considérer (*v.t.*), to consider.

consignataire (dépositaire) (pers.) (*n.m.*), depositary ; trustee.

consignataire (Dr. mar. & Com.) (*n.m.*), consignee :
consignataire de la (*ou* à la) cargaison, consignee of the cargo.

consignataire du navire *ou* consignataire de la coque, consignee of the ship ; ship's broker.

consignateur, -trice (pers.) (*n.*), consignor ; consigner.

consignation (dépôt à titre de garantie, etc.) (*n.f.*), deposit :
consignation d'un cautionnement, deposit of a security (surety).

consignation (Douanes) (*n.f.*), deposit; deposit of cash (in lieu of bond) :
consignation de droits de douane, deposit of customs duties.

consignation (dépôt de marchandises) (*n.f.*), consignment :
marchandises en consignation (*f.pl.*), goods on consignment.

consigne (*n.f.*) *ou* consigne des bagages (bureau de gare), cloak room :
bagages déposés (*ou* mis) à la consigne (*m.pl.*), luggage deposited in (*or* put into) the cloak room.

consigne des bagages (action) (*f.*), deposit of luggage in cloak room.

consigner (mettre en dépôt) (*v.t.*), to deposit :
consigner une somme d'argent chez quelqu'un, to deposit a sum of money with someone.
consigner en papier, to deposit paper security.
les marchandises ne peuvent être retirées des douanes qu'après les droits ont été payés, consignés, ou garantis (*f.pl.*), the goods can only be cleared after the duties have been paid, deposited, or secured.

consigner (Dr. mar. & Com.) (*v.t.*), to consign :
consigner un navire aux agents de l'affréteur, to consign a ship to the charterer's agents.
marchandises consignées à un pays étranger (*f.pl.*), goods consigned to a foreign country.

consigner (citer, rapporter dans un écrit) (*v.t.*), to record :
les agents de change doivent consigner sur des livres spéciaux toutes les opérations faites par leur ministère (*m.pl.*), stockbrokers must record in special books all the deals done through their agency.

consolidation (*n.f.*), consolidation; unification; funding; strengthening :
consolidation de la dette flottante, consolidation of the floating debt.

consolidation d'un marché à prime (Bourse) (*f.*), exercise of, taking up, an option.

consolidé (*n.m.*), consolidated government stock.
Consolidés (*n.m.pl.*), Consols.

consolider (*v.t.*), to consolidate; to unify; to fund; to strengthen :
dette consolidée (*f.*) (opp. à *dette flottante*), consolidated debt; unified debt. See example under flottant, -e.
consolider des arrérages, to fund interest.
consolider une situation, to strengthen a position.

consolider un marché à prime (Bourse) (opp. à *abandonner une prime*), to exercise, to take up, an option.

consolider (se) (*v.r.*), to strengthen :
les valeurs bancaires se consolident (Bourse) (*f.pl.*), bank shares strengthened.

consommateur, -trice (pers.) (*n.*) (Ant. : *producteur*), consumer.

consommation (*n.f.*), consumption; use :
la consommation journalière de charbon, the daily consumption of coal.

consommation intérieure *ou simplement* consommation, home consumption; home use :
marchandises mises en consommation (Douanes) (*f.pl.*), goods for home consumption (*or* home use).

consommer (*v.t.*), to consume; to use. See example under produire.

consortium (association en participation pour une opération déterminée) (*n.m.*), syndicate; consortium :
un consortium de banquiers, a syndicate of bankers.

constatation (*n.f.*), ascertainment; verification; proof; establishment; declaration; fixing; attestation; recording; noting; mention :
constatation d'identité, proof of indentity.

constater (*v.t.*). See examples :
constater les profits, l'importance des avaries, to ascertain the profits, the extent of the damage.
constater un fait, to ascertain, to establish, to verify, to note, to attest, a fact.
certificat qui constate l'existence d'hypothèques (*m.*), certificate which proves (*or* shows) (*or* mentions) the existence of mortgages.
constater l'adoption d'une résolution, to declare a resolution carried.
les agents de change ont seuls le droit de constater les cours des valeurs cotées (*m.pl.*), the brokers (on the Paris Bourse) have the exclusive right of fixing the prices of quoted securities.
en France, le refus de paiement d'un effet de commerce doit être constaté le lendemain du jour de l'échéance par un acte que l'on nomme protêt faute de paiement, in France, dishonour by non payment of a bill of exchange should be attested (*or* noted) the day after the day of maturity by an act called protest for non payment.
constater les naissances et décès qui se produisent à bord d'un navire, to record the births and deaths which occur on board a ship.
gouvernements qui ont une tendance à satisfaire, quelquefois au mépris de la vérité, leur désir de constater des résultats qui font honneur à leur administration (*m.pl.*), governments which have a tendency, sometimes in defiance of truth, to satisfy their desire to record results which do credit to their administration.
constater sur le récépissé la nature et l'importance des avaries, to note on the receipt the nature and extent of the damage.
nous avons constaté que le bilan présenté par le conseil d'administration est l'expression exacte de la situation active et passive de la société (rapport des commissaires aux comptes, formule française), we are of opinion that (*or* in our opinion) such balance sheet is properly drawn up so as to exhibit a true and correct view of the state of the company's affairs (auditors' report, English formula).

contrat d'affrètement constaté par un connaissement (m.), contract of affreightment evidenced by a bill of lading.

constituer (v.t.), to constitute; to form; to incorporate:
assemblée régulièrement constituée (f.), meeting regularly constituted.
constituer un syndicat, to form a syndicate.
constituer une société, to form, to incorporate, a company.

se constituer (v.r.), to be constituted; to be formed; to be incorporated; to form:
une nouvelle société se constitua au capital de tant, a new company was formed (or incorporated) with a capital of so much.
financiers qui se constituent en syndicat pour garantir une émission (m.pl.), financiers who form a syndicate to underwrite an issue.

constituer (Dr.) (v.t.), to settle:
constituer une annuité à quelqu'un, to settle an annuity on someone.

constituer avocat, to instruct, to brief, counsel.

constituer avoué, to instruct, to appoint, a solicitor.

constitution (n.f.), constitution; formation; incorporation:
constitution d'une banque en société anonyme, formation of a bank into a limited company.
constitution d'un fonds de réserve, formation of a reserve fund.

constitution (Dr.) (n.f.), settlement:
constitution d'une annuité à quelqu'un, settlement of an annuity on someone.

constitution d'avocat (f.), instructions to, instructing, briefing, counsel.

constitution d'avoué (f.), instructions to, instructing, appointment of, appointing, a solicitor.

constructeur de navires (pers.) (m.), shipbuilder.

construction (n.f.), building; construction:
construction de navires ou construction navale ou construction maritime, shipbuilding.

construire (v.t.), to build; to construct:
navires construits à l'étranger (m.pl.), ships built abroad.

consul (pers.) (n.m.), consul:
consul de France ou consul français, French consul.
le consul britannique à Marseille, the British consul at Marseilles.
consul général, consul general.

consulaire (qui appartient au consul) (adj.), consular:
rapport consulaire (m.), consular report.

consulaire (qui appartient à la justice commerciale) (adj.), commercial:
tribunal consulaire (m.), commercial court.

consulat (n.m.), consulate:
consulat général, consulate general.

consulat (Mar.) (n.m.), captain's report (of extraordinary incidents during the voyage), made by a French master to a French consul abroad. It is called **consulat** when it is complete (normal arrival) and **petit consulat** when it is abridged, as for example, in case of a call of distress.

consultatif, -ive (adj.), consultative:
voix consultative (f.), consultative voice.

consultation (conférence) (n.f.), consultation.

consultation (avis motivé) (Dr.) (n.f.), opinion; advice:
consultation d'avocat, counsel's opinion; opinion of counsel; counsel's advice.
les avocats ont le droit de donner des consultations, counsel have the right to give opinions.

consultation (mémoire adressé à un avocat) (n.f.), case for counsel.

consulter (v.t.), to consult; to refer to:
consulter un avocat, to consult counsel.
consulter un prix courant, to consult a price list; to refer to a price current.

consulter (v.i.), to consult:
consulter avec quelqu'un, to consult with someone.

contenant (opp. à contenu) (n.m.), container:
les boîtes, les étuis, et les contenants similaires, boxes, cases, and like (or similar) containers.

contenir (v.t.), to contain; to hold; to comprise; to include:
la proposition doit contenir: le nom du navire, celui du capitaine, etc., the proposal should contain: the name of the ship, that of the master, etc.

contentieux, -euse (Dr.) (adj.), contentious; law (used as adj.):
affaire contentieuse (f.), contentious matter; law case.

contentieux (agence d'affaires) (n.m.), law offices.

contentieux (d'une administration) (n.m.), solicitor's department; law department; solicitor's office.

contenu (n.m.), contents:
le contenu d'un colis, d'une lettre, d'un connaissement, the contents of a package, of a letter, of a bill of lading.

contestation (n.f.), dispute; difference:
contestations entre employeurs et employés, entre la douane et le commerce, disputes between employers and employees, between the customs and traders.

continent (n.m.), continent.

continental, -e, -aux (adj.), continental.

contingence (n.f.), contingency; contingence.

contingent, -e (adj.), contingent:
annuité contingente (f.), contingent annuity.

contingent (contingentement de la production) (n.m.), quota:
un contingent de tant de tonnes, a quota of so many tons.

contingentement (de la production) (n.m.), curtailment; curtailing (of the output).

contingenter (v.t.), to curtail:
contingenter la production du caoutchouc, de l'étain, to curtail the output of rubber, of tin.

continuer (v.t.), to continue:
navire hors d'état de continuer son voyage (m.), ship unable to continue her voyage.

contractable (adj.), contractable:
obligation contractable (f.), contractable obligation.

contractant, -e (*adj.*), contracting:
parties contractantes (*f.pl.*), contracting parties.
contractant, -e (pers.) (*n.*), contractant.
contracter (*v.t.*), to contract; to enter into; to
take out:
celui qui accepte une lettre de change contracte
l'obligation d'en payer le montant, the
person who accepts a bill of exchange contracts the obligation (*or* engages) to pay the
amount of it.
contracter un bail, to enter into a lease.
contracter des dettes, un emprunt, to contract
debts, a loan.
l'assurance contractée seulement après l'arrivée
du navire est nulle, insurance contracted
only after arrival of the ship is null.
contracter une police d'assurance, une assurance
en son propre nom ou au nom et pour compte
de tierces personnes, to take out an insurance
policy, an insurance in one's own name or in
the name and for account of third persons.
contracter (*v.i.*), to contract; to covenant:
les mineurs ne sont pas aptes à contracter (*m.pl.*
ou *f.pl.*), minors are not capable of contracting.
contractuel, -elle (*adj.*), contractual:
obligations contractuelles (*f.pl.*), contractual
obligations. (*Cf.* services contractuels.)
contractuellement (*adv.*), contractually; by
contract.
contradictoire (*adj.*), check; control (*used as
adjs*); joint:
pesage contradictoire (*m.*), check weighing.
expertise contradictoire (*f.*), joint survey;
check survey; control survey.
contradictoirement (*adv.*), jointly:
les vices d'emballage doivent être constatés
contradictoirement avant le départ du
navire (*m.pl.*), defects in packing should be
ascertained jointly (i.e., as between shipowner
and shipper) before the sailing of the ship.
contrainte (Dr. mar.) (*n.f.*), restraint:
contraintes de princes, de gouvernants,
restraints of princes, of rulers.
contraire (en parlant des changes) (*adj.*), unfavourable; unfavorable; against. See
change for example.
contrat (*n.m.*), contract; agreement; deed;
indenture; articles; letter; bond:
contrat à forfait, contract at an agreed price (*or*
at a fixed price); contract with a fixed and
determined consideration.
contrat à la grosse *ou* contrat de grosse,
bottomry or respondentia bond.
contrat à la grosse sur corps, bottomry bond.
contrat à la grosse sur facultés, respondentia
bond.
contrat à titre gratuit *ou* contrat de bienfaisance (opp. à *contrat à titre onéreux*), bare
contract; naked contract; nude contract.
contrat à titre onéreux, onerous contract.
contrat accessoire, accessory contract.
contrat aléatoire, aleatory contract:
le contrat d'assurance est un contrat aléatoire
qui a pour but d'indemniser l'assuré d'un
dommage résultant d'un cas fortuit, a contract of insurance is an aleatory contract

which has as its object the indemnification
of the insured for (*or* contract whereby the
insured is indemnified against) a damage
resulting from a fortuitous event.
contrat bilatéral *ou* contrat synallagmatique,
bilateral contract; synallagmatic contract.
contrat commutatif, commutative contract.
contrat consensuel, consensual contract.
contrat d'affrètement, contract of affreightment.
contrat d'agence, agency agreement (agreement enumerating the conditions under which
representation is granted).
contrat d'assurance maritime, contract of
marine (*or* of sea) insurance:
le contrat d'assurance maritime est le contrat
par lequel l'assureur s'engage à indemniser
l'assuré de la manière et dans les limites qui
y sont convenues, contre les pertes maritimes,
c'est-à-dire les pertes qui se rapportent aux
aventures maritimes, a contract of marine
insurance is a contract whereby the insurer
undertakes to indemnify the assured, in
manner and to the extent thereby agreed,
against marine losses, that is to say, the
losses incident to marine adventure.
contrat d'engagement des gens de l'équipage
ou contrat de travail des gens de mer, agreement with crew.
contrat d'hypothèque *ou* contrat hypothécaire,
mortgage deed.
contrat d'indemnité, contract of indemnity.
contrat d'union, (in France) a contract between
several creditors, agreeing collectively to take
steps to recover debts due to them by the
same debtor.
contrat de commission (Bourse de marchandises) (opp. à *contrat direct*), commission
contract; broker's contract.
contrat de fret, freight contract.
contrat de garantie, underwriting contract;
underwriting letter.
contrat de gérance, management agreement.
contrat de mandat (Dr.), agency contract
(contract of trust; mandatory contract).
contrat de passage *ou* contrat de transport des
passagers, passenger contract (sea or air).
contrat de société *ou* contrat d'association,
partnership deed; deed (*or* articles) of
partnership.
contrat de transport *ou* contrat d'expédition,
contract of carriage:
le contrat de transport est la convention par
laquelle un voiturier se charge, moyennant
un prix convenu et suivant un mode de
transport déterminé, de porter d'un lieu
dans un autre une personne ou une chose,
a contract of carriage is an agreement
whereby a carrier undertakes, in consideration of an agreed price and by a certain
method of conveyance, to carry from one
place to another a person or a thing.
contrat de vente, contract for sale; sale
contract; agreement for sale.
contrat de voyage *ou* contrat de transport des
voyageurs, passenger contract (land, sea, or
air).

contrat direct (Bourse de marchandises), direct contract; principal contract.

contrat direct (Opérations sur valeurs mobilières), outside broker's contract.

contrat entre le capitaine et le propriétaire *ou* contrat de préposition, agreement between master and owner.

contrat principal, principal contract; principal agreement.

contrat réel, real contract.

contrat résoluble, determinable contract; avoidable contract; voidable contract.

contrat solonnel, solemn contract.

contrat translatif de propriété, conveyance.

contrat unilatéral, unilateral contract.

contravention (infraction aux règlements) (*n.f.*), contravention; breach; breach of the regulations; infringement:

contravention à un monopole, infringement of a monopoly.

contre (Dr.) (*prép.*), versus [Abbrev.: v. *or* vs]: X. contre Y., X. versus (*or* v.) Y.

contre-balancer (*v.t.*), to counterbalance.

se contre-balancer (*v.r.*), to counterbalance each other; to be counterbalanced.

contrebande, contrebandier. See below.

contre-caution [**contre-cautions** *pl.*] (*n.f.*), counter surety; counter security.

contre-changer (*v.t.*), to counterchange.

contre-dater (*v.t.*), to alter the date of.

contre-déclaration [**contre-déclarations** *pl.*] (*n.f.*), counter declaration.

contre-expertise. See under **contre-visite.**

contrefaçon, contrefaire. See below.

contre-mandat [**contre-mandats** *pl.*] (*n.m.*), counter mandate; counter instructions.

contremandement, contremander, contremarque. See below.

contre-opération [**contre-opérations** *pl.*] (*n.f.*), counter operation.

contre-ordre [**contre-ordres** *pl.*] (*n.m.*), counter order.

contre-partie [**contre-parties** *pl.*] (*n.f.*), counterpart:

la vente est la conséquence et la contre-partie de l'achat, a sale is the consequence and the counterpart of a purchase.

contre-partie (*n.f.*) *ou* **contre-partiste** (*n.m.*) (pers.), other side; other party; another dealer:

vendeur qui a dû satisfaire au versement avant de livrer les titres à sa contre-partie (*m.*), seller who has to pay the call before delivering the stock to the other side (i.e., the buyer). *Cf.* faire la contre-partie.

généralement, ces intermédiaires s'interposent comme un écran entre l'acheteur et le vendeur; ils traitent entre eux, entre intermédiaires, entre collègues, sans que leur contre-partie connaisse le nom de leur client, ni leur client celui de la contre-partie, generally, these intermediaries (i.e., brokers) interpose like a screen between the buyer and the seller; they deal between themselves, between intermediaries, between colleagues,

without the other side knowing the name of their client, or their client that of the other side.

agent qui ne peut pas trouver une contre-partie sur le marché, broker who cannot find another dealer on the market. *Note :*—In Paris, broker deals with broker and the other broker dealt with is the *contre-partie.* In London, broker deals with dealer *or* jobber, consequently *contre-partie* in this sense has no technical equivalent in English.

contre-partie (contrat direct) (*n.f.*), running stock (against one's client). *Cf.* faire la contre-partie, se faire la contre-partie *and* maison de contre-partie.

contre-partie (Comptab.) (*n.f.*), contra:

la partie simple consiste dans l'inscription des articles au fur et à mesure dans un seul compte, sans aucune contre-partie, single entry consists in entering up items one after another in one account, without any contra.

le compte *ayants compte d'acceptations* a sa contre-partie au passif dans le compte *acceptations pour compte de clients* (bilan de banque), the account *liability* (or *liabilities*) *of customers for acceptance* (or *acceptances*) has its contra among the liabilities in the account *acceptances on account of* (or *for*) *customers* (bank balance sheet).

les comptes crédités en contre-partie (*m.pl.*), the accounts credited per contra.

compte contre-partie (*m.*), contra account.

contre-partiste [**contre-partistes** *pl.*] (banquier marron) (pers.) (*n.m.*), runner (of stock against his client):

le contre-partiste est celui qui opère lui-même contre son donneur d'ordre : le client veut-il vendre une valeur quelconque, le contre-partiste achète, et réciproquement, the runner is one who operates himself against his principal : should the client wish to sell a security, the runner buys, and vice versa.

contre-passement [**contre-passements** *pl.*] (*n.m.*) *ou* **contre-passation** [**contre-passations** *pl.*] (*n.f.*) (Comptab.), writing back; reversal; reversing; contraing; transfer.

contre-passer (Comptab.) (*v.t.*), to write back; to reverse; to contra; to transfer:

contre-passer un article, une écriture, to write back, to reverse, to contra, to transfer, an item, an entry.

contre-passer une balance au compte pertes et profits, to transfer a balance to profit and loss account.

contre-passer une écriture d'ordre à la réouverture des livres, to reverse a suspense entry on the reopening of the books.

le crédit n'est que provisoire et peut être contre-passé au cas de non paiement, the credit is only provisional and can be written back (*or* reversed) (*or* contraed) in case of non payment.

se contre-passer (*v.r.*), to contra each other.

contre-passer une lettre de change, to endorse back a bill of exchange.

contre-poser (Comptab.) (*v.t.*), to misenter.

contre-position [contre-positions *pl.*] (Comptab.)
(*n.f.*), misentry :
contre-position d'un article sur les livres,
misentry of an item in the books.

contre-proposition [contre-propositions *pl.*] (*n.f.*),
counter proposal ; counter proposition.

contresigner, contrestaries, contresurestaries. See
below.

contre-valeur [contre-valeurs *pl.*] (*n.f.*), value in
exchange ; exchange value :
lettres de change fournies en contre-valeur de
marchandises (*f.pl.*), bills of exchange given
as value in exchange (*or* as exchange value)
for goods.

contre-visite [contre-visites *pl.*] *ou* contre-vérification [contre-vérifications *pl.*] (Douanes) (*n.f.*),
reexamination :
contre-visite (*ou* contre-vérification) des marchandises déjà vérifiées, reexamination of
goods already examined.

contre-visite *ou* contre-expertise [contre-expertises
pl.] (de navires) (*n.f.*), resurvey.

contrebande (*n.f.*), smuggling ; contraband :
contrebande absolue *ou* contrebande par nature,
absolute contraband.
contrebande de guerre, contraband of war.
contrebande relative, occasional contraband.
marchandises de contrebande (*f.pl.*), smuggled
goods ; contraband goods.

contrebandier, -ère (pers.) (*n.*), smuggler ; con-
trabandist.

contrefaçon *ou* contrefaction (action) (*n.f.*),
counterfeiting ; forging ; infringement ;
imitation :
contrefaçon littéraire *ou* contrefaçon de (*ou*
en) librairie, infringement of copyright.

contrefaçon *ou* contrefaction (ouvrage contrefait)
(*n.f.*), counterfeit ; forgery ; infringement ;
imitation.

contrefaire (*v.t.*), to counterfeit ; to forge ; to
infringe ; to imitate :
contrefaire des monnaies, to counterfeit coin.
contrefaire des billets de banque, une signature,
to forge bank notes, a signature.
contrefaire un objet breveté, to infringe a
patented article.
contrefaire une marque de fabrique, to forge,
to imitate, a trade mark.

contremandement (action) (*n.m.*), counter-
manding.

contremandement (révocation) (*n.m.*), countermand.

contremander (*v.t.*), to countermand.

contremarque (*n.f.*) (Abrév. : cque), countermark.

contresigner (*v.t.*), to countersign :
contresigner un double comme preuve
d'acceptation, to countersign a duplicate
as evidence of acceptance.

contresurestaries *ou* contrestaries (Dr. mar.)
(*n.f.pl.*), damages for detention.

contribuable (*adj.*), liable to contribute ; contributable ; liable to taxation.

contribuable (pers.) (*n.m.* ou *f.*), taxpayer ;
ratepayer.

contribuant, -e (*adj.*), contributing :

les parties contribuantes (*f.pl.*), the contributing
parties.

contribuant (pers.) (*n.m.*), contributor.

contribuer (*v.t.*), to contribute :
contribuer ce qui est nécessaire pour satisfaire
aux besoins de quelqu'un, to contribute what
is necessary to satisfy someone's needs.

contribuer (*v.i.*), to contribute :
contribuer pour un tiers, to contribute one
third (*or* a third).
contribuer à une dépense, à une perte
proportionnellement au montant dont on
est responsable aux termes de son contrat,
to contribute to an expense, to a loss in
proportion to the amount for which one is
liable under one's contract.
tout qui tire profit du sacrifice commun est
tenu de contribuer à indemniser les dommages
subis (Avarie commune), everything which
benefits by the common sacrifice is liable
to contribute to indemnify the damage
sustained.

contributaire (*adj.*), contributory.

contributaire (pers.) (*n.m.* ou *f.*), contributory.

contributeur, -trice (pers.) (*n.*), contributor.

contributif, -ive (*adj.*), contributive ; contributory :
la part contributive de chacun, the contributory share of each.

contribution (part d'une dépense) (*n.f.*), contribution :
contribution aux dépenses d'une entreprise,
contribution to the expenses of an enterprise.
contribution à l'avarie commune (*ou* en avarie
commune) (*ou* d'avarie commune) (*ou* aux
avaries communes), contribution to (*or*
in) general average ; general average contribution :
contribution, c'est-à-dire participation aux
dommages, pertes, ou frais extraordinaires
provenant d'un sacrifice pour le salut
commun du navire et de la cargaison,
contribution, that is to say, participation
in the extraordinary damage, losses, or
expenses arising from a sacrifice for the
common safety of the ship and cargo.

contribution (impôt) (*n.f.*), tax ; rate ; duty :
contribution directe, direct tax.
contribution indirecte, indirect tax.
contribution foncière sur la propriété bâtie,
property tax on buildings.
contribution foncière sur les propriétés non
bâties, tax on property not built upon ;
land tax.
contribution extraordinaire sur les bénéfices de
guerre, excess profits duty.
contributions et impôts, rates and taxes.

contribution (répartition entre créanciers) (*n.f.*),
distribution :
contribution amiable, distribution to creditors
by agreement among themselves without the
intervention of the Court.
contribution judiciaire, distribution to creditors
under the supervision of the Court.

contributoire (*adj.*), contributory.

contrôlable (*adj.*), controllable.

contrôle (*n.m.*), control; inspection; check; supervision; superintendence:
contrôle de la caisse, control of the cash.
contrôle des reports du grand livre, check on ledger postings.

contrôler (*v.t.*), to control; to inspect; to check; to verify; to examine; to supervise; to superintend:
branche d'industrie contrôlé par un trust (*f.*), branch of industry controlled by a trust.
contrôler la dépense (*ou* les dépenses), to control the expenditure.
contrôler le poids et, dès lors, accepter d'en répondre, to check the weight and, thereafter, accept responsibility for it.
le service du contrôle (d'une banque, ou analogue) ne peut donner de bons résultats que s'il est indépendant des services contrôlés, the inspection department (of a bank, or the like) cannot show good results unless it is independent of the departments inspected.

contrôleur, -euse (pers.) (*n.*), controller; comptroller; inspector; checker; examiner; supervisor; superintendent:
contrôleur des contributions directes, inspector of taxes.
contrôleur général (service public), controller general; comptroller general.

contrôleurs (faillite) (*n.m.pl.*), committee of inspection.

convenio (*n.m.*), scheme of composition; arrangement with creditors.

convenir (*v.i.*), to agree:
convenir d'un prix *ou* convenir sur un prix, to agree upon a price.

convention (traité) (*n.f.*), convention:
règles imposées par des conventions internationales (*f.pl.*), rules laid down by international conventions.
convention monétaire, monetary convention.

convention (accord; contrat) (*n.f.*), agreement; contract:
la convention des parties suffit à valider l'opération, the agreement of the parties is sufficient to validate the operation.
convention de vente, agreement for sale; sale contract.
convention ducroire, del credere agreement.
convention expresse, express agreement.
convention par écrit, agreement in writing; written agreement.
convention syndicale, underwriting contract; underwriting letter.
convention tacite, tacit agreement.
convention verbale, verbal agreement.

convention (stipulation; clause) (*n.f.*), covenant.

conventionnel, -elle (*adj.*), conventional; agreement (*used as adj.*):
clause conventionnelle (*f.*), agreement clause.

convenu, -e (*adj. & p.p.*), agreed; agreed upon; stipulated:
la somme convenue, the sum agreed upon; the agreed sum.

convenu (langage convenu) (Télégr.) (*n.m.*), code; code language:
mot en convenu (*m.*), word in code.

conversation (Téléph.) (*n.f.*), conversation; call:
la taxe d'une conversation de trois minutes, the charge for a three minutes' conversation.
conversation interurbaine, trunk call.
conversation interurbaine de jour, de nuit, day, night, trunk call.
conversation locale, local call.
conversation régionale, toll call.
conversations à heures fixes par abonnement, subscription calls.

conversion (*n.f.*), conversion:
conversion du trois pour cent, du franc-or dans la monnaie d'un autre pays, des titres nominatifs en titres au porteur, conversion of the three per cents, of the gold franc into the money of another country, of registered securities to bearer securities.

conversion (Bourse) (*n.f.*), going on the other tack (going a bear after going a bull, or vice versa).

convertibilité (*n.f.*), convertibility.

convertible *ou* **conversible** *ou* **convertissable** (*adj.*), convertible:
papier convertible (*m.*), convertible paper.
les billets de banque sont dits convertibles quand les porteurs ont le droit d'en demander le remboursement à vue à la banque d'émission (*m.pl.*), bank notes are said to be convertible when the holders have the right to demand repayment of them at sight at the bank of issue.

convertir (*v.t.*), to convert; to turn:
cubage converti en poids (*m.*), measurement converted into weight.
convertir le 5 p. 100 en 4 1/2, to convert the 5 per cents into 4½ per cents.
convertir un billet de banque en espèces, to convert, to turn, a bank note into cash.
conv. (*abrév.*), converti, -e.

convertissement (*n.m.*), conversion:
convertissement des valeurs en espèces, conversion of securities into cash.

convertisseur, -euse (pers.) (*n.*), converter.

convocation (action) (*n.f.*), calling; convening; calling together:
convocation d'une assemblée, calling, convening, a meeting.
convocation des actionnaires, calling the shareholders together.

convocation (*n.f.*) *ou* **convocation d'assemblée** *ou* **convocation en assemblée** (avis), notice; notice of meeting:
recevoir une convocation (*ou* une convocation d'assemblée), to receive a notice (*or* a notice of meeting).
convocations d'assemblées générales *ou* convocations en assemblées générales, notices of general meetings.
une seule convocation pour deux assemblées, a single notice for two meetings.

convoi (Mar.) (*n.m.*), convoy; convoying:
le convoi des navires marchands par des bâtiments de guerre, the convoy (*or* convoying) of merchant ships by war vessels.
navigation en convoi (*f.*), navigation under convoy.

convoi (train de chemin de fer) (*n.m.*), train :
convoi de marchandises, goods train ; merchandise train ; freight train.
convoi de voyageurs, passenger train.

convoquer (*v.t.*), to call ; to convene ; to call together :
convoquer une assemblée d'actionnaires, to call, to convene, a meeting of shareholders.
MM. les actionnaires sont convoqués en assemblée générale annuelle, pour le . . . 19 . ., rue . . ., nº . . ., à . . heures du . . ., notice is hereby given that the annual general meeting of the company will be held at . . . Street, on . . . 19 . ., at . . o'clock in the . . .
convoquer les créanciers, les intéressés, to call the creditors, the interested parties, together.

convoyer (Mar.) (*v.t.*), to convoy.

convoyeur (Ch. de f.) (pers.) (*n.m.*), man in charge : (Cf. **conducteur.**)
lorsque le chemin de fer autorise l'escorte d'un transport sur ses lignes, le convoyeur est transporté gratuitement, when the railway authorizes attendance while travelling on its lines, the man in charge is carried free of charge.

coobligation (*n.f.*), joint liability ; joint obligation.

coopératif, -ive (*adj.*), cooperative :
société coopérative (*f.*), cooperative society.

coopération (*n.f.*), cooperation.

coopérative (*n.f.*), cooperative society.

coopérative de placement (*f.*), investment trust ; securities trust.

coopérer (*v.i.*), to cooperate :
coopérer à une entreprise avec quelqu'un, to cooperate in an enterprise with someone.

cooptation (*n.f.*), cooption ; cooptation.

coopter (*v.t.*), to coopt ; to cooptate :
coopter un administrateur, to coopt a director.

copartageant, -e (pers.) (*n.*), joint sharer.

copartager (*v.t.*), to share jointly.

coparticipant, -e (pers.) (*n.*), partner in joint account ; member of a *société en participation*.

copie (*n.f.*), copy :
copie d'une lettre, copy of a letter.
copie à la presse, press copy.
copie au net, clean copy ; fair copy :
mettre au net une lettre *ou* copier une lettre au propre, to make a clean copy of a letter.
copie au papier carboné, carbon ; carbon copy.
copie de change, copy of exchange.
copie du capitaine *ou* copie du vapeur (connaissement), captain's copy (bill of lading). *See note under* connaissement-chef.
copie fidèle, true copy.
copie certifiée conforme à l'original *ou* pour copie conforme, certified copy ; certified a true copy.
copie certifiée conforme au télégramme reçu par téléphone, certified copy of telegram received by telephone.
copie authentique d'un acte, true copy, certified copy, of a deed.

copie d'effets (Banq.) (*m.*), bills received register.

copie d'inventaire (*m.*), balance sheet book.

copie de factures (*m.*), invoice book.

copie de lettres (*m.*), letter book ; copy letter book.

copier (*v.t.*), to copy ; to make a copy of :
copier une lettre, to copy a letter.

copieux, -euse (*adj.*), copious ; full :
le très copieux rapport du conseil d'administration, the very full report of the directors.

copiste (pers.) (*n.m.* ou *f.*), copier ; copyist.

copreneur, -euse (pers.) (*n.*), colessee.

copropriétaire (pers.) (*n.m.* ou *f.*), coproprietor ; joint proprietor ; part owner ; joint owner.

copropriété (*n.f.*), joint ownership :
copropriété d'un navire, joint ownership of a ship.

copyright (*n.m.*), copyright.

coque (d'un navire) (*n.f.*), hull, body (of a ship).

corbeille (*n.f.*), basket :
corbeille à papier, waste paper basket.
corbeille pour lettres à classer, filing basket.

corbeille (Bourse) (*n.f.*). *See under* marché des valeurs.

cordage (Douanes) (*n.m.*), taping.

corde (*n.f.*), tape.

corder (*v.t.*), to tape.

cordons de la bourse (*m.pl.*), purse strings :
tenir les cordons de la bourse, tenir serrés les cordons de la bourse, to hold the purse strings, to hold the purse strings tight.

corporation (*n.f.*), corporation.

corps (d'un chèque, d'un effet, d'une police d'assurance, ou analogue) (*n.m.*), body (of a cheque, of a bill, of an insurance policy, or the like) :
mettre la somme en toutes lettres dans le corps du chèque, to put the amount in words at length in the body of the cheque.

corps (d'un navire) (*n.m.*), hull, body (of a ship).

corps et biens (*m.pl.*), crew and cargo ; life and property :
navire qui a péri corps et biens (*m.*), ship which is lost, crew and cargo.
navire qui dévie de sa route dans le but de sauver corps et biens (*m.*), ship which deviates from her course for the purpose of saving life and property.

correction (*n.f.*), correction :
correction d'adresse, d'une date erronée, correction of address, of a wrong date.

correspondance (commerce de lettres ; des lettres ; une lettre ; envoi postal) (*n.f.*), correspondence ; letters ; letter ; post ; postal packet ; packet : (See note under **objet de correspondance.**)
avoir avec quelqu'un une correspondance active, to have an active correspondence with someone.
dépouiller sa correspondance, to go through one's correspondence ; to look through one's letters ; to go through one's post.
papiers ayant le caractère d'une correspondance personnelle (Poste) (*m.pl.*), papers having the character of personal correspondence (*or* having the nature of letters [*or* of a letter]).
une correspondance adressée poste restante, a postal packet addressed poste restante.

réexpédition des correspondances (*f.*), re-direction of postal packets.

correspondance-avion [correspondances-avion *pl.*] (*n.f.*), air packet; air mail packet.

correspondances-avion (*n.f.pl.*), air packets; air mail packets; air mail correspondence.

correspondance (relations d'affaires) (*n.f.*), connection :
maison qui a des correspondances partout (*f.*), house which has connections everywhere.

correspondance (communication, relations entre deux localités, deux pays) (*n.f.*), connection; correspondence :
Paris-Prague-Varsovie, avec correspondance à Prague sur Budapest (Aviation), Paris-Prague-Warsaw, with connection (*or* correspondence) at Prague for Budapest.
si par suite du retard d'un train, la correspondance avec un autre train est manquée, if owing to lateness of one train, connection (*or* correspondence) with another train is missed.

correspondance pour (en transbordement pour), transhipping for :
départs de Marseille pour Colombo, correspondance à Colombo pour Pondichéry (*m.pl.*), sailings from Marseilles for Colombo, transhipping at Colombo for Pondicherry.

correspondancier, -ère (pers.) (*n.*), correspondence clerk.

correspondant, -e (*adj.*), corresponding. See example under **année.**

correspondant (pers.) (*n.m.*), correspondent :
correspondant particulier, private correspondent.

correspondre (*v.i.*), to correspond :
correspondre avec ses amis, to correspond with one's friends.

corriger (*v.t.*), to correct :
corriger une épreuve d'imprimerie, les fautes d'impression, to correct a printer's proof, printers' errors.

corsaire (pers. ou navire) (*n.m.*), corsair.

corsaire de la finance (pers.) (*m.*), financial shark.

cosignataire (pers.) (*n.m.* ou *f.*), cosignatory.

cotable (*adj.*), quotable :
valeur cotable (*f.*), quotable security.

cotation (*n.f.*), quotation :
cotation de cours (Bourse), quotation of prices.
cotation de fret, quotation for freight; freight quotation.

cotation (de navires) (*n.f.*), classing; classification.

cote (part) (*n.f.*), quota; share; contribution :
payer sa cote, to pay one's quota (*or* share).

cote (part assignée à chaque contribuable dans les impôts) (*n.f.*), assessment; rating :
cote foncière, assessment on, rating of, landed property.
cote mobilière, assessment on income.

cote (cotation; prix) (*n.f.*), quotation :
cote de fret, quotation for freight; freight quotation.

cote (indication des valeurs, des marchandises, négociées sur le marché public) (*n.f.*), quotation; quotations; price; prices; rates; marking; mark; marks; list; table :

cote des cours (Bourse de valeurs), quotation, marking, of prices.

cote de clôture, closing quotation.

cote officielle du disponible (Bourse de marchandises), official spot quotation.

admission à la cote (Bourse de valeurs) (*f.*), admission to quotation.

mettre des oppositions à la cote (Bourse de valeurs), to lodge objections to marks.

valeurs mobilières sujettes aux fluctuations de la cote (*f.pl.*), stocks and shares subject to fluctuations of price (*or* of prices).

cote des changes (prix de négociation des effets de commerce sur l'étranger), exchange rates; foreign exchange rates; foreign exchanges; on 'change table.

ouverture sans animation, mais la cote est résistante (*f.*), opening without liveliness, but prices are strong (*or* the list is strong).

cote de la bourse *ou* cote officielle des valeurs de bourse *ou simplement* cote officielle, stock exchange daily official list; official list; quoted list :
valeurs inscrites à la cote officielle (*f.pl.*), securities quoted in the official list.

cote en banque. In France, the daily list of the *coulisse* or *marché en banque. See explanation under* marché des valeurs. The *cote en banque* is divided into two portions, called respectively *cote du marché des banquiers en valeurs au comptant* and *cote du marché des banquiers en valeurs à terme.*

Note :—On the London Stock Exchange there are two kinds of prices, viz. :—
(1) prices of stocks admitted to official quotation (*or* prices of quoted securities), and
(2) prices of stocks not admitted to official quotation (*or* prices of unquoted securities).
The lists recording these prices are called :—
(1) in full.—*Stock Exchange daily official list ;* in short and in newspaper parlance.—*official list ;* colloquially.—*quoted list.*
(2) in full.—*Stock Exchange record of bargains in securities which have not received a quotation in the Stock Exchange official list ;* in newspaper parlance.—*supplementary list ;* colloquially.—*unquoted list.*

cote (criée) (Bourse de marchandises) (*n.f.*), call.

cote (d'un effet) (*n.f.*), due dating (of a bill).

cote (des navires) (*n.f.*), character; class; classing; classification :
les cotes sont représentées de la manière suivante : (Veritas) 3/3 1.1., etc., (Lloyd's) 100 A1, etc., the characters are represented in the following manner : (Veritas) 3/3 1.1., etc., (Lloyd's) 100 A1, etc.
navire de première cote (*m.*), first class vessel.

côte (rivage de la mer) (*s'emploie souvent au pluriel*) (*n.f.*), coast; seacoast; shore; seaboard :
les côtes d'Angleterre, the English coast.
les côtes de l'Atlantique, the Atlantic seaboard.

côté (*n.m.*), side :
côté droit, côté gauche, côté le plus fort, côté le plus faible, côté opposé, d'un compte,

right hand side, left hand side, stronger side, weaker side, opposite side, of an account.

côté de l'adresse (d'une enveloppe, d'une carte postale, d'un paquet), address side (of an envelope, of a postcard, of a packet).

coter (numéroter) (*v.t.*), to number ; to letter ; to mark (with letters or numbers) ; to page :
coter un registre, to number, to page, a register.
coter des pièces, to mark, to letter, documents.
coter un effet, to due date a bill.
coter un livre de comptabilité, to folio a book of account in words ; to write the numbers of the pages on a book of account in words (required by law in some cases).
coter des notes en marge d'un livre, to make notes in the margin of a book.

coter (fixer l'impôt) (*v.t.*), to assess ; to rate.

coter (fixer le prix, le taux, la cote) (*v.t.*), to quote ; to mark :
coter un prix (Com.), to quote a price.
coter le fret à tel taux, poids ou cube, to quote the freight at such a rate, weight or measurement.
coter un cours (Bourse), to quote, to mark, a price.
coter un emprunt, une valeur (Bourse), to quote a loan, a security.
les valeurs cotées en bourse, à la Bourse de Bruxelles (*f.pl.*), the securities quoted on the stock exchange, on the Brussels Bourse.
actions cotées (*f.pl.*), quoted shares.
coter le certain, l'incertain, to quote certain, uncertain. *See example and explanation under syns* donner le certain, l'incertain.

se coter (*v.r.*) *ou* **coter** (*v.t.*) *ou* **être coté, -e,** to be quoted :
actions qui se cotent à tant *ou* actions qui cotent tant *ou* actions qui sont cotées tant (*f.pl.*), shares which are quoted at so much.
le prix se cote par tonne, the price is quoted per ton.
les prix doivent être cotés autant que possible dans la monnaie du pays importateur (*m.pl.*), prices should be quoted as far as possible in the currency of the importing country.

coter (navires) (*v.t.*), to class :
vapeur coté 100 A1 au Lloyd, 3/3 1.1. au Veritas (*m.*), steamer classed 100 A1 at Lloyd's, 3/3 1.1. at Veritas.

coteur (Bourse de valeurs) (pers.) (*n.m.*), marking clerk.

coteur du Syndicat (Bourse de marchandises) (*m.*), chairman of the clearing house call.

côtier, -ère (*adj.*), coast (*used as adj.*) ; coasting :
fleuve côtier (*m.*), coast river.
station côtière (*f.*), coast station.
navire côtier (*m.*), coasting ship ; coaster.

cotisable (*adj.*), assessable :
bénéfice exonéré comme n'étant pas cotisable à l'impôt (*m.*), profit exempt as not being assessable to tax.

cotisation (quote-part) (*n.f.*), quota ; share ; contribution ; subscription ; fee ; assessment :

payer sa cotisation, to pay one's quota (or share) (*or* contribution) (*or* subscription).
cotisation patronale (retraites ouvrières, etc.), employer's share.
un fonds formé au moyen de cotisations, a fund formed by means of contributions.
cotisation payable à une association, subscription payable to an association.
cotisation d'admission (à une association), entrance fee.
en cas d'assurance mutuelle, la rémunération peut être donnée sous la forme de cotisation, in case of mutual insurance, the remuneration may be given in the form of assessment.

cotiser (*v.t.*), to assess :
les bénéfices cotisés à la cédule des revenus commerciaux (*m.pl.*), the profits assessed under the schedule of income from trade.

cotiser (se) (*v.r.*), to club together ; to subscribe.

cotransporteur (pers.) (*n.m.*), joint carrier.

couchette (lit de bord) (*n.f.*), berth :
les couchettes occupées par des passagers d'entrepont pendant le voyage, the berths occupied by steerage passengers during the voyage.

coulage (*n.m.*), leakage :
le fret est dû entièrement pour les marchandises diminuées par coulage, full freight is due on goods diminished by leakage.
coulages et même détournements, leakages and even embezzlements.

couler (*v.t.*), to sink ; to run down :
couler un navire (en le sabordant), to sink a ship.
couler un navire (en l'abordant), to run a ship down.

couler (*v.i.*) *ou* **couler bas** *ou* **couler à fond,** to sink ; to founder ; to go down :
navire qui coula et se perdit (*m.*), ship which sank (*or* foundered) (*or* went down) and was lost.

coulisse (*n.f.*), **coulissier** (pers.) (*n.m.*). *See under* marché des valeurs.

coup (*n.m.*), coup ; stroke :
faire un coup sur la bourse, to bring off a coup on the stock exchange.
coup de fortune, stroke of fortune (*or* of good luck).
coup d'accordéon (argot financier), reduction of the nominal value of a company's shares followed by a new issue at the reduced price. (*coup d'accordéon* is a picturesque reference to the deflation and inflation of an accordion.)

coupe-papier [**coupe-papier** *pl.*] (*n.m.*), paper knife.

coupement de débris (*m.*), cutting away wreck.

couper la connexion au cours d'une conversation (Téléph.), to cut off connection during a conversation.

couper les dépenses, to cut down expenses.

se couper un bras, to cut one's loss.

coupon (Fin.) (*n.m.*) (Abrév. : **c.** *ou* **coup.** *ou* **cp.**), coupon :
coupon d'intérêt (*Abrév. :* **c. int.**) *ou* coupon d'arrérages, interest coupon.
coupon de dividende (*Abrév. :* **c. div.** *ou* **c. de div.**), dividend coupon.

coupon attaché (opp. à *coupon détaché* ou *ex-coupon*) (*Abrév. :* c. att. *ou* c. at.), with coupon ; cum coupon.

coupon détaché, ex coupon ;   ex dividend. See example under **détacher.**

coupon arriéré (*Abrév. :* coup. arr.), coupon in arrear.

coupon domicilié, domiciled coupon.

coupon (d'un carnet de voyage, ou billet analogue) (*n.m.*), coupon (of a tour ticket, or the like).

coupon (d'un billet aller et retour) (*n.m.*), half : les deux coupons d'un billet aller et retour, the two halves of a return ticket.

coupon d'aller, outward half.

coupon de retour, return half.

coupon d'action (*m.*), subshare. See note under **coupure d'action.**

coupon-réponse international [**coupons-réponse internationaux** *pl.*] (Poste) (*m.*), international reply coupon.

couponnier (pers.) (*n.m.*), coupon clerk.

coupure (*n.f.*) (Abrév. : c. *ou* C. *ou* **coup.**), denomination :

société qui émet ses actions en unités et en coupures de 5, 10, 25, 50, ou 100 (*f.*), company which issues its shares in ones and in denominations of 5, 10, 25, 50, or 100.

c. 25 *ou* C. 25 *ou* c. de 25 (*abrév.*), coupures de 25.

billets de banque de petites coupures (*m.pl.*), bank notes of small denominations.

toutes coupures, any denominations.

coupures de poids, de 0 à 5 kilos, de 5 à 10 kilos, denominations of weight, of 0 to 5 kilos, of 5 to 10 kilos.

coupure d'action (*f.*),   subshare. *Note :*—In France, *sociétés par actions* cannot divide their capital into shares of less than 25 francs each, when the capital does not exceed fr. 200,000, and less than 100 francs each when the capital is above fr. 200,000, but they can split the shares into **coupures d'actions** (also called **coupons d'actions** and **tantièmes d'actions**). In England, there is no limitation imposed on the amount of the share in limited companies. 2s. and 1s. shares are not uncommon. Companies have been registered with 1d. shares, and even with ¼d. shares. All or any of the shares of a company limited by shares, if so authorized by its articles, can be split or subdivided into shares of smaller amount than is fixed by the memorandum, but they then become whole shares and not subshares. Likewise an English company can, if so authorized by its articles, consolidate and divide all or any of its share capital into shares of larger amount than its existing shares. Subshares are not provided for by the English law. There is no need for them inasmuch as no limitation on the amount of the share is imposed. The word subshare is used in England of the *coupures* of foreign companies.

cour (Dr.) (*n.f.*), court :

cour d'arbitrage, court of arbitration ; arbitration court.

cour de justice, court of justice ; law court.

cour d'appel, court of appeal ; appeal court.

Cour de cassation, Court of Cassation.

cour d'accès (Ch. de f.) (*f.*), station yard.

courant, -e (qui est en cours, en parlant des divisions du temps) (*adj.*) (Abrév. : c. *ou* **cour.** *ou* ct *ou* ct), current ; present ; instant :

mois courant (*m.*), current month ; present month ; instant month.

année courante (*f.*), current year ; present year.

le 10 courant, the 10th instant.

courant, -e (qui a un cours légal) (*adj.*), current :

monnaie courante (*f.*), current money.

courant, -e (qui a une application continue) (*adj.*), current :

les intérêts courants (*m.pl.*),   the current interest.

courant (succession du temps) (*n.m.*), course :

dans le courant de l'année, in the course of the year.

courant (mois actuel) (*n.m.*),   current month ; present month ; instant month :

paiement à faire fin courant *ou* payement à faire fin du courant (*m.*), payment to be made at the end of the present month.

fin courant (Bourse). See under **fin.**

courant (*n.m.*) *ou* **courant de mois** (Bourse de marchandises), current month :

acheter du courant et non du disponible,   to buy the current month and not spot.

le courant peut être livré jusqu'au dernier jour du mois en cours, the current month can be delivered up to the last day of the instant month.

courant d'affaires (*m.*),   turnover :

les obligations X. 6 0/0 clôturent à 517 contre 520 fr. avec un courant d'affaires assez suivi,   X.   6% debentures closed at 517 against 520 francs with a fairly continuous turnover.

courant du marché (*m.*), market price.

courir (encourir) (*v.t.*), to run ; to incur :

courir un risque, to run, to incur, a risk.

courir (passer, en parlant du temps) (*v.i.*), to run :

l'effet a tant de jours à courir (*m.*), the bill has so many days to run.

courir (avoir son cours ; s'accroître ; s'acquérir) (*v.i.*), to run ; to accrue ; to attach :

intérêts qui courent depuis le 1er mars (*m.pl.*), interest which runs from 1st March ; interest which accrues from March 1.

intérêt couru (*m.*) *ou* intérêts courus (*m.pl.*), accrued interest.

le fret court du jour où le navire a fait voile, the freight runs from the day the ship sailed.

police qui est censée courir d'une certaine date (*f.*),   policy which is deemed to run from a certain date.

le risque couvert par la présente police court dès le moment du chargement à bord du navire d'exportation,   the risk under this policy attaches from the time of loading on board the export vessel.

courir après, to run after :

le banquier est quelquefois obligé de chercher des capitaux, et quelquefois de courir après les placements, the banker is sometimes obliged to look for money, and sometimes to run after investments.

courir franc, to get something done for nothing.

courir sur la place, to be hawked about the place (said of bills of exchange which have depreciated owing to many attempts to discount them, or the like).

courir sur le marché de quelqu'un, to improve on someone's offer; to go one better.

courrier (*n.m.*) *ou* **courrier postal** (totalité des lettres que porte le même courrier), post; mail:

le premier courrier, le dernier courrier, le courrier du matin, le courrier du soir, the first post, the last post, the morning post, the evening post.

par le même courrier, by the same post.

répondre par retour (*ou* par le retour) du courrier, to reply by return of post.

les lettres tirées à trois exemplaires sont destinées à être envoyées par des courriers différents (*f.pl.*), bills drawn in sets of three are intended to be sent by different mails.

courriers maritimes (Poste). *English equivalent is* imperial and foreign mails.

courrier (correspondance) (*n.m.*), post; correspondence; letters; mail:

lire son courrier, to read, to go through, one's post (*or* one's correspondence) (*or* one's letters).

le chef du service préside à l'ouverture du courrier (*ou* des courriers), the head of the department superintends the opening of the letters.

cours (marche; progression) (*n.m.*), course; currency:

projet en cours d'exécution (*m.*), plan in course of execution.

pendant le cours de l'assurance, during the currency of the insurance.

en cours (en usage; courant), current; present; instant:

monnaies en cours (*f.pl.*), current monies; current coins.

intérêts en cours (*m.pl.*), current interest.

année en cours (*f.*), current year; present year.

mois en cours (*m.*), current month; present month; instant month.

au taux de change en cours à Paris à la date de la remise, at the rate of exchange current in Paris at (*or* on) the date of remittance.

cours (Navig.) (*n.m.*), course:

navire qui reprend son cours (*m.*), ship which resumes her course.

cours (circulation des monnaies, des billets de banque, etc.) (*n.m.*), currency; circulation:

cours forcé, forced currency:

gouvernement qui accorde le cours forcé aux billets d'une banque (*m.*), government which grants forced currency to a bank's notes.

les billets de banque ont cours forcé quand la banque émettrice est dispensée de rembourser ses billets en espèces (*m.pl.*), bank notes have forced currency when the issuing bank is dispensed from repaying its notes in cash.

papier à cours forcé (*m.*), forced currency paper.

avoir cours, to be current; to be tender; to pass:

cette pièce a cours en France, this coin is current (*or* this coin passes) in France.

à l'exception de l'or, les monnaies étrangères n'ont pas cours, with the exception of gold, foreign moneys are not current.

les monnaies d'or et le dollar d'argent ont cours illimité, gold coins and the silver dollar are tender to any amount (*or* are unlimited tender).

cours légal, lawful currency; legal tender; legal tender currency:

on a retiré le cours légal à ces pièces, the lawful currency of these coins has been withdrawn.

avoir cours légal, to have lawful currency; to be lawfully current; to be legal tender:

les billets émis ont cours légal (*m.pl.*), the notes issued have lawful currency (*or* are lawfully current) (*or* are legal tender).

les pièces d'or ont cours légal illimité (*f.pl.*), the gold coins are legal tender to any amount (*or* are unlimited legal tender).

les monnaies divisionnaires d'argent ont cours légal jusqu'à concurrence de 10 dollars par paiement (*f.pl.*), the silver fractional coins are legal tender up to 10 dollars per payment.

billets à cours légal (*m.pl.*), lawfully current notes; legal tender notes.

cours (valeur morale accordée au papier d'un négociant) (*n.m.*), currency:

le cours d'une signature sur la place de Paris, the currency of a signature on the Paris market.

cours (prix; taux) (*n.m.*) (Abrév.: **c.** *ou* **C.**), price; rate; quotation:

bulletin de cours (*m.*), list of prices (*or* of rates) (*or* of quotations).

cours à terme (Bourse de valeurs), settlement price; price for the account.

cours à terme (Marché des changes), forward rate.

cours à vue (Marché des changes), demand rate.

cours au comptant, price for cash; cash price.

cours commerciaux, commodity prices.

cours d'achat, cost:

les actions sont estimées aux cours d'achat (*f.pl.*), the shares are valued at cost.

cours d'après-bourse, street price; price after hours.

cours d'introduction (Bourse), opening price (price at which shares are introduced on the market).

cours d'ouverture (*Abrév.:* ouv. *ou* ouvert.) *ou* cours du début, opening price (first price quoted at commencement of day's market).

cours de change *ou* cours du change [cours des changes *pl.*] *ou* cours de place *ou* cours de devise [cours des devises *pl.*], rate of exchange; exchange rate; exchange; foreign exchange rate; foreign exchange:

le cours du change du jour sur Paris, the rate of exchange of the day on Paris.

cours des changes (*ou* des devises) à terme, forward exchange rates.

cours de clôture, closing price.

cours de compensation [cours des compensations *pl.*] (*Abrév. :* c/c.), making up price ; make up price :
les opérations de report sont réglées au cours de compensation (*f.pl.*), contango dealings are settled at the making up price.

cours de conversion d'une monnaie, rate of conversion of a money.

cours de déport, backwardation rate.

cours de l'intérêt, rate of interest.

cours de l'option *ou* cours du stellage, put and call price ; price of put and call ; price of double option.

cours de l'ou, put price ; price of put.

cours de la réponse des primes, price at time for declaration of options. See explanation under **prime.**

cours de prime, option price ; price of option.

cours de rachat, buying in price.

cours de report, contango rate ; contango ; carry over rate ; continuation rate.

cours de résiliation (Bourse de marchandises), cancelling price ; invoicing back price ; default price ; settlement price (fixed for defaulted contract).

cours demandé(s) (acheteurs) *ou* cours acheteur(s) *ou* cours Argent (*Abrév. :* cours A. *ou simplement* A.), price(s) bid (buyers) ; buying rate(s).

cours des actions, share prices ; prices of shares.

cours du chèque, cheque rate.

cours du comptant (Marché des changes), spot price ; spot rate.

cours du disponible (Bourse de marchandises), spot price ; spot rate ; price ex store ; price ex warehouse.

cours du dont, call price ; price of call.

cours du ferme (opp. à *cours de prime*), price of firm stock.

cours du (*ou* de) fret, rate of freight ; freight rate.

cours du jour, price (*or* rate) of the day.

cours du livrable (Bourse de marchandises), forward price ; terminal price.

cours du marché *ou* cours de bourse *ou* cours de la place, market price.

cours en Bourse, House price.

cours extrêmes, highest and lowest prices.

cours hors Bourse *ou* cours hors cote *ou* cours hors Banque, unofficial price. *Cf.* marché hors cote.

cours le plus bas (*Abrév. :* p.b.), lowest price ; bottom price.

cours le plus haut (*Abrév. :* p.h.), highest price ; top price.

cours limité, limited price :
acheter au cours limité, to buy at a limited price.

cours moyen (*Abrév. :* C/M. *ou* c/m. *ou* c/.m/.), middle price ; middle ; average price :

au cours moyen, at the middle price ; at middle ; at the average price.

Note :—In France, orders are frequently given to be executed at middle, which is the arithmetical mean between the highest and lowest prices of the day. This price is not known until the close of the Bourse. This method does not obtain on the London Stock Exchange.

cours nul (cote de la bourse) (*Abrév. :* c.n. *ou* cn.), business done should not have been marked :
Actions X. Hier, cours nul (*Abrév. :* Act. X. h.c.n. *ou* h.cn.), Erratum.—In yesterday's List the business done in X. Shares should not have been marked ——. Cf. **lire** & **hier.**

cours offert(s) (vendeurs) *ou* cours vendeur(s) *ou* cours Papier (*Abrév. :* cours P. *ou simplement* P.), price(s) offered (sellers) ; selling rate(s).

cours plus élevé, higher price.

cours plus faible, lower price.

cours pratiqués *ou* cours faits, bargains done ; business done. See **pratiqué, -e.**

cours précédent (*Abrév. :* c. préc.), previous price.

cours tel quel, tel quel rate ; tale quale rate. See **parité** for example.

cours unique (*Abrév. :* C. uni.). On the Paris Bourse when it is not possible to obtain the quantity of stock that one would wish to buy for want of offers and when it is not possible to sell the quantity of shares offered for want of bids, there is made a *cours unique*, which is in this case marked with an asterisk on the list, or the list may mention " demandes réduites," q.v., or " offres réduites," q.v. *Cours unique* has no equivalent on the London Stock Exchange.

cours authentique et officiel (cote officielle) (*m.*), stock exchange daily official list.

course (prix de déplacement) (*n.f.*), fare (petty expense) :
la course est de tant, the fare is so much.

course aux titres (*f.*), run on the shares :
on est à la veille d'assister à une course aux titres de plusieurs sociétés de mines d'or, it will not be long before we shall see a run on the shares of several gold mining companies.

course des vendeurs (Bourse) (*f.*), bear panic ; stampede of bears.

course en foule aux guichets (d'une banque) (descente sur une banque) (*f.*), run (on a bank). Cf. **accourir en foule.**

court, -e (*adj.*) (Ant. : *long*), short :
placement à court terme (*m.*), short term investment ; short dated investment.

dépôt à court terme (*m.*), deposit at short notice.

valeurs réalisables à court terme (*f.pl.*), securities realizable at short notice.

effets à courtes échéances (*m.pl.*), short dated bills ; short bills.

être court, -e *ou* **être à court,** to be short ; to run short ; to run out :
être court d'argent *ou* être à court d'argent, to be short, to run short, to run out, of money.

courtage (profession) (*n.m.*), broking ; brokerage :
courtage des affrètements, freight broking ; freight brokerage.
courtage (prime) (*n.m.*) (Abrév. : **ctg.** *ou* **cᵍᵉ**), brokerage ; commission :
courtage d'achat, buying brokerage ; buying commission.
courtage de change, exchange brokerage.
courtage de vente, selling brokerage ; selling commission.
courtage des reports (Bourse), commission on contangoes.
courter (*v.t.*), to sell ; to offer for sale :
courter des marchandises, to offer goods for sale.
courter (*v.i.*), to broke ; to buy and sell on commission.
courtier, -ère (pers.) (*n.*), broker :
courtier d'assurances, insurance broker.
courtier d'assurances maritimes, marine insurance broker :
en Angleterre, le courtier d'assurances maritimes n'est pas un officier ministériel ; son ministère n'est nullement obligatoire, mais on y recourt habituellement, in England, a marine insurance broker is not a legal officer ; his services are in no way obligatory, but they are generally made use of. *See note under* courtier maritime.
courtier de change *ou* courtier d'escompte, exchange broker ; exchange dealer ; foreign exchange broker ; bill broker.
courtier en grains, grain broker.
courtier en (*ou* de) marchandises, produce broker :
les courtiers en marchandises remplissent à la bourse des marchandises les mêmes fonctions que les agents de change à la bourse des valeurs, produce brokers perform on the produce exchange the same functions as stockbrokers on the stock exchange.
See note under marché commercial.
courtier maritime *ou* courtier de navires, ship broker.
Note :—In France, *courtiers maritimes* are divided into two classes, viz. :—*courtiers interprètes et conducteurs de navires* (commonly called simply *courtiers maritimes*), and *courtiers d'assurances maritimes*.
    Courtiers maritimes are public officers, and monopolists.
    Courtiers interprètes et conducteurs de navires have the exclusive right to act :—
    (1) as translators and interpreters,
    (2) in the fulfilment of port and customs formalities, and giving assistance to captains and crews as to local usages, or the like,
    (3) as ship brokers (but ship broking is not always a de facto monopoly), and
    (4) in the buying and selling of ships.
    Courtiers d'assurances maritimes have the monopoly of marine insurance broking. They draw up, in concurrence with *notaires*, the insurance policies, and officially fix rates of premium.
    In England, a ship broker is a broker or

agent who finds freight, and often passengers, for vessels, and vessels for freight, sometimes acting as sole agent and/or manager for a ship or ships or line of ships, and who also, in many cases, acts as *agent for the purchase and sale of ships* (in that case usually describing himself as such). Accessorily, ship brokers, often if not generally, act for merchants and shippers as shipping (i.e., forwarding) agents, customs agents, and marine insurance brokers (in that case often describing themselves as *ship and insurance brokers*).
courtier marron, outside broker.
coût (*n.m.*), cost :
coût de l'assurance, de la vie, de notre dépêche, cost of the insurance, of living, of our telegram.
coût-assurance-fret *ou* coût, fret, et assurance (*Abrév. :* c.a.f. *ou* C.A.F. *ou* caf. *ou* CAF. *ou* c.f.a. *ou* c.i.f. *ou* C.I.F. *ou* cif.), cost, insurance, freight ; cost, freight, and insurance :
caf. Royaume-Uni, c.i.f. U.K.
contrat CAF. (*m.*), C.I.F. contract.
coût-fret (*Abrév. :* c.f. *ou* C.F. *ou* cf.), cost and freight.
coûtant (*adj.m.*), cost (*used as adj.*) :
prix coûtant (*m.*), cost price ; cost.
coûter (*v.i.*), to cost :
coûter cher, to be dear ; to be expensive ; to be costly :
les marchandises coûtent très cher (*f.pl.*), the goods are very dear.
coûteusement (*adv.*), expensively.
coûteux, -euse (*adj.*), costly ; expensive ; dear.
coutume (*n.f.*), custom ; usage :
selon les coutumes de la place (*ou* du port) d'Anvers, according to the customs (*or* usages) of the port of Antwerp.
couvert, -e (*p.p.*), covered :
être à couvert, to be covered (to be guaranteed).
l'emprunt n'a pas été couvert (*m.*), the loan was undersubscribed.
couvert (abri) (*n.m.*), cover :
marchandises placées sous couvert (*f.pl.*), goods placed under cover.
couverture (garantie fournie) (*n.f.*), cover ; security ; deposit.
couverture (Fin., Banq. et Bourse) (*n.f.*), cover ; margin :
somme remise à un agent à titre de couverture d'opérations de bourse (*f.*), amount remitted to a broker by way of cover (*or* margin) on stock exchange transactions.
agent de change qui exige une couverture de 25 0/0 en espèces (*m.*), stockbroker who requires a cover (*or* a margin) of 25 % in cash.
opérer avec couverture, sans couverture, to operate with cover (*or* with a margin), without cover (*or* without margin).
couverture (arbitrage) (Bourse) (*n.f.*), covering ; hedging ; hedge :
les cotons ont avancé sur des couvertures sur les rapprochés (*m.pl.*), cottons have advanced on coverings on near positions.

acheter, vendre, à long terme comme une couverture, to buy, to sell, at long date as a hedge.

couverture (Assce) (*n.f.*), cover ; covering :
couverture d'abonnement, open cover.
la couverture des risques terrestres, des risques de mer, the covering of land risks, of sea risks.

couvrir (*v.t.*), to cover :
couvrir des marchandises contre les risques de mer, to cover goods against sea risks.
police qui couvre le risque de perte totale du navire (*f.*), policy which covers the risk of total loss of the ship.
couvrir des risques que les polices ordinaires laissent à découvert, to cover risks which ordinary policies leave uncovered.
couvrir son banquier, son agent du montant d'une opération, to cover one's banker, one's broker for the amount of a transaction.
couvrir ses frais, to cover, to make, one's expenses.
couvrir un découvert (Bourse), to cover a short account (*or* a bear account).
la période couverte par la présente police, the period covered by this policy.
on dit que la souscription est couverte quand le nombre des titres souscrits est au moins égal au nombre des titres offerts, an application is said to be covered when the number of shares applied for is at least equal to the number of shares offered.
émission couverte plusieurs fois (*f.*), issue covered several times over.

se couvrir (*v.r.*), to cover ; to cover oneself ; to hedge :
se couvrir du montant d'une remise par une traite, to cover oneself for the amount of a remittance by a draft.
se couvrir en rachetant (Bourse), to cover (*or* to cover oneself) by buying back.
se couvrir par des réassurances, to cover oneself by reinsurance.
se couvrir en achetant à long terme (Bourse), to cover, to hedge, by buying at long date.

cover-system (Bourse) (*n.m.*), cover system ; cutting limit system.

crayon (*n.m.*), pencil :
indications inscrites au crayon (*f.pl.*), particulars entered in pencil.
crayon à copier *ou* crayon à encre *ou* crayon-encre [crayons-encre *pl.*] (*n.m.*), copying pencil.
crayon de couleur, crayon bleu, crayon rouge, coloured pencil, blue pencil, red pencil.

crayonner (*v.t.*), to pencil :
crayonner des notes, to pencil notes.

créance (*n.f.*) (Ant. : *dette*), debt ; indebtedness ; book debt ; claim ; debt and rights :
titre de créance (*m.*), proof of debt ; evidence of indebtedness.
créance chirographaire, unsecured debt.
créance douteuse, doubtful debt.
créance garantie, secured debt.
créance hypothécaire, debt on mortgage ; mortgage debt.

créance litigieuse, litigious claim.
créance ordinaire, ordinary debt.
créance privilégiée, preferential debt ; privileged debt ; preferred debt.
mauvaise créance *ou* créance véreuse *ou* créance amortie, bad debt.
créances et dettes *ou* dettes et créances. See under **dette**.

créancier, -ère (pers.) (*n.*), creditor :
créancier à la grosse, creditor on bottomry or respondentia. *Cf.* prêt à la grosse.
créancier chirographaire, unsecured creditor :
les créanciers privilégiés et hypothécaires sont d'abord désintéressés ; la répartition a lieu ensuite entre les créanciers chirographaires au prorata de leurs créances admises et affirmées, the preferential and mortgage creditors are first paid off ; a distribution than takes place among the unsecured creditors in proportion to their debts admitted and proved.
créancier gagiste [créanciers gagistes *pl.*], lienor ; pledgee :
chemin de fer qui a sur la marchandise les droits d'un créancier gagiste (*m.*), railway which has on the goods the rights of a lienor (*or* pledgee).
créancier hypothécaire, mortgagee ; mortgage creditor ; creditor on mortgage.
créancier nanti, secured creditor.
créancier partiellement nanti, partly secured creditor.
créancier entièrement (*ou* complètement) nanti, fully secured creditor.
créancier ordinaire, ordinary creditor.
créancier privilégié, preferential creditor.

créateur, -trice (fondateur) (pers.) (*n.*), founder ; creator :
créateur d'une maison de commerce, founder of a house of business.

créateur (*n.m.*) *ou* **créateur de la filière** (pers.) (Bourse de marchandises), first seller ; deliverer.

création (*n.f.*), creation ; establishment ; foundation ; making ; making out ; writing out ; starting. See **créer** (*v.t.*) for examples.

crédit (réputation de solvabilité) (*n.m.*), credit :
qui dit crédit, dit confiance, who says credit, says confidence.

crédit (délai pour le paiement) (*n.m.*), credit :
le commerce vit de crédit, trade lives on credit.
obtenir un mois de crédit, to obtain a month's credit.
acheter à crédit, to buy on (*or* upon) credit.
crédit à court terme *ou* crédit à (*ou* de) courte durée *ou* court crédit, short credit.
crédit à long terme *ou* crédit à (*ou* de) longue durée *ou* long crédit, long credit.
crédit foncier *ou* crédit immobilier, credit based on the value of real property, buildings, houses, farms, land, in fact any property which can be mortgaged.
crédit mobilier, credit based on any personal property, such as stocks and shares.

crédit (Banq.) (*n.m.*), credit : (*Cf.* **accréditif**.)
crédit de banque *ou* crédit bancaire, bank credit.

crédit en banque *ou* crédit à la banque, credit at the bank; credit with the bank.

avoir crédit en banque (*ou* à la banque), to have a credit (*or* to be in credit) at the bank.

avoir un crédit chez un banquier, to have a credit with a banker.

crédit à découvert *ou* crédit libre *ou* crédit en blanc *ou* crédit par caisse *ou* crédit sur notoriété, open credit; blank credit; cash credit.

crédit confirmé *ou* crédit à l'exportation, confirmed credit; confirmed banker's credit; export credit.

crédit documentaire, documentary credit:
le crédit documentaire repose notamment sur les connaissements à l'ordre du chargeur, documentary credit is based particularly on bills of lading to shipper's order.

crédit non confirmé *ou* crédit simple, unconfirmed credit; simple credit.

crédit par acceptation, acceptance credit.

crédit par acceptation renouvelable, revolving credit.

crédit personnel, personal credit:
le crédit personnel est basé sur la réputation du commerçant, personal credit is based on the reputation of the trader.

crédit (Comptab.) (*n.m.*) (Abrév.: **Cr** *ou* **C.**), credit; creditor; credit side; creditor side.

crédit (établissement de crédit) (*n.m.*), credit institution; bank:
crédit foncier, a bank or credit institution which makes loans on the security of real estate.

crédit mobilier, a bank or financial institution which finds capital for industrial enterprises, places and launches issues of stocks and shares, grants loans on the security of personal property, and the like.

crédit municipal, pawnshop.

crédité, -e (pers.) (*n.*), credited party.

créditer (*v.t.*), to credit; to place money to the credit of:
créditer un compte, une somme à quelqu'un, quelqu'un d'une somme, to credit an account, an amount to someone, someone with an amount.

créditer quelqu'un chez un banquier, to place money to someone's credit with a banker.

créditeur, -trice (*adj.*) (Abrév.: **Cr** *ou* **C.**), credit (*used as adj.*): creditor (*used as adj.*); in credit:
compte créditeur (*m.*), creditor account; account in credit.

balance créditrice (*f.*), credit balance.

créditeur, -trice (pers.) (*n.*), creditor:
créditeurs divers, sundry creditors.

créer (*v.t.*), to create; to establish; to found; to start; to make; to make out; to write out:
créer une hypothèque, une nouvelle série d'actions, un fonds de réserve, to create a mortgage, a new series of shares, a reserve fund.

créer une industrie, to create, to establish, an industry.

créer une maison de commerce, to found, to establish, a house of business.

créer une filière (Bourse de marchandises), to start a string.

créer un marché, to make a market:
M. X. était le détenteur du stock entier, et sa première opération fut de créer un marché, Mr X. was the holder of the entire stock, and his first operation was to make a market.

créer un chèque, to make out, to write out, a cheque.

créer une atmosphère de hausse autour d'une valeur (Bourse), to talk up, to boost, the value of a stock.

connaissement créé à l'ordre du chargeur (*m.*), bill of lading made to the shipper's order.

crête (caisse à claire-voie) (*n.f.*), crate.

creux, -euse (*adj.*). *See* titres creux *and* papier creux.

criée (*n.f.*), auction:
vente à la criée (*f.*), sale by auction.

crieur (Bourse) (pers.) (*n.m.*), crier who calls out the prices of certain public stocks dealt in.

crise (*n.f.*), crisis:
crise financière, financial crisis.

croisement (d'un chèque) (*n.m.*), crossing.

croiser un chèque, to cross a cheque.

croisière (*n.f.*), cruise:
une croisière en Méditerranée, a cruise in the Mediterranean.

transatlantique en croisière autour du monde (*m.*), transatlantic boat cruising (*or* on a cruise) round the world.

cubage (*n.m.*) *ou* **cube** (*n.m.*), cubic measurement; measurement:
payer au cubage les marchandises dont la densité est inférieure à un chiffre donné, to pay by measurement for cargo whose density is lower than a given figure.

coter le fret à tel taux, poids ou cube, to quote the freight at such a rate, weight or measurement.

cubage converti en poids, measurement converted into weight.

cueillette (*n.f.*). *See* affrètement à cueillette, charge à la cueillette, chargement en cueillette, charger un navire en cueillette, fret à la cueillette.

cuivre (monnaie de cuivre) (*n.m.*), copper.

cumul (*n.m.*), lumping.

cumulatif, -ive (*adj.*) (Abrév.: **cum.**), cumulative:
dividende cumulatif (*m.*), cumulative dividend.

cumuler (*v.t.*), to lump:
le poids cumulé du contenant et du contenu, the lumped (*or* the lump) weight of the container and the contents.

cuprifères (*n.f.pl.*) *ou* **valeurs cuprifères** (*f.pl.*), coppers; copper shares.

curateur, -trice (pers.) (*n.*), curator (*m.*); curatrix (*f.*); guardian; trustee.

cylindre (d'une machine à écrire) (*n.m.*), cylinder (of a typewriter).

D

dactylographe (*adj.*), typewriting; of or pertaining to a typewriter:
jeune fille dactylographe, girl typewriter; girl typist.

dactylographe (*n.m.*) *ou* **dactylotype** (*n.f.*), typewriter; typewriting machine; writing machine. See syn. **machine à écrire** for varieties.

dactylographe *ou simplement* **dactylo** (pers.) (*n.m.* ou *f.*), typewriter; typist:
dactylo féminin, girl typewriter; girl typist.

dactylographie (*n.f.*), typewriting; typing.

dactylographier (*v.t.*), to typewrite; to type:
dactylographier une lettre, to typewrite, to type, a letter.

dactylographique (*adj.*), typewriting:
signes dactylographiques (*m.pl.*), typewriting signs.

danger (*n.m.*), danger:
danger imminent rendant nécessaire le déchargement immédiat de la cargaison, imminent danger rendering necessary the immediate discharge of the cargo.
grave danger qui menace le navire et la cargaison, grave danger which threatens the ship and the cargo.

dangereux, -euse (*adj.*), dangerous:
marchandises dangereuses (*f.pl.*), dangerous goods.

dans l'espace de tant de jours, dans un délai raisonnable, within so many days, within a reasonable time.

darse (*n.f.*), camber; darsena (basin or dock for boats).

date (*n.f.*), date: (Cf. **millésime**.)
date d'une lettre, de départ d'un navire, date of a letter, of sailing of a ship.
date d'envoi, date of dispatch.
date de l'échéance, due date.
date de valeur *ou* date d'entrée en valeur, value date; value; as at. See example under **valeur**.
date du départ (d'un compte courant), starting date.
de date (effets), after date; from date (bills):
à 3 mois de date veuillez payer, etc., 3 months after (*or* from) date pay, etc.
effet payable à 3 jours de date (*m.*), bill payable 3 days after (*or* from) date; bill payable at 3 days' date.

dater (*v.t.*), to date:
le connaissement doit être daté, the bill of lading should be dated.

dateur (*n.m.*), dater; date stamp.

de droit *ou* **de jure** (Dr.), de jure:
en vertu du principe de jure, by virtue of the de jure principle.
contrat résolu de jure (*m.*), contract voided de jure.

de fait *ou* **de facto** (Dr.), de facto:
monopole de fait (*m.*), de facto monopoly.

débâchage (*n.m.*), unsheeting (removing sheets from railway wagons).

débâcher (*v.t.*), to unsheet:
débâcher un wagon de chemin de fer, to unsheet a railway wagon.

débâcle (chute financière) (*n.f.*), crash; smash; collapse; slide; slump:
mais après ce boom, c'est la débâcle, but after this boom, there was a slump.

déballage (*n.m.*), unpacking.

déballer (*v.t.*), to unpack.

débaptiser un compte, to change the name of an account.

débarcadère (*n.m.*), landing; landing place; landing platform; wharf.

débardage (*n.m.*), unloading; unlading; unshipment; landing.

débarder (*v.t.*), to unload; to unlade; to unship; to land.

débardeur (pers.) (*n.m.*), docker.

débarquement (*n.m.*) (Ant.: *embarquement*), landing; disembarking; disembarkment; disembarcation; discharge; unloading; unlading; unshipment.
vente au débarquement. *See under* **vente**, *and cf.* bordereau de débarquement.
en débarquement, unloading:
en débarquement dans les docks: 000 tonnes, unloading in the docks: 000 tons.

débarquer (*v.t.*), to land; to disembark; to discharge; to unload; to unlade; to unship:
débarquer les marchandises au port le plus voisin, en tout autre port, to land, to discharge, the goods at the nearest port, at any other port.
débarquer des marchandises sur des embarcations ou des chalands, sur le quai, to discharge, to unload, to unship, goods into craft or barges, on the quay.
débarquer des passagers, to land, to disembark, passengers.

débarquer (*v.i.*), to land; to disembark:
débarquer dans un port étranger, to land, to disembark, in a foreign port.

débats de compte (*m.pl.*), discussion of an account.

débattre (*v.t.*). See examples:
débattre un compte, les conditions d'un marché, to discuss an account, the conditions of a bargain.
les conditions d'escompte sont à débattre entre client et banquier (*f.pl.*), the conditions of discounting are a matter for arrangement between customer and banker.
prix à débattre (*m.*), price a matter for negotiation (*or* a matter for arrangement).
à prix débattu, at an arranged price.
moyennant surprime à débattre, in consideration of additional premium to be arranged.

débit (Comptab.) (*n.m.*) (Abrév.: **Dt** *ou* **déb.** *ou* **D.**), debit; debtor; debit side; debtor side.

débiter (*v.t.*), to debit:
débiter un compte, quelqu'un d'une somme, to debit an account, someone with an amount.

débiteur, -trice (*adj.*) (Abrév.: **Dt** *ou* **débit.**), debtor; debit:

compte débiteur (*m.*), debtor account; debit account.

colonne débitrice (*f.*), debit column.

la société débitrice, the debtor company.

débiteur, -trice (pers.) (*n.*) (Abrév.: **Dr**), debtor:

débiteurs divers, sundry debtors.

débiteur délégué (Dr.), delegated debtor.

débiteur hypothécaire, mortgagor; debtor on mortgage; mortgage debtor.

débiteur insolvable, insolvent debtor.

débiteurs par acceptation (bilan de banque), liability (*or* liabilities) of customers for acceptances (*or* for acceptance).

débiteur principal (Dr.), principal debtor.

débiteur solvable, solvent debtor.

débouché (à l'industrie) (*n.m.*), outlet (for trade); market:

port qui sert de débouché aux produits fabriqués d'un pays (*m.*), port which serves as an outlet for the manufactured products of a country.

l'encouragement le plus utile pour l'industrie agricole et manufacturière est de lui assurer le débouché de ses productions (*m.*), the most useful encouragement for agricultural and manufacturing industry is to assure to it an outlet (*or* a market) for its productions.

débours *ou* **déboursé** *ou* **déboursement** (*s'emploient surtout au pluriel*) (*n.m.*), disbursement; out of pocket expense; outgoing; outlay.

débours (*n.m.pl.*) *ou* **déboursés** (*n.m.pl.*) (Ch. de f.), paid-on charges:

débours sur les envois en port dû, paid-on charges on carriage forward consignments.

les débours (*ou* déboursés) sont des sommes avancées par les administrations des chemins de fer à la charge de la marchandise, soit lors de la remise au transport, soit en cours de route, paid-on charges are sums advanced by the railway companies at the expense of the goods, either when collecting, or while in transit.

déboursement (action) (*n.m.*), disbursement.

débourser (*v.t.*), to disburse; to lay out; to spend:

débourser beaucoup d'argent, to lay out a lot of money.

débris (épaves) (*n.m.pl.*), wreck; wreckage:

coupement de débris (*m.*), cutting away wreck.

sauvetage des débris (*m.*), salvage of wreck (*or* of wreckage).

débrouiller (*v.t.*), to unravel; to clear up:

débrouiller la situation d'un failli, to unravel, to clear up, the affairs of a bankrupt.

début (d'une assurance) (*n.m.*), commencement (of an insurance).

décacheter (*v.t.*), to unseal; to open:

décacheter une lettre, to open, to unseal, a letter.

décaissement (*n.m.*), withdrawal.

décaisser (*v.t.*), to withdraw:

décaisser une somme d'argent, to withdraw a sum of money.

décéder (*v.i.*), to decease; to die:

personne décédée (*f.*), deceased person.

décès (*n.m.*), decease; death.

décharge (*n.f.*), discharge; release:

donner décharge par un reçu, to give discharge by a receipt.

décharge d'une soumission (Douanes), discharge of a bond.

obtenir la décharge ou la réduction de ses impôts, to obtain the discharge or the reduction of one's taxes.

décharge (concordat) (*n.f.*), composition:

décharge de 25 0/0, composition of 5s. in the £.

décharge (débarquement) (*n.f.*), discharge; unloading; unlading; unshipment.

déchargement (débarquement) (*n.m.*), discharge; unloading; unlading; unshipment:

le déchargement final du navire, the final discharge of the vessel.

déchargement sans désemparer (d'un navire), continuous discharge.

le déchargement des wagons s'effectuera immédiatement après l'arrivée des convois, the unloading of the trucks is to take place immediately after arrival of the trains.

décharger (*v.t.*), to discharge; to release:

décharger quelqu'un d'une obligation, to discharge, to release, someone from an obligation.

décharger un compte, to discharge an account.

décharger (débarquer) (*v.t.*), to discharge; to unload; to unlade; to unship:

décharger la cargaison dans (*ou* sur) des embarcations, les marchandises au port de destination, to discharge the cargo into craft, the goods at the port of destination.

navire qui commence à décharger sa cargaison (*m.*), ship which begins to discharge (*or* unload) her cargo.

déchargeur (ouvrier des docks) (*n.m.*), docker.

déchéance (Dr.) (*n.f.*), loss, forfeiture (of rights). Cf. **déchu**.

déchet (*s'emploie souvent au pluriel*) (*n.m.*), waste; wastage; loss:

déchets en volume, en poids, wastage, loss, in bulk, in weight.

déchet de route, loss in transit.

il y a quelques déchets sans grande importance (Bourse), there have been several losses without much importance.

déchiffrable (*adj.*), decipherable.

déchiffrement (action) (*n.m.*), deciphering; decoding; translating.

déchiffrement (écrit déchiffré) (*n.m.*), translation: déchiffrement d'un câblogramme, translation of a cable.

déchiffrer (*v.t.*), to decipher; to decode; to translate:

déchiffrer une dépêche télégraphique, to decode, to translate, a telegram.

déchirer (*v.t.*), to tear up:

déchirer une convention, to tear up an agreement.

déchu (-e) d'un droit (être) (Dr.), to lose, to forfeit, a right:

porteur d'un effet qui est déchu de tous droits contre les endosseurs (*m.*), holder of a bill who loses (*or* forfeits) all rights against the endorsers. See also example under **avenant**.

assurance qui est déchue si l'assuré exagère
sciemment le montant du dommage (f.),
insurance which is forfeited if the insured
knowingly exaggerates the amount of the
damage.

décider (v.t.), to decide: to settle; to resolve;
to resolve on:
décider les différends qui peuvent s'élever, to
decide, to settle, disputes which may arise.
l'assemblée générale extraordinaire a décidé
d'augmenter le capital social d'une somme de
0 fr. par la création de 0 actions de 0 fr.
chacune (f.), it was resolved at the extraordinary general meeting to increase the
company's capital by an amount of 0 francs
by the creation of 0 shares of 0 francs each.

décimal, -e, -aux (adj.), decimal:
système décimal (m.), decimal system.

décimale (n.f.), decimal.

décision (n.f.), decision; resolution:
les décisions prises par l'assemblée générale,
the resolutions passed at the general meeting.
décision arbitrale, arbitration award; award.

déclarant, -e (pers.) (n.), declarant:
déclaration que le déclarant doit déposer à
la douane pour permettre au service de
vérifier la marchandise importée (f.), entry
which the declarant must lodge with the
customs to allow the service to examine the
goods imported.

déclaration (n.f.), declaration; statement;
note; return:
déclaration d'aliment (Assce mar.), declaration
on the policy; declaration of interest (or
of risk) (or of value):
la police flottante assure les marchandises
dès leur embarquement et non pas seulement à partir de la déclaration d'aliment,
a floating policy insures the goods as and
when they are shipped and not only from
the time of declaration of interest.
déclaration d'expédition, consignment note.
déclaration d'hypothèque, declaration of mortgage.
déclaration de guerre, declaration of war.
déclaration de revenu (Impôt sur le revenu),
return of income; income tax return:
article qui doit être compris dans la déclaration
des revenus de l'année (m.), item which
ought to be included in the return of
income (or in the income tax return) for the
year.
le contribuable doit remettre au contrôleur
des contributions directes une déclaration
de son bénéfice net, the taxpayer must
send in to the inspector of taxes a return
of his net profit.
faire la déclaration de ses bénéfices, de son
revenu global, to make a return of one's
profits, of one's total income.
déclaration patronale (impôt sur les traitements et salaires), employer's return.
la déclaration à faire au greffier, the return to
be made to the registrar.
déclaration de souscription et de versement.
See explanation under assemblée constitutive.

déclaration de transfert. *See under* feuille de
transfert.
déclaration de valeur des marchandises à
assurer, declaration of value of goods for
insurance.
l'administration est responsable jusqu'à concurrence du montant de la déclaration des
valeurs insérées dans les chargements (Poste)
(f.), the authorities are liable for an amount
not exceeding the declaration of values
inserted in the insurances.
toute déclaration de valeur supérieure à la
valeur réelle du contenu d'un colis est
considérée comme frauduleuse (Poste), any
declaration of value over and above the actual
value of the contents of a parcel is considered
as fraudulent.
déclaration de versement (d'un mandat de
poste), certificate of issue (of a money order).
déclaration fausse *ou* fausse déclaration *ou*
déclaration inexacte, false (or untrue)
declaration (or statement); misstatement;
misrepresentation.

déclaration (Douanes) (n.f.), declaration; entry;
report:
déclaration de douane *ou* déclaration en douane,
customs declaration; customs entry;
customs report:
déclaration en douane (Poste), customs
declaration.
déclaration du contenu d'un bagage, declaration of the contents of an article of luggage.
faire une déclaration en douane d'un navire,
de marchandises, to pass a customs entry
of a ship, of goods.
toute opération de douane comporte une
déclaration préalable, a preliminary entry
(or declaration) is required in every customs
operation.
déclaration d'acquittement de droits *ou*
déclaration pour l'acquittement des droits,
duty-paid entry.
déclaration d'embarquement *ou* déclaration
d'exportation, export specification.
déclaration d'entrée, entry inwards; declaration inwards; clearance inwards.
déclaration d'entrepôt *ou* déclaration d'entrée
en entrepôt *ou* déclaration de mise en
entrepôt, warehousing entry; entry for
warehousing.
déclaration de consommation *ou* déclaration
de mise en consommation, entry for home use;
home use entry.
déclaration de (*ou* en) détail (opp. à *déclaration
de gros*), entry; bill of entry (opp. to *report*).
déclaration de (*ou* en) gros *ou* déclaration
générale *ou* déclaration sommaire, report;
report of the whole cargo. Also applied in
France to train loads of goods arriving at
French frontier stations.
déclaration de réexportation d'entrepôt,
shipping bill.
déclaration de sortie, entry outwards;
declaration outwards.
déclaration de soumission, declaration for
bond.

déclaration de transbordement, transhipment entry.

déclaration de transit, transit entry.

déclaration définitive, perfect entry ; perfected entry.

déclaration pour produits exempts de droits, entry for duty-free goods ; free entry.

déclaration provisoire, sight entry ; bill of sight.

déclarer (*v.t.*), to declare ; to state ; to report ; to return ; to certify ; to disclose :

déclarer un dividende, la valeur pour l'assurance, une séance levée, to declare a dividend, the value for insurance, a meeting closed.

la valeur déclarée dans la police, the value declared in the policy.

aggravation de risque que l'assuré est tenu de déclarer (*f.*), increase of risk which the insured is bound to declare.

déclarer la somme en risque sur chaque navire, to declare, to report, the amount at risk on each ship.

l'assuré s'oblige à déclarer en aliment, pendant la durée de la police, en tant qu'elles y sont applicables, toutes les expéditions faites pour son compte (*m.*), the insured binds himself to declare (*or* to report) as attaching interest, during the term of the policy, in so far as they are applicable to it, all shipments made on his account.

le chiffre à déclarer pour chaque employé (impôts), the figure to return (*or* to be returned) for each employee.

cession qui doit être enregistrée, ou déclarée au bureau de l'enregistrement (*f.*), transfer which must be registered, or returned to the registry office.

je soussigné Paul X. déclare que . . ., I, the undersigned Paul X., declare (*or* certify) that . . .

déclarer toute circonstance essentielle, to disclose every material circumstance.

colis avec valeur déclarée (colis chargé) (*m.*), insured parcel.

valeur déclarée fr. 0 (inscription sur un objet chargé), insured for 0 francs.

colis sans valeur déclarée (colis non chargé) (*m.*), uninsured parcel.

déclarer (Douanes) (*v.t.*), to declare ; to enter ; to report :

déclarer la valeur au bureau de la douane, to declare the value at the custom house.

bagages de voyageurs déclarés en douane (*m.pl.*), passengers' luggage declared at the customs.

déclarer des marchandises pour la consommation, le transit, l'entrepôt, le transbordement, la réexportation, ou l'admission temporaire, pour l'acquittement des droits, to enter goods for home consumption, transit, warehousing, transhipment, reexport, or temporary admission, for the payment of duty.

déclarer (se) **acheteur** (Opérations à prime) (Bourse), to call :

le cours ayant haussé, nous nous déclarons acheteurs des titres, the price having risen, we call the stock.

déclarer (se) **vendeur** (Opérations à prime), to put :

le cours ayant baissé, je me déclare vendeur des actions, the price having fallen, I put the shares.

déclassé, -e (non bancable) (*adj.*), unbankable : papier déclassé (*m.*), unbankable paper. See note under **bancable**.

déclassé, -e (en parlant de valeurs de bourse) (*adj.*) (Ant. : *classé, -e*), displaced (i.e., held by the speculative public ; not as investment) :

actions déclassées (*f.pl.*), displaced shares.

déclassement (Bourse) (*n.m.*), displacement :

le déclassement provenant de la conversion du 3 1/2 0/0, the displacement arising from the conversion of the $3\frac{1}{2}\%$.

déclassement (voyages par ch. de f., etc.) (*n.m.*), change of class :

déclassement à (*ou* en) 1re, change of class to 1st.

décliner (*v.t.*), to decline :

décliner une offre, la responsabilité d'un sinistre, to decline an offer, responsibility for an accident.

décomposer (analyser ; dépouiller) (*v.t.*), to analyze ; to analyse.

décomposition (analyse) (*n.f.*), analysis :

décomposition du prix de revient en ses principaux éléments, analysis of the cost price into its chief components.

décompte (*n.m.*), working out the charges ; working out ; reckoning ; calculation :

décompte d'un bordereau d'encaissement, working out the charges on a list of bills for collection.

décompte des intérêts dus, working out, reckoning, calculation, of the interest due.

décompte du temps (débarquement d'un navire), time sheet.

décompter (*v.t.*), to work out the charges on ; to work out ; to reckon ; to calculate :

décompter un effet, un bordereau d'escompte, to work out the charges on a bill, on a list of bills for discount.

le bordereau est décompté par le banquier, the list is worked out by the banker.

décompter les jours de l'ouverture jusqu'à la fermeture du compte, to reckon, to calculate, the days from the opening to the closing of the account.

déconfiture (*n.f.*), insolvency (of a non trading debtor).

découper (*v.t.*), to cut out :

découper une annonce et la coller dans un album, to cut out an advertisement and stick it in a guard book.

découpure de journal (*f.*), newspaper cutting.

découvert (déficit) (*n.m.*), deficit ; deficiency ; shortage :

combler un découvert, to make up a deficit (*or* a shortage).

à découvert (sans couverture ; sans garantie), uncovered ; without cover ; unsecured ; without security :
le assuré qui est à découvert d'un quart, d'un tiers (*m.*), insured who is uncovered by a quarter, by a third.
couvrir des risques que les polices ordinaires laissent à découvert, to cover risks which ordinary policies leave uncovered.
la banque n'accepte aucune opération de bourse à découvert, the bank does not undertake any stock exchange transaction without cover.
avances à découvert (*f.pl.*), unsecured advances ; advances without security ; uncovered advances.

découvert (Banq.) (*n.m.*), overdraft :
le découvert d'un compte de banque est la somme dont le débit surpasse le crédit, the overdraft of a bank account is the amount by which the debit exceeds the credit.
découvert en blanc *ou* découvert sur notoriété, unsecured overdraft.
découvert moyen, average overdraft.

à découvert, overdrawn :
compte de banque qui est à découvert (*m.*), banking account which is overdrawn.
dépôt à découvert (*m.*). *See under* dépôt libre.

découvert (Bourse) (*n.m.*), bear account ; bears ; short account ; short interest ; shorts :
vendre à découvert; to sell a bear ; to sell short.
le découvert sur la Rente est étendu, there is a big bear account (*or* short account) (*or* short interest) open in Rentes.
il n'y a pas de découvert, there are no bears (*or* shorts).
le découvert se rachète, the bears (*or* the shorts) are buying back.
vente à découvert (*f.*), bear sale ; short sale ; short.
être à découvert, to be caught short.
baissier à découvert (*m.*), uncovered bear.

découvrir une erreur dans les livres, to find a mistake in the books.

décrochage (Téléph.) (*n.m.*), removing the receiver.

décrocher le récepteur (*ou* l'écouteur) (*ou* l'appareil) *ou simplement* **décrocher** (*v.t.*) (Téléph.) (Ant. : *raccrocher*), to remove the receiver :
l'abonné décroche et attend (*m.*), the subscriber removes the receiver and waits.

dédit (*n.m.*), penalty ; forfeit :
dédits en cas d'inexécution du contrat, forfeits, penalties, for non performance of the agreement.

dédommagement (*n.m.*), damages ; compensation ; indemnification ; indemnity.

dédommager (*v.t.*), to compensate ; to recoup ; to indemnify :
dédommager quelqu'un de ses pertes, to compensate, to recoup, to indemnify, someone for his losses.

se dédommager (*v.r.*), to compensate oneself ; to recoup oneself.

dédouanement *ou* **dédouanage** (*n.m.*), clearance ; clearing ; clearance through the customs (of goods) :
l'agent en douane remplit, pour les expéditeurs ou les destinataires, les formalités de dédouanement des marchandises (*m.*), the customs agent fulfils, for shippers or consignees, the formalities of clearing the goods through the customs.

dédouaner (*v.t.*), to clear ; to clear through the customs :
dédouaner les marchandises dans les dix jours qui suivent la présentation de la déclaration en douane, to clear the goods within the ten days following the presentation of the customs entry.

déductible (*adj.*), deductible :
perte déductible (*f.*), deductible loss.

déduction (*n.f.*), deduction ; allowance ; relief :
déduction pour dépenses (Impôt sur le revenu), deduction, allowance, relief, for expenses.
déduction personnelle (Impôt sur le revenu), personal allowance.
déduction pour différence du vieux au neuf (Assce mar.), deduction new for old.

déduction faite de *ou* **après déduction de,** after deducting :
déduction faite (*ou* après déduction) de l'impôt, des frais, after deducting tax, the expenses.

sous déduction d'escompte, less discount :
prix d'achat, sous déduction d'escompte (*m.*), purchase price, less discount.

sous déduction d'impôt *ou* **sous déduction d'impôt sur le revenu** *ou* **impôts déduits,** less tax ; less income tax :
intérêt payable par semestre, sous déduction d'impôt (*m.*), interest payable half yearly, less tax.
les intérêts, impôts déduits, sont payables par semestre, the interest, less tax, is payable half yearly.

déduire (*v.t.*), to deduct :
déduire les acomptes payés, ses frais, l'impôt sur le revenu, to deduct the amounts paid on account, one's expenses, income tax.

à déduire, to be deducted ; less ; deduct :
dépenses du mois, à déduire, expenses of the month, to be deducted.
à déduire : dépenses du mois, deduct (*or* less) : expenses for the month.

défaillance (*n.f.*), default :
être responsable de la livraison des titres à l'acheteur en cas de défaillance du vendeur, to be responsible for the delivery of the stock to the buyer in case of default of the seller.

défaillant, -e (*adj.*), defaulting :
partie défaillante (*f.*), defaulting party.

défaillant, -e (pers.) (*n.*), defaulter.

défaire (*v.t.*), to undo ; to cancel :
défaire un marché, to undo, to cancel, a bargain.

défaire (se), to unload :
porteur de titres qui veut se défaire d'un gros paquet d'actions (*m.*), stockholder who wants to unload a big block of shares.

défalcation (*n.f.*), deduction.

défalquer (*v.t.*), to deduct :
défalquer le poids de l'emballage, les centimes sur les factures dépassant 100 francs, to deduct the weight of the packing, the centimes on invoices exceeding 100 francs.

défaut (vice) (*n.m.*), defect ; fault :
défaut apparent, apparent defect ; apparent fault.
défaut caché, latent defect ; latent fault.

défaut (manque ; absence) (*n.m.*), default ; failure ; want ; lack ; absence :
défaut de versement des termes appelés, failure to pay, default in paying, the instalments called up.
défaut de déclaration (Impôts cédulaires), failure to make a return.
défaut de jugement, de confiance dans la solvabilité d'une banque, want, lack, of judgment, of confidence in the solvency of a bank.
défaut de nouvelles (d'un navire), absence of news (of a ship).
défaut d'acceptation ou de paiement (d'un effet), dishonour (of a bill). *See example under synonymous expression* non acceptation ou non paiement.
défaut d'acceptation (d'un effet), dishonour ; dishonour by non acceptance ; failure to accept.
défaut de paiement (d'un effet), dishonour ; dishonour by non payment ; failure to pay ; default in paying.
défaut d'avis, no advice ; no orders ; want of advice.
défaut de provision (Banq.), no funds ; no effects.
défaut de provision (lettre de change), absence of consideration.

à défaut de, failing ; in default of ; for want of :
à défaut de paiement dans les trente jours, failing payment within thirty days.
à défaut d'accord (*ou* d'entente) entre tous les intéressés, failing agreement between all the interested parties ; in default of agreement between all the parties concerned.
je donne, par les présentes, pouvoir à M. A., et, à son défaut, à M. B., I hereby appoint as my proxy Mr A., and, failing him, Mr B.

défavorable (*adj.*), unfavourable ; unfavorable :
change défavorable (*m.*), unfavourable exchange ; exchange against us.

défectible (Comptab.) (*adj.*) (Ant. : *indéfectible*), wasting :
actif défectible (*m.*) *ou* valeurs défectibles (*f.pl.*), wasting assets.

défendeur, -eresse (Dr.) (pers.) (*n.*), defendant :
suivant que la société est demanderesse ou défenderesse, according as the company is plaintiff or defendant.

défendre (*v.t.*), to protect ; to maintain :
défendre une position (Bourse), to protect a book.
les métallurgiques défendent assez bien leurs cours (*f.pl.*), irons and steels maintain their prices fairly well.

défendre (se) (*v.r.*), to hold up ; to be maintained :
l'action X. se défend bien, X. shares held up well (*or* were well maintained).

déficit [**déficits** *pl.*] (*n.m.*) (Ant. : *excédent*), deficit ; deficiency ; shortage ; short :
le déficit d'une entreprise est exprimé par le solde débiteur du compte de pertes et profits, the deficiency of a business is expressed by the debit balance of the profit and loss account.
déficit de caisse (*ou* dans l'encaisse), de poids, shortage in the cash, in weight.
déficits et excédents de caisse (*ou* dans l'encaisse) (Banq.), cash shorts and overs.

déficitaire (*adj.*) (opp. à *bénéficiaire*), debit (*used as adj.*) ; showing a loss ; adverse :
apurer un solde déficitaire, to wipe off a debit balance.
bilan déficitaire (*m.*), balance sheet showing a loss.
suivant que le résultat de l'exercice est bénéficiaire ou déficitaire, according as the result of the trading shows (*or* is) a profit or a loss.
balance commerciale déficitaire (*f.*), adverse trade balance. *See example under* balance du commerce.

définitif, -ive (*adj.*), definitive ; definite :
titre définitif (*m.*) (opp. à *titre provisoire*), definitive (*or* definite) certificate.

déflation (*n.f.*), deflation :
déflation monétaire, monetary deflation.
déflation de crédit, deflation of credit.

défrayer (*v.t.*), to defray.
se défrayer (*v.r.*), to pay one's expenses :
n'avoir pas de quoi se défrayer, not to have enough money to pay one's expenses.

dégagement (*n.m.*), redemption ; getting out of pawn ; relief.

dégager (retirer ce qui avait été donné comme gage) (*v.t.*), to redeem ; to get out of pawn : dégager son bien, to redeem one's property.

dégager (soustraire à une obligation) (*v.t.*), to relieve :
syndicataire qui se trouve dégagé de l'engagement pris (*m.*), underwriter who is relieved from the engagement contracted.
la place (*ou* la position de place) est dégagée (Bourse) (opp. à *la place est chargée*), the market is all bears (*or* is all takers) ; sellers over.

dégât (*n.m.*) *ou* **dégâts** (*n.m.pl.*), damage :
dégâts et pertes provenant d'incendie, damage and loss by fire.

dégonflement (*n.m.*), deflation ; reduction :
dégonflement du poste « effets à payer » (bilan), reduction of the item " bills payable."

degré de liquidité (Comptab.) (*m.*), ratio of liquid assets to current liabilities.

dégrèvement (*n.m.*), disencumbrance ; relief ; reduction ; cut :
projets de dégrèvements d'impôts (*m.pl.*), plans for tax reductions (*or* tax cuts).
demande en dégrèvement (impôts) (*f.*), application (*or* claim) for relief.

dégrever (*v.t.*),   to disencumber; to relieve; to cancel:
dégrever une propriété,   to disencumber a property (to free it from mortgage).
abattement dégrevant la tranche inférieure du revenu (*m.*),   abatement relieving the lower portion of the income.
les colis réexpédiés sur leur point d'origine sont généralement dégrevés des droits de douane (*m.pl.*), the customs duty raised on a parcel abroad is generally cancelled if the parcel is returned.
dégringolade (*n.f.*), slump; heavy fall:
dégringolade des cours, slump in prices.
délai (temps accordé) (*n.m.*),   time; extension; extension of time:
traite tirée à un court délai de vue (*f.*), draft drawn a short time after sight.
stipuler un délai d'enlèvement, de livraison, to stipulate a time of (*or* for) collection, of (*or* for) delivery.
dans un délai raisonnable,   within a reasonable time.
délai prescrit *ou* délai réglementaire, prescribed time.
délai d'attente, time of waiting.
délai de planche *ou* délais de planche, laytime:
usage d'après lequel le délai de planche ne court (*ou* les délais de planche ne courent) que d'un certain jour (*m.*), custom according to which laytime only runs from a certain date.
obtenir un délai,   to get time; to obtain an extension (*or* an extension of time).
délai (retardement) (*n.m.*), delay:
livraison sans délai (*f.*), delivery without delay.
délai-congé [**délais-congé** *pl.*] (*n.m.*) *ou* **délai de congé**, notice (period of notice):
un délai-congé d'une semaine, a week's notice.
délaissé, -e (en parlant des valeurs de bourse) (*p.p.*), neglected:
les fonds mexicains demeurent délaissés (*m.pl.*), Mexican stocks remain neglected.
délaissement (Assce mar.) (*n.m.*), abandonment:
délaissement d'un navire, de facultés assurées, abandonment of a ship, of insured goods.
assuré qui fait à ses assureurs le délaissement du chargement (*m.*), insured who makes to his underwriters abandonment of the cargo.
le délaissement est la faculté à l'assuré d'exiger le montant entier de la somme assurée moyennant le transfert à l'assureur de la propriété de la chose assurée dans l'état où l'a laisser le sinistre, abandonment is the option to the insured to claim the whole amount of the sum insured in consideration of the transfer to the insurer of the property of the thing insured in the state in which the casualty left it.
délaisser (Assce mar.) (*v.t.*), to abandon.
délégant, -e *ou* **délégateur, -trice** (pers.) (*n.*), delegant; delegator.
délégataire (pers.) (*n.m.* ou *f.*), delegatee.
délégation (Dr.) (*n.f.*), delegation:
délégation de pouvoir, d'une dette, delegation of power, of a debt.

délégation (Com.) (*n.f.*), delegation; letter of delegation.
délégation (Bourse) (*n.f.*) (Abrév.: **délég.**), delegation.
délégué, -e (pers.) (*n.*), delegate:
le délégué officiel du comité,   the official delegate of the committee.
Cf. administrateur-délégué.
délégué, -e (Dr.) (pers.) (*n.*), delegated debtor.
déléguer (*v.t.*), to delegate:
déléguer son autorité, un fonds pour le paiement d'un créancier, to delegate one's authority, funds for the payment of a creditor.
après leur nomination les administrateurs se réunissent en conseil pour choisir parmi eux un président et déléguer une partie de leurs pouvoirs à l'un ou à plusieurs d'entre eux qui dirigeront les affaires de la société et feront exécuter les délibérations du conseil: ces membres prennent le titre d'administrateurs délégués, after their appointment, the directors meet as a board to choose one of their number to be chairman and to delegate a part of their powers to one or more of their number who will manage the company's business and will cause the decisions of the board to be carried out: these members take the title of managing directors.
délestage (*n.m.*), unballasting.
délester (*v.t.*), to unballast.
délibération (discussion) (*n.f.*),   deliberation; consideration; proceedings; transaction; business:
faute de rapport des commissaires, les délibérations de l'assemblée sur les comptes et le bilan seraient nulles, failing a report of the auditors, the consideration by the meeting of the accounts and the balance sheet would be null.
après délibération (*ou* après en avoir délibéré), le conseil prend la résolution suivante (procès-verbal), after consideration, It was resolved that; after consideration, Resolved that.
délibérations d'une assemblée,   proceedings, transactions, business, of a meeting.
délibération (résolution) (*n.f.*),   resolution; decision:
les délibérations prises par l'assemblée générale, the resolutions passed at the general meeting.
délibérer (*v.t.*) *ou* **délibérer sur**, to consider; to consider, and if thought fit, to pass; to deliberate on; to transact:
assemblée convoquée à l'effet de délibérer sur l'ordre du jour suivant (*f.*),   meeting convened to consider the following agenda (or to transact the following business).
mettre à l'ordre du jour les questions à délibérer, to put down on the agenda the business to be transacted.
M.M. les actionnaires sont convoqués en assemblée générale extraordinaire (*lieu, date, et heure*) à l'effet de délibérer sur l'ordre du jour suivant, notice is hereby given that an extraordinary general meeting of the company will be held (*place, date, and time*) for the purpose of considering and, if thought fit, of passing the following resolution (*or* resolutions).

delivery-order [**delivery-orders** *pl.*] (bon de livraison à valoir sur connaissement) (*n.m.*), delivery order.

délivrable (*adj.*), deliverable.

délivrance (*n.f.*), delivery ; handing over :
délivrance des marchandises au destinataire, entre les mains des consignataires, delivery of the goods to the consignee, into the hands of the consignees.
la délivrance du chèque transfère au bénéficiaire la propriété de la provision, delivery of a cheque transfers to the payee the property in the consideration.

délivrer (*v.t.*), to deliver ; to hand over ; to hand :
délivrer de la marchandise, des titres, to deliver goods, stock.
délivrer les papiers à quelqu'un, to hand over, to hand, the papers to someone.
navire prêt à délivrer sa cargaison, ship ready to deliver her cargo.
le billet délivré au passager, the ticket delivered (*or* handed) to the passenger.
délivrez à l'ordre de M. X., deliver to the order of Mr X.

déloyal, -e, -aux (*adj.*), dishonest ; unfair :
cassier déloyal (*m.*), dishonest cashier.
concurrence déloyale (*f.*), unfair competition.

demandable (*adj.*), demandable ; claimable.

demande (*n.f.*), request ; application ; enquiry ; inquiry ; demand ; call ; claim :
demande d'emploi [demandes d'emplois *pl.*] (opp. à *offre d'emploi*), situation wanted.
demande d'indemnité (Assce), claim :
une demande d'indemnité dépassant la valeur de la marchandise, a claim exceeding the value of the goods.
demande de chèques (Banq.), request for cheques.
demande de prix, enquiry, inquiry, for price (*or* for quotation).
il y a encore de nombreuses demandes de fret sur l'Algérie, there are still numerous enquiries for freight to Algeria.
l'action X. est l'objet de demandes (*ou* est demandée) à 3 910, X. shares are in demand at 3,910 francs.
demande de remboursement (Caisse d'épargne), notice of withdrawal.
demande de renseignements, request for information.
demande en dégrèvement, en décharge (impôts), application, claim, for relief, for discharge.
demande en dommages-intérêts, en paiement de la valeur des marchandises non délivrées, claim for damages, for payment of the value of undelivered goods.
demande en remboursement de droits, claim, application, for repayment of duties.

sur demande, on application :
prix sur demande (*m.pl.*), prices on application.

sur demande (à présentation), on demand ; on presentation ; at sight ; at call ; on call ; call (*used as adj.*) :
emprunt remboursable sur demande (*m.*), loan repayable on demand.

dépôt remboursable sur demande (*m.*), deposit repayable at call (*or* on demand).
argent remboursable sur demande (*m.*) *ou* prêts remboursables sur demande (*m.pl.*) (Marché monétaire), money at (*or* on) call ; call money ; loans at call.

demande (Économie) (*n.f.*), demand :
la demande d'effets sur l'étranger, the demand for foreign bills.
l'offre et la demande, supply and demand ; demand and supply :
la loi de l'offre et de la demande, the law of supply and demand (*or* of demand and supply). See examples under **loi.**

demande (commande) (Com.) (*n.f.*), order :
demande de marchandises, order for goods.

demande (Bourse) (*n.f.*) (opp. à *offre*), bid.
demandes réduites (Bourse) (*Abrév.* : dem. réd. *ou* dem. r.), (in France, on a quotation list) means that the stock has only been able to be quoted by reducing the buying orders to be executed. Bids exceeding offers are officially reduced on the basis of about 40%, e.g., 10 shares reduced to 4. *Cf.* cours unique. Marking a quotation *demandes réduites* is sometimes only a surreptitious means of boosting the shares. One may come across remarks like the following in the French press.—C'est la seule explication plausible de la cotation demandes réduites à 895 contre 840, This is the only plausible explanation of the quotation bids reduced at 895 against 840, i.e., the foregoing is the only plausible explanation of the marking of the shares bids reduced, thus causing them to rise from 840 to 895 francs.

demande reconventionnelle (Dr.) (*f.*), counter-claim ; set off.

demandé (Téléph.) (pers.) (*n.m.*), called subscriber ; distant subscriber.

demander (prier) (*v.t.*), to ask ; to ask for ; to request ; to pass a request for ; to book ; to enquire ; to inquire ; to apply for :
demander des conseils, to ask for, to ask, advice.
demander une faveur, to ask a favour.
M. le président demande ensuite aux actionnaires s'ils ont des observations à présenter ou des explications à réclamer, the chairman then asked the shareholders whether they had any comments to make or questions to put.
demander une conversation téléphonique (au bureau central), to pass a request for, to book, a telephone call (at the exchange) :
les conversations à heure fixe doivent être demandées au moins une heure à l'avance (*f.pl.*), fixed time calls should be booked at least one hour in advance.

demander (exiger) (*v.t.*), to demand ; to claim :
demander ce qui est dû, to demand, to claim, what is due.
demander compensation à celui dont la faute a occasionné le sinistre, to claim compensation from the person whose fault has caused the accident.

demander (avoir besoin de) (*v.t.*), to want :
demander un emploi, to want a situation.

demander dans les journaux, to advertise for :
demander dans les journaux un commis,   to
advertise for a clerk.
demander (Bourse) (*v.t.*), to bid; to bid for; to
want :
l'agent demande :   je prends (*ou* je donne) 100
(actions) X. tel prix, the broker (*in England,
it would be the* jobber) bids :   buy (*short for*
I will buy) 100 X. (shares) such or such a
price.   *Cf.* l'agent offre, *under* **offrir.**
cours demandés (acheteurs) (Bourse) (*m.pl.*),
prices bid (buyers).
action X. :   80 fr. demandé; 82 fr. offert, X.
shares :   80 fr. bid; 82 fr. offered.
valeurs demandées (*f.pl.*),   stocks bid for;
stocks wanted; shares in demand.
demandeur, -euse (pers.) (*n.*), applicant :
demandeur en concession,   applicant for
licence (*or* for concession).
demandeur (abonné demandeur) (Téléph.) (pers.)
(*n.m.*), caller; calling subscriber.
demandeur, -eresse (Dr.) (pers.) (*n.*), plaintiff :
suivant que la société est demanderesse ou
défenderesse,   according as the company is
plaintiff or defendant.
démarchage (*n.m.*), canvassing; running; share
pushing :   (See notes under **démarcheur.**)
démarchage à domicile,   house to house
canvassing.
démarche (*n.f.*), step; measure; service :
démarche conseillable, advisable step.
parts de fondateurs attribuées aux apporteurs
en rémunération de leurs démarches (*f.pl.*),
founders' shares allotted to the vendors as
consideration for their services.
démarcheur (pers.) (*n.m.*), canvasser; runner;
share pusher. (The *démarcheur,* in France
and Belgium, is a canvasser or traveller
employed by the banks [even the big first
class banks], outside brokers, and other
financial houses, to go round soliciting custom
or pushing shares : he is in finance what the
commercial traveller is in trade.   English
banks and financial houses do not practise
this form of visitation.)
Note :—In English, the words *runner* and
especially *share pusher* are used in an unfavourable sense.
démettre de (se), to resign; to throw up :
se démettre de son emploi,   to resign one's
position; to throw up one's situation.
demeurer couvert, -e (Assce), to be held covered :
en cas d'autres modifications non prévues par la
présente police, dans le voyage, l'itinéraire, ou
les conditions de transport, les effets assurés
n'en demeurent pas moins couverts sans
interruption, sauf surprime à payer aux
assureurs,   in case of other variations not
provided for in this policy, in the voyage,
route, or conditions of carriage, the insured
effects are nevertheless held covered without
interruption, subject to an extra premium to
be paid to the underwriters.
Cf. facultés de toutes déviations, etc.
demi-courtage (*n.m.*), half brokerage; half commission.

demi-fret (*n.m.*), (In France) half freight (*or*
forfeit freight) payable in certain cases on
throwing up a charter or cancelling a freight
booking.
demi-gros (*n.m.*) *ou* **commerce de demi-gros** (*m.*),
wholesale trade; wholesale commerce :
faire le demi-gros, to do a wholesale trade.
vente en demi-gros (*f.*), wholesale sale.
See note under **gros** *ou* **gros commerce.**
demi-net, demi-nette (*adj.*), (In France) free of
income tax but not of *droit* (or *impôt*) (or *taxe*)
de transmission (transfer duty).   *See note
under* droit de transmission.
demi-place (*n.f.*), half fare. See example under
place.
demi pour cent (*m.*), half per cent :
une ristourne de demi pour cent,   an allowance of half per cent.
demi-shilling [**demi-shillings** *pl.*] (monnaie anglaise)
(*n.m.*), sixpence.
demi-tarif (*n.m.*), half fare; half rates :
billet de demi-tarif pour les enfants (*m.*), child's
half fare ticket.
demi-terme (moitié d'un terme de location) (*n.m.*),
half a quarter :
ne passer qu'un demi-terme dans un bureau,
to stay only half a quarter in an office.
demi-terme (époque) (*n.m.*), half quarter; half
quarter day :
déménager au demi-terme,   to move on half
quarter day.
demi-terme (loyer) (*n.m.*), half quarter's rent :
payer un demi-terme d'avance,   to pay a half
quarter's rent in advance.
démission (*n.f.*), resignation :
je vous prie d'accepter ma démission, pour
raison de santé, d'administrateur de la
société, I ask you to accept my resignation,
for reasons of health, as director of the
company.
démissionnaire (*adj.*), resigned; to have resigned :
administrateur réputé démissionnaire (*m.*),
director deemed to have resigned.
démissionnaire (pers.) (*n.m.* ou *f.*),   resigner;
resignor.
démissionner (*v.i.*), to resign :
le cabinet a démissionné,   the cabinet has
resigned.
démolir un navire, to break up a ship.
démolisseur de navires (pers.) (*m.*), ship breaker.
démolition (d'un navire) (*n.f.*),   breaking up (a
ship).
démonétisation (*n.f.*), demonetization :
démonétisation des anciennes pièces, demonetization of old coins.
démonétiser (*v.t.*), to demonetize :
refondre des pièces d'argent démonétisées, to
remint demonetized silver coins.
démontrer (*v.t.*), to demonstrate; to prove; to
show; to shew :
il y a des espoirs de profits futurs pour les
brevets ou procédés dont la productivité est
possible mais mon démontrée,   there are
hopes of future profits for the patents or
processes whose productivity is possible but
not proved.

dénantir (*v.t.*), to take away security from ; to deprive of collateral :
dénantir un créancier, to take away a creditor's security.
se dénantir (*v.r.*), to give up one's security.
deniers publics (*m.pl.*), public money.
à beaux deniers comptants. See under **comptant.**
dénigrement (*n.m.*), running down.
dénigrer (*v.t.*), to run down (to speak disparagingly of) :
dénigrer les produits d'un concurrent, to run down the goods of a competitor.
dénomination (*n.f.*), denomination ; name ; naming :
la société a pour dénomination : *ou* la société prend la dénomination de : (status d'une société par actions), the name of the company is : .
dénommer (*v.t.*), to denominate ; to name :
dénommer une personne dans un acte, to name a person in a deed.
dénoncer (faire connaître) (*v.t.*), to give notice of :
dénoncer l'avarie à l'armateur, to give notice of damage to the shipowner.
denrée (*n.f.*), commodity ; food ; produce :
denrées destinées à l'exportation, commodities, produce, intended for export.
denrée alimentaire, foodstuff.
denrées coloniales, colonial produce.
départ (*n.m.*), departure :
départ du courrier, d'un train, departure of the mail, of a train.
au départ *ou* **de départ** (opp. à *à l'arrivée* ou *d'arrivée*), outgoing :
courrier au départ (*m.*), outgoing mail.
communication de départ (Téléph.) (*f.*), outgoing call.
départ (Navig.) (*n.m.*), departure ; sailing :
port de départ (*m.*), port of departure.
date de départ d'un navire (*f.*), date of sailing of a ship.
départs de Bordeaux tous les 14 jours, sailings from Bordeaux every fortnight.
arrivages (*ou* arrivées) et départs, arrivals and sailings.
départ (d'un compte, d'un compte courant) (*n.m.*), starting date (of an account, of an account current).
départ usines, ex works ; ex mill :
cours : départ usines, tant : sur wagon, tant, prices : ex works (*or* ex mill), so much ; on rail, so much.
dépassement (*n.m.*), excess.
dépasser (*v.t.*), to exceed : to be above :
la demande dépasse l'offre, the demand exceeds the supply.
dépasser le pair, to be above, to exceed, par.
dépasser un crédit, to exceed a credit.
Cf. **ne dépassant pas,** under **ne,** and **jusqu'à concurrence de,** under **jusqu'à.**
dépècement *ou* **dépeçage** (*n.m.*), breaking up.
dépecer (*v.t.*), to break up :
dépecer un vieux bateau, to break up an old boat.
dépêche (*n.f.*) *ou* **dépêche télégraphique,** message ; telegraphic message ; telegram ; wire.

dépêche (sac à dépêches) (Poste) (*n.f.*), mail bag.
dépêcher (*v.t.*), to dispatch ; to despatch.
dépens (frais de justice) (*n.m.pl.*), costs ; law costs :
être condamné (-e) aux dépens, to be ordered to pay the costs.
dépense (*n.f.*), expense ; charge ; cost ; expenditure : (See also **frais.**)
dépenses au port de relâche *ou* dépenses de relâche, expenses at port of refuge ; port of refuge expenses.
dépense d'avarie commune, general average expense.
dépenses d'exploitation, working expenses ; operating costs.
dépenses de maison, establishment charges ; standing expenses ; overhead charges (*or* expenses) ; expenses.
dépenses de publicité, advertising expenses.
dépenses directes *ou* dépenses proportionnelles (Établissement des prix de revient), direct expenses ; establishment charges ; departmental charges.
dépenses diverses, general expenses ; sundry expenses.
dépenses en immobilisations *ou* dépenses d'établissement, capital expenditure.
dépenses indirectes *ou* dépenses fixes (Établissement des prix de revient), indirect expenses (*or* charges) ; fixed charges ; overhead charges ; on-cost charges.
dépenses substituées (Avarie commune), substituted expenses.
la dépense excède la recette, the expenditure exceeds the receipts.
dépenser (*v.t.*), to spend ; to expend :
dépenser son revenu par anticipation, to spend one's income in advance.
déperdition (*n.f.*), loss :
déperdition de capital, loss of capital.
dépérissement (de capital) (*n.m.*), dwindling (of assets).
déplacé, -e (en parlant des effets, du papier de commerce) (*adj.*) *ou* **déplacé** (*n.m.*). *See under* effets sur place.
déplacement (*n.m.*), displacement ; shifting ; shift ; movement :
déplacement de richesses, de fonds, displacement of wealth, of funds.
déplacement de cours (Bourse), shift, movement, of prices.
déplacement (d'un navire) (*n.m.*), displacement (of a ship) :
déplacement en charge, load displacement.
déplacement lège, light displacement.
déplacer (*v.t.*), to displace ; to shift ; to move ; to send elsewhere :
déplacer les richesses, to displace wealth.
déplacer le fardeau de la preuve, to shift the burden of proof.
déplacer des marchandises, to send goods elsewhere (in order to find a better market).
déplacer (avoir un déplacement de) (*v.t.*), to displace :
navire qui déplace 10 000 tonnes (*m.*), ship which displaces 10,000 tons.
déplacer (se) (*v.r.*), to shift ; to move :

cours qui se déplace un peu (*m.*), price which shifts (*or* moves) slightly.

dépliant (*n.m.*), folder:
dépliants pour la publicité, folders for advertising.

déport (prolongement de livraison par le vendeur) (Bourse) (*n.m.*), backwardation; backwardization:
lorsqu'il y a un déport, le vendeur paye pour reporter, when there is a backwardation (*or* a backwardization), the seller pays to continue.

déport (bonification) (Bourse) (*n.m.*) (Abrév.: **D.** *ou* **B.** *ou* **b.**), backwardation; backwardization; back:
vendeur à découvert qui paye un déport (*m.*), bear seller who pays a backwardation (*or* a backwardization) (*or* a back).
See also example under **report** (loyer).

déport (bénéfice) (Négociations de change à terme) (*n.m.*) (Abrév.: **D.** *ou* **B.** *ou* **b.**), premium; under spot. See examples under **report**.

déporté, -e (Bourse) (*adj.* ou *p.p.*), backwardized:
titres déportés (*m.pl.*), backwardized stock.

déposant, -e (pers.) (*n.*), depositor; customer:
(The word *déposant* in French is not only applied to a *depositor* proper or customer on bank deposit account, but also to a customer on bank current account. See notes under **dépôt**.)
déposant de la caisse nationale d'épargne, post office savings bank depositor.

déposer (*v.t.*), to deposit; to place; to lodge; to hand in; to file; to lay:
déposer des fonds chez un banquier, une somme en main tierce, to deposit funds with a banker, a sum in the hands of a third party.
MM. les possesseurs (*ou* MM. les propriétaires) d'actions au porteur sont priés de déposer leurs titres au siège social 0 jours au moins avant la réunion, holders of bearer shares are requested to deposit their warrants at the company's office 0 days at least before the meeting.
déposer des titres en garde, to deposit, to place, securities in safe custody.
déposer à la douane une copie du manifeste, to deposit, to lodge, at the customs a copy of the manifest.
déposer un paquet au guichet du bureau de poste, to hand in a packet over the counter of the post office.
déposer à la poste *ou* déposer dans la boîte *ou* simplement déposer, to post:
lettres déposées dans les boîtes aux lettres particulières (*f.pl.*), letters posted in private letter boxes.
déposer en nantissement, to lodge as collateral; to hypothecate; to pledge:
titres déposés en nantissement (*m.pl.*), securities lodged as collateral; securities hypothecated (*or* pledged).
actions déposées en nantissement en garantie de fonds avancés (*f.pl.*), shares hypothecated (*or* pledged) as security for money advanced.

déposer une déclaration au greffe, to file a return at the registry.
déposer sur le bureau (à une assemblée), to lay on the table:
bilan déposé sur le bureau (*m.*), balance sheet laid on the table.
déposer son bilan, to submit a statement of one's affairs; to file a statement of one's affairs at the *Tribunal de Commerce* (a procedure required of a trader stopping payment: analogous to *filing one's petition* in England).

déposit *ou* **deposit** (Bourse de marchandises) (*n.m.*). See *under* caisse de liquidation.

dépositaire (pers.) (*n.m.* ou *f.*) (correlatif de *déposant*), depositary; trustee:
le banquier est le dépositaire des fonds de ses clients, the banker is the depositary of the funds of his customers.

dépôt (action de déposer; chose déposée) (*n.m.*), deposit; placing; lodgment; handing in; filing:
dépôt de marchandises à quai ou sous tente, deposit of goods on wharf or in bonded sheds.
dépôt de numéraire, de valeurs (Douanes), deposit of cash, of stock (in lieu of bond).
dépôt de garantie (Fin.), deposit of security.
dépôt de garantie (provision), deposit:
dépôt de garantie télégraphique, telegraph deposit.
dépôt de garantie téléphonique, telephone deposit.
abonné qui a versé un dépôt de garanti (*m.*), subscriber who has paid a deposit.
dépôt des télégrammes (Poste), handing in of telegrams.
le dépôt au guichet est obligatoire pour des objets chargés ou recommandés, handing in over the counter is compulsory for insured or registered packets.
dépôt à la poste *ou* dépôt dans la boîte *ou* simplement dépôt, posting:
heure limite de dépôt (*f.*) *ou* dernière limite d'heure de dépôt (*f.*), latest time for posting.
dépôt d'un acte au bureau de l'enregistrement, filing a deed at the registry office.
dépôt en banque: *Note:*—It should be borne in mind that the meaning of the word *dépôt* in French banking is not confined to the restricted acceptation of the word *deposit* in English banking (i.e., money lodged with a bank, bearing interest, and subject to notice of withdrawal), but that it is used indifferently of money placed on deposit or on current account. Thus, the big French joint stock banks are called *sociétés de dépôt*, and the following sentence, for example: *la société est autorisée à recevoir, avec ou sans intérêts, des capitaux en dépôt* means: *the company is authorized to receive money on deposit or current account, at or without interest.* The sentence *the bank also receives money on deposit* would be rendered in French as follows:—*la banque reçoit aussi des fonds en dépôts exigibles à terme ou à préavis.* *Cf.* compte de dépôt.

dépôt remboursable sur demande, deposit at call.

dépôt à préavis *ou* dépôt avec préavis *ou* dépôt à délai de préavis (dépôt à un certain nombre de jours de vue, c'est-à-dire remboursable quelques jours après que la demande en a été faite au banquier, par conséquent toujours avec préavis), deposit at notice :

dépôt à 7 jours de préavis, deposit at 7 days' notice.

dépôt à terme *ou* dépôt à terme fixe *ou* dépôt à échéance *ou* dépôt à échéance fixe, fixed deposit ; deposit for a fixed period.

dépôt à court terme, deposit at short notice.

dépôt à vue *ou* dépôt à vue ou avec préavis, placing money on current account. (The words *avec préavis* [*at notice*] used here are explained by the fact that French and Belgian banks require one or more days' notice for the withdrawal of large amounts from current account. In England, no notice is required, however large the amount. The continental banks, however, do not apply these notice rules rigorously : similarly the English banks do not insist on 7 days' notice for the withdrawal of short deposits, although of course they have the right to do so.)

dépôt en coffre-fort, safe deposit.

Note :—In England, safe deposit, i.e., keeping of securities, money, or other valuables, in individual strong room compartments, is undertaken by companies called *safe deposit companies* (there are 5 in London).

In France, this service (*service de coffres-forts*) is run by the big banks (*établissements de crédit*), who have a right of inspection (not so in England) of what is to be lodged in the safes. In France, persons or companies hiring out safes are legally bound (there is a special law on safe hiring [*location de coffres-forts*]) to keep an alphabetical index (*répertoire alphabétique*) of their customers' names and addresses, and also a register containing the date and time of each visit to the safe, together with the signature of the visiting person. These books are open to inspection by government officials. If the visiting person is not the actual hirer, but only a duly authorized representative (*fondé de pouvoirs*), he has to sign a declaration that to the best of his knowledge and belief the hirer, and other persons, if any, having rights to the contents of safe, are still alive. On the death of the hirer, the safe can only be opened in the presence of a duly appointed *notaire*, charged with making an inventory of the contents. Any person, having knowledge of the death of the hirer, visiting the safe unauthorizedly renders himself personally liable to the death duties payable by the estate of the deceased hirer and to other penalties.

In England, safe deposits are not subject to direct government control. Moreover, banks will accept, free of charge, for their customers the safe custody (*see* dépôt libre) of small locked boxes or sealed packets, but the customer has no right of access to the strong room ; the box or packet is brought to him in the manager's office.

dépôt libre *ou* dépôt en garde *ou simplement* dépôt, safe custody :

placer des titres en dépôt libre *ou* mettre des titres en dépôt, to place securities in safe custody.

Note :—Unlike the English banks, which keep their customers' securities in safe custody gratuitously, the French and Belgian banks make a charge for this service, called **droit de garde,** calculated at a rate of so much on the value of the securities deposited. If the securities are lodged open or unsealed, it is called a **dépôt à découvert** ; if in a sealed packet, a **dépôt cacheté,** in which case the charge is calculated on the declared value.

dépôt de bilan, submission of a statement of one's affairs. *See* déposer son bilan.

dépôt (magasin) (*n.m.*), depot ; store ; stores ; storehouse ; warehouse :

dépôt de douane. *The French equivalent of the English* King's warehouse. Cf. **mise en dépôt** and **entrepôt frauduleux.**

dépouillement (*n.m.*), examination ; scrutiny ; looking into ; looking through ; going through ; analysis :

la journée commence par le dépouillement de la correspondance, the day begins by going through the letters.

dépouillement des frais, du compte divers, analysis of expenses, of sundries account.

dépouiller (*v.t.*), to examine ; to look into ; to look through ; to go through ; to analyze ; to analyse ; to make an analysis of :

dépouiller un compte, to examine, to look into, to go through, to analyze, to make an analysis of, an account.

dépouiller la colonne Divers, to analyze the Sundries column.

dépouiller sa correspondance, to go through, to look through, one's correspondence (*or* one's letters) (*or* one's post).

dépréciation (*n.f.*) (Ant. : *amélioration*), depreciation :

dépréciation de matériel, de l'argent, des valeurs fournies en nantissement, depreciation of plant, of money, of securities lodged as collateral.

la dépréciation de diverses monnaies nationales par rapport à l'or a eu pour conséquence la hausse générale des prix, the depreciation of various national currencies in relation to gold has had as a consequence a general rise of prices.

déprécier (*v.t.*), to depreciate :

déprécier la valeur des actions, to depreciate the value of shares.

se déprécier (*v.r.*), to depreciate ; to go worse :

avec le temps, certaines valeurs s'améliorent, d'autres se déprécient, in time, certain stocks appreciate (*or* go better), others depreciate (*or* go worse).

dépression (*n.f.*), depression :
dépression d'une valeur, depression of a stock.

déprimer (*v.t.*), to depress :
nouvelle qui a eu un effet déprimant sur le marché (*f.*), news which has had a depressing effect on the market.

dérangement (*n.m.*), derangement ; disturbance :
dérangement des affaires, disturbance of business.

déranger (*v.t.*), to derange ; to disturb ; to upset :
déranger ses plans, to derange, to disturb, to upset, one's plans.

dératisation (*n.f.*), destruction of rats :
dératisation des navires provenant des pays contaminés de peste, destruction of rats on ships coming from countries contaminated by plague.

dératiser un navire, to destroy the rats on a ship.

dernier acheteur (Bourse de marchandises) (*m.*), last buyer ; receiver.

dernier cours (Bourse) (*m.*) [Abrév. : **d**r **c.** *ou* **c.(d**r**)**], closing price.
derniers cours cotés (*m.pl.*) (bulletin de cours), latest closing.

dernier port de reste (*m.*), last, final, port of discharge.

dernière limite d'heure de dépôt (Poste) (*f.*), latest time for posting.

dernière répartition (entre créanciers—société en liquidation) (*f.*), final dividend ; final distribution :
troisième et dernière répartition, third and final dividend (*or* distribution). *Cf.* première et unique répartition.

dernières nouvelles (*f.pl.*) *ou* **dernière heure** (*f.*) *ou* **dernière minute** (*f.*) (rubrique dans un journal), latest news ; stop press news ; stop press.

dérobade (*n.f.*), break (in prices) :
les stannifères n'ont pas cherché à réagir contre la dérobade de la semaine dernière (*f.pl.*), tins did not attempt to react from last week's break.

dérogation (*n.f.*), derogation :
révocabilité qui est une dérogation au droit commun (*f.*), revocability which is a derogation from (*or* to) (*or* of) the common law.

dérogatoire (*adj.*), derogatory :
clause dérogatoire au droit commun (*f.*), clause derogatory to the common law.

déroger (*v.i.*), to derogate :
déroger à la loi par des conventions contraires, to derogate from the law by agreements to the contrary.

déroutement (Navig.) (*n.m.*), change of route ; change of voyage ; change of route or of voyage ; deviation :
déroutement forcé ou volontaire, forced or voluntary change of route or of voyage.

dérouter (*v.t.*), to lead astray ; to upset :
le résultat a dérouté ses combinaisons, the result has upset his calculations.

désabonnement (*n.m.*), discontinuance of subscription.

désabonner (se) (*v.r.*), to discontinue to subscribe ; to discontinue one's subscription :

se désabonner à un journal, to discontinue one's subscription to a newspaper.

désaccord (*n.m.*), disagreement :
désaccord entre les experts, disagreement between experts.
être en désaccord, to disagree.

désapprovisionné, -e (à découvert) (Banq.) (*adj.*), overdrawn :
compte désapprovisionné (*m.*), overdrawn account.

désarmement (*n.m.*), laying up :
la période de désarmement, the laying up period.

désarmer (*v.t.*), to lay up :
navire désarmé au port pour réparations (*m.*), ship laid up in port for repairs.

désarrimage (rupture de charge) (*n.m.*), breaking bulk ; breaking the stowage.

désarrimage (dérangement accidentel de la cargaison) (*n.m.*), shifting (of cargo) :
bris à la suite de désarrimage (*m.*), breakage as a consequence of shifting.

désarrimer (rompre la charge) (*v.t.*), to break bulk ; to break the stowage.

désarrimer (déranger accidentellement) (*v.t.*), to shift :
le roulis présente le grave inconvénient de tendre à désarrimer les marchandises dans les cales et à les rejeter à un côté, rolling has the grave inconvenience of tending to shift the cargo in the holds and to throw it to one side.

se désarrimer (*v.r.*), to shift.

désastre (*n.m.*), disaster.

descendre (*ou* **descendre en masse**) **sur une banque,** to run on a bank.

descente (*n.f.*) *ou* **descente en masse** (sur une banque), run (on a bank).

déshabiller saint Pierre pour habiller saint Paul, to rob Peter to pay Paul.

déshypothéquer (*v.t.*), to free from mortgage ; to disencumber :
déshypothéquer une propriété, to free a property from mortgage ; to disencumber a property.

désignation (*n.f.*), description ; naming ; nomination ; appointment :
désignation des titres, description of securities.
désignation du contenu, description, nature, of contents :
désignation inexacte du contenu d'une caisse, incorrect description of contents of a case.
chargements assurés sans désignation du navire ni du capitaine (*m.pl.*), shipments insured without naming (*or* nomination) of the ship or master.

désigner (*v.t.*), to describe ; to name ; to nominate ; to appoint :
faculté de désigner le navire porteur de la marchandise (*f.*), option of naming (*or* nominating) the ship which is to carry the goods.
si un navire déterminé a été désigné, les marchandises ne peuvent être embarquées

que sur ce navire, if a certain ship has been named (or nominated) the goods can only be shipped on that vessel.

désigner un arbitre, to appoint an arbitrator.

désinfecter (v.t.), to disinfect.

désinfection (n.f.), disinfection :
désinfection de tout ou partie du navire, disinfection of whole or part of the ship.

désintéressement (n.m.), buying out ; satisfying ; paying off.

désintéresser (v.t.), to buy out ; to satisfy ; to pay off :
désintéresser un associé, to buy out a partner.
désintéresser un créancier, to satisfy, to pay off, a creditor.

despatch (n.), **despatch money.** Syn. de **dispatch, dispatch money.**

desserte (n.f.), service :
la desserte d'un port par les voies ferrées, des fleuves, ou des canaux, the service of a port by railroads, rivers, or canals.

desservir (faire le service de) (v.t.), to serve :
les principales lignes de navigation desservant l'Amérique du Sud (f.pl.), the principal shipping lines serving South America.
ligne de chemin de fer qui dessert le Centre et le Midi (f.), railway line which serves the Midlands and the South.

destinataire (pers.) (n.m. ou f.), consignee ; receiver ; recipient :
destinataire qui se présente à la gare pour enlever sa marchandise, consignee who calls at the station to collect his goods.

destinataire (Poste) (pers.) (n.m. ou f.), addressee :
si l'expéditeur d'un objet chargé veut recevoir un avis de réception du destinataire, if the sender of an insured article wishes to receive an advice of delivery to the addressee.

destinateur, -trice (pers.) (n.), sender ; consignor ; consigner.

destination (n.f.), destination :
conduire les marchandises au lieu de leur destination, le voyageur sain et sauf à destination, to convey the goods to the place of their destination, the passenger safe and sound to destination.
à destination de, bound for :
navire venant d'Anvers, à destination de Londres (m.), ship coming from Antwerp and bound for London.

destruction des rats (f.), destruction of rats.

détachement (n.m.), detachment ; cutting off ; tearing out.
détachement du coupon en bourse, going ex coupon. See example under **se détacher.**

détacher (v.t.), to detach ; to cut off ; to tear out :
coupon qui est détaché chaque fois les arrérages sont payés (m.), coupon which is cut off (or detached) each time the interest is paid.
détacher un chèque du carnet, un reçu d'un livre à souches, to tear a cheque out of the book, a receipt out of a counterfoil book.
quand une valeur détache un coupon, un droit de souscription, when a stock goes ex coupon, ex rights.

lorsqu'un coupon est détaché à la cote, le cours baisse normalement du montant de ce coupon, when a stock goes ex coupon, the price drops normally by the amount of the coupon.

dét. (abrév.), détaché, -e.

se détacher (en parlant des coupons, des droits) (v.r.). See example :
pour les valeurs au porteur les coupons se détachent à la cote (ou à la bourse) (ou en bourse) le jour de leur mise en paiement, c'est a partir de ce moment que les titres se négocient ex-coupon ou ex-dividende, (on certain exchanges) bearer securities go ex coupon on the day the dividend is payable : from this moment the securities are dealt in ex coupon or ex dividend.

détail (énumération) (n.m.), detail ; details ; particular ; particulars :
détails d'un compte, details, particulars, of an account.
paiements dont détail au livre de caisse (m.pl.), payments as per details (or as per particulars) in cash book.
en attendant réception de plus amples détails, pending receipt of further particulars.

détail (n.m.) ou **commerce de détail** (m.), retail ; retail trade :
faire le détail, to do a retail trade.
vente en détail (f.), retail sale.
See note under **gros** ou **gros commerce.**

détaillant, -e (pers.) (n.) ou **marchand au détail** (m.) ou **marchand détaillant** (m.), retailer ; retail dealer ; retail trader.

détailler (exposer avec détail) (v.t.), to detail :
détailler la liste des valeurs mobilières détenues en portefeuille, to detail the list of stocks and shares held in the box.
un état détaillé de compte, a detailed statement of account.

détailler (vendre en détail) (v.t.), to retail.

détaxe (n.f.), return, remission (partial or total), or reduction of customs duties, railway charges, postal charges, or the like, e.g., détaxes de distance des sucres des colonies françaises means remission of part of the duty on sugar exported from say French West Indian Colonies in view of the long distance away of these colonies from the home country, in order to allow it to compete with sugar produced nearer home which would bear smaller freight charges.
la réclamation pour détaxe doit être adressée au bureau de poste, the claim for return of charges should be sent to the post office.

détaxer (v.t.), to untax ; to return (or remit) the duties (or charges) on :
la douane détaxe les denrées destinées à l'exportation, the customs untax (or remit [or return] the duties on) commodities intended for export.
surtaxer les riches, détaxer les pauvres, to surtax the rich, to untax the poor.

détendre (se) (v.r.), to ease off. See example under **tendre (se).**

détenir (v.t.), to detain ; to hold :

détenir un gage, des actions, to hold a security, shares.
les titres détenus en garantie (*m.pl.*), the stocks held as security.
détente (des reports) (Bourse) (*n.f.*), easing off (of contangoes).
détenteur, -trice (pers.) (*n.*), holder:
détenteur d'un gage, d'un effet de commerce, d'une traite, d'un chèque, holder of a security, of a bill of exchange, of a draft, of a cheque. Cf. **porteur.**
détenteur d'obligations, debenture holder.
détenteur de titres, stockholder; scripholder.
détenteur de bonne foi, bona fide holder.
détenteur de mauvaise foi, mala fide holder.
détention (*n.f.*), detention; detainment; holding:
détention d'un navire, detention, detainment, of a ship.
détention de titres, holding stock.
détérioration (*n.f.*), deterioration; damage.
détourné, -e (*adj.*), circuitous:
remise détournée sur Londres (arbitrage composé) (*f.*), circuitous remittance on London.
détourné, -e (en parlant des effets, du papier de commerce) (*adj.*). *See under* effets sur place.
détournement (*n.m.*), misappropriation; misapplication; embezzlement; making away with; abstraction; diversion; fraudulent conversion (of funds).
détourner (*v.t.*), to misappropriate; to misapply; to embezzle; to make away with; to abstract; to divert:
détourner des fonds, to misappropriate, to misapply, to embezzle, to divert, money.
détourner des livres, to make away with, to abstract, books.
détresse (*n.f.*), distress:
navire en mer en détresse (*m.*), ship at sea in distress.
détroit (Géogr.) (*n.m.*), straits:
le détroit de Gibraltar, du Pas de Calais, the Straits of Gibraltar, of Dover.
dette (*n.f.*) (Ant.: *créance*), debt; indebtedness:
le montant de ma dette, the amount of my debt (*or* of my indebtedness).
dette active *ou simplement* dette (opp. à *dette passive*), book debt; debt; debt due to the trader; active debt.
dette caduque, statute barred debt; debt barred by limitation.
dette chirographaire, unsecured debt.
dette consolidée *ou* dette unifiée (opp. à *dette flottante*), consolidated debt; unified debt. See example under **flottant, -e.**
dette d'honneur, debt of honour.
dette de jeu, gambling debt; gaming debt.
dette de société, partnership debt.
dette flottante, floating debt. See example under **flottant, -e.**
dette fondée, funded debt.
dette hypothécaire, mortgage debt; debt on mortgage.
dette inexigible, debt not due:
dette inexigible présentement, debt not due at the present time.
dette liquide *ou* dette claire, liquid debt.

dette obligataire, debenture debt.
dette passive *ou simplement* dette, debt due by the trader; passive debt; debt.
dette privilégiée, preferential debt.
dette publique *ou* dette nationale, national debt; public debt.
dette simulée, simulated debt; fictitious debt.
dettes et créances, debts due by the trader and debts due to the trader; indebtedness:
il. faut distinguer les dettes d'après leur exigibilité et les créances d'après leur disponibilité et la manière dont elles sont garanties, debts due by the trader must be distinguished according to their repayability and debts due to the trader according to their liquidness and the way in which they are secured.
les dettes et créances internationales sont considérées comme la base principale des changes, international indebtedness is considered as the chief basis of the exchanges.
comme il est très rare que les créances et les dettes réciproques de deux pays se balancent exactement, les changes sont rarement au pair, as it is very rare that the mutual indebtedness of two countries exactly balances, the exchanges are rarely at par.
deuxième (*en abrégé* **2e**) (*adj.*), second; 2nd:
deuxième hypothèque (*f.*), second (*or* 2nd) mortgage.
deuxième de change (*f.*), second of exchange. See **première de change** for example.
dévalorisation (*n.f.*), devalorization:
la dévalorisation du franc, the devalorization of the franc.
dévaloriser (*v.t.*), to devalorize.
dévaluation (*n.f.*), devaluation:
dévaluation du franc-papier, devaluation of the paper franc.
devenir (*v.i.*), to become:
devenir propriétaire par achat ou échange, to become proprietor by purchase or exchange.
déviation (*n.f.*), deviation; change of route:
déviation du voyage envisagé par la police, deviation from the voyage contemplated by the policy.
dévier (*v.i.*), to deviate:
faculté de dévier par n'importe quelle route (*f.*), leave to deviate by any route.
navire qui dévie de sa route pour sauver des vies humaines ou des biens (*m.*), ship which deviates from her course to save lives or property.
devis de chargement (*m.*), stowage manifest.
devise (*n.f.*) *ou* **devise étrangère**, currency; foreign currency; bill (in foreign currency); foreign bill; exchange; foreign exchange:
chaque devise a deux cours: l'un pour le papier court, l'autre pour le papier long, each currency has two rates: one for short exchange, the other for long exchange.
effet en devise (*m.*), bill in currency (*or* in foreign currency).
tenir un compte en devise (*ou* en devise étrangère), to keep an account in currency (*or* in foreign currency).

devise étrangère *ou* devise sur l'étranger *ou simplement* devisé, foreign bill ; foreign exchange.

cours des devises à terme (*m.pl.*), forward exchange rates.

devises en report, foreign exchange on continuation account.

le compte Effets étrangers est débité des devises reçues, the account Foreign Bills is debited with the bills received.

Note :—The word *Devise* or *Devises* as a column heading in a foreign exchange quotation list, bill book, or the like, is rendered in English by the word *Centre* or *Place ;* thus *Devise : New-York, Centre* (or *Place*) : *New York ; Devises : Bruxelles, Lisbonne, Centre* (or *Place*) : *Brussels, Lisbon.*

dévoiler (*v.t.*), to disclose :
dévoiler les noms des parties contractantes, to disclose the names of the contracting parties.

devoir (*n.m.*), duty :
les devoirs des neutrés en cas de guerre, the duties of neutrals in case of war.

devoir (être tenu de payer) (*v.t.*), to owe :
devoir tant de francs, to owe so many francs.

devoir (*v.i.*), to owe ; to owe money :
devoir de tous côtés, to owe money all round.

diamantifères (*n.f.pl.*) *ou* **valeurs diamantifères** (*f.pl.*), diamonds ; diamond shares.

dictée (*n.f.*), dictation :
dictée de la réponse à une lettre, dictation of the reply to a letter.

dicter (*v.t.*), to dictate :
dicter une lettre à son secrétaire, un télégramme à une opératrice téléphonique, to dictate a letter to one's secretary, a telegram to a telephone operator.

dicteur, -euse (pers.) (*n.*), dictator.

différé, -e (*adj.*), deferred :
paiement différé (*m.*), deferred payment.
actions différées (*f.pl.*) (*Abrév. :* act. dif.), deferred shares ; deferred stock.

différence (*n.f.*), difference :
différence entre le débit et le crédit d'un compte, difference between the debit and the credit of an account.
rechercher une différence dans les écritures (*ou* dans les livres), to look for a difference in the books.
différence de caisse, difference in the cash ; cash difference.
différence de change, difference of (*or* on) exchange.
différence du vieux au neuf (Assce mar.), new for old :
les avaries communes seront remboursables sans déductions pour différence du vieux au neuf (*f.pl.*), general average payable without deductions new for old.

différence (Bourse) (*n.f.*), difference :
différences de bourse, stock exchange differences.
différence à payer ou à recevoir, difference to pay or to receive.

différend (*n.m.*), difference ; dispute.

différentiel, -elle (*adj.*), differential :

droits différentiels (Douanes) (*m.pl.*), differential duties.
tarif différentiel frappant les produits étrangers plus lourdement que les marchandises d'origine nationale (*m.*), differential tariff hitting foreign products more heavily than goods of national origin.

différer (*v.t.*), to defer ; to delay ; to put off ; to postpone ; to hold over :
différer un paiement, to defer, to put off, to hold over, a payment.

digraphie (*n.f.*) (opp. à *unigraphie*), double entry bookkeeping.

dilapider sa fortune, to squander one's fortune.

diminuer (*v.t.*), to diminish ; to decrease ; to lessen ; to reduce ; to lower :
diminuer les ressources d'un pays, to diminish the resources of a country.
diminuer sa dépense, to lessen, to reduce, one's expenses.
diminuer le taux officiel d'escompte, to reduce, to lower, the bank rate.

diminuer (*v.i.*), to diminish ; to decrease ; to lessen.

diminution (amoindrissement) (*n.f.*), diminution ; decrease ; lessening ; reduction ; lowering :
diminution de valeur, de prix, decrease of, decrease in, reduction in, lowering of, value, price.

diminution (rabais) (*n.f.*), reduction ; allowance ; rebate :
faire une diminution sur un compte, to make a reduction (*or* an allowance), to allow a rebate, on an account.

direct, -e (*adj.*), direct :
impôt direct (*m.*) *ou* contribution directe (*f.*), direct tax.

directeur, -trice (*adj.*), managing ; directing :
comité directeur (*m.*), managing committee.
puissance directrice (*f.*), directing power.
Cf. valeurs directrices.

directeur (pers.) (*n.m.*) (Abrév. : **Dᴿ**), manager ; master ; leader :
directeur d'une société (*ou* d'une compagnie), d'un syndicat de garantie, d'un syndicat de placement, manager of a company, of an underwriting syndicate, of a pool.
directeur de succursale, branch manager.
directeur des contributions directes, special commissioner of taxes.
directeur des postes, postmaster.
directeur général des Douanes, chairman of the Board of Customs.
directeur général des postes, postmaster general.
directeur intérimaire, acting manager.
directeur régional, district manager.
directeurs du marché (Bourse), leaders of the market. *Cf.* valeurs directrices.

directrice (pers.) (*n.f.*), manageress.

direction (emploi de directeur) (*n.f.*) (Abrév. : **dᴏⁿ**), management ; direction :
direction d'une affaire, du personnel, management of an affair, of the staff.

direction (bureau) (*n.f.*), manager's office.

direction de créanciers (faillite) (*f.*), committee of creditors ; committee of inspection.

directorat (*n.m.*), managership :
aspirer au directorat d'une banque, to aspire to the managership of a bank.
pendant son directorat, during his managership.

dirigeable (*n.m.*), dirigible ; airship.

dirigeants (du marché) (Bourse) (pers.) (*n.m.pl.*), leaders (of the market). *Cf.* valeurs dirigeantes.

diriger (*v.t.*), to manage ; to direct :
diriger une entreprise, to manage, to direct, an enterprise.

discordance (*n.f.*), disagreement :
discordance du journal et du grand livre, disagreement between the journal and the ledger.

discours (*n.m.*), speech ; address :
discours du président, chairman's speech.
prononcer un discours, to deliver a speech.

discrédit (*n.m.*), discredit.

discréditer (*v.t.*), to discredit.

discussion (*n.f.*), discussion :
après la discussion, M. le président met aux voix les résolutions, after the discussion, the chairman put the resolutions to the meeting.

discuter (*v.t.*), to discuss :
discuter un amendement, to discuss an amendment.
être discuté (-e) *ou* **se discuter** (*v.r.*), to be enquired for :
les valeurs d'étain sont plus discutées, sont un peu plus discutées, cette semaine (*f.pl.*), tin shares were more, were a little more, enquired for this week ; there were more, a few more, enquiries for tin shares this week.

disette (*n.f.*), want ; dearth ; scarcity ; lack :
nous apprenons maintenant que la pénurie devient disette, we learn now that scarcity is becoming want.
disette de fret, du numéraire, du titre, dearth, scarcity, of freight, of coin, of stock.

dispache (*n.f.*) *ou* **dispache d'avarie**, average adjustment ; average statement ; adjustment ; statement :
dispache d'avarie commune, general average adjustment (*or* statement).
les avaries communes et les frais de sauvetage se régleront suivant dispache étrangère, general average and salvage charges payable according to foreign statement (*or* adjustment).

dispacheur (pers.) (*n.m.*), average adjuster ; average stater ; average taker ; adjuster :
les dispacheurs font un rapport sur l'avarie ; c'est la dispache, the average adjusters make a report on the damage : this report is the average adjustment (*or* statement).

disparition (*n.f.*), disappearance :
disparition ou destruction totale du navire, disappearance or total destruction of the ship.

dispatch (jours sauvés) (*n.f.*), dispatch ; despatch ; days saved.

dispatch money (prime de rapidité) (*f.*) (Ant. : *surestaries*), dispatch money ; despatch money :
l'armateur bénéficie d'une prime appelée dispatch money lorsque la cargaison du navire est embarquée ou débarquée dans un délai

moindre que le délai de planche (*m.*), the shipowner benefits by a premium called dispatch money when the ship's cargo is loaded or unloaded in less time than laytime.

dispendieusement (*adv.*), expensively.

dispendieux, -euse (*adj.*), expensive ; costly.

dispenser (se) de payer une somme, to escape payment of a sum.

disponibilité (*n.f.*), availability ; disposableness ; power of disposal ; liquidness :
disponibilité des capitaux, availability of capital ; liquidness of assets.
il faut distinguer les dettes d'après leur exigibilité et les créances d'après leur disponibilité et la manière dont elles sont garanties, debts due by the trader must be distinguished according to their repayability and debts due to the trader according to their liquidness and the way in which they are secured.

disponibilités (fonds disponibles) (*n.f.pl.*), available funds (*or* assets) ; disposable funds ; liquid assets :
disponibilités en quête d'emploi, available funds in quest of employment.
les disponibilités forment ce qu'on appelle le fonds de roulement, the available assets form what is called working capital.
avoir de nombreuses disponibilités, to have plenty of available funds (*or* liquid assets).
le bilan fait ressortir que les disponibilités sont plus que suffisantes pour faire face aux exigibilités, the balance sheet shows that the liquid assets are more than sufficient to meet the current liabilities.

disponibilités en caisse et banque(s) (*f.pl.*) *ou* **disponible en caisse et banque(s)** (*m.*), cash in (*or* on) hand and at (*or* in) bank ; cash at bankers and in (*or* on) hand.

disponible (*adj.*), available ; disposable ; liquid :
fonds disponibles (*m.pl.*), available funds ; disposable funds.
valeurs disponibles (*f.pl.*) *ou* **disponible** (*n.m.*), liquid assets.

disponible (Bourse de marchandises) (*n.m.*) (Abrév. : **disp.** *ou* **dispon.**) (opp. à *livrable*), spot ; on the spot ; ex store ; ex warehouse :
cours : disponible tant ; livrable tant, prices : spot (*or* on the spot) so much ; shipment (*or* for shipment) so much.
cours du disponible (*m.*), spot price ; spot rate ; price ex store (*or* ex warehouse).
cote officielle du sucre disponible (*f.*), official quotation for spot sugar.

disponible (Opérations de change) (*n.m.*), spot :
acheter un disponible de 100 dollars, to buy 100 spot dollars.

disposé, -e (*p.p.*). See example :
les valeurs sud-africaines ont été mieux disposées cette semaine (*f.pl.*), South African shares were better in tone (*or* were more cheerful) this week.

disposer (faire ce qu'on veut de quelque chose) (*v.t.*), to dispose :
disposer de son bien, to dispose of one's property.

disposer (fournir ; tirer) (*v.t.*), to draw :
disposer un effet, un chèque sur son banquier,
to draw a bill, a cheque on one's banker.
disposer (prescrire) (*v.i.*), to provide :
la loi ne dispose que pour l'avenir, the law only
provides for the future.
disposer (fournir ; tirer) (*v.i.*), to draw :
le tireur d'une traite dispose sur le tiré, the
drawer of a draft draws on the drawee.
il n'est disposé sur les comptes de dépôts que
par des chèques, current accounts can only
be drawn on by cheques.
disposition (pouvoir de disposer) (*n.f.*), disposal ;
disposition :
mettre une somme d'argent à la disposition
d'un ami, to put a sum of money at the
disposal of a friend.
disposition de son bien, disposal of one's
property.
disposition (traite ; mandat) (*n.f.*), draft :
banque qui paie les dispositions faites sur elle
(*f.*), bank which pays the drafts made on it.
disposition à vue, sight draft ; draft at sight.
dispositions (d'une loi, d'une police d'assurance)
(*n.f.pl.*), provisions (of an act, of an insurance
policy).
dispositions (caractère) (*n.f.pl.*), tone :
les dispositions d'ensemble du marché, the
general tone of the market.
disque d'appel *ou simplement* **disque** (*n.m.*)
(Téléph. automatique), dial. Cf. **composer**
sur son disque d'appel.
dissection (*n.f.*), dissection ; analysis.
disséquer (*v.t.*), to dissect ; to analyze ; to analyse :
disséquer un compte, un bilan, to dissect, to
analyze, an account, a balance sheet.
dissident, -e (*adj.*), dissenting ; dissentient :
créanciers dissidents (*m.pl.*), dissentient
creditors.
dissimulation d'actif (faillite) (*f.*), concealment
of assets.
dissiper (*v.t.*), to squander :
dissiper sa fortune, to squander one's fortune.
dissolution (*n.f.*), dissolution :
dissolution d'une société, dissolution of a
company (*or* of a partnership). See note
under **social.**
dissoudre (*v.t.*), to dissolve. See example under
société.
distance (*n.f.*), distance :
distance à vol d'oiseau entre bureaux (Téléph.),
direct distance between exchanges.
distinct, -e (*adj.*), distinct ; separate :
chaque embarcation, radeau, ou allège sera
censé l'objet d'une assurance distincte, each
craft, raft, or lighter to be deemed the
subject of a separate insurance.
distraction (prélèvement d'argent) (*n.f.*), appropriation ; setting aside :
faire une distraction pour être distribuée aux
employés, to make an appropriation for
distribution among the employees ; to set
aside a sum for distribution among the staff.
distraction (détournement) (*n.f.*), abstraction ;
diversion ; embezzlement ; fraudulent conversion (of funds).

distraire (prélever) (*v.t.*), to appropriate ; to set
aside :
distraire tant sur ses économies, to appropriate,
to set aside, so much out of one's
savings.
distraire (séparer une partie d'un tout) (*v.t.*), to
take away ; to take off :
somme distraite d'une autre somme (*f.*),
amount taken away from another amount ;
sum taken off another sum.
distraire (détourner à son profit) (*v.t.*), to
abstract ; to divert ; to embezzle :
caissier infidèle qui a distrait des valeurs (*m.*),
dishonest cashier who has abstracted securities.
distraire de l'argent, to abstract, to divert, to
embezzle, money.
distribuable (*adj.*), distributable ; deliverable :
bénéfice distribuable (*m.*), distributable profit.
objet de correspondance distribuable par
exprès (*m.*), postal packet deliverable by
express.
distribuer (*v.t.*), to distribute ; to deliver :
distribuer un dividende aux actionnaires, to
distribute a dividend to the shareholders.
distribution (*n.f.*), distribution ; delivering ;
delivery :
distribution des richesses, distribution of
wealth.
distribution postale, postal delivery.
distribution des correspondances (Poste), delivery of letters.
distribution au guichet, à domicile, par exprès,
delivery to callers (*or* at post office), to place
of residence, by express.
distribution gratuite (Poste), free delivery.
zone de distribution gratuite des télégrammes
(*f.*), free delivery area of telegrams.
distribution par contribution (*f.*), distribution (to
creditors).
dito (*n.m. & adv.*) (Abrév. : D⁰ *ou* d⁰), ditto.
divers, -e (*adj.*), sundry ; general ; miscellaneous :
frais divers (*m.pl.*) *ou* dépenses diverses (*f.pl.*),
sundry expenses ; general expenses.
valeurs diverses (*f.pl.*) *ou simplement* diverses
ou divers, miscellaneous shares ; miscellaneous.
divers (*n.m.pl.*), sundries :
Divers à Divers (Comptab.), Sundries Dr To
Sundries.
Pertes et Profits à Divers (Comptab.), Profit
and Loss Dr To Sundries.
divertissement (détournement) (*n.m.*), diversion ;
abstraction ; misapplication ; embezzle-
ment ; fraudulent conversion :
divertissement de fonds, diversion, misapplication, embezzlement, fraudulent conversion, of funds.
dividend-warrant (*n.m.*), dividend warrant.
dividende (portion de bénéfice) (*n.m.*) (Abrév. :
div. *ou* **divid.** *ou* **divde** *ou* **d.**), dividend :
payer un dividende de 5 0/0, to pay a dividend
of 5% ; to pay a 5% dividend.
dividende sur l'exercice 19—, dividend for the
year 19—.

dividendes d'actions *ou* dividendes des actions, dividends on shares.

société payant (*ou* donnant) des dividendes (*f.*), dividend paying company.

dividende cumulatif, cumulative dividend.

dividende non cumulatif, non cumulative dividend.

dividende privilégié, preferential dividend; preferred dividend.

dividende fictif, fictitious dividend; sham dividend.

dividende prélevé sur le capital, dividend paid out of capital.

dividende intercalaire *ou* dividende statutaire, interest on capital during construction.

dividende intérimaire *ou* dividende provisoire, interim dividend. *Cf.* acompte de dividende.

dividende final, final dividend. *Cf.* solde de dividende.

dividende non réclamé, unclaimed dividend.

dividende (la) (Abrév.: **div.**). In French market news, *actions de dividende*, q.v., are often referred to as *la dividende*, i.e., l' (action de *understood*) dividende. *Cf. note under* actions de capital.

dividende (part dans le partage du fonds d'un failli) (*n.m.*), dividend.

dividende (Arith.) (*n.m.*), dividend.

dividende d'avarie (répartition d'avaries communes) (*m.*), average payment.

diviser (*v.t.*), to divide:

diviser une feuille en de nombreuses colonnes, to divide a sheet into numerous columns.

huit divisé par deux égale quatre (*Abrév.:* 8 : 2 = 4), eight divided by two equals four (*Abbrev.:* 8 ÷ 2 = 4).

capital social de 0 millions de francs, divisé en 0 000 actions de 0 000 francs chacune (*m.*), authorized capital of 0,000,000 francs, divided into 0,000 shares of 0,000 francs each.

se diviser (*v.r.*), to be divided:

les comptes se divisent en autant de catégories qu'il y a de natures d'opérations (*m.pl.*), accounts are divided into as many classes as there are kinds of transactions.

diviseur (*n.m.*), divisor.

divisibilité (*n.f.*), divisibility.

divisible (*adj.*), divisible; dividable.

division (*n.f.*), division:

division d'une propriété, division of a property.

division des nombres entiers, des fractions (Arith.), division of whole numbers, of fractions.

division du travail (Écon.), division of labour; division of employment.

divisionnaire (*adj.*), divisional:

monnaie divisionnaire (*f.*), divisional coins; fractional coins; subsidiary coins.

dock (Navig.) (*n.m.*), dock:

dock flottant, floating dock.

dock-entrepôt [**docks-entrepôts** *pl.*] *ou simplement* **dock** (*n.m.*), dock warehouse; warehouse; store:

dock frigorifique, cold store.

docker (pers.) (*n.m.*), docker.

document (*n.m.*), document:

documents de valeur, sans valeur intrinsèque (*ou* dépourvus de valeur intrinsèque), documents of value, without intrinsic value (*or* of no intrinsic value).

documents d'embarquement *ou* documents d'expédition *ou* documents maritimes, shipping documents.

documents qui accompagnent les marchandises, documents which accompany goods.

connaissement, police d'assurance, copies de factures, etc., constituent ce que l'on appelle les documents, bill of lading, insurance policy, copies of invoices, etc., constitute what are called the documents.

comptant contre documents (*m.*), cash against documents.

documents contre acceptation (*Abrév.:* D.A.), documents against (*or* on) acceptance.

documents contre paiement (*Abrév.:* D.P.), documents against (*or* on) payment.

documentaire (appuyé sur des documents) (*adj.*), documentary:

preuve documentaire (*f.*), documentary proof.

documentaire (accompagné de documents) (*adj.*), documentary; with documents attached:

traite documentaire (*f.*) *ou* traite accompagnée de documents (*f.*) *ou* effet documentaire (*m.*) *ou* effet accompagné par des documents (*m.*), documentary bill; document bill; draft with documents attached.

crédit documentaire (*m.*), documentary credit.

doit *ou* **Doit** (Abrév.: **Dt** *ou* **D.**) (Comptab.) (*n.m.*), debit; debit side; debtor; debtor side; Dr:

doit d'un compte, debit, debit side, debtor, debtor side, of an account.

doit et avoir *ou* Doit et Avoir, debit and credit; debtor and creditor; Dr and Cr:

le carnet de compte donne par Doit et Avoir la situation en banque du client, the pass book shows by Dr and Cr the customer's position at the bank.

Doit *ou* **Dt** (formule sur une facture de débit), Dr to; To; Bought of:

A.B. (*vendeur*) Doit Monsieur C. D. (*acheteur*), Mr C. D. (*buyer*) Dr to A. B. (*seller*); Mr C. D. To A. B.; Mr C. D. Bought of A. B.

doitage (*n.m.*), putting Dr and Cr.

doiter (un grand livre) (*v.t.*), to put (the words) Dr and Cr (on a ledger heading).

dollar (*n.m.*) (Abrév.: **$** *ou* **dol.** [**dols** *pl.*] *ou* **doll.** [**dolls** *pl.*]), dollar.

domaine (*n.m.*) *ou* **compte domaine** (*m.*) (poste de bilan), property; property account.

domicile (*n.m.*), domicile; residence; house; premises; trader's premises; address:

effet payable au domicile d'un tiers (*m.*), bill payable at the domicile of a third party.

domicile légal, legal domicile.

domicile réel, place of residence.

le nom et le domicile du destinataire, the consignee's name and address.

livraison à mon domicile (*f.*), delivery at my residence (*or* house) (*or* address) (*if one lives there*); delivery at my premises (*if made to one's place of business*).

livraison à domicile ou en gare (*f.*), delivery at residence (*or* at trader's premises) or at railway station, to be called for.

domiciliataire (pers.) (*n.m.*), paying agent.

domiciliation (*n.f.*), domiciliation.

domicilier (*v.t.*), to domicile :
domicilier un effet à une banque, to domicile a bill at a bank.

dommage (*n.m.*) *ou* **dommages** (*n.m.pl.*), damage ; injury ; loss :
dommages occasionnés par la pluie, par les rats, damage caused by rain, by rats.
constatation des pertes et dommages (*f.*), ascertainment of losses and damage.
dommages indirects, consequential damages.
dommages matériels d'incendie (Assce-incendie), loss or damage by fire.
une bonne année répare les dommages de deux mauvaises, a good year makes up for the losses of two bad ones.

dommageable (*adj.*), damageable :
conséquences dommageables (*f.pl.*), damageable consequences.

dommages-intérêts (*n.m.pl.*) *ou* **dommages et intérêts** (*m.pl.*) (Dr.), damages :
être tenu (-e) des dommages-intérêts, to be liable for damages.

don (*n.m.*) *ou* **donation** (*n.f.*), gift ; donation.

données (*n.f.pl.*), data.

donner (*v.t.*). See examples :
donner à bail, to lease :
donner une maison à bail, to lease a house.
donner assignation sur ses biens, to give a charge on one's property.
donner avis, to give notice :
donner avis un jour d'avance, to give notice a day beforehand.
donner immédiatement avis à la compagnie de tout sinistre qui parviendrait à sa connaissance, to give notice immediately to the company of any accident that may come to one's knowledge.
donner des conseils, des renseignements, to give advice, information.
donner des instructions à un avoué, to instruct, to give instructions to, an *avoué*.
donner en report (Bourse) (*v.t.*), to give on ; to give the rate on ; to lend :
titres donnés en report (*m.pl.*), stock given on ; stock lent.
donner la monnaie de tant de francs, to give change for so many francs.
donner le certain, to quote fixed (*or* certain) (*or* direct) exchange ; to quote in home currency :
donner l'incertain, to quote movable (*or* uncertain) (*or* indirect) (*or* variable) exchange ; to quote in foreign currency :
on dit qu'une place donne le certain à une autre lorsque c'est la monnaie de la première qui sert de terme de comparaison entre les deux places. Londres donne donc le certain à Paris, et réciproquement Paris lui donne l'incertain, one says that a place quotes the other fixed exchange when it is the money of the former which serves as term of com-

parison between the two places. Thus London quotes Paris fixed (*or* certain) (*or* direct) exchange (*or* quotes Paris in home currency) [viz. :—London quotes Paris so many francs to the £1 (basis), the £ being the home currency of London—exchange called *fixed* or *certain* because the basis (£1) does not vary], and conversely Paris quotes it movable (*or* uncertain) (*or* indirect) (*or* variable) exchange (*or* in foreign currency) [viz. :—so many francs to the £1 being to Paris a foreign currency—exchange called *movable*, or *uncertain*, or *variable*, because the rate, i.e., the number of francs to the £1 varies].

donner le signal de fin (Téléph.), to clear a connection.

donner lecture de, to read :
puis M. le président donne lecture du rapport, the chairman then read the report.

donner pouvoir à, to appoint as proxy :
je soussigné (*nom*) donne, par les présentes, pourvoir à M. A., et, à son défaut, à M. B., I the undersigned (*name*) hereby appoint as my proxy Mr A., and, failing him, Mr B.

donner reçu *ou* donner récépissé *ou* donner acquit *ou* donner quittance, to give a receipt ; to give receipt :
donner reçu à l'expéditeur, to give a receipt to the sender.

donner quittance des paiements faits, to give receipt for payments made.

donner rendez-vous (*ou* un rendez-vous) à quelqu'un, to make an appointment with someone.

se donner rendez-vous, to make an appointment (to agree to meet each other).

donner sa démission, to tender, to send in, to give in, to hand in, one's resignation.

donner son aval à un effet, to guarantee, to back, a bill.

donner un ordre au cours moyen, to give an order at middle price.

donner un poste à un navire, to berth a ship.

donner une compensation (Bourse), to have made up.

donner une moyenne de, to give an average of ; to average :
total de tant de millions de francs pour tant de prêts, ce qui donne une moyenne d'environ tant par prêt (*m.*), total of so many loans, which gives an average of (*or* which averages) about so much per loan.

le carnet de compte donne la situation en banque du client, the pass book shows the customer's position at the bank.

à un cours donné, at a given price.

société donnant des dividendes (*f.*), dividend paying company.

donneur à la grosse (pers.) (*m.*), lender on bottomry or respondentia.

donneur d'aval (d'un effet de commerce) (pers.) (*m.*), guarantor, surety, guarantee, backer (of a bill of exchange).

donneur d'option *ou* **donneur de stellage** (Bourse) (*m.*), taker for a put and call.

donneur d'ordre (pers.) (*m.*), principal:
donneur d'ordre et commissionnaire, principal and agent.
l'agent de change est en droit d'exiger que son donneur d'ordre lui remette, avant toute négociation, les effets à négocier ou les fonds destinés à acquitter le montant de la négociation (*m.*), the stockbroker is entitled to require his principal to hand him, before dealing, the stock to be dealt in or the money to pay for the amount of the deal.

donneur de caution (pers.) (*m.*), surety; security; guarantor; guarantee.

donneur de faculté de lever double (Bourse) (*m.*), taken for a call of more.

donneur de faculté de livrer double (Bourse) (*m.*), taken for a put of more.

dont (*pronom*). See examples:
paiements dont détail au livre de caisse (*m.pl.*), payments as per details (*or* as per particulars) in cash book.
dont quittance, receipt whereof is hereby acknowledged; which is hereby acknowledged to have been received.
dont un accompli, les autres restent (*ou* demeurent) sans valeur (*ou* les autres seront de nulle valeur) (connaissement), one of which being accomplished, the others to stand (*or* shall stand) void (*or* the others shall be void).

dont (Bourse) (*n.m.*) (Abrév.: **dt** *ou* **d**/ *ou* /) (opp. à *ou*), call; call option; buyer's option:
marché où on traite le dont et l'ou (*m.*), market on which calls and puts are dealt in.
acheter dont, to give for the call; to buy a call option.
spéculateur qui est acheteur de 100 actions X.Y.Z. à 403 dont 3 (*m.*), speculator who is giver of 3 francs (per share) for the call of 100 X.Y.Z. shares at 400.
vendre dont, to take for the call; to sell a call option.
le mot *dont* se remplace souvent par les lettres « dt » ou par la lettre « d » et une barre « / » ou même simplement par une barre « / » suivi de la prime; ainsi, dt 0,25 *ou* d/0,25 *ou* /0,25, the word *dont* (in French) is often replaced by the letters " dt " or by the letter " d " and a stroke " / " or even simply by a stroke " / " followed by the option rate; thus, dt 0,25 *or* d/0,25 *or* /0,25 (dt *or* d/ *or* / = option rate; 0,25 = 25 centimes).
Abbreviated examples of French call option orders:—A/. 12 000 3% français à 84,60/0,25 fin juillet = Give 25 centimes (*per 3 francs of rente*) for the call of 12,000 French 3 per cents at 84 francs 60 centimes for end July account. (*See* **rente** *for explanation of how rentes are dealt in.*)
Le 3/8: A/. 50 Rio d/40 fr. au 15/8 mx = Le 3 août: Achetez 50 Rio dont 40 francs, au 15 courant, au mieux = 3rd August (*date of order*): Give 40 francs (per share) for the call of 50 Rio Tintos, for mid August account, at best.

Note further :—
dont un *ou* dont 1f. *ou* dont 20 sous = option rate 1 franc.
dont 10 sous = option rate 50 centimes.
,,   5 sous = ,,   ,,   25 ,,
,,   1 sou = ,,   ,,   5 ,,
,,   2 liards = ,,   ,, $2\frac{1}{2}$,,
See also full explanation of option dealing setting out differences between French and English practice, under **prime.**

doré (-e) sur tranche, gilt-edged:
papier doré sur tranche (effets de commerce) (*m.*), gilt-edged paper.

dormant, -e (*adj.*), dormant:
comptes dormants (*m.pl.*), dormant accounts.

dos (*n.m.*), back:
dos d'une lettre de change, d'un titre, back of a bill of exchange, of a certificate.
comme son nom l'indique, l'endossement se met au dos de l'effet, as its name indicates, the endorsement is put on the back of the bill.

dossier (*n.m.*), dossier; bundle (of papers).

dossier (d'une procédure) (Dr.) (*n.m.*), brief; dossier.

dotation (*n.f.*), endowment; appropriation:
dotation à la réserve, appropriation to the reserve.

doter (*v.t.*), to endow; to appropriate to:
entreprises puissantes dotées de larges moyens de trésorerie (*f.pl.*), powerful concerns endowed with ample financial means.
doter un fonds spécial pour amortissements d'une somme de tant de francs, to appropriate to a special fund for depreciation a sum of so many francs.

douane (*n.f.*) *ou* **douanes** (*n.f.pl.*) (administration) (Abrév.: **dne**), customs.

douane (lieux où sont perçus les droits) (*n.f.*), customs; custom house:
déposer un manifeste en douane, to lodge a manifest with (*or* at) the customs (*or* at the custom house).

douane (droits de douane) (*n.f.*), customs; customs duty; customs duties:
marchandises qui ne payent pas de douane (*f.pl.*), goods which do not pay customs (*or* customs duty) (*or* customs duties).

douanier, -ère (*adj.*), customs (*used as adj.*):
union douanière (*f.*), customs union.

douanier (pers.) (*n.m.*), customs officer; officer of custom:
douanier convoyeur, train customs officer (i.e., a customs officer travelling on the train in the interests of the service).

double (*adj.*), double:
tenir des livres en partie double, to keep books by double entry.
double assurance (*f.*), double insurance.
doubles colonnes (*f.pl.*), double columns.
double emploi (*m.*), duplication; amount entered twice:
s'assurer qu'il n'y a ni omission ni double emploi dans l'enregistrement des articles, to ascertain that there is neither omission

nor duplication (*or* nor amount entered twice) in the entering up of the items. *Cf.* faire double emploi.

double étalon (étalon monétaire), double standard.

double fret (*m.*), double freight.

double prime (Bourse) (*f.*), double option; put and call; put and call option.

double (*adv.*), double:

payer double, to pay double.

double (*adv.*) *ou* **en double** *ou* **en double exemplaire**, in duplicate:

fait double (*ou* fait en double) à Paris le 1ᵉʳ juin 19—, done (*or* made) in duplicate at Paris, the 1st June 19—.

dresser un acte en double *ou* en double exemplaire, to draw up a deed in duplicate.

double (copie) (*n.m.*), duplicate; counterpart:

double d'un acte, duplicate, counterpart, of a deed.

doublé (*n.m.*) *ou* **doublure** (*n.f.*) (Bourse), option to double:

doublé à la baisse *ou* doublure à la baisse, put of more; put o' more; seller's option to double.

doublé à la hausse *ou* doublure à la hausse, call of more; call o' more; buyer's option to double.

doubler (*v.t.*), to double:

doubler sa mise, to double one's stake.

douteux, -euse (*adj.*), doubtful:

créance douteuse (*f.*), doubtful debt.

drainage (*n.m.*), drainage; drain:

drainage de l'or par l'étranger, drainage of gold by the foreigner.

drainage de capitaux, drain of money.

drainer (*v.t.*), to drain:

dès le début de la guerre, l'or a été chassé de la circulation et drainé vers l'encaisse des banques, from the beginning of the war, gold was driven out of circulation and drained towards the cash in hand of the banks.

drawback (remboursement à la sortie des droits perçus à l'entrée) (Douanes) (*n.m.*), drawback:

produits admis au bénéfice du drawback (*m.pl.*), commodities admitted to the benefit of drawback; drawback goods.

drawbacks à l'exportation des produits français, drawbacks on exportation of French products.

dressement (*n.m.*), drawing up; drawing; making out; preparation:

dressement d'une liste, drawing up, making out, preparation of, a list.

dresser (rédiger) (*v.t.*), to draw up; to draw; to make out; to prepare:

dresser un bilan, un contrat, les statuts d'une société, procès-verbal d'une réunion, to draw up, to draw, to prepare, a balance sheet, a contract, the articles of a company, the minutes of a meeting.

dresser l'inventaire de son portefeuille, de son actif et de son passif, to make out a list of one's investments, of one's assets and liabilities.

droit, -e (en parlant des monnaies) (*adj.*), standard; standard weight; full weight; of standard weight and fineness:

pièce droite (*f.*), standard coin; standard weight coin; full weight coin; coin of standard weight and fineness. See example under **pièce.**

monnaie droite (*f.*), standard money.

droit (des monnaies) (*n.m.*), standard weight, standard weight and fineness (of monies *or* of coins).

droit (faculté) (*n.m.*), right:

la liberté ne perd jamais ses droits, liberty never loses her rights.

droit à un bail, right to a lease.

droits civils, civil rights.

droit d'entrée, right of admission. See example under **qualité de membre.**

droit de préférence *ou* droit préférentiel, preferential right.

droit de rétention *ou* droit de gage, lien:

armateur qui a un droit de rétention (*ou* droit de gage) pour le paiement du fret (*m.*), owner who has a lien on the cargo for payment of the freight.

droit (*ou* droits) de souscription *ou* *simplement* droit *ou* droits (*Abrév.:* dr.), right of application; application rights; right; rights:

le droit de souscription s'exerce: 1⁰ par les porteurs d'actions anciennes; 2⁰ par les personnes qui, ne possédant pas d'actions anciennes, achètent des droits, application rights are exercised (1) by the holders of old shares; (2) by the persons who, not possessing old shares, buy rights.

avec droit (*Abrév.:* av.-dt) *ou* droit attaché (opp. à *ex-droit* *ou* *droit détaché*), with rights; cum rights; cum new.

ex-droit (*Abrév.:* ex-dr. *ou* ex-d. *ou* ex-dt) *ou* droit détaché, ex rights; ex new.

droit de vote, rights of voting; voting right; right to vote.

droits des créanciers, rights of creditors.

droits patrimoniaux d'auteur, copyright.

droit (*n.m.*) *ou* **droits** (*n.m.pl.*) (imposition; taxe), duty; duties; due; dues; fee; fees:

droit ad valorem [droits ad valorem *pl.*] (Douanes), ad valorem duty.

droit compensateur (Douanes), countervailing duty.

droit d'amarrage *ou* droit d'ancrage, berthage; anchorage.

droits d'arbitrage, arbitration fees.

droit d'assurance (Poste), insurance fee; fee for insurance.

droit d'avarie (contribution accessoire aux frais de navigation), average:

chapeau et droit d'avarie, primage and average.

droit d'enregistrement (taxe additionnelle) (Transports, etc.), booking fee.

droits d'enregistrement (immatriculation au greffe, ou analogue), registration duties; registration dues.

droit d'entrée (cotisation d'admission à une association), entrance fee.

droits d'entrée *ou* droits d'importation (Douanes), import duty.

droit d'industrie-clé, key industry duty.

droits de balisage *ou* droits de balise, beaconage.

droits de bassin *ou* droits de dock, dock dues; dockage.

droits de chancellerie, legation fees; consular fees.

droit de commission (des mandats-poste), poundage (on money orders).

droit de constitution, capital duty. *Note :*— In France, a *droit de timbre à la charge des sociétés* (stamp duty on companies) is payable in addition to the *droit de constitution* (*lit.* incorporation duty).

droit de douane *ou* droits de douane, customs duty; customs duties; customs.

droit de garde (Banq.), charge for safe custody. *See note under* dépôt libre *ou* dépôt en garde.

droit de garde (taxe de dépôt des bagages), cloak room fee.

droit de garde *ou* droit de magasinage (Douanes), rent on goods deposited in King's warehouse. *Cf.* dépôt de douane *and* **mise en dépôt.**

droits de mutation (mutations entre vifs), transfer duty; conveyance duty.

droits de mutation (mutations par décès), succession duty; succession tax.

droits de navigation, navigation dues.

droit de péage, toll.

droits de phare *ou* droits de feux et fanaux, light dues.

droits de pilotage, pilotage dues; pilotage.

droit de police (Assce), policy duty.

droits de port, port dues; harbour dues.

droits de quai, wharf dues; wharfage.

droit de recommandation (Poste), registration fee; fee for registration.

droit de régie, excise duty :
 boissons et autres marchandises sujettes aux droits de régie (*f.pl.*), liquors and other goods liable to excise duties.

droits de sauvegarde, safeguarding duties.

droit de signature, indemnity of one half per cent of the sum insured, claimable by French underwriters on cancelment of a policy of insurance.

droits de sortie *ou* droits d'exportation, export duty.

droit de stationnement (Ch. de f.), demurrage charge; demurrage (for detention or non use of vehicles).

droit de statistique, statistical tax (In France, a customs tax to cover the cost of preparing Government statistics of trade).

droit de timbre, stamp duty.

droit de timbre à quittance, receipt stamp duty.

droit de tonnage, tonnage duty; tonnage.

droit de transmission *ou* droit de transfert, transfer duty.

Note :—In France, the *droit de transmission* on registered securities is charged on the amount of the consideration for sale. On bearer securities the duty is leviable annually on the basis of the amounts distributed as dividend or interest. The annual duty is calculated by means of a percentage on the basis of the average price of the stock during the preceding year. The company paying the dividend or interest deducts the duty paid from the value of the coupon (unless paid *demi-net*, q.v.), and accounts for the duty in a total amount to the revenue authorities.

It will be seen that this *droit de transmission* on bearer securities is payable whether the stock changes hands or not, and is therefore not a *transfer duty* proper, but is of the nature of an additional income tax. Added to this is the fact that the tax is cumulative, so that a company not paying dividends for some years might see its first dividend entirely wiped out by arrears of tax. A purely speculative share never paying a dividend would not have to pay the tax at all.

droit de visite, inspection fee; survey fee.

droit fiscal, revenue duty.

droit fixe (droit d'enregistrement), fixed duty.

droits McKenna, McKenna duties.

droit plein, full duty.

droit prohibitif, prohibitive duty :
 les droits sont prohibitifs quand leur quotité est telle qu'ils rendent l'importation impossible, duties are prohibitive when their amount is such that they render importation impossible.

droit proportionnel (droit d'enregistrement), ad valorem duty.

droit protecteur, protective duty :
 les droits protecteurs ont, pour but principal, de défendre la production nationale contre la concurrence étrangère, the principal object of protective duties is to secure national production against foreign competition.

droit spécifique (Douanes), specific duty.

droit (ensemble des lois) (*n.m.*), law :
 droit civil *ou* droit privé, civil law; private law.
 droit commercial, commercial law; law merchant.
 droit commun, common law.
 droit de l'avarie commune *ou* droit des avaries communes, law of general average.
 droit français, French law.
 droit international *ou* droit des gens, international law; law of nations.
 droit international privé, private international law; international private law.
 droit international public, public international law.
 droit maritime, maritime law; shipping law.
 droit national, national law.
 droit public, public law.

droiture (en), directly; direct; straight :
 importation en droiture (*f.*), direct importation (i.e., from a foreign port to a home port, the ship not calling at intermediate port or ports).

produits qui arrivent en droiture de Buenos-Ayres (*m.pl.*), produce which arrives directly (*or* direct) (*or* straight) from Buenos Ayres.

dû, due [dus, dues *pl.*] (échu) (*p.p.* & *adj.*), due; owing :
aucun fret n'est dû pour les augmentations de poids résultant d'avaries de mer (*m.*), no freight is due on any increase in weight resulting from sea damage.
décompte des intérêts dus (*m.*), working out the interest due.
toutes primes échues, dues par l'assuré (*f.pl.*), all outstanding premiums, due by the insured ; all premiums due, owing by the insured.

dû, due (attribuable) (*adj.*), due; attributable; ascribable :
inéxecution due à la force majeure (*f.*), non performance due to force majeure.

dû, due (régulier) (*adj.*), due; proper :
traduction en due forme (*f.*), translation in due (*or* proper) form.

dû (*n.m.*), due :
réclamer sou dû, to claim one's due.

ducroire (convention) (*n.m.*), del credere :
les agents de change sont ducroire, c'est-à-dire responsables de la livraison des titres à l'acheteur en cas de défaillance du vendeur, et du paiement au vendeur en cas de défaillance de l'acheteur (*m.pl.*), stockbrokers are del credere, that is to say, responsible for delivery of the stock to the buyer in case of default of the seller, and for payment to the seller in case of default of the buyer.

ducroire (prime) (*n.m.*), del credere commission.

ducroire (commissionnaire) (pers.) (*n.m.*), del credere agent.

dûment (*adv.*), duly; properly :
connaissement dûment timbré, dûment accompli (*m.*), bill of lading duly stamped, duly accomplished.

dumping (*n.m.*), dumping :
le dumping consiste en établissant, pour le même produit, deux prix ou deux échelles de prix : un prix relativement élevé sur le marché intérieur ; des prix plus bas, variables suivant les cas, sur les marchés extérieurs, dumping consists in establishing, for the same commodity, two prices or two scales of prices : one price relatively high on the home market ; lower prices, variable according to circumstances, on foreign markets.

duplicata [duplicata *pl.*] (*n.m.*), duplicate :
duplicata de change, duplicate of exchange.
duplicata de la lettre de voiture, duplicate of the consignment note ; duplicate consignment note.
duplicata de quittance, de facture, duplicate receipt, invoice.
le copie de lettres est un registre exclusivement constitué par des duplicata, the letter book is a register formed exclusively of duplicates.

en duplicata *ou* **par duplicata,** in duplicate :
dresser un acte en duplicata *ou* rédiger un acte par duplicata, to draw up a deed in duplicate.

duplicateur (*n.m.*), duplicator ; duplicating machine :
duplicateur à plat, flat duplicating machine.
duplicateur au stencil, stencil duplicator.
duplicateur rotatif, rotary duplicating machine.

dur (-e) à la vente (être), to be hard to sell :
cette marchandise est dure à la vente, these goods are hard to sell.

durée (*n.f.*), duration ; term :
durée d'un bail, term, duration, of a lease.
police qui exprime la durée pour laquelle elle est souscrite (*f.*), policy which expresses the term for which it is written.

E

eau (*n.f.*) *ou* **eaux** (*n.f.pl.*), water ; waters :
réexpédition par fer ou eau à destination de l'intérieur (*f.*), reforwarding by rail or water to inland destination.
eaux à marée, tidal water.
eau de mer *ou* eaux marines, sea water.
eau douce, fresh water.
eau profonde, deep water :
canal maritime en eau profonde (*m.*), deep-water ship canal.
eaux intérieures, inland waters.
eaux lui servant d'accès, waters leading thereto :
navire naufragé dans un port ou les eaux lui servant d'accès (*m.*), ship wrecked in a port or the waters leading thereto.

eaux territoriales, territorial waters :
navire saisi dans les eaux territoriales françaises (*m.*), ship seized in French territorial waters.

ébranler (*v.t.*), to shake :
ébranler la confiance du public dans la sécurité de la circulation fiduciaire, to shake the confidence of the public in the security of the paper currency.

écart (variation) (*n.m.*), difference :
écarts de prix, des taux, differences in price, in rates.
écart entre le prix de revient et le prix de vente, difference between the cost price and the selling price.
écart entre le cours acheteur et le cours vendeur,

difference between buying price and selling
price ; turn of the market.

écart (*n.m.*) *ou* **écart de prime** (Bourse), écart
(difference between the prices for firm stock
and option stock).

écarter (s') (*v.r.*), to deviate :
navire qui s'écarte de sa route pour sauver
des vies humaines ou des biens (*m.*), ship
which deviates from her course to save lives
or property.

échange (troc) (*n.m.*), exchange ; barter :
le commerce est fondé sur l'échange, commerce
is founded on exchange.
commerce d'échange (*m.*), trade by barter (*or*
by exchange).
l'échange d'un objet contre un autre, des billets
contre espèces, the exchange of one article
for another, of notes for coin.
échange de correspondance, de ratifications,
exchange of correspondence, of ratifications.
échange d'observations, exchange of remarks ;
discussion :
après échange d'observations, et personne
ne demandant plus la parole, M. le président
met aux voix les résolutions suivantes,
after discussion, and there being no further
questions, the chairman put the following
resolutions to the meeting.

échangeable (*adj.*), exchangeable :
billet de banque échangeable contre de l'or
(*m.*), bank note exchangeable for gold.

échanger (*v.t.*), to exchange ; to barter :
échanger une valeur contre une autre, des
actions privilégiées contre des actions
ordinaires, to exchange one security for
another, preference shares for ordinary
shares.
la correspondance échangée entre les parties,
the correspondence exchanged between the
parties.

s'échanger (*v.r.*), to be exchanged ; to exchange ;
to change hands :
les deux monnaies doivent s'échanger au pair,
the two moneys should be exchanged at
par.
l'action X. s'échange à 2 560 *ou* on échange
l'action X. à 2 560, X. shares changed
hands (*or* exchanged) at 2,560 francs.

échangiste (*n.m.*) *ou* **échangeur, -euse** (pers.),
exchanger.

échantillon (*n.m.*), sample :
échantillon cacheté, sealed sample.
échantillon de valeur *ou* échantillon de prix,
sample of value.
échantillons sans valeur marchande, samples
of no commercial value (*or* without saleable
value).
échantillons des voyageurs de commerce,
commercial travellers' samples.

échantillonnage (*n.m.*), sampling.

échantillonner (*v.t.*), to sample :
les marchandises passibles de droits peuvent
être échantillonnées en vue des transactions
commerciales ; les échantillons sont soumis
aux droits lors de leur enlèvement de
l'entrepôt, dutiable goods can be sampled

with a view to commercial transactions ;
the samples are subject to duty when being
removed from the warehouse.

échantillonneur (pers.) (*n.m.*), sampler.

échapper (*v.i.*), to escape :
échapper à la poursuite de l'ennemi ou des
pirates, to escape (*or* to escape from) the
pursuit of the enemy or pirates.
échapper au paiement d'une somme, to escape
payment of a sum.

échauffement de la cargaison (*m.*), heating of cargo.

échéable *ou* **échéant, -e** (*adj.*), falling due ; due ;
payable :
billet échéable à telle date (*m.*), bill falling due
(*or* bill due) (*or* bill payable) on such a date.

échéance (expiration) (*n.f.*), expiration ; expiry :
date d'échéance de location (*f.*), date of
expiration of tenancy.
échéance d'un marché à prime (Bourse),
expiration of an option.
à son échéance, la présente police se
renouvellera pour une année entière, on
expiry, this policy will be renewed for a full
year.

échéance (date d'exigibilité) (*n.f.*), due date ;
date payable ; date :
échéance d'un coupon, due date of a coupon ;
date a coupon is payable.
obligations remboursables à échéances fixes
(*f.pl.*), debentures redeemable at fixed dates.

échéance (date d'entrée en valeur d'intérêts)
(*n.f.*), value ; value date ; as at. See syn.
valeur for example.

échéance (époque à laquelle le paiement d'un effet
de commerce doit être effectué) (*n.f.*),
maturity ; due date ; date :
l'effet sera payé à l'échéance, à la date de son
échéance (*m.*), the bill will be paid at
maturity, at its maturity date.
billet dont l'échéance tombe un jour férié
(*m.*), bill of which the due date falls on a non
business day.
effets payables à des échéances déterminées
(*m.pl.*), bills payable at fixed dates.
échéance moyenne *ou* échéance commune,
average due date ; mean due date.
papier à échéance (*m.*), bills to mature.
effet à longue échéance (*m.*), long dated bill ;
long bill.
bons à échéance rapprochée (*m.pl.*), shortly
maturing bonds.

échéance (terme d'échéance ; délai qui s'écoule
entre la date de l'engagement et son
exigibilité) (*n.f.*), tenor ; term ; currency ;
time of payment :
l'échéance de la lettre de change est 3 mois
de vue, the tenor (*or* the term) (*or* the
currency) (*or* the time of payment) of the
bill of exchange is 3 months after sight.
il ne sera admis à l'escompte aucun **effet d'une**
échéance de moins de cinq jours, no bill of
less than five days' tenor (*or* currency) will
be discounted.

échéance (billet) (*n.f.*), bill ; draft ; note :
faire face à une échéance, payer des échéances,
to meet a bill, to pay bills.

échéance à terme, time bill; time draft; time note.

échéancier (*n.m.*), diary (any book for recording in order of due date payments to be made or amounts to be collected).

échéancier (d'effets de commerce) (*n.m.*), bill diary.

échelle (*n.f.*), scale:
échelle mobile des salaires, sliding wage scale.

échelle (escale) (Navig.) (*n.f.*), call; calling:
(See **escale**, synonymous with *échelle* in this sense, for complete list of translations and examples. *échelle* is not very often used, *escale* being the commoner word.)
échelle directe, direct call; forward call.
échelle rétrograde, indirect call; backward call; call behind the named port.

échelles du Levant (*f.pl.*), Levantine ports.

échelon (Cotation en bourse) (*n.m.*), step:
la cotation se fait habituellement par échelons ou multiples de 0,25 pour les titres au-dessous de 100 francs, quotation is usually made by steps or multiples of 25 centimes for shares under 100 francs.

échelonnement (*n.m.*), spreading.

échelonner (*v.t.*), to spread:
échelonner une souscription en plusieurs verse-ments, to spread a subscription into several instalments.
versements échelonnés sur plusieurs mois (*m.pl.*), instalments (*or* calls) spread over several months.

échiquier (*n.m.*), exchequer.

échoir *ou* **écheoir** (*v.i.*), to fall due; to mature; to expire:
le billet échoit demain, the bill falls due (*or* matures) (*or* expires) to-morrow.
intérêts à échoir (*m.pl.*), accruing interest.

échouement (Navig.) (*n.m.*), stranding; ground-ing; running aground; running on shore; beaching:
échouement d'un navire sur les rochers, stranding of a ship on the rocks.
échouement fortuit *ou* échouement accidentel, accidental stranding.
échouement volontaire *ou* **échouage** (*n.m.*), voluntary stranding.
Note:—According to French maritime law, **échouement** may be (1) **simple** (not preventing the continuation of the voyage), or (2) **échouement avec bris** (stranding with break): this may be (*a*) **partiel** (in this case, after repairs the ship continues on her voyage), or (*b*) **absolu** (giving rise to abandonment). (See under **bris**.)

échouer (*v.t.*), to strand; to ground; to run aground (*or* on shore); to beach:
échouer un navire sur le rivage pour éviter la perte totale, to beach a ship in order to escape total loss.

échouer (*v.i.*), to strand; to ground; to run aground (*or* on shore); to beach:
navire qui échoua sur un écueil (*m.*), ship which stranded on a reef.
navire échoué (*m.*), stranded ship; vessel aground.

s'échouer (*v.r.*), to strand; to ground; to run aground (*or* on shore); to beach:
navire qui s'échoua sur une île (*m.*), ship which stranded on an island.

échouer (ne pas réussir) (*v.i.*), to fail:
échouer dans ses entreprises, to fail in one's enterprises.

échu, -e (*adj.*), due; outstanding; owing; matured:
l'acquittement des termes échus d'annuités (*m.*), the payment of instalments of annuities due (*or* outstanding).
toutes primes échues, dues par l'assuré (*f.pl.*), all premiums due, owing by the insured; all outstanding premiums, due by the insured.
frais échus (*m.pl.*) *ou* dépenses échues (*f.pl.*), outstanding expenses.
intérêts échus (*m.pl.*), outstanding interest; interest due.

éclairage des locaux (*m.*), lighting the premises.

éclatement (d'un incendie, de la guerre) (*n.m.*), breaking out (of a fire, of war).

éclatement (de chaudières, de conduites) (*n.m.*), bursting, explosion (of boilers, of pipes).

écluse (de canal ou de bassin) (*n.f.*), lock (canal or dock):
les dénivellations du terrain sont compensées par des écluses (*f.pl.*), drops in the ground are compensated by locks.

économat (d'une banque, ou établissement analogue) (*n.m.*), stationery department.

économe (*adj.*), economical; economic; thrifty; saving.

économe (d'une banque, ou établissement analogue) (pers.) (*n.m.*), stationery clerk.

économie (*n.f.*), economy; thrift; saving:
économie politique *ou simplement* économie, political economy; economics.
économie de temps procuré par l'emploi de l'avion, saving of time effected by the use of the aeroplane.

économies (argent amassé par l'épargne) (*n.f.pl.*), savings:
prendre sur ses économies, to draw on one's savings.

économique (qui a rapport à l'administration des dépenses) (*adj.*), economical; economic.

économique (qui coûte peu) (*adj.*), economical; economic; inexpensive; cheap.

économique (qui a rapport à l'économie politique) (*adj.*), economic:
le cours du change dépend, dans une large mesure, de la situation économique du pays, the rate of exchange depends, to a large extent, on the economic situation of the country.

économiquement (*adv.*), economically.

économiser (*v.t.*), to economize; to save:
économiser ses revenus, l'usage du numéraire, to economize one's income, the use of coin.
économiser le travail, to save labour.

économiste (pers.) (*n.m.*), economist.

écoulé (*adj.*) *ou* de **l'écoulé** (du mois dernier), ultimo. (*Cf.* exercice écoulé.)

écoulement (*n.m.*), placing; sale:

écoulement de produits indigènes sur les marchés étrangers, placing of home products on foreign markets.

écouler (*v.t.*), to place; to sell:
écouler des actions dans le public, to place shares with, to sell shares to, the public.

s'écouler (*v.r.*), to sell; to be sold; to be placed:
objets qui s'écoulent bien (*m.pl.*), articles which sell well.

écouteur (Téléph.) (*n.m.*), receiver:
décrocher, raccrocher, l'écouteur, to remove, to replace, the receiver.

écoutille (*n.f.*), hatch; hatchway:
la fermeture des écoutilles, battening down the hatches.

écrire (*v.t.*), to write; to write up:
écrire une lettre, to write a letter.
écrire très lisiblement, please write clearly.
écrire à la machine, to typewrite; to type:
écrire une lettre à la machine, to typewrite, to type, a letter.
écrire une note sur un agenda, to write, to make, a note in a diary.
employé qui écrit la comptabilité (*m.*), clerk who writes up the books (*or* the accounts).

écrit (*n.m.*), writing.
en écrit *ou* **par écrit** *ou* **à l'écrit** *ou* **écrit, -e,** in writing; written:
convention en écrit (*ou* par écrit) (*ou* à l'écrit) (*ou* écrite) (*f.*), agreement in writing; written agreement.
confirmation verbale ou écrite (*f.*), verbal or written confirmation.

écrit (convention écrite) (*n.m.*), written agreement; agreement in writing:
la nécessité d'un écrit en matière de vente de navire, the need of a written agreement when selling a ship.

écriture (*n.f.*), writing; handwriting; writing up:
écriture à la machine, typewriting; typing.
écriture courante, current handwriting.
écriture illisible, illegible writing.

écriture (Comptab.) (*n.f.*), entry: (See also **article.**)
les écritures faites sur le journal, the entries made in the journal.
écriture comptable, book entry.
écriture d'inventaire *ou* écriture de clôture, closing entry.
écriture d'ordre, suspense entry.
écriture d'ouverture, opening entry; starting entry.
écriture de banque, bank transfer (transfer from one customer's account to another, effected by means of instructions to the bank).
écriture de journal, journal entry.
écriture de redressement *ou* écriture rectificative, correcting entry.
écriture de virement *ou* écriture de contre-passement, transfer entry.
écriture inverse *ou* écriture de contre-passement, reverse entry; reversing entry; contra entry.

écritures (*n.f.pl.*) *ou* **écritures comptables,** accounts; books; records:
les écritures d'une banque, the accounts (*or* the books) (*or* the records) of a bank.
tenir les écritures d'une maison, to keep a firm's accounts (*or* a firm's books).
rechercher une différence dans les écritures, to look for a difference in the books.
falsification d'écritures comptables (*f.*), falsification of accounts.
bénéfices d'écritures (*m.pl.*) (opp. à *bénéfices réalisés*), book profits.

écu (*n.m.*), 5 franc piece (silver).

effacement de marques (*m.*), obliteration of marks.

effectif, -ive (*adj.*), effective; real; actual; in cash; in coin:
monnaie effective (*f.*), effective (*or* real) money.
avoir tant de francs effectifs dans sa caisse, to have so many francs in cash (*or* in coin) in one's cash.
valeur effective au moment de la perte (*f.*), actual value at the time of the loss.

effectivement (*adv.*), effectively; really; actually:
bénéfice effectivement réalisé (*m.*), profit actually realized.

effectuer (*v.t.*), to effect; to make; to execute:
effectuer un paiement, to effect, to make, a payment.
effectuer un transfert (de titres mobiliers), to execute a transfer.

s'effectuer (*v.r.*), to be effected; to be made; to be executed:
le paiement s'effectue comme suit, payment is made as follows.

effet (d'une assurance) (*n.m.*), attachment; on risk:
l'effet de l'assurance a cessé, the attachment of the insurance has ceased; the insurance has ceased to attach (*or* to be on risk).

effet (*n.m.*) *ou* **effet de commerce** *ou* **effet commercial,** bill; bill of exchange; exchange; bill or note (*see* Note 2 below); draft:
(*Note 1 :—bill of exchange* is the equivalent of *effet de commerce* in the general and legal senses of the term, and must be distinguished from the restricted meaning of the term, viz.: an acceptable draft, which in French is *lettre de change.*)
(*Note 2 :*—In France, a *billet à ordre* (promissory note) is an *effet de commerce.* In England, a *promissory note* is not a *bill of exchange,* hence the translation *bill or note* which is a very common expression in English, especially in text books.)
(*Note 3 :*—In France, a dock or warehouse warrant is also an *effet de commerce.*)
(*Note 4 :*—See also **papier.**)
effet à courte échéance *ou* effet à courts jours *ou* effet à courts-jours, short dated bill; short bill.
effets à l'escompte, à l'encaissement, bills for discount, for collection.
effet à longue échéance [effets à longues échéances *pl.*], long dated bill; long bill.

effet à payer (*Abrév.*: E. à P.), bill payable.
effet à recevoir (*Abrév.*: E. à R.), bill receivable.
effet à renouvellement, kite; windmill.
effet à vue, sight bill; draft at sight.
effet au pair. In France, bill on which no *change de place* (see this expression in vocabulary) is chargeable.
effet au porteur, bill payable to bearer.
effet avalisé, guaranteed bill; backed bill.
effet bancable, bankable bill. See note under **bancable**.
effets brûlants, hot bills; bills maturing in a few days; bills that have only a few days to run.
effets creux, house bills; pig on pork.
effet de finance, finance bill.
effet documentaire *ou* effet accompagné de (*ou* par des) documents (opp. à *effet libre*), documentary bill; document bill; bill with documents attached.
effet en devise, bill in foreign currency (or in currency).
effets en pension *ou* effets en (*ou* à la) nourrice, pawned bills; bills in pawn (bills lodged with a bank as collateral against advances and retired before maturity).
effets en souffrance (*ou* en suspens), bills in suspense; bills held over.
effet escomptable, discountable bill.
effets escomptés, bills discounted.
effet étranger *ou* effet sur l'étranger, foreign bill; foreign exchange.
effet impayé *ou* effet retourné (*ou* rendu) (*ou* renvoyé) impayé, dishonoured bill; bill dishonoured by non payment; bill returned dishonoured; unpaid bill.
effet innégociable *ou* effet incommerçable, unnegotiable bill.
effet libre, clean bill.
effet négociable *ou* effet commerçable, negotiable bill.
effet non accepté *ou* effet retourné (*ou* rendu) (*ou* renvoyé) faute d'acceptation *ou* effet retourné (*ou* rendu) (*ou* renvoyé) par défaut d'acceptation, dishonoured bill; bill dishonoured by non acceptance; bill returned dishonoured; unaccepted bill.
effet retourné *ou* effet rendu *ou* effet renvoyé, dishonoured bill; bill returned dishonoured.
effet sur l'intérieur, inland bill; home-trade bill.
effets sur place, town bills; local bills; bills payable in the same locality as that in which the collecting bank is situated: opposed to *effets sur le dehors* or *effets déplacés* or *déplacé* (*n.m.*) or *effets détournés*, that is, bills payable in other places, especially in small localities. The English equivalents, applied chiefly to cheques are as follows:— in London, *town*, *metropolitan*, and *country*; out of London:—*local*, *country*, and *London*.
effets (biens) (*n.m.pl.*), effects; property; estate; articles:
effets immobiliers, real property; real estate; realty; immovable effects; fixed property.

effets mobiliers *ou* effets personnels, personal effects; personal property; personal estate; movables; personals; personalty; movable effects.
effets personnels des voyageurs, des gens de mer, personal effects of passengers, of seamen.
effets servant à l'usage personnel du passager, articles for the personal use of the passenger.
effets (valeurs; titres) (*n.m.pl.*), securities; stocks; stock; stocks and shares:
effets au porteur, bearer securities; bearer stocks; bearer stock.
effets nominatifs, registered securities; registered stocks; registered stock.
effets publics, government securities; government stocks; public securities.
effleurer (Bourse) (*v.t.*), to touch:
cours qui n'a été qu'effleuré (*m.*), price which has only been touched.
effondrement (Bourse) (*n.m.*), slump:
effondrement des cours, slump in prices.
effondrer (s') (*v.r.*), to slump:
l'action X. s'effondre de 4 500 à 4 000, X. shares slumped from 4,500 to 4,000 francs.
effritement (des cours) (Bourse) (*n.m.*), crumbling (of prices).
effriter (s') (*v.r.*), to crumble.
égal, -e, -aux (*adj.*), equal:
colonnes présentant des totaux égaux (*f.pl.*), columns showing equal totals.
également (*adv.*), equally.
égaler (*v.t.*), to equal:
dix moins quatre égale six (*Abrév.*: 10−4=6), ten minus four equals six (*Abbrev.*: 10 − 4 = 6).
égalisation (*n.f.*), equalization.
égaliser (*v.t.*), to equalize:
égaliser les totaux, to equalize the totals.
égalité (*n.f.*), equality:
égalité de deux nombres, de voix pour une proposition, de traitement, equality of two numbers, of votes for a resolution, of treatment.
égaré, -e (*adj.*), mislaid; lost; miscarried.
égarement (*n.m.*), mislaying; loss; miscarriage.
égarer (*v.t.*), to mislay; to lose:
égarer des papiers, to mislay, to lose, papers.
s'égarer (*v.r.*), to be mislaid; to be lost; to miscarry.
élan (en parlant des cours de bourse) (*n.m.*), buoyancy.
élection (*n.f.*), election:
élection d'un président, de domicile, election of a president (*or* of a chairman), of domicile.
électrification (*n.f.*), electrification:
électrification d'un chemin de fer, electrification of a railway.
électrifier (*v.t.*), to electrify.
élévation (hausse) (*n.f.*), raising; rise; increase:
élévation des tarifs, du taux officiel d'escompte, raising, rise, of rates, of the bank rate.
élevé, -e (*adj.*), high:
emprunter à un taux d'intérêt élevé, to borrow at a high rate of interest.
par suite du prix élevé de l'argent, owing to the high price of money.

élever (hausser) (*v.t.*), to raise ; to increase :
armateur qui élève les taux des frets (*m.*),
shipowner who raises (or increases) freight
rates.

s'élever (*v.r.*), to rise ; to reach ; to amount
to ; to increase ; to arise :
le prix s'élevait à tant, the price rose to (or
reached) so much.
les bénéfices s'élèvent à 100 000 fr. (*m.pl.*),
the profits amount to 100,000 francs.
s'il s'élève des difficultés, if difficulties arise.

éligibilité (*n.f.*), eligibility.

éligible (*adj.*), eligible.

élimination (*n.f.*), elimination :
élimination d'erreurs, elimination of errors.

éliminer (*v.t.*), to eliminate.

élire (*v.t.*), to elect :
élire un administrateur, to elect a director.
élire domicile chez son notaire, to elect domicile
with one's notary.

éloigné (Bourse de marchandises) (*n.m.*) (opp. à
rapproché), distant position :
achats sur les éloignés par suite de la fermeté
des marchés des grains et des valeurs (*m.pl.*),
purchases on distant positions in consequence of the firmness of the grain and stock
markets.

émargement (*n.m.*), signature ; signing :
remettre un colis au destinataire contre
émargement au carnet de livraison, to deliver
a parcel to the addressee against signature
in the delivery book.

émarger le carnet, to sign the book (to append
one's signature or initials in a delivery book,
wages book or sheet, or the like, as acknowledgment of receipt).

emballage (*n.m.*), packing ; package :
emballage en caisse pleine, en caisse à claire-
voie, packing in close cases, in crates.
emballage extérieur, external packing.
emballage intérieur, internal packing.
emballage maritime *ou* emballage pour transport outre-mer, packing for shipment.
les marchandises sont livrables en caisses
d'origine ou tous autres emballages d'origine
(*f.pl.*), goods to be delivered in original
cases or any other original packages.

emballement à la hausse *ou simplement* **emballement** (des cours) (Bourse) (*n.m.*), boom (in
prices).

emballer (*v.t.*), to pack :
emballer des marchandises, to pack goods.

embarcadère (*n.m.*), landing ; landing place ;
landing platform ; wharf :
embarcadère flottant, landing stage ; floating
stage ; floating wharf ; float.

embarcation (*n.f.*), craft ; boat : (See also
bateau and **canot**.)
embarcations et allèges employées au chargement ou au déchargement des navires,
craft and lighters used in the loading or
unloading of ships.
les allèges sont des embarcations servant au
chargement et au déchargement de la
marchandise (*f.pl.*), lighters are craft used
for loading and unloading cargo.

les embarcations du bord, the ship's boats.
embarcation de sauvetage, lifeboat.

embargo (*n.m.*), embargo :
lever l'embargo sur un navire, to raise the
embargo on a ship.

embarquement (*n.m.*) (Abrév. : **emb.**) (Ant. :
débarquement), shipping ; shipment ;
embarking ; embarkation ; embarcation :
embarquement sur premier vapeur, sur
navire suivant, shipment on first steamer,
on following ship.
fret payable à destination suivant poids
déclaré à l'embarquement (*m.*), freight
payable at destination as per weight
declared on shipment.
on cote le sucre de Cuba, embarquement mars-
avril à 7 sh. 4 1/2d. caf. Royaume-Uni,
Cuban sugar quoted, for March-April shipment at 7s. 4½d. c.i.f. U.K.
embarquement de passagers, embarking
passengers.

embarquer (*v.t.*), to ship ; to embark :
embarquer la marchandise dans la période de
temps convenue, to ship the goods within
the agreed period of time.
embarqué (-e) en moins, short shipped :
quantité embarquée en moins (*f.*), amount
short shipped.

s'embarquer (*v.r.*), to embark ; to go on board ;
to sail ; to be shipped ; to be embarked.
la marchandise en vrac s'embarque généralement au moyen d'appareils spéciaux, goods
in bulk are generally embarked by means
of special apparatus.

embouchure (d'un fleuve) (*n.f.*), mouth (of a river).

embranchement particulier (Ch. de f.) (*m.*),
private siding.

émetteur, -trice (*adj.*), issuing :
le banquier émetteur, the issuing banker.
la société émettrice, the issuing company.

émetteur (pers.) (*n.m.*), issuer.

émetteur (*n.m.*) *ou* **émetteur de la filière** (pers.)
(Bourse de marchandises), first seller ;
deliverer.

émettre (*v.t.*), to issue ; to start :
émettre des billets de banque, un chèque,
des obligations pour une somme égale au
maximum des prêts, to issue bank notes,
a cheque, debentures for an amount equal
to the maximum of the loans.
émettre des actions au pair (*ou* au pair nominal)
(*ou* à leur valeur nominale), to issue shares
at par.
émettre des actions au-dessus du pair (*ou*
au-dessus du pair nominal) (*ou* au-dessus
de leur valeur nominale), to issue shares at
a premium.
émettre des actions au-dessous du pair (*ou*
au-dessous du pair nominal) (*ou* au-dessous
de leur valeur nominale), to issue shares
at a discount :
l'émission des actions au-dessous du pair
nominal serait illégale (*f.*), issuing shares at
a discount would be illegal.
actions émises contre espèces (*f.pl.*), shares
issued for cash.

actions émises dans le public (*f.pl.*), shares issued to the public.

émettre une filière (Bourse de marchandises), to start a string.

émeute (*n.f.*), riot.

émeutier, -ère (pers.) (*n.*), rioter.

émigrant, -e (pers.) (*n.*), emigrant.

émigration (*n.f.*), emigration.

émigrer (*v.i.*), to emigrate.

émission (*n.f.*), issue; issuing; coming out; starting:
émission de valeurs, de billets de banque, issue of securities, of bank notes.
les émissions sont publiques ou privées, issues are public or private.
opérations en actions à émission (Bourse) (*f.pl.*), dealings in shares for the coming out.
émission d'une filière (Bourse de marchandises), starting a string.

emmagasinage *ou* **emmagasinement** (*n.m.*), storing; storage; warehousing.

emmagasiner (*v.t.*), to store; to put into store; to warehouse.

emménagement (d'un navire) (*n.m.*), fitting; accommodation; appointments. See examples under syn. **aménagement**.

emménager (*v.t.*), to fit; to accommodate. See example under syn. **aménager**.

émolument (*n.m.*), emolument:
les traitements et autres émoluments (*m.pl.*), salaries and other emoluments.

empire (*n.m.*), empire:
empire d'outre-mer, oversea empire.

emplacement (sur une feuille de papier) (*n.m.*), space; room:
emplacement réservé aux mentions de service, space for service instructions.
au cas où l'emplacement réservé sur la feuille serait insuffisant pour l'inscription des mentions nécessaires, celles-ci peuvent être reportées au verso, if the space provided on the sheet is inadequate for entering (*or* if there is not room on the sheet to enter) the necessary particulars, they can be put on the back.
emplacement du timbre-poste, affix stamp here.

emplacement (poste de mouillage) (Navig.) (*n.m.*), berth; berthage:
emplacement de chargement, loading berth.

emplacement des machines (dans un navire) (*m.*), engine room space.

emploi (usage) (*n.m.*), employment; use:
emploi d'une somme d'argent, des capitaux dans la production, des capitaux en report, employment, use, of a sum of money, of capital in production, of money on contango.

emploi (occupation) (*n.m.*), employment; employ; situation; place; post; position; job; berth:
chercher de l'emploi, to look for a place; to seek employment.

employé (pers.) (*n.m.*), clerk; employee; employé; servant; assistant; man:
employé de banque, bank clerk.
employé de chemin de fer, railwayman; railway servant.

employé de la régie, exciseman.
employé de magasin, shop assistant.

employée (pers.) (*n.f.*), lady clerk; clerk; employee; assistant.

employer (*v.t.*), to employ; to use:
employer un commis, to employ a clerk.
code employé (*m.*), code used.

employer (Comptab.) (*v.t.*), to put; to enter:
employer une somme en recette, en dépense, to put, to enter, an amount in the receipts, in the expenditure.

employeur, -euse (pers.) (*n.*), employer; principal.

empocher (*v.t.*), to pocket:
navire abandonné en haute mer dans le but d'empocher une somme considérable (*m.*), ship abandoned on the high seas with the object of pocketing a considerable sum.

emprunt (obtention à titre de prêt) (*n.m.*), borrowing:
emprunt d'une somme d'argent, borrowing a sum of money.
toutes les opérations du banquier peuvent se résumer, en définitive, en emprunts et en prêts, all the transactions of the banker may be summed up, shortly, in borrowing and in lending.

emprunt (secours étranger) (*n.m.*), use; making use:
transport direct par terre sans emprunt de la mer (*m.*), direct transport by land without use of the sea.

emprunt (somme empruntée) (*n.m.*), loan: (Cf. **prêt**.)
emprunt à la grosse, bottomry or respondentia loan; loan on bottomry or respondentia; marine loan; maritime loan.
emprunts de colonies, colonial stocks.
emprunt de conversion, conversion loan.
emprunts de départements, county stocks.
emprunt de la Défense nationale, War loan.
emprunt de réparation, reparation loan.
emprunt de rescision, rescission loan.
emprunts de villes, corporation stocks; municipal loans.
emprunt extérieur, external loan; foreign loan.
emprunt forcé, forced loan.
emprunt funding *ou* emprunt de consolidation, funding loan.
emprunt garanti *ou* emprunt gagé, secured loan.
emprunt hypothécaire, loan on mortgage; mortgage loan.
emprunt intérieur, internal loan.
emprunt national, national loan.
emprunt-obligations (*n.m.*) *ou* emprunt obligataire, loan on debentures; debenture loan.
emprunt public, public loan.
emprunt remboursable sur demande, loan repayable on demand.
emprunt sur titres, loan on stock.

emprunter (obtenir à titre de prêt) (*v.t.*), to borrow:
emprunter de l'argent à gros intérêt, sur (*ou* à) hypothèque, sur nantissement, to borrow money at high interest, on mortgage, on security (*or* on collateral).
emprunter des titres (Bourse), to borrow stock.

emprunter (s'aider d'un secours étranger) (*v.t.*), to make use of ; to use :
les navires qui empruntent le canal de Suez (*m.pl.*), the ships which make use of (*or* which use) the Suez canal.
remonter la Seine au lieu d'emprunter la voie ferrée, to go up the Seine instead of using (*or* making use of) the railway.

emprunteur, -euse (*adj.*), borrowing :
État emprunteur (*m.*), borrowing State.
société emprunteuse (*f.*), borrowing company.

emprunteur, -euse (pers.) (*n.*), borrower :
emprunteur à la grosse, borrower on bottomry or respondentia.

En Banque *or* **En Coulisse.** *See note under* marché des valeurs.

en bloc, en bloc ; in one lot :
opérations inscrites en bloc à la fin de la journée (*f.pl.*), transactions entered en bloc at the end of the day.

En Bourse (rubrique de journal), Round the House ; Round the Markets ; Market News.

en charge. See under **charge.**

en dedans ou en dehors de la route ordinaire, in or out of the customary route.

en fûts *ou* **en barils** (se dit des huiles) (opp. à *nu, -e*), in barrels.

en gare (gare restante), at railway station, to be called for ; to be called for :
livraison en gare (*f.*), delivery at railway station, to be called for.

en mer, at sea :
navire en mer (*m.*), ship at sea.

en tambours (se dit des huiles) (opp. à *nu, -e*), in drums.

en-tête [en-têtes *pl.*] (*n.m.*), heading ; head :
en-tête de facture, bill head ; bill heading.
en-tête de grand livre, ledger heading.
en-tête de lettre, letter heading.

en une fois, en une seule fois, en une ou plusieurs fois. See under **fois.**

enarrher (*v.t.*), to leave a deposit with ; to give earnest money to ; to pay a deposit to :
enarrher son propriétaire, to leave a deposit with one's landlord.

enarrheur (pers.) (*n.m.*), depositor.

encaissable (*adj.*), cashable ; encashable ; collectable ; collectible :
coupons encaissables à Paris (*m.pl.*), coupons collectable in Paris.

encaisse (*n.f.*), cash in hand ; cash balance ; cash ; till money :
l'encaisse d'une banque, the cash in hand of a bank.
une encaisse de tant de francs, cash in hand, a cash balance, cash, of so many francs.
s'il y a excédent ou déficit dans l'encaisse, if there is an over or a short in the cash (*or* in the till money).
encaisse métallique *ou* encaisse or et argent (Banq.), cash and bullion in hand ; gold and silver coin and bullion :
la banque est tenue d'avoir une encaisse métallique égale au tiers du montant de ses billets et de ses autres engagements à vue,

the bank is bound to have cash and bullion in hand (*or* to have gold and silver coin and bullion) equal to one third of the amount of its notes and of its other sight commitments.

encaisse-or (Banq.), gold coin and bullion.

encaisse-argent (Banq.), silver coin and bullion.

encaissement (*n.m.*), cashing ; encashment ; collection ; payment ; receipt ; cash receipt :
la remise d'un effet à l'encaissement, the remittance of a bill for collection.
présenter un chèque à l'encaissement, to present a cheque for payment.
encaissements et paiements, receipts and payments ; cash receipts and payments.

sauf encaissement. See under **sauf.**

encaisser (*v.t.*), to cash ; to encash ; to collect :
encaisser un chèque, to cash, to encash, to collect, a cheque.
la banque a encaissé les fonds, the bank has collected the money.
compte effets à encaisser (*m.*), bills for collection account.

encaisseur, -euse (*adj.*), collecting :
le banquier encaisseur, the collecting banker.

encaisseur (pers.) (*n.m.*), collector :
l'encaisseur d'un effet, the collector of a bill.

encaisseur (guichetier encaisseur) (Banq.) (pers.) (*n.m.*), receiver ; receiving cashier.

enchère (mise) (*n.f.*), bid :
mettre enchère, to make a bid.

enchère (*n.f.*) *ou* **enchères** (*n.f.pl.*) *ou* **encan** (*n.m.*) (manière de vendre), auction ; sale :
vendre une maison à l'enchère (*ou* aux enchères) (*ou* à l'encan), to sell a house by (*or* at) auction.

enchérir (mettre une enchère sur) (*v.t.*), to bid for :
enchérir un immeuble, to bid for a property.

enchérir (rendre plus cher) (*v.t.*), to raise, to advance, to increase, to enhance, the price of :
enchérir des marchandises, to raise the price of goods.

enchérir (*v.i.*), to rise in price ; to advance in price ; to increase in price ; to enhance in price ; to get dearer ; to rise ; to improve :
le blé enchérit, wheat is rising in price.
enchérir sur les prix offerts, to overbid, to outbid, to improve upon, the prices offered ; to overbid.

enchérir de, to bid :
enchérir de tant, to bid so much (at an auction).

enchérissement (*n.m.*), rise in price ; rise in cost ; advance in price ; increase in price ; enhancement of price :
enchérissement du coût de la vie, des vivres, rise in the cost of living ; increase in the price of necessaries.

enchérisseur, -euse (pers.) (*n.*), bidder.

encoffrer (s'approprier) (*v.t.*), to appropriate ; to pocket :
encoffrer de l'argent donné en dépôt, to appropriate money left on deposit.

encombrant, -e (en parlant d'un colis, ou analogue) (*adj.*), bulky ; of exceptional bulk in proportion to weight :

colis encombrant (*m.*), bulky parcel.

le droit de garde est majoré pour certains objets encombrants (bicyclettes, voitures d'enfants, etc.), the cloak room fee is increased for certain articles of exceptional bulk in proportion to weight (bicycles, perambulators, etc.).

encombrement (d'un marché) (*n.m.*), glutting, glut (of a market).

marché encombré (*m.*), glutted market.

encombrement (d'un port, des quais) (*n.m.*), congestion, crowded state (of a port, of the wharves).

encombrement (autour des guichets) (*n.m.*), crowding (round the ticket windows).

encombrement (arrimage) (*n.m.*), space occupied; space taken up; measurement:

l'encombrement d'un chargement, the space occupied by a cargo.

coter le fret à tel taux, poids ou encombrement, to quote the freight at such a rate, weight or measurement.

tonneau d'encombrement (*m.*), measurement ton.

encourir (*v.t.*), to incur; to run:

encourir une responsabilité, to incur a liability.

encourir un risque, to incur, to run, a risk.

frais spéciaux encourus (*m.pl.*), special expenses incurred.

encours (Banq.) (*n.m.*), (the) total (of bills remitted by the client to the banker) running (at any particular time).

encre (*n.f.*), ink:

encre à écrire, writing ink.

encre communicative *ou* encre à copier *ou* encre copiant, copying ink.

encre de couleur, coloured ink.

encre noire *ou* encre ordinaire, black ink; ordinary ink.

encre rouge, red ink:

les sommes ressorties à l'encre rouge (*f.pl.*), the amounts shown in red ink.

encrier (*n.m.*), inkstand; inkpot; ink bottle:

encrier de bureau, office inkstand; squat ink bottle.

encrier inversable, safety inkpot.

endetter (*v.t.*), to cause to run into debt; to get into debt.

s'endetter (*v.r.*), to get into debt; to run into debt.

endommager (*v.t.*), to damage; to injure:

navire endommagé qui doit être réparé (*m.*), damaged ship which should be repaired.

être endommagé (-e) par l'eau de mer, to be damaged by sea water; to be sea damaged.

endossable (*adj.*), endorsable; indorsable:

chèque endossable (*m.*), endorsable cheque.

endossataire (pers.) (*n.m.* ou *f.*), endorsee.

endossement *ou* **endos** (*n.m.*), endorsement; indorsement:

endossement d'un billet, d'un connaissement, endorsement of a bill, of a bill of lading.

endossement à forfait, endorsement without recourse.

endossement en blanc *ou* endos en blanc, blank endorsement; indorsement in blank.

endossement régulier, regular endorsement.

endossement irrégulier, irregular endorsement.

endosser (*v.t.*), to endorse; to indorse:

endosser une lettre de change, to endorse, to indorse, a bill of exchange.

en général, il est d'usage d'endosser la police en blanc, in general, it is the custom to endorse the policy in blank.

endosseur (pers.) (*n.m.*), endorser; indorser.

enfant trouvé (passager clandestin) (*m.*), stowaway.

enfreindre (*v.t.*), to infringe; to violate; to break:

enfreindre la règle, to infringe, to break, the rule.

engagement (*n.m.*), engagement; booking; commitment; liability; undertaking; pledging; pledge; hypothecation; pawning; signing on:

faire honneur à ses engagements, to carry out one's engagements.

limiter le montant de son engagement, to limit the amount of one's commitment (*or* liability) (*or* undertaking).

engagement pris, engagement contracted; undertaking: (*Cf.* prendre l'engagement.)

réclamer l'exécution de l'engagement pris par quelqu'un, to claim performance of someone's undertaking (*or* of the engagement contracted by someone).

négociations pour les engagements de frets (*f.pl.*), negotiations for freight bookings.

sans engagement de dates. See under **sans.**

engagement cautionné (Douanes), bond. *See syn.* soumission cautionnée *for example.*

engagement (Bourse) (*n.m.*), checking slip.

engager (lier par une promesse) (*v.t.*), to engage; to pledge; to bind:

engager sa parole, to engage, to pledge, one's word.

les marchés fermes engagent à la fois le vendeur et l'acheteur; un marché à prime engage le vendeur sans engager l'acheteur (Bourse), firm bargains bind both the seller and the buyer; an option bargain binds the taker without binding the giver.

l'antidate d'un connaissement engage la responsabilité du capitaine (*f.*), the ante-dating of a bill of lading pledges the responsibility of the master.

le capitaine en signant les connaissements engage l'armateur, the master by signing the bills of lading binds the shipowner.

chaque assureur n'est engagé que dans la limite de la somme par lui souscrite, each insurer is bound only within the limit of the amount subscribed by him.

engager (prendre à forfait) (*v.t.*), to book:

engager un passage, un fret avec une ligne de navigation, to book a passage, a freight with a shipping line.

engager (faire entrer; aventurer) (*v.t.*), to put in; to engage:

engager du capital dans une entreprise, to put capital into, to engage capital in, a business.

capital engagé (*m.*), trading capital.

engager (mettre en gage) (*v.t.*), to pledge; to hypothecate; to pawn:
engager des valeurs, to pledge, to hypothecate, securities.

engager (attacher à son service) (*v.t.*), to engage; to sign on:
engager un employé, to engage an employee.
engager l'équipage d'un navire, to engage, to sign on, the crew of a ship.

s'engager (*v.r.*), to engage; to sign on.

engager (s') (*v.r.*), to engage; to undertake; to agree; to promise; to bind oneself; to pledge oneself; to take upon oneself:
s'engager dans des spéculations hasardeuses, to engage in risky speculations.
s'engager à payer une somme déterminée, une traite à l'échéance, to undertake to pay a certain sum, a bill at maturity.
s'engager par cautionnement, to bind oneself under, to pledge oneself by, a surety bond.
les administrateurs qui ont agi dans la limite de leurs pouvoirs engagent la société sans s'engager eux-mêmes (*m.pl.*), directors who have acted within the limit of their powers bind the company without binding themselves.
part pour laquelle l'assureur s'engage dans le risque assuré (*f.*), share for which the insurer binds himself (*or* share which the underwriter takes upon himself) in the risk insured.

enlevé (-e) par la mer (*ou* **par les lames**) (**être**), to be washed overboard:
pontée enlevée par la mer en cours de route (*f.*), deck cargo washed overboard in course of transit.

enlèvement (retrait) (*n.m.*), removal; collection; taking away:
enlèvement des marchandises avant paiement des droits, removal of goods before payment of duty.
enlèvement à domicile, collection at residence (*or* at trader's premises).

enlèvement par la mer (*ou* **par les lames**) (*m.*), washing overboard.

enlever (retirer) (*v.t.*), to remove; to collect; to take away:
destinataire qui se présente à la gare pour enlever sa marchandise (*m.*), consignee who calls at the station to collect (*or* to remove) his goods.

enlever (émission de titres) (*v.t.*), to take up:
si les titres ne sont pas enlevés par le public, le syndicat de garantie est réputé souscripteur, if the shares are not (*or* if the stock is not) taken up by the public, the underwriting syndicate is deemed applicant.

enlever (gagner) (*v.t.*), to put on:
l'action X. enlève 120 fr. à 12 850, X. shares put on 120 fr. at 12,850 francs.

enliassement (*n.m.*), bundling (papers); tying into a bundle (*or* into bundles).

enliasser (*v.t.*), to bundle (papers); to tie into a bundle (*or* into bundles).

ennemi, -e (*adj.*), enemy (*used as adj.*):
navire ennemi (*m.*), enemy ship.

ennemi, -e (*n.*), enemy:
ennemis du pays (*expression used in French bills of lading*), King's enemies (*expression used in English bills of lading*).

énoncer (*v.t.*), to enunciate; to state; to express; to word; to name; to specify; to provide; to stipulate; to contain; to give:
énoncer une somme en chiffres, en lettres, en toutes lettres, to express an amount in figures, in words, in words at length.
ce que la police doit énoncer, what the policy must specify (*or* should contain) (*or* should provide) (*or* ought to state) (*or* ought to stipulate).
une police doit énoncer: le nom de l'assuré, etc., an insurance policy must specify: the name of the insured, etc.
les marchandises énoncées sur le connaissement (*f.pl.*), the goods named in the bill of lading.
énoncer la valeur des marchandises dans les déclarations de douane, to give the value of the goods in the customs entries.

énonciation (*n.f.*), enunciation; statement; expression; wording; naming; specification; provision; stipulation; particular:
l'énonciation des marchandises doit être faite suivant les termes du tarif (Douanes), the specification of the goods should be made according to the terms of the tariff.
assurance avec énonciation de la somme assurée (*f.*), insurance with specification of the sum insured.
récuser les énonciations d'un connaissement, to challenge the stipulations (*or* the provisions) of a bill of lading.
loi qui exige que le connaissement porte les énonciations essentielles suivantes: le nom du navire et celui du chargeur, etc., law which requires that the bill of lading should contain the following essential particulars: the name of the ship and that of the shipper, etc.

enquête (*n.f.*), enquiry; inquiry:
naufrage suivi d'une enquête (*m.*), wreck followed by an enquiry.

enquêter sur, to enquire into; to inquire into:
enquêter sur la position actuelle d'une industrie, to enquire into the present position of an industry.

enrayer (arrêter, suspendre l'action de) (*v.t.*), to stop; to check:
enrayer un procès (Dr.), to stop a case.
enrayer la concurrence, to check competition.

enregistrement (action) (*n.m.*), registration; registry; filing; entering; entering up; entry; recording; booking:
enregistrement direct de bagages, through registration of luggage.

enregistrement (bureaux) (*n.m.*), registry:
aller à l'enregistrement, to go to the registry.

enregistrer (*v.t.*), to register; to file; to enter; to enter up; to record; to book:
enregistrer un acte, une déclaration, to register, to file, a deed, a return.
enregistrer des bagages, to register luggage.

enregistrer une opération, to enter, to record, to book, a transaction.

les opérations enregistrées au (ou sur le) journal (f.pl.), the transactions entered (or entered up) in the journal.

enregistreur (pers.) (n.m.), registrar.

enrichir (v.t.), to enrich.

s'enrichir (v.r.), to get rich; to grow rich; to thrive:

s'enrichir à bon compte, to get rich easily.

enrichissement (n.m.), enrichment.

enseigne lumineuse (Publicité) (f.), illuminated sign.

entamer (v.t.), to begin; to commence; to institute; to encroach upon:

entamer des poursuites contre un débiteur, to commence, to institute, proceedings against a debtor.

entamer son capital, to encroach upon one's capital.

entendre (s') (s'accorder) (v.r.), to agree on; to agree upon:

s'entendre sur un prix, to agree on (or upon) a price.

entente (n.f.), understanding; agreement:

à défaut d'entente entre tous les intéressés, failing agreement between all the interested parties; in default of agreement between all the parties concerned.

entier (n.m.) ou **nombre entier** (m.), whole number.

entier (en), in full:

payer le fret en entier, to pay the freight in full.

entièrement libéré, -e ou **entièrement versé, -e,** fully paid; fully paid up:

actions entièrement libérées (f.pl.), fully paid shares.

capital entièrement versé (m.), fully paid capital.

capital: 10 millions entièrement versés, capital: 10 millions fully paid up.

entièrement nanti, -e, fully secured:

créancier entièrement nanti (m.), fully secured creditor.

entourer (s') de garanties suffisantes, to surround oneself with sufficient guarantees.

entrain (n.m.), buoyancy:

les valeurs de caoutchouc se sont progressivement raffermies pendant la première moitié de la semaine, puis elles ont fait preuve, dans la séance de jeudi, d'un entrain très net (f.pl.), rubber shares hardened progressively during the first half of the week, then, during Thursday's session, they showed very distinct buoyancy (or were distinctly buoyant).

seul, le marché de New-York fait à nouveau preuve d'allant et d'entrain, mais son influence ne se fait pas sentir de manière tangible sur notre place, alone, the market of New York showed renewed signs of activity and buoyancy, but its influence did not make itself felt in a tangible manner on our market.

entrée (pénétration) (n.f.), entrance; entry; entering:

entrée d'un navire dans un port, entrance, entry, of a ship into a port.

à l'entrée ou à la sortie des ports, on entering or leaving ports.

entrée (des voyageurs) (gare de ch. de f.) (n.f.), way in (for passengers) (railway station).

entrée (importation) (n.f.), importation; import:

les droits de douane perçus pour l'entrée des marchandises (m.pl.), the customs duties collected for the importation of goods.

le trafic total, entrées et sorties réunies, the total traffic, imports and exports combined.

entrée (n.f.) ou **entrée en douane,** clearance inwards; clearing inwards; entry inwards.

entrée (droit de douane) (n.f.), import duty.

entrée (recette) (n.f.), receipt:

entrées et sorties de caisse, cash receipts and payments.

entrée en (ou **au**) **bassin** (f.), docking; dockage; going into dock.

entrée en cale sèche ou **entrée en forme** (f.), drydocking; dry-dockage; going into dry dock.

entrée en valeur (f.), coming into value:

les intérêts ne courent qu'a partir des dates d'entrée en valeur des capitaux (m.pl.), interest only runs from the dates of coming into value (or from the value dates) of the capital sums. See also example under entrer en valeur.

entrée en vigueur (d'une convention, d'un traité) (f.), coming into force (of an agreement, of a treaty).

entremise (n.f.), agency:

le commerce des assurances est généralement traité par l'entremise de courtiers, insurance business is generally done through the agency of brokers.

entrepont (n.m.), steerage.

entreposage ou **entrepôt** (n.m.), warehousing; bonding; storing; storage:

l'entreposage (ou l'entrepôt) des marchandises importées, the warehousing (or the bonding) of imported goods.

déclarer des marchandises pour l'entreposage (ou pour l'entrepôt) (Douanes), to enter goods for warehousing (or for bonding).

entreposer (v.t.), to warehouse; to bond; to store:

les marchandises entreposées (ou les marchandises d'entrepôt) n'acquittent les droits, le cas échéant, qu'au moment où elles sont retirées de l'entrepôt pour la consommation (f.pl.), warehoused goods (or bonded goods) only pay duty, if any, when they are taken out of bond for home use.

entreposeur (pers.) (n.m.), warehouse keeper; bonded storekeeper.

entrepositaire (pers.) (n.m.), bonder:

l'entrepositaire est tenu de fournir caution pour garantir les droits et les amendes qui pourraient devenir exigibles, the bonder is obliged to give security to guarantee the duties and fines which may become payable.

entrepôt (local dans lequel sont déposées des marchandises) (n.m.), warehouse; store.

entrepôt (n.m.) ou **entrepôt légal** ou **entrepôt de douane** (local où sont placées régulièrement les marchandises passibles de droits), warehouse; store; bonded warehouse; bonded store ; bond ; customs warehouse *or* store : *Note :*—In France, *entrepôts de douane* are distinguished as to (*a*) **entrepôts réels,** which are public bonded warehouses, (*b*) **entrepôts fictifs,** i.e., private bonded warehouses, and (*c*) **entrepôts spéciaux,** viz., bonded warehouses for special purposes or commodities, such as the warehousing of dangerous or noxious goods, cold storage, etc. There is also in France the **entrepôt frauduleux,** in which are deposited goods introduced fraudulently into the country. *Cf.* dépôt de douane *and* magasins généraux.

le droit de magasinage dans l'entrepôt, the right of warehousing in bond (*or* of storing in a bonded warehouse).

entrepôt frigorifique, cold store.

à l'entrepôt *ou* **en entrepôt** *ou* **en E.** *ou simplement* **E.** (opp. à *à l'acquitté*), in bond; in bonded warehouse :

marchandises vendues à l'entrepôt (*f.pl.*), goods sold in bond.

vente en entrepôt *ou* vente en E. *ou* vente E. (*f.*), sale in bonded warehouse.

entreprendre (*v.t.*), to undertake; to take in hand; to contract :

entreprendre le transport des marchandises pour un prix déterminé à forfait, to undertake the carriage of goods for a fixed contract price; to contract for through booking of goods.

une société ne peut entreprendre aucune opération non prévue par ses statuts, a company may not undertake any business not provided for under its memorandum.

entrepreneur (pers.) (*n.m.*), contractor :

entrepreneur de chargement *ou* entrepreneur de déchargement *ou* entrepreneur de chargement et de déchargement, master porter.

entrepreneur de publicité, advertising contractor.

entrepreneur de quai, wharfinger.

entrepreneur de remorquage, towage contractor.

entrepreneur de roulage *ou* entrepreneur de transports, cartage contractor; haulage contractor; carrier.

entrepreneur de roulages publics, common carrier (goods).

entrepreneur de voitures publiques, common carrier (passengers).

entrepreneur de voitures et de roulages publics, common carrier (goods and passengers).

entreprise (*n.f.*), enterprise; undertaking; venture; business; concern :

entreprise commerciale, commercial enterprise; commercial undertaking; trading concern.

entreprise rémunératrice, remunerative undertaking; paying concern; profitable business.

les aléas d'une entreprise (*m.pl.*), the chances of a venture.

entrer (*v.i.*), to enter; to go; to go in: to go into; to come :

entrer dans la finance, to go in for finance; to take up financial business; to become a financier.

entrer dans un port, dans une rade, dans un fleuve, to enter a port, a roadstead, a river.

entrer en (*ou* au) bassin, to go into dock; to dock :

avec faculté d'entrer en bassin et d'en sortir, with leave to dock and undock.

entrer en cale sèche *ou* entrer dans la forme, to go into dry dock; to dry-dock :

navire qui entre en cale sèche (*ou* qui entre dans la forme) avec l'assistance de remorqueurs (*m.*), ship which goes into dry dock (*or* which dry-docks) with the help of tugs.

entrer en collision, to come into collision :

navire qui entre en collision avec un autre navire (*m.*), ship which comes into collision with another ship.

entrer en fonction, to enter upon one's duties.

entrer en liquidation, to go into liquidation :

société qui entre en liquidation (*f.*), company which goes into liquidation.

entrer en valeur, to come into value :

on appelle valeur (*ou* date de valeur) (*ou* date d'entrée en valeur) l'époque à laquelle une somme en compte courant devient productive d'intérêt, ou entre en valeur, value (*or* value date) is the date on which an amount in account current becomes interest-bearing, or comes into value.

entrer en vigueur, to come into force :

ce n'est qu'après l'acquittement de la police qu'elle entre en vigueur, it is only after acquittance of the policy that it comes into force.

entretenir (*v.t.*), to maintain.

entretenir quelqu'un de quelque chose, to speak to someone about something; to report something to someone :

M. le président entretien le conseil des affaires courantes, the chairman reported current matters to the board.

entretien (*n.m.*), maintenance; upkeep :

entretien des routes, upkeep of roads; road maintenance.

les vivres nécessaires à l'entretien de l'équipage (*m.pl.*), the provisions necessary for the maintenance of the crew.

entrevue (*n.f.*), interview :

solliciter une entrevue avec son banquier, to ask for an interview with one's banker.

enveloppe (*n.f.*), envelope :

enveloppe à bords coloriés, envelope with coloured borders.

enveloppe à panneau *ou* enveloppe à fenêtre *ou* enveloppe fenestrée, panel envelope; window envelope; outlook envelope.

enveloppe à panneau transparent, envelope with transparent panel.

enveloppe affranchie pour la réponse, stamped addressed envelope.

enveloppe ajourée, cut-out panel envelope.

enveloppe commerciale, commercial envelope (In France, of a size [nearly square] to take business paper folded in four. In England, of a size [oblong] to take business paper folded in six).

enveloppe de lettre chargée ou recommandée, registered letter envelope.

enveloppe deuil, black-bordered envelope.

enveloppe entièrement transparente, wholly transparent envelope.

envie (désir) (*n.f.*), desire; wish:
envie de frustrer ses créanciers, desire, wish, to defraud one's creditors.

environ (Bourse) (*adv.*) (Abrév.: **env/.**), about:
achetez tant d'actions à tel cours environ, buy so many shares at about such a price; buy so many shares at such a price about.
Note :—On the Paris Bourse a specific latitude is generally recognized by *environ*, varying with the nature of the stock. **grand environ** or **environ large** is double the margin implied by *environ*. On the London Stock Exchange no definite margin is understood by *about*, consequently orders given at an about price (à un cours environ) are liable to lead to disputes and dissatisfaction.

envoi (action) (*n.m.*), sending; forwarding; consignment; remittance; dispatch; despatch; sending in; sending out:
envoi contre remboursement *ou* envois contre remboursement, cash on delivery.
envoi de circulaires, sending out circulars.
envoi de fonds, remittance of funds.
envoi des comptes, sending out, sending in, accounts.
date d'envoi d'avis d'arrivée (*f.*), date of dispatch of advice of arrival.

envoi (chose envoyée) (*n.m.*), consignment; parcel; package; packet; article:
la valeur d'un envoi de marchandises, the value of a consignment (*or* parcel) of goods.
envoi à couvert (Transport), packed consignment.
envoi à découvert (Transport), unpacked consignment.
les envois autres que les lettres et cartes postales, packets other than letters and postcards.
envoi avec (*ou* de) valeur déclarée *ou* envoi chargé (Poste), insured packet.
envoi d'échantillons (Poste), sample packet.
envoi d'imprimés (Poste), packet of printed papers.
envoi exprès (Poste), express packet.
envoi postal, postal packet; postal article.
envoi recommandé (Poste), registered packet (*or* article).
See note under **objet** *ou* **objet de correspondance.**

envoyer (*v.t.*), to send; to forward; to remit; to dispatch; to despatch; to send in; to send out; to tender:
envoyer une lettre par la poste, un câblogramme, une remise, to send, to dispatch, a letter by post, a cable, a remittance.
envoyer de l'argent, to send, to remit, money.
envoyer sa démission, to send in, to tender, one's resignation.

envoyeur, -euse (pers.) (*n.*), sender; remitter:

envoyeur d'un mandat-poste, sender, remitter, of a money order.

épargnant, -e (pers.) (*n.*), saver.

épargne (économie) (*n.f.*), saving; economy.

épargnes (somme économisée) (*n.f.pl.*), savings: vivre de ses épargnes, to live on one's savings.

épargner (*v.t.*), to save; to save up; to lay by; to economize; to husband:
un sou épargné est un sou gagné, a penny saved is a penny earned.

épave (carcasse de navire échoué sur une côte) (*n.f.*), wreck.

épave (navire abandonné) (*n.f.*), derelict.

épave (*n.f.*) *ou* **épaves** (*n.f.pl.*) (débris d'un naufrage, en général, ou débris que la mer rejette sur les rivages), wreck; wreckage; jetsam:
les marchandises sauvées des naufrages ou rejetées par les flots sur le littoral constituent des épaves (*f.pl.*), goods salved from wrecks or cast by the waves on the shore constitute wreck (*or* wreckage).

épave (objets abandonnés à la mer et flottant au gré des flots) (*n.f.*), flotsam.

épave (objet abandonné marqué d'une bouée) (*n.f.*), lagan; ligan.
Note :—In English, goods cast or swept from a vessel into the sea and found floating are called *flotsam*.
Jettisoned goods, especially when washed ashore, are called *jetsam* or *wreck*.
Goods cast adrift with a buoy attached, as evidence of ownership, are called *lagan* or *ligan*.
In French, *épave* has all these meanings, collectively or individually.

épeler (*v.t.*), to spell:
épeler les mots (Téléph., etc.), to spell the words.

épingle (*n.f.*), pin.

épingler (*v.t.*), to pin:
fiche épinglée au documents, police épinglée au connaissement (*f.*), slip pinned to the documents, policy pinned to the bill of lading.

époque (*n.f.*) (Abrév.: **Ép.** ou **ép.**), time; date; period:
à l'époque de la livraison, du paiement, at the time of delivery, of payment.
obligations remboursables à époques déterminées (*ou* à époques fixes) (*f.pl.*), debentures redeemable at fixed dates.
un acompte de dividende de tant, en comparaison de tant l'an dernier à pareille époque, an interim dividend of so much, as compared with so much for the corresponding period of last year.
époque de jouissance. See under **jouissance.**

époque (date d'arrêté d'un compte courant) (*n.f.*) (Abrév.: **Ép.** ou **ép.**), period; base date; zero; zero date; époque.

épreuve (*n.f.*), test:
poids des emballages constaté par épreuves (Douanes) (*m.*), weight of packings ascertained by tests.

épreuve d'imprimerie (*f.*), printer's proof.

éprouver (supporter; souffrir) (*v.t.*), to meet with; to sustain; to suffer; to experience:

éprouver des pertes à la bourse, to meet with losses on the stock exchange.

épuisement (*n.m.*), exhaustion; drain:
épuisement des ressources publiques, exhaustion of the national resources.

épuiser (*v.t.*), to exhaust; to drain:
les coupons sont épuisés, c'est-à-dire ils ont tous été détachés (*m.pl.*), the coupons are exhausted, that is to say, they have all been cut off (*or* detached).

équilibre (*n.m.*), equilibrium; balance:
attendre que l'équilibre entre la production et la consommation se rétablisse par le jeu normal de la loi de l'offre et de la demande, to wait until equilibrium between production and consumption is restored by the normal action of the law of supply and demand.

équilibrer (*v.t.*), to balance:
équilibrer un budget, to balance a budget.

équipage (Mar.) (*n.m.*), crew:
le capitaine et l'équipage, the master and crew.

équipement (*n.m.*), equipment; outfit; fitting out.

équiper (*v.t.*), to equip; to fit out; to outfit:
équiper un navire, to equip, to fit out, to outfit, a ship.

équitable (*adj.*), equitable:
partage équitable (*m.*), equitable division.

équivalent (*n.m.*), equivalent.

équivaloir (*v.i.*), to be equivalent:
partage qui équivaut à 5 0/0 (*m.*), distribution which is equivalent to 5%.

erreur (*n.f.*), error; mistake; slip:
erreur d'addition, de calcul, error, mistake, of (*or* in) addition, of (*or* in) calculation (*or* reckoning).
erreur dans la livraison par suite de l'insuffisance des marques, wrong delivery owing to insufficiency of marks.
erreur de compensation (Comptab.), compensating error.
erreur de jugement, de (*ou* dans la) navigation, error of judgment, of (*or* in) navigation.
erreur de plume *ou* erreur de copiste, slip of the pen; clerical error.
erreurs de report (Comptab.), errors in posting.
erreur typographique, misprint; printer's error.
écriture annulée par erreur (*f.*), entry cancelled in error (*or* in [*or* by] mistake).

erroné, -e (*adj.*), erroneous; wrong:
calcul erroné (*m.*), erroneous calculation; wrong calculation.

erronément (*adv.*), erroneously; by mistake.

escale (arrêt) (*n.f.*), call; call at a named port (i.e., a port in the customary or advertised route); call at intermediate port; calling; calling at named (*or* intermediate) ports: (Cf. **relâche**.)
navire partant du Havre et faisant une escale à Brest (*ou* et escalant à Brest) (*m.*), ship sailing from Havre and making a call at Brest (*or* and calling at Brest).
faire escale (*ou* escaler) dans un port sur la route, to call (*or* to make a call) at a port on the route.
faire escale (*ou* faire échelle), c'est-à-dire s'arrêter dans certains ports intermédiaires

pour y prendre ou laisser des marchandises, to call, that is to say, to stop at certain intermediate ports, there to take or leave cargo.
(*steamer*) X. (pour Londres) a fait escale à Périm le 31 (*date*) (Mouvement des Navires), (*steamer*) X. (for London) called (*or* cld) (*or* c.) Perim 31 (*date*) (Shipping News).
la voie la plus directe et sans escale, the shortest route and without calling at intermediate ports.
escale dans un port étranger pour recevoir des ordres (*f.*), calling, call, in a foreign port to receive orders.
escale directe, direct call; forward call.
escale rétrograde, indirect call; backward call; call behind the named port.
faire toutes escales directes ou rétrogrades, to make any calls, direct or indirect; to proceed backwards or forwards.

escale (lieu d'arrêt) (*n.f.*), port of call; named port (i.e., port in the customary or advertised route); intermediate port; place of call. (Cf. **relâche**.)

escaler (*v.i.*). *Same as* faire escale. See examples under **escale**.

escomptable (*adj.*), discountable:
effet escomptable (*m.*), discountable bill.

escompte (action) (*n.m.*), discounting; discount:
effets remis en banque à l'escompte (*m.pl.*), bills sent to the bank for discount (*or* for discounting).
escompte à forfait, discounting without recourse.

escompte (Com.) (*n.m.*) (Abrév.: **esc.** *ou* **escte** *ou* **esc**te), discount:
faire un escompte de 5 p. cent, to allow a discount of 5%.
escomptes accordés, discounts allowed.
escomptes obtenus, discounts received.
escomptes sur achats, sur ventes, discounts on purchases, on sales.
escompte sur marchandises *ou* escompte sur (*ou* de) facture *ou* escompte-remise [escomptes-remises *pl.*] (*n.m.*) *ou* escompte d'usage, trade discount.
escompte de caisse *ou* escompte au comptant *ou* escompte-intérêt [escomptes-intérêts *pl.*] (*n.m.*) *ou* *simplement* escompte, cash discount; discount for cash.

escompte (*n.m.*) *ou* **escompte de banque**, discount:
escompte en dedans *ou* escompte rationnel, true discount; arithmetical discount.
escompte en dehors *ou* escompte commercial *ou* escompte irrationnel, bank discount.
escompte hors banque *ou* escompte privé (opp. à *escompte officiel*), market rate; market rate of discount; discount rate of the open market; open market discount rate; private rate; private rate of discount.
escompte officiel, bank rate; bank rate of discount; official rate; official rate of discount. *See* taux officiel *for examples.*

escompte (Bourse) (*n.m.*), calling for delivery before the settlement (a right existing in French and other continental stock exchange practice):

l'acheteur à terme a le droit de se faire livrer avant terme les valeurs négociées : cette faculté de l'acheteur s'appelle l'*escompte*, (in France) a buyer for the settlement has the right of calling for delivery before the settlement of the securities dealt in : this option of the buyer is known as *escompte*.

Note :—The exercise of the right of *escompte* is exceptional. Its object is to bring about a temporary rise by forcing the bears to buy and deliver.

escompter (*v.t.*), to discount :
  escompter un effet, to discount a bill.
  escompter une hausse de valeurs, to discount a rise of stocks.
  la spéculation escompte les bonnes nouvelles, speculation discounts good news.

s'escompter (*v.r.*), to be discounted :
  billets qui s'escomptent facilement (*m.pl.*), bills which are easily discounted.

escompter (Bourse) (*v.t.*), to call for delivery before the settlement : See **escompte** (Bourse).
  escompter son vendeur, to call for delivery from one's seller before the settlement.

escompteur, -euse (*adj.*), discounting :
  le banquier escompteur, the discounting banker.

escompteur (pers.) (*n.m.*), discounter.

espèces (*n.f.pl.*) (Abrév. : **esp.**), cash ; coin ; specie :
  payer en espèces, to pay in cash (*or* in specie).
  espèces en caisse et en (*ou* et à la) banque, cash in (*or* on) hand and at (*or* in) bank ; cash at bankers and in (*or* on) hand.
  actions souscrites en espèces (*f.pl.*), shares subscribed (*or* subscribed for) in cash.
  actions émises contre espèces (*f.pl.*), shares issued for cash.
  versement espèces (*m.*), cash payment.
  espèces en compte, cash on account.
  espèces pour solde, cash to balance ; cash in settlement.
  l'échange des billets contre espèces (*m.*), the exchange of notes for coin.
  espèces monnayées, coined money ; minted money ; specie ; coin.
  espèces sonnantes et trébuchantes, hard cash ; hard money.

espéré, -e (*adj.*), anticipated :
  profit espéré (*m.*), anticipated profit.

esquiver (*v.t.*), to evade ; to escape ; to elude :
  esquiver ses créanciers, to evade one's creditors.

essai (*n.m.*), trial :
  essai à la mer, sea trial.
  essai de vitesse, speed trial.
  un mois à l'essai (emploi, etc.), a month on trial.

essence (nature) (*n.f.*), essence :
  la délivrance de la marchandise au destinataire est de l'essence du contrat de transport, the delivery of the goods to the consignee is of the essence of the contract of carriage.

essor (*n.m.*), progress :
  l'essor économique de l'Amérique du Nord, the economic progress of North America.

essuie-plume *ou* **essuie-plumes** [essuie-plume *ou* essuie-plumes *pl.*] (*n.m.*), penwiper.

estampillage (*n.m.*), stamping ; marking.

estampille (*n.f.*), stamp ; mark :
  estampille sur un titre constatant une réduction de capital, stamp on a certificate mentioning a reduction of capital.
  estampille de contrôle, denoting stamp.

estampiller (*v.t.*), to stamp ; to mark :
  titres estampillés du paiement d'un coupon (*m.pl.*), certificates stamped (*or* marked) with the payment of a coupon.
  actions estampillées (*f.pl.*), stamped shares ; marked shares (i.e., certificates marked with notice that rights have been exercised, or the like).
  est. *ou* Est. *ou* estamp. *ou* Estamp. (*abrév.*), estampillé, -e.

estarie (*n.f.*), lay day.

estimatif, -ive (*adj.*), estimated :
  imputations estimatives (*f.pl.*), estimated charges.

estimation (*n.f.*), estimate ; valuation :
  estimation des choses assurées, des biens offerts en garantie, valuation of property insured, of property offered as security.
  estimation de tout repos, reliable estimate ; safe estimate.

estimer (*v.t.*), to estimate ; to value :
  estimer les actions au cours de bourse, to value the shares at market price.

estuaire (*n.m.*), estuary :
  l'estuaire de la Tamise, the estuary of the Thames ; the Thames estuary.

établir (fonder ; créer ; instituer) (*v.t.*), to establish ; to found :
  établir une industrie, to establish, to found, an industry.
  établir une communication téléphonique, to establish a telephone call.

établir (fixer) (*v.t.*), to fix :
  établir un prix, to fix a price.

établir (dresser) (*v.t.*), to draw up ; to draw ; to make out ; to make ; to strike :
  établir un compte, to draw up, to make out, an account.
  connaissement établi en quatre originaux (*m.*), bill of lading made in four originals.
  établir une balance, to strike a balance.
  établir la moyenne de, to average :
    établir la moyenne des bénéfices de plusieurs années, to average the profits of several years.

établir le prix de revient (Comptab.), to ascertain the cost ; to cost (*v.i.*) :
  établir le prix de revient par tonne de fonte produite, par tonne de charbon extrait, to ascertain the cost, to cost, per ton of metal produced, per ton of mineral raised.
  là où on fabrique une foule d'objets, le prix de revient comptable est souvent très difficile à établir, where a great number of articles are manufactured, it is often very difficult to ascertain the book cost.

établir le prix de revient de (Comptab.), to ascertain the cost of ; to cost (*v.t.*) :
  établir le prix de revient des deux qualités d'après ces prix, to cost the two qualities according to these prices.

établissement (action d'instituer) (*n.m.*), establishment; foundation.

établissement (fixation) (*n.m.*), fixing.

établissement (dressement) (*n.m.*), drawing up; drawing; making out; striking:
établissement d'un bilan, drawing up a balance sheet.

établissement (exploitation commerciale ou industrielle) (*n.m.*), establishment; institution:
un établissement de banque, a banking establishment.
établissement de crédit, credit institution; bank.

établissement (dépenses en immobilisations) (Comptab.) (*n.m.*), capital expenditure.

établissement des prix de revient (Comptab.) (*m.*), costing.

étagère (*n.f.*), pen rack.

étalon (*n.m.*), standard:
étalon-argent (*n.m.*) *ou* étalon d'argent, silver standard.
étalon boiteux, limping standard.
étalon de valeur, standard of value:
la monnaie est, à la fois, l'étalon des valeurs et un instrument d'échange, money is, at the same time, the standard of values and an instrument of exchange.
étalon métallique, metallic standard.
étalon monétaire, monetary standard. *See example under* pièce type.
étalon-or (*n.m.*) *ou* étalon d'or, gold standard:
pays à étalon-or (*ou* à étalon d'or) (*m.*), gold standard country.
étalon-or de change *ou* étalon de change-or, gold exchange standard; gold bullion standard.
étalon-papier (monnaie) (*n.m.*), paper standard.
double étalon (or et argent), double standard.

étape (*n.f.*), stage:
voyage en plusieurs étapes (*m.*), journey in several stages.

état (manière d'être; situation) (*n.m.*), state; condition:
l'état du marché, the state (*or* the condition) of the market.
état d'innavigabilité, unseaworthiness.
en état d'innavigabilité, unseaworthy.
état de navigabilité *ou* état de tenir la mer, seaworthiness.
en état de navigabilité *ou* en état de naviguer *ou* en état de tenir la mer, seaworthy. V. exemple sous syn. **bon état de navigabilité (en)**.

état (*n.m.*) *ou* **état de situation**, position:
banquier qui juge de la solvabilité de ses habitués d'après l'état de leur compte chez lui (*m.*), banker who judges of the solvency of his customers according to the position of their account with him.
examiner l'état de situation d'une caisse, to examine a cash position.

état (tableau; mémoire) (*n.m.*), statement; account; return:
état de caisse, cash statement.

état de dépenses *ou* état de frais, statement, account, return, of expenses.
état de finances, financial statement; finance statement; statement of the finances.
état détaillé de ses opérations, de son compte, detailed account of one's transactions, of one's account.
état sommaire de la situation, summary statement of the position.
état d'inscription hypothécaire négatif, certificate of the non existence of mortgages.
état d'inscription hypothécaire positif, certificate of the existence of mortgages.

État (*n.m.*), state; State; government; Government:
l'État libre d'Irlande, the Irish Free State.
banque d'État, State bank; government bank.

état-major [états-majors *pl.*] (d'un paquebot) (*n.m.*), senior officers, executive (of a liner).

étatisation (*n.f.*), nationalization:
étatisation d'une industrie, des chemins de fer, nationalization of an industry, of railways.

étatiser (*v.t.*), to nationalize.

été (*n.m.*), summer.

éteindre (*v.t.*), to extinguish; to pay off:
éteindre un incendie (*ou* le feu) à bord, to extinguish a fire on board.
l'acceptation de la marchandise éteint toute action contre le chemin de fer provenant du contrat de transport (*f.*), the acceptance of the goods extinguishes any action against the railway arising out of the contract of carriage.
éteindre une dette en remboursant le capital, to extinguish a debt by repaying the capital.

étendre (*v.t.*), to extend:
étendre son champ d'action, le cercle de ses opérations, to extend one's field of action, the circle of one's operations.

étendue (*n.f.*), extent:
la nature et l'étendue d'un risque, du dommage résultant d'un sinistre, the nature and extent of a risk, of the damage resulting from an accident.

étiquetage (*n.m.*), labelling; labeling.

étiqueter (*v.t.*), to label.

étiquette (*n.f.*), label:
étiquette indiquant la gare de destination, label showing the destination station.
les anciennes étiquettes doivent être enlevées ou oblitérées (bagages), old labels must be removed or obliterated.
étiquette « annexe » [étiquettes « annexes » *pl.*], " enclosure " label; duplicate enclosure check.
étiquette d'adresse, address label.
étiquette de recommandation (Poste), registration label.
étiquette gommée, gummed label.
étiquette volante, tie-on label; tag label.

étranger, -ère (*adj.*), foreign:
monnaie étrangère (*f.*), foreign money.
en principe toute marchandise importée de l'étranger est réputée étrangère et par suite soumise aux droits, in principle all merchandise imported from abroad is deemed to

be foreign and in consequence subject to duty.

à l'étranger, in a foreign country; abroad: biens à l'étranger (*m.pl.*), property abroad.

étranglement (Bourse) (*n.m.*), squeeze: étranglement de la spéculation à découvert, bear squeeze.

étrangler les vendeurs à découvert (Bourse), to squeeze the bears.

être (*v. substantif*). See examples:
être aux appointements, to receive a salary: il n'est aux appointements que depuis six mois, he has received a salary for the last six months only.
être dans les affaires, to be in business.
être de moitié dans une affaire, to go halves in a deal.
être en argent *ou* être en fonds, to be well provided with money; to be in funds.
être en faillite, to be bankrupt; to be insolvent.
être en hausse, à la hausse, en baisse, à la baisse. See under **hausse, baisse.**
être loin de compte, to be a long way out; to be far from agreeing.
être mal dans ses affaires *ou* être mal dans ses finances, to be in financial difficulties; to be in Queer Street.
être sur ses gardes, to be on one's guard.

étroit, -e (en parlant d'un marché) (*adj.*) (opp. à *large*), limited:
titres qui n'ont qu'un marché étroit (*m.pl.*), shares which have only a limited market.

étroitesse (d'un marché) (*n.f.*), limitedness, limited condition (of a market).

étude (cabinet) (*n.f.*), office; lawyer's office; chambers:
étude de notaire, notaire's office.

étude (clientèle d'un notaire, d'un avoué, etc.) (*n.f.*), practice:
vendre son étude, to sell one's practice.

évaluation (*n.f.*), valuation; estimate:
évaluation de marchandises, des choses assurées, valuation of goods, of insured property.
évaluation des pertes, estimate of the losses.

évaluer (*v.t.*), to value; to estimate:
évaluer une propriété, son portefeuille, les titres au cours de bourse, to value a property, one's investments, the stocks at market price.
évaluer une perte, to estimate a loss.

évasion d'impôt (*f.*), evasion of tax.

éventualité (*n.f.*), eventuality; contingency:
réserver une marge pour les éventualités, to reserve a margin for contingencies.

éventuel, -elle (*adj.*), eventual; contingent:
titres d'une valeur douteuse ou éventuelle (*m.pl.*), securities of a doubtful or eventual value.
passif éventuel (*m.*) [passif éventuel *ou* passifs éventuels *pl.*], contingent liability [contingent liabilities *pl.*].

éventuellement (*adv.*), eventually; contingently.

évidence (*n.f.*), evidence:
attendu qu'il résulte à l'évidence que . . ., whereas it appears from the evidence that . . .

ex-bonus (Abrév.: **ex-bon.**) *ou* **ex-répartition bonus** (Abrév.: **ex-rép. bon.**) *ou simplement* **ex-répartition** (Abrév.: **ex-rép.** *ou* **ex-répart.**), ex-bonus.

ex-coupon (Abrév.: **ex-c.** *ou* **ex-coup.** *ou* **e-c.** *ou* **x-c.**) (opp. à *coupon attaché*), ex coupon. See example under **se détacher.**

ex-dividende (Abrév.: **ex-div.** *ou* **ex-d.**) *ou* **ex-exercice** (Abrév.: **ex-ex.**) (opp. à *jouissance ou exercice—attaché*), ex dividend; dividend off:
actions cotées ex-dividende (*f.pl.*), shares quoted ex dividend.
ex-exercice 19—, ex dividend 19—.

ex-droit (Abrév.: **ex-dr.** *ou* **ex-d.** *ou* **ex-dt**) (opp. à *avec droit* ou *droit attaché*), ex rights; ex new:
titre ex-droit (*m.*), stock ex rights (*or* ex new).

ex-nom (d'un navire) (*n.m.*), late name (of a ship).

ex-remboursement (de capital) (Abrév.: **ex-remb.**), ex repayment.

ex-répartition (d'actions nouvelles) (Abrév.: **ex-rép.** *ou* **ex-répart.** *ou* **ex-r.**), ex allotment.

ex steamer (Abrév.: **ex st.**), ex steamer:
en transbordement ex steamer B., transhipping ex steamer B.

exact, -e (juste) (*adj.*), exact; accurate; correct:
nombre exact de jours (*m.*), exact number of days.
calcul exact (*m.*), accurate calculation; correct reckoning.

exact, -e (ponctuel) (*adj.*), punctual:
être exact (-e) à payer ses dettes, to be punctual in paying one's debts.
employé exact (*m.*), punctual employee.

exactement (*adv.*), exactly; accurately; correctly.

exaction (*n.f.*), exaction; extortion.

exactitude (justesse) (*n.f.*), exactness; exactitude; accuracy; correctness.

exactitude (ponctualité) (*n.f.*), punctuality:
exactitude dans les affaires, dans les paiements, punctuality in business, in paying.

exagération (*n.f.*), exaggeration:
exagération de valeur, exaggeration of value.
exagération d'imposition, overassessment.

exagérer (*v.t.*), to exaggerate:
assurance qui est déchue si l'assuré exagère sciemment le montant du dommage (*f.*), insurance which is forfeited if the insured knowingly exaggerates the amount of the damage.

examen (*n.m.*), examination; inspection; looking into; looking through; going into; going through:
examen des marchandises (Douanes, etc.), examination of the goods.
examen des titres de propriété, inspection of title deeds of property.

examen (épreuve que subit un candidat) (*n.m.*), examination:
passer l'examen préliminaire, l'examen final, to pass the preliminary examination, the final examination.

examinateur, -trice (pers.) (*n.*), examiner; inspector.

examiner (*v.t.*), to examine; to inspect; to look into; to look through; to go into; to go through:
  examiner des livres, to examine, to inspect, to look through, to go through, books.
  examiner la situation de la caisse, to examine, to look into, to go into, the cash position.

excédent (*n.m.*) (Ant.: *déficit*), excess; surplus; over:
  excédents de bagages (opp. à *franchise de poids*), excess luggage:
  les excédents de bagages sont taxés ainsi qu'il suit, excess luggage is charged for as follows.
  excédent de caisse (*ou* dans l'encaisse), surplus in the cash.
  déficits et excédents de caisse (*ou* dans l'encaisse) (Banq.), cash shorts and overs.
  excédent de poids, excess weight.
  excédent de recettes, de l'actif sur le passif, surplus, excess, of receipts, of assets over liabilities.
  réassurance d'excédent (*f.*), excess reinsurance.

excéder (*v.t.*), to exceed:
  dépense qui excède la recette (*f.*), expenditure which exceeds the receipts.

exception (*n.f.*), exception:
  les exceptions confirment la règle, the exception proves the rule.

excès (*n.m.*), excess:
  excès d'un nombre sur un autre, excess of one number over another.

excessif, -ive (*adj.*), excessive.

excessivement (*adv.*), excessively.

exclure (*v.t.*), to exclude; to shut out:
  police qui exclut les risques de grève (*f.*), policy which excludes strike risks.
  sont exclus tous recours provenant de retards, excluding all claims arising from delay.
  cargaison exclue (*f.*), shut out cargo.

exclusif, -ive (*adj.*), exclusive; sole:
  droit exclusif (*m.*), exclusive right; sole right.
  agent exclusif pour la France et ses Colonies (*m.*), sole agent for France and Colonies.

exclusion (*n.f.*), exclusion; shutting out.

excursion (*n.f.*), excursion; trip:
  excursion à terre, land excursion.

excursionniste (pers.) (*n.m. ou f.*), excursionist.

exécuter (*v.t.*), to execute; to carry out; to perform:
  exécuter un contrat, to execute, to carry out, to perform, a contract.
  exécuter un ordre, to execute an order.
  exécuter une convention de bonne foi, to carry out an agreement in good faith.

exécuter (Bourse) (*v.t.*), to buy in or sell out against; to buy in or sell out:
  agent qui a le droit d'exécuter son client dans le courant de la liquidation (*m.*), broker who has the right to buy in or sell out against his client during the settlement.
  valeurs exécutées (*f.pl.*), stock bought in or sold out.
  exécuter un acheteur, to sell out against a buyer.
  exécuter un vendeur, to buy in against a seller.
  exécuter un souscripteur retardataire, to sell

the shares of a subscriber in arrears with his calls. (In France, the practice is to sell such shares, on the Bourse if quoted, or by public auction if unquoted, and sue for any deficiency: in England such shares must first be forfeited.)

s'exécuter (*v.r.*), to pay up:
  opérateur sous la menace de liquidation d'office s'il ne s'exécute pas (Bourse) (*m.*), operator under the threat of official closing if he does not pay up.
  tous les actionnaires s'exécutent sauf l'un d'eux, all the shareholders pay up except one of them.

exécuteur testamentaire (pers.) (*m.*), executor.

exécutrice testamentaire (pers.) (*f.*), executrix.

exécution (*n.f.*), execution; carrying out; performance:
  exécution d'un ordre d'assurance, execution of an order of insurance.
  exécution d'un projet, execution of a project; carrying out a plan.
  exécution d'un marché, carrying out a bargain.
  tout le commerce de la banque est fondé sur l'exécution exacte et précise des engagements pris, all banking trade is founded on the punctual and strict performance of undertakings.

en exécution de, in pursuance of:
  en exécution des articles — et — de la loi de 24 juillet 1867 sur les sociétés, in pursuance of sections — and — of the Companies Act of 24th July 1867.

exécution (*n.f.*) *ou* **exécution en bourse,** buying in and selling out; buying in or selling out:
  exécution d'un vendeur, buying in against a seller.
  exécution d'un acheteur, selling out against a buyer.

exemplaire (*n.m.*), copy; specimen:
  deux exemplaires des statuts, two copies of the articles of association.
  connaissement qui est rédigé en trois, en quatre, exemplaires (*m.*), bill of lading which is drawn in three, in four, copies.
  exemplaire du capitaine (connaissement), captain's copy. *See note under* connaissement-chef.
  exemplaire justificatif *ou* exemplaire de justification (d'un journal), voucher copy (of a newspaper).

exemplaires de lettres de change. See examples:
  lettre de change à plusieurs exemplaires (*f.*) *ou* traite en plusieurs exemplaires (*f.*), bill of exchange in a set; bill in a set.
  les lettres tirées à trois exemplaires (*ou* en triple exemplaire) sont destinées à être envoyées par des courriers différents, afin que, si l'une s'égare, l'autre parvienne à destination (*f.pl.*), bills drawn in sets of three are intended to be sent by different mails, in order that, if one should go astray, the other may reach its destination.
  on rencontre aussi la pluralité d'exemplaires dans le cas où le tireur désire présenter l'effet à l'acceptation tout en voulant se

réserver une négociation immédiate : dans ce cas il en dresse deux exemplaires, the set (or plurality of copies) is also met with when the drawer wishes to present the bill for acceptance intending meanwhile to negotiate it : in this case he makes two vias (or copies) of it.

exempt, -e (*adj.*), exempt ; free :
reçus exempts du droit de timbre à quittance (*m.pl.*), receipts exempt from receipt stamp duty.
exempt (·e) d'impôt (*ou* impôts), free of tax ; tax free :
tous les coupons de rentes françaises sont exempts de tout impôt, à l'exception de ceux de la rente 3 0/0 amortissable, all coupons of French rentes are free of all tax, with the exception of those of the 3% redeemable rente.
exempt (-e) de droits, duty-free ; free of duty ; free ; exempt from duty ; uncustomed :
marchandises exemptes de droits (*f.pl.*), duty-free goods ; free goods ; uncustomed goods.
toutes les marchandises importées ou exportées, qu'elles soient sujettes à des droits ou qu'elles soient exemptes, all goods imported or exported, whether dutiable or free.

exempter (*v.t.*), to exempt ; to exonerate.

exemption (*n.f.*), exemption ; exoneration :
exemption d'impôt, de visite de douane, exemption from tax, from customs examination.

exercer (faire usage) (*v.t.*), to exercise ; to make :
exercer un droit, son droit d'option, la faculté de souscrire, to exercise a right, one's right of option, the option of subscribing.
exercer un recours contre quelqu'un pour préjudice subi, to make a claim against someone for damage sustained.

exercice (action de faire valoir) (*n.m.*), exercise :
exercice d'une faculté, d'un pouvoir, d'un privilège, de ses fonctions, exercise of an option, of a power, of a privilege, of one's duty.

exercice (action de pratiquer une profession) (*n.m.*), practice ; office :
avocat en exercice (*m.*), barrister in practice ; practising barrister.
les administrateurs en exercice (*m.pl.*), the directors in office.

exercice (action de pratiquer une industrie) (*n.m.*), trading :
quel que soit le résultat de l'exercice, whatever may be the result of the trading.
imputer une dette sur l'exercice du mois précédent, to charge a debt against the previous month's trading.

exercice (*n.m.*) *ou* **exercice financier** (période d'exécution des services d'un budget), financial year ; trading year ; trading period ; year ; period ; accounting period ; account :
exercice social (d'une société par actions), company's year ; company's financial year (*or* trading year) (*or* trading period) (*or* accounting period).
si l'année sociale comprend deux exercices semestriels, if the company's year comprises

two half yearly trading periods (*or* two six monthly accounting periods).
exercice prenant fin (*ou* clôturant) le 31 décembre, financial year, year, trading year, accounting period, ending 31st December.
exercice ayant pris fin (*ou* exercice clôturé *ou* clos) le 31 décembre, financial year, year, trading year, accounting period, ended 31st December.
dividende de l'exercice 19— (*m.*), dividend for the year 19—.
solde reporté de l'exercice précédent (*m.*) *ou* solde de l'exercice précédent (*m.*) *ou* report de l'exercice précédent (*m.*) (poste du bilan ou du compte profits et pertes), balance brought forward from last account ; balance of (*or* from) last account.
solde des bénéfices reporté à nouveau sur l'exercice suivant (*m.*), balance of profits carried forward to next account.
inventaire de fin d'exercice (*m.*), accounts to the end of the financial year.
les dépenses non payées en fin d'exercice (*f.pl.*), the expenses unpaid at the end of the financial year.
combler les pertes des mauvais exercices, to make good the losses of bad years.

exercice — attaché (Abrév. : **ex. — at.** *ou* **ex. — att.**) (opp. à *ex-exercice* —), cum dividend — :
exercice 19— attaché, cum dividend 19—.

exhiber (*v.t.*), to exhibit ; to produce ; to show ; to shew :
exhiber ses livres, to exhibit, to produce, one's books.
exhiber un billet de chemin de fer, to produce, to show, a railway ticket.

exhibition (*n.f.*), exhibition ; production ; showing ; shewing.

exigence (*n.f.*), exigence ; requirement ; demand ; call ; claim :
se conformer aux exigences des assureurs, to comply with the underwriters' requirements.

exiger (*v.t.*), to exact ; to require ; to demand ; to call for ; to claim :
exiger le paiement dans un certain délai, to require, to claim, to demand, payment within a certain time.
exiger l'impôt, to demand the taxes.
exiger le montant entier de la somme assurée, to claim the whole amount of the sum insured.
exiger communication des pièces, to call for production of documents.

exigibilité (*n.f.*), repayability ; payability ; demand ; claim ; current liability :
l'exigibilité d'une dette commence au jour de l'échéance, the repayability of a debt begins on the day it becomes due. See also example under **disponibilité**.
banques obligées de faire face chaque jour à des exigibilités énormes (*f.pl.*), banks called upon daily to meet enormous demands.
le bilan fait ressortir que les disponibilités sont plus que suffisantes pour faire face aux exigibilités, the balance sheet shows that

the liquid assets are more than sufficient to meet the current liabilities.

exigible (*adj.*), repayable; payable; demandable; requirable; claimable; current:
l'émission des billets à vue et au porteur (billets de banque) constitue, au profit des banques, un dépôt exigible sur demande (*f.*), the issue of notes at sight and to bearer (bank notes) constitutes, for the use of the banks, a deposit repayable (*or* payable) on demand.
si aucune échéance n'est indiquée, le droit de timbre exigible sera de tant 0/0, if no time of payment is stated, the stamp duty payable is so much per cent.
les fonds déposés en comptes de chèques sont toujours exigibles, c'est-à-dire que le déposant peut en réclamer le montant à tout moment par la présentation de chèques (*m.pl.*), the money placed on current account is always demandable, that is to say, the customer can claim the amount of it at any time by presenting cheques.
passif exigible *ou* passif exigible à court terme (*m.*), current liabilities.

existence (*n.f.*) *ou* **existant** (*n.m.*), stock: (See also **stock**.)
existence (*ou* existant) en magasin (Com.), stock in warehouse; stock in trade.
existence (*ou* existant) en or, en espèces, en billets de banque, en effets de commerce (Banq.), stock of gold, of cash, of bank notes, of bills of exchange.
existences (*ou* existants) de la (*ou* dans la) (*ou* en) caisse (Banq.), stocks in the till.

exode (*n.m.*), flight:
l'exode de capitaux nationaux en période de troubles monétaires, the flight of national capital in time of monetary troubles.

exonération (*n.f.*), exoneration; exemption; relief:
l'exonération de la taxe dont jouissent ces marchandises, the exemption from the tax which these goods enjoy.

exonérer (*v.t.*), to exonerate; to exempt; to relieve:
exonérer les transporteurs, en tout ou en partie, de leur responsabilité légale, to exonerate, to relieve, the carriers, wholly or partly, from their legal liability.
exonérer quelqu'un de ses fautes ou de celles de ses préposés, to exonerate, to exempt, someone from his faults or those of his servants.
exonérer un minimum de revenu, considéré comme nécessaire à l'existence, to exempt a minimum of income, considered as necessary to existence.

s'exonérer (*v.r.*), to exonerate oneself; to be exonerated:
prétendre s'exonérer de toute responsabilité, to claim to exonerate oneself (*or* to claim to be exonerated) (*or* to claim exoneration) from all liability.
nul ne pouvant s'exonérer de ses fautes personnelles, no one being able to exonerate himself from his personal faults.

exorbitamment (*adv.*), exorbitantly.
exorbitance (*n.f.*), exorbitance:
l'exorbitance des prétentions d'un vendeur, the exorbitance of the claims of a seller.
exorbitant, -e (*adj.*), exorbitant:
demander un prix exorbitant, to ask an exorbitant price.
expédier (envoyer à destination) (*v.t.*), to send; to dispatch; to despatch; to forward; to ship:
expédier une dépêche, une lettre par la poste, to send, to dispatch, a telegram, a letter by post.
expédier les marchandises à leur port de destination, to forward, to ship, the goods to their port of destination.
avant d'expédier le courrier, bien relire les adresses, before dispatching the post, read over the addresses carefully.
expédier (*v.t.*) *ou* **expédier en douane**, to clear; to clear out; to clear outwards:
on dit que le navire est expédié quand il est muni de tous ses papiers, one says that the ship is cleared when she is provided with all her papers.
expédier un acte, to make a copy of a deed and authenticate it. Cf. **expédition**.
expéditeur, -trice (envoyeur) (pers.) (*n.*), sender:
mentionner l'adresse de l'expéditeur au verso de l'enveloppe, to mention the address of the sender on the back of the envelope.
expéditeur (chargeur) (pers.) (*n.m.*), shipper; consignor; consigner.
expéditeur (agent de transport) (*n.m.*), forwarding agent.
expédition (envoi) (*n.f.*) (Abrév.: **expⁿ**), sending; dispatch; despatch; forwarding; shipping; shipment; consignment; transit:
la prompte expédition des marchandises, prompt forwarding (*or* dispatch) (*or* shipment) of the goods.
on cote le sucre de Cuba, expédition en mars-avril à 7 sh. 4 1/2d. caf. Royaume-Uni, Cuban sugar quoted, for March-April shipment at 7s. 4½d. c.i.f. U.K.
expédition par chemin de fer, forwarding by rail.
expédition du connaissement au destinataire des marchandises, dispatch of the bill of lading to the consignee of the goods.
la présente expédition est faite aux conditions portées ci-après, the present shipment is made on the following conditions.
le nombre de caisses composant une expédition, the number of cases making up a shipment (*or* a consignment).
risque de séjour à terre en cours normal d'expédition (*m.*), risk whilst on quays, wharves, or in sheds during the ordinary course of transit.
expédition (aventure) (*n.f.*), adventure:
la sauvegarde de marchandises exposées aux périls d'une expédition maritime, the safeguarding of goods exposed to the perils of a marine adventure.
expédition (*n.f.*) *ou* **expédition en douane**,

clearance; clearing; clearance out (or out-wards); clearing out (or outwards):
expédition du navire, clearance of ship; clearing the ship outwards.

expédition (copie authentique d'un acte judiciaire ou notarié) (*n.f.*), copy:
en France, les notaires ont seuls le droit de délivrer des expéditions des actes dont ils possèdent les minutes, in France, *notaires* have the exclusive right of supplying copies of deeds of which they possess the originals.

expédition (papier de bord) (*n.f.*) (*s'emploie généralement au pluriel*), paper; ship's paper; clearance paper:
le bâtiment est censé prêt à faire voile lorsque le capitaine est muni de ses expéditions pour son voyage, the vessel is reputed to be ready to sail when the master is provided with his papers (or clearance papers) for his voyage.
expéditions de douane, customs papers (such as ships' clearance papers, transires, bond notes, receipts, and the like).

expéditionnaire (expéditeur) (pers.) (*n.m. ou f.*), sender.

expéditionnaire (commis expéditeur de marchandises) (*n.m.*), forwarding clerk; dispatch clerk; shipping clerk.

expéditionnaire (employé chargé de recopier) (*n.m.*), copying clerk.

expérience (*n.f.*), experience; skill.

expérimenté, -e (*adj.*), experienced; skilled:
commis expérimenté (*m.*), experienced clerk.

expert, -e (*adj.*), expert.

expert (pers.) (*n.m.*), expert; valuer; surveyor:
marchandises examinées par des experts (*f.pl.*), goods examined by experts.
expert nommé par le Lloyd, surveyor appointed by Lloyds.
expert-comptable [experts-comptables *pl.*] (*n.m.*), professional accountant.
expert-comptable diplômé, qualified accountant. *See note under* brevet d'expert-comptable reconnu par l'État.
expert écrivain [experts écrivains *pl.*] (*m.*) ou expert en écritures, handwriting expert. *Also, in France*—expert appointed by the Court to pronounce an opinion on the way books of account have been kept.
expert répartiteur d'avaries [experts répartiteurs d'avaries *pl.*] ou expert-dispacheur [experts-dispacheurs *pl.*] (*n.m.*), average adjuster; average stater; average taker; adjuster.

expertise (*n.f.*), survey; examination; valuation:
l'expertise fixe le montant de l'indemnité, the survey fixes the amount of the indemnity.
l'échantillon destiné à l'expertise est prélevé par le service (des douanes) en présence du déclarant (*m.*), the sample for examination is drawn by the (customs) service in presence of the declarant.

expertiser (*v.t.*), to survey; to examine; to value:
expertiser la marchandise et déterminer la nature de l'avarie, to survey the goods and determine the nature of the damage.

expiration (*n.f.*), expiration; expiry:
expiration d'un bail, d'une concession, du temps du risque, de la présente police, des jours de planche, expiration, expiry, of a lease, of a concession, of the time of the risk, of this policy, of the lay days.

expirer (*v.i.*), to expire.

exploit (Dr.) (*n.m.*), writ.

exploitation (action d'exploiter des biens) (*n.f.*), working; operation; running; exploitation; trading:
exploitation d'un brevet, working, running, exploitation of, a patent.
l'exploitation commerciale du navire sous la forme d'affrètement revêt plusieurs formes, the commercial exploitation of the ship in the form of affreightment assumes several forms.
bénéfice d'exploitation (*m.*), trading profit.

exploitation (compte d'exploitation) (Comptab.) (*n.f.*), trading account; working account.

exploitation (entreprise) (*n.f.*), undertaking; concern:
une exploitation commerciale ou industrielle, a commercial or industrial undertaking (or concern).

exploitation (abus) (*n.f.*), exploitation:
exploitation d'un client confiant, exploitation of an unsuspecting client.

exploiter (faire valoir) (*v.t.*), to work; to operate; to run; to exploit:
exploiter un brevet, to work, to run, to exploit, a patent.
exploiter un navire à profit, à perte, to operate, to run, a ship at a profit, at a loss.

s'exploiter (*v.r.*), to be carried on:
les magasins où s'exploite le commerce, the shops where business is carried on.

exploiter (abuser) (*v.t.*), to exploit:
exploiter la crédulité publique, to exploit the credulity of the public.

explosion (*n.f.*), explosion; bursting:
explosion de chaudières, ou de conduites, explosion, bursting, of boilers, or pipes.

exportable (*adj.*), exportable:
marchandises exportables (*f.pl.*), exportable goods.

exportateur, -trice (*adj.*), exporting; export (*used as adj.*):
pays exportateur (*m.*), exporting country.
négociant exportateur (*m.*), export merchant.

exportateur, -trice (pers. ou pays) (*n.*), exporter:
exportateurs des produits français, exporters of French products.
pays qui est gros exportateur de charbon (*m.*), country which is a big exporter of coal.
la Grande-Bretagne est une grande exportatrice de houille, Great Britain is a big exporter of coal.

exportation (action) (*n.f.*) (Ant.: *importation*), export; exportation:
l'exportation des capitaux est parfois interdite, the export (or exportation) of money is sometimes forbidden.

exportation (marchandises exportées) (*n.f.*), export; exportation:

exportations d'Angleterre en Amérique, exports from England to America.

exportations visibles, visible exports.

exportations invisibles, invisible exports.

exporter (*v.t.*), to export :
exporter de l'or, des marchandises, to export gold, goods.

exposant, -e (pers.) (*n.*), exhibitor.

exposant de charge (d'un navire) (*m.*), wind and water line.

exposé (*n.m.*), statement ; account ; return :
exposé de la situation d'une banque, statement of the position of a bank.

exposé de ses opérations, account of one's transactions.

exposition (*n.f.*), exhibition :
expositions et foires commerciales, commercial exhibitions and fairs.

exprès, -esse (*adj.*), express :
envois exprès (Poste) (*m.pl.*), express packets.

stipulation expresse (*f.*), express stipulation.

exprès (*n.m.*), express :
l'exprès s'entend de tout mode de distribution plus rapide que la poste, express is understood to mean any method of delivery quicker than the post.

taxe supplémentaire pour livraison par exprès (Poste) (*f.*), extra charge for delivery by express.

exprès (pers.) (*n.m.*), express messenger.

express (*adj. invar.*), express ; fast :
train express *ou simplement* **express** [**express** *pl.*] (*n.m.*), express train ; express.

bateau express [bateaux express *pl.*] (*m.*), fast boat.

exprimer (*v.t.*), to express :

police qui exprime la durée pour laquelle elle est souscrite (*f.*), policy which expresses the term for which it has been written.

extinction (*n.f.*), extinction ; extinguishing ; paying off :
extinction du feu (*ou* d'incendie) à bord, extinguishing fire on board.

extinction graduelle d'une dette publique, gradual extinction of a national debt.

extourne (Comptab.) (*n.f.*), contraing ; reversal ; reversing ; writing back.

extourner (*v.t.*), to contra ; to reverse ; to write back :
extourner un débit, to contra, to reverse, to write back, a debit.

Note :—*extourner* is to write back the whole of, opposed to *ristourner*, to write back or transfer a part of.

extra-européen, -enne (*adj.*), extra-European :
régime extra-européen (Poste, etc.) (*m.*), extra-European system.

extraire (*v.t.*), to extract ; to abstract.

extrait (*n.m.*), extract ; abstract :
extrait d'un livre, d'un rapport, extract from a book, from a report.

extrait de compte, abstract of account.

extraordinaire (*adj.*) (Abrév. : **extr.**), extraordinary :
assemblée générale extraordinaire (*f.*), extraordinary general meeting.

Extrême Orient (*m.*) (opp. à *Proche Orient*), Far East.

extrinsèque (*adj.*) (Ant. : *intrinsèque*), extrinsic :
la valeur extrinsèque d'une pièce de monnaie, the extrinsic value of a coin.

extrinsèquement (*adv.*), extrinsically.

F

fabricant (pers.) (*n.m.*), manufacturer ; maker.

fabrication (*n.f.*), manufacture.

fabrique (*n.f.*), manufactory ; factory ; works ; mill.

fabriquer (*v.t.*), to manufacture ; to make :
fabriquer des marchandises, to manufacture goods.

fabriqué en France, en Angleterre (mention d'origine), made in France, in England.

facile (Fin.) (*adj.*) (opp. à *serré*), easy :
l'escompte est facile lorsque le taux privé est bien plus faible que le taux officiel de l'escompte (*m.*), discount is easy when the market rate is much lower than the bank rate of discount.   Cf. **serré** and **nominal**.

le marché monétaire français est toujours très facile, the French money market is still very easy.

facilité (Fin.) (*n.f.*), easiness ; ease :
reprise stimulée par la facilité de l'argent (*f.*), recovery stimulated by the easiness of money.

factage (Ch. de f.) (*n.m.*), cartage ; parcels cartage (collection or delivery of parcels sent or received by passenger train, in distinction to **camionnage**, q.v.).

factage (prix du transport) (*n.m.*), cartage.

facteur (*n.m.*), factor :
le plus important facteur à considérer, the most important factor to be considered.

facteur (*n.m.*) *ou* **facteur de la poste** *ou* **facteur des postes** (pers.), postman :
facteur rural, rural postman.

facteur cycliste, postman on cycle.

facteur enfant [facteurs enfants *pl.*] (*m.*) *ou* facteur-télégraphiste [facteurs-télégraphistes *pl.*] (*n.m.*) *ou* facteur des télégraphes, telegraph boy ; telegraph messenger.

facteur en douane (pers.) (*m.*), custom's agent ; custom house broker.

factorerie (comptoir, bureau des agents d'une compagnie de commerce en pays étranger) (*n.f.*), agency ; foreign agency.

facturation (*n.f.*), invoicing ; billing.

facture (*n.f.*) (Abrév. : **fre**), invoice; bill; note:
  facture consulaire, consular invoice.
  facture d'achat, purchase invoice.
  facture d'avoir *ou* facture de crédit, credit note.
  facture d'ordre, departmental invoice (i.e., invoice rendered from one department to another for accountancy or record purposes).
  facture d'origine, invoice of origin.
  facture de débit (opp. à *facture d'avoir*), invoice; debit note.
  facture de la cargaison, manifest.
  facture de vente, sale invoice.
  facture fictive *ou* facture simulée *ou* facture pro forma, pro forma invoice.
  facture finale, final invoice.
  facture générale, statement (of account).
  facture originale, original invoice.
  facture provisoire, provisional invoice.
  facture rectificative, corrected invoice; amended invoice.
facturer (*v.t.*), to invoice; to bill:
  facturer des marchandises, to invoice, to bill, goods.
facturier (pers.) (*n.m.*), invoice clerk.
facturier (copie des factures) (*n.m.*), invoice book.
facturier d'entrée (*m.*), purchases book; purchases day book; purchases journal; purchase book; purchase journal; bought book; bought journal; invoice book.
facturier de sortie (*m.*), sales book; day book; sales day book; sales journal.
facultatif, -ive (*adj.*), optional:
  le sauvetage est facultatif et ne peut être imposé, salvage is optional and cannot be imposed.
faculté (droit) (*n.f.*), option; right; leave; liberty:
  exercer la faculté de souscrire, to exercise the option of subscribing.
  faculté de rachat *ou* faculté de réméré, option of repurchase:
  vendre avec faculté de rachat, to sell with the option of repurchase.
  faculté d'émission de billets de banque, de disposer de ses biens, right of issuing bank notes, of disposing of one's property.
  avec faculté de naviguer avec ou sans pilotes, with leave to sail with or without pilots.
  avec toutes les facultés mentionnées aux connaissements, with all liberties as per bills of lading.
  facultés de toutes déviations ou changements de voyage, moyennant surprime à débattre (Assce mar.), held covered at an additional premium to be arranged in case of deviation or change of voyage.
facultés (Assce mar.) (*n.f.pl.*), cargo; goods (as distinguished from the *hull* or *ship*):
  assurance sur corps et facultés (*f.*), insurance of hull and cargo (*or* of ship and goods).
  les facultés assurées sont couvertes depuis le moment où elles quittent le magasin de l'expéditeur jusqu'à celui de leur entrée dans les magasins des réceptionnaires, the insured goods are covered from the time of leaving the shipper's warehouse until deposited in consignees' warehouses.

facultés à la baisse (Bourse) (*f.pl.*). See phrases:
  faculté de livrer double, put of more; put o' more; seller's option to double.
  faculté de livrer triple, put of twice more; seller's option to treble.
  faculté de livrer quadruple, put of three times more; seller's option to quadruple.
  Note :—The above kinds of puts are known generically in French as facultés à la baisse.
facultés à la hausse (Bourse) (*f.pl.*). See phrases:
  faculté de lever double, call of more; call o' more; buyer's option to double.
  faculté de lever triple, call of twice more; buyer's option to treble.
  faculté de lever quadruple, call of three times more; buyer's option to quadruple.
  Note :—The above kinds of calls *are known generically in French as* facultés à la hausse.
faiblage (*n.m.*) *ou* **faiblage de poids** (Monnayage), tolerance of weight; tolerance for error in weight; remedy of (*or* for) weight.
faiblage d'aloi (*m.*), tolerance of (*or* for error in) fineness; remedy of (*or* for) fineness.
faible (*adj.*), weak; low; small; slender; light:
  la tendance du marché a été très faible, the tendency of the market has been very weak.
  faible revenu (*m.*), low (*or* small) (*or* slender) income.
  faible somme d'argent (*f.*), small sum of money.
  pièce faible (*f.*), light coin. See example under **pièce**.
faiblesse (*n.f.*), weakness; lowness; smallness; slenderness; lightness.
faiblir (*v.i.*), to weaken:
  l'action X. faiblit de 435 à 400, X. shares weakened from 435 to 400 francs.
failli, -e (*adj.*), bankrupt; insolvent:
  commerçant failli (*m.*), bankrupt trader; insolvent merchant.
failli, -e (pers.) (*n.*), bankrupt; insolvent debtor; insolvent:
  failli non réhabilité, undischarged bankrupt.
faillir (faire faillite) (*v.i.*), to fail; to become bankrupt; to become insolvent.
faillite (*n.f.*), failure; bankruptcy; insolvency. See note under **banqueroute**.
fair-trade (Écon. polit.) (*n.m.*), fair trade.
faire (*v.t.*). See examples:
  faire accorder les livres (Comptab.), to make the books agree; to agree, to reconcile, the books.
  faire accueil à une traite, à une disposition, à une lettre, to honour, to meet, a draft, a bill.
  faire affaire, to do business:
  nous espérons faire affaire ensemble, we hope to do business together.
  faire apparaître des bénéfices mensongers en majorant les valeurs d'échange, to show illusory profits by overvaluing the exchange.
  faire appel, to appeal; to call; to invite:
  le fait que l'État n'a pas fait appel au crédit public est la preuve tangible de la restauration des finances publiques, the fact that the government has not appealed to public

credit is the tangible proof of the restoration of the public finances.

sentence arbitrale contre laquelle appel a été faite (*f.*), arbitration award appealed from.

faire appel à une garantie, to call on a guarantee.

faire appel aux actionnaires pour souscrire le capital d'une nouvelle société, to invite the shareholders to subscribe the capital of a new company.

faire apport, to transfer; to assign. See examples under syn. **apporter.**

faire argent d'une chose, to turn a thing into money.

faire argent d'une opération, to make money out of a transaction.

faire assembler, to call together :
faire assembler les actionnaires, to call the shareholders together.

faire assurer, to insure; to assure; to make insurance of :
faire assurer son mobilier, la cargaison d'un navire, to insure one's furniture, a ship's cargo.
faire assurer sur sa vie, to insure, to assure, one's life.
l'assuré peut faire assurer la prime de l'assurance. En matière d'assurance maritime, on peut faire assurer la prime et la prime de la prime, the insured can insure the premium of insurance. In marine insurance, one can insure the premium and the premium on the premium.
les grandes compagnies de navigation font rarement assurer leurs navires, et restent ainsi leurs propres assureurs, the big shipping companies seldom insure (*or* make insurance of) their ships, and so are their own insurers.

faire banqueroute, to go, to become, bankrupt.

faire bon accueil à une traite, à une disposition, à une lettre, to honour, to meet, a draft, a bill.

faire bon compte, to sell cheap.

faire bonne figure, to make a good showing.

faire cadeau de quelque chose à quelqu'un, to make a present of something to someone.

faire cadrer un compte, to make an account agree; to agree, to reconcile, an account.

faire circuler des capitaux, to circulate capital.

faire collision, to come into collision ; to collide; to foul; to run foul :
navire qui fait collision avec un autre navire *m.*), ship which comes into collision with *or* collides with) (*or* fouls) (*or* runs foul of) another ship.

faire commerce de métaux précieux, to trade in precious metals.

faire compenser (Bourse), to have made up :
faire compenser son achat et sa vente avec tel ou tel agent ou banquier, to have one's purchase and one's sale made up with such or such broker.

faire concurrence à quelqu'un, to compete, to be in competition, with someone.

faire connaître toute circonstance essentielle, to disclose every material circumstance.

faire courir, to attach :
lorsque le règlement d'un port fait courir les surestaries pendant l'arrêt du steamer, when the regulation of a port attaches demurrage during the stoppage of the steamer.

faire courir le découvert (Bourse), to frighten the bears.

faire crédit, to give credit :
le détenteur d'un billet de banque fait crédit à la banque qui l'a émis, the holder of a bank note gives credit to the bank which has issued it.

faire de bonnes affaires, to do good business.

faire de l'argent, to make money.

faire de l'argent d'une chose, to turn a thing into money.

faire déduction des sommes payées d'avance, to deduct the amounts paid in advance.

faire défaut (*v.i.*), to fail; to be missing :
faire défaut à ses engagements, to fail in one's engagements.
faire défaut à l'acceptation d'un effet, to dishonour a bill; to dishonour a bill by non acceptance; to fail to accept a bill.
faire défaut au paiement d'un effet, to dishonour a bill ; to dishonour a bill by non payment; to fail to pay a bill.
si une partie des objets fait défaut à la livraison, if a part of the articles is missing on delivery.

faire des affaires avec quelqu'un, to do business, to transact business, to deal, with someone.

faire des arbitrages (*ou* des couvertures) (Bourse), to hedge.

faire des avances à quelqu'un, en compte courant, to make advances to someone, on account current.

faire des dettes, to run (*or* to get) into debt.

faire des économies, to save ; to husband one's resources.

faire des frais, to go to expense.

faire des pertes à la bourse, to make losses on the stock exchange.

faire des placements, to invest; to make investments :
faire des placements en valeurs de bourse, to invest, to make investments, in stocks and shares.

faire des sondages dans (vérifications comptables), to challenge :
faire des sondages dans les titres en dépôt, à bâtons rompus, mais en prenant des dispositions pour qu'une vérification totale de tous les dossiers ait eu lieu dans le courant de chaque année, to challenge the securities in safe custody, not the whole lot straightaway, but arranging matters in such a way that a complete check is made of every bundle in the course of each year.

faire diminuer le prix des valeurs, to lower the price of stocks.

faire double emploi, to duplicate:
commission qui fait double emploi avec une autre commission déjà prélevée (*f.*), commission which duplicates with another commission already charged. *Cf.* double emploi.

faire du charbon, to coal; to bunker; to take in coal:
faire du charbon en route est fort cher, to coal en route (*or* bunkering en route) is very expensive.
relâcher pour faire du charbon, to call for bunkering.

faire écouler des actions, to place, to sell, shares.

faire écriture d'un article au grand livre, d'un article en compte courant, de quelque chose sur un livre, to enter, to enter up, an item in the ledger, an item in current account, something in a book.

faire enregistrer ses bagages en temps voulu, to have one's baggage registered in proper time.

faire entrer en (*ou* au) bassin, to dock:
faire entrer au bassin un navire, to dock a ship.
faire entrer un navire en cale sèche '(*ou* dans la forme), to dry-dock a ship.

faire entrer en compte, to bring into account.

faire escale *ou* faire échelle, to call; to call at; to call at a named port (*or* at an intermediate port) (*or* at intermediate ports); to make a call. See examples under **escale.**

faire face à, to meet:
faire face à une échéance, à une demande, aux dépenses courantes, aux retraits quotidiens, to meet a bill, a demand, current expenses, daily withdrawals.

faire faillite, to fail; to go bankrupt; to become insolvent.

faire figurer, to show; to shew:
faire figurer la réserve au passif, to show the reserve among the liabilities.

faire foi, to be evidence:
le procès-verbal fait foi jusqu'à preuve contraire, the minutes are evidence until the contrary is proved.

faire fortune, to make a fortune:
faire fortune à la bourse, to make a fortune on the stock exchange.

faire grâce à quelqu'un d'une dette, to forgive someone a debt.

faire grève (se mettre en grève), to go on strike; to strike; to walk out.

faire honneur à, to honour; to meet:
faire honneur à une lettre de change, to honour, to meet, a bill of exchange.
faire honneur à sa signature, to honour one's signature.
faire honneur à ses engagements, to meet one's engagements.

faire inscrire un navire au bureau de l'inscription maritime, to enter a ship at the marine registry office.

faire l'abandon. *See under* faire le délaissement.

faire l'acquit de sa charge, to fulfil one's trust.

faire l'affaire, to bring a thing off; to do the business:
nous espérons faire l'affaire, we hope to bring the thing off; we hope to do the business.

faire l'application (ordres de bourse), to cross; to match; to marry. See example under **application.**

faire l'appoint, to make up an amount with small coin (*or* with minor coin) (*or* with small change). See example under **appoint.**

faire l'appréciation de *ou* faire l'évaluation de, to make a valuation (*or* an estimate) of; to value; to estimate:
faire l'appréciation des marchandises, to make a valuation of (*or* to value) goods.
faire l'évaluation des pertes occasionnées par un incendie, to make an estimate of (*or* to estimate) the losses caused by a fire.

faire l'entrée en douane d'un navire, to enter, to clear, a ship inwards.

faire l'escompte de, to discount:
faire l'escompte des effets de commerce, to discount bills of exchange.

faire l'examen d'un compte, to make an examination of, to examine, to go into, an account.

faire l'historique d'une négociation, to write an account of a transaction.

faire l'impossible *ou* faire tout son possible, to do one's utmost (*or* one's very utmost):
en cas de péril, le capitaine est tenu de faire l'impossible pour sauver l'argent et les marchandises les plus précieuses de son chargement, in case of peril, the master is bound to do his utmost (*or* his very utmost) to save the money and the most valuable goods of his cargo.
l'assuré doit faire tout son possible pour sauver la chose assurée (*m.*), the insured must do his utmost to save the property insured.

faire l'inventaire de ses marchandises, to take stock, to make an inventory, of one's goods.

faire la balance des affaires de l'année, to balance, to balance up, the books for the year.

faire la balance entre l'actif et le passif, to strike the balance between the assets and the liabilities.

faire la banque, to do banking business.

faire la caisse, to make up the cash:
le caissier doit faire sa caisse tous les jours; on entend par là, vérifier si le montant des espèces en caisse correspond bien à celui qui ressort du livre de caisse, the cashier should make up his cash every day; this means, seeing whether the amount of cash in hand agrees with that shown by the cash book.

faire la contre-partie (Bourse), to carry stock; to run stock (against one's client):
lorsque le prix du report devient assez rémunérateur pour tenter le capital disponible, les banquiers et capitalistes viennent s'offrir pour faire la contre-partie de l'acheteur qui veut se faire reporter, when the contango rate becomes sufficiently

remunerative to tempt available capital, the bankers and capitalists come along and offer to carry the stock for the buyer who wishes to give on.

banquier marron qui se présente faussement à ses clients comme intermédiaire pour l'exécution de leurs ordres de bourse, dont il fait la contre-partie (*m.*), outside broker who holds himself out falsely to his clients as intermediary for the execution of their stock exchange orders, in respect of which he runs the stock.

Cf. se faire la contre-partie, **contre-partie, contre-partiste,** *and* maison de contre-partie.

faire la contrebande, to smuggle (*v.i.*).

faire la correspondance, to do, to attend to, the correspondence.

faire la déclaration de ses bénéfices, de son revenu global (Impôts cédulaires), to make a return of one's profits, of one's total income.

faire la délivrance du chargement contre paiement du fret, to make delivery of the shipment against payment of the freight.

faire la minute de, to make a draft of; to draft:
  faire la minute d'une lettre, to make a draft of, to draft, a letter.

faire la paie, to pay the wages.

faire la place, to do the place; to canvass the town.

faire la preuve du chargé, d'un sinistre, de la valeur de la chose assurée, de la quantité chargée, que la perte de sa marchandise est due à un vol à bord, to prove shipment, a loss, the value of the thing insured, the quantity shipped, that the loss of one's goods is due to a theft on board.

faire la transcription au net d'un manuscrit, to make a fair copy of a manuscript.

faire le commerce, to trade; to deal:
  faire le commerce de métaux précieux, to trade in precious metals.

les spéculateurs qui font le commerce des primes (*m.pl.*), speculators who deal in options.

faire le compte de, to count; to count up; to reckon; to reckon up:
  faire le compte de son argent, to count, to count up, one's money.

faire le courtage, to be a broker; to do broking; to broke; to buy and sell on commission:
  faire le courtage des assurances maritimes, c'est-à-dire de mettre en rapport assureurs et assurés, to broke in marine insurance, that is to say, to put into communication insurers and insured.

faire le délaissement *ou* faire l'abandon, to make abandonment; to abandon:
  assuré qui n'est plus recevable à faire le délaissement (*m.*), assured who no longer has the right to make abandonment (*or* to abandon). See also example under **délaissement.**

faire le dépôt de, to deposit:
  faire le dépôt d'un testament chez un banquier, to deposit a will with a banker.

faire le dépouillement d'un compte, to make an analysis of, to analyze, to examine, to look into, to go through, an account.

faire le double d'un acte, to make a duplicate of, to duplicate, a deed.

faire le nécessaire, to do the necessary:
  nous vous prions de vouloir bien faire le nécessaire pour notre compte pour le recouvrement de cette créance (*ou* pour recouvrer cette créance), we beg you to have the kindness to do the necessary for the recovery of this debt (*or* to recover this debt).

faire le placement des actions, to place shares.

faire le pourcentage des frais généraux, to work out the percentage of establishment charges.

faire le protêt d'une lettre de change, to note protest of a bill of exchange.

faire le relevé de *ou* faire le relèvement de, to make out, to draw up, a statement of:
  faire le relevé d'un compte, de son actif et de son passif, to make out a statement, to draw up a statement, of an account, of one's assets and liabilities.

faire le reportage des délibérations d'une assemblée d'actionnaires, to report the proceedings of a shareholders' meeting.

faire les fonds, to find the money:
  A. fait les fonds pour moitié, B. et C. chacun pour un quart, A. finds half the money, B. and C. each a quarter.

faire les frais de, to bear the cost (*or* the expense) of:
  faire les frais d'une entreprise, to bear the cost of an undertaking.

faire monter (*v.t.*), to raise; to force up:
  faire monter les grains en les accaparant, to force up the price of grain by cornering it.

faire naufrage, to be wrecked; to be shipwrecked; to be lost:
  navire qui fait naufrage sans laisser de trace (*m.*), ship which is wrecked (*or* lost) without leaving a trace.

faire naviguer (*v.t.*), to navigate; to sail; to run:
  le droit de faire naviguer ledit navire sous pavillon français, the right to sail the said ship under the French flag.
  faire naviguer un navire à profit, à perte, to run a ship at a profit, at a loss.

faire partie de, to form part of; to belong to; to be a member of:
  faire partie d'un comité, to be a member of, to belong to, a committee.
  somme qui fait partie des frais (*f.*), amount which forms part of the expenses.

faire passer au bassin un navire (*v.t.*), to dock a ship.

faire perte (opp. à *faire prime*), to stand at a discount. See example under **perte.**

faire peser puis enregistrer ses bagages, to have one's luggage weighed and then registered.

faire place nette, to dismiss, to discharge, all the staff; to sack the lot (*slang*).

faire preuve de, to show; to shew; to display: le marché des valeurs continue à faire preuve de résistance, à faire preuve d'une grande animation, the stock market continues to show (*or* to display) strength, to show (*or* display) a good deal of liveliness.

faire prime, to stand at a premium. See examples under **prime.**

faire protester, to protest: porteur d'un effet qui fait protester faute d'acceptation, faute de paiement (*m.*), holder of a bill who protests for non acceptance, for non payment.

faire relâche, to call; to put in (for supplies or shelter). See examples under syn. **relâcher.**

faire remarquer une erreur, une omission, to call attention to a mistake, an omission.

faire remise d'une somme d'argent, to make a remittance of, to remit, a sum of money.

faire rentrer une créance, to collect, to recover, a debt.

faire reporter (Bourse) (*v.t.*) (*Abrév.*: f.r. *ou* fr. *ou* v/a.), to give on; to give the rate on; to give on stock for; to lend: faire reporter une position à la liquidation prochaine, to give on, to give the rate on, a position (*or* a book) for the next account (*or* for new time).

faire reporter des titres, to give on, to give the rate on, to lend, stock.

faire reporter un prêteur, to give on stock for a lender.

Cf. **reporter** (opérer un report sur).

faire ressortir (*v.t.*), to show; to shew: faire ressortir des bénéfices mensongers en majorant les valeurs d'échange, to show illusory profits by overvaluing the exchange.

compte qui fait ressortir une perte (*m.*), account which shows a loss.

colonne faisant ressortir la balance de chaque compte (*f.*), column showing the balance of each account.

faire rouler des capitaux, to turn over capital: le commerce consiste non à placer mais à faire rouler des capitaux, trade consists not in investing but in turning over capital.

faire sa fortune, to make one's fortune.

faire ses affaires *ou* faire son affaire, to succeed in business; to make a fortune: une société qui ne fait pas ses affaires entre en liquidation, a company which does not succeed in business goes into liquidation.

faire ses affaires (*ou* son affaire) sur la bourse, to make a fortune on the stock exchange.

faire ses frais, to make, to cover, one's expenses.

faire son inventaire tous les six mois, au moins une fois l'an, to make up one's accounts every six months, at least once a year.

faire son testament, to make one's will.

faire sortir de (*ou* d'en) (*ou* du) bassin (*v.t.*), to undock: faire sortir de bassin un navire, to undock a ship.

faire suivre (*v.t.*), to forward; to send on; to redirect: faire suivre la marchandise par un autre bateau, to send on, to forward, the goods by another boat.

donner l'ordre de faire suivre des télégrammes par la voie télégraphique, par la voie postale, to give orders to redirect telegrams by telegraph, by post.

si le destinataire est parti à l'étranger, ne pas faire suivre, if the addressee has gone abroad, do not forward.

faire suivre (mention sur un objet de correspondance), please forward; to be forwarded.

faire table rase, to make a clean sweep: faire table rase des considérations qui précèdent, to make a clean sweep of former considerations.

faire tenir (*v.t.*), to remit; to send: je vous fais tenir par la poste un mandat de tant de francs, I am remitting (*or* sending) you by post an order for so many francs.

faire timbrer un acte à l'extraordinaire, to get an instrument stamped at the Revenue Office.

faire titre, to confer title: tous les écrits privés susceptibles de faire titre sont soumis au droit de timbre, all private written agreements capable of conferring title are liable to stamp duty.

faire tout son possible. *See under* faire l'impossible.

faire traite sur quelqu'un, to draw, to draw a bill, on someone.

faire un appel de fonds, to make a call.

faire un arbitrage de portefeuille, de valeurs, to make a change of investments, of stocks.

faire un bon placement, to make a good investment.

faire un brouillon de lettre, to make a draft of a letter.

faire un compromis, to make a compromise; to compromise.

faire un contre-passement (Comptab.), to make, to pass, a transfer.

faire un coup sur la bourse, to bring off a coup on the stock exchange.

faire un emprunt (*ou* un prêt), to make a loan.

faire un escompte, to allow a discount: faire un escompte de 5 p. 100, to allow a discount of 5%.

faire un escompte (Bourse), to call for delivery before the settlement. See **escompte** (Bourse).

faire un faux calcul, to make a wrong calculation; to make a mistake in calculation.

faire un marché, un marché avantageux, to do, to make, to enter into, to transact, a bargain, a good bargain. Cf. **fait, -e** and **pratiqué, -e.**

faire un paiement, to make a payment.

faire un prix, to quote, to price.

faire un rapport, to make a report; to report: faire un rapport sur les comptes, sur la situation d'une société, to make a report (*or* to report) on the accounts, on the position of a company.

faire un recouvrement, to recover, to collect, a debt.

faire un report (Comptab.), to carry over a total.

faire un report (Bourse) (*v.i.*), to carry over; to continue; to contango:

le capitaliste ou l'agent qui fait un report ne spécule point à proprement parler: il prête sur dépôt de titres, the capitalist or the broker who carries over (*or* continues) (*or* contangoes) does not speculate properly speaking: he lends on deposit of stock.

faire un versement (*ou* un envoi) (*ou* une remise) de fonds, to make a remittance of funds.

faire un versement sur des titres non libérés, to pay an instalment (*or* a call) on partly paid shares.

faire un voyage, to go on a voyage (*or* a trip); to make a journey.

faire une annonce dans un journal, to put an advertisement, to advertise, in a newspaper.

faire une application, to call upon (*or* on) the underwriters (to take up shares). Cf. **application.**

faire une bonne affaire, to make a good bargain; to do a good piece of business.

faire une commande de marchandises, to give an order for goods.

faire une déclaration au greffier, to make a return to the registrar.

faire une déclaration en douane d'un navire, de marchandises, to pass a customs entry of a ship, of goods.

faire une distraction pour être distribuée aux employés, to make an appropriation, to set aside a sum, for distribution among the staff.

faire une écriture sur le journal, to make an entry in the journal.

faire une erreur de calcul, to make a mistake in calculation; to make a wrong calculation.

faire une fausse spéculation, to make a bad speculation.

faire une fraude, to commit a fraud.

faire une moyenne (Bourse), to average:
faire une moyenne de ses achats, de ses ventes, to average one's purchases, one's sales.

faire une proposition à quelqu'un, to make a proposal (*or* a proposition) to someone.

faire une proposition à une assemblée, to propose a resolution to, to move a resolution at, a meeting.

faire une remise de 5 0/0 sur le montant brut d'une facture, to allow a discount of 5% on the gross amount of an invoice.

faire une remise de fonds, to make a remittance of, to remit, funds.

faire une visite, to pay a visit; to make a call.

faire valoir (*v.t.*), to turn to account (*or* to profit) (*or* to advantage); to employ:

faire valoir son bien, to turn one's property to account.

faire valoir son argent, to employ one's money.

faire-valoir (*n.m.*), turning to account (*or* to profit) (*or* to advantage).

faire varier (*v.t.*), to cause to vary:
l'abondance ou la rareté de marchandises fait varier le prix (*f.*), the abundance or scarcity of goods causes the price to vary.

faire voile (*v.i.*), to sail:
lorsque le navire a fait voile, il était hors d'état de naviguer, when the ship sailed, she was unseaworthy.

navire prêt à faire voile (*m.*), ship ready (*or* about) to sail.

faire (prononcer le cours de) (Bourse) (*v.t.*), to be called; to call:

la Rente fait tant; les actions X.Y.Z. font tant, Rentes are called so much *or* they call Rentes so much; X.Y.Z. shares are called so much *or* they call X.Y.Z. shares so much.

on a introduit aujourd'hui le nouvel emprunt de conversion qui fait 1/4 0/0 de prime, there was introduced to-day the new conversion loan which is called $\frac{1}{4}$% premium.

faire (demander un prix) (*v.t.*), to ask for; to offer at:

faire une chose — francs, to ask — francs for a thing; to offer a thing at — francs.

faire (ne) que changer son argent, only to get one's money back; to make nothing out of it:

je n'ai fait que changer mon argent, I have only got my money back; I have made nothing out of it.

faire (se) (*v.r.*). See examples:
l'émission se fait au pair (*f.*), the issue is made at par.

les opérations au comptant sont celles qui se font argent contre titres, ou titres contre argent (*f.pl.*), dealings for cash are those which are done money against stock, or stock against money.

se faire assurer, to insure; to assure:
se faire assurer contre l'incendie, contre toutes fautes ou prévarications du capitaine et de l'équipage, to insure against fire, against any wrongful acts or defaults of the master and crew.

se faire escompter un billet, to get a bill discounted:
le capitaine d'un navire peut tirer une lettre de change sur l'armateur et se la faire escompter, the master of a ship can draw a bill of exchange on the owner and get it discounted.

se faire faire des avances (d'argent), to get, to obtain, advances (of money).

se faire indemniser par l'assureur pour la totalité de la perte, to recover from the insurer the whole of the loss.

se faire la contre-partie, to run stock, to speculate, against each other:
dans le report acheteurs et vendeurs se font la contre-partie pour le plus grand nombre

de transactions engagées, in contangoing buyers and sellers run stock against each other (or speculate against each other) in most of the dealings engaged in.

Cf. faire la contre-partie, **contre-partie, contre-partiste,** *and* maison de contre-partie.

se faire livrer des titres négociés à terme, to call for delivery of shares dealt in for the settlement.

se faire ouvrir un compte, to open an account (for oneself):
commerçant qui veut se faire ouvrir un compte à une banque, chez un banquier (*m.*), trader who wishes to open an account at a bank, with a banker.

se faire réassurer, to reinsure:
se faire réassurer auprès d'un autre assureur, to reinsure with another underwriter.

se faire rembourser **par** l'assureur une partie de la prime versée, to recover from the underwriter a part of the premium paid.

se faire remorquer, to be towed:
navire qui se fait remorquer par un autre navire (*m.*), ship which is towed by another ship.

se faire reporter (*Abrév.:* f.r. *ou* fr. *ou* v/a.), to give on; to give the rate; to lend stock. See examples under **reporter** (prendre en report), and under **report** (loyer).

se faire représenter, to be represented:
les actionnaires ont le droit de se faire représenter par des mandataires dans toutes les assemblées (*m.pl.*), the shareholders have the right to be represented at all meetings by proxies.

se faire un joli revenu, to make a fine income (for oneself).

se faire une moyenne (Bourse), to average:
gens qui se font une moyenne après une forte baisse (*m.pl.*), people who average after a heavy fall.

se faire une opinion du risque auquel une cargaison est exposée, to form an opinion of the risk to which a cargo is exposed.

faiseur d'affaires (pers.) (*m.*), shady financier.

faiseur de moyenne (Bourse) (pers.) (*m.*), averager.

fait, -e (*p.p.*), done; made:
fait double (*ou* fait en double) à Paris, le 1ᵉʳ janvier 19—, done (*or* made) in duplicate at Paris, the 1st January 19—.
cours faits (Bourse) (*m.pl.*), bargains done; business done; prices made.

fait, -e (en parlant des effets, du papier de commerce) (*adj.*), guaranteed; backed:
papier fait (*m.*) *ou* valeurs faites (*f.pl.*), guaranteed bills; backed bills.

fait (*n.m.*), fact; act:
fait matériel, material fact.
ce sera une simple question de fait que de distinguer dans chaque cas les conséquences directes et les conséquences indirectes, it is a simple question of fact to distinguish in each case the direct consequences and the indirect consequences.
fait ou faute de l'assuré, d'un tiers, act or fault of the insured, of a third party.

fait de Dieu, act of God.

fait du prince *ou* fait du souverain (Dr. internat.), act of a prince:
les conséquences résultant du fait du prince (*f.pl.*), the consequences resulting from the act of a prince.

faits de guerre, acts of war.

faits de heurt de digues, quais, etc. (police d'assurance sur corps), injury to piers, wharves, etc. (hull insurance policy).

faits de mort ou de blessures de personnes, loss of life or personal injury:
responsabilité pour faits de mort ou de blessures de personnes (*f.*), responsibility for loss of life or personal injury.

falsificateur, -trice (pers.) (*n.*), falsifier; forger.

falsification (*n.f.*), falsification:
falsification d'écritures comptables, falsification of accounts.

falsifier (*v.t.*), to falsify; to tamper with; to forge:
falsifier un registre, to falsify, to tamper with, a book.
falsifier une signature, to forge a signature.

fardage (d'arrimage) (*n.m.*), dunnage.

farde (Papeterie) (*n.f.*), folder.

fardeau de la preuve (*m.*), burden of proof (or of proving); onus of proof (or of proving):
fardeau de la preuve qui incombe à l'assureur, burden (*or* onus) of proof which falls on the insurer.
mettre à la charge de quelqu'un le fardeau de la preuve d'une faute, to throw on someone the burden (*or* onus) of proving a wrongful act.

farder (*v.t.*), to dunnage.

faussaire (pers.) (*n.m.* ou *f.*), forger.

faussement (*adv.*), falsely; wrongly; erroneously.

fausser (*v.t.*), to falsify:
fausser un bilan, to falsify a balance sheet.

fausseté (*n.f.*), falsity; falseness; untruth:
fausseté des énonciations d'un connaissement, falsity, falseness, of the particulars of a bill of lading.

faute (*n.f.*), fault; wrongful act; error; blame:
responsabilité des fautes et négligences des capitaine, pilote, marins, agent, préposé, ou autres personnes, liability for the wrongful acts (*or* faults) and defaults (*or* negligence) of the master, pilot, crew, agent, servant, or other persons.
navire en faute (*m.*), ship in (*or* at) fault (*or* to blame).
aucune faute ne peut être imputée au préposé de la compagnie, no blame can be imputed to the company's servant.
faute d'arrimage, fault of stowing.
faute d'impression, printer's error; misprint.
faute de copiste, clerical error.

faute de, failing; in default of; for want of:
faute de paiement dans les trente jours, failing, in default of, payment in thirty days.
le groupe bancaire est irrégulier, faute d'affaires (Bourse), the bank group is irregular, for want of business.

fauteuil de la présidence (assemblée) (*m.*), chair:

M. X. occupe le fauteuil de la présidence,
Mr X. was in the chair.

faux, fausse (*adj.*),   false;   wrong;   untrue;
erroneous; base; bad; forged :
faux bilan (*m.*), false balance sheet.
faux chèque (*m.*), forged cheque.
calcul faux (*m.*), wrong (*or* erroneous) calculation.
faux emploi (Comptab.) (*m.*), wrong entry.
faux frais (Dr.) (*m.pl.*), untaxable costs.
faux frais (petites dépenses imprévues) (*m.pl.*),
incidental expenses.
faux fret (*m.*), (In France) half freight or forfeit freight payable in certain cases on
throwing up a charter or cancelling a freight
booking.
faux numéro *ou* faux numéro d'appel (Téléph.)
(*m.*), wrong number.
fausse adresse (*f.*), wrong address.
fausse déclaration (*f.*), false (*or* untrue) declaration (*or* statement) ; misstatement ; misrepresentation.
fausse marque de fabrique (*f.*),   false trade
mark.
fausse monnaie (*f.*), bad money; base coin ;
counterfeit coin.
fausse spéculation (*f.*), bad speculation.

faux (*n.m.*), falsification ; forgery :
faux en écritures comptables, falsification of
accounts.

faveur (*n.f.*), favour; favor :
l'action X. est en faveur (Bourse), X. shares
are in favour.

favorable (*adj.*), favourable ; favorable :
change favorable (*m.*), favourable exchange ;
exchange for us.

femme mariée commerçante (*f.*), married woman
engaged in business ;   feme sole trader ;
feme sole merchant.

fenêtre de viseur (d'une machine à calculer) (*f.*),
dial opening.

fer (*abrév. de* chemin de fer) (*n.m.*), rail ; railway ;
railroad :
réexpédition par fer ou par eau à destination
de l'intérieur (*f.*), reforwarding by rail or
water to inland destination.

fermage (*n.m.*), rent :
au point de vue économique, le fermage des
terres et le loyer des maisons ne sont que des
variétés de l'intérêt du capital, from the
economic point of view, rent on lands and
rent on houses are only varieties of interest on
capital. (*Cf.* **affermage** and **affermer.**)

fermant à clef, lockup :
tiroir fermant à clef (*m.*), lockup drawer.

ferme (opp. à *conditionnel*) (Com. et Fin.) (*adj.*),
firm :
offre ferme (*f.*), firm offer.
garantie de prise ferme (*f.*), firm underwriting.

ferme (opp. à *à prime*) (Bourse) (*adj.*), firm :
marché ferme [marchés fermes *pl.*] (*m.*) (opp. à
marché à prime), firm bargain ; firm deal.
See examples under **prime** (marché à prime).

ferme (soutenu à un taux élevé) (Bourse et Com.)
(*adj.*), firm :
le marché est ferme, the market is firm.

les valeurs de sucre sont plus fermes dans
l'ensemble (*f.pl.*), sugar shares were firmer
generally.

ferme (*adv.*), firm :
achetez 100 actions ferme, buy 100 shares firm.
titres achetés ferme (*m.pl.*), stock bought firm.
je suis acheteur ferme, nous sommes vendeurs
ferme, I am a firm buyer, we are firm sellers.
Note :—The French construction is adverbial,
hence *ferme* is invariable : the English is
adjectival.
maison qui a pris un emprunt moitié ferme
moitié à option (*f.*), house which has taken
a loan half firm half on option.

ferme (*n.f.*), lease :
prendre une propriété à ferme, to take a
property on lease.

ferme (Bourse) (*n.m.*), firm stock :
je préfère acheter plutôt du ferme que des
primes, I would rather buy firm stock than
options (*or* than give for options).
le vendeur se couvre en rachetant son ferme
vendu, the seller covers himself by buying
back his firm stock sold.

fermer (*v.t.*), to close; to do up; to shut; to
shut up :
fermer une lettre, to close, to do up, a letter.
fermer un compte, to close an account.
fermer boutique, to shut up shop.

fermer (*v.i.*), to close; to shut :
bureaux qui ferment à cinq heures (*m.pl.*),
offices which close at five o'clock.

fermer (Bourse) (*v.i.*), to close :
valeur qui ferme à tel ou tel cours (*f.*), stock
which closes at such or such a price.

fermeté (*n.f.*), firmness :
fermeté du marché, firmness of the market.

fermeture (*n.f.*), closing :
fermeture de la bourse, closing of the stock
exchange.
fermeture d'un compte, closing an account.

fermier, -ère (*adj.*), leasing :
concéder le droit d'exploitation d'une ligne de
chemin de fer à des sociétés fermières
moyennant des redevances, to grant the right
of working a railway line to leasing companies in consideration of rents.

fermier, -ère (pers.) (*n.*), leaseholder.

ferré, -e *ou* **ferroviaire** (*adj.*), rail (*used as adj.*) ;
railway (*used as adj.*) ; by rail :
transport ferré (*m.*), rail transport; railway
transport; transport by rail.
une compagnie de transports, ferrée ou maritime,
a carrying company, rail or sea.
service ferroviaire (*m.*), railway service.

ferroviaires (actions ou valeurs de chemins de fer)
(*n.m.pl.*), railways ; railway stocks ; railway
shares ; rails.

ferry-boat [**ferry-boats** *pl.*] (bac transbordeur)
(*n.m.*), ferry boat.

fête légale (*f.*), legal holiday ; public holiday ;
bank holiday.

feu (*n.m.*), fire :
feu à terre ou en magasin, à bord ou dans les
allèges, fire on shore or in warehouses, on
board or in craft.

dommage causé par le feu à des marchandises sujettes à l'inflammation spontanée (*m.*), damage caused by fire to goods liable to spontaneous inflammation.

navire (*m.*), cargaison (*f.*), en feu, ship, cargo, on fire.

feuille (*n.f.*), sheet; leaf; slip; list; roll:

feuille de papier, de coupons, sheet of paper, of coupons.

feuille d'appointements, salaries list; list of salaries.

feuille d'émission, application and allotment sheet.

feuille de gros (Douanes), report; report of the whole cargo.

feuille de liquidation (Bourse de valeurs), clearing sheet.

feuille de paie *ou* feuille des salaires, pay roll; pay sheet; wages sheet.

feuille de pointage (contrôle de chargement, déchargement, pesage, etc.), tally sheet.

feuille de pointage (d'un navire), outturn report.

feuille de présence (des personnes dans un bureau), time sheet; time book.

feuille de présence (des personnes dans une réunion), list of those present; attendance sheet:

feuille de présence des actionnaires assistant à l'assemblée générale, list of shareholders present at the general meeting.

feuille de route *ou* feuille de voyage, waybill.

feuille de transfert, transfer deed; deed of transfer; transfer:

le transfert des actions nominatives donne lieu à la signature d'une feuille de transfert par l'actionnaire, the transfer of registered shares requires the signature of a transfer deed by the shareholder.

Note :—In France seller and buyer do not as a rule sign one and the same deed, as in England: the seller signs a **feuille de transfert** or **déclaration de transfert** and the buyer a **feuille d'acceptation de transfert** or **acceptation de transfert.**

feuille de versement (Banq.), paying in slip; credit slip; deposit slip.

feuille des passagers, list of passengers; passenger list.

feuille mobile, loose leaf:

grand livre à feuilles mobiles (*m.*), loose leaf ledger.

feuille volante, loose sheet:

contrat rédigé sur des feuilles volantes (*m.*), agreement written on loose sheets.

feuille (Bourse) (*n.f.*), the membership list of the Paris *coulissiers* (*see explanation of this word under* marché des valeurs): thus a firm who is a member of the *coulisse* is said to be **une maison inscrite à la feuille** or simply **une maison à la feuille.**

ficelage (Douanes) (*n.m.*), taping.

ficeler (Douanes) (*v.t.*), to tape.

ficelle (*n.f.*), string; twine; tape:

une pelote (*ou* un peloton) de ficelle, a ball of string.

fiche (feuillet isolé) (*n.f.*), slip (of paper):

fiche épinglée au document, slip pinned to the document.

fiche de pesage, weight slip.

fiche de rappel, reference slip.

fiche mobile *ou* fiche-carton [fiches-cartons *pl.*] (*n.f.*) *ou simplement* fiche, loose card; index card; card.

fiche (Bourse) (*n.f.*), ticket.

fichier (répertoire sur fiches) (*n.m.*), card index.

fichier (meuble-fichier) (*n.m.*), card index; card index cabinet.

fictif, -ive (*adj.*), fictitious; sham; pro forma:

régime qui avait le grand inconvénient de surcharger les budgets de recettes et de dépenses fictives (*m.*), system which had the great drawback of overloading the budgets with fictitious receipts and expenditure.

actif fictif (*m.*), fictitious assets.

dividende fictif (*m.*), fictitious (*or* sham) dividend.

facture fictive (Com.) (*f.*), pro forma invoice.

fidèle (probe envers son maître) (*adj.*), trustworthy; honest:

caissier fidèle (*m.*), trustworthy cashier; honest cashier.

fidélité (probité) (*n.f.*), fidelity; trustworthiness; honesty:

assurance sur la fidélité du personnel (*f.*), fidelity insurance.

fiduciaire (*adj.*), fiduciary:

circulation fiduciaire (*f.*), fiduciary circulation (*or* currency).

See also monnaie fiduciaire, titres fiduciaires, valeurs fiduciaires, *and* certificat fiduciaire.

figurer (*v.i.*), to appear; to figure; to show; to shew; to be shown:

article qui figure au passif d'un bilan, au débit d'un compte, sur les livres, item which appears (*or* figures) (*or* is shown) among the liabilities on a balance sheet, in (*or* to) the debit of an account, in the books.

emprunt qui figure à la cote (*m.*), loan which appears (*or* figures) (*or* is shown) in the list.

les amortissements figurent en rouge (*m.pl.*), the amounts written off are shown in red.

figurine (*n.f.*) *ou* **figurine postale**, stamp; postage stamp:

figurine d'affranchissement, stamp in prepayment of postage.

figurines détériorées, spoiled stamps.

fil (Télégr.) (*n.m.*) (opp. à *sans fil*), wire:

acheminement par fil (*m.*), routing by wire.

ordre transmis par fil (*m.*), order sent by wire.

filial, -e, -aux (*adj.*), subsidiary:

entreprises filiales (*f.pl.*), subsidiary concerns.

filiale (*n.f.*), subsidiary: subsidiary company:

l'envergure de la Société est mondiale, elle possède des filiales aux États-Unis, en Grande-Bretagne, en France, en Allemagne, et en Russie (*f.*), the range of the Company is world wide, it owns subsidiaries in the United States, in Great Britain, in France, in Germany, and in Russia.

filière (Bourse de marchandises) (*n.f.*), string :
réaliser le marché par filière consiste à déclarer qu'on prend livraison en arrêtant la filière ou à se substituer un acheteur, to close a connected contract consists in declaring for delivery by ending the string or by substituting a buyer for oneself.

filière (Bourse de valeurs) (*n.f.*), trace.

filiériste (Bourse de marchandises) (pers.) (*n.m.*), clearing house clerk.

filiériste (Bourse de valeurs) (pers.) (*n.m.*), settling room clerk.

filigrane (*n.m.*), watermark :
les filigranes des billets de banque, the watermarks of bank notes.

filigraner (*v.t.*), to watermark.

fin (*n.f.*), end ; close ; finish ; termination :
fin de l'année, du mois, end, close, of the year, of the month :
l'encaisse en fin d'année (*f.*), the cash balance at the end of the year.
ristourne de fin d'année (*f.*), end year rebate.
l'action X. faiblit en fin de séance (Bourse), X. shares weakened at the close (*or* at the finish).
fin d'un risque, end, close, termination, of a risk.
fin du contrat de transport, end of the contract of carriage.
les dépenses non payées en fin d'exercice (*f.pl.*), the expenses unpaid at the end of the financial year.
paiement fin courant, fin prochain (*m.*), payment at the end of the present month, at the end of next month.
fin courant *ou simplement* fin (Bourse) (*Abrév. :* f.c. *ou* fc. *ou* fin c. *ou* fin ct *ou* fin cour. *ou simplement* fin), end this ; end this account ; end current account.
fin prochain (Bourse) (*Abrév. :* f.p. *ou* fp. *ou* fin pr.), end next ; end next account.
fin (*mois*) (Bourse) (opp. à 15 [*quinze*]), end (*month*) ; end (*month*) account :
achetez tant d'actions pour fin avril, buy so many shares for end April (*or* for end April account).
See note under **quinze** (*mois*), under Q.
fin de mois (relevé de fin de mois), monthly statement.

final, -e, -als (*adj.*), final :
compte final (*m.*), final account.

finance (*n.f.*), finance :
conseil d'administration composé d'hommes ayant une grande position dans la finance (*ou* dans le monde de la finance) (*m.*), board composed of men occupying a big position in finance (or in the world of finance).
personnes versées dans la question de finances (*f.pl.*), persons versed in the question of finance.
la finance accordée au commerce et à l'industrie par les banques, the finance granted to trade and industry by the banks.

finances (*n.f.pl.*), finances ; cash ; money ; gold and silver coin or (*or* and) bullion :
ses finances sont en baisse, his finances are low.
le transport par chemin de fer des finances, valeurs, objets d'art, etc., the transport by

railway of gold and silver coin and bullion, valuable papers, works of art, etc.
colis finances et valeurs (*m.*), value parcel.

financement (*n.m.*), financing :
le financement d'entreprises nouvelles, the financing of new concerns.

financer (*v.t.*), to finance ; to financier :
le passif exprime avant tout comment l'affaire a été financée, the liabilities express above all how the business has been financed.

financer (*v.i.*), to finance ; to financier.

financier, -ère (*adj.*), financial ; finance (*used as adj.*) :
crise financière (*f.*), financial crisis.
comité financier (*m.*), finance committee.

financier (pers.) (*n.m.*), financier :
un habile financier, a clever financier.

financièrement (*adv.*), financially.

finir (*v.i.*), to finish :
l'action X. qui avait quelque peu repris la semaine dernière jusqu'à 682, a fléchit à 657 pour se relever légèrement ensuite à 665 et finir à 665, X. shares which recovered somewhat last week to 682, sagged to 657 to rise slightly afterwards to 665 and finish at 665 francs.

firme (raison sociale) (*n.f.*), firm ; firm name ; style of firm.

fisc (trésor de l'État) (*n.m.*), Treasury ; Treasury Board ; Treasury Department ; fisc.

fisc (administration) (*n.m.*), Revenue ; Revenue authorities ; Inland Revenue ; Commissioners of Inland Revenue.

fiscal, -e, -aux (*adj.*), fiscal ; revenue (*used as adj.*) :
loi fiscale (*f.*), fiscal law.
timbre fiscal (*m.*), revenue stamp.

fiscalement (*adv.*), fiscally.

fixation (*n.f.*), fixing :
fixation d'un prix, d'une date, fixing a price, a date.

fixe (*adj.*), fixed :
revenu fixe (*m.*), fixed income.

fixe (*n.m.*), fixed salary :
vous aurez tant de fixe, you will have so much fixed salary ; you will have a fixed salary of so much.

fixer (*v.t.*), to fix :
fixer une limite, le taux de l'intérêt, la rémunération (*ou* l'allocation) des commissaires, le quantum des dommages-intérêts à allouer, to fix a limit, the rate of interest, the remuneration of the auditors, the amount of damages to be allowed.

fléchir (*v.i.*), to sag ; to droop ; to give way :
après avoir fléchi, les cours se sont relevés en fin de semaine, after having sagged (*or* drooped) (*or* given way), prices rose at the end of the week.

fléchissement (*n.m.*), sagging ; drooping ; giving way.

fleuve (*n.m.*), river.

flot (à), afloat :
la jauge totale des navires à flot, the total tonnage of ships afloat.
marchandises emmagasinées à terre ou à flot (*f.pl.*), goods stored ashore or afloat.

flottant, -e (Fin.) (*adj.*), floating :
dette flottante (*f.*) (opp. à *dette consolidée*),
floating debt :
la dette flottante d'un État est la partie
variable de la dette publique, elle forme une
portion du fonds de roulement du Trésor
essentiellement temporaire ; elle est représentée par des bons du Trésor, etc. : la dette
consolidée est une dette perpétuelle ou à
long terme, the floating debt of a State is
the variable part of the national debt, it
forms a portion of the working capital of the
Treasury essentially temporary ; it is represented by Treasury bonds, etc. : the consolidated debt is a perpetual or long term debt.

flottant, -e (*adj.*) *ou* **en cargaison flottante** *ou* **sous
voile** (Bourse de marchandises), afloat ;
on passage :
vente de marchandises flottantes (*ou* en
cargaison flottante) (*ou* sous voile), sale of
goods afloat (*or* on passage).
cours : disponible tant ; flottant tant, prices :
spot so much ; afloat so much.

flottant (*n.m.*) *ou* **titres flottants** (*m.pl.*) (Bourse),
shares (*or* stock) on the market :
public qui absorbe les titres flottants (*ou* le
flottant) (*m.*), public which absorbs the
shares (*or* the stock) on the market.

flotte (*n.f.*), fleet :
une flotte de vapeurs, une flotte aérienne, a
fleet of steamers, an air fleet.

fluctuant, -e (*adj.*), fluctuating.

fluctuation (*n.f.*), fluctuation :
fluctuations brusques des prix, dans le cours du
change, sudden fluctuations of prices, in the
rate of exchange.

fluctuer (*v.i.*), to fluctuate :
le câble sur Londres a fluctué entre — et —,
London cables fluctuated between — and —.

foi (*n.f.*), faith ; witness :
un contrat d'assurance est basé sur la bonne
foi la plus absolue, et si la bonne foi la plus
absolue n'est pas été observée par l'une des
parties, le contrat peut être annulé par l'autre
partie, an insurance contract is based upon
the utmost good faith, and if the utmost good
faith be not observed by either party, the
contract may be avoided by the other party.
acheteur de bonne foi (*m.*), bona fide buyer ;
purchaser in good faith.
détenteur de mauvaise foi (*m.*), mala fide
holder.
en foi de quoi, in witness whereof.

foire (marché) (*n.f.*), fair :
expositions et foires commerciales, commercial exhibitions and fairs.

fois (*n.f.pl.*), times ; times over :
neuf fois sur dix, nine times out of ten.
emprunt souscrit plusieurs fois (*m.*), loan
applied for several times over.
en une fois *ou* **en une seule fois,** in full ; in one
amount ; all at one time :
le paiement peut se faire en une fois ou par
versements échelonnés, payment can be
made in full (*or* in one amount) or in (*or* by)
instalments.

abonnement payable en une seule fois (*m.*), subscription payable in full (*or* in one amount).
émission en une fois de 60 000 actions nouvelles
de 100 fr. chacune (*f.*), issue in one amount
of 60,000 new shares of 100 francs each.
l'assemblée ordinaire, tenue le 29 avril, a
autorisé le conseil d'administration à
procéder, en une ou plusieurs fois, à toute
époque qu'il jugera convenable et dans les
conditions qu'il décidera, à l'émission
d'obligations pour un montant maximum de
200 millions de francs, étant entendu que
le produit en pourra être utilisé au remboursement anticipé d'obligations en circulation
(*f.*), at the ordinary meeting held on 29th
April the board were authorized to proceed,
in one or more amounts, whenever they may
deem fit (*or* to proceed as and when required)
and under the conditions they may resolve on,
to the issue of debentures to a maximum
amount of 200 million francs, it being understood that the proceeds may be used for
redemption in advance of debentures in
circulation.

une fois payé, -e, in a single payment :
moyennant une somme une fois payée, in
consideration of a sum in a single payment.
au lieu de mille francs de rente, il a préféré
donner vingt mille francs une fois payés,
instead of an annual payment of a thousand
francs, he preferred to give twenty thousand
francs in a single payment.

folio [**folios** *pl.*] (*n.m.*) (Abrév. : **Fo** *ou* **fo** *ou* **fo**)
folio ; page :
folio du grand livre, ledger folio.
inscription du folio du journal d'après lequel
l'article est rapporté (*f.*), putting in the
journal folio from which the item is posted.

foliotage (*n.m.*), folioing ; foliation ; paging ;
pagination. Cf. **pagination** (*n.f.*).

folioter (*v.t.*), to folio ; to page : (Cf. **paginer.**)
folioter un registre, to folio, to page, a book.
folioter le journal, c'est-à-dire indiquer dans la
colonne *ad hoc* le folio de chaque compte au
grand livre, to folio the journal, that is to
say, to indicate in the column provided for
this purpose the folio of each account in the
ledger.

foncier, -ère (*adj.*), landed ; land (*used as adj.*) ;
ground (*used as adj.*) :
propriétaire foncier (*m.*), landed proprietor.
impôt foncier (*m.*), land tax.
rente foncière (*f.*), ground rent.

fonction (*s'emploie souvent au pl.*) (*n.f.*), function ;
duty ; office :
confier les fonctions de secrétaire du conseil à
l'un des directeurs, to intrust the duties (*or*
functions) of secretary to the board to one
of the managers.
le conseil restera (*ou* demeurera) en fonctions
jusqu'à l'assemblée annuelle, the board will
remain in office until the annual meeting.

fonctionnaire (pers.) (*n.m.* *ou* *f.*), official ;
functionary :
fonctionnaire public, government official.
fonctionnaire de douane, customs official.

fond (*n.m.*), bottom ; undertone :
  le fond de la baisse a été atteint, the bottom of
  the fall has been reached.
  la rubrique des étrangères ne présente pas de
  tendance uniforme ; toutefois, on y note un
  certain fond de résistance dans l'ensemble
  (Bourse), the foreign section did not show any
  uniform tendency ; however, it was noted
  that there was in it a certain undertone of
  strength generally.
fondateur, -trice (pers.) (*n.*), founder :
  fondateur d'une maison de commerce, founder
  of a house of business.
  part de fondateur (*f.*), founder's share.
fondateur (**la**) (*abrév. de* la part de fondateur, *en
  bourse*) (Abrév. : **fond.**), founders (*abbrev. of*
  founders' shares, *in market news*) :
  la fondateur X. clôture à 513,   X. founders
  closed at 513 francs.
fondation (*n.f.*), foundation ; establishment ;
  basis ; base.
fondé de pouvoir *ou* **fondé de pouvoirs** (pers.) (*m.*),
  attorney ;   private attorney ;   attorney in
  fact ;   proxy ;   duly authorized representative :
  la personne qui vient prendre livraison d'une
  lettre adressée poste restante doit justifier
  qu'elle est le destinataire ou son fondé
  de pouvoirs, the person who comes to take
  delivery of a letter addressed poste restante
  must prove that he is the addressee or his
  duly authorized representative.
fonder (établir) (*v.t.*), to found ; to establish ;
  to base :
  fonder une maison de commerce, to found a
  house of business.
  compagnie d'assurance fondée à Londres en
  1720 (*f.*), insurance company established in
  London in 1720.
  recours fondé sur une perte (*m.*), claim based
  upon a loss.
fonder (assigner un fonds) (*v.t.*), to fund :
  fonder une dette publique, to fund a public
  debt.
fonds (somme d'argent [*souvent au pl. en ce sens*] ;
  capital d'un bien) (*n.m.*), fund ; funds ;
  money ; cash ; capital :
  être en fonds, to be in funds.
  les fonds sont bas, funds are low.
  actions remises en nantissement en garantie de
  fonds avancés (*f.pl.*), shares hypothecated
  as security for money advanced.
  un fonds dont le revenu sera plus que suffisant
  pour me faire passer agréablement le reste
  de mes jours, a capital the income from which
  will be more than enough to enable me to pass
  the remainder of my life in comfort.
  les fonds nécessaires à la construction de la
  ligne, the funds (*or* the capital) required to
  construct the line.
  fonds d'amortissement, sinking fund.
  fonds d'assurance, insurance fund.
  fonds de garantie, guarantee fund.
  fonds de prévoyance, contingency fund.
  fonds de réserve *ou* fonds de prévision,   reserve fund.

  fonds de roulement, working capital :
  les disponibilités forment ce qu'on appelle
  le fonds de roulement (*f.pl.*), the available
  assets form   what   is   called   working
  capital.
  fonds en caisse et en banque, cash in (*or* on)
  hand and at (*or* in) bank ;   cash at bankers
  and in (*or* on) hand.
  fonds perdu, life annuity :
  placer son argent à fonds perdu, to invest one's
  money in a life annuity.
  fonds social (d'une société anonyme),   company's funds. See note under **social.**
  fonds social (d'une société en nom collectif),
  partnership funds (*or* capital) :
  après la dissolution de la société, les associés
  se partagent le fonds social, after dissolution
  of the partnership, the partners divide the
  partnership funds.
fonds (fonds publics ; valeurs de bourse portées à
  la cote officielle) (*n.m.pl.*), funds ; stock ;
  stocks ; securities :
  fonds coloniaux, colonial stocks.
  fonds consolidés, Consols.
  fonds d'État, government stocks ; government
  securities.
  fonds d'États étrangers,   foreign stocks and
  bonds ;   foreign   government   stocks   (*or*
  securities).
  fonds garantis, guaranteed stock ; guaranteed
  stocks.
  fonds indigènes, home stocks ; home securities.
  fonds publics, public funds ; public securities.
fonds de commerce *ou simplement* **fonds** (*n.m.*),
  goodwill ; business (goodwill, premises, stock
  in trade, etc.) :
  acheter un fonds (*ou* un fonds de commerce), to
  buy a goodwill (*or* a business).
  un fonds de boulanger, a baker's business.
  le nom sous lequel un fonds de commerce a
  été créé est la propriété du créateur de ce
  fonds,   the name under which a goodwill
  has been established is the property of the
  founder of that goodwill.
fonds de terre (*m.*), land ; piece of land.
forban (pers.) (*n.m.*), rover.
force (*n.f.*), force :
  la force des choses, the force of circumstances.
  force probante de la lettre de voiture, probatory force of the consignment note.
  force libératoire. See under **libératoire.**
  force majeure, force majeure ; cause beyond
  control.
forcé, -e (*adj.*), forced ; compulsory :
  emprunt forcé (*m.*), forced loan.
  relâche forcée (d'un navire) (*f.*),   forced (*or*
  compulsory) call.
forcement de voiles (Navig.) (*m.*), carrying press
  of sail.
forclore (Dr.) (*v.t.*), to foreclose.
forclusion (Dr.) (*n.f.*), foreclosure.
forfait (*n.m.*), contract ; contract at an agreed
  (*or* fixed) price (*or* sum) ; contract with a
  fixed and determined consideration ; agreed
  price ;   agreed consideration ; fixed price ;
  fixed consideration ; specific amount :

prévenir, par un forfait (*ou* par un contrat à forfait), toutes contestations judiciaires, to prevent, by a contract (*or* by a contract at an agreed [*or* fixed] price) (*or* by a contract with a fixed and determined consideration), all legal disputes.

accepter un forfait d'indemnité réglé à l'avance, to accept an agreed sum as indemnity settled in advance; to accept a penalty agreed on beforehand.

un forfait (*ou* une indemnité forfaitaire) de demi pour cent fixé(e) par une clause du contrat, an agreed consideration of half per cent fixed by a clause of the contract.

à forfait *ou* **forfaitaire** (*adj.*), on contract; by contract; contract (*used as adj.*); contractual; at an agreed (*or* fixed) price (*or* sum) (*or* rate); for a fixed (*or* agreed) consideration; for a specific amount; fixed; fixed in advance; agreed; through; standard; without recourse:

acheter des marchandises à forfait, to buy goods on contract.

entreprendre le transport des marchandises pour un prix déterminé à forfait, to undertake the carriage of goods for a fixed contract price (*or* for a price determined by contract) (*or* at an agreed price); to contract for through booking of goods.

prix à forfait *ou* prix forfaitaire (*m.*), contract price; agreed price; fixed price.

limitation forfaitaire de responsabilité (*f.*), contract (*or* contractual) limitation of liability.

moyennant paiement d'une somme forfaitaire, in consideration of the payment of an agreed sum (*or* of an amount fixed in advance).

police à forfait sur valeurs (Assce) (*f.*), open policy on valuables for a specific amount.

taux à forfait (*ou* taux forfaitaires) pour Londres domicile, et l'intérieur de l'Angleterre (*m.pl.*), through rates to address in London, and the interior of England.

transports à forfait (*ou simplement* forfaits) pour toutes destinations (*m.pl.*), through bookings to all parts.

taxe (*ou* redevance) forfaitaire pour l'enlèvement et la réinstallation des organes essentiels d'un poste téléphonique (*f.*), standard charge for the removal and re-installation of a telephone line and apparatus.

endossement à forfait (effets) (Banq.) (*m.*), endorsement without recourse.

forfaitairement (*adv.*) *ou* **à forfait,** contractually; by contract; at an agreed price (*or* sum) (*or* rate):

frais généraux fixés forfaitairement à 5 0/0 du capital (*m.pl.*), expenses fixed at an agreed rate of 5% on the capital.

forger (*v.t.*), to forge:
forger une signature, to forge a signature.

formalité (*n.f.*), formality:
formalité d'enregistrement, formality of registration.

formalités de douane, customs formalities.

justifier de l'accomplissement de toutes les formalités requises, to show that all the necessary formalities have been complied with.

formation (*n.f.*), formation:
formation d'une société, d'un fonds de réserve, formation of a company, of a reserve fund.

forme (*n.f.*), form:
forme d'une quittance, form of a receipt.

forme de radoub *ou* **forme sèche** *ou simplement* **forme** (*n.f.*), graving dock; dry dock.

forme flottante (*f.*), floating dock.

formel, -elle (*adj.*), formal:
démenti formel (*m.*), formal denial.

formellement (*adv.*), formally.

former (*v.t.*), to form:
former une association, to form an association.

se former (*v.r.*), to form (for oneself); to be formed:
se former une opinion du risque auquel une cargaison est exposée, to form an opinion of the risk to which a cargo is exposed.

une nouvelle banque se forma au capital de tant, a new bank was formed with a capital of so much.

formule (modèle) (*n.f.*), form:
remplir une formule imprimée, to fill up a printed form.

formule d'acquit, form of receipt; receipt form.

formule d'approbation (d'un relevé de compte), form of confirmation.

formule d'effet de commerce, bill form; form of bill of exchange.

formule de chèque, cheque form.

formule de connaissement, bill of lading form; form of bill of lading.

formule de mandat (Poste), requisition form; form of requisition (for money order).

formule de pouvoir *ou* formule de mandat, form of proxy; proxy form.

formule de proposition (Assce), proposal form.

formule de réclamation, claim form.

formule de télégramme, telegram form.

formule de transfert, transfer form; form of transfer.

formule type (*ou* formule-type) de connaissement [formules types *ou* formules-types *pl.*], standard form of bill of lading.

formule (façon de s'exprimer) (*n.f.*), form; formula:
compliments, félicitations, remerciements, et autres formules de politesse, compliments, congratulations, thanks, and other formulas of courtesy.

formuler (*v.t.*), to formulate:
formuler une réclamation contre quelqu'un, to formulate a claim against someone.

fort, -e (considérable) (*adj.*), large; big; heavy; full; considerable; overweight:
une forte somme d'argent, a large amount, a big sum, of money.

un forte commande de marchandises, a large order, a big order, for goods.

forte hausse (de cours, de prix) (*f.*), big rise.

forte baisse (de cours, de prix) (*f.*), heavy fall ; big fall.

les deux plus forts actionnaires, the two largest (*or* biggest) shareholders.

piè_e forte (*f.*), overweight coin. See example under **pièce.**

prix fort (*m.*), full price.

fortuit, -e (*adj.*), fortuitous :
cas fortuit (*m.*), fortuitous event.
une cause fortuite de sacrifice, a fortuitous cause of sacrifice.

fortuitement (*adv.*), fortuitously.

fortune (*n.f.*), fortune :
faire fortune, to make a fortune.

fortune de mer (patrimoine de mer) (Dr.) (*f.*). In France, the *fortune de mer* (possessions on the sea) is the part of the property of the ship-owner engaged in the exploitation of his ship, and is, by virtue of a legal fiction, distinguished from his **fortune de terre** (possessions on land). The object of this distinction is to limit, by reason of the special risks of navigation, the liability of the sea carrier to his *fortune de mer*. This limitation finds its practical application in the option given to the carrier of absolving himself from all further liability by abandonment of the ship and freight.

fortune de mer (*f.*) *ou* **fortunes de mer** (*f.pl.*) (péril maritime), maritime perils ; maritime peril ; marine perils (*or* peril) ; perils of the seas (*or* sea) ; peril of the sea ; sea peril :
choses perdues par fortune de mer (*f.pl.*), property lost by perils of the seas.

fourgon (Ch. de f.) (*n.m.*), brake van ; brake ; guard's van ; van.

fourgon à bagages (Ch. de f.) (*m.*), luggage van ; luggage vehicle.

fourgon à bestiaux (Ch. de f.) (*m.*), cattle truck.

fourgon de livraison (voiture routière) (*m.*), delivery van.

fourgon pour train à marchandises (*m.*), goods brake.

fournir (pourvoir) (*v.t.*), to furnish ; to supply ; to provide ; to give ; to find ; to lodge ; to deposit :
fournir des renseignements, to furnish, to supply, to give, information.
fournir de l'argent à quelqu'un, to provide, to supply, someone with money ; to supply money to someone ; to find money for someone.
fournir bonne et valable caution pour la garantie du paiement d'une contribution, to give, to find, good and valid security for the guarantee of the payment of a contribution.
l'entrepositaire est tenu de fournir caution pour garantir les droits et les amendes qui pourraient devenir exigibles (*m.*), the bonder is bound to give security to guarantee the duties and fines which may become payable.
porteur d'un effet qui prouve qu'il en a fourni la valeur (*m.*), holder of a bill who proves that he has given value for it.
fournir en nantissement, to lodge as collateral ; to hypothecate ; to pledge :
valeurs fournies en nantissement (*f.pl.*),

securities lodged as collateral ; securities hypothecated (*or* pledged).
actions fournies en nantissement en garantie de fonds avancés (*f.pl.*), shares hypothecated (*or* pledged) as security for money advanced.

fournir une couverture (Bourse et Banq.), to margin ; to deposit a margin :
donneur d'ordre qui doit fournir une couverture (*m.*), principal who must margin (*or* must deposit a margin). Cf. **compléter la couverture fournie antérieurement.**

fournir la preuve que les valeurs assurées ont été expédiées de la manière déclarée dans la proposition d'assurance, to furnish evidence that the insured securities have been dispatched in the manner declared in the proposal of insurance.

fournir (disposer ; tirer) (*v.t.*), to draw :
fournir une traite, un chèque sur son banquier, to draw a bill, a cheque on one's banker.

fournir (pourvoir) (*v.i.*), to provide ; to contribute :
vente d'une partie de la cargaison afin de fournir aux besoins pressants du navire (*f.*), sale of a part of the cargo in order to provide for the pressing needs of the ship.
fournir à la dépense, to contribute to the expenses.

fournir (disposer ; tirer) (*v.i.*), to draw :
fournir sur quelqu'un à trois mois (tirer un effet sur quelqu'un), to draw on someone at three months.
fournir sur son banquier (tirer un chèque sur son banquier), to draw on one's banker.

fournissement (fonds que chaque associé apporte dans une société) (*n.m.*), contribution.

fournisseur (pers.) (*n.m.*), supplier ; dealer :
fournisseur de navires *ou* fournisseur maritime, ship store dealer ; ship chandler ; marine store dealer.

fourniture (*n.f.*), supply ; supplying ; store ; requisite :
fournitures pour navires *ou* fournitures maritimes, ship stores ; ship chandlery ; marine stores.
fournitures de bureau *ou* *simplement* fournitures, office requisites ; stationery :
imprimés et fournitures, printing and stationery.

fraction (*n.f.*), fraction :
fraction décimale, decimal fraction.
fraction ordinaire, common fraction ; vulgar fraction.
valeur qui a perdu une fraction (Bourse) (*f.*), stock which has lost a fraction.
une fraction de rente, a fraction of rente.
fractions d'actions nouvelles, fractions of new shares.

par fraction indivisible de . . ., for every . . . or fraction (*or* fractional part) of . . . :
par fraction indivisible de 1 000 francs jusqu'à 10 000 francs *tant*, et par fraction indivisible de 1 000 francs en excédent *tant*, for every 1,000 francs or fraction of 1,000 francs up to 10,000 francs *so much*, and for every additional 1,000 francs or fractional part of 1,000 francs *so much*.

fractionnaire (*adj.*), fractional :
nombre fractionnaire (*m.*), fractional number.
fractionnement (*n.m.*), splitting.
fractionner (*v.t.*), to split :
fractionner des actions, to split shares.
fragile (*adj.*), fragile :
objets fragiles tels que la verrerie (*m.pl.*), fragile articles such as glassware.
fragile (annotation sur un colis), fragile ; with care ; glass, with care ; glass.
frai (d'une pièce d'argent) (*n.m.*), wear, abrasion (of a coin).
frais (*n.m.pl.*), expenses ; expense ; charges ; cost ; costs : (See also **dépense**.)
frais accessoires, accessory expenses ; expenses in connection :
le prix de revient est le résultat d'un prix d'achat majoré d'une foule de frais accessoires, transports, commission, etc., the cost price is the result of a purchase price increased by a multitude of accessory expenses, transport, commission, etc.
les frais accessoires de correspondance, d'envoi de fonds, etc., the expenses in connection with the correspondence, remittance of funds, etc.
frais accidentels *ou* faux frais, incidental expenses.
frais consulaires, consular charges.
frais d'administration, management expenses ; administration expenses.
frais d'assurance, insurance charges.
frais d'entretien, cost of upkeep ; upkeep expenses.
frais d'escompte, discount charges.
frais d'expédition, forwarding charges ; shipping charges.
frais d'exploitation, working expenses ; cost of working ; operating costs.
frais d'hôtel, hotel expenses.
frais d'impression, cost of printing ; printing.
frais de banque, bank charges (note, however, that *frais de banque* generally means petty charges, such as postages, telegrams, or the like, whereas *bank charges* in England means any charge made by a bank, whether for interest, discount, commission, or petties).
frais de bureau, office expenses.
frais de chômage (de wagons de ch. de f.), demurrage charges ; demurrage.
frais de commerce, trade expenses.
frais de constitution, preliminary expenses ; formation expenses.
frais de contentieux, legal charges.
frais de course, fares (petty expense).
frais de déplacement (des personnes), travelling expenses :
frais de déplacement des experts, travelling expenses of the experts.
frais de déplacement (des choses), removal expenses :
frais de déplacement du mobilier, removal expenses of the furniture.
frais de dispache, adjustment charges.
frais de douane, customs charges.
frais de gérance, management expenses.

frais de magasinage *ou* frais d'emmagasinage, warehouse charges ; warehousing charges ; storage charges.
frais de mise à terre *ou* frais de débarquement, landing charges.
frais de premier établissement. See note :
Note :—*frais de premier établissement* or simply *premier établissement* is a loose and indeterminate term in French and fortunately has no general equivalent in English : sometimes it means merely preliminary or formation expenses (properly called *frais de constitution* in French), sometimes it means initial capital expenditure made to start the concern or further expenditure to develop it, or again it may include the whole of the capital expenditure. As will be seen, the vagrancy of the term can lead to abuse, as for instance the inclusion thereunder of fruitless expenditure or losses incurred during the initial stages of an enterprise.
frais de relâche *ou* frais du port de relâche, expenses at port of refuge ; port of refuge expenses.
frais de sauvetage, salvage charges ; salvage.
frais de vente, expenses of selling.
frais de voyage, travelling expenses.
frais divers, general expenses ; sundry expenses.
frais échus *ou* frais à payer, outstanding expenses.
frais et charges de l'entreprise (*ou* de l'exploitation), cost and expenses of the business ; cost and expenses of carrying on the business.
frais généraux (*Abrév. :* F.G.), standing expenses ; standing charges ; establishment charges ; overhead expenses (or charges) ; expenses.
frais généraux *ou* frais fixes *ou* frais indirects (Établissement des prix de revient), overhead charges ; on-cost charges ; fixed charges ; indirect charges (or expenses).
frais spéciaux *ou* frais directs *ou* frais proportionnels (Établissement des prix de revient), direct expenses ; establishment charges ; departmental charges.
aux frais de, at the expense of ; at . . . . .'s expense :
manutention faite aux frais et risque de la marchandise, aux frais de la compagnie (*f.*), handling done at the expense and risk of the goods, at the company's expense.
sans frais. See under **sans.**
frais (Dr.) (*n.m.pl.*), costs ; expenses :
être condamné (-e) aux frais d'un procès, to be ordered to pay the costs of an action.
frais de justice, law costs ; law expenses.
franc, franche (*adj.*), free :
Note :—Such expressions as *franc de port, franc d'avaries,* can, at will, vary or remain invariable ; as, *envoyer franche de port une lettre* (to send a letter post free) [here, *franche* is an adjective, qualifying the feminine noun *lettre*], or *envoyer franc de port une lettre* [here, *franc de port* is an adverbial phrase, and consequently is invariable].

franc d'avarie *ou* franc d'avaries,   free of average ; free from average :

franc d'avaries au-dessous de la franchise énoncée dans la police, free from average under the franchise specified in the policy.

franc d'avarie commune *ou* franc d'avaries communes (*Abrév. :* f.a.c.), free of (*or* from) general average.

franc d'avarie particulière *ou* franc d'avaries particulières (*Abrév. :* f.a.p.),   free of (*or* from) particular average.

franc d'avaries particulières absolument, free of particular average absolutely.

franc d'avaries particulières sauf en cas d'échouement, free from particular average unless the vessel be stranded.

franc de droits de douane,   free of customs duties.

franc de perte totale, free of total loss.

franc de port (Ch. de f., etc.), carriage paid.

franc de port (Poste), post free.

franc de tous droits (franco de tous frais), free of all charges.

marchandise franche de tout droit (*f.*) *ou* marchandises franches de tout droit (*f.pl.*), duty-free goods ; free goods ; uncustomed goods.

franc de tout recours pour perte partielle, de tout recours provenant de retard, free from all claim in respect of partial loss, of any claim arising from delay.

franc (monnaie) (*n.m.*) (Abrév. : **f.** *ou* **F.** [**f.** *ou* **F.** *pl.*] *ou* **fr.** [**fr.** *ou* **frs** *pl.*] *ou* **Fr.** [**Fr.** *ou* **Frs** *pl.*], franc :

franc français, French franc.

franc belge, Belgian franc.

franc suisse, Swiss franc.

franc international, international franc.

franc-argent [francs-argent *pl.*] (*n.m.*),   silver franc.

franc-or [francs-or *pl.*] (*n.m.*), gold franc :

franc-papier [francs-papier *pl.*] (*n.m.*),   paper franc :

5 000   francs-or   ou   25 000   francs-papier français, 5,000 gold francs or 25,000 French paper francs.

ramener les prix dans les différents pays en francs-or, seul moyen rationnel d'effectuer une comparaison pratique, to bring the prices in the different countries to gold francs, the only rational means of effecting a practical comparison.

franc-bord [**francs-bords** *pl.*] (d'un navire) (*n.m.*), freeboard.

franchir (passer ; traverser) (*v.t.*), to pass ; to cross :

franchir la frontière, la barre d'un fleuve, to cross the frontier, the bar of a river.

franchir (dépasser) (*v.t.*), to exceed :

franchir la limite normale du crédit, to exceed the normal limit of credit.

franchise (*n.f.*), exemption ; free (*used adjectivally*) :

la franchise de la taxe dont jouissent ces marchandises, the exemption from the tax which these goods enjoy.

franchise absolue d'avaries particulières, free of particular average absolutely.

franchise de poids *ou* franchise de bagages (opp. à *excédents de bagages*), weight allowed free ; free allowance ; free allowance of luggage :

il est alloué à chaque voyageur, pour ses bagages, une franchise de poids de — kilos pour les 1res classes, — kilos pour les 2es classes, et — kilos pour les 3es classes, each passenger is granted, for his luggage, a free allowance of — kilos 1st class, — kilos 2nd class, and — kilos 3rd class.

admission en franchise (Douanes),   free admission.

marchandises admissibles en franchise de droits sur justification d'origine (*f.pl.*),   goods admissible duty free (*or* free of duty) on proof of origin.

franchise (limites apportées à la responsabilité des assureurs) (*n.f.*), franchise (analogous to the English *percentage*) : See note under **tableau** (de franchises).

franc d'avaries au-dessous de la franchise énoncée dans la police, free from average under the franchise specified in the policy.

par franchise on entend le pourcentage minimum que le dommage admis en avarie particulière doit atteindre pour être mis à la charge des assureurs, by franchise is understood the minimum percentage that damage admitted in particular average must reach in order to be thrown on the underwriters.

avaries payables sans égard à la franchise (*f.pl.*), average irrespective of franchise.

franchise (Poste) (*n.f.*), franking :

la franchise est l'exemption de taxe accordée, franking is the exemption from charge granted.

lettre en franchise (*ou* en franchise de port) (*f.*), franked letter.

francisation (*n.f.*), registration (*or* registry) (in France, of a ship of French nationality). *Cf.* acte de francisation.

franciser un navire, (In France) to register a ship (of French nationality).

franco (*adv.*) (Abrév. : **fco** *ou* **fo** *ou* **F.F.**), free ; free of charge ; free of expense :

franco à quai, free at wharf ; free on quay ; ex wharf ; ex quay.

franco bord *ou* franco à bord (*Abrév. :* f.o.b. *ou* F.O.B. *ou* fob. *ou* f. à b. *ou* F.B.), free on board :

marchandises rendues franco à bord du navire dans le port de départ (*f.pl.*), goods delivered free on board the ship in the port of departure.

franco courtage *ou* franco de courtage *ou* franco commission *ou* simplement franco, free of brokerage ; free of commission ; free :

opération de bourse faite franco courtage (*ou* faite franco) (*f.*), stock exchange transaction done free of commission (*or* done free).

franco de douane, free of customs duties.

franco de port (Ch. de f., etc.), carriage paid.

franco de port (Poste), post free.

franco de tous frais, free of all charges.

franco le long du bord du navire *ou* franco le long du navire (*Abrév.* : F.A.S.), free along-side ship.

franco wagon *ou* franco gare *ou simplement* sur wagon, free on rail; free on truck; on rail.

les chèques sont encaissés franco (*m.pl.*), cheques are collected free of charge.

franco (Bourse) (*n.m.*), single commission (on double operation of purchase and sale):
profiter du franco, to benefit by the single commission.

frappe (*n.f.*), stamping; impressing; striking; coinage; minting:
frappe de l'or, coinage, minting, of gold.

frapper (donner un ou plusieurs coups à) (*v.t.*), to strike:
frapper les touches d'une machine à écrire, to strike the keys of a typewriter.

frapper (donner une empreinte à) (*v.t.*), to stamp; to impress; to strike; to coin; to mint:
les obligations remboursées sont frappées d'un timbre d'annulation (*f.pl.*), the redeemed debentures are stamped with a calcellation stamp.

frapper de la monnaie, to coin, to mint, money; to strike coins:
pièces d'or frappées par la Monnaie (*f.pl.*), gold coins struck by the mint.

frapper (atteindre par une décision juridique administrative) (*v.t.*), to hit; to lay on (*or* upon); to be laid upon; to fall upon:
impôt qui frappe tous les revenus (*m.*), tax which hits (*or* which is laid upon) (*or* which falls on) all incomes.

frapper d'un impôt *ou* frapper de taxes, to tax; to lay a tax (*or* taxes) upon:
en France l'affichage est frappé d'un impôt, in France bill posting is taxed.

frapper de taxes les produits de l'industrie étrangère, to tax, to lay taxes upon, the products of foreign industry.

frapper (être établi sur) (*v.t.*), to be secured on:
hypothèque qui frappe des biens (*f.*), mortgage which is secured on property.

frapper de nullité, to render void:
la loi a frappé de nullité toute clause qui dispenserait le créancier de se conformer à ces formalités, the statute has rendered void any clause which relieves the creditor from complying with these formalities.

l'assurance maritime est, comme toutes les conventions, frappée de nullité quand elle est entachée de fraude (*f.*), marine insurance, like all agreements, is rendered void when it is tainted by fraud.

fraude (*n.f.*), fraud:
commettre (*ou* faire) une fraude, to commit a fraud.
la fraude vicie un contrat, fraud vitiates a contract.

frauder (*v.t.*), to defraud; to cheat:
frauder la douane, to defraud, to cheat, the customs.

fraudeur, -euse (pers.) (*n.*), defrauder; smuggler.
frauduleusement (*adv.*), fraudulently.
frauduleux, -euse (*adj.*), fraudulent:

moyens frauduleux (*m.pl.*), fraudulent means.
déclaration frauduleuse de la valeur d'un colis (*f.*), fraudulent declaration of the value of a parcel.

free-trade (libre-échange) (*n.m.*), free trade.

freinte (*n.f.*), wastage; waste; loss:
freinte en volume, en poids, wastage, loss, in bulk, in weight.
freinte de route, loss in transit.

fréquenter (*v.t.*), to frequent:
fréquenter un marché, to frequent a market.

frère (navire frère) (*n.m.*), sister; sister ship; twin ship:
s/s. *A.* frère du s/s. *B.*, s/s. *A.* sister to s/s. *B.*

fret (prix de transport par mer des marchandises; prix de louage d'un navire) (*n.m.*), freight:
le fret est payé suivant la nature des marchandises, freight is paid according to the nature of the cargo.

fret à faire *ou* fret en risque, freight at risk.
fret à forfait *ou* fret forfaitaire, through freight.
fret à la cueillette *ou* fret à cueillette, berth terms; liner rate.
fret à temps *ou* fret à terme, time freight.
fret acquis, freight earned; freight not repayable. See examples under **acquis.**
fret anticipé, anticipated freight.
fret au long cours, ocean freight.
fret au voyage, voyage freight.
fret brut, gross freight.
fret brut réel à faire, actual gross freight at risk.
fret convenu par charte-partie *ou* fret à gagner en exécution de la charte-partie, chartered freight:
fret convenu par charte-partie à faire, à terme, au voyage, chartered freight at risk, for time, for voyage.
fret d'aller *ou* fret de sortie, outward freight.
fret de distance *ou* fret proportionnel *ou* fret proportionnel à la distance, distance freight; freight pro rata; freight pro rata itineris peracti.
fret de retour, homeward freight; return freight.
fret entier, full freight.
fret espéré, anticipated freight.
fret net, net freight.
fret par contrat, contract freight (freight at reduced rates, according to an agreement).
fret payable à destination suivant poids déclaré à l'embarquement, freight payable at destination as per weight declared on shipment.
fret payé d'avance *ou simplement* fret payé, freight paid in advance; advanced freight; advance freight; prepaid freight.
fret supplémentaire, additional freight; extra freight.
fret sur le vide *ou* fret mort, dead freight.

fret (cargaison) (*n.m.*), freight; cargo:
navire qui débarque la totalité ou une partie de son fret (*m.*), ship which lands the whole or a part of her freight (*or* cargo).
navire qui ne peut pas trouver un fret de retour (*m.*), ship which cannot find a homeward freight.

fret léger, light freight.
fret lourd, heavy freight.
rètement (*n.m.*), freighting; affreightment;
chartering; charterage; charter.
réter (*v.t.*), to freight; to affreight; to charter.
réteur (pers.) (*n.m.*), charterer; freighter;
affreighter; owner; shipowner:
charte-partie qui énonce les noms du fréteur et
de l'affréteur, charter party which specifies
the names of the owner and charterer. (See
note under **armateur**.)
rontière (*n.f.*), frontier:
marchandises visitées à la frontière (*f.pl.*), goods
examined at the frontier.
frontière de mer, sea frontier.
frontière de terre, land frontier.
ructueusement (*adv.*), profitably.
ructueux, -euse (*adj.*), profitable:
placement fructueux (*m.*), profitable investment.
ruits (revenu) (*n.m.pl.*), profits; benefit:
fruits casuels, casual profits.
rustration (*n.f.*), frustration:
frustration du voyage assuré, frustration of the
insured voyage.
rustrer (*v.t.*), to frustrate; to defeat; to
defraud; to deprive:
frustrer ses créanciers, to defeat, to defraud,
one's creditors.

frustrer un associé de sa part de bénéfice, to
defraud, to deprive, a partner of his share of
profit.
fuite (exode) (*n.f.*), flight:
la fuite de capitaux nationaux en période de
troubles monétaires, the flight of national
capital in time of monetary troubles.
funding (consolidation) (Fin.) (*n.m.*), funding:
emprunt funding (*m.*), funding loan.
fusion (*n.f.*) *ou* **fusionnement** (*n.m.*), amalgamation; merging; merger; fusion:
fusion de plusieurs banques, amalgamation (*or*
fusion) (*or* merging) (*or* merger) of several
banks.
fusionner (*v.t.*), to amalgamate; to merge; to
fuse:
fusionner deux compagnies de chemins de fer,
to amalgamate two railway companies.
fusionner (*v.i.*), to amalgamate; to merge; to
fuse:
lorsque plusieurs sociétés fusionnent, when
several companies amalgamate (*or* merge).
les deux sociétés fusionnantes, the two
amalgamating companies.
se fusionner (*v.r.*), to amalgamate; to merge;
to fuse.
fût (tonneau) (*n.m.*), barrel; cask; drum.
futaille (*n.f.*), cask; barrel.

G

gabarage *ou* **gabariage** (*n.m.*), lighterage.
gabare (*n.f.*), lighter; barge.
gabarier (pers.) (*n.m.*), lighterman; bargeman;
bargee.
gâché, -e (*adj.*), spoiled; spoilt:
formule gâchée (*f.*), spoilt form.
gage (*n.m.*), pledge; pawn; security:
titres détenus en gage (*m.pl.*), securities held in
pledge (*or* in pawn); stocks held as security.
en effet, les marchandises importées sont le
gage des droits auxquels elles sont soumises,
et ne peuvent être mises à la disposition des
importateurs sans garantie, in fact, the goods
imported are the pledge of the duties to which
they are liable, and cannot be put at the
disposal of the importers without security.
gager (*v.t.*), to pledge; to pawn; to hypothecate:
gager des valeurs, to pledge, to pawn, to
hypothecate, securities.
actions gagées en garantie de fonds avancés
(*f.pl.*), shares pledged (*or* pawned) (*or*
hypothecated) as security for money
advanced.
être gagé (-e) sur, to be secured on:
hypothèque qui est gagée sur des biens (*f.*),
mortgage which is secured on property.
emprunt gagé, secured loan.

gages (*n.m.pl.*), wages:
gages des gens de mer, seamen's wages.
gageur, -euse (pers.) (*n.*), pledger; pawner;
pawnor; hypothecator; lienee.
gagiste (pers.) (*n.m.*), pledgee; pawnee; lienor.
gagnant, -e (*adj.*), winning:
numéro gagnant (*m.*), winning number.
gagner (*v.t.*), to gain; to put on; to make; to
earn; to win; to save:
l'action X. gagne quelques points, X. shares
gained (*or* put on) a few points.
l'action X. gagne du terrain à 673, X. shares
gained ground at 673 francs.
gagner des richesses, to gain wealth.
à vouloir tout gagner, on risque de tout perdre,
by wanting to gain (*or* to win) all, one risks
losing all.
gagner une fortune en rien de temps, to make
a fortune in no time.
la société n'a jamais gagné d'argent, the
company has never made money.
un sou épargné est un sou gagné, a penny saved
is a penny earned.
gagner un procès, un pari, to win a case, a bet.
gagneur, -euse (pers.) (*n.*), gainer; winner.
gain (*n.m.*), gain; profit; earning (*commonly in
plural*); saving:

en assurance, ce qui est gain pour l'un est perte pour l'autre, in insurance, what is gain for one is loss for the other.

valeur qui marque un gain de plusieurs points (*f.*), stock which shows a gain of several points.

réaliser des gains énormes, to make enormous profits.

gain de temps procuré par l'emploi de l'avion, saving of time effected by the use of the aeroplane.

garage (lieu où l'on remise les automobiles) (*n.m.*), garage.

garant, -e (pers.) (*n.*), guarantor; surety; guarantee; security:

se rendre garant (-e) pour un ami, to become surety for a friend.

garanti, -e (pers.) (*n.*), guarantee (person guaranteed).

garantie (*n.f.*), guarantee; guaranty; warranty; security; surety; indemnity:

garantie de banque, bank guarantee.

garantie de solvabilité, de l'exécution d'un engagement, guarantee of solvency, of the fulfilment of an engagement.

garantie de qualité, guaranty, guarantee, warranty, of quality.

garantie de navigabilité, warranty of seaworthiness.

garantie expresse, express warranty:

une garantie expresse n'exclut pas une garantie implicite, sauf le cas d'incompatibilité (Dr. mar. anglais), an express warranty does not exclude an implied warranty, unless it be inconsistent therewith.

garantie implicite, implied warranty:

il y a garantie implicite que l'aventure assurée est licite, et qu'autant que cela dépend de l'assuré, elle sera accomplie d'une manière licite (Dr. mar. anglais), there is an implied warranty that the adventure insured is a lawful one, and that, so far as the assured can control the matter, the adventure shall be carried out in a lawful manner.

avance contre garantie (*f.*), advance against security; secured advance.

titres détenus en garantie, déposés en garantie d'avances, déposés en nantissement en garantie des fonds avancés (*m.pl.*), stocks held as security, lodged as security for advances, hypothecated (*or* pledged) as security for money advanced.

lettre de garantie (*f.*), letter of indemnity.

sans garantie. See under **sans.**

garantie (engagement à prendre le capital non souscrit par le public) (*n.f.*), underwriting:

garantie de prise ferme, firm underwriting.

garantir (*v.t.*), to guarantee; to warrant; to secure:

garantir une émission de titres, une créance, un minimum d'intérêt à des actions, un caissier, to guarantee an issue of stock, a debt, a minimum interest on shares, a cashier.

l'entrepositaire est tenu de fournir caution pour garantir les droits et les amendes qui pour-

raient devenir exigibles, the bonder is bound to give security to guarantee the duties and fines which may become payable.

garantir par hypothèque une créance, to secure a debt by mortgage.

créance garantie (*f.*), secured debt.

avances garanties (*f.pl.*), secured advances; advances against security.

valeur garantie (*f.*) *ou* valeurs garanties (*f.pl.*) *ou* titre garanti (*m.*) *ou* titres garantis (*m.pl.*) *ou* fonds garantis (*m.pl.*), guaranteed stock; guaranteed stocks.

se garantir (*v.r.*), to secure oneself:

se garantir par hypothèque, to secure oneself by mortgage.

garantir (s'engager à prendre le capital non souscrit par le public) (*v.t.*), to underwrite:

garantir une émission, to underwrite an issue.

le syndicataire profite de la commission de garantie (*ou* commission syndicale), qui correspond au nombre de titres garantis par lui, the underwriter profits by the underwriting commission, which corresponds with (*or* to) the number of shares underwritten by him.

garçon de bureau (*m.*), messenger; commissionaire.

garçon de recette (Banq.) (*m.*), walk clerk; walks clerk.

garde (*n.f.*) *ou* **garde en dépôt**, keeping; custody; safe custody:

laisser une somme d'argent à la garde d'un ami, to leave a sum of money in keeping (*or* in the custody) of a friend.

délai de garde des télégrammes (par l'administration des postes) (*m.*), time of keeping telegrams.

la garde (*ou* la garde en dépôt) des titres, the safe custody of securities.

déposer des titres en garde, to place securities in safe custody. *See note under* dépôt libre *ou* dépôt en garde.

garde (Douanes) (pers.) (*n.m.*), watcher:

placer des gardes à bord d'un navire, to put watchers on board a ship.

garde-côte [**garde-côte** *ou* **garde-côtes** *pl.*] (*n.m.*), coast-defence ship.

garde de convoi de marchandises (pers.) (*m.*), goods guard.

garder (*v.t.*), to keep; to retain; to take care of:

garder copie d'une lettre, to keep a copy of a letter.

garder une somme d'argent à quelqu'un, to keep, to take care of, a sum of money for someone.

quelles valeurs sont à garder ? which stocks are to be kept (*or* are to be retained) ?

gare (*n.f.*) *ou* **gare de chemin de fer**, station; railway station:

gare d'arrivée, station of arrival; arrival station.

gare d'attache (d'un wagon de ch. de f.), home station.

gare d'eau, waterside station.

gare d'échange *ou* gare de transbordement, exchange station.

gare d'embranchement *ou* gare de bifurcation, junction station.

gare d'évitement, sidings.

gare de départ, station of departure; departure station; starting station.

gare de destination *ou* gare destinataire, destination station; station of destination.

gare de douane, customs station.

gare de jonction, joint station.

gare de (*ou* des) marchandises *ou* gare de petite vitesse, goods station.

gare de passage *ou* gare intermédiaire *ou* gare d'escale, way station; intermediate station.

gare de (*ou* des) voyageurs *ou* gare de grande vitesse, passenger station.

gare expéditrice *ou* gare d'expédition, sending station; forwarding station.

gare frontière [gares frontière *pl.*], frontier station.

gare maritime, marine station.

gare réceptrice *ou* gare de réception, receiving station; delivering station.

gare terminus *ou* gare de tête de ligne *ou* gare en cul-de-sac, terminus; terminal; terminal station.

en gare *ou* **gare restante,** at railway station, to be called for; to be called for:
livraison en gare *ou* remise gare restante (*f.*), delivery at railway station, to be called for.

garnir (*v.t.*), to fill:
carnet de commandes largement garni (*m.*), well filled order book.

gaspillage (*n.m.*), waste:
gaspillage de temps, waste of time.

gaspiller (*v.t.*), to waste; to squander:
gaspiller du temps et de l'argent, to waste time and money.
gaspiller sa fortune, to squander one's fortune.

général, -e, -aux (*adj.*) (Abrév.: **gal, gale**), general:
assemblée générale (*f.*), general meeting.

gens de l'équipage (*m.pl.*), crew; members of the crew.

gens de mer (*m.pl.*), seamen; seafaring men; seafarers; mariners; sailors:
loyers des gens de mer (*m.pl.*), seamen's wages.

gérance (fonction) (*n.f.*), management:
gérance d'une entreprise, management of an undertaking.

gérance (temps que dure la fonction) (*n.f.*), managership:
pendant sa gérance, during his managership.

gérant, -e (*adj.*), managing:
administrateur gérant (*m.*), managing director.

gérant (pers.) (*n.m.*), manager:
gérant d'une société (*ou* d'une compagnie), d'un syndicat de garantie, d'un syndicat de placement, manager of a company, of an underwriting syndicate, of a pool.
gérant d'affaires, business manager.
gérant (-e) de cabine (Téléph.), call office attendant.

gérante (pers.) (*n.f.*), manageress.

gérer (*v.t.*), to manage; to conduct: to administer:

l'association est gérée par deux administrateurs, the association is managed by two directors.

gestion (*n.f.*), management; care; . conduct; administration:
gestion d'affaires, conduct, management, of affairs.
gestion financière d'un pays, financial administration of a country.

gestionnaire (*adj.*), managing; management (*used as adj.*):
compte gestionnaire (*m.*), management account.

gestionnaire (pers.) (*n.m.*), manager.

glace (*n.f.*) *ou* **glaces** (*n.f.pl.*), ice:
navigation interrompue par la glace (*ou* par les glaces) (*f.*), navigation stopped by ice.

glisser (*v.i.*), to slip back:
l'action X. glisse de 105 à 100, X. shares slipped back from 105 to 100 francs.

global, -e, -aux (*adj.*), total; grand; sum (*used as adj.*):
somme globale (*f.*) *ou* montant global (*m.*), total amount.
total global (*m.*), grand total; sum total.

gogo (pers.) (*n.m.*), simpleton; gull.

gold-point [gold-points *pl.*] (*n.m.*), gold point; bullion point; specie point:
gold-point d'entrée *ou* gold-point d'importation, import (*or* incoming) gold point (*or* bullion point) (*or* specie point):
gold-point de sortie *ou* gold-point d'exportation, export (*or* outgoing) gold point (*or* bullion point) (*or* specie point):
dans deux pays ayant l'étalon de l'or, le change réciproque oscille, autour du pair, entre les gold-points d'entrée et de sortie, in two countries having the gold standard, the reciprocal exchange oscillates, around par, between the import and export gold points.

gommage (*n.m.*), gumming.

gomme (*n.f.*), gum.

gomme (*n.f.*) *ou* **gomme élastique** *ou* **gomme à effacer,** indiarubber; rubber; eraser:
gomme pour le crayon *ou* gomme à crayon, pencil eraser.
gomme pour l'encre (*ou* à encre), ink eraser.
gomme pour machines à écrire, typewriter's eraser.

gommer (*v.t.*), to gum:
étiquette gommée (*f.*), gummed label.

gonflement (*n.m.*), swelling; inflation; increase:
un gonflement du poste « portefeuille-effets » (bilan de banque), an increase of the item " bills of exchange."

gonfler (*v.t.*), to swell; to inflate; to increase:
trusts qui, en gonflant leur capital à l'excès, veulent donner l'impression de la puissance, et masquer, par une réduction apparente, leurs énormes bénéfices (*m.pl.*), trusts which, by inflating their capital to excess, wish to give the impression of power, and conceal, by an apparent reduction, their enormous profits.

gouvernement *ou* **Gouvernement** (*n.m.*), government; Government:
le Gouvernement est préféré à tous créanciers, the Government is preferred over all creditors.

gouverner (*v.t.*), to govern:

c'est l'état des récoltes dans les grands pays producteurs qui gouverne le prix du blé sur le marché général, it is the condition of the crops in the great producing countries which governs the price of wheat on the general market.

gouverneur (pers.) (*n.m.*), governor:

le gouverneur de la Banque de France, de la Banque d'Angleterre, the governor of the Bank of France, of the Bank of England.

« Je consens à ce que le chef de la Banque [de France] soit appelé *gouverneur*, si cela peut lui faire plaisir, car les titres ne coûtent rien.

« Je consens également à ce que son traitement soit aussi élevé qu'on voudra, puisque c'est la Banque qui doit payer.» NAPOLÉON Ier dans la séance du 27 mars 1806 du Conseil d'État.

" I consent to the head of the Bank [of France] being called *governor*, if it please him, because titles cost nothing.

" I likewise consent to his salary being as high as you please, as the Bank will have to pay it." NAPOLEON I at the sitting of 27th March 1806 of the Council of State.

grâce à, thanks to:

grâce à l'absence de concurrence, thanks to the absence of competition.

gradué, -e (*adj.*), graduated:

échelle graduée (*f.*), graduated scale.

droit de timbre gradué (*m.*), graduated stamp duty.

graduer (*v.t.*), to graduate:

graduer les cotisations suivant l'importance du revenu, to graduate the assessments according to the amount of the income.

grand cabotage (*m.*). See explanatory note under **cabotage.**

grand détail (*m.*), departmental store business (*or* trade).

grand environ (Bourse). See under **environ.**

grand livre [grands livres *pl.*] (*m.*), ledger; register:

grand livre à feuilles mobiles, loose leaf ledger; perpetual ledger.

grand livre auxiliaire *ou* grand livre fractionnaire *ou* grand livre analytique *ou* grand livre originaire *ou* grand livre de développement, subsidiary ledger; subledger; departmental ledger; sectional ledger.

grand livre auxiliaire de frais, expenses ledger.

grand livre des achats, bought ledger; purchases ledger; credit ledger.

grand livre des clients, customers' ledger; clients' ledger.

grand livre des comptes particuliers, personal ledger.

grand livre des fournisseurs, suppliers' ledger.

grand livre des obligataires, register of debenture holders.

grand livre des titres *ou* grand livre des actionnaires, share ledger; share register; stock register; register of members.

grand livre des valeurs, securities ledger.

grand livre des ventes, sales ledger; sold ledger; debit ledger.

grand livre divers, sundries ledger.

grand livre double, double ledger (account on a page; paged).

grand livre général *ou* grand livre des comptes généraux *ou* grand livre synthétique, general ledger; impersonal ledger; nominal ledger.

grand livre simple, single ledger (account on an opening; folioed).

grand-livre (*ou* **grand livre**) **de la dette publique** (*m.*), register of the national debt. See note under **rente.**

grand magasin (*m.*), store; stores; departmental store.

grande ligne *ou* **grande artère** (Ch. de f.) (*f.*), main line; trunk line:

les grandes lignes partant de Paris, the main lines out of Paris.

les grandes artères du réseau français, the trunk lines of the French system.

grande navigation (*f.*), ocean carrying trade.

grande vitesse (Ch. de f.) (*f.*) (Abrév.: **g.v.** *ou* **G.V.**), fast train; fast trains; passenger train (*or* trains):

marchandises expédiées en grande vitesse (*f.pl.*), goods sent by passenger train.

grands réseaux *ou* **grands chemins de fer** (Bourse) (*m.pl.*), heavy rails; heavies.

gratification (*n.f.*), gratuity; bonus:

gratification au personnel, bonus to the staff.

appointements et gratifications, salaries and bonuses.

grattage (*n.m.*), scratching out; erasure.

gratter (*v.t.*), to scratch out; to erase.

gratter (*v.i.*), to scratch out:

on ne doit pas gratter sur les livres, one should not scratch out in the books.

grattoir (de bureau) (*n.m.*), eraser; knife eraser.

gratuit, -e (*adj.*), gratuitous; free; bonus (*used as adj.*):

remise gratuite (*f.*), free delivery.

actions gratuites (*f.pl.*), bonus shares.

gratuité (*n.f.*), gratuitousness.

gré (*n.m.*), discretion:

absolument au gré du capitaine, in the absolute discretion of the captain.

gré à gré (de), by negotiation; by mutual agreement; by private treaty:

le règlement de gré à gré est employé dans les sinistres de minime importance (Assce), settlement by negotiation is resorted to in small losses.

vente de gré à gré (*f.*), sale by private treaty.

greffe (*n.m.*), registry.

greffier (pers.) (*n.m.*), registrar.

grenier (d'arrimage) (*n.m.*), dunnage.

grenier (en), in bulk:

charger des grains en grenier, to ship grain in bulk.

grève (plage) (*n.f.*), beach; shore; sea beach; seashore:

grève de galets, shingle beach; pebble beach.

grève de sable, sandy beach.

grève (cessation concertée du travail) (*n.f.*) (opp. à *lock-out* ou *grève patronale*), strike; walkout:

se mettre en grève, to go on strike ; to strike ; to walk out.

grève d'agents de chemins de fer, railway strike.

grève dans les charbonnages, coal strike.

grève de sympathie *ou* grève de solidarité, sympathetic strike.

grève des (*ou* de) dockers, dock strike.

grève générale, general strike.

grève perlée, ca'canny strike :

cheminots qui font la grève perlée par suite du rejet de leur demande d'augmentation de salaires (*m.pl.*), railwaymen who go on ca'canny strike in consequence of the rejection of their demand for increase of wages.

grève patronale (*f.*), lockout.

grever (*v.t.*), to burden ; to weight ; to encumber ; to put on ; *or by ellipsis* on ; upon :

grever d'une hypothèque une propriété, to encumber a property with a mortgage.

grever le budget de dépenses d'un exercice d'une somme exceptionnellement grosse, to weight, to burden, the budget of expenses of one accounting period with an exceptionally heavy sum.

les produits nationaux se trouvant ainsi grevés plus lourdement que par le passé (*m.pl.*), the national products thus finding themselves more heavily burdened than in the past.

l'expéditeur peut grever son envoi d'un remboursement jusqu'à concurrence de la valeur de la marchandise (*m.*), the sender can put a trade charge on his consignment not exceeding the value of the goods.

la marchandise peut être grevée d'un remboursement jusqu'à concurrence de sa valeur, the trade charge on (*or* upon) the goods may not exceed their value.

les colis peuvent être grevés de remboursements jusqu'à concurrence de tant de francs (*m.pl.*), the trade charge on (*or* upon) parcels may not exceed so many francs.

expédition grevée de remboursement (*f.*), consignment on (*or* upon) which a trade charge is to be collected.

les frais grevant l'envoi (*m.pl.*), the charges on (*or* upon) the consignment.

gréviste (pers.) (*n.m.* ou *f.*), striker.

griffe (timbre) (*n.f.*), stamp ; signature stamp ; facsimile stamp :

griffe à date, date stamp ; dater.

griffe (empreinte imitant une signature) (*n.f.*), imprinted *or* stamped signature ; facsimile signature.

griffer (*v.t.*), to print, to stamp, a signature on.

gril (de carénage) (*n.m.*), gridiron ; grid.

grippe-argent [**grippe-argent** *pl.*] (pers.) (*n.m.*), money grubber ; money grub.

grise (ligne légère tracée sur du papier à écrire) (*n.f.*), faint line ; faint ; feint line ; feint.

gros, grosse (important) (*adj.*), large ; big ; great ; heavy ; high :

une grosse somme d'argent, a large amount (*or* a big sum) of money.

gros banquiers, gros chargeurs (*m.pl.*), big bankers, big shippers.

gros bagages (*m.pl.*), heavy luggage.

emprunter à gros intérêt, to borrow at high interest.

grosses avaries (Assce mar.) (*f.pl.*), general average ; gross average. See **avarie** for examples.

grosses coupures (d'actions, etc.) (*f.pl.*) (*Abrév. :* gr. coup. *ou* gr. c:), big denominations (of shares, etc.).

gros (*n.m.*) *ou* **gros commerce** (*m.*) *ou* **commerce de** (*ou* **en**) **gros** (*m.*), direct trade ; direct commerce :

faire le gros, to do a direct trade.

vente en gros (*f.*), direct sale.

Note :—(*a*) *direct* (i.e., producing or manufacturing), (*b*) *wholesale* (buying from the producer or manufacturer and selling to the retailer), and (*c*) *retail* (selling to consumer) are technical terms, and have as equivalents in French (*a*) *gros,* (*b*) *demi-gros,* and (*c*) *détail.*

In a looser or more general sense, in English as in French, *wholesale* (*gros*) is merely contrasted with *retail* (*détail*). This is particularly the case in the mere sense of selling in large quantities, thus, to *sell wholesale* (*vendre en gros*), as contrasted with selling in small quantities, thus *selling retail* (*vente en détail*).

The three grades are thus frequently denominated (*a*) *producer* (*producteur*), (*b*) *wholesale* (*gros*), and (*c*) *retail* (*détail*).

Furthermore, *producer* (*producteur*) can be contrasted merely with *consumer* or *user* (*consommateur*), thus, producer who sells direct to the consumer, producteur qui vend directement au consommateur.

grosse (Dr.) (*n.f.*), engrossment ; copy.

grosse (*n.f.*) *ou* **grosse aventure** (Dr. mar.), bottomry or respondentia.

grosse sur corps *ou* **grosse aventure sur corps** (Dr. mar.) (*f.*), bottomry.

grosse sur facultés *ou* **grosse aventure sur facultés** (Dr. mar.) (*f.*), respondentia.

grossier, -ère (*adj.*), rough :

calcul grossier (*m.*), rough (*or* approximate) calculation.

grossièrement (*adv.*), roughly.

grossir un compte, to inflate an account.

grossiste (pers.) (*n.m.*), wholesaler. (See note under **gros** *ou* **gros commerce**.)

group (*n.m.*), bag (of money).

groups *ou* articles de valeur (comme cargaison d'un navire), gold, silver, jewellery, or precious stones.

groupage *ou* **groupement** (*n.m.*), grouping ; batching :

groupage des lots sur un même connaissement, grouping lots on the same bill of lading.

un groupage est la réunion dans un même envoi de plusieurs petits colis, a grouping is the bundling in one and the same consignment of several small parcels.

groupe (*n.m.*), group ; batch :

groupe de comptes, d'actionnaires, group of accounts, of shareholders.

groupe de colis, group, batch, of parcels.

groupe de lettres, de chiffres (Télégr.), group of letters, of figures.

le groupe caoutchoutier (Bourse), the rubber group.

groupement (*n.m.*) *ou* **groupement pour opérations en commun** (Fin.), pool.

grouper (*v.t.*), to group; to batch :
grouper les marchandises appartenant à plusieurs expéditeurs, to group the goods belonging to several shippers.

grue (*n.f.*), crane.

guelte (*n.f.*), commission on sale.

guerre (*n.f.*) (Ant.: *paix*), war :
guerre de tarifs, rate war; tariff war.

guichet (d'une banque, d'un bureau de poste, ou analogue) (*n.m.*), counter (of a bank, of a post office, or the like) :
échanger des billets au guichet d'une banque, to exchange notes over (*or* at) the counter of a bank.
guichet télégraphique (bureau de poste), telegrams counter.
distribution au guichet (Poste), delivery to callers (*or* at post office).
Note :—French banks, post offices, and the like, generally serve the public through a *guichet* (little window), like the ticket window of a railway booking office. In England, similar business is generally done on a counter from behind a grill, or over an open counter. Hence the translation of *guichet* by *counter* in this sense.

à guichet ouvert, on demand; on presentation : payer à guichet ouvert, to pay on demand (*or* on presentation).

guichet d'enregistrement des bagages *ou* **guichet bagages** (Ch. de f., etc.) (*m.*), luggage registration office; luggage office.

guichet de distribution des billets *ou simplement* **guichet** (*n.m.*) (Ch. de f., etc.), booking office; ticket window.

guichetier (d'une banque) (pers.) (*n.m.*), cashier; teller :
guichetier encaisseur, receiving cashier; receiver.
guichetier payeur, paying cashier; payer.

guide (pers.) (*n.m.*), guide :
le service d'un guide compétent, the services of a competent guide.

guide (livre) (*n.m.*), guide; guide book :
guide de voyage, travel guide (*or* guide book).

guide (carte-guide) (répertoire sur fiches) (*n.m.*), guide card.

guide-papier (d'une machine à écrire) (*n.m.*), paper guide.

guinée (monnaie de compte d'Angleterre) (*n.f.*), guinea :
la guinée est employée pour le calcul des honoraires, et pour l'établissement des prix dans certains commerces de luxe (la guinée n'est qu'une monnaie de compte), (in England) the guinea is used in the reckoning of fees, and for fixing prices in certain luxury trades (the guinea is only a money of account).

H

'**halle aux marchandises** (Ch. de f.) (*f.*), goods shed.

'**halte** (Ch. de f.) (*n.f.*), halt.

'**handicap** (*n.m.*), handicap.

'**handicaper** (*v.t.*), to handicap :
complications qui handicapent les concurrents (*f.pl.*), complications which handicap competitors.

'**hangar** (*n.m.*), shed :
hangar de dock, dock shed.

'**hangar** (pour remiser les avions) (*n.m.*), hangar; shed.

'**harasse** (*n.f.*), crate.

'**hardes** (des gens de mer) (*n.f.pl.*), effects (of seamen) (clothing, and the like).

'**hasard** (*n.m.*), hazard; chance; risk; venture : un hasard heureux, a happy chance.

'**hasarder** (*v.t.*), to hazard; to risk; to venture : hasarder sa fortune dans une entreprise, to risk one's fortune in an enterprise.

'**hasardeux, -euse** (*adj.*), hazardous; risky : spéculation hasardeuse (*f.*), risky (*or* hazardous) speculation.

'**hausse** (augmentation de prix) (*n.f.*), rise; rise in price; advance in price; increase in price :
la hausse ou la baisse des titres de bourse, des frets, the rise or the fall of stocks and shares, of freights.
tendance à la hausse (dans les cours) (*f.*), upward tendency (in prices).
hausse du taux officiel d'escompte, rise in the bank rate.
opération à la hausse (Bourse) (*f.*), dealing for a rise; bull transaction.
mouvement de hausse des valeurs (*m.*), upward movement of stocks.

être en hausse *ou* **être à la hausse** (Bourse), to be rising; to be a rising market; to be up; to be on :
les valeurs pétrolifères sont en hausse (*ou* sont à la hausse), oil shares are rising (*or* are a rising market) (*or* are up).
vendre en hausse et acheter en baisse, to sell on a rising market and to buy on a falling market.

cuivre en hausse de 1/4 à £69 15sh. (*ou*
£69 3/4), copper up 5s. at £69 15s.;
copper 5s. on at £69 15s.

être à la hausse (en parlant des personnes), to
go for a rise :
spéculateur qui est à la hausse (*m.*), speculator
who is going for a rise.

'hausser (*v.t.*), to raise ; to advance ; to increase :
hausser le prix de quelque chose, to raise, to
advance, to increase, the price of something.

'hausser (augmenter de prix) (*v.i.*), to rise ;
to rise in price ; to go up ; to advance in
price ; to be rising ; to improve :
le blé hausse, wheat is rising (*or* is going up).
hausser sur une offre, to improve on an offer.

'haussier (Bourse) (pers.) (*n.m.*) (opp. à *baissier*),
bull ; long :
les haussiers achètent à terme des valeurs qu'ils
espèrent revendre à un cours plus élevé,
bulls buy for the settlement stocks which
they hope to resell at a higher price.

'haut, -e (*adj.*). See examples :
le taux du change est haut, the rate of exchange
is high.
haut commerce (*m.*), business ; trade (of an
important nature).
haute banque *ou* haute finance (*f.*), big banks ;
high finance :
les maisons de haute banque (*f.pl.*), the big
banking houses.
haute mer (*f.*), high sea ; deep sea :
vapeur de haute mer (*m.*), deep-sea steamer.
hautes parties contractantes (traités) (*f.pl.*),
high contracting parties (treaties).

'haut (partie supérieure) (*n.m.*), top :
le haut d'une page, the top of a page.

'hauts et bas (*n.m.pl.*), ups and downs :
avoir des hauts et des bas de fortune, to have
ups and downs of fortune.

'hâvre (*n.m.*), haven.

hebdomadaire (*adj.*), weekly :
carte d'abonnement hebdomadaire (*f.*), weekly
season ticket.

héritier (pers.) (*n.m.*), heir.

héritière (pers.) (*n.f.*), heiress.

hésitant, -e (*adj.*), hesitating ; undecided :
l'action X. est plutôt hésitante à 178, X. shares
are rather undecided at 178 francs.

hésiter (*v.i.*), to hesitate ; to be undecided :
l'action X. hésite autour de 1 383, X. shares
were undecided around 1,383 francs.

heure (*n.f.*), hour ; time :
train qui marche à (*ou* qui parcourt) — kilomètres à l'heure (*ou* par heure) (*m.*), train
which runs (*or* which travels) at — kilometres
an hour (*or* per hour).
à toute heure de jour ou de nuit, at any hour
(or time) of the day or night.
heure d'été, summer time.
heures d'ouverture *ou* heures d'ouverture et de
clôture, hours of business ; business hours ;
hours of attendance :
heures réglementaires d'ouverture et de clôture
des bureaux télégraphiques, usual hours of
business (or of attendance) at telegraph
offices.

heures de bourse, stock exchange hours.
heure de chargement (d'un navire), loading
hour.
heure de départ, d'arrivée, time of departure,
of arrival.
heure de dépôt (d'un télégramme), time
handed in.
heures de distribution (Poste), hours, times, of
delivery.
heures de douane, customs hours.
heures de jour, daytime :
pendant les heures de jour, during the daytime.
heure de l'Europe Occidentale *ou* heure de
Greenwich (midi) (*Abrév.*: H. E. Occ. *ou*
H^re E. Occ.), West European time ; Western
European time ; West Europe time ; Greenwich time (12 noon in relation to Amsterdam,
Central, and East European times).
heure d'Amsterdam (midi 20) (*Abrév.*: H.
holl.), Amsterdam time (12.20 p.m. in
relation to West European time).
heure de l'Europe Centrale (13 heures) (*Abrév.*:
H.E.C. *ou* H. E. Cent. *ou* H^re E. Cent.),
Central European time ; Mid European time ;
Mid Europe time (1 p.m. in relation to
West European time).
heure de l'Europe Orientale (14 heures)
(*Abrév.*: H.E.Or. *ou* H^re E.Or.), East European time ; Eastern European time ; East
Europe time (2 p.m. in relation to West
European time).
heure de la réponse des primes (Bourse), time
for declaration of options. See explanation
under **prime**.
heures de travail, working hours ; hours of
labour.
heure-limite de dépôt [heures-limite de dépôt
pl.], latest time for posting.
heure sauvée (dispatch), hour saved.
heures supplémentaires, overtime :
les heures supplémentaires, quand on ne peut
pas les éviter, sont payées à part, overtime,
when it cannot be avoided, is paid extra.
la somme payée pour les heures supplémentaires, the amount paid for overtime.
travailler en heures supplémentaires, to work
overtime.

heureuse arrivée (d'un navire à destination) (*f.*),
safe arrival (of a ship at destination).
Cf. vente à l'heureuse arrivée.

hier (mention dans la cote) (Bourse) (*adv.*) (Abrév. :
h.), bargain done on the previous day.

hier, cours nul (Abrév. : **h.c.n.** *ou* **h.cn.**). See
under **cours.**

hier lire (Abrév. : **hl.**). See under **lire.**

'hisser une valeur (Bourse), to run up a stock.

historique (*n.m.*), history ; account :
faire l'historique d'une négociation, to write an
account of a transaction.

hiver (*n.m.*), winter.

hiverner (*v.i.*), to winter :
navire bloqué par les glaces et obligé d'hiverner
(*m.*), ship blockaded by ice and obliged to
winter.

'holding [**holding** *pl.*] (trust de valeurs) (*n.f.*),
holding company.

homme (*n.m.*), man :
  homme d'affaires,   business man ; man of business.
  homme d'affaires (agent d'affaires), agent ; business agent.
  homme d'argent, money grubber ; money grub.
  hommes d'équipage, crew ; members of the crew.
  homme de confiance *ou* homme de commerce sûr *ou* homme sur lequel on peut compter, reliable man.
  homme de finance, financial man ; financier.
  homme de loi, lawyer.
  homme de mer, seaman ; seafaring man ; seafarer ; mariner ; sailor.
  homme de paille, man of straw :
    prête-nom qui cache un homme de paille (*m.*), dummy who masks a man of straw.
  homme de parole, man of his word.
  homme qui en a la garde, man in charge.
  homme rangé, steady man.
  homme-sandwich [hommes-sandwichs   *pl.*] (Publicité) (*n.m.*), sandwich man.
honnête (*adj.*), honest ; upright.
honnêtement (*adv.*), honestly ; uprightly.
honnêteté (*n.f.*), honesty ; uprightness ; integrity.
honneur (*n.m.*), honour :
  tiers qui accepte un effet, à défaut du tiré, pour l'honneur de la signature du tireur (*m.*), third party who accepts a bill, in default of the drawee, for the honour of the signature of the drawer.
honoraire (*adj.*), honorary :
  membre honoraire (*m.*), honorary member.
honoraires (*n.m.pl.*), fee ; fees :
  honoraires d'avocat, counsel's fees.
  honoraires d'expert, expert's fee ; surveyor's fees.
  honoraires d'expertise, survey fees.
  honoraires des administrateurs, directors' fees.
honorariat (*n.m.*), honorary membership :
  association qui confère l'honorariat à ses anciens membres (*f.*), association which confers honorary membership on its old members.
honorer (*v.t.*), to honour ; to meet ; to take up ; to lift ; to redeem :
  le premier point qui intéresse l'escompteur c'est la certitude que l'effet escompté sera honoré à l'échéance, the first point that interests the discounter is the certainty that the dis- counted bill will be honoured (*or* met) (*or* taken up) (*or* lifted) (*or* redeemed) at maturity.
horaire (*n.m.*), time table.
'hors banque. *See* escompte hors banque *&* papier hors banque.
'hors cote (Bourse). *See* marché hors cote.
'hors d'état de naviguer, unseaworthy :
  lorsque le navire a fait voile, il était hors d'état de naviguer, when the ship sailed, she was unseaworthy.
'hors de vente, unsaleable ; unsalable :

marchandise hors de vente (*f.*), unsaleable goods.
hostilité (*n.f.*), hostility :
  hostilités ou opérations belliqueuses, hostilities or warlike operations.
hôtel (*n.m.*), hotel :
  hôtel ouvert toute l'année, hotel open all the year round.
hôtel des Monnaies *ou* **hôtel de la Monnaie** (*m.*), mint.
hôtel des postes (*m.*), general post office.
'houille (*n.f.*), coal.
hydroaéroplane *ou* **hydravion** *ou* **hydroavion** (*n.m.*), hydroaeroplane.
hypothécable (*adj.*), mortgageable :
  biens hypothécables (*m.pl.*), mortgageable property.
hypothécaire (*adj.*) (Abrév. : hyp. *ou* hypoth. *ou* h.), mortgage (*used as adj.*) ; of or pertaining to a mortgage ; created by a mortgage ; secured by mortgage :
  contrat hypothécaire (*m.*), mortgage deed.
  inscription hypothécaire (*f.*), registration of mortgage.
  créancier hypothécaire (*m.*), creditor on mort- gage ; mortgage creditor.
hypothécairement (*adv.*), by mortgage ; on mortgage :
  être obligé (-e) hypothécairement, to be bound by mortgage.
  créance garantie hypothécairement (*f.*), debt secured by mortgage.
  emprunter hypothécairement, to borrow on mortgage.
hypothèque (*n.f.*) (Abrév. : hyp. *ou* hypoth. *ou* h.), mortgage :
  avoir hypothèque sur un bien, to have a mortgage on a property.
  première hypothèque *ou* hypothèque de premier rang, first mortgage.
  hypothèque générale, general mortgage ; blanket mortgage.
  le *mortgage* du droit anglais correspond, avec de grandes différences toutefois, à l'hypo- thèque du droit français, the mortgage of English law corresponds, with wide differences however, to the *hypothèque* of French law.
hypothéquer (soumettre à l'hypothèque) (*v.t.*), to mortgage :
  hypothéquer une maison, un navire, sa part dans un navire, le navire en cours de route pour les besoins de l'expédition, to mortgage a house, a ship, one's share in a ship, the ship during the voyage for the needs of the adventure.
s'hypothéquer (*v.r.*), to be mortgaged ; to become mortgaged.
hypothéquer (garantir par hypothèque) (*v.t.*), to secure by mortgage :
  hypothéquer une créance, to secure a debt by mortgage.

I

ici (Téléph.) (*adv.*), speaking (*p.pr.*) :
à l'appel : « Ici A.B., » on calling : " A.B.
speaking."

il (en parlant d'un navire) (*pron.m.*), she ; it :
Note :—In French, a ship is grammatically
masculine. In English, a ship is generally
personified as feminine, and is then referred
to as *she*. The use of *it*, while not incorrect,
is unusual. Similarly *navire frère* becomes
in English *sister ship*.
on dit que le navire est expédié quand il est
muni de tous ses papiers, one says that the
ship is cleared when she is provided with all
her papers.

île (*n.f.*), island ; isle :
les îles Britanniques, the British Isles.

illégal, -e, -aux (*adj.*), illegal ; unlawful :
actes illégaux (*m.pl.*), illegal acts ; unlawful acts.

illégalement (*adv.*), illegally ; unlawfully.

illégalité (*n.f.*), illegality ; unlawfulness :
illégalité d'un contrat, illegality of a contract.

illicite (*adj.*), illicit ; unlawful :
gain illicite (*m.*), illicit gain.

illicitement (*adv.*), illicitly ; unlawfully.

illimité, -e (*adj.*), unlimited :
responsabilité illimitée (*f.*), unlimited liability.
une somme illimitée sans toutefois dépasser un
maximum par navire ou voyage de tant, an
unlimited amount but not to exceed a maximum per ship or voyage of so much.

illisibilité (*n.f.*), illegibleness ; illegibility ; unreadableness.

illisible (*adj.*), illegible ; unreadable :
écriture illisible (*f.*), illegible writing ; unreadable handwriting.

illisiblement (*adv.*), illegibly :
écrire illisiblement, to write illegibly.

illusoire (*adj.*), illusory :
bénéfice illusoire (*m.*), illusory profit.

immatériel, -elle (en parlant d'immobilisations)
(*adj.*), intangible :
valeurs immatérielles (*f.pl.*), intangible assets.

immatriculation *ou* **immatricule** (*n.f.*), registration ; registry ; entering ; entry :
immatriculation (*ou* immatricule) d'un acte,
registration, registry, of a deed.
tout navire doit être attaché à un port sous la
forme d'une immatriculation sur un registre
spécial tenu au bureau de l'inscription
maritime, every ship must belong to a port
under the form of an entry in a special
register kept at the marine registry office.

immatriculer (*v.t.*), to register ; to enter :
ces valeurs sont immatriculées au nom de la
société (*f.pl.*), these securities are registered
in the name of the company.
navire immatriculé dans les colonies (*m.*), ship
registered in the colonies.

immeuble (Dr.) (*adj.*), real ; immovable ; fixed :
biens immeubles (*m.pl.*), real property ; real
estate ; realty ; immovable property ; fixed
property.

immeuble (*n.m.*) *ou* **immeubles** (*n.m.pl.*) (Dr.),
real property ; real estate ; realty ; immovable property ; fixed property ; property :
droit au bail d'un immeuble sis à Paris, rue X.,
n° 29, servant de bureaux et de dépôt à la
société (*m.*), right to the lease of a property
situated in Paris, at No. 29 X. Street, used as
offices and stores by the company.

immeuble (*n.m.*) *ou* **immeubles** (*n.m.pl.*) (terrains,
bâtiments, etc.), premises :
immeuble commercial, business premises.
immeuble (*ou* immeubles) de la banque, bank
premises.

immigrant, -e (pers.) (*n.*), immigrant.

immigration (*n.f.*), immigration :
l'immigration présente pour les pays neufs de
très réels avantages, immigration is of very
real benefit to new countries.

immigrer (*v.i.*), to immigrate.

immiscer (s') (*v.r.*), to meddle ; to interfere :
s'immiscer dans la direction d'une entreprise,
to interfere in the management of a
concern.

immobilier, -ère (*adj.*), real ; immovable ; fixed :
biens immobiliers (*m.pl.*) *ou* valeurs immobilières
(*f.pl.*), real property ; real estate ; realty ;
immovable property ; fixed property.

immobilier (*n.m.*), real property ; real estate ;
realty ; immovable property ; fixed property.

immobilisation (*n.f.*), immobilization ; lockup ;
tie up ; capitalization :
immobilisation d'un stock d'or, immobilization
of a stock of gold.
immobilisation de capital (*ou* de capitaux), lockup, tie up, immobilization, of capital (*or* of
money).
immobilisation de dépenses, capitalization of
expenditure.

immobilisations (*n.f.pl.*) *ou* **dépenses en immobilisations** (*f.pl.*), capital expenditure :
les immobilisations représentent tous les
capitaux correspondant au capital fixe, et par
opposition au capital circulant, capital
expenditure represents all capital (*or* assets)
corresponding to fixed capital (*or* assets) and
as opposed to floating capital (*or* circulating
assets).

immobiliser (*v.t.*), to immobilize ; to lock up ; to
tie up ; to capitalize :
le capital immobilisé dans une lettre de change
est mobilisé dès que la lettre est payée, the
money locked up (*or* tied up) (*or* immobilized)
in a bill of exchange is set free (*or* mobilized)
as soon as the bill is paid.
le vendeur est astreint à immobiliser ses
capitaux dans le crédit qu'il fait à son client :
la lettre de change lui permet de mobiliser sa
créance, d'en obtenir par l'escompte, le
montant avant son échéance, the seller is
compelled to lock up (*or* to tie up) (*or* to
immobilize) his capital in the credit he gives
to his customer : the bill of exchange enables

him to mobilize his debt, to obtain the amount of it by discount before its due date.

dépenses immobilisées (*f.pl.*), capitalized expenditure.

valeurs immobilisées (*f.pl.*) *ou* actif immobilisé (*m.*) *ou* capital immobilisé (*m.*), fixed assets; permanent assets; capital assets; fixed capital.

impair, -e (*adj.*), uneven; odd:
3, 5, 7, sont des nombres impairs, 3, 5, 7, are uneven (*or* odd) numbers.

impayé, -e (*adj.*), unpaid; dishonoured:
somme impayée (*f.*), unpaid amount.
chèque impayé (*m.*), unpaid cheque; dishonoured cheque.

impayé (*n.m.*) (Abrév.: **imp.**) *ou* **effet impayé** (*m.*) *ou* **impayé retourné** *ou* **impayé rendu** *ou* **impayé renvoyé**, dishonoured bill; bill dishonoured by non payment; unpaid bill; bill returned dishonoured.

impécunieux, -euse (*adj.*), impecunious.

impécuniosité (*n.f.*), impecuniosity.

impermutabilité (*n.f.*), inexchangeability.

impermutable (*adj.*), inexchangeable; unexchangeable:
valeurs impermutables (*f.pl.*), inexchangeable (*or* unexchangeable) securities.

implaçable (*adj.*), unplaceable:
l'argent au jour le jour est pour ainsi dire implaçable sur notre marché à 2 1/4 0/0 (*m.*), daily money is so to speak unplaceable on our market at $2\frac{1}{4}\%$.

implacé, -e (*adj.*), unplaced:
titres implacés (*m.pl.*), unplaced shares.

implicite (*adj.*), implied. *See example under* garantie implicite.

impliquer (*v.t.*), to imply:
le silence n'implique pas toujours consentement tacite, silence does not always imply tacit consent.

importance (*n.f.*), importance; amount; size; magnitude:
affaire de peu d'importance (*f.*), matter of small importance; unimportant matter.
dépenses proportionnées à l'importance des affaires de la maison (*f.pl.*), expenses in proportion to the amount (*or* the size) (*or* the magnitude) of the firm's business.

importateur, -trice (*adj.*), importing; import (*used as adj.*):
pays importateur (*m.*), importing country.
négociant importateur (*m.*), import merchant.

importateur, -trice (pers. ou pays) (*n.*), importer:
marchandises à la disposition des importateurs (*f.pl.*), goods at the disposal of the importers.
pays qui est gros importateur de matières d'alimentation (*m.*), country which is a big importer of foodstuffs.
la Grande-Bretagne est une grande importatrice de produits coloniaux, Great Britain is a big importer of colonial produce.

importation (action) (*n.f.*) (Ant.: *exportation*), importation; import:
importation en France de marchandises étrangères, importation of foreign goods into France.

importation (ce qui est importé) (*n.f.*), import; importation:
importations d'Amérique en Angleterre, imports into England from America.

importer (*v.t.*), to import:
importer de l'or, des marchandises, to import gold, goods.
en principe, toute marchandise importée de l'étranger est réputée étrangère et par suite soumise aux droits, in principle, all merchandise imported from abroad is deemed to be foreign and in consequence subject to duty.

imposable (*adj.*), taxable; ratable; rateable; assessable; chargeable with duty:
revenu imposable (*m.*), taxable (*or* assessable) income:
en principe, le revenu imposable est le chiffre déclaré par le contribuable (Impôts cédulaires), in principle, the assessable income is the figure returned by the taxpayer.
marchandises imposables à la valeur (*f.pl.*), goods taxable (*or* chargeable with duty) on value.
le poids imposable, the weight chargeable with duty.

imposé, -e (pers.) (*n.*), taxpayer; ratepayer.

imposer (fixer; établir) (*v.t.*), to impose:
imposer des droits nouveaux, to impose new duties.
pouvoir être imposé (-e) en paiement. See under **pouvoir.**

imposer (frapper d'un impôt) (*v.t.*), to tax; to rate; to assess; to charge with duty:
imposer le revenu, to tax income.
marchandises imposées au brut (*ou* au poids brut), au net (*ou* au poids net), autrement qu'au poids (*f.pl.*), goods charged with duty (*or* rated) on the gross weight, on the net weight, otherwise than by weight.
marchandises imposées à des droits différents (*f.pl.*), goods charged with different duties.

imposition (*n.f.*), imposition; impost; tax; assessment:
multiples impositions sur le même revenu, multiple impositions on the same income.
le revenu de l'année immédiatement antérieure à l'année d'imposition, the income of the year preceding the year of assessment.
imposition d'office, arbitrary assessment.
imposition supplémentaire (Impôts cédulaires), additional assessment.

impôt (*n.m.*), tax; duty; impost; taxation; taxes:
impôt cédulaire, schedule tax; tax on income; income tax:
l'*income-tax* anglais se compose de cinq impôts cédulaires, cédules A, B, C, D, et E (*m.*), English income tax is composed of five schedule taxes, schedules A, B, C, D, and E.
biens qui acquittent déjà l'impôt cédulaire à un autre titre (*m.pl.*), property which already pays income tax under another head.
l'impôt cédulaire et général, income tax and surtax.
Note:—The plural *impôts cédulaires* is equivalent to the English expression *income tax*

in the general sense of taxes on incomes of various natures, as defined in the different schedules.

impôt de capitation, capitation tax; head tax; poll tax.

impôt de superposition *ou* impôt complémentaire, supertax.

impôt de transmission, transfer duty. *See note under syn.* droit de transmission.

impôt dégressif, degressive tax.

impôt direct, direct tax.

impôt du timbre, stamp duty; stamp tax.

impôt foncier, land tax; tax on landed property; property tax.

impôt général sur le revenu *ou* impôt global sur le revenu, surtax. *Note :*—The present *surtax* in England was formerly called *supertax*.

impôt indirect, indirect tax.

impôt progressif, progressive tax.

impôt sur le chiffre d'affaires, turnover tax. In France, a tax on the turnover of the business of those who buy to resell, habitually or occasionally, on those liable to the tax on incomes derived from trade and manufacture, and on those carrying on the business of mines and quarries. Agriculturalists, fishermen, artisans, and professional men are not liable to the tax.

impôt sur le revenu *ou* impôt sur revenu, income tax; tax on income.

impôt sur le revenu des valeurs mobilières, stockholder's tax.

impôt sur les bénéfices agricoles, farmer's tax.

impôt sur les bénéfices industriels et commerciaux, tax on incomes derived from trade and manufacture.

impôt sur les traitements, salary tax.

impôts et contributions, rates and taxes.

payer l'impôt, to pay taxes.

répartition inéquitable des impôts (*f.*), inequitable distribution of taxation.

impression (*n.f.*), printing :
impression de titres, printing certificates.
impressions en relief à l'usage des aveugles (Poste), blind literature.

imprimé (*n.m.*) *ou* **formule imprimée** (*f.*) *ou* **imprimés** (*n.m.pl.*), printed form; printed matter :
un jeu complet de tous les imprimés, a complete set of all the printed forms (*or* printed matter).
lettre sur formule imprimée (*f.*), letter on a printed form.

imprimé (Poste) (*n.m.*), printed paper.

imprimés (Poste) (*n.m.pl.*), printed papers; printed matter.
imprimés en relief pour aveugles (Poste), blind literature.

imprimés (frais d'impression : nom de compte de grand livre ou de poste de compte pertes et profits), printing :
imprimés et fournitures, printing and stationery.

imprimer (*v.t.*), to print :
la police d'assurance peut être manuscrite ou imprimée ; ou en partie manuscrite et en partie imprimée, an insurance policy may be written or printed ; or partly written and partly printed.

imprimeur (pers.) (*n.m.*), printer.

improductif, -ive (*adj.*), unproductive :
capitaux improductifs (*m.pl.*), unproductive capital.

improductivement (*adv.*), unproductively.

improductivité (*n.f.*), unproductivity; unproductiveness.

improfitable (*adj.*), unprofitable; unremunerative.

imputable (*adj.*), chargeable :
frais imputables à un compte, sur une dette (*m.pl.*), expenses chargeable to an account, on a debt.
la proportion de la somme imputable à la chose assurée, the proportion of the amount chargeable to the property insured.

imputation (Comptab.) (*n.f.*), charge; charging :
rectifier les erreurs dans l'imputation des dépenses, to rectify errors in the charging of expenses.

imputation (*n.f.*) *ou* **imputation de paiement** (Dr.), appropriation (application of the property of a debtor to one of several debts) :
imputation sur une dette, appropriation to a debt.

imputer (Comptab.) (*v.t.*), to charge :
imputer une dépense sur un compte, une somme sur l'exercice du mois précédent, to charge an expense to an account, an amount to the previous month's trading.

inacquitté, -e (*adj.*), undischarged; unreceipted :
dette inacquittée (*f.*), undischarged debt.
mémoire inacquitté (*m.*), unreceipted bill.

inactif, -ive (*adj.*), dull :
les mines sont inactives (Bourse) (*f.pl.*), mines are dull.

inactivité (d'un marché) (*n.f.*), dullness (*or* dulness) (of a market).

inaliénable (*adj.*), inalienable; unalienable; untransferable :
droit inaliénable (*m.*), inalienable right.

inanimé, -e (en parlant des valeurs de bourse) (*adj.*), lifeless.

inattendu, -e (*adj.*), unexpected.

inautorisé, -e (*adj.*), unauthorized.

incalculable (*adj.*), incalculable :
pertes incalculables (*f.pl.*), incalculable losses.

incalculablement (*adv.*), incalculably.

incapacité (Assurance-accidents) (*n.f.*), disablement :
incapacité permanente, permanent disablement.
incapacité temporaire, temporary disablement.

incendie (*n.m.*), fire.

incendié, -e (*adj.*), burnt.

incertain, -e (*adj.*), uncertain.

incertain (Changes) (*n.m.*), movable exchange (i.e., rate of exchange); uncertain exchange; indirect exchange; variable exchange. *See* donner l'incertain *for example.*

incertifié, -e (*adj.*), uncertified.

incertitude (*n.f.*), uncertainty.

incessible (*adj.*), inalienable; unalienable; untransferable :
droit incessible (*m.*), inalienable right.

inchangé, -e (*adj.*), unchanged ; unaltered :
le cours reste inchangé, the price remains unchanged (*or* unaltered).
incidence (*n.f.*), incidence :
incidence d'un impôt, incidence of a tax.
income-tax (*n.m.*), income tax.
incommerçable (*adj.*), unnegotiable :
effet incommerçable (*m.*), unnegotiable bill.
inconnu, -e (*adj. & p.p.*), unknown :
risque inconnu (*m.*), unknown risk.
poids, valeur, et contenu inconnus, weight, value, and contents unknown.
inconvertible *ou* **inconvertissable** (*adj.*), inconvertible ; unconvertible :
papier-monnaie inconvertible en espèces (*m.*), paper money inconvertible (*or* unconvertible) into coin.
incorporation (*n.f.*), incorporation :
l'incorporation des frais généraux aux prix de revient, incorporation of overhead charges with costs.
incorporer (*v.t.*), to incorporate :
incorporer les écritures de chaque succursale dans celles du siège, to incorporate the accounts of each branch with those of the head office.
incoté, -e (*adj.*), unquoted :
valeurs incotées (*f.pl.*), unquoted securities.
incourant, -e (inescomptable) (*adj.*), undiscountable :
billet incourant (*m.*), undiscountable bill.
indéchiffrable (*adj.*), undecipherable ; illegible :
écriture indéchiffrable (*f.*), illegible writing.
indéchiffrablement (*adv.*), illegibly.
indécis, -e (*adj.*), undecided :
la tendance, tout d'abord indécise, s'est raffermie en séance, the tendency, undecided at first, hardened later on.
indéfectible (Comptab.) (*adj.*), non wasting :
actif indéfectible (*m.*) *ou* valeurs indéfectibles (*f.pl.*), non wasting assets.
indemnisation (*n.f.*), indemnification ; compensation ; recovery :
indemnisation des expropriés, indemnification, compensation, of expropriated persons.
droit d'indemnisation en vertu d'une assurance (*m.*), right of indemnification (*or* of recovery) under an insurance.
indemniser (*v.t.*), to indemnify ; to compensate :
indemniser le possesseur d'une propriété expropriée pour cause d'utilité publique, to indemnify, to compensate, the owner of a property taken for public use.
indemniser l'assuré d'une perte, les armateurs de certaines conséquences ou responsabilités qui peuvent se soulever, to indemnify the assured for a loss, the shipowners for certain consequences or liabilities that may arise.
indemnitaire (*adj.*), indemnificatory :
le caractère indemnitaire de l'assurance, the indemnificatory character of insurance.
indemnitaire (pers.) (*n.m. ou f.*), indemnitee.
indemnité (*n.f.*), indemnity ; compensation ; claim ; loss ; allowance ; consideration ; remuneration :
indemnité de guerre, war indemnity.

indemnité pour cause d'expropriation, indemnity, compensation, for expropriation.
fixer l'indemnité au montant du dommage, to fix the indemnity (*or* the claim) at the amount of the damage.
le montant de l'indemnité reconnue (Assce), the amount of the ascertained claim (*or* loss).
le règlement de l'indemnité a lieu dans les trois mois du sinistre, settlement of the claim takes place within three months of the accident.
les indemnités dues par les assureurs sont payables comptant (*f.pl.*), the losses due by the underwriters are payable in cash.
indemnité convenue en cas de retard, compensation, allowance, indemnity, agreed in case of delay.
indemnités dues aux victimes d'un accident, compensation due to the victims of an accident.
réclamer une indemnité en cas de congédiement, to claim compensation in case of dismissal.
une indemnité forfaitaire de demi pour cent fixée par une clause du contrat, an agreed consideration of half per cent fixed by a clause of the contract.
indemnité d'assistance maritime, remuneration for assistance (at sea).
indemnité de sauvetage, remuneration for salvage ; salvage.
indent (commande ; ordre) (*n.m.*), indent.
indépensé, -e (*adj.*), unexpended ; unspent :
balance indépensée (*f.*), unexpended (*or* unspent) balance.
index (*n.m.*), index :
index d'un livre, index of a book.
index de finales de mots (code télégraphique), terminals index.
index-number (Écon.) (*n.m.*), index number.
indexation (*n.f.*), indexing.
indicateur (livre ou brochure qui sert de guide) (*n.m.*), guide ; guide book :
indicateur de voyage, travel guide (*or* guide book).
indicateur des chemins de fer, railway guide.
indicateur universel des postes, télégraphes, et téléphones (*Abrév. :* indicateur universel des P.T.T.), post office guide.
indication (*n.f.*), indication ; information ; particular ; instruction :
colonnes pour l'inscription des indications suivantes (*f.pl.*), columns for entering the following information (*or* particulars).
indications de service, service instructions.
indice (*n.m.*), index ; figure ; number :
le prix auquel une maison d'exportation peut vendre ses lettres de change est considéré comme un indice infaillible du crédit dont cette maison jouit dans le monde commercial, the price at which an export house can sell its bills of exchange is considered as an infallible index of the credit which that house enjoys in the commercial world.
indice du coût de la vie, cost of living figure.
indice économique, index number.
indirect, -e (*adj.*), indirect :

impôt indirect (*m.*) *ou* contribution indirecte (*f.*), indirect tax.

indisponibilité (*n.f.*), unavailability; unavailableness.

indisponible (*adj.*), unavailable:
fonds indisponibles (*m.pl.*), unavailable funds.

individuel, -elle (*adj.*), individual; several:
responsabilité individuelle (*f.*), several liability; individual liability.

individuellement (*adv.*), individually; severally:
administrateurs qui sont responsables individuellement ou solidairement, suivant les cas, envers la société ou envers les tiers, des fautes qu'ils auraient commises dans leur gestion (*m.pl.*), directors who are liable severally or jointly and severally, as the case may be, to the company or to third parties, for wrongful acts which they may have done in their management.

indivis, -e (qui n'est pas divisé) (*adj.*), undivided:
biens indivis (*m.pl.*), undivided property.

indivis, -e (qui possède une propriété non divisée) (*adj.*), joint:
propriétaire indivis (*m.*), joint proprietor.
actions indivises (*f.pl.*), joint shares (shares held jointly).

indivisément (*adv.*) *ou* **par indivis**, jointly:
propriété possédée indivisément (*ou* possédée par indivis) (*f.*), property owned jointly.

indivisibilité (*n.f.*), indivisibility.

indivisible (*adj.*), indivisible:
un tout indivisible, an indivisible whole.

indivisiblement (*adv.*), indivisibly.

indivision (*n.f.*), joint ownership; joint possession.

indu, -e (*adj.*), undue; not due:
somme indue (*f.*), undue amount; amount not due.

indu (*n.m.*), what is not due:
réclamer l'indu, to claim what is not due.

indûment (*adv.*), unduly:
taxe indûment perçue (*f.*), charge unduly collected.

industrie (*n.f.*), industry:
industrie-clef [industries-clefs *pl.*] *ou* industrie-clé [industries-clés *pl.*] (*n.f.*), key industry.
industrie de l'armement *ou* industrie des transports maritimes, shipping industry:
l'industrie de l'armement est de plus en plus entre les mains de sociétés, the shipping industry is more and more in the hands of companies.
industrie des constructions navales, shipbuilding industry.
industrie ferroviaire, railway industry.

industriel, -elle (*adj.*), industrial:
centre industriel (*m.*), industrial centre.
valeurs industrielles (*f.pl.*) *ou* **industrielles** (*n.f.pl.*), industrial shares; industrials.

industriel (pers.) (*n.m.*), manufacturer.

industriellement (*adv.*), industrially.

inéchangeable (*adj.*), inexchangeable; unexchangeable:
valeurs inéchangeables (*f.pl.*), unexchangeable securities.

inégal, -e, -aux (*adj.*), unequal.

inégalement (*adv.*), unequally.

inégalité (*n.f.*), inequality:
inégalités de prix, inequalities of (*or* in) price.

inemployé, -e (*adj.*), unemployed; unused:
capitaux inemployés (*m.pl.*), unemployed capital.

inéquitable (*adj.*), inequitable; unequitable:
répartition inéquitable des impôts (*f.*), inequitable (*or* unequitable) distribution of taxation.

inéquitablement (*adv.*), inequitably; unequitably.

inescomptable (*adj.*), undiscountable:
billet inescomptable (*m.*), undiscountable bill.

inévalué, -e (*adj.*), unvalued.

inexact, -e (faux) (*adj.*), inaccurate; incorrect; wrong; false:
calcul inexact (*m.*), wrong calculation.

inexact, -e (qui manque de ponctualité) (*adj.*), unpunctual:
employé inexact (*m.*), unpunctual employee.

inexactement (*adv.*), inaccurately; incorrectly; wrongly; wrong; unpunctually.

inexactitude (*n.f.*), inaccuracy; incorrectness; unpunctuality.

inexécution (*n.f.*), non performance; non execution:
inexécution totale ou partielle d'un contrat d'affrètement, total or partial non performance of a contract of affreightment.

inexigible (*adj.*), not due; undue; not payable; not demandable:
dette présentement inexigible (*f.*), debt not due at the present time.

infidèle (*adj.*), unfaithful; inaccurate; dishonest:
caissier infidèle (*m.*), dishonest cashier.

infidèlement (*adv.*), unfaithfully; inaccurately; dishonestly.

infidélité (*n.f.*), infidelity; unfaithfulness; inaccuracy; dishonesty; breach of trust:
infidélité d'une traduction, inaccuracy of a translation.
infidélité d'un dépositaire, breach of trust on the part of a trustee.

infirmer (*v.t.*) (Ant.: *confirmer*), to cancel:
infirmer une lettre, to cancel a letter.

infirmité permanente (Assurance-accidents) (*f.*), permanent disablement.

inflation (*n.f.*), inflation:
inflation monétaire, monetary inflation.
inflation de crédit, inflation of credit.
inflation d'or, inflation of gold.

infléchir (s') (*v.r.*), to dip:
l'action X. s'infléchit à 1 815, X. shares dipped to 1,815 francs.

influent, -e (*adj.*), influential:
un groupe de personalités influentes, a group of influential people.

informations (recherches) (*n.f.pl.*), enquiries; inquiries:
prendre des informations sur quelqu'un, to make enquiries about someone.

informe (*adj.*), informal.

informer (*v.t.*), to inform:
informer quelqu'un de ce qui passe, to inform someone of what is going on.

infraction (*n.f.*), infraction; infringement; breach; contravention; violation:

infraction aux conditions et engagements, breach, violation, of the conditions and undertakings.

infraction aux règlements, de garantie, breach of the regulations, of warranty.

initial, e, -als (*adj.*), initial; opening:
capital initial (*m.*), initial capital; opening capital.

initiale (*n.f.*), initial:
signer une lettre de ses initiales, to initial, to put one's initials to, a letter.

innavigabilité (*n.f.*), innavigability; unnavigability; unseaworthiness:
louer un second navire au cas d'innavigabilité du premier, to hire a second ship in case of unseaworthiness of the first.

innavigable (*adj.*), innavigable; unnavigable; unseaworthy.

innégociable (*adj.*), unnegotiable:
billet innégociable (*m.*), unnegotiable bill.

inofficiel, -elle (*adj.*), unofficial:
communication inofficielle (*f.*), unofficial communication.

inofficiellement (*adv.*), unofficially.

inopérant, -e (*adj.*), inoperative:
clause inopérante (*f.*), inoperative clause.

insatisfait, -e (*adj.*), unsatisfied:
dette insatisfaite (*f.*), unsatisfied debt.

inscriptible (se dit des rentes) (*adj.*), inscribable.

inscription (*n.f.*), inscription; inscribing; registration; registry; entering; entering up; entry; putting in; recording; record:
inscription d'hypothèque ou inscription hypothécaire, registration of mortgage.
inscription maritime, marine registry.
inscription des abonnés à l'annuaire (Téléph.), entry of subscribers in directory.
inscription du folio du journal d'après lequel l'article est rapporté, putting in, entering, the journal folio from which the entry is posted.
effet transmis au caissier pour l'inscription sur le livre d'effets à payer (*m.*), bill handed to the cashier for entry in the bills payable book.
inscription digraphique (Comptab.), double entry:
toutes des formules des articles du journal général sont des inscriptions digraphiques, all forms of journal entries are double entries.
inscription unigraphique (Comptab.), single entry.

inscription à la cote (Bourse de valeurs) (*f.*), quotation in the list.

inscription de rente ou **inscription sur le grand-livre** (*f.*), inscribed rente.

inscrire (*v.t.*), to inscribe; to register; to enter; to enter up; to put in; to record; to make; to write:
la valeur nominale est celle inscrite sur un titre de bourse, the nominal (or face) value is that inscribed on a stock or share certificate.
inscrire une hypothèque sur un navire, to register a mortgage on a ship.
les articles inscrits sur le journal (*m.pl.*), the items entered in the journal; the entries made in the journal.

les opérations inscrites au jour le jour sur le journal (*f.pl.*), the transactions recorded (or entered up) from day to day in the journal.

inscrire quelque chose sur un livre, to enter, to enter up, to record, to write, something in a book.

inscrire une souscription, une somme au carnet de banque, to enter, to enter up, a subscription, an amount in the bank pass book.

inscrire (Bourse de valeurs) (*v.t.*), to quote (to admit and enter on the official list; not to be confused with quotations of prices by dealers):
valeurs inscrites à la cote officielle (*f.pl.*), securities quoted in the official list. *Cf.* valeurs inscrites.

inscrire (s') (inscrire son nom) (*v.r.*), to put one's name down:
s'inscrire sur une liste, to put one's name down on a list.

inscrire (s') (Dr.) (*v.r.*), to register (one's mortgage).

inscrire (s') (*v.r.*) ou **être inscrit, -e** (être porté), to appear; to stand:
les actions s'inscrivent (ou sont inscrites) au bilan pour tant de francs (*f.pl.*), the shares appear (or stand) in the balance sheet at so many francs.

inscrire (s') (se coter) (Bourse) (*v.r.*), to be quoted; to be marked:
l'action X. s'inscrit à tant (*f.*), X. shares are quoted at so much.
s'inscrire en hausse (ou en reprise) (ou en avance) (ou en progrès), to be marked up:
l'action X. s'inscrit en reprise, X. shares were marked up.
s'inscrire en baisse (ou en recul) (ou en réaction), to be marked down:
les cours se sont de nouveau inscrits en baisse (*m.pl.*), prices have again been marked down.

inscrivant, -e (pers.) (*n.*), registrant.

insérer (*v.t.*), to insert; to put in:
insérer une annonce dans un journal, to insert (or to put) an advertisement, to advertise, in a newspaper.
insérer une clause dans un contrat, to insert, to put, a clause in a contract.

insertion (*n.f.*), insertion; putting in.

insolvabilité (*n.f.*), insolvency:
insolvabilité d'un débiteur, insolvency of a debtor.

insolvable (*adj.*), insolvent:
débiteur insolvable (*m.*), insolvent debtor.

insolvable (pers.) (*n.m.* ou *f.*), insolvent.

inspecter (*v.t.*), to inspect; to examine:
inspecter les livres d'un négociant, to inspect, to examine, a merchant's books.

inspecteur, -trice (pers.) (*n.*), inspector; examiner:
inspecteur d'une compagnie d'assurance, inspector of an insurance company.

inspection (*n.f.*), inspection; examination.

instabilité (*n.f.*), instability; unsteadiness:
les graves conséquences de l'instabilité monétaire (*f.pl.*), the grave consequences of monetary instability.

instable (*adj.*), unstable; unsteady:
les frets maritimes sont essentiellement instables

et varient fréquemment (*m.pl.*), maritime freights are essentially unstable and vary frequently.

cours instables (*m.pl.*), unsteady prices.

installation (*n.f.*) *ou* **installation et agencement,** fixtures; fittings; fixtures and fittings; installation.

institution (*n.f.*), institution:
les banques sont des institutions de crédit (*f.pl.*), banks are credit institutions.

instructions (*n.f.pl.*), instructions:
se renfermer dans ses instructions, to confine oneself to one's instructions.

instructions relatives à l'embarquement (*ou* aux embarquements), shipping instructions.

instruire (informer) (*v.t.*), to inform:
instruisez-moi de ce qui passe, inform me of what is going on.

instrument (Dr.) (*n.m.*), instrument:
le billet à ordre est un instrument de crédit, alors que le chèque est un instrument de paiement, the promissory note is an instrument of credit, whereas the cheque is an instrument of payment.

insuccès (*n.m.*), failure:
insuccès de lancement d'un navire, failure of launch of a ship.

insuffisamment (*adv.*), insufficiently:
correspondances insuffisamment affranchies (*f.pl.*), insufficiently prepaid postal packets; underpaid postal packets.

insuffisance (*n.f.*), insufficiency:
insuffisance d'actif, insufficiency of assets.
insuffisance d'emballage, de marques, insufficiency of packing, of marks.
insuffisance de provision (Banq.), insufficient funds; not sufficient funds.
insuffisance d'imposition, underassessment.

insuffisant, -e (*adj.*), insufficient:
emballage insuffisant (*m.*), insufficient packing.

intact, -e (*adj.*), intact:
retrouver un dépôt intact, to find a deposit intact.

intangible (*adj.*), intangible:
valeurs intangibles (*f.pl.*), intangible assets.

intégral, -e, -aux (*adj.*), full; in full:
prime intégrale (*f.*), full premium.
des paiements intégraux (*m.pl.*), payments in full.

intégralement (*adv.*), fully; in full:
actions intégralement libérées (*f.pl.*), fully paid shares.
capital intégralement versé (*m.*), fully paid capital; capital fully paid up.
acquitter intégralement le montant de son passif, to discharge one's liabilities in full.

intégralité (*n.f.*), whole:
l'intégralité du capital, the whole of the capital.

intègre (*adj.*), upright; honest.

intègrement (*adv.*), uprightly; honestly.

intégrité (*n.f.*), integrity; uprightness; honesty.

intenter (Dr.) (*v.t.*), to enter; to bring; to institute; to take; to commence; to begin:
intenter une action (*ou* intenter action) à (*ou* contre) quelqu'un, to bring (*or* to enter) an action, to institute (*or* to take) (*or* to commence) proceedings, against someone.

intercalaire (*adj.*). *See* intérêt intercalaire *and* dividende intercalaire.

intercolonial, -e, -aux (*adj.*), intercolonial.

interdiction (*n.f.*), interdiction; prohibition:
interdiction de commerce, interdiction of commerce.
interdiction d'exportation, d'importation, prohibition of export, of import.
interdictions postales, postal prohibitions.

interdire (*v.t.*), to interdict; to prohibit.

intéressé, -e (pers.) (*n.*), interested party; party concerned:
convoquer les intéressés, to call the interested parties together.

intéresser (conquérir la coopération de) (*v.t.*), to interest:
intéresser quelqu'un à une affaire, to interest someone in a matter.

s'intéresser (*v.r.*), to interest oneself; to take an interest:
s'intéresser dans une entreprise, to interest oneself, to take an interest, in an enterprise.

intéresser (donner un intérêt à) (*v.t.*), to give a share (*or* an interest); to give a share (*or* an interest) to:
intéresser un employé aux bénéfices, to give an employee a share in the profits; to give an interest in the profits to an employee.

intérêt (ce qui importe à l'utilité de quelqu'un) (*n.m.*), interest:
sauvegarder les intérêts des actionnaires, to protect the shareholders' interests.
capitaine qui se réfugie dans un port, dans l'intérêt commun (*m.*), master who takes refuge in a port, in the common interest.

intérêt (droit éventuel à un bénéfice) (*n.m.*), interest:
avoir un intérêt dans une entreprise, to have an interest in an undertaking.
intérêt à la livraison (Transports ferroviaires). In France and Belgium, the senders of goods by railway can ensure compensation for proved loss or damage larger than that ordinarily paid, or (and chiefly) for delay in delivery. This is called *intérêt à la livraison,* and has, of course, to be paid extra for, the fee being called *taxe d'intérêt à la livraison.* On the continent, delay in conveyance and delivery, beyond statutory limits, is damageable in law. In England, this is not so, but the time taken for conveyance and delivery must be reasonable.

intérêt (risque; aliment) (Assce mar.) (*n.m.*), interest; risk; value:
chaque intérêt fera l'objet d'une police séparée, each interest (*or* risk) to form the subject of a separate policy.
les intérêts assurables qui sont l'objet de l'assurance, the insurable interests which are the subject matter of the insurance.
omission ou erreur dans la description de l'intérêt, du navire, ou du voyage (*f.*), omission or error in the description of the interest, vessel, or voyage.
l'assuré doit avoir intérêt à l'assurance; sinon il n'y a pas de risque pour lui (*m.*), the

insured must have interest in the insurance; otherwise there is no risk for him.

intérêt (bénéfice qu'on retire de l'argent prêté) (*s'emploie très souvent au pluriel*) (*n.m.*) (Abrév.: **int.** *ou* **intér.**), interest:
intérêts à échoir, accruing interest.
intérêts à recevoir, interest receivable.
intérêt alloué aux dépôts, interest allowed on deposits.
intérêt composé (opp. à *intérêt simple*), compound interest.
intérêt couru *ou* intérêts accrus, accrued interest.
intérêt de prêt *ou* intérêt sur prêt, interest on loan.
intérêts de prêts *ou* intérêts des prêts *ou* intérêts sur prêts, interest on loans:
intérêts de prêts sur fonds publics, interest on loans on public securities.
intérêts de retard *ou* intérêts moratoires, interest in arrears.
intérêts des fonds déposés en garantie, interest on money lodged as security.
le taux de l'intérêt de l'argent, the rate of interest on money.
intérêt du capital *ou* intérêts des capitaux, interest on capital.
intérêts et bénéfice du portefeuille, interest and profit on investments.
intérêt différé, deferred interest.
intérêts échus, outstanding interest.
intérêt intercalaire *ou* intérêt statutaire, interest on capital during construction. *Note :—* The term *intérêt intercalaire* or *statutaire* is also applied in France to a fixed interest or dividend paid on share capital whether earned or not. *See fuller particulars under* actions de dividende.
intérêt nautique (prêt à la grosse aventure), marine interest; maritime interest.
intérêts noirs (comptes courants, ou analogues), black interest; interest in black.
intérêts prélevés sur le capital, interest paid out of capital.
intérêts rouges (comptes courants, ou analogues), red interest; interest in red.
intérêt simple, simple interest.

intérimaire (qui a lieu par intérim) (*adj.*), interim:
dividende intérimaire (*m.*), interim dividend.

intérimaire (qui remplit un intérim) (*adj.*), acting:
directeur intérimaire (*m.*), acting manager.

intérimaire (pers.) (*n.m.* ou *f.*), substitute ad interim.

interligne (*n.m.*) *ou* **interlinéation** (*n.f.*) *ou* **interlignage** (*n.m.*), interlineation.

intermédiaire (*adj.*), intermediate:
acheteurs et vendeurs intermédiaires (*m.pl.*), intermediate buyers and sellers.
vapeur intermédiaire (*m.*), intermediate steamer.

intermédiaire (pers.) (*n.m.*), intermediary; middleman:
simples intermédiaires qui achètent pour revendre, mere intermediaries (or middlemen) who buy to resell (or to sell again).

banquier qui reçoit des souscriptions à une émission en qualité d'intermédiaire entre le public et l'émetteur (*m.*), banker who receives applications for an issue in the capacity of intermediary between the public and the issuer.

international, -e, -aux (*adj.*), international:
droit international (*m.*), international law.
Cf. régime international, télégramme du régime international, & mandat de poste international.

interprétation (*n.f.*), interpretation:
interprétation d'une convention, de la loi, interpretation of an agreement, of the law.

interprète (pers.) (*n.m.* ou *f.*), interpreter:
interprètes en uniforme à la disposition des voyageurs dans les gares et ports, interpreters in uniform at the service of travellers in the railway stations and ports.

interpréter (*v.t.*), to interpret:
on peut interpréter diversement ces données numériques, these numerical data can be variously interpreted.

interrompre (*v.t.*), to interrupt; to break:
interrompre son voyage en cours de route, to break one's journey.

interruption (*n.f.*), interruption; breaking; break:
télégramme retardé par interruption de communication (*m.*), telegram delayed by interruption of communication.
interruption de voyage, break of journey.

interurbain, -e (Téléph.) (*adj.*), trunk:
communication interurbaine (*f.*), trunk call.
Interurbain, qui demandez-vous? Trunks, what number are you calling? ; Trunks, number, please?

intervenant (pers.) (*n.m.*), acceptor for honour; acceptor supra (*or* suprà) protest.

intervenir (*v.i.*), to intervene; to enter:
tiers qui intervient pour accepter une lettre de change protestée faute d'acceptation (*m.*), third party who intervenes to accept a bill of exchange protested for non acceptance.
intervenir dans un contrat, to enter into a contract.
traité intervenu entre la Société et M. X. (*m.*), agreement entered into between the Company and Mr X.

intervention (*n.f.*), intervention; honour:
intervention à protêt, intervention on protest.
acceptation par intervention (*f.*), acceptance for honour; acceptance supra (*or* suprà) protest.

interversion (*n.f.*), transposition:
lorsqu'il y a une interversion de chiffres, la différence est toujours un multiple de 9, when there is a transposition of figures, the difference is always a multiple of 9.

intervertir le fardeau de la preuve, to shift the burden of proof.

interview (*n.f.* ou *m.*), interview:
solliciter une (*ou* un) interview avec son banquier, to ask for an interview with one's banker.

interviewer (*v.t.*), to interview:
interviewer quelqu'un, to interview someone.

intitulé (d'un compte, d'un compte du grand livre) (*n.m.*), name (of an account, of a ledger account).

intitulé (d'un acte) (*n.m.*), premises (of a deed).

intrinsèque (*adj.*) (Ant.: *extrinsèque*), intrinsic : la valeur intrinsèque d'une pièce de monnaie dépend de la quantité de métal précieux qu'elle renferme, the intrinsic value of a coin depends on the quantity of precious metal it contains. (*Cf.* monnaie intrinsèque.)

intrinsèquement (*adv.*), intrinsically : intrinsèquement, cette valeur vaut mieux que les cours actuellement cotés, intrinsically, this stock is worth more than the prices at present quoted.

introducteurs (Bourse) (pers.) (*n.m.pl.*), introducers ; shop. See example under **introduction**.

introduction (*n.f.*), introduction ; bringing out : lettre d'introduction (*f.*), letter of introduction. pour réussir une introduction de valeurs sur le marché et amener un public acheteur, les introducteurs s'assurent, d'habitude, le concours des organes financiers à grands tirages, qui prônent les mérites des valeurs introduites, to succeed in a bringing out (*or* in an introduction) of shares on the market and bring in a buying public, the shop generally secures the help of widely circulating financial organs which extol the merits of the shares brought out (*or* introduced).

actions à l'introduction (*f.pl.*), shop shares.

introduire (*v.t.*), to introduce ; to bring out : nous avons l'honneur d'introduire auprès de vous Monsieur un tel, we have much pleasure in introducing to you Mr So-and-so.

invalide (*adj.*), invalid.

invalider (*v.t.*), to invalidate : invalider un testament, to invalidate a will.

invalidité (*n.f.*), invalidity : invalidité d'un contrat, invalidity of a contract.

invendable (*adj.*), unsaleable ; unsalable : marchandises invendables (*f.pl.*), unsaleable goods.

invendu, -e (*adj.*), unsold : marchandises invendues (*f.pl.*) *ou* **invendus** (*n.m.pl.*), unsold goods.

inventaire (état détaillé) (*n.m.*), inventory ; list : dresser un inventaire des biens d'un particulier, to draw up an inventory of the property of a private person.

dresser l'inventaire de son portefeuille, de son actif et de son passif, to make out a list of one's investments, of one's assets and liabilities.

inventaire de bord, ship's inventory.

l'inventaire est une sorte de manifeste permanent du matériel accessoire du navire, the inventory is a kind of permanent manifest of the accessory appliances of the ship.

inventaire des agrès et du mobilier du navire, inventory of ship's tackle and furniture.

inventaire (*n.m.*) *ou* **inventaire des marchandises** (Com.), stock taking : l'inventaire comporte deux opérations : le relevé des quantités et leur évaluation, stock taking comprises two operations : noting (*or* recording) the quantities and their valuation.

inventaire (évaluation) (Fin.) (*n.m.*), valuation : inventaire des titres, du portefeuille (*ou* du portefeuille-titres), des marchandises restant en magasin, valuation of securities, of investments, of goods remaining in stock.

inventaire comptable *ou* **inventaire intra-comptable** *ou* *simplement* **inventaire** (*n.m.*), accounts ; balance sheet and schedules : *Note :*—*inventaire* is the detailed accounts ; the balance sheet, profit and loss account, trading account, stock sheets, list and valuation of investments, or the like, such as would be placed before say the directors and auditors of a company, as opposed to *bilan*, the condensed balance sheet, such as would be printed and published.

faire son inventaire tous les six mois, au moins une fois l'an, to make up one's accounts every six months, at least once a year.

inventaire de fin d'exercice, accounts to the end of the financial year.

l'inventaire de 19— fait apparaître un bénéfice de tant, the accounts for 19— show a profit of so much.

inventaire extra-comptable (*m.*), stock sheets.

inventeur d'épave (pers.) (*m.*), finder of wreckage.

inventorier (Com., etc.) (*v.t.*), to make an inventory of ; to inventory ; to take stock of ; to list : inventorier ses marchandises, to make an inventory of, to inventory, to take stock of, one's goods.

inventorier (Fin.) (*v.t.*), to value : inventorier les titres au cours de bourse, des marchandises au prix d'achat, to value the stocks at the market price, goods at cost.

investir (*v.t.*), to invest : administrateurs régulièrement investis de leurs fonctions (*m.pl.*), directors properly invested with their office.

conseil d'administration investi du pouvoir de contracter des emprunts (*m.*), board empowered to contract loans (*or* invested with the power of contracting loans).

le capital investi dans une affaire, the capital invested in a business.

investissement (*n.m.*), investment : investissement momentané des fonds de roulement, temporary investment of working capital.

invisible (*adj.*), invisible : exportations invisibles (*f.pl.*), invisible exports.

invitation (*n.f.*), invitation ; taking : invitation au public pour la souscription d'une émission, d'un emprunt, invitation to the public to subscribe to an issue, to a loan.

inviter (*v.t.*), to invite ; to take : inviter des soumissions pour la réparation des dommages, to invite, to take, tenders for the repair of the damage.

ipso facto, ipso facto : la qualité de membre du comité ne confère pas, ipso facto, le droit d'entrée dans les locaux du comité, membership of the committee does not confer, ipso facto, the right of admission to the committee's premises.

irrachetable (*adj.*), irredeemable; unredeemable: obligations irrachetables (*f.pl.*), irredeemable bonds; unredeemable debentures.

irracheté, -e (*adj.*), unredeemed.

irréalisable (*adj.*), unrealizable: valeurs irréalisables (*f.pl.*), unrealizable securities.

irrécouvrable (*adj.*), irrecoverable; unrecoverable: créance irrécouvrable (*f.*), irrecoverable (*or* unrecoverable) debt.

irréductible (*adj.*), irreducible. souscrire à titre irréductible. See under **souscrire.**

irrégularité (*n.f.*), irregularity: irrégularité d'un titre de propriété, irregularity of a title to property. commettre des irrégularités, to commit irregularities.

irrégulier, -ère (*adj.*), irregular; bad: tendance irrégulière du marché (*f.*), irregular tendency (*or* trend) of the market.

endossement irrégulier (*m.*), irregular endorsement. livrer un titre régulier en remplacement d'un titre irrégulier (Bourse), to deliver a good certificate in replacement of a bad certificate.

irrégulièrement (*adv.*), irregularly.

irremboursable (*adj.*), irredeemable; unredeemable: obligations irremboursables (*f.pl.*), irredeemable bonds; unredeemable debentures.

irrémunéré, -e (*adj.*), unremunerated.

irresponsabilité (*n.f.*), irresponsibility; non liability.

irresponsable (*adj.*), irresponsible; not liable: les assureurs sont irresponsables de tous dommages et pertes provenant du vice propre de la chose (*m.pl.*), the underwriters are not liable for any damage or loss arising from inherent vice of the thing.

item [**item** *pl.*] (*n.m.*), item: il y a beaucoup de petits item dans le compte, there are a lot of small items in the account.

itinéraire (*n.m.*), itinerary; route: itinéraire le plus court, shortest route.

J

j'écoute (Téléph.), number, please?; what number are you calling?: dès que l'opératrice a dit « j'ecoute, » formulez lentement et distinctement le numéro demandé, as soon as the operator has said "number, please?" give her slowly and distinctly the number required.

jauge (capacité d'un navire) (*n.f.*), burden; tonnage; register tonnage; registered tonnage; register: (Cf. **tonnage.**) le principe de la taxation sur la jauge du navire, the principle of charging on the tonnage (*or* on the register tonnage) (*or* on the register) of the ship. jauge brute, gross register tonnage; gross registered tonnage; gross register. jauge de Panama, Panama canal register; Panama canal tonnage. jauge de Suez, Suez canal register; Suez canal tonnage. jauge nette, net register tonnage; net registered tonnage; net register.

jaugeage (*n.m.*), measurement: le tonnage d'un navire résulte d'une opération technique, le jaugeage: le jaugeage des navires est l'opération qui a pour objet de déterminer la capacité cubique des cales, the tonnage of a ship results from a technical operation, measurement: measurement of ships is the operation which has for its object to determine the cubic capacity of the holds.

jauger (mesurer la capacité de) (*v.t.*), to measure: jauger un navire, to measure a ship.

jauger (avoir tel tonnage) (*v.i.*), to be of; to be of . . . burden: navire qui jauge 800 tonneaux (*m.*), ship which is of 800 tons (*or* which is of 800 tons burden). Cf. **port.**

je regrette de vous avoir dérangé (Téléph.), I am sorry you have been troubled; sorry you've been troubled.

jet à la mer *ou simplement* **jet** (*n.m.*), jettison; casting away: jet de marchandises à la mer *ou* jet de cargaison, jettison, casting away, of cargo. jet de pontée *ou* jet à la mer de la pontée *ou* jet de marchandises chargées sur le pont, jettison of deck cargo; jettison of goods shipped on deck.

jeté (-e) par les flots sur le rivage (être), to be washed ashore (*or* on shore).

jetée (*n.f.*), jetty; pier.

jeter (*v.t.*), to throw; to cast; to put: jeter des marchandises sur le marché, une lettre au panier, to throw goods on the market, a letter into the waste paper basket. jeter par-dessus bord des marchandises d'une nature dangereuse, to throw overboard goods of a dangerous nature. jeter dans la boîte aux lettres, to put into the letter box; to post: lettres jetées dans les boîtes aux lettres particulières (*f.pl.*), letters posted in private letter boxes. jeter à la mer *ou* jeter en mer *ou simplement* jeter, to jettison; to cast away:

marchandises jetées (*ou* jetées à la mer) pour le salut commun (*f.pl.*), goods jettisoned (*or* cast away) for the common safety.

jeter en mer une partie du chargement (*ou* jeter une partie de la cargaison à la mer) afin d'alléger le navire en cas de péril, to jettison, to cast away, a part of the cargo in order to lighten the ship in case of peril.

eton (*n.m.*), token :
jeton de monnaie *ou* jeton-monnaie [jetons-monnaie *pl.*] (*n.m.*), money token.
See also example under **appoint**.

eton (*n.m.*) *ou* **jeton de présence**, in France, metal counter or tally given to a director, or the like, each time he attends a board meeting : these counters serve as evidence of number of attendances when drawing fees, which are usually reckoned at so much an attendance. In practice, there is usually no material distribution of these tokens, the word being applied to the fee :
toucher de beaux jetons de présence, to draw some handsome fees.

jetons de présence des administrateurs *ou* jetons des administrateurs, directors' fees.

en France, la rémunération des administrateurs consiste généralement en jetons de présence et dans l'allocation d'une part des bénéfices de la société, in France, the remuneration of the directors generally consists of fees and the allocation of a share of the company's profits.

Note :—In France, *jetons de présence* are sometimes offered and paid to shareholders as an inducement to attend general meetings, in order to get a quorum, which is generally very high.

jeu (agiotage) (*n.m.*), game ; gaming ; gambling ; speculation :
jeu de hasard, game of chance.
le jeu ne vaut pas la chandelle, the game is not worth the candle.
plaider (*ou* invoquer) l'exception de jeu, to plead the Gaming Act.
jeu sur les différences et les reports, gambling in differences and contangoes.
jeux de bourse, gambling on the stock exchange ; stock exchange speculations.

jeu (série) (*n.m.*), set :
jeu complet de livres, de connaissements, de lettres de change, d'imprimés, complete (*or* full) set of books, of bills of lading, of bills of exchange, of printed forms.

jeune fille dactylographe (*f.*), girl typewriter ; girl typist.

joindre (*v.t.*). See examples :
joindre à la lettre de voiture les documents qui sont nécessaires à l'accomplissement des formalités de douane, to attach to the consignment note the documents which are required to comply with the customs formalities.
joindre l'intérêt au capital, to add the interest to the capital.
joindre les deux bouts (*ou* les deux bouts de l'année), to make both ends meet.

jouer (*v.i.*), to play ; to gamble ; to speculate ; to operate ; to job :
jouer gros jeu, to play, to gamble, for high stakes.
jouer à la bourse, sur les valeurs de bourse, to speculate, to gamble, on the stock exchange, in stocks and shares.
jouer à la hausse, à la baisse (Bourse), to operate (*or* to speculate) for a rise, for a fall ; to go a bull, a bear.
jouer les allées et venues (Bourse), to job in and out.

joueur, -euse (pers.) (*n.*), gambler ; speculator ; operator.

jouir de, to enjoy ; to receive ; to have :
jouir d'un droit (*ou* d'un privilège), to enjoy, to have, a right :
banque qui jouit du privilège exclusif d'émettre des billets (*f.*), bank which has the exclusive right of issuing notes.
jouir d'une bonification d'escompte sur des versements par anticipation, to receive a discount on payments in advance of calls.

jouissance (Dr.) (*n.f.*), enjoyment :
avoir la propriété et la jouissance des biens et droits, to have the ownership and enjoyment of properties and rights.

jouissance (la) (Abrév. : **jouiss.**). In French market news, *actions de jouissance*, q.v., are often referred to as *la jouissance*, i.e., l'(action de *understood*) jouissance. *Cf.* note *under* actions of capital.

jouissance (*n.f.*) *ou* **époque de jouissance** (*f.*) (échéance de l'intérêt, du dividende), due date of coupon (*or* of interest) ; date coupon (*or* interest) is due (*or* payable) ; *or elliptically* : interest due (*or* payable) ; dividend payable :
Rente 3 0/0.—jouissance : 1er janvier, 1er avril, 1er juillet, 1er octobre, cotée ex-coupon de 75 centimes, les 16 décembre, 16 mars, 16 juin, et 16 septembre, Rentes 3%.— interest due : 1st January, 1st April, 1st July, 1st October, quoted ex coupon of 75 centimes on 16th December, 16th March, 16th June, and 16th September.
les arrérages du 3 0/0 se payent aux époques de jouissance qui sont : les 1er janvier, 1er avril, 1er juillet, et 1er octobre de chaque année (*m.pl.*), interest on the 3 per cents is paid on the due dates of the coupons which are : 1st January, 1st April, 1st July, and 1st October of each year.
époques de jouissance (en-tête de colonne 5 du bulletin de la cote de la Compagnie des Agents de change de Paris), interest due (heading of column 3 of the London Stock Exchange Daily Official List).

jouissance (date de paiement du dernier coupon) (*n.f.*) (Abrév. : **J.** *ou* **j.** *ou* **jouiss.** *ou* **jouis.** *ou* **jce**), date last interest (*or* dividend) (*or* coupon) paid ; last interest (*or* dividend) (*or* coupon) paid (*followed by date*) ; bearing interest from ; cum dividend ; cum coupon ; with coupon ; cum ; dividend on :
Note :—In France, in speaking of dividend

rights, they mention the date of the last payment. In England, the date of the next payment is stated.

le dernier coupon du 3 0/0 ayant été détaché le 1er janvier 19—, on dit (*en France*) que le 3 0/0 se négocie « jouissance janvier 19—, » c.-à-d. avec tous les coupons à toucher après cette date, the last coupon of the 3% having been detached on 1st January 19—, one says (*in England*) that the 3% is being dealt in " cum (*or* with) April 19— coupon," i.e., with all coupons to be collected commencing with the one due on 1st April (following).

titre qui est jouissance coupon N° 8 (*m.*), stock which is cum (*or* with) coupon No. 8.

actions X.Y.Z. ex-coupon N° 6 jouissance 1er février 19— (*ou en abrév.:* X.Y.Z. ex-c. 6 J. 1 fév. '—), X.Y.Z. shares ex coupon No. 6 last coupon paid 1st February 19—.

la société émettra le 1er décembre 19— 10 000 obligations de 500 fcs chacune 6 0/0, jouissance du 1er janvier prochain, the company will issue on 1st December 19— 10,000 debentures of 500 francs each 6%, bearing interest from 1st January next.

jour (*n.m.*) (Abrév.: **j.** *ou* **jr** [**jrs** *pl.*]), day : tant de jours d'intérêt à tant pour cent, so many days' interest at so much per cent.

jour courant, running day.

jour de calendrier (minuit à minuit), calendar day.

jour de chargement, loading day.

jours de date. See under **date.**

jour de grâce *ou* jour de faveur, day of grace.

jour de la liquidation (Bourse), account day ; settlement day ; settling day ; pay day.

jour de la réponse des primes *ou simplement* jour de la réponse (Bourse), option declaration day ; option day.

jour de paiement *ou* jour de paie, pay day.

jour de place *ou* jour de bourse, market day ; business day ; working day : deux jours de bourse francs, two clear business days.

jour de planche, lay day.

jour de pont (Bourse), (in France) a working or business day coming between a Sunday and a public holiday: the Paris Bourse is closed on a *jour de pont.*

jour de repos, day of rest.

jour de surestarie [jours de surestaries *pl.*], day of demurrage.

jours de vue. See under **vue.**

jour des reports *ou* jour de reports (Bourse), contango day.

jour du terme, quarter day.

jour férié *ou* jour de fête *ou* jour de fête légale *ou* jour de chômage, non business day ; holiday ; legal holiday ; public holiday ; bank holiday.

jour franc *ou* jour plein, clear day : donner un préavis de 7 jours francs, to give seven clear days' notice.

jour non férié *ou* jour ouvrable *ou* jour ouvrier *ou* jour de travail, business day ; working day ; work day.

jour pendant lequel le temps permet de travailler [jours pendant lesquels le temps permet de travailler *pl.*], weather working day.

jours réversibles, reversible days : jours réversibles pour l'embarquement et le débarquement, reversible days for loading and discharging.

jours sauvés, days saved ; dispatch ; despatch.

à ce jour, to date : intérêts à ce jour (*m.pl.*), interest to date.

à jour, up to date : tenir à jour les écritures d'une maison, to keep a firm's books up to date.

au jour le jour, from day to day : les opérations inscrites au jour le jour sur le journal (*f.pl.*), the transactions entered up from day to day in the journal.

au jour le jour (Marché monétaire), day to day ; daily : prêts au jour le jour (*m.pl.*) *ou* argent au jour le jour (*m.*), day to day loans (*or* money) ; daily loans ; daily money.

journal (publication périodique) (*n.m.*), newspaper ; paper ; journal : journal illustré, illustrated paper.

Journal officiel, Gazette. The *Journal officiel de la République française* is the official organ of the French Government, of which the English equivalent is the *London Gazette,* the Scotch the *Edinburgh Gazette,* the Northern Irish the *Belfast Gazette,* the Belgian the *Moniteur Belge :* notice à publier au Journal officiel (*f.*), notice to be advertised in the Gazette.

journal quotidien, daily paper ; daily.

journal (Mar.) (*n.m.*), log ; log book ; journal ; report : journal de bord, log ; log book.

journal de la machine, engine room log.

journal de mer, captain's report (of extraordinary incidents during the voyage).

journal de route *ou* journal de voyage, sea journal.

journal (Comptab.) (*n.m.*), journal ; day book ; book ; register : (See also **livre** and **registre.**)

journal *ou* journal général *ou* journal synthétique, journal ; journal proper. *See note under* balance cumulée.

journaux auxiliaires *ou* journaux fractionnaires *ou* journaux analytiques, subsidiary journals.

journal d'effets, bill book ; bill journal.

journal de caisse, cash journal. In France, a book additional and supplemental to the cash book, in which the cash book items are journalized. *See note under* livres de commerce *as to compulsory keeping of the* journal *or* livre journal. Use of the cash journal does not obtain in England.

journal des achats, purchases book ; purchases day book ; purchases journal ; purchase book ; purchase journal ; bought book ; bought journal ; invoice book.

journal des divers *ou* journal d'opérations diverses, sundries journal.

journal des effets à payer, bills payable book; bills payable journal.

journal des effets à recevoir, bills receivable book; bills receivable journal.

journal des rendus *ou* journal de retours, returns book.

journal des rendus sur achats *ou* journal des rendus aux fournisseurs, returns outwards book.

journal des rendus sur ventes *ou* journal des rendus par les clients, returns inwards book.

journal des transferts, transfer register.

journal des ventes *ou* journal des débits, sales book; day book; sales day book; sales journal.

journal-grand-livre [journaux-grands-livres *pl.*] (*n.m.*) *ou* journal grand livre *ou* journal américain, combined journal and ledger; journal and ledger combined.

journal légal. In France, one of the books which the law requires a trader to keep. *See note under* livres de commerce.

journal originaire, book of original entry.

ournalisation (Comptab.) (*n.f.*), journalization.

ournaliser (*v.t.*), to journalize:
journaliser une opération, to journalize a transaction.

ournalisme (Presse) (*n.m.*), journalism.

ournaliste (Presse) (pers.) (*n.m.*), journalist.

ournaliste (Comptab.) (pers.) (*n.m.*), journalizer.

ournée (*n.f.*), day:
journée de travail, working day:
journée de travail de huit heures, working day of eight hours; 8-hour working day.

diciaire (*adj.*), judicial.

diciairement (*adv.*), judicially.

ge (pers.) (*n.m.*), judge; justice; magistrate; master:
juge taxateur, taxing master.

gement (Dr.) (*n.m.*), judgment; judgement; adjudication; decree; award: (En France, les tribunaux de commerce et de première instance prononcent des *jugements*, tandis que les décisions des cours d'appel et de la Cour de cassation s'appellent des *arrêts*.)

jugement arbitral, arbitration award.

jugement contradictoire, judgment after trial.

jugement par défaut, judgment by default.

jugement déclaratif de faillite, adjudication in bankruptcy; decree in bankruptcy.

umelage (Bourse de marchandises) (*n.m.*), contra account. *See* caisse de liquidation.

urer (*v.i.*), to swear:
les témoins jurent de dire la vérité, toute la vérité, et rien que la vérité (*m.pl.*), witnesses swear to speak the truth, the whole truth, and nothing but the truth.

usqu'à concurrence de *ou* **jusqu'à . . . inclusivement** *ou simplement* **jusqu'à** *ou* **à concurrence d'un maximum de,** up to; not exceeding:
les colis postaux peuvent être assurés jusqu'à concurrence de tant (*m.pl.*), postal packets can be insured up to so much.

indemnité pour perte ou avarie jusqu'à concurrence de tant (*f.*), compensation for loss or damage not exceeding so much.

jusqu'à tant de grammes inclusivement, not exceeding so many grammes. Cf. **ne dépassant pas,** under ne.

jusqu'à nouvel avis, until (*or* till) further advice.

jusqu'à preuve contraire, in the absence of evidence to the contrary; until the contrary is proved.

juste (*adj.*), accurate.

justement (*adv.*), accurately.

justesse (*n.f.*), accuracy.

justice (Dr.) (*n.f.*), justice; law:
cour de justice (*f.*), court of justice; law court.

action en justice (*f.*), action at law.

justificatif, -ive (*adj.*), voucher (*used as adj.*):
numéro justificatif *ou* exemplaire justificatif *ou* exemplaire de justification (d'un journal) (*m.*), voucher copy (of a newspaper).

pièce justificative (*f.*), voucher.

justification (*n.f.*), justification; proof:
justification d'une exception, justification of an exception.

justification de perte, d'origine, de réclamation, du paiement des droits, d'un droit à la propriété des titres, proof of loss, of origin, of claim, of the payment of the duties, of a right to the ownership of shares.

demander la justification de la valeur réelle, to ask for proof of the actual value.

justifier (*v.t.*), to justify; to prove:
justifier la vérité de ses prédictions par les événements, to justify, to prove, the truth of one's predictions by events.

la personne qui vient prendre livraison d'une lettre adressée poste restante doit justifier qu'elle est le destinataire ou son fondé de pouvoirs, the person who comes to take delivery of a letter addressed poste restante must prove that he is the addressee or his duly authorized representative.

l'assurance est nulle s'il est justifié que la nouvelle d'un sinistre était connue (*f.*), the insurance is void if it is proved that the news of an accident was known.

le coût justifié des objets remplaçant ceux perdus ou endommagés par fortune de mer, the proved cost of the things replacing those lost or damaged by sea peril.

justifier de (*v.i.*), to prove; to give proof of; to show that:
justifier de son identité, to prove one's identity.

l'assuré est tenu de justifier de la non arrivée (*m.*), the insured is bound to prove the non arrival.

justifier de l'accomplissement de toutes les formalités requises, to show that all the necessary formalities have been complied with.

K

kaffiriques (valeurs sud-africaines) (Bourse) (*n.m.pl.*), Kaffirs; South Africans; South African shares.
kilomètre-train [kilomètres-trains *pl.*] (*n.m.*) *ou* **kilomètre de train** [kilomètres de trains *pl.*], train kilometre, analogous to English *tra* *mile* (mille de train).

krach *ou* **krack** (*n.m.*), crash; smash: le krack d'une banque, a bank crash (smash).

L

l'un, l'une, each:
prix des outils de rechange : poinçons, l'un, fr. —, matrices, l'une, fr. —, prices of spare tools : punches, each, — francs ; dies, each — francs.
là-bas (Bourse), end next month account : for instance, *du 5 sous là-bas* means a bid or an offer for options at 25 centimes option rate for the account at the end of the following month, for example, for end May if one is in April.
la pièce, each :
marteaux, la pièce, fr. —, hammers, each — francs.
affrètement à la pièce (*m.*), freighting by the case.
lacune (*n.f.*), blank; blank space.
laissé pour compte [laissés pour compte *pl.*] (*n.m.*), on hand, refused ; goods (*or* parcel, or the like) on hand, refused (*or* left on hand, refused) :
ne pas confondre le « laissé pour compte » avec « l'abandon, » do not confuse " on hand, refused " with " abandonment."
un laissé pour compte au transporteur, goods (*or* a parcel) left on hand, refused, with the carrier.
laisser (*v.t.*), to leave ; to let ; to allow :
laisser un blanc dans une lettre, to leave a blank in a letter.
laisser à un homme sûr la manutention de ses affaires, to leave the management of one's affairs in the hands of a reliable man.
laisser pour compte, to leave on hand, refused :
laisser la marchandise pour compte à la compagnie de chemins de fer, to leave the goods on hand, refused, with the railway company.
laisser dormir une affaire, to let a matter rest.
laisser dormir ses capitaux, to allow one's money to remain idle.
laisser protester un effet, to allow a bill to be protested.
laisser-passer [laisser-passer *pl.*] (Douanes) (*n.m.*), cart note.
lamanage (*n.m.*), branch piloting.

lamaneur (pers.) (*n.m.*), branch pilot. See no under **pilote.**
lancement (d'une entreprise) (*n.m.*), launchir (of an enterprise).
lancement (d'une compagnie) (*n.m.*), floatatio flotation, bringing out (of a company).
lancement (d'un prospectus) (*n.m.*), issu sending out (of a prospectus).
lancer (*v.t.*). See examples :
lancer un navire, to launch a ship.
lancer une affaire, to launch an enterprise.
lancer un prospectus, des circulaires, to issu to send out, a prospectus, circulars.
lancer une compagnie, to float, to bring out, company.
lancer des titres sur le marché, to throw shar on the market.
lancer un ballon d'essai, to put out a feeler.
lanceur (pers.) (*n.m.*), launcher.
langage (*n.m.*), language :
langage chiffré, cipher language; cipher cypher :
le langage chiffré est formé de groupes d chiffres ou de lettres ayant un sens secre (*ou* une signification secrète), ou de mot ne remplissant pas les conditions exigée pour la formation du langage convenu cipher language is composed of groups o series of figures or letters having a secre meaning, or of words not fulfilling th conditions applicable to code language.
langage clair (Télégr.), plain language.
langage convenu (*Abrév. :* L. conv.), cod language ; code :
télégramme en langage convenu (*m.*), tele gram in code.
langage mixte, combinations in plain language code, and/or cipher.
langage secret (*Abrév. :* LS.), secret language.
large (en parlant d'un marché) (*adj.*) (opp. *étroit*), free:
large marché animé en actions X. vers 160 fr. lively free market in X. shares round abou 160 francs.
pétroles.—transactions sensiblement plus larges, et avance générale des cours, oils.—dealings

appreciably freer, and general advance of prices.

rgement (*adv.*), freely :
lorsqu'une valeur est largement offerte avec peu ou pas de demandes, when a stock is freely offered with few or no bids.

vage de titres (*m.*), faking the numbers of stolen share certificates, or other fraudulent alterations, so as to make them saleable. *Also means* fraudulent conversion of stocks by a broker to his own use.

zaret (*n.m.*), lazaret; lazaretto :
déposer les marchandises au lazaret en cas de quarantaine, to lodge the goods in a lazaret (*or* lazaretto) in case of quarantine.
séjour des personnes dans un lazaret (*m.*), stay of persons in a lazaret (*or* lazaretto).

cas échéant, if any; if there be occasion.

Lloyd, Lloyd's :
agent du Lloyd (*m.*), Lloyd's agent.

long du bord *ou simplement* **le long,** alongside :
marchandises reçues ou livrées le long du bord (*ou* le long du bord du navire) (*ou* le long du navire) (*f.pl.*), goods received or delivered alongside (*or* alongside the ship).
navire le long du quai (*m.*), ship alongside the quay.

temps le permettant, weather permitting.

cture (*n.f.*), reading :
la lecture d'un bilan n'est pas chose aisée, reading a balance sheet is not easy.
Cf. donner lecture de.

gal, -e, -aux (*adj.*), legal; lawful.

galement (*adv.*), legally; lawfully.

galisation (*n.f.*), legalization :
légalisation d'un certificat d'origine, legalization of a certificate of origin.
la légalisation n'a pour effet que de certifier l'authenticité de la signature apposée au bas de l'acte, elle n'en a aucun sur le contenu de l'acte, legalization has for effect only to certify the authenticity of the signature appended at the foot of the document, it has none on the contents of the document.

galiser (*v.t.*), to legalize :
signature légalisée par l'autorité diplomatique ou consulaire française (*f.*), signature legalized by the French diplomatic or consular authority.

galité (*n.f.*), legality; lawfulness.

gataire (pers.) (*n.m. ou f.*), legatee :
légataire universel, -elle, sole legatee.

gation (*n.f.*), legation.

ge (*adj.*) (opp. à *en charge*), light :
déplacement lège (*m.*), light displacement.

gislation (*n.f.*), legislation.

gs (*n.m.*), legacy; bequest.

ser (*v.t.*), to injure :
décision qui paraît léser ses intérêts (*f.*), decision which would seem to injure one's interests.

sion (*n.f.*), injury.

st (*n.m.*), ballast :
navire sur (*ou* en) lest (*m.*), ship in ballast.
lest d'eau *ou* lest liquide, water ballast.

stage (*n.m.*), ballasting :

sable pour le lestage des navires (*m.*), sand for the ballasting of ships.

lester (*v.t.*), to ballast.

lettre (*n.f.*), letter; note :
écrire une lettre, to write a letter.
lettre avec (*ou* de) valeur déclarée *ou* lettre chargée (*Abrév.:* lettre V.D. *ou* LVD.), insured letter.
lettre-avion [lettres-avion *pl.*] (*n.f.*), air letter; air mail letter.
lettre bénéficiant du délai supplémentaire, late fee letter.
lettre circulaire, circular letter.
lettre d'adhésion (garantie d'émission) (Fin.), letter of acceptance.
lettre d'avis, advice note; advice; letter of advice.
lettre d'avis de répartition, allotment letter ; letter of allotment; letter of acceptance. See **attribuer.**
lettre d'avis de report (Bourse), continuation contract.
lettre d'avis de retour de souscription, letter of regret.
lettre d'introduction, letter of introduction.
lettre de change *ou simplement* lettre, bill of exchange; bill; exchange : (an acceptable draft. Cf. **effet de commerce.**) See **première de change.**
lettre de change à l'extérieur, foreign bill; foreign exchange.
lettre de change à plusieurs exemplaires, bill of exchange in a set.
lettre de confirmation, letter of confirmation.
lettre de convocation, notice of meeting :
la lettre de convocation adressée aux actionnaires, the notice of meeting addressed to the shareholders. See **convoquer & délibérer.**
lettre de crédit *ou* lettre de créance (*Abrév.:* l/c. *ou* l/cr.), letter of credit :
lettre de crédit circulaire, circular letter of credit.
lettre de crédit circulaire mondiale *ou* lettre de crédit circulaire valable dans le monde entier, world wide circular letter of credit; world letter of credit.
lettre de crédit collective, general letter of credit.
lettre de crédit confirmé, confirmed letter of credit.
lettre de crédit simple, special letter of credit.
lettre de gage, bond issued by the Crédit foncier, corresponding to an agreed loan on mortgage : these bonds are negotiable.
lettre de garantie *ou* lettre d'indemnité, letter of indemnity :
éviter l'insertion d'une clause restrictive en délivrant une lettre de garantie, to avoid the insertion of a restrictive clause by giving a letter of indemnity.
lettre de garantie de commission, commission note.
lettres de marque, letters of marque; letters of mart.
lettre de mer, sea letter; sea brief.

lettre de mer (Belgique), certificate of registry ; ship's register (in Belgium, of a ship of Belgian nationality). *Cf.* acte de francisation.

lettre de poursuite *ou* lettre de rappel (poursuite du client), follow up letter :

circulaires suivies de lettres de poursuite (*ou* de rappel) (*f.pl.*), circulars followed by follow up letters.

lettre de rappel (réclamation de paiements en retard, etc.), letter of reminder.

lettre de recommandation, letter of recommendation.

lettres de rencontre (Comptab.), keying up letters (letters of the alphabet placed against items on one side of a ledger account as references to corresponding items on the other side).

lettre de signatures autorisées (Banq.), mandate form.

lettre de voiture, consignment note.

lettre morte, dead letter :

loi qui est lettre morte (*f.*), law which is a dead letter.

lettre ouverte (Poste), open letter.

lettre par exprès, express letter.

lettre passe-partout [lettres passe-partout *pl.*], set form of letter.

lettre recommandée, registered letter.

lettre remise à la poste, post letter ; letter sent through the post.

lettre renvoyée (Poste), returned letter.

lettre surtaxée *ou* lettre taxée (Poste), surcharged letter.

en lettres *ou* **en toutes lettres,** in words ; in words at length :

la concordance de la somme en lettres avec la somme en chiffres, the agreement of the amount in words with the amount in figures.

énoncer une somme en toutes lettres, to express an amount in words at length.

Levant (*n.m.*), Levant.

levée (Poste) (*n.f.*), clearing (a letter box) ; collection (of letters) :

l'heure de la dernière levée (*f.*), the time of the last collection.

levée exceptionnelle *ou* levée supplémentaire, late fee collection.

levée (d'une séance) (*n.f.*), closing (of a meeting).

levée (de titres) (Bourse) (*n.f.*), taking up, taking delivery (of stock).

levée (des documents) (*n.f.*), lifting, taking up, retiral, retirement (of documents).

levée (d'une prime) (Bourse) (*n.f.*), taking up, exercise (of an option).

levée (des contributions) (*n.f.*), levy, collection (of taxes).

levée (*n.f.*) *ou* **levée de compte** (prélèvement), drawing :

les levées personnelles du commerçant représentant des retraits de fonds opérés en cours d'exercice, doivent être, à l'inventaire, virées à capital, the personal drawings of the trader representing withdrawals of money effected during the year, should be transferred to capital at balance sheet time.

lever (*v.t.*). See examples :

lever des documents, to lift, to take up, to retire, documents.

lever des impôts (*ou* des taxes), to levy, to collect, taxes :

lever une taxe sur les opérations de jeu, c'est reconnaître leur existence légale, to levy a tax on gaming transactions is to acknowledge their legal existence.

lever ferme tant de titres (contrat de garantie), to take firm so many shares.

lever l'embargo sur un navire, to raise, to take off, the embargo on a ship.

lever les titres que l'on a achetés, to take up, to take delivery of, the stock which one has bought.

lever protêt d'un effet en cas de non paiement, to make protest of a bill in case of dishonour.

lever une boîte aux lettres, to clear a letter box :

les boîtes aux lettres sont levées aux heures fixes (*f.pl.*), letter boxes are cleared at fixed times.

lever une option (Fin.), to take up, to exercise an option.

lever une prime (Bourse), to take up, to exercise, an option.

lever une prohibition, to raise a prohibition (i.e., to put an end to it).

lever une séance, to close a meeting :

déclarer une séance levée, to declare a meeting closed.

levier d'interligne (d'une machine à écrire) (*m.*), carriage lever.

levier porte-caractères (d'une machine à écrire) (*m.*), type bar.

lévrier de la mer (*fig.*) (*m.*), ocean greyhound.

liard (Négociations à prime) (Bourse) (*n.m.*), 1¼ centimes. See **dont.**

liasse (de papiers, de lettres) (*n.f.*), bundle (of papers, of letters).

liasse (pli) (Chambre de compensation de banquiers) (*n.f.*), charge (bundle of paid vouchers).

libellé (rédaction) (*n.m.*), drawing ; drawing up ; making ; wording :

la régularité de l'effet au point de vue du libellé, the regularity of the bill from the point of view of the wording.

libellé (*n.m.*) *ou* **libellés** (*n.m.pl.*) (indications), particulars ; description ; narration :

inscrire dans le libellé la date, le numéro, la somme, l'échéance de l'effet, to enter in the particulars, the date, the number, the amount, the due date of the bill.

colonnes pour l'inscription des libellés suivants (*f.pl.*), columns for entering the following particulars.

colonne du libellé (*f.*), particulars column ; description column.

le libellé d'un article (*ou* d'une écriture) dans le grand livre, the particulars of an entry (or of an item) in the ledger.

le libellé d'un article (*ou* d'une écriture) du journal (Comptab.), the narration of a journal entry.

libeller (*v.t.*), to draw up ; to draw ; to make ; to word :

libeller un exploit (Dr.), to draw a writ.

libeller une lettre de change comme suit, to make, to word, a bill of exchange as follows.

un ordre doit toujours être libellé d'une façon claire et précise, pour éviter toute contestation ou toute erreur d'interprétation, an order should always be worded in a clear and precise manner, to avoid any dispute or mistake in interpretation.

libeller un chèque au porteur, à ordre, to make a cheque payable to bearer, to order.

libération (*n.f.*), discharge; release; relief; payment; paying up; payment in full:

libération d'une soumission (Douanes), discharge of a bond.

la libération d'une action se fait par voie d'appels de fonds, the paying up of a share is done by way of calls.

libération entière (*ou* complète) (*ou* intégrale) *ou* simplement libération (d'une action), payment in full (of a share):

libération à la répartition, payment in full on allotment.

les actions doivent être nominatives jusqu'à leur complète libération (*f.pl.*), shares must be registered (i.e., not bearer) until their payment in full (*or* until they are fully paid).

libératoire (*adj.*). See phrases:

paiement, reçu, libératoire (*m.*), payment, receipt, in full discharge.

pouvoir libératoire (*m.*) *ou* force libératoire (*f.*), legal tender; legal tender currency:

le pouvoir libératoire de ces pièces est limité (*ou* la force libératoire de ces pièces est limitée) à tant, the legal tender (*or* the legal tender currency) of these coins is limited to so much.

avoir pouvoir libératoire *ou* avoir force libératoire *ou* être libératoire, to be legal tender:

l'étalon monétaire est le métal précieux qui entre dans la composition des pièces types, lesquelles ont force libératoire illimitée (*m.*), the monetary standard is the precious metal which enters into the composition of standard coins, which are unlimited legal tender.

l'or a le pouvoir libératoire illimité *ou* l'or a force libératoire sans limitation de quantité (*m.*), gold is legal tender to any amount (*or* is unlimited legal tender).

les pièces divisionnaires n'ont pouvoir libératoire que jusqu'à (*ou* n'ont force libératoire qu'à) concurrence de tant (*f.pl.*), the fractional coins are only legal tender up to so much.

les paiements en or sont libératoires (*m.pl.*), payments in gold are legal tender.

monnaie libératoire (*f.*), legal tender; legal tender currency; lawful money.

libérer (*v.t.*), to discharge; to release; to relieve; to pay up; to pay up in full; to pay:

libérer un débiteur, to discharge, to release, a debtor.

libérer une grosse quantité de capitaux en abaissant les réserves des banques, to release a large amount of money by lowering the reserves of the banks.

libérer quelqu'un d'une responsabilité, to relieve someone from a liability.

libérer une action *ou* libérer entièrement (*ou* complètement) (*ou* intégralement) une action, to pay up a share; to pay up a share in full.

actions entièrement (*ou* complètement) (*ou* intégralement) libérées *ou* simplement actions libérées (*f.pl.*), fully paid shares.

actions non libérées *ou* actions non entièrement (*ou* non complètement) (*ou* non intégralement) libérées (*f.pl.*), partly paid shares. See note as to methods of quoting partly paid shares under **action**.

quand on dit que tel titre de 500 francs est libéré de 200 francs, cela signifie que 200 francs ont été versés et qu'il en reste encore 300 francs à verser, when we say that such or such a share of 500 francs is 200 francs paid, it means that 200 francs has been paid and that there still remains 300 francs to be paid.

lib. (*abrév.*), libéré, -e; libéré (-e) de.

se libérer (*v.r.*), to absolve oneself from further liability; to clear oneself; to free oneself; to pay up; to pay up in full; to pay up one's calls:

se libérer d'une dette, to clear oneself, to free oneself, from a debt.

donner à quelqu'un la faculté de se libérer (*ou* de se libérer entièrement) avant l'échéance, to give someone the option of paying up (*or* of paying up in full) before due date.

les débiteurs ont le droit de se libérer par anticipation, en tout ou en partie (*m.pl.*), the debtors have the right of paying (*or* of paying up) in advance, wholly or partly.

liberté (*n.f.*), liberty; leave:

le principe de la liberté des conventions, the principle of the liberty of agreements.

si le capitaine a la liberté d'entrer dans différents ports, if the master has the liberty (*or* has leave) to enter different ports.

libre (*adj.*). See examples:

libre à l'entrée (exempt de droits) (Douanes), duty-free; free; uncustomed:

marchandises libres à l'entrée (*f.pl.*), duty-free goods; free goods; uncustomed goods.

libre des droits de douane (à l'acquitté), duty paid:

marchandise vendue libre des droits de douane (*f.*), goods sold duty paid.

libre frappe (*f.*) *ou* libre monnayage (*m.*), free coinage.

libre pratique (*f.*), pratique; free pratique:

lorsque la patente de santé est nette, le navire est admis en libre pratique, when the bill of health is clean, the ship is admitted in pratique (*or* in free pratique).

à son arrivée, le navire stationne en rade ou dans l'avant-port jusqu'à ce que l'officier de santé lui accorde la libre pratique, on her arrival, the ship lies in the roads or in the outer harbour until the officer of health gives her the pratique.

crédit libre (m.), open credit; blank credit.

papier libre (m.) (opp. à papier timbré), un-stamped paper.

traite libre (f.) ou effet libre (m.) (opp. à traite [ou effet] documentaire), clean bill.

libre-échange (n.m.), free trade:
de vives discussions entre les champions du libre-échange et du protectionnisme, lively discussions between the champions of free trade and protectionism.

libre-échangiste (adj.), free-trade (used as adj.):
doctrines libre-échangistes (f.pl.), free-trade doctrines.

libre-échangiste [libre-échangistes pl.] (pers.) (n.m. ou f.), free trader; free tradist:
par principe, les libre-échangistes apprécient avant tout le bon marché des produits importés, tandis que les protectionnistes considèrent comme un mal l'importation de tout article que l'on peut fabriquer dans leur pays, in principle, free traders value above all cheapness of imported products, while protectionists consider as an evil the importation of any article that can be made in their country. (See also example under **protectionniste**.)

librement (adv.), freely:
en principe, les conventions sont réputées se former librement entre les parties con-tractantes, in principle, agreements are reputed to be made freely between the con-tracting parties.

licence (n.f.), licence:
licence d'exportation, export licence.
licence d'importation, import licence.
licence de fabrication, manufacturing licence.
licence de vente, selling licence.

lier (v.t.), to bind:
décision arbitrale sans appel qui lie les deux parties (f.), arbitration award without appeal which binds both parties.
l'assureur n'est lié qu'après acceptation du risque (m.), the underwriter is only bound after acceptance of the risk.
ordre lié (Bourse). See under **ordre**.
affaires liées, opérations liées. See under **affaire, opération**.

se lier (v.r.), to bind oneself:
se lier par serment, to bind oneself under oath.

lieu (n.m.), place:
lieu de paiement d'un effet, du règlement d'avarie, place of payment of a bill, of adjustment of average.
lieu d'escale, place of call. Cf. **escale**.
lieu de relâche, place of call. See **relâche** for explanation of distinction between this and next entry.
lieu de relâche ou lieu de relâche forcée ou lieu de refuge ou lieu de salut, place of necessity; place of distress; place of refuge.
les lieux de départ et de destination, the places of sailing and destination.

See also phrases under **port**, some of which are often associated with lieu instead of port, thus lieu de décharge, place of discharge.

ligne (n.f.), line:
tirer une ligne sur le papier, to draw a line on the paper.
souscrire une ligne (Assce), to underwrite a line.
ligne à service régulier (navires), regular service line.
ligne aérienne ou ligne d'avion, air line.
ligne d'abonné (Téléph.), subscriber's line.
ligne d'artère (Ch. de f.), main line; trunk line.
ligne d'intérêt privé (Ch. de f. ou Téléph.), private line.
ligne de charge (d'un navire), load line.
ligne de chemin de fer ou ligne ferrée, railway line; line of railway.
ligne de côte [lignes de côtes pl.] (Géogr.), coast line.
ligne de flottaison (d'un navire), water line:
ligne de flottaison en charge, load water line.
ligne de flottaison lège, light water line.
ligne de navigation, shipping line.
ligne de tramway, tramway line; tram line.
ligne de vapeurs, line of steamers.
ligne interrompue (Téléph.), line out of order.
ligne principale (Ch. de f.), main line:
le point de jonction avec la ligne principale, the point of junction with the main line.
ligne principale (Téléph.), direct exchange line; exchange line. See note under poste principal.
ligne supplémentaire (Téléph.), extension line; extension. See note under poste principal.
ligne terrestre (Télégr.), land line.

limitation (n.f.), limitation:
limitation de responsabilité des armements, des engagements des assureurs, limitation of liability (or responsibility) of shipowners, of liability of the underwriters.

limite (n.f.), limit:
toute émission de billets de banque a ses limites, every issue of bank notes has its limits.
acheter ou vendre dans des limites de prix, to buy or sell within price limits.
limite d'âge pour la mise à la retraite des fonctionnaires civils, age limit for pensioning civil functionaries.
limites de dimensions ou de volume, de poids (des colis postaux), limits of size, of weight (of postal parcels).
limite de la prime ou simplement limite (Bourse), limit price at which option is abandoned. See explanation under **prime**.

limité, -e (adj.), limited:
responsabilité limitée (f.), limited liability.

limité (télégramme déposé en dernière limite d'heure) (n.m.), telegram handed in near closing time.

limiter (v.t.), to limit:
limiter ses chances de perte, la responsabilité de l'armateur à ses propres lignes de naviga-tion, to limit one's chances of loss, the

responsibility of the shipowner to his own lines of shipping.

liner (navire desservant une ligne régulière) (*n.m.*), liner.

lingot (*n.m.*), ingot :
  lingots au titre légal, ingots of legal fineness.

liquidateur (pers.) (*n.m.*), liquidator :
  liquidateur d'une société, liquidator of a company.

liquidateur (Bourse de marchandises) (pers.) (*n.m.*), clearing house clerk.

liquidateur (Bourse de valeurs) (pers.) (*n.m.*), settling room clerk.

liquidation (*n.f.*) (Abrév. : **liq.** *ou* **liquid.**), liquidation ; winding up :
  liquidation d'une société, liquidation, winding up, of a company.
  société en liquidation (*f.*) (*Abrév. :* S^{te} en liq. *ou* Soc. en liquid.), company in liquidation.
  liquidation judiciaire, liquidation, winding up, subject to supervision of court.
  liquidation volontaire, voluntary liquidation ; voluntary winding up.

liquidation (d'une opération, d'un marché, d'une position) (Bourse) (*n.f.*), closing (a transaction, a bargain, a position [*or* a book]).

liquidation (terme) (Bourse de valeurs) (*n.f.*) (Abrév. : **liq.** *ou* **liquid.**), settlement ; account :
  primes en liquidation au 15 du mois prochain (*f.pl.*), options till the account on the 15th of next month.
  liquidation courante *ou simplement* liquidation (*Abrév. :* liq. ct *ou* liquid. c^t *ou simplement* liq. *ou* liquid.), current account ; current settlement ; this account :
    cours en liquidation courante *ou* cours en liquidation (*m.*), price for current (*or* for this) account.
  liquidation prochaine (*Abrév. :* liq. pr. *ou* liq. proch.), next account ; new time.
  liquidation suivante, following account ; ensuing settlement ; succeeding account.
  liquidation de fin de mois, on the Paris Bourse, the end month settlement (*or* account). See note under **quinze.**
  liquidation de quinzaine *ou* liquidation du quinze, on the Paris Bourse, the mid month settlement (*or* account). See note under **quinze.**

liquidation (Bourse de marchandises) (*n.f.*), settlement (i.e., fixing the price in case of default) :
  des liquidations d'office peuvent être faites en cas de défaillance des contractants, official settlements can be made in case of default of contractants.

liquidation (vente à bas prix des marchandises, en vue d'un écoulement rapide) (*n.f.*), sale ; selling off.

liquide (*adj.*), liquid ; wet :
  dette liquide (*f.*), liquid debt.
  marchandises liquides (*f.pl.*) (opp. à *marchandises sèches*), wet goods.

liquidé, -e (pers.) (*n.*), debtor (one whose affairs are being liquidated).

liquider (*v.t.*). See examples :
  liquider une compagnie, ses affaires, to liquidate, to wind up, a company, one's affairs.
  liquider une dette, to liquidate, to discharge, to pay off, a debt.
  liquider une opération, un marché, une position, une valeur (Bourse), to close a transaction, a bargain, a position (*or* a book), a stock :
    acheteur qui doit ou liquider sa position ou se faire reporter (*m.*), buyer who must either close his position (*or* his book) or give on.
  liquider une opération (par virement au comptoir de liquidation) (Bourse de valeurs), to settle a transaction.

liquider (*v.i.*), to liquidate ; to close :
  société qui liquide (*f.*), company which liquidates.
  spéculateur qui liquide (*m.*), speculator who closes.

se liquider (*v.r.*), to liquidate ; to close ; to be closed :
  société qui se liquide (*f.*), company which liquidates.
  spéculateur qui se liquide (*m.*), speculator who closes.
  opérations qui se liquident par un mouvement de titres ou de fonds (*f.pl.*), transactions which are closed by the passing of stock or of money.

liquidité (*n.f.*), liquidness. Cf. coefficient de liquidité *ou* **degré de liquidité.**

lire (*v.t.*), to read :
  il importe que l'on lise attentivement les documents que l'on est appelé à signer, it is important that one should read carefully the documents one is called upon to sign.
  lire entre les lignes (*fig.*), to read between the lines.
  le procès-verbal de la dernière séance est lu et adopté, the minutes of the last meeting were read and confirmed.
  lu et approuvé (*invar.*), read and approved.

lire (cote de la bourse) (Abrév. : **l.**), business done should have been :
  Actions X. Hier, lire — (*Abrév. :* Act. X. hl. —), Erratum.—In yesterday's List the business done in X. shares at — should have been —. *Cf.* cours nul *&* **hier.**

liste (*n.f.*), list :
  liste de départs (navires), list of sailings ; sailings list.
  liste de présence, list of those present.
  liste de sinistres maritimes *ou* liste noire, list of marine casualties ; casualty list ; black list.
  liste de souscripteurs, list of subscribers (*or* of applicants).
  liste de souscription, list of applications ; subscription list.
  liste des passagers, passenger list ; list of passengers.
  liste nominative des actionnaires, list of names, nominal list, of shareholders.

litige (*n.m.*), litigation.

litigieux, -euse (*adj.*), litigious :
  droits litigieux (*m.pl.*), litigious rights.

littoral (*n.m.*), littoral; coast; shore; seacoast; seaboard:
littoral atlantique, Atlantic seaboard.

livrable (*adj.*), deliverable:
marchandises en cours de production livrables à une époque ultérieure (*f.pl.*), goods in course of production deliverable at a later date.

livrable (Bourse de marchandises) (Abrév.: **liv.**) (*n.m.*) (opp. à *disponible*), forward; terminal; shipment; for shipment:
cours du livrable (*m.*), forward price; terminal price.
cours: disponible tant; livrable tant, prices: spot (*or* on the spot) so much; shipment (*or* for shipment) so much.

livrable (Marché aux grains) (*n.m.*) (opp. à *disponible*), futures; options:
en livrable sur la future campagne, les affaires quoique un peu plus actives que la semaine précédente, n'ont eu encore que peu d'importance, in futures (*or* options) on the coming campaign, business although a little more active than the previous week, was still only small.

livraison (*n.f.*), delivery; delivering:
livraison à domicile, delivery at residence; delivery at trader's premises; delivery:
la livraison à domicile est, en règle générale, suspendue les dimanches, as a general rule, delivery is suspended on Sundays.
gares fermées les dimanches tant à la réception qu'à la livraison des marchandises (*f.pl.*), stations closed on Sundays both for the receiving (*or* receipt) and delivering (*or* delivery) of goods.
livraison de la cargaison, delivery of the cargo; delivering the cargo.
livraison par erreur, misdelivery.
livraison par exprès (Poste), express delivery.
titres qui sont de bonne livraison (Bourse) (*m.pl.*), shares which are (*or* stock which is) good delivery.
livraison à terme (Bourse), forward delivery; future delivery. *Cf.* opérations de change à terme.

livre (*n.f.*) *ou* livre sterling [livres sterling *pl.*] (Abrév.: **£** *ou* **L.** *ou* **l.** *ou* **liv.** *ou* **l.s.** *ou* **Ls.** *ou* **liv. st.** *ou* **liv. sterl.**), pound; pound sterling.

livre (registre) (*n.m.*), book; journal; day book; register: (See also **registre, journal,** and **carnet.**)
livre à feuilles fixes (*ou* à feuillets fixes) *ou* livre relié, bound book.
livre à feuilles mobiles (*ou* à feuillets mobiles), loose leaf book.
livre à marchés, bargain book.
livre à souche *ou* livre à souches, counterfoil book; stub book.
livre auxiliaire (Comptab.), subsidiary book.
livre d'achats *ou* livre des achats *ou* livre d'achat, purchases book; purchases day book; purchases journal; purchase book; purchase journal; bought book; bought journal; invoice book.

livre d'actionnaires, share register; share ledger; register of members.
livre d'adresses, address book.
livre d'échéances, bill diary.
livre d'effets, bill book; bill journal.
livre d'entrée des effets *ou* livre d'entrée *ou* livre copie d'effets *ou* livre des numéros (Banq.), bills received register.
livre d'entrées (en magasin), stock received book.
livre d'inventaire *ou* livre des inventaires, balance sheet book.
livre d'ordre *ou* livre de statistique (opp. à *livre de report*), memorandum book; statistical book; registry book.
livre d'ordres *ou* livre de commandes, order book.
livre de balance *ou* livre de soldes *ou* livre des balances de vérification, balance book; trial balance book.
livre de bord (Mar.), log; log book.
livres de bord (Mar.), ship's books.
livre de caisse, cash book.
livre de comptabilité *ou* livre de compte *ou* livre de comptes *ou* livre comptable, account book; book of account.
livre de copie de lettres *ou* livre de copies de lettres *ou* livre copies de lettres, copy letter book; letter book.
livre de dépouillement, analysis book.
livre de magasin, warehouse book.
livre de petite caisse, petty cash book.
livre de positions, position book.
livre de réclamations, claims book.
livre de renseignements, opinion list.
livre de report, financial book; account book.
livre de risques, risks book.
livre de signatures (Banq.), signature book; autograph book.
livre de sorties (de magasin), stock issued book.
livre de stock *ou* livre de magasin (Com.), stock book.
livre de ventes *ou* livre des ventes *ou* livre de vente *ou* livre de (*ou* des) débits, sales book; day book; sales day book; sales journal.
livre des effets à payer, bills payable book; bills payable journal.
livre des effets à recevoir *ou* livre du portefeuille, bills receivable book; bills receivable journal.
livre des entrées, receipts book.
livre des rendus, returns book.
livre des rendus sur achats *ou* livre des rendus aux fournisseurs, returns outwards book.
livre des rendus sur ventes *ou* livre des rendus par les clients, returns inwards book.
livre des timbres-poste *ou* livre d'entrée et de sortie des timbres, postage book; stamp book.
livre des transferts, transfer register.
livre fermé, livre ouvert. *See* **paginer à livre fermé, à livre ouvert.**
livre fractionnaire, subsidiary book.
livre-journal [livres-journaux *pl.*] (*n.m.*) *ou* livre journal [livres journaux *pl.*] (Comptab.),

journal (journal proper or subsidiary journal).
Cf. **journal.**

livres (écritures ; comptabilité) (*n.m.pl.*), books ;
accounts :
tenir les livres d'une maison, to keep a firm's
books (*or* accounts).
rechercher une différence dans les livres, to
look for a difference in the books.
livres de commerce, in France, books which
everyone in business is bound to keep : they
are 3 in number, viz. :—**journal** *or* **livre
journal** *or* **journal légal** (journal), **copie de
lettres** *or* **livre de copie de lettres** (letter book),
and **copie d'inventaire** *or* **livre d'inventaires**
(balance sheet book). *Cf.* sociétés commerciales.

livrer (*v.t.*), to deliver :
livrer des marchandises, les titres que l'on a
vendus, to deliver goods, the stock which
one has sold.
le capitaine n'est pas obligé de livrer les
marchandises toutes à la fois ; il a la faculté
d'en faire la livraison par séries, the master is
not obliged to deliver the goods all together ;
he has the right to make delivery of them
in series.
livrer par erreur, to misdeliver :
correspondance livrée par erreur à une personne
autre que le véritable destinataire (*f.*), postal
packet misdelivered to a person other than
the real addressee.
livrez à l'ordre de M. X., deliver to the order of
Mr X.

livret (*n.m.*), booklet ; book.

livret d'identité (accompagnant une lettre de
crédit, ou analogue) (*m.*), letter of indication.

livret de déposant *ou* **livret nominatif** *ou* **livret de
caisse d'épargne** *ou* *simplement* **livret** (*n.m.*),
depositor's book ; deposit book ; savings
bank book.

livret-horaire [**livrets-horaires** *pl.*] (*n.m.*), time
table.

livret indicateur de la marche des trains (*m.*),
railway guide.

livreur (pers.) (*n.m.*), deliverer.

livreur (Bourse de marchandises) (pers.) (*n.m.*),
deliverer ; first seller.

livreuse (*n.f.*), delivery van ; van.

Lloyd (le), Lloyd's :
agent du Lloyd (*m.*), Lloyd's agent.

local, -e, -aux (*adj.*), local :
directeurs locaux (*m.pl.*), local managers.

local (*n.m.*), place ; premises :
la valeur locative annuelle des locaux occupés
par l'assuré, the annual rental value of the
premises occupied by the insured.
locaux commerciaux, business premises.

localité (*n.f.*), locality ; place :
localité agréée (pour un entrepôt légal),
approved place (for a bonded warehouse).
localité non agréée, unapproved place.

locataire (pers.) (*n.m.* ou *f.*), tenant ; renter ;
hirer :
locataire d'un coffre-fort, renter, hirer, of
a safe.
locataire à bail, lessee ; leaseholder.

locateur, -trice (pers.) (*n.*), lessor.

locatif, -ive (*adj.*), tenant's ; tenants' ; rental ;
renting ; letting ; hiring :
réparations locatives, tenant's (*or* tenants')
repairs.
risque locatif (*m.*), tenant's third party risk.
valeur locative (*f.*), rental value ; letting value ;
rental :
la valeur locative annuelle des locaux occupés
par l'assuré, the annual rental value of the
premises occupied by the insured.

location (action de donner à loyer) (*n.f.*), letting.

location (action de prendre à loyer) (*n.f.*), renting ; hiring ; hire ; reservation ; booking ;
tenancy :
location de coffres-forts, renting, hiring, of
safes.
location de chalands, barge hire.
bâches en location (Ch. de f.) (*f.pl.*), sheets on
hire.
location de places (Ch. de f., etc.), reservation,
booking, of seats.
date d'échéance de location (*f.*), date of expiration of tenancy.

location (prix du loyer) (*n.f.*), rent :
payer sa location, to pay one's rent.

lock-out [**lock-outs** *pl.*] (fermeture temporaire des
usines et ateliers, décidée par les patrons)
(*n.m.*) (opp. à *grève*), lockout.

locman (pers.) (*n.m.*), branch pilot. See note
under **pilote.**

locomotive (*n.f.*), locomotive ; engine ; railway
engine :
locomotive à voyageurs, passenger engine.
locomotive à marchandises, goods engine ;
freight locomotive.

logées fûts (c.-à-d. logées dans des fûts) (se dit des
huiles) (opp. à *nu, -e*), in barrels.

loi (règle) (*n.f.*), law :
loi de Gresham (Écon. polit.), Gresham's law :
« la mauvaise monnaie chasse la bonne, »
" bad money drives out good."
loi de l'offre et de la demande, law of supply
and demand ; law of demand and supply :
« la valeur monte quand la demande dépasse
l'offre, et réciproquement, » "the value rises
when the demand exceeds the supply, and
vice versa."
les cours des frets varient dans des proportions
énormes suivant la loi de l'offre et de la
demande (*m.pl.*), freight rates vary in
enormous proportions according to the law
of supply and demand.
loi des moyennes, law of averages.
loi du pavillon *ou* loi du pavillon du navire,
law of the flag ; law of the ship's flag.

loi (acte de l'autorité souveraine) (*n.f.*), act :
loi de finances *ou* loi des finances, finance act.
loi sur le timbre, stamp act.
loi sur les sociétés, companies act.

loin de compte (être), to be a long way out ; to be
far from agreeing.

lombard (*n.m.*) *ou* **prêt lombard** (*m.*), lombard
loan ; loan on collateral.

long, longue (*adj.*) (Ant. : *court*), long :
une longue lettre, a long letter.

placement à long terme (*m.*), long term investment; long dated investment.

effets à longues échéances (*m.pl.*), long dated bills; long bills.

long cours (*m.*) (opp. à *cabotage*), deep-sea navigation; ocean navigation; deep-sea voyage; ocean voyage; foreign voyage:

navire partant pour le long cours (*m.*), ship sailing on an ocean voyage (*or* on a deep-sea voyage); ship leaving for a foreign voyage.

Note :—Specifically, in France, *long cours* is navigation between European ports of the one part and all foreign and colonial ports outside Europe of the other part, with the exception of Mediterranean ports. Cf. note under **cabotage**, and *cf.* fret, marchandises, navire, voyage, au long cours.

le long du bord. See under **le**.

long-courrier [long-courriers *pl.*] (*n.m.*), foreign-going ship; ocean-going vessel.

lot (partie) (*n.m.*), lot; parcel:

lot de marchandises, lot, parcel, of goods.

lot (Bourse de marchandises) (*n.m.*), load:

le nombre d'unités renfermées dans un lot, the number of units contained in a load.

lot (Fin.) (*n.m.*), prize:

obligations à lots (*f.pl.*), prize bonds.

loterie (*n.f.*), lottery.

louage (*n.m.*), letting; renting; hiring; hire:

louage d'un navire, de services, hiring, hire, of a vessel, of services.

louer (*v.t.*), to let; to rent; to hire; to reserve; to book:

louer au mois une maison, to let, to rent, a house by the month.

louer à bail *ou simplement* louer, to let on lease; to lease:

le preneur est tenu de restituer la chose louée à la fin du bail, the lessee is bound to restore the leased property at the end of the lease.

louer une place dans un train, to reserve, to book, a seat in a train.

à louer, to let; to be let; for hire:

locaux à louer (*m.pl.*), premises to let (*or* to be let).

lourd, -e (*adj.*), heavy:

marchandises lourdes (*f.pl.*), heavy goods.

les diamantifères sont lourdes (Bourse) (*f.pl.*), diamonds are heavy.

lourdeur (*n.f.*), heaviness.

loyal, -e, -aux (*adj.*), fair:

qualité loyale et marchande (*f.*), fair average quality.

loyer (*n.m.*), hire; rent:

loyer de l'argent (*ou* des capitaux), price (*or* hire) (*or* rent) of money:

l'abaissement du loyer de l'argent a certainement contribué au maintien de la prospérité économique (*m.*), the lowering of the price of money has certainly contributed to the maintenance of economic prosperity.

payer un loyer élevé (*ou* des loyers élevés), to pay a high rent.

loyer de bureau, rent of office; office rent.

loyer d'avance, rent in advance.

See also example under **fermage**.

loyers des gens de mer (*m.pl.*), seamen's wages.

lu et approuvé (*invar.*), read and approved.

lucratif, -ive (*adj.*), lucrative; profitable:

commerce lucratif (*m.*), lucrative (*or* profitable) trade.

lutter (*v.i.*), to fight:

lutter contre la concurrence étrangère, to fight (*or* to fight against) foreign competition.

M

M. [**MM.** *ou* **Mrs** *pl.*] (Monsieur [Messieurs *pl.*]), Mr (written before the surname); Esq. (form of epistolary address, written after the surname) [Messrs *pl.* (written before the surname)]:

M. X., Mr X.; X. Esq.

MM. X. & Cie, Messrs X. & Co.

machine (locomotive) (*n.f.*), engine; railway engine; locomotive.

machine à additionner (*f.*), adding machine; adder:

machine à additionner pour tous travaux d'analyse, adding machine for all analysis work.

machine à additionner visible, visible adding machine.

machine à additionner et à soustraire (*f.*), adding-subtracting machine.

machine à adresses *ou* **machine à faire les adresses** (*f.*), addressing machine.

machine à affranchir *ou* **machine à timbrer** *ou* **machine pour l'affranchissement du courrier** (*f.*), stamp affixing machine.

machine à calculer (*f.*), calculating machine.

machine à copier le courrier (*f.*), letter copying machine.

machine à dicter (*f.*), dictating machine.

machine à écrire (*f.*), typewriter; typewriting machine; writing machine:

machine à écrire à plat, flat writing machine.

machine à écrire comptable, typewriter accounting machine:

machine à écrire comptable pour tous travaux de comptabilité, typewriter accounting machine for all bookkeeping work.

machine à écrire comptable pour travaux de facturation, typewriter accounting machine for invoicing work.

machine à écrire portative, portable typewriter.

machine à écrire silencieuse, noiseless typewriter.

machine à écrire standard, standard typewriter.

machine à écrire visible, visible writing machine.

à la machine, typewritten:
factures à la machine (f.pl.), typewritten invoices.

machine à facturer (f.), invoicing machine; billing machine.

machine à multiplier ou machine multiplicatrice (f.), multiplying machine.

machine à sténographier (f.), shorthand machine; stenograph.

machine comptable (f.), accounting machine; bookkeeping machine:

machine comptable automatique-coupons, automatic bookkeeping machine for dividend work.

machine comptable automatique pour compagnies de distribution d'énergie, automatic bookkeeping machine for public utility consumers' accounting.

machine comptable automatique pour comptes courants banque et relevés, automatic bookkeeping machine for bank ledgers and statements.

machine comptable automatique pour comptes courants et relevés, automatic bookkeeping machine for posting ledgers and statements.

machine comptable automatique pour inventaire permanent, automatic bookkeeping machine for stores records work.

machine comptable automatique pour travaux de paie, automatic bookkeeping machine for pay roll work.

machine comptable écrivant à plat, flat writing accounting machine.

machine marine (f.), marine engine.

machines (n.f.pl.), machinery:
chaudières, machines, et tout ce qui s'y rattache, boilers, machinery, and everything connected therewith.

magasin (n.m.), warehouse; store; stores.

magasins généraux. In France, general warehouses which receive goods which any merchant or manufacturer likes to deposit in them, with the object of facilitating sales or loans on the security of the goods so deposited. *Magasins généraux* are nearly all public bonded warehouses. They are then sometimes called **magasins généraux-entrepôts**. Cf. **entrepôt** and **warrant** (n.m.).

magasin (compte du grand livre), stock.

magasin-cale [magasins-cales pl.] (Douanes) (n.m.), bonded shed; sufferance wharf. See note under **cale**.

magasin d'approvisionnement (m.), storeroom.

magasinage (n.m.), storing; storage; warehousing:

le droit de magasinage dans l'entrepôt, the right of warehousing in bond (or of storing) (or of storage) in a bonded warehouse.

magasinage (frais d'emmagasinage) (n.m.), warehouse charges; warehousing charges; storage charges.

magasiner (v.t.), to store; to warehouse.

magasinier (pers.) (n.m.), storekeeper; warehouseman.

magnat (pers.) (n.m.), magnate:
un magnat de la finance, a financial magnate.

main courante (f.), rough book; waste book; blotter.

main courante de caisse (Banq.), counter cash book; teller's cash book.

main courante de recettes ou main courante d'entrée (Banq.), received cash book; received (counter) cash book.

main courante de dépenses ou main courante de sortie (Banq.), paid cash book; paying cashier's counter cash book.

main-d'œuvre [mains-d'œuvre pl.] (n.f.), labour:
le prix de main-d'œuvre et celui des matières premières, the cost of labour and that of raw materials.

maintenir (v.t.), to maintain; to keep:
maintenir le dividende à 5 0/0, to maintain the dividend at 5%.

se maintenir (v.r.), to be maintained (or kept); to keep:
l'action X. se maintien à 262, X. shares were maintained (or X. shares kept) at 262 francs.

maintien (n.m.), maintenance; keeping:
maintien de la prospérité économique, maintenance of economic prosperity.

maison (édifice) (n.f.), house:
prendre une maison à bail, to take a house on lease.

maison (établissement de commerce) (n.f.), house; firm:

maison à succursales multiples, multiple firm.

maison d'armement, shipping house; shipping firm.

maison d'émission, issuing house.

maison d'escompte, discount house.

maison de banque, banking house; banking firm; bank.

maison de commerce, business house; house of business; commercial house; firm.

maison de commission, commission house.

maison de contre-partie, bucket shop; cover snatching firm. Cf. **contre-partie, contre-partiste**, faire la contre-partie, *and* se faire la contre-partie.

maison mère, parent house.

maison succursale, branch house.

maître (pers.) (n.m.), master; captain:
le capitaine est maître de son navire après Dieu, the captain is master of his ship under God.

« Ah ! si j'avais été Maître de la Mer ! . . . » NAPOLÉON, à Sainte-Hélène, " Ah ! if I had been Master of the Sea ! . . ." NAPOLEON, at Saint Helena.

maître au cabotage, master of coasting vessel.

maître clerc (*m.*), managing clerk (in a lawyer's office).

maître de poste, postmaster.

maître et préposé, master and servant.

se trouver maître de la situation, to find oneself master of the situation.

maître (titre donné aux gens de robe) (Abrév. : **Me** [**Mes** *pl.*]), Mr :

maître un tel, Mr So-and-so.

majeure partie (*f.*), major part :

association composée en majeure partie d'étrangers (*f.*), association composed for the major part of foreigners.

majoration (*n.f.*), increase ; overvaluation ; overestimate ; overcharge :

valeur de facture sans aucune majoration (*f.*), invoice value without any increase.

majoration des valeurs formant l'actif d'un bilan, overvaluation of the assets in a balance sheet.

majorer (*v.t.*), to increase ; to add something to ; to overvalue ; to overestimate ; to overcharge in :

majorer le prix d'achat pour couvrir ses frais, to increase, to add something to, the purchase price to cover one's expenses.

majorer les valeurs d'échange, to overvalue the exchange.

majorer une facture, to overcharge in an invoice.

majorité (*n.f.*), majority :

être élu (-e) à la majorité des suffrages (*ou* des voix), to be elected by a majority of votes.

malhonnête (*adj.*), dishonest.

malhonnêtement (*adv.*), dishonestly.

malhonnêteté (*n.f.*), dishonesty :

malhonnêteté d'un dépositaire, dishonesty of a trustee.

mali [**malis** *pl.*] (*n.m.*) (Ant. : *boni*), shortage ; short ; deficit ; deficiency :

malis et bonis de caisse (*ou* dans l'encaisse), cash shorts and overs.

malle (Poste) (*n.f.*), mail ; post :

la malle de l'Inde *ou* la malle des Indes, the Indian mail.

malle de nuit, night mail.

malle (paquebot-poste) (*n.f.*), mail steamer ; mail boat ; mail packet.

malversation (*n.f.*), embezzlement :

malversation de fonds, embezzlement of money.

mandant (pers.) (*n.m.*), principal ; mandator :

mandant et mandataire, principal and agent ; mandator and mandatary. See example under **mandat**.

mandat (fonctions, obligations déléguées) (*n.m.*), mandate ; order ; instructions ; trust :

pays placé sous mandat français (*m.*), country placed under French mandate.

l'assemblée doit, chaque année, nommer des commissaires ; elle peut aussi renouveler leur mandat (*f.*), the meeting must, every year, appoint auditors ; it can also renew their mandate.

l'obligation pour le mandataire de justifier de l'exécution de son mandat cesse lorsque le mandant lui a donné décharge (*f.*), the

obligation of the agent to prove the per formance of his trust (*or* the carrying out of his instructions) ceases when the principal ha discharged him.

mandat d'assurer donné avant la connaissanc du sinistre, order (*or* instructions) to insur given before knowledge of the accident.

mandat (procuration) (*n.m.*) (Abrév. : **mat** *o* **mdt** *ou* **m.**), procuration ; power ; power c attorney ; proxy :

un mandat suppose un contrat par lequel un personne est chargée par une autre de l représenter et d'agir au mieux des intérêt qui lui sont confiés, a power of attorne supposes a contract by which a person i charged by another to represent him and t act in the best of the interests entrusted t him.

mandat général, general power.

mandat spécial, special power ; particula power.

formule de mandat pour une assemblée général d'actionnaires (*f.*), form of proxy for general meeting of shareholders.

mandat (effet de commerce) (*n.m.*), bill ; draft.

mandat (*n.m.*) *ou* **mandat de paiement** (Banq. order ; order to pay ; order for payment cheque ; withdrawal notice ; notice of with drawal of funds :

le chèque est un mandat de paiement adress au banquier, a cheque is an order to pa addressed to the banker.

mandat de versement, mandat-lettre de crédi *See under* compte courant postal.

mandat de virement (Banq.). See unde **virement** (Banq.).

mandat de voyage, traveller's cheque ; chequ for travellers ; circular note.

mandat de poste *ou* **mandat-poste** [**mandats-post** *pl.*] (*n.m.*) *ou* **mandat postal** *ou* *simplemer* **mandat** (*n.m.*), money order ; post offic order ; order : [*See note* (*last paragraph*) *und* compte courant postal.]

mandat-carte [mandats-cartes *pl.*] (*n.m.*), car money order.

mandat-contribution [mandats-contribution *pl.*] (*n.m.*), free money order for payment c taxes.

mandat d'abonnement. In France, a specia inland money order for payment of sub scriptions to newspapers.

mandat de poste international *ou* *simplemer* mandat international, international mone order ; imperial or foreign money order.

mandat de recouvrement. In France, a del collecting order—the French post offic undertakes the collection of amounts payabl on invoices, bills of exchange, etc.

mandat de remboursement, trade charg money order.

mandat-lettre [mandats-lettres *pl.*] (*n.m.*). I France, a letter money order, having a spac for correspondence.

mandat télégraphique, telegraph money orde

mandataire (pers.) (*n.m.* ou *f.*), mandatary ; mandatory ; agent ; attorney ; proxy :

les administrateurs sont les mandataires de la
société chargés de la gestion des affaires
sociales (*m.pl.*), the directors are the mandataries of the company, entrusted with the
management of its business.

la compagnie agit seulement à titre de mandataire des autres compagnies, the company
acts only as agent for the other companies.

le capitaine est le mandataire légal qui
représente l'armement pour tout ce qui
concerne le navire qu'il commande, the
captain is the legal agent who represents the
shipowners in all that concerns the ship he
commands.

l'assuré ou son mandataire (*m.*), the insured or
his agent.

les actionnaires ont le droit de se faire représenter par des mandataires dans toutes les
assemblées (*m.pl.*), the shareholders have the
right to be represented at all meetings by
proxies.

mandater (*v.t.*), to issue an order for the payment
of; to authorize the payment of:
mandater des frais de voyage, to authorize the
payment of travelling expenses.

mande (on), a message states:
on mande de Lisbonne que . . ., a message
from Lisbon states that . . .

manger (*employé métaphoriquement*) (*v.t.*), to eat;
to eat up:
dissipateur qui mange le fonds et le revenu (*m.*),
spendthrift who eats up the capital and the
income.

maniement *ou* **maniment** (*n.m.*), handling;
management; conduct; care:
confier à quelqu'un le maniement de sommes
importantes, to entrust the handling of large
sums of money to someone.
maniement des deniers publics, care, handling,
of public money.

manier (*v.t.*), to handle; to manage; to conduct:
manier des affaires, to handle, to manage, to
conduct, business.
manier des fonds considérables, to handle
considerable sums of money.

manifeste (*n.m.*), manifest:
le manifeste est l'état détaillé des marchandises
formant le chargement d'un navire, a
manifest is a detailed statement of the goods
forming a ship's cargo.
manifeste d'entrée, inward manifest.
manifeste de cabotage, coasting manifest.
manifeste de douane, customs manifest.
manifeste de fret, freight manifest.
manifeste de sortie, outward manifest.
manifeste de transit, transit manifest.

manifester (*v.t.*), to manifest:
marchandises régulièrement manifestées (*f.pl.*),
cargo properly manifested.

manifold (*n.m.*), manifold book.

manipulation (maniement) (*n.f.*), handling:
les fonctions du caissier consistent dans la
manipulation des fonds (*f.pl.*), the work of
the cashier consists in the handling of the
cash.

manipulation (tripotage) (*n.f.*), manipulation.

manipuler (*v.t.*), to handle; to manipulate.

manœuvre (d'un navire) (*n.f.*), handling:
ce qu'on demande avant tout au capitaine,
c'est la manœuvre du navire, what is
required above all of the captain is the
handling of the ship.

manœuvrer un navire, to handle a ship.

manquant, -e (*adj.*), missing:
colis manquants (*m.pl.*), missing packages.

manquant (*s'emploie souvent au pluriel*) (*n.m.*),
shortage; short; deficiency; loss:
manquant en caisse, shortage, short, deficiency, in the cash.
armateur responsable des manquants (*m.*),
owner liable for shortage (*or* shortages) (*or*
loss).
manquant en poids, en nombre, par coulage à
la suite de fortune de mer, loss in weight, in
number, by leakage as a consequence of a
peril of the sea.
manquants provenant de l'insuffisance des
emballages, loss arising from insufficient
packing.

manque (*n.m.*), want; lack; shortage; short;
deficiency:
manque d'argent, de fonds, de confiance, de
diligence, de soins, d'affaires, want, lack, of
money, of funds, of confidence, of diligence,
of care, of business.
manque en caisse, shortage, short, deficiency,
in the cash.
manque de fonds (Banq.), no funds; no effects.

de manque, wanting; missing; short:
trouver 20 francs de manque dans un sac de
1 000 francs, to find 20 francs missing in a
1,000 franc bag; to find a 1,000 franc bag
20 francs short.

manque (sans affaires) (Bourse de marchandises)
(Abrév.: **M.**), no dealings.

manquer (laisser échapper) (*v.t.*), to miss:
manquer un train, un bateau, une correspondance, une occasion, to miss a train, a
boat, a connection, an opportunity.

manquer (ne pas faire honneur à ses engagements;
faire faillite) (*v.i.*), to default; to fail:
commerçant qui est obligé de manquer (*m.*),
merchant who is compelled to default.
banque qui a manqué (*f.*), bank which has failed.
manquer à ses engagements, à son devoir, to
fail in one's engagements, in one's duty.

manquer (être de moins) (*v.i.*), to be missing:
si une partie des objets manque à la livraison,
if a part of the articles is missing on delivery.

manquer de, to want; to be in want of; to be in
need of; to lack:
manquer d'argent, to want, to be in want of,
to lack, money.
manquer de capacité pour les affaires, to lack
capacity for business.

manufacture (fabrique) (*n.f.*), manufactory;
factory; works.

manufacturer (*v.t.*), to manufacture.

manufacturier, -ère (pers.) (*n.*), manufacturer.

manuscrit, -e (*adj.*), manuscript; written; in
writing:
formule imprimée qui porte les indications

manuscrites suivantes (*f.*), printed form which contains the following written particulars (*or* the following particulars in writing).

manutention (gestion) (*n.f.*), handling; management; care:
manutention de la cargaison, handling cargo.
manutentions maritimes, stevedoring.
manutention des deniers publics, care, handling, of public money.
laisser à un homme sûr la manutention de ses affaires, to leave the management of one's affairs in the hands of a reliable man.

manutentionner (*v.t.*), to handle; to manage:
la valeur des marchandises manutentionnées dans le port, the value of the goods handled in the port.
le tonnage manutentionné pendant l'année, the tonnage handled during the year.

marasme (*n.m.*), stagnation; dullness; dulness:
le marasme général des affaires, the general stagnation (*or* dullness) of business.

marc le franc (au) *ou* **marc la livre (au)**, pro rata; in proportion; proportionally:
répartir le prix des biens d'un débiteur entre ses créanciers au marc le franc de leurs créances, to distribute the amount realized by a debtor's property among his creditors pro rata to their debts.
les assureurs contribueront au marc le franc (*m.pl.*), the underwriters will contribute pro rata (*or* proportionally).
les avaries communes sont supportées par le chargement, par le navire, et par le fret, au marc le franc de leur valeur (*f.pl.*), general average is borne by the cargo, the ship, and the freight, in proportion to their value.

marchand, -e (*adj.*), merchantable; merchant; mercantile; commercial; marketable; market (*used as adj.*); saleable; salable; sale (*used as adj.*):
marine marchande (*f.*), mercantile marine; commercial marine; merchant marine.
valeur marchande (*f.*), sale value; saleable value; market value; marketable value.
qualité loyale et marchande (*f.*), fair average quality.

marchand, -e (pers.) (*n.*), dealer; trader:
marchand au détail *ou* marchand détaillant, retail dealer (*or* trader); retailer.
marchand de journaux, newsagent.
marchand en (*ou* de) demi-gros, wholesale trader (*or* dealer); wholesaler. See note under **gros** *ou* **gros commerce**.
marchand en (*ou* de) gros, direct trader. See note under **gros** *ou* **gros commerce**.

marchandage (*n.m.*), bargaining; haggling.

marchander (*v.i.*), to bargain; to haggle.

marchandise (*n.f.*) *ou* **marchandises** (*n.f.pl.*), goods; merchandise; commodity; commodities; cargo; freight:
marchandises acquittées, duty-paid goods.
marchandises d'entrepôt *ou* marchandises entreposées, bonded goods.
marchandises d'origine (*ou* de provenance) étrangère, goods of foreign origin.
marchandises dangereuses, inflammables, *ou*

explosibles, dangerous, inflammable, or explosive goods.
marchandises de cabotage, coasting cargo.
marchandises de grande vitesse *ou* marchandises de la messagerie, parcels; parcels and other merchandise by passenger train, passenger steamer, or aeroplane.
marchandises de long cours, foreign cargo.
marchandises de retour (réadmission en franchise) (Douanes), returned goods; goods returned; goods brought back.
marchandises destinées à l'exportation, goods, merchandise, commodities, intended for export.
marchandises du pont, deck cargo.
marchandises faiblement taxées (*ou* tarifées) (Douanes), low-duty goods.
marchandises fortement taxées (*ou* tarifées), high-duty goods.
marchandise(s) franche(s) de tout droit *ou* marchandise(s) exempte(s) de droits *ou* marchandise(s) libre(s) à l'entrée *ou* marchandise(s) exempte(s), duty-free goods; free goods; uncustomed goods.
marchandises légères *ou* marchandises de cubage *ou* marchandises d'encombrement, measurement goods; measurement cargo; measure goods; light goods; light freight.
marchandises liquides, wet goods.
marchandises lourdes *ou* marchandises pondéreuses, weight goods; weight cargo; dead weight; dead-weight cargo; heavy goods; heavy freight.
marchandises mises en consommation (Douanes), goods for home use.
marchandises non acquittées, uncustomed goods (having paid no duty).
marchandise(s) passible(s) de droits *ou* marchandise(s) sujette(s) à des droits *ou* marchandise(s) payant des droits de douane *ou* marchandise(s) tarifée(s) *ou* marchandise(s) taxée(s), dutiable goods.
marchandises périssables, perishable goods; perishable merchandise.
marchandises sèches, dry goods.
les bagages des voyageurs ne sont pas considérés comme marchandises (*m.pl.*), passengers' luggage is not considered as merchandise.
les lettres de change n'étant que le signe représentatif des monnaies, peuvent être considérées comme une marchandise que l'on vend où que l'on achète à un prix plus ou moins élevé (*f.pl.*), bills of exchange being but the representative sign of money, can be considered as merchandise, which is sold or bought at a greater or less price.

marchandises *ou* **marchandises générales** (compte de marchandises) (Comptab.), goods; goods account.

marche (*n.f.*), running; sailing:
charbon destiné à la marche de la machine (*m.*), coal for running the engine.
marche des trains, running of trains.
renseignements sur la marche des navires à travers les mers (*m.pl.*), information on the sailing of ships across the seas.

navire en marche (*m.*), ship under way.

marche à la vapeur *ou simplement* marche (d'un navire), steaming.

marche à la voile *ou simplement* marche (d'un navire), sailing.

marche à suivre (*f.*), procedure.

marché (convention en général) (*n.m.*), agreement; contract:

rompre un marché, to break an agreement.

marché (convention d'achat ou de vente) (*n.m.*), contract; bargain; transaction; dealing; deal:

administrateur qui a passé des marchés avec la société (*m.*), director who has entered into contracts with the company.

faire un marché avantageux, to make a good bargain; to do a good deal.

marché à prime *ou* marché libre *ou* marché conditionnel (Bourse), option bargain; option. See examples under **prime** (marché à prime).

marché à prime pour lever, call; call option; buyer's option.

marché à prime pour livrer, put; put option; seller's option.

marché à terme *ou* marché à livrer (Com.), transaction on (*or* upon) credit; time bargain.

marché à terme *ou* marché à livrer (Bourse de marchandises), forward transaction.

Note :—Properly, *marché à terme* refers to a forward transaction done on the *marché réglementé* and *marché à livrer* to a transaction on the *marché libre*. (*See these terms under* marché commercial.) The difference between transactions done on the *marché réglementé* and those done on the *marché libre* is that whereas on the latter the type and quality of the goods, as also the terms and conditions, are as may be mutually agreed and not subject to set and uniform regulations, on the former, with the sole exception of the price, everything is regulated according to fixed and uniform rules.

marché à terme *ou* marché à livrer (Bourse de valeurs), settlement bargain; dealing for the settlement; transaction for the settlement; bargain for account; time bargain.

marché à terme ferme (Bourse de marchandises), transaction for future delivery during specified periods.

marché au comptant (opp. à *marché à terme*), cash bargain; bargain for cash; bargain for money; cash transaction; transaction for cash; cash deal; dealing for money.

marché de spéculation, speculative bargain.

marché en (*ou* par) filière (Bourse de marchandises), connected contract. See example under **filière**.

marché ferme, firm bargain; firm deal. See examples under **prime** (marché à prime).

marché hors caisse (Bourse de marchandises), contract not registered with the clearing house. *See* caisse de liquidation.

marché par caisse, contract registered with the clearing house. *See* caisse de liquidation.

marché (état de l'offre et de la demande) (Bourse) (*n.m.*), market:

le marché a haussé, the market has risen.

il n'y en a pas sur le marché, there are none on the market.

marché étroit, limited market:

titres qui n'ont qu'un marché étroit (*m.pl.*), shares which have only a limited market.

marché large, free market:

large marché animé en actions X. vers 160 fr., lively free market in X. shares round about 160 francs.

marché (emplacement où l'on offre les produits à vendre; ville; contrée; compartiment de bourse) (*n.m.*), market:

marché à terme *ou* marché du terme (Marché des produits coloniaux) (Bourse de marchandises), terminal market.

marché à (*ou* du) terme (Marché aux grains) (Bourse de marchandises), futures market; options market.

marché à (*ou* du) terme (Bourse de valeurs). *See note under* marché des valeurs.

marché après-bourse, street market.

marché au (*ou* du) comptant, cash market.

marché aux bestiaux, cattle market.

marché aux (*ou* des) grains, corn market; corn exchange; grain market (*or* exchange).

marché commercial, produce market.

Note :—The French produce markets, held on the produce exchanges, consist of two distinct markets, (1) a **marché réglementé** (regulated or official market under the control of a *syndicat* [committee] — in Paris, called Syndicat général de la Bourse de commerce de Paris), and (2) a **marché libre** (open market). (*See note under* marché à terme *ou* marché à livrer, *above.*) Public sales (*ventes publiques*) are also held.

Moreover, on the French produce exchanges there exist the **marché au comptant,** and the **marché à terme.**

In principle, goods of any kind can be dealt in on any *bourse de marchandises,* but in practice, each important commercial centre is specialized and deals principally in certain goods. Thus, coffee and general colonial produce is dealt in at Marseilles, Bordeaux, and Havre; wool at Havre, Roubaix and Tourcoing. At Paris, dealings take place in grain, flour, rice, seeds, alcohols, oils, sugar, rubber, hides, minerals, metals, etc.

The French term *bourse de marchandises* or *bourse de commerce* has a very much wider application than the English term *produce exchange.* As a matter of fact, no exchange in London is nominally designated produce exchange. Produce such as tea, sugar, spices, dried fruits, essential oils, chemicals, etc., is dealt in at the London Commercial Sale Rooms (often called Mincing Lane, from the name of the street in which it is situated). Wheat and other grain, flour, seeds, oilseeds, oils, and the like, on the Baltic Exchange, which is also the Shipping

Exchange (*full title* Baltic Mercantile and Shipping Exchange). Wheat and other grain, flour, seeds, oilseeds, and the like, are also dealt in on the London Corn Exchange (often called Mark Lane, being situate in that street), where samples are exhibited. (No samples are exhibited in the Baltic Exchange.) Coal is dealt in on the Coal Exchange, metals on the Metal Exchange, rubber on the Rubber Exchange, wool on the Wool Exchange, furs on the Fur Exchange, hops on the Hop Exchange, fruit on the London Fruit Exchange, etc.

The term *produce broker* (translated in this dictionary as *courtier de marchandises*) is, however, used in London, but is practically confined to a colonial produce broker, a Mincing Lane broker. A broker on a corn exchange is called a *grain broker*, one on the metal exchange a *metal broker*, and so on with each in turn.

marchés d'outre-mer, oversea markets.

marché de l'argent *ou* marché monétaire *ou* marché des monnaies *ou* marché des capitaux, money market.

les banques d'émission sont le régulateur du marché de l'argent (*f.pl.*), the banks of issue are the governors of the money market.

marché de l'escompte, discount market.

marché de l'escompte hors banque, open discount market.

marché de l'étain, tin market.

marché de la matière première, commodity market.

marché des actions *ou* marché des actions . . . *ou* marché des titres (*ou* du titre) *ou* marché de la valeur, market in the shares; market in . . . shares; market in the stock:

le marché des actions X. s'améliore légèrement, the market in X. shares improved slightly.

cela a suffit pour impressionner le marché du titre, that was sufficient to make an impression on the market in the stock.

marché des affrètements, chartering market; charter market.

marché des affrètements en retour, homeward charter market.

marché des changes *ou* marché cambiste *ou* marché des devises, foreign exchange market.

marché des changes à terme, forward exchange market.

marché des cotons *ou* marché du coton *ou* marché cotonnier, cotton market.

marché des droits de souscription, rights market.

marché des émissions, issue market.

marché des frets, freight market.

marché des métaux, metal market.

marché des pétrolifères (Bourse), oil market.

marché des « Pieds Humides. » See under **pieds humides.**

marché des valeurs *ou* marché des titres, stock market; share market:

la Bourse de Paris se compose de deux grands marchés, le **marché officiel** (*ou* le **marché en**

Bourse) (*ou* le **parquet**), à la tête duquel sont les *agents de change* nommés par le gouvernement et qui se réunissent au *parquet* dans une partie close par des barrières et appelée la *corbeille* (le nombre des agents de change près de la Bourse de Paris est soixante-dix); le second marché porte le nom de **coulisse** (*ou* **marché en banque**) (*ou* **marché des valeurs en banque**) (*ou* **marché libre**) (*ou* **syndicat de banquiers**); il se tient en dehors du palais de la Bourse sous le péristyle; il est libre, mais ce sont des banquiers spéciaux appelés **coulissiers** (*ou* **banquiers en valeurs**), réunis en syndicat, qui y traitent la plus grande partie des opérations. Ils sont subdivisés l'un et l'autre en trois marchés spéciaux : le *marché du* (ou *au*) *comptant*, le *marché du* (ou *à*) *terme*, et le *marché de la rente*. Pendant les heures de bourse, le *marché* (ou le *syndicat*) *des banquiers en rente* ou *coulisse des rentes* est toléré à l'intérieur de la Bourse à gauche de la *corbeille*. (*Nota :*—En *coulisse* le *marché du comptant* s'appelle aussi *syndicat des banquiers en valeurs au comptant*, et le *marché du terme* s'appelle aussi *marché des valeurs à terme* ou *syndicat des banquiers en valeurs à terme*), the Paris Bourse (stock exchange) consists of two big markets, the **marché officiel** (or the **marché en bourse**) (or the **parquet**), at the head of which are the *agents de change* (stockbrokers) nominated by the government and who meet in the *parquet* in a part enclosed by barriers and called the *corbeille* (the number of *agents de change* accredited to the Paris Bourse is seventy); the second market bears the name of **coulisse** (or **marché en banque**) (or **marché des valeurs en banque**) (or **marché libre**) (or **syndicat de banquiers**); it is held outside the House under the peristyle (colonnade); it is free, but special brokers called **coulissiers** (or **banquiers en valeurs**), united to form a syndicate, do most of the business. Both are subdivided into three special markets: the *marché du* (or *au comptant* (cash market), the *marché du* (or *à*) *terme* (settlement market), and the *marché de la rente* (rente market). During stock exchange hours, the *marché* (or the *syndicat*) *des banquiers en rente* or *coulisse des rentes* is tolerated inside the House to the left of the *corbeille*. (*Note :*—In the *coulisse*, the *marché du comptant* is also called *syndicat des banquiers en valeurs au comptant*, and the *marché du terme* is also called *marché des valeurs à terme* or *syndicat des banquiers en valeurs à terme*.) *Cf.* marché hors cote.

Note :—As newspaper headings, and the like, *Au Parquet* means *On the Marché officiel*, *En Banque* or *En Coulisse* means *On the Marché en Banque* or *Coulisse*. *Sous le péristyle* also means *On the Coulisse*, but is sometimes used to refer to the prices on the *marché hors cote*, in contradistinction to *Au Parquet* and *En Banque*.

Note :—Unlike in London, where *broker* deals
with *jobber* (or *dealer*), in Paris, *broker* deals
with *broker*, and the other broker dealt with
is called the *contre-partie*, q.v.

marché du caoutchouc *ou* marché des caoutchoucs, rubber market.

marché du crédit, credit market :
 capital qui s'offre sur le marché du crédit (*m.*),
 capital on offer in the credit market.

marché du cuivre, copper market.

marché du travail, labour market.

marché extérieur *ou* marché étranger, foreign
market.

marché fermé *ou* marché contrôlé, one man
market.

marché hors cote, unofficial market ; market in
securities which have not received a quotation
in an official list (i.e., in Paris, in the *cote
officielle* or in the *cote en banque*).

Note :—The *marché hors cote* in Paris is distinct
from both the *parquet* and the *coulisse*. It is,
so to speak, a *coulisse* of the *coulisse*.
Hundreds of stocks are dealt in on the
marché hors cote, especially in the early days
of their speculative activity, which by reason
of its greater freedom and less onerous
conditions and formalities of quotation offers
greater facilities for a free market. Some of
these stocks are destined at a later date to
be quoted on the *marché officiel* or on the
marché en banque, especially after they have
quieted down, and are more established.
 Securities dealable on the London Stock
Exchange are of two kinds, *quoted* and
unquoted. To deal in either of these it is
necessary to obtain *permission to deal*. It is
not permitted to a member of the London
Stock Exchange to deal on the Stock Exchange in any security for which permission
to deal has not been granted.
 For information concerning the kinds of
prices quoted on the London Stock Exchange,
and the names of the lists recording them,
see note under **cote.**

marché intérieur *ou* marché métropolitain,
home market.

marché libre *ou* marché ouvert, open market ;
free market :
 banque qui a pu acquérir de l'or sur le marché
 libre (*f.*), bank which has been able to buy
 gold on the open market.

emprunts contractés sur le marché libre des
 capitaux (*m.pl.*), loans contracted on the
 open money market.

ce qui caractérise le marché libre c'est l'absence
 de toute réglementation, what characterizes a free market is the absence of all
 regulation.

marché (réunion de marchands) (*n.m.*), market :
 ville où il n'y a qu'un marché par semaine (*f.*),
 town where there is only one market a
 week.

marcher (*v.i.*), to run ; to travel ; to go ; to sail :
 marcher à — kilomètres à l'heure (se dit
 d'un train, etc.), to run at, to travel at, —
 kilometres an hour.

navire destiné à marcher à grande vitesse (*m.*),
 ship designed to travel (*or* to sail) at high
 speed.

marcher à vide, to go light :
 si le navire marche à vide, if the vessel goes
 light.

marée (*n.f.*), tide :
 une marée exceptionnellement haute, an
 exceptionally high tide.
 la Méditerranée n'a pas de marée, the Mediterranean has no tide.

marge (blanc autour d'une page) (*n.f.*), margin :
 connaissement qui présente (*ou* qui indique) en
 marge les marques et numéros des colis, des
 marchandises à transporter (*m.*), bill of
 lading which shows in the margin the marks
 and numbers of the packages, of the goods to
 be carried.
 marchandises marquées et numérotées comme
 en marge (*f.pl.*), goods marked and numbered
 as per margin (*or* as in the margin hereof).

marge (surplus ; excès) (*n.f.*), margin :
 marge de bénéfice *ou* marge bénéficiaire,
 margin of profit.
 la marge entre la somme avancée et la valeur
 des titres au moment de l'opération, the
 margin between the amount advanced and
 the value of the securities at the time of the
 transaction.
 réserver une marge pour les éventualités, to
 reserve a margin for contingencies.

marge (couverture ; provision) (Fin., Banq., et
 Bourse) (*n.f.*), margin ; cover :
 agent de change qui exige une marge de 25 0/0
 en espèces (*m.*), stockbroker who requires a
 margin (*or* a cover) of 25% in cash.
 déposer une marge en espèces comme couverture proportionnée à ses engagements, to
 deposit a margin in cash as cover in proportion to one's engagements.
 marge supplémentaire, further margin (*or* cover).

marginal, -e, -aux (*adj.*), marginal :
 notes marginales (*f.pl.*), marginal notes.

marin, -e (*adj.*), marine ; sea (*used as adj.*) ;
 nautical :
 mille marin (*m.*), sea mile ; nautical mile.

marin (pers.) (*n.m.*), seaman ; sailor ; mariner ;
 seafaring man ; seafarer.

marine (*n.f.*), marine ; shipping ; maritime
 navigation :
 marine marchande, mercantile marine ; commercial marine ; merchant marine ; merchant
 shipping ; merchant service :
 la marine marchande d'un pays est l'ensemble
 des bâtiments de mer consacrés aux transactions commerciales, the mercantile marine
 of a country is the collection of seagoing
 vessels employed in trade.
 loi sur la marine marchande (*f.*), merchant
 shipping act.
 en marine, on évalue toutes les distances en
 milles, in maritime navigation, all distances
 are reckoned in miles.

maritime (*adj.*) (Abrév. : **mar.** *ou* **marit.**), maritime ; marine ; sea (*used as adj.*) ; shipping
 (*used as adj.*) :

assurance maritime (*f.*), marine (*or* maritime) (*or* sea) insurance.

commerce maritime (*m.*), maritime commerce; sea trade.

agence maritime (*f.*), shipping agency.

marquage (*n.m.*), marking.

marque (*n.f.*), mark; brand:
marques et numéros des colis, marks and numbers of packages.
marque de commerce *ou* marque de fabrique, commercial mark; trade mark.
marques ordinaires (métaux), ordinary brands.
marque principale, leading mark.

marqué, -e (*adj.*), marked; decided:
une reprise marquée, a marked (*or* decided) recovery.

marquer (*v.t.*), to mark; to show; to shew:
les colis doivent être marqués distinctement, et porter, outre les marques et numéros, le nom du port de destination (*m.pl.*), the packages should be marked distinctly, and bear, besides the marks and numbers, the name of the port of destination.
marquer une bonne résistance (en parlant des cours de bourse), to show strength.
Cf. valeurs marquantes.

marron, -onne (*adj.*), outside:
banquier marron *ou* courtier marron (*m.*), outside broker.

marronnage (*n.m.*), outside broking. *Note :—*
In France, *marronnage* (outside broking, i.e., exercising the functions of a broker by one who is not an accredited broker) is illegal.

masse (*n.f.*). See examples:
réduire peu à peu la masse écrasante de la dette flottante, to reduce little by little the crushing mass of the floating debt.
droit éminemment favorable à la masse des créanciers (*m.*), right highly advantageous to the mass (*or* body) of creditors.
masse active (Fin.), assets.
masse débitrice *ou* masse passive *ou* masse contribuable (Avarie commune), contributing values; contributing interests and values; contributory mass; interests liable to contribute:
l'évaluation des biens profitant du sacrifice s'appelle masse débitrice (*f.*), the valuation of the property benefiting by the sacrifice is called contributing values.
masse capital, capital and premiums received on shares.
masse créancière *ou* masse active (Avarie commune), amounts (*or* values) (*or* mass) (*or* loss, damage, and expense) to be made good:
les dommages et dépenses qui constituent l'avarie commune s'appellent masse créancière, the damage and expenses which constitite the general average are called amounts to be made good.
masse des espèces monnayées en circulation, aggregate, mass, of coin in circulation.
masses indivisibles *ou* masses indivisibles et objets de dimensions exceptionnelles (Transport ferroviaire), long, heavy, or bulky articles:

transport des masses indivisibles (*m.*), conveyance of long, bulky, or heavy articles.

masse passive (Fin.), liabilities.

masse sociale (d'une société), funds of a (*or* of the) company.

mât de charge *ou* **mât de chargement** (*m.*), derrick.

matador de la finance (pers.) (*m.*), financial magnate.

matelot (pers.) (*n.m.*), sailor; seaman; mariner; seafaring man; seafarer.

matériel, -elle (*adj.*), material; tangible:
fait matériel (*m.*), material fact.
valeurs matérielles (*f.pl.*), tangible assets.

matériel remorqueur (Ch. de f.) (*m.*), hauling stock.

matériel roulant (Ch. de f.) (*m.*), rolling stock.

matière (*n.f.*) *ou* **matière première** (en terme de bourse), commodity; raw material:
caoutchoutières lourdes malgré la hausse de la matière (*ou* de la matière première) (*f.pl.*), rubbers heavy in spite of the rise in the commodity (*or* in the raw material).
les valeurs d'étain sont mieux en général, à la faveur de la reprise de la matière (*f.pl.*), tin shares are better in general, favoured by the recovery of the commodity.

matière brute *ou* **matière première** (*f.*), raw material:
les matières premières consommées par la fabrication d'un article, the raw materials used in the manufacture of an article.

matière d'alimentation (*f.*), foodstuff.

matières d'or et d'argent *ou* *simplement* **matières** (*n.f.pl.*), bullion; gold and silver bullion:
commerce des matières d'or et d'argent (*m.*), bullion trade; trade in gold and silver bullion.
matières d'or, gold bullion.
matières d'argent, silver bullion.

maussade (*adj.*), dull:
l'action X. est maussade à 510, X. shares are dull at 510 francs.

maussaderie (*n.f.*), dullness; dulness:
la maussaderie générale des affaires, the general dullness of business.

mauvais, -e (*adj.*), bad:
mauvais état de navigabilité (*m.*) (opp. à bon état de navigabilité), unseaworthiness.
en mauvais état de navigabilité, unseaworthy See example under **bon état de navigabilité (en)**.
mauvais papier (effets de commerce) (*m.*), bad paper.
mauvais temps (*m.*), bad weather.
mauvaise créance (*f.*), bad debt.
titres qui sont de mauvaise livraison (Bourse (*m.pl.*), shares which are (*or* stock which is bad delivery.

maximum [maxima *ou* maximums *pl.*] (*adj* invar. pour les deux genres), maximum:
le montant maximum de l'émission, the maximum amount of the issue.
les bons titres n'ont pas de cours maximum (*m.pl.*), good stocks have no maximum price
risque maximum [risques maxima *ou* risques maximums *pl.*], maximum risk.

valeur maximum (*f.*) [valeurs maxima *ou* valeurs maximums *pl.*], maximum value.

maximum [**maxima** *ou* **maximums** *pl.*] (*n.m.*), maximum :
perte qui atteint son maximum (*f.*), loss which reaches its maximum.
rechercher des placements judicieux, présentant un minimum de risque et assurant un maximum de revenu, to look for judicious investments, presenting a minimum of risk and assuring a maximum of revenue.

au maximum *ou* **à concurrence d'un maximum de,** at most ; not exceeding :
amende de tant de francs au maximum (*f.*), fine not exceeding so many francs.

maximum de charge (d'un navire) (*m.*), burden, burthen (of a ship).

mécanicien (d'un navire) (pers.) (*n.m.*), engineer (of a ship).

mécanicien (*n.m.*) *ou* **mécanicien conducteur de locomotive,** driver ; engine driver.

mécanographie (*n.f.*), typewriting ; typing.

mécompte (*n.m.*), miscalculation ; mistake ; error :
addition dans laquelle il y a du mécompte (*f.*), addition in which there is a mistake.

se mécompter (*v.r.*), to miscalculate ; to make a mistake.

médecin (pers.) (*n.m.*), doctor.

médecin sanitaire maritime (*m.*), medical officer of health (at a port).

médical, -e, -aux (*adj.*), medical :
visite médicale des passagers et de l'équipage (*f.*), medical inspection of passengers and crew.

meilleur, -e (*adj.*), better :
la tendance du marché est meilleure, the tendency (*or* trend) of the market is better.

meilleur marché (*invar.*) *ou* **à meilleur marché** *ou* **à meilleur compte,** cheaper :
ces actions sont meilleur marché (*f.pl.*), these shares are cheaper.
obtenir du crédit à meilleur marché (*ou* à meilleur compte), to obtain cheaper credit.

membre (pers.) (*n.m.*), member :
les membres d'un comité, du conseil d'administration, de l'équipage, the members of a committee, of the board, of the crew.

mémoire (état de sommes dues) (*n.m.*), bill ; account :
payer un mémoire, to pay a bill (*or* an account).

mémoire (état de ce qui est dû à un homme de loi) (*n.m.*), bill ; bill of costs :
mémoire taxé, taxed bill of costs.

mémoire (mention dans la colonne francs et centimes d'un bilan, d'un compte), „ „ „ (i.e., dits in the £ s. d. column) ; not valued ; no value.

pour mémoire, as a memorandum ; as a record ; to place it on record ; not valued ; no value :
les amortissements ne figurent que pour mémoire (*m.pl.*), the amounts written off are shown only as a memorandum (*or* record).
nous signalons cette exception pour mémoire, we mention this exception to place it on record.

les concessions et permis de recherches sont portés dans le bilan pour mémoire, the claims and prospecting licences stand in the balance sheet not valued ; no value is shown in the balance sheet for the claims and prospecting licences.

mémorandum [**mémorandums** *pl.*] (note) (*n.m.*), memorandum ; note :
pour la correspondance de détail, on se sert du mémorandum, sur papier de petit format, for minor correspondence, the memorandum is used, on small sized paper.

mémorandum (carnet) (*n.m.*), memorandum book.

mémorial (brouillard) (*n.m.*), rough book ; waste book ; blotter.

menace (*n.f.*), threat ; menace :
menace de ruine, de renvoi, threat, menace, of ruin, of dismissal.

menacer (*v.t.*), to threaten ; to menace.

ménager (disposer pour un certain but) (*v.t.*), to make :
ménager une réserve en dehors de ses opérations courantes, to make a reserve outside (*or* apart from) one's current transactions.

ménager (employer avec économie) (*v.t.*), to make good use of ; to husband ; to economize :
ménager son argent, to make good use of one's money ; to husband one's resources.
ménager ses revenus, l'usage du numéraire, to economize one's income, the use of coin.

mener (*v.t.*), to conduct :
mener ses affaires avec sagesse, to conduct one's affairs wisely.

meneurs (du marché) (Bourse) (pers.) (*n.m.pl.*), leaders (of the market).

mensonger, -ère (*adj.*), lying ; false ; untrue ; illusory :
prospectus mensonger (*m.*), lying prospectus.
bénéfice mensonger (*m.*), illusory profit.

mensualité (*n.f.*), monthly cheque, payment, drawing, or the like :
mensualités des associés, monthly drawings of partners.

mensuel, -elle (*adj.*), monthly :
rapport mensuel (*m.*), monthly report.

mensuellement (*adv.*), monthly :
le règlement des primes se fait, en règle générale, trimestriellement ou mensuellement, settlement of the premiums is made, as a general rule, quarterly or monthly.

mention (*n.f.*), mention ; naming ; notice ; words ; word ; particular ; instruction :
mention sur le connaissement du nom du capitaine, mention on the bill of lading of the name of the master.
quoique cette loi n'en fasse pas mention dans les indications que doit porter le connaissement, la date est un élément important, although this law makes no mention of it in the particulars that a bill of lading should contain, the date is an important element.
les mentions imprimées de la facture, the notices printed on the invoice.
connaissement portant la mention *fret payé* (*m.*), bill of lading bearing the notice (*or* the words) *freight prepaid*.

le billet portait la mention *à l'ordre de*, la mention *accepté*, the bill bore the words *to the order of*, the word *accepted*.

la loi exige que le connaissement porte les mentions essentielles suivantes, the law requires that the bill of lading should contain the following essential particulars.

colonnes pour l'inscription des mentions suivantes (*f.pl.*), columns for entering the following particulars.

télégrammes déposés sans mention de voie, avec une mention de voie (*m.pl.*), telegrams handed in without route instructions, with a route instruction.

mentions de service (sur une formule imprimée), service instructions.

mentionner (*v.t.*), to mention; to name:

la quantité mentionnée au connaissement, the quantity mentioned (*or* named) in the bill of lading.

menu, -e (*adj.*), small; petty:

menue monnaie (*f.*), small money; small change.

menus dépôts (*m.pl.*), small deposits.

menus frais (*m.pl.*) *ou* menues dépenses (*f.pl.*), petty expenses; petties.

mer (*n.f.*), sea:

navire en mer (*m.*), ship at sea.

mer libre, open sea.

mercantile (*adj.*), mercantile; commercial:

opérations mercantiles (*f.pl.*), mercantile business.

mercantilisme (*n.m.*), mercantilism.

mercantiliste (*adj.*), mercantilistic:

politique mercantiliste (*f.*), mercantilistic policy.

mercantiliste (pers.) (*n.m.*), mercantilist.

mercuriale (*n.f.*), official list (of corn or produce exchange prices).

mère (*adj.f.*), mother; parent:

mère patrie (*f.*), mother country:

le lien naturel entre la mère patrie et ses possessions d'outre-mer, the natural bond between the mother country and her oversea possessions.

société mère (*f.*), parent company.

Mesdames, Messieurs (préambule à l'allocution du président), Ladies and Gentlemen:

Mesdames, Messieurs, vous avez entendu le très copieux rapport de votre conseil d'administration et le rapport de vos commissaires aux comptes, Ladies and Gentlemen, you have heard the very full report of your board and the report of your auditors.

mésestimation (*n.f.*), undervaluation; underestimation; underestimate.

mésestimer (*v.t.*), to undervalue; to underestimate.

mésoffrir (*v.i.*), to underbid.

message (*n.m.*), message:

un message de l'agent du Lloyd à Lisbonne annonce que . . ., a message from Lloyd's agent at Lisbon states that . . .

message téléphoné (Poste), telephoned message.

message téléphoné d'une cabine publique, message telephoned from a public call office.

messager, -ère (pers.) (*n.*), messenger:

messager spécial (Poste, etc.), special messenger.

messagerie (*n.f.*) *ou* **messageries** (*n.f.pl.*) (service de transport des voyageurs et des marchandises de grande vitesse) (Ch. de f. & Navig.), passenger and parcels service; mail, passenger, and parcel service.

messagerie (service de transport des marchandises de grande vitesse) (*n.f.*), parcels service; parcel service.

messagerie (bâtiment des messageries) (*n.f.*), parcels office; parcel office.

messageries (marchandises de grande vitesse) (*n.f.pl.*), parcels; parcels and other merchandise by passenger train, passenger boat, or aeroplane; parcels traffic; parcel traffic: tonnage des messageries (*m.*), parcels tonnage.

Messieurs *ou* **Messieurs les Actionnaires** (préambule à l'allocution du président), Gentlemen. Cf. **Mesdames, Messieurs.**

mesure (précaution; démarche) (*n.f.*), measure; step:

mesures prises pour le salut commun du navire et de la cargaison, measures, steps, taken for the common safety of the ship and cargo.

métal (*n.m.*), metal:

métal-étalon (*n.m.*), standard metal:

pays dans lequel l'argent était le métal-étalon (*m.*), country in which silver was the standard metal.

métal jaune (or), métal blanc (argent), métal rouge (cuivre), yellow metal (gold), white metal (silver), red metal (copper).

métal précieux, precious metal:

le métal précieux qui entre dans la composition des pièces types, the precious metal which enters into the composition of standard coins.

métallique (*adj.*), metallic; metal (*used as adj.*):

monnaie métallique *ou* circulation métallique (*f.*), metallic money; metallic currency.

navire métallique (*m.*), metal vessel.

méthode (*n.f.*), method:

méthode des nombres (comptes courants et d'intérêts), product method.

méthode hambourgeoise *ou* méthode par soldes (c^{tes} c^{ts} et d'int.), steps method; balance method.

méthode progressive *ou* méthode directe (c^{tes} c^{ts} et d'int.), forward method.

méthode rétrograde *ou* méthode indirecte (c^{tes} c^{ts} et d'int.), backward method; époque method.

métrique (*adj.*), metric:

système métrique (*m.*), metric system.

métropole (capitale) (*n.f.*), metropolis:

Londres est la plus puissante métropole bancaire, commerciale et industrielle du globe, London is the most powerful banking, commercial and industrial metropolis of the globe.

métropole (contrée considérée par rapport aux colonies qu'elle a fondées) (*n.f.*), home; home country; mother country:

le lien naturel entre la métropole et ses possessions d'outre-mer, the natural bond between the mother country and her oversea

possessions (*or* between the home country
and its oversea possessions).

port de la métropole *ou* port métropolitain (*m.*),
home port.

métropolitain, -e (qui appartient à la capitale
d'un État) (*adj.*), metropolitan :
chemin de fer métropolitain (*m.*) (*Abrév.* :
métro.), metropolitan railway.

métropolitain, -e (qui a le caractère d'une métropole) (*adj.*), home (*used as adj.*) ; domestic :
service métropolitain ou colonial (*m.*), home or
colonial service.

commerce métropolitain (*m.*), home trade ;
domestic trade.

mettre (*v.t.*). See examples :
mettre à bord, to put on board.

mettre à contribution, to draw on :
mettre à contribution les réserves, to draw
on the reserves.

banque qui a été mise à contribution par l'État
dans des fortes proportions (*f.*), bank which
has been drawn on by the Government for
heavy amounts.

mettre à découvert (Banq.), to overdraw :
mettre un compte à découvert, to overdraw
an account.

mettre à flot (*v.t.*), to float.

mettre [de l'argent] à l'écart, to put [money]
by.

mettre à l'ordre du jour les questions à
délibérer, to put (*or* to put down) on the
agenda the business to be transacted.

mettre [son argent] à la caisse d'épargne, to
put [one's money] in (*or* into) the savings
bank.

mettre à la charge de *ou* mettre à charge de,
to charge to ; to charge with ; to put on (*or*
upon) ; to throw on (*or* upon) :
mettre le port à la charge (*ou* à charge) du
client, to charge the postage to the
customer ; to charge the customer with the
carriage.

mettre à la charge de quelqu'un le fardeau de
la preuve d'une faute, l'obligation de contribuer à une dépense, to throw, to put, on
someone the burden of proving a wrongful
act, the obligation to contribute to an
expense.

le remboursement consiste dans la somme mise
à charge de la marchandise par l'expéditeur,
a trade charge is the sum put upon the goods
by the sender.

mettre [une lettre] à la poste, to post [a letter].

mettre à la retraite, to pension ; to pension off.

mettre à la voile (se dit d'un navire) (*v.i.*), to
sail.

mettre à profit, to turn to account (*or* to
profit) (*or* to advantage).

mettre à quai un navire, to wharf a ship.

mettre à terre des marchandises, to land
goods ; to put goods ashore.

mettre au net la situation d'un failli, to
elucidate, to unravel, to clear up, the position
(*or* the affairs) of a bankrupt.

mettre au net une lettre, to make a clean copy
of a letter.

mettre aux voix une résolution (*ou* une proposition), to put a resolution to a meeting.

mettre [une annonce] dans un journal, to put
[an advertisement], to advertise, in a paper.

mettre des oppositions à la cote (Bourse), to
lodge objections to marks.

mettre du bon argent contre du mauvais, to
throw good money after bad.

mettre en bassin (*v.t.*), to dock.

mettre en chantier (*ou* en construction) un
navire, to lay down a ship ; to lay a ship on
the stocks.

mettre en commun, to pool :
mettre des fonds, des risques, en commun, to
pool funds, risks.

mettre en distribution un dividende, to distribute a dividend.

mettre en entrepôt, to put into warehouse ; to
warehouse.

mettre [un navire] en état de tenir la mer, to
make [a ship] seaworthy.

mettre en faillite, to make bankrupt ; to
bankrupt :
négociant qui est sur le point d'être mis en
faillite (*m.*), merchant who is on the point
of being made bankrupt (*or* of being
bankrupted).

mettre en filière (Bourse de marchandises),
to connect up :
client qui charge son courtier de mettre en
filière la marchandise (*m.*), client who
instructs his broker to connect up the goods.

mettre en gage, to pledge ; to hypothecate ;
to pawn ; to put in pawn :
le capitaine peut faire vendre ou mettre en
gage les marchandises pour les besoins de
l'expédition, the master can sell or pledge
the cargo for the needs of the adventure.

mettre [des titres] en garde (*ou* en dépôt), to
place, to deposit, [securities] in safe custody.

mettre en liquidation, to put into liquidation :
·société mise en liquidation judiciaire (*f.*), company put into liquidation under supervision
of the court.

mettre [des papiers] en ordre, to put [papers]
in order.

mettre en paiement un coupon, un acompte,
un solde, de dividende, to pay a coupon, an
interim, a final, dividend.

mettre en pension (Banq. et Bourse), to pawn :
mettre des titres en pension, to pawn stock.

mettre en rapports vendeurs et acheteurs, to
put in touch sellers and buyers.

'mettre [des capitaux] en report, to lend, to
employ, [money] on contango.

mettre en réserve, to put to reserve :
bénéfices mis en réserve (*m.pl.*), profits put to
reserve.

mettre en service un navire, to put a ship into
service (*or* into commission).

mettre en syndicat, to pool :
mettre en syndicat des titres, to pool shares.

mettre en valeur, to turn to account (*or* to
profit) (*or* to advantage) :
mettre en valeur son portefeuille, to turn one's
investments to account.

mettre en vente, to put up, to expose, for sale :
mettre une chose en vente, to put a thing up
for sale.

mettre l'embargo sur un navire, to lay, to put,
an embargo on (or upon) a ship ; to embargo a
ship.

mettre la date sur un chèque, to put the date
on a cheque.

mettre opposition sur un titre en cas de perte
ou de fraude, to stop a bond in case of loss or
fraud.

mettre ordre à ses affaires ou mettre l'ordre
dans ses affaires, to put one's affairs in order.

mettre tant à quelque chose, to give, to pay,
so much for something.

mettre tous ses œufs dans le même panier (fig.),
to put all one's eggs in one basket.

se mettre (v.r.). See examples :
se mettre d'accord, to come to an agreement.
se mettre dans les affaires, to engage in, to
go into, business.
se mettre de moitié dans une affaire, to go
halves in a deal.
se mettre en grève, to go on strike ; to strike ;
to walk out.
se mettre en liquidation, to go into liquidation.

meuble (Dr.) (adj.), personal ; movable ; moveable :
biens meubles (m.pl.), personal property ;
personal estate ; personalty ; personals ;
chattels personal ; movable property ;
movables ; moveables.

meubles (Dr.) (n.m.pl.), personal property ;
personal estate ; personalty ; personals ;
chattels personal ; movable property ;
movables ; moveables.

meubles (objets servant à garnir une habitation)
(n.m.pl.), furniture.
meuble-classeur [meubles-classeurs pl.] (n.m.),
filing cabinet.
meuble à classement vertical (m.), vertical filing
cabinet.
meuble-fichier [meubles-fichiers pl.] (n.m.), card
index cabinet.

mévendre (v.t.), to sell at a low price ; to sell at a
loss ; to sell at a sacrifice ; to sacrifice ; to
slaughter :
il y a des moments où l'on se voit forcé de
mévendre, there are times when one is forced
to sell at a sacrifice.
mévendre ses titres, to sacrifice, to slaughter,
one's stocks.

mévente (n.f.), selling at a loss ; sacrifice ;
slaughter.

mi-terme (à), on half quarter day ; at half
quarter.

mieux (adj. & adv.), better ; best :
valeurs petrolières mieux ; l'action X. est
mieux à 305, oil shares better ; X. shares
were better at 305 francs.
au mieux (Abrév. : **mx** ou **m x**), at best :
on donne fréquemment des ordres d'acheter ou
de vendre au mieux ; les ordres donnés
sans stipulation relative au cours à appliquer
sont aussi exécutés au mieux, orders are
frequently given to buy or to sell at best ;

orders given without stipulation relative to
the price to be applied are also executed at
best.

sauf mieux, or better :
achetez tant de telles actions à tant, sauf
mieux, buy so many such or such shares at
so much, or better.

mieux (n.m.), improvement :
léger mieux en valeurs bancaires, slight improvement in bank stocks.

milieu (sphère sociale) (n.m.), circle :
dans les milieux bien informés, in well informed
circles.

mille marin (m.), nautical mile ; sea mile ;
geographical mile :
les distances parcourues sur mer s'expriment en
milles marins (f.pl.), the distances travelled
over (or covered) on the sea are expressed in
nautical miles.
en marine, on évalue toutes les distances en
milles, in maritime navigation, all distances
are reckoned in miles.

millésime (n.m.), date ; year :
le millésime d'une pièce de monnaie, the date
of a coin (i.e., the year it was struck).
l'exercice est désigné par son millésime : on dit
l'exercice 19—, ou par les millésimes des deux
années successives, lorsqu'il y a chevauchement sur l'année civile : exercice 19— - 19—,
the financial year is designated by its date :
one says the year 19—, or by the dates of two
successive years, when there is overlapping
on the calendar year : year 19— - 19—.
quantième, mois, et millésime, day, month,
and year.

milliard (n.m.), milliard ; thousand millions
(1,000,000,000).

millionnaire (adj.), millionary.

millionnaire (pers.) (n.m. ou f.), millionaire ;
millionnaire :
un millionnaire américain, an American
millionaire.

mine d'or (au propre et au figuré) (f.), gold mine.

mines (n.f.pl.) ou **valeurs minières** (f.pl.), mines ;
mining shares :
les mines étaient soutenues (Bourse), mines
were supported.

mines pour porte-mines (f.pl.), leads for pencil
cases.

mineur, -e (pers.) (n.), minor ; infant :
les mineurs ne sont pas aptes à contracter,
minors are not capable of contracting.
mineur commerçant, infant trader.

minimum [minima ou minimums pl.] (adj. invar. pour les deux genres), minimum :
le nombre minimum d'actions fixé par les
statuts, the minimum number of shares fixed
by the articles.
intérêt minimum (m.) ou intérêts minima (m.pl.)
ou intérêts minimums (m.pl.), minimum
interest.
valeur minimum (f.) [valeurs minima ou valeurs
minimums pl.], minimum value.

minimum [minima ou minimums pl.] (n.m.),
minimum :
tant par 100 francs avec un minimum de tant

par effet, so much per 100 francs with a minimum of so much per bill.

banque où le minimum des effets admissibles est de tant de francs, bank where the minimum of admissible bills is so many francs.

ministère (charge) (*n.m.*), office :
remplir les devoirs de son ministère, to fulfil the duties of one's office.

ministère (entremise ; concours) (*n.m.*), agency ; services ; good offices :
courtiers qui doivent consigner sur des livres spéciaux toutes les opérations faites par leur ministère (*m.pl.*), brokers who must record in special books all the deals done through their agency.
offrir son ministère, to offer one's services (*or* good offices).

minoration (*n.f.*), undervaluation ; underestimation ; underestimate :
minoration des valeurs formant l'actif d'un bilan, undervaluation of the assets in a balance sheet.

minorer (*v.t.*), to undervalue ; to underestimate :
minorer les valeurs d'échange, to undervalue the exchange.

minorité (*n.f.*), minority :
la minorité se conforme à la décision prise par la majorité, the minority conforms to the resolution passed by the majority.

minute (écrit original sur lequel se fait une copie) (*n.f.*), draft :
faire la minute d'une lettre, to make a draft of, to draft, a letter.

minute (original d'un acte notarié, d'un jugement) (*n.f.*), original :
minute d'un acte, original of a deed.

minute (formule originale) (*n.f.*), form :
expéditeur d'un télégramme qui doit mentionner son adresse sur la minute, qui doit indiquer la route sur la minute (*m.*), sender of a telegram who must mention his address on the form, who should write the route in the form.

minuter *ou* **minuer** (*v.t.*), to draw up ; to draw ; to draft ; to make a draft of :
minuter un contrat, to draw up, to draw, to draft, a contract.

mise (action de mettre) (*n.f.*), putting, etc. See the phrases given below, and see the verb **mettre** for other phrases.

mise (*n.f.*) *ou* **mise de fonds** (ce qu'on met dans une société de commerce), putting up of money ; amount of money invested ; money (*or* capital) invested (*or* put up) ; investment ; capital ; stake :
objet social qui n'exige qu'une mise de fonds graduelle (*m.*), objects of the company which only require the gradual putting up of money.
bénéfice qui correspond à tant pour cent de la mise de fonds (*m.*), profit which is equal to so much per cent on the amount of money invested (*or* on the capital invested) (*or* on the money put up) (*or* on the investment) (*or* on the capital).
réaliser de bons bénéfices avec une mise de fonds fort peu élevée, to make good profits with a very small capital.

chaque mise de 1 000 francs, every 1,000 francs put up.

dans une société anonyme aucun des associés n'est tenu au delà de sa mise, in a limited company no member is liable beyond his stake.

mise (ce qu'on expose au jeu) (*n.f.*), stake :
doubler sa mise, to double one's stake.

mise (aux enchères) (*n.f.*), bid :
la dernière mise a été de tant, the last bid was so much.

mise (**être de**) (en parlant d'une monnaie), to be current :
les anciens louis ne sont plus de mise (*m.pl.*), the old louis are no longer current.

mise à bord (*f.*), putting on board.

mise à la charge *ou* **mise à charge** (*f.*), charging :
mise à la charge (*ou* à charge) de l'acheteur du droit de timbre, charging the buyer with the stamp duty.

mise à la poste (des lettres, etc.) (*f.*), posting.

mise à la retraite (*f.*), pensioning ; pensioning off.

mise à prix (enchères) (*f.*), reserve price ; upset price.

mise à terre (*f.*), landing :
la mise temporaire à terre de la cargaison pour la réparation des avaries du navire, temporary landing of the cargo in order to repair damage to the ship.

mise dehors (*f.*). See **mises dehors**.

mise en bassin (*f.*), docking.

mise en chantier (d'un navire) (*f.*), laying down ; laying on the stocks.

mise en commun de fonds (*f.*), pooling of funds.

mise en dépôt des marchandises non déclarées (*f.*), deposit in King's warehouse of goods not entered. *Cf.* dépôt de douane.

mise en distribution (*f.*), distribution.

mise en entrepôt (*f.*), putting into warehouse ; warehousing.

mise en gage (*f.*), pledging ; hypothecation ; pawning.

mise en liquidation d'une société (*f.*), putting into liquidation of a company.

mise en paiement (*f.*), payment :
mise en paiement d'un dividende, payment of a dividend.

mise en possession (Dr.) (*f.*), putting in possession.

mise en risques (Assce) (*f.*), attachment of risk.

mise en syndicat de titres (*f.*), pooling of shares.

mise en valeur *ou* **mise à profit** (*f.*), turning to account (*or* to profit) (*or* to advantage) :
mise en valeur de son portefeuille, turning one's investments to account.

mise en vente (*f.*), putting up for sale.

mise hors (*f.*), disbursement.

miser (*v.i.*), to bid :
vente aux enchères où personne ne mise (*f.*), auction sale where no one bids.

mises dehors (*f.pl.*), disbursements ; ship's disbursements (money advanced and disbursements incurred for the voyage).

mixte (formé d'éléments de différente nature) (*adj.*), mixed :

cargaison mixte (*f.*), mixed cargo.
risques mixtes maritimes et terrestres (*m.pl.*), mixed sea and land risks.
See also
> abordage mixte,
> actions mixtes,
> certificat mixte,
> langage mixte,
> navigation mixte,
> navire mixte,
> paquebot mixte,
> spéculation mixte,
> titre mixte,
> trafic mixte,
> train mixte,
> transport mixte,
> valeurs mixtes,
> voyage mixte.

mobilier, -ère (Dr.) (*adj.*), personal; movable; moveable :
biens mobiliers (*m.pl.*), personal property; personal estate; personalty; personals; chattels personal; movable property; movables; moveables.

mobilier, -ère (qui concerne, qui a pour objet un meuble) (*adj.*), of or relating to personal *or* movable property :
vente mobilière (*f.*), sale of personal property.

mobilier, -ère (en parlant de valeurs) (*adj.*), transferable :
valeurs mobilières (*f.pl.*), transferable securities; stocks and shares.

mobilier (objets servant à garnir une habitation) (*n.m.*), furniture :
mobilier et agencement, furniture and fittings; furniture, fixtures and fittings.
le mobilier d'un navire, the furniture of a ship.

mobilisable (*adj.*), mobilizable :
les capitaux placés en valeurs industrielles ne sont pas toujours facilement mobilisables (*m.pl.*), money (*or* capital) invested in industrials is not always easily mobilizable.

mobilisation (*n.f.*), mobilization; setting free :
mobilisation de capital (*ou* de capitaux) (Fin.), setting free, mobilization, of capital (*or* of money).
mobilisation d'immeubles (Dr.), mobilization of realty.

mobiliser (*v.t.*), to mobilize; to set free :
le capital immobilisé dans une lettre de change est mobilisé dès que la lettre est payée, the money locked up (*or* immobilized) in a bill of exchange is set free (*or* mobilized) as soon as the bill is paid.
le vendeur est astreint à immobiliser ses capitaux dans le crédit qu'il fait à son client : la lettre de change lui permet de mobiliser sa créance, d'en obtenir par l'escompte, le montant avant son échéance, the seller is compelled to lock up (*or* to immobilize) his capital in the credit he gives to his customer : the bill of exchange enables him to mobilize his debt, to obtain the amount of it by discount, before its due date.

se mobiliser (*v.r.*), to be mobilized; to be set free :

les immeubles peuvent se mobiliser dans certains cas (*m.pl.*), immovable property is capable of being mobilized (i.e., converted into movable property) in certain cases.

mode (*n.m.*), mode; method :
mode annuitaire d'acquittement, mode of paying off by annual instalments.

modèle (*n.m.*), specimen :
modèle de chèque, de lettre de crédit, de bilan, specimen of cheque, of letter of credit, of balance sheet; specimen cheque, letter of credit, balance sheet.

modeste (*adj.*), modest :
une dépense modeste, une fortune modeste, a modest expenditure, a modest fortune.

modicité (*n.f.*), smallness; moderateness; lowness :
modicité d'un prix, lowness of a price.

modification (*n.f.*), modification; alteration; variation :
modification d'un contrat, modification, alteration, of a contract.
modifications suggérées par l'expérience, modifications, alterations, suggested by experience.
modification aux statuts, alteration in the articles of association.
modification de risque, variation of risk.

modifier (*v.t.*), to modify; to alter; to vary; to curtail; to reduce :
modifier les clauses d'un contrat, to modify, to vary, the terms of a contract.
modifier sa dépense, to curtail, to reduce, one's expenditure.

modique (*adj.*), moderate :
revenus modiques (*m.pl.*), moderate income.

moi-même [**nous-mêmes** *pl.*] (*pronom*), myself; self :
payez à moi-même, payez à nous-mêmes (écrit sur un chèque), pay self, pay selves.

moins (Arith.) (*n.m.*), minus; minus sign :
il fallait un plus, vous avez mis un moins, you should have put a plus, you have put a minus sign.

moins (Arith.) (*prép.*), minus; less :
dix moins quatre égale six (*Abrév.* : $10 - 4 = 6$), ten minus (*or* less) four equals six (*Abbrev.* : $10 - 4 = 6$).
montant de la vente, moins le courtage, amount of the sale, less brokerage.
dividende, moins les impôts (*m.*), dividend, less tax.
constructions (tant), moins amortissements (tant) (poste de bilan) (*f.pl.*), buildings (so much), less depreciation (so much).

en moins ou en plus, under or over :
toute différence en moins ou en plus (*f.*), any difference under or over.

moins cher, -ère, cheaper.

moins-value [**moins-values** *pl.*] (*n.f.*) (Ant. : *plus-value*), depreciation; decrease of value; decrease in value; decrease; deficit; deficiency :
moins-value du matériel, de l'argent, des valeurs fournies en nantissement, sur les cours des actions, depreciation of plant, of money, of securities lodged as collateral, in the prices of shares.

moins-value résultant des conséquences d'un échouement, depreciation, decrease of (or in) value, resulting from the consequences of a stranding.
moins-value des contributions, deficit in taxes.
être en moins-value, to be down :
l'action X. est en moins-value à 620 contre 645, X. shares were down at 620 against 645 francs.
mois (n.m.) (Abrév. : **m.**), month (one of the 12 parts into which the calendar year is divided) ; calendar month (period equivalent to a month, as from Jan. 15 to Feb. 15) :
obtenir un mois de crédit, to obtain a month's credit.
papier à trois mois ou papier à 3 mois d'échéance (m.), three months' paper ; bills at 3 months.
mois chauds. See under **quatre mois.**
mois civil ou mois commun, calendar month (a month as defined in a calendar ; *distinguished from a* lunar month).
mois courant ou mois en cours, present month ; current month ; instant month.
mois courant (Bourse de marchandises), current month :
le mois courant peut être livré jusqu'au dernier jour du mois en cours, the current month can be delivered up to the last day of the instant month.
mois prochain, next month.
du mois dernier, ultimo.
du mois prochain, proximo.
mois légal, thirty days.
mois (prix convenu pour un mois de travail) (n.m.), month's pay ; month's salary :
toucher son mois, to draw one's month's pay.
môle (jetée) (n.m.), mole.
mollesse (Bourse) (n.f.), easiness ; ease.
mollir (Bourse) (v.i.), to ease :
les actions X. ont molli, les ordinaires à 305 et les privilégiées à 282, X. shares eased, the ordinaries to 305 and the preference to 282 francs.
moment (n.m.), moment ; time :
le cours pratiqué au moment de la réponse des primes, the price ruling at the moment of the declaration of options.
les facultés assurées sont couvertes depuis le moment où elles quittent le magasin de l'expéditeur (f.pl.), the insured goods are covered from the time of leaving the shipper's warehouse.
monde (n.m.), world :
le monde de finance ou le monde financier, the world of finance ; the financial world.
monde des affaires, business world.
les diverses corporations et individualités qui constituent le monde maritime, the diverse corporations and individualities which constitute the shipping world.
monétaire (adj.), monetary ; money (used as adj.) :
l'unité monétaire française est le franc (f.), the French monetary unit is the franc.
marché monétaire (m.), money market.
monétairement (adv.), monetarily.

monétisation (n.f.), monetization.
monétiser (v.t.), to monetize :
monétiser de l'argent, to monetize silver.
Moniteur belge ou **Moniteur Belge** ou *simplement* **Moniteur** (n.m.), the official organ of the Belgian Government, of which the English equivalent is the *London Gazette*, the Scotch the *Edinburgh Gazette*, the Northern Irish the *Belfast Gazette*, the French the *Journal officiel*, q.v.
monnaie (n.f.) ou **monnaies** (n.f.pl.) (argent en général), money ; currency : (See examples below.)
monnaie (pièce) (n.f.), coin ; piece of money : (See examples below.)
monnaie (n.f.) ou **monnaies** (n.f.pl.) ou **monnaie de métal** ou **monnaies de métal** ou **monnaie métallique** (pièces en général), money ; coin ; coins ; coinage ; metallic money ; metallic currency :
monnaies au titre légal, coins of legal fineness.
monnaie banco ou monnaie de banque, banco ; bank money.
monnaie courante ou monnaies en cours, current money ; current coins.
monnaie d'argent ou monnaie-argent (n.f.), silver money ; silver coin ; silver currency ; silver.
monnaie d'or ou monnaie-or (n.f.), gold money ; gold coin ; gold currency ; gold :
les affaires financières internationales qui se traitent à Londres, grâce au prestige d'une monnaie-or inattaquable (f.pl.), the international financial business which is done in London, thanks to the prestige of an unassailable gold currency.
monnaie de billon, copper or nickel coin.
monnaie de change ou monnaie d'échange, money of exchange. *See* monnaie de compte *for example.*
monnaie de compte, money of account :
la monnaie de compte est celle par laquelle les sommes sont exprimées dans les transactions et dans les écritures de commerce : ainsi, en France, la monnaie de compte se compose de la pièce de 1 franc et de la pièce de 1 centime, ou, comme on dit, on compte en France par francs et centimes, money of account is that in which sums are expressed in transactions and in commercial accounts : thus, in France, the money of account consists of the 1 franc piece, and of the 1 centime piece, or, as is said, in France they reckon in francs and centimes.
en France, le franc est à la fois monnaie réelle, monnaie de compte, et monnaie de change, in France, the franc is at the same time real money, money of account, and money of exchange.
la guinée anglaise n'est qu'une monnaie de compte, the English guinea is only a money of account.
monnaie de cuivre ou monnaie de bronze, copper money ; copper coin ; copper.
monnaie de nickel, nickel money ; nickel coin ; nickel.

monnaie de papier, paper money; paper currency; convertible paper money. Cf. **papier-monnaie.**

monnaie divisionnaire *ou* monnaie d'appoint, fractional coins; divisional coins; subsidiary coins (*or* money):

monnaie divisionnaire d'argent, silver fractional (*or* divisional) (*or* subsidiary) coins (*or* money).

le montant du chèque doit être indiqué en toutes lettres. Le montant de la monnaie divisionnaire peut toutefois être indiqué en chiffres seulement, the amount of the cheque must be stated in words at length. The amount of the fractional money can however be stated in figures only.

monnaie droite, standard money.

monnaie effective *ou* monnaie réelle, effective money; effective; real money:

on compte parfois en Angleterre en guinées (de 21 schellings), mais il n'y a plus de monnaie réelle représentant effectivement une guinée, in England we (*or* they) reckon sometimes in guineas (of 21 shillings), but there is no longer any real money actually representing a guinea.

monnaie-étalon (*n.f.*), standard money.

monnaie étrangère, foreign money (*or* currency).

monnaie faible *ou* monnaie légère (opp. à *monnaie forte*), light money; light coin. See example under **pièce.**

monnaie fictive *ou* monnaie fiduciaire *ou* monnaie conventionnelle (opp. à *monnaie droite* ou *intrinsèque*), token money.

monnaie fictive ou monnaie fiduciaire (papier-monnaie), inconvertible paper money; fiat money; fiat paper money; paper money; paper currency.

monnaie forte, overweight money; overweight coin.

monnaie intrinsèque, standard money.

monnaie légale *ou* monnaie libératoire, lawful money; legal tender; legal tender currency:

billets qui sont remboursables en or ou en monnaie légale (*m.pl.*), notes which are redeemable in gold or in lawful money (*or* in gold or in legal tender) (*or* in gold or in legal tender currency).

monnaie nationale, home currency.

monnaie scripturale (opp. à *monnaie effective* ou *monnaie réelle*), representative money.

une lettre de change doit être payée dans la monnaie qu'elle indique, a bill of exchange must be paid in the currency which it names.

la production moderne a besoin d'une monnaie stable, modern production has need of a stable currency.

abaissement du titre de la monnaie (*ou* des monnaies) (*ou* de la monnaie de métal) (*ou* des monnaies de métal) (*m.*), lowering the fineness of the coinage.

monnaie (pièces données en échange) (*n.f.*), change; money:

donner la monnaie de mille francs, to give change for a thousand francs.

Monnaie (l'hôtel des Monnaies) (*n.f.*), mint:

il n'y a qu'une Monnaie en Angleterre, c'es celle de Londres, there is only one mint i England, namely the one in London.

monnayable (*adj.*), coinable:

métaux monnayables (*m.pl.*), coinable metals.

monnayage (*n.m.*), coinage; minting:

monnayage de l'or, coinage, minting, of gold.

monnayer (*v.t.*), to coin; to mint:

monnayer des lingots, to coin, to mint, ingots.

argent monnayé, coined money; minted money

monométallisme (*n.m.*), monometalism; mono metallism.

monométalliste (*adj.*), monometallic:

suivant qu'un État adope un étalon unique o un étalon double il est dit monométalliste o bimétalliste, according as a State adopts single standard or a double standard it is sai to be monometallic or bimetallistic.

pays monométalliste-or (*m.*), gold standar country.

pays monométalliste-argent (*m.*), silver standar country.

monométalliste (pers.) (*n.m.*), monometalist monometallist.

monoplan (*n.m.*), monoplane.

monopole (*n.m.*), monopoly:

monopole qui rend toute concurrence im possible, monopoly which makes an competition impossible.

le monopole est la négation de la concurrence monopoly is the negation of competition.

monopole d'État, Government monopoly.

monopole de fait, de facto monopoly.

monopoleur *ou* **monopolisateur** (pers.) (*n.m.*) monopolist.

monopolisation (*n.f.*), monopolization.

monopoliser (*v.t.*), to monopolize:

monopoliser la vente du tabac, to monopoliz the sale of tobacco.

montant (*n.m.*), amount; total:

montant brut d'une facture, gross amount o an invoice.

montant d'un effet de commerce, amount contents, of a bill of exchange.

montant global, total amount; sum total.

montant des dépenses, amount of the ex penses; total expenses.

montant de la prime (Bourse), option money

spéculateur qui abandonne la prime et limit sa perte à tant, le montant de la prime (*m.*) speculator who abandons the option and limits his loss at so much, the option money

monter (atteindre un total de) (*v.i.*), to amount

la dépense monte à tant, the expenses amount t so much.

monter (atteindre un prix plus élevé) (*v.i.*), t rise; to go up:

valeur qui va monter (*f.*), stock which is going to rise (*or* which is going to go up).

monter à bord d'un navire, to go on board a ship

montrer (*v.t.*), to show; to shew:

la différence de ces deux sommes montre l'importance du bénéfice ou de la perte, th difference between these two sums shows th amount of the profit or of the loss.

moratoire (*adj.*), moratory. *Cf.* intérêts de retard *ou* intérêts moratoires.

moratorium [**moratoria** *pl.*] (*n.m.*), moratorium: établissements de crédit qui se prévalurent du moratorium pour ne pas rembourser leurs dépôts dans les premiers mois de la guerre (*m.pl.*), credit institutions who took advantage of the moratorium in order not to repay their deposits during the first months of the war.

mort (*n.f.*), death; decease.

morte-saison [**mortes-saisons** *pl.*] (*n.f.*), dead season.

mot (*n.m.*), word:
mot artificiel (Télégr.), artificial word (pronounceable group of letters having the appearance of a real word).
mot convenu *ou* mot de code (Télégr.), code word.
mot convenu de contrôle, check code word; check word.
mot en clair, en convenu, en chiffré (Télégr.), word in plain language, in code, in cipher.
mot mutilé (Télégr.), mutilated word.
mot réel (Télégr.), real word.
mot taxé (Télégr.), word charged for.
mots guides (vérification par analogie) (Téléph.), identification words:

Français		Anglais	
A	Anatole	A	Alfred
B	Benjamin	B	Benjamin
C	Célestin	C	Charlie
D	Désiré	D	David
E	Édouard	E	Edward
F	François	F	Frederick
G	Gaston	G	George
H	Henri	H	Harry
I	Isidore	I	Isaac
J	Joseph	J	Jack
K	Kléber	K	King
L	Lazare	L	Lucy
M	Marie	M	Mary
N	Nicolas	N	Nellie
O	Oscar	O	Oliver
P	Pierre	P	Peter
Q	Québec	Q	Queenie
R	Robert	R	Robert
S	Samuel	S	Sally
T	Théodor	T	Tommy
U	Ursule	U	Uncle
V	Victor	V	Victor
W	William	W	William
X	Xavier	X	Xmas
Y	Yvonne	Y	Yellow
Z	Zoé	Z	Zebra

moteur-citerne [**moteurs-citernes** *pl.*] (*n.m.*) *ou* **bateau-citerne à moteur** (*m.*) *ou* **navire-citerne à moteur** (*m.*), motor tanker.

motocyclette (*n.f.*), motor bicycle.

mou, mol (*devant une voyelle*), **molle** (Bourse) (*adj.*), easy:
l'action X. est molle à 728, X. shares are easy at 728 francs.

mouillage (manœuvre) (*n.m.*), anchoring; mooring; berthing.

mouillage (lieu de mouillage) (*n.m.*), anchorage; moorings; berth; berthage:
navire en mouillage dans un port (*m.*), ship at anchorage in a port.

mouiller (*v.t.*), to anchor; to moor; to berth.

mouiller (*v.i.*), to anchor; to moor; to berth.

mouilleur (pour timbres-poste, étiquettes, etc.) (*n.m.*), damper (for postage stamps, labels, etc.).

mouillure (*n.f.*), wetting:
mouillure par eau de mer, par eau douce (cause d'avaries), wetting by sea water, by fresh water.

mousse (pers.) (*n.m.*), boy; ship boy.

mouvement (*n.m.*). See examples:
mouvements de capitaux tels que les émissions à l'étranger ou le remboursement de crédits, movements of money such as issues abroad or the repayment of credits.
un mouvement ascensionnel (*ou* un mouvement de hausse) des valeurs, an upward movement of stocks.
mouvement des valeurs, de l'argent, du papier, circulation of securities, of money, of paper.
mouvement de bourse, stock exchange fluctuation.
le mouvement des ports maritimes français, the traffic of French seaports.
mouvement (circulation; ventes) (Bourse de marchandises), turnover; sales:
mouvement: 000 tonnes, turnover (*or* sales): 000 tons.
Mouvement des Navires (rubrique de journal), Shipping News; Shipping Intelligence; Shipping; Movements of Ships.
mouvement populaire, civil commotion.
tous les mouvements d'espèces sont inscrits sur un registre appelé livre de caisse, all the cash transactions are entered in a book called cash book.
les mouvements des valeurs de la banque, the bank's transactions in securities.

moyen, -enne (calculé en faisant la moyenne) (*adj.*), average; mean; middle:
cours moyen (*m.*), average price; middle price.
échéance moyenne (*f.*), average due date; mean due date.

moyennant (*prép.*), in consideration of; on; at:
moyennant le versement (*ou* moyennant paiement) d'une somme convenue, in consideration of the payment of an agreed sum.
moyennant l'attribution de 0 actions entièrement libérées, in consideration of the allotment of 0 fully paid shares.
moyennant prime à débattre, at a premium to be arranged.

moyenne (*n.f.*), average; mean:
prendre la moyenne, to take the average.
moyenne entre le plus haut et le plus bas cours, average between the highest and the lowest price.
moyenne d'achat (Bourse), purchase average.
moyenne de vente (Bourse), sale average.

moyennes (Bourse) (*n.f.pl.*), averaging:
les moyennes se pratiquent pour défendre une

mauvaise position, averaging is done to protect a bad position.

réduire la perte par des moyennes, to reduce the loss by averaging.

Cf. faire une moyenne *and* se faire une moyenne.

moyennement (*adv.*) *ou* **en moyenne**, on an average :
objets vendus de 10 à 15 francs moyennement (*ou* en moyenne) (*m.pl.*), articles sold from 10 to 15 francs on an average.

moyens (ressources) (*n.m.pl.*), means :
avoir des moyens, to have means.
moyens de production, means of production.

multiplan (*n.m.*), multiplane.

multiple (*n.m.*), multiple :
beaucoup de sociétés émettent des actions dites multiples, c'est-à-dire des unités et des coupures de 5, 10, 25, 50, ou 100 actions, many companies issue shares called multiples, that is to say, ones and denominations of 5, 10, 25, 50, or 100 shares.
les bons sont du nominal de 20 francs et multiples (*m.pl.*), the bonds are of the nominal value of 20 francs and multiples.

multiplication (*n.f.*), multiplication.

multiplier (*v.t.*), to multiply :
deux multiplié par trois égale six (*Abrév. :* $2 \times 3 = 6$), two multiplied by three equals six (*Abbrev. :* $2 \times 3 = 6$).

munir (*v.t.*), to provide :
navire muni de tous ses papiers (*m.*), ship provided with all her papers.
le voyageur doit, lorsqu'il commence son voyage, être muni d'un billet, the traveller

should, when be begins his journey, be provided with a ticket.

se munir (*v.r.*), to provide oneself :
se munir d'argent, to provide oneself with money.

munitions de bouche (*f.pl.*), provisions ; food ; victuals.

munitions de guerre (*f.pl.*), munitions of war.

mutation (Dr.) (*n.f.*), transfer ; conveyance ; transmission :
mutation de biens *ou* mutation de propriété, transfer, conveyance, of property.
mutation d'hypothèque, transfer of mortgage.
mutation en douane, transfer (of ownership of vessel) at the registry of shipping.
mutation entre vifs, transfer inter vivos.
mutation par décès (succession), transmission on death.

mutation d'entrepôt (Douanes) (*f.*), removal (of goods) under bond.

mutatis mutandis, mutatis mutandis :
les conditions sont les mêmes, mutatis mutandis (*f.pl.*), the conditions are the same, mutatis mutandis.

mutilé, -e (*adj.*), mutilated ; damaged :
titre mutilé (*m.*), mutilated certificate ; damaged bond.

mutinerie (*n.f.*), mutiny.

mutuel, -elle (*adj.*), mutual :
assurance mutuelle (*f.*), mutual insurance ; mutual assurance.

mutuelliste *ou* **mutualiste** (pers.) (*n.m.* ou *f.*), member of a mutual company (*or* society) (e.g. a mutual insurance company or society).

N

nantir (donner des gages pour garantir une dette, un prêt) (*v.t.*), to secure ; to give as security ; to hypothecate ; to pledge :
nantir un prêteur par hypothèque, to secure a lender by a mortgage ; to give a lender a mortgage as security.
dans le report, le prêteur est nanti d'un titre, in contangoing, the lender is secured by a stock.
nantir des valeurs, to hypothecate, to pledge, securities.
actions nanties en garantie de fonds avancés (*f.pl.*), shares hypothecated (*or* pledged) as security for money advanced.
créancier nanti (*m.*), secured creditor.
créancier partiellement nanti (*m.*), partly secured creditor.
créancier entièrement (*ou* complètement) nanti (*m.*), fully secured creditor.

se nantir (*v.r.*), to secure oneself :
se nantir par hypothèque, to secure oneself by mortgage.

nantir (pourvoir ; munir) (*v.t.*), to provide :
être nanti (-e) des fonds destinés au paiement d'un effet, to be provided with the money to pay a bill.

se nantir (*v.r.*), to provide oneself :
se nantir de l'argent, to provide oneself with money.

nantissement (action) (*n.m.*), hypothecation ; pledging :
nantissement en garantie d'avances, hypothecation as security for advances.

nantissement (ce qui est remis en garantie) (*n.m.*), security ; collateral security ; collateral ; pledge :
prêter de l'argent sur nantissement, to lend money on security (*or* on collateral) (*or* on collateral security).
prêt sur nantissement de marchandises (*m.*), loan on security of goods.
titres remis (*ou* déposés) (*ou* fournis) en nantissement (*m.pl.*) *ou* valeurs remises (*ou* déposées) (*ou* fournies) en nantissement

(*f.pl.*), securities lodged as collateral; hypothecated securities; securities pledged.

donner un effet à titre de nantissement, to give a bill by way of collateral security (*or* as collateral).

nantissement (acte de nantissement) (*n.m.*), letter of hypothecation; hypothecation certificate.

nation (*n.f.*), nation:

nation la plus favorisée (Écon. polit.), most favoured nation.

national, -e, -aux (*adj.*), national.

nationalisation (*n.f.*), nationalization:

nationalisation d'une industrie, des chemins de fer, nationalization of an industry, of railways.

nationaliser (*v.t.*), to nationalize.

nationalité (*n.f.*), nationality:

navire de nationalité française, britannique (*m.*), ship of French, British, nationality.

la nationalité permet au navire de porter le pavillon national, et de réclamer la protection de son gouvernement ou de ses représentants, nationality enables the ship to carry the national flag, and to claim the protection of her government or its representatives.

nature (en), in kind:

rémunérations en nature (logement, nourriture, etc.) (*f.pl.*), remuneration in kind (lodging, food, etc.).

naufrage (*n.m.*), wreck; shipwreck:

le naufrage de la *Lutine* qui se perdit le 10 octobre 1799, à l'entrée du Zuyderzée, the wreck of the *Lutine* which was lost on the 10th October 1799, at the entrance to the Zuider Zee.

sauver quelque chose du naufrage, to save something from the wreck.

naufragé, -e (*adj.*), wrecked; shipwrecked:

navire naufragé (*m.*), wrecked (*or* shipwrecked) vessel.

marchandises naufragées (*f.pl.*), wrecked cargo.

personnes naufragées (*f.pl.*) *ou* **naufragés** (*n.m.pl.*), shipwrecked persons.

nautique (*adj.*), nautical:

science nautique (*f.*), nautical science.

navigabilité (*n.f.*), navigability; navigableness; seaworthiness:

garantie de navigabilité (*f.*), warranty of seaworthiness.

navigabilité (d'un aéroplane) (*n.f.*), airworthiness.

navigable (*adj.*), navigable; seaworthy; airworthy:

fleuve navigable (*m.*), navigable river.

navigation (*n.f.*), navigation; sailing; shipping:

navigation entre la France et l'Algérie, navigation between France and Algeria.

les difficultés de la navigation du Rhin (*ou* de la navigation rhénane) (*f.pl.*), the difficulties of the navigation of the Rhine (*or* of navigating the Rhine) (*or* of Rhine navigation).

fausse navigation du navire, improper navigation of the ship.

l'arrimage se lie à la stabilité du navire et intéresse ainsi la sécurité de la navigation (*m.*), stowing is bound up with the stability of the

ship and thus concerns the safety of the navigation.

compagnie de navigation (*f.*), shipping company; navigation company.

navigation à vapeur, steam navigation; steaming.

navigation à voile, sail navigation; sailing.

navigation aérienne, aerial navigation; air navigation; aviation.

navigation au (*ou* de) cabotage *ou* navigation de côte, coasting navigation; coastwise navigation.

navigation au long cours, deep-sea navigation; ocean navigation.

navigation au tramping, tramp navigation.

navigation d'escale, port of call navigation.

navigation de plaisance, pleasure navigation.

navigation fluviale *ou* navigation intérieure, inland navigation; inside navigation; internal navigation:

la supériorité économique du chemin de fer sur la navigation intérieure, the economic superiority of the railway over inland navigation.

navigation maritime, maritime navigation.

navigation mixte, maritime and internal navigation.

naviguer (*v.i.*), to navigate; to sail:

navire inapte à naviguer (*m.*), ship incapable of navigating.

avec faculté de naviguer avec ou sans pilotes, with leave to sail with or without pilots.

naviguer sur, to navigate (*v.t.*); to sail (*v.t.*); to sail on:

un navire n'existe dans le vrai sens du terme que s'il est apte à naviguer sur mer, a ship does not exist in the true sense of the term unless she is capable of navigating (*or* sailing) (*or* sailing on) the sea (*or* fit to sail the sea) (*or* fit to sail on the sea).

navire (*n.m.*), ship; vessel; boat; bottom: (See also **bateau, bâtiment, bord, paquebot, steamer,** and **vapeur.**)

navire à deux hélices, twin screw ship.

navire à émigrants, emigrant ship.

navire à moteur, motorship; motor vessel; power vessel.

navire à ordre, ship under orders.

navire à passagers *ou* navire à voyageurs, passenger ship; passenger boat; passenger vessel.

navire à passagers (*ou* à voyageurs) et à marchandises, cargo and passenger ship.

navire à vapeur, steamship; steamer.

navire à vapeur au long cours, ocean-going steamer; foreign-going steamer.

navire à voiles, sailing ship; sailing vessel; sailer.

navire abandonné, derelict.

navire abordé, ship collided with:

navire abordeur *ou* navire abordant, colliding ship:

le dommage occasionné par le navire abordeur au navire abordé, the damage caused by the colliding ship to the ship collided with.

navire affrété *ou* navire frété, chartered vessel.

navire au cabotage *ou* navire de cabotage *ou*

navire caboteur *ou* navire côtier, coasting vessel; coasting ship; coaster; home-trade ship.

navire au long cours *ou* navire long-courrier [navires long-courriers *pl.*], foreign-going ship; ocean-going vessel.

navire charbonnier, coal ship; collier.

navire chargé, laden ship:
navire chargé ou sur lest, ship laden or in ballast.

navire-citerne [navires-citernes *pl.*] (*n.m.*), tank ship; tank vessel; tanker.

navire-citerne à moteur, motor tanker.

navire composé *ou* navire composite (fer et bois), composite vessel.

navire courrier postal [navires courriers postaux *pl.*], mail steamer.

navire de charge *ou* navire à cargaison, cargo boat; cargo vessel; freighter.

navire de commerce *ou* navire marchand, trading vessel; merchant vessel; merchant-man.

navire de haute mer, deep-sea vessel.

navire de mer, seagoing vessel.

navire de plaisance, pleasure vessel.

navire de première cote, first class vessel (i.e., rated in the first class).

navire des Grands Lacs, Lake vessel.

navire désigné, named ship; nominated ship.

navire en acier, steel ship.

navire en béton, concrete ship.

navire en bois, wooden vessel.

navire en construction, ship in course of building.

navire en détresse, ship in distress.

navire en fer, iron ship.

navire en mer, ship at sea.

navire en partance *ou* navire effectuant son voyage d'aller, outward bound vessel; outbound vessel; outward bounder. Cf. **partance.**

navire en retour *ou* navire effectuant son voyage de retour, homeward bound vessel; home bound vessel; inward bound vessel; inbound vessel.

navire ennemi, enemy ship.

navire excursionniste, excursion ship.

navire exportateur *ou* navire d'exportation, exporting ship; export ship.

navire frigorifique, refrigerated vessel.

navire garde-côte, coast-defence ship.

navire importateur *ou* navire d'importation, importing ship; import ship.

navire indemne (Quarantaine), clean ship.

navire infecté (Quarantaine), infected ship.

navire jumeau *ou* navire frère, twin ship; sister ship.

navire lent *ou* navire omnibus, slow boat.

navire marchant à vide, ship going light; light vessel.

navire métallique, metal vessel.

navire mixte (voyageurs et marchandises), cargo and passenger ship.

navire mixte (moitié en bois, moitié en fer), composite vessel.

navire neutre, neutral ship.

navire pétrolier, oil ship; oiler.

navire rapide *ou* navire express *ou* navire de grande vitesse, fast boat.

navire régulier *ou* navire à parcours régulier *ou* navire de ligne régulière, regular boat; liner.

navire relâcheur, calling ship:
navires relâcheurs qui charbonnent, calling ships which coal.

navire sans nouvelles *ou* navire perdu sans nouvelles, missing ship.

navire sauveteur, salvage vessel.

navire sur (*ou* en) lest, ship in ballast.

navire suspect (Quarantaine), suspected ship.

navire tramp [navires tramps *pl.*] *ou* navire de tramping *ou* navire vagabond *ou* navire irrégulier, tramp; tramp steamer; ocean tramp.

navire type [navires types *pl.*], standard ship.

ne dépassant pas, not exceeding:
taxe: ne dépassant pas 1 kilogramme, tant; au-dessus de 1 kilo jusqu'à 2 kilos, tant, charge: not exceeding 1 kilogramme, so much; exceeding 1 kilo but not exceeding 2 kilos, so much.

Cf. **jusqu'à concurrence de,** under **jusqu'à.**

ne répond pas (Téléph.), sorry, there's no reply; I am sorry there is no reply; no reply.

ne répondant pas des marques, de la casse (mention de connaissement), ship not responsible for marks, for breakages.

néant (*n.m.*), none; nil:
mettre le mot « néant » sur un article de compte, to put the word " none " (*or* " nil ") against an item of account (in order to show that there is no income or expenditure under that head).

nécessaire (*adj.*), necessary.

nécessaire (*n.m.*), necessary:
nous vous prions de vouloir bien faire le nécessaire pour le recouvrement de cette créance (*ou* pour recouvrer cette créance), we beg you to have the kindness to do the necessary for the recovery of this debt (*or* to recover this debt).

nécessairement (*adv.*), necessarily.

nécessité (*n.f.*), necessity:
marchandises sacrifiées pour les nécessités du bord (*f.pl.*), cargo sacrificed for the necessities of the ship.

négatif, -ive (*adj.*), negative.

négativement (*adv.*), negatively; in the negative.

négligé, -e (*adj. & p.p.*), neglected:
les fonds mexicains demeurent négligés (Bourse) (*m.pl.*), Mexican stocks remain neglected.

négligence (*n.f.*) (*s'emploie quelquefois au pluriel*), negligence; neglect; default:
négligence (*ou* négligences) du capitaine ou des gens de mer, negligence, neglect, default, of master or mariners.

négligence-clause (Assce mar.) (*n.f.*), negligence clause.

négligent, -e (*adj.*), negligent.

négoce (*n.m.*), trade; trading; commerce; business:
le négoce enrichit une nation, trade enriches a nation.

négociabilité (*n.f.*), negotiability :
négociabilité d'un billet, negotiability of a bill.
négociable (*adj.*), negotiable ; dealable ; marketable :
papier négociable (effets) (*m.*), negotiable paper.
titres négociables en bourse (*m.pl.*), stocks negotiable (*or* dealable) (*or* marketable) on the stock exchange.
mandat qui n'est pas négociable et ne peut donc être endossé (*m.*), order which is not negotiable and cannot therefore be endorsed.
négociant, -e (pers.) (*n.*), trader ; merchant :
négociant-commissionnaire [négociants-commissionnaires *pl.*] (*n.m.*), commission merchant.
négociateur, -trice (pers.) (*n.*), negotiator :
les négociateurs d'un traité, the negotiators of a treaty.
négociation (action) (*n.f.*), negotiation ; transaction ; dealing : (See also **opération**.)
négociation d'un emprunt, negotiation of a loan.
négociation (affaire) (*n.f.*) (Abrév. : **négoc.**),
negotiation ; transaction ; dealing ; deal ; bargain :
négociation à prime (Bourse), option bargain ; option deal ; option.
négociations à prime (Bourse), option dealing ; dealing in options ; option dealings ; option bargains ; option deals.
négociation à terme (Bourse de valeurs), dealing for the settlement ; bargain for account.
négociation au comptant, cash transaction ; cash deal ; dealing for cash ; bargain for cash ; bargain for money.
négociations de change à terme, forward exchange transactions (*or* dealings) ; exchange for forward (*or* future) delivery.
négociations de change au comptant, spot exchange transactions (*or* dealings) ; exchange for spot delivery.
négociation (vente ou transmission des effets de commerce ou lettres de change) (*n.f.*), negotiation :
négociation d'un effet, negotiation of a bill.
négocier (traiter une affaire) (*v.t.*), to negotiate :
négocier un emprunt, une vente, to negotiate a loan, a sale.
négocier (passer un effet de commerce) (*v.t.*), to negotiate :
négocier une lettre de change, to negotiate a bill of exchange.
négocier (*v.i.*), to negotiate ; to deal ; to treat ; to trade :
il refuse de négocier avec lui, he refuses to deal (*or* to negotiate) (*or* to treat) with him.
négocier en Amérique, to trade in America.
se négocier (*v.r.*), to be negotiated ; to be dealt in :
le papier à plus de trois mois se négocie difficilement, paper at more than three months is negotiated with difficulty.
il se négocie à la Bourse de Paris des titres de toutes sortes, all kinds of securities are dealt in on the Paris Bourse.
nemine contradicente, nemine contradicente, *usually abbreviated* nem. con.

net, nette (*adj.*) (Ant. : *brut*), net ; nett :
prix net (*m.*), net price.
net produit (*ou* produit net) d'une vente (*m.*), net proceeds of a sale.
net produit (*ou* produit net) d'un effet (*m.*), proceeds, net avails, of a bill.
somme nette (*f.*) *ou* montant net (*m.*), net amount.
net (nette) d'impôt (*ou* **d'impôts**), free of tax ; tax free :
dividende de 5 0/0 net d'impôt (*m.*), dividend of 5% free of tax.
intérêts nets d'impôts (*m.pl.*), interest free of tax ; tax free interest.
net (nette) d'impôt sur le revenu, free of income tax. *Cf.* demi-net.
net (*n.m.*), net ; net amount, result, proceeds, weight, or the like :
le net à porter au crédit du client, the net amount to be carried to the customer's credit.
le net d'une vente, the net proceeds of a sale.
le net de l'opération, the net result of the transaction.
net d'un effet, proceeds, net avails, of a bill.
marchandises imposées au net (*f.pl.*), goods charged with duty on the net weight (*or* on the net).
net légal, net réel. *Same as* poids net légal, poids net réel, *q.v.*
neutralité (*n.f.*), neutrality :
neutralité d'un navire, neutrality of a ship.
neutre (*adj.*), neutral :
pavillon neutre (*m.*), neutral flag.
neutre (*n.m.*), neutral :
les devoirs des neutres en cas de guerre (*m.pl.*), the duties of neutrals in case of war.
nigériennes (*n.f.pl.*) *ou* **valeurs nigériennes** (*f.pl.*), Nigerians ; Nigerian shares.
nitratières (*n.f.pl.*) *ou* **valeurs nitratières** (*f.pl.*), nitrates ; nitrate shares.
niveau (*n.m.*), level :
maintenir les prix à un niveau élevé, to maintain prices at a high level.
niveau d'ensemble des cours, general level of prices.
niveler (*v.t.*), to level :
niveler des taux, des cours, to level rates, prices :
rétablir l'équilibre de l'offre et de la demande sur les deux places, et de niveler les cours, to reestablish the equilibrium of demand and supply on the two markets, and level prices.
niveler les cours (Arbitrage sur des lettres de change), to bring the rates to level time (*or* to the same level).
nivellement des cours (*m.*), bringing the rates to level time (*or* to the same level).
no cure no pay. *See* clause « no cure no pay. »
nœud (Navig.) (*n.m.*), knot :
la vitesse des navires s'exprime en nœuds, the speed of ships is expressed in knots.
un cargo de 10 nœuds, a cargo boat of 10 knots ; a 10-knot cargo boat.

nolis *ou* **nolage** (terme employé surtout dans la Méditerranée) (*n.m.*), freight.

nolisement *ou* **nolissement** (*n.m.*), freighting; chartering; charterage; charter; affreightment.

noliser (*v.t.*), to freight; to charter; to affreight.

nom (*n.m.*), name:

nom du porteur, de l'envoyeur, du titre, de la valeur, d'un compte, name of bearer, of sender, of stock, of the security, of an account.

tout navire doit avoir un nom, every ship must have a name.

nom actuel (d'un navire), present name (of a ship).

nom ancien *ou* ex-nom (d'un navire), late name.

prendre le nom et l'adresse (*ou* les nom et adresse) de quelqu'un, to take someone's name and address.

les nom, prénoms, adresse, et profession (*ou* et qualités) du souscripteur, the full name (*or* the name in full), address, and profession or business (*or* and occupation) (*or* and description) of the applicant.

nom commercial, business name; trade name.

nom de baptême, Christian name.

nom de convention *ou* nom conventionnel (Télégr.), arbitrary name.

nom de famille *ou* nom patronymique, surname.

nom social, name of firm; corporate name; style; name and style.

sous un nom interposé, in a nominee's name.

nombre (*n.m.*), number:

nombre de colis, number of packages; quantity.

nombre cardinal, cardinal number; cardinal.

nombre décimal, decimal number.

nombre des adhérents *ou* nombre des adhésions, membership:

la durée de cette association est illimitée ainsi que le nombre des adhérents, qui peuvent être recrutés aussi bien en province qu'à Paris, the duration of this association is unlimited as well as the membership, which may be recruited as well in the country as in Paris.

nombre entier, whole number.

nombre fractionnaire, fractional number.

nombre-indice [nombres-indices *pl.*] *ou* nombre indicateur (Écon.), index number.

nombre ordinal, ordinal number; ordinal.

nombre pair, even number.

nombre impair, odd number; uneven number.

en nombre rond, in round numbers.

nous avons un grand nombre de ces titres en portefeuille, we have a large number of these shares in our box; we have a big holding of these shares.

nombre (comptes courants, ou analogues) (*n.m.*), product; number:

nombre rouge, red product.

nombre noir, black product.

méthode des nombres (*f.*), product method.

nomenclature (*n.f.*), nomenclature; name:

récépissé qui porte la nomenclature complète de la valeur déposée (*m.*), receipt which contains the full name of the security lodged.

nominal, -e, -aux (*adj.*), nominal:

société au capital nominal de tant (*f.*), company with a nominal (*or* an authorized) (*or* a registered) capital of so much.

valeur nominale (*f.*) *ou* **nominal** (*n.m.*), nominal value; face value:

la valeur nominale (*ou* le nominal) d'une action, the nominal value (*or* the face value) of a share.

les bons sont de la valeur nominale (*ou* sont du nominal) de 250 francs et multiples; la valeur nominale (*ou* le nominal) des obligations est de 500 francs, the bonds are of the nominal value (*or* are of the face value) of 250 francs and multiples; the nominal value (*or* the face value) of the debentures is 500 francs.

la valeur nominale (*ou* le nominal) d'un effet, the face value of a bill.

un taux purement nominal, a purely nominal rate.

en clôture, les cours restent nominaux, at the close, prices remained nominal.

sucre de Java.—mars-avril 10/10 1/2d. nominal (*ou* en abrév.: 10/10 1/2 nom. *ou* 10/10 1/2 n.) caf., Java sugar.—March-April 10/10½d. nominal c.i.f.

l'escompte est nominal lorsque les effets négociables sont rares sur le marché, ou lorsqu'ils sont peu ou pas demandés (*m.*), discount is nominal when negotiable bills are scarce on the market, or when there is little or no demand. Cf. **facile** and **serré**.

nominalement (*adv.*), nominally.

nominatif, -ive (en parlant des titres) (*adj.*) (opp. à au porteur) (Abrév.: **nom.**), registered:

actions nominatives (*f.pl.*) *ou* titres nominatifs (*m.pl.*) *ou* valeurs nominatives (*f.pl.*) *ou* effets nominatifs (*m.pl.*), registered shares; registered stock; registered securities.

nominatif, -ive (qui contient des noms) (*adj.*), nominal; of names; of the names:

liste nominative des actionnaires (*f.*), list of names, nominal list, of shareholders.

nomination (*n.f.*), nomination; appointment; election.

nommer (choisir) (*v.t.*), to nominate; to appoint; to elect; to choose:

nommer un comité, les premiers administrateurs d'une société, to appoint a committee, the first directors of a company.

être nommé (-e) à la présidence d'une assemblée, to be elected (*or* to be chosen) chairman, to be elected to the presidency, of a meeting.

L'emploi du trait d'union entre la particule négative **non** *et le mot suivant est facultatif, tant en français qu'en anglais.*

non acceptable (*adj.*), unacceptable; not acceptable.

non acceptation (d'un effet) (*n.f.*), dishonour; dishonour by non acceptance; non acceptance.

non acceptation ou non paiement (d'un effet), dishonour:
pour les effets documentaires le remetteur doit indiquer à la banque un correspondant auquel elle doit remettre les documents en cas de non acceptation ou de non paiement, as to documentary bills the remitter should mention to the bank a correspondent to whom it should send the documents in case of dishonour.

non accepté, -e (*adj.*), unaccepted:
effet non accepté (*m.*), dishonoured bill; bill dishonoured by non acceptance; unaccepted bill.

non accomplissement (*n.m.*), non fulfilment.

non acquitté, -e (Douanes) (*adj.*), uncustomed (having paid no duty):
marchandises non acquittées (*f.pl.*), uncustomed goods.

non affranchi, -e (Poste ou colis) (*adj.*), unpaid:
taxer une lettre comme non affranchie, to charge a letter as unpaid.

non affrété, -e (*adj.*), unchartered.

non amorti, -e (*adj.*), unredeemed.

non amortissable (*adj.*), unredeemable; irredeemable:
obligations non amortissables (*f.pl.*), unredeemable bonds; irredeemable debentures.

non appelé, -e (*adj.*), uncalled; not called:
capital non appelé (*m.*) ou **non appelé** (*n.m.*), uncalled capital.

non arrivée (*n.f.*), non arrival.

non assuré, -e (*adj.*), uninsured.

non avarié, -e ou **non endommagé, -e** (*adj.*), undamaged.

non bancable (*adj.*), unbankable:
effet non bancable (*m.*), unbankable bill.

non chargé, -e (Poste) (*adj.*), uninsured:
colis non chargé (*m.*), uninsured parcel.

non commerçant, -e (*adj.*), non trading.

non commerçant, -e (pers.) (*n.*), non trader.

non concordance (*n.f.*), disagreement.

non cotation (Bourse) (*n.f.*), non quotation.

non coté, -e (Bourse) (*adj.*) (Abrév.: **n.c.**), unquoted; not quoted:
valeurs non cotées (*f.pl.*), unquoted securities (*or* stocks).
valeurs non cotées officiellement (*f.pl.*), securities (*or* stocks) not quoted officially.

non coté, -e (navires) (*adj.*), not classed.

non cumulatif, -ive (*adj.*), non cumulative:
dividende non cumulatif (*m.*), non cumulative dividend.

non daté, -e (*adj.*), undated; not dated:
lettre non datée (*f.*), undated letter.

non déclaré, -e (*adj.*), undeclared; unentered; not entered (at customs):
expédition non déclarée (*f.*), unentered shipment; shipment not entered.

non distribué, -e (Poste) (*adj.*), undelivered:
correspondances non distribuées (*f.pl.*), undelivered postal packets.

non emballé, -e (*adj.*), unpacked.

non embarquement (*n.m.*), non shipment.

non enregistré, -e (*adj.*), unregistered.

non exécution (*n.f.*), non execution; non performance:
non exécution des clauses d'un contrat, non execution of the terms of a contract.

non expiré, -e ou **non échu, -e** ou **non couru, -e** (*adj.*), unexpired:
temps non expiré (ou non couru) (d'une police d'assurance) (*m.*), unexpired time (of a policy of insurance).
effet non échu (*m.*), unexpired bill.

non franco de port, carriage forward; carriage to pay.

non garanti, -e (*adj.*), unsecured:
créance non garantie (*f.*), unsecured debt.

non garantie (*n.f.*), non warranty.

non gréviste (pers.) (*n.m.* ou *f.*), non striker.

non imposition (*n.f.*), non assessment.

non libéré, -e (*adj.*) (Abrév.: **non lib.**) ou **non entièrement** (ou **non complètement**) (ou **non intégralement**) **libéré, -e** ou **non entièrement versé, -e,** partly paid; partly paid up:
actions non libérées ou actions non entièrement (ou non complètement) (ou non intégralement) libérées (*f.pl.*) ou titres non libérés (*m.pl.*), partly paid shares. See note as to methods of quoting partly paid shares under **action**.
capital non entièrement versé ou capital non libéré (*m.*), partly paid capital; capital partly paid up.

non livraison ou **non remise** (*n.f.*), non delivery:
non livraison de titres, non delivery of stock.

non livré, -e (*adj.*), undelivered:
colis non livré (*m.*), undelivered parcel.

non membre (pers.) (*n.m.*), non member.

non navigabilité (*n.f.*), non navigability; unseaworthiness.

non négociable (*adj.*), non negotiable; not negotiable:
billet non négociable (*m.*), non negotiable note.
chèque revêtu de la mention non négociable (*m.*), cheque bearing the words not negotiable. *See full example under* chèque barré « non négociable. »
Cf. example under **négociable**.

non officiel, -elle (*adj.*), unofficial.

non ouvert, -e (*adj.*), unopened:
lettre non ouverte (*f.*), unopened letter.

non paiement ou **non payement** (*n.m.*), non payment:
non paiement d'une prime échue, non payment of a premium due.

non paiement (d'un effet) (*n.m.*), dishonour; dishonour by non payment (of a bill).

non parvenu, -e (*p.p.* ou *adj.*), miscarried:
réclamations concernant les mandats non parvenus, concernant les mandats présumés non parvenus (*f.pl.*), applications concerning money orders which have miscarried, concerning orders presumed to have miscarried.

non payé, -e (*adj.*), unpaid:
droits non payés (*m.pl.*), unpaid duties.

non périmé, -e (*adj.*), unexpired:
carte d'abonnement non périmée (*f.*), unexpired season ticket.

non pesé, -e (*adj.*), unweighed.
non professionnel, -elle (*adj.*), non professional.
non professionnel, -elle (pers.) (*n.*), non professional. See example under **professionnel**.
non prohibé, -e (*adj.*), unprohibited.
non prononçable (*adj.*), unpronounceable:
groupe de lettres non prononçable (Télégr.) (*m.*), unpronounceable group of letters.
non protesté, -e (*adj.*), unprotested:
effet non protesté (*m.*), unprotested bill.
non réalisé, -e (*adj.*), unrealized.
non réclamé, -e (*adj.*), unclaimed:
dividende non réclamé (*m.*), unclaimed dividend.
bagages non réclamés (*m.pl.*), unclaimed luggage.
non recommandé, -e (Poste) (*adj.*), unregistered:
lettre non recommandée (*f.*), unregistered letter.
non réhabilité, -e (*adj.*), undischarged:
failli non réhabilité (*m.*), undischarged bankrupt.
non responsabilité (*n.f.*), non liability.
non restituable *ou* **non remboursable** (*adj.*), not returnable; non returnable; not repayable; earned:
fret payé d'avance et non restituable en cas de sinistre (*m.*), freight paid in advance and not (*or* non) returnable in case of loss.
non signé, -e (*adj.*), unsigned:
lettre non signée (*f.*), unsigned letter.
non timbré, -e (*adj.*), unstamped:
effet non timbré (*m.*), unstamped bill.
non utilisé, -e *ou* **non employé, -e** (*adj.*), unused:
timbres non utilisés (*ou* non employés) (*m.pl.*), unusued stamps.
non valeur (état d'une propriété qui ne produit rien) (*n.f.*), unproductiveness; unproductivity:
la non valeur d'une propriété, the unproductiveness of a property.
non valeur [**non valeurs** *pl.*] (mauvaise créance) (*n.f.*), bad debt.
non valeur (titre de bourse sans valeur) (*n.f.*), worthless security; valueless stock.
non valeurs (choses dépourvues de valeur, par exemple, figurines détériorées) (*n.f.pl.*), valueless stock.
non vente (*n.f.*), no sale:
les jours de non vente (*m.pl.*), the no sale days.
non versé, -e (*adj.*), unpaid:
montant non versé (*m.*) *ou* **non versé** (*n.m.*), unpaid amount; amount unpaid.
non versement (*n.m.*), non payment.
nonobstant (*prép.*), notwithstanding:
nonobstant ce qui précède *ou* nonobstant les dispositions qui précèdent *ou* nonobstant les dispositions ci-dessus, notwithstanding the foregoing.
nonobstant toute clause contraire, toute disposition contraire du présent contrat, notwithstanding any provision to the contrary, anything to the contrary contained in this contract.
normalisation (dans la fabrication) (*n.f.*), standardization (of manufacture).

normaliser (*v.t.*), to standardize.
nota [**nota** *pl.*] (*n.m.*), note; remark.
nota bene (Abrév.: **N.-B.**), nota bene.
notaire (pers.) (*n.m.*), notaire; notary. *Note :—*
In France, a *notaire* exercises many of the functions of a solicitor, including conveyancing and company work.
notarial, -e, -aux (*adj.*), notarial:
fonctions notariales (*f.pl.*), notarial functions.
notarié, -e (*adj.*), notarially authenticated; notarially certified; notarial; done by a *notaire*:
pièce notariée (*f.*), notarially certified document; document certified by a *notaire*.
notarier (*v.t.*), to draw up:
le notaire X. a notarié le contrat, the *notaire* X. has drawn up the contract.
note (observation écrite) (*n.f.*), note; memorandum:
prendre note d'une chose sur son carnet, to make a note of something in one's pocketbook.
note marginale, marginal note.
note (mémoire) (*n.f.*), note; bill; account:
note d'assurance, insurance account; underwriting account (debit note of insurance charges).
note d'honoraires, note of fees.
note de débit, debit note.
note de chargement, shipping note.
note de commission, commission order form; commission order (the written and/or printed instrument).
note de couverture (Assce-incendie), cover note; covering note; cover.
note de crédit *ou* note d'avoir, credit note.
note de dépenses, note, account, of expenses.
note de détail (Compagnie de navigation), consignment note.
note de fret, freight note.
note de poids, weight note.
note de remise (Ch. de f.), consignment note.
noter (*v.t.*), to note:
notez bien que . . ., please note that . . .
manquant en caisse qui résulte d'une dépense qui n'a pas été notée (*m.*), shortage in the cash resulting from an expense which has not been noted.
notice (*n.f.*), notice:
notice à publier au Journal officiel, notice to be advertised in the Gazette.
notification (*n.f.*), notification; notice:
notification devra être donnée dès la réception des avis, notice (*or* notification) must be given immediately on receipt of advices.
notifier (*v.t.*), to notify:
notifier à l'assureur (*ou* notifier l'assureur de) tous les renseignements afférents à l'expédition, to notify to the underwriter (*or* to notify the insurer of) all information concerning the adventure.
notoriété (**sur**), unsecured; without security:
avances sur notoriété (*f.pl.*), unsecured advances; advances without security.
compte ouvert sur notoriété (*m.*), account opened without security.

notre sieur (en parlant d'un associé d'une maison de commerce) (Abrév.: **n.s.** *ou* **N.S.**), Mr; our Mr:
  notre sieur X. signera: . . ., Mr X. will sign: . . .
nouer les deux bouts *ou* **nouer les deux bouts de l'année** (*fig.*), to make both ends meet.
nourrice (en) (*ou* **à la**). *See* effets en (*ou* à la) nourrice.
nourrir (*v.t.*), to nurse:
  nourrir une affaire, une industrie, to nurse a business, an industry.
nourriture (*n.f.*), food; provisions; victuals.
nous-mêmes (*pronom pl.*). *See* **moi-même.**
nouveau *ou* **nouvel** (devant une voyelle ou un *h* muet), **-elle** (*adj.*) (Abrév.: **nouv.** *ou* **n.**), new; further:
  nouvelle émission d'actions, new issue of shares.
  une action nouvelle contre deux anciennes de la Société X., one new share for two old ones in the X. Company.
  nouvelle feuille de coupons (*Abrév.*: n.f.c. *ou* nouv. f. coup.), new sheet of coupons.
  nouvel avis (*m.*), further advice:
    jusqu'à nouvel avis, until (*or* till) further advice.
  à nouveau, carried forward to next account; carried forward. *See* solde à nouveau, report à nouveau, *and* reporter à nouveau.
nouvelle (*n.f.*) *ou* **nouvelles** (*n.f.pl.*), news; piece of news:
  nouvelle d'un sinistre, de l'arrivée, de la perte, d'un navire, news of a casualty, of the arrival, of the loss, of a ship.
  téléphoner une importante nouvelle, to telephone an important piece of news.
sans nouvelles. See under **sans.**
novice (pers.) (*n.m.*), apprentice.
nu, -e (se dit des huiles) (*adj.*) (opp. à en *fûts* ou *logées fûts* ou *en tambours*), naked:
  huiles de coprahs,—les 100 kilos nues gare Marseille, copra oil.—per 100 kilos naked f.o.r. Marseilles.
  à nu (non emballé), unprotected:
    marchandises transportées en vrac ou à nu (*f.pl.*), goods carried in bulk or unprotected.
nuit (*n.f.*), night.
nul, nulle (*adj.*), no; null; nil (*n.*); void; invalid:
  si le solde est nul *ou* si la balance est nulle, if there is no balance; if the balance is nil.
  marché nul au début, acheteurs et vendeurs faisant défaut (*m.*), market nil at the start, buyers and sellers being wanting.
  bref, tendance un peu meilleure, mais affaires presque nulles, briefly, tendency a little better, but business almost nil.
  l'assurance est nulle s'il est justifié que la nouvelle d'un sinistre était connue (*f.*), the insurance is void if it is proved that the news of an accident was known.
  nul (nulle) et non avenu, -e, null and void:
    considérer l'opposition comme nulle et non avenue, to treat the objection as null and void.

à l'expiration du terme de deux ans, les titres seront considérés comme nuls et non avenus, s'ils n'ont pas été renouvelés, at the expiration of the term of two years, the titles will be considered as null and void, if they have not been renewed.
nullité (*n.f.*), nullity:
  la conséquence de la réticence sera la nullité de l'assurance, the consequence of concealment is nullity of the insurance.
numéraire (espèces sonnantes) (*n.m.*), coin; cash; specie; hard cash; hard money:
  actions souscrites en numéraire (*f.pl.*), shares subscribed (*or* subscribed for) in cash.
numéraire (masse des espèces monnayées en circulation) (*n.m.*), coin; coinage; specie; money; currency:
  numéraire d'argent, silver coin; silver coinage; silver money; silver currency; silver.
  numéraire fictif, inconvertible paper money; fiat money; fiat paper money; paper money; paper currency.
numéro (*n.m.*) (Abrév.: **no** *ou* **No**), number:
  marques et numéros des colis, marks and numbers of packages.
  numéro d'habitation, house number.
  numéro d'ordre, running number; rotation number:
    lorsque l'emploi de plusieurs feuilles est nécessaire, donner un numéro d'ordre à chacune d'elles, when the use of several sheets is necessary, give a running number to each of them.
  numéros d'ordre de débarquement (séries), running landing numbers.
  numéro de commande, order number.
  numéro de débarquement, landing number.
  numéro de l'abonné (Téléph.), subscriber's number.
  numéro de lot, lot number.
  numéro de renvoi *ou* numéro de référence, reference number.
  numéro de téléphone *ou* numéro d'appel *ou* *simplement* numéro, telephone number; call number; number:
    il faut toujours demander les abonnés par leur numéro d'appel, one should always ask for subscribers by their call number.
  faux numéro d'appel, wrong number.
  numéros des pages d'un livre, numbers of the pages of a book.
  numéros des pièces justificatives, voucher numbers.
  numéro justificatif (d'un journal), voucher copy (of a newspaper).
numérotage (*n.m.*), numbering.
numéroter (*v.t.*), to number:
  numéroter un effet, les pages d'un livre, to number a bill, the pages of a book.
  marchandises marquées et numérotées comme ci-après (*f.pl.*), goods marked and numbered as follows.
  10 000 actions numérotées de 1 à 10 000, 10,000 shares numbered 1 to 10,000.

O

objet (chose quelconque) (*n.m.*), object; article; goods:
  objets de valeur, objects of value; valuable articles; valuable goods; value goods; valuables.
  objets affectés à l'usage personnel du voyageur, articles for the personal use of the passenger.
  objets de dimensions exceptionnelles (Ch. de f.), long, heavy, or bulky articles.
  objet de longueur exceptionnelle (Ch. de f.), long article.

objet (*n.m.*) *ou* **objet de correspondance** *ou* **objet postal,** article; postal article; packet; postal packet:
  Note :—In English, *packet* or *postal packet* has two meanings, specific and general.
    Specifically, it means a packet unclassifiable as a letter, newspaper, box, sample, or the like, such as a roll, or small parcel of papers or other articles. This in French is *paquet* or *paquet-poste.*
    Generally,. it means any packet of whatever kind, a letter, newspaper, box, sample, or what not. This in French is *objet, objet de correspondance, objet postal, correspondance, envoi.*
  lettres ou autres objets de correspondance, letters or other postal packets.
  objets de correspondance de toute nature, postal packets of every (*or* of any) kind.
  objet de correspondance pour l'intérieur, inland postal packet.
  objet de correspondance pour l'étranger, foreign postal packet.
  objet avec valeur déclarée *ou* objet chargé, insured article.
  objets interdits, prohibited articles.
  objet postal recommandé *ou* objet recommandé, registered postal packet; registered article.

objet (d'une société) (*n.m.*), objects (of a company):
  la société a pour objet: l'achat, la vente, la prise à bail, etc. (statuts), the objects for which the company is established are: to purchase, to sell, to take on lease, etc. (memorandum of association).

objet (d'une assurance) (*n.m.*), subject matter; subject (of an insurance):
  objet assuré *ou* objets assurés, subject matter insured; property insured.
  on désigne par l'objet du contrat d'assurance la chose assurée, one designates by the subject matter (*or* the subject) of a contract of insurance the thing (*or* the property) insured.

obligataire (*adj.*), debenture (*used as adj.*):
  dette obligataire (*f.*), debenture debt.

obligataire *ou* obligationnaire (Fin.) (pers.) (*n.m. ou f.*), debenture holder; bondholder.

obligataire (Dr.) (pers.) (*n.m. ou f.*), obligee.

obligation (engagement; lien) (*n.f.*), obligation; liability:

l'obligation de contribuer aux sacrifices faits pour la conservation de l'aventure (Assce mar.), the obligation (*or* the liability) to contribute to the sacrifices made for the preservation of the adventure.
l'obligation principale de l'assuré consiste dans le paiement de la prime, the chief obligation of the insured consists in the payment of the premium.

obligation (*n.f.*) *ou* **obligation de garantie** (acte de cautionnement), bond; indemnity bond; surety bond:
  l'obligation de garantie dont l'association de cautionnement est tenue envers le Trésor, the bond under which the guarantee society is bound to the Treasury.

obligation (Fin.) (*n.f.*) (Abrév.: **oblig.** *ou* **obl.** *ou* **ob.**), debenture; bond; *obligation:*
  qui dit obligation, dit gage durable et service régulier, who says debenture, says durable pledge and regular payment of interest.
  obligations à la souche, unissued debentures.
  obligations à lots, prize bonds; lottery bonds.
  obligations à primes, premium bonds.
  obligation amortissable *ou* obligation remboursable *ou* obligation rachetable, redeemable bond; redeemable debenture.
  obligation au porteur, bearer bond; bearer debenture.
  obligation chirographaire (opp. à *obligation hypothécaire*), simple debenture; naked debenture.
  obligation garantie, guaranteed bond.
  obligation nominative, registered debenture; registered bond.
  obligation non amortissable *ou* obligation irremboursable *ou* obligation irrachetable, irredeemable bond; unredeemable debenture.
  obligations de premier, de deuxième, de troisième, rang *ou* obligations de priorité, 1er rang, 2e rang, 3e rang *ou* obligations privilégiées, 1er rang, 2e rang, 3e rang, first, second, third, debentures.
  obligation hypothécaire, mortgage debenture; mortgage bond.
  obligations de première, de deuxième, de troisième, hypothèque (Abrév.: obl. 1re 2e, 3e, h.), first, second, third, mortgage debentures (*or* bonds):
  obligations 5 0/0 1re hypothèque, 5% 1st mortgage debentures (*or* bonds).
  obligations-or, gold bonds:
  obligations 5 0/0-or 19—, 5% gold bonds 19—.

obligé, -e (Dr.) (pers.) (*n.*), obligor.

obliger (*v.t.*), to oblige; to obligate; to bind:
  être obligé, -e, to be obliged; to be bound; to be liable:

la banque est obligée d'avoir une encaisse métallique égale au tiers du montant de ses billets et de ses autres engagements à vue, the bank is obliged (or bound) to have gold and silver coin and bullion equal to one third of the amount of its notes and of its other sight commitments.

être personnellement obligé (-e) envers l'assureur du paiement de la prime, to be personally liable to the insurer for the payment of the premium.

s'obliger (v.r.), to bind oneself; to be obligated; to undertake:
propriétaire qui ne s'oblige que sur son navire et sur le fret, owner who is only obligated on his ship and the freight.
je m'oblige à verser le surplus (bulletin de souscription), I undertake to pay the balance.

oblitérateur (n.m.), cancelling stamp.

oblitération (n.f.), obliteration; cancellation; cancelation:
oblitération de marques, obliteration of marks.

oblitérer (v.t.), to obliterate; to cancel:
oblitérer un timbre-poste, to cancel a postage stamp.

observation (n.f.), observation; remark; comment:
colonne pour les observations (f.), remarks column.

observer (v.t.), to observe; to remark; **to respect**:
observer une clause dans un contrat, to observe, to respect, a clause in a contract.

obstacles de princes et peuples (Assce mar.) (m.pl.), restraints of princes and people.

obtenir (v.t.), to obtain; to secure; to get:
obtenir un délai, to obtain an extension of time; to get time.
obtenir l'agence d'une compagnie, to secure, to get, the agency of a company.

occulte (adj.), hidden; secret:
rémunération occulte (f.), secret remuneration.

occuper (v.t.), to occupy:
occuper un emploi, to occupy a situation.

occuper le fauteuil de la présidence, to be in the chair:
M. X. occupe le fauteuil de la présidence, Mr X. was in the chair.

océan (n.m.), ocean.

œillet (n.m.), eyelet.

office (devoir; fonction) (n.m.), office; duty; post; functions.

office (charge) (n.m.), membership; seat:
agent de change qui achète l'office à son prédécesseur (m.), stockbroker who buys membership (or the seat) from his predecessor.

office (bureau) (n.m.), office; bureau; agency:
office de publicité, advertising agency; publicity bureau.

d'office (en vertu de sa charge), official; officially; arbitrary; arbitrarily:
rachat d'office (Bourse) (m.), official buying in; buying in officially.
exécution d'office d'un vendeur (f.), buying in officially against a seller.

télégramme collationné d'office (m.), telegram repeated officially.

la formalité de recommandation est appliquée d'office, c'est-à-dire sans taxe spéciale, à une nombreuse catégorie d'objets dont il est utile de garder trace de transmission, the formality of registration is applied officially, that is to say, without special charge, to a large class of packets of which it is advisable to keep trace of transmission.

imposition d'office ou taxation d'office (Impôts cédulaires) (f.), arbitrary assessment.

être taxé (-e) d'office pour défaut de déclaration, to be assessed arbitrarily for having failed to make a return.

d'office (sans en être requis), automatically; necessarily; as a matter of course; of one's own accord:
emprunt renouvelé d'office (m.), loan renewed automatically.
lorsque le capital d'une société n'a pas été entièrement libéré, les titres sont nominatifs d'office, when the capital of a company has not been fully paid up, the certificates are necessarily registered.
les spéculateurs qui ont refusé de renouveler ou de parfaire leur couverture sont liquidés d'office (m.pl.), the speculators who have refused to renew or to complete their cover are closed as a matter of course.
il l'a fait d'office, he did it of his own accord.

à titre d'office, ex officio.

officiel, -elle (adj.), official:
document officiel (m.), official document.
rachat officiel (Bourse) (m.), official buying in.
l'Officiel, short for Journal officiel, which see.

officiellement (adv.), officially:
actions cotées officiellement (f.pl.), shares quoted officially.

officier (pers.) (n.m.), officer:
les officiers et l'équipage, the officers and crew.
officier de santé, officer of health; health officer.

officine (n.f.), shop; stable:
société véreuse émanant d'une officine de moralité douteuse (f.), shady company emanating from a stable of doubtful morality.
officine de contre-partie, bucket shop.

offre (n.f.), offer; tender:
offre ferme, firm offer.
offre labiale ou offre verbale, verbal offer.
offre réelle (Dr.), tender.
offre d'emploi [offres d'emploi pl.] (opp. à demande d'emploi), situation vacant.

offre (Bourse) (n.f.) (opp. à demande), offer.
offres réduites (Abrév.: off. réd. ou off. r.), (in France, on a quotation list) means that the stock has only been able to be quoted by reducing the selling orders to be executed. Cf. demandes réduites and cours unique.

offre (Écon.) (n.f.), supply:
la loi de l'offre et de la demande, the law of supply and demand. See examples under **loi.**

offreur (pers.) (n.m.), offerer.

offrir (v.t.), to offer; to tender:
offrir des marchandises, de vendre quelque chose, to offer goods, to sell something.

offrir ses services, to offer, to tender, one's services.

l'agent offre : j'ai (c.-à-d. j'ai à vendre) 100 (actions) X. tel prix, the broker (*in England, it would be the* jobber) offers : sell (i.e., I will sell) 100 X. (shares) such or such a price. *Cf.* l'agent demande, *under* **demander.**

cours offerts (vendeurs) (Bourse) (*m.pl.*), prices offered (sellers).

action X. : 80 fr. demandé ; 82 fr. offert, X. shares : 80 fr. bid ; 82 fr. offered.

l'action X. est offerte à 800 contre 900, X. shares came on offer at 800 against 900 francs (market news).

quant à la monnaie de nickel et de bronze, elle ne peut que servir d'appoint à la pièce de 5 francs, c'est-à-dire être offerte jusqu'à 4 f. 95, as to nickel and copper money, (in France) it can only serve as change for the 5 franc piece, that is to say, be tendered up to fr. 4·95.

pouvoir être offert (-e) en paiement, to be legal tender :

la monnaie divisionnaire d'argent ne peut être offerte en paiement que jusqu'à tant, silver fractional coins are only legal tender up to so much.

offrir la parole (à une assemblée d'actionnaires), to ask for questions :

M. le président offre ensuite la parole à ceux des actionnaires qui ont des explications à réclamer, the chairman then asked if there were any shareholders who had questions to put.

oisif, -ive (*adj.*), idle :

capital oisif (*m.*), idle capital.

omnibus (*adj.*), slow :

bateau omnibus (*m.*), slow boat.

omnibus (*n.m.*), omnibus ; bus :

omnibus automobile, motor omnibus ; motor bus.

omnium (*n.m.*) *ou* **omnium de valeurs** (société), omnium ; omnium investment company.

omnium (ensemble des diverses sortes de fonds) (*n.m.*), omnium.

onéreux, -euse (*adj.*), onerous ; for a valuable consideration :

contrat à titre onéreux (*m.*), onerous contract.

propriété acquise à titre onéreux (*f.*), property acquired by onerous title (*or* for a valuable consideration).

onglet (*n.m.*), tab :

répertoire divisé par des onglets entre toutes les lettres de l'alphabet (*m.*), index divided by tabs between all the letters of the alphabet.

opérateur, -trice (pers.) (*n.*), operator :

opérateur à la hausse, à la baisse (Bourse), operator for a rise, for a fall.

opératrice téléphonique, telephone operator (girl).

opératrice des renseignements (Téléph.), enquiry operator ; directory enquiry operator.

opératrice interurbaine (Téléph.), trunk operator.

opération (*n.f.*), operation ; transaction ; dealing ; deal :

opération à cheval (Bourse), straddle ; spread ; cross book.

opération à court terme, short term transaction ; short dated deal.

opération à émission (Bourse), dealing for the coming out.

opération à la baisse *ou* opération à découvert (Bourse), dealing for a fall ; bear transaction.

opération à la hausse (Bourse), dealing for a rise ; bull transaction.

opération à long terme, long term transaction ; long dated deal.

opérations à prime (Bourse), option dealing ; dealing in options ; option dealings. Explanations of option dealing in France and in England are contained in a note under **prime.**

opération à terme *ou* opération à livrer (Com.), transaction on (*or* upon) credit.

opération à terme *ou* opération à livrer (Bourse de valeurs), dealing for the settlement ; transaction for the account.

opération au comptant, cash transaction ; transaction for cash ; cash deal ; dealing for cash.

opérations de banque, banking transactions ; banking operations ; banking business.

opérations de bourse *ou* opérations boursières, stock exchange transactions ; market transactions.

opérations de change, exchange transactions ; foreign exchange transactions (*or* dealings) ; exchange ; foreign exchange :

opérations de change à terme, forward exchange transactions (*or* dealings) ; exchange for forward (*or* future) delivery.

opérations de change au comptant, spot exchange transactions (*or* dealings) ; exchange for spot delivery.

opérations liées (Bourse), combined deal, i.e., selling a stock cum rights and simultaneous buying of the same stock ex rights.

opéré (*n.m.*), deal ; execution :

avis d'opéré (Bourse) (*m.*), advice of deal ; advice of purchase (*or* of sale).

exiger l'opéré d'un ordre, to claim execution of an order.

opérer (*v.t.*), to operate ; to effect ; to make ; to do :

opérer un versement, to effect, to make, a payment.

opérer (*v.i.*), to operate ; to deal ; to go :

opérer à la hausse, à la baisse (Bourse), to operate for a rise, for a fall ; to go a bull, a bear.

il refuse d'opérer avec lui, he refuses to deal with him.

en France, il est rigoureusement interdit aux agents de change d'opérer pour leur compte personnel et de s'intéresser dans aucune affaire commerciale, directement ou indirectement, in France, it is strictly forbidden for *agents de change* to deal (*or* to operate) for their personal account and to interest themselves in any commercial transaction, directly or indirectly.

s'opérer (*v.r.*), to be done ; to be effected :

les retraits de fonds s'opèrent par chèques (*m.pl.*), withdrawals of money are effected by cheques.

opinion (*n.f.*), opinion:
se faire (*ou* se former) une opinion du risque auquel une cargaison est exposée, to form an opinion of the risk to which a cargo is exposed.

opposition à la cote (Bourse) (*f.*), objection to mark:
mettre des oppositions à la cote, to lodge objections to marks.
Cf. mettre opposition sur un titre, *under* **mettre**.

optant (Fin.) (pers.) (*n.m.*), taker; taker of an (*or* of the) option.

opter (*v.i.*), to choose; to decide; to declare; to exercise an (*or* the) option:
opter entre deux alternatives, entre l'abandon de la marchandise et le paiement d'indemnités pécuniaires, to choose between two alternatives, between abandonment of the goods and payment of pecuniary compensation.
optant qui opte pour la livraison (*m.*), taker who exercises his option for delivery.

option (faculté) (*n.f.*), option:
exercer son droit d'option, to exercise one's right of option.
résiliation de la police pouvant se faire à l'option de l'assuré (*f.*), cancellation of the policy being at the option of the assured.
option de change, option of exchange.

option (Fin.) (*n.f.*), option; call:
donner aux courtiers qui font le placement des titres une option de tant d'actions à tant, to give to the brokers who place the shares an option (*or* a call) on so many shares at so much.
négociations à option (*f.pl.*), option dealings.
maison qui a pris un emprunt moitié ferme moitié à option (*f.*), house which has taken a loan half firm half on option.
les marchandises en option (*f.pl.*), the goods on (*or* under) option.

option (double prime; stellage) (Bourse) (*n.f.*), put and call; put and call option; double option:
l'option est la réunion de l'ou et du dont, the put and call is the combination of the put and of the call.
Note:—put and call is sometimes called **double option** in French (probably the English term *double option* borrowed).

option du double (faculté de lever double) (Bourse) (*f.*) (Abrév.: **op. d.**), call of more; call o' more; buyer's option to double.

optionnaire (Fin.) (pers.) (*n.m.*), giver; giver of an (*or* of the) option.

or (*n.m.*), gold:
or en barre, bar gold.
or standard, standard gold.
or, argent, métaux précieux, numéraire, titres, bijoux, œuvres d'art, et objets (*ou* articles) de valeur analogues (comme cargaison), gold, silver, precious metals, coin, securities, jewellery, works of art, and similar valuables.
une pièce d'or, a gold coin.

être payé (-e) en or, to be paid in gold.
francs-or (*n.m.pl.*), gold francs.

ordinaire (*adj.*) (Abrév.: **ord.**), ordinary:
actions ordinaires (*f.pl.*) (*Abrév.:* ord.), ordinary shares; ordinary stock.
créancier ordinaire (*m.*), ordinary creditor.

ordre (disposition méthodique) (*n.m.*), order:
mettre des papiers en ordre, to put papers in order.
l'ordre de sortie est déterminé par un tirage au sort, the order of retirement shall be determined by lot.

ordre (commandement d'une autorité supérieure) (*n.m.*), order; direction:
escale dans un port étranger pour recevoir des ordres (*f.*), calling at a foreign port to receive orders.
transmettre des ordres à un navire par T.S.F., to transmit orders to a ship by wireless.

ordre (directions pour paiement, pour livraison) (*n.m.*) (Abrév.: **o/**), order:
le chèque est un ordre de payer adressé au banquier, a cheque is an order to pay addressed to the banker.
dans la pratique, le connaissement est établi à l'ordre du chargeur, in practice, the bill of lading is made to the shipper's order.
mettre son ordre au dos d'un billet, to put one's order on the back of a bill.
payez à l'ordre de M. X. (*Abrév.:* payez o/ M. X.), pay to the order of Mr X. See further examples under **payez**.
chèque à ordre (*m.*) (opp. à *chèque au porteur*), order cheque; cheque to order.

ordre (commande) (*n.m.*), order:
exécution d'un ordre d'assurance (*f.*), execution of an order of insurance.
ordres de bourse, stock exchange orders.
ordre à prime (Bourse), option order.
ordre à terme (Bourse de valeurs), order for the settlement (*or* for the account).
ordre d'achat, buying order.
ordre de vente, selling order.
ordre ferme, firm order.
ordre lié (Bourse), contingent order (i.e., selling shares of one kind and buying shares of another, the one transaction not to be effected without the other).
ordre permanent *ou* ordre à perpétuité, standing order.
ordre stop (Bourse de valeurs), stop order; cutting limit order.
ordres en carnet (*ou* en portefeuille), orders in hand; unfilled orders.

ordre du jour (*m.*), agenda; business; business before the meeting:
les objets sur lesquels les administrateurs, ou les actionnaires, sont appelés à se prononcer constituent l'ordre du jour (*m.pl.*), the matters on which the directors, or the shareholders, are called on to decide make up the agenda.
assemblée générale convoquée à l'effet de délibérer sur l'ordre du jour suivant (*f.*), meeting convened to consider the following agenda (*or* to transact the following business).

mettre à l'ordre du jour les questions à délibérer, to put down on the agenda the
business to be transacted.

rien n'étant plus à l'ordre du jour, la séance est
levée, there being no other business, the meeting was closed ; there being no further business
before the meeting, the sitting was closed.

ordre public (*m.*), public policy :
clause contraire à l'ordre public (*f.*), clause
contrary to public policy.

orientation (*n.f.*), trend ; tendency :
la bonne orientation des valeurs de pétrole cette
semaine s'explique par la situation générale
du marché du pétrole en Amérique, the
favourable trend (*or* the brightness) of oil
shares this week is explained by the general
condition of the oil market in America.

meilleure orientation en stannifères en fin de
séance, better trend (*or* brighter tendency) in
tins at the finish.

les actions X. sont en bonne (*ou* excellente)
orientation à 728, X. shares were a bright
spot at 728 francs.

original, -e, -aux *ou* **originaire** (*adj.*), original :
facture originale (*f.*), original invoice.
capital originaire (*m.*), original capital.
original déposit (Bourse de marchandises) (*m.*).
See caisse de liquidation.

original (manuscrit primitif) (*n.m.*), original :
original d'un acte, original of a deed.
comparer la traduction à l'original, to compare
the translation with the original.

connaissement établi en quatre originaux (*m.*),
bill of lading made in four originals.

origine (*n.f.*), origin :
marchandises d'origine étrangère (*f.pl.*), goods
of foreign origin.

pays d'origine (*m.*), country of origin.
Cf. emballages d'origine, *under* **emballage.**

origine (bulletin de la cote), with coupon No. 1 ;
coupon No. 1 attached. (*origine* is a word
used in quotation lists : it means that no
dividend has yet been paid and therefore
coupon No. 1 is still attached.)

oscillant, -e (*adj.*), fluctuating.

oscillation (*n.f.*), fluctuation :
oscillations dans le cours du change, fluctuations in the rate of exchange.

osciller (*v.i.*), to fluctuate ; to move :
action qui oscille entre 12 francs et 14 francs (*f.*),
share which fluctuates (*or* moves) between
12 francs and 14 francs.

ou (Bourse) (*n.m.*) (opp. à *dont*), put ; put option ;
seller's option :

marché où on traite le dont et l'ou (*m.*), market
on which calls and puts are dealt in.

spéculateur qui est vendeur de 100 actions
X.Y.Z. à 517 ou 3 (*m.*), speculator who is
giver of 3 francs (per share) for the put of
100 X.Y.Z. shares at 520.

See explanations under **prime.**

ouest-africaines (*n.f.pl.*) *ou* **valeurs ouest-africaines**
(*f.pl.*), West Africans ; West African shares ;
jungles.

outre-mer (*adv.*), oversea ; overseas :
s'établir outre-mer, to settle oversea (*or* overseas).

outre-mer (d') (*adj.*), oversea :
colonies d'outre-mer (*f.pl.*), oversea colonies.

ouvert, -e (*adj.*), open :
compte ouvert (*m.*), open account.
ouvert en permanence (se dit de certains
bureaux de poste, etc.), open always.

ouverture (*n.f.*), opening :
ouverture des panneaux (d'un navire), opening
the hatches.

ouverture de la souscription, opening of the
subscription list.

le chef du service préside à l'ouverture du
courrier, the head of the department superintends the opening of the letters.

ouv. *ou* ouvert. (Bourse) (*abrév.*), cours
d'ouverture.

ouvre-lettres [ouvre-lettres *pl.*] *ou* **ouvre-courrier**
[ouvre-courrier *pl.*] (*n.m.*), letter opener.

ouvrir (*v.t.*), to open ; to open up :
ouvrir une lettre, une séance, un compte à la
banque, les livres d'une nouvelle société, to
open a letter, a meeting, an account at the
bank, the books of a new company.

ouvrir sur le grand livre un compte à quelqu'un,
to open an account for someone in the ledger.

ouvrir un crédit en banque (*ou* dans une maison
de banque), chez un banquier, auprès d'un
correspondant, à un voyageur, to open a
credit with (*or* at) a bank, with a banker,
with a correspondent, for a traveller.

ouvrir un pays au commerce, to open a country
to commerce ; to open up a country to trade.

ouvrir (*v.i.*), to open :
valeur qui ouvre à tel ou tel cours (Bourse) (*f.*),
stock which opens at such or such a price.

bureau qui n'ouvre pas le dimanche (*m.*), office
which does not open on Sunday.

s'ouvrir (*v.r.*), to open :
le compte s'ouvre par un solde débiteur de
tant, the account opens with a debit balance
of so much.

P

page (*n.f.*) (Abrév. : **p.**), page ; folio :
les pages d'un livre, the pages of a book.
page de droite, right hand page.
page de gauche, left hand page.

pagination (*n.f.*), paging ; pagination ; folioing ;
foliation.

pagination à livre fermé (Comptab.) (*f.*), paging ;
pagination. See example under **paginer à
livre fermé.**

pagination à livre ouvert (Comptab.) (*f.*), folioing ;
foliation. See example under **paginer à
livre ouvert.**

paginer (*v.t.*), to page; to folio:
paginer un livre, to page a book.
paginer à livre fermé (Comptab.), to page:
en comptabilité, le journal est paginé à livre
fermé, c'est-à-dire que chaque page porte un
numéro différent, in bookkeeping, the
journal is paged, that is to say, each page
bears a different number.
paginer à livre ouvert (Comptab.), to folio:
le grand livre est généralement paginé à livre
ouvert, c'est-à-dire que la page à gauche et
la page à droite portent le même numéro, the
ledger is generally folioed, that is to say, the
left hand page and the right hand page bear
the same number.
paie (*n.f.*), pay; wages; wage:
la paie d'un ouvrier, the pay, the wages, of a
workman.
paiement (*n.m.*) (Abrév.: **paiem**ᵗ), payment:
paiement à compte, payment on account;
instalment; installment.
paiement contre documents, payment against
documents.
paiement d'avance *ou* paiement par anticipation *ou* paiement anticipé, payment in
advance; payment in anticipation; prepayment.
paiement en trop, overpayment.
paiement fin courant, payment at the end of
the present month.
paiement fractionné, payment in driblets.
paiement intégral, payment in full.
paiement libératoire, payment in full discharge.
paiement par intervention (effets de commerce), payment for honour.
pain à cacheter (*m.*), wafer; wafer seal;
signet wafer.
pair, -e (exactement divisible par deux) (*adj.*),
even:
nombre pair (*m.*), even number.
pair (*n.m.*) (Abrév.: **P.** *ou* **p.**), par:
pair commercial, commercial par:
le pair commercial est le prix de revient de la
pièce (métal précieux et frais de monnayage),
the commercial par is the cost of the coin
(precious metal and minting expenses).
pair intrinsèque *ou* pair métallique *ou* pair du
change *ou simplement* pair, mint par; mint
par of exchange; par of exchange; par:
le pair intrinsèque (*ou* métallique) (*ou* le pair
du change) de la livre sterling comparée au
franc français est 124 fr. 21 (plus exactement 124,2134), the mint par (*or* par of
exchange) of the pound sterling compared
with the French franc is 124 fr. 21 (more
exactly 124·2134).
change au pair (*m.*), exchange at par.
pair politique *ou* pair proportionnel, arbitrated
par; arbitrated par of exchange.
pair des effets, par of stocks:
une action de 500 fr. est au pair lorsque son
prix courant est de 500 fr., a share of 500
francs is at par when its current price is
500 francs.
le pair d'un titre est la valeur nominale de ce

titre, fixée lors de l'émission, the par of a
stock is the nominal value of that stock fixed
at the time of issue.
Cf. émettre des actions au pair, au-dessus du
pair, au-dessous du pair, *under* **émettre** (*v.t.*).
au pair (reports en Bourse), even:
le report (*ou* le taux du report) est au pair,
the contango (*or* the contango rate) is
even.
See also example under **report** (loyer de
l'argent).
pair de place (*m.*), cost of collection (of bills of
exchange); bank charges (on bills). *See
note under syn.* change de place.
paix (*n.f.*) (Ant.: *guerre*), peace.
palais de justice (*m.*), courts of justice; law
courts.
Palais de la Bourse (*m.*). Full designation of the
Bourse (Stock Exchange) building in Paris.
palans du navire (*m.pl.*), ship's tackles:
marchandises amenées le long du bord par les
palans du navire (*f.pl.*), goods lowered alongside by the ship's tackles.
sous palan. See under **sous**.
panier à lettres (*m.*), letter basket.
panier au papier *ou simplement* **panier** (*n.m.*),
waste paper basket:
jeter un journal au panier, to throw a newspaper into the waste paper basket.
panique (*n.f.*), panic:
panique sur la bourse, panic on the stock
exchange.
cours de panique (*m.pl.*), panic prices.
panneau (ouverture, écoutille, d'un navire) (*n.m.*),
hatch; hatchway:
la fermeture des panneaux, battening down the
hatches.
panneau (couvercle de cale) (*n.m.*), hatch.
panneau-réclame [panneaux-réclame *pl.*] (*n.m.*),
hoarding; advertisement hoarding.
paperasse (*n.f.*), old paper; old papers; waste
paper:
l'accumulation d'une paperasse, de vieilles
paperasses (*f.*), the accumulation of old
papers, of waste paper.
papeterie (fournitures de bureau) (*n.f.*), stationery.
papeterie (boîte) (*n.f.*), stationery case; paper
case.
papier (*n.m.*), paper:
titres ne valant plus que le prix du papier
(*m.pl.*), stock not worth more than the price
of the paper.
pour le moment, nul ne se plaint; tout le monde
gagne de l'argent, sur le papier, just now,
nobody is complaining; everybody is making
money, on paper.
papier à écrire, writing paper.
papier à lettre *ou* papier à lettres, letter
paper:
papier à lettre avec en-tête imprimé, headed
letter paper.
papier à lettres deuil, black-bordered letter
paper.
papier blanc (vierge d'écrit), blank paper.
papier buvard (blanc, rose), blotting paper
(white, pink).

papier carbone [papiers carbone *pl.*] *ou* papier carboné [papiers carbonés *pl.*], carbon paper; carbon.

papiers d'affaires, business papers.

papier d'emballage, packing paper.

papiers de bord *ou* papiers d'expédition, ship's papers; clearance papers.

papiers de commerce *ou* papiers d'affaires (Poste), commercial papers.

papier de la débite, stamped paper on sale (paper stamped before execution of the instrument, such as bill forms). *Cf.* timbrer à l'extraordinaire.

papier de rebut, waste paper.

papier glacé, glazed paper.

papier-journal. See below.

papier libre *ou* papier mort, unstamped paper (i.e., not bearing inland revenue stamps).

papier pour machines à écrire *ou* papier machine à écrire *ou* simplement papier machine, typewriting paper.

papier timbré, stamped paper.

papier (*n.m.*) *ou* **papiers** (*n.m.pl.*) (effets de commerce), paper; bills; exchange: (See also **effet.**)

le papier est recherché sur notre marché monétaire et il est insuffisant pour satisfaire les demandes, paper is in request on our money market and it is insufficient to satisfy the demand.

papier à courte échéance, short bills; short dated bills.

papier à échéance, bills to mature.

papier à vue, sight bills.

papier bancable, bankable paper. See note under **bancable.**

papier brûlant, hot bills; bills maturing in a few days; bills that have only a few days to run.

papier court (*Abrév. :* p.c.), short exchange.

papier creux, house bills; pig on pork.

papier de banque, bank paper; bank bills.

papier de commerce *ou* papier commercial, commercial paper; commercial bills; trade paper (*or* bills); mercantile paper (*or* bills); ordinary bills.

papier de complaisance, accommodation paper; accommodation bills.

papier de haut commerce *ou* papier hors banque, fine trade bills; prime trade paper; white paper.

papier de haute banque, fine bank bills.

papier doré sur tranche, gilt-edged paper.

papier en l'air *ou* papiers de circulation, kites; windmills.

papier fait, guaranteed bills; backed bills.

papier long (*Abrév. :* p.l.), long exchange.

papier négociable *ou* papier commerçable, negotiable paper.

papier non bancable *ou* papier déclassé, unbankable paper. See note under **bancable.**

papier sur place (*ou* papier de place), déplacé, détourné. *Same as* effets sur place, déplacés, détournés, *q.v.*

Papier (cours Papier) (cote) (Abrév. : **P.**) (opp. à *Argent*), price(s) offered (sellers).

papier-journal [**papiers-journaux** *pl.*] (*n.m.*), account book; book of account.

papier-monnaie (*n.m.*), paper money; paper currency; inconvertible paper money; fiat money; fiat paper money:

les billets de banque à cours forcé sont du papier-monnaie (*m.pl.*), forced currency bank notes are inconvertible paper money (*or* fiat money).

Cf. monnaie de papier.

papiers de valeur (*m.pl.*), value papers; valuable papers.

papiers-valeurs (*n.m.pl.*), paper securities; securities for money; paper money.

papillon (*n.m.*), slip; attachment (a small piece of paper stuck on a bill of lading or on an insurance policy and containing a clause or reservation):

papillon spécial collé sur un connaissement se référant à la clause d'irresponsabilité, special slip (*or* attachment) stuck on a bill of lading referring to the non liability clause.

paquebot (*n.m.*) *ou* **paquebot à voyageurs** *ou* **paquebot à passagers** *ou* **paquebot à vapeur** (opp. à *cargo-boat*), passenger ship; passenger boat; passenger vessel; passenger steamer; steamer; steamship; liner; packet:

paquebot à classe unique, one class liner.

paquebot à grande vitesse, fast passenger steamer.

paquebot à moteur, motor liner.

paquebot aérien, airship; dirigible.

paquebot mixte, cargo and passenger steamer.

paquebot-poste [paquebots-poste *pl.*] (*n.m.*) *ou* paquebot postal, mail steamer; mail boat; mail packet.

paquebot transatlantique, Atlantic liner; transatlantic liner.

paquet (*n.m.*), packet; parcel; lot; block:

il est permis de réunir, en un même paquet, des échantillons et des imprimés (Poste), it is permissible to enclose in the same packet samples and printed matter.

paquet avec (*ou* de) valeur déclarée *ou* paquet chargé (Poste) (*Abrév. :* paquet V.D. *ou* PVD.), insured packet.

paquet-lettre [paquets-lettres *pl.*] (Poste) (*n.m.*), letter packet.

paquet-poste [paquets-poste *pl.*] (*n.m.*), postal packet.

See note under **objet** *ou* **objet de correspondance.**

vendre ses titres par petits paquets, to sell one's shares in small parcels (*or* lots).

offrir sur le marché de gros paquets d'actions, to offer on the market big blocks of shares.

par (reports du grand livre) (Comptab.) (*prép.*) (opp. à **à**), By:

par Marchandises, By Goods.

par an (Abrév. : **p. an**), per annum:

5 0/0 par an, 5% per annum.

par avion (inscription sur une lettre, un paquet, etc.) (Transport par voie aérienne), by air mail.

par-dessus bord, overboard:

jeter par-dessus bord des marchandises d'une nature dangereuse, to throw overboard goods of a dangerous nature.

par les présentes *ou* **par le présent acte,** hereby :
je donne, par les présentes, pouvoir à M. X.,
I hereby appoint as my proxy Mr X.

par procuration *ou par abrév.* **P. P**on *ou* **Par p**on,
per (*or* by) procuration ; per procurationem ;
per pro. ; per proc. ; p.p. See example
under **procuration.**

**par train de grande vitesse, par train de petite
vitesse,** by (*or* per) passenger train, by (*or*
per) goods train.

par vapeur direct (sans transbordement),   by
direct steamer.

parafe *ou* **paraphe** (*n.m.*),   initials :
apposer son parafe, to put one's initials.

parafer *ou* **parapher** (*v.t.*), to initial :
parafer un renvoi, to initial an alteration.

se parafer (*v.r.*), to be initialed :
pièce qui doit se parafer (*f.*), document which
ought to be initialed.

paraître (*v.i.*), to appear :
paraître devant un tribunal, to appear before a
court.

parc (*n.m.*), yard ; park :
parc à charbon, coal yard.
parc à matières *ou* parc de stockage,   stock
yard.
parc à voitures, car park.

parcelle (de blé, etc.) (Bourse de marchandises)
(*n.f.*), parcel (of wheat, etc.) :
parcelles de Manitoba nord mars 42/6d.
vendeur, parcels of Northern Manitoba
March sellers at 42/6d.

parcontre (*n.m.*), contra ; offset :
ces courtages sont perçus sur chaque opération,
achat et vente, et sans parcontre,   these
brokerages are charged on each deal,
purchase and sale, and without contra
(*or* offset) (i.e., brokerage charged both
ways).

parcourir (*v.t.*), to travel over ; to cover ;   to
travel at ; to run at :
les distances parcourues sur mer s'expriment
en milles marins (*f.pl.*), the distances
travelled over (*or* covered) on the sea are
expressed in nautical miles.
parcourir — kilomètres à l'heure (se dit d'un
train, etc.), to travel at, to run at, — kilometres an hour.

parcours (chemin suivi) (*n.m.*), distance ; stretch ;
run ; haul :
parcours de — km. et au-dessous, parcours au
delà de — km., distances (*or* stretches) (*or*
runs) (*or* hauls) of — kilometres and under,
distances (*or* stretches) (*or* runs) (*or* hauls)
over — km.
parcours par voie ferrée, railroad haul.

parcours (trajet) (*n.m.*), journey ; voyage ; transit :
parcours à charge (d'un wagon de ch. de f.),
journey when loaded ;   journey loaded ;
loaded journey.
parcours à vide (d'un wagon de ch. de f.),
journey when empty ;   journey empty ;
empty journey.
parcours aérien, air journey ; air transit.
parcours en chemin de fer, railway journey.
parcours maritime, sea voyage ; sea transit.

parcours moyen d'un voyageur,   average
journey of a passenger.
parcours terrestre *ou* parcours territorial, land
journey ; land transit.

pardon de vous avoir dérangé (Téléph.),   sorry
you've been troubled ; I am sorry you have
been troubled.

parfaire (*v.t.*),, to complete ; to make up :
parfaire une somme, la différence, to make up
an amount, the difference.

pari passu, pari passu :
actions nouvelles qui participent aux bénéfices
pari passu avec les actions anciennes (*f.pl.*),
new shares which participate in the profits
pari passu with the old shares.

paritaire (*adj.*), one for one :
échange paritaire d'actions (*m.*), exchange of
shares one for one.

parité (équivalence des cours du change sur deux
places) (*n.f.*), parity :
parité entre deux cours, parity between two
rates.
change à la parité *ou* change à parité, exchange
at parity :
lorsque le cours du change de deux places sur
leurs cotes respectives—Paris sur la cote de
Londres, Londres sur la cote de Paris—
ou celui d'une même place sur différentes
cotes, donnent une somme équivalente, on
dit que les cotes sont à la parité ; dans le
cas contraire, elles sont dites telles quelles
(*ou* quand la prime de l'un au-dessus du
pair est exactement proportionnelle à la
perte de l'autre, l'on dit que les deux changes
sont à parité ; dans le cas contraire, ils sont
dits tels quels), when the rate of exchange
of two markets on their respective lists—
Paris on the London list, London on the
Paris list—or that of the same market
on different lists, give an equivalent sum,
the quotations are said to be at parity (*or*
when the premium of one above par is in
exact proportion to the discount of the
other, the two exchanges are said to be at
parity) ; when the reverse is the case, they
are said to be tel quel.

parité (Bourse de marchandises) (*n.f.*), equivalent :
rendu gare (de chemin de fer) X. ou parité,
delivered X. (railway) station or equivalent.

parquet (Bourse) (*n.m.*).   *See under* marché des
valeurs.

parquet de chargement (arrimage) (*m.*), dunnage.

parrain (pers.) (*n.m.*), recommender :
candidat présenté par trois parrains (*m.*),
candidate introduced by three recommenders.

parrainage (*n.m.*), recommendation :
le parrainage de deux courtiers déjà admis, the
recommendation of two brokers already
admitted.

part (*n.f.*), part ; share ; portion :
convention entre Monsieur A. d'une part et
Monsieur B. d'autre part (*f.*), agreement
between Mr A. of the one part and Mr B. of
the other part.

de seconde part, de troisième part, of the second part, of the third part.

prendre une part dans une affaire, une part des bénéfices, to take a share in a deal, a share of the profits.

capitaine qui a une part dans le navire (*m.*), master who holds a share in the vessel.

lorsqu'il y a plusieurs assureurs, chacun d'eux inscrit au bas de la police la part pour laquelle il s'engage dans le risque assuré, where there are several underwriters, each of them writes down at the bottom of the policy the share he takes upon himself in the risk insured.

part de lion (*fig.*), lion's share.

part de prise (Dr. mar. internat.), prize money.

part syndicale *ou* part syndicataire *ou* part de syndicat, share of underwriting.

part de fondateur (*Abrév. :* fond.) *ou* part bénéficiaire, founder's share ; management share.

Note :—Unlike in England, where founders' or management shares form part of the company's capital, in France, *parts de fondateurs* or *parts bénéficiaires* are not represented by any capital value. They are merely profit sharing rights after certain distributions on the ordinary shares, and can be likened to directors' percentages of profits. The fact of not representing any capital value is the essential difference between a *part* and an *action*. *parts de fondateur* like *actions d'apport* are not negotiable for 2 years. *See note under* actions à la souche. *Cf.* actions industrielles.

parts d'apport, vendors' shares in a *société à responsabilité limitée*, q.v.

part d'intérêt, share of a partner in a *société par intérêts* (or *de personnes*), q.v.

pts (*abrév.*), parts.

partage (action) (*n.m.*), division ; distribution ; sharing ; splitting :

partage des bénéfices, division, distribution, sharing, of profits.

le partage du butin, the sharing of the spoil.

avoir avec quelqu'un un bureau en partage, to share an office with someone.

partage des voix *ou simplement* **partage** (*n.m.*), equality of votes ; equal voting :

en cas de partage des voix *ou* en cas de partage, in case of equality of votes ; if the voting is equal.

partageable (*adj.*), divisible ; dividable ; distributable :

les bénéfices partageables (*m.pl.*), the divisible profits.

partageant (pers.) (*n.m.*), sharer.

partager (*v.t.*), to divide ; to distribute ; to share ; to split :

partager une terre, to divide a piece of land.

partager un bénéfice, to divide a profit.

partager un dividende, to distribute a dividend.

nous partageons tous également, we all share alike.

partager le différend (*ou* la différence) *ou* partager le différend en deux *ou* partager le différend par la moitié, to split the difference.

partageur (pers.) (*n.m.*), liquidator.

partance (*n.f.*), sailing ; readiness to sail : visite de partance (*f.*), survey on sailing.

en partance, in readiness to sail ; about to sail ; outward bound ; outbound :

navire en partance pour un voyage au long cours (*m.*), ship about to sail (*or* outward bound) (*or* outbound) on a foreign voyage.

participant, -e (pers.) (*n.*), participant ; sharer : participant à une répartition, participant in a distribution.

participation (*n.f.*), participation ; sharing ; share ; joint venture ; joint adventure :

participation aux bénéfices, profit sharing ; share (*or* participation) in profits.

prendre une participation dans l'affaire, to take a share in the deal.

compte de participation (*m.*), joint venture account ; joint adventure account ; joint account.

en participation, on joint account :

opérations en participation (*f.pl.*), transactions on joint account.

participer (*v.i.*), to participate ; to share :

obligations qui participent à des tirages au sort périodiques (*f.pl.*), bonds which participate in periodical drawings.

participer aux pertes, to participate in losses ; to share in the losses ; to share the loss.

particulier, -ère (*adj.*), private :

intérêts particuliers (*m.pl.*), private interests.

banque particulière (*f.*), private bank.

partie (portion d'un tout) (*n.f.*), part ; portion :

somme divisée en un certain nombre de parties égales (*f.*), amount divided into a certain number of equal parts.

partie d'un risque, part of a risk.

partie de chargement de wagon, part truck load.

partie (quantité de marchandises, de titres, qu'on vend ou qu'on achète) (*n.f.*), parcel ; lot ; block :

partie de marchandises, parcel, lot, of goods.

offrir sur le marché de fortes parties d'actions, to offer on the market big blocks (*or* parcels) of shares.

partie (manière de tenir les livres) (Comptab.) (*n.f.*), entry :

partie double, double entry :

tenir des livres en partie double (*ou* à parties doubles), to keep books by double entry.

partie simple, single entry :

tenue des livres en partie simple (*ou* à partie simple) (*f.*), single entry bookkeeping.

See also example under **contre-partie** (Comptab.).

partie (pers.) (*n.f.*), party :

se rendre partie dans un procès, to become party to an action.

parties contractantes, contracting parties.

parties intéressées, interested parties ; parties concerned.

partiel, -elle (*adj.*), partial :

perte partielle (Assce) (*f.*), partial loss.

partiellement (*adv.*), partially; partly:
titres partiellement libérés (*m.pl.*), partly paid shares.
créancier partiellement nanti (*m.*), partly secured creditor.

partir (*v.i.*), to depart; to start; to go; to leave; to sail:
heure à laquelle le train part (*f.*), time at which the train goes (*or* leaves) (*or* starts) (*or* departs).
partir à l'étranger, to go abroad:
si le destinataire est parti à l'étranger, ne pas faire suivre, if the addressee has gone abroad, do not forward.
partir de Paris, to leave Paris.
partir pour Londres, to leave for London.
partir sans laisser d'adresse, to go away without leaving an address.
parti sans laisser d'adresse (mention sur un objet de correspondance), gone away, no address.
le moment où le navire part, the time at which the ship sails.
navire prêt à partir pour un voyage au long cours (*m.*), ship ready (*or* about) to sail on an ocean voyage.
(*steamer*) X. parti de Cuxhaven le 31 (*date*) pour Anvers (Mouvement des Navires), (*steamer*) X. (for Antwerp) left (*or* l.) (*or* sailed [*or* s.]) Cuxhaven 31 (*date*) (Shipping News).

parvenir (*v.i.*), to reach; to arrive; to get to:
en vertu de cette clause, quoi qu'il arrive, que les marchandises parviennent ou non à leur destination, l'armateur touchera son fret, by virtue of this clause, whatever happens, whether the goods reach (*or* arrive at) (*or* get to) their destination or not, the shipowner receives his freight.

pas (détroit) (Géogr.) (*n.m.*), strait; straits:
Pas de Calais, Straits of Dover.

pas coté (sans cotation) (Bourse) (Abrév.: **p.c.**), no quotation.

pas de changement, no change:
pas de changements en valeurs bancaires, no changes in bank stocks.

pas demandé (Bourse), no bid.

pas libre (Téléph.), sorry, number's engaged; I am sorry the number is engaged; number engaged.

pas traité (sans transaction) (Bourse), no dealings.

passage (*n.m.*), passage; crossing; going; transit:
le passage entre l'Angleterre et le continent, the passage (*or* crossing) between England and the continent.
prix de passage (*m.*), passage money.
le coût du déchargement et du passage en douane, the cost of unloading and passage through the customs.
passage en (*ou* au) bassin, docking; going into dock.

passage souterrain (Ch. de f.) (*m.*), subway:
passage souterrain, desservi par des escaliers, par le moyen duquel le public accède aux quais, subway, served by stairs, by means of which the public has access to the platforms.

passager, -ère (pers.) (*n.*), passenger:
(*Note:—passager* is confined to boat, boat train, and air, passengers. Cf. **voyageur.**)
tous ces vapeurs prennent un nombre limité de passagers, all these steamers take a limited number of passengers.
passager clandestin, stowaway.
passager d'entrepont, steerage passenger.
passager de cabine *ou* passager de chambre, cabin passenger.
passager de troisième en cabine, third cabin passenger.

passager-kilomètre [**passagers-kilomètre** *pl.*] (*n.m.*) *ou* **passager kilométrique** (service aérien), passenger kilometre, analogous to English *passenger mile* (passager-mille).

passation (d'un dividende) (*n.f.*), passing:
sur l'annonce de la passation de son dividende, l'action s'est alourdie, on the announcement of the passing of the dividend, the shares became heavy.

passation (Dr.) (*n.f.*), drawing up; drawing:
passation d'un acte, drawing up, drawing, a deed.

passation (enregistrement) (*n.f.*), filing. See example under **passer.**

passation (Comptab.) (*n.f.*), passing; making; entering; entering up; entry; posting:
passation d'écritures *ou* passation des articles en compte, passing, making, entries; entering items.
passation des écritures au journal, making entries in the journal.

passation d'ordres (*f.*), giving, placing, orders.

passavant *ou* **passe-avant** (Douanes) (*n.m.*), transire:
passavant de cabotage, coasting transire.

passe (*n.f.*), odd money:
ajouter à des billets de banque deux francs pour la passe, to add to some bank notes two francs for the odd money.

passeport (certificat pour la libre circulation des personnes) (*n.m.*), passport:
les préposés des douanes sont chargés d'exiger des voyageurs la représentation de leurs passeports (*m.pl.*), the customs officials are directed to require travellers to show their passports.

passeport (permis de mettre en mer) (*n.m.*), passport; clearance: (See note under **congé.**)
le passeport est pour un navire étranger ce que le congé est pour un navire français, (in France) the *passeport* is for a foreign ship what the *congé* is for a French ship.

passer (faire; conclure) (*v.t.*), to make; to enter into:
passer un marché, to make, to enter into, a bargain.
passer un bail, un contrat (*ou* un marché), to enter into a lease, a contract:
administrateur qui a passé des marchés avec la société (*m.*), director who has entered into contracts with the company.

passer (mettre en circulation) (*v.t.*), to pass; to utter:

passer une pièce fausse, un faux chèque, to pass, to utter, a counterfeit coin, a forged cheque.

passer (transmettre) (*v.t.*), to give ; to place : passer un ordre, to give, to place, an order. valeur reçue que passerez en compte suivant avis de (*signature*) (lettre de change), value received which place to account as advised.

se passer (*v.r.*), to be given ; to be placed : ordres qui se passent par écrit (*m.pl.*), orders which are given in writing.

passer (transmettre par endossement) (*v.t.*), to endorse over : passer une lettre de change à l'ordre d'un tiers, to endorse over a bill of exchange to the order of a third party.

passer (rédiger en forme légale) (*v.t.*), to draw up ; to draw : passer un acte, to draw up, to draw, a deed.

passer (enregistrer, déposer au greffe) (*v.t.*), to file : passer une déclaration au bureau d'enregistrement, to file a return at the registration office.

passer (inscrire) (Comptab.) (*v.t.*), to pass ; to make ; to enter ; to post : passer une écriture *ou* passer un article en compte, to pass, to make, an entry ; to enter, to enter up, an item. passer écriture de, to enter ; to enter up : passer écriture d'une opération, to enter, to enter up, a transaction. passer un article en compte courant, to pass an item to, to enter an item in, current account. passer un article aux profits et pertes, to post an item to profit and loss account.

passer (traverser un lieu sans s'y arrêter) (*v.i.*), to pass ; to cross : (*steamer*) X. passé Ouessant le 31 (*date*) pour Anvers (Mouvement des Navires), (*steamer*) X. (for Antwerp) passed (*or* psd) (*or* p.) Ushant 31 (*date*) (Shipping News). passer de France en Angleterre, to cross from France to England.

passer (en parlant des cours de bourse) (*v.i.*), to shade : l'action X. passe de 1 610 à 1 595, X. shares shaded from 1,610 to 1,595 francs.

passer après (prendre rang après), to rank after : privilège qui passe immédiatement après un autre (*m.*), right which ranks immediately after another.

passer au bassin (se dit d'un navire), to dock (*v.i.*).

passer avant (prendre rang avant), to rank before ; to take precedence of : les créanciers privilégiés passent avant les créanciers ordinaires (*m.pl.*), preferential creditors rank before ordinary creditors.

passer en contrebande, to smuggle (*v.t.*).

passer un dividende (ne pas le déclarer), to pass a dividend. See example under **passation**.

passible (*adj.*), liable : être passible de dommages-intérêts, to be liable for damages. personne passible de l'impôt (*f.*), person liable for tax.

les lettres de change sont passibles du droit de timbre (*f.pl.*), bills of exchange are liable to stamp duty. passible de droits, dutiable ; liable to duty : marchandises passibles de droits (*f.pl.*), dutiable goods ; goods liable to duty.

passif (*n.m.*) (opp. à *actif*), liabilities ; liability : l'excédent de l'actif sur le passif (*m.*), the excess of assets over liabilities. passif éventuel [passif éventuel *ou* passifs éventuels *pl.*], contingent liability [contingent liabilities *pl.*]. passif à long terme, long term liabilities. passif exigible à court terme *ou simplement* passif exigible, current liabilities. passif non exigible (capital-actions, obligations, réserves), non current liabilities.

patente de santé (*f.*), bill of health : patente de santé brute *ou simplement* patente brute, foul bill of health ; foul bill. patente (de santé) nette, clean bill (of health) ; pratique. patente (de santé) suspecte, suspected bill, touched bill (of health).

patron, -onne (pers.) (*n.*), employer ; principal ; master (*m.*) : le patron d'une maison de commerce, the principal of a business house. patron et préposé, master and servant. patron d'un bateau, master, captain, skipper, of a boat.

le patronat et le salariat, employers and employed.

patronner (*v.t.*), to father : émission patronnée par une banque (*f.*), issue fathered by a bank.

pauvre (*adj.*), poor.

pavillon (*n.m.*), flag : le navire porte un pavillon qui est le signe de la nationalité du navire, the ship carries a flag which is the sign of the ship's nationality. navire naviguant sous pavillon français (*m.*), ship sailing under the French flag. le commerce suit le pavillon *ou* le pavillon précède la marchandise, trade follows the flag. pavillon ami, friendly flag. pavillon de quarantaine, quarantine flag. pavillon ennemi, enemy flag. pavillon neutre, neutral flag.

payable (*adj.*), payable : droit payable par anticipation (*m.*), duty payable in advance. traite payable à vue, à présentation (*f.*), draft payable at sight, on presentation (*or* on demand). les intérêts et dividendes sont payables le 1er janvier (acompte) et le 1er juillet (solde), interest and dividends are payable 1st January (interim) and 1st July (final). actions de 500 fr., payables 100 fr. en souscrivant (*ou* à la souscription), 100 fr. à la (*ou* lors de la) répartition, tant de francs au (*date*) (*f.pl.*), shares of fr. 500, payable fr. 100 on application, fr. 100 on allotment, so many francs on (*date*).

payable comptant (annulation du barrement d'un chèque), pay cash.

payant, -e (*adj.*), paying:
entreprise payante (*f.*), paying concern.

paye (*n.f.*), pay; wages; wage:
paye d'un ouvrier, pay, wages, of a workman.

payement (*n.m.*). Same as **paiement**, *q.v.*

payer (*v.t.*), to pay:
payer des contributions, ses dettes, un dividende aux actionnaires, to pay taxes, one's debts, a dividend to the shareholders.
si le fret n'est pas payé, le destinataire le règle, if the freight is not paid, the consignee settles it.
payer à l'échéance, to pay at due date; to pay at maturity:
payer une lettre de change à l'échéance, to pay a bill of exchange at maturity.
ne pas payer un effet, to dishonour a bill; to dishonour a bill by non payment; not to pay a bill:
effets qui ne sont pas payés (*m.pl.*), bills which are dishonoured (*or* which are dishonoured by non payment) (*or* which are not paid). *Cf.* ne pas accepter un effet, *under* **accepter**.
payer à présentation *ou* payer à bureau ouvert *ou* payer à guichet ouvert, to pay on demand; to pay on presentation; to pay over the counter:
payer un billet à présentation, to pay a bill on presentation.
payer au comptant *ou* payer comptant *ou* payer en espèces, to pay in cash:
payer comptant fin courant, fin prochain, to pay in cash at the end of the present month, at the end of next month.
payer au comptant-compté, to pay cash down; to pay spot cash; to pay on or before delivery.
payer d'avance *ou* payer par avance *ou* payer par anticipation, to pay in advance; to pay in anticipation; to prepay:
payer une somme d'avance, to pay an amount in advance; to prepay an amount.
payer en trop, to overpay:
ristourne d'une somme payée en trop (*f.*), return of an amount overpaid.
payer intégralement, to pay in full.
payer recta, to pay on the nail.
payer une lettre de change par intervention, to pay a bill of exchange for honour.
actions de 500 francs, 200 francs payés (*Abrév.* : act. f. 500 f. 200 p.), shares of 500 francs, 200 francs paid.
orges : parcelles Azoff mer noire, mars-avril, 17/6d. payé et acheteur (*ou en abrév.* : 17/6 P. & A. *ou* P. & ach.), barley : parcels Azoff/ Black Sea, March-April, 17/6d. paid and buyers.

à payer, payable:
effets à payer (*m.pl.*), bills payable.

une fois payé, -e. See under **fois.**

se payer (*v.r.*), to be paid; to pay each other:
le dividende se paye annuellement en avril ou mai, the dividend is paid yearly in April or May.

les différences qu'ils ont à se payer (*f.pl.*), the differences they have to pay each other.

payeur, -euse (*adj.*), paying:
banquier payeur (*m.*), paying banker.

payeur, -euse (pers.) (*n.*), payer:
payeur par intervention (effets de commerce), payer for honour.

payeur (guichetier payeur) (Banq.) (*n.m.*), payer; paying cashier.

payeur (tiré d'une lettre de change) (*n.m.*), drawee (of a bill of exchange).

payeur de la prime (Opérations à prime) (Bourse) (*m.*) (opp. à *receveur de la prime*), giver of the rate.

payez à *ou* **veuillez payer à** (*v. à l'impératif*), pay; pay to:
à trois jours de vue payez (*ou* veuillez payer) à l'ordre de MM. X. & Cⁱᵉ, à l'ordre de nous-mêmes, la somme de tant (lettre de change), three days after sight pay to the order of Messrs X. & Co., to our order, so much. See also example under **première de change.**
payez à l'ordre de MM. X. & Cⁱᵉ (écrit endossé sur un effet, une lettre de change, etc.), pay to the order of Messrs X. & Co.
payez à l'ordre de M. X. *ou* payez à M. X. ou ordre (écrit sur un chèque), pay X. Esq. or order; pay Mr X. or order.
payez à moi-même, payez à nous-mêmes (chèque), pay self, pay selves.
payez à l'ordre de moi-même, de nous-mêmes (chèque), pay self, selves, or order.
payez au porteur, pay bearer; pay to bearer.
payez au porteur M. X. *ou* payez à M. X. ou au porteur (chèque), pay X. Esq. or bearer; pay Mr X. or bearer.

pays (*n.m.*), country; territory:
pays à étalon d'or *ou* pays monométalliste-or, gold standard country.
pays d'origine, country of origin.
pays de mandat, mandated territory.
pays de protectorat, protectorate.
pays de provenance, last country of exportation; country from which the goods have been directly imported, as opposed to the *pays d'origine*, i.e., the country where the product has been grown or manufactured. In France, goods coming from a *pays de provenance* are subject to the *surtaxe de provenance*. As this surtax does not exist in English customs, there is no specific technical equivalent in English of the French word *provenance* in this sense, *and cf.* port de provenance:
pour l'application du tarif, les importateurs doivent indiquer dans leurs déclarations l'origine et la provenance de la marchandise, c'est-à-dire le pays où la marchandise a été produite et celui d'où elle est directement importée, (In France) for the application of the tariff, the importers must state in their entries the origin and the *provenance* of the goods, that is to say, the country where the goods have been produced and that from which they have been directly imported.

pays faisant partie de l'Union postale universelle, Union country; country in the
Universal Postal Union.
pays hors l'Union postale universelle, non
Union country.

péage (*n.m.*), toll.

pécuniaire (*adj.*), pecuniary:
pertes pécuniaires (*f.pl.*), pecuniary losses.

pécuniairement (*adv.*), pecuniarily.

pécunieux, -euse (*adj.*), moneyed; flush of
money.

peine (pénalité) (*n.f.*), penalty:
cette déclaration doit être effectuée dans les
vingt-quatres heures de l'arrivée du navire
sous peine de 500 francs d'amende, this
entry must be made within twenty four hours
of the arrival of the ship on (*or* under) penalty
of 500 francs fine.
peines encourues pour fausse déclaration en cas
de fraude, ou de contravention, penalties
incurred for false declaration, in case of
fraud, or breach of the regulations.

pelote (*n.f.*) *ou* **peloton** (*n.m.*) (de ficelle), ball (of
string).

pénalité (*n.f.*), penalty; forfeit:
être passible des pénalités prononcées par les
lois, to be liable to the penalties imposed by
law.
pénalités encourues pour fausse déclaration,
en cas de fraude, ou de contravention,
penalties incurred for false declaration, in
case of fraud, or breach of the regulations.
pénalités en cas d'inexécution du contrat,
penalties, forfeits, for non performance of the
agreement.
une pénalité de tant par jour de retard en cas
de non livraison à la date convenue, a
penalty of so much per day of delay in
case of non delivery on the agreed date.
pénalité: confiscation de la marchandise faussement déclarée et amende de tant de francs
au maximum, penalty: confiscation of the
goods falsely entered and a fine not exceeding
so many francs.

péniche (*n.f.*), lighter; barge.

penny [pence *pl.*] (monnaie anglaise) (*n.m.*)
(Abrév.: **d.**), penny.

pension (*n.f.*) *ou* **pension de retraite,** pension;
retiring allowance:
pension à vie *ou* pension viagère, pension for
life; life pension.

pension (Banq. & Bourse) (*n.f.*), pawning; pawn:
titres en pension (*m.pl.*), pawned stock; stock
in pawn.
valeurs en report ou en pension (*f.pl.*), stocks
on contango or in pawn.

pensionnaire (pers.) (*n.m.* ou *f.*), pensioner.

pensionner (*v.t.*), to pension; to pension off:
pensionner un employé, to pension, to pension
off, an employee.

pénurie (manque) (*n.f.*), scarcity; dearth; want;
lack:
pénurie d'argent, want, lack, of money.
pénurie de fret, scarcity, lack, of freight.

percepteur (pers.) (*n.m.*), collector; collector of
taxes; tax collector; rate collector:

percepteur des contributions directes, collector
of taxes (income tax, or the like).

perception (*n.f.*), collection:
perception des impôts, des droits de douane,
collection of taxes, of customs duties.

percevable (*adj.*), collectable; collectible:
taxe percevable (*f.*), collectable tax.

percevoir (*v.t.*), to collect; to charge:
percevoir une taxe, to collect a tax.
la commission perçue par la banque est de 1 0/0,
the commission charged by the bank is 1%.
port perçu (*m.*), carriage paid; postage paid.

perdant, -e (*adj.*), losing:
les numéros perdants (*m.pl.*), the losing numbers.

perdant, -e (pers.) (*n.*), loser:
les perdants payent, the losers pay.

perdre (*v.t.*), to lose:
perdre un procès, son argent, tous ses droits
à une indemnité, to lose an action, one's
money, all one's rights to an indemnity.
perdre de vue une considération importante, to
lose sight of an important consideration.
perdre du terrain, to lose ground:
l'action X. perd du terrain à 3 375, X. shares
lost ground at 3,375 francs.
marchandises perdues par naufrage ou échouement (*f.pl.*), goods lost by wreck or stranding.
perdu sans nouvelles (en parlant d'un navire),
missing. See examples under syn. **sans
nouvelles.**

se perdre (faire naufrage) (*v.r.*), to be lost;
to be wrecked:
navire qui coula et se perdit corps et biens
(*m.*), ship which sank and was lost crew
and cargo.

perforateur (classement de lettres) (*n.m.*), perforator; punch.

perforer (*v.t.*), to perforate:
perforer des timbres aux initiales de la raison
sociale, to perforate stamps with the firm's
initials.

perforeuse de chèques (*f.*), cheque perforator;
cheque protector.

péril (*n.m.*), peril:
péril de mer *ou* péril de la mer *ou* péril maritime
maritime peril; marine peril; peril of the
sea; sea peril.
péril imminent, imminent peril.

périmé, -e (*adj.*), lapsed; expired; out of date:
mandat périmé (mandat de poste) (*m.*), lapsed
order (money order).
coupon de retour périmé (billet de chemin de
fer) (*m.*), return half out of date.

périmer (*v.i.*), to lapse; to expire.

périmètre de distribution gratuite (Poste) (*m.*),
limit of free delivery.

période (*n.f.*), period:
pendant une période de tant d'années, during
a period of so many years.
See also example under **année.**

périodique (*adj.*), periodic; periodical:
tirages au sort périodiques (*m.pl.*), periodical
drawings.

périodique (journal) (*n.m.*), periodical.

périr (*v.i.*), to perish; to be lost:
navire qui a péri, corps et biens, sans laisser

aucune trace (*m.*), ship which is lost, crew and cargo, without leaving any trace.

périssable (*adj.*), perishable:
marchandises périssables (*f.pl.*), perishable goods; perishable merchandise.

péristyle (*n.m.*). *See notes under* marché des valeurs.

permanent, -e (*adj.*) (Ant.: *temporaire*), permanent; standing:
placement permanent (*m.*), permanent investment.
ordre permanent (*m.*), standing order.

permis (*n.m.*), permit; licence; order; note; bill:
permis d'embarquement, shipping note.
permis d'entrée (marchandises), import permit.
permis de conduire (voitures automobiles), driver's licence.
permis de débarquement *ou* permis de débarquer, landing order.
permis de douane, customs permit.
permis de navigation, navigation permit.
permis de provisions de bord, victualling bill.
permis de sortie (navire), clearance.
permis de sortie (marchandises), export permit.
permis de sortie d'entrepôt, warehouse keeper's order (delivery order addressed to bonded storekeeper).
permis de transbordement, transhipment permit.

permission (*n.f.*), permission; leave:
permission de s'absenter, leave of absence.

perpétuel, -elle (*adj.*) (Abrév.: **perp.** *ou* **perpét.**), perpetual:
les rentes françaises sont ou perpétuelles ou amortissables (*f.pl.*), French rentes are either perpetual or redeemable.

perpétuité (*n.f.*), perpetuity.

personne (*n.f.*), person:
personne interposée, nominee.
sous un nom interposé, in a nominee's name.

personne ne demandant plus la parole, M. le président met aux voix les résolutions suivantes; personne ne demandant plus la parole, les résolutions suivantes ont été mises aux voix et adoptées à l'unanimité, there being no further questions, the chairman put the following resolutions to the meeting; there being no further questions, the following resolutions were put to the meeting and carried unanimously.

personne? personne? (Téléph.), have you finished?:
la téléphoniste, si elle n'entend aucune conversation, coupe après avoir interrogé « Personne? Personne? » the telephonist, if she hears no conversation, cuts off after having asked " Have you finished? "

personnel, -elle (*adj.*), personal:
compte personnel (*m.*), personal account.
les lettres sont ouvertes, abstraction faite de celles portant la mention « personnelle, » qui sont remises aux destinataires (*f.pl.*), the letters are opened except those marked " personal," which are handed to the addressees.

personnel (*n.m.*), staff:
personnel de bureau, office staff.
personnel sédentaire, indoor staff.

personnellement (*adv.*), personally:
être personnellement responsable du paiement d'une somme, to be personally liable for the payment of an amount.

perspective (*n.f.*), prospect:
perspectives d'avenir, future prospects; prospects for the future.

perte (opp. à *profit* ou *bénéfice*) (*n.f.*) (Abrév.: p^{te}), loss:
perte d'argent, de temps, de marché (*ou* de débouché), d'un navire, des bagages du voyageur, loss of money, of time, of market, of a ship, of the passenger's luggage.
perte au change *ou* perte à la monnaie *ou* perte au cours *ou* perte sur le change *ou* perte sur change, loss on exchange.
perte brute, gross loss.
perte d' (*ou* par) avarie commune, general average loss.
perte d'exploitation, trading loss.
perte de place *ou* pertes de place, cost (*or* costs) of collection (of bills of exchange); bank charges (on bills). *See note under* syn. change de place.
perte de vie ou blessures corporelles, loss of life or personal injury.
perte des loyers (Assce-incendie), loss of rent.
perte en poids, loss in weight.
pertes et profits (pertes et gains), profit and loss.
pertes et profits *ou* compte des pertes et profits (*Abrév.:* P. & P. *ou* P.P.), profit and loss; profit and loss account:
passer un article aux pertes et profits, to post an item to profit and loss.
perte maritime, marine loss.
perte nette, net loss.
perte nette pour balance (compte pertes et profits), balance being net loss.
pertes ou avaries résultant des négligences, fautes, ou défauts, loss or damage arising from negligence, fault, or failure.
perte partielle (Assce), partial loss.
perte sèche, dead loss.
perte totale (Assce), total loss:
perte totale du navire, de la marchandise, total loss of the ship, of the cargo.
steamer qui s'est échoué, et qui sera probablement une perte totale (*m.*), steamer which stranded, and which will probably be a total loss.
perte totale partielle, partial total loss.
perte totale seulement, total loss only.

à perte, at a loss:
vendre à perte, to sell at a loss.

perte (différence en moins entre le pair d'un titre et son cours) (*n.f.*) (opp. à *prime*), discount:
une action de 500 fr. qui se vend 400 fr., se négocie à 100 fr. de perte, a share of 500 francs which sells at 400 francs, is dealt in at 100 francs discount.
emprunt qui fait 1/4 0/0 de perte (Bourse) (*m.*), loan which is called ¼% discount.

être en perte *ou* faire perte, to be at a discount ;
to stand at a discount :

actions qui sont en perte (*ou* qui font perte)
sur le marché (*f.pl.*), shares which are at
a discount (*or* which stand at a discount)
on the market.

pays où l'or se cote en prime ou en perte sur
la base de tant de francs pour un kilogramme
d'or pur (*m.*), country where gold is quoted
at a premium or at a discount on the basis
of so many francs for a kilogramme of pure
gold.

pesage (*n.m.*) *ou* **pesée** (*n.f.*), weighing :
pesage contradictoire, check weighing.
pesée d'épreuve, test weighing.

pèse-lettre [**pèse-lettres** *pl.*] (*n.m.*), letter scales ;
letter scale.

peser (*v.t.*), to weigh :
peser au décigramme près (Douanes), to weigh
to the nearest decigramme.
marchandises pesées jusqu'au gramme (*f.pl.*),
goods weighed to the gramme.

peser (*v.i.*), to weigh.

peseur (pers.) (*n.m.*), weigher :
peseurs et mesureurs jurés, sworn weighers
and measurers.

petit bleu (*m.*), telegram.

petit cabotage (*m.*). See explanatory note under
cabotage.

petit clerc (*m.*), junior clerk (in a lawyer's office).

petit commerce (*m.*), retail trade.

petit commis (*m.*), office boy.

petit consulat (*m.*), captain's report (of extraordinary incidents during the voyage).
See explanation under **consulat.**

petit employé (*m.*), junior clerk (in a commercial
office, or the like).

petite annonce (*f.*), small advertisement ; classified
advertisement.

petite avarie (Assce mar.) (*f.*), petty average ;
petit average.

petite caisse (*f.*), petty cash.

petite monnaie (*f.*), small change.

petite prime pour le lendemain *ou* **petite prime au
lendemain** (Bourse) (*f.*), day to day option ;
one day option ; option till the next day.

petite vitesse (Ch. de f.) (*f.*) (Abrév. : **p.v.** *ou*
P.V.), slow train ; slow trains ; goods
train (*or* trains) ; freight train (*or* trains) ;
merchandise train (*or* trains) :
marchandises expédiées en petite vitesse (*f.pl.*),
goods sent by goods train.

petites coupures (*f.pl.*) (Abrév. : **p.cp.**), small
denominations.

petites dépenses (*f.pl.*), petty expenses ; petties.

pétroles (*n.m.pl.*) *ou* **valeurs de pétrole** (*f.pl.*) *ou*
valeurs pétrolières *ou* **valeurs pétrolifères**
(*f.pl.*) *ou* **pétrolières** (*n.f.pl.*) *ou* **pétrolifères**
(*n.f.pl.*), oils ; oil shares.

pétrolier (*n.m.*), oiler ; oil ship.

peu d'affaires (*m.*), little doing ; little business :
l'action X. eut peu d'affaires, there was little
doing in X. shares.

peu important, -e *ou* **de peu d'importance,** small :
ordre de peu d'importance (*m.*), small order.

phare (*n.m.*), lighthouse.

pièce (*n.f.*) *ou* **pièce d'argent** *ou* **pièce de monnaie**
piece ; coin ; piece of money :
une pièce de 5 francs, a 5 franc piece.

une pièce d'or (*ou* une pièce en or), une pièce
d'argent (*ou* une pièce en argent), a gold
coin, a silver coin.

pièces d'or *ou* pièces en or, gold coins ; gold
coin.

pièce droite, standard coin ; full weight coin ;
standard weight coin ; coin of standard
weight and fineness :

pièce faible *ou* pièce légère, light coin :

pièce forte, overweight coin :

une pièce est dite droite, quand son poids
et son titre sont bien exacts : elle est dite
faible ou forte suivant qu'elle est au-dessous
ou au-dessus, a coin is said to be standard
(*or* to be of standard weight and fineness)
when its weight and its fineness are quite
correct : it is said to be light or overweight
according as it is under or over.

pièce type, standard coin :

l'étalon monétaire est le métal précieux qu
entre dans la composition des pièces types
lesquelles ont force libératoire illimitée (*m.*),
the monetary standard is the precious metal
which enters into the composition of standard
coins, which are unlimited legal tender.

pièce usée, worn coin.

pièce (document) (*n.f.*), document ; voucher
paper :

pièces d'embarquement, shipping documents.

pièces de bord, ship's papers.

pièce de caisse *ou* pièce justificative de caisse
cash voucher.

pièce de compatibilité *ou* pièce comptable
bookkeeping voucher.

pièce de dépense, voucher for payment.

pièce de recette, voucher for receipt.

pièce jointe *ou* pièce annexe, enclosure.

pièce justificative *ou* pièce à l'appui *ou* pièce
justificative à l'appui *ou* pièce certificativ
ou *simplement* pièce, voucher ; vouche
in support ; document in support :

comptes accompagnés de pièces justificative
(*m.pl.*), accounts accompanied by vouchers

pièces à l'appui d'un compte, vouchers i
support of an account.

pièce justificative de perte (Assce), proof o
loss (voucher) :

les indemnités dues par les assureurs son
payables comptant, trente jours après l
remise complète des pièces justificative
(*f.pl.*), losses due by the underwriters ar
payable in cash, thirty days after complet
delivery of proofs.

pièces probantes, documentary evidence.

la pièce, à la pièce. See under **la.**

pied (*n.m.*) (Ant. : *tête*), foot ; bottom ; footing :
pied d'un état, foot, bottom, of a statement.
les marchandises seront payées sur le pied d
leur valeur réelle (*f.pl.*), the goods will b
paid for on the footing of their actual value.

pied de la prime *ou* *simplement* **pied** (*n.m.*) (Bourse)
limit price at which option is abandoned
(See explanation under **prime.**)

pied de l'ou, limit price at which put option
is abandoned.

pied du dont, limit price at which call option
is abandoned.

pieds humides (*m.pl.*), pushers who stand outside
a Bourse (and get *wet feet* when it is raining)
selling scrip of non existent or defunct
companies : the buyers are either swindlers
or fools.

pillage (*n.m.*), pilfering ; pilferage ; plundering :
pillage des effets naufragés,   plundering of
wrecked effects.

piller (*v.t.*), to pilfer ; to plunder.

pilotage (*n.m.*), pilotage ; piloting :
le pilotage est obligatoire dans une zone
délimitée pour chaque port,   pilotage is
compulsory within a zone prescribed for
each port.

pilotages le long des côtes ou à l'entrée des
ports,   pilotings along coasts or at the
entrance of ports.

pilotage d'entrée, pilotage inwards.

pilotage de sortie, pilotage outwards.

pilotage (droit) (*n.m.*), pilotage ; pilotage dues.

pilote (pers.) (*n.m.*), pilot :
avec faculté de naviguer avec ou sans pilotes,
with leave to sail with or without pilots.

pilote aérien, air pilot.

pilote hauturier *ou* pilote de mer, sea pilot.

pilote lamaneur, branch pilot.

Note :—The French distinguish between (1)
pilote hauturier who pilots ships on the high
seas ; very rarely used and never obligatorily,
and (2) the *pilote* or *pilote côtier* or *pilote
lamaneur* or *locman* who pilots ships in or
out of ports.

Trinity House (English) pilots are of
two classes, *sea pilots* and *river pilots*. The
sea pilot brings the vessel to the " entrance "
of the port. The *river pilot* takes charge of the
vessel from the time the sea pilot leaves her
until she arrives at the entrance of the dock
where she will discharge, when the *dock pilot*
takes charge until the vessel is safely moored
at her berth. As an instance, a ship coming
into the Port of London is usually boarded
by the sea pilot at Dungeness or Beachy
Head and piloted by him as far as
Gravesend, where the river pilot takes
charge.

piloter (*v.t.*), to pilot.

pince à poser les œillets *ou* pince à œillets (*f.*),
eyelet pliers ; eyelet punch.

pince-notes [pince-notes *pl.*] (*n.m.*), letter clip.

pique-notes [pique-notes *pl.*] (*n.m.*), bill file.

pirate (pers.) (*n.m.*), pirate.

piraterie (*n.f.*), piracy.

place (ville ; endroit) (*n.f.*), place ; town ; spot :
place bancable *ou* place bancale, bank place.
See note under **bancable.**

place médiate *ou* place intermédiaire (change
indirect) (Arbitrage de banque),   intermediate place.

faire la place, to do the place ; to canvass the
town.

chèque sur place (*m.*), town cheque.

sur place, on the spot :
marchandises achetées et revendues sur place
(*f.pl.*), goods bought and sold again on the
spot.

place (marché) (*n.f.*), market :
jour de place (*m.*), market day.

place de change *ou* place cambiste, foreign
exchange market.

la place française est gros acheteur de portefeuille anglais, the French market is a big
buyer of English bills.

quand la place est acheteur, when the market
is a buyer.

place chargée, place dégagée (*ou* soulagée)
(Bourse).   See under **charger, dégager** *or*
soulager.

place (pour un navire) (*n.f.*), berth ; berthage :
place à quai, quay berth.

place (pour un passager de navire, pour un
voyageur dans un wagon-lit ; couchette) (*n.f.*),
berth :
place de 1ʳᵉ classe, 1st class berth.

compartiment à une place, à deux places
(wagon-lit) (*m.*), one-berth, two-berth, compartment.

place (pour un voyageur de chemin de fer, ou
analogue) (*n.f.*), seat ; fare :
(en France) de trois à sept ans, les enfants
paient demi-place et ont droit à une place
distincte ; au-dessus de sept ans, les enfants
paient place entière, (in France) from three
to seven years old, children pay half fare
and have the right to a separate seat ; over
seven years children pay full fare.

place (emploi) (*n.f.*), place ; situation ; post ;
position ; employment ; job ; berth ; office :
perdre sa place, to lose one's place.

si une place d'administrateur devient vacante,
if a director's office becomes vacant.

placement (action de placer) (*n.m.*), placing :
placement des commandes chez les fournisseurs,
placing orders with suppliers.

placement d'actions dans le public, placing
shares with the public.

marchandise de placement sûr (*f.*), goods which
can easily be placed.

placement (des navires) (*n.m.*), berthing (of ships).

placement (disposition d'un capital) (*n.m.*), investment ; lending :
placement de fonds, investment of funds (*or* of
money).

placement de fonds, de titres, en report,
lending money, stock, on contango.

placements en actions de chemins de fer, investments in railway shares.

faire un bon placement, to make a good investment.

placement à court terme, short term investment ; short dated investment.

placement à long terme *ou* placement de
longue haleine, long term **investment** ; long
dated investment.

placement sûr *ou* placement de tout repos, safe
investment.

placements de père de famille, gilt-edged
(*or* gilt-edge) investments.

placements à revenus fixes, fixed yield investments.

placements à revenus fixes et à lots, fixed yield investments with rights of participation in drawings for cash prizes, such as *obligations à lots* (prize bonds).

placements à revenus variables, variable yield investments.

placements temporaires, temporary investments.

placement (*n.m.*) *ou* **placement à échéance** (dépôt à terme fixe) (Banq.), fixed deposit; deposit for a fixed period.

placer (mettre dans un lieu; déposer) (*v.t.*), to place; to put; to deposit:
placer des titres en garde, to place, to deposit, securities in safe custody.

placer (passer; donner; écouler) (*v.t.*), to place:
placer une assurance supplémentaire sur une cargaison assurée, to place an additional insurance on an insured cargo.
placer des actions dans le public, to place shares with the public.

se placer (*v.r.*), to be placed:
une partie seulement de l'emprunt parvint à se placer, a part only of the loan came to be placed.

placer (prêter ou céder à intérêt) (*v.t.*), to invest; to put; to lend:
placer de l'argent, tous ses fonds disponibles sur les valeurs réalisables, to invest money, all one's available money in realizable securities.
placer en rentes viagères le restant de sa fortune, to invest, to put, the remainder of one's fortune in life annuities.
placer des capitaux en report, to lend, to employ, money on contango.
placer des titres en report, to lend stock on contango.

placer (procurer un emploi à) (*v.t.*), to find a place for; to get a situation for; to place:
placer un jeune homme dans une maison de commerce, to find a place for a young man in a business house.

se placer (*v.r.*), to find a place; to get a situation.

placeur, -euse (pers.) (*n.*), placer.

placier, -ère (pers.) (*n.*), canvasser; town traveller.

plage (*n.f.*), beach; sea beach; shore; seashore:
une plage de sable, a sandy beach.

plainte (*n.f.*), complaint:
plaintes formulées par le public à raison des incidents de l'exploitation des lignes, complaints formulated by the public by reason of incidents of working the lines.

plan (*n.m.*), plan; project; scheme; table:
le plan Dawes, le plan Young, the Dawes plan, the Young plan.
plan d'amortissement, redemption table.
plan d'arrimage *ou* plan de chargement, stowage plan.
plan de campagne, plan of campaign.

planche (délai de planche) (*n.f.*), laytime:
usage d'après lequel la planche ne court que d'un certain jour (*m.*), custom according

to which laytime only runs from a certain day.

plaque-support de papier (d'une machine à écrire) (*f.*), paper shelf.

plein, -e (*adj.*), full:
plein tarif (*m.*), full rates; full fare:
télégrammes à plein tarif (*m.pl.*), telegrams at full rates.
billet à plein tarif (*m.*), full fare ticket.
pleine mer (*f.*), open sea; high seas:
navires en pleine mer (*m.pl.*), ships on the high seas.
pleine prime (Assce) (*f.*), full premium.

plein (Assce) (*n.m.*), full (*adj.*); full up (*adj.*); line; limit; office limit:
compagnie qui a son plein sur un certain risque (*f.*), company which is full (or is full up) (or which has its line or its limit or its office limit) on a certain risk.
assureur qui n'est pas responsable pour une somme supérieure au plein maximum souscrit par lui dans la police (*m.*), insurer who is not liable for an amount above the maximum line subscribed by him in the policy.
pour chaque expédition effectuée sur un navire à désigner, il est fixé un plein au delà duquel l'assureur ne répond pas, for each shipment made on a ship to be named, there is fixed a limit (or an office limit) beyond which the underwriter is not liable.

pléthore (*n.f.*), plethora; glut:
pléthore de capitaux, glut of money; plethora of funds.

pli (enveloppe de lettre) (*n.m.*), cover; envelope:
deux lettres sous le même pli, two letters under the same cover.
expédier des titres sous pli recommandé, to send certificates under registered cover.
une lettre sous pli cacheté, a letter in a sealed envelope.

pli (lettre) (*n.m.*), letter:
envoyer des billets de banque par pli chargé, to send bank notes by insured letter.

pli (liasse) (Chambre de compensation des banquiers) (*n.m.*), charge (bundle of paid vouchers).

pliage (*n.m.*), folding; folding up.

plier (*v.t.*), to fold; to fold up:
plier une lettre, to fold, to fold up, a letter.

plomb (Douanes) (*n.m.*), plomb.

plombage (*n.m.*), plombing.

plomber (*v.t.*), to plomb:
plomber un colis, un wagon contenant des marchandises, to plomb a package, a truck containing goods.

plume (*n.f.*), pen; nib:
plume d'acier *ou* plume métallique, steel pen.
plume en or, à bec d'iridium, gold pen, with iridium point.

plumier (*n.m.*), pen tray.

pluralité d'assurances (*f.*), double insurance.

pluralité d'exemplaires (*f.*), plurality of copies; set:
en raison de la pluralité d'exemplaires du connaissement, il peut y avoir entre les divers exemplaires des divergences, owing

to the plurality of copies of the bill of lading, there may be divergencies between the different copies. See also example under **exemplaire.**

plus (Arith.) (*n.m.*), plus; plus sign:
il fallut un plus, vous avez mis un moins, you should have put a plus, you have put a minus.

plus (Arith.) (*prép.*), plus (*adj.*):
trois plus quatre égale sept (*Abrév.:* $3 + 4 = 7$), three plus four equals seven (*Abbrev.:* $3 + 4 = 7$).
prix d'achat, plus le courtage (*m.*), purchase price, plus brokerage.

en plus ou en moins, over or under; plus or minus:
toute différence en plus ou en moins (*f.*), any difference over or under; any plus or minus difference.

plus d'affaires, more doing; more business:
plus d'affaires aux industrielles (Bourse), more doing in industrials.

plus haut et plus bas cours (Bourse) (*m.pl.*), highest and lowest prices.

plus offrant enchérisseur *ou* **plus fort enchérisseur** (aux enchères) (*m.*), highest bidder:
le dernier et plus offrant enchérisseur, the last and highest bidder.

plus-payé [plus-payés *pl.*] (*n.m.*), overpayment.

plus prochain courrier (*m.*), next post (*or* mail).

plus-value [plus-values *pl.*] (*n.f.*) (Ant.: *moins-value*), appreciation; increase of value; increase in value; increase; surplus:
plus-value d'actif, des apports, appreciation of assets, of assets brought into a business.
plus-value sur les cours des actions, appreciation in the prices of shares.
plus-value des contributions, surplus in taxes.

être en plus-value, to be up:
l'action X. est en plus-value à 510, X. shares were up at 510 francs.

plusieurs colis réunis sous une enveloppe commune (Douanes) (*m.pl.*), omnibus package.

poche (*n.f.*), pocket:
vider ses poches, to empty one's pockets.

poids (*n.m.*), weight:
poids à l'embarquement, shipping weight.
poids brut, gross weight:
le poids brut est celui qui résulte du pesage du contenu et du contenant, gross weight is that which results from weighing the contents and the container.
poids demi-brut, net weight, i.e., weight of goods including inner packings, but excluding outer cases. In very technical connections such as customs weighings, the translations of the three French expressions (1) poids brut, (2) poids demi-brut, and (3) poids net réel (*or* effectif) are in English (1) gross weight, (2) net weight, and (3) net net weight.
poids net (opp. à *poids brut*), net weight.
poids net légal, net weight without taring (assumed by the customs in accordance with their regulations, in certain cases).

poids net réel *ou* poids net effectif, net net weight. *See note under* poids demi-brut.
poids ou cube *ou* poids ou volume *ou* poids ou encombrement, weight or measurement:
coter le fret à tel taux, poids ou cube, to quote the freight at such a rate, weight or measurement.
poids, valeur, et contenu inconnus, weight, value, and contents unknown.

point (question; matière) (*n.m.*), point:
point de droit, de fait, point of law, of fact.
point en faveur (des haussiers), bull point.
plan qui n'a qu'un point faible (*m.*), plan which has only one weak point.

point (Bourse) (*n.m.*), point:
valeur qui a perdu un demi-point, plusieurs points (*f.*), stock which has lost half a point, several points.
valeur qui est cotée à Londres 1/2 point plus bas qu'à la Bourse de Paris (*f.*), stock which is quoted half a point lower in London than on the Paris Bourse.
point d'entrée de l'or, import (*or* incoming) gold point (*or* bullion point) (*or* specie point).
point de sortie de l'or, export (*or* outgoing) (gold point) (*or* bullion point) (*or* specie point).

point (marque) (*n.m.*), tick.

pointage (*n.m.*), ticking; ticking off; checking; tallying; tally. *Cf.* feuille de pointage.

pointer (*v.t.*), to tick; to tick off; to check; to tally:
pointer les articles d'un compte, to tick, to tick off, to check, the items in an account.
pointer un relevé avec un compte, to check, to tick off, a statement with an account.
pointer un compte (Bourse), to check an account.

pointeur (pers.) (*n.m.*), tally clerk.

pointillé (*n.m.*) *ou* **pointillé perforé,** dotted line; perforation:
détacher un volant de la souche suivant pointillé, to tear off a leaf from the counterfoil along the dotted line (*or* perforation).

police (agents de la sécurité publique) (*n.f.*), police:
police des côtes à terre, coast police; coast-guards.
police des voies ferrées, railway police.

police (Assce) (*n.f.*), policy:
police à forfait *ou* police en bloc *ou* police-bloc [polices-bloc *pl.*] *ou* police globale, open policy for a specific amount:
police à forfait sur valeurs, open policy on valuables for a specific amount.
police à ordre, policy to order.
police à temps *ou* police à terme, time policy.
police à tous risques *ou* police tous risques, all risks policy.
police ajustable (Assce-incendie), floating policy; floater.
police au porteur, policy to bearer.
police au voyage, voyage policy.
police d'abonnement *ou* police flottante *ou* police ouverte (Assce mar.), floating policy; floater; open policy; declaration policy:

une police flottante maritime est celle qui décrit l'assurance en termes généraux et laisse à préciser par des déclarations ultérieures le nom du ou des navires et les autres détails, a marine floating policy is a policy which describes the insurance in general terms, and leaves the name of the ship or ships and other particulars to be defined by subsequent declaration.

police d'assurance, insurance policy; policy of insurance; assurance policy; policy of assurance.

police d'assurance contre l'incendie *ou* police-incendie [polices-incendie *pl.*], fire insurance policy; fire policy.

police d'assurance sur la vie, life insurance policy; life assurance policy.

police d'honneur, honour policy.

police distincte *ou* police séparée, separate policy. See example under **distinct, -e.**

police du Lloyd, Lloyd's policy:
le premier original de la police du Lloyd date d'environ 1613, the first original of Lloyd's policy dates from about 1613.

police évaluée, valued policy.

police franc d'avarie, free of average policy.

police maritime *ou* police d'assurance maritime, marine policy; marine insurance policy; policy of sea insurance:
police française d'assurance maritime sur corps de navires à vapeur, sur marchandises ou facultés, French marine insurance policy on steamship hulls, on goods or cargo.

police nominative *ou* police à bénéficiaire désigné, policy to a named person.

police non évaluée, unvalued policy.

police sur corps, hull policy; ship policy.

police sur facultés, cargo policy.

police terrestre, non marine policy.

police type [polices types *pl.*], standard policy; common policy.

police de chargement (terme employé dans les ports de la Méditerranée) (*f.*), bill of lading; bill.

politique (*n.f.*), policy:
la politique financière des grandes banques, the financial policy of the big banks.
politique de libre-échange, free trade policy.

polycopie (*n.f.*), manifold.

polycopier (*v.t.*), to manifold:
polycopier une lettre, to manifold a letter.

ponctualité (*n.f.*), punctuality:
ponctualité dans ses engagements, punctuality in one's engagements.

ponctuel, -elle (*adj.*), punctual;
réponse ponctuelle (*f.*), punctual reply.

ponctuellement (*adv.*), punctually:
répondre ponctuellement aux lettres que l'on reçoit, to reply punctually to the letters one receives.

pont (d'un navire) (*n.m.*), deck:
pont de tonnage, tonnage deck.
pont inférieur, lower deck.
pont principal, main deck.
pont-promenade [ponts-promenade *pl.*] (*n.m.*), promenade deck.

pont supérieur, upper deck.

pont tente *ou* pont des embarcations, boat deck.

pont à bascule (*m.*) *ou* **pont-bascule** [ponts-bascules *pl.*] (*n.m.*) *ou* **pont à peser** (*m.*), weighbridge.

pontée (*n.f.*), deck cargo; deck load:
pontée au risque des expéditeurs, deck cargo at shippers' risk. *Cf.* charger en pontée.

ponton (*n.m.*), pontoon; hulk.

pool (*n.m.*), pool (combination to fix rates or prices):
pool des blés, wheat pool.

port (transport) (*n.m.*), carriage; carrying.

port (prix payé pour faire porter) (*n.m.*), carriage; postage:
port d'un colis, carriage on a parcel (if conveyed by carrier); postage on a parcel (if sent through the post).
port d'une lettre, postage on a letter.
port dû (*Abrév.:* P.D.) *ou* port à recevoir, carriage forward; carriage to pay:
marchandises expédiées en port dû (*f.pl.*), goods consigned carriage forward.
port payé (*Abrév.:* P.P.) *ou* port perçu, carriage paid; postage paid:
si l'expédition est faite en port payé, l'expéditeur doit régler le montant de la taxe, the consignment is made carriage paid, the sender must pay the amount of the charge.

port (maximum de charge d'un navire) (*n.m.*), burden; burthen:
un navire du port de 1 000 tonneaux, a ship of 1,000 tons burden (*or* burthen). *Cf.* **jauger** (*v.i.*).
port en lourd, dead-weight capacity; dead-weight tonnage; dead weight; capacity:
le port en lourd est le poids exprimé en tonnes (en France, tonnes métriques de 1 000 kilos; en Angleterre, tonnes de 1 016 kilos) qu'un navire déterminé peut porter dead-weight capacity is the weight expressed in tons (in France, metric tons = 0·9842 ton *or* 2,204·6 lbs; in England tons of 20 cwt *or* 2,240 lbs) that a certain ship can lift.
port en marchandises, dead-weight cargo capacity; capacity.

port (retrait d'une côte maritime) (*n.m.*), port; harbour:
le port de Marseille, the port of Marseilles.
port à marée *ou* port d'échouage, tidal harbour.
port aérien, air port.
port autonome, (In France) an autonomous port, i.e., a port administered by a civil port authority, as opposed to a *port non autonome*, i.e., a port, nominally at least, under government authority.
port charbonnier, coal port.
port commercial *ou* port de commerce, commercial port; mercantile port.
port côtier, coast port.
port d'armement (d'un navire), home port.
port d'arrivée, port of arrival.

port d'attache *ou* port d'immatriculation *ou* port d'immatricule, port of registry:
le navire doit avoir un domicile, qui est le port d'attache, a ship must have a domicile, which is the port of registry.

port d'atterrissage, port of landing.

port d'entrepôt (Douanes), warehousing port.

port d'escale *ou* port d'échelle *ou* port intermédiaire, port of call; named port (i.e., port in the customary or advertised route); intermediate port:
Boulogne est un port d'escale (*ou* un port intermédiaire) où les transatlantiques viennent ancrer quelques heures pour prendre les passagers, Boulogne is a port of call (*or* an intermediate port) where the transatlantic boats come to anchor some hours to pick up passengers.

port d'expédition (en douane), port of clearance.

port d'hivernage, wintering port.

port d'ordres, port of call for orders:
port d'ordres situé sur la route du navire et où il trouvera ses instructions, port of call for orders situated on the ship's route and where she will find her instructions.

port de cabotage, coasting port.

port de charge *ou* port de chargement *ou* port d'embarquement *ou* port d'expédition *ou* port expéditeur, port of shipment; shipping port; port of loading; loading port; port of lading; lading port; port of embarcation. (See note under **embarquement**.)

port de construction, building port.

port de décharge *ou* port de déchargement *ou* port de débarquement *ou* port de reste *ou* port de livraison, port of discharge; port of delivery. (*Note:*—port de reste is not strictly correct in this sense, but is often so used in French: *port of destination* is its proper signification.)

port de départ, port of departure.

port de destination *ou* port de reste, port of destination.

ports de l'océan, ocean ports (in France, ports on North Sea, Channel, and Atlantic ocean; distinguished from *ports de la Méditerranée*).

port de la Baltique, Baltic port.

port de la Manche, Channel port.

port de la Méditerranée, Mediterranean port.

port de la Mer du Nord, North Sea port.

port de la Mer Noire, Black Sea port.

port de la métropole *ou* port métropolitain (opp. à *port étranger*), home port.

port de mer *ou* port maritime, seaport; outport.

port de pêche, fishing port.

port de prime abord, port first touched at.

port de provenance, port arrived from (i.e., last loading port). (*Cf.* pays de provenance.)

port de relâche, port of call. See **relâche** for explanation of distinction between this and next entry.

port de relâche *ou* port de relâche forcée *ou* port de refuge *ou* port de salut, port of necessity; port of distress; port of refuge:

port de relâche où le navire s'est réfugié pour se préserver d'un danger qui le menaçait, port of refuge where the ship took shelter (*or* port of necessity [*or* port of distress] where the ship took refuge) to save herself from a danger which threatened her.

port de relèvement, nearest safe port. Cf. **relèvement.**

port de réparation (*ou* de réparations), repairing port.

port de retour, port of return.

port de tête de ligne, terminal port.

port de transbordement, port of transhipment; transhipping port.

port de transit, port of transit.

port de visite, port of survey.

port désigné, named port; nominated port.

ports du Levant, Levantine ports.

port ennemi, enemy port.

port étranger, foreign port.

port final de déchargement *ou* dernier port de reste, final, last, port of discharge.

port franc, free port (where no duties are levied on articles of commerce).

port intérieur *ou* port en rivière *ou* port fluvial (opp. à *port de mer*), close port.

port intermédiaire. *See under* port d'escale.

port le plus convenable, most convenient port.

port le plus voisin *ou* port le plus proche *ou* port le plus rapproché, nearest port.

port libre, open port (open to navigation; not closed, as by ice, or sanitary regulations).

port marchand, mercantile port; commercial port.

port neutre, neutral port.

port ouvert, free port (free for use by trading vessels of all nations).

port pétrolier, oil port.

porte-copie [porte-copie *pl.*] (*n.m.*), copy holder.

portecrayon. See below.

portefeuille. See below.

porte-mine [porte-mine *pl.*] *ou* **porte-mines** [porte-mines *pl.*] (*n.m.*), pencil case.

porte-monnaie [porte-monnaie *pl.*] (*n.m.*), purse.

porte ouverte (Politique internationale) (*f.*), open door:
principe de la porte ouverte (*m.*), open door principle.

porte-plume [porte-plume *pl.*] (*n.m.*), penholder.

porte-plume à réservoir *ou* **porte-plume réservoir** (*m.*), fountain pen.

porte-timbres [porte-timbres *pl.*] (*n.m.*), stamp rack.

portecrayon (*n.m.*), pencil holder.

portecrayon à étui (*m.*), pencil protector.

portée en lourd (*f.*). Same as **port en lourd.**

portefeuille (*n.m.*), portfolio; box; case; bill case; wallet; holding; hand:
nous avons une grande quantité de ces actions en portefeuille, we have a large quantity of these shares in portfolio (*or* in our portfolio) (*or* in our box) (*or* in the box); we have a big holding of these shares.

valeur gardée en portefeuille et encaissée à l'échéance (*f.*), security kept in the portfolio (*or* in the box) and cashed at due date.

la banque publie tous les ans le détail des titres qu'elle a en portefeuille, the bank publishes every year the details of the securities which it has in its portfolio (*or* publishes every year particulars of its holdings).

les effets en portefeuille (*m.pl.*), the bills in the bill case (*or* in the portfolio).

ordres en portefeuille (*m.pl.*) *ou* commandes en portefeuille (*f.pl.*), orders in hand; unfilled orders.

portefeuille-effets (*n.m.*) *ou* **portefeuille d'effets** *ou simplement* **portefeuille** (*n.m.*), bills; bills of exchange:

réescompter le portefeuille d'autres banques, to rediscount other banks' bills.

la place française a été gros acheteur de portefeuille anglais, the French market has been a big buyer of English bills.

service du portefeuille (*m.*) *ou* service du portefeuille-effets (*m.*) *ou simplement* portefeuille, bills department:

le chef du service du portefeuille *ou* le chef du portefeuille, the head of the bills department.

un gonflement du poste « portefeuille-effets » (bilan de banque), an increase of the item " bills of exchange."

portefeuille-titres (*n.m.*) *ou* **portefeuille de titres** (*m.*) *ou* **portefeuille-valeurs** (*n.m.*) *ou* **portefeuille de valeurs** (*m.*) *ou simplement* **portefeuille** (*n.m.*), investments; investment; securities; paper securities; securities for money; paper holdings; holdings; stocks and shares:

le portefeuille de la société comprend des titres appartenant à tous les genres d'industries, notamment des titres d'affaires pétrolifères, the company's investments (*or* holdings) include (*or* the company's portfolio comprises) shares pertaining to all kinds of industries, notably shares in oil concerns.

valeur attrayante, à ce cours, pour le portefeuille (*f.*), stock attractive, at this price, as an investment.

l'action X. semble intéressante pour le portefeuille à son cours actuel sur la seule base du dernier dividende, X. shares seem interesting as an investment at their present price on the basis of the last dividend alone.

la spéculation montre moins de timidité et la clientèle de portefeuille paraît susceptible de s'intéresser de nouveau aux affaires, speculation shows less nervousness and the investing public seems inclined to interest itself again in business.

prévision pour moins-value du portefeuille (*ou* du portefeuille-titres) (*f.*), provision for depreciation of investments (*or* of securities).

articles qui sont bloqués dans le chapitre portefeuille (*ou* qui sont réunis sous la rubrique portefeuille-titres) (*m.pl.*), items

which are lumped under the heading investments.

avoir toute sa fortune en portefeuille, to have all one's fortune invested in paper securities (*or* in stocks and shares).

portefeuilliste (pers.) (*n.m.*), investor.

porter (*v.t.*), to carry; to convey; to lift; to bear; to contain; to take; to carry out; to extend:

porter une somme d'argent (l'avoir sur soi), to carry a sum of money (to have it on one's person).

porter en lourd, to carry dead weight:

navire qui ne peut pas porter en lourd plus de 1 000 tonneaux (*m.*), ship which cannot carry more than 1,000 tons dead weight.

compte qui porte intérêt (*m.*), account which carries interest.

somme portée en réserve (*f.*), amount carried to reserve.

le port en lourd est le poids que le navire peut porter sans immerger sa ligne de charge, dead-weight capacity is the weight a ship will lift without putting her load line under water.

capital qui porte intérêt (*m.*), capital which bears interest.

les titres nominatifs portent le nom de la personne à laquelle ils appartiennent (*m.pl.*), registered share certificates bear the name of the person to whom they belong.

le chèque porte l'endos suivant, the cheque bears the following endorsement.

connaissement qui porte les énonciations suivantes (*m.*), bill of lading which contains the following particulars.

porter une lettre à la poste, to take a letter to the post.

porter la balance des intérêts dans la colonne des capitaux, to carry out, to extend, the balance of interest in the principal column.

porter secours à un navire en détresse, to assist a vessel in distress.

porter sur le fond, to strike, to hit, the bottom:

navire qui porte sur le fond et qui ne revient pas à flot (*m.*), ship which strikes (*or* hits) the bottom and does not get off.

porté (-e) ci-contre, as per contra; per contra:

amortissements sur l'actif porté ci-contre, reserves for depreciation of assets as per contra (*or* for depreciation on assets per contra).

être porté (-e) (figurer), to be shown; to appear; to stand:

valeurs portées à la cote officielle (*f.pl.*), securities shown (*or* appearing) in the official list.

fournisseur qui est porté comme créancier sur les livres (*m.*), supplier who appears as a creditor on the books.

actions qui sont portées dans l'inventaire du portefeuille au cours de la bourse au 31 décembre (*f.pl.*), shares which stand in the list of investments at the market price on 31st December.

la société possède des titres portés dans ses livres pour tant, the company owns securities standing in its books at so much.

se porter caution *ou* **se porter garant, -e,** to become surety; to go surety; to be surety; to be security; to stand surety; to hold oneself liable; to guarantee :

personne qui se porte caution d'une (*ou* pour une) autre personne (*ou* qui se porte garante d'une autre personne), des engagements pris par une autre personne, du paiement d'une dette (*f.*), person who becomes surety for another person, for the engagements contracted by another person, for the payment of a debt.

porter (inscrire) (*v.t.*), to enter; to put; to mark; to show; to shew; to pass; to post :

porter un nom sur une liste, to put, to enter, a name on a list.

porter d'une façon très apparente sur l'enveloppe la mention « Exprès, » mark, put, boldly on the envelope the word " Express."

les envois à distribuer par exprès doivent porter la mention « Exprès, » packets to be delivered by express must be marked " Express."

porter en passif la réserve, to show the reserve among the liabilities.

porter une somme au crédit du compte de réserve, un article en compte courant, to pass an amount to the credit of reserve account, an item to current account.

porter un article au grand livre, to post, to enter, an item in the ledger.

porter (augmenter) (*v.t.*) (Ant. : *ramener*), to increase; to raise :

la circulation autorisée des billets qui, primitivement, était de tant de millions de francs, a été augmentée successivement et portée, l'année dernière, à tant, the authorized note currency which, originally, was so many million francs, has been increased successively, and was raised, last year, to so much.

dividende porté de 5 à 10 p. cent (*m.*), dividend raised (*or* increased) from 5 to 10%.

porteur (pers.) (*n.m.*), bearer; holder; messenger :

le porteur d'une lettre, the bearer of a letter.

porteur d'un chèque, d'une lettre de crédit, bearer, holder, of a cheque, of a letter of credit.

porteur d'un effet de commerce, d'une lettre de change, d'une traite, d'une action, d'une obligation, d'un connaissement, holder of a bill of exchange, of a draft, of a share, of a debenture, of a bill of lading.

porteur de titres, stockholder; scripholder.

porteur pour valeur fournie, holder for value.

tiers porteur, holder in due course.

porteur-exprès [porteurs-exprès *pl.*] (Poste) (*n.m.*), express messenger.

porteur spécial, special messenger.

au porteur, to bearer; bearer (*used as adj.*) :

billet payable au porteur (*m.*), bill payable to bearer.

chèque au porteur (*m.*) (opp. à *chèque à ordre*), bearer cheque; cheque to bearer.

actions au porteur (*f.pl.*) *ou* titres au porteur (*m.pl.*) *ou* valeurs au porteur (*f.pl.*) *ou* effets au porteur (*m.pl.*) (opp. à *actions*, ou *valeurs*, *nominatives*, ou *titres*, ou *effets*, *nominatifs*), bearer shares; bearer stock; bearer securities.

portion (*n.f.*), portion; part; share.

portionnaire (pers.) (*n.m.*), owner (of a share in a ship). Cf. **quirat.**

pose de la quille (*f.*), laying of keel.

pose-plumes [pose-plumes *pl.*] (*n.m.*), pen rack.

position (situation) (*n.f.*), position; book; account :

banquier qui juge de la solvabilité de ses clients d'après la position de leur compte chez lui (*m.*), banker who judges of the solvency of his customers according to the position of their account with him.

acheteur qui doit ou liquider sa position ou se faire reporter (Bourse) (*m.*), buyer who must either close his position (*or* his book) or give on.

position de place (Bourse), market position; market :

le taux des reports est généralement le baromètre de la position de place, the contango rate is generally the barometer of the market position (*or* of the market).

position de place chargée, dégagée *ou* soulagée (Bourse). See under **charger, dégager** *or* **soulager.**

position acheteur *ou* position à la hausse (Bourse), bull position (*or* book) (*or* account).

position vendeur (*ou* à la baisse), bear (*or* short) position (*or* book) (*or* account) :

opérateur qui a une grosse position vendeur de telle valeur (*m.*), operator who has a big bear account in such a stock.

position (emploi) (*n.f.*), position; post; situation; place; job; employment; berth.

posséder (*v.t.*), to possess; to own; to have; to hold :

posséder de grands biens, to possess, to own, to have, a lot of property.

le nombre d'actions qu'il est nécessaire de posséder, the number of shares which it is necessary to hold.

possesseur (pers.) (*n.m.*), possessor; owner; holder :

être possesseur d'une propriété, to be the owner of a property.

possesseur d'une action, d'une obligation, holder of a share, of a debenture.

possession (jouissance) (*n.f.*), possession; owning; having; holding :

possession vaut titre (adage), possession is nine points of the law.

possession (chose possédée) (*n.f.*), possession; holding :

ses possessions en terres, one's possessions in land; one's holdings of land.

les colonies et possessions d'outre-mer, oversea colonies and possessions.

post-scriptum [post-scriptum *pl.*] (*n.m.*) (Abrév.:
P.-S.), postscript; P.S.:
mettre un post-scriptum, to put a postscript.

postal, -e, -aux (*adj.*), postal:
services postaux (*m.pl.*), postal services.

postaliser (*v.t.*), to forward by post (what would
normally have been forwarded by other
means):
postaliser un télégramme, to forward a telegram
by post.

postdate (*n.f.*) (Ant.: *antidate*), postdate; postdating.

postdater (*v.t.*), to postdate:
postdater une lettre, to postdate a letter.

poste (administration publique chargée du transport des lettres, etc.) (*n.f.*), post; postal
service:
la poste est exploitée par l'État, the post is
run by the government.

poste (courrier) (*n.f.*), post; mail:
la poste vient de partir, the post has just gone;
the mail has just left.
poste aérienne *ou* poste-avion [postes-avion *pl.*]
(*Abrév.*: PAV.), air mail.
poste aux lettres, letter post.
poste recommandée (*Abrév.*: PR.), registered
post.

poste (bureau) (*n.f.*), post; post office:
aller à la poste, to go to the post.
poste restante (*Abrév.*: P.R.), poste restante;
to be called for:
adresser une lettre « poste restante, » to
address a letter " poste restante; " to address
a letter " to be called for."

poste (station) (*n.m.*), station:
poste de douane, customs station.
poste de T.S.F., wireless station.
poste émetteur (Télégr.), transmitting station.
poste récepteur (Télégr.), receiving station.

poste (Téléph.) (*n.m.*). See examples:
poste central *ou* poste central téléphonique,
exchange; telephone exchange:
poste central automatique, automatic exchange.
poste central de rattachement, home exchange.
poste central interurbain, trunk exchange.
poste central manuel, manual exchange.
poste central régional, toll exchange.
poste d'abonné *ou* poste d'abonnement, subscriber's line. (*See note under* poste principal
and cf. ligne d'abonné.)
poste principal, direct exchange line; exchange line; main station.
Note :—The literal and proper English translation of *poste* is *station*, and of *ligne* is *line*. In
England, however, while the telephone
engineer will speak of the *main station*
(*poste principal*), meaning the principal
installation or apparatus on the subscriber's premises (as opposed to the
extension), the subscriber will speak of his
telephone installation as his *line*. Thus in
the English Tariff Rates for Telephone
Service, the charges are referred to as being
for *Direct Exchange Lines* and *Extension*

Lines, while in France they are referred to
as for *Postes principaux* and *Postes supplémentaires*, or as *Abonnements principaux*
and *Abonnements supplémentaires*.
poste supplémentaire, extension line; extension; extension station; additional
line.
poste public, call office; public call office.

poste (*n.m.*) *ou* **poste de mouillage** *ou* **poste d'amarrage**, berth; berthage:
poste à quai, quay berth.
poste d'embarquement, loading berth.

poste (rubrique) (*n.m.*), heading; head; item:
un poste spécial à l'actif du bilan, a special
heading on the assets side of the balance
sheet.
la caractéristique du bilan est l'importance du
poste obligations, the feature of the balance
sheet is the amount of the item debentures.

poste (emploi; fonction) (*n.m.*), post; employment; situation; place; position; job; berth.

postulant, -e (pers.) (*n.*), candidate; applicant.

pour (*prép.*) (Abrév.: **p.** *ou* **pr**), for; for and on
behalf of; pro:
l'effet est signé pour et non par procuration (*m.*),
the bill is signed for (*or* for and on behalf of) (*or*
pro) and not per pro. (*or* per procuration).

pour acquit (formule apposée sur un reçu),
received.

pour aval. Same as **bon pour aval.** See under **bon.**
pourboire. See below.

pour cent (Abrév.: **0/0** *ou* **%** *ou* **p.c.** *ou* **p. cent** *ou*
p. 100 *ou* **p. 0/0**), per cent (*without full stop*);
per cent. (*with full stop*); per centum:
tant pour cent, so much per cent.
Note :—In French insurance, a rate of so much
per cent means a rate of so much per 100
francs. Thus, for example, 1/8% on 10,000
francs is 12 fr. 50.
In English insurance, a rate (usually quoted
in shillings and pence) of so much per cent
means a rate of so much per £100. Thus, for
example, 2s. 6d.% (*or* ⅛%) on £1,000 is
£1 5s.

pour-cent (*n.m.*), percentage; rate per cent:
quel est le pour-cent qu'on vous offre? what
percentage are you offered?
à quel pour-cent avez-vous placé ? at what rate
per cent. have you invested ?
le — pour cent (rente sur l'État), — per cents:
acheter du trois pour cent, to buy three per
cents.

pourcentage. See below.

pour-compte [pour-compte *pl.*] (*n.m.*), on hand,
refused; goods (*or* parcel, or the like) on
hand, refused (*or* left on hand, refused). See
examples under syn. **laissé pour compte.**

pour copie conforme (formule apposée sur une
copie) (Abrév.: **P.C.C.**), a true copy;
certified a true copy.

pour et contre, pros and cons; for and against:
peser le pour et le contre, to consider (*or* to
weigh) the pros and cons.
différentes opinions : les unes, pour ; les autres,
contre, different opinions : the ones, for ;
the others, against.

pour mémoire. See under **mémoire.**

pour mille (Abrév.: **0/00** *ou* %o), per mille; per mil; per thousand.

pourboire (*n.m.*), tip.

pourcentage (*n.m.*), percentage:
faire le pourcentage des frais généraux, to work out the percentage of standing expenses.
franc d'avaries au-dessous du pourcentage spécifié dans la police, free from average under the percentage specified in the policy. See note under **tableau** (de franchises).

pourcenté, -e (*adj.*), percentage (*used as adj.*); percentaged:
quote-parts fixes ou pourcentées (*f.pl.*), fixed or percentage contributions.

pourchasser le découvert (Bourse), to squeeze the bears.

pourcompte [**pourcompte** *pl.*] (*n.m.*), on hand, refused; goods (*or* parcel, or the like) on hand, refused (*or* left on hand, refused). See examples under syn. **laissé pour compte.**

poursuite (Dr.) (*n.f.*), proceedings; action:
entamer des poursuites contre un débiteur, to commence proceedings against a debtor.
poursuite civile, civil action; civil proceedings.

poursuite du client (Com.) (*f.*), follow up system.

poursuivre (*v.t.*), to proceed on (*or* upon); to follow up:
navire rendu prêt à poursuivre son voyage (*m.*), ship made ready to proceed upon her voyage.
poursuivre une entreprise, to follow up an enterprise.

poursuivre (agir en justice) (*v.t.*), to proceed against; to sue; to sue for:
poursuivre un débiteur, to proceed against, to sue, a debtor.
poursuivre le paiement d'un reliquat, to sue for a balance (*or* for the payment of the balance of an account).
être poursuivi (-e) par ses créanciers, to be sued by one's creditors.

pourvoir (*v.t.*), to provide; to supply; to furnish.

pourvoir (*v.i.*), to provide:
vente d'une partie de la cargaison afin de pourvoir aux besoins pressants du navire (*f.*), sale of a part of the cargo in order to provide for the pressing needs of the ship.

se pourvoir (*v.r.*), to provide oneself:
se pourvoir d'argent, to provide oneself with money.

pousser (*v.t.*), to push:
on pousse les Mines X. un peu vite, semble-t-il, bien que l'affaire soit très sérieuse, X. Mines (shares) are being pushed rather fast, it seems, although the concern is quite genuine.

pouvoir (faculté de faire) (*n.m.*), power:
le pouvoir d'achat de la monnaie, de l'or, the purchasing power of money, of gold.
pouvoir libératoire. See under **libératoire.**

pouvoir (mandat; procuration) (*n.m.*), power; authority; power of attorney; proxy:
les pouvoirs d'un liquidateur, du capitaine en matière de vente ou de mise en gage des marchandises, the powers of a liquidator, of the master in matters of sale or pledging of the cargo.

gérant ayant pouvoir de signer pour la société, ayant les pouvoirs les plus étendus pour administrer les affaires de la société (*m.*), manager having power to sign for the company, having the widest powers to administer the affairs of the company.
montrer ses pouvoirs, to show one's authority (*or* one's powers).
donner un pouvoir par-devant notaire, to give a power of attorney before a notary.
donner pouvoir à. See under **donner.**
formule de pouvoir pour une assemblée générale d'actionnaires (*f.*), form of proxy for a general meeting of shareholders.
pouvoir général, general power.
pouvoir impératif, special proxy.
pouvoir spécial, special power; particular power.

pouvoir être imposé (-e) en paiement *ou* **pouvoir être offert (-e) en paiement,** to be legal tender:
les pièces d'argent ne peuvent pas être imposées (*ou* offertes) en paiement pour plus de tant (*f.pl.*), silver coins are not legal tender for more than so much.

pouvoirs publics (*m.pl.*), public authorities.

pratique (*n.f.*). *See* libre pratique.

pratiqué, -e (en parlant de cours) (Bourse) (*p.p.* ou *adj.*), made; done; ruling:
les cours pratiqués *ou* les cours qu'on a pratiqués (*m.pl.*), the prices at which bargains were made (*or* done); the ruling prices; *hence* (*on the Stock Exchange*) bargains done:
cours pratiqués au comptant, à terme, bargains done for cash, for the settlement (*or* for the account).
les cours pratiqués quotidiennement sur ces marchés sont enregistrés sur des cotes *ad hoc*, the bargains done daily on these markets are recorded in lists expressly intended for this purpose.
le cours pratiqué au moment de la réponse des primes, the price ruling at the moment of the declaration of options.

se pratiquer (*v.r.*), to rule; to be made; to be done:
les prix qui se pratiquent simultanément sur les différents marchés (*m.pl.*), the prices which rule at the same time on the different markets.
ces cours se pratiquaient hier (Bourse) (*m.pl.*), these bargains were done yesterday.

pratiquer (*v.t.*), to make; to do:
pratiquer un amortissement, to make a reserve for depreciation.

préavis (*n.m.*), notice:
donner un préavis de 7 jours francs, to give 7 clear days' notice.
dépôt à 7 jours de préavis (*m.*), deposit at 7 days' notice.

précieux, -euse (*adj.*), precious; valuable:
métal précieux (*m.*), precious metal.
temps précieux (*m.*), valuable time.

précis (*n.m.*), précis:
le précis d'une affaire, the précis of a matter.

précisions (détails; indications) (*n.f.pl.*), particulars.

prédénommé, -e (*adj.*), aforesaid; aforementioned; above-named.

préemption (*n.f.*), preemption.

préféré, -e (*adj.* ou *p.p.*), preferred; preferential: le dernier emprunt sera toujours préféré à celui qui l'aura précédé, the last loan is always preferred over (*or* preferential to) that which preceded it.

préférence (Fin.) (*n.f.*) (Abrév.: **préf.**), preference: actions de préférence (*f.pl.*), preference shares.

préférence (traitement de faveur) (Écon.) (*n.f.*), preference: préférence impériale (britannique), imperial preference.

préférentiel, -elle (*adj.*) *ou* **de préférence**, preferential: droit préférentiel *ou* droit de préférence (*m.*), preferential right.

préférer (*v.t.*), to prefer: préférer un créancier à (*ou* sur) des autres, to prefer one creditor over others. le Gouvernement est préféré à tous créanciers, the Government is preferred over all creditors.

préjudice (*n.m.*), prejudice; damage; injury; loss: préjudice résultant d'une livraison tardive, causé par sa négligence, loss, damage, resulting from a late delivery, caused by one's negligence.

sans préjudice de, without prejudice to: action prescrite par un an, sans préjudice des cas de fraude ou d'infidélité (*f.*), action statute barred after one year, without prejudice to cases of fraud or breach of trust.

prélèvement (*n.m.*), drawing; charging; taking; setting aside; appropriation; payment: les prélèvements personnels du commerçant, représentant des retraits de fonds opérés en cours d'exercice, doivent être, à l'inventaire, virés à capital, the personal drawings of the trader, representing withdrawals of money effected during the year, should be transfered to capital at balance sheet time. prélèvements sur compte courant, drawings on current account. prélèvement d'échantillons, taking samples; drawing samples; sampling. faire un prélèvement pour être distribué aux employés, pour former un fonds de réserve, to make an appropriation for distribution among the staff, to form a reserve fund. prélèvement d'intérêts, de dividendes, sur le capital, payment of interest, of dividends, out of capital.

prélever (*v.t.*), to draw; to charge; to take; to set aside; to appropriate; to pay: commerçant qui prélève dans sa caisse, pour ses besoins personnels, une somme de tant (*m.*), trader who draws from his cash, for his personal requirements, a sum of so much. intérêts sur les sommes prélevées (*m.pl.*), interest on the amounts drawn.

prélever des échantillons pour reconnaître l'espèce, la qualité, la valeur, etc., des marchandises, to take samples in order to find out the kind, the quality, the value, etc., of the goods.
échantillon prélevé en présence du déclarant (Douanes) (*m.*), sample drawn in presence of the declarant.
prélever une commission sur une opération, to charge, to draw, a commission on a transaction: la commission prélevée par la banque est de 1 0/0, the commission charged by the bank is 1%.
somme prélevée sur la réserve pour amortir le montant d'un détournement (*f.*), sum taken (*or* appropriated) from the reserve to write off the amount of an embezzlement.
quand le bilan est achevé, le conseil d'administration détermine l'importance des réserves à prélever sur les bénéfices et le dividende à proposer aux actionnaires, when the balance sheet is completed, the board decides the amount of the reserves to be set aside (*or* to be appropriated) out of profits and the dividend to be recommended to the shareholders.
intérêt, dividende, prélevé sur le capital (*m.*), interest, dividend, paid out of capital.

premier, -ère (*adj.*) (Abrév.: **1er, 1re**), first; 1st; premier:
premiers administrateurs (*m.pl.*), first directors.
premier cours (Bourse) (*m.*) [*Abrév.:* 1er c. *ou* c. (1er) *ou simplement* 1er], opening price.
premier établissement (*m.*). *See* frais de premier établissement.
premier port d'escale (*m.*), first port of call.
premier vendeur (Bourse de marchandises) (*m.*), first seller; deliverer.
première et unique répartition (*f.*) (entre créanciers—société en liquidation), first and final dividend (*or* distribution). Cf. **dernière répartition.**
première hypothèque (*f.*), first mortgage.
première prime (Assce) (opp. à *prime de renouvellement*), first premium.
billet de première (*ou* de 1re) classe (*m.*), first (*or* 1st) class ticket.
Londres sur la Tamise, premier port anglais et premier port européen, London on Thames, premier English port and premier European port.
la flotte commerciale anglaise est la première du monde, the English mercantile fleet is the premier fleet of the world.

première de change (*f.*), first of exchange:
à dix jours de vue, payez par (*ou* veuillez payer contre) cette première de change (la seconde et la troisième n'étant payées) *ou* (la deuxième et la troisième ne l'étant *ou* ne l'étant pas) à l'ordre de M. X., à l'ordre de nous-mêmes, la somme de tant, ten days after sight of this first of exchange (second and third of the same tenor and date unpaid [*or* being unpaid] [*or* not paid]) pay to the order of Mr X., to our order, so much.

prémunir (se) contre la hausse, la baisse, to provide against a rise, a fall.

prendre (*v.t.*). See examples:

prendre à bail *ou* prendre à ferme, to take on lease; to lease:

prendre une maison à bail, to take a house on lease; to lease a house.

prendre à bord des marchandises, to take goods on board.

prendre à compte *ou* prendre à valoir, to take on account:

prendre tant à compte (*ou* à valoir), to take so much on account.

prendre des marchandises à compte (*ou* à crédit), to take goods on account (*or* on credit).

prendre à l'escompte un effet de commerce, to discount a bill of exchange.

prendre [un navire] à la remorque, to take [a ship] in tow.

prendre à option, to take on option. *See example under* prendre ferme.

prendre à sa charge *ou* prendre en charge *ou* prendre la charge de *ou* prendre charge de, to take charge of; to take care of; to take upon oneself; to take over; to undertake to pay:

prendre à sa charge (*ou* prendre en charge) une somme d'argent pour quelqu'un, to take charge of, to take care of, a sum of money for someone.

c'est, en effet, le capitaine qui, au nom de l'armateur, prend charge de la marchandise, it is, in effect, the master who, in the name of the owner, takes charge of the goods.

assureur qui prend à sa charge (assureurs qui prennent à leur charge *pl.*) un certain risque (*m.*), insurer who takes upon himself (insurers who take upon themselves *pl.*) a certain risk.

la société prendra la charge du passif (*ou* prendra le passif à sa charge), the company will take over (*or* will undertake to pay) the liabilities.

la nouvelle société prend en charge l'actif et le passif, the new company takes over the assets and the liabilities.

prendre les droits à sa charge, to undertake to pay the duty.

prendre [quelqu'un] au mot, to take [someone] at his word.

prendre charge (recevoir la charge), to load; to lade; to take cargo:

navire prêt à prendre charge (*m.*), ship ready to load.

prendre charge pour un ou plusieurs ports, to take cargo for one or several ports.

prendre communication des livres. See under communication.

prendre conseil, to take advice.

prendre copie d'une lettre, to take a copy of a letter.

prendre cours, to run; to attach:

le délai de livraison prend cours à partir de l'heure de minuit, the time of delivery runs from the hour of midnight.

le risque couvert par la présente police prend cours dès le moment du chargement à bord du navire d'exportation, the risk under this policy attaches from the time of loading on board the export vessel.

prendre des bureaux à Londres, to take offices in London.

prendre des notes à une assemblée, to take notes at a meeting.

prendre des passagers, to take, to pick up, passengers.

Boulogne est un port d'escale où les transatlantiques viennent ancrer quelques heures pour prendre les passagers, Boulogne is a port of call where the transatlantic boats come to anchor some hours to pick up passengers.

prendre des renseignements *ou* prendre des informations *ou* prendre connaissance, to make enquiries; to make inquiries; to enquire; to inquire:

prendre des renseignements (*ou* des informations) sur quelqu'un, to make enquiries, to enquire, about someone.

prendre connaissance de la situation de quelqu'un, to enquire into someone's position.

prendre des sûretés avant de prêter de l'argent, to obtain security before lending money.

prendre en charge. *See under* prendre à sa charge.

prendre en ligne de compte, to take into account:

prendre en ligne de compte les fluctuations du change, to take the fluctuations of exchange into account.

prendre en report (Bourse) (*v.t.*), to take in; to take the rate on; to borrow (stock); to carry (stock):

titres pris en report (*m.pl.*), stock taken in; stock borrowed; stock carried. See example under **report** (renouvellement).

prendre ferme, to take firm:

maison qui a pris un emprunt moitié ferme moitié à option (*f.*), house which has taken a loan half firm half on option.

prendre fin, to end:

le transport terrestre prend fin par la livraison de la marchandise au destinataire, land carriage ends by the delivery of the goods to the consignee.

l'exercice prenant fin le 31 décembre (*m.*), the year (*or* the financial year) ending 31st December.

l'exercice ayant pris fin le 31 décembre (*m.*), the year (*or* the financial year) ended 31st December.

prendre hypothèque sur un bien, to take a mortgage on a property.

prendre l'engagement, to undertake: (*Cf.* engagement pris.)

prendre l'engagement de fournir une somme d'argent, de payer une traite à l'échéance, to undertake to provide a sum of money, to pay a bill at maturity.

prendre la direction d'une affaire, to take over the management of an affair.

prendre la mer, to put, to proceed, to sea :
navire en état de prendre la mer (*m.*), ship in
a condition to put (*or* to proceed) to sea.

prendre la moyenne entre le plus haut et le
plus bas cours, to take the average between
the highest and the lowest price.

prendre la suite des affaires d'une société en
liquidation, to take over the business of a
company in liquidation.

prendre le nom et l'adresse (*ou* les nom et
adresse) de quelqu'un, to take someone's
name and address.

prendre les mesures (*ou* les dispositions) (*ou*
les démarches) nécessaires à la conservation
de ses droits, pour protéger les marchandises
de toute avarie, pour conserver les objets
assurés, to take the necessary steps to protect
one's rights, to protect goods from any
damage, to preserve the insured property.

prendre livraison des titres, to take delivery
of, to take up, stock.

prendre note d'une chose sur son carnet, to
take, to make, a note of something in one's
pocketbook.

prendre ou laisser, to take or leave :
c'est à prendre ou à laisser, you can take it or
leave it ; take it or leave it.

prendre ou requérir toutes mesures conserva-
toires (Assce mar.), to sue, labour, and travel.

prendre part à une entreprise, aux délibérations
d'une assemblée, to take part in an enterprise,
in the proceedings of a meeting.

prendre part à une répartition, to share in a
distribution.

prendre possession, to take possession :
compagnie d'assurances qui a le droit de
prendre possession, en totalité ou en partie,
des marchandises assurées et de les traiter
comme sa propriété (*f.*), insurance company
which has the right to take possession,
wholly or partly, of the insured goods and
to treat them as its property.

prendre rang, to rank :
hypothèques qui prennent rang suivant leur
date d'inscription (*f.pl.*), mortgages which
rank according to the date of their
registration.

les créanciers privilégiés prennent rang avant
les créanciers ordinaires (*m.pl.*), preferential
creditors rank before ordinary creditors.

privilège qui prend rang immédiatement après
un autre (*m.*), right which ranks immediately after another.

nouvelles actions qui prennent le même rang
que les anciennes (*f.pl.*), new shares which
rank pari passu with the old.

les porteurs d'obligations chirographaires
prennent rang concurremment avec les
créanciers ordinaires (*m.pl.*), the holders
of naked debentures rank equally (*or*
concurrently) with the ordinary creditors.

prendre sur ses économies, to draw on one's
savings.

prendre un arrangement avec ses créanciers,
to come to an arrangement with one's
creditors.

prendre un billet (des billets) pour (*ou* à
destination de), to take a ticket (tickets)
for ; to book to :
prendre un billet direct pour Londres (*ou* un
billet direct à destination de Londres),
to book through to London.

prendre un intérêt dans une entreprise, to
take an interest in an undertaking.

prendre une commande, to take an order.

prendre une perte, to take a loss :
savoir prendre une perte, c'est-à-dire perdre
une certaine somme, mais liquider avant
de perdre davantage, to know how to take
a loss, that is to say, to lose a certain
amount, but to close before losing more.

prendre une résolution (*ou* une délibération) (*ou*
une décision) (à une assemblée), to pass,
to carry, to adopt, a resolution.

après en avoir délibéré le conseil prend (*ou*
a pris) la résolution suivante (procès-
verbal), after consideration, It was resolved
that ; after consideration, Resolved that.

preneur, -euse (personne qui prend ; acheteur) (*n.*),
taker ; buyer ; purchaser :
le papier négociable trouve toujours preneur,
negotiable paper always finds a taker (*or* a
buyer).

les fonds publics trouvent facilement preneurs
en bourse (*m.pl.*), public funds easily find
buyers on the stock exchange.

preneur, -euse (*adj.*), buying ; purchasing :
la société preneuse, the purchasing company.

preneur, -euse (qui prend à bail) (pers.) (*n.*),
lessee ; taker :
le bailleur et le preneur, the lessor and the
lessee.

preneur, -euse (bénéficiaire) (*n.*), payee :
preneur d'un effet de commerce (*ou* d'une
lettre de change), d'un billet à ordre, payee
of a bill of exchange, of a promissory note.

preneur à la grosse (*m.*), borrower on bottomry
or respondentia.

preneur d'assurance (*m.*), placer of insurance.

preneur d'option *ou* **preneur de stellage** (Bourse)
(*m.*), giver for a put and call.

preneur de faculté de lever double (Bourse) (*m.*),
giver for a call of more.

preneur de faculté de livrer double (Bourse) (*m.*),
giver for a put of more.

prénom (*n.m.*), Christian name ; forename ;
first name.

les nom, prénoms, adresse, et profession, the
full name (*or* the name in full), address, and
occupation.

préposant (pers.) (*n.m.*), master :
préposant et préposé, master and servant.

préposé, -e (pers.) (*n.*), official ; servant :
un préposé de la douane, a customs official.

armateur qui est responsable des fautes commises par ses préposés dans la manutention
de la cargaison (*m.*), shipowner who is
liable for the faults committed by his
servants in the handling of the cargo.

le capitaine est à la fois le préposé et le
mandataire du propriétaire du navire qu'il
commande, the master is both the servant

and the agent of the owner of the ship he commands.

prescription (Dr.) (*n.f.*), prescription; barring by limitation; finality; bar of the statute of limitations.

prescription (ordre formel et détaillé) (*n.f.*), provision:
les prescriptions d'une loi, the provisions of an act.

prescrire (*v.t.*), to prescribe; to specify; to provide:
les formalités prescrites par la loi (*f.pl.*), the formalities prescribed by law.
délai prescrit (*m.*), prescribed time.
ce que la police doit prescrire, what the policy should provide.
l'expéditeur est libre de prescrire ou non la voie que doit suivre son télégramme (*m.*), the sender is at liberty to specify or not the route by which his telegram should be sent.

se prescrire (*v.r.*), to be barred by statute of limitations; to be statute barred; to be barred by limitation:
les arrérages des rentes françaises se prescrivent par cinq ans (*m.pl.*), interest on French rentes is statute barred after five years.

présent, -e (*adj.*), present:
biens présents et à venir (*m.pl.*), property present and future.
tous les propriétaires, présents et futurs, de la chose assurée, all the owners, present and future, of the property insured.
sont présents (*ou* étaient présents): M. A., président, et MM. B., C., administrateurs (procès-verbal d'assemblée), present: A., chairman, B., C., directors.

présentateur, -trice (*adj.*), presenting:
banque présentatrice (*f.*), presenting bank.

présentateur, -trice (pers.) (*n.*), presenter:
présentateur d'un billet, presenter of a bill.

présentation (*n.f.*), presentation; presentment; production; showing; shewing:
présentation à l'acceptation, au paiement (d'un effet de commerce), presentation, presentment, for acceptance, for payment.
présentation d'une déclaration en douane, presentation of a customs entry.
présentation de billets (en voyage), production of tickets; showing tickets.

à présentation, on presentation; on demand; at sight:
payer un billet à présentation, to pay a note on presentation (*or* on demand) (*or* at sight).

présente (*n.f.*), present:
au reçu de la présente (la lettre que voici), on receipt of the present.
savoir faisons par ces présentes *ou* à tous ceux qui ces présentes verront (Dr.), know all men by these presents; to all to whom these presents shall come.

par les présentes *ou* **par le présent acte,** hereby:
je donne, par les présentes, pouvoir à M. X., I hereby appoint as my proxy Mr X.

présenter (*v.t.*), to present; to shew; to offer; to produce; to show; to shew; to pass:

présenter un chèque au paiement (*ou* à l'encaissement), un effet à l'acceptation, à l'escompte à la banque, to present a cheque for payment, a bill for acceptance, for discount at the bank.
présenter des comptes, un rapport à l'assemblée générale des actionnaires, to present accounts, a report to the general meeting of shareholders.
établissement de banque qui est obligé d'acheter toutes matières d'or qui lui sont présentées (*m.*), banking establishment which is obliged to buy all the gold bullion offered to it.
compte qui présente un solde de tant de francs au crédit (*m.*), account which shows a balance of so many francs to the credit.
les voyageurs doivent présenter leurs billets à toute réquisition des préposés de la compagnie (*m.pl.*), passengers must produce (*or* show) their tickets whenever required to do so by the company's servants.
présenter une demande de communication téléphonique (au bureau central), to pass a request for a telephone call (to the exchange).

préserver (*v.t.*), to preserve; to keep:
préserver d'un péril commun imminent les biens en risque dans une expédition maritime, to preserve the property at risk in a maritime adventure from a common imminent peril.

présidence (*n.f.*), chairmanship; presidency:
être nommé (-e) à la présidence d'une assemblée, to be elected chairman, to be elected to the presidency, of a meeting.
pendant la présidence de M. X., during Mr X's chairmanship.

président, -e (pers.) (*n.*), chairman; president:
président d'une assemblée, chairman, president, of a meeting.

présider (*v.t.*), to preside at; to preside over; to be chairman of:
présider une assemblée, to preside at (*or* over) a meeting.
l'assemblée est présidée par le président du conseil d'administration (*f.*), the meeting is presided over by the chairman of the board.
il préside la compagnie, he is chairman of the company.

présider (*v.i.*), to preside; to be in the chair; to take the chair:
M. X. préside, Mr X. presided; Mr X. was in (*or* took) the chair.
présider à une assemblée, to preside at a meeting.

présomption (*n.f.*), presumption:
présomption de faute, de fortune de mer, de perte de la marchandise, presumption of fault, of sea peril, of loss of the goods.

presse (les journaux) (*n.f.*), press:
campagne de presse (*f.*), press campaign.

presse à copier (*f.*), copying press.

presse-agrafes [presse-agrafes *pl.*] (*n.m.*), staple press.

presse-papiers [presse-papiers *pl.*] (*n.m.*), paper weight.

prestation (*n.f.*), furnishing; provision; contribution; lending; loaning; loan:
prestation de capitaux, provision, lending, loaning, loan, of capital.

prestation de serment (*f.*), taking oath; swearing.

présumer (*v.t.*), to presume:
envois contenant ou présumés contenir des objets passibles de droits de douane (*m.pl.*), packets containing or presumed to contain articles liable to customs duty.

prêt, -e (*adj.*), ready:
navire prêt à prendre charge, à délivrer (*m.*), ship ready to load, to deliver.

prêt (action) (*n.m.*), loan; lending; loaning:
un prêt d'argent, a loan of money.
toutes les opérations du banquier peuvent se résumer, en définitive, en emprunts et en prêts, all the transactions of the banker may be summed up, shortly, in borrowing and in lending.

prêt (chose, somme prêtée) (*n.m.*), loan; advance: (Cf. **emprunt**.)
prêt à court terme, short loan.
prêt à découvert (Banque), loan on overdraft.
prêt à intérêt *ou* prêt à intérêts, loan at interest.
prêt à la grosse *ou* prêt à la grosse aventure *ou* prêt à (*ou* de) retour de voyage *ou* prêt maritime, bottomry or respondentia loan; loan on bottomry or respondentia; marine loan; maritime loan.
prêt à la grosse sur corps, bottomry loan; loan on bottomry.
prêt à la grosse sur facultés, respondentia loan; loan on respondentia.
prêt à long terme, long period loan.
prêts à sept jours (Marché monétaire), seven day loans; weekly loans; weekly fixtures.
prêt à terme, loan at notice.
prêts au jour le jour (Marché monétaire), day to day loans (*or* money); daily loans; daily money.
prêts au mois (Marché monétaire), monthly loans (*or* money) (*or* fixtures).
prêt garanti *ou* prêt gagé, secured loan.
prêt hypothécaire, loan on mortgage; mortgage loan.
prêts remboursables sur demande (Marché monétaire), loans at call; money at call; call money.
prêt sur nantissement *ou* prêt lombard, loan on collateral; lombard loan.
prêt sur titres, loan on stock; advance on stocks.

prêtable (*adj.*), lendable; loanable:
fonds prêtables (*m.pl.*), lendable funds; loanable money.

prête-nom [prête-noms *pl.*] (*n.m.*), dummy:
prête-nom qui cache un homme de paille, dummy who masks a man of straw.

prétendre (*v.t.*) *ou* **prétendre à** (*v.i.*) (réclamer comme un droit), to claim; to lay claim to:
prétendre (*ou* prétendre à) une part dans les bénéfices, une commission pour sa peine, une indemnité pour le retard, des privilèges spéciaux, to claim a share in the profits, a commission for one's trouble, an indemnity for delay, special privileges.

prétention (*n.f.*), claim; pretension:
l'exorbitance des prétentions d'un vendeur (*f.*), the exorbitance of the claims of a seller.

prêter (*n.m.*), lending; loaning; loan:
le prêter est quelquefois plus onéreux que le donner, lending is sometimes more burdensome than giving.

prêter (*v.t.*), to lend:
prêter de l'argent sur nantissement, sur hypothèque, to lend money on security, on mortgage.
prêter des titres, des capitaux en report (Bourse), to lend stock, money on contango.
prêter son nom, to lend one's name.

prêter (*v.i.*), to lend:
prêter à intérêt, au taux de 5 0/0, to lend at interest, at the rate of 5%.

prêter serment, to take oath; to be sworn; to swear:
prêter serment devant un tribunal, to take oath, to be sworn, before a court.

prêteur, -euse (*adj.*), lending:
banquier prêteur (*m.*), lending banker.
banque prêteuse (*f.*), lending bank.

prêteur, -euse (pers.) (*n.*), lender:
prêteur à la grosse, lender on bottomry or respondentia.
prêteur sur gage *ou* prêteur sur gages *ou* prêteur sur nantissement, pledgee; pawnee; lender on security (*or* on collateral).

preuve (*n.f.*), proof; evidence:
la preuve des causes de l'abordage est souvent difficile, proof of the causes of collision is often difficult.
l'écrit qui sert de preuve au contrat d'assurance est appelé police d'assurance (*m.*), the written agreement which serves as evidence of the contract of insurance is called policy of insurance.
jusqu'à preuve contraire, in the absence of evidence to the contrary; until the contrary is proved.

prévaloir (se) d'un droit, to avail oneself of a right.

prévarication (*n.f.*), breach of trust; default:
fautes ou prévarications du capitaine ou de l'équipage (*f.pl.*), wrongful acts or defaults of the master or crew.

prévenir (informer) (*v.t.*), to give notice; to give notice to; to inform; to acquaint:
prévenir l'assureur dans les trois jours de la réception de la nouvelle d'un sinistre, to give the insurer notice (*or* to give notice to the insurer) within three days of the receipt of the news of an accident.

prévision (*n.f.*) *ou* **prévision d'avenir,** forecast.

prévision (réserve) (*n.f.*), provision; reserve:
prévision pour moins-value du portefeuille, provision for depreciation of investments.
prévision pour créances douteuses, reserve for doubtful debts.

prévision de caisse (Banq.) (*f.*), cash requirement; cover for the day.

prévu (-e) par les statuts, provided by the articles (or by the articles of association) (or by the memorandum of association):
modification de capital prévue par les statuts (f.), alteration of capital provided by the articles of association.

prier (v.t.), to ask; to request:
prier le bureau du télégraphe de faire répéter le ou les mots mutilés, to ask, to request, the telegraph office to repeat the mutilated word or words.

prière (n.f.), request.
prière d'adresser la réponse au secrétaire, all communications to be addressed to the secretary.

prima facie ou **prime face (de),** prima facie:
preuve prima facie (f.) ou évidence de prime face (f.), prima facie evidence.

primage (chapeau du capitaine) (n.m.), primage:
le primage est un supplément de fret calculé à raison de tant pour cent sur le fret principal, primage is an additional freight calculated at a rate of so much per cent on the principal freight.

primata de change (m.), first of exchange.
primata de quittance (m.), original receipt.
prime (bénéfice réalisé sur une opération quelconque) (n.f.), premium; profit; interest; remuneration; money:
prime de grosse, marine interest; maritime interest.
prime de rapidité, dispatch money; despatch money.
prime de sauvetage, remuneration for salvage; salvage.
prime du change, exchange premium; premium on exchange; exchange; agio.

prime (somme accordée à titre d'encouragement) (n.f.), premium; bounty; bonus:
prime de remboursement, redemption premium.
primes à la production, à l'exportation, bounties on production, on exports.
salaire avec prime, wages with bonus.

prime (Assce) (n.f.), premium:
prime à débattre ou prime à arbitrer, premium to be arranged.
prime annuelle, annual premium; yearly premium.
prime au temps, time premium.
prime au voyage, voyage premium.
prime brute, gross premium; office premium. See example under **chargement** (de la prime).
prime d'assurance, insurance premium; premium of assurance.
prime d'assurance contre l'incendie, fire insurance premium; fire premium.
prime d'été, summer premium.
prime d'hiver, winter premium.
prime de la première année, first year's premium.
prime de pontée, deck cargo premium.
prime de renouvellement (opp. à première prime), renewal premium.
prime en cours à la date de la police, current premium on date of policy.
prime entière ou prime intégrale, full premium.

prime liée, round voyage premium.
prime nette, net premium; pure premium; mathematical premium; risk premium. See example under **chargement** (de la prime).
prime supplémentaire ou prime additionnelle, additional premium.
prime unique, single premium.

prime (plus-value acquise par un titre sur son cours d'émission ou au delà du pair) (n.f.) (opp. à perte), premium:
une action de 500 fr. qui se vend 600 fr., se négocie à 100 fr. de prime, a share of 500 francs which sells at 600 francs, is dealt in at 100 francs premium.
emprunt qui fait 1/4 0/0 de prime (Bourse) (m.), loan which is called $\frac{1}{4}$% premium.
primes d'émission ou primes sur émissions ou primes sur actions, premiums on shares.
être en prime ou faire prime, to be at a premium; to stand at a premium:
actions qui sont en prime (ou qui font prime) sur le marché (f.pl.), shares which are at a premium (or which stand at a premium) on the market.
l'or fait prime sur le marché des monnaies (m.), gold is at a premium on the money market.
pays où l'or se cote en prime ou en perte sur la base de tant de francs pour un kilogramme d'or pur (m.), country where gold is quoted at a premium or at a discount on the basis of so many francs for a kilogramme of pure gold.

prime (marché à prime) (Bourse) (n.f.) (Abrév.: **pr.** ou **p.**), option: (See note under prime directe.)
les marchés fermes engagent à la fois le vendeur et l'acheteur; un marché à prime engage le vendeur sans engager l'acheteur, firm bargains bind both the seller and the buyer; an option bargain binds the taker without binding the giver.
le cours d'une même valeur, au même moment, est plus élevé à prime que ferme, the price of the same stock, at the same moment, is higher on option than firm.
prime à longue échéance, long dated option.
prime au 15, au 31 (Abrév.: pr. au 15, pr. au 31), option till the 15th, till the 31st (of the current month).
prime directe ou prime dont ou simplement dont ou prime pour lever ou prime pour prendre ou non ou prime acheteur ou prime pour l'acheteur ou prime simple à la hausse ou prime plus, call; call option; buyer's option.
Note :—On a market where only calls are dealt in, and not puts, or where puts are exceptional, the word prime alone means call or call option. Consequently, all such expressions as acheter à prime, vente à prime, without any further qualification, may be understood to refer to calls, though literally, prime alone means option, without specifying whether call or put.
prime double, double option; put and call; put and call option.

prime indirecte *ou* prime ou *ou simplement* ou *ou* prime renversée *ou* prime inverse *ou* prime pour livrer *ou* prime pour livrer ou non *ou* prime vendeur *ou* prime pour le vendeur *ou* prime simple à la baisse *ou* prime moins, put; put option; seller's option.

prime pour demain (*Abrév.:* pr. dem. *ou* p. dem.), option till to-morrow.

prime pour le lendemain *ou* prime au lendemain, day to day option; one day option; option till the next day.

Note:—The **call option** in French is called **dont** = *of which*, i.e., the price quoted for the stock on call option is so much per share *dont* (of which) so much per share is option rate. (See examples of call option orders under **dont.**)

The **put option** in French is called **ou** = *or*, i.e., the price quoted for the stock on put option is so much per share *ou* (or) so much put option rate per share has to be paid. (See example of put option order under **ou.**)

The limit price at which the option is abandoned is called the **pied de la prime** or **limite de la prime**—**pied du dont** in case of a call, **pied de l'ou** in case of a put; thus, supposing the option prices to be

    call: 33,50 francs dont 1
    put: 31,50 francs ou 1

32 francs 50 centimes represents the *pied du dont* and likewise the *pied de l'ou.*

In London, the option rate is independent of the option price quoted for the stock.

The following examples will serve to illustrate the above explanations :—

London example.—I decide to give for the call for current account on 1,000 XYZ shares. My broker says to me, I have a taker of 1s. at 25s., and I have a taker of 9d. at 25s. 6d. I decide on the former. I pay down the option money of £50 (= 1,000 shares at 1s.), and cover, if required. I now have the right to call 1,000 shares at 25s. up to the time for declaration of options. (In London, 2.45 on the day before contango day.) If the price of the shares does not exceed 25s., I abandon the option and lose my £50, plus charges for brokerage and stamp duty; if it exceeds 25s., I sell, provided I do not wish to take the shares firm. If after I have sold at a profit the stock should fall below my option price, I abandon the option, and buy the stock on the market. If the stock should rise again, I repeat the operation, always being protected by my option.

Paris example.—The call option prices of X.Y.Z. shares are quoted at fr. 33,50 dont 1 f., that is to say, of which price of fr. 33·50, one franc is option rate; or, fr. 33 dont 50, i.e., of which price of 33 francs, 50 centimes is option rate. The *pied* or *limite de la prime* is therefore fr. 32·50. I give 1 franc per share for the call of 100 shares and pay down 100 francs option money, and cover, if required. If by the time

for the declaration of options the price of the shares does not exceed fr. 32·50, I abandon the option and lose my 100 francs option money, and charges for brokerage and duties. If the price reaches say fr. 34·50, I sell and make 100 francs profit, less charges. If I sell at fr. 33·50 I only lose the charges, as the 1 franc realized above the *pied* is exactly balanced by the option money paid. If I sell at fr. 33, I lose 50 centimes per share, viz., the difference between my 1 franc option rate and the 50 centimes excess over the *pied*, plus charges. Supposing I do not want to sell, I can of course call the shares and take them firm by paying fr. 32·50 per share, viz., fr. 33·50 less 1 franc option money already paid, plus charges.

Another term in French option dealing that needs explanation is **cours de la réponse des primes** (price at time for declaration of options). This has no counterpart in English practice, the reason for which will be apparent from the following explanations. In London, if I do not sell, or declare that I abandon, before the time for declaration of options, I have necessarily to take the stock firm at the option price. In Paris, if I have not sold before the **heure de la réponse,** my broker either abandons the option for me, if the ruling price is at my *pied* or (in the case of a call option) under, or, if the price is (in the case of a call option) above my *pied*, he sells for me without waiting to be asked to do so. This sale of my option stock is put through to me at the *cours de la réponse*, which is the price ruling at the *heure de la réponse* (1.30 on the day before contango day in Paris). This *cours de la réponse* is not a more or less conventional price, like say a making up price. In fact, during the quarter of an hour preceding the *heure de la réponse*, there is a veritable battle between the various interests involved, and fluctuations, often very violent, take place, according as greater or less quantities of options are exercised or abandoned.

Option dealings are very popular in France and take place on an enormous scale. Many interesting combinations are practised which are unknown, or at least uncommon, in England, where comparatively option bargains are dealt in to only a limited extent.

prime (taux unitaire de la prime) (Bourse) (*n.f.*) (*Abrév.:* **pr.** *ou* **p.**), option rate; rate of option; rate:

payeur, receveur, de la prime (*m.*), giver, taker, of the rate.

primer (Dr.) (*v.t.*), to rank before; to take precedence of:

primer quelqu'un en hypothèque, to rank before someone by virtue of a prior mortgage.

les créanciers privilégiés priment les créanciers ordinaires, preferential creditors rank before ordinary creditors.

être primé (-e) par, to rank after:

les créances ordinaires sont primées par les créances hypothécaires (*f.pl.*), ordinary debts rank after mortgage debts.

primer (Fin.) (*v.t.*), to premium :
monnaie qui prime le franc ou qui est primée par lui (*f.*), money which premiums the franc or is premiumed by it.

primitif, -ive (*adj.*), original :
manuscrit primitif (*m.*), original manuscript.
souscripteur primitif (*m.*), original subscriber.

principal, -e, -aux (*adj.*), principal ; chief :
principal créancier (*m.*), principal (*or* chief) creditor.

principal (capital d'une dette) (*n.m.*), principal :
principal d'une lettre de change, principal of a bill of exchange.
principal et intérêts, principal and interest.

prioritaire (*adj.*), prior :
un prélèvement prioritaire sur les bénéfices nets, a prior appropriation on the net profits.

priorité (*n.f.*), priority ; preference :
priorité d'hypothèque, de date, priority of mortgage, of date.
actions de priorité (*f.pl.*), preference shares ; preferred shares.

prise (action de prendre) (*n.f.*), taking, etc. See the phrases given below, and see the verb **prendre** for other phrases.

prise (prélèvement) (*n.f.*), drawing :
prises d'espèces, cash drawings.

prise (capture) (*n.f.*), taking ; capture :
prises en mer, takings at sea.

prise (navire pris) (*n.f.*), prize.

prise à domicile (Ch. de f., etc.) (*f.*), collection at residence ; collection at trader's premises ; collection :
aucune prise à domicile n'est effectuée les dimanches, no collection is made on Sundays.

prise de bénéfice (*f.*) *ou* **prises de bénéfice** (*ou* **de bénéfices**) (*f.pl.*), profit taking :
malgré les prises de bénéfices et de grosses réalisations, les cours ont fait preuve de résistance, in spite of profit taking and heavy realizations, prices showed strength.
reprise marquée de tout le groupe caoutchoutier que des prises de bénéfice empêchent, toutefois, de clôturer au plus haut (*f.*), marked recovery in all the rubber group which profit taking prevented, however, from closing at best.
l'action X. qui s'était redressée à 1 110 est remenée à 1 080, sur prises de bénéfice, X. shares which had hardened to 1,110 francs were lowered to 1,080, on profit taking.

prise usine (départ usine), ex works ; ex mill :
cours : prise usine, tant ; sur wagon, tant, prices : ex works (*or* ex mill), so much ; on rail, so much.

prisée (*n.f.*), appraisement ; valuation ; estimate.

priser (*v.t.*), to appraise ; to value ; to estimate :
priser des meubles, to value furniture.

priseur (pers.) (*n.m.*), appraiser ; valuer.

privation de jouissance (Dr.) (*f.*), deprivation of enjoyment.

privé, -e (*adj.*), private :

intérêts privés (*m.pl.*), private interests.
banque privée (*f.*), private bank.

privilège (droit ; avantage) (*n.m.*), privilege ; right :
banque qui jouit du privilège exclusif d'émettre des billets (*f.*), bank which has the exclusive right to issue notes.
privilège de souscription, application rights.

privilège (droit de préférence) (*n.m.*), privilege ; lien ; charge ; preferential claim :
avoir un privilège (*ou* être privilégié, -e) sur les meubles d'un débiteur, to have a lien (*or* a charge) on the personal property of a debtor.
le paiement du fret est garanti par un privilège sur les marchandises chargées, payment of the freight is secured by a lien on (*or* upon) (*or* over) the goods shipped.
privilège d'hypothèque, mortgage charge.
le salaire des ouvriers est l'objet d'un privilège, workmen's wages constitute a preferential claim.
privilège du vendeur, vendor's lien.
privilège général, general lien.
privilège maritime, maritime lien.
privilège spécial, particular lien ; specific lien.

privilège (acte) (*n.m.*), charge :
enregistrer un privilège, to register a charge.

privilégié, -e (*adj.*) (Abrév. : **priv.** *ou* **privil.**), preferential ; preferred ; privileged :
créance privilégiée (*f.*), preferential debt ; preferred debt ; privileged debt.
action privilégiée (*f.*), preferred share ; preference share.

prix (*n.m.*) (Abrév. : **Px**), price ; rate ; quotation ; charge ; money ; consideration ; consideration money : (Cf. **cours**.)
le prix de l'or, de l'argent, the price of gold, of money.
les prix sont l'expression monétaire des valeurs, prices are the monetary expression of values.
demande de prix (*f.*), enquiry for price (*or* for quotation).
prix raisonnable, reasonable price (*or* charge).
prix courant (Abrév. : P.C.) *ou* prix du marché (prix réglé par la balance de l'offre et de la demande), current price ; market price ; price current.
prix courant (bulletin), price current ; price list ; current price list :
consulter un prix courant, to consult a price list.
prix d'achat *ou* prix d'acquisition, purchase price ; purchase consideration ; cost :
prix d'achat (*ou* prix d'acquisition) de l'immeuble, purchase price, cost, of the premises.
les actions sont estimées aux prix d'acquisition (*ou* aux prix d'achat) (*f.pl.*), the shares are valued at cost.
prix d'apport, consideration (*or* purchase consideration) for transfer (vendors' assets acquired).
prix d'émission (des actions, etc.), issue price.
prix d'un transfert (de valeurs mobilières), consideration money for a transfer.
prix de barème, scale rate ; scale charge.
prix de base, basis price.

prix de demi-gros, wholesale price; trade price. See note under **gros** *ou* **gros commerce.**

prix de détail, retail price.

prix de (*ou* de la) facture, invoice price.

prix de gros, direct price (*technical sense*); wholesale price (*general sense*). See note under **gros** *ou* **gros commerce.**

prix de la place *ou* prix de (*ou* du) transport *ou simplement* prix (par voie de terre, ou par voie d'air), fare:

voyageur qui paie le prix de sa place (*m.*), passenger who pays his fare.

le transport des voyageurs est effectué moyennant le paiement préalable du prix de la place, the carriage of passengers is effected in consideration of the prepayment of the fare.

prix des places des voyageurs *ou* prix de transport des voyageurs, passenger fares.

enfants transportés à moitié prix (*m.pl.*), children carried at half fare (*or* at half price).

prix de la prime *ou* prix de base de la prime (Bourse), option price; price of option.

prix de la voiture *ou* prix de (*ou* du) transport, charge (*or* charges) for carriage; carriage charge (*or* charges); carriage; cartage:

le fret est le prix de transport des marchandises par mer, freight is the charge for carriage of goods by sea.

le prix du transport par voie ferrée en France, the charges for railway carriage in France.

prix de passage *ou* prix du voyage *ou* prix de (*ou* du) transport *ou simplement* prix (par voie de mer, ou par voie d'air), passage money; fare.

prix de revient *ou* prix coûtant *ou simplement* prix, cost; cost price; prime cost; flat cost; first cost:

Note :—cost, prime cost, flat cost, and *first cost* are costing (i.e., industrial or manufacturing) terms.

   cost and *cost price* are commercial or financial (i.e., buying or selling) terms.

le prix de revient d'un objet se compose des matières consommées par sa fabrication, des salaires payés, et d'un tantième de frais généraux, the cost of an article is composed of the material used in its manufacture, of the wages paid, and of a proportion of overhead charges (Costing).

prix coûtant des matières premières, cost of the raw material (Costing).

le prix de main-d'œuvre et celui des matières premières, the cost of labour and that of raw materials (Costing).

prix de revient des objets fabriqués, prime cost, flat cost, first cost, of manufactured articles (Costing).

prix de revient total (*ou* global), total cost (Costing).

prix de revient brut, gross cost (Costing).

prix de revient final, final cost (Costing).

prix de revient (*ou* prix coûtant) du stock en magasin, cost price, cost, of the stock in trade (commercial).

les actions sont évaluées aux prix coûtants (*ou*

aux prix de revient) (*f.pl.*), the shares are valued at cost (financial).

prix de vente, selling price; consideration for sale.

prix des reports *ou* prix du report (Bourse), contango rate; contango; carry over rate; continuation rate.

prix des tarifs, tariff rates.

prix du change (différence entre le pair intrinsèque et le cours actuel) (Banq.), premium; exchange premium; premium or exchange; exchange; agio.

prix du fret, charge (*or* charges) for freight; freight charge (*or* charges); freight:

le connaissement énonce le prix du fret, the bill of lading specifies the charges for freight.

prix fort, full price.

prix marqué, marked price.

de prix, of value; valuable; precious:

·échantillon de prix (*m.*), sample of value.

objet de prix (*m.*), valuable article.

pro forma, pro forma:

facture pro forma (*f.*), pro forma invoice.

pro tempore, pro tempore.

probabilité (*n.f.*), probability:

probabilités moyennes de pertes ou de dommages (Assce), average probabilities of losses or damage.

probant, -e (*adj.*), probatory; documentary:

force probante de la lettre de voiture (*f.*), probatory force of the consignment note.

pièces probantes (*f.pl.*), documentary evidence.

procédure (*n.f.*), procedure; proceeding; proceedings:

la procédure du règlement d'avarie, the procedure of the adjustment of average.

procédure civile (Dr.), civil proceedings.

procédure sommaire (Dr.), summary proceeding.

procès (Dr.) (*n.m.*), action; case; lawsuit:

procès civil, civil action.

gagner son procès, to win one's case.

procès-verbal [procès-verbaux *pl.*] (compte rendu) (*n.m.*) (Abrév. : **P.-V.**), minute; minutes; report:

dresser procès-verbal des délibérations d'une assemblée (*ou* d'une réunion), to draw up the minutes of proceedings of a meeting.

procès-verbaux d'assemblées, minutes of meetings.

procès-verbal des délibérations du conseil d'administration, minutes of proceedings of the board of directors; board minutes.

le procès-verbal de la dernière séance est lu et adopté, the minutes of the last meeting were read and confirmed.

Note :—Recordings of formal proceedings in minutes, reports, and the like, always in the past tense in English, are usually in the present tense in French.

procès-verbal d'ouverture des panneaux, report of stowage.

procès-verbal constatant l'état de la marchandise, report establishing the condition of the goods.

processus (*n.m.*), process:

le processus du règlement d'avarie, the process of the adjustment of average.

prochain (Bourse de valeurs) (*n.m.*) (Abrév.: **pain**), next account; next settlement. *Cf.* fin prochain.

prochain mois (*m.*) *ou simplement* **prochain** (*n.m.*) (Bourse de marchandises), next month; next.

Proche Orient (*m.*) (opp. à *Extrême Orient*), Near East.

procuration (*n.f.*), procuration; power; power of attorney; proxy:
agir par procuration, to act by procuration.
procuration rédigée par-devant notaire, power of attorney drawn up before a notary.
assister à une assemblée soit personnellement, soit par procuration pour le compte d'autres créanciers, to be present at a meeting either personally, or by proxy (*or* by procuration) for the account of other creditors.
procuration générale, general power.
procuration spéciale, special power; particular power.

par procuration (*en abrégé* **P. Pon** *ou* **Par pon**), per procuration; per procurationem; (*generally abbreviated* per pro. *or* per proc. *or* p.p.):
si le représentant a une procuration, il fait précéder sa signature des mots: P. Pon de M. un tel, if the representative has a power of attorney, he precedes his signature with the words: p.p. So-and-So.

procurer (*v.t.*), to procure; to obtain; to get; to find; to raise:
procurer des capitaux à une industrie, to find, to raise, to get, money for an industry.
procurer une place à quelqu'un sans emploi, to find a place for someone out of employ.

se procurer (*v.r.*), to procure; to obtain; to get; to find; to raise:
se procurer de l'argent (*ou* des capitaux), to find, to raise, to get, money (*or* capital):
société qui émet des actions pour se procurer des capitaux (*f.*), company which issues shares in order to raise capital.

producteur, -trice *ou* **productif, -ive** (*adj.*), producing; productive; bearing:
industrie productrice (*f.*), producing industry.
capital productif d'intérêt (*m.*), interest-bearing capital; capital bearing interest.
somme de tant productive d'intérêts à quatre pour cent l'an (*f.*), sum of so much bearing interest at four per cent per annum.

producteur, -trice (pers.) (*n.*), producer:
le producteur et le consommateur, the producer and the consumer.

production (*n.f.*), production; output:
les productions du sol, the productions of the soil.
l'exportation stimule la production (*f.*), exportation stimulates production.
production en masse, mass production.
contingenter la production du caoutchouc, to curtail the output of rubber.

production (exhibition) (*n.f.*), production; exhibition:
production des titres (faillite), production of evidence (to prove a debt) (bankruptcy).

productivité (*n.f.*), productivity; productiveness.

produire (*v.t.*), to produce; to bear; to yield:
aucune nation ne produit tout ce dont elle a besoin, aucune ne peut consommer tout ce qu'elle est en mesure de produire, no nation produces all it needs, none can consume all it is able to produce.
capital qui produit 5 0/0 par an (*m.*), capital which yields 5% per annum.

produire (exhiber) (*v.t.*), to produce; to exhibit:
produire un titre, ses livres, des pièces de nature à justifier sa prétention, to produce, to exhibit, a certificate, one's books, documents of a nature to prove one's claim.

produit (*n.m.*) *ou* **produits** (*n.m.pl.*) (production; matière; denrée), product; produce; commodity:
produits coloniaux *ou* produits des colonies, colonial produce.
produits de l'industrie, products of industry.
produits destinés à l'exportation, commodities, produce, intended for export.
produits du sol, produce, products, of the soil.
produits étrangers *ou* produits exotiques, foreign products (*or* produce).
produits métropolitains *ou* produits de la métropole *ou* produits indigènes, home products; home produce; home-grown produce.
le coton est le produit principal du Soudan, cotton is the staple commodity (*or simply* the staple) of the Sudan.
les résultats démontrent, une fois de plus, que quels que soient les cours du produit, les grandes sociétés pétrolières, qui non seulement produisent, mais raffinent, transportent et distribuent le pétrole et ses dérivés, conservent une marge bénéficiaire unitaire très large (*m.pl.*), results show, once again, that whatever the prices of the commodity may be, the big oil companies, who not only produce, but refine, carry and distribute the petroleum and its derivatives, have a very large unit margin of profit left over.

produit (rapport; bénéfice) (*n.m.*), product; proceeds; yield; profit:
multiplier le capital par les jours et porter le produit dans la colonne des intérêts, to multiply the principal by the days and carry out the product in the interest column.
le produit brut, le produit net, d'une vente, the gross proceeds, the net proceeds, of a sale.
net produit (*ou* produit net) d'un effet, proceeds, net avails, of a bill.
le produit d'un capital, the yield of a capital.
opération qui laisse un produit avantageux (*f.*), transaction which leaves a good profit.

produit (recette) (*n.m.*), takings; receipts:
vérifier le produit de la journée, to check the day's takings; to verify the day's receipts.

profession (qualités) (*n.f.*) *ou* **qualité ou profession**, profession; profession or business; occupation; description:
les nom, prénoms, adresse (*ou* domicile), et profession (*ou* qualité ou profession) du souscripteur, the full name (*or* the name in

full), address, and profession or business (*or* and occupation) (*or* and description) of the applicant.

sans profession. See under **sans**.

professionnel, -elle (*adj.*) *ou* **de profession,** professional ; by profession :
l'élément professionnel (*m.*), the professional element.

comptable professionnel *ou* comptable de profession (*m.*), professional accountant; accountant by profession.

professionnel, -elle (pers.) (*n.*), professional :
si le professionnel peut être accidentellement spéculateur, le non professionnel l'est toujours et nécessairement, whereas the professional may be accidentally a speculator, the non professional is always and necessarily so.

profit (*s'emploie souvent au pl.*) (*n.m.*), profit ; benefit ; interest :
profit sur l'opération, sur une vente, profit on the transaction, on a sale.

vendre à profit, to sell at a profit.

profit espéré, anticipated profit :
si le profit espéré est compris dans l'assurance, if the anticipated profit is included in the insurance.

assurance qui couvre aussi des frais et un profit espéré (*f.*), insurance which also covers expenses and an anticipated profit.

profits et pertes (gains et pertes), profit and loss.

profits et pertes *ou* compte des profits et pertes (*Abrév.* : P. & P. *ou* P.P.), profit and loss ; profit and loss account :
passer un article aux profits et pertes, to post an item to profit and loss.

profit maritime *ou* profit nautique, marine interest ; maritime interest.

profitable (*adj.*), profitable :
commerce profitable (*m.*), profitable trade.

profitablement (*adv.*), profitably.

profiter (tirer un profit) (*v.i.*), to profit ; to gain ; to benefit :
profiter sur une marchandise vendue, to profit by goods sold.

dans la plupart des marchés, une seule des parties profite, in most bargains, only one of the parties benefits.

profiter de la plus-value du change, to benefit, to profit, by the appreciation of the exchange.

profiter (rapporter) (*v.i.*), to be profitable ; to benefit :
ce marché lui a peu profité, that bargain was not very profitable to him.

programme (*n.m.*), programme :
programme des excursions à terre, programme of land excursions.

progrès (*n.m.pl.*), progress :
faire de grands progrès, to make great progress.

progresser (*v.i.*), to progress ; to go ahead :
l'action X. progresse de 1 670 à 1 700, X. shares went ahead from 1,670 to 1,700 francs.

prohiber (*v.t.*), to prohibit :
loi qui prohibe l'importation et la vente de certaines marchandises (*f.*), law which prohibits the importation and sale of certain goods.

prohiber l'entrée (*ou* l'importation) de marchandises de fabrication étrangère, d'armes de toutes espèces, de munitions de guerre, de la poudre et d'autres matières explosibles, to prohibit the importation of goods of foreign make, of arms of all kinds, of munitions of war, of powder and other explosive substances.

prohibitif, -ive (*adj.*), prohibitive :
droit prohibitif (*m.*), prohibitive duty. *See example under* droit prohibitif, *under* **droit**.

prohibition (*n.f.*), prohibition :
prohibition d'entrée (*ou* sur importation), prohibition of import (*or* on importation) ; import prohibition.

prohibition de sortie (*ou* sur exportation), prohibition of export (*or* on exportation) ; export prohibition.

prohibitionniste (*adj.*), prohibitionist :
mesures prohibitionnistes (*f.pl.*), prohibitionist measures.

prohibitionniste (pers.) (*n.m.*), prohibitionist.

projet (dessein) (*n.m.*), project ; scheme ; plan :
projet ambitieux, ambitious scheme.

projet (première rédaction) (*n.m.*), draft :
le bilan, tant qu'il n'est pas approuvé par l'assemblée générale, n'est qu'un projet, the balance sheet, so long as it is not approved by the general meeting, is only a draft.

projet de convention *ou* projet d'acte, draft agreement.

projet de marché *ou* projet de contrat, draft contract.

projet de statuts, draft articles.

projet de chargement (d'un navire) (*m.*), stowage manifest.

projeter (former le plan, le dessin de) (*v.t.*), to plan ; to intend ; to contemplate :
projeter un voyage, to plan, to contemplate, a journey.

donner avis des expéditions projetées, to give notice of intended shipments.

promesse (*n.f.*), promise :
promesse d'actions, promise of shares.

le billet de banque est une promesse de payer une certaine somme à vue et au porteur, a bank note is a promise to pay a certain sum on demand and to bearer.

promesses d'inscriptions, (in France) uninscribable fractions of *rente* arising from conversions.

promesse (billet) (*n.f.*). *Same as* billet simple.

prometteur, -euse (*adj.*), promising.

promettre (*v.t.*), to promise :
promettre de payer, to promise to pay.

promoter (*v.t.*), to promote :
promoter une société, to promote a company.

promoteur (pers.) (*n.m.*), promoter :
promoteur d'un syndicat, promoter of a syndicate.

promotion (*n.f.*), promotion.

prompt, -e (*adj.*) (Abrév. : ppt), prompt :
la prompte expédition des marchandises, prompt forwarding (*or* shipment) of the goods.

embarquement prompt (*ou* prompt embarquement) (*ou* chargement prompt) dans les 21 jours francs de la date du contrat (m.), prompt shipment within 21 clear days of the date of the contract.

vente en expédition prompte (f.), sale for prompt delivery (or for prompt shipment).

promptitude (n.f.), promptitude; promptness; dispatch; despatch.

prononçable (adj.), pronounceable:
groupe de lettres prononçable (Télégr.) (m.), pronounceable group of letters.

prononcer (v.t.), to pronounce; to deliver:
prononcer un discours, to deliver a speech.

proportion (n.f.), proportion; ratio:
la proportion du prêt diffère suivant la nature du titre (avances sur titres), the proportion of the loan differs according to the nature of the security.

frais d'administration hors de toute proportion avec l'importance des affaires de la maison (m.pl.), administration expenses out of all proportion with (or to) the size of the firm's business.

proportionnel, -elle (adj.), proportional; pro rata; proratable; ratable; rateable:
réclamer une indemnité proportionnelle au dommage subi, to claim compensation proportional to the damage sustained.

perte bonifiée par voie de contribution proportionnelle (f.), loss made good by ratable (or by pro rata) (or by proratable) contribution.

Cf. droit proportionnel and règle proportionnelle.

proportionnellement (adv.), proportionally; proportionately; pro rata; ratably:
assureurs qui contribuent à la valeur réelle proportionnellement aux sommes assurées par eux (m.pl.), underwriters who contribute to the actual value proportionally (or ratably) to the amounts insured by them.

fret payé proportionnellement (m.), freight paid pro rata.

proportionner (v.t.), to proportion:
proportionner ses dépenses à ses revenus, ses engagements au capital dont on dispose, to proportion one's expenditure to one's income, one's commitments to the capital at one's disposal.

proposant, -e (pers.) (n.), proposer.

proposer (présenter; soumettre) (v.t.), to propose; to recommend; to move:
proposer un amendement, to move, to propose, an amendment.

le conseil d'administration propose la répartition d'un dividende, the board recommends the distribution of a dividend.

proposer (offrir comme prix) (v.t.), to offer:
proposer tant de francs d'un objet, to offer so many francs for an article.

se proposer (v.r.), to offer oneself:
se proposer pour un emploi, to offer oneself for a situation.

proposition (n.f.), proposition; proposal; recommendation; resolution:
faire une proposition à quelqu'un, to make a proposal (or a proposition) to someone.

proposition d'assurance, proposal of insurance.

soumettre une proposition de dividende, to submit a recommendation of dividend.

faire une proposition à une assemblée, to propose a resolution to, to move a resolution at, a meeting.

propriétaire (personne à qui une chose appartient) (n.m. ou f.), proprietor (m. or f.); proprietress (f.); owner (m. or f.); holder (m. or f.):
propriétaire de la marchandise, owner, proprietor, of the goods.

propriétaire de navire, shipowner: (See note under **armateur**.)

capitaine qui est lui-même propriétaire du navire (m.), captain who is himself the shipowner (or who is himself owner of the ship).

propriétaire qui ne s'oblige que sur son navire et sur le fret, owner who is only obligated on his ship and the freight.

propriétaire de quai, wharfinger.

propriétaire foncier, landed proprietor.

propriétaire d'une action, d'une obligation, holder, proprietor, of a share, of a debenture.

être propriétaire d'un nombre d'actions (de garantie). See under **cautionnement**.

propriétaire (personne qui possède un immeuble occupé par un ou plusieurs locataires) (n.m. ou f.), landlord (m. or f.); landlady (f.).

propriété (n.f.), property; estate; ownership:
navire qui est la propriété d'une société d'armement (m.), ship which is the property of a shipping company.

propriété foncière, landed property; landed estate.

propriétés immobilières, real property; real estate; realty.

propriété littéraire ou simplement propriété, copyright.

justification d'un droit à la propriété des titres (f.), proof of a right to the ownership of stock.

prorata [**prorata** pl.] (n.m.), proportion; share:
recevoir son prorata des bénéfices, to receive one's proportion (or share) of the profits.

prorata d'intérêts en cours, proportion of current interest.

au prorata, pro rata; proratable; in proportion:
la perte fut partagée au prorata, the loss was shared pro rata.

une répartition au prorata, a pro rata (or a proratable) distribution.

au prorata de, pro rata to; in proportion to:
dans une liquidation, chaque créancier reçoit au prorata de sa créance, in a liquidation, each creditor receives pro rata to his debt.

avoir part à un bénéfice au prorata de sa mise de fonds, to share in a profit in proportion to one's holding.

prorata temporis, on the capital for the time being paid up thereon:
les bénéfices permettent de répartir le dividende de 5 0/0 prorata temporis aux actions privilégiées (m.pl.), the profits allow of

the distribution on the preference shares of the dividend of 5% per annum on the capital for the time being paid up thereon.

prorogation (*n.f.*), prolongation; extension; putting off.

proroger (*v.t.*), to prolong; to extend; to put off: proroger l'échéance d'un billet, to prolong, to extend, the time of payment of a bill.

prospectus [**prospectus** *pl.*] (*n.m.*) *ou* **prospectus d'émission**, prospectus:
lancer un prospectus d'une société, to issue a prospectus of a company.

prospère (*adj.*), prosperous:
homme prospère (*m.*), prosperous man.

prospèrement (*adv.*), prosperously.

prospérer (*v.i.*), to prosper; to be prosperous; to thrive.

prospérité (*n.f.*), prosperity.

protecteur, -trice (Écon. polit.) (*adj.*), protective:
tarif protecteur (*m.*), protective tariff. *See example under* droit protecteur.

protection (Écon. polit.) (*n.f.*) (opp. à *libre-échange*), protection:
droits de douane destinés à assurer à la production nationale une protection efficace sur le marché intérieur contre la concurrence étrangère (*m.pl.*), customs duties designed to assure to the national production an effective protection on the home market against foreign competition.

protectionnisme (*n.m.*), protectionism:
cartels favorisés par le protectionnisme douanier (*m.pl.*), cartels favoured by customs protectionism.

protectionniste (*adj.*), protectionist:
le port franc est une brèche dans le système protectionniste, the free port is a breach in the protectionist system.

protectionniste (pers.) (*n.m.*), protectionist:
que veulent les protectionnistes ? Empêcher l'importation étrangère de concurrencer nos produits; assurer aux producteurs nationaux le marché national, what do protectionists want? To prevent foreign importation from competing with our products; to assure to the national producers the national market. (See also example under libre-échangiste.)

protectorat (*n.m.*), protectorate.

protège-mine [**protège-mine** *pl.*] (*n.m.*) *ou* **protège-pointe** [**protège-pointe** *pl.*] (*n.m.*), pencil protector.

protéger (*v.t.*), to protect:
protéger une industrie contre la concurrence déloyale par des droits de douane, to protect an industry against unfair competition by customs duties.

protestable (*adj.*), protestable:
en France, le chèque est protestable comme la lettre de change, in France, a cheque is protestable like a bill of exchange.

protestataire (pers.) (*n.m. ou f.*), protester.

protestation (*n.f.*), protestation; protest:
avis d'opéré reçu sans protestation (*m.*), advice of deal received without protest (*or* protestation).

protester (faire un protêt) (*v.t.*), to protest:
pourquoi (*ou* ce que vu) j'ai protesté ledit effet (acte de protêt), wherefore I now do protest the said bill. *Cf.* faire protester.
protester contre refus de payer, to protest against refusal to pay.

protester (faire un protêt contre le billet de) (*v.t.*), to protest against:
protester un négociant, to protest against a merchant.

protêt (*n.m.*), protest; protestation:
ne prendre livraison des marchandises que sous protêt formel, to take delivery of the goods only under formal protest.
protêt du capitaine du navire, protest of the ship's master.
protêt faute d'acceptation, protest for non acceptance.
protêt faute de paiement, protest for non payment. *See example under* refus de paiement.

prouver (*v.t.*), to prove:
prouver l'existence d'une société, to prove the existence of a company.
obliger le destinataire à prouver une faute du transporteur, c'est l'exposer le plus souvent à prouver l'impossible, to make the consignee prove a fault of the carrier is, in most cases, to expose him to prove the impossible.
que prouve le connaissement? what does the bill of lading prove?

provenance (*n.f.*), origin:
marchandises de provenance étrangère (*f.pl.*), goods of foreign origin.

provenance (Douanes) (*n.f.*). *See* pays de provenance, surtaxe de provenance, *and* port de provenance.

provincial, -e, -aux (*adj.*) *ou* **de province**, provincial; country (*used as adj.*):
banque de province *ou* banque provinciale (*f.*), country bank; provincial bank.

provision (amas de choses) (*n.f.*), provision; store; stock; supply:
une provision d'imprimés, a supply (*or* a stock) of printed forms.
provisions de bord, ship's stores.
provisions de bouche, provisions; food; victuals.

provision (ce qu'un client dépose préalablement) (*n.f.*), provision; funds; deposit:
espèces reçues par un banquier en provision d'une lettre de crédit (*f.pl.*), cash received by a banker as provision for a letter of credit.
avoir une provision chez un banquier, to have funds with a banker.
personne qui émet un chèque sans provision préalable et disponible (*f.*), person who issues a cheque without sufficient funds to meet it. *Cf.* chèque sans provision.
une provision peut être demandée pour garantir le paiement, a deposit may be asked for to secure payment.
provision télégraphique *ou* provision de garantie télégraphique, telegraph deposit.
provision téléphonique *ou* provision de garantie téléphonique *ou* provision téléphone, telephone deposit (deposit for calls).

provision insuffisante *ou* insuffisance de provision (Banq.), insufficient funds ; not
sufficient funds.
défaut de provision (Banq.), no funds ; no
· effects.

provision (couverture ; marge) (Fin., Banq., et
Bourse) (*n.f.*), cover ; margin :
agent de change qui exige une provision de
25 0/0 en espèces (*m.*), stockbroker who requires a cover (*or* a margin) of 25% in cash.

provision (prévision ; réserve) (Comptab.) (*n.f.*),
provision ; reserve :
provision pour créances douteuses, reserve
for doubtful debts ; bad debts reserve.
provision pour impôts, reserve for taxation.
Note :—Properly, in French, *provision* is a
temporary reserve, a necessary provision
against what is practically sure to happen in
the ordinary course of events, such as a
reserve for bad debts or taxation, while
réserve is a more or less permanent reserve,
an amount put by out of earnings, such as the
réserve légale, a bank reserve, or the like.

provision (d'une lettre de change, ou analogue)
(*n.f.*), consideration (for a bill of exchange,
or the like) :
l'acceptation d'une lettre suppose la provision
(*f.*), acceptance of a bill implies consideration.
la délivrance du chèque transfère au bénéficiaire la propriété de la provision, delivery
of a cheque transfers to the payee the
property in the consideration.
défaut de provision (lettre de change) (*m.*),
absence of consideration.
Cf. **cause** and **causer.**

provisionnel, -elle (*adj.*), provisional.
provisionnellement (*adv.*), provisionally.
provisionner (effets de commerce) (*v.t.*), to give
consideration for :
les effets non provisionnés (*ou* les effets qui ne
sont pas provisionnés) sont dits effets de complaisance (*m.pl.*), bills for which no consideration has been given are called accommodation bills.

provisoire (*adj.*), provisional :
assurance provisoire dans laquelle l'évaluation
n'est qu'approximative (*f.*), provisional
insurance in which the valuation is only
approximate.
Cf. titre provisoire.

provisoirement (*adv.*), provisionally :
couvrir un risque provisoirement, to cover a
risk provisionally.

provoquer (*v.t.*), to instigate ; to engineer :
provoquer une enquête, to instigate an
enquiry.
provoquer une hausse (Bourse), to engineer a
rise.

public, -ique (*adj.*), public ; national :
vente publique (*f.*), public sale.
dette publique (*f.*), public (*or* national) debt.

public (*n.m.*), public :
émettre des actions dans le public, to issue
shares to the public.
placer des actions dans le public, to place
shares with the public.

publication (*n.f.*), publication.

publicité (*n.f.*), publicity ; advertising :
la publicité coûte fort cher, advertising is very
expensive.

publier (*v.t.*), to publish ; to advertise :
publier un bilan, l'inventaire détaillé du portefeuille, to publish a balance sheet, a detailed
list of the investments.
publier une notice au Journal officiel, to
advertise a notice in the Gazette.

pupitre (*n.m.*), desk :
pupitre fermant à clef, lockup desk.

purge (*n.f.*), redemption ; paying off :
purge d'hypothèque *ou* purge légale, redemption, paying off, of mortgage.

purger (*v.t.*), to redeem ; to pay off ; to free ;
to rid ; to clear :
purger une hypothèque, to redeem, to pay off,
a mortgage.
purger son bien de dettes, to free, to clear,
one's property from debt ; to rid one's
property of debts.

Q

quadruplé (Bourse) (*n.m.*), option to quadruple :
quadruplé à la baisse, put of three times more ;
seller's option to quadruple.
quadruplé à la hausse, call of three times
more ; buyer's option to quadruple.

quai (Mar.) (*n.m.*), quay ; wharf :
quai aux charbons, coal wharf.
quai d'embarquement, landing ; landing place ;
landing platform.
quai à quai, wharf to wharf.

quai (Ch. de f.) (*n.m.*), platform :
quai d'arrivée, arrival platform.
quai de départ, departure platform.

qualité (*n.f.*) (Abrév.: **Qté**), quality :
qualité à tel type, quality about as per such
or such type sample.
qualité à telle marque, quality according to
such or such a mark.
qualité à type standard, quality about as per
lodged standard sample.

qualité conforme aux échantillons *ou* qualité sur échantillon de références, quality about as per samples, sealed or in possession of buyers.

qualité loyale et marchande *ou* qualité courante *ou* qualité commerciale, fair average quality.

qualité vue et agréée, quality subject to approval.

qualité de membre *ou simplement* **qualité** (*n.f.*), membership :

acquérir la qualité de membre d'une association, to acquire membership (*or* to become a member) of an association.

la qualité de membre du comité ne confère pas, ipso facto, le droit d'entrée dans les locaux du comité, membership of the committee does not confer, ipso facto, the right of admission to the committee's premises.

tout membre quittant l'association ou perdant sa qualité, any member leaving the association or losing his membership.

qualités (*n.f.pl.*) *ou* **qualité ou profession**, description ; profession or business ; occupation :

les nom, prénoms, adresse (*ou* domicile), et qualités (*ou* qualité ou profession) du souscripteur, the full name (*or* the name in full), address, and description (*or* and profession or business) (*or* and occupation) of the applicant.

quantième (*n.m.*) *ou* **quantième du mois,** day ; day of the month :

quantième, mois, et millésime, day, month, and year.

la date doit être inscrite en toutes lettres, quant au quantième du mois et au mois lui-même, the date should be written in words at length, as to the day of the month and the month itself.

quantité (*n.f.*), quantity.

quantité (nombre de colis) (*n.f.*), quantity ; amount ; number of packages.

quantité embarquée en moins, amount short shipped.

quantité en portefeuille *ou simplement* **quantité** (*n.f.*), quantity in portfolio (*or* in the box) ; holding :

nous avons une grande quantité de ces actions en portefeuille, we have a large quantity of these shares in portfolio (*or* in our portfolio) (*or* in the box) ; we have a big holding of these shares.

quantum (quantité ; somme qu'on ne précise pas ; tant pour cent ; marc le franc) (*n.m.*), amount ; quantum ; proportion ; percentage ; ratio :

fixer le quantum des dommages-intérêts à allouer, to fix the amount of damages to be allowed.

toucher son quantum de bénéfices, to draw one's proportion of profits.

répartir les frais accidentels d'après un quantum à déterminer, to apportion the incidental expenses according to a proportion to be determined.

appliquer à la fabrication le quantum de frais généraux qui lui incombe, to charge against the cost of manufacture the percentage of overhead expenses properly applicable thereto.

quantum (quorum) (*n.m.*), quorum : (See also **quorum**.)

le quantum n'est pas atteint, a quorum is not present.

quarantaine (*n.f.*), quarantine :

pertes que causent les quarantaines aux compagnies de navigation (*f.pl.*), losses which quarantines cause to shipping companies.

quartier (*n.m.*), quarter :

le quartier commerçant d'une ville, the business quarter of a town.

quasi-contrat [**quasi-contrats** *pl.*] (*n.m.*), quasi contract :

les quasi-contrats diffèrent des contrats en ce qu'il n'y a pas un accord de volonté entre les parties, quasi contracts differ from contracts in that there is no accord of will between the parties.

quatre chiffres (Banq.) (*m.pl.*), bills of exchange running into four figures, viz., of the value of 1,000 francs and over. Cf. **broche.**

quatre mois *ou simplement* **quatre** *ou* **4** (*n.m.pl.*) (Bourse de marchandises), four months ; four (months over which delivery may be spread) :

quatre premiers (*Abrév. :* 4 prem.) *ou* quatre de janvier (janvier, février, mars, avril), first four ; first 4 (January, February, March, April).

(les) quatre de mars (mars, avril, mai, juin), (the) four months, March, April, May, June.

(les) quatre de mai *ou* (les) quatre chauds *ou* (les) mois chauds *ou* (les) chauds (mai, juin, juillet, août), (the) middle four (May, June, July, August).

(les) quatre d'octobre (octobre, novembre, décembre, janvier), (the) four months, October, November, December, January.

(les) quatre de novembre (novembre, décembre, janvier, février), (the) four months, November, December, January, February.

quatre derniers (*Abrév. :* 4 dern.) (septembre, octobre, novembre, décembre), last four (September, October, November, December).

quatre mois de septembre (les), the four months, September, October, November, and December.

que dit être (clause de connaissement), said to contain.

questions à délibérer (à une assemblée) *ou simplement* **questions** (*n.f.pl.*), business :

mettre à l'ordre du jour les questions à délibérer, to put down on the agenda the business to be transacted.

questions diverses, general business.

qui de droit, those whom it may concern :

les animaux, dont il n'est pas pris livraison à l'arrivée, sont mis en fourrière, aux frais, risques et périls de qui de droit (*m.pl.*), animals, of which delivery is not taken on arrival, are impounded, at the expense and risk of those whom it may concern.

qui demandez vous ? (Téléph.), number, please? ;
    what number are you calling?
quille (d'un navire) (n.f.), keel (of a ship).
quinze (mois) ou 15 (Bourse) (n.m.), mid (month) ;
    mid (month) account :
    achetez tant d'actions pour le 15 août ou
    achetez tant d'actions au 15/8, buy so many
    shares for mid August (or for mid August
    account).
    les liquidations au parquet ont lieu le 15 et
    le dernier jour de chaque mois. En coulisse,
    les liquidations n'ont lieu qu'à fin de mois,
    (in Paris) settlements on the parquet take
    place on the 15th and the last day of each
    month. On the coulisse, settlements take
    place only at the end of the month. See
    marché des valeurs for explanation of the
    words parquet and coulisse.
    Note :—On the Paris Bourse, mid month
    contango day is always on the 15th day of
    the month (or the first business day after
    the 15th, if the 15th falls on a non business
    day), and the end month contango day is on
    the last day of the month (or the first business
    day after, if the last day of the month falls
    on a non business day).
    On the London Stock Exchange, settlement
    dates are fixed periodically by the Stock
    Exchange Committee. Settlements now take
    place in London every fortnight, with
    occasional variations, as at holiday times,
    consequently the terms mid account and end
    account are no longer used.
quirat (n.m.), share (in a ship) :
    le navire est supposé se diviser, sous le rapport
    de la propriété, en un certain nombre de
    parts égales, appelées quirats ; en France
    ordinairement vingt-quatre quirats, en
    Angleterre soixante-quatre, the ship, with
    respect to ownership, is supposed to be
    divided into a certain number of equal
    parts, called shares ; in France generally
    twenty four shares, in England sixty four.
quirataire (pers.) (n.m.), owner (of a share or
    shares in a ship) :
    navire qui est la propriété de plusieurs
    quirataires (m.), ship which is the property
    of several owners.
quittance (n.f.), receipt ; discharge : (See also
    acquit, récépissé, and reçu.)
    quittance comptable, accountable receipt.
    quittance de consignation (Douanes), deposit
    receipt.
    quittances de droit, des paiements faits, receipts
    for duty, for payments made.
    quittance de loyer, receipt for rent ; rent
    receipt.
    quittance finale, receipt in full discharge ;
    receipt for the balance.
    quittance valable, valid receipt ; good receipt.
    dont quittance, receipt whereof is hereby
    acknowledged ; which is hereby acknow-
    ledged to have been received.
quittancer (v.t.), to receipt :
    quittancer un mémoire, to receipt a bill.
quitter (se retirer de quelque lieu) (v.t.), to leave :

quitter Paris, to leave Paris.
    le train express quittant Bruxelles-Midi à
    23 h. 3, the express train leaving Brussels
    Midi at 11.3 p.m.
    (steamer) X. a quitté Marseille le 31 (date)
    pour Londres (Mouvement des Navires),
    (steamer) X. (for London) left (or l.) Marseilles
    31 (date) (Shipping News).
    le capitaine ne doit quitter son bord que le
    dernier, the captain should be the last to
    leave his ship.
quitter (décharger) (v.t.), to discharge ; to
    release :
    quitter quelqu'un d'une dette, to discharge
    someone from a debt.
quitus (n.m.), quietus ; quittance ; discharge
    (from liability) :
    obtenir son quitus, to obtain one's quietus (or
    quittance) (or discharge).
    donner quitus à un caissier, to give quietus (or
    quittance) to a cashier.
    Note :—It is customary in France for cashiers,
    collectors, and the like, to receive a formal
    quitus. This is also the case with retiring
    directors. (In the case of a deceased director
    the quitus would be given to his heirs.)
    Thus in a directors' report to the shareholders
    one may find the following : « M. X. nous
    a prié d'accepter sa démission d'adminis-
    trateur de la Société : le Conseil vous prie de
    lui donner quitus de sa gestion. » And in the
    report of proceedings of the meeting the
    following resolution : « L'assemblée générale
    donne à M. X. quitus de sa gestion. » In
    the case of a deceased director, the resolution
    would read : « L'assemblée générale donne
    quitus de gestion aux successions de feu
    M. un tel » (to the heirs of the late Mr So-
    and-So).
quorum [quorum pl.] (n.m.), quorum :
    si l'assemblée générale ne réunit pas un quorum,
    une nouvelle assemblée est convoquée,
    if at the general meeting a quorum is not
    present, a new meeting is convened.
    le quorum n'est pas atteint, a quorum is not
    present.
    un quorum de trois quarts du capital, a quorum
    of three quarters of the capital.
quote-part [quotes-parts pl.] (n.f.), quota ; share ;
    proportion ; contribution :
    payer sa quote-part, to pay one's quota (or
    share) (or proportion) (or contribution).
    recevoir sa quote-part des bénéfices, to receive
    one's proportion (or one's share) of the profits.
    quotes-parts revenant à chacun dans le con-
    tingentement des ventes, quotas falling to
    each in the curtailment of sales.
quotidien, -enne (adj.), daily.
quotidien (n.m.) ou journal quotidien (m.), daily ;
    daily paper.
quotité (n.f.), amount ; proportion ; quantity ;
    shape :
    la quotité à prélever sur les bénéfices pour
    composer le fonds de réserve, the amount
    to be appropriated out of profits to form
    the reserve fund.

la quotité du prêt diffère suivant la nature du titre (avances sur titres), the amount (or proportion) of the loan differs according to the nature of the security.

on ne peut opérer que sur une certaine quotité (appelée la quotité négociable) de ces titres ou sur un multiple de cette quotité (Bourse de valeurs), one can only deal in a certain quantity (or shape) (called the marketable quantity or dealable shape) of this stock or in a multiple of this quantity (or shape).

R

rabais (remise) (*n.m.*), allowance; discount; rebate :
accorder un rabais, to allow a discount; to make an allowance.
rabais de fret, rebate of freight; freight rebate.
rabais de prime, rebate of premium.

rabais (diminution de prix) (*n.m.*), reduction; reduction of price; discount :
vendre au rabais, to sell at a reduction (or at a discount).

rabaissement (*n.m.*), lowering; reduction.

rabaisser (diminuer) (*v.t.*), to lower; to reduce :
rabaisser un prix, to lower, to reduce, a price.

rabaisser (déprécier) (*v.t.*), to depreciate; to underrate.

rabat *ou* **rabattage** (*n.m.*), reduction :
il y a un grand rabat de prix, there is a big reduction in price.

rabatteur d'affaires (pers.) (*m.*), tout; touter.

rabattre (retrancher de prix) (*v.t.*), to deduct; to take off; to knock off :
rabattre les centimes, to knock off the centimes.

rabattre (se) (*v.r.*), to fall back; to fall away; to go back; to relapse :
l'action X. s'est rabattue de 91 à 87, X. shares fell back (or fell away) (or went back) (or relapsed) from 91 to 87 francs.

raccrochage (Téléph.) (*n.m.*), replacing the receiver.

raccrocher le récepteur (*ou* l'écouteur) (*ou* l'appareil) *ou simplement* **raccrocher** (*v.t.*) (Téléph.) (Ant. : *décrocher*), to replace the receiver :
raccrochez dès que la conversation est terminée, replace the receiver when conversation is finished.

rachat (recouvrement d'une chose vendue) (*n.m.*), repurchase; buying back :
vendre avec faculté de rachat, to sell with option of repurchase.

rachat (achat de ce qu'on a vendu) (Bourse) (*n.m.*), buying back :
rachats des vendeurs à découvert, buying back of bear sellers.

rachat (exécution) (Bourse de valeurs) (*n.m.*) (opp. à *revente*), buying in; buying in against : [Cf. **exécution** (Bourse).]
rachat de titres, de valeurs, buying in stock, securities.
rachat d'un vendeur, buying in against a seller.

rachat (exécution) (Bourse de marchandises) (*n.m.*) (opp. à *revente*), repurchase; purchasing against. (See examples under the verb.)

rachat (extinction d'une obligation) (*n.m.*), redemption :
rachat d'une obligation, redemption of a debenture (or of a bond).

rachat (Assce) (*n.m.*), surrender :
valeur de rachat d'une police d'assurance sur la vie, surrender value of a life insurance policy.

rachetable (*adj.*), repurchasable; redeemable :
objet rachetable par le vendeur (*m.*), article repurchasable by the seller.
obligation rachetable (*f.*), redeemable bond.

racheter (acheter ce qu'on a vendu) (*v.t.*), to repurchase; to buy back :
racheter un objet vendu, to buy back an article sold.
l'acheteur revend les titres qu'il ne peut pas lever et le vendeur rachète les titres qu'il ne peut livrer (*m.*), the buyer sells out the stock he cannot take up and the seller buys back the stock he cannot deliver. See note under **revendre.**

se racheter (Bourse) (*v.r.*), to buy back :
vendeur obligé de se racheter pour faire face à sa livraison (*m.*), seller obliged to buy back in order to meet his delivery.
je me rachète à tel cours, I buy back at such or such a price.
le découvert se rachète, the bears (or the shorts) are buying back.

racheter (exécution) (Bourse de valeurs) (*v.t.*) (opp. à *revendre*), to buy in; to buy in against : [Cf. **exécuter** (Bourse).]
racheter des titres, des valeurs, to buy in stock, securities.
racheter un vendeur, to buy in against a seller.

racheter (exécution) (Bourse de marchandises) (*v.t.*) (opp. à *revendre*), to repurchase; to purchase against :
racheter des marchandises, to repurchase goods.
racheter un défaillant, to purchase against a defaulter.

racheter (se libérer à prix d'argent de) (*v.t.*), to redeem :
racheter une obligation, to redeem a debenture (or a bond).

racheteur, -euse (pers.) (n.), repurchaser; redeemer.

rade (n.f.), roadstead; roads; road:
navire qui séjourne (ou qui stationne) en rade (m.), ship which is lying in a roadstead (or which lies in the roads).
rade foraine, open roadstead.

radeau (n.m.), raft.

radiation (n.f.), striking out; crossing out:
radiation d'un article d'un compte, striking out, crossing out, an item in an account.
radiation d'inscription hypothécaire ou radiation d'hypothèque, entry of satisfaction of mortgage.

radier (v.t.), to strike out; to cross out:
radier une clause dans un contrat, to strike out a clause in a contract.
radier une inscription hypothécaire par une mention sur le registre (mention faite par le conservateur), to enter a memorandum of satisfaction of mortgage on the register.

radiodiffusion (n.f.), broadcasting.

radiotélégramme ou **radiogramme** ou **simplement radio** (n.m.), radiotelegram; radiogram; radio; wireless message:
les radiotélégrammes sont échangés avec les navires en mer au moyen des stations côtières, radiotelegrams are exchanged with ships at sea by means of coast stations.
radiotélégramme à grande distance, long distance radiotelegram.
d'après un radio de l'Agence X., according to a wireless message of the X. Agency.

radiotélégraphie (n.f.), radiotelegraphy; wireless telegraphy.

radiotélégraphique ou **simplement radio** (adj.), radiotelegraphic; radio; wireless:
station radiotélégraphique ou station radio [stations radios pl.] (f.), radiotelegraphic station; radio station; wireless station.

radiotéléphonie (n.f.), radiotelephony; wireless telephony.

radouber un navire endommagé, to repair a damaged ship.

raffermi, -e (adj.), firm; hard.
se raffermir (v.r.), to firm; to firm up; to harden; to harden up:
les actions X. se raffermissent (f.pl.), X. shares hardened.
la tendance, tout d'abord indécise, s'est raffermie en séance, the tendency, undecided at first, hardened later on.

raffermissement (n.m.), firmness; hardness.

raison de commerce ou **raison commerciale** (f.), business name; trade name.

raison sociale ou **simplement raison** (n.f.), firm; firm name; name; style; style of firm; style of the firm; name of company; company's name:
les initiales de la raison sociale (f.pl.), the firm's initials.
signer son nom ou sa raison sociale, to sign one's name or one's firm name.
maison de banque connue sous la raison X. & Cie (f.), banking house known under the style of X. & Co.

la raison sociale est . . . (statuts), the name of the company is . . . (memorandum of association).

raisonnable (adj.), reasonable:
prix raisonnable (m.), reasonable price (or charge).
dans un délai raisonnable, within a reasonable time.

raisonner un arbitrage, to compute an arbitrage.

ralentir (v.i.), to slacken; to fall off.

ralentissement (n.m.), slackening; falling off:
ralentissement saisonnier de commandes, seasonal falling off (or slackening) of orders.

ramener (réduire) (Ant.: porter) (v.t.), to reduce; to lower; to bring:
dividende ramené de 8 à 4 0/0 (m.), dividend reduced from 8 to 4%.
l'action X. qui s'était redressée à 1 110 est ramenée à 1 080, sur des prises de bénéfice, X. shares which had hardened to 1,110 francs were lowered to 1,080, on profit taking.
ramener les prix dans les différents pays en francs-or, seul moyen rationnel d'effectuer une comparaison pratique, to bring the prices in the different countries to gold francs, the only rational means of effecting a practical comparison.

rang (n.m.), rank:
rang assigné à une créance, rank assigned to a debt.
entre les créanciers hypothécaires le rang s'établit par la date, between mortgagees rank is established by date.
Cf. prendre rang.

ranimer (se) (v.r.), to recover:
l'action X. se ranime de 1 505 à 1 540, X. shares recovered from 1,505 to 1,540 francs.

rapatriement (n.m.), repatriation; sending home.

rapatrier (v.t.), to repatriate; to send home:
on dit que la place de Paris a rapatrié des montants très importants d'emprunts français contractés aux États-Unis pendant la guerre, it is said that the Paris market has repatriated very large amounts of French loans contracted in the United States during the war.
rapatrier l'équipage, to send the crew home.

rapidité usitée (f.), customary dispatch:
décharger avec la rapidité usitée pour un steamer, to discharge with the customary dispatch for a steamer.

rappel (n.m.), recalling; calling in; calling over. See the verb for examples.

rappel (n.m.) ou **rappel de compte**, reminder:
rappel de commande, d'échéance, reminder of order, of due date.
envoyer à quelqu'un un rappel de compte (invitation de payer), to send someone a reminder.

rappel de cours (Bourse) (m.), marking of omitted bargain.

rappeler (v.t.), to recall; to call in; to call over:
rappeler le bureau, l'opératrice (Téléph.), to recall the exchange, the operator.

vous serez rappelé dès qu'un circuit sera
disponible (Téléph.), you will be recalled as
soon as a line becomes available.

rappeler une avance, to call in an advance.

rappeler un compte avec les livres, to call over
an account with the books.

à rappeler *ou* à rappeler, s.v.p. (mention à l'en-
tête d'une lettre), reference ; for reference
please quote.

rapport (récit) (*n.m.*), report :

faire un rapport sur la situation d'une société,
to make a report on the position of a company.

rapport d'arrimage, report of stowage.

rapport d'expertise, survey report.

rapport de mer *ou* rapport du capitaine,
captain's report (of extraordinary incidents
during the voyage).

rapport des administrateurs *ou* rapport du
conseil d'administration, directors' report ;
report of the directors :

approuver les rapports et les comptes de
l'exercice au 31 décembre 19—, to approve
the report and accounts for the year to
31st December 19—.

rapport des commissaires (*ou* des commissaires
aux comptes), auditors' report ; report of
the auditors.

rapport en douane, entry ; bill of entry.

rapport (revenu) (*n.m.*), yield ; return ; revenue ;
income :

rapport d'un capital, yield of (*or* return on) a
capital.

installation d'un **rapport** fructueux (*f.*), installation yielding a profitable return.

emploi de grand rapport (*ou* d'un grand rapport)
(*m.*), post bringing in a big income.

maison de rapport (*f.*), revenue-earning house.

capitaux en rapport (*m.pl.*), productive (*or*
revenue-earning) capital.

rapport (relation) (*n.m.*), ratio :

le rapport entre l'or et l'argent, entre l'émission
de billets de banque et la réserve métallique,
the ratio between gold and silver, between the
issue of bank notes and the bullion reserve.

rapporter (faire le récit de) (*v.t.*), to report :

rapporter les décisions d'un comité, to report
the decisions of a committee.

rapporter (donner comme produit) (*v.t.*), to bring
in ; to bear ; to produce ; to yield :

maison qui rapporte tant par an (*f.*), house that
brings in so much a year.

titres rapportant tant d'intérêt par an (*m.pl.*),
stock yielding so much interest per annum.

rapporter (Comptab.) (*v.t.*), to post :

inscription du folio du journal d'après lequel
l'article est rapporté (*f.*), putting in the
journal folio from which the item is posted.

rapproché (Bourse de marchandises) (*n.m.*) (opp. à
éloigné), near position :

les cotons ont avancé sur des couvertures sur les
rapprochés (*m.pl.*), cottons have advanced
on coverings on near positions.

rapprochement (comparaison) (*n.m.*), comparison :

résultat du rapprochement entre le bénéfice
brut et le montant des ventes exprimé en
pourcentage (*m.*), result of the comparison

between the gross profit and the amount of
the sales expressed in percentage.

rapprocher (mettre en parallèle) (*v.t.*), to compare.

rare (*adj.*) (Ant. : *abondant*), scarce :

l'argent est rare (*m.*) *ou* les capitaux sont rares
(*m.pl.*), money is scarce.

rareté *ou* **raréfaction** (*n.f.*), scarcity ; dearth :

rareté (*ou* raréfaction) du numéraire, du titre,
de fret, scarcity, dearth, of coin, of stock, of
freight :

la hausse est l'œuvre de la rareté (*ou* de la
raréfaction) du titre, a rise is the consequence of a scarcity (*or* a dearth) of stock.

ratification (*n.f.*), ratification ; confirmation.

ratifier (*v.t.*), to ratify ; to confirm :

ratifier une nomination, to confirm, to ratify,
an appointment (to a post).

ratifier la décision d'une assemblée, to confirm
the resolution of a meeting.

rationalisation (*n.f.*), rationalization :

rationalisation de l'industrie, rationalization of
industry.

rationaliser (*v.t.*), to rationalize.

rattraper le temps perdu, to make up for lost time.

raturage (*n.m.*), scratching out.

rature (*n.f.*), erasure :

registre bien tenu, sans ratures ni surcharges
(*m.*), register well kept, without erasures or
corrections (*or* alterations).

raturer (*v.t.*), to erase ; to scratch out.

ravitaillement (*n.m.*), victualling ; revictualling.

ravitailler (*v.t.*), to victual ; to revictual.

rayer (*v.t.*), to cross out ; to strike out ; to delete ;
to expunge :

rayer un mot, to cross out, to strike out, to
delete, a word.

rayer les mentions qui ne conviennent pas,
delete, strike out, words not applicable ;
delete as required.

valeur rayée de la cote (*f.*), stock expunged from
the list.

rayure (*n.f.*), crossing out ; striking out ; deletion ;
expunction.

réacquérir (*v.t.*), to reacquire :

réacquérir un bien, to reacquire a property.

réaction (*n.f.*), reaction :

le fait saillant de la journée a été la vive réaction
du franc, the outstanding event of the day
was the sharp reaction of the franc.

réactionner (*v.i.*), to react :

valeur qui réactionne de tel cours à tel cours (*f.*),
stock which reacts from such a price to such
a price.

réadmettre (*v.t.*), to readmit.

réadmission (*n.f.*), readmission :

réadmission en franchise des marchandises
exportées par erreur à l'étranger, free
readmission of goods exported abroad in
mistake.

réaffrètement (*n.m.*), rechartering ; reaffreightment.

réaffréter (*v.t.*), to recharter ; to reaffreight :

profit réalisé pour un affréteur qui aurait réaffrété un navire à un prix plus élevé (*m.*),
profit made by a charterer who has rechartered a ship at a higher price.

réagir (*v.i.*), to react :
les stannifères n'ont pas cherché à réagir contre la dérobade de la semaine dernière (*f.pl.*), tins did not attempt to react from last week's break.

réalisable (*adj.*), realizable :
valeurs réalisables (*f.pl.*), realizable assets (*or* securities).

réalisation (*n.f.*), realization ; closing ; making :
la réalisation d'un bénéfice est le but de tout échange commercial, making (*or* to make) a profit is the object of every commercial exchange.

réaliser (*v.t.*), to realize ; to close ; to make :
réaliser un placement, un stock de marchandises, to realize an investment, a stock of goods.
réaliser un marché, une affaire, to close a contract (*or* a bargain), a transaction :
achat à prime réalisé avant le jour de la réponse (*m.*), option purchase closed before option day.
bénéfice effectivement réalisé (*m.*), profit actually realized (*or* made).

réaliseur (pers.) (*n.m.*), realizer.

réappréciation (*n.f.*), revaluation.

réapprécier (*v.t.*), to revalue.

réarrimage (*n.m.*), restowing.

réarrimer (*v.t.*), to restow :
réarrimer la cargaison dans la cale d'un navire, to restow the cargo in the hold of a ship.

réassurance (*n.f.*), reinsurance ; reassurance :
réassurance d'excédent *ou* réassurance de trop-plein, excess reinsurance.
réassurance de partage, share reinsurance ; participating reinsurance.

réassuré, -e (pers.) (*n.*), reinsured.

réassurer (*v.t.*), to reinsure ; to reassure :
réassurer auprès d'autres compagnies tout ou partie d'un risque, le surplus (*ou* l'excédent) de son risque, to reinsure with other companies the whole or part of a risk, the surplus (*or* the excess) of one's risk.

se réassurer (*v.r.*), to reinsure :
l'assureur peut à son tour se réassurer auprès d'un autre assureur pour la totalité ou une partie du risque qu'il assume directement vis-à-vis de l'assuré (*m.*), the underwriter in his turn can reinsure with another underwriter for the whole or part of the risk he assumes directly towards the assured.

réassureur (pers.) (*n.m.*), reinsurer.

rebut (Poste) (*n.m.*), dead letter ; dead postal packet :
les objets de correspondance qui ne peuvent être ni distribués, ni réexpédiés, ni renvoyés aux expéditeurs, sont dénommés rebuts (*m.pl.*), postal packets which cannot be delivered, nor redirected, nor returned to the senders, are called dead postal packets.

rebut (bureau des rebuts) (Poste) (*n.m.*), dead letter office ; returned letter office :
objets de correspondance rendus aux expéditeurs ou versés au rebut (*m.pl.*), postal packets returned to the senders or sent to the dead letter office.

recacheter (*v.t.*), to reseal.

récapitulatif, -ive (*adj.*), recapitulative.

récapitulation (*n.f.*), recapitulation ; summary.

récapituler (*v.t.*), to recapitulate ; to summarize.

recensement (vérification de marchandises) (*n.m.*), stock taking :
recensement d'entrepôt de douane, stock taking of customs warehouse.

récépissé [**récépissés** *pl.*] (*n.m.*), receipt : (See also **reçu, quittance**, and **acquit.**)
récépissé de dépôt, deposit receipt (receipt for a lodgment, as a security. *Cf.* bon de caisse *and* bon à échéance).
récépissé de dépôt d'un télégramme, receipt for a telegram.
récépissé de souscription, application receipt.
récépissé de versement d'appel de fonds, call receipt ; receipt for payment of call.
récépissé à l'expéditeur, au destinataire. In France, the *récépissé à l'expéditeur* (the receipt for the sender) is given to the sender of goods by railway, and the *récépissé au destinataire* (receipt for the consignee) accompanies the consignment and is given to the consignee on arrival of the goods. These *récépissés* are duplicates and take the place of the railway consignment note :
la lettre de voiture n'est plus guère employée que pour les transports internationaux. Pour les expéditions à l'intérieur du pays, elle est remplacée par le récépissé, (In France) the consignment note is not much used now except for international transports. For inland dispatches, it is replaced by the *récépissé*.

récépissé-warrant [**récépissés-warrants** *pl.*] (*n.m.*), warrant (for goods deposited in a public or dock warehouse).

récepteur, -euse (pers.) (*n.*), receiver.

récepteur (Téléph.) (*n.m.*) (opp. à *transmetteur*), receiver :
décrocher, raccrocher, le récepteur, to remove, to replace, the receiver.

réception (*n.f.*), receipt ; receiving ; reception :
accuser réception d'une lettre, to acknowledge receipt of a letter.
réception des avis, de la nouvelle d'un sinistre, de la marchandise à bord, receipt, reception, of advices, of the news of an accident, of the goods on board.
gares fermées les dimanches tant à la réception qu'à la livraison des marchandises (*f.pl.*), stations closed on Sundays both for the receiving (*or* receipt) (*or* reception) and delivering (*or* delivery) of goods.

réceptionnaire (pers.) (*n.m.* ou *f.*), receiver ; consignee :
l'expéditeur et le réceptionnaire, the sender and the receiver.
réceptionnaire du chargement, receiver, consignee, of the shipment.

réceptionnaire (Bourse de marchandises) (pers.) (*n.m.*), receiver ; last buyer.

recette (recouvrement de ce qui est dû) (*n.f.*), receiving :
faire la recette d'une maison de commerce, to do the receiving of a business house.

recette (*n.f.*) *ou* **recettes** (*n.f.pl.*) (ce qui est reçu),
receipt; receipts; takings; returns;
revenue :
recettes et dépenses de caisse, cash receipts
and payments.
compter la recette et la dépense, to reckon up
the receipts and the expenditure (*or* the
takings and the expenses).
la recette brute, the gross receipts (*or* returns).
recettes des douanes, customs receipts.
recettes fiscales *ou* recettes provenant d'impôts,
inland revenue; internal revenue; revenue
derived from taxes.
recettes voyageurs (Ch. de f.), passenger
receipts.
recette (bureau d'un receveur) (*n.f.*), collector's
office; office :
recette des douanes, office of collector of
customs.
receveur, -euse (pers.) (*n.*), collector; receiver :
receveur des contributions, tax collector;
collector of taxes; rate collector.
receveur des contributions directes, collector
of taxes (income tax, and the like).
receveur des douanes, collector of customs.
receveur (pour la distribution des billets aux
voyageurs) (pers.) (*n.m.*), booking clerk.
receveur de la prime (Opérations à prime) (Bourse)
(*m.*) (opp. à *payeur de la prime*), taker of the
rate.
recevoir (*v.t.*), to receive; to get; to accept :
recevoir une lettre, to receive, to get, a letter.
recevoir des appointements, de l'argent en
dépôt, tant à compte, to receive a salary,
money on deposit, so much on account.
recevez mes civilités, mes respects, accept my
compliments, my respects.
Recevez, Monsieur (Messieurs), mes (nos)
meilleures salutations (*ou* salutations empressées) (formule de politesse précédant
signature), Yours faithfully; Yours truly.
à recevoir, receivable :
intérêts à recevoir (*m.pl.*), interest receivable.
rechange (opération) (*n.m.*), reexchange :
rechange d'une lettre de change, reexchange
of a bill of exchange.
rechange (prix du nouveau change) (*n.m.*), reexchange :
payer le change et le rechange, to pay the
exchange and the reexchange.
rechargement (*n.m.*), reloading; reshipping.
recharger (*v.t.*), to reload; to reship :
marchandise rechargée sur un autre navire (*f.*),
goods reloaded on another ship (*or* reshipped
on another boat).
recherche (*n.f.*), search; searching; searching
for; looking for; rummaging :
recherche d'une différence, des erreurs dans les
écritures, looking for a difference, mistakes
in the books.
recherches à bord (des navires) (Douanes),
rummaging; searching; search on board.
rechercher (s'efforcer de trouver) (*v.t.*), to search;
to search for; to solicit; to look for; to seek
after :

rechercher la cause des discordances, to look
for the cause of disagreements.
rechercher des commandes, to solicit orders.
être recherché, -e, to be in request :
l'action X. est recherchée à 729 fr., X. shares
were in request at 729 francs.
réciprocité (*n.f.*), reciprocity :
réciprocité de traitement, reciprocity of treatment.
certains produits importés à cette colonie sont
admis en franchise, et, par réciprocité, les
produits coloniaux, à quelques exceptions
près, sont exempts de taxes douanières à
leur entrée dans la métropole (*m.pl.*), certain
products imported into that colony are
admitted free, and, by reciprocity, the
colonial products, with a few exceptions,
exempt from customs charges on their
importation into the home country.
réciproque (*adj.*), reciprocal :
concessions réciproques (*f.pl.*), reciprocal concessions.
réclamant, -e (pers.) (*n.*), claimant; claimer.
réclamateur (pers.) (*n.m.*), claimant; claimer;
receiver :
réclamateur du chargement, receiver of the
shipment (*or* of the cargo).
réclamation (*n.f.*), claiming; claim; application :
réclamation d'indemnité, claim for indemnity
(*or* for compensation); claim.
une réclamation de pertes ou d'avaries, a claim
for losses or damage.
les assureurs ne feront aucune réclamation pour
fret (*m.pl.*), no claim to be made by the
underwriters for freight.
adresser une réclamation au contrôleur des
contributions directes, to send in a claim
to the inspector of taxes.
réclamations concernant les mandats non
parvenus, applications concerning money
orders which have miscarried.
réclame (*n.f.*), advertisement; advertising.
réclamer (*v.t.*), to claim; to apply :
réclamer son dû, l'indu, le paiement dans un
délai de quelques jours, le payement d'un effet
au jour de l'échéance, le paiement à ses
assureurs, une lettre au bureau de poste,
une indemnité en cas de congédiement, to
claim one's due, what is not due, payment
within several days, payment of a bill on the
day of maturity, payment from one's
insurers, a letter at the post office, compensation in case of dismissal.
si les marchandises ne sont pas réclamées, ou
plusieurs porteurs de connaissements réclament la même marchandise, if the goods are
not claimed, or if several holders of bills of
lading claim the same goods.
les réclamer par télégraphe s'ils ne sont pas
transmis par le retour du courrier, apply for
them by telegraph if they are not sent by
return of post.
reclouer (*v.t.*), to renail :
caisses reclouées (réservation sur un connaissement, sur une lettre de voiture), cases
renailed.

récolte (*n.f.*), crop :
arrivée de la nouvelle récolte (*f.*), arrival of the new crop.

recommandable (*adj.*), recommendable :
placement recommandable (*m.*), recommendable investment.

recommandataire (celui sur lequel une lettre de change est tirée « au besoin ») (pers.) (*n.m.*), referee in case of need ; case of need. See examples under **besoin.**

recommandation (*n.f.*), recommendation :
lettre de recommandation (*f.*), letter of recommendation.

recommandation (Poste) (*n.f.*), registration :
la recommandation ou le chargement est un traitement spécial appliqué aux objets de correspondance dont les expéditeurs veulent assurer la remise, contre reçu, aux destinataires, ou garantir le contenu desdits objets, registration or insurance is a special treatment applied to postal packets of which the senders wish to ensure delivery, against receipt, to the addressees, or to protect the contents of the said packets.

recommandé, -e (Poste) (*adj.*) (Abrév. : **R.**), registered :
lettre recommandée (*f.*), registered letter.

recommander (prier d'être favorable à) (*v.t.*), to recommend :
recommander un ami à quelqu'un, to recommend a friend to someone.

recommander (Poste) (*v.t.*), to register :
recommander une lettre, to register a letter.

récompense (*n.f.*), recompense ; compensation ; indemnity.

récompenser (*v.t.*), to recompense ; to compensate ; to indemnify :
récompenser quelqu'un d'une perte, to compensate, to recompense, to indemnify, someone for a loss.

se récompenser (*v.r.*), to recompense oneself ; to compensate oneself ; to make up :
se récompenser de ses pertes, to compensate oneself for, to make up, one's losses.

recomptage (*n.m.*), recount :
recomptage des votes, recount of votes.

recompter (*v.t.*), to recount ; to count again.

reconduction ou **réconduction** (Dr.) (*n.f.*), reconduction ; relocation ; renewal of lease :
les concessions se renouvellent de mois en mois par tacite reconduction (*f.pl.*), the concessions are to be renewed from month to month by tacit reconduction.

reconnaissance (*n.f.*), acknowledgment ; acknowledgement ; receipt :
le capitaine est responsable des marchandises dont il se charge. Il en fournit une reconnaissance. Cette reconnaissance se nomme connaissement, the master is responsible for the cargo entrusted to his care. He gives an acknowledgment of (or receipt for) them. This acknowledgment is called bill of lading.
reconnaissance de consignation (Douanes), deposit receipt.
reconnaissance de dette, acknowledgment of debt.

reconvention (*n.f.*) ou **demande reconventionnelle** (*f.*) (Dr.), counterclaim ; set off.

recopier (*v.t.*), to recopy :
recopier une lettre, to recopy a letter. .

record (*adj.*), record ; record-breaking :
exportations qui atteignent le chiffre record de tant de millions (*f.pl.*), exports which reach the record figure (or the record-breaking figure) of so many millions.
actions qui ont atteint des cours records (*f.pl.*), shares which have reached record prices.

record (*n.m.*), record :
compagnie qui détient le record de la vitesse dans l'Atlantique-Nord (*f.*), company which holds the speed record in the North Atlantic.

recotation (de navires) (*n.f.*), reclassification.

recouponnement (*n.m.*), renewal of coupons.

recouponner (*v.t.*), to renew the coupons of :
recouponner un titre, to renew the coupons of a certificate.

recourir (avoir recours) (*v.i.*), to have recourse :
recourir à une garantie, to have recourse to a guarantee.

recours (*n.m.*), recourse ; claim :
État qui a recours au papier-monnaie (*m.*), State which has recourse to inconvertible paper money.
avoir recours contre l'endosseur d'un effet, to have recourse to the endorser of a bill.
recours de l'assureur contre l'auteur du dommage, recourse of the insurer against the author of the damage.
chargeur qui se trouve privé de tout recours contre l'armateur (*m.*), shipper who finds himself deprived of any recourse (or claim) against the shipowner.
s'assurer contre le recours des tiers, to insure against a third party claim.

recouvrable (*adj.*), recoverable ; collectable ; collectible :
sommes recouvrables (*f.pl.*), recoverable sums ; collectable amounts.

recouvrement (action de recouvrer ce qui était perdu) (*n.m.*), recovery :
recouvrement de trésor perdu, recovery of lost treasure.

recouvrement (perception de sommes dues) (*n.m.*), recovery ; collection :
recouvrement des taxes, collection of taxes.
la remise d'un effet en recouvrement, the remittance of a bill for collection.

recouvrements (dettes actives) (*n.m.pl.*), book debts :
recouvrements restant à faire au moment de la vente d'un fonds de commerce, book debts outstanding at the time of sale of a business.

recouvrer (acquérir de nouveau) (*v.t.*), to recover :
marchandises jetées recouvrées par les propriétaires (*f.pl.*), jettisoned goods recovered by the owners.

recouvrer (percevoir) (*v.t.*), to recover ; to collect :
recouvrer une créance, to recover, to collect, a debt.

recta (*adv.*), punctually ; on the nail :
payer recta, to pay on the nail.

rectificatif, -ive (*adj.*), correcting; corrected; amending; amended:
article rectificatif (*m.*) *ou* écriture rectificative (*f.*) (Comptab.), correcting entry.
facture rectificative (*f.*), corrected (*or* amended) invoice.
rectification (*n.f.*), rectification; correction; amendment:
rectification de cours (Bourse), correction of price.
rectifier (*v.t.*), to rectify; to correct; to amend:
toute erreur de poids peut être rectifiée par une nouvelle pesée, any error of weight can be rectified (*or* corrected) by a new weighing.
rectifier un calcul, to correct a calculation.
rectifier un compte, to amend, to correct, to rectify, an account.
recto [**rectos** *pl.*] (d'un livre) (*n.m.*) (Abrév.: **R**⁰) (Ant.: *verso*), right hand page (*or* side) (of a book). See **verso** for example.
recto (d'un effet, d'un chèque, ou analogue) (*n.m.*) (Ant.: *verso*), face (of a bill, of a cheque, or the like):
indiquer la somme à payer au recto d'un effet, to state the sum to be paid on the face of a bill.
recto (d'une enveloppe, d'une carte postale, d'un paquet) (*n.m.*) (Ant.: *verso*), address side, face (of an envelope, of a postcard, of a packet).
reçu (*n.m.*), receipt; acknowledgment: (See also **récépissé, quittance, acquit,** and **reconnaissance.**)
en France, les reçus de sommes supérieures à dix francs doivent porter un timbre de quittance; en Angleterre, sont assujettis au droit de timbre les reçus de sommes de £2 et au-dessus, in France, receipts for amounts over ten francs have to bear a receipt stamp; in England, receipts for £2 and upwards are subject to stamp duty.
Note:—In France, receipt stamp duty is ad valorem; in England, it is fixed.
reçu à valoir, receipt on account.
reçu de bord *ou* reçu de navire *ou* reçu provisoire *ou* reçu pour (*ou* d') embarquement, mate's receipt.
reçu de consignation (Douanes), deposit receipt.
reçu de souscription (à des titres), application receipt.
reçu libératoire, receipt in full discharge.
reçu motivé *ou* reçu causé, receipt with consideration for payment stated.
reçu simple, receipt with consideration for payment not stated.
reçu, -e (*p.p.*), received: (*Note:*—reçu is invariable if placed before the sum named, but not if it follows it.)
reçu mille francs, received one thousand francs.
mille francs reçus à valoir, one thousand francs received on account.
recueillir des commandes (*ou* **des ordres**), to get orders.
recul (*n.m.*), setback; recession; relapse; giving way:

campagne de hausse entrecoupée de quelques reculs (Bourse) (*f.*), bull campaign interrupted by a few setbacks.
reculer (*v.i.*), to recede; to relapse; to give way; to fall back; to fall away; to go back; to drop; to have a setback:
l'action X. recule d'un point de 91 à 90, X shares receded (*or* relapsed) (*or* gave way) (*or* fell back) (*or* went back) (*or* fell away) (*or* dropped) a point from 91 to 90 francs.
récupérable (*adj.*), recoverable; collectable; collectible:
créance récupérable (*f.*), recoverable debt.
récupération (*n.f.*), recovery; collection:
récupération d'une créance, recovery, collection, of a debt.
récupérer (*v.t.*), to recover; to collect; to recoup:
récupérer ses déboursés, to recoup one's disbursements; to recover one's out of pockets.
il est impossible aux importateurs de récupérer cette dépense sur leurs acheteurs, it is impossible for the importers to recover this expense from their buyers.
se récupérer (*v.r.*), to recover; to recoup oneself; to retrieve:
se récupérer de ses pertes, to recoup oneself for, to retrieve, one's losses.
rédacteur (d'un traité, d'un décret) (pers.) (*n.m.*), draughtsman (of an agreement, of a decree).
rédacteur (d'un journal) (pers.) (*n.m.*), editor (of a newspaper).
rédaction (*n.f.*), drawing up; drawing; writing out; writing up; making out; preparation. (See the verb **rédiger** for examples.)
rédaction en langage convenu (Télégr.) (*f.*), coding; putting into code.
reddition (*n.f.*), rendering:
reddition de comptes, rendering of accounts.
redevable (*adj.*), indebted; liable:
être redevable de, to be indebted for; to owe; to owe a balance of; to be liable for; to be liable to:
je ne vous suis redevable de rien, I am not indebted (*or* liable) to you for anything; I owe you nothing.
être redevable de tant de francs sur un compte, to owe a balance of so many francs on an account.
personne redevable de l'impôt (*f.*), person liable for tax.
redevable (pers.) (*n.m.* ou *f.*), person liable; debtor:
redevables (*ou* personnes redevables) des droits de douane, persons liable for customs duties.
redevance (*n.f.*), royalty; rent; rental; duty; charge:
concéder le droit d'exploitation d'une mine moyennant des redevances, d'une ligne de chemin de fer moyennant des redevances, to grant the right of working a mine in consideration of royalties, a railway line in consideration of rents.
redevance d'abonnement (Téléph.), subscription rental; rental.
redevance des mines, mineral rights duty.

redevance forfaitaire pour l'enlèvement et la réinstallation des organes essentiels d'un poste téléphonique, standard charge for the removal and reinstallation of a telephone line and apparatus.

redevoir (*v.t.*), to owe a balance of:
redevoir tant sur un compte, to owe a balance of so much on an account.

rédhibition (Dr.) (*n.f.*), redhibition.

rédhibitoire (*adj.*), redhibitory:
vice rédhibitoire (*m.*), redhibitory defect.

rédiger (*v.t.*), to draw up; to draw; to write out; to write up; to write; to make out; to prepare; to make:
rédiger un acte, to draw up, to draw, to prepare, a deed.
rédiger des livres, le journal, to write up books, the journal.
rédiger un mémoire, to make out, to write out, a bill.
contrat rédigé sur des feuilles volantes (*m.*), agreement written on loose sheets.
connaissement rédigé à ordre (*m.*), bill of lading made to order.
rédiger un télégramme en langage convenu, to code a telegram; to put a telegram into code; to prepare a telegram in code language.

redressement (rectification) (*n.m.*), rectification; correction.

redresser (*v.t.*), to rectify; to correct:
redresser une erreur, to rectify, to correct, an error.

redresser (se) (*v.r.*), to harden; to firm up:
l'action X., un moment faible, se redresse en clôture à 1 115, X. shares, weak at one time, hardened (*or* firmed up) at the close to 1,115 francs.

redû (*n.m.*), balance; balance due:
solder le redû, to pay the balance.

réductible (*adj.*), reducible.
souscrire à titre réductible. See under **souscrire**.

réduction (*n.f.*), reduction; cut; deduction:
réduction de capital, reduction of capital.
réduction de salaires, reduction, cut, in wages; wages cut.
on envisage une réduction du dividende qui serait vraisemblablement ramené de 5 à 4 0/0, there is a likelihood of a cut in the dividend which would probably be reduced from 5 to 4%.
réduction pour différence du vieux au neuf (Assce mar.), deduction new for old.

réduire (*v.t.*), to reduce; to cut down; to curtail:
réduire le coût de la vie, le taux officiel de l'escompte, to reduce the cost of living, the bank rate.
réduire ses dépenses, to reduce, to cut down, to curtail, one's expenses.
tarif réduit (*m.*), reduced tariff; reduced rates.

réel, -elle (*adj.*), real; actual; effective:
change réel (*m.*), real exchange.
droit réel (Dr.) (*m.*), real right.
les marchandises seront payées sur le pied de leur valeur réelle (*f.pl.*), the goods will be paid for on the footing of their actual value.

réélection (*n.f.*), reelection.

rééligibilité (*n.f.*), reeligibility.

rééligible (*adj.*), reeligible:
tout administrateur sortant est rééligible, a retiring director shall be reeligible.

réélire (*v.t.*), to reelect:
réélire un administrateur, to reelect a director.

réembarquement, réembarquer. Same as **rembarquement, rembarquer.**

réenregistrement (*n.m.*), reregistration.

réenregistrer (*v.t.*), to reregister.

réentreposage (*n.m.*), rewarehousing.

réentreposer (*v.t.*), to rewarehouse.

réescompte (*n.m.*), rediscount; rediscounting.

réescompte du portefeuille (poste de bilan et de compte profits et pertes) (Banq.) (*m.*), rebate on bills not due:
après déduction du réescompte du portefeuille et des frais généraux, il reste un bénéfice net de . . ., after deducting rebate on bills not due and establishment charges, there remains a net profit of . . . .

réescompter (*v.t.*), to rediscount:
réescompter le portefeuille d'autres banques, to rediscount other banks' bills.

réescompteur (pers.) (*n.m.*), rediscounter.

réévaluation (*n.f.*), revaluation.

réévaluer (*v.t.*), to revalue:
réévaluer les immeubles, to revalue the premises.

réexpédier (*v.t.*), to reforward; to reship; to redirect:
réexpédier les marchandises à leur destination, to reforward the goods to their destination.
marchandises réexpédiées par mer au delà du point de destination indiqué au connaissement (*f.pl.*), goods reshipped beyond the point of destination shown on the bill of lading.
réexpédier une lettre, un colis postal, à une nouvelle adresse, to redirect a letter, a postal parcel, to a new address.
donner l'ordre de réexpédier des télégrammes par la voie télégraphique, par la voie postale, to give orders to redirect telegrams by telegraph, by post.

réexpédition (*n.f.*), reforwarding; reshipment; reshipping; redirection:
réexpédition des marchandises par un autre navire, reforwarding goods by another ship.
réexpédition des matières premières de nos entrepôts sur les places étrangères de consommation, reshipment of (*or* reshipping) raw materials from our warehouses to foreign places of consumption.
réexpédition des correspondances, redirection of postal packets.

réexportateur, -trice (pers.) (*n.*), reexporter.

réexportation (*n.f.*), reexport; reexportation:
réexportation d'échantillons importés dans un pays par des voyageurs de commerce, reexportation of samples imported into a country by commercial travellers.

réexporter (*v.t.*), to reexport:
marchandises réexportées à l'étranger (*f.pl.*), goods reexported abroad.

réfaction (Com.) (*n.f.*), allowance.; rebate :
réfaction pour écart de qualité, allowance for
difference of quality.
référence (attestation) (*n.f.*), reference :
employé qui a d'excellentes références (*m.*),
employee who has excellent references.
référence de banquier, banker's reference.
référence de fournisseur, trade reference.
référence (renvoi) (*n.f.*) (Abrév. : **réf.** *ou* **réfce**),
reference :
référence croisée, cross reference.
référence (à rappeler, s.v.p.—mention à l'en-tête
d'une lettre), reference ; for reference please
quote.
reflux (*n.m.*), reflux :
reflux d'or, reflux of gold.
refondre (Monnayage) (*v.t.*), to recoin ; to remint :
refondre des pièces d'argent démonétisées, to
remint demonetized silver coins.
refondre un navire, to rebuild a ship.
refonte (*n.f.*) *ou* refonte des monnaies, recoinage ;
recoinage of moneys ; reminting ; reminting
coins.
refonte d'un navire (*f.*), rebuilding a ship.
refrappage (*n.m.*) *ou* refrappement (*n.m.*) *ou* refrappage (*ou* refrappement) des monnaies,
recoinage ; recoinage of moneys ; reminting ;
reminting coins.
refrapper (*v.t.*) *ou* refrapper des monnaies, to
recoin ; to recoin moneys ; to remint ; to
remint coins.
refuge (*n.m.*), refuge ; shelter.
réfugier (se) (*v.r.*), to take refuge ; to take
shelter :
se réfugier dans un port de relâche, to take
refuge in a port of necessity (*or* in a port of
distress) ; to take shelter in a port of refuge.
refus (*n.m.*), refusal :
refus de la marchandise, refusal of goods.
refus d'acceptation ou de paiement (d'un effet),
dishonour (of a bill). See example under
synonymous expression **non acceptation ou
non paiement.**
refus d'acceptation (d'un effet), dishonour ;
dishonour by non acceptance ; refusal to
accept.
refus de paiement (d'un effet), dishonour ;
dishonour by non payment ; refusal to
pay :
en France, le refus de paiement d'un effet de
commerce doit être constaté le lendemain du
jour de l'échéance par un acte que l'on
nomme protêt faute de paiement, in France,
dishonour by non payment of a bill of
exchange should be attested (*or* noted) the
day after the day of maturity by an act
called protest for non payment.
refuser (*v.t.*) *ou* se refuser (*v.r.*), to refuse :
refuser de prendre livraison, to refuse to take
delivery.
assureur qui, après avoir examiné le risque,
l'accepte ou le refuse (*m.*), underwriter who,
after having examined the risk, accepts or
refuses it.
colis refusés ou non réclamés (*m.pl.*), refused or
unclaimed parcels.

refuser d'accepter un effet *ou* se refuser à
accepter un effet, to dishonour a bill ; to
dishonour a bill by non acceptance ; to refuse
to accept a bill.
refuser de payer un effet *ou* se refuser à payer
un effet, to dishonour a bill ; to dishonour
a bill by non payment ; to refuse to pay a bill.
tirage refusé (*m.*), dishonoured draft.
regagner (*v.t.*), to regain ; to recover :
regagner l'argent perdu, to regain, to recover
the money lost.
régie (administration) (*n.f.*), excise.
régie (bureau) (*n.f.*), excise office.
régime (*n.m.*), system :
régime de l'entrepôt (Douanes), warehousing
system.
régime européen (Poste, etc.), European system.
régime extra-européen, extra-European system.
régime intérieur, inland system :
télégramme du régime intérieur (*m.*), inland
telegram.
régime international (Poste). *English equivalent is* imperial and foreign system :
télégramme du régime international (*m.*),
imperial or foreign telegram (*collective plural*
imperial and foreign telegrams).
régime de faveur (Douanes) (*m.*), preference :
le régime de faveur accordé aux produits
coloniaux, the preference granted to colonial
produce.
marchandises ayant droit à un régime de
faveur (*f.pl.*), goods entitled to a preference
(*or* to preferential duty).
régional, -e, -aux (*adj.*), regional ; district (*used as*
adj.) :
directeur régional (*m.*), district manager.
régional, -e, -aux (Téléph.) (*adj.*), toll (*used as*
adj.) :
communication régionale (*f.*), toll call.
Régional, qui demandez-vous ? Toll, what
number are you calling ? ; Toll, number,
please ?
registre (*n.m.*), register ; book ; record : (See also
livre and **journal.**)
registre à souche *ou* registre à souches, counterfoil book ; stub book.
registre d'ordre, memorandum book ; statistical
book ; registry book.
registre de bord, log ; log book.
registre de classification de navires, ships'
classification register :
Registre du Lloyd, Lloyd's Register (*full*
title Lloyd's Register of Shipping).
Registre Veritas, Veritas Register.
registre de comptabilité, account book ; book
of account.
registre de dépôt (Douanes), King's warehouse
register. *Cf.* dépôt de douane.
registre de livraison (colis), delivery book.
registre de présence, attendance book.
registre de transferts, transfer register.
registre de visite, inspection register.
registre des actionnaires, share register ; share
ledger ; register of members.
registre des déclarations de construction et
soumissions de francisation *ou* registre de

l'état civil des navires, *the French equivalent of the English* register book :

tout navire doit être attaché à un port sous la forme d'une immatriculation sur un registre spécial tenu au bureau de l'inscription maritime, *every ship must belong to a port under the form of an entry in a special register kept at the marine registry office.*

registre des délibérations *ou* registre des procès-verbaux, *minute book.*

registre des inscriptions (hypothèques maritimes), *register book.*

registre des réclamations, *requests book; claims book.*

registre du commerce. *In France, a State register akin to the English register of business names, but differing in the respect that whereas the English registration applies only in cases where a person is trading or practising under a name different from his own, or the partnership includes persons other than those mentioned in the firm name, and contains these particulars only, the French registre du commerce applies to everyone carrying on business in France, whether an individual trader, a partnership, a company or other body corporate, and whether of French or foreign nationality.   Particulars of every imaginable nature have to be furnished. Every paper, invoice, letter, order, catalogue, prospectus, etc., must contain the name of the tribunal de commerce where the entry is registered, and the number of the registration.   This is done in the following form, for example, Registre du Commerce (or abbreviated: Reg. du Com. or Reg. Com. or R.C.): Seine 000 000.*

registre extra-comptable, *separate book (i.e., a book, as a bill book, not forming an integral part of a bookkeeping system).*

églage (*n.m.*), *ruling* :

réglage d'une feuille de papier, *ruling of a sheet of paper.*

ègle (principe) (*n.f.*), *rule* :

règle conjointe *ou* règle de chaîne, *chain rule.*

règles d'York et d'Anvers, *York-Antwerp rules* :

les avaries communes ont fait l'objet d'une sorte de codification internationale établie par des congrès et connue sous le nom de règles d'York et d'Anvers, *general average has formed the subject of a kind of international codification settled by congresses and known by the name of York-Antwerp rules.*

règles de bourse *ou* règles boursières (Bourse de valeurs), *stock exchange rules.*

règle de change, *rule of exchange.*

règles de la Haye (Transport maritime), *Hague rules.*

règle de trois (Arith.), *rule of three.*

règle proportionnelle (Assurance-incendie), *average* :

quand il y a application de la règle proportionnelle, on dit que l'assuré est son propre assureur pour la différence entre la somme

assurée et la valeur réelle de la chose assurée, *when there is application of average, it is said that the insured is his own insurer for the difference between the sum insured and the actual value of the thing insured.*

les assurances partielles sont des assurances proportionnelles, *partial insurances are average insurances.*

en général, le report est la règle et le déport l'exception, *in general, contango is the rule and backwardation the exception.*

règle (instrument) (*n.f.*), *rule* ; *ruler* :

règle de bureau, *office ruler.*

règlement (acquittement) (*n.m.*) (Abrév.: **règlt**), *settlement* ; *paying* ; *paying off* :

règlement du passif, *settlement of, paying off, the liabilities.*

le règlement de l'indemnité a lieu dans les trois mois du sinistre, *settlement (or payment) of the claim takes place within three months of the accident.*

règlement à terme, *credit settlement.*

règlement au comptant, *cash settlement.*

règlement (action d'arrêter) (*n.m.*), *settlement* ; *adjustment* ; *statement* ; *assessment* :

règlement d'une contestation, *settlement of a dispute.*

règlement d'un compte, *adjustment, settlement, of an account.*

le cours de compensation sert de base pour les reports et pour le règlement des différences, *the making up price serves as a basis for contangoes and for the settlement of differences.*

règlement d'avarie (*ou* d'avaries) (*ou* des avaries) (Assce mar.), *adjustment of average* ; *average adjustment* ; *average statement* :

le règlement des avaries communes est basé sur un principe de justice qui veut que tout sacrifice fait dans l'intérêt commun soit supporté par tous ceux qui ont profité par ce sacrifice, *the adjustment of general average is based on a principle of justice which requires that any sacrifice in the common interest should be supported by all those who have profited by this sacrifice.*

règlement d'avarie grosse sur corps, *adjustment of general average on hull; general average adjustment on hull.*

règlement d'avarie particulière, *adjustment of particular average* ; *particular average adjustment.*

règlement d'un sinistre (Assurance-incendie), *assessment of a loss.*

règlement (solde d'un compte) (*n.m.*), *balance* ; *balance of account.*

règlement (ordonnance) (*n.m.*), *regulation* :

règlements ayant pour objet de prévenir les abordages en mer, *collision regulations.*

règlements consulaires, *consular regulations.*

règlements de bourse *ou* règlements boursiers (Bourse de valeurs), *stock exchange regulations.*

règlements de douane *ou* règlements douaniers, *customs regulations.*

règlements de port, *port regulations.*

réglementation *ou* **règlementation** (*n.f.*), regulation; regulating:
réglementation du travail à bord des navires de commerce, regulation of labour on board merchant ships.

réglementer *ou* **règlementer** (*v.t.*), to regulate:
l'État intervient presque dans tous les pays pour réglementer et limiter l'émission et la circulation des billets (*m.*), the Government intervenes nearly in all countries to regulate and limit the issue and the circulation of notes.

régler (tirer des lignes sur) (*v.t.*), to rule:
régler une page, un registre, to rule a page, a book.

régler (acquitter) (*v.t.*), to settle; to pay; to pay off:
régler un solde, un compte en espèces, to settle, to pay, a balance, an account in cash.
régler au comptant, c'est se libérer immédiatement de sa dette, to settle in cash is to free oneself immediately from one's debt.
les opérations de report sont réglées au cours de compensation (*f.pl.*), contango dealings are settled at the making up price.
si le fret n'est pas payé, le destinataire le règle, if the freight is not paid, the consignee settles it.
régler les avaries sur chaque évaluation, to pay average on each valuation.
régler compte, to settle up; to square accounts:
supposons que, le 31 mars, on veuille liquider l'opération et régler compte, suppose that, on the 31st March, one wishes to close the transaction and settle up (*or* and square accounts).

régler (modifier) (*v.t.*), to settle; to adjust; to regulate; to state:
régler un compte, to settle, to adjust, an account (to bring it into agreement; to settle differences on it).
régler l'avarie commune et le sauvetage d'après les lois et les usages du lieu où finit l'aventure, to adjust, to state, general average and salvage according to the law and practice obtaining at the place where the adventure ends.

se régler (*v.r.*), to be settled; to be adjusted; to be regulated:
les avaries communes se régleront conformément aux règles d'York et d'Anvers, general average will be adjusted (*or* to be adjusted) (*or* adjustable) according to York-Antwerp rules.
le taux du fret se règle sur (*ou* est réglé par) l'offre et la demande, the rate of freight is regulated by supply and demand.

régler (modérer) (*v.t.*), to regulate; to restrict; to reduce:
régler sa dépense, to regulate, to restrict, one's expenses.

régler (arrêter; faire l'inventaire de) (*v.t.*), to close; to make up; to rule off:
régler ses comptes une fois l'an, tous les six mois, to close, to make up, to rule off, one's accounts once a year, every six months.

réglure (*n.f.*), ruling:
réglure d'une page, ruling of a page.

régularisation (de dividende) (*n.f.*), equalization:
réserve pour régularisation de dividende (*f.*), reserve for equalization of dividend.

régularité (*n.f.*), regularity:
régularité d'un chèque, d'un titre de propriété, regularity of a cheque, of a title to property.

régulier, -ère (*adj.*), regular; due; proper; good:
endossement régulier (*m.*), regular endorsement.
livrer un titre régulier en remplacement d'un titre irrégulier (Bourse), to deliver a good certificate in replacement of a bad certificate.

régulièrement (*adv.*), regularly; duly; properly:
prêteur régulièrement nanti (*m.*), lender duly (*or* properly) secured.

réhabilitation (d'un failli) (*n.f.*), discharge.

réhabiliter (*v.t.*), to discharge:
réhabiliter un failli, to discharge a bankrupt.

réimportateur, -trice (pers.) (*n.*), reimporter.

réimportation (*n.f.*), reimport; reimportation.

réimporter (*v.t.*), to reimport.

réinscription (*n.f.*), reentry.

réinscrire (*v.t.*), to reenter:
réinscrire un article sur un compte, to reenter an item in an account.

réinvestir (*v.t.*), to reinvest:
réinvestir des capitaux, to reinvest capital.

réinvestissement (*n.m.*), reinvestment.

rejaugeage (d'un navire) (*n.m.*), remeasurement (of a ship). Cf. **jaugeage**.

rejauger (*v.t.*), to remeasure.

rejet (*n.m.*), rejection; throwing out; disallowance.

rejeter (*v.t.*), to reject; to throw out; to disallow:
rejeter une offre, to reject an offer.
rejeter un amendement, to reject, to throw out, an amendment.
rejeter une dépense, un article de dépense, to disallow an expense; to throw out an item of expenditure.

relâche (action) (*n.f.*), call; calling; putting in (for supplies or shelter, in or out of the customary or advertised route); *Hence.*— refuge; necessity; distress: (Cf. **escale**.)
relâches occasionnées soit par la perte fortuite de câbles, ancres, voiles, mâts, etc., soit par le besoin de ravitaillement, soit par voie d'eau à réparer, calls occasioned whether by the fortuitous loss of cables, anchors, sails, masts, etc., or by the need of victualling, or by a leak to be repaired.
relâche rendue nécessaire par une fortune de mer, call, putting in, rendered necessary by a peril of the sea.
port de relâche (*m.*), port of refuge; port of necessity; port of distress.
navire qui rentre dans le port de départ en relâche (*m.*), ship which puts back into the port of sailing for refuge (*or* of necessity) (*or* in distress).
relâche forcée, forced call; compulsory call; compulsory putting in.

la relâche est volontaire ou forcée, a call (or putting in) is voluntary or forced (or compulsory).

le navire X. en relâche forcée dans ce port pour avaries éprouvées dans la coque et la machine, the ship X. having been compelled to put into this port on account of damage sustained by the hull and the engine.

relâche (port ou place où entre un capitaine par suite des besoins ou nécessités du navire tels que manque de charbon ou de provisions, ou bien après avarie) (*n.f.*), port of call; place of call:

Singapour est une relâche fréquente, Singapore is a frequent port (or place) of call.

relâche (*n.f.*) *ou* **relâche forcée** (port ou place où le capitaine est obligé de rentrer de toute nécessité, pour la sauvegarde des intérêts dont il a la charge), port (or place) of distress; port (or place) of refuge; port (or place) of necessity.

relâcher (*v.i.*), to call; to put in (for supplies or shelter):

relâcher pour faire du charbon (*ou* pour charbonner), pour prendre des ordres, pour se ravitailler, to call for bunkering (or to put in to coal), to take orders, to revictual.

le navire est libre de relâcher (*ou* de faire relâche) dans les ports qui se trouvent même en dehors de sa route habituelle ou de son itinéraire annoncé, dans n'importe quel ordre, et dans n'importe quel but, the ship shall have liberty to call at ports even out of the customary or advertised route, in any order, and for any purpose.

relâcher forcément par suite d'une tempête, to put in of necessity (or compulsorily) owing to a storm.

voie d'eau qui obligea le navire à relâcher (*ou* à faire relâche) dans un port de refuge, à relâcher à Marseille (*f.*), leak which obliged the ship to put into a port of refuge, to put into Marseilles.

relance du client (Com.) (*f.*), follow up system.

relevage (Poste) (*n.m.*), clearing (a letter box); collection (of letters).

relevé *ou* **relèvement** (action) (*n.m.*), making out a statement; drawing up a statement; taking out; abstracting; noting; recording:

relèvement d'un compte, making out a statement of account; drawing up a statement of account; abstracting an account.

vérifier le relevé de la balance, to check the taking out of the trial balance.

l'inventaire comporte deux opérations: le relevé des quantités et leur évaluation (*m.*), stock taking comprises two operations: noting (or recording) the quantities and their valuation.

relevé *ou* **relèvement** (état) (*n.m.*), statement; abstract; return:

faire le relevé (*ou* le relèvement) d'un compte, to make out a statement (or an abstract) of account.

les relevés des comptes (*ou* les relevés de

factures) des fournisseurs, the suppliers' statements of account.

relevé de fin de mois, monthly statement.

un relevé de son actif et de son passif, a statement of one's assets and liabilities.·

relevé de caisse, cash statement.

relevé de dispache contenant seulement les données sommaires, abstract of average adjustment containing only summary data.

relevés de trafic, traffic returns.

relèvement (élévation; reprise) (*n.m.*), raising; rise; recovery; revival:

relèvement du taux officiel de l'escompte, des salaires, des taxes postales, des tarifs de chemin de fer, raising, rise, of the bank rate, of wages, of postal charges, of railway rates.

relèvement des affaires, recovery, revival, of business.

relèvement des cours, recovery of prices.

relèvement (Navig.) (*n.m.*), proceeding:

surprime de relèvement de La Havane sur le Brésil et La Plata (*f.*), additional premium for proceeding from Havana to Brazil and the Plate.

Cf. port de relèvement.

relever (élever; hausser) (*v.t.*), to raise:

relever un navire échoué, to raise a stranded ship.

relever un tarif, to raise a tariff.

se relever (*v.r.*), to rise; to recover; to move up:

la perspective presque certaine de voir les cours se relever, the almost certain prospect of seeing prices rise (or recover).

l'action X. se relève de 885 à 935, X. shares rose (or recovered) (or moved up) from 885 to 935 francs.

relever (dresser l'état de; copier; prendre note de) (*v.t.*), to make out a statement of; to draw up a statement of; to take out; to abstract; to note; to record:

relever un compte, to make out a statement of account; to draw up a statement of account; to abstract an account.

relever une liste d'actionnaires, les soldes du grand livre, la balance de chaque compte sur le livre de soldes, to take out a list of shareholders, the ledger balances, the balance of each account on the balance book.

relever un fait, to note, to record, a fact.

relever (faire remarquer) (*v.t.*), to call attention to:

relever une erreur, une omission, to call attention to a mistake, an omission.

relever (libérer; dispenser) (*v.t.*), to relieve:

relever quelqu'un de ses engagements, quelqu'un d'une responsabilité, to relieve someone from his engagements, someone from a liability.

relever (Poste) (*v.t.*), to clear; to collect:

les boîtes aux lettres sont relevées aux heures fixes (*f.pl.*), letter boxes are cleared at fixed times.

relever (aller autre part) (Navig.) (*v.i.*), to proceed:

augmentation de prime applicable au cas où un navire trouvant son port de destination bloqué, séjourne devant ce port ou relève pour d'autres (f.), increase of premium applicable to the case where a ship finding her port of destination blocked, lies before that port or proceeds to others.

reliquat (n.m.), balance (remainder):
poursuivre le payement d'un reliquat, to sue for payment of the balance.

reporter à nouveau le reliquat du compte de profits et pertes, to carry forward the balance of profit and loss account.

reliquataire (pers.) (n.m. ou f.), debtor for the balance (of an account).

relocat on (n.f.), reletting; relocation.

relouer (v.t.), to relet.

remballage (n.m.), repacking.

remballer (v.t.), to repack.

rembarquement (n.m.), reshipment; reshipping.

rembarquer (v.t.), to reship:
rembarquer une cargaison, to reship a cargo.

remboursabilité (n.f.), repayability; redeemability; redeemableness:
remboursabilité d'un billet de banque, repayability, redeemability, of a bank note.

remboursable (adj.) (Abrév.: **remb.** ou **rembour.** ou **rb.** ou **r.**), repayable; reimbursable; returnable; redeemable:
emprunt remboursable sur demande, à terme (ou à des échéances fixes), au pair par voie de tirage au sort, en or (ou contre de l'or), en espèces (m.), loan repayable on demand, at fixed dates, at par by drawings, in gold, in cash.

obligation remboursable (f.), redeemable bond; redeemable debenture.

remboursement (n.m.) (Abrév.: **remb.** ou **rembour.** ou **rb.** ou **r.**), repayment; reimbursement; paying off; payment; refund; return; redemption; retiral; retirement:
exiger le remboursement d'une créance, to require the repayment of a debt.

remboursement de capital, d'une somme payée en trop, repayment, return, of capital, of an amount overpaid.

remboursement des pertes, des avaries (Assce), payment of losses, of damage.

remboursement des obligations, redemption of bonds (or of debentures).

remboursement après attribution, return on allotment.

remboursement d'un effet, retiral, retirement, of a bill.

remboursement (Caisse d'épargne) (n.m.), withdrawal:
remboursement à vue, withdrawal on demand.

remboursement intégral des fonds déposés, withdrawal of the whole of a deposit.

remboursement partiel des fonds déposés, withdrawal of a portion of a deposit.

remboursement (Envois contre remboursement) (n.m.), trade charge (Cash on delivery):
le remboursement consiste dans la somme mise à charge de la marchandise par l'expéditeur et qui doit lui être payée après réception de la marchandise par le destinataire, a trade charge is the sum put upon the goods by the

sender and which must be paid to him after receipt of the goods by the consignee.

le remboursement représente la valeur ou une partie de la valeur de la marchandise, the trade charge represents the value or a part of the value of the goods.

le colis postal peut être grevé d'un remboursement jusqu'à concurrence de tant de francs, the trade charge on any one postal parcel must not exceed so many francs.

rembourser (v.t.), to repay; to reimburse; to pay off; to pay back; to pay; to refund; to return; to redeem; to retire:
rembourser un emprunt, le capital, to repay, to pay off, to pay back, to return, a loan, the capital.

rembourser intégralement ses créanciers, to repay, to pay off, to pay, one's creditors in full.

payez pour moi, je vous rembourserai, pay for me, I will reimburse you.

rembourser une obligation, to redeem a bond (or a debenture).

rembourser un effet, to retire a bill.

se rembourser (v.r.), to reimburse oneself; to repay oneself; to be reimbursed.

remède (Monnayage) (n.m.), remedy; remedy of the mint; tolerance; tolerance of the mint.

remède d'aloi, tolerance of fineness; tolerance for error in fineness; remedy of (or for) fineness.

Cf. **faiblage** and **tolérance**.

remercier un employé, to dismiss, to discharge, to sack, an employee.

réméré (n.m.), repurchase; redemption:
vente à réméré (f.), sale with option of repurchase.

remetteur, -euse (adj.), remitting; sending:
le banquier remetteur, the remitting banker.

remetteur ou **remettant** (pers.) (n.m.), remitter; sender.

remettre (faire tenir; livrer) (v.t.), to remit; to send; to send in; to put; to lodge; to hand; to hand over; to deliver:
remettre de l'argent, to remit, to send, money.

remettre des effets en recouvrement ou remettre des effets à l'encaissement, to remit bills for collection.

effets remis en banque à l'escompte (m.pl.), bills sent (or remitted) to the bank for discount.

remettre au contrôleur des contributions directes une déclaration de son revenu, to send in to the inspector of taxes a return of one's income.

argent remis en dépôt à terme (m.), money put on fixed deposit.

l'armement est tenu de remettre le connaissement au titulaire du reçu provisoire (m.), the shipowners are bound to hand (or hand over) (or deliver) the bill of lading to the holder of the mate's receipt.

remettre de l'argent en main propre, to hand over money personally.

remettre une lettre, to deliver a letter.

lettre remise à la poste (*f.*), letter sent through the post.

remettre à 0 (*zéro*) le viseur d'une machine à calculer, to clear the dial of a calculating machine.

remettre à flot (*v.t.*), to refloat :
remettre à flot un navire échoué, to refloat a stranded ship.

remettre en nantissement, to lodge as collateral ; to hypothecate ; to pledge :
valeurs remises en nantissement (*f.pl.*), securities lodged as collateral ; securities hypothecated (*or* pledged) :
actions remises en nantissement en garantie de fonds avancés (*f.pl.*), shares hypothecated (*or* pledged) as security for money advanced.

remettre un navire en bon état de navigabilité, to make a ship seaworthy again.

emettre (différer) (*v.t.*), to put off ; to defer ; to postpone ; to adjourn :
remettre une affaire à un autre jour, to put off, to postpone, a matter to another day.
remettre une cause à huitaine, to adjourn a case for a week.

emettre (assigner une époque plus éloignée à) (*v.t.*), to put off :
remettre ses créanciers, to put off one's creditors.

emettre (faire grâce de) (*v.t.*), to remit ; to allow :
remettre une dette, to remit a debt.
remettre 5 0/0 sur le montant d'une facture, to allow 5% on the amount of an invoice.

emettre (mettre en dépôt) (*v.t.*), to entrust ; to intrust :
je lui ai remis mes fonds, I have entrusted my money to him ; I have intrusted him with my funds.

emettre (se) (rétablir ses affaires) (*v.r.*), to start again ; to make a fresh start :
se remettre d'une faillite, to start again, to make a fresh start, after a failure.

emise (envoi de valeurs à un correspondant) (*n.f.*) (Abrév. : **rse**), remittance :
envoyer une remise, to send a remittance.
faire une remise de fonds, to make a remittance of, to remit, funds.
la remise d'un effet en recouvrement *ou* la remise d'un effet à l'encaissement, the remittance of a bill for collection.

emise (effet de commerce) (*n.f.*), bill (of exchange) :
porter une remise au compte courant, to enter a bill in current account.

emise (livraison) (*n.f.*), delivery ; handing ; handing over :
remise d'un colis, d'actions, delivery of a parcel, of shares.
la responsabilité du transporteur cesse dès la remise de la marchandise au destinataire, the responsibility of the carrier ceases on handing over the goods (*or* on delivery of the goods) to the consignee.
remise à domicile, delivery at residence ; delivery at trader's premises ; delivery :

la remise à domicile est, en règle générale suspendue les dimanches, as a general rule, delivery is suspended on Sundays.
remise des télégrammes, delivery of telegrams.
remise gratuite (*Abrév.* : RG.), free delivery.
remise par exprès (Poste), express delivery.

remise (délai ; ajournement) (*n.f.*), delay ; putting off ; postponement ; adjournment.

remise (rabais ; escompte) (*n.f.*), allowance ; discount ; reduction :
faire une remise de 5 0/0 sur le montant brut d'une facture, to allow a discount, to make an allowance, of 5% on the gross amount of an invoice.
remise sur le prix convenu, allowance, reduction, on the agreed price.
remise sur marchandises *ou simplement* remise (opp. à *escompte de caisse*), trade discount ; discount.

remise (commission) (*n.f.*), commission :
la remise accordée à un agent, the commission allowed to an agent.

remise (commission d'un remisier) (Bourse) (*n.f.*), half commission ; commission (of a remisier *or* half commission man).

remise (grâce) (*n.f.*), remission :
remise d'une dette, de droits de douane, de pénalité, remission of a debt, of customs duty, of penalty.

remise à flot (*f.*), refloating.

remise à 0 (*zéro*) (du viseur d'une machine à calculer) (*f.*), clearance (of the dial of a calculating machine).

remisier (Bourse) (pers.) (*n.m.*), half commission man ; remisier.

remorquage (*n.m.*) *ou* **remorque** (*n.f.*), towage ; towing ; tow :
remorquage d'un navire en danger, towage of, towing, a ship in danger.
prendre un navire à la remorque, to take a ship in tow.

remorque (véhicule routier remorqué) (opp. à *tracteur*) (*n.f.*), trailer.

remorqué (*n.m.*), tow :
l'abandon du remorqué par le remorqueur (*m.*), the abandonment of the tow by the tug.

remorquer (*v.t.*), to tow ; to haul ; to draw :
remorquer un navire à destination, to tow a ship to destination.
avec faculté de remorquer ou se faire remorquer (Assce), with leave to tow or be towed.
locomotive qui remorque une lourde charge (*f.*), locomotive which hauls (*or* draws) a heavy load.

remorqueur (*n.m.*), tug ; tug boat.

remplaçable (*adj.*), replaceable.

remplacement (*n.m.*), replacement :
la valeur de remplacement doit être calculée d'après la valeur que représentait l'intérêt assuré au moment du sinistre, the value of replacement should be calculated according to the value that the insured interest represented at the time of the casualty.

remplacer (*v.t.*), to replace.

remplir (exécuter ; réaliser) (*v.t.*), to fulfil ; to comply with :

remplir une condition, ses obligations, to fulfil a condition, one's obligations:

dans tout contrat, il existe des obligations à remplir pour chacune des parties contractantes, in every contract, there are obligations to fulfil for each of the contracting parties.

remplir les formalités imposées par la loi, les conditions exigées par les statuts, to comply with the legal formalities, the conditions required by the articles of association.

remplir (combler les lacunes, les vides de) (*v.t.*), to fill up; to fill in:

remplir un livre, to fill up a book.

remplir une formule, un chèque, une souche, to fill up a form, a cheque, a counterfoil.

remplir les blancs dans une formule, to fill in the blanks in a form.

remplissage (*n.m.*), filling up; filling in.

remprunter (*v.t.*), to borrow again; to reborrow.

rémunérateur, -trice *ou* **rémunérant, -e** (*adj.*), remunerative; paying; profitable:

entreprise rémunératrice (*f.*), remunerative undertaking; paying concern; profitable business.

rémunération (*n.f.*), remuneration; payment; consideration; purchase consideration; return:

recevoir la juste rémunération de son travail, to receive an adequate remuneration for one's work.

fixer la rémunération des commissaires, to fix the remuneration of the auditors.

la rémunération du travail et la rémunération du capital, payment for services and return on capital.

en rémunération (*ou* en représentation) des apports il a été attribué aux apporteurs 0 000 actions de 0 chacune, entièrement libérées, de la société, as payment for (*or* as consideration for) (*or* as purchase consideration for) the transfer there has been allotted to the vendors 0,000 shares of 0 each, fully paid, in the company.

rémunérer (*v.t.*), to remunerate; to pay; to make a return on:

rémunérer des services, to remunerate, to pay, for services.

bénéfices suffisants pour permettre de rémunérer le capital-actions (*m.pl.*), sufficient profits to enable a return to be made on the share capital.

rencaissage *ou* **rencaissement** (*n.m.*), recashing.

rencaisser (*v.t.*), to recash.

renchérir (*v.t.*), to raise, to advance, to increase, to enhance, the price of:

renchérir des marchandises, to raise the price of goods.

renchérir (*v.i.*), to rise in price; to advance in price; to increase in price; to enhance in price; to get dearer; to rise; to improve:

le blé renchérit, wheat is rising.

renchérissement (*n.m.*), rise in price; advance in price; increase in price; enhancement of price:

renchérissement des matières premières, rise in price of raw materials.

renchérisseur, -euse (pers.) (*n.*), runner up (of prices).

rencontre (collision) (*n.f.*), collision.

rencontre (Comptab.) (*n.f.*), posting folio; folio (in folio column).

rencontrer (se heurter à) (*v.t.*), to collide with; to run into.

se rencontrer (*v.r.*), to collide; to run into each other.

rendement (*n.m.*), yield; return; output; capacity:

rendement d'un capital, yield of (*or* return on) a capital.

valeurs à gros rendement (*f.pl.*), high yield stocks.

rendement des impôts, d'un titre, yield of taxes, of a stock.

rendement du personnel, output of the staff.

rendement d'un port, d'un bassin, capacity of a port, of a dock.

rendement (poids net des marchandises débarquées à l'arrivée d'un navire) (*n.m.*), outturn.

rendez-vous (convention) (*n.m.*), appointment:

donner rendez-vous (*ou* un rendez-vous) à quelqu'un, to make an appointment with someone.

rendez-vous (lieu) (*n.m.*), place of meeting.

rendre (restituer) (*v.t.*), to return; to give back; to repay; to pay back; to give up:

rendre un prêt, to return, to repay, to pay back, a loan.

acquitter une facture et la rendre à l'acheteur, to receipt an invoice and give it back (*or* and return it) to the buyer.

wagons rendus vides (*m.pl.*), wagons returned empty.

rendre son billet à la fin du voyage, to give up one's ticket at the end of the journey.

à rendre, returnable:

fûts à rendre (*m.pl.*), casks returnable.

rendre (accorder) (*v.t.*), to render:

les services rendus au public par le banquier (*m.pl.*), the services rendered to the public by the banker.

rendre (prononcer) (*v.t.*), to make:

rendre une sentence (Arbitrage), to make an award.

rendre (faire devenir) (*v.t.*), to render; to make:

la négligence-clause rend l'armateur irresponsable, the negligence clause renders the shipowner not liable.

rendre (voiturer; porter; livrer) (*v.t.*), to deliver:

marchandise rendue franco bord (*f.*), goods delivered free on board.

marchandises rendues chez l'acheteur (*f.pl.*), goods delivered buyer.

rendre (délivrer; donner) (*v.t.*), to render; to give:

rendre un compte, to render an account.

rendre compte de, to render an account of; to give account of; to account for; to report:

rendre compte de sa gestion, to give, to render an, account of one's management.

rendre compte à une assemblée générale des décisions d'un comité, to report the decisions of a committee to a general meeting.

rendre la monnaie d'une pièce de cinq francs, to give change for a five franc piece.

rendre une moyenne de, to give an average of ; to average :

total de tant de millions de francs pour tant de prêts, ce qui rend une moyenne d'environ tant par prêt (m.), total of so many million francs for so many loans, which gives an average of (or which averages) about so much per loan.

rendre (rapporter) (v.t.), to yield ; to produce ; to bring in :

valeur qui rend 5 0/0 par an (f.), security which yields (or which brings in) 5% per annum.

rendre (se) (v.r.). See examples :

se rendre à bord d'un navire, to go on board a ship.

le navire aura la faculté de se rendre et de séjourner à tout port ou lieu, vessel to have liberty to proceed and to stay at any port or place.

se rendre caution ou se rendre garant, -e, to become surety ; to go surety ; to be surety ; to be security ; to stand surety ; to hold oneself liable ; to guarantee :

se rendre caution (ou se rendre garant, -e) d'une obligation contractée par un débiteur, to become surety for an obligation contracted by a debtor.

se rendre compte de, to ascertain ; to find out :

se rendre compte de sa situation, to ascertain one's position ; to find out how one stands.

se rendre partie, to become party :

se rendre partie dans un procès, to become party to an action.

rendu (objet retourné par l'acheteur ou le vendeur) (n.m.), return :

rendus sur achats ou rendus sous achats, purchase returns ; returns outwards.

rendus sur ventes ou rendus sous ventes, sales returns ; returns inwards.

renfermer (comprendre ; contenir) (v.t.), to comprise ; to include ; to contain :

contrat qui renferme toutes les mentions prescrites par la loi (m.), contract which contains all the particulars prescribed by the law.

renfermer (se) (v.r.), to confine oneself :

se renfermer dans ses instructions, to confine oneself to one's instructions.

renflouage ou **renflouement** (n.m.), refloating ; floating :

renflouer (v.t.), to refloat ; to float :

renflouer un navire échoué, to refloat a stranded ship ; to float a vessel aground.

un remorqueur passe un contrat avec un navire échoué et entreprend de le renflouer, a tug enters into a contract with a stranded ship and undertakes to refloat her.

rengagement (mise de nouveau en gage) (n.m.), repledging ; repawning.

rengagement (nouvel embauchage) (n.m.), re-engagement.

rengager (mettre de nouveau en gage) (v.t.), to repledge ; to repawn ; to pledge again.

rengager (embaucher de nouveau) (v.t.), to re-engage :

rengager un employé, to reengage an employee.

se rengager (contracter un nouvel engagement) (v.r.), to reengage ; to reenter an employment.

renoncer à, to renounce ; to waive :

renoncer à son droit, to waive, to renounce, one's right.

les chargeurs renonçant à toute réclamation de ce chef (m.pl.), the shippers waiving any claim hereunder.

renonciation (n.f.), renunciation ; waiving ; waiver :

renonciation de droits, renunciation of rights.

acte considéré comme renonciation au délaissement (m.), act considered as waiver of abandonment.

renouvelable (adj.), renewable :

l'accord est valable pour un an et il est renouvelable automatiquement chaque année (m.), the agreement is valid for one year and it is renewable automatically each year.

renouveler (v.t.), to renew :

renouveler un bail, un effet, une police d'assurance, to renew a lease, a bill, an insurance policy.

renouveleur (pers.) (n.m.), renewer.

renouvellement (n.m.), renewal :

renouvellement de coupons d'un titre, renewal of coupons of a certificate.

renouvellement (n.m.) ou **prime de renouvellement** (f.) (Assce) (opp. à première prime), renewal ; renewal premium.

renseignement (s'emploie surtout au pluriel) (n.m.), information ; particulars ; enquiry ; inquiry :

demande de renseignements (f.), request for information (or particulars).

fournir des renseignements complémentaires, to furnish (or to give) further information (or particulars).

pour frets et autres renseignements s'adresser aux agents, for freights and further particulars apply to the agents.

prendre des renseignements sur quelqu'un, to make enquiries, to inquire, about someone.

renseigner (v.t.), to give information ; to inform :

renseigner quelqu'un sur une affaire, to give someone information, to inform someone, about a matter.

se renseigner (v.r.), to make enquiries ; to enquire ; to inquire :

se renseigner sur la situation de quelqu'un, to make enquiries about, to enquire as to, someone's position.

rente (n.f.) ou **rentes** (n.f.pl.) ou **rente sur l'État,** rente ; rentes :

les fonds d'États étrangers se négocient ou en capital ou en rentes (m.pl.), foreign stocks are dealt in either in capital or in rentes.

acheter de la rente française, to buy some French rentes.

les rentes françaises sont ou perpétuelles ou amortissables, French rentes are either perpetual or redeemable.

Note :—*rente* is the interest payable by a Government on a national debt, it is not *capital stock ;* consequently, unless the State has contracted to redeem the principal, as in the case of *rente amortissable,* it does not owe any capital at all; it has merely contracted in perpetuity to pay so much *rente* (*interest*) periodically.

The prices of *rentes* go up and down in the same way as the prices of capital stocks and shares.

The price quoted is the cost of so many francs of annual rente ; thus, if the French 3% Rentes are quoted at 80, 80 francs will buy the property in an inscription in the Register of the National Debt (*Grand-Livre de la Dette publique*) yielding 3 francs of rente annually : if the price of the 3½% is fr. 97·50, fr. 195 will buy 7 francs of annual rente, and so on.

To ascertain the amount of a purchase or sale of so many *francs de rente* (a buying or a selling order is given in these terms), the amount of the order should be divided by the rate per cent of interest and multiplied by the price ; thus, a purchase of 1 500 *francs de rente* 3 0/0 *à* 58 *fr.* would cost 29,000 francs (viz. :—1,500 ÷ 3 × 58) ; 500 *francs de rente* 4 0/0 *à* 60 would cost 7,500 francs (viz. :— 500 ÷ 4 × 60).

To ascertain the amount of rente a sum of money will buy, multiply the sum of money by the rate of interest and divide by the price ; thus (taking the above examples) :

29,000 × 3 = 87,000 ÷ 58 = 1,500.

7,500 × 4 = 30,000 ÷ 60 = 500.

rente (recette annuellement renouvelée) (*s'emploie souvent au pl.*) (*n.f.*), income; annual income; yearly income; revenue; annuity; rent :

six mille livres de rente bien venantes, an income of six thousand pounds coming in regularly.

vivre de ses rentes, to live on one's income.

rente à terme, annuity.

rente foncière, ground rent.

rente viagère, life annuity.

rente viagère avec réversion, survivorship annuity; reversionary annuity.

rentes, actions, et obligations (*f.pl.*), stocks and shares.

rentier, -ère (possesseur de fonds publics ; portefeuilliste) (*n.*), stockholder; fundholder; investor.

rentier, -ère (personne qui a une annuité) (*n.*), annuitant :

rentier viager (*m.*), rentière viagère (*f.*), life annuitant.

rentier, -ère (personne qui vit uniquement de ses rentes) (*n.*), person of independent means :

travailler dans l'espoir de devenir rentier, -ère, to work in the hope of becoming independent.

rentrée (action de porter ou de reporter à l'intérieur ce qui était dehors) (*n.f.*) (opp. à *sortie*), inflow; influx :

une rentrée d'or, richesse durable et supérieure aux autres richesses, an inflow (*or* an influx) of gold, durable wealth and better than other riches.

rentrée (perception ; recouvrement) (*n.f.*), collection; return; returns; receipt :

la rentrée des impôts, the collection, the receipt, of taxes.

rentrées et sorties de caisse, cash receipts and payments.

les rentrées journalières, the daily returns (*or* receipts).

rentrées diverses, sundry receipts.

rentrées fiscales, revenue receipts; inland revenue receipts.

c'était une rentrée difficile, it was a difficult debt to collect (*or* to get in).

les honoraires des agents de recouvrements sont basés sur les rentrées de fonds qu'ils réussissent à opérer (*m.pl.*), the fees of debt recovery agents are based on the amount of money they succeed in collecting.

rentrées (effets, etc., mis en liasse après payement) (*n.f.pl.*), paid bills (of exchange), cheques, etc. :

les rentrées de juin, the paid bills of June.

rentrer (Comptab.) (*v.t.*), to reenter :

rentrer un article sur un compte, to reenter an item in an account.

rentrer (Navig.) (*v.i.*), to put back :

navire qui rentre dans le port de départ en relâche (*m.*), ship which puts back into the port of sailing for refuge (*or* of necessity) (*or* in distress).

rentrer (être reçu) (*v.i.*), to come in :

fonds qui rentrent mal (*m.pl.*), money which is coming in badly.

rentrer dans ses débours, to be reimbursed one's out of pocket expenses.

rentrer dans un bien par réversion, to regain possession of a property by reversion.

renverser le fardeau de la preuve, to shift the burden of proof.

renvoi (action de retourner) (*n.m.*), return; sending back :

renvoi de marchandises, d'un effet impayé, des wagons de particulier après déchargement, return of goods, of a dishonoured bill, of private owner's wagons after unloading.

renvoi (congé) (*n.m.*), dismissal; discharge.

renvoi (ajournement) (*n.m.*), adjournment; postponement; putting off :

renvoi d'une cause à huitaine, adjournment of a case for a week.

renvoi d'une discussion, postponement of a discussion.

renvoi (rapport) (*n.m.*), reference :

numéro de renvoi (*m.*), reference number.

renvoi (*n.m.*) *ou* **renvoi en marge,** alteration; alteration in the margin (marginal modification or addition to a document) :

parafer un renvoi, to initial an alteration.

renvoyer (faire retourner) (*v.t.*), to return; to send back :
renvoyer un colis à l'expéditeur, to return a parcel to the sender.
wagons renvoyés vides (*m.pl.*), wagons returned empty.

renvoyer (congédier) (*v.t.*), to dismiss; to discharge; to sack (*slang*) :
renvoyer un employé, to dismiss, to discharge, to sack, an employee.
renvoyer des ouvriers en masse, to lock out workmen.

renvoyer (ajourner) (*v.t.*), to adjourn; to postpone; to put off :
renvoyer une affaire au lendemain, to postpone a matter to the following day; to put a matter off till the next day.

renvoyer (adresser, reporter pour obtenir une décision, des renseignements) (*v.t.*), to refer :
renvoyer une affaire devant un tribunal compétent, quelqu'un à son banquier, to refer a matter to a competent tribunal, someone to one's banker.

renvoyer (se rapporter) (*v.i.*), to refer :
les chiffres renvoient aux pages de l'ouvrage (*m.pl.*), the figures refer to the pages of the work.

réorganisateur, -trice (*adj.*), reorganizing.
réorganisateur, -trice (pers.) (*n.*), reorganizer.
réorganisation (*n.f.*), reorganization :
réorganisation du personnel, reorganization of the staff.

réorganiser (*v.t.*), to reorganize :
réorganiser l'administration d'une maison de commerce, to reorganize the management of a business house.

réouverture (*n.f.*), reopening :
réouverture d'un marché, des livres, reopening of a market, of the books.

réparateur de navires (pers.) (*m.*), ship repairer.
réparation (*n.f.*), repairing; repair; reparation :
réparations locatives, tenant's (*or* tenants') repairs.
réparations maritimes, ship repairs.
réparations provisoires, temporary repairs.
réparations allemandes, German reparations.

réparer (*v.t.*), to repair :
réparer un navire endommagé, to repair a damaged ship.

répartir (*v.t.*), to divide; to distribute; to apportion; to assess; to spread; to allot; to appropriate :
répartir une somme entre des créanciers au prorata de (*ou* au marc le franc de) leurs créances, to divide, to distribute, an amount among creditors pro rata to their debts.
répartir un dividende, to distribute a dividend.
répartir les frais accidentels d'après un quantum à déterminer, les avaries d'après la loi et les conventions des parties, to apportion the incidental expenses according to a proportion to be determined, the average according to law and as agreed by the parties.
répartir un risque, to spread a risk.
perte répartie sur un nombre d'années (*f.*), loss spread over a number of years.

répartissable (*adj.*), divisible; dividable; distributable; apportionable; assessable; allottable.

répartiteur (de contributions) (pers.) (*n.m.*), assessor (of taxes); district commissioner.
répartiteur d'avaries (pers.) (*m.*), average adjuster; average stater; average taker.

répartition (*n.f.*) (Abrév. : rép. *ou* Rép. *ou* répart.), division; distribution; dividend; apportionment; assessment; spreading; allotment; appropriation :
répartition des richesses, distribution of wealth.
répartition entre les actionnaires d'un dividende, d'actif au cas de liquidation, distribution of a dividend among the shareholders, of assets in case of liquidation.
répartition entre créanciers (société en liquidation), distribution among creditors; dividend to creditors :
première et unique répartition, troisième et dernière répartition, etc., first and final dividend (*or* distribution), third and final dividend (*or* distribution), etc.
actions de 500 fr., payables 100 fr. en souscrivant (*ou* à la souscription), 100 fr. à la (*ou* lors de la) répartition, tant de francs au (*date*) (*f.pl.*), shares of fr. 500, payable fr. 100 on application, fr. 100 on allotment, so many francs on (*date*).
libération à la répartition (*f.*), payment in full on allotment.
répartition du bénéfice net conformément aux prescriptions statutaires ou aux décisions de l'assemblée des actionnaires, appropriation of the net profit, in accordance with the provisions of the articles or the resolutions of the shareholders' meeting.
seules les avaries communes donnent lieu à répartition; les avaries particulières sont supportées et payées par le propriétaire de la chose qui a essuyé le dommage ou occasionné la dépense, only general averages give rise to apportionment; particular averages are borne and paid by the owner of the thing which has sustained the damage or occasioned the expense.
répartition proportionnelle entre les intéressés des pertes résultant du sacrifice (règlement d'avaries communes), pro rata apportionment between the parties concerned of the losses resulting from the sacrifice.
répartition de contributions, assessment of taxes.

repasser (examiner de nouveau) (*v.t.*), to re-examine; to go into again :
repasser un compte, to reexamine an account; to go into an account again.

repayement (*n.m.*), paying again; paying over again; repayment.

repayer (*v.t.*), to pay again; to pay over again; to repay.

répertoire (*n.m.*), index; directory :
un répertoire, placé au commencement du livre, permet de se reporter immédiatement à chaque compte, an index, placed in front of the book, enables one to refer immediately to every account.

répertoire sur fiches, card index.

répertoire maritime, shipping directory.

répertoire des opérations de bourse (*m.*). In France, a register that stockbrokers, produce brokers, bankers, money dealers, and other intermediaries, are legally bound to keep, giving full particulars of purchases and sales effected through their agency. An extract of the record in the *répertoire* has to be sent by the broker to his client. In practice, the particulars of the *répertoire* are shown in the contract note sent by the broker to his client and the law is thus respected. The entries in the *répertoire* give rise to assessment of the *impôt sur les opérations de bourse*.

répertoire des opérations de change (*m.*). In France, a register in which persons who deal in foreign exchange are legally bound to record their transactions.

répertoire des transitaires (*m.*). In France, a register in which customs agents and agencies, transport companies, shipbrokers, and, in general, all intermediaries who professedly clear goods through the customs, are legally bound to enter their transactions.

répertorier (*v.t.*), to index :

chaque écriture est répertoriée alphabétiquement par nom de navire (*f.*), each entry is indexed alphabetically under name of ship.

répéter (*v.t.*), to repeat :

répéter le numéro (Téléph., etc.), to repeat the number.

prier le bureau du télégraphe de faire répéter le ou les mots mutilés, to ask the telegraph office to repeat (*or* to have repeated) the mutilated word or words.

radiotélégramme répété le lendemain (*m.*), radiotelegram repeated the next day.

répéter (Dr.) (*v.t.*), to claim back :

répéter contre le bénéficiaire un billet à ordre que l'on a souscrit, to claim back from the payee a promissory note that one has made.

répétition (*n.f.*), repetition :

répétition de mots supposés erronés, du télégramme de bureau à bureau, repetition of words supposed to be wrong, of the telegram from office to office.

répétition (Dr.) (*n.f.*), claiming back :

répétition de dividendes contre les actionnaires, claiming back of dividends from the shareholders.

replacement (*n.m.*), reinvestment.

replacer (*v.t.*), to reinvest :

replacer des capitaux, to reinvest capital.

replier (se) (*v.r.*), to fall back ; to fall away ; to go back :

l'action X. s'est repliée de 1 873 à 1 835, X. shares fell back (*or* fell away) (*or* went back) from 1,873 to 1,835 francs.

répondant (caution) (pers.) (*n.m.*), surety ; security :

être le répondant de quelqu'un, to be someone's surety.

répondre (faire une réponse) (*v.i.*), to answer ; to reply :

répondre à une lettre, to answer, to reply to, a letter.

répondre affirmativement, négativement, to reply in the affirmative, in the negative.

répond pas *ou* ne répond pas (Téléph.), sorry, there's no reply ; I am sorry there is no reply ; no reply.

répondre (se porter garant) (*v.i.*), to answer ; to be security ; to guarantee ; to be liable :

répondre pour quelqu'un, de la solvabilité de quelqu'un, to answer for, to be security for, to guarantee, someone, someone's solvency.

répondre des avaries occasionnées par la pluie, par les rats, to be liable for damage caused by rain, by rats.

avarie dont les assureurs ont à répondre (*f.*), average for which the assurers are liable.

l'assureur ne répondra pas, du chef d'un seul et même accident, de plus de tant de francs (*m.*), the underwriter shall not be liable in respect of any one accident for more than so many francs.

ne répondant pas. See under **ne.**

répondre à (Bourse), to declare :

répondre à une prime, to declare an option.

ces primes sont répondues à 1 h. 30 (*f.pl.*), these options are declared at 1.30.

réponse (*n.f.*), answer ; reply :

réponse à une lettre, answer, reply, to a letter.

en réponse à un actionnaire, il a été déclaré que . . ., in reply to a shareholder, it was stated that . . .

réponse payée (télégramme) (*Abrév.:* R.P.), reply paid.

réponse type [réponses types *pl.*], set form of reply.

réponse des primes (Bourse) (*f.*), declaration of options. See note under **prime.**

report (action de transporter un total) (Comptab.) (*n.m.*), carrying ; carrying forward ; carrying over ; bringing forward ; carrying out ; extension :

report d'un total au haut de la page suivante, d'un compte d'un folio à un autre, carrying forward, carrying, carrying over, a total to the top of the next page, an account from one folio to another.

report d'un total du bas de la page précédente, bringing forward a total from the bottom of the previous page.

report d'une somme dans la colonne extérieure, carrying out, extension, of an amount in the outer column.

report (somme transportée ; balance transportée) (Comptab.) (*n.m.*), amount (*or* balance) carried forward (*or* carried down) ; carry forward ; carry over ; amount (*or* balance) brought forward (*or* brought down) :

le report est de tant de francs, the amount (*or* the balance) carried forward (*or* carried down) is so many francs ; the carry forward (*or* the carry over) is so many francs ; the amount (*or* the balance) brought forward (*or* brought down) is so many francs.

report à nouveau, balance carried forward to next account; balance to next account; carry forward.

report antérieur *ou* report de l'exercice précédent *ou* report à nouveau de l'exercice précédent, balance brought forward from last account; balance from last (*or* from previous) account.

report (inscription en haut d'une colonne) Comptab.) (opp. à *à reporter* ou *reporté*), brought forward; forward: (*Note :*—If two amounts are brought forward, as in a journal, *brought forward* remains invariable in English, but in French the plural *reports* must be used.)
report du folio . . ., brought forward from folio . . .

report (transport au débit ou au crédit) (Comptab.) (*n.m.*), posting:
le report des écritures du journal aux comptes du grand livre, the posting of journal entries to the ledger accounts.
les reports du grand livre, les reports du journal aux comptes du grand livre, the ledger postings, the postings from the journal to the ledger accounts.

report (renouvellement d'une position et sa prorogation jusqu'à la liquidation suivante) (Bourse) (*n.m.*), contango; contangoing; continuation; continuation account; carrying over; carry over:
mettre (*ou* placer) (*ou* employer) des capitaux en report, c'est effectuer un placement temporaire de quinze ou de trente jours, garanti par les titres pris en report, to lend (*or* to employ) money on contango, that is to make a temporary investment for a fortnight or a month, secured by the stock taken in.
devises en report (*f.pl.*), foreign exchange on continuation account.
reports sur devises, continuations (*or* continuation accounts) on foreign exchanges.
dans le report, le prêteur est nanti d'un titre, in contangoing (*or* in carrying over), the lender is secured by a stock.

report (loyer de l'argent immobilisé par le capitaliste pendant l'espace d'une liquidation) (Bourse) (*n.m.*) (Abrév.: **R.** *ou* rep.), contango; contango rate; carry over rate; continuation rate:
il arrive parfois que le report est au pair, c'est-à-dire qu'il n'en coûte rien que le courtage pour se faire reporter, ou même que, par suite de la rareté exceptionnelle d'un titre, l'acheteur a droit à une bonification s'il se fait reporter: cette bonification porte le nom de déport, it sometimes happens that the contango (*or* the contango rate) (*or* the carry over rate) (*or* the continuation rate) is even, that is to say, there is nothing to pay except the brokerage to enable one to lend stock, or even that, owing to an exceptional scarcity of a stock, the buyer has right to an allowance if he lends stock: this allowance bears the name of backwardation (*or* back) (*or* backwardization).

report (Négociations de change à terme) (*n.m.*) (Abrév.: **R.**), discount; over spot:

pour la détermination des cours à terme, on cote le report ou le déport, c.-à-d. la somme qu'il y a lieu d'ajouter (R.) au cours du comptant ou d'en soustraire (B.) pour obtenir la valeur de la base cotée, for the determination of the forward rates there is quoted a discount or a premium, i.e., the amount that there is occasion to add (d.) to the spot rate or to subtract from it (p.) to obtain the value of the basis quoted.
Devise: Londres, 1 mois, 0 15 B. à 0 05 B., Centre: London, 1 month, (p.) 15–5c.

report (écart entre le comptant et le terme) (Bourse) (*n.m.*), difference between cash and settlement prices.

reportable (Bourse) (*adj.*), contangoable; continuable:
valeurs reportables (*f.pl.*), contangoable stocks; continuable securities.

reportage (*n.m.*), reporting; press work:
reportage d'une réunion, reporting a meeting.
Cf. faire le reportage de.

reporté (Bourse) (pers.) (*n.m.*) (opp. à *reporteur*), giver. See example under **reporteur.**

reporter (journaliste) (pers.) (*n.m.*), reporter;
le reporter d'un journal, the reporter of a newspaper; a press reporter.

reporter *ou* reporter à nouveau (transporter un total) (Comptab.) (*v.t.*), to carry; to carry forward; to carry over; to bring forward; to carry out; to extend:
reporter une somme à une autre page, les totaux à la page suivante, to carry forward, to carry, to carry over, an amount to another page, the totals to the following page.
solde des bénéfices reporté à nouveau sur l'exercice suivant (*m.*), balance of profits carried forward to next account.
reporter une somme d'une autre page, to bring forward an amount from another page.
nous avons l'honneur de vous adresser ci-joint le relevé de votre compte arrêté au . . . 19—, et présentant un solde de fr. —— en votre faveur, que nous reportons à votre crédit à nouveau, we have pleasure in sending you herewith statement of your account made up to the . . . 19—, showing a balance in your favour of fr. ——, which we carry forward to your credit.
reporter la balance des intérêts dans la colonne des capitaux, to carry out, to extend, the balance of interest in the principal column.

à reporter *ou* reporté (inscription en bas d'une colonne), carried forward; forward:
reporté au folio . . ., carried forward to folio . . .

reporter (porter au débit, au crédit) (Comptab.) (*v.t.*), to post; to post up:
sommes reportées au débit et au crédit des comptes du grand livre (*f.pl.*), amounts posted to the debit and to the credit of the ledger accounts.
reporter un compte, to post, to post up, an account.

reporter (faire le report de) (Bourse) (*v.t.*) (Abrév.: **r.** *ou* **rep.** *ou* **rp.** *ou* **a/v.**), to carry over; to continue; to contango:

reporter une position d'une liquidation à la prochaine, to carry over, to continue, to contango, a position (or a book) from one account (or settlement) to the next.

reporter (opérer un report sur) (Bourse) (*v.t.*), to take in; to take in stock for; to take the rate on; to borrow; to carry:

reporter des titres, to take in, to take the rate on, to borrow, to carry, stock.

reporter un emprunteur, to take in stock for a borrower.

titres reportés (*m.pl.*), stock taken in; stock borrowed; stock carried.

Cf. faire reporter, *under* **faire.**

reporter (faire un report) (Bourse) (*v.i.*), to carry over; to contango; to continue:

les agents de change refusent de reporter (*m.pl.*), the stockbrokers refuse to carry over (or to continue) (or to. contango). *See also example under* faire un report, *under* **faire.**

reporter (prendre en report) (*v.i.*), to take in; to take the rate; to borrow stock; to carry stock:

c'est au cours de compensation que l'acheteur se fait reporter et que le vendeur reporte, it is at the making up price that the buyer gives on and the seller takes in.

le plus souvent sur un grand marché, comme celui de Paris, il se rencontre qu'il y a d'un côté beaucoup d'acheteurs qui, ne pouvant lever leurs titres achetés en liquidation, c'est-à-dire en prendre livraison, se font reporter, et, d'un autre côté, beaucoup de vendeurs qui, n'étant pas en possession des titres vendus en liquidation, reportent, generally on a big market, like the Paris market, there are to be found on the one hand many buyers who, being unable to take up their stock, bought for the account (or for the settlement), that is to say, to take delivery of it, give on (or give the rate) (or lend stock), and, on the other hand, many sellers who, not being in possession of stock sold for the account (or settlement), take in (or take the rate) (or borrow stock) (or carry stock).

en se faisant reporter à chaque liquidation l'acheteur peut rester indéfiniment à la hausse, moyennant paiement régulier des reports et règlement des différences, et le vendeur à découvert peut prolonger à volonté sa position à la baisse, en reportant également à chaque liquidation, by giving on (or by giving the rate) (or by lending stock) at each settlement the buyer can remain a bull indefinitely, in consideration of the regular payment of contangoes and settlement of differences, and the bear seller can prolong at will his bear position, by taking in (or by taking the rate) (or by borrowing or carrying stock) likewise at each settlement.

reporter (se) (se référer) (*v.r.*), to refer:

un répertoire permet de se reporter immédiatement à chaque compte, an index enables one to refer immediately to every account.

reporteur (Bourse) (pers.) (*n.m.*), taker:

en rémunération du prêt, le reporteur touche du reporté une prime, qui s'appelle report, as remuneration for the loan, the taker receives from the giver a premium, which is called contango.

capital reporteur (*m.*) *ou* **capitaux reporteurs** (*m.pl.*), money lent (on stock taken in).

repos (de tout), safe; reliable:

estimation de tout repos (*f.*), safe estimate; reliable estimate.

repoussement (*n.m.*), rejection; voting down.

repousser (*v.t.*), to reject; to vote down:

repousser une offre, to reject an offer.

repousser l'ajournement d'une assemblée, to vote down the adjournment of a meeting.

reprendre (Dr.) (*v.t.*), to resume possession:

le propriétaire a le droit de refuser de renouveler le bail s'il reprend les locaux, soit pour lui, soit pour reconstruire l'immeuble, the landlord has the right to refuse to renew the lease if he resumes possession, either for his own use, or to rebuild the property.

reprendre (se charger de) (*v.t.*), to take over:

la Société A. absorbera par fusion la Société B. en reprenant tout son actif, à charge par elle de payer tout son passif, le tout à dater du 1er janvier écoulé, the A. Company will absorb by amalgamation the B. Company by taking over all its assets and liabilities, the whole to date from 1st January last.

reprendre (*v.i.*) *ou* **se reprendre** (*v.r.*) (se relever), to recover; to rally; to pick up:

les valeurs minières reprennent (*ou* se reprennent) vigoureusement (*ou* vivement) (*f.pl.*), mining shares recovered (or rallied) (or picked up) sharply (or smartly).

représaille (*n.f.*), reprisal.

représentant (pers.) (*n.m.*), representative; agent:

représentant attitré, accredited representative.

les sociétés d'assurances maritimes nomment en général des agents ou des représentants dans les ports principaux (*f.pl.*), marine insurance companies usually appoint agents or representatives in the principal ports.

le capitaine est le représentant de l'armateur. Est-il le représentant des chargeurs? the master is the owner's representative. Is he the shippers' representative?

représentant de commerce, commercial agent; business agent; trade representative.

représentation (exhibition) (*n.f.*), production; showing; shewing; exhibition:

représentation de billets, production of tickets; showing tickets.

représentation (état d'une personne qui remplace une autre) (*n.f.*), representation; agency.

représentation (rémunération) (*n.f.*), consideration; purchase consideration. See example under syn. **rémunération.**

représenter (présenter de nouveau) (*v.t.*), to represent:

représenter un effet à l'acceptation, un chèque au paiement, to represent a bill for acceptance, a cheque for payment.

représenter (exhiber) (*v.t.*), to produce; to show; to shew; to exhibit:

représenter un titre, les pièces, to produce, to exhibit, a certificate, the documents.

le voyageur est tenu de représenter son billet à toute réquisition des préposés de la compagnie, the passenger is bound to produce (or show) his ticket whenever required to to do so by the company's servants.

représenter (tenir la place de quelqu'un) (*v.t.*), to represent :
représenter une maison de commerce, un actionnaire, les parties devant les cours, to represent a firm, a shareholder, the parties before the courts.

reprêter (*v.t.*), to relend.

reprise (relèvement ; recrudescence) (*n.f.*), recovery ; rally ; revival ; resumption :
reprise des affaires, recovery, revival, resumption, of business.

reprise des cours, recovery of, rally in, prices.

reprise des dividendes, resumption of dividends.

une vigoureuse (*ou* vive) reprise du groupe caoutchoutier à la séance de mercredi a été compensée par la faiblesse des autres séances, a sharp rally (or a smart recovery) in the rubber group at Wednesday's session was offset by weakness in the other sessions.

être en reprise, to recover ; to rally ; to pick up :
l'action X. est en reprise de 675 à 695, X. shares recovered (or rallied) (or picked up) from 675 to 695 francs.

reprise (de locaux) (Dr.) (*n.f.*), resumption of possession :
droit de reprise par le propriétaire (*m.*), right of resumption of possession by the landlord. See also example under **reprendre.**

reprise (prime de location) (*n.f.*), premium :
local à louer, sans reprise (*Abrév.:* ss repr.), petite reprise (*m.*), premises to let, no premium, small premium.

bureaux à louer, 4 pièces, loyer 35 000, reprise 50 000 francs (*m.pl.*), offices to let, 4 rooms, rent 35,000, premium 50,000 francs.

réputation (*n.f.*), reputation :
le crédit personnel est basé sur la réputation du commerçant, personal credit is based on the reputation of the trader.

réputé, -e (*adj.*), reputed ; deemed :
usage bien établi qui est réputé faire partie de la police (*m.*), well established practice which is deemed to form part of the policy.

navire qui est réputé perdu (*m.*), ship which is deemed to be lost.

requête des créanciers (*f.*), petition of creditors.

requin (pers.) (*n.m.*), shark :
requin financier, financial shark.

requis, -e (*adj.*), required ; necessary :
formalités requises (*f.pl.*), necessary formalities.

réquisition (*n.f.*), requisition.

réquisitionner (*v.t.*), to requisition :
en cas de guerre, les navires de commerce peuvent être réquisitionnés par l'État, in case of war, merchant ships can be requisitioned by the Government.

rescapé, -e (pers.) (*n.*), survivor (one who escapes from a wreck, or the like).

rescision (*n.f.*), rescission :
emprunt de rescision (*m.*), rescission loan.

réseau (*n.m.*), system ; network :
réseau de chemins de fer (*ou* de voies ferrées), de canaux, system, network, of railways, of canals :
le réseau de chemins de fer de la Grande-Bretagne, the railway system of Great Britain.

réseau national postal aérien, national postal air system.

réservation (*n.f.*) *ou* **réserve** (*n.f.*), reservation ; reserve ; exception :
réservation d'un droit, reservation of a right.

les réserves stipulées dans un contrat, the reservations (*or* the reserves) (*or* the exceptions) stipulated in a contract.

connaissement portant la réserve poids inconnu (*m.*), bill of lading bearing the reservation weight unknown.

en réserve, in reserve ; by :
mettre une somme en réserve, to put an amount in reserve ; to put a sum by.

sous les réserves d'usage (Banq.), under usual reserves ; under reserve :
le montant du chèque est porté à votre crédit sous les réserves d'usage, the amount of the cheque is passed to your credit under usual reserves.

sous réserve, under reserve ; subject ; on condition ; qualified :
sous réserve de modifications, de toute disposition (*ou* stipulation) expresse de la police, des termes de la présente police, des clauses suivantes, de certaines exceptions, des dispositions de la présente loi, des dispositions qui précèdent, des conditions ci-après mentionnées, subject to alteration, to any express provision in the policy, to the terms of this policy, to the following clauses, to certain exceptions, to the provisions of this Act, to the foregoing provisions, to the conditions hereinafter mentioned.

en certains pays, les télégrammes en langage convenu ne sont admis que sous réserve que le code employé soit déposé aux bureaux de destination, in certain countries, telegrams in code are admitted only on condition that the code used has deposited with the authorities.

acceptation sous réserves (lettres de change) (*f.*), qualified acceptance.

réserve (Fin. & Comptab.) (*n.f.*), reserve :
réserve cachée *ou* réserve occulte *ou* réserve latente, secret reserve ; hidden reserve ; inner reserve :
la plupart des postes de l'actif sont évalués avec une telle prudence qu'ils recèlent des réserves occultes très importantes, most of the items on the assets side are valued with such caution that they conceal very material secret reserves.

réserve d'or (Banq.), gold reserve.

réserve de la banque, bank reserve.

réserve de prévoyance, contingency reserve.

réserve des primes (Assce), reserve for premiums paid in advance.

réserve extraordinaire, extraordinary reserve.

réserve générale, general reserve.

réserve légale, legal reserve :

en France, la réserve legale est obligatoire dans les sociétés par actions ; elle est de 5 p. 100 des bénéfices nets jusqu'à concurrence du dixième du capital social, in France, the legal reserve is obligatory in joint stock companies ; it is 5% of the net profits until it amounts to one tenth of the nominal capital.

réserve métallique (Banq.), bullion reserve ; metallic reserve.

réserve pour régularisation de dividende, pour éventualités, reserve for equalization of dividend, for contingencies.

réserve prime d'émission *ou* réserve prime sur actions, premium reserve ; premiums on shares reserve.

réserve statutaire, reserve provided by the articles (*or* by the articles of association).

réserve visible, visible reserve.

See note under **provision.**

réserver (garder pour un autre temps) (*v.t.*), to reserve ; to put by ; to lay by :

réserver une place à l'avance dans un train, to reserve a seat in advance in a train.

réserver quelque argent pour les cas imprévus, to reserve, to put by, to lay by, some money for unforeseen contingencies.

réserver (mettre à part) (*v.t.*), to reserve :

réserver une partie des bénéfices, une marge pour les éventualités, to reserve a part of the profits, a margin for contingencies.

réserver (se) (*v.r.*), to reserve ; to reserve to oneself :

assureur qui se réserve la faculté de résilier la police en certains cas (*m.*), insurer who reserves the right to cancel (*or* reserves to himself the option of cancelling) the policy in certain cases.

la compagnie se réserve le droit de vérifier le poids de tout colis faisant partie du chargement, the company reserves the right to check the weight of any package forming part of the shipment.

résidence (*n.f.*), residence.

résidu (rompu ; fraction) (*n.m.*), fraction (incomplete unit of a share or of stock) :

les résidus se négocient en bourse, fractions are dealt in on the stock exchange.

résignation (*n.f.*), resignation.

résigner (*v.t.*), to resign :

résigner un emploi, to resign a position.

résiliation (*n.f.*) *ou* **résiliement** (*n.m.*) *ou* **résilîment** (*n.m.*), cancellation ; annulment ; avoidance ; termination ; determination ; rescission :

résiliation d'un bail, cancellation of a lease.

résilier (*v.t.*), to cancel ; to annul ; to avoid ; to void ; to terminate ; to determine ; to rescind :

résilier un contrat, to cancel, to annul, to avoid, to void, to terminate, to determine, to rescind, a contract.

résistance (en parlant des cours de bourse) (*n.f.*), strength :

l'action X. fait preuve de résistance, X. shares showed strength.

résistant, -e (*adj.*), strong :

les valeurs de banques sont résistantes (Bourse) (*f.pl.*), bank shares are strong.

résoluble (qui peut être annulé) (*adj.*), determinable ; terminable ; voidable ; avoidable ; cancellable ; annullable ; rescindable.

résolution (proposition ; décision) (*n.f.*), resolution ; business :

après la discussion, M. le président met aux voix les résolutions, after the discussion, the chairman put the resolutions to the meeting.

les résolutions prises par l'assemblée générale, the resolutions passed at the general meeting.

personne ne demandant plus la parole, les résolutions sont adoptées à l'unanimité (compte rendu), there being no further questions, the resolutions were passed unanimously.

résolutions diverses (ordre du jour), general business.

résolution (destruction d'un contrat valable) (*n.f.*), termination ; determination ; rescission ; avoidance ; cancellation ; annulment.

résolutoire (*adj.*). *See* clause résolutoire.

résoudre (déterminer ; décider) (*v.t.*), to resolve ; to resolve on :

un emprunt de tant fut résolu, a loan of so much was resolved on.

résoudre (annuler) (*v.t.*), to terminate ; to determine ; to rescind ; to avoid ; to void ; to cancel ; to annul :

résoudre un contrat, to terminate, to determine, to rescind, to avoid, to void, to cancel, to annul, a contract.

se résoudre (*v.r.*), to be cancelled ; to be determined ; to be terminated ; to be terminated :

un bail se résout par l'expiration du terme fixé, a lease is determined by the expiration of the term fixed.

respecter (*v.t.*), to respect ; to observe ; to comply with :

respecter une clause dans un contrat, to respect, to observe, to comply with, a clause in a contract.

responsabilité (*n.f.*), responsibility ; liability :

la signature du capitaine engage la responsabilité du navire, the captain's signature pledges the liability of the ship.

la responsabilité du navire cesse dès le débarquement dans ledit port, the liability of the ship ceases on discharging in the said port.

responsabilité des patrons *ou* responsabilité patronale, employers' liability.

responsabilité limitée, limited liability.

responsabilité illimitée, unlimited liability.

responsable (*adj.*), responsible ; liable :

le propriétaire est responsable du capitaine et de l'équipage ; le capitaine est responsable des marchandises dont il se charge, the owner is responsible for the master and the crew; the master is responsible for the goods entrusted to his care.

l'armateur est responsable de ses fautes et de celles de ses préposés (*m.*), the shipowner is responsible (*or* liable) for his faults and those of his servants.

ressaisir (se) (*v.r.*), to pick up; to rally; to recover :
l'action X. se ressaisit vivement, X. shares picked up (*or* rallied) (*or* recovered) sharply (*or* smartly).

resserrement (*n.m.*), tightness; tightening:
resserrement d'argent, de crédit, tightness of money, of credit.

ressortir (*v.i.*), to show; to shew; to appear:
la somme ressortie à la colonne de caisse, les sommes sont ressorties à l'encre rouge, the amount shown in the cash column, the amounts are shewn in red ink.
le résultat de l'opération ressortira de la comparaison du débit et du crédit, the result of the transaction will appear on comparing the debit with the credit.

ressource (*n.f.*), resource; commodity:
l'agriculture est la principale ressource économique française (*f.*), agriculture is the chief French economic resource.
le coton est la principale ressource du Soudan, cotton is the staple commodity (*or simply* the staple) of the Sudan.

restant (*n.m.*) *ou* **reste** (*n.m.*), remainder; balance; surplus:
placer en rentes viagères le restant (*ou* le reste) de sa fortune, to invest the remainder of one's fortune in life annuities.
restant de compte, balance of account.
le restant en caisse à la fin de la journée, the balance (*of cash*) in hand at the end of the day.
restants de provisions de bord, surplus ship's stores.

restauration (*n.f.*), restoration:
restauration des finances publiques, restoration of the public finances.

restaurer (*v.t.*), to restore.

reste (Arith.) (*n.m.*), remainder:
15 soustrait de 27 donne pour reste 12, 15 subtracted from 27 gives as a remainder 12.

rester (*v.i.*), to remain:
la présente convention restera en vigueur pendant une période de tant d'années, the present agreement to remain in force during a period of so many years.
reste à reporter à nouveau fr. . . . ., there remains to be carried forward fr. . . . .
rester le dernier, to be the last:
le capitaine a le devoir d'honneur de rester le dernier à son bord, the captain has the duty of honour to be the last to leave his ship.

restituable (*adj.*), returnable:
taxe restituable (*f.*), returnable tax.

restituer (*v.t.*), to return; to restore:
armateur qui est tenu de restituer le fret qui lui

aura été avancé (*m.*), shipowner who is obliged to return the freight advanced to him.
le preneur est tenu de restituer la chose louée à la fin du bail, the lessee is bound to restore the leased property at the end of the lease.

restitution (*n.f.*), return; restoration:
restitution de taxes indûment perçues, return of taxes unduly collected.

restreindre (*v.t.*), to restrict:
restreindre ses dépenses *ou* se restreindre (*v.r.*), to restrict one's expenses; to retrench.
transactions très restreintes (*f.pl.*), dealings very restricted.

restrictif, -ive (*adj.*), restrictive:
clause restrictive (*f.*), restrictive clause.

restriction (*n.f.*), restriction:
restriction de la production, des crédits, restriction of production (*or* of output), of credits.
restrictions d'entrée (*ou* à l'entrée), de sortie (*ou* à la sortie), restrictions on importation, on exportation.
restrictions de quarantaine, quarantine restrictions.
restriction des loyers, rent restriction.

résultat (*n.m.*), result:
quel que soit le résultat de l'exercice, whatever may be the result of the trading.
résultats de l'exercice *ou* résultats de l'exploitation, trading results.

résultat (ce que l'on obtient à la répartition d'une souscription) (*n.m.*), result:
acheter en bourse le résultat d'une souscription de tant d'actions, to buy on the stock exchange the result of an application for so many shares.

résumé (*n.m.*), résumé; recapitulation; summary; abstract.

résumer (*v.t.*), to recapitulate; to summarize.

retard (*n.m.*), delay; lateness:
retard à la livraison, dans l'exécution d'un ordre, dans l'acheminement de la marchandise, delay in delivery, in the execution of an order, in forwarding (*or* in the dispatch of) the goods.
retard dans l'arrivée des trains, lateness, delay, in the arrival of trains.

retardataire (*adj.*) *ou* **en retard**, in arrear; in arrears; late:
contribuable retardataire *ou* contribuable en retard (*m. ou f.*), taxpayer in arrears.
actionnaires en retard de versements (*m.pl.*), shareholders in arrear with calls.
le train est en retard, the train is late.

retarder (*v.t.*), to retard; to delay; to defer; to put off:
retarder un paiement, to delay, to defer, to put off, a payment.

retélégraphier (*v.t.*), to retelegraph.

retenir (prélever) (*v.t.*), to retain; to keep back; to withhold; to stop:
retenir les services de quelqu'un, to retain someone's services.
retenir tant sur la paye d'un employé, to retain, to stop, to withhold, so much out of an employee's pay.

retenir (Arith.) (*v.t.*), to carry :
retenir un chiffre, to carry a figure.
4 fois 9, 36, je pose 6 et je retiens 3, 4 times 9,
36, I put down 6 and carry 3.

retenir (s'assurer par précaution) (*v.t.*), to engage ;
to book :
retenir une chambre dans un hôtel, une price
dans un train, to engage, to book, a room
in an hotel, a seat in a train.

retenue (prélèvement) (*n.f.*), retention ; stoppage ;
amount retained :
retenues opérées sur les salaires, stoppages
made on wages ; amounts retained out of
wages ; retentions on wages.

retenue (Arith.) (*n.f.*), carry :
porter la retenue sous chaque colonne, to put
the carry under each column.

réticence (*n.f.*), concealment :
assurance qui est nulle en cas de réticence ou
fausse déclaration de l'assuré, insurance
which is null in case of concealment or misrepresentation by the insured.

retirer (reprendre) (*v.t.*), to withdraw ; to retire ;
to take out ; to take away ; to remove ;
to collect :
retirer des pièces de la circulation, to withdraw,
to retire, coins from circulation.
retirer un dépôt, to withdraw a deposit.
retirer un effet, to retire a bill.
retirer le navire du service des affréteurs, to
withdraw the ship from the service of the
charterers.
destinataire qui se présente à la gare pour retirer
sa marchandise (*m.*), consignee who calls at
the station to collect (*or* to remove) (*or* to
take away) his goods.
retirer de l'entrepôt, to take out of bond (*or*
warehouse) ; to clear :
marchandises retirées de l'entrepôt pour la
consommation (*f.pl.*), goods taken out of
bond for home use.
retirer des douanes, to clear ; to remove from
the customs :
les marchandises ne peuvent être retirées des
douanes qu'après les droits ont été payés,
consignés, ou garantis (*f.pl.*), the goods can
only be cleared (*or* removed from the
customs) after the duties have been paid,
deposited, or secured.

retirer (recueillir) (*v.t.*), to draw ; to get ; to
make ; to derive :
retirer tant d'un bien, un profit d'une entreprise, to draw, to get, to make, so much out
of a property, a profit out of an enterprise ;
to derive so much from a property, a profit
from an undertaking.

retirer (se) (quitter sa profession) (*v.r.*), to retire :
se retirer d'une association, des affaires, to
retire from an association, from business.

être retiré (-e) **des affaires,** to be retired from
business.

retirer (se) (se rétrécir) (*v.r.*), to shrink :
l'action X. se retire de 5 250 à 5 175, X.
shares shrank from 5,250 to 5,175 francs.

retour (*n.m.*), return :

retour de marchandises, d'un effet accepté,
d'un effet impayé, return of goods, of an
accepted bill, of a dishonoured bill.
retours sur achats, purchase returns ; returns
outwards.
retours sur ventes, sales returns ; returns inwards.
répondre par retour (*ou* par le retour) du
courrier, to reply by return of post.
retour sans frais (avis sur un effet de commerce),
protest waived in case of dishonour ; incur
no expenses ; notarial charges not to be
incurred ; no noting ; retour sans frais ;
sans frais.

retour (effet non payé à l'échéance) (*n.m.*), dishonoured bill ; bill returned dishonoured.

retour (voyage de retour) (*n.m.*), return ; return
journey (*or* voyage) (*or* passage) ; homeward
voyage. See example under **aller.**

retour (billet de retour) (*n.m.*), return ; return
ticket.

retourner (*v.t.*), to return :
retourner un colis à l'expéditeur, to return
a parcel to the sender.
wagons retournés vides (*m.pl.*), wagons returned
empty.
retourner un effet *ou* retourner un effet impayé,
to return a bill dishonoured. *Cf.* effet
retourné.

se retourner (Bourse) (*v.r.*), to go on the other
tack :
opérateur qui se retourne (*m.*), operator who
goes on the other tack.

retrait (action de retirer) (*n.m.*), withdrawal ;
retirement ; retiral ; removal ; collection :
retrait d'une demande, d'un dépôt, d'argent
d'une banque, withdrawal of a request, of a
deposit, of money from a bank.
retrait d'un effet, retirement, retiral, of a
bill.
retrait des marchandises à destination, collection, removal, of the goods, at destination.

retraite (traite à nouveau) (*n.f.*), redraft ; reexchange ; renewal bill ; renewed bill.

retraite (pension de retraite) (*n.f.*), pension ;
retiring allowance :
retraite pour la vieillesse, old age pension.

retraité (pers.) (*n.m.*), pensioner.

retrancher (Arith.) (*v.t.*), to deduct ; to subtract ; to take away :
retrancher un nombre d'un autre, to deduct,
to subtract, to take away, one number from
another.

se retrancher (*v.r.*), to be deducted ; to be
subtracted ; to be taken away :
le courtage s'ajoute aux achats ou se retranche
des ventes, brokerage is added to purchases
or deducted from sales.

retransférer (*v.t.*), to retransfer.

retransmission (Radiotélégr., etc.) (*n.f.*) (Abrév. :
RM.), retransmission.

rétrécir (se) (*v.r.*), to shrink :
l'action X. se rétrécit de 5 325 à 5 250, X.
shares shrank from 5,325 to 5,250 francs.

rétrograder (*v.i.*), to relapse ; to fall back ; to
fall away ; to go back :

l'action X. rétrograde de 20 050 à 19 965, X. shares relapsed (*or* fell back) (*or* fell away) (*or* went back) from 20,050 to 19,965 francs.

retrouver (*v.t.*), to find :
retrouver une erreur dans les livres, un dépôt intact, to find a mistake in the books, a deposit intact.

réunion (assemblée) (*n.f.*), meeting :
réunion d'actionnaires, meeting of shareholders ; shareholders' meeting.
réunion de créanciers, meeting of creditors.
la prochaine réunion du conseil (*ou* du conseil d'administration), the next board meeting.

réunion (assemblage ; blocage) (*n.f.*), combination ; lumping.

réunir (assembler ; bloquer) (*v.t.*), to combine ; to lump :
le trafic total, entrées et sorties réunies, the total traffic, imports and exports combined.
articles qui sont réunis sous la rubrique portefeuille-titres (*m.pl.*), items which are lumped under the heading investments.

réunir (se) (*v.r.*), to meet :
après leur nomination, les administrateurs se réunissent en conseil pour choisir parmi eux un président, after their appointment, the directors meet as a board to choose some one of their number to be chairman.

revalorisation (*n.f.*), revalorization :
revalorisation du franc-papier, revalorization of the paper franc.
Note :—The French franc having been revalorized at 124·21 (more exactly 124·2134) to the £1 sterling, viz., at about one fifth of its former value, it follows that very large, indeed enormous, sets of figures are constantly met with. Share values of, for instance, 5,000 francs are common ; sometimes 10,000, 20,000, and even 40,000 occur, and founders' shares may reach a very much higher figure. Profits of companies often run into millions, and of large companies into tens of millions of francs (a million francs is roughly £8,000). Capitals of large concerns run into thousands of millions. A thousand millions (called a *milliard* in French) of francs is about £8,000,000.

révéler (*v.t.*), to reveal ; to disclose :
révéler toute circonstance essentielle, to disclose every material circumstance.

revenant-bon [**revenants-bons** *pl.*] (profit éventuel) (*n.m.*), casual profit ; unexpected gain ; perquisite :
les revenants-bons d'un marché, the unexpected profits resulting from a bargain.
les revenants-bons d'une charge, the perquisites of an office.

revenant-bon (boni) (*n.m.*), surplus ; unexpended balance.

revendable (*adj.*), resalable.

revendeur, -euse (pers.) (*n.*), reseller.

revendicable (*adj.*), claimable.

revendicateur (pers.) (*n.m.*), claimant ; claimer.

revendication (*n.f.*), claiming ; claim.

revendiquer (*v.t.*), to claim ; to lay claim to :

revendiquer un droit, to claim, to lay claim to, a right.

revendre (vendre ce qu'on a acheté) (*v.t. & v.i.*), to resell ; to sell again ; to sell out :
simples intermédiaires qui achètent pour revendre (*m.pl.*), mere intermediaries (*or* middlemen) who buy to resell (*or* to sell again).
revendre une chose plus cher qu'elle n'a coûté, to resell a thing at a higher price than it cost.
revendre avec bénéfice, to.resell, to sell again, to sell out, at a profit.
l'acheteur revend les titres qu'il ne peut pas lever et le vendeur rachète les titres qu'il ne peut livrer (*m.*), the buyer sells out the stock he cannot take up and the seller buys back the stock he cannot deliver.
saisir un cours favorable pour revendre, to take advantage of a favourable price to sell out.
Note :—An English stockbroker would not use the expression to *sell out* in this sense ; he would say *to sell* simply. With him *to sell out* is the opposing term to *to buy in* (*racheter*, *exécuter*). Outside the Stock Exchange, however, *to sell out*, meaning to *dispose of wholly or entirely*, is correct English.

revendre (vendre de nouveau) (*v.t.*), to resell :
revendre plusieurs fois le même objet, to resell the same article several times over.

revendre (exécution) (Bourse de valeurs) (*v.t.*) (opp. à *racheter*), to sell out ; to sell out against : [Cf. **exécuter** (Bourse).]
revendre des titres, des valeurs, to sell out stock, securities.
revendre un acheteur, to sell out against a buyer.

revendre (exécution) (Bourse de marchandises) (*v.t.*) (opp. à *racheter*), to resell ; to sell against :
revendre des marchandises, to resell goods.
revendre un défaillant, to sell against a defaulter.

revenir (coûter) (*v.i.*), to come to ; to cost :
achat qui revient à tant (*m.*), purchase which comes to so much.

revente (*n.f.*), resale ; selling out :
revente d'un fonds de commerce, resale of a business.

revente (exécution) (Bourse de valeurs) (*n.f.*) (opp. à *rachat*), selling out ; selling out against : [Cf. **exécution** (Bourse).]
revente des titres, des valeurs, selling out stock, securities.
revente d'un acheteur, selling out against a buyer.

revente (exécution) (Bourse de marchandises) (*n.f.*) (opp. à *rachat*), resale ; selling against. (See examples under verb.)

revenu (*s'emploie souvent au pl.*) (*n.m.*), revenue ; income :
revenu de portefeuille-titres, income on investments.
revenu imposable, taxable income ; assessable revenue.

revenu viager, income for life; life income.

revenus de l'État ou revenus publics, government revenue; public revenue.

revenus fixes (*Abrév.:* r.f.), income from fixed yield investments.

revenus fixes avec lots, income from prize bonds (obligations à lots).

revenus variables (*Abrév.:* rev. var.), income from variable yield investments.

revenus temporaires, income from temporary investments.

réversion (Dr.) (*n.f.*), reversion:
rentrer dans un bien par réversion, to regain possession of a property by reversion.

revêtir d'une signature, to sign:
nous vous prions de nous retourner l'accusé de réception ci-joint, revêtu de votre signature, please sign and return the enclosed acknowledgment.

être revêtu (-e) de, to contain; to bear:
effets revêtus de signatures de premier ordre (*m.pl.*), bills containing first class signatures.
chèque revêtu de la mention non négociable (*m.*), cheque bearing (*or* containing) the words not negotiable.

revirement (*n.m.*), change; turn:
revirement en hausse (Bourse), change, turn, for the better:
si le commencement de la huitaine a été mauvais, il y a fréquemment un revirement en hausse pour les derniers jours de la semaine, if the beginning of the week has been bad, there is frequently a change (*or* turn) for the better towards the end of the week.
revirement en baisse, change, turn, for the worse.

revirement de fonds *ou* **revirement de deniers** *ou* **simplement revirement** (*n.m.*), making over a debt.

reviser *ou* **réviser** (*v.t.*), to revise:
reviser un tarif, to revise a tariff.

révocable (*adj.*), revocable:
procuration révocable (*f.*), revocable procuration.

révocation (*n.f.*), revocation:
révocation d'un testament, revocation of a will.

révoquer (*v.t.*), to revoke:
révoquer une donation, to revoke a grant.

rhodésiennes (*n.f.pl.*) *ou* **valeurs rhodésiennes** (*f.pl.*), Rhodesians; Rhodesian shares.

richard, -e (pers.) (*n.*), rich man (woman); very rich person; moneyed man (woman); capitalist.

riche (*adj.*), rich; wealthy:
un riche propriétaire, a rich property owner; a wealthy landlord.
un pays riche en forêts, a country rich in forests.

riche (pers.) (*n.m.*), rich person; rich man.

les riches (*m.pl.*), the rich; rich people:
les banques anglaises ne prêtent qu'aux riches (*f.pl.*), English banks only lend to rich people.

richement (*adv.*), richly.

richesse (*n.f.*) *ou* **richesses** (*n.f.pl.*), riches; wealth:

la richesse d'un État, the wealth of a State.

amasser d'immenses richesses, to amass immense riches (*or* wealth).

la vigne constitue la principale richesse du Portugal, the vine constitutes Portugal's chief wealth.

rien n'étant plus à l'ordre du jour, la séance est levée, there being no further business before the meeting, the sitting was closed; there being no other business, the meeting was closed.

ripage (désarrimage) (*n.m.*), shifting (of cargo).

riper (se désarrimer) (*v.i.*), to shift.

risque (aléa; hasard; danger; péril) (*n.m.*), risk; adventure:
à quoi bon courir des risques, lorsqu'on peut opérer à coup sûr? why run risks, when one can operate safely?
les risques inhérents aux pièces créées au porteur, the risks inherent in documents made to bearer.
aux risques du navire, at ship's risk.
aux risques et périls (*ou simplement* aux risques) de l'expéditeur, du destinataire, at sender's (*or* consignor's), at receiver's (*or* consignee's) risk.
aux risques et périls des chargeurs, des propriétaires de la marchandise, ou des consignataires, at the risk of the shippers, of the owners of the goods, or of the consignees.

risque (dangers auxquels sont exposés les choses assurées; événement fortuit ou de force majeure) (*n.m.*), risk:
les risques inséparables d'une expédition maritime, the risks inseparable from a marine adventure.
maison qui est assurée contre le risque d'incendie (*f.*), house which is insured against the risk of fire.
risque à temps *ou* risque à terme, time risk.
risque d'abordage *ou* risque de collision, collision risk; running down risk.
risque d'allèges, craft risk; risk of craft; lighterage risk:
tous risques d'allèges pour transport immédiat de terre à bord et de bord à terre, all risks of craft to and from the vessel.
risque d'ennemis, enemy risk.
risque d'escales, calls risk.
risque d'explosion, explosion risk.
risque d'hiver, winter risk.
risque d'incendie *ou* risque de feu, fire risk.
risque de baraterie, barratry risk.
risque de casse, breakage risk; risk of breakage.
risque de chargement, loading risk.
risque de déchargement, unloading risk.
risque de déviation, deviation risk.
risque de drômes, raft risk.
risque de glaces, ice risk.
risque de guerre, war risk.
risque de paix, peace risk.
risque de perte ou d'endommagement par exposition aux intempéries, risk of loss or damage by exposure to weather.
risque de pontée, deck cargo risk.

risque de port, port risk.
risque de port sur corps, hull port risk.
risque de quarantaine, quarantine risk.
risque de séjour à terre, shore risk.
risque de séjour à terre en cours normal
d'expédition, risk whilst on quays, wharves,
or in sheds during the ordinary course of
transit.
risque de séjour sur allèges, risk of storage in
craft.
risque de transbordement, transhipment risk.
risque de vol, theft risk.
risque du recours de tiers, third party risk.
risque locatif, tenant's third party risk.
risque maritime *ou* risque de mer,   marine
risk ; maritime risk ; sea risk.
risques mixtes maritimes et terrestres, mixed
sea and land risks.
risque terrestre *ou* risque de terre, land risk ;
non marine risk.
risque (objet de l'assurance ; aliment ; valeur)
(*n.m.*), risk ; interest ; value :
l'assurance, étant un contrat d'indemnité,
n'est valable que s'il existe un risque (*f.*),
insurance, being a contract of indemnity, is
valid only if there is a risk.
la part pour laquelle l'assureur s'engage dans
le risque assuré, the share for which the
insurer binds himself in the risk (*or* interest)
(*or* value) insured.
chaque risque fera l'objet d'une police distincte,
each risk (*or* interest) to form the subject of
a separate policy.
risque (personne ou chose exposée à un sinistre)
(*n.m.*), risk :
personne qui, maison qui, est un bon risque (*f.*),
person who, house which, is a good risk.
risqué, -e (*adj.*), risky.
risquer (*v.t.*), to risk ; to venture :
risquer sa fortune, to risk one's fortune.
ristournable (*adj.*), returnable :
prime ristournable à l'assuré (*f.*), premium
returnable to the insured.
ristourne *ou* **ristorne** (restitution) (*n.f.*), return ;
refund ; rebate ; allowance :
ristourne d'une somme payée en trop, return of
an amount overpaid.
ristourne de capital, return of capital.
ristourne de fret, rebate of freight ; freight rebate.
ristourne de prime (Assce), return of premium.
si l'effet est réclamé, la banque ne fait pas de
ristourne des agios qu'elle a prélevés, if the
bill is claimed back, the bank makes no
return (*or* refund) of the discount charges
which it has drawn.
banquier qui a, comme bénéfice, la ristourne que
fait l'agent sur le tarif officiel des courtages
(*m.*), banker who has, as profit, the allowance
(*or* the rebate) which the broker makes on the
official commission rates.
ristourne *ou* **ristorne** (Comptab.) (*n.f.*), transfer ;
writing back.
ristourner *ou* **ristorner** (restituer) (*v.t.*), to return ;
to refund :
ristourner l'excédent, to return, to refund, the
excess.

ristourner *ou* **ristorner** (Comptab.) (*v.t.*), to transfer ; to write back :
ristourner partie d'un débit, to transfer, to
write back, part of a debit.
Note :—*ristourner* is to transfer or write back
part of, opposed to *extourner*, to write back
the whole of ; to contra ; to reverse.
rivage (de la mer, d'un lac, d'un fleuve) (*n.m.*),
shore, beach (of the sea, of a lake, of a
river).
rive (*n.f.*), bank ; shore :
rive d'un fleuve, bank, shore, of a river.
quais convenablement aménagés sur les deux
rives du fleuve (*m.pl.*), wharves conveniently
arranged (*or* laid out) on both banks of the
river.
la rive droite, la rive gauche, d'un fleuve, the
right bank, the left bank, of a river.
rive de la mer, seashore.
rivière (*n.f.*), river.
robinet ouvert (*argot financier*) (*m.*), on tap.
rôle (liste) (*n.m.*), list ; bill :
rôle d'appointements, salaries list ; list of
salaries.
rôle d'équipage *ou* rôle de l'équipage *ou* rôle
d'armement, crew list ; list of the crew ;
shipping articles ; ship's articles ; articles.
rôle de désarmement, portage bill.
à tour de rôle, in turn ; in (*or* by) rotation :
sortir à tour de rôle, to retire in (*or* by)
rotation.
rôle de cotisation *ou* *simplement* **rôle** (*n.m.*) (Impôts
cédulaires), assessment book :
les rôles sont établis par le contrôleur d'après
les déclarations faites par les intéressés,
après vérification et rectification s'il y a lieu,
the assessment books are made out by the
inspector in accordance with the returns made
by the parties concerned, after examination
and amendment if necessary.
rompre (*v.t.*), to break ; to break up ; to cut off ;
to cancel :
rompre un marché, to break an agreement.
rompre charge, to break bulk :
réexpédition des wagons sans rompre charge
(*f.*), reforwarding of wagons without
breaking bulk.
rompre un voyage, to break up a voyage.
rompre un voyage avant le départ du vaisseau,
to cancel a booking before departure of the
vessel.
rompre la connexion au cours d'une conversation
(Téléph.), to cut off connection during a
conversation.
rompu (*n.m.*), fraction (incomplete unit of a
share or of stock) :
les rompus se négocient en bourse, fractions
are dealt in on the stock exchange.
rond, -e (*adj.*), round :
les billets de banque ne sont émis que pour des
sommes rondes, dites coupures (*m.pl.*),
bank notes are only issued in round sums,
called denominations.
une somme ronde de mille francs, a round sum
of a thousand francs.
rouage (*fig.*) (*n.m.*), machinery :

le rouage de la vie commerciale, the machinery of commercial life.

roulage (*n.m.*), haulage ; hauling.

roulant, -e (en parlant de capitaux) (*adj.*), circulating ; floating :
capitaux roulants (*m.pl.*), circulating capital ; circulating assets ; floating capital (*or* assets) ; revenue assets.

rouleau (de papiers) (*n.m.*), roll (of papers).

roulement (succession de personnes qui se remplacent alternativement dans certaines fonctions) (*n.m.*), rotation :
roulement établi par le sort, rotation determined by lot.

roulement (de capital) (*n.m.*), turnover (of capital).

fonds de roulement (*m.*), working capital.

rouler (se dit d'un navire) (*v.i.*), to roll.

rouler (osciller ; varier) (*v.i.*), to fluctuate ; to vary :
un revenu qui roule, bon an mal an, entre 50 000 et 60 000 francs, an income which fluctuates (*or* varies), taking one year with another, between 50,000 and 60,000 francs.

rouler (abonder ; avoir une circulation active) (*v.i.*), to be plentiful ; to circulate freely :
l'argent roule en Amérique (*m.*), money circulates freely in America.
Cf. faire rouler des capitaux.

roulette (de timbres-poste) (*n.f.*), roll (of postage stamps).

roulis (*n.m.*) (opp. à *tangage*), rolling. See example under **désarrimer.**

route (voie de terre) (*n.f.*), road ; way.

route (direction suivie) (*n.f.*), route ; itinerary ; course ; way :
route aérienne, airway ; air route.
route commerciale, trade route.
route de terre, overland route ; land route.
faculté de se rendre dans tous les ports en dedans ou en dehors de la route ordinaire (*f.*), liberty to proceed to any ports in or out of the customary route.
par n'importe quelle route, by any route.
navire qui reprend sa route (*m.*), ship which resumes her course.

route (cheminement) (*n.f.*), transit ; voyage ; way ; journey ; route :
avaries de route (*f.pl.*), damage in transit.
marchandise avariée en cours de route (*f.*), goods damaged in course of transit (*or* damaged in transit) (*or* damaged in transitu).
prêt contracté par le capitaine en cours de route (*m.*), loan contracted by the master during the voyage.
reprendre sa route, to resume one's journey.

le steamer *X.* a fait escale à Périm le 31 (*date*), en route d'Anvers à Kobe, the steamer *X.* called at Perim 31 (*date*), en route from Antwerp to Kobe.
navire faisant route (*m.*), ship under way.

router (*v.t.*), to route.

routier, -ère (*adj.*), route ; road (*used as adjs*) :
carte routière (*f.*), route map ; road map.

rouvrir (*v.t.*), to reopen :
rouvrir un compte, to reopen an account.

Royaume-Uni de Grande-Bretagne et Irlande du Nord (*m.*), United Kingdom of Great Britain and Northern Ireland.

ruban (*n.m.*), ribbon ; riband :
ruban bleu, blue ribbon ; blue riband :
la lutte pour le ruban bleu de l'Atlantique (le ruban bleu est le symbole du record de la vitesse), the fight for the blue ribbon of the Atlantic (the blue ribbon is the symbol of the speed record).
ruban pour machines à écrire, typewriting ribbon (*or* riband) :
ruban à copier *ou* ruban copiant, copying ribbon.
ruban fixe, non copying ribbon ; record ribbon.

rubrique (*n.f.*), heading ; head ; section :
rubrique de journal, newspaper heading.
articles qui sont réunis sous la rubrique portefeuille (*m.pl.*), items which are lumped under the heading investments.
rubrique de la cote, section of the list (i.e., the quotation list of a Stock or other Exchange) :
pas de changements à la rubrique des étrangères, no change in the foreign section.

ruée (*n.f.*), rush ; run :
une ruée sur les valeurs minières, a rush (*or* a run) on mining shares.

ruine (*n.f.*), ruin.

ruiner (*v.t.*), to ruin.

se ruiner (*v.r.*), to ruin oneself :
se ruiner en spéculations hasardeuses, to ruin oneself in risky speculations.

rumeur (*n.f.*), rumour ; rumor :
démenti de rumeurs défavorables (*m.*), denial of unfavourable rumours.

rupture (*n.f.*), breakage ; breaking ; breaking up ; breaking off ; rupture :
rupture de communication (Téléph.), cut off.
rupture des objets fragiles, d'arbre, breakage of fragile articles, of shaft.
rupture de charge, breaking bulk.
rupture d'un voyage, breaking up of a voyage.
rupture de relations diplomatiques, rupture, breaking off, of diplomatic relations.

rural, -e, -aux (*adj.*), rural :
facteur rural (*m.*), rural postman.

S

S.O.S. (signal) (*m.*), S.O.S. :
   lancer un S.O.S., to send out an S.O.S.
sabordement *ou* **sabordage** (*n.m.*), scuttling.
saborder (*v.t.*), to scuttle :
   saborder un navire en feu, to scuttle a burning
   ship.
sac (*n.m.*), sack ; bag :
   un sac de sucre, de tant de francs, a bag of
   sugar, of so many francs.
   sac à dépêches (Poste), mail bag.
sacrifice (*n.m.*), sacrifice :
   sacrifice volontaire fait pour le salut commun
   du navire et du chargement,   voluntary
   sacrifice made for the common safety of the
   ship and cargo.
sacrifier (*v.t.*), to sacrifice :
   sacrifier une partie ou la totalité de la cargaison
   pour sauver le navire, to sacrifice a part or
   the whole of the cargo to save the ship.
   sacrifier ses titres, to sacrifice one's stocks
   (to sell them at a big loss).
sain, -e (*adj.*), sound :
   papier sain (effets de commerce) (*m.*), sound
   paper.
   une saine organisation comptable,   a sound
   system of bookkeeping.
   des valeurs saines et réalisables (*f.pl.*), sound
   and realizable securities.
   une monnaie saine, c'est-à-dire non dépréciée
   par rapport à l'or, a sound currency, that is
   to say, undepreciated in relation to gold.
   la valeur saine de la propriété au moment du
   sinistre (Assce),   the sound value of the
   property at the time of the accident.
   la différence entre la valeur saine et la valeur
   assurée du navire, the difference between
   the vessel's sound and insured values.
   conduire les voyageurs sains et saufs à
   destination, to carry the passengers safe
   and sound to destination.
saisie (*n.f.*), seizure :
   saisie d'un navire, de marchandises non
   déclarées à la douane, seizure of a ship, of
   goods not declared to the customs.
   saisie judiciaire, seizure under legal process.
saisir (opérer la saisie de) (*v.t.*), to seize :
   navire qui est saisi et vendu (*m.*), ship which is
   seized and sold.
saisir (ne pas laisser échapper) (*v.t.*), to take
   advantage of ; to avail oneself of :
   saisir un cours favorable pour revendre, to
   take advantage of a favourable price to
   sell out.
salaire (*n.m.*), wages ; wage ; pay :
   salaire d'un ouvrier, wages, pay, of a workman.
   salaires des gens de mer, seamen's wages.
salarié, -e (*adj.*), salaried ; paid :
   un secrétaire salarié,   a salaried (*or* a paid)
   secretary.
salarié, -e (pers.) (*n.*),   wage earner ; salaried
   man ; salaried woman.

salle (*n.f.*), room ; hall ; office :
   salle d'attente (Ch. de f.), waiting room.
   salle de coffres-forts, strong room.
   salle de liquidation (Bourse de valeurs), settling
   room.
   salle de ventes publiques, public sale room.
   salle des bagages (Ch. de f.), luggage office.
   salle des dactylographes, typewriters' room.
   salle des pas perdus (Ch. de f.), booking hall.
salon d'attente (d'un bureau commercial) (*m.*),
   waiting room.
Salon de l'Automobile (*m.*),   Motor Show.
salut (*n.m.*), safety :
   opérer un jet pour le salut commun, to make
   a jettison for the common safety.
sanction (*n.f.*), sanction ; approbation ; approval.
sanctionner (*v.t.*),   to sanction ; to approve :
   usage sanctionné par la pratique (*m.*),   custom
   sanctioned by practice.
   sanctionner les actes d'un mandataire,   to
   approve the acts of an agent.
sans affaires (Bourse), no dealings ; idle :
   l'action X. est sans affaires à 6,   X. shares are
   idle at 6 francs.
sans arrêt (Ch. de f., etc.), non stop :
   trajet sans arrêt (*m.*), non stop journey.
sans avis *ou* **sans autre avis** (mention sur une
   lettre de change) (opp. à *suivant avis*),
   without advice ; without other advice.
sans cotation (Bourse), no quotation.
sans date, without day ; sine die ; undated :
   s'ajourner sans date, to adjourn without day
   (*or* sine die).
   lettre sans date (*f.*), undated letter.
sans engagement de dates (Navig.) (Abrév. :
   s.e.d.d.), all sailings subject to change without notice ; all sailings subject to change
   with or without notice.
sans fil (Télégr.), wireless :
   acheminement par sans fil (*m.*) (opp. à
   acheminement par fil), routing by wireless.
sans frais (Abrév. : **S.F.**) *ou* **retour sans frais** *ou*
   sans compte de retour *ou* **sans protêt** (effets
   de commerce), no noting ; incur no expenses ;
   notarial charges not to be incurred ; protest
   waived in case of dishonour ; sans frais ;
   retour sans frais.
sans garantie (à découvert), unsecured :
   créance sans garantie (*f.*), unsecured debt.
sans garantie des marques, de la casse (clause de
   connaissement),   ship not responsible for
   marks, for breakages.
sans nouvelles *ou* **perdu sans nouvelles** (en parlant
   d'un navire), missing :
   navire sans nouvelles *ou* navire perdu sans
   nouvelles (*m.*), missing ship.
   navire réputé perdu sans nouvelles (*m.*), ship
   deemed to be missing.
   perte du navire sans nouvelles (*f.*), loss of the
   ship as missing.
sans préjudice, without prejudice. See example
   under **préjudice.**

sans profession, no occupation; gentleman:
Paul X., sans profession, demeurant à . . .,
Paul X., no occupation (or Paul X., gentleman) residing at . . .

sans reprise (Relocation) (Abrév.: **ss repr.**), no premium. See example under **reprise.**

sans transaction (Bourse), no dealings.

sans-travail (pers.) (*n.m.pl.*), unemployed.

sans valeur (Abrév.: **s.v.**), valueless; worthless:
titres sans valeur (*m.pl.*), valueless securities; worthless stocks.
c. 2 à 7 s.v. (cote de la bourse), coupons 2 to 7 valueless.

sans valeur déclarée (Poste), uninsured:
colis sans valeur déclarée (*m.*), uninsured parcel.

sans voie (Télégr.), unrouted:
télégramme sans voie (*m.*), unrouted telegram.

satisfaire (*v.t.*) *ou* **satisfaire à,** to satisfy:
satisfaire ses créanciers, to satisfy one's creditors.
satisfaire aux besoins de quelqu'un, to satisfy someone's needs.

satisfaisant, -e (*adj.*), satisfactory:
réponse satisfaisante (*f.*), satisfactory reply.

sauf, sauve (*adj.*), safe. See example under **sain, -e.**

sauf bonne fin (Abrév.: **s.b.f.**) *ou* **sauf encaissement** (Banq.), under reserve; under usual reserves:
le montant du chèque est porté à votre crédit sauf bonne fin (*ou* sauf encaissement), the amount of the cheque is passed to your credit under reserve (*or* under usual reserves).

sauf-conduit [**sauf-conduits** *pl.*] (*n.m.*), safe-conduct.

sauf convention (*ou* stipulation) **contraire,** unless otherwise agreed.

sauf dispositions contraires des statuts, save as otherwise provided in the articles.

sauf erreur ou omission (Abrév.: **S.E. ou O.** *ou* **S.E.O.**), errors and omissions excepted.

sauf imprévu (Abrév.: **s.i.**), unless prevented by unforeseen circumstances; circumstances permitting.

sauf indication contraire expresse dans les présentes, unless expressly otherwise stated herein.

sauf livraison (Bourse) (Abrév.: **s.l.**), against delivery.

sauf mieux (Bourse), or better. See example under **mieux.**

saut (*n.m.*), jump; spurt.

sauter (*v.i.*), to jump; to spurt:
l'action X. saute de 1 400 à 1 512 1/2, X. shares jumped (*or* spurted) from 1,400 to 1,512 fr. 50 c.

sauvegarde (*n.f.*), safeguard; safeguarding; protection:
la sauvegarde de marchandises exposées aux périls d'une expédition maritime, the safeguarding of goods exposed to the perils of a marine adventure.
sauvegarde d'industries, safeguarding of industries.

sauvegarder (*v.t.*), to safeguard; to protect:
sauvegarder la vie des matelots et des passagers, les intérêts des actionnaires, to safeguard, to protect, the lives of the sailors and passengers, the interests of the shareholders.

sauver (*v.t.*), to save; to salve; to salvage:
sauver le navire d'un péril imminent, to save the ship from an imminent peril.
navire qui s'écarte de sa route pour sauver des vies humaines ou des biens (*m.*), ship which deviates from her course to save lives or property.
l'assuré doit faire tout son possible pour sauver la chose assurée (*m.*), the insured must do his utmost to save the property insured.
la valeur des biens sauvés, the value of the salved (*or* salvaged) property.

sauvetage (*n.m.*), saving; salvage:
sauvetage des personnes en cas de sinistre, saving persons in case of disaster.
sauvetage des épaves, salvage of wreck.
le sauvetage a pour objet, une fois le navire a fait naufrage ou a échoué, de le sauver ainsi que la cargaison, ou ce qui reste de l'un ou de l'autre, the purpose of salvage is, once the ship is wrecked or has stranded, to salve her along with the cargo, or whatever remains of one or the other.

sauveteur (pers.) (*n.m.*), salvor; salver; salvager.

savoir faisons par ces présentes (Dr.), know all men by these presents.

sceau (*n.m.*), seal:
sceau de la douane, customs seal.

scellage (*n.m.*), sealing.

sceller (*v.t.*), to seal; to seal up:
sceller un acte, to seal a deed.
sceller une lettre, to seal, to seal up, a letter.
sceller une lettre avec un cachet de cire, to seal a letter with a wax seal.
colis scellés des plombs de douane (*m.pl.*), packages sealed with customs plombs.

schelling (monnaie anglaise) (*n.m.*) (Abrév.: **sh.**), shilling.

scindement (*n.m.*), division; splitting.

scinder (*v.t.*), to divide; to split.
se scinder (*v.r.*), to be divided; to be split.

script (*n.m.*), scrip; deferred interest certificate.

scrutateur (pers.) (*n.m.*), scrutineer.

scrutin (*n.m.*), ballot; balloting; poll:
l'élection est faite à la majorité des suffrages et au scrutin secret (*f.*), the election is made by a majority of votes and at a secret ballot.

scrutiner (*v.i.*), to ballot.

séance (réunion) (*n.f.*), sitting; meeting; session:
ouvrir la séance, to open the meeting (*or* the sitting).
le procès-verbal de la dernière séance est lu et adopté, the minutes of the last meeting were read and confirmed.
séance de bourse, stock exchange session.

sec, sèche (*adj.*), dry:
marchandises sèches (*f.pl.*) (opp. à *marchandises liquides*), dry goods.

sec (être à) (n'avoir plus d'argent), to be dry:
je suis tout à fait à sec, I am quite dry.

second, -e (*adj.*) (Abrév.: **2e**), second; 2nd:
 billet de seconde (*ou* de 2e) classe (*m.*), second
 (*or* 2nd) class ticket.
second officier *ou simplement* **second** (*n.m.*) (pers.)
 (Navig.), mate.
seconde de change (*f.*), second of exchange. See
 première de change for example.
secourir (*v.t.*), to help; to aid; to assist; to
 rescue; to relieve:
 secourir un navire en détresse, to assist a vessel
 in distress.
secours (*n.m.*), help; aid; assistance; rescue;
 relief:
 banque qui vient au secours du marché (*f.*),
 bank which comes to the rescue of the
 market.
 caisse de secours (*f.*), relief fund.
secret, -ète (*adj.*), secret:
 langage secret (Télégr.) (*m.*), secret language.
secret (*n.m.*), secret; secrecy:
 les agents de change sont tenus au secret
 professionnel et ne doivent pas dévoiler les
 noms des parties contractantes (*m.pl.*),
 stockbrokers are bound to professional
 secrecy and may not disclose the names of
 the contracting parties.
secrétaire (pers.) (*n.m.*), secretary:
 secrétaire du conseil d'administration, secretary
 to the board of directors.
 secrétaire adjoint, assistant secretary.
 secrétaire femme, lady secretary.
 secrétaire particulier, private secretary.
secrétariat (fonction de secrétaire) (*n.m.*),
 secretaryship.
secrétariat (bureau du secrétaire) (*n.m.*),
 secretary's office:
 siège social et secrétariat (*suivi d'une adresse*),
 secretary and offices (*followed by an address*).
sécurité (*n.f.*), security; safety:
 compagnie qui donne à ses assurés toute la
 sécurité sur laquelle ils sont en droit de
 compter (*f.*), company which affords to its
 insured all the security they are entitled to
 expect.
 la sécurité de ses fonds, the safety of one's
 money.
 danger de nature à compromettre la sécurité
 du navire, des personnes à bord du navire
 (*m.*), danger of a nature to imperil the safety
 of the ship, of the persons on board the ship.
seing (*n.m.*), sign manual; signature (on a deed,
 or the like).
seing privé (*m.*), private seal:
 acte sous seing privé (*m.*), deed under private
 seal.
séjour (*n.m.*), stay; lying:
 pendant le séjour du navire dans les docks,
 dans un port de relâche, during the stay of
 the ship in the docks, in a port of refuge;
 while the ship is in dock, in a port of distress.
 séjour forcé dans un port, compulsory stay in
 a port.
 séjour à terre. *See* risque de séjour à terre.
 séjour sur allèges. *See* risque de séjour sur
 allèges.
 taxe de séjour (*f.*), visitors' tax.

séjourner (*v.i.*), to stay; to lie:
 personnes séjournant temporairement en France
 (*f.pl.*), persons staying temporarily in
 France.
 avec faculté de toucher et séjourner à tous
 ports ou lieux quelconques, with liberty to
 touch and stay at any ports or places whatsoever.
 navire qui séjourne en rade (*m.*), vessel which
 lies (*or* is lying) in a roadstead (*or* in the roads).
sélection (*n.f.*), selection.
sélectionné, -e (*adj.*), selected:
 placements sélectionnés (*m.pl.*), selected
 investments.
selon le cas, as the case may be; according to
 circumstances.
semaine (*n.f.*), week.
semestre (espace de six mois) (*n.m.*), half year;
 half; six months:
 premier semestre *ou* semestre de janvier *ou*
 semestre d'hiver, first half year; first half;
 first six months (six months commencing
 January 1):
 le premier semestre de l'intérêt, the first six
 months' interest.
 second semestre *ou* deuxième semestre *ou*
 semestre de juillet *ou* semestre d'été, second
 half year; second half; second six months
 (six months commencing July 1).
semestre (rente, traitement qui se paye tous les
 six mois) (*n.m.*), half year's (*or* half yearly)
 (*or* six months') income, dividend, interest,
 drawings, salary, payment, instalment, or
 the like:
 toucher son semestre, to draw one's half year's
 pay; to receive one's half yearly dividend.
 les annuités sont payables par semestre: tout
 semestre non payé à l'échéance porte intérêt
 de plein droit, the annuities are payable half
 yearly: every half yearly instalment not
 paid at due date bears interest of right.
 semestre sur £1 000 à 5 0/0, half year's (*or*
 six months') interest on £1,000 at 5%.
semestriel, -elle (*adj.*), half yearly; semiannual:
 assemblée semestrielle (*f.*), half yearly meeting.
semestriellement (*adv.*) *ou* **par semestre**, half
 yearly; semiannually:
 intérêt payé semestriellement (*ou* par semestre)
 (*m.*), interest paid half yearly.
sensible (*adj.*), appreciable:
 une sensible augmentation de prix, an appreciable rise in price.
sentence arbitrale *ou* **sentence d'arbitrage** (*f.*),
 arbitration award.
 sentence partielle, partial award.
séparé, -e (*adj.*), separate; distinct:
 chaque expédition sera considérée comme
 faisant l'objet d'un contrat séparé (*f.*),
 each shipment to be regarded as a separate
 contract.
séquestration (*n.f.*), sequestration.
série (*n.f.*) (Abrév.: **srie**), series; set:
 une nouvelle série d'actions, a new series of
 shares.
 valeurs remboursables par séries (*f.pl.*),
 securities redeemable in series.

le capitaine a la faculté de livrer les marchandises par séries, the master has the option of delivering the goods in series.

chaque série se règle séparément et c'est sur chaque série que se feront le calcul et l'application de la franchise, each series is adjusted separately and it is upon each series that the calculation and application of the franchise will be made.

les marchandises chargées en vrac ne sont pas divisées en séries, goods shipped in bulk are not divided into series.

série pleine (marchandises), full series.

série de solde (marchandises), tail series.

série complète de connaissements, full set of bills of lading.

serment (*n.m.*), oath :
prêter serment devant un tribunal, to take oath, to be sworn, before a court.
sous serment, on oath.

serre-notes [serre-notes *pl.*] (*n.m.*), letter clip.

serré, -e (Fin.) (*adj.*) (opp. à *facile*), tight :
l'escompte ou l'argent est dit serré lorsque par suite des besoins en capitaux du marché, le taux de l'escompte privé se rapproche du taux officiel de l'escompte (*m.*), discount or money is said to be tight when owing to the market's requirements of money, the market rate of discount approximates to the bank rate of discount. Cf. **facile** and **nominal.**

serrer (se) (*v.r.*), to tighten :
l'escompte se serre à l'approche des grands emprunts (*m.*), discount tightens on the approach of heavy borrowing.

service (assistance ; bon office) (*n.m.*), service :
offrir ses services, to offer one's services.
services rendus, services rendered.
services de sauvetage, salvage services.

service (fonctionnement organisé) (*n.m.*), service ; booking :
service accéléré, accelerated service.
service aérien, air service.
service aérien de messageries, air parcel service.
service automobile de voyageurs, motor passenger service.
service circulant toute l'année, all the year round service.
services contractuels (transports à forfait), through bookings.
service de camionnage, cartage service (of goods sent or received by goods train).
service de factage, cartage service (of parcels or other merchandise sent or received by passenger train) ; parcels cartage service.
service de chemins de fer *ou* service ferroviaire, railway service.
service de la messagerie *ou* service de (*ou* des) messageries, parcels service ; parcel service :
service ferroviaire de messageries *ou* service de messageries par voie ferrée, railway parcels service.
service de marchandises, goods service ; freight service.
service de passagers, passenger service.

service de réexpédition (Ch. de f.), delivery outside prescribed boundaries.
service de renseignements (Téléph.), directory enquiry.
service de vapeurs de charge, cargo service.
service de voyageurs, passenger service.
service des colis postaux, parcel post.
  Note :—In most parts of France, the parcel post is run by the railway and shipping companies on behalf of the Government. In England, it is run by the Government post office.
service des douanes *ou* service douanier, customs service.
service des postes *ou* service postal, postal service ; mail service.
service express *ou* service rapide (Ch. de f. ou Navig.), express service.
service (ensemble d'un personnel) (*n.m.*), department ; service ; establishment ; staff :
chef du service de la publicité (*m.*), manager of the advertising department.
service actif (Douanes, etc.), outdoor establishment ; outdoor staff.
service de l'exploitation (Ch. de f.), traffic department.
service de la caisse (*m.*) *ou simplement* caisse (*n.f.*), cash department.
service de la comptabilité (*m.*) *ou simplement* comptabilité (*n.f.*), accounts department.
service de la voie et des bâtiments (Ch. de f.), way and works department.
service des titres (*m.*) *ou simplement* titres (*n.m.pl.*) (Banq.), security department ; stock department.
service du contentieux (*m.*) *ou simplement* contentieux (*n.m.*), solicitor's department ; law department.
service du matériel et traction (Ch. de f.), rolling stock and locomotive department.
service du portefeuille *ou* service du portefeuille-effets *ou simplement* portefeuille (*n.m.*) (Banq.), bills department :
le chef du service du portefeuille *ou* le chef du portefeuille, the head of the bills department.
service sédentaire, indoor establishment ; clerical staff.
service d'intérêt *ou simplement* **service** (*n.m.*), service ; payment of interest :
emprunts dont le service d'intérêt est garanti par l'État (*m.pl.*), loans on which the payment of interest (or loans the service of which) is guaranteed by the Government.
somme nécessaire au service de l'emprunt (*f.*), amount required for the service of the loan ; amount required for the payment of (or sum required to pay) the interest on the loan.
servir (payer les intérêts sur) (*v.t.*), to serve ; to pay the interest on ; to pay :
somme suffisante pour servir les obligations (*f.*), sum sufficient to serve (or to pay the interest on) the bonds.
l'intérêt servi à l'obligataire (*m.*), the interest paid to the bondholder.

servir de (se), to use; to make use of :
comment il faut se servir du téléphone, how to use the telephone.
beaucoup de personnes médisent du téléphone parce qu'elles ne savent pas bien s'en servir, many people speak ill of the telephone because they do not know how to use it properly.

serviteur (pers.) (*n.m.*), servant.

seul propriétaire (*m.*), **seule propriétaire** (*f.*), sole owner; sole proprietor.

seule de change (*f.*), sola of exchange; sole of exchange.

shilling (monnaie anglaise) (*n.m.*) (Abrév.: **sh.**), shilling.

si le temps le permet, weather permitting.

siège (*n.m.*) *ou* **siège social**, offices; office; registered office; registered office of the company :
siège social et secrétariat (*suivi d'une adresse*), secretary and offices (*followed by an address*).
une société sans siège (*ou* sans siège social), a company without a registered office.
le siège social est établi à . . . (status d'une société), the registered office of the company will be situated in . . . (memorandum of association of a company).
siège principal *ou simplement* siège *ou* siège social (opp. à *succursale*), head office :
la Banque X. a six succursales (son siège [*ou* son siège social] est à Paris), the X. Bank has six branches (its head office is in Paris).

siéger (*v.i.*), to sit :
le tribunal siège toute l'année, the tribunal sits all the year round.

signal de manœuvre (bourdonnement continu) (Téléph. automatique) (*m.*), dialling tone (continuous purring sound).

signal distinctif du code international des signaux (Navig.) (*m.*), call sign.

signal lumineux (Publicité) (*m.*), illuminated sign.

signal pas libre (Téléph.) (*m.*), engaged tone.

signataire (pers.) (*n.m.* ou *f.*), signatory; signatary; signer :
signataire d'un contrat, signer of, signatory to, a contract.

signature (action) (*n.f.*), signing :
la signature du contrat aura lieu demain, the signing of the contract will take place to-morrow.

signature (autographe) (*n.f.*), signature :
faire légaliser une signature, to legalize a signature.

signer (*v.t.*), to sign :
signer une lettre, to sign a letter.
connaissement signé du capitaine (*m.*), bill of lading signed by the master.
personnes ayant pouvoir de signer pour la société (*f.pl.*), persons having power to sign for the company.
notre sieur X. signera : . . ., Mr. X. will sign : . . .
Note :—In France, when an official of a Company, Bank, or other institution, signs a letter, or other document, his description precedes his signature, thus :—

Le Président,
A. B.
L'Administrateur délégué,
C. D.
Un Administrateur,
E. F.
Le Directeur,
G. H.
Le Secrétaire,
I. J.
Le Chef de Bureau,
K. L.

In England, the reverse is the case, thus :—
A. B.,
Chairman.
C. D.,
Managing Director.
E. F.,
Director.
G. H.,
Manager.
I. J.,
Secretary.
K. L.,
Chief Clerk.

signer à, to witness; to witness the signature on :
signer à une convention, to witness an agreement.

se signer (*v.r.*), to be signed :
document qui doit se signer (*m.*), document which ought to be signed.

silo (*n.m.*), silo.

silver-point [silver-points *pl.*] (*n.m.*), silver point.

simple tradition. See under **tradition.**

simulé, -e (Com.) (*adj.*), pro forma :
facture simulée (*f.*), pro forma invoice.

sine die, sine die; without day :
s'ajourner sine die, to adjourn sine die; to adjourn without day.

sinistre (*n.m.*), disaster; casualty; accident; wreck; loss; claim :
la réception de la nouvelle du sinistre (Assce), the receipt of news of the casualty (*or* accident) (*or* loss) (*or* claim).
sinistre qui a causé une perte, casualty which has caused a loss.
fret remboursable en cas de sinistre (*m.*), freight repayable in case of loss.
le règlement de petits sinistres (Assce), the settlement of small losses (*or* claims).
preuve de sinistre (Assce) (*f.*), proof of loss.
sinistre majeure, major casualty :
sinistre majeure entraînant la perte totale du navire, major casualty involving the total loss of the ship.
sinistre partiel, partial loss :
sinistre total, total loss :
le mode de règlement des sinistres partiels ou totaux (Assce mar.), the method of adjustment of partial or total losses.

sinistré, -e (*adj.*), wrecked; lost; burnt; damaged :

navire sinistré (naufragé) (*m.*), wrecked ship.

maison sinistrée (incendiée) (*f.*), burnt house.

situation (état où se trouve une caisse, etc.) (*n.f.*), position :

examiner la situation de la caisse, to examine the cash position.

le carnet de compte donne la situation en banque du client, the pass book shows the customer's position at the bank.

le taux des reports est généralement le baromètre de la situation de place, the contango rate is generally the barometer of the market position.

situation financière bien assise, strong financial position.

situation (état écrit ou imprimé) (*n.f.*), statement ; return :

situation de la banque, bank return ; bank statement.

situation de trésorerie, financial statement ; finance statement ; statement of finances.

slogan (formule synthétique heureuse, de style lapidaire) (*n.m.*), slogan.

smogler (*v.i.*), to smuggle.

social, -e, -aux (*adj.*), corporate ; of or relating to a firm *or* partnership *or* company, *often translatable by*: of a firm ; of the firm ; the firm's ; of a partnership ; of a company ; of the company ; the company's :

cachet social (*m.*), corporate seal.

les actionnaires, en principe, sont maîtres de la marche dans la société anonyme ; en pratique, leur action sociale est assez limitée (*m.pl.*), the shareholders, in principle, are the controlling body in a public company ; in practice, their corporate action is somewhat limited.

la raison sociale est X. & Cie, the name of the firm (*or* the firm's name) is X. & Co.

année sociale (*f.*) *ou* exercice social (*m.*) (d'une société par actions), company's year ; company's trading year (*or* trading period) (*or* accounting period).

créanciers sociaux (d'une société par actions) (*m.pl.*), creditors of the company ; company's creditors.

Cf. capital social *and* **siège social.**

Note :—As in the case of the noun *société*, which means either a *company* or a *partnership*, the adjective *social* also pertains to either, and its correct translation can only be determined by context, as, for instance, in the following cases :—(1) en cas de dissolution, l'actif social, après paiement du passif, est réparti entre les actionnaires, in case of dissolution, the company's assets, after payment of the liabilities, are divided amongst the shareholders. (2) après la dissolution de la société, les associés se partagent le fonds social, after dissolution of the partnership, the partners divide the partnership assets (*or* the firm's assets) amongst themselves.

sociétaire (*n.m. ou f.*), member ; member of the company ; shareholder ; stockholder :

commissaire qui est aussi sociétaire (*m.*),

auditor who is also a member of the company (*or* who is also a shareholder).

société (*n.f.*) (Abrév.: **Sté** *ou* **Soc.** *ou* **S.**), company ; firm ; partnership ; society : (See notes under **compagnie** and under **association** for distinctions between those words and *société.*)

société à capital variable, in France, any company, whatever may be its form, can stipulate in its memorandum of association (*statuts*) that its nominal capital will be liable to increase or reduction : it is then a *société à capital variable* (company with variable capital). Cooperative societies, mutual credit companies, and the like, take this form.

société à responsabilité limitée, limited company ; limited liability company ; company limited by shares ; private company.

Note :—société à responsabilité limitée is translated here as *private company,* as to all intents and purposes it fills the same function as an English private company. It is, however, more in the nature of a partnership with limited liability. The directors are called *gérants.* The shares are called *parts* (see this word in vocabulary) or *parts sociales,* and there are no share certificates. The capital of the company must be 25,000 francs at least. It cannot be reduced below this figure. It is divided into *parts sociales* of 100 francs, or multiples of 100 francs. The *parts* must be paid up in full. There may exist *parts ordinaires, parts privilégiées,* and *parts de jouissance* (*Cf.* actions de jouissance). Like *parts de fondateur,* q.v., and *actions d'apport,* q.v., the *parts* can only be transferred according to civil law, and are not dealable on the Stock Exchange. The right to transfer *parts* is restricted. The minimum number of members is 2, but there is no maximum. If the membership is below 20, no annual meeting need be held. No public issue can be made. It is not assimilated to a public company (*société anonyme*), as an English private company is to a public company, but is the subject of separate and distinct legislation.

The English *private company,* with the exception of a few vital differences, is practically the same as a public company. These differences are notably : Minimum number of subscribers 2. Maximum (exclusive of persons who are in the employment of the company) 50. Restriction of the right to transfer its shares. Prohibition of any invitation to the public to subscribe for any shares or debentures of the company. Not required to include in the annual summary the statement in the form of a balance sheet. Not required to hold a statutory meeting, nor to present a statutory report. Not required to file a statement in lieu of prospectus. Have no regard to minimum subscription, may commence business without any restriction, and requires no certificate entitling to do so. The shares of an English private company are not dealable on the London Stock Exchange.

société anonyme (*Abrév.*: Sté anme *ou* Soc. anme *ou* S.A.) *ou* société anonyme par actions, limited company; limited liability company; company limited by shares; public company : (*Note* :—Inasmuch as a *société anonyme* is a creation of French law and a *limited company* a creation of English law, these French and English terms are of course only equivalent in a general way. The designation *anonyme* (anonymous) has reference to the fact that a *société anonyme* is not, or is not necessarily, in the name or names of the principal interested parties.) la constitution d'une banque en société anonyme, the formation of a bank into a limited company.

société apporteuse, vendor company.

société approuvée (société de secours mutuels), approved society.

sociétés commerciales et sociétés civiles. In France, companies and partnerships are denominated *commerciales* or *civiles* according to their objects or the nature of their habitual transactions. *Sociétés commerciales* are those which habitually perform *actes de commerce*, such as buying and selling of goods, manufacturing, commission, transport, banking or market transactions, constructional work, shipping, insurance, etc. There are four kinds of *sociétés commerciales*, viz. :—
    (1) société en nom collectif,
    (2) société en commandite,
    (3) société anonyme,
    (4) société à responsabilité limitée.
They are subject to special fiscal laws, they are obliged to keep the *livres de commerce* (q.v.), they are subjected to certain formalities of publicity, and they come under the jurisdiction of the *tribunaux de commerce*. (*See* tribunal de commerce.)
All other *sociétés* are *civiles*, and, in principle, are regulated by the *code civil*. A *société* is *civile* when the acts it habitually performs are not *actes de commerce*. Companies having as their objects agricultural or mining operations are, in principle, *civiles*. A *société commerciale* can transact *opérations civiles*, and similarly a *société civile* can engage in a few *opérations commerciales*, without these isolated acts changing the nature of the *société*.
Owing to legal difficulties, however, it has been enacted that all *sociétés*, whatever their objects, formed since 1st August 1893 under the *Code de commerce* or the Act of 24th July 1867 are *commerciales* and subject to the laws and usages of *commerce*.

société consistant d'un individu, one man company.

société coopérative *ou* société de coopération, cooperative society.

société d'assurance *ou* société d'assurances, insurance company; assurance company; office.

société d'assurance à primes (*ou* à prime fixe), proprietary insurance (*or* assurance) company; proprietary office.

société d'assurances mutuelles, mutual insurance (*or* assurance) company (*or* society); mutual office.

société d'utilité publique, public utility company.

société de banque, banking company.

sociétés de capitaux (opp. à *sociétés de personnes*). *sociétés de capitaux* (associations of capital) are the *sociétés par actions* (joint stock companies).

société de caution, guarantee society.

société de classification de navires, ships' classification society :
    le Bureau Veritas est une société française de classification, the Bureau Veritas is a French classification society.

société de construction de navires *ou* société de construction navale, shipbuilding company

sociétés de crédit. In France, name under which are known the big joint stock banks.

société de dépôt. See note under **dépôt.**

société de finance *ou* société financière, finance company.

société de gérance (société de gestion de portefeuille), investment trust; securities trust.

société de navigation *ou* société d'armement *ou* société de transports maritimes, shipping company; navigation company :
    société de navigation à vapeur, steam navigation company.

sociétés de personnes *ou* sociétés par intérêts (opp. à *sociétés par actions*). *sociétés de personnes* (associations of persons) are the *société en nom collectif* and the *société en commandite simple. Cf.* part d'intérêt.

société de placement *ou* société de portefeuille, investment company.

société de prévoyance, provident society.

société de secours mutuels, friendly society.

Société des Nations (*Abrév.*: S.D.N.), League of Nations.

société donnant (*ou* payant) des dividendes, dividend paying company.

société en commandite, commandite; partnership en commandite; limited partnership. (In France, a partnership contracted between one or several persons called *commandités*, who manage the business and whose liability is unlimited, and one or several persons called *commanditaires* or *associés en commandite* or *associés commanditaires*, who only contribute money and whose liability is limited to the amount of capital they have undertaken to provide. The name of a *société en commandite* must contain one or several of the names of the *commandités*. The capital can be divided into shares, in which case the company is called a **société en commandite par actions.** If the capital is not divided into shares it is known as a **société en commandite simple.**

société en formation. *See note under* assemblée constitutive.

société en nom collectif, firm; partnership; partnership firm; general partnership.

société en participation, particular partnership; special partnership.

société filiale, subsidiary company.

société holding [sociétés holding *pl.*] *ou* société de contrôle, holding company.

société mère, parent company.

société par actions, joint stock company: en France, les sociétés par actions se divisent en deux classes: la société en commandite par actions et la société anonyme, in France, joint stock companies are divided into two classes: the *société en commandite par actions* and the *société anonyme.*

société pétrolière *ou* société de pétroles, oil company.

société privée *ou* société particulière, private company. *See note under* compagnie privée *which applies here also.*

société sœur, sister company.

société stannifère, tin company.

société verbale en nom collectif, verbal partnership.

nous avons l'honneur de porter à votre connaissance que la société qui a existé entre nous est dissoute à partir de ce jour, we have to inform you that the partnership which has existed between us is dissolved from to-day. *See also example under* **social.**

soigner un compte, to nurse an account.

soin (*n.m.*) (*s'emploie souvent au pluriel*), care: en ce qui concerne les soins à donner aux marchandises dont le capitaine se charge, as regards the care of the goods entrusted to the master.

aux soins de, care of; c/o.: M. A., aux soins de M. B., Mr A., care of (*or, and usually*, c/o.) Mr B.

solde (différence entre le débit et le crédit d'un compte) (*n.m.*) (Abrév.: **Sde**), balance: (See also **balance.**)

solde de compte, de fret, balance of account, of freight.

les soldes du grand livre, the ledger balances.

solde à nouveau (Comptab.), balance carried forward to next account; balance to next account.

solde à nouveau (montant des factures précédentes) (Com.), account rendered.

solde à reporter, balance carried forward; balance carried down.

solde ancien, old balance.

solde créditeur, credit balance.

solde de caisse, cash balance.

solde de dividende (opp. à *acompte de dividende*), final dividend: déclarer un solde de dividende, to declare a final dividend.

les dividendes sont payables le 1er janvier (acompte) et le 1er juillet (solde) (*m.pl.*), dividends are payable 1st January (interim) and 1st July (final).

solde débiteur, debit balance.

solde en banque *ou* solde à la banque, bank balance; balance at (*or* in) bank.

solde en bénéfice, en perte, du compte de (*ou* des) profits et pertes (bilan), balance, being profit, being loss, as per profit and loss account (balance sheet).

solde en caisse, balance in (*or* on) hand.

solde formant le bénéfice net, la perte nette, reporté au bilan (compte profits et pertes), balance, being net profit, being net loss, carried to balance sheet.

solde reporté, balance brought forward; balance brought down.

solde reporté de l'exercice précédent *ou* solde de l'exercice précédent *ou* solde précédent, balance brought forward from last account; balance from last (*or* from previous) account.

solde (reliquat d'une somme à payer) (*n.m.*), balance; settlement: le solde d'une facture, the balance of an invoice.

espèces pour solde (*f.pl.*) (opp. à *espèces en compte*), cash to balance; cash in settlement (opp. *to cash on account*).

pour solde de tout compte, in full settlement.

solder (acquitter) (*v.t.*), to pay; to pay off; to settle: solder un mémoire, le redû, to pay, to settle, a bill, the balance.

solder intégralement, to pay in full.

solder un découvert, to pay off an overdraft.

solder (Comptab.) (*v.t.*), to balance: solder un compte, to balance an account.

se solder (*v.r.*), to balance; to be balanced; to balance each other; to show a balance: compte qui se solde (*m.*), account which balances.

s'assurer si le budget de cet État se solde en équilibre ou en déficit, to ascertain whether the budget of this State balances or shows a deficit.

compte qui se solde par tant de francs au crédit (*m.*), account which shows a balance of so many francs to the credit.

le compte courant se solde habituellement en sa faveur par un crédit, the current account usually shows a credit balance in his favour.

les comptes se soldent par un bénéfice net de tant (*m.pl.*), the accounts show a net profit of so much.

solidaire (*adj.*) *ou* **conjoint (-e) et solidaire,** joint and several; liable; responsible; answerable: (Cf. **individuel, -elle.**)

responsabilité solidaire *ou* responsabilité conjointe et solidaire (*f.*), joint and several liability.

créance solidaire (*f.*), joint and several debt.

codébiteurs solidaires (*m.pl.*), joint and several codebtors.

le mari est solidaire des actes de sa femme, the husband is responsible for the acts of his wife.

solidairement (*adv.*) *ou* **conjointement et solidairement,** jointly and severally: (Cf. **individuellement.**)

associés qui sont solidairement responsables (*ou* qui sont conjointement et solidairement responsables) de tous les actes sociaux (*m.pl.*), partners who are jointly and severally liable for all the firm's acts.

le chargeur et le consignataire garantissent solidairement la compagnie de toutes les conséquences dommageables. Ils se portent garants solidaires du paiement de tous droits, amendes de douane, etc., the shipper and the consignee, jointly and severally, are liable to the company for all damageable consequences. They hold themselves liable, jointly and severally, for the payment of all dues, customs fines, etc.

olidariser (*v.t.*), to make jointly and severally liable :
on devrait solidariser tous les membres de l'association, all the members of the association should be made jointly and severally liable.

olidarité (*n.f.*), joint and several liability. *Cf.* grève de solidarité.

olliciter (*v.t.*), to solicit ; to ask ; to apply for :
solliciter des commandes, to solicit orders.
solliciter son congé, to ask for leave of absence.
solliciter un emploi, to apply for a situation.

olvabilité (*n.f.*), solvency ; solvability :
solvabilité d'un négociant, du tireur et de l'accepteur d'une lettre de change, solvency, solvability, of a merchant, of the drawer and of the acceptor of a bill of exchange.

olvable (*adj.*), solvent :
débiteur solvable (*m.*), solvent debtor.

ombrer (*v.i.*), to founder ; to sink ; to go down :
navire qui sombra et se perdit (*m.*), ship which foundered (*or* sank) (*or* went down) and was lost.

ommaire (*adj.*), summary :
état sommaire de la situation (*m.*), summary statement of the position.
procédure sommaire (*f.*) *ou* cause sommaire (*f.*) (Dr.), summary proceeding.

omme (*n.f.*), sum ; amount :
somme d'argent payée d'avance, sum, amount, of money paid in advance.
déclarer la somme en risque dès la réception d'avis (Assce), to declare (*or* to report) the amount at risk on receipt of advices.
somme grosse, lump sum.
somme partielle, partial amount ; short ; subtotal :
les sommes partielles qui composent le total (Comptab.), the shorts (*or* subtotals) which make up the total.
somme totale *ou* somme globale, total amount ; sum total.

sommes (inscription en haut d'une colonne de caisse) (*n.f.pl.*), amount :
colonne des sommes (*f.*), amount column.

ommer (*v.t.*), to summon ; to call on ; to call upon :
sommer un débiteur de payer, to call on (*or* upon) a debtor to pay.

ommier d'entrepôt (*m.*), warehouse book.

ondage (Vérifications comptables) (*n.m.*),

challenge. *See* faire des sondages dans *for example.*

sondage (Douanes) (*n.m.*), spitting :
sondage des colis pour la vérification de l'espèce ou de la qualité des marchandises, spitting packages for verification of the kind or quality of the goods.

sonde (*n.f.*), spit.

sonder (*v.t.*), to spit.

sonnant la casse (réserve sur un connaissement, une lettre de voiture), rattles ; apparently broken.

sonner (*v.t.*), to ring :
sonner le bureau (Téléph.), to ring the exchange.

sort (*n.m.*), lot :
choisir par le sort, to choose by lot.

sortant, -e (en parlant des administrateurs, des commissaires des comptes) (*adj.*), retiring :
administrateur sortant (*m.*), retiring director.

sortie (action de quitter) (*n.f.*), going out ; leaving :
à l'entrée ou à la sortie des ports, on entering or leaving ports.
sortie de (*ou* d'en) (*ou* de) (*ou* du) bassin, undocking ; going out of dock.

sortie (mouvement hors du pays) (*n.f.*) (opp. à *rentrée*), outflow ; efflux :
une sortie d'or, ou tout au moins de capitaux, qui pourrait entraîner l'appauvrissement du pays, an outflow (*or* an efflux) of gold, or at least of capital, which might bring about the impoverishment of the country.

sortie (des voyageurs) (Ch. de f.) (*n.f.*), way out (for passengers).

sortie (d'un administrateur, d'un commissaire) (*n.f.*), retirement ; retiral.

sortie (paiement) (*n.f.*), payment :
entrées et sorties de caisse, cash receipts and payments.

sortie (exportation) (*n.f.*), exportation ; export :
le trafic total, entrées et sorties réunies, the total traffic, imports and exports combined.

sortir (passer du dedans au dehors) (*v.i.*), to go out ; to leave :
sortir de (*ou* d'en) (*ou* du) bassin, to undock ; to go out of dock :
avec faculté d'entrer en bassin et d'en sortir, with leave to dock and undock.
sortir de (*ou* de la) cale sèche, to go out of dry dock.
aucun bâtiment ne peut sortir du port sans congé, no vessel may leave port without clearance.

sortir (cesser d'être employé quelque part) (*v.i.*), to leave ; to retire :
sortir du service, to leave, to retire from, the service.
sortir à tour de rôle, to retire in rotation.
les administrateurs qui doivent sortir cette année sont MM. A. et B., the directors who have to retire this year are Messrs A. and B.

sou (*n.m.*), 5 centimes. *See* **dont.**

souche (*n.f.*), counterfoil ; stub ; stump ; butt ; block :

la souche du carnet de chèques, the counter-foil of the cheque book.

livre à souche (*m.*) *ou* registre à souche (*m.*) *ou* carnet à souches (*m.*), counterfoil book; stub book.

actions, obligations, à la souche. See under **action, obligation.**

souffrance (suspens) (*n.f.*), suspense:
intérêts en souffrance (*m.pl.*), interest in suspense.

effets en souffrance (*m.pl.*), bills in suspense; bills held over.

souffrance (détention d'un wagon de ch. de f., ou de marchandises) (*n.f.*), demurrage:
souffrance de matériel roulant, demurrage of rolling stock.

quand les marchandises en souffrance sont sujettes à détérioration, elles sont, en général, vendues, when goods on demurrage are liable to deteriorate, they are generally sold.

laisser les marchandises en souffrance sur les quais, to leave the goods on demurrage on the wharves.

souffrance (non livraison) (*n.f.*), non delivery:
expéditeur qui demande qu'il soit avisé directe-ment de la livraison ou de la souffrance de sa marchandise (*m.*), sender who asks to be advised direct of the delivery or non delivery of his goods.

colis postaux en souffrance (*m.pl.*), undeliver-able postal parcels.

soulagement (*n.m.*), relief; lightening:
opération qui apporte un grand soulagement au marché (*f.*), transaction which brings a great relief to the market.

soulager (*v.t.*), to relieve; to lighten:
soulager un navire en débarquant tout ou partie de sa cargaison, to lighten a ship by unloading all or part of her cargo.

la place (*ou* la position de place) est soulagée (Bourse) (opp. à *la place est chargée*), the market is all bears (*or* is all takers); sellers over.

soulever une question, to raise a question.

soulignement (*n.m.*), underlining.

souligner (*v.t.*), to underline:
souligner les mots ou les passages du texte sur lesquels on désire attirer l'attention, to underline the words or the passages of the text to which one wishes to draw attention.

soulte (*n.f.*) *ou* **soulte d'échange** *ou* **soute** (*n.f.*), balance; balance in cash; cash adjust-ment; cash distribution (in an exchange, the difference in value payable in cash):
bel et vaste immeuble à vendre, tant au comptant, délai pour soulte (*m.*), fine and spacious premises for sale, so much cash, balance can remain.

ledit échange est fait moyennant une soulte de la part de La Compagnie X. de tant de francs, the said exchange is made in con-sideration of a balance in cash payable by The X. Company of so many francs.

l'échange est à raison de 0 actions nouvelles plus une soulte de 00 francs par action,

contre 0 actions anciennes (*m.*), the exchange is at the rate of 0 new shares plus a cash distribution of 00 francs per share, for 0 old shares.

soumettre (*v.t.*), to submit:
soumettre des échantillons, to submit samples.

soumettre à l'examen les livres d'un négociant, une proposition à l'approbation d'une assemblée, to submit a merchant's books to an examination, a proposal to the approval of a meeting.

soumis (-e) à (être), to be liable to:
les lettres de change sont soumises au droit de timbre, au droit proportionnel (*f.pl.*), bills of exchange are liable to stamp duty, to ad valorem duty.

dividendes soumis à l'impôt sur le revenu (*m.pl.*), dividends liable to income tax.

soumission (*n.f.*), tender:
soumissions d'emprunts publics, pour la réparation des dommages, tenders for public loans, for the repair of the damage.

soumission cachetée, sealed tender.

soumission cautionnée *ou* soumission de crédit (Douanes), bond:
droits garantis par des soumissions cautionnées (*m.pl.*), duties secured by bonds.

sous la garantie d'une soumission cautionnée renouvelable chaque année, les déclarants peuvent être autorisés à enlever les mar-chandises aussitôt après la vérification, c'est-à-dire avant le paiement des droits, under security of a bond renewable each year, the declarants may be authorized to take the goods away immediately after examination, that is to say, before payment of the duties.

soumissionnaire (pers.) (*n.m.*), tenderer.
soumissionnaire cautionné *ou simplement* soumissionnaire (Douanes), bond.

soumissionner (*v.t.*), to tender; to tender for:
soumissionner au gouvernement un emprunt de tant de millions de francs, to tender to the government for a loan of so many million francs.

source (*n.f.*), source:
source d'informations, de revenu, source of information, of income.

la maison X. & Cie déclare tenir de source sûre que . . ., the firm X. & Co. states it has learned from a reliable source that . . .

sous-affrètement [**sous-affrètements** *pl.*] (*n.m.*), subcharter.

sous-affréter (*v.t.*), to subcharter.

sous-affréteur [**sous-affréteurs** *pl.*] (pers.) (*n.m.*), subcharterer.

sous-agence [**sous-agences** *pl.*] (*n.f.*), subagency.

sous-agent [**sous-agents** *pl.*] (pers.) (*n.m.*), sub-agent.

sous-agent comptable [**sous-agents comptables** *pl.*] (*m.*), assistant accountant.

sous-assurance [**sous-assurances** *pl.*] (*n.f.*), under-insurance.

sous-assurer (*v.t.*), to underinsure.

sous-bail [**sous-baux** *pl.*] (*n.m.*), sublease; under-lease.

sous-bailleur [sous-bailleurs *pl.*] (pers.) (*n.m.*), sublessor; underlessor.

sous-caissier [sous-caissiers *pl.*] (pers.) (*n.m.*), under cashier; assistant cashier.

sous charge. See under **charge.**

sous-chef [sous-chefs *pl.*] (pers.) (*n.m.*), submanager; under manager; assistant manager.

sous-chef de gare (*m.*), assistant station master.

sous-comité [sous-comités *pl.*] (*n.m.*), subcommittee.

sous-compte [sous-comptes *pl.*] (*n.m.*), subsidiary account; subaccount.

souscripteur, souscription, souscrire. See below.

sous déduction d'impôt, less tax:
intérêt payable par semestre, sous déduction d'impôt (*m.*), interest payable half yearly, less tax.

sous-directeur [sous-directeurs *pl.*] (pers.) (*n.m.*) (Abrév.: **S/Dr**), submanager; under manager; assistant manager.

sous-directrice [sous-directrices *pl.*] (*n.f.*), submanageress; under manageress; assistant manageress.

sous-diviser, sous-division. Same as **subdiviser, subdivision.**

sous-estimation [sous-estimations *pl.*] *ou* **sous-évaluation** [sous-évaluations *pl.*] (*n.f.*), underestimation; underestimate; undervaluation:
sous-évaluation d'actif, undervaluation of assets.

sous-estimer *ou* **sous-évaluer** (*v.t.*), to underestimate; to undervalue.

sous-gouverneur [sous-gouverneurs *pl.*] (pers.) (*n.m.*), deputy governor:
un sous-gouverneur de la Banque de France, de la Banque d'Angleterre, a deputy governor of the Bank of France, of the Bank of England.

Sous le péristyle. *See notes under* marché des valeurs.

sous les réserves d'usage (Banq.). See under **réserve.**

sous-locataire [sous-locataires *pl.*] (pers.) (*n.m. ou f.*), subtenant; under tenant.

sous-locataire (à bail) (*n.m. ou f.*), sublessee; underlessee.

sous-location [sous-locations *pl.*] (*n.f.*), subletting; underletting.

sous-louer (*v.t.*), to sublet; to underlet:
preneur qui a le droit de sous-louer (*m.*), lessee who has the right to sublet (or to underlet).

sous-main [sous-mains *pl.*] (*n.m.*) *ou* **sous-main buvard** [sous-mains buvards *pl.*] (*m.*), writing pad; blotting pad.

sous palan *ou* **sous vergues,** under ship's derrick; under ship's tackle; under ship's slings; over ship's side; at ship's rail:
le débarquement s'effectuera à quai ou sous palan (*ou* sous vergues), discharge will be made on quay or under ship's derrick (or tackle) (or slings) (or on quay or over ship's side) (or on quay or at ship's rail).
prendre les marchandises sur le quai ou sous le hangar et les amener sous palan, to take the goods on the wharf or in the shed and bring them under the ship's derrick (or tackle) (or slings).

sous-preneur [sous-preneurs *pl.*] (pers.) (*n.m.*). Same as **sous-locataire.**

sous protêt, supra protest; suprà protest. See acceptation sous protêt.

sous réserve. See under **réserve.**

sous-secrétaire [sous-secrétaires *pl.*] (pers.) (*n.m.*), assistant secretary; under secretary:
sous-secrétaire d'État, under secretary of State.

soussigner, soustraction, soustraire. See below.

sous-syndicataire [sous-syndicataires *pl.*] (pers.) (*n.m.*), subunderwriter.

sous vapeur. See under **charge** (sous charge *ou* sous vapeur).

sous voile, on passage; afloat. See example under **flottant.**

souscripteur (celui qui prend part à une souscription) (pers.) (*n.m.*), subscriber; applicant:
souscripteur à un emprunt, subscriber to a loan.
souscripteur en numéraire *ou* souscripteur en espèces, cash subscriber.
le souscripteur remplit et signe un bulletin de souscription, the applicant fills up and signs an application form.

souscripteur (d'une lettre de change, d'un chèque) (*n.m.*), drawer (of a bill of exchange, of a cheque).

souscripteur (d'un billet à ordre) (*n.m.*), maker (of a promissory note, of a note of hand).

souscripteur (assureur) (pers.) (*n.m.*), underwriter; subscriber:
les souscripteurs de chacune des assurances convenant de payer leur proportion, the underwriters (or subscribers) on each insurance agreeing to pay their proportion.

souscription (action de signer) (*n.f.*), signing; subscription:
contrat auquel il ne manque que la souscription (*m.*), contract which only wants signing.

souscription (signature) (*n.f.*), signature; subscription.

souscription (engagement) (*n.f.*), subscription; application:
souscription à une émission, subscription to an issue.
souscription à des actions, application for shares.
actions payables entièrement lors de la souscription (*f.pl.*), shares payable in full on application.
actions de 500 fr., payables 100 fr. à la souscription (*ou* en souscrivant), 100 fr. à la (*ou* lors de la) répartition, tant de francs au (*date*) (*f.pl.*), shares of fr. 500, payable fr. 100 on application, fr. 100 on allotment, so many francs on (*date*).

souscription (somme qui doit être versée par le souscripteur) (*n.f.*), subscription:
verser une souscription de tant de francs, to pay a subscription of so many francs.

souscription (liste de souscription) (*n.f.*), list of applications; subscription list; list; lists:
la souscription sera ouverte le jeudi 9 janvier 19— et close le même jour, the list of applications (*or* the subscription list) (*or* the list) (*or* the lists) will be opened on Thursday the 9th January 19— and closed the same day.

souscription (Assce) (*n.f.*), underwriting; writing; subscription:
souscription d'un risque, underwriting, subscription of, a risk.

souscrire (*v.t.*). See examples:
souscrire le capital, un emprunt, l'intégralité (*ou* la totalité) du capital, d'un emprunt, to subscribe, to subscribe for, to apply for, the capital, a loan, the whole of the capital, of a loan.
souscrire à titre irréductible, to apply as of right:
souscrire à titre réductible, to apply for excess shares:
les actionnaires actuels ont le droit de souscrire, à titre irréductible, à une action nouvelle pour chaque action ancienne, moyennant un versement de 000 francs par action: ils ont également la faculté de présenter des souscriptions à titre réductible en versant 000 francs par action, the present shareholders are entitled to apply as of right for one new share for each old share, in consideration of the payment of 000 francs per share: they also have the option of presenting applications for excess shares by paying 000 francs per share.
souscrire un acte, to sign a deed.
souscrire une obligation, to subscribe, to sign, to enter into, a bond.
souscrire une soumission cautionnée (Douanes), to enter into a bond.
souscrire un effet de commerce, un chèque, to draw a bill of exchange, a cheque.
souscrire un billet à ordre, to make a promissory note.
souscrire un effet, un chèque, à ordre, au porteur, to draw a bill, a cheque, to order, to bearer; to make a bill, a cheque, payable to order, to bearer.
souscrire un risque maritime, une ligne, to underwrite a marine risk, a line.
la somme souscrite par chaque assureur est la limite de son engagement, the amount subscribed by each underwriter (*or* the sum underwritten by each insurer) is the limit of his commitment.
police souscrite à Londres (*f.*), policy underwritten (*or* written) in London.
avant tout les Lombards étaient banquiers, et ce n'était qu'accessoirement qu'ils souscrivaient des assurances, above all the Lombards were bankers, and it was only accessorily that they wrote assurances.

souscrire (consentir) (*v.i.*), to consent; to agree:
souscrire à un arrangement, to consent to, to agree to, an arrangement.

souscrire (prendre part à une souscription) (*v.i.*), to subscribe; to apply:
souscrire à une émission, à un emprunt, t⟨ subscribe to an issue, to a loan.
souscrire à tant d'actions d'une société, t⟨ apply for, to subscribe for, so many shares i⟨ a company.

souscrire pour (Assce), to subscribe for; to under⟨ write (*v.t.*):
d'habitude, chaque compagnie souscrit pou⟨ une partie du risque proposé par le courtier usually, each company underwrites a par⟨ of the risk proposed by the broker.

soussigné, -e (*adj.*), undersigned:
les témoins soussignés (*m.pl.*), the undersigned witnesses.
je soussigné Paul X. déclare que . . ., I, the undersigned Paul X. declare (*or* certify that . . .

le soussigné, la soussignée (pers.), the under⟨ signed:
le soussigné déclare . . ., the undersigned declares (*or* certifies) . . .

soussigner (*v.t.*), to undersign.

soustraction (Arith.) (*n.f.*), subtraction:
le résultat de la soustraction se nomme reste, excès, ou différence, the result of a subtraction is called remainder, excess, o⟨ difference.

soustraction (enlevage par ruse ou par fraude) (*n.f.*), abstraction:
soustraction de papiers, abstraction of papers.

soustraire (Arith.) (*v.t.*), to subtract; to take away:
soustraire 10 de 15, to subtract, to take away, 10 from 15.

soustraire (ôter par adresse ou par fraude) (*v.t.*) to abstract:
soustraire des documents, to abstract documents.

soustraire (arracher) (*v.t.*), to tear out:
soustraire une feuille d'un livre, to tear a leaf out of a book.

soustraire (libérer) (*v.t.*), to relieve:
soustraire quelqu'un à une responsabilité, to relieve someone from a liability.

soute (*n.f.*), bunker:
soute à charbon, coal bunker.

soute (soulte). See under **soulte.**

soutenir (*v.t.*), to support:
soutenir les cours en achetant, to support prices by buying.
les mines étaient soutenues (Bourse) (*f.pl.*), mines were supported.

souterrain (*n.m.*), tunnel; subway:
le souterrain du mont Cenis, the Mont Cenis tunnel.
souterrain, desservi par des escaliers, par le moyen duquel le public accède aux quais, subway, served by stairs, by means of which the public has access to the platforms.

soutirer (*v.t.*), to get; to extract; to squeeze:
soutirer de l'argent à quelqu'un, to get, to extract, to squeeze, money out of (*or* from) someone.

spécial, -e, -aux (*adj.*), special:
procuration spéciale (*f.*) *ou* mandat spécial

(*m.*) (opp. à *procuration générale* ou *mandat général*), special power; particular power.

pécialités (*n.f.pl.*) *ou* **valeurs de spécialités** (*f.pl.*) (Bourse), specialities.

pécification (*n.f.*), specification:
l'espace réservé sur la lettre de voiture pour la spécification des marchandises (*m.*), the space reserved on the consignment note for the specification of the goods.

pécifier (*v.t.*), to specify:
les marchandises ci-dessous spécifiées (*f.pl.*), the goods specified below.

pécimen (*n.m.*), specimen:
spécimen de sa signature, specimen of one's signature.

péculateur, -trice (pers.) (*n.*), speculator:
un spéculateur sur les blés, a speculator in wheat.

péculatif, -ive (*adj.*) *ou* **de spéculation,** speculative:
valeurs spéculatives *ou* valeurs de spéculation (*f.pl.*), speculative stocks.

péculation (*n.f.*), speculation; venture:
spéculations de bourse *ou* spéculations en bourse, stock exchange speculations; speculations on the stock exchange.
spéculation mixte *ou* spéculation à cheval, straddle; spread; cross book.

péculer (*v.i.*), to speculate:
spéculer sur la bourse, sur les valeurs de bourse, sur les changes, to speculate on the stock exchange, in stocks and shares, in exchanges.
spéculer à la hausse *ou* spéculer en hausse, to speculate for (*or* on) a rise; to go a bull.
spéculer à la (*ou* en) baisse, to speculate for (*or* on) a fall; to go a bear.

tabilisateur, -trice (*adj.*), stabilizing.

tabilisation (*n.f.*), stabilization:
stabilisation de la monnaie, du franc, des prix à un niveau raisonnable, stabilization of the currency, of the franc, of prices at a reasonable level.

tabiliser (*v.t.*), to stabilize:
on ne peut stabiliser les prix qu'en stabilisant le change, prices can only be stabilized by stabilizing the exchange.

tabilité (*n.f.*), stability; steadiness:
la stabilité est une qualité indispensable de tout étalon de valeur (*f.*), stability is an indispensable quality of every standard of value.

table (*adj.*), stable; steady:
la production moderne a besoin d'une monnaie stable, modern production has need of a stable currency.
l'action X. est stable, est plus stable, à 103, X. shares are steady, are steadier, at 103 francs.

tage (*n.m.*), articles:
stage de cinq années chez un expert-comptable, five years' articles with a professional accountant.

tagiaire (pers.) (*n.m.* ou *f.*), articled clerk.

tagnant, -e (*adj.*), stagnant:
l'état stagnant des affaires (*m.*), the stagnant state of business.

stagnation (*n.f.*), stagnation:
stagnation des cours, des affaires, stagnation of prices, of business.

stand (dans une exposition) (*n.m.*), stand (in an exhibition).

standard de Saint-Pétersbourg *ou simplement* **standard** (*n.m.*) (Abrév.: **std**) (bois), St Petersburg standard; Petersburg standard hundred; standard.

standardisation (normalisation) (*n.f.*), standardization:
standardisation dans la fabrication, standardization in manufacture.

standardiser (*v.t.*), to standardize.

stannifères (*n.f.pl.*) *ou* **valeurs stannifères** (*f.pl.*), tins; tin shares.

starie (*n.f.*), lay day:
staries réversibles, reversible lay days.

station (*n.f.*), station:
station côtière (Radiotélégr.), coast station.
station de bord (Radiotélégr.), ship station.
station de commerce, trading station:
stations de commerce en Afrique-Equatoriale française, trading stations in French Equatorial Africa.
station de radiodiffusion, broadcasting station.
station de T.S.F. *ou* station radiotélégraphique *ou* station radio [stations radios *pl.*], wireless station; radiotelegraphic station; radio station.
station émettrice *ou* station d'émission (Télégr.), transmitting station.
station réceptrice *ou* station de réception (Télégr.), receiving station.

station (*n.f.*) *ou* **station intermédiaire** (Ch. de f.), station; intermediate station; way station: (See also **gare.**)
station de chemin de fer, railway station.

stationnaire (*adj.*), stationary:
cours qui reste stationnaire (*m.*), price which remains stationary.

stationnement (d'un train) (*n.m.*), holding (a train).

stationnement (des wagons) (Ch. de f.) (*n.m.*), detention or non use of vehicles:
chargement, déchargement, et stationnement des wagons dont la manutention est faite par le commerce, loading, unloading, and detention or non use of vehicles the handling of which is done by traders.

stationner en rade (se dit d'un navire), to lie in a roadstead (*or* in the roads).

statisticien, -enne (pers.) (*n.*), statistician.

statistique (*adj.*), statistical:
rapports statistiques (*m.pl.*), statistical reports.

statistique (*n.f.*) *ou* **statistiques** (*n.f.pl.*), statistics; return; returns:
l'appréciation des risques d'assurance est fondée sur l'expérience, c'est-à-dire sur la statistique (*f.*), the valuation of insurance risks is based on experience, that is to say, on statistics.
les statistiques hebdomadaires donnent (*ou* la statistique hebdomadaire donne) le total des

stocks à 0 000 tonnes, the weekly returns give the total stocks at 0,000 tons.

statu quo (*n.m.*), status quo; status in quo; no change:
en France, certains courtiers ont un statut
maintenir le statu quo,   to maintain the status quo.
statu quo aux valeurs d'étain (Bourse),   no change in tin shares.

statuer sur, to decide; to resolve:
statuer sur les différends qui peuvent s'élever, to decide disputes which may arise.
convoquer l'assemblée générale pour statuer sur la liquidation de la société, to call a general meeting to resolve to wind up the company.

statut (Dr.) (*n.m.*), status:
en France, certains courtiers ont un statut légal,   in France, certain brokers have a legal status.
statuts. See below.

statutaire (prévu par les statuts) (*adj.*),   provided by the articles (*or* by the articles of association) (*or* by the memorandum of association); of the articles; intra vires:
réserve statutaire (*f.*),   reserve provided by the articles.
prescriptions statutaires (*f.pl.*),   provisions of the articles.
intérêt statutaire, dividende statutaire. See under **intérêt, dividende.**

statutaire (désigné par les statuts) (*adj.*),   appointed by the articles (*or* by the articles of association):
gérant statutaire (*m.*),   manager appointed by the articles.

statutairement (*adv.*),   in accordance with the articles (*or* memorandum);   under the articles:
tantièmes attribués statutairement (*m.pl.*), percentage of profits apportioned in accordance with the articles.

statuts (d'une société) (*n.m.pl.*),   articles of association, articles, memorandum of association, memorandum, memorandum and articles (of a company): (*Note :*—In France, the *memorandum and articles* are all in one and are called *statuts.* In England, the *memorandum of association* is the charter of the company and defines its powers, whilst the *articles of association* form a code of regulations for the internal management of its affairs.)
les pouvoirs du conseil d'administration sont définis par les statuts sociaux (*m.pl.*),   the powers of the board are defined by the company's articles.
une société ne peut entreprendre aucune opération non prévue par ses statuts,   a company may not undertake any business not provided for under its memorandum.

steam-boat *ou* **steamboat** (*n.m.*),   steamboat.

steamer (*n.m.*) (Abrév.: **s.s.** *ou* **S.S.** *ou* **s/s.** *ou* **ss.** *ou* **st.** *ou* **St.** *ou* **steam.** *ou* **Steam.**), steamer; steamship: (See also **bâtiment, navire, paquebot,** and **vapeur.**)

steamer au long cours, ocean-going steamer; foreign-going steamer.
steamer fluvial, river steamer.

stellage (Bourse) (Abrév.: **stell.** *ou* **stel.**) (*n.m.*), put and call; put and call option; double option.

stellionat (Dr.) (*n.m.*), stellionate.

stencil (*n.m.*), stencil:
stencil à la cire, wax stencil.
stencil chiffonnable, indestructible stencil.

sténodactylographe *ou* **sténodactylo** (pers.) (*n.m.* ou *f.*), shorthand-typist.

sténodactylographie (*n.f.*), shorthand and typewriting.

sténogramme (Sténographie) (*n.m.*),   grammalogue.

sténographe (*adj.*), shorthand; stenographic:
reporter sténographe (*m.*), shorthand reporter.

sténographe *ou* simplement **sténo** (pers.) (*n.m.* ou *f.*), shorthand writer; stenographer.

sténographie (*n.f.*),   shorthand;   shorthand writing; stenography.

sténographier (*v.t.*),   to take down;   to take down in shorthand:
sténographier une lettre, un discours, to take down a letter, a speech; to take down a letter, a speech, in shorthand.

sténographique (*adj.*), shorthand; stenographic:
signes sténographiques (*m.pl.*),   shorthand signs.

sténographiquement (*adv.*), in shorthand; stenographically.

sténotype (*n.f.*),   stenograph;   shorthand machine.

sterling (*adj. invar.*), sterling:
livre sterling (*f.*), pound sterling.
10 000 *l.* sterling, £10,000 sterling.

stipulation (*n.f.*),   stipulation;   provision; covenant:
les stipulations et exceptions insérées dans le connaissement,   the stipulations and exceptions inserted in the bill of lading.
stipulation expresse, express stipulation.
récuser les stipulations d'un connaissement, to challenge the provisions of a bill of lading.

stipuler (*v.t.*), to stipulate; to provide:
stipuler une garantie, un délai de livraison, to stipulate a guarantee, a time of (*or* for) delivery.
armateur qui stipule qu'il ne répondra pas des fautes du capitaine (*m.*),   owner who stipulates (*or* provides) that he will not be liable for the wrongful acts of the master.

stock (existence) (*n.m.*), stock:
stock de marchandises, stock of goods.
stock d'or (Banq.), stock of gold.
stock de titres, stock of shares.
stock en magasin (Com.), stock in warehouse; stock in trade.
stock au début de l'exercice (Com.), opening stock.
stock à l'inventaire (Com.), closing stock.
stocks visibles, visible stocks.

stock (compte du grand livre), stock.

stockage (*n.m.*), stocking.

stocker (*v.t.*), to stock:
magasin où on peut stocker mille tonnes de marchandises (*m.*), warehouse where one can stock a thousand tons of goods.

stoppage à la source (Income-tax) (*m.*), collection at the source.

stylographe (*n.m.*) (Abrév.: **stylo.**), fountain pen.

subdiviser (*v.t.*), to subdivide:
compte général subdivisé en une série de comptes et sous-comptes (*m.*), general account subdivided into a series of accounts and subaccounts.

se subdiviser (*v.r.*), to be subdivided.

subdivisible (*adj.*), subdivisible.

subdivision (*n.f.*), subdivision:
subdivision d'actions, subdivision of shares.

subir (*v.t.*), to suffer; to sustain:
subir une perte, to suffer, to sustain, a loss.
valeur qui subit une dépréciation (*f.*), security which suffers a depreciation.

subrécargue (pers.) (*n.m.*), supercargo.

subrogation (Dr.) (*n.f.*), subrogation:
subrogation des droits de l'assuré à la compagnie, subrogation of the rights of the insured to the company.

subroger (*v.t.*), to subrogate:
assureur qui est subrogé aux droits de l'assuré contre le capitaine ou l'armement (*m.*), underwriter who is subrogated to the rights of the assured against the master or the owners.
par le paiement de l'indemnité, l'assureur est subrogé dans tous les droits de recours contre des tiers appartenant à l'assuré, by the payment of the indemnity, the underwriter is subrogated to all rights of recourse against third parties belonging to the insured.

subséquent, -e (successif) (Transports) (*adj.*), succeeding; on:
transporteur subséquent (*m.*), succeeding carrier; on-carrier.

subside (*n.m.*), subsidy.

subsidiaire (*adj.*), subsidiary.

substitution (*n.f.*), substitution:
substitution d'un autre navire à un navire assuré, substitution of another ship for an insured ship.

subvenir (*v.i.*), to provide:
vente d'une partie de la cargaison afin de subvenir aux besoins pressants du navire (*f.*), sale of a part of the cargo in order to provide for the pressing needs of the ship.

subvention (*n.f.*), subsidy; subvention.

subventionner (*v.t.*), to subsidize:
subventionner un service postal, to subsidize a postal service.

successif, -ive (*adj.*), successive; succeeding:
la question de la responsabilité des voituriers successifs, the question of the responsibility of succeeding carriers.
la compagnie et les entrepreneurs de transport qui lui succéderont, the company and any succeeding carrier.

succursale (*adj.*), branch:
maison succursale (*f.*), branch house.

succursale (*n.f.*) (Abrév.: **succle** *ou* **sle**) (opp. à *siège* ou *siège social* ou *siège principal*), branch; branch office:
succursale d'une banque, branch of a bank.
succursale de province, country branch.

sucrer (se) (Bourse) (*v.r.*), to pick up shares (with a view to engineering a rise).

sud-africaines (*n.f.pl.*) *ou* **valeurs sud-africaines** (*f.pl.*), South Africans; South African shares; Kaffirs.

suffire (satisfaire à) (*v.i.*), to suffice; to be sufficient; to be enough; to be adequate; to be able to meet:
cent francs suffiront, a hundred francs will be sufficient (*or* will be enough).
suffire à toutes ses obligations, to be able to meet all one's obligations.

suffisamment (*adv.*), sufficiently; enough; adequately:
être suffisamment pourvu (-e) d'argent, to be sufficiently provided with money.

suffisance (*n.f.*), sufficiency; adequacy.

suffisant, -e (qui est en quantité assez grande) (*adj.*), sufficient; enough; adequate:
somme suffisante (*f.*), sufficient sum; adequate amount.
achats pour lesquels tant de francs est suffisant (*m.pl.*), purchases for which so many francs is enough.

suffisant, -e (qui a des ressources) (*adj.*), able:
débiteur suffisant pour payer (*m.*), debtor able to pay.

suffrage (*n.m.*), vote:
donner son suffrage, to give one's vote.

suite de lettre *ou* simplement **suite** (*n.f.*) (seconde ou subséquente feuille de papier à lettres), follower.

suivant (*prép.*), according to; as per:
suivant avis (mention sur une lettre de change) (opp. à *sans avis* ou *sans autre avis*), as per advice.
suivant vos instructions, according to, as per, your instructions.
suivant inventaire, as per list.
suivant celui de ces événements qui s'accomplira le premier, whichever event may first happen.
suivant les usages. See under usage.

suivants (Comptab.) (*n.m.pl.*), sundries:
Pertes et Profits aux suivants, Profit and Loss Dr To Sundries.
Les suivants aux suivants, Sundries Dr To Sundries.

suivi, -e (*adj.*), consistent; continuous:
achats suivis (*m.pl.*), consistent buying.

suivre (*v.t.*), to follow; to follow up; to carry out:
suivre un conseil, les avis de quelqu'un, les instructions d'une lettre, to follow an advice, the advice of someone, the instructions contained in a letter.
suivre une entreprise, to carry out, to follow up, an enterprise.

sujet, -ette (*adj.*), subject; liable:

marchandises sujettes à la casse (*f.pl.*), goods subject (*or* liable) to breakage.

sujet (-ette) à des droits, dutiable; subject (*or* liable) to duty:

toutes les marchandises importées ou exportées, qu'elles soient sujettes à des droits ou qu'elles soient exemptes, all goods imported or exported, whether dutiable or free.

marchandises sujettes à des droits d'entrée (*f.pl.*), goods liable to import duty.

sujet (d'une assurance) (*n.m.*), subject, subject matter (of an insurance):

le sujet du risque est la chose assurée, the subject (*or* the subject matter) of the risk is the thing insured.

sujet, -ette (pers.) (*n.*), subject:

sujet né (sujette née) britannique, British born subject.

Note :—France being a republic, its citizens are not *subjects* (*sujet* is a subject of a kingdom): they are simply *Français* (Frenchmen). Thus the counterpart of the sentence " to acquire membership (*or* to become a member) of the syndicate, it is necessary to be a British subject, or to be a naturalized British subject " would be in French « pour acquérir la qualité de membre du syndicat, il faut être Français, ou être naturalisé Français. »

superbénéfice (*n.m.*), surplus profit:

les actions privilégiées sont assimilées aux actions ordinaires dans le partage des superbénéfices (*f.pl.*), the preference shares are assimilated to the ordinary shares in the sharing of surplus profits.

superdividende (*n.m.*), surplus dividend:

superdividende en sus d'un premier dividende de tant, surplus dividend over and above a first dividend of so much. *See note under* actions de dividende.

suppléer (*v.t.*), to make up:

suppléer un déficit, to make up a deficit.

supplément (*n.m.*), supplement; addition; extra; excess:

supplément de fret, additional freight; extra freight.

supplément de prime (Assce), additional premium; extra premium.

supplément (*n.m.*) *ou* **supplément de taxe** *ou* **supplément du prix de la place** (Ch. de f., etc.), supplement; supplementary charge; extra fare; excess fare:

supplément à acquitter pour admission dans une voiture Pullman, supplement, supplementary charge, extra fare, to pay for admittance to a Pullman car.

supplément (à un journal) (*n.m.*), supplement (to a newspaper).

supplémentaire (*adj.*), supplementary; additional; extra; further:

prime supplémentaire (*f.*), additional premium; extra premium.

demander un crédit supplémentaire *ou* demander un supplément de crédit, to ask for a further credit.

supporter (*v.t.*), to support; to bear:

supporter une perte, les frais encourus pour la conservation de son propre bien, to bear a loss, the expenses incurred for the preservation of one's own property.

suppression (*n.f.*), suppression; abolishing; doing away with:

le caractère distinctif de tout monopole réside dans la suppression de la concurrence, the distinctive character of every monopoly lies in the suppression of competition.

supprimer (*v.t.*), to suppress; to abolish; to do away with:

supprimer un train, to suppress a train (to withdraw it from the service).

supprimer un droit de douane, to abolish, to do away with, a customs duty.

supputation (*n.f.*), computation; reckoning; calculation; working out.

supputer (*v.t.*), to compute; to reckon; to reckon up; to calculate; to work out:

supputer le nombre d'années, to calculate, to reckon, the number of years.

supputer les dépenses, to work out, to reckon up, the expenses.

supputer les résultats probables d'une nouvelle vraie ou fausse sur le cours des fonds, to calculate the probable results of a true or false piece of news on the price of the funds.

sûr, -e (*adj.*), safe:

placement sûr (*m.*), safe investment.

port sûr (*m.*), safe port.

bassin ou autre place sûre de chargement (*m.*), dock or other safe loading place.

sur-arbitre [**sur-arbitres** *pl.*] (pers.) (*n.m.*), umpire.

sur bonnes ou mauvaises nouvelles (Assce mar.), lost or not lost:

assurance faite sur bonnes ou mauvaises nouvelles (*f.*), insurance made lost or not lost.

Sur Mer (Mouvement des Navires) (rubrique de journal), Shipping News; Shipping Intelligence; Shipping.

sur-souscrit, -e (*adj.*), oversubscribed:

l'émission fut sur-souscrite (*f.*), the issue was oversubscribed.

sur wagon, on rail; free on rail; free on truck.

suractivité (*n.f.*), overactivity.

surassurance (*n.f.*), overinsurance.

surassurer (*v.t.*), to overinsure:

assuré qui est surassuré par assurances cumulatives (*m.*), assured who is overinsured by double insurance.

surcapitalisation (*n.f.*), overcapitalization.

surcapitaliser (*v.t.*), to overcapitalize.

surcharge (*n.f.*), surcharge; overcharge; overloading; overload; loading:

surcharge d'un navire, overloading a ship.

surcharge de la prime (Assce), loading of the premium. *See example under syn.* **chargement** (de la prime).

surcharge (mot écrit sur un autre mot comme émendation) (*n.f.*), correction; alteration:

faire une surcharge, to make a correction (*or* an alteration).

registre bien tenu, sans ratures ni surcharges (*m.*), register well kept, without erasures or corrections (*or* alterations).

surcharger (imposer une charge excessive) (*v.t.*), to surcharge ; to overcharge ; to overload ; to load :
surcharger un timbre-poste, to surcharge a postage stamp.
les contributions se règlent certains mois qui sont ainsi surchargés (*f.pl.*), taxes are paid in certain months which are thus overcharged.
surcharger un navire au-dessus de la ligne de flottaison, to overload a ship above the water line.
marché surchargé de titres (*m.*), market overloaded with stock.
surcharger la prime (Assce), to load the premium.

surcharger (imposer des travaux excessifs) (*v.t.*), to overwork :
surcharger ses employés, to overwork one's clerks.

surcharger (faire une surcharge sur l'écriture) (*v.t.*), to correct ; to alter :
les lettres de voiture surchargées ou grattées ne sont pas admises (*f.pl.*), corrected (*or* altered) or scratched consignment notes are not accepted.

surélévation (*n.f.*), rise ; increase ; forcing up.
surélever (*v.t.*), to raise ; to increase ; to force up :
surélever un prix, to force up a price.
surenchère (*n.f.*), higher bid ; outbidding.
surenchérir (*v.i.*), to bid higher ; to rise higher in price.
surenchérissement (*n.m.*), higher bidding ; further rise in price :
surenchérissement des denrées, further rise in the price of provisions.
surenchérisseur, -euse (pers.) (*n.*), outbidder.
surestarie (temps au delà de celui stipulé pour le chargement et le déchargement) (*n.f.*), demurrage :
navire en surestarie (*m.*), ship on demurrage.
surestarie (jour de surestarie) (*n.f.*), day of demurrage.
surestaries (rémunération) (*n.f.pl.*) (opp. à *dispatch money*), demurrage :
paiement des surestaries (*m.*), payment of demurrage.
surestimation *ou* **surévaluation** (*n.f.*), overestimate ; overvaluation.
surestimer *ou* **surévaluer** (*v.t.*), to overestimate ; to overvalue.
sûreté (éloignement de tout péril) (*n.f.*), safety ; security :
la sûreté de ses fonds, the safety of one's money.
sûreté (caution ; garantie) (*s'emploie aussi au pl.*) (*n.f.*), security ; surety :
sûreté d'une créance, security, surety, for a debt.
prendre des sûretés avant de prêter de l'argent, to obtain security before lending money.
surfaire (demander un prix trop élevé de) (*v.t.*), to overcharge ; to overcharge for ; to ask too much for ; to charge too much for :

surfaire un objet, to ask too much for an article.
surfaire (vanter à l'excès) (*v.t.*), to overrate :
surfaire la valeur d'une action, to overrate the value of a share.
surfaire (*v.i.*), to overcharge ; to charge too much ; to ask too much :
ce marchand surfait, this shopkeeper overcharges.
surfret (*n.m.*), extra freight ; additional freight.
surhaussement (*n.m.*), rise ; increase ; forcing up.
surhausser (*v.t.*), to raise ; to increase ; to force up :
surhausser un prix, to force up a price.
surmenage (*n.m.*), overworking.
surmener (*v.t.*), to overwork :
surmener ses employés, to overwork one's clerks.
suroffre (*n.f.*), overbid ; higher offer ; better bid.
surpassé, -e (sur-souscrit) (*adj.*), oversubscribed :
l'émission fut surpassée (*f.*), the issue was oversubscribed.
surpaye (action) (*n.f.*), overpayment.
surpaye (gratification) (*n.f.*), extra pay ; bonus.
surpayer (*v.t.*), to overpay ; to overpay for ; to pay too much for :
surpayer un employé, to overpay an employee.
pays qui étaient obligés de surpayer les charbons anglais (*m.pl.*), countries which were obliged to overpay for English coal.
surpayer un objet, to pay too much for an article.
surplus (*n.m.*), surplus ; overplus ; excess ; balance :
surplus des bénéfices, surplus profits ; excess profits.
je m'oblige à verser le surplus (bulletin de souscription), I undertake to pay the balance.
surprendre une signature, to obtain a signature by fraud.
surprime (Assce) (*n.f.*), additional premium ; extra premium :
surprime à débattre *ou* surprime à arbitrer, additional (*or* extra) premium to be arranged.
surprime d'âge (du navire), additional premium for age (of vessel).
surprime de relèvement. See under **relève-ment**.
surprix (*n.m.*), excess price.
surproduction (*n.f.*), overproduction.
sursalaire (*n.m.*), extra pay ; bonus.
sursurestaries (*n.f.pl.*), damages for detention.
surtare (*n.f.*), supertare.
surtaux (*n.m.*), overassessment.
surtaxe (*n.f.*), surtax ; surcharge ; fee ; duty :
surtaxe aérienne (Poste), air fee ; air mail fee.
surtaxe d'entrepôt. In France, surtax on commodities produced outside Europe but imported from a European country, e.g., Australian produce imported from England. The word *entrepôts* in this connection means

European countries, which countries are legally regarded as merely warehouses for the produce coming from abroad. This surtax is additional to the ordinary customs duty, if any, applicable to the particular product.

surtaxe d'origine. In France, surtax on produce of European origin imported from somewhere other than the country of production, e.g., Italian produce imported from Switzerland. This surtax is additional to the ordinary customs duty, if any, applicable to the particular product.

Note :—The *surtaxe d'entrepôt* and the *surtaxe d'origine* were instituted with the object of favouring direct relationship with producing countries.

surtaxe de levée exceptionnelle (Poste), late fee.

surtaxe de pavillon, alien duty.

surtaxe de poste restante, poste restante fee.

surtaxe de provenance. In France, surtax on goods coming from a *pays de provenance*. See this phrase in vocabulary for explanation.

surtaxer (*v.t.*), to surtax; to surcharge:
surtaxer les riches, détaxer les pauvres, to surtax the rich, to untax the poor.
lettre surtaxée (*f.*), surcharged letter.

surveillance (*n.f.*), superintendence; supervision.

surveillant, -e (pers.) (*n.*), superintendent; supervisor:
endroit où est prélevé l'échantillon choisi par les réceptionnaires ou par les surveillants des vendeurs (*m.*), place where sample is drawn chosen by receivers or by sellers' superintendents.

surveiller (*v.t.*), to superintend; to supervise; to look after.

survendre (*v.t.*), to overcharge for; to sell too dear:
survendre sa marchandise, to overcharge for one's goods.

survendre (*v.i.*), to overcharge; to sell too dear:
marchand qui a l'habitude de survendre (*m.*), shopkeeper who is in the habit of overcharging.

survente (*n.f.*), overcharge; sale at an excessive price; selling at inflated prices:
la survente est une conséquence du monopole, inflated prices are a consequence of monopoly.

survivant, -e (rescapé) (pers.) (*n.*), survivor.

survivant, -e (Dr.) (pers.) (*n.*), survivor.

suscription (d'une lettre) (*n.f.*), superscription.

susceptible (*adj.*), susceptible; capable:
valeurs susceptibles d'être cotées (*f.pl.*), securities capable of being quoted.

susdénommé, -e *ou* **susnommé, -e** (*adj.*), abovenamed; aforenamed:
la personne susdénommée (*ou* susnommée), the above-named person.

susdénommé, -e *ou* **susnommé, -e** *ou* **susdit, -e** (pers.) (*n.*), above-named; aforenamed:

entre les susnommés il a été convenu . . ., it has been agreed between the above-named . . .

susdit, -e *ou* **susmentionné, -e** (*adj.*), aforesaid; said; above-mentioned; aforementioned:
la susdite partie, the aforesaid party.
la convention susmentionnée, the above-mentioned agreement.

suspendre (*v.t.*), to suspend; to stop:
suspendre ses payements, to suspend, to stop, one's payments.

suspens (en), in suspense; in abeyance; held over:
cette affaire est en suspens, this matter is in abeyance (*or* in suspense) (*or* held over).
écritures en suspens (Comptab.) (*f.pl.*), items in suspense.
effets en suspens (*m.pl.*), bills in suspense; bills held over.

suspension (*n.f.*), suspension; stoppage:
suspension de paiements, suspension, stoppage, of payment.

sympathie (*n.f.*), sympathy:
la Banque X. fléchit en (*ou* par) sympathie avec les fonds turcs, X. Bank (shares) drooped in sympathy with Turkish funds.

syndic (pers.) (*n.m.*), syndic (in France, a manager of the affairs of a community or body of men engaged in a business or professional enterprise, particularly the chairman of a disciplinary committee; as, le *syndic des notaires*).
syndic de faillite, trustee, assignee, in bankruptcy.
syndic des naufrages, receiver of wreck.

syndical, -e, -aux (*adj.*), syndical; underwriting; of underwriting:
acte syndical (*m.*), underwriting contract; underwriting letter.
part syndicale *ou* part syndicataire *ou* part de syndicat (*f.*), share of underwriting.

syndicat (fonctions, exercice des fonctions, etc., d'un syndic) (*n.m.*), trusteeship:
accepter le syndicat d'une faillite, to accept the trusteeship of a bankruptcy.
durant le syndicat d'un tel, during the trusteeship of So-and-so.

syndicat (consortium) (*n.m.*), syndicate:
un syndicat de banquiers, a syndicate of bankers.
syndicat-animateur [syndicats-animateurs *pl.*] (Bourse) (*n.m.*), shop.
syndicat d'émission, issue syndicate.
syndicat d'introduction (Bourse), introducing syndicate.
syndicat de banquiers, syndicat des banquiers en valeurs au comptant, en valeurs à terme. *See under* marché des valeurs.
syndicat de bourse, market syndicate.
syndicat de finance *ou* syndicat financier, finance syndicate; financial syndicate.
syndicat de garantie, underwriting syndicate.
syndicat parisien, syndicat à la lyonnaise. A *syndicat parisien* is an underwriting syndicate

in which, if the public do not subscribe the full amount required to complete the issue, each underwriter is called upon to take up shares to the extent of the proportion of the amount underwritten by him and not taken up by the public : distinguished from *syndicat à la lyonnaise*, in which the underwriter is wholly relieved when he has placed an amount equal to his share of underwriting, or is partly relieved to the extent of the shares placed by him.

 syndicat de placement *ou* syndicat de vente, pool.

syndicataire (pers.) (*n.m.*), syndicator ; member of a (*or* the) syndicate.

syndicataire (membre d'un syndicat de garantie) (*n.m.*), underwriter.

syndiquer (*v.t.*), to syndicate :
 syndiquer une industrie, to syndicate an industry.
 actions syndiquées (*f.pl.*), syndicated shares.

se syndiquer (*v.r.*), to syndicate ; to form a syndicate ; to unite to form a syndicate :

financiers qui se syndiquent pour garantir une émission (*m.pl.*), financiers who form a syndicate to underwrite an issue.

systématique (*adj.*), systematic ; systematical.

systématiquement (*adv.*), systematically :
 des faits systématiquement groupés (*m.pl.*), facts systematically grouped.

systématisation (*n.f.*), systematization.

systématiser (*v.t.*), to systematize.

se systématiser (*v.r.*), to be systematized ; to be reduced to a system.

systématiseur (pers.) (*n.m.*), systematizer.

système (*n.m.*), system :
 le système fiscal français, the French fiscal system.
 les avantages d'un système monétaire décimal (*m.pl.*), the advantages of a decimal monetary system.
 un vaste système de bassins, hangars, et entrepôts, a vast system of docks, sheds, and warehouses.
 système des entrepôts (Douanes), warehousing system.

T

T.S.F. (*abrév. de* télégraphie sans fil) (*f.*), wireless ; wireless telegraphy :
 navire pourvu de T.S.F. (*m.*), ship provided with wireless (*or* with wireless telegraphy).

table (meuble) (*n.f.*), table :
 tables et chaises, tables and chairs.

table (tableau) (*n.f.*), table :
 table alphabétique (d'un livre), index (of a book).
 table d'amortissement, redemption table.
 table d'intérêts, interest table.
 table de multiplication *ou* table de Pythagore, multiplication table.
 table de parités, parity table ; table of par values.

tableau (*n.m.*), table ; list :
 tableau comparatif, comparative table.
 tableau d'amortissement, redemption table.
 tableau de marche (liste de départs de navires), list of sailings ; sailings list.

tableau (de franchises) (police d'assce mar.) (*n.m.*), table, memorandum (of franchises) :
 les marchandises désignées comme franc d'avarie particulière au tableau (*f.pl.*), the goods designated as free of particular average in the memorandum.
 Note :—In French policies the *franchises* figure in the form of a table or list (called *tableau*) ; in English policies the *percentages* are given in the form of a memorandum or note (called *memorandum*).

tableau commutateur *ou simplement* **tableau** (*n.m.*) (Téléph.), switch board.

tabulateur (*n.m.*), tabulator.

tacite (*adj.*), tacit ; implied.

taille-crayon [**taille-crayon** *pl.*] *ou* **taille-crayons** [**taille-crayons** *pl.*] (*n.m.*), pencil sharpener.

talon (souche) (*n.m.*), counterfoil ; stub ; stump ; butt ; block :
 talon de récépissé, counterfoil of receipt.
 viser le talon d'un chèque, to initial the counterfoil of a cheque. See also example under **volant.**

talon (certificat attaché à un titre pour obtenir une nouvelle feuille de coupons) (*n.m.*), talon :
 talon donnant droit à une nouvelle feuille de coupons, talon conferring the right to a new sheet of coupons.

tambour (*n.m.*) (Abrév. : **tamb.**), drum.

tampon (coussin impregné d'encre) (*n.m.*), stamp pad ; inking pad ; pad.

tangage (d'un navire) (*n.m.*) (opp. à *roulis*), pitching.

tangible (*adj.*), tangible :
 valeurs tangibles (*f.pl.*), tangible assets.

tanguer (se dit d'un navire) (*v.i.*), to pitch.

tant (une si grande quantité, un si grand nombre) (*adv.*), so much ; so many :
 tant de jours d'intérêt à tant pour cent, so many days' interest at so much per cent.

tant pour cent (*m.*), percentage :
 prix diminué d'un tant pour cent (*m.*), price reduced by a certain percentage.
 capitaine qui reçoit un tant pour cent sur le fret (*m.*), master who receives a percentage on the freight.
 prime fixée à un tant pour cent des valeurs

assurées (f.), premium fixed at a percentage of the values insured. See note under **pour cent.**

tantième (adj.), proportional :
soit à trouver la tantième partie des bénéfices qui revient à un associé, to find the proportional part of the profits accruing to a partner.

tantième (n.m.), proportion ; percentage ; share ; interest ; percentage of profits :
la banque leur alloue un tantième du produit, the bank allows them a proportion of (or a percentage of) (or a share of) (or an interest in) the proceeds.
le tantième de chaque associé dans les bénéfices est proportionnel à ce qu'il apporte, the interest (or share) of each partner in the profits is proportional to what he brings in.
tantièmes des administrateurs, directors' percentage of profits.
tantième d'action, subshare. See note under **coupure d'action.**

taper (v.t.) ou **taper à la machine** ou **taper à la machine à écrire,** to typewrite ; to type :
taper une lettre ou taper une lettre à la machine, to typewrite, to type, a letter.

tarage (n.m.), taring :
le tarage des wagons vides, taring empty trucks.

tardif, -ive (adj.), late :
livraison tardive (f.), late delivery.

tare (n.f.) (Abrév. : **T.**), tare :
la tare est le poids des emballages servant au transport des marchandises ; la différence entre le poids brut et la tare donne le poids net, the tare is the weight of the packages used in the carrying of the goods ; the difference between the gross weight and the tare gives the net weight.
tare conventionnelle ou tare d'usage, customary tare.
tare inscrite, painted tare :
les marchandises en vrac peuvent être pesées sur pont-bascule et leur poids net obtenu en déduisant du poids total reconnu la tare inscrite sur le wagon (f.pl.), goods in bulk can be weighed on a weighbridge and their net weight obtained by deducting from the total weight found the tare painted on the wagon.
tare intégrale, lump tare.
tare légale, tare assumed by the customs (in arriving at a net weight without taring). Cf. poids net légal.
tare proportionnelle, average tare.
tare réelle, real tare ; actual tare.

tare de caisse (f.), shortage in the cash.

tarer (v.t.), to tare.

tarif (n.m.), tariff ; rate ; rates ; scale ; price list ; list ; fare :
tarif colonial (des droits de douane), preferential rates (of customs duties) (on goods imported from colonies). Cf. tarif minimum.
tarif combiné, combined rate.
tarif d'annonces, advertisement rates.
tarif d'assurances, insurance tariff ; insurance rates.

tarif d'entrée (Douanes), import list.
tarif d'urgence (télégrammes), urgent rate.
tarifs de base, basis rates.
tarif de (ou des) courtages (Bourse), scale of commissions ; commission rates :
tarif de courtages établi par la chambre syndicale des agents de change, scale of commissions fixed by the stock exchange committee.
banquier qui a comme bénéfice la ristourne que fait l'agent sur le tarif officiel des courtages (m.), banker who has, as profit, the rebate which the broker makes on the official commission rates.
tarif de douane ou tarif des douanes ou tarif douanier, customs tariff.
tarif de faveur ou tarif de préférence ou tarif préférentiel, preferential tariff :
Note :—When speaking of French preferential tariffs, it is better to use the words tarif de faveur, when of British (i.e., imperial), the words tarif de préférence or tarif préférentiel.
un tarif de faveur concédé aux nations qui nous accordent des avantages corrélatifs, a preferential tariff conceded to nations who grant us correlative privileges.
les tarifs préférentiels dont bénéficient les transactions interimpériales, the preferential tariffs under which interimperial transactions benefit.
tarif de la messagerie, parcels rate(s).
tarif (ou tarifs) de marchandises, goods rates ; freight rates.
tarif de sortie (Douanes), export list.
tarif (ou tarifs) de voyageurs, passenger rates.
tarifs des chemins de fer ou tarif ferroviaire, railway rates.
tarif des échantillons ou tarif d'affranchissement des échantillons, sample rate ; prepaid rate of postage for samples.
tarif des impressions en relief à l'usage des aveugles (Poste), blind literature rate.
tarif des imprimés (Poste), printed paper rate.
tarif des lettres (Poste), letter rate.
tarif des périodiques ou tarif des imprimés périodiques ou tarif des publications périodiques (Poste), newspaper rate.
tarif du régime intérieur (affranchissement postal), inland rate.
tarif général ou tarif maximum (des droits de douane), full rates (of customs duties).
tarif McKinley, McKinley tariff.
tarif minimum ou tarif spécial (des droits de douane), preferential rates (of customs duties) (on goods imported from foreign countries under reciprocity agreements) : (Cf. tarif colonial.)
marchandises étrangères qui bénéficient du tarif minimum sur justification d'origine (f.pl.), foreign goods which benefit by preferential rates on proof of origin.
tarif ordinaire (télégrammes, etc.), ordinary rate.

tarifs postaux, postal rates; postage rates.

billet à plein tarif, à demi-tarif (*m.*), full fare, half fare, ticket; ticket at full fare (*or* at full rate), at half fare.

tarifaire (*adj.*), tariff (*used as adj.*); rating: régime tarifaire (*m.*), tariff system; rating system.

tarifer (*v.t.*), to tariff; to rate; to price; to charge with duty: marchandises tarifées autrement qu'au poids (Douanes) (*f.pl.*), goods rated (*or* charged with duty) otherwise than by weight.

marchandise tarifée (payant des droits de douane) (*f.*), dutiable goods.

tarification (*n.f.*), tariffication; rating: tarification douanière au poids, au volume, customs tariffication by weight, by measurement.

tarification ferroviaire sur la base exclusivement kilométrique, railway tariffication (*or* rating) on an exclusively kilometric basis.

tassement (recul) (Bourse) (*n.m.*), setback: campagne de hausse entrecoupée de quelques tassements (*f.*), bull campaign interrupted by a few setbacks.

tasser (se) (*v.r.*), to have a setback: aux industrielles, l'action X. s'est encore tassée de 3 180 à 3 150, among industrials, X. shares had another setback from 3,180 to 3,150 francs.

taux (prix fixé ou réglé par une convention ou par l'usage) (*n.m.*), rate; price: le taux du salaire, the rate of wages.

le taux d'émission des actions, the issue price of shares.

taux à forfait *ou* taux forfaitaire, through rate(s): taux à forfait pour Londres domicile, et l'intérieur de l'Angleterre (*m.pl.*), through rates to address in London, and the interior of England.

taux à vue (Marché des changes), demand rate.

taux d'escompte *ou* taux de l'escompte, rate of discount; discount rate.

taux d'intérêt *ou* taux de l'intérêt *ou simplement* taux, rate of interest; rate: taux d'intérêt des avances *ou* taux des avances, rate of interest on advances; rate for advances.

le taux de l'intérêt de l'argent, the rate of interest on money.

prêter au taux de 5 pour cent, to lend at the rate of 5 per cent.

taux légal, legal rate of interest (rate of interest fixed by the law in the absence of agreement, etc.).

taux de capitalisation (d'un titre), rate of capitalization, yield (of a stock).

taux de (*ou* du) change, rate of exchange; exchange: au taux de change en cours à Paris à la date de la remise, at the rate of exchange current in Paris on the date of the remittance.

taux de conversion, rate of conversion.

taux de (*ou* du) fret, freight rate; rate of freight.

taux de l'argent *ou* taux monétaires, money rates.

taux de prime *ou* taux de la prime (Assce), rate of premium.

taux des déports *ou* taux du déport (Bourse), backwardation rate.

taux des renouvellements (de l'argent), renewal rate.

taux des reports *ou* taux du report (Bourse), contango rate; contango; carry over rate; continuation rate. See example under **cherté.**

taux du trois mois, three months' bills rate.

taux hors banque (*Abrév.:* THB.) *ou* taux privé *ou* taux d'escompte hors banque *ou* taux d'escompte privé *ou* taux de l'escompte privé (opp. à *taux officiel*), market rate; market rate of discount; discount rate of the open market; open market discount rate; private rate; private rate of discount.

taux officiel *ou* taux officiel d'escompte *ou* taux officiel de l'escompte *ou* taux de la Banque régulatrice, bank rate; bank rate of discount; official rate; official rate of discount: intérêt à 1 0/0 au-dessus du taux officiel (*ou* au-dessus du taux officiel d'escompte) (*ou* au-dessus du taux de la Banque régulatrice) (*m.*), interest at 1% above bank rate.

l'escompte ou l'argent est dit serré lorsque par suite des besoins en capitaux du marché, le taux de l'escompte privé se rapproche du taux officiel de l'escompte, c'est-à-dire, en France, du taux de la Banque de France (*m.*), discount or money is said to be tight when owing to the market's requirements of money, the market rate of discount approximates to the bank rate of discount, that is to say, in France, to the rate of the Bank of France.

taux officiel de la Banque d'Angleterre *ou* taux d'escompte de la Banque d'Angleterre, Bank rate; Bank of England minimum rate of discount.

taux officiel de la Banque de France *ou* taux d'escompte de la Banque de France *ou* taux Banque de France (*Abrév.:* TB.), French bank rate; Bank of France rate of discount.

taux officiel (*ou* taux d'escompte) de la Banque nationale (*ou* de la Banque Nationale de Belgique), Belgian bank rate; National Bank of Belgium rate of discount.

taux pour cent, rate per cent.

taux unitaire de la prime (Bourse), option rate.

taxable *ou* **taxatif, -ive** (*adj.*), taxable; assessable; chargeable with duty.

taxateur (pers.) (*n.m.*), taxer.

taxateur (*n.m.*) *ou* **juge taxateur** (*m.*), taxing master.

taxation (*n.f.*), taxation; rating; assessment; charging; charging with duty; charges; fixing of maximum price(s):

répartition inéquitable de taxation (f.), inequitable distribution of taxation.

taxation des frais d'un procès, taxation of the costs of an action.

taxation d'office (Impôts cédulaires), arbitrary assessment.

mode de taxation des excédents de bagages (m.), method of charging for excess luggage.

taxation des télégrammes internationaux, charges for imperial and foreign telegrams.

essais de taxation par l'État pendant la guerre de 1914–1918 (m.pl.), attempts at fixing of maximum prices by the government during the war of 1914–1918.

taxe (impôt; droit) (n.f.) ou **taxes** (n.f.pl.), tax; taxes; rate; rates; duty; due; dues; taxation:

payer sa taxe, to pay one's taxes (or one's rates).

taxe d'abonnement au timbre, composition for stamp duty.

taxe d'importation, import duty.

taxe de luxe, luxury tax.

taxes de pilotage, pilotage dues; pilotage.

taxe de séjour, visitors' tax.

taxe de transmission, transfer duty. *See* note under syn. droit de transmission.

taxe des pauvres, poor rate; poor rates.

taxe hypothécaire, mortgage duty.

taxes intérieures, inland duties.

taxe sur le revenu ou taxe sur revenu, income tax.

taxe (prix officiellement fixé pour certains services) (n.f.), charge; fee:

taxe arrondie au décime supérieur, charge rounded up to the next higher *décime*; fractions of a penny charged as a penny.

taxe d'exprès (Poste), express fee.

taxe d'intérêt à la livraison. *See* intérêt à la livraison.

taxe de bord (radiotélégrammes), ship charge.

taxe de chômage (Ch. de f.), demurrage; demurrage charge.

taxe de communication (Téléph.), charge for call; call charge.

taxe de dédouanement (Poste), fee for clearance through customs.

taxe de dépôt des bagages, cloak room fee.

taxe de factage, porterage charge.

taxe de jour (Téléph.), day charge.

taxe de location (de places), reservation fee (for seats).

taxe de nuit (Téléph.), night charge.

taxe de prise à domicile (Ch. de f., etc.), charge for collection.

taxe de rapprochement, quay handling charges.

taxe de recommandation (Poste), registration fee; fee for registration.

taxe de réexpédition (Poste), charge for redirection.

taxe de remboursement, cash on delivery fee.

taxe de remise à domicile (Ch. de f., etc.), charge for delivery.

taxe de stationnement (Ch. de f.), demurrage charge; demurrage (for detention or non use of vehicles).

taxe de transmission téléphonique (télégrammes), writing down fee.

taxe forfaitaire pour l'enlèvement et la réinstallation des organes essentiels d'un poste téléphonique, standard charge for the removal and reinstallation of a telephone line and apparatus.

taxe maritime (radiotélégrammes), marine charge (land charge or ship charge).

taxe-minute (Téléph.) (n.f.), minute charge:

la taxe-minute est le tiers de la taxe appliquée pour trois minutes, the minute charge is a third of the charge made for three minutes.

taxes postales, postal charges.

taxe supplémentaire, supplementary charge.

taxe terrestre (radiotélégrammes), land charge.

taxe unitaire (de conversation téléphonique), unit charge.

taxe (Dr.) (n.f.), taxation:

taxe des dépens ou taxe des frais et actes, taxation of costs.

taxer (mettre un impôt sur) (v.t.), to tax; to rate, to assess; to charge with duty (Customs):

taxer les objets de luxe, to tax luxuries.

marchandises taxées au brut (ou au poids brut), au net (ou au poids net), autrement qu'au poids (f.pl.), goods charged with duty on the gross weight, on the net weight, otherwise than by weight.

se taxer (v.r.), to be taxed:

tout se taxe, everything is taxed.

taxer (régler le prix de) (v.t.), to charge; to charge for; to fix the maximum price(s) of:

taxer une lettre comme non affranchie, to charge a letter as unpaid.

les excédents de bagages sont taxés ainsi qu'il suit (m.pl.), excess luggage is charged (or is charged for) as follows.

marchandises taxées à la tonne (f.pl.), goods charged by the ton.

État qui intervient de taxer le pain et la viande (m.), government which invervenes to fix the maximum prices of bread and meat.

taxer (Dr.) (v.t.), to tax:

taxer les dépens d'un procès, to tax the costs of an action.

mémoire taxé (m.), taxed bill of costs.

taxeur (pers.) (n.m.), taxer.

tel quel, telle quelle (Abrév.: **T.Q.**), tel quel; tale quale:

cours tel quel (m.), tel quel rate; tale quale rate. See **parité** for example.

cote telle quelle (f.), tel quel quotation; tale quale quotation.

télégramme (n.m.), telegram; wire:

expédier un télégramme, to send a telegram (or a wire).

télégramme à adresses multiples ou simplement télégramme multiple (Abrév.: TM.), multiple address telegram; multiple telegram.

télégramme à distribuer même pendant la nuit (Abrév.: Nuit), telegram to be delivered at once, if in the normal course it would be retained until the daytime.

télégramme (qui parvient à destination la nuit) à distribuer seulement pendant les heures de jour (*Abrév.: * Jour), telegram (arriving at night) to be delivered only in the daytime.

télégramme à faire suivre *ou* télégramme à réexpédier (*Abrév.: * FS.), telegram to follow the addressee; telegram to be redirected.

télégramme à remise retardée (*Abrév.: * DLT.), daily letter telegram.

télégramme adressé poste restante (*Abrév.: * GP.), telegram addressed poste restante.

télégramme adressé poste restante recommandée (*Abrév.: * GPR.), telegram addressed poste restante registered.

télégramme adressé télégraphe restant (*Abrév.: * TR.), telegram to be called for; telegram addressed télégraphe restant.

télégramme avec accusé de réception (télégraphique) (*Abrév.: * PC.), telegram with notice of delivery (by telegraph).

télégramme avec accusé de réception postal (*Abrév.: * PCP.), telegram with notice of delivery by post.

télégramme avec collationnement (*Abrév.: * TC.), telegram with repetition.

télégramme avec réponse payée (*Abrév.: * RP.), reply paid telegram.

télégramme chiffré, telegram in cipher.

télégramme de fin de semaine (*Abrév.: * WLT.), week-end letter telegram.

télégramme de mer, telegram from ship at sea.

télégramme de presse (*Abrév.: * Presse), press telegram.

télégramme de service, service telegram.

télégramme déposé en dernière limite d'heure (*Abrév.: * limité), telegram handed in near closing time.

télégramme destiné à (*ou* à destination d') un navire en mer, telegram for transmission to ship at sea.

télégramme différé (*Abrév.: * LCO., LCF., *ou* LCD.), deferred telegram. *Note : —* For meanings of LCO., etc., see Abréviations en usage ordinaire.

télégramme du régime intérieur *ou simplement* télégramme intérieur, inland telegram.

télégramme du régime international *ou simplement* télégramme international. *English equivalent is* imperial or foreign telegram (*collective plural* imperial and foreign telegrams).

télégramme en compte (provision de garantie), telegram in account :

les télégrammes en compte sont ceux dont la taxe n'est pas perçue au moment du dépôt, telegrams in account are those on which the charge is not collected at the time of handing in.

télégramme en langage clair, telegram in plain language.

télégramme en langage convenu, telegram in code.

télégramme-lettre [télégrammes-lettres *pl.*] (*n.m.*), letter telegram.

télégramme-mandat [télégrammes-mandats *pl.*] (*n.m.*), money order telegram.

télégramme maritime, marine telegram (telegram to or from ship at sea) :

télégrammes maritimes échangés au moyen des stations côtières avec les navires en mer, marine telegrams exchanged through coast stations with ships at sea.

télégramme officiel, official telegram.

télégramme ordinaire, ordinary telegram.

télégramme privé, private telegram.

télégramme-réponse [télégrammes-réponse *pl.*], (*n.m.*), reply telegram.

télégramme sans voie, unrouted telegram.

télégramme sémaphorique (*Abrév.: * Sem.), telegram to be signalled when vessel (not equipped for wireless telegraphy) is passing (a signalling station); semaphoric telegram.

télégramme téléphoné, telephoned telegram.

télégramme urgent (*Abrév.: * D.), urgent telegram.

télégramme via T.S.F., telegram via wireless.

télégraphe (appareil) (*n.m.*), telegraph :

recevoir des nouvelles par le télégraphe, to receive news by telegraph.

télégraphe imprimeur, tape machine; printing telegraph; ticker.

télégraphe (bureau) (*n.m.*), telegraph office :

aller au télégraphe, to go to the telegraph office.

télégraphe restant (mots inscrits sur un télégramme), to be called for (at a telegraph office); télégraphe restant.

télégraphie (*n.f.*), telegraphy :

télégraphie avec fil (*f.*) *ou simplement* fil (*n.m.*), wire telegraphy; wire :

acheminement par fil (*m.*), routing by wire.

télégraphie sans fil *ou* T.S.F. *ou simplement* sans fil, wireless telegraphy; wireless; radiotelegraphy :

acheminement par sans fil (*m.*), routing by wireless.

télégraphier (*v.t.*), to telegraph; to wire :

télégraphier une nouvelle, to telegraph a piece of news.

télégraphier (*v.i.*), to telegraph; to wire.

télégraphique (*adj.*), telegraphic; telegraph (*used as adj.*) :

adresse télégraphique (*f.*), telegraphic address.

bureau télégraphique (*m.*), telegraph office.

télégraphiquement (*adv.*), telegraphically.

télégraphiste (pers.) (*n.m.* ou *f.*), telegraphist.

téléphone (*n.m.*), telephone.

téléphoner (*v.t.*), to telephone :

téléphoner une importante nouvelle, to telephone an important piece of news.

téléphoner (*v.i.*), to telephone.

téléphonie (*n.f.*), telephony :

téléphonie avec fil, wire telephony.

téléphonie sans fil (*Abrév.: * T.S.F.), wireless telephony; radiotelephony.

téléphonique (*adj.*), telephonic; telephone (*used as adj.*) :

appel téléphonique (*m.*), telephonic call; telephone call; ring up.

téléphoniquement (*adv.*), telephonically.

téléphoniste (pers.) (*n.m.* ou *f.*), telephonist.

témoin (pers.) (*n.m.*), witness:
les témoins soussignés, the undersigned witnesses.
en témoin de quoi, in witness whereof.
tempête (*n.f.*), storm.
temporaire (*adj.*) (Ant.: *permanent*), temporary: placements temporaires (*m.pl.*), temporary investments.
temps (*n.m.*), time:
le temps est de l'argent *ou* le temps, c'est de l'argent, time is money.
les temps auxquels les risques doivent commencer et finir, the times at which the risks are to commence and close.
nous ne manquerons pas de vous en aviser en temps utile, we will not fail to advise you of it in good (*or* proper) (*or* due) time.
temps gagné (dispatch), time gained.
temps perdu (dispatch), time lost.
demander du temps (délai; remise), to ask for time.
accordez-moi du temps (délai; remise), give me time.
temps le permettant *ou* **le temps le permettant,** weather permitting.
tendance (*n.f.*), tendency; trend:
les tendances du marché, the tendencies (*or* the trend) of the market.
tendance à la baisse (Bourse), downward tendency (*or* trend); bearish tendency.
tendance à la hausse (Bourse), upward tendency (*or* trend); bullish tendency.
tendre (**se**) (*v.r.*), to stiffen; to harden; to harden up; to firm; to firm up:
les reports sont chers ou se tendent si l'argent est rare et le titre abondant; les reports sont bon marché ou se détendent si l'argent est abondant et le titre rare (*m.pl.*), contangoes are high (*or* heavy) or stiffen (*or* harden *or* harden up) (*or* firm *or* firm up) if money is scarce and stock plentiful; contangoes are low (*or* light) or ease off if money is plentiful and stock scarce.
la livre et le dollar se tendent, the pound and the dollar hardened.
tendu, -e (*adj.*), stiff; hard; firm.
teneur (*n.f.*), tenor; terms; contents:
teneur et forme de la lettre de voiture, tenor and form of the consignment note.
en foi de quoi le capitaine a signé quatre connaissements, tous d'une même (*ou* de même) teneur et date, in witness whereof the master has signed four bills of lading, all of same tenor and date.
modifications apportées à la teneur d'un traité (*f.pl.*), alterations made in the terms of an agreement.
teneur d'une lettre, contents of a letter.
teneur de carnet (Bourse) (pers.) (*m.*), authorized clerk.
teneur de livres (pers.) (*m.*), bookkeeper. Cf. **comptable,** and example thereunder.
teneuse de livres (*f.*), bookkeeper; lady bookkeeper.
tenir (*v.t.*). See examples:
tenir à bail, to hold on (*or* under) lease:

tenir une maison à bail, to hold a house on (*or* under) lease.
tenir à la disposition de, to hold at the disposal of:
solde tenu à la disposition du bénéficiaire (*m.*), balance held at the disposal of the beneficiary.
tenir compte de, to take into account; to make allowance for; to have regard to; to account:
tenir compte des fluctuations du change, to take the fluctuations of exchange into account; to make allowance for the fluctuations in the exchange.
tenir compte des conseils de quelqu'un, to have regard to someone's advice.
tenir compte à l'acheteur de l'intérêt, to account to the buyer for the interest.
tenir conseil, to hold a meeting (*or* a consultation). *Cf.* tenir une assemblée.
tenir couvert, -e (Assce), to hold covered:
nous vous tenons couvert, vous êtes tenu couvert, en attendant réception de plus amples détails, we hold you covered, pending receipt of further particulars.
tenir des livres *ou* tenir des écritures *ou* tenir la comptabilité *ou* tenir des comptes, to keep books; to keep accounts:
tenir les livres (*ou* les écritures) (*ou* la comptabilité) (*ou* les comptes) d'une maison, to keep a firm's books (*or* accounts).
tenir des livres en partie double (*ou* à parties doubles), to keep books by double entry.
tenir des livres en partie simple (*ou* à partie simple), to keep books by single entry.
tenir ses écritures d'une manière irrégulière, to keep one's accounts in an irregular manner.
tenir à jour les écritures, to keep the books (*or* the accounts) up to date.
tenir la bourse, to hold the purse.
tenir la caisse, to keep the cash (to have the care of the cash):
employé qui tient la caisse et écrit la comptabilité (*m.*), clerk who keeps the cash and writes up the books.
tenir la mer, to keep at sea:
aptitude d'un navire à tenir la mer (*f.*), fitness of a ship to keep at sea.
tenir les cordons de la bourse, to hold the purse strings.
tenir serrés les cordons de la bourse, to hold the purse strings tight.
tenir note de (*ou* tenir registre de) ses dépenses, to keep a note of, to jot down, one's expenses.
tenir sa position, to hold on:
disposer d'un capital suffisant pour tenir sa position, to have at command a sufficient capital to enable one to hold on.
tenir ses engagements, to keep one's engagements.
tenir son argent sous clef, to keep one's money under lock and key.
tenir un emploi, to hold, to occupy, a situation.
tenir un livre propre, to keep a book clean.

tenir une assemblée générale d'actionnaires, to hold a general meeting of shareholders.

tenir (suivre son cours) (*v.i.*), to hold up; to be sustained; to be firm; to be hard:
notre marché tient toujours (*m.*), our market holds up very well (*or* is still firm) (*or* is still hard).

tenir (siéger) (*v.i.*), to sit:
les tribunaux tiennent toute l'année (*m.pl.*), the tribunals sit all the year round.

tenir (**se**) (être tenu) (*v.r.*), to be kept; to be held:
les comptes courants avec intérêts peuvent se tenir suivant plusieurs méthodes (*m.pl.*), accounts current with interest can be kept according to several methods.
si une assemblée extraordinaire doit se tenir à la suite d'une assemblée ordinaire, if an extraordinary meeting is intended to be held following an ordinary meeting.

tenir (**se**) (se maintenir) (*v.r.*), to keep; to keep oneself; to be:
l'action X. se tient à 262, X. shares kept at 262 francs.
se tenir dans les marges du code, to keep within the law.
se tenir renseigné (-e) sur une certaine affaire, to keep oneself posted on a certain matter.
se tenir sur ses gardes, to be on one's guard.

tenir (**se**) (ne vouloir pas céder) (*v.r.*), to hold out:
se tenir à vingt francs sur un marché de mille écus, to hold out for a few shillings on a transaction involving hundreds of pounds.

tension (*n.f.*), stiffness; hardness; firmness:
tension des reports, stiffness, hardness, firmness, of contangoes. See example under **tendre (se).**

tente (magasin-cale) (Douanes) (*n.f.*), bonded shed; sufferance wharf:
dépôt de marchandises à quai ou sous tente (*m.*), deposit of goods on wharf or in bonded shed (*or* sheds).

tenu, -e (ferme dans le prix) (*adj.*), firm; hard:
valeurs tenues (*f.pl.*), firm stocks.
les fonds turcs sont mieux tenus dans l'ensemble (*m.pl.*), Turkish funds were firmer (*or* harder) generally.

tenu (-e) à (être) *ou* **tenu (-e) de** (être) *ou* **tenu (-e) pour** (être), to be bound to; to be obliged to; to be liable for:
être tenu (-e) de remplir une obligation, to be bound to fulfil an obligation.
la banque est tenue d'avoir une encaisse métallique égale au tiers du montant de ses billets et de ses autres engagements à vue, the bank is bound (*or* obliged) to have gold and silver coin and bullion equal to one third of the amount of its notes and of its other sight commitments.
plusieurs personnes qui sont tenues à une dette (*f.pl.*), several people who are liable for a debt.
être tenu (-e) des dommages-intérêts, to be liable for damages.
être tenu (-e) pour le tout, to be liable for the whole.

tenue (action d'être tenu) (*n.f.*), holding:
la tenue d'une réunion du conseil, de l'assemblée générale, the holding of a board meeting, of the general meeting.

tenue (dispositions; ton) (*n.f.*), tone:
la Bourse de Paris était favorablement influencée par la bonne tenue de Wall Street hier, the Paris Bourse was favourably influenced by the good tone (*or* firmness) of Wall Street yesterday.

tenue (fermeté dans la valeur des fonds) (*n.f.*), firmness:
la tenue de la rente, the firmness of rentes.

tenue des livres *ou* **tenue de livres** *ou* **tenue des** (*ou* **de**) **comptes** (*f.*), bookkeeping; keeping books; keeping accounts: (See also **comptabilité.**)
tenue des livres en partie double *ou* tenue des livres à parties doubles, double entry bookkeeping.
tenue des livres en partie simple (*ou* à partie simple), single entry bookkeeping.

terme (durée; époque) (*n.m.*), term; time; date:
terme d'un bail, term of a lease.
le terme est l'essence du contrat, time is the essence of the contract.
terme de grâce, time to pay.
terme fatal *ou* terme de rigueur, latest time; latest date; final date; at the latest (after which no further time will be given, as for payment):
le terme fatal de la liquidation en bourse, the final date of the settlement on the stock exchange.
terme d'échéance (d'un effet, d'une lettre de change), term; time of payment; tenor; currency:
le terme d'échéance de la lettre de change est trois mois de vue, the term (*or* the time of payment) (*or* the tenor) (*or* the currency) of the bill of exchange is three months after sight.

à terme. See
achat à terme,
achat à terme ferme,
acheter à terme,
affrètement à terme,
assurance à terme,
crédit à court terme,
crédit à long terme,
dépôt à court terme,
dépôt à terme,
dépôt à terme fixe,
'ret à terme,
marché à terme,
marché à terme ferme,
négociation à terme,
négociations de change à terme,
opération à court terme,
opération à long terme,
opération à terme,
opérations de change à terme,
passif à long terme,
passif exigible à court terme,
placement à court terme,

placement à long terme,
police à terme,
prêt à court terme,
prêt à long terme,
prêt à terme,
règlement à terme,
remboursable à terme,
rente à terme,
risque à terme,
valeurs réalisables à court terme,
vendre à terme,
vente à terme,
vente à terme ferme.

terme (clause; teneur) (*n.m.*), term:
les termes d'un contrat, the terms of a contract.

terme (Bourse de valeurs) (*n.m.*), account; settlement.

terme (fin) (*n.m.*), end:
le terme d'un procès, the end of an action.

terme (durée de 3 mois) (*n.m.*), quarter:
occuper un bureau pendant un terme, to occupy an office for one quarter.

terme (époque à laquelle on doit effectuer le payement du prix d'un loyer) (*n.m.*), quarter day.

terme (somme à payer pour la location d'un terme) (*n.m.*), quarter's rent; rent:
payer un terme, to pay a quarter's rent.
à Paris, le payement du terme est dû au 1er janvier, au 1er avril, au 1er juillet, et au 1er octobre, in Paris, payment of rent is due on 1st January, 1st April, 1st July, and 1st October.

terme (versement; acompte) (*n.m.*), instalment; installment; call:
verser le premier, le second, terme, to pay the first, the second, instalment (*or* call) (on shares, or the like).
l'acquittement (*ou* le versement) des termes échus d'annuités, d'intérêts (*m.*), the payment of instalments of annuities, of interest, due.

terminer (accommoder) (*v.t.*), to settle:
terminer un différend à l'amiable, to settle a difference amicably.

terminer (clôturer) (*v.i.*), to finish; to close:
l'action X. termine à 573 sans grand changement sur son cours d'il y a huit jours, X. shares finished (*or* closed) at 573 francs without much change in their price of a week ago.

terminus (Ch. de f.) (*n.m.*), terminus; terminal; terminal station.

terne (*adj.*), dull:
c'est encore une semaine bien terne que nous avons à passer en revue, again it is a very dull week that we have to pass in review.

terrain (*n.m.*) *ou* **terre** (*n.f.*), land; ground; piece of land; piece of ground:
le terrain se vend cher à Paris, land (*or* ground) is dear in Paris.
terrains et bâtiments, land and buildings.
la bourse est, par excellence, le terrain de l'inconnu et des surprises, the stock exchange is, preeminently, the land of the unknown and of surprises.

acheter une terre, to buy a piece of land (*or* a piece of ground).

terre (opp. à *mer*) (*n.f.*), land; shore.
à terre, on land; on shore; ashore:
feu à terre ou à bord (*m.*), fire on shore or on board.
marchandises emmagasinées à terre ou à flot (*f.pl.*), goods stored ashore or afloat.

terre-plein [terre-pleins *pl.*] (*n.m.*), open space (as, for instance, on a wharf, as opposed to *covered space*, as sheds or warehouses).

terrestre (*adj.*) *ou* **de terre**, land (*used as adj.*); non marine:
risque terrestre *ou* risque de terre (Assce) (*m.*), land risk; non marine risk.

territoire de (*ou* à) **mandat** (*m.*), mandated territory.

testament (*n.m.*), will; testament; will and testament; last will and testament:
faire son testament, to make one's will.
ceci est mon testament, this is my last will and testament.

testamentaire (*adj.*), testamentary.

testateur (pers.) (*n.m.*), testator.

testatrice (pers.) (*n.f.*), testatrix.

tester (*v.i.*), to make a will; to make one's will

tête (première ligne d'une feuille; haut) (*n.f.*), head; top:
être en tête d'une liste de souscription, to be at the head of, to be at the top of, to head to top, a subscription list.

tête (principale direction) (*n.f.*), head:
être à la tête des affaires, to be at the head of affairs.

tête (en-tête) (*n.f.*), heading; head:
tête de facture, bill head; bill heading.
tête de grand livre, ledger heading.
tête de lettre, letter heading.

tête de ligne (Ch. de f.) (*f.*), terminus; terminal terminal station:
la tête de ligne du réseau P.-L.-M., the terminus of the P.L.M. system.

texte (*n.m.*), text; wording:
texte d'une police d'assurance, d'un télégramme, text, wording, of an insurance policy, of a telegram.

théorie métallique (*f.*), currency principle.

thésaurisation (*n.f.*), hoarding; hoarding up:
pénurie de numéraire due à la thésaurisation (*f.*), scarcity of coin due to hoarding.

thésauriser (*v.t.*), to hoard; to hoard up; to treasure up:
thésauriser l'or, to hoard gold.

thésauriseur, -euse (pers.) (*n.*), hoarder.

ticker (*n.m.*), ticker; tape machine; printing telegraph.

ticket (*n.m.*), ticket: (See also **billet**.)
ticket d'entrée en gare, platform ticket.
ticket de chemin de fer *ou* ticket de place, railway ticket.
ticket de location de place *ou* ticket garde place, reserved seat ticket.

tickler (mémorial) (*n.m.*), tickler; memorial tickler.

tiers, tierce (*adj.*), third; of a third party:
une tierce personne, a third person.

déposer une somme en main tierce, to deposit a sum in the hands of a third party.

tiers (tierce personne) (*n.m.*), third person; third party:
avoir recours à un tiers, to have recourse to a third person.
risque du recours de tiers (*m.*), third party risk.

tiers arbitre (pers.) (*m.*), third arbitrator; umpire.

tiers porteur (d'un effet, etc.) (*m.*), holder in due course (of a bill, etc.):
police d'assurance transmise à un tiers porteur de bonne foi régulièrement nanti du connaissement (*f.*), insurance policy transferred to a bona fide holder in due course duly secured by bill of lading.

tillac (*n.m.*), deck.

timbrage (*n.m.*), stamping:
timbrage des titres au porteur, stamping bearer warrants.
formules présentées au timbrage (*f.pl.*), forms presented for stamping.

timbre (marque imprimée; vignette; figurine) (*n.m.*), stamp:
un timbre d'un franc (*ou* de 1 franc), un timbre d'un demi-centime, a franc stamp (*or* a 1 fc stamp), a half centime stamp.
timbre à l'extraordinaire, stamp impressed by a revenue office (on an instrument submitted to it). See example under **timbrer.**
timbre ayant déjà servi, used stamp.
timbre chemin de fer [timbres chemins de fer *pl.*], railway charges stamp.
timbre d'affranchissement (Poste), stamp in prepayment of postage.
timbre d'effet de commerce *ou* timbre des effets de commerce *ou* timbre des effets, bill stamp.
timbre de chèque *ou* timbre-chèque [timbres-chèques *pl.*] (*n.m.*), cheque stamp.
timbre de connaissement, bill of lading stamp.
timbre de dimension. In France, stamp representing duty paid, applicable to certain legal or formal instruments, and proportioned on the size of the paper used.
timbre de police, policy stamp.
timbre de quittance *ou* timbre à quittance *ou* timbre-quittance [timbres-quittances *pl.*] (*n.m.*) *ou* timbre d'acquit *ou* timbre proportionnel d'acquit [timbres proportionnels d'acquits *pl.*] *ou* timbre spécial pour quittances, reçus et décharges, receipt stamp.
timbre de virement. In France, revenue stamp on a *mandat, bon,* or *chèque, de virement.*
timbre-épargne [timbres-épargne *pl.*] (*n.m.*), coupon (post office savings bank).
timbre fiscal, revenue stamp; inland revenue stamp.
timbre humide, pad stamp; *can be translated as* rubber stamp *or* indiarubber stamp.
timbre mobile *ou* timbre adhésif, adhesive stamp.
timbre non employé *ou* timbre non utilisé, unused stamp.

timbre-poste [timbres-poste *pl.*] (*n.m.*), postage stamp.
timbre proportionnel, ad valorem stamp.
timbre sec *ou* timbre fixe *ou* timbre imprimé, impressed stamp; embossed stamp.
timbre-taxe [timbres-taxe *pl.*] (*n.m.*), postage due stamp.

timbre (marque particulière que chaque bureau de poste imprime sur les lettres) (*n.m.*), postmark:
cette lettre porte le timbre de Paris, this letter bears the Paris postmark.

timbre (marque d'une administration, d'une maison de commerce) (*n.m.*), stamp:
apposer le timbre de la maison sur une lettre, to put the firm's stamp on a letter.

timbre (instrument servant à apposer une marque) (*n.m.*), stamp; press:
timbre à date *ou* timbre dateur, date stamp; dater.
timbre à main, hand stamp.
timbre composteur, office printing outfit (interchangeable rubber-faced type).
timbre d'annulation *ou* timbre oblitérateur, cancelling stamp.
timbre de réception, received stamp.
timbre en caoutchouc, rubber stamp; indiarubber stamp.
timbre horaire *ou* timbre horo-dateur, time stamp.
timbre humide, pad stamp; endorsing stamp; *can be translated as* rubber stamp *or* indiarubber stamp:
clauses ajoutées à la main ou au timbre humide (*f.pl.*), clauses added by hand or with a rubber stamp.
timbre numéroteur automatique, self-acting numbering machine.
timbre sec, embossing press.

timbre (bureau où l'on timbre le papier) (*n.m.*), stamp office:
aller au timbre, to go to the stamp office.

timbre (clochette) (*n.m.*), bell:
timbre d'appel, call bell.

timbre-chef [timbres-chefs *pl.*] (*n.m.*), original stamped bill of lading. *See note under syn.* connaissement-chef.

timbré, -e (*adj.*), stamped:
papier timbré (*m.*), stamped paper.

timbrer (*v.t.*), to stamp:
timbrer un acte, un effet, une lettre, un reçu, to stamp a deed, a bill, a letter, a receipt.
timbrer à l'extraordinaire, to stamp at the revenue office (or at the Inland Revenue Office) (or, as one would say in London, at Somerset House, or at Telegraph Street):
pour être réguliers, les chèques doivent être timbrés à l'extraordinaire, to be regular, cheques should be stamped at the revenue office.
faire timbrer un acte à l'extraordinaire, to get an instrument stamped at the revenue office.
Cf. papier de la débite.

timbreur, -euse (pers.) (*n.*), stamper.

tirage (*n.m.*), drawing; making out; writing out; draft:
le tirage d'une lettre de change, d'un chèque, the drawing (*or* the draft) of a bill of exchange, of a cheque.
tirage refusé, dishonoured draft.
tirage croisé (effets de commerce), cross firing.
tirage en l'air *ou* tirage en blanc *ou* tirage à découvert, kite flying; flying a kite; kiting.
tirage (*n.m.*) *ou* **tirage au sort**, drawing; drawing lots; lot:
obligations amortissables par des tirages au sort périodiques (*f.pl.*), bonds redeemable by periodical drawings.
l'ordre de sortie est déterminé par un tirage au sort (*m.*), the order of retirement is determined by lot.
tirage à lots, prize drawing.
tirage (d'un journal) (*n.m.*), circulation (of a newspaper):
les tarifs des annonces de journaux sont proportionnels à leur tirage et à leur influence (*m.pl.*), advertisement rates of newspapers are proportional to their circulation and to their influence.
tirant d'eau (d'un bateau) (*m.*), draught (of a boat):
tirant d'eau en charge, load draught; laden draught.
tirant d'eau lège, light draught.
tiré (pers.) (*n.m.*), drawee:
tiré d'une lettre de change, drawee of a bill of exchange.
tirer (tracer) (*v.t.*), to draw:
tirer une ligne sur le papier, une double barre sous une addition, to draw a line on the paper, a double line under an addition.
tirer (en parlant des effets de commerce) (*v.t.*), to draw:
tirer une lettre de change, to draw a bill of exchange.
tirer en l'air *ou* tirer en blanc *ou* tirer à découvert, to kite; to fly a kite.
tirer (en parlant des chèques) (*v.t.*), to draw; to make out; to write out:
tirer un chèque, to draw, to make out, to write out, a cheque.
tirer sur son banquier, sur Londres, to draw on one's banker, on London.
tirer (retirer; recueillir) (*v.t.*), to draw; to derive; to make:
tirer un bénéfice d'une opération, to draw (*or* to derive) a profit from, to make a profit out of, a transaction.
tirer (obtenir avec des efforts) (*v.t.*), to extract; to squeeze; to get; to draw:
tirer de quelqu'un de l'argent, to extract money from someone; to squeeze (*or* to get) money out of someone.
tirer (*v.t.*) *ou* **tirer au sort**, to draw; to draw lots; to draw lots for:
tirer des numéros, to draw numbers.
les bons destinés à être remboursés sont tirés au sort (*m.pl.*), the bonds for redemption are drawn.

tirer un coup de fusil (en bourse) (*fig.*), to have a little flutter.
tireur, -euse (pers.) (*n.*), drawer:
tireur d'une lettre de change, d'un chèque, drawer of a bill of exchange, of a cheque.
tireur en l'air *ou* tireur en blanc *ou* tireur à découvert, kite flier.
tiroir (*n.m.*), drawer:
tiroir fermant à clef, lockup drawer.
tiroir de caisse, till.
titre (acte, pièce authentique établissant un droit) (*n.m.*), title; title deed; deed; muniment; document; proof; evidence:
nul ne peut se créer un titre à soi-même, no one can create a title (to property) for himself.
propriété acquise à titre onéreux (*f.*), property acquired by onerous title (*or* for a valuable consideration).
le bulletin de bagages constitue un titre qui donne le droit au voyageur de réclamer ses colis à l'arrivée, the baggage ticket constitutes a title which gives the passenger the right to claim his packages on arrival.
titre de propriété, title to property; title deed of property; document of title; muniment of title; proof of ownership.
titre de créance, proof of debt; evidence of indebtedness.
souscrire à titre irréductible, à titre réductible. See under **souscrire**.
titre (degré de fin des matières monnayées ou des matières d'or ou d'argent) (*n.m.*), fineness:
le titre est le rapport du poids du métal fin au poids total de l'alliage, the fineness is the ratio of the weight of fine metal to the total weight of the alloy.
abaissement du titre des monnaies (*m.*), lowering the fineness of the coinage.
monnaies au titre légal (*f.pl.*), coins of legal fineness.
titre (certificat) (*n.m.*) (Abrév.: **tit.**), certificate; scrip; warrant; bond: (See also **certificat**.)
titre de bourse, stock or share certificate:
la valeur nominale est celle inscrite sur un titre de bourse, the nominal (*or* face) value is that inscribed on a stock or share certificate.
titre d'actions *ou* titre d'action (*s'il s'agit d'une action seulement*), share certificate.
titre d'obligation(s), debenture certificate; debenture bond.
titre au porteur (opp. à *titre nominatif*), bearer certificate; bearer warrant; share warrant; share warrant to bearer; warrant to bearer; stock warrant; bearer scrip; bearer bond.
titre définitif (opp. à *titre provisoire*), definitive (*or* definite) certificate.
titre mixte, registered certificate with coupons attached.
titre multiple (opp. à *titre unitaire*), multiple certificate; certificate for more than one share.

titre nominatif, registered certificate (or scrip).

titre provisoire, scrip; scrip certificate; provisional certificate; interim certificate.

titre unitaire, certificate for one share; one. See example under **unité.**

titre (valeur mobilière; rente; action; obligation) (*n.m.*) (Abrév.: **tit.**), security; stock; share; bond; holding: (See also **valeur** *ou* **valeurs,** and **action.**)

titres qui sont de bonne livraison (Bourse), stock which is (or shares which are) good delivery.

le placement de ses disponibilités en titres, the investment of one's available capital in stocks and shares.

échange, titre pour titre, des actions de 500 francs contre des actions de 250 francs (*m.*), exchange, share for share, of shares of 500 francs for shares of 250 francs.

titre à lots, prize bond; lottery bond.

titres à ordre, registered shares transferable by endorsement of the certificate.

titres à prime, option stock; stock on option.

titres au porteur, bearer securities; bearer bonds; bearer shares; bearer stock; bearer stocks.

titres creux, (in France) shares or stock issued before the requirements of the law in respect thereto have been complied with, the principal of these requirements being that the capital of the company must be fully subscribed and the shares paid up to at least one quarter of their nominal value. The putting into circulation of *titres creux* is fraudulent.

titre d'arbitrage, arbitrage share:

titres d'arbitrage avec Londres, arbitrage shares with London.

titres de bourse, stock exchange securities; stocks and shares:

la valeur réelle d'un titre de bourse peut être supérieure, égale, ou inférieure à la valeur nominale, the actual value of a stock or share may be higher than, equal to, or lower than the nominal value.

titre de père de famille, gilt-edged (or gilt-edge) security.

titres de placement *ou* titres de portefeuille (opp. à *titres de spéculation*), investment securities; investment shares; investment stocks:

valeur qui offre tous les caractères du titre de portefeuille (*f.*), stock which offers all the qualities of an investment security.

titres de spéculation *ou* titres spéculatifs, speculative securities; speculative shares; speculative stocks.

titres en pension, pawned stock (or stocks); stock (or stocks) in pawn.

titres fiduciaires, paper securities; securities for money; paper holdings; paper money.

titres flottants. See under **flottant.**

titre funding [titres funding *pl.*], funding certificate.

titre garanti *ou* titres garantis, guaranteed stock; guaranteed stocks.

titres libérés, fully paid stock; fully paid shares.

titres nominatifs, registered securities; registered shares; registered stock; registered stocks.

titres non libérés *ou* titres partiellement libérés, partly paid shares.

service des titres (*m.*) *ou simplement* titres (*n.m.pl.*) (Banq.), security department; stock department:

le chef du service des titres *ou* le chef des titres, the head of the security department.

titulaire (pers.) (*n.m.* ou *f.*), holder:

titulaire d'un compte, d'une lettre de crédit, d'une action, d'une obligation, d'un billet de chemin de fer, holder of an account, of a letter of credit, of a share, of a debenture, of a railway ticket.

tolérance (Transport) (*n.f.*), allowance:

une tolérance de 2 p. cent du poids est accordée, pour déchet de route, sur le poids des marchandises liquides ou sèches, an allowance of 2 per cent of the weight is made, for wastage in transit, on the weight of wet or dry goods.

tolérance (Monnayage) (*n.f.*), tolerance; tolerance of the mint; remedy; remedy of the mint:

tolérance de poids *ou* tolérance de fabrication, tolerance of weight; tolerance for error in weight; remedy of (or for) weight.

tolérance de titre, tolerance of (or for error in) fineness; remedy of (or for) fineness.

tolérance de frai, tolerance for loss of weight (or for abrasion) in circulation.

tomber (*v.i.*), to fall:

valeur qui a tombé à zéro (*f.*), share which has fallen to zero (or to nothing).

tomber d'accord, to come to an agreement; to agree:

deux experts qui tombent d'accord, two experts who come to an agreement (or who agree).

tomber en souffrance, to come on demurrage.

ton (*n.m.*), tone:

dans son examen de la situation du marché des valeurs durant le mois dernier, la banque signale un ton meilleur, dû au relâchement des taux monétaires et à un ralentissement très sensible dans le rythme des nouvelles émissions, in its examination of the position of the stock market during last month, the bank signalizes a better tone, due to the relaxation of money rates and to a very appreciable slackening in the stream of new issues.

tonnage (poids en tonnes) (*n.m.*), tonnage:

tonnage des messageries, parcels tonnage.

Note:—It must be borne in mind that in speaking of *tonnage* in French, the weight in French *tonnes* is ordinarily meant, and in speaking of *tonnage* in English, the weight in English *tons* is ordinarily meant. See equivalents of French *tonne* and English *ton* in Tables of Weights at end of this volume.

tonnage (jauge d'un navire) (*n.m.*), tonnage; burden; burthen: (*Cf.* **jauge.**)

le tonnage du navire est l'expression de la capacité intérieure du navire, the tonnage of the ship is the expression of the internal capacity of the ship.

tonnage brut (*Abrév.: t.br.*), gross tonnage.

tonnage de jauge *ou simplement* tonnage, register tonnage; registered tonnage; register:

tonnage de jauge brute, gross register tonnage; gross registered tonnage; gross register.

tonnage de jauge nette, net register tonnage; net registered tonnage; net register.

tonnage canal de Panama, Panama canal tonnage; Panama canal register.

tonnage canal de Suez, Suez canal tonnage; Suez canal register.

tonnage dead weight (*Abrév.: t.d.w.*), dead-weight tonnage.

tonnage net, net tonnage.

tonnage sous le pont, underdeck tonnage; tonnage under deck.

tonnage (l'affrètement d'un ensemble de navires) (*n.m.*), tonnage; shipping:

là où il y a abondance de tonnage et peu de marchandises, le fret est bas, et inversement, where there is an abundance of tonnage (*or* of shipping) and little cargo, freight is low, and vice versa.

le tonnage-vapeur de différents pays, the steamer tonnage of various countries.

tonnage (droit de tonnage) (*n.m.*), tonnage; tonnage duty.

tonne (unité de poids) (*n.f.*), ton. See **tonneau** *ou* **tonne** for specific terms, and see Table of Weights at end of volume for equivalents.

tonne-kilomètre [**tonnes-kilomètres** *pl.*] (*n.f.*) *ou* **tonne kilométrique** (Ch. de f.) (Abrév.: **T.K.**), kilometre ton, = the transport of 1 *tonne* (1,000 kg.) of freight 1 kilometre, analogous to the English *ton mile* (tonne millénaire) = transport of 1 ton (2,240 lbs) 1 mile.

tonneau (fût; baril) (*n.m.*), cask; barrel; drum.

tonneau (*n.m.*) *ou* **tonne** (*n.f.*) (unité de poids), ton:

tonneau d'affrètement *ou* tonneau de fret *ou* tonneau de portée *ou* tonne de portée en lourd, freight ton; shipping ton; ton dead weight. In France, 1,000 kilogrammes, or 1·44 cubic metres, usually. In England, the *freight ton* is 20 cwt, or 40 cubic feet (= 1·132 cubic metres), usually.

tonneau d'encombrement *ou* tonne d'encombrement *ou* tonneau à l'encombrement *ou* tonneau de capacité *ou* tonneau de mer *ou* tonne de mer, measurement ton.

tonneau de jauge *ou simplement* tonneau *ou* tonne de jauge *ou simplement* tonne *ou* tonneau de registre *ou* tonneau-registre

[tonneaux-registres *pl.*] (*n.m.*) *ou* tonne de registre *ou* tonne-registre [tonnes-registres *pl.*] (*n.f.*), register ton; ton register; ton, = 100 cubic feet or 2·8317 cubic metres—same in France as in England.

tonneau de jauge brute (*Abrév.: t.j.b.*), ton gross register; gross register ton:

vapeurs d'au moins 100 tonneaux de jauge brute (*m.pl.*), steamers of at least 100 tons gross register.

tonneau de jauge nette, ton net register; net register ton:

voiliers d'au moins 50 tonneaux de jauge nette (*m.pl.*), sailing ships of at least 50 tons net register.

tonneau-poids [tonneaux-poids *pl.*] (*n.m.*) *ou* tonneau de déplacement *ou* tonne de déplacement, displacement ton; ton displacement.

tx (*abrév.*), tonneaux.

tort (à), wrong; wrongly:

taxe perçue à tort (*f.*), charge wrongly collected.

total, -e, -aux (*adj.*), total:

somme totale (*f.*), total sum; total amount; sum total.

total (assemblage de plusieurs parties formant un tout) (*n.m.*), total; whole:

le total de l'actif, du passif, the total assets, liabilities; the whole of the assets, of the liabilities.

total (somme obtenue par l'addition) (*n.m.*), total:

le total d'une addition, the total of an addition.

total global, grand total; sum total.

totalement (*adv.*), totally.

totalisateur *ou* **totaliseur** (*n.m.*), totalizator; totalizer.

totalisation (*n.f.*), totalization; summing up:

la totalisation des recettes, the totalization of receipts.

totaliser (*v.t.*), to totalize; to sum up; to total.

totalité (*n.f.*), totality; whole:

la totalité des recettes, the whole of the receipts.

accepter soit la totalité, soit une partie du risque à couvrir, to accept either the whole, or a part of the risk to be covered.

la presque totalité de, almost the whole of; nearly all:

la presque totalité des recettes, nearly all the receipts.

en totalité, in full:

versements faits en totalité ou à valoir (*m.pl.*), payments made in full or on account.

touche (d'une machine à écrire, d'une machine à calculer, d'une caisse enregistreuse) (*n.f.*), key (of a typewriter, of a calculating machine, of a cash register):

les touches du clavier, the keys of the keyboard.

toucher (atteindre) (*v.t.*), to touch:

baisse qui a touché le fond (*ou* le tuf) (Bourse) (*f.*), fall which has touched bottom (*or* which has bottomed).

toucher (percevoir; recevoir; encaisser) (*v.t.*), to draw; to receive; to cash:

toucher le montant d'un billet, to receive the amount of a bill.

toucher de l'argent, ses appointements, un traitement fixe, son quantum des bénéfices, to draw, to receive, money, one's salary, a fixed salary, one's proportion of the profits.

toucher un chèque, to cash a cheque.

obligataires qui touchent leurs coupons (*m.pl.* ou *f.pl.*), debenture holders who receive (*or* cash) their coupons.

toucher (*v.i.*), to touch:
toucher à un port (*ou* en un port), à tous ports (*ou* en tout port), to touch at a port, at any ports.

avec faculté de toucher et séjourner à tous ports ou lieux quelconques, with liberty to touch and stay at any ports or places whatsoever.

toujours à flot *ou* **toujours en flot** (se dit d'un navire—dans une charte-partie), always afloat.   See **aussi près qu'il pourra**, etc., under **aussi**.

tour (voyage; excursion) (*n.m.*), tour:
compagnie de navigation qui organise des tours en Méditerranée (*f.*), shipping company which organizes Mediterranean tours.

tour de rôle (à).   See under **rôle**.

tourisme (*n.m.*), touring. (*Cf.* bureau de tourisme.)

touriste (pers.) (*n.m.* ou *f.*), tourist:
les revenus provenant de l'entretien de touristes étrangers (*m.pl.*),   the revenues accruing from the maintenance of foreign tourists.

touristique (*adj.*), touring (*used as adj.*); tourist (*used as adj.*);   touristic:
trafic touristique (*m.*), tourist traffic.

tournée (*n.f.*), round; walk:
facteur, voyageur, en tournée (*m.*), postman, traveller, on his round (*or* on his walk).

tourner à compte, to turn out well.

tous droits des parties réservés (*m.pl.*), all rights of the parties reserved.

tous les départs sans engagement de date (Navig.) (*m.pl.*), all sailings subject to change without notice; all sailings subject to change with or without notice.

tous risques (*m.pl.*), all risks:
assurance contre tous risques (*f.*), insurance against all risks.

tout payé (*invar.*) (Abrév.: **t.p.**), fully paid (*used chiefly in the abbreviated form* t.p. *in quotation lists, and the like. English equivalent* f.p.).

toute l'année, all the year; all the year round:
hôtel ouvert toute l'année (*m.*), hotel open all the year round.

toutes coupures (d'actions) (*f.pl.*) (Abrév.: **t.c.** *ou* **t.coup.**), any denominations (of shares):
t.c.p. 25, toutes coupures par 25 (les négociations se font par 25 titres livrables en toutes coupures).

traçage (*n.m.*), drawing; draft; writing out; making out.   See the verb **tracer** for example.

tracé (*n.m.*), sketch:
tracé d'un livre de compte, sketch of an account book (to show ruling, etc.).

tracer (*v.t.*), to draw; to write out; to make out: tracer un chèque, to draw, to write out, to make out, a cheque.

tracteur (*n.m.*) (opp. à *remorque*), tractor.

traction (*n.f.*), traction; haulage; hauling.

tradition (Dr.) (*n.f.*), delivery; tradition:
le billet de banque se transmet de la main à la main, on dit par tradition, the bank note is transmitted from hand to hand, one says by delivery (*or* by tradition).

la cession des actions au porteur s'opère par simple tradition du titre, the transfer of bearer shares is effected by mere (*or* by simple) delivery of the scrip.

tradition manuelle *ou* tradition matérielle, manual delivery.

traducteur (pers.) (*n.m.*),   translator:
traducteur assermenté, sworn translator.

traduction (*n.f.*), translation.

traduire (*v.t.*), to translate:
traduire du français en anglais, to translate from French into English.

traduire un câblogramme, to translate a cable.

traduire (se) (*v.r.*), to show; to shew:
les comptes du dernier exercice se traduisent par une perte de tant (*m.pl.*), last year's accounts show a loss of so much.

trafic (mouvement) (*n.m.*), traffic:
le trafic des ports maritimes français,   the traffic of French seaports.

trafic de transit, transit traffic.

trafic des émigrants, emigrant traffic.

trafic des marchandises, goods traffic; freight traffic;   merchandise traffic.

trafic des messageries, parcels traffic; parcel traffic.

trafic des passagers *ou* trafic passagers, passenger traffic (sea, air, or boat train).

trafic des voyageurs *ou* trafic voyageurs, passenger traffic (land, sea, or air).

trafic lourd, heavy traffic.

trafic mixte, sea and land traffic.

trafic touristique, tourist traffic.

trafic (négoce) (*n.m.*), traffic; trading; trade:
le trafic des vins, the trade in wines; the wine trade.

trafiquant (pers.) (*n.m.*), trader:
les Hollandais sont un peuple de trafiquants (*m.pl.*), the Dutch are a nation of traders.

trafiquer (*v.t.*), to negotiate:
trafiquer une lettre de change, to negotiate a bill of exchange.

trafiquer (*v.i.*), to trade; to traffic:
le commerce de banque consiste à trafiquer de la monnaie et du crédit, the business of banking consists in trading in money and credit.

train (*n.m.*), train:
train bleu, blue train.

train d'ouvriers, workmen's train.

train de chalands, string of barges.

train de chemin de fer, railway train.

train de grand parcours, long distance train.

train de luxe, train de luxe:
train de luxe composé de voitures-salons, train de luxe composed of saloon carriages.

train de marchandises *ou* train de petite vitesse, goods train; merchandise train; freight train.

train de marchandises à marche rapide, fast goods train.

train de messagerie *ou* train de messageries, parcels train.

train de nuit, night train.

train de paquebot *ou* train de correspondance avec le paquebot [trains de correspondance avec les paquebots *pl.*] *ou* train de passagers, boat train.

train de plaisir, excursion train; cheap train.

train de voyageurs *ou* train de grande vitesse, passenger train.

train désigné, fast goods train (for farm produce, fish traffic, etc.).

train direct, through train.

train express [trains express *pl.*], express train; express.

train impair *ou* train descendant, down train.

train local, local train.

train mixte, passenger and goods train; composite train; mixed train.

train omnibus *ou* train de petite vitesse, slow train.

train pair *ou* train montant, up train.

train-poste [trains-poste *pl.*] (*n.m.*), mail train.

train pour le service des colis de grande vitesse, express parcels train.

train rapide *ou* train de grande vitesse, fast train.

train spécial, special train.

train supplémentaire, relief train:
trains supplémentaires doublant, triplant, le train utile, relief trains, doubling, tripling, the booked train.

traîner (*v.t.*), to draw; to haul:
locomotive qui traîne une lourde charge (*f.*), locomotive which draws (*or* hauls) a heavy load.

trait de plume (*m.*), stroke of the pen.

traite (*n.f.*) (Abrév.: **tr.** [**trs** *pl.*] *ou* **T**/), draft; bill; exchange: (See also **effet.**)
un chèque est une traite sur un banquier, a cheque is a draft on a banker.

traite à vue *ou* traite payable à vue, draft at sight; sight draft; draft payable at sight.

traite documentaire *ou* traite accompagnée de (*ou* par des) documents (opp. à *traite libre*), documentary bill; document bill; bill with documents attached.

traite documents contre acceptation (*Abrév.*: traite D.A.), documents against acceptance bill; bill for acceptance; acceptance bill.

traite documents contre paiement (*Abrév.*: traite D.P.), documents against payment bill; bill for payment; payment bill.

traite en l'air, kite; windmill.

traite en plusieurs exemplaires, bill in a set.

traite libre, clean bill.

traite sur l'étranger, foreign bill; foreign exchange.

traité (*n.m.*), treaty; agreement; contract:

traité d'agence, agency agreement.

traité de commerce, treaty of commerce; commercial treaty.

traité de direction, management agreement.

traité de fusion, amalgamation agreement.

traité de réassurance, reinsurance pool; reinsurance exchange.

traité particulier, private treaty:
traité particulier qui a pour effet d'accorder une réduction sur les prix des tarifs, private treaty which has the effect of making a reduction on tariff rates.

traitement (manière d'agir) (*n.m.*), treatment:
traitement de la nation la plus favorisée (Écon. polit.), most favoured nation treatment.

traitement de faveur (Douanes), preference:
le traitement de faveur accordé aux produits coloniaux, the preference granted to colonial produce.

traitement (appointements d'un fonctionnaire) (*n.m.*), salary; stipend:
directeur qui touche un traitement fixe (*m.*), manager who receives (*or* draws) a fixed salary.

traiter (négocier) (*v.t.*), to negotiate; to transact:
traiter un marché, to negotiate, to transact, a bargain.

traiter (*v.i.*), to treat; to deal; to negotiate; to transact business; to do business:
il refuse de traiter avec lui, he refuses to deal (*or* to transact, *or* to do, business) (*or* to treat) with him.

se traiter (être vendu) (*v.r.*), to be dealt in; to sell; to be sold:
le blé se traite à tant, wheat is being dealt in (*or* is selling) (*or* is being sold) at so much.
il se traite à la Bourse de Paris des titres de toutes sortes, all sorts of securities are dealt in on the Paris Bourse.

trajet (*n.m.*), passage; journey; transit; trip; haul:

trajet avec chargement, cargo passage.

trajet d'aller, outward journey; outward passage; outward trip.

trajet d'aller et de retour, journey, passage, trip, there and back.

trajet de retour, homeward (*or* return) journey (*or* passage) (*or* trip).

trajet par chemin de fer (*ou* par voie ferrée), railway journey (*or* trip); rail transit; railroad haul.

trajet par mer *ou* trajet maritime, sea passage; sea transit.

trajet sur (*ou* en) lest, ballast passage.

tramp *ou* **tramp-steamer** [**tramp-steamers** *pl.*] (navire vagabond) (*n.m.*), tramp; tramp steamer; ocean tramp.

tramping (vagabondage d'un navire) (*n.m.*), tramping.

tramway [**tramways** *pl.*] (voie) (*n.m.*), tramway; street railroad; street railway.

tramway (voiture) (*n.m.*), tram; tram car; car; street car.

tranche (*n.f.*), block; set; portion; each:
bloquer une tranche d'actions, to tie up a block of shares.

tranche de trois chiffres, set of three figures.

abattement dégrevant la tranche inférieure du revenu (*m.*), abatement relieving the lower portion of the income.

et ainsi de suite, en augmentant d'un vingt-cinquième par tranche de 10 000 francs jusqu'à 100 000 francs, and so on, rising by one twentyfifth for each 10,000 francs (*or* by one twentyfifth per portion of 10,000 francs) up to 100,000 francs.

trancher une contestation (*ou* **un différend**), **une question,** to settle a dispute, a question.

transaction (opération) (*n.f.*), transaction; deal; dealing:
transaction commerciale, commercial transaction (*or* deal).

pas de (*ou* aucune) transaction sur l'action, no dealings in the shares.

transaction (acte par lequel on transige sur un différend, un procès, etc.) (*n.f.*), compromise; arrangement:
une médiocre transaction est parfois préférable à un bon procès, a poor compromise is sometimes preferable to a successful action.

transatlantique (*adj.*), transatlantic.

transatlantique (*n.m.*) *ou* **paquebot transatlantique** (*m.*), Atlantic liner; transatlantic liner (*or* boat).

transbordement (*n.m.*), transhipment; transshipment.

en transbordement pour, transhipping for:
départs du Havre pour Rio de Janeiro, en transbordement pour Pernambuco (*m.pl.*), sailings from Havre for Rio de Janeiro, transhipping for Pernambuco.

transborder (*v.t.*), to tranship; to transship:
marchandises transbordées au cours du voyage, sur un autre navire dans un port intermédiaire (*f.pl.*), goods transhipped during the voyage, on another ship in an intermediate port.

transcription (action) (*n.f.*), copying; transcription.

transcription (copie) (*n.f.*), copy; transcript; transcription:
faire la transcription au net d'un manuscrit, to make a fair copy of a manuscript.

transcription (Comptab.) (*n.f.*), posting.

transcrire (*v.t.*), to copy; to transcribe:
transcrire une lettre, to copy, to transcribe, a letter.

transcrire (Comptab.) (*v.t.*), to post; to post up:
transcrire le journal au grand livre, to post the journal into the ledger; to post up the ledger from the journal.

transférable (*adj.*), transferable:
valeur transférable (*f.*), transferable security.

transfèrement (*n.m.*), transfer; transference:
le transfèrement d'une créance, the transfer of a debt.

transférer (transmettre) (*v.t.*), to transfer:
transférer une inscription de rente, ses biens

to transfer some inscribed rente, one's property.

se transférer (*v.r.*), to be transferred.

transférer (Comptab.) (*v.t.*), to transfer:
transférer un article d'un compte à un autre, une balance au compte pertes et profits, to transfer an item from one account to another, a balance to profit and loss account.

transfert (*n.m.*), transfer:
transfert d'actions, de propriété, d'hypothèque, transfer of shares, of property, of mortgage.

le transfert est la transmission de propriété d'un titre nominatif d'une personne à une autre, a transfer is a conveyance of property in a registered stock or share from one person to another.

transferts d'entrepôt (Douanes), transfers in warehouse.

transfert télégraphique (Opérations de change) (*Abrév.:* T.T.), telegraphic transfer; telegraph transfer; cable transfer; cable.

transfert (feuille de transfert) (*n.m.*), transfer; transfer deed; deed of transfer:
transfert d'une action nominative signé par le cédant et le cessionnaire, transfer of a registered share signed by the transferor and the transferee.

Note:—In France, seller and buyer do not as a rule sign one and the same deed, as in England: the seller signs a **feuille de transfert** or **déclaration de transfert** and the buyer a **feuille d'acceptation de transfert** or **acceptation de transfert.**

transfert d'ordre *ou* transfert provisoire (Bourse), (in France), a provisional or intermediate transfer drawn up and executed, if desired, by *agents de change* (*stockbrokers*) in order that the name of the client shall not be disclosed. The seller of the stock signs a *transfert d'ordre* in the name of his broker; the selling broker a *transfert d'ordre* in the name of the buying broker; finally the last named, a *transfert réel* in the name of his buying client.

transferts d'ordre are not liable to stamp duty, on condition however that the *transfert réel* is executed within 10 days of the first transfer.

transfert d'ordre *ou* transfert gratuit, nominal transfer (transfer for a nominal consideration, or where no consideration passes, as in the case of a gift or succession. In France, such a transfer is not liable to stamp duty. In England, liable to a fixed stamp duty of 10s.)

transfert de forme, (in France) a notification in the form of a transfer of a change in civil status of the shareholder or stockholder, such as a change of name, profession, occupation, business, or description. Such a transfer is not liable to stamp duty.

transfert de (*ou* en) garantie *ou* transfert à titre de garantie, blank transfer; transfer in blank. (In France, a *transfert de garantie* is not subject to stamp duty if property does not pass.)

Note :—These French and English terms do not correspond exactly, as the practice in France is not the same as in England. In England, the law provides that " no notice of any trust, expressed, implied, or constructive, shall be entered on the register." When shares are pledged, the usual practice is to hand over the share certificate to the pledgee, accompanied by a blank transfer (i.e., transfer signed by the transferor, but undated and not containing the name of the transferee). French law allows a company to recognize a trust, the shareholder executing a *transfert de garantie,* which the company enters on its register.

transfert réel, (in France) a real transfer, i.e., a transfer conveying ownership of shares, stock, or the like, sold for a valuable consideration, as distinguished from a *transfert d'ordre* or a *transfert de forme.*

transformer (*v.t.*), to transform ; to change ; to turn :
transformer une société en nom collectif en société anonyme, to turn a partnership into a limited company.

transit (*n.m.*), transit :
marchandises en transit de ou pour d'autres ports ou lieux, à travers la Suisse, goods in transit from or for other ports or places, through (*or* across) Switzerland.
marchandises de transit (*f.pl.*), transit goods.

transitaire (pers.) (*n.m.*), transit agent.

transiter (*v.t.*), to pass in transit :
transiter des marchandises, to pass goods in transit.

transiter (*v.i.*), to pass in transit :
marchandises transitant par la France, par le canal de Panama (*f.pl.*), goods passing in transit through France, through the Panama canal.

translation (*n.f.*), transfer ; conveyance :
translation de propriété, transfer, conveyance, of property.

transmetteur (Téléph.) (*n.m.*) (opp. à *récepteur*), transmitter.

transmettre (faire parvenir) (*v.t.*), to transmit ; to forward ; to send on :
transmettre un ordre, to transmit, to send on, an order.

transmettre (faire passer par mutation) (*v.t.*), to transmit ; to transfer ; to convey :
transmettre une propriété, to transfer, to convey, a property.
transmettre par voie d'endossement une lettre de change à l'ordre d'un tiers, to endorse over a bill of exchange to the order of a third party.

se transmettre (*v.r.*), to be transferred ; to be conveyed :
le connaissement à ordre se transmet par endossement comme une lettre de change, a bill of lading to order is transferred by endorsement like a bill of exchange.

transmission (action de faire parvenir) (*n.f.*), transmission ; forwarding ; sending on.

transmission (action de faire passer par muta-

tion) (*n.f.*), transmission ; transfer ; conveyance :
transmission de biens par testament, transmission of property by will.
transmission d'actions, transfer of shares.

transpacifique (*adj.*), transpacific.

transport (action de transporter d'un lieu dans un autre) (*n.m.*), transport ; transportation ; conveyance ; conveying ; carriage ; carrying ; haulage ; hauling ; transit ; booking :
chemin de fer qui accepte au transport des marchandises présentant des signes manifestes d'avarie (*m.*), railway which accepts for conveyance (*or* for booking) goods showing evident signs of damage.
transports à forfait, through bookings.
transport fluvial, river transport.
transport immédiat de terre à bord et de bord à terre, transit to and from the vessel.
transport maritime *ou* transport par mer, sea carriage ; carriage by sea ; marine transport ; shipping.
transport mixte, sea and land carriage.
transport par chemin de fer *ou* transport par voie ferrée *ou* transport par fer *ou* transport ferré, railway carriage ; railway transport ; rail transport ; rail transit.
transport par eau, carriage by water ; water carriage.
transport par roulage *ou* transport par voiture, haulage ; hauling ; cartage ; carting.
transport routier, road transport.
transport terrestre, land carriage ; land conveyance.

transport (Dr.) (*n.m.*), transfer ; making over :
transport d'une créance, transfer of a debt.

transport (contre-passement) (Comptab.) (*n.m.*), transfer :
transport d'une somme d'un compte à un autre, transfer of an amount from one account to another.

transport (report) (Comptab.) (*n.m.*), carrying out ; extension :
transport de la balance des intérêts dans la colonne des capitaux, carrying out, extension, of the balance of interest in the principal column.

transport-cession [**transports-cessions** *pl.*] (*n.m.*), assignment (of debts or other incorporeal property).

transporter (porter d'un lieu dans un autre) (*v.t.*), to transport ; to convey ; to carry :
transporter des marchandises par chemin de fer, to transport, to convey, to carry, goods by rail.
l'obligation essentielle de l'armateur est de transporter le passager au port de destination (*f.*), the essential obligation of the shipowner is to carry the passenger to the port of destination.

transporter (Dr.) (*v.t.*), to transfer ; to make over :
transporter une créance, to transfer, to make over, a debt.

se transporter (*v.r.*), to be transferred (*or* made over).

transporter (contre-passer) (Comptab.) (*v.t.*), to transfer :
transporter une balance au compte pertes et profits, to transfer a balance to profit and loss account.

transporter (porter ; reporter) (Comptab.) (*v.t.*), to carry out ; to extend.

transporteur (pers.) (*n.m.*), carrier :
transporteur subséquent, succeeding carrier ; on-carrier.

transposition (*n.f.*), transposition :
transposition de chiffres, transposition of figures.

transvaaliennes (*n.f.pl.*) *ou* **valeurs transvaaliennes** (*f.pl.*), South Africans ; South African shares ; Kaffirs.

travail (*n.m.*), work ; labour :
travail de bureau, office work ; clerical work.
travaux en cours, works in progress.
vivre de son travail, to live by one's labour.

travailler (Bourse) (*v.t.*), to deal in :
on travaille activement la privilégiée X., X. preference were actively dealt in.

travailler (*v.i.*), to work ; to labour ; to endeavour :
travailler pour gagner son pain, dans l'espoir de devenir rentier, to work to earn one's bread, in the hope of becoming independent.
travailler en heures supplémentaires, to work overtime.
travailler au recouvrement d'une somme, to endeavour to recover an amount.

travailler (Bourse) (*v.i.*), to deal :
il est maintenant possible de travailler sur notre place sans risque de surpayer quand on achète ou de casser les cours quand on vend, it is now possible to deal on our market without risk of paying too much when one buys or of banging the market when one sells.

être travaillé, -e, to be dealt in :
l'ordinaire X. a été l'un des titres les plus activement travaillés au marché, X. ordinary was one of the most actively dealt in stocks on the market.

traversée (*n.f.*), passage ; voyage ; crossing :
une traversée mouvementée, a rough passage (*or* voyage) (*or* crossing).
la traversée entre l'Angleterre et le continent, the crossing (*or* passage) between England and the continent.
traversée maritime, sea passage.
traversée sur lest, ballast passage.

traverser (*v.t.*), to cross :
traverser l'Atlantique, to cross the Atlantic.

trésor (bureaux, caisse d'un trésorier public) (*n.m.*), treasury ; exchequer.

trésor public *ou* *simplement* **Trésor** (*n.m.*) (administration chargée de la gestion des deniers publics), Treasury ; Exchequer ; Treasury Board ; Treasury Department.

trésorerie (fonctions de trésorier public) (*n.f.*), treasurership.

trésorerie (bureaux) (*n.f.*), treasury :
aller à la trésorerie, to go to the treasury.

trésorerie (finances de l'État) (*n.f.*), treasury ; exchequer :
la trésorerie nationale, the national exchequer.

trésorerie (finances d'une administration, d'une société) (*n.f.*), finances :
situation de trésorerie (*f.*), statement of finances ; finance statement ; financial statement.

trésorier, -ère (*adj.*), treasury ; exchequer (*used as adjs*) :
les autorités trésorières (*f.pl.*), the treasury authorities.

trésorier, -ère (pers.) (*n.*), treasurer.

tri *ou* **triage** (*n.m.*), sorting :
le tri (*ou* le triage) des lettres, des papiers, the sorting of letters, of papers.

tribord (Naut.) (*n.m.*) (opp. à *bâbord*), starboard.

tribunal (juridiction) (*n.m.*), tribunal ; court :
comparaître devant le tribunal, to appear before the tribunal.
tribunal civil, civil court.
tribunal de commerce *ou* tribunal consulaire, commercial court (in France, a tribunal or court composed of elected members or traders exercising judicial functions in commercial cases). *See explanation of* sociétés commerciales et sociétés civiles, *under* **société**.
tribunal de prise *ou* tribunal des prises, prize court.

tribunal (les magistrats qui composent le tribunal) (*n.m.*), tribunal ; court :
le tribunal se déclare suffisamment éclairé, the court has heard sufficient evidence.

tributaire de (être), to be dependent on (*or* upon) ; to depend on (*or* upon) :
être tributaire de l'étranger, to be dependent upon, to depend on, foreign supplies.
être tributaire pour la matière première de l'Extrême Orient, to be dependent upon the Far East for raw material.

trier (*v.t.*), to sort.

trimestre (espace de trois mois) (*n.m.*), quarter ; three months :
un trimestre de loyer, a quarter's rent ; three months' rent.
être payé (-e) par trimestre, to be paid by the quarter ; to be paid quarterly.

trimestre (rente, traitement qui se paye tous les trois mois) (*n.m.*), quarter's (*or* quarterly) income, dividend, interest, drawings, salary, money, payment, instalment, or the like :
recevoir son trimestre, to receive one's quarter's money.

trimestriel, -elle (*adj.*), quarterly :
appointements trimestriels (*m.pl.*), quarterly salary.

trimestriellement (*adv.*), quarterly :
somme payée trimestriellement (*f.*), sum paid quarterly.

triplan (*n.m.*), triplane.

triple (*adj.*), treble ; triple ; three times :
triple droit (Douanes) (*m.*), treble duty.
triple taxe (télégrammes urgents) (*f.*), three times the ordinary rates.

triple *ou* **triplicata** [**triplicata** *pl.*] (*n.m.*), treble ; triplicate :

triple de la valeur à l'acquitté (amende de douane), treble the duty-paid value.

en triple *ou* **en triple exemplaire** *ou* **en triple expédition** *ou* **en triplicata** *ou* **par triplicata,** in triplicate :

dresser un acte en triple *ou* en triple exemplaire, to draw up a deed in triplicate.

connaissement en triplicata (*m.*), bill of lading in triplicate.

triplicata de change (*m.*), third of exchange. See **première de change** for example.

triplé (Bourse) (*n.m.*), option to treble :

triplé à la baisse, put of twice more ; seller's option to treble.

triplé à la hausse, call of twice more ; buyer's option to treble.

tripotage de bourse (*m.*), jobbery ; market manipulation ; market jobbery ; rigging the market.

triptyque (automobiles en douane) (*n.m.*), pass sheet :

le triptyque se compose de trois volants : une *souche*, un *volant d'entrée*, et un *volant de sortie*, the pass sheet is made up of three leaves : a *counterfoil*, an *importation voucher*, and an *exportation voucher*.

troc (*n.m.*), barter ; exchange :

le troc fut sans doute la première forme du commerce, barter was without doubt the first form of trade.

le simple troc des marchandises exportées contre les marchandises importées ne constitue pas le seul élément de la balance économique d'un pays, the simple exchange of exported goods for imported goods does not constitute the only element of the balance of indebtedness of a country.

trois (les) (Bourse de marchandises) (*m.pl.*), the three months, e.g., les trois (*ou* les 3) d'avril, the three months April, May, June. Cf. **quatre.**

trois mois *ou*, *et généralement*, **3 mois** (Marché des métaux) (opp. à *comptant*), three months ; 3 months.

troisième (Abrév. : **3e**) (*adj.*), third ; 3rd :

billet de troisième (*ou* de 3ᵉ) classe (*m.*), third (*or* 3rd) class ticket.

passager de troisième classe en cabine (*m.*), third cabin passenger.

troisième de change (*f.*), third of exchange. See **première de change** for example.

tromper (*v.t.*), to deceive ; to upset :

tromper le public, l'acheteur sur l'origine de produits de fabrication étrangère, to deceive the public, the buyer on the origin of products of foreign make.

le résultat a trompé notre calcul, the result has upset our calculations.

trop payé (*n.m.*), overpayment.

trop payer (*v.t.*), to overpay :

ristourne d'une somme trop payée (*f.*), return of an amount overpaid.

trop taxer (*v.t.*), to overcharge :

objets de correspondance taxés à tort ou trop taxés (*m.pl.*), postal packets wrongly charged or overcharged.

troquer (*v.t.*), to barter ; to exchange :

troquer un objet contre un autre, to exchange, to barter, one thing for another.

troubles ouvriers (*m.pl.*), labour troubles ; labour disturbances.

trousseau de clefs (*m.*), bunch of keys.

trouver (*v.t.*), to find :

trouver du bon dans une affaire, to find a transaction profitable.

truc (*n.m.*), trick :

des trucs de métier, tricks of the trade.

truc pour duper le public, trick to deceive the public.

trust (réunion d'entreprises) (*n.m.*), trust :

trust de l'acier, steel trust.

trust de pétrole, oil trust.

trust de placement, investment trust ; securities trust.

trust de valeurs, holding company.

tunnel (*n.m.*), tunnel :

le tunnel du Saint-Gothard, the St Gothard tunnel.

tunnel sous la Manche, Channel tunnel.

tuyau (renseignement confidentiel) (*n.m.*), tip :

donner un tuyau de bourse, to give a stock exchange tip.

tuyauter (*v.t.*), to give a tip to ; to tip :

tuyauter quelqu'un, to give someone a tip ; to tip someone.

U

un (l'), une (l'), each. See example under **l'un, l'une,** at commencement of letter **L.**

unanime (*adj.*), unanimous :

le consentement unanime de tous les actionnaires, the unanimous consent of all the shareholders.

unanimement (*adv.*) *ou* **à l'unanimité,** unanimously :

administrateur réélu à l'unanimité (*m.*), director reelected unanimously.

une contre une, one for one :

échange d'actions une contre une (*m.*), exchange of shares one for one.

une fois payé, -e, en une fois, en une seule fois, en une ou plusieurs fois. See under **fois.**

unification (*n.f.*), unification ; consolidation ; standardization :

unification d'emprunts différents, unification of different loans.

unifié, -e (*adj.*) (opp. à *flottant*), unified; consolidated:
dette unifiée (*f.*), unified debt; consolidated debt.

unifier (*v.t.*), to unify; to consolidate; to standardize:
congrès internationaux réunis pour tenter d'unifier le droit de l'avarie commune (*m.pl.*), international congresses assembled to try to standardize the law of general average.

unigraphie (*n.f.*) (opp. à *digraphie*), single entry bookkeeping.

unilatéral, -e, -aux (Dr.) (*adj.*), unilateral:
contrat unilatéral (*m.*), unilateral contract.

union (*n.f.*), union:
union douanière, customs union.
Union latine *ou* Union monétaire latine, Latin Union; Latin Monetary Union (now abandoned).
Union monétaire scandinave, Scandinavian Monetary Union.
Union postale universelle, Universal Postal Union.

unique (*adj.*), sole:
propriétaire unique (*m.* ou *f.*), sole proprietor.

unité (terme de comparaison) (*n.f.*), unit:
le franc était l'unité monétaire de l'Union latine, the franc was the monetary unit of the Latin Union.
le nombre d'unités renfermées dans un lot (Bourse de marchandises), the number of units contained in a load.

unité (*n.f.*) *ou* **titre unitaire** (*m.*) (Abrév.: **u.** *ou* **un.**), one; certificate for one share:
société qui émet ses actions en unités et en coupures de 5, 10, 25, 50, ou 100 (*f.*), company which issues its shares in ones and in denominations of 5, 10, 25, 50, or 100.

urgence (*n.f.*), urgency.

urgent, -e (*adj.*), urgent:
ordre urgent (*m.*), urgent order.

usage (*s'emploie souvent au pluriel*) (*n.m.*), use; usage; custom:
l'usage des routes est gratuit dans la plupart des pays, use of the roads is free in most countries.
objets affectés à l'usage personnel du voyageur (*m.pl.*), articles for the personal use of the passenger.
usages de place *ou* usages des lieux *ou* usages locaux *ou* usages du port, usage (*or* custom) of the port; local custom:
d'après (*ou* suivant) (*ou* selon) les usages de la place (*ou* du port) d'Anvers, according to the usage (*or* the custom) of the port of Antwerp; as customary at the port of Antwerp.
usages du port de chargement, du lieu de déchargement, usage, custom, of the port of loading, of the place of unloading.

usager (pers.) (*n.m.*), user:
les principaux usagers du port, the principal users of the port.

usance (*n.f.*), usance:
avoir sur quelqu'un une lettre de change à usance, à une usance, à double usance, à usance de trente jours, to have a bill of exchange on someone at usance, at one usance, at double usance, at thirty days' usance.

user d'un droit, de la faculté de souscrire, to exercise a right, the option of subscribing.

usine (*n.f.*), works; factory; mill.

usité, -e (*adj.*), customary. See example under **rapidité usitée**.

usuraire *ou* **usurier, -ère** (*adj.*), usurious:
prêt usuraire (*m.*), usurious loan.

usurairement (*adv.*), usuriously.

usure (détérioration) (*n.f.*), wear:
usure normale *ou* simplement usure, wear and tear:
l'usure d'un navire n'est pas une avarie, wear and tear of a ship is not an average.
l'usure des avions dépend moins du vol que du nombre des atterrissages, surtout forcés, wear and tear of aeroplanes depends less on flight than on the number of landings, especially forced.

usure (intérêt excessif) (*n.f.*), usury.

usurier, -ère (pers.) (*n.*), usurer.

V

vacance (état d'une charge qui n'est pas occupée) (*n.f.*), vacancy:
en cas de vacance dans l'intervalle de deux assemblées générales, le conseil peut pourvoir au remplacement (statuts), any casual vacancy may be filled up by the directors.
combler une vacance accidentelle, to fill, to fill up, a casual vacancy.

vacances (intervalle de repos) (*n.f.pl.*), holiday; holidays:
prendre quelques jours de vacances, to take a few days holiday.
vacances de Pâques, Easter holidays.

vacances (*n.f.pl.*) *ou* **vacation** (*n.f.*) (Dr.), vacation; recess.

vacant, -e (*adj.*), vacant:
si une place d'administrateur devient vacante, if a director's office becomes vacant.

vagon (*n.m.*). Same as **wagon**.

vague (*n.f.*), wave:

vague de spéculation, de baisse, wave of speculation, of depression.

vaisseau (*n.m.*), vessel; ship; boat.

Note :—The word *vaisseau* is sometimes restricted to the meaning of Government vessel, especially a war vessel, as distinguished from *navire*, a merchant vessel.

valable (*adj.*), valid; good; available:

quittance valable (*f.*), valid receipt; good receipt.

billet qui n'est valable que dans certains trains (*m.*), ticket which is only available (*or* valid) for certain trains.

valablement (*adv.*), validly.

vale (*n.m.*), scrip; deferred interest certificate.

valeur (ce que vaut une chose) (*n.f.*), value; valuableness; worth; interest:

la valeur d'une chose est la puissance d'échange qu'elle possède, the value (*or* the worth) of a thing is the power of exchange it possesses.

les prix sont l'expression monétaire des valeurs (*m.pl.*), prices are the monetary expression of values.

valeur à l'état avarié (Assce), damaged value.

valeur actuelle (d'un effet), proceeds, net avails (of a bill).

valeur agréée de l'objet d'une assurance, agreed value of the subject matter of an insurance.

valeur assurable *ou* valeur d'assurance, insurable value; insurable interest; insurable risk; insurance value:

la valeur assurable (*ou* la valeur d'assurance) de la chose assurée, the insurable (*or* insurance) value of the thing insured.

les valeurs assurables qui sont l'objet de l'assurance, the insurable interests (*or* risks) which are the subject matter of the insurance.

valeur assurée à prendre en cas d'avaries, en cas de perte totale, insured value for average purposes, for total loss purposes.

valeur comptable, book value.

valeurs créancières *ou* valeurs actives (Avarie commune), values (*or* amounts) (*or* mass) (*or* loss, damage, and expense) to be made good.

valeur d'achat *ou* valeur d'acquisition, cost:

les actions sont estimées pour leur valeur d'achat (*f.pl.*), the shares are valued at cost.

valeur d'usage, value as a going concern.

valeur de facture, invoice value.

valeur de rachat d'une police d'assurance sur la vie, surrender value of a life insurance policy.

valeurs débitrices *ou* valeurs passives *ou* valeurs contributives (Avarie commune), contributing values; contributory interests and values; contributory mass; interests liable to contribute.

valeur déclarée, declared value. *Cf.* colis avec valeur déclarée.

valeur déclarée: fr. 0 (inscription sur un objet chargé) (*Abrév.:* V.D.: fr. 0), insured for: 0 francs.

valeur des marchandises à assurer, value of goods for insurance.

valeur en capital, capital value:

la valeur en capital des titres calculée au cours moyen du jour, the capital value of the stock calculated at the middle price of the day.

valeur en compte, value in account.

valeur en douane, customs value; value for customs purposes.

valeur entière, full value.

valeur faciale (d'un timbre-poste, d'un timbre fiscal), face value (of a postage stamp, of a revenue stamp).

valeur fournie (lettres de change), value given.

valeur locative, rental value.

valeur marchande *ou* valeur vénale, sale value; saleable value; market value; marketable value:

la valeur marchande des pièces de monnaie, comme celle de toute autre marchandise, dépend de la loi de l'offre et de la demande, the sale value of pieces of money (*or* of coins), like that of any other merchandise, depends on the law of supply and demand.

pour le service postal international, les échantillons ne doivent pas avoir de valeur marchande, for the international postal service, samples must not have a saleable value.

valeur marchande à l'état sain (Assce), sound market value.

si la valeur vénale du titre est supérieure à sa valeur nominale, if the marketable value of the stock is higher than its face value.

valeur nette à l'état sain *ou* valeur saine nette (Assce), net sound value.

valeur nominale (d'une action), nominal value, face value (of a share):

la valeur nominale est celle inscrite sur un titre de bourse, the nominal (*or* face) value is that inscribed on a stock or share certificate.

valeur nominale (d'un effet), face value (of a bill).

valeur reçue que passerez en compte suivant avis de (*signature*) (lettre de change), value received which place to account as advised.

valeur réelle *ou* valeur effective, actual value:

la valeur réelle d'un titre de bourse peut être supérieure, égale, ou inférieure à la valeur nominale, the actual value of a stock or share may be higher than, equal to, or lower than (*or* over, equal to, or under) the nominal value.

de valeur, of value; valuable; precious:

un objet de valeur, an article of value (*or* of worth); a valuable article.

documents de valeur, de grande valeur, dépourvus de valeur intrinsèque (*m.pl.*), documents of value, of great value, of no intrinsic value.

valeurs (objets, etc., de valeur) (*n.f.pl.*), valuables; valuable goods; value goods:

police pour l'assurance de valeurs, telles que : titres, coupons, papier-monnaie, effets de commerce, métaux précieux (or et argent monnayés et non monnayés), platine, pierres précieuses, perles fines, etc. (*f.*), policy for the insurance of valuables, such as : securities, coupons, paper money, bills of exchange, precious metals (gold and silver coined and not coined), platinum, precious stones, fine pearls, etc.

valeur (*n.f.*) *ou* **date de valeur** (*f.*) *ou* **date d'entrée en valeur** (*f.*) (Abrév. : **v**/ *ou* **val.**), value ; value date ; as at : la valeur (*ou* la date de valeur) (*ou* la date d'entrée en valeur) (*ou* l'échéance) d'une somme est la date à laquelle elle commence à porter intérêt ; ainsi, si nous remettons à un banquier le 1er novembre, un chèque sur Londres, il nous créditera de son montant valeur (*ou* échéance) 6 novembre, date à laquelle il considère qu'il l'aura encaissé et à partir de laquelle il nous en doit par conséquent les intérêts, the value (*or* the value date) of an amount is the date on which it commences to bear interest ; thus, if we remit to a banker on 1st November, a cheque on London, he will credit us with its amount value 6th November (*or* as at 6th November), the date by which he reckons he will have collected it and from which consequently he owes us interest on it. See also example under **capital**.

valeur compensée (Changes), here and there.

valeur (*n.f.*) *ou* **valeurs** (*n.f.pl.*) (valeurs mobilières, titres, actions, obligations, effets de commerce, etc., représentant une certaine somme d'argent), security ; securities ; stock ; stocks ; share ; shares ; bond ; bonds ; investment ; investments ; holding ; holdings ; asset ; assets ; bill ; bills ; draft ; drafts ; paper ; papers ; valuable paper(s) ; value paper(s) ; money, or its equivalent in any form : (See also **titre** and **action**.)

valeur à lots, prize bond ; lottery bond.

valeurs à ordre, registered shares transferable by endorsement of the certificate.

valeurs à prime, option stock ; stock on option.

valeurs à revenu fixe, fixed yield securities.

valeurs à revenu variable, variable yield securities.

valeur à vue, sight draft ; bill at sight.

valeur active (opp. à *valeur passive*), asset.

valeurs admises. *See under* valeurs inscrites.

valeurs au porteur, bearer securities ; bearer stock ; bearer stocks ; bearer shares ; bearer bonds.

valeurs brûlantes, hot bills ; bills maturing in a few days ; bills that have only a few days to run.

valeur cotée, quoted security (stock for which there is a market price).

valeurs d'alimentation, food shares.

valeurs d'allumettes, match shares.

valeur d'appoint *ou* valeur de second ordre, second rate stock (*or* share).

valeurs d'apport, vendor's assets ; vendors' assets.

valeurs d'assurances, insurance shares.

valeurs d'attractions, amusement shares.

valeurs d'automobiles, motor shares ; motors.

valeurs d'eaux, water shares.

valeurs d'échange *ou* valeurs de roulement (opp. à *valeurs immobilisées*), floating assets ; circulating assets ; revenue assets.

valeurs d'électricité, electricity shares.

valeurs d'étain *ou* valeurs stannifères, tin shares ; tins.

valeurs d'hôtels, hotel shares.

valeurs d'or *ou* valeurs aurifères, gold shares.

valeurs de banques *ou* valeurs bancaires, bank shares.

valeurs de bourse, stock exchange securities ; stocks and shares.

valeurs de caoutchouc *ou* valeurs caoutchoutières, rubber shares ; rubbers.

valeurs de charbonnages *ou* valeurs de mines de charbon, coal shares.

valeurs de chemins de fer, railway shares ; railway stocks ; railways ; rails.

valeurs de ciments, cement shares.

valeurs de cinéma, cinema shares.

valeurs de circulation, kites ; windmills.

valeurs de complaisance, accommodation bills ; accommodation paper.

valeurs de constructions mécaniques, engineering shares.

valeurs de corbeille. *See under* valeurs inscrites.

valeurs de coulisse. *See under* valeurs non inscrites.

valeurs de cuivre *ou* valeurs cuprifères, copper shares ; coppers.

valeurs de diamants *ou* valeurs diamantifères, diamond shares ; diamonds.

valeurs de fantaisie (*fig. ou sarcastique*), bazaar shares ; shares in a bazaar.

valeurs de gaz *ou* valeurs gazières, gas shares ; gas stocks.

valeurs de gramophones, gramophone shares.

valeurs de grands magasins, stores shares.

valeurs de mines *ou* valeurs minières, mining shares ; mines.

valeurs de navigation, shipping shares.

valeurs de nitrate *ou* valeurs nitratières, nitrate shares ; nitrates.

valeurs de parquet. *See under* valeurs inscrites.

valeurs de père de famille, gilt-edged (*or* gilt-edge) securities.

valeurs de pétrole *ou* valeurs pétrolières *ou* valeurs pétrolifères, oil shares ; oils.

valeurs de placement *ou* valeurs de portefeuille (opp. à *valeurs de spéculation*), investment securities ; investment shares ; investment stocks.

valeurs de roulement. *See under* valeurs d'échange.

valeurs de services publics, public utility stocks.

valeurs de soie artificielle, artificial silk shares.

valeurs de spécialités, specialities.

valeurs de spéculation *ou* valeurs spéculatives, speculative securities; speculative shares; speculative stocks.

valeurs de tabacs, tobacco shares.

valeurs de textiles *ou* valeurs textiles, textile shares.

valeurs de tout repos *ou* valeurs à couverture de tout repos, safe investments.

valeurs défectibles, wasting assets.

valeurs dirigeantes *ou* valeurs directrices *ou* valeurs marquantes, leading shares; leading counters; leading favourites; leaders:
    les valeurs dirigeantes (*ou* directrices) (*ou* marquantes) ont regagné une partie du terrain abandonné, the leading shares (*or* leading counters) (*or* leading favourites) (*or* leaders) have regained a part of the ground lost.

valeurs disponibles, available (*or* liquid) assets.

valeurs diverses, miscellaneous shares.

valeurs effectives, effective money; effective; real money.

valeurs en banque. *See under* valeurs non inscrites.

valeurs en or et en argent (encaisse métallique) (Banq.), gold and silver coin and bullion.

valeurs engagées, trading assets.

valeurs étrangères (opp. à *valeurs indigènes* ou, en France, à *valeurs françaises*), foreign stocks; foreign securities.

valeurs faites, guaranteed bills; backed bills.

valeurs fiduciaires, paper securities; securities for money; paper holdings; paper money.

valeurs formant l'actif d'un bilan, assets in a balance sheet:
    majoration des valeurs formant l'actif du bilan (*f.*), overvaluation of the assets in the balance sheet.

valeur garantie *ou* valeurs garanties, guaranteed stock; guaranteed stocks.

valeurs immatérielles *ou* valeurs intangibles, intangible assets.

valeurs immobilières, real property; real estate; realty; immovable property; fixed property:

valeurs immobilisées, fixed assets; permanent assets; capital assets.

valeurs indigènes, home stocks; home securities.

valeurs industrielles, industrial shares; industrials.

valeurs inscrites *ou* valeurs admises à la cote officielle *ou* valeurs figurant à la cote officielle *ou* valeurs de parquet *ou* valeurs de corbeille, listed securities; quoted securities; stocks and shares officially quoted on a French Bourse. *See* marché des valeurs, **inscrire**, *and cf.* valeur cotée.

valeurs irréalisables, unrealizable securities; unrealizable assets.

valeurs matérielles, tangible assets.

valeurs mixtes, registered stocks with coupons attached to the certificates.

valeurs mobilières, stocks and shares; transferable securities.

valeurs nigériennes, Nigerian shares; Nigerians.

valeurs nominatives, registered securities; registered stock; registered stocks; registered shares.

valeurs non cotées *ou* valeurs incotées, unquoted securities (stocks for which there are no market prices).

valeurs non inscrites *ou* valeurs non admises à la cote officielle *ou* valeurs en banque *ou* valeurs du marché en banque *ou* valeurs de coulisse, unlisted securities; unquoted securities; stocks and shares not officially quoted on a French Bourse. *See* marché des valeurs, **inscrire**, *and cf.* valeurs non cotées.

valeurs ouest-africaines, West African shares; West Africans; jungles.

valeurs-papiers (*n.f.pl.*), paper securities; securities for money; paper holdings; paper money.

valeur passive, liability:
    la nouvelle société prendra en charge les valeurs passives, the new company will take over the liabilities.

valeurs réalisables, realizable securities; realizable assets:
    valeurs réalisables à court terme, securities realizable at short notice.

valeurs rhodésiennes, Rhodesian shares; Rhodesians.

valeurs sidérurgiques *ou* valeurs métallurgiques *ou* valeurs du groupe forges et fonderies, iron and steel shares.

valeurs sud-africaines *ou* valeurs transvaaliennes, South African shares; South Africans; Kaffirs.

valeurs tangibles, tangible assets.

valeurs territoriales, land shares.

valide (*adj.*), valid:
    testament valide (*m.*), valid will.

validement (*adv.*), validly.

validité (*n.f.*), validity; availability:
    la formalité de l'écriture n'est exigée que pour la validité du contrat, the formality of writing is only required for the validity of the contract.
    validité des billets d'aller et retour, availability, validity, of return tickets.

valoir (avoir une valeur de) (*v.i.*), to be worth:
    objet qui vaut de l'argent, qui vaut tant de francs (*m.*), article which is worth money, which is worth so many francs.
    les actions X. ont valu tant (en Bourse), X. shares were worth so much.

    à valoir, on account:
    reçu tant de francs à valoir sur mes déboursés, received so many francs on account of my disbursements.

valorisation (*n.f.*), valorization.

valoriser (*v.t.*), to valorize:
    coupons d'un emprunt étranger valorisés à 55 0/0-or (*m.pl.*), coupons of a foreign loan valorized at 55% gold.

vapeur (*n.f.*), steam.

vapeur (*n.m.*) (Abbrev.: **vap.**), steamer; steamship; steamboat: (See also **bateau, bâtiment, navire, paquebot,** and **steamer.**)

vapeur à deux hélices, twin screw steamer.

vapeur à hélice, screw steamer.

vapeur charbonnier, steam collier.

vapeur-citerne [vapeurs-citernes *pl.*] *ou* vapeur-tank [vapeurs-tanks *pl.*] (*n.m.*),   tank steamer.

vapeur de charge, cargo steamer.

vapeur de haute mer,   deep-sea steamer.

vapeur de ligne régulière *ou simplement* vapeur de ligne, liner.

vapeur fluvial, river steamer.

vapeur océanique *ou* vapeur transocéanique, ocean steamer.

vapeur postal [vapeurs postaux *pl.*] (*Abrév.:* m/s. *ou* m.s.),   mail steamer; mail boat; mail packet.

variable (*adj.*) (opp. à *fixe*), variable :

valeurs à revenu variable (*f.pl.*),   variable yield securities.

vedette (*n.f.*) *ou*   **principale vedette** (valeur marquante), leader; leading counter; leading share; leading favourite :

ce groupe est actuellement la vedette du marché (Bourse), this group is at present the leader of the market.

les principales vedettes du group caoutchoutier, the leading counters of the rubber group.

être en vedette, to be prominent :

les valeurs de caoutchouc ont été en vedette pendant toute la semaine (*f.pl.*),   rubber shares have been prominent all the week.

véhicule (*n.m.*), vehicle ; car :

véhicule automobile, motor vehicle.

véhicule routier, road vehicle.

véhicules de chemins de fer roulant sur leurs propres roues (*ou* roulant sur essieux), railway vehicles running on their own wheels :

le transport de véhicules de chemins de fer roulant sur leurs propres roues, the conveyance of railway vehicles running on their own wheels.

veille (jour précédent) (*n.f.*), day before ; eve ; yesterday :

spéculateur qui a acheté la veille de la baisse, vendu la veille de la hausse (*m.*), speculator who has bought the day before the fall, sold the day before the rise ; speculator who has bought on the eve of the fall, sold on the eve of the rise.

sur la Bourse de Paris, les opérations à primes se résolvent à 1h. 30, la veille de la liquidation, appelé pour cela jour de la réponse des primes,   on the Paris Bourse, dealings in options are resolved at 1.30 p.m., on the day before the settlement, called on that account option declaration day.

clôture de la veille (bulletin de cours) (*f.*), yesterday's closing.

veiller (*v.i.*). See examples :

veiller à ce que quelqu'un fait quelque chose, to see that someone does something.

veiller à l'exécution des réparations, to see that the repairs are carried out ; to look after the carrying out of the repairs.

veiller à la conservation de la marchandise avec

tous les soins d'un bon père de famille, to take due and proper care of the goods.

veiller au sauvetage et à la conservation des objets assurés, to sue, labour, and travel for the saving and preserving of the property insured.

veilleur de nuit (d'une banque) (pers.) (*m.*), night watchman.

vénal, -e, -aux (pécuniaire) (*adj.*),   marketable ; market (*used as adj.*) ; saleable ; sale (*used as adj.*). See example *under* valeur marchande *ou* valeur vénale.

venant de . . ., à destination de . . ., sailing from . . . and bound for . . . :

navire venant d'Anvers, à destination de Londres (*m.*),   ship sailing from Antwerp and bound for London.

vendable (*adj.*) *ou* **de vente,** saleable ; marketable : marchandises vendables (*f.pl.*) *ou* marchandise de vente (*f.*), saleable goods ; marketable goods.

vendeur, -euse (personne dont la profession est de vendre) (*n.*) (Ant. : *acheteur*), seller :

vendeur à découvert (Bourse),   bear seller ; short seller.

vendeur d'un dont (*ou* d'une prime directe) (Bourse), taker for a call ; seller of a call option.

vendeur d'un ou (*ou* d'une prime indirecte) (Bourse), giver for a put ; buyer of a put option :

spéculateur qui est vendeur de 100 actions X.Y.Z. à 517 ou 3 (*m.*), speculator who is giver of 3 francs (per share) for the put of 100 X.Y.Z. shares at 520.

Note :—The French envisage the sale of the shares by the putter (*vendeur de 0 actions*). The English envisage the giver of the rate for the option to put or sell the shares, or, and which is the same thing, the buyer of the option to put or sell the shares. Hence *vendeur* has to be translated by *giver* or *buyer* in this case. *Cf.* acheteur d'un ou.

cours offerts (vendeurs) (Bourse) (*m.pl.*) (*Abrév.:* V.), prices offered (sellers).

parcelles de (blé) Manitoba nord mars 42/6d. vendeur (*ou en abrév.:* 42/6 vend. *ou* 42/6 V.) (*f.pl.*), parcels of Northern Manitoba (wheat) March sellers at 42/6d.

quand la place est vendeur, when the market is a seller.

pendant la guerre les grandes nations productrices sont restées, jusqu'à un certain point, absentes des marchés comme vendeuses,   during the war the great producing nations kept away, to a certain point, from the markets as sellers.

vendeur, -eresse (personne qui fait un acte de vente) (*n.*), vendor.

vendre (faire le commerce de) (*v.t.*) (Ant. : *acheter*), to sell :

vendre des marchandises, des actions, un navire, to sell goods, shares, a ship.

vendre à bon compte, cher (*ou* chèrement), à l'amiable, à l'enchère (*ou* aux enchères), à la commission, à perte, à tout prix,   to sell cheap, at a high price, privately (*or* by private treaty), by auction (*or* at auction), on commission, at a loss, at any price.

vendre à couvert (Bourse), to sell for delivery.

vendre à découvert (Bourse), to sell a bear; to sell short; to short; to bear; to bear the market; to hammer; to hammer the market:

spéculer sur la bourse, c'est-à-dire acheter ou vendre à découvert, to speculate on the stock exchange, that is to say, to buy a bull or sell a bear (*or* to bull or to bear) (*or* to bull or bear the market).

vendre de la Rente à découvert, to sell a bear of Rente; to sell Rentes short; to short Rentes.

vendre à terme *ou* vendre à crédit (Com.), to sell upon (*or* on) credit:

on sait assez que chaque espèce de marchandise se vend habituellement à tel ou tel terme, sous tel ou tel escompte, we know well enough that every kind of merchandise is usually sold upon such or such credit, at such or such discount.

vendre à terme (Bourse de valeurs), to sell for the settlement (*or* for the account).

vendre à terme (Bourse de marchandises), to sell forward.

vendre comptant *ou* vendre au comptant, to sell for cash.

vendre dont (Bourse), to take for the call; to sell a call option:

vendre 25 Rio dont 40 francs, to take 40 francs (per share) for the call on 25 Rios.

See explanation of option dealing under **prime.**

vendre par échelons de hausse (Bourse), to average sales.

V. *ou* V/. (ordres de bourse) (*abrév.*), vendez; vendre; vendu; vente.

à vendre, to be sold; for sale:

à vendre.—immeuble de banque, to be sold.— banking premises.

vendre (céder moyennant un prix convenu) (*v.t.*), to sell for; to sell at:

vendre un article tant de francs, to sell an article for (*or* at) so many francs.

vendre (Dr.) (*v.t.*), to sell up:

vendre quelqu'un, to sell someone up.

vendre (se) (être vendu) (*v.r.*), to be sold; to be sold for; to be sold at; to sell for; to sell at; *hence:* to be:

le marché où se vendent les actions et autres titres semblables, the market where shares and other similar securities are sold.

action qui se vend tant (*f.*), share which is sold at (*or* which sells at) so much.

le terrain, à Paris, se vend cher, ground, in Paris, is dear.

vendre (se) (avoir de la vente) (*v.r.*), to sell:

objets qui se vendent bien (*m.pl.*), articles which sell well.

Vendredi noir (panique financière) (*m.*), Black Friday.

venir en concurrence *ou* **venir en concours,** to rank equally; to rank concurrently;

to rank pari passu. See examples under syn. **concourir.**

vente (*n.f.*) (Abrév.: **vte**) (Ant.: *achat*), sale; selling:

la vente de marchandises, de monnaie, the sale of goods, of money.

marchandise de bonne vente (*f.*), goods which will command a ready sale; goods which will sell well.

vente à découvert (Bourse), bear sale; short sale; short.

vente à l'acquitté *ou* vente à l'A., duty-paid sale; sale ex bond. *Note:—In Marseilles the* vente à l'acquitté *is termed* vente à la consommation.

vente à l'amiable *or* vente de gré à gré, sale by private treaty.

vente à l'enchère *ou* vente aux enchères *ou* vente à la criée *ou* vente à l'encan, sale by auction.

vente à l'heureuse arrivée, sale to arrive; sale subject to safe arrival (of ship).

vente à livrer (Bourse de valeurs), sale for delivery.

vente à réméré, sale with option of repurchase.

vente à tempérament *ou* vente par abonnement, hire purchase; instalment plan.

vente à terme *ou* vente à crédit (Com.) (opp. à *vente au comptant*), credit sale; sale on credit.

vente à terme (Bourse de valeurs), sale for the settlement; sale for the account.

vente à terme *ou* vente à livrer (Bourse de marchandises) (opp. à *vente en disponible*), forward sale. *See note under* marché à terme.

vente à terme ferme (Bourse de marchandises), sale for future delivery during specified periods.

vente au comptant *ou* vente comptant, cash sale; sale for money.

vente au débarquement, sale delivered ex ship (*or* ex steamer); sale on ex ship terms; sale on landed terms; sale free overside.

vente caf., sale c.i.f. ; c.i.f. sale; sale on c.i.f. terms.

vente comptant-compté, cash down sale.

vente contre remboursement, cash on delivery sale.

vente d'une prime (Bourse), taking for an option; selling an option.

vente de marchandises flottantes (*ou* en cargaison flottante) (*ou* sous voile) avec faculté d'option entre plusieurs destinations, sale of goods afloat (*or* on passage) on optional bill of lading.

vente dont *ou* vente à prime directe (Bourse), taking for the call; selling a call option.

vente en demi-gros, wholesale sale. See note under **gros** *ou* **gros commerce.**

vente en détail, retail sale.

vente en (*ou* de) disponible (Bourse de marchandises), spot sale.

vente en entrepôt *ou* vente en E. *ou* vente E., sale in bonded warehouse.

vente en expédition prompte, sale for prompt delivery (*or* for prompt shipment).

vente en gros, direct sale. See note under
gros *ou* **gros commerce.**
vente par échelons de hausse (Bourse),
averaging sales.
vente par navire désigné, sale by named
vessel.
ventes professionnelles (Bourse), professional
sales ; shop selling.
vente publique, public sale.
vente sur échantillon, sale on sample.
vente sur embarquement, sale on shipment ;
sale at port of shipment.
ventes : 000 tonnes (Bourse de marchandises),
sales (*or* turnover) : 000 tons.
ventilation (Comptab.) (*n.f.*), apportionment ;
analysis.
ventiler (Comptab.) (*v.t.*), to apportion ; to
analyze ; to analyse :
ventiler les frais accidentels d'après un quantum
à déterminer, to apportion the incidental
expenses according to a proportion to be
determined.
ventiler la colonne Divers, to analyze the
Sundries column.
verbal, -e, -aux (*adj.*), verbal :
confirmation verbale ou écrite (*f.*), verbal or
written confirmation.
verbalement (*adv.*), verbally :
ordres donnés verbalement (*m.pl.*), orders
given verbally.
véreux, -euse (*adj.*), shady ; bad :
financier véreux (*m.*), shady financier.
société véreuse émanant d'une officine (*ou*
d'une boutique) de moralité douteuse (*f.*),
shady company emanating from a stable
of doubtful morality.
créance véreuse (*f.*), bad debt.
vergues (sous). See under **sous palan.**
vérificateur (pers.) (*n.m.*), examiner.
vérificateur comptable (pers.) (*m.*), auditor.
vérification (*n.f.*), verification ; examination ;
checking :
marchandises soumises à la vérification des
préposés des douanes (*f.pl.*), goods submitted to the examination (*or* verification)
of the customs officials.
vérification d'un compte, verification, checking, of an account.
vérification comptable *ou simplement* vérification, auditing ; audit.
vérification des pièces justificatives, vouching ; checking vouchers.
vérifier (*v.t.*), to verify ; to examine ; to check ;
to audit :
vérifier le contenu d'un paquet, le produit de
la journée, to verify, to check, the contents
of a packet, the day's receipts (*or* takings).
vérifier les livres (*ou* les écritures), les encaisses,
to check, to audit, the books (*or* the accounts),
the cash in hand.
vérifier un fait, to verify a fact.
les agents des douanes ont le droit de vérifier
les marchandises qui leur sont déclarées
(*m.pl.*), customs officers have the right to
examine the goods declared to them.
Veritas (*n.m.*) *ou* **Bureau Veritas** (*m.*) (société de

classification de navires), Veritas ; Bureau
Veritas :
la cote d'un vapeur au Veritas, the class of
a steamer at Veritas. See also example under
Bureau Veritas.
versement (*n.m.*), payment ; remittance ; paying in ; paying up ; instalment ; installment ; call :
versement d'appels de fonds, en compte
courant, par chèque d'une somme convenue,
payment of calls, on current account, by
cheque of an agreed sum.
versements à la banque, à la petite caisse,
payments into the bank, into petty cash.
faire un versement de fonds, to make a remittance of funds.
échelonner une souscription en plusieurs versements, to spread a subscription into several
instalments.
le paiement peut se faire en une fois ou par
versements échelonnés, payment can be
made in full or in (*or* by) instalments.
versement de souscription (à des actions, des
obligations), application money.
versement de répartition (répartition d'actions,
d'obligations), allotment money.
versement par anticipation *ou* versement anticipatif (appel de fonds), payment in
advance ; payment in advance of calls ; call
paid in advance.
versement de libération *ou* dernier versement,
final instalment ; final call (on shares, or
the like).
Warning.—Essential diversity of meaning or
purport exists in the French expressions
premier, second, troisième, etc., *versements,*
and also in their English equivalents *first,
second, third,* etc., *instalments ;* thus, *application money* is often referred to in French as
the *premier versement* and the *first call* sometimes as the *deuxième versement* and sometimes as the *troisième versement,* according
as it constitutes the second or the third
payment or parting with money. The precise application can only be determined by
context. While *instalment* in English Company practice may be equivocal, *call* is not.
Calls are assessments demanded after application money and allotment money ; thus,
first call is the first money payable after
amount due on allotment.
versement (Opérations de change) (*n.m.*), telegraphic transfer ; telegraph transfer ; cable
transfer ; cable.
versement (Caisse d'épargne) (*n.m.*), deposit.
verser (*v.t.*), to pay ; to pay in ; to deposit ;
to pay up :
verser un appel de fonds, to pay a call.
verser au comptant *ou* verser comptant, to
pay in cash.
verser à la banque tant de francs, to pay so
many francs into the bank ; to pay in so
many francs to the bank ; to bank so many
francs.
fonds versés en banque (*m.pl.*), money paid
into the bank.

verser des fonds à la caisse nationale d'épargne, to deposit money in the post office savings bank.

société au capital nominal de tant, dont tant a été versé (*f.*), company with an authorized capital of so much, of which so much has been paid up (*or* paid).

se verser (*v.r.*), to be paid:
les impôts se versent chez les percepteurs (*m.pl.*), taxes are paid to the collectors.

verso [**versos** *pl.*] (d'un livre) (*n.m.*) (Abrév.: **Vo**) (Ant.: *recto*), left hand page (*or* side) (of a book):
dès leur réception, les ordres sont inscrits sur un livre spécial, les achats au verso, les ventes au recto, as soon as they are received, the orders are entered in a special book, the purchases on the left hand page (*or* side), the sales on the right hand page (*or* side).

verso (d'un effet, d'un chèque, ou analogue, d'une enveloppe, d'une carte postale, d'un paquet) (*n.m.*) (Ant.: *recto*), back (of a bill, of a cheque, or the like, of an envelope, of a postcard, of a packet):
comme son nom l'indique, l'endossement se met au verso de l'effet, as its name indicates, the endorsement is put on the back of the bill.
donner un reçu sur le verso du connaissement, to give a receipt on the back of the bill of lading.

vertu de (en), in pursuance of:
en vertu des articles — et — de la loi de 24 juillet 1867 sur les sociétés, in pursuance of sections — and — of the Companies Act of 24th July 1867.

veuillez faire suivre (mention sur un objet de correspondance), please forward.

veuillez payer à. See under **payez à.**

veuillez répéter le numéro (Téléph.), please repeat the number; will you please repeat the number?

via (*prép.*), via:
départ pour New-York via Le Havre, sailing for New York via Havre.
télégramme acheminé « Via Impérial » (*m.*), telegram routed " Via Imperial."

viager, -ère (*adj.*), life (*used as adj.*); for life:
rente viagère (*f.*), life annuity.
revenu viager (*m.*), income for life; life income.

viager (*n.m.*), life income; life annuity; life annuities:
placer son argent en viager, to invest one's money in life annuities.

viagèrement (*adv.*), for life:
bien cédé viagèrement (*m.*), property given up for life.

vice (*n.m.*), vice; defect; fault; error:
vice apparent, apparent defect.
vice caché, latent defect; hidden defect:
vices cachés échappant à une diligence raisonnable, latent defects not discoverable by due diligence.
vice d'adresse, wrong address.
vice d'arrimage, improper stowage; bad stowage; fault of stowing:
avaries résultant d'un vice d'arrimage (*f.pl.*),

damage resulting from improper (*or* bad) stowage.
vice de clerc, clerical error.
vice de construction, constructional defect.
vice de forme (dans un acte), informality; irregularity.
vice propre (*Abrév.*: **VP**), inherent vice; vice propre:
par vice propre de la marchandise on entend la détérioration de la marchandise par sa nature ou par l'influence d'agents naturels extérieurs, by inherent vice (*or* by vice propre) is understood deterioration of the goods by their nature or by the influence of external natural agents.
vice rédhibitoire, redhibitory defect.

vice-consul [**vice-consuls** *pl.*] (pers.) (*n.m.*), vice consul.

vice-consulat [**vice-consulats** *pl.*] (*n.m.*), vice consulate.

vice-gérance [**vice-gérances** *pl.*] (*n.f.*), vice managership.

vice-gérant [**vice-gérants** *pl.*] (pers.) (*n.m.*), vice manager; deputy manager.

vice-présidence [**vice-présidences** *pl.*] (*n.f.*), vice chairmanship; vice presidency.

vice-président [**vice-présidents** *pl.*] (pers.) (*n.m.*), vice chairman; deputy chairman; vice president.

victime (*n.f.*), victim:
la victime d'un accident, the victim of an accident.

victuailles (*n.f.pl.*), victuals; provisions; food.

vide (*adj.*), empty:
pots à lait vides en retour (*m.pl.*), returned empty milk churns.

à vide (opp. à *à charge*), empty; when empty:
navire avec la perspective de retourner à vide (*m.*), ship with the prospect of returning empty.
parcours à vide (d'un wagon de ch. de f.) (*m.*), journey empty; empty journey; journey when empty.

vide (wagon vide, caisse vide, etc.) (*n.m.*), empty:
vide en retour, returned empty.

vider (*v.t.*), to empty:
vider ses poches, to empty one's pockets.

vider une contestation, to settle a dispute.

vie (*n.f.*), life; living:
navire qui dévie de sa route pour sauver des vies humaines ou des biens (*m.*), ship which deviates from her course to save lives or property.
pension à vie (*f.*), pension for life; life pension.
vie moyenne (Assce), average life.
vie chère, dear living.

vierge (*adj.*), blank:
si, sur telle ou telle valeur, il n'a été fait aucune opération, la ligne reste vierge (bulletin de cours), if, in such or such stock, no deal has been done, the line is left blank (list of quotations).

vierge de, free from:
connaissements vierges de toute clause d'exonération de responsabilité (*m.pl.*), bills of lading free from any clause relieving from liability.

vignette « pièces jointes » (*f.*), " enclosure "
label; duplicate enclosure check.

vigueur (en), in force:
règlements, police, encore en vigueur, regulations, policy, still in force.

la taxe à percevoir est toujours celle qui est
en vigueur au moment où les marchandises
sont déclarées pour l'acquittement des
droits, the duty to be collected is always
that which is in force at the time when the
goods are entered for payment of duty.

vil prix (*m.*), knock out price.

ville (*n.f.*), town:
ville de province, country town; provincial
town.

violation de dépôt, de dépôts publics (*f.*), misappropriation of trust funds, of public
funds.

violation de garantie (*f.*), breach of warranty.

virement (Fin. et Comptab.) (*n.m.*) (Abrév.:
virt), transfer:
le plus souvent, les opérations de change se
font par simples virements entre banquiers
correspondants, for the most part, exchange transactions are done by simple
transfers between corresponding bankers.

virement d'un compte, d'un compte à un
autre, transfer of an account, from one
account to another.

virement au débit du 1er compte *ou* pour
virement au 1er compte (libellé d'une écriture de journal) (Comptab.), transfer to
debit of former account; for amount transferred to former a/c.

virement au crédit du 2e compte *ou* pour virement au 2e compte (Comptab.), transfer
to credit of latter account; for amount
transferred to latter a/c.

virement (Banq.) (*n.m.*), bank transfer; transfer
from one account to another in the bank's
books.
[*Note*:—In France, this is not effected by
passing an ordinary cheque, as in England,
but by a *mandat de virement* or *bon de virement* (*order to transfer*). *Cf. remarks under*
compte courant postal.]

virer (*v.t.*), to transfer (from one account to
another):
virer une somme au compte intérêts, à pertes
et profits, to transfer an amount to interest
account, to profit and loss.

visa [**visas** *pl.*] (*n.m.*), visa; visé; initials *or*
signature (put to a document, account, or
the like, as evidence of identification or
approval); marking; certification:
le visa d'un consul sur un passeport, the visa
(*or* the visé) of a consul on a passport.

visa de transit, transit visa.

visa pour timbre, stamping authentication.
In France, official written mention on a
document, taking the place of a revenue
stamp, in certain cases.

visa (d'une lettre de change) (*n.m.*), sighting (of
a bill of exchange).

viser (*v.t.*), to visa; to visé; to initial; to sign;
to mark; to certify:

viser un passeport, to visa (*or* to visé) a passport.

viser le talon d'un chèque, to initial the
counterfoil of a cheque.

chèque visé (Banq.) (*m.*), marked cheque;
certified cheque.

viser des livres de commerce. In France, to
enter upon the first page of the *livres de
commerce* (q.v.) a formula stating the number
of pages the book contains. This formula
has to be certified by a *juge du tribunal de
commerce*, or by the *maire* in small places.

viser pour timbre, to authenticate as stamped.
See explanation under visa pour timbre.

viser une lettre de change, to sight a bill of
exchange.

viseur (d'une machine à calculer) (*n.m.*), dial
(of a calculating machine).

visible (*adj.*), visible:
exportations visibles (*f.pl.*), visible exports.

visite (*n.f.*), visit; call; inspection; examination; survey:
faire une visite, to pay a visit; to make a
call.

visite de la douane (*ou* visite douanière) des
marchandises, des bagages, customs examination of goods, of luggage (*or* baggage):

visite douanière des bagages à main qui a
lieu (*ou* qui se fait) dans le train en cours
de route, customs examination of hand
luggage which takes place in the train
during the journey.

tout colis adressé à un ambassadeur, chargé
d'affaires, ou ministre, accrédités auprès du
Gouvernement français, est admis en
franchise de droit de douane et sans visite,
any package addressed to an ambassador,
chargé d'affaires, or minister, accredited
to the French Government, is admitted
free of customs duty and without examination.

visite de mise en service (navire), survey on
being put into service.

visite de partance (navire), survey on sailing.

visite médicale des passagers et de l'équipage,
medical inspection of passengers and crew.

visite périodique de la coque d'un navire,
periodical inspection (*or* survey) of the hull
of a ship.

visite à bord (des navires) (Douanes) (*f.*), rummaging (ships).

visiter (*v.t.*), to visit; to inspect; to examine;
to survey:
les bagages des voyageurs seront visités à la
frontière (*m.pl.*), passengers' luggage will
be examined at the frontier.

les armateurs peuvent toujours demander que
leurs navires soient visités (*m.pl.*), shipowners can always insist upon their ships
being surveyed.

visiteur, -euse (personne qui est en visite) (*n.*),
visitor; caller:
exposition qui attire en très grand nombre
les visiteurs étrangers (*f.*), exhibition which
attracts foreign visitors in very great
numbers.

visiteur (personne chargée d'une inspection) (*n.m.*), inspector; examiner.

vitesse (*n.f.*), speed:
la vitesse des navires s'exprime en nœuds, the speed of ships is expressed in knots.
le grand avantage de l'avion sur les autres moyens de transport est la vitesse, the great advantage of the aeroplane over other means of transport is speed.

vivres (*n.m.pl.*), provisions; victuals; food.

voie (*n.f.*), way; road; route:
voie aérienne *ou* voie d'air, airway; air route.
voie de mer *ou* voie maritime, sea route.
voie de terre, overland route; land route.
voie ferrée *ou* voie de fer, railway; railroad; rail.
voie fluviale, inland route (river or canal); interior waterway.
voie navigable *ou* voie d'eau, waterway; water route:
on distingue deux sortes de voies navigables: les rivières et les canaux, there are two kinds of waterways: rivers and canals.
expéditeur qui prescrit la voie que doit suivre son télégramme (*m.*), sender who specifies the route by which his telegram is to be sent.

par la voie, by the route; via:
télégramme acheminé par la « Voie Impérial » (*m.*), telegram routed "Via Imperial."

sans voie. See under **sans.**

voie de garage (Ch. de f.) (*f.*), siding.

voie de tramway (*f.*), tram track.

voilier (*n.m.*), sailer; sailing ship; sailing vessel.

voir (effets de commerce) (*v.t.*), to sight:
effet vu le (*date*), bill sighted (*date*).
voir le tireur (Banq.), refer to drawer.

voiture (véhicule routier) (*n.f.*), carriage; cart; car; vehicle; van; wagon; waggon:
voiture automobile, motor vehicle.
voiture de livraison, delivery van.
voiture de tramway, tram car; tram.

voiture (wagon de chemin de fer) (*n.f.*), carriage; coach; car; wagon; waggon: (See also **wagon.**)
voiture à voyageurs, passenger carriage; passenger coach; passenger car.
voiture automotrice, rail motor car.
voiture directe, through carriage.
voiture-lit [voitures-lits *pl.*] (*n.f.*), sleeping car.
voiture Pullman, Pullman car; Pullman.
voiture-salon [voitures-salons *pl.*] (*n.f.*), saloon; saloon carriage; saloon car; parlour car.
voiture salon-restaurant [voitures salons-restaurants *pl.*], parlour restaurant car.

voiture (transport) (*n.f.*), carriage; carrying; transport; transportation.

voiture (prix du transport) (*n.f.*), carriage.

voiture-kilomètre [voitures-kilomètre *pl.*] (*n.f.*) *ou* **voiture kilométrique** (*f.*), car kilometre, analogous to the English car mile (voiture-mille).

voiturer (*v.t.*), to cart; to carry; to convey; to transport.

voiturier (pers.) (*n.m.*), carrier; carman; carter: voiturier successif, succeeding carrier; on-carrier.

voix (*n.f.*), voice; vote:
voix consultative, consultative voice.
chaque membre de l'assemblée a une voix (*m.*), each member present has one vote.
voix prépondérante, casting vote:
président qui a voix prépondérante en cas de partage (*m.*), chairman who has a casting vote if the voting is equal.

vol (progression dans l'air sur un aéroplane) (*n.m.*), flying; flight; aviation:
trajet effectué d'un seul vol (*m.*), passage effected in one flight.
vol d'essai, trial flight.
vol de nuit, night flying; night flight.

vol (action de celui qui dérobe) (*n.m.*), theft; robbery:
vol à main armée, robbery by force.

volant (*n.m.*) (opp. à *talon*), leaf:
remplir un des feuillets du carnet de chèques, talon et volant, détacher le volant et le présenter à l'encaissement, to fill up one of the leaves of the cheque book, counterfoil and leaf, to detach the leaf and present it for payment.
volant d'entrée (d'un triptyque), importation voucher (of a pass sheet).
volant de sortie (d'un triptyque), exportation voucher.

voler (se mouvoir dans l'air) (*v.i.*), to fly.

voleur, -euse (pers.) (*n.*), thief; robber:
voleurs à main armée (Assce mar.), assailing thieves; sturdy thieves.

volontaire (*adj.*), voluntary:
échouement volontaire (*m.*), voluntary stranding.

volontairement (*adv.*), voluntarily:
dommages soufferts volontairement pour le bien et le salut commun du navire et de la cargaison (*m.pl.*), damage suffered voluntarily for the welfare and common safety of the ship and cargo.

volume (*n.m.*), volume; bulk; measurement:
le volume des affaires, des ordres, the volume of business, of orders.
freinte en volume (*f.*), wastage in bulk.
fret calculé d'après le volume des marchandises (*m.*), freight calculated according to the measurement of the goods.

votant, -e (pers.) (*n.*), voter.

votation (*n.f.*), voting:
mode de votation (*m.*), method of voting.

vote (*n.m.*), vote.

voter (*v.t.*), to vote; to pass a vote:
voter l'ajournement d'une assemblée, une résolution à main levée (*ou* à mains levées), to vote the adjournment of a meeting, a resolution by a show of hands.
voter des remerciements aux administrateurs, to pass a vote of thanks to the directors.

voter (*v.i.*), to vote:
voter sur une proposition, to vote on a resolution.
cette résolution est adoptée à l'unanimité des

actionnaires présents, à l'exception de M.
X., apporteur, qui s'est abstenu de voter
(ou qui n'a pas pris part au vote), the resolution was carried unanimously by the
shareholders present, with the exception of
Mr X., vendor, who did not vote (or who
abstained from voting) (or who did not take
part in the voting).

Votre dévoué [Vos dévoués *pl.*] (formule de
politesse précédant signature), Yours faithfully ; Yours truly.

voyage (*n.m.*), travel ; travelling ; traveling ;
voyage ; passage ; journey ; tour ; trip ;
transit ; booking :
agence de voyages (*f.*), travel agency.
voyages à forfait, through bookings.
voyage au cabotage, coasting voyage.
voyage au (ou de) long cours, ocean voyage ;
foreign voyage ; deep-sea voyage.
voyage avec chargement, cargo passage.
voyage circulaire, circular tour.
voyage d'aller, outward voyage (or journey)
(or passage) (or trip) ; outward bound
voyage ; outbound voyage.
voyage d'aller et de retour, round voyage ;
journey (or passage) there and back.
voyage d'essai, trial trip.
voyage d'excursion, excursion trip.
voyage de (ou par) mer, sea voyage ; sea
passage.
voyage de retour, homeward (or return)
voyage (or journey) (or passage) (or trip) ;
homeward bound voyage ; home bound
voyage ; inward bound voyage ; inbound
voyage.
voyage intermédiaire d'un port à un autre,
intermediate voyage from one port to
another.
voyage mixte, river and sea voyage.
voyage par chemin de fer, railway journey
(or trip) ; rail transit.
voyage par terre, overland journey ; overland travel ; land journey.
voyage sur (ou en) lest, ballast passage.
marchandise avariée en cours de voyage (*f.*),
goods damaged in course of transit (or
damaged in transit) (or damaged in transitu).
rompre un voyage avant le départ du vaisseau,
to cancel a booking before departure of the
vessel.

voyager (*v.i.*), to travel ; to journey ; to sail :

voyager en Europe, to travel in Europe.
la marchandise voyage, sauf convention contraire, aux risques et périls de l'acheteur,
the goods travel, unless otherwise agreed,
at buyer's risk.

voyageur, -euse (pers.) (*n.*), traveller ; traveler ;
passenger ; fare : (*Note :—voyageur* can be
used of a passenger using any means of
locomotion, whether on land or sea, or in the
air. Cf. **passager.**)
voyageur à la commission, traveller on commission.
voyageur de commerce, commercial traveller.
train de voyageurs (*m.*), passenger train.

voyageur-kilomètre [voyageurs-kilomètre *pl.*]
(*n.m.*) ou **voyageur kilométrique,** passenger
kilometre, analogous to English *passenger
mile* (voyageur-mille).

vrac (en) ou **vrague (en),** in bulk :
expédier en vrac, to ship in bulk.
la marchandise en vrac s'embarque généralement au moyen d'appareils spéciaux, goods
in bulk are generally embarked by means
of special apparatus.

vu (*n.m.*), sight :
payer une traite au vu du connaissement, to
pay a bill on sight of the bill of lading.

vue (*n.f.*), sight :
à vue, at sight ; on demand ; on presentation ; at (or on) call ; sight (*used as adj.*) ;
demand (*used as adj.*) ; call (*used as adj.*) :
traite à vue ou traite payable à vue (*f.*),
draft at sight ; sight draft ; draft payable
at sight (or on presentation).
cours à vue (Opérations de change) (*m.*),
demand rate.
le billet de banque est une promesse de
payer une certaine somme à vue et au
porteur, a bank note is a promise to pay
a certain sum on demand and to bearer.
argent à vue (*m.*), money (or loans) at (or
on) call ; call money.
de vue ou **à .. de vue,** after sight ; at .. sight :
le nombre de jours de vue, the number of
days after sight.
à trois jours de vue veuillez payer, etc.
(lettre de change), three days after sight
pay, etc. See **première de change** for full
example.
effet payable à trente jours de vue (*m.*), bill
payable thirty days after sight ; bill payable at thirty days' sight.

W

wagon (Ch. de f.) (*n.m.*), wagon ; waggon ;
truck ; car ; carriage ; coach ; van : (See also
voiture.)
wagon à bestiaux ou wagon à bétail, cattle
truck ; cattle wagon.
wagon à charbons ou wagon à houille, coal
truck ; coal wagon.

wagon à couloir, corridor carriage.
wagon à (ou de) marchandises, goods wagon ;
goods truck ; goods van ; freight car.
wagon appartenant à un particulier ou wagon
de particulier ou wagon particulier, owner's
wagon.
wagon chargé, loaded wagon (or truck).

wagon-citerne [wagons-citernes *pl.*] *ou* wagon-réservoir [wagons-réservoirs *pl.*] (*n.m.*), tank car.

wagon complet, truck load; full truck load: le minimum de poids par wagon complet, the minimum weight per truck load.

marchandises pondéreuses expédiées en wagon complet (*f.pl.*), heavy goods consigned in truck loads.

tarif des wagons complets (*m.*), truck load rates.

wagon couvert *ou* wagon fermé, covered wagon; covered truck; covered van; box wagon; box car.

wagon de chemin de fer, railway truck (*or* wagon) (*or* car) (*or* van) (*goods*); railway carriage (*or* coach) (*or* car) (*passengers*).

wagon découvert *ou* wagon ouvert, open wagon; open truck.

wagon découvert bâché, sheeted open wagon.

wagon découvert non bâché, unsheeted open wagon.

wagon-écurie [wagons-écuries *pl.*] (*n.m.*) *ou* wagon-boxe pour le transport de chevaux [wagons-boxes *pl.*] (*m.*), horse box.

wagon frigorifique *ou* wagon réfrigérant, refrigerated van.

wagon incomplet, part truck load.

wagon isotherme, insulated van.

wagon-laitière [wagons-laitières *pl.*] (*n.m.*), milk van.

wagon-lit [wagons-lits *pl.*] (*n.m.*), sleeping car.

wagon-poste [wagons-poste *pl.*] (*n.m.*), sorting carriage; sorting tender; mail car.

wagon-restaurant [wagons-restaurants *pl.*] (*n.m.*), dining car; restaurant car.

wagon-salon [wagons-salons *pl.*] (*n.m.*), saloon carriage; saloon car; saloon; parlour car.

wagon-truck [wagons-trucks *pl.*] (*n.m.*), carriage truck (railway wagon for carrying a road vehicle).

franco wagon *ou simplement* **sur wagon,** free on rail; free on truck; on rail.

wagon-kilomètre [**wagons-kilomètre** *pl.*] (*n.m.*) *ou* **wagon kilométrique** (*m.*), car kilometre, analogous to English *car mile* (wagon-mille).

warrant (*n.m.*) *ou* **récépissé-warrant** [**récépissés-warrants** *pl.*] (*n.m.*), warrant; deposit warrant: (for goods deposited in a public or dock warehouse.)

le warrant est un billet à ordre gagé par des marchandises déposées dans des magasins généraux ou dans des docks, (in France) a *warrant* is a note of hand pledged by goods deposited in *magasins généraux* or in dock warehouses.

warrantage (*n.m.*), securing (goods) by warrant.

warranter (des marchandises) (*v.t.*), to secure (goods) by warrant.

water-ballast (*n.m.*), water ballast.

Z

Zeppelin (*n.m.*), Zeppelin.

zéro (absolument rien) (*n.m.*), zero: fortune réduite à zéro (*f.*), fortune reduced to zero.

zollverein (*n.m.*), zollverein.

zone (*n.f.*), zone; area:

zones franches dans les ports maritimes (Douanes), free zones in maritime ports.

zone de distribution (*ou* de remise) gratuite des télégrammes, free delivery area of telegrams.

zone de remise à domicile (Ch. de f., etc.), delivery area; delivering area.

ADDENDUM

abréviation (*n.f.*), abbreviation.
accalmie (*n.f.*), lull.
accès (*n.m.*), access.
accompagnement (*n.m.*), accompaniment:
feuille d'accompagnement, covering letter.
achalander (*v.t. & i.*), to procure:
bien achalandé, well connected, well attended,
with a large custom.
achat (*n.m.*):
achat à tempérament, hire-purchase.
contrat à tempérament, hire-purchase agreement.
vente à tempérament, hire-purchase sale,
instalment sale.
acte (*n.m.*):
acte additionnel, rider, codicil.
acte d'aliénation, transfer of property, conveyance.
acte d'attribution, act of assignment.
acte de complaissance, act of accommodation.
acte consensuel, contract by mutual arrangement.
acte constitutif de gage, debenture bond,
mortgage bond.
acte fiduciaire, contract of trusteeship.
acte de nationalité, ship's registry of nationality.
acte public, official document.
acte de société, deed of partnership.
faire acte d'authorité, to act with full powers.
affichage (*n.m.*), bill sticking, placarding.
agio (*n.m.*), agio, exchange premium.
à l'amiable (*adjectival*), by private arrangement,
'gentleman's agreement'.
amplification (*n.f.*), amplification, certified copy.
amputer (*v.t.*), (un crédit), to curtail, to reduce.
ancienneté (*f.*), seniority.
ancillaire (*adj.*), ancillary.
annoter (*v.t.*), to annotate.
antarcie (*n.f.*), self-sufficiency.
antichèse (*n.f.*), assignment of the revenue of real
estate, given in security of a debt.
anti-inflationnist, -e (*adj.*), anti-inflationary.
appareil (*n.m.*), apparatus (camera):
appareil administratif, administrative machine.
apprentissage (*n.m.*), apprenticeship.
arrêté municipal (*n.m.*), bye-law.
arrière-caution (*n.f.*), counter surety.
article (*n.m.*), computer record.
artisan (*n.m.*), craftsman, artisan.
assainir (*v.t. & i.*), to reorganize:
assainissement (*n.m.*), reorganization, (financial) reconstruction, (financial) rehabilita-
tion.
assurance (*n.f.*):
assurance dotale, dowry insurance.
assurance obligatoire, compulsory insurance.

assurance pluie vacances, weather insurance.
assurance supplémentaire, additional insurance.
astreinte (*n.f.*), demurrage.
voir: **souffrance.**
attaché (*p.p.*), attached:
avec document attaché, with document
attached.
attaché (*n.m.*), attaché (military, naval, etc.).
attestation (*n.f.*), certificate, testimonial.
autofinancement (*n.m.*), self-financing.
automation (*n.f.*), automation.
autrui (*pron. indef.*), other persons, third party.
voir: **tiers** (tierce personne).
avancement (*n.m.*), promotion.
avantageux (*adj.*), advantageous, profitable.
avant-projet (*n.m.*), draft.
voir: **projet** (*n.m.*).
avenu (*adj. or n.m.*), null and void.

bague (*n.m.*) **fiscale**, revenue band.
baux (*n.pl.*):
voir: **bail** (*n.m.*).
biens (*n.m.pl.*):
biens à l'abandon, property without an owner.
bimensuel (*adj.*), fortnightly.
bimestriel (*adj.*), bi-monthly.
binaire (*adj.*), binary:
échelle binaire, binary scale.

$$
\begin{aligned}
2^0 &= 1 & 2^3 &= 8 \\
2^1 &= 2 & 2^4 &= 16 \\
2^2 &= 4 & 2^5 &= 32
\end{aligned}
$$

therefore: 51 is represented in the binary scale
by:—
$$2^0 + 2^1 + 2^4 + 2^5$$
bloc (*n.m.*), block
bon (*adj.*):
bons offices, good offices.
brancher (*v.t.*), to connect, to connect up (elec.).
See also: **raccordement.**
brevet (*n.m.*), patent:
demander un brevet, to apply for a patent.
bottin (*n.m.*), directory:
le Bottin, the telephone directory.
boule de neige (*n.f.*), snowball:
faire boule de neige, to snowball.
les ventes font boule de neige, sales are snowballing.
breveté (*p.p.*), patented.
breveter (*v.t.*), to patent.
reproduction interdite, copyright reserved.

calquer (*v.t.*), to trace, to copy, to imitate
closely:
papier à calquer, tracing paper.
camelote (*n.f.*), cheap goods, rubbish, trash.
camoufler (*v.t.*), to camouflage (more often: to

i

conceal, to fake):
nous avons reconnu que les comptes ont été camouflés, we have found the accounts to be faked.
carte (*n.f.*):
carte donnée (*n.f.*), data card.
carte paramètre (*n.f.*), parameter card.
carte perforée (*n.f.*), punched card.
système à carte perforée, punched card system.
carte récapitulative (*n.f.*), summary card.
carte vierge (*n.f.*), blank card.
case (*n.f.*), stacker (for punched-card machine).
cas (*n.m.*), case:
le cas échéant, should the case arise.
casier (*n.m.*), pigeon-hole cabinet, filing cabinet.
chiffre (*n.m.*), digit.
catégorie (*n.f.*), category.
cheptel (*n.m.*), livestock.
chevalier d'industrie (*n.m.*), swindler (industrial, commercial).
Voir: **escroc**
ci-apres (*adv.*), hereafter, further on.
ci-contre, opposite.
ci-dessous, hereunder, below.
ci-dessus, above.
ci-inclus, ci-joint, enclosed herewith, sub-joined, conjoined.
clerc (*n.m.*), clerk:
clerc d'homme de loi (apprentis), articled clerk.
commise (*f.*), female clerk.
codicille (*n.f.*), codicille.
commoda (*n.m.*), free loan.
comparant (*n.m.*), party:
le comparant de première part, the party of the first.
compétence (*n.f.*), competency, authority.
les autorités compétentes, the Authorities.
'utilisation des compétences', staff selection, i.e., 'putting square pegs into square holes and round pegs into round holes'.
compression (*n.f.*), compression, retrenchment, curtailment.
comprimer (*v.t.*), to retrench, to curtail.
concevoir (*v.t.*), to draft.
condition (*n.f.*):
conditions d'embarquement, ship's articles.
condoléance (*n.f.*), condolence.
conflit (*n.m.*), conflict:
un conflit d'intérêts, a conflict of interests.
conjoncture (*n.f.*), situation, market condition:
basse, slump.
haute, boom,
connexion, connexite (*n.f.*), two or more actions, an overall action comprising two or more actions.
conseiller municipal (*n.m.*), alderman.
contester (*v.t.*), to contest.
contigu à . . ., contiguous to . . .
contremaître (*n.m.*), foreman.
contumace, *voir:* **défaillant.**
convaincre (*v.t.*), to convince.
coulant (*adj.*), (accommodant), accommodating.
coulissier (*n.m.*), outside broker.
courbe (*n.f.*), curve (on a graph):
courbe du chomage, unemployment chart.

curatelle (*n.f.*), guardianship.
curriculum vitae (*n.m.*), personal record, *curriculum vitae.*
cycle (*n.m.*), cycle:
durée du cycle, cycle time.
déblocage (*n.m.*), unblocking, release:
fonds débloqués, released funds.
débordé (*p.p.*), overwhelmed.
débutant, -e (*n.m. & f.*), beginner.
décommander (*v.t.*), to countermand.
défaillant (*n.m.*), contumace (*n.m.*), absconder.
défectueux (*adj.*), defective.
défense (*imp.*) (**de, d'**), (it is) forbidden:
défense d'afficher, Stick no bills.
défense de fumer, No smoking.
défense d'entrer, No admittance.
Voir: **interdiction interdir** (*v.*).
démarrage (*n.m.*), start.
démarrer (*v.t.*) démarré (*p.p.*), to start (usually mechanical):
démarrer la voiture, to start the car.
déménagement (*n.m.*), removal, a move:
usually referring to the removal of furniture (from one house to another).
démonstrateur (*n.m.*), demonstrator.
dépendance (*n.f.*), annex, outbuildings.
dérouleur de bande (or 'ruban') **magnétique,** magnetic tape unit.
désachalander (*v.t.*), to take away the custom/ trade.
déséquilibrer (*v.t.*), to unbalance.
déterminer (*v.t.*), to determine, ascertain:
déterminer le coût, to determine the cost, ascertain the cost.
devanture (*n.m.*), shop window, shop display.
devis (*n.m.*), estimate:
we shall be glad to have your estimate for the cost of all the printing work, nous serons heureux de reçevoir votre devis pour le coût de tout travail d'imprimerie.
devise (*n.f.*):
devises convertibles, convertible currency.
dictaphone (*n.m.*), dictaphone.
domaine (*n.m.*), domain, field.
ce n'est pas dans son domaine, it is not in his field.
données (*n.f.pl.*), data.
drapeau (*n.m.*), flag, marker (in a business machine).
drawback (*n.m.*), drawback (amount of excise or import duty paid back or remitted on goods exported).
dû, due, due:
en dû temps, in due course.
en due forme, in due form.
économe (*n.m.*), bursar, treasurer.
électrique (*adj.*), electric.
électricien (*n.m.*), electrician.
électricité (*n.f.*), electricity.
electrisation (*n.f.*), electrification.
électronique (*adj.*), electronic.
calculateur (*n.m.*) électronique, electronic calculating-machine.
système à cartes perforées, **punched-card** machine.

élément (*n.m.*), element, component part.
élément d'entrée, input element.
élément de sortie, output element.
élément périphérique, peripheral unit.
être dans son élément, to be in one's element.

élevage (*n.m.*), breeding, stock-breeding, raising, rearing (of cattle).

embarras (*n.m.*), embarrassment, hindrance, impediment, difficulty, straits:
embarras de finances, financial difficulties.

embouteillage (*n.m.*), traffic block, congestion, 'bottle-neck'.

empêcher (*v.t.*), to prevent, to impede:
s'empêcher (*v.t.*), to refrain from.

emphytéose (*n.f.*), long lease.

emphytéote (*n.m.*), leaseholder.

encaissable (*adj.*), collectable (usually in respect of cash).

en cours, courant (*adj.*), current:
en cours de fabrication, in the process of manufacture.

engrais (*m.pl.*), manure:
engrais chimique(s), fertilizer(s).

en tête (*n.m.*), heading:
en tête de lettre, letterhead.

entrer (*v.i.*), to enter, to come in.
entrer en vigueur, to come into force.
entrer en considération, to be taken into account.

équipe (*n.f.*), shift, team, crew.

escroc (*n.m.*), swindler, sharper, blackleg.
escroquer (*v.t.*), to swindle.
escroquerie (*n.f.*), a swindle.
Voir aussi: **chevalier d'industrie.**

essence (*n.f.*), petrol.

étalage (*n.m.*), (shop) window:
mettre à l'étalage, to display.

exécutoir (*adv.*), executary.

ex-magazin, ex works.

exploitant (*n.m.*), operator, owner.

exploitation (*n.f.*), working, cultivating.
Note:—In English the words 'exploitation', 'to exploit,' etc. quite often carry a derogatory meaning or suggestion; 'exploitation of labour' tends to suggest 'sweated labour'. In French, the word carries no such implications.

expropriation (*n.f.*), expropriation.

extrinsèque (*adj.*), extrinsic; proceeding or operating from without, not inherent (opposite of intrinsic).

extension (*n.f.*), extension:
extension (tel.), extension line.

extincteur (*n.m.*), fire extinguisher.

éviction (*n.f.*), eviction, dispossession.

façon (*n.f.*), (prix), manufacturing cost, workmanship, labour.

façonner (*v.t.*), to form, to fashion, to make, to mould, to shape.

familial (*adj.*), family:
allocation familiale, family allowance.

famille (*n.f.*), family:
chef (*n.m.*) de famille, head of the house, householder.

père de famille, head of the family.

félicitation(s), congratulation(s):
présenter nos félicitations, to offer our congratulations.

ferme (*n.f.*), farm.

fermier (*n.m.*), farmer.

fermière (*n.f.*), farmer's wife, lady-farmer.

ferraille (*n.f.*), scrap-iron.

feu, le feu (*adj.*), late, the late, deceased:
le feu Monsieur . . ., the late Mr. . . .
le feu Roi, the late King.

fidéicommis (*n.m.*), trust.

fidéicommissaire (*n.m.*), beneficiary of a trust.

fidéjusseur (*n.m.*), surety.

florin (*n.m.*), florin.

fongie (*adj.*), When material, or a mechanical device has suffered normal wear and tear (but not damaged or broken) it is in a state of 'fongie'.

format (*n.m.*), size, form, format (of a book, sheet), layout.

frère (*n.m.*), brother.

gabarit (*n.m.*), loading gauge.

garçon de course(s) (*n.m.*), errand boy, messenger boy.

garde-meuble (*n.m.*), furniture repository.

gâter (*v.t.*), to spoil:
gâter le marché, to spoil the market.

gaz (*n.m.*), gas:
gaz domestique, domestic gas.

gelé (*p.p.*), frozen:
crédit gelé, frozen assets, funds.

gêne (*n.m.*), embarrassment, awkwardness, impediment, handicap:
gêne pécuniaire, financial embarrassment.

genre (*n.m.*), kind, type:
du dernier genre, of the latest style/fashion.

goulot (*n.m.*), d'étranglement, bottle-neck:
la production a été retardée par un goulot d'étranglement, production has been delayed by a bottle-neck.
Voir: **embouteillage,** traffic jam.

goût (*n.m.*), taste.

gracieux (*adj.*), gracious, kindly, etc.:
à titre gracieux, gratuitously.

graphique (*n.m.*), graph.

gratis (*adj.*), gratis, free, for nothing, without charge.

greffier (*n.m.*), clerk of the court.

groupe de travail (*n.m.*), working party.

habitude (*n.m.*), habit, custom.

haler (*v.t.*), to tow (usually a ship).
(*Note:*—to tow a motor car, remorquer une voiture.)

halle (*n.f.*), market, covered market:
Les Halles, The Market.
(*Note:*—Not used in the singular.)

heritage (*n.m.*), inheritance:
heriter de . . ., to inherit from . . .

heure-homme (*n.f.*), man hour.

heures-homme (*pl.*), man hours.

honoré (*adj.*), esteemed:
honoré Monsieur, esteemed Sir, honoured Sir.
nous avons l'honneur, we have the honour.

hôtel (*n.m.*), hotel, town mansion, large house, inn, hall.
  hôtel de ville, Town Hall.
  hôtel des monnaies, Mint.
  hôtel des postes, General Post Office.
  hôtel Dieu, the (chief) hospital of a town.
houille (*n.f.*), coal, pit coal:
  mine de houille, houillère, coal mine, colliery.
huile (*n.f.*), oil.
huis clos (*adj.*), in camera.
huissier (*n.m.*), usher, bailiff, sheriff's officer, process-server.

identification (*n.m.*), identification.
identifier (*v.t.*), to identify.
identique (*adj.*), identical.
identité (*n.f.*), identify.
imitation (*n.f.*), imitation:
  contrefaçon (*n.f.*), imitation.
  imiter/contrefaire une signature, to forge a signature.
impasse (*n.f.*), deadlock.
importance (*n.f.*), importance:
  l'importance du crédit, the amount of the credit.
  quelle est l'importance de ses ventes? what is the volume of his sales?
inconnu, -e (*n., adj. & adv.*), unknown.
incontestable (*adj.*), incontestable.
indexé (*p.p.*), indexed, index-linked.
inébranlé (*p.p.*), inébranlée, unshaken:
  inébranlable, unshakable.
ingénieur (*n.m.*), engineer:
  Ingénieur diplômé, qualified engineer, (engineer with degree).
  ingénieur, *ou*, ingénieur-mécanicien, -ne, mechanic.
ingérence (*n.f.*), interference.
ininflammable (*adj.*), non-inflammable.
inopportun (*adj.*), inopportune, inconvenient.
inscription (*n.f.*), inscription, entry.
insu:
  à notre insu, without our knowledge.
inutile (*adj.*), useless.
investisseur (*n.m.*), investor.
investisseuse, (*n.f.*), investor.
irrévocable (*adj.*), irrevocable.
italique (*n.m.*), italic:
  en italiques, in italics.

juridiction (*n.f.*), jurisdiction.

kiosque (*n.m.*), kiosk.

lecteur de bande perforée (*m.*), paper tape reader (mechanical).
lecteur de cartes (*m.*), card reader (mechanical).
léger (*adj.*), light, thin, flimsy, buoyant, thoughtless, wanton, trifling:
  une perte légère, a trivial loss.
lez (lès), near (a town):
  lez Dieppe, near Dieppe.
  Voir: **près.**
licenciement (*n.m.*), dismissal:
  licenciement de personnel, laying off.
  licenciement sans préavis, dismissal without notice.

licencier (*v.t.*), to dismiss, to lay off.
licitation (*n.f.*), sale by auction of property held *indivisum*.
location-vente (*n.f.*), hire purchase.
logement (*n.m.*), housing.
loup (*n.m.*), (lit. wolf), stag, premium hunter.
lubrifiants (*m.pl.*), lubricants.

machine à écrire a ruban magnétique (*f.*), magnetic tape typewriter.
machine-outil (*n.f.*), machine-tool.
machiniste (*n.m. & f.*), machine operator.
magasin (*n.m.*):
  magasin d'alimentation, hopper (for punched card systems, etc.).
magistrat (*n.m.*), magistrate, alderman.
magnétophone (*n.m.*), tape recorder.
main (*n.f.*), hand:
  changer de mains, to change hands.
  remettre en main propre, to deliver personally.
  main-forte, assistance, help, aid.
  mainlevée (*n.f.*), withdrawal.
  mainmorte (*n.f.*), mortmain.
malaise (*n.m.*), uneasiness.
manteau (*n.m.*), coat, overcoat:
  manteau de titre (*n.m.*), certificate.
margeur (*n.m.*), marginal stop.
matériaux (*n.m.pl.*), material(s).
matériel (*n.m.*), material (the).
matériel, -le (*adj.*), materially (minded).
mécanique (*adj.*), mechanical:
  électro-mécanique, electro-mechanical.
  mécanisation, mechanization.
  mécaniser (*v.t.*), to mechanize.
mécanographie (*n.f.*), machine posting.
méfiance (*n.f.*), distrust, suspicion.
  se méfier de, to distrust (someone—something).
  méfiant -e (*adj.*), distrustful.
  soupçonneux -euse (*adj.*), suspicious.
mémoire (*n.f.*), memory (memory store):
  mémoire a accès aléatoire, random access store.
  mémoire a disque magnétique, disk store.
  mémoire a disques magnétiques, disk store.
  mémoire a tores magnétiques, core store.
  mémoire tambour (*n.m.*), drum store.
  mémoire tambour magnétique, drum store.
  mémoire tampon (*n.m.*), buffer store.
mérite (*n.m.*), merit, worth, attainments:
  en reconnaissance de ses mérites, in recognition of his services.
mériter (*v.t.*), to merit, to deserve:
  il mérite une augmentation, he deserves a rise.
métallurgie (*n.f.*), metallurgy.
metayage (*n.m.*), share cropping (leasing of farms under conditions of sharing produce with owner).
métier (*n.m.*), trade, calling (profession).
militaire (*n.m. & adj.*), military:
  il est militaire, he is a soldier.
  militaire et civile, military & civil(ian).
milliard (*n.m.*), American 'billion'.
mine (*n.f.*), mine:
  concession minière, mining concession.
mineur (*n.m.*), (ouvrier), miner.

ministre (*n.m.*), Minister:
Ministre des affaires étrangères, Foreign Minister.
(American: Secretary of State.)
moderniser (*v.t.*), to modernize.
motiver (*v.t.*), to give reason for.
multilatéral (*adj.*), multilateral.

né, née (*p.p. & adj.*), born:
Mme Dubois, née Lemercier, Mrs. Dubois, maiden name Lemercier.
neuf, neuve (*adj.*), new:
voir: **nouveau** (*adj.,m.*)
     nouvel (*adj.,m.*)
     nouvelle (*adj.,f.*)
Noël (*n.m.*), Christmas:
les fêtes de Noël, the Christmas holidays.
noir (*adj.*), black:
marché noir, black market.
liste noir, blacklist.
boule noir,* black-ball.
*usually more politely expressed as: 'Rejeté au scrutin'.
norme (*n.f.*), norm, standard.
nuitée (*n.f.*), one night's lodging.
nu-propriétaire (*n.m. & f.*), absentee landlord, 'bare owner', i.e. 'not enjoying the actual use of his property'.

obligatoire (*adj.*), compulsory.
obligeance (*n.f.*), courtesy, kindness:
. . . ayez, s.v.p., l'obligeance de . . . . . . please be so kind as to . . .
occasion (*n.f.*), occasion, opportunity:
à la première occasion, at the first opportunity.
voiture d'occasion, second-hand car.
occupation (*n.f.*), occupation, job, situation, position:
Voir aussi: **métier.**
occurence:
en l'occurence, in the present case.
octroi (*n.m.*), granting.
octroyer (*v.t.*), to grant:
Aussi: accorder, to grant.
    concéder, to grant.
officieux (*adj.*), semiofficial.
once (*n.f.*), ounce.
onéreux -euse (*adj.*), onerous.
ordinateur (*n.m.*), computer:
ensemble électronique   } to describe *any*
appareil électronique   } electronic device.
machine à calculer électronique, computer.
outillage (*n.m.*), plant, equipment:
l'outillage de, the tooling up of.
outiller (*v.t.*), to equip with plant equipment, to tool up.
ouvrier (*n.m.*), workman, worker.
ouvrière (*n.f.*), worker (female).

Pâques (*n.m.*), Easter:
les fêtes de Pâques, the Easter holidays.
paramètre (*n.m.*), parameter.
parquage (*n.m.*), parking (*n.m.*), le, parking.
parquer (*v.t.*), to park:
défense de parquer, de stationner, No Parking.
stationner, to park (police term).

'stationnement interdit', no waiting (police notice).
patrimoine (*n.m.*), patrimony.
patronage (*n.m.*), patronage.
patte (*n.f.*), flap (of an envelope).
Pentecôte (*n.f.*), Whitsun, Pentecost.
péréquation (*n.f.*), equalization:
faire la péréquation, to equalize.
perforateur (*n.m.*) **de bande** (*n.f.*), paper tape punch.
perforateur (*n.m.*) **de carte,** card perforator, card punch.
permettre (*v.t. & i.*), to permit, to allow:
permission (*n.f.*), a permit, permission.
Permission de congé, leave of absence.
permis (*n.m.*), permit:
permis de conduire, driving licence.
personalité (*n.f.*), personality:
personalité civile, incorporation, legal status.
acquérir la personalité, to acquire legal status, to be incorporated.
personne déplacée (*n.f.*), displaced person.
pétrolifères (*n.m.pl.*), oils, oil shares.
photographie (*n.f.*), photograph:
(photo) . . . (*abbr.*), (photo).
photocopie (*n.f.*), photostat.
photolithographie (*n.f.*), photolithography.
phototypographie (*n.f.*), half-tone engraving.
pince-notes (*n.m.*), paper clip.
plafond (*n.m.*), ceiling, limit:
j'ai des dettes jusqu'au plafond, I am up to the 'eyebrows' in debt.
planification (*f.*) **économique,** economic planning.
plastique (*n.f.*), plastic:
matières plastiques, plastics.
plénier, -ère (*adj.*), plenary:
séance (*f.*) plénière, plenary session.
poinçonner (*v.t.*), to punch (file holes).
poinçonneuse (*n.f.*), punch.
porte-mines (*n.m.*), propelling pencil.
porteur (*n.m.*), porter, railway station.
poste (station) (*n.m.*):
poste d'interrogation, enquiry station.
préachat (*n.m.*), prepayment.
préalable (*adj.*), previous.
préalablement (*adv.*), previously.
précédent (*n.m.*), precedent.
préciser (*v.t. & i.*), to specify.
précompter (*v.t.*), to deduct (beforehand).
préfabriquer (*v.t.*), to prefabricate:
préfabriqué, prefabricated.
préfinancement (*n.m.*), prefinancing.
près, près de (*adj.*), near.
voir aussi: lez.
pression (*n.f.*), pressure:
pression inflationniste, inflationary pressure.
prévoyance (*n.f.*), foresight, precaution:
prévoyance sociale, State Insurance.
prix (*n.m.*):
majorer le prix d'achat pour couvrir les frais, établir le bénéfice, mark-up.
procédé (*n.m.*), (industrie), process (industrial).
programmation (*n.f.*), programming.
programme (*n.m.*):
programme de service, service routine.

programme enregistré, stored programme.
programme standard, standard routine.
multiprogrammation, multiprogrammation.
sous-programme, subroutine.
prolonger (*v.t.*), to prolong, to extend:
la banque a consentit de prolonger le crédit pour un mois, the Bank has agreed to extend the credit for one month.
propagande (*n.f.*), propaganda.
prospecter (*v.t.*), to prospect.
prospecteur (*n.m.*), prospector, canvasser.
publicitaire (*adj.*), advertising:
cadeau, gift.
valeur, value.
publicitaire (*n.m. or f.*), publicity man (or woman).
pupille (*n.m. & f.*), ward.

quadriennale (*adj.*), four yearly.
quaiage:
voir: quayage.
qualifié (*adj.*), qualified, competent:
ingénieur qualifié, qualified engineer, person holding an engineering degree, or equivalent.
quayage (*n.m.*), wharfage.
quitte et libre, free and unencumbered, free and clear.
quota (*n.m.*), quota.

raccordement (*n.m.*), joining, union, junction:
voies de raccordement, loop line, railway lines in a factory area.
raccordement électrique, electrical connexion; see also: **brancher.**
rajustement (*n.m.*), adjustment, readjustment.
rajustement d'un différend, settling of a difference.
rationnement (*n.m.*), rationing.
rayon (*n.m.*), department (of a shop):
chef (*m.*) de rayon, departmental manager.
réapprovisionner (*v.t.*), to restock.
récession (*n.f.*), recession.
récognition (*n.f.*), recognition, acknowledgement:
acte (*m.*) récognitif, act of acknowledgement.
récolte (*n.f.*), harvest.
réforme (*n.f.*), reform.
réformer (*v.t.*), to reform:
réforme monétaire, reorganization of (the) currency.
régisseur (*n.m.*), agent, manager, steward.
régression (*n.f.*), regression, drop, decrease.
réimpression (*n.f.*), reprint.
réinstallation (*n.f.*), reinstallation, resettlement.
réintégrer (*v.t.*), to reinstate.
relation (*n.f.*), relation, connection:
relations tendues, strained relations.
rester en relation avec, to keep in touch with
rentabilité, -ée (*n.f.*), profitability, productiveness, productivity, earning capacity.
répercussion (*n.f.*), repercussion, impact.
répit (*n.m.*), respite:
jours de répit, days of grace.
Voir aussi: **sursis**
reproduction (*n.f.*), reproduction:
reproduction interdite, copyright (reserved).
Also means: reprinting, and republication.

répudiation (*n.f.*), repudiation, renunciation.
répudier (*v.t. & i.*), to repudiate, to renounce, to relinquish.
ressortir à to belong to.
rétribuer (*v.t.*), to remunerate, to requite.
rétribution (*n.f.*), remuneration:
Note:—Rarely used in French in the sense of vengeance (or 'just retribution').
revenir (*v.i.*), to come back (to):
revenir sur une decision, to reconsider a decision.
reviseur (*n.m.*), auditor.
rodage:
en rodage (*adjectival*), running in, i.e. a motor-car engine.
rotation (*n.f.*), rotation, circulation, turnover (of stocks).
rouille et oxydation, rust and oxydization.
'rubis sur ongle', to the last cent/sou/farthing.

sabotage (*n.m.*), sabotage.
sabotager (*v.t.*), to sabotage.
saisissable (*adj.*), distrainable.
saison (*n.f.*), season:
demande (*f.*) saisonnière, seasonal demands.
en pleine saison, at the height of the season.
saturation (*n.f.*), saturation.
saut (*n.m.*), (machine à écrire, ordinateur, etc.), skip, jump.
secteur (*n.m.*), sector.
section (*n.f.*), section, branch.
servitude (*n.f.*), servitude, right of way.
signal (on Telex, etc.) (*n.m.*), message, signal.
simulé (*adj.*), simulated, sham.
simultanéité (*n.f.*), simultaneity.
soit (*adv.*), be it so, well and good:
soit 200 francs, say 200 francs.
sommation (*n.f.*), summons.
standard (*n.m.*) (tel.), switchboard (tel.).
stimulant (*n.m.*), stimulant.
stimulant, -e (*adj.*), stimulating.
stimuler (*v.t.*), to stimulate:
stimuler les ventes, to stimulate sales.
stylo (*n.m.*), **stylographe** (*n.m.*), fountain pen:
Note:—The expression 'plume réservoir' is no longer used.
subir (*v.t. & i.*), to suffer, to undergo, to experience:
subir une perte, to suffer a loss.
subordonné, -ée (*n.*), subordinate.
supplément (*n.m.*), supplement, addenda, addendum.
surcapacité (*n.f.*), over-capacity.
surcroît (*n.m.*), increase.
sur-emploi (*n.m.*), over-employment.
surévaluation (*n.f.*), over-valuation.
surpoids (*n.m.*), over weight, excess weight.
sursis (*n.m.*), respite:
sursis de payement, respite of payment.
la sentence a été mise en sursis, the sentence has been suspended.
sur-souscrit (*adj.*), over-subscribed.
synthèse (*n.f.*), synthesis, composition.

tabulaire (*adj.*), tabular.

tabulateur (*n.m.*), tabulator (typewriter mechanism).
tabulateur (*n.m.*), tabulator (male operator).
tabulatrice (*n.f.*), tabulator (female operator).
télécommunication (*n.f.*), telecommunication:
satellite de télécommunication, telecommunication satellite.
téléscripteur (*n.m.*), teleprinter.
Telex (*n.m.*), Telex.
tempérament (*n.m.*), temperament:
achat à tempérament, hire purchase.
temps (*n.m.*), time:
quel temps fait il? what is the weather like?
je n'ai pas le temps, I haven't got time.
en temps voulu/ utile, in due course.
temps d'accès (*n.m.*), access time.
textile -s (*n.m.*), textile -s.
traitement (*n.m.*), processing.
transitoire (*adj.*), transitory.
transmissible (*adj.*), transferable.
travail à domicile (m.), free-lance (work):
Aussi: travailler à son propre compte, working on one's own account.
traveller-chèque (*n.m.*), traveller's cheque.
triennal (*adj.*), triennial, every third year.
trieur, -euse (*n.m. & f.*), sorter.
trieuse (*n.f.*), sorting machine.
tutelle (*n.f.*), guardianship.

tuteur (*n.m.*), guardian.

unité centrale (*f.*), central processor.
usufructuaire (*n.m.*), usufructuary (one who has the use of).
Voir: **nu-propriétaire.**
usufruitier (*adj.*), usufructuary.
Note:—usufruct (*n. & v.t.*) right of enjoying the use and advantage of another's property, short of destruction or waste of its substance.
utilisable (*adj.*) useable.
utilisation (*n.f.*), utilisation:
utilisation des compétences, staff selection, selection of talent; 'putting round pegs in round holes, and square pegs in square holes'.
utiliser (*v.t.*), to use.
utilité (*n.f.*), utility:
l'utilité, the usefulness.

vacations (*n.f.pl.*), attendance fee.
vente (*n.f.*):
vente à tempérament, hire purchase sale.
véritable (*adj.*), real, genuine.
vetusté (*n.f.*), wear and tear
voir: **fongie**
volant (*n.m.*), steering wheel (of car).
volumineux (*adj.*), bulky.

ABRÉVIATIONS EN USAGE ORDINAIRE

A. (Comptab.), avoir.

A. (cote de la bourse et des changes), Argent; cours Argent.

A. (cote de la bourse de marchandises), acheteurs; cours demandés.

A. *ou* **A/.** (ordres de bourse), achetez; acheter; acheté; achat.

A/ *ou* **à l'A.** (Douanes), à l'acquitté.

a.c. (Assce mar.), avarie(s) commune(s).

a.p. (Assce mar.), avarie(s) particulière(s).

a/v. (Bourse) (opp. à *v/a*. ou *f.r*.), reporter. (*a/v*. veut dire *acheté-vendu*.)

ab. (primes) (Bourse), abandonné, -e.

ac., acompte.

acc., acceptation.

ach. (Bourse de marchandises), acheteur(s).

act. *ou* **a/.** *ou* **a.,** action(s).

adm. *ou* **admin.,** administration.

am. *ou* **amort.,** amortissable; amortissement.

anc., ancien, -enne.

Anten. (Télégr.), acheminement par sans fil.

AR. (Poste), avis de réception.

art., article.

ass. extr., assemblée extraordinaire.

ass. ord., assemblée ordinaire.

au 15 (Bourse de valeurs), au 15 courant.

auj., aujourd'hui.

Av. (Comptab.), Avoir.

A/, avarie de mer.

av.-dt, avec droit.

B., balle.

B. *ou* **b.** (Bourse de valeurs), bonification; déport.

B. *ou* **b.** (Négociations de change à terme), bénéfice; déport.

B/, billet à ordre.

B.P.F. *ou* **B.P.Fr.,** bon pour francs. See note under **bon pour** in dictionary.

Banq., Banque.

Bⁱⁿ, bassin.

b^{ot}, ballot.

b^{qe}, barrique.

BVD. (Poste), boîte(s) de valeur(s) déclarée(s).

C. *ou* **c.,** compte.

C. (Comptab.), crédit; créditeur.

c., caisse.

c. *ou* **ct** [**cts** *pl*.], cent(s).

c., centime(s).

c., coupon.

c. *ou* **C.,** coupure; coupures: c. 25 *ou* C. 25 *ou* c. de 25, coupures de 25.

c., courant: fin c. *ou* f.c., fin courant.

c. *ou* **C.,** cours.

c/, contre.

c.a.f. *ou* **C.A.F.** *ou* **caf.** *ou* **c.f.a.** *ou* **c.i.f.** *ou* **C.I.F.** *ou* **cif.,** coût-assurance-fret; coût, fret, et assurance (*cost, insurance, freight; cost, freight, and insurance*).

c. att. *ou* **c. at.,** coupon attaché.

C/C. *ou* **c.c.** *ou* **c/c.** *ou* **c/c/** *ou* **C.C^t,** compte courant: c/c. postal, compte courant postal.

c/c. *ou* **c/c/** (Bourse de valeurs), cours de compensation.

C. civ., Code civil.

C. Co. *ou* **C. com.** *ou* **C. de com.,** Code de Commerce.

c.(d^r), dernier cours.

c. du jour, cours du jour.

c.f. *ou* **C.F.** *ou* **cf.,** coût-fret.

C.I.M. (Transports internationaux), convention internationale des marchandises.

C.I.V., convention internationale des voyageurs.

c/j. (effets de commerce), courts jours.

C/M. *ou* **c/m.** *ou* **c/.m/.,** cours moyen.

c.n. *ou* **cn.,** cours nul.

C.N.E., caisse nationale d'épargne.

C.O., compte ouvert.

C.P., colis postal.

c.préc., cours précédent.

c.(1er), premier cours.

c. uni., cours unique.

Caire, commissionnaire.

Cap. *ou* **Capit.** *ou* **C.,** capitaine.

cap., capital.

cap., action(s) de capital.

c^{de}, commande.

c^{ge}, courtage.

ch., chèque.

ch. de f., chemin(s) de fer.

ch. f. *ou* **ch. fixe,** change fixe.

Cie *ou* **Cie,** Compagnie.

clôt. préc. *ou* **clôt. pr.** (bulletin de cours), clôture précédente.

com. *ou* **com** *ou* **con** *ou* **commis.** *ou* **c^{ion},** commission.

comp. (Bourse), compensation.

compt, comptant.

conv., converti, -e.

coup. *ou* **coup. de** *ou* **cp. de,** coupure(s); coupure(s) de.

coup. *ou* **cp.,** coupon.

coup. arr., coupon arriéré.

cour. *ou* **c^t** *ou* **ct,** courant.

cpt, comptant.

cpte *ou* **c^{te},** compte.

cpte c^t *ou* **c^{te} c^t** *ou* **c^{te} c.,** compte courant.

c^{que}, contremarque.

C^r, crédit; créditeur.

C^{re}, commissionnaire.

ctg., courtage.

cum., cumulatif, -ive.

319

D. (Comptab.), débit; Doit.
D. (Bourse), déport; bonification.
D. (Négociations de change à terme), déport; bénéfice.
D., télégramme urgent.
d. (monnaie anglaise), pence; penny.
d/ *ou* **dt** *ou simplement une barre* / (Bourse), dont. See this word in dictionary.
D.A., documents contre acceptation.
D.C.V. (convention internationale des voyageurs), dispositions complémentaires uniformes.
D.P., documents contre paiement.
D.P.L.G. (se dit des experts-comptables reconnus par l'État), Diplômé par le Gouvernement. *See* brevet d'expert-comptable.
déb., débit.
débit., débiteur.
délég., délégation.
dem. (Bourse), demandé.
dem. réd. *ou* **dem. r.** (Bourse), demandes réduites.
dét., détaché, -e.
dif., différé, -e.
disp. *ou* **dispon.,** disponible.
div. *ou* **divid.** *ou* **divde** *ou* **d.,** dividende.
div., action(s) de dividende.
DLT., télégramme à remise retardée.
dne, douane.
Do *ou* **do,** dito.
dol. [**dols** *pl.*] *ou* **doll.** [**dolls** *pl.*] *ou* **$,** dollar.
don, direction.
Dr, débiteur.
Dr, directeur.
dr. (Bourse), droit(s) (de souscription).
dr c., dernier cours.
Dt, débit; débiteur; Doit.
DW., tonneau(x) [*ou* tonne(s)] de portée en lourd (*dead weight*).

E. *ou* **en E.** (*dans la locution* vente en E. *ou* vente E.), entrepôt; en entrepôt.
E. à P., effet(s) à payer.
E. à R., effet(s) à recevoir.
E.V. (Correspondance), En ville.
emb., embarquement.
en liq. *ou* **en liquid.,** en liquidation.
env/. (Bourse), environ.
Ép. *ou* **ép.,** époque.
esc. *ou* **escte** *ou* **escte,** escompte: esc. 10/2½, escompte 10 et 2½%.
esp., espèces.
est. *ou* **Est.** *ou* **estamp.** *ou* **Estamp.,** estampillé, -e.
ex., exercice:
 ex. préc., exercice précédent.
ex. — at. *ou* **ex. — att.,** exercice — attaché: ex. 19— at., exercice 19— attaché.
ex-bon. *ou* **ex-rép. bon.,** ex-bonus; ex-répartition bonus.
ex-c. *ou* **ex-coup.** *ou* **e-c.,** ex-coupon.
ex-c. div. *ou* **ex-c. de div.,** ex-coupon de dividende: ex-c. 15 div., ex-coupon n° 15 de dividende.
ex-c. int. *ou* **ex-c. d'int.,** ex-coupon d'intérêt.
ex-div. *ou* **ex-d.,** ex-dividende.
ex-dr. *ou* **ex-d.** *ou* **ex-dt,** ex-droit.
ex-ex., ex-exercice: ex-ex. 19—, ex-exercice 19—.

ex-remb., ex-remboursement.
ex-rép. *ou* **ex-répart.** *ou* **ex-r.,** ex-répartition.
ex st., ex steamer.
expn, expédition.

f. *ou* **F.,** franc(s).
f.a.c., franc d'avarie(s) commune(s).
f.a.p., franc d'avarie(s) particulière(s).
F.A.S., franco le long du navire (*free alongside ship*).
f.c. *ou* **fc.** *ou* **fin c.** *ou* **fin ct** *ou* **fin cour.** *ou simplement* **fin,** fin courant.
F.G., frais généraux.
f.o.b. *ou* **F.O.B.** *ou* **fob.** *ou* **f. à b.** *ou* **F.B.,** franco bord; franco à bord (*free on board*).
f.p. *ou* **fp.** *ou* **fin pr.,** fin prochain.
f.r. *ou* **fr.** (Bourse) (opp. à *r.* ou *a/v.*), faire reporter; se faire reporter.
fco *ou* **fo** *ou* **F.F.,** franco.
Fil (Télégr.), acheminement par fil.
Fo *ou* **fo** *ou* **f°,** folio.
fond., part(s) de fondateur.
fr. [**fr.** *ou* **frs** *pl.*] *ou* **Fr.** [**Fr.** *ou* **Frs** *pl.*], franc.
fre, facture.
FS., télégramme à faire suivre.

g.v. *ou* **G.V.,** grande vitesse.
gal, gale, général, -e.
GP., télégramme adressé poste restante.
GPR., télégramme adressé poste restante recommandée.
gr. coup. *ou* **gr. c.,** grosses coupures.

h., hier:
 h.c.n. *ou* h.cn., hier, cours nul. *See* cours nul *in dictionary*.
 hl., hier lire. See **lire** (cote de la bourse) in dictionary.
 h.d.c., hier, dernier cours.
 h.s.c., hier, seul cours.
H.E.C. *ou* **H. E. Cent.** *ou* **Hre E. Cent.,** heure de l'Europe Centrale.
H. E. Occ. *ou* **Hre E. Occ.,** heure de l'Europe Occidentale.
H. E. Or. *ou* **Hre E. Or.,** heure de l'Europe Orientale.
H. holl., heure d'Amsterdam.
hyp. *ou* **hypoth.** *ou* **h.,** hypothécaire; hypothèque.

imp. (effet de commerce), impayé.
int. *ou* **intér.,** intérêt(s).
int. (Poste), service international.
Italcable (Télégr.), Compagnia Italiana dei Cavi Telegrafici Sottomarini.

J. *ou* **j.** *ou* **jouiss.** *ou* **jce,** jouissance.
j. *ou* **jr** [**jrs** *pl.*], jour.
jouiss., action(s) de jouissance.
Jour, télégramme (qui parvient à destination la nuit) à distribuer seulement pendant les heures de jour.

l., lire. See **lire** (cote de la bourse) in dictionary.
£ *ou* **L.** *ou* **l.** *ou* **liv.** *ou* **l.s.** *ou* **Ls.** *ou* **liv. st.** *ou* **liv. sterl.,** livre(s); livre(s) sterling.
L/C., leur compte.

l/c. *ou* l/cr., lettre de crédit.
L. conv. (Télégr.), langage convenu.
l/o/, à leur ordre.
L.P.D. (tarif de transport), le plus réduit.
LCD. (télégrammes différés), télégramme rédigé en langue admise par le pays de destination.
LCF. (télégrammes différés), télégramme rédigé en langue française.
LCO. (télégrammes différés), télégramme rédigé en langue admise par le pays d'origine.
lib., libéré, -e ; libéré (-e) de.
limité, télégramme déposé en dernière limite d'heure.
liq. *ou* liquid., liquidation.
liq. ct *ou* liquid. ct *ou simplement* liq. *ou* liquid. (Bourse), liquidation courante.
liq. pr. *ou* liq. proch. (Bourse), liquidation prochaine.
liv., livrable.
LS. (Télégr.), langage secret.
LVD. (Poste), lettre(s) de valeur(s) déclarée(s).

M. (Bourse de marchandises), manque (sans affaire).
M. *ou* Mr [MM. *ou* Mrs *pl.*], Monsieur [Messieurs *pl.*].
m., mois.
M/C., mon compte.
m/m., moi-même.
M/O., mon ordre.
m/s. *ou* m.s., vapeur postal (*mail steamer*).
mar., marine.
mar. *ou* marit., maritime.
mat *ou* mdt *ou* m., mandat.
Me [Mes *pl.*], maître.
MP., télégramme à remettre en mains propres.
ms., moins.
mx *ou* m x (Bourse), au mieux.

N. (cote de la bourse de marchandises), nominal.
N.B., nota bene.
N/C., notre compte.
n.c. (Bourse), non coté, -e.
n. est., non estampillé, -e.
n.f.c. *ou* nouv. f. coup., nouvelle feuille de coupons.
n.s. *ou* N/S., notre sieur.
nég. ch. fixe *ou* n. ch. fixe, négociable au change fixe.
négoc., négociation.
no *ou* No, numéro.
nom., nominatif, -ive.
non lib., non libéré, -e.
nouv. *ou* n., nouveau, -elle.
9bre, novembre.
Nuit, télégramme à distribuer même pendant la nuit.

o/, ordre.
o/, à l'ordre de.
o/ m/m., à l'ordre de moi-même.
0/0 *ou* %, pour cent.
0/00 *ou* %₀, pour mille.
O.P.R. (Poste), objets admis à circuler à prix réduit (papiers d'affaires affranchis comme tels, imprimés périodiques ou non, échantillons).

oblig. *ou* obl. *ou* ob., obligation(s).
8bre, octobre.
off. (Bourse), offert.
off. réd. *ou* off. r. (Bourse), offres réduites.
op.d. (Bourse), option du double.
ord., ordinaire ; action(s) ordinaire(s).
ouv. *ou* ouvert. (Bourse), cours d'ouverture.

P. *ou* p., pair.
P. (cote de la bourse et des changes), Papier ; cours Papier.
P. (cote de la bourse de marchandises), paye.
p., page.
p. (en parlant du montant versé sur des titres, des actions), payé, -e.
p., pour.
p., prime.
p., prochain, -e.
P. & P., Profits et Pertes ; Pertes et Profits.
p. an, par an.
p.b. (Bourse), plus bas ; au plus bas ; cours le plus bas.
P.C., prix courant.
p.c. *ou* p. cent *ou* p. 100 *ou* p. 0/0, pour cent.
p.c., papier court.
p.c. (Bourse), pas coté.
P.C.C., pour copie conforme.
p.cp., petites coupures.
P.D., port dû.
p. dem., etc. *Syn. de* pr. dem., etc., V. ci-après.
p.dt, prime dont.
p.h. (Bourse), plus haut ; au plus haut ; cours le plus haut.
P.I.V. (convention internationale des voyageurs), prescriptions communes d'expédition.
p.l., papier long.
P.-L.-M., Paris-Lyons-Méditerranée ; Chemins de fer de Paris à Lyon et à la Méditerranée ; Compagnie des chemins de fer de Paris à Lyon et à la Méditerranée.
P.-O., Paris-Orléans ; Chemin de fer de Paris à Orléans ; Compagnie du chemin de fer de Paris à Orléans.
P.P. (Comptab.), Profits et Pertes ; Pertes et Profits.
P.P. (Transport), port payé.
P.Pon *ou* Par pon, par procuration.
P.R., poste restante.
P.-S., post-scriptum.
P.T.T., Postes, Télégraphes et Téléphones.
P.-V., procès-verbal.
p.v. *ou* P.V., petite vitesse.
paiemt, paiement.
pain, prochain.
PAV., poste-avion.
PC., télégramme avec accusé de réception télégraphique.
PCP., télégramme avec accusé de réception postal.
perp. *ou* perpét., perpétuel, -elle.
ppt, prompt.
PQ (Télégr.), Compagnie française des câbles télégraphiques.
PR., poste recommandée.
pr, pour.

pr., prime :

pr. dem., prime pour demain.

pr. fin c. *ou* pr. f. c., prime fin courant.

pr. fin pr. *ou* pr. fin p. *ou* pr. f. p., prime fin prochain.

pr., prochain, -e.

préc., précédent, -e.

préf., préférence.

1er c. *ou simplement* **1er,** premier cours.

Presse, télégramme de presse.

prior., action(s) de priorité.

priv. *ou* **privil.,** privilégié, -e.

pte, perte.

pts, parts.

PU., télégramme partiellement urgent.

PVD. (Poste), paquet(s) de valeur(s) déclarée(s).

Px, prix.

Qté, qualité.

R. (Bourse), report ; taux du report ; prix du report.

R. (Négociations de change à terme), report.

R. (Poste), recommandé, -e.

r. (Bourse) (opp. à *f.r.* ou *v/a.*), reporter.

r.f., revenu fixe.

R.P. (télégrammes), réponse payée.

réf. *ou* **réfce,** référence.

Reg. du Com. *ou* **Reg. Com.** *ou* **R.C.,** Registre du Commerce.

règlt, règlement.

remb. *ou* **rembour.** *ou* **rb.** *ou* **r.,** remboursement ; remboursable :

r. au pair, remboursable au pair.

rep. (Bourse), report ; taux du report ; prix du report.

rep. *ou* **rp.** (Bourse), reporter.

rép. *ou* **Rép.** *ou* **répart.,** répartition.

rev. var., revenu variable.

RG. (Transport), remise gratuite.

RM. (Radiotélégr.), retransmission.

Ro, recto.

rse, remise.

s/, sur.

s.b.f., sauf bonne fin.

S/C., son compte.

s.c. (Bourse), seul cours.

S.D.N., Société des Nations.

S/Dr, sous-directeur.

s.e.d.d., sans engagement de date(s).

S.E. ou O. *ou* **S.E.O.,** sauf erreur ou omission.

S.F., sans frais.

S.I., sans intérêt.

s.i, sauf imprévu.

s.l. (Bourse), sauf livraison.

s.s. *ou* **S.S.** *ou* **s/s.** *ou* **ss.,** steamer ; vapeur ; navire à vapeur (*steamship*).

S.S.P., sous seing privé.

s.v., sans valeur :

c. 2 à 7 s.v., coupons 2 à 7 sans valeur.

s.v.p., s'il vous plaît.

Sde, solde.

Sem., télégramme sémaphorique.

7bre, septembre.

sh. (monnaie anglaise), schelling(s) ; shilling(s).

srie, série.

ss. repr., sans reprise.

st. *ou* **St.** *ou* **steam.** *ou* **Steam.,** steamer ; vapeur ; navire à vapeur.

std (commerce des bois), standard.

Sté *ou* **Soc.** *ou* **S.,** Société.

Sté anme *ou* **Soc. anme** *ou* **S.A.,** Société anonyme.

stell. *ou* **stel.** (Bourse), stellage.

succle *ou* **sle,** succursale.

T., tare.

T. (Poste), taxe à percevoir.

T/, traite.

t.br., tonnage brut.

t.c. *ou* **t.cp.** *ou* **t.coup.,** toutes coupures.

t.c. p. 25, toutes coupures par 25 (les négociations se font par 25 titres livrables en toutes coupures).

t.d.w., tonnage dead weight.

t.g. (Ch. de f.), tarifs généraux.

t.j.b., tonneau(x) de jauge brute.

T.K., tonne(s)-kilomètre(s) ; tonne(s) kilométrique(s).

t.p., tout payé.

T.Q., tel quel, telle quelle.

T.S. (Ch. de fer), tarif spécial.

T.S.F., télégraphie sans fil.

T.S.F., téléphonie sans fil.

t.s.v.p., tournez, s'il vous plaît.

T.T., transfert télégraphique.

tamb., tambour.

TB. (escompte), taux Banque de France.

TC., télégramme avec collationnement.

Tél., téléphone.

THB. (escompte), taux hors banque.

tit., titre(s).

TM., télégramme multiple ; télégramme à adresses multiples.

TR., télégramme adressé télégraphe restant.

tr. [**trs** *pl.*], traite.

TT., télégramme téléphoné.

tx, tonneaux.

u. *ou* **un.,** unité.

V. (cote de la bourse de marchandises), vendeurs ; cours offerts.

V. *ou* **V/.** (ordres de bourse), vendez ; vendre ; vendu ; vente.

V/ *ou* **val.,** valeur.

v/a. (Bourse) (opp. à *a/v.* ou *r.*), faire reporter ; se faire reporter (*v/a.* veut dire *vendu-acheté*).

V/C., votre compte.

V.D. (Poste), valeur(s) déclarée(s).

v/v., de votre ville.

vap., vapeur ; navire à vapeur.

vend. (Bourse), vendeur(s).

virt, virement.

Vo, verso.

Vp, vice propre.

vte, vente.

WLT., télégramme de fin de semaine.

x-c., ex-coupon.

xbre, décembre.

XP. (Poste), exprès payé.

SIGNES CONVENTIONNELS

La SÉPARATION DES DÉCIMALES, indiquée en français par une virgule ; ainsi 0,005 1,005 est indiquée en anglais par un point ; ainsi ·005 *ou* 0·005 1·005

Les TRANCHES DE TROIS CHIFFRES, séparées en français par des espaces ; ainsi 1 005 1 000 000 ou par des points ; ainsi **1.005 1.000.000** sont séparées en anglais par des virgules ; ainsi **1,005 1,000,000**
La séparation par des espaces s'emploie aussi en Amérique.

Les FRACTIONS et le **SIGNE DU POUR CENT,** fréquemment imprimés en français en gros caractères ; ainsi 2 1/2 0/0 sont généralement imprimés en anglais en petits caractères, ainsi 2½%

Les VALEURS MONÉTAIRES sont exprimées ainsi :—
En France.—
    1 fr. *ou* fr. 1 *ou* Fr. 1 *ou* 1 f. *ou* f. 1 *ou* 1f *ou* 1,00 *ou* 1 00 *ou* 1.— *ou* 1 — *ou* 1. , *ou* 1 , , *ou* 1 franc
    1 fr. 05 *ou* fr. 1,05 *ou* Fr. 1,05 *ou* frs 1,05 *ou* Frs 1,05 *ou* 1,05 fr. *ou* 1,05 f. *ou* 1f05 *ou* 1,05 *ou* 1 05
      ou 1 franc 5 centimes
    0 fr. 05 *ou* fr. 0,05 *ou* Fr. 0,05 *ou* 0f05 *ou* 0,05 fr. *ou* 0,05 f. *ou* 0,05 *ou* 0 05 *ou* 5 c. *ou* 5 centimes

    £1 *ou* 1£ *ou* 1l. *ou* 1 livre *ou* 1 liv. sterl. *ou* 1 livr. sterl. *ou* 1 l.s.
    £1 5sh. *ou* 1£ 5sh. *ou* £1 5sh. 0d. *ou* 1£ 5sh. 0d. *ou* 1l. 5s. 0d. *ou* £1 5 0 *ou* £1 1/4 *ou* 1 1/4
    £1 1sh. 1d. *ou* 1£ 1sh. 1d. *ou* 1l. 1s. 1d. *ou* £1 1 1
    1sh. *ou* 1sh. 0d. *ou* 1s. 0d. *ou* 1 schelling *ou* 1 shilling
    1sh. 1d. *ou* 1sh. 1 *ou* 1s. 1d.
    6d. *ou* 6 pence *ou* 1/2 shilling *ou* demi-shilling
    1d. *ou* 1 penny
En Angleterre.—
    1 fr. *ou* Fr. 1 *ou* 1f. *ou* 1 fc *ou* 1 franc
    1 fr. 5c. *ou* Fr. 1·05 *ou* frs 1·05 *ou* Frs 1·05 *ou* fcs 1·05 *ou* Fcs 1·05 *ou* 1 franc 5 centimes
    5 c. *ou* 5 centimes

    £1 *ou* 1l. *ou* 1 pound
    £1 5s. *ou* £1 5s. 0d. *ou* £1 5 0 *ou* £1 5/ *ou* 1 5 0 *ou* 1¼
    £1 1s. 1d. *ou* £1 1 1 *ou* 1 1 1
    1s. *ou* 1s. 0d. *ou* 1/- *ou* 0 1 0 *ou* 1 0 *ou* 1 shilling
    1s. 1d. *ou* 1/1d. *ou* 1/1 *ou* 0 1 1 *ou* 1 1
    6d. *ou* 6 pence *ou* sixpence
    1d. *ou* 1 penny

MONNAIE DÉCIMALE BRITANNIQUE (Effectif depuis le 15 février, 1971).
Le système a pour base deux unités seulement, la livre et le nouveau penny ; la livre vaut 100 nouveau pennies.
    £1 *ou* £1.00, une livre
    £1.25, une livre et vingt-cinq nouveau pennies
    £1.00½, une livre et un nouveau halfpenny
    £0.57 *ou* 57p, cinquante-sept nouveau pennies
    £0.00½ *ou* ½p, un nouveau halfpenny

Note.— In France, the figure 1 is generally written with an upstroke; thus 1 or ⏤ (this is never done in England).

As a consequence, the figure 7, in France, is crossed; thus, 7 (never in England), as otherwise it might be confused with a 1.

The figure 5 is either written as in England 5, or thus ſ or ʄ. This is frequently joined on in a flowing style to the preceding figure, thus 25 may be written 25 or 2ʃ or 2ʃ or 2ʃ.

DIVISION OF FRENCH WORDS INTO SYLLABLES

In French, words are divided into syllables according to the following rules :—

(1) *A consonant between two vowels commences a new syllable :*
ca-pi-tal, ca-pi-ta-li-sa-ble, ca-pi-ta-li-ser, ca-pi-ta-lis-me, ca-pi-ta-lis-te, mo-no-mé-tal-lis-te, li-bé-ra-toi-re, dé-sap-pro-vi-si-on-ne-ment, a-rith-mé-ti-que-ment, an-tis-ta-tu-tai-re-ment, pri-vi-lè-ge, su-bor-don-né, su-res-ta-ries, é-ti-que-ta-ge, e-xa-mi-na-teur, e-xer-ci-ce, e-xis-ten-ce, e-xo-né-rer, i-ne-xac-te-ment, in-de-xa-ti-on, i-nu-ti-le, u-ne, u-na-ni-me-ment, vi-gueur, vi-gou-reux, vi-gou-reu-se, paie-ment, pa-ral-lé-lé-pi-pé-di-que.

(2) *Two adjoining consonants (except Rule 4 digraphs) between two vowels separate into two syllables :*
ac-com-mo-der, ac-quit-te-ment, at-ter-ris-sa-ge, bail-le-res-se, chan-geant, chan-gean-te, con-cur-ren-ti-el-le, cor-res-pon-dan-ce, des-cen-dre, ex-cep-ti-on-nel-le-ment, ex-pé-di-ti-on-nai-re, in-na-vi-ga-ble, in-te-ro-cé-a-ni-que, in-ter-val-le, ir-res-pon-sa-bi-li-té, os-cil-ler, ras-seoir, re-con-nais-san-ce, res-ti-tu-er, sub-di-vi-ser, sur-taux, veil-le.

(3) *A vowel can only begin a syllable, other than an initial syllable, when preceded by another vowel :*
ac-cue-il-lir, a-é-ro-pla-ne, a-gré-er, an-ci-en, ar-ri-è-re, ba-la-yu-res, bé-né-fi-ci-ai-re, ca-mi-on, ca-out-chouc, co-as-so-ci-é, co-ef-fi-ci-ent, co-ïn-ci-der, dé-pou-il-le-ment, ex-tra-or-di-nai-re, feu-il-le, in-né-go-ci-a-ble, li-er, mi-eux, na-ti-on, ou-est, ré-é-va-lu-er, ré-u-ni-on, ro-yau-me, vic-tu-ail-les, vi-e-il-lir, vi-eux, voi-li-er, vo-ya-ge.

(4) *The following digraph consonants are inseparable :*
bl : câ-blo-gram-me, chan-gea-ble, o-bli-té-rer, pu-bli-que. *Exception :* sub-lu-nai-re.
br : dé-brou-il-ler, li-bre, su-bré-car-gue. *Exception :* sub-ro-ger *and derivatives.*
ch : dis-pa-cheur, é-chan-til-lon, é-chauf-fer, gui-chet, ré-cher-che.
cl : ac-cla-mer, ac-cli-ma-ter, é-clai-ra-ge, é-clu-se, ex-clu-sif.
cr : des-crip-ti-ve, é-cri-tu-re, ma-nus-crit, pres-cri-re, sous-cri-re.
dh : ré-dhi-bi-toi-re.
dr : a-dres-ser, cor-res-pon-dre, en-tre-pren-dre, or-dre.
fl : af-flux, ef-fleu-rer, in-fla-ti-on, in-flu-ent.
fr : af-fran-chir, en-cof-frer, in-dé-chif-fra-ble, ré-af-frè-te-ment, re-frap-pa-ge.
gl : ag-glo-mé-rer, a-veu-gle, é-tran-gle-ment, né-gli-gen-ce, rè-gle-ment.
gn : com-pa-gnie, é-par-gnant, ren-sei-gne-ment, si-gnal, vi-gnet-te.
gr : ag-gra-va-ti-on, dé-gros-sir, dé-ni-grer, in-té-gral, re-gret.
ph : chi-ro-gra-phai-re, dac-ty-lo-gra-phi-er, té-lé-pho-ne, u-ni-gra-phi-que.
pl : ac-com-plis-se-ment, ap-pli-ca-ti-on, com-plè-te-ment, ex-ploit.
pr : an-ti-pro-tec-ti-on-nis-te, ap-pren-dre, ex-pri-mer, pro-pri-é-té.
rh : ar-rhe-ment, ar-rhes, bi-blo-rhapt, e-nar-rher, trans-rhé-na-ne.
th : au-then-ti-que, dés-hy-po-thé-quer, hy-po-thé-cai-re, mé-tho-de.
tr : ad-mi-nis-tra-tif, cen-tre, co-di-rec-tri-ce, con-tre-si-gner, con-tres-ta-ries, il-lus-trée.
vr : a-vril, li-vrai-son, li-vre, ma-nœu-vrer, ou-vri-er.

(5) (*a*) **ns, bs,** *and* **rs** *are separable if followed by a vowel :*
con-sa-crer, con-seil-la-ble, con-si-dé-rer, in-sé-rer, in-sol-va-ble, in-suf-fi-sant, tran-sac-ti-on, tran-sat-lan-ti-que, tran-si-ter ; ab-sor-ber, ob-ser-ver ; per-su-a-der.
(*b*) **ns, bs,** *and* **rs** *are inseparable if followed by a consonant :*
cons-pi-rer, cons-ta-ter, cons-ti-tu-er, ins-pec-ter, ins-tal-ler, trans-cen-dant, trans-fè-re-ment, trans-port ; no-nobs-tant, obs-ta-cles, subs-tan-ce ; in-ters-ti-ce, pers-pec-ti-ve.
(*c*) **ns** *and* **bs** *are inseparable if followed by a consonant coupled with* **r :**
cons-trui-re, ins-cri-re, trans-cri-re, trans-gres-ser ; abs-trac-ti-on, obs-truc-ti-on.
(*d*) **ns** *and* **bs** *are separable before* **ci :** con-sci-en-ci-eux, in-sci-em-ment ; ab-scis-se.

(6) (*a*) **mp** *and* **nc** *followed by* **t** *are inseparable :*
a-comp-te, comp-ta-ble, es-comp-ter, pré-emp-ti-on ; fonc-ti-on, sanc-ti-on.
(*b*) *In all other combinations* **mp** *and* **nc** *are separable :*
em-plo-yer, em-prun-ter, im-por-tant ; a-van-cer, fran-çais, fran-che, fran-co.

(7) *In writing or in print no syllable is separable which does not include a vowel ;* thus, trigraph consonants are inseparable initially : **scru-tin,** but separable medially : **ins-cru-ta-ble.**

Some of the small syllables, especially initial vowel uniliterals and final biliterals beginning with a vowel, are not usually separated from the body of the word in writing or print, but they are of importance in the pronunciation ; thus, **émission** is pronounced *é-mis-si-on*, but the written or printed word is ordinarily only divided émis- (*end of line*) **sion**, not é- (*end of line*) **mission**, nor émissi- (*end of line*) **on**, though d'é- (*end of line*) **mission**, l'é- (*end of line*) **mission**, are better than d' (*end of line*) **émission**, l' (*end of line*) **émission**.

Divisions of words at the ends of lines should of course be avoided as far as possible, and not be carried to extremes.

ENGLISH-FRENCH DICTIONARY

A

abandon (*v.t.*), abandonner :
to abandon an undertaking, a ship to her fate, abandonner une entreprise, un navire à son sort.
to abandon an option (Fin.), abandonner une option.
to abandon an option (Stock Exch.), abandonner une prime.

abandon (Mar. Insce) (*v.t.*), délaisser ; abandonner.

abandon (Mar. Insce) (*v.i.*), faire le délaissement ; faire l'abandon :
insured who no longer has the right to abandon, assuré qui n'est plus recevable à faire le délaissement (*m.*).

abandonment (*n.*), abandon (*m.*) ; abandonnement (*m.*) :
abandonment of a voyage, of the ship and cargo at sea, abandon d'un voyage, d'un navire et de la cargaison en mer.
abandonment to creditors of the ship and freight, abandon aux créanciers du navire et du fret.
abandonment of goods in customs, abandon des marchandises en douane.
abandonment of an option (Stock Exch.), abandon d'une prime.

abandonment (Mar. Insce) (*n.*), délaissement (*m.*) ; abandon (*m.*) :
abandonment of a ship, of insured goods, délaissement, abandon, d'un navire, de facultés assurées.
insured who makes to his underwriters abandonment of the cargo, assuré qui fait à ses assureurs le délaissement du chargement (*m.*).
abandonment is the option to the insured to claim the whole amount of the sum insured in consideration of the transfer to the insurer of the property of the thing insured in the state in which the casualty left it, le délaissement est la faculté à l'assuré d'exiger le montant entier de la somme assurée moyennant le transfert à l'assureur de la propriété de la chose assurée dans l'état où l'a laisser le sinistre.

abatement (Income Tax) (*n.*), abattement (*m.*) :
abatement relieving the lower portion of the income, abattement dégrevant la tranche inférieure du revenu.

abbreviated address (Teleg.), adresse abrégée (*f.*).

abeyance (in), en suspens :
the matter is in abeyance, l'affaire est en suspens (*f.*).

able (having sufficient resources) (*adj.*), suffisant, -e :
debtor able to pay, débiteur suffisant pour payer (*m.*).
to be able to meet all one's obligations, suffire à toutes ses obligations.

aboard (*adv.*), à bord ; à bord de :
loading goods aboard the ship, chargement de la marchandise à bord le navire (*ou* à bord du navire) (*m.*).

abolish (*v.t.*), abolir ; supprimer :
to abolish a customs duty, abolir, supprimer, un droit de douane.

about (Stock Exch.) (*adv.*), environ :
buy so many shares at about such a price *or* buy so many shares at such a price about, achetez tant d'actions à tel cours environ.
Note :—On the Paris Bourse a specific latitude is generally recognized by *environ*, varying with the nature of the stock. **grand environ** or **environ large** is double the margin implied by *environ*. On the London Stock Exchange no definite margin is understood by *about*, consequently orders given at an about price (*à un cours environ*) are liable to lead to disputes and dissatisfaction.

above (*prep.*), au-dessus de :
to be above par, être au-dessus du pair ; dépasser le pair.

above-mentioned (*adj.*), susmentionné, -e :
the above-mentioned agreement, la convention susmentionnée.

above-named (*adj.*), susnommé, -e ; susdénommé, -e ; susdit, -e ; prédénommé, -e :
the above-named party, la partie susnommée (*ou* susdénommée) (*ou* susdite) (*ou* prédénommée).

above-named (pers.) (*n.*), susnommé, -e ; susdénommé, -e :
it has been agreed between the above-named . . ., entre les susnommés il a été convenu . . .

abrasion (of a coin) (*n.*), frai (d'une pièce d'argent) (*m.*).

abroad (in foreign parts) (*adv.*), à l'étranger :
property abroad, biens à l'étranger (*m.pl.*).
V. aussi exemple sous **foreign**.

absence of consideration (for a bill of exchange), défaut de provision (*m.*).

absence of news (of a ship), défaut de nouvelles (*m.*).

absolute contraband (distinguished from *occasional contraband*), contrebande absolue (*f.*) ; contrebande par nature (*f.*).

absolve oneself from further liability (to), se
libérer.

abstract or abstracting (n.), extrait (m.); relevé
(m.); relèvement (m.); résumé (m.):
abstract of account, extrait de compte;
relevé de compte; relèvement de compte.
abstract of average adjustment containing
only summary data, relevé de dispache
contenant seulement les données sommaires.
abstracting an account, relèvement d'un
compte.

abstract (to epitomize) (v.t.), extraire; relever:
to abstract an account, the results of an
account, relever un compte, les résultats
d'un compte.

abstract (to embezzle; to purloin; to make
away with) (v.t.), distraire; soustraire;
détourner:
dishonest cashier who has abstracted securities,
caissier infidèle qui a distrait des valeurs
(m.).
to abstract papers, books, soustraire, détourner, des papiers, des livres.

abstraction (purloining) (n.), distraction (f.);
soustraction (f.); détournement (m.).

abundance (n.), abondance (f.).

abundant (adj.), abondant, -e.

abuse (n.), abus (m.):
abuse of confidence, abus de confiance.

accelerated service (Transport), service accéléré
(m.).

accept (to consent to receive) (v.t.), accepter;
agréer; recevoir:
to accept either the whole, or a part of the
risk to be covered, accepter soit la totalité,
soit une partie du risque à couvrir.
an insurance contract is deemed to be concluded when the proposal of the insured is
accepted by the insurer, un contrat d'assurance est censé conclu lorsque la proposition de l'assuré est acceptée par l'assureur.
accept my compliments, my respects, agréez,
acceptez, recevez, mes civilités, mes respects.

accept (bills of exchange) (v.t.), accepter:
to accept a bill of exchange, accepter une
lettre de change.

acceptability or acceptableness (n.), acceptabilité
(f.):
acceptableness of a proposal, acceptabilité
d'une proposition.

acceptable (adj.), acceptable:
acceptable offer, offre acceptable (f.).

to be acceptable, s'accepter; s'agréer:
proposals which may be acceptable, propositions qui peuvent s'agréer (f.pl.).

acceptance (n.), acceptation (f.); agréage (m.);
agrégation (f.):
acceptance of certain conditions, acceptation
de certaines conditions.
acceptance of abandonment (Mar. Insce), acceptation de délaissement.
acceptance of the goods at departure station,
agréage, agrégation, de la marchandise en
gare de départ.

acceptance (bills of exchange) (n.), acceptation
(f.):

to present a bill for acceptance, présenter un
effet à l'acceptation.
acceptance against documents, acceptation
contre documents.
an accepted bill of exchange is called an acceptance: also the word acceptances occurs in
bank balance sheets, la lettre de change
acceptée s'appelle une acceptation: on
trouve aussi dans les bilans des banques,
le mot acceptations.
acceptance for honour or acceptance supra (or
suprà) protest (Abrev.: acceptance S.P.),
acceptation par intervention; acceptation
par honneur; acceptation sous protêt.
blank acceptance, acceptation en blanc.
acceptances on account of (or acceptances for)
customers (Banking), acceptations pour
compte de clients.

acceptance bill (opp. to payment bill), traite
documents contre acceptation (f.).

acceptance credit, crédit par acceptation (m.).

accepted (formula used in accepting a bill of
exchange) (p.p.), accepté (invar.):
acceptance is expressed by the word accepted,
l'acceptation est exprimée par le mot accepté
(f.).

accepting officer (of telegraph office), agent
taxateur (m.).

acceptor (pers.) (n.), accepteur (m.):
acceptor of a bill, accepteur d'une lettre.

acceptor for honour or acceptor supra (or suprà)
protest, intervenant (m.).

access (to books) (n.), communication (f.):
the auditors have a right of access at all times
to the books of the company, les commissaires ont droit, toutes les fois qu'ils le
jugent convenable, de prendre communication des livres de la société (m.pl.).

accessory (adj.), accessoire:
accessory contract (Law), contrat accessoire
(m.).
accessory expenses, frais accessoires (m.pl.):
the cost price is the result of a purchase
price increased by a multitude of accessory
expenses, transport, commission, etc., le
prix de revient est le résultat d'un prix
d'achat majoré d'une foule de frais acces
soires, transports, commission, etc.

accident (n.), accident (m.); sinistre (m.):
railway accident, accident de chemin de
fer.
accident of navigation, of the sea, accident
de navigation, de mer.
the receipt of news of the accident, la récep
tion de la nouvelle du sinistre.

accident insurance, assurance contre les acci
dents (f.); assurance contre les accident
corporels (f.); assurance-accidents (f.).

accidental (adj.), accidentel, -elle; fortuit, -e
accidental collision (opp. to negligent collision)
abordage fortuit (m.).
accidental stranding (opp. to voluntary strand
ing), échouement fortuit (m.); échouemen
accidentel (m.).

accommodate (to fit out) (v.t.), aménager; em
ménager:

to accommodate a ship for the carriage of
steerage passengers as an emigrant ship,
aménager, emménager, un navire pour le
transport de passagers d'entrepont comme
navire à émigrants.

ccommodation (fitting out) (*n.*), aménagement
(*m.*); emménagement (*m.*):
this steamer has splendid accommodation for
passengers, ce steamer a de splendides
aménagements pour passagers.

ship which has accommodation for 800 passengers, navire qui a des aménagements (*ou*
emménagements) pour 800 passagers (*m.*).

the accommodation of the port with a view to
tourist traffic, l'aménagement du port en
vue du trafic touristique.

ccommodation acceptance, acceptation de complaisance (*f.*).

ccommodation bill *or* **accommodation note,**
billet de complaisance (*m.*).

ccommodation paper *or* **accommodation bills,**
papier de complaisance (*m.*); valeurs de
complaisance (*f.pl.*).

ccompany (*v.t.*), accompagner:
consignment note accompanying the goods,
lettre de voiture accompagnant la marchandise (*f.*),
accompanied luggage, bagages accompagnés
(*m.pl.*).

ccomplish (*v.t.*), accomplir:
one of the bills of lading being accomplished,
the others to stand void, l'un des connaissements étant accompli, les autres restent
sans valeur.

ccomplishment (*n.*), accomplissement (*m.*).

ccord (*n.*), accord (*m.*):
quasi contracts differ from contracts in that
there is no accord of will between the parties,
les quasi-contrats diffèrent des contrats en
ce qu'il n'y a pas un accord de volonté entre
les parties (*m.pl.*).

of one's own accord, de son plein gré; d'office:
he did it of his own accord, il l'a fait d'office.

ccord (*v.t.*), accorder.

ccording to circumstances, selon le cas.

ccording to usage. V. sous **usage.**

ccording to your instructions, suivant vos
instructions.

ccount (*n.*) (Abbrev.: **a/c.** [**a/cs** *pl.*] *or* **A/c.**
[**A/cs** *pl.*] *or* **acct**), compte (*m.*); état (*m.*);
exposé (*m.*); mémoire (*m.*); note (*f.*):
(Cf. **accounts.**)
to have an account at the bank, avoir un
compte à la banque.
capital account, compte de capital; compte
capital.
cash account, compte de caisse.
account of expenses, état de dépenses; état
de frais; note de dépenses.
account of goods purchased (opp. to *account
sales*), compte d'achat.
account of one's transactions, exposé, état,
de ses opérations.
account of proceedings (report), compte rendu.

in account, en compte:
value in account, valeur en compte (*f.*).

on account, à compte; d'acompte; à bon
compte; à valoir; en compte:
to take so many francs on account, prendre
tant de francs à compte (*ou* d'acompte)
(*ou* à bon compte).
received £10 on account of my disbursements,
reçu £10 à valoir sur mes déboursés.
cash on account (opp. to *cash to balance*),
espèces en compte (*f.pl.*).
to take goods on account (i.e., on credit),
prendre des marchandises à compte.

on (*or* **for**) **account of,** pour le compte de;
à l'acquit de:
to pay money on account of a third party,
verser des fonds pour le compte (*ou* à
l'acquit) d'un tiers.
on clients' account, pour le compte d'autrui.
for one's own account, pour son compte;
pour son propre compte:
in France, an *agent de change* (stockbroker) is
not allowed to operate for his own account,
en France, un agent de change ne
peut faire d'opérations pour son propre
compte.
acting for account of whom it may concern,
agissant pour le compte de qui il appartiendra; agissant pour compte de qui il
peut appartenir.

account (the balance sheet or the profit and loss
account) (*n.*), exercice (*m.*): (Cf. **accounts.**)
balance brought forward from last account *or*
balance from last account (item in balance
sheet or in profit and loss account), solde
reporté de l'exercice précédent (*m.*); solde
de l'exercice précédent (*m.*); report de
l'exercice précédent (*m.*).
balance of profits carried forward to next
account, solde des bénéfices reporté à
nouveau sur l'exercice suivant (*m.*).

account (history) (*n.*), historique (*m.*):
to write an account of a transaction, faire
l'historique d'une négociation.

account (position; book) (Stock Exch.) (*n.*),
position (*f.*). V. exemple sous **bear account.**

account (the fortnightly or monthly reckoning
between buyers and sellers; the settlement)
(Stock Exch.) (*n.*), terme (*m.*); liquidation
(*f.*):
dealings for the account, négociations à terme
(*f.pl.*); opérations à terme (*f.pl.*).
current account *or* this account, liquidation
courante; liquidation:
price for current (*or* for this) account, cours en
liquidation courante (*m.*); cours en liquidation (*m.*).
options till the account on the 15th of next
month, primes en liquidation au 15 du mois
prochain (*f.pl.*).

account (*v.t.*), rendre compte; tenir compte:
to account to the buyer for the interest, rendre
compte (*ou* tenir compte) à l'acheteur de
l'intérêt.

account book, livre de comptabilité (*m.*); registre
de comptabilité (*m.*); livre comptable
(*m.*); livre de compte (*m.*); livre de comptes
(*m.*); papier-journal (*m.*).

account books (financial books—as opp. to *memorandum, statistical,* or *registry books*), livres de report (*m.pl.*).

account current [accounts current *pl.*] (Abbrev.: **A/C.**), compte courant (*m.*).

account current with interest, compte courant et d'intérêts.

account day (Stock Exch.), jour de la liquidation (*m.*).

account rendered (Com.), solde à nouveau (*m.*).

account sales [account sales *pl.*] (Abbrev.: **A/S.**), compte de vente (*m.*).

account settled *or* **account stated,** arrêté de compte (*m.*).

accountable (*adj.*), comptable:
to be accountable for a sum of money, être comptable d'une somme d'argent.
accountable receipt, quittance comptable (*f.*).

accountancy (*n.*), comptabilité (*f.*):
for a long time past the art of bookkeeping has made way for the science of accountancy, depuis longtemps déjà l'art de la tenue de livres a fait place à la science de la comptabilité.

accountant (pers.) (*n.*), comptable (*m.*); agent comptable (*m.*):
professional accountant, comptable professionnel; comptable de profession; expert-comptable (*m.*).
whereas the accountant organizes, advises, and directs, the bookkeeper performs the work, under the former's directions, alors que le comptable organise, conseille, et dirige, le teneur de livres exécute, sur les indications du premier.

accounting (*n.*), comptabilité (*f.*):
cost accounting, comptabilité de prix de revient.

accounting machine, machine comptable (*f.*). V. automatic bookkeeping machine *pour variétés.*

accounting period, exercice (*m.*):
accounting period ending 31st December, exercice prenant fin (*ou* clôturant) le 31 décembre.
accounting period ended 31 December, exercice ayant pris fin (*ou* exercice clôturé *ou* clos) le 31 décembre.
if the company's year comprises two half yearly accounting periods, si l'année sociale comprend deux exercices semestriels.

accounting system, comptabilité (*f.*):
in certain accounting systems a combined journal and ledger is used, on utilise dans certaines comptabilités le journal-grand-livre.

accounts (records of pecuniary transactions; books) (*n.pl.*), comptes (*m.pl.*); écritures (*f.pl.*); écritures comptables (*f.pl.*); comptabilité (*f.*); livres (*m.pl.*):
to have one's accounts up to date, avoir ses comptes à jour.
the accounts presented by the directors, les comptes présentés par les administrateurs.
to keep a firm's accounts, tenir les comptes (*ou* les écritures) (*ou* la comptabilité) (*ou* les livres) d'une maison.

falsification of accounts, falsification d'écriture comptables (*f.*).

accounts (detailed accounts; balance sheet and schedules; balance sheet, profit and loss account, trading account, stock sheets list and valuation of investments, or the like such as would be placed before say the directors and auditors of a company) (*n.pl.*) inventaire (*m.*); inventaire comptable (*m.*); inventaire intra-comptable (*m.*):
to make up one's accounts once a year, every six months, faire son inventaire une fois l'an, tous les six mois.
accounts to the end of the financial year, inventaire de fin d'exercice.
the accounts for 19— show a profit of so much, l'inventaire de 19— fait apparaître un bénéfice de tant.

accounts department, service de la comptabilité (*m.*); comptabilité (*f.*).

accredited (*adj.*), accrédité, -e; attitré, -e:
accredited banker, banquier accrédité (*m.*).
accredited broker, courtier attitré (*m.*).
accredited party, accrédité, -e:
letters of credit bear the following particulars date of creation, name of the accredited party, etc., les lettres de crédit portent les indications suivantes: date de création nom de l'accrédité, etc. (*f.pl.*).
accredited representative, représentant attitré (*m.*).

accrue (*v.i.*), courir; accroître; s'accroître; s'acquérir:
interest which accrues from the 1st March, which accrues day by day, intérêts qui courent depuis le 1er mars, qui s'acquièrent jour par jour (*m.pl.*).

accrued interest, intérêt couru (*m.*); intérêts accrus (*m.pl.*).

accruing interest, intérêts à échoir (*m.pl.*).

accumulate (*v.t.*), accumuler; amonceler:
to accumulate wealth, capital, accumuler, amonceler, des richesses, des capitaux.
the orders accumulated over the week end, les ordres accumulés durant la fin de la semaine (*m.pl.*).

accumulate (*v.i.*), s'accumuler; s'amonceler.

accumulation (*n.*), accumulation (*f.*); amoncellement (*m.*):
to avoid the accumulation of useless old papers, the bane of every office, éviter l'accumulation d'une paperasse inutile, fléau de toutes les administrations.

accuracy (*n.*), exactitude (*f.*); justesse (*f.*).

accurate (*adj.*), exact, -e; juste:
accurate calculation, calcul exact (*m.*).

accurately (*adv.*), exactement; justement.

acknowledge receipt (to), accuser réception:
to acknowledge receipt of a letter, accuser réception d'une lettre.

acknowledgment *or* **acknowledgement** (*n.*), reconnaissance (*f.*); accusé de réception (*m.*); reçu (*m.*); avis (*m.*):
acknowledgment of debt, reconnaissance de dette.
the master is responsible for the cargo entrusted

to his care. He gives an acknowledgment of
them. This acknowledgment is called bill
of lading, le capitaine est responsable des
marchandises dont il se charge. Il en fournit
une reconnaissance. Cette reconnaissance se
nomme connaissement.

acknowledgment of delivery (Post),   avis de
réception.

acquire (*v.t.*),   acquérir :
to acquire a piece of land, acquérir une terre.

acquisition (*n.*),   acquisition (*f.*).

acquit (*v.t.*),   acquitter :
to acquit someone from an obligation, acquitter
quelqu'un d'une obligation.

acquittance (*n.*), acquittement (*m.*) ; acquit (*m.*) :
it is only after acquittance of the policy that
it comes into force,   ce n'est qu'après
l'acquittement de la police qu'elle entre en
vigueur.

act (action ; manifestation of will) (*n.*),   acte
(*m.*) ; fait (*m.*) :
sacrifice emanating from a voluntary act of
the master,   sacrifice émanant d'un acte
volontaire du capitaine (*m.*).
act or fault of the insured, of a third party,
fait ou faute de l'assuré, d'un tiers.
act of a prince (Internat. Law), fait du prince ;
fait du souverain :
the consequences resulting from the act of a
prince, les conséquences résultant du fait
du prince (*f.pl.*).
act of God, acte de Dieu ; fait de Dieu.
acts of war, faits de guerre.

act (of parliament) (*n.*),   loi (*f.*) :
finance act, loi de finances ; loi des finances.
companies act, loi sur les sociétés.

act (*v.i.*),   agir :
to act according to circumstances, agir selon
le cas.
agent who is authorized to act for the company,
agent qui est autorisé à agir pour la compagnie (*m.*).
acting for account of whom it may concern,
agissant pour le compte de qui il appartiendra ; agissant pour compte de qui il
peut appartenir.

acting (*adj.*),   intérimaire :
acting manager,   directeur intérimaire (*m.*).

acting partner (opp. to *sleeping*, or *dormant*, or
silent, or *secret*, *partner*),   commandité, -e.

action (Law) (*n.*),   action (*f.*) ;   procès (*m.*) ;
affaire (*f.*) ;   poursuite (*f.*) ;   poursuites
(*f.pl.*) ;   cause (*f.*) :
to bring an action against someone,   intenter
une action contre quelqu'un.
action at law,   action en justice :
protestation followed by an action at law
within so many days,   protestation suivie
d'une action en justice dans le délai de
tant de jours (*f.*).
action for damages,   action en dommages-
intérêts.
civil action,   action civile ; procès civil ; affaire
civile ;   poursuite civile ;   cause civile.

actionable (Law) (*adj.*),   actionnable.

active (*adj.*),   actif, -ive ; allant, -e :

active market,   marché actif (*m.*).
active dealings in stocks,   transactions actives
en valeurs (*f.pl.*).
Mexican shares are very active,   les valeurs
mexicaines sont très allantes (*f.pl.*).
active debt (opp. to *passive debt*),   dette active
(*f.*).

actively (*adv.*),   activement :
securities actively dealt in,   valeurs activement
traitées (*f.pl.*).

activity [**activities** *pl.*] (*n.*),   activité (*f.*) ; allant
(*m.*).

actual (*adj.*),   actuel, -elle ; réel, -elle ; effectif,
-ive :
actual gross freight at risk,   fret brut réel à
faire (*m.*).
actual tare,   tare réelle (*f.*).
actual total loss (Mar. Insce) (opp. to *constructive
total loss*),   perte totale absolue (*f.*) ;   perte
totale réelle (*f.*).   *Note :*—Translation only ;
does not obtain in French Law.
the actual value of a stock or share may be
higher than, equal to, or lower than (*or
over, equal to, or under*) the nominal value,
la valeur réelle d'un titre de bourse peut
être supérieure, égale, ou inférieure à la
valeur nominale.
actual value at the time of the loss,   valeur
effective au moment de la perte (*f.*).
the goods will be paid for on the footing of
their actual value, les marchandises seront
payées sur le pied de leur valeur réelle
(*f.pl.*).

actually (*adv.*),   actuellement ;   réellement ;
effectivement :
profit actually realized,   bénéfice effectivement
réalisé (*m.*).

actuarial (*adj.*),   actuarial, -e, -aux :
actuarial science,   science actuariale (*f.*).

actuarially (*adv.*),   actuarialement.

actuary [**actuaries** *pl.*] (pers.) (*n.*),   actuaire
(*m.*).

ad valorem duty (Customs) (distinguished from
specific duty),   droit ad valorem (*m.*).

ad valorem duty (registration duty) (distinguished
from *fixed duty*),   droit proportionnel (*m.*).

ad valorem stamp,   timbre proportionnel (*m.*).

add (*v.t.*),   ajouter ; additionner ; joindre :
to add the interest to the capital, the freight
to the value of the goods,   ajouter, joindre,
l'intérêt au capital, le fret à la valeur des
marchandises.
to be added,   être ajouté, -e, additionné, -e,
joint, -e ;   s'ajouter ;   s'additionner ;   se
joindre :
the brokerage is added to purchases or deducted
from sales,   le courtage s'ajoute aux achats
ou se retranche des ventes.

add *or* **add up** (Arith.) (*v.t.*),   additionner :
to add up a column of figures, additionner une
colonne de chiffres.

add a postscript to a letter (to) *or* **add a footnote to
a letter (to),**   apostiller une lettre.

add back (to) (Income Tax),   ajouter :
inspector who adds back a partner's salary to
the profit shown by the business,   contrôleur

qui ajoute les appointements d'un associé au bénéfice accusé par l'entreprise (*m.*).

add something to the purchase price to cover one's expenses (to), majorer le prix d'achat pour couvrir ses frais.

addable *or* **addible** (*adj.*), additionnable : addable sums, sommes additionnables (*f.pl.*).

adder (pers.) (*n.*), additionneur, -euse.

adding machine *or* **adder** (*n.*), machine à additionner (*f.*) ; additionneuse (*f.*) : adding machine for all analysis work, machine à additionner pour tous travaux d'analyse.

adding-subtracting machine, machine à additionner et à soustraire (*f.*).

addition *or* **adding** *or* **adding up** (*n.*), addition (*f.*).

additional (*adj.*), additionnel, -elle ; supplémentaire : additional assessment (Income Tax), imposition supplémentaire (*f.*). additional freight, surfret (*m.*) ; fret supplémentaire (*m.*) ; supplément de fret (*m.*). additional insurance, assurance supplémentaire (*f.*). additional line (Teleph.), poste supplémentaire (*m.*). *V. note sous* direct exchange line. additional premium (Insce), surprime (*f.*) ; prime supplémentaire (*f.*) ; supplément de prime (*m.*) ; prime additionnelle (*f.*) : additional premium to be arranged, surprime à débattre ; surprime à arbitrer. additional premium for age (of vessel), surprime d'âge (du navire).

additionally (*adv.*), additionnellement.

address (*n.*), adresse (*f.*) ; domicile (*m.*) : address on a letter, adresse sur une lettre. to take someone's name and address, prendre le nom et l'adresse (*ou* les nom et adresse) de quelqu'un. the consignee's name and address, le nom et l'adresse (*ou* et le domicile) du destinataire. the address only to be written on this side (postcard), ce côté est exclusivement réservé à l'adresse ; ce côté réservé à l'adresse.

address (directing or consigning, as a ship or cargo) (*n.*), adresse (*f.*).

address (speech) (*n.*), allocution (*f.*) ; discours (*m.*).

address (*v.t.*), adresser : to address a letter to someone, adresser une lettre à quelqu'un.

address book, livre d'adresses (*m.*).

address card, carte d'adresse (*f.*).

address clause (charter party), clause d'adresse (*f.*).

address commission, commission d'adresse (*f.*).

address label, étiquette d'adresse (*f.*).

address side (of an envelope, of a postcard, of a packet), côté de l'adresse (*m.*), recto (*m.*) (d'une enveloppe, d'une carte postale, d'un paquet).

addressee (Post) (pers.) (*n.*), destinataire (*m.* ou *f.*) : if the sender of an insured article wishes to receive an advice of delivery to the addressee, si l'expéditeur d'un objet chargé veut recevoir un avis de réception du destinataire.

addressing machine, machine à adresses (*f.*) machine à faire les adresses (*f.*).

addressing office, bureau d'adresses (*m.*) ; burea d'écritures (*m.*).

adhesive stamp (opp. to *impressed stamp*), timbr mobile (*m.*) ; timbre adhésif (*m.*).

adhesive transparent paper tape, bande gommé en papier transparent (*f.*).

adjourn (*v.t.*), ajourner ; renvoyer ; remettre : to adjourn the proceedings, ajourner le délibérations. to adjourn a case for a week, ajourner renvoyer, remettre, une cause à huitaine.

adjourn (*v.i.*), s'ajourner : the members have adjourned sine die, le membres se sont ajournés sine die (*m.pl.*).

adjournable (*adj.*), ajournable.

adjourned meeting, assemblée ajournée (*f.*) réunion ajournée (*f.*).

adjournment (*n.*), ajournement (*m.*) ; renvo (*m.*) ; remise (*f.*).

adjudication in bankruptcy, jugement déclarati de faillite (*m.*).

adjust (*v.t.*), ·ajuster ; régler : to adjust a difference, an account, ajuster régler, un différend, un compte.

adjust (Mar. Insce) (*v.t.*), régler : to adjust general average and salvage according to the law and practice obtaining at the plac where the adventure ends, régler l'avari commune et le sauvetage d'après les loi et les usages du lieu où finit l'aventure.

to be adjusted, être réglé, -e ; se régler : general average to be adjusted (*or* adjustable according to York-Antwerp rules, les avarie communes se régleront conformément aux règles d'York et d'Anvers.

adjuster (of average) (pers.) (*n.*), dispacheur (*m.*) répartiteur (*m.*) ; expert répartiteur (*m.*) expert-dispacheur (*m.*).

adjustment (*n.*), ajustement (*m.*) ; règlemen (*m.*).

adjustment account (Bkkpg), compte collecti (*m.*).

adjustment of average (Mar. Insce), règlement d'avaries (*m.*) ; dispache (*f.*) : adjustment of general average on hull *o* general average adjustment on hull, règle ment d'avarie grosse sur corps. the adjustment of general average is based o a principle of justice which requires that any sacrifice in the common interest should be supported by all those who have profited by this sacrifice, le règlement des avaries communes est basé sur un principe de justice qui veut que tout sacrifice fait dans l'intérêt commun soit supporté par tous ceux qui ont profité par ce sacrifice. adjustment of particular average, règlement d'avarie particulière. general average and salvage charges payable according to foreign adjustment, les avaries communes et les frais de sauvetage se régleront suivant dispache étrangère (*f.pl.*). adjustment charges, frais de dispache (*m.pl.*).

administer (*v.t.*), administrer ; gérer :

to administer the affairs of a company, administrer, gérer, les affaires d'une compagnie.

dministration (n.), administration (f.); gestion (f.):
administration of a country, administration, gestion, d'un pays.
the administration of the post office in England, l'administration des postes en Angleterre.

dministration expenses, frais d'administration (m.pl.).

dministrative (adj.), administratif, -ive:
administrative power, pouvoir administratif (m.).

dministratively (adv.), administrativement.

dmissibility (n.), admissibilité (f.).

dmissible (adj.), admissible.

dmission (n.), admission (f.):
admission to quotation (Stock Exch.), admission à la cote.

dmission ticket, bulletin d'admission (m.).

dmit (v.t.), admettre; bonifier:
to admit a claim, admettre un recours.
to admit as general average the damage done to a ship or her cargo, admettre, bonifier, en avarie commune le dommage causé à un navire ou à sa cargaison.

to admit of, admettre:
this affair admits of no delay, cette affaire n'admet aucun retard.

dopt (v.t.), adopter; prendre:
to adopt a resolution, adopter une proposition; prendre une résolution (ou une délibération) (ou une décision).

doption (n.), adoption (f.); prise (f.).

dult's ticket, billet d'adulte (m.).

dulterate the coinage (to), adultérer, altérer, les monnaies.

dulteration of the coinage, adultération (f.), altération (f.), des monnaies.

dvance (n.), avance (f.); anticipation (f.); à-valoir (m.); à-bon-compte (m.); prêt (m.):
advance of freight, avance de fret.
advance of money, avance d'argent (ou de fonds).
advance on current account, avance en compte courant.
advances on documents, avances sur documents.
advances on securities (or on stocks), avances sur valeurs; prêts sur titres.
advance against security or secured advance, avance contre garantie; avance garantie.
advances on a contract, on consignment of goods, avances, anticipations, sur un contrat, sur consignation de marchandises.
advances to crew on wages, avances à l'équipage sur gages.
sharp advance of X. shares, vive avance de l'action X.

in advance, en avance; à l'avance; d'avance; par avance; par anticipation; anticipatif, -ive; anticipé, -e:
to pay in advance, payer par avance (ou par anticipation).
rent paid in advance or simply rent in advance

loyer payé d'avance (m.); loyer d'avance (m.).

advance (v.t.), avancer:
to advance money to employees, avancer de l'argent à des employés.

advance (v.i.), s'avancer:
X. shares advanced from 2s. to 2s. 3d., l'action X. s'avance de 2 sh. à 2 sh. 3d.

advance in price, augmentation de prix (f.); augmentation (f.); 'hausse (f.); renchérissement (m.); enchérissement (m.).

advance in price (to), augmenter de prix; 'hausser; renchérir; enchérir.

advance the price of (to), augmenter le prix de; 'hausser le prix de; renchérir; enchérir:
to advance the price of goods, augmenter le prix, hausser le prix, renchérir, enchérir, des marchandises.

advanced freight or **advance freight,** fret payé d'avance (m.); fret payé (m.).

advantage (n.), avantage (m.); bénéfice (m.); compte (m.).

adventure (n.), expédition (f.); aventure (f.); risque (m.):
the safeguarding of goods exposed to the perils of a marine adventure, la sauvegarde de marchandises exposées aux périls d'une expédition maritime.
common danger threatening the adventure with loss, danger commun menaçant de perte l'aventure (m.).
lawful marine adventure, aventure maritime licite.

adverse trade balance (opp. to favourable trade balance), balance commerciale déficitaire (f.). V. exemple sous balance of trade.

advertise (v.t.), annoncer; faire annoncer; publier:
to advertise the payment of a coupon, annoncer le paiement d'un coupon.
to advertise a notice in the Gazette, publier une notice au Journal officiel.

advertise for a clerk (to), demander dans les journaux un commis.

advertise in a newspaper (to), faire, mettre, insérer, une annonce dans un journal.

advertisement (n.) (Abbrev.: advt or ad.), annonce (f.); réclame (f.):
advertisement of a sale, annonce d'une vente.
advertisement required by law, annonce judiciaire.

advertisement hoarding, panneau-réclame (m.).

advertisement rates, tarif d'annonces (m.).

advertiser (pers.) (n.), annoncier (m.).

advertising (n.), publicité (f.); réclame (f.):
advertising is very expensive, la publicité coûte fort cher.

advertising agency, agence de publicité (f.); bureau de publicité (m.); office de publicité (m.).

advertising campaign, campagne de publicité (f.).

advertising contractor, entrepreneur de publicité (m.).

advertising expenses, dépenses de publicité (f.pl.).

advice (notification) (*n.*), avis (*m.*) :
  advice of arrival, of receipt, avis d'arrivée, de réception.
  advice of deal (Stock Exch.), avis d'opéré ; avis d'opération.
  advice of delivery (Post), avis de réception :
  advice of delivery of insured articles, avis de réception d'objets chargés.
  advice of draft, avis de traite.
  advice of non delivery, avis de non livraison ; avis de souffrance.
  advice of payment of money orders, avis de paiement de mandats-poste.
  advice of shipment *or* advice of dispatch, avis d'expédition ; avis d'embarquement.
  no advice, défaut d'avis.
advice (counsel ; recommendations) (*n.*), avis (*m.*) ; avis (*m.pl.*) ; conseil (*m.*) ; conseils (*m.pl.*) :
  to give good advice, donner un bon avis (*ou* des bons conseils).
  he is fond of giving advice, il aime à donner des avis.
  to take advice, prendre conseil.
  to ask for advice, demander des conseils.
advice boat, aviso (*m.*).
advice note *or simply* **advice** (*n.*), lettre d'avis (*f.*).
advisable (*adj.*), conseillable :
  advisable step, démarche conseillable (*f.*).
advise (to inform) (*v.t.*), aviser :
  to advise one's correspondent of a shipment of goods, aviser son correspondant d'une expédition de marchandises.
advise (to counsel) (*v.t.*), conseiller.
aerial (*adj.*), aérien, -enne :
  aerial navigation, navigation aérienne (*f.*) ; aviation (*f.*).
aerodrome (*n.*), aérodrome (*m.*).
aeronaut (pers.) (*n.*), aéronaute (*m.*) ; aviateur (*m.*).
aeronautic *or* **aeronautical** (*adj.*), aéronautique.
aeronautics (*n.*), aéronautique (*f.*).
aeroplane (*n.*) (Abbrev. : 'plane), aéroplane (*m.*) ; avion (*m.*).
aeroplane ticket, billet d'avion (*m.*).
affair (*n.*), affaire (*f.*).
affidavit (*n.*), affidavit (*m.*).
affiliate (*v.t.*), affilier :
  to affiliate several societies to a central society, affilier plusieurs sociétés à une société centrale.
affiliate (*v.i.*), s'affilier :
  to affiliate with a society, s'affilier à une société.
affiliated (*adj.*), affilié, -e :
  affiliated societies, sociétés affiliées (*f.pl.*).
affiliated member *or* **affiliate** (*n.*), affilié, -e.
affiliation (*n.*), affiliation (*f.*).
affirmative (*adj.*), affirmatif, -ive :
  affirmative answer *or* affirmative reply, réponse affirmative (*f.*).
affirmatively (*adv.*), affirmativement.
affix (*v.t.*), apposer :
  to affix a seal, a stamp to a receipt, apposer un sceau, un timbre sur un reçu.

affix stamp here, emplacement du timbre poste.
affixing (*n.*), apposition (*f.*) :
  affixing a seal, an adhesive stamp, apposition d'un sceau, d'un timbre mobile.
affreight (*v.t.*), affréter ; fréter ; noliser.
affreighter (pers.) (*n.*), affréteur (*m.*) ; fréteur (*m.*).
affreightment (*n.*), affrètement (*m.*) ; frètement (*m.*) ; nolisement (*m.*) :
  the commercial exploitation of the ship in the form of affreightment assumes several forms, l'exploitation commerciale du navire sous la forme d'affrètement revêt plusieurs formes (*f.*).
  contract of affreightment, contrat d'affrètement (*m.*).
  affreightment by bill of lading, affrètement-transport (*m.*).
  affreightment by charter, affrètement-location (*m.*).
afloat (Produce Exch.) (*adj. & adv.*) (Abbrev. : **aflt**), flottant, -e ; en cargaison flottante ; sous voile :
  sale of goods afloat, vente de marchandises flottantes (*ou* en cargaison flottante) (*ou* sous voile) (*f.*).
  prices : spot so much ; afloat so much, cours : disponible tant ; flottant tant.
afloat (*adv.*), à flot :
  the total tonnage of ships afloat, la jauge totale des navires à flot.
  goods stored ashore or afloat, marchandises emmagasinées à terre ou à flot (*f.pl.*).
aforesaid *or* **aforementioned** (*adj.*), susdit, -e ; prédénommé, -e :
  the aforesaid person, la susdite personne ; la personne prédénommée.
after hours (in the street) (Stock Exch.), après-bourse :
  X. shares remained after hours at 2½ bid, l'action X. reste après-bourse à 2 1/2 demandé.
  price after hours, cours d'après-bourse (*m.*).
against delivery (Stock Exch.), sauf livraison.
against or for (said of exchanges). V. **exchange** (rate of exchange).
age (*n.*), âge (*m.*) :
  age of a ship, âge d'un navire.
  age limit for pensioning civil functionaries, limite d'âge pour la mise à la retraite des fonctionnaires civils (*f.*).
agency (instrumentality) (*n.*), entremise (*f.*) ; ministère (*m.*) :
  insurance business is generally done through the agency of brokers, le commerce des assurances est généralement traité par l'entremise de courtiers.
  brokers who must record in special books all the deals done through their agency, courtiers qui doivent consigner sur des livres spéciaux toutes les opérations faites par leur ministère (*m.pl.*).
agency [agencies *pl.*] (bureau) (*n.*), agence (*f.*) ; bureau (*m.*) ; cabinet (*m.*) ; comptoir (*m.*) ; factorerie (*f.*) :

employment agency, agence de placement; bureau de placement.

agency (position or business of an agent,—duration of such an office) (*n.*), agence (*f.*); représentation (*f.*) :
to obtain the agency of a company, obtenir l'agence d'une compagnie.
during his agency, pendant son agence.

agency account, compte agence (*m.*).

agency agreement *or* **agency contract** (agreement enumerating the conditions under which representation is granted), traité d'agence (*m.*); contrat d'agence (*m.*).

agency contract (contract of trust; mandatory contract) (Law), contrat de mandat (*m.*).

agency trade, commerce de représentation (*m.*).

agenda (*n.pl. or collective pl.*), ordre du jour (*m.*) :
the matters on which the directors, or the shareholders, are called on to decide make up the agenda, les objets sur lesquels les administrateurs, ou les actionnaires, sont appelés à se prononcer constituent l'ordre du jour (*m.pl.*).
meeting convened to consider the following agenda, assemblée convoquée à l'effet de délibérer sur l'ordre du jour suivant (*f.*).
to put down on the agenda the business to be transacted, mettre à l'ordre du jour les questions à délibérer.

agent (representative) (pers.) (*n.*) (Abbrev. : **Agt**), agent (*m.*); commissionnaire (*m.*); représentant (*m.*) :
the company's agent at Liverpool, l'agent de la compagnie à Liverpool.
sole agent for France and Colonies, agent exclusif pour la France et ses Colonies.
insurance agent, agent d'assurances.
shipping agent, agent maritime; commissionnaire-chargeur; commissionnaire-expéditeur.

agent (as distinguished from *principal*) (*n.*), mandataire (*m.* ou *f.*); commissionnaire (*m.*) :
the company acts only as agent for the other companies, la compagnie agit seulement à titre de mandataire des autres compagnies.
the captain is the legal agent who represents the shipowner in all that concerns the ship he commands, le capitaine est le mandataire légal qui représente l'armement pour tout ce qui concerne le navire qu'il commande.
the insured or his agent, l'assuré ou son mandataire (*m.*).
the agent receives from his principal a retribution called commission, le commissionnaire reçoit de son commettant une rétribution appelée commission.

aggravation (*n.*), aggravation (*f.*) :
aggravation of the risk necessitating an indorsement to the insurance, aggravation du risque nécessitant un avenant à l'assurance.

aggregate (*n.*), masse (*f.*) :
aggregate of coin in circulation, masse des espèces monnayées en circulation.

agio (difference between mint par and present price; exchange premium) (*n.*), agio (*m.*); prix du change (*m.*); prime du change (*f.*).

agiotage (*n.*), agiotage (*m.*).

agree (*v.t.*), faire accorder; apurer; faire cadrer :
to agree the books, faire accorder les livres.
to agree an account, apurer, faire accorder, faire cadrer, un compte.

agree (to be in concord) (*v.i.*), s'accorder; tomber d'accord; être en accord; être d'accord; concorder :
two experts who agree, deux experts qui tombent d'accord.
the books agree, les livres sont en accord (*ou* sont d'accord) (*m.pl.*).
the amount in words agrees with the amount in figures, la somme en lettres concorde avec la somme en chiffres.

agree on (to) *or* **agree upon (to),** s'accorder sur; convenir sur; convenir de; s'entendre sur; arrêter :
to agree on (*or* upon) a price, s'accorder sur, convenir sur, convenir d', s'entendre sur, arrêter, un prix.

agree to (to), consentir; consentir à; souscrire à; s'engager à :
to agree to a sale, a loan, consentir, consentir à, une vente, un prêt.
to agree to an arrangement, consentir à, souscrire à, un arrangement.

agreed price (*or* **sum**) (*or* **rate**) *or* **agreed consideration,** prix convenu (*m.*); prix à forfait (*m.*); prix forfaitaire (*m.*); somme forfaitaire (*f.*); indemnité forfaitaire (*f.*); forfait (*m.*) :
to undertake the carriage of goods at an agreed price, entreprendre le transport des marchandises pour un prix déterminé à forfait.
in consideration of the payment of an agreed sum, moyennant paiement d'une somme forfaitaire.
to accept an agreed sum as indemnity settled in advance, accepter un forfait d'indemnité réglé à l'avance.
an agreed consideration of half per cent fixed by a clause of the contract, un forfait (*ou* une indemnité forfaitaire) de demi pour cent fixé(e) par une clause du contrat.
at an agreed sum (*or* price) (*or* rate), à forfait; forfaitairement :
expenses fixed at an agreed rate of 5% on the capital, frais généraux fixés forfaitairement à 5 0/0 du capital (*m.pl.*).

agreed valuation clause (Mar. Insce), clause valeur agréée (*f.*); clause vaille que vaille (*f.*); clause vaille plus, vaille moins (*f.*).

agreed value of the subject matter of an insurance, valeur agréée de l'objet d'une assurance (*f.*).

agreement *or* **agreeing** (accord; correspondence) (*n.*), accord (*m.*); entente (*f.*); convention (*f.*); concordance (*f.*); apurement (*m.*) :
to come to an agreement, tomber d'accord.
failing agreement between all the interested parties *or* in default of agreement between all the parties concerned, à défaut d'accord (*ou* d'entente) entre tous les intéressés.
the agreement of the parties is sufficient to validate the operation, la convention des parties suffit à valider l'opération.

agreement between the journal and the ledger, accord, concordance, du journal et du grand livre.

agreement of the cash in hand with the balance shown by the cash book, concordance des espèces en caisse avec le solde accusé par le livre de caisse.

in case of transfer, the deposit will be repaid to the transferor after agreeing the account, en cas de cession, le dépôt de garanti est remboursé au cédant après apurement du compte.

agreeing manifests (Customs), apurement des manifestes.

agreement (contract) (*n.*),   convention (*f.*); acte (*m.*); contrat (*m.*); marché (*m.*); traité (*m.*):

agreement in writing,   convention par écrit; acte à l'écrit.

agreement for sale,   convention de vente; acte de vente; contrat de vente.

agreement between master and owner, contrat entre le capitaine et le propriétaire; contrat de préposition.

agreement with crew,   contrat d'engagement des gens de l'équipage; contrat de travail des gens de mer.

to break an agreement, rompre un marché.

to enter into an agreement with a company, passer un traité avec une compagnie.

agreement clause, clause conventionnelle (*f.*).

agricultural show, concours agricole (*m.*).

aground (*adj. & adv.*), échoué, -e:

vessel aground, navire échoué (*m.*).

aid (assistance) (*n.*), aide (*f.*); assistance (*f.*); secours (*m.*):

financial aid, aide financière.

aid (*v.t.*), aider; assister; secourir.

air (*n.*), air (*m.*).

aircraft. V. ci-après.

air fee *or* **air mail fee** (Post), surtaxe aérienne (*f.*).

air journey *or* **air transit,** parcours aérien (*m.*).

air letter *or* **air mail letter,** lettre-avion (*f.*).

air line, ligne aérienne (*f.*); ligne d'avion (*f.*).

air liner, avion de ligne régulière (*m.*).

air mail, poste aérienne (*f.*); poste-avion (*f.*).

by air mail (inscription on a letter, a packet, etc., sent by airway), par avion.

air mail correspondence *or* **air packets** *or* **air mail packets,** correspondances-avion (*f.pl.*).

airman. V. ci-après.

air navigation, navigation aérienne (*f.*); aviation (*f.*).

air packet *or* **air mail packet,** correspondance-avion (*f.*).

air parcel, colis-avion (*m.*).

air parcel service, service aérien de messageries (*m.*).

air pilot, pilote aérien (*m.*).

airplane. V. ci-après.

air port, aéroport (*m.*); port aérien (*m.*):

the air port of London, of Paris, l'aéroport de Londres, de Paris.

air port of delivery, aéroport de débarquement.

air port of lading, aéroport d'embarquement.

air service, service aérien (*m.*).

airship. V. ci-après.

air station, aérogare (*f.*):

Croydon, Le Bourget, air station,   l'aérogare de Croydon, du Bourget.

air ticket, billet aérien (*m.*).

airway, airworthiness, airworthy. V. ci-après.

aircraft (*n.*),   aéronef (*m.*).

airman [**airmen** *pl.*] (*n.*),   aviateur (*m.*); aéronaute (*m.*).

airplane (*n.*), avion (*m.*); aéroplane (*m.*).

airship (*n.*),   paquebot aérien (*m.*); dirigeable (*m.*).

airway (*n.*) *or* **air route,** voie aérienne (*f.*); voie d'air (*f.*); route aérienne (*f.*).

airworthiness (of an aeroplane) (*n.*), navigabilité (*f.*).

airworthy (*adj.*), navigable.

aleatory (*adj.*), aléatoire:

a contract of insurance is an aleatory contract which has as its object the indemnification of the insured for (*or* contract whereby the insured is indemnified against) a damage resulting from a fortuitous event,   le contrat d'assurance est un contrat aléatoire qui a pour but d'indemniser l'assuré d'un dommage résultant d'un cas fortuit.

alien duty, surtaxe de pavillon (*f.*).

all (**one's**) (the whole of one's fortune), tout son avoir (*m.*):

obstinate gamblers lose their all,   les joueurs obstinés perdent tout leur avoir (*m.pl.*).

all communications to be addressed to the secretary, prière d'adresser la réponse au secrétaire.

all rights of the parties reserved, tous droits des parties réservés (*m.pl.*).

all risks (Insce) (Abbrev.: **A.R.**),   tous risques (*m.pl.*):

insurance against all risks, assurance contre tous risques (*f.*).

all risks policy,   police à tous risques (*f.*); police tous risques (*f.*).

all sailings subject to change without notice *or* **all sailings subject to change with or without notice** (Shipping),   tous les départs sans engagement de date (*m.pl.*); sans engagement de dates.

all the year *or* **all the year round,** toute l'année:

hotel open all the year round, hôtel ouvert toute l'année (*m.*).

all the year round service, service circulant toute l'année (*m.*).

allocation (*n.*), allocation (*f.*):

allocation of a share of the profits, allocation d'une part des bénéfices.

allonge (rider on a bill of exchange) (*n.*), allonge (*f.*).

allot (*v.t.*), attribuer; répartir:

to allot shares to an applicant, attribuer des actions à un souscripteur.

to allot the shares in full, attribuer intégralement les actions.

in response to your application, you have been allotted so many shares of the X. Company. The amount payable on application and allotment is so much, you have already paid so much, making amount due from you on allotment so much. Payment of the amount due from you should be made to . . ., nous avons l'honneur de vous informer que sur votre souscription à tant d'actions de la Compagnie X., pour laquelle vous avez versé tant, il vous a été attribué tant d'actions qui, à raison de tant pour le montant des versements de souscription et de répartition, exigent un versement de tant, soit une différence de tant, que vous voudrez bien verser à . . .

a quarter of the profits in excess of 4% on the bank's capital, is allotted to the State, le quart des bénéfices excédant 4 0/0 sur le capital de la banque, est attribué à l'État.

allotment (*n.*), attribution (*f.*); répartition (*f.*):

allotment to the founders of so many fully paid shares, attribution aux fondateurs de tant d'actions entièrement libérées.

shares of 10s., payable 2s. 6d. on application, 2s. 6d. on allotment, so many shillings on (*date*), actions de 10sh., payables 2sh. 6d. en souscrivant (*ou* à la souscription), 2sh. 6d. à la (*ou* lors de la) répartition, tant de schellings au (*date*) (*f.pl.*).

payment in full on allotment, libération à la répartition (*f.*).

allotment letter, avis d'attribution (*m.*); avis de répartition (*m.*); lettre d'avis de répartition (*f.*).

allotment money, versement de répartition (*m.*).

allottable (*adj.*), attribuable; répartissable.

allottee (pers.) (*n.*), attributaire (*m.* ou *f.*).

allow (*v.t.*). V. exemples :

to allow an expense appearing in an account, allouer une dépense portée dans un compte.

to allow a claim, admettre un recours.

to allow a bill to be protested, laisser protester un effet.

to allow one's money to remain idle, laisser dormir ses capitaux.

to allow one's debtor time to pay, accorder un délai à son débiteur.

to allow someone a discount, accorder (*ou* faire) un escompte à quelqu'un ; bénéficier (*ou* bonifier) quelqu'un d'une remise (*ou* d'un rabais).

to allow a discount of 5% on the gross amount of an invoice, accorder un escompte, faire une remise, de 5 p. 100 sur le montant brut d'une facture.

to allow 5% interest on deposits, bonifier (*ou* allouer) 5 0/0 d'intérêt aux dépôts.

allowable (*adj.*), allouable ; accordable :

allowable expense, dépense allouable (*f.*).

allowance (*n.*), allouance (*f.*); allocation (*f.*); tolérance (*f.*); bonification (*f.*); boni (*m.*); réfaction (*f.*); remise (*f.*); rabais (*m.*); déduction (*f.*); diminution (*f.*); ristourne (*f.*); ristorne (*f.*); indemnité (*f.*):

allowance of an expense appearing in an account, allouance, allocation, d'une dépense portée dans un compte.

a monthly allowance of so much, une allouance (*ou* une allocation) mensuelle de tant.

allowance for difference of quality, bonification, réfaction, pour écart de qualité.

an allowance of 2 per cent of the weight is made, for wastage in transit, on the weight of wet or dry goods, une tolérance de 2 p. cent du poids est accordée, pour déchet de route, sur le poids des marchandises liquides ou sèches.

the expression net indicates that there is no allowance of discount, l'expression net indique qu'il n'y a pas de bonification d'escompte (*f.*).

allowance for expenses (Income Tax), déduction pour dépenses.

banker who has, as profit, the allowance which the broker makes on the official commission rates, banquier qui a, comme bénéfice, la ristourne que fait l'agent sur le tarif officiel des courtages (*m.*).

allowance agreed in case of delay, indemnité convenue en cas de retard.

alloy (*n.*), alliage (*m.*).

alluring (*adj.*), alléchant, -e :

alluring proposition, proposition alléchante (*f.*).

almanac (*n.*), almanach (*m.*).

alongside (Abbrev.: **a/s.**), le long du bord ; le long :

goods received or delivered alongside (*or* alongside the ship), marchandises reçues ou livrées le long du bord (*ou* le long du bord du navire) (*ou* le long du navire) (*f.pl.*).

ship alongside the quay, navire le long du quai (*m.*).

alphabetical (*adj.*), alphabétique :

alphabetical index, répertoire alphabétique (*m.*).

alter (*v.t.*), changer ; modifier :

to alter one's plans, changer ses projets.

alter (to make a correction on a writing) (*v.t.*), surcharger :

altered or scratched consignment notes are not accepted, les lettres de voiture surchargées ou grattées ne sont pas admises (*f.pl.*).

alteration (*n.*), changement (*m.*); modification (*f.*) :

alteration in the articles of association, modification aux statuts.

alteration (word written over another as emendation; correction) (*n.*), surcharge (*f.*) :

to make an alteration, faire une surcharge.

register well kept, without erasures or alterations, registre bien tenu, sans ratures ni surcharges (*m.*).

alteration (marginal modification or addition to a document) (*n.*), renvoi (*m.*); renvoi en marge (*m.*) :

to initial an alteration, parafer un renvoi.

alternate (*adj.*), alternatif, -ive :

alternate director, administrateur alternatif (*m.*).

alternate (pers.) (*n.*), alternatif (*m.*).

alternative (*adj.*), alternatif, -ive :

alternative offer, offre alternative (*f.*).

alternative (*n.*), alternative (*f.*).

alternatively (*adv.*), alternativement:
account alternatively debtor and creditor, compte alternativement débiteur et créditeur (*m.*).

always afloat (said of a ship—in a charter party) (Abbrev.: **a.a.**), toujours à flot; toujours en flot. V. **so near thereunto,** etc., sous **so.**

amalgamate (*v.t.*), fusionner:
to amalgamate two railway companies, fusionner deux compagnies de chemins de fer.
the two amalgamating companies, les deux sociétés fusionnantes.

amalgamate (*v.i.*), fusionner; se fusionner:
when several companies amalgamate, lorsque plusieurs sociétés fusionnent.

amalgamation (*n.*), fusion (*f.*); fusionnement (*m.*):
amalgamation of several banks, fusion de plusieurs banques.

amalgamation agreement, traité de fusion (*m.*).

amass (*v.t.*), amasser; accumuler:
to amass money, a fortune, amasser, accumuler, de l'argent, une fortune.

ambassador (pers.) (*n.*), ambassadeur (*m.*).

ambition (*n.*), ambition (*f.*).

ambitious (*adj.*), ambitieux, -euse:
ambitious scheme, projet ambitieux (*m.*).

amend (*v.t.*), amender; rectifier; changer:
to amend a resolution, amender une proposition.
to amend an account, rectifier un compte.

amended (corrected) (*adj.*), rectificatif, -ive:
amended invoice, facture rectificative (*f.*).

amendment (modification of a resolution) (*n.*), amendement (*m.*):
to move an amendment, proposer un amendement.

amendment (of an account) (*n.*), rectification (*f.*).

amendments to entries (Customs), changements aux déclarations (*m.pl.*).

amicable (*adj.*), amiable:
amicable division, partage amiable (*m.*).

amortizable (*adj.*), amortissable.

amortization *or* **amortizement** (*n.*), amortissement (*m.*):
amortization of a loan, amortissement d'un emprunt.

amortize (*v.t.*), amortir.

amount (*n.*) (Abbrev.: **amt**), montant (*m.*); somme (*f.*); chiffre (*m.*); importance (*f.*); quantum (*m.*); quotité (*f.*); quantité (*f.*):
amount of an invoice, of a bill of exchange, montant d'une facture, d'un effet de commerce.
amount of money, somme d'argent.
amount at risk (Insce), somme en risque:
to declare (*or* to report) the amount at risk on receipt of advices, déclarer la somme en risque dès la réception d'avis.
amount brought forward *or* amount brought down (Bkkpg), somme reportée (*f.*); report (*m.*).
amount carried forward *or* amount carried down (Bkkpg), somme à reporter (*f.*); report (*m.*).

amount paid in advance, somme payée d'avance.
amount paid on account, acompte payé (*m.*); acompte versé (*m.*):
to deduct the amount paid on account from the total to be paid, déduire l'acompte versé du total à payer.
£000,000 (amount of the capital), £000 000 (chiffre du capital).
expenses in proportion to the amount of the firm's business, dépenses proportionnées à l'importance des affaires de la maison (*f.pl.*).
to fix the amount of damages to be allowed, fixer le quantum des dommages-intérêts à allouer.
the amount to be appropriated out of profits to form the reserve fund, la quotité à prélever sur les bénéfices pour composer le fonds de réserve.
amount short shipped, quantité embarquée en moins.

in one amount, en une fois; en une seule fois:
payment can be made in one amount or in (*or* by) instalments, le paiement peut se faire en une fois ou par versements échelonnés.
subscription payable in one amount, abonnement payable en une seule fois (*m.*).
issue in one amount, in one or more amounts, of 60,000 shares of £1 each, émission en une fois, en une ou plusieurs fois, de 60 000 actions de £1 chacune (*f.*).

amount (inscription at the head of a cash column) (*n.*), sommes (*f.pl.*):
amount column, colonne des sommes (*f.*).

amount (*v.i.*), monter; se chiffrer; s'élever:
the expenses amount to so much, la dépense monte à tant.
transactions which amount to several million pounds, opérations qui se chiffrent par (*ou* qui s'élèvent à) plusieurs millions de livres (*f.pl.*).

amounting to *or* **to the amount of,** s'élevant à; à concurrence de:
there are reserves amounting to £100,000, il existe des réserves à concurrence de 100 000 livres.

amount entered twice (Bkkpg), double emploi (*m.*):
to ascertain that there is neither omission nor amount entered twice in the entering up of the items, s'assurer qu'il n'y a ni omission ni double emploi dans l'enregistrement des articles.

amount of money invested, mise de fonds (*f.*); mise (*f.*):
profit which is equal to so much per cent on the amount of money invested, bénéfice qui correspond à tant pour cent de la mise de fonds (*m.*).

amount written off, amortissement (*m.*):
amount written off premises, amortissement sur immeuble (*ou* sur immeubles).
the amounts written off are shown in red, les amortissements figurent en rouge.

amounts to be made good (opp. to *contributing values*) (General Average), masse créancière (*f.*); masse active (*f.*); valeurs créancières (*f.pl.*); valeurs actives (*f.pl.*):
the damage and expenses which constitute the general average are called amounts to be made good, les dommages et dépenses qui constituent l'avarie commune s'appellent masse créancière.

Amsterdam time (Abbrev.: **A.T.**), heure d'Amsterdam (*f.*). (12.20 p.m. [midi 20] in relation to **West European time,** q.v.).

amusement shares, valeurs d'attractions (*f.pl.*).

analysis [**analyses** *pl.*] (*n.*), analyse (*f.*); dépouillement (*m.*); ventilation (*f.*); dissection (*f.*); décomposition (*f.*):
analysis of expense items, analyse des articles de dépenses.
analysis of expenses, of sundries account, dépouillement des frais, du compte divers.
analysis of the cost price into its chief components, décomposition du prix de revient en ses principaux éléments.

analysis book, livre de dépouillement (*m.*).

analysis column, colonne de dépouillement (*f.*); colonne de ventilation (*f.*).

analytic *or* **analytical** (*adj.*), analytique:
analytical table, table analytique (*f.*).

analytically (*adv.*), analytiquement.

analyzable *or* **analysable** (*adj.*), analysable.

analyze *or* **analyse** (*v.t.*), analyser; dépouiller; ventiler; faire le dépouillement de; disséquer; décomposer:
to analyze a transaction, a position, analyser une opération, une situation.
to analyze an account, dépouiller, faire le dépouillement d', disséquer, un compte.
to analyze the Sundries column, dépouiller, ventiler, la colonne Divers.

anchor (*n.*), ancre (*f.*).

anchor (*v.t.*), mouiller.

anchor (*v.i.*), mouiller.

anchorage (*n.*), mouillage (*m.*):
ship at anchorage in a port, navire en mouillage dans un port (*m.*).

anchorage (charges) (*n.*), droit d'ancrage (*m.*); droit d'amarrage (*m.*).

anchoring (*n.*), mouillage (*m.*).

angaria (Mar. Law) (*n.*), angarie (*f.*).

announce (*v.t.*), annoncer:
to announce the payment of a coupon, annoncer le paiement d'un coupon.

announcement (*n.*), annonce (*f.*):
announcement of a sale, annonce d'une vente.

annual (*adj.*), annuel, -elle:
annual accounts, comptes annuels (*m.pl.*).
annual charge *or* annual expense, dépense annuelle (*f.*).
annual income, revenu annuel (*m.*); rente (*f.*); année (*f.*).
annual ordinary general meeting, assemblée générale ordinaire annuelle (*f.*).
annual premium (Insce), prime annuelle (*f.*).
repayable by annual instalments. V. sous **repayable.**

annual (year book) (*n.*), annuaire (*m.*).

annually (*adv.*), annuellement.

annuitant (pers.) (*n.*), rentier, -ère.

annuity [**annuities** *pl.*] (*n.*), annuité (*f.*); rente à terme (*f.*); rente (*f.*):
life annuity, annuité à vie; rente viagère.

annul (*v.t.*), annuler; résilier; résoudre:
to annul a contract, annuler, résilier, résoudre, un contrat.

annullable (*adj.*), annulable; résoluble.

annulment (*n.*), annulation (*f.*); résiliation (*f.*); résiliement (*m.*); résilîment (*m.*); résolution (*f.*).

annum (*only in the phrase* per annum) (*n.*), an (*m.*):
5 per cent per annum, 5 pour cent l'an (*ou* par an).

answer (*n.*), réponse (*f.*):
answer to a letter, réponse à une lettre.

answer (to reply to) (*v.t.*), répondre à:
to answer a letter, répondre à une lettre.

answer for (**to**) (to be security for), répondre pour; répondre de; cautionner:
to answer for someone's honesty, répondre pour, répondre de, cautionner, la probité de quelqu'un.

antedate *or* **antedating** (*n.*) (Ant.: *postdate* or *postdating*), antidate (*f.*):
the antedating of a bill of lading pledges the responsibility of the master, l'antidate d'un connaissement engage la responsabilité du capitaine.

antedate (*v.t.*), antidater:
to antedate a contract, antidater un contrat.

anticipate (*v.t.*), anticiper:
to anticipate a payment by a week, anticiper un paiement de huit jours.

anticipated (*adj.*), anticipé, -e; espéré, -e:
anticipated freight, fret espéré (*m.*); fret anticipé (*m.*).
anticipated profit, profit espéré (*m.*); bénéfice espéré (*m.*):
if the anticipated profit is included in the insurance, si le profit espéré (*ou* le bénéfice espéré) est compris dans l'assurance.
insurance which also covers expenses and an anticipated profit, assurance qui couvre aussi des frais et un profit (*ou* un bénéfice) espéré (*f.*).

anticipation (*n.*), anticipation (*f.*):
anticipation of payment, anticipation de paiement.

antidumping (*n.*), antidumping (*m.*).

any denominations (of shares), toutes coupures (d'actions) (*f.pl.*).

apparel (of a ship) (*n.*), apparaux (d'un navire) (*m.pl.*).

apparent (*adj.*), apparent, -e:
apparent damage (to the contents of a package) (opp. to *hidden damage*), avaries apparentes (*f.pl.*).
apparent defect (opp. to *latent,* or *hidden, defect*), défaut apparent (*m.*); vice apparent (*m.*).
goods in apparent good order and condition, marchandises en bon état et conditionnement apparents (*f.pl.*).

apparently broken (reservation on a bill of lading, a consignment note), sonnant la casse.
appeal (Law) (*n.*), appel (*m.*).
appeal (*v.i.*), appeler ; faire appel :
to appeal from a judgment, appeler d'un jugement.
arbitration award appealed from, sentence arbitrale contre laquelle appel a été faite (*f.*).
the fact that the government has not appealed to public credit is the tangible proof of the restoration of the public finances, le fait que l'État n'a pas fait appel au crédit public est la preuve tangible de la restauration des finances publiques.
appeal court, cour d'appel (*f.*).
appealable (*adj.*), appelable.
appear (to be seen) (*v.i.*), apparaître ; figurer ; ressortir ; être porté, -e ; être inscrit, -e ; s'inscrire ; chiffrer :
item which appears among the liabilities on a balance sheet, in (*or* to) the debit of an account, in the books, article qui apparaît (*ou* qui figure) (*ou* qui ressort) au passif d'un bilan, au débit d'un compte, sur les livres (*m.*).
supplier who appears as a creditor on the books, fournisseur qui est porté comme créancier sur les livres (*m.*).
the value appearing in the books, la valeur chiffrée sur les livres.
the shares appear in the balance sheet at so much, les actions figurent (*ou* sont portées) (*ou* sont inscrites) (*ou* s'inscrivent) au bilan pour tant (*f.pl.*).
appear (Law) (*v.i.*), comparaître ; paraître :
to appear before a court, comparaître devant un tribunal ; paraître devant une cour.
appellant (*adj.*), appelant, -e.
appellant (pers.) (*n.*), appelant, -e.
append (*v.t.*), apposer :
endorser who appends his signature to a bill, endosseur qui appose sa signature sur un effet (*m.*).
appending (*n.*), apposition (*f.*).
applicant (petitioner) (pers.) (*n.*), demandeur, -euse :
applicant for licence *or* applicant for concession, demandeur en concession.
applicant (for an employment) (pers.) (*n.*), postulant, -e.
applicant (subscriber) (pers.) (*n.*), souscripteur (*m.*) :
the applicant fills up and signs an application form, le souscripteur remplit et signe un bulletin de souscription.
application (capacity of being applied or used) (*n.*), application (*f.*) ; affectation (*f.*) :
applications to a floating policy (declarations), applications à une police d'abonnement.
the worth of a building independent of its industrial application, la valeur d'un bâtiment indépendante de son affectation industrielle.
application (formal request ; claim) (*n.*), demande (*f.*) ; réclamation (*f.*) :

application for repayment of duties, demande en remboursement de droits.
application for relief, for discharge (Taxation), demande en dégrèvement, en décharge.
prices on application, prix sur demande (*m.pl.*).
applications concerning money orders which have miscarried, réclamations concernant les mandats non parvenus.
application (subscription) (*n.*), souscription (*f.*) :
application for shares, souscription à des actions.
shares payable in full on application, actions payables entièrement lors de la souscription (*f.pl.*).
shares of 10s., payable 2s. 6d. on application, 2s. 6d. on allotment, so many shillings on (*date*), actions de 10sh., payables 2sh. 6d. en souscrivant (*ou* à la souscription), 2sh. 6d. à la (*ou* lors de la) répartition, tant de schellings au (*date*) (*f.pl.*).
application and allotment sheet, feuille d'émission (*f.*).
application form, bulletin de souscription (*m.*).
application money, versement de souscription (*m.*).
application receipt, reçu de souscription (*m.*) ; récépissé de souscription (*m.*).
application rights, droits de souscription (*m.pl.*) ; privilège de souscription (*m.*). V. exemple sous **right.**
apply (*v.t. & v.i.*). V. exemples :
the names of two firms to which the bank can apply for information, les noms de deux maisons auxquelles la banque peut s'adresser pour obtenir des renseignements (*m.pl.*).
for freights and further particulars apply to the agents, pour frets et autres renseignements s'adresser aux agents.
apply for them by telegraph if they are not sent by return of post, les réclamer par télégraphe s'ils ne sont pas transmis par le retour du courrier.
to apply an instalment to a certain debt, affecter un paiement à compte à une certaine dette.
to apply for a situation, solliciter un emploi.
to apply for so many shares in a company, souscrire à tant d'actions d'une société.
to apply for the whole of the loan, of a capital, souscrire l'intégralité de l'emprunt, du capital.
to apply as of right, souscrire à titre irréductible : .
to apply for excess shares, souscrire à titre réductible :
the present shareholders are entitled to apply as of right for one new share for each old share, in consideration of the payment of so much per share : they also have the option of presenting applications for excess shares by paying so much per share, les actionnaires actuels ont le droit de souscrire à titre irréductible à une action nouvelle pour chaque action ancienne, moyennant un versement de tant par action : ils ont également la faculté de présenter des souscriptions à titre réductible en versant tant par action.

to apply oneself to business, s'appliquer aux affaires.

appoint (*v.t.*), nommer; désigner; constituer: to appoint a committee, the first directors of a company, nommer un comité, les premiers administrateurs d'une société.

to appoint an arbitrator, désigner un arbitre.

to appoint a solicitor, constituer avoué.

appoint as proxy (to), donner pouvoir à: I the undersigned (*name*) hereby appoint as my proxy Mr A., and, failing him, Mr B., je soussigné (*nom*) donne, par les présentes, pouvoir à M. A., ou, à son défaut, à M. B.

appointed by the articles (*or* **by the articles of association**), statutaire: manager appointed by the articles, gérant statutaire (*m.*).

appointment *or* **appointing** (nomination) (*n.*), nomination (*f.*); désignation (*f.*); constitution (*f.*).

appointment (agreement to meet) (*n.*), rendez-vous (*m.*): to make an appointment with someone, donner rendez-vous (*ou* un rendez-vous) à quelqu'un.

appointments (accommodation) (*n.pl.*), aménagement (*m.*); emménagement (*m.*): the appointments of the ship are magnificent, l'aménagement (*ou* l'emménagement) du navire est luxueux.

apportion (*v.t.*), répartir; ventiler: to apportion the incidental expenses according to a proportion to be determined, répartir, ventiler, les frais accidentels d'après un quantum à déterminer.

to apportion the average according to law and as agreed by the parties, répartir les avaries d'après la loi et les conventions des parties.

apportionable (*adj.*), répartissable.

apportionment (*n.*), répartition (*f.*); ventilation (*f.*): only general averages give rise to apportionment; particular averages are borne and paid by the owner of the thing which has sustained the damage or occasioned the expense, seules les avaries communes donnent lieu à répartition; les avaries particulières sont supportées et payées par le propriétaire de la chose qui a essuyé le dommage ou occasionné la dépense.

pro rata apportionment between the parties concerned of the losses resulting from the sacrifice (adjustment of general average), répartition proportionnelle entre les intéressés des pertes résultant du sacrifice.

appraise (*v.t.*), priser.

appraisement (*n.*), prisée (*f.*).

appraiser (pers.) (*n.*), priseur (*m.*); commissaire-priseur (*m.*).

appreciable (marked) (*adj.*), appréciable; sensible: an appreciable rise in price, une sensible (*ou* appréciable) augmentation de prix.

hardly appreciable changes, changements peu appréciables (*m.pl.*).

appreciate (*v.t.*), améliorer.

appreciate (*v.i.*), s'améliorer: in time, certain stocks appreciate, others depreciate, avec le temps, certaines valeurs s'améliorent, d'autres se déprécient.

appreciation (*n.*) (Ant.: *depreciation*), amélioration (*f.*); plus-value (*f.*): appreciation of (*or* in) prices, amélioration des cours; plus-value sur les cours.

appreciation of assets, of assets brought into a business, plus-value d'actif, des apports.

apprentice (pers.) (*n.*), novice (*m.*).

approbation (*n.*), approbation (*f.*); agrément (*m.*); sanction (*f.*): to ask for someone's approbation, solliciter l'agrément de quelqu'un.

appropriate (to set apart for a particular purpose) (*v.t.*), consacrer; distraire; affecter; prélever; répartir; attribuer; doter: to appropriate funds to the redemption of an annuity, consacrer, affecter, des fonds au rachat d'une annuité.

to appropriate so much out of one's savings, distraire, prélever, tant sur ses économies.

sum appropriated from the reserve to write off the amount of an embezzlement, somme prélevée sur la réserve pour amortir le montant d'un détournement (*f.*).

when the balance sheet is completed, the board decides the amount of the reserves to be appropriated out of profits and the dividend to be recommended to the shareholders, quand le bilan est achevé, le conseil d'administration détermine l'importance des réserves à prélever sur les bénéfices et le dividende à proposer aux actionnaires.

to appropriate to a special fund for depreciation a sum of so many pounds, doter un fonds spécial pour amortissements d'une somme de tant de livres.

appropriate (to take for one's own use) (*v.t.*), s'approprier; encoffrer: to appropriate money left on deposit, encoffrer de l'argent donné en dépôt.

appropriation (setting apart to a specific use, or money so set apart) (*n.*), distraction (*f.*); affectation (*f.*); prélèvement (*m.*); répartition (*f.*); attribution (*f.*); dotation (*f.*): to make an appropriation for distribution among the staff, faire une distraction pour être distribuée (*ou* un prélèvement pour être distribué) aux employés.

appropriation of the net profit, in accordance with the provisions of the articles or the resolutions of the shareholders' meeting, répartition (*ou* affectation) du bénéfice net, conformément aux prescriptions statutaires ou aux décisions de l'assemblée des actionnaires.

appropriation to the reserve, dotation, attribution, à la réserve.

appropriation (application of the property of a debtor to one of several debts) (Law) (*n.*), imputation (*f.*); imputation de paiement (*f.*): appropriation to a debt, imputation sur une dette.

approval (*n.*), approbation (*f.*); agrément (*m.*); sanction (*f.*) :
approval of the report and accounts by the shareholders, approbation des rapports et des comptes par les actionnaires.
the approval of the board is required in order to become a shareholder in certain companies, il faut l'agrément du conseil pour devenir actionnaire de certaines sociétés.
on approval (Com.) (often contracted to : **on appro.**), à condition ; sous condition.
approve *or* **approve of** (*v.t.*), approuver ; agréer ; sanctionner :
to approve a proposal, approuver, agréer, une proposition.
to approve the acts of an agent, approuver, sanctionner, les actes d'un mandataire.
securities approved by the bank, valeurs agréées par la banque (*f.pl.*).
approved place (for a bonded warehouse), localité agréée (pour un entrepôt légal) (*f.*).
approved society (friendly society), société approuvée (*f.*).
approximate (*adj.*), approximatif, -ive :
approximate calculation, calcul approximatif (*m.*).
approximately (*adv.*), approximativement.
approximation (*n.*), approximation (*f.*).
Arabic numerals *or* **Arabic figures,** chiffres arabes (*m.pl.*).
arbitrage *or* **arbitraging** (Banking) (*n.*), arbitrage (*m.*) ; arbitrage de banque (*m.*) :
arbitrage (*or* arbitraging) in bills (*or* in exchange), in bullion, arbitrage sur les lettres de change, sur les matières d'or et d'argent.
arbitrage of exchange, arbitrage de change.
arbitrage *or* **arbitraging** (Stock Exch.) (*n.*), arbitrage (*m.*) ; arbitrage de place à place (*m.*) (entre son propre pays et une place à l'étranger.—Cf. **shunting**) :
arbitrage (*or* arbitraging) in stocks, arbitrage sur des valeurs.
arbitrage has as effect the levelling of prices on all the markets of the world, les arbitrages ont pour effet de niveler les cours sur tous les marchés du monde.
arbitrage share, titre d'arbitrage (*m.*) :
arbitrage shares with Paris, titres d'arbitrage avec Paris.
arbitrage syndicate, syndicat arbitragiste (*m.*).
arbitrager *or* **arbitrageur** *or* **arbitragist** (*n.*) *or* **arbitrage dealer** (pers.), arbitragiste (*m.*).
arbitrary address (Teleg.), adresse de convention (*f.*) ; adresse conventionnelle (*f.*).
arbitrary assessment (Income Tax), imposition d'office (*f.*) ; taxation d'office (*f.*) :
to be assessed arbitrarily for having failed to make a return, être taxé (-e) d'office pour défaut de déclaration.
arbitrary name (Teleg.), nom de convention (*m.*) ; nom conventionnel (*m.*).
arbitrary price, prix arbitraire (*m.*).
arbitrate (*v.t.*), arbitrer.
to be arbitrated upon, être arbitré, -e ; s'arbitrer :

these damages can be arbitrated upon, ces dommages peuvent s'arbitrer (*m.pl.*).
arbitrated par *or* **arbitrated par of exchange,** pair politique (*m.*) ; pair proportionnel (*m.*).
arbitration (*n.*), arbitrage (*m.*) :
arbitration in case of strikes, for settlement of disputes which may arise on the subject of the interpretation or application of the said arrangements, arbitrage en cas de grèves, pour le règlement des contestations qui peuvent s'élever au sujet de l'interprétation et de l'application desdits arrangements.
arbitration for quality, for condition (Produce Exch.), arbitrage de qualité, de conditionnement.
amount awarded by arbitration, somme adjugée par arbitrage (*f.*).
arbitration of exchange, arbitrage du change.
arbitration award, décision arbitrale (*f.*) ; sentence arbitrale (*f.*) ; sentence d'arbitrage (*f.*) ; jugement arbitral (*m.*) ; arbitrage (*m.*).
arbitration board, conseil d'arbitrage (*m.*).
arbitration bond, compromis d'arbitrage (*m.*).
arbitration clause, clause compromissoire (*f.*) ; clause d'arbitrage (*f.*) ; clause arbitrale (*f.*) :
an arbitration clause authorizing the submission to arbitrators of eventual disputes, une clause compromissoire permettant de soumettre à des arbitres les contestations éventuelles.
arbitration court, cour d'arbitrage (*f.*).
arbitration fees, droits d'arbitrage (*m.pl.*).
arbitrator *or* **arbiter** (pers.) (*n.*), arbitre (*m.*) :
any dispute between parties to be settled by arbitrators whose award shall be final, toute contestation entre parties sera tranchée par des arbitres statuant en dernier ressort (*f.*).
archives (*n.pl.*), archives (*f.pl.*) :
documents kept in the archives, documents conservés dans les archives (*m.pl.*).
are you there ? (Teleph.), allô !
area (*n.*), zone (*f.*) ; circonscription (*f.*) :
delivery area (Rly., etc.), zone, circonscription, de remise à domicile.
arise (*v.i.*), s'élever ; survenir :
if difficulties arise, s'il s'élève des difficultés.
arithmetic (*n.*), arithmétique (*f.*).
arithmetical *or* **arithmetic** (*adj.*), arithmétique :
arithmetical calculation, calcul arithmétique (*m.*).
arithmetical discount (opp. to *bank discount*), escompte en dedans (*m.*) ; escompte rationnel (*m.*).
arithmetically (*adv.*), arithmétiquement.
arithmetician (pers.) (*n.*), arithméticien, -enne.
arrange (*v.t.*), arranger ; accommoder ; débattre ; arbitrer :
to arrange a matter amicably, arranger, accommoder, une affaire à l'amiable.
to arrange one's papers, arranger ses papiers.
at an arranged price, à prix débattu.
in consideration of additional premium to be arranged, moyennant surprime à débattre (*ou* à arbitrer).

arrangement (*n.*),   arrangement (*m.*) ;   accommodement (*m.*) :
  to make an arrangement with someone,   faire un arrangement avec quelqu'un.
to be a matter for arrangement, être à débattre :
  the conditions of discounting are a matter for arrangement between customer and banker, les conditions d'escompte sont à débattre entre client et banquier (*f.pl.*).
  price a matter for arrangement,   prix à débattre (*m.*).
arrangement with creditors,   concordat (*m.*) ; convenio (*m.*) ; transaction (*f.*).
arrears (*n.pl.*),   arriéré (*m.*) :
  arrears of rent, of work,   arriéré de loyer, de travail.
in arrears *or* **in arrear,** en arrière ; arriéré, -e ; en retard ; retardataire :
  to be in arrear with one's rent,   être en arrière pour ses loyers.
  rent in arrear,   loyer en arrière (*m.*) ; loyer arriéré (*m.*).
  taxpayer in arrears,   contribuable en retard (*m.* ou *f.*) ;   contribuable retardataire (*m.* ou *f.*).
  shareholders in arrear with calls,   actionnaires en retard de versements (*m.pl.*).
arrest (Internat. Law) (*n.*),   arrêt (*m.*) :
  arrests of princes, of rulers, of a foreign power, arrêts de princes, de gouvernants, d'une puissance étrangère.
arrest (*v.t.*),   arrêter :
  ship which is arrested on the voyage by order of a foreign power,   navire qui est arrêté en voyage par ordre d'une puissance étrangère (*m.*).
arrival (*n.*),   arrivée (*f.*) ; arrivage (*m.*) :
  arrival of goods, of a stock of Australian gold, arrivage, arrivée, de marchandises, d'un stock d'or australien.
  arrival of a train, of the ship with her cargo at the port of destination,   arrivée d'un train, du navire avec sa cargaison au port de destination.
  arrivals and sailings,   arrivages et départs ; arrivées et départs.
arrival platform (Rly.) (opp. to *departure platform*),   quai d'arrivée (*m.*).
arrival station,   gare d'arrivée (*f.*).
arrive (*v.i.*),   arriver ; parvenir :
  to arrive safely,   arriver à bon port :
  whether the ship arrives safely or is lost on the voyage,   que le navire arrive à bon port ou se perde pendant le voyage.
  goods arriving by sea from abroad,   marchandises arrivant par mer de l'étranger (*f.pl.*).
  whether the goods arrive at their destination or not,   que les marchandises parviennent ou non à leur destination.
  (*steamer*) *X.,* from Batavia, arrived (*or* arrd) (*or* a.) Marseilles 31 (*date*) (Shipping News), (*steamer*) *X.* arrivé à Marseille le 31 (*date*), de Batavia (Mouvement des Navires).
  sale to arrive *or* sale subject to safe arrival, vente à l'heureuse arrivée (*f.*).

article (object) (*n.*),   article (*m.*) ;   objet (*m.*) ; effets (*m.pl. seulement*) ;   envoi (*m.*) :
  article of merchandise,   article de marchandise.
  article of luggage (*or* of baggage),   article de bagage ;   bagage (*m.*) :
  declaration of the contents of an article of luggage,   déclaration du contenu d'un bagage (*f.*).
  articles of stationery,   articles de papeterie.
  registered article (Post),   objet recommandé ; envoi recommandé.
  articles for the personal'use of the passenger, objets affectés à l'usage personnel du voyageur ; effets servant à l'usage personnel du passager.
article (division ; head) (*n.*),   article (*m.*) :
  the articles of an agreement, of a treaty,   les articles d'un contrat, d'un traité.
  a newspaper article,   a financial article,   un article de journal, un article financier.
articled clerk,   stagiaire (*m.* ou *f.*).
articles (list of the crew) (*n.pl.*),   rôle d'équipage (*m.*) ; rôle de l'équipage (*m.*) ; rôle d'armement (*m.*).
articles (apprenticeship) (*n.pl.*),   stage (*m.*) :
  five years' articles with a professional accountant,   stage de cinq années chez un expert-comptable.
articles of association *or simply* **articles** (*n.pl.*), statuts (*m.pl.*) :   (*Note :*—In France, the *memorandum and articles* are all in one and are called *statuts.*   Cf. **memorandum of association** and note thereunder.)
  the powers of the board are defined by the company's articles,   les pouvoirs du conseil d'administration sont définis par les statuts sociaux (*m.pl.*).
  of the articles (*or* **the articles of association**), des statuts ; statutaire :
  provisions of the articles of association, prescriptions statutaires (*f.pl.*).
  appointed by the articles (*or* **by the articles of association**),   statutaire :
  manager appointed by the articles,   gérant statutaire (*m.*).
  provided by the articles (*or* **by the articles of association**),   statutaire :
  reserve provided by the articles,   réserve statutaire (*f.*).
  in accordance with the articles *or* **under the articles,**   statutairement :
  percentage of profits apportioned in accordance with the articles,   tantièmes attribués statutairement (*m.pl.*).
articles of partnership,   contrat de société (*m.*) ; contrat d'association (*m.*).
artificial silk shares,   valeurs de soie artificielle (*f.pl.*).
artificial word (pronounceable group of letters having the appearance of, and opposed to, a *real word*) (Teleg.),   mot artificiel (*m.*).
artillery (*n.*),   artillerie (*f.*).
as at (value in account as at),   valeur (*f.*) ; date de valeur (*f.*) ;   date d'entrée en valeur (*f.*) ; échéance (*f.*) :

we have debited your account with £000 as at 1st March, nous avons débité votre compte de £000 valeur (*ou* échéance) 1er mars.

as at (balance sheet heading). V. sous **balance sheet.**

as customary. V. sous **customary.**

as fast as steamer can deliver according to the custom of the port, aussi vite que le vapeur pourra délivrer d'après les usages de place.

as per, suivant; dont:
as per advice (notice on a bill of exchange) (opp. to *without advice* or *without other advice*), suivant avis.
as per list, as per your instructions, suivant inventaire, suivant vos instructions.
payments as per details (*or* as per particulars) in cash book, paiements dont (*ou* suivant) détail au livre de caisse (*m.pl.*).

as per contra. V. sous **contra.**

as required *or* **as and when required,** au fur et à mesure des besoins; en une ou plusieurs fois, à toute époque:
board authorized to borrow a sum of £2,000,000 as required (*or* as and when required), conseil d'administration autorisé à emprunter une somme de £ 2 millions au fur et à mesure des besoins.
at the ordinary meeting, held on 29th April, the board were authorized to proceed, as and when required, and under the conditions they may resolve on, to the issue of debentures to a maximum amount of £100,000, it being understood that the proceeds may be used for redemption in advance of debentures in circulation, l'assemblée ordinaire, tenue le 29 avril, a autorisé le conseil d'administration à procéder, en une ou plusieurs fois, à toute époque qu'il jugera convenable et dans les conditions qu'il décidera, à l'émission d'obligations pour un montant maximum de £100 000, étant entendu que le produit en pourra être utilisé au remboursement anticipé d'obligations en circulation (*f.*).

as the case may be, selon le cas.

ascertain (*v.t.*), constater; se rendre compte de:
to ascertain a fact, the profits, the extent of the damage, constater un fait, les profits, l'importance des avaries.
to ascertain one's position, se rendre compte de sa situation.
to ascertain the cost, the cost of (Accountancy). V. sous **cost** (*v.i.*) & **cost** (*v.t.*).

ashore (on land) (*adv.*), à terre:
goods stored ashore or afloat, marchandises emmagasinées à terre ou à flot (*f.pl.*).

ask *or* **ask for** (*v.t.*), prier; demander; solliciter:
to ask the telegraph office to repeat the mutilated word or words, prier le bureau du télégraphe de faire répéter le ou les mots mutilés.
to ask a favour, demander une faveur.
to ask advice *or* to ask for advice, demander des conseils.
to ask for leave of absence, solliciter son congé.

to ask so much for a thing, demander tant pour une chose; faire une chose tant.
to ask too much for an article, demander trop pour, surfaire, un article.
the chairman then asked the shareholders whether they had any comments to make or questions to put *or* the chairman then asked if there were any shareholders who had questions to put, M. le président demande ensuite aux actionnaires s'ils ont des observations à présenter ou des explications à réclamer; M. le président offre ensuite la parole à ceux des actionnaires qui ont des explications à réclamer.

assailing thieves (Mar. Insce), voleurs à main armée (*m.pl.*).

assemble (*v.t.*), assembler.

assemble (*v.i.*), s'assembler.

assess (Taxation) (*v.t.*), coter; cotiser; imposer; répartir; taxer:
the profits assessed under the schedule of income from trade, les bénéfices cotisés à la cédule des revenus commerciaux (*m.pl.*).

assessable (*adj.*), cotisable; imposable; répartissable; taxable; taxatif, -ive:
profit exempt as not being assessable to tax, bénéfice exonéré comme n'étant pas cotisable à l'impôt (*m.*).
in principle, the assessable income is the figure returned by the taxpayer (Income Tax), en principe, le revenu imposable est le chiffre déclaré par le contribuable.

assessment (Taxation) (*n.*), cote (*f.*); cotisation (*f.*); imposition (*f.*); répartition (*f.*); taxation (*f.*):
assessment on landed property, cote foncière.
assessment on income, cote mobilière.
assessment of taxes, répartition de contributions.
the income of the year preceding the year of assessment, le revenu de l'année immédiatement antérieure à l'année d'imposition.
arbitrary assessment (Income Tax), imposition d'office; taxation d'office.

assessment (apportionment of a contribution) (*n.*), cotisation (*f.*):
in case of mutual insurance, the remuneration may be given in the form of an assessment, en cas d'assurance mutuelle, la rémunération peut être donnée sous la forme de cotisation.

assessment (of a loss) (Fire Insce) (*n.*), règlement (d'un sinistre) (*m.*).

assessment book (Income Tax), rôle de cotisation (*m.*); rôle (*m.*):
the assessment books are made out by the inspector in accordance with the returns made by the parties concerned, after examination and amendment if necessary, les rôles sont établis par le contrôleur d'après les déclarations faites par les intéressés, après vérification et rectification s'il y a lieu.

assessor (of taxes) (pers.) (*n.*), répartiteur (*m.*), commissaire répartiteur (*m.*) (de contributions).

assessor (expert adviser) (pers.) (*n.*), assesseur (*m.*).

asset (*n.*) (opp. to *liability*), actif (*m.*); valeur (*f.*); valeur active (*f.*); capital (*m.*): [*In the pl.* **assets**:—actif; actifs; valeurs actives; valeurs formant l'actif; masse active (*f.*); capitaux]:

contingent asset [contingent assets *pl.*], actif éventuel [actif éventuel *ou* actifs éventuels *pl.*].

the excess of assets over liabilities, l'excédent de l'actif sur le passif (*m.*).

overvaluation of the assets in a balance sheet, majoration des valeurs formant l'actif d'un bilan (*f.*).

fixed assets *or* permanent assets *or* capital assets, capitaux fixes; capital fixe; capital immobilisé; actif immobilisé; valeurs immobilisées. V. exemple sous **fixed.**

Note :—In French balance sheets, the assets appear on the left hand side and the liabilities on the right. This is the reverse of English practice.

asset accounts (Bkkpg), comptes de valeurs (*m.pl.*); comptes du gérant (*m.pl.*); comptes de l'exploitation (*m.pl.*).

assets brought in (*or* **into a business**) *or* **assets transferred** *or* **assets taken over from vendor,** apport (*m.*); apports (*m.pl.*):

appreciation of assets brought into a business, plus-value des apports (*f.*).

Cf. **vendors' shares.**

assets in kind or money brought in (*or* taken over) (*or* transferred), apports en nature ou en numéraire.

assets transferred to company for a valuable consideration, apport en société fait à titre onéreux.

assign (pers.) (*n.*), ayant cause (*m.*); ayant droit (*m.*):

bill of lading to order or assigns, connaissement à ordre ou aux ayants droit (*m.*).

assign (*v.t.*), céder.

assign (to make over vendor assets) (*v.t.*), apporter; faire apport :

Mr X. assigns to the company the patents taken out or applied for in his name, M. X. apporte (*ou* fait apport) à la société des brevets pris ou demandés à son nom.

assignee (of a debt) (pers.) (*n.*), cessionnaire (d'une créance) (*m.* ou *f.*).

assignee in bankruptcy, syndic de faillite (*m.*).

assignment (*n.*), cession (*f.*); cession-transport (*f.*); transport-cession (*m.*):

assignment of property (to creditors), cession de biens.

assignment of debts (or other incorporeal property), cession-transport, transport-cession, cession, de créances.

assignment (of assets by a vendor) (*n.*), apport (*m.*):

assignment of a patent, of a mining licence, apport d'un brevet, d'une concession de mines.

Cf. **transfer** (of assets by a vendor) and note thereunder.

assignor (pers.) (*n.*), cédant, -e.

assist (*v.t.*), assister; aider; secourir; porter secours à :

to assist a vessel in distress, assister, secourir, porter secours à, un navire en détresse.

assistance (*n.*), assistance (*f.*); aide (*f.*); secours (*m.*):

assistance at sea, to a ship in distress, assistance en mer, à un navire en détresse.

assistance is the help given by one ship to another ship in case of danger; danger is an essential condition of assistance; in the absence of danger, it is not assistance, but towage, l'assistance est le secours prêté par un navire à un autre en cas de danger; le danger est une condition essentielle de l'assistance; en l'absence de danger, il y a non pas assistance, mais remorquage.

to come to someone's assistance, venir en aide à quelqu'un.

assistant (pers.) (*n.*), aide (*m.* ou *f.*). Cf. **shop assistant.**

assistant accountant, aide-comptable (*m.* ou *f.*); sous-agent comptable (*m.*).

assistant cashier, sous-caissier (*m.*).

assistant manager, sous-directeur (*m.*); sous-chef (*m.*).

assistant manageress, sous-directrice (*f.*).

assistant managing director, administrateur sous-délégué (*m.*).

assistant member of a committee, membre adjoint à un comité (*m.*).

assistant secretary, sous-secrétaire (*m.*); secrétaire adjoint (*m.*).

assistant station master, sous-chef de gare (*m.*).

association (*n.*), association (*f.*):

commercial travellers' association, association des voyageurs de commerce.

Cf. **guarantee association.**

association not for profit, association (*f.*). *Note :*—In France, the word *association* in the legal sense means an *association not for profit*, and is opposed to *société*, a company for the acquisition of gain.

assurance (Insce) (*n.*), assurance (*f.*): (*Note :*—The words *assurance*, *assure*, etc., are the older forms of *insurance*, *insure*, etc., and are now used only, but not exclusively, for life and marine insurance. Cf. **insurance, insure,** etc.)

life assurance, assurance sur la vie; assurance-vie.

assurance company, compagnie d'assurance (*f.*); compagnie d'assurances (*f.*); société d'assurance (*ou* d'assurances) (*f.*).

assurance policy, police d'assurance (*f.*).

assure (to insure) (*v.t.*), faire assurer; assurer :

to assure one's life, faire assurer sur sa vie.

assure (to insure) (*v.i.*), s'assurer; se faire assurer.

assured [**assured** *pl.*] (pers.) (*n.*), assuré, -e.

assurer (pers.) (*n.*), assureur (*m.*).

at a premium to be arranged, moyennant prime à débattre.

at railway station, to be called for, en gare ; gare restante ; bureau restant :
delivery at railway station, to be called for, livraison en gare (*f.*) ; remise gare restante (*f.*).

at sea, en mer :
ship at sea, navire en mer (*m.*).

at ship's rail, sous palan ; sous vergues. V. exemple sous syn. **under ship's derrick.**

Atlantic liner, paquebot transatlantique (*m.*) ; transatlantique (*m.*).

attach (to annex) (*v.t.*), annexer ; joindre :
to attach to the consignment note the documents which are required to comply with the customs formalities, annexer, joindre, à la lettre de voiture les documents qui sont nécessaires à l'accomplissement des formalités de douane.

attach (to cause to come into operation) (*v.t.*), faire courir :
when the regulation of a port attaches demurrage during the stoppage of the steamer, lorsque le règlement d'un port fait courir les surestaries pendant l'arrêt du steamer.

attach (to come into operation) (*v.i.*), commencer à courir ; prendre cours ; courir :
the risk under this policy attaches from the time of loading on board the export vessel, le risque couvert par la présente police commence à courir (*ou* prend cours) (*ou* court) dès le moment du chargement à bord du navire d'exportation.
Cf. exemple sous **attachment** (of an insurance).

attaché (pers.) (*n.*), attaché (*m.*) :
commercial attaché, attaché commercial.

attachment (a slip or small piece of paper stuck on a bill of lading or an insurance policy and containing a clause or reservation) (*n.*), papillon (*m.*) :
special attachment stuck on a bill of lading referring to the non liability clause, papillon spécial collé sur un connaissement se référant à la clause d'irresponsabilité.

attachment (of an insurance) (commencement or duration ; on risk) (*n.*), effet (d'une assurance) (*m.*) :
the attachment of the insurance has ceased *or* the insurance has ceased to attach, l'effet de l'assurance a cessé.

attachment of risk (Insce), mise en risques (*f.*).

attack (to impugn) (*v.t.*), attaquer :
to attack a contract, attaquer un contrat.

attain (*v.t.*), atteindre.

attend (to be present at) (*v.t.*), assister à :
to attend a board meeting, assister à un conseil des administrateurs.

attend to the correspondence (to), faire la correspondance.

attendance (audience) (*n.*), assistance (*f.*) :
there was a good attendance at the general meeting, il y avait une nombreuse assistance à l'assemblée générale.

attendance book, registre de présence (*m.*).

attendance sheet, feuille de présence (*f.*).

attendant (man travelling in charge of animals sent by railway) (*n.*), conducteur (*m.*) :
race horses accompanied by an attendant, chevaux de course accompagnés d'un conducteur (*m.pl.*).

attendant of call office (Teleph.), gérant (-e) de cabine.

attest (*v.t.*), attester ; constater :
to attest a fact, attester, constater, un fait.
in France, dishonour by non payment of a bill of exchange should be attested the day after the day of maturity by an act called protest for non payment, en France, le refus de paiement d'un effet de commerce doit être constaté le lendemain du jour de l'échéance par un acte que l'on nomme protêt faute de paiement.

attorney [**attorneys** *pl.*] (*n.*) *or* **attorney in fact** (pers.), fondé de pouvoir (*m.*) ; fondé de pouvoirs (*m.*) ; mandataire (*m.* ou *f.*).

attorney (*n.*) *or* **attorney at law** (U.S.A.), avocat (*m.*).

attract (*v.t.*), attirer :
to be attracted by big profits, être attiré (-e) par de gros bénéfices.
to attract capital, attirer les capitaux.

auction (*n.*), enchère (*f.*) ; enchères (*f.pl.*) ; encan (*m.*) ; criée (*f.*) :
to sell a house by (*or* at) auction, vendre une maison à l'enchère (*ou* aux enchères) (*ou* à l'encan) (*ou* à la criée).

auctioneer (pers.) (*n.*), commissaire-priseur (*m.*).

audit *or* **auditing** (*n.*), vérification (*f.*) ; vérification comptable (*f.*) :
audit of accounts, vérification des comptes.

audit (*v.t.*), vérifier :
to audit the books (*or* the accounts), the cash in hand, vérifier les livres (*ou* les écritures), les encaisses.

audit committee, comité de censure (*m.*).

auditor (pers.) (*n.*), commissaire des comptes (*m.*) ; commissaire aux comptes (*m.*) ; commissaire-vérificateur (*m.*) ; commissaire vérificateur des comptes (*m.*) ; commissaire de surveillance (*m.*) ; commissaire (*m.*) ; censeur (*m.*) ; commissaire-censeur (*m.*) ; vérificateur comptable (*m.*).

auditors' report, rapport des commissaires (*ou* des commissaires aux comptes) (*m.*).

auditorship (*n.*), commissariat de comptes (*m.*).

augment (*v.t.*), augmenter.

augment (*v.i.*), augmenter ; s'augmenter.

augmentation (*n.*), augmentation (*f.*).

authenticate (*v.t.*), authentiquer :
to authenticate a document, authentiquer un acte.

authority [**authorities** *pl.*] (legal or rightful power) (*n.*), autorité (*f.*) :
the authority of the laws, of a manager, l'autorité des lois, d'un directeur.

authority (government) (*n.*), autorité (*f.*) ; pouvoir (*m.*) :
port sanitary authority, autorité sanitaire du port.
public authorities, pouvoirs publics.

authorization (*n.*), autorisation (*f.*).

authorize (*v.t.*), autoriser.

authorize the payment of (to), mandater :
to authorize the payment of travelling expenses, mandater des frais de voyage.

authorized (*adj.*), autorisé, -e :
the authorized note currency of a bank, la circulation autorisée des billets d'une banque.

authorized capital, capital social (*m.*) ; capital nominal (*m.*) :
the authorized capital of a company, le capital social (*ou* le capital nominal) d'une société (*ou* d'une compagnie).
company with an authorized capital of so much, société au capital nominal de tant (*f.*).

authorized clerk (Stock Exch.), teneur de carnet (*m.*) ; commis principal (*m.*).

autograph book (Banking), livre de signatures (*m.*).

automatic (*adj.*), automatique :
automatic bookkeeping machine for bank ledgers and statements, machine comptable automatique pour comptes courants banque et relevés (*f.*).
automatic bookkeeping machine for dividend work, machine comptable automatique-coupons (*f.*).
automatic bookkeeping machine for pay roll work, machine comptable automatique pour travaux de paie (*f.*).
automatic bookkeeping machine for posting ledgers and statements, machine comptable automatique pour comptes courants et relevés (*f.*).
automatic bookkeeping machine for public utility consumers' accounting, machine comptable automatique pour compagnies de distribution d'énergie (*f.*).
automatic bookkeeping machine for stores records work, machine comptable automatique pour inventaire permanent (*f.*).
automatic exchange (Teleph.) (opp. to *manual exchange*), bureau central automatique (*m.*) ; bureau automatique (*m.*) ; poste central automatique (*m.*).

automatically (*adv.*), automatiquement ; d'office :
loan renewed automatically, emprunt renouvelé automatiquement (*ou* d'office) (*m.*).

automobile (*n.*), automobile (*m.* ou *f.*) ; auto (*m.* ou *f.*).

avail oneself of a right (to), se prévaloir d'un droit.

availability (disposability) (*n.*), disponibilité (*f.*) :
availability of capital, disponibilité des capitaux.

availability (validity) (*n.*), validité (*f.*) :
availability of return tickets, validité des billets d'aller et retour.

available (at one's disposal) (*adj.*), disponible :
available funds *or* available assets, fonds disponibles (*m.pl.*) ; disponibilités (*f.pl.*) :
available funds in quest of employment, disponibilités en quête d'emploi.

the available assets form what is called working capital, les disponibilités forment ce qu'on appelle le fonds de roulement.

available (valid) (*adj.*), valable :
ticket which is only available for certain trains, billet qui n'est valable que dans certains trains (*m.*).

average (*adj.*), moyen, -enne :
average due date, échéance moyenne (*f.*) ; échéance commune (*f.*).
average life (Insce), vie moyenne (*f.*).
average overdraft, découvert moyen (*m.*).
average price (Stock Exch.), cours moyen (*m.*) :
at the average price, au cours moyen.
average tare, tare proportionnelle (*f.*).

average (mean) (*n.*), moyenne (*f.*) :
to take the average, prendre la moyenne.
average between the highest and lowest prices, moyenne entre le plus haut et le plus bas cours.
purchase average (Stock Exch.), moyenne d'achat.
sale average (Stock Exch.), moyenne de vente.

on an average, en moyenne ; moyennement :
articles sold from £2 to £3 on an average, objets vendus de £2 à £3 en moyenne (*ou* moyennement) (*m.pl.*).

average (stipulation that in the event of loss the sum payable shall not exceed the proportion that the face value of the policy bears to the actual value of the property covered) (Fire Insce) (*n.*), règle proportionnelle (*f.*) :
when there is application of average, it is said that the insured is his own insurer for the difference between the sum insured and the actual value of the thing insured, quand il y a application de la règle proportionnelle, on dit que l'assuré est son propre assureur pour la différence entre la somme assurée et la valeur réelle de la chose assurée.
partial insurances are average insurances, les assurances partielles sont des assurances proportionnelles.

average (Mar. Law) (*n.*), avarie (*f.*) ; avaries (*f.pl.*) :
wages and maintenance of crew not admissible in average, ne sont pas admis en avarie les loyers et la nourriture de l'équipage.
wear and tear of a ship is not an average, l'usure d'un navire n'est pas une avarie (*f.*).
average payable on each valuation, whether the average be particular or general, les avaries seront remboursables sur chaque évaluation, qu'il s'agisse d'avaries particulières ou d'avaries communes.
ship under average, navire en état d'avarie (*m.*).

average (gratuity, formerly allowed to masters of ships, in consideration of care of goods) (*n.*), avarie (*f.*) ; avaries (*f.pl.*) ; droit d'avarie (*m.*) :
primage and average, avaries et chapeau ; chapeau et droit d'avarie.

average (*v.t.*), établir la moyenne de :

to average the profits of several years, établir la moyenne des bénéfices de plusieurs années.

average (Stock Exch.) (*v.t.*), faire une moyenne : to average purchases, faire une moyenne d'achats ; acheter par échelons de baisse.

to average sales, faire une moyenne de ventes ; vendre par échelons de hausse.

average (*v.i.*), donner une moyenne de ; rendre une moyenne de :
total of so many pounds for so many loans, which averages about so much per loan, total de tant de livres pour tant de prêts, ce qui donne (*ou* ce qui rend) une moyenne d'environ tant par prêt (*m.*).

average (Stock Exch.) (*v.i.*), se faire une moyenne : people who average after a heavy fall, gens qui se font une moyenne après une forte baisse (*m.pl.*).

average adjuster *or* **average stater** *or* **average taker** (pers.), dispacheur (*m.*) ; répartiteur d'avaries (*m.*) ; expert répartiteur d'avaries (*m.*) ; expert-dispacheur (*m.*) :
the average adjusters make a report on the damage : this report is the average adjustment (*or* statement), les dispacheurs font un rapport sur l'avarie : c'est la dispache.

average adjustment *or* **average statement**, dispache (*f.*) ; dispache d'avarie (*f.*) ; règlement d'avaries (*m.*).

average bond, compromis d'avaries (*m.*) ; acte de compromis (*m.*) :
an average bond by which the interested parties bind themselves to contribute to the amount to be fixed by the average adjusters, un compromis d'avaries par lequel les intéressés s'obligent à contribuer pour le montant qui sera établi par les dispacheurs.

average damage (opp. to *average expenses*),

avarie-dommages (*f.*) ; avaries matérielles (*f.pl.*).

average expenses, avarie-frais (*f.*) ; avaries en frais (*f.pl.*).

average payment (apportionment of general average), dividende d'avarie (*m.*).

average surveyor, commissaire d'avarie (*m.*) ; commissaire d'avaries (*m.*).

averager (Stock Exch.) (pers.) (*n.*), faiseur de moyenne (*m.*).

averaging (Stock Exch.) (*n.*), moyennes (*f.pl.*) ; communes (*f.pl.*) :
averaging is done to protect a bad position, les moyennes (*ou* les communes) se pratiquent pour défendre une mauvaise position.

to reduce the loss by averaging, réduire la perte par des moyennes (*ou* par des communes).

averaging purchases, achat par échelons de baisse (*m.*).

averaging sales, vente par échelons de hausse (*f.*).

aviation (*n.*), aviation (*f.*) ; navigation aérienne (*f.*) ; vol (*m.*).

aviator (pers.) (*n.*), aviateur (*m.*) ; aéronaute (*m.*).

avoid (Law) (*v.t.*), résoudre ; résilier ; annuler :
to avoid a contract, résoudre, résilier, annuler, un contrat.

avoidable (Law) (*adj.*), résoluble ; annulable.

avoidance (Law) (*n.*), résolution (*f.*) ; résiliation (*f.*) ; résiliement (*m.*) ; resiliment (*m.*) ; annulation (*f.*).

avoidance clause (Law), clause résolutoire (*f.*).

award (arbitration) (*n.*), décision (arbitrale) (*f.*) ; sentence (arbitrale) (*ou* d'arbitrage) (*f.*) ; jugement (arbitral) (*m.*) ; arbitrage (*m.*).

award (*v.t.*), adjuger :
amount awarded by arbitration, somme adjugée par arbitrage (*f.*).

B

back (*n.*), verso (*m.*) ; dos (*m.*) :
back of a cheque, of a bill of exchange, of a bill of lading, of a certificate, of an envelope, of a postcard, of a packet, verso, dos, d'un chèque, d'une lettre de change, d'un titre, d'une enveloppe, d'une carte postale, d'un paquet :
as its name indicates, the endorsement is put on the back of the bill, comme son nom l'indique, l'endossement se met au verso (*ou* au dos) de la lettre.

to give a receipt on the back of a bill of lading, donner un reçu sur le verso du connaissement.

back (to guarantee) (*v.t.*), donner son aval à ; avaliser ; avaler :

surety who undertakes to back a bill, donneur de caution qui s'engage à donner son aval à (*ou* à avaliser) (*ou* à avaler) un effet (*m.*).

back rent, loyer arriéré (*m.*).

backed bills, effets avalisés (*m.pl.*) ; papier fait (*m.*) ; valeurs faites (*f.pl.*).

backer (guarantor of a bill) (pers.) (*n.*), donneur d'aval (*m.*) ; avaliste (*m.*).

backward call (of a ship at an intermediate port) (opp. to *forward call*), escale rétrograde (*f.*) ; échelle rétrograde (*f.*).

backward method (accounts current with interest), méthode rétrograde (*f.*) ; méthode indirecte (*f.*).

backwardation *or* **backwardization** (seller's postponement of delivery) (Stock Exch.) (*n.*), déport (*m.*) :

when there is a backwardation (*or* a back-wardization), the seller pays to continue, lorsqu'il y a un déport, le vendeur paye pour reporter.

backwardation *or* **backwardization** *or* **back** (premium) (Stock Exch.) (*n.*) (opp. to *contango*), déport (*m.*); bonification (*f.*) :
bear seller who pays a backwardation (*or* a backwardization) (*or* a back), vendeur à découvert qui paie un déport (*ou* une bonification) (*m.*).
V. aussi exemple sous **contango** *or* **contango rate.**

backwardation rate, cours de déport (*m.*); taux des déports (*m.*); taux du déport (*m.*).

backwardized (Stock Exch.) (*adj. & p.p.*), déporté, -e :
backwardized stock, titres déportés (*m.pl.*).

bad (*adj.*), mauvais, -e; faux, fausse; irrégulier, -ère :
bad debt, mauvaise créance (*f.*); créance véreuse (*f.*); créance amortie (*f.*); non valeur (*f.*).
bad debts reserve, provision pour créances douteuses (*f.*); amortissement des créances douteuses (*m.*).
bad coin (base coin), fausse monnaie (*f.*).
bad paper (bills of exchange), mauvais papier (*m.*).
bad speculation, fausse spéculation (*f.*).
bad stowage, vice d'arrimage (*m.*) :
damage resulting from bad stowage, avaries résultant d'un vice d'arrimage (*f.pl.*).
bad weather, mauvais temps (*m.*).
shares which are (*or* stock which is) bad delivery, titres qui sont de mauvaise livraison (*m.pl.*).
to deliver a good certificate in replacement of a bad certificate (Stock Exch.), livrer un titre régulier en remplacement d'un titre irrégulier.

bag (*n.*) (Abbrev.: **b.** *or* **B/** *or* **B/-** *or* **bg** [**bgs** *pl.*]), sac (*m.*) :
a bag of sugar, un sac de sucre.

bag (of money) (*n.*), sac (*m.*); group (*m.*).

baggage (*n.*), bagage (*m.*); bagages (*m.pl.*).
See note and word groups under syn. **luggage.**

balance (difference between debit and credit; remainder) (*n.*) (Abbrev.: **bal.** *or* **Bal.** *or* **blce** *or* **Blce**), balance (*f.*); solde (*m.*); restant (*m.*); reste (*m.*); reliquat (*m.*); surplus (*m.*); règlement (*m.*); redû (*m.*); soulte (*f.*); soute (*f.*).
balance of an account (Bkkpg), solde, balance, d'un compte.
balance of an invoice, solde d'une facture.
balance of freight, solde de fret.
bank balance *or* balance at (*or* in) bank, solde en banque; solde à la banque.
balance in (*or* on) hand (of cash), solde en caisse; restant en caisse.
to carry forward the balance of profit and loss account, reporter à nouveau le solde (*ou* le reliquat) du compte profits et pertes.
to sue for the balance, poursuivre le paiement d'un reliquat.

to pay the balance, verser le surplus; payer le reliquat; solder le redû :
I undertake to pay the balance (letter of application), je m'oblige à verser le surplus.
fine and spacious premises for sale, so much cash, balance can remain, bel et vaste immeuble à vendre, tant au comptant, délai pour soulte (*m.*).
debit balance, solde débiteur; balance débitrice.
balance brought forward *or* balance brought down, solde reporté; report (*m.*).
balance brought forward from last account *or* balance from last (*or* from previous) account, solde reporté de l'exercice précédent; balance de l'exercice précédent; solde précédent; report antérieur; report de l'exercice précédent; report à nouveau de l'exercice précédent.
balance carried forward *or* balance carried down, solde à reporter; report (*m.*).
balance carried forward to next account *or* balance to next account, solde à nouveau; balance à nouveau; report à nouveau.
balance, being profit, being loss, as per profit and loss account (balance sheet), solde en bénéfice, en perte, du compte de profits et pertes (*ou* du compte des pertes et profits).
balance, being net profit, being net loss, carried to balance sheet (profit and loss account), solde formant le bénéfice net, la perte nette, reporté au bilan; bénéfice net pour balance reporté au bilan, perte nette pour balance reportée au bilan.

balance (equilibrium) (*n.*), balance (*f.*); équilibre (*m.*) :
balance of indebtedness (Polit. Econ.), balance des comptes; balance économique :
the simple exchange of exported goods for imported goods does not constitute the only element of the balance of indebtedness of a country, le simple troc des marchandises exportées contre les marchandises importées ne constitue pas le seul élément de la balance économique d'un pays.
balance of trade (Polit. Econ.), balance du commerce; balance commerciale :
the balance is favourable to (*or* in favour of) a country when the amount of its exports exceeds that of its imports; if not it is unfavourable (*or* adverse) to it, la balance est favorable à un pays lorsque le montant de ses exportations dépasse celui de ses importations; sinon elle lui est défavorable.

balance (trial balance) (Bkkpg) (*n.*), balance (*f.*); balance de vérification (*f.*); balance d'ordre (*f.*) :
monthly balance, balance mensuelle.

balance *or* **balance up** (Bkkpg) (*v.t.*), balancer; solder; faire la balance :
to balance an account, balancer, solder, un compte.
to balance (*or* to balance up) the books for the year, balancer les livres pour l'année; faire la balance des affaires de l'année.
in the trial balance, the total of the debit

balances should balance that of the credit balances, dans la balance de vérification, l'ensemble des soldes débiteurs doit balancer celui des soldes créditeurs.

balance (to bring into or keep in equilibrium) (*v.t.*), balancer; équilibrer:
drawback balanced by advantages, inconvénient balancé par des avantages (*m.*).
to balance a budget, équilibrer un budget.

balance (*v.i.*) *or* **to balance each other,** se balancer; se solder; se solder en équilibre:
columns which balance, colonnes qui se balancent (*f.pl.*).
account which balances, compte qui se solde (*m.*).
to ascertain whether the budget of this State balances or shows a deficit, s'assurer si le budget de cet État se solde en équilibre ou en déficit.
two items which balance each other, deux articles qui se balancent (*m.pl.*).
cash to balance (opp. to *cash on account*), espèces pour solde (*f.pl.*).

balance account (Bkkpg), compte collectif (*m.*).

balance book, livre de balance (*m.*); livre de soldes (*m.*); livre des balances de vérification (*m.*).

balance in cash *or simply* **balance** (*n.*) (in an exchange, the difference in value payable in cash), soulte (*f.*); soulte d'échange (*f.*); soute (*f.*):
the said exchange is made in consideration of a balance in cash payable by the X. Company of £0,000, ledit échange est fait moyennant une soulte de la part de la Compagnie X. de £0 000.

balance method (accounts current with interest), méthode par soldes (*f.*); méthode hambourgeoise (*f.*).

balance sheet (Abbrev.: **B/S.** *or* **b.s.**), bilan (*m.*); bilan d'exploitation (*m.*); inventaire (*m.*); inventaire comptable (*m.*); inventaire intra-comptable (*m.*):
balance sheet at (*or* as at) (*or* on) (*or* made up to) 31st December 19—, bilan au (*ou* arrêté au) 31 décembre 19—.
balance sheet at commencement of business, bilan d'entrée.
to make up one's balance sheet once a year, faire son inventaire une fois l'an.
Note :—inventaire is the **balance sheet and schedules,** the detailed accounts; the balance sheet, profit and loss account, trading account, stock sheets, list and valuation of investments, or the like, such as would be placed before say the directors and auditors of a company. *bilan* is the condensed balance sheet, such as would be printed and published. *bilan d'exploitation* is the opposing term to *bilan de liquidation* (statement of affairs in a bankruptcy). The full expression is used only when it is necessary to distinguish the one *bilan* from the other.
*Note :—*In French balance sheets, the assets appear on the left hand side and the liabilities

on the right. This is the reverse of English practice.

balance sheet book, livre d'inventaire (*m.*); copie d'inventaire (*m.*); livre des inventaires (*m.*).

bale (*n.*) (Abbrev.: **b.** *or* **B/** *or* **B/-**), balle (*f.*); ballot (*m.*).

ball (of string) (*n.*), pelote (*f.*), peloton (*m.*) (de ficelle).

ballast (*n.*), lest (*m.*):
ship in ballast, navire sur (*ou* en) lest (*m.*).

ballast (*v.t.*), lester.

ballast passage (opp. to *cargo passage*), voyage sur (*ou* en) lest (*m.*); trajet sur lest (*m.*); traversée sur lest (*f.*).

ballasting (*n.*), lestage (*m.*):
sand for the ballasting of ships, sable pour le lestage des navires (*m.*).

ballot *or* **balloting** (*n.*), scrutin (*m.*):
the election is made by a majority of votes and at a secret ballot, l'élection est faite à la majorité des suffrages et au scrutin secret (*f.*).

ballot (*v.i.*), scrutiner.

Baltic port, port de la Baltique (*m.*).

banco (*adj.*), banco:
two hundred florins banco, deux cents florins banco.

banco (*n.*), monnaie banco (*f.*); monnaie de banque (*f.*).

bang the market (**to**), casser les cours. V. exemple sous **deal** (*v.i.*).

bank (of a river) (*n.*), rive (*f.*), berge (*f.*), bord (*m.*) (d'un fleuve *ou* d'une rivière):
wharves conveniently arranged (*or* laid out) on both banks of the river, quais convenablement aménagés sur les deux rives du fleuve (*m.pl.*).

bank (Fin.) (*n.*) (Abbrev.: **bk** *or* **Bk**), banque (*f.*); maison de banque (*f.*); caisse (*f.*); crédit (*m.*); établissement de crédit (*m.*):
bank of commerce, banque de commerce; banque commerciale.
bank of deposit, banque de dépôt.
bank of discount, banque d'escompte.
bank of issue *or* bank of circulation, banque d'émission; banque de circulation.
savings bank, caisse d'épargne.

bank (to pay into the bank) (*v.t.*), verser à la banque:
to bank so many pounds, verser à la banque tant de livres.

bank account, compte de banque (*m.*); compte en banque (*m.*).

bank balance, solde en banque (*m.*); solde à la banque (*m.*).

bank charges, frais de banque (*m.pl.*). (Note, however, that *frais de banque* generally means petty expenses, such as postages, telegrams, or the like, whereas *bank charges* in England means any charge made by a bank, whether for interest, discount, commission, or petties: *bank charges* should therefore be translated into French by one or more of the following expressions, according to circumstances: intérêts, commissions, agios, changes (*ou* pertes de place), commission de caisse, frais de recouvrement (*ou* frais d'encaissement), frais, frais de banque.)

ank cheque, chèque de banque (*m.*); chèque bancaire (*m.*).

ank clerk, employé de banque (*m.*); commis de banque (*m.*).

ank commission, commission de banque (*f.*); commission bancaire (*f.*).

ank credit, crédit de banque (*m.*); crédit bancaire (*m.*).

ank discount (opp. to *true*, or *arithmetical*, *discount*), escompte en dehors (*m.*); escompte commercial (*m.*); escompte irrationnel (*m.*).

ank guarantee, caution de banque (*f.*); garantie de banque (*f.*).

ank holiday, jour de fête légale (*m.*); fête légale (*f.*); jour férié (*m.*).

ank money, monnaie de banque (*f.*); monnaie banco (*f.*).

ank note, billet de banque (*m.*).

ank paper or **bank bills** (bills of exchange) (opp. to *trade paper* or *bills*), papier de banque (*m.*).

ank pass book, carnet de banque (*m.*); carnet de compte (*m.*).

ank place, place bancable (*f.*); place bancale (*f.*).

ank rate or **bank rate of discount** (opp. to *market*, or *private*, *rate*), taux officiel (*m.*); taux officiel d'escompte (*m.*); taux officiel de l'escompte (*m.*); taux de la Banque régulatrice (*m.*); escompte officiel (*m.*):
interest at 1% above bank rate, intérêt à 1 0/0 au-dessus du taux officiel (*ou* au-dessus du taux officiel d'escompte) (*ou* au-dessus du taux de la Banque régulatrice) (*m.*).

discount or money is said to be tight when owing to the market's requirements of money, the market rate of discount approximates to the bank rate of discount, that is to say, in France, to the rate of the Bank of France, l'escompte ou l'argent est dit serré lorsque par suite des besoins en capitaux du marché, le taux de l'escompte privé se rapproche du taux officiel de l'escompte, c'est-à-dire, en France, du taux de la Banque de France (*m.*).

Bank rate or Bank of England minimum rate of discount, taux officiel de la Banque d'Angleterre; taux d'escompte de la Banque d'Angleterre.

French bank rate or Bank of France rate of discount, taux officiel de la Banque de France; taux d'escompte de la Banque de France; taux Banque de France.

Belgian bank rate or National Bank of Belgium rate of discount, taux officiel (*ou* taux d'escompte) de la Banque nationale (*ou* de la Banque Nationale de Belgique).

bank reserve, réserve de la banque (*f.*).

bank return or **bank statement**, situation de la banque (*f.*).

bank shares, valeurs de banques (*f.pl.*); valeurs bancaires (*f.pl.*).

bank transfer, virement (*m.*); écriture de banque (*f.*).

bankable (*adj.*), bancable; banquable: bankable bills or bankable paper, effets bancables (*m.pl.*); papier bancable (*m.*).

banker (pers.) (*n.*), banquier, -ère.

banker's reference, référence de banquier (*f.*).

banker's ticket (on dishonoured bill), compte de retour (*m.*).

bankers' clearing house, chambre de compensation des banquiers (*f.*).

banking (*n.*) (Abbrev. **bkg**) or **banking business** or **banking transactions** or **banking operations**, banque (*f.*); opérations de banque (*f.pl.*):
banking is trade in money, la banque est le commerce d'argent (*ou* des capitaux).
to do banking business, faire la banque.
banking and finance, banque et finances.
banking in all its forms, la banque sous toutes ses formes.

banking account, compte de banque (*m.*); compte en banque (*m.*).

banking company, société de banque (*f.*).

banking customs, coutumes banquières (*f.pl.*).

banking house or **banking firm** or **banking establishment**, maison de banque (*f.*); établissement bancaire (*m.*).

bankrupt (*adj.*) (Abbrev.: **bkrpt**), banqueroutier, -ère; failli, -e:
bankrupt merchant or bankrupt trader, commerçant banqueroutier (*m.*); commerçant failli (*m.*).

bankrupt (pers.) (*n.*), banqueroutier, -ère; failli, -e.

bankrupt (*v.t.*), mettre en faillite.

bankruptcy [**bankruptcies** *pl.*] (*n.*), banqueroute (*f.*); faillite (*f.*).
Note:—In France, *banqueroute* is the failure of a trader occasioned by his own fault and is a punishable offence. Failure brought about by misfortune is called *faillite*.

bar (at the mouth of a river) (*n.*), barre (à l'embouchure d'un fleuve) (*f.*).

bar gold, or en barre (*m.*).

bar of division (between the numerator and the denominator of a fraction), barre de fraction (*f.*).

bar of the statute of limitations or **barring by limitation**, prescription (*f.*).
to be barred by limitation or **to be barred by statute of limitations** or **to be statute barred**, se prescrire; être prescrit, -e:
interest on French rentes is statute barred after five years, les arrérages des rentes françaises se prescrivent par cinq ans (*m.pl.*).

bare boat charter, affrètement coque nue (*m.*).

bare contract (opp. to *onerous contract*), contrat à titre gratuit (*m.*); contrat de bienfaisance (*m.*).

bargain (*n.*), marché (*m.*); négociation (*f.*); affaire (*f.*):
to make a good bargain, faire un marché avantageux (*ou* une bonne affaire) (*ou* une négociation heureuse).

bargain for cash *or* bargain for money, marché au comptant; négociation au comptant.

bargain for account (Stock Exch.), marché à terme; marché à livrer; négociation à terme.

bargains done (Stock Exch.), cours pratiqués (*m.pl.*); cours faits (*m.pl.*). *V. exemples sous* to do a bargain.

bargain done on the previous day (mention in a quotation list) (Stock Exch.), hier.

bargain (to haggle) (*v.i.*), marchander.

bargain book, livre à marchés (*m.*).

bargain book (stockbroker's), carnet à marchés (*m.*); carnet (*m.*); carnet d'agent de change (*m.*).

bargaining (*n.*), marchandage (*m.*).

barge (*n.*), chaland (*m.*); chalan (*m.*); gabare (*f.*); allège (*f.*); péniche (*f.*); barge (*f.*).

barge hire, location de chalands (*f.*).

bargee *or* **bargeman** [**bargemen** *pl.*] (*n.*), gabarier (*m.*).

bark *or* **barque** (*n.*), barque (*f.*).

barratry (*n.*), baraterie (*f.*):

barratry of the master and mariners, baraterie de patron; baraterie du patron et de l'équipage.

Note :—The French distinguish between **baraterie criminelle** which is *barratry* in the English sense, and **baraterie civile** (or **baraterie simple**) which is a *fault* or *wrongful act* for which the master is responsible.

the word *baraterie* in French, includes all the wrongful acts of the master, of whatever nature they may be; the English word *barratry* includes only intentionally fraudulent or criminal acts, and does not apply to faults of negligence, incapacity, or the like, le mot *baraterie* en français, comprend toutes les fautes du capitaine, de quelque nature qu'elles soient; le mot anglais *barratry* ne comprend que les seuls actes intentionnellement frauduleux ou criminels, et ne s'entend pas aux fautes de négligence, incapacité, ou autres semblables.

barratry risk, risque de baraterie (*m.*).

barrel (cask) (*n.*) (Abbrev.: **bar.** *or* **bbl** *or* **brl**), baril (*m.*); barrique (*f.*); fût (*m.*); futaille (*f.*); tonneau (*m.*).

barrier (*n.*), barrière (*f.*):

country closed by customs barriers, pays fermé par des barrières de douanes (*m.*).

barrister (*n.*) *or* **barrister at law** (pers.), avocat (*m.*).

barter (*n.*), échange (*m.*); troc (*m.*); change (*m.*):

trade by barter, commerce d'échange (*m.*).

barter was without doubt the first form of trade, le troc fut sans doute la première forme de commerce.

barter (*v.t.*), échanger; troquer.

base (*n.*), base (*f.*); fondation (*f.*).

base (*v.t.*), baser; asseoir; fonder:

to base one's calculations on present prices, baser ses calculs sur les prix actuels.

to base taxation on income, asseoir l'impôt sur le revenu.

the tax is based on the capital of the deb la taxe est assise sur le capital de la créanc

claim based upon a loss, recours fondé su une perte (*m.*).

base coin, fausse monnaie (*f.*).

base date (accounts current with interest époque (*f.*).

basin (Navig.) (*n.*), bassin (*m.*):

basin for small craft, bassin de batellerie.

basis [**bases** *pl.*] (*n.*), base (*f.*); assiette (*f.*) fondation (*f.*):

basis of a contract, of credit, base d'un con trat, du crédit.

basis of a mortgage, assiette d'une hypo thèque.

basis of assessment (Income Tax), base d'im position; base de cotisation; assiette d l'impôt.

basis of exchange, base du change.

basis of taxation, of contribution (*to taxation* by landed property, base, assiette, de l'im pôt, de la contribution foncière.

the basis of the valuation of the merchandis declared is, for the purpose of this insuranc agreed to be at . . ., la base d'évaluatio des marchandises déclarées est, aux fins d la présente assurance, fixée par accor mutuel à . . .

bank which has a firm basis, banque qui une assiette solide (*f.*).

basis price, prix de base (*m.*).

basis rates, tarifs de base (*m.pl.*).

basket (*n.*), corbeille (*f.*); panier (*m.*):

waste paper basket, panier au papier; cor beille à papier.

batch (*n.*), groupe (*m.*):

a batch of parcels, un groupe de colis.

batch (*v.t.*), grouper.

batching (*n.*), groupage (*m.*).

bazaar shares *or* **shares in a bazaar** (*fig. or sarcastic* valeurs de fantaisie (*f.pl.*).

be (*v.i.*), être:

to be a long way out *or* to be far from agree ing, être loin de compte.

to be bankrupt, être en faillite.

to be in business, être dans les affaires.

to be in credit at the bank, avoir crédit e banque (*ou* à la banque).

to be in financial difficulties *or* to be i Queer Street, être mal dans ses affaire (*ou* dans ses finances).

to be in funds, être en fonds.

to be in the chair, occuper le fauteuil de l présidence; présider:

Mr X. was in the chair, M. X. occupe l fauteuil de la présidence; M. X. préside

to be of . . . *or* to be of . . . burden, jauger ship which is of 800 tons (*or* which is of 80 tons burden), navire qui jauge 800 tonneau (*m.*). (Cf. **burden.**)

to be on one's guard, être, se tenir, sur se gardes.

to be out of work, chômer d'ouvrage chômer:

10,000 seamen are out of work, 10 000 gen de mer chôment.

each (of the sea, of a lake, of a river) (n.), plage (f.), grève (f.), rivage (m.) (de la mer, d'un lac, d'un fleuve):
sandy beach, plage (ou grève) de sable.
shingle beach or pebble beach, grève de galets.

each (v.t.), échouer; échouer sur le rivage:
to beach a ship to escape total loss, échouer un navire sur le rivage pour éviter la perte totale.

each (v.i.), échouer; s'échouer.

eaching (n.), échouement (m.).

eacon (n.), balise (f.).

eaconage (n.), droits de balisage (m.pl.); droits de balise (m.pl.).

ear (Stock Exch.) (pers.) (n.) (opp. to bull), baissier (m.): (Cf. **bears** sous **bear account.**)
bears sell for the settlement stocks which they hope to repurchase at a lower price, les baissiers vendent à terme des valeurs qu'ils espèrent racheter à un cours plus faible.

ear (to carry; to contain) (v.t.), porter; être revêtu (-e) de:
registered share certificates bear the name of the person to whom they belong, les titres nominatifs portent le nom de la personne à laquelle ils appartiennent (m.pl.).
the cheque bears the following endorsement, the words not negotiable, le chèque porte (ou est revêtu de) l'endos suivant, la mention non négociable.

ear (to be answerable for) (v.t.), supporter; faire:
to bear a loss, the expenses incurred for the preservation of one's own property, supporter une perte, les frais encourus pour la conservation de son propre bien.
to bear the cost of an undertaking, faire les frais d'une entreprise.
Cf. to be borne by, sous **borne.**

ear (to produce) (v.t.), porter; rapporter; produire; être productif (-ive) de:
capital which bears interest or interest-bearing capital, capital qui porte intérêt (m.); capital productif d'intérêts (m.).
sum of so much bearing interest at four per cent per annum, somme de tant productive d'intérêts à quatre pour cent l'an (f.).
the company will issue on 1st December 19— 10,000 debentures of £10 each 6%, bearing interest from 1st January next, la société émettra le 1er décembre 19— 10 000 obligations de £10 chacune 6 0/0, jouissance du 1er janvier prochain.

ear (v.t.) or to bear the market, vendre à découvert:
to speculate on the stock exchange, that is to say, to bull or to bear (or to bull or to bear the market), spéculer sur la bourse, c'est-à-dire acheter ou vendre à découvert.

ear account or bear position or bears (pers.) (n.pl.) (Stock Exch.), position vendeur (f.); position à la baisse (f.); découvert (m.):
operator who has a big bear account in such a stock, opérateur qui a une grosse position vendeur de telle valeur (m.).

there is a big bear account open in Mexican Eagles, le découvert sur la Mexican Eagle est étendu.
there are no bears, il n'y a pas de découvert.
the bears are buying back, le découvert se rachète.
the market is all bears, la place (ou la position de place) est dégagée (ou est soulagée).

bear campaign, campagne de baisse (f.).

bear panic or bear stampede, course des vendeurs (f.).

bear raid, attaque du découvert (f.); attaque des baissiers (f.):
a hot bear raid on X., aroused by the news that this concern had reduced its output, caused this stock to give way, carrying with it the whole of the list, une vive attaque des baissiers sur X., provoquée par la nouvelle que cette entreprise avait réduit sa production, fait fléchir cette valeur, entraînant l'ensemble de la cote.

bear sale, vente à découvert (f.).

bear seller, vendeur à découvert (m.).

bear squeeze, étranglement de la spéculation à découvert (m.); chasse au découvert (f.).

bear transaction, opération à découvert (f.); opération à la baisse (f.).

bearer (pers.) (n.), porteur (m.):
bearer of a letter, of a cheque, of a letter of credit, porteur d'une lettre, d'un chèque, d'une lettre de crédit.
bill payable to bearer, billet payable au porteur (m.).

bearer bond (opp. to registered bond), obligation au porteur (f.); bon au porteur (m.); titre au porteur (m.); valeur au porteur (f.).

bearer certificate or bearer warrant or bearer scrip or bearer bond, titre au porteur (m.).

bearer cheque or cheque to bearer (opp. to order cheque or cheque to order), chèque au porteur (m.).

bearer debenture, obligation au porteur (f.).

bearer shares or bearer stock or bearer stocks or bearer securities, actions au porteur (f.pl.); titres au porteur (m.pl.); valeurs au porteur (f.pl.); effets au porteur (m.pl.).

bearish tendency (Stock Exch.), tendance à la baisse (f.).

beat a record (to), battre un record:
economic activity which has beaten the records of the previous year, activité économique qui a battu les records de l'année précédente (f.).

become (v.i.). V. exemples:
to become affiliated to a certain society, s'affilier à une certaine société.
to become bankrupt, to become insolvent, faire banqueroute; faire faillite; faillir.
to become party to an action, se rendre partie dans un procès.
to become surety for, se rendre garant (-e) pour; se rendre caution de; se porter caution de; cautionner:
to become surety for a friend, a cashier, se rendre garant (-e) pour, cautionner, un ami, un caissier.

to become surety for an obligation contracted by a debtor, se rendre caution d', se porter caution d', une obligation contractée par un débiteur.

to become the proprietor by purchase or exchange, devenir propriétaire par achat ou échange.

before hours (Stock Exch.), avant-bourse. Cf. **after hours.**

begin (v.t.), commencer; entamer.

beginning (n.), commencement (m.):
beginning of the year, commencement de l'année.

behalf of (on) (on account of), à l'acquit de; au compte de:
to pay money, to negotiate bills, on behalf of a third party, verser des fonds, négocier des effets, à l'acquit (ou au compte) d'un tiers.
for and on behalf of. V. sous **for.**

behindhand (adv. & adj.), en arrière; arriéré, -e:
to be behindhand with one's rent, être en arrière pour ses loyers.

belga (n.), belga (m.). Note :—The belga, which is nominally equivalent to 5 Belgian francs, is only a money of exchange. The franc retains its place in the national economy and continues to be used and to circulate in Belgium.

Belgian bank rate or **National Bank of Belgium rate of discount,** taux officiel (ou taux d'escompte) de la Banque nationale (ou de la Banque Nationale de Belgique) (m.).

Belgian franc, franc belge (m.).

bell (n.), timbre (m.):
call bell, timbre d'appel.

belong (said of a ship in relation to her port of registry) (v.i.), être attaché:
every ship must belong to a port, called the port of registry, tout navire doit être attaché à un port, appelé le port d'attache (ou port d'immatriculation).

below (adv.), au-dessous de:
below the average, au-dessous de la moyenne.

beneficiary [**beneficiaries** pl.] (pers.) (n.), bénéficiaire (m. ou f.):
beneficiary of an insurance policy, bénéficiaire d'une police d'assurance.
beneficiary of a letter of credit, bénéficiaire d'une lettre de crédit; accrédité, -e.

benefit (n.), bénéfice (m.); avantage (m.); profit (m.); compte (m.):
benefit of salvage, of temporary admission, bénéfice de sauvetage, de l'admission temporaire.

benefit (v.i.), profiter; bénéficier:
in most bargains, only one of the parties benefits, dans la plupart des marchés, une seule des parties profite.
to benefit by appreciation of the exchange, bénéficier, profiter, de la plus-value du change.

benefit of a fall (in price) **clause,** clause de parité (f.).

bequest (n.), legs (m.).

berth (employ) (n.), place (f.); position (f.); poste (m.); emploi (m.):
to lose one's berth, perdre sa place.

berth or **berthage** (place where a ship lies at anchor, or at a wharf) (n.), poste de mouillage (m.); poste d'amarrage (m.); poste (m.); mouillage (m.); place (f.); emplacement (m.):
quay berth, poste à quai; place à quai.
loading berth, emplacement de chargement.

berth (bunk or bed in a vessel, or sleeping car) (n.), couchette (f.); place (f.):
the berths occupied by steerage passengers during the voyage, les couchettes occupées par des passagers d'entrepont pendant la voyage.
1st class berth, place de 1re classe.
one-berth, two-berth, compartment (sleeping car), compartiment à une place, à deux places (m.).

berth (a ship) (v.t.), donner un poste à, amarrer, mouiller (un navire).

berth (v.i.), s'amarrer; mouiller.

berth freighting, affrètement à cueillette (m.).

berth terms (Abbrev.: **b.t.**), fret à la cueillette (m.); fret à cueillette (m.).

berthage (charges) (n.), droit d'amarrage (m.); droit d'ancrage (m.).

berthing (of ships) (n.), placement (m.); mouillage (m.).

better (to be), être mieux; être meilleur, -e; être amélioré, -e; s'améliorer:
oil shares better; X. shares were better at 2¾, valeurs petrolières mieux; l'action X est mieux (ou l'action X. s'améliore) à 2 3/4.
the tendency of the market is better, la tendance du marché est meilleure (ou s'améliore).

better, best (Stock Exch.), mieux (V. les locutions):
or better, sauf mieux:
buy so many such or such shares at so much or better, achetez tant de telles actions à tant, sauf mieux.
at best, au mieux:
orders are frequently given to buy or to sell at best; orders given without stipulation relative to the price to be applied are also executed at best, on donne fréquemment des ordres d'acheter ou de vendre au mieux; les ordres donnés sans stipulation relative au cours à appliquer sont aussi exécutés au mieux.

better (v.t.), améliorer:
to better the financial position of a bank, améliorer la situation financière d'une banque.

bettering or **betterment** (n.), amélioration (f.):
betterment of the lot of the staff, amélioration du sort du personnel.

bid (Stock Exch.) (n.) (opp. to offer), demande (f.).

bid (auction) (n.), enchère (f.); mise (f.):
to make a bid, mettre enchère.
the last bid was so much, la dernière mise a été de tant.

bid (auction) (v.t.), enchérir de:
to bid so much, enchérir de tant.

bid or **bid for** (Stock Exch.) (v.t.), demander:
the jobber (in France, it would be the broker

bids : buy (*short for* I will buy) 100 X. (shares) such or such a price, l'agent demande : je prends (*ou* je donne) 100 (actions) X. tel prix. *Cf.* the jobber offers, *sous* **offer.**

X. shares : 1s. 6d. bid ; 1s. 4½d. offered, l'action X. 1sh. 6d., demandé ; 1sh. 4 1/2d. offert.

prices bid (buyers) (Stock Exch.), cours demandés (acheteurs) (*m.pl.*).

stocks bid for, valeurs demandés (*f.pl.*).

d (*v.i.*), miser :
auction sale where no one bids, vente aux enchères où personne ne mise (*f.*).

d for (to) (auction), enchérir :
to bid for a property, enchérir un immeuble.

dder (at auctions) (pers.) (*n.*), enchérisseur, -euse.

g (*adj.*), gros, grosse ; grand, -e ; fort, -e ; considérable ; 'haut, -e :
big denominations (of shares, or the like), grosses coupures (*f.pl.*).
big sum, grosse somme (*f.*) ; forte somme (*f.*) ; somme considérable (*f.*).
big rise, big fall (of prices), forte hausse (*f.*), forte baisse (*f.*) (de cours, de prix).
big shippers, gros chargeurs (*m.pl.*).
the big bankers, les gros banquiers (*m.pl.*).
the big banks, les grandes banques (*f.pl.*) ; la haute banque ; la haute finance.
the big banking houses, les maisons de haute banque (*f.pl*).
big five. En Angleterre, l'ensemble de cinq grandes banques (Barclays, Lloyds, Midland, National Provincial & Westminster Banks).
the two biggest shareholders, les deux plus forts actionnaires.

dlateral contract, contrat bilatéral (*m.*) ; contrat synallagmatique (*m.*).

ll (bill of exchange ; draft) (*n.*), effet (*m.*) ; billet (*m.*) ; mandat (*m.*) ; échéance (*f.*) ; traite (*f.*) ; remise (*f.*) ; lettre (*f.*) ; valeur (*f.*) : [Cf. **bill of exchange** et **bills** *or* **bills of exchange** (collectively) ci-après.]

bill receivable [bills receivable *pl.*] (*Abbrev. :* B.R. *or* b.r. *or* b. rec.), effet à recevoir.

bill payable [bills payable *pl.*] (*Abbrev. :* B.P. *or* b.p.), effet à payer.

bill payable to bearer, billet au porteur ; effet au porteur.

bills payable account, bills receivable book, etc. V. ci-après.

bill in a set *or* bill of exchange in a set, traite en plusieurs exemplaires ; lettre de change à plusieurs exemplaires.

documentary bill *or* document bill *or* bill with documents attached (opp. to *clean bill*), traite documentaire ; effet documentaire ; traite accompagnée de documents ; effet accompagné par des documents.

documents against acceptance bill (*Abbrev. :* D/A. bill) *or* bill for acceptance, traite documents contre acceptation.

documents against payment bill (*Abbrev. :* D/P. bill) *or* bill for payment, traite documents contre paiement.

foreign bill (opp. to *inland bill*), effet étranger ; effet sur l'étranger ; traite sur l'étranger ; lettre de change à l'extérieur ; devise (*f.*) ; devise étrangère ; devise sur l'étranger :
the account Foreign Bills is debited with the bills received, le compte Effets étrangers est débité des devises reçues.

dishonoured bill *or* bill returned dishonoured, effet retourné ; retour (*m.*) ; effet rendu ; effet renvoyé.

dishonoured bill *or* bill dishonoured by non payment *or* bill returned dishonoured, effet impayé ; impayé (*m.*) ; effet retourné (*ou* rendu) (*ou* renvoyé) impayé ; impayé retourné ; impayé rendu ; impayé renvoyé.

dishonoured bill *or* bill dishonoured by non acceptance *or* bill returned dishonoured, effet non accepté ; effet retourné (*ou* rendu) (*ou* renvoyé) faute d'acceptation ; effet retourné (*ou* rendu) (*ou* renvoyé) par défaut d'acceptation.

bill (invoice) (*n.*), facture (*f.*) ; mémoire (*m.*) ; note (*f.*).

bill (such as may be given to a customer in a shop or store) (*n.*), note (*f.*) ; bulletin (*m.*) ; bulletin de vente (*m.*).

bill (bank note) (U.S.A.) (*n.*), billet (*m.*) ; billet de banque (*m.*).

bill (to invoice) (*v.t.*), facturer :
to bill goods, facturer des marchandises.

bill book (Bkkpg), livre d'effets (*m.*) ; journal d'effets (*m.*).

bill broker, courtier d'escompte (*m.*) ; courtier de change (*m.*).

bill case, portefeuille (*m.*) :
the bills in the bill case, les effets en portefeuille (*m.pl.*).

bill diary, échéancier (*m.*) ; livre d'échéances (*m.*) ; carnet d'échéance (*ou* d'échéances) (*m.*).

bill exchange (opp. to *money exchange*), change tiré (*m.*) ; change commercial (*m.*).

bill file, pique-notes (*m.*).

bill form, formule d'effet de commerce (*f.*).

bill head *or* **bill heading,** en-tête de facture (*m.*) ; tête de facture (*f.*).

bill of costs *or* simply **bill** (*n.*) (Law), mémoire (*m.*) :
taxed bill of costs, mémoire taxé.

bill of entry (Abbrev. : B/E.) (Customs), déclaration de (*ou* en) détail (*f.*) ; rapport en douane (*m.*). [V. **entry** (Customs) pour exemples.]

bill of exchange [bills of exchange *pl.*] *or* bill *or* note *or* simply bill (*n.*) (as a general and legal term) (Abbrev. : B/E. *or* b.e.), effet de commerce (*m.*) ; effet commercial (*m.*) ; effet (*m.*).
Note :—In England a *promissory note* is not a *bill of exchange* ; hence the expression *bill or note.* In France, however, a *billet à ordre* (promissory note) is an *effet de commerce.*

bill of exchange *or* simply **bill** (*n.*) (an acceptable draft) (Abbrev. : B/E. *or* b.e.), lettre de change (*f.*) ; lettre (*f.*) ; traite (*f.*).

bill of health (Abbrev. : B.H.), patente de santé (*f.*).

bill of lading [bills of lading *pl.*] *or sometimes simply* bill (*n.*) (Abbrev.: **B/L.** [**Bs/L.** *pl.*] *or* **b.l.** *or* **B/Ldg** [**Bs/Ldg** *pl.*]), connaissement (*m.*) : (*V. note sous* original stamped bill of lading.)

bill of lading to a named (*or* specified) person, connaissement à personne dénommée ; connaissement nominatif.

bill of lading to bearer, connaissement au porteur.

bill of lading to (*or* unto) order, connaissement à ordre.

bill of lading clause, clause de connaissement (*f.*).

bill of lading form, formule de connaissement (*f.*).

bill of lading stamp, timbre de connaissement (*m.*).

bill of sight (Customs), déclaration provisoire (*f.*).

bill stamp, timbre d'effet de commerce (*m.*) ; timbre des effets de commerce (*m.*) ; timbre des effets (*m.*).

billing (invoicing) (*n.*), facturation (*f.*).

billing machine, machine à facturer (*f.*).

bills (*n.pl.*) *or* **bills of exchange** (collectively), portefeuille (*m.*) ; portefeuille-effets (*m.*) ; portefeuille d'effets (*m.*) ; papier (*m.*) ; papiers (*m.pl.*) ; valeurs (*f.pl.*) ; effets (*m.pl.*) ; devises (*f.pl.*) :

to rediscount other banks' bills, réescompter le portefeuille d'autres banques.

the French market has been a big buyer of English bills, la place française a été gros acheteur de portefeuille anglais.

an increase of the item " bills of exchange " (bank balance sheet), un gonflement du poste « portefeuille-effets. »

guaranteed bills *or* backed bills, effets avalisés ; papier fait ; valeurs faites.

bills for discount, for collection, effets à l'escompte, à l'encaissement.

bills discounted, effets escomptés.

hot bills *or* bills maturing in a few days *or* bills that have only a few days to run, effets brûlants ; papier brûlant ; valeurs brûlantes.

bills to mature, papier à échéance.

bills in pawn *or* pawned bills, effets en pension (*ou* en [*ou* à la] nourrice).

bills in suspense *or* bills held over, effets en souffrance (*ou* en suspens).

foreign bills. V. sous **bill.**

bills department (Banking), service du portefeuille (*m.*) ; service du portefeuille-effets (*m.*) ; portefeuille (*m.*) :

the head of the bills department, le chef du service du portefeuille ; le chef du portefeuille.

bills payable account, compte d'effets à payer (*m.*).

bills payable book *or* **bills payable journal,** livre des effets à payer (*m.*) ; journal des effets à payer (*m.*).

bills receivable account, compte d'effets à recevoir (*m.*).

bills receivable book *or* **bills receivable journ:** livre des effets à recevoir (*m.*) ; journal d effets à recevoir (*m.*) ; livre du portefeui (*m.*).

bills received register (Banking), livre d'entr des effets (*m.*) ; livre d'entrée (*m.*) ; liv copie d'effets (*m.*) ; copie d'effets (*m* livre des numéros (*m.*).

bimetalism *or* **bimetallism** (*n.*), bimétallisme (*m* **bimetalist** *or* **bimetallist** (pers.) (*n.*), bimétallis (*m.*).

bimetallic (*adj.*), bimétallique :

bimetallic system, système bimétallique (*m*

bimetallistic (*adj.*), bimétalliste :

according as a State adopts a single standa or a double standard it is said to be mon metallic or bimetallistic, suivant qu' État adope un étalon unique ou un étal double il est dit monométalliste ou bimét: liste.

bind (*v.t.*), lier ; engager ; obliger :

arbitration award without appeal which bin both parties, décision arbitrale sans app qui lie les deux parties (*f.*).

the master by signing the bills of lading bin the shipowner, le capitaine en signant l connaissements engage l'armateur.

firm bargains bind both the seller and t buyer ; an option bargain binds the tak without binding the giver (Stock Exch.), l marchés fermes engagent à la fois le vende et l'acheteur ; un marché à prime enga le vendeur sans engager l'acheteur.

to be bound, être lié (-e), engagé (-e), obli (-e), tenu (-e) :

the underwriter is only bound after accep ance of the risk, l'assureur n'est lié qu' près acceptation du risque (*m.*).

each insurer is bound only within the lim of the amount subscribed by him, chaq assureur n'est engagé que dans la limi de la somme par lui souscrite.

the bank is bound to have gold and silv coin and bullion equal to one third of t amount of its notes and of its other sigl commitments, la banque est tenue (*c* obligée) d'avoir une encaisse métalliqu égale au tiers du montant de ses bille et de ses autres engagements à vue.

to be bound to fulfil an obligation, êt tenu (-e) de remplir une obligation.

to bind oneself, se lier ; s'engager ; s'engag soi-même ; s'obliger :

to bind oneself under oath, se lier p serment.

to bind oneself under a surety bond, s'e gager, s'obliger, par cautionnement.

share for which the insurer binds himself the risk insured, part pour laquelle l'ass reur s'engage dans le risque assuré (*f.*).

directors who have acted within the limi of their powers bind the company withou binding themselves, les administrateu qui ont agi dans la limite de leurs pouvoir engagent la société sans s'engager eu mêmes (*m.pl.*).

nder (file for papers) (*n.*), biblorhapte (*m.*).

plane (*n.*), biplan (*m.*).

rth certificate, bulletin de naissance (*m.*).

ack-bordered envelope, enveloppe deuil (*f.*).

ack-bordered letter paper, papier à lettres deuil (*m.*).

lack Friday (financial panic), Vendredi noir (*m.*).

ack ink, encre noire (*f.*).

ack interest (current accounts, or the like) (opp. to *red interest*), intérêts noirs (*m.pl.*).

ack list, liste noire (*f.*); liste de sinistres maritimes (*f.*).

ack product (current accounts, or the like), nombre noir (*m.*).

lack Sea port, port de la Mer Noire (*m.*).

ame (*n.*), blâme (*m.*); faute (*f.*):
ship to blame, navire en faute (*m.*).
no blame can be imputed to the company's servant, aucune faute ne peut être imputée au préposé de la compagnie.

lank (*adj.*), blanc, blanche; en blanc; vierge:
blank acceptance, acceptation en blanc (*f.*).
blank credit, crédit en blanc (*m.*); crédit à découvert (*m.*); crédit libre (*m.*); crédit par caisse (*m.*); crédit sur notoriété (*m.*).
blank endorsement, endossement en blanc (*m.*); endos en blanc (*m.*).
blank paper, papier blanc (*m.*).
blank signature (Law), blanc-seing (*m.*).
blank transaction *or* blank deal, opération blanche (*f.*); affaire en blanc (*f.*).
if, in such or such stock, no deal has been done, the line is left blank (list of quotations), si, sur telle ou telle valeur, il n'a été fait aucune opération, la ligne reste vierge (bulletin de cours).
blank transfer *or* transfer in blank, transfert de (*ou* en) garantie (*m.*); transfert à titre de garantie (*m.*).
Note :—These English and French terms do not correspond exactly, as the practice in France is not the same as in England. In England, the law provides that " no notice of any trust, expressed, implied, or constructive, shall be entered on the register." When shares are pledged, the usual practice is to hand over the share certificate to the pledgee, accompanied by a blank transfer (i.e., transfer signed by the transferor but undated and not containing the name of the transferee). French law allows a company to recognize a trust, the shareholder executing a *transfert de garantie*, which the company enters on its register.

lank (*n.*) *or* blank space, blanc (*m.*); lacune (*f.*):
to leave a blank in a letter, laisser un blanc dans une lettre.

in blank, en blanc:
cheque signed in blank, chèque signé en blanc (*m.*).

lanket mortgage, hypothèque générale (*f.*).

lind entry (Bkkpg), article borgne (*m.*).

lind literature (Post), impressions en relief à l'usage des aveugles (*f.pl.*); imprimés en relief pour aveugles (*m.pl.*).

blind literature rate, tarif des impressions en relief à l'usage des aveugles (*m.*).

bloc (en). V. sous en.

block (counterfoil) (*n.*), souche (*f.*); talon (*m.*).

block (Printing) (*n.*), cliché (*m.*).

block (parcel; lot) (*n.*), partie (*f.*); paquet (*m.*); tranche (*f.*):
to offer on the market big blocks of shares, offrir sur le marché de fortes parties (*ou* de gros paquets) d'actions.
to tie up a block of shares, bloquer une tranche d'actions.

blockade (*n.*), blocus (*m.*).

blockade *or* block (*v.t.*), bloquer:
port blockaded (*or* blocked) by the enemy, port bloqué par l'ennemi (*m.*).

blotter (*n.*) *or* blotting pad *or* blotting case, buvard (*m.*); sous-main (*m.*); sous-main buvard (*m.*); carton buvard (*m.*); cartable (*m.*).

blotter (waste book) (*n.*), brouillard (*m.*); main courante (*f.*); mémorial (*m.*); chiffrier (*m.*); brouillon (*m.*).

blotting dabber, buvard (tampon) (*m.*).

blotting paper (white, pink), papier buvard (blanc, rose) (*m.*).

blue pencil, crayon bleu (*m.*).

blue ribbon *or* blue riband, ruban bleu (*m.*):
the fight for the blue ribbon of the Atlantic (the blue ribbon is the symbol of the speed record), la lutte pour le ruban bleu de l'Atlantique (le ruban bleu est le symbole du record de la vitesse).

blue train (Rly.), train bleu (*m.*).

bluff (*n.*), bluff (*m.*).

bluff (*v.t.*), bluffer:
to bluff someone, bluffer quelqu'un.

bluff (*v.i.*), bluffer.

bluffer (pers.) (*n.*), bluffeur, -euse.

board (*n.*) *or* board of directors, conseil (*m.*); conseil d'administration (*m.*); administration (*f.*):
a company is administered by a board of directors elected by shareholders. The board chooses a manager, la société est administrée par le conseil d'administration élu par les actionnaires. Le conseil d'administration choisit le directeur.
board of customs, conseil d'administration des douanes.
board of management, conseil de gérance.
By order of the Board, So-and-so, Secretary (subscription to a notice of meeting, or the like), Le Conseil d'administration.

board (on), à bord; à bord de:
loading the goods on board the ship, chargement de la marchandise à bord le navire (*ou* à bord du navire) (*m.*).
expenses until on board the vessel, frais jusqu'à bord du navire (*m.pl.*).

board (to go on board) (*v.t.*), aborder:
customs officials who board a ship, agents des douanes qui abordent un navire (*m.pl.*).

board meeting, conseil des administrateurs (*m.*); réunion du conseil (*f.*); réunion du conseil d'administration (*f.*):

to attend a board meeting, assister à un conseil des administrateurs.

the next board meeting, la prochaine réunion du conseil (ou du conseil d'administration).

board minutes, procès-verbal des délibérations du conseil d'administration (m.).

boat (n.), bateau (m.); canot (m.); embarcation (f.); navire (m.); bâtiment (m.); vaisseau (m.):

lifeboat, bateau de sauvetage; canot de sauvetage; embarcation de sauvetage.

the ship's boats, les embarcations du bord.

boat deck, pont tente (m.); pont des embarcations (m.).

boat train, train de paquebot (m.); train de correspondance avec le paquebot (m.); train de passagers (m.).

body [**bodies** pl.] (of a ship) (n.), corps (m.), coque (f.) (d'un navire).

body (of a cheque, of a bill, of an insurance policy) (n.), corps (m.):

to put the amount in words at length in the body of a cheque, mettre la somme en toutes lettres dans le corps d'un chèque.

body of creditors (the major portion), masse des créanciers (f.):

right highly advantageous to the body of creditors, droit éminemment favorable à la masse des créanciers (m.).

boiler (n.), chaudière (f.).

bona fide, de bonne foi; bona fide:

bona fide holder, détenteur de bonne foi (m.).

bona fide purchaser, acquéreur de bonne foi (m.); acheteur de bonne foi (m.).

to act bona fide, agir de bonne foi; agir bona fide.

bond (debt certificate) (n.) (Abbrev.: **bd** [**bds** pl.]), bon (m.); obligation (f.); titre (m.); valeur (f.):

prize bond or lottery bond, bon à lots; obligation à lots; titre à lots; valeur à lots.

bond (obligation in writing) (n.), obligation (f.); acte (m.); contrat (m.):

bottomry bond, contrat à la grosse sur corps.

bond (of indemnity) (n.), cautionnement (m.); obligation (f.); obligation de garantie (f.); acte de caution (m.); acte de cautionnement (m.):

bond of a guarantee society to insure the fidelity of a person about to be appointed to a post, cautionnement d'une association de cautionnement pour assurer la fidélité d'une personne sur le point d'être nommée à un poste.

the bond under which the guarantee society is bound to the Treasury, l'obligation de garantie dont l'association de cautionnement est tenue envers le Trésor.

salvage bond, obligation de garantie d'indemnité de sauvetage.

bond (contract by which two persons agree to submit to the arbitration of a third) (n.), compromis (m.):

arbitration bond, compromis d'arbitrage.

bond (Customs) (n.), soumission cautionnée (f.); soumission de crédit (f.); engagement cautionné (m.): (Cf. **bonded warehouse** o simply **bond.**)

duties secured by bonds, droits garantis pa des soumissions cautionnées (m.pl.).

under security of a bond renewable each yea the declarants may be authorized to take th goods away immediately after examinatior that is to say, before payment of the dutie sous la garantie d'une soumission cautionné renouvelable chaque année, les déclarant peuvent être autorisés à enlever les mar chandises aussitôt après la vérification c'est-à-dire avant le paiement des droits.

bond (Customs) (v.t.), entreposer.

bondholder. V. ci-après.

bond note (Customs), acquit à caution (m.); acquit-à-caution (m.).

bonded goods, marchandises d'entrepôt (f.pl.); marchandises entreposées (f.pl.):

bonded goods only pay duty, if any, when the are taken out of bond for home use, le marchandises entreposées (ou les mar chandises d'entrepôt) n'acquittent les droits le cas échéant, qu'au moment où elles son retirées de l'entrepôt pour la consommation

bonded shed, tente (f.); magasin-cale (m.):

deposit of goods on wharf or in bonded she (or sheds), dépôt de marchandises à qua ou sous tente (m.).

Note :—A bonded place is deemed by the Frenc Customs as a cale or hold of a ship, hence magasin-cale.

bonded warehouse or **bonded store** or simply **bond** (n.), entrepôt (m.); entrepôt légal (m.) entrepôt de douane (m.):

the right of warehousing in bond (or of storin in a bonded warehouse), le droit d magasinage dans l'entrepôt.

goods taken out of bond for home use, mar chandises retirées de l'entrepôt pour la consommation (f.pl.).

in bond or **in bonded warehouse** (opp. to duty paid), à l'entrepôt; en entrepôt; en E. E. :

goods sold in bond, marchandises vendues à l'entrepôt (f.pl.).

sale in bonded warehouse, vente en entrepôt (f.); vente en E. (f.); vente E. (f.).

bonder (pers.) (n.), entrepositaire (m.); sou-missionnaire cautionné (m.); soumission-naire (m.):

the bonder is obliged to give security to guarantee the duties and fines which may become payable, l'entrepositaire est tenu de fournir caution pour garantir les droits et les amendes qui pourraient devenir exigibles.

bondholder (pers.) (n.), obligataire (m. ou f.); obligationnaire (m. ou f.).

bonding (n.), entreposage (m.); entrepôt (m.):

the bonding of imported goods, l'entreposage (ou l'entrepôt) des marchandises importées.

to enter goods for bonding, déclarer des marchandises pour l'entreposage (ou pour l'entrepôt).

bonus [**bonuses** pl.] (n.), gratification (f.);

sursalaire (*m.*); surpaye (*f.*); prime (*f.*); boni (*m.*); bonification (*f.*); bonus (*m.*):
bonus to the staff, gratification, sursalaire, prime, au personnel.
salaries and bonuses, appointements et gratifications.
to distribute a bonus in new shares, répartir un bonus en actions nouvelles.
Cf. **ex bonus.**

onus shares, actions gratuites (*f.pl.*):
the shareholders will receive one bonus share for five old shares, les actionnaires toucheront une action gratuite pour cinq anciennes (*m.pl.*).

ook (*n.*), livre (*m.*); registre (*m.*); livret (*m.*); journal (*m.*); carnet (*m.*); cahier (*m.*): [Cf. **books** (accounts).]
account book or book of account, livre de compte; livre de comptes; livre de comptabilité; livre comptable; registre de comptabilité; papier-journal (*m.*).
pocketbook, carnet de poche.
book of certificates *or* certificate book, cahier de certificats.
book of forms, carnet de formules.
book of original entry (Bkkpg), journal originaire.
book of stamps (Post), carnet de timbres.

ook (stockbroker's bargain book) (*n.*), carnet (*m.*).

ook (position) (Stock Exch.) (*n.*), position (*f.*):
buyer who must either close his book or give on, acheteur qui doit ou liquider sa position ou se faire reporter (*m.*).

ook (to record in a book) (*v.t.*), enregistrer:
to book a transaction, enregistrer une opération.

ook (to engage) (*v.t.*), engager; retenir; louer; demander:
to book a passage, a freight with a shipping line, engager un passage, un fret avec une ligne de navigation.
to book a room in an hotel, retenir une chambre dans un hôtel.
to book a seat in a train, retenir, louer, une place dans un train.
to book a telephone call, demander une conversation téléphonique:
fixed time calls should be booked at least three hours in advance, les conversations à heure fixe doivent être demandées au moins trois heures à l'avance.

ook (*v.i.*), prendre un billet (des billets):
to book through to Paris, prendre un billet direct pour Paris (*ou* un billet direct à destination de Paris).

ook debt, dette active (*f.*); créance (*f.*); recouvrement (*m.*):
book debts outstanding at the time of sale of a business, recouvrements restant à faire au moment de la vente d'un fonds de commerce.

ook entry, écriture comptable (*f.*).

ook profits (opp. to *realized profits*), bénéfices d'écritures (*m.pl.*).

ook ticket (ticket in book form, as a tour ticket), billet-livret (*m.*).

book value, valeur comptable (*f.*).

booking (recording) (*n.*), enregistrement (*m.*).

booking (engagement of passage or transportation) (*n.*), engagement (*m.*); location (*f.*):
negotiations for freight bookings, négociations pour engagements de fret (*f.pl.*).
booking seats (in a train, or the like), location de places.

booking (conveyance; service) (*n.*), transport (*m.*); voyage (*m.*); service (*m.*):
railway which accepts for booking goods showing evident signs of damage, chemin de fer qui accepte au transport des marchandises présentant des signes manifestes d'avarie (*m.*).
to cancel a booking before departure of the vessel, rompre un voyage avant le départ du vaisseau.
through bookings, transports à forfait; voyages à forfait; forfaits (*m.pl.*); services contractuels:
through bookings to all parts, forfaits pour toutes destinations.
to contract for through booking of goods, entreprendre le transport des marchandises pour un prix déterminé à forfait.

booking clerk, receveur (pour la distribution des billets aux voyageurs) (*m.*).

booking fee, droit d'enregistrement (*m.*).

booking hall (Rly.), salle des pas perdus (*f.*).

booking office (Rly., etc.), guichet de distribution de billets (*m.*); guichet (*m.*).

bookkeeper (pers.) (*n.*), teneur de livres (*m.*); teneuse de livres (*f.*); comptable (*m.*). Cf. exemple sous **accountant.**

bookkeeping (*n.*), tenue des livres (*f.*); tenue de livres (*f.*); comptabilité (*f.*); comptabilisation (*f.*):
double entry bookkeeping, tenue des livres en partie double; comptabilité en partie double; comptabilisation en partie double.
commercial bookkeeping, comptabilité commerciale.
bank bookkeeping, comptabilité de banque.
company bookkeeping, comptabilité de (*ou* des) sociétés.
Cf. exemple sous **accountancy.**

bookkeeping difficulties *or* **difficulties of** (*or* **in**) **bookkeeping,** difficultés comptables (*f.pl.*); difficultés comptabiliaires (*f.pl.*).

bookkeeping machine, machine comptable (*f.*).
V. automatic bookkeeping machine *pour variétés*.

bookkeeping voucher, pièce de comptabilité (*f.*); pièce comptable (*f.*).

booklet (*n.*), brochure (*f.*); livret (*m.*).

books (accounts) (*n.pl.*), livres (*m.pl.*); écritures (*f.pl.*); écritures comptables (*f.pl.*); comptabilité (*f.*):
to keep a firm's books, tenir les livres (*ou* les écritures) (*ou* la comptabilité) d'une maison.
to look for a difference in the books, rechercher une différence dans les livres (*ou* dans les écritures).

boom (in prices) (Stock Exch.) (*n.*) (Ant.: *slump*),

emballement à la hausse (*m.*) ; emballement (des cours) (*m.*).

boom (feverish excitement or enthusiasm) (*n.*), boom (*m.*) :
but after this boom, there was a slump, mais après ce boom, c'est la débâcle.

booming (*adj.*), booming :
the market is booming (Stock Exch.), le marché est booming.

boost the value of a share (to), créer une atmosphère de hausse autour d'une valeur.

bordereau [**bordereaux** *pl.*] (*n.*), bordereau (*m.*).

borne by (to be), être à la charge de ; être supporté (-e) par :
all charges shall be borne by the consignee, tous les frais sont à la charge du destinataire.

borrow (*v.t.*), emprunter :
to borrow money from someone at high interest, on mortgage, on security (*or* on collateral), emprunter de l'argent à quelqu'un à gros intérêt, sur (*ou* à) hypothèque, sur nantissement.

borrow (to take in) (Stock Exch.) (*v.t.*), emprunter ; reporter ; prendre en report :
to borrow stock, emprunter des titres ; reporter des titres ; prendre des titres en report ; reporter (*v.i.*) :
stock borrowed, titres empruntés (*m.pl.*) ; titres reportés (*m.pl.*) ; titres pris en report (*m.pl.*).
Pour exemples de reporter (*v.i.*), V. *sous* to take in (*v.i.*).

borrower (pers.) (*n.*), emprunteur, -euse :
borrower on bottomry or respondentia, emprunteur à la grosse ; preneur à la grosse (*m.*).

borrowing (*adj.*), emprunteur, -euse :
borrowing State, État emprunteur (*m.*).
borrowing company, société emprunteuse (*f.*).

borrowing (*n.*), emprunt (*m.*) ; emprunts (*m.pl.*) :
borrowing a sum of money, emprunt d'une somme d'argent.
all the transactions of the banker may be summed up, shortly, in borrowing and in lending, toutes les opérations du banquier peuvent se résumer, en définitive, en emprunts et en prêts.

bottom (*n.*) (Ant. : *top*), fond (*m.*) ; bas (*m.*) ; pied (*m.*) :
the bottom of the fall has been reached, le fond de la baisse a été atteint.
bottom of a page, bas, pied, d'une page.

bottom (of a ship) (*n.*), carène (*f.*) :
sighting the bottom after stranding, examen de la carène après échouement (*m.*).

bottom (ship) (*n.*), navire (*m.*).

bottom (*v.i.*), toucher le fond (*ou* le tuf) :
price which has bottomed, prix qui a touché le fond (*ou* le tuf) (*m.*).

bottom left hand corner, angle gauche inférieur (*m.*).

bottom price (Stock Exch.), cours le plus bas (*m.*).

bottom right hand corner, angle droit inférieur (*m.*). Cf. exemple sous **top right hand corner**.

bottomry (Mar. Law) (*n.*), grosse sur corps (*f.*) grosse aventure sur corps (*f.*) ; bomeri (*f.*). (Cf. **respondentia**.)

bottomry bond, contrat à la grosse sur corp (*m.*).

bottomry loan, prêt à la grosse sur corps (*m.*).

bottomry or respondentia, grosse (*f.*) ; gross aventure (*f.*).

bottomry or respondentia bond, contrat à l grosse (*m.*) ; contrat de grosse (*m.*).

bottomry or respondentia loan, prêt à la gross (*m.*) ; prêt à (*ou* de) retour de voyage (*m.*) emprunt à la grosse (*m.*).

bought book *or* **bought journal** (Bkkpg), livr d'achats (*m.*) ; livre des achats (*m.*) ; livr d'achat (*m.*) ; journal des achats (*m.*) facturier d'entrée (*m.*).

bought contract (Stock Exch.) (opp. to *sol contract*), bordereau d'achat (*m.*).

bought ledger, grand livre des achats (*m.*).

Bought of (formula on an invoice). V. sous sy **Dr to**.

bound (to be). V. sous **bind**.

bound book, livre relié (*m.*) ; livre à feuille fixes (*ou* à feuillets fixes) (*m.*).

bound for, à destination de :
ship coming from Antwerp and bound fc London, navire venant d'Anvers, à destina tion de Londres (*m.*).

bounty [**bounties** *pl.*] (*n.*), prime (*f.*) :
bounties on production, on exports, primes la production, à l'exportation.

bourse (*n.*), bourse (*f.*) :
the Paris Bourse, la Bourse de Paris.
Note :—The full designation of the Paris Bours building is *Palais de la Bourse.*
For information concerning the Paris Bours see under marché des valeurs.

box [**boxes** *pl.*] (*n.*), boîte (*f.*) :
box of nibs *or* box of pens, boîte de plumes.

box (portfolio) (*n.*), portefeuille (*m.*) :
security kept in the box and cashed at du date, valeur gardée en portefeuille e encaissée à l'échéance (*f.*).
we have a large quantity of these shares i our (*or* in the) box, nous avons une grand quantité de ces actions en portefeuille.

box wagon *or* **box car** (Rly.) (opp. to *open wagon* wagon couvert (*m.*) ; wagon fermé (*m.*).

boy (ship boy) (pers.) (*n.*), mousse (*m.*).

boycott *or* **boycotting** (*n.*), boycottage (*m.*).

boycott (*v.t.*), boycotter.

brake van *or* simply **brake** (*n.*) (Rly.), fourgo (*m.*).

branch (division ; department) (*n.*), branch (*f.*) :
branch of industry, of commerce (*or* of trade branche de l'industrie, du commerce.

branch (*n.*) *or* **branch office** (Abbrev. : **B.O.**) (su ordinate local office, store, etc.) (opp. t *head office*), succursale (*f.*) ; bureau succu sale (*m.*).

branch (of a bank) (*n.*), succursale (*f.*), compto (*m.*) (d'une banque).

branch account (opp. to *head office account* compte succursale (*m.*).

anch house (opp. to *parent house*), maison
  succursale (*f.*).
anch manager, directeur de succursale (*m.*).
anch pilot, lamaneur (*m.*); pilote lamaneur
  (*m.*); locman (*m.*). V. note sous **pilot.**
anch piloting, lamanage (*m.*).
and (*n.*), marque (*f.*).
each (violation of official duty) (*n.*), infraction
  (*f.*); violation (*f.*); contravention (*f.*):
breach of the conditions and undertakings,
  infraction aux conditions et engagements.
breach of the regulations, infraction aux
  règlements; contravention.
breach of trust, infidélité (*f.*); prévarication
  (*f.*); abus de confiance (*m.*).
breach of warranty, violation (*ou* infraction)
  de garantie.
eak (in prices) (*n.*), dérobade (*f.*):
tins did not attempt to react from last week's
  break, les stannifères n'ont pas cherché
  à réagir contre la dérobade de la semaine
  dernière (*f.pl.*).
eak (*v.t.*), rompre; briser; enfreindre:
to break a record, battre un record. V. exemple
  sous syn. **beat a record (to).**
to break a seal, briser un cachet.
to break an agreement, rompre un marché.
to break bulk *or* to break the stowage, rompre
  charge; désarrimer:
reforwarding wagons without breaking bulk,
  réexpédition des wagons sans rompre charge
  (*f.*).
to break the rule, enfreindre la règle.
eak of journey (Rly., etc.), arrêt en cours de
  route (*m.*); interruption de voyage (*f.*).
eak one's journey (to), interrompre son voyage
  en cours de route.
eak up *or* break *or* breaking (wreck of a ship)
  (*n.*), bris (*m.*).
eak up (*v.t.*), briser; démolir; dépecer;
  rompre:
ship which is broken up (wrecked), navire qui
  est brisé (*m.*).
to break up an old boat (to take it to pieces),
  démolir, dépecer, un vieux bateau.
to break up a voyage, rompre un voyage.
eakage (*n.*), casse (*f.*); rupture (*f.*); bris (*m.*):
breakage of fragile articles, casse, rupture,
  bris, des objets fragiles.
breakage of shaft, rupture d'arbre.
eakage risk, risque de casse (*m.*).
eaking bulk *or* breaking the stowage, rupture
  de charge (*f.*); désarrimage (*m.*).
eaking off of diplomatic relations, rupture de
  relations diplomatiques (*f.*).
eaking out of a fire, of war, éclatement d'un
  incendie, de la guerre (*m.*).
eaking up an old boat, démolition (*f.*), dépècement (*m.*), dépeçage (*m.*) d'un vieux bateau.
eaking up of a voyage, rupture d'un voyage (*f.*).
ief (of a case) (Law) (*n.*), dossier (d'une
  procédure) (*m.*).
ief counsel (to), constituer avocat.
iefing counsel, constitution d'avocat (*f.*).
ightness (*n.*), bonne orientation (*f.*):
the brightness of oil shares this week is explained

by the general condition of the oil market
  in America, la bonne orientation des valeurs
  de pétrole cette semaine s'explique par la
  situation générale du marché du pétrole en
  Amérique.
brighter tendency in tins at the finish, meilleure
  orientation en stannifères en fin de séance.
X. shares were a bright spot at 1¾, les actions
  X. sont en bonne (*ou* excellente) orientation
  à 1 3/4.
bring a ship into a port, to destination (to), conduire un navire dans un port, à destination.
bring a thing off (to) (to do the business), faire
  l'affaire:
we hope to bring the thing off, nous espérons
  faire l'affaire.
bring an action against someone (to), intenter
  une action à (*ou* contre) quelqu'un; actionner
  quelqu'un; attaquer quelqu'un en justice.
bring down (*v.t.*), abaisser:
to bring down a price, abaisser un prix.
bring forward (Bkkpg) (*v.t.*) (opp. to *carry forward*), reporter:
to bring forward an amount from another
  page, reporter une somme d'une autre
  page.
bring in (to yield) (*v.t.*), rapporter; rendre:
house that brings in so much a year, maison
  qui rapporte tant par an (*f.*).
security which brings in 5% per annum,
  valeur qui rend 5 0/0 l'an (*f.*).
bring in (to) *or* bring into (a business) (to),
  apporter:
the interest (*or* share) of each partner in the
  profits is proportional to what he brings in,
  le tantième de chaque associé dans les
  bénéfices est proportionnel à ce qu'il apporte.
bring into account (to), faire entrer en compte.
bring off a coup on the stock exchange (to), faire
  un coup sur la bourse.
bring out (Stock Exch.) (*v.t.*), introduire. V.
  exemple sous **bringing out.**
bring out a company (to), lancer une compagnie.
bring the interested parties together (to), aboucher
  les intéressés.
bring the rates to level time (*or* to the same level)
  (to) (Arbitrage of exchange), niveler les
  cours.
bring to (to) (to reduce to), ramener à:
to bring the prices in the different countries to
  gold francs, the only rational means of
  effecting a practical comparison, ramener
  les prix dans les différents pays en francs-
  or, seul moyen rationnel d'effectuer une
  comparaison pratique.
bringing forward (Bkkpg), report (*m.*):
bringing forward a total from the bottom of
  the previous page, report d'un total du bas
  de la page précédente.
bringing out (Stock Exch.), introduction (*f.*):
to succeed in a bringing out of shares on the
  market and bring in a buying public, the
  shop generally secures the help of widely
  circulating financial organs, which extol the
  merits of the shares brought out, pour réussir
  une introduction de valeurs sur le marché

et amener un public acheteur, les introducteurs s'assurent, d'habitude, le concours des organes financiers à grands tirages, qui prônent les mérites des valeurs introduites.

bringing out (a company), lancement (d'une compagnie) (*m.*).

bringing the rates to level time (*or* **to the same level**) (Arbitrage), nivellement des cours (*m.*).

broadcasting (*n.*), radiodiffusion (*f.*).

broadcasting station, station de radiodiffusion (*f.*).

broke (*v.i.*) *or* **to do broking** *or* **to be a broker,** courter; faire le courtage:

to broke in marine insurance, that is to say, to put into communication insurers and insured, faire le courtage des assurances maritimes, c'est-à-dire mettre en rapport assureurs et assurés.

broker (pers.) (*n.*), courtier, -ère; agent (*m.*): insurance broker, courtier d'assurances.

broker *or* **stockbroker** (Stock Exch.) (pers.) (*n.*), agent (*m.*); agent de change (*m.*); banquier (*m.*); banquier en valeurs (*m.*); courtier (*m.*):

Note :—These English and French terms do not correspond exactly, the French Bourse practice differing materially from English Stock Exchange practice. The *agent de change* is a State nominated broker. He operates in a separate market, known as the *parquet*, and is distinguished from the *coulissier* or *banquier*, who deals in the market known as the *coulisse* or *marché en banque.* See *fuller explanation of Paris Bourse system under* marché des valeurs.

outside broker, banquier marron (*m.*); courtier marron (*m.*).

broker's account *or* **brokers' account** (settlement a/c.) (Stock Exch.), compte de liquidation (*m.*).

broker's contract (commission contract) (Produce Exch.) (opp. to *direct contract* or *principal contract*), contrat de commission (*m.*).

broker's contract note (Stock Exch.), bordereau d'agent de change (*m.*); bordereau de bourse (*m.*).

broker's note, bordereau de courtage (*m.*).

brokerage (commission) (*n.*), courtage (*m.*).

brokerage (commission paid to stockbrokers, or others, for introducing applicants for shares) (*n.*), commission de placement (*f.*).

broking *or* **brokerage** (*n.*), courtage (*m.*):

freight broking *or* freight brokerage, courtage des affrètements.

brought forward *or* *simply* **forward** (inscription at the top of a page) (Bkkpg) (Abbrev.: **b/f.** *or* **brot fwd** *or* **bt fwd** *or* *simply* **fwd** *or* **fd**) (opp. to *carried forward*), report: (*Note :*— If two amounts are brought forward, as in a journal, *brought forward* remains invariable in English, but in French the plural *reports* must be used.)

brought forward from folio . . ., report du folio . . .

bucket shop, maison de contre-partie (*f.*); officine de contre-partie (*f.*).

budge (*v.i.*), bouger:

the price does not budge, le cours ne boug pas.

budget (*n.*), budget (*m.*):

the budget of this State balances, le budget d cet État se solde en équilibre.

budget for (to), budgéter:

to budget for expenses, budgéter des dépenses

budgetary (*adj.*), budgétaire:

budgetary receipts, recettes budgétaires (*f.pl.*)

budla operation *or* **budlaing** (*n.*), vente au comp tant contre rachat à terme.

build *or* **build up** (*v.t.*), bâtir; construire:

ships built abroad, navires construits l'étranger (*m.pl.*).

to build up one's fortune, bâtir sa fortune.

builder (pers.) (*n.*), constructeur (*m.*):

shipbuilder, constructeur de navires.

builder's certificate (ships'), certificat de cons tructeur (*m.*).

building (edifice) (*n.*), bâtiment (*m.*); constructio (*f.*).

building port, port de construction (*m.*).

bulk (*n.*), volume (*m.*):

wastage in bulk, freinte en volume (*f.*).

bulk (**in**), en vrac; en vrague; en grenier:

to ship grain in bulk, charger des grains e vrac (*ou* en grenier).

goods in bulk are generally embarked by mean of special apparatus, la marchandise e vrac s'embarque généralement au moye d'appareils spéciaux.

bulkhead (*n.*), cloison étanche (*f.*).

bulky (*adj.*) *or* **of exceptional bulk in proportio to weight** (said of a parcel, or the like) encombrant, -e:

bulky parcel, colis encombrant (*m.*).

the cloak room fee is increased for certai articles of exceptional bulk in proportio to weight (bicycles, perambulators, etc.) le droit de garde est majoré pour certain objets encombrants (bicyclettes, voitures d'enfant, etc.).

Cf. long, heavy, or bulky articles.

bull (Stock Exch.) (pers.) (*n.*) (opp. to *bear*) 'haussier (*m.*):

bulls buy for the settlement stocks which they hope to resell at a higher price, les haussiers achètent à terme des valeurs qu'ils espèrent revendre à un cours plus élevé.

the market is all bulls, la place (*ou* la position de place) est chargée.

bull (*v.t.*) *or* **to bull the market,** acheter à découvert:

to speculate on the stock exchange, that is to say, to bull or to bear (*or* to bull or to bear the market), spéculer sur la bourse, c'est-à-dire acheter ou vendre à découvert.

bull account (*or* **position**), position acheteur (*ou* à la hausse) (*f.*). V. exemple sous **bear account.**

bull campaign, campagne de hausse (*f.*).

bull point, point en faveur (des haussiers) (*m.*).

bull purchase, achat à découvert (*m.*).

bull transaction, opération à la hausse (*f.*).

bulletin (*n.*), bulletin (*m.*).

bullion (*n.*), matières d'or et d'argent (*f.pl.*); matières (*f.pl.*).

bullion point, gold-point (*m.*).

bullion reserve (Banking), réserve métallique (*f.*).

bullion trade, commerce des matières d'or et d'argent (*m.*).

bullish tendency (Stock Exch.), tendance à la hausse (*f.*).

bunch (of keys) (*n.*), trousseau (de clefs) (*m.*).

bundle (*n.*), liasse (*f.*):
bundle of letters, liasse de lettres.
bundle of papers, liasse de papiers (*f.*); dossier (*m.*).

bundle (papers) (*v.t.*), enliasser.

bundling (papers) (*n.*), enliassement (*m.*).

bunker (*n.*), soute (*f.*):
coal bunker, soute à charbon.

bunker (*v.i.*), faire du charbon; charbonner:
to bunker en route (*or* bunkering on the voyage) is very expensive, faire du charbon (*ou* charbonner) en route est fort cher.
to call to bunker (*or* for bunkering), relâcher pour faire du charbon; faire relâche pour charbonner.

bunker coal *or* **bunkers** (*n.pl.*), charbon de soute (*m.*).

bunkering (*n.*), charbonnage (*m.*):
the speed of bunkering is limited by the trimming in the bunkers, la rapidité du charbonnage est limitée par l'arrimage dans les soutes.

buoy (*n.*), bouée (*f.*).

buoyancy (*n.*), élan (*m.*); entrain (*m.*):
rubber shares hardened during the first half of the week, then, during Thursday's session, they showed very distinct buoyancy (*or* were distinctly buoyant), les valeurs de caoutchouc se sont progressivement raffermies pendant la première moitié de la semaine, puis elles ont fait preuve, dans la séance de jeudi, d'un entrain très net (*f.pl.*).
alone, the market of New York showed renewed signs of activity and buoyancy, but its influence did not make itself felt in a tangible manner on our market, seul, le marché de New-York fait à nouveau preuve d'allant et d'entrain, mais son influence ne se fait pas sentir de manière tangible sur notre place.

burden *or* **burthen** (of a ship) (*n.*), port (*m.*); maximum de charge (*m.*):
a ship of 1,000 tons burden (*or* burthen), un navire du port de 1 000 tonneaux. (*Cf.* to be of . . . burden, *sous* be.)

burden (to weight) (*v.t.*), grever:
to burden the budget of expenses of one accounting period with an exceptionally heavy sum, grever le budget de dépenses d'un exercice d'une somme exceptionnellement grosse.
the national products thus finding themselves more heavily burdened than in the past, les produits nationaux se trouvant ainsi plus lourdement grevés que sur le passé (*m.pl.*).

burden of proof *or* **burden of proving,** charge de la preuve (*f.*); fardeau de la preuve (*m.*):
burden of proof which falls on the insurer, charge (*ou* fardeau) de la preuve qui incombe à l'assureur.
to throw on someone the burden of proving a wrongful act, mettre à la charge de quelqu'un le fardeau de la preuve d'une faute.

bureau [bureaus *or* bureaux *pl.*] (*n.*), bureau (*m.*); agence (*f.*); office (*m.*):
publicity bureau, bureau (*ou* agence) (*ou* office) de publicité.
bureau de change (exchange office), bureau de change; change (*m.*).
Bureau Veritas *or simply* Veritas (*n.*) (ships' classification society), Bureau Veritas (*m.*); Veritas (*m.*):
the register of the Bureau Veritas is called the *Veritas Register* from the emblem Truth adopted by the Society, le registre du Bureau Veritas est appelé le *Registre Veritas* du nom de l'emblème Vérité adopté par la Société.

burglary insurance, assurance contre le vol (*f.*).

burnt (*adj.* or *p.p.*), incendié, -e; sinistré, -e:
burnt house, maison incendiée (*f.*); maison sinistrée (*f.*).

bursting of boilers, of pipes, éclatement (*m.*), explosion (*f.*) de chaudières, de conduites.

bus [buses *or* busses *pl.*] (*n.*), omnibus (*m.*).

business (commercial affairs; trade) (*n.*), affaires (*f.pl.*); commerce (*m.*); 'haut commerce (*m.*); négoce (*m.*):
to do business with someone, faire des affaires avec quelqu'un. [**business done** (Stock Exch.), V. ci-après.]
to be in business, être dans les affaires.
business is bad, les affaires vont mal; le commerce va mal.
banking business *or* business of banking, commerce de banque.

business (a commercial enterprise or establishment; goodwill) (*n.*), affaire (*f.*); entreprise (*f.*); fonds (*m.*); fonds de commerce (*m.*):
to take a share in the business, prendre une participation dans l'affaire.
a profitable business, une entreprise rémunératrice.
to buy a business, acheter un fonds.
a baker's business, un fonds de boulanger.

business (occupation; profession) (*n.*), qualité (*f.*). V. exemple sous **profession or business.**

business (transactions at a meeting; matters to be considered; agenda) (*n.*), délibérations (*f.pl.*); questions à délibérer (*f.pl.*); questions (*f.pl.*); résolutions (*f.*); ordre du jour (*m.*):
the business of a meeting, les délibérations d'une assemblée.
to put down on the agenda the business to be transacted, mettre à l'ordre du jour les questions à délibérer.
there being no other business, the meeting was closed *or* there being no further business before the meeting, the sitting **was**

closed, rien n'étant plus à l'ordre du jour, la séance est levée.

general business (last item on agenda), questions diverses ; résolutions diverses.

meeting convened to transact the following business, assemblée convoquée à l'effet de délibérer sur l'ordre du jour suivant (*f.*).

business agent, représentant de commerce (*m.*).

business card, carte d'adresse (*f.*).

business centre, centre des affaires (*m.*).

business day (opp. to *non business day*), jour non férié (*m.*); jour ouvrable (*m.*); jour de travail (*m.*).

business day (Stock Exch.), jour non férié (*m.*); jour ouvrable (*m.*); jour de travail (*m.*); bourse (*f.*); jour de bourse (*m.*):

five clear business days before the date fixed for the drawing, cinq jours de bourse francs (*ou* cinq bourses pleines) avant la date fixée pour le tirage.

the stock must be delivered within ten business days of the sale, les titres doivent être livrés dans les dix bourses qui suivent la vente (*ou* livrés avant la dixième bourse qui suit celle de la vente) (*m.pl.*).

business done (Stock Exch.), cours pratiqués (*m.pl.*); cours faits (*m.pl.*). V. *exemples sous* to do a bargain.

business done should have been (Stock Exchange List), lire :
Erratum.—In yesterday's List the business done in X. Shares at ⸺ should have been ⸺, Actions X. Hier, lire ⸺.

business done should not have been marked (Stock Exchange List), cours nul :
Erratum.—In yesterday's List the business done in X. Shares should not have been marked ⸺, Actions X. Hier, cours nul.

business enterprise, entreprise commerciale (*f.*).

business hours, heures d'ouverture (*f.pl.*); heures d'ouverture et de clôture (*f.pl.*).

business house, maison de commerce (*f.*).

business man, homme d'affaires (*m.*).

business manager, gérant d'affaires (*m.*).

business name, raison de commerce (*f.*); raison commerciale (*f.*); nom commercial (*m.*).

business papers, papiers d'affaires (*m.pl.*).

business premises, locaux commerciaux (*m.pl.*); immeuble commercial (*m.*).

business quarter, quartier commerçant (*m.*).

business world, monde des affaires (*m.*).

butt (counterfoil) (*n.*), souche (*f.*); talon (*m.*).

buy (*v.t.*) (Ant.: *sell*), acheter; acquérir :

to buy a house, acheter une maison.

ships bought from foreign owners, navires achetés à des armateurs étrangers (*m.pl.*).

to buy a bull (Stock Exch.), acheter à découvert :

to speculate on the stock exchange, that is to say, to buy a bull or sell a bear, spéculer sur la bourse, c'est-à-dire acheter ou vendre à découvert.

to buy a pig in a poke, acheter chat en poche.

to buy at a high price, acheter cher ; acheter chèrement.

to buy cheap, acheter à bon compte.

to buy direct, wholesale, retail, acheter en gros, en demi-gros, en détail (V. note sous **wholesale**).

to buy for a rise (Stock Exch.), acheter à la hausse.

to buy for cash (*or* for money), acheter comptant ; acheter au comptant.

to buy for the settlement (*or* for the account) (Stock Exch.), acheter à terme.

to buy on a fall (Stock Exch.), acheter à la baisse.

to buy on commission, acheter à la commission.

to buy on credit, acheter à crédit (*ou* à terme).

bt (*abbrev.*), bought.

buy and sell on commission (to), faire le courtage ; courter.

buy back (*v.t.*), racheter :

to buy back an article sold, racheter un objet vendu.

buy back (to cover bear sales) (Stock Exch.) (*v.t.*), racheter :

the buyer sells out (*or* sells) the stock he cannot take up and the seller buys back the stock he cannot deliver, l'acheteur revend les titres qu'il ne peut pas lever et le vendeur rachète les titres qu'il ne peut livrer (*m.*). V. note sous **sell out**.

buy back (Stock Exch.) (*v.i.*), se racheter :

seller obliged to buy back in order to meet his delivery, vendeur obligé de se racheter pour faire face à sa livraison (*m.*).

I buy back at such or such a price, je me rachète à tel cours.

the bears (*or* the shorts) are buying back, le découvert se rachète.

buy in (Stock Exch.) (*v.t.*). V. exemples :

to buy in against a seller, exécuter (*ou* racheter) un vendeur.

to buy in stock, securities, racheter des titres, des valeurs.

to buy in or sell out against *or* **to buy in or sell out,** exécuter :

broker who has the right to buy in or sell out against his client during the settlement, agent qui a le droit d'exécuter son client dans le courant de la liquidation (*m.*).

stock bought in or sold out, valeurs exécutées (*f.pl.*).

Cf. **sell out**.

buy out (*v.t.*), désintéresser :

to buy out a partner, désintéresser un associé.

buyable (*adj.*), achetable.

buyer (pers.) (*n.*), acheteur, -euse; acquéreur -eure *ou* -euse; preneur, -euse :

an Oriental proverb says : " The buyer needs a hundred eyes, the seller only one," un proverbe oriental dit : « Il faut cent yeux à l'acheteur, un seul au vendeur. »

prices bid (buyers) (Stock Exch.), cours demandés (acheteurs) (*m.pl.*).

when the market is a buyer, quand la place est acheteur.

X. preference found buyers at 2¼, la privilégiée X. trouve acquéreur à 2 1/4.

barley :   parcels Azoff/Black Sea, March-April, 17/6d. paid and buyers (*or abbreviated* 17/6 p. & b.),   orges : parcelles Azoff mer noire, mars-avril, 17/6d. payé et acheteur.

negotiable paper always finds a buyer,   le papier négociable trouve toujours preneur.

public funds easily find buyers on the stock exchange,   les fonds publics trouvent facilement preneurs en bourse (*m.pl.*).

uyer of a call option (giver for a call) (Stock Exch.),   acheteur d'un dont (*m.*) ;   acheteur d'une prime directe (*m.*).

uyer of a put option (giver for a put) (Stock Exch.),   vendeur d'un ou (*m.*) ;   vendeur d'une prime indirecte (*m.*).   V. note sous syn. **giver for a put.**

uyer's option (call) (Stock or other Exch.),   prime pour l'acheteur (*f.*) ;   prime acheteur (*f.*) ;   prime pour lever (*f.*) ;   marché à prime pour lever (*m.*) ;   prime pour lever ou non (*f.*) ;   prime directe (*f.*) ;   dont (*m.*) ;   prime dont (*f.*) ;   prime plus (*f.*) ;   prime simple à la hausse (*f.*).

uyer's option to double,   doublé à la hausse (*m.*) ;   doublure à la hausse (*f.*) ;   faculté de lever double (*f.*) ;   option du double (*f.*).

uyer's option to quadruple,   quadruplé à la hausse (*m.*) ;   faculté de lever quadruple (*f.*).

uyer's option to treble,   triplé à la hausse (*m.*) ;   faculté de lever triple (*f.*).

uyers over (Stock Exch.), la place (*ou* la position de place) est chargée.

uying (*n.*), achat (*m.*) ;   acquisition (*f.*) :   the act of commerce is essentially buying to sell again, l'acte de commerce est essentiellement l'achat pour revendre (*m.*).

buying a call (Stock Exch.),   achat dont ; achat à prime directe.

buying for cash (*or* for money), achat au comptant ; achat comptant.

buying for the settlement (*or* for the account) (Stock Exch.),   achat à terme.

buying back, rachat (*m.*) :   buying back of bear sellers (Stock Exch.), rachats des vendeurs à découvert.

buying brokerage, courtage d'achat (*m.*).

buying commission, commission d'achat (*f.*).

buying in and selling out *or* **buying in or selling out** (Stock Exch.), exécution (*f.*) ; exécution en bourse (*f.*).   buying in against a seller (Stock Exch.), exécution (*f.*),   rachat (*m.*) d'un vendeur.   Cf. **selling out against a buyer.**   buying in stock, securities (Stock Exch.), rachat de titres, de valeurs (*m.*).

buying in price (Stock Exch.),   cours de rachat (*m.*).

buying order, ordre d'achat (*m.*).

buying out a partner, désintéressement d'un associé (*m.*).

buying rate (Foreign Exchange), cours acheteur (*m.*) ; cours Argent (*m.*) ; A.

By (ledger posting) (Bkkpg) (*prep.*) (opp. to *To*), par :   By Goods, par Marchandises.

by direct steamer (without transhipment),   par vapeur direct.

By order of the Board. V. sous **board.**

by passenger train, by goods train, by air mail, par train de grande vitesse,   par train de petite vitesse, par avion.

C

a'canny strike, grève perlée (*f.*) :   railwaymen who go on ca'canny strike in consequence of the rejection of their demand for increase of wages, cheminots qui font la grève perlée par suite du rejet de leur demande d'augmentation de salaires (*m.pl.*).

abin (of a ship) (*n.*), cabine (*f.*), chambre (*f.*) (d'un navire).

abin baggage (opp. to *hold baggage*), bagages de cabine (*m.pl.*).

abin passenger, passager de cabine (*m.*) ; passager de chambre (*m.*).

able (submarine telegraph) (*n.*), câble (*m.*) :   transatlantic cable, câble transatlantique.

able *or* **cablegram** (*n.*), câble (*m.*) ; câblogramme (*m.*) :   to send a cable (*or* a cablegram), envoyer un câble (*ou* un câblogramme).

able (*v.t.*), câbler :   the manager has cabled that . . ., le directeur a câblé que . . .

cable (*v.i.*), câbler :   to cable to someone, câbler à quelqu'un.

cable company, compagnie de câbles (*f.*).

cable transfer *or* simply **cable** (*n.*) (Foreign Exchange), câble transfert (*m.*) ; câble (*m.*) ; transfert télégraphique (*m.*) ; versement (*m.*) :   on the foreign exchange market, Paris cables were (*or* the Paris cable *or* the cable on Paris was) dealt in at . . ., au marché dès changes, le câble sur Paris se traite à . . .

calculable (*adj.*), calculable ; computable ; chiffrable.

calculate (*v.t.*), calculer ; supputer ; compter ; décompter :   to calculate the interest, the days, calculer, supputer, compter, décompter, les intérêts, les jours.   to calculate the probable results of a true or false piece of news on the price of the funds, supputer les résultats probables d'une nouvelle vraie ou fausse sur le cours des fonds.

to be calculated, être calculé, -e, supputé, -e, compté, -e, décompté, -e ; se calculer ; se supputer ; se compter :
the tax is calculated on the amount of the capital, la taxe se calcule sur le montant des capitaux.

calculate (*v.i.*), compter ; chiffrer.

calculating (*adj.*), calculateur, -trice ; calculant -e.

calculating machine, machine à calculer (*f.*).

calculation (act of reckoning) (*n.*), calcul (*m.*) ; supputation (*f.*) ; comptage (*m.*) ; compte (*m.*) ; décompte (*m.*).

calculation (plan) (*n.*), calcul (*m.*) :
the result has upset our calculations, le résultat a trompé notre calcul.

calculator (pers.) (*n.*), calculateur, -trice ; chiffreur, -euse.

calendar (*n.*), calendrier (*m.*).

calendar day (midnight to midnight), jour du calendrier (*m.*).

calendar month (a month as defined in a calendar ; distinguished from a *lunar month*), mois civil (*m.*) ; mois commun (*m.*).

calendar month (period equivalent to a month, as from Jan. 15 to Feb. 15), mois (*m.*).

calendar year, année civile (*f.*) :
period of twelve months which does not coincide with the calendar year, période de douze mois qui ne coïncide pas avec l'année civile (*f.*).

call (appeal) (*n.*), appel (*m.*) :
call for help of a ship in distress, appel de secours d'un navire en détresse.

call (demand) (*n.*), appel (*m.*) ; demande (*f.*) ; exigence (*f.*) :
call of margin, appel de marge.
deposit repayable at call, dépôt remboursable sur demande (*m.*).
money at (*or* on) call *or* call money *or* loans at call (Money Market), argent remboursable sur demande (*m.*) ; argent à vue (*m.*) ; prêts remboursables sur demande (*m.pl.*).

call (Teleph.) (*n.*), appel (*m.*) ; communication (*f.*) ; conversation (*f.*) :
reply without delay to calls from the exchange, répondez sans retard aux appels du bureau central.
trunk call, communication interurbaine ; conversation interurbaine.

call (Clearing House quotation) (Produce Exch.) (*n.*), cote (*f.*).

call (visit) (*n.*), visite (*f.*) :
to make a call, faire une visite.

call (*n.*) *or* **call at intermediate port** *or* **calling** (*n.*) *or* **calling at intermediate ports** (putting into a named port, i.e., a port in the customary or advertised route), escale (*f.*) :
direct call *or* forward call, escale directe ; échelle directe :
indirect call *or* backward call *or* call behind the named port, escale rétrograde ; échelle rétrograde :

to make any calls, direct or indirect, faire toutes escales (*ou* échelles) directes ou rétrogrades.
ship sailing from Havre and making a call at Brest (*or* and calling at Brest), navire partant du Havre et faisant une escale à Brest (*ou* et escalant à Brest) (*m.*).
calling (*or* call) at a foreign port to receive orders, escale dans un port étranger pour recevoir des ordres.
to call (*or* to make a call) at a port on the route, faire escale (*ou* escaler) dans un port sur la route.
to call, that is to say, to stop at certain intermediate ports, there to take or leave cargo, faire escale (*ou* faire échelle), c'est-à-dire s'arrêter dans certains ports intermédiaires pour y prendre ou laisser des marchandises.
the shortest route and without calling at intermediate ports, la voie la plus directe et sans escale.
(*steamer*) X. (for London) called (*or* cld) (*or* c. Perim 31 (*date*) (Shipping News), (*steamer* X. (pour Londres) a fait escale à Périm le 31 (*date*) (Mouvement des Navires).

call *or* **calling** (putting in for supplies or shelter in or out of the customary or advertised route) (*n.*), relâche (*f.*) :
call rendered necessary by a peril of the sea, relâche rendue nécessaire par une fortune de mer.
calls occasioned whether by the fortuitous loss of cables, anchors, sails, masts, etc., or by the need of revictualling or by a leak to be repaired, relâches occasionnées soit par la perte fortuite de câbles, ancres, voiles, mâts, etc., soit par le besoin de ravitaillement, soit par voie d'eau à réparer.
a call is voluntary or compulsory, la relâche est volontaire ou forcée.

call (instalment on partly paid shares, or the like) (*n.*), appel (*m.*) ; appel de fonds (*m.*) ; versement (*m.*) ; terme (*m.*) :
to make a call, a call of capital, faire un appel de fonds, un appel de capitaux.
payment of calls, versement d'appels de fonds (*m.*).
call paid in advance, versement par anticipation.
final call, versement de libération ; dernier versement ; dernier terme.

Warning :—Essential diversity of meaning or purport exists in the French expressions *premier*, *second*, *troisième*, etc., *versements* ; thus, *application money* (*versement de souscription*) is often referred to in French as the *premier versement*, and the *first call* sometimes as the *deuxième versement* and sometimes as the *troisième versement*, according as it constitutes the second or the third *payment* or parting with money. The precise application can only be determined by context.
Call in English company practice is not equivocal. *Calls* are assessments demanded after application money and allotment

money ; thus, *first call* is the first money
payable after amount due on allotment.

call (option) (Fin.) (*n.*), option (*f.*); faculté
(*f.*):
to give to the brokers who place the shares a
call on so many shares at so much, donner
aux courtiers qui font le placement des
titres une option de tant d'actions à tant.

call (*n.*) *or* **call option** (Stock or other Exch.)
(opp. to *put* or *put option*), dont (*m.*); prime
directe (*f.*); prime dont (*f.*); prime pour
lever (*f.*); prime pour prendre ou non (*f.*);
prime acheteur (*f.*); prime pour l'acheteur
(*f.*); marché à prime pour lever (*m.*);
prime simple à la hausse (*f.*); prime plus (*f.*):
Note :—On a market where only *calls* are dealt
in, and not *puts*, or where *puts* are exceptional, the word *prime* alone means *call* or
call option. Consequently, all such expressions as *acheter à prime, vente à prime,*
without any further qualification, may be
understood to refer to *calls*, though literally,
prime alone means *option*, without specifying *call* or *put*.
Note :—See explanation of option dealing,
under **option**.
market on which calls and puts are dealt in,
marché où on traite le dont et l'ou (*m.*).
to give for the call *or* to buy a call option,
acheter dont :
speculator who is giver of 1s. (per share) for
the call of 100 X.Y.Z. shares at 25s., spéculateur qui est acheteur de 100 actions
X.Y.Z. à 26 schellings dont 1 schelling (*m.*).
to take for the call *or* to sell a call option,
vendre dont.

call (Option dealings) (Stock Exch.) (*v.t.*), se
déclarer acheteur :
the price having risen I (we) call the stock,
le cours ayant haussé, je me déclare acheteur
(nous nous déclarons acheteurs) des titres.

call (to utter the price of) (*v.t.*) *or* **called (to be)**
(Stock Exch.), faire :
Rentes are called so much *or* they call Rentes
so much ; X.Y.Z. shares are called so
much *or* they call X.Y.Z. shares so much,
la Rente fait tant ; les actions X.Y.Z.
font tant.
there was introduced to-day the new conversion loan which is called ¼% premium,
on a introduit aujourd'hui le nouvel emprunt de conversion qui fait 1/4 0/0 de
prime.

call (*v.i.*) *or* **call at** *or* **call at a named port** (*or*
at an intermediate port) (*or* **at intermediate
ports**) (**to**), faire escale ; faire échelle ;
escaler. V. exemples sous **call** (*n.*).

call (to put in for supplies or shelter) (*v.i.*),
relâcher ; faire relâche :
to call for bunkering, to take orders, to revictual, relâcher pour charbonner (*ou* pour
faire du charbon), pour prendre des ordres,
pour se ravitailler.
the ship shall have liberty to call at ports
even out of the customary or advertised
route, in any order, and for any purpose,

le navire est libre de faire relâche (*ou* de
relâcher) dans les ports qui se trouvent en
dehors de sa route habituelle ou de son
itinéraire annoncé, dans n'importe quel
ordre, et dans n'importe quel but.

call (*v.*) (miscellaneous meanings). V. exemples :
to call a meeting of shareholders, convoquer
une assemblée d'actionnaires.
to call attention to a mistake, an omission,
appeler l'attention sur, relever, faire remarquer, une erreur, une omission.
to call for delivery of shares dealt in for the
settlement, se faire livrer des titres négociés à terme.
to call for production of documents, exiger
communication des pièces.
to call in an advance, rappeler une avance.
to call on (*or* upon) a debtor to pay, sommer un débiteur de payer.
to call on a guarantee, faire appel à une
garantie.
to call on (*or* upon) the underwriters (to take
up shares), faire une application. Cf.
calling upon the underwriters.
to call over an account with the books,
rappeler un compte avec les livres.
to call the exchange, the operator (Teleph.),
appeler le bureau, l'opératrice.
to call the shareholders, the interested parties,
together, convoquer, faire assembler,
assembler, appeler, les actionnaires, les
intéressés.
to call up (*or simply* to call) an instalment on
partly paid shares, appeler un versement
sur des titres non libérés.

call charge (Teleph.), taxe de communication
(*f.*).

call money (Money Market), argent remboursable sur demande (*m.*); argent à vue (*m.*);
prêts remboursables sur demande (*m.pl.*).

call number (Teleph.), numéro d'appel (*m.*):
one should always ask for subscribers by their
call number, il faut toujours demander les
abonnés par leur numéro d'appel.

call of more *or* **call o' more** (Stock Exch.),
doublé à la hausse (*m.*); doublure à la
hausse (*f.*); faculté de lever double (*f.*);
option du double (*f.*).

call of three times more (Stock Exch.), quadruplé à la hausse (*m.*); faculté de lever
quadruple (*f.*).

call of twice more (Stock Exch.), triplé à la
hausse (*m.*); faculté de lever triple (*f.*).

call office (Teleph.), cabine (*f.*); poste public
(*m.*).

call office attendant (Teleph.), gérant (-e) de
cabine.

call price (Stock Exch.), cours du dont (*m.*).

call receipt, récépissé de versement d'appel
de fonds (*m.*).

call sign (Shipping), signal distinctif du code
international des signaux (*m.*).

called subscriber (Teleph.), abonné demandé
(*m.*); demandé (*m.*).

called up capital, capital appelé (*m.*).

caller (visitor) (pers.) (*n.*), visiteur, -euse.

caller (*n.*) *or* **calling subscriber** (Teleph.) (pers.) (opp. to *called*, or *distant, subscriber*), demandeur (*m.*); abonné demandeur (*m.*); abonné appelant (*m.*).

calling (Teleph.) (*n.*), appel (*m.*):
on calling: " A.B. speaking," à l'appel: « Ici A.B. »

calling (Navig.). V. **call** *or* **calling**, ci-avant.

calling (*n.*) *or* **calling together**, convocation (*f.*):
calling the shareholders together, convocation des actionnaires.

calling (*n.*) *or* **calling up**, appel (*m.*):
calling up the final instalment on a partly paid share, appel du dernier versement d'un titre non libéré.

calling clause (Navig.), clause d'échelle (*f.*).

calling for orders bill of lading, connaissement à ordres (*m.*).

calling in *or* **calling over,** rappel (*m.*). V. le verbe pour exemples.

calling ship, navire relâcheur (*m.*):
calling ships which coal, navires relâcheurs qui charbonnent.

calling upon the underwriters *or* **calling on the underwriters to take up shares,** application (*f.*):
being called upon to take up the shares is the chief risk run in taking a share of the underwriting, l'application est le plus grand risque que comporte la prise d'une part syndicale.

if the amount taken firm by the underwriting syndicate is not placed, that is to say, if the underwriters are called on, each underwriter is allotted a fraction of the number of shares unplaced proportional to the amount of his underwriting commitment, en cas de non placement du montant pris ferme par le syndicat de garantie, c'est-à-dire en cas d'application, il est attribué à chaque syndicataire une fraction du nombre de titres non placés proportionnelle au montant de son engagement syndical.

calls risk (Mar. Insce), risque d'escales (*m.*).

camber (basin or dock for boats) (*n.*), darse (*f.*).

cambist (pers.) (*n.*), cambiste (*m.*).

campaign (*n.*), campagne (*f.*):
press campaign, campagne de presse.

canal (*n.*), canal (*m.*):
the Suez canal, the Panama canal, the Manchester ship canal, le canal de Suez, le canal de Panama, le canal maritime de Manchester.

canal boat, bateau de charge (*m.*).

canal boats *or* **canal and/or river boats** (collectively), batellerie (*f.*).

cancel (*v.t.*), annuler; résilier; résoudre; défaire; infirmer; rompre; oblitérer:
to cancel a contract, annuler, résilier, résoudre, un contrat.
to cancel a bargain, a sale, annuler, résilier, résoudre, défaire, un marché, une vente.
to cancel a stamp, annuler, oblitérer, un timbre.
to cancel a letter (opp. to *to confirm a letter*), infirmer une lettre.

to cancel a booking before departure of the vessel, rompre un voyage avant le départ du vaisseau.

cancel each other (to) (said of contra entries) (Bkkpg), s'annuler; se contre-passer.

cancel the customs duty on (to), dégrever des droits de douane:
the customs duty on a parcel abroad is generally cancelled if the parcel is returned, les colis réexpédiés sur leur point d'origine sont généralement dégrevés des droits de douane (*m.pl.*).

cancellable *or* **cancelable** (*adj.*), annulable; résoluble.

cancellation *or* **cancelation** (*n.*), annulation (*f.*); résiliation (*f.*); résiliement (*m.*): résiliment (*m.*); résolution (*f.*); oblitération (*f.*):
cancellation of a lease, annulation, résiliation, résolution, d'un bail.

cancelling price (Produce Exch.), cours de résiliation (*m.*).

cancelling stamp *or* **canceling stamp,** timbre d'annulation (*m.*); timbre oblitérateur (*m.*); oblitérateur (*m.*).

candidate (pers.) (*n.*), candidat (*m.*); postulant, -e:
examination of candidates, examen de candidats (*m.*).

canvass the town (to), faire la place.

canvasser (pers.) (*n.*), placier, -ère; démarcheur (*m.*).

canvassing (*n.*), démarchage (*m.*):
house to house canvassing, démarchage à domicile.

capable (*adj.*), capable; apte; susceptible:
ship which is not capable of making the agreed voyage, navire qui n'est pas apte à faire le voyage convenu (*m.*).
minors are not capable of contracting, les mineurs ne sont pas aptes à contracter (*m.pl.*).
securities capable of being quoted, valeurs susceptibles d'être cotées (*f.pl.*).

capacity [**capacities** *pl.*] (*n.*), capacité (*f.*):
to estimate the purchasing capacity of a country, évaluer la capacité d'achat d'un pays.
to lack capacity for business, manquer de capacité pour les affaires.

capacity (of a port, of a dock) (*n.*), rendement (d'un port, d'un bassin) (*m.*).

capacity (dead-weight capacity of a ship) (*n.*), port en lourd (*m.*); portée en lourd (*f.*).

capacity (dead-weight cargo capacity) (*n.*), port en marchandises (*m.*).

capital (*n.*), capital (*m.*); capitaux (*m.pl.*); fonds (*m.*); fonds (*m.pl.*); mise de fonds (*f.*); mise (*f.*):
in order to engage in this kind of transaction, it is necessary to have a certain capital at command, pour se livrer à ce genre d'opérations, il faut disposer d'un certain capital.
the capital required to construct the line, les capitaux (*ou* les fonds) nécessaires à la construction de la ligne.

a capital the income from which will be more than enough to enable me to pass the remainder of my life in comfort, un fonds dont le revenu sera plus qui suffisant pour me faire passer agréablement le reste de mes jours.

to make good profits with a very small capital, réaliser de bons bénéfices avec une mise de fonds fort peu élevée.

capital invested, capital investi;   mise de fonds.

profit which is equal to so much per cent on the capital (or on the capital invested), bénéfice qui correspond à tant pour cent de la mise de fonds (m.).

working capital, capital de roulement; fonds de roulement.

fixed capital,   capitaux fixes;   capital fixe; capital immobilisé. V. exemple sous **fixed.**

capital (of a company) (n.),   capital (m.):
the capital of the company is £ . . . divided into . . . shares of £ . . each (memorandum of association),   le capital social est fixé à . . . livres et divisé en . . . actions de . . livre(s) chacune.

called up capital or capital called up (opp. to uncalled capital), capital appelé.

paid up capital or capital paid up (opp. to authorized, or nominal, or registered, capital), capital versé;   capital effectif;   capital réel.

fully paid capital or capital fully paid up, capital entièrement (ou complètement) (ou intégralement) versé.

partly paid capital or capital partly paid up, capital non entièrement versé;   capital non libéré.

capital issued as fully paid up otherwise than in cash (opp. to cash capital),   capital-apports (m.).

capital (brought into a business) (n.),   apport (m.):
to withdraw, to lose, one's capital,   retirer, perdre, son apport.

capital account, compte de capital (m.); compte capital (m.); compte d'apport (m.).

capital assets (opp. to revenue, or floating, or circulating assets),   capitaux fixes (m.pl.); capital fixe (m.);   capital immobilisé (m.); actif immobilisé (m.);   valeurs immobilisées (f.pl.).

capital charges, charges du capital (f.pl.).

capital duty, droit de constitution (m.).
Note :—In France, a droit de timbre à la charge des sociétés (stamp duty on companies) is payable in addition to the droit de constitution (lit. incorporation duty).

capital expenditure, immobilisations (f.pl.); dépenses en immobilisations (f.pl.); établissement (m.); dépenses d'établissement (f.pl.):
capital expenditure represents all capital (or assets) corresponding to fixed capital (or assets), and as opposed to floating capital (or assets),   les immobilisations représentent tous les capitaux correspondant au capital fixe, et par opposition au capital circulant.

capital expenditure account,   compte d'immobilisations (m.);   compte immobilisations (m.); compte d'établissement (m.).

capital sum, capital (m.):
date from which a capital sum begins to bear interest, date à partir de laquelle un capital commence à porter intérêt (f.).
interest only runs from the value dates of the capital sums, les intérêts ne courent qu'à partir des dates d'entrée en valeur des capitaux (m.pl.).

capital value, valeur en capital (f.):
the capital value of the stock calculated at the middle price of the day, la valeur en capital des titres calculée au cours moyen du jour.

capitalism (n.),   capitalisme (m.).

capitalist (pers.) (n.),   capitaliste (m. ou f.); richard, -e.

capitalistic (adj.), capitaliste.

capitalizable (adj.), capitalisable:
capitalizable interest,   intérêts capitalisables (m.pl.).

capitalization (n.),   capitalisation (f.);   immobilisation (f.):
capitalization of interest, capitalisation d'intérêts (f.);   anatocisme (m.).
capitalization of stocks, of the average income for the previous two years, capitalisation des valeurs, du revenu moyen des deux années précédentes.
the market capitalization of a concern is obtained by multiplying the price of the share by the number of shares, la capitalisation boursière d'une entreprise s'obtient en multipliant le prix de l'action par le nombre de titres.
capitalization of expenditure,   immobilisation de dépenses.

capitalize (v.t.),   capitaliser;   immobiliser:
to capitalize interest, an income, capitaliser des intérêts, une rente.
to capitalize at 5% the average of the last four years' dividends, capitaliser à 5 0/0 la moyenne des dividendes des quatre dernières années.
the share capitalizes at about $4\frac{1}{2}\%$ its last dividend of 6d., l'action capitalise à 4 1/2 0/0 environ son dernier dividende de 6 pence (f.).
capitalized expenditure,   dépenses immobilisées (f.pl.).

to be capitalized,   être capitalisé, -e;   se capitaliser:
the interest is capitalized at the end of the year, at each rest, l'intérêt se capitalise en fin d'année, à chaque arrêté (m.).

capitalize (v.i.), se capitaliser:
shares which capitalize at 4%, actions qui se capitalisent à 4 0/0 (f.pl.).

capitation tax, impôt de capitation (m.).

capsize (v.i.), chavirer:
ship which, after a collision, capsizes, navire qui, après un abordage, chavire (m.).

capsizing (n.), chavirement (m.).

captain (pers.) (*n.*) (Abbrev.: **Capt.**), capitaine (*m.*); maître (*m.*); patron (*m.*): (V. aussi **master.**)
captain of foreign-going vessel, capitaine au long cours.

captain's copy (of bill of lading), exemplaire du capitaine (*m.*); copie du capitaine (*f.*); copie du vapeur (*f.*). V. *note sous* original stamped bill of lading.

captain's report (of extraordinary incidents during the voyage), rapport de mer (*m.*); journal de mer (*m.*); rapport du capitaine (*m.*).

captor (pers.) (*n.*), capteur (*m.*).

capture (*n.*), capture (*f.*); prise (*f.*).

car (*n.*), wagon (*m.*); voiture (*f.*); chariot (*m.*).

car (motor car) (*n.*), auto (*m. ou f.*); automobile (*m. ou f.*).

car (tram car) (*n.*), voiture (de tramway) (*f.*); tramway (*m.*).

car kilometre, wagon-kilomètre (*m.*); wagon kilométrique (*m.*); voiture-kilomètre (*f.*); voiture kilométrique (*f.*), analogue au *car mile* anglais (wagon-mille *ou* voiture-mille).

car park, parc à voitures (*m.*).

carbon copy or *simply* **carbon** (*n.*) *or* **copy** (*n.*), copie au papier carboné (*f.*); copie (*f.*).

carbon paper or *simply* **carbon** (*n.*), papier carbone (*m.*); papier carboné (*m.*); carbone (*m.*).

card (*n.*), carte (*f.*):
postcard, carte postale.

card (loose card; index card) (*n.*), fiche (*f.*); carte-fiche (*f.*); fiche mobile (*f.*); fiche-carton (*f.*).
cardboard. V. ci-après.

card index, répertoire sur fiches (*m.*); fichier (*m.*); cartothèque (*f.*).

card index or **card index cabinet,** fichier (*m.*); meuble-fichier (*m.*); cartothèque (*f.*).

card money order (Post), mandat-carte (*m.*).

cardboard (*n.*), carton (*m.*):
corrugated cardboard, carton ondulé.

cardboard box, carton (*m.*).

cardinal number or *simply* **cardinal** (*n.*) (opp. to *ordinal number* or *ordinal*), nombre cardinal (*m.*).

care (charge, oversight, or management) (*n.*), soin (*m.*); soins (*m.pl.*); conservation (*f.*):
as regards the care of the goods entrusted to the master, en ce qui concerne les soins à donner aux marchandises dont le capitaine se charge.
care of the property insured, conservation des objets assurés.

care (of public money) (*n.*), maniement (*m.*), manutention (*f.*), gestion (*f.*) (des deniers publics).

care of (Abbrev.: **c/o.**), aux soins de:
Mr A., care of (*or, and usually*, c/o.) Mr B., M. A., aux soins de M. B.

care of general delivery (Post) (U.S.A.), poste restante; bureau restant.

careen (*v.t.*), caréner.

careen (*v.i.*), caréner.

careenage (*n.*), carénage (*m.*).

career (*n.*), carrière (*f.*):
to take up a career, embrasser une carrière.

cargo [**cargoes** *pl.*] (*n.*), cargaison (*f.*); chargement (*m.*); charge (*f.*); marchandises (*f.pl.*); fret (*m.*):
ship which lands the whole or a part of her cargo, navire qui débarque la totalité ou une partie de sa cargaison (*ou* de son chargement) (*ou* de son fret) (*m.*).
the quantity of goods which constitute the cargo of a ship, la quantité de marchandises qui constitue la charge d'un navire.
a wood cargo *or* a cargo of timber, an oil cargo *or* a cargo of oil, une cargaison, un chargement, de bois, de pétrole.

cargo (as distinguished from the *hull* or *ship*) (Mar. Insce) (*n.*), facultés (*f.pl.*):
insurance of hull and cargo, assurance sur corps et facultés (*f.*).

cargo and passenger steamer (*or* **vessel**), cargo mixte (*m.*); paquebot mixte (*m.*); navire mixte (*m.*); vapeur à passagers (*ou* à voyageurs) et à marchandises (*m.*).

cargo boat *or* **cargo vessel** (opp. to *passenger boat* or *vessel*), navire de charge (*m.*); bâtiment de charge (*m.*); cargo-boat (*m.*); cargo (*m.*); navire à cargaison (*m.*); chargebot (*m.*).

cargo insurance (distinguished from *hull insurance*), assurance sur facultés (*f.*).

cargo liner, cargo-liner (*m.*).

cargo passage (opp. to *ballast passage*), voyage avec chargement (*m.*); trajet avec chargement (*m.*).

cargo policy (distinguished from *hull policy*), police sur facultés (*f.*).

cargo service, service de vapeurs de charge (*m.*).

cargo steamer, vapeur de charge (*m.*).

cargo underwriter, assureur sur facultés (*m.*).

carman [**carmen** *pl.*] (*n.*), charretier (*m.*); voiturier (*m.*); charroyeur (*m.*); camionneur (*m.*).

carman's delivery sheet, bordereau de factage (*m.*).

carriage (vehicle) (*n.*), voiture (*f.*); wagon (*m.*).

carriage or **carrying** (transport) (*n.*), transport (*m.*); voiture (*f.*); port (*m.*); charriage (*m.*); charroi (*m.*); camionnage (*m.*):
carriage by sea, transport par mer; transport maritime.
carriage by water, transport par eau.

carriage (the charge for, or expense of, carrying) (*n.*), port (*m.*); prix du transport (*m.*); prix de la voiture (*m.*); voiture (*f.*); charriage (*m.*); charroi (*m.*); camionnage (*m.*); affranchissement (*m.*):
carriage on a parcel, port d'un colis.
carriage forward or carriage to pay, port dû; port à recevoir; non franco de port:
goods consigned carriage forward, marchandises expédiées en port dû (*f.pl.*).
carriage paid, port payé; port perçu; franco de port; franc de port; affranchi, -e:
if the consignment is made carriage paid, the sender must pay the amount of the charge, si l'expédition est faite en port

payé, l'expéditeur doit régler le montant de la taxe.

carriage paid parcel, colis affranchi (m.).

carriage (of a typewriter, of a calculating machine) (n.), chariot (d'une machine à écrire, d'une machine à calculer) (m.).

carriage lever (of a typewriter), levier d'interligne (m.).

carriage truck (railway vehicle for carrying a road vehicle), wagon-truck (m.).

carried (said of a resolution), adopté (invar.): carried unanimously, adopté à l'unanimité.

carried forward or simply **forward** (inscription at the bottom of a page) (Bkkpg) (Abbrev.: **c/f.** or **cd fwd** or simply **fwd** or **fd**) (opp. to brought forward), à reporter; reporté: carried forward to folio . . ., reporté au folio . . .

carried on (to be), être exploité, -e; s'exploiter: the shops where business is carried on, les magasins où s'exploite le commerce (m.pl.).

carrier (pers.) (n.), voiturier (m.); transporteur (m.); camionneur (m.); charroyeur (m.); entrepreneur de transports (m.); entrepreneur de roulage (m.).

carry [**carries** pl.] (Arith.) (n.), retenue (f.): to put the carry under each column, porter la retenue sous chaque colonne.

carry (to bear) (v.t.), porter: to carry a sum of money (on one's person), porter une somme d'argent (l'avoir sur soi). ship which cannot carry more than 1,000 tons dead weight, navire qui ne peut pas porter en lourd plus que 1 000 tonneaux (m.). Cf. **dead-weight capacity.** account which carries interest, compte qui porte intérêt (m.). amount carried to reserve, somme portée en réserve (f.).

carry (to convey; to transport) (v.t.), porter; transporter; conduire; charrier; charroyer; voiturier; camionner: the essential obligation of the shipowner is to carry the passenger to the port of destination, l'obligation essentielle de l'armateur est de transporter le passager au port de destination (f.). to carry the goods to the place of their destination, the passenger safe and sound to destination, transporter, conduire, les marchandises au lieu de leur destination, le voyageur sain et sauf à destination.

carry (Arith.) (v.t.), retenir: to carry a figure, retenir un chiffre. 4 times 9, 36, I put down 6 and carry 3, 4 fois 9, 36, je pose 6 et je retiens 3.

carry (Stock Exch.) (v.t.), reporter; prendre en report: to carry stock, reporter des titres; prendre des titres en report; reporter (v.i.); faire la contre-partie: stock carried, titres reportés (m.pl.); titres pris en report (m.pl.). Pour exemples de reporter (v.i.), V. sous to take in (v.i.). when the contango rate becomes sufficiently

remunerative to tempt available capital, the bankers and capitalists come along and offer to carry the stock for the buyer who wishes to give on, lorsque le prix du report devient assez rémunérateur pour tenter le capital disponible, les banquiers et capitalistes, viennent s'offrir pour faire la contre-partie de l'acheteur qui veut se faire reporter.

carry a resolution (to), adopter une proposition; prendre une résolution (ou une délibération) (ou une' décision): the resolution was carried unanimously, with the exception of Mr X., vendor, who did not vote, cette résolution est adoptée à l'unanimité, à l'exception de M. X., apporteur, qui s'est abstenu de voter.

carry forward (amount carried forward) (Bkkpg), report (m.); report à nouveau (m.).

carry forward or simply **carry** (Bkkpg) (v.t.), reporter; reporter à nouveau: to carry forward (or simply to carry) an amount to another page, the totals to the following page, reporter une somme à une autre page, les totaux à la page suivante. balance of profits carried forward to next account, solde des bénéfices reporté à nouveau sur l'exercice suivant (m.). we have pleasure in sending you herewith statement of your account made up to the . . . 19—, showing a balance in your favour of £——, which we carry forward to your credit, nous avons l'honneur de vous adresser ci-joint le relevé de votre compte arrêté au . . . 19——, présentant un solde de £—— en votre faveur, que nous reportons à votre crédit à nouveau.

carry out a contract, an agreement in good faith (to), exécuter un contrat, une convention de bonne foi.

carry out an enterprise (to), suivre une entreprise.

carry out the balance of interest in the principal column (to), porter, reporter, transporter, la balance des intérêts dans la colonne des capitaux.

carry over (amount carried over) (Bkkpg), report (m.): the carry over is £——, le report est de £——.

carry over or **carrying over** (Stock Exch.), report (m.): in carrying over the lender is secured by a stock, dans le report le prêteur est nanti d'un titre.

carry over (Bkkpg) (v.t.), reporter: to carry over a total, reporter un total; faire un report.

carry over (Stock Exch.) (v.t.), reporter: to carry over a position (or a book) from one account (or settlement) to the next, reporter une position d'une liquidation à la prochaine.

carry over (v.i.), reporter; faire un report: the stockbrokers refuse to carry over, les agents de change refusent de reporter (m.pl.). the capitalist or the broker who carries over does not speculate properly speaking: he lends on deposit of stock, le capitaliste ou l'agent qui fait un report ne spécule point à proprement parler : il prête sur dépôt de titres.

carry over rate, report (*m.*) ; taux des reports (*m.*) ; taux du report (*m.*) ; prix des reports (*m.*) ; prix du report (*m.*) ; cours de report (*m.*). V. exemple sous **contango** *or* **contango rate**.

carrying (transport) (*n.*). V. **carriage** *or* **carrying**.

carrying (a resolution) (*n.*), adoption (d'une résolution) (*f.*).

carrying capacity (of a barge), capacité de charge (d'un chaland) (*f.*).

carrying forward *or* **carrying over** *or* *simply* **carrying** (*n.*) (Bkkpg), report (*m.*) :
carrying forward (*or* carrying over) (*or* carrying) a total to the top of the next page, an account from one folio to another, report d'un total au haut de la page suivante, d'un compte d'un folio à un autre.

carrying out (a plan, a bargain), exécution (d'un projet, d'un marché) (*f.*).

carrying out (extension into another column), report (*m.*) ; transport (*m.*).

carrying press of sail (Navig.), forcement de voiles (*m.*).

cart (*n.*), charrette (*f.*) ; voiture (*f.*).

cart (*v.t.*), charrier ; charroyer ; voiturer ; camionner.

cart note (Customs), laisser-passer (*m.*) ; congé (*m.*).

cartage *or* **carting** (*n.*), charroi (*m.*) ; charriage (*m.*) ; camionnage (*m.*) ; factage (*m.*) ; transport par voiture (*m.*) ; transport par roulage (*m.*) :
Note :—Specifically, in French, cartage (i.e., collection or delivery) of goods received or sent by goods train is called *camionnage*. Cartage of parcels or other merchandise received or sent by passenger train is called *factage*.
cartage to the steamer, from the station to quay, camionnage au vapeur, de la gare à quai.

cartage (price paid for carting) (*n.*), charriage (*m.*) ; charroi (*m.*) ; camionnage (*m.*) ; factage (*m.*) ; prix du transport (*m.*).

cartage contractor, entrepreneur de roulage (*m.*) ; entrepreneur de transports (*m.*).

cartage service, service de camionnage (*m.*) ; service de factage (*m.*). V. note sous **cartage**.

cartel (*n.*), cartel (*m.*) :
cartel of banks, cartel de banques.

carter (pers.) (*n.*), charretier (*m.*) ; voiturier (*m.*) ; charroyeur (*m.*) ; camionneur (*m.*).

cartload (*n.*), charretée (*f.*).

case (box) (*n.*) (Abbrev.: **C.** *or* **c.** [**c/s** *pl.*]), caisse (*f.*) :
case of goods, caisse de marchandises.
freighting by the case, affrètement à la pièce (*m.*).

case (portfolio ; wallet) (*n.*), portefeuille (*m.*).

case (Law) (*n.*), cause (*f.*) ; procès (*m.*) :
to win one's case, gagner son procès.

case for counsel, consultation (*f.*).

case of need (notice on a bill of exchange), besoin (*m.*) :
a case of need is a notice by which the drawer, or one of the endorsers, indicates that in case of dishonour of the bill of exchange by the drawee, the bill should be presented to a third person who is instructed to pay the amount of it : this notice is called a case of need and the person who it is intended should intervene is designated under the name of referee in case of need, le besoin est la mention par laquelle le tireur, ou l'un des endosseurs, indique que dans le cas de non paiement de la lettre de change par le tiré, l'effet devra être présenté à une tierce personne qui est chargée d'en acquitter le montant : cette mention s'appelle un besoin et la personne qui doit intervenir est désignée sous le nom de recommandataire.

in case of need (wording on bills of exchange), au besoin ; et au besoin :
in case of need apply to Mr X., au besoin chez M. X. ; et au besoin à M. X.

case of need (bills of exchange) (pers.), besoin (*m.*) ; recommandataire (*m.*) :
a case of need or referee in case of need is a contingent payer that the drawer or an endorser names on the bill of exchange to whom the holder may resort in case of need, that is to say, in case the bill is dishonoured by non acceptance or non payment, le besoin ou recommandataire est un payeur éventuel que le tireur ou un endosseur indique sur la lettre de change comme pouvant payer en cas de besoin, c'est-à-dire en cas de non acceptation ou de non paiement de la lettre.
holder of a bill who is not bound to note protest to all the cases of need indicated, porteur d'une lettre qui n'est pas obligé de faire le protêt à tous les besoins indiqués (*m.*).

cash (ready money) (*n.*), espèces (*f.pl.*) ; numéraire (*m.*) ; argent (*m.*) ; finances (*f.pl.*) ; comptant (*m.*) :
hard cash, espèces sonnantes et trébuchantes ; argent liquide ; numéraire.
cash on account, espèces en compte.
cash to balance *or* cash in settlement, espèces pour solde.
the transport of cash by railway, le transport des finances par chemin de fer.
net cash, comptant net.
cash against documents, comptant contre documents.
cash less discount, comptant avec escompte.
cash on the usual terms, comptant d'usage ; comptant simple.
cash on delivery. V. ci-après.
cash on or before delivery *or* cash with order, comptant à livrer ; comptant contre remboursement ; comptant-compté (*m.*) ; comptant sur balle.

in cash *or* **for cash** *or* **cash** (*used as adj.*), en espèces ; contre espèces ; espèces ; en numéraire ; au comptant ; comptant (*adv.*) ; à beaux deniers comptants :

to pay in cash, payer en espèces (ou en numéraire); payer comptant; payer à beaux deniers comptants.

the premium is payable in cash on delivery of the policy, la prime est payable comptant au moment de la livraison de la police.

shares subscribed (or subscribed for) in cash, actions souscrites en espèces (ou en numéraire) (f.pl.).

shares issued for cash, actions émises contre espèces (f.pl.).

purchase paid for in cash at the end of the month, achat réglé au comptant fin de mois (m.).

to buy for cash, acheter comptant.

the money changer neither buys nor sells credit, all his transactions are for cash, le changeur n'achète ni ne vend du crédit, toutes ses opérations sont au comptant.

cash bonus (opp. to share bonus), bonus en espèces (m.).

cash payments or payments in cash, paiements comptant (m.pl.); paiements au comptant (m.pl.); versements espèces (m.pl.).

cash purchase (opp. to credit purchase) (Com.), achat au comptant (m.); achat comptant (m.).

cash sale (opp. to credit sale) (Com.), vente au comptant (f.); vente comptant (f.).

cash settlement (opp. to credit settlement), règlement au comptant (m.).

cash subscriber, souscripteur en numéraire (ou en espèces) (m.).

cash transaction or cash deal or cash bargain, opération au comptant (f.); négociation au comptant (f.); marché au comptant (m.).

cash transactions, mouvements d'espèces (m.pl.):

all the cash transactions are entered in a book called cash book, tous les mouvements d'espèces sont inscrits sur un registre appelé livre de caisse.

cash (Metal Market) (n.) (opp. to three months), comptant (m.).

cash (funds in cash or at the disposal of the cashier; cash in hand) (n.), caisse (f.); encaisse (f.); fonds (m.pl.); espèces (f.pl.); finances (f.pl.):

the employee entrusted with the important department of the cash is called cashier, l'employé chargé de l'important service de la caisse est appelé caissier (m.).

if there is an over or a short in the cash, s'il y a excédent ou déficit dans l'encaisse.

cash in (or on) hand, encaisse; fonds en caisse; espèces en caisse; caisse:

the cash in hand of a bank, l'encaisse d'une banque.

cash in hand and at the Bank of England, caisse et Banque d'Angleterre.

cash in hand of so many pounds, une encaisse de tant de livres.

to check the cash or notes in hand, vérifier les espèces ou billets en caisse.

cash in (or on) hand and at (or in) bank or

cash at bankers and in (or on) hand, fonds en caisse et en banque; espèces en caisse et à la banque; caisse(s) et banque(s); disponibilités en caisse et banque(s) (f.pl.); disponible en caisse et banque(s) (m.).

cash and bullion in hand (Banking), encaisse métallique; encaisse or et argent:

the bank is bound to have cash and bullion in hand equal to one third of the amount of its notes and of its other sight commitments, la banque est tenue d'avoir une encaisse métallique égale au tiers du montant de ses billets et de ses autres engagements à vue.

cash (v.t.), encaisser; toucher:

to cash a cheque, a coupon, encaisser, toucher, un chèque, un coupon.

cash account (Bkkpg), compte de caisse (m.).

cash account (account settled promptly in ready money, as opposed to a credit account), compte d'espèces (m.).

cash accounting or **cash bookkeeping** (opp. to store, or stock, accounting, or bookkeeping), comptabilité-espèces (f.).

cash adjustment, soulte (f.); soulte d'échange (f.); soute (f.).

cash balance, solde de caisse (m.); balance de caisse (f.); encaisse (f.).

cash book (Abbrev.: **C.B.**), livre de caisse (m.); caisse (f.).

cash box, caisse (f.); cassette (f.).

cash capital (opp. to capital issued as fully paid up otherwise than in cash), capital-espèces (m.); capital-numéraire (m.); capital de numéraire (m.); capital en numéraire (m.).

cash column, colonne de caisse (f.); colonne caisse (f.).

cash credit, crédit par caisse (m.); crédit à découvert (m.); crédit libre (m.); crédit en blanc (m.); crédit sur notoriété (m.).

cash department, service de la caisse (m.); caisse (f.).

cash desk, caisse (f.).

cash difference, différence de caisse (f.).

cash discount (distinguished from trade discount), escompte de caisse (m.); escompte au comptant (m.); escompte-intérêt (m.); escompte (m.).

cash distribution (in an exchange of shares, the balance payable in cash), soulte (f.); soulte d'échange (f.); soute (f.):

the exchange is at the rate of 0 new shares plus a cash distribution of £0 per share, for 0 old shares, l'échange est à raison de 0 actions nouvelles plus une soulte de 0£ par action, contre 0 actions anciennes (m.).

cash down, argent comptant (m.); argent sur table (m.); argent clair (m.); comptant-compté.

cash down sale, vente comptant-compté (f.).

cash drawings, prises d'espèces (f.pl.).

cash market (Corn or other Exch.), marché au comptant (m.); marché du comptant (m.).

cash on delivery (Abbrev.: **C.O.D.**), envoi contre remboursement (m.); envois contre remboursement (m.pl.).

cash on delivery fee, taxe de remboursement (f.).

cash on delivery letter, bulletin de remboursement (m.).

cash on delivery parcel, colis contre remboursement (m.); colis grevé de remboursement (m.).

cash on delivery sale, vente contre remboursement (f.).

cash receipts and payments, recettes et dépenses de caisse (f.pl.); entrées et sorties de caisse (f.pl.); rentrées et sorties de caisse (f.pl.); encaissements et paiements (m.pl.).

cash register, caisse enregistreuse (f.); caisse contrôleuse (f.).

cash requirement (cover for the day) (Banking), prévision de caisse (f.).

cash shares (opp. to *vendors' shares*), actions de numéraire (f.pl.); actions en numéraire (f.pl.); actions financières (f.pl.).

cash shorts and overs, déficits et excédents de caisse (*ou* dans l'encaisse) (m.pl.); malis et bonis (m.pl.).

cash statement, état de caisse (m.); relevé de caisse (m.); bordereau de caisse (m.):
the cashier should, each day, draw up a cash statement, to prove his cash in hand, le caissier devrait, chaque jour, établir un bordereau de caisse, pour justifier son encaisse.

cash voucher (receipt for money), pièce de caisse (f.); pièce justificative de caisse (f.).

cash voucher (for the delivery of a sum of money), bon de caisse (m.).

cashable (*adj.*), encaissable.

cashier (pers.) (n.), caissier, -ère.

cashier (of a bank) (n.), caissier (m.); guichetier (m.).

cashier and bookkeeper, caissier-comptable (m.).

cashier's desk *or* cashier's office, caisse (f.).

cashing (encashment) (n.), encaissement (m.).

cask (n.), tonneau (m.); barrique (f.); baril (m.); fût (m.); futaille (f.).

cast (addition) (n.), addition (f.).

cast *or* cast up (to add up) (*v.t.*), additionner:
to cast (*or* to cast up) a column of figures, additionner une colonne de chiffres.

cast away (to jettison) (*v.t.*), jeter à la mer; jeter en mer; jeter. V. syn. jettison (*v.t.*) pour exemples.

caster (pers.) (n.), additionneur, -euse.

casting *or* casting up (n.), addition (f.).

casting away (jettison), jet à la mer (m.); jet (m.). V. syn. jettison pour exemples.

casting vote, voix prépondérante (f.):
chairman who has a casting vote if the voting is equal, président qui a voix prépondérante en cas de partage (m.).

casual profit, fruit casuel (m.); revenant-bon (m.).

casual vacancy, vacance accidentelle (f.).

casualty [casualties *pl.*] (n.), sinistre (m.):
the receipt of news of the casualty, la réception de la nouvelle du sinistre.
casualty which has caused a loss, sinistre qui a causé une perte.

casualty list, liste de sinistres (f.).

catalogue (n.), catalogue (m.):
illustrated catalogues and prices on application, catalogues illustrés et prix sur demande.

catalogue (*v.t.*), cataloguer:
an article catalogued at so much, un objet catalogué à tant.

cataloguing *or* cataloging (n.), cataloguement (m.).

cattle market, marché aux bestiaux (m.).

cattle truck *or* cattle wagon, wagon à bestiaux (m.); wagon à bétail (m.); fourgon à bestiaux (m.).

caught (to be), être accroché, -e :
speculator on 'change who is caught, spéculateur en bourse qui est accroché (m.).

caught short (to be) (Stock Exch.), être à découvert.

causa proxima *or* immediate (*or* proximate) (*or* final) cause (of a sea accident), cause immédiate (f.).

causa remota *or* remote cause, cause première (f.); cause primitive (f.).

cause (Law) (n.), cause (f.).

cause beyond control, force majeure (f.).

cause to vary (to), faire varier:
the abundance or scarcity of goods causes the price to vary, l'abondance ou la rareté de marchandises fait varier le prix (f.).

caution money, cautionnement (m.); caution (f.).

cede (*v.t.*), céder:
to cede a right, céder un droit.

cedula (n.), cédule (f.).

cellar (n.), cave (f.):
the stock of gold in the bank's cellars, le stock d'or dans les caves de la banque.

cement shares, valeurs de ciments (f.pl.).

censor (pers.) (n.), censeur (m.).

censor (*v.t.*), censurer.

censorship (n.), censure (f.):
all telegrams exchanged with that country are liable to censorship, tous les télégrammes échangés avec ce pays-là sont soumis à la censure.

cent (money) (n.) (Abbrev.: c. *or* ct [cts *pl.*]), cent (m.).

centime (money) (n.) (Abbrev.: c.), centime (m.).

Central European time (Abbrev.: C.E.T.), heure de l'Europe centrale (f.) (1 p.m. [13 heures]) in relation to West European time, q.v.).

centre (n.), centre (m.):
business centre *or* centre of business, centre des affaires:
the heart of London is the City, the business centre, le cœur de Londres est la City, centre des affaires.
Note:—The word *Centre* (meaning *Place*) as a column heading in a foreign exchange quotation list, bill book, or the like, is rendered in French by the word *Devise* or *Devises*; thus, *Centre: New York, Devise: New-York*; *Centre: Brussels, Lisbon, Devises: Bruxelles, Lisbonne*.

certain exchange, certain (m.). V. to quote certain exchange *pour exemple.*

certificate (n.) (Abbrev.: **cert.**), certificat (m.):
certificate of airworthiness (of an aeroplane), certificat de navigabilité.
certificate of clearing inwards (Customs), certificat d'arrivée.
certificate of clearing outwards (Customs), certificat de sortie.
certificate of damage, certificat d'avarie (ou d'avaries).
certificate of insurance, certificat d'assurance. V. exemple sous syn. **insurance certificate.**
certificate of issue (of a post office money order), déclaration de versement (f.).
certificate of measurement (of a ship), certificat de jauge; certificat de jaugeage.
certificate of origin (of goods), certificat d'origine.
certificate of registration of mortgage, certificat d'inscription hypothécaire.
certificate of registry (of a ship), certificat d'immatriculation; certificat d'attache. *Note :*—These are literal translations. The equivalent of *certificate of registry*, in France, of a ship of French nationality, is *acte de francisation* (m.) or *brevet de francisation* (m.), and in Belgium, of a ship of Belgian nationality, *lettre de mer* (f.).
certificate of satisfaction (*or* reduction) (of a mortgage), certificat de radiation (d'une hypothèque).
certificate of seaworthiness, certificat de navigabilité.
certificate of shipment, certificat d'embarquement.

certificate (voucher to the ownership of shares, or the like) (n.) (Abbrev.: **cert.**), titre (m.); certificat (m.):
share certificate, titre d'actions (*ou* titre d'action *s'il s'agit d'une action seulement*); certificat d'action(s).
certificate for one share, titre unitaire (m.); unité (f.). V. exemple sous **one.**
certificate for more than one share, certificat multiple.

certificate book, cahier de certificats (m.).

certification (n.), certification (f.); visa (m.):
certification of signatures, certification de signatures.

certificatory (adj.), certificatif, -ive.

certified broker, courtier attitré (m.).

certified cheque (U.S.A. Banking), chèque visé (m.).

certified copy (of a deed), copie authentique (d'un acte) (f.).

certified copy *or* **certified a true copy,** copie certifiée conforme à l'original; pour copie conforme :
certified copy of telegram received by telephone, copie certifiée conforme au télégramme reçu par téléphone.

certify (v.t.), certifier; authentiquer; viser; déclarer :
copy of the minutes certified by the directors, copie des procès-verbaux certifiée par les administrateurs (f.).

I, the undersigned Paul X., certify that . . ., je soussigné Paul X. déclare que . . .

certifying (adj.), certificateur, -trice :
certifying notary, notaire certificateur (m.).

cessation (n.), cessation (f.).

cession of property (Law), cession de biens (f.).

chain rule, règle conjointe (f.); règle de chaîne (f.).

chair (n.), chaise (f.):
tables and chairs, tables et chaises.

chair (at a meeting) (n.), fauteuil de la présidence (m.).
to be in the chair, occuper le fauteuil de la présidence; présider :
Mr X. was in the chair, M. X. occupe le fauteuil de la présidence; M. X. préside.

chairman [**chairmen** pl.] (pers.) (n.), président, -e :
chairman of a meeting, président d'une assemblée.
to be chairman of a company, être le président d', présider, une compagnie.
chairman of the Board of Customs, directeur général des Douanes (m.). *Note :*—The full appellation of the English Board is Board of Customs and Excise.
chairman of the clearing house call (Produce Exch.), coteur du Syndicat (m.).

chairmanship (n.), présidence (f.):
during Mr X's chairmanship, pendant la présidence de M. X.

challenge (Auditing) (n.), sondage (m.).

challenge (Auditing) (v.t.), faire des sondages dans :
to challenge the securities in safe custody, not the whole lot straightaway, but arranging matters in such a way that a complete check is made of every bundle in the course of each year, faire des sondages dans les titres en dépôt, à bâtons rompus, mais en prenant des dispositions pour qu'une vérification totale de tous les dossiers ait eu lieu dans le courant de chaque année.

chamber counsel, avocat consultant (m.).

chamber of commerce, chambre de commerce (f.).

chambers (office) (n.pl.), cabinet (m.); étude (f.):
chambers of a barrister, cabinet d'un avocat.

chance (adj.), aléatoire :
chance gain, gain aléatoire (m.).

chance (n.), chance (f.); aléa (m.); 'hasard (m.):
the chances are in his favour, les chances sont en sa faveur.
the chances of a venture, les aléas d'une entreprise.
a happy chance, une chance heureuse; un hasard heureux.

change (alteration) (n.), changement (m.):
change of address, of residence, of offices, in (*or* of) the bank rate, changement d'adresse, de résidence, de siège, du taux officiel.
change of class (travel by railway, etc.), changement de classe; déclassement (m.):
change of class to 1st, déclassement à (*ou* en) 1re.

change of route, changement de route; déroutement (*m.*); déviation (*f.*).

change of route or of voyage, changement de route ou de voyage; déroutement (*m.*):
forced or voluntary change of route or of voyage, déroutement forcé ou volontaire.

change of train, of vessel, changement de train, de vaisseau.

change of voyage, changement de voyage; déroutement (*m.*).

change for the better, for the worse (Stock Exch.), revirement en hausse, en baisse (*m.*). *V. exemple sous syn.* turn for the better, for the worse.

change (*n.*) *or* **change of investments,** arbitrage (*m.*); arbitrage de portefeuille (*m.*):
to make a change of investments, of stocks, faire un arbitrage de portefeuille, de valeurs.

change (small money) (*n.*), change (*m.*); monnaie (*f.*); appoint (*m.*):
change for a silver coin, change d'une pièce d'argent.

to give change for five pounds, donner la monnaie de cinq livres.

country in which the legal tender of nickel is limited to change for so much, pays dans lequel le pouvoir libératoire du nickel est limité à l'appoint de tant (*m.*).

change *or* **'change** (exchange) (*n.*), bourse (*f.*) (*s'emploie surtout dans la locution* **on 'change,** sur la bourse; à la bourse; en bourse).

change *or* **'change** (session) (*n.*), bourse (*f.*):
two deals done during the same change, deux opérations effectuées dans la même bourse.

change (*v.t.*), changer; transformer:
to change one's plans, changer ses projets.

to change a bank note, French money for English money, changer un billet de banque, la monnaie française contre la monnaie anglaise.

to change the name of an account, changer le nom d', débaptiser, un compte.

change (to exchange one investment for another by sale of the one and purchase of the other; to hedge) (*v.t.*), arbitrager; arbitrer:
to change one stock for another, if the first is dearer than the second, that is to say, if at their present prices, it yields less than the other, arbitrager (*ou* arbitrer) une valeur contre une autre, si la première est plus chère que la seconde, c'est-à-dire si à leurs cours actuels elle rapporte moins que l'autre.

change hands (to), changer de mains; s'échanger:
X. shares changed hands at 2, l'action X. change de mains (*ou* s'échange) à 2; on échange l'action X. à 2.

changer (money changer) (pers.) (*n.*), changeur, -euse.

Channel port, port de la Manche (*m.*).

Channel tunnel, tunnel sous la Manche (*m.*).

charabanc (*n.*), autocar (*m.*).

character (figure; class of a ship) (*n.*), caractère (*m.*); cote (*f.*):
the characters used for the classification of ships, les caractères employés pour la classification des navires.

the characters are represented in the following manner: (Lloyd's) 100 A1, etc., (Veritas) 3/3 1.1., etc., les cotes sont représentées de la manière suivante: (Lloyd's) 100 A1, etc., (Veritas) 3/3 1.1., etc.

character (reputation) (*n.*), caractère (*m.*):
to have a good character, avoir bon caractère.

charge (*n.*) *or* **charges** (*n.pl.*) (price; expense) (Abbrev.: **chge** [**chges** *pl.*]), prix (*m.*); taxe (*f.*); taxes (*f.pl.*); taxation (*f.*); frais (*m.pl.*); dépense (*f.*); dépenses (*f.pl.*); redevance (*f.*):
reasonable charge, prix raisonnable.

postal charges, taxes postales.

discount charges, frais d'escompte.

establishment charges, frais généraux; dépenses de maison.

charge for call (Teleph.), taxe de communication.

charge (*or* charges) for carriage *or* carriage charge (*or* charges), prix de (*ou* du) transport; prix de la voiture:
freight is the charge for carriage of goods by sea, le fret est le prix de transport des marchandises par mer..

the charges for railway carriage in England, le prix du transport par voie ferrée en Angleterre.

charge for collection (Rly., etc.), taxe de prise à domicile.

charge for delivery (Rly., etc.), taxe de remise à domicile.

charge (*or* charges) for freight *or* freight charge (*or* charges), prix du fret:
the bill of lading specifies the charges for freight, le connaissement énonce le prix du fret.

charges for imperial and foreign telegrams, taxation des télégrammes internationaux.

charge for redirection (Post), taxe de réexpédition.

standard charge for the removal and reinstallation of a telephone line and apparatus, taxe, redevance, forfaitaire pour l'enlèvement et la réinstallation des organes essentiels d'un poste téléphonique.

charge (encumbrance; lien; expense) (*n.*) (Abbrev.: **chge**), charge (*f.*); privilège (*m.*); affectation (*f.*); assignation (*f.*):
assets encumbered with a charge, valeurs grevées d'une charge (*f.pl.*).

the debenture charges, les charges des obligations.

interest on capital constitutes a charge on production, les intérêts du capital constituent une charge de la production (*m.pl.*).

to have a charge on the personal property of a debtor, avoir un privilège (*ou* être privilégié, -e) sur les meubles d'un débiteur.

mortgage charge, affectation hypothécaire; privilège d'hypothèque.

charge on one's property present and future, assignation sur ses biens présents et à venir.

charge (instrument) (*n.*) (Abbrev.: **chge**), privilège (*m.*):
to register a charge, enregistrer un privilège.

charge (Bkkpg) (*n.*) (Abbrev.: **chge**), imputation (*f.*); affectation (*f.*).

charge (bundle of paid vouchers) (Bankers' Clearing House) (*n.*), liasse (*f.*); pli (*m.*).

charge (*v.t.*), charger; mettre à la charge; mettre à charge; taxer; prélever; percevoir; imputer; affecter; appliquer:

to charge an account with all the expenses, charger un compte de tous les frais.

to charge the postage to the customer *or* to charge the customer with the carriage, mettre le port à la charge (*ou* à charge) du client.

to charge a letter as unpaid, taxer une lettre comme non affranchie.

excess luggage is charged (*or* charged for) as follows, les excédents de bagages sont taxés ainsi qu'il suit (*m.pl.*).

goods charged by the ton, marchandises taxées à la tonne (*f.pl.*).

the commission charged by the bank is 1%, la commission prélevée (*ou* perçue) par la banque est de 1 0/0.

to charge an expense to an account, an amount to the previous month's trading, imputer une dépense sur un compte, une somme sur l'exercice du mois précédent.

property charged as security for a debt, immeuble affecté à la garantie d'une créance (*m.*).

to charge against the cost of manufacture the percentage of overhead expenses properly applicable thereto, appliquer à la fabrication le quantum de frais généraux qui lui incombe.

fractions of a penny charged as a penny (i.e., charge rounded up to the next higher penny), taxe arrondie au décime supérieur (*f.*).

charge with duty (**to**) (Customs), taxer; imposer; tarifer; taxer (*ou* imposer) à des droits:

goods charged with duty on the gross weight, on the net weight, otherwise than by weight, marchandises taxées (*ou* imposées) (*ou* tarifées) au brut (*ou* au poids brut), au net (*ou* au poids net), autrement qu'au poids (*f.pl.*).

goods charged with different duties, marchandises imposées à des droits différents (*f.pl.*).

chargeable (*adj.*), à la charge; imputable; affectable; applicable:

the duty is chargeable to the seller, le droit est à la charge du vendeur.

the proportion of the amount chargeable to the property insured, la proportion de la somme imputable à la chose assurée.

losses chargeable against (*or* to) the year, pertes imputables à (*ou* affectables à) (*ou* applicables à) (*ou* à la charge de) l'année (*f.pl.*).

chargeable lands, terres affectables (*f.pl.*).

chargeable with duty, imposable; taxable; taxatif, -ive:

the weight chargeable with duty, le poids imposable.

charging (*n.*), mise à la charge (*f.*); mise à charge (*f.*); taxation (*f.*); prélèvement

(*m.*); imputation (*f.*); affectation (*f.*); application (*f.*):

charging the buyer with the stamp duty, mise à la charge (*ou* à charge) de l'achetéur du droit de timbre.

method of charging for excess luggage, mode de taxation des excédents de bagages (*m.*).

to rectify errors in the charging of expenses, rectifier les erreurs dans l'imputation des dépenses.

charging an amount to a certain expense, affectation d'une somme à une telle dépense.

charitable donations *or* **charity** (*n.*) *or* **charities** (*n.pl.*), bienfaisance (*f.*).

chart (*n.*), carte (*f.*); carte marine (*f.*).

charter (Shipping) (*n.*).   V. **charter-party** *or* **charter** & **chartering** *or* **charter**, ci-après.

charter (*v.t.*), affréter; fréter; noliser:

to charter a ship, wholly or in part, for the carriage of goods, to load cargo in a port of call for orders, affréter un navire, en tout ou en partie, pour le transport de marchandises, pour charger de la marchandise dans un port d'ordres.

to be chartered, être affrété, -e; s'affréter:

in practice, tramps are chartered, either by the voyage, or by time, les tramps s'affrètent pratiquement, soit au voyage, soit au temps (*m.pl.*).

charter party [**charter parties** *pl.*] *or* **charterparty** *or* simply **charter** (*n.*) (Abbrev.: **C/P.**), charte-partie (*f.*):

the charter party is the contract of hiring a ship. It derives its name from the fact that formerly contracts of affreightment were written on a single sheet (charter) which was afterwards torn in two (charte-partie *literally translated means* divided charter), each of the contractants keeping one of the parts, la charte-partie est le contrat de louage d'un navire. Elle tire son nom de ce qu'autrefois les contrats d'affrètement étaient écrits sur une pièce (charte) qu'on déchirait ensuite en deux, chacun des contractants conservant une des parties.

a charter party is a written agreement drawn to prove a contract of affreightment, la charte-partie est un écrit dressé pour constater le contrat d'affrètement.

grain charter, charte-partie de grain.

ore charter, charte-partie de minerai.

chartered company, compagnie à charte (*f.*); compagnie privilégiée (*f.*) (does not exist in France).

chartered freight, fret convenu par charte-partie (*m.*); fret à gagner en exécution de la charte-partie (*m.*):

chartered freight at risk, for time, for voyage, fret convenu par charte-partie à faire, à terme, au voyage.

chartered vessel, navire affrété (*m.*); navire frété (*m.*).

charterer (pers.) (*n.*), affréteur (*m.*); fréteur (*m.*).

chartering *or* **charterage** *or* **charter** (*n.*), affrètement (*m.*); affrètement-location (*m.*); frètement (*m.*); nolisement (*m.*):

chartering a ship for a full and entire cargo, affrètement d'un navire pour un plein et entier chargement.

charter for a series of voyages, affrètement pour une série de voyages.

chartering market *or* **charter market,** marché des affrètements (*m.*).

chattels personal [chattel personal *sing.*], biens meubles (*m.pl.*); biens mobiliers (*m.pl.*); biens personnels (*m.pl.*); meubles (*m.pl.*); effets mobiliers (*m.pl.*); effets personnels (*m.pl.*).

chauffeur (pers.) (*n.*), chauffeur (*m.*); conducteur (*m.*).

cheap (*adj.*), bon marché (*invar.*); à bon marché; à bon compte; à prix réduit:
money is cheap, l'argent est bon marché (*ou* est à bon marché) (*m.*).
the goods are cheap, les marchandises sont bon marché (*f.pl.*).
cheap ticket, billet à prix réduit (*m.*).
cheap train, train de plaisir (*m.*).

cheap *or* **cheaply** (*adv.*), à bon marché; à bon compte:
to buy cheap (*or* cheaply), acheter à bon marché (*ou* à bon compte).

cheaper (*adj.*), meilleur marché (*invar.*); à meilleur marché; à meilleur compte; moins cher, -ère:
these shares are cheaper, ces actions sont meilleur marché (*ou* sont moins chères) (*f.pl.*).
to obtain cheaper credit, obtenir du crédit à meilleur marché (*ou* à meilleur compte).

cheapness (*n.*), bon marché (*m.*):
the cheapness of money, of credit, le bon marché de l'argent (*ou* des capitaux), du crédit.
customer who allows himself to be tempted by cheapness, client qui se laisse tenter par le bon marché (*m.*).

cheat (*v.t.*), frauder.

check (used as *adj.*), contradictoire; de contrôle:
check code word *or* simply check word (Teleg.), mot convenu de contrôle (*m.*).
check survey, expertise contradictoire (*f.*).
check weighing, pesage contradictoire (*m.*).

check *or* **checking** (*n.*), vérification (*f.*); pointage (*m.*); contrôle (*m.*):
check on ledger postings, contrôle des reports du grand livre.

check (Banking) (U.S.A.) (*n.*). Syn. de **cheque.**

check (*v.t.*), vérifier; pointer; contrôler:
to check the day's takings, the contents of a packet, the cash in hand, vérifier le produit de la journée, le contenu d'un paquet, les encaisses.
to check the items in an account, a statement with an account, vérifier, pointer, contrôler, les articles d'un compte, un relevé avec un compte.
to check an account (Stock Exch.), pointer un compte.
to check the weight and, thereafter, accept responsibility for it, contrôler le poids et, dès lors, accepter d'en répondre.

check competition (to), enrayer la concurrence.

checking slip (Stock Exch.), engagement (*m.*).

cheerful (to be), être bien disposé, -e:
South African shares were more cheerful this week, les valeurs sud-africaines ont été mieux disposées cette semaine (*f.pl.*).

cheque (*n.*) (Abbrev.: **chq.**), chèque (*m.*); mandat (*m.*):
bearer cheque *or* cheque to bearer, chèque au porteur.
order cheque *or* cheque to order, chèque à ordre.
cheque crossed generally, chèque à barrement général. V. exemple sous **crossing.**
cheque crossed specially, chèque à barrement spécial. V. exemple sous **crossing.**
cheque crossed "not negotiable," chèque barré « non négociable: »
a cheque bearing the words "not negotiable" does not cease to be transferable by endorsement like an ordinary cheque, but the transferee in good faith has no better title to it than his transferor, le chèque revêtu de la mention « non négociable » ne cesse pas d'être transmissible par endossement comme un chèque ordinaire, mais le cessionnaire de bonne foi n'a pas plus de droits que son cédant. (N.B.—Same practice in France as in England.)
cheque for travellers *or* traveller's cheque, mandat de voyage; chèque de voyage; billet de crédit circulaire (*m.*).
cheque with receipt form attached, chèque-récépissé (*m.*).
the Paris cheque (*or* Paris cheques) (*or* cheques on Paris) (Foreign Exchange), le chèque sur Paris:
the Paris cheque (*or* Paris cheques) (*or* cheques on Paris) fluctuated between —— and ——, le chèque sur Paris a fluctué entre —— et ——.

cheque book, carnet de chèques (*m.*); chéquier (*m.*).

cheque form, formule de chèque (*f.*).

cheque perforator *or* **cheque protector,** perforeuse de chèques (*f.*).

cheque rate (Foreign Exchange), cours du chèque (*m.*).

cheque stamp, timbre de chèque (*m.*); timbre-chèque (*m.*).

chief (*adj.*), principal, -e, -aux:
chief accountant, chef de comptabilité (*m.*); chef comptable (*m.*).
chief cashier, caissier principal (*m.*).
chief clerk, commis principal (*m.*); commis chef (*m.*); chef de bureau (*m.*).
chief creditor, principal créancier (*m.*).

child's half-fare ticket (Rly.), billet de demi-tarif pour les enfants (*m.*).

choice paper (bills of exchange), papier de choix (*m.*).

choose (to elect) (*v.t.*), nommer:
to be chosen chairman of a meeting, être nommé (-e) à la présidence d'une assemblée.

choose (*v.i.*), opter:
to choose between two alternatives, between abandonment of the goods and payment of pecuniary compensation, opter entre deux

alternatives, entre l'abandon de la marchandise et le paiement d'indemnités pécuniaires.

Christian name, prénom (*m.*); nom de baptême (*m.*).

Christmas card, carte de Noël (*f.*).

cinema shares, valeurs de cinéma (*f.pl.*).

cipher (conventional character) (*n.*), chiffre (*m.*): to write in cipher, écrire en chiffres.

cipher (*n.*) *or* **cipher language** (Teleg.), chiffré (*m.*); langage chiffré (*m.*):
word in cipher, mot en chiffré (*m.*).
telegram in cipher, télégramme en langage chiffré (*m.*).
cipher language is composed of groups or series of figures or letters having a secret meaning, or of words not fulfilling the conditions applicable to code language, le langage chiffré est formé de groupes de chiffres ou de lettres ayant un sens secret (*ou* une signification secrète), ou de mots ne remplissant pas les conditions exigées pour la formation du langage convenu.

cipher (Teleg.) (*v.t.*), chiffrer:
to cipher a telegram, chiffrer un télégramme.

cipher (to calculate arithmetically) (*v.i.*), chiffrer.

cipher code, code chiffré (*m.*).

ciphering (*n.*), chiffrage (*m.*).

circle (social sphere) (*n.*), milieu (*m.*):
in well informed circles, dans les milieux bien informés.

circuitous (*adj.*), détourné, -e:
circuitous remittance on Paris (compound arbitration of exchange), remise détournée sur Paris (*f.*).

circular (*adj.*), circulaire:
circular letter, lettre circulaire (*f.*).
circular letter of credit (*Abbrev.* : c.l.c.), lettre de crédit circulaire (*f.*).
circular note (cheque for travellers), billet de crédit circulaire (*m.*); mandat de voyage (*m.*); chèque de voyage (*m.*).
circular ticket, billet circulaire (*m.*).
circular tour ticket, carnet de voyage circulaire (*m.*).

circular (*n.*), circulaire (*f.*):
circular calling the shareholders together, circulaire convocatrice des actionnaires.
a circular is understood to mean any communication drawn in letter form and of which the text, reproduced in a certain number of copies by a means of mechanical impression, is addressed indifferently to all the persons to whom the circular is sent, la circulaire s'entend de toute communication en forme de lettre et dont le texte, reproduit à un certain nombre d'exemplaires par un moyen d'impression mécanique, s'adresse indifféremment à toutes les personnes auxquelles la circulaire est envoyée.

circulate (*v.t.*), faire circuler:
to circulate capital, faire circuler des capitaux.

circulate (*v.i.*), circuler:
capital which does not circulate yields nothing, tout capital qui ne circule pas ne rapporte pas.

circulate freely (to), rouler:
money circulates freely in America, l'argent roule en Amérique (*m.*).

circulating (*adj.*), circulant, -e; roulant, -e:
circulating capital *or* circulating assets (opp. to *fixed capital*, or *fixed assets*, or *permanent assets*, or *capital assets*), capitaux circulants (*m.pl.*); capitaux roulants (*m.pl.*); capitaux mobiles (*m.pl.*); capitaux mobiliers (*m.pl.*); capitaux flottants (*m.pl.*); valeurs d'échange (*f.pl.*); valeurs de roulement (*f.pl.*). *V. exemple sous* fixed capital *or* fixed assets.

circulation (*n.*), circulation (*f.*); cours (*m.*); mouvement (*m.*):
circulation of money, of paper, circulation, mouvement, de l'argent, du papier.
to withdraw coins from circulation, retirer des pièces de la circulation.
the number of bank notes in circulation, le nombre de billets de banque en circulation.

circulation (of a newspaper) (*n.*), tirage (d'un journal) (*m.*):
advertisement rates of newspapers are proportional to their circulation and to their influence, les tarifs des annonces de journaux sont proportionnels à leur tirage et à leur influence (*m.pl.*).

circulatory (*adj.*), circulatoire:
the circulatory power of the bank note, le pouvoir circulatoire du billet de banque.

circumstances permitting, sauf imprévu.

civil (Law) (*adj.*), civil, -e:
civil action *or* civil proceedings, action civile (*f.*); procès civil (*m.*); cause civile (*f.*); affaire civile (*f.*); poursuite civile (*f.*); procédure civile (*f.*).
civil code, code civil (*m.*).
civil court, tribunal civil (*m.*).
civil law, droit civil (*m.*); droit privé (*m.*).
civil rights, droits civils (*m.pl.*).
civil year, année civile (*f.*).

civil commotion, mouvement populaire (*m.*).

claim (*n.*), réclamation (*f.*); revendication (*f.*); recours (*m.*); prétention (*f.*); exigence (*f.*); demande (*f.*); demande d'indemnité (*f.*); indemnité (*f.*); sinistre (*m.*):
a claim for losses or damage, une réclamation de pertes ou d'avaries.
no claim to be made by the underwriters for freight, les assureurs ne feront aucune réclamation pour fret (*m.pl.*).
to send in a claim to the inspector of taxes, adresser une réclamation au contrôleur des contributions directes.
claim for indemnity, réclamation d'indemnité; demande d'indemnité.
to insure against a third party claim, s'assurer contre le recours des tiers.
shipper who finds himself deprived of any claim against the shipowner, chargeur qui se trouve privé de tout recours contre l'armateur (*m.*).
the exorbitance of the claims of a seller, l'exorbitance des prétentions d'un vendeur (*f.*).

claim for damages, for payment of the value of undelivered goods, for repayment of duties, demande en dommages-intérêts, en paiement de la valeur des marchandises non délivrées, en remboursement de droits.

claim for relief, for discharge (Taxation), demande en dégrèvement, en décharge.

a claim exceeding the value of the goods, une demande d'indemnité dépassant la valeur de la marchandise.

to fix the claim at the amount of the damage, fixer l'indemnité au montant du dommage.

the amount of the ascertained claim, le montant de l'indemnité reconnue.

settlement of the claim takes place within three months of the accident, le règlement de l'indemnité a lieu dans les trois mois du sinistre.

the receipt of news of the claim (Insce), la réception de la nouvelle du sinistre.

the settlement of small claims (Insce), le règlement de petits sinistres.

claim (debt) (*n.*), créance (*f.*) :
litigious claim, créance litigieuse.

claim (*v.t.*), réclamer ; revendiquer ; prétendre ; prétendre à ; exiger ; demander :
to claim a right, revendiquer, réclamer, un droit.

to claim one's due, what is not due, payment within several days, payment of a bill on the day of maturity, payment from one's insurers, réclamer, exiger, demander, son dû, l'indu, le paiement dans un délai de quelques jours, le payement d'un effet au jour de l'échéance, le paiement à ses assureurs.

to claim a letter from the post office, réclamer une lettre au bureau de poste.

if the goods are not claimed, or if several holders of bills of lading claim the same goods, si les marchandises ne sont pas réclamées, ou si plusieurs porteurs de connaissements réclament la même marchandise.

to claim compensation in case of dismissal, réclamer une indemnité (*ou* demander compensation) en cas de congédiement.

to claim a share in the profits, a commission for one's trouble, an indemnity for delay, special privileges, prétendre (*ou* prétendre à) une part dans les bénéfices, une commission pour sa peine, une indemnité pour le retard, des privilèges spéciaux.

to claim the whole amount of the sum insured, exiger le montant entier de la somme assurée.

claim back (*v.t.*), répéter :
to claim back from the payee a promissory note that one has made, répéter contre le bénéficiaire un billet à ordre que l'on a souscrit.

claim form, formule de réclamation (*f.*).

claimable (*adj.*), revendicable ; exigible ; demandable.

claimant *or* **claimer** (pers.) (*n.*), réclamateur (*m.*) ; revendicateur (*m.*) ; réclamant, -e.

claiming (*n.*), réclamation (*f.*) ; revendication (*f.*).

claiming back, répétition (*f.*) :

claiming back of dividends from the shareholders, répétition de dividendes contre les actionnaires.

claims book, livre de réclamations (*m.*) ; registre des réclamations (*m.*).

clandestine (*adj.*), clandestin, -e :
prohibited or clandestine trade, commerce prohibé ou clandestin (*m.*).

class (*n.*), classe (*f.*) ; cote (*f.*) :
first class ticket, billet de première classe (*m.*).
first class vessel, navire de première cote (*m.*).

class *or* **classify** (*v.t.*), classer ; classifier ; coter :
to classify the items under as many heads as there are accounts, classer les articles en autant de chefs qu'il y en a de comptes.
steamer classed 100 A1 at Lloyd's, 3/3 1.1. at Veritas, vapeur classé (*ou* coté) 100 A1 au Lloyd, 3/3 1.1. au Veritas (*m.*).

classification *or* **classing** (*n.*), classification (*f.*) ; classement (*m.*) ; cotation (*f.*) ; cote (*f.*) :
classification of accounts, classification des comptes.

classification certificate (ship's), certificat de classification (*m.*) ; certificat de cote (*m.*).

classification clause (ship's), clause de classification (de navires) (*f.*).

classification register (ships'), registre de classification (de navires) (*m.*).

classification society (ship's), société de classification (de navires) (*f.*) :
the Bureau Veritas is a French classification society, le Bureau Veritas est une société française de classification.

classified advertisement, annonce classée (*f.*) ; petite annonce (*f.*).

clause (*n.*), clause (*f.*) ; article (*m.*) :
the clauses of an agreement, of a bill of lading, of an insurance policy, of the articles of association of a company, les clauses d'une convention, d'un connaissement, d'une police d'assurance, des statuts d'une société.

clean acceptance (of a bill of exchange), acceptation sans réserves (*f.*).

clean bill (bill of exchange) (opp. to *documentary bill*), effet libre (*m.*) ; traite libre (*f.*).

clean bill (of health) (opp. to *foul bill*), patente (de santé) nette (*f.*).

clean bill of lading (opp. to *foul,* or *dirty, bill of lading*), connaissement net (*m.*) ; connaissement sans réserve (*m.*).

clean copy, copie au net (*f.*) ; transcription au net (*f.*). *Cf.* to make a clean copy of a letter.

clean ship (Quarantine), navire indemne (*m.*).

clean up a balance sheet (to) (to eliminate bad debts, or the like), assainir un bilan.

clear (plain ; lucid) (*adj.*), clair, -e :
a clear system of accounts, une comptabilité claire.
« Tout ce qui n'est pas clair n'est pas français » (RIVAROL), " What is not clear is not French."

clear (said of days) (*adj.*), franc ; plein :
clear day, jour franc (*m.*) ; jour plein (*m.*) :
to give 7 clear days' notice, donner un préavis de 7 jours francs.

clear (*v.t.*) *or* **clear through the customs (to)**

(to free [goods] from customs charges; to take out of bond) (*v.t.*), dédouaner; retirer des douanes; retirer de l'entrepôt:
to clear the goods within the ten days following the presentation of the customs entry, dédouaner les marchandises dans les dix jours qui suivent la présentation de la déclaration en douane.
the goods can only be cleared after the duties have been paid, deposited, or secured, les marchandises ne peuvent être retirées des douanes qu'après les droits ont été payés, consignés, ou garantis (*f.pl.*).

clear *or* **clear out** *or* **clear outwards** (*v.t.*), expédier; expédier en douane:
one says that the ship is cleared when she is provided with all her papers, on dit que le navire est expédié quand il est muni de tous ses papiers.

clear (Post) (*v.t.*), lever; relever:
letter boxes are cleared at fixed times, les boîtes aux lettres sont levées (*ou* relevées) aux heures fixes (*f.pl.*).

clear (Banking) (*v.t.*), compenser:
to clear a cheque, compenser un chèque.

clear a connection (to) (Teleph.), donner le signal de fin.

clear a ship inwards (to), faire l'entrée en douane d'un navire.

clear one's property from debt (to), purger son bien de dettes.

clear oneself from a debt (to), se libérer d'une dette.

clear the dial of a calculating machine (to), remettre à 0 (*zéro*) le viseur d'une machine à calculer.

clear up the affairs of a bankrupt (to), mettre au net (*ou* débrouiller) la situation d'un failli.

clearance *or* **clearing** (*n.*) *or* **clearance through the customs** (of goods), dédouanement (*m.*); dédouanage (*m.*):
the customs agent fulfils, for shippers or consignees, the formalities of clearing the goods through the customs, l'agent en douane remplit, pour les expéditeurs ou les destinataires, les formalités de dédouanement des marchandises (*m.*).

clearance *or* **clearing** (*n.*) *or* **clearance out** *or* **clearing out** *or* **clearance** (*or* **clearing**) **outwards**, expédition (*f.*); expédition en douane (*f.*):
clearance of ship *or* clearing the ship outwards, expédition du navire.

clearance (permission for a ship to leave port) (*n.*), congé (*m.*); congé maritime (*m.*); congé de navigation (*m.*); certificat de sortie (*m.*); permis de sortie (*m.*); passeport (*m.*):
Note:—French ships leaving a French port have to be provided with a **congé**. It states that the master has complied with the necessary formalities to have the right to sail under the French flag. It is available for one year.
Foreign ships leaving a French port have to be provided with a **passeport**. The *passeport*

is for foreign ships what the *congé* is for French ships.
no vessel may leave port without clearance, aucun bâtiment ne peut sortir du port sans congé.

clearance (of the dial of a calculating machine) (*n.*), remise à 0 (*zéro*) (*f.*).

clearance inwards *or* **clearing inwards** (of a ship) (Customs), entrée (*f.*); entrée en douane (*f.*); déclaration d'entrée (*f.*).

clearance papers, expéditions (*f.pl.*); papiers d'expédition (*m.pl.*):
the vessel is reputed to be ready to sail when the master is provided with his clearance papers for his voyage, le bâtiment est censé prêt à faire voile lorsque le capitaine est muni de ses expéditions pour son voyage.

clearing (a letter box) (Post) (*n.*), levée (*f.*); relevage (*m.*).

clearing (Banking) (*n.*), compensation (*f.*):
cheques presented for clearing, chèques présentés à la compensation (*m.pl.*).

clearing bank, banque de compensation (*f.*).

clearing house (Abbrev.: C/H.), chambre de compensation (*f.*); clearing-house (*m.*):
bankers' clearing house, chambre de compensation des banquiers.

clearing house *or* *simply* **clearing** (*n.*) (Stock Exch.), comptoir de liquidation (*m.*).

clearing house (of a guarantee association) (Produce Exch.), caisse de liquidation (*f.*).
See note under caisse de liquidation *in French-English section.*

clearing house clerk (Produce Exch.), liquidateur (*m.*); filiériste (*m.*).

clearing sheet (Stock Exch.), feuille de liquidation (*f.*).

clearness (*n.*), clarté (*f.*):
clearness of an account, clarté d'un compte.

clerical error (a mistake in copying or writing), erreur de plume (*f.*); erreur de copiste (*f.*); faute de copiste (*f.*).

clerical error (Law), vice de clerc (*m.*).

clerical staff, service sédentaire (*m.*).

clerical work, travail de bureau (*m.*).

clerk (pers.) (*n.*), employé, -e; commis, -e; commis (-e) de bureau; commis (-e) sédentaire:
bank clerk, employé de banque; commis de banque.

clerk (in a lawyer's office) (*n.*), clerc (*m.*):
notary's clerk, clerc de notaire.

client (pers.) (*n.*), client, -e:
clients of a notary, clients d'un notaire.

clientele (*n.*), clientèle (*f.*).

clients' ledger, grand livre des clients (*m.*).

cloak room (Rly.), consigne (*f.*); consigne des bagages (*f.*):
luggage deposited in (*or* put into) the cloak room, bagages déposés (*ou* mis) à la consigne (*m.pl.*).

cloak room fee, droit de garde (*m.*); taxe de dépôt des bagages (*f.*).

cloak room ticket, bulletin de consigne (*m.*).

close *or* **closing** (*n.*), fin (*m.*); bout (*m.*); clôture (*f.*):

close of the year, fin, bout, de l'année.

close of a risk, fin d'un risque.

close (*or* closing) of navigation, clôture de la navigation.

at the close (at the finish of the day's market), en clôture ; en fin de séance :

X. shares weakened at the close, l'action X. faiblit en clôture (*ou* en fin de séance).

close (*v.t.*). V. exemples :

to close a letter, fermer une lettre.

to close a bargain, arrêter, clore, un marché.

to close a meeting, lever, clore, une séance :

to declare a meeting closed, déclarer une séance levée.

to close a transaction, a bargain, a position (*or* a book), a stock (Stock Exch.), liquider, réaliser, une opération, un marché, une position, une valeur :

buyer who must either close his position (*or* his book) or give on, acheteur qui doit ou liquider sa position ou se faire reporter (*m.*).

option purchase closed before option day, achat à prime réalisé avant le jour de la réponse (*m.*).

to be closed (Stock Exch.), être liquidé, -e ; se liquider :

transactions which are closed by the passing of stock or of money, opérations qui se liquident par un mouvement de titres ou de fonds (*f.pl.*).

to close an account, arrêter, régler, clore, clôturer, fermer, un compte :

to close an account current at 30th June, arrêter un compte courant au 30 juin.

to close one's accounts once a year, every six months, arrêter, régler, clore, clôturer, ses comptes une fois l'an, tous les six mois.

one closes an account when one ceases to have business relations with the customer, on ferme un compte lorsqu'on cesse d'avoir avec le client des relations d'affaires.

to close the books of an old company, clôturer les livres d'une ancienne société.

close (*v.i.*), fermer ; clôturer ; terminer :

offices which close at 5 o'clock, bureaux qui ferment à 5 heures (*m.pl.*).

X. shares closed at 2 without much change in their price of a week ago, l'action X. clôture (*ou* termine) (*ou* ferme) à £2 sans grand changement sur son cours d'il y a huit jours.

close (to liquidate a position) (Stock Exch.) (*v.i.*), liquider ; se liquider :

speculator who closes, spéculateur qui liquide (*ou* qui se liquide) (*m.*).

close case (opp. to *crate*), caisse pleine (*f.*).

close port (inland port) (opp. to *outport*), port intérieur (*m.*) ; port en rivière (*m.*) ; port fluvial (*m.*).

closing (*n.*), fermeture (*f.*) ; clôture (*f.*) ; arrêté (*m.*) :

closing of the stock exchange, fermeture de la bourse.

closing of the application list, clôture de la souscription.

closing of a liquidation, clôture d'une liquidation.

closing (stoppage of work) (*n.*), chômage (*m.*) :

Sunday closing, chômage du dimanche.

stock exchange closing.—Upon the occasion of . . ., the stock exchange will be closed on Monday and Tuesday next, chômage boursier.—A l'occasion de . . ., la bourse sera fermée lundi et mardi prochains.

closing (of a meeting) (*n.*), levée (*f.*), clôture (*f.*) (d'une séance).

closing (a transaction, a bargain, a position [*or* a book]) (Stock Exch.) (*n.*), liquidation (*f.*), réalisation (*f.*) (d'une opération, d'un marché, d'une position).

closing entry (Bkkpg) (opp. to *opening*, or *starting*, *entry*), article d'inventaire (*m.*) ; écriture d'inventaire (*f.*) ; écriture de clôture (*f.*).

closing price *or* **closing quotation** (Stock Exch.) (opp. to *opening price*), dernier cours (*m.*) ; cours de clôture (*m.*) ; cote de clôture (*f.*).

clsoing stock (opp. to *opening stock*) (Com.), stock à l'inventaire (*m.*).

closure (*v.t.*), clôturer :

to closure the debate, clôturer les débats.

club together (to), se cotiser.

coach (Rly.) (*n.*), voiture (*f.*) ; wagon (*m.*).

coadventurer (pers.) (*n.*), co-intéressé, -e.

coal (*n.*), charbon (*m.*) ; 'houille (*f.*).

coal (*v.i.*), faire du charbon ; charbonner :

to coal en route is very expensive, faire du charbon, charbonner, en route est fort cher.

coal bunker, soute à charbon (*f.*).

coal dock, bassin aux charbons (*m.*) ; bassin à charbon (*m.*) ; bassin charbonnier (*m.*).

coal port, port charbonnier (*m.*).

coal shares, valeurs de charbonnages (*f.pl.*) ; valeurs de mines de charbon (*f.pl.*).

coal ship, navire charbonnier (*m.*) ; bateau charbonnier (*m.*) ; charbonnier (*m.*).

coal strike, grève dans les charbonnages (*f.*).

coal truck *or* **coal wagon** (Rly.), wagon à charbons (*m.*) ; wagon à houille (*m.*).

coal wharf, quai aux charbons (*m.*).

coal yard, chantier à charbon (*m.*) ; parc à charbon (*m.*).

coaling (*n.*), charbonnage (*m.*) :

the speed of coaling is limited by the trimming in the bunkers, la rapidité du charbonnage est limitée par l'arrimage dans les soutes.

coast (*n.*), côte (*f.*) ; côtes (*f.pl.*) ; littoral (*m.*) ; bords (*m.pl.*) :

the English coast, les côtes d'Angleterre.

the Baltic coast, les bords de la mer Baltique.

coast (*v.i.*), caboter.

coast-defence ship, navire garde-côte (*m.*) ; garde-côte (*m.*).

coast line, ligne de côte (*f.*).

coast police *or* **coastguards** (*n.pl.*), police des côtes à terre (*f.*). (Pour le singulier **coast-guard,** v. ci-après).

coast port, port côtier (*m.*).

coast river, fleuve côtier (*m.*).

coast station (Radioteleg.), station côtière (*f.*).

coaster (*n.*) *or* **coasting vessel** *or* **coasting ship,**

navire au cabotage (*m.*); navire de cabotage (*m.*); navire caboteur (*m.*); bateau caboteur (*m.*); caboteur (*m.*); cabotier (*m.*); navire côtier (*m.*).

coaster (pers.) (*n.*),   caboteur (*m.*); cabotier (*m.*).

coastguard (pers.) (*n.*),   agent de police des côtes à terre (*m.*).

coasting (*n.*) *or* **coasting trade** *or* **coastwise trade,** cabotage (*m.*); commerce de cabotage (*m.*); commerce caboteur (*m.*):

coasting from one English port to another English port, between English ports, between home ports,   cabotage d'un port anglais à un autre port anglais, entre ports anglais, entre ports de la métropole.

coasting cargo (opp. to *foreign cargo*), marchandises de cabotage (*f.pl.*).

coasting manifest, manifeste de cabotage (*m.*).

coasting navigation *or* **coastwise navigation,** navigation au (*ou* de) cabotage (*f.*); navigation de côte (*f.*).

coasting port, port de cabotage (*m.*).

coasting voyage, voyage au cabotage (*m.*).

cocontractant (pers.) (*n.*), cocontractant, -e.

cocontracting (*adj.*), cocontractant, -e.

cocreditor (pers.) (*n.*), cocréancier, -ère.

code (Teleg.) (*n.*), code (*m.*):

the codes used for the preparation of telegrams in code language *or* the codes used for the coding of telegrams,   les codes employés pour la rédaction des télégrammes en langage convenu.

code (*v.t.*), rédiger en langage convenu; codifier; coder:

to code a telegram,   rédiger un télégramme en langage convenu; codifier, coder, un télégramme.

code address, adresse convenue (*f.*).

code language *or* *simply* **code** (*n.*),   langage convenu (*m.*); convenu (*m.*):

telegram in code,   télégramme en langage convenu (*m.*).

word in code,   mot en convenu (*m.*).

code word, mot convenu (*m.*); mot de code (*m.*).

codebtor (pers.) (*n.*), codébiteur, -trice.

coding (Teleg.) (*n.*), rédaction en langage convenu (*f.*); codification (*f.*).

codirector (pers.) (*n.*), coadministrateur, -trice.

coffer (*n.*), coffre (*m.*); caisse (*f.*):

the coffers of the State,   les coffres de l'État.

the coffers of a bank, of a company,   les caisses d'une banque, d'une société.

coin (a single piece of money) (*n.*),   pièce (*f.*); pièce d'argent (*f.*); pièce de monnaie (*f.*); monnaie (*f.*):

a gold coin,   une pièce d'or.

coins of legal fineness,   monnaies au titre légal.

coin (coined money collectively or in general) (*n.*),   monnaie (*f.*);   monnaies (*f.pl.*); monnaie de métal (*f.*); monnaies de métal (*f.pl.*); monnaie métallique (*f.*);   pièces (*f.pl.*); numéraire (*m.*); espèces (*f.pl.*); espèces monnayées (*f.pl.*):

gold coin,   monnaie d'or;   monnaies d'or; pièces d'or.

the exchange of notes for coin,   l'échange des billets contre espèces (*ou* contre numéraire) (*m.*).

in coin,   en espèces; en numéraire; effectif, -ive:

to have £—— in coin in one's cash,   avoir £—— effectives dans sa caisse.

coin (*v.t.*),   monnayer; frapper; battre:

to coin ingots,   monnayer des lingots.

to coin money,   frapper de la, battre, monnaie:

« je dois être le maître dans tout ce dont je me mêle, et surtout dans ce qui regarde la Banque [de France], qui est bien plus à l'empereur qu'aux actionnaires, puisqu'elle bat monnaie. » NAPOLÉON 1er dans la séance du 2 avril 1806 du Conseil d'État, "I intend to be the master in everything in which I am concerned, and above all in that which concerns the Bank [of France], which is much more to the emperor than to the shareholders, because it coins money." NAPOLEON I at the sitting of 2nd April 1806 of the Council of State.

coinable (*adj.*),   monnayable:

coinable metals,   métaux monnayables (*m.pl.*).

coinage (coining) (*n.*),   monnayage (*m.*); frappe (*f.*):

coinage of gold,   monnayage, frappe, de l'or.

coinage (the system of coins used in a country) (*n.*),   monnaie (*f.*);   monnaies (*f.pl.*); monnaie de métal (*f.*); monnaies de métal (*f.pl.*); monnaie métallique (*f.*); numéraire (*m.*):

lowering the fineness of the coinage,   abaissement du titre de la monnaie (*ou* des monnaies) (*ou* de la monnaie de métal) (*ou* des monnaies de métal) (*ou* de la monnaie métallique) (*ou* du numéraire) (*m.*).

coined money, argent monnayé (*m.*); espèces monnayées (*f.pl.*).

coinsurance (*n.*), coassurance (*f.*).

coinsured [**coinsured** *pl.*] (pers.) (*n.*), coassuré, -e.

cold store,   entrepôt frigorifique (*m.*); dock frigorifique (*m.*).

colessee (pers.) (*n.*), copreneur, -euse.

collapse (heavy fall of prices) (Stock Exch.) (*n.*), chute (*f.*); débâcle (*f.*).

collateral (*n.*) *or* **collateral security,** nantissement (*m.*):

securities lodged as collateral,   titres remis (*ou* déposés) (*ou* fournis) en nantissement (*m.pl.*); valeurs remises (*ou* déposées) (*ou* fournies) en nantissement (*f.pl.*).

to lend on collateral (*or* on collateral security),   prêter sur nantissement.

to give a bill by way of collateral security (*or* as collateral),   donner un effet à titre de nantissement.

collation (Teleg.) (*n.*), collationnement (*m.*).

colleague (pers.) (*n.*), collègue (*m.*).

collect (to recover; to encash) (*v.t.*), recouvrer; récupérer; percevoir; faire rentrer; lever; encaisser:

to collect a debt,   recouvrer, récupérer, faire rentrer, une créance; faire un recouvrement:

lawyer's office where there are many debts to collect, étude où il y a beaucoup de recouvrements à faire (f.).

to collect the freight, percevoir le fret.

to collect rates and taxes, percevoir, lever, recouvrer, des impôts et contributions.

to collect a cheque, encaisser un chèque.

the bank has collected the money, la banque a encaissé les fonds.

collect (to remove) (v.t.), enlever; retirer; prendre :
consignee who calls at the station to collect his goods, destinataire qui se présente à la gare pour enlever (ou pour retirer) sa marchandise (m.).

collect (letters) (Post) (v.t.), lever; relever.

collectable or **collectible** (adj.), recouvrable; récupérable; percevable; encaissable :
collectable amounts, sommes recouvrables (ou récupérables) (f.pl.).
collectable tax, taxe percevable (f.).
coupons collectible in Paris, coupons encaissables à Paris (m.pl.).

collecting (adj.), encaisseur, -euse :
the collecting banker, le banquier encaisseur.

collection (recovery; encashment) (n.), recouvrement (m.); récupération (f.); perception (f.); rentrée (f.); levée (f.); encaissement (m.) :
collection of a sum due, recouvrement d'une somme due.
collection of customs duties, perception des droits de douane.
collection of taxes, perception, recouvrement, levée, rentrée, des impôts (ou des contributions) (ou des taxes).
the remittance of a bill for collection, la remise d'un effet en recouvrement; la remise d'un billet à l'encaissement.
bills for collection account, compte effets à encaisser (m.).

collection (removal by the consignee; taking to the station by the railway company) (n.), enlèvement (m.); retrait (m.); prise (f.); apport à la gare (m.) :
collection of the goods, enlèvement, retrait, de la marchandise.
collection at residence or collection at trader's premises or simply collection, prise à domicile; enlèvement à domicile :
no collection is made on Sundays, aucune prise à domicile n'est effectuée les dimanches.
additional charge for collection, taxe supplémentaire pour apport à la gare (f.).

collection (of letters) (Post) (n.), levée (f.); relevage (m.) :
the time of the last collection, l'heure de la dernière levée (f.).

collection at the source (Income Tax), stoppage à la source (m.).

collective (adj.), collectif, -ive :
collective liability of railways, responsabilité collective des chemins de fer (f.).

collector (pers.) (n.) (Abbrev.: **Collr**), receveur (m.); percepteur (m.); encaisseur (m.) :
collector of customs, receveur des douanes.

tax collector, percepteur des impôts; receveur des contributions.

collector of taxes (income tax, or the like), percepteur des contributions directes; receveur des contributions directes.

collector of a cheque, of a bill, encaisseur d'un chèque, d'un billet.

collector's office, recette (f.); bureau du receveur (m.) :
office of collector of customs, recette des douanes.

collide (Navig.) (v.i.), s'aborder; faire collision; se rencontrer.

collide with (to) (Navig.), aborder; faire collision avec; rencontrer :
ship which collides with another ship, navire qui aborde (ou qui fait collision avec) un autre navire (m.).

colliding ship, navire abordeur (m.); navire abordant (m.); abordeur (m.) :
the damage caused by the colliding ship to the ship collided with, le dommage occasionné par le navire abordeur (ou par l'abordeur) au navire abordé (ou à l'abordé).

collier (coal-carrying ship) (n.), charbonnier (m.); navire charbonnier (m.); charbonnier (m.).

collision (Navig.) (n.), abordage (m.); collision (f.); rencontre (f.) :
collision with another ship, abordage à un autre bâtiment.
ship which comes into collision with another ship, navire qui entre en collision avec un autre navire (m.).
collision due to inevitable accident, abordage douteux; abordage mixte.
collision due to inscrutable accident, abordage fortuit.

collision clause, clause collision (f.); clause d'abordage (f.).

collision regulations, règlements ayant pour objet de prévenir les abordages en mer (m.pl.).

collision risk, risque de collision (m.); risque d'abordage (m.).

collusion (n.), collusion (f.) :
fraud or collusion, fraude ou collusion.

collusive or **collusory** (adj.), collusoire.

collusively (adv.), collusoirement.

colonial (adj.), colonial, -e, -aux :
colonial bank, banque coloniale (f.).
colonial produce, produits coloniaux (m.pl.); produits des colonies (m.pl.); denrées coloniales (f.pl.).
colonial stocks, fonds coloniaux (m.pl.); emprunts de colonies (m.pl.).

colony [**colonies** pl.] (n.), colonie (f.).

coloured ink, encre de couleur (f.).

coloured pencil, crayon de couleur (m.).

column (n.) (Abbrev.: **col.**), colonne (f.) :
the columns of a register, of a newspaper, a separate column, a column of figures, an inner column, an outer column, a cash column, a double cash column, a francs and centimes column, a pounds, shillings, and pence column, debit column, credit column, folio column, detail column, particulars

column (*or* description column), remarks column, analysis column, amounts column, shorts column, sundries column, principal column, interest column, les colonnes d'un registre, d'un journal, une colonne à part, une colonne de chiffres, une colonne intérieure, une colonne extérieure, une colonne de caisse (*ou* une colonne caisse), une double colonne de caisse, une colonne francs et centimes, une colonne livres, schellings, et pence, colonne débitrice, colonne créditrice, colonne des folios, colonne de détail, colonne du libellé, colonne pour les observations (*ou* colonne remarques), colonne de dépouillement (*ou* colonne de ventilation), colonne des sommes, colonne pour les sommes partielles, colonne divers, colonne des capitaux, colonne des intérêts (*ou* colonne d'intérêts).

columnar (*adj.*), à colonnes :
   columnar cash book, livre de caisse à colonnes (*m.*).

combination (*n.*), combinaison (*f.*) :
   financial combinations, combinaisons financières.

combinations in plain language, code, and/or cipher (Teleg.), langage mixte (*m.*).

combine (Com.) (*n.*), coalition (*f.*) ; combinaison (*f.*) :
   combine of big producers, coalition de grands producteurs.

combine (*v.t.*), combiner ; réunir :
   the total traffic, imports and exports combined, le trafic total, entrées et sorties réunies.

combined entry (journal entry), article collectif (*m.*) ; article récapitulatif (*m.*) ; article composé (*m.*).

combined journal and ledger, journal-grand-livre (*m.*) ; journal grand livre (*m.*) ; journal américain (*m.*).

combined rate, tarif combiné (*m.*).

combined ticket (Travel), billet combiné (*m.*).

come alongside (to), accoster ; accoster à :
   barge which comes alongside a ship, a wharf, chaland qui accoste un navire, un quai (*m.*).
   ship which comes alongside the quay or the wharves, navire qui accoste à quai ou aux appontements (*m.*).

come in (to) (to be received), rentrer :
   money which is coming in badly, fonds qui rentrent mal (*m.pl.*).

come into collision (to) (*v.i.*), entrer en collision ; faire collision ; s'aborder.

come into collision with (to), entrer en collision avec ; faire collision avec ; aborder :
   ship which comes into collision with another ship, navire qui entre en (*ou* qui fait) collision avec (*ou* qui aborde) un autre navire.

come into force (to), entrer en vigueur :
   it is only after acquittance of the policy that it comes into force, ce n'est qu'après l'acquittement de la police qu'elle entre en vigueur.

come into value (to), entrer en valeur :
   value (*or* value date) is the date on which an amount in account current becomes interest-bearing, or comes into value, on appelle valeur (*ou* date de valeur) (*ou* date d'entrée en valeur) l'époque à laquelle une somme en compte courant devient productive d'intérêt, ou entre en valeur.

come on demurrage (to), tomber en souffrance.

come on offer (to), être offert, -e :
   X. shares came on offer at 1 against 1¼, l'action X. est offerte à 1 contre 1 1/4.

come to (to) (to cost), revenir :
   purchase which comes to so much, achat qui revient à tant (*m.*).

come to an agreement (to), tomber d'accord ; se mettre d'accord :
   two experts who come to an agreement, deux experts qui tombent (*ou* qui se mettent) d'accord.

come to an arrangement with one's creditors (to), prendre un arrangement avec ses créanciers ; s'atermoyer.

coming alongside, accostage (*m.*).

coming campaign (Produce Exch.), campagne future (*f.*).

coming in regularly, bien venant, -e :
   an income of six thousand pounds coming in regularly, six mille livres de rente bien venantes.

coming into force (of an agreement, of a treaty), entrée en vigueur (d'une convention, d'un traité) (*f.*).

coming into value, entrée en valeur (*f.*) :
   interest only runs from the dates of coming into value of the capital sums, les intérêts ne courent qu'à partir des dates d'entrée en valeur des capitaux (*m.pl.*).

coming out (Stock Exch.), émission (*f.*) :
   dealings in shares for the coming out, opérations en actions à émission (*f.pl.*).

command (*v.t.*), commander :
   steamer commanded by captain So-and-so, vapeur commandé par le capitaine un tel (*m.*).

commander (of a ship) (pers.) (*n.*), commandant (d'un navire) (*m.*).

commence (*v.t.*), commencer ; intenter ; entamer :
   to commence business, commencer les affaires (*ou* les opérations sociales).
   to commence proceedings, intenter une action ; entamer des poursuites :
   to commence proceedings against a debtor, intenter une action à (*ou* contre), entamer des poursuites contre, un débiteur.

commencement (*n.*), commencement (*m.*) ; début (*m.*) :
   commencement and end of a risk, commencement (*ou* début) et fin d'un risque.

comment (*n.*), commentaire (*m.*) ; observation (*f.*) :
   press comments, commentaires de la presse.

comment on (to), commenter :
   to comment on a decision, commenter une décision.

commentary [commentaries *pl.*] (*n.*), commentaire (*m.*).

commerce (*n.*), commerce (*m.*) ; négoce (*m.*) :
   commerce enriches a nation, le commerce (*ou* le négoce) enrichit une nation.

commercial (*adj.*), commercial, -e, -aux; commerçant, -e; marchand, -e; de commerce;
d'affaires:
commercial agent, représentant de commerce
(*m.*).
commercial bank, banque commerciale (*f.*);
banque de commerce (*f.*).
commercial bookkeeping, comptabilité commerciale (*f.*).
commercial code (Law), code de commerce
(*m.*).
commercial court (Law), tribunal de commerce (*m.*); tribunal consulaire (*m.*).
commercial envelope, enveloppe commerciale
(*f.*). (In France, of a size [nearly square]
to take business paper folded in four. In
England, of a size [oblong] to take business
paper folded in six.)
commercial exchange, change commercial
(*m.*); change tiré (*m.*).
commercial house, maison de commerce (*f.*).
commercial law, droit commercial (*m.*).
commercial marine, marine marchande (*f.*).
commercial mark, marque de commerce (*f.*).
commercial paper *or* commercial bills (bills
of exchange), papier de commerce (*m.*);
papier commercial (*m.*).
commercial papers (Post), papiers de commerce
(*m.pl.*); papiers d'affaires (*m.pl.*).
commercial par, pair commercial (*m.*):
the commercial par is the cost of the coin
(precious metal and minting expenses),
le pair commercial est le prix de revient de
la pièce (métal précieux et frais de
monnayage).
commercial port, port commercial (*m.*);
port marchand (*m.*); port de commerce (*m.*).
commercial sale rooms, bourse de (*ou* des)
marchandises (*f.*); bourse de commerce
(*f.*). *V. note sous* marché commercial.
commercial traveller, voyageur de commerce
(*m.*); commis voyageur (*m.*).
commercial travellers' samples, échantillons
des voyageurs de commerce (*m.pl.*).
commercial treaty, traité de commerce (*m.*).
commercialize (*v.t.*), commercialiser.
commercially (*adv.*), commercialement.
commission (charge; trust; transaction for
others) (*n.*), commission (*f.*):
to execute a commission for the account of
one's principal, exécuter une commission
pour le compte de son commettant.
commission (compensation allowed to a factor or
agent) (*n.*) (Abbrev.: **com.** *or* **commn**),
commission (*f.*); remise (*f.*); courtage (*m.*):
commission allowed to an agent, commission,
remise, accordée à un agent.
commission for collection (of bills), commission
d'encaissement.
commission (*charged*) for keeping account
(Banking), commission de compte; commission de caisse.
commission on contangoes (Stock Exch.),
courtage des reports.
commission on sale, commission sur vente;
guelte (*f.*).

travellers' commissions, commissions des
voyageurs.
commission (of a remisier or half commission man)
(Stock Exch.) (*n.*), remise (*f.*).
commission (*v.t.*), commissioner.
commission agent *or* **commission merchant**
commissionnaire (*m.*); négociant-commissionnaire (*m.*):
the commission agent receives from his principal
a retribution called commission, le commissionnaire reçoit de son commettant une
rétribution appelée commission.
commission contract (Produce Exch.) (opp. to
direct contract or *principal contract*), contrat
de commission (*m.*).
commission house, maison de commission (*f.*).
commission note, lettre de garantie de commission
(*f.*).
commission order form *or simply* **commission order**
(the written and/or printed instrument),
bon de commission (*m.*); note de commission
(*f.*).
commission rates, tarif des courtages (*m.*).
commissionaire (messenger) (pers.) (*n.*), garçon de bureau (*m.*).
Commissioners of Inland Revenue, fisc (*m.*).
commissoria lex (Law), clause commissoire (*f.*).
commit (*v.t.*), commettre; faire:
to commit irregularities, a fraud, commettre,
faire, des irrégularités, une fraude.
commitment (*n.*), engagement (*m.*):
to limit the amount of one's commitment,
limiter le montant de son engagement.
committee (*n.*), comité (*m.*):
committee for general purposes, comité de
réglementation.
Cf. **stock exchange committee**.
committee of creditors *or* **committee of inspection**
(Bankruptcy), direction de créanciers (*f.*);
contrôleurs (*m.pl.*).
commodity [**commodities** *pl.*] (*n.*), produit (*m.*);
denrée (*f.*); marchandise (*f.*); matière
(*f.*); matière première (*f.*); article (*m.*);
ressource (*f.*):
commodities intended for export, produits
destinés (*ou* denrées destinées) (*ou* marchandises destinées) à l'exportation.
rubbers heavy in spite of the rise in the commodity, caoutchoutières lourdes malgré
la hausse de la matière (*ou* de la matière
première) (*f.pl.*).
tin shares are better in general, favoured by
the recovery of the commodity, les valeurs
d'étain sont mieux en général, à la faveur
de la reprise de la matière (*f.pl.*).
recovery in the prices of the commodity (tea,
for example), reprise des cours de l'article
(thé, par exemple) (*f.*).
cotton is the staple commodity of the Sudan,
le coton est le produit principal (*ou* la
ressource principale) du Soudan.
results show, once again, that whatever the
prices of the commodity may be, the big
oil companies, who not only produce, but
refine, carry and distribute the petroleum
and its derivatives, have a very large unit

margin of profit left over, les résultats démontrent, une fois de plus, que quels que soient les cours du produit, les grandes sociétés pétrolières, qui non seulement produisent, mais raffinent, transportent et distribuent le pétrole et ses dérivés, conservent une marge bénéficiaire unitaire très large (*m.pl.*).

commodity market (distinguished from *share market*), marché de la matière première (*m.*).

commodity prices, cours commerciaux (*m.pl.*).

common (*adj.*), commun, -e ; ordinaire :
a common fund, un fonds commun.
common average (Mar. Insce) (opp. to *general average*), avarie particulière (*f.*) ; avaries particulières (*f.pl.*) ; avarie simple (*f.*) ; avaries simples (*f.pl.*).
common carrier (goods), entrepreneur de roulages publics (*m.*).
common carrier (passengers), entrepreneur de voitures publiques (*m.*).
common carrier (goods and passengers), entrepreneur de voitures et roulages publics (*m.*).
common fraction (Arith.), fraction ordinaire (*f.*).
common law, droit commun (*m.*).
common policy (Insce), police type (*f.*).
common safety, salut commun (*m.*) :
voluntary sacrifice made for the common safety of the ship and cargo, sacrifice volontaire fait pour le salut commun du navire et du chargement (*m.*).

communicate (*v.t.*), communiquer :
to communicate to the insurers all information concerning the adventure, communiquer aux assureurs tous renseignements relatifs à l'expédition.

communicate (*v.i.*), communiquer :
to communicate by telephone, communiquer par le téléphone.

communication (*n.*), communication (*f.*) :
long distance communication (Radioteleg.), communication à grande distance.

community [communities *pl.*] (*n.*), communauté (*f.*) :
community of interest, communauté d'intérêts.

commutative contract, contrat commutatif (*m.*).

company [companies *pl.*] (*n.*) (Abbrev.: **Co.** or **Coy** or **Compy**), compagnie (*f.*) ; société (*f.*) :
a railway company, une compagnie de chemins de fer.
banking company, société de banque.
Note :—In France, concerns such as railways, mines, water, gas or electric light companies, and insurance companies, are usually, though not necessarily, called *compagnies*, and ordinary commercial, industrial, or financial concerns are usually called *sociétés*. Legally, there is no difference between *compagnie* and *société*.
and company (*usually abbreviated* & Co.) (crossing of a cheque), et compagnie (*généralement en abrégé* & Cie). V. exemple sous **crossing**.

company's or **of the company**, social, -e, -aux :
de la société ; de la compagnie :

the company's creditors or the creditors of the company, les créanciers sociaux (*m.pl.*).
the company's bankers, les banquiers de la société (*m.pl.*).
company's year or company's financial year (or trading year), année sociale (*f.*) ; exercice social (*m.*).

companies act, loi sur les sociétés (*f.*).

company bookkeeping, comptabilité de (*ou* des) sociétés (*f.*).

company director, administrateur de société(s) (*m.*).

company's sheet (Rly.) (opp. to *owner's*, or *trader's*, *sheet*), bâche appartenant au chemin de fer (*f.*) ; bâche du chemin de fer (*f.*).

comparative (*adj.*), comparatif, -ive :
comparative table, tableau comparatif (*m.*).

compare (*v.t.*), comparer ; rapprocher ; collationner :
to compare a copy, a translation, with the original, comparer une copie, une traduction, à, collationner une copie, une traduction, sur, l'original.
to compare one year's expenses with the other's, Monday's prices with those of last week, comparer les frais d'une année à l'autre, les cours de lundi avec ceux de la semaine dernière.

comparison or **comparing** (*n.*), comparaison (*f.*) ; rapprochement (*m.*) ; collationnement (*m.*) :
result of the comparison between the gross profit and the amount of the sales expressed in percentage, résultat du rapprochement entre le bénéfice brut et le montant des ventes exprimé en pourcentage (*m.*).

compartment (of a passenger carriage) (Rly.) (*n.*), compartiment (d'une voiture à voyageurs) (*m.*).

compass (*n.*), compas (*m.*) ; boussole (*f.*) ; boussole marine (*f.*).

compensate (*v.t.*), compenser ; indemniser ; récompenser ; dédommager :
profits which compensate one's losses, bénéfices qui compensent ses pertes (*m.pl.*).
reduction allowed to compensate possible errors, réduction accordée pour compenser les erreurs possibles (*f.*).
to compensate the owner of a property taken for public use, indemniser le possesseur d'une propriété expropriée pour cause d'utilité publique.
to compensate someone for a loss, récompenser, dédommager, quelqu'un d'une perte.

to compensate oneself or **to compensate each other**, se compenser ; s'indemniser ; se récompenser ; se dédommager :
to compensate oneself for one's losses, se récompenser, se dédommager, de ses pertes.
differences which compensate each other, différences qui se compensent (*f.pl.*).

compensating error (Bkkpg), erreur de compensation (*f.*).

compensation (*n.*), compensation (*f.*) ; indemnisation (*f.*) ; indemnité (*f.*) ; récompense (*f.*) ; dédommagement (*m.*) :
compensation agreed in case of delay, indemnité convenue en cas de retard.

compensation due to the victims of an accident, indemnités dues aux victimes d'un accident.
to claim compensation in case of dismissal, réclamer une indemnité en cas de congédiement.
compete for (to), concourir pour ; concourir à :
to compete for an issue of stock, concourir à une émission de titres.
compete with (to), faire concurrence à ; concurrencer :
to compete with someone, faire concurrence à, concurrencer, quelqu'un.
to prevent foreign importation from competing with national production, empêcher l'importation étrangère de concurrencer la production nationale.
competing or **competitive** (adj.), concurrent, -e ; concurrentiel, -elle :
competing industries, industries concurrentes (f.pl.).
competitive products of foreign origin, produits concurrents d'origine étrangère (m.pl.).
competitive companies, compagnies concurrentielles (f.pl.).
competition (n.), concurrence (f.) ; compétition (f.) :
the competition of the motor and the railway, la concurrence de l'automobile et du chemin de fer.
to buy or sell in competition with someone, acheter ou vendre en concurrence avec quelqu'un.
competitor (pers.) (n.), concurrent, -e.
complaint (n.), plainte (f.) :
complaints formulated by the public by reason of incidents of working the lines, plaintes formulées par le public à raison des incidents de l'exploitation des lignes.
comply with (to), se conformer à ; remplir ; accomplir ; respecter :
to comply with the clauses in an agreement, the legal formalities, the conditions required by the articles of association, se conformer aux, remplir les, accomplir les, respecter les, clauses dans un contrat, formalités imposées par la loi, conditions exigées par les statuts.
to comply with quarantine or other regulations, with all the consular regulations in force, with the underwriters' requirements, se conformer à des règlements de quarantaine ou autres, à tous les règlements consulaires en vigueur, aux exigences des assureurs.
composite train (passengers and goods), train mixte (m.).
composite vessel (iron and wood), navire composé (m.) ; navire composite (m.) ; navire mixte (m.).
composition (to creditors) (n.), décharge (f.) ; concordat (m.) :
composition of 5s. in the £, décharge, concordat, de 25 0/0.
composition for stamp duty, abonnement au timbre (m.).
composition for stamp duty (sum payable), taxe d'abonnement au timbre (f.).
compound (adj.), composé, -e :

compound arbitration or compound arbitrage (distinguished from simple arbitration or arbitrage), arbitrage composé (m.).
compound entry (journal entry), article composé (m.) ; article collectif (m.) ; article récapitulatif (m.).
compound interest (opp. to simple interest), intérêt composé (m.) ; intérêts composés (m.pl.).
compound (v.i.), concorder ; arriver à un concordat :
to compound with one's creditors, concorder, arriver à un concordat, avec ses créanciers.
compound for stamp duty (to), s'abonner au timbre.
comprise (v.t.), comprendre ; renfermer ; contenir :
if the anticipated profit is comprised in the insurance, si le bénéfice espéré est compris dans l'assurance.
compromise (n.), compromis (m.) ; transaction (f.) :
to prefer a compromise to a lawsuit, préférer un compromis à un procès.
a poor compromise is sometimes preferable to a successful action, une médiocre transaction est parfois préférable à un bon procès.
compromise (v.t.), compromettre.
compromise (v.i.), compromettre ; faire un compromis :
arbitration clause under which the parties bind themselves to compromise, that is to say, to submit to arbitration disputes which may arise on the contract, clause compromissoire pour laquelle les parties s'obligent à compromettre, c'est-à-dire à soumettre à l'arbitrage les contestations pouvant naître du contrat (f.).
comptroller (pers.) (n.), contrôleur (m.).
comptroller general [**comptrollers general** pl.], contrôleur général (m.).
compulsory (adj.), forcé, -e ; obligatoire :
compulsory call or compulsory putting in (of a ship), relâche forcée (f.) :
a call (or putting in) is voluntary or compulsory, la relâche est volontaire ou forcée.
the ship X. having been compelled to put into this port on account of damage sustained by the hull and the engine, le navire X. en relâche forcée dans ce port pour avaries éprouvées dans la coque et la machine.
computable (adj.), calculable.
computation (n.), supputation (f.) ; calcul (m.).
compute (v.t.), supputer ; calculer ; raisonner :
to compute an arbitrage, raisonner un arbitrage.
concealment (n.), réticence (f.) ; dissimulation (f.) :
insurance which is null in case of concealment or misrepresentation by the insured, assurance qui est nulle en cas de réticence ou fausse déclaration de l'assuré (f.).
concealment of assets (bankruptcy), dissimulation d'actif.
concede (v.t.), concéder :
to concede a privilege, concéder un privilège.

concern (enterprise) (*n.*), entreprise (*f.*) ; exploitation (*f.*) ; affaire (*f.*) :
a commercial or industrial concern, une entreprise (*ou* une exploitation) (*ou* une affaire) commerciale ou industrielle.

concessible (*adj.*), concessible :
concessible lands, terrains concessibles (*m.pl.*).

concession (*n.*), concession (*f.*) :
railway concession, concession de chemin de fer.
concession of land, concession de terrain.

concessionaire *or* **concessionary** [**concessionaries** *pl.*] *or* **concessioner** (pers.) (*n.*), concessionnaire (*m.* ou *f.*).

concessionary (*adj.*), concessionnaire :
concessionary company, société concessionnaire (*f.*).

conclude (*v.t.*), conclure ; arrêter ; clore :
to conclude a contract of insurance, conclure un contrat d'assurance.
to conclude a bargain, arrêter, clore, un marché.

concrete ship, navire en béton (*m.*).

condition (*n.*), condition (*f.*) ; état (*m.*) ; conditionnement (*m.*) :
conditions of a contract, conditions d'un contrat.
the condition of the market, l'état (*ou* la condition) du marché.
goods in apparent good order and condition, marchandises en bon état et conditionnement apparents (*f.pl.*).

on condition, sous réserve :
in certain countries, telegrams in code are admitted only on condition that the code used has been deposited with the authorites, en certains pays, les télégrammes en langage convenu ne sont admis que sous réserve que le code employé soit déposé aux bureaux de destination.

conditional (*adj.*), conditionnel, -elle :
conditional acceptance, acceptation conditionnelle (*f.*).

conditionally (*adv.*), conditionnellement.

conduct (*n.*), conduite (*f.*) ; gestion (*f.*) ; maniement (*m.*) ; manîment (*m.*) :
conduct of affairs, conduite, gestion, des affaires.

conduct (*v.t.*), conduire ; gérer ; manier ; mener :
to conduct business, conduire, gérer, manier, mener, des affaires.

conductor (of an omnibus) (pers.) (*n.*), conducteur (d'un omnibus) (*m.*).

confer (*v.i.*), conférer ; s'aboucher :
to confer with one's counsel, conférer avec son avocat.

confer title (to), faire titre :
all private written agreements capable of conferring title are liable to stamp duty, tous les écrits privés susceptibles de faire titre sont soumis au droit de timbre.

conference (*n.*), conférence (*f.*) ; abouchement (*m.*) :
conference of counsel, conference des avocats.
shipping conference (ring), conférence maritime.

confide (*v.t.*), confier.

confide (*v.i.*), se confier.

confidence (confidential communication) (*n.*), confidence (*f.*).

confidence (reliance) (*n.*), confiance (*f.*) :
the whole worth of a bank lies in the confidence which it inspires, toute la valeur d'une banque réside dans la confiance qu'elle inspire.

confidential (*adj.*), confidentiel, -elle :
confidential report, rapport confidentiel (*m.*).

confidentially (*adv.*), confidentiellement.

confine oneself to one's instructions (to), se renfermer dans ses instructions.

confirm (*v.t.*) (Ant. : *cancel*), confirmer ; ratifier ; approuver ; adopter :
to confirm a letter, to confirm by letter the contents of a telegram, confirmer une lettre, confirmer par lettre le contenu d'un télégramme.
to confirm in writing orders given verbally, confirmer par écrit les ordres passés verbalement.
to confirm an appointment (to a post), ratifier une nomination.
to confirm the resolution of a meeting, ratifier la décision d'une assemblée.
the minutes of the last meeting were read and confirmed, le procès-verbal de la dernière séance est lu et adopté (*ou* et approuvé).

confirmation (*n.*), confirmation (*f.*) ; ratification (*f.*) ; approbation (*f.*) ; adoption (*f.*) :
confirmation of credit, of a piece of news, confirmation de crédit, d'une nouvelle.

confirmed credit *or* **confirmed banker's credit,** crédit confirmé (*m.*) ; crédit à l'exportation (*m.*).

confirmed letter of credit, lettre de crédit confirmé (*f.*).

confiscate (*v.t.*), confisquer.

confiscation (*n.*), confiscation (*f.*) :
confiscation of smuggled goods, of falsely entered goods, for breach of the laws, confiscation de marchandise de contrebande, de marchandise faussement déclarée, pour contravention aux lois.

congestion (*n.*), encombrement (*m.*) :
congestion of a port, of the wharves, encombrement d'un port, des quais.

connect up (to) (Produce Exch.), mettre en filière :
client who instructs his broker to connect up the goods, client qui charge son courtier de mettre en filière la marchandise.

connected contract (Produce Exch.), marché en (*ou* par) filière (*m.*). V. exemple sous **string.**

connection (business relations) (*n.*), correspondance (*f.*) :
house which has connections everywhere, maison qui a des correspondances partout (*f.*).

connection (clientele) (*n.*), clientèle (*f.*).

connection (transfer or continuation in transit from one route to another) (*n.*), correspondance (*f.*) :
if owing to lateness of one train, connection with another train is missed, si par suite du retard d'un train, la correspondance avec un autre train est manquée.

Paris-Prague-Warsaw, with connection at Prague for Budapest (Aviation), Paris-Prague-Varsovie, avec correspondance à Prague sur Budapest.

conscientious (*adj.*), consciencieux, -euse.

conscientiously (*adv.*), consciencieusement.

consensual contract, contrat consensuel (*m.*).

consent (*n.*), consentement (*m.*); accord (*m.*); agrément (*m.*) :
consent of the parties, consentement des parties.
consent in writing, consentement par écrit.
to obtain someone's consent to do a thing, obtenir l'agrément de quelqu'un à (*ou* pour) faire une chose.

consent to (to), consentir ; consentir à ; souscrire à :
to consent to a sale, consentir, consentir à, une vente.
to consent to an arrangement, consentir à, souscrire à, un arrangement.

consequential damages, dommages indirects (*m.pl.*).

conservative estimate, appréciation réservée (*f.*).

consider (to deliberate) (*v.t.*), considérer ; délibérer ; délibérer sur :
meeting convened to consider the following agenda, assemblée convoquée à l'effet de délibérer sur l'ordre du jour suivant (*f.*).

consider and, if thought fit, to pass the resolution(s) (to), délibérer sur l'ordre du jour :
notice is hereby given that an extraordinary general meeting of the company will be held (*place, date, and time*) for the purpose of considering and, if thought fit, of passing the following resolution (*or* resolutions), MM. les actionnaires sont convoqués en assemblée générale extraordinaire (*lieu, date, et heure*) à l'effet de délibérer sur l'ordre du jour suivant.

considerable (*adj.*), considérable :
considerable expense, dépense considérable (*f.*).

consideration *or* **considering** (*n.*), considération (*f.*); délibération (*f.*) :
that is worth considering (*or* merits consideration), cela mérite considération.
failing a report of the auditors, the consideration by the meeting of the accounts and the balance sheet would be null, faute de rapport des commissaires, les délibérations de l'assemblée sur les comptes et le bilan seraient nulles.
after consideration, It was resolved that *or* after consideration, Resolved that (board minutes), après délibération (*ou* après en avoir délibéré), le conseil prend la résolution suivante.

consideration (*n.*) *or* **consideration money,** prix (*m.*); rémunération (*f.*); représentation (*f.*); indemnité (*f.*) :
consideration for sale, prix de vente.
consideration money for a transfer (of stock or shares), prix d'un transfert.
consideration (*or* purchase consideration) for transfer (vendors' assets acquired), prix d'apport; rémunération des apports :

as consideration for the transfer there has been allotted to the vendors 0,000 shares of 0 each, fully paid, in the company, en rémunération (*ou* en représentation) des apports il a été attribué aux apporteurs 0 000 actions de 0 chacune, entièrement libérées, de la société.
an agreed consideration of half per cent fixed by a clause of the contract, une indemnité forfaitaire de demi pour cent fixée par une clause du contrat.

in consideration of, moyennant :
in consideration of the payment of a certain sum, moyennant le versement (*ou* moyennant paiement) d'une certaine somme.
in consideration of the allotment of 0 fully paid shares, moyennant l'attribution de 0 actions entièrement libérées.

for a valuable consideration. V. sous **valuable.**

consideration (Law) (*n.*), provision (*f.*); cause (*f.*) :
acceptance of a bill implies consideration, l'acceptation d'une lettre suppose la provision (*f.*).
delivery of a cheque transfers to the payee the property in the consideration, la délivrance du chèque transfère au bénéficiaire la propriété de la provision.
absence of consideration (bill of exchange), défaut de provision (*m.*).
the consideration in the contract of affreightment, la cause dans le contrat d'affrètement.
in a sale, the consideration for the sale is the payment of the price by the purchaser, dans une vente, la cause de la vente est le paiement du prix par l'acquéreur.
bill of exchange which states the consideration for its creation, that is to say, if value for it has been given in cash, in goods, or in account, effet de commerce qui énonce la cause de sa création, c'est-à-dire si la valeur en a été fournie en espèces, en marchandises, ou en compte. Cf. **to state the consideration.**
accommodation bills have no commercial transaction as consideration, les valeurs de complaisance n'ont pour cause aucune opération commerciale (*f.pl.*).
the consideration for the insurance must be legal, la cause de l'assurance doit être licite.

consign (*v.t.*), consigner :
to consign a ship to the charterer's agents, consigner un navire aux agents de l'affréteur.
goods consigned to a foreign country, marchandises consignées à un pays étranger (*f.pl.*).

consignee (pers.) (*n.*), consignataire (*m.*); destinataire (*m.*); réceptionnaire (*m.*) :
consignee of the cargo, consignataire de la (*ou* à la) cargaison.
consignee of the ship, consignataire du navire ; consignataire de la coque.
consignee of the shipment, réceptionnaire du chargement.
consignee who calls at the station to collect his goods, destinataire qui se présente à la gare pour enlever sa marchandise.

onsignment (act of consigning) (n.), consignation (f.); expédition (f.); envoi (m.):
goods on consignment, marchandises en consignation (f.pl.).

onsignment (that which is consigned; shipment; parcel) (n.), consignation (f.); expédition (f.); chargement (m.); envoi (m.):
the number of cases making up a consignment, le nombre de caisses composant une expédition.
the value of a consignment of goods, la valeur d'un envoi de marchandises.
the name of the ship and the value of the consignment, le nom du navire et la valeur du chargement (ou de l'envoi).
package forming part of the consignment, colis faisant partie du chargement (m.).

onsignment account, compte de consignation (m.).

onsignment note (Rly.), lettre de voiture (f.); déclaration d'expédition (f.); bulletin de remise (m.); note de remise (f.).

onsignment note (Shipping), bordereau d'expédition (m.); bordereau de chargement (m.); bulletin de chargement (m.); déclaration d'expédition (f.); note de détail (f.).

onsignor or **consigner** (pers.) (n.), consignateur, -trice; expéditeur, -trice; destinateur, -trice.

onsistent (adj.), suivi, -e:
consistent buying, achats suivis (m.pl.).

onsolidate (v.t.), consolider; unifier.

onsolidated debt (opp. to floating debt), dette consolidée (f.); dette unifiée (f.). V. exemple sous **floating.**

onsolidation (n.), consolidation (f.); unification (f.):
consolidation of the floating debt, consolidation de la dette flottante.

onsolidation act (of Parliament), loi coordonnée (f.).

onsols (n.pl.), Consolidés (m.pl.); fonds consolidés (m.pl.).

onsortium (syndicate) (n.), consortium (m.).

onstitute (v.t.), constituer:
meeting regularly constituted, assemblée régulièrement constituée (f.).

onstitution (n.), constitution (f.).

onstructional defect, vice de construction (m.).

onstructive total loss (Mar. Insce) (Abbrev.: c.t.l.) (opp. to actual total loss), perte totale relative (f.); perte réputée (ou censée) totale (f.). Note:—Translation only; does not obtain in French Law.

onsul (pers.) (n.), consul (m.):
French consul, consul de France; consul français.
the British consul at Marseilles, le consul britannique à Marseille.
consul general [consuls general pl.], consul général.

onsular (adj.), consulaire:
consular agent, agent consulaire (m.).
consular charges or consular fees, frais consulaires (m.pl.); droits de chancellerie (m.pl.).
consular invoice, facture consulaire (f.).

consular regulations, règlements consulaires (m.pl.).
consular report, rapport consulaire (m.).

consulate (n.), consulat (m.):
consulate general [consulates general pl.], consulat général.

consult (v.t.), consulter:
to consult counsel, a price list, consulter un avocat, un prix courant.

consult (v.i.), consulter:
to consult with someone, consulter avec quelqu'un.

consultation (n.), consultation (f.); conseil (m.).

consultative (adj.), consultatif, -ive:
consultative voice, voix consultative (f.).

consume (v.t.), consommer. V. exemple sous **produce.**

consumer (pers.) (n.), consommateur, -trice:
the producer and the consumer, le producteur et le consommateur.

consumption (n.), consommation (f.):
the daily consumption of coal, la consommation journalière de charbon.

contain (v.t.), contenir; porter; comprendre; renfermer; énoncer; être revêtu (-e) de:
the proposal should contain: the name of the ship, that of the master, etc., la proposition doit contenir: le nom du navire, celui du capitaine, etc.
bill of lading which contains the following particulars, connaissement qui porte les énonciations suivantes (m.).
contract which contains all the particulars prescribed by the law, contrat qui renferme toutes les mentions prescrites par la loi (m.).
what the policy should contain, ce que la police doit énoncer.
bills containing first class signatures, effets revêtus de signatures de premier ordre (m.pl.).
cheque containing the words not negotiable, chèque revêtu de la mention non négociable (m.).

container (opp. to contents) (n.), contenant (m.):
boxes, cases, and like (or similar) containers, les boîtes, les étuis, et les contenants similaires.

contango [**contangoes** pl.] or **contangoing** (Stock Exch.) (n.), report (m.):
to lend (or to employ) money on contango, that is to make a temporary investment for a fortnight or a month, secured by the stock taken in, mettre (ou placer) des capitaux en report, c'est effectuer un placement temporaire de quinze ou de trente jours, garanti par les titres pris en report.
in contangoing the lender is secured by a stock, dans le report le prêteur est nanti d'un titre.

contango (n.) or **contango rate,** report (m.); taux des reports (m.); taux du report (m.); prix des reports (m.); prix du report (m.); cours de report (m.):
it sometimes happens that the contango (or the contango rate) (or the carry over rate) (or the continuation rate) is even, that is to say,

there is nothing to pay except the brokerage
to enable one to lend stock, or even that
owing to an exceptional scarcity of a stock,
the buyer has right to an allowance if he lends
stock : this allowance bears the name of
backwardation (*or* back) (*or* backwardization),
il arrive parfois que le report est au pair,
c'est-à-dire qu'il n'en coûte rien que le
courtage pour se faire reporter, ou même
que par suite de la rareté exceptionnelle
d'un titre, l'acheteur a droit à une bonification s'il se fait reporter : cette bonification
porte le nom de déport.
V. aussi exemple sous **highness.**

contango (*v.t.*), reporter :
to contango (*or* to continue) a position (*or* a
book) from one account (*or* settlement) to
the next, reporter une position d'une
liquidation à la prochaine.

contango (*v.i.*), reporter ; faire un report :
the stockbrokers refuse to contango (*or* to
continue), les agents de change refusent de
reporter (*m.pl.*).
the capitalist or the broker who contangoes
(*or* continues) does not speculate properly
speaking : he lends on deposit of stock, le
capitaliste ou l'agent qui fait un report ne
spécule point à proprement parler : il prête
sur dépôt de titres.

contango day, jour des reports (*m.*) ; jour de
reports (*m.*).

contangoable (*adj.*), reportable :
contangoable stocks, valeurs reportables (*f.pl.*).

contemplate a journey (to), projeter un voyage.

contentious (*adj.*), contentieux, -euse :
contentious matter, affaire contentieuse (*f.*).

contents (*n.pl.*), contenu (*m.*) ; teneur (*f.*) :
the contents of a package, of a bill of lading,
le contenu d'un colis, d'un connaissement.
contents of a letter, contenu, teneur, d'une
lettre.
contents of a bill of exchange, montant d'un
effet de commerce (*m.*).

continent (*n.*), continent (*n.*).

continental (*adj.*), continental, -e, -aux.

contingency [**contingencies** *pl.*] *or* **contingence**
(*n.*), contingence (*f.*) ; aléatoire (*m.*) ;
éventualité (*f.*) :
to reserve a margin for contingencies, réserver
une marge pour les éventualités.

contingency fund, fonds de prévoyance (*m.*).

contingency reserve, réserve de prévoyance (*f.*).

contingent (*adj.*), contingent, -e ; aléatoire ;
éventuel, -elle ; lié, -e :
contingent annuity, annuité contingente (*f.*).
contingent gain *or* contingent profit, gain
aléatoire (*m.*) ; profit aléatoire (*m.*).
contingent liability [contingent liabilities *pl.*],
passif éventuel (*m.*) [passif éventuel *ou* passifs
éventuels *pl.*].
contingent order (i.e., selling shares of one kind
and buying shares of another, the one transaction not to be effected without the other)
(Stock Exch.), ordre lié (*m.*).

contingently (*adv.*), aléatoirement ; éventuellement.

continuable (Stock Exch.) (*adj.*), reportable :
continuable stocks, valeurs reportables (*f.pl.*).

continuation (*n.*) *or* **continuation account** (Stoc.
Exch.), report (*m.*) :
continuations (*or* continuation accounts) o
foreign exchanges, reports sur devises.
foreign exchange on continuation accoun
devises en report (*f.pl.*).

continuation contract, lettre d'avis de report (*f.*)

continuation rate (Stock Exch.), report (*m.*)
taux des reports (*m.*) ; taux du report (*m.*)
prix des reports (*m.*) ; prix du report (*m.*)
cours de report (*m.*). V. exemple sous syr
contango *or* **contango rate.**

continue (*v.t.*), continuer :
ship unable to continue her voyage, navi
hors d'état de continuer son voyage (*m.*).

continue (Stock Exch.) (*v.t.*), reporter. V
exemple sous syn. **contango.**

continue (Stock Exch.) (*v.i.*), reporter ; faire u
report. V. exemples sous syn. **contango.**

continuous discharge (unloading a ship), décharge
ment sans désemparer (*m.*).

contra (*n.*), contre-partie (*f.*) ; parcontre (*m.*) :
single entry consists in entering up items on
after another in one account, without an
contra, la partie simple consiste dan
l'inscription des articles au fur et à mesur
dans un seul compte, sans aucune contre
partie.
the account liability (or *liabilities*) of *customer*
for acceptance (or *acceptances*) has its contr
among the liabilities in the accoun
acceptances on account of (or *for*) *customer*
(bank balance sheet), le compte *ayant*
compte d'*acceptations* a sa contre-partie a
passif dans le compte *acceptations pou*
compte de clients.
these brokerages are charged on each dea
purchase and sale, and without contra (i.e
brokerage charged both ways), ces courtage
sont perçus sur chaque opération, acha
et vente, et sans parcontre.

per contra *or* **as per contra** (Bkkpg), en contre
partie ; porté (-e) ci-contre :
the accounts credited per contra, les compte
crédités en contre-partie (*m.pl.*).
reserves for depreciation of assets per contr
(*or* on assets as per contra), amortissement
sur l'actif porté ci-contre (*m.pl.*).

contra (Bkkpg) (*v.t.*), annuler ; contre-passer
extourner :
to contra an item, an entry, annuler, contre
passer, extourner, un article, une écriture.

to contra each other, s'annuler ; se contre
passer.

contra account (Bkkpg), compte contre-parti
(*m.*).

contra account (Produce Exch.), jumelage (*m.*).

contra entry (Bkkpg), article inverse (*m.*)
écriture inverse (*f.*) ; article (*ou* écriture) d
contre-passement.

contraband (*n.*), contrebande (*f.*) :
contraband of war, contrebande de guerre.

contraband goods, marchandises de contre
bande (*f.pl.*).

ontrabandist (pers.) (*n.*), contrebandier, -ère.
ontract (*n.*), contrat (*m.*); convention (*f.*);
acte (*m.*); marché (*m.*); traité (*m.*):
sale contract *or* contract for sale, contrat de
vente; convention de vente; acte de vente.
director who has entered into contracts with
the company, administrateur qui a passé
des marchés avec la société (*m.*).
contract of affreightment, contrat d'affrètement.
contract of carriage, contrat de transport;
contrat d'expédition:
a contract of carriage is an agreement whereby
a carrier undertakes, in consideration of an
agreed price and by a certain method of
conveyance, to carry from one place to
another a person or a thing, le contrat de
transport est la convention par laquelle
un voiturier se charge, moyennant un prix
convenu et suivant un mode de transport
déterminé, de porter d'un lieu dans un
autre une personne ou une chose.
contract of indemnity, contrat d'indemnité.
contract of marine (*or* of sea) insurance,
contrat d'assurance maritime:
a contract of marine insurance is a contract
whereby the insurer undertakes to indemnify
the assured, in manner and to the extent
thereby agreed, against marine losses, that
is to say, the losses incident to marine adventure, le contrat d'assurance maritime est le
contrat par lequel l'assureur s'engage à
indemniser l'assuré de la manière et dans les
limites qui y sont convenues, contre les
pertes maritimes, c'est-à-dire les pertes qui
se rapportent à une aventure maritime.
contract registered with the clearing house
(Produce Exch.), marché par caisse.
contract not registered with the clearing house
(Produce Exch.), marché hors caisse.
contract at an agreed (*or* fixed) price *or* contract
with a fixed and determined consideration
or simply contract, forfait (*m.*); contrat à
forfait (*m.*):
to prevent, by a contract (*or* by a contract
at an agreed [*or* a fixed] price) (*or* by a
contract with a fixed and determined
consideration), all legal disputes, prévenir,
par un forfait (*ou* par un contrat à forfait),
toutes contestations judiciaires.
on contract *or* **by contract** *or* **contract** (*used as
adj.*), à forfait; forfaitaire; par contrat:
to buy goods on contract, acheter des marchandises à forfait.
to undertake the carriage of goods for a fixed
contract price (*or* for a price determined
by contract), entreprendre le transport des
marchandises pour un prix déterminé à
forfait.
contract freight (freight at reduced rates,
according to an agreement), fret par
contrat (*m.*).
contract limitation of liability, limitation
forfaitaire de responsabilité (*f.*).
contract price, prix à forfait (*m.*); prix
forfaitaire (*m.*); prix du contrat (*m.*).

contract (*n.*) *or* **contract note** (Stock Exch.),
bordereau (*m.*):
broker's contract note *or* stockbroker's contract,
bordereau d'agent de change; bordereau
de bourse.
purchase contract, bordereau d'achat.
sale contract, bordereau de vente.
contract (*v.t.*), contracter; prendre; entreprendre:
the person who accepts a bill of exchange
contracts the obligation to pay the amount
of it, celui qui accepte une lettre de change
contracte l'obligation d'en payer le montant.
insurance contracted only after arrival of the
ship is null, l'assurance contractée seulement
après l'arrivée du navire est nulle (*f.*).
to contract an engagement, prendre, contracter,
un engagement.
to contract debts, a loan, contracter des
dettes, un emprunt.
contract (*v.i.*), contracter:
minors are not capable of contracting, les
mineurs ne sont pas aptes à contracter
(*m.pl.*).
contractable (*adj.*), contractable:
contractable obligation, obligation contractable (*f.*).
contractant (pers.) (*n.*), contractant, -e.
contracting (*adj.*), contractant, -e:
contracting parties, parties contractantes (*f.pl.*).
contractor (pers.) (*n.*), entrepreneur (*m.*):
advertising contractor, entrepreneur de
publicité.
contractual (*adj.*), contractuel, -elle; forfaitaire:
contractual obligations, obligations contractuelles (*f.pl.*).
contractual limitation of liability, limitation
forfaitaire de responsabilité (*f.*).
contractually (*adv.*), contractuellement; forfaitairement; à forfait.
contraing (Bkkpg) (*n.*), annulation (*f.*); contre-
passement (*m.*); contre-passation (*f.*);
extourne (*f.*). V. l'exemple sous le verbe
to contra.
contravention (*n.*), contravention (*f.*); infraction
(*f.*).
contributable (*adj.*), contribuable.
contribute (*v.t.*), contribuer pour:
to contribute a third (*or* one third), contribuer
pour un tiers.
contribute (*v.i.*), contribuer; fournir:
to contribute to the expenses, contribuer aux
dépenses; fournir à la dépense.
to contribute to a loss in proportion to the
amount for which one is liable under one's
contract, contribuer à une perte proportionnellement au montant dont on est responsable
aux termes de son contrat.
everything which benefits by the common
sacrifice is liable to contribute to indemnify
the damage sustained (General Average),
tout qui tire profit du sacrifice commun est
tenu de contribuer à indemniser les dommages
subis.
contributing (*adj.*), contribuant, -e:

contributing parties, parties contribuantes (*f.pl.*).

contributing values *or* **contributing interests and values** *or* **contributory mass** *or* **interests liable to contribute** (opp. to *values* [or *amounts*] [or *mass*] *to be made good*) (General Average), masse débitrice (*f.*) ; valeurs débitrices (*f.pl.*) ; masse passive (*f.*) ; valeurs passives (*f.pl.*) ; masse contribuable (*f.*) ; valeurs contributives (*f.pl.*) :
the valuation of the property benefiting by the sacrifice is called contributing values, l'évaluation des biens profitant du sacrifice s'appelle masse débitrice (*f.*).

contribution (*n.*), contribution (*f.*) ; prestation (*f.*) ; quote-part (*f.*) ; cote (*f.*) ; cotisation (*f.*) ; fournissement (*m.*) :
contribution to the expenses of an enterprise, contribution aux dépenses d'une entreprise.
contribution to (*or* in) general average *or* general average contribution, contribution à l'avarie commune (*ou* en avarie commune) (*ou* d'avarie commune) (*ou* aux avaries communes) :
contribution, that is to say, participation in the extraordinary damage, losses, or expenses arising from a sacrifice for the common safety of the ship and cargo, contribution, c'est-à-dire participation aux dommages, pertes, ou frais extraordinaires provenant d'un sacrifice pour le salut commun du navire et de la cargaison.
a fund formed by means of contributions, un fonds formé au moyen de cotisations.

contributor (pers.) (*n.*), contribuant (*m.*) ; contributeur, -trice :
contributor in arrears, contribuant en retard ; contributeur retardataire.

contributory *or* **contributive** (*adj.*), contributoire ; contributaire ; contributif, -ive :
the contributory share of each, la part contributive de chacun.

contributory [**contributories** *pl.*] (pers.) (*n.*), contributaire (*m.* ou *f.*).

control (*used as adj.*), contradictoire :
control survey, expertise contradictoire (*f.*).

control (*n.*), contrôle (*m.*) :
control of the cash, contrôle de la caisse.

control (*v.t.*), contrôler :
to control the expenditure, contrôler les dépenses (*ou* la dépense).
branch of industry controlled by a trust, branche d'industrie contrôlé par un trust (*f.*).

controllable (*adj.*), contrôlable.

controller (pers.) (*n.*), contrôleur, -euse :
controller general [controllers general *pl.*], contrôleur général.

convene (*v.t.*), convoquer :
to convene a meeting of shareholders, convoquer une assemblée d'actionnaires.

convening (a meeting) (*n.*), convocation (d'une assemblée) (*f.*).

convention (*n.*), convention (*f.*) :
monetary convention, convention monétaire (*f.*).

rules laid down by international conventions, règles imposées par des conventions internationales (*f.pl.*).

conventional (*adj.*), conventionnel, -elle.

conversation (*n.*), conversation (*f.*) :
the charge for a three minutes' conversation (Teleph.), la taxe d'une conversation de trois minutes.

conversion (*n.*) (Abbrev. : **conv.**), conversion (*f.*) ; convertissement (*m.*) :
conversion of the three per cents, of registered securities to bearer, conversion du trois pour cent, des titres nominatifs au porteur.
conversion of the gold franc into the money of another country, conversion du franc-or dans la monnaie d'un autre pays.
conversion of securities into cash, convertissement des valeurs en espèces.

conversion loan, emprunt de conversion (*m.*).

convert (*v.t.*), convertir :
to convert the 5 per cents into 4½ per cents, convertir le 5 p. 100 en 4 1/2.
to convert a bank note into cash, convertir un billet de banque en espèces.
measurement converted into weight, cubage converti en poids (*m.*).

converter (pers.) (*n.*), convertisseur, -euse.

convertibility (*n.*), convertibilité (*f.*).

convertible (*adj.*), convertible ; convertissable ; convertissable :
convertible paper, papier convertible (*m.*).
convertible paper money, monnaie de papier convertible (*f.*).
Cf. inconvertible paper money.
bank notes are said to be convertible when the holders have the right to demand repayment of them at sight at the bank of issue, les billets de banque sont dits convertibles quand les porteurs ont le droit d'en demander le remboursement à vue à la banque d'émission (*m.pl.*).

convey (to carry) (*v.t.*), porter ; transporter ; conduire ; charrier ; voiturer :
to convey goods by rail, transporter des marchandises par chemin de fer.
to convey the goods to the place of their destination, the passenger safe and sound to destination, conduire les marchandises au lieu de leur destination, le voyageur sain et sauf à destination.

convey (Law) (*v.t.*), transmettre.

conveyance *or* **conveying** (transport) (*n.*), transport (*m.*) ; charriage (*m.*).

conveyance (act) (Law) (*n.*), transmission (*f.*) ; translation (*f.*) ; mutation (*f.*) :
conveyance of property, transmission, translation, mutation, de biens (*ou* de propriété).

conveyance (deed) (*n.*), acte de transmission (*m.*) ; acte de cession (*m.*) ; acte de mutation (*m.*) ; acte translatif de propriété (*m.*) ; contrat translatif de propriété (*m.*).

conveyance duty, droits de mutation (*m.pl.*).

convoy *or* **convoying** (*n.*), convoi (*m.*) :
the convoy (*or* convoying) of merchant ships by war vessels, le convoi des navires marchands par des bâtiments de guerre.

navigation under convoy, navigation en convoi (*f.*).

convoy (*v.t.*), convoyer.

cooperate (*v.i.*), coopérer:
to cooperate in an enterprise with someone, coopérer à une entreprise avec quelqu'un.

cooperation (*n.*), coopération (*f.*).

cooperative (*adj.*), coopératif, -ive:
cooperative society, société coopérative (*f.*); société de coopération (*f.*); coopérative (*f.*).

coopt *or* **cooptate** (*v.t.*), coopter:
to coopt a director, coopter un administrateur.

cooptation *or* **cooption** (*n.*), cooptation (*f.*).

copartner (pers.) (*n.*), coassocié, -e.

copier (pers.) (*n.*), copiste (*m.* ou *f.*).

copper (*n.*) *or* **copper coin**, cuivre (*m.*); monnaie de cuivre (*f.*); bronze (*m.*); monnaie de bronze (*f.*); billon (*m.*); monnaie de billon (*f.*).

copper market, marché du cuivre (*m.*).

copper *or* **nickel coin**, billon (*m.*); monnaie de billon (*f.*).

copper shares *or* **coppers** (*n.pl.*), valeurs de cuivre (*f.pl.*); valeurs cuprifères (*f.pl.*); cuprifères (*f.pl.*).

coproprietor (pers.) (*n.*), copropriétaire (*m.* ou *f.*).

copy [**copies** *pl.*] (*n.*), copie (*f.*); transcription (*f.*):
copy of a letter, copie d'une lettre.
copy of exchange, copie de change.
to make a fair copy of a manuscript, faire la transcription au net d'un manuscrit.
copy of memorandum of satisfaction (of a mortgage), certificat de radiation (d'une hypothèque) (*m.*).

copy (of a deed) (*n.*), expédition (*f.*); grosse (*f.*).

copy (specimen) (*n.*), exemplaire (*m.*):
two copies of the articles of association, deux exemplaires des statuts.
bill of lading which is drawn in three, in four, copies, connaissement qui est rédigé en trois, en quatre, exemplaires (*m.*).

copy (*v.t.*), copier; transcrire:
to copy a letter (to make a transcript of a letter), copier, transcrire, une lettre.
to copy a letter (press copy), copier une lettre.

copy holder, porte-copie (*m.*).

copy letter book, livre de copie de lettres (*m.*); livre de copies de lettres (*m.*); livre copies de lettres (*m.*); copie de lettres (*m.*).

copying (*n.*), transcription (*f.*).

copying clerk, commis expéditionnaire (*m.*); expéditionnaire (*m.*).

copying ink, encre communicative (*f.*); encre à copier (*f.*); encre copiant (*f.*).

copying pencil, crayon à copier (*m.*); crayon à encre (*m.*); crayon-encre (*m.*).

copying press, presse à copier (*f.*).

copying ribbon (typewriting) (distinguished from *non copying*, or *record, ribbon*), ruban à copier (*m.*); ruban copiant (*m.*).

copyist (pers.) (*n.*), copiste (*m.* ou *f.*).

copyright (*n.*), droits patrimoniaux d'auteur (*m.pl.*); copyright (*m.*); propriété littéraire (*f.*); propriété (*f.*). *Cf.* infringement of copyright.

corn market *or* **corn exchange**, marché aux (*ou* des) grains (*m.*).

corner (*v.t.*), accaparer:
to corner the major part of the stocks to be found on the market, accaparer la majeure partie des titres se trouvant sur le marché.

cornerer (*n.*) *or* **corner man**, accapareur (*m.*).

cornering *or* **corner** (*n.*), accaparement (*m.*):
cornering the market, products of prime necessity, l'accaparement du marché, de produits de première, nécessité.

corporate (*adj.*), social, -e, -aux:
corporate name, nom social (*m.*).
corporate seal, cachet social (*m.*).
the shareholders, in principle, are the controlling body in a public company; in practice, their corporate action is somewhat limited, les actionnaires, en principe, sont maîtres de la marche dans la société anonyme; en pratique leur action sociale est assez limitée (*m.pl.*).

corporation (*n.*) (Abbrev.: **corpn** *or* **corp.** *or* **cpn**), corporation (*f.*).

corporation stocks, emprunts de villes (*m.pl.*).

correct (*adj.*), exact, -e:
correct calculation, calcul exact (*m.*).

correct (*v.t.*), corriger; rectifier; redresser:
to correct a printer's proof, printers' errors, corriger une épreuve d'imprimerie, les fautes d'impression.
to correct an error, rectifier, redresser, une erreur.

correct (to make an alteration on a writing) (*v.t.*), surcharger:
corrected or scratched consignment notes are not accepted, les lettres de voiture surchargées ou grattées ne sont pas admises (*f.pl.*).

correcting *or* **corrected** (*adj.*), rectificatif, -ive; de redressement:
correcting entry (Bkkpg), écriture rectificative (*f.*); écriture de redressement (*f.*); article rectificatif (*ou* de redressement) (*m.*).
corrected invoice, facture rectificative (*f.*).

correction (*n.*), correction (*f.*); rectification (*f.*); redressement (*m.*):
correction of address, of a wrong date, correction d'adresse, d'une date erronée.
correction of an account, rectification, redressement, d'un compte.
correction of price (Stock Exch.), rectification de cours.

correction (word written over another as emendation; alteration) (*n.*), surcharge (*f.*):
to make a correction, faire une surcharge.
register well kept, without erasures or corrections, registre bien tenu, sans ratures ni surcharges (*m.*).

correctly (*adv.*), exactement.

correctness (*n.*), exactitude (*f.*).

correspond (*v.i.*), correspondre:
to correspond with one's friends, correspondre avec ses amis.

correspondence (exchange of letters) (*n.*), correspondance (*f.*):

to have an active correspondence with someone, avoir avec quelqu'un une correspondance active.

papers having the character of personal correspondence (Post), papiers ayant le caractère
d'une correspondance personnelle (*m.pl.*).

correspondence (letters) (*n.*),   correspondence
(*f.*);   courrier (*m.*);   lettres (*f.pl.*):
to go through one's correspondence, dépouiller sa correspondance.

correspondence (connection) (Travel) (*n.*),   correspondance (*f.*):
if owing to lateness of one train, correspondence
with another train is missed, si par suite
du retard d'un train, la correspondance avec
un autre train est manquée.

Paris-Prague-Warsaw, with correspondence at
Prague for Budapest (Aviation),   Paris-
Prague-Varsovie,   avec   correspondance   à
Prague sur Budapest.

correspondence clerk, correspondancier, -ère.

correspondent (pers.) (*n.*), correspondant (*m.*).

corresponding (*adj.*), correspondant, -e ; pareil,
-eille :
corresponding period, période correspondante
(*f.*); pareille époque (*f.*). V. exemples sous
year et sous **period.**

corridor carriage (Rly.), wagon à couloir (*m.*).

corrugated cardboard, carton ondulé (*m.*).

corsair (pers. or ship) (*n.*), corsaire (*m.*).

cosignatory [**cosignatories** *pl.*] (pers.) (*n.*),   cosignataire (*m.* ou *f.*).

cost (*n.*),   coût (*m.*);   frais (*m.pl.*);   dépense
(*f.*): [Cf. **cost price** *or simply* **cost** & **costs**
(Law).]
cost of the insurance, of living, of our telegram,
coût de l'assurance, de la vie, de notre
dépêche.
cost of printing, of upkeep and repairs, frais
d'impression, d'entretien et réparations.
cost and expenses of the business *or* cost and
expenses of carrying on the business, frais
et charges de l'entreprise (*ou* de l'exploitation).
operating costs,   dépenses d'exploitation ;
frais d'exploitation.

cost (*v.t.*) *or* **to ascertain the cost of** (Accountancy), établir le prix de revient de :
to cost the two qualities according to these
prices, établir le prix de revient des deux
qualités d'après ces prix.

cost (to be of the price of) (*v.i.*), coûter :
to cost a great deal, coûter cher ; coûter fort
cher ; coûter bon.

cost (*v.i.*) *or* **to ascertain the cost** (Accountancy),
établir le prix de revient :
to cost (*or* to ascertain the cost) per ton of
metal produced, per ton of mineral raised,
établir le prix de revient par tonne de fonte
produite, par tonne de charbon extrait.
where a great number of articles are manufactured, it is often very difficult to ascertain
the book cost, là où on fabrique une foule
d'objets, le prix de revient comptable est
souvent très difficile à établir.

cost account, compte de revient (*m.*).

cost accounting, comptabilité de prix de revient
(*f.*).

cost and freight (Abbrev.:   **c. & f.** *or* **C. & F.**
or **c.f.** *or* **C.F.** *or* **c.fr.**), coût-fret.

cost, insurance, freight (Abbrev.: **c.i.f.** *or* **C.I.F.**)
or **cost, freight, and insurance** (Abbrev.:
c.f. & i.),   coût-assurance-fret ; coût, fret,
et assurance :
C.I.F. contract, contrat CAF. (*m.*).
c.i.f. sale, vente caf. (*f.*).
c.i.f. U.K., caf. Royaume-Uni.

cost of living figure, indice du coût de la vie (*m.*).

cost price *or simply* **cost** (*n.*), prix de revient
(*m.*); prix coûtant (*m.*);   prix (*m.*);   prix
d'acquisition (*m.*);   prix d'achat (*m.*);
cours d'achat (*m.*);   valeur d'achat (*f.*);
valeur d'acquisition (*f.*):
cost price (*or* cost) of the stock in trade, prix
de revient, prix coûtant, du stock en magasin.
the cost of an article is composed of the
materials used in its manufacture, of the
wages paid, and of a proportion of overhead charges, le prix de revient d'un objet
se compose des matières consommées par
sa fabrication, des salaires payés, et d'un
tantième de frais généraux.
the shares are valued at cost, les actions sont
estimées (*ou* évaluées) aux prix d'acquisition (*ou* aux prix de revient) (*ou* aux prix
coûtants) (*ou* aux cours d'achat) (*ou* pour
leur valeur d'achat *ou* d'acquisition) (*f.pl.*).
cost of the premises, prix d'acquisition, prix
d'achat, de l'immeuble.
cost of the raw material (Costing), prix coûtant
des matières premières.
the cost of labour and that of raw material
(Costing), le prix de main-d'œuvre et celui
des matières premières.

costing (*n.*) (Accountancy),   établissement de
prix de revient (*m.*).

costly (*adj.*), coûteux, -euse ;   cher, -ère ; dispendieux, -euse.

costs (Law) (*n.pl.*), frais (*m.pl.*); dépens (*m.pl.*):
to be ordered to pay the costs of an action,
être condamné (-e) aux frais (*ou* aux dépens)
d'un procès.

cosurety [**cosureties** *pl.*] (pers.) (*n.*), cocaution (*f.*)

cotenant (pers.) (*n.*), colocataire (*m.* ou *f.*).

cotton market, marché des cotons (*m.*);   marché
du coton (*m.*);   marché cotonnier (*m.*).

council (*n.*), conseil (*m.*):
council of the League of Nations, conseil de
la Société des Nations.

counsel [**counsel** *pl.*] (pers.) (*n.*),   avocat (*m.*);
conseil (*m.*);   avocat-conseil (*m.*):
counsel have the right to give opinions, les
avocats ont le droit de donner des consultations.

counsel's fees, honoraires d'avocat (*m.pl.*).

counsel's opinion *or* **counsel's advice,** consultation d'avocat (*f.*).

count *or* **count up** (*v.t.*),   compter ;   faire le
compte de :
to count one's money *or* to count up one's
money, compter, faire le compte de, son
argent.

to be counted, être compté, -e ; se compter :
outside the frontiers of the country which
has issued it, money is not counted, it is
weighed, en dehors des frontières du pays
qui l'a émise, la monnaie ne se compte
pas, elle se pèse.

count (*v.i.*), compter :
in telegrams, a sign of punctuation counts as
one word, dans les télégrammes un signe de
ponctuation compte pour un mot.

count on *or* **upon** (*v.i.*), compter sur :
to count on (*or* upon) someone, compter sur
quelqu'un.

counter (of a bank, a post office, or the like)
(*n.*), guichet (d'une banque, d'un bureau
de poste, ou analogue) (*m.*) ; caisse (*f.*) :
to exchange notes over (*or* at) the counter of
a bank, échanger des billets au guichet
d'une banque.
paying counter (of a bank), caisse des paiements.

counter (pers.) (*n.*), compteur, -euse :
the cashier is not only a counter of money,
le caissier n'est pas seulement un compteur
d'argent.

counterbalance. V. ci-après.

counter cash book (Banking), main courante
de caisse (*f.*) ; chiffrier de caisse (*m.*) ; brouillard de caisse (*m.*).

counterchange, counterclaim. V. ci-après.

counter declaration, contre-déclaration (*f.*).

counterfeit, counterfoil. V. ci-après.

counter instructions, contre-mandat (*m.*).

countermand, countermark. V. ci-après.

counter operation, contre-opération (*f.*).

counter order, contre-ordre (*m.*).

counterpart. V. ci-après.

counter proposal *or* **counter proposition,** contre-
proposition (*f.*).

countersign. V. ci-après.

counter surety *or* **counter security** (guarantee),
contre-caution (*f.*).

counter surety *or* **counter security** (pers.), contre-caution (*f.*) ; certificateur de caution
(*m.*).

countervailing. V. ci-après.

counterbalance (*v.t.*), contre-balancer.

to counterbalance each other, se contre-
balancer.

counterchange (*v.t.*), contre-changer.

counterclaim (Law) (*n.*), demande reconventionnelle (*f.*) ; reconvention (*f.*).

counterfeit (*n.*), contrefaçon (*f.*).

counterfeit (*v.t.*), contrefaire :
to counterfeit coin, contrefaire des monnaies.

counterfeit coin, fausse monnaie (*f.*).

counterfoil (*n.*), souche (*f.*) ; talon (*m.*) :
the counterfoil of the cheque book, la souche
du carnet de chèques.
counterfoil of receipt, talon de récépissé.
to initial the counterfoil of a cheque, viser le
talon d'un chèque. V. aussi exemple sous
leaf.

counterfoil book, livre à souche (*m.*) ; livre à
souches (*m.*) ; registre à souche (*m.*) ; carnet
à souches (*m.*).

countermand (*n.*), contremandement (*m.*).

countermand (*v.t.*), contremander.

countermark (*n.*), contremarque (*f.*).

counterpart (*n.*), contre-partie (*f.*) ; double (*m.*) :
a sale is the consequence and the counterpart
of a purchase, la vente est la conséquence
et la contre-partie de l'achat.
counterpart of a deed, double d'un acte.

countersign (*v.t.*), contresigner :
to countersign a duplicate as evidence of
acceptance, contresigner un double comme
preuve d'acceptation.

countervailing duty (Economics), droit compensateur (*m.*).

counting (*n.*), comptage (*m.*) ; compte (*m.*) :
the counting and the weighing of the cases,
of the quantities delivered, le comptage
et le pesage des caisses, des quantités
délivrées.
counting of words (Teleg.), compte des mots.

counting house, bureau (*m.*).

country [countries *pl.*] (*n.*), pays (*m.*) :
country of origin, pays d'origine.
gold standard country, pays à étalon d'or ;
pays monométalliste-or.

country bank, banque de province (*f.*) ; banque
provinciale (*f.*).

country branch, succursale de province (*f.*).

country cheque, chèque de place à place (*m.*).

county stocks, emprunts de départements (*m.pl.*).

coup (*n.*), coup (*m.*) :
to bring off a coup on the stock exchange,
faire un coup sur la bourse.

coupon (*n.*), coupon (*m.*) :
coupon of a tour ticket, or the like, coupon
d'un carnet de voyage, ou billet analogue.
interest coupon, coupon d'intérêt.
coupon in arrear, coupon arriéré.

coupon (post office savings bank) (*n.*), timbre-
épargne (*m.*).

coupon book (post office savings bank), bulletin
d'épargne (*m.*).

coupon clerk, couponnier (*m.*).

course (*n.*), cours (*m.*) ; courant (*m.*) :
plan in course of execution, projet en cours
d'exécution (*m.*).
in the course of the year, dans le courant de
l'année.

as a matter of course (necessarily ; automatically), d'office :
the speculators who have refused to renew
or to complete their cover are closed as a
matter of course, les spéculateurs qui ont
refusé de renouveler ou de parfaire leur
couverture sont liquidés d'office (*m.pl.*).

course (Navig.) (*n.*), cours (*m.*) ; route (*f.*) :
ship which resumes her course, navire qui
reprend son cours (*ou* sa route) (*m.*).

court (Law) (*n.*), cour (*f.*) ; tribunal (*m.*) ;
conseil (*m.*) :
court of appeal, cour d'appel.
court of arbitration, cour d'arbitrage.
court of inquiry, conseil d'enquête.
court of justice, cour de justice.
commercial court, tribunal de commerce ;
tribunal consulaire.

courts of justice, palais de justice (*m.*).

covenant (*n.*), stipulation (*f.*); convention (*f.*).

cover (shelter) (*n.*), couvert (*m.*) :
goods placed under cover, marchandises placées sous couvert (*f.pl.*).

cover (envelope) (*n.*), pli (*m.*) :
two letters under the same cover, deux lettres sous le même pli.
to send certificates under registered cover, expédier des titres sous pli recommandé.

cover (Insce) (*n.*), couverture (*f.*). Cf. **cover note** *or* **cover.**

cover (margin) (Fin., Banking, & Stock Exch.) (*n.*), couverture (*f.*); provision (*f.*); marge (*f.*); acompte (*m.*) :
amount remitted to a broker by way of cover on stock exchange transactions, somme remise à un agent à titre de couverture d'opérations de bourse (*f.*).
stockbroker who requires a cover of 25% in cash, agent de change qui exige une couverture (*ou* une provision) (*ou* une marge) (*ou* un acompte) de 25 0/0 en espèces (*m.*).

with cover, avec couverture :
to operate with cover, opérer avec couverture.

without cover, à découvert ; sans couverture :
the bank does not undertake any stock exchange transaction without cover, la banque n'accepte aucune opération de bourse à découvert (*ou* sans couverture).

cover (*v.t.*), couvrir :
to cover goods against sea risks, couvrir des marchandises contre les risques de mer.
policy which covers the risk of total loss of the ship, police qui couvre le risque de perte totale du navire (*f.*).
to cover risks which ordinary policies leave uncovered, couvrir des risques que les polices ordinaires laissent à découvert.
to cover one's banker, one's broker for the amount of a transaction, couvrir son banquier, son agent du montant d'une opération.
to cover one's expenses, couvrir (*ou* faire) ses dépenses.
to cover a short account (*or* a bear account) (Stock Exch.), couvrir un découvert.
the period covered by this policy, la période couverte par la présente police.
an application is said to be covered when the number of shares applied for is at least equal to the number of shares offered, on dit que la souscription est couverte quand le nombre des titres souscrits est au moins égal au nombre des titres offerts.
issue covered several times over, émission couverte plusieurs fois (*f.*).

to be covered (to be guaranteed), être à couvert.

cover (to pass or travel over) (*v.t.*), parcourir :
the distances covered on the sea are expressed in nautical miles, les distances parcourues sur mer s'expriment en milles marins (*f.pl.*).

cover (*v.i.*) *or* **cover oneself** (to), se couvrir :
to cover (*or* to cover oneself) by buying back (Stock Exch.), se couvrir en rachetant.

to cover by buying at long date (Produce or other Exch.), se couvrir en achetant à long terme.
to cover oneself for the amount of a remittance by a draft, se couvrir du montant d'une remise par une traite.
to cover oneself by reinsurance, se couvrir par des réassurances.

cover for the day (cash requirement) (Banking), prévision de caisse (*f.*).

cover note *or* **covering note** *or* *simply* **cover** (*n.*), (Mar. Insce), arrêté (*m.*); arrêté d'assurance (*m.*); arrêté provisoire (*m.*).

cover note *or* **covering note** *or* *simply* **cover** (*n.*) (Fire Insce), note de couverture (*f.*).

cover snatching firm, maison de contre-partie (*f.*). Cf. **to run stock.**

cover system (cutting limit system), cover-system (*m.*).

covered wagon *or* **covered truck** *or* **covered van** (Rly.) (opp. to *open wagon* or *truck*), wagon couvert (*m.*); wagon fermé (*m.*).

covering (*n.*), couverture (*f.*) :
the covering of land risks, of sea risks, la couverture des risques terrestres, des risques de mer.

covering (hedging) (*n.*), couverture (*f.*) :
cottons have advanced on coverings on near positions, les cotons ont avancé sur les couvertures sur les rapprochés (*m.pl.*).

Cr (abbreviation of *creditor*) (Bkkpg), Avoir ; avoir ; Av. ; A. ; Crédit ; crédit ; Cr ; C. :
to divide the page into Dr and Cr, diviser la page en Doit et Avoir.
Cr. by (formula on a credit note). V. sous **Credited.**

craft (*n. sing.* or *pl.*), embarcation (*f.sing.*); embarcations (*f.pl.*); allège (*f.sing.*); allèges (*f.pl.*) :
craft or lighters used in the loading or unloading of ships, embarcations ou allèges employées au chargement ou au déchargement des navires.
lighters are craft used for loading and unloading cargo, les allèges sont des embarcations servant au chargement et au déchargement de la marchandise (*f.pl.*).

craft risk, risque d'allèges (*m.*). *V. exemple sous* risk of craft.

crane (*n.*), grue (*f.*).

crash (*n.*), krach (*m.*); krack (*m.*); débâcle (*f.*); chute (*f.*) :
a bank crash, le krach d'une banque.

crate (opp. to *open case*) (*n.*), caisse à claire-voie (*f.*); 'harasse (*f.*); crête (*f.*).

create (*v.t.*), créer :
to create an industry, a reserve fund, a mortgage, a new series of shares, créer une industrie, un fonds de réserve, une hypothèque, une nouvelle série d'actions.

creation (*n.*), création (*f.*).

credit (*used as adj.*), créditeur, -trice :
credit account, compte créditeur (*m.*).
credit balance, solde créditeur (*m.*); balance créditrice (*f.*).
credit column, colonne créditrice (*f.*).

credit (reputation of solvency) (*n.*), crédit (*m.*):
who says credit, says confidence, qui dit crédit, dit confiance.

credit (time to pay) (*n.*), crédit (*m.*):
trade lives on credit, le commerce vit de crédit.
to obtain a month's credit, obtenir un mois de crédit.

upon credit *or* **on credit** *or* **credit** (*used as adj.*),
à crédit; à terme; à livrer; à compte:
to buy on (*or* upon) credit, acheter à crédit (*ou* à terme).

we know well enough that every kind of merchandise is usually sold upon such or such credit, at such or such discount, on sait assez que chaque espèce de marchandise se vend habituellement à tel ou tel terme, sous tel ou tel escompte.

transaction upon credit, opération à terme (*f.*); opération à livrer (*f.*); marché à terme (*m.*); marché à livrer (*m.*).

to take goods on credit, prendre des marchandises à compte.

credit purchase (opp. to *cash purchase*) (Com.), achat à crédit (*m.*); achat à terme (*m.*).

credit sale (opp. to *cash sale*) (Com.), vente à crédit (*f.*); vente à terme (*f.*).

credit settlement (opp. to *cash settlement*), règlement à terme (*m.*).

credit (Banking) (*n.*), crédit (*m.*); accréditif (*m.*); avoir (*m.*):
credit at the bank *or* credit with the bank, crédit en banque; crédit à la banque; avoir en banque.
to have a credit (*or* to be in credit) at the bank, avoir crédit en banque (*ou* à la banque).
to have a credit with a banker, avoir un crédit chez un banquier.
credits opened by correspondence, at the request of the beneficiaries, and utilized by them, on proof of their identity, accréditifs ouverts par correspondance, sur la demande des bénéficiaires, et utilisés par ceux-ci, sous constation de leur identité.
documentary credit, crédit documentaire; accréditif documentaire.

credit (Bkkpg) (*n.*) (Abbrév.: **Cr**), crédit (*m.*); avoir (*m.*):
debit and credit, débit et crédit; doit et avoir.
to enter an amount to the credit of an account, inscrire une somme à l'avoir d'un compte.
to deduct from the statement the various credits allowed, déduire du relevé les divers avoirs accordés.

credit (*v.t.*), créditer; bonifier:
to credit an account, créditer un compte.
to credit someone with an amount *or* to credit an amount to someone, créditer quelqu'un d'une somme; créditer une somme à quelqu'un.
the interest credited to depositors, l'intérêt bonifié aux déposants (*m.*).

credit institution, institution de crédit (*f.*); établissement de crédit (*m.*); crédit (*m.*):
banks are credit institutions, les banques sont des institutions de crédit (*f.pl.*).

credit insurance, assurance de crédit (*f.*).

credit ledger, grand livre des achats (*m.*).

credit note (Abbrev.: **C/N.**), note de crédit (*f.*); note d'avoir (*f.*); facture d'avoir (*f.*); facture de crédit (*f.*).

credit side (of an account) (Bkkpg), crédit (*m.*), avoir (*m.*) (d'un compte).

credit slip (Banking), bordereau de versement (*m.*); feuille de versement (*f.*).

Credited *or* **Credit** *or* **Cr** (formula on a credit note), Avoir:
Mr A. B. (*buyer*) Credited by (*or* Credit by) (*or* Cr. by) C. D. (*seller*) *or* C. D. (*seller*) Credited to Mr A. B. (*buyer*), C. D. (*vendeur*) Avoir à Monsieur A. B. (*acheteur*).

credited party, crédité, -e.

creditor (pers.) (*n.*), créditeur, -trice; créancier, -ère:
sundry creditors, créditeurs divers.
creditor on bottomry or respondentia, créancier à la grosse. (Cf. **bottomry** and **respondentia**.)
creditor on mortgage *or* mortgage creditor, créancier hypothécaire:
the preferential and mortgage creditors are first paid off; a distribution then takes place among the unsecured creditors in proportion to their debts admitted and proved, les créanciers privilégiés et hypothécaires sont d'abord désintéressés; la répartition a lieu ensuite entre les créanciers chirographaires, au prorata de leurs créances admises et affirmées.

creditor (*n.*) *or* **creditor side** (of an account) (Bkkpg) (Abbrev.: **Cr**), crédit (*m.*); avoir (*m.*):
debtor and creditor, débit et crédit; doit et avoir.

creditor account *or* **account in credit,** compte créditeur (*m.*).

creditors' meeting, assemblée de créanciers (*f.*).

crew (Naut.) (*n.*), équipage (*m.*); hommes d'équipage (*m.pl.*); gens de l'équipage (*m.pl.*):
the master and crew, le capitaine et l'équipage.

crew and cargo (life and property), corps et biens (*m.pl.*):
ship which is lost, crew and cargo, navire qui a péri, corps et biens (*m.*).

crew list, rôle d'équipage (*m.*); rôle de l'équipage (*m.*); rôle d'armement (*m.*).

crisis [**crises** *pl.*] (*n.*), crise (*f.*):
financial crisis, crise financière.

crop (*n.*), récolte (*f.*):
arrival of the new crop, arrivée de la nouvelle récolte (*f.*).

cross (to pass from one side to the other) (*v.t.*), traverser; passer; franchir:
to cross the Atlantic, traverser l'Atlantique.
to cross from England to France, passer d'Angleterre en France.
to cross the frontier, the bar of a river, franchir la frontière, la barre d'un fleuve.

cross (a cheque) (*v.t.*), barrer; croiser:
the person who issues a cheque, or a holder, can cross it, la personne qui émet un chèque, ou un porteur, peut le barrer.

cross (Stock Exch. orders) (*v.t.*), faire l'application de :
a banker receives an order to sell 10 X. shares for Y's account and to buy 8 of them for Z's account : the banker sells 2 shares through his stockbroker and crosses (*or* matches) (*or* marries) the 8 others, un banquier reçoit ordre de vendre 10 actions X. pour le compte d'Y. et d'en acheter 8 pour le compte de Z. : le banquier fait vendre 2 actions par son agent de change et fait l'application des 8 autres.

cross book (Stock Exch.), opération à cheval (*f.*) ; spéculation à cheval (*f.*) ; spéculation mixte (*f.*).

cross firing (bills of exchange), circulation croisée (*f.*) ; tirage croisé (*m.*).

cross out (*v.t.*), rayer ; radier ; biffer ; barrer :
to cross out a clause in an agreement, rayer, radier, biffer, barrer, une clause dans une convention.

cross reference, référence croisée (*f.*).

crossed cheque (opp. to *open cheque*), chèque barré (*m.*) ; chèque croisé (*m.*) :
a crossed cheque can only be presented for payment by a banker, le chèque barré ne peut être présenté au paiement que par un banquier.

crossing (passing) (*n.*), traversée (*f.*) ; passage (*m.*) :
a rough crossing, une traversée mouvementée.
the crossing between England and the continent, la traversée (*ou* le passage) entre l'Angleterre et le continent.

crossing (of a cheque) (*n.*), barrement (*m.*) ; croisement (*m.*) :
the crossing is general if it bears no wording between the two lines, or only the words " & Co. ; " it is special if the name of a banker is written between the two lines. A general crossing can be converted into a special crossing by the drawer or by a holder, le barrement est général s'il ne porte entre les deux barres aucune désignation, ou seulement la mention « & Cⁱᵉ ; » il est spécial si le nom d'un banquier est inscrit entre les deux barres. Le barrement général peut être transformé en barrement spécial par le tireur ou par un porteur. (*Note :—* Same practice in France as in England.)

crossing (Stock Exch. orders) (*n.*), application (*f.*).

crossing out, radiation (*f.*) ; rayure (*f.*) ; biffage (*m.*) ; biffement (*m.*) ; biffure (*f.*).

crowded state (of a port, of the wharves), encombrement (d'un port, des quais) (*m.*).

crowding round the ticket windows, encombrement autour des guichets (*m.*).

Crown Colony, Colonie de la Couronne (*f.*).

cruise (*n.*), croisière (*f.*) :
a cruise in the Mediterranean, une croisière en Méditerranée.
transatlantic boat cruising (*or* on a cruise) round the world, transatlantique en croisière autour du monde (*m.*).

crumble (*v.i.*), s'effriter.

crumbling (of prices) (Stock Exch.) (*n.*), effritement (des cours) (*m.*).

cum coupon *or* **cum dividend** (Abbrev. : **cum div.** *or* **cum d.** *or* **c. div.** *or* **c.d.**) (opp. to *ex coupon* or *ex dividend*), coupon attaché ; exercice — attaché ; jouissance :
cum coupon No. 8 (*or* with coupon No. 8), coupon Nᵒ 8 attaché ; jouissance coupon Nᵒ 8.
stock which is cum (*or* with) coupon No. 8, titre qui est jouissance coupon Nᵒ 8 (*m.*).
cum 19— dividend, exercice 19— attaché.
*Note :—*In France, in speaking of dividend rights, they mention the date of the last payment—*jouissance*. In England, the date of the next payment is stated.
the last coupon of the 3% having been detached on 1st January 19—, one says (*in England*) that the 3% is being dealt in " cum (*or* with) April 19— coupon," i.e., with all coupons to be collected commencing with the one due 1st April (following), le dernier coupon du 3 0/0 ayant été détaché le 1ᵉʳ janvier 19—, on dit (*en France*) que le 3 0/0 se négocie « jouissance janvier 19—, » c.-à-d. avec tous les coupons à toucher après cette date.

cum rights *or* **cum new** (opp. to *ex rights* or *ex new*), avec droit ; droit attaché :
shares cum rights, titres avec droit (*m.pl.*).

cumulative (*adj.*) (Abbrev. : **cum.** *or* **cm.** *or* **c.**), cumulatif, -ive :
cumulative dividend, dividende cumulatif (*m.*).
cumulative preference shares, actions de priorité cumulatives (*f.pl.*).

currency [**currencies** *pl.*] (state of being current ; passing from hand to hand ; circulation) (*n.*), cours (*m.*) ; circulation (*f.*) :
during the currency of the insurance, pendant le cours de l'assurance.
the currency of money, le cours (*ou* la circulation) de l'argent.
forced currency, cours forcé.
legal tender currency, cours légal. V. exemples sous **legal.**

currency (money ; medium of exchange ; total sum or amount of such medium of exchange) (*n.*), monnaie (*f.*) ; numéraire (*m.*) ; circulation (*f.*) :
modern production has need of a stable currency, la production moderne a besoin d'une monnaie stable.
a bill of exchange must be paid in the currency which it names, une lettre de change doit être payée dans la monnaie qu'elle indique.
silver currency, monnaie d'argent ; numéraire d'argent.
legal tender currency, monnaie légale ; monnaie libératoire. V. exemple sous **legal.**
the authorized note currency of a bank, la circulation autorisée des billets d'une banque.

foreign currency *or* simply **currency,** devise étrangère (*f.*) ; devise (*f.*) ; monnaie étrangère (*f.*) :
bill in foreign currency (*or* in currency), effet en devise (*m.*).

to keep an account in currency (*or* in foreign currency) (Bkkpg), tenir un compte en devise (*ou* en devise étrangère) (*ou* en monnaie étrangère).

each currency has two rates : one for short exchange, the other for long exchange, chaque devise a deux cours ; l'un pour le papier court, l'autre pour le papier long.

currency (current value or estimation ; acceptance) (*n.*), cours (*m.*) :
the currency of a signature on the Paris market, le cours d'une signature sur la place de Paris.

currency (of a bill of exchange) (*n.*), échéance (*f.*) ; terme d'échéance (*m.*) :
no bill of less than five days' currency will be discounted, il ne sera admis à l'escompte aucun effet d'une échéance de moins de cinq jours.

the currency of the bill of exchange is 3 months after sight, l'échéance (*ou* le terme d'échéance) de la lettre de change est 3 mois de vue.

currency principle, théorie métallique (*f.*).

current (*adj.*), courant, -e ; en cours :
current account (account current ; running account), compte courant (*m.*) :
advance on current account, avance en compte courant (*f.*).
current account with interest, compte courant et d'intérêts.
current account (drawing account) (Banking), compte de dépôt (*m.*) ; compte de dépôts (*m.*) ; compte de dépôts à vue (*m.*) ; compte de chèques (*m.*) ; compte-chèque (*m.*) ; compte d'espèces (*m.*) ; compte de dépôt d'espèces (*m.*) :
current accounts can only be drawn on by cheques, il n'est disposé sur les comptes de dépôt que par des chèques.
current account *or* current settlement (Stock Exch.), liquidation courante (*f.*) ; liquidation (*f.*) :
price for current account, cours en liquidation courante (*m.*) ; cours en liquidation (*m.*).
current handwriting, écriture courante (*f.*).
current interest, intérêts courants (*m.pl.*) ; intérêts en cours (*m.pl.*).
current liabilities (opp. to *long term liabilities*), exigibilités (*f.pl.*) ; passif exigible à court terme (*m.*) ; passif exigible (*m.*) :
the balance sheet shows that the liquid assets are more than sufficient to meet the current liabilities, le bilan fait ressortir que les disponibilités sont plus que suffisantes pour faire face aux exigibilités.
current money *or* current coins, monnaie courante (*f.*) ; argent courant (*m.*) ; monnaies en cours (*f.pl.*).
current month, mois courant (*m.*) ; mois en cours (*m.*) ; courant (*m.*).
current month (Produce Exch.), courant (*m.*) ; courant du mois (*m.*) ; mois courant (*m.*) :
the current month can be delivered up to the last day of the instant month, le courant (*ou* le mois courant) peut être livré jusqu'au dernier jour du mois en cours.

to buy the current month and not spot, acheter du courant et non du disponible.
current premium on date of policy, prime en cours à la date de la police (*f.*).
current price, prix courant (*m.*) ; prix du marché (*m.*).
current price list, prix courant (*m.*).
current year, année courante (*f.*) ; année en cours (*f.*).
at the rate of exchange current in London at (*or* on) the date of the remittance, au taux de change en cours à Londres à la date de la remise.

to be current, avoir cours ; être de mise :
this coin is current in France, cette pièce a cours en France.
with the exception of gold, foreign moneys are not current, à l'exception de l'or, les monnaies étrangères n'ont pas cours.
guineas are no longer current, les guinées ne sont plus de mise (*f.pl.*).

curtail (*v.t.*), modifier ; réduire ; contingenter :
to curtail one's expenses, modifier, réduire, ses dépenses.
to curtail the output of rubber, ot tin, contingenter la production du caoutchouc, de l'étain.

curtailment *or* **curtailing** (of the output) (*n.*), contingentement (de la production) (*m.*).

custody (*n.*), garde (*f.*) :
to leave a sum of money in the custody of a friend, laisser une somme d'argent à la garde d'un ami.

custom (usage) (*n.*), usage (*m.*) ; coutume (*f.*) :
local customs, usages (*ou* coutumes) de place ; usages locaux ; coutumes locales.
according to the custom of the port of Antwerp, d'après (*ou* selon) (*ou* suivant) les usages de la place (*ou* du port) d'Anvers.

custom (business support ; patronage) (*n.*), clientèle (*f.*) ; achalandage (*m.*).

custom house, custom house broker. V. ci-après.

customary (*adj.*), usité, -e ; d'usage ; d'après (*ou* selon) (*ou* suivant) les usages ; conventionnel, -elle ; ordinaire :
to discharge with the customary dispatch for a steamer, décharger avec la rapidité usitée pour un steamer.
as customary at the port of London, d'après (*ou* suivant) (*ou* selon) les usages de la place (*ou* du port) de Londres.
customary route, route ordinaire (*f.*). V. exemple sous **route.**
customary tare, tare conventionnelle (*f.*) ; tare d'usage (*f.*).

customer (pers.) (*n.*), client, -e ; ayant compte (*m.*) ; déposant, -e :
the customers of a business house, les clients (*ou* la clientèle) d'une maison de commerce.
a banker's customers, les ayants compte (*ou* les déposants) d'un banquier.

customers' ledger, grand livre des clients (*m.*).

customs (the customs authorities or administration) (*n.pl.*) (Abbrev. : **Cstms**), douane (*f.*) ; douanes (*f.pl.*).

customs (*n.pl.*) *or* **custom house** (Abbrev.: **C.H.**), douane (*f.*); bureau de (*ou* de la) douane (*m.*):
to lodge a manifest with (*or* at) the customs (*or* at the custom house), déposer un manifeste en douane.

customs (*n.pl.*) *or* **customs duty** *or* **customs duties,** douane (*f.*); droit de douane (*m.*); droits de douane (*m.pl.*):
goods which do not pay customs (*or* customs duty) (*or* customs duties), marchandises qui ne payent pas de douane (*ou* de droit de douane) (*ou* des droits de douane) (*f.pl.*).

customs agency, agence en douane (*f.*).

customs agent *or* **custom house broker,** agent en douane (*m.*); commissionnaire en douane (*m.*); facteur en douane (*m.*):
the customs agent fulfils, for shippers or consignees, the formalities of clearing the goods through the customs, l'agent en douane remplit, pour les expéditeurs ou les destinataires, les formalités de dédouanement des marchandises.

customs charges, frais de douane (*m.pl.*).

customs code (Abbrev.: **C.C.**), code des douanes (*m.*).

customs declaration *or* **customs entry** *or* **customs report,** déclaration de douane (*f.*); déclaration en douane (*f.*). V. exemples sous **entry.**

customs declaration (Post), déclaration en douane (*f.*).

customs examination of baggage, visite de la douane (*ou* visite douanière) des bagages (*f.*).

customs hours, heures de douane (*f.pl.*).

customs lock, clef de la douane (*f.*).

customs manifest, manifeste de douane (*m.*).

customs officer, agent de douane (*m.*); douanier (*m.*).

customs permit, permis de douane (*m.*).

customs receipts, recettes des douanes (*f.pl.*).

customs regulations, règlements de douane (*m.pl.*); règlements douaniers (*m.pl.*).

customs service, service des douanes (*m.*); service douanier (*m.*).

customs station, poste de douane (*m.*); gare de douane (*f.*).

customs tariff, tarif de douane (*m.*); tarif des douanes (*m.*); tarif douanier (*m.*).

customs union, union douanière (*f.*).

customs value (value for customs purposes), valeur en douane (*f.*).

customs warehouse *or* **customs store,** entrepôt de douane (*m.*).

cut (reduction) (*n.*), réduction (*f.*); dégrèvement (*m.*):
there is a likelihood of a cut in the dividend which would probably be reduced from 5 to 4%, on envisage une réduction du dividende qui serait vraisemblement ramené de 5 à 4 0/0.
cut in wages *or* wages cut, réduction de salaires.
plans for tax cuts, projets de dégrèvements d'impôts (*m.pl.*).

cut down expenses (to), couper, réduire, les dépenses.

cut off (Teleph.) (*n.*), rupture de communication (*f.*).

cut off (to) (to detach), détacher:
coupon which is cut off each time interest is paid, coupon qui est détaché chaque fois que les arrérages sont payés (*m.*).

cut off connection during a conversation (to) (Teleph.), couper, rompre, la connexion au cours d'une conversation.

cut one's loss (to), se couper un bras.

cut out (*v.t.*), découper:
to cut out an advertisement and stick it in a guard book, découper une annonce et la coller dans un album.

cut out (Produce Exch.) (*v.t.*), compenser.

cut-out panel envelope, enveloppe ajourée (*f.*).

cutting (from newspaper) (*n.*), découpure (de journal) (*f.*).

cutting away wreck, coupement de débris (*m.*).

cutting limit order (Stock Exch.), ordre stop (*m.*).

cutting limit system (Stock Exch.), cover-system (*m.*).

cutting off, détachement (*m.*).

cutting out *or* **cut out** (Produce Exch.) (*n.*), compensation (*f.*):
to close a transaction by cutting out (*or* by cut out), liquider une affaire par compensation.

cylinder (of a typewriter) (*n.*), cylindre (d'une machine à écrire) (*m.*).

cypher, cyphering. Syn. de **cipher, ciphering.**

D

dabble on the stock exchange (to), boursicoter.

dabbler on the stock exchange (pers.), boursicoteur, -euse; boursicotier, -ère.

daily (*adj.*), quotidien, -enne.

daily [dailies *pl.*] (*n.*) *or* **daily paper,** quotidien (*m.*); journal quotidien (*m.*).

daily letter telegram (Abbrev.: **DLT.**), télégramme à remise retardée (*m.*).

daily loans *or* **daily money** (Money Market), prêts au jour le jour (*m.pl.*); argent au jour le jour (*m.*).

damage (*n.*), dommage (*m.*); dommages (*m.pl.*); avarie (*f.*); avaries (*f.pl.*); dégât (*m.*); dégâts (*m.pl.*); détérioration (*f.*); préjudice (*m.*):
damage caused by rain, by rats, by sea water,

avaries occasionnées (*ou* dommages [*ou* dégâts] occasionés) par la pluie, par les rats, par eau de mer.

damage and loss by fire,   dégâts et pertes provenant d'incendie.

damage in transit, avaries de route.

damage (i.e., *loss*) resulting from a late delivery, caused by one's negligence,   préjudice résultant d'une livraison tardive, causé par sa négligence.

damage (*v.t.*), endommager ; avarier :
contents of a case slightly damaged by sea water,   contenu d'une caisse légèrement endommagé par l'eau de mer (*ou* avarié d'eau de mer) (*m.*).
suppose that instead of being lost, the goods are simply damaged, supposons qu'au lieu d'être perdues, les marchandises soient simplement avariées.

damage report, certificat d'avarie (*m.*) ; certificat d'avaries (*m.*).

damageable (*adj.*), dommageable :
damageable consequences, conséquences dommageables (*f.pl.*).

damaged (*adj.*), endommagé, -e ; avarié, -e ; sinistré, -e ; mutilé, -e :
damaged ship which should be repaired, navire endommagé qui doit être réparé (*m.*).
damaged certificate, titre mutilé (*m.*).
damaged goods, marchandises avariées (*f.pl.*).
damaged value (opp. to *sound value*) (Insce), valeur à l'état avarié (*f.*).

damages (*n.pl.*),   dommages-intérêts (*m.pl.*) ; dommages et intérêts (*m.pl.*) ; dédommagement (*m.*) :
to be liable for damages,   être tenu (-e) des dommages-intérêts.

damages for detention (Mar. Law), sursurestaries (*f.pl.*) ; contresurestaries (*f.pl.*) ; contrestaries (*f.pl.*).

damper (for postage stamps, labels, etc.) (*n.*), mouilleur (pour timbres-poste, étiquettes, etc.) (*m.*).

danger (*n.*), danger (*m.*) :
imminent danger rendering necessary the immediate discharge of the cargo,   danger imminent rendant nécessaire le déchargement immédiat de la cargaison.
grave danger which threatens the ship and the cargo, grave danger qui menace le navire et la cargaison.

dangerous (*adj.*), dangereux, -euse :
dangerous, inflammable, or explosive goods, marchandises dangereuses, inflammables, ou explosibles (*f.pl.*).

darsena (basin or dock for boats) (*n.*), darse (*f.*).

data [**datum** *sing.*] (*n.pl.*), données (*f.pl.*).

date (*n.*), date (*f.*) :
date of a letter, of sailing of a ship,   date d'une lettre, de départ d'un navire.
3 months after date pay, etc. *or* 3 months from date pay, etc. (bills), à 3 mois de date veuillez payer, etc.
bill payable 3 days after (*or* from date) *or* bill payable at 3 days' date (*Abbrev.* : bill

payable 3 d.d.),   effet payable à 3 jours de date (*m.*).

date of dispatch, date d'envoi.

to date, à ce jour :
interest to date, intérêts à ce jour (*m.pl.*).

up to date, à jour :
to keep a firm's books up to date, tenir à jour les écritures d'une maison.

date (year) (*n.*), millésime (*m.*) :
the date of a coin (i.e., the year it was struck), le millésime d'une pièce de monnaie.
the financial year is, designated by its date : one says the year 19—, or by the dates of two successive years, when there is overlapping on the calendar year :   year 19—-19—, l'exercice est désigné par son millésime : on dit l'exercice 19—, ou par les millésimes des deux années successives, lorsqu'il y a chevauchement sur l'année civile : exercice 19—-19—.
Cf. example under **year** (regarded as mere date).

date (due date) (*n.*), échéance (*f.*) ; époque (*f.*) :
bills payable at fixed dates, effets payables à des échéances fixes (*ou* déterminées) (*m.pl.*).
debentures redeemable at fixed dates, obligations remboursables à échéances fixes (*ou* à époques déterminées) (*f.pl.*).
date interest (*or* coupon) is due (*or* payable) *or* due date of coupon (*or* of interest) *or* elliptically interest due (*or* payable) *or* dividend payable, jouissance (*f.*) ; époque de jouissance :
Rentes 3%.—interest due : 1st January, 1st April, 1st July, 1st October, quoted ex coupon of 75 centimes on 16th December, 16th March, 16th June, and 16th September, Rente 3 0/0.—jouissance : 1er janvier, 1er avril, 1er juillet, 1er octobre, cotée ex-coupon de 75 centimes les 16 décembre, 16 mars, 16 juin, et 16 septembre.
interest on the 3 per cents is paid on the due dates of the coupons which are : 1st January, 1st April, 1st July, and 1st October of each year, les arrérages du 3 0/0 se payent aux époques de jouissance qui sont : les 1er janvier, 1er avril, 1er juillet, et 1er octobre de chaque année (*m.pl.*).
interest due (heading of column 3 of the London Stock Exchange Daily Official List), époques de jouissance (en-tête de colonne 5 du bulletin de la cote de la Compagnie des Agents de change de Paris).

date (*v.t.*), dater :
the bill of lading should be dated, le connaissement doit être daté.

date back (*v.t.*), antidater :
to date a contract back, antidater un contrat.

date stamp *or* **dater** (*n.*), timbre à date (*m.*) ; griffe à date (*f.*) ; timbre dateur (*m.*) ; dateur (*m.*).

day (*n.*), jour (*m.*) ; journée (*f.*) :
so many days' interest at so much per cent, tant de jours d'intérêt à tant pour cent.
day of demurrage [days of demurrage *pl.*], surestarie (*f.*) ; jour de surestarie (*m.*).

day of grace, jour de grâce ; jour de faveur.

day of rest, jour de repos.

days after (or from) date or days' date (Abbrev. : d.d.). V. sous **date.**

days after sight or days' sight (Abbrev. : d.s.). V. sous **sight.**

days saved, jours sauvés (m.pl.) ; dispatch (f.) ; despatch (f.).

8-hour working day, journée de travail de 8 heures.

from day to day, au jour le jour :
the transactions entered from day to day in the journal, les opérations inscrites au jour le jour sur le journal (f.pl.).

day (business day ; working day) (Stock Exch.) (n.), jour (m.) ; bourse (f.) ; jour de bourse (m.) :
two deals done the same day, deux opérations effectuées dans la même bourse.

day before, veille (f.) ; jour précédent (m.) :
speculator who has bought the day before the fall, sold the day before the rise, spéculateur qui a acheté la veille de la baisse, vendu la veille de la hausse (m.).

on the Paris Bourse, dealings in options are resolved at 1.30 p.m., on the day before the settlement, called on that account option declaration day, sur la Bourse de Paris, les opérations à primes se résolvent à 1h. 30, la veille de la liquidation, appelé pour cela jour de la réponse des primes.

two days before, avant-veille (f.).

day book (Bkkpg) (Abbrev. : **d.b.**), journal (m.) ; livre (m.) ; facturier (m.) :
purchases day book, livre d'achats ; livre des achats ; livre d'achat ; journal des achats ; facturier d'entrée.

sales day book or simply day book, livre de ventes ; livre des ventes ; livre de vente ; journal des ventes ; livre de (ou des) débits ; journal des débits ; facturier de sortie.

day charge (Teleph.) (opp. to night charge), taxe de jour (f.).

day of the month or simply **day** (n.), quantième du mois (m.) ; quantième (m.) :
the date should be written in words at length, as to the day of the month and the month itself, la date doit être inscrite en toutes lettres, quant au quantième du mois et au mois lui-même.

day, month, and year, quantième, mois, et millésime.

day to day loans or **day to day money** (Money Market), prêts au jour le jour (m.pl.) ; argent au jour le jour (m.).

day to day option (Stock Exch.), petite prime pour le lendemain (f.) ; prime au (ou pour le) lendemain (f.).

day trunk call (Teleph.), communication (ou conversation) interurbaine de jour (f.).

daytime (n.), heures de jour (f.pl.) :
during the daytime, pendant les heures de jour.

de facto (Law) (opp. to de jure), de fait ; de facto :
de facto monopoly, monopole de fait (m.).

de jure (Law), de droit ; de jure :

by virtue of the de jure principle, en vertu du principe de jure.

contract voided de jure, contrat résolu de jure (m.).

dead freight, fret sur le vide (m.) ; fret mort (m.).

dead letter, lettre morte (f.) :
law which is a dead letter, loi qui est lettre morte (f.).

dead letter or **dead postal packet** (Post), rebut (m.) :
postal packets which cannot be delivered, nor redirected, nor returned to the senders, are called dead postal packets, les objets de correspondance qui ne peuvent être ni distribués, ni réexpédiés, ni renvoyés aux expéditeurs, sont dénommés rebuts (m.pl.).

dead letter office, bureau des rebuts (m.) ; bureau du rebut (m.) ; rebut (m.) :
postal packets returned to the sender or sent to the dead letter office, objets de correspondance rendus aux expéditeurs ou versés au rebut (m.pl.).

dead loss, perte sèche (f.).

dead money, argent mort (m.) ; argent qui dort (m.).

dead season, morte-saison (f.).

dead-weight capacity (Abbrev. : **d.w.c.**) or **dead-weight tonnage** or simply **dead weight,** port en lourd (m.) ; portée en lourd (f.) ; tonnage dead weight (m.) : (Cf. to carry dead weight.)

dead-weight capacity is the weight expressed in tons (in England, tons of 20 cwt or 2,240 lbs ; in France, metric tons = 0·9842 ton or 2,204·6 lbs) that a certain ship can lift, le port (ou la portée) en lourd est le poids exprimé en tonnes (en Angleterre, tonnes de 1 016 kilos ; en France, tonnes métriques de 1 000 kilos) qu'un navire déterminé peut porter.

dead-weight cargo or simply **dead weight** (opp. to measurement goods), marchandises lourdes (f.pl.).

dead-weight cargo capacity, port en marchandises (m.).

dead-weight charter, affrètement en lourd (m.).

deal (n.), affaire (f.) ; négociation (f.) ; opération (f.) ; opéré (m.) ; transaction (f.) ; marché (m.) :
to make a hundred pounds profit out of a deal, avoir cent livres de boni dans une affaire.

cash deal, négociation au comptant ; opération au comptant ; marché au comptant.

advice of deal, avis d'opéré (ou d'opération) (m.).

deal (v.i.), traiter ; négocier ; travailler ; opérer ; commercer ; faire le commerce :
he refuses to deal with him, il refuse de traiter (ou de négocier) (ou d'opérer) avec lui.

in France, it is strictly forbidden for agents de change to deal for their personal account and to interest themselves in any commercial transaction, directly or indirectly, en France, il est rigoureusement interdit aux agents de change d'opérer pour leur compte personnel et de s'intéresser dans aucune affaire commerciale, directement ou indirectement.

it is now possible to deal on our market without
risk of paying too much when one buys or
of banging the market when one sells, il
est maintenant possible de travailler sur
notre place sans risque de surpayer quand
on achète ou de casser les cours quand on
vend.
to deal in everything, commercer de tout.
speculators who deal in options, les spéculateurs
qui font le commerce des primes (*m.pl.*).
to be dealt in, se traiter ; se négocier :
wheat is being dealt in at so much, le blé se
traite à tant.
all sorts of securities are dealt in on the Paris
Bourse, il se négocie (*ou* se traite) à la
Bourse de Paris des titres de toutes sortes.
X. preference were actively dealt in, on
travaille activement la privilégiée X.
dealable (*adj.*), négociable ; commerçable :
stocks dealable on the stock exchange, titres
négociables en bourse (*m.pl.*).
dealer (pers.) (*n.*), marchand, -e ; fournisseur
(*m.*) :
retail dealer, marchand au détail.
dealer (London Stock Exchange) (pers.) (*n.*),
banquier de placement et de spéculation
(*m.*). (*Note :*—Descriptive translation only—
these English and French terms do not
correspond, as *dealers* do not exist in France
as an integral part of the Bourse system.
In London, *broker* deals with *dealer* ; in
Paris, *broker* deals with *broker*, and the other
broker dealt with is called the *contre-partie*.
*See explanation of Paris Bourse system
under* marché des valeurs.)
dealing (*n.*), négociation (*f.*) ; opération (*f.*) ;
transaction (*f.*) ; affaire (*f.*) ; marché (*m.*) :
dealing for a rise (Stock Exch.), opération à
la hausse.
dealing for a fall (Stock Exch.), opération à
la baisse.
dealing for the coming out (Stock Exch.),
opération à émission.
dealings for cash (*or* for money), négociations
au comptant, opérations au comptant ;
affaires au comptant ; marchés au comptant.
dealings for the settlement (*or* for the account)
(Stock Exch.), négociations à terme ;
opérations à terme ; affaires à terme ;
marchés à terme ; marchés à livrer.
no dealings in the shares, pas de (*ou* aucune)
transaction sur l'action.
dear (expensive) (*adj.*), cher, -ère ; coûteux, -euse :
money is dear, l'argent est cher (*m.*).
dear year, chère année (*f.*).
to be dear, être cher, -ère ; coûter cher :
the goods are very dear, les marchandises sont
très chères (*ou* coûtent très cher) (*f.pl.*).
dearly (*adv.*), chèrement ; cher.
dearness (*n.*), cherté (*f.*) :
the dearness of money, of credit, of rents, of
living, la cherté des capitaux, du crédit,
des loyers, de la vie.
dearth (*n.*), rareté (*f.*) ; raréfaction (*f.*) ; pénurie
(*f.*) ; disette (*f.*) :
dearth of coin, of stock, of freight, rareté,

raréfaction, pénurie, disette, du numéraire,
du titre, de fret.
death (*n.*), mort (*f.*) ; décès (*m.*).
debase the coinage (**to**), altérer, adultérer,
amenuiser, la monnaie.
debasement (of the coinage) (*n.*), altération (*f.*),
adultération (*f.*), amenuisement (*m.*), changement (*m.*) (des monnaies).
debenture (*n.*) (Abbrev.: **deb.**), obligation (*f.*) :
who says debenture, says durable pledge and
regular payment of interest, qui dit
obligation, dit gage durable et service
régulier.
debenture capital, capital-obligations (*m.*).
debenture certificate *or* **debenture bond,** titre
d'obligation(s) (*m.*) ; certificat d'obligation(s)
(*m.*).
debenture debt, dette obligataire (*f.*).
debenture holder, obligataire (*m.* ou *f.*) ; obligationnaire (*m.* ou *f.*) ; détenteur d'obligation
(*m.*) ; titulaire d'obligations (*m.*) ; porteur
d'obligations (*m.*).
debenture holders' association, association
d'obligataires (*f.*).
debenture loan, emprunt obligataire (*m.*) ;
emprunt-obligations (*m.*).
debit (*used as adj.*), débiteur, -trice ; déficitaire :
debit account, compte débiteur (*m.*).
debit balance (Bkkpg), solde débiteur (*m.*) ;
balance débitrice (*f.*).
debit balance (balance being loss), solde
débiteur (*m.*) ; solde déficitaire (*m.*) :
to wipe off a debit balance, apurer un solde
déficitaire.
debit column, colonne débitrice (*f.*).
debit (Bkkpg) (*n.*) (Abbrev.: **Dr**), débit (*m.*) ;
doit (*m.*) :
debit of an account, débit, doit, d'un compte.
debit and credit, débit et crédit ; doit et avoir.
debit (*v.t.*), débiter :
to debit an account, someone with an amount,
débiter un compte, quelqu'un d'une somme.
debit ledger, grand livre des ventes (*m.*).
debit note (Abbrev.: **D/N.**), note de débit (*f.*) ;
facture de débit (*f.*).
debit side (of an account) (Bkkpg), débit (*m.*),
doit (*m.*) (d'un compte).
debt (*n.*) *or* **debt due by the trader,** dette (*f.*) ;
dette passive (*f.*) :
to run into debt, faire des dettes.
debts due by the trader must be distinguished
according to their repayability and debts
due to the trader according to their liquidness
and the way in which they are secured, il
faut distinguer les dettes d'après leur
exigibilité et les créances d'après leur disponibilité et la manière dont elles sont
garanties.
debt (*n.*) *or* **debt due to the trader,** créance (*f.*) ;
dette active (*f.*) ; dette (*f.*) :
recoverable debt, créance recouvrable ; dette
récupérable.
debt and rights, créance (*f.*).
debt collecting agency *or* **debt recovery agency,**
agence de recouvrements (*f.*).
debt collector, agent de recouvrements (*m.*).

debt of honour, dette d'honneur (f.).
debtor (pers.) (n.), débiteur, -trice; redevable (m. ou f.):
  debtor on mortgage, débiteur hypothécaire.
  debtor for the balance (of an account), reliquataire (m. ou f.).
debtor (one whose affairs are being liquidated) (n.), liquidé, -e.
debtor (n.) or **debtor side** (Bkkpg) (Abbrev.: Dr), débit (m.); doit (m.):
  debtor and creditor, débit et crédit, doit et avoir.
  Dr To, Dr to. V. sous **Dr.**
debtor account, compte débiteur (m.).
debtor company, société débitrice (f.).
decease (n.), décès (m.); mort (f.).
decease (v.i.), décéder:
  deceased person, personne décédée (f.).
deceive (v.t.), tromper:
  to deceive the public, the buyer on the origin of products of foreign make, tromper le public, l'acheteur sur l'origine de produits de fabrication étrangère.
decide (v.t.), décider; statuer sur:
  to decide disputes which may arise, décider les, statuer sur les, différends qui peuvent s'élever.
decided (marked) (adj.), marqué, -e:
  a decided recovery, une reprise marquée.
decimal (adj.), décimal, -e, -aux:
  decimal fraction, fraction décimale (f.).
  decimal number, nombre décimal (m.).
  decimal system, système décimal (m.).
decimal (n.), décimale (f.).
decipher (v.t.), déchiffrer.
decipherable (adj.), déchiffrable.
deciphering (n.), déchiffrement (m.).
decision (n.), décision (f.); délibération (f.).
deck (of a ship) (n.), pont (m.); tillac (m.).
deck cabin, cabine de pont (f.).
deck cargo or **deck load,** pontée (f.); chargement du pont (m.); chargé sur le pont (m.); màrchandises du pont (f.pl.):
  deck cargo at shippers' risk, pontée au risque des expéditeurs.
deck cargo premium, prime de pontée (f.).
deck cargo risk, risque de pontée (m.).
deck chair, chaise de pont (f.).
deck shipment, chargement sur le pont (m.); chargement sur le tillac (m.); chargement en pontée (m.); chargé sur le pont (m.).
declarant (pers.) (n.), déclarant, -e:
  entry which the declarant must lodge with the customs to allow the service to examine the goods imported, déclaration que le déclarant doit déposer à la douane pour permettre au service de vérifier la marchandise importée.
declaration (n.), déclaration (f.); constatation (f.):
  declaration of mortgage, déclaration d'hypothèque.
  declaration of war, déclaration de guerre.
declaration (Customs) (n.), déclaration (f.):
  a preliminary declaration is required in every customs operation, toute opération de douane comporte une déclaration préalable.

declaration of the contents of an article of luggage, déclaration du contenu d'un article de bagage.
  declaration inwards, déclaration d'entrée.
  declaration outwards, déclaration de sortie.
  declaration for bond, déclaration de soumission.
declaration (Insce) (n.), déclaration (f.); application (f.):
  declaration of value of goods for insurance, déclaration de valeur des marchandises à assurer.
  the authorities are liable for an amount not exceeding the declaration of values inserted in the insurances (Post), l'administration est responsable jusqu'à concurrence du montant de la déclaration des valeurs insérées dans les chargements (f.).
  any declaration of value over and above the actual value of the contents of a parcel is considered as fraudulent (Post), toute déclaration de valeur supérieure à la valeur réelle du contenu d'un colis est considérée comme frauduleuse.
  declaration . on the policy or declaration of interest (or of risk) (or of value), application à la police; déclaration d'aliment:
  declarations on a floating policy, applications à une police d'abonnement.
  a floating policy insures the goods as and when they are shipped and not only from the time of declaration of interest, la police flottante assure les marchandises dès leur embarquement et non pas seulement à partir de la déclaration d'aliment.
declaration of options (Stock Exch.), réponse des primes (f.).
declaration policy (Insce), police d'abonnement (f.); police flottante (f.); police ouverte (f.).
declare (v.t.), déclarer; constater:
  to declare a dividend, the value for insurance, a meeting closed, déclarer un dividende, la valeur pour l'assurance, une séance levée.
  to declare a resolution carried, constater l'adoption d'une résolution.
  I, the undersigned Paul X., declare that . . ., je soussigné Paul X. déclare que . . .
  the value declared in the policy, la valeur déclarée dans la police.
  increase of risk which the insured is bound to declare, aggravation de risque que l'assuré est tenu de déclarer (f.).
  to declare the amount at risk on each ship, déclarer la somme en risque sur chaque navire.
  to declare the value at the custom house, déclarer la valeur au bureau de la douane.
  passengers' luggage declared at the customs, bagages de voyageurs déclarés en douane (m.pl.).
declare (Stock Exch.) (v.t.), répondre à:
  to declare an option, répondre à une prime.
  these options are declared at 2.45, ces primes sont répondues à 2h. 45 (f.pl.).
declare as attaching interest (to) (Insce), déclarer en aliment; alimenter:

the insured binds himself to declare (or to report) as attaching interest, during the term of the policy, in so far as they are applicable to it, all shipments made on his account, l'assuré s'engage à déclarer en aliment, pendant la durée de la police, en tant qu'elles y sont applicables, toutes les expéditions faites pour son compte (m.).

the insured undertakes to declare as interest attaching to the present floating policy all the exports and/or imports for which it has been concluded, l'assuré s'engage à alimenter la présente police d'abonnement par toutes les exportations et/ou importations pour lesquelles elle a été conclue (m.).

declared value, valeur déclarée (f.).

decline (fall in prices) (n.), baisse (f.):
decline in foreign stocks, baisse des fonds étrangers.

decline (v.t.), décliner:
to decline an offer, responsibility for an accident, décliner une offre, la responsabilité d'un accident.

decline (v.i.), baisser.

decode (v.t.), déchiffrer:
to decode a telegram, déchiffrer une dépêche télégraphique.

decoding (n.), déchiffrement (m.).

decrease (n.), diminution (f.); amoindrissement (m.):
decrease in the receipts, of price, diminution, amoindrissement, des recettes, de prix.
decrease in value or decrease of value or simply decrease, diminution de valeur; moins-value (f.):
decrease in value of shares, moins-value des actions.

decrease (v.t.), diminuer; amoindrir.

decrease (v.i.), diminuer; se diminuer; amoindrir; s'amoindrir.

decree (Law) (n.), arrêt (m.); jugement (m.):
decree in bankruptcy, jugement déclaratif de faillite.

deduct (v.t.), déduire; faire déduction de; retrancher; défalquer; rabattre:
to deduct one's expenses, income tax, déduire ses frais, l'impôt sur le revenu.
to deduct the amounts paid in advance, déduire les, faire déduction des, retrancher les, sommes payées d'avance.
to deduct the weight of the packing, the pence on invoices exceeding five pounds, déduire, défalquer, rabattre, le poids de l'emballage, les pence sur les factures dépassant cinq livres.

to be deducted, être déduit, -e, retranché, -e, etc.; se déduire; se retrancher; se défalquer:
brokerage is added to purchases or deducted from sales, le courtage s'ajoute aux achats ou se retranche des ventes.

deduct or **to be deducted,** à déduire:
deduct: expenses for the month, à déduire: dépenses du mois.
expenses of the month, to be deducted, dépenses du mois, à déduire.

deductible (adj.), déductible:
deductible loss, perte déductible (f.).

deduction (n.), déduction (f.); défalcation (f.); réduction (f.):
deduction for expenses (Income Tax), déduction pour dépenses.
deduction new for old (Mar. Insce), déduction, réduction, pour différence du vieux au neuf.

after deducting, déduction faite de; après déduction de:
after deducting tax, the expenses, déduction faite (ou après déduction) de l'impôt, des frais.

deed (Law) (n.), acte (m.); contrat (m.); titre (m.):
deed under private seal, acte sous seing privé.
partnership deed or deed of partnership, contrat de société; contrat d'association.
deed of transfer (conveyance) (Law), acte de cession; acte de transmission; acte de mutation; acte (ou contrat) translatif de propriété.

deed of transfer (stocks and shares), feuille de transfert (f.). V. note sous **transfer** (n.) or **transfer deed.**

deemed (p.p.), censé, -e; réputé, -e:
each craft, raft, or lighter, to be deemed the subject of a separate insurance, chaque embarcation, radeau, ou allège, sera censé l'objet d'une assurance distincte.
well established practice which is deemed to form part of the policy, usage bien établi qui est réputé faire partie de la police (m.).
ship which is deemed to be lost, navire qui est réputé perdu (m.).

deep-sea captain, capitaine au long cours (m.).

deep-sea navigation, navigation au long cours (f.); long cours (m.).

deep-sea steamer, vapeur de haute mer (f.).

deep-sea voyage, voyage au (ou de) long cours (m.); long cours (m.):
ship sailing on a deep-sea voyage, navire partant pour le long cours (m.).

deep water, eau profonde (f.).

deep-water ship canal, canal maritime en eau profonde (m.).

default (n.), défaut (m.); défaillance (f.); prévarication (f.); négligence (f.):
default in paying a note, défaut de paiement d'un billet.
wrongful acts or defaults of the master or crew, fautes ou prévarications (ou négligences) du capitaine ou de l'équipage (f.pl.).
to be responsible for the delivery of the stock to the buyer in case of default of the seller, être responsable de la livraison des titres à l'acheteur en cas de défaillance du vendeur.

in default of, à défaut de; faute de:
in default of agreement between all the parties concerned, à défaut d' (ou faute d') accord (ou d'entente) entre tous les intéressés.

default (v.i.), manquer:
merchant who is compelled to default, commerçant qui est obligé de manquer (m.).

default price (Produce Exch.), cours de résiliation (*m.*).
defaulter (pers.) (*n.*), défaillant, -e.
defaulting (*adj.*), défaillant, -e :
defaulting party, partie défaillante (*f.*).
defeat one's creditors (to), frustrer ses créanciers.
defect (*n.*), défaut (*m.*) ; vice (*m.*) :
latent defect, défaut caché ; vice caché.
defendant (Law) (pers.) (*n.*), défendeur, -eresse :
according as the company is plaintiff or defendant, suivant que la société est demanderesse ou défenderesse.
defer (*v.t.*), différer ; remettre ; arriérer ; retarder :
to defer the payment of interest, différer le paiement des, arriérer le paiement des, retarder le paiement des, attermoyer les, intérêts.
deferred (*adj.*) (Abbrev. : **def.** *or* **defd**), différé, -e :
deferred annuity, annuité différée (*f.*).
deferred interest, intérêt différé (*m.*).
deferred interest certificate, script (*m.*) ; vale (*m.*) ; bon (*m.*).
deferred shares *or* deferred stock *or* deferred stocks, actions différées (*f.pl.*).
deferred telegram (*Abbrev.* : LCO., LCF., *or* LCD.), télégramme différé (*m.*). *Note* :— For meaning of LCO., etc., see Abbreviations in common use.
deficit *or* **deficiency** [**deficiencies** *pl.*] (*n.*), déficit (*m.*) ; moins-value (*f.*) ; mali (*m.*) ; manquant (*m.*) ; manque (*m.*) ; découvert (*m.*) :
to make up a deficit (*or* a deficiency), suppléer (*ou* combler) (*ou* bonifier) un déficit (*ou* un découvert).
deficit in taxes (Ant. : *surplus*), moins-value des contributions.
the deficiency of a business is expressed by the debit balance of the profit and loss account (Ant. : *surplus*), le déficit d'une entreprise est exprimé par le solde débiteur du compte de pertes et profits.
definitive *or* **definite** (*adj.*), définitif, -ive :
definitive (*or* definite) certificate (opp. to *scrip* or *scrip certificate* or *provisional*, or *interim*, *certificate*), titre définitif (*m.*).
deflation (*n.*), déflation (*f.*) ; dégonflement (*m.*) :
monetary deflation, déflation monétaire.
deflation of credit, déflation de crédit.
defraud (*v.t.*), frauder ; frustrer :
to defraud the customs, frauder la douane.
to defraud one's creditors, a partner of his share of profit, frustrer ses créanciers, un associé de sa part de bénéfice.
defrauder (pers.) (*n.*), fraudeur, -euse.
defray (*v.t.*), défrayer.
degressive tax, impôt dégressif (*m.*).
del credere, ducroire (*m.*) :
stockbrokers are del credere, that is so say, responsible for delivery of the stock to the buyer in case of default of the seller, and for payment to the seller in case of default of the buyer, les agents de change sont ducroire, c'est-à-dire responsables de la livraison des titres à l'acheteur en cas de défaillance du vendeur, et du paiement

au vendeur en cas de défaillance de l'acheteur (*m.pl.*).
del credere agent, commissionnaire ducroire (*m.*) ; ducroire (*m.*).
del credere agreement, convention ducroire (*f.*).
del credere commission, commission ducroire (*f.*) ; ducroire (*m.*).
del credere export agent, commissionnaire-exportateur ducroire (*m.*).
delay (*n.*), retard (*m.*) ; délai (*m.*) ; remise (*f.*) :
delay in the arrival of trains, in delivery, in the execution of an order, in forwarding (*or* in the dispatch of) the goods, retard dans l'arrivée des trains, à la livraison, dans l'exécution d'un ordre, dans l'acheminement de la marchandise.
delivery without delay, livraison sans retard (*ou* sans délai) (*f.*).
delay (*v.t.*), retarder ; différer :
to delay a payment, retarder, différer, un paiement.
delegant *or* **delegator** (pers.) (*n.*), délégant, -e ; délégateur, -trice.
delegate (pers.) (*n.*), délégué, -e :
the official delegate of the committee, le délégué officiel du comité.
delegate (*v.t.*), déléguer :
to delegate one's authority, funds for the payment of a creditor, déléguer son autorité, un fonds pour le paiement d'un créancier.
V. aussi exemple sous **managing director**.
delegated debtor (Law), débiteur délégué (*m.*) ; délégué, -e.
delegatee (pers.) (*n.*), délégataire (*m.* ou *f.*).
delegation (Law) (*n.*), délégation (*f.*) :
delegation of power, of a debt, délégation de pouvoir, d'une dette.
delegation (letter of delegation) (Com.) (*n.*), délégation (*f.*).
delegation (share certificate) (*n.*), délégation (*f.*).
delete (*v.t.*), biffer ; rayer :
delete words not applicable *or* delete as required, biffez la mention inutile ; rayer les mentions qui ne conviennent pas.
deletion (*n.*), biffage (*m.*) ; biffement (*m.*) ; biffure (*f.*) ; rayure (*f.*).
deliver (*v.t.*), livrer ; délivrer ; remettre ; rendre ; distribuer :
to deliver goods, livrer, délivrer, des marchandises (*ou* de la marchandise).
the master is not obliged to deliver the goods all together ; he has the right to make delivery of them in series, le capitaine n'est pas obligé de livrer les marchandises toutes à la fois ; il a la faculté d'en faire la livraison par séries.
deliver to the order of Mr X., délivrez, livrez, à l'ordre de M. X.
goods delivered free on board, marchandise rendue franco bord (*f.*).
goods delivered buyer, marchandises rendues chez l'acheteur (*f.pl.*).
ship ready to deliver her cargo, navire prêt à délivrer sa cargaison (*m.*).
to deliver stock, livrer, délivrer, remettre, des titres :

to deliver the stock which one has sold, livrer les titres que l'on a vendus.

the ticket delivered to the passenger, le billet délivré au passager.

deliver a speech (to), prononcer un discours.

deliverable (*adj.*), livrable; délivrable; distribuable:

goods in course of production deliverable at a later date, marchandises en cours de production livrables à une époque ultérieure (*f.pl.*).

postal packet deliverable by express, objet de correspondance distribuable par exprès (*m.*).

deliverer (pers.) (*n.*), livreur (*m.*).

deliverer (Produce Exch.) (pers.) (*n.*), livreur (*m.*); créateur (*m.*); créateur de la filière (*m.*); émetteur (*m.*); émetteur de la filière (*m.*); premier vendeur (*m.*).

delivering. V. **delivery** *or* **delivering**.

delivering area *or* **delivery area**, zone (*ou* circonscription) de remise (*ou* de distribution) à domicile (*f.*):

free delivery area of telegrams, zone, circonscription, de distribution (*ou* de remise) gratuite des télégrammes.

delivering office *or* **delivery office** (opp. to *dispatching office*) (Post), bureau distributeur (*m.*); bureau de distribution (*m.*).

delivering station (Rly.), gare réceptrice (*f.*); gare de réception (*f.*).

delivery [**deliveries** *pl.*] (*n.*) (Abbrev.: **dely**), livraison (*f.*); délivrance (*f.*); remise (*f.*); distribution (*f.*):

delivery of a parcel, of shares, livraison, délivrance, remise, d'un colis, d'actions.

delivery of the goods to the consignee, into the hands of the consignees, délivrance des marchandises au destinataire, entre les mains des consignataires.

shares which are (*or* stock which is) good delivery (Stock Exch.), titres qui sont de bonne livraison (*m.pl.*).

delivery at residence *or* delivery at trader's premises *or* *simply* delivery *or* delivering, livraison à domicile (*f.*); remise à domicile (*f.*); livraison (*f.*); remise (*f.*):

as a general rule, delivery is suspended on Sundays, la livraison (*ou* la remise) à domicile est, en règle générale, suspendue les dimanches.

stations closed on Sundays both for the receiving (*or* reception) (*or* receipt) and delivering (*or* delivery) of goods, gares fermées les dimanches tant à la réception qu'à la livraison des marchandises (*f.pl.*).

delivery outside prescribed boundaries (Rly.), service de réexpédition (*m.*).

postal delivery, distribution postale.

delivery of letters (Post), distribution des correspondances.

delivery of telegrams, remise, distribution, des télégrammes.

delivery to callers (*or* at post office), to place of residence, by express (Post), distribution au guichet, à domicile, par exprès.

on or before delivery, comptant-compté; comptant à livrer; comptant contre remboursement; comptant sur balle:

to pay on or before delivery, payer comptant-compté.

delivery (Law) (*n.*), tradition (*f.*); délivrance (*f.*):

the transfer of bearer shares is effected by mere (*or* by simple) delivery of the scrip, la cession des actions au porteur s'opère par simple tradition du titre.

the bank note is transmitted from hand to hand, one says by delivery, le billet de banque se transmet de la main à la main, on dit par tradition.

delivery of a cheque transfers to the payee the property in the consideration, la délivrance du chèque transfère au bénéficiaire la propriété de la provision.

delivery area, delivery office. V. sous **delivering**.

delivery book (parcels), carnet de livraison (*m.*); registre de livraison (*m.*).

delivery order (Abbrev.: **D/O.**), bon de livraison (*m.*); bon d'enlèvement (*m.*); bon à enlever (*m.*); bon à délivrer (*m.*); delivery-order (*m.*); bon de livraison à valoir sur connaissement (*m.*).

Note:—If a bill of lading is split up into several delivery orders, these being regarded as separate bills of lading, it is preferable to use the term *delivery-order* in French, or *bon de livraison à valoir sur connaissement.*

delivery sheet (carman's), bordereau de factage (*m.*).

delivery van, voiture de livraison (*f.*); fourgon de livraison (*m.*); livreuse (*f.*).

demand (*n.*), demande (*f.*); exigence (*f.*):

X. shares are in demand at 1¾, l'action X. est l'objet de demandes (*ou* est demandée) à 1 3/4.

on demand, sur demande; à vue; à bureau ouvert; à guichet ouvert; à présentation:

loan repayable on demand, emprunt remboursable sur demande (*m.*).

bank note repayable on demand, billet de banque remboursable à vue (*ou* à bureau ouvert) (*ou* à guichet ouvert) (*ou* à présentation) (*m.*).

demand (Economics) (*n.*), demande (*f.*):

the demand for foreign bills, la demande d'effets sur l'étranger.

supply and demand *or* demand and supply, l'offre et la demande:

the law of supply and demand, la loi de l'offre et de la demande. N. exemples sous **law.**

demand (*v.t.*), demander; exiger:

to demand the taxes, what is due, demander, exiger, l'impôt, ce qui est dû.

demand rate (Foreign exchange market), cours à vue (*m.*); taux à vue (*m.*).

demandable (*adj.*), demandable; exigible:

the money placed on current account is always demandable, that is to say, the customer can claim the amount of it at any time by presenting cheques, les fonds déposés en comptes de chèques sont toujours exigibles, c'est-à-dire que le déposant peut en réclamer le montant à tout moment par la présentation de chèques (*m.pl.*).

demonetization (*n.*), démonétisation (*f.*):
demonetization of old coins, démonétisation des anciennes pièces.

demonetize (*v.t.*), démonétiser:
to remint demonetized silver coins, refondre des pièces d'argent démonétisées.

demurrage (detention of a ship beyond specified time) (*n.*), surestarie (*f.*):
ship on demurrage, navire en surestarie (*m.*).
day of demurrage, jour de surestarie (*m.*); surestarie (*f.*).

demurrage (detention of a railway vehicle) (*n.*), souffrance (*f.*); chômage (*m.*):
demurrage of rolling stock, souffrance, chômage, de matériel roulant.

demurrage (detention of goods) (*n.*), souffrance (*f.*):
when goods on demurrage are liable to deteriorate, they are generally sold, quand les marchandises en souffrance sont sujettes à détérioration elles sont, en général, vendues.
to leave the goods on demurrage on the wharves, laisser les marchandises en souffrance sur les quais.

demurrage (*n.*) or **demurrage charges** (Shipping) (Ant.: *dispatch money*), surestaries (*f.pl.*):
payment of demurrage, paiement des surestaries (*m.*).

demurrage (*n.*) or **demurrage charge** (or **charges**) (for detention or non use of railway vehicles), droit de stationnement (*m.*); taxe de stationnement (*f.*); taxe de chômage (*f.*); frais de chômage (*m.pl.*).

denomination (*n.*), coupure (*f.*):
company which issues its shares in ones and denominations of 5, 10, 25, 50, or 100, société qui émet ses actions en unités et en coupures de 5, 10, 25, 50, ou 100 (*f.*).
bank notes of small denominations, billets de banque de petites coupures (*m.pl.*).
any denominations, toutes coupures.
denominations of weight, of 0 to 5 lbs, of 5 to 10 lbs, coupures de poids, de 0 à 5 livres, de 5 à 10 livres.

denoting stamp, estampille de contrôle (*f.*).

depart (*v.i.*), partir.

department (*n.*) (Abbrev.: **dept**), service (*m.*):
manager of the advertising department, chef du service de la publicité (*m.*).

departmental charges (Costing) (opp. to *overhead*, or *on-cost*, or *fixed*, *charges*, or *indirect charges* or *expenses*), frais spéciaux (*m.pl.*); frais directs (*m.pl.*); frais proportionnels (*m.pl.*); dépenses directes (*ou* proportionnelles) (*f.pl.*).

departmental invoice (i.e., invoice rendered from one department to another for accountancy or record purposes), facture d'ordre (*f.*).

departmental ledger, grand livre fractionnaire (*m.*); grand livre auxiliaire (*m.*); grand livre analytique (*m.*); grand livre originaire (*m.*); grand livre de développement (*m.*).

departmental store, grand magasin (*m.*).

departmental store business (*or* **trade**), grand détail (*m.*).

departure (*n.*), départ (*m.*):
departure of the mail, of a train, départ du courrier, d'un train.
port of departure, port de départ (*m.*).

departure platform (Rly.) (opp. to *arrival platform*), quai de départ (*m.*).

departure station, gare de départ (*f.*).

depend (on *or* upon) (*v.i.*) *or* **dependent** (on *or* upon) (to be) (to rely upon as a source of supply), être tributaire (de):
to depend upon foreign supplies, être tributaire de l'étranger.
to be dependent upon the Far East for raw material, être tributaire pour la matière première de l'Extrême Orient.

dependent on (*or* **upon**) (**to be**) (to rely upon for support), être à la charge de:
to be dependent on (*or* upon) someone, être à la charge de quelqu'un.
persons dependent on the taxpayer (Income Tax), personnes à la charge du contribuable (*f.pl.*).
dependent person, personne à charge (*f.*).

deposit (placing for safe keeping or profit) (*n.*), dépôt (*m.*); mise en dépôt (*f.*); consignation (*f.*); consigne (*f.*):
deposit of a security, dépôt (*ou* consignation) d'une garantie (*ou* d'un cautionnement).
deposit of goods on wharf or in bonded sheds, dépôt de marchandises à quai ou sous tente.
deposit in King's warehouse of goods not entered, mise en dépôt des marchandises non déclarées (Cf. **King's warehouse**.)
deposit of luggage in cloak room, dépôt des bagages à la consigne; consigne des bagages.

deposit (Banking) (*n.*), dépôt (*m.*):
Note:—It should be borne in mind that the meaning of the word *dépôt* in French banking is not confined to the restricted acceptation of the word *deposit* in English banking (i.e., money lodged with a bank, bearing interest, and subject to notice of withdrawal), but that it is used indifferently of money placed on deposit or current account. Thus the big French joint stock banks are called *sociétés de dépôt*, and the following sentence, for example: *la société est autorisée à recevoir, avec ou sans intérêts, des capitaux en dépôt* means: *the company is authorized to receive money on deposit or current account, at or without interest. Placing money on current account* is *dépôt à vue.* (Cf. **current account** *and* **deposit account**.) The sentence *the bank also receives money on deposit* would be rendered in French as follows:— *la banque reçoit aussi des fonds en dépôts exigibles à terme ou à préavis.*
deposit at call, dépôt remboursable sur demande.
deposit at notice, dépôt à préavis; dépôt avec préavis; dépôt à délai de préavis.
deposit at 7 days' notice, dépôt à 7 jours de préavis.

deposit at short notice, dépôt à court terme.

fixed deposit *or* deposit for a fixed period, dépôt à terme ; dépôt à terme fixe ; dépôt à échéance ; dépôt à échéance fixe ; placement (*m.*) ; placement à échéance (*m.*).

deposit (Savings Bank) (*n.*), versement (*m.*) ; dépôt (*m.*).

deposit (Customs) (*n.*), consignation (*f.*) ; dépôt (*m.*) :

deposit of customs duties, consignation de droits de douane.

deposit of cash (in lieu of bond), consignation ; dépôt de numéraire.

deposit of stock (securities), dépôt de valeurs.

deposit (pledge ; security ; earnest ; cover) (*n.*), cautionnement (*m.*) ; ·dépôt de garantie (*m.*) ; provision (*f.*) ; provision de garantie (*f.*) ; arrhes (*f.pl.*) ; couverture (*f.*) :

deposit with gas company, cautionnement au gaz.

telephone deposit (deposit for calls), dépôt de garantie téléphonique ; provision de garantie téléphonique ; provision téléphone :

subscriber who has paid a deposit, abonné qui a versé un dépôt de garantie (*m.*).

a deposit may be asked for to secure payment, une provision peut être demandée pour garantir le paiement.

promise of sale made with deposit, promesse de vente faite avec des arrhes (*f.*).

deposit (*v.t.*), déposer ; faire le dépôt de ; consigner ; placer ; mettre ; fournir :

to deposit at the customs a copy of the manifest, déposer à la douane une copie du manifeste.

to deposit a sum in the hands of a third party, déposer, faire le dépôt d', placer, consigner, une somme en main tierce.

to deposit funds with a banker, déposer, faire le dépôt, consigner, des fonds chez un banquier.

to deposit securities in safe custody, déposer, placer, mettre, des titres en garde ; mettre des valeurs en dépôt.

to deposit paper security, consigner en papier.

the goods can only be cleared after the duties have been paid, deposited, or secured, les marchandises ne peuvent être retirées des douanes qu'après les droits ont été payés, consignés, ou garantis (*f.pl.*).

holders of bearer shares are requested to deposit their warrants at the company's office 0 days at least before the meeting, MM. les possesseurs (*ou* MM. les propriétaires) d'actions au porteur sont priés de déposer leur titres au siège social 0 jours au moins avant la réunion.

principal who must deposit a margin (Stock Exch.), donneur d'ordre qui doit fournir une couverture (*m.*).

deposit (Savings Bank) (*v.t.*), verser ; déposer :

to deposit money in the post office savings bank, verser des fonds à la caisse nationale d'épargne.

deposit account (Banking) (Abbrev. :   **D.A.**), compte de dépôts à terme ou à préavis (*m.*) ;

compte de dépôts à terme ou avec préavis (*m.*) :

fixed deposit account, compte de dépôts à terme (*m.*).

deposit account at notice, compte de dépôts à préavis (*ou* avec préavis) (*ou* à délai de préavis).

deposit account at 7 days' notice, compte de .dépôts à 7 jours de préavis.

deposit bank, banque de dépôt (*f.*).

deposit book (Savings Bank, etc.), livret (*m.*) ; livret nominatif (*m.*).

deposit receipt (receipt for a lodgment, as of securities), récépissé de dépôt (*m.*).

deposit receipt (Banking), bon de caisse (*m.*). *Cf.* fixed deposit receipt *and note thereunder.*

deposit receipt (Customs), reçu de consignation (*m.*) ; quittance de consignation (*f.*) ; reconnaissance de consignation (*f.*).

deposit slip (U.S. Banking), bordereau de versement (*m.*) ; feuille de versement (*f.*).

deposit warrant (dock warrant), warrant (*m.*) ; récépissé-warrant (*m.*).

depositary [depositaries *pl.*] (pers.) (*n.*) (correlative of *depositor*), dépositaire (*m. ou f.*) ; consignataire (*m.*) :

the banker is the depositary of the funds of his customers, le banquier est le dépositaire des fonds de ses clients.

depositor (pers.) (*n.*), déposant, -e ; enarrheur (*m.*) :

post office savings bank depositor, déposant de la caisse nationale d'épargne.

depositor's book (savings bank, etc.), livret de déposant (*m.*) ; livret nominatif (*m.*) ; livret (*m.*).

depot (*n.*), dépôt (*m.*).

depreciate (*v.t.*), déprécier ; avilir ; rabaisser ; amortir :

to depreciate the value of shares, déprécier la valeur des actions.

to depreciate the furniture by 10% per annum, amortir le mobilier de 10 0/0 par an.

depreciate (*v.i.*), se déprécier ; s'avilir :

in time, certain stocks appreciate, others depreciate, avec le temps, certaines valeurs s'améliorent, d'autres se déprécient.

perishable goods depreciate rapidly, les marchandises périssables s'avilissent rapidement.

depreciation (*n.*) (Ant. : *appreciation*), dépréciation (*f.*) ; moins-value (*f.*) ; avilissement (*m.*) ; amortissement (*m.*) :

depreciation of plant, of money, of securities lodged as collateral, dépréciation, moins-value, du matériel, de l'argent, des valeurs fournies en nantissement.

the depreciation of various national currencies in relation to gold has had as a consequence a general rise of prices, la dépréciation de diverses monnaies nationales par rapport à l'or a eu pour conséquence la hausse générale des prix.

depreciation resulting from the consequences of a stranding, moins-value résultant des conséquences d'un échouement.

depreciation in the prices of shares, moins-value sur les cours des actions.

overproduction brings about a depreciation in prices, la surproduction amène l'avilissement des prix.

depreciation on premises, amortissement sur immeuble (*ou* sur immeubles).

depreciation on diminishing values (opp. to *fixed depreciation*), amortissement dégressif.

depress (*v.t.*), déprimer :
news which has had a depressing effect on the market, nouvelle qui a eu un effet déprimant sur le marché (*f.*).

depression (*n.*), dépression (*f.*) :
depression of a stock, dépression d'une valeur.

deprivation of enjoyment (Law), privation de jouissance (*f.*).

deputy chairman, vice-président (*m.*).

deputy governor, sous-gouverneur (*m.*) :
a deputy governor of the Bank of England, of the Bank of France, un sous-gouverneur de la Banque d'Angleterre, de la Banque de France.

deputy manager, vice-gérant (*m.*).

derange (*v.t.*), déranger :
to derange one's plan, déranger ses plans.

derangement (*n.*), dérangement (*m.*).

derelict (*n.*), navire abandonné (*m.*) ; épave (*f.*).

derive (*v.t.*), tirer ; retirer :
to derive a profit from an enterprise, a profit from a transaction, a profit from differences in price, tirer, retirer, un profit d'une entreprise, du profit d'une opération, un bénéfice des écarts de prix.

derogate (*v.i.*), déroger :
to derogate from the law by agreements to the contrary, déroger à la loi par conventions contraires.

derogation (*n.*), dérogation (*f.*) :
revocability which is a derogation from (*or* to) (*or* of) the common law, révocabilité qui est une dérogation au droit commun (*f.*).

derogatory (*adj.*), dérogatoire :
clause derogatory to the common law, clause dérogatoire au droit commun (*f.*).

derrick (ship's) (*n.*), mât de charge (*m.*) ; mât de chargement (*m.*).
under ship's derrick. V. sous **under.**

description (particulars) (*n.*), désignation (*f.*) ; libellé (*m.*) ; libellés (*m.pl.*) :
incorrect description of contents of a case, désignation inexacte du contenu d'une caisse.
description of securities, désignation des titres.
description column, colonne du libellé (*f.*).

description (profession or business ; occupation) (*n.*), qualités (*f.pl.*) ; profession (*f.*) :
the full name (*or* the name in full), address, and description of the applicant, les nom, prénoms, adresse (*ou* domicile), et qualités (*ou* profession) du souscripteur.

design to contain (to), consacrer à :
page of the ledger divided into vertical columns each designed to contain a subsidiary account, page du grand livre divisée en colonnes verticales consacrées chacune à un sous-compte (*f.*).

desire to defraud one's creditors, envie de frustrer ses créanciers (*f.*).

desk (*n.*), pupitre (*m.*) :
lockup desk, pupitre fermant à clef.

despatch (*n. & v.*). Syn. de **dispatch.**

destination (*n.*), destination (*f.*) :
to convey the goods to the place of their destination, the passenger safe and sound to destination, conduire les marchandises au lieu de leur destination, le voyageur sain et sauf à destination.

destination station, gare de destination (*f.*) ; gare destinataire (*f.*).

destroy the rats on a ship (to), dératiser un navire.

destruction of rats, dératisation (*f.*) ; destruction des rats (*f.*) :
destruction of rats on ships coming from countries contaminated by plague, dératisation des navires provenant des pays contaminés de peste.

detach (*v.t.*), détacher :
to detach a coupon, détacher un coupon.

detachment (*n.*), détachement (*m.*).

detail (*n.*), détail (*m.*) :
details of an account, détails d'un compte.
payments as per details in cash book, paiements dont détail au livre de caisse (*m.pl.*).

detail (*v.t.*), détailler :
to detail the list of stocks and shares held in the box, détailler la liste des valeurs mobilières détenues en portefeuille.
a detailed statement of account, un état détaillé de compte.

detail column, colonne de détail (*f.*).

detain (*v.t.*), détenir.

detention *or* **detainment** (*n.*), détention (*f.*) :
detention, detainment, of a ship, détention d'un navire.

detention or non use of vehicles (Rly.), stationnement (*m.*) :
loading, unloading, and detention or non use of vehicles the handling of which is done by traders, chargement, déchargement, et stationnement des wagons dont la manutention est faite par le commerce.

deterioration (*n.*), détérioration (*f.*).

determinable (Law) (*adj.*), résoluble :
determinable contract, contrat résoluble (*m.*).

determination (Law) (*n.*), résolution (*f.*) ; résiliation (*f.*) ; résiliement (*m.*) ; résiliment (*m.*).

determination clause (Law), clause résolutoire (*f.*).

determine (to annul) (Law) (*v.t.*), résoudre ; résilier :
to determine a contract, résoudre, résilier, un contrat.

determine (*v.i.*) *or* **to be determined** (Law), se résoudre :
a lease is determined by the expiration of the term fixed, un bail se résout par l'expiration du terme fixé.

devalorization (*n.*), dévalorisation (*f.*) :
the devalorization of the franc, la dévalorisation du franc.

devalorize (*v.t.*), dévaloriser.
devaluation (*n.*), dévaluation (*f.*) :
 devaluation of the paper franc, dévaluation
 du franc-papier.
deviate (*v.i.*), dévier ; s'écarter :
 ship which deviates from her course to save
 lives or property, navire qui dévie (*ou* qui
 s'écarte) de sa route pour sauver des vies
 humaines ou des biens (*m.*).
 leave to deviate by any route, faculté de
 dévier par n'importe quelle route (*f.*).
deviation (*n.*), déviation (*f.*) ; déroutement
 (*m.*) ; changement de route (*m.*) :
 deviation from the voyage contemplated by
 the policy, déviation du voyage envisagé
 par la police.
deviation clause (Abbrev. : **D/C.**), clause déviation (*f.*).
deviation risk, risque de déviation (*m.*).
devise (*v.t.*), combiner :
 to devise a plan, combiner un plan.
devote (*v.t.*), consacrer :
 the manager must devote his whole time to
 the company's business, le gérant doit
 consacrer tout son temps aux affaires
 sociales.
 the thirty years he has devoted to his business, les trente années qu'il a consacrées
 à son commerce.
dial (of a calculating machine) (*n.*), viseur
 (d'une machine à calculer) (*m.*).
dial (Automatic Teleph.) (*n.*), disque d'appel
 (*m.*) ; disque (*m.*).
dial (Automatic Teleph.) (*v.t.*), composer ; composer sur son disque d'appel :
 the subscriber, in the first place, dials the
 first three letters of the exchange name
 wanted, printed in heavy type ; he then
 dials the four numerals of the number required, l'abonné compose d'abord sur son
 disque d'appel les trois premières lettres du
 nom du bureau demandé, indiquées en
 caractères majuscules ; il compose à la
 suite les quatre chiffres du numéro demandé
 (*m.*).
dial opening (of a calculating machine), fenêtre
 de viseur (*f.*).
dialling tone (continuous purring sound) (Automatic Teleph.), signal de manœuvre
 (bourdonnement continu) (*m.*).
diamond shares *or* **diamonds** (*n.pl.*), valeurs de
 diamants (*f.pl.*) ; valeurs diamantifères
 (*f.pl.*) ; diamantifères (*f.pl.*).
diary [**diaries** *pl.*] (journal) (*n.*), agenda (*m.*) :
 to make a note in a diary, faire une note sur
 un agenda.
diary (a book for recording in order of due date
 payments to be made or amounts to be
 collected, specifically a **bill diary**) (*n.*),
 échéancier (*m.*) ; carnet d'échéance (*m.*) ;
 carnet d'échéances (*m.*).
dictate (*v.t.*), dicter :
 to dictate a letter to one's secretary, a telegram to a telephone operator, dicter une
 lettre à son secrétaire, un télégramme à une
 opératrice téléphonique.

dictating machine, machine à dicter (*f.*).
dictation (*n.*), dictée (*f.*) :
 dictation of the reply to a letter, dictée de la
 réponse à une lettre.
dictator (pers.) (*n.*), dicteur, -euse.
difference (dissimilarity) (*n.*), différence (*f.*) ;
 écart (*m.*) :
 difference between the debit and credit of an
 account, différence entre le débit et le
 crédit d'un compte.
 to look for a difference in the books, rechercher une différence dans les écritures (*ou*
 dans les livres).
 difference in the cash, différence de caisse.
 difference between the cost price and the
 sale price, écart entre le prix de revient et
 le prix de vente.
 differences in price, in rates, écarts de prix,
 des taux.
 difference of (*or* on) exchange, différence de
 change.
difference (Stock Exch.) (*n.*), différence (*f.*) :
 difference to pay or to receive, différence à
 payer ou à recevoir.
 stock exchange differences, différences de
 bourse.
difference (disagreement in opinion) (*n.*), différend (*m.*) ; contestation (*f.*).
differential (*adj.*), différentiel, -elle :
 differential duties (Customs), droits différentiels (*m.pl.*).
 differential tariff hitting foreign products more
 heavily than goods of national origin, tarif
 différentiel frappant les produits étrangers
 plus lourdement que les marchandises
 d'origine nationale (*m.*).
diminish (*v.t.*), diminuer ; amoindrir :
 to diminish the resources of a country, diminuer les ressources d'un pays.
diminish (*v.i.*), diminuer ; se diminuer ; amoindrir ; s'amoindrir.
diminution (*n.*), diminution (*f.*) ; amoindrissement (*m.*).
dining car (Rly.), wagon-restaurant (*m.*).
dip (*v.i.*), s'infléchir :
 X. shares dipped to 1¾, l'action X. s'infléchit
 à 1 3/4.
direct (*adj.*), direct, -e :
 direct call (of a ship at an intermediate port),
 escale directe (*f.*) ; échelle directe (*f.*).
 direct contract (Produce Exch.) (opp. to *commission contract* or *broker's contract*), contrat
 direct (*m.*).
 direct distance between exchanges (Teleph.),
 distance à vol d'oiseau entre bureaux (*f.*).
 direct exchange (the exchange of one currency
 directly for another without intervention of
 a third currency), change direct (*m.*).
 direct exchange (rate of exchange), certain
 (*m.*). *V.* to quote direct exchange *pour
 exemple.*
 direct exchange line (Teleph.) (distinguished
 from *extension line*), poste principal (*m.*) ;
 ligne principale (*f.*).
 Note :—The literal and proper English translation of *poste* is *station,* and of *ligne* is

line. In England, however, while the telephone engineer will speak of the *main station* (*poste principal*), meaning the principal installation or apparatus on the subscriber's premises, the subscriber will always speak of his telephone installation as his *line.* Thus, in the English Tariff Rates for Telephone service, the charges are referred to as being for *Direct Exchange Lines* and *Extension Lines*, while in France they are referred to as for *Postes principaux* and *Postes supplémentaires*, or as *Abonnements principaux* and *Abonnements supplémentaires.*

direct expenses (Costing) (opp. to *indirect expenses* or *charges*, or *overhead*, or *on-cost*, or *fixed*, *charges*), frais spéciaux (*m.pl.*); frais directs (*m.pl.*); frais proportionnels (*m.pl.*); dépenses directes (*ou* proportionnelles) (*f.pl.*).

direct importation (i.e., from a foreign port to a home port, the ship not calling at intermediate port or ports), importation en droiture (*f.*); importation directe (*f.*):
produce which arrives direct (*or* directly) (*or* straight) from Buenos Ayres, produits qui arrivent en droiture de Buenos-Ayres (*m.pl.*).

direct tax, impôt direct (*m.*); contribution directe (*f.*).

direct (without the intermediation of a wholesaler) (*adj.*), de gros; en gros:
direct trade *or* direct commerce, commerce de (*ou* en) gros (*m.*); gros commerce (*m.*); gros (*m.*):
to do a direct trade, faire le gros.
direct sale, vente en gros (*f.*).
direct trader, marchand en gros (*m.*).
V. note sous **wholesale.**

direct (to control; to manage) (*v.t.*), diriger; administrer:
to direct an enterprise, diriger une entreprise.

direct (to instruct) (*v.t.*), charger:
to direct someone to reply to a letter, charger quelqu'un de répondre à une lettre.

directing (*adj.*), directeur, -trice:
the directing power, la puissance directrice.

direction (*n.*), direction (*f.*); administration (*f.*); prescription (*f.*):
direction for routing appearing on the consignment note, prescription d'acheminement figurant sur la lettre de voiture.

director (of a company) (pers.) (*n.*), administrateur, -trice (d'une société). (Cf. **directors,** ci-après.)

directorate (*n.*), administration (*f.*).

directors (board of directors) (*n.pl.*), administrateurs (*m.pl.*); conseil d'administration (*m.*).

directors' fees, jetons de présence des administrateurs (*m.pl.*); jetons des administrateurs (*m.pl.*); honoraires des administrateurs (*m.pl.*). V. exemple sous **fees.**

directors' percentage of profits, tantièmes des administrateurs (*m.pl.*).

directors' report, rapport des administrateurs (*m.*); rapport du conseil d'administration (*m.*).

directorship (*n.*), administration (*f.*).

directory [**directories** *pl.*] (*n.*), annuaire (*m.*); répertoire (*m.*):
telephone directory, annuaire des abonnés au téléphone.
shipping directory, répertoire maritime.

directory enquiry (Teleph.), service de renseignements (*m.*).

directory enquiry operator (Teleph.), opératrice des renseignements (*f.*).

dirigible (airship) (*n.*), dirigeable (*m.*); paquebot aérien (*m.*).

dirty bill of lading (opp. to *clean bill of lading*), connaissement avec réserves (*m.*); connaissement portant des réserves (*m.*).

disablement (Accident Insurance) (*n.*), incapacité (*f.*).

disagree (*v.i.*), n'être pas d'accord; être en désaccord.

disagreement (*n.*), désaccord (*m.*); discordance (*f.*); non concordance (*f.*):
disagreement between the experts, désaccord entre les experts.
disagreement between the journal and the ledger, discordance du journal et du grand livre.

disallow (*v.t.*), rejeter:
to disallow an expense, rejeter une dépense.

disallowance (*n.*), rejet (*m.*).

disappearance (*n.*), disparition (*f.*):
disappearance or total destruction of the ship, disparition ou destruction totale du navire.

disaster (*n.*), désastre (*m.*); sinistre (*m.*).

disburse (*v.t.*), débourser.

disbursement (act) (*n.*), déboursement (*m.*); mise hors (*f.*).

disbursement (expense) (*n. generally used in the plural*), débours (*m.*); déboursé (*m.*); déboursement (*m.*); mise hors (*f.*).

disbursements (ship's) (money advanced and expenses incurred for the voyage) (Mar. Insce) (*n.pl.*), mises dehors (*f.pl.*).

discharge (an unloading of vessel or cargo) (*n.*), décharge (*f.*); déchargement (*m.*); débarquement (*m.*):
the final discharge of the vessel, le déchargement final du navire.

discharge (acquittal) (*n.*), décharge (*f.*); libération (*f.*); affranchissement (*m.*); acquit (*m.*); acquittement (*m.*); quittance (*f.*); quitus (*m.*):
discharge of a bond (Customs), décharge, libération, d'une soumission.
to give discharge by a receipt, donner décharge par un reçu.
to obtain the discharge or the reduction of one's taxes, obtenir la décharge ou la réduction de ses impôts.
in full discharge, libératoire:
receipt in full discharge, reçu libératoire (*m.*); quittance finale (*f.*).

discharge (of a bankrupt) (*n.*), réhabilitation (d'un failli) (*f.*).

discharge (dismissal from an employment) (*n.*),

renvoi (*m.*) ; congé (*m.*) ; congédiement (*m.*).

discharge (to unload) (*v.t.*), décharger ; débarquer :
to discharge the cargo into craft or barges, on the quay, décharger, débarquer, la cargaison dans (*ou* sur) des embarcations ou des chalands, sur le quai.
to discharge the goods at the port of destination, at the nearest port, at any other port, décharger, débarquer, les marchandises au port de destination, au port le plus voisin, en tout autre port.

discharge (to acquit) (*v.t.*), décharger ; libérer ; affranchir ; acquitter ; quitter ; liquider :
to discharge an account, décharger un compte.
to discharge someone from an obligation, from a debt, acquitter, quitter, libérer, quelqu'un d'une obligation, d'une dette.
to discharge one's liabilities in full, acquitter intégralement le montant de son passif.
to discharge a debt, liquider une dette.

discharge (Bankruptcy) (*v.t.*), réhabiliter :
to discharge a bankrupt, réhabiliter un failli.

discharge (to dismiss from employment) (*v.t.*), renvoyer ; congédier ; remercier :
to discharge an employee, renvoyer, congédier, remercier, un employé.
to discharge all the staff, congédier tout le personnel ; faire place nette.

disciplinary board, conseil de discipline (*m.*).
disciplinary committee, chambre de discipline (*f.*).

disclose (*v.t.*), faire connaître ; révéler ; déclarer ; dévoiler :
to disclose every material circumstance, faire connaître, révéler, déclarer, toute circonstance essentielle.
to disclose the names of the contracting parties, dévoiler les noms des parties contractantes.

discontinuance of business, cessation d'entreprise (*f.*).
discontinuance of subscription, désabonnement (*m.*).
discontinue to subscribe (to) *or* **discontinue one's subscription (to),** se désabonner :
to discontinue one's subscription to a newspaper, se désabonner à un journal.

discount (act) (*n.*), escompte (*m.*) :
bills sent to the bank for discount, effets remis en banque à l'escompte (*m.pl.*).

discount (interest retained for advancing money on negotiable securities not yet due) (Banking & Fin.) (*n.*) (Abbrev.: **dis.** *or* **disc.** *or* **disct**), escompte (*m.*) ; escompte de banque (*m.*) ; commission d'escompte (*f.*).

discount (allowance ; rebate) (Com. & Fin.) (*n.*) (Abbrev.: **dis.** *or* **disc.** *or* **disct**), escompte (*m.*) ; remise (*f.*) ; rabais (*m.*) :
to allow a discount of 5% on the gross amount of an invoice, faire, accorder, un escompte (*ou* une remise) (*ou* un rabais) de 5 0/0 sur le montant brut d'une facture.
discounts on purchases, on sales, escomptes, remises, sur achats, sur ventes.

trade discount, remise ; remise sur marchandises ; escompte sur marchandises ; escompte sur (*ou* de) facture ; escompte-remise (*m.*) ; escompte d'usage.
cash discount *or* discount for cash, escompte de caisse ; escompte au comptant ; escompte-intérêt (*m.*) ; escompte.
discounts allowed, escomptes accordés.
discounts received, escomptes obtenus.

discount (sum less than par value) (*n.*) (opp. to *premium*) (Abbrev.: **dis.** *or* **disc.** *or* **disct**), perte (*f.*) :
a share of £1 which sells at 15/-, is dealt in at 5/- discount, une action de 1*l.* qui se vend 15*sh.*, se négocie à 5*sh.* de perte.
loan which is called ¼% discount (Stock Exch.), emprunt qui fait 1/4 0/0 de perte (*m.*).
to be at a discount *or* to stand at a discount, être en perte ; faire perte :
shares which are at a discount (*or* which stand at a discount) on the market, actions qui sont en perte (*ou* qui font perte) sur le marché (*f.pl.*).
country where gold is quoted at a premium or at a discount on the basis of so many francs for a kilogramme of pure gold, pays où l'or se cote en prime ou en perte sur la base de tant de francs pour un kilogramme d'or pur (*m.*).
Cf. to issue shares at a discount, *sous* **issue** (*v.t.*).

discount (over spot) (*n.*) (Forward exchange rates) (Abbrev.: **d.**), report (*m.*) :
for the determination of the forward rates there is quoted a discount or a premium, i.e., the amount there is occasion to add (d.) to the spot rate or to subtract from it (p.) to obtain the value of the basis quoted, pour la détermination des cours à terme, on cote le report ou le déport, c.-à-d. la somme qu'il y a lieu d'ajouter (R.) au cours du comptant ou d'en soustraire (B.) pour obtenir la valeur de la base cotée.
Centre : Paris, 1 month, (p.) 15–5c., Devise : Paris, 1 mois, 0 15 B. à 0 05 B.

discount (*v.t.*), escompter ; faire l'escompte de ; prendre à l'escompte :
to discount a bill, escompter, faire l'escompte d', prendre à l'escompte, un effet.
to discount a rise of stocks, escompter une hausse de valeurs.
speculation discounts good news, la spéculation escompte les bonnes nouvelles.
to be discounted, être escompté, -e ; s'escompter.

discount bank, banque d'escompte (*f.*).
discount charges, agio (*m.*) ; frais d'escompte (*m.pl.*).
discount house, maison d'escompte (*f.*).
discount market, marché de l'escompte (*m.*).
discount rate, taux d'escompte (*m.*) ; taux de l'escompte (*m.*).
discount rate of the open market (opp. to *bank rate*), taux hors banque (*m.*) ; taux privé (*m.*) ; taux d'escompte hors banque (*m.*) ;

taux d'escompte privé (*m.*); taux de l'escompte privé (*m.*); escompte hors banque (*m.*); escompte privé (*m.*). Cf. **bank rate.**

discountable (*adj.*), escomptable: discountable bill, effet escomptable (*m.*).

discounter (pers.) (*n.*), escompteur (*m.*).

discounting (*adj.*), escompteur, -euse: the discounting banker, le banquier escompteur.

discounting (*n.*), escompte (*m.*): discounting a bill, escompte d'un effet. discounting without recourse, escompte à forfait.

discovery (Law) (*n.*), communication (*f.*): discovery of documents, communication de pièces.

discredit (*n.*), discrédit (*m.*).

discredit (*v.t.*), discréditer.

discrepancy report (unloading of a ship), bordereau des litiges (*m.*).

discretion (*n.*), gré (*m.*): in the absolute discretion of the captain, absolument au gré du capitaine.

discretionary order, ordre à appréciation (*m.*).

discuss (*v.t.*), discuter; débattre: to discuss an amendment, discuter un amendement. to discuss an account, the conditions of a bargain, débattre un compte, les conditions d'un marché.

discussion (*n.*), discussion (*f.*); débats (*m.pl.*); échange d'observations (*f.*): after discussion, and there being no further questions, the chairman put the following resolutions to the meeting, après discussion (*ou* après échange d'observations), et personne ne demandant plus la parole, M. le président met aux voix les résolutions suivantes. discussion of an account, débats de compte.

disembark (*v.t.*), débarquer: to disembark passengers, débarquer des passagers.

disembark (*v.i.*), débarquer: to disembark in a foreign port, débarquer dans un port étranger.

disembarking *or* **disembarkation** *or* **disembarcation** (*n.*), débarquement (*m.*).

disencumber (to free from mortgage) (*v.t.*), dégrever; déshypothéquer: to disencumber a property, dégrever, déshypothéquer, une propriété.

disencumbrance (*n.*), dégrèvement (*m.*).

dishonest (*adj.*), malhonnête; infidèle; déloyal, -e, -aux: dishonest cashier, caissier malhonnête (*ou* infidèle) (*ou* déloyal) (*m.*).

dishonestly (*adv.*), malhonnêtement.

dishonesty (*n.*), malhonnêteté (*f.*); infidélité (*f.*).

dishonour (*n.*), non acceptation ou non paiement; défaut d'acceptation ou de paiement (*m.*); refus d'acceptation ou de paiement (*m.*): as to documentary bills, the remitter should mention to the bank a correspondent to whom it should send the documents in case of dishonour, pour les effets documentaires le remetteur doit indiquer à la banque un correspondant auquel elle doit remettre les documents en cas de non acceptation ou de non paiement.

dishonour (*n.*) *or* **dishonour by non acceptance,** non acceptation (*f.*); défaut d'acceptation (*m.*); refus d'acceptation (*m.*).

dishonour (*n.*) *or* **dishonour by non payment,** non paiement (*m.*); défaut de paiement (*m.*); refus de paiement (*m.*): in France, dishonour by non payment of a bill of exchange should be attested (*or* noted) the day after the day of maturity by an act called protest for non payment, en France le refus de paiement d'un effet de commerce doit être constaté le lendemain du jour de l'échéance par un acte que l'on nomme protêt faute de paiement.

dishonour (*v.t.*) *or* **to dishonour by non acceptance,** ne pas accepter; faire défaut à l'acceptation de; refuser d'accepter; se refuser à accepter.

dishonour (*v.t.*) *or* **to dishonour by non payment,** ne pas payer; faire défaut au paiement de refuser de payer; se refuser à payer: bills which are dishonoured (*or* which are dishonoured by non payment), effets qui ne sont pas payés (*m.pl.*).

dishonoured bill. V. sous **bill.**

dishonoured cheque, chèque impayé (*m.*).

dishonoured draft, tirage refusé (*m.*).

disinfect (*v.t.*), désinfecter.

disinfection (*n.*), désinfection (*f.*): disinfection of whole or part of the ship, désinfection de tout ou partie du navire.

dismiss (to discharge from service) (*v.t.*), renvoyer; congédier; remercier: to dismiss an employee, renvoyer, congédier remercier, un employé. to dismiss all the staff, congédier tout le personnel; faire place nette.

dismissal (*n.*), renvoi (*m.*); congé (*m.*); congédiement (*m.*).

dispatch (forwarding) (*n.*), expédition (*f.*) envoi (*m.*); acheminement (*m.*): dispatch of a telegram, of the bill of lading, to the consignee of the goods, expédition envoi, d'une dépêche, du connaissement au destinataire des marchandises. delay in the dispatch of the goods, retard dans l'acheminement de la marchandise (*m.*). date of dispatch of advice of arrival, date d'envoi d'avis d'arrivée (*f.*).

dispatch (speed) (*n.*), promptitude (*f.*); rapidité (*f.*): with dispatch, avec promptitude. with customary dispatch, avec la rapidité usitée.

dispatch (days saved) (Shipping) (*n.*) (opp. to demurrage), dispatch (*f.*); despatch (*f.*) jours sauvés (*m.pl.*).

dispatch (*v.t.*), expédier; envoyer; acheminer dépêcher: before dispatching the post, read over the

addresses carefully, avant d'expédier le
courrier, bien relire les adresses.
letters dispatched by weekly mails, lettres
acheminées par courriers hebdomadaires
(*f.pl.*).
ispatch boat *or* **dispatch vessel,** aviso (*m.*).
ispatch clerk, expéditionnaire (*m.*).
ispatch money (opp. to *demurrage*), dispatch
money (*f.*); despatch money (*f.*); prime
de rapidité (*f.*):
the shipowner benefits by a premium called
dispatch money when the ship's cargo is
loaded or unloaded in less time than laytime, l'armateur bénéficie d'une prime
appelée dispatch money lorsque la cargaison
est embarquée ou débarquée dans un délai
moindre que le délai de planche (*m.*).
ispatch note, bulletin d'envoi (*m.*); bulletin
d'expédition (*m.*).
ispatch note (Parcel Post), bulletin d'expédition (*m.*); bulletin postal (*m.*).
ispatching office (Post) (opp. to *delivering office*),
bureau de départ (*m.*).
isplace (*v.t.*), déplacer :
to displace wealth, déplacer les richesses.
ship which displaces 10,000 tons, navire qui
déplace 10 000 tonnes (*m.*).
isplaced (i.e., held by the speculative public ;
not as investment) (*adj.*) (Ant. : *placed*),
déclassé, -e :
displaced shares, actions déclassées (*f.pl.*).
isplacement (*n.*), déplacement (*m.*):
displacement of wealth, of funds, déplacement de richesses, de fonds.
displacement of a ship, déplacement d'un
navire. V. **light displacement** & **load displacement.**
isplacement (Stock Exch.) (*n.*), déclassement
(*m.*):
the displacement arising from the conversion
of the 3%, le déclassement provenant de la
conversion du 3 0/0.
isplacement ton, tonneau-poids (*m.*); tonneau
de déplacement (*m.*); tonne de déplacement (*f.*).
isplay (*v.t.*), faire preuve de :
the stock market continues to display strength,
weakness, le marché des valeurs continue
à faire preuve de résistance, faiblesse.
isplay advertisement, annonce de fantaisie (*f.*);
annonce courante (*f.*).
isposable (*adj.*), disponible :
disposable funds, fonds disponibles (*m.pl.*);
disponibilités (*f.pl.*).
isposal (*n.*), disposition (*f.*):
disposal of one's property, disposition de son
bien.
to put a sum of money at the disposal of a
friend, mettre une somme d'argent à la
disposition d'un ami.
ispose of (to), disposer de ; céder :
to dispose of a property, a goodwill, disposer
d', céder, une propriété, un fonds de commerce.
ispute (*n.*), contestation (*f.*); différend (*m.*):
disputes between employers and employees,

between the customs and traders, contestations, différends, entre employeurs et employés, entre la douane et le commerce.
dissect (*v.t.*), disséquer :
to dissect an account, a balance sheet, disséquer un compte, un bilan.
dissection (*n.*), dissection (*f.*).
dissenting *or* **dissentient** (*adj.*), dissident, -e :
dissentient creditors, créanciers dissidents
(*m.pl.*).
dissolution (Law) (*n.*), dissolution (*f.*):
dissolution of a company (*or* of a partnership),
dissolution d'une société.
dissolve (*v.t.*), dissoudre. V. exemple sous
partnership.
distance (*n.*), distance (*f.*); parcours (*m.*):
direct distance between exchanges (Teleph.),
distance à vol d'oiseau entre bureaux.
distances of — miles and under, distances
over — miles (travelling over), parcours de
— milles et au-dessous, parcours au delà
de — milles.
distance freight, fret de distance (*m.*); fret
proportionnel (*m.*); fret proportionnel à la
distance (*m.*).
distant position (Corn or other Exchange) (opp.
to *near position*), éloigné (*m.*):
purchases on distant positions in consequence
of the firmness of the grain and stock
markets, achats sur les éloignés par suite
de la fermeté des marchés des grains et des
valeurs (*m.pl.*).
distant subscriber (Teleph.) (opp. to *caller* or
calling subscriber), abonné demandé (*m.*);
demandé (*m.*).
distinct (*adj.*), distinct, -e ; séparé, -e.
distress (*n.*), détresse (*f.*); relâche (*f.*):
ship at sea in distress, navire en mer en
détresse (*m.*).
port of distress, port de relâche (*m.*).
ship which puts back into the port of sailing
in distress, navire qui rentre dans le port
de départ en détresse (*ou* en relâche) (*m.*).
distributable (*adj.*), distribuable ; répartissable ;
partageable :
distributable profit, bénéfice distribuable (*m.*).
distribute (*v.t.*), distribuer ; mettre en distribution ; répartir ; partager :
to distribute a dividend, distribuer, mettre
en distribution, répartir, partager, un
dividende.
to distribute the amount realized by a debtor's
property pro rata among his creditors,
répartir le prix des biens d'un débiteur entre
ses créanciers au marc le franc de leurs
créances.
distribution (*n.*), distribution (*f.*); mise en
distribution (*f.*); répartition (*f.*); partage
(*m.*):
distribution of profits, of wealth, distribution,
répartition, partage, des bénéfices, des
richesses.
distribution among creditors, répartition entre
créanciers; contribution (*f.*); distribution par contribution.
district bank, banque régionale (*f.*).

district commissioner (of taxes), répartiteur (m.), commissaire répartiteur (m.) (de contributions).

district manager, directeur régional (m.).

district office, bureau régional (m.).

disturbance (n.), dérangement (m.) :
disturbance of business, dérangement des affaires.

ditto (adv.), dito.

ditto [dittos pl.] (n.) (Abbrev.: **do** or **Do**), dito (m.).

diversion (misappropriation) (n.), détournement (m.); distraction (f.).

divert (v.t.), détourner; distraire :
to divert money to one's own uses, détourner, distraire, de l'argent à son profit.

dividable (adj.). Syn. de **divisible.**

divide (to split up) (v.t.), diviser; partager; scinder :
to divide a sheet into numerous columns, diviser une feuille en de nombreuses colonnes.
to divide a piece of land, diviser, partager, une terre.
to be divided, être divisé, -e, partagé, -e; se diviser; se partager; se scinder :
accounts are divided into as many classes as there are kinds of transactions, les comptes se divisent en autant de catégories qu'il y a de natures d'opérations (m.pl.).

divide (Arith.) (v.t.), diviser :
eight divided by two equals four (Abbrev.: $8 \div 2 = 4$), huit divisé par deux égale quatre (Abrév.: $8 : 2 = 4$).
authorized capital of £0,000,000 divided into 0,000,000 shares of £0 each, capital social de 0 millions de livres, divisé en 0 000 000 actions de £0 chacune (m.).

divide (to distribute in shares; to apportion) (v.t.), répartir; partager :
to divide a profit, répartir, partager, un bénéfice.
to divide an amount among creditors pro rata to their debts, répartir, partager, une somme entre des créanciers au prorata de leurs créances.

dividend (share of profits as apportioned among shareholders) (n.) (Abbrev.: **div.** or **divd** or **d.**), dividende (m.) :
dividends on shares, dividendes d'actions; dividendes des actions.
to pay a dividend of 5% or to pay a 5% dividend, payer un dividende de 5 0/0.
dividend for the year 19—, dividende de l'exercice 19—.
dividend paying company, société payant (ou donnant) des dividendes (f.).
fictitious dividend or sham dividend, dividende fictif.
dividend paid out of capital, dividende prélevé sur le capital.

dividend (share in the division of funds of a bankrupt) (n.), dividende (m.).

dividend (distribution among creditors—company in liquidation) (n.) (Abbrev.: **div.** or **divd**), répartition (f.) :

first and final dividend, third and final dividend, etc., première et unique répartition, troisième et dernière répartition, etc.

dividend (Arith.) (n.), dividende (m.).

dividend coupon, coupon de dividende (m.).

dividend off (U.S.A.), ex-dividende.

dividend on (U.S.A.), jouissance. V. exemple et explications sous syn. **cum dividend.**

dividend payable (followed by dates) (ellipsis fo dates dividend payable), jouissance (f.) époque de jouissance (f.) :
dividend payable : 1st January and 1st July jouissance : 1er janvier et 1er juillet.

dividend warrant, dividend-warrant (m.) chèque-dividende (m.).

divisibility (n.), divisibilité (f.).

divisible (capable of being separated into part (adj.), divisible; partageable.

divisible (distributable in shares; apportionable (adj.), répartissable; partageable :
divisible profits, profits répartissables (m.pl.) bénéfices partageables (m.pl.).

division (separation into parts) (n.), divisio (f.); partage (m.); scindement (m.) :
division of a property, division d'une propriété division of labour or division of employmen (Economics), division du travail.

division (Arith.) (n.), division (f.) :
division of whole numbers, of fractions, divisio des nombres entiers, des fractions.

division (distribution) (n.), répartition (f. partage (m.) :
division of the profits, répartition, partag des bénéfices.

divisional (adj.), divisionnaire :
divisional coins, monnaie divisionnaire (f. monnaie d'appoint (f.) :
silver divisional coins, monnaie divisionnai d'argent.

divisor (n.), diviseur (m.).

do (v.t.). V. exemples :
to do a bargain, faire un marché.
to be done (said of bargains) (Stock Exch. être fait, -e; être pratiqué, -e; se fair se pratiquer :
bargains done or business done, cou pratiqués (m.pl.); cours faits (m.pl.).
bargains (or business) done for cash (for money), for the settlement (or f the account), cours pratiqués au comptan à terme.
the bargains done daily on these marke are recorded in lists expressly intend for this purpose, les cours pratiqu quotidiennement sur ces marchés sor enregistrés sur des cotes ad hoc.
dealings for cash are those which are do money against stock, or stock again money, les opérations au comptant so celles qui se font argent contre titre ou titres contre argent (f.pl.).
these bargains were done yesterday, c cours se pratiquaient hier (m.pl.).
to do away with a customs duty, supprime abolir, un droit de douane.
to do banking business, faire la banque.

o do business, faire des affaires; faire
affaire; traiter:
to do business with someone, faire des affaires
(*ou* traiter) avec quelqu'un.
we hope to do business together, nous
espérons faire affaire ensemble.
to do good business, faire de bonnes affaires.
to do one's utmost (*or* one's very utmost),
faire tout son possible; faire l'impossible:
the insured must do his utmost to save the
property insured, l'assuré doit faire tout
son possible pour sauver la chose assurée
(*m.*).
in case of peril, the master is bound to do his
utmost (*or* his very utmost) to save the
money and the most valuable goods of his
cargo, en cas de péril, le capitaine est
tenu de faire l'impossible pour sauver
l'argent et les marchandises les plus
précieuses de son chargement.
to do the business, faire l'affaire:
we hope to do the business, nous espérons
faire l'affaire.
to do the correspondence, faire la correspondance.
to do the necessary, faire le nécessaire:
we beg you to have the kindness to do the
necessary for the recovery of this debt
(*or* to recover this debt), nous vous prions
de vouloir bien faire le nécessaire pour le
recouvrement de cette créance (*ou* pour
recouvrer cette créance).
to do the place (to canvass the town), faire
la place.
to do up a letter, fermer, cacheter, une lettre.
ck (Navig.) (*n.*), bassin (*m.*); dock (*m.*);
forme (*f.*); cale (*f.*).
ck (*v.t.*), faire entrer en (*ou* au) bassin; faire
passer au bassin; mettre en bassin.
ck (*v.i.*), entrer, passer, en (*ou* au) bassin:
with leave to dock and undock, avec faculté
d'entrer en bassin et d'en sortir.
ck company, compagnie des docks (*f.*).
ck dues *or* **dockage** (*n.*), droits de bassin (*m.pl.*);
droits de dock (*m.pl.*).
ck shed, 'hangar de dock (*m.*).
ck strike, grève des (*ou* de) dockers (*f.*).
ck warehouse, dock-entrepôt (*m.*); dock
(*m.*).
cker (pers.) (*n.*), docker (*m.*); déchargeur
(*m.*); débardeur (*m.*).
cking *or* **dockage** (*n.*), entrée en (*ou* au) bassin
(*f.*); passage en (*ou* au) bassin (*m.*); mise
en bassin (*f.*).
ctor (pers.) (*n.*), médecin (*m.*).
ctor's certificate, certificat de médecin (*m.*);
certificat médical (*m.*).
cument (*n.*), document (*m.*); pièce (*f.*); acte
(*m.*); titre (*m.*):
documents of value, without intrinsic value
(*or* of no intrinsic value), documents de
valeur, sans valeur intrinsèque (*ou* dépourvus
de valeur intrinsèque).
documents which accompany goods, documents
qui accompagnent les marchandises.
bill of lading, insurance policy, copies of

invoices, etc., constitute what are called the
documents, connaissement, police d'assurance, copies de factures, etc., constituent
ce que l'on appelle les documents.
cash against documents, comptant contre
documents (*m.*).
documents against (*or* on) acceptance (*Abbrev.*:
D/A.), documents contre acceptation.
documents against acceptance bill (*Abbrev.*:
D/A. bill), traite documents contre acceptation (*f.*).
documents against (*or* on) payment (*Abbrev.*:
D/P.), documents contre paiement.
documents against payment bill (*Abbrev.*:
D/P. bill), traite documents contre paiement (*f.*).
bill with documents attached. V. sous
documentary.
documents in support, pièces à l'appui;
pièces certificatives.
to legalize a document, légaliser un acte.
document of title, acte de propriété; titre
de propriété.
document cabinet, cartonnier (*m.*).
documentary (certified in writing) (*adj.*), documentaire; probant, -e:
documentary proof, preuve documentaire (*f.*).
documentary evidence, pièces probantes (*f.pl.*).
documentary (*adj.*) *or* **with documents attached**
(opp. to *clean*), documentaire; accompagné
(-e) de (*ou* par des) documents:
documentary bill *or* document bill *or* bill with
documents attached, traite documentaire
(*f.*); effet documentaire (*m.*); traite accompagnée de documents (*f.*); effet accompagné
par des documents (*m.*).
documentary credit, crédit documentaire
(*m.*); accréditif documentaire (*m.*):
documentary credit is based particularly on
bills of lading to shipper's order, le crédit
documentaire repose notamment sur les
connaissements à l'ordre du chargeur.
dollar (*n.*) (Abbrev.: **$** *or* **dol.** [**dols** *pl.*] *or* **doll.**
[**dolls** *pl.*]), dollar (*m.*).
domestic trade (opp. to *foreign trade*), commerce
intérieur (*m.*); commerce métropolitain
(*m.*).
domicile (Law) (*n.*), domicile (*m.*):
bill payable at the domicile of a third party,
effet payable au domicile d'un tiers (*m.*).
legal domicile, domicile légal.
domicile (*v.t.*), domicilier:
to domicile a bill at a bank, domicilier un
effet à une banque.
domiciled bill, billet à domicile (*m.*).
domiciled coupon, coupon domicilié (*m.*).
domiciliary clause, clause attributive de juridiction (*ou* de compétence) (*f.*); clause de
compétence (*f.*).
domiciliation (*n.*), domiciliation (*f.*).
donation (gift) (*n.*), don (*m.*); donation (*f.*).
donations (charitable) (*n.pl.*), bienfaisance (*f.*).
done (executed) (*p.p.*), fait, -e:
done in duplicate at London, the 1st January
19—, fait double (*ou* fait en double) à
Londres, le 1er janvier 19—.

done (said of bargains) (Stock Exch.) (*p.p.*). *V. sous* to do a bargain.

dormant (*adj.*), dormant, -e :
dormant accounts, comptes dormants (*m.pl.*).
dormant partner (opp. to *acting partner*), commanditaire (*m.* ou *f.*); associé commanditaire (*m.*); bailleur de fonds (*m.*).

dossier (*n.*), dossier (*m.*) :
dossier of a case (Law), dossier d'une procédure.

dotted line, pointillé (*m.*) :
to tear off a leaf from the counterfoil along the dotted line, détacher un volant de la souche suivant pointillé.

double (*adj.*), double :
double columns, doubles colonnes (*f.pl.*).
double entry (Bkkpg) (opp. to *single entry*), partie double (*f.*); inscription digraphique (*f.*) :
to keep books by double entry, tenir des livres en partie double.
double entry bookkeeping, tenue des livres en partie double (*ou* à parties doubles) (*f.*); comptabilité (*ou* comptabilisation) en partie double (*f.*); digraphie (*f.*).
all forms of journal entries are double entries, toutes les formules des articles du journal général sont des inscriptions digraphiques.
double freight, double fret (*m.*).
double insurance, assurance cumulative (*f.*); double assurance (*f.*); pluralité d'assurances (*f.*) :
assured who is overinsured by double insurance, assuré qui est surassuré par assurances cumulatives (*m.*).
double ledger (account on a page; paged) (opp. to *single ledger*), grand livre double (*m.*).
double option (put and call) (Stock Exch.), double prime (*f.*); prime double (*f.*); option (*f.*); stellage (*m.*).
double standard (monetary standard—gold and silver), double étalon (*m.*).

double (*adv.*), double :
to pay double, payer double.

double (*n.*), double (*m.*).

double (*v.t.*), doubler :
to double one's stake, doubler sa mise.

doubtful (*adj.*), douteux, -euse :
doubtful debt, créance douteuse (*f.*).
doubtful collision (of ships), abordage fautif (*m.*); abordage mixte (*m.*).

down (to be), être en moins-value ; être en baisse :
X. shares were down at 1s. 6d. against 1s. 9d., l'action X. est en moins-value à 1sh. 6d. contre 1sh. 9d.
copper down 5s. at £69 15s., cuivre en baisse 1/4 à £69 15sh. (*ou* à £69 3/4).

down train (opp. to *up train*), train impair (*m.*); train descendant (*m.*). V. note sous **up train.**

downward movement of stocks, mouvement de baisse des valeurs (*m.*).

downward tendency *or* **downward trend** (in prices), tendance à la baisse (*f.*).

Dr (abbreviation of *debtor*) (Bkkpg), Doit ; doit ; Débit ; débit ; Déb. ; D^t ; D. :
the pass book shows by Dr and Cr the customer's position at the bank, le carnet de compte donne par Doit et Avoir la situation en banque du client.

Dr To (journalizing), à (*abréviation de* doit à) when securities are deposited, the entry to be passed is : Deposits Dr To Depositors, lors du dépôt de titres, l'article à passer est : Dépôts à Déposants.
Sundries Dr To Sundries, Divers à Divers, Les suivants aux suivants.
Dr to *or simply* To *or* Bought of (*Abbrev.* Bot of) (formula on an invoice), Doit :
Mr A. B. (*buyer*) Dr to C. D. (*seller*) *or* Mr A. B. To C. D. *or* Mr A. B. Bought of C. D., C. D. (*vendeur*) Doit Monsieur A. B. (*acheteur*).

draft (outline ; original writing) (*n.*), projet (*m.*); brouillon (*m.*); minute (*f.*) :
the balance sheet, so long as it is not approved by the general meeting, is only a draft, le bilan, tant qu'il n'est pas approuvé par l'assemblée générale, n'est qu'un projet.
draft agreement, projet de convention ; projet d'acte.
draft articles, projet de statuts.
draft contract, projet de marché ; projet de contrat.
draft of a letter *or* draft letter, brouillon d'une (*ou* de) lettre ; minute d'une (*ou* de) lettre :
to make a draft of a letter, faire la minute d'une lettre.

draft (act of drawing) (*n.*), tirage (*m.*); traçage (*m.*) :
the draft of a bill, of a cheque, le tirage d'un effet, d'un chèque.

draft (bill ; cheque) (*n.*) (Abbrev. : dft), traite (*f.*); tirage (*m.*); disposition (*f.*); effet (*m.*); mandat (*m.*); bon (*m.*), échéance (*f.*); valeur (*f.*) :
a cheque is a draft on a banker, un chèque est une traite sur un banquier.
draft at sight *or* draft payable at sight *or* sight draft, traite à vue ; traite payable à vue ; disposition à vue ; effet à vue ; valeur vue ; bon à vue.
a draft on the Bank of England, un bon sur la Banque d'Angleterre.
bank which pays the drafts made on it, banque qui paie les dispositions faites sur elle (*f.*).
dishonoured draft, tirage refusé.

draft (*v.t.*), minuter ; minuer ; faire la minute de :
to draft a contract, a letter, minuter, faire la minute d', un contrat, une lettre.

drain *or* **drainage** (*n.*), drainage (*m.*); épuisement (*m.*) :
drain of money, drainage de capitaux.
drainage of gold by the foreigner, drainage de l'or par l'étranger.

drain (*v.t.*), drainer ; épuiser :
from the beginning of the war, gold was driven out of circulation and drained towards the cash in hand of the banks, dès le début de la guerre, l'or a été chassé de la circulation et drainé vers l'encaisse des banques.

draught (of a boat) (*n.*), tirant d'eau (d'un bateau) (*m.*).

aughtsman [draughtsmen *pl.*] (of an agreement, of a decree) (*n.*), rédacteur (d'un traité, d'un décret) (*m.*).

·aw (to delineate) (*v.t.*), tirer :
to draw a line on the paper, a double line under an addition, tirer une ligne sur le papier, une double barre sous une addition.

·aw (to haul) (*v.t.*), traîner ; remorquer :
locomotive which draws a heavy load, locomotive qui traîne (*ou* qui remorque) une lourde charge (*f.*).

·aw (to attract) (*v.t.*), attirer :
to draw attention to a fact, attirer l'attention sur un fait.

·aw (to derive) (*v.t.*), tirer ; retirer :
to draw a profit from a transaction, so much out of a property, tirer, retirer, du profit d'une opération, tant d'un bien.

·aw (to obtain means or receive supplies from a source) (*v.t. & i.*), prélever ; prendre ; mettre à contribution :
trader who draws from his cash, for his personal requirements, a sum of so much, commerçant qui prélève dans sa caisse, pour ses besoins personnels, une somme de tant (*m.*).
interest on the amounts drawn, intérêts sur les sommes prélevées (*m.pl.*).
to draw a commission on a transaction, prélever une commission sur une opération.
to draw on one's savings, prendre sur ses économies.
to draw on the reserves, mettre à contribution les réserves.
bank which has been drawn on by the Government for heavy amounts, banque qui a été mise à contribution par l'État dans des fortes proportions (*f.*).

lraw (to call for and take into possession) (*v.t.*), toucher :
to draw money, a salary, one's proportion of profits, toucher de l'argent, des appointements, son quantum de bénéfices.

lraw (samples) (*v.t.*), prélever :
sample drawn in presence of the declarant, échantillon prélevé en présence du déclarant (*m.*).

lraw (*v.t.*) *or* **to draw lots** *or* **to draw lots for,** tirer ; tirer au sort :
to draw numbers, tirer des numéros.
the bonds for redemption are then drawn, les bons destinés à être remboursés sont alors tirés au sort (*m.pl.*).

draw (to write out) (*v.t.*), tirer ; fournir ; disposer ; tracer ; souscrire :
to draw a bill, a cheque, tirer, souscrire, fournir, disposer, tracer, un effet, un chèque.
to draw a cheque on one's banker, tirer, fournir, disposer, tracer, un chèque sur son banquier.
to draw a cheque to order, to bearer, souscrire un billet à ordre, au porteur.

draw (to make out, as a cheque ; to make a draft) (*v.i.*), tirer ; fournir ; disposer ; faire traite.
to draw on someone, on one's banker, tirer, fournir, disposer, faire traite, sur quelqu'un, sur son banquier.

the drawer of a draft draws on the drawee, le tireur d'une traite dispose sur le tiré.
current accounts can only be drawn on by cheques, il n'est disposé sur les comptes de dépôts que par des chèques.
drawback. V. ci-après.

draw up *or* simply **draw** (to prepare in writing) (*v.t.*), dresser ; rédiger ; minuter ; minuer ; passer ; établir ; faire ; libeller :
to draw up a deed *or* to draw a deed, dresser, rédiger, minuter, passer, un acte.
to draw up (*or* to draw) the articles of a company, rédiger, dresser, établir, les statuts d'une société.
to draw up a balance sheet, dresser, établir, un bilan.
to draw up an account, établir un compte.
to draw a writ, libeller un exploit.

draw up a statement of account (to), faire le relevé d', relever, un compte.

drawback (Customs) (*n.*) (Abbrev. : **dbk**), drawback (*m.*) :
commodities admitted to the benefit of drawback *or* drawback goods, produits admis au bénéfice du drawback (*m.pl.*).
drawbacks on exportation of English products, drawbacks à l'exportation des produits anglais.

drawee (pers.) (*n.*), tiré (*m.*) ; payeur (*m.*) :
drawee of a bill of exchange, tiré, payeur, d'une lettre de change.

drawer (pers.) (*n.*), tireur, -euse ; souscripteur (*m.*) :
drawer of a bill of exchange, of a cheque, tireur, souscripteur, d'une lettre de change, d'un chèque.

drawer (furniture) (*n.*), tiroir (*m.*) :
lockup drawer, tiroir fermant à clef.

drawer (of a document cabinet) (*n.*), carton (*m.*).

drawing (an amount of money taken) (*n. usually pl.*), prélèvement (*m.*) ; levée (*f.*) ; levée de compte (*f.*) ; prise (*f.*) :
the personal drawings of the trader representing withdrawals of money effected during the year should be transferred to capital at balance sheet time, les prélèvements personnels du commerçant représentant des retraits de fonds opérés en cours d'exercice, doivent être, à l'inventaire, virés à capital (*ou* les levées personnelles . . . doivent être . . . virées à capital).
drawings on current account, prélèvements sur compte courant.
cash drawings, prises d'espèces.

drawing (samples) (*n.*), prélèvement (d'échantillons) (*m.*).

drawing (*n.*) *or* **drawing lots,** tirage (*m.*) ; tirage au sort (*m.*) :
bonds redeemable by periodical drawings, obligations amortissables par des tirages au sort périodiques (*f.pl.*).

drawing (of cheques, bills, or the like) (*n.*), tirage (*m.*) ; traçage (*m.*).

drawing *or* **drawing up** (*n.*), dressement (*m.*) ; rédaction (*f.*) ; établissement (*m.*) ; passation (*f.*) ; libellé (*m.*). V. exemples sous le verbe.

drawing up a statement of account, relevé (m.), relèvement (m.) d'un compte.

drawing account (current account) (Banking), compte de dépôt (m.); compte de dépôts (m.); compte de dépôts à vue (m.); compte de chèques (m.); compte-chèque (m.); compte d'espèces (m.); compte de dépôt d'espèces (m.).

drawings account or **drawing account** (account of amounts drawn out of the business by the trader), compte prélèvements (m.); compte de levées (m.).

driver (of a locomotive) (pers.) (n.), mécanicien (m.).

driver (of a motor vehicle) (n.), conducteur (m.), chauffeur (m.) (d'une voiture automobile) (m.).

driver's licence (motor vehicles), permis de conduire (m.).

droop (v.i.), fléchir:
after having drooped, prices rose at the end of the week, après avoir fléchi, les cours se sont relevés en fin de semaine.

drooping (n.), fléchissement (m.).

drop (n.), baisse (f.); chute (f.):
drop in wheat, in foreign stocks, in the rate of discount, baisse des blés, des fonds étrangers, du taux de l'intérêt.

drop (v.i.), baisser; reculer:
X. shares dropped from 1¼ to 1, l'action X. baisse de 1 1/4 à 1.
X. shares dropped a point, l'action X. recule d'un point.

drum (n.) (Abbrev.: **drm** [**drms** pl.]), tambour (m.); tonneau (m.); fût (m.).

dry (adj.), sec, sèche:
dry dock (opp. to wet dock), cale sèche (f.); bassin sec (m.); bassin à sec (m.); forme de radoub (f.); forme sèche (f.); forme (f.); bassin de radoub (m.); cale de radoub (f.).
dry goods (opp. to wet goods), marchandises sèches (f.pl.).
dry money (hard cash), argent sec (m.); argent liquide (m.); argent liquide et sec (m.).

dry (to be) (to have no more money), être à sec:
I am quite dry, je suis tout à fait à sec.

dry-dock (v.t.), faire entrer en cale sèche; faire entrer dans la forme:
to dry-dock a ship, faire entrer un navire en cale sèche.

dry-dock (v.i.), entrer en cale sèche; entrer dans la forme:
ship which dry-docks with the help of tugs, navire qui entre en cale sèche (ou qui entre dans la forme) avec l'assistance de remorqueurs (m.).

dry-docking or **dry-dockage** (n.), entrée en cale sèche (f.); entrée en forme (f.).

dud cheque (Slang), chèque sans provision (m.).

due (ascribable) (adj.), dû, due:
non performance due to force majeure, non exécution due à force majeure (f.).

due (regular) (adj.), dû, due; régulier, -ère:
translation in due form, traduction en due forme (f.).

due (payable forthwith) (adj.), dû, due; éch -e:
no freight is due on any increase in weig' resulting from sea damage, aucun fret n'e dû pour les augmentations de poids résulta d'avaries de mer (m.).
working out the interest due, décompte d intérêts dus (m.).
the payment of instalments of annuities du l'acquittement des termes échus d'annuit (m.).
all premiums due, owing by the insured or a outstanding premiums, due by the insure toutes primes échues, dues par l'assu (f.pl.).

not due, inexigible:
debt not due at the present time, det présentement inexigible (f.).

due (falling due) (adj.), échéable; échéant, -e bill due on such a date, billet échéable à tel date (m.).

due (n.), dû (m.):
to claim one's due, réclamer son dû.

what is not due, indu (m.):
to claim what is not due, réclamer l'indu.

due (duty) (n.) or **dues** (n.pl.), droit (m.); droi (m.pl.); taxe (f.); taxes (f.pl.):
pilotage dues, droits (ou taxes) de pilotage.

due date, échéance (f.); date de l'échéance (f.) bill of which the due date falls on a non busine day, billet dont l'échéance tombe un jou férié.
average due date, échéance moyenne; échéanc commune.
due date of coupon (or of interest). V. sou **date.**

due date (v.t.), coter:
to due date a bill, coter un effet.

due dating (of a bill), cote (f.).

dull (adj.), maussade; inactif, -ive; terne:
X. shares are dull at 1½, l'action X. es maussade (ou inactive) à 1 1/2.
again it is a very dull week that we have to pas in review, c'est encore une semaine bie terne que nous avons à passer en revue.

dullness or **dulness** (n.), maussaderie (f.); in activité (f.); marasme (m.); atonie (f.):
the general dullness of business, la maussaderi générale (ou le marasme général) des affaires

duly (in proper manner) (adv.), dûment; régulière ment:
bill of lading duly stamped, duly accomplished connaissement dûment timbré, dûment ac compli (m.).
lender duly secured, prêteur régulièremen nanti (m.).

duly (in proper time) (adv.), bien:
we have duly received your letter, nous avon bien reçu votre lettre.

duly authorized representative, fondé de pouvoi (m.); fondé de pouvoirs (m.):
the person who comes to take delivery of a lette addressed poste restante must prove that h is the addressee or his duly authorized repre sentative, la personne qui vient prendr livraison d'une lettre adressée poste restant

doit justifier qu'elle est le destinataire ou son fondé de pouvoirs.

immy [dummies pl.] (pers.) (n.), prête-nom (m.) :
dummy who masks a man of straw, prête-nom qui cache un homme de paille.

imping (n.), dumping (m.) :
dumping consists in establishing, for the same commodity, two prices or two scales of prices : one price relatively high on the home market ; lower prices, variable according to circumstances, on foreign markets, le dumping consiste en établissant, pour le même produit, deux prix ou deux échelles de prix : un prix relativement élevé sur le marché intérieur ; des prix plus bas, suivant les cas, sur les marchés extérieurs.

innage (n.), fardage (m.) ; grenier (m.) ; parquet de chargement (m.).

innage (v.t.), farder.

uplicate (n.), double (m.) ; duplicata (m.) :
duplicate of a deed, double d'un acte.
duplicate of exchange, duplicata de change.
duplicate of the consignment note or duplicate consignment note, duplicata de la lettre de voiture.
duplicate receipt, invoice, duplicata de quittance, de facture.
the letter book is a register formed exclusively of duplicates, le copie de lettres est un registre exclusivement constitué par des duplicata.
duplicate enclosure check, étiquette « annexe » (f.) ; vignette « pièces jointes » (f.).
in duplicate, en double ; en double exemplaire ; double ; en duplicata ; par duplicata :
to draw up a deed in duplicate, dresser un acte en double (ou en double exemplaire) (ou en ou par duplicata).
done in duplicate at London, the 1st June 19—, fait double (ou fait en double) à Londres, le 1er juin 19—.

uplicate (v.t.), faire le double de :
to duplicate a deed, faire le double d'un acte.

uplicate (v.i.), faire double emploi :
commission which duplicates with another commission already charged, commission qui fait double emploi avec une autre commission déjà prélevée (f.).

uplication (n.), double emploi (m.) :
to ascertain that there is neither omission nor duplication in the entering up of the items, s'assurer qu'il n'y a ni omission ni double emploi dans l'enregistrement des articles.

uplicator (n.) or **duplicating machine,** duplicateur (m.).

uration (n.), durée (f.) :
duration of a lease, durée d'un bail.

dutiable (adj.), passible de droits ; sujet (-ette) à des droits ; payant des droits de douane ; tarifé, -e ; taxé, -e :
dutiable goods, marchandises passibles de droits (f.pl.) ; marchandises sujettes à des droits (f.pl.) ; marchandises payant des droits de douane (f.pl.) ; marchandise tarifée (f.) ; marchandises taxées (f.pl.).
all goods imported or exported, whether dutiable or free, toutes les marchandises importées ou exportées, qu'elles soient sujettes à des droits ou qu'elles soient exemptes.

duty [duties pl.] (obligation) (n.), devoir (m.) ; fonction (f.) ; fonctions (f.pl.) ; office (m.) :
the duties of neutrals in case of war, les devoirs des neutres en cas de guerre.
to entrust the duties of secretary to the board to one of the managers, confier les fonctions du secrétaire du conseil à l'un des directeurs.

duty (due ; tax) (n.), droit (m) ; droits (m.pl.) ; taxe (f.) ; impôt (m.) ; redevance (f.) :
registration duty, droit d'enregistrement.
customs duties, droits de douane.
transfer duty, droit de transmission ; taxe de transmission ; impôt de transmission ; droit de transfert ; droits de mutation. See note under droit de transmission.
mineral rights duty, redevance des mines.

duty-free (adj.) (opp. to dutiable), franc (franche) de tout droit ; exempt (-e) de droits ; exempt, -e ; libre à l'entrée :
duty-free goods, marchandise franche de tout droit (f.) ; marchandises franches de tout droit (f.pl.) ; marchandises exemptes de droits (f.pl.) ; marchandise exempte (f.) ; marchandises libres à l'entrée (f.pl.).

duty free (adv.), en franchise de droits ; en franchise :
goods admissible duty free on proof of origin, marchandises admissibles en franchise de droits sur justification d'origine (f.pl.).

duty-paid (Customs) (adj.), acquitté, -e :
duty-paid goods, marchandises acquittées (f.pl.).

duty paid (opp. to in bond) (adv.), à l'acquitté ; libre des droits de douane :
goods sold duty paid, marchandises vendues à l'acquitté (f.pl.) ; marchandise vendue libre des droits de douane (f.).
duty-paid sale, vente à l'acquitté (f.) ; vente à l'A. (f.).
treble the duty-paid value (customs fine), triple de la valeur à l'acquitté (m.).

duty-paid entry, déclaration d'acquittement de droits (f.) ; déclaration pour l'acquittement des droits (f.).

dwindling (of assets) (n.), dépérissement (de capital) (m.).

E

each (every) (*adj.*), chaque ; l'un, l'une ; la pièce :
stamps of — lbs each, pilons de — livres poids chaque.
prices of spare tools : punches, each, £— ;
dies, each, £—, prix des outils de rechange :
poinçons, l'un £— ; matrices, l'une, £—.
hammers, each, —s., marteaux, la pièce, — schellings.
each (for) (per portion), par tranche de :
and so on, rising by one twentyfifth for each £100 up to £500, et ainsi de suite, en augmentant d'un vingt-cinquième par tranche de 100£ jusqu'à 500£.
Cf. **for every . . . or fraction of . . .,** sous **fraction.**
earmark (*v.t.*), affecter :
to earmark a certain amount for payment of the interest on the capital, affecter une certaine somme au paiement de l'intérêt du capital.
earmarking (*n.*), affectation (*f.*).
earn (*v.t.*), gagner ; acquérir :
a penny saved is a penny earned, un sou épargné est un sou gagné.
earned (*adj. or p.p.*), acquis, -e ; non restituable ; non remboursable ; gagné, -e :
the profit earned on a sale, le bénéfice acquis sur une vente.
the freight, whether paid in advance or payable at destination, is always deemed earned or due, whether the ship or the goods arrive safely or are lost on the voyage, le fret, qu'il ait été payé d'avance ou soit payable à destination, est toujours censé acquis ou dû, que le navire ou la marchandise arrive à bon port ou se perde pendant le voyage.
earnest (*n.*) *or* **earnest money,** arrhes (*f.pl.*) :
promise of sale made with earnest (*or* with earnest money), promesse de vente faite avec des arrhes (*f.*).
earning (act or process of earning) (*n.*), acquisition (*f.*) :
earning of freight, acquisition du fret.
earning (that which is earned) (*n. commonly used in plural*), gain (*m.*).
earthquake clause (Insce), clause relative aux tremblements de terre (*f.*).
ease (Stock Exch.) (*v.i.*), mollir :
X. shares eased, the ordinaries to 1½ and the preference to 1¼, les actions X. ont molli, les ordinaires à 1 1/2 et les privilégiées à 1 1/4.
ease off (*v.i.*), se détendre. V. exemple sous **stiffen** (*v.i.*).
easiness *or* **ease** (Fin.) (*n.*), facilité (*f.*) ; aisance (*f.*) :
recovery stimulated by the easiness of money, reprise stimulée par la facilité de l'argent (*f.*).
the approach of the end of the month exerted no restraining influence on the monetary easiness of the Paris market, l'approche du fin de mois n'exerçait aucune influence sur l'aisance monétaire du marché de Paris (*f.*).
easiness *or* **ease** (Stock Exch.) (*n.*), mollesse (*f.*).

easing off (*n.*), détente (*f.*) :
easing off of contangoes, détente des reports.
East European time *or* **Eastern European time** **East Europe time** (Abbrev. : **E.E.T.**), heu de l'Europe Orientale (*f.*) (2 p.m. [14 heures in relation to **West European time,** q.v.).
easy (Fin.) (*adj.*) (opp. to *tight*), facile :
the London money market is still very eas le marché monétaire de Londres est toujou très facile.
discount is easy when the market rate is mu lower than the bank rate of discoun l'escompte est facile lorsque le taux pri est bien plus faible que le taux officiel l'escompte (*m.*). Cf. **tight** & **nominal.**
easy (Stock Exch.) (*adj.*), mou, mol (*deva une voyelle*), molle :
X. shares are easy at 1¼, l'action X. est mo à 1 1/4.
eat *or* **eat up** (*used metaphorically*) (*v.t.*), mange spendthrift who eats up the capital and t income, dissipateur qui mange le fonds le revenu (*m.*).
écart (difference between the prices for firm stoc and option stock) (Stock Exch.) (*n.*), éca (*m.*) ; écart de prime (*m.*).
economic (relating to the science of economic (*adj.*), économique :
the rate of exchange depends, to a large exten on the economic situation of the countr le cours du change dépend, dans une lar; mesure, de la situation économique du pays
economical *or* **economic** (careful and providen saving) (*adj.*), économe ; économique.
economically (*adv.*), économiquement.
economics (*n.*) *or* **political economy,** économ (*f.*) ; économie politique (*f.*).
economist (pers.) (*n.*), économiste (*m.*).
economize (*v.t.*), économiser ; ménager :
to economize one's income, the use of coi économiser, ménager, ses revenus, l'usa; du numéraire.
economy [economies *pl.*] (*n.*), économie (*f.*).
editor (of a newspaper) (pers.) (*n.*), rédacte (d'un journal) (*m.*).
effect (*v.t.*), effectuer ; faire ; opérer :
to effect a payment, effectuer, faire, opére un paiement.
to effect a compromise, effectuer, faire, u compromis.
to be effected, être effectué, -e, fait, -e, opér -e ; s'effectuer ; se faire ; s'opérer :
withdrawals of money are effected by cheque les retraits de fonds s'oppèrent par chèque (*m.pl.*).
effective (*adj.*), effectif, -e ; réel, -elle :
effective money *or* simply **effective** (n (distinguished from *paper money*), monna effective (*f.*) ; monnaie réelle (*f.*) ; valeu effectives (*f.pl.*).
effectively (*adv.*), effectivement ; réellement.
effects (*n.pl.*), effets (*m.pl.*) ; 'hardes (*f.pl.*) :

movable effects, effets mobiliers.

personal effects of passengers, effets personnels des voyageurs.

effects of seamen (clothing, and the like), effets, hardes, des gens de mer.

flux (*n.*) (opp. to *influx*), sortie (*f.*) :

an efflux of gold, or at least of capital, which might bring about the impoverishment of the country, une sortie d'or, ou tout au moins de capitaux, qui pourrait entraîner l'appauvrissement du pays.

ght-hour working day, journée de travail de huit heures (*f.*).

astic band, bande en caoutchouc (*f.*) ; bracelet en caoutchouc (*m.*) ; caoutchouc (*m.*).

ect (*v.t.*), élire ; nommer :

to elect a director, élire un administrateur.

to elect domicile with one's solicitor, élire domicile chez son solicitor.

to be elected chairman of a meeting *or* to be elected to the presidency of a meeting, être nommé (-e) à la présidence d'une assemblée.

lection (*n.*), élection (*f.*) ; nomination (*f.*).

lectricity shares, valeurs d'électricité (*f.pl.*).

lectrification (*n.*), électrification (*f.*) :

electrification of a railway, électrification d'un chemin de fer.

lectrify (*v.t.*), électrifier.

ligibility (*n.*), éligibilité (*f.*).

ligible (*adj.*), éligible.

liminate (*v.t.*), éliminer :

to eliminate errors, éliminer des erreurs.

limination (*n.*), élimination (*f.*).

lucidate (*v.t.*), mettre au net :

to elucidate the position of a bankrupt, mettre au net la situation d'un failli.

mbargo [embargoes *pl.*] (*n.*), embargo (*m.*) :

to raise the embargo on a ship, lever l'embargo sur un navire.

mbargo (*v.t.*), mettre l'embargo sur :

to embargo a ship, mettre l'embargo sur un navire.

mbark (*v.t.*), embarquer.

to be embarked, être embarqué, -e ; s'embarquer :

goods in bulk are generally embarked by means of special apparatus, la marchandise en vrac s'embarque généralement au moyen d'appareils spéciaux.

mbark (*v.i.*), s'embarquer.

mbarking *or* **embarkation** *or* **embarcation** (*n.*), embarquement (*m.*) :

embarking passengers, embarquement de passagers.

mbassy [embassies *pl.*] (*n.*), ambassade (*f.*).

mbezzle (*v.t.*), détourner ; distraire :

to embezzle money, funds, détourner, distraire, de l'argent, des fonds.

mbezzlement (*n.*), détournement (*m.*) ; distraction (*f.*) ; divertissement (*m.*) ; malversation (*f.*).

mbossed stamp, timbre sec (*m.*) ; timbre fixe (*m.*) ; timbre imprimé (*m.*).

mbossing press, timbre sec (*m.*).

migrant (pers.) (*n.*), émigrant, -e.

migrant ship, navire à émigrants (*m.*).

emigrant traffic, trafic des émigrants (*m.*).

emigrate (*v.i.*), émigrer.

emigration (*n.*), émigration (*f.*).

emigration agent, agent d'émigration (*m.*).

emigration officer, commissaire d'émigration (*m.*).

emolument (*n.*), émolument (*m.*) :

salaries and other emoluments, traitements et autres émoluments (*m.pl.*).

empire (*n.*), empire (*m.*) :

oversea empire, empire d'outre-mer.

employ (*n.*), emploi (*m.*).

employ (to turn to account ; to put ; to place) (*v.t.*), employer ; faire valoir ; mettre ; placer :

to employ one's money, employer, faire valoir, son argent.

to employ money on contango, employer, mettre, placer, des capitaux en report.

employ (to engage) (*v.t.*), employer :

to employ a clerk, employer un commis.

employ (to occupy) (*v.t.*), consacrer :

vessels employed in trade, bâtiments (de mer) consacrés au commerce (*m.pl.*).

employé (pers.) (*n.*), employé (*m.*).

employee (pers.) (*n.*), employé, -e.

employer (pers.) (*n.*), patron, -onne ; employeur, -euse.

employers and employed, employeurs et employés ; le patronat et le salariat.

employer's return (salary tax), déclaration patronale (*f.*).

employer's share (workmen's pensions, or the like), cotisation patronale (*f.*).

employers' liability, responsabilité des patrons (*f.*) ; responsabilité patronale (*f.*).

employers' liability insurance *or* **employers' indemnity insurance,** assurance contre les accidents de travail (*f.*) ; assurance accidents du travail (*f.*).

employment (use) (*n.*), emploi (*m.*) :

employment of a sum of money, of capital in production, emploi d'une somme d'argent, des capitaux dans la production.

employment (occupation) (*n.*), emploi (*m.*) ; place (*f.*) ; position (*f.*) ; poste (*m.*) :

to seek employment, chercher de l'emploi.

employment agency *or* **employment bureau,** agence de placement (*f.*) ; bureau de placement (*m.*).

empower (*v.t.*), investir du pouvoir :

board empowered to contract loans, conseil d'administration investi du pouvoir de contracter des emprunts (*m.*).

empty (Abbrev. : **emty** *or* **ety**) (*adj.*), vide :

returned empty milk churns, pots à lait vides en retour (*m.pl.*).

empty (*adj.*) *or* **when empty,** à vide :

ship with the prospect of returning empty, navire avec la perspective de retourner à vide (*m.*).

empty journey *or* journey empty *or* journey when empty (of a railway wagon) (opp. to *loaded journey*), parcours à vide (*m.*).

empty [empties *pl.*] (empty wagon, empty case, etc.) (*n.*), vide (*m.*) :

returned empty, vide en retour.

empty (*v.t.*), vider:
to empty one's pockets, vider ses poches.
en bloc, en bloc:
transactions entered en bloc at the end of the day, opérations inscrites en bloc à la fin de la journée (*f.pl.*).
encash (*v.t.*), encaisser:
to encash a cheque, encaisser un chèque.
encashable (*adj.*), encaissable.
encashment (*n.*), encaissement (*m.*).
enclosure (*n.*) (Abbrev.: **encl.**), annexe (*f.*); pièce annexe (*f.*); pièce jointe (*f.*):
any enclosure should be pinned to the letter, chaque annexe doit être épinglée à la lettre.
" enclosure " label, étiquette « annexe » (*f.*); vignette « pièces jointes » (*f.*).
encroach on *or* **upon** (*v.i.*), entamer; anticiper sur:
to encroach upon one's capital, entamer son capital.
to encroach on one's income, anticiper sur ses revenus.
encumber (*v.t.*), grever:
to encumber a property with a mortgage, grever d'une hypothèque une propriété.
encumbrance (*n.*), charge (*f.*).
end (*n.*), fin (*f.*); bout (*m.*); terme (*m.*):
end of a risk (Insce), fin d'un risque.
end of the contract of carriage, fin du contrat de transport.
end of the month, of the year, fin, bout, du mois, de l'année.
end this *or* end this account *or* end current account (Stock Exch.), fin courant; fin.
end next *or* end next account (Stock Exch.), fin prochain.
end (*month*) *or* end (*month*) account (Stock Exch.) (opp. to *mid*), fin (*mois*):
buy so many shares for end April (*or* for end April account), achetez tant d'actions pour fin avril.
See note under **mid** (*month*) *or* **mid** (*month*) **account.**
the end of an action, le terme d'un procès.
at the end of, en fin de; fin; à bout de:
the cash balance at the end of the year, l'encaisse en fin d'année (*f.*).
the expenses unpaid at the end of the financial year, les dépenses non payées en fin d'exercice (*f.pl.*).
payment at the end of the present month, at the end of next month, paiement fin courant, fin prochain (*m.*).
to be at the end of one's resources, être à bout de ses ressources.
end (*v.i.*), finir; prendre fin; clôturer:
land carriage ends by the delivery of the goods to the consignee, le transport terrestre prend fin par la livraison de la marchandise au destinataire.
the year (*or* the financial year) ending 31st December, l'exercice prenant fin (*ou* clôturant) le 31 décembre (*m.*).
the year (*or* the financial year) ended 31st December, l'exercice ayant pris fin (*ou* l'exercice clôturé *ou* clos) le 31 décembre (*m.*).

end a string (to) (Produce Exch.), arrêter u filière.
end year rebate, ristourne de fin d'année (*f.*).
endeavour (*v.i.*), s'efforcer; tâcher; essaye chercher; travailler:
to endeavour to recover an amount, travaill au recouvrement d'une somme.
endorsable (*adj.*), endossable:
endorsable cheque, chèque endossable (*m.*).
endorse (*v.t.*), endosser:
to endorse a bill of exchange, endosser u lettre de change.
in general, it is the custom to endorse the poli in blank, en général, il est d'usage d'endoss la police en blanc.
endorse back (*v.t.*), contre-passer:
to endorse back a bill of exchange, contr passer une lettre de change.
endorse over (*v.t.*), passer; transmettre par vo d'endossement:
to endorse over a bill of exchange to the ord of a third party, passer, transmettre p voie d'endossement, une lettre de change l'ordre d'un tiers.
endorsee (pers.) (*n.*), endossataire (*m. ou f.*).
endorsement (*n.*), endossement (*m.*); endos (*m.*
endorsement of a bill of exchange, of a bill lading, endossement d'un effet de commerc d'un connaissement.
blank endorsement *or* endorsement in blan endossement en blanc; endos en blanc.
endorsement without recourse, endossement forfait.
endorsement (Insce) (*n.*), avenant (*m.*):
changes occurring in the risk necessarily for the subject of endorsements or of new policie failing which the insured may forfeit h rights, les changements survenus dans risque font obligatoirement l'objet d'avenan ou de nouvelles polices, faute de quoi l'assu peut être déchu de ses droits.
endorsement of interest declared (Floatin policy insurance), avenant d'aliment (*m.*).
endorsement of interest declared (Insuranc steamer or steamers to be declared Floating policy insurance), avenant d'appl cation (*m.*); avenant de déclaration (*m.*).
endorser (pers.) (*n.*), endosseur (*m.*).
endorsing stamp, timbre humide (*m.*).
endow (*v.t.*), doter:
powerful concerns endowed with ample financi means, entreprises puissantes dotées d larges moyens de trésorerie (*f.pl.*).
endowment (*n.*), dotation (*f.*).
endowment insurance (distinguished from *who life insurance*), assurance en cas de vi (*f.*); assurance à capital différé (*f.*); assuranc à rente différée (*f.*).
enemy [**enemies** *pl.*] (*n.*), ennemi, -e:
King's enemies (*expression used in Englis bills of lading*), ennemis du pays (*expressio used in French bills of lading*).
enemy flag (opp. to *friendly flag*), pavillo ennemi (*m.*).
enemy port, port ennemi (*m.*).
enemy risk, risque d'ennemis (*m.*).

emy ship, navire ennemi (*m*.).

gage (*v.t.*), engager; retenir:
to engage an employee, engager un employé.
to engage capital in a business, engager du capital dans une entreprise.
to engage one's word, engager sa parole.
to engage a room in an hotel, retenir une chambre dans un hôtel.

gage (*v.i.*), s'engager; se mettre:
to engage in business, s'engager, se mettre, dans les affaires.

gaged tone (Teleph.), signal pas libre (*m*.).

gagement (*n*.), engagement (*m*.):
to carry out one's engagements, faire honneur à ses engagements.

gine (railway engine) (*n*.), machine (*f*.); locomotive (*f*.).

gine driver, mécanicien conducteur de locomotive (*m*.).

gine room log, journal de la machine (*m*.).

gine room space (in a ship), emplacement des machines (*m*.).

gineer (of a ship) (pers.) (*n*.), mécanicien (d'un navire) (*m*.).

gineer a rise (to) (Stock Exch.), provoquer une hausse.

gineering shares, valeurs de constructions mécaniques (*f.pl.*).

grossment (Law) (*n*.), grosse (*f*.).

hance in price (to), augmenter de prix; renchérir; enchérir.

hance the price of (to), augmenter le prix de; renchérir; enchérir:
to enhance the price of goods, augmenter le prix, renchérir, enchérir, des marchandises.

hancement of price, augmentation de prix (*f*.); renchérissement (*m*.); enchérissement (*m*.).

joy (Law) (*v.t.*), jouir de:
to enjoy a right, jouir d'un droit.

joyment (Law) (*n*.), jouissance (*f*.):
to have the ownership and enjoyment of properties and rights, avoir la propriété et la jouissance des biens et droits.

quire (*v.t.*), demander.

quire (*v.i.*), se renseigner; prendre des renseignements; prendre des informations; prendre connaissance:
to enquire into someone's position, se renseigner sur, prendre des renseignements sur, prendre des informations sur, prendre connaissance de, la situation de quelqu'un.

quire into (to) (officially or publicly), enquêter sur:
to enquire into the present position of an industry, enquêter sur la position actuelle d'une industrie.

quired for (to be), être discuté, -e; se discuter:
tin shares were more, were a little more, enquired for this week *or* there were more, a few more, enquiries for tin shares this week, les valeurs d'étain sont plus discutées, un peu plus discutées, cette semaine (*f.pl.*).

quiry [enquiries *pl.*] (*n*.), enquête (*f*.); demande (*f*.); renseignements (*m.pl.*); renseignement (*m*.); informations (*f.pl.*); information (*f*.):

wreck followed by an enquiry, naufrage suivi d'une enquête (*m*.).
enquiry for price (*or* for quotation), demande de prix.
there are still numerous enquiries for freight to Algeria, il y a encore de nombreuses demandes de fret sur l'Algérie.
to make enquiries about someone, prendre des renseignements (*ou* des informations) sur quelqu'un.

enquiry agency, agence de renseignements (*f*.).

enquiry form, bulletin de renseignements (*m*.).

enquiry office, bureau de renseignements (*m*.).

enquiry operator (Teleph.), opératrice des renseignements (*f*.).

enrich (*v.t.*), enrichir.

enrichment (*n*.), enrichissement (*m*.).

ensuing account *or* **ensuing settlement** (Stock Exch.), liquidation suivante (*f*.).

ensure (*v.t.*), assurer:
to ensure the safety of a marine adventure, assurer le salut d'une expédition maritime.

enter (to pass into the interior of) (*v.t.*), entrer dans:
to enter a port, a roadstead, a river, entrer dans un port, dans une rade, dans un fleuve.

enter *or* **enter up** (*v.t.*), inscrire; faire inscrire; enregistrer; immatriculer; comptabiliser; porter; passer; passer écriture de; faire écriture de; employer:
to enter a name on a list, an item in the ledger, an item in current account, something in a book, inscrire, enregistrer, porter, passer, faire (*ou* passer) écriture d' (de), un nom sur une liste, un article au grand livre, un article en compte courant, quelque chose sur un livre.
to enter a ship at the marine registry office, faire inscrire un navire au bureau de l'inscription maritime.
to enter an amount in the receipts, in the expenditure, employer une somme en recette, en dépense.
the transactions entered (*or* entered up) from day to day in the journal, les opérations inscrites (*ou* enregistrées) (*ou* comptabilisées) au jour le jour sur le (*ou* au) journal (*f.pl.*).

enter (goods) (Customs) (*v.t.*), déclarer:
to enter goods for home use (*or* for home consumption), transit, warehousing, transhipment, reexport, or temporary admission, for payment of duty, déclarer des marchandises pour la consommation, le transit, l'entrepôt, le transbordement, la réexportation, ou l'admission temporaire, pour l'acquittement des droits.

enter a memorandum of satisfaction of mortgage on the register (to) (memorandum made by the registrar), radier une inscription hypothécaire par une mention sur le registre.

enter an action against someone (to), intenter une action à (*ou* contre) quelqu'un.

enter into (to), faire; passer; contracter; souscrire; intervenir dans:
to enter into a bargain, faire, passer, un marché.

to enter into a lease, passer, contracter, un bail.

to enter into a bond (Customs), souscrire une soumission cautionnée.

to enter into an agreement (*or* a contract), passer, intervenir dans, un contrat (*ou* un traité) (*ou* un marché):

director who has entered into contracts with the company, administrateur qui a passé des marchés avec la société (*m.*).

agreement entered into between the Company and Mr X., traité intervenu entre la Société et M. X. (*m.*).

enter inwards (to) (ship) (Customs), faire l'entrée en douane:

to enter a ship inwards, faire l'entrée en douane d'un navire.

enter upon one's duties (to), entrer en fonction.

entering *or* **entrance** *or* **entry** (passing into the interior of) (*n.*), entrée (*f.*):

on entering or leaving ports, à l'entrée ou à la sortie des ports.

entrance (*or* entry) of a ship into a port, entrée d'un navire dans un port.

entering *or* **entering up** (*n.*), inscription (*f.*); enregistrement (*m.*); immatriculation (*f.*); comptabilisation (*f.*); passation (*f.*):

entering the journal folio from which the item is posted, inscription du folio du journal d'après lequel l'article est rapporté.

enterprise (*n.*), entreprise (*f.*).

entertain a proposal (to), accueillir favorablement une proposition.

entrance fee (to an association), cotisation d'admission (*f.*); droit d'entrée (*m.*).

entrust (*v.t.*), confier; remettre:

to entrust the handling of large sums of money to someone, one's goods to a transport agent, confier à quelqu'un le maniement de sommes importantes, sa marchandise à un commissionnaire de transports.

I have entrusted my money to him, je lui ai remis mes fonds.

to be entrusted with, avoir charge de:

to be entrusted with the selling of a property, avoir charge de vendre une propriété.

entry [**entries** *pl.*] (entering up) (*n.*), inscription (*f.*); enregistrement (*m.*); immatriculation (*f.*); passation (*f.*):

entry of subscribers in directory, inscription des abonnés à l'annuaire.

bill handed to the cashier for entry in the bills payable book, effet transmis au caissier pour l'inscription sur le livre d'effets à payer (*m.*).

every ship must belong to a port under the form of an entry in a special register kept at the marine registry office, tout navire doit être attaché à un port sous la forme d'une immatriculation sur un registre spécial tenu au bureau de l'inscription maritime.

entry (method of bookkeeping) (*n.*), inscription (*f.*); partie (*f.*). *V. exemples sous* double entry *et* single entry.

entry (item) (Bkkpg) (*n.*), article (*m.*); écriture (*f.*):

the entries made in the journal, les articl[es] inscrits sur le journal; les écritures faite[s] sur le journal.

entry (Customs) (*n.*), déclaration (*f.*); déclaratio[n] de (*ou* en) détail (*f.*):

a preliminary entry is required in every custom[s] operation, toute opération de douan[e] comporte une déclaration préalable.

to pass a customs entry of a ship, of good[s] faire une déclaration en douane d'un navir[e] de marchandises.

entry inwards, déclaration d'entrée; entré[e] (*f.*); entrée en douane (*f.*).

entry for duty-free goods, déclaration pou[r] produits exempts de droits.

entry for home use, déclaration de conson[m]mation; déclaration de mise en co[n]sommation.

entry for warehousing, déclaration d'entrepôt déclaration d'entrée en entrepôt; déclaratio[n] de mise en entrepôt.

entry outwards, déclaration de sortie.

entry of satisfaction of mortgage, radiatio[n] d'inscription hypothécaire (*f.*); radiatio[n] d'hypothèque (*f.*).

envelope (*n.*), enveloppe (*f.*); pli (*m.*):

envelope with coloured borders, enveloppe bords coloriés.

envelope with transparent panel, enveloppe panneau transparent.

a letter in a sealed envelope, une lettre sou[s] pli cacheté.

envelope addressing agency, bureau d'adresse[s] (*m.*); bureau d'écritures (*m.*).

époque (base date) (accounts current wit[h] interest) (*n.*), époque (*f.*).

époque method, méthode rétrograde (*f.*); métho[de] indirecte (*f.*).

equal (*adj.*), égal, -e, -aux:

columns showing equal totals, colonne[s] présentant des totaux égaux (*f.pl.*).

equal (*v.t.*), égaler:

ten minus four equals six (*Abbrev.*: 10 − 4 = 6), dix moins quatre égale six. (*Abrév.* 10 − 4 = 6).

equality [**equalities** *pl.*] (*n.*), égalité (*f.*):

equality of two numbers, of treatment, égalit[é] de deux nombres, de traitement.

equality (*n.*) *or* **equality of rank** (Law), concou[rs] (*m.*); concurrence (*f.*):

equality of rights, concours de privilèges.

equality (*or* equality of rank) between creditor[s] concours entre créanciers.

equality of votes *or* **equal voting,** partage de[s] voix (*m.*); partage (*m.*); égalité de voi[x] (*f.*):

in case of equality of votes *or* if the voting [is] equal, en cas de partage des voix; en ca[s] de partage.

equality of votes for a resolution, égalité d[e] voix pour une proposition.

equalization (*n.*), égalisation (*f.*).

equalization (of dividend) (*n.*), régularisatio[n] (*f.*):

reserve for equalization of dividend, réserv[e] pour régularisation de dividende (*f.*).

ualize (*v.t.*), égaliser :
to equalize the totals, égaliser les totaux.
ually (*adv.*), également.
uilibrium (*n.*), équilibre (*m.*) :
to wait until equilibrium between production and consumption is restored by the normal action of the law of supply and demand, attendre que l'équilibre entre la production et la consommation se rétablisse par le jeu normal de la loi de l'offre et de la demande.
uip (*v.t.*), équiper ; armer :
to equip a ship, équiper un navire.
boats equipped for the coasting trade, equipped for fishing, bateaux armés au cabotage, armés pour la pêche (*m.pl.*).
uipment (*n.*), équipement (*m.*) ; armement (*m.*) :
character giving the qualities of the hull and of the equipment, cote donnant les qualités de la coque et de l'armement (*f.*).
uitable (*adj.*), équitable :
equitable division, partage équitable (*m.*).
uivalent (*n.*), équivalent (*m.*) ; parité (*f.*) :
delivered X. (railway) station or equivalent, rendu gare (de chemin de fer) X. ou parité.
quivalent (to be), équivaloir :
distribution which is equivalent to 5%, partage qui équivaut à 5 0/0 (*m.*).
rase (*v.t.*), raturer ; gratter ; effacer.
raser (knife eraser) (*n.*), grattoir (*m.*).
raser (indiarubber) (*n.*), gomme à effacer (*f.*) ; gomme (*f.*) :
pencil eraser, gomme pour le crayon ; gomme à crayon.
rasure (*n.*), rature (*f.*) ; grattage (*m.*) :
register well kept, without erasures or corrections (*or* alterations), registre bien tenu, sans ratures ni surcharges (*m.*).
rroneous (*adj.*), erroné, -e ; faux, fausse :
erroneous calculation, calcul erroné (*m.*) ; calcul faux (*m.*).
rroneously (*adv.*), erronément ; faussement.
rror (*n.*), erreur (*f.*) ; faute (*f.*) ; mécompte (*m.*) :
error of (*or* in) addition, of (*or* in) calculation, erreur d'addition, de calcul.
error of (*or* in) navigation, erreur de (*ou* dans la) navigation.
error of judgment, erreur de jugement.
errors in posting (Bkkpg), erreurs de report.
errors and omissions excepted (*Abbrev. :* E. & O.E.), sauf erreur ou omission.
entry cancelled in error, écriture annulée par erreur (*f.*).
scape (*v.t.*) *or* **escape from**, échapper à :
to escape (*or* escape from) the pursuit of the enemy or pirates, échapper à la poursuite de l'ennemi ou des pirates.
to escape payment of a sum, échapper au paiement d', se dispenser de payer, une somme.
sq. (*abbrev. of* Esquire) (form of epistolary address written after the surname) [*pl.* **Messrs** (written before the surname)], M. ; M^r [MM. *ou* M^rs *pl.*] :
X. Esq., M. X.
ssence (substance) (*n.*), essence (*f.*) :

the delivery of the goods to the consignee is of the essence of the contract of carriage, la délivrance de la marchandise au destinataire est de l'essence du contrat de transport.
establish (*v.t.*), établir ; créer ; fonder ; asseoir :
to establish an industry, établir, créer, une industrie.
insurance company established in London in 1720, compagnie d'assurance fondée à Londres en 1720 (*f.*).
to establish a telephone call, établir une communication téléphonique.
to establish public credit, asseoir le crédit public.
establishment (act of founding) (*n.*), établissement (*m.*) ; création (*f.*) ; fondation (*f.*).
establishment (institution) (*n.*), établissement (*m.*) :
a banking establishment, un établissement de banque.
establishment (staff) (*n.*), service (*m.*) :
indoor establishment, service sédentaire.
establishment charges (standing expenses), frais généraux (*m.pl.*) ; dépenses de maison (*f.pl.*).
establishment charges (Costing) (opp. to *overhead*, or *on-cost*, or *fixed*, *charges*, or *indirect charges* or *expenses*), frais spéciaux (*m.pl.*) ; frais directs (*m.pl.*) ; frais proportionnels (*m.pl.*) ; dépenses directes (*ou* proportionnelles) (*f.pl.*).
estate (Law) (*n.*), bien (*m.*) ; biens (*m.pl.*) ; effets (*m.pl.*) ; propriété (*f.*) ; propriétés (*f.pl.*) :
real estate, biens immeubles ; effets immobiliers ; propriétés immobilières.
estimate (*n.*), estimation (*f.*) ; appréciation (*f.*) ; évaluation (*f.*) ; prisée (*f.*) :
estimate of the losses, évaluation des pertes.
details influencing the estimate of the risk (Insce), détails influant sur l'appréciation du risque (*m.pl.*).
estimate (*v.t.*), estimer ; apprécier ; faire l'appréciation de ; évaluer ; faire l'évaluation de ; priser.
estimated (*adj.*), estimatif, -ive :
estimated charges, imputations estimatives (*f.pl.*).
estuary [**estuaries** *pl.*] (*n.*), estuaire (*m.*) :
the estuary of the Thames *or* the Thames estuary, l'estuaire de la Tamise.
European system (Post, etc.) (distinguished from *extra-European system*), régime européen (*m.*).
evade (*v.t.*), esquiver :
to evade one's creditors, esquiver ses créanciers.
evasion of tax, évasion d'impôt (*f.*).
eve (*n.*), veille (*f.*) :
speculator who has bought on the eve of the fall, sold on the eve of the rise, spéculateur qui a acheté la veille de la baisse, vendu la veille de la hausse (*m.*).
even (*adj.*), pair, -e :
even number, nombre pair (*m.*).
even money, compte rond (*m.*) :
one hundred and fifty thousand three hundred pounds, is a hundred and fifty thousand

pounds even money, cent cinquante mille trois cents livres, c'est cent cinquante mille livres, compte rond.

even (said of contangoes) (Stock Exch.) (*adj.*), au pair:

the contango (*or* the contango rate) is even, le report (*ou* le taux du report) est au pair. V. aussi exemple sous **contango** *or* **contango rate.**

eventual (*adj.*), éventuel, -elle:

securities of a doubtful or eventual value, titres d'une valeur douteuse ou éventuelle (*m.pl.*).

eventuality [eventualities *pl.*] (*n.*), éventualité (*f.*).

eventually (*adv.*), éventuellement.

evidence (*n.*), évidence (*f.*); preuve (*f.*); titre (*m.*):

whereas it appears from the evidence that . . ., attendu qu'il résulte à l'évidence que . . .

the written agreement which serves as evidence of the contract of insurance is called policy of insurance, l'écrit qui sert de preuve au contrat d'assurance est appelé police d'assurance (*m.*).

in the absence of evidence to the contrary, jusqu'à preuve contraire.

evidence of indebtedness, titre de créance.

to be evidence, faire foi:

the minutes are evidence until the contrary is proved, le procès-verbal fait foi jusqu'à preuve contraire.

evidence (*v.t.*), constater:

contract of affreightment evidenced by a bill of lading, contrat d'affrètement constaté par un connaissement (*m.*).

ex allotment (of new shares), ex-répartition.

ex bond (opp. to *in bond*), à l'acquitté; à l'A.:

goods sold ex bond, marchandises vendues à l'acquitté (*f.pl.*).

sale ex bond, vente à l'acquitté (*f.*); vente à l'A. (*f.*).

ex bonus, ex-bonus; ex-répartition bonus; ex-répartition.

ex coupon (opp. to *with coupon* or *cum coupon*) (Abbrev.: **ex cp.** *or* **xcp.**), ex-coupon; coupon détaché. *V. exemple sous* to go ex coupon.

ex dividend (opp. to *cum dividend* or *dividend on*) (Abbrev.: **ex div.** *or* **xdiv.** *or* **xd.** *or simply* **ex** *or* **x**), ex-dividende; ex-exercice:

shares quoted ex dividend, actions cotées ex-dividende (*f.pl.*).

ex dividend 19—, ex-exercice 19—.

ex officio, à titre d'office.

ex repayment (of capital), ex-remboursement.

ex rights *or* **ex new** (opp. to *with rights* or *cum rights* or *cum new*) (Abbrev.: **ex n.** *or* **x-n.**), ex-droit; droit détaché:

stock ex rights (*or* ex new), titre ex-droit (*m.*).

ex ship (sales) (Abbrev.: **x-ship** *or* **x-shp** *or* **x-sh.**) *or* **ex steamer** (Abbrev.: **ex ss.**), au débarquement:

sale delivered ex ship (*or* ex steamer) *or* sale on ex ship terms, vente au débarquement (*f.*).

ex steamer (transhipment) (Abbrev.: **ex ss.**), e steamer:

transhipping ex steamer B., en transbordemer ex steamer B.

ex store (Abbrev.: **ex stre** *or* **x-stre**) *or* **ex war house** (Abbrev.: **ex whse** *or* **x-whse**) (Produc Exch.), disponible (*m.*):

price ex store *or* price ex warehouse, cours d disponible (*m.*).

ex wharf (Abbrev.: **ex whf** *or* **x-whf**), franc à quai.

ex works (Abbrev.: **x-wks**) *or* **ex mill** (Abbrev. **x-mill** *or* **x-mll** *or* **x-ml**), départ usines prise usine:

prices: ex works (*or* ex mill), so much; o rail, so much, cours: départ usines (*o* prise usine), tant; sur wagon, tant.

exact (*adj.*), exact, -e:

exact number of days, nombre exact de jou (*m.*).

exact (*v.t.*), exiger.

exaction (*n.*), exaction (*f.*).

exaggerate (*v.t.*), exagérer:

insurance which is forfeited if the insure knowingly exaggerates the amount of th damage, assurance qui est déchue si l'assur exagère sciemment le montant du dommag (*f.*).

exaggeration (*n.*), exagération (*f.*):

exaggeration of value, exagération de valeur.

examination (*n.*), examen (*m.*); inspection (*f.*) visite (*f.*); vérification (*f.*); expertise (*f.*):

examination of a merchant's books, examen inspection, des livres d'un négociant.

examination of the goods (Customs), visite vérification, examen, des marchandises.

goods submitted to the examination of th customs officials, marchandises soumise à la vérification des préposés des douane (*f.pl.*).

customs examination of hand luggage whic takes place in the train during the journey visite douanière des bagages à main qu a lieu (*ou* qui se fait) dans le train en cour de route.

any package addressed to an ambassador chargé d'affaires, or minister, accredited t the British Government, is admitted fre of customs duty and without examination tout colis adressé à un ambassadeur, charg d'affaires, ou ministre, accrédités auprè du Gouvernement britannique, est admi en franchise de droit de douane et sans visite

the sample for examination is drawn by th (customs) service in presence of the declarant l'échantillon destiné à l'expertise est prélev par le service (des douanes) en présence du déclarant (*m.*).

examination (test of a candidate) (*n.*), examer (*m.*):

to pass the preliminary examination, the fina examination, passer l'examen préliminaire l'examen final.

examine (*v.t.*), examiner; faire l'examen de inspecter; visiter; vérifier; dépouiller faire le dépouillement de; compulser:

to examine the cash position, examiner la situation d'une caisse.

passengers' luggage will be examined at the frontier, les bagages des voyageurs seront visités à la frontière (*m.pl.*).

customs officers have the right to examine the goods declared to them, les agents des douanes ont le droit de vérifier les marchandises qui leur sont déclarées (*m.pl.*).

to examine an account, examiner, faire l'examen d', dépouiller, faire le dépouillement d', compulser, un compte.

exd *or* ex. (*abbrev.*), examined.

examiner (pers.) (*n.*), examinateur, -trice; inspecteur, -trice; visiteur, -euse; vérificateur (*m.*).

exceed (*v.t.*), excéder; dépasser; franchir; aller au delà de :.

to exceed the normal limit of credit, dépasser, excéder, franchir, la limite normale du crédit.

the demand exceeds the supply, la demande dépasse l'offre.

to exceed one's instructions, aller au delà de sa charge.

Cf. **not exceeding**, sous **not**.

exception (*n.*), exception (*f.*); réserve (*f.*):

the exception proves the rule, les exceptions confirment la règle.

the exceptions stipulated in a contract, les réserves stipulées dans un contrat.

excess (*n.*), excès (*m.*); excédent (*m.*); surplus (*m.*); dépassement (*m.*):

excess of one number over another, excès d'un nombre sur un autre.

excess of receipts over expenses, of assets over liabilities, excédent des recettes sur les dépenses, de l'actif sur le passif.

excess fare, supplément (*m.*); supplément de taxe (*m.*); supplément du prix de la place (*m.*).

excess luggage (opp. to *free allowance*), excédents de bagages (*m.pl.*):

excess luggage is charged for as follows, les excédents de bagages sont taxés ainsi qu'il suit.

excess price, excédent de prix (*m.*); surprix (*m.*).

excess profits, surplus des bénéfices (*m.*).

excess profits duty (Abbrev.: **E.P.D.**), contribution extraordinaire sur les bénéfices de guerre (*f.*).

excess reinsurance (distinguished from *share,* or *participating, reinsurance*), réassurance d'excédent (*f.*); réassurance de trop-plein (*f.*).

excess shares (to apply for). V. sous **apply.**

excess weight, excédent de poids (*m.*).

excessive (*adj.*), excessif, -ive.

excessively (*adv.*), excessivement.

exchange (barter) (*n.*), échange (*m.*); change (*m.*); troc (*m.*):

commerce is founded on exchange, le commerce est fondé sur l'échange.

the exchange of one article for another, of notes for coin, l'échange d'un objet contre un autre, des billets contre espèces.

exchange of correspondence, of ratifications, échange de correspondance, de ratifications.

money of exchange, monnaie de change (*f.*); monnaie d'échange (*f.*).

the simple exchange of exported goods for imported goods does not constitute the only element of the balance of indebtedness of a country, le simple troc des marchandises exportées contre les marchandises importées ne constitue pas le seul élément de la balance économique d'un pays.

exchange (*n.*) *or* **exchange transactions** (trade in monies and the securities representing them) (Abbrev.: **exch.**), change (*m.*); opérations de change (*f.pl.*); négociations de change (*f.pl.*):

the exchange of moneys, of bank notes, le change des monnaies, des billets de banque.

to speculate in exchanges, spéculer sur les changes.

the collection of foreign bills raises questions of exchange, l'encaissement des traites sur l'étranger soulève des questions de change (*m.*).

foreign exchange *or* external exchange *or simply* exchange, change extérieur; change étranger; change; opérations de change; négociations de change :

exchange for forward (*or* future) delivery, opérations (*ou* négociations) de change à terme.

exchange for spot delivery, opérations (*ou* négociations) de change au comptant.

exchange (instrument of transfer; a bill of exchange) (*n.*), change (*m.*); effet (*m.*); traite (*f.*); lettre (*f.*); lettre de change (*f.*); devise (*f.*):

to buy exchange, acheter du change.

foreign exchange, effet étranger; effet sur l'étranger; traite sur l'étranger; lettre de change à l'extérieur; devise; devise étrangère; devise sur l'étranger. Cf. **first of exchange.**

Exchange for £ (formula on top of a foreign bill of exchange), *expressed in French bills (supposing the bill to be drawn in francs and not in pounds sterling) by* : B.P.F. *or* Bon Pour Fr.

exchange (bills of exchange) (*n.*), change (*m.*); effets (*m.pl.*); effets de commerce (*m.pl.*); effets commerciaux (*m.pl.*); traites (*f.pl.*); lettres (*f.pl.*); lettres de change (*f.pl.*); papier (*m.*):

to buy exchange, acheter du change.

foreign exchange, devises (*f.pl.*); devises étrangères (*ou* sur l'étranger); effets étrangers (*ou* sur l'étranger); effets (*ou* traites) sur l'étranger; lettres de change à l'extérieur :

foreign exchange on continuation account, devises en report.

short exchange, papier court.

exchange (commission of money changer) (*n.*) (Abbrev.: **exch.**), change (*m.*).

exchange (*n.*) (Abbrev.: **exch.**) *or* **rate of exchange** *or* **exchange rate,** change (*m.*); cours de change (*m.*); cours du change (*m.*); cours

de place (*m.*); cours de devise (*m.*); taux
du change (*m.*):
remittance in foreign money converted into
francs at the exchange of the day, remise
en monnaie étrangère convertie en francs
au change du jour (*f.*).
the exchange of London on Paris is the price
in pounds sterling, in London, of securities
payable in Paris in French francs, le change
de Londres sur Paris est le prix en livres
sterling, à Londres, des titres payables à
Paris en francs français.
favourable exchange *or* exchange for us,
change favorable.
unfavourable exchange *or* exchange against us,
change défavorable; change contraire:
the exchange (*or* the rate of exchange) is
against us (*or* unfavorable to [*or* for] our
market), le change (*ou* le taux du change)
est défavorable (*ou* contraire) à notre
place.
fixed exchange (opp. to *exchange of the day*),
change fixe.
exchange at par, change au pair. V. **par.**
exchange at parity, change à la parité; change
à parité. V. **parity** pour exemple.
exchange (*n.*) (Abbrev.: **exch.**) *or* **exchange**
premium (difference between the mint par
and the present price) (Banking), agio (*m.*);
prix du change (*m.*); prime du change (*f.*).
exchange (ledger account) (Bkkpg), change.
exchange (*n.*) *or* **exchange office,** change (*m.*);
bureau de change (*m.*).
exchange (sign on an exchange office) (*n.*), change
(*m.*); bureau de change (*m.*).
exchange (public edifice) (*n.*) (Abbrev.: **Exch.**
or **Ex.** *or* **E.**), bourse (*f.*):
stock exchange, bourse de (ou des) valeurs;
bourse d'effets publics; bourse.
exchange (Teleph.) (*n.*), bureau (*m.*); bureau
central (*m.*); poste (*m.*); poste central (*m.*);
central (*m.*):
to call the exchange, appeler le bureau.
exchange (*v.t.*), échanger; changer; troquer:
to exchange one security for another, preference
shares for ordinary shares, échanger une
valeur contre une autre, des actions
privilégiées contre des actions ordinaires.
the correspondence exchanged between the
parties, la correspondance échangée entre
les parties.
to exchange English for French money,
changer de la monnaie anglaise contre de
la monnaie française.
exchange (*v.i.*) *or* **to be exchanged,** s'échanger;
être échangé, -e; changer de mains:
X. shares exchanged (i.e., changed hands)
at 2, l'action X. s'échange (*ou* change de
mains) à 2.
the two moneys should be exchanged at par,
les deux monnaies doivent s'échanger au
pair.
exchange broker *or* **exchange dealer,** courtier
de change (*m.*); cambiste (*m.*).
exchange brokerage, courtage de change (*m.*).
exchange business, agiotage (*m.*).

exchange contract,' bordereau de change (*m.*);
aval de change (*m.*).
exchange line (Teleph.), poste principal (*m.*);
ligne principale (*f.*). *V.* note *sous syn.* direct
exchange line.
exchange rates (on 'change table), cote des
changes (*f.*). Cf. **exchange** *or* **exchange rate,**
above.
exchange station (Rly.), gare d'échange (*f.*);
gare de transbordement (*f.*).
exchange value, contre-valeur (*f.*):
bills of exchange given as exchange value for
goods, lettres de change fournies en contre-
valeur de marchandises (*f.pl.*).
exchangeable (*adj.*), échangeable:
bank note exchangeable for gold, billet de
banque échangeable contre de l'or (*m.*).
exchanger (pers.) (*n.*), échangiste (*m.*); échangeur,
-euse.
exchequer (*n.*), échiquier (*m.*); trésor (*m.*);
trésor public (*m.*); trésorerie (*f.*):
the national exchequer, la trésorerie nationale.
Exchequer bond, bon du Trésor (*m.*).
excise (*n.*), régie (*f.*); accise (*f.*); excise (*f.*).
(*Note:*—*accise* and *excise*, in French, are only
used when reference is made to English excise.)
excise duty, droit de régie (*m.*); droit d'accise
(*ou* d'excise) (*m.*):
liquors and other goods liable to excise duties,
boissons et autres marchandises sujettes
aux droits de régie (*f.pl.*).
excise office, bureau de la régie (*m.*).
exciseman [**excisemen** *pl.*] (*n.*), employé de la
régie (*m.*).
exclude (*v.t.*), exclure:
policy which excludes strike risks, police qui
exclut les risques de grève (*f.*).
excluding all claims arising from delay, sont
exclus tous recours provenant de retards.
exclusion (*n.*), exclusion (*f.*).
exclusive (*adj.*), exclusif, -ive:
exclusive right, droit exclusif (*m.*).
excursion (*n.*), excursion (*f.*):
land excursion, excursion à terre.
excursion ship, navire excursionniste (*m.*).
excursion ticket, billet d'excursion (*m.*).
excursion train, train de plaisir (*m.*).
excursion trip, voyage d'excursion (*m.*).
excursionist (pers.) (*n.*), excursionniste (*m.* ou *f.*).
execute (*v.t.*), exécuter; effectuer:
to execute a plan, an order, a contract, exécuter
un projet, un ordre, un contrat.
to execute a transfer (of shares, or the like),
effectuer un transfert.
execution (*n.*), exécution (*f.*); opéré (*m.*):
to claim execution of an order, exiger
l'exécution (*ou* l'opéré) d'un ordre.
executive (senior officers) (of a liner) (*n.*), état-
major (d'un paquebot) (*m.*).
executor (pers.) (*n.*) (Abbrev.: **exor**), exécuteur
testamentaire (*m.*).
executrix [**executrixes** *or* **executrices** *pl.*] (pers.)
(*n.*) (Abbrev.: **exrx**), exécutrice testamen-
taire (*f.*).
exempt (*adj.*), exempt, -e:
receipts exempt from receipt stamp duty,

reçus exempts du droit de timbre à quittance (*m.pl.*).

exempt (*v.t.*), exempter; exonérer; affranchir: to exempt someone from liability, exonérer quelqu'un de responsabilité.

to exempt a minimum of income, considered as necessary to existence, exonérer un minimum de revenu, considéré comme nécessaire à l'existence.

in France, if wreck is claimed by its owners, it is exempted from all customs duties when it is of French origin, en France, si les épaves sont réclamées par leurs propriétaires, elles sont affranchies de tous droits de douane lorsqu'elles sont d'origine française.

exemption (*n.*), exemption (*f.*); exonération (*f.*); affranchissement (*m.*); franchise (*f.*): exemption from customs examination, exemption de visite de douane.

the exemption from the tax which these goods enjoy, l'exemption (*ou* l'exonération) (*ou* la franchise) de la taxe dont jouissent ces marchandises.

exemption clause, clause d'exonération (*f.*); clause exonératoire (*f.*).

exercise (*n.*). V. exemples: exercise of an option, of a power, of a privilege, of one's duty, exercice d'une faculté, d'un pouvoir, d'un privilège, de ses fonctions (*m.*).

exercise of an option (Stock Exch.), consolidation d'un marché à prime (*f.*); levée d'une prime (*f.*).

exercise (*v.t.*). V. exemples: to exercise a right, one's right of option, exercer un droit, son droit d'option; user d'un droit, de son droit d'option.

to exercise an (*or* the) (*or* one's) option (Fin.), exercer une (*ou* la) (*ou* sa) faculté; user d'une (*ou* de la) (*ou* de sa) faculté; lever une (*ou* l') (*ou* son) option; opter:

to exercise the option of subscribing, exercer, user de, la faculté de souscrire.

taker who exercises his option for delivery, optant qui opte pour la livraison (*m.*).

to exercise an option (Stock Exch.), consolider un marché à prime; lever une prime.

exhaust (*v.t.*), épuiser: the coupons are exhausted, that is to say, they have all been cut off (*or* detached), les coupons sont épuisés, c'est-à-dire ils ont tous été détachés (*m.pl.*).

exhaustion (*n.*), épuisement (*m.*): exhaustion of the national resources, épuisement des ressources publiques.

exhibit (to produce) (*v.t.*), exhiber; représenter; produire: to exhibit one's books, exhiber ses livres.

exhibition (production of documents) (*n.*), exhibition (*f.*); représentation (*f.*); production (*f.*).

exhibition (show) (*n.*), exposition (*f.*): commercial exhibitions and fairs, expositions et foires commerciales.

exhibitor (at a show) (pers.) (*n.*), exposant, -e.

exonerate (*v.t.*), exonérer; exempter; affranchir: to exonerate someone from liability, from his faults or from those of his servants, exonérer quelqu'un de responsabilité, de ses fautes ou de celles de ses préposés.

to exonerate the carriers, wholly or partly, from their legal responsibility, exonérer les transporteurs, en tout ou en partie, de leur responsabilité légale.

to exonerate oneself, s'exonérer: to claim to exonerate oneself (*or* to claim to be exonerated) (*or* to claim exoneration) from all liability, prétendre s'exonérer de toute responsabilité.

no one being able to exonerate himself from his personal faults, nul ne pouvant s'exonérer de ses fautes personnelles.

exoneration (*n.*), exonération (*f.*); exemption (*f.*); affranchissement (*m.*).

exoneration clause, clause d'exonération (*f.*); clause exonératoire (*f.*).

exorbitance (*n.*), exorbitance (*f.*): exorbitance of the claims of a seller, exorbitance des prétentions d'un vendeur.

exorbitant (*adj.*), exorbitant, -e: to ask an exorbitant price, demander un prix exorbitant.

exorbitantly (*adv.*), exorbitamment.

expect (to wait for) (*v.t.*), attendre: ships expected at London, navires attendus à Londres (*m.pl.*).

expend (*v.t.*), dépenser.

expenditure (*n.*) (Abbrev.: **expre**), dépense (*f.*); dépenses (*f.pl.*): the expenditure exceeds the receipts, la dépense excède la recette.

capital expenditure, dépenses en immobilisations; dépenses d'établissement; immobilisations (*f.pl.*); établissement (*m.*).

expense (*n.*) *or* **expenses** (*n.pl.*), frais (*m.pl.*); dépense (*f.*); dépenses (*f.pl.*); charge (*f.*); charges (*f.pl.*): expenses at port of refuge, dépenses au port de relâche; dépenses de relâche; frais de relâche; frais du port de relâche.

working expenses, frais d'exploitation; dépenses d'exploitation; charges d'exploitation.

cost and expenses of carrying on the business, frais et charges de l'exploitation.

expenses of selling, frais de vente.

expenses in connection, frais accessoires: the expenses in connection with the correspondence, remittance of funds, etc., les frais accessoires de correspondance, d'envoi de fonds, etc.

at the expense of *or* **at . . .'s expense,** aux frais de; à la charge de: handling done at the expense and risk of the goods, at the company's expense, manutention faite aux frais et risque de la marchandise, aux frais de la compagnie (*f.*).

expenses (standing expenses; establishment charges) (*n.pl.*), frais généraux (*m.pl.*); dépenses de maison (*f.pl.*).

expenses ledger, grand livre auxiliaire de frais (*m.*).

expensive (*adj.*), cher, -ère; coûteux, -euse; dispendieux, -euse.
to be expensive, être cher, -ère; coûter cher: the goods are very expensive, les marchandises coûtent très cher (*f.pl.*).
expensively (*adv.*), chèrement; coûteusement; dispendieusement.
experience (*n.*), expérience (*f.*).
experience (*v.t.*), éprouver:
to experience a loss, éprouver une perte.
experienced (skilled) (*adj.*), expérimenté, -e: experienced clerk, commis expérimenté (*m.*).
expert (*adj.*), expert, -e.
expert (pers.) (*n.*), expert (*m.*):
goods examined by experts, marchandises examinées par des experts (*f.pl.*).
expiration *or* **expiry** (*n.*), expiration (*f.*); échéance (*f.*):
expiration of a lease, of a concession, expiration d'un bail, d'une concession.
date of expiration of tenancy, date d'échéance de location (*f.*).
expiration of an option (Stock Exch.), échéance d'un marché à prime.
expiration, expiry, of the time of the risk, of this policy, of the lay days, expiration du temps du risque, de la présente police, des jours de planche.
on expiry, this policy will be renewed for a full year, à son échéance, la présente police se renouvellera pour une année entière.
expire (*v.i.*), expirer; échoir; écheoir; périmer:
the bill expires to-morrow, le billet échoit demain.
exploit (to work) (*v.t.*), exploiter:
to exploit a patent, exploiter un brevet.
exploit (to abuse) (*v.t.*), exploiter:
to exploit the credulity of the public, an unsuspecting client, exploiter la crédulité publique, un client confiant.
exploitation (*n.*), exploitation (*f.*):
the commercial exploitation of the ship in the form of affreightment assumes several forms, l'exploitation commerciale du navire sous la forme d'affrètement revêt plusieurs formes.
explosion (*n.*), explosion (*f.*); éclatement (*m.*):
explosion of boilers, of pipes, explosion, éclatement, de chaudières, de conduites.
explosion risk, risque d'explosion (*m.*).
export (*n.*) (Ant.: *import*), exportation (*f.*); sortie (*f.*):
the export of money is sometimes forbidden, l'exportation des capitaux est parfois interdite.
exports from England to America, exportations d'Angleterre en Amérique.
the total traffic, imports and exports combined, le trafic total, entrées et sorties réunies.
export (*v.t.*), exporter:
to export gold, goods, exporter de l'or, des marchandises.
export commission agent *or simply* **export agent,** commissionnaire-exportateur (*m.*).
export credit, crédit à l'exportation (*m.*); crédit confirmé (*m.*).

export duty, droits d'exportation (*m.pl.*); droits de sortie (*m.pl.*).
export gold point *or* **export bullion point** *or* **export specie point,** gold-point de sortie (*m.*); gold-point d'exportation (*m.*); point de sortie de l'or (*m.*). V. exemple sous **gold point.**
export licence *or* **export permit,** licence d'exportation (*f.*); permis de sortie (*m.*).
export list (Customs), tarif de sortie (*m.*).
export merchant, négociant exportateur (*m.*).
export prohibition, prohibition de sortie (*f.*).
export ship, navire exportateur (*m.*); navire d'exportation (*m.*).
export specification (Customs), déclaration d'embarquement (*f.*); déclaration d'exportation (*f.*).
export trade, commerce d'exportation (*m.*).
exportable (*adj.*), exportable:
exportable goods, marchandises exportables (*f.pl.*).
exportation (*n.*), exportation (*f.*); sortie (*f.*).
exportation voucher (of a pass sheet), volant de sortie (d'un triptyque) (*m.*).
exporter (pers. or country) (*n.*), exportateur, -trice:
exporters of English products, exportateurs des produits anglais.
country which is a big exporter of coal, pays qui est gros exportateur de charbon (*m.*).
Great Britain is a big exporter of coal, la Grande-Bretagne est une grande exportatrice de houille.
exporting (*adj.*), exportateur, -trice; d'exportation:
exporting country, pays exportateur (*m.*).
exporting ship, navire exportateur (*m.*); navire d'exportation (*m.*).
express (*adj.*), exprès, -esse:
express agreement (opp. to *tacit agreement*), convention expresse (*f.*).
express stipulation, stipulation expresse (*f.*).
express warranty (Mar. Insce) (opp. to *implied warranty*), garantie expresse (*f.*):
an express warranty does not exclude an implied warranty, unless it be inconsistent therewith, une garantie expresse n'exclut pas une garantie implicite, sauf le cas d'incompatibilité. V. *aussi exemple sous* implied warranty.
express (Post) (*n.*), exprès (*m.*):
express is understood to mean any method of delivery quicker than the post, l'exprès s'entend de tout mode de distribution plus rapide que la poste.
extra charge for delivery by express, taxe supplémentaire pour livraison par exprès (*f.*).
express (express train) (*n.*), express (*m.*); train express (*m.*).
express (*v.t.*), exprimer; énoncer:
policy which expresses the term for which it is written, police qui exprime la durée pour laquelle elle est souscrite (*f.*).
to express an amount in figures, in words, in words at length, énoncer une somme en chiffres, en lettres, en toutes lettres.

express delivery, livraison par exprès (*f.*) ; remise par exprès (*f.*).

express fee (Post), taxe d'exprès (*f.*).

express letter, lettre par exprès (*f.*).

express messenger, porteur-exprès (*m.*) ; exprès (*m.*).

express packet (Post), envoi exprès (*m.*).

express parcel (Post), colis à livrer par exprès (*m.*).

express parcel (Rly.), colis messageries à grande vitesse (*m.*).

express parcels train, train pour le service des colis de grande vitesse (*m.*).

express service (Rly. or Shipping), service express (*m.*) ; service rapide (*m.*).

express train, train express (*m.*) ; express (*m.*).

expunction (*n.*), rayure (*f.*).

expunge (*v.t.*), rayer :
stock expunged from the list, valeur rayée de la cote (*f.*).

extend (to widen) (*v.t.*), étendre :
to extend one's field of action, the circle of one's operations, étendre son champ d'action, le cercle de ses opérations.

extend (to prolong) (*v.t.*), proroger :
to extend the time of payment of a bill, proroger l'échéance d'un billet.

extend (to carry out into another column) (*v.t.*), porter ; reporter ; transporter :
to extend the balance of interest in the principal column, porter, reporter, transporter, la balance des intérêts dans la colonne des capitaux.

extension (*n.*) *or* **extension of time,** prorogation (*f.*) ; délai (*m.*) :
to get an extension (*or* an extension of time), obtenir un délai.

extension (carrying out into another column) (*n.*), report (*m.*) ; transport (*m.*).

extension line *or simply* **extension** (*n.*) (Teleph.) (distinguished from *direct exchange line* or *exchange line*), poste supplémentaire (*m.*) ; ligne supplémentaire (*f.*). *V. note sous* direct exchange line.

extent (*n.*), étendue (*f.*) :
the nature and extent of a risk, of the damage resulting from an accident, la nature et l'étendue d'un risque, du dommage résultant d'un sinistre.

external (*adj.*), extérieur, -e :
external exchange, change extérieur (*m.*) ; change étranger (*m.*) ; change (*m.*).
external loan, emprunt extérieur (*m.*).
external packing, emballage extérieur (*m.*).

extinction *or* **extinguishing** (*n.*), extinction (*f.*) :
extinction of a national debt, extinction d'une dette publique.
extinguishing fire on board, extinction du feu (*ou* d'incendie) à bord.

extinguish (*v.t.*), éteindre :
to extinguish a debt by repaying the capital, éteindre une dette en remboursant le capital.
the acceptance of the goods extinguishes any action against the railway arising out of the contract of carriage, l'acceptation de la marchandise éteint toute action contre le chemin de fer provenant du contrat de transport (*f.*).

extra (further) (*adj.*), supplémentaire :
extra fare, supplément (*m.*) ; supplément de taxe (*m.*) ; supplément du prix de la place (*m.*) :
extra fare to pay for admission in a Pullman car, supplément à payer pour admission dans une voiture Pullman.
extra freight, surfret (*m.*) ; supplément de fret (*m.*) ; fret supplémentaire (*m.*).
extra pay, surpaye (*f.*) ; sursalaire (*m.*).
extra premium (Insce), surprime (*f.*) ; supplément de prime (*m.*) ; prime supplémentaire (*f.*) :
extra premium to be arranged, surprime à débattre ; surprime à arbitrer.

extra-European (*adj.*), extra-européen, -enne :
extra-European system (Post, etc.), régime extra-européen (*m.*).

extra vires (opp. to *intra vires*), antistatutaire. V. exemple sous syn. **ultra vires.**

extract (*n.*), extrait (*m.*) :
extract from a book, from a report, extrait d'un livre, d'un rapport.

extract (*v.t.*), extraire.

extract money from (*or* out of) **someone** (to), arracher, tirer, soutirer, de l'argent à (*ou* de) quelqu'un.

extraordinary (*adj.*), extraordinaire :
extraordinary general meeting, assemblée générale extraordinaire (*f.*).
extraordinary reserve, réserve extraordinaire (*f.*).

extrinsic (*adj.*) (Ant. : *intrinsic*), extrinsèque :
the extrinsic value of a coin, la valeur extrinsèque d'une pièce de monnaie.

extrinsically (*adv.*), extrinsèquement.

eyelet (*n.*), œillet (*m.*).

eyelet pliers *or* **eyelet punch,** pince à poser les œillets (*f.*) ; pince à œillets (*f.*).

F

face (of a bill, of a cheque, of an envelope, of a postcard, of a packet) (*n.*) (Ant. : *back*), recto (d'un effet, d'un chèque, d'une enveloppe, d'une carte postale, d'un paquet) (*m.*) :

to state the sum to be paid on the face of a bill, indiquer la somme à payer au recto d'un effet.

face value (of a share, or the like, of a bill). valeur nominale (*f.*), nominal (*m.*) (d'une action, ou analogue, d'un effet) :

the bonds are of the face value of £10 and multiples; the face value of the debentures is £100, les bons sont de la valeur nominale (*ou* sont du nominal) de £10; la valeur nominale (*ou* le nominal) des obligations est de £100.

the face value is that inscribed on a stock or share certificate, la valeur nominale est celle inscrite sur un titre de bourse.

if the marketable value of the stock is higher than its face value, si la valeur vénale du titre est supérieure à sa valeur nominale.

face value (of a postage stamp, of a revenue stamp), valeur faciale (d'un timbre-poste, d'un timbre fiscal) (*f.*).

facsimile signature, griffe (*f.*).

facsimile stamp, griffe (*f.*).

fact (*n.*), fait (*m.*) :
it is a simple question of fact to distinguish in each case the direct consequences and the indirect consequences, ce sera une simple question de fait que de distinguer dans chaque cas les conséquences directes et les conséquences indirectes.

factor (*n.*), facteur (*m.*) :
the most important factor to be considered, le plus important facteur à considérer.

factor (pers.) (*n.*), commissionnaire (*m.*).

factory [**factories** *pl.*] (*n.*), manufacture (*f.*); fabrique (*f.*); usine (*f.*).

fail (to be found wanting) (*v.i.*), manquer; faire défaut :
to fail in one's duty, manquer à son devoir.
to fail in one's engagements, manquer, faire défaut, à ses engagements.

fail (to come short of a result) (*v.i.*), échouer :
to fail in one's enterprises, échouer dans ses entreprises.

fail (to become insolvent) (*v.i.*), faillir; faire faillite; manquer :
bank which has failed, banque qui a failli (*ou* qui a fait faillite) (*ou* qui a manqué) (*f.*).

failing (*prep.*), à défaut de; faute de :
failing payment within thirty days, à défaut de (*ou* faute de) paiement dans les trente jours.
I hereby appoint as my proxy Mr A., and, failing him, Mr B., je donne, par les présentes, pouvoir à M. A., et, à son défaut, à M. B.

failure (insuccess) (*n.*), insuccès (*m.*) :
failure of launch of a ship, insuccès de lancement d'un navire.

failure (default) (*n.*), défaut (*m.*) :
failure to accept, to pay, a bill, défaut d'acceptation, de paiement, d'un effet.
failure to make a return (Income Tax), défaut de déclaration.

failure (insolvency) (*n.*), faillite (*f.*).

faint line *or simply* **faint** (*n.*), grise (*f.*).

fair (market) (*n.*), foire (*f.*) :
commercial exhibitions and fairs, expositions et foires commerciales.

fair average quality (Produce Exch.) (Abbrev.: **f.a.q.**), qualité loyale et marchande (*f.*); qualité courante (*f.*); qualité commerciale (*f.*).

fair copy (of a letter, or the like), copie au net (*f.*); transcription au net (*f.*). *Cf.* to make a fair copy of a manuscript.

fair trade (Polit. Econ.), fair-trade (*m.*).

faith (*n.*), foi (*f.*) :
purchaser in good faith, acquéreur de bonne foi (*m.*).
an insurance contract is based upon the utmost good faith, and if the utmost good faith be not observed by either party, the contract may be avoided by the other party, un contrat d'assurance est basé sur la bonne foi la plus absolue, et si la bonne foi la plus absolue n'est pas observée par l'une des parties, le contrat peut être annulé par l'autre partie.

fall (precipitation) (*n.*), chute (*f.*) :
fall of packages into the water in the course of shipping or unshipping operations, chute de colis à (*ou* dans) l'eau au cours des opérations d'embarquement ou de débarquement.

fall (decline) (*n.*), baisse (*f.*); abaissement (*m.*) :
fall in wheat, in foreign stocks, in the rate of interest, baisse des blés, des fonds étrangers, du taux de l'intérêt.
the rise or the fall of freights, of stocks and shares, la hausse ou la baisse des frets, des titres de bourse.
competition causes a fall in prices, la concurrence produit l'abaissement des prix.
dealing for a fall (Stock Exch.), opération à la baisse (*f.*).
to buy on a fall (Stock Exch.), acheter à la baisse.
speculator who goes for a fall, spéculateur qui est en baisse (*m.*).

fall (*v.i.*) *or* **to be falling** *or* **to be a falling market**, tomber; baisser; s'abaisser; être en baisse; être à la baisse :
share which has fallen to zero (*or* to nothing), valeur qui a tombé à zéro (*ou* à rien) (*f.*).
railway shares are falling (*or* are a falling market), les valeurs de chemins de fer baissent (*ou* sont en baisse) (*ou* sont à la baisse) (*f.pl.*).
to sell on a rising market and to buy on a falling market, vendre en hausse et acheter en baisse.
the price of silver has fallen, le prix de l'argent a baissé (*ou* s'est abaissé).

fall back (to) *or* **fall away (to)**, se replier; se rabattre; reculer; rétrograder :
X. shares fell back (*or* fell away) from 1¼ to 1, l'action X. s'est repliée (*ou* s'est rabattue) (*ou* recule) (*ou* rétrograde) de 1 1/4 à 1.
X. preference fell back a point to so much, la privilégiée X. recule d'un point à tant.

fall clause (benefit of a fall in price clause), clause de parité (*f.*).

fall due (to), échoir; écheoir :
the bill falls due to-morrow, le billet échoit demain.

fall in value (to), se déprécier.

fall into arrear (to), arrérager.

fall off (to slacken) (*v.i.*), ralentir.
falling due, échéable ; échéant, -e :
  bill falling due on such a date, billet échéable
  à telle date (*m.*).
falling off in value, baisse de valeur (*f.*).
falling off of orders, ralentissement de commandes
  (*m.*).
false (*adj.*), faux, fausse ; inexact, -e :
  false balance sheet, faux bilan (*m.*).
  false declaration *or* false statement, fausse
    déclaration (*f.*) ; déclaration fausse (*f.*) ;
    déclaration inexacte (*f.*).
  false trade mark, fausse marque de fabrique
    (*f.*).
falsely (*adv.*), faussement.
falsification (*n.*), falsification (*f.*) ; faux (*m.*) :
  falsification of accounts, falsification d'écritures
    comptables ; faux en écritures comptables.
falsifier (pers.) (*n.*), falsificateur, -trice.
falsify (*v.t.*), falsifier ; fausser :
  to falsify a book, a balance sheet, falsifier,
    fausser, un registre, un bilan.
falsity [**falsities** *pl.*] *or* **falseness** (*n.*), fausseté (*f.*) :
  falsity (*or* falseness) of the particulars of a
    bill of lading, fausseté des énonciations d'un
    connaissement.
family ticket, billet de famille (*m.*).
Far East (opp. to *Near East*), Extrême Orient
  (*m.*).
fare (by land or air) (*n.*), prix de la place (*m.*) ;
  prix de (*ou* du) transport (*m.*) ; prix (*m.*) ;
  place (*f.*) ; tarif (*m.*) :
  the carriage of passengers is effected in con-
    sideration of the prepayment of the fare,
    le transport des voyageurs est effectué
    moyennant le paiement préalable du prix
    de la place.
  passenger who pays his fare, voyageur qui
    paie le prix de sa place (*m.*).
  passenger fares, prix des places des voyageurs ;
    prix de transport des voyageurs.
  children carried at half fare, enfants trans-
    portés à moitié prix (*m.pl.*).
  (in France) from three to seven years old,
    children pay half fare and have the right to
    a separate seat ; over seven years, children
    pay full fare, (en France) de trois à sept ans,
    les enfants paient demi-place et ont droit
    à une place distincte ; au-dessus de sept
    ans, les enfants paient place entière.
  full fare, half fare, ticket *or* ticket at full fare,
    at half fare, billet à plein tarif, à demi-
    tarif (*m.*).
fare (by sea or air) (*n.*), prix de passage (*m.*) ;
  prix du voyage (*m.*) ; prix (*m.*) ; tarif (*m.*).
fare (petty expense) (*n.*), course (*f.*) : [*in the pl.*
  fares, courses (*f.pl.*) *or* frais de course (*m.pl.*).]
  the fare is so much, la course est de tant.
fare (pers.) (*n.*), voyageur, -euse.
farmer's tax, impôt sur les bénéfices agricoles
  (*m.*).
fast boat (opp. to *slow boat*), navire rapide (*m.*) ;
  bateau express (*m.*) ; navire de grande
  vitesse (*m.*).
fast goods train, train de marchandises à marche
  rapide (*m.*).

fast passenger steamer, paquebot à grande vitesse
  (*m.*).
fast train, train rapide (*m.*) ; train de grande
  vitesse (*m.*) ; grande vitesse (*f.*).
fasten (to attach together by means of a staple
  press, or the like) (*v.t.*), agrafer :
  to fasten several sheets of paper, agrafer
    plusieurs feuilles de papier.
fastening (*n.*), agrafage (*m.*).
fatal accident, accident mortel (*m.*).
father (*v.t.*), patronner :
  issue fathered by a bank, émission patronnée
    par une banque (*f.*).
fault (*n.*), faute (*f.*) ; défaut (*m.*) ; vice (*m.*) :
  fault of the master, faute du capitaine.
  fault of stowing, faute d'arrimage ; vice
    d'arrimage.
  latent fault, défaut caché ; vice caché.
  ship in (*or* at) fault, navire en faute (*m.*).
favour *or* **favor** (*n.*), faveur (*f.*) :
  X. shares are in favour (Stock Exch.), l'action
    X. est en faveur.
favourable *or* **favorable** (*adj.*), favorable :
  favourable exchange, change favorable (*m.*).
  favourable trade balance (opp. to *unfavourable,*
    or *adverse, trade balance*), balance com-
    merciale favorable (*f.*). *V. exemple sous*
    balance of trade.
feature (*n.*), caractéristique (*f.*) :
  the feature of the balance sheet is the amount
    of the item debentures, la caractéristique du
    bilan est l'importance du poste obligations.
fee (*n.*) *or* **fees** (*n.pl.*), honoraires (*m.pl.*) ; jeton
  (*m.*) ; jeton de présence (*m.*) ; jetons de
  présence (*m.pl.*) ; cotisation (*f.*) ; droit (*m.*) ;
  droits (*m.pl.*) ; taxe (*f.*) ; taxes (*f.pl.*) :
  expert's fee *or* surveyor's fees, honoraires
    d'expert.
  counsel's fees, honoraires d'avocat.
  directors' fees, jetons de présence, jetons,
    honoraires, des administrateurs :
    in France, the remuneration of the directors
      generally consists of fees and the allocation
      of a share of the company's profits, en
      France, la rémunération des administrateurs
      consiste généralement en jetons de présence
      et dans l'allocation d'une part des bénéfices
      de la société.
  entrance fee (to an association), cotisation
    d'admission ; droit d'entrée.
  fee for clearance through customs (Post),
    taxe de dédouanement.
  fee for insurance (Post), droit d'assurance.
  fee for registration (Post), droit de recom-
    mendation ; taxe de recommendation.
feeder (branch railway) (*n.*), affluent (*m.*) :
  local lines destined to serve as feeders to the
    main lines, lignes d'intérêt local destinées
    à servir d'affluents aux grandes lignes
    (*f.pl.*).
feint line *or* simply **feint** (*n.*), grise (*f.*).
feme sole trader *or* **feme sole merchant,** femme
  mariée commerçante (*f.*).
ferry boat, ferry-boat (*m.*) ; bac transbordeur
  (*m.*).
fiat money *or* **fiat paper money,** papier-monnaie

(*m.*) ; monnaie fictive (*f.*) ; monnaie fiduciaire (*f.*) ; numéraire fictif (*m.*) :
forced currency bank notes are fiat money, les billets de banque à cours forcé sont du papier-monnaie (*m.pl.*).

fictitious (*adj.*), fictif, -ive :
fictitious assets, actif fictif (*m.*).
fictitious dividend, dividende fictif (*m.*).
system which had the great drawback of overloading the budgets with fictitious receipts and expenditure, régime qui avait le grand inconvénient de surcharger les budgets de recettes et de dépenses fictives (*m.*).
fictitious accounts (Bkkpg), comptes de (*ou* des) résultats (*m.pl.*).

fidelity (*n.*), fidélité (*f.*) :
fidelity of a cashier, fidélité d'un caissier.

fidelity insurance, assurance sur la fidélité du personnel (*f.*).

fiduciary (*adj.*), fiduciaire :
fiduciary circulation *or* fiduciary currency, circulation fiduciaire (*f.*).

field (*n.*), champ (*m.*) :
field of operations, of activity, champ d'opérations, d'activité.

fight (*v.t.*) *or* **fight against** (**to**), lutter contre :
to fight (*or* to fight against) foreign competition, lutter contre la concurrence étrangère.

figure (*n.*), chiffre (*m.*) :
to express an amount in figures, énoncer une somme en chiffres.

figure (to appear) (*v.i.*), figurer ; chiffrer :
loan which figures in the list, emprunt qui figure à la cote (*m.*).
the value figuring in the books, la valeur chiffrée sur les livres.

figure out (*v.t.*), chiffrer.

figure out (*v.i.*), se chiffrer.

figuring out, chiffrage (*m.*).

file (for letters, etc.) (*n.*), classeur (*m.*) ; biblorhapt (*m.*) :
letter file, classeur de lettres.

file (to put on a file for preservation and reference) (*v.t.*), classer :
letters filed in alphabetical order, in order of date, under subjects, lettres classées par ordre alphabétique (*ou* dans l'ordre alphabétique), par ordre (*ou* dans l'ordre) chronologique, par ordre (*ou* dans l'ordre) idéologique (*f.pl.*).

file (to register with a public registrar) (*v.t.*), déposer ; passer ; enregistrer :
to file a return at the registry, déposer, passer, enregistrer, une déclaration au greffe.

filing (letters, papers, etc.) (*n.*), classement (de lettres, de papiers, etc.) (*m.*).

filing (registration) (*n.*), dépôt (*m.*) ; passation (*f.*) ; enregistrement (*m.*).

filing basket, corbeille pour lettres à classer (*f.*).

filing cabinet, meuble-classeur (*m.*) ; classeur (*m.*).

filing clerk, classier, -ère.

fill (an order book) (*v.t.*), garnir :
well filled order book, carnet de commandes largement garni (*m.*).

fill (*or* **fill up**) **a casual vacancy** (**to**), combler une vacance accidentelle. V. aussi autre exemple sous **vacancy.**

fill up *or* **fill in** (*v.t.*), remplir :
to fill up a book, remplir un livre.
to fill up a form, a cheque, a counterfoil, remplir une formule, un chèque, une souche.
to fill in the blanks in a form, remplir les blancs dans une formule.

filling up *or* **filling in,** remplissage (*m.*).

final (*adj.*), final, -e, -als ; dernier, -ère :
final account, compte final (*m.*).
final cause (of a sea accident), cause immédiate (*f.*).
final cost (Costing), prix de revient final (*m.*).
final date (as for payment, after which no further time will be given), terme fatal (*m.*) ; terme de rigueur (*m.*) :
the final date of the settlement on the stock exchange, le terme fatal de la liquidation en bourse.
final dividend (distribution of profits to shareholders) (distinguished from *interim dividend*), solde de dividende (*m.*) ; dividende final (*m.*) :
to declare a final dividend, déclarer un solde de dividende (*ou* un dividende final).
dividends are payable 1st January (interim) and 1st July (final), les dividendes sont payables le 1er janvier (acompte) et le 1er juillet (solde) (*m.pl.*).
final dividend *or* final distribution (distribution among creditors—company in liquidation), dernière répartition (*f.*) :
third and final dividend (*or* distribution), troisième et dernière répartition. *Cf.* first and final dividend (*or* distribution).
final instalment (on shares, or the like), versement de libération (*m.*) ; dernier versement (*m.*).
final invoice (opp. to *provisional invoice*), facture finale (*f.*).
final port of discharge, port final de déchargement (*m.*) ; dernier port de reste (*m.*).

finality (barring by limitation) (*n.*), prescription (*f.*).

finance (conduct of monetary affairs) (*n.*), finance (*f.*) ; finances (*f.pl.*) :
board composed of men occupying a big position in finance (*or* in the world of finance), conseil d'administration composé d'hommes ayant une grande position dans la finance (*ou* dans le monde de la finance) (*m.*).
persons versed in the question of finance, personnes versées dans la question de finances (*f.pl.*).

finance (money in hand or coming in) (*n.*), finance (*f.*) ; commandite (*f.*) ; trésorerie (*f.*) :
the finance granted to trade and industry by the banks, la finance (*ou* la commandite) accordée au commerce et à l'industrie par les banques.
statement of finances, état de finances (*m.*) ; situation de trésorerie (*f.*).
his finances are low, ses finances sont en baisse.

finance (*v.t.*), financer ; commanditer :
the liabilities express above all how the business

has been financed, le passif exprime avant
tout comment l'affaire a été financée.

should the banker finance commercial and
industrial undertakings ? le banquier doit-
il commanditer des entreprises commerciales
et industrielles ?

finance (*v.i.*), financer ; se commanditer :
a bankrupt cannot finance, un banqueroutier
ne saurait se commanditer.

finance act, loi de finances (*f.*) ; loi des finances
(*f.*).

finance bill (bill of exchange), effet de finance
(*m.*).

finance committee, comité de finance (*m.*) ;
comité financier (*m.*).

finance company, société de finance (*f.*) ; société
financière (*f.*).

finance statement, état de finances (*m.*) ;
situation de trésorerie (*f.*).

finance syndicate, syndicat de finance (*m.*) ;
syndicat financier (*m.*).

financial (*adj.*), financier, -ère :
financial books (account books — opp. to
memorandum, statistical, or *registry, books*),
livres de report (*m.pl.*).

financial crisis, crise financière (*f.*).

financial magnate, magnat (*ou* matador) de la
finance (*m.*).

financial statement, état de finances (*m.*) ;
situation de trésorerie (*f.*).

financial syndicate, syndicat financier (*m.*) ;
syndicat de finance (*m.*).

the financial world, le monde financier ; le
monde de (*ou* de la) finance.

financial year, exercice (*m.*) ; exercice financier (*m.*) ; année financière (*f.*) :
financial year ending 31st December, exercice
prenant fin (*ou* clôturant) le 31 décembre.

the financial year ended 31st December,
l'exercice ayant pris fin (*ou* l'exercice
clôturé *ou* clos) le 31 décembre.

the payment of taxes at the end of the financial year, le paiement des impôts à la fin
de l'année financière.

financially (*adv.*), financièrement.

financier (*n.*) *or* **financial man,** financier (*m.*) ;
homme de finance (*m.*) :
a clever financier, un habile financier.

financier (*v.t.*), commanditer ; financer.

financier (*v.i.*), se commanditer ; financer.

financing (*n.*), financement (*m.*) :
the financing of new concerns, le financement
d'entreprises nouvelles.

financing company, compagnie de financement
(*f.*).

financing expenses, charges financières (*f.pl.*).

find (*v.t.*), trouver ; retrouver ; découvrir ; procurer ; se procurer ; fournir :
to find a transaction profitable, trouver du
bon dans une affaire.

to find a deposit intact, retrouver un dépôt
intact.

to find a mistake in the books, découvrir,
retrouver, une erreur dans les livres.

to find a place (for someone), procurer une
place ; placer :

to find a place for a young man in a business
house, placer, procurer une place à, un
jeune homme dans une maison de commerce.

to find a place (for oneself), se placer ; se
procurer une place.

to find money, procurer des capitaux ;
fournir de l'argent ; faire les fonds :
to find money for an industry, procurer des
capitaux, fournir de l'argent, à une
industrie.

A. finds half the money, B. and C. each a
quarter, A. fait les fonds pour moitié,
B. et C. chacun pour un quart.

to find money (for oneself), se procurer de
l'argent ; battre monnaie.

to find good and valid security for the guarantee
of the payment of a contribution, fournir
bonne et valable caution pour la garantie
du paiement d'une contribution.

find out how one stands (to), se rendre compte
de sa situation.

finder of wreckage (pers.), inventeur d'épave
(*m.*).

fine (*adj.*), beau (bel *before a vowel or silent* h),
belle ; magnifique :
fine bills, beau papier (*m.*).

fine bank bills, papier de haute banque (*m.*).

fine trade bills, papier de haut commerce
(*m.*) ; papier hors banque (*m.*).

fine piece of business, affaire d'or (*f.*) ; affaire
magnifique (*f.*).

fine (pecuniary penalty) (*n.*), amende (*f.*) :
every breach of the customs regulations results
in a fine, toute infraction aux règlements
douaniers se traduit par une amende.

fine not exceeding so many pounds, amende
de tant de livres au maximum.

fineness (Minting) (*n.*), titre (*m.*) :
the fineness is the ratio of the weight of fine
metal to the total weight of the alloy, le
titre est le rapport du poids du métal fin au
poids de l'alliage.

lowering the fineness of the coinage, abaissement du titre des monnaies (*m.*).

coins of legal fineness, monnaies au titre légal
(*f.pl.*).

finish (at the) (at the close of the day's market),
en fin de séance ; en clôture :
X. shares weakened at the finish, l'action X.
faiblit en fin de séance (*ou* en clôture).

finish (*v.i.*), finir ; terminer :
X. shares which recovered somewhat last
week to 22s. sagged to 21s. to rise slightly
afterwards to 21s. 6d. and finish at 21s. 6d.,
l'action X. qui avait quelque peu repris la
semaine dernière jusqu'à 22sh. a fléchit à
21sh. pour se relever légèrement ensuite à
21sh. 6d. et finir (*ou* terminer) à 21sh. 6d.

fire (*n.*), incendie (*m.*) ; feu (*m.*) :
fire on shore or in warehouses, on board or in
craft, feu à terre ou en magasin, à bord ou
dans les allèges.

damage caused by fire to goods liable to
spontaneous inflammation, dommage causé
par le feu à des marchandises sujettes à
l'inflammation spontanée (*m.*).

ship, cargo, on fire, navire (m.), cargaison (f.), en feu.

fire insurance, assurance contre l'incendie (f.); assurance-incendie (f.); assurance contre le feu (f.).

fire insurance company or **fire office,** compagnie d'assurance (ou d'assurances) contre l'incendie (f.).

fire insurance policy or **fire policy,** police d'assurance contre l'incendie (f.); police-incendie (f.).

fire insurance premium or **fire premium,** prime d'assurance contre l'incendie (f.); prime-incendie (f.).

fire risk, risque d'incendie (m.); risque de feu (m.).

fire underwriter, assureur contre l'incendie (m.).

fireman [firemen pl.] (of a ship) (n.), chauffeur (d'un navire) (m.).

firm (Com. & Fin.) (adj.), ferme:
firm offer (opp. to conditional offer), offre ferme (f.).
firm underwriting, garantie de prise ferme (f.).

firm (opp. to optional) (Stock Exch.) (adj.), ferme:
firm bargain or firm deal, marché ferme (m.) [marchés fermes pl.]. V. **option bargain** pour exemples.
I am a firm buyer, we are firm sellers, je suis acheteur ferme, nous sommes vendeurs ferme. Note:—The English construction is adjectival: the French is adverbial, hence ferme is invariable.

firm stock (opp. to option stock), ferme (m.):
I would rather buy firm stock than options (or than give for options), je préfère acheter plutôt du ferme que des primes.
the seller covers himself by buying back his firm stock sold, le vendeur se couvre en rachetant son ferme vendu.

firm (steady; without downward tendencies) (Stock Exch. and Com.) (adj.), ferme; raffermi, -e; tenu, -e; tendu, -e:
firm stocks, valeurs fermes (f.pl.); valeurs tenues (f.pl.).

firm (to be), être ferme; être tenu, -e; tenir:
cinema shares were firmer generally, les valeurs de cinéma sont plus fermes (ou sont mieux tenues) dans l'ensemble (f.pl.).
our market is still firm, notre marché tient toujours (m.).

firm (stiff; hard—said of contango rates) (adj.), tendu, -e.

firm (adv.), ferme:
buy 100 shares firm, achetez 100 actions ferme.
shares bought firm (Stock Exch.), titres achetés ferme (m.pl.).
house which has taken a loan half firm, half on option, maison qui a pris un emprunt moitié ferme, moitié à option (f.).

firm (n.), maison (f.); maison de commerce (f.); société (f.); société en nom collectif (f.); firme (f.).
firm's capital, capital social (m.).

firm (n.) or **firm name,** raison sociale (f.); raison (f.); firme (f.); nom de la firme (m.):

the firm's initials, les initiales de la raison sociale (f.pl.).
to sign one's name or one's firm name, signer son nom ou sa raison sociale.

firm or **firm up** (v.i.), se raffermir; se tendre; se redresser:
X. shares, weak at one time, firmed up at the close to 1¾, l'action X., un moment faible, se raffermit (ou se redresse) en clôture à 1 3/4. V. aussi exemple sous syn. **stiffen.**

firmness (n.), fermeté (f.); raffermissement (m.); tenue (f.); tension (f.):
firmness of the market, of South Africans, fermeté, raffermissement, tenue, du marché, des valeurs sud-africaines.
firmness of contangoes, tension des reports.

first or abbreviated **1st** (adj.), premier, -ère; 1er, 1re:
first and final dividend (or distribution) (to creditors—company in liquidation), première et unique répartition (f.). Cf. final dividend or final distribution, sous **final.**
first (or 1st) class ticket, billet de première (ou de 1re) classe (m.).
first class vessel (i.e., rated in the first class), navire de première cote (m.).
first cost (of manufactured articles) (Costing), prix de revient (des objets fabriqués) (m.).
first directors, premiers administrateurs (m.pl.).
first four or first 4 (January, February, March, April) (Produce Exch.), quatre premiers (m.pl.); 4 premiers (m.pl.) (janvier, février, mars, avril).
first half year or first half or first six months (six months commencing January 1), premier semestre (m.); semestre de janvier (m.); semestre d'hiver (m.):
the first six months' interest, le premier semestre de l'intérêt.
first mortgage, première hypothèque (f.); hypothèque de premier rang (f.).
first name (Christian name), prénom (m.).
first port of call, premier port d'escale (m.).
first premium (Insce) (opp. to renewal premium), première prime (f.).
first, second, preference shares (Abbrev.: 1st, 2nd, prefs), actions de priorité de premier rang, de deuxième rang (f.pl.).
first, second, third, debentures, obligations de premier, de deuxième, de troisième, rang (f.pl.); obligations de priorité, 1er rang, 2e rang, 3e rang (f.pl.); obligations privilégiées, 1er rang, 2e rang, 3e rang (f.pl.).
first, second, third, mortgage debentures (or bonds), obligations de première, de deuxième, de troisième, hypothèque (f.pl.):
5% 1st mortgage debentures (or bonds), obligations 5 0/0 1re hypothèque.
first seller (Produce Exch.), premier vendeur (m.); créateur (m.); créateur de la filière (m.); émetteur (m.); émetteur de la filière (m.); livreur (m.).
first trial balance, balance préparatoire (f.); balance préparatoire d'inventaire (f.); balance de vérification avant inventaire (f.).

first year's premium (Insce), prime de la première année (*f.*).

first of exchange, première de change (*f.*); primata de change (*m.*):
ten days after sight of this first of exchange (second and third of the same tenor and date unpaid [*or* being unpaid] [*or* not paid]) pay to the order of Mr X., to our order, so much, à dix jours de vue, payez par (*ou* veuillez payer contre) cette première de change (la seconde et la troisième n'étant payées) *ou* (la deuxième et la troisième ne l'étant *ou* ne l'étant pas) à l'ordre de M. X., à l'ordre de nous-mêmes, la somme de tant.

fisc (*n.*), fisc (*m.*); trésor public (*m.*).

fiscal (*adj.*), fiscal, -e, -aux:
fiscal law, loi fiscale (*f.*).

fiscally (*adv.*), fiscalement.

fishing port, port de pêche (*m.*).

fit (capable) (*adj.*), apte; approprié, -e:
ship which is not fit to make the agreed voyage, navire qui n'est pas apte à faire le voyage convenu (*m.*).

fit (to adapt) (*v.t.*), aménager; emménager:
to fit a ship for the carriage of steerage passengers as an emigrant ship, aménager, emménager, un navire pour le transport de passagers d'entrepont comme navire à émigrants.

fit out (*v.t.*), armer; équiper.

fit up *or simply* **fit** (*v.t.*), agencer:
to fit up an office, premises, agencer un bureau, un local.

fitting (adaptation) (*n.*), aménagement (*m.*); emménagement (*m.*).

fitting out (*n.*), armement (*m.*); équipement (*m.*):
building and fitting out a ship, la construction et l'armement d'un navire.

fitting up *or simply* **fitting** (an office, or the like) (*n.*), agencement (*m.*).

fittings (*n.pl.*) *or* **fixtures** (*n.pl.*) *or* **fixtures and fittings,** agencement (*m.*); agencements (*m.pl.*); installation (*f.*); installation et agencement:
furniture and fittings *or* furniture, fixtures and fittings, mobilier et agencement.

fix (*v.t.*), fixer; établir; constater; asseoir:
to fix a limit, the rate of interest, the remuneration of the auditors, the amount of damages to be allowed, fixer une limite, le taux de l'intérêt, la rémunération (*ou* l'allocation) des commissaires, le quantum des dommages-intérêts à allouer.
to fix a price, fixer, établir, un prix; constater un cours:
the brokers (on the Paris Bourse) have the exclusive right of fixing the prices of quoted securities, les agents de change ont seuls le droit de constater les cours des valeurs cotées (*m.pl.*).
to fix the maximum price(s) of, taxer:
government which intervenes to fix the maximum prices of bread and meat, État qui intervient de taxer le pain et la viande.
the government has fixed the income tax at so many shillings in the pound, le gouvernement a assis l'impôt sur le revenu à tant pour cent.

fixed (*adj.*), fixe; à forfait; forfaitaire:
fixed capital *or* fixed assets (opp. to *floating*, or *circulating*, *capital* or *assets*, or *revenue assets*), capitaux fixes (*m.pl.*); capital fixe (*m.*); capital immobilisé (*m.*); actif immobilisé (*m.*); valeurs immobilisées (*f.pl.*):
capital expenditure represents all capital (*or* assets) corresponding to fixed capital (*or* assets), and as opposed to floating capital (*or* circulating assets), les immobilisations représentent tous les capitaux correspondant au capital fixe, et par opposition au capital circulant.
fixed charges, charges fixes (*f.pl.*).
fixed charges (Costing) (opp. to *direct expenses* or *establishment charges* or *departmental charges*), frais fixes (*m.pl.*); frais indirects (*m.pl.*); frais généraux (*m.pl.*); dépenses fixes (*ou* indirectes) (*f.pl.*).
fixed deposit (Banking), dépôt à terme (*m.*); dépôt à terme fixe (*m.*); dépôt à échéance (*m.*); dépôt à échéance fixe (*m.*); placement (*m.*); placement à échéance (*m.*).
fixed deposit account, compte de dépôts à terme (*m.*).
fixed deposit receipt, bon à échéance (*m.*); bon à échéance fixe (*m.*); bon de caisse (*m.*). *Note :*—In France, *bons à échéance* can be made payable to bearer, to depositor's order, or to the order of a third party. If the deposit is for several years the *bon de capital* is accompanied by *bons d'intérêts* (interest coupons). In England, banks do not give receipts for deposits, unless they are asked for. Nor do they issue deposit pass books, unless asked for. The usual practice of the customer being to transfer money to deposit account from current account, the transaction is shown in the current account pass book. In England, a deposit receipt is not a negotiable instrument.
fixed depreciation (opp. to *depreciation on diminishing values*), amortissement fixe (*m.*).
fixed duty (registration duty) (opp. to *ad valorem duty*), droit fixe (*m.*).
fixed exchange (opp. to *exchange of the day*), change fixe (*m.*).
fixed exchange (rate of exchange), certain (*m.*). *V.* to quote fixed exchange *pour exemple.*
fixed in advance, fixé (-e) à l'avance; forfaitaire; à forfait:
in consideration of the payment of an amount fixed in advance, moyennant paiement d'une somme forfaitaire.
fixed income, revenu fixe (*m.*).
fixed price *or* fixed consideration, prix fixe (*m.*); prix à forfait (*m.*); prix forfaitaire (*m.*); prix déterminé à forfait (*m.*); forfait (*m.*):
to undertake the carriage of goods at a fixed price, entreprendre le transport des marchandises pour un prix déterminé à forfait.

fixed property, biens immeubles (*m.pl.*); effets immobiliers (*m.pl.*); immeubles (*m.pl.*); immeuble (*m.*); immobilier (*m.*); valeurs immobilières (*f.pl.*).

fixed time trunk call, communication interurbaine à heure fixe (*f.*).

fixed yield investments (opp. to *variable yield investments*), placements à revenus fixes (*m.pl.*).

fixed yield securities, valeurs à revenu fixe (*f.pl.*).

fixed by arbitration (to be), être fixé (-e) par l'arbitrage; s'arbitrer :
these damages can be fixed by arbitration, ces dommages peuvent s'arbitrer (*m.pl.*).

fixing (*n.*), fixation (*f.*); établissement (*m.*); constatation (*f.*) :
fixing a price, a date, fixation d'un prix, d'une date.

fixing of maximum price(s), taxation (*f.*) :
attempts at fixing of maximum prices by the government during the war 1914–1918, essais de taxation par l'État pendant la guerre 1914–1918 (*m.pl.*).

fixtures (*n.pl.*). V. **fittings**.

flag (*n.*), pavillon (*m.*) :
the ship carries a flag which is the sign of the ship's nationality, le navire porte un pavillon qui est le signe de la nationalité du navire.
ship sailing under the British flag, navire naviguant sous pavillon britannique (*m.*).
trade follows the flag, le commerce suit le pavillon ; le pavillon précède la marchandise.

flat cost (of manufactured articles) (Costing), prix de revient (des objets fabriqués) (*m.*).

flat duplicating machine, duplicateur à plat (*m.*).

flat writing accounting machine, machine comptable écrivant à plat (*f.*).

flat writing machine, machine à écrire à plat (*f.*).

fleet (*n.*), flotte (*f.*) :
a fleet of steamers, an air fleet, une flotte de vapeurs, une flotte aérienne.

flight (Aviation) (*n.*), vol (*m.*) :
trial flight, vol d'essai.
passage effected in one flight, trajet effectué d'un seul vol (*m.*).

flight (exodus) (*n.*), fuite (*f.*); exode (*m.*) :
the flight of national capital in time of monetary troubles, la fuite (*ou* l'exode) de capitaux nationaux en période de troubles monétaires.

float (Navig.) (*v.t.*), mettre à flot ; renflouer :
to float a vessel aground, renflouer un navire échoué.

float (Fin.) (*v.t.*), lancer :
to float a company, lancer une compagnie.

floatation *or* **flotation** (of a company) (*n.*), lancement (*m.*).

floating (*adj.*), flottant, -e :
floating capital *or* floating assets (opp. to *fixed capital*, or *assets*, or *permanent*, or *capital, assets*), capitaux mobiles (*m.pl.*); capitaux mobiliers (*m.pl.*); capitaux circulants (*m.pl.*); capitaux roulants (*m.pl.*); capitaux flottants (*m.pl.*); valeurs d'échange (*f.pl.*); valeurs de roulement (*f.pl.*). *V. exemple sous* fixed capital *or* fixed assets.

floating debt (opp. to *consolidated debt*), dette flottante (*f.*) :
the floating debt of a State is the variable part of the national debt, it forms a portion of the working capital of the Treasury essentially temporary ; it is represented by Treasury bonds, etc. : the consolidated debt is a perpetual or long term debt, la dette flottante d'un État est la partie variable de la dette publique, elle forme une portion du fonds de roulement du Trésor essentiellement temporaire ; elle est représentée par des bons du Trésor, etc. : la dette consolidée est une dette perpétuelle ou à long terme.

floating dock, bassin flottant (*m.*); dock flottant (*m.*); forme flottante (*f.*); cale flottante (*f.*).

floating policy (*Abbrev.* : F.P.) *or* **floater** (Fire Insce), police ajustable (*f.*).

floating policy (*Abbrev.* : F.P.) *or* **floater** (*n.*) (Mar. Insce), police d'abonnement (*f.*); police flottante (*f.*); police ouverte (*f.*) :
a marine floating policy is a policy which describes the insurance in general terms, and leaves the name of the ship or ships and other particulars to be defined by subsequent declaration, une police flottante maritime est celle qui décrit l'assurance en termes généraux et laisse à préciser par des déclarations ultérieures le nom du ou des navires et les autres détails.

floating policy insurance (Mar. Insce), assurance d'abonnement (*f.*); assurance flottante (*f.*).

floating stage *or* floating wharf *or* **float** (*n.*), embarcadère flottant (*m.*).

floating (Navig.) (*n.*), mise à flot (*f.*); renflouage (*m.*); renflouement (*m.*).

flotsam (*n.*), épave (*f.*).

fluctuate (*v.i.*), fluctuer ; osciller ; rouler :
Paris cables fluctuated between — and —, le câble sur Paris a fluctué entre — et —.
share which fluctuates between 2s. and 3s., action qui oscille entre 2sh. et 3sh. (*f.*).
an income which fluctuates, taking one year with another, between £1,000 and £1,500, un revenu qui roule, bon an mal an, entre £1 000 et £1 500.

fluctuating (*adj.*), fluctuant, -e ; oscillant, -e.

fluctuation (*n.*), fluctuation (*f.*); oscillation (*f.*); mouvement (*m.*) :
sudden fluctuations of prices, in the rate of exchange, fluctuations, oscillations, mouvements, brusques des prix, dans le cours du change.

flush of money, pécunieux, -euse.

fly (a national flag) (*v.t.*), battre :
ship flying the Belgian flag, navire battant pavillon belge (*m.*).

fly (Aviation) (*v.i.*), voler.

fly a kite (to) (Fin.), tirer en l'air ; tirer en blanc ; tirer à découvert.

flying (*n.*), vol (*m.*); aviation (*f.*) :
night flying, vol de nuit.

flying a kite (Fin.), tirage en l'air (*m.*); tirage en blanc (*m.*); tirage à découvert (*m.*).

fold or **fold up** (*v.t.*), plier:
    to fold (*or* to fold up) a letter, plier une lettre.
folder (Stationery) (*n.*), chemise (*f.*); farde (*f.*).
folder (Publicity) (*n.*), dépliant (*m.*):
    folders for advertising, dépliants pour la publicité.
folding or **folding up** (*n.*), pliage (*m.*).
folio (*n.*) (Abbrev.: **f.** [**ff.** *pl.*] or **Fo** or **fo** or **Fol.** or **fol.**), folio (*m.*); page (*f.*):
    folio of the ledger, folio du grand livre.
    putting in the journal folio from which the item is posted, inscription du folio du journal d'après lequel l'article est rapporté (*f.*).
folio (posting folio) (Bkkpg) (*n.*), rencontre (*f.*).
folio (*v.t.*), folioter; paginer:
    to folio a book, folioter, paginer, un registre.
    to folio the journal, that is to say, to indicate in the column provided for this purpose the folio of each account in the ledger, folioter le journal, c'est-à-dire indiquer dans la colonne *ad hoc* le folio de chaque compte au grand livre.
folio (to number the two opposite pages alike, as distinguished from *to page*) (*v.t.*), paginer à livre ouvert:
    the ledger is generally folioed, that is to say, the left hand page and the right hand page bear the same number, le grand livre est généralement paginé à livre ouvert, c'est-à-dire que la page à gauche et la page à droite portent le même numéro. Cf. **page** (*v.t.*).
folio column, colonne des folios (*f.*).
folioing or **foliation** (paging) (*n.*), foliotage (*m.*); pagination (*f.*).
folioing or **foliation** (numbering of two opposite pages alike) (*n.*), pagination à livre ouvert (*f.*).
follow (*v.t.*), suivre:
    to follow an advice, someone's advice, the instructions contained in a letter, suivre un conseil, les avis de quelqu'un, les instructions d'une lettre.
follow up (*v.t.*), suivre; poursuivre:
    to follow up an enterprise, suivre, poursuivre, une entreprise.
follow up letter (Com.), lettre de poursuite (*f.*); lettre de rappel (*f.*):
    circulars followed by follow up letters, circulaires suivies de lettres de poursuite (*ou* de rappel) (*f.pl.*).
follow up system, poursuite du client (*f.*); relance du client (*f.*).
follower (second or subsequent sheet of letter paper) (*n.*), suite (*f.*); suite de lettre (*f.*).
following account or **following settlement** (Stock Exch.), liquidation suivante (*f.*).
food (*n.*), nourriture (*f.*); vivres (*m.pl.*); provisions de bouche (*f.pl.*); munitions de bouche (*f.pl.*); victuailles (*f.pl.*).
food shares, valeurs d'alimentation (*f.pl.*).
foodstuff (*n.*), matière d'alimentation (*f.*); denrée alimentaire (*f.*).
foot (*n.*) (Ant.: *head*), pied (*m.*); bas (*m.*):
    foot of a page, pied, bas, d'une page.
foot up or **foot** (Arith.) (*v.t.*), additionner:

to foot up a column of figures, additionner une colonne de chiffres.
footing (*n.*), pied (*m.*):
    the goods will be paid for on the footing of their actual value, les marchandises seront payées sur le pied de leur valeur réelle (*f.pl.*).
footing up or **footing** (Arith.) (*n.*), addition (*f.*).
footnote (*n.*), apostille (*f.*).
for or **for and on behalf of,** pour:
    the bill is signed for (*or* for and on behalf of) and not per pro. (*or* per procuration), l'effet est signé pour et non par procuration (*m.*).
for and against, pour et contre:
    different opinions: the ones, for; the others, against, différentes opinions: les unes, pour; les autres, contre.
for or **against** (said of exchanges). V. **exchange** (rate of exchange).
for the account (Stock Exch.). V. sous **account**.
force (*n.*), force (*f.*):
    the force of circumstances, la force des choses.
    probatory force of the consignment note, force probante de la lettre de voiture.
in force, en vigueur:
    regulations, policy, still in force, règlements (*m.pl.*), police (*f.*), encore en vigueur.
    the duty to be collected is always that which is in force at the time when the goods are entered for payment of duty, la taxe à percevoir est toujours celle qui est en vigueur au moment où les marchandises sont déclarées pour l'acquittement des droits.
force majeure (cause beyond control), force majeure (*f.*).
force up (*v.t.*), faire monter; surélever; surhausser:
    to force up prices, faire monter, surélever, surhausser, les prix.
forced (*adj.*), forcé, -e:
    forced call (of a ship at a port of call), relâche forcée (*f.*):
        a call is voluntary or forced, la relâche est volontaire ou forcée.
    forced currency, cours forcé (*m.*):
        government which grants forced currency to a bank's notes, gouvernement qui accorde le cours forcé aux billets d'une banque (*m.*).
        bank notes have forced currency when the issuing bank is dispensed from repaying its notes in cash, les billets de banque ont cours forcé quand la banque émettrice est dispensée de rembourser ses billets en espèces (*m.pl.*).
    forced currency paper, papier à cours forcé (*m.*).
    forced landing (of an aeroplane), atterrissage forcé (*m.*).
    forced loan, emprunt forcé (*m.*).
    forced or voluntary change of route or of voyage, changement de route ou de voyage forcé ou volontaire (*m.*); déroutement forcé ou volontaire (*m.*).
forecast (*n.*), prévision (*f.*); prévision d'avenir (*f.*).

foreclose (Law) (*v.t.*), forclore.

foreclosure (Law) (*n.*), forclusion (*f.*).

foreign (*adj.*), étranger, -ère ; extérieur, -e :
foreign agency, factorerie (*f.*).
foreign bill (opp. to *inland bill*). V. sous **bill**.
foreign cargo (opp. to *coasting cargo*), marchandises de long cours (*f.pl.*).
foreign company (opp. to *British company*), société étrangère (*f.*).
foreign currency (opp. to *home currency*). V. sous **currency**.
foreign exchange. V. sous **exchange** (a bill of of exchange) & **exchange** (bills of exchange).
foreign exchange *or* foreign exchange transactions (*or* dealings), change étranger (*m.*) ; change extérieur (*m.*) ; change (*m.*) ; opérations de change (*f.pl.*) ; négociations de change (*f.pl.*) ; cambisme (*m.*).
foreign exchange (*or* monies) bought and sold *or* foreign moneys exchanged *or* simply foreign exchange (sign on an exchange office), achat et vente de monnaies étrangères ;´ change (*m.*) ; bureau de change (*m.*).
foreign exchange broker, courtier de change (*m.*) ; cambiste (*m.*).
foreign exchange market, marché des changes (*m.*) ; marché cambiste (*m.*) ; marché des devises (*m.*) ; place de change (*f.*) ; place cambiste (*f.*).
foreign exchange rates *or* foreign exchanges (the prices themselves), cours des changes (*m.pl.*) ; cours de place (*m.pl.*) ; cours des devises (*m.pl.*).
foreign exchange rates *or* foreign exchanges (on 'change table), cote des changes (*f.*).
foreign-going ship (opp. to *home-trade ship*), navire au long cours (*m.*) ; navire long-courrier (*m.*) ; long-courrier (*m.*) ; bâtiment au long cours (*m.*).
foreign-going steamer, steamer au long cours (*m.*) ; navire à vapeur au long cours (*m.*).
foreign loan, emprunt extérieur (*m.*).
foreign market (opp. to *home market*), marché extérieur (*m.*) ; marché étranger (*m.*).
foreign money, monnaie étrangère (*f.*).
foreign port (opp. to *home port*), port étranger (*m.*).
foreign postal packet (opp. to *inland postal packet*), objet de correspondance pour l'étranger (*m.*). Cf. **imperial and foreign system**.
foreign products *or* foreign produce (opp. to *home products* or *produce*), produits étrangers (*m.pl.*) ; produits exotiques (*m.pl.*).
foreign securities *or* foreign stocks, valeurs étrangères (*f.pl.*) ; fonds étrangers (*m.pl.*).
foreign stocks and bonds *or* foreign government stocks (*or* securities), fonds d'État étrangers (*m.pl.*).
foreign trade (opp. to *home trade* or *domestic trade*), commerce extérieur (*m.*) ; commerce international (*m.*).
foreign voyage (ocean voyage) (opp. to *coasting voyage*), voyage au (*ou* de) long cours (*m.*) ; long cours (*m.*) :

ship leaving for a foreign voyage, navire partant pour le long cours (*m.*).
in principle, all merchandise imported from abroad is deemed to be foreign and in consequence subject to duty, en principe, toute marchandise importée de l'étranger est réputée étrangère et par suite soumise aux droits.

forename (*n.*), prénom (*m.*).

forfeit (penalty for non performance) (*n.*), dédit (*m.*) ; pénalité (*f.*) :
forfeits for non performance of the agreement, dédits, pénalités, en cas d'inexécution du contrat.

forfeit (*v.t.*), être déchu (-e) de :
to forfeit a right, être déchu (-e) d'un droit.
insurance which is forfeited if the insured knowingly exaggerates the amount of the damage, assurance qui est déchue si l'assuré exagère sciemment le montant du dommage (*f.*).
V. aussi exemple sous **endorsement** (Insce).

forfeiture (*n.*), déchéance (*f.*).

forge (*v.t.*), forger ; falsifier ; contrefaire :
to forge a signature, forger, falsifier, contrefaire, une signature.
to forge bank notes, contrefaire des billets de banque.

forged cheque, faux chèque (*m.*) ; chèque forgé (*m.*).

forger (pers.) (*n.*), faussaire (*m.*) ; falsificateur, -trice.

forgery [**forgeries** *pl.*] (*n.*), faux (*m.*) ; contrefaçon (*f.*).

forgive someone a debt (to), faire grâce à quelqu'un d'une dette.

form (prescribed order of words) (*n.*), forme (*f.*) :
form of a receipt, forme d'une quittance.

form (instrument of manifestation) (*n.*), minute (*f.*) :
sender of a telegram who must mention his address on the form, who should write the route in the form, expéditeur d'un télégramme qui doit mentionner son adresse sur la minute, qui doit indiquer la route sur la minute (*m.*).

form (a paper with spaces left to be filled) (*n.*), formule (*f.*) ; bulletin (*m.*) :
to fill up a printed form, remplir une formule imprimée.
cheque form, formule de chèque.
telegram form, formule de télégramme.
form of application *or* application form (for shares or stock), bulletin de souscription.
form of bill of exchange *or* bill form, formule d'effet de commerce.
form of bill of lading *or* bill of lading form, formule de connaissement.
form of confirmation (of a statement of account), formule d'approbation.
form of proxy *or* proxy form, formule de pouvoir ; formule de mandat.
form of receipt *or* receipt form, formule d'acquit.
form of requisition *or* requisition form (for money order), formule de mandat.

form of transfer *or* transfer form (stocks and shares), formule de transfert.

form (*v.t.*), former; constituer; faire; se former; se constituer; se faire:
to form a company, a syndicate, constituer, former, une société, un syndicat.
amount which forms part of the expenses, somme qui fait partie des frais (*f.*).
financiers who form a syndicate to underwrite an issue, financiers qui se syndiquent (*ou* se constituent en syndicat) pour garantir une émission (*m.pl.*).
to form an opinion of the risk to which a cargo is exposed, se faire, se former, une opinion du risque auquel une cargaison est exposée.

to be formed, être formé (-e), constitué, -e; se former; se constituer:
a new company was formed with a capital of so much, une nouvelle société se constitua (*ou* se forma) au capital de tant.

formal (*adj.*), formel, -elle:
formal denial, démenti formel (*m.*).

formality [**formalities** *pl.*] (*n.*), formalité (*f.*):
formality of registration, formalité d'enregistrement.
customs formalities, formalités de douane.
to show that all the necessary formalities have been complied with, justifier de l'accomplissement de toutes les formalités requises.

formally (*adv.*), formellement.

formation (*n.*), formation (*f.*); constitution (*f.*):
formation of a reserve fund, constitution, formation, d'un fonds de réserve.
formation of a bank into a limited company, constitution, formation, d'une banque en société anonyme.

formation expenses, frais de constitution (*m.pl.*).

formula [**formulas** *or* **formulæ** *pl.*] (*n.*), formule (*f.*):
compliments, congratulations, thanks, and other formulas of courtesy, compliments, félicitations, remerciements, et autres formules de politesse.

formulate (*v.t.*), formuler:
to formulate a claim against someone, formuler une réclamation contre quelqu'un.

fortuitous (*adj.*), fortuit, -e:
fortuitous event, cas fortuit (*m.*).
a fortuitous cause of sacrifice, une cause fortuite de sacrifice.

fortuitously (*adv.*), fortuitement.

fortune (*n.*), fortune (*f.*); avoir (*m.*):
to make a fortune, faire fortune.

forward (Bkkpg). V. **brought forward** & **carried forward.**

forward (Produce Exch.) (*adj.* & *n.*) (opp. to *spot*), livrable (*m.*).

forward (to dispatch) (*v.t.*), expédier; acheminer; faire suivre; transmettre:
to forward the goods to their port of destination, expédier les marchandises à leur port de destination.
to forward the goods by another boat, faire suivre la marchandise par un autre bateau.
letters forwarded by weekly mails, lettres acheminées par des courriers hebdomadaires (*f.pl.*).
to forward a telegram by post, postaliser, acheminer par poste, un télégramme.
to be forwarded *or* please forward (inscription on a postal packet), faire suivre; veuillez faire suivre.
if the addressee has gone abroad, do not forward, si le destinataire est parti à l'étranger, ne pas faire suivre.

forward call (of a ship at an intermediate port) (opp. to *backward call*), escale directe (*f.*); échelle directe (*f.*).

forward delivery, livraison à terme (*f.*).

forward exchange market, marché des changes à terme (*m.*).

forward exchange transactions (*or* **dealings**) *or* **exchange for forward delivery** (opp. to *spot exchange transactions*), négociations (*ou* opérations) de change à terme (*f.pl.*).

forward method (accounts current with interest), méthode progressive (*f.*); méthode directe (*f.*).

forward price (Produce Exch.) (opp. to *spot price*), cours du livrable (*m.*).

forward rate (Foreign Exchange Market), cours à terme (*m.*):
forward exchange rates, cours des changes (*ou* des devises) à terme (*m.pl.*).

forward sale (Produce Exch.) (opp. to *spot sale*), vente à terme (*f.*); vente à livrer (*f.*).

forward transaction (Produce Exch.), marché à terme (*m.*); marché à livrer (*m.*).

forwarding (*n.*), expédition (*f.*); acheminement (*m.*); transmission (*f.*):
prompt forwarding of the goods, la prompte expédition des marchandises.
forwarding by rail, expédition par chemin de fer.
delay in forwarding the goods, retard dans l'acheminement de la marchandise (*m.*).
forwarding telegrams by post, acheminement des télégrammes par la poste.

forwarding agent, commissionnaire de transport (*ou* de transports) (*m.*); commissionnaire-messager (*m.*); agent de transport (*m.*); expéditeur (*m.*); agent metteur à bord (*m.*).

forwarding charges, frais d'expédition (*m.pl.*).

forwarding clerk, expéditionnaire (*m.*).

forwarding station (Rly.), gare expéditrice (*f.*); gare d'expédition (*f.*).

foul (to collide with) (Navig.) (*v.t.*), aborder; faire collision avec.

foul (*v.i.*), s'aborder; faire collision.

foul bill (of health) (opp. to *clean bill*), patente (de santé) brute (*f.*).

foul bill of lading (opp. to *clean bill of lading*), connaissement avec réserves (*m.*); connaissement portant des réserves (*m.*).

fouling (*n.*), abordage (*m.*); collision (*f.*).

found (to establish) (*v.t.*), fonder; créer; établir:
to found a house of business, fonder, créer, établir, une maison de commerce.

foundation (*n.*), fondation (*f.*); création (*f.*); établissement (*m.*).

founder (pers.) (*n.*), fondateur, -trice; créateur, -trice :
founder of a house of business, fondateur, créateur, d'une maison de commerce.
founder (*v.i.*), sombrer; couler bas; couler à fond; couler :
ship which foundered and was lost, navire qui sombra (*ou* qui coula) et se perdit (*m.*).
founder's share [**founders' shares** *pl.*], part de fondateur (*f.*); part bénéficiaire (*f.*).
Note :—Unlike in England, where founders' or management shares form part of the company's capital, in France, *parts de fondateurs* or *parts bénéficiaires* are not represented by any capital value. They are merely profit sharing rights after certain distributions on the ordinary shares, and can be likened to directors' percentages of profits. The fact of not representing any capital value is the essential difference between a *part* and an *action*. *parts de fondateur*, like *actions d'apport*, are not negotiable for two years. See note under **vendors' shares.**
founders (*abbrev. of* founders' shares—*in market news*), la fondateur (*abrév. de* la part de fondateur—*en bourse*) :
X. founders closed at 1½, la fondateur X. clôture à 1 1/2.
fountain pen, stylograph (*m.*); stylo (*m.*); porteplume à réservoir (*m.*); porte-plume réservoir (*m.*).
four months *or simply* **four** (*n.*) (Produce Exch.), quatre mois (*m.pl.*); quatre (*m.pl.*) :
the first four *or* the first 4 (January, February, March, April), les quatre premiers; les 4 premiers (janvier, février, mars, avril).
fraction (*n.*), fraction (*f.*) :
decimal fraction, fraction décimale (*f.*).
stock which has lost a fraction, valeur qui a perdu une fraction (*f.*).
fractions of a penny charged as a penny, taxe arrondie au décime supérieur (*f.*).
for every . . . or fraction (*or* **fractional part) of . . .,** par fraction indivisible de . . . :
for every £50 or fraction of £50 up to £250 *so much,* and for every additional £50 or fractional part of £50 *so much,* par fraction indivisible de 50£ jusqu'à 250£ *tant,* et par fraction indivisible de 50£ en excédent *tant.*
Cf. **each (for).**
fraction (incomplete unit of a share or of stock) (*n.*), fraction (*f.*); rompu (*m.*); résidu (*m.*) :
fractions of new shares, fractions d'actions nouvelles.
a fraction of rente, une fraction de rente.
fractions are dealt in on the Stock Exchange, les rompus (*ou* les résidus) se négocient en bourse.
fractional (*adj.*), fractionnaire :
fractional number, nombre fractionnaire (*m.*).
fractional coins *or* fractional money, monnaie divisionnaire (*f.*); monnaie d'appoint (*f.*) :
silver fractional coins, monnaie divisionnaire d'argent.
the amount of the cheque must be stated in

words at length. The amount of the fractional money can however be stated in figures only, le montant du chèque doit être indiqué en toutes lettres. Le montant de la monnaie divisionnaire peut toutefois être indiqué en chiffres seulement.
fragile (*adj.*), fragile :
fragile articles such as glassware, objets fragiles tels que la verrerie (*m.pl.*).
fragile (notice on a parcel), fragile.
frame (compartment of a ruled page) (*n.*), cadre (*m.*); case (*f.*) :
frame for service instructions, cadre réservé (*ou* case réservée) aux mentions de service.
franc (money) (*n.*) (Abbrev.: **f.** *or* **F.** [**f.** *or* **F.** *pl.*] *or* **fr.** [**fr.** *or* **frs** *pl.*] *or* **Fr.** [**Fr.** *or* **Frs** *pl.*] *or* **fc** [**fcs** *pl.*]), franc (*m.*).
franchise (Mar. Insce) (*n.*), franchise (*f.*) :
by franchise is understood the minimum percentage that damage admitted in particular average must reach in order to be thrown on the underwriters, par franchise on entend le pourcentage minimum que le dommage admis en avarie particulière doit atteindre pour être mis à la charge des assureurs.
average irrespective of franchise, avaries payables sans égard à la franchise (*f.pl.*).
V. note sous **memorandum** (of percentages), et cf. **percentage.**
franked letter, lettre en franchise (*ou* en franchise de port) (*f.*).
franking (Post) (*n.*), franchise (*f.*) :
franking is the exemption from charge granted, la franchise est l'exemption de taxe accordée.
fraud (*n.*), fraude (*f.*) :
to commit a fraud, commettre une fraude.
fraud vitiates a contract, la fraude vicie un contrat.
fraudulent (*adj.*), frauduleux, -euse :
fraudulent means, moyens frauduleux (*m.pl.*).
fraudulent declaration of the value of a parcel, déclaration frauduleuse de la valeur d'un colis (*f.*).
fraudulent conversion (of funds), détournement (*m.*), divertissement (*m.*), distraction (*f.*) (de fonds).
fraudulently (*adv.*), frauduleusement.
free allowance *or* **free allowance of luggage** (opp. to *excess luggage*), franchise de poids (*f.*); franchise de bagages (*f.*) :
each passenger is granted, for his luggage, a free allowance of — lbs 1st class, — lbs 2nd class, and — lbs 3rd class, il est alloué à chaque voyageur, pour ses bagages, une franchise de poids de — livres pour les 1ʳᵉˢ classes, — livres pour les 2ᵉˢ classes, et — livres pour les 3ᵉˢ classes.
free alongside ship (Abbrev.: **f.a.s.** *or* **F.A.S.**), franco le long du bord du navire; franco le long du navire.
free at wharf, franco à quai.
freeboard. V. ci-après.
free coinage, libre frappe (*f.*); libre monnayage (*m.*).
free delivery, remise gratuite (*f.*); distribution gratuite (*f.*).

free delivery area (of telegrams, parcels, or the like), zone de distribution (*ou* de remise) gratuite (*f.*); circonscription de remise (*ou* de distribution) gratuite (*f.*).

free from. V. sous **free of.**

free from mortgage (to), déshypothéquer :
to free a property from mortgage, déshypothéquer une propriété.

free luggage (no excess charges to pay), bagages en franchise (*m.pl.*).

free market (unrestricted by regulations), marché libre (*m.*); marché ouvert (*m.*) :
what characterizes a free market is the absence of all regulation, ce qui caractérise le marché libre c'est l'absence de toute réglementation.

free market (characterized by plentiful dealings) (opp. to *limited market*), marché large (*m.*) :
lively free market in X. shares round about 1¼, large marché animé en actions X. vers 1 1/4.

oils.—dealings appreciably freer, and general advance of prices, pétroles.—transactions sensiblement plus larges, et avance générale des cours.

free money order for payment of taxes, mandat-contribution (*m.*).

free of *or* **free from** *or simply* **free** (*adj. & adv.*), franc (franche) de (*adj.*); franc de (*adj. invar.*); exempt (-e) de (*adj.*); net (nette) de (*adj.*); franco (*adv.*); franco de; en franchise de (*adv.*); en franchise (*adv.*); *ou par ellipse* franchise (*adv.*); vierge de : (Cf. **warranted free of.**)

Note :—Such expressions as *franc de port, franc d'avaries,* can, at will, vary or remain invariable ; as, *envoyer franche de port une lettre* (to send a letter post free) [here, *franche* is an adjective, qualifying the feminine noun *lettre*], or *envoyer franc de port une lettre* [here, *franc de port* is an adverbial phrase, and consequently is invariable].

free of all charges, franco de tous frais ; franc de tous droits.

free of (*or* from) all claim in respect of partial loss, of (*or* from) any claim arising from delay, franc de tout recours pour perte partielle, de tout recours provenant de retard.

free of average *or* free from average, franc d'avarie ; franc d'avaries :
free from average under the franchise specified in the policy, franc d'avaries au-dessous de la franchise énoncée dans la police.

free of average policy, police franc d'avarie (*f.*).

free of brokerage *or* free of commission *or simply* free, franco courtage ; franco de courtage ; franco commission ; franco :
stock exchange transaction done free of commission (*or* done free), opération de bourse faite franco courtage (*ou* faite franco) (*f.*).

free of charge *or* free of expense *or simply* free, franco :
cheques are collected free of charge, les chèques sont encaissés franco (*m.pl.*).

free of customs duties, franc de droits de douane ; franco de douane.

free of duty *or* duty-free (*adj.*) *or* duty free (*adv.*) *or simply* free, franc (franche) de tout droit (*adj.*); exempt (-e) de droits (*adj.*); exempt, -e (*adj.*); libre à l'entrée (*adj.*); en franchise de droits (*adv.*); en franchise (*adv.*) :
duty-free goods *or simply* free goods (Customs), marchandises franches de tout droit (*f.pl.*); marchandises exemptes de droits (*f.pl.*); marchandise exempte (*f.*); marchandises libres à l'entrée (*f.pl.*).

all goods imported or exported, whether dutiable or free, toutes les marchandises importées ou exportées, qu'elles soient sujettes à des droits ou qu'elles soient exemptes.

goods admissible free of duty (*or* duty free) on proof of origin, marchandises admissibles en franchise de droits sur justification d'origine (*f.pl.*).

free admission (Customs), admission en franchise (*f.*).

entry for duty-free goods *or simply* free entry (Customs), déclaration pour produits exempts de droits (*f.*).

free of (*or* from) general average (Mar. Insce) (*Abbrev. :* f.g.a. *or* F.G.A.), franc d'avarie commune ; franc d'avaries communes :
free of general average clause (*Abbrev. :* f.g.a. clause), clause franc d'avaries communes (*f.*); clause de franchise d'avaries communes (*f.*).

free of income tax, net (nette) d'impôt sur le revenu.

free of (*or* from) particular average (*Abbrev. :* f.p.a. *or* F.P.A.) (Mar. Insce) (opp. to *with particular average or simply with average*), franc d'avarie particulière ; franc d'avaries particulières :
free from particular average unless the vessel be stranded, franc d'avaries particulières sauf en cas d'échouement.

free of particular average absolutely, franc d'avaries particulières absolument ; franchise absolue d'avaries particulières.

free of particular average clause (*Abbrev. :* f.p.a. clause), clause franc d'avaries particulières (*f.*).

free of tax *or* tax free, net (nette) d'impôt (*ou* d'impôts); exempt (-e) d'impôt (*ou* d'impôts) :
dividend of 5% free of tax, dividende de 5 0/0 net d'impôt (*m.*).

interest free of tax, intérêts nets d'impôts (*m.pl.*).

all coupons of French rentes are free of all tax, with the exception of those of the 3% redeemable, tous les coupons de rentes françaises sont exempts de tout impôt, à l'exception de ceux de la rente 3 0/0 amortissable.

free of total loss, franc de perte totale.

bills of lading free from any clause relieving from liability, connaissements vierges de toute clause d'exonération de responsabilité (*m.pl.*).

free on board (Abbrev.: **f.o.b.** *or* **F.O.B.**), franco bord; franco à bord:

goods delivered free on board the ship in the port of departure, marchandises rendues franco à bord du navire dans le port de départ (*f.pl.*).

free on board (*or* f.o.b.) to ex ship's sling, bord à bord:

freight paid f.o.b. to ex ship's sling, fret payé bord à bord (*m.*).

free on board (*or* f.o.b.) to landing on quay, bord à quai.

free on quay (Abbrev.: **f.o.q.**), franco à quai.

free on rail (Abbrev.: **f.o.r.** *or* **F.O.R.**) *or* **free on truck** (Abbrev.: **f.o.t.** *or* **F.O.T.**) *or* *simply* **on rail,** franco wagon; franco gare; sur wagon.

free one's property from debt (**to**), purger son bien de dettes.

free oneself from a debt (**to**), se libérer d'une dette.

free overside, au débarquement:

sale free overside, vente au débarquement (*f.*).

free port (where no duties are levied on articles of commerce), port franc (*m.*).

free port (free for use by trading vessels of all nations), port libre (*m.*); port ouvert (*m.*).

free pratique, libre pratique (*f.*). V. exemple sous **pratique.**

free trade (*adj.*), libre-échangiste; de libre-échange:

free trade doctrines, doctrines libre-échangistes (*f.pl.*).

free trade policy, politique de libre échange (*f.*).

free trade, libre-échange (*m.*); free-trade (*m.*):

lively discussions between the champions of free trade and protectionism, de vives discussions entre les champions du libre-échange et du protectionnisme.

free trader *or* **free tradist,** libre-échangiste (*m.* ou *f.*); antiprotectionniste (*m.* ou *f.*):

in principle, free traders value above all cheapness of imported products, while protectionists consider as an evil the importation of any article that can be made in their country, par principe, les libre-échangistes apprécient avant tout le bon marché des produits importés, tandis que les protectionnistes considèrent comme un mal l'importation de tout article que l'on peut fabriquer dans leur pays. (V. aussi exemple sous **protectionist.**)

freeboard (of a ship) (*n.*), franc-bord (d'un navire) (*m.*).

freely (*adv.*), librement; largement:

in principle, agreements are reputed to be made freely between the contracting parties, en principe, les conventions sont réputées se former librement entre les parties contractantes.

when a stock is freely offered with few or no bids, lorsqu'une valeur est largement offerte avec peu ou pas de demandes.

freeness (of a market) (*n.*), ampleur (d'un marché) (*f.*). Cf. **free market** (characterized by plentiful dealings).

freight (price paid for transport by sea) (*n.*) (Abbrev.: **frt**), fret (*m.*); prix du fret (*m.*); nolis (*m.*); nolage (*m.*):

freight is paid according to the nature of the cargo, le fret est payé suivant la nature des marchandises.

freight at risk, fret à faire; fret en risque.

freight earned *or* freight not repayable, fret acquis. V. exemples sous **earned** & **not repayable.**

freight paid in advance, fret payé d'avance; fret payé.

freight payable at destination as per weight declared on shipment, fret payable à destination suivant poids déclaré à l'embarquement.

freight pro rata *or* freight pro rata itineris peracti, fret proportionnel; fret proportionnel à la distance; fret de distance.

freight (cargo; goods) (*n.*), fret (*m.*); charge (*f.*); chargement (*m.*); cargaison (*f.*); marchandises (*f.pl.*):

ship which lands the whole or part of her freight, navire qui débarque la totalité ou une partie de son fret (*ou* de son chargement) (*ou* de sa cargaison) (*m.*).

ship which cannot find a homeward freight, navire qui ne peut pas trouver un fret de retour (*m.*).

heavy freight, fret lourd; marchandises lourdes.

freight (*v.t.*), affréter; fréter; noliser.

freight account, compte de fret (*m.*).

freight bookings, engagements de fret (*m.pl.*).

freight broking *or* **freight brokerage,** courtage des affrètements (*m.*).

freight contract, contrat de fret (*m.*).

freight insurance, assurance sur fret (*f.*).

freight locomotive, locomotive à marchandises (*f.*).

freight manifest, manifeste de fret (*m.*).

freight market, marché des frets (*m.*).

freight note, note de fret (*f.*).

freight office (of a shipping company), bureau du fret (d'une compagnie de navigation) (*m.*).

freight quotation, cote de fret (*f.*); cotation de fret (*f.*).

freight rate (Shipping), taux de fret (*m.*); taux du fret (*m.*); cours de (*ou* du) fret (*m.*).

freight rates (Rly.), tarif (*m.*) [*ou* tarifs (*m.pl.*)] de marchandises (*m.*).

freight rebate, ristourne de fret (*f.*); rabais de fret (*m.*).

freight service, service de marchandises (*m.*).

freight ton, tonneau d'affrètement (*m.*); tonneau de fret (*m.*); tonneau de portée (*m.*); tonne de portée en lourd (*f.*). In France, 1,000 kilogrammes, or 1·44 cubic metres, usually.

In England, the freight ton is 20 cwt, or 40 cubic feet (= 1·132 cubic metres), usually.

freight traffic, trafic des marchandises (*m.*).

freight train, train de marchandises (*m.*); train de petite vitesse (*m.*); petite vitesse (*f.*).

freighter (pers.) (*n.*), affréteur (*m.*); fréteur (*m.*):
the essential obligation of the freighter, whatever may be the kind of freighting, is the payment of the freight, l'obligation essentielle de l'affréteur, quel que soit le genre d'affrètement, est le paiement du fret (*f.*).
freighter (freight carrying vessel) (*n.*), navire de charge (*m.*); bâtiment de charge (*m.*); cargo-boat (*m.*); cargo (*m.*); navire à cargaison (*m.*); chargebot (*m.*).
freighting (*n.*), affrètement (*m.*); frètement (*m.*); nolisement (*m.*):
freighting ad valorem, affrètement ad valorem.
freighting by contract, affrètement à forfait.
freighting by the case, affrètement à la pièce.
freighting on measurement, affrètement au volume.
freighting on weight, affrètement au poids.
freighting per head (cattle), affrètement à la tête (bétail).
freighting per ton, affrètement au tonneau; affrètement à la tonne.
French (*adj.*), français, -e:
French bank rate, taux officiel de la Banque de France (*m.*); taux d'escompte de la Banque de France (*m.*); taux Banque de France (*m.*).
French consul, consul de France (*m.*); consul français (*m.*).
French fiscal system, système fiscal français (*m.*).
French franc, franc français (*m.*).
French rente *or* French rentes, rente française (*f.*); rentes françaises (*f.pl.*).
frequent (*v.t.*), fréquenter:
to frequent a market, fréquenter un marché.
fresh money (opp. to *old money*), argent frais (*m.*):
the company which, having need of fresh money, does not wish to increase its capital, can have recourse to the issue of debentures, la société qui, ayant besoin d'argent frais, ne veut pas augmenter son capital, peut recourir à l'émission d'obligations.
fresh water (opp. to *sea water*), eau douce (*f.*).
friendly (*adj.*), amical, -e, -aux; amicable; amiable:
friendly arbitrator, arbitre amiable compositeur (*m.*); amiable compositeur (*m.*).
friendly flag (opp. to *enemy flag*), pavillon ami (*m.*).
friendly reception, accueil amical (*ou* amicable) (*m.*).
friendly society, société de secours mutuels (*f.*).
frighten the bears (to) (Stock Exch.), faire courir le découvert.
frontier (*n.*), frontière (*f.*):
goods examined at the frontier, marchandises visitées à la frontière (*f.pl.*).
frontier station, gare frontière (*f.*).
frustrate (*v.t.*), frustrer.
frustration (*n.*), frustration (*f.*):
frustration of the insured voyage, frustration du voyage assuré.
fulfil (*v.t.*), remplir; faire l'acquit de; accomplir:

to fulfil a condition, one's obligations, remplir une condition, ses obligations.
in every contract, there are obligations to fulfil for each of the contracting parties, dans tout contrat, il existe des obligations à remplir pour chacune des parties contractantes.
to fulfil one's trust, faire l'acquit de sa charge.
fulfilment (*n.*), accomplissement (*m.*):
fulfilment of a contract, accomplissement d'un contrat.
full (*adj.*), plein, -e; entier, -ère; complet, -ète; copieux, -euse; intégral, -e, -aux:
full address, adresse complète (*f.*).
full cargo, chargement complet (*m.*); cargaison complète (*f.*); entière cargaison (*f.*).
full cargo charter (distinguished from *part cargo charter*), affrètement total (*m.*).
full duty, droit plein (*m.*).
full fare, plein tarif (*m.*); place entière (*f.*). V. exemple sous **fare.**
full fare ticket, billet à plein tarif (*m.*); billet à place entière (*m.*).
full freight, fret entier (*m.*).
full name *or* name in full, nom et prénoms:
the full name (*or* the name in full), address, and profession or business (*or* and occupation) (*or* and description) of the applicant, les nom, prénoms, adresse, et profession (*ou* et qualités) du souscripteur.
full premium, prime entière (*f.*); prime intégrale (*f.*); pleine prime (*f.*).
full price, prix fort (*m.*).
full rates, plein tarif (*m.*):
telegrams at full rates, télégrammes à plein tarif (*m.pl.*).
full rates (of customs duties) (distinguished from *preferential rates*), tarif général (*m.*), tarif maximum (*m.*) (des droits de douane).
full report (comprehensive statement), rapport copieux (*m.*):
the very full report of the directors, le très copieux rapport du conseil d'administration.
full series (Shipping) (opp. to *tail series*), série pleine (*f.*).
full set (of bills of lading), jeu complet (*m.*), série complète (*f.*) (de connaissements).
full trial balance, balance préparatoire (*f.*); balance préparatoire d'inventaire (*f.*); balance de vérification avant inventaire (*f.*).
full truck load (Rly.) (opp. to *part truck load*), charge complète de wagon (*f.*); wagon complet (*m.*).
full value, valeur entière (*f.*).
full weight coin, pièce droite (*f.*).
full (to be) *or* **full up (to be)** (Insce), avoir son plein:
company which is full (*or* full up) on a certain risk, compagnie qui a son plein sur un certain risque (*f.*).
fully (*adv.*) *or* **in full**, entièrement; complètement; intégralement; tout; en entier; en totalité; en une fois; en une seule fois:
fully paid *or* fully paid up (opp. to *partly paid or partly paid up*) (*Abbrev.:* **f.p.** *or* **f.pd** *or*

fy pd), entièrement libéré, -e ; complètement libéré, -e ; intégralement libéré, -e ;
libéré, -e ; entièrement (ou complètement)
(ou intégralement) versé, -e ; tout payé :
fully paid shares or fully paid stock, actions
entièrement (ou complètement) (ou intégralement) libérées (f.pl.) ; actions libérées
(f.pl.) ; titres libérés (m.pl.).
tout payé (invar.) is used in the abbreviated
form t.p. in quotation lists, and the like.
English equivalent : f.p.
fully paid capital, capital entièrement (ou
complètement) (ou intégralement) versé (m.).
capital : 10 millions fully paid up, capital :
10 millions entièrement versés.
fully secured creditor (opp. to partly secured
creditor), créancier entièrement (ou complètement) nanti (m.).
to discharge one's liabilities in full, acquitter
intégralement le montant de son passif.
to pay the freight in full, payer le fret en
entier.
payments made in full or on account, versements faits en totalité ou à valoir (m.pl.).
payment can be made in full or in (or by)
instalments, le paiement peut se faire en
une fois ou par versements échelonnés.
subscription payable in full, abonnement
payable en une seule fois (m.).
fumes from hold, buée de cale (f.).
function (n.), fonction (f.) ; office (m.) :
the functions of a secretary, les fonctions
d'un secrétaire.
functionary [**functionaries** pl.] (pers.) (n.), fonctionnaire (m. ou f.).
fund (n.), fonds (m.) ; caisse (f.) : (Pour le
pluriel **funds,** V. ci-après.)
reserve fund, fonds de réserve.
pension fund, caisse des retraites.
fund (v.t.), fonder ; consolider :
to fund a public debt, fonder une dette
publique.
to fund interest, consolider des arrérages.
funded debt, dette fondée (f.).
funded property, biens en rentes (m.pl.).
fundholder (pers.) (n.), rentier, -ère.
funding (n.), funding (m.) ; consolidation (f.).
funding certificate, titre funding (m.).
funding loan, emprunt funding (m.) ; emprunt
de consolidation (m.).
funds (n.pl.), fonds (m.pl.) ; fonds (m.) ; masse
(f.) ; provision (f.) :
to be in funds, être en fonds.
funds are low, les fonds sont bas.
funds of a company, fonds social ; masse
sociale.
to have funds with a banker, avoir une provision chez un banquier.
person who issues a cheque without sufficient
funds to meet it, personne qui émet un

chèque sans provision préalable et disponible
(f.).
no funds (Banking), défaut de provision.
insufficient funds or not sufficient funds (Banking), provision insuffisante ; insuffisance de
provision.
funds (public securities) (n.pl.), fonds (m.pl.) :
public funds, fonds publics.
furnish (v.t.), fournir ; pourvoir :
to furnish information, fournir des renseignements.
to furnish evidence that the insured securities
have been dispatched in the manner declared in the proposal of insurance, fournir
la preuve que les valeurs assurées ont été
expédiées dans la manière déclarée dans la
proposition d'assurance.
furniture (n.), mobilier (m.) ; meubles (m.pl.) :
furniture and fittings or furniture, fixtures
and fittings, mobilier et agencement.
furniture (of a ship) (n.), accessoires (m.pl.) ;
mobilier (m.) (d'un navire) :
hull, tackle, apparel, furniture, etc., corps,
agrès, apparaux, accessoires (ou mobilier),
etc.
further (adj.), supplémentaire ; complémentaire ; nouveau (or nouvel before a vowel or
silent h), -elle :
to ask for a further credit, demander un
crédit supplémentaire ; demander un
supplément de crédit.
further advice, nouvel avis (m.) :
until (or till) further advice, jusqu'à nouvel
avis.
further information, renseignements complémentaires (m.pl.).
further margin or further cover, marge supplémentaire (f.).
fuse (to amalgamate) (v.t.), fusionner.
fuse (v.i.), fusionner ; se fusionner.
fusion (n.), fusion (f.) ; fusionnement (m.) :
fusion of several banks, fusion de plusieurs
banques.
future delivery, livraison à terme (f.).
for future delivery, à terme :
exchange for future delivery, opérations (ou
négociations) de change à terme (f.pl.).
transaction for future delivery during specified
periods, marché à terme fixe (m.).
future prospects or **prospects for the future,**
perspectives d'avenir (f.pl.).
futures (Corn Exchange) (n.pl.) (opp. to spot),
livrable (m.) :
in futures on the coming campaign, business
although a little more active than the previous
week, was still only small, en livrable sur la
future campagne, les affaires quoique un
peu plus actives que la semaine précédente,
n'ont eu encore que peu d'importance.
futures market (Corn Exchange), marché à
terme (m.) ; marché du terme (m.).

G

gain (*n.*), gain (*m.*):
in insurance, what is gain for one is loss for the other, en assurance, ce qui est gain pour l'un est perte pour l'autre.
stock which shows a gain of several points, valeur qui marque un gain de plusieurs points (*f.*).

gain (*v.t.*), gagner:
to gain wealth, gagner des richesses.
by wanting to gain all, one risks losing all, à vouloir tout gagner, on risque de tout perdre.
X. shares gained a few points, l'action X. gagne quelques points.
X. preference gained ground at 1½, la privilégiée X. gagne du terrain à 1 1/2.

gain (*v.i.*), profiter.

gainer (pers.) (*n.*), gagneur, -euse.

gamble (*v.i.*), jouer; agioter:
to gamble on the stock exchange, jouer à la bourse; agioter.

gambler (pers.) (*n.*), joueur, -euse; agioteur, -euse.

gambling (*n.*), jeu (*m.*); jeux (*m.pl.*); agiotage (*m.*):
gambling in differences and contangoes, jeu sur les différences et les reports.
gambling on the stock exchange, jeux de bourse; agiotage.

gambling debt, dette de jeu (*f.*).

game *or* **gaming** (*n.*), jeu (*m.*):
game of chance, jeu de hasard.
the game is not worth the candle, le jeu ne vaut pas la chandelle.
to plead the Gaming Act, plaider (*ou* invoquer) l'exception de jeu.

gaming debt, dette de jeu (*f.*).

garage (for motors) (*n.*), garage (*m.*).

gas shares *or* **gas stocks,** valeurs de gaz (*f.pl.*); valeurs gazières (*f.pl.*).

Gazette (*n.*), Journal officiel (*m.*); l'Officiel (*m.*): The *Journal officiel de la République française* is the official organ of the French Government, of which the English equivalent is the *London Gazette*.
notice to be advertised in the Gazette, notice à publier au Journal officiel (*f.*).

general (*adj.*), général, -e, -aux:
general acceptance (of a bill of exchange), acceptation sans réserves (*f.*).
general average (Mar. Insce) (*Abbrev.*: g.a. *or* G.A.) (opp. to *particular average*), avarie commune (*f.*); avaries communes (*f.pl.*); avarie grosse (*f.*); avaries grosses (*f.pl.*); grosses avaries (*f.pl.*).
general average act, acte d'avarie commune (*m.*).
general average adjustment *or* general average statement, dispache d'avarie commune (*f.*).
general average bond, compromis d'avaries grosses (*m.*).
general average clause, clause avarie commune (*f.*).

general average contribution, contribution à l'avarie commune (*ou* en avarie commune) (*ou* d'avarie commune) (*ou* aux avaries communes) (*f.*).
general average expense, dépense d'avarie commune (*f.*).
general average loss, perte d' (*ou* par) avarie commune (*f.*).
general average sacrifice, sacrifice d'avarie commune (*m.*).
general balance sheet, bilan général (*m.*); bilan d'ensemble (*m.*).
general bill of lading, connaissement collectif (*m.*).
general business (last item on agenda), questions diverses (*f.pl.*); résolutions diverses (*f.pl.*).
general cargo, charge à la cueillette (*f.*); chargement en cueillette (*m.*):
to load a ship with general cargo, charger un navire à (*ou* en) cueillette.
general crossing (of a cheque) (opp. to *special crossing*), barrement général (*m.*). V. exemple sous **crossing.**
general expenses, frais divers (*m.pl.*); dépenses diverses (*f.pl.*).
general ledger, grand livre général (*m.*); grand livre des comptes généraux (*m.*); grand livre synthétique (*m.*).
general letter of credit, lettre de crédit collective (*f.*).
general level of prices, niveau d'ensemble des cours (*m.*).
general lien (opp. to *particular*, or *specific*, *lien*), privilège général (*m.*).
general meeting, assemblée générale (*f.*).
general mortgage, hypothèque générale (*f.*).
general partnership (opp. to *particular*, or *special, partnership*), société en nom collectif (*f.*).
general post office (*Abbrev.*: G.P.O.), hôtel des postes (*m.*).
general power (Law) (distinguished from *special power* or *particular power*), procuration générale (*f.*); pouvoir général (*m.*); mandat général (*m.*).
general railway classification of goods, classification ferroviaire générale des marchandises (*f.*).
general reserve (Fin.), réserve générale (*f.*).
general strike, grève générale (*f.*).
general trial balance (Bkkpg), balance générale (*f.*).

gentleman (no occupation), sans profession:
Paul X., gentleman, residing at . . ., Paul X., sans profession, demeurant à . . .

Gentlemen (preamble to chairman's speech), Messieurs; Messieurs les Actionnaires. Cf. **Ladies and Gentlemen.**

geographical mile, mille marin (*m.*).

get (to obtain; to procure; to receive) (*v.t.*), obtenir; recueillir; procurer; se procurer; se faire faire; recevoir; acquérir:

to get time (extension of time, as for payment), obtenir un délai.

to get orders, recueillir des commandes (ou des ordres).

to get money (for oneself), se procurer de l'argent; battre monnaie.

to get money for an industry, procurer des capitaux à une industrie.

to get an advance (of money), se faire faire une avance (d'argent).

to get a letter, recevoir une lettre.

to get a situation for someone, placer quelqu'un.

to get a situation (for oneself), se placer.

get a bill discounted (to), se faire escompter un billet:

the master of a ship can draw a bill of exchange on the owner and get it discounted, le capitaine d'un navire peut tirer une lettre de change sur l'armateur et se la faire escompter.

get a bond note discharged (or cancelled) (to), apurer un acquit-à-caution.

get an instrument stamped at the revenue office (to), faire timbrer un acte à l'extraordinaire.

get dearer (to), renchérir; enchérir:

wheat is getting dearer, le blé renchérit.

get into arrears (to), s'arriérer; s'arrérager.

get into debt (to) (to get someone else into debt), endetter.

get into debt (to), (to get oneself into debt), s'endetter; faire des dettes.

get one's money's worth (to) or get value for one's money (to), en avoir pour son argent.

only to get one's money back, ne faire que changer son argent:

I have only got my money back, je n'ai fait que changer mon argent.

get out of (to) (to extract from), retirer de; tirer à; soutirer à; arracher à:

to get so much out of a property, retirer tant d'un bien.

to get money (or some money) out of someone, soutirer, tirer, arracher, de l'argent à quelqu'un.

get rich (to), s'enrichir:

to get rich easily, s'enrichir à bon compte.

get something for nothing (to), courir franc.

gift (n.), don (m.); donation (f.).

gilt-edged or gilt-edge (adj.), doré (-e) sur tranche; de père de famille:

gilt-edged paper (bills of exchange), papier doré sur tranche (m.).

gilt-edged securities or gilt-edge investments, valeurs de père de famille (f.pl.); titres de père de famille (m.pl.); placements de père de famille (m.pl.).

girl typewriter or girl typist, jeune fille dactylographe (f.); dactylo féminin (m.).

give (v.). V. exemples:

to give a charge on one's property, donner assignation sur ses biens.

to give a good security, fournir une bonne caution.

to give a lender a mortgage as security, nantir un prêteur par hypothèque.

to give a receipt or to give receipt, donner reçu; donner récépissé; donner acquit; donner quittance:

to give a receipt to the sender, donner reçu à l'expéditeur.

to give receipt for payments made, donner quittance des paiements faits.

to give a rise to a clerk, augmenter un commis.

to give a salary to an employee, donner des appointements à, appointer, un employé.

to give a tip to (to give confidential information to), tuyauter; donner un tuyau à:

to give someone a tip, tuyauter quelqu'un.

to give account of one's management, rendre compte de sa gestion.

to give advice, donner des conseils.

to give an average of, donner (ou rendre) une moyenne de:

total of so many pounds for so many loans, which gives an average of about so much per loan, total de tant de livres pour tant de prêts, ce qui donne (ou ce qui rend) une moyenne d'environ tant par prêt (m.).

to give an earnest to (to pay a deposit), donner des arrhes à; arrher:

to give an earnest to one's landlord, donner des arrhes à, arrher, son propriétaire.

to give an employee a share (or an interest) in the profits, intéresser un employé aux bénéfices.

to give an order at middle price, donner, passer, un ordre au cours moyen.

to give an order for goods, faire, passer, une commande de marchandises.

to be given (speaking of orders), être donné, -e, passé, -e; se donner; se passer:

orders which are given verbally, orders which are given in writing, ordres qui sont donnés verbalement, ordres qui se passent par écrit (m.pl.).

to give back, rendre:

to receipt an invoice and give it back to the buyer, acquitter une facture et la rendre à l'acheteur.

to give change for so many pounds, donner, rendre, la monnaie de tant de livres.

to give consideration for (bills of exchange), provisionner:

bills for which no consideration has been given are called accommodation bills, les effets non provisionnés (ou les effets qui ne sont pas provisionnés) sont dits effets de complaisance (m.pl.).

to give credit, faire crédit:

the holder of a bank note gives credit to the bank which has issued it, le détenteur d'un billet de banque fait crédit à la banque qui l'a émis.

to give for the call (Stock Exch.), acheter dont:

to give 1s. for the call of 100 X.Y.Z. shares, acheter 100 actions X.Y.Z. dont un schelling. V. aussi exemple sous **giver for the call.**

to give instructions to a solicitor, donner des instructions à un solicitor.

to give notice a day beforehand, donner avis un jour d'avance.

to give notice immediately to the company of any accident that may come to one's knowledge, donner immédiatement avis à la compagnie de tout sinistre qui parviendrait à sa connaissance.

to give notice of damage to the shipowner, dénoncer l'avarie à l'armateur.

to give notice to the insurer (or to give the insurer notice) within three days of the receipt of the news of an accident, prévenir, donner avis à, l'assureur dans les trois jours de la réception de la nouvelle d'un sinistre.

to give on (v.t.) or to give the rate on (Stock Exch.), faire reporter; donner en report:

to give on (or to give the rate on) a position (or a book) for the next account (or for new time), faire reporter une position à la liquidation prochaine.

to give on stock or to give the rate on stock, faire reporter des titres; donner des titres en report.

stock given on, titres donnés en report (m.pl.).

to give on (v.i.) or to give the rate (Stock Exch.), se faire reporter. V. exemples sous antonyme to take in (v.i.) or to take the rate.

to give on stock for (Stock Exch.), faire reporter:

to give on stock for a lender, faire reporter un prêteur.

to give one's debtor time to pay, accorder un délai à son débiteur.

to give security, fournir caution; cautionner:

to give good and valid security for the guarantee of the payment of a contribution, fournir bonne et valable caution pour la garantie du paiement d'une contribution.

the bonder is bound to give security to guarantee the duties and fines which may become payable, l'entrepositaire est tenu de fournir caution pour garantir les droits et les amendes qui pourraient devenir exigibles (m.).

to give security for customs duties, cautionner des droits de douane.

to give so many pounds to someone, donner, compter, payer, tant de livres à quelqu'un.

to give so much for something, donner tant pour, mettre tant à, quelque chose.

to give someone information about a matter, donner des renseignements à, renseigner, quelqu'un sur une affaire.

to give the value of the goods in the customs entries, énoncer la valeur des marchandises dans les déclarations de douane.

to give up one's property, céder, abdiquer, ses biens.

to give up one's security, se dénantir.

to give up one's ticket at the end of the journey, rendre son billet à la fin du voyage.

to give value (bills of exchange), fournir valeur:

holder of a bill who proves that he has given value for it, porteur d'un effet qui prouve qu'il en a fourni la valeur (m.).

to give way, reculer; fléchir:

share which gives way several fractions, action qui recule (ou qui fléchit) de quelques fractions (f.).

at a given price, à un cours donné.

giver (contangoes) (Stock Exch.) (pers.) (n.) (opp. to taker), reporté (m.):

as remuneration for the loan, the taker receives from the giver a premium, which is called contango, en rémunération du prêt, le reporteur touche du reporté une prime, qui s'appelle report.

the market is all givers, la place (ou la position de place) est chargée.

giver for a call (Stock Exch.), acheteur d'un dont (ou d'une prime directe):

speculator who is giver of 1s. (per share) for the call of 100 X.Y.Z. shares at 25s., spéculateur qui est acheteur de 100 actions X.Y.Z. à 26 schellings dont 1 schelling (m.). V. explication des opérations à prime sous option dealing.

giver for a call of more (Stock Exch.), preneur de faculté de lever double (m.).

giver for a put (Stock Exch.), vendeur d'un ou (ou d'une prime indirecte):

speculator who is giver of 1s. (per share) for the put of 100 X.Y.Z. shares at 25s., spéculateur qui est vendeur de 100 actions X.Y.Z. à 24 schellings ou 1 schelling.

Note:—The French envisage the sale of the shares by the putter (vendeur de 0 actions). The English envisage the giver of the rate for the option to put or sell the shares, or, and which is the same thing, the buyer of the option to put or sell the shares. Hence giver or buyer has to be translated by vendeur in this case. Cf. note under **taker**.

giver for a put and call (Stock Exch.), preneur d'option (m.); preneur de stellage (m.).

giver for a put of more (Stock Exch.), preneur de faculté de livrer double (m.).

giver of an (or of the) option or simply **giver** (n.) (Fin.) (opp. to taker), optionnaire (m.).

giver of the rate (Option dealings) (Stock Exch.), payeur de la prime (m.).

giving an earnest, arrhement (m.).

giving for an option, achat d'une prime (m.).

giving for the call, achat dont (m.); achat à prime directe (m.).

giving orders, passation d'ordres (f.).

giving way, recul (m.); fléchissement (m.).

glass partition, cloison de verre (f.).

glass, with care or simply **glass** (notice on a parcel), fragile.

glazed paper, papier glacé (m.).

glut or **glutting** (n.), encombrement (m.); pléthore (f.):

glut of money, pléthore de capitaux.

glut (v.t.), encombrer:

glutted market, marché encombré (m.).

go (v.i.). V. exemples:

to go a bear (Stock Exch.), jouer à la baisse; opérer à la baisse; spéculer à la (ou en) baisse.

to go a bull (Stock Exch.), jouer à la hausse;

opérer à la hausse ; spéculer à la (*ou* en) hausse.

to go abroad, partir à l'étranger :

if the addressee has gone abroad, do not forward, si le destinataire est parti à l'étranger, ne pas faire suivre.

to go ahead, progresser :

X. shares went ahead from 1 to 1¼, l'action X. progresse de 1 à 1 1/4.

to go away without leaving an address, partir sans laisser d'adresse.

to go back, reculer ; rétrograder ; se replier ; se rabattre :

X. shares went back from 2s. to 1s. 9d., l'action X. recule (*ou* rétrograde) (*ou* s'est repliée) (*ou* s'est rabattue) de 2sh. à 1sh. 9d.

to go bankrupt, faire banqueroute ; faire faillite ; faillir.

to go better (said of prices, of stocks and shares, or the like), s'améliorer :

in time, certain stocks go better, others go worse, avec le temps, certaines valeurs s'améliorent, d'autres se déprécient.

to go beyond one's instructions, aller au delà de sa charge.

to go down (to fall in price), baisser ; s'abaisser :

the shares are going down, les actions baissent (*f.pl.*).

the price of silver has gone down, le prix de l'argent s'est abaissé.

to go down (to sink ; to founder), sombrer ; couler bas ; couler à fond ; couler :

ship which went down and was lost, navire qui coula (*ou* qui sombra) et se perdit (*m.*).

to go ex coupon *or* to go ex dividend, to go ex rights. V. exemples :

(on certain exchanges) bearer securities go ex coupon on the day the dividend is payable : from this moment the securities are dealt in ex coupon or ex dividend, pour les valeurs au porteur les coupons se détachent à la cote (*ou* à la bourse) (*ou* en bourse) le jour de leur mise en paiement, c'est à partir de ce moment que les titres se négocient ex-coupon ou ex-dividende.

when a stock goes ex coupon, ex rights, quand une valeur détache un coupon, un droit de souscription.

when a stock goes ex coupon, the price drops normally by the amount of the coupon, lorsqu'un coupon est détaché à la cote, le cours baisse normalement du montant de ce coupon.

to go for a rise, for a fall (Stock Exch.), être à la hausse, à la baisse :

speculator who is going for a rise, spéculateur qui est à la hausse (*m.*).

to go halves in a deal, être, se mettre, de moitié dans une affaire.

to go in for finance, entrer dans la finance.

to go into an account, examiner, faire l'examen d', un compte.

to go into an account again, repasser un compte.

to go into business (to engage in business), entrer, se mettre, dans les affaires.

to go into dock, entrer en (*ou* au) bassin.

to go into dry dock, entrer en cale sèche ; entrer dans la forme :

ship which goes into dry dock with the help of tugs, navire qui entre en cale sèche (*ou* qui entre dans la forme) avec l'assistance de remorqueurs (*m.*).

to go into liquidation, entrer, se mettre, en liquidation :

company which goes into liquidation, société qui entre en liquidation (*f.*).

to go light, marcher à vide :

if the vessel goes light, si le navire marche à vide.

to go on a trial trip, faire un voyage d'essai.

to go on board a ship, aller, se rendre, monter, à bord d'un navire ; s'embarquer dans un navire.

to go on strike, se mettre en grève ; faire grève.

to go on the other tack (Stock Exch.), se retourner :

operator who goes on the other tack, opérateur qui se retourne (*m.*).

to go one better (to improve on someone's offer), courir sur le marché de quelqu'un.

to go out of dock, sortir d'en (*ou* du) bassin.

to go out of dry dock, sortir de (*ou* de la) cale sèche.

to go surety for someone, se porter caution, se rendre caution, se porter garant (-e), se rendre garant (-e), de quelqu'un.

to go through an account, dépouiller, faire le dépouillement, d'un compte.

to go through one's correspondence (*or* one's post), dépouiller sa correspondance ; lire son courrier.

to go through the books, compulser, examiner, les livres.

to go to expense, faire des frais.

to go to the help of a ship in peril, aller au secours d'un navire en péril.

to go up (to rise in price), monter ; 'hausser :

stock which is going to go up, valeur qui va monter (*ou* qui va hausser) (*f.*).

to go worse, se déprécier. *V. exemple sous* to go better.

time at which the train goes, heure à laquelle le train part (*f.*).

going concern, affaire roulante (*f.*).

going ex coupon, détachement du coupon en bourse (*m.*). *V. exemples sous* to go ex coupon.

going into dock, entrée en (*ou* au) bassin (*f.*); passage en (*ou* au) bassin (*m.*).

going on the other tack (Stock Exch.), conversion (*f.*).

going out of dock, sortie d'en (*ou* du) bassin (*f.*).

going through one's correspondence, dépouillement de sa correspondance (*m.*) :

the day begins by going through the correspondence, la journée commence par le dépouillement de la correspondance.

gold (*n.*), *or* (*m.*) :

to be paid in gold, être payé (-e) en or.

a gold coin, une pièce d'or ; une pièce en or.

gold (*n.*) *or* **gold money** *or* **gold coin** *or* **gold**

currency (*collectively*), or (*m.*); monnaie d'or (*f.*); monnaie-or (*f.*); numéraire d'or (*m.*); pièces en or (*f.pl.*):
the international financial business which is done in London, thanks to the prestige of an unassailable gold currency, les affaires financières internationales qui se traitent à Londres, grâce au prestige d'une monnaie-or inattaquable.

gold and silver bullion, matières d'or et d'argent (*f.pl.*); matières (*f.pl.*).

gold and silver coin and bullion (Banking), encaisse métallique (*f.*); encaisse or et argent (*f.*); valeurs en or et en argent (*f.pl.*):
the bank is bound to have gold and silver coin and bullion equal to one third of the amount of its notes and of its other sight commitments, la banque est tenue d'avoir une encaisse métallique égale au tiers du montant de ses billets et de ses autres engagements à vue.

gold and silver coin or (*or* and) **bullion** (considered as merchandise while in course of transport), finances (*f.pl.*); or et argent monnayés ou (*ou* et) en lingots :
the transport by railway of gold and silver coin or uullion, valuable papers, works of art, etc., le transport par chemin de fer des finances, valeurs, objets d'art, etc.

gold bonds, obligations-or (*f.pl.*):
5% gold bonds 19—, obligations 5 0/0-or 19—.

gold bullion, matières d'or (*f.pl.*).

gold certificate (U.S.A.), certificat-or (*m.*).

gold coin and bullion (Banking), encaisse-or (*f.*).

gold exchange standard *or* **gold bullion standard,** étalon-or de change (*m.*); étalon de change-or (*m.*).

gold franc, franc-or (*m.*):
to bring the prices in the different countries to gold francs, the only rational means of effecting a practical comparison, ramener les prix dans les différents pays en francs-or, seul moyen rationnel d'effectuer une comparaison pratique.
5,000 gold francs or 25,000 French paper francs, 5 000 francs-or ou 25 000 francs-papier français.

gold mine (*literally and figuratively*), mine d'or (*f.*).

gold pen, with iridium point, plume en or, à bec d'iridium (*f.*).

gold point, gold-point (*m.*):
in two countries having the gold standard, the reciprocal exchange oscillates, around par, between the import and export gold points, dans deux pays ayant l'étalon de l'or, le change réciproque oscille, autour du pair, entre les gold-points d'entrée et de sortie.

gold reserve (Banking), réserve d'or (*f.*).

gold shares, valeurs d'or (*f.pl.*); valeurs aurifères (*f.pl.*).

gold, silver, precious metals, coin, securities, jewellery, works of art, and similar valuables (as cargo), or, argent, métaux précieux, numéraire, titres, bijoux, œuvres d'art, et objets analogues (*m.pl.*); groups ou articles de valeur (*m.pl.*).

gold standard, étalon-or (*m.*); étalon d'or (*m.*).

gold standard country, pays à étalon d'or (*m.*); pays monométalliste-or (*m.*).

gone away, no address (Post), parti sans laisser d'adresse.

good (*adj.*), bon, bonne; avantageux, -euse; régulier, -ère; valable :
a good house always has good clerks, une bonne maison a toujours de bons employés.
it is good business, c'est une bonne affaire.
we have had a good year, nous avons eu une bonne année.
it was a good opportunity, c'était une bonne occasion.
to find a good security, fournir une bonne caution.
good average quality, bonne qualité moyenne (*f.*).
good bargain, marché avantageux (*m.*).
good brands (metals), bonnes marques (*f.pl.*).
good debt, bonne créance (*f.*).
good paper (bills of exchange), bon papier (*m.*).
shares which are (*or* stock which is) good delivery (Stock Exch.), titres qui sont de bonne livraison (*m.pl.*).
to deliver a good certificate in replacement of a bad certificate (Stock Exch.), livrer un titre régulier en remplacement d'un titre irrégulier.
good receipt, quittance valable (*f.*).
to be good for an amount, être bon (bonne) pour payer une somme; être bon (bonne) pour en répondre.
to be good at arithmetic, chiffrer rapidement :
he is very good at arithmetic, il chiffre très rapidement.

goods (*n.pl. only*), marchandises (*f.pl.*); marchandise (*f.*):
goods for home use (Customs), marchandises mises en consommation.
goods of foreign origin, marchandises d'origine (*ou* de provenance) étrangère.
goods on hand, refused. V. sous **on hand, refused.**
goods returned *or* goods brought back (free readmission) (Customs), marchandises de retour.

goods (cargo, as distinguished from the *ship* or *hull*) (Mar. Insce) (*n.pl.*), facultés (*f.pl.*); marchandises (*f.pl.*):
insurance of ship and goods, assurance sur corps et facultés (*ou* sur navire et marchandises) (*f.*).
the insured goods are covered from the time of leaving the shipper's warehouse until deposited in consignee's warehouses, les facultés (*ou* les marchandises) assurées sont couvertes depuis le moment où elles quittent le magasin de l'expéditeur jusqu'à celui de leur entrée dans les magasins des réceptionnaires.

goods account *or simply* **goods** (Bkkpg), compte de marchandises (*m.*); marchandises; marchandises générales.

goods brake, fourgon pour train à marchandises (*m.*).

goods engine, locomotive à marchandises (*f.*).

goods guard, garde de convoi de marchandises (*m.*).

goods rates, tarif (*m.*) [*ou* tarifs (*m.pl.*)] de marchandises.

goods service, service de marchandises (*m.*).

goods shed (Rly.), 'halle aux marchandises (*f.*).

goods station, gare de (*ou* des) marchandises (*f.*); gare de petite vitesse (*f.*).

goods traffic, trafic des marchandises (*m.*).

goods train, train de marchandises (*m.*); convoi de marchandises (*m.*); train de petite vitesse (*m.*); petite vitesse (*f.*):
goods sent by goods train, marchandises expédiées en petite vitesse (*f.pl.*).

goods wagon *or* **goods truck** *or* **goods van** (Rly.), wagon à (*ou* de) marchandises (*m.*).

goodwill (*n.*), fonds de commerce (*m.*); fonds (*m.*); clientèle (*f.*):
the name under which a goodwill has been established is the property of the founder of that goodwill, le nom sous lequel un fonds de commerce a été créé est la propriété du créateur de ce fonds.

govern (*v.t.*), gouverner; régir:
it is the condition of the crops in the great producing countries which governs the price of wheat on the general market, c'est l'état des récoltes dans les grands pays producteurs qui gouverne le prix du blé sur le marché général.

government *or* **Government** (*n.*) (Abbrev.: **gov.** *or* **govt** *or* **Gov.** *or* **Govt**), gouvernement (*m.*); Gouvernement (*m.*); État (*m.*):
the Government is preferred over all creditors, le Gouvernement est préféré à tous créanciers.

government bank, banque d'État (*f.*).

government banker, banquier de l'État (*m.*).

government bill of lading, connaissement de l'État (*m.*).

government monopoly, monopole d'État (*m.*).

government revenue, revenus de l'État (*m.pl.*); revenus publics (*m.pl.*).

government stocks *or* **government securities,** fonds d'État (*m.pl.*); effets publics (*m.pl.*).

governor (pers.) (*n.*), gouverneur (*m.*):
the governor of the Bank of England, of the Bank of France, le gouverneur de la Banque d'Angleterre, de la Banque de France.
« Je consens à ce que le chef de la Banque [de France] soit appelé *gouverneur,* si cela peut lui faire plaisir, car les titres ne coûtent rien.
« Je consens également à ce que son traitement soit aussi élevé qu'on voudra, puisque c'est la Banque qui doit payer. » NAPOLÉON 1er dans la séance du 27 mars 1806 du Conseil d'État.
" I consent to the head of the Bank [of France] being called *governor,* if it please him, because titles cost nothing.

" I likewise consent to his salary being as high as you please, as the Bank will have to pay it." NAPOLEON I at the sitting of 27th March 1806 of the Council of State.

gradual (*adj.*), graduel, -elle:
gradual extinction of a debt, extinction graduelle d'une dette (*f.*).

graduate (*v.t.*), graduer:
to graduate the assessments according to the amount of the income, graduer les cotisations suivant l'importance du revenu.

graduated (*adj.*), gradué, -e:
graduated stamp duty, droit de timbre gradué (*m.*).
graduated scale, échelle graduée (*f.*).

grain broker, courtier en grains (*m.*).

grain charter, charte-partie de grain (*f.*).

grain market *or* **grain exchange,** marché aux (*ou* des) grains (*m.*).

grain trade, commerce des grains (*m.*).

grammalogue (Shorthand) (*n.*), sténogramme (*m.*).

gramophone shares, valeurs de gramophones (*f.pl.*).

grand total, total global (*m.*).

grant (*n.*), accord (*m.*); concession (*f.*); allouance (*f.*):
grant of a patent, accord d'un brevet.
grant of land, concession de terrain.

grant (*v.t.*), accorder; consentir; concéder; allouer:
to grant an overdraft, accorder, consentir, un découvert.
to grant a monopoly, concéder un monopole.
to grant compensation, allouer une indemnité.

grantable (*adj.*), accordable; concessible; allouable.

grantee (pers.) (*n.*), cessionnaire (*m.* ou *f.*); concessionnaire (*m.* ou *f.*).

grantor (pers.) (*n.*), cédant, -e.

gratuitous (*adj.*), gratuit, -e.

gratuitousness (*n.*), gratuité (*f.*).

gratuity [**gratuities** *pl.*] (*n.*), gratification (*f.*).

graving dock, forme de radoub (*f.*); forme sèche (*f.*); forme (*f.*); bassin de radoub (*m.*); cale de radoub (*f.*); bassin à sec (*m.*); bassin sec (*m.*); cale sèche (*f.*).

Greenwich time, heure de Greenwich (*f.*); heure de l'Europe occidentale (*f.*). Cf. **West European time.**

Gresham's law, loi de Gresham (*f.*):
" bad money drives out good," « la mauvaise monnaie chasse la bonne. »

gridiron *or* **grid** (Careening) (*n.*), gril (de carénage) (*m.*).

gross (*adj.*) (Ant.: *net*), brut, -e:
the gross amount of an invoice is its total without discount, le montant brut d'une facture est son total sans escompte.

gross average (Mar. Insce), avarie grosse (*f.*); avaries grosses (*f.pl.*); grosses avaries (*f.pl.*); avarie commune (*f.*); avaries communes (*f.pl.*). *V. syn.* general average *pour exemples.*

gross cost (Costing), prix de revient brut (*m.*).

gross freight, fret brut (*m.*).

gross loss, perte brute (*f.*).

gross premium (Insce) (opp. to *net*, or *pure*, or *mathematical*, or *risk, premium*), prime brute (*f.*). V. exemple sous **loading** (of the premium).

gross price, prix brut (*m.*).

gross proceeds, produit brut (*m.*); brut (*m.*).

gross profit *or* gross profits, bénéfice brut (*m.*); profit brut (*m.*); bénéfices bruts (*m.pl.*); profits bruts (*m.pl.*).

gross receipts, recette brute (*f.*).

gross register ton, tonneau de jauge brute (*m.*).

gross register tonnage *or* gross registered tonnage *or* simply gross register, tonnage de jauge brute (*m.*); jauge brute (*f.*).

gross tonnage, tonnage brut (*m.*).

gross weight *or* simply **gross** (*n.*), poids brut (*m.*); brut (*m.*):

  gross weight is that which results from weighing the contents and the container, le poids brut est celui qui résulte du pesage du contenu et du contenant.

  goods charged with duty on the gross weight (*or* on the gross), marchandises imposées au poids brut (*ou* au brut) (*f.pl.*).

ground (land) (*n.*), terrain (*m.*); terre (*f.*):

  ground is dear in London, le terrain se vend cher à Londres. Cf. **piece of ground.**

ground (to run on shore) (*v.t.*), échouer.

ground (*v.i.*), échouer; s'échouer.

ground rent, rente foncière (*f.*).

grounding (*n.*), échouement (*m.*).

group (*n.*), groupe (*m.*):

  group of accounts of shareholders, groupe de comptes, d'actionnaires.

  group of letters, of figures (Teleg.), groupe de lettres, de chiffres.

  the rubber group (Stock Exch.), le groupe caoutchoutier.

group (*v.t.*), grouper; agrouper:

  to group figures, grouper, agrouper, des chiffres.

  to group the goods belonging to several shippers, grouper les marchandises appartenant à plusieurs expéditeurs.

grouping (*n.*), groupement (*m.*); agroupement (*m.*):

  grouping lots on the same bill of lading, groupage des lots sur le même connaissement.

  a grouping is the bundling in one and the same consignment of several small parcels, un groupage est la réunion dans un même envoi de plusieurs petits colis.

guarantee *or* **guaranty** [guaranties *pl.*] (*n.*), garantie (*f.*); caution (*f.*):

  guarantee of the fulfilment of an engagement, of solvency, garantie de l'exécution d'un engagement, de solvabilité.

  guaranty (*or* guarantee) of quality, garantie de qualité.

  bank guarantee, caution de banque; garantie de banque.

guarantee *or* **guaranty** (of a bill of exchange) (*n.*), aval (*m.*).

guarantee (person guaranteed) (*n.*), garanti, -e; cautionné, -e.

guarantee (*v.t.*), garantir; cautionner; assurer; répondre pour; répondre de:

  to guarantee an issue of stock, garantir une émission de titres.

  the bonder is bound to give security to guarantee the duties and fines which may become payable, l'entrepositaire est tenu de fournir caution pour garantir les droits et les amendes qui pourraient devenir exigibles (*m.*).

  to guarantee the payment of a debt, garantir le, répondre pour le, répondre du, assurer le, paiement d'une créance.

  to guarantee a minimum interest on shares, garantir, assurer, un minimum d'intérêt à des actions.

  to guarantee a cashier, cautionner, répondre pour, garantir, un caissier.

guarantee (bills of exchange) (*v.t.*), donner son aval à; avaliser; avaler:

  surety who undertakes to guarantee a bill, donneur de caution qui s'engage à donner son aval à (*ou* à avaliser) (*ou* à avaler) un effet (*m.*).

guarantee association (Produce Exch.), caisse de garantie (*f.*).

guarantee fund, fonds de garantie (*m.*).

guarantee insurance, assurance de cautionnement (*f.*); assurance de garantie (*f.*).

guarantee society, association de cautionnement (*f.*); société de caution (*f.*).

guaranteed bills, effets avalisés (*m.pl.*); papier fait (*m.*); valeurs faites (*f.pl.*).

guaranteed bond, obligation garantie (*f.*).

guaranteed stock (Abbrev.: **guar.** *or* **gtd**) *or* **guaranteed stocks,** valeur garantie (*f.*); valeurs garanties (*f.pl.*); titre garanti (*m.*); titres garantis (*m.pl.*); fonds garantis (*m.pl.*).

guaranteeing (*n.*), cautionnement (*m.*).

guarantor *or* **guarantee** (pers.) (*n.*), garant, -e; caution (*f.*); donneur de caution (*m.*); accréditeur (*m.*).

guarantor (of a bill of exchange) (pers.) (*n.*), donneur d'aval (*m.*); avaliste (*m.*).

guard (of a train) (pers.) (*n.*), conducteur (d'un train) (*m.*).

guard book, album (*m.*):

  to cut out an advertisement and stick it in a guard book, découper une annonce et la coller dans un album.

guard's van (Rly.), fourgon (*m.*).

guide (pers.) (*n.*), guide (*m.*):

  the services of a competent guide, le service d'un guide compétent.

guide (*n.*) *or* **guide book,** guide (*m.*); indicateur (*m.*):

  travel guide, guide de voyage; indicateur de voyage.

guide card (card index), carte-guide (*f.*); guide (*m.*).

guinea (money of account) (*n.*) (Abbrev.: **g.** *or* **G.** [**g.** *or* **G.** *or* **gs** *or* **Gs** *pl.*] *or* **gu.** *or* **gua.** [**guas** *pl.*]), guinée (*f.*):
the guinea is used in the reckoning of fees, and for fixing prices in certain luxury trades (the guinea is only a money of account), (en Angleterre) la guinée est employée pour le calcul des honoraires, et pour l'établissement des prix dans certains commerces de luxe (la guinée n'est qu'un monnaie de compte).

gum (*n.*), gomme (*f.*).

gum (*v.t.*), gommer.

gummed label (opp. to *tie-on,* or *tag,* *label*) étiquette gommée (*f.*).

gumming (*n.*), gommage (*m.*).

H

haggle (*v.i.*), marchander.

haggling (*n.*), marchandage (*m.*).

Hague rules (Carriage by sea), règles de la Haye (*f.pl.*).

half [**halves** *pl.*] (of a return ticket) (*n.*), coupon (*m.*):
the two halves of a return ticket, les deux coupons d'un billet aller et retour.

half a quarter, demi-terme (*m.*):
to stay only half a quarter in an office, ne passer qu'un demi-terme dans un bureau.

half brokerage *or* **half commission,** demi-courtage (*m.*).

half commission (of a half commission man) (Stock Exch.), remise (*f.*).

half commission man (Stock Exch.), remisier (*m.*).

half fare, demi-place (*f.*); moitié prix (*m.*). V. exemples sous **fare.**

half-fare ticket (child's), billet de demi-place (*ou* de demi-tarif) (pour les enfants) (*m.*).

half per cent, demi pour cent (*m.*):
an allowance of half per cent, une ristourne de demi pour cent.

half quarter day *or simply* **half quarter,** demi-terme (*m.*); mi-terme (*m.*):
to move on half quarter day, déménager au demi-terme (*ou* à mi-terme).

half quarter's rent, demi-terme (*m.*):
to pay a half quarter's rent in advance, payer un demi-terme d'avance.

half year, semestre (*m.*):
the first half year's interest, le premier semestre de l'intérêt.

half yearly (*adj.*), semestriel, -elle:
half yearly meeting, assemblée semestrielle (*f.*).

half yearly (*or* **half year's**) **income, dividend, interest, drawings, salary, payment, instalment,** or the like, semestre (*m.*):
to draw one's half yearly dividend, one's half year's pay, toucher son semestre.
the annuities are payable half yearly: every half yearly instalment not paid at due date bears interest of right, les annuités sont payables par semestre: tout semestre non payé à l'échéance porte intérêt de plein droit.
half year's interest on £1,000 at 5%, semestre sur £1 000 à 5 0/0.

half yearly (*adv.*), semestriellement; par semestre:

interest paid half yearly, intérêt payé semestriellement (*ou* par semestre) (*m.*).

halt (Rly.) (*n.*), 'halte (*f.*).

hammer (*v.t.*) *or* **to hammer the market** (U.S.A.), vendre à découvert.

hand (in) (*or* **on**) (speaking of cash), en caisse balance in (*or* on) hand, solde en caisse (*m.*) restant en caisse (*m.*).
Cf. cash in (*or* on) hand.

hand (in) (speaking of orders), en carnet; en portefeuille:
orders in hand, ordres en carnet (*ou* en portefeuille) (*m.pl.*); commandes en carnet (*ou* en portefeuille) (*f.pl.*).

hand *or* **hand over** (*v.t.*), remettre; délivrer:
to hand over money personally, remettre de l'argent en main propre.
the shipowners are bound to hand (*or* hand over) the bill of lading to the holder of the mate's receipt, l'armement est tenu de remettre (*ou* de délivrer) le connaissement au titulaire du reçu provisoire (*m.*).

hand in (*v.t.*), déposer; donner:
to hand in a packet over the counter of the post office, déposer un paquet au guichet du bureau de poste.
to hand in one's resignation, donner sa démission.

hand luggage, bagages à main (*m.pl.*); bagages à la main (*m.pl.*).

hand package, colis à la main (*m.*).

hand stamp, timbre à main (*m.*).

handicap (*n.*), 'handicap (*m.*).

handicap (*v.t.*), 'handicaper:
complications which handicap competitors, complications qui handicapent les concurrents (*f.pl.*).

handing in, dépôt (*m.*):
handing in of telegrams (Post), dépôt des télégrammes.
handing in over the counter is compulsory for insured or registered packets, le dépôt au guichet est obligatoire pour des objets chargés ou recommandés.

handing over, remise (*f.*); délivrance (*f.*):
the responsibility of the carrier ceases on handing over the goods to the consignee, la responsabilité du transporteur cesse dès la remise de la marchandise au destinataire.

handle (*v.t.*), manier; manutentionner; manipuler:

to handle business, considerable sums of money, manier des affaires, des fonds considérables.

the value of the goods handled in the port, la valeur des marchandises manutentionnées dans le port.

the tonnage handled during the year, le tonnage manutentionné pendant l'année.

handle a ship (to), manœuvrer un navire.

handling (n.), maniement (m.); maniment (m.); manutention (f.); manipulation (f.): to entrust the handling of large sums of money to someone, confier à quelqu'un le maniement (ou la manutention) de sommes importantes.

handling cargo, manutention de la cargaison.

the work of the cashier consists in the handling of the cash, les fonctions du caissier consistent dans la manipulation des fonds (f.pl.).

handling (a ship) (n.), manœuvre (f.): what is required above all of the captain is the handling of the ship, ce qu'on demande avant tout au capitaine, c'est la manœuvre du navire.

handsome (adj.), beau (bel *devant une voyelle ou un h muet*), belle: to realize handsome profits, réaliser de beaux bénéfices.

handwriting (n.), écriture (f.).

hangar (for aeroplanes) (n.), 'hangar (m.).

harbour (n.), port (m.).

harbour dues, droits de port (m.pl.).

harbour master, capitaine de port (m.).

hard (stiff; firm—said of contango rates, stocks, or the like) (adj.), tendu, -e; tenu, -e; raffermi, -e: De Beers are harder than yesterday, la De Beers est mieux tenue qu'hier.

hard cash or **hard money**, espèces sonnantes et trébuchantes (f.pl.); argent liquide (m.); argent sec (m.); argent liquide et sec (m.); numéraire (m.).

hard to sell (to be), être dur (-e) à la vente: these goods are hard to sell, cette marchandise est dure à la vente.

harden or **harden up** (v.i.), se tendre; se raffermir; se redresser: X. shares hardened, les actions X. se tendent (ou se raffermissent) (f.pl.). X. shares, weak at one time, hardened at the close to 1½, l'action X., un moment faible, se redresse en clôture à 1 1/2. the tendency, undecided at first, hardened later on, la tendance, tout d'abord indécise, s'est raffermie en séance. V. aussi exemple sous **stiffen** (v.i.).

hardness (n.), tension (f.); raffermissement (m.); redressement (m.): hardness of contangoes, tension des reports.

hatch (of a ship) (cover) (n.), panneau (m.).

hatch or **hatchway** (opening) (n.), panneau (m.); écoutille (f.): battening down the hatches, la fermeture des panneaux (ou des écoutilles).

haul (n.), parcours (m.); trajet (m.):

railroad haul, parcours par voie ferrée; trajet par voie ferrée.

haul (to draw) (v.t.), remorquer; traîner: locomotive which hauls a heavy load, locomotive qui remorque (ou qui traîne) une lourde charge (f.).

haulage or **hauling** (n.), roulage (m.); traction (f.); transport (m.); transport par roulage (m.).

haulage contractor, entrepreneur de roulage (m.); entrepreneur de transports (m.).

hauling stock (Rly.) (distinguished from *rolling stock*), matériel remorqueur (m.).

have (v.t.). V. exemples: to have a good character, avoir bon caractère.

to have a little flutter (on the stock exchange), tirer un coup de fusil.

to have a lot of property, avoir, posséder, de grands biens.

to have a mortgage on a property, avoir hypothèque sur un bien.

to have a right, avoir, jouir d', un droit (ou un privilège): bank which has the exclusive right of issuing notes, banque qui jouit du privilège exclusif d'émettre des billets (f.).

to have a talk or to have an interview, s'aboucher.

to have an account at the bank, avoir compte en banque (ou à la banque).

to have an account open with someone, avoir un compte ouvert chez quelqu'un.

to have enough money, avoir suffisamment d'argent.

to have made up (Stock Exch.), faire compenser; donner une compensation: to have one's purchase and one's sale made up with such or such broker, faire compenser son achat et sa vente avec tel ou tel agent ou banquier.

to have means, avoir des moyens.

to have money (to be well off), avoir de la monnaie.

to have one's accounts up to date, avoir ses comptes à jour.

to have one's limit (or one's office limit) (or one's line). V. sous **limit**.

to have one's luggage registered in proper time, faire enregistrer ses bagages en temps voulu.

to have one's luggage weighed and then registered, faire peser puis enregistrer ses bagages.

to have other strings to one's bow, avoir d'autres cordes à son arc.

to have plenty of available funds, avoir de nombreuses disponibilités.

to have regard to someone's advice, tenir compte des conseils de quelqu'un.

to have the exclusive (or the sole) right, avoir seul le droit: on the Paris Bourse, the brokers have the exclusive right of fixing the prices of quoted securities, sur la Bourse de Paris les agents de change ont seuls le droit de constater les cours des valeurs cotées.

have you finished ? (Teleph.),   personne ? personne ? :

the telephonist, if she hears no conversation, cuts off after having asked " Have you finished ? "   la téléphoniste, si elle n'entend aucune conversation, coupe après avoir interrogé « Personne ? Personne ? »

haven (*n.*),   'havre (*m.*).

hawk (*v.t.*),   colporter.

hawked about the place (to be),   courir sur la place.

hawking (*n.*),   colportage (*m.*) :

share hawking, colportage de titres.

hazard (*n.*),   'hasard (*m.*).

hazard (*v.t.*),   'hasarder.

hazardous (*adj.*),   'hasardeux, -euse :

hazardous speculation, spéculation hasardeuse (*f.*).

head (pers.) (*n.*),   chef (*m.*) :

the heads of industrial and commercial undertakings,   les chefs d'entreprises industrielles et commerciales.

head of department,   chef de service.

head clerk *or* head of counting house,   chef de bureau (*m.*); commis chef (*m.*); commis principal (*m.*).

head accountant,   chef de comptabilité ; chef comptable.

head (the position occupied by a leader) (*n.*),   tête (*f.*) :

to be at the head of affairs,   être à la tête des affaires.

head (first line of a list) (*n.*),   tête (*f.*) :

to be at the head of a subscription list,   être en tête d'une liste de souscription.

head *or* **heading** (upper part of a printed paper) (*n.*),   en-tête (*m.*) ;   tête (*f.*) :

bill head *or* bill heading,   en-tête de facture ; tête de facture.

head *or* **heading** (a caption, title, or the like) (*n.*),   chef (*m.*) ; rubrique (*f.*) ; poste (*m.*) ; chapitre (*m.*) :

to classify the items under as many heads as there are accounts,   classer les articles en autant de chefs qu'il y a de comptes.

a special heading on the assets side of the balance sheet,   une rubrique spéciale (*ou* un poste spécial) (*ou* un chapitre spécial) à l'actif du bilan.

items which are lumped under the heading investments,   articles qui sont bloqués dans le chapitre portefeuille (*ou* qui sont réunis sous la rubrique portefeuille-titres) (*m.pl.*).

head (*v.t.*),   être en tête de :

to head a subscription list,   être en tête d'une liste de souscription.

head office (Abbrev.:   **H.O.**) (opp. to *branch office*),   siège principal (*m.*) ; siège social (*m.*) ; siège (*m.*) :

the X. Bank has six branches (its head office is in London),   la Banque X. a six succursales (son siège [*ou* son siège social] est à Londres).

head office (Post) (opp. to *branch office*),   bureau principal (*m.*).

head office account (opp. to *branch account*),   compte siège (*m.*).

head tax,   impôt de capitation (*m.*).

headed letter paper,   papier à lettre avec en-tête imprimé (*m.*).

health officer,   agent du service sanitaire (*m.*) ; officier de santé (*m.*).

heap of money,   amas d'argent (*m.*).

hearing (*n.*),   audition (*f.*) :

hearing of an appeal,   audition d'un appel.

heating of cargo,   échauffement de la cargaison (*m.*).

heating the premises,   chauffage des locaux (*m.*).

heaviness (of a market) (*n.*),   lourdeur (*f.*) ; alourdissement (*m.*).

heavy (*adj.*),   lourd, -e ; pondéreux, -euse ; gros, grosse ; fort, -e ; cher, -ère :

heavy fall (of prices on 'change),   forte baisse (*f.*), chute (*f.*), dégringolade (*f.*) (de cours sur la bourse).

heavy freight *or* heavy goods (opp. to *light freight* or *light goods*),   fret lourd (*m.*) ; marchandises lourdes (*f.pl.*) ; marchandises pondéreuses (*f.pl.*).

heavy luggage,   gros bagages (*m.pl.*).

heavy rails *or* **heavies** (*n.pl.*) (Stock Exch.),   grands réseaux (*m.pl.*) ; grands chemins de fer (*m.pl.*).

heavy traffic,   trafic lourd (*m.*).

diamonds are heavy (Stock Exch.),   les diamantifères sont lourdes (*f.pl.*).

contangoes are heavy,   les reports sont chers (*m.pl.*). V. exemple sous **stiffen** (*v.i.*).

to become heavy (speaking of stock exch. prices),   s'alourdir.

hedge (*n.*),   arbitrage (*m.*) ; arbitrage de portefeuille (*m.*) ; couverture (*f.*) :

to buy, to sell, at long date as a hedge,   acheter, vendre, à long terme comme une couverture.

hedge (*v.t.*),   arbitrager ;   arbitrer :

to hedge one stock against another, if the first is dearer than the second, that is to say, if at their present prices, it yields less than the other,   arbitrager (*ou* arbitrer) une valeur contre une autre, si la première est plus chère que la seconde, c'est-à-dire si à leurs cours actuels, elle rapporte moins que l'autre.

hedge (*v.i.*),   faire un arbitrage ;   faire des arbitrages (*ou* des couvertures) ; se couvrir :

to hedge by buying at long date,   se couvrir en achetant à long terme.

hedging (*n.*) *or* **hedging transactions**,   arbitrage (*m.*) ; arbitrage de portefeuille (*m.*) ; affaires d'arbitrage (*f.pl.*) ; couverture (*f.*) ; affaires de couverture (*f.pl.*) :

hedging for the settlement, hedging between cash and settlement,   arbitrage à terme, arbitrages entre le comptant et le terme.

heir (pers.) (*n.*),   héritier (*m.*).

heiress (pers.) (*n.*),   héritière (*f.*).

held covered. V. sous **hold**.

held over,   en souffrance ; en suspens :

bills held over,   effets en souffrance (*ou* en suspens) (*m.pl.*).

hello ! (Teleph.) (*interj.*),   allô !

help (*n.*), secours (*m.*); aide (*f.*); assistance (*f.*).
help (*v.t.*), secourir; aider; assister.
here and there (Foreign Exchange), valeur compensée.
hereby (Law) (*adv.*), par les présentes; par le présent acte:
　I hereby appoint as my proxy Mr X., je donne, par les présentes, pouvoir à M. X.
hidden (*adj.*), caché, -e; occulte; latent, -e:
　hidden damage (to the contents of a package) (opp. to *apparent damage*), avaries occultes (*f.pl.*).
　hidden defect (opp. to *apparent defect*), vice caché (*m.*).
　hidden reserve (opp. to *visible reserve*), réserve cachée (*f.*); réserve occulte (*f.*); réserve latente (*f.*).
high (*adj.*) (Ant.: *low*), 'haut, -e; élevé, -e:
　the rate of exchange is high, le taux du change est haut.
　high contangoes, reports chers (*m.pl.*). V. exemples sous **stiffen** (*v.i.*) et sous **highness**.
　high contracting parties (treaties), hautes parties contractantes (*f.pl.*).
　high-duty goods, marchandises fortement taxées (*ou* tarifées) (*f.pl.*).
　high finance, haute finance (*f.*); haute banque (*f.*).
　high interest *or* high rate of interest, gros intérêt (*m.*); taux d'intérêt élevé (*m.*):
　to borrow at high interest (*or* at a high rate of interest), emprunter à gros intérêt (*ou* à un taux d'intérêt élevé).
　high price, prix élevé (*m.*); cherté (*f.*):
　high price of money, prix élevé, cherté, de l'argent.
　high priced goods, marchandises chères (*f.pl.*).
　high seas, hautes mers (*f.pl.*); pleine mer (*f.*):
　ships on the high seas, navires en pleine mer (*m.pl.*).
higher price (Stock Exch.), cours plus élevé (*m.*).
highest and lowest prices (Stock Exch.), plus haut et plus bas cours; cours extrêmes (*m.pl.*).
highest bidder, plus offrant enchérisseur (*m.*); plus fort enchérisseur (*m.*):
　the last and highest bidder, le dernier et plus offrant enchérisseur.
highest price (Stock Exch.), cours le plus haut (*m.*).
highness (of contangoes) (Stock Exch.) (*n.*), cherté (des reports) (*f.*):
　the contango rate is variable and its highness or lowness is dependent on greater or less plentifulness of available capital, as also on the greater or less plentifulness of stock to be given on, le taux des reports est variable et sa cherté ou son bon marché sont subordonnés à la plus ou moins grande abondance de capitaux disponibles, comme aussi à la plus ou moins grande quantité de titres à faire reporter.
hire *or* **hiring** (act) (*n.*), louage (*m.*); location (*f.*):

hire (*or* hiring) of a vessel, of services, louage d'un navire, de services.
　hiring of safes, location de coffre-forts.
　sheets on hire (Rly.), bâches en location (*f.pl.*).
for hire (to be let), à louer.
hire (pecuniary consideration) (*n.*), loyer (*m.*):
　hire of money, loyer de l'argent (*ou* des capitaux).
hire (*v.t.*), louer.
hire purchase, vente à temperament (*f.*); vente par abonnement (*f.*).
hirer (pers.) (*n.*), locataire (*m.* ou *f.*):
　hirer of a safe, locataire d'un coffre-fort.
hit (to be laid upon) (*v.t.*), frapper:
　tax which hits all incomes, impôt qui frappe tous les revenus (*m.*).
hit the bottom (to), porter sur le fond:
　ship which hits the bottom and does not get off, navire qui porte sur le fond et ne revient pas à flot (*m.*).
hoard *or* **hoard up** (*v.t.*), thésauriser:
　to hoard gold, thésauriser l'or.
hoarder (pers.) (*n.*), thésauriseur, -euse.
hoarding *or* **hoarding up** (*n.*), thésaurisation (*f.*):
　scarcity of coin due to hoarding, pénurie de numéraire due à la thésaurisation (*f.*).
hoarding (advertisement) (*n.*), panneau-réclame (*m.*).
hold (of a ship) (*n.*), cale (d'un navire) (*f.*):
　cargo is stowed in the hold, les marchandises sont arrimées dans la cale (*f.pl.*).
hold (*v.t.*), tenir; détenir; contenir; posséder; avoir:
　to hold a house on (*or* under) lease, tenir une maison à bail.
　to hold a meeting (*or* a consultation), tenir conseil.
　to hold a general meeting of shareholders, tenir une assemblée générale d'actionnaires.
　to hold a security, shares, détenir un gage, des actions:
　the stocks held as security, les titres détenus en garantie (*m.pl.*).
　the number of shares which it is necessary to hold, le nombre d'actions qu'il est nécessaire de posséder.
　to hold a situation, tenir un emploi.
　to hold at the disposal of, tenir à la disposition de:
　balance held at the disposal of the beneficiary, solde tenu à la disposition du bénéficiaire (*m.*).
　to hold covered (Insce), tenir couvert, -e:
　we hold you covered, you are held covered, pending receipt of further particulars, nous vous tenons couvert, vous êtes tenu couvert, en attendant réception de plus amples détails.
to be held covered (Insce), être tenu (-e) couvert, -e; demeurer couvert, -e:
　in case of other variations not provided for in this policy, in the voyage, route, or conditions of carriage, the insured effects are nevertheless held covered without interruption, subject to an extra premium to be paid to the underwriters, en cas

d'autres modifications non prévues par la présente police, dans le voyage, l'itinéraire, ou les conditions de transport, les effets assurés n'en demeurent pas moins couverts sans interruption, sauf surprime à payer aux assureurs.

held covered at an additional premium to be arranged in case of deviation or change of voyage, facultés de toutes déviations ou changements de voyage, moyennant surprime à débattre.

to hold the purse, tenir, avoir, la bourse.

to hold the purse strings, tenir les cordons de la bourse.

to hold the purse strings tight, tenir serrés les cordons de la bourse.

to be held, être tenu, -e ; se tenir :

if an extraordinary meeting is intended to be held following an ordinary meeting, si une assemblée extraordinaire doit se tenir à la suite d'une assemblée ordinaire.

hold baggage (opp. to *cabin baggage*), bagages de cale (*m.pl.*).

hold on (to), tenir sa position :

to have at command a sufficient capital to enable one to hold on, disposer d'un capital suffisant pour tenir sa position.

hold oneself liable for the payment of a debt (to), se porter garant (-e) du paiement. d'une dette.

hold out (to) (not to give way), se tenir :

to hold out for a few shillings on a transaction involving hundreds of pounds, se tenir à vingt francs sur un marché de mille écus.

hold over a payment (to), arriérer, différer, un paiement.

bills held over, effets en souffrance (*ou* en suspens) (*m.pl.*).

hold up (to be firm) (*v.i.*), tenir ; se défendre :

our market holds up well, notre marché tient toujours (*m.*).

X. shares held up well, l'action X. se défend bien.

holder (pers.) (*n.*), détenteur, -trice ; titulaire (*m. ou f.*); porteur (*m.*); propriétaire (*m. ou f.*); possesseur (*m.*) :

holder of a security, détenteur d'un gage.

holder of a share, of a debenture, détenteur, titulaire, porteur, propriétaire, possesseur, d'une action, d'une obligation.

holder of an account, titulaire d'un compte.

holder of a letter of credit, of a bill of lading, of a ticket, titulaire, porteur, d'une lettre de crédit, d'un connaissement, d'un billet.

holder of a bill of exchange, of a draft, of a cheque, porteur, détenteur, d'un effet de commerce, d'une traite, d'un chèque.

holder in due course, tiers porteur (*m.*) :

insurance policy transferred to a bona fide holder in due course duly secured by bill of lading, police d'assurance transmise à un tiers porteur de bonne foi régulièrement nanti du connaissement (*f.*).

holder for value, porteur pour valeur fournie.

holder (one employed in the hold of a vessel) (*n.*), calier (*m.*).

holding (*n.*), tenue (*f.*); détention (*f.*); possession (*f.*) :

holding a board meeting, of the general meeting, tenue d'une réunion du conseil, de l'assemblée générale.

holding stock, détention de titres.

holding of a share qualification. V. sous **qualification.**

holding (property owned ; quantity possessed ; stock ; security) (*n.*), possession (*f.*); avoir (*m.*); valeur (*f.*); titre (*m.*); quantité en portefeuille (*f.*); quantité (*f.*); nombre (*m.*); titres en portefeuille (*m.pl.*); portefeuille (*m.*) :

one's holdings of land, ses possessions (*ou* son avoir) en terres.

paper holdings, papiers-valeurs (*m.pl.*); valeurs-papiers (*f.pl.*); valeurs fiduciaires (*f.pl.*); titres fiduciaires (*m.pl.*); portefeuille-titres (*m.*); portefeuille de titres (*m.*); portefeuille (*m.*).

we have a large holding of these shares, nous avons une grande quantité (*ou* un grand nombre) de ces actions en portefeuille.

the company's holdings include shares pertaining to all kinds of industries, notably shares in oil concerns, le portefeuille de la société comprend des titres appartenant à tous genres d'industries, notamment des titres d'affaires pétrolifères.

the bank publishes every year particulars of its holdings, la banque publie tous les ans le détail des titres qu'elle a en portefeuille.

holding (a train) (detention) (*n.*), stationnement (d'un train) (*m.*).

holding company, 'holding (*f.*); société holding (*f.*); société de contrôle (*f.*); trust de valeurs (*m.*).

holiday (public holiday) (*n.*), jour de fête (*m.*); jour férié (*m.*); fête (*f.*).

holiday (*n.*) or **holidays** (*n.pl.*) (interval of rest), vacances (*f.pl.*); congé (*m.*) :

to take a few days holiday, prendre quelques jours de vacances.

Easter holidays, vacances de Pâques.

home bound (*adj.*). Syn. de **homeward bound,** q.v.

home consumption (Abbrev. : **h.c.**) *or* **home use,** consommation intérieure (*f.*); consommation (*f.*) :

goods for home consumption (*or* home use) (Customs), marchandises mises en consommation (*f.pl.*).

home country *or simply* **home** (*n.*), métropole (*f.*) :

the natural bond between the home country and its oversea possessions, le lien naturel entre la métropole et ses possessions d'outre-mer.

home currency (opp. to *foreign currency*), monnaie nationale (*f.*).

home exchange (Teleph.), bureau d'attache (*m.*); poste central de rattachement (*m.*).

home market (opp. to *foreign market*), marché intérieur (*m.*); marché métropolitain (*m.*).

home or colonial service, service métropolitain ou colonial (*m.*).

home port (opp. to *foreign port*), port de la métropole (*m.*); port métropolitain (*m.*).

home port (of a ship), port d'armement (*m.*).

home products *or* **home produce** *or* **home-grown produce,** produits métropolitains (*m.pl.*); produits de la métropole (*m.pl.*); produits indigènes (*m.pl.*).

home station (of a railway wagon), gare d'attache (*f.*).

home stocks *or* **home securities** (opp. to *foreign stocks* or *securities*), valeurs indigènes (*f.pl.*); fonds indigènes (*m.pl.*).

home trade (opp. to *foreign trade*), commerce intérieur (*m.*); commerce métropolitain (*m.*).

home trade (coasting trade) (Shipping), cabotage (*m.*).

home-trade bill (opp. to *foreign bill*), effet sur l'intérieur (*m.*).

home-trade ship (opp. to *foreign-going ship*), navire au (*ou* de) cabotage (*m.*); navire caboteur (*m.*); bateau caboteur (*m.*); caboteur (*m.*); cabotier (*m.*); navire côtier (*m.*).

home use entry (Customs), déclaration de consommation (*f.*); déclaration de mise en consommation (*f.*).

homeward bill of lading (opp. to *outward bill of lading*), connaissement d'entrée (*m.*).

homeward bound vessel *or* **home bound vessel** (opp. to *outward bound*, or *outbound*, *vessel*), navire en retour (*m.*); navire effectuant son voyage de retour (*m.*).

homeward charter market, marché des affrètements en retour (*m.*).

homeward freight (opp. to *outward freight*), fret de retour (*m.*).

homeward journey *or* **homeward trip** *or* **homeward passage** *or* **homeward voyage** *or* **homeward bound voyage** *or* **home bound voyage** (opp. to *outward journey*, or *trip*, or *passage*, or *voyage*), trajet de retour (*m.*); voyage de retour (*m.*); retour (*m.*).

honest (*adj.*), honnête; fidèle; intègre: honest cashier, caissier fidèle (*m.*).

honestly (*adv.*), honnêtement; fidèlement; intègrement.

honesty (*n.*), honnêteté (*f.*); fidélité (*f.*); intégrité (*f.*).

honorary (*adj.*), honoraire: honorary member, membre honoraire (*m.*). honorary membership, honorariat (*m.*): association which confers honorary membership on its old members, association qui confère l'honorariat à ses anciens membres (*f.*).

honour *or* **honor** (*n.*), honneur (*m.*); accueil (*m.*); intervention (*f.*): third party who accepts a bill, in default of the drawee, for the honour of the signature of the drawer, tiers qui accepte un effet, à défaut du tiré, pour l'honneur de la signature du tireur (*m.*).

acceptance for honour, acceptation par intervention (*ou* par honneur) (*ou* sous protêt) (*f.*).

honour *or* **honor** (*v.t.*), faire honneur à; honorer; faire bon accueil à; faire accueil à; accueillir:

to honour one's signature, faire honneur à sa signature.

to honour a draft, a bill of exchange, faire honneur à, faire bon accueil à, faire accueil à, accueillir, une traite, une disposition, une lettre de change.

the first point that interests the discounter is the certainty that the discounted bill will be honoured at maturity, le premier point qui intéresse l'escompteur c'est la certitude que l'effet escompté sera honoré à l'échéance.

honour policy (Insce), police d'honneur (*f.*).

horse box (Rly.), wagon-écurie (*m.*); wagon-boxe pour le transport de chevaux (*m.*).

hostility [**hostilities** *pl.*] (*n.*), hostilité (*f.*): hostilities or warlike operations, hostilités ou opérations belliqueuses (*f.pl.*).

hot (maturing in a few days; that have only a few days to run—said of bills) (*adj.*), brûlant, -e: hot bills, effets brûlants (*m.pl.*); papier brûlant (*m.*); valeurs brûlantes (*f.pl.*).

hotel (*n.*), hôtel (*m.*): hotel open all the year round, hôtel ouvert toute l'année.

hotel expenses, frais d'hôtel (*m.pl.*).

hotel shares, valeurs d'hôtels (*f.pl.*).

hour (*n.*), heure (*f.*): at any hour of the day or night, à toute heure de jour ou de nuit.

business hours *or* hours of business *or* hours of attendance, heures d'ouverture; heures d'ouverture et de clôture:

usual hours of business (*or* of attendance) at telegraph offices, heures réglementaires d'ouverture et de clôture des bureaux télégraphiques.

stock exchange hours, heures de bourse.

hours of delivery (Post), heures de distribution.

hours of labour, heures de travail.

hours saved (dispatch) (Shipping), heures sauvées.

train which runs at (*or* which travels at) — miles an hour (*or* per hour), train qui marche à (*ou* qui parcourt) — milles à l'heure (*ou* par heure) (*m.*).

house (*n.*), maison (*f.*): to take a house on lease, prendre une maison à bail.

house of business, maison de commerce.

house (stock exchange) (*n.*), bourse (*f.*): notice posted in the House, avis affiché en Bourse (*m.*).

Round the House (newspaper heading), En Bourse; Ce qui se dit en Bourse; Ce qu'on dit en Bourse.

house bills, effets creux (*m.pl.*); papier creux (*m.*).

house number, numéro d'habitation (*m.*).

House price, cours en Bourse (*m.*).

house property, biens-fonds (*m.pl.*): to invest one's money in house property, placer son argent en biens-fonds.

hulk (n.), ponton (m.).
hull (of a ship) (n.), coque (f.), corps (m.) (d'un navire).
hull insurance, assurance sur corps (f.).
hull policy, police sur corps (f.).
hull port risk, risque de port sur corps (m.).
hull underwriter, assureur sur corps (m.).
hullo ! (Teleph.) (interj.), allô !
husband one's resources (to), ménager son argent ; faire des économies.
hydroaeroplane (n.), hydroaéroplane (m.); hydravion (m.); hydroavion (m.).
hypothecate (Fin.) (v.t.), remettre en nantissement ; fournir en nantissement ; déposer en nantissement ; nantir ; gager ; engager ; mettre en gage :

to hypothecate securities, remettre en nantissement, fournir en nantissement, déposer en nantissement, nantir, gager, engager, des valeurs (ou des titres).
shares hypothecated as security for money advanced, actions remises (ou fournies) (ou déposées) en nantissement en garantie d fonds avancés (f.pl.); actions nanties (ou gagées) (ou mises en gage) en garantie de fonds avancés (f.pl.).
hypothecation (n.), nantissement (m.); engagement (m.) ; mise en gage (f.) :
hypothecation as security for advances, nantissement en garantie d'avances.
hypothecation certificate, acte de nantissement (m.); nantissement (m.).
hypothecator (pers.) (n.), gageur, -euse.

I

I am sorry the number is engaged (Teleph.), pas libre.
I am sorry there is no reply (Teleph.), répond pas ; ne répond pas.
I am sorry you have been troubled (Teleph.), je regrette de vous avoir dérangé ; pardon de vous avoir dérangé.
ice (n.), glace (f.); glaces (f.pl.) :
navigation stopped by ice, navigation interrompue par la glace (ou par les glaces) (f.).
ice risk (Mar. Insce), risque de glaces (m.).
identification words (verification by analogy) (Teleph.), mots guides (m.pl.) :

English	French
A Alfred	A Anatole
B Benjamin	B Benjamin
C Charlie	C Célestin
D David	D Désiré
E Edward	E Édouard
F Frederick	F François
G George	G Gaston
H Harry	H Henri
I Isaac	I Isidore
J Jack	J Joseph
K King	K Kléber
L Lucy	L Lazare
M Mary	M Marie
N Nellie	N Nicolas
O Oliver	O Oscar
P Peter	P Pierre
Q Queenie	Q Québec
R Robert	R Robert
S Sally	S Samuel
T Tommy	T Théodor
U Uncle	U Ursule
V Victor	V Victor
W William	W William
X Xmas	X Xavier
Y Yellow	Y Yvonne
Z Zebra	Z Zoé

identity card, carte d'identité (f.).
idle (adj.), oisif, -ive ; sans affaires :
idle capital, capital oisif (m.).
X. shares are idle at 1s., l'action X. est sans affaires à 1sh.
if any or if there be occasion, le cas échéant.
illegal (adj.), illégal, -e, -aux :
illegal acts, actes illégaux (m.pl.).
illegality [illegalities pl.] (n.), illégalité (f.):
illegality of a contract, illégalité d'un contrat.
illegally (adv.), illégalement.
illegibility or illegibleness (n.), illisibilité (f.).
illegible (adj.), illisible ; indéchiffrable :
illegible writing, écriture illisible (ou indéchiffrable) (f.).
illegibly (adv.), illisiblement ; indéchiffrablement :
to write illegibly, écrire illisiblement.
illicit (adj.), illicite :
illicit gain, gain illicite (m.).
illuminated sign (Publicity), enseigne lumineuse (f.) ; affiche lumineuse (f.) ; signal lumineux (m.).
illusory (adj.), illusoire ; mensonger, -ère :
illusory profit, profit illusoire (m.); bénéfice mensonger (m.).
illustrated advertisement, annonce illustrée (f.).
illustrated catalogue or illustrated price list, catalogue illustré (m.); album-tarif (m.).
illustrated paper, journal illustré (m.).
immediate cause (of an accident of the sea) (opp. to remote cause), cause immédiate (f.).
immigrant (pers.) (n.), immigrant, -e.
immigrate (v.i.), immigrer.
immigration (n.), immigration (f.) :
immigration is of real benefit to new countries, l'immigration présente pour les pays neufs de très réels avantages.
imminent peril (Navig.), péril imminent (m.).

immobilization (*n.*), immobilisation (*f.*):
immobilization of capital (*or* of money), of a stock of gold, immobilisation de capital (*ou* des capitaux), d'un stock d'or.

immobilize (*v.t.*), immobiliser:
the money immobilized (i.e., locked up) in a bill of exchange is mobilized (i.e., set free) as soon as the bill is paid, le capital immobilisé dans une lettre de change est mobilisé dès que la lettre est payée.

the seller is compelled to immobilize (*or* to lock up) his capital in the credit he gives to his customer: the bill of exchange enables him to mobilize his debt, to obtain the amount of it by discount before its due date, le vendeur est astreint à immobiliser ses capitaux dans le crédit qu'il fait à son client: la lettre de change lui permet de mobiliser sa créance, d'en obtenir par l'escompte, le montant avant son échéance.

immovable (Law) (*adj.*), immeuble; immobilier, -ère:
immovable property, biens immeubles (*m.pl.*); effets immobiliers (*m.pl.*); immeubles (*m.pl.*); immeuble (*m.*); immobilier (*m.*); valeurs immobilières (*f.pl.*).

impecuniosity (*n.*), impécuniosité (*f.*).

impecunious (*adj.*), impécunieux, -euse.

imperial and foreign mails (Post). *French equivalent is* courriers maritimes (*m.pl.*).

imperial and foreign system (Post). *French equivalent is* régime international (*m.*).

imperial or foreign money order [imperial and foreign money orders *collective plural*]. *French equivalent is* mandat de poste international *or simply* mandat international (*m.*).

imperial or foreign telegram [imperial and foreign telegrams *collective plural*]. *French equivalent is* télégramme du régime international *or simply* télégramme international (*m.*).

imperial preference (Econ.), préférence impériale (*f.*).

impersonal accounts (real or property accounts) (Bkkpg) (opp. to *personal accounts*), comptes de choses (*m.pl.*).

impersonal accounts (recording gains and losses) (Bkkpg), comptes de (*ou* des) résultats (*m.pl.*).

impersonal ledger, grand livre des comptes généraux (*m.*); grand livre général (*m.*); grand livre synthétique (*m.*).

implied (*adj.*) (opp. to *express*), implicite; tacite:
implied warranty (Mar. Insce), garantie implicite (*f.*):
there is an implied warranty that the adventure insured is a lawful one, and that, so far as the assured can control the matter, the adventure shall be carried out in a lawful manner, il y a garantie implicite que l'aventure assurée est licite, et qu'autant que cela dépend de l'assuré, elle sera accomplie d'une manière licite. *V. aussi exemple sous* express warranty.

imply (*v.t.*), impliquer:

silence does not always imply tacit consent, le silence n'implique pas toujours consentement tacite.

import (*n.*) (Ant.: *export*), importation (*f.*); entrée (*f.*):
imports into England from America, importations d'Amérique en Angleterre.
the total traffic, imports and exports combined, le trafic total, entrées et sorties réunies.

import (*v.t.*), importer:
to import gold, goods, importer de l'or, des marchandises.
in principle, all merchandise imported from abroad is deemed to be foreign and in consequence subject to duty, en principe, toute marchandise importée de l'étranger est réputée étrangère et par suite soumise aux droits.

import duty, droits d'entrée (*m.pl.*); entrée (*f.*); droits d'importation (*m.pl.*); taxe d'importation (*f.*).

import gold point *or* **import bullion point** *or* **import specie point,** gold-point d'entrée (*m.*); gold-point d'importation (*m.*); point d'entrée de l'or (*m.*). V. exemple sous **gold point.**

import (*or* importation) **licence** *or* **import permit,** licence d'importation (*f.*); bon d'importation (*m.*); permis d'entrée (*m.*).

import list (Customs), tarif d'entrée (*m.*).

import merchant, négociant importateur (*m.*).

import prohibition, prohibition d'entrée (*f.*).

import ship, navire importateur (*m.*); navire d'importation (*m.*).

import trade, commerce d'importation (*m.*).

importation (*n.*), importation (*f.*); entrée (*f.*):
importation of foreign goods into England, importation en Angleterre de marchandises étrangères.
the customs duties collected for the importation of goods, les droits de douane perçus pour l'entrée des marchandises (*m.pl.*).

importation voucher (of a pass sheet), volant d'entrée (d'un triptyque) (*m.*).

importer (pers. or country) (*n.*), importateur, -trice:
goods at the disposal of the importers, marchandises à la disposition des importateurs (*f.pl.*).
country which is a big importer of foodstuffs, pays qui est gros importateur de matières d'alimentation (*m.*).
Great Britain is a big importer of colonial produce, la Grande-Bretagne est une grande importatrice de produits coloniaux.

importing (*adj.*), importateur, -trice:
importing country, pays importateur (*m.*).
importing ship, navire importateur (*m.*); navire d'importation (*m.*).

impose (*v.t.*), imposer:
to impose new duties, imposer des droits nouveaux.

impost *or* **imposition** (*n.*), impôt (*m.*); imposition (*f.*):
multiple impositions no the same income, multiples impositions sur le même revenu.

impressed stamp, timbre sec (*m.*); timbre fixe (*m.*); timbre imprimé (*m.*).

improper stowage, vice d'arrimage (*m.*):
damage resulting from improper stowage, avaries résultant d'un vice d'arrimage (*f.pl.*).

improve (*v.t.*), améliorer:
to improve the financial position of a bank, améliorer la situation financière d'une banque.

improve (*v.i.*), s'améliorer:
some stocks improved slightly, quelques titres s'améliorent faiblement (*m.pl.*).

improve on (*or* upon) (to), enchérir sur; 'hausser sur; courir sur:
to improve upon the prices offered, enchérir sur les prix offerts.
to improve on someone's offer, hausser sur l'offre de quelqu'un; courir sur le marché de quelqu'un.

improvement (*n.*), amélioration (*f.*); mieux (*m.*):
improvement of (*or* in) prices, amélioration des cours.
slight improvement in bank stocks, légère amélioration (*ou* léger mieux) en valeurs bancaires.
lessee who has made improvements, preneur qui a fait des améliorations (*m.*).

impugn (*v.t.*), attaquer:
to impugn a contract, attaquer un contrat.

in any event, à tout événement.

in barrels (said of oils) (opp. to *naked*), en fûts; en barils; logées fûts.

in bond *or* **in bonded warehouse.** V. sous **bonded warehouse.**

in drums (said of oils) (opp. to *naked*), en tambours.

in full. V. sous **fully.**

in one amount, in one or more amounts. V. sous **amount.**

in or out of the customary route (Navig.), en dedans ou en dehors de la route ordinaire.

in port and at sea, au port et en mer.

in the absence of evidence to the contrary, jusqu'à preuve contraire.

inaccuracy [**inaccuracies** *pl.*] (*n.*), inexactitude (*f.*); infidélité (*f.*):
inaccuracy of a translation, inexactitude, infidélité, d'une traduction.

inaccurate (*adj.*), inexact, -e; infidèle.

inaccurately (*adv.*), inexactement; infidèlement.

inalienable (*adj.*), inaliénable; incessible:
inalienable right, droit inaliénable (*ou* incessible) (*m.*).

inbound (*adj.*). Syn. de **inward bound,** q.v.

incalculable (*adj.*), incalculable:
incalculable losses, pertes incalculables (*f.pl.*).

incalculably (*adv.*), incalculablement.

incidence (*n.*), incidence (*f.*):
incidence of a tax, incidence d'un impôt.

incidental expenses, faux frais (*m.pl.*); frais accidentels (*m.pl.*).

include (*v.t.*), comprendre; renfermer; contenir:
if the anticipated profit is included in the insurance, si le bénéfice espéré est compris dans l'assurance.

income (*n.*), revenu (*m.*); revenus (*m.pl.*); rapport (*m.*); rente (*f.*); rentes (*f.pl.*); année (*f.*):
income on investments, revenu de portefeuille-titres.
income from fixed yield investments, revenus fixes.
income from variable yield investments, revenus variables.
income from temporary investments, revenus temporaires.
income for life *or* life income, revenu viager.
post bringing in a big income, emploi de grand rapport (*ou* d'un grand rapport) (*m.*).
an income of six thousand pounds coming in regularly, six mille livres de rente bien venantes.
to live on one's income, vivre de ses rentes.

income tax, impôt sur le revenu (*m.*); taxe sur le revenu (*f.*); impôt sur revenu (*m.*); taxe sur revenu (*f.*); impôt cédulaire (*m.*); impôts cédulaires (*m.pl.*); income-tax (*m.*):
Note:—impôts cédulaires is equivalent to the English expression *income tax* in the general sense of taxes on incomes of various natures, as defined in the different schedules.
property which already pays income tax under another head, biens qui acquittent déjà l'impôt cédulaire à un autre titre (*m.pl.*).
income tax and surtax, l'impôt cédulaire et général.

income tax return, déclaration de revenu (*f.*). V. **return** pour exemple.

incoming (*adj.*) (opp. to *outgoing*), à l'arrivée; d'arrivée; d'entrée:
incoming call (Teleph.), communication d'arrivée (*f.*).
incoming gold point *or* incoming bullion point *or* incoming specie point, gold-point d'entrée (*m.*); gold-point d'importation (*m.*); point d'entrée de l'or (*m.*).
incoming mail, courrier à l'arrivée (*m.*).

inconvertible (*adj.*), inconvertible; inconvertissable:
paper money inconvertible into coin, papier-monnaie inconvertible en espèces (*m.*).
inconvertible paper money, papier-monnaie (*m.*); monnaie fictive (*f.*); monnaie fiduciaire (*f.*); numéraire fictif (*m.*):
forced currency bank notes are inconvertible paper money, les billets de banque à cours forcé sont du papier-monnaie (*m.pl.*).
Cf. convertible paper money.

incorporate (*v.t.*), incorporer:
to incorporate the accounts of each branch with those of the head office, incorporer les écritures de chaque succursale dans celles du siège.

incorporate (Law) (*v.t.*), constituer:
to incorporate a company, constituer une société.

incorporation (*n.*), incorporation (*f.*):
incorporation of overhead charges with costs, incorporation des frais généraux aux prix de revient.

incorporation (Law) (*n.*), constitution (*f.*).

incorrect (*adj.*), inexact, -e.
incorrectly (*adv.*), inexactement.
incorrectness (*n.*), inexactitude (*f.*).
increase (*n.*), augmentation (*f.*); accroissement (*m.*); majoration (*f.*); élévation (*f.*); aggravation (*f.*); gonflement (*m.*):
increase of capital, augmentation de capital.
increase in weight resulting from sea damage, augmentation de poids résultant d'avaries de mer.
increase in the wealth of a nation, accroissement de la richesse d'une nation.
increase in price, augmentation de prix (*f.*); augmentation (*f.*); accroissement de prix (*m.*); élévation de prix (*f.*); enchérissement (*m.*); renchérissement (*m.*); 'hausse (*f.*).
invoice value without any increase, valeur de facture sans aucune majoration (*f.*).
increase of the risk necessitating an endorsement to the insurance, aggravation du risque nécessitant un avenant à l'assurance.
an increase of the item " bills of exchange " (bank balance sheet), un gonflement du poste « portefeuille-effets. »
increase in (or of) value or simply increase, augmentation de valeur (*f.*); plus-value (*f.*):
increase in the value of shares, plus-value des actions.
increase (*v.t.*), augmenter; accroître; majorer; élever; porter; aggraver; gonfler:
to increase one's fortune, augmenter, accroître, sa fortune.
to increase a clerk's salary, augmenter un commis.
to increase the price of goods, augmenter le prix, élever le prix, enchérir, renchérir, 'hausser le prix, des marchandises.
to increase the purchase price to cover one's expenses, majorer le prix d'achat pour couvrir ses frais.
dividend increased from 5 to 10%, dividende porté de 5 à 10 p. cent (*m.*).
to increase the taxes, aggraver les impôts.
increase (*v.i.*), augmenter; accroître; s'augmenter; s'accroître; s'élever:
to increase in price, augmenter de prix; enchérir; renchérir; 'hausser.
incur (*v.t.*), encourir; courir:
to incur a liability, encourir une responsabilité.
to incur a risk, encourir, courir, un risque.
special expenses incurred, frais spéciaux encourus (*m.pl.*).
incur no expenses (notice on a bill of exchange), sans frais; sans protêt; retour sans frais; sans compte de retour.
indebted (*adj.*), redevable:
I am not indebted to you for anything, je ne vous suis redevable de rien.
indebtedness (the sum owed) (*n.*), dette (*f.*); créance (*f.*):
the amount of my indebtedness, le montant de ma dette.
evidence of indebtedness (proof of debt), titre de créance (*m.*).

indebtedness (debts colléctively) (*n.*), dettes et créances (*f.pl.*); créances et dettes (*f.pl.*):
international indebtedness is considered as the chief basis of the exchanges, les dettes et créances internationales sont considérées comme la base principale des changes.
as it is very rare that the mutual indebtedness of two countries exactly balances, the exchanges are rarely at par, comme il est très rare que les créances et dettes réciproques de deux pays se balancent exactement, les changes sont rarement au pair.
Cf. balance of indebtedness (Polit. Econ.).
indemnification (*n.*), indemnisation (*f.*); dédommagement (*m.*):
indemnification of expropriated persons, indemnisation des expropriés.
indemnificatory (*adj.*), indemnitaire:
the indemnificatory character of insurance, le caractère indemnitaire de l'assurance.
indemnify (*v.t.*), indemniser; dédommager; récompenser:
to indemnify the assured for a loss, the shipowners for certain consequences or liabilities that may arise, indemniser l'assuré d'une perte, les armateurs de certaines conséquences ou responsabilités qui peuvent se soulever.
to indemnify the owner of a property taken for public uses, indemniser le possesseur d'une propriété expropriée pour cause d'utilité publique.
to indemnify someone for his losses, indemniser, dédommager, récompenser, quelqu'un de ses pertes.
indemnitee (pers.) (*n.*), indemnitaire (*m.* ou *f.*).
indemnity [**indemnities** *pl.*] (compensation or reimbursement for a loss) (*n.*), indemnité (*f.*); dédommagement (*m.*); récompense (*f.*):
indemnity agreed in case of delay, for expropriation, indemnité convenue en cas de retard, pour cause d'expropriation.
to fix the indemnity at the amount of the damage, fixer l'indemnité au montant du dommage.
war indemnity, indemnité de guerre.
indemnity (*n.*) or **indemnity bond** or **letter of indemnity** (undertaking or contract to make good to another a loss or to protect him against liability), caution (*f.*); cautionnement (*m.*); acte de caution (*m.*); acte de cautionnement (*m.*); garantie (*f.*); obligation de garantie (*f.*); lettre de garantie (*f.*); lettre d'indemnité (*f.*):
to obtain a duplicate of a lost certificate by giving an indemnity (or by giving a letter of indemnity), obtenir un duplicata d'un certificat perdu en donnant caution (ou en donnant une lettre de garantie).
indemnities required for the delivery of duplicates of lost scrip, cautionnements exigés pour la délivrance de duplicata de titres perdus.
indent (order) (*n.*), indent (*m.*).
indenture (Law) (*n.*), acte (*m.*); contrat (*m.*).

independent (of independent means) (*adj.*), indépendant, -e; *also rendered in French by the noun* rentier, -ère:
to work in the hope of becoming independent, travailler dans l'espoir de devenir rentier.
indestructible stencil, stencil chiffonnable (*m.*).
index [**indexes** *or* **indices** *pl.*] (indication; guide) (*n.*), indice (*m.*):
the price at which an export house can sell its bills of exchange is considered as an infallible index of the credit which that house enjoys in the commercial world, le prix auquel une maison d'exportation peut vendre ses lettres de change est considéré comme un indice infaillible du crédit dont cette maison jouit dans le monde commercial.
index [**indexes** *pl.*] (alphabetical list) (*n.*), index (*m.*); répertoire (*m.*); table alphabétique (*f.*):
index of a book, index, répertoire, table alphabétique, d'un livre (*ou* d'un registre).
an index, placed in front of the book, enables one to refer immediately to every account, un répertoire, placé au commencement du livre, permet de se reporter immédiatement à chaque compte.
index (*v.t.*), répertorier:
each entry is indexed alphabetically under name of ship, chaque écriture est répertoriée alphabétiquement par nom de navire (*f.*).
index card, carte-fiche (*f.*); fiche-carton (*f.*); fiche mobile (*f.*); fiche (*f.*).
index number (Economics), nombre-indice (*m.*); nombre indicateur (*m.*); chiffre-indice (*m.*); indice économique (*m.*); index-number (*m.*).
indexing (*n.*), indexation (*f.*).
indiarubber (eraser) (*n.*), gomme (*f.*); gomme élastique (*f.*).
indiarubber ring *or* **indiarubber band,** bande en caoutchouc (*f.*); bracelet en caoutchouc (*m.*); caoutchouc (*m.*).
indiarubber stamp, timbre en caoutchouc (*m.*); timbre humide (*m.*).
indirect (*adj.*), indirect, -e:
indirect call (of a ship at an intermediate port), escale rétrograde (*f.*); échelle rétrograde (*f.*).
indirect charges (*or* expenses) (Costing) (opp. to *direct expenses* or *establishment charges* or *departmental charges*), frais indirects (*m.pl.*); frais fixes (*m.pl.*); frais généraux (*m.pl.*); dépenses indirectes (*ou* fixes) (*f.pl.*).
indirect exchange (making use of one or more intermediate currencies), change indirect (*m.*).
indirect exchange (rate of exchange), incertain (*m.*). *V.* to quote indirect exchange *pour exemple.*
indirect tax, impôt indirect (*m.*); contribution indirecte (*f.*).
indivisibility (*n.*), indivisibilité (*f.*).
indivisible (*adj.*), indivisible:
an indivisible whole, un tout indivisible.
indivisibly (*adv.*), indivisiblement.

indoor establishment *or* **indoor staff** (opp. to *outdoor establishment* or *staff*), service sédentaire (*m.*); personnel sédentaire (*m.*).
indorsable, indorse, indorsement, indorser. Syn. de **endorsable, endorse,** etc.
inducement (Shipping) (*n.*), aliment (*m.*):
these steamers will call at X. if sufficient inducement for this port, ces vapeurs feront escale à X. en cas d'aliment suffisant pour ce port.
industrial (*adj.*), industriel, -elle:
industrial bookkeeping, comptabilité industrielle (*f.*).
industrial insurance, assurance industrielle (*f.*); assurance ouvrière (*f.*).
industrial shares *or* **industrials** (*n.pl.*), valeurs industrielles (*f.pl.*); industrielles (*f.pl.*).
industrially (*adv.*), industriellement.
industry [**industries** *pl.*] (*n.*), industrie (*f.*):
the shipbuilding industry, l'industrie des constructions navales.
inequality [**inequalities** *pl.*] (*n.*), inégalité (*f.*):
inequalities of (*or* in) price, inégalités de prix.
inequitable (*adj.*), inéquitable:
inequitable distribution of taxation, répartition inéquitable des impôts (*f.*).
inequitably (*adv.*), inéquitablement.
inexchangeability (*n.*), impermutabilité (*f.*).
inexchangeable (*adj.*), inéchangeable; impermutable:
inexchangeable securities, valeurs inéchangeables (*ou* impermutables) (*f.pl.*).
infant trader, mineur commerçant (*m.*).
infected ship (Quarantine), navire infecté (*m.*).
infidelity (*n.*), infidélité (*f.*).
inflate (*v.t.*), gonfler; grossir; charger:
to inflate an account, gonfler, grossir, charger, un compte.
trusts which, by inflating their capital to excess, wish to give the impression of power, and conceal, by an apparent reduction, their enormous profits, trusts qui, en gonflant leur capital à l'excès, veulent donner l'impression de la puissance, et masquer par une réduction apparente, leurs énormes bénéfices (*m.pl.*).
inflation (*n.*), gonflement (*m.*); inflation (*f.*):
monetary inflation, inflation monétaire.
inflation of credit, inflation de crédit.
inflation of gold, inflation d'or.
inflow *or* **influx** (*n.*) (opp. to *outflow* or *efflux*), rentrée (*f.*); afflux (*m.*):
an inflow (*or* an influx) of gold, durable wealth and better than other riches, une rentrée d'or, richesse durable et supérieure aux autres richesses.
inflow (*or* influx) of gold brought by foreign visitors, afflux d'or apporté par les visiteurs étrangers.
influential (*adj.*), influent, -e:
a group of influential people, un groupe de personalités influentes.
inform (*v.t.*), informer; instruire; renseigner; prévenir:
to inform someone about a matter, of what is

going on, informer, instruire, renseigner, quelqu'un sur une affaire, de ce qui passe.

informal (*adj.*), informe.

informality [**informalities** *pl.*] (*n.*), vice de forme (*m.*).

information (*n.*), renseignements (*m.pl.*); renseignement (*m.*); indications (*f.pl.*); indication (*f.*):
request for further information, demande de renseignements complémentaires.
to furnish information, fournir des renseignements.
form which contains the following information, formule qui porte les indications suivantes (*f.*).

infringe (*v.t.*), enfreindre; contrefaire:
to infringe the rule, enfreindre la règle.
to infringe a patented article, contrefaire un objet breveté.

infringement *or* **infraction** (*n.*), infraction (*f.*); contravention (*f.*); contrefaçon (*f.*):
infringement of a monopoly, contravention à un monopole.
infringement of copyright, contrefaçon littéraire; contrefaçon de (*ou* en) librairie.

ingot (*n.*), lingot (*m.*):
ingots of legal fineness, lingots au titre légal.

inherent vice, vice propre (*m.*):
by inherent vice (*or* by vice propre) of the goods is understood deterioration of the goods by their nature or by the influence of external natural agents, par vice propre de la marchandise on entend la détérioration de la marchandise par sa nature ou par l'influence d'agents naturels extérieurs.
V. aussi exemple sous **liable**.

initial (*adj.*), initial, -e, -als:
initial capital, capital initial (*m.*); capital d'apport (*m.*); capital d'établissement (*m.*).
initial capital expenditure, frais de premier établissement (*m.pl.*); premier établissement (*m.*).

initial (*n.*), initiale (*f.*). Pour le pluriel **initials**, V. ci-après.

initial (*v.t.*), parafer; parapher; apposer son parafe à; signer de ses initiales; viser:
to initial an alteration, parafer un renvoi.
to initial a letter, signer une lettre de ses initiales.
to initial the counterfoil of a cheque, viser le talon d'un chèque.
to be initialed, être parafé, -e, visé, -e; se parafer:
document which ought to be initialed, pièce qui doit se parafer (*f.*).

initials (*n.pl.*), parafe (*m.*); paraphe (*m.*); initiales (*f.pl.*); visa (*m.*):
to put one's initials, apposer son parafe (*ou* ses initiales) (*ou* son visa).

injure (*v.t.*), léser; avarier; endommager:
decision which would seem to injure one's interests, décision qui paraît léser ses intérêts (*f.*).

injury [**injuries** *pl.*] (*n.*), lésion (*f.*); dommage (*m.*); avarie (*f.*); avaries (*f.pl.*); préjudice (*m.*);

injury to piers, wharves, etc. (hull insurance policy), faits de heurt de digues, quais, etc. (*m.pl.*).

ink (*n.*), encre (*f.*).

ink eraser, gomme pour l'encre (*f.*); gomme à encre (*f.*).

inking pad (stamp pad), tampon (*m.*).

inkpot (*n.*) *or* **inkstand** (*n.*) *or* **ink bottle,** encrier (*m.*).

inland (*adj.*), intérieur, -e:
inland bill (opp. to *foreign bill*), effet sur l'intérieur (*m.*).
inland duties, taxes intérieures (*f.pl.*).
inland navigation *or* inside navigation, navigation intérieure (*f.*); navigation fluviale (*f.*); batellerie (*f.*); batellerie fluviale (*f.*):
the economic superiority of the railway over inland navigation, la supériorité économique du chemin de fer sur la navigation intérieure.
the costs of railway carriage are higher than those of inland navigation, les prix de revient des transports par chemins de fer sont plus élevés que ceux de la batellerie (*m.pl.*).
inland parcel, colis postal du régime intérieur (*m.*).
inland postal packet, objet de correspondance pour l'intérieur (*m.*).
inland rate (of postage), tarif du régime intérieur (*m.*).
inland revenue (revenue derived from taxes), recettes fiscales (*f.pl.*); recettes provenant d'impôts (*f.pl.*).
Inland Revenue (Revenue authorities) (*Abbrev.*: I.R.), fisc (*m.*).
inland revenue receipts, rentrées fiscales (*f.pl.*).
inland revenue stamp, timbre fiscal (*m.*).
inland route (river or canal), voie fluviale (*f.*).
inland system (Post) (opp. to *imperial and foreign system*), régime intérieur (*m.*).
inland telegram, télégramme du régime intérieur (*m.*); télégramme intérieur (*m.*).
inland waters, eaux intérieures (*f.pl.*).

innavigability (*n.*), innavigabilité (*f.*).

innavigable (*adj.*), innavigable.

inner column (opp. to *outer column*), colonne intérieure (*f.*).

inner reserve (opp. to *visible reserve*), réserve cachée (*f.*); réserve occulte (*f.*); réserve latente (*f.*).

inoperative (*adj.*), inopérant, -e:
inoperative clause, clause inopérante (*f.*).

inquire (*v.i.*). Syn. de **enquire**.

inquiry [**inquiries** *pl.*] (*n.*). Syn. de **enquiry**.

inscribable (said of stocks) (*adj.*), inscriptible.

inscribe (*v.t.*), inscrire:
the nominal (*or* face) value is that inscribed on a stock or share certificate, la valeur nominale est celle inscrite sur un titre de bourse.

inscribed rente (Abbrev.: **insc. rente**), inscription de rente (*f.*); inscription sur le grand-livre (*f.*).

inscription *or* **inscribing** (*n.*), inscription (*f.*).

insert (*v.t.*), insérer; apposer:

to insert a clause in a contract, insérer une clause dans un contrat ; apposer une clause à un acte.

insertion (*n.*), insertion (*f.*) ; apposition (*f.*) : insertion of an advertisement in a newspaper, insertion d'une annonce dans un journal.

inside navigation. *V. sous* inland navigation.

insolvency [**insolvencies** *pl.*] (*n.*), insolvabilité (*f.*) ; déconfiture (*f.*) ; faillite (*f.*) : insolvency of a debtor, insolvabilité d'un débiteur.

insolvent (*adj.*), insolvable ; failli, -e : insolvent debtor, débiteur insolvable (*m.*) ; débiteur failli (*m.*) ; failli, -e. to be insolvent, être insolvable ; être en faillite.

insolvent (pers.) (*n.*), insolvable (*m.* ou *f.*) ; failli, -e.

inspect (*v.t.*), inspecter ; examiner ; compulser ; visiter ; contrôler : to inspect a merchant's books, inspecter, examiner, compulser, les livres d'un négociant. the inspection department (of a bank, or the like) cannot show good results unless it is independent of the departments inspected, le service du contrôle (d'une banque, ou analogue) ne peut donner de bons résultats que s'il est indépendant des services contrôlés.

inspection (*n.*), inspection (*f.*) ; examen (*m.*) ; visite (*f.*) ; contrôle (*m.*) : inspection of title deeds of property, examen des titres de propriété. periodical inspection of the hull of a ship, visite périodique de la coque d'un navire.

inspection committee, comité de surveillance (*m.*).

inspection fee, droit de visite (*m.*).

inspection order *or* **inspecting order** (Customs), bon d'ouverture (*m.*).

inspection register, registre de visite (*m.*).

inspector (pers.) (*n.*), inspecteur, -trice ; examinateur, -trice ; visiteur, -euse ; contrôleur, -euse : inspector of an insurance company, inspecteur d'une compagnie d'assurance. inspector of taxes, contrôleur des contributions directes.

instability [**instabilities** *pl.*] (*n.*), instabilité (*f.*) : the grave consequences of monetary instability, les graves conséquences de l'instabilité monétaire (*f.pl.*).

instalment *or* **installment** (*n.*), acompte (*m.*) ; paiement à compte (*m.*) ; versement (*m.*) ; terme (*m.*) : to pay an instalment, verser un acompte ; faire un versement. loan repayable by (*or* in) instalments, prêt remboursable par acomptes (*m.*). to spread a subscription into several instalments, échelonner une souscription en plusieurs versements. payment can be made in full or in (*or* by) instalments, le paiement peut se faire en une fois ou par versements échelonnés. issue of debentures in full or in instalments,

émission d'obligations en une ou plusieurs fois (*f.*). first, second, third, etc., instalment (on shares, or the like), premier, second, troisième, etc., versement ; premier, second, troisième, etc., terme : to pay the first, the second, instalment, faire le premier, le second, versement ; verser le premier, le deuxième, terme. final instalment (on shares, or the like), versement de libération ; dernier versement. the payment of instalments of annuities, of interest, due, l'acquittement (*ou* le versement) des termes échus d'annuités, d'intérêts (*m.*).

instalment plan (hire purchase), vente à tempérament (*f.*) ; vente par abonnement (*f.*).

instant (of the present month) (*adj.*) (Abbrev. : **inst.**), courant ; en cours : instant month, mois courant (*m.*) ; mois en cours (*m.*) ; courant (*m.*). the 10th instant, le 10 courant.

instigate (*v.t.*), provoquer : to instigate an enquiry, provoquer une enquête.

institute proceedings against someone (to), intenter une action à (*ou* contre), entamer des poursuites contre, quelqu'un.

institution (*n.*), institution (*f.*) ; établissement (*m.*) : credit institution, institution de crédit (*f.*) ; établissement de crédit (*m.*) ; crédit (*m.*).

instruct (*v.t.*), charger ; donner des instructions à : to instruct someone to reply to a letter, charger quelqu'un de répondre à une lettre. to instruct a solicitor, charger un avoué ; constituer avoué ; donner des instructions à un solicitor. to instruct counsel, constituer avocat.

instructing counsel (*or* **instructions to**) **counsel,** constitution d'avocat (*f.*).

instructions (*n.pl.*), instructions (*f.pl.*) ; charge (*f.*) ; mandat (*m.*) ; mentions (*f.pl.*) ; mention (*f.*) : to confine oneself to one's instructions, se renfermer dans ses instructions. to go beyond one's instructions, aller au delà de sa charge. instructions to insure given before knowledge of the accident, mandat d'assurer donné avant la connaissance du sinistre. the obligation of the agent to prove the carrying out of his instructions ceases when the principal has discharged him, l'obligation pour le mandataire de justifier de l'exécution de son mandat cesse lorsque le mandant lui a donné décharge (*f.*). service instructions (on a printed form), mentions de service. telegrams handed in without route instructions, with a route instruction, télégrammes déposés sans mention de voie, avec une mention de voie (*m.pl.*).

instrument (Law) (*n.*), instrument (*m.*) ; acte (*m.*) :

the promissory note is an instrument of credit, whereas the cheque is an instrument of payment, le billet à ordre est un instrument de crédit, alors que le chèque est un instrument de paiement.

instrument in writing, acte à l'écrit.

instrument of transfer, acte de cession; acte de transmission; acte de mutation; acte translatif de propriété.

insufficiency (*n.*), insuffisance (*f.*) :

insufficiency of assets, of packing, of marks, insuffisance d'actif, d'emballage, de marques.

insufficient (*adj.*), insuffisant, -e :

insufficient address, adresse insuffisante (*f.*).

insufficient funds (Banking) (*Abbrev. :* I/F), provision insuffisante; insuffisance de provision.

insufficient packing, emballage insuffisant (*m.*).

insufficiently prepaid postal packets, correspondances insuffisamment affranchies (*f.pl.*).

insulated van (Rly.), wagon isotherme (*m.*).

insurable (*adj.*), assurable :

theoretically every risk is insurable, théoriquement tout risque est assurable.

insurable interest *or* insurable value, intérêt assurable (*m.*); valeur assurable (*f.*). V. exemples sous **interest** & **value.**

insurance (*n.*) (Abbrev. : **ins.** *or* **insce** *or* **insur.**), assurance (*f.*) :

the insurance of a cargo is made on the foundation of the bill of lading which evidences it, l'assurance d'un chargement est faite sur le fondement du connaissement qui le constate.

insurance against risks of redemption at par, assurance contre les risques de remboursement au pair.

insurance for account of whom it may concern, assurance pour le compte de qui il appartiendra; assurance pour compte de tiers; assurance pour compte.

insurance of premium, assurance de la prime.

insurance on cargo *or* insurance on (*or* of) goods (*or* merchandise), assurance sur facultés; assurance sur (*ou* des) marchandises.

insurance on (*or* of) freight, assurance sur (*ou* du) fret.

insurance on hull *or* insurance on (*or* of) ship, assurance sur corps; assurance sur (*ou* du) navire.

insurance, steamer or steamers to be declared (floating policy insurance), assurance in quovis (*ou* in quo vis); assurance par navire à désigner; assurance sur navire indéterminé.

insurance subject to safe arrival (Mar. Insce), assurance sur bonne arrivée.

insurance (Post) (*n.*), chargement (*m.*) :

registration or insurance is a special treatment applied to postal packets of which the senders wish to ensure delivery, against receipt, to the addressees, or to protect the contents of the said packets, la recommendation ou le chargement est un traitement spécial appliqué aux objets de corres-

pondance dont les expéditeurs veulent assurer la remise, contre reçu, aux destinataires, ou de garantir le contenu desdits objets.

insurance account (debit note of insurance charges), note d'assurance (*f.*).

insurance agent, agent d'assurances (*m.*).

insurance broker, courtier d'assurances (*m.*). *See note under* courtier maritime.

insurance card, carte d'assuré (*f.*).

insurance certificate, certificat d'assurance (*m.*) : the insurance certificate often replaces the insurance policy, or is its indispensable complement, in the course of commercial transactions, le certificat d'assurance remplace souvent la police d'assurance, ou en est le complément indispensable, au cours d'opérations commerciales.

insurance charges, frais d'assurance (*m.pl.*).

insurance company, compagnie d'assurance (*f.*); compagnie d'assurances (*f.*); société d'assurance (*ou* d'assurances) (*f.*).

insurance fee (Post), droit d'assurance (*m.*).

insurance fund, fonds d'assurance (*m.*).

insurance note, arrêté d'assurance (*m.*); arrêté provisoire (*m.*); arrêté (*m.*).

insurance policy, police d'assurance (*f.*).

insurance premium, prime d'assurance (*f.*).

insurance shares, valeurs d'assurances (*f.pl.*).

insurance value, valeur d'assurance (*f.*) : the insurance value of the thing insured, la valeur d'assurance de la chose assurée.

insure (to make sure or secure) (*v.t.*), assurer : to insure the carrying out of a bargain, the safety of a marine adventure, assurer l'exécution d'un marché, le salut d'une expédition maritime.

insure (to make insurance of) (*v.t.*), faire assurer ; faire assurer sur ; assurer : to insure one's furniture, a ship's cargo, faire assurer, assurer, son mobilier, la cargaison d'un navire.

the insured can insure the premium of insurance. In marine insurance, one can insure the premium and the premium on the premium, l'assuré peut faire assurer la prime de l'assurance. En matière d'assurance maritime, on peut faire assurer la prime et la prime de la prime.

the big shipping companies seldom insure their ships, and so are their own insurers, les grandes compagnies de navigation font rarement assurer leurs navires, et restent ainsi leurs propres assureurs.

to insure one's life, faire assurer sur sa vie.

to be insured, être assuré, -e ; s'assurer : these certificates are not insured because they are registered, ces titres ne s'assurent pas puisqu'ils sont nominatifs (*m.pl.*).

insure (to guarantee to make good a loss) (*v.t.*), assurer : company which insures a house against the risk of fire, compagnie qui assure une maison contre le risque d'incendie (*f.*).

insure (Post) (*v.t.*), charger : to insure a letter, charger une lettre.

insure (*v.i.*), s'assurer ; se faire assurer :

to insure against fire, against the risks for which one is liable, against a third party claim, against any wrongful acts or defaults of the master and crew, s'assurer, se faire assurer, contre l'incendie, contre les risques dont on est responsable, contre le recours des tiers, contre toutes fautes ou prévarications du capitaine et de l'équipage.

insured [**insured** *pl.*] *or* **insuree** (pers.) (*n.*), assuré, -e :

the premium is the remuneration due by the insured to the insurer, la prime est la rémunération due par l'assuré à l'assureur.

insured box (Post), boîte avec (*ou* de) valeur déclarée (*f.*) ; boîte chargée (*f.*).

insured for : £0 (inscription on an insured article), valeur déclarée : 0£.

insured letter, lettre avec (*ou* de) valeur déclarée (*f.*) ; lettre chargée (*f.*).

insured packet *or* **insured article,** objet (*ou* envoi) (*ou* paquet) avec (*ou* de) valeur déclarée (*m.*) ; objet chargé (*m.*) ; envoi chargé (*m.*) ; paquet chargé (*m.*). *V. note sous* postal packet.

insured parcel (Post), colis avec valeur déclarée (*m.*) ; colis chargé (*m.*).

insured value, valeur assurée (*f.*) :

insured value for average purposes, for total loss purposes, valeur assurée à prendre en cas d'avaries, en cas de perte totale.

insurer (pers.) (*n.*), assureur (*m.*) :

in case of partial insurance, the insured is deemed to be his own insurer for the excess, en cas d'assurance partielle, l'assuré est réputé être son propre assureur pour l'excédent.

intact (*adj.*), intact, -e :

to find a deposit intact, retrouver un dépôt intact.

intangible assets, valeurs immatérielles (*f.pl.*) ; valeurs intangibles (*f.pl.*).

intended shipment, expédition projetée (*f.*).

intercolonial (*adj.*), intercolonial, -e, -aux.

interdict (*v.t.*), interdire.

interdiction (*n.*), interdiction (*f.*) :

interdiction of commerce, interdiction de commerce.

interest (personal concern) (*n.*), intérêt (*m.*) ; profit (*m.*) :

to protect the shareholders' interests, sauvegarder les intérêts des actionnaires.

master who takes refuge in a port, in the common interest, capitaine qui se réfugie dans un port, dans l'intérêt commun (*m.*).

interest (risk ; value) (Insce) (*n.*), aliment (*m.*) ; intérêt (*m.*) ; risque (*m.*) ; valeur (*f.*) :

each interest to form the subject of a separate policy, chaque aliment (*ou* intérêt) (*ou* risque) fera l'objet d'une police distincte.

the insurable interests which are the subject matter of the insurance, les valeurs (*ou* intérêts) assurables qui sont l'objet de l'assurance.

omission or error in the description of the interest, vessel, or voyage, omission ou

erreur dans la description de l'intérêt, du navire, ou du voyage (*f.*).

the insured must have interest in the insurance ; otherwise there is no risk for him, l'assuré doit avoir intérêt à l'assurance ; sinon il n'y a pas de risque pour lui (*m.*).

the vessel by which the interest is, or is intended to be, shipped, le navire dans lequel l'aliment est embarqué, ou destiné à l'être.

the declaration of interest should be made to the underwriter within the time specified in the contract, la déclaration d'aliment doit être faite à l'assureur dans le délai fixé au contrat.

the company agrees to insure the goods as interest attaching to a floating policy specially taken out for this purpose, la compagnie accepte de faire assurer les marchandises en aliment à une police flottante spécialement contractée à cet effet.

interests liable to contribute (General Average), V. syn. **contributing interests.**

interest (proprietary right or share ; part ownership) (*n.*), intérêt (*m.*) ; tantième (*m.*) ; commandite (*f.*) : (Cf. **share.**)

to have an interest in an undertaking, avoir un intérêt dans une entreprise.

the interest of each partner in the profits is proportional to what he brings in, le tantième de chaque associé dans les bénéfices est proportionnel à ce qu'il apporte.

the bank allows them an interest in the proceeds, la banque leur alloue un tantième du produit.

his interest is three thousand pounds, sa commandite est de trois mille livres.

interest (payment for the use of money) (*n.*) (Abbrev. : **int.** *or* **in.** *or* **i.**), intérêt (*m.*) ; intérêts (*m.pl.*) ; arrérages (*m.pl.*) : (*Note :—arrérages* is usually said of interest on rentes, Government stocks, Treasury bonds, or the like.)

interest allowed on deposits, intérêt alloué aux dépôts.

interest in arrears, intérêts de retard ; intérêts moratoires.

interest in black (accounts current, or the like), intérêts noirs.

interest in red, intérêts rouges.

interest on capital, intérêt du capital ; intérêts des capitaux.

interest on capital during construction, dividende intercalaire (*m.*) ; dividende statutaire (*m.*) ; intérêt intercalaire ; intérêt statutaire.

interest on loan, intérêts de prêt ; intérêt sur prêt.

interest on loans, intérêts de prêts ; intérêts des prêts ; intérêts sur prêts :

interest on loans on public securities, intérêts de prêts sur fonds publics.

interest on money lodged as security, intérêts des fonds déposés en garantie.

the rate of interest on money, le taux de l'intérêt de l'argent.

interest and profit on investments, intérêts et bénéfice du portefeuille.

interest paid out of capital, intérêts prélevés sur le capital.

interest receivable, intérêts à recevoir.

the interest on the national debt, les arrérages de la dette nationale.

French bearer rentes have an interest coupon attached to the certificate, which is cut off each time interest is paid, les rentes françaises au porteur ont un coupon d'arrérages joint au titre, qui est détaché chaque fois que les arrérages sont payés (*f.pl.*). See **date** (due date).

interest (*v.t.*), intéresser :
to interest someone in a matter, intéresser quelqu'un à une affaire.

to interest oneself, s'intéresser :
to interest oneself in a commercial undertaking, s'intéresser dans une entreprise commerciale.

interest account, compte d'intérêts (*m.*); compte d'intérêt (*m.*).

interest-bearing, productif (-ive) d'intérêt :
interest-bearing capital, capital productif d'intérêt (*m.*).

interest coupon, coupon d'intérêt (*m.*); coupon d'arrérages (*m.*).

interest due *or* **interest payable** (*ellipsis for* date interest is due or payable). V. sous **date** (due date).

interest table, table d'intérêts (*f.*).

interested party, intéressé, -e; partie intéressée (*f.*) :
to call the interested parties together, convoquer les intéressés.

interfere (*v.i.*), s'immiscer :
to interfere in the management of a concern, s'immiscer dans la direction d'une entreprise.

interim certificate (opp. to *definitive,* or *definite, certificate*), titre provisoire (*m.*); certificat provisoire (*m.*).

interim dividend (distinguished from *final dividend*), acompte de dividende (*m.*); acompte sur dividende (*m.*); acompte sur le dividende (*m.*); dividende intérimaire (*m.*); dividende provisoire (*m.*) :
to declare an interim dividend, déclarer un acompte de dividende (*ou* un dividende intérimaire) (*ou* un dividende provisoire).

dividends are payable 1st January (interim) and 1st July (final), les dividendes sont payables le 1er janvier (acompte) et le 1er juillet (solde) (*m.pl.*).

interior waterway, voie fluviale (*f.*).

interlineation (*n.*), interligne (*m.*); interlinéation (*f.*); interlignage (*m.*).

intermediary [**intermediaries** *pl.*] (pers.) (*n.*), intermédiaire (*m.*) :
banker who receives applications for an issue in the capacity of intermediary between the public and the issuer, banquier qui reçoit des souscriptions à une émission en qualité d'intermédiaire entre le public et l'émetteur (*m.*).

mere intermediaries who buy to resell (*or* to

sell again), simples intermédiaires qui achètent pour revendre.

intermediate (*adj.*), intermédiaire :
intermediate buyers and sellers, acheteurs et vendeurs intermédiaires (*m.pl.*).

intermediate place (indirect foreign exchange), place médiate (*f.*); place intermédiaire (*f.*).

intermediate port, port intermédiaire (*m.*); port d'escale (*m.*); escale (*f.*); port d'échelle (*m.*); échelle (*f.*).

intermediate station (Rly.), station intermédiaire (*f.*); station (*f.*); gare de passage (*f.*); gare intermédiaire (*f.*); gare d'escale (*f.*).

intermediate steamer, vapeur intermédiaire (*m.*).

intermediate voyage from one port to another, voyage intermédiaire d'un port à un autre (*m.*).

internal (*adj.*), intérieur, -e :
internal exchange, change intérieur (*m.*).

internal loan, emprunt intérieur (*m.*).

internal navigation, navigation intérieure (*f.*); navigation fluviale (*f.*); batellerie (*f.*); batellerie fluviale (*f.*). V. *exemples sous syn.* inland navigation.

internal packing, emballage intérieur (*m.*).

internal revenue, recettes fiscales (*f.pl.*); recettes provenant d'impôts (*f.pl.*).

international (*adj.*), international, -e, -aux :
International Chamber of Commerce, Chambre de commerce internationale (*f.*).

international franc, franc international (*m.*).

International Labour Office (*Abbrev.:* I.L.O.), Bureau international du travail (*m.*).

international law, droit international (*m.*); droit des gens (*m.*).

international money order, mandat de poste international (*m.*).

international private law, droit international privé (*m.*).

international reply coupon, coupon-réponse international (*m.*).

international travelling pass, certificat international de route (*m.*).

interpret (*v.t.*), interpréter :
these numerical data can be variously interpreted, on peut interpréter diversement ces données numériques.

interpretation (*n.*), interprétation (*f.*) :
interpretation of an agreement, of the law, interprétation d'une convention, de la loi.

interpreter (pers.) (*n.*), interprète (*m.* ou *f.*) :
interpreters in uniform at the service of travellers in the railway stations and ports, interprètes en uniforme à la disposition des voyageurs dans les gares et ports.

interruption (*n.*), interruption (*f.*) :
telegram delayed by interruption of communication, télégramme retardé par interruption de communication (*m.*).

intervene (*v.i.*), intervenir :
third party who intervenes to accept a bill of exchange protested for non acceptance, tiers qui intervient pour accepter une lettre de change protestée faute d'acceptation (*m.*).

intervention (*n.*), intervention (*f.*) :
intervention on protest, intervention à protêt.
interview (*n.*), entrevue (*f.*) ; interview (*f.* ou
m.) ; abouchement (*m.*) :
to ask for an interview with one's banker,
solliciter une entrevue (*ou* une *ou* un
interview) avec son banquier.
interview (*v.t.*), interviewer :
to interview someone, interviewer quelqu'un.
intra vires (opp. to *ultra vires* or *extra vires*),
statutaire.
intrinsic (*adj.*) (Ant. : *extrinsic*), intrinsèque :
the intrinsic value of a coin depends on the
quantity of precious metal it contains,
la valeur intrinsèque d'une pièce de monnaie
dépend de la quantité de métal précieux
qu'elle renferme.
intrinsically (*adv.*), intrinsèquement :
intrinsically, this stock is worth more than
the prices at present quoted, intrinsèquement, cette valeur vaut mieux que les cours
actuellement cotés.
introduce (*v.t.*), introduire :
we have much pleasure in introducing to you
Mr So-and-So, nous avons l'honneur d'introduire auprès de vous Monsieur un tel.
introducer (pers.) (*n.*), introducteur, -trice.
introducing syndicate (Stock Exch.), syndicat
d'introduction (*m.*).
introduction (*n.*), introduction (*f.*) :
introduction of shares on the market, introduction de titres sur le marché.
letter of introduction, lettre d'introduction
(*f.*).
intrust (*v.t.*). Syn. de **entrust**.
invalid (*adj.*), invalide ; nul, nulle.
invalidate (*v.t.*), invalider :
to invalidate a will, invalider un testament.
invalidity (*n.*), invalidité (*f.*) :
invalidity of a contract, invalidité d'un contrat.
inventory [**inventories** *pl.*] (*n.*), inventaire (*m.*) :
to draw up an inventory of the property of a
private person, dresser un inventaire des
biens d'un particulier.
inventory of ship's tackle and furniture,
inventaire des agrès et du mobilier du navire.
the inventory is a kind of permanent manifest
of the accessory appliances of the ship,
l'inventaire est une sorte de manifeste permanent du matériel accessoire du navire.
inventory (*v.t.*), inventorier :
to inventory goods, inventorier des marchandises.
invest (to entrust) (*v.t.*), investir ; confier :
directors properly invested with their office,
administrateurs régulièrement investis de
leurs fonctions (*m.pl.*).
board invested with the power of contracting
loans, conseil d'administration investi du
pouvoir de contracter des emprunts (*m.*).
to invest the management of a bank in a
governor, confier la direction d'une banque
à un gouverneur.
invest (to lay out in business) (*v.t.*), placer ;
investir :
to invest money, all one's available money in

realizable securities, placer de l'argent,
tous ses fonds disponibles sur les valeurs
réalisables.
to invest the remainder of one's fortune in
life annuities, placer en rentes viagères le
restant de sa fortune.
capital invested, capital investi (*m.*) ; mise
de fonds (*f.*).
the capital invested in a business, le capital
investi dans une affaire.
invest (*v.i.*), faire un placement ; faire des
placements :
to invest in stocks and shares, faire des placements en valeurs de bourse.
investing public, clientèle de portefeuille (*f.*) :
speculation shows less nervousness and the
investing public seems inclined to interest
itself again in business, la spéculation
montre moins de timidité et la clientèle de
portefeuille paraît susceptible de s'intéresser
de nouveau aux affaires.
investment (*n.*), placement (*m.*) ; investissement
(*m.*) ; valeur (*f.*) ; portefeuille (*m.*) ; mise
de fonds (*f.*) ; mise (*f.*) : (Pour le pluriel
investments, V. ci-après.)
temporary investment of funds (*or* of money),
of working capital, placement, investissement, momentané de fonds, des fonds de
roulement.
to make a good investment, faire un bon
placement.
safe investment, placement sûr ; valeur de
tout repos.
stock attractive, at this price, as an investment, valeur attrayante, à ce cours, pour
le portefeuille (*f.*).
X. shares seem interesting as an investment
at their present price on the basis of the
last dividend alone, l'action X. semble
intéressante pour le portefeuille à son cours
actuel sur la seule base du dernier dividende.
profit which is equal to so much per cent on
the investment (*or* on the amount of money
invested) (*or* on the money, *or* capital, invested), bénéfice qui correspond à tant pour
cent de la mise de fonds (*m.*).
investment capital, capitaux de placement (*m.pl.*).
investment company, société de placement (*f.*) ;
société de portefeuille (*f.*).
investment securities *or* **investment shares** *or*
investment stocks (opp. to *speculative
securities*), valeurs de placement (*f.pl.*) ;
titres de placement (*m.pl.*) ; valeurs de portefeuille (*f.pl.*) ; titres de portefeuille (*m.pl.*) :
stock which offers all the qualities of an investment security, valeur qui offre tous les
caractères du titre de portefeuille (*f.*).
investment trust, trust de placement (*m.*) ; coopérative de placement (*f.*) ; société de
gérance (*f.*).
investments (*n.pl.*), placements (*m.pl.*) ; portefeuille (*m.*) ; portefeuille-titres (*m.*) ; portefeuille de titres (*m.*) ; portefeuille-valeurs
(*m.*) ; portefeuille de valeurs (*m.*) ; valeurs
(*f.pl.*) :

investments in railway shares, placements
en actions de chemins de fer.

the company's investments include shares pertaining to all kinds of industries, notably
shares in oil concerns, le portefeuille de la
société comprend des titres appartenant à
tous genres d'industries, notamment des
titres d'affaires pétrolifères.

provision for depreciation of investments,
prévision pour moins-value du portefeuille
(*ou* du portefeuille-titres) (*f.*).

items which are lumped under the heading
investments, articles qui sont bloqués dans
le chapitre portefeuille (*ou* qui sont réunis
sous la rubrique portefeuille-titres) (*m.pl.*).

investor (pers.) (*n.*), rentier, -ère; portefeuilliste
(*m.*).

invisible (*adj.*), invisible:
invisible exports, exportations invisibles (*f.pl.*).

invitation (*n.*), invitation (*f.*); appel (*m.*):
invitation to the public to subscribe to an issue,
to a loan, appel, invitation, au public pour
la souscription d'une émission, d'un emprunt.

invite (*v.t.*), inviter; appeler; faire appel à:
to invite tenders for repair of the damage,
inviter des soumissions pour la réparation
des dommages.

to invite the shareholders to subscribe the
capital of a new company, faire appel aux
actionnaires pour souscrire le capital d'une
nouvelle société.

invoice (*n.*) (Abbrev.: **inv.**), facture (*f.*); facture
de débit (*f.*):
invoice of origin, facture d'origine.
invoice of goods bought (opp. to *account sales*),
compte d'achat (*m.*).

invoice (*v.t.*), facturer:
to invoice goods, facturer des marchandises.

invoice book (purchase journal), livre d'achats
(*m.*); livre des achats (*m.*); livre d'achat
(*m.*); journal des achats (*m.*); facturier
d'entrée (*m.*).

invoice book (press copy book of sales invoices),
copie des factures (*m.*); facturier (*m.*).

invoice clerk, facturier (*m.*).

invoice price, prix de (*ou* de la) facture (*m.*).

invoice value, valeur de facture (*f.*).

invoicing (*n.*), facturation (*f.*).

invoicing back price (Produce Exch.), cours de
résiliation (*m.*).

invoicing machine, machine à facturer (*f.*).

inward bill of lading (opp. to *outward bill of
lading*), connaissement d'entrée (*m.*).

inward bound vessel *or* **inbound vessel** (opp. to
outward bound, or *outbound*, *vessel*), navire
en retour (*m.*); navire effectuant son
voyage de retour (*m.*).

inward bound voyage *or* **inbound voyage**, voyage
de retour (*m.*).

inward manifest, manifeste d'entrée (*m.*).

ipso facto, ipso facto:
membership of the committee does not confer,
ipso facto, the right of admission to the
committee's premises, la qualité de membre
du comité ne confère pas, ipso facto, le
droit d'entrée dans les locaux du comité.

iron and steel shares, valeurs sidérurgiques
(*f.pl.*); valeurs métallurgiques (*f.pl.*);
valeurs du groupe forges et fonderies (*f.pl.*).

iron ship, navire en fer (*m.*).

irrecoverable (*adj.*), irrécouvrable:
irrecoverable debt, créance irrécouvrable (*f.*).

irredeemable (*adj.*), non amortissable; irremboursable; irrachetable:
irredeemable bonds *or* irredeemable debentures,
obligations non amortissables (*ou* irremboursables) (*ou* irrachetables) (*f.pl.*).

irreducible (*adj.*), irréductible.

irregular (*adj.*), irrégulier, -ère:
irregular tendency (*or* trend) of the market,
tendance irrégulière du marché (*f.*).
irregular endorsement, endossement irrégulier
(*m.*).

irregularity [**irregularities** *pl.*] (*n.*), irrégularité
(*f.*); vice de forme (*m.*):
irregularity of a title to property, irrégularité
d'un titre de propriété.
to commit irregularities, commettre des
irrégularités.

irregularly (*adv.*), irrégulièrement.

island *or* **isle** (*n.*), île (*f.*):
the British Isles, les îles Britanniques.

issue *or* **issuing** (*n.*), émission (*f.*):
issue of bank notes, of securities, émission de
billets de banque, de valeurs.
issues are public or private, les émissions sont
publiques ou privées.

issue *or* **issuing** (of a prospectus) (*n.*), lancement (d'un prospectus) (*m.*).

issue (*v.t.*), émettre:
to issue bank notes, a cheque, debentures for
a sum equal to the maximum of the loans,
émettre des billets de banque, un chèque,
des obligations pour une somme égale au
maximum des prêts.
to issue shares at par, émettre des actions
au pair (*ou* au pair nominal) (*ou* à leur valeur
nominale).
to issue shares at a premium, émettre des
actions au-dessus du pair (*ou* au-dessus du
pair nominal) (*ou* au-dessus de leur valeur
nominale).
to issue shares at a discount, émettre des
actions au-dessous du pair (*ou* au-dessous
du pair nominal) (*ou* au-dessous de leur
valeur nominale):
issuing shares at a discount would be illegal,
l'émission des actions au-dessous du pair
nominal serait illégale (*f.*).
shares issued for cash, actions émises contre
espèces (*f.pl.*).
shares issued to the public, actions émises
dans le public (*f.pl.*).

issue a prospectus (to), lancer un prospectus.

issue market, marché des émissions (*m.*).

issue price (of shares, or the like), prix d'émission
(*m.*); taux d'émission (*m.*).

issue syndicate, syndicat d'émission (*m.*).

issuer (pers.) (*n.*), émetteur (*m.*).

issuing (*adj.*), émetteur, -trice:
the issuing banker, le banquier émetteur.
the issuing company, la société émettrice.

issuing house, maison d'émission (*f.*); banque de placement (*f.*); banque de placement et de spéculation (*f.*); banque de spéculation et de placement (*f.*).

issuing office (money orders, etc.) (opp. to *paying office*), bureau d'émission (*m.*).

item (*n.*), item (*m.*); article (*m.*); poste (*m.*); chapitre (*m.*):
there are a lot of small items in the account, il y a beaucoup de petits item dans le compte.

items of expense (in an account), articles de dépense.

cash item, article de caisse.

the feature of the balance sheet is the amount of the item debentures, la caractéristique du bilan est l'importance du poste obligations.

explanations on an item in the balance sheet, explications sur un poste (*ou* un chapitre) du bilan (*f.pl.*).

itinerary [**itineraries** *pl.*] (*n.*), itinéraire (*m.*); route (*f.*).

J

jetsam (*n.*), épave (*f.*).

jettison (*n.*), jet à la mer (*m.*); jet (*m.*):
jettison of cargo, jet de marchandises à la mer; jet de cargaison.
jettison of deck cargo *or* jettison of goods shipped on deck, jet de pontée; jet à la mer de la pontée; jet de marchandises chargées sur le pont.

jettison (*v.t.*), jeter à la mer; jeter en mer; jeter:
to jettison a part of the cargo in order to lighten the ship in case of peril, jeter en mer une partie du chargement (*ou* jeter une partie de la cargaison à la mer) afin d'alléger le navire en cas de péril.
goods jettisoned for the common safety, marchandises jetées (*ou* jetées à la mer) pour le salut commun (*f.pl.*).

jetty [**jetties** *pl.*] (*n.*), jetée (*f.*).

job (employment; situation) (*n.*), emploi (*m.*); place (*f.*); poste (*m.*); position (*f.*):
to throw up one's job, se démettre de son emploi.

job in and out (to) (Stock Exch.), jouer les allées et venues.

jobber (London Stock Exch.) (pers.) (*n.*), banquier de placement et de spéculation (*m.*). (*Note:* —Descriptive translation only—these English and French terms do not correspond, as *jobbers* do not exist in France as an integral part of the Bourse system. In London, *broker* deals with *jobber*; in Paris, *broker* deals with *broker*, and the other broker dealt with is called the *contre-partie. See explanation of Paris Bourse system under* marché des valeurs.)

jobbery [**jobberies** *pl.*] (*in an unfavourable sense*) (Stock Exch.) (*n.*), tripotage de bourse (*m.*); agiotage (*m.*); agio (*m.*).

jobbing in contangoes (Stock Exch.), arbitrage en reports (*m.*).

joint (*adj.*), conjoint, -e; indivis, -e:
joint account (an account, as of shares in a share register, pertaining to two or more persons), compte conjoint (*m.*); compte-joint (*m.*).

joint adventure *or* joint venture, participation (*f.*).

joint adventure account *or* joint venture account *or* simply joint account (in a commercial or financial transaction), compte de (*ou* en) participation (*m.*).
on joint account, en participation:
transactions on joint account, opérations en participation (*f.pl.*).

joint adventure account *or* simply joint account *or* joint account, half shares, compte à demi (*m.*); compte à 1/2 (*m.*).

joint adventure account, ⅓, ¼, shares *or* joint account ⅓, ¼, shares, compte à 1/3, à 1/4 (*m.*).

joint and several, solidaire; conjoint (-e) et solidaire: (Cf. **several.**)
joint and several codebtors, codébiteurs solidaires (*m.pl.*).
joint and several debt, créance solidaire (*f.*).
joint and several liability, solidarité (*f.*); responsabilité solidaire (*f.*); responsabilité conjointe et solidaire (*f.*).

V. aussi exemple sous jointly and severally.

joint attorney, comandataire (*m.* ou *f.*).
joint carrier, cotransporteur (*m.*).
joint creditor, cocréancier, -ère.
joint debtor, codébiteur, -trice.
joint founder, cofondateur, -trice.
joint holder, codétenteur, -trice.
joint liability *or* joint obligation, obligation conjointe (*f.*); coobligation (*f.*).
joint liquidator, coliquidateur (*m.*).
joint management, codirection (*f.*); cogérance (*f.*).
joint manager, codirecteur (*m.*); cogérant (*m.*).
joint manageress, codirectrice (*f.*); cogérante (*f.*).
joint owner *or* joint proprietor, copropriétaire (*m.* ou *f.*); propriétaire indivis (*m.*).

joint ownership *or* joint possession, copropriété (*f.*); indivision (*f.*):
joint ownership of a ship, copropriété d'un navire.
joint partner, coassocié, -e.
joint purchaser, coacquéreur, -euse *ou* -esse.
joint sharer, copartageant, -e.
joint shares (shares in a company held jointly), actions indivises (*f.pl.*).
joint station (Rly.), gare de jonction (*f.*).
joint stock bank, banque par actions (*f.*); société de crédit (*f.*):
in France, the big joint stock banks are known under the name of *sociétés de crédit*, en France, les grandes banques par actions sont connues sous le nom de sociétés de crédit.
joint stock company, société par actions (*f.*); compagnie par actions (*f.*).
joint surety *or* joint security *or* joint guarantor (pers.), cocaution (*f.*).
joint tenant, colocataire (*m.* ou *f.*).
joint venture. *V. sous* joint adventure.
joint (for the purpose of check or control) (*adj.*), contradictoire:
joint survey, expertise contradictoire (*f.*).
jointly (*adv.*), conjointement; indivisément; par indivis:
to own a property jointly with others, posséder une propriété conjointement (*ou* indivisément) (*ou* par indivis) avec des autres.
jointly and severally, solidairement; conjointement et solidairement: (Cf. **severally.**)
partners who are jointly and severally liable for all the firm's acts, associés qui sont solidairement (*ou* qui sont conjointement et solidairement) responsables de tous les actes sociaux (*m.pl.*).
the shipper and the consignee, jointly and severally, are liable to the company for all damageable consequences. They hold themselves liable, jointly and severally, for the payment of all dues, customs fines, etc., le chargeur et le consignataire garantissent solidairement la compagnie de toutes les conséquences dommageables. Ils se portent garants solidaires du paiement de tous droits, amendes de douane, etc.
to make jointly and severally liable, solidariser; rendre solidaire:
all the members of the association should be made jointly and severally liable, on devrait solidariser (*ou* rendre solidaires) tous les membres de l'association.
jointly (as a check or control) (*adv.*), contradictoirement:
defects in packing should be ascertained jointly (i.e., as between shipowner and shipper) before the sailing of the ship, les vices d'emballage doivent être constatés contradictoirement avant le départ du navire (*m.pl.*).
jot down (*v.t.*), tenir note de: tenir registre de:
to jot down one's expenses, tenir note de, tenir registre de, ses dépenses.
journal (subsidiary journal or book) (Bkkpg)

(*n.*) (Abbrev.: **J.**), journal (*m.*); livre (*m.*); livre-journal (*m.*); livre journal (*m.*):
purchases journal *or* bought journal, journal des achats; livre des achats; livre d'achats; livre d'achat; facturier d'entrée (*m.*).
journal (*n.*) *or* **journal proper** (Bkkpg) (Abbrev.: **J.**), journal (*m.*); livre-journal (*m.*); livre journal (*m.*); journal général (*m.*); journal synthétique (*m.*).
journal (newspaper) (*n.*), journal (*m.*).
journal and ledger combined, journal-grand-livre (*m.*); journal grand livre (*m.*); journal américain (*m.*).
journal entry (Bkkpg), article de journal (*m.*); écriture de journal (*f.*).
journalism (Press) (*n.*), journalisme (*m.*).
journalist (Press) (pers.) (*n.*), journaliste (*m.*).
journalization (Bkkpg) (*n.*), journalisation (*f.*).
journalize (*v.t.*), journaliser:
to journalize a transaction, journaliser une opération.
journalizer (pers.) (*n.*), journaliste (*m.*).
journey [**journeys** *pl.*] (*n.*), voyage (*m.*); trajet (*m.*); parcours (*m.*); route (*f.*):
overland journey *or* land journey, voyage par terre; parcours terrestre.
journey there and back, trajet d'aller et de retour; voyage d'aller et de retour; aller et retour (*m.*).
average journey of a passenger, parcours moyen d'un voyageur.
journey empty *or* journey when empty *or* empty journey (of a railway wagon), parcours à vide.
journey loaded *or* journey when loaded *or* loaded journey, parcours à charge.
to resume one's journey, reprendre sa route.
journey (*v.i.*), voyager.
judge (pers.) (*n.*), juge (*m.*).
judgment *or* **judgement** (Law) (*n.*), jugement (*m.*); arrêt (*m.*): (en France, les tribunaux de commerce et de première instance prononcent des *jugements*, tandis que les décisions des cours d'appel et de la Cour de cassation s'appellent des *arrêts*.)
judgment after trial, jugement contradictoire.
judgment by default, jugement par défaut.
judgment of the court of appeal, arrêt de la cour d'appel.
judicial (*adj.*), judiciaire.
judicially (*adv.*), judiciairement.
jump (*n.*), saut (*m.*); bond (*m.*).
jump (*v.i.*), sauter; bondir:
X. shares jumped from 2 to 2½, l'action X. saute (*ou* bondit) de 2 à 2 1/2.
junction station (Rly.) (*n.*), gare d'embranchement (*f.*); gare de bifurcation (*f.*).
jungles (West African shares) (Stock Exch.) (*n.pl.*), ouest-africaines (*f.pl.*); valeurs ouest-africaines (*f.pl.*).
junior clerk (in a merchant's office, or the like), petit employé (*m.*).
junior clerk (in a lawyer's office), petit clerc (*m.*).
jurisdiction clause, clause attributive de

juridiction (*ou* de compétence) (*f.*); clause de compétence (*f.*).

justice (Law) (*n.*), justice (*f.*):
court of justice, cour de justice (*f.*).

justice (Law) (pers.) (*n.*), juge (*m.*).

justification (*n.*), justification (*f.*):

justification of an exception, justification d'une exception.

justify (*v.t.*), justifier:
to justify the truth of one's predictions by events, justifier la vérité de ses prédictions par les événements.

K

Kaffirs (South African shares) (Stock Exch.) (*n.pl.*), kaffiriques (*m.pl.*); sud-africaines (*f.pl.*); transvaaliennes (*f.pl.*); valeurs sud-africaines (*f.pl.*); valeurs transvaaliennes (*f.pl.*).

keel (of a ship) (*n.*), quille (d'un navire) (*f.*).

keep (*v.*). V. exemples:
to keep a copy of, garder copie de:
to keep a copy of a letter, garder copie d'une lettre.
which stocks are to be kept? quelles valeurs sont à garder?
X. shares kept at 1¾, l'action X. se maintien (*ou* se tient) à 1 3/4.
to keep a note, tenir note; tenir registre:
to keep a note of one's expenses, tenir note, tenir registre, de ses dépenses.
to keep at sea, tenir la mer:
fitness of a ship to keep at sea, aptitude d'un navire à tenir la mer (*f.*).
to keep back, retenir:
to keep back so much out of an employee's pay, retenir tant sur la paie d'un employé.
to keep books *or* to keep accounts, tenir des livres; tenir des écritures; tenir la comptabilité; tenir des comptes:
to keep books by double entry, tenir des livres en partie double (*ou* à parties doubles).
to keep books by single entry, tenir des livres en partie simple (*ou* à partie simple).
to keep a firm's books (*or* accounts), tenir les livres (*ou* les écritures) (*ou* la comptabilité) (*ou* les comptes) d'une maison.
to keep one's accounts in an irregular manner, tenir ses écritures d'une manière irrégulière.
to keep the books (*or* the accounts) up to date, tenir les écritures à jour.
to be kept, être tenu, -e; se tenir:
accounts current with interest can be kept according to several methods, les comptes courants avec intérêts peuvent se tenir suivant plusieurs méthodes (*m.pl.*).
to keep certain books and documents for 5, 10, years (i.e., not to destroy them), conserver certains registres et documents pendant 5, 10, ans.
to keep clean, tenir propre:
to keep a book clean, tenir un livre propre.
to keep one's engagements, tenir ses engagements.

to keep oneself posted on a certain matter, se tenir renseigné (-e) sur une certaine affaire.
to keep the cash (to have the care of the cash), tenir la caisse:
clerk who keeps the cash and writes up the books, employé qui tient la caisse et écrit la comptabilité (*m.*).
to keep under lock and key, tenir sous clef:
to keep one's money under lock and key, tenir son argent sous clef.
to keep within the law, se tenir dans les marges du code.

keeping (custody) (*n.*), garde (*f.*):
to leave a sum of money in the keeping of a friend, laisser une somme d'argent à la garde d'un ami.
time of keeping telegrams (by the postal authorities), délai de garde des télégrammes (*m.*).

keeping books *or* **keeping accounts**, tenue des livres (*f.*); tenue de livres (*f.*); tenue des (*ou* de) comptes (*f.*).

keg (*n.*), barillet (*m.*); barriquaut (*m.*); baricaut (*m.*); baril (*m.*).

key (of a typewriter, of a calculating machine, of a cash register) (*n.*), touche (d'une machine à écrire, d'une machine à calculer, d'une caisse enregistreuse) (*f.*):
the keys of the keyboard, les touches du clavier.

key industry, industrie-clef (*f.*); industrie-clé (*f.*).

key industry duty, droit d'industrie-clé (*m.*).

keyboard (of a typewriter, of a calculating machine, of a cash register) (*n.*), clavier (d'une machine à écrire, d'une machine à calculer, d'une caisse enregistreuse) (*m.*).

keyed advertisement, annonce à clef (*f.*).

keying up letters (letters of the alphabet placed against items on one side of a ledger account as references to corresponding items on the other side), lettres de rencontre (*f.pl.*).

kilometre ton (Rly.), tonne-kilomètre (*f.*); tonne kilométrique (*f.*) = le transport d'une tonne (1 000 kg.) de marchandises à une distance d'un kilomètre: analogue à la *tonne millénaire* anglaise (*ton mile*) = le transport d'une *ton* (1 016 kg.) un *mile* (1,6093 kil.).

kind (in), en nature:
remuneration in kind (lodging, food, etc.),

rémunérations en nature (logement, nourriture, etc.) (*f.pl.*).

King's warehouse (Customs). *The French equivalent is called* dépôt de douane (*m.*). *Cf.* deposit in King's warehouse.

King's warehouse register, registre de dépôt (*m.*).

kite (fictitious commercial paper) (*n.*), cerf-volant (*m.*); traite en l'air (*f.*); effet à renouvellement (*m.*). *In the pl.* **kites,** traites en l'air (*f.pl.*); papier en l'air (*m.*); papier de circulation (*m.*); valeurs de circulation (*f.pl.*); cerfs-volants (*m.pl.*); cavalerie (*f.*); effets à renouvellement (*m.pl.*).

kite (*v.i.*), tirer en l'air; tirer en blanc; tirer à découvert.

kite flier (pers.), tireur en l'air (*m.*); tireur en blanc (*m.*); tireur à découvert (*m.*).

kite flying *or* **kiting** (*n.*), tirage en l'air (*m.*); tirage en blanc (*m.*); tirage à découvert (*m.*).

knife eraser, grattoir (*m.*).

knock off (to deduct) (*v.t.*), rabattre : to knock off the centimes, rabattre les centimes.

knock out price, vil prix (*m.*).

knot (Navig.) (*n.*), nœud (*m.*) : the speed of ships is expressed in knots, la vitesse des navires s'exprime en nœuds. a cargo boat of 10 knots *or* a 10-knot cargo boat, un cargo de 10 nœuds.

know all men by these presents (Law), savoir faisons par ces présentes; à tous ceux qui ces présentes verront.

known (*adj.*), connu, -e : known risk, risque connu (*m.*).

L

label (*n.*), étiquette (*f.*) : label showing the destination station, étiquette indiquant la gare de destination. old labels must be removed or obliterated (luggage), les anciennes étiquettes doivent être enlevées ou oblitérées.

label (*v.t.*), étiqueter.

labelling *or* **labeling** (*n.*), étiquetage (*m.*).

labour (*n.*), travail (*m.*); main-d'œuvre (*f.*) : to live by one's labour, vivre de son travail. the cost of labour and that of raw materials, le prix de main-d'œuvre et celui des matières premières.

labour exchange, bureau municipal de placement gratuit (*m.*).

labour government, gouvernement travailliste (*m.*).

labour market, marché du travail (*m.*).

labour party (parliamentary), parti travailliste (*m.*).

labour troubles *or* **labour disturbances,** troubles ouvriers (*m.pl.*).

lack (*n.*), manque (*m.*); défaut (*m.*); pénurie (*f.*); disette (*f.*) : lack of business, manque d'affaires. lack of money (*or* of funds), manque, pénurie, disette, d'argent (*ou* de fonds). lack of judgment, of confidence, défaut, manque, de jugement, de confiance.

lack (*v.t.*), manquer de : to lack money, capacity for business, manquer de l'argent, de capacité pour les affaires.

lade (*v.t.*), charger : ship laden or in ballast, navire chargé ou sur lest (*m.*). V. aussi exemples sous syn. **load.**

lade (*v.i.*), prendre charge.

laden draught (opp. to *light draught*), tirant d'eau en charge (*m.*).

Ladies and Gentlemen (preamble to chairman's speech), Mesdames, Messieurs : Ladies and Gentlemen, you have heard the very full report of your board and the report of your auditors, Mesdames, Messieurs, vous avez entendu le très copieux rapport de votre conseil d'administration et le rapport de vos commissaires aux comptes.

lading (act of loading) (*n.*), charge (*f.*); chargement (*m.*).

lading (load; cargo) (*n.*), charge (*f.*); chargement (*m.*); cargaison (*f.*) : the quantity of goods which constitutes the lading of a ship, la quantité de marchandises qui constitue la charge d'un navire.

lading port, port de charge (*m.*); port de chargement (*m.*); port d'embarquement (*m.*); port d'expédition (*m.*); port expéditeur (*m.*).

lady bookkeeper, teneuse de livres (*f.*).

lady cashier, caissière (*f.*).

lady clerk, employée (*f.*); commise (*f.*).

lady secretary, secrétaire femme (*m.*).

lagan (*n.*), épave (*f.*).

laid up return (Mar. Insce), chômage (*m.*).

Lake vessel (ship navigating on the North American Great Lakes), navire des Grands Lacs (*m.*).

land (real estate; piece of ground) (*n.*), terre (*f.*); terres (*f.pl.*); fonds de terre (*m.*); fonds de terre (*m.pl.*); terrain (*m.*); terrains (*m.pl.*); biens-fonds (*m.pl.*); bien-fonds (*m.*) : to buy some land, acheter des terres. land is dear in London, le terrain se vend cher à Londres. land and buildings, terrains et bâtiments. land and house property, biens-fonds (*m.pl.*).

land (as opposed to the *sea*) (*n.*), terre (*f.*) : on land, à terre.

land (region) (*n.*), terrain (*m.*) :
the stock exchange is, preeminently, the land
of the unknown and of surprises, la bourse
est, par excellence, le terrain de l'inconnu et
des surprises.

land (*v.t.*), débarquer ; mettre à terre ; débarder :
to land passengers, the goods at the nearest
port, débarquer, mettre à terre, des passagers,
les marchandises au port le plus voisin.

land (*v.i.*), débarquer ; aborder ; atterrir :
to land in a foreign port, débarquer, aborder,
dans un port étranger.

land agent (shipping agent ashore), agent
terrestre (*m.*).

land bank, banque territoriale (*f.*) ; banque
agraire (*f.*) ; banque hypothécaire (*f.*).

land carriage *or* **land conveyance,** transport
terrestre (*m.*).

land charge (radiotelegrams) (opp. to *ship charge*),
taxe terrestre (*f.*).

land excursion, excursion à terre (*f.*).

land frontier, frontière de terre (*f.*).

land journey *or* **land transit,** parcours terrestre
(*m.*) ; parcours territorial (*m.*) ; voyage
par terre (*m.*).

land line (Teleg.), ligne terrestre (*f.*).

land risk (Insce), risque terrestre (*m.*) ; risque
de terre (*m.*).

land route, voie de terre (*f.*) ; route de terre
(*f.*).

land shares, valeurs territoriales (*f.pl.*).

land tax, contribution foncière sur les propriétés
non-bâties (*f.*) ; impôt foncier (*m.*).

landed (*adj.*), foncier, -ère :
landed estate *or* landed property, propriété
foncière (*f.*) ; bien-fonds (*m.*) ; biens-fonds
(*m.*).
landed proprietor, propriétaire foncier (*m.*).

landed terms. *V.* sale on landed terms.

landing (*n.*), mise à terre (*f.*) ; débarquement
(*m.*) ; débardage (*m.*) ; atterrissage (*m.*) :
temporary landing of the cargo in order to
repair damage to the ship, la mise temporaire
à terre de la cargaison pour la réparation
des avaries du navire.
port of landing of a ship, port d'atterrissage
d'un navire (*m.*).
forced landing of an aeroplane, atterrissage
forcé d'un aéroplane.

landing (*n.*) *or* **landing place** *or* **landing platform,**
débarcadère (*m.*) ; embarcadère (*m.*) ; quai
d'embarquement (*m.*).

landing charges, frais de mise à terre (*m.pl.*) ;
frais de débarquement (*m.pl.*).

landing number, numéro de débarquement (*m.*).

landing order, permis de débarquement (*m.*) ;
permis de débarquer (*m.*).

landing stage, embarcadère flottant (*m.*).

landlady [**landladies** *pl.*] (pers.) (*n.*), propriétaire
(*f.*).

landlord (pers.) (*n.*), propriétaire (*m.*).

language (*n.*), langage (*m.*) :
code language, langage convenu.

lapse (*v.i.*), périmer ; devenir caduc, -uque :
lapsed order (money order), mandat périmé
(*m.*).

if the insurance has lapsed, si l'assurance est
caduque.

large (*adj.*), gros, grosse ; fort, -e ; considérable :
large amount of money *or* large sum of money
grosse somme d'argent (*f.*) ; forte somme
d'argent (*f.*) ; somme considérable d'argent
(*f.*).
large order for goods, forte commande de
marchandises (*f.*).
the two largest shareholders, les deux plus
forts actionnaires.

last buyer (Produce Exch.), dernier acheteur
(*m.*) ; arrêteur (*m.*) ; arrêteur de la filière
(*m.*) ; réceptionnaire (*m.*).

last four *or* **last 4** (September, October, November,
December) (Produce Exch.), quatre dernier
(*m.pl.*) ; 4 derniers (*m.pl.*) (septembre,
octobre, novembre, décembre).

last port of discharge, dernier port de reste (*m.*) ;
port final de déchargement (*m.*).

late (delayed) (*adj.*), tardif, -ive ; en retard :
late delivery, livraison tardive (*f.*).
the train is late, le train est en retard.

late fee (Post), surtaxe de levée exceptionnelle
(*f.*).

late fee collection, levée exceptionnelle (*f.*) ; levée
supplémentaire (*f.*).

late fee letter, lettre bénéficiant du délai supplémentaire (*f.*).

late fee letter box, boîte aux lettres réservée
aux levées exceptionnelles (*f.*).

late name (of a ship) (opp. to *present name*),
ex-nom (*m.*), nom ancien (*m.*) (d'un navire).

lateness (*n.*), retard (*m.*) :
lateness in the arrival of trains, retard dans
l'arrivée des trains.

latent fault *or* **latent defect,** vice caché (*m.*) :
défaut caché (*m.*) :
latent defects not discoverable by due diligence,
défauts cachés échappant à une diligence
raisonnable.

latest closing (list of quotations), derniers cours
cotés (*m.pl.*).

latest date *or* **latest time** (after which no time will
be given, as for payment), terme de rigueur
(*m.*) ; terme fatal (*m.*).

latest news (heading in a newspaper), dernières
nouvelles (*f.pl.*) ; dernière heure (*f.*) ;
dernière minute (*f.*).

latest time for posting, heure-limite de dépôt
(*f.*) ; dernière limite d'heure de dépôt (*f.*).

Latin Union *or* **Latin Monetary Union,** Union
latine (*f.*) ; Union monétaire latine (*f.*)
(now abandoned).

launch (longboat) (*n.*), chaloupe (*f.*).

launch (*v.t.*), lancer :
to launch a ship, lancer un navire.
to launch an enterprise, lancer une affaire.

launcher (pers.) (*n.*), lanceur (*m.*).

launching (*n.*), lancement (*m.*).

law (*n.*), loi (*f.*) ; droit (*m.*) ; justice (*f.*) :
law merchant, droit commercial.
law of general average, droit de l'avarie
commune ; droit des avaries communes.
law of nations, droit des gens ; droit international.

law of supply and demand *or* law of demand and supply, loi de l'offre et de la demande :
" the value rises when the demand exceeds the supply, and vice versa," « la valeur monte quand la demande dépasse l'offre, et réciproquement. »
freight rates vary in enormous proportions according to the law of supply and demand, les cours des frets varient dans des proportions énormes suivant la loi de l'offre et de la demande (*m.pl.*).

law of the flag *or* law of the ship's flag, loi du pavillon ; loi du pavillon du navire.

English law, droit anglais.

action at law, action en justice (*f.*).

aw case, affaire contentieuse (*f.*).

aw costs *or* **law expenses,** frais de justice (*m.pl.*) ; dépens (*m.pl.*).

aw court, cour de justice (*f.*).

aw courts, palais de justice (*m.*).

aw department, service du contentieux (*m.*) ; contentieux (*m.*).

aw offices, contentieux (*m.*).

awful (*adj.*), légal, -e, -aux :
lawful currency, cours légal (*m.*) : (*Cf.* legal tender.)
the lawful currency of these coins has been withdrawn, on a retiré le cours légal à ces pièces.
to have lawful currency *or* to be lawfully current, avoir cours légal :
the notes issued have lawful currency (*or* are lawfully current), les billets émis ont cours légal (*m.pl.*).
lawfully current notes, billets à cours légal (*m.pl.*).
lawful money, monnaie légale (*f.*) ; monnaie libératoire (*f.*) :
notes which are redeemable in gold or in lawful money, billets qui sont remboursables en or ou en monnaie légale (*m.pl.*).

awfully (*adv.*), légalement.

awfulness (*n.*), légalité (*f.*).

awsuit (*n.*), procès (*m.*).

awyer (pers.) (*n.*), homme de loi (*m.*).

awyer's office, étude (*f.*).

ay a tax on (to) *or* **lay taxes upon** (to), frapper d'un impôt ; frapper de taxes :
in France, a tax is laid upon bill posting, en France, l'affichage est frappé d'un impôt.
to lay taxes upon the products of foreign industry, frapper de taxes les produits de l'industrie étrangère.

ay an embargo on a ship (to), mettre l'embargo sur un navire.

ay by (*v.t.*), réserver :
to lay by some money for unforeseen contingencies, réserver quelque argent pour les cas imprévus.

lay claim to (to), revendiquer ; prétendre à ; prétendre :
to lay claim to a right, revendiquer un droit.

lay day (Shipping), jour de planche (*m.*) ; starie (*f.*) ; estarie (*f.*). Cf. laytime.

lay down a ship (to) *or* **lay down a ship on the**

stocks (to), mettre en chantier (*ou* en construction) un navire.

lay on the table (to) (at a meeting), déposer sur le bureau :
balance sheet laid on the table, bilan déposé sur le bureau (*m.*).

lay out (*v.t.*), débourser :
to lay out a lot of money, débourser beaucoup d'argent.

lay up (to) (*v.t.*), désarmer :
ship laid up in port for repairs, navire désarmé au port pour réparations (*m.*).

laying down *or* **laying on the stocks,** mise en chantier (*m.*).

laying of keel, pose de la quille (*f.*).

laying up, désarmement (*m.*) ; chômage (*m.*) :
the laying up period, la période de désarmement (*ou* de chômage).
laying up caused by a collision, chômage causé par un abordage.

laytime (Shipping) (*n.*), planche (*f.*) ; délai de planche (*m.*) ; délais de planche (*m.pl.*) : (Cf. **lay day**.)
custom according to which laytime only runs from a certain day, usage d'après lequel la planche (*ou* le délai de planche) ne court (*ou* les délais de planche ne courent) que d'un certain jour (*m.*).

lazaret *or* **lazaretto** (*n.*), lazaret (*m.*) :
to lodge the goods in a lazaret (*or* lazaretto) in case of quarantine, déposer les marchandises au lazaret en cas de quarantaine.
stay of persons in a lazaret (*or* lazaretto), séjour des personnes dans un lazaret (*m.*).

leader (pers.) (*n.*), meneur (*m.*) ; directeur (*m.*) ; dirigeant (*m.*) ; chef de file (*m.*) :
leaders of the market, meneurs, directeurs, dirigeants, du marché.
banks who tend more or less to draw closer to their leader, banques qui tendent plus ou moins à se rapprocher de leur chef de file (*f.pl.*).

leading article (in a newspaper), article de fond (*m.*).

leading mark, marque principale (*f.*).

leading underwriter (Mar. Insce), apériteur (*m.*).

leading share *or* **leading counter** *or* **leading favourite** *or* **leader** (*n.*), valeur dirigeante (*f.*) ; valeur directrice (*f.*) ; valeur marquante (*f.*) ; principale vedette (*f.*) ; vedette (*f.*) :
the leading shares (*or* leading counters) (*or* leading favourites) (*or* leaders) regained a part of the ground lost, les valeurs dirigeantes (*ou* directrices) (*ou* marquantes) (*ou* les principales vedettes) ont regagné une partie du terrain abandonné.
this group is at present the leader of the market, ce groupe est actuellement la vedette du marché.

leads for pencil cases, mines pour porte-mines (*f.pl.*).

leaf [**leaves** *pl.*] (*n.*) (opp. to *counterfoil*), volant (*m.*) :
to fill up one of the leaves of the cheque book, counterfoil and leaf, to detach the leaf and to present it for payment, remplir un des

feuillets du carnet de chèques, talon et volant, détacher le volant et le présenter à l'encaissement.

League of Nations, Société des Nations (*f.*).

leakage (*n.*), coulage (*m.*) :
full freight is due on goods diminished by leakage, le fret est dû entièrement pour les marchandises diminuées par coulage.
leakages and even embezzlements, coulages et même des détournements.

leap year, année bissextile (*f.*).

lease (*n.*), bail (*m.*) ; ferme (*f.*) :
to take a house on lease, prendre une maison à bail.
to take a property on lease, prendre une propriété à ferme.

lease (to grant on lease) (*v.t.*), donner à bail ; louer à bail ; louer ; affermer :
to lease a house, donner une maison à bail.
the lessee is bound to restore the leased property at the end of the lease, le preneur est tenu de restituer la chose louée à la fin du bail.
to lease a railway line to another company, affermer une ligne de chemin de fer à une autre compagnie.
if the properties are leased, their gross income is constituted by the amount of the rents collected, si les propriétés sont affermées, leur revenu brut est constitué par le montant des fermages perçus. (V. aussi exemple sous **rent.**)

lease (to take on lease) (*v.t.*), prendre à bail ; prendre à ferme :
to lease a house, prendre une maison à bail.

leaseholder (pers.) (*n.*), locataire à bail (*m.*) ; fermier, -ère.

leasing (*adj.*), fermier, -ère :
to grant the right of working a railway line to leasing companies in consideration of rents, concéder le droit d'exploitation d'une ligne de chemin de fer à des sociétés fermières moyennant des redevances.

leasing (*n.*), prise à bail (*f.*) ; affermage (*m.*).

leave (permission) (*n.*), faculté (*f.*) ; liberté (*f.*) :
with leave to sail with or without pilots, avec faculté de naviguer avec ou sans pilotes.
if the master has leave to enter different ports, si le capitaine a la liberté d'entrer dans différents ports.

leave (*n.*) **or leave of absence,** congé (*m.*) ; permission de s'absenter (*f.*) ; autorisation de s'absenter (*f.*) :
three months' leave, trois mois de congé.

leave (to allow to remain) (*v.t.*), laisser :
to leave a blank in a letter, laisser un blanc dans une lettre.
to leave the management of one's affairs in the hands of a reliable man, laisser à un homme sûr la manutention de ses affaires.

leave (to quit) (*v.t.*), partir de ; sortir de ; quitter :
to leave London, partir de, quitter, Londres.
the express train leaving Brussels Midi at 11.3 p.m., le train express quittant (*ou* partant de) Bruxelles-Midi à 23h. 3.

(*steamer*) X. (for London) left (*or* l.) Marseille 31 (*date*) (Shipping News), (*steamer*) X parti de Marseille (*ou* a quitté Marseille) 31 (*date*) pour Londres (Mouvement de Navires).
no vessel may leave port without clearance aucun bâtiment ne peut sortir du port sans congé.
to leave the service, sortir du service.
the captain should be the last to leave his ship le capitaine ne doit quitter son bord qu le dernier ; le capitaine doit rester le dernie à son bord.
to leave on hand, refused, goods left on hand refused, etc. V. sous **on hand, refused.**

leave (to depart) (*v.i.*), partir :
to leave for Paris, partir pour Paris.
time at which the train leaves, heure à laquell le train part (*f.*).

leave a deposit with (to), arrher ; enarrher :
to leave a deposit with one's landlord, arrher enarrher, son propriétaire.

leaving (departure) (*n.*), sortie (*f.*) :
on entering or leaving ports, à l'entrée ou la sortie des ports.

ledger (*n.*), grand livre (*m.*).

ledger account, compte du grand livre (*m.*).

ledger balances, soldes du grand livre (*m.pl.*).

ledger heading, en-tête de grand livre (*m.*) ; tête de grand livre (*f.*).

ledger postings, reports du grand livre (*m.pl.*).

left bank (of a river) (opp. to *right bank*), riv gauche (d'un fleuve) (*f.*).

left hand page (*or* side) (of a book), verso (*m.*) page de gauche (*f.*), côté gauche (*m.*) (d'ur livre) :
as soon as they are received, the orders ar entered in a special book, the purchases o the left hand page (*or* side), the sales on th right hand page (*or* side), dès leur réception les ordres sont inscrits sur un livre spécial les achats au verso, les ventes au recto.

left hand side of an account, côté gauche d'ur compte (*m.*).

legacy [legacies *pl.*] (*n.*), legs (*m.*).

legal (*adj.*), légal, -e, -aux ; licite :
legal chargès, frais de contentieux (*m.pl.*).
legal consideration, cause licite (*f.*). V. **con-sideration** (Law).
legal holiday, fête légale (*f.*) ; jour de fête légale (*m.*).
legal tender *or* legal tender currency (legally current value of coin or other money that may be offered in payment of a debt) cours légal (*m.*) ; pouvoir libératoire (*m.*) force libératoire (*f.*) :
the legal tender (*or* the legal tender currency of these coins is limited to so much, le pouvoir libératoire de ces pièces est limité (*ou* la force libératoire de ces pièces est limitée) à tant.
to be legal tender, avoir cours légal ; avoir pouvoir libératoire ; avoir force libératoire être libératoire ; pouvoir être imposé (-e) en paiement ; pouvoir être offert (-e) en paiement :

the notes issued by this bank are legal tender, les billets émis par cette banque ont cours légal (*ou* ont pouvoir libératoire) (*ou* ont force libératoire) (*ou* peuvent être imposés en paiement) (*m.pl.*).

the monetary standard is the precious metal which enters into the composition of standard coins, which are unlimited legal tender, l'étalon monétaire est le métal précieux qui entre dans la composition des pièces types, lesquelles ont force libératoire illimitée (*m.*).

the gold coins are legal tender to any amount (*or* are unlimited legal tender), les pièces d'or ont cours légal illimité (*f.pl.*).

gold is legal tender to any amount (*or* is unlimited legal tender), l'or a le pouvoir libératoire illimité (*m.*) ; l'or a force libératoire sans limitation de quantité (*m.*).

silver fractional coins are only legal tender up to so much, les pièces divisionnaires d'argent n'ont cours légal que jusqu'à (*ou* n'ont pouvoir libératoire que jusqu'à) (*ou* n'ont force libératoire qu'à) concurrence de tant (*f.pl.*).

payments in gold are legal tender, les paiements en or sont libératoires (*m.pl.*).

silver coins are not legal tender for more than so much, les pièces d'argent ne peuvent pas être imposées (*ou* offertes) en paiement pour plus de tant (*f.pl.*).

legal tender *or* legal tender currency (legally current money ; lawful money ; coin or other money that may legally be offered in payment of a debt), monnaie légale (*f.*) ; monnaie libératoire (*f.*) :

notes which are redeemable in gold or in legal tender (*or* in gold or in legal tender currency), billets qui sont remboursables en or ou en monnaie légale (*m.pl.*).

legal tender notes, billets à cours légal (*m.pl.*).

legal year, année civile (*f.*).

gality [legalities *pl.*] (*n.*), légalité (*f.*).

galization (*n.*), légalisation (*f.*) :

legalization of a certificate of origin, légalisation d'un certificat d'origine.

legalization has for effect only to certify the authenticity of the signature appended at the foot of the document, it has none on the contents of the document, la légalisation n'a pour effet que de certifier l'authenticité de la signature apposée au bas de l'acte, elle n'en a aucun sur le contenu de l'acte.

galize (*v.t.*), légaliser ; authentiquer :

to legalize a document, légaliser, authentiquer, un acte.

signature legalized by the British diplomatic or consular authority, signature légalisée par l'autorité diplomatique ou consulaire britannique (*f.*).

gally (*adv.*), légalement.

gatee (pers.) (*n.*), légataire (*m. ou f.*).

gation (*n.*), légation (*f.*).

gation fees, droits de chancellerie (*m.pl.*).

gislation (*n.*), législation (*f.*).

end (*v.t.*), prêter ; placer :

to lend money on security, on mortgage, prêter de l'argent sur nantissement, sur hypothèque.

to lend one's name, prêter son nom.

to lend money on contango, prêter, mettre, placer, des capitaux en report.

money lent (on stock taken in) (Stock Exch.), capital reporteur (*m.*) ; capitaux reporteurs (*m.pl.*).

to lend stock (Stock Exch.), prêter des titres ; faire reporter des titres ; donner des titres en report ; placer des titres en report ; se faire reporter. *V. exemples sous* to take in *or* to take the rate *et sous* **contango** *or* **contango rate.**

lend (*v.i.*), prêter :

to lend at interest, at the rate of 5%, prêter à intérêt, au taux de 5 0/0.

lendable (*adj.*), prêtable :

lendable funds, fonds prêtables (*m.pl.*).

lender (pers.) (*n.*), prêteur, -euse :

lender on security, prêteur sur nantissement (*ou* sur gage) (*ou* sur gages).

lender on bottomry or respondentia, prêteur à la grosse ; donneur à la grosse (*m.*). Cf. **bottomry,** & **respondentia.**

lending (*adj.*), prêteur, -euse :

lending banker, banquier prêteur (*m.*).

lending bank, banque prêteuse (*f.*).

lending (*n.*), prêter (*m.*) ; prêt (*m.*) ; prestation (*f.*) ; placement (*m.*) :

lending is sometimes more burdensome than giving, le prêter est quelquefois plus onéreux que le donner.

all the transactions of the banker may be summed up, shortly, in borrowing and in lending, toutes les opérations du banquier peuvent se résumer, en définitive, en emprunts et en prêts.

lending capital, prestation de capitaux.

lending money, stock, on contango, prêt, placement, mise, de fonds, de titres, en report.

less (minus ; deduct) (*adj.*), moins (*prép.*) ; sous déduction de ; déduit, -e ; à déduire :

16 less 4 equals 12, 16 moins 4 égale 12.

amount of the sale, less brokerage, montant de la vente, moins le courtage.

buildings (so much), less depreciation (so much) (balance sheet item), constructions (tant), moins amortissements (tant) (*f.pl.*).

purchase price, less discount, prix d'achat, sous déduction d'escompte (*m.*).

interest payable half yearly, less tax, intérêt payable par semestre, sous déduction d'impôt (*ou* moins les impôts) (*m.*).

the interest, less tax, is payable half yearly, les intérêts, impôts déduits (*ou* moins les impôts), sont payables par semestre (*m.pl.*).

less : expenses for the month, à déduire : dépenses du mois.

lessee (pers.) (*n.*), preneur, -euse ; locataire à bail (*m. ou f.*).

lessen (*v.t.*), diminuer ; amoindrir :

to lessen one's expenses, diminuer, amoindrir, sa dépense.

lessen (*v.i.*), diminuer ; se diminuer ; amoindrir ; s'amoindrir.

lessening (*n.*), diminution (*f.*); amoindrissement (*m.*).

lessor (pers.) (*n.*), bailleur, -eresse; locateur, -trice.

let (to allow) (*v.t.*), laisser:
to let a matter rest, laisser dormir une affaire.

let (to put to hire or rent) (*v.t.*), louer:
to let a house by the month, louer au mois une maison.
to let on lease, louer à bail.
to let *or* **to be let**, à louer:
premises to let (*or* to be let), locaux à louer (*m.pl.*).

letter (*n.*). lettre (*f.*):
to write a letter, écrire une lettre.
registered letter, lettre recommandée (*f.*); pli recommandé (*m.*).
letter of acceptance (underwriting) (Fin.), lettre d'adhésion.
letter of acknowledgment, ·accusé de réception (*m.*).
letter of advice, lettre d'avis.
letter of allotment *or* letter of acceptance (opp. to *letter of regret*), avis d'attribution (*m.*); avis de répartition (*m.*); lettre d'avis de répartition (*f.*). V. **allot** (*v.t.*).
letter of application, bulletin de souscription (*m.*).
letter of confirmation, lettre de confirmation.
letter of credit (*Abbrev.*: L.C. *or* l.c.), lettre de crédit; lettre de créance.
letter of delegation, délégation (*f.*).
letter of hypothecation, acte de nantissement (*m.*); nantissement (*m.*).
letter of indemnity, lettre de garantie (*f.*); caution (*f.*); acte de caution (*m.*); cautionnement (*m.*); acte de cautionnement (*m.*); lettre d'indemnité (*f.*):
to obtain a duplicate of a lost certificate by giving a letter of indemnity, obtenir un duplicata d'un certificat perdu en donnant une lettre de garantie (*ou* en donnant caution).
letter of indication (accompanying a letter of credit, or the like), livret d'identité (*m.*); carte d'identité (*f.*).
letter of introduction, lettre d'introduction.
letters of marque *or* letters of mart, lettres de marque.
letter of recommendation, lettre de recommandation.
letter of regret, avis de retour de souscription (*m.*); lettre d'avis de retour de souscription (*f.*).
letter of reminder, lettre de rappel.
letters (collectively) (*n.pl.*), lettres (*f.pl.*); courrier (*m.*); correspondance (*f.*):
the head of the department superintends the opening of the letters, le chef du service préside à l'ouverture du courrier (*ou* des courriers).
papers having the nature of letters (or of a letter) (Post), papiers ayant le caractère d'une correspondance personnelle (*m.pl.*).

letter (to mark with letters) (*v.t.*), coter:
to letter documents, coter des pièces.

letter basket, panier à lettres (*m.*).
letter book, copie de lettres (*m.*); livre de copie de lettres (*m.*); livre de copies de lettres (*m.*); livre copies de lettres (*m.*).
letter box, boîte aux lettres (*f.*).
letter card, carte-lettre (*f.*).
letter clip, serre-notes (*m.*); pince-notes (*m.*).
letter copying machine, machine à copier le courrier (*f.*).
letter file, classeur de lettres (*m.*).
letter heading, en-tête de lettre (*m.*); tête de lettre (*f.*).
letter opener, ouvre-lettres (*m.*); ouvre-courrier (*m.*).
letter packet, paquet-lettre (*m.*).
letter paper, papier à lettres (*m.*); papier à lettre (*m.*).
letter post, poste aux lettres (*f.*).
letter rate (Post), tarif des lettres (*m.*).
letter scale *or* **letter scales,** pèse-lettre (*m.*).
letter sealing wax, cire fine à cacheter (*f.*).
letter telegram, télégramme-lettre (*m.*).
letting (*adj.*), locatif, -ive:
letting value, valeur locative (*f.*).
letting (*n.*), location (*f.*); louage (*m.*).
Levant (*n.*), Levant (*m.*).
Levantine ports, échelles du Levant (*f.pl.*) ports du Levant (*m.pl.*).
level (*n.*), niveau (*m.*):
to maintain prices at a high level, maintenir les prix à un niveau élevé.
level (*v.t.*), niveler:
to level rates, prices, niveler des taux, de cours:
to reestablish the equilibrium of demand and supply on the two markets, and level prices, rétablir l'équilibre de l'offre et de la demande sur les deux places, et de niveler les cours.
levy (of taxes) (*n.*), levée (des contributions) (*f.*).
levy (*v.t.*), lever:
to levy a tax on gaming transactions is to acknowledge their legal existence, lever une taxe sur les opérations de jeu, c'est reconnaitre leur existence légale.
liability [liabilities *pl.*] (obligation) (*n.*), obligation (*f.*); engagement (*m.*); responsabilité (*f.*):
the liability to contribute to the sacrifices made for the preservation of the adventure (Mar. Insce), l'obligation de contribuer aux sacrifices faits pour la conservation de l'aventure.
the captain's signature pledges the liability of the ship, la signature du capitaine engage la responsabilité du navire.
the liability of the ship ceases on discharging in the said port, la responsabilité du navire cesse dès le débarquement dans ledit port.
to limit the amount of one's liability, limiter le montant de sa responsabilité (*ou* de son engagement).
limited liability, responsabilité limitée.
liability (or liabilities) of customers for acceptances (*or* for acceptance) (bank balance sheet), débiteurs par acceptations (*m.pl.*); ayants compte d'acceptations (*m.pl.*).
liability (*n.*) (opp. to *asset*), passif (*m.*); valeur

passive (*f.*) : [*Au pl.* **liabilities** :—passif ; pasifs ; valeurs passives ; masse passive (*f.*)] :

contingent. liability [contingent liabilities *pl.*], passif éventuel. [passif éventuel *ou* passifs éventuels *pl.*].

the excess of assets over liabilities, l'excédent de l'actif sur le passif (*m.*).

the new company will take over the liabilities, la nouvelle société prendra le passif à sa charge ; la nouvelle société prendra en charge les valeurs passives.

iable for (to be) *or* liable to (to be), être tenu (-e) à ; être tenu (-e) de ; être tenu (-e) pour ; être soumis (-e) à ; être sujet (-ette) à ; être assujetti (-e) à ; être assujéti (-e) à ; être passible de ; être redevable de ; être responsable de ; répondre de ; être solidaire de ; être obligé (-e) de (*ou* à) :

several people who are liable for a debt, plusieurs personnes qui sont tenues à une dette.

to be liable for damages, être tenu (-e) des dommages-intérêts ; être passible de dommages-intérêts.

to be liable for the whole, être tenu (-e) pour le tout.

person liable for tax, personne passible de (*ou* redevable de) (*ou* assujettie à) l'impôt (*f.*).

dividends liable to income tax, dividendes soumis à l'impôt sur le revenu (*m.pl.*).

bills of exchange are liable to stamp duty, les lettres de change sont soumises au (*ou* sont assujetties au) (*ou* sont passibles du) droit de timbre (*f.pl.*).

the husband is liable for the acts of his wife, le mari est solidaire (*ou* est responsable) des actes de sa femme.

goods liable to import duty, marchandises sujettes à des (*ou* passibles des) droits d'entrée (*f.pl.*).

goods liable to breakage, marchandises sujettes à la casse (*f.pl.*).

the shipowner is liable for his faults and those of his servants, l'armateur est responsable de ses fautes et de celles de ses préposés (*m.*).

the underwriters are not liable for any loss or damage arising from inherent vice of the thing, les assureurs ne sont pas responsables (*ou* les assureurs sont irresponsables) de tous dommages et pertes provenant du vice propre de la chose (*m.pl.*).

to be liable for damage caused by rain, by rats, répondre des avaries occasionnées par la pluie, par les rats.

average for which the assurers are liable, avarie dont les assureurs ont à répondre (*f.*).

the underwriter shall not be liable in respect of any one accident for more than so many pounds, l'assureur ne répondra pas, du chef d'un seul et même accident, de plus de tant de livres (*m.*).

to be personally liable to the insurer for the payment of the premium, être personnellement obligé (-e) envers l'assureur du paiement de la prime.

liberty [**liberties** *pl.*] (*n.*),   liberté (*f.*) ; faculté (*f.*) :

the principle of the liberty of agreements, le principe de la liberté des conventions.

if the master has the liberty to enter different ports, si le capitaine a la liberté d'entrer dans différents ports.

with all liberties as per bills of lading, avec toutes les facultés mentionnées aux connaissements.

licence (*n.*), licence (*f.*) ; permis (*m.*) ; brevet (*m.*) ; bon (*m.*).

license a pilot (to), breveter un pilote.

lie (to occupy a certain place) (*v.i.*), séjourner ; stationner :

vessel which lies (*or* is lying) in a roadstead (*or* in the roads), navire qui séjourne (*ou* qui stationne) en rade (*m.*).

lien (*n.*), privilège (*m.*) ; droit de rétention (*m.*) ; droit de gage (*m.*) :

to have a lien on the personal property of a debtor, avoir un privilège (*ou* être privilégié, -e) sur les meubles d'un débiteur.

vendor's lien, privilège du vendeur.

payment of the freight is secured by a lien on (*or* upon) (*or* over) the goods shipped, le paiement du fret est garanti par un privilège sur les marchandises chargées.

owner who has a lien on the cargo for payment of the freight, armateur qui a un droit de rétention (*ou* droit de gage) sur la cargaison pour le paiement du fret (*m.*).

lienee (pers.) (*n.*), gageur, -euse.

lienor (pers.) (*n.*), gagiste (*m.* ou *f.*) ; créancier gagiste (*m.*) :

railway which has on the goods the rights of a lienor, chemin de fer qui a sur la marchandise les droits d'un créancier gagiste (*m.*).

life [**lives** *pl.*] (*n.*), vie (*f.*).

for life, à vie ; viager, -ère ; viagèrement :

income for life *or* life income, revenu à vie (*m.*) ; revenu viager (*m.*) ; viager (*m.*).

pension for life *or* life pension, pension à vie (*f.*) ; pension viagère (*f.*).

property given up for life, bien cédé viagèrement (*m.*).

life and property (passengers, crew, and cargo), corps et biens (*m.pl.*) ; vies humaines et biens :

ship which deviates from her course for the purpose of saving (*or* from her course to save) life and property, navire qui dévie de sa route dans le but de sauver corps et biens (*ou* de sa route pour sauver des vies humaines et des biens) (*m.*).

life annuitant, rentier viager (*m.*) ; rentière viagère (*f.*).

life annuity, rente viagère (*f.*) ; viager (*m.*) ; annuité à vie (*f.*) ; fonds perdu (*m.*) :

to invest one's money in a life annuity, placer son argent en viager (*ou* à fonds perdu).

life assurance *or* **life insurance**, assurance sur la vie (*f.*) ; assurance-vie (*f.*).

life assurance company *or* **life insurance company** *or* **life office**, compagnie d'assurance (*ou* d'assurances) sur la vie (*f.*).

life assurance policy *or* **life insurance policy,** police d'assurance sur la vie (*f.*).

lifeboat (*n.*), bateau de sauvetage (*m.*); canot de sauvetage (*m.*); embarcation de sauvetage (*f.*).

lifeless (speaking of stocks and shares) (*adj.*), inanimé, -e.

lift (to carry) (*v.t.*), porter:
dead-weight capacity is the weight a ship will lift without putting her load line under water, le port en lourd est le poids que le navire peut porter sans immerger sa ligne de charge.

lift (to take up; to honour) (*v.t.*), lever; honorer: to lift documents, lever des documents.
the first point that interests the discounter is the certainty that the discounted bill will be lifted at maturity, le premier point qui intéresse l'escompteur c'est la certitude que l'effet escompté sera honoré à l'échéance.

lifting (of documents) (*n.*), levée (des documents) (*f.*).

ligan (*n.*), épave (*f.*).

light coin (single coin) (opp. to *overweight coin*), pièce faible (*f.*); pièce légère (*f.*). V. exemple sous **standard coin.**

light money *or* **light coin,** monnaie faible (*f.*); monnaie légère (*f.*).

light contangoes (opp. to *heavy contangoes*), reports bon marché (*m.pl.*). V. exemple sous **stiffen** (*v.i.*).

light displacement (opp. to *load displacement*), déplacement lège (*m.*).

light draught (opp. to *load*, or *laden, draught*), tirant d'eau lège (*m.*).

light dues, droits de phare (*m.pl.*); droits de feux et fanaux (*m.pl.*).

light freight *or* **light goods** (opp. to *heavy freight* or *heavy goods*), fret léger (*m.*); marchandises légères (*f.pl.*).

lighthouse, lightship *or* **light vessel.** V. ci-après.

light vessel (ship going light—opp. to *laden vessel*), navire marchant à vide (*m.*).

light water line (opp. to *load water line*), ligne de flottaison lège (*f.*).

lighten (*v.t.*), alléger; soulager:
cargo which is discharged into craft to lighten a stranded ship, cargaison qui est déchargée dans des embarcations pour alléger (*ou* soulager) un navire échoué (*f.*).
it is agreed that the ship going up to Nantes shall lighten at Saint-Nazaire and that the expense of lightening shall be paid by the receiver of the goods, il est convenu que le navire remontant à Nantes doit alléger à Saint-Nazaire et que les frais d'allègement sont à la charge du réceptionnaire de la marchandise.

lightening (*n.*), allégement (*m.*); allègement (*m.*).

lighter (barge) (*n.*), allège (*f.*); chaland (*m.*); chalan (*m.*); gabare (*f.*); péniche (*f.*):
lighters are craft used for loading and unloading cargo, les allèges sont des embarcations servant au chargement et au déchargement de la marchandise.

lighterage (*n.*), chalandage (*m.*); gabarage (*m.*); gabariage (*m.*); batelage (*m.*).

lighterage risk, risque d'allèges (*m.*).

lighterman [**lightermen** *pl.*] (*n.*), gabarier (*m.*); batelier (*m.*).

lighthouse (*n.*), phare (*m.*).

lighting the premises, éclairage des locaux (*m.*).

lightship (*n.*) *or* **light vessel** (Abbrev.: **Lt V.**), bateau-feu (*m.*); bateau-phare (*m.*).

limit (*n.*), limite (*f.*):
limits of size, of weight (of postal parcels), limites de dimensions ou de volume, de poids (des colis postaux).
every issue of bank notes has its limits, toute émission de billets de banque a ses limites.
to buy or sell within price limits, acheter ou vendre dans des limites de prix.
limit of free delivery (Post), périmètre de distribution gratuite (*m.*).

limit (*n.*) *or* **office limit** *or* **line** (*n.*) (Insce), plein (*m.*):
company which has its limit (*or* its office limit) (*or* its line) on a certain risk, compagnie qui a son plein sur un certain risque (*f.*).
for each shipment made on a ship to be named, there is a limit (*or* an office limit) beyond which the underwriter is not liable, pour chaque expédition effectuée sur un navire à désigner, il est fixé un plein au delà duquel l'assureur ne répond pas.
insurer who is not liable for an amount in excess of the maximum line subscribed by him in the policy, assureur qui n'est pas responsable pour une somme supérieure au plein maximum souscrit par lui dans la police (*m.*).

limit (*v.t.*), limiter:
to limit one's chances of loss, the responsibility of the shipowner to his own lines of shipping, limiter ses chances de perte, la responsabilité de l'armateur à ses propres lignes de navigation.

limitation (*n.*), limitation (*f.*):
limitation of liability (*or* responsibility) of shipowners, of liability of the underwriters, limitation de responsabilité des armements, des engagements des assureurs.

limited (*adj.*), limité, -e:
limited coasting trade, bornage (*m.*).
limited company *or* limited liability company *or* company limited by shares *or* public company, société anonyme (*f.*); société anonyme par actions (*f.*):
Note :—Inasmuch as a *limited company* is a creation of English law and a *société anonyme* a creation of French law, these English and French terms are of course only equivalent in a general way. The word *anonyme* [anonymous] has reference to the fact that a *société anonyme* is not, or is not necessarily, in the name or names of the principal interested parties.
the formation of a bank into a limited company, la constitution d'une banque en société anonyme.
limited company *or* limited liability company

or company limited by shares *or* private company, société à responsabilité limitée (*f.*).

Note :—société à responsabilité limitée is given here as a translation of *private company*, as to all intents and purposes it fills the same function as an English private company.

The *société à responsabilité limitée* is, however, more in the nature of a partnership with limited liability. The directors are called *gérants*. The shares are called *parts* (See this word in vocabulary) or *parts sociales*, and there are no share certificates. The capital of the company must be 25,000 francs at least. It cannot be reduced below this figure. It is divided into *parts sociales* of 100 francs, or multiples of 100 francs. The *parts* must be paid up in full. There may exist *parts ordinaires*, *parts privilégiées*, and *parts de jouissance* (*Cf.* actions de jouissance). Like *parts de fondateur*, q.v., and *actions d'apport*, q.v., the *parts* can only be transferred according to civil law, and are not dealable on the Stock Exchange. The right to transfer *parts* is restricted. The minimum number of shares is 2, but there is no maximum. No public issue can be made. If the membership is below 20, no annual meeting need be held. It is not assimilated to a public company (*société anonyme*), as an English private company is to a public company, but is the subject of separate and distinct legislation.

The English *private company*, with the exception of a few vital differences, is practically the same as a public company. These differences are notably :—Minimum number of subscribers 2. Maximum (exclusive of persons who are in the employment of the company) 50. Restriction of the right to transfer its shares. Prohibition of any invitation to the public to subscribe for any shares or debentures of the company. Not required to include in the annual summary the statement in the form of a balance sheet. Not required to hold a statutory meeting, nor to present a statutory report. Not required to file a statement in lieu of prospectus. Have no regard to a minimum subscription, may commence business without any restriction, and requires no certificate entitling to do so. The shares of an English private company are not dealable on the London Stock Exchange.

limited liability, responsabilité limitée (*f.*).
limited partner, commanditaire (*m.* ou *f.*).
limited partnership, société en commandite (*f.*); commandite (*f.*).
limited price (Stock Exch.), cours limité (*m.*): to buy at a limited price, acheter au cours limité.
limited (speaking of a market) (*adj.*) (opp. to *free*), étroit, -e :

shares which have only a limited market, titres qui n'ont qu'un marché étroit (*m.pl.*).
limitedness (*n.*) *or* **limited condition** (of a market), étroitesse (d'un marché) (*f.*).
limping standard (monetary standard), étalon boiteux (*m.*).
line (*n.*), ligne (*f.*) :
to draw a line on the paper, tirer une ligne sur le papier.
to underwrite a line (Insce), souscrire une ligne.
line of railway, ligne de chemin de fer; ligne ferrée.
line of steamers, ligne de vapeurs.
line out of order (Teleph.), ligne interrompue.
line (office limit) (Insce) (*n.*).   V. sous **limit**.
liner (*n.*) (opp. to *tramp*), vapeur de ligne (*f.*); paquebot (*m.*); navire régulier (*m.*); navire à parcours régulier (*m.*); vapeur de ligne régulière (*m.*); liner (*m.*).
liner company, compagnie de lignes régulières (*f.*).
liner freighting, affrètement à cueillette (*m.*).
liner rate (berth terms), fret à la cueillette (*m.*); fret à cueillette (*m.*).
lion's share (*fig.*), part du lion (*f.*).
liquid (*adj.*), liquide; disponible :
liquid assets, disponibilités (*f.pl.*); valeurs disponibles (*f.pl.*); disponible (*m.*); actif disponible (*m.*); actif liquide (*m.*):
the balance sheet shows that the liquid assets are more than sufficient to meet the current liabilities, le bilan fait ressortir que les disponibilités sont plus que suffisantes pour faire face aux exigibilités.
liquid debt, dette liquide (*f.*); dette claire (*f.*).
liquidate (*v.t.*), liquider :
to liquidate a company, liquider une société.
to liquidate a debt, one's affairs, liquider une dette, ses affaires.
liquidate (*v.i.*), liquider; se liquider :
company which liquidates, société qui liquide (*ou* qui se liquide) (*f.*).
liquidation (*n.*) (Abbrev.: **liq.** *or* **liqn**), liquidation (*f.*) :
company in liquidation (*Abbrev. :* Co. in liq. *or* Coy in liqn), société en liquidation (*f.*).
voluntary liquidation, liquidation volontaire.
liquidation subject to supervision of court, liquidation judiciaire.
liquidator (pers.) (*n.*), liquidateur (*m.*); partageur (*m.*).
liquidness (*n.*), liquidité (*f.*); disponibilité (*f.*).
debts due by the trader must be distinguished according to their repayability and debts due to the trader according to their liquidness and the way in which they are secured, il faut distinguer les dettes d'après leur exigibilité et les créances d'après leur disponibilité et la manière dont elles sont garanties.
list (*n.*), liste (*f.*); bordereau (*m.*); feuille (*f.*); rôle (*m.*); tableau (*m.*); inventaire (*m.*); bulletin (*m.*); catalogue (*m.*):

list of applicants *or* list of subscribers, liste de souscripteurs.

list of applications *or* subscription list *or simply* list *or* lists, souscription (*f.*); liste de souscription :
the list of applications (*or* the subscription list) (*or* the list) (*or* the lists) will be opened on Thursday the 9th January 19— and closed the same day, la souscription sera ouverte le jeudi 9 janvier 19— et close le même jour.

list of bills for collection (Banking), bordereau d'encaissement; bordereau d'effets à l'encaissement.

list of bills for discount (Banking), bordereau d'escompte; bordereau d'effets à l'escompte.

company which publishes a list of its investments, société qui publie un bordereau de son portefeuille (*f.*).

to make out a list of one's investments, of one's assets and liabilities, dresser l'inventaire de son portefeuille, de son actif et de son passif.

list of marine casualties *or* black list, liste de sinistres maritimes ; liste noire.

list of names (*or* nominal list) of shareholders, liste nominative des actionnaires.

list of passengers *or* passenger list, liste des passagers ; feuille des passagers.

list of prices (*or* of quotations), bulletin de cours.

list of sailings *or* sailings list, liste de départs ; tableau de marche.

list of salaries *or* salaries list, feuille d'appointements ; rôle d'appointements.

list of the crew *or* crew list, rôle de l'équipage ; rôle d'armement.

list of those present, feuille de présence ; liste de présence :
list of shareholders present at the general meeting, feuille de présence des actionnaires assistant à l'assemblée générale.

illustrated lists and prices on application, catalogues illustrés et prix sur demande.

list (Stock Exch.) (*n.*), bulletin (*m.*); cote (*f.*) :
stock exchange daily official list, bulletin de la cote ; cote officielle des valeurs de bourse ; cote de la bourse.
opening without liveliness, but the list is strong, ouverture sans animation, mais la cote est résistante (*f.*).

list (to catalogue ; to inventory) (*v.t.*), cataloguer ; inventorier :
an article listed at so much, un article catalogué à tant.

listed securities (Stock Exch.) (opp. to *unlisted securities*), valeurs inscrites (*f.pl.*); valeurs admises à la cote officielle (*f.pl.*); valeurs figurant à la cote officielle (*f.pl.*); valeurs de parquet (*f.pl.*); valeurs de corbeille (*f.pl.*).

listing (*n.*), cataloguement (*m.*).

litigation (*n.*), litige (*m.*).

litigious (*adj.*), litigieux, -euse :
litigious claim, créance litigieuse (*f.*).
litigious rights, droits litigieux (*m.pl.*).

little doing *or* **little business,** peu d'affaires (*m.*) :
there was little doing in X. shares, l'action X. eut peu d'affaires.

littoral (*n.*), littoral (*m.*).

live animals *or* **live stock,** animaux vivants (*m.pl.*).

live weight (opp. to *dead weight*), charge utile (*f.*) :
railway truck which can carry a live weight of 10 tons, wagon de chemin de fer qui peut transporter une charge utile de 10 tonnes (*m.*).

liveliness (*n.*), animation (*f.*) :
the stock market continues to show a good deal of liveliness, le marché des valeurs continue à faire preuve d'une grande animation.

lively (*adj.*), animé, -e :
market lively, bourse animée (*f.*).

living (*n.*), vie (*f.*) :
dear living, vie chère.

Lloyd's (Shipping & Mar. Insce), le Lloyd.

Lloyd's agent, agent du Lloyd (*m.*).

Lloyd's policy (Insce), police du Lloyd (*f.*) :
the first original of Lloyd's policy dates from about 1613, le premier original de la police du Lloyd date d'environ 1613.

Lloyd's Register (*full title* **Lloyd's Register of Shipping**), Registre du Lloyd (*m.*).

load (*n.*), charge (*f.*); chargement (*m.*) :
the quantity of goods which constitutes the load of a ship, la quantité de marchandises qui constitue la charge d'un navire.

load (Corn or other Exch.) (*n.*), lot (*m.*) :
the number of units contained in a load, le nombre d'unités renfermées dans un lot.

load (*v.t.*), charger :
to load a railway truck, grain in bulk, a ship with general cargo, charger un wagon de chemin de fer, des grains en vrac, un navire en (*ou* à) cueillette.
ship which begins to load her cargo, navire qui commence à charger sa cargaison (*m.*).

load (Insce) (*v.t.*), charger ; surcharger :
to load the premium, charger, surcharger, la prime. V. exemple sous **loading** (of the premium).

load (*v.i.*), prendre charge :
ship ready to load, navire prêt à prendre charge (*m.*).

load displacement (opp. to *light displacement*), déplacement en charge (*m.*).

load draught (opp. to *light draught*), tirant d'eau en charge (*m.*).

load line (of a ship), ligne de charge (*f.*).

load water line (opp. to *light water line*), ligne de flottaison en charge (*f.*).

loaded (*adj.*) *or* **when loaded,** chargé, -e ; à charge :
loaded wagon *or* loaded truck, wagon chargé (*m.*).
loaded journey *or* journey loaded *or* journey when loaded (of a railway wagon) (opp. to *empty journey*), parcours à charge (*m.*).

loading (*n.*), charge (*f.*); chargement (*m.*) :
the place and time agreed upon for loading and unloading, le lieu et le temps convenus pour la charge et la décharge (*ou* pour le chargement et le déchargement).

to proceed with the loading of the goods and their stowage, procéder au chargement des marchandises et à leur arrimage.

loading (Abbrev.: **ldg**) *or* now **loading** *or* **on the berth** *or* **now on the berth**, en charge :
s/s. *X.*, now loading (*or* now on the berth) for Havre, sailing 31 January, circumstances permitting, s/s. *X.*, en charge pour le Havre, partant le 31 janvier, sauf imprévu.

loading *or* **loading, loaded, or about to be loaded** (speaking of Produce Exch. prices), sous charge ; sous vapeur :
prices : spot *so much* ; afloat *so much* ; loading *so much*, cours : disponible *tant* ; flottant *tant* ; sous charge *tant*.

loading (of the premium) (Insce) (*n.*), chargement (*m.*), surcharge (*f.*) (de la prime) :
the premiums paid by the insured are gross premiums, that is to say, premiums increased by a percentage called loading, serving to cover administration expenses, to leave a profit to the underwriter, to form a reserve fund in case losses exceed probabilities, etc., les primes versées par les assurés sont des primes brutes, c'est-à-dire des primes nettes majorées d'un pourcentage appelé chargement, servant à couvrir les frais d'administration, à laisser un bénéfice à l'assureur, à constituer un fonds de réserve au cas où les sinistres dépassent les probabilités, etc.

loading berth, poste d'embarquement (*m.*) ; emplacement de chargement (*m.*).

loading day, jour de chargement (*m.*).

loading hour, heure de chargement (*f.*).

loading on the berth (liner freighting), affrètement à cueillette (*m.*).

loading port, port de charge (*m.*) ; port de chargement (*m.*) ; port d'embarquement (*m.*) ; port d'expédition (*m.*) ; port expéditeur (*m.*).

loading risk (Mar. Insce), risque de chargement (*m.*).

loan (act of lending) (*n.*), prêt (*m.*) ; prêter (*m.*) ; prestation (*f.*) ; avance (*f.*) :
a loan of money, un prêt, une prestation, une avance, d'argent.

loan (sum lent or borrowed) (*n.*) (Abbrev.: **ln**), prêt (*m.*) ; emprunt (*m.*) ; avance (*f.*) :
loans at call (Banking), prêts remboursables sur demande (*m.pl.*) ; argent remboursable sur demande (*m.*) ; argent à vue (*m.*).

loan at interest, prêt à intérêt (*ou* à intérêts).

loan at notice, prêt à terme.

loan on bottomry, prêt à la grosse sur corps.

loan on bottomry or respondentia, prêt à la grosse ; prêt à (*ou* de) retour de voyage ; emprunt à la grosse.

loan on collateral, prêt sur nantissement ; prêt lombard ; lombard (*m.*).

loan on debentures, emprunt-obligations (*m.*).

loan on mortgage, prêt hypothécaire ; emprunt hypothécaire.

loan on overdraft, prêt à découvert.

loan on respondentia, prêt à la grosse sur facultés.

loan on stock, prêt sur titres ; emprunt sur titres ; avance sur titres.

loan repayable on demand, emprunt remboursable sur demande.

loan account, compte d'avances (*m.*).

loan capital, capital d'emprunt (*m.*).

loanable (*adj.*), prêtable :
loanable funds, fonds prêtables (*m.pl.*).

loaning (*n.*), prêter (*m.*) ; prêt (*m.*) ; prestation (*f.*).

local (*adj.*), local, -e, -aux :
local bank, banque locale (*f.*).
local call (Teleph.), communication locale (*f.*) ; conversation locale (*f.*).
local custom, usages de place (*m.pl.*) ; usages des lieux (*m.pl.*) ; usages locaux (*m.pl.*).
local exchange (Teleph.), bureau local (*m.*).
local managers, directeurs locaux (*m.pl.*).
local train, train local (*m.*).

locality [localities *pl.*] (*n.*), localité (*f.*).

lock (canal or dock) (*n.*), écluse (de canal ou de bassin) (*f.*) :
drops in the ground are compensated by locks, les dénivellations du terrain sont compensées par des écluses (*f.pl.*).

lock out workmen (to), renvoyer des ouvriers en masse.

lockout (*n.*). V. ci-après.

lock up (Fin.) (*v.t.*), immobiliser ; bloquer :
Pour exemples du mot *immobiliser*, V. sous **immobilize.**
it may be admitted that the cost of the plant should be increased by the interest on the capital which it has locked up during its construction, on peut admettre que le prix de revient des installations doit être grossi de l'intérêt des capitaux qu'elles ont bloqués pendant leur établissement.

lockup. V. ci-après.

locked canal, canal éclusé (*m.*).

lockout (*n.*) (opp. to *strike* or *walkout*), lock-out (*m.*) ; grève patronale (*f.*).

lockup (of capital, of money) (*n.*), immobilisation (*f.*) ; blocage (*m.*) ; bloquage (*m.*).

lockup desk, pupitre fermant à clef (*m.*).

locomotive (*n.*), locomotive (*f.*) ; machine (*f.*).

lodge (*v.t.*), déposer ; remettre ; fournir ; mettre :
to lodge at the customs a copy of the manifest, déposer à la douane une copie du manifeste.
securities lodged as collateral, titres déposés (*ou* remis) (*ou* fournis) en nantissement (*m.pl.*) ; valeurs déposées (*ou* remises) (*ou* fournies) en nantissement (*f.pl.*).
to lodge objections to marks (Stock Exch.), mettre des oppositions à la cote.

lodgment (*n.*), dépôt (*m.*) ; remise (*f.*) ; fournissement (*m.*) ; mise (*f.*).

log (*n.*) *or* **log book** (Navig.), livre de bord (*m.*) ; journal de bord (*m.*) ; registre de bord (*m.*).

lombard loan, prêt lombard (*m.*) ; lombard (*m.*) ; prêt sur nantissement (*m.*).

long (*adj.*) (Ant.: *short*), long, longue :
a long letter, une longue lettre.
long article (Railway Transport), objet de longueur exceptionnelle (*m.*).
long bill *or* long dated bill, effet à longue échéance (*m.*).
long credit, crédit à long terme (*m.*) ; crédit

à (*ou* de) longue durée (*m.*); long crédit (*m.*).
long dated option, prime à longue échéance (*f.*).
long distance radiotelegram, radiotélégramme à grande distance (*f.*).
long distance train, train de grand parcours (*m.*).
long exchange, papier long (*m.*).
long, heavy, or bulky articles (Railway Transport), masses indivisibles (*f.pl.*); masses indivisibles et objets de dimensions exceptionnelles ; objets de dimensions exceptionnelles (*m.pl.*):
   conveyance of long, heavy, or bulky articles, transport des masses indivisibles (*m.*).
long period loan, prêt à long terme (*m.*).
long term investment *or* long dated investment, placement à long terme (*m.*); placement de longue haleine (*m.*).
long term liabilities (opp. to *current liabilities*), passif à long terme (*m.*).
long (Stock Exch. U.S.A.) (pers.) (*n.*) (opp. to *short*), 'haussier (*m.*).
long way out (to be) (to be far from agreeing), être loin de compte.
longest in office. V. exemple :
   the directors to retire shall be those who have been longest in office since their last election (articles of association), le renouvellement a lieu par ancienneté de nomination.
look after (to), veiller à ; surveiller :
   to look after the carrying out of the repairs, veiller à l'exécution des réparations.
look for (to), chercher ; rechercher :
   to look for a place, chercher un emploi ; chercher de l'emploi.
   to look for the cause of disagreements, rechercher la cause des discordances.
look into (to) *or* look through (to), examiner ; compulser ; dépouiller ; faire le dépouillement de :
   to look into the cash position, examiner la situation de la caisse.
   to look into an account, dépouiller, faire le dépouillement d', un compte.
   to look through one's letters, dépouiller sa correspondance.
looking for, recherche (*f.*) :
   looking for a difference, mistakes, in the books, recherche d'une différence, des erreurs, dans les écritures.
looking into *or* looking through, examen (*m.*); dépouillement (*m.*).
loose card, fiche mobile (*f.*) ; carte-fiche (*f.*); fiche-carton (*f.*) ; fiche (*f.*).
loose leaf book (opp. to *bound book*), livre à feuilles mobiles (*ou* à feuillets mobiles) (*m.*).
loose leaf ledger, grand livre à feuilles mobiles (*m.*).
loose leaf pocketbook, carnet de poche à feuillets mobiles (*m.*).
loose sheet (of paper), feuille volante (*f.*) :
   agreement written on loose sheets, contrat rédigé sur des feuilles volantes (*m.*).
loro account, compte loro (*m.*).

lorry [lorries *pl.*] (*n.*), camion (*m.*):
   motor lorry, camion automobile.
lose (*v.t.*), perdre ; abandonner ; céder ; égarer ; adirer :
   to lose an action, one's money, all one's rights to an indemnity, perdre un procès, son argent, tous ses droits à une indemnité.
   X. shares lost a fraction, l'action X. perd (*ou* abandonne) une fraction.
   to lose ground, perdre, abandonner, céder, du terrain :
      X. shares lost ground at 1½, l'action X. perd du terrain à 1 1/2.
   to lose a certificate, a cheque, a draft, perdre, égarer, adirer, un certificat (*ou* un titre), un chèque, une traite.
   to lose papers, perdre, égarer, des papiers.
   to lose sight of an important consideration, perdre de vue une considération importante.
   to lose a right (Law), être déchu (-e) d'un droit ; perdre un droit :
      holder of a bill who loses all rights against the endorsers, porteur d'un effet qui est déchu de tous droits contre les endosseurs (*m.*).
   goods lost by wreck or stranding, marchandises perdues par naufrage ou échouement (*f.pl.*).
   ship which is lost, crew and cargo, without leaving any trace, navire qui se perd (*ou* qui a péri) (*ou* qui a fait naufrage), corps et biens, sans laisser aucune trace (*m.*).
loser (pers.) (*n.*), perdant, -e :
   the losers pay, les perdants payent.
losing (*adj.*), perdant, -e :
   the losing numbers, les numéros perdants (*m.pl.*).
loss (failure to keep or win) (*n.*), perte (*f.*); pertes (*f.pl.*) ; déperdition (*f.*):
   loss of money, of time, of market, of a ship, of the passenger's luggage, perte d'argent, de temps, de marché (*ou* de débouché), d'un navire, des bagages du voyageur.
   loss of capital, perte, déperdition, de capital.
   loss of life or personal injury, perte de vie ou blessures corporelles ; faits de mort ou de blessures de personnes (*m.pl.*):
      responsibility for loss of life or personal injury, responsabilité pour faits de mort ou de blessures de personnes (*f.*).
   loss of rent (Fire Insce), perte des loyers.
   loss on exchange, perte au change ; perte à la monnaie ; perte au cours ; perte sur le change ; perte sur change.
   loss of a right (Law), déchéance (*f.*), perte d'un droit. *Cf.* to lose a right.
   according as the result of the trading is (*or* shows) a profit or a loss, suivant que le résultat de l'exercice accuse un bénéfice ou une perte ; suivant que le résultat de l'exercice est bénéficiaire ou déficitaire.
   balance sheet showing a loss, bilan déficitaire (*m.*).
at a loss, à perte :
   to sell at a loss, vendre à perte.
loss (going astray) (*n.*), perte (*f.*); égarement (*m.*) ; adirement (*m.*):

loss of a certificate, perte, égarement, adirement, d'un titre.

oss (damage) (*n.*), perte (*f.*); pertes (*f.pl.*); dommage (*m.*); dommages (*m.pl.*); préjudice (*m.*):

loss resulting from a late delivery, caused by one's negligence, perte, pertes, préjudice, résultant d'une livraison tardive, causée (causées) (causé) par sa négligence.

damage and loss by fire *or* loss or damage by fire (Fire Insce), dégâts et pertes provenants d'incendie [dégâts *m.pl.*]; dommages matériels d'incendie.

a good year makes up for the losses of two bad ones, une bonne année répare les dommages de deux mauvaises.

oss (waste; wastage; falling away) (*n.*), perte (*f.*); pertes (*f.pl.*); manquant (*m.*); manquants (*m.pl.*); déchet (*m.*); déchets (*m.pl.*); freinte (*f.*):

loss in weight, in bulk, perte, manquant, déchets, freinte, en poids, en volume.

loss by leakage as a consequence of a peril of the sea, manquant par coulage à la suite de fortune de mer.

loss arising from insufficient packing, manquants provenant de l'insuffisance des emballages.

loss in transit, déchet de route; freinte de route.

there have been several losses without much importance (Stock Exch.), il y a quelques déchets sans grande importance.

loss (diminution of value) (Insce) (*n.*), perte (*f.*); pertes (*f.pl.*):

total loss, perte totale. *V. exemples sous* **total.**

loss or damage arising from negligence, fault, or failure, pertes ou avaries résultant des négligences, fautes, ou défauts.

loss, damage, and expense to be made good (General Average). V. syn. **amounts to be made good.**

loss (casualty) (Insce) (*n.*), sinistre (*m.*):

total loss, sinistre total. V. exemple sous **total.**

proof of loss, preuve de sinistre (*f.*).

the receipt of news of the loss, la réception de la nouvelle du sinistre.

freight repayable in case of loss, fret remboursable en cas de sinistre (*m.*).

the settlement of small losses, le règlement de petits sinistres.

loss (sum payable) (Insce) (*n.*), indemnité (*f.*):

the losses due by the underwriters are payable in cash, les indemnités dues par les assureurs sont payables comptant (*f.pl.*).

lost (*adj.*), perdu, -e; égaré, -e; adiré, -e; sinistré, -e:

lost ticket, billet perdu (*m.*).

lost bond, obligation perdue (*f.*); obligation égarée (*f.*); bon adiré (*m.*).

Cf. ship which is lost, *sous* **lose.**

lost or not lost (Mar. Insce), sur bonnes ou mauvaises nouvelles:

insurance made lost or not lost, assurance faite sur bonnes ou mauvaises nouvelles (*f.*).

lot (parcel) (*n.*), lot (*m.*); partie (*f.*); paquet (*m.*):

lot of goods, lot, partie, de marchandises.

to sell one's shares in small lots, vendre ses titres par petits paquets.

lot (the use of lots as a means of deciding anything) (*n.*), sort (*m.*):

to choose by lot, choisir par le sort.

lot (drawing lot) (*n.*), tirage au sort (*m.*); tirage (*m.*):

the order of retirement is determined by lot, l'ordre de sortie est déterminé par un tirage au sort (*m.*).

lot number, numéro de lot (*m.*).

lottery [lotteries *pl.*] (*n.*), loterie (*f.*).

lottery bond, bon à lots (*m.*); obligation à lots (*f.*): titre à lots (*m.*); valeur à lots (*f.*).

lottery ticket, billet de loterie (*m.*).

low (*adj.*) (Ant.: *high*), bas, basse; faible; bon marché:

low price, bas prix (*m.*).

low income, faible revenu (*m.*).

low-duty goods, marchandises faiblement taxées (*ou* tarifées) (*f.pl.*).

the low grades of service in an administration, les bas emplois d'une administration (*m.pl.*).

the rate of exchange is low, le taux du change est bas.

contangoes are low, les reports sont bon marché (*m.pl.*). V. exemple sous **stiffen** (*v.i.*).

lower (*v.t.*), baisser; abaisser; rabaisser; diminuer; faire diminuer; ramener:

to lower the price of stocks, baisser, abaisser, rabaisser, faire diminuer, le prix des valeurs.

to lower the bank rate, abaisser, diminuer, le taux officiel d'escompte.

X. shares which had hardened to 8s. 9d. were lowered to 8s. 6d., on profit taking, l'action X. qui s'était redressée à 8sh. 9d. est ramenée à 8sh. 6d., sur prises de bénéfices.

lower deck, pont inférieur (*m.*).

lower price, cours plus faible (*m.*).

lowering (*n.*), abaissement (*m.*); rabaissement (*m.*); diminution (*f.*):

lowering the fineness of the coinage, abaissement du titre des monnaies.

lowest price (Stock Exch.), cours le plus bas (*m.*).

lowness (of a price) (*n.*), modicité (d'un prix) (*f.*).

lowness (of contangoes) (*n.*), bon marché (des reports) (*m.*). V. exemple sous **highness.**

luck (*n.*), chance (*f.*):

good luck, bad luck, to bring luck, to have luck (*or* to be lucky), bonne chance, mauvaise chance, porter chance, avoir de la chance.

lucky (*adj.*), chanceux, -euse:

lucky man, homme chanceux (*m.*).

lucrative (*adj.*), lucratif, -ive:

lucrative trade, commerce lucratif (*m.*).

lucrative transaction, transaction lucrative (*f.*); affaire d'or (*f.*); affaire magnifique (*f.*).

luggage (*n.*), bagage (*m.*); bagages (*m.pl.*).

Note :—luggage and *baggage* are synonymous words. *luggage* is the English word; *baggage* is the American word, but it is largely used in England.

luggage registration office *or simply* **luggage office,** guichet d'enregistrement des bagages (*m.*) ; guichet bagages (*m.*) ; salle des bagages (*f.*).

luggage registration ticket (*or* **voucher**) *or simply* **luggage ticket** *or* **luggage voucher,** bulletin d'enregistrement des bagages (*m.*) ; bulletin de bagages (*m.*).

luggage van *or* **luggage vehicle** (Rly.), fourgon à bagages (*m.*).

lump (*v.t.*), cumuler ; bloquer ; réunir :
the lumped (*or* the lump) weight of the container

and the contents, le poids cumulé du con tenant et du contenu.

items which are lumped under the heading investments, articles qui sont bloqués dans le chapitre portefeuille (*ou* qui sont réunis sous la rubrique portefeuille-titres) (*m.pl.*).

lump sum, somme grosse (*f.*).

lump tare, tare intégrale (*f.*).

lumping (*n.*), cumul (*m.*) ; blocage (*m.*) ; bloquage (*m.*) ; réunion (*f.*).

luxury tax, taxe de luxe (*f.*).

luxury trade, commerce de luxe (*m.*).

lying (false) (*adj.*), mensonger, -ère :
lying prospectus, prospectus mensonger (*m.*).

M

machine (*n.*), machine (*f.*) :
calculating machine, machine à calculer.

machinery (*n.*), machines (*f.pl.*) :
boilers, machinery, and everything connected therewith, chaudières, machines, et tout ce qui s'y rattache.

machinery (*fig.*) (*n.*), rouage (*m.*) :
the machinery of commercial life, le rouage de la vie commerciale.

made (*p.p.*), fait, -e ; pratiqué, -e :
the prices at which bargains were made, les cours pratiqués (*m.pl.*) ; les cours qu'on a pratiqués (*m.pl.*) ; les cours faits (*m.pl.*).
made in duplicate at London, the 1st January 19—, fait double (*ou* fait en double) à Londres, le 1er janvier 19—.

made in England, in France (statement of origin), fabriqué en Angleterre, en France.

magnate (pers.) (*n.*), magnat (*m.*) ; matador (*m.*) :
a financial magnate, un magnat (*ou* un matador) de la finance.

mail (Post) (*n.*), malle (*f.*) ; poste (*f.*) ; courrier (*m.*) ; courrier postal (*m.*) :
the Indian mail, la malle de l'Inde (*ou* des Indes).
the mail has just left, la poste vient de partir.
bills drawn in sets of three are intended to be sent by different mails, les lettres tirées à trois exemplaires sont destinées à être envoyées par des courriers différents (*f.pl.*).

mail bag (Post), dépêche (*f.*) ; sac à dépêches (*m.*).

mail carriage *or* **mail car** (Rly.), wagon-poste (*m.*).

mail, passenger, and parcel service, messagerie (*f.*) ; messageries (*f.pl.*).

mail service, service des postes (*m.*) ; service postal (*m.*).

mail steamer (Abbrev. : **m/s.** *or* **m.s.**) *or* **mail boat** *or* **mail packet,** paquebot-poste (*m.*) ; paquebot postal (*m.*) ; vapeur postal (*m.*) ; malle (*f.*).

mail train, train-poste (*m.*).

main deck, pont principal (*m.*).

main line (Rly.), ligne principale (*f.*) ; grande ligne (*f.*) ; grande artère (*f.*) ; ligne d'artère (*f.*) :
the point of junction with the main line, le point de jonction avec la ligne principale.
the main lines out of London, les grandes lignes partant de Londres.

maintain (*v.t.*), maintenir ; entretenir ; défendre ; alimenter :
irons and steels maintain their prices fairly well, les métallurgiques maintiennent (*ou* défendent) assez bien leurs cours (*f.pl.*).
to maintain the dividend at 5%, maintenir le dividende à 5 0/0.
reserve maintained by the excess of receipts, réserve alimentée par l'excédent de recettes (*f.*).

to be maintained, être maintenu, -e ; être défendu, -e ; se maintenir ; se défendre :
prices were well maintained, prices were fairly well maintained, les cours se maintiennent bien, les cours sont assez défendus (*m.pl.*).
X. shares were well maintained, l'action X. se défend bien.

maintenance (*n.*), maintien (*m.*) ; entretien (*m.*) ; alimentation (*f.*) :
maintenance of economic prosperity, maintien de la prospérité économique.
maintenance of roads, entretien des routes.
the provisions necessary for the maintenance of the crew, les vivres nécessaires à l'entretien de l'équipage (*m.pl.*).
stoppages on wages for the maintenance of relief or provident funds, retenus sur les salaires pour l'alimentation des caisses de secours ou de prévoyance (*m.pl.*).

major (*adj.*), majeur, -e :
major casualty involving the total loss of the ship, sinistre majeur entraînant la perte totale du navire (*m.*).

association composed for the major part of foreigners, association composée en majeure partie des étrangers (*f.*).

majority [**majorities** *pl.*] (*n.*), majorité (*f.*) :
to be elected by a majority of votes, être élu (-e) à la majorité des suffrages (*ou* des voix).

make (*v.t.*). V. exemples :
to make a bad spec. (*Colloquial*), boire, avaler, un bouillon.
to make a bad speculation, faire une fausse spéculation.
to make a bargain (to enter into a bargain), faire, passer, un marché. *Cf.* to make a good bargain.
to make a bill, a cheque, payable to order, to bearer, souscrire, libeller, un effet, un chèque, à ordre, au porteur.
to make a bill of exchange in the following terms, libeller une lettre de change dans les termes suivants.
to make a bill of lading, établir, créer, rédiger, un connaissement :
bill of lading made in four originals, connaissement établi en quatre originaux (*m.*).
bill of lading made to the shipper's order, connaissement créé (*ou* rédigé) à l'ordre du chargeur (*m.*).
to make a call (to pay a visit), faire une visite.
to make a call (Shipping), faire escale ; faire échelle. V. exemples sous **call** (*n.*).
to make a call (Fin.), faire un appel de fonds.
to make a change of investments, of stocks, faire un arbitrage de portefeuille, de valeurs.
to make a claim against someone for damage sustained, exercer un recours contre quelqu'un pour préjudice subi.
to make a clean copy of a letter, copier une lettre au propre ; mettre au net une lettre.
to make a clean sweep, faire table rase :
to make a clean sweep of former considerations, faire table rase des considérations qui précèdent.
to make a draft of a letter, faire un brouillon de lettre ; faire la minute d'une lettre.
to make a fair copy of a manuscript, faire la transcription au net d'un manuscrit.
to make a fine income (for oneself), se faire un joli revenu.
to make a fortune, faire fortune ; gagner une fortune ; faire ses affaires ; faire son affaire :
to make a fortune on the stock exchange, faire fortune, gagner une fortune, faire ses affaires, faire son affaire, sur (*ou* à) la bourse.
to make a fresh start after a failure in business, se remettre d'une faillite.
to make a good bargain, faire un marché avantageux (*ou* une bonne affaire) (*ou* une négociation heureuse).
to make a good investment, faire un bon placement.
to make a good showing, faire bonne figure.
to make a journey, faire un voyage.
to make a loan, faire un prêt (*ou* un emprunt).
to make a marginal note on a deed, apostiller, mettre une apostille à la marge d', un acte.

to make a market, créer un marché :
Mr X. was the holder of the entire stock, and his first operation was to make a market, M. X. était le détenteur du stock entier, et sa première opération fut de créer un marché.
to make a mistake, faire une faute (*ou* une erreur) ; se mécompter :
to make a mistake in the calculation, faire une erreur de calcul ; faire un faux calcul.
to make a note, faire une note ; écrire une note ; coter une note ; prendre note :
to make a note in a diary, faire, écrire, coter, une note sur un agenda.
to make a note of something in one's pocket-book, prendre note d'une chose sur son carnet.
to make a payment, faire un paiement ; effectuer un payement ; opérer un versement.
payment is made as follows, le paiement s'effectue comme suit.
to make a payment a week in advance, anticiper un paiement de huit jours.
to make a present of something to someone, faire cadeau de quelque chose à quelqu'un.
to make a price, faire un prix.
to make a profit, réaliser, tirer, retirer, un bénéfice (*ou* un profit) ; bénéficier :
to make large profits, enormous gains, réaliser de hauts bénéfices, des gains énormes.
to make a profit out of an undertaking, on a line of goods, tirer un bénéfice, retirer un profit, bénéficer, d'une entreprise, sur une marchandise.
to make a promissory note, souscrire un billet à ordre.
to make a remittance of a sum of money, faire remise d', remettre, une somme d'argent.
to make a remittance of funds, faire une remise (*ou* un envoi) (*ou* un versement) de fonds.
to make a report on the accounts, on the position of a company, faire un rapport sur les comptes, sur la situation d'une société.
to make a reserve for depreciation, faire, pratiquer, un amortissement.
to make a reserve outside (*or* apart from) one's current transactions, ménager une réserve en dehors de ses opérations courantes.
to make a return of one's profits, of one's total income (Income Tax), faire la déclaration de ses bénéfices, de son revenu global.
to make a return on (to pay a dividend on, or the like), rémunérer :
sufficient profits to enable a return to be made on the share capital, bénéfices suffisants pour permettre de rémunérer le capital-actions (*m.pl.*).
to make a return to the registrar, faire une déclaration au greffier.
to make a transfer (Bkkpg), faire un contre-passement.
to make a valuation of goods, faire l'appréciation, faire l'évaluation, des marchandises.
to make abandonment (Mar. Insce), faire le délaissement ; faire l'abandon :

insured who no longer has the right to make abandonment, assuré qui n'est plus recevable à faire le délaissement (*m.*). V. exemple sous **abandonment**.

to make advances to someone, on account current, faire des avances à quelqu'un, en compte courant.

to make [an account] [the books] agree, faire accorder, faire cadrer [un compte], [les livres].

to make allowance for fluctuations in exchange, tenir compte des fluctuations du change.

to make an abstract of an account, faire le relevé d', faire le relèvement d', relever, un compte.

to make an analysis of an account, faire le dépouillement d', dépouiller, un compte.

to make an appointment (to agree to meet each other), se donner rendez-vous.

to make an appointment with someone, donner rendez-vous (*ou* un rendez-vous) à quelqu'un.

to make an appropriation for distribution among the employees, faire une distraction pour être distribuée aux employés.

to make an award (Arbitration), rendre une sentence.

to make an entry (Bkkpg), faire une écriture ; passer une écriture ; passer un article en compte ; inscrire un article :
the entries made in the journal, les écritures faites sur le journal (*f.pl.*) ; les articles inscrits sur le journal (*m.pl.*).

to make an estimate of the losses caused by a fire, faire l'évaluation, faire l'appréciation, des pertes occasionnées par un incendie.

to make an inventory of one's goods, faire l'inventaire de, inventorier, ses marchandises.

to make an investment, faire un placement.

to make away with books, détourner des livres.

to make bankrupt, mettre en faillite :
marchant who is on the point of being made bankrupt, négociant qui est sur le point d'être mis en faillite (*m.*).

to make both ends meet (*fig.*), joindre, nouer, les deux bouts ; joindre, nouer, les deux bouts de l'année.

to make delivery of the shipment against payment of the freight, faire la délivrance du chargement contre paiement du fret.

to make enquiries (*or* inquiries) about someone, about someone's position, prendre des renseignements, prendre des informations, se renseigner, sur quelqu'un, sur la situation de quelqu'un.

to make fast (Navig.) (*v.t.*), amarrer.

to make fast (Navig.) (*v.i.*), s'amarrer.

to make good a loss, bonifier une perte.

to make good as general average the damage done to a ship or her cargo, bonifier, admettre, en avarie commune le dommage causé à un navire ou à sa cargaison.

to make good the losses of bad years, combler les pertes des mauvais exercices.

to make good use of one's money, ménager son argent.

to make insurance (*or* assurance) of, faire assurer ; assurer :
the big shipping companies seldom make insurance of their ships, and so are their own insurers, les grandes compagnies de navigation font rarement assurer leurs navires, et restent ainsi leurs propres assureurs.

to make jointly and severally liable. V. *sous* jointly and severally.

to make losses on the stock exchange, faire des pertes à la bourse.

to make money out of a transaction, faire argent, faire (*ou* gagner) de l'argent, d'une opération.

the company has never made money, la société n'a jamais gagner d'argent.

to make nothing out of it, ne faire que changer son argent :
I have made nothing out of it, je n'ai fait que changer mon argent.

to make one's expenses, faire, couvrir, ses frais.

to make one's fortune, faire sa fortune ; faire ses affaires ; faire son affaire.

to make one's will, faire son testament ; tester.

to make out a bill, dresser, rédiger, un mémoire.

to make out a cheque, créer, tirer, tracer, un chèque.

to make out a list of one's investments, of one's assets and liabilities, dresser l'inventaire de son portefeuille, de son actif et de son passif.

to make out a statement of account, faire le relevé d', faire le relèvement d', relever, un compte.

to make out an account, établir un compte.

to make over a debt, transporter une créance.

to make protest of a bill in case of dishonour, lever protêt d'un effet en cas de non paiement.

to make [a ship] seaworthy, mettre [un navire] en état de tenir la mer.

to make [a ship] seaworthy again, remettre [un navire] en bon état de navigabilité.

to make so much out of a deal, avoir tant de boni dans une affaire.

make up (*n.*). V. sous **making up**, ci-après.

to make up (to put into a fit condition) (*v.t.*), conditionner ; confectionner :
to make up a balance sheet, statistics, letters for the post, confectionner un bilan, des statistiques, des lettres pour la poste.

printed papers and commercial papers must be made up in such a way that they can be easily examined, les imprimés et papiers de commerce doivent être confectionnés (*ou* conditionnés) de telle sorte qu'ils puissent être facilement vérifiés (*m.pl.*).

to make up (Stock Exch.), compenser :
to give the order to the broker A. to make up with the broker B., donner l'ordre à l'agent A. de compenser avec l'agent B.

the stock must be taken up or delivered at the settlement, unless the transaction is made up, les titres doivent être levés ou livrés en liquidation, à moins que l'opération ne soit compensée (*m.pl.*).

X. shares which were made up at the last settlement at 1¼, were quoted at 1½, l'action X., qui a été compensée à la dernière liquidation à 1 1/4, s'inscrit à 1 1/2.

to be made up, être compensé, -e ; se compenser :

two deals which are made up the one by the other, deux opérations qui se compensent l'une par l'autre (*f.pl.*).

to make up a deficit (*or* a shortage), suppléer un déficit ; combler un déficit (*ou* un découvert) ; bonifier un déficit :

to make up a shortage in weight, suppléer, combler, bonifier, un déficit de poids.

to make up an account current to the 30th June, arrêter, régler, un compte courant au 30 juin.

the accounts are made up at (*or* on) the 30th June and 31st December in (*or* of) each year, les comptes sont arrêtés le 30 juin et le 31 décembre de chaque année (*m.pl.*).

to make up an amount, the difference, parfaire une somme, la différence.

to make up an amount with small coin (*or* with minor coin) (*or* with small change), faire l'appoint. *V. exemple sous* small coin.

to make up for, compenser ; rattraper :

profits which make up for one's losses, bénéfices qui compensent ses pertes (*m.pl.*).

to make up for lost time, rattraper le temps perdu.

to make up one's accounts every six months, at least once a year, faire son inventaire, arrêter ses comptes, régler ses comptes, tous les six mois, au moins une fois l'an.

to make up one's losses, se récompenser de ses pertes.

to make up the cash (to balance up the cash book), faire, arrêter, la caisse :

the cashier should make up his cash every day ; this means, seeing whether the amount of cash in hand agrees with that shown by the cash book, le caissier doit faire sa caisse tous les jours ; on entend par là, vérifier si le montant des espèces en caisse correspond bien à celui qui ressort du livre de caisse.

to make use of, se servir de ; emprunter :

the ships which make use of the Suez canal, les navires qui empruntent le canal de Suez (*m.pl.*).

to go up the Thames instead of making use of the railway, remonter la Tamise au lieu d'emprunter la voie ferrée.

maker (of a promissory note, of a note of hand) (pers.) (*n.*), souscripteur (d'un billet à ordre) (*m.*).

making a profit, réalisation d'un bénéfice (*f.*) :

making (*or* to make) a profit is the object of every commercial exchange, la réalisation d'un bénéfice est le but de tout échange commercial.

making an entry (Bkkpg), passation d'une écriture (*f.*) ; passation d'un article en compte (*f.*) :

making entries in the journal, passation des écritures au journal.

making out a cheque, création (*f.*), tirage (*m.*), traçage (*m.*) d'un chèque.

making out a list, dressement (*m.*), rédaction (*f.*) d'une liste.

making out a statement of account, relevé (*m.*), relèvement (*m.*) d'un compte.

making over a debt, revirement (*m.*) ; revirement de fonds (*m.*) ; revirement de deniers (*m.*).

making up *or* **make up** (putting into a fit condition), confection '(*f.*) ; confectionnement (*m.*) ; conditionnement (*m.*) :

making up a balance sheet, letters for the post, confection d'un bilan, des lettres pour la poste.

make up of packets (Post), conditionnement des envois.

making up *or* **make up** (Stock Exch.), compensation (*f.*).

making up price *or* **make up price** (Stock Exch.) (Abbrev. : **M/U.**), cours de compensation (*m.*) :

contango dealings are settled at the making up price, les opérations de report sont réglées au cours de compensation (*f.pl.*).

making up the cash, the trial balance (balancing up), arrêté de la caisse, de la balance de vérification (*m.*) :

the date of the making up of the trial balance, la date de l'arrêté de la balance de vérification.

mala fide, de mauvaise foi :

mala fide holder, détenteur de mauvaise foi (*m.*).

mala fide purchaser, acquéreur de mauvaise foi (*m.*) ; acheteur de mauvaise foi (*m.*).

to act mala fide, agir de mauvaise foi.

man [men *pl.*] (*n.*), homme (*m.*) :

man in charge, homme qui en a la garde ; convoyeur (*m.*) : (Cf. **attendant.**)

when the railway authorizes attendance while travelling on its lines, the man in charge is carried free of charge, lorsque le chemin de fer autorise l'escorte d'un transport sur ses lignes, le convoyeur est transporté gratuitement.

man of business, homme d'affaires.

man of his word, homme de parole.

man of straw, homme de paille :

dummy who masks a man of straw, prête-nom qui cache un homme de paille (*m.*).

man (*v.t.*) *or* **man and supply (to),** armer :

to man a boat, armer un canot.

the owner mans and supplies the ship, that is to say, puts her in a state to set out on a voyage, by providing her with all that is necessary ; master, crew, victuals, fuel, l'armateur arme le navire, c'est-à-dire le met en état d'entreprendre un voyage, en le munissant de tout ce qui est nécessaire ; capitaine, équipage, provisions de bouche, combustibles (*m.*).

man, equip, and supply (to), armer ; armer et équiper :

to man, equip, and supply a ship, armer un navire; armer et équiper un navire.

Note :—The word *équiper* is really not necessary in the French phrase, but is often used.

manage (*v.t.*), diriger; administrer; gérer; conduire; manier; manutentionner:

to manage affairs, diriger, gérer, administrer, conduire, manier, des affaires.

the master manages the ship on behalf of the owner, le capitaine conduit le navire pour le compte de l'armateur.

the association is managed by two directors, l'association est gérée par deux administrateurs (*f.*).

management (*n.*), direction (*f.*); gérance (*f.*); gestion (*f.*); administration (*f.*); conduite (*f.*); maniement (*m.*); maniment (*m.*); manutention (*f.*):

every captain entrusted with the management of a ship is responsible for his wrongful acts in the exercise of his functions, tout capitaine chargé de la conduite (*ou* de l'administration) d'un navire est garant de ses fautes dans l'exercice de ses fonctions.

the captain is not only entrusted with the technical management of the ship and with the commandership of the crew, le capitaine n'est pas seulement préposé de la conduite technique du navire et du commandement de l'équipage.

to leave the management of one's affairs in the hands of a reliable man, laisser à un homme sûr la manutention de ses affaires.

management account, compte gestionnaire (*m.*).

management agreement, traité de direction (*m.*); contrat de gérance (*m.*).

management expenses, frais d'administration (*m.pl.*); frais de gérance (*m.pl.*).

management share, part bénéficiaire (*f.*); part de fondateur (*f.*).

manager (pers.) (*n.*) (Abbrev.: **mgr**), directeur (*m.*); gérant (*m.*); gestionnaire (*m.*); chef (*m.*):

manager of a company, directeur, gérant, d'une société (*ou* d'une compagnie).

manager of an underwriting syndicate, of a pool, gérant, directeur, d'un syndicat de garantie, d'un syndicat de placement.

manager of department, chef de service.

manager's office, cabinet du directeur (*m.*); bureau de directeur (*m.*); direction (*f.*).

manageress (pers.) (*n.*), directrice (*f.*); gérante (*f.*).

managership (*n.*), directorat (*m.*); gérance (*f.*):

to aspire to the managership of a bank, aspirer au directorat d'une banque.

during his managership, pendant son directorat; durant sa gérance.

managing (*adj.*), directeur, -trice; gérant, -e; gestionnaire:

managing agent, agent gérant (*m.*).

managing clerk (in a merchant's office, a bank, or the like), chef de bureau (*m.*); commis principal (*m.*); commis chef (*m.*).

managing clerk (in a lawyer's office), maître clerc (*m.*).

managing committee, comité de direction (*m.*); comité directeur (*m.*).

managing director, administrateur délégué (*m.*); administrateur directeur (*m.*); administrateur gérant (*m.*):

after their appointment, the directors meet as a board to choose one of their number to be chairman and to delegate a part of their powers to one or more of their number who will manage the company's business and will cause the decisions of the board to be carried out : these members take the title of managing directors, après leur nomination, les administrateurs se réunissent en conseil pour choisir parmi eux un président et déléguer une partie de leurs pouvoirs à l'un ou à plusieurs d'entre eux qui dirigeront les affaires de la société et feront exécuter les délibérations du conseil : ces membres prennent le titre d'administrateurs délégués.

managing owner (Shipping), armateur-gérant (*m.*); armateur-titulaire (*m.*).

mandatary *or* **mandatory** [**mandataries** *or* **mandatories** *pl.*] (pers.) (*n.*), mandataire (*m. ou f.*):

the directors are the mandataries of the company, entrusted with the management of its business, les administrateurs sont les mandataires de la société, chargés de la gestion des affaires sociales (*m.pl.*).

mandate (*n.*), mandat (*m.*):

country placed under British mandate, pays placé sous mandat britannique (*m.*).

the meeting must, every year, appoint auditors; it can also renew their mandate, l'assemblée doit, chaque année, nommer des commissaires; elle peut aussi renouveler leur mandat (*f.*).

mandate form (Banking), lettre de signatures autorisées (*f.*).

mandated territory, pays de mandat (*m.*); territoire de (*ou* à) mandat (*m.*).

mandator (pers.) (*n.*), mandant (*m.*):

mandator and mandatary, mandant et mandataire.

manifest (Shipping) (*n.*), manifeste (*m.*); facture de la cargaison (*f.*):

a manifest is a detailed statement of the goods forming a ship's cargo, le manifeste est l'état détaillé des marchandises formant le chargement d'un navire.

manifest (*v.t.*), manifester:

cargo properly manifested, marchandises régulièrement manifestées (*f.pl.*).

manifold (*n.*), polycopie (*f.*).

manifold (*v.t.*), polycopier:

to manifold a letter, polycopier une lettre.

manifold book, carnet genre manifold (*m.*); manifold (*m.*).

manipulation (jobbery) (*n.*), manipulation (*f.*); tripotage (*m.*).

manning (*n.*) *or* **manning and supplying,** armement (*m.*). V. **man** (*v.t.*) pour exemples.

manning, equipping, and supplying, armement
(*m.*) ; armement et équipement (*m.pl.*).   V.
exemple et note sous **man, equip, and supply
(to).**
manual delivery (Law), tradition manuelle (*f.*) ;
tradition matérielle (*f.*).
manual exchange (Teleph.) (opp. to *automatic
exchange*), bureau central manuel (*m.*) ;
bureau manuel (*m.*) ; poste central manuel
(*m.*).
manufactory [manufactories *pl.*] (*n.*), fabrique
(*f.*) ; manufacture (*f.*).
manufacture (*n.*), fabrication (*f.*).
manufacture (*v.t.*), fabriquer ; manufacturer :
to manufacture goods, fabriquer, manufacturer,
des marchandises.
manufacturer (pers.) (*n.*), fabricant (*m.*) ; industriel (*m.*) ; manufacturier, -ère.
manufacturing licence, licence de fabrication
(*f.*).
margin (space on the edge of a sheet) (*n.*), marge
(*f.*) :
bill of lading which shows in the margin the
marks and numbers of the packages, of the
goods to be carried, connaissement qui
présente (*ou* qui indique) en marge les
marques et numéros des colis, des marchandises à transporter (*m.*).
goods marked and numbered as per margin
(*or* as in the margin hereof), marchandises
marquées et numérotées comme en marge
(*f.pl.*).
margin (excess ; surplus) (*n.*), marge (*f.*) :
margin of profit, marge de bénéfice ; marge
bénéficiaire.
the margin between the amount advanced and
the value of the securities at the time of the
transaction, la marge entre la somme avancée
et la valeur des titres au moment de
l'opération.
to reserve a margin for contingencies, réserver
une marge pour les éventualités.
margin (cover) (Fin., Banking, and Stock Exch.)
(*n.*), marge (*f.*) ; couverture (*f.*) ; provision
(*f.*) ; acompte (*m.*) :
stockbroker who requires a margin of 25% in
cash, agent de change qui exige une marge
(*ou* une couverture) (*ou* une provision)
(*ou* un acompte) de 25 0/0 en espèces
(*m.*).
to deposit a margin in cash as cover in proportion to one's engagements, déposer une
marge en espèces comme couverture proportionnée à ses engagements.
margin (*v.i.*), fournir une couverture :
principal who must margin, donneur d'ordre
qui doit fournir une couverture (*m.*).
to margin up, compléter la couverture fournie
antérieurement :
principal who is bound to margin up, if
necessary, donneur d'ordre qui est tenu de
compléter, s'il y a lieu, la couverture par
lui fournie antérieurement (*m.*).
marginal (*adj.*), marginal, -e, -aux :
marginal note, note marginale (*f.*) ; apostille
(*f.*).

marine (*adj.*), maritime ; marin, -e :
marine charge (land charge or ship charge)
(radiotelegrams), taxe maritime (*f.*).
marine engine, machine marine (*f.*).
marine insurance *or* marine assurance, assurance maritime (*f.*).
marine insurance broker, courtier d'assurances
maritimes (*m.*).   V. note *sous* courtier maritime.
marine insurance clauses, clauses d'assurances
maritimes (*f.pl.*).
marine insurance company, compagnie d'assurance maritime (*ou* d'assurances maritimes)
(*f.*).
marine interest, change maritime (*m.*) ; profit
maritime (*m.*) ; profit nautique (*m.*) ; intérêt
nautique (*m.*) ; prime de grosse (*f.*).
marine loan (Law). *Syn. de* maritime loan.
marine loss, perte maritime (*f.*).
marine peril. *Syn. de* maritime peril.
marine policy *or* marine insurance policy,
police maritime (*f.*) ; police d'assurance
maritime (*f.*).
marine registry, inscription maritime (*f.*).
marine registry office, bureau de l'inscription
maritime (*m.*).
marine risk, risque maritime (*m.*) ; risque de
mer (*m.*).
marine station (Rly.), gare maritime (*f.*).
marine store dealer, fournisseur de navires
(*m.*) ; fournisseur maritime (*m.*).
marine stores, fournitures pour navires (*f.pl.*) ;
fournitures maritimes (*f.pl.*).
marine superintendent, capitaine d'armement
(*m.*).
marine telegram (telegram to or from ship
at sea), télégramme maritime (*m.*) :
marine telegrams exchanged through coast
stations with ships at sea, télégrammes
marines échangés au moyen des stations
côtières avec les navires en mer.
marine transport, transport maritime (*m.*) ;
transport par mer (*m.*).
marine (shipping) (*n.*), marine (*f.*) :
merchant marine, marine marchande.
mariner (pers.) (*n.*), marin (*m.*) ; homme de
mer (*m.*) ; gens de mer (*m.pl. only*) ; matelot (*m.*).
maritime (*adj.*), maritime :
maritime and internal navigation, navigation
mixte (*f.*).
maritime commerce *or* maritime trade, commerce maritime (*m.*).
maritime insurance *or* maritime assurance,
assurance maritime (*f.*).
maritime interest. *Syn. de* marine interest.
maritime law, droit maritime (*m.*).
maritime lien, privilège maritime (*m.*).
maritime loan (Law), prêt maritime (*m.*) ;
prêt à la grosse (*m.*) ; prêt à la grosse aventure (*m.*) ; prêt à (*ou* de) retour de voyage
(*m.*) ; emprunt à la grosse (*m.*). Cf. **bottomry,
& respondentia.**
maritime navigation, navigation maritime
(*f.*) ; marine (*f.*) :
in maritime navigation, all distances are

reckoned in miles, en marine, on évalue toutes les distances en milles.

maritime peril, péril de mer (*m.*); fortune de mer (*f.*); péril maritime (*m.*). *Note :— fortune de mer is also a collective plural thus, choses perdues par fortune de mer, property lost by maritime perils. The plural, fortunes de mer, is sometimes used.*

maritime risk, risque maritime (*m.*); risque de mer (*m.*).

mark (Com., etc.) (*n.*), marque (*f.*):
marks and numbers of packages, marques et numéros des colis.

mark (imprint of a stamp) (*n.*), estampille (*f.*).

mark (*n.*) *or* **marks** (*n.pl.*) *or* **marking** (*n.*) *or* **markings** (*n.pl.*) (Stock Exch.), cote (*f.*):
to lodge objections to marks, mettre des oppositions à la cote.
marking of prices, cote des cours.
marking of omitted bargain, rappel de cours (*m.*).

mark (*v.t.*), marquer; coter; porter; porter la mention; estampiller:
the packages should be marked distinctly, and bear, besides the marks and numbers, the name of the port of destination, les colis doivent être marqués distinctement, et porter, outre les marques et numéros, le nom du port de destination (*m.pl.*).
to mark a price (Stock Exch.), coter un cours.
to mark documents (to distinguish them with letters or numbers), coter des pièces.
mark boldly on the envelope the word "Express," porter d'une façon très apparente sur l'enveloppe la mention « Exprès. »
packets to be delivered by express must be marked "Express," les envois à distribuer par exprès doivent porter la mention « Exprès. »
certificates marked with the payment of a coupon, titres estampillés du paiement d'un coupon (*m.pl.*).

marked (decided) (*adj.*), marqué, -e:
a marked recovery, une reprise marquée.

marked (to be) (to be quoted) (Stock Exch.), s'inscrire; être inscrit, -e; se coter; coter; être coté, -e:
to be marked up, s'inscrire en hausse (*ou* en reprise) (*ou* en avance) (*ou* en progrès):
X. shares were marked up, l'action X. s'inscrit en reprise.
to be marked down, s'inscrire en baisse (*ou* en recul) (*ou* en réaction):
prices have again been marked down this week, les cours se sont de nouveau inscrits en baisse cette semaine (*m.pl.*).

marked cheque, chèque visé (*m.*).

marked price, prix marqué (*m.*).

marked shares (i.e., certificates stamped with notice that rights have been exercised, or the like), actions estampillées (*f.pl.*).

market (*n.*), marché (*m.*); place (*f.*); bourse (*f.*); débouché (*m.*):
the stock market *or* the share market, le marché des valeurs; le marché des titres.
market in the shares *or* market in . . . shares

or market in the stock, marché des actions; marché des actions . . .; marché des titres (*ou* du titre); marché de la valeur:
the market in X. shares improved slightly, le marché des actions X. s'améliore légèrement.
that was sufficient to make an impression on the market in the stock, cela a suffit pour impressionner le marché du titre.

oil market (Stock Exch.), marché des pétrolifères.

oversea markets, marchés d'outre-mer.
the French market is a big buyer of English bills, la place française est gros acheteur de portefeuille anglais.
capital on offer in the credit market, capital qui s'offre sur le marché du crédit (*m.*).
there are none on the market, il n'y en a pas sur le marché.
shares (*or* stock) on the market (Stock Exch.), titres flottants (*m.pl.*); flottant (*m.*):
public which absorbs the shares (*or* the stock) on the market, public qui absorbe les titres flottants (*ou* le flottant) (*m.*).
the market has risen, le marché a haussé; la bourse est en hausse.
market quiet, market lively, bourse calme, bourse animée.
town where there is only one market a week, ville où il n'y a qu'un marché par semaine (*f.*).
shares sold at to-day's market, actions vendues à la bourse de ce jour (*f.pl.*).
the market is all bears (*or* is all takers) (Stock Exch.), la place (*ou* la position de place) est dégagée (*ou* est soulagée).
the market is all bulls (*or* is all givers) (Stock Exch.), la place (*ou* la position de place) est chargée.
when the market is a buyer, quand la place est acheteur.
the contango rate is generally the barometer of the market (*or* of the market position), le taux des reports est généralement le baromètre de la position de place (*ou* de la situation de place).
the most useful encouragement for agricultural and manufacturing industry is to assure to it a market for its productions, l'encouragement le plus utile pour l'industrie agricole et manufacturière est de lui assurer le débouché de ses productions (*m.*).

market day, jour de place (*m.*); jour de bourse (*m.*).

market jobbery (in an unfavourable sense) (Stock Exch.), tripotage de bourse (*m.*); agiotage (*m.*); agio (*m.*).

Market News (newspaper heading), En Bourse; Ce qui se dit en Bourse; Ce qu'on dit en Bourse; A travers les Marchés.

market price, cours du marché (*m.*); prix du marché (*m.*); cours de la place (*m.*); cours de bourse (*m.*); courant du marché (*m.*); prix courant (*m.*).

market rate *or* **market rate of discount** (opp. to *bank rate*), taux hors banque (*m.*); taux privé (*m.*); taux d'escompte hors banque (*m.*); taux d'escompte privé (*m.*); taux de l'escompte privé (*m.*); escompte hors banque (*m.*); escompte privé (*m.*). V. exemple sous **bank rate.**

market syndicate, syndicat de bourse (*m:*).

market transactions, transactions boursières (*f.pl.*); opérations de bourse (*f.pl.*).

market value, valeur marchande (*f.*); valeur vénale (*f.*).

marketable (*adj.*), marchand, -e; vendable; de vente; vénal, -e, -aux; négociable:
  marketable goods, marchandises vendables (*f.pl.*); marchandise de vente (*f.*).
  the marketable value of an article, la valeur marchande (*ou* vénale) d'un objet.
  if the marketable value of the stock is higher than its face value, si la valeur vénale du titre est supérieure à sa valeur nominale.
  stocks marketable on the stock exchange, titres négociables en bourse (*m.pl.*).

marking (Com., etc.) (*n.*), marquage (*m.*).

marking (stamping) (*n.*), estampillage (*m.*).

marking (Stock Exch.) (*n.*). V. **mark** *or* **marking.**

marking clerk (Stock Exch.), coteur (*m.*).

married woman engaged in business, femme mariée commerçante (*f.*).

marry (Stock Exch. orders) (*v.t.*), faire l'application. V. exemple sous syn. **cross.**

marrying (Stock Exch. orders) (*n.*), application (*f.*).

mass (aggregate) (*n.*), masse (*f.*):
  mass of coin in circulation, masse des espèces monnayées en circulation.
  right highly advantageous to the mass of creditors, droit éminemment favorable à la masse des créanciers (*m.*).
  to reduce little by little the crushing mass of the floating debt, réduire peu à peu la masse écrasante de la dette flottante.
  mass to be made good (opp. to *contributory mass*) (General Average), masse créancière (*f.*); masse active (*f.*); valeurs créancières (*f.pl.*); valeurs actives (*f.pl.*). V. exemple sous syn. **amounts to be made good.**

mass production, production en masse (*f.*).

master (pers.) (*n.*), maître (*m.*); capitaine (*m.*); patron (*m.*); préposant (*m.*): (V. aussi **captain.**)
  the captain is master of his ship under God, le capitaine est maître de son navire après Dieu.
  « Ah ! si j'avais été Maître de la Mer ! . . . » NAPOLÉON, à Sainte-Hélène, "Ah ! if I had been Master of the Sea ! . . ." NAPOLEON, at Saint Helena.
  the master and the crew, le capitaine et l'équipage.
  master of coasting vessel, maître au cabotage; capitaine au cabotage.
  master of foreign-going vessel, capitaine au long cours.
  to find oneself master of the situation, se trouver maître de la situation.
  master and servant, maître et préposé; patron et préposé; préposant et préposé.

master porter (Shipping), entrepreneur de chargement (*m.*); entrepreneur de déchargement (*m.*); entrepreneur de chargement et de déchargement (*m.*).

match (Stock Exch. orders) (*v.t.*), faire l'application. V. exemple sous syn. **cross.**

match shares, valeurs d'allumettes (*f.pl.*).

matching (Stock Exch. orders) (*n.*), application (*f.*).

mate (pers.) (Navig.) (*n.*), second officier (*m.*); second (*m.*).

mate's receipt (Abbrev.: **m/r.** *or* **M.R.**), bon de bord (*m.*); bon de chargement (*m.*); reçu de bord (*m.*); reçu provisoire (*m.*); reçu de navire (*m.*); reçu pour (*ou* d') embarquement (*m.*); billet de bord (*m.*); billet d'embarquement (*m.*); bulletin de chargement (*m.*); certificat de chargement (*m.*); mate's receipt (*m.*).

material fact, fait matériel (*m.*).

mathematical premium (Insce) (opp. to *gross*, or *office*, *premium*), prime nette (*f.*).

matter (*n.*), affaire (*f.*):
  current matters, affaires courantes.

matter of course (as a). V. sous **course.**

mature (*v.i.*), échoir; écheoir:
  the bill matures to-morrow, le billet échoit demain.
  bills to mature, papier à échéance (*m.*).

matured (*adj.*), échu, -e.

maturity [**maturities** *pl.*] (*n.*), échéance (*f.*):
  to pay a bill of exchange at maturity, at its maturity date, payer une lettre de change à l'échéance, à la date de son échéance.

maximum (*adj.*), maximum:
  the maximum amount of the issue, le montant maximum de l'émission.
  maximum line (Insce), plein maximum (*m.*).
  good stocks have no maximum price, les bons titres n'ont pas de cours maximum (*m.pl.*).
  maximum risk, risque maximum (*m.*) [risques maxima *ou* risques maximums *pl.*].
  maximum value, valeur maximum (*f.*) [valeurs maxima *ou* valeurs maximums *pl.*].

maximum [**maxima** *or* **maximums** *pl.*] (*n.*), maximum (*m.*):
  loss which reaches its maximum, perte qui atteint son maximum (*f.*).
  to look for judicious investments presenting a minimum of risk and assuring a maximum of revenue, rechercher des placements judicieux, présentant un minimum de risque et assurant un maximum de revenu.

McKenna duties, droits McKenna (*m.pl.*).

mean (*adj.*), moyen, -enne:
  mean due date, échéance moyenne (*f.*); échéance commune (*f.*).

means (resources) (*n.pl.*), moyens (*m.pl.*):
  means of production, moyens de production.
  to have means, avoir des moyens.

measure (step) (*n.*), mesure (*f.*); démarche (*f.*):
  measures taken for the common safety of the ship and cargo, mesures prises pour le salut commun du navire et de la cargaison.

measure (to gauge) (*v.t.*), jauger :
to measure a ship, jauger un navire.

measurement (gauging) (*n.*), jaugeage (*m.*) :
the tonnage of a ship results from a technical operation, measurement : measurement of ships is the operation which has for its object to determine the cubic capacity of the holds, le tonnage d'un navire résulte d'une opération technique, le jaugeage : le jaugeage des navires est l'opération qui a pour objet de déterminer la capacité cubique des cales.

measurement (cubic measurement) (*n.*), cubage (*m.*) ; cube (*m.*) ; volume (*m.*) ; encombrement (*m.*) :
to pay by measurement for cargo whose density is lower than a given figure, payer au cubage (*ou* au volume) (*ou* à l'encombrement) les marchandises dont la densité est inférieure à un chiffre donné.

measurement converted into weight, cubage converti en poids.

to quote the freight at such a rate, weight or measurement, coter le fret à tel taux, poids ou encombrement (*ou* poids ou cube).

measurement goods *or* **measurement cargo** *or* **measure goods** (opp. to *weight cargo* or *deadweight cargo*), marchandises légères (*f.pl.*) ; marchandises de cubage (*f.pl.*) ; marchandises d'encombrement (*f.pl.*).

measurement ton, tonneau d'encombrement (*m.*) ; tonne d'encombrement (*f.*) ; tonneau à l'encombrement (*m.*) ; tonneau de capacité (*m.*) ; tonneau de mer (*m.*) ; tonne de mer (*f.*).

medical (*adj.*), médical, -e, -aux :
medical certificate, certificat médical (*m.*) ; certificat de médecin (*m.*).

medical inspection of passengers and crew, visite médicale des passagers et de l'équipage (*f.*).

medical officer of health (at a port) (*Abbrev. :* M.O.H.), médecin sanitaire maritime (*m.*) ; agent du service sanitaire (*m.*).

Mediterranean port, port de la Méditerranée (*m.*).

meet (to satisfy ; to answer) (*v.t.*), faire face à ; faire honneur à :
to meet a demand, current expenses, daily withdrawals, faire face à une demande, aux dépenses courantes, aux retraits quotidiens.

to meet one's engagements, faire honneur à ses engagements.

meet (bills of exchange) (*v.t.*), faire face à ; accueillir ; faire bon accueil à ; faire accueil à ; faire honneur à ; honorer :
to meet a bill, a draft, faire face à une échéance ; accueillir, faire bon accueil à, faire accueil à, faire honneur à, un effet, une traite, une disposition.

the first point that interests the discounter is the certainty that the discounted bill will be met at maturity, le premier point qui intéresse l'escompteur c'est la certitude que l'effet escompté sera honoré à l'échéance.

meet (*v.i.*), s'assembler ; se réunir :
after their appointment the directors meet as a board to choose some one of their number to be chairman, après leur nomination les administrateurs se réunissent en conseil pour choisir entre eux un président.

meet with (to) (to experience), éprouver :
to meet with losses on the stock exchange, éprouver des pertes à la bourse.

meeting (satisfying ; discharging) (*n.*), bonne fin (*f.*) :
to become surety for someone is to guarantee the meeting of the engagements contracted by him with a third party, se porter caution pour quelqu'un, c'est garantir la bonne fin des engagements pris par lui envers un tiers.

the endorsers are jointly and severally liable for meeting the bills to which they have appended their signature, les endosseurs sont solidairement responsables de la bonne fin des effets sur lesquels ils ont apposé leur signature (*m.pl.*).

meeting (assembly) (*n.*), assemblée (*f.*) ; réunion (*f.*) ; conseil (*m.*) ; conférence (*f.*) :
meeting of shareholders, of creditors, assemblée, réunion, d'actionnaires, de créanciers.

board meeting *or* meeting of directors, réunion du conseil d'administration ; conseil des administrateurs.

to hold a meeting, tenir conseil.

meeting of heads (*or* managers) of departments, conférence de chefs de service.

meeting (sitting) (*n.*), séance (*f.*) :
to open the meeting, ouvrir la séance.

the minutes of the last meeting were read and confirmed, le procès-verbal de la dernière séance est lu et adopté.

member (pers.) (*n.*), membre (*m.*) ; adhérent (*m.*) :
the members of a committee, of the board, les membres d'un comité, du conseil d'administration.

member of a mutual company (*or* society) (e.g., a mutual insurance company or society), mutuelliste (*m. ou f.*) ; mutualiste (*m. ou f.*).

member of a (*or* of the) syndicate, membre, adhérent, d'un (*ou* du) syndicat ; syndicataire (*m.*).

member of the company *or simply* member, membre de la société (*m.*) ; associé, -e ; sociétaire (*m. ou f.*) :
a shareholder is a member of the company, a debenture holder is a lending creditor of the company, l'actionnaire est un associé, l'obligataire est un créancier prêteur de la société (*m.*).

auditor who is also a member of the company, commissaire qui est aussi associé (*ou* sociétaire) (*m.*).

members of the crew, membres de l'équipage (*m.pl.*) ; gens de l'équipage (*m.pl.*) ; hommes d'équipage (*m.pl.*).

to be a member of, faire partie de :
he is a member of the committee, il fait partie du comité.

membership (state of being a member) (n.),
qualité de membre (f.) ;   qualité (f.) :
to acquire membership (or to become a member)
of a syndicate,   acquérir la qualité de
membre d'un syndicat.
membership of the committee does not confer,
ipso facto, the right of admission to the
committee's premises, la qualité de membre
du comité ne confère pas, ipso facto, le
droit d'entrée dans les locaux du comité.
any member leaving the association or losing
his membership,   tout membre quittant
l'association ou perdant sa qualité.

membership (joining) (n.), adhésion (f.) :
the conditions of membership of an association, les conditions d'adhésion à une association.

membership (seat) (n.), charge (f.) ;   office (m.) :
stockbroker who buys membership from his
predecessor, agent de change qui achète la
charge (ou l'office) à son prédécesseur (m.).

membership (number of adherents) (n.), nombre
des adhérents (m.) ;   nombre des adhésions
(f.) :
the duration of this association is unlimited
as well as the membership, which may be
recruited as well in the country as in London,
la durée de cette association est illimitée
ainsi que le nombre des adhérents, qui
peuvent être recrutés aussi bien en province
qu'à Londres.

memorandum [**memorandums** or **memoranda** pl.]
(n.) (Abbrev.: **memo.**), mémorandum (m.) ;
note (f.) :
for minor correspondence, the memorandum
is used, on small sized paper, pour la correspondance de détail, on se sert du mémorandum, sur papier de petit format.

memorandum (as a), pour mémoire :
the amounts written off are shown only as a
memorandum,   les amortissements ne
figurent que pour mémoire (m.pl.).

memorandum (of percentages) (Mar. Insce policy)
(n.), mémorandum (m.), tableau (m.) (de
pourcentages) :
the goods designated as free of particular
average in the memorandum,   les marchandises désignées comme franc d'avarie
particulière au tableau (f.pl.).
Note :—In French policies the franchises figure
in the form of a table or list (called tableau) :
in English policies the percentages are given
in the form of a memorandum or note (called
memorandum).

memorandum book, carnet (m.) ; mémorandum
(m.) ;   calepin (m.).

memorandum books (opp. to financial, or account,
books), livres d'ordre (m.pl.) ;   livres de
statistique (m.pl.) ; registres d'ordre (m.pl.).

memorandum of association or simply **memorandum** (n.) or **memorandum and articles,**
statuts (m.pl.) :   (Note :—In France, the
memorandum and articles are all in one and
are called statuts.   In England, the memorandum of association is the charter of the
company and defines its powers, whilst the

articles of association (q.v.) form a code of
regulations for the internal management of
its affairs.)
a company may not undertake any business not
provided for under its memorandum, une
société ne peut entreprendre aucune opération
non prévue par ses statuts.

memorandum of insurance, arrêté d'assurance
(m.) ;   arrêté provisoire (m.) ;   arrêté (m.).

memorandum pad, bloc-notes (m.) ;   block-notes
(m.).

memory tickler, tickler (m.).

menace (n.), menace (f.) :
menace of ruin, of dismissal, menace de ruine,
de renvoi.

menace (v.t.), menacer.

mental arithmetic, arithmétique mentale (f.).

mention (n.), mention (f.) ;   constation (f.) :
mention on the bill of lading of the name of
the master, mention sur le connaissement
du nom du capitaine.
although this law makes no mention of it in
the particulars that a bill of lading should
contain, the date is an important element,
quoique cette loi n'en fasse pas mention
dans les indications que doit porter le connaissement, la date est un élément important.

mention (v.t.), mentionner ;   constater :
the quantity mentioned in the bill of lading,
la quantité mentionnée (ou constatée) au
connaissement.

mercantile (adj.), mercantile ;   marchand, -e ;
commercial, -e, -aux ;   commerçant, -e :
mercantile agency, agence de renseignements
(f.).
mercantile business,   opérations mercantiles
(ou commerciales) (f.pl.).
mercantile marine, marine marchande (f.) :
the mercantile marine of a country is the
collection of seagoing vessels employed in
trade, la marine marchande d'un pays est
l'ensemble des bâtiments de mer consacrés
aux transactions commerciales.
mercantile paper or mercantile bills (bills of
exchange), papier de commerce (m.) ;   papier
commercial (m.).
mercantile port, port marchand (m.) ;   port
commercial (m.) ;   port de commerce (m.).

mercantilism (n.), mercantilisme (m.).

mercantilist (pers.) (n.), mercantiliste (m.).

mercantilistic (adj.), mercantiliste :
mercantilistic policy, politique mercantilis
(f.).

merchandise (n.sing.), marchandise (f.) ;   marchandises (f.pl.) :   (Note :—The plural mer-
chandises is obsolete, but is still retained in
Lloyd's marine insurance policy.)
passengers' luggage is not considered as
merchandise, les baggages des voyageurs
ne sont pas considérés comme marchandises
(m.pl.).
bills of exchange being but the representative
sign of money, can be considered as merchandise, which is sold or bought at a greater
or less price, les lettres de change n'étant

que le signe représentatif des monnaies, peuvent être considérées comme une marchandise, que l'on vend ou que l'on achète à un prix plus ou moins élevé (*f.pl.*).

merchandise traffic, trafic des marchandises (*m.*).

merchandise train, train de marchandises (*m.*); convoi de marchandises (*m.*); train de petite vitesse (*m.*); petite vitesse (*f.*).

merchant (*adj.*), marchand, -e:
merchant marine *or* merchant service *or* merchant shipping, marine marchande (*f.*).
merchant shipping act, loi (anglaise) sur la marine marchande (*f.*).
merchant vessel, navire marchand (*m.*); bâtiment marchand (*m.*); navire de commerce (*m.*); bâtiment de commerce (*m.*); bateau de commerce (*m.*).

merchant (pers.) (*n.*), négociant, -e; commerçant, -e:
commission merchant, négociant-commissionnaire.
shippers are merchants engaging in import trade and export trade, les chargeurs sont des commerçants se livrant au commerce d'exportation et au commerce d'importation (*m.pl.*).

merchantable (*adj.*), marchand, -e.

merchantman [**merchantmen** *pl.*] (*n.*). *Syn. de* merchant vessel.

mere delivery. V. sous **delivery** (Law).

merge (*v.t.*), fusionner.

merge (*v.i.*), fusionner; se fusionner.

merging *or* **merger** (*n.*), fusion (*f.*); fusionnement (*m.*):
merging (*or* merger) of several banks, fusion de plusieurs banques.

message (*n.*), message (*m.*); dépêche (*f.*):
a message states, on mande; un message annonce:
a message from Lisbon states that . . ., on mande de Lisbonne que . . .
a message from Lloyd's agent at Lisbon states that . . ., un message de l'agent du Lloyd à Lisbonne annonce que . . .
message telephoned from a public call office, message téléphoné d'une cabine publique.

messenger (pers.) (*n.*), messager, -ère; porteur (*m.*):
special messenger, messager spécial; porteur spécial.

messenger (commissionaire) (pers.) (*n.*), garçon de bureau (*m.*).

Messrs. V. **Mr.**

metal (*n.*), métal (*m.*):
precious metal, métal précieux.
yellow metal (gold), white metal (silver), red metal (copper), métal jaune (or), métal blanc (argent), métal rouge (cuivre).

metal market, marché des métaux (*m.*).

metal vessel, navire métallique (*m.*).

metallic (*adj.*), métallique:
metallic money *or* metallic currency, monnaie métallique (*f.*); circulation métallique (*f.*); monnaies de métal (*f.pl.*).
metallic reserve (Banking), réserve métallique (*f.*).

metallic standard (money) (opp. to *paper standard*), étalon métallique (*m.*).

method (*n.*), méthode (*f.*); mode (*m.*).

metric (*adj.*), métrique:
metric system, système métrique (*m.*).

metropolis (*n.*), métropole (*f.*):
London is the most powerful banking, commercial and industrial metropolis of the globe, Londres est la plus puissante métropole bancaire, commerciale et industrielle du globe.

metropolitan (*adj.*), métropolitain, -e:
metropolitan railway (*Abbrev.:* metro. *or simply* met.), chemin de fer métropolitain (*m.*).

mid (*month*) *or* **mid** (*month*) **account** (Stock Exch.), 15 (*m.*) (= le quinze du mois—the fifteenth of the month):
buy so many shares for mid August (*or* for mid August account), achetez tant d'actions pour le 15 août; achetez tant d'actions au 15/8.
(in Paris) settlements on the *parquet* take place on the 15th and the last day of each month. On the *coulisse* settlements take place only at the end of the month, les liquidations au parquet ont lieu le 15 et le dernier jour de chaque mois. En coulisse, les liquidations n'ont lieu qu'à fin de mois. *See* marché des valeurs *for explanation of the words* parquet *and* coulisse.
Note:—On the Paris Bourse, mid month contango day is always on the 15th day of the month (or on the first business day after the 15th, if the 15th falls on a non business day), and the end month contango day is on the last day of the month (or the first business day after, if the last day of the month falls on a non business day).
On the London Stock Exchange, settlement dates are fixed periodically by the Stock Exchange Committee. Settlements now take place in London every fortnight with occasional variations, as at holiday times, consequently the terms *mid account* and *end account* are no longer used.

Mid European time *or* **Mid Europe time** (Abbrev.: **M.E.T.**), heure de l'Europe Centrale (*f.*). (1 p.m. [13 heures] in relation to **West European time,** q.v.).

middle (average) (*adj.*), moyen, -enne:
at the middle price *or* at middle, au cours moyen.
Note:—In France, orders are frequently given to be executed at middle, which is the arithmetical mean between the highest and lowest prices of the day. This price is not known until the close of the Bourse. This method does not obtain on the London Stock Exchange.

middle four *or* **middle 4** (May, June, July, August) (Produce Exch.), quatre (*ou* 4) de mai (*m.pl.*); quatre chauds (*m.pl.*); **mois chauds** (*m.pl.*); chauds (*m.pl.*).

middleman [**middlemen** *pl.*] (*n.*), intermédiaire (*m.*):
mere middlemen who buy to resell (*or* to sell

again), simples intermédiaires qui achètent
pour revendre.

mile (nautical) (*n.*), mille (marin) (*m.*) :
in maritime navigation, all distances are
reckoned in miles, en marine, on évalue
toutes les distances en milles.

milk van (Rly.), wagon-laitière (*m.*).

mill (*n.*), usine (*f.*) ; fabrique (*f.*).

millionaire *or* **millionnaire** (pers.) (*n.*), millionnaire (*m.* ou *f.*) :
an American millionaire, un millionnaire
américain.

millionary (*adj.*), millionnaire.

mineral rights duty, redevance des mines (*f.*).

minimize a loss (to), atténuer une perte.

minimum (*adj.*), minimum :
the minimum number of shares fixed by the
articles, le nombre minimum d'actions
fixé par les statuts.

minimum interest, intérêt minimum (*m.*) ;
intérêts minima (*m.pl.*) ; intérêts minimums
(*m.pl.*).

minimum value, valeur minimum (*f.*). [valeurs
minima *ou* valeurs minimums *pl.*]

minimum [minima *or* minimums *pl.*] (*n.*), minimum (*m.*) :
so much per 100 francs with a minimum of so
much per bill, tant par 100 francs avec un
minimum de tant par effet.

bank where the minimum of admissible bills
is so many pounds, banque où le minimum
des effets admissibles est de tant de livres.

mining shares *or* **mines** (*n.pl.*), valeurs de mines
(*f.pl.*) ; valeurs minières (*f.pl.*) ; mines
(*f.pl.*) :
mines were supported (Stock Exch.), les
mines étaient soutenues.

minor (pers.) (*n.*), mineur, -e :
minors are not capable of contracting, les
mineurs ne sont aptes à contracter.

minor coin, appoint (*m.*). *V. exemple sous syn.*
small coin.

minority [minorities *pl.*] (*n.*), minorité (*f.*) :
the minority conforms to the resolution passed
by the majority, la minorité se conforme à
la décision prise par la majorité.

mint (*n.*), hôtel de la Monnaie (*m.*) ; hôtel des
Monnaies (*m.*) ; Monnaie (*f.*) :
there is only one mint in England, namely the
one in London, il n'y a qu'un seul hôtel
des Monnaies (*ou* il n'y a qu'une Monnaie)
en Angleterre, c'est celui (*ou* celle) de
Londres.

mint (*v.t.*), monnayer ; frapper ; battre :
to mint gold, monnayer, frapper, l'or.

mint par *or* **mint par of exchange,** pair intrinsèque (*m.*) ; pair métallique (*m.*) ; pair du
change (*m.*) ; pair (*m.*) :
the mint par of the pound sterling compared
with the French franc is 124 fr. 21 (more
exactly 124·2134), le pair intrinsèque (*ou*
métallique) de la livre sterling comparée
au franc français est 124 fr. 21 (plus exactement 124,2134).

minted money, argent monnayé (*m.*) ; espèces
monnayées (*f.pl.*).

minting (*n.*), monnayage (*m.*) ; frappe (*f.*).

minus (Arith.) (*adj.*), moins (*prép.*) :
ten minus four equals six (*Abbrev.* : 10 − 4 =
6), dix moins quatre égale six (*Abbrev.* :
10 − 4 = 6).

minus (*n.*) *or* **minus sign,** moins (*m.*) :
you should have put a plus, you have put a
minus, il fallut un plus, vous avez mis un
moins.

minus or plus difference, différence en moins
ou en plus (*f.*).

minute (*n.*) *or* **minutes** (*n.pl.*), procès-verbal (*m.*) :
to draw up the minutes of proceedings of a
meeting, dresser procès-verbal des délibérations d'une assemblée (*ou* d'une réunion).

minutes of meetings, procès-verbaux d'assemblées.

board minutes *or* minutes of proceedings of
the board of directors, procès-verbal des
délibérations du conseil d'administration.

the minutes of the last meeting were read and
confirmed, le procès-verbal de la dernière
séance est lu et adopté.

Note :—Recordings of formal proceedings in
minutes, reports, and the like, always in
the past tense in English, are usually in
the present tense in French.

minute book, registre des délibérations (*m.*) ;
registre des procès-verbaux (*m.*).

minute charge (Teleph.), taxe-minuti (*f.*) :
the minute charge is a third of the charge
made for three minutes, la taxe-minute est
le tiers de la taxe appliquée pour trois
minutes.

misappropriate *or* **misapply** (*v.t.*), détourner.

misappropriation *or* **misapplication** (*n.*), détournement (*m.*) ; divertissement (*m.*) ; violation
(*f.*) :
misappropriation (*or* misapplication) of funds,
détournement, divertissement, de fonds.

misappropriation of trust funds, violation de
dépôt.

misapplication of public funds, violation de
dépôts publics.

miscalculate (*v.i.*), se mécompter.

miscalculation (*n.*), mécompte (*m.*).

miscarriage (failure to transport properly) (*n.*),
égarement (*m.*).

miscarried (*p.p.* or *adj.*), non parvenu, -e ;
égaré, -e :
applications concerning money orders which
have miscarried, concerning orders presumed to have miscarried, réclamations
concernant les mandats non parvenus, concernant les mandats présumés non parvenus
(*f.pl.*).

miscarry (*v.i.*), s'égarer.

miscellaneous shares *or simply* **miscellaneous,**
valeurs diverses (*f.pl.*) ; diverses ; divers.

misdeliver (*v.t.*), livrer par erreur :
postal packet misdelivered to a person other
than the real addressee, correspondance
livrée par erreur à une personne autre que
le véritable destinataire (*f.*).

misdelivery [misdeliveries *pl.*] (*n.*), livraison
par erreur (*f.*).

misenter (Bkkpg) (*v.t.*), contre-poser.
misentry [**misentries** *pl.*] (Bkkpg) (*n.*), contre-position (*f.*) :
    misentry of an item in the books, contre-position d'un article sur les livres.
mislay (*v.t.*), égarer :
    to mislay papers, égarer des papiers.
mislaying (*n.*), égarement (*m.*).
misprint (*n.*), faute d'impression (*f.*) ; erreur typographique (*f.*).
miss (*v.t.*), manquer :
    to miss a train, a boat, a connection, an opportunity, manquer un train, un bateau, une correspondance, une occasion.
missing (*adj.*), manquant, -e ; de manque :
    missing packages, colis manquants (*m.pl.*).
    to find two shillings missing in a five pound bag, trouver deux schellings de manque dans un sac de cinq livres.
missing (to be), manquer ; faire défaut :
    if a part of the articles is missing on delivery, si une partie des objets manque (*ou* fait défaut) à la livraison.
missing (said of a ship) (*p.pr.* & *adj.*), sans nouvelles ; perdu sans nouvelles :
    ship deemed to be missing, navire réputé perdu sans nouvelles (*m.*).
    loss of the ship as missing, perte du navire sans nouvelles (*f.*).
    missing ship, navire sans nouvelles (*m.*) ; navire perdu sans nouvelles (*m.*).
misstatement *or* **misrepresentation** (*n.*), déclaration inexacte (*f.*) ; fausse déclaration (*f.*) ; déclaration fausse (*f.*).
mistake (*n.*), erreur (*f.*) ; mécompte (*m.*) :
    mistake in calculation, in addition, erreur de calcul, d'addition.
    addition in which there is a mistake, addition dans laquelle il y a du mécompte (*f.*).
    entry cancelled in (*or* by) mistake, écriture annulée par erreur (*f.*).
mixed (*adj.*), mixte :
    mixed cargo, cargaison mixte (*f.*).
    mixed sea and land risks, risques mixtes maritimes et terrestres (*m.pl.*).
    mixed train (passengers and goods), train mixte (*m.*).
mobilizable (*adj.*), mobilisable :
    money (*or* capital) invested in industrials is not always easy mobilizable, les capitaux placés en valeurs industrielles ne sont pas toujours facilement mobilisables (*m.pl.*).
mobilization (*n.*), mobilisation (*f.*) :
    mobilization of capital (*or* of money), mobilisation de capital (*ou* de capitaux).
    mobilization of realty (Law), mobilisation d'immeubles.
mobilize (*v.t.*), mobiliser :
    the money immobilized (i.e., locked up) in a bill of exchange, is mobilized (i.e., set free) as soon as the bill is paid, le capital immobilisé dans une lettre de change est mobilisé dès que la lettre est payée.
    the seller is compelled to immobilize (*or* to lock up) his capital in the credit he gives to his customer : the bill of exchange enables

him to mobilize his debt, to obtain the amount of it by discount before its due date, le vendeur est astreint à immobiliser ses capitaux dans le crédit qu'il fait à son client : la lettre de change lui permet de mobiliser sa créance, d'en obtenir par l'escompte, le montant avant son échéance.
to be mobilized, se mobiliser :
    immovable property is capable of being mobilized (i.e., converted into movable property) in certain cases, les immeubles peuvent se mobiliser dans certains cas (*m.pl.*).
mode (*n.*), mode (*m.*) :
    mode of paying off by annual instalments, mode annuitaire d'acquittement.
moderate (*adj.*), modique :
    moderate income, revenus modiques (*m.pl.*).
modest (*adj.*), modeste :
    a modest expenditure, a modest fortune, une dépense modeste, une fortune modeste.
modification (*n.*), modification (*f.*) :
    modification of the terms of a contract, modification des clauses d'un contrat.
    modifications suggested by experience, modifications suggérées par l'expérience.
modify (*v.t.*), modifier.
mole (pier) (*n.*), môle (*m.*).
moment (*n.*), moment (*m.*) :
    the price ruling at the moment of declaration of options, le cours pratiqué au moment de la déclaration des primes.
monetarily (*adv.*), monétairement.
monetary (*adj.*), monétaire :
    monetary standard, étalon monétaire (*m.*). V. exemple sous **standard coin.**
    the French monetary unit is the franc, l'unité monétaire française est le franc (*f.*).
monetization (*n.*), monétisation (*f.*).
monetize (*v.t.*), monétiser :
    to monetize silver, monétiser de l'argent.
money [**moneys** *or* **monies** *pl.*] (*n.*), argent (*m.*) ; monnaie (*f.*) ; numéraire (*m.*) ; fonds (*m.pl.*) ; capital (*m.*) ; capitaux (*m.pl.*) ; valeurs (*f.pl.*) ; finances (*f.pl.*) :
    money is scarce, l'argent est rare ; les capitaux sont rares.
    foreign money, monnaie étrangère.
    silver money, monnaie d'argent ; numéraire d'argent ; argent.
    shares hypothecated as security for money advanced, actions remises en nantissement en garantie de fonds avancés (*f.pl.*).
    money at (*or* on) call (Banking), argent remboursable sur demande ; argent à vue ; prêts remboursables sur demande (*m.pl.*).
    money lent (on stock taken in) (Stock Exch.), capital reporteur ; capitaux reporteurs.
    money lying idle, argent qui dort ; argent mort.
    money of account, monnaie de compte :
    money of account is that in which sums are expressed in transactions and in commercial accounts : thus, in France, the money of account consists of the 1 franc piece and of the 1 centime piece, or, as is said,

in France they reckon in francs and centimes, la monnaie de compte est celle par laquelle les sommes sont exprimées dans les transactions et dans les écritures de commerce : ainsi, en France, la monnaie de compte se compose de la pièce de 1 franc et de la pièce de 1 centime, ou, comme on dit, on compte en France par francs et centimes.

in France, the franc is at the same time real money, money of account, and money of exchange, en France, le franc est à la fois monnaie réelle, monnaie de compte, et monnaie de change.

the English guinea is only a money of account, la guinée anglaise n'est qu'une monnaie de compte.

money of exchange, monnaie de change ; monnaie d'échange.

real money or **effective money,** monnaie réelle ; monnaie effective ; valeurs effectives.

money put up or **money invested** or **amount of money invested,** mise de fonds (*f.*) ; mise (*f.*) :

profit which is equal to so much per cent on the money put up, bénéfice qui correspond à tant pour cent de la mise de fonds (*m.*).

the transport of money by railway, le transport des finances par chemin de fer.

for money (for cash) (Stock Exch.), au comptant :

dealing for money (cash bargain), négociation au comptant (*f.*) ; marché au comptant (*m.*).

money changer or **money dealer** or **money jobber,** changeur, -euse ; changeur de monnaie (*m.*) :

money changers were the ancestors of modern bankers, les changeurs ont été les ancêtres des banquiers modernes.

money exchange (opp. to *bill exchange*), change réel (*m.*) ; change manuel (*m.*) ; change menu (*m.*) ; change local (*m.*).

money grubber or **money grub,** grippe-argent (*m.*) ; homme d'argent (*m.*).

money lender, bailleur de fonds (*m.*).

money market, marché de l'argent (*m.*) ; marché monétaire (*m.*) ; marché des monnaies (*m.*) ; marché des capitaux (*m.*) :

the banks of issue are the governors of the money market, les banques d'émission sont le régulateur du marché de l'argent (*f.pl.*).

money market or **money market intelligence** (article in a newspaper), bulletin de la bourse (*m.*).

money order (Abbrev. : **M.O.**), mandat de poste (*m.*) ; mandat-poste (*m.*) ; mandat postal (*m.*) ; mandat (*m.*) :

free money order for payment of taxes, mandat-contribution (*m.*).

money order telegram, télégramme-mandat (*m.*).

money rates, taux monétaires (*m.pl.*) ; taux de l'argent (*m.pl.*).

money token, jeton-monnaie (*m.*).

moneyed (flush of money) (*adj.*), pécunieux, -euse :

moneyed man, homme pécunieux (*m.*) ; richard (*m.*).

monometalism or **monometallism** (*n.*), monométallisme (*m.*).

monometalist or **monometallist** (pers.) (*n.*), monométalliste (*m.*).

monometallic (*adj.*), monométalliste :

according as a State adopts a single standard or a double standard it is said to be monometallic or bimetallistic, suivant qu'un État adopte un étalon unique ou un étalon double il est dit monométalliste ou bimétalliste.

monoplane (*n.*), monoplan (*m.*).

monopolist (pers.) (*n.*), monopoleur (*m.*) ; monopolisateur (*m.*).

monopolization (*n.*), monopolisation (*f.*).

monopolize (*v.t.*), monopoliser :

to monopolize the sale of tobacco, monopoliser la vente de tabac.

monopoly [**monopolies** *pl.*] (*n.*), monopole (*m.*) :

monopoly which makes any competition impossible, monopole qui rend toute concurrence impossible.

monopoly is the negation of competition, le monopole est la négation de la concurrence.

month (*n.*) (Abbrev. : **m.** or **mo.** [**mos** *pl.*] or **mth**), mois (*m.*) :

to obtain a month's credit, obtenir un mois de crédit.

three months' paper or bills at 3 months, papier à trois mois (*m.*) ; papier à 3 mois d'échéance (*m.*).

month's pay or **month's salary** or **month's wages,** mois (*m.*) :

to draw one's month's pay, toucher son mois.

monthly (*adj.*), mensuel, -elle ; au mois :

monthly report, rapport mensuel (*m.*).

monthly cheque, drawings, payment, or the like, mensualité (*f.*) :

monthly drawings of partners, mensualités des associés.

monthly statement, relevé de fin de mois (*m.*) ; fin de mois (*f.*).

monthly money or monthly loans or monthly fixtures (Money. Market), argent au mois (*m.*) ; prêts au mois (*m.pl.*).

monthly (*adv.*), mensuellement :

settlement of the premiums is made, as a rule, quarterly or monthly, le règlement des primes se fait, en règle générale, trimestriellement ou mensuellement.

moor (Navig.) (*v.t.*), amarrer ; mouiller.

moor (Navig.) (*v.i.*), s'amarrer ; mouiller.

mooring (Navig.) (*n.*), amarrage (*m.*) ; mouillage (*m.*).

moorings (*n.pl.*), mouillage (*m.*).

moratorium [**moratoria** *pl.*] (*n.*), moratorium (*m.*) :

credit institutions who took advantage of the moratorium in order not to repay their deposits during the first months of the war, établissements de crédit qui se prévalurent du moratorium pour ne pas rembourser leurs dépôts dans les premiers mois de la guerre (*m.pl.*).

moratory (*adj.*), moratoire.

more doing *or* **more business,** plus d'affaires:
more doing in industrials (Stock Exch.), plus
d'affaires aux industrielles.

mortgage (*n.*) (Abbrev.: **mort.** *or* **mortg.** *or*
mge *or* **mt.**), hypothèque (*f.*):
to have a mortgage on a property, avoir
hypothèque sur un bien.
the mortgage of English law corresponds, with
wide differences however, to the *hypothèque*
of French law, le *mortgage* du droit anglais
correspond, avec de grandes différences
toutefois, à l'hypothèque du droit français.
by mortgage *or* **on mortgage,** hypothécairement:
to be bound by mortgage, être obligé (-e)
hypothécairement.
debt secured by mortgage, créance garantie
hypothécairement (*f.*).
to borrow on mortgage, emprunter hypothécairement.

mortgage (*v.t.*), hypothéquer:
to mortgage a house, a ship, one's share in a
ship, the ship during the voyage for the
needs of the adventure, hypothéquer une
maison, un navire, sa part dans un navire,
le navire en cours de route pour les besoins
de l'expédition.

mortgage charge, affectation hypothécaire (*f.*);
privilège d'hypothèque (*m.*).

mortgage creditor *or* **creditor on mortgage,**
créancier hypothécaire (*m.*). V. exemple
sous **creditor.**

mortgage debenture *or* **mortgage bond** (opp. to
simple, or *naked*, *debenture*), obligation
hypothécaire (*f.*). Cf. first mortgage debentures.

mortgage debt *or* **debt on mortgage,** dette
hypothécaire (*f.*); créance hypothécaire (*f.*).

mortgage debtor, débiteur hypothécaire (*m.*).

mortgage deed, contrat d'hypothèque (*m.*);
contrat hypothécaire (*m.*); acte d'hypothèque (*m.*).

mortgage duty, taxe hypothécaire (*f.*).

mortgage loan *or* **loan on mortgage,** emprunt
hypothécaire (*m.*); prêt hypothécaire (*m.*).

mortgage registry, bureau des hypothèques
(*m.*).

mortgageable (*adj.*), hypothécable:
mortgageable property, biens hypothécables
(*m.pl.*).

mortgagee (pers.) (*n.*), créancier hypothécaire
(*m.*).

mortgagor (pers.) (*n.*), débiteur hypothécaire
(*m.*).

most convenient port, port le plus convenable
(*m.*).

most favoured nation (Polit. Econ.), nation la
plus favorisée (*f.*).

most favoured nation clause, clause de la nation
la plus favorisée (*f.*).

most favoured nation treatment, traitement de
la nation la plus favorisée (*f.*).

mother country (as opposed to *colonies* or *foreign
possessions*), mère patrie (*f.*); métropole
(*f.*):

the natural bond between the mother country
and her overseas possessions, le lien naturel
entre la mère patrie (*ou* la métropole) et
ses possessions d'outre-mer.

motor bicycle, motocyclette (*f.*).

motor bus *or* **motor omnibus,** autobus (*m.*);
omnibus automobile (*m.*).

motor car *or* *simply* **motor** (*n.*), automobile
(*m.* ou *f.*); auto (*m.* ou *f.*).

motor car insurance *or* **motor insurance,** assurance des véhicules automobiles (*f.*).

motor liner, paquebot à moteur (*m.*).

motor lorry, camion automobile (*m.*).

motor passenger service, service automobile de
voyageurs (*m.*).

motor shares *or* **motors** (*n.pl.*), valeurs d'automobiles (*f.pl.*); automobiles (*f.pl.*).

motorship. V. ci-après.

Motor Show, Salon de l'Automobile (*m.*).

motor tanker, bateau-citerne à moteur (*m.*);
navire-citerne à moteur (*m.*); moteur-
citerne (*m.*).

motor vehicle, véhicule automobile (*m.*); voiture
automobile (*f.*).

motoring (*n.*), automobilisme (*m.*).

motorist (pers.) (*n.*), automobiliste (*m.* ou *f.*).

motorship (*n.*) *or* **motor vessel** (Abbrev.: **m.v.** *or*
M.V.), navire à moteur (*m.*).

mouth (of a river) (*n.*), bouche (*f.*), embouchure
(*f.*) (d'un fleuve).

movable (Law) (*adj.*), meuble; mobilier, -ère:
movable property *or* movable effects *or*
movables (*n.pl.*), biens meubles (*m.pl.*);
biens mobiliers (*m.pl.*); biens personnels
(*m.pl.*); effets mobiliers (*m.pl.*); effets
personnels (*m.pl.*); meubles (*m.pl.*).
movable exchange, incertain (*m.*). V. to
quote movable exchange *pour exemple*.

move (to propose) (*v.t.*), proposer; faire:
to move an amendment, proposer un amendement.
to move a resolution at a meeting, faire une
proposition à une assemblée.

move (to stir; to budge) (*v.i.*), bouger; se
déplacer:
X. preference moved slightly round about
1¾, la privilégiée X. bouge un peu (*ou* se
déplace légèrement) aux environs de 1 3/4.

move (to fluctuate) (*v.i.*), osciller:
share which moves between 1 and 1¼, action
qui oscille entre 1 et 1 1/4.

move up (**to**), se relever:
X. shares moved up from 1s. to 1s. 3d., l'action X. se relève de 1sh. à 1sh. 3d.

moveable (*adj.* & *n.*). Syn. de **movable.**

movement (*n.*), mouvement (*m.*); déplacement
(*m.*):
movements of money such as issues abroad
or the repayment of credits, mouvements
de capitaux tels que les émissions à l'étranger ou le remboursement de crédits.
an upward movement of stocks, un mouvement de hausse des valeurs.
Movements of Ships (Shipping News), Mouvement des Navires.

moving spirit (pers.), animateur (*m.*):

our chairman, Mr X., the moving spirit of the establishment, notre président, M. X., l'animateur de l'établissement.

Mr [**Messrs** *pl.*] (Mister ; Esquire), M. (Monsieur) [MM. *ou* Mʳˢ (Messieurs) *pl.*] :
Mr X., M. X.
Messrs X. & Co., MM. X. & Cⁱᵉ.

Mr *or* **our Mr** (in speaking of a partner in a firm), notre sieur :
Mr X. will sign : . . ., notre sieur X. signera : . . .

Mr (title given to barristers, etc.), maître :
Mr So-and-so, maître un tel.

multiplane (*n.*), multiplan (*m.*).

multiple (*n.*), multiple (*m.*) :
many companies issue shares called multiples, that is to say, ones and denominations of 5, 10, 25, 50, and 100, shares, beaucoup de sociétés émettent des actions dites multiples, c'est-à-dire des unités et des coupures de 5, 10, 25, 50, et 100, actions.
the bonds are of the nominal value of £10 and multiples, les bons sont du nominal de £10 et multiples (*m.pl.*).

multiple address telegram *or simply* **multiple telegram** (Abbrev. : **TM**.), télégramme à adresses multiples (*m.*) ; télégramme multiple (*m.*).

multiple certificate *or* **certificate for more than one share,** titre multiple (*m.*).

multiple firm, maison à succursales multiples (*f.*).

multiple shares, actions multiples (*f.pl.*).

multiplication (*n.*), multiplication (*f.*).

multiplication table, table de multiplication (*f.*) ; table de Pythagore (*f.*).

multiply (*v.t.*), multiplier :
two multiplied by three equals six (*Abbrev. :* 2 × 3 = 6), deux multiplié par trois égale six (*Abrév. :* 2 × 3 = 6).

multiplying machine, machine à multiplier (*f.*) ; machine multiplicatrice (*f.*).

municipal loans, emprunts de villes (*m.pl.*).

muniment of title, acte de propriété (*m.*) ; titre de propriété (*m.*).

munitions of war, munitions de guerre (*f.pl.*).

mutatis mutandis, mutatis mutandis :
the conditions are the same, mutatis mutandis, les conditions sont les mêmes, mutatis mutandis (*f.pl.*).

mutilated (*adj.*), mutilé, -e :
mutilated certificate, titre mutilé (*m.*).
mutilated word (Teleg.), mot mutilé (*m.*).

mutiny [**mutinies** *pl.*] (*n.*), mutinerie (*f.*).

mutual (*adj.*), mutuel, -elle :
mutual guarantee society, association de cautionnement mutuel (*f.*).
mutual insurance *or* mutual assurance, assurance mutuelle (*f.*).
mutual insurance (*or* assurance) company (*or* society) *or* mutual office (opp. to *proprietary insurance company* or *proprietary office*), compagnie d'assurances mutuelles (*f.*) ; société d'assurances mutuelles (*f.*).
mutual indebtedness. V. sous **indebtedness.**

N

nail (on the) (punctually), recta :
to pay on the nail, payer recta.

naked (loose) (said of oils) (*adj.*) (Abbrev. : **nked** *or* **nkd**) (opp. to *in barrels* or *in drums*), nu, -e :
copra oil.—per 100 kilos naked f.o.r. Marseilles, huiles de coprah.—les 100 kilos nues gare Marseille.

naked debenture (opp. to *mortgage debenture*), obligation chirographaire (*f.*).

naked contract (opp. to *onerous contract*), contrat à titre gratuit (*m.*) ; contrat de bienfaisance (*m.*).

name (*n.*), nom (*m.*) ; dénomination (*f.*) ; raison (*f.*) ; nomenclature (*f.*) ; intitulé (*m.*) :
every ship must have a name, tout navire doit avoir un nom.
name of bearer, of sender, nom du porteur, de l'envoyeur.
to take someone's name and address, prendre le nom et l'adresse (*ou* les nom et adresse) de quelqu'un.
the full name (*or* the name in full), address,

and profession or business (*or* and occupation) (*or* and description) of the applicant, les nom, prénoms, adresse, et profession (*ou* et qualités) du souscripteur.
name of firm, raison sociale ; nom social.
the name of the company is . . . (memorandum of association), la raison sociale est . . . ; la société a pour dénomination . . . ; la société prend la dénomination de . . .
name of stock, of the security, nom, nomenclature, du titre, de la valeur :
receipt which contains the full name of the security lodged, récépissé qui porte la nomenclature complète de la valeur déposée (*m.*).
name of an account, of a ledger account, nom, intitulé, d'un compte, d'un compte du grand livre.

name (*v.t.*), dénommer ; désigner ; énoncer ; mentionner :
to name a person in a deed, dénommer une personne dans un acte.
option of naming (*or* nominating) the ship which is to carry the goods, faculté de

désigner le navire porteur de la marchandise (*f.*).

if a certain ship has been named (*or* nominated) the goods can only be shipped on that vessel, si un navire déterminé a été désigné, les marchandises ne peuvent être embarquées que sur ce navire.

the goods named in the bill of lading, les marchandises énoncées sur le (*ou* mentionnées au) connaissement (*f.pl.*).

named port (a port in the customary or advertised route), port désigné (*m.*); escale (*f.*); port d'escale (*m.*); échelle (*f.*); port d'échelle (*m.*).

named ship, navire désigné (*m.*).

naming (*n.*), dénomination (*f.*); désignation (*f.*); énonciation (*f.*); mention (*f.*):
shipments insured without naming (*or* nomination) of the ship or master, chargements assurés sans désignation du navire ni du capitaine (*m.pl.*).

narration (Bkkpg) (*n.*), libellé (*m.*):
the narration of a journal entry, le libellé d'un article (*ou* d'une écriture) de journal.

nation (*n.*), nation (*f.*):
most favoured nation (Polit. Econ.), nation la plus favorisée.

national (*adj.*), national, -e, -aux; public, -ique:
national bank, banque nationale (*f.*); banque publique (*f.*).
national debt, dette publique (*f.*); dette nationale (*f.*).
national law, droit national (*m.*).
national loan, emprunt national (*m.*).

nationality [**nationalities** *pl.*] (*n.*), nationalité (*f.*):
ship of British, French, nationality, navire de nationalité britannique, française (*m.*).
nationality enables the ship to carry the national flag, and to claim the protection of her government or its representatives, la nationalité permet au navire de porter le pavillon national, et de réclamer la protection de son gouvernement ou de ses représentants.

nationalization (*n.*), nationalisation (*f.*); étatisation (*f.*):
nationalization of an industry, of railways, nationalisation, étatisation, d'une industrie, des chemins de fer.

nationalize (*v.t.*), nationaliser; étatiser.

nature of contents (description of contents of a parcel), désignation du contenu (*f.*).

nautical mile, mille marin (*m.*):
the distances travelled over (*or* covered) on the sea are expressed in nautical miles, les distances parcourues sur mer s'expriment en milles marins (*f.pl.*).

nautical science, science nautique (*f.*).

navigability *or* **navigableness** (*n.*), navigabilité (*f.*).

navigable (*adj.*), navigable:
navigable river, fleuve navigable (*m.*).

navigate (*v.t.*), faire naviguer; naviguer sur:
a ship does not exist in the true sense of the term unless she is capable of navigating the

sea, un navire n'existe dans le vrai sens du terme que s'il est apte à naviguer sur mer.

navigate (*v.i.*), naviguer:
ship incapable of navigating, navire inapte à naviguer (*m.*).

navigation (*n.*), navigation (*f.*):
navigation between England and America, navigation entre l'Angleterre et l'Amérique.
the difficulties of the navigation of the Rhine (*or* of navigating the Rhine) (*or* of Rhine navigation), les difficultés de la navigation du Rhin (*ou* de la navigation rhénane) (*f.pl.*).
stowing is bound up with the stability of the ship and thus concerns the safety of the navigation, l'arrimage se lie à la stabilité du navire et intéresse ainsi la sécurité de la navigation (*m.*).
improper navigation of the ship, fausse navigation du navire.

navigation (a canal) (*n.*), canal (*m.*); canal de navigation (*m.*).

navigation company (shipping company), compagnie (*ou* société) de navigation (*f.*); compagnie (*ou* société) d'armement (*f.*); compagnie (*ou* société) de transports maritimes (*f.*).

navigation dues, droits de navigation (*m.pl.*).

navigation permit, permis de navigation (*m.*).

Near East (opp. to *Far East*), Proche Orient (*m.*).

near position (Corn or other Exchange) (opp. to *distant position*), rapproché (*m.*):
cottons have advanced on coverings on near positions, les cotons ont avancé sur des couvertures sur les rapprochés (*m.pl.*).

nearest port, port le plus voisin (*m.*); port le plus proche (*m.*); port le plus rapproché (*m.*).

nearest safe port, port de relèvement (*m.*).

necessarily (*adv.*), nécessairement; d'office:
when the capital of a company has not been fully paid up, the certificates are necessarily registered, lorsque le capital d'une société n'a pas été entièrement libéré, les titres sont nominatifs d'office.

necessary (*adj.*), nécessaire.

necessary (*n.*), nécessaire (*m.*):
we beg you to have the kindness to do the necessary for the recovery of this debt (*or* to recover this debt), nous vous prions de vouloir bien faire le nécessaire pour le recouvrement de cette créance (*ou* pour recouvrer cette créance).

necessity [**necessities** *pl.*] (*n.*), nécessité (*f.*):
cargo sacrificed for the necessities of the ship, marchandises sacrifiées pour les nécessités du bord (*f.pl.*).

necessity (Navig.) (*n.*), relâche (*f.*):
port of necessity, port de relâche (*m.*).
ship which puts back into the port of sailing of necessity, navire qui rentre dans le port de départ en relâche (*m.*).

need (*n.*), besoin (*m.*):
present needs, besoins actuels.

case of need, in case of need. V. sous **case.**

negative (*adj.*), négatif, -ive :
negative answer *or* negative reply, réponse négative (*f.*).

negatively (*adv.*), négativement.

neglected (*p.p.*), négligé, -e ; délaissé, -e :
Mexican stocks remain neglected (Stock Exch.), les fonds mexicains demeurent négligés (*ou* délaissés) (*m.pl.*).

negligence *or* **neglect** (*n.*), négligence (*f.*) ; négligences (*f.pl.*) :
negligence (*or* neglect) of master or mariners, négligence (*ou* négligences) du capitaine ou des gens de mer.

negligence clause (Mar. Insce), clause de négligence (*f.*) ; clause négligence (*f.*) ; négligence-clause (*f.*).

negligent (*adj.*), négligent, -e ; fautif, -ive :
negligent collision, abordage fautif (*m.*) :
negligent collision embraces collision caused by the fault of one of the ships and that due to the fault of both ships, l'abordage fautif embrasse l'abordage causé par la faute de l'un des navires et celui dû à la faute des deux navires.

negotiability (*n.*), négociabilité (*f.*) ; commercialité (*f.*) :
negotiability of a bill, négociabilité, commercialité, d'un effet.

negotiable (*adj.*), négociable ; commerçable :
negotiable bill, effet négociable (*m.*) ; effet commerçable (*m.*).
negotiable paper, papier négociable (*m.*) ; papiers commerçables (*m.pl.*).
stocks negotiable on the stock exchange, titres négociables en bourse (*m.pl.*).
order which is not negotiable and cannot therefore be endorsed, mandat qui n'est pas négociable et ne peut donc être endossé (*m.*).

negotiate (to treat for by bargain) (*v.t.*), négocier ; traiter :
to negotiate a loan, a sale, négocier un emprunt, une vente.
to negotiate a bargain, traiter un marché.

negotiate (to transfer for value received) (*v.t.*), négocier ; trafiquer :
to negotiate a bill of exchange, négocier, trafiquer, une lettre de change.

to be negotiated, être négocié, -e, traité, -e, trafiqué, -e ; se négocier ; se traiter ; se trafiquer :
paper at more than three months is negotiated with difficulty, le papier à plus de trois mois se négocie difficilement.

negotiate (*v.i.*), négocier ; traiter.

negotiation (*n.*), négociation (*f.*) ; gré à gré :
negotiation of a bill, négociation d'un effet.
settlement by negotiation is resorted to in small losses (Insce), le règlement de gré à gré est employé dans les sinistres de minime importance.
price a matter for negotiation, prix à débattre (*m.*).

negotiator (pers.) (*n.*), négociateur, -trice :
the negotiators of a treaty, les négociateurs d'un traité.

nemine contradicente : *usually abbreviated* **nem. con.,** nemine contradicente.

net *or* **nett** (*adj.*) (Ant. : *gross*), net, nette :
net amount, somme nette (*f.*) ; montant net (*m.*) ; net (*m.*) :
the net amount to be carried to the customer's credit, le net à porter au crédit du client.
net assets, actif net (*m.*).
net avails (of a bill), net produit (*m.*), produit net (*m.*), net (*m.*), valeur actuelle (*f.*) (d'un effet).
net cash *or* net prompt cash, comptant net (*m.*). V. exemple sous **prompt.**
net charter *or* net form charter, affrètement coque nue (*m.*).
net freight, fret net (*m.*).
net income *or* net revenue, revenu net (*m.*).
net loss, perte nette (*f.*).
net premium (Insce) (opp. to *gross*, or *office, premium*), prime nette (*f.*). V. exemple sous **loading** (of the premium).
net price, prix net (*m.*).
net proceeds of a sale, net produit (*m.*), produit net (*m.*), net (*m.*) d'une vente.
net profit *or* net profits, bénéfice net (*m.*) ; profit net (*m.*) ; bénéfices nets (*m.pl.*) ; profits nets (*m.pl.*).
net register ton, tonneau de jauge nette (*m.*).
net register tonnage *or* net registered tonnage *or simply* net register, tonnage de jauge nette (*m.*) ; jauge nette (*f.*).
net result, résultat net (*m.*) ; net (*m.*) :
the net result of a transaction, le net d'une opération.
net sound value (Insce), valeur nette à l'état sain (*f.*) ; valeur saine nette (*f.*).
net tonnage, tonnage net (*m.*).
net weight *or simply* net (*n.*) (gross weight, less the tare—the common meaning), poids net (*m.*) ; net (*m.*) :
goods charged with duty on the net weight (*or* on the net), marchandises imposées au poids net (*ou* au net) (*f.pl.*).
net weight (weight of goods including inner packings, but excluding outer cases), poids demi-brut (*m.*).
net net weight (weight of the bare goods), poids net réel (*m.*) ; poids net effectif (*m.*) ; net réel (*m.*).
Note :—In very technical connections such as customs weighings, the three weights are in English (1) *gross weight* (goods and tare) (2) *net weight* (goods plus inner packings), and (3) *net net weight* (bare goods). The French for these expressions is (1) *poids brut,* (2) *poids demi-brut,* and (3) *poids net réel* (ou *effectif*).
net weight without taring (assumed by the customs in accordance with their regulations, in certain cases), poids net légal (*m.*).

network (system) (*n.*), réseau (*m.*) :
network of railways, of canals, réseau de chemins de fer (*ou* de voies ferrées), de canaux.

neutral (*adj.*), neutre :
neutral flag, pavillon neutre (*m.*).

neutral port, port neutre (*m.*).

neutral ship, navire neutre (*m.*).

neutral (*n.*), neutre (*m.*):
the duties of neutrals in case of war, les devoirs des neutres en cas de guerre (*m.pl.*).

neutrality [**neutralities** *pl.*] (*n.*), neutralité (*f.*):
neutrality of a ship, neutralité d'un navire.

new (*adj.*), nouveau *or* nouvel (before a vowel or a silent *h*), -elle:
new issue of shares, nouvelle émission d'actions (*f.*).
one new share for two old ones in the X. Company, une action nouvelle contre deux anciennes de la Société X.
new time (Stock Exch.), liquidation prochaine (*f.*).
New year card, carte du Nouvel An (*f.*).

new for old (Mar. Insce), différence du vieux au neuf (*f.*):
general average payable without deductions new for old, les avaries communes seront remboursables sans déductions pour différence du vieux au neuf.

news (*n.sing.*), nouvelle (*f.*); nouvelles (*f.pl.*); bruit (*m.*):
news of a casualty, of the arrival, of the loss, of a ship, nouvelle d'un sinistre, de l'arrivée, de la perte, d'un navire.

newsagent (*n.*), marchand de journaux (*m.*).

newspaper (*n.*), journal (*m.*).

newspaper advertisement, annonce de journal (*f.*).

newspaper cutting, découpure de journal (*f.*).

newspaper heading, rubrique de journal (*f.*).

newspaper rate (Post), tarif des périodiques (*m.*); tarif des imprimés périodiques (*m.*); tarif des publications périodiques (*m.*).

newspaper wrapper, bande de journal (*f.*).

next account *or* **next settlement** (Stock Exch.), liquidation prochaine (*f.*); prochain (*m.*).

next month *or simply* **next** (*n.*) (Produce Exch.), prochain mois (*m.*); mois prochain (*m.*); prochain (*m.*).

next post *or* **next mail,** plus prochain courrier (*m.*).

nib (*n.*), bec (*m.*); plume (*f.*).

nickel money, monnaie de nickel (*f.*).

Nigerian shares *or* **Nigerians** (*n.pl.*), valeurs nigériennes (*f.pl.*); nigériennes (*f.pl.*).

night (*n.*) (opp. to *day*), nuit (*f.*).

night charge (Teleph.), taxe de nuit (*f.*).

night mail, malle de nuit (*f.*).

night train, train de nuit (*m.*).

night trunk call (Teleph.), communication (*ou* conversation) interurbaine de nuit (*f.*).

night watchman (of a bank), veilleur de nuit (*m.*).

nil (*n.*), nul, nulle (*adj.*); néant (*m.*):
if the balance is nil, si le solde est nul; si la balance est nulle.
briefly, tendency a little better, but business almost nil, bref, tendance un peu meilleure, mais affaires presque nulles.
market nil at the start, buyers and sellers being wanting, marché nul au début, acheteurs et vendeurs faisant défaut (*m.*).

to put the word "nil" against an item of account (in order to show that there is no income or expenditure under that head), mettre le mot « néant » sur un article de compte.

nitrate shares *or* **nitrates** (*n.pl.*), valeurs de nitrate (*f.pl.*); valeurs nitratières (*f.pl.*); nitratières (*f.pl.*).

no advice (Abbrev.: **N/A.**) *or* **no orders** (Abbrev.: **N/O.**) (Banking), défaut d'avis.

no agents (mention in a small advertisement), agents s'abstenir.

no bid (Stock or other Exch.), pas demandé.

no change, pas de changement; statu quo:
no changes in bank shares, pas de changements en valeurs de banques; statu quo aux valeurs bancaires.

no cure no pay clause (Salvage), clause « no cure no pay » (*f.*); clause « pas de résultat, pas de paiement » (*f.*); clause « aucune rémunération n'est due, si le secours prêté reste sans résultat utile » (*f.*).

no dealings (Stock or other Exch.), sans transaction; pas traité.

no dealings (Produce Exch.), manque; sans affaires.

no dealings in the shares, pas de (*ou* aucune) transaction sur l'action.

no funds (Abbrev.: **N.F.**) *or* **no effects** (Banking), manque de fonds; défaut de provision.

no noting (notice on a bill of exchange) (Abbrev.: **N/N.**), sans compte de retour; sans frais; retour sans frais; sans protêt.

no occupation, sans profession:
Paul X, no occupation, residing at . . ., Paul X, sans profession, demeurant à . . .

no premium (Reletting), sans reprise. V. exemple sous **premium.**

no quotation (Stock or other Exchange), sans cotation; pas coté.

no reply (Teleph.), répond pas; ne répond pas.

no sale, non vente (*f.*):
the no sale days, les jours de non vente (*m.pl.*).

no value. V. sous syn. **not valued.**

noiseless typewriter, machine à écrire silencieuse (*f.*).

noisy (*adj.*), bruyant, -e:
noisy meeting, réunion bruyante (*f.*).

nominal (*adj.*), nominal, -e, -aux:
nominal accounts (real or property accounts) (Bkkpg) (opp. to *personal accounts*), comptes de choses (*m.pl.*).
nominal accounts (recording gains and losses) (Bkkpg), comptes de (*ou* des) résultats (*m.pl.*).
nominal capital, capital nominal (*m.*); capital social (*m.*):
company with a nominal capital of so much, société au capital nominal de tant (*f.*).
the nominal capital of a company, le capital nominal d'une société; le capital social d'une compagnie.
nominal exchange, change nominal (*m.*).
nominal fine (Customs), amende de principe (*f.*).
nominal ledger, grand livre des comptes

généraux (*m.*);   grand livre général (*m.*); grand livre synthétique (*m.*).

nominal list of shareholders (i.e., list of names), liste nominative des actionnaires (*f.*).

nominal transfer (transfer for a nominal consideration, or where no consideration passes, as in the case of a gift or succession), transfert d'ordre (*m.*);   transfert gratuit (*m.*). (In England, such a transfer is liable to a fixed stamp duty of 10s. In France, not liable to stamp duty.)

nominal value of a share, or the like, valeur nominale (*f.*), nominal (*m.*) d'une action, ou analogue:

   the bonds are of the nominal value of £10 and multiples; the nominal value of the debentures is £100, les bons sont de la valeur nominale (*ou* sont du nominal) de £10 et multiples; la valeur nominale (*ou* le nominal) des obligations est de £100.

   the nominal value is that inscribed on a stock or share certificate, la valeur nominale est celle inscrite sur un titre de bourse.

at the close, prices remained nominal, en clôture, les cours restent nominaux.

a purely nominal rate, un taux purement nominal.

discount is nominal when negotiable bills are scarce on the market, or when there is little or no demand, l'escompte est nominal lorsque les effets négociables sont rares sur le marché, ou lorsqu'ils sont peu ou pas demandés (*m.*). Cf. **easy** and **tight.**

Java sugar.—March-April 10/10½d. nominal (*or abbreviated* 10/10½ nom. *or* 10/10½ n.) c.i.f., sucre de Java.—mars-avril 10/10 1/2d. nominal caf.

nominally (*adv.*), nominalement.

nominate (*v.t.*), nommer; désigner.

nominated ship, navire désigné (*m.*). V. exemples sous **name, naming.**

nomination (*n.*), nomination (*f.*); désignation (*f.*).

nominee (pers.) (*n.*), personne interposée (*f.*).

   in a nominee's name, sous un nom interposé.

The use of the hyphen between the prefix non *and the following word is optional, both in English and French.*

non acceptance (*n.*), non acceptation (*f.*):

   non acceptance of a bill, non acceptation d'un effet.

non arrival (*n.*), non arrivée (*f.*).

non assessment (*n.*), non imposition (*f.*).

non business day, jour férié (*m.*); jour de fête (*m.*); jour de chômage (*m.*).

non copying ribbon (typewriter), ruban fixe (*m.*).

non cumulative (*adj.*) (Abbrev.: **non cum.**), non cumulatif, -ive:

   non cumulative dividend, dividende non cumulatif (*m.*).

   non cumulative 7% preference shares, actions de priorité 7 0/0 non cumulatives (*f.pl.*).

non current liabilities (share capital, debentures, reserves), passif non exigible (*m.*).

non delivery (*n.*), non livraison (*f.*); non remise (*f.*); souffrance (*f.*): (Cf. **undeliverable postal parcels.**)

   non delivery of stock, non livraison de titres.

   sender who asks to be advised direct of the delivery or the non delivery of his goods, expéditeur qui demande qu'il soit avisé directement de la livraison ou de la souffrance de sa marchandise.

non interest bearing account, compte plat (*m.*); compte non productif d'intérêts (*m.*).

non liability (*n.*), non responsabilité (*f.*); irresponsabilité (*f.*).

non liability clause, clause de non responsabilité (*f.*); clause d'irresponsabilité (*f.*).

non marine (*adj.*), terrestre:

   non marine insurance, assurance terrestre (*f.*).

   non marine policy, police terrestre (*f.*).

   non marine risk, risque terrestre (*m.*); risque de terre (*m.*).

   non marine underwriter, assureur terrestre (*m.*).

non member (pers.) (*n.*), non membre (*m.*).

non negotiable (*adj.*), non négociable:

   non negotiable note, billet non négociable (*m.*).

non payment (*n.*), non paiement (*m.*); non payement (*m.*); non versement (*m.*):

   non payment of a bill, of a premium due, non paiement d'un effet, d'une prime échue.

non performance *or* **non execution** *or* **non fulfilment** (*n.*), non exécution (*f.*); inexécution (*f.*); non accomplissement (*m.*):

   total or partial non performance of a contract of affreightment, inexécution totale ou partielle d'un contrat d'affrètement.

non professional (*adj.*), non professionnel, -elle.

non professional (pers.) (*n.*), non professionnel, -elle. V. exemple sous **professional.**

non quotation (Stock Exch.) (*n.*), non cotation (*f.*).

non returnable (*adj.*). V. sous **not returnable** ci-après.

non shipment (*n.*), non embarquement (*m.*).

non stop (Rly., etc.), sans arrêt:

   non stop journey, trajet sans arrêt (*m.*).

non striker (pers.) (*n.*), non gréviste (*m.* ou *f.*).

non trader (pers.) (*n.*), non commerçant, -e.

non trading (*adj.*), non commerçant, -e.

non Union country, pays hors l'Union postale universelle (*m.*).

non warranty clause, clause de non garantie (*f.*).

non wasting (*adj.*), indéfectible:

   non wasting assets, actif indéfectible (*m.*); valeurs indéfectibles (*f.pl.*).

none (not any; nil) (*pron.*), néant (*n.m.*):

   to put the word " none " against an item of account (in order to show that there is no income or expenditure under that head), mettre le mot « néant » sur un article de compte.

North Sea port, port de la mer du Nord (*m.*).

nostro account, compte nostro (*m.*).
not acceptable, non acceptable.
not classed (ships), non coté, -e.
not entered (at customs—said of goods), non déclaré, -e.
not exceeding (up to; at most), jusqu'à concurrence de; ne dépassant pas; jusqu'à ... inclusivement; jusqu'à; au maximum; à concurrence d'un maximum de :
compensation for loss or damage not exceeding so much, indemnité pour perte ou avarie jusqu'à concurrence de tant (*f.*).
charge : not exceeding 1 lb., so much; exceeding 1 lb. but not exceeding 2 lbs, so much, taxe : ne dépassant pas 1 livre poids, tant; au-dessus de 1 livre jusqu'à 2 livres, tant.
not exceeding so many lbs, jusqu'à tant de livres poids inclusivement.
fine not exceeding so many pounds, amende de tant de livres au maximum (*f.*).
not negotiable, non négociable :
cheque bearing the words not negotiable, chèque revêtu de la mention non négociable (*m.*). *See full example under* cheque crossed "not negotiable," & cf. example under **negotiable.**
not repayable *or* **not returnable** *or* **non returnable** (*adj.*), non remboursable; non restituable; acquis, -e :
freight paid in advance and not (*or* non) returnable in case of loss, fret payé d'avance et non restituable en cas de sinistre (*m.*).
freight not repayable under any circumstances, fret acquis à tout événement (*m.*).
insurance premium which is not returnable if the risk has attached, prime d'assurance qui est acquise s'il a commencé à courir les risques (*f.*).
not sufficient funds (Banking) (Abbrev.: **N/S.** *or* **n/s.**), insuffisance de provision; provision insuffisante.
not valued *or* **no value** *or* **,, ,, ,,** (i.e., dits in the £ s. d. column of a balance sheet, of an account), mémoire; pour mémoire :
the claims and prospecting licences stand in the balance sheet not valued *or* no value is shown in the balance sheet for claims and prospecting licences, les concessions et permis de recherches sont portés dans le bilan pour mémoire.
nota bene (*usually abbreviated* **N.B.**), nota bene.
notarial (*adj.*), notarial, -e, -aux :
notarial functions, fonctions notariales (*f.pl.*).
notarial (*adj.*) *or* **notarially authenticated** *or* **notarially certified,** notarié, -e :
notarially authenticated document, acte notarié (*m.*).
notarial charges not to be incurred (notice on a bill of exchange), sans compte de retour; sans frais; retour sans frais; sans protêt.
notarial ticket *or* **notarial charges** (on dishonoured bill), compte de retour (*m.*).
notary [notaries *pl.*] (pers.) (*n.*), notaire (*m.*).
Note :—In France, a *notaire* exercises many of the functions of a solicitor, including conveyancing and company work.

notary's clerk, clerc de notaire (*m.*).
notary's office, étude de notaire (*f.*).
note (memorandum) (*n.*), note (*f.*); mémorandum (*m.*) :
to make a note of something in one's pocketbook, prendre note d'une chose sur son carnet.
note (a brief letter) (*n.*), billet (*m.*); lettre (*f.*); bulletin (*m.*) :
advice note, lettre d'avis.
dispatch note, bulletin d'envoi; bulletin d'expédition.
note (bill; account) (*n.*), note (*f.*); facture (*f.*); bulletin (*m.*); bordereau (*m.*) :
note of expenses, of fees, note de dépenses, d'honoraires.
credit note, note de crédit; note d'avoir; facture d'avoir.
broker's contract note, bordereau d'agent de change; bordereau de bourse.
note (bank note) (*n.*), billet (*m.*); billet de banque (*m.*).
note (exchange) (*n.*), billet (*m.*); mandat (*m.*); échéance (*f.*) :
promissory note *or* note of hand, billet à ordre.
note (voucher; permit) (*n.*), bon (*m.*); permis (*m.*) :
receiving note, bon à embarquer.
shipping note, permis d'embarquer.
note (issued by a company, repayable at a fixed date) (*n.*), bon de caisse (*m.*).
note (nota bene) (*n.*), nota (*m.*).
note (*v.t.*), noter; relever; constater :
please note that . . ., notez bien que . . .
shortage in the cash which results from an expense which has not been noted, manquant en caisse qui résulte d'une dépense qui n'a pas été notée (*m.*).
to note a fact, relever, constater, un fait.
to note on the receipt the nature and extent of the damage, constater sur le récépissé la nature et l'importance des avaries.
in France, dishonour by non payment of a bill of exchange should be noted the day after the day of maturity by an act called protest for non payment, en France, le refus de paiement d'un effet de commerce doit être constaté le lendemain du jour de l'échéance par un acte que l'on nomme protêt faute de paiement.
to note protest of a bill of exchange, faire le protêt d'une lettre de change.
notebook (*n.*), carnet (*m.*); calepin (*m.*).
notebook (shorthand) (*n.*), bloc-sténo (*m.*).
notice (advice) (*n.*), avis (*m.*); préavis (*m.*); avertissement (*m.*); notification (*f.*); notice (*f.*); mention (*f.*); bulletin (*m.*); terme (*m.*) :
notice of abandonment (Mar. Insce), avis de délaissement.
notice of assessment (Taxation), avertissement.
notice of delivery (telegrams), accusé de réception (*m.*). *V.* telegram with notice of delivery.

notice of interest declared (Floating policy insurance), bulletin d'aliment.

notice of interest declared (Insurance, steamer or steamers to be declared—Floating policy insurance, bulletin d'application.

notice of meeting *or simply* notice, avis de convocation (*m.*); lettre de convocation (*f.*); convocation (*f.*); convocation d'assemblée (*f.*); convocation en assemblée (*f.*):
 a copy of the newspaper containing the notice of meeting, or of the notice addressed to the shareholders, un exemplaire du journal contenant l'avis de convocation, ou de la lettre de convocation adressée aux actionnaires.
 to receive a notice (*or* a notice of meeting), recevoir une convocation (*ou* une convocation d'assemblée).

notice of general meeting, avis de convocation à l'assemblée générale.

notices of general meetings, convocations d'assemblées générales, convocations en assemblées générales.

a single notice for two meetings, une seule convocation pour deux assemblées.

notice is hereby given that the annual general meeting of the company will be held at . . . Street, on . . . 19 . ., at . . o'clock in the . . ., MM. les actionnaires sont convoqués en assemblée générale pour . . . 19 . ., rue . . ., nº . . ., à . . heures du . . . V. aussi exemple sous **consider.**

notice of receipt, avis de réception.

notice of withdrawal (Savings Bank), demande de remboursement (*f.*).

notice of withdrawal of funds (Banking), mandat (*m.*).

notice must be given immediately on receipt of advices, notification devra être donnée dès la réception des avis.

notice to be advertised in the Gazette, notice à publier au Journal officiel.

to give notice a day beforehand, donner avis un jour d'avance.

to give 7 clear days' notice, donner un préavis de 7 jours francs.

deposit at 7 days' notice, dépôt a 7 jours de préavis (*m.*).

the notices printed on the invoice, les mentions imprimées de la facture.

bill of lading bearing the notice *freight prepaid*, connaissement portant la mention *fret payé* (*m.*).

loan at notice, prêt à terme (*m.*).

deposit at short notice, dépôt à court terme (*m.*).

securities realizable at short notice, valeurs réalisables à court terme (*f.pl.*).

notice (*n.*) *or* **notice to quit**, congé (*m.*):
 tenant who has given notice, locataire qui a donné congé (*m.*).
 the notice given by the employer, by the employee, le congé donné par l'employeur, par l'employé.

notice (period of notice) (*n.*), délai-congé (*m.*); délai de congé (*m.*):
 a week's notice, un délai-congé d'une semaine.

notification (*n.*), notification (*f.*); avertissement (*m.*); avis (*m.*).

notify (*v.t.*), notifier; avertir; aviser:
 to notify to the underwriter (*or* to notify the insurer of) all information concerning the adventure, notifier à l'assureur (*ou* notifier l'assureur de) tous les renseignements afférents à l'expédition.

noting (recording) (*n.*), relèvement (*m.*); relevé (*m.*); constatation (*f.*):
 stock taking comprises two operations: the noting of the quantities and their valuation, l'inventaire comporte deux opérations: le relevé des quantités et leur évaluation (*m.*).

notwithstanding (*prep.*), nonobstant:
 notwithstanding any provision to the contrary, anything to the contrary contained in this contract, nonobstant toute clause contraire, toute disposition contraire du présent contrat.
 notwithstanding the foregoing, nonobstant ce qui précède; nonobstant les dispositions qui précèdent; nonobstant les dispositions ci-dessus.

now loading *or* **now on the berth**, en charge. V. exemple sous **loading.**

nude contract (opp. to *onerous contract*), contrat à titre gratuit (*m.*); contrat de bienfaisance (*m.*).

null and void, nul (nulle) et non avenu, -e:
 to treat the objection as null and void, considérer l'opposition comme nulle et non avenue.
 at the expiration of the term of two years, the titles will be considered as null and void, if they have not been renewed, à l'expiration du terme de deux ans, les titres seront considérés comme nuls et non avenus, s'ils n'ont pas été renouvelés.

nullity (*n.*), nullité (*f.*):
 the consequence of concealment is the nullity of the insurance, la conséquence de la réticence sera la nullité de l'assurance.

number (*n.*) (Abbrev.: Nº [Nos *pl.*] *or* No [Nos *pl.*]), nombre (*m.*); numéro (*m.*); chiffre (*m.*):
 2 is an even number, 2 est un nombre pair.
 number of packages (quantity), nombre de colis (*m.*); quantité (*f.*).
 total number of shares, chiffre total des actions.
 marks and numbers of packages, marques et numéros des colis.
 voucher numbers, numéros des pièces justificatives.
 the numbers of the pages of a book, les numéros des pages d'un livre.
 to put the number on the top of a page, mettre le chiffre au haut d'une page.

number (product—accounts current, or the like) (*n.*), nombre (*m.*).

number (*n.*) *or* **call number** (Teleph.), numéro (*m.*); numéro d'appel (*m.*):

wrong number, faux numéro d'appel.
number engaged, pas libre.
number, please? qui demandez-vous?; j'écoute:
as soon as the operator has said "number,
please?" give her slowly and distinctly
the number required, dès que l'opératrice
a dit « j'écoute, » formulez lentement et
distinctement le numéro demandé.

number (*v.t.*), numéroter; chiffrer; coter:
to number a bill, numéroter un effet.
to number an account book, numéroter, chiffrer, coter, un livre de comptabilité.
goods marked and numbered as follows,

marchandises marquées et numérotées comme ci-après (*f.pl.*).
10,000 shares numbered 1 to 10,000, 10 000
actions numérotées de 1 à 10 000.

numbering (*n.*), numérotage (*m.*).
numbering machine (self-acting), timbre numéroteur (automatique) (*m.*).
numeral (*n.*), chiffre (*m.*):
Arabic numerals, chiffres arabes.
nurse (*v.t.*), nourrir; soigner:
to nurse a business, an industry, nourrir une
affaire, une industrie.
to nurse an account, soigner un compte.

O

oath (*n.*), serment (*m.*):
to take the oath before a tribunal, prêter
serment devant un tribunal.
on oath, sous serment.
objection to mark (Stock Exch.), opposition à
la cote (*f.*):
to lodge objections to marks, mettre des
oppositions à la cote.
objects (of a company) (*n.pl.*), objet (*m.*), but
(*m.*) (d'une société):
the objects for which the company is established are: to purchase, to sell, to take on
lease, etc. (memorandum of association),
la société a pour objet (*ou* pour but): l'achat,
la vente, la prise à bail, etc.
obligation (*n.*), obligation (*f.*):
the obligation to contribute to the sacrifices
made for the preservation of the adventure
(Mar. Insce), l'obligation de contribuer
aux sacrifices faits pour la conservation de
l'aventure.
the chief obligation of the insured consists in
the payment of the premium, l'obligation
principale de l'assuré consiste dans le
paiement de la prime.
oblige *or* **obligate** (*v.t.*), obliger.
to be obliged *or* **to be obligated**, être obligé, -e;
s'obliger; être tenu, -e:
the bank is obliged to have gold and silver
coin and bullion equal to one third of its
notes and of its other sight commitments,
la banque est obligée (*ou* tenue) d'avoir
une encaisse métallique égale au tiers du
montant de ses billets et de ses autres
engagements à vue.
owner who is only obligated on his ship and
the freight, propriétaire qui ne s'oblige
que sur son navire et sur le fret.
obligee (Law) (pers.) (*n.*), obligataire (*m.* ou *f.*).
obligor (Law) (pers.) (*n.*), obligé, -e.
obliteration (*n.*), oblitération (*f.*); effacement
(*m.*):
obliteration of marks, oblitération, effacement, de marques.

observe (*v.t.*), observer; respecter:
to observe a clause in an agreement, observer,
respecter, une clause dans une convention.
obtain (*v.t.*). V. exemples:
to obtain a signature by fraud, surprendre
une signature.
to obtain advances of money, procurer (*ou*
se faire faire) des avances de fonds.
to obtain an extension of time for payment,
obtenir un délai dans le paiement; s'atermoyer.
to obtain security before lending money,
prendre des sûretés avant de prêter de
l'argent.
occasional contraband (distinguished from *absolute contraband*), contrebande relative (*f.*).
occupation (profession or business; description)
(*n.*), profession (*f.*); qualités (*f.pl.*):
the full name (*or* the name in full), address,
and occupation of the applicant, les nom,
prénoms, adresse (*ou* domicile), et profession
(*ou* qualités) du souscripteur.
occupy a situation (to), occuper (*ou* tenir) un
emploi.
ocean (*n.*), océan (*m.*).
ocean carrying trade, grande navigation (*f.*).
ocean freight, fret au long cours (*m.*).
ocean-going steamer, steamer au long cours
(*m.*); navire à vapeur au long cours
(*m.*).
ocean-going vessel, navire au long cours (*m.*);
navire long-courrier (*m.*); bâtiment long-
courrier (*m.*); long-courrier (*m.*).
ocean greyhound (*fig.*), lévrier de la mer (*m.*).
ocean navigation, navigation au long cours (*f.*);
long cours (*m.*).
ocean steamer, vapeur océanique (*m.*); vapeur
transocéanique (*m.*).
ocean tramp, tramp (*m.*); tramp-steamer (*m.*);
navire tramp (*m.*); navire de tramping
(*m.*); navire vagabond (*m.*); navire
irrégulier (*m.*).
ocean voyage, voyage au (*ou* de) long cours
(*m.*); long cours (*m.*):

ship sailing on an ocean voyage,   navire partant pour le long cours (m.).

odd money, appoint (m.); passe (f.):
to add to some bank notes two shillings for the odd money, ajouter à des billets de banque deux schellings pour la passe.

odd number, nombre impair (m.):
3, 5, 7, are odd numbers, 3, 5, 7, sont des nombres impairs.

off (to be) (Stock or other Exch.) (opp. to **to be on**), être en baisse:
copper 5s. off at £69 15s., cuivre en baisse de 1/4 à £69 15sh. (ou £69 3/4).

offer (n.), offre (f.):
verbal offer, offre labiale; offre verbale.

offer (Stock Exch.) (n.) (opp. to bid), offre (f.).

offer (v.t.), offrir; proposer; faire; présenter:
to offer goods for sale, offrir en vente, courter, des marchandises.
to offer to sell something, one's services, offrir de vendre quelque chose, ses services.
the jobber (in France, it would be the broker) offers: sell (i.e., I will sell) 100 X. (shares) such or such a price, l'agent offre: j'ai (c.-à-d. j'ai à vendre) 100 (actions) X. tel prix. Cf. the jobber bids, sous **bid.**
prices offered (sellers) (Stock Exch.), cours offerts (vendeurs) (m.pl.).
X. shares: 1s. 6d. bid; 1s. 4½d. offered, action X.: 1sh. 6d. demandé; 1sh. 4 1/2d. offert.
to offer so much for an article, proposer tant d'un objet.
to offer a thing at so much, faire une chose tant.
banking establishment which is obliged to buy all the gold bullion offered to it, établissement de banque qui est obligé d'acheter toutes les matières d'or qui lui sont présentées (m.).
to offer oneself for a situation, s'offrir, se proposer, pour un emploi.

offerer (pers.) (n.), offreur (m.).

office (charge; functions) (n.), charge (f.); office (m.); exercice (m.); fonctions (f.pl.); place (f.); ministère (m.):
in virtue of his office, en vertu de sa charge.
to fulfil the duties of one's office, remplir les devoirs de sa charge (ou son office) (ou son ministère).
the directors in office, les administrateurs en exercice (m.pl.).
longest in office. V. sous **longest.**
the board will remain in office until the annual meeting, le conseil restera (ou demeurera) en fonctions jusqu'à l'assemblée annuelle.
if a director's office becomes vacant, si une place d'administrateur devient vacante.

office (room or building) (n.), bureau (m.); cabinet (m.); étude (f.); office (m.):
office of destination (Post), bureau de destination; bureau destinataire.
office of issue (money orders, etc.), bureau d'émission.
office of origin (Post), bureau d'origine.
office of payment (money orders, etc.), bureau payeur.

office of posting (Post), bureau de dépôt.
office open always, bureau à service permanent; bureau ouvert en permanence.

office (n.) or **offices** (n.pl.) (seat of administration; head office; registered office), siège (m.); siège social (m.):
secretary and offices (followed by an address), siège social et secrétariat (suivi d'une adresse).

office (the cashier's office, the coffers of a bank, or the like) (n.), caisse (f.); recette (f.):
generally bearer shares must be lodged in the company's office before the meeting, généralement les titres au porteur doivent être déposés dans la caisse sociale avant l'assemblée.
office of collector of customs, recette des douanes.

office (insurance or assurance company) (n.), compagnie d'assurance (f.); compagnie d'assurances (f.); société d'assurance (ou d'assurances) (f.):
fire office, compagnie (ou société) d'assurance (ou d'assurances) contre l'incendie.

office boy, petit commis (m.).

office expenses, frais de bureau (m.pl.).

office limit (Insce). V. sous **limit.**

office premium (Insce) (opp. to net, or pure, or mathematical, or risk, premium), prime brute (f.).

office printing outfit (interchangeable rubber-faced type), composteur (m.); timbre composteur (m.).

office rent, loyer de bureau (m.).

office requisites, fournitures de bureau (f.pl.).

office staff, personnel de bureau (m.).

office work, travail de bureau (m.).

officer (of a ship) (pers.) (n.), officier (d'un navire) (m.):
the officers and crew, les officiers et l'équipage.

officer of custom or **customs officer,** agent de douane (m.); douanier (m.).

officer of health or **health officer,** agent du service sanitaire (m.); officier de santé (m.).

officer of taxes, agent des contributions directes (m.).

official (adj.), officiel, -elle; d'office:
official buying (in Stock Exch.), rachat officiel (m.); rachat d'office (m.).
official document, document officiel (m.).
official list (of stock exchange quotations), cote officielle (f.):
securities quoted in the official list, valeurs inscrites à la cote officielle (f.pl.).
official rate or official rate of discount (bank rate) (opp. to private, or market, rate), taux officiel (m.); taux officiel d'escompte (m.); escompte officiel (m.). V. **bank rate.**
official telegram, télégramme officiel (m.).

official (pers.) (n.), fonctionnaire (m. ou f.); préposé, -e:
government official, fonctionnaire public.
a customs official, un préposé (ou un fonctionnaire) de la douane.

officially (*adv.*), officiellement; d'office: shares quoted officially, actions cotées officiellement (*f.pl.*).

buying in officially against a seller, exécution d'office d'un vendeur (*f.*).

telegram repeated officially, télégramme répété d'office (*m.*).

the formality of registration is applied officially, that is to say, without special charge, to a large class of packets of which it is advisable to keep trace of transmission, la formalité de recommandation est appliquée d'office, c'est-à-dire sans taxe spéciale, à une nombreuse catégorie d'objets dont il est utile de garder trace de transmission.

offset (*n.*), compensation (*f.*); parcontre (*m.*): the new shares will be paid up by offset against the amount of the debentures converted, les actions nouvelles seront libérées par compensation avec le montant des obligations converties (*f.pl.*).

these brokerages are charged on each deal, purchase and sale, and without offset (i.e., brokerage charged both ways), ces courtages sont perçus sur chaque opération, achat et vente, et sans parcontre.

offset (*v.t.*), compenser: profits which offset one's losses, bénéfices qui compensent ses pertes (*m.pl.*).

oil company, société pétrolière (*f.*); société de pétroles (*f.*).

oil dock, bassin aux pétroles (*m.*); bassin à pétrole (*m.*); bassin pétrolier (*m.*).

oil market (Stock Exch.), marché des pétrolifères (*m.*).

oil port, port pétrolier (*m.*).

oil shares *or* **oils** (*n.pl.*), valeurs de pétrole (*f.pl.*); valeurs pétrolières (*f.pl.*); pétroles (*m.pl.*); pétrolières (*f.pl.*); pétrolifères (*f.pl.*); valeurs pétrolifères (*f.pl.*).

oil ship *or* **oiler** (*n.*) (a vessel for the transportation of oil), navire pétrolier (*m.*); bateau pétrolier (*m.*); pétrolier (*m.*).

oil trust, trust de pétrole (*m.*).

oil yard, chantier pétrolier (*m.*).

old age pension, retraite pour la vieillesse (*f.*).

old age pension fund, caisse des retraites pour la vieillesse (*f.*).

old balance, solde ancien (*m.*).

old money (opp. to *fresh money*), argent ancien (*m.*).

old paper *or* **old papers,** paperasse (*f.*); vieilles paperasses (*f.pl.*): the accumulation of old papers, l'accumulation d'une paperasse, de vieilles paperasses (*f.*).

old shares, actions anciennes (*f.pl.*): one new share for two old ones in the X. Company, une action nouvelle contre deux anciennes de la Société X.

omnibus [**omnibuses** *pl.*] (*n.*), omnibus (*m.*).

omnibus package (Customs), plusieurs colis réunis sous une enveloppe commune.

omnium (aggregate of different kinds of stock) (*n.*), omnium (*m.*).

omnium (*n.*) *or* **omnium investment company,** omnium (*m.*); omnium de valeurs (*m.*).

on (to be) (Stock or other Exch.) (opp. to **to be off**), être en hausse: copper 5s. on at £69 15s., cuivre en hausse de 1/4 à £69 15sh. (*ou* £69 3/4).

on *or* **upon** (ellipsis for *put on* or *upon*; at the charge or door of; encumbering) (*prep.*). V. exemples: the trade charge on (*or* upon) parcels may not exceed so many pounds, les colis peuvent être grevés de remboursements jusqu'à concurrence de tant de livres (*m.pl.*).

the trade charge on (*or* upon) the goods may not exceed their value, la marchandise peut être grevée d'un remboursement jusqu'à concurrence de sa valeur.

consignment on (*or* upon) which a trade charge is to be collected, expédition grevée de remboursement (*f.*).

the charges on (*or* upon) the consignment, les frais grevant l'envoi (*m.pl.*).

on *or* **upon** (borne by). V. sous **upon.**

on approval (Com.) (often contracted to: **on appro.**), à condition; sous condition.

on-carrier (succeeding carrier) (pers.) (*n.*), voiturier successif (*m.*); transporteur subséquent (*m.*).

on 'change, sur la bourse; à la bourse; en bourse.

on 'change table, cote des changes (*f.*).

on condition that. V. sous **condition.**

on-cost charges (Costing) (opp. to *direct expenses* or *establishment charges* or *departmental charges*), frais généraux (*m.pl.*); frais fixes (*m.pl.*); frais indirects (*m.pl.*); dépenses fixes (*ou* indirectes) (*f.pl.*).

on hand, refused *or* **goods** (*or* **parcel,** or the like) **on hand, refused** (*or* **left on hand refused**), laissé pour compte (*m.*); pour-compte (*m.*); pourcompte (*m.*): do not confuse "on hand, refused" with abandonment, ne pas confondre le « laissé pour compte » avec « l'abandon. »

goods (*or* a parcel) left on hand, refused, with the carrier, un laissé pour compte au transporteur.

to leave the goods on hand, refused, with the railway company, laisser la marchandise pour compte à la compagnie de chemins de fer.

on passage (said of goods), sous voile; en cargaison flottante; flottant, -e.

on rail, sur wagon; franco wagon; franco gare.

on risk (Insce.). V. exemple: the insurance has ceased to be on risk, l'effet de l'assurance a cessé (*m.*).

on tap (*financial slang*), robinet ouvert (*m.*).

on the berth, en charge. V. exemple sous **loading** *or* **on the berth.**

one (*n.*) *or* **certificate for one share,** unité (*f.*); titre unitaire (*m.*): company which issues its shares in ones and in denominations of 5, 10, 25, 50, or 100, société qui émet ses actions en unités ou en coupures de 5, 10, 25, 50, ou 100 (*f.*).

one class liner, paquebot à classe unique (*m.*).

one day option (Stock Exch.), petite prime pour le lendemain (*f.*); prime au (*ou* pour le) lendemain (*f.*).

one for one, une contre une; paritaire:
exchange of shares one for one, échange d'actions une contre une; échange paritaire d'actions (*m.*).

one man company, société consistant d'un individù (*f.*).

one man market, marché fermé (*m.*); marché contrôlé (*m.*).

one of which being accomplished, the others to stand (*or* **shall stand**) **void** (*or* **the others shall be void**) (bill of lading), dont un accompli, les autres restent (*ou* demeurent) sans valeur (*ou* les autres seront de nulle valeur).

one way traffic, circulation à sens unique (*f.*).

onerous (*adj.*), onéreux, -euse:
onerous contract (opp. to *bare*, or *naked*, or *nude, contract*), contrat à titre onéreux (*m.*).
property acquired by onerous title, propriété acquise à titre onéreux (*f.*).

onus of proof *or* **onus of proving,** charge de la preuve (*f.*); fardeau de la preuve (*m.*):
onus of proof which falls on the insurer, charge (*ou* fardeau) de la preuve qui incombe à l'assureur.
to throw on someone the onus of proving a wrongful act, mettre à la charge de quelqu'un le fardeau de la preuve d'une faute.

open (*adj.*), ouvert, -e:
open account (an account in which some item is not settled between the parties), compte ouvert (*m.*).
open account (running account), compte courant (*m.*).
open always (said of certain post offices, etc.), ouvert en permanence; à service permanent:
office open always, bureau à service permanent (*m.*); bureau ouvert en permanence (*m.*).
open cheque (opp. to *crossed cheque*), chèque ouvert (*m.*); chèque non barré (*m.*).
open cover (Insce), couverture d'abonnement (*f.*).
open credit, crédit à découvert (*m.*); crédit libre (*m.*); crédit en blanc (*m.*); crédit par caisse (*m.*); crédit sur notoriété (*m.*).
open discount market, marché de l'escompte hors banque (*m.*).
open door (International Politics), porte ouverte (*f.*):
open door principle, principe de la porte ouverte (*m.*).
open letter (not sealed up) (Post), lettre ouverte (*f.*).
open market, marché libre (*m.*); marché ouvert (*m.*):
bank which has been able to buy gold on the open market, banque qui a pu acquérir de l'or sur le marché libre (*f.*).
loans contracted on the open money market, emprunts contractés sur le marché libre des capitaux (*m.pl.*).

oper. market discount rate (opp. to *bank rate*), taux hors banque (*m.*); taux privé (*m.*); taux d'escompte hors banque (*m.*); taux d'escompte privé (*m.*); escompte hors banque (*m.*); escompt privé (*m.*). Cf. **bank rate.**

open policy (Mar. Insce) (*Abbrev.:* O.P.), police d'abonnement (*f.*); police flottante (*f.*); police ouverte (*f.*).
open policy for a specific amount, police à forfait (*f.*); police en bloc (*f.*); police globale (*f.*):
open policy on valuables for a specific amount, police à forfait sur valeurs (*f.*).

open port (open to navigation; not closed, as by ice, or sanitary regulations), port libre (*m.*).

open roadstead, rade foraine (*f.*).

open sea, pleine mer (*f.*); mer libre (*f.*).

open space (as for instance on a wharf, as opposed to *covered space*, as sheds or warehouses), terre-plein (*m.*).

open wagon *or* open truck (opp. to *covered wagon* or *truck*, or *box wagon*), wagon découvert (*m.*); wagon ouvert (*m.*).

open (*v.t.*), ouvrir:
to open (*or* to open up) a country to trade, ouvrir un pays au commerce.
to open a credit for a traveller, ouvrir un crédit à, accréditer, un voyageur.
to open a credit with (*or* at) a bank, with a banker, with a correspondent, ouvrir un crédit en banque (*ou* dans une maison de banque), chez un banquier, auprès d'un correspondant.
to open a letter, ouvrir, décacheter, une lettre.
to open a meeting, ouvrir une séance.
to open an account at the bank, the books of a new company, ouvrir un compte à la banque, les livres d'une nouvelle société.
to open an account for someone in the ledger, ouvrir sur le grand livre un compte à quelqu'un.
to open an account (for oneself), se faire ouvrir un compte:
trader who wishes to open a current account at a bank, with a banker, commerçant qui veut se faire ouvrir un compte de chèques à une banque, chez un banquier (*m.*).

open (*v.i.*), ouvrir; s'ouvrir:
stock which opens at such or such a price, valeur qui ouvre à tel ou tel cours (*f.*).
office which does not open on Sunday, bureau qui n'ouvre pas le dimanche (*m.*).
the account opens with a debit balance of so much, le compte s'ouvre par un solde débiteur de tant.

opening (*n.*), ouverture (*f.*):
the head of the department superintends the opening of the letters, le chef du service préside à l'ouverture du courrier.
opening of the list of applications, ouverture de la souscription.
opening the hatches, ouverture des panneaux.

opening balance sheet (statement of affairs at commencement of business), bilan d'entrée (*m.*).

opening capital, capital initial (*m.*); capital d'apport (*m.*); capital d'établissement (*m.*).

opening entry (Bkkpg) (opp. to *closing entry*), article d'ouverture (*m.*); écriture d'ouverture (*f.*).

opening price (first price quoted at opening of day's market) (Stock Exch.) (opp. to *closing price*), premier cours (*m.*); cours d'ouverture (*m.*); cours du début (*m.*).

opening price (price at which shares are introduced on the market) (Stock Exch.), cours d'introduction (*m.*).

opening stock (Com.) (opp. to *closing stock*), stock au début de l'exercice (*m.*).

operate (*v.t.*), opérer; exploiter:
to operate a ship at a profit, at a loss, exploiter un navire à profit, à perte.

operate (*v.i.*), opérer:
agent who operates for his personal account, agent qui opère pour son compte personnel (*m.*).
to operate for a rise (Stock Exch.), opérer à la hausse; jouer à la hausse.

operating costs *or* **operating expenses,** dépenses d'exploitation (*f.pl.*); frais d'exploitation (*m.pl.*).

operation (*n.*), opération (*f.*); exploitation (*f.*):
financial operation, opération financière.

operator (pers.) (*n.*), opérateur, -trice; joueur, -euse; boursier, -ère:
telephone operator (girl), opératrice téléphonique.
operator for a rise, for a fall, opérateur (*ou* joueur) à la hausse, à la baisse.
many operators prefer to deal from day to day by means of one day options, nombre de boursiers préfèrent opérer au jour le jour à l'aide des primes pour le lendemain (*m.*).

opinion (*n.*), opinion (*f.*); avis (*m.*):
to form an opinion of the risk to which a cargo is exposed, se faire (*ou* se former) une opinion du risque auquel une cargaison est exposée.

to be of opinion, être d'avis; constater:
we are of opinion that (*or* in our opinion) such balance sheet is properly drawn up so as to exhibit a true and correct view of the state of the company's affairs (auditors' report, English formula), nous avons constaté que le bilan présenté par le conseil d'administration est l'expression exacte de la situation active et passive de la société (rapport des commissaires aux comptes, formule française).

opinion (of counsel) (*n.*), consultation (d'avocat) (*f.*):
counsel have the right to give opinions, les avocats ont le droit de donner des consultations.

opinion list, livre de renseignements (*m.*).

opposite side of an account, côté opposé d'un compte (*m.*).

option (*n.*), faculté (*f.*); option (*f.*):
to exercise the option of subscribing, exercer la faculté de souscrire.
to exercise one's right of option, exercer son droit d'option.
cancellation of the policy being at the option of the assured, résiliation de la police pouvant se faire à l'option de l'assuré (*f.*).
option of exchange, option de change.
option of repurchase, faculté de rachat; faculté de réméré:
to sell with option of repurchase, vendre avec faculté de rachat; vendre à réméré.

option (call on shares) (Fin.) (*n.*), option (*f.*):
to give to the brokers who place the shares an option on so many shares at so much, donner aux courtiers qui font le placement des titres une option de tant d'actions à tant.
option dealings, négociations à option (*f.pl.*).
house which has taken a loan half firm half on option, maison qui a pris un emprunt moitié ferme moitié à option (*f.*).
the goods on (*or* under) option, les marchandises en option (*f.pl.*).

option (*n.*) *or* **option bargain** (Stock or Produce Exch.), prime (*f.*); marché à prime (*m.*); négociation à prime (*f.*); marché libre (*m.*); marché conditionnel (*m.*):
firm bargains bind both the seller and the buyer; an option bargain binds the taker without binding the giver, les marchés fermes engagent à la fois le vendeur et l'acheteur; un marché à prime engage le vendeur sans engager l'acheteur.
the price of the same stock, at the same moment, is higher on option than firm, le cours d'une même valeur, au même moment, est plus élevé à prime que ferme.
option till the 5th, till the 19th (of the present month), prime au 5, au 19.
option till the next day, prime au (*ou* pour le) lendemain; petite prime au (*ou* pour le) lendemain.
option till to-morrow, prime pour demain.
option dealing, opérations à prime (*f.pl.*); négociations à prime (*f.pl.*); affaires à primes (*f.pl.*).
Note:—The **call option** in French is called **dont** = *of which*, i.e., the price quoted for the stock on call option is so much per share *dont* (of which) so much per share is option rate. (See examples of call option orders under **call** *or* **call option,** and under **dont** in French-English section of the dictionary.)
The **put option** in French is called **ou** = *or*, i.e., the price quoted for the stock on put option is so much per share *ou* (or) so much put option rate per share has to be paid. (See example of put option order under **put** *or* **put option.**)
The limit price at which the option is abandoned is called the **pied de la prime** or **limite de la prime—pied du dont** in case of

a call, **pied de l'ou** in case of a put; thus, supposing the option prices to be

        call: 33,50 francs dont 1
        put: 31,50 francs ou 1

32 francs 50 centimes represents the *pied du dont* and likewise the *pied de l'ou*.

In London, the option rate is independent of the option price quoted for the stock.

The following examples will serve to illustrate the above explanations:—

London example.—I decide to give for the call for current account on 1,000 XYZ shares. My broker says to me, I have a taker of 1s. at 25s., and I have a taker of 9d. at 25s. 6d. I decide on the former. I pay down the option money of £50 (= 1,000 shares at 1s.), and cover, if required. I now have the right to call 1,000 shares at 25s. up to the time for declaration of options. (In London, 2.45 on the day before contango day.) If the price of the shares does not exceed 25s., I abandon the option and lose my £50, plus charges for brokerage and stamp duty; if it exceeds 25s., I sell, provided I do not wish to take the shares firm. If after I have sold at a profit the stock should fall below my option price, I abandon the option and buy the stock on the market. If the stock should rise again, I repeat the operation, always being protected by my option.

Paris example.—The call option prices of X.Y.Z. shares are quoted at fr. 33,50 dont 1 f., that is to say, of which price of fr. 33·50 one franc is option rate; or, fr. 33 dont 50, i.e., of which price of 33 francs, 50 centimes is option rate. The *pied* or *limite de la prime* is therefore fr. 32·50. I give 1 franc per share for the call of 100 shares and pay down 100 francs option money, and cover, if required. If by the time for the declaration of options the price of the shares does not exceed fr. 32·50, I abandon the option and lose my 100 francs option money, and charges for brokerage and duties. If the price reaches say fr. 34·50, I sell and make 100 francs profit, less charges. If I sell at fr. 33·50 I only lose the charges, as the 1 franc realized above the *pied* is exactly balanced by the option money paid. If I sell at fr. 33, I lose 50 centimes per share, viz., the difference between my 1 franc option rate and the 50 centimes excess over the *pied*, plus charges. Supposing I do not want to sell, I can of course call the shares and take them firm by paying fr. 32·50 per share, viz., fr. 33·50, less 1 franc option money already paid, plus charges.

Another term in French option dealing that needs explanation is **cours de la réponse des primes** (price at time for declaration of options). This has no counterpart in English practice, the reason for which will be apparent from the following explanations. In London, if I do not sell, or declare that I abandon, before the time for declaration of options, I have necessarily to take the stock firm at the option price. In Paris, if I have not sold before the **heure de la réponse,** my broker either abandons the option for me, if the ruling price is at my *pied* or (in case of a call option) under, or, if the price is (in case of a call option) above my *pied*, he sells for me without waiting to be asked to do so. This sale of my option stock is put through to me at the *cours de la réponse*, which is the price ruling at the *heure de la réponse* (1.30 on the day before contango day in Paris). This *cours de la réponse* is not a more or less conventional price, like say a making up price. In fact, during the quarter of an hour preceding the *heure de la réponse* there is a veritable battle between the various interests involved, and fluctuations, often very violent, take place, according as greater or less quantities of options are exercised or abandoned.

Option dealings are very popular in France and take place on an enormous scale. Many interesting combinations are practised which are unknown, or at least uncommon, in England, where comparatively option bargains are dealt in to only a limited extent.

option (Corn Exchange) (*n.*). V. **options,** ci-après.

option declaration day *or* **option day** (Stock Exch.), jour de la réponse des primes (*m.*); jour de la réponse (*m.*).

option money (on a property), acompte de préférence (sur un immeuble) (*m.*).

option money (Stock Exch.), montant de la prime (*m.*):
speculator who abandons the option and limits his loss at so much, the option money, spéculateur qui abandonne la prime et limite sa perte à tant, le montant de la prime (*m.*).

option order (Stock Exch.), ordre à prime (*m.*).

option price (Stock Exch.), cours de prime (*m.*); prix de la prime (*m.*); base de la prime (*f.*); prix de base de la prime (*m.*).

option rate *or* **rate of option** *or simply* **rate** (*n.*) *or commonly, but incorrectly,* **option money** (Stock Exch.), prime (*f.*); taux unitaire de la prime (*m.*):
giver, taker, of the rate, payeur, receveur, de la prime (*m.*).

option stock *or* **stock on option** (opp. to *firm stock*), valeurs à prime (*f.pl.*); titres à prime (*m.pl.*).

option to double (Stock Exch.), doublé (*m.*); doublure (*f.*).

option to quadruple (Stock Exch.), quadruplé (*m.*).

option to treble (Stock Exch.), triplé (*m.*).

optional (*adj.*), facultatif, -ive:
salvage is optional and cannot be imposed, le sauvetage est facultatif et ne peut être imposé.

options (Corn Exchange) (*n.pl.*) (opp. to *spot*), livrable (*m.*):
in options on the coming campaign, business

although a little more active than the previous week was still only small, en livrable les affaires sur la future campagne, quoique un peu plus actives que la semaine précédente n'ont eu encore que peu d'importance.

options market (Corn Exchange), marché à terme (*m.*); marché du terme (*m.*).

or better (Stock Exch.), sauf mieux. V, exemple sous **better.**

order (direction; command; instructions) (*n.*), ordre (*m.*):
calling at a foreign port to receive orders, escale dans un port étranger pour recevoir des ordres (*f.*).
to transmit orders to a ship by wireless, transmettre des ordres à un navire par T.S.F.

order (methodical arrangement) (*n.*), ordre (*m.*):
to put papers in order, mettre des papiers en ordre.
the order of retirement shall be determined by lot, l'ordre de sortie est déterminé par un tirage au sort.

order (commission to buy, sell, obtain, or supply) (*n.*), commande (*f.*); demande (*f.*); ordre (*m.*); mandat (*m.*):
to give a large order for goods, faire une forte commande (*ou* demande) de marchandises.
execution of an order of insurance, exécution d'un ordre d'assurance (*f.*).
order to insure given before knowledge of the accident, mandat d'assurer donné avant la connaissance du sinistre.
stock exchange orders, ordres de bourse.
order for the settlement or for the account (Stock Exch.), ordre à terme.
orders in hand *or* unfilled orders, commandes (*ou* ordres) en carnet (*ou* en portefeuille).

order (direction as to payment or delivery) (*n.*), ordre (*m.*); mandat (*m.*); bon (*m.*); permis (*m.*):
order to pay *or* order for payment, ordre de payer; mandat; mandat de paiement:
a cheque is an order to pay addressed to the banker, le chèque est un ordre de payer (*ou* un mandat de paiement) adressé au banquier.
to put one's order on the back of a bill, mettre son ordre au dos d'un billet.
pay to the order of Mr X., payez à l'ordre de M. X.
money order *or* post office order, mandat de poste; mandat-poste (*m.*); mandat postal; mandat.
in practice, the bill of lading is made to the shipper's order, dans la pratique, le connaissement est établi à l'ordre du chargeur.
delivery order, bon de livraison.
landing order, permis de débarquement.

By order of the Board. V. sous **board.**

order (*v.t.*), commander:
to order goods, commander des marchandises.
to order each party to pay its own costs (Law), compenser les dépens.
to be ordered to pay the costs (Law), être condamné (-e) aux dépens (*ou* aux frais).

order book, livre de commandes (*m.*); livre d'ordres (*m.*); carnet de commandes (*m.*)

order cheque (opp. to *bearer cheque*), chèque à ordre (*m.*).

order form *or* simply **order** (*n.*) (the written and/or printed instrument), bon de commande (*m.*); bulletin de commande (*m.*).

order number, numéro de commande (*m.*).

ordinal number *or* simply **ordinal** (*n.*) (opp. to *cardinal number* or *cardinal*), nombre ordinal (*m.*).

ordinary (*adj.*) (Abbrev.: **ord.** *or* **ordy**), ordinaire:
ordinary average (Mar. Insce), avarie particulière (*f.*); avaries particulières (*f.pl.*); avarie simple (*f.*); avaries simples (*f.pl.*).
ordinary bills (trade paper), papier de commerce (*m.*); papier commercial (*m.*).
ordinary brands (metals), marques ordinaires (*f.pl.*).
ordinary creditor, créancier ordinaire (*m.*).
ordinary debt, créance ordinaire (*f.*).
ordinary general meeting, assemblée générale ordinaire (*f.*).
ordinary rate (telegrams, etc.), tarif ordinaire (*m.*).
ordinary season ticket, carte d'abonnement ordinaire (*f.*).
ordinary share certificate, certificat d'action(s) ordinaire(s) (*m.*).
ordinary shareholder *or* ordinary stockholder, actionnaire ordinaire (*m.* ou *f.*).
ordinary shares *or* simply shares *or* ordinary stock (*Abbrev.*: ord. *or* ordy), actions ordinaires (*f.pl.*); actions (*f.pl.*).
ordinary telegram, télégramme ordinaire (*m.*)

ordnance (*n.*), armement (*m.*).

ore charter, charte-partie de minerai (*f.*).

origin (*n.*), origine (*f.*); provenance (*f.*):
goods of foreign origin, marchandises d'origine (*ou* de provenance) étrangère (*f.pl.*).
country of origin, pays d'origine (*m.*).

original (*adj.*), original, -e, -aux; originaire; primitif, -ive:
original capital, capital originaire (*m.*); capital primitif (*m.*); capital d'origine (*m.*).
original cases, caisses d'origine (*f.pl.*):
goods to be delivered in original cases or any other original packages, les marchandises sont livrables en caisses d'origine ou tous autres emballages d'origine (*f.pl.*).
original invoice, facture originale (*f.*).
original manuscript, manuscrit original (*ou* primitif) (*m.*).
original receipt, primata de quittance (*m.*).
original stamped bill of lading, connaissement-chef (*m.*); timbre-chef (*m.*).
Note :—In French practice the *connaissement-chef* or *timbre-chef* (this being the bill of lading which is impressed with the stamp duty paid, the other copies bearing a denoting stamp) is given to the captain, and this is the copy which accompanies the goods, i.e., the *captain's copy.* The captain presents this *connaissement-chef* to the consignee on arrival, who endorses his

receipt on the back to accomplish it. The consignee can however, if he wishes, give to the captain, duly endorsed, the copy he has received from the shipper. This latter is the English method; the *captain's copy* (*exemplaire* [ou *copie*] *du capitaine*) being marked *not negotiable*.

original subscriber, souscripteur primitif (*m.*).

original (*n.*), original (*m.*); minute (*f.*) :
original of a deed, original, minute, d'un acte.
to compare the translation with the original, comparer la traduction à l'original.
bill of lading made in four originals, connaissement établi en quatre originaux (*m.*).

other side *or* **other party** (pers.), contre-partie (*f.*) :
seller who has to pay the call before delivering the stock to the other side (i.e., the buyer), vendeur qui a dû satisfaire au versement avant de livrer les titres à sa contre-partie.
generally, these intermediaries (i.e., brokers) interpose like a screen between the buyer and the seller; they deal between themselves, between intermediaries, between colleagues, without the other side knowing the name of their client, or their client that of the other side, généralement, ces intermédiaires s'interposent comme un écran entre l'acheteur et le vendeur; ils traitent entre eux, entre intermédiaires, entre collègues, sans que leur contre-partie connaisse le nom de leur client, ni leur client celui de la contre-partie.

out of date (lapsed), périmé, -e :
return half out of date (railway ticket), coupon de retour périmé (*m.*).

out of pocket expenses *or* **out of pockets** *or* **outgoings** (*n.pl.*) *or* **outlay** (*n.*), débours (*m.pl.*); déboursés (*m.pl.*); déboursements (*m.pl.*).

outbid the prices offered (to), enchérir sur les prix offerts.

outbound (*adj.*). Syn. de **outward bound**, q.v.

outdoor establishment *or* **outdoor staff** (Customs, etc.) (opp. to *indoor establishment* or *staff*), service actif (*m.*).

outer column (opp. to *inner column*), colonne extérieure (*f.*).

outer port *or* **outer harbour**, avant-port (*m.*).

outfit (*n.*), équipement (*m.*).

outfit (*v.t.*), équiper.

outflow (*n.*) (opp. to *inflow*), sortie (*f.*) :
an outflow of gold, or at least of capital, which might bring about the impoverishment of the country, une sortie d'or, ou tout au moins, de capitaux, qui pourrait entraîner l'appauvrissement du pays.

outgoing (*adj.*) (opp. to *incoming*), au départ; de départ; de sortie :
outgoing mail, courrier au départ (*m.*).
outgoing call (Teleph.), communication de départ (*f.*).
outgoing gold point *or* outgoing bullion point *or* outgoing specie point, gold-point de sortie (*m.*); gold-point d'exportation (*m.*); point de sortie de l'or (*m.*).

outgoings, outlay. V. sous **out of pocket expenses.**

outlet (*n.*), débouché (*m.*) :
outlet for trade, débouché à l'industrie.
port which serves as an outlet for the manufactured products of a country, port qui sert de débouché aux produits fabriqués d'un pays (*m.*).
the most useful encouragement for agricultural and manufacturing industry is to assure to it an outlet for its productions, l'encouragement le plus utile pour l'industrie agricole et manufacturière est de lui assurer le débouché de ses productions (*m.*).

outlook envelope, enveloppe à fenêtre (*f.*); enveloppe fenestrée (*f.*); enveloppe à panneau (*f.*).

outport (seaport) (*n.*) (opp. to *close port*), port de mer (*m.*); port maritime (*m.*).

output (*n.*), rendement (*m.*); production (*f.*) :
output of the staff, rendement du personnel.
to curtail the output of rubber, contingenter la production du caoutchouc.

outside broker, banquier marron (*m.*); courtier marron (*m.*).

outside broker's contract, contrat direct (*m.*).

outside broking, marronnage (*m.*). *Note :*—In France, *marronnage* (outside broking, i.e., exercising the functions of a broker by one who is not an accredited broker, is illegal.

outstanding (*adj.*), échu, -e; arriéré, -e; à payer :
outstanding expenses, frais échus (*m.pl.*); frais à payer (*m.pl.*); dépenses échues (*f.pl.*).
outstanding interest, intérêts échus (*m.pl.*).
outstanding matter, affaire arriérée (*f.*).
outstanding payment, paiement arriéré (*m.*).
all outstanding premiums, due by the insured, toutes primes échues, dues par l'assuré (*f.pl.*).

outturn (net weight of cargo unloaded on arrival of a ship) (*n.*), rendement (*m.*).

outturn report (unloading a ship), bordereau de débarquement (*m.*); feuille de pointage (*f.*).

outward bill of lading (opp. to *inward*, or *homeward, bill of lading*), connaissement de sortie (*m.*).

outward bound vessel *or* **outbound vessel** *or* **outward bounder** (opp. to *homeward bound*, or *home bound*, or *inward bound*, or *inbound, vessel*), navire en partance (*m.*); navire effectuant son voyage d'aller (*m.*).
Note :—*en partance* should be used in the sense of *about to sail; effectuant son voyage d'aller* in the sense of *outbound while proceeding on her voyage at sea*, as for example, in the question asked about a ship at sea : Is this ship outward bound or inward bound? Ce navire effectue-t-il son voyage d'aller ou son voyage de retour?

outward freight (opp. to *homeward*, or *return, freight*), fret d'aller (*m.*); fret de sortie (*m.*).

outward half (of a return ticket) (opp. to *return half*), coupon d'aller (*m.*).

outward journey *or* **outward trip** *or* **outward passage** *or* **outward voyage** *or* **outward bound voyage** *or* **outbound voyage** (opp. to *homeward*, or *return*, *journey*, *trip*, *passage*, or *voyage*), trajet d'aller (*m.*); voyage d'aller (*m.*); aller (*m.*).

outward manifest (opp. to *inward manifest*), manifeste de sortie (*m.*).

over (Banking) (*n.*), excédent (*m.*); boni (*m.*): cash shorts and overs, déficits et excédents de caisse (*ou* dans l'encaisse) (*m.pl.*).

over or under, en plus ou en moins: any difference over or under, toute différence en plus ou en moins (*f.*).

over ship's side, sous palan; sous vergues. V. exemple sous syn. **under ship's derrick.**

over spot (discount) (Forward exchange rates) (Abbrev.: **d.**), report (*m.*). V. exemples sous syn. **discount.**

overactivity (*n.*), suractivité (*f.*).

overassessment (*n.*), surtaux (*m.*); exagération d'imposition (*f.*).

overbid (*n.*), suroffre (*f.*).

overbid (*v.i.*) *or* **to overbid the prices offered,** enchérir sur les prix offerts.

overboard (*adv.*), par-dessus bord: to throw overboard goods of a dangerous nature, jeter par-dessus bord des marchandises d'une nature dangereuse.

overcapitalization (*n.*), surcapitalisation (*f.*).

overcapitalize (*v.t.*), surcapitaliser.

overcharge (*n.*) (Abbrev.: **o/c.**), survente (*f.*); surcharge (*f.*); majoration (*f.*).

overcharge (*v.t.*), surcharger; trop taxer: taxes are paid in certain months which are thus overcharged, les contributions se règlent certains mois qui sont ainsi surchargés (*f.pl.*).
postal packets wrongly charged or overcharged, objets de correspondance taxés à tort ou trop taxés (*m.pl.*).

overcharge (*v.i.*), surfaire; survendre: shopkeeper who is in the habit of overcharging, marchand qui a l'habitude de surfaire (*ou* de survendre) (*m.*).

overcharge for (to), survendre; surfaire: to overcharge for one's goods, survendre, surfaire, sa marchandise.

overcharge in (to), majorer; compter en trop sur: to overcharge in an invoice, majorer une facture.
goods overcharged in our invoice, marchandises comptés en trop sur notre facture (*f.pl.*).

overdraft (Banking) (*n.*) (Abbrev.: **o/d.**), découvert (*m.*); avance à découvert (*f.*): the overdraft of a bank account is the amount by which the debit exceeds the credit, le découvert d'un compte de banque est la somme dont le débit surpasse le crédit.
average overdraft, découvert moyen.

overdraw (*v.t.*), mettre à découvert: to overdraw an account, mettre un compte à découvert.

overdrawn (to be) *or* **overdrawn at the bank (to be),** être à découvert; avoir débit en banque; avoir débit à la banque.

overdrawn account, compte à découvert (*m.*); compte désapprovisionné (*m.*).

overdue (*adj.*), arriéré, -e: overdue payment, paiement arriéré (*m.*).

overestimate (*n.*), surestimation (*f.*); surévaluation (*f.*); majoration (*f.*).

overestimate (*v.t.*), surestimer; surévaluer; majorer.

overhead charges (Costing) (opp. to *direct expenses* or *establishment charges* or *departmental charges*), frais généraux (*m.pl.*); frais fixes (*m.pl.*); frais indirects (*m.pl.*); dépenses fixes (*ou* indirectes) (*f.pl.*).

overhead expenses *or* **overhead charges** (standing expenses), frais généraux (*m.pl.*); dépenses de maison (*f.pl.*).

overinsurance (*n.*), surassurance (*f.*).

overinsure (*v.t.*), surassurer: assured who is overinsured by double insurance, assuré qui est surassuré par assurances cumulatives (*m.*).

overland journey *or* **overland travel,** voyage par terre (*m.*).

overland route, voie de terre (*f.*); route de terre (*f.*).

overload (*v.t.*), surcharger: to overload a ship above the water line, surcharger un navire au-dessus de la ligne de flottaison.
market overloaded with stock, marché surchargé de titres (*m.*).

overloading *or* **overload** (*n.*), surcharge (*f.*): overloading a ship, surcharge d'un navire.

overpay (*v.t.*) *or* **overpay for** (to), surpayer; payer en trop; trop payer: to overpay an employee, surpayer un employé.
return of an amount overpaid, ristourne d'une somme payée en trop (*ou* d'une somme trop payée) (*f.*).
countries which were obliged to overpay for English coal, pays qui étaient obligés de surpayer les charbons anglais (*m.pl.*).

overpayment (*n.*), plus-payé (*m.*); trop payé (*m.*); surpaye (*f.*); paiement en trop (*m.*).

overproduction (*n.*), surproduction (*f.*).

overrate (*v.t.*), surfaire: to overrate the value of a share, surfaire la valeur d'une action.

overriding commission, commission syndicale additionnelle (*f.*).

oversea (*adj.*), d'outre-mer: oversea colonies, colonies d'outre-mer (*f.pl.*).

oversea *or* **overseas** (*adv.*), outre-mer: to settle oversea (*or* overseas), s'établir outre-mer.

oversubscribed (*adj.*), surpassé, -e; sur-souscrit, -e: the issue was oversubscribed, l'émission fut surpassée (*ou* sur-souscrite) (*f.*).

overtime (*n.*), heures supplémentaires (*f.pl.*): overtime, when it cannot be avoided, is paid extra, les heures supplémentaires, quand on ne peut pas les éviter, sont payées à part.

the amount paid for overtime, la somme payée pour les heures supplémentaires.
to work overtime, travailler en heures supplémentaires.

overvaluation (*n.*), surestimation (*f.*); surévaluation (*f.*); majoration (*f.*):
overvaluation of the assets in a balance sheet, majoration des valeurs formant l'actif d'un bilan.

overvalue (*v.t.*), surestimer; surévaluer; majorer:
to overvalue the exchange, majorer les valeurs d'échange.

overweight coin (single coin), pièce forte (*f.*). V. exemple sous **standard coin.**

overweight money or **overweight coin**, monnaie forte (*f.*).

overwork (*v.t.*), surmener; surcharger:
to overwork one's clerks, surmener, surcharger, ses employés.

overworking (*n.*), surmenage (*m.*).

owe (*v.t.*), devoir; être redevable de:
to owe so many pounds, devoir tant de livres.
I owe you nothing, je ne vous suis redevable de rien.
to owe a balance of, devoir un reliquat de; être redevable de; redevoir:
to owe a balance of so much on an account, redevoir tant sur un compte.

owe (*v.i.*), devoir:
to owe all round, devoir de tous côtés.

owing (*adj.*), dû, due; échu, -e; arriéré, -e:
all premiums due, owing by the insured, toutes primes échues, dues par l'assuré (*f.pl.*).
rent owing, loyer arriéré (*m.*).

own (*v.t.*), posséder:
to own a house, a lot of property, posséder une maison, de grands biens.

owner (pers.) (*n.*), possesseur (*m.*); propriétaire (*m. ou f.*):
to be the owner of a property, être possesseur d'une propriété.
owner of the goods, propriétaire de la marchandise.

owner (shipowner) (*n.*), armateur (*m.*); propriétaire (*m.*); fréteur (*m.*):
Note :—The reasons for translation of the French words *propriétaire*, *armateur*, and *fréteur*, by the single English word *owner* (or *shipowner*) are the following:—
In French law and practice the person concerned with the ship is considered in three qualities, viz.—
(1) As the actual proprietor of the ship. In this case he is known as the *propriétaire*.
(2) As the person who mans, equips, and supplies the ship, when he is known as the *armateur*, or if he owns her as well, as the *armateur-propriétaire*.
(3) As the person letting out a contract of affreightment (charter or bill of lading), when he is still known as the *armateur*, or less commonly, as the *fréteur*.
The uniformity of expression in English, viz., *owner*, is due to the fact that in English law and practice the person presented in

any of these three qualities is considered for the time being as the owner, and the possession of the ship is considered for the time as being vested in him.
In England, the position and duties of the *armateur* are usually discharged by the ship's *managers*, so that, according to circumstances or context the word *armateur* may have to be translated as *owner or his manager or agent*, as for instance in the translation of an Act of Parliament, or the like, or by one or both of the words *manager or/and agent*, as for instance in the translation of the sentence *le propriétaire du navire ou son armateur loue au chargeur, the shipowner or his manager (or/and agent) lets to the shipper*.
In the large majority of cases, however, *owner* will be found to be the correct and sufficient translation of *armateur*.

a contract of affreightment conjoins an owner and a shipper, un contrat d'affrètement unit un armateur et un chargeur.
the obligation of the owner to provide a seaworthy vessel fit to carry the cargo, l'obligation pour l'armateur de fournir un navire en bon état de navigabilité et approprié au transport de la cargaison (*f.*).
captain who is himself owner of the ship, capitaine qui est lui-même propriétaire du navire (*m.*).
owner who is only obligated on his ship and the freight, propriétaire qui ne s'oblige que sur son navire et le fret.
charter party which specifies the names of the owner and charterer, charte-partie qui énonce les noms du fréteur et de l'affréteur.
Note :—**owners** collectively may be rendered by armement (*m.*), as,
the difficulties encountered by owners, les difficultés que rencontrent l'armement (*f.pl.*).
a charterer is a person who contracts with the owners, l'affréteur est une personne qui contracte avec l'armement (*m.*).
the owners are bound to hand the bill of lading to the holder of the mate's receipt, l'armement est tenu de remettre le connaissement au titulaire du reçu provisoire.

owner (of a share or shares in a ship) (*n.*), quirataire (*m.*); portionnaire (*m.*): [Cf. **share** (in a ship).]
ship which is the property of several owners, navire qui est la propriété de plusieurs quirataires (*m.*).

owner-charterer [**owner-charterers** *pl.*] (*n.*), armateur-affréteur (*m.*).

owner's sheet (Rly.) (opp. to *company's sheet*), bâche appartenant à l'expéditeur (*f.*); bâche particulière (*f.*).

owner's wagon (Rly.), wagon appartenant à un particulier (*m.*); wagon de particulier (*m.*); wagon particulier (*m.*).

ownership (*n.*), propriété (*f.*):
proof of a right to the ownership of stock, justification d'un droit à la propriété des titres (*f.*).

P

pack (v.t.), emballer :
to pack goods, emballer des marchandises.
package (parcel) (n.) (Abbrev. : pkg. [pkgs pl.]
or pk. [pks pl.]), colis (m.) ; envoi (m.).
package (packing) (n.), emballage (m.). V.
exemple sous original cases.
packed consignment (Transport), envoi à couvert
(m.).
packet (n.), paquet (m.) ; envoi (m.) ; objet (m.) :
postal packet, paquet-poste (m.) ; envoi postal ;
objet postal ; objet de correspondance ;
correspondance (f.). V. note sous postal
packet, sous postal.
it is permissible to enclose in the same packet
samples and printed matter, il est permis
de réunir, en un même paquet, des
échantillons et des imprimés.
packet of printed papers, envoi d'imprimés.
packets other than letters and postcards, les
envois autres que les lettres et cartes
postales.
packet (passenger steamer) (n.), paquebot (m.).
packing (n.), emballage (m.) :
packing in close cases, in crates, emballage
en caisse pleine, en caisse à claire-voie.
packing for shipment, emballage maritime ;
emballage pour transport outre-mer.
packing paper, papier d'emballage (m.).
pad (memorandum pad) (n.), bloc-notes (m.) ;
block-notes (m.).
pad (stamp pad) (n.), tampon (m.).
pad stamp, timbre humide (m.).
paddle boat, bateau à roues (m.).
page (n.), page (f.) ; folio (m.) :
the pages of a book, les pages d'un livre.
page or paginate (v.t.), paginer ; folioter ;
coter ; chiffrer :
to page a book, a register, a book of account,
paginer, folioter, coter, chiffrer, un livre,
un registre, un livre de comptabilité.
page (to number the pages consecutively, as
opposed to to folio) (v.t.), paginer à livre
fermé :
in bookkeeping, the journal is paged, that is
to say, each page bears a different number,
en comptabilité, le journal est paginé à
livre fermé, c'est-à-dire que chaque page
porte un numéro différent. Cf. folio (v.t.).
paging or pagination (n.), pagination (f.) ; foliotage (m.).
paging or pagination (as opposed to folioing or
foliation) (n.), pagination à livre fermé (f.).
paid (salaried) (adj.), salarié, -e :
a paid secretary, un secrétaire salarié.
paid (said of shares) (p.p.) (Abbrev. : p. or pd).
V. sous pay (v.t.).
paid bills, paid cheques, etc. (bills of exchange,
cheques, etc. put up into bundles after
payment), rentrées (f.pl.) :
the paid bills of June, les rentrées de juin.
paid cash book (Banking), main courante de
dépenses (f.) ; main courante de sortie (f.) ;

chiffrier de dépenses (ou de sortie) (m.) ;
brouillard de dépenses (ou de sortie) (m.).
paid-on charges (Rly.), débours (m.pl.) ; déboursés (m.pl.) :
paid-on charges on carriage forward consignments, débours sur envois en port dû.
paid-on charges are sums advanced by the
railway companies at the expense of the
goods, either when collecting, or while in
transit, les débours (ou déboursés) sont des
sommes avancées par les administrations des
chemins de fer à la charge de la marchandise,
soit lors de la remise au transport, soit en
cours de route.
paid up capital (opp. to authorized, or nominal,
or registered, capital), capital versé (m.) ;
capital effectif (m.) ; capital réel (m.).
paid up share capital, capital-actions versé (m.).
painted tare, tare inscrite (f.) :
goods in bulk can be weighed on a weighbridge
and their net weight obtained by deducting
from the total weight found the tare painted
on the wagon, les marchandises en vrac
peuvent être pesées sur pont-bascule et
leur poids net obtenu en déduisant du poids
total reconnu la tare inscrite sur le wagon.
pamphlet (n.), brochure (f.).
Panama canal register or Panama canal tonnage,
jauge de Panama (f.) ; tonnage canal de
Panama (m.).
panel envelope, enveloppe à panneau (f.) ; enveloppe à fenêtre (f.) ; enveloppe fenestrée
(f.).
panic (n.), panique (f.) :
panic on the stock exchange, panique sur la
bourse.
panic prices, cours de panique (m.pl.).
paper (n.), papier (m.) :
writing paper, papier à écrire.
stock not worth more than the price of the
paper, titres ne valant plus que le prix du
papier (m.pl.).
just now, nobody is complaining ; everybody
is making money, on paper, pour le moment,
nul ne se plaint ; tout le monde gagne de
l'argent, sur le papier.
paper (written or printed pledges or promises
to pay) (n.), papier (m.) ; papiers (m.pl.) ;
valeurs (f.pl.) :
negotiable paper, papier négociable ; papiers
commerçables.
paper is in request on our money market and
it is insufficient to satisfy the demand, le
papier est recherché sur notre marché
monétaire et il est insuffisant pour satisfaire les demandes.
paper (ship's) (used chiefly in the plural) (n.),
papier (de bord) (m.) ; pièce (de bord) (f.) ;
expédition (f.) :
the vessel is reputed to be ready to sail when
the master is provided with his papers for
his voyage, le bâtiment est censé prêt à

faire voile lorsque le capitaine est muni
de ses expéditions pour son voyage.

customs papers (such as ships' clearance papers,
transires, bond notes, receipts, and the like),
expéditions de douane.

paper (newspaper) (*n.*), journal (*m.*) :
to advertise in a paper, faire une annonce,
insérer une annonce, dans un journal.

paper case, papeterie (*f.*).

paper fastener or **paper clip,** attache (de bureau)
(*f.*).

paper franc, franc-papier (*m.*) :
5,000 gold francs or 25,000 French paper
francs, 5 000 francs-or ou 25 000 francs-
papier français.

paper guide (of a typewriter), guide-papier (*m.*).

paper knife, coupe-papier (*m.*).

paper money or **paper currency** (convertible),
monnaie de papier (*f.*).

paper money or **paper currency** (inconvertible),
papier-monnaie (*m.*) ; monnaie fictive (*f.*) ;
monnaie fiduciaire (*f.*) ; numéraire fictif
(*m.*) :
the currency of (inconvertible) paper money is
forced, le cours du papier-monnaie est forcé.

paper securities or **paper holdings** or, *but less
correctly,* **paper money,** papiers-valeurs
(*m.pl.*) ; valeurs-papiers (*f.pl.*) ; valeurs
fiduciaires (*f.pl.*) ; titres fiduciaires (*m.pl.*) ;
portefeuille-titres (*m.*) ; portefeuille de titres
(*m.*) ; portefeuille-valeurs (*m.*) ; portefeuille
de valeurs (*m.*) ; portefeuille (*m.*) :
to have all one's fortune invested in paper
securities, avoir toute sa fortune en portefeuille.

paper shelf (of a typewriter), plaque-support
de papier (*f.*).

paper standard (money) (opp. to *metallic standard*),
étalon-papier (*m.*).

paper weight, presse-papiers (*m.*).

par (*n.*), pair (*m.*) :
mint par or mint par of exchange or par of
exchange or *simply* par, pair intrinsèque ;
pair métallique ; pair du change ; pair :
the mint par (or the par of exchange) of the
pound sterling compared with the French
franc is 124 fr. 21 (more exactly 124·2134),
le pair intrinsèque (*ou* métallique) (*ou* le
pair du change) de la livre sterling comparée
au franc français est 124 fr. 21 (plus exactement 124,2134).

exchange at par, change au pair (*m.*).

par of stocks, pair des effets :
a share of £1 is at par when its current price
is £1, une action de 1 *l.* est au pair lorsque
son prix courant est de 1 *l.*

the par of a stock is the nominal value of that
stock fixed at the time of issue, le pair
d'un titre est la valeur nominale de ce titre
fixé lors de l'émission.

parcel (package) (*n.*) (Abbrev. : **pcl** [**pcls** *pl.*]),
colis (*m.*) : (Cf. **parcels,** ci-après.)
postal parcel, colis postal.
parcel on which a trade charge is to be
collected, colis grevé de remboursement ;
colis contre remboursement.

parcel on hand, refused. V. sous **on hand,
refused.**

parcel (collection ; group ; mass ; lot) (*n.*),
envoi (*m.*) ; partie (*f.*) ; lot (*m.*) ; paquet
(*m.*) :
parcel of goods, envoi, partie, lot, de marchandises :
the value of a parcel of goods, la valeur d'un
envoi de marchandises.
to offer on the market big parcels of shares,
offrir sur le marché de fortes parties d'actions.
to sell one's shares in small parcels, vendre
ses titres par petits paquets.

parcel (of wheat) (Corn Exch.) (*n.*), parcelle
(de blé) (*f.*) :
parcels of Northern Manitoba March sellers
at 42/6d., parcelles de Manitoba nord
mars 42/6d. vendeur.

parcel post, service des colis postaux (*m.*).
Note :—In England, the parcel post is run
by the Government post office. In most
parts of France, it is run by the railway
and shipping companies on behalf of the
Government.

parcels (*n.pl.*) or **parcels and other merchandise
by passenger train, passenger boat, or aeroplane,** messageries (*f.pl.*) ; articles de
messagerie (*m.pl.*) ; marchandises de la
messagerie (*f.pl.*) ; marchandises de grande
vitesse (*f.pl.*) :
parcels tonnage, tonnage des messageries
(*m.*).
parcels and goods, articles de messagerie et
marchandises.

parcels cartage (collection or delivery of parcels
in towns) (Rly.), factage (*m.*).

parcels cartage service, service de factage (*m.*).

parcels office or **parcel office,** bâtiment des
messageries (*m.*) ; bureau de messageries
(*m.*) ; messagerie (*f.*).

parcels rate(s) (Rly.), tarif de la messagerie
(*m.*).

parcels service or **parcel service,** service de la
messagerie (*m.*) ; service de (*ou des*) messageries (*m.*) ; messagerie (*f.*) :
railway parcel service, service ferroviaire des
messageries ; service de messageries par
voie ferrée.

parcels traffic or **parcel traffic,** trafic des messageries (*m.*) ; messageries (*f.pl.*).

parcels train, train de messagerie (*m.*) ; train
de messageries (*m.*).

parent (*adj.*), mère (*f.*) :
parent company (opp. to *subsidiary company*),
société mère (*f.*) ; compagnie mère (*f.*).
parent house (opp. to *branch house*), maison
mère (*f.*).

pari passu, pari passu :
new shares which participate in the profits
pari passu with the old shares, actions
nouvelles qui participent aux bénéfices pari
passu avec les actions anciennes (*f.pl.*).
to rank pari passu. V. sous **rank.**

parity [**parities** *pl.*] (equivalence of the rates of
exchange on two markets) (*n.*), parité (*f.*) :

parity between two rates, parité entre deux cours.

exchange at parity, change à la parité ; change à parité (*m.*) :

when the rate of exchange of two markets on their respective lists—London on the Paris list, Paris on the London list—or that of the same market on different lists, give an equivalent sum, the quotations are said to be at parity (*or* when the premium of one above par is in exact proportion to the discount of the other, the two exchanges are said to be at parity) ; when the reverse is the case, they are said to be tel quel, lorsque le cours du change de deux places sur leurs cotes respectives— Londres sur la cote de Paris, Paris sur la cote de Londres—ou celui d'une même place sur différentes cotes, donnent une somme équivalente, on dit que les cotes sont à la parité ; dans le cas contraire, elles sont dites telles quelles (*ou* quand la prime de l'un au-dessus du pair est exactement proportionnelle à la perte l'autre, l'on dit que les deux changes sont à parité ; dans le cas contraire, ils sont dits tels quels).

parity table, table des parités (*f.*).

parlour car (Rly.), voiture-salon (*f.*) ; wagon-salon (*m.*).

parlour restaurant car (Rly.), voiture salon-restaurant (*f.*).

part (*n.*), partie (*f.*) ; portion (*f.*) ; part (*f.*) :
part of a risk, partie d'un risque.

amount divided into a certain number of equal parts, somme divisée en un certain nombre de parties égales (*f.*).

agreement between Mr A. of the one part and Mr B. of the other part, convention entre Monsieur A. d'une part et Monsieur B. d'autre part (*f.*).

of the second part, of the third part, de seconde part, de troisième part.

part cargo charter (distinguished from *whole cargo charter*), affrètement partiel (*m.*).

part owner, copropriétaire (*m.* ou *f.*).

part truck load (Rly.) (distinguished from *truck load* or *full truck load*), wagon incomplet (*m.*) ; charge incomplète de wagon (*f.*) ; charge incomplète (*f.*) ; partie de chargement de wagon (*f.*).

part truck load rates, tarif des wagons incomplets (*ou* des charges incomplètes) (*m.*).

part with (to), céder :
to part with a property, céder une propriété.

partial (*adj.*), partiel, -elle :
partial acceptance (of a bill of exchange), acceptation partielle (*f.*) ; acceptation restreinte (*f.*).

partial award (Arbitration), sentence partielle (*f.*).

partial loss (Insce) (*Abbrev. :* p.l.) (opp. to *total loss*), perte partielle (*f.*) ; sinistre partiel (*m.*) :
partial loss of the goods, perte partielle de la marchandise.

the method of adjustment of partial or total losses, le mode de règlement des sinistres partiels ou totaux.

partial total loss (Insce), perte totale partielle (*f.*).

partially (*adv.*), partiellement.

participant (pers.) (*n.*), participant, -e :
participant in a distribution, participant à une répartition.

participate (*v.i.*), participer :
to participate in losses, participer aux pertes.
bonds which participate in periodical drawings, obligations qui participent à des tirages au sort périodiques (*f.pl.*).

participating reinsurance (distinguished from *excess reinsurance*), réassurance de partage (*f.*).

participation (*n.*), participation (*f.*) :
participation in profits, participation aux bénéfices.

particular average (Mar. Insce) (Abbrev. : **p.a.** or **P.A.**) (opp. to *general average*), avarie particulière (*f.*) ; avaries particulières (*f.pl.*) ; avarie simple (*f.*) ; avaries simples (*f.pl.*).

particular average adjustment, règlement d'avarie particulière (*m.*).

particular lien (opp. to *general lien*), privilège spécial (*m.*).

particular partnership (opp. to *general partnership*), société en participation (*f.*) ; association commerciale en participation (*f.*) ; association en participation (*f.*).

particular power (Law) (opp. to *general power*), procuration spéciale (*f.*) ; pouvoir spécial (*m.*) ; mandat spécial (*m.*).

particulars (*n.pl.*), détails (*m.pl.*) ; détail (*m.*) ; indications (*f.pl.*) ; mentions (*f.pl.*) ; énonciations (*f.pl.*) ; libellé (*m.*) ; libellés (*m.pl.*) ; renseignements (*m.pl.*) ; précisions (*f.pl.*) :
particulars of an account, détails d'un compte.

payments as per particulars in cash book, paiements dont détail au livre de caisse (*m.pl.*).

pending receipt of further particulars, en attendant réception de plus amples détails.

law which requires that the bill of lading should contain the following essential particulars : the name of the ship and that of the shipper, etc., loi qui exige que le connaissement porte les mentions (*ou* les énonciations) (*ou* les indications) essentielles suivantes : le nom du navire et celui du chargeur, etc.

columns for entering the following particulars, colonnes pour l'inscription des indications (*ou* des mentions) suivantes (*ou* des libellés suivants) (*f.pl.*).

to enter in the particulars the date, the number, the amount, the due date of the bill, inscrire dans le libellé la date, le numéro, la somme, l'échéance de l'effet.

the particulars of an entry (*or* of an item) in the ledger, le libellé d'un article (*ou* d'une écriture) dans le grand livre.

for freights and further particulars apply to the agents, pour frets et autres renseignements s'adresser aux agents.

particulars column, colonne de libellé (*f.*).
partition (office fitting) (*n.*), cloison (*f.*) :
   glass partition, cloison de verre.
partly paid (Abbrev.: **ptly pd**) *or* **partly paid up**
   (opp. to *fully paid* or *fully paid up*), non
   libéré, -e ; non entièrement (*ou* non complètement) (*ou* non intégralement) libéré, -e ; non
   entièrement versé, -e ; partiellement libéré, -e :
   partly paid shares, actions non libérées (*f.pl.*) ;
   actions non entièrement (*ou* non complètement) (*ou* non intégralement) libérées
   (*f.pl.*) ; titres non libérés (*m.pl.*) ; titres
   partiellement libérés (*m.pl.*).
Warning:—The methods of quoting partly
   paid shares in France and England are
   different. In England, the actual price
   is quoted, in France, the nominal value
   plus the premium, or minus the discount,
   is quoted. Thus, in England, a 5s. share
   2s. 6d. paid, being dealt in at 1s. premium,
   would be quoted 3s. 6d. In France, a 500
   franc share, 300 francs paid, being dealt in
   at 100 francs premium, would be quoted
   600 francs, but the actual price would of
   course be 400 francs, viz. :—fr. 600 (quoted
   price) less fr. 200 (uncalled) = fr. 400.
   In France, as in England, if a share is
   only partly paid, the amount paid up is
   stated against the share in the quotation
   list.
   partly paid capital *or* capital partly paid up,
   capital non entièrement versé (*m.*) ; capital
   non libéré (*m.*).
partly secured creditor (opp. to *fully secured
   creditor*), créancier partiellement nanti
   (*m.*).
partner (pers.) (*n.*), associé, -e ; associé (-e) en
   nom collectif :
   partner in a bank, associé d'une maison de
   banque.
partner in joint account, coparticipant, -e.
partnership (*n.*) *or* **partnership firm,** société (*f.*) ;
   société en nom collectif (*f.*) ; association
   (*f.*) :
   after dissolution of the partnership, the
   partners divide the partnership funds,
   après la dissolution de la société, les associés
   se partagent le fonds social.
   we have to inform you that the partnership
   which has existed between us is dissolved
   from to-day, nous avons l'honneur de
   porter à votre connaissance que la société
   qui a existé entre nous est dissoute à
   partir de ce jour.
   verbal partnership, société verbale en nom
   collectif.
   limited partnership, société en commandite.
   particular partnership *or* special partnership,
   société en participation ; association (*ou*
   association commerciale) en participation.
partnership capital *or* **partnership funds,** capital
   social (*m.*) ; fonds social (*m.*). V. exemple
   sous **partnership.**
partnership debt, dette de société (*f.*).
partnership deed, contrat de société (*m.*) ; contrat d'association (*m.*).

party [**parties** *pl.*] (pers.) (*n.*), partie (*f.*) ; ayant
   droit (*m.*) :
   to become party to an action, se rendre partie
   dans un procès.
   to secure the consent of all parties, obtenir
   le consentement de tous les ayants droit.
party concerned *or* **interested party,** intéressé,
   -e ; partie intéressée (*f.*).
party entitled, ayant droit (*m.*) :
   the interest on the debentures and the dividends on the shares are paid to the
   parties entitled against surrender of the
   coupons, l'intérêt des obligations et les
   dividendes des actions sont payés aux ayants
   droit contre remise des coupons.
party named (in a letter of credit, or the like),
   accrédité, -e :
   to enable the correspondent to identify the
   party named, pour permettre au correspondant de reconnaître l'identité de l'accrédité.
party ticket (Rly.), billet collectif (*m.*).
pass (*v.t. & v.i.*). V. exemples :
   to pass a counterfeit coin, a forged cheque,
   passer une pièce fausse, un faux chèque.
   to pass a cheque through the clearing house,
   compenser un chèque.
   to pass a customs entry of a ship, of goods,
   faire une déclaration en douane d'un navire,
   de marchandises.
   to pass a dividend (not to declare one), passer
   un dividende. V. exemple sous **passing.**
   to pass a request for a telephone call (to the
   exchange), présenter une demande de
   communication téléphonique ; demander
   une conversation téléphonique.
   to pass a resolution, prendre une résolution
   (*ou* une délibération) (*ou* une décision) ;
   adopter une proposition.
   to pass a transfer (Bkkpg), faire un contre-
   passement.
   to pass a vote of thanks to the directors,
   voter des remerciements aux administrateurs.
   to pass an entry (Bkkpg), passer une écriture ; passer un article en compte.
   to pass an item to current account, passer,
   porter, un article en compte courant.
   to pass in transit (*v.t.*), transiter ; passer
   en transit :
   to pass goods in transit, transiter des marchandises.
   to pass in transit (*v.i.*), transiter ; passer
   en transit :
   goods passing in transit through France,
   through the Panama canal, marchandises
   transitant par la France, par le canal de
   Panama (*f.pl.*).
   (*steamer*) X. (for Antwerp) passed (*or* psd)
   (*or* p.) Ushant 31 (*date*) (Shipping News),
   (*steamer*) X. passé Ouessant le 31 (*date*)
   pour Anvers (Mouvement des Navires).
   this coin passes in France, cette pièce a cours
   en France.
pass book (Banking), carnet de compte (*m.*) ;
   carnet de banque (*m.*).

pass book (motor cars at customs), carnet de passages en douane (*m.*).

pass sheet (motor cars at customs), triptyque (*m.*):
the pass sheet is made up of three leaves : a *counterfoil*, an *importation voucher*, and an *exportation voucher*, le triptyque se compose de trois volants : une *souche*, un *volant d'entrée*, et un *volant de sortie*.

passage (*n.*), passage (*m.*); traversée (*f.*); trajet (*m.*); voyage (*m.*):
the passage between England and the continent, le passage (*ou* la traversée) entre l'Angleterre et le continent.
a rough passage, une traversée mouvementée.
the cost of unloading and passage through the customs, le coût du déchargement et du passage en douane.

passage money, prix de passage (*m.*); prix du voyage (*m.*).

passage ticket, billet de passage (*m.*); billet de voyage (*m.*).

passenger (pers.) (*n.*), voyageur, -euse; passager, -ere : (*Note :*—*voyageur* can be used of a passenger using any means of locomotion, whether on land or sea, or in the air. *passager* is confined to boat, boat train, and air, passengers.)
all these steamers take a limited number of passengers, tous ces vapeurs prennent un nombre limité de passagers.

passenger and goods train, train mixte (*m.*).

passenger and parcels service, messagerie (*f.*); messageries (*f.pl.*).

passenger carriage *or* **passenger coach** *or* **passenger car** (Rly.), voiture à voyageurs (*f.*).

passenger certificate (ship's), certificat à passagers (*m.*).

passenger contract (land, sea, or air), contrat de voyage (*m.*); contrat de transport des voyageurs (*m.*).

passenger contract (sea or air only), contrat de passage (*m.*); contrat de transport des passagers (*m.*).

passenger engine, locomotive à voyageurs (*f.*).

passenger kilometre, voyageur-kilomètre (Rly.) (*m.*); passager-kilomètre (air) (*m.*); voyageur kilométrique (Rly.) (*m.*); passager kilométrique (air) (*m.*), analogue au *passenger mile* anglais (voyageur mille *ou* passager mille).

passenger list, liste des passagers (*f.*); feuille des passagers (*f.*).

passenger rates, tarif (*m.*) (*ou* tarifs [*m.pl.*]) de voyageurs.

passenger receipts, recettes voyageurs (*f.pl.*).

passenger service, service de voyageurs (*ou* de passagers) (*m.*).

passenger ship *or* **passenger boat** *or* **passenger vessel** *or* **passenger steamer** (opp. to *cargo boat*), paquebot (*m.*); paquebot à voyageurs (*m.*); paquebot à passagers (*m.*); paquebot à vapeur (*m.*); navire à passagers (*m.*).

passenger station, gare de (*ou* des) voyageurs (*f.*); gare de grande vitesse (*f.*).

passenger ticket, billet de voyageur (*m.*).

passenger traffic (land, sea, or air), trafic des voyageurs (*m.*); trafic voyageurs (*m.*).

passenger traffic (sea, air, or boat train), trafic des passagers (*m.*); trafic passagers (*m.*).

passenger train, train de voyageurs (*m.*); convoi de voyageurs (*m.*); train de grande vitesse (*m.*); grande vitesse (*f.*):
goods sent by passenger train, marchandises expédiées en grande vitesse (*f.pl.*).

passengers' luggage (*or* **baggage**), bagages des voyageurs (*ou* des passagers) (*m.pl.*).

passing (of a dividend) (*n.*), passation (*f.*):
on the announcement of the passing of the dividend, the shares became heavy, sur l'annonce de la passation de son dividende, l'action s'est alourdie.

passing (a resolution) (*n.*), adoption (d'une résolution) (*f.*).

passing entries (Bkkpg), passation d'écritures (*f.*); passation des articles en compte (*f.*).

passive (*adj.*) (opp. to *active*), passif, -ive : passive debt, dette passive (*f.*).

passport (certificate for free passage of persons) (*n.*), passeport (*m.*):
the customs officials are directed to require travellers to show their passports, les préposés des douanes sont chargés d'exiger des voyageurs la représentation de leurs passeports (*m.pl.*).

passport (permission to a ship to proceed on her voyage) (*n.*), passeport (*m.*): (Cf. **clearance.**)
(in France) the *passeport* is for a foreign ship what the *congé* is for a French ship, le passeport est pour un navire étranger ce que le congé est pour un navire français.

past year (financial year), exercice écoulé (*m.*); exercice révolu (*m.*).

paste (*n.*), colle (*f.*); colle de pâte (*f.*):
office paste, colle de bureau.

pawn (*n.*), gage (*m.*); pension (*f.*):
securities held in pawn, titres détenus en pension (*m.pl.*); valeurs détenues en gage (*f.pl.*).
stock (*or* stocks) on contango or in pawn, titres (*ou* valeurs) en report ou en pension.

pawn (*v.t.*), engager; gager; mettre en gage; mettre en pension :
to pawn one's property, engager son bien.
to pawn securities (*or* stock), mettre des titres en pension (*ou* en gage); gager des valeurs.
pawned bills *or* bills in pawn (bills lodged with a bank as collateral against advances and retired before maturity), effets en pension (*m.pl.*); effets en (*ou* à la) nourrice (*m.pl.*).
pawned stock (Banking and Stock Exch.), titres en pension (*m.pl.*).

pawnee (pers.) (*n.*), gagiste (*m.* ou *f.*); prêteur sur gage (*m.*); prêteur sur gages (*m.*).

pawner *or* **pawnor** (pers.) (*n.*), gageur, -euse.

pawning (*n.*), engagement (*m.*); mise en gage (*f.*); pension (*f.*).

pawnshop (*n.*), crédit municipal (*m.*).
pay (*n.*), paye (*f.*); paie (*f.*); salaire (*m.*):
  pay of a workman, paye, paie, salaire, d'un
  ouvrier.
pay (*v.t.* & *v.i.*), payer; verser; acquitter;
  solder; régler; libérer; se libérer; compter;
  donner; mettre; mettre en paiement;
  rémunérer; rembourser; prélever:
  to pay one's debts, a bill, payer, acquitter,
  solder, régler, ses dettes, un mémoire.
  to pay the balance, payer le reliquat; verser
  le solde; solder le redû.
  to pay so many pounds to someone, payer,
  verser, compter, tant de livres à quelqu'un.
  to pay so much for something, payer, donner,
  tant pour, mettre tant à, quelque chose.
  to pay a bill of exchange for honour, payer
  une lettre de change par intervention.
  to pay a call (*or* an instalment) on partly
  paid shares, verser un appel de fonds, faire
  un versement, sur des titres non libérés.
  to pay a coupon, an interim, a final, dividend, mettre en paiement, payer, un
  coupon, un acompte, un solde, de dividende.
  to pay a dividend to the shareholders, payer
  un dividende aux actionnaires.
  to pay a salary to an employee, payer des
  appointements à, appointer, un employé.
  to pay at due date (*or* at maturity), payer à
  l'échéance:
  to pay a bill of exchange at maturity, payer
  une lettre de change à l'échéance.
  to pay average on each valuation, régler les
  avaries sur chaque évaluation.
  to pay cash down *or* to pay spot cash *or* to
  pay on or before delivery, payer comptant-
  compté.
  to pay each other, se payer:
  the differences they have to pay each other,
  les différences qu'ils ont à se payer (*f.pl.*).
  to pay for services, payer, rémunérer, des
  services.
  to pay in advance (*or* in anticipation), payer
  d'avance; verser par avance; acquitter
  par anticipation; libérer par anticipation;
  se libérer par anticipation:
  to pay an amount in advance, payer (*ou*
  verser) une somme d'avance.
  the debtors have the right of paying in advance, wholly or partly, les débiteurs ont
  le droit de se libérer par anticipation, en
  tout ou en partie (*m.pl.*).
  to pay in cash, payer au comptant; payer
  comptant; verser comptant; payer en
  espèces:
  to pay in cash at the end of the present
  month, at the end of next month, payer
  comptant fin courant, fin prochain.
  to pay in full, payer, verser, solder, intégralement.
  to pay on demand *or* to pay on presentation
  or to pay over the counter, payer à présentation; payer à bureau ouvert; payer
  à guichet ouvert:
  to pay a bill on presentation, payer un
  billet à présentation.

to pay on the nail, payer recta.
to pay one's expenses, payer ses frais; se
  défrayer:
  not to have enough to pay one's expenses,
  n'avoir pas de quoi se défrayer.
to pay taxes, payer des contributions (*ou*
  des impôts); contribuer.
to pay the interest on. V. ci-après.
to pay the wages, faire la paie.
to pay too much for an article, payer trop
  pour, surpayer, un article.
if the freight is not paid, the consignee settles
  it, si le fret n'est pas payé, le destinataire
  le règle.
shares of £10, £2 paid, actions de 10£, 2£
  payées; actions de £10, libérées de £2.
when we say that such or such a share of £1
  is 15/- paid, it means that 15/- has been
  paid and that there still remains 5/- to be
  paid, quand on dit que tel titre de £1 est
  libéré de 15 schellings, cela signifie que
  15sh. ont été versés et qu'il reste encore
  5sh. à verser.
barley: parcels Azoff/Black Sea, March-April,
  17/6d. paid and buyers (*or* abbreviated
  17/6 p. & b.), orges: parcelles Azoff mer
  noire, mars-avril, 17/6d. payé et acheteur.
interest, dividend, paid out of capital, intérêt
  dividende, prélevé sur le capital (*m.*).
**on the capital for the time being paid up there-
  on**, prorata temporis:
  the profits allow of the distribution on the
  preference shares of the dividend of 5%
  per annum on the capital for the time
  being paid up thereon, les bénéfices permettent de répartir le dividende de 5 0/0
  prorata temporis aux actions privilégiées
  (*m.pl.*).
to be paid, être payé, -e, versé, -e; se payer;
  se verser:
  the dividend is paid yearly in April or May,
  le dividende se paye annuellement en avril
  ou mai.
  taxes are paid to the collectors, les impôts
  se versent chez les percepteurs (*m.pl.*).
pay *or* **pay to** (*v. in the imperative*), payez à;
  veuillez payer à:
  three days after sight pay to the order of
  Messrs X. & Co., to our order, so much (bill
  of exchange), à trois jours de vue payez
  (*ou* veuillez payer) à l'ordre de MM. X. & Cie,
  à l'ordre de nous-mêmes, la somme de tant.
  V. aussi exemple sous **first of exchange.**
  pay bearer *or* pay to bearer, payez au porteur.
  pay to the order of Messrs X. & Co. (endorsement on a bill of exchange, etc.),
  payez à l'ordre de MM. X. & Cie.
  pay X. Esq. or order *or* pay Mr X. or order
  (enfacement on a cheque), payez à l'ordre
  de M. X.; payez à M. X. ou ordre.
  pay X. Esq. or bearer *or* pay Mr X. or bearer
  (on cheque), payez au porteur M. X.;
  payez M. X. ou au porteur.
  pay self, pay selves (cheque), payez à moi-
  même, payez à nous-mêmes.

pay self, selves, or order (cheque),   payez à l'ordre de moi-même, de nous-mêmes.

pay cash (cancellation of crossing of a cheque), payable comptant.

pay a deposit on or **to (to)** (to give an earnest), arrher; donner des arrhes sur ou à; enarrher: to pay a deposit on goods,   arrher des marchandises.

pay a visit (to),   faire une visite.

pay back (to),   rembourser; rendre: to pay back a loan,   rembourser, rendre, un prêt.

pay bill or **pay voucher,**   bon de paye (m.).

pay day,   jour de paiement (m.);   jour de paie (m.).

pay day (Stock Exch.),   jour de la liquidation (m.).

pay in (to),   verser: to pay in so many pounds to the bank,   verser à la banque tant de livres.

money paid into the bank,   fonds versés en banque (m.pl.).

pay off (to),   acquitter; solder; régler; rembourser; liquider; désintéresser; éteindre; amortir; purger: to pay off a debt,   acquitter, rembourser, régler, liquider, éteindre, amortir, une dette.

to pay off an overdraft,   solder un découvert.

to pay off a creditor,   désintéresser, rembourser, un créancier.

to pay off a mortgage,   purger une hypothèque.

pay out (to),   payer; verser; compter: to pay out so many francs to someone,   payer, verser, compter, tant de francs à quelqu'un.

pay over again (to),   repayer.

pay roll or **pay sheet,**   feuille de paie (f.); feuille des salaires (f.).

pay the interest on (to) or simply **to pay** (to provide the interest on; to serve),   servir: sum sufficient to pay the interest on the bonds, somme suffisante pour servir les obligations (f.).

the interest paid to the bondholder,   l'intérêt servi à l'obligataire (m.).

pay up (to) (v.t.),   libérer; verser: to pay up a share,   libérer une action.

company with an authorized capital of so much, of which so much has been paid up, société au capital nominal de tant, dont tant a été versé (f.). Cf. **paid up capital,** sous **paid.**

pay up (to) (v.i.),   se libérer; s'exécuter: to give someone the option of paying up before due date,   donner à quelqu'un la faculté de se libérer avant l'échéance.

all the shareholders pay up except one of them,   tous les actionnaires s'exécutent sauf l'un d'eux.

operator under the threat of official closing if he does not pay up (Stock Exch.),   opérateur sous la menace de liquidation d'office s'il ne s'exécute pas (m.).

pay up in full (to) (v.t.),   libérer entièrement; libérer complètement;   libérer intégralement;   libérer:

to pay up a share in full,   libérer entièrement, libérer complètement,   libérer intégralement, libérer, une action.

pay up in full (to) (v.i.),   se libérer entièrement; se libérer complètement;   se libérer intégralement;   se libérer.

payability (n.),   exigibilité (f.).

payable (adj.),   payable;   échéable;   échéant, -e;   exigible;   à payer;   à la charge: duty payable in advance,   droit payable par anticipation (ou exigible d'avance) (m.).

interest and dividends are payable 1st January (interim) and 1st July (final),   les intérêts et dividendes sont payables le 1er janvier (acompte) et le 1er juillet (solde).

shares of 10s., payable 2s. 6d. on application, 2s. 6d. on allotment, so many shillings on (date),   actions de 10sh., payables 2sh. 6d. en souscrivant (ou à la souscription), 2sh. 6d. à la (ou lors de la) répartition, tant de schellings au (date) (f.pl.).

bills payable,   effets à payer (m.pl.).

bill payable at sight, on such a date,   effet payable (ou échéable) (ou exigible) à vue, à telle date (m.).

the issue of notes at sight and to bearer (bank notes) constitutes, for the use of the banks, a deposit payable on demand,   l'émission des billets à vue et au porteur (billets de banque) constitue, au profit des banques, un dépôt exigible sur demande (f.).

if no time of payment is stated, the stamp duty payable is so much per cent,   si aucune échéance n'est indiquée, le droit de timbre exigible sera de tant 0/0.

the stamp duty is payable by the seller,   le droit de timbre est à la charge du vendeur.

payee (pers.) (n.),   bénéficiaire (m. ou f.); preneur, -euse: payee of a cheque, of a money order, of a letter of credit,   bénéficiaire d'un chèque, d'un mandat de poste, d'une lettre de crédit.

payee of a bill of exchange, of a promissory note,   preneur, bénéficiaire, d'un effet de commerce (ou d'une lettre de change), d'un billet à ordre.

the name of the payee to whose order the bill is drawn,   le nom du bénéficiaire à l'ordre duquel le billet est souscrit.

payer (pers.) (n.),   payeur, -euse: payer for honour (bills of exchange),   payeur par intervention.

paying (who pays) (adj.),   payeur, -euse; payant, -e: the paying banker,   le banquier payeur.

paying cashier or **payer** (n.) (Banking),   caissier payeur (m.);   caissier des paiements (m.); guichetier payeur (m.);   payeur (m.).

paying cashier's counter cash book.   Syn. de **paid cash book.**

paying agent (for a bill of exchange),   domiciliataire (m.).

paying (remunerative) (adj.),   rémunérateur, -trice;   rémunérant, -e;   payant, -e: paying concern,   entreprise rémunératrice (f.);   entreprise payante (f.).

paying counter (Banking), caisse des paiements (*f.*).

paying in (Banking), versement (*m.*).

paying in slip (Banking), bordereau de versement (*m.*); feuille de versement (*f.*).

paying off a mortgage, purge d'hypothèque (*f.*); purge légale (*f.*).

paying off creditors, désintéressement (*m.*), remboursement (*m.*) des créanciers.

paying office (money orders, etc.) (opp. to *issuing office*), bureau payeur (*m.*).

paying over again, repayement (*m.*).

paying up, libération (*f.*); versement (*m.*):
the paying up of a share is done by way of calls, la libération d'une action se fait par voie d'appels de fonds.

payment (*n.*) (Abbrev.: **payt** or **paymt** or **pt**), paiement (*m.*); payement (*m.*); paîment (*m.*); mise en paiement (*f.*); versement (*m.*); acquittement (*m.*); libération (*f.*); rémunération (*f.*); remboursement (*m.*); sortie (*f.*); encaissement (*m.*); prélèvement (*m.*):
payment against documents, paiement contre documents.
payment at the end of the present month, paiement fin courant.
payment by cheque of an agreed sum, versement par chèque d'une somme convenue.
payment by sender of customs charges (Post), affranchissement préalable des frais de douane (*m.*).
payment for honour, paiement par intervention.
payment for services, paiement, rémunération, du travail (*ou* des services).
as payment for the transfer there has been allotted to the vendors 0,000 shares of 0 each, fully paid, in the company, en rémunération des apports il a été attribué aux apporteurs 0 000 actions de 0 chacune, entièrement libérées, de la société.
payment in advance (*or* in anticipation), payement d'avance; paiement par anticipation; paiement anticipé; versement par anticipation; versement anticipatif; à-valoir (*m.*); à-bon-compte (*m.*).
payment in advance of calls, versement par anticipation.
payment in driblets, payement fractionné.
payment in full, paiement intégral; libération entière; libération complète; libération:
payment in full of a share, libération entière, libération complète, libération intégrale, libération, d'une action.
payment in full on allotment, libération à la répartition.
shares must be registered (i.e., not bearer) until their payment in full (*or* until they are fully paid), les actions doivent être nominatives jusqu'à leur complète libération (*f.pl.*).
payment in full discharge, paiement libératoire.

payment into the bank, into petty cash, versement à la banque, à la petite caisse.
payment of a dividend, mise en paiement, paiement, d'un dividende.
payment of calls, versement d'appels de fonds.
payment of interest (service), service d'intérêt (*m.*); service (*m.*):
loans on which the payment of interest is guaranteed by the Government, emprunts dont le service d'intérêt est garanti par l'État (*m.pl.*). Cf. **to pay the interest on.**
amount required for payment of (*or* amount required to pay) the interest on the loan, somme nécessaire au service de l'emprunt (*f.*).
payment of interest, of dividends, out of capital, prélèvement d'intérêt, de dividendes, sur le capital.
payment of losses, of damage (Insce), remboursement des pertes, des avaries.
payment of the claim takes place within three months of the accident, le règlement de l'indemnité a lieu dans les trois mois du sinistre.
payment on account, acompte (*m.*); paiement à compte (*m.*); à-valoir (*m.*); à-bon-compte (*m.*):
payment on account of capital, acompte sur le capital.
payment on current account, versement en compte courant.
to present a cheque for payment, présenter un chèque au paiement (*ou* à l'encaissement).
cash receipts and payments, entrées et sorties de caisse (*f.pl.*); rentrées et sorties de caisse (*f.pl.*).

payment bill (opp. to *acceptance bill*), traite documents contre paiement (*f.*).

peace (*n.*) (Ant.: *war*), paix (*f.*).

peace risk (opp. to *war risk*), risque de paix (*m.*).

pecuniarily (*adv.*), pécuniairement.

pecuniary (*adj.*), pécuniaire:
pecuniary losses, pertes pécuniaires (*f.pl.*).

pen (*n.*), plume (*f.*).

penholder, penknife, penwiper. V. ci-après.

pen rack, étagère (*f.*); pose-plumes (*m.*).

pen tray, plumier (*m.*).

penalty [**penalties** *pl.*] (*n.*), pénalité (*f.*); peine (*f.*); dédit (*m.*); forfait d'indemnité (*m.*):
to be liable to the penalties imposed by law, être passible des pénalités prononcées par les lois.
a penalty of so much per day of delay in case of non delivery on the agreed date, une pénalité de tant par jour de retard en cas de non livraison à la date convenue.
penalties for non performance of the agreement, pénalités, dédits, en cas d'inexécution du contrat.
penalties incurred for false declaration, in case of fraud or breach of the regulations, pénalités, peines, encourues pour fausse déclaration, en cas de fraude ou de contravention.

this entry must be made within twenty four hours of the arrival of the ship on (*or* under) penalty of 500 francs fine, cette déclaration doit être effectuée dans les vingt-quatre heures de l'arrivée du navire sous peine de 500 francs d'amende.

penalty: confiscation of the goods falsely entered and a fine not exceeding so many pounds, pénalité: confiscation de la marchandise faussement déclarée et amende de tant de livres au maximum.

to accept a penalty agreed on beforehand, accepter un forfait d'indemnité réglé à l'avance.

penalty clause (in a contract), clause pénale (*f.*).

pencil (*n.*), crayon (*m.*):
particulars entered in pencil, indications inscrites au crayon (*f.pl.*).

pencil (*v.t.*), crayonner:
to pencil notes, crayonner des notes.

pencil case, porte-mine (*m.*); porte-mines (*m.*).

pencil eraser, gomme pour le crayon (*f.*); gomme à crayon (*f.*).

pencil holder, portecrayon (*m.*).

pencil protector, protège-mine (*m.*); protège-pointe (*m.*); portecrayon à étui (*m.*).

pencil sharpener, taille-crayon (*m.*); taille-crayons (*m.*).

penholder (*n.*), porte-plume (*m.*).

penknife (*n.*), canif (*m.*).

penny [**pennies** *pl.* for coins by number; **pence** *pl.* for amount of value] (*n.*) (Abbrev.: **d.**), penny (*m.*).

pension (*n.*), pension (*f.*); retraite (*f.*); pension de retraite (*f.*):
pension for life, pension à vie; pension viagère.
old age pension, retraite pour la vieillesse.

pension *or* **pension off** (*v.t.*), pensionner; mettre à la retraite:
to pension (*or* to pension off) an employee, pensionner un employé.

pension fund, caisse de retraites (*f.*); caisse des retraites (*f.*).

pensioner (pers.) (*n.*), pensionnaire (*m.* ou *f.*); retraité (*m.*).

pensioning *or* **pensioning off** (*n.*), mise à la retraite (*f.*).

penwiper (*n.*), essuie-plume (*m.*); essuie-plumes (*m.*).

per annum (Abbrev.: **p.a.** *or* **p.an.** *or* **per an.**), par an; l'an:
5% per annum, 5 0/0 par an (*ou* l'an).

per cent (*without full stop*) *or* **per cent.** (*with full stop*) *or* **per centum** (Abbrev.: % *or* **p.c.** *or* **pc.**), pour cent:
so much per cent, tant pour cent.
Note:—In English insurance, a rate (usually quoted in shillings and pence) of so much per cent means a rate of so much per £100. Thus, for example, 2s. 6d.% (*or* ⅛%) on £1,000 is £1 5s.
In French insurance, a rate of so much per cent means a rate of so much per 100 francs. Thus, for example, 1/8% on 10,000 francs is 12 fr. 50.

— per cents (government stock), le — pour cent:

to buy three per cents, acheter du trois pour cent.

per contra. V. sous **contra.**

per mille *or* **per mil** *or* **per thousand** (Abbrev.: ‰), pour mille.

per passenger train, per goods train, per air mail, par train de grande vitesse, par train de petite vitesse, par avion.

per procuration *or* **per procurationem,** *generally abbreviated* **per pro.** *or* **per proc.** *or* **p.p.,** par procuration; P.Pᵒⁿ; Par pᵒⁿ. V. exemple sous **power of attorney.**

percentage (*n.*), pourcentage (*m.*); pour-cent (*m.*); tant pour cent (*m.*); tantième (*m.*); quantum (*m.*):
to work out the percentage of establishment charges, faire le pourcentage des frais généraux.
free from average under the percentage specified in the policy, franc d'avaries au-dessous du pourcentage énoncé dans la police. [V. note sous **memorandum** (of percentages), & cf. **franchise.**]
what percentage are you offered? quel est le pour-cent qu'on vous offre?
price reduced by a certain percentage, prix diminué d'un tant pour cent (*m.*).
master who receives a percentage on the freight, capitaine qui reçoit un tant pour cent sur le fret (*m.*).
premium fixed at a percentage of the values insured, prime fixée à un tant pour cent des valeurs assurées (*f.*). V. note sous **per cent.**
the bank allows them a percentage of the proceeds, la banque leur alloue un tantième du produit.
to charge against the cost of manufacture the percentage of overhead expenses properly applicable thereto, appliquer à la fabrication le quantum de frais généraux qui lui incombe.

percentage of profits (allowed under the articles to directors, or the like), tantième (*m.*); tantièmes (*m.pl.*):
directors' percentage of profits, tantièmes des administrateurs.

percentaged (*adj.*) *or* **percentage** (*used as adj.*), pourcenté, -e:
fixed or percentage contributions, quote-parts fixes ou pourcentées (*f.pl.*).

perfect entry *or* **perfected entry** (Customs) (distinguished from *sight entry*), déclaration définitive (*f.*).

perforate (*v.t.*), perforer:
to perforate stamps with the firm's initials, perforer des timbres aux initiales de la raison sociale.

perforation (dotted line) (*n.*), pointillé (*m.*); pointillé perforé (*m.*):
to tear off a leaf from the counterfoil along the perforation, détacher un volant de la souche suivant pointillé.

perforator (punch for letter filing) (*n.*), perforateur (*m.*).

perforator (for cheques) (*n.*), perforeuse (*f.*).

perform (*v.t.*), exécuter; accomplir:

to perform a contract, exécuter un contrat.
to perform a duty, accomplir un devoir.
performance (*n.*), exécution (*f.*); accomplissement (*m.*):
all banking trade is founded on the punctual and strict performance of undertakings, tout le commerce de la banque est fondé sur l'exécution exacte et précise des engagements pris.
peril (*n.*), péril (*m.*):
imminent peril, péril imminent.
peril of the sea, péril de la mer (*m.*); fortune de mer (*f.*); péril maritime (*m.*). *Note :— fortune de mer* is also a collective plural, thus, *choses perdues par fortune de mer* (*f.pl.*), *property lost by perils of the seas* (or *sea*). The plural, *fortunes de mer*, is sometimes used.
period (*n.*), période (*f.*); époque (*f.*); terme (*m.*):
during a period of so many years, pendant une période de tant d'années. V. aussi exemple sous **year**.
an interim dividend of so much, as compared with so much for the corresponding period of last year, un acompte de dividende de tant, en comparaison de tant l'an dernier à pareille époque.
deposit for a fixed period, dépôt à terme fixe (*m.*).
period (base date of an account current) (*n.*), époque (*f.*).
period (accounting period) (*n.*), exercice (*m.*):
period under review (past financial period), exercice écoulé; exercice révolu.
periodic *or* **periodical** (*adj.*), périodique:
periodical drawings, tirages au sort périodiques (*m.pl.*).
periodical inspection, visite périodique (*f.*).
periodical (publication) (*n.*), périodique (*m.*).
perish (*v.i.*), périr.
perishable (*adj.*), périssable:
perishable goods *or* perishable merchandise, marchandises périssables (*f.pl.*).
permanent (*adj.*), permanent, -e:
permanent assets (opp. to *floating*, or *circulating*, or *revenue*, *assets*), actif immobilisé (*m.*); valeurs immobilisées (*f.pl.*); capitaux fixes (*m.pl.*); capital fixe (*m.*); capital immobilisé (*m.*).
permanent disablement (Accident Insurance) (opp. to *temporary disablement*), infirmité permamente (*f.*); incapacité permanente (*f.*).
permanent investment (opp. to *temporary investment*), placement permanent (*m.*).
permission (*n.*), permission (*f.*).
permit (*n.*), permis (*m.*):
customs permit, permis de douane.
perpetual (*adj.*) (Abbrev.: **perp.**), perpétuel, -elle:
French rentes are either perpetual or redeemable, les rentes françaises sont ou perpétuelles ou amortissables (*f.pl.*).
perpetual ledger, grand livre à feuilles mobiles (*m.*).

perpetuity (*n.*), perpétuité (*f.*).
perquisite (*n.*), revenant-bon (*m.*):
the perquisites of an office, les revenants-bons d'une charge.
person (*n.*), personne (*f.*).
person liable (for tax), redevable (*m. ou f.*), personne redevable (*f.*) (de l'impôt).
person named (in a letter of credit, or the like), accrédité, -e:
to enable the correspondent to identify the person named, pour permettre au correspondant de reconnaître l'identité de l'accrédité.
person of independent means, rentier, -ère:
to work in the hope of becoming independent, travailler dans l'espoir de devenir rentier.
personal (*adj.*), personnel, -elle:
personal accident insurance, assurance contre les accidents corporels (*f.*); assurance contre les accidents (*f.*); assurance-accidents (*f.*).
personal accounts (Bkkpg) (opp. to *impersonal accounts*), comptes de personnes (*m.pl.*); comptes personnels (*m.pl.*); comptes des particuliers (*m.pl.*); comptes particuliers (*m.pl.*).
personal allowance (Income Tax), déduction personnelle (*f.*).
personal credit, crédit personnel (*m.*):
personal credit is based on the reputation of the trader, le crédit personnel est basé sur la réputation du commerçant.
personal ledger, grand livre des comptes particuliers (*m.*).
the letters are opened, except those marked "personal," which are handed to the addressees, les lettres sont ouvertes, abstraction faite de celles portant la mention « personelle, » qui sont remises aux destinataires (*f.pl.*).
personal (Law) (*adj.*) (opp. to *real*), meuble; mobilier, -ère; personnel, -elle:
personal property *or* personal estate *or* personal effects *or* **personals** (*n.pl.*) *or* **personalty** (*n.*), biens meubles (*m.pl.*); biens mobiliers (*m.pl.*); biens personnels (*m.pl.*); meubles (*m.pl.*); effets mobiliers (*m.pl.*); effets personnels (*m.pl.*).
personally (*adv.*), personellement:
to be personally liable for the payment of an amount, être personnellement responsable du paiement d'une somme.
Petersburg standard hundred (timber), standard de Saint-Pétersbourg (*m.*).
petition of creditors, requête des créanciers (*f.*).
petty average *or* **petit average** (Mar. Insce), petite avarie (*f.*).
petty cash (Abbrev.: **P.C.**), petite caisse (*f.*).
petty cash book, livre de petite caisse (*m.*); carnet de petite caisse (*m.*).
petty expenses *or* **petties** (*n.pl.*), menus frais (*m.pl.*); menues dépenses (*f.pl.*); petites dépenses (*f.pl.*).
pick up (to), se ressaisir; se reprendre; reprendre; être en reprise:
mining shares picked up smartly, les valeurs

minières se ressaisissent (*ou* se reprennent)
(*ou* reprennent) vivement.
X. shares picked up from 1 to 1¼, l'action X.
est en reprise de 1 à 1 1/4.

pick up passengers (to), prendre des passagers :
Boulogne is a port of call where the transatlantic boats come to anchor some hours
to pick up passengers, Boulogne est un
port d'escale où les transatlantiques viennent ancrer quelques heures pour prendre
les passagers.

pick up shares (to) (with a view to engineering
a rise), se sucrer.

picture postcard, carte postale illustrée (*f.*).

piece (coin) (*n.*),   pièce (*f.*) :
a two shilling piece,   une pièce de deux
schellings.
piece of money,   pièce d'argent ;   pièce de
monnaie ;   monnaie (*f.*).

piece of business, affaire (*f.*) :
a fine piece of business,   une affaire d'or ;
une affaire magnifique.

piece of land *or* **piece of ground,** terre (*f.*) ; fonds
de terre (*m.*) ;   terrain (*m.*) :
to buy a piece of land,   acheter une terre (*ou*
un fonds de terre) (*ou* un terrain).

piece of news, nouvelle (*f.*) :
to telephone an important piece of news,
téléphoner une importante nouvelle.

pier (*n.*),   jetée (*f.*).

pig on pork, papier creux (*m.*) ;   effets creux
(*m.pl.*).

pile (*n.*),   amas (*m.*) :
pile of money,   amas d'argent.

pile up (*v.t.*),   amasser ;   amonceler :
to pile up a fortune,   amasser une fortune.

pilfer (*v.t.*),   piller.

pilfering *or* **pilferage** (*n.*),   pillage (*m.*).

pilot (Navig.) (pers.) (*n.*),   pilote (*m.*) :
with leave to sail with or without pilots,
avec faculté de naviguer avec ou sans
pilotes.
Note :—The French distinguish between (1)
pilote hauturier who pilots ships on the
high seas ;   very rarely used and never
obligatorily, and (2) the *pilote* or *pilote
côtier* or *lamaneur* or *locman* who pilots
ships in or out of ports.
Trinity House (English) pilots are of two
classes, *sea pilots* and *river pilots*.   The sea
pilot brings the vessel to the " entrance "
of the port.   The river pilot takes charge
of the vessel from the time the sea pilot
leaves her until she arrives at the entrance
of the dock where she will discharge, when
the *dock pilot* takes charge until the vessel
is safely moored at her berth.   As an instance,
a ship coming into the Port of London is
usually boarded by the sea pilot at Dungeness or Beachy Head and piloted by him
as far as Gravesend, where the river pilot
takes charge.

pilot (*v.t.*),   piloter.

pilot boat, bateau-pilote (*m.*).

pilot licence, brevet de pilote (*m.*).

pilotage *or* **piloting** (*n.*),   pilotage (*m.*) :

pilotage is compulsory within a zone prescribed for each port,   le pilotage est obligatoire dans une zone délimitée pour chaque
port.
pilotings along coasts or at the entrance of
ports,   pilotages le long des côtes ou à
l'entrée des ports.
pilotage inwards,   pilotage d'entrée.
pilotage outwards,   pilotage de sortie.

pilotage dues *or simply* **pilotage** (*n.*),   droits de
pilotage (*m.pl.*) ;   taxes de pilotage (*f.pl.*) ;
pilotage (*m.*).

pin (*n.*),   épingle (*f.*).

pin (*v.t.*),   épingler :
slip pinned to the documents, policy pinned
to the bill of lading,   fiche épinglée au
documents,   police épinglée au connaissement (*f.*).

piracy [**piracies** *pl.*] (*n.*),   piraterie (*f.*).

pirate (pers.) (*n.*),   pirate (*m.*).

pitch (said of a ship) (*v.i.*),   tanguer.

pitching (opp. to *rolling*) (*n.*),   tangage (*m.*).

place (locality) (*n.*),   lieu (*m.*) ;   place (*f.*) ;   local
(*m.*) :
place of payment of a bill,   lieu de paiement
d'un effet.
to do the place (to canvass the town),   faire
la place.
the places of sailing and destination,   les lieux
de départ et de destination.
place of adjustment of average,   lieu du règlement d'avarie.
place of call (of a ship in customary or advertised route),   lieu d'escale (*m.*) ;   escale
(*f.*) ;   échelle (*f.*).   Cf. **call.**
place of call (for supplies or shelter),   lieu de
relâche (*m.*) ;   relâche (*f.*).   Cf. **call.**
place of meeting,   rendez-vous (*m.*).
place of necessity *or* place of distress *or* place
of refuge,   lieu de relâche ;   lieu de relâche
forcée ;   relâche (*f.*) ;   lieu de refuge ;   lieu
de salut.
See also phrases under **port** some of which are
often associated with *place* instead of *port*,
thus, place of discharge, lieu de décharge.
Note :—The word *Place* (meaning *Centre*) as
a column heading in a foreign exchange
quotation list, bill book, or the like, is
rendered in French by the word *Devise* or
Devises ;   thus, *Place : New York*, *Devise :
New-York ;   Place : Brussels, Lisbon,
Devises : Bruxelles, Lisbonne.*

place (situation ; employment) (*n.*),   place (*f.*) ;
poste (*m.*) ;   position (*f.*) ;   emploi (*m.*) :
to lose one's place,   perdre sa place.

place (to deposit ; to lodge) (*v.t.*),   placer ;   mettre ;
déposer :
to place securities in safe custody,   placer,
mettre, déposer, des titres en garde ;   mettre
des valeurs en dépôt.

place (to dispose of [a thing] in a desired
or selected way) (*v.t.*),   placer ;   passer ;
donner :
to place an order,   placer, passer, donner, un
ordre.

to place an additional insurance on an insured cargo, placer une assurance supplémentaire sur une cargaison assurée.
value received which place to account as
advised (bill of exchange), valeur reçue
que passerez en compte suivant avis de
(*signature*).
place (to dispose of by selling) (*v.t.*), placer;
faire le placement de; écouler; faire écouler:
to place shares, placer, faire le placement,
écouler, faire écouler, des actions.
goods which can easily be placed, marchandises de placement sûr (*f.pl.*).
to be placed, être placé, -e; se placer; s'écouler:
a part only of the loan came to be placed,
une partie seulement de l'emprunt parvint
à se placer.
place money to someone's credit with a banker
(to), créditer quelqu'un chez un banquier.
place of residence (Law), domicile réel (*m.*).
placed (held by the public as investment) (*adj.*)
(Ant.: *displaced*), classé, -e; placé, -e:
well placed shares, valeurs bien classées
(*f.pl.*); actions bien placées (*f.pl.*).
placer (pers.) (*n.*), placeur, -euse.
placer (of insurance) (pers.) (*n.*), preneur (d'assurance) (*m.*).
placing (lodging) (*n.*), mise (*f.*); dépôt (*m.*):
placing money on current account, dépôt à
vue.
placing (giving) (*n.*), placement (*m.*); passation (*f.*):
placing orders, placement, passation, d'ordres
(*ou* de commandes):
placing orders with suppliers, placement
des commandes chez les fournisseurs.
placing (disposing of by selling) (*n.*), placement
(*m.*); écoulement (*m.*):
placing of home products on foreign markets,
placement, écoulement, de produits indigènes
sur les marchés étrangers.
placing shares with the public, placement,
écoulement, d'actions dans le public.
placing (state of being held by the public as
investment—said of stocks and shares) (*n.*),
classement (*m.*); placement (*m.*).
plain language (Teleg.), langage clair (*m.*);
clair (*m.*):
telegram in plain language, télégramme en
langage clair (*m.*).
word in plain language, mot en clair (*m.*).
plaintiff (Law) (pers.) (*n.*), demandeur, -eresse:
according as the company is plaintiff or defendant, suivant que la société est demanderesse ou défenderesse.
plan (*n.*), plan (*m.*); projet (*m.*):
plan of campaign, plan de campagne.
the Dawes plan, the Young plan, le plan
Dawes, le plan Young.
plan (to scheme) (*v.t.*), projeter:
to plan a journey, projeter un voyage.
plate glass insurance, assurance contre le bris
de glaces (*f.*).
platform (Rly.) (*n.*), quai (*m.*).
platform ticket, ticket d'entrée en gare (*m.*).

play (to gamble) (*v.i.*), jouer:
to play for high stakes, jouer gros jeu.
please forward (inscription on a postal packet),
veuillez faire suivre; faire suivre.
please repeat the number (Teleph.), veuillez
répéter le numéro.
please write clearly, écrire très lisiblement.
pleasure boat, bateau de plaisance (*m.*).
pleasure navigation, navigation de plaisance
(*f.*).
pleasure vessel (opp. to *trading vessel*), navire
de plaisance (*m.*); bâtiment de plaisance
(*m.*).
pledge (*n.*), gage (*m.*); nantissement (*m.*);
engagement (*m.*):
securities held in pledge, titres détenus en
gage (*m.pl.*).
in fact, the goods imported are the pledge of
the duties to which they are liable, and
cannot be put at the disposal of the importers without security, en effet, les marchandises importées sont le gage des droits
auxquels elles sont soumises, et ne peuvent
être mises à la disposition des importateurs
sans garantie.
pledge (*v.t.*), gager; engager; mettre en gage;
remettre en nantissement; fournir en
nantissement; déposer en nantissement;
nantir:
to pledge one's property, gager, engager,
son bien.
to pledge securities, gager, remettre en nantissement, fournir en nantissement, déposer en nantissement, engager, nantir,
des valeurs (*ou* des titres).
shares pledged as security for money advanced,
actions gagées (*ou* mises en gage) (*ou* nanties) en garantie de fonds avancés (*f.pl.*);
actions remises (*ou* fournies) (*ou* déposées)
en nantissement en garantie de fonds
avancés (*f.pl.*).
to pledge one's word, engager sa parole.
the antedating of a bill of lading pledges the
responsibility of the master, l'antidate
d'un connaissement engage la responsabilité du capitaine (*f.*).
the master can sell or pledge the cargo for the
needs of the adventure, le capitaine peut
faire vendre ou mettre en gage les marchandises pour les besoins de l'expédition.
pledge oneself (to), s'engager:
to pledge oneself by a surety bond, s'engager par cautionnement.
pledgee (pers.) (*n.*), gagiste (*m.* ou *f.*); créancier
gagiste (*m.*); prêteur sur gage (*m.*); prê-
teur sur gages (*m.*):
railway which has on the goods the rights of
a pledgee, chemin de fer qui a sur la marchandise les droits d'un créancier gagiste
(*m.*).
pledger (pers.) (*n.*), gageur, -euse.
pledging (*n.*), engagement (*m.*); mise en gage
(*f.*); nantissement (*m.*).
plentiful (*adj.*) (Ant.: *scarce*), abondant, -e:
money is plentiful, l'argent est abondant (*m.*).
plentifulness *or* **plenty** (*n.*), abondance (*f.*).

plethora (*n.*), pléthore (*f.*) :
plethora of money, pléthore de capitaux.
plomb (Customs) (*n.*), plomb (*m.*).
plomb (*v.t.*), plomber :
to plomb a package, a truck containing goods,
plomber un colis, un wagon contenant des
marchandises.
plombing (*n.*), plombage (*m.*).
plunder (*v.t.*), piller.
plundering (*n.*), pillage (*m.*) :
plundering of wrecked effects, pillage des
effets naufragés.
plurality [**pluralities** *pl.*] (*n.*), pluralité (*f.*) :
owing to the plurality of copies of the bill of
lading, there may be divergencies between
the different copies, en raison de la pluralité d'exemplaires du connaissement, il
peut y avoir entre les divers exemplaires
des divergences.
plus (*adj.*), plus (*prep.*) :
three plus four equals seven (*Abbrev. :* 3 + 4
= 7), trois plus quatre égale sept (*Abbrev. :*
3 + 4 = 7).
purchase price, plus brokerage, prix d'achat,
plus le courtage (*m.*).
plus (*n.*) *or* **plus sign,** plus (*m.*) :
you should have put a plus, you have put a
minus, il fallut un plus, vous avez mis un
moins.
plus or minus difference, différence en plus ou
en moins (*f.*).
pocket (*n.*), poche (*f.*) :
to empty one's pockets, vider ses poches.
pocket (*v.t.*), empocher ; encoffrer :
ship abandoned on the high seas with the
object of pocketing a considerable sum,
navire abandonné en haute mer dans le
but d'empocher une somme considérable (*m.*).
pocket money, argent de poche (*m.*).
pocketbook (*n.*), carnet de poche (*m.*).
point (item) (*n.*), point (*m.*) :
plan which has only one weak point, plan
qui n'a qu'un point faible (*m.*).
point of law, of fact, point de droit, de fait.
point (a unit of variation in price per share)
(Stock Exch.) (*n.*), point (*m.*) :
stock which has lost half a point, several points,
valeur qui a perdu un demi-point, plusieurs
points (*f.*).
stock which is quoted half a point lower in
London than on the Paris Bourse, valeur
qui est cotée à Londres 1/2 point plus bas
qu'à la Bourse de Paris (*f.*).
police (*n.*), police (*f.*) :
railway police, police des voies ferrées.
policy [**policies** *pl.*] (Insce) (*n.*), police (*f.*) :
marine insurance policy *or* policy of sea
insurance, police d'assurance maritime :
French marine insurance policy on steamship
hulls, on goods or cargo, police française
d'assurance maritime sur corps de navires à
vapeur, sur marchandises ou facultés.
policy to a named person, police nominative ;
police à bénéficiaire désigné.
policy to bearer, police au porteur.
policy to order, police à ordre.

policy (course or plan of action) (*n.*), politique
(*f.*) :
the financial policy of the big banks, la politique
financière des grandes banques.
free trade policy, politique de libre-échange.
policy duty, droit de police (*m.*).
policy stamp, timbre de police (*m.*).
political economy, économie politique (*f.*).
poll (*n.*), scrutin (*m.*).
poll tax, impôt de capitation (*m.*).
pond (timber dock) (*n.*), bassin aux (*ou* à) bois
de flottage (*m.*).
pontoon (*n.*), ponton (*m.*).
pool (combination to fix rates or prices) (*n.*),
pool (*m.*) :
wheat pool, pool des blés.
pool (share placing syndicate) (*n.*), syndicat de
placement (*m.*) ; syndicat de vente (*m.*) ;
groupement (*m.*) ; groupement pour
opérations en commun (*m.*).
pool (*v.t.*), mettre en commun ; mettre en
syndicat :
to pool funds, risks, mettre des fonds, des
risques, en commun.
to pool shares, mettre en syndicat des titres.
pooling (*n.*), mise en commun (*f.*) ; mise en
syndicat (*f.*).
poor (*adj.*), pauvre.
poor rate *or* **poor rates,** taxe des pauvres (*f.*).
port (harbour) (*n.*), port (*m.*) :
the port of London, le port de Londres.
port arrived from (i.e., last loading port), port
de provenance.
port first touched at, port de prime abord.
port of arrival, port d'arrivée.
port of call (a named port, i.e., a port in the
customary or advertised route), port d'escale
(*m.*) ; escale (*f.*) ; port d'échelle (*m.*) ; échelle
(*f.*) ; port intermédiaire (*m.*) :
Boulogne is a port of call where the transatlantic boats come to anchor some hours
to pick up passengers, Boulogne est un port
d'escale (*ou* un port intermédiaire) où les
transatlantiques viennent ancrer quelques
heures pour prendre les passagers.
port of call (a port of supplies or shelter, in
or out of the customary or advertised route),
port de relâche (*m.*) ; relâche (*f.*) :
Singapore is a frequent port of call, Singapour est une relâche fréquente.
port of call for orders, port d'ordres :
port of call for orders situated on the ship's
route and where she will find her instructions, port d'ordres situé sur la route du
navire et où il trouvera ses instructions.
port of clearance, port d'expédition.
port of departure, port de départ.
port of destination, port de destination ;
port de reste.
port of discharge *or* port of delivery, port
de décharge ; port de déchargement ; port
de débarquement ; port de reste ; port de
livraison.
Note :—port de reste is not strictly correct
in this sense, but is often so used in French :
port of destination is its proper signification.

port of embarcation, port d'embarquement.
port of landing, port d'atterrissage.
port of necessity *or* port of distress *or* port of refuge, port de relâche ; port de relâche forcée ; relâche (*f.*) ; relâche forcée (*f.*) ; port de refuge ; port de salut :
port of refuge where the ship took shelter (*or* port of necessity [*or* port of distress] where the ship took refuge) to save herself from a danger which threatened her, port de relâche où le navire s'est réfugié pour se préserver d'un danger qui le menaçait.
port of registry, port d'attache ; port d'immatriculation ; port d'immatricule :
a ship must have a domicile, which is the port of registry, le navire doit avoir un domicile, qui est le port d'attache.
port of return, port de retour.
port of shipment *or* port of loading *or* port of lading, port de charge ; port de chargement ; port d'expédition ; port expéditeur ; port d'embarquement.
port of survey, port de visite.
port of transhipment, port de transbordement.
port of transit, port de transit.
port (Naut.) (*n.*) (opp. to *starboard*), bâbord (*m.*).
port dues, droits de port (*m.pl.*).
port of call navigation, navigation d'escale (*f.*).
port of refuge expenses, frais de relâche (*m.pl.*) ; frais du port de relâche (*m.pl.*) ; dépenses de relâche (*f.pl.*) ; dépenses au port de relâche (*f.pl.*).
port regulations, règlements de port (*m.pl.*).
port risk, risque de port (*m.*).
port sanitary authority, autorité sanitaire du port (*f.*).
portable typewriter, machine à écrire portative (*f.*).
portage bill (Shipping), rôle de désarmement (*m.*).
porterage (*n.*), factage (*m.*).
porterage charge, taxe de factage (*f.*).
portfolio (*n.*), portefeuille (*m.*) :
security kept in the portfolio and cashed at due date, valeur gardée en portefeuille et encaissée à l'échéance (*f.*).
we have a large quantity of these shares in portfolio (*or* in our portfolio), nous avons une grande quantité de ces actions en portefeuille.
the bank publishes every year the details of the securities which it has in its portfolio, la banque publie tous les ans le détail des titres qu'elle a en portefeuille.
the company's portfolio includes shares pertaining to all kinds of industries, notably shares in oil concerns, le portefeuille de la société comprend des titres appartenant à tous les genres d'industries, notamment des titres d'affaires pétrolifères.
portion (*n.*), portion (*f.*) ; part (*f.*) ; partie (*f.*) ; tranche (*f.*) :
and so on, rising by one twentyfifth per portion of £100 (i.e., for each £100) up to £500, et ainsi de suite, en augmentant d'un vingt-cinquième par tranche de 100£ jusqu'à 500£.
abatement relieving the lower portion of the

income, abattement dégrevant la tranche inférieure du revenu (*m.*).
position (relative situation) (*n.*), position (*f.*) ; état (*m.*) ; situation (*f.*) ; état de situation (*m.*) :
banker who judges of the solvency of his customers according to the position of their account with him, banquier qui juge de la solvabilité de ses clients (*ou* habitués) d'après la position (*ou* l'état) de leur compte chez lui (*m.*).
the pass book shows the customer's position at the bank, le carnet de compte donne la situation en banque du client.
to examine the cash position, examiner la situation (*ou* l'état de situation) de la caisse.
strong financial position, situation financière bien assise.
buyer who must either close his position or give on (Stock Exch.), acheteur qui doit ou liquider sa position ou se faire reporter (*m.*).
the contango rate is generally the barometer of the market position, le taux des reports est généralement le baromètre de la position de place (*ou* de la situation de place).
position (employment ; situation) (*n.*), position (*f.*) ; poste (*m.*) ; place (*f.*) ; emploi (*m.*).
position book, livre de positions (*m.*).
possess (*v.t.*), posséder :
to possess a lot of property, posséder de grands biens.
possession (*n.*), possession (*f.*) :
possession is nine points of the law (adage), possession vaut titre.
possessions (*n.pl.*), possessions (*f.pl.*) ; avoir (*m.*) :
oversea colonies and possessions, les colonies et possessions d'outre-mer.
one's possessions in land, ses possessions, son avoir, en terres.
possessor (pers.) (*n.*), possesseur (*m.*).
post (post office) (*n.*), poste (*f.*) ; bureau de poste (*m.*) :
to go to the post, aller à la poste.
post (mail) (*n.*), poste (*f.*) ; malle (*f.*) :
the post has just left, la poste vient de partir.
post (postal service) (*n.*), poste (*f.*) :
the post is run by the government, la poste est exploitée par l'État.
post (correspondence) (*n.*), courrier (*m.*) ; correspondance (*f.*) ; lettres (*f.pl.*) :
to go through one's post, lire son courrier ; dépouiller sa correspondance.
post (dispatch of postal matter) (*n.*), courrier (*m.*) ; courrier postal (*m.*) :
the first post, the last post, the morning post, the evening post, le premier courrier, le dernier courrier, le courrier du matin, le courrier du soir.
by the same post, par le même courrier.
to reply by return of post, répondre par retour (*ou* par le retour) du courrier.
post (employment ; situation) (*n.*), poste (*m.*) ; position (*f.*) ; office (*m.*) ; place (*f.*) ; emploi (*m.*).
post (Post) (*v.t.*), mettre à la poste ; déposer à la poste ; déposer dans la boîte ; déposer ; jeter dans la boîte aux lettres :

to post a letter, mettre, déposer, une lettre à la poste.

letters posted in private letter boxes, lettres déposées (*ou* jetées) dans les boîtes aux lettres particulières (*f.pl.*).

post (to placard) (*v.t.*), afficher :
notice posted in the House, avis affiché en Bourse (*m.*).

post *or* **post up** (Bkkpg) (*v.t.*), porter ; rapporter ; reporter ; passer ; transcrire :
to post an item in the ledger, an item to profit and loss account, porter, rapporter, reporter, passer, un article au grand livre, un article aux profits et pertes.

to post (*or* to post up) an account, reporter un compte.

to post the journal into the ledger *or* to post up the ledger from the journal, transcrire le journal au grand livre.

putting in the journal folio from which the item is posted, inscription du folio du journal d'après lequel l'article est rapporté (*f.*).

postcard, postdate. V. ci-après.

post free, franc de port ; franco de port.

post letter, lettre remise à la poste (*f.*).

postman, postmark, postmaster. V. ci-après.

post office (Abbrev.: **P.O.**), bureau de poste (*m.*) ; poste (*f.*).

post office box (Abbrev.: **P.O.B.**), boîte postale (*f.*) ; boîte de commerce (*f.*).

post office guide, indicateur universel des postes, télégraphes et téléphones (*m.*).

post office order (money order) (Abbrev.: **P.O.O.**), mandat de poste (*m.*) ; mandat-poste (*m.*) ; mandat postal (*m.*) ; mandat (*m.*).

post office savings bank, caisse nationale d'épargne (*f.*) ; caisse d'épargne postale (*f.*) ; caisse nationale d'épargne postale (*f.*).

post paid, affranchi, -e :
post paid letter, lettre affranchie (*f.*).

post-war (*adj.*) (opp. to *pre-war*), d'après-guerre :
to reduce our crushing post-war debt, réduire notre écrasante dette d'après-guerre.

postage (*n.*), port (*m.*) ; affranchissement (*m.*) :
postage on a letter, port d'une lettre.

postage book, livre des timbres-poste (*m.*) ; livre d'entrée et de sortie des timbres (*m.*).

postage due stamp, timbre-taxe (*m.*) ; chiffre-taxe (*m.*).

postage paid, port payé.

postage rates, tarifs postaux (*m.pl.*).

postage stamp, timbre-poste (*m.*) ; figurine postale (*f.*).

postal (*adj.*), postal, -e, -aux :
postal article, objet postal (*m.*) ; envoi postal (*m.*).

postal authorities, administration des postes (*f.*).

postal order (*Abbrev.*: P.O.), bon de poste (*m.*). *Note :*—postal orders have been abolished in France following the creation of the *chèque postal*, and the simplification of the use of low value money orders.

postal packet, paquet-poste (*m.*) ; envoi postal (*m.*) ; objet postal (*m.*) ; objet de correspondance (*m.*) ; correspondance (*f.*) :

Note :—In English, *packet* or *postal packet* has two meanings, specific and general.

Specifically, it means a packet unclassifiable as a letter, newspaper, box, sample, or the like, such as a roll, or small parcel of papers or other articles. This in French is *paquet* or *paquet-poste*.

Generally, it means any packet of whatever kind, a letter, newspaper, box, sample, or what not. This in French is *objet*, *objet de correspondance*, *objet postal*, *correspondance*, *envoi*.

postal packets of every (*or* of any) kind, objets de correspondance de toute nature.

letters or other postal packets, lettres ou autres objets de correspondance.

a postal packet addressed poste restante, une correspondance adressée poste restante.

redirection of postal packets, réexpédition des correspondances (*f.*).

postal parcel, colis postal (*m.*).

postal rates, tarifs postaux (*m.pl.*).

postal savings bank, caisse nationale d'épargne (*f.*) ; caisse d'épargne postale (*f.*) ; caisse nationale d'épargne postale (*f.*).

postal service, service des postes (*m.*) ; service postal (*m.*) ; poste (*f.*).

Postal Union, Union postale (*f.*).

postcard (*n.*) (Abbrev.: **p.c.**), carte postale (*f.*).

postdate *or* **postdating** (*n.*) (Ant.: *antedate*), postdate (*f.*).

postdate (*v.t.*), postdater :
to postdate a letter, postdater une lettre.

poste restante, poste restante ; bureau restant :
to address a letter " poste restante," adresser une lettre « poste restante. »

poste restante fee, surtaxe de poste restante (*f.*).

posting (letters, etc.) (Post) (*n.*), mise à la poste (*f.*) ; dépôt à la poste (*m.*) ; dépôt dans la boîte (*m.*) ; dépôt (*m.*) :
latest time for posting, heure-limite de dépôt (*f.*) ; dernière limite d'heure de dépôt (*f.*).

posting (Bkkpg) (*n.*), report (*m.*) ; passation (*f.*) ; transcription (*f.*) :
the posting of journal entries to the ledger accounts, le report des écritures du journal aux comptes du grand livre.

the ledger postings, the postings from the journal to the ledger accounts, les reports du grand livre, les reports du journal aux comptes du grand livre.

posting box, boîte aux lettres (*f.*).

posting folio (Bkkpg), rencontre (*f.*).

postman [**postmen** *pl.*] (*n.*), facteur (*m.*) ; facteur de la poste (*ou* des postes) (*m.*) :
postman on cycle, facteur cycliste.

postmark (*n.*), timbre (*m.*) :
this letter bears the Paris postmark, cette lettre porte le timbre de Paris.

postmaster (pers.) (*n.*), maître de poste (*m.*) ; directeur des postes (*m.*).

postmaster general [**postmasters general** *pl.*] (Abbrev.: **P.M.G.**), directeur général des postes (*m.*).

postponable (*adj.*), ajournable.

postpone (*v.t.*), remettre; renvoyer; ajourner; différer:

to postpone a matter for a week, remettre, renvoyer, une affaire à huitaine.

to postpone the payment of, différer le paiement de; atermoyer:

to pay the capital and postpone payment of the interest, payer le capital et atermoyer les intérêts.

postponement (*n.*), remise (*f.*); renvoi (*m.*); ajournement (*m.*):

postponement of a discussion, renvoi d'une discussion.

postscript (*n.*) (Abbrev.: **P.S.**), post-scriptum (*m.*); P.-S.; apostille (*f.*):

to put a postscript, mettre un post-scriptum.

pound (*n.*) (Abbrev.: **£** *or* **L.** *or* l.) *or* **pound sterling** [**pounds sterling** *pl.*] (Abbrev.: **£ stg** *or* **L. ster.** *or* l. stg), livre (*f.*); livre sterling (*f.*).

poundage (on money orders) (*n.*), droit de commission (des mandats-poste) (*m.*).

pounds, shillings, and pence column (Abbrev.: **£ s. d. col.**), colonne livres, schellings, et pence (*f.*).

power (capacity to act) (*n.*), pouvoir (*m.*):

the powers of a liquidator, of the master in matters of sale or pledging of the cargo, les pouvoirs d'un liquidateur, du capitaine en matière de vente ou de mise en gage des marchandises.

manager having power to sign for the company, having the widest powers to administer the affairs of the company, gérant ayant pouvoir de signer pour la société, ayant les pouvoirs les plus étendus pour administrer les affaires de la société (*m.*).

power of attorney [**powers of attorney** *pl.*] *or simply* **power** (*n.*) (Abbrev.: **P/A.**), procuration (*f.*); pouvoir (*m.*); mandat (*m.*):

power of attorney drawn up before a notary, procuration rédigée (*ou* mandat rédigé) par-devant notaire.

if the representative has a power of attorney, he precedes his signature with the words: p.p. So-and-so, si le représentant a une procuration, il fait précéder sa signature des mots: P.Pᵒⁿ de M. un tel.

a power of attorney supposes a contract by which a person is charged by another to represent him and to act in the best of the interests entrusted to him, un mandat suppose un contrat par lequel une personne est chargée par une autre de la représenter et d'agir au mieux des intérêts qui lui sont confiés.

power vessel, navire à moteur (*m.*).

practice (in) *or* **practising**, en exercice:

barrister in practice *or* practising barrister, avocat en exercice (*m.*).

pratique (intercourse or communication with the shore) (*n.*), libre pratique (*f.*):

when the bill of health is clean, the ship is admitted in pratique (*or* in free pratique), lorsque la patente de santé est nette, le navire est admis en libre pratique.

on her arrival, the ship lies in the roads or in the outer habour until the officer of health gives her the pratique, à son arrivée, le navire stationne en rade ou dans l'avant-port jusqu'à ce que l'officier de santé lui accorde la libre pratique.

pratique (clean bill of health) (*n.*), patente nette (*f.*).

pre-war (*adj.*) (opp. to *post-war*), d'avant-guerre:

pre-war figures, chiffres d'avant-guerre (*m.pl.*).

precious (*adj.*), précieux, -euse; de valeur; de prix:

precious metal, métal précieux (*m.*):

the precious metal which enters into the composition of standard coins, le métal précieux qui entre dans la composition des pièces types.

précis (*n.*), précis (*m.*):

the précis of a matter, le précis d'une affaire.

preemption (*n.*), préemption (*f.*).

prefer (*v.t.*), préférer:

to prefer one creditor over others, préférer un créancier à (*ou* sur) des autres.

the Government is preferred over all creditors, le Gouvernement est préféré à tous créanciers.

preference (*n.*), préférence (*f.*).

preference (Economics) (*n.*), régime de faveur (*m.*); traitement de faveur (*m.*); préférence (*f.*):

Note :—When referring to French preference, it is better to use the word *faveur*, when to imperial (i.e., British), the word *préférence*.

goods entitled to a preference (*or* to preferential duty), marchandises ayant droit à un régime de faveur (*f.pl.*).

the preference granted to colonial produce, le traitement de faveur (*ou* le régime de faveur) accordé aux produits coloniaux.

imperial preference, préférence impériale.

preference share certificate, certificat d'action(s) de priorité (*m.*).

preference shareholder *or* **preference stockholder**, actionnaire de priorité (*m.* ou *f.*).

preference shares *or* **preference stock** *or* **preference stocks** (Abbrev.: **pref.** *or* **prefs** *or* **prefce** *or* **prf.** *or* **pf.**) *or* **preferred shares** *or* **preferred stock** *or* **preferred stocks** (Abbrev.: **pfd** *or* **pref.** *or* **prefs** *or* **prf.** *or* **pf.**), actions de priorité (*f.pl.*); actions privilégiées (*f.pl.*); actions de préférence (*f.pl.*):

X. preference (*or* X. prefs) were better (Stock Exch.), la privilégiée X. s'améliore.

preferential *or* **preferred** (Law) (*adj.*), privilégié, -e; préféré, -e; préférentiel, -elle:

preferential claim, privilège (*m.*):

workmen's wages constitute a preferential claim, le salaire des ouvriers est l'objet d'un privilège.

preferential creditor, créancier privilégié (*m.*). V. exemple sous **creditor**.

preferential debt *or* preferred debt, créance privilégiée (*f.*); dette privilégiée (*f.*).

preferential right, droit de préférence (*m.*); droit préférentiel (*m.*).

the last loan is always preferred over (*or*

preferential to) that which preceded it, le dernier emprunt est toujours préféré à celui qui l'aura précédé.

preferential dividend *or* **preferred dividend,** dividende privilégié (*m.*).

preferential rates (of customs duties) (on goods imported from foreign countries under reciprocity agreements) (distinguished from *full rates*), tarif minimum (*m.*), tarif spécial (*m.*) (des droits de douane) :
foreign goods which benefit by preferential rates on proof of origin, marchandises étrangères qui bénéficient du tarif minimum sur justification d'origine (*f.pl.*).

preferential rates (of customs duties) (on goods imported from colonies), tarif colonial (*m.*).

preferential tariff (of customs duties), tarif de faveur (*m.*) ; tarif de préférence (*m.*) ; tarif préférentiel (*m.*) : (V. note sous **preference.**)
a preferential tariff conceded to nations who grant us correlative privileges, un tarif de faveur concédé aux nations qui nous accordent des avantages corrélatifs.
the preferential tariffs under which inter-imperial transactions benefit, les tarifs préférentiels dont bénéficient les transactions interimpériales.

prejudice (*n.*), préjudice (*m.*) :
without prejudice to, sans préjudice de :
action statute barred after one year, without prejudice to cases of fraud or breach of trust, action prescrite par un an, sans préjudice des cas de fraude ou d'infidélité (*f.*).

preliminary expenses, frais de constitution (*m.pl.*).

premier (*adj.*), premier, -ère :
London on Thames, premier English port and premier European port, Londres sur la Tamise, premier port anglais et premier port européen.
the English mercantile fleet is the premier fleet of the world, la flotte commerciale anglaise est la première du monde.

premises (land and buildings) (*n.pl.*), immeuble (*m.*) ; immeubles (*m.pl.*) ; locaux (*m.pl.*) :
bank premises, immeuble (*ou* immeubles) de la banque.
business premises, locaux commerciaux ; immeuble commercial.
the annual rental value of the premises occupied by the insured, la valeur locative annuelle des locaux occupés par l'assuré.

premises (address ; legal domicile) (*n.pl.*), domicile (*m.*) :
delivery at my premises, livraison à mon domicile (*f.*).

premises (of a deed) (*n.pl.*), intitulé (d'un acte) (*m.*).

premium (bounty or bonus) (*n.*), prime (*f.*) :
redemption premium, prime de remboursement.

premium (Letting) (*n.*), reprise (*f.*) :
premises to let, no premium, small premium, local à louer, sans reprise, petite reprise (*m.*).

offices to let, 4 rooms, rent £240, premium £400, bureaux à louer, 4 pièces, loyer £240, reprise £400 (*m.pl.*).

premium (*n.*) (Abbrev. : **pm** *or* **prm**) *or* **premium on exchange** (difference between mint par and present price), prime du change (*f.*) ; prix du change (*m.*) ; agio (*m.*).

premium (sum in advance of par value) (*n.*) (opp. to *discount*) (Abbrev. : **pm** *or* **prm**), prime (*f.*) :
a share of £1 which sells at £1 5s. 0d. (*or* 25/-), is dealt in at 5/- premium, une action de 1*l.* qui se vend 1*l.* 5*sh.* 0*d.* (*ou* 25*sh.*), se négocie à 5*sh.* de prime.
loan which is called ¼% premium (Stock Exch.), emprunt qui fait 1/4 0/0 de prime (*m.*).
to be at a premium *or* to stand at a premium, être en prime ; faire prime :
shares which are at a premium (*or* which stand at a premium), actions qui sont en prime (*ou* qui font prime) (*f.pl.*).
gold is at a premium on the money market, l'or fait prime sur le marché des monnaies (*m.*).
country where gold is quoted at a premium or at a discount on the basis of so many francs for a kilogramme of pure gold, pays où l'or se cote en prime ou en perte sur la base de tant de francs pour un kilogramme d'or pur (*m.*).
premiums on shares, primes d'émission ; primes sur émissions ; primes sur actions.
Cf. to issue shares at a premium, *sous* **issue** (*v.t.*).

premium (Forward exchange rates) (*n.*) (Abbrev. : **p.**) (opp. to *discount*), déport (*m.*) ; bénéfice (*m.*). V. exemples sous **discount.**

premium (Insce) (*n.*) (Abbrev. : **pm** *or* **prm**), prime (*f.*) :
insurance premium *or* premium of insurance, prime d'assurance.
premium to be arranged, prime à débattre ; prime à arbitrer.

premium (*v.t.*), primer :
money which premiums the franc or which is premiumed by it, monnaie qui prime le franc ou qui est primée par lui (*f.*).

premium bonds, obligations à primes (*f.pl.*).

premium reserve *or* **premiums on shares reserve,** réserve prime d'émission (*f.*) ; réserve prime sur actions (*f.*).

prepaid freight, fret payé d'avance (*m.*) ; fret payé (*m.*).

prepaid letter, lettre affranchie (*f.*).

prepaid parcel, colis affranchi (*m.*).

prepaid rate of postage, tarif d'affranchissement (*m.*) :
prepaid rate of postage for samples, tarif d'affranchissement des échantillons.

preparation (drawing up) (*n.*), dressement (*m.*) ; rédaction (*f.*).

prepare (to draw up) (*v.t.*), dresser ; rédiger :
to prepare a contract, dresser, rédiger, un contrat.

prepay (*v.t.*), payer d'avance ; payer par anticipation ; acquitter préalablement ; affranchir :

rent prepaid, loyer payé d'avance (*m.*); loyer d'avance (*m.*).

to prepay the freight, affranchir le fret.

prepay the postage (*or* **carriage**) **on** (**to**), affranchir :
to prepay the postage on a letter, affranchir une lettre.

postage on parcels must be prepaid, les colis postaux doivent être obligatoirement affranchis au départ (*m.pl.*).

packets posted unpaid or underpaid.—if posted unpaid charged with double postage, if posted underpaid, with double the amount short paid, objets non ou insuffisamment affranchis.—taxe double du montant de l'affranchissement manquant ou de l'insuffisance d'affranchissement.

prepayment (*n.*), paiement d'avance (*m.*); payement par anticipation (*m.*); paiement anticipé (*m.*); acquittement préalable (*m.*); affranchissement (*m.*); affranchissement préalable (*m.*) :
prepayment of customs charges, affranchissement préalable des frais de douane.

prepayment call office, cabine téléphonique publique à encaissement automatique (*f.*); cabine taxiphone publique (*f.*).

prepayment of postage (*or* **carriage**), affranchissement (*m.*).

prescribe (*v.t.*), prescrire :
the formalities prescribed by law, les formalités prescrites par la loi (*f.pl.*).
prescribed time, délai prescrit (*m.*); délai réglementaire (*m.*).

prescription (bar of the statute of limitations) (*n.*), prescription (*f.*).

present (*adj.*), présent, -e ; courant, -e ; en cours ; actuel, -elle :
all the owners, present and future, of the property insured, tous les propriétaires, présents et futurs, de la chose assurée.
property present and future, biens présents et à venir (*m.pl.*).
present : A., chairman, B., C., directors (minutes of meeting), sont présents (*ou* étaient présents) : M. A., président, et MM. B., C., administrateurs.
present campaign (Corn Exchange), campagne actuelle (*f.*); campagne en cours (*f.*).
present month, mois courant (*m.*); mois en cours (*m.*); courant (*m.*) :
payment to be made at the end of the present month, paiement à faire fin courant (*ou* fin du courant) (*m.*).
present name (of a ship) (opp. to *late name*), nom actuel (d'un navire) (*m.*).

present (present writing) (*n.*), présente (*f.*) :
on receipt of the present (the present letter), au reçu de la présente.
know all men by these presents *or* to all to whom these presents shall come, savoir faisons par ces présentes ; à tous ceux qui ces présentes verront.

present (*v.t.*), présenter :
to present a cheque for payment, a bill for acceptance, for discount at the bank,

présenter un chèque au paiement (*ou* à l'encaissement), un effet à l'acceptation, à l'escompte à la banque.

to present accounts, a report to the general meeting of shareholders, présenter des comptes, un rapport à l'assemblée générale des actionnaires.

present (to be), assister :
to be present at a meeting of shareholders, assister à une assemblée des actionnaires.
he was present at the board meeting, il a assisté au conseil des administrateurs.

presentation *or* **presentment** (*n.*), présentation (*f.*) :
presentation of a customs entry, présentation d'une déclaration en douane.
presentation (*or* presentment) for acceptance, for payment (of a bill), présentation à l'acceptation, au paiement.

on presentation, à présentation ; à bureau ouvert ; à guichet ouvert ; à vue ; sur demande :
to pay on presentation, payer à présentation (*ou* à bureau ouvert) (*ou* à guichet ouvert).

presenter (pers.) (*n.*), présentateur, -trice :
presenter of a bill, présentateur d'un billet.

presenting (*adj.*), présentateur, -trice :
presenting bank, banque présentatrice (*f.*).

preservation *or* **preserving** (*n.*), préservation (*f.*); conservation (*f.*) :
preservation of (*or* preserving) the property insured, conservation des objets assurés.

preserve (*v.t.*), préserver ; conserver :
to preserve the property at risk in a maritime adventure from a common imminent peril, préserver d'un péril commun imminent les biens en risque dans une expédition maritime.

preside (*v.i.*), présider :
Mr X. presided, M. X. préside.

preside at (**to**) *or* **preside over** (**to**), présider à ; présider :
to preside at (*or* over) a meeting, présider à, présider, une assemblée.
the meeting is presided over by the chairman of the board, l'assemblée est présidée par le président du conseil d'administration (*f.*).

presidency [**presidencies** *pl.*] (*n.*), présidence (*f.*) :
to be elected to the presidency of a meeting, être nommé (-e) à la présidence d'une assemblée.

president (pers.) (*n.*), président, -e.

press (copying) (*n.*), presse (à copier) (*f.*).

press (the newspapers) (*n.*), presse (*f.*).

press agency, agence d'information (*f.*).

press campaign, campagne de presse (*f.*).

press copy, copie à la presse (*f.*).

press telegram (Abbrev.: **Press**), télégramme de presse (*m.*).

press work (reporting in newspapers), reportage (*m.*).

presume (*v.t.*), présumer :
packets containing or presumed to contain articles liable to customs duties, envois contenant ou présumés contenir des objets passibles de droits de douane (*m.pl.*).

presumption (*n.*), présomption (*f.*) :
  presumption of fault, of sea peril, of loss of the goods, présomption de faute, de fortune de mer, de perte de la marchandise.
previous closing *or* **previous close** (Abbrev.: **prev. close**) (list of quotations), clôture précédente (*f.*).
previous price (Stock Exch.), cours précédent (*m.*).
previous year, année précédente (*f.*) ; année antérieure (*f.*). V. exemple sous **year.**
price (*n.*), prix (*m.*) :
  the price of gold, le prix de l'or.
  prices are the monetary expression of values, les prix sont l'expression monétaire des valeurs.
  price of money, prix de l'argent ; loyer de l'argent (*m.*) :
    the lowering of the price of money has certainly contributed to the maintenance of economic prosperity, l'abaissement du loyer de l'argent a certainement contribué au maintien de la prospérité économique (*m.*).
price (rate of quotation) (*n.*), prix (*m.*) ; cours (*m.*) ; taux (*m.*) ; cote (*f.*) :
  price current (the current or market price), prix courant ; prix du marché.
  list of prices (quotations), bulletin de cours (*m.*).
  issue price (of shares, or the like), prix d'émission ; taux d'émission.
  prices of shares, cours des actions.
  price(s) bid (buyers), cours demandé(s) (acheteurs) ; cours acheteur(s) ; cours Argent ; Argent.
  price(s) offered (sellers), cours offert(s) (vendeurs) ; cours vendeur(s) ; cours Papier ; Papier.
  price of the day, cours du jour.
  price for cash (on 'change), cours au comptant.
  price for the settlement *or* price for the account (Stock Exch.) (opp. to *price for cash*), cours à terme.
  price of call (Stock Exch.), cours du dont.
  price of option (Stock Exch.), cours de prime ; prix de la prime ; base de la prime (*f.*) ; prix de base de la prime.
  price of put (Stock Exch.), cours de l'ou.
  price of put and call *or* price of double option (Stock Exch.), cours de l'option ; cours du stellage.
  spot price *or* price ex store *or* price ex warehouse (Produce or Corn Exch.), cours du disponible.
  stocks and shares subject to fluctuations of price (*or* of prices), valeurs mobilières sujettes aux fluctuations des cours (*ou* de la cote) (*f.pl.*).
price (*v.t.*), tarifer.
price list *or* **price current** (Abbrev.: **P.C.**), prix courant (*m.*) ; tarif (*m.*) :
  to consult a price list, consulter un prix courant.
prima facie, prima facie ; de prime face :
  prima facie evidence, preuve prima facie (*f.*) ; évidence de prime face (*f.*).
primage (*n.*), chapeau (*m.*) ; chapeau du capitaine (*m.*) ; primage (*m.*) :

primage is an additional freight calculated at a rate of so much per cent on the principal freight, le chapeau du capitaine (*ou* le primage) et un supplément de fret calculé à raison de tant pour cent sur le fret principal.
prime cost (of manufactured articles) (Costing), prix de revient (des objets fabriqués) (*m.*).
prime trade bills, papier de haut commerce (*m.*) ; papier hors banque (*m.*).
principal (*adj.*), principal, -e, -aux :
  principal agreement (*or* contract), contrat principal (*m.*).
  principal contract (direct contract) (Produce or Corn Exch.) (opp. to *commission contract* or *broker's contract*), contrat direct (*m.*).
  principal creditor, principal créancier (*m.*).
  principal debtor, débiteur principal (*m.*).
principal (capital of a debt) (*n.*), capital (*m.*) ; capitaux (*m.pl.*) ; principal (*m.*) :
  principal and interest, capital et intérêt ; capitaux et intérêts ; principal et intérêts :
  the interest is added to the principal, les intérêts s'ajoutent aux capitaux (*m.pl.*).
  principal of a bill of exchange, capital, principal, d'une lettre de change.
principal (as distinguished from *agent*) (pers.) (*n.*), mandant (*m.*) ; commettant (*m.*) ; donneur d'ordre (*m.*) :
  principal and agent, mandant et mandataire ; commettant et commissionnaire ; donneur d'ordre et commissionnaire.
  the obligation of the agent to prove the carrying out of his instructions ceases when the principal has discharged him, l'obligation pour le mandataire de justifier de l'exécution de son mandat cesse lorsque le mandant lui a donné décharge (*f.*).
  the agent receives from his principal a retribution called commission, le commissionnaire reçoit de son commettant une rétribution appelée commission.
  the stockbroker is entitled to require his principal to hand him, before dealing, the stock to be dealt in or the money to pay for the amount of the deal, l'agent de change est en droit d'exiger que son donneur d'ordre lui remette, avant toute négociation, les effets à négocier ou les fonds destinés à acquitter le montant de la négociation (*m.*).
principal (the real purchaser at a sale, as distinguished from his agent) (*n.*), command (*m.*).
principal (employer) (pers.) (*n.*), patron, -onne ; employeur, -euse :
  principal of a business house, patron d'une maison de commerce.
print (*v.t.*), imprimer :
  an insurance policy may be written or printed ; or partly written and partly printed, la police d'assurance peut être manuscrite ou imprimée ; ou en partie manuscrite et en partie imprimée.
printed clause (opp. to *written clause*), clause imprimée (*f.*).
printed form *or* **printed matter,** formule imprimée (*f.*) ; imprimé (*m.*) ; imprimés (*m.pl.*) :

letter on a printed form, lettre sur formule imprimée (*f.*).

a complete set of all the printed forms (*or* printed matter), un jeu complet de tous les imprimés.

printed matter (Post), imprimés (*m.pl.*).

printed paper (Post), imprimé (*m.*).

printed paper rate (Post), tarif des imprimés (*m.*).

printer (pers.) (*n.*), imprimeur (*m.*).

printer's block, cliché d'imprimerie (*m.*).

printer's error, faute d'impression (*f.*); erreur typographique (*f.*).

printer's proof, épreuve d'imprimerie (*f.*).

printing (*n.*), impression (*f.*):
printing certificates, impression des titres.

printing (cost of printing; name of ledger account or of item in profit and loss account) (*n.*), imprimés (*m.pl.*); frais d'impression (*m.pl.*):
printing and stationery, imprimés et fournitures.

printing telegraph, télégraphe imprimeur (*m.*); ticker (*m.*).

prior (*adj.*), prioritaire; antérieur, -e:
a prior appropriation on the net profits, un prélèvement prioritaire sur les bénéfices nets.
prior contract, contrat antérieur (*m.*).

priority (*n.*), priorité (*f.*); antériorité (*f.*):
priority of date, of mortgage, priorité, antériorité, de date, d'hypothèque.

private (*adj.*) (Ant.: *public*), privé, -e; particulier, -ère:
private account (*Abbrev.:* P/A.), compte particulier (*m.*).
private attorney, fondé de pouvoir (*m.*); fondé de pouvoirs (*m.*).
private bank, banque privée (*f.*); banque particulière (*f.*).
private cabin, cabine particulière (*f.*).
private code, code privé (*m.*).
private company (*ordinary meaning*), compagnie privée (*f.*); compagnie particulière (*f.*); société privée (*ou* particulière) (*f.*):
construction of a railway by the State with working concession to private companies, construction d'un chemin de fer par l'État avec concession de l'exploitation à des compagnies privées (*f.*).
private company (limited liability company), société à responsabilité limitée (*f.*). *V. note sous* limited company *or* private company.
private correspondent, correspondant particulier (*m.*).
private interests, intérêts privés (*m.pl.*); intérêts particuliers (*m.pl.*).
private international law, droit international privé (*m.*).
private issue (of shares), émission privée (*f.*).
private law, droit privé (*m.*); droit civil (*m.*).
private letter box *or* private posting box, boîte aux lettres particulière (*f.*).
private line (Rly. or Teleph.), ligne d'intérêt privé (*f.*).
private rate *or* private rate of discount (opp. to *official,* or *bank, rate*), taux privé (*m.*); taux d'escompte (*ou* de l'escompte) privé

(*m.*); escompte privé (*m.*); taux hors banque (*m.*); taux d'escompte hors banque (*m.*); escompte hors banque (*m.*).

private seal, seing privé (*m.*):
deed under private seal, acte sous seing privé (*m.*).

private secretary, secrétaire particulier (*m.*).

private siding (Rly.), embranchement particulier (*m.*).

private telegram, télégramme privé (*m.*).

private treaty, traité particulier (*m.*):
private treaty which has the effect of making a reduction on tariff rates, traité particulier qui a pour effet d'accorder une réduction sur les prix des tarifs.
Cf. sale by private treaty.

privilege (Law) (*n.*), privilège (*m.*).

privileged (*adj.*), privilégié, -e:
privileged debt, créance privilégiée (*f.*); dette privilégiée (*f.*).

prize (Fin.) (*n.*), lot (*m.*).

prize (ship captured) (Internat. Law) (*n.*), prise (*f.*).

prize bond, bon à lots (*m.*); obligation à lots (*f.*); titre à lots (*m.*); valeur à lots (*f.*).

prize court, conseil des prises (*m.*); tribunal des (*ou* de) prises (*m.*).

prize drawing, tirage à lots (*m.*).

prize money, part de prise (*f.*).

pro (for; for and on behalf of) (used before a signature), pour.

pro forma, fictif, -ive; simulé, -e; pro forma:
pro forma invoice, facture fictive (*f.*); facture simulée (*f.*); facture pro forma (*f.*).

pro rata, au prorata; au marc le franc; au marc la livre; proportionnel, -elle; proportionnellement:
the underwriters will contribute pro rata, les assureurs contribueront au prorata (*ou* au marc le franc) (*m.pl.*).
pro rata contribution, contribution au prorata (*f.*); contribution proportionnelle (*f.*).
pro rata freight, fret proportionnel (*m.*); fret proportionnel à la distance (*m.*); fret de distance (*m.*).
freight paid pro rata, fret payé proportionnellement (*m.*).

pro rata to, au prorata de; au marc le franc de; au marc la livre de:
in a liquidation each creditor receives pro rata to his debt, dans une liquidation chaque créancier reçoit au prorata de sa créance.
to distribute the amount realized by a debtor's property among his creditors pro rata to their debts, répartir le prix des biens d'un débiteur entre ses créanciers au marc le franc de leurs créances.

pro tempore (Abbrev.: **pro tem.**), pro tempore.

probability [**probabilities** *pl.*] (*n.*), probabilité (*f.*):
average probabilities of losses or damage (Insce), probabilités moyennes de pertes ou de dommage.

probatory (*adj.*), probant, -e:
probatory force of the consignment note, force probante de la lettre de voiture (*f.*).

procedure (*n.*), procédure (*f.*) ; marche à suivre (*f.*) :
the procedure of the adjustment of average, la procédure du règlement d'avarie.
proceed (*v.i.*). V. exemples :
to proceed backwards or forwards (i.e., to make any calls, direct or indirect—said of a ship), faire toutes escales directes ou rétrogrades.
ship in a condition to proceed to sea, navire en état de prendre la mer (*m.*).
ship made ready to proceed upon her voyage, navire rendu prêt à poursuivre son voyage (*m.*).
vessel to have liberty to proceed and to stay at any port or place, le navire aura la faculté de se rendre et de séjourner à tout port ou lieu.
increase of premium applicable to the case where a ship finding her port of destination blocked, lies before that port or proceeds to others, augmentation de prime applicable au cas où un navire trouvant son port de destination bloqué, séjourne devant ce port ou relève pour d'autres (*f.*).
proceed against (to), poursuivre :
to proceed against a debtor, poursuivre un débiteur.
proceeding (to another port) (Navig.) (*n.*), relèvement (*m.*) :
additional premium for proceeding from Havana to Brazil and the Plate, surprime de relèvement de la Havane sur le Brésil et La Plata.
proceedings (transactions) (*n.pl.*), délibérations (*f.pl.*) :
proceedings of a meeting, délibérations d'une assemblée.
proceedings (Law) (*n.pl.*), procédure (*f.*) ; poursuites (*f.pl.*) ; poursuite (*f.*) ; cause (*f.*) ; action (*f.*) ; affaire (*f.*) :
civil proceedings, procédure civile ; poursuite civile ; cause civile ; action civile ; affaire civile.
to commence proceedings against a debtor, entamer des poursuites contre un débiteur.
proceeds (*n.pl.*), produit (*m.*) :
the gross proceeds, the net proceeds, of a sale, le produit brut, le produit net, d'une vente.
proceeds (of a bill) (*n.pl.*), net produit (*m.*), produit net (*m.*), net (*m.*), valeur actuelle (*f.*) (d'un effet).
process (*n.*), processus (*m.*) :
the process of the adjustment of average, le processus du règlement d'avarie.
procuration (*n.*), procuration (*f.*) ; mandat (*m.*) :
to act by procuration, agir par procuration (*ou* par mandat).
procuration drawn up before a notary, procuration rédigée (*ou* mandat rédigé) par-devant notaire.
per (*or* by) procuration *or* per procurationem, *generally abbreviated* per pro. *or* per proc. *or* p.p., par procuration ; P.Pon ; Par pon.
V. exemple sous **power of attorney.**

produce (*n.*), produit (*m.*) ; produits (*m.pl.*) ; denrées (*f.pl.*) :
produce of the soil, produits du sol.
produce intended for export, produits destinés (ou denrées destinées) à l'exportation.
produce (to bring forth) (*v.t.*), produire :
no nation produces all it needs, none can consume all it is able to produce, aucune nation ne produit tout ce dont elle a besoin, aucune ne peut consommer tout ce qu'elle est en mesure de produire.
produce (to bring in) (*v.t.*), produire ; rapporter ; rendre.
produce (to exhibit ; to show) (*v.t.*), produire ; exhiber ; présenter ; représenter ; communiquer :
to produce a certificate, one's books, produire, exhiber, représenter, un titre, ses livres.
to produce documents of a nature to prove one's claim, produire des pièces de nature à justifier sa prétention.
passengers must produce their tickets whenever required to do so by the company's servants, les voyageurs doivent présenter (*ou* représenter) (*ou* exhiber) leurs billets à toute réquisition des préposés de la compagnie (*m.pl.*).
produce broker, courtier de (*ou* en) marchandises (*m.*) :
produce brokers perform on the produce exchange the same functions as stockbrokers on the stock exchange, les courtiers en marchandises remplissent à la bourse des marchandises les mêmes fonctions que les agents de change à la bourse des valeurs. *V. note sous* marché commercial.
produce exchange, bourse de (*ou* des) marchandises (*f.*) ; bourse de commerce (*f.*).
Note :—According to French law, *bourse de commerce* means either a *bourse de marchandises* or a *bourse de valeurs,* but in common usage *bourse de commerce* means *bourse de marchandises.* See note *under* marché commercial.
produce market, marché commercial (*m.*). See note *under* marché commercial.
producer (pers.) (*n.*), producteur, -trice :
the producer and the consumer, le producteur et le consommateur.
producing *or* **productive** (*adj.*), producteur, -trice ; productif, -ive ; en rapport :
producing industry, industrie productrice (*f.*).
capital productive of interest, capital productif d'intérêt (*m.*).
productive capital, capitaux en rapport (*m.pl.*).
product (anything produced) (*n.*), produit (*m.*) :
products of the soil, of industry, produits du sol, de l'industrie.
product (current accounts, or the like) (*n.*), produit (*m.*) ; nombre (*m.*) :
to multiply the principal by the days and carry out the product in the interest column, multiplier le capital par les jours et porter le produit dans la colonne des intérêts.
red product, nombre rouge.
product method, méthode des nombres (*f.*).

production (*n.*), production (*f.*):
the productions of the soil, les productions du sol.
exportation stimulates production, l'exportation stimule la production (*f.*).
production (exhibition; showing) (*n.*), production (*f.*); exhibition (*f.*); présentation (*f.*); représentation (*f.*); communication (*f.*):
auditor who calls for production of titles to property, commissaire qui exige communication des titres de propriété (*m.*).
productivity *or* **productiveness** (*n.*), productivité (*f.*).
profession (*n.*) *or* **profession or business** (occupation; description), profession (*f.*); qualités (*f.pl.*); qualité ou profession:
the full name (*or* the name in full), address, and profession or business of the applicant, les nom, prénoms, adresse (*ou* domicile), et qualité ou profession (*ou* qualités) (*ou* profession) du souscripteur.
professional (*adj.*) *or* **by profession**, professionnel, -elle; de profession:
the professional element, l'élément professionnel (*m.*).
professional accountant *or* accountant by profession, comptable professionnel (*m.*); comptable de profession (*m.*); expert-comptable (*m.*).
professional (pers.) (*n.*), professionnel, -elle:
whereas the professional may be accidentally a speculator, the non professional is always and necessarily so, si le professionnel peut être accidentellement spéculateur, le non professionnel l'est toujours et nécessairement.
professional risks indemnity insurance, assurance contre le risque professionnel (*f.*).
profit (*used as adj.*) *or* **being a profit** *or* **showing a profit,** bénéficiaire:
profit balance, solde bénéficiaire (*m.*).
balance sheet showing a profit, bilan bénéficiaire (*m.*).
according as the result of the trading is (*or* shows) a profit or a loss, suivant que le résultat de l'exercice est bénéficiaire ou déficitaire.
profit (*n.*), bénéfice (*m.*); profit (*m.*); boni (*m.*); gain (*m.*); prime (*f.*); produit (*m.*); fruit (*m.*):
profit on a sale, on the transaction, on exchange, bénéfice, profit, sur une vente, sur l'opération, au change.
profit on charter, bénéfice d'affrètement.
profit on investments, bénéfice du portefeuille.
net profit *or* net profits, bénéfice net; bénéfices nets; profit net; profits nets.
to make a hundred pounds profit out of a deal, avoir cent livres de boni dans une affaire.
to make enormous profits, réaliser des gains énormes.
transaction which leaves a good profit, opération qui laisse un produit avantageux (*f.*).
casual profits (Law), fruits casuels.

profit (*v.i.*), bénéficier; profiter:
to profit by goods sold, by appreciation of the exchange, bénéficier, profiter, sur une marchandise vendue, de la plus-value du change.
profit and loss (gains and losses), profits et pertes; pertes et profits.
profit and loss *or* **profit and loss account** (Bkkpg) (Abbrev.: **P. & L.** *or* **P. & L. A/c.**), profits et pertes; pertes et profits; compte des (*ou* de) profits et pertes (*m.*); compte pertes et profits (*m.*):
to post an item to profit and loss, passer un article aux profits et pertes.
profit sharing, participation aux bénéfices (*f.*).
profit taking, prise de bénéfice (*f.*); prises de bénéfice (*ou* de bénéfices) (*f.pl.*):
in spite of profit taking and heavy realization, prices showed strength, malgré les prises de bénéfices et de grosses réalisations, les cours ont fait preuve de résistance.
X. shares which had hardened to 8s. 9d. were lowered to 8s. 6d., on profit taking, l'action X. qui s'était redressée à 8sh. 9d. est ramenée à 8sh. 6d., sur des prises de bénéfice.
marked recovery in all the rubber group which profit taking prevented, however, from closing at best, reprise marquée de tout le groupe caoutchoutier que des prises de bénéfice empêchent, toutefois, de clôturer au plus haut (*f.*).
profitable (*adj.*), rémunérateur, -trice; profitable; fructueux, -euse; bénéficiel, -elle; lucratif, -ive:
profitable business, entreprise rémunératrice (*f.*); affaire profitable (*ou* lucrative) (*f.*).
profitable investment, placement fructueux (*m.*).
profitable (to be), être rémunérateur, -trice, profitable, fructueux, -euse, bénéficiel, -elle; profiter:
that bargain was not very profitable to him, ce marché lui a peu profité.
profitably (*adv.*), profitablement; fructueusement.
programme (*n.*), programme (*m.*):
programme of land excursions, programme des excursions à terre.
progress (*n.*), progrès (*m.pl.*); essor (*m.*):
to make great progress, faire de grands progrès.
the economic progress of North America, l'essor économique de l'Amérique du Nord.
progress (*v.i.*), progresser.
progressive tax, impôt progressif (*m.*).
prohibit (*v.t.*), prohiber; interdire:
to prohibit the importation of goods of foreign make, of arms of all kinds, of munitions of war, of powder and other explosive substances, prohiber l'entrée (*ou* l'importation) de marchandises de fabrication étrangère, d'armes de toutes espèces, de munitions de guerre, de la poudre et d'autres matières explosibles.
law which prohibits the importation and sale

of certain goods, loi qui prohibe l'importation et la vente de certaines marchandises (*f.*).

prohibited articles (Post), objets interdits (*m.pl.*).

prohibition (*n.*), prohibition (*f.*); interdiction (*f.*):
prohibition of export (*or* on exportation), prohibition, interdiction, de sortie (*ou* sur exportation).
prohibition of import (*or* on importation), prohibition, interdiction, d'entrée (*ou* sur importation).
postal prohibitions, interdictions postales.

prohibitionist (*adj.*), prohibitionniste :
prohibitionist measures, mesures prohibitionnistes (*f.pl.*).

prohibitionist (pers.) (*n.*), prohibitionniste (*m.*).

prohibitive (*adj.*), prohibitif, -ive :
prohibitive duty, droit prohibitif (*m.*) :
duties are prohibitive when their amount is such that they render importation impossible, les droits sont prohibitifs quand leur quotité est telle qu'ils rendent l'importation impossible.

project (*n.*), projet (*m.*); plan (*m.*).

prolong (*v.t.*), proroger :
to prolong the time of payment of a bill, proroger l'échéance d'un billet.

prolongation (*n.*), prorogation (*f.*).

promenade deck, pont-promenade (*m.*).

prominent (to be), être en vedette :
rubber shares have been prominent all the week, les valeurs de caoutchouc ont été en vedette pendant toute la semaine (*f.pl.*).

promise (*n.*), promesse (*f.*) :
promise of shares, promesse d'actions.
a bank note is a promise to pay a certain sum on demand and to bearer, le billet de banque est une promesse de payer une certaine somme à vue et au porteur.

promise (*v.t.*), promettre ; s'engager :
to promise to pay, promettre de payer.

promising (*adj.*), prometteur, -euse.

promissory note (Abbrev.: **P/N.** *or* **p.n.**), billet à ordre (*m.*).

promote (*v.t.*), promoter :
to promote a company, promoter une société.

promoter (pers.) (*n.*), promoteur (*m.*) :
promoter of a syndicate, promoteur d'un syndicat.

promotion (*n.*), promotion (*f.*).

promotion shares, actions de primes (*f.pl.*).

prompt (*adj.*) (Abbrev.: **ppt**), prompt, -e :
prompt cash, argent comptant (*m.*); comptant (*m.*) :
prompt cash against documents, comptant contre documents.
prompt cash less discount, comptant avec escompte.
payment : net prompt cash without discount on presentation of documents, paiement : comptant net sans escompte à présentation des documents.
prompt forwarding (*or* shipment) of the goods, la prompte expédition des marchandises.
prompt shipment within 21 clear days of the

date of the contract, embarquement prompt (*ou* prompt embarquement) (*ou* chargement prompt) dans les 21 jours francs de la date du contrat (*m.*).
sale for prompt delivery (*or* for prompt shipment), vente en expédition prompte (*f.*).

promptitude *or* **promptness** (*n.*), promptitude (*f.*).

pronounceable (*adj.*), prononçable :
pronounceable group of letters (Teleg.), groupe de lettres prononçable (*m.*).

proof (evidence) (*n.*), preuve (*f.*); justification (*f.*); constatation (*f.*) :
proof of the causes of collision is often difficult, la preuve des causes de l'abordage est souvent difficile.
proof of origin, of claim, of the payment of the duties, of a right to the ownership of stock, justification d'origine, de réclamation, de paiement des droits, d'un droit à la propriété des titres.
to ask for proof of the actual value, demander la justification de la valeur réelle.
proof of loss (act) (Insce), justification de perte. Cf. proof of loss (voucher), ci-après.
proof of identity, constatation d'identité.

proof (printer's) (*n.*), épreuve (d'imprimerie) (*f.*).

proof of indebtedness, titre de créance (*m.*).

proof of loss (voucher) (Insce), pièce justificative de perte (*f.*) :
losses due by the underwriter are payable in cash, thirty days after complete delivery of proofs, les indemnités dues par les assureurs sont payables comptant, trente jours après la remise complète des pièces justificatives (*f.pl.*). Cf. proof of loss (act) ci-avant.

proof of ownership (muniment of title), titre de propriété (*m.*); acte de propriété (*m.*).

proper (due; regular) (*adj.*), dû, due; régulier -ère :
translation in proper form, traduction en due forme (*f.*).

properly (duly; regularly) (*adv.*), dûment ; régulièrement :
cargo properly manifested, marchandises régulièrement manifestées (*f.pl.*).

property [**properties** *pl.*] (*n.*) (Abbrev.: **ppty**), bien (*m.*); biens (*m.pl.*); effets (*m.pl.*); chose (*f.*); objets (*m.pl.*); avoir (*m.*); avoirs (*m.pl.*); propriété (*f.*); propriétés (*f.pl.*) :
real property *or* simply property, biens immeubles; propriétés immobilières; immeubles (*m.pl.*); immeuble (*m.*).
right to the lease of a property situated in London, at No 29 X. Street, used as offices and stores by the company, droit au bail d'un immeuble sis à Londres, rue X., n° 29, servant de bureaux et de dépôt à la société (*m.*).
property present and future, biens présents et à venir.
property lodged with a bank, avoirs déposés en banque.

ship which is the property of a shipping company, navire qui est la propriété d'une société d'armement (*m.*).

the value of the property insured, la valeur de la chose assurée (*ou* des objets [*ou* biens] assurés). V. aussi exemple sous **subject matter.**

property (*n.*) *or* **property account** (item in balance sheet), domaine (*m.*); compte domaine (*m.*).

property accounts (Bkkpg), comptes de valeurs (*m.pl.*); comptes du gérant (*m.pl.*); comptes de l'exploitation (*m.pl.*).

property tax, contribution foncière sur les propriétés bâties (*f.*); impôt foncier (*m.*).

proportion (*n.*), proportion (*f.*); quote-part (*f.*); quotité (*f.*); quantum (*m.*); tantième (*m.*); prorata (*m.*):

the proportion of the loan differs according to the nature of the security (advances on securities), la proportion (*ou* la quotité) du prêt diffère suivant la nature du titre.

to receive one's proportion of the profits, recevoir sa quote-part (*ou* son quantum) (*ou* son tantième) (*ou* son prorata) des bénéfices.

proportion of current interest, prorata d'intérêts en cours.

in proportion, en proportion; au prorata.

in proportion to, en proportion de; au prorata de; proportionné (-e) à; au marc le franc de; au marc la livre de:

to share in a profit in proportion to one's capital invested, avoir part à un bénéfice au prorata de sa mise de fonds.

general average is borne by the cargo, the ship, and the freight, in proportion to their value, les avaries communes sont supportées par le chargement, par le navire, et par le fret, au marc le franc de leur valeur (*f.pl.*).

out of proportion with (*or* **to**), 'hors de proportion avec; disproportionné (-e) à:

administration expenses out of all proportion with (*or* to) the size of the firm's business, frais d'administration hors de toute proportion avec l'importance des affaires de la maison (*m.pl.*).

proportion (*v.t.*), proportionner:

to proportion one's expenditure to one's income, one's commitments to the capital at one's disposal, proportionner ses dépenses à ses revenus, ses engagements au capital dont on dispose.

proportional (*adj.*), proportionnel, -elle; tantième:

to claim compensation proportional to the damage sustained, réclamer une indemnité proportionnelle au dommage subi.

to find the proportional part of the profits accruing to a partner, soit à trouver la tantième partie des bénéfices qui revient à un associé.

proportionally *or* **proportionately** (*adv.*), proportionnellement; au marc le franc; au marc la livre:

underwriters who contribute to the actual value proportionally to the amounts insured

by them, assureurs qui contribuent à la valeur réelle proportionnellement aux sommes assurées par eux (*m.pl.*).

the underwriters will contribute proportionally, les assureurs contribueront au marc le franc (*m.pl.*).

proposal *or* **proposition** .(*n.*), proposition (*f.*); affaire (*f.*):

to make a proposal (*or* a proposition) to someone, faire une proposition à quelqu'un.

proposal of insurance, proposition d'assurance.

a copper proposition, une affaire de cuivre.

proposal form, forme de proposition (*f.*).

propose (*v.t.*), proposer; faire:

to propose an amendment, proposer un amendement.

to propose a resolution to a meeting, faire une proposition à une assemblée.

proposer (pers.) (*n.*), proposant, -e.

proprietary accounts (Bkkpg), comptes de (*ou* des) résultats (*m.pl.*).

proprietary insurance *or* **proprietary assurance** (opp. to *mutual insurance*), assurance à prime (*f.*); assurance à prime fixe (*f.*).

proprietary insurance (*or* **assurance**) **company** *or* **proprietary office,** compagnie d'assurances à primes (*f.*); société d'assurance à prime fixe (*f.*).

proprietor (pers.) (*n.*), propriétaire (*m.* ou *f.*):

proprietor of a share, of a debenture, of the goods, propriétaire d'une action, d'une obligation, de la marchandise.

proprietress (pers.) (*n.*), propriétaire (*f.*).

proratable (*adj.*), au prorata; proportionnel, -elle:

proratable contribution, contribution au prorata; contribution proportionnelle (*f.*).

pros and cons, pour et contre:

to consider (*or* to weigh) the pros and cons, peser le pour et le contre.

prospect (*n.*), perspective (*f.*):

future prospects *or* prospects for the future, perspectives d'avenir.

prospectus [**prospectuses** *pl.*] (*n.*), prospectus (*m.*); prospectus d'émission (*m.*):

to issue a prospectus of a company, lancer un prospectus d'une société.

prosper (*v.i.*), prospérer.

prosperity (*n.*), prospérité (*f.*).

prosperous (*adj.*), prospère:

prosperous man, homme prospère (*m.*).

prosperously (*adv.*), prospèrement.

protect (to guard; to safeguard; to defend) (*v.t.*), protéger; sauvegarder; défendre:

to protect an industry against unfair competition by customs duties, protéger une industrie contre la concurrence déloyale par des droits de douane.

to protect the lives of the sailors and passengers, sauvegarder la vie des matelots et des passagers.

to protect the interests of the shareholders, sauvegarder, défendre, les intérêts des actionnaires.

to protect a book (Stock Exch.), défendre une position.

protect (to see that a note, draft, or the like, is paid or satisfied at maturity) (Com.) (*v.t.*), garantir la bonne fin de ; être responsable de la bonne fin de :
the endorsers are jointly and severally liable to protect the bills to which they have appended their signature, les endosseurs sont solidairement responsables de la bonne fin des effets sur lesquels ils ont apposé leur signature (*m.pl.*).

protection (Com.) (*n.*), bonne fin (*f.*) :
it is important for the drawer to ensure the protection of the bill, il est important pour le tireur d'assurer la bonne fin de l'effet.

protection (Polit. Econ.) (*n.*) (opp. to *free trade*), protection (*f.*) :
customs duties designed to assure to the national production an effective protection on the home market against foreign competition, droits de douane destinés à assurer à la production nationale une protection efficace sur le marché intérieur contre la concurrence étrangère (*m.pl.*).

protection and indemnity club (Mar. Insce), club d'indemnité (*m.*).

protectionism (*n.*), protectionnisme (*m.*) :
cartels favoured by customs protectionism, cartels favorisés par le protectionnisme douanier (*m.pl.*).

protectionist (*adj.*), protectionniste :
the free port is a breach in the protectionist system, le port franc est une brèche dans le système protectionniste.

protectionist (pers.) (*n.*), protectionniste (*m.*) :
what do protectionists want? To prevent foreign importation from competing with our products ; to assure to the national producers the national market, que veulent les protectionnistes? Empêcher l'importation étrangère de concurrencer nos produits ; assurer aux producteurs nationaux le marché national. (V. aussi exemple sous **free trader.**)

protective (Polit. Econ.) (*adj.*), protecteur, -trice :
protective duty (opp. to *revenue duty*), droit protecteur (*m.*) :
the principal object of protective duties is to secure national production against foreign competition, les droits protecteurs ont, pour but principal, de défendre la production nationale contre la concurrence étrangère.
protective tariff, tarif protecteur (*m.*).

protectorate (*n.*), protectorat (*m.*); pays de protectorat (*m.*).

protest *or* **protestation** (*n.*), protêt (*m.*); protestation (*f.*) :
protest for non acceptance, protêt faute d'acceptation.
protest for non payment, protêt faute de paiement. V. exemple sous **dishonour for non payment.**
protest of the ship's master, protêt du capitaine du navire.
to take delivery of the goods only under formal protest, ne prendre livraison de marchandises que sous protêt formel.
advice of deal received without protest (protestation), avis d'opéré reçu sans protestation (*m.*).

protest (*v.t.*), protester ; faire protester :
wherefore I now do protest the said bill (notarial protest), pourquoi (*ou* ce que vu) j'ai protesté ledit effet.
holder of a bill who protests for non acceptance, for non payment, porteur d'un effet qui fait protester faute d'acceptation, faute de paiement.

to protest against, protester contre ; protester :
to protest against refusal to pay, protester contre refus de payer.
to protest against a merchant (to make protest against the bill of a merchant), protester un négociant.

protest waived in case of dishonour, sans frais retour sans frais ; sans compte de retour sans protêt.

protestable (*adj.*), protestable :
in France, a cheque is protestable like a bill of exchange, en France, le chèque est protestable comme la lettre de change.

prove (*v.t.*), prouver ; faire la preuve de ; justifier ; justifier de ; démontrer ; constater :
to prove the existence of a company, prouver l'existence d'une société.
to make the consignee prove a fault of the carrier is, in most cases, to expose him to prove the impossible, obliger le destinataire à prouver une faute du transporteur, c'est l'exposer le plus souvent à prouver l'impossible.
what does the bill of lading prove? que prouve le connaissement?
to prove a loss, the value of the thing insured, shipment, the quantity shipped, that the loss of one's goods is due to a theft on board, faire la preuve d'un sinistre, de la valeur de la chose assurée, du chargé, de la quantité chargée, que la perte de sa marchandise est due à un vol à bord.
to prove the truth of one's predictions by events, justifier la vérité de ses prédictions par les événements.
the person who comes to take delivery of a letter addressed poste restante must prove that he is the addressee or his duly authorized representative, la personne qui vient prendre livraison d'une lettre adressée poste restante doit justifier qu'elle est le destinataire ou son fondé de pouvoirs.
the insurance is void if it is proved that the news of an accident was known, l'assurance est nulle s'il est justifié que la nouvelle d'un sinistre était connue (*f.*).
to prove one's identity, justifier de son identité.
the insured is bound to prove the non arrival, l'assuré est tenu de justifier de la non arrivée (*m.*).
the proved cost of the things replacing those lost or damaged by sea peril, le coût justifié

des objets remplaçant ceux perdus ou endommagés par fortune de mer.

there are hopes of future profits for the patents
or processes, whose productiveness is possible
but not proved, il y a des espoirs de profits
futurs pour les brevets ou procédés dont la
productivité est possible mais non démontrée.

until the contrary is proved, jusqu'à preuve
contraire.

certificate which proves the existence of mortgages, certificat qui constate l'existence
d'hypothèques (m.).

prove acceptable (to), s'agréer :
proposals which may prove acceptable, propositions qui peuvent s'agréer (f.pl.).

provide (to furnish) (v.t.), pourvoir ; fournir ;
munir ; nantir :
to provide someone with money, fournir de
l'argent à quelqu'un.

ship provided with all her papers, navire
muni de tous ses papiers (m.).

the traveller should, when he begins his
journey, be provided with a ticket, le
voyageur doit, lorsqu'il commence son
voyage, être muni d'un billet.

to be provided with the money to pay a bill,
être nanti (-e) des fonds destinés au paiement d'un effet.

provide (to specify ; to stipulate) (v.t.), énoncer ;
prescrire ; stipuler :
what the policy should provide, ce que la
police doit énoncer (ou prescrire).

owner who provides that he is not liable for
the wrongful acts of the master, armateur
qui stipule qu'il ne répondra pas des fautes
du capitaine (m.).

provide (v.i.), pourvoir ; fournir ; subvenir ;
disposer :
sale of a part of the cargo in order to provide
for the pressing needs of the ship, vente
d'une partie de la cargaison afin de pourvoir aux (ou de fournir aux) (ou de subvenir
aux) besoins pressants du navire (f.).

the law only provides for the future, la loi
ne dispose que pour l'avenir.

provide against a rise, a fall (to), se prémunir
contre la hausse, la baisse.

provide oneself (to), se pourvoir ; se munir ;
se nantir :
to provide oneself with money, se pourvoir,
se munir, se nantir, d'argent.

provided by the articles (or **by the articles of
association**) (or **by the memorandum of
association**), prévu (-e) par les statuts ;
statutaire : (V. note sous **articles of association**.)
alteration of capital provided by the articles
of association, modification de capital
prévue par les statuts (f.).

reserve provided by the articles, réserve
statutaire (f.).

provident fund, caisse de prévoyance (f.).

provident society, société de prévoyance (f.).

provincial (adj.), provincial, -e, -aux ; de province :

provincial bank, banque de province (f.) ;
banque provinciale (f.).

provision (act of providing) (n.), prestation (f.) :
provision of capital, prestation de capitaux.

provision (funds with a bank, or the like) (n.),
provision (f.) :
cash received by a banker as provision for a
letter of credit, espèces reçues par un
banquier en provision d'une lettre de crédit
(f.pl.).

provision (reserve) (n.), provision (f.) ; prévision (f.) :
provision for depreciation of investments, prévision pour moins-value du portefeuille.

provision for redemption of premises, amortissement sur immeuble (ou sur immeubles)
(m.).

provision (stipulation) (n.), énonciation (f.) ;
disposition (f.) ; stipulation (f.) ; prescription (f.) ; clause (f.) :
to challenge the provisions of a bill of lading,
of an insurance policy, récuser les énonciations (ou les dispositions) (ou les stipulations) d'un connaissement, d'une police
d'assurance.

provisions of an act, prescriptions, dispositions, d'une loi.

notwithstanding any provision to the contrary, nonobstant toute clause contraire.

provision (v.t.), approvisionner ; avitailler :
to provision a ship, approvisionner, avitailler,
un navire.

provisional (adj.), provisionnel, -elle ; provisoire :
provisional account, compte provisoire (m.).

provisional certificate (of stocks or shares)
(opp. to definitive, or definite, certificate),
titre provisoire (m.) ; certificat provisoire
(m.).

provisional certificate (interim certificate of
registry of a ship), acte provisoire (m.).

provisional insurance in which the valuation
is only approximate, assurance provisoire
dans laquelle l'évaluation n'est qu'approximative.

provisional invoice (opp. to final invoice),
facture provisoire (f.).

provisional note (Mar. Insce), arrêté provisoire (m.) ; arrêté d'assurance (m.) ;
arrêté (m.).

provisionally (adv.), provisoirement :
to cover a risk provisionally, couvrir un
risque provisoirement.

provisioning (n.), approvisionnement (m.).

provisions (food) (n.pl.), provisions de bouche
(f.pl.) ; munitions de bouche (f.pl.) ; vivres
(m.pl.) ; victuailles (f.pl.) ; nourriture (f.) ;
approvisionnements (m.pl.).

proximate cause (of an accident of the sea) (opp.
to remote cause), cause immédiate (f.).

proximo (adv.) (Abbrev. : **prox.**), du mois
prochain.

proxy [**proxies** pl.] (pers.) (n.), mandataire (m.
ou f.) ; fondé de pouvoir (m.) ; fondé de
pouvoirs (m.) ; procuration (f.) :

the shareholders have the right to be represented at all meetings by proxies, les actionnaires ont le droit de se faire représenter par des mandataires dans toutes les assemblées (*m.pl.*).

to be present at a meeting either personally, or by proxy for the account of other creditors, assister à une assemblée soit personnellement, soit par procuration pour le compte d'autres créanciers.

Cf. **appoint as proxy (to).**

proxy [**proxies** *pl.*] (instrument) (*n.*), pouvoir (*m.*); mandat (*m.*); procuration (*f.*):

form of proxy (*or* proxy form) for a general meeting of shareholders, formule de pouvoir (*ou* de mandat) (*ou* de procuration) pour une assemblée générale d'actionnaires (*f.*).

public (*adj.*) (Ant.: *private*), public, -ique:
public attorney (U.S.A.), avocat (*m.*).
public authorities, pouvoirs publics (*m.pl.*).
public call office (Teleph.), poste public (*m.*); cabine publique (*f.*).
public company (limited liability), société anonyme (*f.*). *V.* note *sous* limited company *or* public company.
public debt, dette publique (*f.*); dette nationale (*f.*).
public funds *or* public securities, fonds publics (*m.pl.*); effets publics (*m.pl.*).
public holiday, fête légale (*f.*); jour de fête légale (*m.*); jour férié (*m.*).
public international law, droit international public (*m.*).
public issue (of shares), émission publique (*f.*).
public liability insurance, assurance de responsabilité civile (*f.*).
public loan, emprunt public (*m.*).
public money, deniers publics (*m.pl.*).
public policy, ordre public (*m.*):
clause contrary to public policy, clause contraire à l'ordre public (*f.*).
public revenue, revenus publics (*m.pl.*); revenus de l'État (*m.pl.*).
public sale, vente publique (*f.*).
public sale room, salle de ventes publiques (*f.*).
public utility company, compagnie (*ou* société) d'utilité publique (*f.*).
public utility stocks, valeurs de services publics (*f.pl.*).

public (*n.*), public (*m.*); clientèle (*f.*):
to issue shares to the public, émettre des actions dans le public.
to place shares with the public, placer des actions dans le public.
market down, for want of orders from the public, marché en réaction, faute d'ordres de la clientèle (*m.*).

publication (*n.*), publication (*f.*).

publicity (*n.*), publicité (*f.*).

publicity bureau, bureau de publicité (*m.*); agence de publicité (*f.*); office de publicité (*m.*).

publish (*v.t.*), publier:
to publish a balance sheet, a detailed list of the investments, publier un bilan, l'inventaire détaillé du portefeuille.

puff paragraph (in a newspaper), annonce-article (*f.*).

Pullman car *or simply* **Pullman** (*n.*), voiture Pullman (*f.*).

punch (letter filing) (*n.*), perforateur (*m.*).

punctual (*adj.*), ponctuel, -elle; exact, -e:
punctual employee, employé ponctuel (*m.*); employé exact (*m.*).
punctual reply, réponse ponctuelle (*f.*).

punctuality (*n.*), ponctualité (*f.*); exactitude (*f.*):
punctuality in business, in one's engagements, in paying, ponctualité, exactitude, dans les affaires, dans ses engagements, dans les paiements.

punctually (*adv.*), ponctuellement; recta:
to reply punctually to the letters that one receives, répondre ponctuellement aux lettres que l'on reçoit.

punter (speculator on a rising or falling market) (pers.) (*n.*), accompagnateur (*m.*).

purchasable (*adj.*), achetable.

purchase *or* **purchasing** (*n.*) (Ant.: *sale* or *selling*), achat (*m.*); acquisition (*f.*):
purchase of securities (*or* of stocks), achat de valeurs.
purchase of premises, acquisition d'immeubles.
purchase for future delivery during specified periods (Produce Exch.), achat à terme ferme.
purchase for money (*or* for cash) *or* cash purchase, achat au comptant; achat comptant.
purchase for the settlement (*or* for the account) (Stock Exch.), achat à terme.

purchase (*v.t.*), acheter; acquérir.

purchase against (to) (Produce Exch.) (opp. to *sell against*), racheter:
to purchase against a defaulter, racheter un défaillant.

purchase contract (Stock Exch.), bordereau d'achat (*m.*).

purchase invoice, facture d'achat (*f.*).

purchase price *or* **purchase consideration,** prix d'achat (*m.*); prix d'acquisition (*m.*); rémunération (*f.*); représentation (*f.*):
purchase price of the premises, prix d'achat, prix d'acquisition, de l'immeuble.
purchase consideration for transfer (of vendors' assets), prix d'apport (*m.*); rémunération des apports (*f.*):
as purchase consideration for the transfer there has been allotted to the vendors 0,000 shares of 0 each, fully paid, in the company, en rémunération (*ou* en représentation) des apports il a été attribué aux apporteurs 0 000 actions de 0 chacune, entièrement libérées de la société.

purchase returns, rendus sur achats (*m.pl.*); rendus sous achats (*m.pl.*); retours sur achats (*m.pl.*).

purchaser (pers.) (*n.*), acheteur, -euse; acquéreur, -eure *ou* -euse; preneur, -euse:
purchaser in good faith, in bad faith, acheteur, acquéreur, de bonne foi, de mauvaise foi.

purchases account, compte d'achats (*m.*).

purchases book *or* **purchases day book** *or* **purchase book** *or* **purchases journal** *or* **purchase journal** (Bkkpg), livre d'achats (*m.*) ; livre des achats (*m.*) ; livre d'achat (*m.*) ; journal des achats (*m.*) ; facturier d'entrée (*m.*).

purchases ledger, grand livre des achats (*m.*).

purchasing (*adj.*), acquéreur, -euse ; preneur, -euse :

the purchasing stockbroker, l'agent de change acquéreur (*m.*).

the purchasing company, la société preneuse.

purchasing power, pouvoir d'achat (*m.*) :

the purchasing power of money, of gold, le pouvoir d'achat de la monnaie, de l'or.

purchasing against a defaulter (Produce Exch.), rachat d'un défaillant (*m.*).

pure premium (Insce) (opp. to *gross,* or *office, premium*), prime nette (*f.*).

purse (*n.*), bourse (*f.*) ; porte-monnaie (*m.*).

purse strings, cordons de la bourse (*m.pl.*) :

to hold the purse strings, to hold the purse strings tight, tenir les cordons de la bourse, tenir serrés les cordons de la bourse.

purser (pers.) (*n.*), commissaire (*m.*) ; commissaire de la marine marchande (*m.*) :

the purser of a liner, le commissaire d'un paquebot.

pursuance of (**in**), en vertu de ; en exécution de :

in pursuance of sections —— and —— of the Companies Act 1929, en vertu (*ou* en exécution) des articles —— et —— de la loi de 1929 sur les sociétés.

push (*v.t.*), pousser :

X. Mines (shares) are being pushed rather fast, it seems, although the concern is quite genuine, on pousse les Mines X. un peu vite, semble-t-il, bien que l'affaire soit très sérieuse.

put (*n.*) *or* **put option** (Stock or other Exch.) (opp. to *call* or *call option*), ou (*m.*) ; prime ou (*f.*) ; prime indirecte (*f.*) ; prime renversée (*f.*) ; prime inverse (*f.*) ; prime pour livrer (*f.*) ; prime pour livrer ou non (*f.*) ; prime vendeur (*f.*) ; prime pour le vendeur (*f.*) ; marché à prime pour livrer (*m.*) ; prime simple à la baisse (*f.*) ; prime moins (*f.*) :

market on which calls and puts are dealt in, marché où on traite le dont et l'ou (*m.*).

speculator who is giver of 1s. (per share) for the put of 100 X.Y.Z. shares at 25s., spéculateur qui est vendeur de 100 actions X.Y.Z. à 24 schellings ou 1 schelling (*m.*).

V. explications sous option dealing.

put (*v.t.*). V. exemples :

to put a clause in a contract, mettre, insérer, une clause dans, apposer une clause à, un contrat.

to put a name on a list, porter un nom sur une liste.

to put a resolution to a meeting, mettre aux voix une résolution (*ou* une proposition).

to put a stamp on a receipt, apposer un timbre sur un reçu.

to put all one's eggs in one basket (*fig.*), mettre tous ses œufs dans le même panier.

to put an advertisement in a newspaper, mettre, insérer, faire, une annonce dans un journal.

to put an embargo on a ship, mettre un embargo sur un navire.

to put [goods] ashore, mettre à terre [des marchandises].

to put [papers] away, caser [des papiers].

to put back (Navig.) (*v.i.*), rentrer :

ship which puts back into the port of sailing for refuge (*or* of necessity) (*or* in distress), navire qui rentre dans le port de départ en relâche (*m.*).

to put by some money for unforeseen contingencies, mettre de l'argent à l'écart, réserver quelque argent, pour les cas imprévus.

to put capital into a business, engager du capital dans une entreprise.

to put in (to enter) (*v.t.*), inscrire :

to put in a folio, inscrire un folio.

to put in (for shelter or supplies—said of a ship) (*v.i.*), relâcher ; faire relâche :

to put in to coal, to take orders, to revictual, relâcher (*ou* faire relâche) pour faire du charbon (*ou* pour charbonner), pour prendre des ordres, pour se ravitailler.

leak which obliged the ship to put into a port of refuge, to put into Dover, voie d'eau qui obligea le navire à relâcher (*ou* à faire relâche) dans un port de refuge, à relâcher à Douvres (*f.*).

to put in of necessity (*or* compulsorily) owing to a storm, relâcher forcément par suite d'une tempête.

to put in order, mettre en ordre ; mettre ordre à ; mettre l'ordre dans :

to put papers in order, mettre des papiers en ordre.

to put one's affairs in order, mettre ordre à ses affaires ; mettre l'ordre dans ses affaires.

to put in pawn, mettre en gage.

to put in touch sellers and buyers, mettre en rapport vendeurs et acheteurs.

to put into code, rédiger en langage convenu ; codifier ; coder :

to put a telegram into code, rédiger un télégramme en langage convenu ; codifier, coder, un télégramme.

to put into liquidation, mettre en liquidation :

company put into liquidation under supervision of the court, société mise en liquidation judiciaire (*f.*).

to put [a ship] into service (*or* into commission), mettre [un navire] en service.

put off (*v.t.*), remettre ; renvoyer ; ajourner ; proroger ; retarder ; différer ; arriérer :

to put off a matter for a week, to another day, remettre, renvoyer, ajourner, une affaire à huitaine, à un autre jour.

to put off payment of interest, arriérer, différer, ajourner, retarder, le paiement des intérêts ; atermoyer les intérêts.

to put off one's creditors, remettre ses créanciers.

to put on (*or* upon) (to encumber with a

charge), mettre à la charge de ; mettre à charge de ; grever :

a trade charge is the sum put upon the goods by the sender, le remboursement consiste dans la somme mise à charge de la marchandise par l'expéditeur.

the sender can put a trade charge on his consignment not exceeding the value of the goods, l'expéditeur peut grever son envoi d'un remboursement jusqu'à concurrence de la valeur de la marchandise (*m.*).

to put on (speaking of stock exchange prices), gagner ; enlever :

X. shares put on ¼, l'action X. gagne (*ou* enlève) 1/4.

to put on board, mettre à bord.

to put on fixed deposit, on deposit at notice, remettre en dépôt à terme, en dépôt à préavis :

money put on fixed deposit, argent remis en dépôt à terme (*m.*).

to put on (*or* to put down) on the agenda the business to be transacted, mettre à l'ordre du jour les questions à délibérer.

to put on the envelope the word " Express," porter sur l'enveloppe la mention « Exprès. »

to put one's initials, apposer son parafe.

to put one's money in (*or* into) the savings bank, mettre, placer, son argent à la caisse d'épargne.

to put one's name down on a list, s'inscrire sur une liste.

to put the date on a cheque, mettre la date sur un chèque.

to put to *or* to put in, mettre en ; employer en :

profits put to reserve, bénéfices mis en réserve (*m.pl.*).

to put an amount in the receipts, in the expenditure, employer une somme en recette, en dépense.

to put to sea, prendre la mer :

ship in a condition to put to sea, navire en état de prendre la mer (*m.*).

to put up (*v.t.*), mettre :

to put up a thing for sale, mettre une chose en vente.

profit which is equal to so much per cent on the money put up, bénéfice qui correspond à tant pour cent de la mise de fonds (*m.*).

every £100 put up, chaque mise de £100.

put (Option dealings) (Stock Exch.) (*v.t.*), se déclarer vendeur :

the price having fallen, I (we) put the stock, le cours ayant baissé, je me déclare vendeur (nous nous déclarons vendeurs) des titres. .

put and call *or* **put and call option** (Stock Exch.), option (*f.*) ; stellage (*m.*) ; double prime (*f.*) ; prime double (*f.*) :

the put and call is the combination of the put and of the call, l'option est la réunion de l'ou et du dont.

put and call price, cours de l'option (*m.*) ; cours du stellage (*m.*).

put and take (budla operation), vente au comptant contre rachat à terme.

put of more *or* **put o' more** (Stock Exch.), doublé à la baisse (*m.*) ; doublure à la baisse (*f.*) ; faculté de livrer double (*f.*).

put of three times more (Stock Exch.), quadruplé à la baisse (*m.*) ; faculté de livrer quadruple (*f.*).

put of twice more (Stock Exch.), triplé à la baisse (*m.*) ; faculté de livrer triple (*f.*).

put option. V. **put** *or* **put option.**

put price (Stock Exch.), cours de l'ou (*m.*).

putting in (entering), inscription (*f.*) :

putting in the journal folio from which an item is posted, inscription du folio du journal d'après lequel l'article est rapporté.

putting in (for shelter or supplies) (Navig.), relâche (*f.*) :

putting in rendered necessary by a peril of the sea, relâche rendue nécessaire par une fortune de mer.

putting in possession (Law), mise en possession (*f.*).

putting into code, rédaction en langage convenu (*f.*) ; codification (*f.*).

putting into liquidation of a company, mise en liquidation d'une société (*f.*).

putting off (postponement), renvoi (*m.*) ; remise (*f.*) ; ajournement (*m.*).

putting on board, mise à bord (*f.*).

putting up for sale, mise en vente (*f.*).

putting up of money, mise de fonds (*f.*) :

objects of the company which only require the gradual putting up of money, objet social qui n'exige qu'une mise de fonds graduelle (*m.*).

Q

qualification (*n.*), cautionnement (*m.*) :

the directors must have a qualification in shares of the company, les administrateurs doivent avoir un cautionnement en actions de la société (*m.pl.*).

the qualification of a director shall be the holding of at least —— share(s) in the company (regulations for management of a company limited by shares [Table A]), les administrateurs doivent être propriétaires, pendant toute la durée de leur mandat, de chacun —— action(s) au moins (wording of French *statuts d'une société par actions*).

qualification shares, actions de garantie (*f.pl.*); actions déposées en garantie (*f.pl.*). *Note :—* In France and Belgium, qualification shares must be lodged with the company, hence *déposées*. They are held by the company as security for the directors' acts of management, hence *de garantie*.

qualified acceptance (of a bill of exchange), acceptation sous réserve (*f.*).

qualified accountant, expert-comptable diplômé (*m.*).

quality [**qualities** *pl.*] (*n.*), qualité (*f.*):
fair average quality (Produce or other Exch.) (*Abbrev. :* f.a.q.), qualité loyale et marchande; qualité courante; qualité commerciale.
quality about as per lodged standard sample, qualité à type standard.
quality about as per samples, sealed or in possession of buyers, qualité conforme aux échantillons; qualité sur échantillon de références.
quality about as per such or such type sample, qualité à tel type.
quality according to such or such a mark, qualité à telle marque.
quality subject to approval, qualité vue et agréée.

quantity [**quantities** *pl.*] (*n.*), quantité (*f.*); quotité (*f.*):
one can only deal in a certain quantity (called the marketable quantity) of this stock or in a multiple of this quantity, on ne peut opérer que sur une certaine quotité (appelée la quotité négociable) de ces titres ou sur un multiple de cette quotité.

quantity (number of packages) (*n.*), quantité (*f.*); nombre de colis (*m.*).

quantum [**quanta** *pl.*] (*n.*), quantum (*m.*).

quarantine (*n.*), quarantaine (*f.*):
losses which quarantines cause to shipping companies, pertes que causent les quarantaines aux compagnies de navigation (*f.pl.*).

quarantine flag, pavillon de quarantaine (*m.*).

quarantine risk, risque de quarantaine (*m.*).

quarter (3 months) (*n.*), trimestre (*m.*); terme (*m.*):
to be paid by the quarter, être payé (-e) par trimestre.
to occupy an office for one quarter, occuper un bureau pendant un terme.

quarter day, jour du terme (*m.*); terme (*m.*).

quarter's (*or* **quarterly) income, dividend, interest, drawings, salary, money, payment, instalment,** or the like, trimestre (*m.*):
to receive one's quarter's money, recevoir son trimestre.

quarter's rent, terme (*m.*); trimestre de loyer (*m.*):
to pay a quarter's rent, payer un terme (*ou* un trimestre de loyer).

quarterly (*adj.*), trimestriel, -elle :
quarterly salary, appointements trimestriels (*m.pl.*).

quarterly (*adv.*), trimestriellement; par trimestre :
to be paid quarterly, être payé (-e) trimestriellement (*ou* par trimestre).

quasi contract, quasi-contrat (*m.*):
quasi contracts differ from contracts in that there is no accord of will between the parties, les quasi-contrats diffèrent des contrats en ce qu'il n'y a pas un accord de volonté entre les parties.

quay (*n.*), quai (*m.*).

quay berth, poste à quai (*m.*); place à quai (*f.*).

quay handling charges, taxe de rapprochement (*f.*).

quiet (*adj.*), calme :
market quiet, bourse calme (*f.*).

quietus (*n.*), quitus (*m.*):
to obtain one's quietus (i.e., final discharge from liability), obtenir son quitus.
to give quietus to a cashier, donner quitus à un caissier.

quittance (*n.*), quittance (*f.*); quitus (*m.*); acquittement (*m.*); acquit (*m.*):
to give quittance to a cashier, donner quitus à un caissier.

quorum (*n.*), quorum (*m.*); quantum (*m.*):
if at the general meeting a quorum is not present, a new meeting is convened, si l'assemblée générale ne réunit pas un quorum, une nouvelle assemblée est convoquée.
a quorum is not present, le quorum (*ou* le quantum) n'est pas atteint.
a quorum of three quarters of the capital, un quorum de trois quarts du capital.

quota (*n.*), quote-part (*f.*); cote (*f.*); cotisation (*f.*):
to pay one's quota, payer sa quote-part (*ou* sa cote) (*ou* sa cotisation).

quota (curtailment of output or sales) (*n.*), quote-part (*f.*); contingent (*m.*):
quotas falling to each, in the curtailment of sales, quote-parts revenant à chacun dans le contingentement des ventes.
a quota of so many tons, un contingent de tant de tonnes.

quotable (*adj.*), cotable :
quotable security, valeur cotable (*f.*).

quotation (*n.*), cote (*f.*); cotation (*f.*); prix (*m.*); cours (*m.*):
quotation for freight, cote de fret; cotation de fret.
official spot quotation (Produce Exch.), cote officielle du disponible.
enquiry for quotation, demande de prix (*f.*).
list of quotations (prices), bulletin de cours (*m.*).
quotation of prices (Stock Exch.), cote, cotation, des cours.
admission to quotation (Stock Exch.), admission à la cote (*f.*).

quotation in the list (Stock Exch.), inscription à la cote (*f.*). V. observations sous **quote** (to admit, etc.) (*v.t.*).

quote (to name the current price of) (*v.t.*), coter ; faire :
to quote a price, faire, coter, un prix.
to quote the freight at such a rate, weight or

measurement, coter le fret à tel taux, poids ou cube.

quote (to give the market price of) (Stock Exch.) (*v.t.*), coter; donner:

to quote a loan, a security, the price of a stock, coter un emprunt, une valeur, le cours d'une valeur.

the securities quoted on the stock exchange, on the Brussels Bourse, les valeurs cotées en bourse, à la Bourse de Bruxelles (*f.pl.*).

to quote fixed (*or* certain) (*or* direct) exchange *or* to quote in home currency, donner, coter, le certain:

to quote movable (*or* uncertain) (*or* indirect) (*or* variable) exchange *or* to quote in foreign currency, donner, coter, l'incertain:

one says that a place quotes the other fixed exchange when it is the money of the former which serves as term of comparison between the two places. Thus London quotes Paris fixed (*or* certain) (*or* direct) exchange (*or* quotes Paris in home currency) [viz.:— London quotes Paris so many francs to the £1 (basis), the £ being the home currency of London—exchange called *fixed* or *certain* because the basis (£1) does not vary], and conversely Paris quotes it movable (*or* uncertain) (*or* indirect) (*or* variable) exchange (*or* in foreign currency) [viz.:— so many francs to the £1 (basis), the £ being to Paris a foreign currency—exchange called *movable*, or *uncertain*, or *variable*, because the rate, i.e., the number of francs to the £1 varies], on dit qu'une place donne

(*ou* cote) le certain à une autre, lorsque c'est la monnaie de la première qui ser de terme de comparaison entre les deu: places. Londres donne donc le certain à Paris, et réciproquement Paris lui donne l'incertain.

quote (to admit and enter on the official list—no to be confused with quotation of prices by dealers) (Stock Exch.) (*v.t.*), inscrire:

securities quoted in the official list, valeur inscrites à la cote officielle (*f.pl.*).

quoted (for which there is a market price) (Stock Exch.) (*adj.*), coté, -e:

quoted shares, actions cotées (*f.pl.*).

quoted (**to be**), être coté, -e; se coter; coter s'inscrire:

prices should be quoted as far as possible in the currency of the importing country, les prix doivent être cotés autant que possible dans la monnaie du pays importateur (*m.pl.*).

the price is quoted per ton, le prix se cote par tonne.

shares which are quoted at so much, actions qui se cotent à tant (*ou* qui cotent tant) (*ou* qui sont cotées tant) (*ou* qui s'inscrivent à tant) (*f.pl.*).

quoted list (Stock Exch.) (opp. to *unquoted list*), cote officielle (*f.*).

quoted securities (listed securities—*see remarks under* **quote**), valeurs inscrites (*f.pl.*); valeurs admises à la cote officielle (*f.pl.*); valeurs figurant à la cote officielle (*f.pl.*); valeurs de parquet (*f.pl.*); valeurs de corbeille (*f.pl.*).

R

radiotelegram *or* **radiogram** *or* simply **radio** (*n.*), radiotélégramme (*m.*); radiogram (*m.*); radio (*m.*):

radiotelegrams are exchanged with ships at sea by means of coast stations, les radiotélégrammes sont échangés avec les navires en mer au moyen des stations côtières.

radiotelegraphic *or* simply **radio** (*adj.*), radiotélégraphique; radio:

radiotelegraphic station *or* radio station, station radiotélégraphique (*f.*); station radio (*f.*); station de T.S.F. (*f.*).

radiotelegraphy (*n.*), radiotélégraphie (*f.*); télégraphie sans fil (*f.*).

radiotelephony (*n.*), radiotéléphonie (*f.*); téléphonie sans fil (*f.*).

raft (*n.*), radeau (*m.*).

raft risk (Mar. Insce), risque de drômes (*m.*).

rail (*abbrev. for* railway or railroad) (*n.*), fer (*m.*); chemin (*m.*); chemin de fer (*m.*); voie ferrée (*f.*); voie de fer (*f.*):

reforwarding by rail or water to inland destination, réexpédition par fer ou par eau à destination de l'intérieur (*f.*).

a carrying company, rail or sea, une compagnie de transports, ferrée ou maritime.

rail transport *or* rail carriage, transport ferré (*m.*); transport par voie ferrée (*ou* par chemin de fer) (*ou* par fer) (*m.*).

Note:—*ferré*, -e is, of course, in French, an adjective: in the English construction *rail* is a noun used adjectivally.

on rail *or* **free on rail**, sur wagon; franco wagon; franco gare.

rail motor car (Rly.), voiture automotrice (*f.*).

railroad (*n.*) (Abbrev.: **R.R.** *or* **RR.**). Syn. de **railway**.

railway (*n.*) (Abbrev.: **Rly** *or* **Ry**), chemin de fer (*m.*); voie ferrée (*f.*); voie de fer (*f.*); chemin (*m.*); fer (*m.*).

railway carriage *or* **railway coach** *or* **railway car**, voiture de chemin de fer (*f.*); wagon de chemin de fer (*m.*).

ailway **carriage** or railway **transport**. *Syn. de* rail carriage or transport.

ailway **charges stamp**, timbre chemin de fer (*m.*).

ailway **company**, compagnie de chemins de fer (*f.*).

ailway **engine**, machine (*f.*); locomotive (*f.*).

ailway **guide**, indicateur des chemins de fer (*m.*); livret indicateur de la marche des trains (*m.*).

ailway **industry**, industrie ferroviaire (*f.*).

ailway **journey** or railway **trip**, voyage (*ou* trajet) (*ou* parcours) en (*ou* par) chemin de fer (*m.*).

ailway **line**, ligne de chemin de fer (*f.*); ligne ferrée (*f.*).

ailwayman. V. ci-après.

ailway **parcels service**, service ferroviaire de messageries (*m.*); service de messageries par voie ferrée (*m.*).

ailway **police**, police des voies ferrées (*f.*).

ailway **rates**, tarif des chemins de fer (*m.*); tarif ferroviaire (*m.*).

ailway **service**, service de chemins de fer (*m.*); service ferroviaire (*m.*).

ailway **shares** or railway **stock** or railway **stocks** or railways (*n.pl.*) or rails (*n.pl.*), actions de chemins de fer (*f.pl.*); valeurs de chemins de fer (*f.pl.*); chemins de fer (*m.pl.*); chemins (*m.pl.*); ferroviaires (*m.pl.*):
Argentine rails, chemins argentins.

railway **station**, gare de chemin de fer (*f.*); station de chemin de fer (*f.*).
delivery at railway station, to be called for, livraison en gare (*f.*); remise gare restante (*f.*).

railway **station office** (Post), bureau-gare (*m.*).

railway **strike**, grève d'agents de chemins de fer (*f.*).

railway **system**, réseau de chemins de fer (*ou* de voies ferrées) (*m.*):
the railway system of Great Britain, le réseau de chemins de fer de la Grande-Bretagne.

railway **ticket**, billet (*ou* ticket) de chemin de fer (*m.*); billet (*ou* ticket) de place (*m.*):
the registration of luggage is effected on production of the passenger's railway ticket, l'enregistrement des bagages est effectué sur la présentation du billet de place du voyageur (*m.*).

railway **train**, train de chemin de fer (*m.*); convoi de chemin de fer (*m.*).

railway **truck** or railway **wagon** or railway **car**, wagon de chemin de fer (*m.*).

railway **vehicles running on their own wheels**, véhicules de chemins de fer roulant sur leurs propres roues (*ou* roulant sur essieux) (*m.pl.*):
the conveyance of railway vehicles running on their own wheels, le transport de véhicules de chemins de fer roulant sur leur propres roues.

railwayman [railwaymen *pl.*] (*n.*), employé de chemin de fer (*m.*); cheminot (*m.*).

raise (*v.t.*), élever; relever; lever; soulever; 'hausser; augmenter; porter:

shipowner who raises freight rates, armateur qui élève (*ou* relève) les taux des frets (*m.*).

to raise the price of goods, élever le prix, hausser le prix, augmenter le prix, relever le prix, enchérir, renchérir, des marchandises.

to raise a clerk's salary, augmenter un commis.

to raise a prohibition, the embargo on a ship, lever une prohibition, l'embargo sur un navire.

to raise a question, soulever une question.

to raise a stranded ship, relever un navire échoué.

dividend raised from 5 to 10%, dividende porté (*ou* élevé) de 5 à 10 p. cent (*m.*).

the authorized note currency which, originally, was so many million pounds, has been increased successively, and was raised, last year, to so much, la circulation autorisée des billets qui, primitivement, était de tant de millions de livres, a été augmentée successivement, et portée, l'année dernière, à tant.

raise **money** (to) (for another), procurer de l'argent (*ou* des capitaux):
to raise money for an industry, procurer des capitaux à une industrie.

raise **money** (to) (for oneself), battre monnaie; se procurer de l'argent (*ou* des capitaux):
to raise money by selling one's securities, by borrowing, battre monnaie, se procurer de l'argent, en vendant ses titres, en empruntant.

company which issues shares in order to raise money, société qui émet des actions pour se procurer des capitaux (*f.*).

raise **the dust (to)** or raise **the wind (to)** (to raise money) (*Slang*), battre monnaie.

raising (*n.*), élévation (*f.*); relèvement (*m.*):
raising of the bank rate, of wages, of postal charges, of railway rates, élévation, relèvement, du taux officiel de l'escompte, des salaires, des taxes postales, de tarifs de chemin de fer.

rally [rallies *pl.*] (*n.*), reprise (*f.*):
a sharp rally in the rubber group at Wednesday's session was offset by weakness in the other sessions, une vigoureuse (*ou* vive) reprise du groupe caoutchoutier à la séance de mercredi a été compensée par la faiblesse des autres séances.

rally (*v.i.*), reprendre; se reprendre; être en reprise; se ressaisir:
mining shares rallied sharply (*or* smartly), les valeurs minières reprennent (*ou* se reprennent) (*ou* se ressaisissent) vigoureusement (*ou* vivement) (*f.pl.*).
X. shares rallied from 1s. to 1s. 3d., l'action X. est en reprise de 1sh. à 1sh. 3d.

rank (*n.*), rang (*m.*):
rank assigned to a debt, rang assigné à une créance.
between mortgages rank is established by date, entre les créanciers hypothécaires le rang s'établit par la date.

rank (*v.i.*), prendre rang:
mortgages which rank according to the date of their registration, hypothèques qui

prennent rang suivant leur date d'inscription (*f.pl.*).

to rank before, prendre rang avant; passer avant; primer :
preferential creditors rank before ordinary creditors, les créanciers privilégiés prennent rang avant (*ou* passent avant) (*ou* priment) les créanciers ordinaires (*m.pl.*).
to rank before someone by virtue of a prior mortgage, primer quelqu'un en hypothèque.
to rank pari passu *or* to rank equally *or* to rank concurrently, prendre le même rang; prendre rang concurremment; concourir; venir en concurrence; venir en concours :
new shares which rank pari passu with the old, nouvelles actions qui prennent le même rang que les anciennes (*f.pl.*).
the holders of naked debentures rank equally (*or* concurrently) with the ordinary creditors, les porteurs d'obligations chirographaires prennent rang concurremment (*ou* concourent) (*ou* viennent en concurrence) (*ou* viennent en concours) avec les créanciers ordinaires (*m.pl.*).
to rank after, prendre rang après; passer après; être primé (-e) par :
ordinary debts rank after mortgage debts, les créances ordinaires prennent rang après (*ou* passent après) (*ou* sont primées par) les créances hypothécaires (*f.pl.*).
right which ranks immediately after another, privilège qui prend rang (*ou* qui passe) immédiatement après un autre (*m.*).
ratable *or* **rateable** (proportional) (*adj.*), proportionnel, -elle :
loss made good by ratable contribution, perte bonifiée par voie de contribution proportionnelle (*f.*).
ratable *or* **rateable** (taxable) (*adj.*), imposable.
ratably (*adv.*), proportionnellement :
underwriters who contribute to the actual value ratably to the amounts insured by them, assureurs qui contribuent à la valeur réelle proportionnellement aux sommes assurées par eux (*m.pl.*).
rate (price) (*n.*), taux (*m.*); cours (*m.*); prix (*m.*) :
rate of conversion of a money, taux, cours, de conversion d'une monnaie.
rate of discount, taux d'escompte; taux de l'escompte.
rate of exchange [rates of exchange *pl.*], cours de change; cours du change; cours de place; cours de devise; taux du change; change (*m.*) :
the rate of exchange of the day on Paris, le cours du change du jour sur Paris.
at the rate of exchange current in London on the date of the remittance, au taux de change en cours à Londres à la date de la remise.
the rate of exchange of London on Paris is the price in pounds sterling, in London, of securities payable in Paris in French francs, le change de Londres sur Paris est le prix en livres sterling, à Londres, des titres payables à Paris en francs français.

rate of freight, taux de fret; taux du fret; cours de (*ou* du) fret.
rate of interest *or simply* rate, taux d'intérêt; taux de l'intérêt; cours de l'intérêt; taux :
rate of interest on advances *or* rate for advances, taux d'intérêt des avances; taux des avances.
the rate of interest on money, le taux de l'intérêt de l'argent.
to lend at the rate of 5%, prêter au taux de 5 0/0.
rate of option *or simply* rate (Stock Exch.), prime (*f.*); taux unitaire de la prime (*m.*) :
giver, taker, of the rate, payeur, receveur, de la prime (*m.*).
rate of premium, taux de (*ou* de la) prime.
rate of wages, taux du salaire.
rate per cent, taux pour cent; pour-cent (*m.*) :
at what rate per cent have you invested ? à quel pour-cent avez-vous placé?
contango rate, taux des reports; taux du report; prix des reports; prix du report; cours du report; report (*m.*).
rate (*n.*) *or* **rates** (*n.pl.*) (tariff), tarif (*m.*); tarifs (*m.pl.*) :
railway rates, tarif des chemins de fer.
commission rates, tarif des courtages. V. exemple sous **rebate**.
rate (tax) (*n.*), contribution (*f.*); taxe (*f.*) :
poor rate, taxe des pauvres.
rates and taxes, contributions et impôts; impôts et contributions.
rate (*v.t.*), tarifer; imposer; taxer; coter :
goods rated otherwise than by weight (Customs), marchandises tarifées (*ou* imposées) autrement qu'au poids (*f.pl.*).
rate collector, receveur des contributions (*m.*); percepteur (*m.*).
rate war, guerre de tarifs (*f.*).
ratepayer (pers.) (*n.*), contribuable (*m.* ou *f.*); imposé, -e.
ratification (*n.*), ratification (*f.*).
ratify (*v.t.*), ratifier :
to ratify an appointment (to a post), ratifier une nomination.
rating (*n.*), tarification (*f.*); cote (*f.*); taxation (*f.*) :
railway rating on an exclusively kilometric basis, tarification ferroviaire sur la base exclusivement kilométrique.
rating system, régime tarifaire (*m.*).
ratio (*n.*), rapport (*m.*); coefficient (*m.*); proportion (*f.*); quantum (*m.*) :
ratio between gold and silver, between the issue of bank notes and the bullion reserve, rapport entre l'or et l'argent, entre l'émission des billets de banque et la réserve métallique.
ratio of liquid assets to current liabilities, coefficient de liquidité; degré de liquidité (*m.*).
rationalization (*n.*), rationalisation (*f.*) :
rationalization of industry, rationalisation de l'industrie.
rationalize (*v.t.*), rationaliser.
rattles (i.e., contents apparently broken—

reservation on a bill of lading, a consignment note), sonnant la casse.

raw material, matière brute (*f.*); matière première (*f.*) :
the raw materials used in the manufacture of an article, les matières premières consommées par la fabrication d'un article.

reach (to come to) (*v.t.*), atteindre; parvenir à; arriver à :
to reach the end of one's journey, atteindre le, parvenir au, arriver au, but de son voyage.
by virtue of this clause, whatever happens, whether the goods reach their destination or not, the shipowner receives his freight, en vertu de cette clause, quoi qu'il arrive, que les marchandises parviennent (*ou* arrivent) ou non à leur destination, l'armateur touchera son fret.

reach (to attain) (*v.t.*), atteindre; s'élever à :
the price reached so much, le prix a atteint (*ou* s'élevait à) tant.

reacquire (*v.t.*), réacquérir :
to reacquire a property, réacquérir une propriété.

react (*v.i.*), réagir; réactionner :
tins did not attempt to react from last week's break, les stannifères n'ont pas cherché à réagir contre la dérobade de la semaine dernière (*f.pl.*).
stock which reacts from such a price to such a price, valeur qui réactionne de tel cours à tel cours (*f.*).

reaction (*n.*), réaction (*f.*) :
the outstanding event of the day was the sharp reaction of the franc, le fait saillant de la journée a été la vive réaction du franc.

read (*v.t.*), lire; donner lecture de :
it is important that one should read carefully the documents one is called upon to sign, il importe que l'on lise attentivement les documents que l'on est appelé à signer.
to read between the lines (*fig.*), lire entre les lignes.
the chairman then read the report, puis M. le président donne lecture du rapport.
the minutes of the last meeting were read and confirmed, le procès-verbal de la dernière séance est lu et adopté.
read and approved, lu et approuvé.

read over (to) (to compare), collationner :
to read over a copy with the original, collationner une copie sur l'original.

reading (*n.*), lecture (*f.*) :
reading a balance sheet is not easy, la lecture d'un bilan n'est pas chose aisée.

reading over (comparing), collationnement (*m.*).

readmission (*n.*), réadmission (*f.*) :
free readmission of goods exported abroad in mistake, réadmission en franchise des marchandises exportées par erreur à l'étranger.

readmit (*v.t.*), réadmettre.

ready (*adj.*), prêt, -e :
ship ready to load, to deliver, navire prêt à prendre charge, à délivrer (*m.*). *Cf.* ready to sail, *sous* **sail** (*v.i.*).

ready money *or Slang* **ready** (*n.*)—often with the,** argent comptant (*m.*); comptant (*m.*); beaux deniers comptants (*m.pl.*); argent clair (*m.*).

ready reckoner, barème (*m.*); barrême (*m.*); comptes faits (*m.pl.*).

reaffreight (*v.t.*), réaffréter.

reaffreightment (*n.*), réaffrètement (*m.*).

real (*adj.*), V. exemples :
real accounts (Bkkpg), comptes de valeurs (*m.pl.*); comptes du gérant (*m.pl.*); comptes de l'exploitation (*m.pl.*).
real contract (Law), contrat réel (*m.*).
real exchange (opp. to *commercial,* or *bill, exchange*), change réel (*m.*); change manuel (*m.*); change menu (*m.*); change local (*m.*).
real money, monnaie réelle (*f.*); monnaie effective (*f.*); valeurs effectives (*f.pl.*) :
in England, we (*or* they) reckon sometimes in guineas (of 21 shillings), but there is no longer any real money actually representing a guinea, on compte parfois en Angleterre en guinées (de 21 schellings), mais il n'y a plus de monnaie réelle représentant effectivement une guinée.
real property *or* real estate *or* **realty** [**realties** *pl.*] (*n.*), biens immeubles (*m.pl.*); biens immobiliers (*m.pl.*); immeubles (*m.pl.*); immeuble (*m.*); immobilier (*m.*); propriétés immobilières (*f.pl.*); effets immobiliers (*m.pl.*); valeurs immobilières (*f.pl.*).
real right (Law), droit réel (*m.*).
real tare, tare réelle (*f.*).
real word (Teleg.) (opp. to *artificial word*), mot réel (*m.*).

realizable (*adj.*), réalisable :
realizable securities, valeurs réalisables (*f.pl.*).
securities realizable at short notice, valeurs réalisables à court terme (*f.pl.*).

realization (*n.*), réalisation (*f.*).

realize (*v.t.*), réaliser :
to realize an investment, a stock of goods, réaliser un placement, un stock de marchandises.
profit actually realized, bénéfice effectivement réalisé (*m.*).

realizer (pers.) (*n.*), réaliseur (*m.*).

realty (*n.*). *V. sous* real property.

reasonable (*adj.*), raisonnable :
reasonable price (*or* charge), prix raisonnable (*m.*).
within a reasonable time, dans un délai raisonnable.

reassurance (*n.*), réassurance (*f.*).

reassure (*v.t.*), réassurer. V. exemples sous syn. **reinsure.**

rebate (*n.*), rabais (*m.*); ristourne (*f.*); ristorne (*f.*); réfaction (*f.*); bonification (*f.*); bonification d'escompte (*f.*); boni (*m.*); diminution (*f.*) :
rebate of freight, ristourne de fret; rabais de fret.
rebate of premium (Insce), rabais de prime.
to receive a rebate on calls paid in advance, jouir d'une bonification d'escompte sur des versements par anticipation.
banker who has, as profit, the rebate which

the broker makes on the official commission rates, banquier qui a, comme bénéfice, la ristourne que fait l'agent sur le tarif officiel des courtages (*m.*).

rebate on bills not due (item in bank balance sheet and profit and loss account), réescompte du portefeuille (*m.*):
after deducting rebate on bills not due and establishment charges, there remains a net profit of . . ., après déduction du réescompte du portefeuille et des frais généraux, il reste un bénéfice net de . . .

reborrow (*v.t.*), remprunter.

rebuild a ship (to), refondre un navire.

rebuilding (a ship) (*n.*), refonte (d'un navire) (*f.*).

recall (*v.t.*), rappeler:
to recall the exchange, the operator (Teleph.), rappeler le bureau, l'opératrice:
you will be recalled as soon as a line becomes available, vous serez rappelé dès qu'un circuit sera disponible.

recapitulate (*v.t.*), récapituler; résumer.

recapitulation (*n.*), récapitulation (*f.*); résumé (*m.*).

recapitulative (*adj.*), récapitulatif, -ive.

recashing (*n.*), rencaissage (*m.*); rencaissement (*m.*).

recede (*v.i.*), reculer:
X. shares receded a point, l'action X. recule d'un point.

receipt (act) (*n.*), réception (*f.*); recette (*f.*):
to acknowledge receipt of a letter, accuser réception d'une lettre.
receipt of advices, of the news of an accident, of the goods on board, réception des avis, de la nouvelle d'un sinistre, de la marchandise à bord.
receipt whereof is hereby acknowledged *or* which is hereby acknowledged to have been received, dont quittance.

receipt (that which is received) (*n.*). V. **receipts.**

receipt (acknowledgment) (*n.*), reçu (*m.*); quittance (*f.*); acquit (*m.*); récépissé (*m.*); reconnaissance (*f.*):
in France, receipts for amounts over ten francs have to bear a receipt stamp; in England, receipts for £2 and upwards are subject to stamp duty, en France, les reçus de sommes supérieures à dix francs doivent porter un timbre de quittance; en Angleterre, sont assujettis au droit de timbre les reçus de sommes de £2 et au-dessus.
Note:—In France, receipt stamp duty is ad valorem; in England, it is fixed.
receipt for payment, reçu (*ou* quittance) (*ou* acquit) (*ou* récépissé) de paiement (*ou* de versement).
receipt for rent, for duty, quittance de loyer, de droit.
receipt on account, reçu à valoir.
receipt for the balance *or* receipt in full discharge, quittance finale; reçu libératoire.
receipt for a telegram, récépissé de dépôt d'un télégramme.
receipt with consideration for payment not stated, reçu simple.

receipt with consideration for payment stated, reçu motivé; reçu causé.

receipt (*v.t.*), acquitter; quittancer:
to receipt a bill of lading, acquitter un connaissement.
to receipt an invoice, a bill, acquitter, quittancer, une facture, un mémoire.

receipt form, formule d'acquit (*f.*).

receipt stamp, timbre de quittance (*m.*); timbre à quittance (*m.*); timbre-quittance (*m.*); timbre d'acquit (*m.*); timbre proportionnel d'acquit (*m.*); timbre spécial pour quittances, reçus et décharges (*m.*).

receipt stamp duty, droit de timbre à quittance (*m.*).

receipts (*n.pl.*), recette (*f.*); recettes (*f.pl.*); entrées (*f.pl.*); rentrées (*f.pl.*); encaissements (*m.pl.*); produit (*m.*):
to reckon up the receipts and the expenditure, compter la recette et la dépense.
the gross receipts, la recette brute.
cash receipts and payments, recettes et dépenses de caisse; entrées et sorties de caisse; rentrées et sorties de caisse; encaissements et paiements.
the daily receipts, les rentrées journalières.
sundry receipts, rentrées diverses.
to check the day's receipts, vérifier le produit de la journée.

receipts book, livre des entrées (*m.*); carnet des recettes (*m.*).

receivable (to be received) (*adj.*), à recevoir:
interest receivable, intérêts à recevoir (*m.pl.*).

receive (*v.t.*), recevoir; toucher; jouir de:
to receive a letter, recevoir une lettre.
to receive money on deposit, recevoir de l'argent en dépôt.
to receive so much on account, recevoir, toucher, tant à compte.
debenture holders who receive their coupons, obligataires qui touchent leurs coupons (*m.pl.* ou *f.pl.*).
to receive a salary, toucher un traitement; recevoir des appointements; être aux appointements:
he has received a salary for the last six months only, il n'est aux appointements que depuis six mois.
to receive a discount on payments in advance of calls, jouir d'une bonification d'escompte sur des versements par anticipation.
to receive a proposal favorably, recevoir favorablement, accueillir favorablement, agréer, une proposition.

received (*p.p.*) (Abbrev.: **rec'd** *or* **recd**), reçu, -e; acquit; pour acquit: (*Note:*—*reçu* is invariable if placed before the sum named, but not if it follows it.)
received one thousand pounds, reçu mille livres.
one thousand pounds received on account, mille livres reçues à valoir.

received cash book *or* **received (counter) cash book** (Banking), main courante de recettes (*f.*); main courante d'entrée (*f.*); chiffrier de recettes (*m.*); brouillard d'entrée (*m.*).

received for shipment bill of lading, connaissement reçu pour embarquement (*ou* reçu pour être embarqué) (*ou* reçu pour charger) (*m.*).

received stamp (rubber stamp), timbre de réception (*m.*).

receiver *or* **recipient** (pers.) (*n.*), réceptionnaire (*m.* ou *f.*); destinataire (*m.* ou *f.*); récepteur, -euse :
the sender and the receiver, l'expéditeur et le réceptionnaire (*ou* et le destinataire).

receiver (of a shipment *or* of a cargo) (pers.) (*n.*), réceptionnaire (*m.* ou *f.*), réclamateur (*m.*), destinataire (*m.* ou *f.*) (d'un chargement).

receiver (Produce Exch.) (pers.) (*n.*), réceptionnaire (*m.*); arrêteur (*m.*); arrêteur de la filière (*m.*); dernier acheteur (*m.*).

receiver (treasurer) (pers.) (*n.*), receveur, -euse.

receiver (pers.) (Banking). V. sous **receiving cashier**.

receiver (Teleph.) (*n.*) (opp. to *transmitter*), récepteur (*m.*); écouteur (*m.*); appareil d'écoute (*m.*); appareil (*m.*) :
to remove, to replace, the receiver, décrocher, raccrocher, le récepteur (*ou* l'écouteur) (*ou* l'appareil).

receiver of wreck (pers.), syndic des naufrages (*m.*).

receiving *or* **reception** (*n.*), réception (*f.*) :
stations closed on Sundays both for the receiving (*or* reception) and delivering (*or* delivery) of goods, gares fermées les dimanches tant à la réception qu'à la livraison des marchandises (*f.pl.*).
reception of advices, of the news of an accident, of the goods on board, réception des avis, de la nouvelle d'un sinistre, de la marchandise à bord.

receiving (collection of money) (*n.*), recette (*f.*) :
to do the receiving of a business house, faire la recette d'une maison de commerce.

receiving cashier *or* **receiver** (*n.*) (Banking), caissier des recettes (*m.*); guichetier encaisseur (*m.*); encaisseur (*m.*).

receiving note, bon à embarquer (*m.*).

receiving office (Rly.), bureau de ville (*m.*); bureau de réception (*m.*) :
the goods received in the receiving offices of the railway companies, les marchandises reçues dans les bureaux de ville des compagnies de chemins de fer (*f.pl.*).

receiving office (for telegrams), bureau de réception (*m.*); bureau récepteur (*m.*); bureau réceptionnaire (*m.*).

receiving order (for goods), bon de réception (*m.*).

receiving station (Rly.) (opp. to *sending station*), gare réceptrice (*f.*); gare de réception (*f.*).

receiving station (Teleg.) (opp. to *transmitting station*), poste récepteur (*m.*); station réceptrice (*f.*); station de réception (*f.*).

recess (vacation) (Law) (*n.*), vacances (*f.pl.*); vacation (*f.*).

recession (*n.*), recul (*m.*). V. le verbe **recede** pour exemple.

recharter (*v.t.*), réaffréter :
profit made by a charterer who has rechartered

a ship at a higher price, profit réalisé par un affréteur qui aurait réaffrété un navire à un prix plus élevé (*m.*).

rechartering (*n.*), réaffrètement (*m.*).

recipient. V. sous **receiver**.

reciprocal (*adj.*), réciproque :
reciprocal concessions, concessions réciproques (*f.pl.*).

reciprocity (*n.*), réciprocité (*f.*) :
reciprocity of treatment, réciprocité de traitement.
certain products imported into that colony are admitted free, and, by reciprocity, the colonial products, with a few exceptions, are exempt from customs charges on their importation into the home country, certains produits importés à cette colonie sont admis en franchise, et, par réciprocité, les produits coloniaux, à quelques exceptions près, sont exempts de taxes douanières à leur entrée dans la métropole (*m.pl.*).

reckon *or* **reckon up** (*v.t.*), compter; faire le compte de; décompter; supputer; calculer :
to reckon the days (i.e., the number of days for an interest calculation), compter, décompter, supputer, calculer, les jours.
to reckon up the receipts and the expenses, compter, supputer, calculer, la recette et la dépense.

reckon (*v.i.*), compter; chiffrer.

reckoner (pers.) (*n.*), compteur, -euse; calculateur, -trice; chiffreur, -euse.

reckoning (*n.*), comptage (*m.*); compte (*m.*); décompte (*m.*); supputation (*f.*); calcul (*m.*).

reclassification (of ships) (*n.*), recotation (*f.*).

recognized (acknowledged or certified) (*adj.*), attitré, -e :
recognized merchant, commerçant attitré (*m.*).

recoin (*v.t.*), refondre; refrapper.

recoinage (*n.*) *or* **recoinage of moneys**, refonte (*f.*); refonte des monnaies (*f.*); refrappage (*m.*); refrappement (*m.*); refrappage (*ou* refrappement) des monnaies (*m.*).

recommend (*v.t.*), recommander; conseiller; proposer :
to recommend a friend to someone, recommander un ami à quelqu'un.
the board recommends the distribution of a dividend, le conseil d'administration propose la répartition d'un dividende.

recommendable (*adj.*), recommandable; conseillable :
recommendable investment, placement recommandable (*m.*).

recommendation (*n.*), recommandation (*f.*); proposition (*f.*); parrainage (*m.*) :
letter of recommendation, lettre de recommandation (*f.*).
to submit a recommendation of dividend, soumettre une proposition de dividende.
the recommendation of two brokers already admitted, le parrainage de deux courtiers déjà admis.

recommender (pers.) (*n.*), parrain (*m.*) :

candidate introduced by three recommenders, candidat présenté par trois parrains (m.).

recompense (n.), récompense (f.).

recompense (v.t.), récompenser :
to recompense someone for a loss, récompenser quelqu'un d'une perte.

reconcile (v.t.), faire accorder ; faire cadrer ; apurer :
to reconcile an account, faire accorder, faire cadrer, apurer, un compte.

reconciliation (n.), accord (m.) ; concordance (f.) ; apurement (m.) :
reconciliation between the journal and the ledger, accord, concordance, entre le journal et le grand livre.

reconciliation account (Bkkpg), compte collectif (m.).

reconduction (Law) (n.), reconduction (f.) ; réconduction (f.) :
the concessions to be renewed from month to month by tacit reconduction, les concessions se renouvellent de mois en mois par tacite reconduction (f.pl.).

recopy (v.t.), recopier :
to recopy a letter, recopier une lettre.

record or **record-breaking** (adj.), record :
exports which reach the record figure (or the record-breaking figure) of so many millions, exportations qui atteignent le chiffre record de tant de millions (f.pl.).
shares which have reached record prices, actions qui ont atteint des cours records (f.pl.).

record (a writing or register) (n.), écriture (f.) ; inscription (f.) ; registre (m.) :
the records of a bank, les écritures d'une banque.

as a record or **to place it on record,** pour mémoire :
the amounts written off are shown only as a record, les amortissements ne figurent que pour mémoire (m.pl.).
we mention this exception to place it on record, nous signalons cette exception pour mémoire.

record (best recorded achievement) (n.), record (m.) :
company which holds the speed record in the North Atlantic, compagnie qui détient le record de la vitesse dans l'Atlantique Nord (f.).

record (v.t.), enregistrer ; inscrire ; consigner ; relever ; constater ; comptabiliser :
the transactions recorded in the journal, les opérations enregistrées (ou inscrites) (ou comptabilisées) sur le journal (f.pl.).
the journal is the medium by which facts are recorded in order of date, le journal est l'organe classificateur par dates des faits à comptabiliser.
to record a fact, consigner, relever, un fait.
stockbrokers must record in special books all the deals done through their agency, les agents de change doivent consigner (ou inscrire) sur des livres spéciaux toutes les opérations faites par leur ministère (m.pl.).
to record the births and deaths which occur on board a ship, constater les naissances et décès qui se produisent à bord d'un navire.

governments which have a tendency, sometimes in defiance of truth, to satisfy their desire to record results which do credit to their administration, gouvernements qui ont une tendance à satisfaire, quelquefois au mépris de la vérité, leur désir de constater des résultats qui font honneur à leur administration (m.pl.).

record ribbon (non copying ribbon for typewriter) (distinguished from copying ribbon), ruban fixe (m.).

recording (n.), enregistrement (m.) ; inscription (f.) ; consignation (f.) ; relèvement (m.) ; relevé (m.) ; constatation (f.) ; comptabilisation (f.) :
stocktaking comprises two operations : recording the quantities and their valuation, l'inventaire comporte deux opérations : le relevé des quantités et leur évaluation (m.).

recount (n.), recomptage (m.) :
recount of votes, recomptage des votes.

recount (v.t.), recompter.

recoup (v.t.), récupérer ; dédommager :
to recoup one's disbursements, récupérer ses déboursés.

recoup oneself (to), se récupérer ; se dédommager :
to recoup oneself for one's losses, se récupérer, se dédommager, de ses pertes.

recourse (n.), recours (m.) :
recourse of the insurer against the author of the damage, recours de l'assureur contre l'auteur du dommage.
shipper who finds himself deprived of any recourse against the shipowner, chargeur qui se trouve privé de tout recours contre l'armateur (m.).

to have recourse, avoir recours ; recourir :
State which has recourse to inconvertible paper money, État qui a recours (ou qui recourt) au papier-monnaie (m.).
to have recourse to the endorser of a bill, avoir recours contre l'endosseur d'un effet.

without recourse, à forfait :
endorsement without recourse, endossement à forfait (m.).

recover (v.t.), recouvrer ; récupérer ; faire rentrer ; regagner ; se faire rembourser ; se faire indemniser :
to recover a debt, recouvrer, récupérer, faire rentrer, une créance ; faire un recouvrement.
jettison goods recovered by the owners, marchandises jetées recouvrées par les propriétaires (f.pl.).
to recover the money lost, regagner l'argent perdu.
it is impossible for the importers to recover this expense from their buyers, il est impossible aux importateurs de récupérer cette dépense sur leurs acheteurs.
to recover from the underwriter a part of the premium paid, se faire rembourser par l'assureur une partie de la prime versée.
to recover from the insurer the whole of the

loss, se faire indemniser par l'assureur pour la totalité de la perte.

recover (*v.i.*), se recouvrer ; se récupérer ; se regagner ; se relever ; reprendre ; se reprendre ; être en reprise ; se ressaisir ; se ranimer :

the almost certain prospect of seeing prices recover, la perspective presque certaine de voir les cours se relever.

mining shares recovered sharply (*or* smartly), les valeurs minières reprennent (*ou* se reprennent) (*ou* se ressaisissent) vivement (*ou* vigoureusement) (*f.pl.*).

X. shares recovered from 1s. to 1s. 3d., l'action X. est en reprise (*ou* se ranime) de 1sh. à 1sh. 3d.

recoverable (*adj.*), recouvrable ; récupérable :

recoverable debt, créance recouvrable (*f.*) ; dette récupérable (*f.*).

recovery [**recoveries** *pl.*] (regaining possession ; collection ; indemnification) (*n.*), recouvrement (*m.*) ; récupération (*f.*) ; indemnisation (*f.*) :

recovery of lost treasure, recouvrement de trésor perdu.

right of recovery under an insurance, droit d'indemnisation en vertu d'une assurance (*m.*).

recovery (revival) (*n.*), reprise (*f.*) ; relèvement (*m.*) :

recovery of business, of prices, reprise, relèvement, des affaires, des cours.

rectification (*n.*), rectification (*f.*) ; redressement (*m.*).

rectify (*v.t.*), rectifier ; redresser :

to rectify an error, rectifier, redresser, une erreur.

any error of weight can be rectified by a new weighing, toute erreur de poids peut être rectifiée par une nouvelle pesée.

red bill of lading, connaissement rouge (*m.*).

red ink, encre rouge (*f.*) :

the amounts shown in red ink, les sommes ressorties à l'encre rouge (*f.pl.*).

red interest (current accounts, or the like) (opp. to *black interest*), intérêts rouges (*m.pl.*).

red pencil, crayon rouge (*m.*).

red product (current accounts, or the like), nombre rouge (*m.*).

redeem (*v.t.*), amortir ; rembourser ; racheter ; purger ; dégager ; honorer :

to redeem a debenture (*or* a bond), amortir, rembourser, racheter, une obligation.

to redeem a mortgage, purger une hypothèque.

to redeem one's property, dégager son bien.

the first point that interests the discounter is the certainty that the discounted bill will be redeemed at maturity, le premier point qui intéresse l'escompteur c'est la certitude que l'effet escompté sera honoré à l'échéance.

redeemability (*n.*), remboursabilité (*f.*).

redeemable (*adj.*) (Abbrev. : **red.**), amortissable ; remboursable ; rachetable :

redeemable bonds (*or* debentures), obligations amortissables (*ou* remboursables) (*ou* rachetables) (*f.pl.*).

redeemer (pers.) (*n.*), racheteur, -euse.

redemption (*n.*), amortissement (*m₁*) ; remboursement (*m.*) ; rachat (*m.*) ; réméré (*m.*) ; purge (*f.*) ; dégagement (*m.*) :

redemption of the national debt, amortissement de la dette publique.

redemption of mortgage, purge d'hypothèque ; purge légale.

redemption premium, prime de remboursement (*f.*).

redemption table, tableau d'amortissement (*m.*) ; table d'amortissement (*f.*) ; plan d'amortissement (*m.*).

redemptional (*adj.*), amortissant, -e.

redhibition (Law) (*n.*), rédhibition (*f.*).

redhibitory (*adj.*), rédhibitoire :

redhibitory defect, vice rédhibitoire (*m.*).

redirect (*v.t.*), réexpédier ; faire suivre :

to redirect a letter, a postal parcel, to a new address, réexpédier une lettre, un colis postal, à une nouvelle adresse.

to give orders to redirect telegrams by telegraph, by post, donner l'ordre de réexpédier (*ou* de faire suivre) des télégrammes par la voie télégraphique, par la voie postale.

redirection (*n.*), réexpédition (*f.*) :

redirection of postal packets, réexpédition des correspondances.

rediscount *or* **rediscounting** (*n.*), réescompte (*m.*).

rediscount (*v.t.*), réescompter :

to rediscount other banks' bills, réescompter le portefeuille d'autres banques.

rediscounter (pers.) (*n.*), réescompteur (*m.*).

redraft (renewed bill of exchange) (*n.*), retraite (*f.*).

reduce (*v.t.*), réduire ; abaisser ; rabaisser ; diminuer ; modifier ; ramener :

to reduce a price, one's expenditure, réduire, abaisser, rabaisser, diminuer, modifier, un prix, sa dépense.

to reduce the bank rate, the cost of living, réduire, abaisser, diminuer, le taux officiel d'escompte, le coût de la vie.

dividend reduced from 8 to 4%, dividende ramené de 8 à 4 0/0 (*m.*).

reduced rate ticket, billet à prix réduit (*m.*).

reduced tariff *or* **reduced rates,** tarif réduit (*m.*).

reducible (*adj.*), réductible.

reduction (*n.*), réduction (*f.*) ; abaissement (*m.*) ; rabaissement (*m.*) ; rabais (*m.*) ; rabat (*m.*) ; rabattage (*m.*) ; remise (*f.*) ; diminution (*f.*) ; dégonflement (*m.*) ; dégrèvement (*m.*) :

reduction of capital, réduction de capital.

reduction on the agreed price, remise sur le prix convenu.

to sell at a reduction, vendre au rabais.

reduction of the item " bills payable " (balance sheet), dégonflement du poste « effets à payer. »

plans for tax reductions, projets de dégrèvements d'impôts (*m.pl.*).

reelect (*v.t.*), réélire :

to reelect a director, réélire un administrateur.

reelection (*n.*), réélection (*f.*).

reeligibility (*n.*), rééligibilité (*f.*).

reeligible (*adj.*), rééligible :

a retiring director shall be reeligible, tout administrateur sortant est rééligible.

reengage (*v.t.*), rengager :
to reengage an employee, rengager un employé.

reengage (to reenter an employment) (*v.i.*), se rengager.

reengagement (*n.*), rengagement (*m.*).

reenter (to record again) (*v.i.*), réinscrire ; rentrer :
to reenter an item in an account, réinscrire, rentrer, un article sur un compte.

reentry [reentries *pl.*] (*n.*), réinscription (*f.*).

reexamination (Customs) (*n.*), contre-visite (*f.*) ; contre-vérification (*f.*) :
reexamination of goods already examined, contre-visite (*ou* contre-vérification) des marchandises déjà vérifiées.

reexamine (*v.t.*), repasser :
to reexamine an account, repasser un compte.

reexchange (operation) (*n.*), rechange (*m.*) :
reexchange of a bill of exchange, rechange d'une lettre de change.

reexchange (renewed bill of exchange) (*n.*), retraite (*f.*).

reexchange (price of the new draft) (*n.*), rechange (*m.*) :
to pay the exchange and the reexchange, payer le change et le rechange.

reexport *or* **reexportation** (*n.*), réexportation (*f.*) :
reexportation of samples imported into a country by commercial travellers, réexportation d'échantillons importés dans un pays par des voyageurs de commerce.

reexport (*v.t.*), réexporter :
goods reexported abroad, marchandises réexportées à l'étranger (*f.pl.*).

reexport trade, commerce intermédiaire (*m.*) ; commerce de réexportation (*m.*).

reexporter (pers.) (*n.*), réexportateur, -trice.

refer (*v.t.*). V. exemple :
to refer a matter to a competent tribunal, renvoyer une affaire devant un tribunal compétent.

refer (*v.i.*). V. exemples :
to refer to a price list, consulter un prix courant.
an index enables one to refer immediately to each account, un répertoire permet de se reporter (*ou* se référer) à chaque compte.
the figures refer to the pages of the work, les chiffres renvoient aux pages de l'ouvrage (*m.pl.*).
refer to drawer (Banking) (*Abbrev. :* R/D.), voir le tireur.

referee in case of need (pers.), recommandataire (*m.*) ; besoin (*m.*). V. exemples sous **case of need**.

reference (testimonial) (*n.*), référence (*f.*) :
banker's reference, référence de banquier.
employee who has excellent references, employé qui a d'excellentes références (*m.*).

reference (direction of the attention) (*n.*) (Abbrev. : **ref.** *or* **refce**), référence (*f.*) ; renvoi (*m.*) :
cross reference, référence croisée.

reference *or* **for reference please quote** (mention on letter heading), référence ; à rappeler ; à rappeler, s.v.p.

reference number, numéro de référence (*m.*) ; numéro de renvoi (*m.*).

reference slip, fiche de rappel (*f.*).

refloat (*v.t.*), remettre à flot ; renflouer :
to refloat a stranded ship, remettre à flot, renflouer, un navire échoué.
a tug enters into a contract with a stranded ship and undertakes to refloat her, un remorqueur passe un contrat avec un navire échoué et entreprend de le renflouer.

refloating (*n.*), remise à flot (*f.*) ; renflouage (*m.*) ; renflouement (*m.*).

reflux (*n.*), reflux (*m.*) :
reflux of gold, reflux d'or.

reforward (*v.t.*), réexpédier :
to reforward the goods to their destination, réexpédier les marchandises à leur destination.

reforwarding (*n.*), réexpédition (*f.*) :
reforwarding goods by another ship, réexpédition des marchandises par un autre navire.

refrigerated van (Rly.), wagon frigorifique (*m.*) ; wagon réfrigérant (*m.*).

refrigerated vessel, navire frigorifique (*m.*).

refuge (*n.*), refuge (*m.*) ; relâche (*f.*) :
port of refuge, port de refuge (*m.*) ; port de relâche (*m.*).
ship which puts back into the port of sailing for refuge, navire qui rentre dans le port de départ en relâche (*m.*).

refund (*n.*), remboursement (*m.*) ; ristourne (*f.*) ; ristorne (*f.*).

refund (*v.t.*), rembourser ; ristourner ; ristorner :
to refund the excess, ristourner l'excédent.

refusal (*n.*), refus (*m.*) :
refusal of goods, refus de la marchandise.
refusal to accept, to pay, a bill, refus d'acceptation, de paiement, d'un effet.

refuse (*v.t.*), refuser ; se refuser :
to refuse to accept, to pay, a bill, refuser d'accepter, de payer, un effet ; se refuser à accepter, à payer, un effet.
to refuse to take delivery, refuser de prendre livraison.
underwriter who, after having examined the risk, accepts or refuses it, assureur qui, après avoir examiné le risque, l'accepte ou le refuse (*m.*).
refused or unclaimed parcels, colis refusés ou non réclamés (*m.pl.*).
on hand, refused. V. sous **on**.

regain (*v.t.*), regagner :
to regain the money lost, regagner l'argent perdu.
to regain possession of a property by reversion, rentrer dans un bien par réversion.

register (*n.*), registre (*m.*) ; livre (*m.*) ; journal (*m.*) ; grand-livre (*m.*) :
every ship must belong to a port under the form of an entry in a special register kept at the marine registry office, tout navire doit être attaché a un port sous la forme d'une immatriculation sur un registre spécial tenu au bureau de l'inscription maritime.

transfer register, registre de transferts ; livre des transferts ; journal des transferts.

register of debenture holders, grand livre des obligataires.

register of members, registre des actionnaires ; livre des actionnaires ; grand livre des actionnaires.

register (tonnage of a ship) (*n.*). V. sous **register tonnage.**

register (*v.t.*), enregistrer ; inscrire ; immatriculer :

to register a deed, enregistrer, immatriculer, un acte.

to register a mortgage on a ship, inscrire une hypothèque sur un navire.

ship registered in the colonies, navire immatriculé dans les colonies (*m.*).

these securities are registered in the name of the company, ces valeurs sont enregistrées (*ou* immatriculées) au nom de la société (*f.pl.*).

to register luggage, enregistrer des bagages.

register (Post) (*v.t.*), recommander :

to register a letter, recommander une lettre.

register book (Marine Registry), livre d'enregistrement (*m.*). *Note :—This is a literal translation only ; the French equivalent of* register book *is* registre des déclarations de construction et soumissions de francisation (*m.*) *or* registre de l'état civil des navires (*m.*).

register book (of mortgages on ships), registre des inscriptions (*m.*).

register ton, tonneau de jauge (*m.*) ; tonne de jauge (*f.*) ; tonneau de registre (*m.*) ; tonneau-registre (*m.*) ; tonne de registre (*f.*) ; tonne-registre (*f.*). = 100 cubic feet or 2·8317 cubic metres—same in France as in England.

register tonnage *or* **registered tonnage** *or simply* **register** (*n.*), tonnage de jauge (*m.*) ; jauge (*f.*) ; tonnage (*m.*) :

the principle of charging on the register tonnage (*or* on the register) of the ship, le principe de la taxation sur la jauge du navire.

registered (Post) (*adj.*) (Abbrev. : **reg.** *or* **reg**d *or* **R.**), recommandé, -e :

registered letter, lettre recommandée (*f.*) ; pli recommandé (*m.*) :

to send bank notes by registered letter, certificates under registered cover, expédier (*ou* envoyer) des billets de banque par lettre recommandée (*ou* par pli recommandé), des titres sous pli recommandé.

registered letter envelope, enveloppe de lettre chargée ou recommandée (*f.*).

registered packet *or* registered article, objet (*ou* envoi) recommandé (*m.*).

registered post, poste recommandée (*f.*).

registered (as opposed to *bearer*) (*adj.*) (Abbrev. : **reg.** *or* **reg**d), nominatif, -ive :

registered certificate *or* registered scrip, titre nominatif (*m.*) ; certificat nominatif (*m.*).

registered certificate with coupons attached, certificat mixte (*m.*) ; titre mixte (*m.*).

registered bond *or* registered debenture, obligation nominative (*f.*).

registered share certificate, certificat nominatif d'action(s) (*m.*).

registered shares *or* registered stock *or* registered stocks *or* registered securities, actions nominatives (*f.pl.*) ; titres nominatifs (*m.pl.*) ; valeurs nominatives (*f.pl.*) ; effets nominatifs (*m.pl.*).

registered shares transferable by endorsement of the certificate, titres à ordre (*m.pl.*).

registered abbreviated address (Teleg.), adresse abrégée enregistrée (*f.*).

registered capital, capital social (*m.*) ; capital nominal (*m.*) :

the registered capital of a company, le capital social d'une compagnie ; le capital nominal d'une société.

company with a registered capital of so much, société au capital nominal de tant (*f.*).

registered luggage, bagages enregistrés (*m.pl.*).

registered office *or* **registered office of the company,** siège (*m.*) ; siège social (*m.*) :

a company without a registered office, une société sans siège (*ou* sans siège social).

the registered office of the company will be situated in . . . (memorandum of association of a company), le siège social est établi à . . . (statuts d'une société).

registrant (pers.) (*n.*), inscrivant, -e.

registrar (pers.) (*n.*), enregistreur (*m.*) ; greffier (*m.*).

registrar of mortgages, conservateur des hypothèques (*m.*).

registrar of transfers, agent comptable des transferts (*m.*).

registration *or* **registry** [**registries** *pl.*] (act) (*n.*), enregistrement (*m.*) ; inscription (*f.*) ; immatriculation (*f.*) ; immatricule (*f.*) :

registration of mortgage, inscription d'hypothèque ; inscription hypothécaire.

registration (Post) (*n.*), recommandation (*f.*) :

registration or insurance is a special treatment applied to postal packets of which the senders wish to ensure delivery, against receipt, to the addressees, or to protect the contents of the said packets, la recommandation ou le chargement est un traitement spécial appliqué aux objets de correspondance dont les expéditeurs veulent assurer la remise, contre reçu, aux destinataires, ou garantir le contenu desdits objets.

registration *or* **registry** (in France, of a ship of French nationality) (*n.*), francisation (*f.*). V. note sous **register book.**

registration dues *or* **registration duties,** droits d'enregistrement (*m.pl.*).

registration fee (Post), droit de recommandation (*m.*) ; taxe de recommandation (*f.*).

registration label (Post), étiquette de recommandation (*f.*).

registration office *or* **registry** (*n.*), bureau d'enregistrement (*m.*) ; bureau d'immatricule (*m.*) ; enregistrement (*m.*) ; greffe (*m.*) :

to go to the registry, aller à l'enregistrement.

registry books (distinguished from *financial*, or *account, books*), livres d'ordre (*m.pl.*) ; livres de statistique (*m.pl.*) ; registres d'ordre (*m.pl.*).

regular (*adj.*), régulier, -ère :
regular boat, navire régulier (*m.*).
regular endorsement, endossement régulier (*m.*).
regular service line, ligne à service régulier (*f.*).
regularity (*n.*), régularité (*f.*) :
regularity of a cheque, of a title to property, régularité d'un chèque, d'un titre de propriété.
regularly (*adv.*), régulièrement.
regulate (to adjust) (*v.t.*), régler ; calculer :
to regulate one's expenses according to one's income, régler, calculer, ses dépenses d'après ses revenus.
the rate of freight is regulated by supply and demand, le taux du fret est réglé par (*ou* se règle sur) l'offre et la demande.
regulate (to make regulations for) (*v.t.*), réglementer ; règlementer :
the Government intervenes nearly in all countries to regulate and limit the issue and the circulation of notes, l'État intervient presque dans tous les pays pour réglementer l'émission et la circulation des billets (*m.*).
regulation *or* **regulating** (making regulations for) (*n.*), réglementation (*f.*) ; règlementation (*f.*) :
regulation of labour on board merchant ships, réglementation du travail à bord des navires de commerce.
regulation (rule) (*n.*), règlement (*m.*) :
stock exchange regulations, règlements de bourse ; règlements boursiers.
reimbursable (*adj.*), remboursable.
reimburse (*v.t.*), rembourser :
pay for me, I will reimburse you, payez pour moi, je vous rembourserai.
reimburse oneself (**to**) *or* **reimbursed** (**to be**), se rembourser ; être remboursé, -e ; rentrer dans :
to be reimbursed one's out of pocket expenses, se rembourser, rentrer dans, ses débours.
reimbursement (*n.*), remboursement (*m.*).
reimport *or* **reimportation** (*n.*), réimportation (*f.*).
reimport (*v.t.*), réimporter.
reimporter (pers.) (*n.*), réimportateur, -trice.
reinsurance (*n.*), réassurance (*f.*).
reinsurance pool *or* **reinsurance exchange**, traité de réassurance (*m.*).
reinsure (*v.t.*), réassurer :
to reinsure with other companies the whole or part of a risk, the surplus (*or* the excess) of one's risk, réassurer auprès d'autres compagnies tout ou partie d'un risque, le surplus (*ou* l'excédent) de son risque.
reinsure (*v.i.*), se réassurer ; se faire réassurer :
the underwriter in his turn can reinsure with another underwriter for the whole or part of the risk he assumes directly towards the assured, l'assureur peut à son tour se réassurer (*ou* se faire réassurer) auprès d'un autre assureur pour la totalité ou une partie du risque qu'il assume directement vis-à-vis de l'assuré (*m.*).
reinsured [reinsured *pl.*] (pers.) (*n.*), réassuré, -e.
reinsurer (pers.) (*n.*), réassureur (*m.*).

reinvest (*v.t.*), replacer ; réinvestir :
to reinvest capital, replacer, réinvestir, des capitaux.
reinvestment (*n.*), replacement (*m.*) ; réinvestissement (*m.*).
reject (*v.t.*), rejeter ; repousser :
to reject an offer, a proposal, an amendment, rejeter, repousser, une offre, une proposition, un amendement.
rejection (*n.*), rejet (*m.*) ; repoussement (*m.*).
relapse (*n.*), recul (*m.*).
relapse (*v.i.*), reculer ; rétrograder ; se rabattre :
X. shares relapsed a point, l'action X. recule d'un point.
X. shares relapsed from 1¼ to 1, l'action X. rétrograde (*ou* s'est rabattue) de 1 1/4 à 1.
release (*n.*), libération (*f.*) ; décharge (*f.*) ; acquittement (*m.*) ; affranchissement (*m.*).
release (*v.t.*), libérer ; décharger ; acquitter ; affranchir :
to release a large amount of money by lowering the reserves of the banks, libérer une grosse quantité de capitaux en abaissant les réserves des banques.
to release someone from an obligation, libérer, décharger, acquitter, affranchir, quelqu'un d'une obligation.
relend (*v.t.*), reprêter.
relet (*v.t.*), relouer.
reletting (*n.*), relocation (*f.*).
reliable bank, banque de tout repos (*f.*).
reliable estimate, estimation de tout repos (*f.*).
reliable man, homme de confiance (*m.*) ; homme d'un commerce sûr (*m.*) ; homme sur lequel on peut compter (*m.*).
relief (*n.*), soulagement (*m.*) ; secours (*m.*) ; dégagement (*m.*) ; exonération (*f.*) ; affranchissement (*m.*) ; libération (*f.*) ; dégrèvement (*m.*) ; déduction (*f.*) :
transaction which brings a great relief to the market, opération qui apporte un grand soulagement au marché (*f.*).
application (*or* claim) for relief (Taxation), demande en dégrèvement (*f.*).
relief for expenses (Income Tax), déduction pour dépenses.
relief fund, caisse de secours (*f.*).
relief train (Rly.), train supplémentaire (*m.*) :
relief trains doubling, tripling, the booked train, trains supplémentaires doublant, triplant, le train utile.
relieve (*v.t.*), soulager ; secourir ; dégager ; relever ; exonérer ; affranchir ; libérer ; soustraire ; dégrever :
underwriter who is relieved from the engagement contracted, syndicataire qui se trouve dégagé (*ou* relevé) de l'engagement pris (*m.*).
to relieve the carriers, wholly or partly, from their legal liability, exonérer, relever, affranchir, libérer, les transporteurs, en tout ou en partie, de, soustraire les transporteurs, en tout ou en partie, à, leur responsabilité légale.
abatement relieving the lower portion of the income, abattement dégrevant la tranche inférieure du revenu (*m.*).

relieving clause, clause d'exonération (*f.*); clause exonératoire (*f.*).
relinquish (*v.t.*), abandonner.
relinquishment (*n.*), abandon (*m.*); abandonnement (*m.*).
reload (*v.t.*), recharger:
goods reloaded on another ship, marchandise rechargée sur un autre navire (*f.*).
reloading (*n.*), rechargement (*m.*).
relocation (*n.*), relocation (*f.*); reconduction (*f.*); réconduction (*f.*).
rely on (*or* **upon**) (**to**), compter sur; se confier en:
to rely on (*or* upon) someone, on (*or* upon) one's friends, compter sur, se confier en, quelqu'un, ses amis.
remain (*v.i.*), rester:
the present agreement to remain in force during a period of so many years, la présente convention restera en vigueur pendant une période de tant d'années.
there remains to be carried forward £ . . ., reste à reporter à nouveau £ . . .
remainder (*n.*), restant (*m.*); reste (*m.*):
to invest the remainder of one's fortune in life annuities, placer en rentes viagères le restant de sa fortune.
remainder (Arith.) (*n.*), reste (*m.*):
15 subtracted from 27 gives as a remainder 12, 15 soustrait de 27 donne pour reste 12.
remarks column, colonne pour les observations (*f.*); colonne remarques (*f.*).
remeasure (a ship) (*v.t.*), rejauger (un navire).
remeasurement (*n.*), rejaugeage (*m.*). Cf. **measurement.**
remedy (*n.*) *or* **remedy of the mint** (Coinage), remède (*m.*); tolérance (*f.*):
remedy of (*or* for) fineness, remède d'aloi; tolérance de titre; faiblage d'aloi (*m.*).
remedy of (*or* for) weight, tolérance de poids; tolérance de fabrication; faiblage (*m.*); faiblage de poids (*m.*).
reminder (*n.*), rappel (*m.*); rappel de compte (*m.*):
reminder of order, of due date, rappel de commande, d'échéance.
to send someone a reminder (request to pay), envoyer à quelqu'un un rappel de compte.
remint (*v.t.*), refondre; refrapper:
to remint demonetized silver coins, refondre, refrapper, des pièces d'argent démonétisées.
reminting (*n.*) *or* **reminting coins,** refonte (*f.*); refonte des monnaies (*f.*); refrappage (*m.*); refrappement (*m.*); refrappage (*ou* refrappement) des monnaies (*f.*).
remisier (half commission man) (Stock Exch.) (*n.*), remisier (*m.*).
remission (*n.*), remise (*f.*):
remission of a debt, of penalty, remise d'une dette, de pénalité.
remission of customs duty, remise de droits de douane; détaxe (*f.*).
remission of charges (*or* **duties**), détaxe (*f.*).
remit (to send; to transmit) (*v.t.*), remettre; faire remise de; faire tenir; envoyer:
to remit a sum of money, remettre, faire

remise d', faire tenir, envoyer, une somme d'argent.
to remit money, remettre, faire remise, faire tenir, envoyer, de l'argent.
to remit bills for collection, remettre des effets en recouvrement; remettre des effets à l'encaissement.
I am remitting you by post an order for so many pounds, je vous fais tenir par la poste un mandat de tant de livres.
remit (to forgive) (*v.t.*), remettre:
to remit a debt, remettre une dette.
remit the charges (*or* **duties**) **on** (**to**), détaxer:
the customs remit the duties on commodities intended for export, la douane détaxe les denrées destinées à l'exportation.
remittance (*n.*), remise (*f.*); envoi (*m.*); versement (*m.*):
to send a remittance, envoyer une remise.
to make a remittance of funds, faire une remise (*ou* un envoi) (*ou* un versement) de fonds.
the remittance of a bill for collection, la remise d'un effet en recouvrement (*ou* à l'encaissement).
remitter (pers.) (*n.*), remetteur (*m.*); remettant (*m.*); envoyeur, -euse:
remitter of a money order, envoyeur d'un mandat-poste.
remitting (*adj.*), remetteur, -euse:
the remitting banker, le banquier remetteur.
remote cause (of an accident of the sea) (opp. to *immediate*, or *proximate*, or *final*, *cause*), cause première (*f.*); cause primitive (*f.*).
removal (taking away; collection) (*n.*), enlèvement (*m.*); retrait (*m.*):
removal of goods before payment of duty, enlèvement, retrait, des marchandises avant paiement des droits.
removal (of goods) under bond, mutation d'entrepôt (*f.*).
removal expenses (change of premises), frais de déplacement (*m.pl.*).
remove (to take away; to collect) (*v.t.*), enlever; retirer:
the goods can only be removed from the customs after the duties have been paid, deposited, or secured, les marchandises ne peuvent être retirées des douanes qu'après les droits ont été payés, consignés, ou garantis (*f.pl.*).
consignee who calls at the station to remove his goods, destinataire qui se présente à la gare pour enlever (*ou* pour retirer) sa marchandise (*m.*).
remove the receiver (**to**) (Teleph.) (opp. to *to replace the receiver*), décrocher le récepteur (*ou* l'écouteur) (*ou* l'appareil); décrocher:
the subscriber removes the receiver and waits, l'abonné décroche et attend (*m.*).
removing the receiver, décrochage (*m.*).
remunerate (*v.t.*), rémunérer:
to remunerate for services, rémunérer des services.
remuneration (*n.*), rémunération (*f.*); allocation (*f.*); indemnité (*f.*); prime (*f.*):

to receive an adequate remuneration for one's work, recevoir la juste rémunération pour son travail.

to fix the remuneration of the auditors, fixer la rémunération (*ou* l'allocation) des commissaires.

remuneration for assistance (at sea), indemnité d'assistance maritime.

remuneration for salvage, indemnité de sauvetage ; prime de sauvetage.

remunerative (*adj.*), rémunérateur, -trice ; rémunérant, -e :

remunerative undertaking, entreprise rémunératrice (*f.*).

renail (*v.t.*), reclouer :

cases renailed (reservation on a bill of lading, on a consignment note), caisses reclouées.

render (*v.t.*), rendre :

to render an account, rendre un compte.

to render an account of one's management, rendre compte de sa gestion.

the negligence clause renders the shipowner not liable, la négligence-clause rend l'armateur irresponsable.

the services rendered to the public by the banker, les services rendus au public par le banquier (*m.pl.*).

to render void, frapper de nullité :

the statute has rendered void any clause which relieves the creditor from complying with these formalities, la loi a frappé de nullité toute clause qui dispenserait le créancier de se conformer à ces formalités.

marine insurance, like all agreements, is rendered void when it is tainted by fraud, l'assurance maritime est, comme toutes les conventions, frappée de nullité quand elle est entachée de fraude (*f.*).

rendering (*n.*), reddition (*f.*) :

rendering of accounts, reddition de comptes.

renew (*v.t.*), renouveler :

to renew a bill, a lease, an insurance policy, renouveler un effet, un bail, une police d'assurance.

to renew the coupons of a certificate, renouveler, les coupons d', recouponner, un titre.

renewable (*adj.*), renouvelable :

the agreement is valid for one year and it is renewable automatically each year, l'accord est valable pour un an et il est renouvelable automatiquement chaque année (*m.*).

renewal (*n.*), renouvellement (*m.*) :

renewal of an insurance, renouvellement d'une assurance.

renewal of coupons, renouvellement de coupons ; recouponnement (*m.*).

renewal of lease, renouvellement de location ; reconduction (*f.*) ; réconduction (*f.*).

renewal bill *or* **renewed bill** (of exchange), retraite (*f.*).

renewal premium *or* simply **renewal** (*n.*) (Insce) (opp. to *first premium*), prime de renouvellement (*f.*) ; renouvellement (*m.*).

renewal rate (of money), taux de renouvellement (*m.*).

renewer (pers.) (*n.*), renouveleur (*m.*).

renounce (*v.t.*), renoncer à ; abdiquer :

to renounce one's right, renoncer à, abdiquer, son droit.

rent (*n.*), loyer (*m.*) ; loyers (*m.pl.*) ; location (*f.*) ; rente (*f.*) ; fermage (*m.*) ; redevance (*f.*) :

rent of office, loyer de bureau.

rent in advance, loyer d'avance.

to pay one's rent, payer son loyer (*ou* ses loyers) (*ou* sa location).

very high rent, location fort chère.

ground rent, rente foncière.

from the economic point of view, rent on lands and rent on houses are only varieties of interest on capital, au point de vue économique, le fermage des terres et le loyer des maisons ne sont que des variétés de l'intérêt du capital.

to grant the right of working a railway line in consideration of rents, concéder le droit d'exploitation d'une ligne de chemin de fer moyennant des redevances.

rent on goods deposited in King's warehouse (Customs), droit de garde (*m.*) ; droit de magasinage (*m.*). Cf. **King's warehouse.**

rent (quarter's rent) (*n.*), terme (*m.*) :

in England, payment of rent is due on 25th March, 24th June, 29th September, and 25th December, en Angleterre, le paiement du terme est dû au 25 mars, au 24 juin, au 29 septembre, et au 25 décembre.

rent (*v.t.*), louer.

rent restriction, restriction des loyers (*f.*).

rental (*n.*), prix de location (*m.*) ; valeur locative (*f.*).

rental (of telephone line) (*n.*), redevance (*f.*) ; redevance d'abonnement (*f.*).

rental value, valeur locative (*f.*) :

the annual rental value of the premises occupied by the insured, la valeur locative annuelle des locaux occupés par l'assuré.

rente (*n.*) or **rentes** (*n.pl.*), rente (*f.*) ; rente sur l'État (*f.*) ; rentes (*f.pl.*) :

to buy some French rentes, acheter de la rente française.

French rentes are either perpetual or redeemable, les rentes françaises sont ou perpétuelles ou amortissables.

foreign stocks are dealt in either in capital or in rentes, les fonds d'États étrangers se négocient ou en capital ou en rentes.

Note :—rente is the interest payable by a Government on a national debt, it is not *capital stock ;* consequently, unless the State has contracted to redeem the principal, as in the case of *rente amortissable,* it does not owe any capital at all ; it has merely contracted in perpetuity to pay so much *rente* (*interest*) periodically.

The prices of *rentes* go up and down in the same way as the prices of capital stocks and shares.

The price quoted is the cost of so many francs of annual rente ; thus, if the French 3% Rentes are quoted at 80, 80 francs will buy the property in an inscription in the

Government Register of the National Debt (Grand-Livre de la Dette publique) yielding 3 francs of rente annually: if the price of the $3\frac{1}{2}$% is fr. 97·50, fr. 195 will buy 7 francs of annual rente, and so on.

To ascertain the amount of a purchase or sale of so many *francs de rente* (a buying or a selling order is given in these terms) the amount of the order should be divided by the rate per cent of interest and multiplied by the price; thus, a purchase of 1 500 *francs de rente* 3 0/0 *à* 58 *fr.* would cost 29,000 francs (viz.:—1,500 ÷ 3 × 58); 500 *francs de rente* 4 0/0 *à* 60 would cost 7,500 francs (viz.:—500 ÷ 4 × 60).

To ascertain the amount of rente a sum of money will buy, multiply the sum of money by the rate of interest and divide by the price; thus (taking the above examples),

$$29,000 \times 3 = 87,000 \div 58 = 1,500.$$
$$7,500 \times 4 = 30,000 \div 60 = 500.$$

renter (pers.) (*n.*), locataire (*m.* ou *f.*):
renter of a safe, locataire d'un coffre-fort.
renting (*n.*), location (*f.*); louage (*m.*):
renting of safes, location de coffres-forts.
renunciation (*n.*), renonciation (*f.*); abdication (*f.*); abandon (*m.*); abandonnement (*m.*):
renunciation of rights, renonciation, abdication, de droits.
reopen (*v.t.*), rouvrir:
to reopen an account, rouvrir un compte.
reopening (*n.*), réouverture (*f.*):
reopening of the books, of a market, réouverture des livres, d'un marché.
reorganization (*n.*), réorganisation (*f.*):
reorganization of the staff, réorganisation du personnel.
reorganize (*v.t.*), réorganiser:
to reorganize the management of a business, réorganiser l'administration d'une maison de commerce.
reorganizer (pers.) (*n.*), réorganisateur, -trice.
reorganizing (*adj.*), réorganisateur, -trice.
repack (*v.t.*), remballer.
repacking (*n.*), remballage (*m.*).
repair a damaged ship (to), réparer, radouber, un navire endommagé.
repairing port, port de réparation (*ou* de réparations) (*m.*).
reparation (*n.*), réparation (*f.*):
German reparations, réparations allemandes.
reparation loan, emprunt de réparation (*m.*).
repatriate (*v.t.*), rapatrier:
it is said that the Paris market has repatriated very large amounts of French loans contracted in the United States during the war, on dit que la place de Paris a rapatrié des montants très importants d'emprunts français contractés aux États-Unis pendant la guerre.
repatriation (*n.*), rapatriement (*m.*).
repawn (*v.t.*), rengager.
repawning (*n.*), rengagement (*m.*).
repay (to pay back something) (*v.t.*), rembourser; rendre:
to repay a loan, rembourser, rendre, un prêt.

to repay the capital, rembourser le capital.
repay (to pay back something to) (*v.t.*), rembourser:
to repay all one's creditors, rembourser tous ses créanciers.
repay (to pay over again) (*v.t.*), repayer.
repay oneself (to), se rembourser.
repayability (*n.*), remboursabilité (*f.*); exigibilité (*f.*):
repayability of a bank note, remboursabilité d'un billet de banque.
the repayability of a debt begins on the day it becomes due, l'exigibilité d'une dette commence au jour de l'échéance.
repayable (*adj.*), remboursable; exigible:
loan repayable on demand, at fixed dates, emprunt remboursable (*ou* exigible) sur demande, à terme (*ou* à des échéances fixes) (*m.*).
bonds repayable at par by drawings, obligations remboursables au pair par voie de tirage au sort (*f.pl.*).
repayable by annual (*or* **by yearly**) **instalments,** annuitaire:
debt repayable by annual instalments, dette annuitaire (*f.*).
repayment (reimbursement; refund) (*n.*), remboursement (*m.*):
to require the repayment of a debt, exiger le remboursement d'une créance.
repayment (paying over again) (*n.*), repayement (*m.*).
repeat (*v.t.*), répéter; collationner:
to repeat the number (Teleph., etc.), répéter, collationner, le numéro.
to repeat the address in full, collationner intégralement l'adresse.
radiotelegram repeated the next day, radiotélégramme répété (*ou* collationné) le lendemain (*m.*).
to ask the telegraph office to repeat (*or* to have repeated) the mutilated word or words, prier le bureau du télégraphe de faire répéter le ou les mots mutilés.
repetition (*n.*), répétition (*f.*); collationnement (*m.*):
repetition of the telegram from office to office, collationnement, répétition, du télégramme de bureau à bureau.
repetition of words supposed to be wrong, répétition de mots supposés erronés.
replace (*v.t.*), remplacer.
replace the receiver (to) (Teleph.) (opp. to *to remove the receiver*), raccrocher le récepteur (*ou* l'écouteur) (*ou* l'appareil); raccrocher:
replace the receiver when conversation is finished, raccrochez dès que la conversation est terminée.
replaceable (*adj.*), remplaçable.
replacement (*n.*), remplacement (*m.*):
the value of replacement should be calculated according to the value that the insured interest represented at the time of the casualty, la valeur de remplacement doit être calculée d'après la valeur que représentait l'intérêt assuré au moment du sinistre.

replacing the receiver (Teleph.), raccrochage (*m.*).
repledge (*v.t.*), rengager.
repledging (*n.*), rengagement (*m.*).
reply [**replies** *pl.*] (*n.*), réponse (*f.*) :
reply to a letter, réponse à une lettre.
in reply to a shareholder, it was stated that . . ., en réponse à un actionnaire, il a été déclaré que . . .
reply (*v.i.*), répondre :
to reply to a letter, répondre à une lettre.
to reply in the affirmative, in the negative, répondre affirmativement, négativement.
reply coupon (Post), coupon-réponse (*m.*).
reply half of reply paid postcard, carte postale-réponse (*f.*).
reply paid (telegram), réponse payée.
reply paid postcard, carte postale avec réponse payée (*f.*).
reply paid telegram (Abbrev. : **RP.**), télégramme avec réponse payée (*m.*).
reply telegram, télégramme-réponse (*m.*).
report (*n.*), rapport (*m.*) ; compte rendu (*m.*) ; procès-verbal (*m.*) :
to make a report on the position of a company, faire un rapport sur la situation d'une société.
report of the directors, rapport, compte rendu, des administrateurs (*ou* du conseil d'administration).
the annual reports presented to the shareholders of a company, les comptes rendus annuels présentés aux actionnaires d'une société.
to approve the report and accounts for the year to 31st December 19—, approuver les rapports et les comptes de l'exercice au 31 décembre 19—.
report of proceedings, compte rendu.
report of stowage, rapport d'arrimage ; certificat de bon arrimage (*m.*) ; procès-verbal d'ouverture des panneaux.
report of the auditors, rapport des commissaires (*ou* des commissaires aux comptes).
report establishing the condition of the goods, procès-verbal constatant l'état de la marchandise.
report (rumour) (*n.*), bruit (*m.*) :
the reports of amalgamation with other establishments are unfounded (*or* are without foundation), les bruits de fusion avec d'autres établissements sont dénués de fondement.
it is reported that . . ., le bruit court que . . .
report (*n.*) *or* **report of the whole cargo** (Customs), déclaration de (*ou* en) gros (*f.*) ; déclaration générale (*f.*) ; déclaration sommaire (*f.*) ; feuille de gros (*f.*).
report (to relate) (*v.t.*), rendre compte de ; rapporter ; entretenir ; faire le reportage de :
to report the decisions of a committee, rendre compte des, rapporter les, décisions d'un comité.
the chairman reported current matters to the board, M. le président entretient le conseil des affaires courantes.
to report the proceedings of a shareholders' meeting, faire le reportage d'une assemblée d'actionnaires.

report (to declare) (Customs and Insce) (*v.t.*), déclarer :
to report the amount at risk on each ship, déclarer la somme en risque sur chaque navire.
to report as attaching interest (under a floating policy), déclarer en aliment ; alimenter. V. exemples sous syn. **declare.**
report (*v.i.*), faire un rapport :
to report on the accounts, faire un rapport sur les comptes.
reporter (journalist) (pers.) (*n.*), reporter (*m.*).
reporter's note book, bloc-sténo (*m.*).
reporting (Journalism) (*n.*), reportage (*m.*).
represent (to present anew) (*v.t.*), représenter :
to represent a bill for acceptance, a cheque for payment, représenter un effet à l'acceptation, un chèque au paiement.
represent (to personate) (*v.t.*), représenter :
to represent a firm, a shareholder, the parties before the courts, représenter une maison de commerce, un actionnaire, les parties devant les cours.
to be represented, se faire représenter :
the shareholders have the right to be represented at all meetings by proxies, les actionnaires ont le droit de se faire représenter par des mandataires dans toutes les assemblées (*m.pl.*).
representation (*n.*), représentation (*f.*).
representative (pers.) (*n.*), représentant (*m.*) :
marine insurance companies usually appoint agents or representatives in the principal ports, les sociétés d'assurances maritimes nomment en général des agents ou des représentants dans les ports principaux (*f.pl.*).
the master is the owner's representative. Is he the shippers' representative ? le capitaine est le représentant de l'armateur. Est-il le représentant des chargeurs?
Cf. **duly authorized representative.**
representative money (opp. to *real*, or *effective*, *money*), monnaie scripturale (*f.*).
reprisal (*n.*), représaille (*f.*).
repurchasable (*adj.*), rachetable :
article repurchasable by the seller, objet rachetable par le vendeur (*m.*).
repurchase (*n.*), rachat (*m.*) ; réméré (*m.*) :
sale with option of repurchase, vente avec faculté de rachat (*f.*) ; vente à réméré (*f.*).
repurchase (on default) (Produce Exch.) (*n.*), rachat (*m.*).
repurchase (*v.t.*), racheter.
repurchase (on default) (Produce Exch.) (*v.t.*) (opp. to *resell*), racheter :
to repurchase goods, racheter des marchandises.
repurchaser (pers.) (*n.*), racheteur, -euse.
reputation (*n.*), réputation (*f.*) :
personal credit is based on the reputation of the trader, le crédit personnel est basé sur la réputation du commerçant.
request (*n.*), demande (*f.*) ; prière (*f.*) :
request for information, demande de renseignements.

request for cheques (Banking), demande de chèques.

request (to be in), être recherché, -e :
X. shares were in request at 2s., l'action X. est recherchée à 2sh.

request (*v.t.*), demander ; prier.

requests book, registre de réclamations (*m.*).

require (*v.t.*), exiger :
to require the repayment of a debt, exiger le remboursement d'une créance.
as required, as and when required. V. sous **as.**

requirement (*n.*), besoin (*m.*) ; exigence (*f.*) :
the market's requirements of money, les besoins en capitaux du marché.
to comply with the underwriters' requirements, se conformer aux exigences des assureurs.

requisite (*n.*), article (*m.*) ; fourniture (*f.*) :
travel requisites, articles de voyage.
office requisites, fournitures de bureau.

requisition (*n.*), réquisition (*f.*).

requisition (*v.t.*), réquisitionner :
in case of war, merchant ships can be requisitioned by the Government, en cas de guerre, les navires de commerce peuvent être réquisitionnés par l'État.

requisition form (for money order), formule de mandat (*f.*).

reregister (*v.t.*), réenregistrer.

reregistration (*n.*), réenregistrement (*m.*).

resalable (*adj.*), revendable.

resale (*n.*), revente (*f.*) :
resale of a business, revente d'un fonds de commerce.

resale (on default) (Produce Exch.) (*n.*), revente (*f.*).

rescind a contract (to), annuler, résoudre, résilier, un contrat.

rescindable (*adj.*), annulable ; résoluble.

rescission (*n.*), annulation (*f.*) ; résolution (*f.*) ; résiliation (*f.*) ; résiliement (*m.*) ; résiliment (*m.*).

rescission loan, emprunt de rescision (*m.*).

rescue (*n.*), secours (*m.*) :
bank which comes to the rescue of the market, banque qui vient au secours du marché (*f.*).

rescue (*v.t.*), secourir.

reseal (*v.t.*), recacheter.

resell (*v.t.*), revendre :
to resell a thing at a higher price than it cost, the same article several times, revendre une chose plus cher qu'elle n'a coûté, plusieurs fois le même objet.
to resell at a profit, revendre avec bénéfice.
mere intermediaries (*or* middlemen) who buy to resell, simples intermédiaires qui achetent pour revendre (*m.pl.*).

resell (on default) (Produce Exch.) (*v.t.*) (opp. to *repurchase*), revendre :
to resell goods, revendre des marchandises.

reseller (pers.) (*n.*), revendeur, -euse.

reservation *or* **reserve** (*n.*), réservation (*f.*) ; réserve (*f.*) :
reservation of a right, réservation d'un droit.
the reservations (*or* the reserves) stipulated

in a contract, les réserves stipulées dans un contrat.

bill of lading bearing the reservation weight unknown, connaissement portant la réserve poids inconnu (*m.*).

in reserve, en réserve :
to put an amount in reserve, mettre une somme en réserve.

under reserve *or* **under usual reserves** (Banking), sous les réserves d'usage ; sauf bonne fin ; sauf encaissement :
the amount of the cheque is passed to your credit under reserve (*or* under usual reserves), le montant du chèque est porté à votre crédit sous les réserves d'usage (*ou* à votre crédit sauf bonne fin *ou* sauf encaissement).

reservation (of seats) (Rly., etc.) (*n.*), location (de places) (*f.*).

reservation fee (for seats), taxe de location (*f.*).

reserve (Fin. and Bkkpg.) (*n.*), réserve (*f.*) ; provision (*f.*) ; prévision (*f.*) ; amortissement (*m.*) :
gold reserve (Banking), réserve d'or.
bank reserve, réserve de la banque.
reserve for doubtful debts, for depreciation of plant, provision (*ou* prévision) pour créances douteuses, pour dépréciation de matériel ; amortissement des créances douteuses, de matériel.
reserve for equalization of dividend, for contingencies, réserve pour régularisation de dividende, pour éventualités.
reserve for premiums paid in advance (Insce), réserve des primes.
reserve for taxation, provision pour impôts.
Note :—Properly, in French, *provision* is a temporary reserve, a necessary provision against what is practically sure to happen in the ordinary course of events, such as a reserve for bad debts or taxation, while *réserve* is a more or less permanent reserve, an amount put by out of earnings, such as the *réserve légale*, a bank reserve, or the like.

reserve (to set aside) (*v.t.*), réserver :
to reserve some money for unforeseen contingencies, réserver quelque argent pour les cas imprévus.
to reserve a part of the profits, a margin for contingencies, réserver une partie des bénéfices, une marge pour les éventualités.

reserve (to arrange for beforehand) (*v.t.*), réserver ; retenir ; louer :
to reserve a seat in advance in a train, réserver, retenir, louer, une place à l'avance dans un train.

reserve (*v.i.*) *or* **reserve to oneself (to)**, se réserver :
insurer who reserves the right to cancel (*or* reserves to himself the option of cancelling) the policy in certain cases, assureur qui se réserve la faculté de résilier la police en certains cas (*m.*).
the company reserves the right to check the weight of any package forming part of the

shipment, la compagnie se réserve le droit de vérifier le poids de tout colis faisant partie du chargement.

reserve account, compte de réserve (m.); compte de prévision (m.).

reserve fund, fonds de réserve (m.); fonds de prévision (m.).

reserve price (Auction), mise à prix (f.).

reserved seat ticket (Rly.), ticket (ou billet) garde-place (m.); ticket (ou billet) de location de place (m.).

reship (v.t.), rembarquer; réembarquer; réexpédier; recharger:
to reship a cargo, rembarquer une cargaison.
goods reshipped beyond the point of destination shown on the bill of lading, marchandises réexpédiées au delà du point de destination indiqué au connaissement (f.pl.).

reshipment or **reshipping** (n.), rembarquement (m.); réembarquement (m.); réexpédition (f.); rechargement (m.):
reshipment of (or reshipping) raw materials from our warehouses to foreign places of consumption, réexpédition des matières premières de nos entrepôts sur les places étrangères de consommation.

residence (n.), résidence (f.); domicile (m.):
delivery at residence or at railway station to be called for, livraison à domicile ou en gare (f.).

resign (v.t.), se démettre de; résigner:
to resign one's position, se démettre de, résigner, son emploi.

resign (v.i.), démissionner:
the cabinet has resigned, le cabinet a démissionné.

resignation (n.), démission (f.); résignation (f.):
I ask you to accept my resignation, for reasons of health, as director of the company, je vous prie d'accepter ma démission, pour raison de santé, d'administrateur de la société.

resigned (adj.) or **to have resigned,** démissionnaire:
director deemed to have resigned, administrateur réputé démissionnaire (m.).

resigner or **resignor** (pers.) (n.), démissionnaire (m. ou f.).

resolution (n.), résolution (f.); délibération (f.); décision (f.); proposition (f.):
after the discussion, the chairman put the resolutions to the meeting, après la discussion, M. le président met aux voix les résolutions (ou les propositions).
there being no further questions, the resolutions were passed unanimously (report of proceedings), personne ne demandant plus la parole, les résolutions sont adoptées à l'unanimité.
the resolutions passed at the general meeting, les résolutions (ou les délibérations) (ou les décisions) prises par l'assemblée générale.
to vote on a resolution, voter sur une proposition.

resolve (v.t.) or **resolve on** (to), résoudre; statuer sur; décider; prendre la résolution:

a loan of so much was resolved on, un emprunt de tant fut résolu.
to call a general meeting to resolve to wind up the company, convoquer l'assemblée générale pour statuer sur la liquidation de la société.
it was resolved at the extraordinary general meeting to increase the company's capital by an amount of £0 by the creation of 0 shares of £1 each, l'assemblée générale extraordinaire a décidé d'augmenter le capital social d'une somme de 0 livres par la création de 0 actions de 1 livre chacune (f.).
after consideration, It was resolved that or after consideration, Resolved that (board minutes), après en avoir délibéré (ou après délibération) le conseil prend (ou a pris) la résolution suivante.

resource (n.), ressource (f.):
agriculture is the chief French economic resource, l'agriculture est la principale ressource économique française (f.).

respect (v.t.), respecter; observer:
to respect a clause in a contract, respecter, observer, une clause dans un contrat.

respondentia (Mar. Law) (n.), grosse sur facultés (f.); grosse aventure sur facultés (f.). Cf. **bottomry.**

respondentia bond, contrat à la grosse sur facultés (m.).

respondentia loan, prêt à la grosse sur facultés (m.).

responsibility [**responsibilities** pl.] (n.), responsabilité (f.).

responsible (adj.), responsable; solidaire:
the shipowner is responsible for his faults and those of his servants, l'armateur est responsable de ses fautes et de celles de ses préposés (m.).
the owner is responsible for the master and the crew; the master is responsible for the goods entrusted to his care, le propriétaire est responsable du capitaine et de l'équipage; le capitaine est responsable des marchandises dont il se charge.
ship not responsible for marks, for breakages (bill of lading clause), sans garantie des marques, de la casse.
the husband is responsible for the acts of his wife, le mari est solidaire des actes de sa femme.

rest (making up; closing) (n.), arrêté (m.):
the date of the rest of the current account, la date de l'arrêté du compte courant.
half yearly rests, arrêtés semestriels.

restaurant car (Rly.), wagon-restaurant (m.).

restoration (n.), restauration (f.); restitution (f.):
restoration of the public finances, restauration des finances publiques.

restore (v.t.), restaurer; restituer:
the lessee is bound to restore the leased property at the end of the lease, le preneur est tenu de restituer la chose louée à la fin du bail.

restow (*v.t.*), réarrimer :
  to restow the cargo in the hold of a ship, réarrimer la cargaison dans la cale d'un navire.
restowing (*n.*), réarrimage (*m.*).
restraint (Mar. Law) (*n.*), contrainte (*f.*) ; obstacle (*m.*) :
  restraints of princes, of rulers, contraintes, obstacles, de princes, de gouvernants.
restrict (*v.t.*), restreindre ; régler :
  to restrict one's expenses, restreindre, régler, ses dépenses.
  dealings very restricted, transactions très restreintes (*f.pl.*).
restriction (*n.*), restriction (*f.*) :
  restriction of production (*or* of output), of credits, restriction de la production, des crédits.
  restrictions on importation, on exportation, restrictions d'entrée (*ou* à l'entrée), de sortie (*ou* à la sortie).
  quarantine restrictions, restrictions de quarantaine.
restrictive (*adj.*), restrictif, -ive :
  restrictive clause, clause restrictive (*f.*).
result (*n.*), résultat (*m.*) :
  result of a deal, résultat d'une opération.
result (that which one obtains on allotment of a subscription) (*n.*), résultat (*m.*) :
  to buy on the stock exchange the result of an application for so many shares, acheter en bourse le résultat d'une souscription de tant d'actions.
resume (*v.t.*), reprendre.
resume possession (to) (Law), reprendre :
  the landlord has the right to refuse to renew the lease if he resumes possession of the premises, either for his own use, or to rebuild the property, le propriétaire a le droit de refuser de renouveler le bail s'il reprend les locaux, soit pour lui, soit pour reconstruire l'immeuble.
résumé (recapitulation) (*n.*), résumé (*m.*).
resumption (*n.*), reprise (*f.*) :
  resumption of business, of dividends, reprise des affaires, des dividendes.
resumption of possession (Law), reprise (*f.*) :
  right of resumption of possession by the landlord, droit de reprise par le propriétaire (*m.*).
resurvey (*n.*), contre-visite (*f.*) ; contre-expertise (*f.*).
retail (*n.*) *or* **retail trade**, détail (*m.*) ; commerce de détail (*m.*) ; petit commerce (*m.*) :
  to do a retail trade, faire le détail.
  V. note sous **wholesale**.
retail (*v.t.*), détailler.
retail dealer *or* **retail trader** *or* **retailer** (pers.) (*n.*), marchand au détail (*m.*) ; marchand détaillant (*m.*) ; détaillant, -e.
retail price, prix de détail (*m.*).
retail sale, vente en détail (*f.*).
retain (*v.t.*), retenir ; arrêter :
  to retain someone's services, retenir, arrêter, les services de quelqu'un.
  to retain so much out of the pay of an

employee, retenir tant sur la paye d'un employé.
retard (*v.t.*), retarder.
retelegraph (*v.t.*), retélégraphier.
retention (*n.*), retenue (*f.*).
retiral *or* **retirement** (of a bill) (*n.*), retrait (*m.*) ; remboursement (*m.*).
retiral *or* **retirement** (of documents) (*n.*), levée (*f.*).
retiral *or* **retirement** (of a director, of an auditor) (*n.*), sortie (*f.*).
retire (*v.t.*), retirer ; rembourser ; lever :
  to retire coins from circulation, retirer des pièces de la circulation.
  to retire a bill, retirer, rembourser, un effet.
  to retire documents, lever des documents.
retire (to quit one's profession) (*v.i.*), se retirer :
  to retire from business, from an association, se retirer des affaires, d'une association.
  to be retired from business, être retiré (-e) des affaires.
retire (to withdraw from office) (*v.i.*), sortir :
  to retire from the service, sortir du service.
  to retire in rotation, sortir à tour de rôle.
  the directors who have to retire this year are Messrs A. and B., les administrateurs qui doivent sortir cette année sont MM. A. et B.
retiring allowance, retraite (*f.*) ; pension (*f.*) ; pension de retraite (*f.*).
retiring director, administrateur sortant (*m.*).
retour sans frais. V. sous **sans frais**.
retransfer (*v.t.*), retransférer.
retransmission (Radioteleg., etc.) (*n.*), retransmission (*f.*).
retrench (*v.i.*), se restreindre.
retrieve one's losses (to), se récupérer de ses pertes.
return (sending or coming back) (*n.*), renvoi (*m.*) ; retour (*m.*) :
  return of goods, of an accepted bill, of a dishonoured bill, renvoi, retour, de marchandises, d'un effet accepté, d'un effet impayé.
  return of private owner's wagons after unloading, renvoi des wagons de particulier après déchargement.
  to reply by return of post, répondre par retour (*ou* par le retour) du courrier.
return (article returned by the buyer to the seller) (*n.*), rendu (*m.*) ; retour (*m.*) :
  returns inwards *or* sales returns, rendus sur ventes ; rendus sous ventes ; retours sur ventes.
  returns outwards *or* purchase returns, rendus sur achats ; rendus sous achats ; retours sur achats.
returns book, livre des rendus (*m.*) ; journal des rendus (*m.*) ; journal de retours (*m.*) :
  returns inwards book, livre (*ou* journal) des rendus sur ventes (*m.*) ; livre (*ou* journal) des rendus par les clients (*m.*).
  returns outwards book, livre (*ou* journal) des rendus sur achats (*m.*) ; livre (*ou* journal) des rendus aux fournisseurs (*m.*).
return (repayment ; refund ; restitution) (*n.*),

remboursement (*m.*); ristourne (*f.*); ristorne (*f.*); restitution (*f.*):
return of capital, of an amount overpaid, remboursement, ristourne, de capital, d'une somme payée en trop.
return of premium (Insce), ristourne de prime.
return on allotment, remboursement après attribution.
if the bill is claimed back, the bank makes no return of the discount charges which it has drawn, si l'effet est réclamé, la banque ne fait pas de ristourne des agios qu'elle a prélevés.
return of taxes unduly collected, restitution de taxes indûment perçues.
return of charges *or* **return of duties,** détaxe (*f.*):
the claim for return of charges should be sent to the post office, la réclamation de détaxe doit être adressée au bureau de poste.
Cf. example *sous* **to return the charges** (*or* **duties**) **on.**
return (that which accrues or is received; receipt) (*n.*) (*often in* *pl.*), rentrée (*f.*); recette (*f.*):
the daily returns, les rentrées (*ou* les recettes) journalières.
return (*n.*) *or* **returns** (*n.pl.*) (statement; set of statistics), état (*m.*); exposé (*m.*); relevé (*m.*); relèvement (*m.*); situation (*f.*); déclaration (*f.*); statistique (*f.*); statistiques (*f.pl.*):
return of expenses, état de dépenses (*ou* de frais).
traffic returns, relevés de trafic.
bank return, situation de la banque.
the return to be made to the registrar, la déclaration à faire au greffier.
to make a return of one's profits, of one's total income, faire la déclaration de ses bénéfices, de son revenu global.
the taxpayer must send in to the inspector of taxes a return of his net profit, le contribuable doit remettre au contrôleur des contributions directes une déclaration de son bénéfice net.
return of income *or* income tax return, déclaration de revenu:
item which ought to be included in the return of income (*or* in the income tax return) for the year, article qui doit être compris dans la déclaration des revenus de l'année (*m.*).
the weekly returns give the total stocks at 0,000 tons, les statistiques hebdomadaires donnent (*ou* la statistique hebdomadaire donne) le total des stocks à 0 000 tonnes.
return (remuneration; yield) (*n.*), rémunération (*f.*); rapport (*m.*); rendement (*m.*):
return on a capital, rémunération, rapport, rendement, d'un capital.
payment for services and return on capital, la rémunération du travail et la rémunération du capital. *Cf.* to make a return on, *sous* **make.**

installation yielding a profitable return, installation d'un rapport fructueux (*f.*).
return (to send back; to restore) (*v.t.*), retourner; renvoyer; rendre; rembourser; ristourner; ristorner; restituer:
to return goods, a parcel to the sender, renvoyer, retourner, des marchandises, un colis à l'expéditeur.
wagons returned empty, wagons renvoyés (*ou* retournés) (*ou* rendus) vides (*m.pl.*).
to return a bill dishonoured, retourner un effet; retourner un effet impayé.
to return a loan, rendre un prêt.
to return the capital, rembourser, ristourner, le capital.
to return the excess, ristourner l'excédent.
shipowner who is bound to return the freight advanced to him, armateur qui est tenu de restituer le fret qui lui aura été avancé (*m.*).
retd (*abbrev.*), returned.
to return the charges (*or* **duties**) **on,** détaxer:
the customs return the duties on commodities intended for export, la douane détaxe les denrées destinées à l'exportation.
return (to report officially) (*v.t.*), déclarer:
transfer which must be registered, or returned to the registry office, cession qui doit être enregistrée, ou déclarée au bureau de l'enregistrement (*f.*).
the figure to return (*or* to be returned) for each employee (Income Tax), le chiffre à déclarer pour chaque employé.
return freight (opp. to *outward freight*), fret de retour (*m.*).
return half (of a return ticket) (opp. to *outward half*), coupon de retour (*m.*).
return journey *or* **return trip** *or* **return passage** *or* **return voyage** *or simply* **return** (*n.*) (opp. to *outward journey*, or *trip*, or *passage*, or *voyage*), trajet de retour (*m.*); retour (*m.*).
return ticket *or simply* **return** (*n.*) (opp. to *single ticket* or simply *single*), billet aller et retour (*m.*); billet d'aller et retour (*m.*); billet de retour (*m.*); retour (*m.*).
returnable (*adj.*), restituable; ristournable; à rendre; remboursable:
returnable tax, taxe restituable (*f.*).
premium returnable to the insured, prime ristournable à l'assuré (*f.*).
casks returnable, fûts à rendre (*m.pl.*).
returned empty, vide en retour (*m.*):
returned empty milk churns, pots à lait vides en retour (*m.pl.*).
returned goods (free readmission) (Customs), marchandises de retour (*f.pl.*).
returned letter (Post), lettre renvoyée (*f.*).
returned letter office (Post), bureau des rebuts (*m.*); bureau du rebut (*m.*); rebut (*m.*).
returns book. V. *sous* **return** (*n.*).
revalorization (*n.*), revalorisation (*f.*):
revalorization of the paper franc, revalorisation du franc-papier.
Note :—The French franc having been revalorized at 124·21 (more exactly, 124·2134) to the £1 sterling, viz., at about one fifth of

its former value, it follows that very large, indeed enormous, sets of figures are constantly met with. Share values of, for instance, 5,000 francs are common; 10,000, 20,000, and even 40,000, occur, and founders' shares may reach a very much higher figure. Profits of companies often run into millions, and of large companies into tens of millions of francs (a million francs is roughly £8,000). Capitals of large concerns run into thousands of millions. A thousand millions (called a *milliard* in French) is about £8,000,000.

revaluation (*n.*), réévaluation (*f.*); réappréciation (*f.*).

revalue (*v.t.*), réévaluer; réapprécier:
to revalue the premises, réévaluer les immeubles.

revenue (*n.*) (Abbrev.: **rev.**), revenu (*m.*); revenus (*m.pl.*); recettes (*f.pl.*); rente (*f.*); rapport (*m.*):
government revenue *or* public revenue, revenus de l'État; revenus publics.
revenue derived from taxes *or* inland revenue *or* internal revenue, recettes provenant d'impôts; recettes fiscales.

Revenue (*n.*) *or* **Revenue authorities,** fisc (*m.*); agents du fisc (*m.pl.*).

revenue assets (opp. to *capital,* or *fixed,* or *permanent, assets*), valeurs d'échange (*f.pl.*); valeurs de roulement (*f.pl.*); capitaux mobiles (*m.pl.*); capitaux mobiliers (*m.pl.*); capitaux circulants (*m.pl.*); capitaux roulants (*m.pl.*); capitaux flottants (*m.pl.*).

revenue duty (opp. to *protective duty*), droit fiscal (*m.*).

revenue-earning (*adj.*), de rapport; en rapport:
revenue-earning house, maison de rapport (*f.*).
revenue-earning capital, capitaux en rapport (*m.pl.*).

revenue receipts (inland revenue receipts), rentrées fiscales (*f.pl.*).

revenue stamp, timbre fiscal (*m.*).

reversal *or* **reversing** (Bkkpg) (*n.*), contre-passement (*m.*); contre-passation (*f.*); annulation (*f.*); extourne (*f.*).

reverse (Bkkpg) (*v.t.*), contre-passer; annuler; extourner:
to reverse a suspense entry, contre-passer, annuler, extourner, une écriture d'ordre.
the credit is only provisional and can be reversed in case of non payment, le crédit n'est que provisoire et peut être contre-passé au cas de non paiement.

reverse entry *or* **reversing entry** (Bkkpg), article inverse (*m.*); écriture inverse (*f.*); article (*ou* écriture) de contre-passement.

reversible days, jours réversibles (*m.pl.*):
reversible days for loading and discharging, jours réversibles pour l'embarquement et le débarquement.

reversion (*n.*), réversion (*f.*):
to regain possession of a property by reversion, rentrer dans un bien par réversion.

reversionary annuity, rente viagère avec réversion (*f.*); annuité réversible (*f.*).

revictual (*v.t.*), ravitailler.

revictualling (*n.*), ravitaillement (*m.*).

revise (*v.t.*), reviser; réviser:
to revise a tariff, reviser un tarif.

revival (*n.*), reprise (*f.*); relèvement (*m.*):
revival of business, reprise, relèvement, des affaires.

revocable (*adj.*), révocable:
revocable procuration, procuration révocable (*f.*).

revocation (*n.*), révocation (*f.*):
revocation of a will, révocation d'un testament.

revoke (*v.t.*), révoquer:
to revoke a grant, révoquer une donation.

revolving chair, chaise tournante (*f.*).

revolving credit, crédit par acceptation renouvelable (*m.*).

rewarehouse (*v.t.*), réentreposer.

rewarehousing (*n.*), réentreposage (*m.*).

Rhodesian shares *or* **Rhodesians** (*n.pl.*), valeurs rhodésiennes (*f.pl.*); rhodésiennes (*f.pl.*).

ribbon *or* **riband** (*n.*), ruban (*m.*):
typewriting ribbon (*or* riband), ruban pour machines à écrire.

rich (*adj.*), riche:
a rich landlord, un riche propriétaire.
a country rich in forests, un pays riche en forêts.

rich person *or* **rich man,** riche (*m.*); richard (*m.*).

rich woman, richarde (*f.*).

the rich *or* **rich people,** les riches (*m.pl.*):
English banks only lend to rich people, les banques anglaises ne prêtent qu'aux riches (*f.pl.*).

riches (*n.pl.*), richesse (*f.*); richesses (*f.pl.*):
to amass immense riches, amasser d'immenses richesses.

richly (*adv.*), richement.

rid one's property of debt (to), purger son bien de dettes.

rider (to a manuscript or other document) (*n.*), ajouté (*m.*).

rider (to a bill of exchange) (*n.*), allonge (*f.*).

rigging the market (Stock Exch.), agiotage (*m.*); agio (*m.*); tripotage de bourse (*m.*).

right (claim or title) (*n.*), droit (*m.*); faculté (*f.*); privilège (*m.*):
liberty never loses her rights, la liberté ne perd jamais ses droits.
civil rights, droits civils.
rights of creditors, droits des créanciers.
right of admission, droit d'entrée. V. exemple sous **membership.**
right of disposing of one's property, of issuing bank notes, droit, faculté, privilège, de disposer de ses biens, d'émission de billets de banque.
right of voting *or* voting right *or* right to vote, droit de vote.
right to a lease, droit à un bail.
right of application *or* application rights *or* simply right *or* rights, droit (*ou* droits) de souscription; privilège de souscription; droit; droits:
application rights are exercised: (1) by the

holders of old shares; (2) by the persons who, not possessing old shares, buy rights, le droit de souscription s'exerce: 1° par les porteurs d'actions anciennes; 2° par les personnes qui, ne possédant pas d'actions anciennes, achètent des droits.

to apply for shares as of right. V. sous **apply**.

ex rights. V. sous **ex**.

right bank (of a river), rive droite (d'un fleuve) (f.).

right hand page (*or* side) (of a book), recto (m.), page de droit (f.), côté droit (m.) (d'un livre). V. **left hand page** (*or* side) pour exemple.

right hand side of an account, côté droit d'un compte (m.).

rights market (Stock Exch.), marché des droits de souscription (m.).

ring (string) (Produce Exch.) (U.S.A.) (n.), filière (f.).

ring (v.t.), sonner:
  to ring the exchange (Teleph.), sonner le bureau.

ring out a transaction (to) (U.S.A.), liquider une affaire.

riot (n.), émeute (f.).

rioter (pers.) (n.), émeutier, -ère.

rise (n.) *or* **rise in price** *or* **rise in cost,** élévation (f.); 'hausse (f.); relèvement (m.); augmentation (f.); élévation de prix (f.); augmentation de prix (f.); enchérissement (m.); renchérissement (m.):
  rise in the bank rate, élévation, hausse, relèvement, du taux officiel de l'escompte.
  rise of wages, of postal charges, of railway rates, relèvement des salaires, des taxes postales, des tarifs de chemin de fer.
  the rise or the fall of freights, of stocks and shares, la hausse ou la baisse des frets, des titres de bourse.
  dealing for a rise (Stock Exch.), opération à la hausse (f.).
  speculator who goes for a rise, spéculateur qui est en hausse (m.).
  rise in the price of raw materials, in the price of wheat, in the cost of living, enchérissement, renchérissement, hausse, élévation du prix, augmentation du prix, des matières premières, du blé, des vivres.

rise (increase of salary) (n.), augmentation (f.).

rise (v.i.) *or* **to rise in price** *or* **to be rising** *or* **to be a rising market,** s'élever; se relever; 'hausser; monter; enchérir; renchérir; augmenter de prix; être en hausse; être à la hausse:
  the price rose to so much, le prix (*ou* le cours) s'élevait (*ou* se relevait) à tant.
  wheat is rising, le blé hausse (*ou* monte) (*ou* enchérit) (*ou* renchérit).
  oil shares are rising (*or* are a rising market), les valeurs pétrolières sont en hausse (*ou* sont à la hausse).
  to sell on a rising market and to buy on a falling market, vendre en hausse et acheter en baisse.

risk (chance; hazard; danger; peril) (n.), risque (m.); risques (m.pl.); risques et périls (m.pl.); aléa (m.); chance (f.); 'hasard (m.); aventure (f.):

why run risks, when one can operate safely? à quoi bon courir des risques (*ou* des aléas), lorsqu'on peut opérer à coup sûr?

the risks inherent in documents made to bearer, les risques inhérents aux pièces créées au porteur.

at ship's risk, aux risques du navire.

at sender's (*or* consignor's), at receiver's (*or* consignee's) risk, aux risques et périls (*ou* simplement aux risques) de l'expéditeur, du destinataire.

at the risk of the shippers, of the owners of the goods, or of the consignees, aux risques et périls des chargeurs, des propriétaires de la marchandise, ou des consignataires.

risk (chance of casualty or loss; peril or danger insured against) (Insce) (n.), risque (m.):
  the risks inseparable from a marine adventure, les risques inséparables d'une expédition maritime.
  house which is insured against the risk of fire, maison qui est assurée contre le risque d'incendie (f.).
  risk of breakage *or* breakage risk, risque de casse.
  risk of craft *or* craft risk, risque d'allèges:
  all risks of craft to and from the vessel, tous risques d'allèges pour transport immédiat de terre à bord et de bord à terre.
  risk of loss or damage by exposure to weather, risque de perte ou d'endommagement par exposition aux intempéries.
  risk of storage in craft, risque de séjour sur allèges.
  risk whilst on quays, wharves, or in sheds during the ordinary course of transit, risque de séjour à terre en cours normal d'expédition.

risk (subject of the insurance; interest; value) (n.), risque (m.); aliment (m.); intérêt (m.); valeur (f.):
  insurance, being a contract of indemnity, is valid only if there is a risk, l'assurance, étant un contrat d'indemnité, n'est valable que s'il existe un risque (f.).
  the share for which the insurer binds himself in the risk insured, la part pour laquelle l'assureur s'engage dans le risque assuré.
  each risk to form the subject of a separate policy, chaque risque (*ou* aliment) (*ou* intérêt) (*ou* valeur) fera l'objet d'une police distincte.

risk (person or thing exposed to a casualty) (n.), risque (m.):
  person who, house which, is a good risk, personne qui, maison qui, est un bon risque (f.).

risk (v.t.), risquer; aventurer; 'hasarder:
  to risk one's fortune in an enterprise, risquer, aventurer, hasarder, sa fortune dans une entreprise.

risk premium (Insce) (opp. to *gross*, *or office*, *premium*), prime nette (f.).

risks book, livre de risques (m.).

risky (adj.), risqué, -e; aléatoire; chanceux, -euse; 'hasardeux, -euse:

risky speculation, spéculation aléatoire (f.); spéculation hasardeuse (f.).

river (a large stream discharging into the sea) (n.), fleuve (m.).

river (a stream discharging into a lake, or into another stream) (n.), rivière (f.).

river and sea voyage, voyage mixte (m.).

river bill of lading, connaissement fluvial (m.).

river boat, bateau fluvial (m.); bateau de rivière (m.); bâtiment de rivière (m.).

river boats or **river and/or canal boats** (collectively), batellerie (f.).

river steamer, vapeur fluvial (m.); steamer fluvial (m.).

river transport, transport fluvial (m.).

road (highway) (n.), route (f.); voie (f.); chemin (m.).

road map, carte routière (f.).

road transport, transport routier (m.).

road vehicle, véhicule routier (m.).

roadstead (n.) or **roads** (n.pl.) or **road** (n.sing.), rade (f.):
ship which is lying in a roadstead (or which lies in the roads), navire qui séjourne (ou qui stationne) en rade (m.).

rob Peter to pay Paul (to), déshabiller saint Pierre pour habiller saint Paul.

robber (pers.) (n.), voleur, -euse.

robbery [**robberies** pl.] (n.), vol (m.):
robbery by force, vol à main armée.

roll (of papers) (n.), rouleau (de papiers) (m.).

roll (of postage stamps) (n.), roulette (de timbres-poste) (f.).

roll (said of a ship) (v.i.), rouler.

roll top desk, bureau américain (m.).

rolling (n.) (opp. to pitching), roulis (m.). V. exemple sous **shift.**

rolling stock (Rly.) (distinguished from hauling stock), matériel roulant (m.).

rolling stock and locomotive department (Rly.), service du matériel et traction (m.).

Roman numerals, chiffres romains (m.pl.).

room (on a sheet of paper) (n.), emplacement (m.):
if there is not room on the sheet to enter the necessary particulars, they can be put on the back, au cas où l'emplacement réservé sur la feuille serait insuffisant pour l'inscription des mentions nécessaires, celles-ci peuvent être reportées au verso.

rotary duplicating machine, duplicateur rotatif (m.).

rotation (succession in office) (n.), roulement (m.):
rotation determined by lot, roulement établi par le sort.

in rotation or **by rotation,** à tour de rôle:
to retire in (or by) rotation, sortir à tour de rôle.

rotation number, numéro d'ordre (m.).

rough (adj.). V. exemples:
rough book, brouillard (m.); main courante (f.); mémorial (m.); chiffrier (m.); brouillon (m.).
rough calculation, calcul grossier (ou approximatif) (m.).

rough draft (of a letter), brouillon (d'une lettre) (m.).

rough estimate of an expense, aperçu (m.), estimation approximative (f.), d'une dépense.

rough guess, approximation (f.).

rough passage or **rough crossing** (on the sea), traversée mouvementée (f.).

roughly (adv.), grossièrement; approximativement.

round (adj.), rond, -e:
in round figures or in round numbers, en chiffres ronds; en nombre rond; compte rond.
a round sum of a thousand pounds, une somme ronde de mille livres.
bank notes are only issued in round sums, called denominations, les billets de banque ne sont émis que pour des sommes rondes, dites coupures (m.pl.).
round voyage, voyage d'aller et de retour (m.); aller et retour (m.):
ship freighted for the round voyage, navire frété pour l'aller et le retour (m.).
round voyage insurance, assurance à prime liée (ou à primes liées) (f.); assurance pour l'aller et le retour (f.).
round voyage premium, prime liée (f.).

round (a course ending where it began) (n.), tournée (f.):
postman, traveller, on his round, facteur, voyageur, en tournée (m.).

Round the House or **Round the Markets** (newspaper heading), A travers les Marchés; En Bourse; Ce qui se dit en Bourse; Ce qu'on dit en Bourse.

round up (to), arrondir:
charge rounded up to the next higher penny, taxe arrondie au penny (ou au décime) supérieur (f.).

route (n.), route (f.); voie (f.); itinéraire (m.):
by any route, par n'importe quelle route.
liberty to proceed to any ports in or out of the customary route, faculté de se rendre dans tous les ports en dedans ou en dehors de la route ordinaire (f.).
the steamer X. called at Perim 31 (date) en route from London to Kobe, le steamer X. a fait escale à Périm le 31 (date), en route de Londres à Kobe.
sender who specifies the route by which his telegram is to be sent, expéditeur qui prescrit la voie que doit suivre son télégramme (m.).
shortest route, itinéraire le plus court.

route (v.t.), acheminer; router.

route instructions (telegrams), mention de voie (f.). V. exemple sous **instructions.**

route map, carte routière (f.).

routing (n.), acheminement (m.):
routing by wire (Teleg.) (Abbrev.: By Wire), acheminement par fil.
routing by wireless (Abbrev.: By Wireless), acheminement par sans fil.

rover (pers.) (n.), forban (m.).

royalty [**royalties** pl.] (n.), redevance (f.):

to grant the right of working a mine in consideration of royalties, concéder le droit d'exploitation d'une mine moyennant des redevances.

rubber (eraser) (*n.*), gomme (*f.*); gomme élastique (*f.*).

rubber group (Stock Exch.), groupe caoutchoutier (*m.*).

rubber market, marché du caoutchouc (*m.*); marché des caoutchoucs (*m.*).

rubber ring *or* **rubber band,** bande en caoutchouc (*f.*); bracelet en caoutchouc (*m.*); caoutchouc (*m.*).

rubber shares *or* **rubbers** (*n.pl.*), valeurs de caoutchouc (*f.pl.*); caoutchoucs (*m.pl.*); caoutchoutières (*f.pl.*); valeurs caoutchoutières (*f.pl.*).

rubber stamp, timbre en caoutchouc (*m.*); timbre humide (*m.*):
clauses added by hand or with a rubber stamp, clauses ajoutées à la main ou au timbre humide (*f.pl.*).

ruin (*n.*), ruine (*f.*).

ruin (*v.t.*), ruiner.

ruin oneself (to), se ruiner:
to ruin oneself in risky speculations, se ruiner en spéculations hasardeuses.

rule (*n.*), règle (*f.*):
rule of exchange, règle de change.
rule of three (Arith.), règle de trois.
stock exchange rules, règles de bourse; règles boursières.
in general, contango is the rule and backwardation the exception, en général, le report est la règle et le déport l'exception.

rule *or* **rule off** (to draw lines) (*v.t.*), régler:
to rule a page, régler une page.
to rule off an account, régler un compte.

rule (said of prices or rates) (*v.i.*), se pratiquer:
the prices which rule at the same time on the different markets, les prix qui se pratiquent simultanément sur les différents marchés (*m.pl.*).

ruling (*adj. & p.pr.*), pratiqué, -e:
the ruling price, le cours pratiqué.
the price ruling at the moment of the declaration of options, le cours pratiqué au moment de la réponse des primes.

rule off (to close; to make up) (*v.t.*), régler; arrêter:
to rule off one's accounts once a year, régler, arrêter, ses comptes une fois l'an.

rule out (*v.t.*), biffer:
to rule out in red ink the wrong amount or name of account, biffer à l'encre rouge la somme ou le nom du compte erroné.

ruler *or* **rule** (*n.*), règle (*f.*):
office ruler, règle de bureau.

ruling (*n.*), réglage (*m.*); réglure (*f.*):
ruling of a sheet of paper, réglage, réglure, d'une feuille de papier.

ruling out, biffage (*m.*); biffement (*m.*); biffure (*f.*).

rummaging (ships) (Customs) (*n.*), recherches à bord (des navires) (*f.pl.*); visite à bord (des navires) (*f.*).

rumour *or* **rumor** (*n.*), rumeur (*f.*); bruit (*m.*):
denial of unfavourable rumours, démenti de bruits (*ou* rumeurs) défavorables (*m.*).
the rumours of amalgamation with other establishments are unfounded (*or* are without foundation), les bruits de fusion avec d'autres établissements sont dénués de fondement.
it is rumoured that . . ., le bruit court que . . .

run (distance travelled over) (*n.*), parcours (*m.*):
runs of — miles and under, runs over — miles, parcours de — milles et au-dessus, parcours au delà de — milles.

run (rush) (*n.*), course (*f.*); ruée (*f.*):
a run on mining shares, une course aux, une ruée sur, les valeurs minières.
it will not be long before we shall see a run on the shares of several gold mining companies, on est à la veille d'assister à une course aux titres de plusieurs sociétés de mines d'or.

run (on a bank) (*n.*), descente (*ou* descente en masse) (sur une banque) (*f.*); course en foule aux guichets (d'une banque) (*f.*).

run (to operate) (*v.t.*), exploiter:
to run a ship at a profit, at a loss, exploiter, faire naviguer, un navire à profit, à perte.

run (to incur) (*v.t.*), courir; encourir:
to run a risk, courir, encourir, un risque.

run (to travel) (*v.i.*), marcher; parcourir; circuler:
to run at — miles an hour (said of a train, etc.), marcher à, parcourir, — milles à l'heure.
train which does not run on Sunday, train qui ne circule pas le dimanche (*m.*).

run (to continue in existence) (*v.i.*), courir:
the bill has so many days to run, l'effet a tant de jours à courir (*m.*).

run (to accrue; to attach) (*v.i.*), courir; prendre cours:
interest which runs from 1st March, intérêts qui courent depuis le 1ᵉʳ mars (*m.pl.*).
policy which is deemed to run from a certain date, police qui est censée courir d'une certaine date (*f.*).
the freight runs from the day the ship sailed, le fret court du jour où le navire a fait voile.
the time of delivery runs from the hour of midnight, le délai de livraison prend cours à partir de l'heure de minuit.

run after (to), courir après:
the banker is sometimes obliged to look for money, and sometimes to run after investments, le banquier est quelquefois obligé de chercher des capitaux, et quelquefois de courir après les placements.

run aground (to) *or* **run ashore (to)** (*v.t.*), échouer.

run aground (to) *or* **run ashore (to)** (*v.i.*), échouer; s'échouer.

run down (to speak disparagingly of) (*v.t.*), dénigrer:
to run down the goods of a competitor, dénigrer les produits d'un concurrent.

run down another ship (to), couler, aborder et couler, un autre navire.

run foul of (to) *or* **run into (to)**, aborder; faire collision avec; rencontrer.

run foul of each other (to) *or* **run into each other (to)**, s'aborder; se rencontrer.

run into debt (to), faire des dettes; s'endetter.

run on a bank (to), descendre (*ou* descendre en masse) sur une banque; accourir en foule aux guichets d'une banque.

run short (to) *or* **run out (to)**, être court, -e; être à court:
to run short (*or* to run out) of money, être court (*ou* être à court) d'argent.

run stock (to) (against one's client), faire la contre-partie:
outside broker who holds himself out falsely to his clients as intermediary for the execution of their stock exchange orders, in respect of which he runs the stock, banquier marron qui se présente faussement à ses clients comme intermédiaire pour l'exécution de leurs ordres de bourse, dont il fait la contre-partie (*m.*).

to run stock against each other, se faire la contre-partie:
in contangoing buyers and sellers run stock against each other (*or* speculate against each other) in most of the dealings engaged in, dans le report acheteurs et vendeurs se font la contre-partie pour le plus grand nombre de transactions engagées.

run up a stock (to) (Stock Exch.), 'hisser une valeur.

runner (of stock against his client) (pers.) (*n.*), contre-partiste (*m.*):
the runner is one who operates himself against his principal: should the client wish to sell a security, the runner buys, and vice versa, le contre-partiste est celui qui opère lui-même contre son donneur d'ordre: le client

veut-il vendre une valeur quelconque, le contre-partiste achète, et réciproquement.

runner (canvasser) (pers.) (*n.*), démarcheur (*m.*).

running (*n.*), marche (*f.*); circulation (*f.*); exploitation (*f.*):
running of trains, marche, circulation, des trains.
coal for running the engine, charbon destiné à la marche de la machine (*m.*).
running a patent, exploitation d'un brevet.

running (canvassing) (*n.*), démarchage (*m.*).

running account, compte courant (*m.*).

running aground *or* **running ashore,** échouement (*m.*).

running day (Abbrev.: **r.d.**), jour courant (*m.*).

running down (decrying), dénigrement (*m.*).

running down clause (Abbrev.: **R.D.C.**), clause d'abordage (*f.*); clause collision (*f.*).

running down risk, risque d'abordage (*m.*); risque de collision (*m.*).

running foul *or* **running into,** abordage (*m.*); collision (*f.*).

running landing numbers (series), numéros d'ordre de débarquement (*m.pl.*).

running number, numéro d'ordre (*m.*):
when the use of several sheets is necessary, give a running number to each of them, lorsque l'emploi de plusieurs feuilles est nécessaire, donner un numéro d'ordre à chacune d'elles.

running stock (against one's client), contre-partie (*f.*).

rupture (*n.*), rupture (*f.*):
rupture of diplomatic relations, rupture de relations diplomatiques.

rural (*adj.*), rural, -e, -aux:
rural postman, facteur rural (*m.*).

rush (*n.*), ruée (*f.*):
a rush on mining shares, une ruée sur les valeurs minières.

S

S.O.S. (signal), S.O.S. (*m.*):
to send out an S.O.S., lancer un S.O.S.

sack (*n.*) (Abbrev.: **sk** [**sks** *pl.*]), sac (*m.*).

sack (to dismiss from employment) (*Slang*) (*v.t.*), congédier; renvoyer; remercier:
to sack an employee, congédier, renvoyer, remercier, un employé.
to sack all the staff *or* to sack the lot, congédier tout le personnel; faire place nette.

sacrifice (General Average) (*n.*), sacrifice (*m.*):
voluntary sacrifice made for the common safety of the ship and cargo, sacrifice volontaire fait pour le salut commun du navire et du chargement.

sacrifice (selling at a loss) (*n.*), sacrifice (*m.*); mévente (*f.*).

sacrifice (General Average) (*v.t.*), sacrifier:
to sacrifice a part or the whole of the cargo to save the ship, sacrifier une partie ou la

totalité de la cargaison pour sauver le navire.

sacrifice (to sell at a loss; to slaughter) (*v.t.*), sacrifier; mévendre:
to sacrifice one's stocks, sacrifier, mévendre, ses titres.

safe (strong box) (*n.*), coffre-fort (*m.*); coffre (*m.*).

safe and sound, sain et sauf. V. exemple sous **sound.**

safe arrival (of a ship at destination), bonne (*ou* heureuse) arrivée (d'un navire à destination) (*f.*).

safe-conduct (*n.*), sauf-conduit (*m.*).

safe custody (Banking), garde (*f.*); garde en dépôt (*f.*); dépôt en garde (*m.*); dépôt libre (*m.*); dépôt (*m.*):
the safe custody of securities, la garde (*ou* la garde en dépôt) des titres.

to place securities in safe custody, déposer
des titres en garde; placer des titres en
dépôt libre; mettre des titres en dépôt.

Note :—Unlike the English banks, which keep
their customers' securities in safe custody
gratuitously, the French and Belgian banks
make a charge for this service, called **droit
de garde,** calculated at a rate of so much
on the value of the securities deposited.
If the securities are lodged open or unsealed, it is called a **dépôt à découvert;** if
in a sealed packet, a **dépôt cacheté,** in which
case the charge is calculated on the declared
value.

safe deposit, dépôt en coffre-fort (*m.*).

Note :—In England, safe deposit, i.e., keeping
of securities, money, or other valuables, in
individual strong room compartments, is
undertaken by companies called **safe deposit
companies** (there are 5 in London).

In France, this service (*service de coffres-
forts*) is run by the big banks (*établissements
de crédit*), who have a right of inspection
(not so in England) of what is to be lodged in
the safes. In France, persons or companies
hiring out safes are legally bound (there is
a special law on safe hiring [*location de
coffres-forts*]) to keep an alphabetical index
(*répertoire alphabétique*) of their customers'
names and addresses, and also a register
containing the date and time of each visit
to the safe, together with the signature of
the visiting person. These books are open
to inspection of government officials. If the
visiting person is not the actual hirer but
only a duly authorized representative (*fondé
de pouvoirs*), he has to sign a declaration
that to the best of his knowledge and belief
the hirer and other persons, if any, having
rights to the contents of the safe, are still
alive. On the death of the hirer, the safe
can only be opened in the presence of a duly
appointed *notaire,* charged with making an
inventory of the contents. Any person
having knowledge of the death of the hirer,
visiting the safe unauthorizedly renders
himself personally liable to the death duties
payable by the estate of the deceased hirer,
and to other penalties.

In England, safe deposits are not subject
to direct government control. Moreover,
banks will accept, free of charge, for their
customers the safe custody (q.v.) of small
locked boxes or sealed packets, but the
customer has no right of access to the strong
room; the box or packet is brought to him
in the manager's office.

safe estimate, estimation de tout repos (*f.*).

safe investment, placement sûr (*m.*); placement de tout repos (*m.*); valeur de tout
repos (*f.*); valeur à couverture de tout
repos (*f.*).

safe port, port sûr (*m.*).

dock or other safe loading place, bassin ou
autre place sûre de chargement.

safeguard (*v.t.*), sauvegarder:

to safeguard the lives of the sailors and passengers, the interests of the shareholders,
sauvegarder la vie des matelots et des
passagers, les intérêts des actionnaires.

safeguarding *or* **safeguard** (*n.*), sauvegarde (*f.*):
the safeguarding of goods exposed to the
perils of a marine adventure, la sauvegarde
de marchandises exposées aux périls d'une
expédition maritime.

safeguarding of industries, sauvegarde d'industries.

safeguarding duties, droits de sauvegarde (*m.pl.*).

safely (*adv.*) *or* **safely into port** *or* **safely into
harbour,** à bon port:

whether the ship arrives safely or is lost on the
voyage, que le navire arrive à bon port ou
se perde pendant le voyage.

to bring an unseaworthy ship safely into port
(or harbour), amener un navire innavigable
à bon port.

safety (*n.*), sûreté (*f.*); sécurité (*f.*); salut (*m.*):
the safety of one's money, la sûreté (*ou* la
sécurité) de ses fonds.

danger of a nature to imperil the safety of the
ship, of the persons on board the ship,
danger de nature à compromettre la sécurité
du navire, des personnes à bord du navire
(*m.*).

to make a jettison for the common safety,
faire un jet pour le salut commun.

safety inkpot, encrier inversable (*m.*).

sag (*v.i.*), fléchir:

after having sagged, prices rose at the end of
the week, après avoir fléchi, les cours se
sont relevés en fin de semaine.

sagging (*n.*), fléchissement (*m.*).

said to contain, que dit être.

said to contain clause, clause que dit être (*f.*).

sail (*v.t.*), faire naviguer; naviguer sur:
the right to sail the said ship under the British
flag, le droit de faire naviguer ledit navire
sous pavillon britannique.

ship fit to sail the sea, navire apte à naviguer
sur mer (*m.*).

sail (*v.i.*), naviguer; faire voile; mettre à la
voile; marcher; voyager; partir; s'embarquer:

a ship does not exist in the true sense of the
term unless she is capable of sailing on the
sea (*or* fit to sail on the sea), un navire
n'existe dans le vrai sens du terme que
s'il est apte à naviguer sur mer.

with leave to sail with or without pilots, avec
faculté de naviguer avec ou sans pilotes.

when the ship sailed, she was unseaworthy,
lorsque le navire a fait voile, il était hors
d'état de naviguer.

ship designed to sail at high speed, navire
destiné à marcher à grande vitesse (*m.*).

the time at which the ship sails, le moment
où le navire part.

(*steamer*) X. (for London) sailed (*or* s.) Mar-
seilles 31 (*date*) (Shipping News), (*steamer*)
X. parti de Marseille le 31 (*date*) pour Londres
(Mouvement des Navires).

in readiness to sail *or* **ready to sail** *or* **about to**

sail, en partance; prêt à partir; prêt à faire voile :
ship about to sail on a foreign voyage, navire en partance (*ou* prêt à partir) (*ou* prêt à faire voile) pour un voyage au long cours (*m.*).

sailing (*n.*) *or* **sail navigation,** navigation (*f.*) ; navigation à voile (*f.*).

sailing (setting forth on or prosecuting a voyage) (*n.*), départ (*m.*); partance (*f.*); marche (*f.*) :
date of sailing, date de départ (*f.*).
arrivals and sailings, arrivages (*ou* arrivées) et départs.
sailings from London every fortnight, départs de Londres tous les 14 jours.
survey on sailing, visite de partance (*f.*).
all sailings subject to change. V. sous **all.**
information on the sailing of ships across the seas, renseignements sur la marche des navires à travers les mers (*m.pl.*).

sailing from . . . and bound for . . ., venant de . . ., à destination de . . . :
ship sailing from Antwerp and bound for London, navire venant d'Anvers, à destination de Londres (*m.*).

sailing collier, bateau charbonnier à voiles (*m.*).

sailing ship *or* **sailing vessel** (Abbrev.: **s.v.** *or* **S.V.**) *or* **sailer** (*n.*), navire à voiles (*m.*); voilier (*m.*); bâtiment à voiles (*m.*); bâtiment voilier (*m.*); bateau à voiles (*m.*).

sailings list, liste de départs (*f.*); tableau de marche (*m.*).

sailor (pers.) (*n.*), marin (*m.*); matelot (*m.*); homme de mer (*m.*); gens de mer (*m.pl. only*).

salable (*adj.*). Syn. de **saleable.**

salaried (*adj.*), salarié, -e :
a salaried secretary, un secrétaire salarié.

salaried man, salaried woman, salarié, -e.

salaries list, rôle d'appointements (*m.*); feuille d'appointements (*f.*).

salary [**salaries** *pl.*] (*n.*), appointements (*m.pl.*); traitement (*m.*) :
salaries of staff, appointements du personnel.
manager who receives (*or* draws) a fixed salary, directeur qui touche un traitement fixe (*m.*).

salary tax, impôt sur les traitements (*m.*).

sale (*n.*) (Ant.: *purchase*), vente (*f.*); écoulement (*m.*) :
sale of goods, of shares, vente, écoulement, de marchandises, d'actions.
goods which will command a ready sale *or* goods which will sell well, marchandise de bonne vente (*f.*).
sale by auction, vente à l'enchère; vente aux enchères; vente à la criée; vente à l'encan.
sale by named vessel, vente par navire désigné.
sale by private treaty, vente à l'amiable; vente de gré à gré.
sale c.i.f. *or* sale on c.i.f. terms, vente caf.
sale delivered ex ship (*or* ex steamer) *or* sale on ex ship terms *or* sale on landed terms *or* sale free overside, vente au débarquement.
sale ex bond, vente à l'acquitté; vente à l'A.

sale for delivery (Stock Exch.), vente à livrer.
sale for future delivery during specified periods (Produce Exch.), vente à terme ferme.
sale for money *or* cash sale, vente au comptant; vente comptant.
sale for prompt delivery (*or* for prompt shipment), vente en expédition prompte.
sale for the settlement *or* sale for the account (Stock Exch.), vente à terme.
sale in bonded warehouse, vente en entrepôt; vente en E.; vente E.
sale of goods afloat (*or* on passage) on optional bill of lading, vente de marchandises flottantes (*ou* en cargaison flottante) (*ou* sous voile) avec faculté d'option entre plusieurs destinations.
sale on sample, vente sur échantillon.
sale on shipment *or* sale at port of shipment (opp. to *sale c.i.f.*), vente sur embarquement.
sale to arrive *or* sale subject to safe arrival, vente à l'heureuse arrivée.
sale with option of repurchase, vente à réméré.

sales (turnover) (Produce Exch.) (*n.pl.*), ventes (*f.pl.*); circulation (*f.*); mouvement (*m.*) :
sales: 000 tons, ventes (*ou* circulation) (*ou* mouvement): 000 tonnes.

for sale (to be sold), à vendre.

on sale or return *or simply* **on sale,** à condition; sous condition :
goods sent on sale or return *or* goods on sale, marchandises remises à condition (*f.pl.*); condition (*f.*).

sale (selling off, as by a shop or store, at a low price) (*n.*), liquidation (*f.*).

sale (auction) (*n.*), enchère (*f.*); enchères (*f.pl.*).

sale contract, contrat de vente (*m.*).

sale contract (Stock Exch.), bordereau de vente (*m.*).

sale invoice, facture de vente (*f.*).

sale room, salle de ventes (*f.*). Cf. commercial sale rooms.

saleable (*adj.*) *or* **sale** (*used as adj.*), vendable; de vente; marchand, -e; vénal, -e, -aux :
saleable goods, marchandises vendables (*f.pl.*); marchandises de vente (*f.pl.*).
saleable value *or* sale value, valeur marchande (*f.*); valeur vénale (*f.*).
for the international postal service, samples must not have a saleable value, pour le service postal international, les échantillons ne doivent pas avoir de valeur marchande.
the sale value of pieces of money (*or* of coins), like that of any other merchandise, depends on the law of supply and demand, la valeur marchande des pièces de monnaie, comme celle de toute autre marchandise, dépend de la loi de l'offre et de la demande.

sales account, compte de ventes (*m.*).

sales book *or* **sales day book** *or* **sales journal** (Bkkpg), livre de ventes (*m.*); livre des ventes (*m.*); livre de vente (*m.*); journal des ventes (*m.*); livre de (*ou* des) débits (*m.*); journal des débits (*m.*); facturier de sortie (*m.*).

sales ledger, grand livre des ventes (*m.*).
sales returns, rendus sur ventes (*m.pl.*); rendus sous ventes (*m.pl.*); retours sur ventes (*m.pl.*).
saloon (*n.*) *or* **saloon carriage** *or* **saloon car** (Rly.), voiture-salon (*f.*); wagon-salon (*m.*).
salvage (*n.*), sauvetage (*m.*):
salvage of wreck, sauvetage des épaves.
the purpose of salvage is, once the ship is wrecked or has stranded, to salve her along with the cargo, or whatever remains of one or the other, le sauvetage a pour objet, une fois le navire a fait naufrage ou a échoué, de le sauver ainsi que la cargaison, ou ce qui reste de l'un ou de l'autre.
salvage (*n.*) *or* **salvage charges,** indemnité de sauvetage (*f.*); prime de sauvetage (*f.*); frais de sauvetage (*m.pl.*).
salvage boat, bateau sauveteur (*m.*).
salvage bond, obligation de garantie d'indemnité de sauvetage (*f.*).
salvage services, services de sauvetage (*m.pl.*).
salvage vessel, navire sauveteur (*m.*).
salve *or* **salvage** (*v.t.*), sauver:
the value of the salved (*or* salvaged) property, la valeur des biens sauvés.
salvor *or* **salver** *or* **salvager** (pers.) (*n.*), sauveteur (*m.*).
sample (*n.*), échantillon (*m.*):
sample of value, échantillon de valeur; échantillon de prix.
samples of no commercial value *or* samples without saleable value, échantillons sans valeur marchande.
sample (*v.t.*). échantillonner:
dutiable goods can be sampled with a view to commercial transactions; the samples are subject to duty when being removed from the warehouse, les marchandises passibles de droits peuvent être échantillonnées en vue des transactions commerciales; les échantillons sont soumis aux droits lors de leur enlèvement de l'entrepôt.
sample packet (Post), envoi d'échantillons (*m.*).
sample rate (Post), tarif des échantillons (*m.*).
sampler (pers.) (*n.*), échantillonneur (*m.*).
sampling (*n.*), échantillonnage (*m.*); prélèvement d'échantillons (*m.*).
sampling order, bon à échantillonner (*m.*).
sanction (*n.*), sanction (*f.*).
sanction (*v.t.*), sanctionner; consacrer:
custom sanctioned by practice, usage sanctionné (*ou* consacré) par la pratique (*m.*).
sandwich man [**sandwich men** *pl.*] (Publicity), homme-sandwich (*m.*).
sanitary authority, autorité sanitaire (*f.*).
sans frais *or* **retour sans frais** (notice on a bill of exchange), sans frais; sans protêt; retour sans frais; sans compte de retour.
satisfactory (*adj.*), satisfaisant, -e:
satisfactory reply, réponse satisfaisante (*f.*).
satisfy (*v.t.*), satisfaire; satisfaire à; désintéresser:
to satisfy one's creditors in full, satisfaire, désintéresser, intégralement ses créanciers.

to satisfy someone's needs, satisfaire aux besoins de quelqu'un.
save (to preserve or rescue) (*v.t.*), sauver:
to save the ship from an imminent peril, sauver le navire d'un péril imminent.
the insured must do his utmost to save the property insured, l'assuré doit faire tout son possible pour sauver la chose assurée (*m.*).
ship which deviates from her course to save lives or property, navire qui s'écarte de sa route pour sauver des vies humaines ou des biens (*m.*).
save (to economize) (*v.t.*), épargner; économiser; gagner:
a penny saved is a penny earned, un sou épargné est un sou gagné.
to save labour, économiser le travail.
save (*v.i.*), faire des économies.
save as otherwise provided in the articles, sauf dispositions contraires des statuts.
saver (a thrifty person) (*n.*), épargnant, -e.
saving (preserving or rescuing) (*n.*), sauvetage (*m.*):
saving persons in case of disaster, sauvetage des personnes en cas de sinistre.
saving (economy; gain) (*n.*), épargne (*f.*); économie (*f.*); gain (*m.*):
saving of time effected by the use of the aeroplane, économie, gain, de temps procuré par l'emploi de l'avion.
saving clause, clause de sauvegarde (*f.*).
savings (*n.pl.*), épargnes (*f.pl.*); économies (*f.pl.*):
to live on one's savings, vivre de ses épargnes.
to draw on one's savings, prendre sur ses économies.
savings account, compte d'épargne (*m.*).
savings bank, caisse d'épargne (*f.*).
savings bank book, livret de caisse d'épargne (*m.*); livret nominatif (*m.*); livret (*m.*).
say (*imperative*), disons; ci:
total: say 000,000, total: disons 000 000; total: ci 000 000.
scale (graded series) (*n.*), échelle (*f.*):
sliding wage scale, échelle mobile des salaires.
scale (Tarification) (*n.*), barème (*m.*); barrême (*m.*); tarif (*m.*):
tarification represented by a scale which gives the rates, tarification représentée par un barème qui donne les prix (*f.*).
scale of charges for carriage, barème des prix de transport.
scale of commissions fixed by the stock exchange committee, tarif de courtages établi par la chambre syndicale des agents de change.
scale rate *or* **scale charge,** prix de barème (*m.*).
scales (office) (*n.pl.*), balance (de bureau) (*f.*).
scalper (Stock Exch.) (pers.) (*n.*), accompagnateur (*m.*).
Scandinavian Monetary Union, Union monétaire scandinave (*f.*).
scarce (*adj.*), rare:
money is scarce, l'argent est rare (*m.*); les capitaux sont rares (*m.pl.*).
scarcity (*n.*), rareté (*f.*); raréfaction (*f.*); pénurie (*f.*); disette (*f.*):

scarcity of coin, of stock, of freight, rareté, raréfaction, pénurie, disette, du numéraire, du titre, de fret:
a rise is the consequence of a scarcity of stock, la hausse est l'œuvre de la rareté (*ou* de la raréfaction) du titre.

schedule (list) (*n.*), annexe (*f.*); bordereau (*m.*):
schedules to a balance sheet,   annexes d'un bilan:
company bound to publish as a schedule to the annual balance sheet details of its investments, société tenue de publier en annexe du bilan annuel le détail de son portefeuille (*f.*).
schedule of documents, of investments,   bordereau de pièces, de portefeuille.

schedule (Income Tax) (*n.*), cédule (*f.*):
profit which is taxed under another schedule, bénéfice qui est taxée dans une autre cédule (*m.*).
if one is assessed under various income tax schedules,   si on est imposé aux diverses cédules des impôts sur les revenus.

schedule tax (Income Tax),   impôt cédulaire (*m.*):
English income tax is composed of five schedule taxes, schedules A, B, C, D, and E, l'*income-tax* anglais se compose de cinq impôts cédulaires, cédules A, B, C, D, et E (*m.*).

scheme (*n.*), projet (*m.*); plan (*m.*).

scheme of composition (arrangement with creditors), concordat (*m.*); convenio (*m.*).

scholar's season ticket,   carte d'abonnement d'élève (*f.*).

scratch out (*v.t.*), gratter; raturer.

scratch out (*v.i.*), gratter:
one should not scratch out in the books, on ne doit pas gratter sur les livres.

scratching out, grattage (*m.*); raturage (*m.*).

screw steamer (Abbrev.: **Sc. Sr**), vapeur à hélice (*m.*).

scrip [**scrip** *collective pl.*] (any certificate or certificates for stock or shares) (*n.*),   titre (*m.*); titres (*m.pl.*); certificat (*m.*); certificats (*m.pl.*):
registered scrip, titre (*ou* certificat) nominatif; titres (*ou* certificats) nominatifs.

scrip [**scrip** *pl.*] (*n.*) *or* **scrip certificate** (a preliminary or provisional certificate, exchangeable for a *definitive* [or *definite*] *certificate* when the stock is paid up in full), titre provisoire (*m.*); certificat provisoire (*m.*).

scrip [**scrip** *pl.*] (deferred interest certificate) (*n.*), script (*m.*); vale (*m.*); bon (*m.*).

scripholder (pers.) (*n.*), détenteur de titres (*m.*); porteur de titres (*m.*).

scrutineer (pers.) (*n.*), scrutateur (*m.*).

scuttle (*v.t.*), saborder:
to scuttle a burning ship, saborder un navire en feu.

scuttling (*n.*), sabordement (*m.*); sabordage (*m.*).

sea (*n.*), mer (*f.*):
ship at sea, navire en mer (*m.*).

sea accident, accident de mer (*m.*).

sea and land carriage, transport mixte (*m.*).

sea beach, plage (*f.*); grève (*f.*); rivage de la mer (*m.*).

seaboard. V. ci-après.

sea carriage (opp. to *land carriage*), transport par mer (*m.*); transport maritime (*m.*).

seacoast. V. ci-après.

sea damage, avaries de mer (*f.pl.*).

sea-damaged (Abbrev.: **S/D.**) (*adj.*), endommagé (-e) par l'eau de mer.

seafarer. V. ci-après.

sea frontier (opp. to *land frontier*), frontière de mer (*f.*).

seagoing. V. ci-après.

sea insurance *or* **sea assurance**, assurance maritime (*f.*).

sea journal, journal de route (*m.*); journal de voyage (*m.*).

sea letter *or* **sea brief**, lettre de mer (*f.*).

seaman, seamanlike. V. ci-après.

sea mile, mille marin (*m.*).

sea peril, péril de (*ou* de la) mer (*m.*); péril maritime (*m.*); fortune de mer (*f.*).

sea pilot, pilote hauturier (*m.*); pilote de mer (*m.*). V. note sous **pilot**.

seaport. V. ci-après.

sea risk (Insce), risque de mer (*m.*); risque maritime (*m.*).

sea route, voie de mer (*f.*).

seashore. V. ci-après.

sea trade, commerce par mer (*m.*); commerce maritime (*m.*).

sea trial, essai à la mer (*m.*).

sea voyage *or* **sea passage** *or* **sea transit**, voyage de (*ou* par) mer (*m.*); trajet par mer (*m.*); trajet maritime (*m.*); parcours maritime (*m.*); traversée maritime (*f.*).

sea water (opp. to *fresh water*), eau de mer (*f.*); eaux marines (*f.pl.*).

seaworthiness, seaworthy. V. ci-après.

seaboard (*n.*), littoral (*m.*); côtes (*f.pl.*):
the Atlantic seaboard, le littoral atlantique; les côtes de l'Atlantique.

seacoast (*n.*), côte (*f.*); littoral (*m.*); bords de la mer (*m.pl.*).

seafarer (*n.*) *or* **seafaring man**, marin (*m.*); homme de mer (*m.*); gens de mer (*m.pl. only*); matelot (*m.*).

seagoing barge, chaland de mer (*m.*); allège de mer (*f.*).

seagoing vessel, bâtiment de mer (*m.*); navire de mer (*m.*):
ships and other seagoing vessels, navires et autres bâtiments de mer (*m.pl.*).

seal (*n.*), cachet (*m.*); sceau (*m.*):
wax seal, cachet à la cire. (Cf. **wafer** *or* **wafer seal**.)
customs seal, sceau de la douane; cachet de douane. (Cf. **plomb**.)

seal *or* **seal up** (*v.t.*), cacheter; sceller:
to seal (*or* to seal up) a letter, cacheter, sceller, une lettre.
to seal a letter with a wax seal, sceller une lettre avec un cachet de cire.
to seal a deed, sceller un acte.
packages sealed with customs plombs, colis scellés des plombs de douane (*m.pl.*).

sealed sample, échantillon cacheté (*m.*).
sealed tender, soumission cachetée (*f.*).
sealing (*n.*), cachetage (*m.*); scellage (*m.*).
sealing wax, cire à cacheter (*f.*); cire d'Espagne (*f.*).
seaman [**seamen** *pl.:*] (*n.*), homme de mer (*m.*); gens de mer (*m.pl. only*); marin (*m.*); matelot (*m.*).
seamanlike manner (in a), en bon marin : to manage a ship in a seamanlike manner, conduire un navire en bon marin.
seamen's wages, salaires (*m.pl.*), loyers (*m.pl.*), gages (*m.pl.*) des gens de mer.
seaport (*n.*), port de mer (*m.*); port maritime (*m.*).
search (*n.*) *or* **searching** (*n.*) *or* **searching for,** recherche (*f.*); recherches (*f.pl.*) : searching (*or* search) on board (a ship), recherches à bord.
search (*v.t.*) *or* **search for,** rechercher.
seashore (*n.*), rivage de la mer (*m.*); plage (*f.*); grève (*f.*); rive de la mer (*f.*); bords de la mer (*m.pl.*).
season ticket *or simply* **season** (*n.*), carte d'abonnement (*f.*); abonnement (*m.*).
seat (place in railway carriage, or the like) (*n.*), place (*f.*). V. exemple sous **fare**.
seat (membership) (*n.*), charge (*f.*); office (*m.*) : stockbroker who buys the seat from his predecessor, agent de change qui achète la charge (*ou* l'office) à son prédécesseur (*m.*).
seaworthiness (*n.*) (Ant.: *unseaworthiness*), bon état de navigabilité (*m.*); état de navigabilité (*m.*); état de tenir la mer (*m.*); navigabilité (*f.*) : warranty of seaworthiness, garantie de navigabilité (*f.*).
seaworthy (*n.*), en bon état de navigabilité; en état de navigabilité (*ou* de naviguer); en état de tenir la mer ; navigable : a ship is deemed to be seaworthy when she is reasonably fit in all respects to encounter the ordinary perils of the seas of the adventure insured, un navire est réputé en bon état de navigabilité quand il est à tous égards raisonnablement en état d'affronter les périls ordinaires des mers où a lieu l'aventure assurée.
second *or abbreviated* **2nd** (*adj.*), second, -e ; deuxième ; 2e : second (*or* 2nd) class ticket, billet de seconde (*ou* de 2e) classe (*m.*).
second debentures, second preference shares. V. sous **first**.
second half year *or* second half *or* second six months (six months commencing July 1), second semestre (*m.*); deuxième semestre (*m.*); semestre de juillet (*m.*); semestre d'été (*m.*) : the second six months' interest, le deuxième semestre de l'intérêt.
second mortgage, deuxième hypothèque (*f.*).
second rate stock (*or* share), titre de second ordre (*m.*); valeur d'appoint (*f.*).
second trial balance, balance d'inventaire (*f.*).
second (*n.*), seconde (*f.*); deuxième (*f.*) :

second of exchange, seconde de change; deuxième de change. V. **first of exchange** pour exemple.
second (*v.t.*), appuyer : to second a resolution, appuyer une proposition.
secrecy [**secrecies** *pl.*] (*n.*), secret (*m.*) : stockbrokers are bound to professional secrecy and may not disclose the names of the contracting parties, les agents de change sont tenus au secret professionnel et ne doivent pas dévoiler les noms des parties contractantes (*m.pl.*).
secret (*adj.*), secret, -ète ; occulte ; caché, -e ; latent, -e : secret agreement, accord occulte (*m.*).
secret language (Teleg.), langage secret (*m.*).
secret partner (opp. to *acting partner*), commanditaire (*m.* ou *f.*); associé commanditaire (*m.*); bailleur de fonds (*m.*).
secret remuneration, rémunération occulte (*f.*).
secret reserve (opp. to *visible reserve*), réserve cachée (*f.*); réserve occulte (*f.*); réserve latente (*f.*) : most of the items on the assets side are valued with such caution that they conceal very material secret reserves, la plupart des postes de l'actif sont évalués-avec une telle prudence qu'ils recèlent des réserves occultes très importantes.
secret (*n.*), secret (*m.*).
secretary [**secretaries** *pl.*] (pers.) (*n.*) (Abbrev.: **Sec.** *or* **Secy**), secrétaire (*m.*) : secretary to the board of directors, secrétaire au conseil d'administration.
secretary and offices (*followed by an address*), siège social et secrétariat (*suivi d'une adresse*).
secretary's office, bureau du secrétaire (*m.*); secrétariat (*m.*).
secretaryship (*n.*), secrétariat (*m.*).
section (of an act of Parliament, or the like) (*n.*) (Abbrev.: **sec.** *or* **sect.**), article (*m.*) : in pursuance of sections — and — of the Companies Act 1929, en vertu des articles — et — de la loi de 1929 sur les sociétés.
section (Stock Exch.) (*n.*), compartiment (*m.*) : the mining section, le compartiment minier.
section (of the list) (i.e., the quotation list of a Stock or other Exchange) (*n.*), rubrique (de la cote) (*f.*) : no change in the foreign section, pas de changement à la rubrique des étrangères.
sectional ledger, grand livre fractionnaire (*m.*); grand livre auxiliaire (*m.*); grand livre analytique (*m.*); grand livre originaire (*m.*); grand livre de développement (*m.*).
secure (to obtain) (*v.t.*), obtenir : to secure the agency of a company, obtenir l'agence d'une compagnie.
secure (to give security for) (*v.t.*), cautionner : to secure a cashier, cautionner un caissier.
secure (to give security to) (*v.t.*), nantir : to secure a lender by mortgage, nantir un prêteur par hypothèque.

in contangoing, the lender is secured by a
stock, dans le report, le prêteur est nanti
d'un titre.

secure (*a debt*) **by mortgage** (**to**), hypothéquer ;
garantir par hypothèque :
to secure a debt by mortgage, hypothéquer,
garantir par hypothèque, une créance.

secure (*goods*) **by warrant** (**to**), warranter (des
marchandises).

secure oneself (**to**), se garantir ; se nantir :
to secure oneself by mortgage, se garantir,
se nantir, par hypothèque.
Cf. **secured on** (**to be**) ci-après.

secured (*adj.*), garanti, -e ; gagé, -e ; nanti, -e :
secured advances, avances garanties (*f.pl.*) ;
avances contre garanties (*f.pl.*).
secured creditor, créancier nanti (*m.*).
secured debt, créance garantie (*f.*).
secured loan, emprunt (*ou* prêt) garanti (*ou*
gagé) (*m.*).

secured on (**to be**), être nanti (e) sur ; être
gagé (-e) sur ; être assis (-e) sur ; frapper :
mortgage which is secured on property, hypothèque qui est nantie sur (*ou* qui est gagée
sur) (*ou* qui est assise sur) (*ou* qui frappe)
des biens (*f.*).

securing (*n.*), nantissement (*m.*) ; cautionnement (*m.*).

securing (*goods*) **by warrant**, warrantage (*m.*).

security [**securities** *pl.*] (surety for payment or
enforcement ; guarantee ; pledge ; cover)
(*n.*), garantie (*f.*) ; caution (*f.*) ; cautionnement (*m.*) ; gage (*m.*) ; nantissement (*m.*) ;
sûreté (*f.*) ; sécurité (*f.*) ; couverture (*f.*) :
advance against security, avance contre
garantie (*f.*) ; avance garantie (*f.*).
stocks held as security, lodged as security for
advances, hypothecated (*or* pledged) as
security for money advanced, titres détenus
en garantie (*ou* en gage), déposés en garantie
d'avances, déposés en nantissement en
garantie de fonds avancés (*m.pl.*).
to ask for security, demander une caution.
V. aussi exemples sous to give security.
one thing is never returned so long as the
business is not closed : that is the security,
une chose ne se restitue jamais tant que
l'affaire n'est pas liquidée : c'est le cautionnement.
security for costs (Law), caution judicatum
solvi (*f.*).
security given by an employee, cautionnement déposé par un employé.
to lend money on security (collateral), prêter
de l'argent sur nantissement.
loan on security of goods, prêt sur nantissement de marchandises (*m.*).
security for a debt, sûreté d'une créance.
to obtain security before lending money,
prendre des sûretés avant de prêter de
l'argent.
company which affords to its insured all the
security they are entitled to expect, compagnie qui donne à ses assurés toute la
sécurité sur laquelle ils sont en droit de
compter (*f.*).

without security, sans garantie ; à découvert ;
sur notoriété :
account opened without security, compte
ouvert sans garantie (*ou* ouvert à découvert)
(*ou* ouvert sur notoriété) (*m.*).

security (pers.) (*n.*), caution (*f.*) ; donneur de
caution (*m.*) ; garant, -e ; répondant (*m.*) ;
accréditeur (*m.*) :
to be security for someone, être caution de, se
porter caution de, se porter garant (-e) de,
se rendre caution de, se rendre garant (-e)
de, être le répondant de, répondre pour,
quelqu'un.

security (stock, share, investment, bill, or the
like) (*n. commonly in pl.*), titre (*m.*) ; valeur
(*f.*) ; effet (*m.*) ; fonds (*m.*) ; portefeuille
(*m.*) :
registered securities, titres nominatifs ; valeurs
nominatives ; effets nominatifs.
securities for money (paper securities), papiers-
valeurs (*m.pl.*) ; valeurs-papiers (*f.pl.*) ;
valeurs fiduciaires ; titres fiduciaires ; portefeuille.
public securities, effets publics ; fonds publics.
provision for depreciation of securities, prévision pour moins-value du portefeuille (*f.*).

security department (Banking), service des
titres (*m.*) ; titres (*m.pl.*) :
the head of the security department, le chef
du service des titres ; le chef des titres.

securities clerk, caissier des titres (*m.*) ;
comptable gardien de valeurs (*m.*).

securities ledger, grand livre des valeurs
(*m.*).

securities trust, trust de placement (*m.*) ;
coopérative de placement (*f.*) ; société de
gérance (*f.*).

see that (**to**) (to look after), veiller à :
to see that someone does something, that the
repairs are carried out, veiller à ce que
quelqu'un fait quelque chose, à l'exécution
des réparations.

seek (*v.t.*), chercher :
to seek employment, chercher de l'emploi.

seize (*v.t.*), saisir :
ship which is seized and sold, navire qui est
saisi et vendu (*m.*).

seizure (*n.*), saisie (*f.*) :
seizure of a ship,' of goods not declared to
the customs, saisie d'un navire, de marchandises non déclarées à la douane.
seizure under legal process, saisie judiciaire.

selected (*adj.*), sélectionné, -e :
selected investments, placements sélectionnés
(*m.pl.*).

selection (*n.*), sélection (*f.*).

self [**selves** *pl.*] (*personal pronoun*), moi-même :
pay self, pay selves (enfacement on a cheque),
payez à moi-même, payez à nous-mêmes.

self-acting numbering machine, timbre numéroteur automatique (*m.*).

sell (*v.t.*) (Ant.: *buy*), vendre ; écouler ; faire
écouler :
to sell a ship, vendre un navire.
to sell goods, shares, vendre, écouler, faire
écouler, des marchandises, des actions.

to sell a bear (Stock Exch.), vendre à découvert :
to sell a bear of Rios, vendre du Rio à découvert.
to speculate on the stock exchange, that is to say, to buy a bull or sell a bear, spéculer sur la bourse, c'est-à-dire acheter ou vendre à découvert.
to sell at a high price, vendre cher ; vendre chèrement.
to sell at a loss or to sell at a low price or to sell at a sacrifice, vendre à perte ; mévendre : there are times when one is forced to sell at a sacrifice, il y a des moments où l'on se voit forcé de mévendre.
to sell at any price, vendre à tout prix.
to sell by auction or to sell at auction, vendre à l'enchère ; vendre aux enchères.
to sell cheap, vendre à bon compte ; faire bon compte.
to sell for cash, vendre comptant ; vendre au comptant.
to sell for delivery (Stock Exch.), vendre à couvert.
to sell for the settlement (or for the account) (Stock Exch.), vendre à terme.
to sell forward (Produce Exch.), vendre à terme.
to sell on commission, vendre à la commission.
to sell privately or to sell by private treaty, vendre à l'amiable.
to sell short (Stock Exch.), vendre à découvert :
to sell Rios short, vendre du Rio à découvert.
to sell upon (or on) credit, vendre à terme ; vendre à crédit.
sell (v.i.) or **to be sold,** se vendre ; s'écouler ; se traiter :
articles which sell well, objets qui se vendent (ou s'écoulent) bien (m.pl.).
wheat is selling (or is being sold) at so much, le blé se traite à tant.
the market where shares and other similar securities are sold, le marché où se vendent les actions et autres titres semblables.
to be sold (for sale), à vendre :
to be sold.—banking premises, à vendre.— immeuble de banque.
sell again (to) (v.t. & v.i.), revendre :
simple intermediaries (or middlemen) who buy to sell again, simples intermédiaires qui achètent pour revendre (m.pl.).
sell against (to) (Produce Exch.) (opp. to *purchase against*), revendre :
to sell against a defaulter, revendre un défaillant.
sell for (to) or **sell at (to)** (v.t.), vendre :
to sell an article for (or at) so many pounds, vendre un objet tant de livres.
sell for (to) or **sell at (to)** (v.i.) or **to be sold for** or **to be sold at,** se vendre :
share which sells at (or which is sold at) so much, action qui se vend tant (f.).
sell out (v.t. & v.i.), revendre :
to sell out one's stocks at a profit, revendre ses titres avec bénéfice.

the buyer sells out the stock he cannot take up and the seller buys back the stock he cannot deliver, l'acheteur revend les titres qu'il ne peut pas lever et le vendeur rachète les titres qu'il ne peut livrer (m.).
to take advantage of a favourable price to sell out, saisir un cours favorable pour revendre.
Note :—An English stockbroker would not use the expression *to sell out* in this sense ; he would say *to sell* simply. With him *to sell out* is the opposing term to *to buy in* (see next entry). Outside the Stock Exchange however, *to sell out,* meaning *to dispose of wholly or entirely,* is correct English.
sell out (opp. to *buy in,* q.v.) (Stock Exch.) (v.t. & v.i.). V. exemples :
to sell out stock, securities, revendre des titres, des valeurs.
to sell out against a buyer, exécuter, revendre, un acheteur.
sell up (Law) (v.t.), vendre :
to sell someone up, vendre quelqu'un.
seller (pers.) (n.) (Ant.: *buyer*), vendeur, -euse : bear seller, vendeur à découvert.
prices offered (sellers) (Stock Exch.), cours offerts (vendeurs) (m.pl.).
parcels of Northern Manitoba (wheat) March sellers at 42/6d. (or *abbreviated* 42/6 s.), parcelles de (blé) Manitoba nord mars 42/6d. vendeur (f.pl.).
when the market is a seller, quand la place est vendeur.
during the war the great producing nations kept away, to a certain point, from the markets as sellers, pendant la guerre les grandes nations productrices sont restées, jusqu'à un certain point, absentes des marchés comme vendeuses.
seller of a call option (taker for a call) (Stock Exch.), vendeur d'un dont (m.) ; vendeur d'une prime directe (m.).
seller of a put option (taker for a put) (Stock Exch.), acheteur d'un ou (m.) ; acheteur d'une prime indirecte (m.). V. note sous syn. **taker for a put.**
seller's option (put) (Stock or other Exch.), prime pour le vendeur (f.) ; prime vendeur (f.) ; prime pour livrer (f.) ; prime pour livrer ou non (f.) ; marché à prime pour livrer (m.) ; prime indirecte (f.) ; prime renversée (f.) ; prime inverse (f.) ; ou (m.) ; prime ou (f.) ; prime moins (f.) ; prime simple à la baisse (f.).
seller's option to double, doublé à la baisse (m.) ; doublure à la baisse (f.) ; faculté de livrer double (f.).
seller's option to quadruple, quadruplé à la baisse (m.) ; faculté de livrer quadruple (f.).
seller's option to treble, triplé à la baisse (m.) ; faculté de livrer triple (f.).
sellers over (Stock Exch.), la place (ou la position de place) est dégagée (ou est soulagée).
selling (n.), vente (f.).
selling against a defaulter (Produce Exch.), revente d'un défaillant (f.).

selling brokerage *or* **selling commission,** courtage de vente (*m.*); commission de vente (*f.*).
selling licence, licence de vente (*f.*).
selling off, liquidation (*f.*).
selling office (of a cartel), comptoir de vente (*m.*).
selling order, ordre de vente (*m.*).
selling out, revente (*f.*). V. le verbe pour exemples.
selling out against a buyer (Stock Exch.), exécution (*f.*), revente (*f.*) d'un acheteur. Cf. **buying in.**
selling out stock, securities (Stock Exch.) (opp. to *buying in*), revente des titres, des valeurs (*f.*).
selling price, prix de vente (*m.*).
selling rate (Foreign Exchange), cours vendeur (*m.*); cours Papier (*m.*); P.
selves (*personal pronoun pl.*). V. **self.**
semaphoric telegram, télégramme sémaphorique (*m.*).
semiannual (*adj.*), semestriel, -elle.
semiannually (*adv.*), semestriellement.
send (*v.t.*), envoyer; expédier; remettre; faire tenir; adresser:
  to send a remittance, envoyer une remise.
  to send a letter by post, a telegram, envoyer, expédier, une lettre par la poste, une dépêche.
  letter sent through the post, lettre remise à la poste (*f.*).
  to send money, remettre, envoyer, faire tenir, de l'argent.
send back (to), renvoyer; faire renvoyer:
  to send the goods back, renvoyer les marchandises.
send elsewhere (to), (in order to find a better market), déplacer:
  to send goods elsewhere, déplacer des marchandises.
send home (to), rapatrier:
  to send the crew home, rapatrier l'équipage.
send in (to), remettre; envoyer; donner:
  to send in to the inspector of taxes a return of one's income, remettre au contrôleur des contributions directes une déclaration de son revenu.
  to send in one's resignation, envoyer, donner, sa démission.
send on (to), faire suivre; transmettre:
  to send on the goods by another boat, faire suivre la marchandise par un autre bateau.
  to send on an order, transmettre un ordre.
send out a prospectus, circulars (to), lancer un prospectus, des circulaires.
send out accounts (to) *or* **send in accounts (to),** envoyer des comptes.
sender (pers.) (*n.*) (Ant.: *receiver*), envoyeur, -euse; expéditeur, -trice; expéditionnaire (*m.* ou *f.*); remetteur (*m.*); remettant (*m.*); destinateur, -trice:
  sender of a money order, envoyeur d'un mandat-poste.
  to mention the address of the sender on the back of the envelope, mentionner l'adresse de l'expéditeur au verso de l'enveloppe.

sending (*n.*), envoi (*m.*); expédition (*f.*).
sending home (of seamen), rapatriement (des gens de mer) (*m.*).
sending out a prospectus, lancement d'un prospectus (*m.*).
sending out accounts *or* **sending in accounts,** envoi des comptes (*m.*).
sending out circulars, envoi, lancement, de circulaires (*m.*).
sending station (Rly.) (opp. to *receiving station*), gare expéditrice (*f.*); gare d'expédition (*f.*).
senior officers (of a liner), état-major (d'un paquebot) (*m.*).
separate (*adj.*), séparé, -e; distinct, -e; à part:
  separate book (a book, as a bill book, not forming an integral part of a bookkeeping system), registre extra-comptable (*m.*).
  separate column (on a page), colonne à part (*f.*).
  each shipment to be regarded as a separate contract, chaque expédition sera considérée comme faisant l'objet d'un contrat séparé (*f.*).
  each craft, raft, or lighter to be deemed the subject of a separate insurance, chaque embarcation, radeau, ou allège sera censé l'objet d'une assurance distincte.
  separate policy (Insce), police distincte (*f.*); police séparée (*f.*).
sequestration (*n.*), séquestration (*f.*).
series [series *pl.*] (*n.*) (Abbrev.: **ser.** or **srs**), série (*f.*):
  a new series of shares, une nouvelle série d'actions.
  securities redeemable in series, valeurs remboursables par séries (*f.pl.*).
  the master has the option of delivering the goods in series, le capitaine a la faculté de livrer les marchandises par séries.
  goods shipped in bulk are not divided into series, les marchandises chargées en vrac ne sont pas divisées en séries.
  each series is adjusted separately and it is upon each series that the calculation and application of the franchise will be made, chaque série se règle séparément et c'est sur chaque série que se feront le calcul et l'application de la franchise.
servant (pers.) (*n.*), employé, -e; préposé, -e; serviteur (*m.*):
  railway servant, employé de chemin de fer.
  shipowner who is liable for the faults committed by his servants in the handling of the cargo, armateur qui est responsable des fautes commises par ses préposés dans la manutention de la cargaison (*m.*).
  the master is both the servant and the agent of the owner of the ship he commands, le capitaine est à la fois le préposé et le mandataire du propriétaire du navire qu'il commande.
serve (to provide a service) (*v.t.*), desservir:
  the principal shipping lines serving South America, les principales lignes de navigation desservant l'Amérique du Sud (*f.pl.*).
  railway line which serves the Midlands and

the South, ligne de chemin de fer qui dessert le Centre et le Midi (*f.*).

serve (to provide or pay the interest on) (*v.t.*), servir :

sum sufficient to serve the bonds, somme suffisante pour servir les obligations (*f.*).

service (provision of service) (*n.*), desserte (*f.*) :

the service of a port by railroads, rivers, or canals, la desserte d'un port par des voies ferrées, des fleuves, ou des canaux.

service (means of supplying some general demand) (*n.*), service (*m.*) :

railway service, service de chemins de fer.

service (labour; office) (*n.*), service (*m.*); démarche (*f.*); ministère (*m.*) :

to offer one's services, offrir ses services (*ou* son ministère).

services rendered, services rendus.

founders' shares allotted to the vendors as consideration for their services, parts de fondateur attribuées aux apporteurs en rémunération de leurs démarches (*f.pl.*).

service (provision or payment of interest) (*n.*), service (*m.*); service de l'intérêt (*m.*) :

amount required for the service of the loan, somme nécessaire au service de l'emprunt (*f.*).

loans the service of which is guaranteed by the Government, emprunts dont le service d'intérêt est garanti par l'État (*m.pl.*).

service instructions (on a printed form), mentions de service (*f.pl.*); indications de service (*f.pl.*).

service telegram, télégramme de service (*m.*).

session (working day) (Stock Exch.) (*n.*), séance (*f.*); bourse (*f.*) :

two deals done during the same session, deux opérations effectuées dans la même séance (*ou* bourse).

set (*n.*), jeu (*m.*); série (*f.*); tranche (*f.*) :

set of books, jeu de livres.

full set of bills of lading, of bills of exchange, of printed forms, jeu complet, série complète, de connaissements, de lettres de change, d'imprimés.

bill of exchange in a set *or* bill in a set, lettre de change à plusieurs exemplaires (*f.*); traite en plusieurs exemplaires (*f.*).

bills drawn in sets of three are intended to be sent by different mails, in order that, if one should go astray, the other may reach its destination, les lettres tirées à trois exemplaires (*ou* en triple exemplaire) sont destinées à être envoyées par des courriers différents, afin que, si l'une s'égare, l'autre parvienne à destination (*f.pl.*).

the set (*or* plurality of copies) is also met with when the drawer wishes to present the bill for acceptance intending meanwhile to negotiate it : in this case, he makes two vias (*or* copies) of it, on rencontre aussi la pluralité d'exemplaires dans le cas où le tireur désire présenter l'effet à l'acceptation tout en voulant se réserver une négociation immédiate : dans ce cas, il en dresse deux exemplaires.

set of three figures, tranche de trois chiffres.

set (to put; to append) (*v.t.*), apposer :

endorser who sets his signature to a bill, endosseur qui appose sa signature sur un effet (*m.*).

set aside (to) *or* **set apart (to)**, affecter; consacrer; distraire; prélever :

to set aside a sum for distribution among the staff, affecter (*ou* consacrer) (*ou* distraire) une somme, faire une distraction, pour être distribuée aux employés.

to set aside so much out of one's savings, distraire tant sur ses économies.

to set apart funds for the redemption of an annuity, affecter, consacrer, des fonds au rachat d'une annuité.

when the balance sheet is completed, the board decides the amount of the reserves to be set aside out of profits and the dividend to be recommended to the shareholders, quand le bilan est achevé le conseil d'administration détermine l'importance des réserves à prélever sur les bénéfices et le dividende à proposer aux actionnaires.

set form of letter, lettre passe-partout (*f.*).

set form of reply, réponse type (*f.*).

set free (to) (Fin.), mobiliser :

the money locked up in a bill of exchange is set free as soon as the bill is paid, le capital immobilisé dans une lettre de change est mobilisé dès que la lettre est payée.

set off (compensation; extinction of debt) (*n.*), compensation (*f.*) :

the new shares will be paid up by set off against the amount of the debentures converted, les actions nouvelles seront libérées par compensation avec le montant des obligations converties (*f.pl.*).

set off (counterclaim) (Law) (*n.*), demande reconventionnelle (*f.*); reconvention (*f.*).

set off (*v.t.*), compenser :

to set off a debt, compenser une dette.

to set off the reparation due against the balance of freight remaining to be paid, compenser la réparation due avec le solde du fret restant à payer.

on payment of a loss or damage, all outstanding premiums due by the insured are set off against the loss due by the underwriters, lors du remboursement d'une perte ou d'une avarie, toutes primes échues dues par l'assuré sont compensées avec l'indemnité due par les assureurs.

setback (*n.*), recul (*m.*); tassement (*m.*) :

bull campaign interrupted by a few setbacks, campagne de hausse entrecoupée de quelques reculs (*ou* tassements) (*f.*).

to have a setback, reculer; se tasser :

among industrials, X. shares had another setback from 2½ to 2¼, aux industrielles, l'action X. s'est encore tassée de 2 1/2 à 2 1/4.

setting aside *or* **setting apart**, affectation (*f.*); distraction (*f.*); prélèvement (*m.*).

setting free (of capital, of money), mobilisation (de capital, de capitaux) (*f.*).

settle (*v.t.*). V. exemples :

to settle a dispute, a matter amicably, arranger, accommoder, trancher, décider, vider, terminer, une contestation (*ou* un différend), une affaire à l'amiable.

contango dealings are settled at the making up price, les opérations de report sont réglées au cours de compensation (*f.pl.*).

to settle a transaction (in the settlement department) (Stock Exch.), liquider une opération.

to settle an account in cash, régler, solder, un compte en espèces.

to settle in cash is to free oneself immediately from one's debt, régler au comptant, c'est se libérer immédiatement de sa dette.

if the freight is not paid, the consignee settles it, si le fret n'est pas payé, le destinataire le règle.

to settle one's account, régler son compte; solder son compte; s'acquitter.

to settle an account (to bring it into agreement; to settle differences on it), régler un compte.

to settle an annuity on someone, constituer une annuité à quelqu'un.

to settle up, régler compte:

suppose that, on the 31st March, one wishes to close the transaction and settle up, supposons que, le 31 mars, on veuille liquider l'opération et régler compte.

settlement (*n.*), règlement (*m.*); solde (*m.*); accommodement (*m.*); arrangement (*m.*):

settlement of a dispute, of a difference, règlement, accommodement, arrangement, d'une contestation, d'un différend.

the making up price serves as a basis for contangoes and the settlement of differences, le cours de compensation sert de base pour les reports et pour le règlement des différences.

settlement of the claim takes place within three months of the accident, le règlement de l'indemnité a lieu dans les trois mois du sinistre.

cash in settlement, espèces pour solde (*f.pl.*).

in full settlement, pour solde de tout compte.

settlement (of an annuity on someone) (*n.*), constitution (d'une annuité à quelqu'un) (*f.*).

settlement (Stock Exch.) (*n.*), terme (*m.*); liquidation (*f.*):

dealings for the settlement, négociations à terme (*f.pl.*); opérations à terme (*f.pl.*); affaires à terme (*f.pl.*).

settlement (fixing the price in case of default) (Produce or Corn Exch.) (*n.*), liquidation (*f.*):

official settlements can be made in case of default of contractants, des liquidations d'office peuvent être faites en cas de défaillance des contractants.

settlement account (Stock Exch.), compte de liquidation (*m.*).

settlement bargain (Stock Exch.), marché a terme (*m.*); marché à livrer (*m.*).

settlement day *or* **settling day** (Stock Exch.), jour de la liquidation (*m.*).

settlement department (Stock Exch.), comité de liquidation (*m.*).

settlement price (fixed for defaulted contract) (Produce Exch.), cours de résiliation (*m.*).

settling room (Stock Exch.), salle de liquidation (*f.*).

settling room clerk (Stock Exch.), liquidateur (*m.*); filiériste (*m.*).

seven day loans (Money Market), prêts à sept jours (*m.pl.*).

several (Law) (*adj.*), individuel, -elle:

several liability, responsabilité individuelle (*f.*).

severally (Law) (*adv.*), individuellement:

directors who are liable severally or jointly and severally, as the case may be, to the company or to third parties, for wrongful acts done in their management, administrateurs qui sont responsables, individuellement ou solidairement, suivant les cas, envers la société ou envers les tiers, des fautes qu'ils auraient commises dans leur gestion (*m.pl.*).

shade (*v.i.*), passer:

X. shares shaded from 1s. 6d. to 1s. 4½d., l'action X. passe de 1sh. 6d. à 1sh. 4 1/2d.

shady (*adj.*), véreux, -euse:

shady company emanating from a stable of doubtful morality, société véreuse émanant d'une officine (*ou* d'une boutique) de moralité douteuse (*f.*).

shady financier, financier véreux (*m.*); brasseur d'affaires (*m.*); faiseur d'affaires (*m.*).

shake (*v.t.*), ébranler:

to shake the confidence of the public in the security of the paper currency, ébranler la confiance du public dans la sécurité de la circulation fiduciaire.

sham dividend, dividende fictif (*m.*).

shape (quantity) (Stock Exch.) (*n.*), quotité (*f.*):

one can only deal in a certain shape (called the dealable shape) of this stock or in a multiple of this shape, on ne peut opérer que sur une certaine quotité (appelée la quotité négociable) de ces titres ou sur un multiple de cette quotité.

share (a single portion of something distributed among or partaken of by several; part ownership; quota) (*n.*), part (*f.*); portion (*f.*); participation (*f.*); quote-part (*f.*); prorata (*m.*); tantième (*m.*); cote (*f.*); cotisation (*f.*):

where there are several underwriters each of them writes down at the bottom of the policy the share he takes upon himself in the risk insured, lorsqu'il y a plusieurs assureurs, chacun d'eux inscrit au bas de la police la part pour laquelle il s'engage dans le risque assuré.

to take a share in the deal, prendre une part (*ou* une participation) dans l'affaire.

founder's share *or* management share, part de fondateur; part bénéficiaire. V. note sous **founder's share**, sous F.

share of underwriting, part syndicale; part syndicataire; part de syndicat.

share in profits, participation aux bénéfices; tantième dans les bénéfices.

to receive one's share of the profits, recevoir sa quote-part (*ou* son prorata) des bénéfices.

the bank allows them a share of the proceeds, la banque leur alloue un tantième du produit.

to pay one's share, payer sa part (*ou* sa quote-part) (*ou* son prorata) (*ou* sa cote) (*ou* sa cotisation).

share (in a ship) (*n.*),   quirat (*m.*);   part (*f.*): [Cf. **owner** (of a share or shares in a ship).]

the ship, with respect to ownership, is supposed to be divided into a certain number of equal parts, called shares; in France, generally twenty four shares, in England, sixty four,   le navire est supposé se diviser, sous le rapport de la propriété, en un certain nombre de parts égales, appelées quirats; en France ordinairement vingt-quatre quirats, en Angleterre, soixante-quatre.

master who holds a share in the vessel, capitaine qui a une part dans le navire (*m.*).

share (one of the equal parts into which the capital stock of a company or corporation is divided) (*n.*),   action (*f.*);   titre (*m.*); valeur (*f.*):

ordinary shares or simply shares (*Abbrev.:* ord.), actions ordinaires; actions.

registered shares, actions nominatives; titres nominatifs; valeurs nominatives.

exchange, share for share, of £1 shares for 10s. shares, échange, titre pour titre, des actions de £1 contre des actions de 10sh. (*m.*).

shares which are good delivery (Stock Exch.), titres qui sont de bonne livraison.

shares issued for cash, actions émises contre espèces; actions de (*ou* en) numéraire; actions financières.

shares issued as fully paid up otherwise than in cash, actions d'apport; actions de fondation.

shares issued as partly paid up otherwise than in cash, actions mixtes.

shares on the market. V. sous **market.**

Note :—In naming shares in French without using the word *action* (which is feminine) they must always be spoken of as masculine; thus, **une action Chartered** or **un Chartered,** a Chartered share or one Chartered; **vendre du Chartered à découvert,** to sell a bear of Chartered.

In the case of stocks or shares referred to collectively under their names, as in market news, the gender is either—

(1) As indicated by the noun itself :—

la Rente italienne est résistante, Italian Rentes are strong.

le Consolidé est faible *ou* les Consolidés sont faibles, Consols are weak.

la Banque de France est ferme, Bank of France stock is firm.

le Nord, Nords (North of France Railway stocks).

le P.-L.-M.,   P.L.M's.

le Rio *ou* le Rio-Tinto, Rios *or* Rio Tintos.

le Gaz de Paris, Paris Gas.

les pétroles roumains (*m.pl.*) *ou* les pétrolifères roumaines (*f.pl.*), Roumanian oils.

les Forces Motrices du Rhône (*f.pl.*), Forces Motrices du Rhône.

les caoutchoucs (*m.pl.*) *ou* les caoutchoutières (*f.pl.*), rubbers.

(2) Where no gender is indicated as in proper names and foreign shares, they are referred to in the feminine singular, as,

la Van Ryn Deep, Van Ryn Deeps or Van Ryn Deep.

la Crown Mines,   Crown Mines.

la Meyer and Charlton, Meyer and Charltons *or* Meyer and Charlton.

la Mexican Eagle, Mexican Eagles *or* Mexican Eagle.

la Shell Transport,   Shell Transports *or* Shell Transport.

la Linggi, Linggis *or* Linggi.

la Tanganika *ou en abrév.* la Tanga, Tanganikas *or* Tanganika *or abbreviated* Tanks.

l'Anglo French,   Anglo-French.

Such expressions in market news concerning ruling prices as **Smith** or **Smiths** (*singular or plural in English*) **rose** (*past tense in English*), **Jones shares** (*plural in English*) **fell,** are rendered in French as follows :—**la Smith** (*singular in French*) **monte** (*generally present tense in French*), **l'action Jones** or **les actions Jones** (*generally singular but sometimes plural in French*) **tombe** (*sing.*), **tombent** (*pl.*).

Note further :—**Robinson founders** (' shares *understood*) **rallied, la** (part de *understood*) **fondateur Robinson est en reprise.**

share (*v.t.*) or **share in,**   partager; participer à; avoir part à; prendre part à; avoir en partage :

we all share alike,   nous partageons tous également.

to share (or to share in) the profits or the losses in proportion to one's holding,   participer, avoir part, prendre part, aux bénéfices ou aux pertes au prorata de sa mise de fonds.

to share an office with someone,   avoir avec quelqu'un un bureau en partage.

share bonus (opp. to *cash bonus*),   bonus en actions (*m.*).

share capital,   capital-actions (*m.*):

company with a share capital of so much, société avec un capital-actions de tant (*f.*).

share capital paid up,   capital-actions versé (*m.*).

share certificate,   titre d'actions (*m.*) (*or* titre d'action *if for* 1 *share only*);   certificat d'action(s) (*m.*).

shareholder. V. ci-après.

share jointly (to),   copartager.

share ledger or **share register,**   grand livre des titres (*m.*);   grand livre des actionnaires (*m.*);   registre des actionnaires (*m.*);   livre d'actionnaires (*m.*).

share market,   marché des valeurs (*m.*);   marché des titres (*m.*).   *For information concerning the Paris Bourse, see under* marché des valeurs.

share prices,   cours des actions (*m.pl.*).

share pusher (pers.),   démarcheur (*m.*).

share pushing,   démarchage (*m.*).

share qualification, cautionnement en actions (*m.*). V. exemples sous **qualification.**

share reinsurance (distinguished from *excess reinsurance*), réassurance de partage (*f.*).

share transfer, transfert d'actions (*m.*).

share warrant *or* **share warrant to bearer,** titre au porteur (*m.*).

shareholder (pers.) (*n.*), actionnaire (*m.* ou *f.*); sociétaire (*m.* ou *f.*):
shareholders' meeting, assemblée d'actionnaires (*f.*); réunion d'actionnaires (*f.*).
auditor who is also a shareholder, commissaire qui est aussi sociétaire (*m.*).

sharer (pers.) (*n.*), partageant (*m.*); participant, -e.

sharing (*n.*), partage (*m.*); participation (*f.*):
sharing of profits *or* profit sharing, partage des bénéfices; participation aux bénéfices.
the sharing of the spoil, le partage du butin.

shark (pers.) (*n.*), requin (*m.*); corsaire (*m.*):
financial shark, requin financier; corsaire de la finance.

she (when speaking of a ship) (*pron.*), il:
Note :—In French, a ship is grammatically masculine. In English, a ship is generally personified as feminine, and is then referred to as *she*. The use of *it*, while not incorrect, is unusual. Similarly, *sister ship* becomes in French *navire frère.*
one says that the ship is cleared when she is provided with all her papers, on dit que le navire est expédié quand il est muni de tous ses papiers.

shed (*n.*), 'hangar (*m.*):
dock shed, hangar de dock.
shed for aeroplanes, hangar pour avions.

shed (*v.t.*), céder:
share which sheds a few fractions, action qui cède quelques fractions (*f.*).

sheet (*n.*), feuille (*f.*):
sheet of paper, of coupons, feuille de papier, de coupons.

sheet (tarpaulin, or the like, for covering railway wagons) (*n.*), bâche (*f.*).

sheet (to cover with a sheet) (Rly.) (*v.t.*), bâcher:
to sheet a railway wagon, bâcher un wagon de chemin de fer.

sheeted open wagon (Rly.), wagon découvert bâché (*m.*).

sheeting (covering railway wagons with sheets) (*n.*), bâchage (*m.*).

shelter (*n.*), refuge (*m.*).

shew (*v.t.*). Syn. de **show.**

shift (to move) (*v.t.*), déplacer:
to shift the burden of proof, déplacer, renverser, intervertir, le fardeau de la preuve.

shift (cargo) (*v.t.*), désarrimer:
rolling has the grave inconvenience of tending to shift the cargo in the holds and to throw it to one side, le roulis présente le grave inconvénient de tendre à désarrimer les marchandises dans les cales et à les rejeter à un côté.

shift (to move) (*v.i.*), se déplacer:
price which shifts slightly, cours qui se déplace un peu.

shift (speaking of cargo) (*v.i.*), se désarrimer; riper.

shifting *or* **shift** (moving) (*n.*), déplacement (*m.*):
shift of prices (Stock Exch.), déplacement de cours.

shifting (of cargo) (*n.*), désarrimage (*m.*); ripage (*m.*):
breakage as a consequence of shifting, bris à la suite de désarrimage (*m.*).

shilling (*n.*) (Abbrev.: **s.** *or* /), schelling (*m.*); shilling (*m.*):
two shillings (*Abbrev. :* 2s. *or* 2s. 0d. *or* 2/-), deux schellings (*Abrév. :* 2sh. *ou* 2sh. 0d. *ou* 2s. 0d.).
two shillings and sixpence *or* two and six (*Abbrev. :* 2s. 6d. *or* 2/6d. *or* 2/6), deux schellings et six pence; deux schellings six (*Abrév. :* 2sh. 6d. *ou* 2s. 6d. *ou* 2sh. 6).

ship (*n.*), navire (*m.*); vaisseau (*m.*); bâtiment (*m.*); bateau (*m.*); bord (*m.*):
sailing ship, navire à voiles; bâtiment à voiles; bateau à voiles.
cargo sacrificed for the necessities of the ship, marchandises sacrifiées pour les nécessités du bord (*f.pl.*).
the ship's boats, les embarcations du bord (*f.pl.*).
the captain should be the last to leave his ship, le capitaine ne doit quitter son bord que le dernier; le capitaine doit rester le dernier à son bord.
ship at sea, navire en mer.
ship collided with, navire abordé; abordé (*m.*):
the damage caused by the colliding ship to the ship collided with, le dommage occasionné par le navire aborduer (*ou* par l'abordeur) au navire abordé (*ou* à l'abordé).
ship going light, navire marchant à vide.
ship in ballast, navire sur (*ou* en) lest.
ship in course of building, navire en construction.
ship in distress, navire en détresse.
ship not responsible, etc. V. ci-après.
ship under orders, navire à ordre.

ship (*v.t.*), charger; embarquer; expédier:
to ship grain in bulk, charger des grains en vrac.
owner who has the right to ship the goods on the following vessel, armateur qui a le droit de charger les marchandises sur le navire suivant (*m.*).
to ship the goods within the agreed period of time, embarquer la marchandise dans la période de temps convenue.
to ship the goods to their port of destination, expédier les marchandises à leur port de destination.
to ship on deck, charger sur le pont; charger sur le tillac; charger en pontée:
goods shipped on deck, marchandises chargées sur le pont (*ou* sur le tillac) (*ou* en pontée) (*f.pl.*).
shipped in apparent good order and condition

. . . the goods marked and numbered as follows (bill of lading), chargé (*ou* ont été chargées) en bon état et conditionnement apparents . . . les marchandises marquées et numerotées comme ci-après.

ship breaker (pers.), démolisseur de navires (*m.*).

ship broker, courtier maritime (*m.*); courtier de navires (*m.*). *See note under* courtier maritime *in French-English section.*

shipbuilder, shipbuilding. V. ci-après.

ship canal, canal maritime (*m.*):
the Manchester ship canal, le canal maritime de Manchester.

ship chandler (pers.), fournisseur de navires (*m.*); fournisseur maritime (*m.*).

ship chandlery, fournitures pour navires (*f.pl.*); fournitures maritimes (*f.pl.*).

ship charge (radiotelegrams) (opp. to *land charge*), taxe de bord (*f.*).

shipmaster. V. ci-après.

ship not responsible for marks, for breakages (bill of lading clause), ne répondant pas des marques, de la casse; sans garantie des marques, de la casse.

shipowner. V. ci-après.

ship policy, police sur corps (*f.*).

ship repairer (pers.), réparateur de navires (*m.*).

ship repairs, réparations maritimes (*f.pl.*).

ship's articles, rôle d'équipage (*m.*); rôle de l'équipage (*m.*); rôle d'armement (*m.*).

ship's books, livres de bord (*m.pl.*).

ship's broker, consignataire du navire (*m.*); consignataire de la coque (*m.*).

ship's captain, capitaine de navire (*m.*).

ship's disbursements, mises dehors (*f.pl.*).

ship's inventory, inventaire de bord (*m.*).

ship's papers, pièces de bord (*f.pl.*); papiers de bord (*m.pl.*); expéditions (*f.pl.*); papiers d'expédition (*m.pl.*).

ship's register, certificat d'immatriculation (*m.*); certificat d'attache (*m.*). *Note :*—These are only literal translations. The equivalent of *ship's register*, in France, of a ship of French nationality, is *acte de francisation* (*m.*) or *brevet de francisation* (*m.*), and in Belgium, of a ship of Belgian nationality, *lettre de mer* (*f.*).

ship's stores, approvisionnements de bord (*m.pl.*); provisions de bord (*f.pl.*).

ship's tackles, palans du navire (*m.pl.*).

under ship's tackle *or* **under ship's derrick** *or* **under ship's slings** *or* **over ship's side** *or* **at ship's rail,** sous palan; sous vergues. V. exemples sous **under ship's derrick.**

ship station (Radioteleg.) (opp. to *coast station*), station de bord (*f.*).

ship store dealer, fournisseur de navires (*m.*); fournisseur maritime (*m.*).

ship stores, fournitures pour navires (*f.pl.*); fournitures maritimes (*f.pl.*).

shipwreck, shipyard. V. ci-après.

shipbuilder (pers.) (*n.*), constructeur de navires (*m.*).

shipbuilding (*n.*), construction de navires (*f.*); construction navale (*f.*); construction maritime (*f.*).

shipbuilding company, société de construction de navires (*f.*); société de construction navale (*f.*).

shipbuilding industry, industrie des constructions navales (*f.*).

shipbuilding yard. Syn. de **shipyard.**

shipmaster (pers.) (*n.*), capitaine de navire (*m.*).

shipment (act of shipping) (*n.*) (Abbrev.: **shipt**), chargement (*m.*); charge (*f.*); chargé (*m.*); embarquement (*m.*); expédition (*f.*):
shipment on first steamer, on following ship, chargement, embarquement, sur premier vapeur, sur navire suivant.

freight payable at destination as per weight declared on shipment, fret payable à destination suivant poids déclaré à l'embarquement (*m.*).

evidence of shipment, preuve de chargement (*ou* de chargé) (*f.*).

the present shipment is made on the following conditions, la présente expédition est faite aux conditions portées ci-après.

prompt shipment. V. sous **prompt.**

Cuban sugar quoted, for March-April shipment at 7s. 4½d. c.i.f. U.K., on cote le sucre de Cuba, embarquement mars-avril (*ou* expédition en mars-avril) à 7sh. 4 1/2d. caf. Royaume-Uni.

shipment on deck, chargement sur le pont; chargement sur le tillac; chargement en pontée.

shipment (a consignment) (*n.*), chargement (*m.*); expédition (*f.*):
the name of the ship and the value of the shipment, le nom du navire et la valeur du chargement.

package forming part of the shipment, colis faisant partie du chargement (*m.*).

the number of cases making up a shipment, le nombre de caisses composant une expédition.

shipment *or* **for shipment** (Produce Exch.) (opp. to *spot* or *on the spot*), livrable:
prices: spot (or on the spot) so much; shipment (or for shipment) so much, cours: disponible tant; livrable tant.

shipowner (pers.) (*n.*), armateur (*m.*); propriétaire de navire (*m.*); fréteur (*m.*). V. exemples et note sous syn. **owner** (shipowner).

shipowners *collectively may be rendered by* armement (*m.*), *as,* the difficulties encountered by shipowners, les difficultés que rencontrent l'armement (*f.pl.*).

shipowners' office, bureau de l'armement (*m.*).

shipowning business. V. sous **shipping business,** ci-après.

shipped bill of lading, connaissement embarqué (*m.*).

shipper (pers.) (*n.*), chargeur (*m.*); expéditeur (*m.*):
shippers are merchants engaging in import trade and export trade, les chargeurs sont des commerçants se livrant au commerce d'importation et au commerce d'exportation.

shipping (act) (*n.*),   chargement (*m.*);   charge (*f.*); embarquement (*m.*); expédition (*f.*).

shipping (business) (*n.*),   navigation (*f.*); transport maritime (*m.*). V. aussi **shipping business** *or simply* **shipping**, ci-après.

shipping (ships collectively;   tonnage) (*n.*), marine (*f.*); tonnage (*m.*):
  merchant shipping, marine marchande.
  where, there is an abundance of shipping and little cargo, freight is low, and vice versa, là où il y a abondance de tonnage et peu de marchandises, le fret est bas, et inversement.

shipping agency,   agence maritime (*f.*); agence d'affrètement (*f.*).

shipping agent, agent maritime (*m.*); commissionnaire-chargeur (*m.*); commissionnaire-expéditeur (*m.*).

shipping articles,   rôle d'équipage (*m.*); rôle de l'équipage (*m.*); rôle d'armement (*m.*).

shipping bill,   déclaration de réexportation d'entrepôt (*f.*).

shipping business *or* **shipping trade** *or* **shipping industry** *or* **shipowning business** *or simply* **shipping** (*n.*),   armement (*m.*); industrie de l'armement (*f.*); industrie des transports maritimes (*f.*):
  steps taken to encourage the national shipping business (*or* to encourage national shipping), mesures prises pour encourager l'armement national (*f.pl.*).
  to consider what can be done to meet the crisis in the shipping trade (*or* to meet the shipping crisis), étudier ce qui peut être fait pour parer à la crise de l'armement.
  the shipping industry is more and more in the hands of companies, l'industrie de l'armement est de plus en plus entre les mains de sociétés.

shipping card, carte de départs (*f.*).

shipping charges, frais d'expédition (*m.pl.*).

shipping clerk, expéditionnaire (*m.*).

shipping company,   compagnie (*ou* société) de navigation (*f.*);   compagnie (*ou* société) d'armement (*f.*);   compagnie (*ou* société) de transports maritimes (*f.*).

shipping conference (ring), conférence maritime(*f.*).

shipping directory, répertoire maritime (*m.*).

shipping documents,   pièces d'embarquement (*f.pl.*); documents d'embarquement (*m.pl.*); documents d'expédition (*m.pl.*), documents maritimes (*m.pl.*).

shipping exchange, bourse maritime (*f.*); bourse des frets (*f.*).

shipping house *or* **shipping firm,** maison d'armement (*f.*).

shipping instructions,   instructions relatives à l'embarquement (*ou* aux embarquements) (*f.pl.*).

shipping law, droit maritime (*m.*).

shipping line (transportation system), ligne de navigation (*f.*).

shipping master, commissaire maritime (*m.*).

Shipping News *or* **Shipping Intelligence** *or simply* **Shipping** (newspaper heading), Mouvement des Navires ; Sur Mer.

shipping note (Abbrev.: **S/N.**),   permis d'embarquement (*m.*); note de chargement (*f.*).

shipping office,   bureau d'armement (*m.*).

shipping port,   port de charge (*m.*); port de chargement (*m.*);   port d'embarquement (*m.*); port d'expédition (*m.*);   port expéditeur (*m.*).

shipping shares, valeurs de navigation (*f.pl.*).

shipping ton, tonneau d'affrètement (*m.*); tonneau de fret (*m.*);   tonneau de portée (*m.*);   tonne de portée en lourd (*f.*).   In France, 1,000 kilogrammes, or 1·44 cubic metres, usually. In England, the shipping ton is 20 cwt or 40 cubic feet (1·132 cubic metres), usually.

shipping weight, poids à l'embarquement (*m.*).

shipwreck (*n.*), naufrage (*m.*).

shipwrecked (*adj.*), naufragé, -e :
  shipwrecked persons,   personnes naufragée. (*f.pl.*); naufragés (*m.pl.*).
  shipwrecked vessel, navire naufragé (*m.*).
  to be shipwrecked, faire naufrage.

shipyard (*n.*),   chantier de construction navale (*m.*);   chantier naval (*m.*);   chantier de construction maritime (*m.*);   chantier de construction de navires (*m.*);   chantier de construction (*m.*).

shop (*n.*), magasin (*m.*); boutique (*f.*); officine (*f.*); maison (*f.*):
  bucket shop, officine de contre-partie ; maison de contre-partie. Cf. **stable.**

shop (Stock Exch.) (pers.) (*n.*),   introducteurs (*m.pl.*); syndicat-animateur (*m.*). V. exemple sous **bringing out** (Stock Exch.).

shop assistant, employé (-e) de magasin ; commis (-e) de magasin.

shop buying (Stock Exch.), achats professionnels (*m.pl.*).

shop selling (Stock Exch.), ventes professionnelles (*f.pl.*).

shop shares, actions à l'introduction (*f.pl.*).

shore (of the sea) (*n.*),   rivage (*m.*); bord (*m.*); littoral (*m.*);   côte (*f.*); grève (*f.*); plage (*f.*); rive (*f.*):
  the shores of the Baltic, les bords de la mer Baltique.

shore (of a lake) (*n.*), rivage (*m.*).

shore (of a river) (*n.*),   rivage (*m.*); rive (*f.*); grève (*f.*).

shore (on), à terre :
  fire on shore or on board, feu à terre ou à bord (*m.*).

shore risk (Mar. Insce), risque de séjour à terre (*m.*).

short (*adj.*) (Ant.: *long*), court, -e :
  deposit at short notice, dépôt à court terme (*m.*).
  securities realizable at short notice,   valeurs réalisables à court terme (*f.pl.*).
  short bill *or* short dated bill, effet à courte échéance (*m.*); effet à courts jours (*m.*); effet à courts-jours (*m.*).
  short credit, crédit à court terme (*m.*); crédit à (*ou* de) courte durée (*m.*); court crédit (*m.*).
  short exchange, papier court (*m.*).
  short loan, prêt à court terme (*m.*).
  short-sea trader, short-sea trading.   V. note sous **cabotage.**

short shipped, embarqué (-e) en moins:
amount short shipped, quantité embarquée
en moins (f.).

short term investment or short dated investment, placement à court terme (m.).

short trial balance, balance d'inventaire (f.).

to be short of money, être à court, être court
(-e), d'argent.

short (missing) (adj.), de manque:
to find two shillings short in a five pound bag,
trouver deux schellings de manque dans
un sac de cinq livres.

short (Stock Exch.) (adj.), à découvert:
short account or short interest or **shorts** (pers.)
(n.pl.), position vendeur (f.); position à la
baisse (f.); découvert (m.):
operator who has a big short account in such
a stock, opérateur qui a une grosse position
vendeur de telle valeur (m.).
there is a big short account (or short interest)
open in Mexican Eagles, le découvert sur la
Mexican Eagle est étendu.
there are no shorts, il n'y a pas de découvert.
the shorts are buying back, le découvert
se rachète.
short sale, vente à découvert (f.).
short seller, vendeur à découvert (m.).

short (Stock Exch.) (adv.), à découvert:
to sell short or **to short** (v.t.), vendre à
découvert:
to sell Rios short or to short Rios, vendre du
Rio à découvert.

short (bear sale) (Stock Exch.) (n.), vente à
découvert (f.).

short (bear) (Stock Exch.) (pers.) (n.), baissier (m.).

short (Banking or Cash keeping) (n.), déficit
(m.); mali (m.); manquant (m.); manque
(m.):
cash shorts and overs, déficits et excédents (ou
malis et bonis) de caisse (ou dans l'encaisse)
(m.pl.).

short (Bkkpg) (n.), somme partielle (f.):
the shorts which make up the total, les
sommes partielles qui composent le total.
shorts column, colonne pour les sommes
partielles (f.).

shortage (n.), manquant (m.); manque (m.);
déficit (m.); découvert (m.); mali (m.):
owner liable for shortage (or shortages),
armateur responsable des manquants (m.).
shortage in weight, déficit de poids; manquant
en poids.
shortage in the cash, déficit de caisse; déficit
dans l'encaisse; manquant en caisse;
manque en caisse; mali de caisse; tare
de caisse (f.).
to make up a shortage, suppléer (ou combler)
(ou bonifier) un déficit (ou un découvert).

shortest route, itinéraire le plus court (m.).

shorthand (adj.), sténographique; sténographe:
shorthand signs, signes sténographiques (m.pl.).
shorthand reporter, reporter sténographe (m.).

shorthand (n.) or **shorthand writing,** sténographie
(f.).

shorthand and typewriting, sténodactylographie
(f.).

shorthand machine, machine à sténographier
(f.); sténotype (f.).

shorthand notebook, bloc-sténo (m.).

shorthand-typist (pers.) (n.), sténodactylographe
(m. ou f.); sténodactylo (m. ou f.).

shorthand writer or **shorthand reporter,** sténographe (m. ou f.); sténo (m. ou f.).

shortly maturing bonds, bons à échéance
rapprochée (m.pl.).

show (v.t.), montrer; accuser; porter; faire
preuve de; marquer; faire ressortir; faire
apparaître; faire figurer; se traduire;
présenter; représenter; exhiber; donner;
constater; justifier:
account which shows a loss, compte qui accuse
(ou qui fait ressortir) (ou qui montre) une
perte (m.); compte qui se solde (ou se traduit)
par une perte (m.).
according as the result of the trading shows
(or is) a profit or a loss, suivant que le
résultat de l'exercice accuse (ou fait ressortir)
un bénéfice ou une perte; suivant que le
résultat de l'exercice est bénéficiaire ou
déficitaire.
balance sheet showing a profit, showing a loss,
bilan bénéficiaire, déficitaire (m.).
the stock market continues to show strength,
to show a good deal of liveliness, le marché
des valeurs continue à faire preuve de
résistance, à faire preuve d'une grande
animation (ou continue à marquer une bonne
résistance, une grande animation).
to show the reserve among the liabilities, porter
en passif la réserve; faire figurer la réserve
au passif.
to show illusory profits by overvaluing the
exchange, faire apparaître (ou faire ressortir)
des bénéfices mensongers en majorant les
valeurs d'échange.
the passenger is bound to show his ticket
whenever required to so do by the company's
servants, le voyageur est tenu de présenter
(ou de représenter) (ou d'exhiber) son billet
à toute réquisition des préposés de la
compagnie.
the pass book shows the customer's position
at the bank, le carnet de compte donne la
situation en banque du client.
certificate which shows the existence of mortgages, certificat qui constate l'existence
d'hypothèques (m.).
to show that all the necessary formalities have
been complied with, justifier de l'accomplissement de toutes les formalités requises.

to show a balance, (said of an account), présenter
un solde; se solder; se balancer; faire
ressortir une balance:
account which shows a balance of so many
pounds to the credit, compte qui présente
un solde de tant de livres au crédit; compte
qui se solde (ou qui se balance) par tant de
livres au crédit (m.).
the current account usually shows a credit
balance in his favour, le compte courant
se solde habituellement en sa faveur par
un crédit.

account which shows a debit balance, compte
qui se solde par un débit (m.); compte qui
se balance par un solde débiteur (m.).
to ascertain whether the budget of this State
balances or shows a deficit, s'assurer si le
budget de cet État se solde en équilibre
ou en déficit.
column showing the balance of each account,
colonne faisant ressortir la balance de
chaque compte (f.).
to be shown or **show** (v.i.), être montré, -e,
accusé, -e, porté, -e, ressorti, -e, etc.;
ressortir; figurer; apparaître:
the balance shown in the cash book, le solde
accusé par le livre de caisse.
the amount shown in the cash column, la
somme ressortie à la colonne de caisse.
the amounts written off are shown in red (or
are shown in red ink), les amortissements
figurent en rouge (ou sont ressortis à l'encre
rouge) (m.pl.).
securities shown in the official list, valeurs
portées à la cote officielle (f.pl.).
showing tickets, présentation (f.), représentation
(f.), exhibition (f.) de billets.
shrink (v.i.), se rétrécir; se retirer:
X. shares shrank from 17/6 to 17/-, l'action X.
se rétrécit (ou se retire) de 17sh. 6d. à 17sh.
shunting (Stock Exch.) (n.), arbitrage (m.);
arbitrage de place à place (m.) (entre deux
villes dans le même pays): [Cf. **arbitrage** or
arbitraging (Stock Exch.)]
shunting stocks, arbitrage de valeurs.
shut out (v.t.), exclure:
shut out cargo, cargaison exclue (f.).
shut up shop (to), fermer boutique.
shutting out, exclusion (f.).
sickness insurance, assurance contre la maladie
(f.).
side (n.), côté (m.):
the left hand side of an account, le côté gauche
d'un compte.
side note (marginal note), apostille (f.).
siding (Rly.) (n.), voie de garage (f.). Cf. private
siding.
sidings (Rly.) (n.pl.), voies de garage (f.pl.);
gare d'évitement (f.).
sight (n.), vu (m.); vue (f.):
to pay a bill on sight of the bill of lading,
payer une traite au vu du connaissement.
at sight or **sight** (used as adj.), à vue; à
présentation; sur demande:
draft at sight or draft payable at sight or
sight draft or sight bill, traite à vue (f.);
disposition à vue (f.); traite payable à vue
(ou à présentation) (f.); effet à vue (m.);
bon à vue (m.).
sight bills, papier à vue (m.).
after sight (Abbrev.: **a/s.**) or **at . . . sight,** de
vue; à . . . de vue:
the number of days after sight, le nombre de
jours de vue.
three days after sight pay, etc. (bill of
exchange), à trois jours de vue veuillez
payer, etc. V. **first of exchange** pour exemple
complet.

bill payable thirty days after sight or bill
payable at thirty days' sight (Abbrev.:
b.p. 30 d.s.), effet payable à trente jours
de vue (m.).
sight (bills of exchange) (v.t.), viser; voir:
to sight a bill of exchange, viser une lettre de
change.
bill sighted (date), effet vu le (date).
sight entry (Customs) (distinguished from perfect,
or perfected, entry), déclaration provisoire
(f.).
sighting (of a bill of exchange) (n.), visa (d'une
lettre de change) (m.).
sign (v.t.), signer; revêtir d'une signature;
souscrire; viser:
to sign a letter, signer une lettre.
bill of lading signed by the master, connaissement signé du capitaine (m.).
please sign and return the enclosed acknowledgment, nous vous prions de nous
retourner l'accusé de réception ci-joint,
revêtu de votre signature.
to sign a contract, signer, souscrire, un contrat.
persons having power to sign for the company,
personnes ayant pouvoir de signer pour la
société (f.pl.).
M. X. will sign: . . ., notre sieur X. signera:
. . .
to be signed, être signé (-e), souscrit (-e);
se signer:
document which ought to be signed, document
qui doit se signer (m.).
Note:—In England, when an official of a
Company, Bank, or other institution, signs
a letter, or other document, his description
follows his signature, thus:—
　A. B.,
　Chairman.
　C. D.,
　Managing Director.
　E. F.,
　Director.
　G. H.,
　Manager.
　I. J.,
　Secretary.
　K. L.,
　Chief Clerk.
In France, the reverse is the case, thus:—
　Le Président,
　　A. B.
　L'Administrateur délégué,
　　C. D.
　Un Administrateur,
　　E. F.
　Le Directeur,
　　G. H.
　Le Secrétaire,
　　I. J.
　Le Chef de Bureau,
　　K. L.

sign manual, seing (m.).
sign on (v.t.), engager:

to sign on the crew of a ship, engager l'équipage d'un navire.

sign on (*v.i.*), s'engager.

sign the book (to) (to append one's signature or initials in a delivery book, wages book or sheet, or the like, as acknowledgment of receipt), émarger le carnet.

signatory [signatories *pl.*] *or* **signatary** [signataries *pl.*] *or* **signer** (pers.) (*n.*), signataire (*m.* ou *f.*): signatory to (*or* signer of) a contract, signataire d'un contrat.

signature (*n.*), signature (*f.*); seing (*m.*); visa (*m.*):
to legalize a signature, faire légaliser une signature.

signature *or* **signing** (of a delivery book, wages book or sheet, or the like) (*n.*), émargement (*m.*):
to deliver a parcel to the addressee against signature in the delivery book, remettre un colis au destinataire contre émargement au carnet de livraison.

signature book (Banking), livre de signatures (*m.*).

signature stamp, griffe (*f.*).

signet wafer, pain à cacheter (*m.*).

signing (*n.*), signature (*f.*); souscription (*f.*):
the signing of the contract will take place to-morrow, la signature du contrat aura lieu demain.
contract which only wants signing, contrat qui ne manque que la souscription (*m.*).

signing on, engagement (*m.*).

silent partner (opp. to *acting partner*), commanditaire (*m.* ou *f.*); associé commanditaire (*m.*); bailleur de fonds (*m.*).

silo (*n.*), silo (*m.*).

silver (the metal) (*n.*), argent (*m.*); argent métal (*m.*); métal argent (*m.*): (*Note :*—The word *argent* alone meaning *money* or *cash*, besides meaning *silver*, the expression *argent métal* or *métal argent* is used when it is not clear from the context that *silver* is meant.)
bar silver, argent en barres.
silver without change yesterday in London, argent métal sans changement hier à Londres.
the revenues of the government of India are collected in rupees, that is to say, in silver: this silver has to be converted into gold, les revenus du gouvernement des Indes sont encaissés en roupies, c'est-à-dire en métal argent : cet argent doit être converti en or.

silver (*n.*) *or* **silver money** *or* **silver coin** *or* **silver currency** (collectively), argent (*m.*); monnaie d'argent (*f.*); monnaie-argent (*f.*); numéraire d'argent (*m.*); pièces en argent (*f.pl.*).

silver bullion, matières d'argent (*f.pl.*).

silver coin (a single coin), pièce d'argent (*f.*); pièce en argent (*f.*).

silver coin and bullion (Banking), encaisse-argent (*f.*).

silver franc, franc-argent (*m.*).

silver point, silver-point (*m.*).

silver standard, étalon-argent (*m.*); étalon d'argent (*m.*).

silver standard country, pays à étalon d'argent (*m.*); pays monométalliste-argent (*m.*).

simple arbitration *or* **simple arbitrage** (distinguished from *compound arbitration* or *arbitrage*), arbitrage simple (*m.*).

simple credit (opp. to *confirmed credit*), crédit simple (*m.*); accréditif simple (*m.*); crédit non confirmé (*m.*).

simple debenture (opp. to *mortgage debenture*), obligation chirographaire (*f.*).

simple interest (opp. to *compound interest*), intérêt simple (*m.*).

simulated debt, dette simulée (*f.*).

sine die, sine die; sans date :
to adjourn sine die, s'ajourner sine die (*ou* sans date).

single (*adj.*), simple; unique :
single commission (on double operation of purchase and sale) (Stock Exch.), franco (*m.*):
to benefit by the single commission, profiter du franco.
single entry (Bkkpg) (opp. to *double entry*), partie simple (*f.*); inscription unigraphique (*f.*): (V. exemple sous **contra**.)
single entry bookkeeping, tenue des livres en partie simple (*ou* à partie simple) (*f.*); comptabilité en partie simple (*ou* à partie simple) (*f.*); comptabilisation en partie simple (*f.*); unigraphie (*f.*).
single ledger (account on an opening; folioed) (opp. to *double ledger*), grand livre simple (*m.*).
in a single payment, une fois payé, -e :
in consideration of a sum in a single payment, moyennant une somme une fois payée.
instead of an annual payment of £100, he preferred to give £1,000 in a single payment, au lieu de £100 de rente, il a préféré donner £1 000 une fois payées.
single premium (Insce) (distinguished from *annual*, or *yearly*, *premium*), prime unique (*f.*).
single stroke staple press, agrafeuse coup de poing (*f.*).
single ticket *or* simply **single** (*n.*) (opp. to *return ticket* or simply *return*), billet simple (*m.*).

sink (to cause to founder by scuttling) (*v.t.*), couler :
to sink a ship, couler un navire.

sink (to amortize) (*v.t.*), amortir :
to sink a loan, the national debt, amortir un emprunt, la dette publique.

sink (to founder) (*v.i.*), couler; couler bas; couler à fond; sombrer :
ship which sank and was lost, navire qui coula (*ou* qui sombra) et se perdit (*m.*).

sinking (amortization) (*n.*), amortissement (*m.*).

sinking fund, fonds d'amortissement (*m.*); caisse d'amortissement (*f.*).

sister company, société sœur (*f.*); compagnie sœur (*f.*).

sister ship *or* simply **sister** (*n.*), navire frère (*m.*); navire jumeau (*m.*); frère (*m.*):
s/s. *A.* sister to s/s. *B.*, s/s. *A.* frère du s/s. *B.*

sit (*v.i.*), siéger; tenir:
the tribunal sits all the year round, le tribunal siège (*ou* tient) toute l'année.
sitting (*n.*), séance (*f.*):
to open the sitting, ouvrir la séance.
situation (employment) (*n.*), position (*f.*); place (*f.*); poste (*m.*); emploi (*m.*).
situation vacant [**situations vacant** *pl.*], offre d'emploi (*f.*).
situation wanted [**situations wanted** *pl.*], demande d'emploi (*f.*).
six months, six mois (*m.pl.*); semestre (*m.*).
V. exemples de l'emploi du mot semestre *sous* **half year.**
sixpence (*n.*), six pence (*m.pl.*); demi-shilling (*m.*).
sketch (*n.*), tracé (*m.*):
sketch of an account book (to show ruling, etc.), tracé d'un livre de compte.
skilled (*adj.*), expérimenté, -e.
skipper (of a boat) (pers.) (*Colloquial*) (*n.*), patron (*m.*); capitaine (*m.*).
slacken (*v.i.*), ralentir.
slackening (*n.*), ralentissement (*m.*):
seasonal slackening of orders, ralentissement saisonnier de commandes.
slaughter (sweeping reduction in prices) (*n.*), mévente (*f.*).
slaughter (*v.t.*), mévendre:
to slaughter one's stocks, mévendre ses titres.
sleeping car, wagon-lit (*m.*); voiture-lit (*f.*).
sleeping partner (opp. to *acting partner*), commanditaire (*m. ou f.*); associé commanditaire (*m.*); bailleur de fonds (*m.*).
slide (collapse of prices) (Stock Exch.) (*n.*), chute (*f.*); débâcle (*f.*).
sliding wage scale, échelle mobile des salaires (*f.*).
slip (of paper) (*n.*), fiche (*f.*); feuille (*f.*); bordereau (*m.*):
slip pinned to the document, fiche épinglée au document.
paying in slip, bordereau (*ou* feuille) de versement.
slip (small piece of paper stuck on a bill of lading or an insurance policy and containing a clause or reservation) (*n.*), papillon (*m.*):
special slip stuck on a bill of lading referring to the non liability clause, papillon spécial collé sur un connaissement se référant à la clause d'irresponsabilité.
slip (memorandum of marine insurance) (*n.*), slip (*m.*).
slip (way for a ship) (*n.*), cale (*f.*).
slip back (to), glisser:
X. shares slipped back from 2s. 6d. to 2s. 3d., l'action X. glisse de 2sh. 6d. à 2sh. 3d.
slip of the pen, erreur de plume (*f.*).
slipway (*n.*), cale de halage (*f.*).
slogan (*n.*), slogan (*m.*).
slow boat (opp. to *fast boat*), navire lent (*m.*); bateau omnibus (*m.*).
slow train, train omnibus (*m.*); train de petite vitesse (*m.*); petite vitesse (*f.*).
slump (Stock Exch.) (*n.*) (Ant.: *boom*), effondrement (*m.*); dégringolade (*f.*); débâcle (*f.*):

slump in prices, effondrement, dégringolade, de cours.
but after this boom, there was a slump, mais après ce boom, c'est la débâcle.
slump (*v.i.*), s'effondrer:
X. shares slumped from 4 to 3, l'action X. s'effondre de 4 à 3.
small (*adj.*), petit, -e; menu, -e; faible; peu important, -e; de peu d'importance:
small advertisement, petite annonce (*f.*); annonce classée (*f.*).
small craft (river and/or canal boats), batellerie (*f.*).
small denominations, petites coupures (*f.pl.*).
small deposits, menus dépôts (*m.pl.*).
small income, faible revenu (*m.*).
small money *or* small change *or* small coin, petite monnaie (*f.*); menue monnaie (*f.*); appoint (*m.*):
gold, silver, small coin, or, argent, appoint.
copper and nickel moneys are only used for making up amounts with small coin (*or* with minor coin) (*or* with small change), that is to say, they are struck for small divisions of the monetary unit which it was impossible to strike in precious metal: they are merely tokens, les monnaies de bronze et de nickel ne servent qu'à faire les appoints, c'est-à-dire qu'on les frappe pour de petites divisions de l'unité monétaire, qu'il était impossible de frapper en métal précieux: elles jouent le rôle de simples jetons.
small order, ordre de peu d'importance (*m.*).
small sum of money, faible somme d'argent (*f.*).
smash (*n.*), krach (*m.*); krack (*m.*); débâcle (*f.*); chute (*f.*):
a bank smash, le krach (*ou* la chute) d'une banque.
smooth away difficulties (to), aplanir des difficultés.
smuggle (*v.t.*), passer en contrebande.
smuggle (*v.i.*), faire la contrebande; smogler.
smuggled goods, marchandises de contrebande (*f.pl.*).
smuggler (pers.) (*n.*), contrebandier, -ère; fraudeur, -euse.
smuggling (*n.*), contrebande (*f.*).
so many *or* **so much,** tant:
so many days' interest at so much per cent, tant de jours d'intérêt à tant pour cent.
so near thereunto as she can safely get, always afloat (charter party), aussi près qu'il pourra en atteindre en sécurité, toujours à flot; aussi près qu'il pourra s'en approcher en sûreté (*ou* s'en approcher sans danger), étant toujours en flot; aussi près de là qu'il pourra approcher en sécurité, le navire restant à flot.
society [**societies** *pl.*] (*n.*) (Abbrev.: **Soc.**), société (*f.*); association (*f.*):
cooperative society, société coopérative; société de coopération; coopérative (*f.*).
commercial travellers' society, association des voyageurs de commerce.

sola of exchange or **sole of exchange,** seule de change (*f.*).

sold (to be) (for sale), à vendre :
to be sold.—banking premises, à vendre.—immeuble de banque.

sold contract (Stock Exch.) (opp. to *bought contract*), bordereau de vente (*m.*).

sold ledger, grand livre des ventes (*m.*).

sole agent, agent exclusif (*m.*) :
sole agent for France and Colonies, agent exclusif pour la France et ses Colonies.

sole arbitrator, arbitre unique (*m.*).

sole director, administrateur unique (*m.*).

sole legatee, légataire universel (*m.*) ; légataire universelle (*f.*).

sole owner or **sole proprietor,** seul propriétaire (*m.*) ; seule propriétaire (*f.*) ; propriétaire unique (*m.* ou *f.*).

sole right, droit exclusif (*m.*).

solemn contract, contrat solennel (*m.*).

solicit (*v.t.*), solliciter ; rechercher :
to solicit orders, solliciter, rechercher, des commandes.

solicitor (pers.) (*n.*) (Abbrev. : **solr**), solicitor (*m.*). (En Angleterre, conseiller légal, qui est en même temps avocat plaidant devant certaines cours.)

solicitor's department or **solicitor's office** (law department or office of an administration), contentieux (*m.*) ; service du contentieux (*m.*) ; bureau du contentieux (*m.*).

solvency or **solvability** (*n.*), solvabilité (*f.*) :
solvency (*or solvability*) of a merchant, of the drawer and of the acceptor of a bill of exchange, solvabilité d'un négociant, du tireur et de l'accepteur d'une lettre de change.

solvent (*adj.*), solvable :
solvent debtor, débiteur solvable (*m.*).

something on account, à-valoir (*m.*) ; à-bon-compte (*m.*).

sorry, number's engaged (Teleph.), pas libre.

sorry, there's no reply (Teleph.), répond pas ; ne répond pas.

sorry you've been troubled (Teleph.), pardon de vous avoir dérangé ; je regrette de vous avoir dérangé.

sort (*v.t.*), trier :
to sort letters, papers, trier des lettres, des papiers.

sorting (*n.*), tri (*m.*) ; triage (*m.*).

sorting carriage or **sorting tender** (Rly.), wagon-poste (*m.*).

sorting office (Post), bureau de tri (*m.*).

sound (*adj.*), sain, -e :
sound paper (bills of exchange), papier sain (*m.*).
sound system of bookkeeping, saine organisation comptable (*f.*).
sound and realizable securities, des valeurs saines et réalisables (*f.pl.*).
a sound currency, that is to say, undepreciated in relation to gold, une monnaie saine, c'est-à-dire non dépréciée par rapport à l'or.
the sound value of the property at the time

of the accident (Insce) (opp. to *damaged value*), la valeur saine de la propriété au moment du sinistre.
the difference between the vessel's sound and insured values, la différence entre la valeur saine et la valeur assurée du navire.
sound market value (Insce), valeur marchande à l'état sain (*f.*).
to carry the passengers safe and sound to destination, conduire les voyageurs sains et saufs à destination.

source (*n.*), source (*f.*) :
source of information, of income, source d'informations, de revenu.
the firm X. & Co. states it has learned from a reliable source that . . ., la maison X. & Cⁱᵉ déclare tenir de source sûre que . . .

South African shares or *simply* **South Africans,** valeurs sud-africaines (*f.pl.*) ; valeurs transvaaliennes (*f.pl.*) ; sud-africaines (*f.pl.*) ; transvaaliennes (*f.pl.*) ; kaffiriques (*m.pl.*).

space (on a sheet of paper) (*n.*), emplacement (*m.*) ; cadre (*m.*) ; case (*f.*) :
space for service instructions, emplacement réservé (*ou* cadre réservé) (*ou* case réservée) aux mentions de service.
if the space provided on the sheet is inadequate for entering the necessary particulars, they can be put on the back, au cas où l'emplacement réservé sur la feuille serait insuffisant pour l'inscription des mentions nécessaires, celles-ci peuvent être reportées au verso.

space bar (typewriter), barre d'espacement (*f.*).

space occupied or **space taken up,** encombrement (*m.*) :
the space occupied by a cargo, l'encombrement d'un chargement. Cf. **measurement** (cubic measurement).

speak to someone about something (to), entretenir quelqu'un de quelque chose.

speaking (Teleph.) (*p.pr.*), ici (*adv.*) :
on calling : " A. B. speaking," à l'appel : « Ici A. B. »

special (*adj.*), spécial, -e, -aux :
special commissioner of taxes, directeur des contributions directes (*m.*).
special crossing (of a cheque) (opp. to *general crossing*), barrement spécial (*m.*). V. exemple sous **crossing.**
special letter of credit, lettre de crédit simple (*f.*).
special messenger (Post, etc.), messager spécial (*m.*) ; porteur spécial (*m.*).
special partnership (opp. to *general partnership*), société en participation (*f.*) ; association (*ou* association commerciale) en participation (*f.*).
special power (Law) (distinguished from *general power*), procuration spéciale (*f.*) ; mandat spécial (*m.*) ; pouvoir spécial (*m.*).
special proxy, pouvoir impératif (*m.*).
special settlement (Stock Exch.), liquidation spéciale (*f.*).
special train, train spécial (*m.*).

specialities (stocks or shares) (*n.pl.*), spécialités (*f.pl.*) ; valeurs de spécialités (*f.pl.*).

specie (*n.*),   espèces (*f.pl.*);   espèces monnayées (*f.pl.*);   numéraire (*m.*):
payment in specie *or* specie payment,   paiement en espèces (*m.*).

specie point,   gold-point (*m.*).

specific amount,   montant déterminé (*m.*);   forfait (*m.*):
open policy on valuables for a specific amount, police à forfait sur valeurs (*f.*).

specific duty (Customs) (distinguished from *ad valorem duty*),   droit spécifique (*m.*).

specific lien (opp. to *general lien*),   privilège spécial (*m.*).

specification (particularization) (*n.*),   énonciation (*f.*);   spécification (*f.*):
insurance with specification of the sum insured, assurance avec énonciation de la somme assurée (*f.*).
the specification of the goods should be made according to the terms of the tariff (Customs), l'énonciation des marchandises doit être faite suivant les termes du tarif.
the space reserved on the consignment note for the specification of the goods, l'espace réservé sur la lettre de voiture pour la spécification des marchandises (*m.*).

specification (document lodged with customs on exportation of goods) (*n.*),   déclaration d'embarquement (*f.*).

specify (*v.t.*),   énoncer;   spécifier;   prescrire:
what the policy must specify, ce que la police doit énoncer.
an insurance policy must specify: the name of the insured, etc., une police d'assurance doit énoncer: le nom de l'assuré, etc.
the goods specified below, les marchandises au-dessous spécifiées (*f.pl.*).
the sender is at liberty to specify or not the route by which his telegram should be sent, l'expéditeur est libre de prescrire ou non la voie que doit suivre son télégramme (*m.*).

specimen (*n.*),   spécimen (*m.*);   exemplaire (*m.*);   modèle (*m.*):
specimen of one's signature, spécimen de sa signature.
specimen of cheque, of letter of credit, of balance sheet *or* specimen cheque, letter of credit, balance sheet,   modèle de chèque, de lettre de crédit, de bilan.

speculate (*v.i.*),   spéculer;   jouer:
to speculate on the stock exchange, spéculer sur la bourse;   jouer à la bourse.
to speculate in stocks and shares, in exchanges, spéculer, jouer, sur les valeurs de bourse, sur les changes.
to speculate for a rise, spéculer à la hausse; spéculer en hausse;   jouer à la hausse.
to speculate for a fall, spéculer à la (*ou* en) baisse;   jouer à la baisse.
to speculate against each other, se faire la contre-partie.   V. exemple sous expression synonyme **to run stock against each other**.

speculation (*n.*),   spéculation (*f.*);   jeu (*m.*):
stock exchange speculations *or* speculations on

the stock exchange, spéculations de bourse; spéculations en bourse;   jeux de bourse.

speculative (*adj.*),   spéculatif, -ive;   de spéculation:
speculative bargain, marché de spéculation (*m.*).
speculative securities *or* speculative shares, *or* speculative stocks (opp. to *investment securities, shares, or stocks*),   valeurs de spéculation (*f.pl.*);   titres de spéculation (*m.pl.*);   valeurs spéculatives (*f.pl.*);   titres spéculatifs (*m.pl.*).

speculator (pers.) (*n.*),   spéculateur, -trice;   joueur, -euse:
a speculator in wheat, un spéculateur sur les blés.

speech (*n.*),   discours (*m.*);   allocution (*f.*):
to deliver a speech, prononcer un discours.
chairman's speech,   discours, allocution, du président.

speed (*n.*),   vitesse (*f.*):
the great advantage of the aeroplane over other means of transport is speed, le grand avantage de l'avion sur les autres moyens de transport est la vitesse.
the speed of ships is expressed in knots, la vitesse des navires s'exprime en nœuds.

speed trial,   essai de vitesse (*m.*).

spell (*v.t.*),   épeler:
to spell the words (Teleph., etc.), épeler les mots.

spend (*v.t.*),   dépenser:
to spend all one's income, one's income in advance,   dépenser tout son revenu, son revenu par anticipation.

spit (Customs) (*n.*),   sonde (*f.*).

spit (*v.t.*),   sonder.

spitting (*n.*),   sondage (*m.*):
spitting packages for verification of the kind or quality of the goods, sondage des colis pour la vérification de l'espèce ou de la qualité des marchandises.

split (*v.t.*),   partager;   fractionner;   scinder:
to split the difference, partager le différend (*ou* la différence);   partager le différend en deux; partager le différend par la moitié.
to split shares, fractionner des actions.

splitting (*n.*),   partage (*m.*);   fractionnement (*m.*);   scindement (*m.*).

spoiled *or* **spoilt** (*adj.*),   gâché, -e;   abîmé, -e;   détérioré, -e:
spoilt form, formule gâchée (*ou* abîmée) (*f.*).
spoiled stamps, figurines détériorées (*f.pl.*).

spontaneous combustion (cause of fire),   combustion spontanée (*f.*).

spot (particular place) (*n.*),   place (*f.*):
goods brought and sold again on the spot, marchandises achetées et revendues sur place (*f.pl.*).

spot (*adj.* & *n.*) *or* **on the spot** (Produce Exch.) (Abbrev.: **spt** *or* **sp.**) (opp to *forward* or *terminal* or *shipment* or *for shipment*),   disponible (*m.*):
official quotation for spot sugar, cote officielle du sucre disponible (*f.*).
prices: spot (*or* on the spot) so much;   shipment (*or* for shipment) so much,   cours: disponible tant;   livrable tant.

spot (*adj.* & *n.*) (Corn Exchange) (opp. to *future* or *option*), disponible (*m.*).

spot (*adj.* & *n.*) (Foreign Exchange) (opp. to *forward* or *future*), comptant (*m.*); disponible (*m.*):
to buy 100 spot dollars, acheter un disponible de 100 dollars.

spot cash, comptant (*m.*); argent comptant (*m.*):
to pay spot cash, payer comptant.

spot exchange transactions (*or* **dealings**) *or* **exchange for spot delivery,** négociations (*ou* opérations) de change au comptant (*f.pl.*).

spot price *or* **spot rate** (Produce or Corn Exch.), cours du disponible (*m.*).

spot price *or* **spot rate** (Foreign Exchange Market), cours du comptant (*m.*).

spot sale, vente en (*ou* de) disponible (*f.*).

spread (Stock Exch.) (*n.*), opération à cheval (*f.*); spéculation à cheval (*f.*); spéculation mixte (*f.*).

spread (*v.t.*), échelonner; répartir:
to spread a subscription into several instalments, échelonner une souscription en plusieurs versements.
instalments (*or* calls) spread over several months, versements échelonnés sur plusieurs mois (*m.pl.*).
to spread a risk, répartir un risque.
loss spread over a number of years, perte répartie sur un nombre d'années (*f.*).

spreading (*n.*), échelonnement (*m.*); répartition (*f.*).

spurt (*n.*), bond (*m.*); saut (*m.*):
X. shares made a fresh spurt from 2 to 2½, thus reaching their top price this year against 1½ bottom, l'action X. fait un nouveau bond (*ou* saut) de 2 à 2 1/2, atteignant ainsi son plus haut cours cette année contre 1 1/2 au plus bas.

spurt (*v.i.*), bondir; sauter.

squander (*v.t.*), dissiper; gaspiller; dilapider:
to squander one's fortune, dissiper, gaspiller, dilapider, sa fortune.

square accounts (to), régler compte:
suppose that, on the 31st March, one wishes to close the transaction and square accounts, supposons que, le 31 mars, on veuille liquider l'opération et régler compte.

squeeze (Stock Exch.) (*n.*), étranglement (*m.*); chasse (*f.*):
bear squeeze, étranglement de la spéculation à découvert; chasse au découvert.

squeeze (to extract) (*v.t.*), soutirer; tirer; arracher:
to squeeze money out of someone, soutirer (*ou* arracher) de l'argent à quelqu'un; tirer de quelqu'un de l'argent.

squeeze (Stock Exch.) (*v.t.*), étrangler; chasser; pourchasser:
to squeeze the bears, étrangler les vendeurs à découvert; chasser, pourchasser, le découvert.

St Petersburg standard *or* **Petersburg standard hundred** (timber), standard de Saint-Pétersbourg (*m.*).

stability (*n.*), stabilité (*f.*):
stability is an indispensable quality of every standard of value, la stabilité est une qualité indispensable de tout étalon de valeur.

stabilization (*n.*), stabilisation (*f.*):
stabilization of the currency, of the franc, of prices at a reasonable level, stabilisation de la monnaie, du franc, des prix à un niveau raisonnable.

stabilize (*v.t.*), stabiliser:
prices can only be stabilized by stabilizing the exchange, on ne peut stabiliser les prix qu'en stabilisant le change.

stabilizing (*adj.*), stabilisateur, -trice.

stable (*adj.*), stable:
modern production has need of a stable currency, la production moderne a besoin d'une monnaie stable.

stable (*financial slang*) (*n.*), officine (*f.*); boutique (*f.*):
shady company emanating from a stable of doubtful morality, société véreuse émanant d'une officine (*ou* d'une boutique) de moralité douteuse (*f.*).

staff (*n.*), personnel (*m.*); service (*m.*):
indoor staff, personnel (*ou* service) sédentaire.

staff provident fund, caisse de prévoyance du personnel (*f.*).

staff salaries, appointements du personnel (*m.pl.*).

staff shares, actions de travail (*f.pl.*).

stag (Fin.) (*v.i.*), souscrire seulement pour vendre avec prime sur le cours d'émission.

stage (one of several stopping places in a route of travel) (*n.*), étape (*f.*):
journey in several stages, voyage en plusieurs étapes (*m.*).

stagnant (*adj.*), stagnant, -e:
stagnant price, prix stagnant (*m.*).

stagnation (*n.*), stagnation (*f.*); marasme (*m.*); atonie (*f.*):
stagnation of business, stagnation, marasme, atonie, des affaires.

stake (*n.*), mise (*f.*):
to double one's stake (at gaming), doubler sa mise.
in a limited company, no member is liable beyond his stake, dans une société anonyme aucun des associés n'est tenu au delà de sa mise.

stamp (postage stamp) (*n.*), timbre (*m.*); timbre-poste (*m.*); figurine (*f.*):
a penny stamp (*or* a 1d. stamp), a halfpenny stamp (*or* a ½d. stamp), un timbre d'un penny (ou de 1 penny), un timbre d'un demi-penny.
stamp in prepayment of postage, timbre d'affranchissement; figurine d'affranchissement.
spoiled stamps, figurines détériorées.

stamp (revenue stamp) (*n.*), timbre (*m.*):
inland revenue stamp, timbre fiscal (*m.*).

stamp (instrument) (*n.*), timbre (*m.*); griffe (*f.*):
rubber stamp, timbre en caoutchouc; timbre humide.

stamp (mark made by stamping) (*n.*), timbre (*m.*); estampille (*f.*):
to put the firm's stamp on a letter, apposer le timbre de la maison sur une lettre.
stamp on a certificate mentioning a reduction of capital, estampille sur un titre constatant une réduction de capital.
stamp (*v.t.*), timbrer; estampiller; frapper:
to stamp a deed, a bill, a receipt, timbrer un acte, un effet, un reçu.
to stamp at the revenue office (*or* at the Inland Revenue Office) (*or, as one would say in London*, at Somerset House, *or* at Telegraph Street), timbrer à l'extraordinaire:
to be regular, cheques should be stamped at the revenue office, pour être réguliers, les chèques doivent être timbrés à l'extraordinaire.
to get an instrument stamped at the revenue office, faire timbrer un acte à l'extraordinaire.
Note:—A stamp impressed by a revenue office on an instrument submitted to it is called a *timbre à l'extraordinaire*. Stamped paper on sale (paper stamped before execution of the instrument), such as bill forms, is called *papier de la débite*.
certificates stamped with the payment of a coupon, titres estampillés du paiement d'un coupon (*m.pl.*).
the redeemed debentures are stamped with a cancellation stamp, les obligations remboursées sont frappées d'un timbre d'annulation (*f.pl.*).
stamp (Post) (*v.t.*), timbrer; affranchir:
to stamp a letter, timbrer, affranchir, une lettre.
stamp a signature on (to), griffer.
stamp act, loi sur le timbre (*f.*).
stamp affixing machine, machine à affranchir (*f.*); machine à timbrer (*f.*); machine pour l'affranchissement du courrier (*f.*).
stamp book, livre des timbres-poste (*m.*); livre d'entrée et de sortie des timbres (*m.*).
stamp duty *or* **stamp tax**, droit de timbre (*m.*); impôt du timbre (*m.*).
stamp office, bureau du timbre (*m.*); timbre (*m.*):
to go to the stamp office, aller au timbre.
stamp pad, tampon (*m.*).
stamp rack, porte-timbres (*m.*).
stamped (*adj.*). V. exemples:
stamped addressed envelope, enveloppe affranchie pour la réponse (*f.*).
stamped paper, papier timbré (*m.*).
stamped paper on sale, papier de la débite (*m.*). V. note sous **stamp** (*v.t.*).
stamped shares (i.e., certificates marked with notice that rights have been exercised, or the like), actions estampillées (*f.pl.*).
stamped signature (facsimile signature imprinted by means of an indiarubber stamp), griffe (*f.*).
stampede of bears (Stock Exch.), course des vendeurs (*f.*).
stamper (pers.) (*n.*), timbreur, -euse.
stamping (*n.*), timbrage (*m.*); estampillage (*m.*):

stamping bearer warrants, timbrage des titres au porteur.
forms presented for stamping (with a revenue stamp), formules présentées au timbrage (*f.pl.*).
stamping (Post) (*n.*), timbrage (*m.*); affranchissement (*m.*).
stand (in an exhibition) (*n.*), stand (dans une exposition) (*m.*).
stand (to appear) (*v.i.*), être porté, -e; être inscrit, -e; s'inscrire:
shares which stand in the list of investments at the market price on 31st December, actions qui sont portées (*ou* sont inscrites) (*ou* s'inscrivent) dans l'inventaire du portefeuille au cours de la bourse au 31 décembre (*f.pl.*).
the company owns securities standing in its books at so much, la société possède des titres portés dans ses livres pour tant.
stand at a discount (to), faire perte. V. exemple sous **discount**.
stand at a premium (to), faire prime. V. exemple sous **premium**.
stand surety for (to), se porter garant (-e) de; se porter caution de; se rendre garant (-e) de; se rendre caution de; répondre pour:
to stand surety for the payment of a debt, se porter garant du, répondre pour le, paiement d'une dette.
standard (type; criterion) (*n.*), étalon (*m.*):
monetary standard, étalon monétaire. V. exemple sous **standard coin**.
standard of value, étalon de valeur:
money is, at the same time, the standard of values and an instrument of exchange, la monnaie est, à la fois, l'étalon des valeurs et un instrument d'échange.
standard (*n.*) (Abbrev.: **std**) *or* **St Petersburg standard** (timber), standard (*m.*); standard de Saint-Pétersbourg (*m.*).
standard charge, taxe forfaitaire (*f.*); redevance forfaitaire (*f.*):
standard charge for the removal and reinstallation of a telephone line and apparatus, taxe, redevance, forfaitaire pour l'enlèvement et la réinstallation des organes essentiels d'un poste téléphonique.
standard coin, pièce type (*f.*):
the monetary standard is the precious metal which enters into the composition of standard coins, which are unlimited legal tender, l'étalon monétaire est le métal précieux qui entre dans la composition des pièces types, lesquelles ont force libératoire illimitée (*m.*).
standard coin *or* **standard weight coin** *or* **coin of standard weight and fineness**, pièce droite (*f.*):
a coin is said to be standard (*or* to be of standard weight and fineness) when its weight and its fineness are quite correct: it is said to be light or overweight according as it is under or over, une pièce est dite droite, quand son poids et son titre sont bien exacts; elle est dite faible ou forte suivant qu'elle est au-dessous ou au-dessus.

standard form of bill of lading, formule type (*ou* formule-type) de connaissement (*f.*).

standard gold, or standard (*m.*).

standard metal, métal-étalon (*m.*) :
country in which silver was the standard metal, pays dans lequel l'argent était le métal-étalon (*m.*).

standard money (opp. to *token money*), monnaie-étalon (*f.*) ; monnaie droite (*f.*) ; monnaie intrinsèque (*f.*).

standard policy (Insce), police type (*f.*).

standard ship, navire type (*m.*).

standard typewriter, machine à écrire standard (*f.*).

standard weight or **standard weight and fineness** (of coins, of monies), droit (des monnaies) (*m.*).

standardization (*n.*), normalisation (*f.*) ; unification (*f.*) ; standardisation (*f.*) :
standardization of manufacture, normalisation, standardisation, dans la fabrication.

standardize (*v.t.*), normaliser ; unifier ; standardiser :
international congresses assembled to try to standardize the law of general average, congrès internationaux réunis pour tenter d'unifier le droit de l'avarie commune (*m.pl.*).

standing expenses or **standing charges,** frais généraux (*m.pl.*) ; dépenses de maison (*f.pl.*).

standing order, ordre permanent (*m.*) ; ordre à perpétuité (*m.*).

standstill (*n.*), arrêt (*m.*).

staple (chief) (*adj.*), principal, -e, -aux :
staple commodity *or simply* **staple** (*n.*), produit principal (*m.*) ; principale ressource (*f.*) :
cotton is the staple commodity (*or* the staple) of the Sudan, le coton est le produit principal (*ou* la principale ressource) du Soudan.

staple (fastener) (*n.*), agrafe (de bureau) (*f.*).

staple (*v.t.*), agrafer :
to staple several sheets of paper, agrafer plusieurs feuilles de papier.

staple press, agrafeuse (de bureau) (*f.*) ; presse-agrafes (*m.*).

stapling (*n.*), agrafage (*m.*).

starboard (Naut.) (*n.*) (opp. to *port*), tribord (*m.*).

start (to depart) (*v.i.*), partir :
time at which the train starts, heure à laquelle le train part (*f.*).

start a string (to) (Produce Exch.), émettre, créer, une filière.

start again after a failure (to), se remettre d'une faillite.

starting a string (Produce Exch.), émission (*f.*), création (*f.*) d'une filière.

starting date (of an account, of an account current), date du départ (*f.*) ; départ (*m.*).

starting entry (Bkkpg) (opp. to *closing entry*), article d'ouverture (*m.*) ; écriture d'ouverture (*f.*).

starting station (Rly.), gare de départ (*f.*).

state (*n.*), état (*m.*) :

the state of the market, l'état du marché.

state *or* **State** (government) (*n.*), État (*m.*) :
the Irish Free State, l'État libre d'Irlande.

state (to specify) (*v.t.*), énoncer ; déclarer :
what the policy should state, ce que la police doit énoncer.

state (to adjust) (*v.t.*), régler :
to state general average and salvage according to the law and practice obtaining at the place where the adventure ends, régler l'avarie commune et le sauvetage d'après les lois et les usages du lieu où finit l'aventure.

State bank, banque d'État (*f.*).

State railway, chemin de fer de l'État (*m.*).

state the consideration (to) (bills of exchange), causer :
bill which states that the consideration received was cash, billet qui a été causé en valeur reçue comptant (*m.*).

statement (act of stating) (*n.*), énonciation (*f.*) ; déclaration (*f.*) :
false statement, fausse déclaration.

statement (abstract of account) (*n.*), relevé (*m.*) ; état (*m.*) ; exposé (*m.*) ; situation (*f.*) ; relèvement (*m.*) ; bordereau (*m.*) :
statement of account, relevé de compte ; état de compte ; relèvement de compte ; bordereau de compte ; relevé de factures ; facture générale (*f.*) :
the suppliers' statements of account, les relevés de comptes (*ou* les relevés de factures) des fournisseurs.
statement of expenses, état de frais ; état de dépenses.
statement of one's assets and liabilities, relevé de son actif et de son passif.
statement of the position of a bank, exposé, état, de la situation d'une banque.
cash statement, état de caisse ; relevé de caisse ; bordereau de caisse.
financial statement *or* finance statement *or* statement of finances, état de finances ; situation de trésorerie.

statement (Mar. Insce) (*n.*), dispache (*f.*) :
general average and salvage charges payable according to foreign statement, les avaries communes et les frais de sauvetage se régleront suivant dispache étrangère.

statement of affairs (in a bankruptcy), bilan (*m.*) ; bilan de liquidation (*m.*) :
to submit a statement of one's affairs, déposer son bilan.

statement of affairs at commencement of business, bilan d'entrée (*m.*).

station (*n.*), gare (*f.*) ; station (*f.*) ; poste (*m.*) :
railway station, gare de chemin de fer ; station de chemin de fer.
station of arrival, gare d'arrivée.
station of departure, gare de départ.
station of destination, gare de destination ; gare destinataire.
wireless station, poste de T.S.F.

station master, chef de gare (*m.*) ; chef de station (*m.*).

station yard (Rly.), cours d'accès (*f.*).

stationary (*adj.*), stationnaire :

price which remains stationary, cours qui reste
stationnaire (*m.*).

stationery (*n.*), papeterie (*f.*); fournitures de
bureau (*f.pl.*); fournitures (*f.pl.*):
printing and stationery, imprimés et fournitures.

stationery case, papeterie (*f.*).

stationery clerk (of a bank, or like establishment),
économe (*m.*).

stationery department (of a bank, or like
institution), économat (*m.*).

stationery rack, classeur de bureau (*m.*).

statistical (*adj.*), statistique:
statistical books (opp. to *financial,* or *account,
books*), livres de statistique (*m.pl.*); livres
d'ordre (*m.pl.*); registres d'ordre (*m.pl.*).
statistical reports, rapports statistiques (*m.pl.*).
statistical tax, droit de statistique (*m.*).

statistician (pers.) (*n.*), statisticien, -enne.

statistics (*n.pl.*). statistique (*f.*); statistiques
(*f.pl.*):
the valuation of insurance risks is based on
experience, that is to say, on statistics,
l'appréciation des risques d'assurance est
fondée sur l'expérience, c'est-à-dire sur la
statistique (*f.*).

status (Law) (*n.*), statut (*m.*):
in France, certain brokers have a legal status,
en France, certains courtiers ont un statut
légal.

status quo *or* **status in quo,** statu quo (*m.*):
to maintain the status quo, maintenir le statu
quo.

statute barred (to be). V. sous **bar.**

statute barred debt, dette caduque (*f.*).

stay (*n.*), séjour (*m.*):
compulsory stay in a port, séjour forcé dans
un port.
during the stay of the ship in the docks, in a
port of refuge, pendant le séjour du navire
dans les docks, dans un port de relâche.

stay (*v.i.*), séjourner:
with liberty to touch and stay at any ports or
places whatsoever, avec faculté de toucher et
séjourner à tous ports ou lieux quelconques.
persons staying temporarily in France, personnes séjournant temporairement en France
(*f.pl.*).

steadiness (*n.*), stabilité (*f.*).

steady (*adj.*) (Abbrev.: **stdy**), stable:
X. shares are steady, are steadier, at 3½,
l'action X. est stable, est plus stable, à
3 1/2.

steady man, homme rangé (*m.*).

steam (*n.*), vapeur (*f.*).
steamboat. V. ci-après.

steam collier, vapeur charbonnier (*m.*).

steam lorry, camion à vapeur (*m.*).

steam navigation, navigation à vapeur (*f.*).

steam navigation company, compagnie (*ou* société) de navigation à vapeur (*f.*).
steamship. V. ci-après.

steamboat (*n.*), bateau à vapeur (*m.*); canot à
vapeur (*m.*); vapeur (*m.*); steam-boat
(*m.*); steamboat (*m.*).

steamer (*n.*) (Abbrev.: **str** *or* **sr** *or* **s.**), vapeur

(*m.*); navire à vapeur (*m.*); bâtiment à
vapeur (*m.*); steamer (*m.*); paquebot (*m.*);
paquebot à vapeur (*m.*).

steamer tonnage, tonnage-vapeur (*m.*):
the steamer tonnage of various countries, le
tonnage-vapeur de différents pays.

steaming (*n.*), navigation à vapeur (*f.*); marche
(*f.*).

steamship (*n.*) (Abbrev.: **s.s.** *or* **S.S.** *or* **s/s.** *or*
ss.), navire à vapeur (*m.*); vapeur (*m.*);
bâtiment à vapeur (*m.*); steamer (*m.*);
paquebot (*m.*); paquebot à vapeur (*m.*).

steel cartel, cartel de l'acier (*m.*).

steel pen, plume métallique (*f.*); plume d'acier
(*f.*).

steel ship, navire en acier (*m.*).

steel trust, trust de l'acier (*m.*).

steerage (*n.*), entrepont (*m.*).

steerage passenger, passager d'entrepont (*m.*).

stellionate (Law) (*n.*), stellionat (*m.*).

stencil (*n.*), cliché (*m.*); stencil (*m.*).

stencil duplicator, duplicateur au stencil (*m.*).

stenograph (*n.*), sténotype (*f.*); machine à
sténographier (*f.*).

stenographer (pers.) (*n.*), sténographe (*m.* ou *f.*);
sténo (*m.* ou *f.*).

stenographic (*adj.*), sténographique; sténographe.

stenographically (*adv.*), sténographiquement.

stenography (*n.*), sténographie (*f.*).

step (measure) (*n.*), démarche (*f.*); mesure (*f.*):
advisable step, démarche conseillable.
steps taken for the common safety of the ship
and cargo, mesures prises pour le salut
commun du navire et de la cargaison.

step (Stock Exch. quotations) (*n.*), échelon (*m.*):
the quotation for these shares is usually made
by steps or multiples of 3d., la cotation pour
ces titres se fait habituellement par échelons
ou multiples de 3 pence.

steps method (accounts current with interest),
méthode hambourgeoise (*f.*); méthode par
soldes (*f.*).

sterling (*adj.*) (Abbrev.: **stg** *or* **ster.**), sterling:
pound sterling (*Abbrev.:* **£** stg *or* L. ster.
or l. stg), livre sterling (*f.*).
£10,000 sterling, 10 000 *l.* sterling.

stevedore (pers.) (*n.*), acconier (*m.*); aconier
(*m.*); arrimeur (*m.*).

stevedoring (*n.*), acconage (*m.*); aconage (*m.*);
arrimage (*m.*); manutentions maritimes
(*f.pl.*).

stick (of sealing wax) (*n.*), bâton (de cire à
cacheter) (*m.*).

stick *or* **stick down** (*v.t.*), coller:
to stick a stamp on a letter, coller un timbre
sur une lettre.

sticking (*n.*) *or* **sticking down,** collage (*m.*):
sticking down envelopes, collage des enveloppes.

stiff (*adj.*), tendu, -e.

stiffen (*v.i.*), se tendre:
contangoes are high (*or* heavy) or stiffen (*or*
harden *or* harden up) (*or* firm *or* firm up)
if money is scarce and stock plentiful;
contangoes are low (*or* light) or ease off if
money is plentiful and stock scarce, les

reports sont chers ou se tendent si l'argent est rare et le titre abondant ; les reports sont bon marché ou se détendent si l'argent est abondant et le titre rare (*m.pl.*).

stiffness (*n.*), tension (*f.*) :
stiffness of contangoes, tension des reports.

stipulate (*v.t.*), stipuler ; énoncer :
to stipulate a guarantee, a time of (*or* for) delivery, stipuler une garantie, un délai de livraison.
owner who stipulates that he will not be liable for the wrongful acts of the master, armateur qui stipule qu'il ne répondra pas des fautes du capitaine (*m.*).

stipulation (*n.*), stipulation (*f.*) ; énonciation (*f.*) :
the stipulations of a bill of lading, les stipulations (*ou* énonciations) d'un connaissement.

stock (supply on hand) (*n.*) (Abbrev. : **stk**), existence (*f.*) ; existant (*m.*) ; stock (*m.*) ; provision (*f.*) ; approvisionnement (*m.*) :
stock of goods, stock de marchandises.
stock in warehouse *or* stock in trade, existence (*ou* existant) en magasin ; stock en magasin.
stock of gold (Banking), stock d'or ; existence (*ou* existant) en or.
stock of cash, of bank notes, of bills of exchange (Banking), existence (*ou* existant) en espèces, en billets de banque, en effets de commerce.
stock of shares, stock de titres.
stocks in the till (Banking), existences de la (*ou* dans la) (*ou* en) caisse.
a stock of printed forms, une provision d'imprimés.

stock (stock account in a ledger), stock ; magasin.

stock (*n.*) (Abbrev. : **stk**) *or* **stocks** (*n.pl.*) (Fin.), valeur (*f.*) ; valeurs (*f.pl.*) ; titre (*m.*) ; titres (*m.pl.*) ; effets (*m.pl.*) ; fonds (*m.pl.*) ; actions (*f.pl.*) :
registered stocks, valeurs nominatives ; titres nominatifs ; effets nominatifs ; actions nominatives.
Government stocks, fonds d'État ; effets publics.
railway stock (*or* stocks), valeurs de chemins de fer ; actions de chemins de fer.
fully paid stock, titres libérés.
stock which is good delivery (Stock Exch.), titres qui sont de bonne livraison.
stock on the market. V. sous **market**.

stocks and shares, valeurs mobilières (*f.pl.*) ; valeurs de bourse (*f.pl.*) ; valeurs (*f.pl.*) ; titres de bourse (*m.pl.*) ; titres (*m.pl.*) ; rentes, actions, et obligations (*f.pl.*) ; effets (*m.pl.*) ; portefeuille (*m.*) ; portefeuille-titres (*m.*) ; portefeuille de titres (*m.*) ; portefeuille-valeurs (*m.*) ; portefeuille de valeurs (*m.*) :
the actual value of a stock or share may be higher than, equal to, or lower than the nominal value, la valeur réelle d'un titre de bourse peut être supérieure, égale, ou inférieure à la valeur nominale.

stock (*v.t.*), stocker ; approvisionner :
warehouse where one can stock a thousand tons of goods, magasin où on peut stocker mille tonnes de marchandises (*m.*).

to stock a market in keeping with its needs, approvisionner un marché en rapport avec ses besoins.

stock accounting *or* **stock bookkeeping** (opp. to *cash accounting* or *bookkeeping*), comptabilité-matière (*f.*) ; comptabilité-matières (*f.*).

stock arbitrage, arbitrage sur des valeurs (*m.*).

stock book (Com.), livre de stock (*m.*) ; livre de magasin (*m.*).

stockbroker. V. ci-après.

stock department (securities department of a bank), service des titres (*m.*) ; titres (*m.pl.*).

stock exchange (Abbrev. : **Stock Exch.** *or* **St. Ex.** *or* **S.E.**), bourse (*f.*) ; bourse de (*ou* des) valeurs (*f.*) ; bourse d'effets publics (*f.*) ; bourse de commerce (*f.*) ; stock-exchange (*m.*) :
Note :—The common French expression for *stock exchange* is simply *bourse. Bourse de valeurs* or *bourse d'effets publics* is used only to distinguish from some other exchange such as a *bourse de marchandises,* or when doubt may exist as to what kind of exchange is meant. See note under **produce exchange.**
the London Stock Exchange, le Stock-Exchange de Londres ; la bourse de Londres.

stock exchange committee, chambre syndicale des agents de change (*f.*).

stock exchange daily official list, bulletin de la cote (*m.*) ; cote officielle des valeurs de bourse (*f.*) ; cote de la bourse (*f.*) ; cours authentique et officiel (*m.*).

stock exchange intelligence (article in a newspaper), bulletin de la bourse (*m.*).

stock exchange official intelligence. *The Paris equivalent of the London manual is* annuaire des valeurs cotées à la bourse de Paris (*m.*).

stock exchange regulations, règlements de bourse (*m.pl.*) ; règlements boursiers (*m.pl.*).

stock exchange securities, valeurs de bourse (*f.pl.*) ; titres de bourse (*m.pl.*).

stock exchange transactions, opérations de bourse (*f.pl.*) ; transactions boursières (*f.pl.*).

stockholder. V. ci-après.

stock issued book, livre de sorties (*m.*).

stockjobber. V. ci-après.

stock market, marché des valeurs (*m.*) ; marché des titres (*m.*). *For information concerning the Paris Bourse, see under* marché des valeurs.

stock or share certificate, titre de bourse (*m.*) :
the nominal (*or* face) value is that inscribed on a stock or share certificate, la valeur nominale est celle inscrite sur un titre de bourse.

stock received book, livre d'entrées (*m.*).

stock register, grand livre des titres (*m.*).

stock sheets, inventaire (*m.*) ; inventaire extra-comptable (*m.*).

stock taking, inventaire (*m.*) ; inventaire des marchandises (*m.*) ; recensement (*m.*) :
stock taking comprises two operations : noting (*or* recording) the quantities and their valuation, l'inventaire comporte deux opérations : le relevé des quantités et leur évaluation.

stock taking of customs warehouse, recensement d'entrepôt de douane.

stock warrant, titre au porteur (*m.*).

stock yard, parc à matières (*m.*) ; parc de stockage (*m.*).

stockbroker (pers.) (*n.*), agent de change (*m.*) ; banquier en valeurs (*m.*). V. note sous **broker** (Stock Exch.).

stockbroker's bargain book, carnet d'agent de change (*m.*) ; carnet à marchés (*m.*).

stockbroker's contract, bordereau d'agent de change (*m.*) ; bordereau de bourse (*m.*).

stockholder (pers.) (*n.*), détenteur de titres (*m.*) ; porteur de titres (*m.*) ; actionnaire (*m.* ou *f.*) ; sociétaire (*m.* ou *f.*) ; rentier, -ère.

stockholder's tax, impôt sur le revenu des valeurs mobilières (*m.*).

stocking (*n.*), stockage (*m.*) ; approvisionnement (*m.*).

stockjobber (pers.) (*n.*), banquier de placement et de spéculation (*m.*). V. note sous **jobber.**

stockjobbing (*n.*), affaires de placement et de spéculation (*f.pl.*).

stop *or* **stoppage** (*n.*), arrêt (*m.*) ; suspension (*f.*) ; cessation (*f.*) ; chômage (*m.*) ; retenue (*f.*) :

the stops of a train at stations, les arrêts d'un train aux stations.

a stopping point for passenger ships, un point d'arrêt pour les paquebots.

stoppages on wages, retenues opérées sur les salaires.

stop (*v.t.*), arrêter ; suspendre ; cesser ; enrayer ; retenir ; mettre opposition sur :

to stop business, arrêter les affaires.

to stop payment (*or* payments), suspendre, cesser, le paiement (*ou* les paiements).

to stop payment of a cheque, arrêter le paiement d'un chèque.

to stop a bond in case of loss or fraud, mettre opposition sur un titre en cas de perte ou de fraude.

to stop a case (Law), arrêter, enrayer, un procès.

to stop so much out of a clerk's wages, retenir tant sur la paye d'un employé.

stop (*v.i.*), s'arrêter ; arrêter ; cesser :

to stop selling, cesser de vendre.

stop order (Stock Exch.), ordre stop (*m.*).

stop press news *or simply* **stop press** (heading in a newspaper), dernière heure ; dernière minute.

storage *or* **storing** (warehousing) (*n.*), emmagasinage (*m.*) ; emmagasinement (*m.*) ; magasinage (*m.*) ; entreposage (*m.*) ; entrepôt (*m.*) :

the right of storing (*or* storage) in a bonded warehouse, le droit de magasinage dans l'entrepôt.

storage in craft. *V.* risk of storage in craft.

storage charges, frais de magasinage (*m.pl.*) ; frais d'emmagasinage (*m.pl.*) ; magasinage (*m.*).

store (supply) (*n.*), approvisionnement (*m.*) ; provision (*f.*) ; fourniture (*f.*) :

ship's stores, approvisionnements de bord ; provisions de bord.

ship stores *or* marine stores, fournitures pour navires ; fournitures maritimes.

store *or* **stores** *or* **storehouse** (*n.*), magasin (*m.*) ; dépôt (*m.*) ; entrepôt (*m.*) ; dock (*m.*) :

cold store, entrepôt frigorifique ; dock frigorifique.

store *or* **stores** (departmental store) (*n.*), grand magasin (*m.*).

store (to warehouse) (*v.t.*), emmagasiner ; magasiner ; entreposer.

store (to supply ; to provision) (*v.t.*), approvisionner.

store accounting *or* **store bookkeeping** (opp. to *cash accounting* or *bookkeeping*), comptabilité-matière (*f.*) ; comptabilité-matières (*f.*).

store ship, bateau-magasin (*m.*).

storekeeper (pers.) (*n.*), garde-magasin (*m.*) ; magasinier (*m.*).

storeroom (*n.*), magasin d'approvisionnement (*m.*).

stores delivery note, bon de livraison du magasin d'approvisionnement (*m.*).

stores requisition note, bon de réquisition du magasin d'approvisionnement (*m.*).

stores shares, valeurs de grands magasins (*f.pl.*).

storing (supplying) (*n.*), approvisionnement (*m.*). Cf. *storage* or *storing* (warehousing).

storm (*n.*), tempête (*f.*).

stow (*v.t.*), arrimer :

to stow the goods on board, that is to say, to arrange them methodically in the hold, arrimer les marchandises à bord, c'est-à-dire les disposer méthodiquement dans la cale.

casks should be stowed lengthwise, les fûts doivent être arrimés en longueur (*m.pl.*).

casks should not be stowed bilge on bilge (*or* bulge on bulge) ; that would be bad stowage, on ne doit pas arrimer les fûts bouge sur bouge ; ce serait un vice d'arrimage.

stowage *or* **stowing** (*n.*), arrimage (*m.*) :

with measurement goods the loss of stowage (room) is considerable, avec les marchandises légères la perte à l'arrimage est considérable.

stowage manifest, devis de chargement (*m.*) ; projet de chargement (*m.*).

stowage plan, plan d'arrimage (*m.*) ; plan de chargement (*m.*).

stowaway (pers.) (*n.*), enfant trouvé (*m.*) ; passager clandestin (*m.*).

stower (pers.) (*n.*), arrimeur (*m.*).

straddle (Stock Exch.) (*n.*), opération à cheval (*f.*) ; spéculation à cheval (*f.*) ; spéculation mixte (*f.*).

Straits of Dover (Geog.), Pas de Calais (*m.*) ; détroit du Pas de Calais (*m.*).

Straits of Gibraltar, détroit de Gibraltar (*m.*).

strand (*v.t.*), échouer.

strand (*v.i.*), échouer ; s'échouer :

ship which stranded on a reef, navire qui échoua (*ou* qui s'échoua) sur un écueil (*m.*).

stranding (*n.*), échouement (*m.*) :

stranding of a ship on the rocks, échouement d'un navire sur les rochers.

street car (U.S.A.), tramway (*m.*).

street market (Stock Exch.), marché après-bourse (*m.*).

street price *or* **price in the street** (Stock Exch.), cours d'après-bourse (*m.*).

street railroad *or* **street railway** (U.S.A.), tramway (*m.*).

strength (speaking of stock exch. prices) (*n.*), résistance (*f.*) :
X. shares showed strength, l'action X. fait preuve de résistance.

strengthen (*v.t.*), consolider :
to strengthen a position, consolider une situation.

strengthen (*v.i.*), se consolider :
bank shares strengthened (Stock Exch.), les valeurs bancaires se consolident (*f.pl.*).

strengthening (*n.*), consolidation (*f.*).

stretch (distance) (*n.*), parcours (*m.*) :
stretches of — miles and under, stretches over — miles, parcours de — milles et au-dessous, parcours au delà de — milles.

strike (of workmen) (*n.*) (opp. to *lockout*), grève (*f.*) :
coal strike, grève dans les charbonnages.

strike (*v.t.*), frapper :
to strike the keys of a typewriter, frapper les touches d'une machine à écrire.
gold coins struck by the mint, pièces d'or frappées par la Monnaie (*f.pl.*).

strike (to go on strike—said of workmen) (*v.i.*), se mettre en grève ; faire grève.

strike a balance (to), établir, faire, une balance :
to strike the balance between the assets and the liabilities, établir, faire, la balance entre l'actif et le passif.

strike clause, clause de grève (*f.*).

strike committee, comité de grève (*m.*).

strike out (to), radier ; rayer ; biffer ; barrer :
to strike out a clause in a contract, an item in an account, radier, rayer, biffer, barrer, une clause dans un contrat, un article dans un compte.

strike the bottom (to) (Navig.), porter sur le fond :
ship which strikes the bottom and does not get off, navire qui porte sur le fond et ne revient pas à flot (*m.*).

striker (pers.) (*n.*), gréviste (*m.* ou *f.*).

striking a balance, établissement d'une balance (*m.*).

striking out, radiation (*f.*) : rayure (*f.*) ; biffage (*m.*) ; biffement (*m.*) ; biffure (*f.*).

string (Produce Exch.) (*n.*), filière (*f.*) :
to close a connected contract consists in declaring for delivery by ending the string or by substituting a buyer for oneself, réaliser le marché par filière consiste à déclarer qu'on prend livraison en arrêtant la filière ou à se substituer un acheteur.

string of barges, train de chalands (*m.*).

stroke of fortune (*or* **of good luck**), coup de fortune (*m.*).

stroke of the pen, trait de plume (*m.*).

strong (speaking of stocks and shares) (*adj.*), résistant, -e :

bank shares are strong, les valeurs de banques sont résistantes.

strong box, coffre-fort (*m.*) ; coffre (*m.*).

strong financial position, situation financière forte (*ou* bien assise) (*ou* bien solide) (*f.*).

strong room (in a bank, or the like), cave forte (*f.*) ; salle de coffres-forts (*f.*).

strong room (in a ship), chambre des valeurs (*f.*).

stronger side of an account, côté le plus fort d'un compte (*m.*).

stub *or* **stump** (counterfoil) (*n.*), souche (*f.*) ; talon (*m.*).

stub book, livre à souche (*m.*) ; livre à souches (*m.*) ; registre à souche (*m.*) ; carnet à souches (*m.*).

stumer cheque (*slang*), chèque sans provision (*m.*).

sturdy thieves (Mar. Insce), voleurs à main armée (*m.pl.*).

style (*n.*) *or* **style of a firm** *or* **style of the firm**, raison sociale (*f.*) ; raison (*f.*) ; nom social (*m.*) ; firme (*f.*) :
banking house known under the style of X. & Co., maison de banque connue sous la raison X. & Cie (*f.*).

subaccount (*n.*), sous-compte (*m.*).

subagency [**subagencies** *pl.*] (*n.*), sous-agence (*f.*).

subagent (pers.) (*n.*), sous-agent (*m.*).

subcharter (*n.*), sous-affrètement (*m.*).

subcharter (*v.t.*), sous-affréter.

subcharterer (*n.*), sous-affréteur (*m.*).

subcommittee (*n.*), sous-comité (*m.*).

subdivide (*v.t.*), subdiviser ; sous-diviser :
general account subdivided into a series of accounts and subaccounts, compte général subdivisé en une série de comptes et sous-comptes (*m.*).

subdivisible (*adj.*), subdivisible.

subdivision (*n.*), subdivision (*f.*) ; sous-division (*f.*) :
subdivision of shares, subdivision d'actions.

subject (liable) (*adj.*), sujet, -ette :
goods subject to breakage, marchandises sujettes à la casse (*f.pl.*).

subject (under reserve) (*adj.*), sous réserve :
subject to alteration, to any express provision in the policy, to the terms of this policy, to the following clauses, to certain exceptions, to the provisions of this Act, to the foregoing provisions, to the conditions hereinafter mentioned, sous réserve de modifications, de toute disposition (*ou* stipulation) expresse de la police, des termes de la présente police, des clauses suivantes, de certaines exceptions, des dispositions de la présente loi, des dispositions qui précèdent, des conditions ci-après mentionnées.

subject (pers.) (*n.*), sujet, -ette :
British born subject, sujet né (sujette née) britannique.

Note :—France being a republic, its citizens are not *subjects* (*sujet* is a subject of a kingdom) : they are simply *Français* (Frenchmen). Thus the counterpart of the sentence " to acquire membership (*or* to become a member) of the syndicate, it is necessary to be a British subject, or to be a naturalized British subject " would be in French « pour acquérir la qualité de membre du syndicat, il faut être Français, ou être naturalisé Français. »

subject matter *or simply* **subject** (*n.*) (of an insurance), objet (*m.*) ; sujet (*m.*) :
one designates by the subject matter (*or* the subject) of a contract of insurance the thing (*or* property) insured, on désigne par l'objet du contrat d'assurance la chose assurée.
the subject (*or* the subject matter) of the risk is the thing insured, le sujet du risque est la chose assurée.
subject matter insured, objet assuré (*m.*).

sublease (*n.*), sous-bail (*m.*).

subledger (*n.*). *Syn. de* subsidiary ledger.

sublessee (pers.) (*n.*), sous-preneur (*m.*) ; sous-locataire (à bail) (*m.* ou *f.*).

sublessor (pers.) (*n.*), sous-bailleur (*m.*).

sublet (*v.t.*), sous-louer :
lessee who has the right to sublet, preneur qui a le droit de sous-louer (*m.*).

subletting (*n.*), sous-location (*f.*).

submanager (pers.) (*n.*), sous-directeur (*m.*) ; sous-chef (*m.*).

submanageress (pers.) (*n.*), sous-directrice (*f.*).

submit (*v.t.*), soumettre :
to submit samples, soumettre des échantillons.
to submit a merchant's books to an examination, a proposal to the approval of a meeting, soumettre à l'examen les livres d'un négociant, une proposition à l'approbation d'une assemblée.
to submit a statement of one's affairs (Bankruptcy), déposer son bilan.

suboffice (*n.*), succursale (*f.*) ; bureau succursale (*m.*).

subrogate (*v.t.*), subroger :
underwriter who is subrogated to the rights of the assured against the master or the owners, assureur qui est subrogé aux droits de l'assuré contre le capitaine ou l'armement (*m.*).
by the payment of the indemnity the underwriter is subrogated to all rights of recourse against third parties belonging to the insured, par le paiement de l'indemnité l'assureur est subrogé dans tous les droits de recours contre les tiers appartenant à l'assuré.

subrogation (*n.*), subrogation (*f.*) :
subrogation of the rights of the insured to the company, subrogation des droits de l'assuré à la compagnie.

subrogation clause, clause subrogatoire (*f.*).

subscribe (to sign) (*v.t.*), souscrire :
to subscribe a bond, souscrire une obligation.

subscribe (to underwrite) (Insce) (*v.t.*), souscrire :
the amount subscribed by each underwriter is the limit of his commitment, la somme souscrite par chaque assureur est la limite de son engagement.

subscribe (*v.t.*) *or* **subscribe for (to)** *or* **subscribe to (to)** (to apply for), souscrire ; souscrire à :
to subscribe (*or* to subscribe for) the capital,

a loan, the whole of the capital, of a loan, souscrire le capital, un emprunt, l'intégralité (*ou* la totalité) du capital, d'un emprunt.
to subscribe for so many shares in a company, souscrire à tant d'actions d'une société.
to subscribe to an issue, to a loan, souscrire à une émission, à un emprunt.

subscribe (to an association) (*v.i.*), se cotiser.

subscribe (for oneself to a newspaper) (*v.i.*), s'abonner :
to subscribe to a newspaper, s'abonner à un journal.

subscribe for (to) (for another to a newspaper), abonner :
subscribe for me to this paper, abonnez-moi à ce journal.

subscriber (to a loan, for capital, on an insurance, or the like) (pers.) (*n.*), souscripteur (*m.*) :
the subscribers on each insurance agreeing to pay their proportion, les souscripteurs de chacune des assurances convenant de payer leur proportion.

subscriber (to a newspaper, to the telephone, or the like) (pers.) (*n.*), abonné, -e :
telephone subscriber, abonné au téléphone.

subscriber's line (Teleph.), poste d'abonné (*m.*) ; poste d'abonnement (*m.*) ; ligne d'abonné (*f.*). *V. note sous* direct exchange line.

subscriber's number (Teleph.), numéro de l'abonné (*m.*).

subscription (for capital) (*n.*), souscription (*f.*) :
subscription to an issue, souscription à une émission.

subscription (payable to an association) (*n.*), cotisation (payable à une association) (*f.*).

subscription (to a newspaper, to the telephone) (*n.*), abonnement (à un journal, au téléphone) (*m.*) :
subscription with calls charged for, abonnement à conversations taxées.

subscription calls (Teleph.), conversations à heures fixes par abonnement (*f.pl.*).

subscription list, souscription (*f.*) ; liste de souscription (*f.*). *V. exemple sous* list.

subscription rental (Teleph.), redevance d'abonnement (*f.*).

subshare (*n.*), coupure d'action (*f.*) ; tantième d'action (*m.*) ; coupon d'action (*m.*). *Note :*—
The word subshare is used in England of the *coupures* of foreign companies. Subshares are not provided for by the English law, inasmuch as no limitation is imposed in England on the amount of a share.

subsidiary (auxiliary) (*adj.*), subsidiaire ; auxiliaire :
subsidiary account, sous-compte (*m.*).
subsidiary books (Bkkpg), livres auxiliaires (*m.pl.*).
subsidiary coins, monnaie divisionnaire (*f.*) ; monnaie d'appoint (*f.*) :
silver subsidiary coins, monnaie divisionnaire d'argent.
subsidiary journals (Bkkpg), journaux auxiliaires (*m.pl.*) ; journaux fractionnaires (*m.pl.*) ; journaux analytiques (*m.pl.*).

subsidiary ledger, grand livre auxiliaire (*m.*);
grand livre fractionnaire (*m.*); grand livre
analytique (*m.*); grand livre originaire (*m.*);
grand livre de développement (*m.*).
subsidiary (opp. to *parent*) (*adj.*), filial, -e, -aux:
subsidiary concerns, entreprises filiales (*f.pl.*).
subsidiary [subsidiaries *pl.*] (*n.*) or **subsidiary
company**, filiale (*f.*); société filiale (*f.*):
the range of the Company is world wide, it
owns subsidiaries in the United States, in
Great Britain, in France, in Germany, and
in Russia, l'envergure de la Société est
mondiale, elle possède des filiales aux États-
Unis, en Grande-Bretagne, en France, en
Allemagne, et en Russie (*f.*).
subsidize (*v.t.*), subventionner:
to subsidize a postal service, subventionner
un service postal.
subsidy [subsidies *pl.*] or **subvention** (*n.*), subvention (*f.*); subside (*m.*).
substitute ad interim (pers.), intérimaire (*m.* ou
f.).
substituted expenses (General Average), dépenses
substituées (*f.pl.*).
substitution (*n.*), substitution (*f.*):
substitution of another ship for an insured ship,
substitution d'un autre navire pour un navire
assuré.
subtenant (pers.) (*n.*), sous-locataire (*m.* ou *f.*).
subtotal (Bkkpg) (*n.*), somme partielle (*f.*):
the subtotals which make up the total, les
sommes partielles qui composent le total.
subtract (*v.t.*), soustraire; retrancher:
to subtract one number from another, soustraire, retrancher, un nombre d'un autre.
subtraction (*n.*), soustraction (*f.*):
the result of a subtraction is called remainder,
excess, or difference, le résultat de la soustraction se nomme reste, excès, ou différence.
subunderwriter (pers.) (*n.*), sous-syndicataire
(*m.*).
subway (Rly.) (*n.*), passage souterrain (*m.*);
souterrain (*m.*):
subway, served by stairs, by means of which
the public has access to the platforms,
souterrain (*ou* passage souterrain) desservi
par des escaliers, par le moyen duquel le
public accède aux quais.
succeed in business (to), faire ses affaires; faire
son affaire:
a company which does not succeed in business
goes into liquidation, une société qui ne
fait pas ses affaires entre en liquidation.
succeeding account (Stock Exch.), liquidation
suivante (*f.*).
succeeding carrier, voiturier successif (*m.*);
transporteur subséquent (*m.*):
the question of the responsibility of succeeding
carriers, la question de la responsabilité
des voituriers successifs.
the company and any succeeding carrier, la
compagnie et les entrepreneurs de transport
qui lui succéderont.
succeeding railway, chemin de fer subséquent
(*m.*).
sue (*v.t.*), poursuivre; actionner:

to sue a debtor, poursuivre, actionner, un
débiteur.
to be sued by one's creditors, être poursuivi
(-e) par ses créanciers.
sue and labour clause (Mar. Insce) (Abbrev.:
S/L.C.), clause autorisant les mesures con-
servatoires (*f.*) (*explanatory translation only*).
**sue, labour, and travel for the saving and
preserving of the property insured** (to),
prendre ou requérir toutes mesures con-
servatoires; veiller au sauvetage et à la
conservation des objets assurés.
Suez canal register *ou* **Suez canal tonnage**, jauge
de Suez (*f.*); tonnage canal de Suez (*m.*).
suffer (*v.t.*), subir; éprouver:
to suffer a loss, subir, éprouver, une perte.
security which suffers a depreciation, valeur
qui subit une dépréciation (*f.*).
sufferance wharf, magasin-cale (*m.*); tente (*f.*).
sufficiency (*n.*), suffisance (*f.*).
sufficient (*adj.*), suffisant, -e.
sufficiently (*adv.*), suffisamment.
sum (*n.*), somme (*f.*):
sum of money paid in advance, somme d'argent
payée d'avance.
sum total, somme totale (*f.*); montant global
(*m.*); total global (*m.*).
summarize (*v.t.*), résumer; récapituler.
summary (*adj.*), sommaire:
summary statement of the position, état
sommaire de la situation (*m.*).
summary proceeding (Law), procédure sommaire (*f.*); cause sommaire (*f.*).
summary [summaries *pl.*] (*n.*), résumé (*m.*);
récapitulation (*f.*).
summer (*n.*), été (*m.*).
summer premium (Insce) (opp. to *winter premium*),
prime d'été (*f.*).
summer time, heure d'été (*f.*).
Sunday closing, chômage du dimanche (*m.*).
sundries (Bkkpg) (*n.pl.*), divers (*m.pl.*); suivants
(*m.pl.*):
Sundries Dr To Sundries, Divers à Divers;
Les suivants aux suivants.
Profit and Loss Dr To Sundries, Pertes et
Profits à Divers; Profits et Pertes aux
suivants.
sundries account, compte de divers (*m.*).
sundries column, colonne divers (*f.*).
sundries journal, journal des divers (*m.*); journal
d'opérations diverses (*m.*).
sundries ledger, grand livre divers (*m.*).
sundry (*adj.*), divers, -e:
sundry creditors, créditeurs divers (*m.pl.*).
sundry debtors, débiteurs divers (*m.pl.*).
sundry expenses, frais divers (*m.pl.*); dépenses
diverses (*f.pl.*).
sundry receipts, rentrées diverses (*f.pl.*).
supercargo (pers.) (*n.*), subrécargue (*m.*).
superintend *or* **supervise** (*v.t.*), surveiller; contrôler.
superintendence *or* **supervision** (*n.*), surveillance
(*f.*); contrôle (*m.*).
superintendent *or* **supervisor** (pers.) (*n.*), surveillant, -e; contrôleur, -euse:
place where sample is drawn chosen by receivers

or by sellers' superintendents, endroit où est prelevé l'échantillon choisi par les réceptionnaires ou par les surveillants des vendeurs (*m.*).

superscription (of a letter) (*n.*), suscription (*f.*).

supertare (*n.*), surtare (*f.*).

supertax (*n.*), impôt de superposition (*m.*); impôt complémentaire (*m.*). Cf. **surtax.**

supplement (*n.*), supplément (*m.*) :
supplement (*or* supplementary charge) to pay for admittance in a Pullman car, supplément à payer pour admission dans une voiture Pullman.
supplement to a newspaper, supplément à un journal.

supplementary (*adj.*), supplémentaire :
supplementary charge, taxe supplémentaire (*f.*); supplément de taxe (*m.*); supplément (*m.*).
supplementary list (Stock Exch.). V. note sous **cote.**

supplier (pers.) (*n.*), fournisseur (*m.*).

suppliers' ledger, grand livre des fournisseurs (*m.*).

supply [supplies *pl.*] (*n.*), provision (*f.*); fourniture (*f.*); approvisionnement (*m.*) :
a supply of printed forms, une provision d'imprimés.

supply (*v.t.*), fournir; approvisionner; pourvoir; alimenter :
to supply a ship (to provision it), approvisionner un navire.
our order books are well supplied, nos carnets de commandes sont bien alimentés.

supply and demand, l'offre et la demande [offre (*n.f.*)] :
the law of supply and demand, la loi de l'offre et de la demande. V. exemples sous **law.**

supplying (*n.*), fourniture (*f.*); approvisionnement (*m.*).

support (*n.*), appui (*m.*) :
vouchers in support of an account, pièces à l'appui d'un compte (*f.pl.*); pièces certificatives d'un compte (*f.pl.*).

support (*v.t.*), appuyer; soutenir :
to support a proposal, an account by vouchers, appuyer une proposition, un compte par des pièces justificatives.
to support prices by buying, soutenir les cours en achetant.
mines were supported (Stock Exch.), les mines étaient soutenues (*f.pl.*).

suppress (*v.t.*), supprimer :
to suppress a train (to withdraw it from the service), supprimer un train.

suppression (*n.*), suppression (*f.*) :
the distinctive character of every monopoly lies in the suppression of competition, le caractère distinctif de tout monopole réside dans la suppression de la concurrence.

supra protest *or* **suprà protest** (Abbrev.: **S.P.**), sous protêt. V. acceptance supra protest.

surcharge (*n.*), surtaxe (*f.*).

surcharge (*v.t.*), surcharger; surtaxer :
to surcharge a postage stamp, surcharger un timbre-poste.

surcharged letter (Post), lettre surtaxée (*f.*); lettre taxée (*f.*).

surety [sureties *pl.*] (pers.) (*n.*), caution (*f.*); donneur de caution (*m.*); garant, -e; répondant (*m.*); accréditeur (*m.*) :
to be (*or* to become) (*or* to go) (*or* to stand) surety for someone, être caution de, se porter caution de *ou* pour, se porter garant (-e) de, se rendre caution de, se rendre garant (-e) de, être le répondant de, répondre pour, quelqu'un :
person who becomes surety for another person, for the engagements contracted by another person, for the payment of a debt, personne qui se porte caution d'une (*ou* pour une) autre personne (*ou* qui se rend garante d'une autre personne), des engagements pris par une autre personne, du paiement d'une dette (*f.*).
bond under which the declarant and one or two sureties undertake to pay the customs duties, soumission cautionnée aux termes de laquelle le déclarant et une ou deux cautions s'engagent à payer le montant des droits de douane.

surety (guarantor of a bill of exchange) (pers.) (*n.*), donneur d'aval (*m.*); avaliste (*m.*).

surety (security for payment or performance) (*n.*), sûreté (*f.*); caution (*f.*); cautionnement (*m.*); garantie (*f.*) :
surety for a debt, sûreté d'une créance.

surety bond, cautionnement (*m.*); obligation de garantie (*f.*) :
to pledge oneself by a surety bond, s'engager par cautionnement.

surname (*n.*), nom de famille (*m.*); nom patronymique (*m.*).

surplus (*n.*), surplus (*m.*); excédent (*m.*); plus-value (*f.*); boni (*m.*); revenant-bon (*m.*) :
surplus in the cash (Ant.: *shortage*), excédent de caisse (*ou* dans l'encaisse).
surplus of assets over liabilities (Ant.: *deficiency*), excédent de l'actif sur le passif.
surplus in taxes (Ant.: *deficit*), plus-value des contributions.

surplus cash shares, actions de numéraire de surplus (*f.pl.*).

surplus dividend, superdividende (*m.*) :
surplus dividend over and above a first dividend of so much, superdividende en sus d'un premier dividende de tant.

surplus profit, superbénéfice (*m.*); surplus de bénéfice (*m.*) :
preference shares which are assimilated to the ordinary shares in the sharing of surplus profits, actions privilégiées qui sont assimilées aux actions ordinaires dans le partage des superbénéfices (*f.pl.*).

surplus shares, actions de surplus (*f.pl.*).

surplus ship's stores, restants de provisions de bord (*m.pl.*).

surrender (*n.*), abdication (*f.*); abandon (*m.*); abandonnement (*m.*) :
surrender of rights, abdication de droits.

surrender (Insce) (*n.*), rachat (*m.*) :
surrender value of a life insurance policy,

valeur de rachat d'une police d'assurance sur la vie (f.).

surrender (v.t.), abdiquer; abandonner; céder.

surround oneself with sufficient guarantees (to), s'entourer de garanties suffisantes.

surtax (extra tax) (n.), surtaxe (f.).

surtax (tax additional to income tax) (n.), impôt général sur le revenu (m.); impôt global sur le revenu (m.): (*Note* :—The present *surtax* in England was formerly called *supertax*.) income tax and surtax, l'impôt cédulaire et général.

surtax (v.t.), surtaxer: to surtax the rich, to untax the poor, surtaxer les riches, détaxer les pauvres.

survey (n.), expertise (f.); visite (f.): the survey fixes the amount of the indemnity, l'expertise fixe le montant de l'indemnité. periodical survey of the hull of a ship, visite périodique de la coque d'un navire. survey on being put into service (ship), visite de mise en service. survey on sailing (ship), visite de partance.

survey (v.t.), expertiser; visiter: to survey the goods and determine the nature of the damage, expertiser la marchandise et déterminer la nature de l'avarie. shipowners can always insist upon their ships being surveyed, les armateurs peuvent toujours demander que leurs navires soient visités (m.pl.).

survey certificate, certificat de visite (m.).

survey fee (inspection of ships, or the like), droit de visite (m.).

survey fees (inspection of goods, or the like), honoraires d'expertise (m.pl.).

survey report, rapport d'expertise (m.).

surveyor (pers.) (n.), expert (m.): surveyor appointed by Lloyd's, expert nommé par le Lloyd.

survivor (Law) (pers.) (n.), survivant, -e.

survivor (one who escapes from a wreck, or the like) (pers.) (n.), rescapé, -e; survivant, -e.

survivorship annuity, rente viagère avec réversion (f.).

suspected bill (of health), patente (de santé) suspecte (f.).

suspected ship (Quarantine), navire suspect (m.).

suspend (v.t.), suspendre; arrêter; cesser: to suspend payment (or payments), suspendre, cesser, le paiement (ou les paiements).

suspense (in), en suspens; en souffrance: the matter is in suspense, l'affaire est en suspens (f.). items in suspense (Bkkpg), écritures en suspens (f.pl.). interest in suspense, intérêts en suspens (ou en souffrance) (m.pl.). bills in suspense, effets en souffrance (ou en suspens) (m.pl.).

suspense account (Bkkpg), compte d'ordre (m.); compte de méthode (m.).

suspense entry (Bkkpg), écriture d'ordre (f.).

suspension (n.), suspension (f.); arrêt (m.); cessation (f.).

sustain (v.t.), éprouver; subir: to sustain a loss, éprouver, subir, une perte.

swear (v.t.), assermenter: to swear a witness, assermenter un témoin.

swear (v.i.), prêter serment; jurer: witnesses swear to speak the truth, the whole truth, and nothing but the truth, les témoins jurent de dire la vérité, toute la vérité, et rien que la vérité (m.pl.).

to be sworn, prêter serment: to be sworn before a tribunal, prêter serment devant un tribunal.

swearing (taking an oath) (n.), prestation de serment (f.).

sweepings (from warehoused goods) (n.pl.), balayures (provenant des marchandises entreposées) (f.pl.).

swell (v.t.), gonfler; charger: to swell an account, gonfler, charger, un compte.

swelling (n.), gonflement (m.).

Swiss franc, franc suisse (m.).

switch board (Teleph.), tableau commutateur (m.); tableau (m.).

sworn (adj.), assermenté, -e; juré, -e: sworn translator, traducteur assermenté (m.). sworn weighers and measurers, peseurs et mesureurs jurés (m.pl.).

sympathetic strike, grève de sympathie (f.); grève de solidarité (f.).

sympathy [sympathies pl.] (n.), sympathie (f.): X. Bank (shares) drooped in sympathy with Turkish funds, la Banque X. fléchit en (ou par) sympathie avec les fonds turcs.

synallagmatic contract, contrat synallagmatique (m.); contrat bilatéral (m.).

syndical (adj.), syndical, -e, -aux.

syndicate (n.), syndicat (m.); consortium (m.): a financial syndicate, un syndicat financier; un syndicat de finance. underwriting syndicate, syndicat de garantie. a syndicate of bankers, un syndicat (ou un consortium) de banquiers.

syndicate (v.t.), syndiquer: to syndicate an industry, syndiquer une industrie. syndicated shares, actions syndiquées (f.pl.).

syndicate (v.i.), se syndiquer.

syndicator (pers.) (n.), syndicataire (m.).

system (n.), système (m.); régime (m.); réseau (m.): the French fiscal system, le système fiscal français. the advantages of a decimal monetary system, les avantages d'un système monétaire décimal (m.pl.). a vast system of docks, sheds, and warehouses, un vaste système de bassins, hangars, et entrepôts. warehousing system (Customs), système des entrepôts; régime de l'entrepôt.

system of bookkeeping *or* system of accounts, comptabilité (*f.*) :
in certain systems of bookkeeping a combined journal and ledger is used, on utilise dans certaines comptabilités le journal-grand-livre.
system of railways, of canals, réseau de chemins de fer (*ou* de voies ferrées), de canaux :
the railway system of Great Britain, le réseau de chemins de fer de la Grande-Bretagne.

national postal air system, réseau national postal aérien.
systematic *or* **systematical** (*adj.*), systématique.
systematically (*adv.*), systématiquement :
facts grouped systematically, des faits systématiquement groupés (*m.pl.*).
systematization (*n.*), systématisation (*f.*).
systematize (*v.t.*), systématiser.
systematizer (pers.) (*n.*), systématiseur (*m.*).

T

tab (*n.*), onglet (*m.*) :
index divided by tabs between all the letters of the alphabet, répertoire divisé par des onglets entre toutes les lettres de l'alphabet (*m.*).
table (furniture) (*n.*), table (*f.*) ; bureau (*m.*) :
tables and chairs, tables et chaises.
balance sheet laid on the table (at a meeting), bilan déposé sur le bureau (*m.*).
table (plan) (*n.*), table (*f.*) ; tableau (*m.*) ; plan (*m.*) :
interest table, table d'intérêts.
table of par values, table des parités.
redemption table, tableau d'amortissement ; table d'amortissement ; plan d'amortissement.
tabulator (*n.*), tabulateur (*m.*).
tacit (*adj.*), tacite :
tacit agreement (opp. to *express agreement*), convention tacite (*f.*).
tackle (gear of a ship, in general) (*n.*), agrès (*m.pl.*) :
tackle and apparel, agrès et apparaux.
tackle (hoisting gear) (*n.*), palan (*m.*) :
goods lowered alongside by the ship's tackles, marchandises amenées le long du bord par les palans du navire (*f.pl.*).
under ship's tackle. V. sous **under.**
tag label (opp. to *gummed label*), étiquette volante (*f.*).
tail series (Shipping) (opp. to *full series*), série de solde (*f.*).
take (*v.t.*). V. exemples :
to take a copy of a letter, prendre copie d'une lettre.
to take a loss, prendre une perte :
to know how to take a loss, that is to say, to lose a certain amount, but to close before losing more, savoir prendre une perte, c'est-à-dire perdre une certaine somme, mais liquider avant de perdre davantage.
to take a mortgage on a property, prendre hypothèque sur un bien.
to take a note of something in one's pocketbook, prendre note d'une chose sur son carnet.

to take advantage of a favourable price to sell out, saisir un cours favorable pour revendre.
to take advice, prendre conseil.
to take an interest in an enterprise, prendre un intérêt, s'intéresser, dans une entreprise.
to take an interest in an enterprise (to finance it), commanditer une entreprise.
to take an order, prendre une commande.
to take [someone] at his word, prendre [quelqu'un] au mot.
to take away a creditor's security, dénantir un créancier.
to take away goods (to remove or collect them), enlever, retirer, des marchandises.
to take away one number from another, retrancher, soustraire, un nombre d'un autre.
to take care of *or* to take charge of, prendre en charge ; prendre à sa charge ; prendre charge ; garder ; veiller à :
to take care of (*or* to take charge of) a sum of money for someone, prendre en charge (*ou* prendre à sa charge) une somme d'argent pour quelqu'un ; garder une somme d'argent à quelqu'un.
it is, in effect, the master who, in the name of the owner, takes charge of the goods, c'est, en effet, le capitaine qui, au nom de l'armateur, prend charge de la marchandise.
to take due and proper care of the goods, veiller à la conservation de la marchandise avec tous les soins d'un bon père de famille.
to take cargo for one or several ports, prendre charge pour un ou plusieurs ports.
to take delivery of stock, prendre livraison, lever, des titres.
to take down a letter, a speech *or* to take down a letter, a speech, in shorthand, sténographier une lettre, un discours.
to take firm, prendre ferme ; lever ferme :
house which has taken a loan half firm half on option, maison qui a pris un emprunt moitié ferme moitié à option (*f.*).
to take firm so many shares (underwriting letter), lever ferme tant de titres.
to take for the call (Stock Exch.), vendre dont :

to take 1s. for the call on 100 X.Y.Z. shares, vendre 100 actions X.Y.Z. dont un schelling. See explanation of option dealing under **option**.

to take from the reserve, prélever sur la réserve : sum taken from the reserve to write off the amount of an embezzlement, somme prélevée sur la réserve pour amortir le montant d'un détournement (*f.*).

to take in (*v.t.*) *or* to take the rate on (Stock Exch.), reporter ; prendre en report :

to take in stock *or* to take the rate on stock, reporter des titres ; prendre des titres en report.

stock taken in, titres reportés (*m.pl.*) ; titres pris en report (*m.pl.*).

to take in (*v.i.*) *or* to take the rate (Stock Exch.), reporter :

it is at the making up price that the buyer gives on and the seller takes in, c'est au cours de compensation que l'acheteur se fait reporter et que le vendeur reporte.

generally on a big market, like the London market, there are to be found on the one hand many buyers who being unable to take up their stock bought for the account (*or* for the settlement), that is to say, to take delivery of it, give on (*or* give the rate) (*or* lend stock), and, on the other hand, many sellers who, not being in possession of the stock sold for the account (*or* for the settlement) take in (*or* take the rate) (*or* borrow stock) (*or* carry stock), le plus souvent sur un grand marché, comme celui de Londres, il se rencontre qu'il y a d'un côté beaucoup d'acheteurs qui, ne pouvant lever leurs titres achetés en liquidation, c'est-à-dire en prendre livraison, se font reporter, et, d'un autre côté, beaucoup de vendeurs qui, n'étant pas en possession des titres vendus en liquidation reportent.

by giving on (*or* by giving the rate) (*or* by lending stock) at each settlement the buyer can remain a bull indefinitely, in consideration of the regular payment of contangoes and settlement of differences, and the bear seller can prolong at will his bear position by taking in (*or* by taking the rate) (*or* by borrowing *or* carrying stock) likewise at each settlement, en se faisant reporter à chaque liquidation l'acheteur peut rester indéfiniment à la hausse, moyennant paiement régulier des reports et règlement des différences, et le vendeur à découvert peut prolonger à volonté sa position à la baisse, en reportant également à chaque liquidation.

to take in coal, faire du charbon ; charbonner.

to take in stock for (Stock Exch.), reporter :

to take in stock for a borrower, reporter un emprunteur.

to take [a ship] in tow, prendre [un navire] à la remorque.

to take into account, tenir compte de ; prendre en ligne de compte :

to take the fluctuations of exchange into account, tenir compte des, prendre en ligne de compte les, fluctuations du change.

to take [a ship] into port, to destination, conduire [un navire] dans un port, à destination.

to take [someone's] name and address, prendre le nom et l'adresse (*ou* les nom et adresse) [de quelqu'un].

to take notes at a meeting, prendre des notes à une assemblée.

to take oath, prêter serment :

to take oath before a tribunal, prêter serment devant un tribunal.

to take off (to deduct), rabattre.

to take off the embargo on a ship, lever l'embargo sur un navire.

to take offices in Paris, prendre des bureaux à Paris.

to take [so much] on account, prendre [tant] à compte (*ou* à valoir).

to take [goods] on board, prendre [des marchandises] à bord.

to take [goods] on credit (*or* on account), prendre [des marchandises] à crédit (*ou* à compte).

to take [a house] on lease, prendre [une maison] à bail.

to take on option, prendre à option. *V. exemple sous* to take firm.

to take or leave, prendre ou laisser :

you can take it or leave it *or simply* take it or leave it, c'est à prendre ou à laisser.

to take out (to copy ; to extract), relever :

to take out a list of shareholders, the ledger balances, the balance of each account on the balance book, relever une liste d'actionnaires, les soldes du grand livre, la balance de chaque compte sur le livre de soldes.

to take out an insurance policy, an insurance in one's own name or in the name and for account of third persons, contracter une police d'assurance, une assurance en son propre nom ou au nom et pour compte de tierces personnes.

to take out of bond (*or* warehouse), retirer de l'entrepôt :

goods taken out of bond for home use, marchandises retirées de l'entrepôt pour la consommation (*f.pl.*).

to take over (assets or liabilities), prendre en charge ; prendre la charge de ; prendre à sa charge ; se charger de ; reprendre :

the new company takes over the assets and liabilities, la nouvelle société prend en charge (*ou* prend à sa charge) l'actif et le passif (*ou* se charge [*ou* prend la charge] de l'actif et du passif).

the A. Company will absorb by amalgamation the B. Company by taking over all its assets and liabilities, the whole to date from 1st January last, la Société A. absorbera par fusion la Société B. en reprenant tout son actif, à charge par elle de payer tout son passif, le tout à dater du 1er janvier écoulé.

to take over the business of a company in

liquidation, prendre la suite des affaires d'une société en liquidation.

to take over the management of an affair, prendre la direction d'une affaire.

to take part in an enterprise, in the proceedings of a meeting, prendre part à une entreprise, aux délibérations d'une assemblée.

to take passengers, prendre des passagers. V. exemple sous syn. **to pick up passengers.**

to take possession, prendre possession :
insurance company which has the right to take possession, wholly or partly, of the insured goods and to treat them as its property, compagnie d'assurances qui a le droit de prendre possession, en totalité ou en partie, des marchandises assurées et de les traiter comme sa propriété (*f.*).

to take proceedings against someone, intenter action à (*ou* contre) quelqu'un.

to take refuge *or* to take shelter, se réfugier :
to take refuge in a port of necessity (*or* in a port of distress) *or* to take shelter in a port of refuge, se réfugier dans un port de relâche.

to take samples in order to find out the kind, the quality, the value, etc., of the goods, prélever des échantillons pour reconnaître l'espèce, la qualité, la valeur, etc., des marchandises.

to take [the necessary] steps to protect one's right, to protect goods from any damage, to preserve the insured property, prendre les mesures (*ou* les dispositions) (*ou* les démarches) [nécessaires] à la conservation de ses droits, pour protéger les marchandises de toute avarie, pour conserver les objets assurés.

to take stock of one's goods, faire l'inventaire de, inventorier, ses marchandises.

to take tenders for the repair of the damage, inviter des soumissions pour la réparation des dommages.

to take the average between the highest and the lowest price, prendre la moyenne entre le plus haut et le plus bas cours.

to take the chair, présider :
Mr X. took the chair, M. X. préside.

to take the rate (Stock Exch.). *V.* to take in *or* to take the rate.

to take the rate on (Stock Exch.). *V.* to take in *or* to take the rate on.

to take to business, s'appliquer aux affaires.

to take [a letter] to the post, porter [une lettre] à la poste.

to take up a bill, honorer un effet :
the first point that interests the discounter is the certainty that the discounted bill will be taken up at maturity, le premier point qui intéresse l'escompteur c'est la certitude que l'effet escompté sera honoré à l'échéance.

to take up an option (Fin.), lever une option.

to take up an option (Stock Exch.) (opp. to *to abandon an option*), lever une prime ; consolider un marché à prime.

to take up documents, lever des documents.

to take up financial business, entrer dans la finance.

to take up stock (*or* shares) (to take delivery), lever, prendre livraison, des titres.

to take up stock (*or* shares) (issue of shares), enlever des titres :
if the stock is not (*or* if the shares are not) taken up by the public, the underwriting syndicate is deemed applicant, si les titres ne sont pas enlevés par le public, le syndicat de garantie est réputé souscripteur.

to take upon oneself, prendre à sa charge ; s'engager :
insurer who takes upon himself (insurers who take upon themselves *pl.*) a certain risk, assureur qui prend à sa charge (assureurs qui prennent à leur charge) un certain risque (*m.*).

share which the insurer takes upon himself in the risk insured, part pour laquelle l'assureur s'engage dans le risque assuré (*f.*).

taker (one who takes ; buyer) (*n.*), preneur, -euse :
negotiable paper always finds a taker, le papier négociable trouve toujours preneur.

taker (lessee) (pers.) (*n.*), preneur, -euse.

taker (contangoes) (Stock Exch.) (pers.) (*n.*) (opp. to *giver*), reporteur (*m.*) :
as remuneration for the loan, the taker receives from the giver a premium, which is called contango, en rémunération du prêt, le reporteur touche du reporté une prime, qui s'appelle report.

the market is all takers, la place (*ou* la position de place) est dégagée (*ou* est soulagée).

taker for a call (Stock Exch.) (opp. to *giver for a call*), vendeur d'un dont (*ou* d'une prime directe) (*m.*).

taker for a call of more (Stock Exch.), donneur de faculté de lever double (*m.*).

taker for a put (Stock Exch.) (opp. to *giver for a put*), acheteur d'un ou (*ou* d'une prime indirecte) (*m.*).

Note :—The French envisage the purchase of the shares from the putter. The English envisage the taker of the rate for the option to have the shares put, or, and which is the same thing, the seller of the option to have the shares put. Hence *taker* or *seller* has to be translated by *acheteur* in this case. Cf. note under **giver.**

taker for a put and call (Stock Exch.), donneur d'option (*m.*) ; donneur de stellage (*m.*).

taker for a put of more (Stock Exch.), donneur de faculté de livrer double (*m.*).

taker of an (*or* **of the**) **option** *or* *simply* **taker** (*n.*) (Fin.) (opp. to *giver*), optant (*m.*) :
taker who exercises his option for delivery, optant qui opte pour la livraison.

taker of the rate (Option dealings) (Stock Exch.), receveur de la prime (*m.*).

taking (act of one that takes) (*n.*), prise (*f.*).
V. le verbe **take** pour une foule de locutions.

taking (capture) (*n.*), prise (*f.*) ; capture (*f.*) :
takings at sea, prises en mer.

taking for an option (Stock Exch.), vente d'une prime (*f.*).

taking for the call (Stock Exch.), vente dont (f.); vente à prime directe (f.).

taking oath, prestation de serment (f.).

taking out (copying; extracting), relevé (m.); relèvement (m.):
to check the taking out of the trial balance, vérifier le relevé de la balance.

taking samples, prélèvement d'échantillons (m.).

taking up or **taking delivery** (of stock) (Stock Exch.), levée (de titres) (f.).

taking up (an option) (Stock Exch.), levée (d'une prime) (f.); consolidation (d'un marché à prime) (f.).

taking up (of documents), levée (des documents) (f.).

takings (receipts) (n.pl.), recette (f.); recettes (f.pl.); produit (m.):
to check the day's takings, vérifier la recette (ou le produit) de la journée.

tale quale (Abbrev.: **t/q.** or **T.Q.**). Syn. de **tel quel.**

talk up the value of a stock (to) (Stock Exch.), créer une atmosphère de hausse autour d'une valeur.

tally [tallies pl.] or **tallying** (n.), pointage (m.).

tally (v.t.), pointer.

tally clerk, pointeur (m.).

tally sheet, feuille de pointage (f.).

talon (n.), talon (m.):
talon conferring the right to a new sheet of coupons, talon donnant droit à une nouvelle feuille de coupons.

tamper with a register (to), falsifier un registre.

tangible assets, valeurs matérielles (f.pl.); valeurs tangibles (f.pl.).

tank car (Rly.), wagon-citerne (m.); wagon-réservoir (m.).

tank ship or **tank vessel** or **tanker** (n.), bateau-citerne (m.); navire-citerne (m.); cargo-citerne (m.).

tank steamer, bateau-citerne à vapeur (m.); vapeur-citerne (m.); vapeur-tank (m.).

tape (paper strip of recording telegraph) (n.), bande (f.).

tape (Customs) (n.), corde (f.); ficelle (f.).

tape (Customs) (v.t.), corder; ficeler.

tape machine, télégraphe imprimeur (m.); ticker (m.).

taping (Customs) (n.), cordage (m.); ficelage (m.).

tare (n.), tare (f.):
the tare is the weight of the packages used in the carrying of the goods; the difference between the gross weight and the tare gives the net weight, la tare est le poids des emballages servant au transport des marchandises; la différence entre le poids brut et la tare donne le poids net.
tare assumed by the customs (in arriving at a net weight without taring), tare légale. Cf. net weight without taring.

tare (v.t.), tarer.

tarer (Customs) (n.), colis taré (m.):
the number of tarers, le nombre de colis tarés.

tariff (used as adj.), tarifaire:
tariff system, régime tarifaire (m.).

tariff (n.), tarif (m.):
insurance tariff, tarif d'assurances.
McKinley tariff, tarif McKinley.

tariff (v.t.), tarifer.

tariff rates, prix des tarifs (m.pl.).

tariff war, guerre de tarifs (f.).

tariffication (n.), tarification (f.):
customs tariffication by weight, by measurement, tarification douanière au poids, au volume.
railway tariffication on an exclusively kilometric basis, tarification ferroviaire sur la base exclusivement kilométrique.

taring (n.), tarage (m.):
taring empty trucks, le tarage des wagons vides.

tax (n.), impôt (m.); taxe (f.); contribution (f.); imposition (f.):
income tax or tax on income, impôt sur le revenu; taxe sur le revenu; impôt sur revenu; taxe sur revenu; impôt cédulaire; income-tax (m.). V. note sous **income tax.**
tax on incomes derived from trade and manufacture, impôt sur les bénéfices industriels et commerciaux.

tax free or **free of tax,** net (nette) d'impôt (ou d'impôts); exempt (-e) d'impôt (ou d'impôts):
tax free interest, intérêts nets d'impôts (m.pl.).
all coupons of French rentes are free of all tax, with the exception of those of the 3% redeemable rente, tous les coupons de rentes françaises sont exemptes de tout impôt, à l'exception de ceux de la rente 3 0/0 amortissable.

tax (v.t.), imposer; taxer; frapper d'un impôt; frapper de taxes:
to tax income, imposer le revenu.
to tax luxuries, taxer les objets de luxe.
in France, bill posting is taxed, en France, l'affichage est frappé d'un impôt.
to tax the products of foreign industry, frapper de taxes les produits de l'industrie étrangère.
to be taxed, être taxé, -e; être frappé (-e) d'un impôt; se taxer:
everything is taxed, tout se taxe.

tax (Law) (v.t.), taxer:
to tax the costs of an action, taxer les dépens d'un procès.

tax collector, percepteur (m.); receveur des contributions (m.).

taxable (adj.), imposable; taxable; taxatif, -ive:
taxable income, revenu imposable (m.).
goods taxable on value, marchandises imposables à la valeur (f.pl.).

taxation (n.), taxation (f.); taxe (f.); impôt (m.); impôts (m.pl.):
inequitable distribution of taxation, répartition inéquitable de taxation (ou des impôts) (f.).

taxation (Law) (n.), taxation (f.); taxe (f.):
taxation of costs, taxation des frais; taxe des dépens; taxe des frais et actes.

taxed bill of costs, mémoire taxé (m.).

taxer (pers.) (n.), taxeur (m.).

taxing master (Law), taxateur (m.); juge taxateur (m.)

taxpayer (pers.) (*n.*), imposé, -e ; contribuable (*m.* ou *f.*).

tear out (*v.t.*), arracher ; soustraire ; détacher :
to tear a leaf out of a book, arracher, soustraire, une feuille d'un livre.
to tear a cheque out of the book, a receipt out of a counterfoil book, détacher un chèque du carnet, un reçu d'un livre à souches.

tear up (*v.t.*), déchirer :
to tear up an agreement, déchirer une convention.

tel quel (Abbrev. : **t/q.** *or* **T.Q.**), tel quel, telle quelle :
tel quel rate, cours tel quel (*m.*).
tel quel quotation, cote telle quelle (*f.*).
V. autre exemple sous **parity**.

telegram (*n.*), télégramme (*m.*) ; dépêche (*f.*) ; dépêche télégraphique (*f.*) :
telegram addressed poste restante (*Abbrev. :* GP.), télégramme adressé poste restante.
telegram addressed poste restante registered (*Abbrev. :* GPR.), télégramme adressé poste restante recommandée.
telegram addressed télégraphe restant (*Abbrev. :* TR.), télégramme adressé télégraphe restant.
telegram for transmission to ship at sea, télégramme destiné à (*ou* à destination d') un navire en mer.
telegram from ship at sea, télégramme de mer.
telegram handed in near closing time, télégramme déposé en dernière limite d'heure ; limité (*m.*).
telegram in account (deposit account), télégramme en compte :
telegrams in account are those on which the charge is not collected at the time of handing in, les télégrammes en compte sont ceux dont la taxe n'est pas perçue au moment du dépôt.
telegram in cipher, télégramme chiffré.
telegram in code, télégramme en langage convenu.
telegram in plain language, télégramme en langage clair.
telegram to be called for (*Abbrev. :* TR.), télégramme adressé télégraphe restant.
telegram to be delivered at once, if in the normal course it would be retained until the daytime (*Abbrev. :* Nuit), télégramme à distribuer même pendant la nuit.
telegram (arriving at night) to be delivered only in the daytime (*Abbrev. :* Jour), télégramme (qui parvient à destination la nuit) à distribuer seulement pendant les heures de jour.
telegram to be signalled when vessel (not equipped for wireless telegraphy) is passing (a signalling station), télégramme sémaphorique.
telegram to follow addressee *or* telegram to be redirected (*Abbrev. :* FS.), télégramme à faire suivre ; télégramme à réexpédier.
telegram via wireless, télégramme via T.S.F.
telegram with notice of delivery (by telegraph) (*Abbrev. :* PC.), télégramme avec accusé de réception (télégraphique) (*m.*).

telegram with notice of delivery by post (*Abbrev. :* PCP.), télégramme avec accusé de réception postal.
telegram with repetition (*Abbrev. :* TC.), télégramme avec collationnement.

telegram form, formule de télégramme (*f.*).

telegrams counter (post office), guichet télégraphique (*m.*).

telegraph (*n.*), télégraphe (*m.*) :
to receive news by telegraph, recevoir des nouvelles par le télégraphe.

telegraph (*v.t.*), télégraphier :
to telegraph a piece of news, télégraphier une nouvelle.

telegraph (*v.i.*), télégraphier.

telegraph boy *or* **telegraph messenger,** facteur enfant (*m.*) ; facteur-télégraphiste (*m.*) ; facteur des télégraphes (*m.*).

telegraph deposit, dépôt de garantie télégraphique (*m.*) ; provision de garantie télégraphique (*f.*) ; provision télégraphique (*f.*).

telegraph office, bureau télégraphique (*m.*) ; bureau du télégraphe (*m.*) ; télégraphe (*m.*) :
to go to the telegraph office, aller au télégraphe.

telegraphic (*adj.*), télégraphique :
telegraphic address (*Abbrev. :* T.A.), adresse télégraphique (*f.*).
telegraphic code, code télégraphique (*m.*).
telegraphic money order, mandat télégraphique (*m.*).
telegraphic transfer *or* telegraph transfer (Foreign Exchange) (*Abbrev. :* T.T.), transfert télégraphique (*m.*) ; câble transfert (*m.*) ; câble (*m.*) ; versement (*m.*).

telegraphically (*adv.*), télégraphiquement.

telegraphist (pers.) (*n.*), télégraphiste (*m.* ou *f.*).

telegraphy (*n.*), télégraphie (*f.*).

telephone (*n.*) (Abbrev. : 'phone), téléphone (*m.*).

telephone (*v.t.*) (Abbrev. : 'phone), téléphoner :
to telephone an important piece of news, téléphoner une importante nouvelle.

telephone (*v.i.*), téléphoner.

telephone call, appel téléphonique (*m.*).

telephone call office *or* **telephone box** *or* **telephone kiosk,** cabine téléphonique (*f.*).

telephone deposit, dépôt de garantie téléphonique (*m.*) ; provision téléphonique (*f.*) ; provision téléphone (*f.*) ; provision de garantie téléphonique (*f.*).

telephone directory, annuaire des abonnés au téléphone (*m.*).

telephone exchange, bureau central téléphonique (*m.*) ; bureau téléphonique (*m.*) ; poste central téléphonique (*m.*) ; central téléphonique (*m.*).

telephone number (Abbrev. : **Tel. No** *or* **T.N.**), numéro de téléphone (*m.*) ; numéro d'appel (*m.*).

telephone subscriber, abonné au téléphone (*m.*).

telephoned message (Post), message téléphoné (*m.*).

telephoned telegram (Post), télégramme téléphoné (*m.*).

telephonic (*adj.*), téléphonique.

telephonically (*adv.*), téléphoniquement.

telephonist (pers.) (*n.*), téléphoniste (*m.* ou *f.*).
telephony (*n.*), téléphonie (*f.*).
teller (Banking) (pers.) (*n.*), caissier (*m.*); guichetier (*m.*).
teller's cash book, main courante de caisse (*f.*); chiffrier de caisse (*m.*); brouillard de caisse (*m.*).
temporary (*adj.*) (Ant.: *permanent*), temporaire; provisoire:
temporary admission (Customs), admission temporaire (*f.*).
temporary disablement (Accident Insurance), incapacité temporaire (*f.*).
temporary investments, placements temporaires (*m.pl.*).
temporary repairs, réparations provisoires (*f.pl.*).
tenancy [tenancies *pl.*] (*n.*), location (*f.*):
date of expiration of tenancy, date d'échéance de location (*f.*).
tenant (pers.) (*n.*), locataire (*m.* ou *f.*).
tenant's (*or* tenants') **repairs,** réparations locatives (*f.pl.*).
tenant's third party risk, risque locatif (*m.*).
tendency [tendencies *pl.*] (*n.*), tendance (*f.*); orientation (*f.*):
the tendencies of the market, les tendances (*ou* l'orientation) du marché.
better (*or* brighter) tendency in tins at the finish, meilleure tendance (*ou* orientation) en stannifères en fin de séance.
tender (*n.*), soumission (*f.*); offre (*f.*):
tenders for public loans, for the repair of the damage, soumissions d'emprunts publics, pour la réparation des dommages.
legal tender. V. sous **legal.**
tender (Law) (*n.*), offre réelle (*f.*).
tender (*v.t.*), offrir:
as to nickel and copper money (in France) it can only serve as change for the 5 franc piece, that is to say, be tendered up to fr. 4·95, quant à la monnaie de nickel et de bronze elle ne peut que servir d'appoint à la pièce de 5 francs, c'est-à-dire être offerte jusqu'à 4f.95.
to tender one's services, offrir ses services.
to tender one's resignation, donner, envoyer, sa démission.
to be tender, avoir cours:
gold coins and the silver dollar are tender to any amount, les monnaies d'or et le dollar d'argent ont cours illimité.
to be legal tender. V. sous **legal.**
tender for (to), soumissionner:
to tender to the government for a loan of so many million pounds, soumissionner au gouvernement un emprunt de tant de millions de livres.
tenderer (pers.) (*n.*), soumissionnaire (*m.*).
tenor (of a bill of lading, or the like) (*n.*), teneur (*f.*):
in witness whereof the master has signed four bills of lading, all of the same tenor and date, en foi de quoi le capitaine a signé quatre connaissements, tous d'une même (*ou* de même) teneur et date.

tenor and form of the consignment note, teneur et forme de la lettre de voiture.
tenor *or* **term** (the period of time after the expiration of which a bill falls due) (*n.*), échéance (*f.*); terme d'échéance (*m.*):
the tenor (*or* the term) of the bill of exchange is 3 months after sight, l'échéance (*ou* le terme d'échéance) de la lettre de change est 3 mois de vue.
no bill of less than five days' tenor will be discounted, il ne sera admis à l'escompte aucun effet d'une échéance de moins de cinq jours.
V. aussi exemple sous **first of exchange.**
term (duration) (*n.*), terme (*m.*); durée (*f.*):
term of a lease, terme, durée, d'un bail.
policy which expresses the term for which it is written, police qui exprime la durée pour laquelle elle est souscrite (*f.*).
long term annuity, annuité à long terme (*f.*).
long term investment, placement à long terme (*m.*); placement de longue haleine (*m.*).
short term transaction, opération à court terme (*f.*).
term (clause; text; purport) (*n.*), clause (*f.*); terme (*m.*); teneur (*f.*):
terms of a contract, clauses, termes, d'un contrat.
alterations made in the terms of an agreement, modifications apportées à la teneur (*ou* aux termes) d'un traité (*f.pl.*).
terminable (Law) (*adj.*), résoluble:
terminable contract, contrat résoluble (*m.*).
terminable annuity, annuité terminable (*f.*).
terminal (forward transaction) (Produce Exch.) (*adj.* & *n.*) (opp. to *spot*), livrable (*m.*).
terminal charges (Transport), charges terminales (*f.pl.*).
terminal market (Produce Exch.), marché à terme (*m.*); marché du terme (*m.*).
terminal port, port de tête de ligne (*m.*).
terminal price (Produce Exch.), cours du livrable (*m.*).
terminals index (telegraphic code), index de finales de mots (*m.*).
terminate (to determine) (*v.t.*), résoudre; résilier:
to terminate a contract, résoudre, résilier, un contrat.
termination (determination) (*n.*), résolution (*f.*); résiliation (*f.*); résiliement (*m.*); résilîment (*m.*).
termination (of a risk) (Insce) (*n.*), fin (d'un risque) (*f.*).
terminus [termini *pl.*] (*n.*) *or* **terminal** (*n.*) *or* **terminal station,** terminus (*m.*); gare terminus (*f.*); gare de tête de ligne (*f.*); tête de ligne (*f.*); gare en cul-de-sac (*f.*):
the terminus of the P.L.M. system, la tête de ligne du réseau P.-L.-M.
territorial waters, eaux territoriales (*f.pl.*):
ship seized in French territorial waters, navire saisi dans les eaux territoriales françaises (*m.*).
test (Customs) (*n.*), épreuve (*f.*):
weight of packings ascertained by tests, poids des emballages constaté par des épreuves (*m.*).

test weighing, pesée d'épreuve (f.).
testament (will) (n.), testament (m.).
testamentary (adj.), testamentaire.
testator (pers.) (n.), testateur (m.).
testatrix [**testatrixes** or **testatrices** pl.] (pers.) (n.), testatrice (f.).
text (n.), texte (m.):
  text of an insurance policy, of a telegram, texte d'une police d'assurance, d'un télégramme.
textile shares, valeurs de textiles (f.pl.); valeurs textiles (f.pl.).
thanks to, grâce à:
  thanks to the absence of competition, grâce à l'absence de concurrence.
theft (n.), vol (m.).
theft risk (Insce), risque de vol (m.).
there ? (short for are you there ?) (Teleph.), allô !
there and back, aller et retour :
  the crossing there and back from Dover to Calais, la traversée aller et retour de Douvres à Calais.
there being no further business before the meeting, the sitting was closed or **there being no other business, the meeting was closed,** rien n'étant plus à l'ordre du jour, la séance est levée.
there being no further questions, the chairman put the following resolutions to the meeting ; there being no further questions, the following resolutions were put to the meeting and carried unanimously, personne ne demandant plus la parole, M. le président met aux voix les résolutions suivantes ; personne ne demandant plus la parole, les résolutions suivantes ont été mises aux voix et adoptées à l'unanimité.
thief [**thieves** pl.] (pers.) (n.), voleur, -euse ; brigand (m.).
thing (matter) (n.), affaire (f.); chose (f.):
  things are going badly, les affaires vont mal.
thing (property) (n.), chose (f.):
  goods, freight, or other things, or interests, marchandises, fret, ou autres choses, ou intérêts.
  the value of the thing insured, la valeur de la chose assurée. V. aussi exemples sous **subject matter.**
third (or abbreviated **3rd**) (adj.), troisième ; 3e :
  third cabin passenger, passager de troisième classe en cabine (m.).
  third (or 3rd) class ticket, billet de troisième (ou de 3e) classe (m.).
  third debenture. V. sous **first.**
third (as applied to persons) (adj.), tiers, tierce :
  third arbitrator, tiers arbitre (m.).
  third party or third person, tiers (m.); tierce personne (f.):
  to have recourse to a third party, avoir recours à un tiers.
  to deposit a sum in the hands of a third party, déposer une somme en main tierce.
third of exchange, troisième de change (f.); triplicata de change (m.). V. **first of exchange** pour exemple.

third party accident insurance, assurance accidents aux tiers (f.).
third party insurance, assurance de responsabilité civile (f.).
third party risk, risque du recours de tiers (m.).
this account (Stock Exch.), liquidation courante (f.); liquidation (f.): (Cf. end this.)
  price for this account, cours en liquidation courante (m.); cours en liquidation (m.).
those present, les assistants (m.pl.):
  those present at the general meeting, les assistants à l'assemblée générale.
those whom it may concern, qui de droit :
  animals, of which delivery is not taken on arrival, are impounded, at the expense and risk of those whom it may concern, les animaux, dont il n'est pas pris livraison à l'arrivée, sont mis en fourrière, aux frais, risques et périls de qui de droit (m.pl.).
threat (n.), menace (f.):
  threat of ruin, of dismissal, menace de ruine, de renvoi.
threaten (v.t.), menacer.
three months, trois mois (m.); trimestre (m.):
  three months' rent, un trimestre de loyer.
three months or, and usually, **3 months** (Metal Market) (opp. to cash), trois mois ; 3 mois.
three months' bills rate, taux du trois mois (m.).
three times the ordinary rates (urgent telegrams), triple taxe (f.).
thrive (v.i.), prospérer.
through bill of lading, connaissement direct (m.); connaissement à forfait (m.).
through bookings, transports à forfait (m.pl.); voyages à forfait (m.pl.); forfaits (m.pl.); services contractuels (m.pl.):
  through bookings to all parts, forfaits pour toutes destinations.
  to contract for through booking of goods, entreprendre le transport des marchandises pour un prix déterminé à forfait.
  Cf. to book through, sous **book** (v.i.).
through carriage (railway car), voiture directe (f.).
through freight, fret à forfait (m.); fret forfaitaire (m.).
through rate, taux à forfait (m.); taux forfaitaire (m.):
  through rates to address in Paris, and the interior of France, taux à forfait pour Paris domicile, et l'intérieur de la France.
through registration of luggage, enregistrement direct de bagages (m.).
through ticket (a ticket through to final destination), billet direct (m.).
through ticket (sea-land-sea), billet global (m.).
through train, train direct (m.).
throw (v.t.). V. exemples :
  to throw a letter into the waste paper basket, jeter une lettre au panier.
  to throw good money after bad, mettre du bon argent contre du mauvais.
  to throw goods on the market, jeter (ou lancer) des marchandises sur le marché.
  to throw on someone the burden of proving a wrongful act, l'obligation to· contribute

to an expense, mettre à la charge de quelqu'un le fardeau de la preuve d'une faute, l'obligation de contribuer à une dépense.

to throw out an amendment, an item of expenditure, rejeter un amendement, un article de dépense.

to throw overboard goods of a dangerous nature, jeter par-dessus bord des marchandises d'une nature dangereuse.

to throw up one's situation, se démettre de son emploi.

tick (*n.*), point (*m.*).

tick or **tick off** (*v.t.*), pointer :

to tick (*or* to tick off) the items in an account, pointer les articles d'un compte.

to tick off a statement with an account, pointer un relevé avec un compte.

ticker (*n.*), ticker (*m.*); télégraphe imprimeur (*m.*).

ticket (*n.*), billet (*m.*); ticket (*m.*); bulletin (*m.*) :

ticket at full fare (*or* at full rate), billet a plein tarif ; billet à place entière.

ticket at reduced rate, billet à prix réduit.

ticket out of date, billet périmé.

platform ticket, ticket d'entrée en gare.

baggage ticket, bulletin de bagages.

ticket (Stock Exch.) (*n.*), fiche (*f.*).

ticket (banker's) (on dishonoured bill) (*n.*), compte de retour (*m.*).

ticket window (Rly., etc.), guichet de distribution des billets (*m.*); guichet (*m.*).

ticking or **ticking off** (*n.*), pointage (*m.*).

tickler (book or set of sheets or cards used as reminders) (*n.*), tickler (*m.*).

tidal basin, bassin de marée (*m.*); bassin d'échouage (*m.*).

tidal harbour, port à marée (*m.*); port d'échouage (*m.*).

tidal water, eaux à marée (*f.pl.*).

tide (*n.*), marée (*f.*) :

the Mediterranean has no tide, la Méditerranée n'a pas de marée.

an exceptionally high tide, une marée exceptionnellement haute.

tie into a bundle (to) *or* **tie into bundles (to)** (papers), enliasser.

tie-on label (opp. to *gummed label*), étiquette volante (*f.*).

tie up (of capital, of money) (*n.*), blocage (*ou* bloquage) (*m.*), immobilisation (*f.*) (de capital, de capitaux).

tie up (*v.t.*), bloquer ; immobiliser :

to tie up a block of shares, bloquer une tranche d'actions.

syndicate which ties up a certain number of shares in order not to flood the market, syndicat qui bloque un certain nombre d'actions pour ne pas inonder le marché (*m.*).

the money tied up in a bill of exchange is set free as soon as the bill is paid, le capital immobilisé dans une lettre de change est mobilisé dès que la lettre est payée.

tight (Fin.) (*adj.*) (opp. to *easy*), serré, -e :

discount or money is said to be tight when owing to the market's requirements of money, the market rate of discount approximates to the bank rate of discount, l'escompte ou l'argent est dit serré lorsque par suite des besoins en capitaux du marché, le taux de l'escompte privé se rapproche du taux officiel d'escompte (*m.*). Cf. **easy** & **nominal**.

tighten (*v.i.*), se serrer :

discount tightens on the approach of heavy borrowing, l'escompte se serre à l'approche des grands emprunts (*m.*).

tightness *or* **tightening** (*n.*), resserrement (*m.*) :

tightness of money, of credit, resserrement d'argent, de crédit.

till (*n.*), caisse (*f.*); tiroir de caisse (*m.*) :

cash in the bank's till, espèces dans la caisse de la banque (*f.pl.*).

the stocks in the till (Banking), les existences de la (*ou* dans la) (*ou* en) caisse (*f.pl.*).

to check the cash and notes in the till, vérifier les espèces et billets en caisse.

till further advice, jusqu'à nouvel avis.

till money, encaisse (*f.*) :

if there is an over or a short in the till money, s'il y a excédent ou déficit dans l'encaisse.

timber dock, bassin aux bois (*m.*); bassin à bois (*m.*).

time (system of reckoning) (*n.*), heure (*f.*) :

Greenwich time, heure de Greenwich.

time (a definite or precise point or moment) (*n.*), heure (*f.*); moment (*m.*) :

time of departure, of arrival, heure de départ, d'arrivée.

time for declaration of options (Stock Exch.), heure de la réponse des primes. *V. explication sous* option dealing.

the insured goods are covered from the time of leaving the shipper's warehouse, les facultés assurées sont couvertes depuis le moment où elles quittent le magasin de l'expéditeur (*f.pl.*).

time handed in (of a telegram), heure de dépôt.

time (space of time; extension of time; delay) (*n.*), temps (*m.*); délai (*m.*) :

time is money, le temps est de l'argent ; le temps, c'est de l'argent.

to ask for time, demander du temps (*ou* un délai).

draft drawn a short time after sight, traite tirée à un court délai de vue (*f.*).

to stipulate a time of (*or* for) collection, of (*or* for) delivery, stipuler un délai d'enlèvement, de livraison.

time gained (dispatch), temps gagné.

time lost (dispatch), temps perdu.

time of waiting, délai d'attente.

within a reasonable time, dans un délai raisonnable.

time (particular period) (*n.*), temps (*m.*); époque (*f.*); terme (*m.*) :

the times at which the risks are to commence and close, les temps auxquels les risques doivent commencer et finir.

we will not fail to advise you of it in good (*or* proper) (*or* due) time, nous ne manquerons pas de vous en aviser en temps utile.

at the time of delivery, of payment, à l'époque de la livraison, du paiement.

time is the essence of the contract, le terme est
l'essence du contrat.

time to pay, terme de grâce.

time bargain, marché à terme (*m.*); marché à
livrer (*m.*).

time bill *or* **time draft** *or* **time note,** échéance à
terme (*f.*).

time charter (distinguished from *voyage charter*),
affrètement à temps (*m.*); affrètement à
terme (*m.*); affrètement pour un temps
déterminé (*m.*); affrètement en « time
charter » (*m.*).

time freight, fret à temps (*m.*); fret à terme (*m.*).

time insurance, assurance à temps (*f.*); assurance
à terme (*f.*).

time of payment (tenor) (*n.*), échéance (*f.*);
terme d'échéance (*m.*):

the time of payment of the bill of exchange is
3 months after sight, l'échéance (*ou* le terme
d'échéance) de la lettre de change est 3 mois
de vue.

time policy (Insce), police à temps (*f.*); police
à terme (*f.*).

time premium (Insce), prime au temps (*f.*).

time risk (Insce), risque à temps (*m.*); risque à
terme (*m.*).

time sheet *or* **time book,** feuille de présence (*f.*).

time sheet (discharging a ship), décompte du
temps (*m.*).

time stamp, chronotimbre (*m.*); timbre horaire
(*m.*); timbre horo-dateur (*m.*).

time table, horaire (*m.*); livret-horaire (*m.*).

times over *or simply* **times** (*n.pl.*), fois (*f.pl.*):
loan applied for several times over, emprunt
souscrit plusieurs fois (*m.*).

nine times out of ten, neuf fois sur dix.

tin company, société stannifère (*f.*).

tin-lined case, caisse doublée de fer-blanc (*f.*).

tin market, marché de l'étain (*m.*).

tin shares *or* **tins** (*n.pl.*), valeurs d'étain (*f.pl.*);
valeurs stannifères (*f.pl.*); stannifères (*f.pl.*).

tip (gratification) (*n.*), pourboire (*m.*).

tip (confidential information) (*n.*), tuyau (*m.*):
to give a stock exchange tip, donner un tuyau
de bourse.

tip (to give confidential information to) (*v.t.*),
tuyauter :
to tip someone, tuyauter quelqu'un.

title (*n.*) *or* **title deed,** titre (*m.*):
title to property *or* title deed of property,
titre de propriété.

the baggage ticket constitutes a title which gives
the passenger the right to claim his packages
on arrival, le bulletin de bagages constitue
un titre qui donne le droit au voyageur de
réclamer ses colis à l'arrivée.

no one can create a title (to property) for himself, nul ne peut se créer un titre à soi-même.

To (abbreviation of *Dr To*) (journalizing) (Bkkpg)
(*prep.*), à (abréviation de *doit à*):
when securities are deposited, the entry to
be passed is : Deposits To Depositors, lors
du dépôt des titres, l'article à passer est :
Dépôts à Déposants.

Sundries to Sundries, Divers à Divers ; Les
suivants aux suivants.

To (ledger posting) (Bkkpg) (*prep.*) (opp. to *By*),
à :
To Cash, à Caisse.

To (formula on an invoice). *V. sous syn.* Dr to.

to be called for (Post), poste restante ; bureau
restant:
to address a letter "'to be called for," adresser
une lettre « poste restante. »

to be called for (at a telegraph office), télégraphe
restant.

to be called for (Rly.), gare restante ; en gare ;
bureau restant.

to-day (i.e., to-day's price) (heading in quotation
list), ce jour.

tobacco shares, valeurs de tabacs (*f.pl.*).

token (*n.*), jeton (*m.*). *V. exemple sous* small coin.

token money (opp. to *standard money*), monnaie
fictive (*f.*); monnaie fiduciaire (*f.*); monnaie
conventionnelle (*f.*).

tolerance (*n.*) *or* **tolerance of the mint** (Coinage),
tolérance (*f.*); remède (*m.*):
tolerance of weight *or* tolerance for error in
weight, tolérance de poids ; tolérance de
fabrication ; faiblage (*m.*); faiblage de poids
(*m.*).

tolerance of (*or* for error in) fineness, tolérance
de titre ; remède d'aloi ; faiblage d'aloi.

tolerance for loss of weight (*or* for abrasion) in
circulation, tolérance de frai.

toll (*n.*), péage (*m.*); droit de péage (*m.*).

toll call (Teleph.), communication régionale
(*f.*); conversation régionale (*f.*).

toll exchange (Teleph.), bureau régional (*m.*);
bureau central régional (*m.*); poste central
régional (*m.*).

Toll, what number are you calling ? *or* **Toll,
number, please ?** (Teleph.), Régional, qui
demandez-vous ?

ton (*n.*) *or* **ton register** (Abbrev.: **t.r.**) (Shipping),
tonneau (*m.*); tonne (*f.*); tonneau de jauge
(*m.*); tonne de jauge (*f.*); tonneau de
registre (*m.*); tonneau-registre (*m.*); tonne
de registre (*f.*); tonne-registre (*f.*), = 100
cubic feet or 2·8317 cubic metres—same in
France as in England.

ton dead weight [**tons dead weight** *pl.*], tonneau
de portée (*m.*); tonne de portée en lourd
(*f.*); tonneau d'affrètement (*m.*); tonneau
de fret (*m.*). In France, 1,000 kilogrammes,
or 1·44 cubic metres, usually. In England,
the ton dead weight is 20 cwt, or 40 cubic
feet (= 1·132 cubic metres), usually.

ton displacement [**tons displacement** *pl.*], tonneau-
poids (*m.*); tonneau de déplacement (*m.*);
tonne de déplacement (*f.*).

ton gross register, tonneau de jauge brute (*m.*):
steamers of at least 100 tons gross register,
vapeurs d'au moins 100 tonneaux de jauge
brute (*m.pl.*).

ton measurement [**tons measurement** *pl.*], tonneau
d'encombrement (*m.*); tonne d'encombre-
ment (*f.*); tonneau à l'encombrement (*m.*);
tonneau de capacité (*m.*); tonneau de mer
(*m.*); tonne de mer (*f.*).

ton mile [**ton miles** *pl.*] (Rly.) (Abbrev.: **T.M.**),
tonne millénaire (*f.*) = le transport d'une

ton (1 016 kg.) de marchandises à une distance d'un *mile* (1,6093 kil.): analogue à la *tonne-kilomètre* française = le transport d'une tonne (1 000 kg.) un kilomètre.

ton net register, tonneau de jauge nette (*m.*):
sailing ships of at least 50 tons net register, voiliers d'au moins 50 tonneaux de jauge nette (*m.pl.*).

tone (*n.*), ton (*m.*); tenue (*f.*); dispositions (*f.pl.*):
in its examination of the position of the stock market during last month, the bank signalizes a better tone, due to the relaxation of money rates and to a very appreciable slackening in the stream of new issues, dans son examen de la situation du marché des valeurs durant le mois dernier, la banque signale un ton meilleur, dû au relâchement des taux monétaires et à un ralentissement très sensible dans le rythme des nouvelles émissions.

the London Stock Exchange was favourably influenced by the good tone of Wall Street yesterday, le Stock-Exchange de Londres était favorablement influencée par la bonne tenue de Wall Street hier.

the general tone of the market, les dispositions d'ensemble du marché.

the market, in spite of some irregularity, was better in tone at the close, le marché, malgré quelques irrégularités, a été mieux disposé en clôture.

tonnage (weight in tons) (*n.*), tonnage (*m.*):
parcels tonnage, tonnage des messageries.
Note:—It must be borne in mind that in speaking of *tonnage* in English, the weight in English *tons* is ordinarily meant, and in speaking of *tonnage* in French, the weight in French *tonnes* is ordinarily meant. See equivalents of English *ton* and French *tonne* in Tables of Weights at end of this volume.

tonnage (internal cubic capacity of a vessel expressed in tons) (*n.*), tonnage (*m.*); jauge (*f.*):
the tonnage of the ship is the expression of the internal capacity of the ship, le tonnage du navire est l'expression de la capacité intérieure du navire.

the principle of charging on the tonnage of the ship, le principe de la taxation sur la jauge du navire.

tonnage under deck, tonnage sous le pont.

tonnage (aggregate freightage of a collection of vessels) (*n.*), tonnage (*m.*):
where there is an abundance of tonnage and little cargo, freight is low, and vice versa, là où il y a abondance de tonnage et peu de marchandises, le fret est bas, et inversement.

tonnage deck, pont de tonnage (*m.*).

tonnage duty *or simply* **tonnage** (*n.*), droit de tonnage (*m.*); tonnage (*m.*).

top (*n.*), 'haut (*m.*); tête (*f.*):
the top of a column, le haut, la tête, d'une colonne.

top (*v.t.*), être en tête de:
to top a subscription list, être en tête d'une liste de souscription.

top left hand corner, angle gauche supérieur (*m.*).

top price (Stock Exch.), cours le plus haut (*m.*).

top right hand corner, angle droit supérieur (*m.*):
stamps in prepayment of postage should, as far as possible, be affixed in the top right hand corner of the address side, les timbres d'affranchissement doivent, autant que possible, être apposés à l'angle droit supérieur du recto (*m.pl.*).

tot up (to) *or* **tot together (to)** *or simply* **tot** (*v.t.*), additionner:
to tot up a column of figures, additionner une colonne de chiffres.

total (*adj.*), total, -e, -aux; global, -e, -aux:
total amount, somme totale (*f.*); somme globale (*f.*); montant global (*m.*).

total assets, liabilities, total de l'actif, du passif (*m.*).

total cost (Costing), prix de revient total (*ou* global) (*m.*).

total expenses, frais totaux (*m.pl.*); montant des dépenses (*m.*).

total loss (Insce) (*Abbrev.*: t.l. *or* T.L.) (opp. to *partial loss*), perte totale (*f.*); sinistre total (*m.*):
total loss of the ship, of the cargo, perte totale du navire, de la marchandise.

steamer which stranded, and which will probably be a total loss, steamer qui s'est échoué, et qui sera probablement une perte totale (*m.*).

the method of adjustment of partial or total losses, le mode de règlement des sinistres partiels ou totaux.

total loss only (Mar. Insce) (*Abbrev.*: t.l.o. *or* T.L.O.), perte totale seulement.

total (*n.*), total (*m.*); montant (*m.*).

total (*v.t.*), totaliser.

total account (adjustment account) (Bkkpg), compte collectif (*m.*).

totality (*n.*), totalité (*f.*).

totalization (*n.*), totalisation (*f.*):
the totalization of receipts, la totalisation des recettes.

totalizator *or* **totalizer** (*n.*), totalisateur (*m.*); totaliseur (*m.*).

totalize (*v.t.*), totaliser.

totally (*adv.*), totalement.

totting up *or* **totting together** *or* **totting** (*n.*), additionnement (*m.*).

touch (speaking of prices on the stock exchange) (*v.t.*), toucher; effleurer:
fall which has touched bottom, baisse qui a touché le fond (*ou* le tuf) (*f.*).

price which has only been touched, cours qui n'a'qu'effleuré (*m.*).

touch (to make an incidental stop) (*v.i.*), toucher; aborder:
to touch at a port, at any ports, toucher à un port (*ou* en un port), à tous ports (*ou* en tout port).

with liberty to touch and stay at any ports or places whatsoever, avec faculté de toucher et séjourner à tous ports ou lieux quelconques.

at the first port where the ship touches, au premier port où le navire aborde.

ouched bill (of health),　　patente (de santé) suspecte (*f.*).

our (*n.*),　tour (*m.*) ;　voyage (*m.*) :
shipping company which organizes Mediterranean tours, compagnie de navigation qui organise des tours en Méditerranée (*f.*).

our ticket,　carnet de voyage (*m.*).

ouring (*n.*),　tourisme (*m.*).

ourist (*used as adj.*) *or* **touristic** (*adj.*) *or* **touring** (*used as adj.*),　touristique ; de tourisme :
tourist centre,　centre de tourisme (*m.*).
tourist office,　bureau de tourisme (*m.*).
tourist traffic,　trafic touristique (*m.*).

ourist (pers.) (*n.*),　touriste (*m.* ou *f.*) :
the revenues accruing from the maintenance of foreign tourists, les revenus provenant de l'entretien de touristes étrangers (*m.pl.*).

out *or* **touter** (pers.) (*n.*),　rabatteur d'affaires (*m.*).

ow (vessel towed) (*n.*),　remorqué (*m.*) :
the abandonment of the tow by the tug, l'abandon du remorqué par le remorqueur (*m.*).

ow (*v.t.*),　remorquer :
to tow a ship to destination,　remorquer un navire à destination.

to be towed, se faire remorquer ; être remorqué, -e :
ship which is towed by another ship,　navire qui se fait remorquer par un autre navire (*m.*).
with leave to tow or be towed (Insce),　avec faculté de remorquer ou se faire remorquer.

owage *or* **towing** *or* **tow** (*n.*),　remorquage (*m.*) ; remorque (*f.*) :
towage of (*or* towing) a ship in danger,　remorquage d'un navire en danger.
to take a ship in tow,　prendre un navire à la remorque.

owage contractor,　entrepreneur de remorquage (*m.*).

own (*n.*),　ville (*f.*) ;　place (*f.*) :
country town *or* provincial town,　ville de province.
to canvass the town,　faire la place.

own cheque,　chèque sur place (*m.*).

own traveller,　placier, -ère.

trace (Stock Exch.) (*n.*),　filière (*f.*).

traction (*n.*),　traction (*f.*).

tractor (*n.*) (opp. to *trailer*),　tracteur (*m.*).

trade (*n.*),　commerce (*m.*) ;　'haut commerce (*m.*) ; négoce (*m.*) ; trafic (*m.*) :
trade is bad,　le commerce va mal.
trade enriches a nation,　le commerce (*ou* le négoce) enrichit une nation.
the trade in wines *or* the wine trade,　le commerce (*ou* le trafic) des vins.

trade (*v.i.*),　commercer ; faire commerce ; faire le commerce ; négocier ; trafiquer :
to trade in America, with other countries,　commercer, négocier, trafiquer, en Amérique, avec d'autres pays.
to trade in precious metals,　faire commerce (*ou* faire le commerce) de métaux précieux.
the business of banking consists in trading in money and credit, le commerce de banque consiste à trafiquer de la monnaie et du crédit.

trade balance (Polit. Econ.),　balance commerciale (*f.*) ;　balance du commerce (*f.*). *V. exemple sous syn.* balance of trade.

trade bank,　banque de commerce (*f.*) ; banque commerciale (*f.*).

trade charge (Cash on delivery),　remboursement (*m.*) :
a trade charge is the sum put upon the goods by the sender and which must be paid to him after receipt of the goods by the consignee, le remboursement consiste dans la somme mise à la charge de la marchandise par l'expéditeur et qui doit lui être payée après réception de la marchandise par le destinataire.
the trade charge represents the value or a part of the value of the goods, le remboursement représente la valeur ou une partie de la valeur de la marchandise.
the trade charge on any one postal parcel must not exceed so many pounds, le colis postal peut être grevé d'un remboursement jusqu'à concurrence de tant de livres.

trade charge letter,　bulletin de remboursement (*m.*).

trade charge money order,　mandat de remboursement (*m.*).

trade discount (distinguished from *cash discount*), remise (*f.*) ; remise sur marchandises (*f.*) ; escompte sur marchandises (*m.*) ; escompte sur (*ou* de) facture (*m.*) ; escompte-remise (*m.*) ; escompte d'usage (*m.*).

trade expenses,　frais de commerce (*m.pl.*).

trade mark,　marque de commerce (*f.*) ; marque de fabrique (*f.*).

trade name,　raison de commerce (*f.*) ; raison commerciale (*f.*) ; nom commercial (*m.*).

trade paper *or* **trade bills** (bills of exchange) (opp. to *bank paper*),　papier de commerce (*m.*) ; papier commercial (*m.*).

trade price,　prix de demi-gros (*m.*).

trade reference,　référence de fournisseur (*f.*).

trade representative,　représentant de commerce (*m.*).

trade route,　route commerciale (*f.*).

trader (pers.) (*n.*),　commerçant, -e ; négociant, -e ; trafiquant (*m.*) ; marchand, -e :
personal credit is based on the reputation of the trader, le crédit personnel est basé sur la réputation du commerçant.
the Dutch are a nation of traders, les Hollandais sont un peuple de trafiquants (*m.pl.*).

traders (*collectively*) (*n.pl.*),　le commerce :
disputes between the customs and traders, contestations entre la douane et le commerce (*f.pl.*).

trader's premises,　domicile (*m.*) :
delivery at trader's premises or at railway station, to be called for, livraison à domicile ou en gare (*f.*).

trader's season ticket,　carte d'abonnement pour associés ou gérants d'entreprises commerciales et industrielles (*f.*).

trader's sheet (Rly.) (opp. to *company's sheet*),　bâche appartenant à l'expéditeur (*f.*) ; bâche particulière (*f.*).

trading (*adj.*), commerçant, -e ; commercial, -e, -aux :
trading concern, entreprise commerciale (*f.*).
trading (*n.*), commerce (*m.*) ; négoce (*m.*) ; trafic (*m.*).
trading (Bkkpg) (*n.*), exercice (*m.*) ; exploitation (*f.*) :
whatever may be the result of the trading, quel que soit le résultat de l'exercice.
to charge an amount against the previous month's trading, imputer une somme sur l'exercice du mois précédent.
trading account, compte d'exploitation (*m.*) ; exploitation (*f.*).
trading assets (sundry debtors, for instance), actif engagé (*m.*) ; valeurs engagées (*f.pl.*).
trading capital, capital engagé (*m.*).
trading loss, perte d'exploitation (*f.*).
trading profit, bénéfice d'exploitation (*m.*).
trading results, résultats de l'exercice (*m.pl.*) ; résultats de l'exploitation (*m.pl.*).
trading station, station de commerce (*f.*) :
trading stations in British East Africa, stations de commerce en Afrique Orientale britannique (*ou* anglaise).
trading vessel, navire de commerce (*m.*) ; navire marchand (*m.*) ; bâtiment de commerce (*m.*) ; bâtiment marchand (*m.*) ; bateau de commerce (*m.*).
trading year *or* **trading period,** exercice (*m.*) :
trading year ending 31st December, exercice prenant fin (*ou* clôturant) le 31 décembre.
trading year ended 31st December, exercice ayant pris fin (*ou* exercice clôturé *ou* clos) le 31 décembre.
if the company's year comprises two half yearly trading periods, si l'année sociale comprend deux exercices semestriels.
tradition (delivery) (Law) (*n.*), tradition (*f.*) :
the bank note is transmitted from hand to hand, one says by tradition, le billet de banque se transmet de la main à la main, on dit par tradition.
traffic (*n.*), trafic (*m.*) ; mouvement (*m.*) ; circulation (*f.*) :
passenger traffic, trafic des voyageurs.
the traffic of British seaports, le trafic, le mouvement, des ports maritimes britanniques.
one way traffic, circulation à sens unique.
traffic (*v.i.*), trafiquer.
traffic department (Rly.), service de l'exploitation (*m.*).
traffic returns, relevés de trafic (*m.pl.*).
trailer (*n.*) (opp. to *tractor*), remorque (*f.*).
train (*n.*), train (*m.*) ; convoi (*m.*) :
passenger train, train de voyageurs ; convoi de voyageurs.
train de luxe, train de luxe :
train de luxe composed of saloon carriages, train de luxe composé de voitures-salons.
train customs officer (i.e., a customs officer travelling on the train in the interests of the service), douanier convoyeur (*m.*).
train kilometre, kilomètre-train (*m.*) ; kilomètre de train (*m.*), analogue au *train mile* anglais (mille de train).

tram (*n.*) *or* **tram car,** tramway (*m.*) ; voiture de tramway (*f.*).
tram track, voie de tramway (*f.*).
tramp (*n.*) *or* **tramp steamer** (opp. to *liner*), tramp (*m.*) ; tramp-steamer (*m.*) ; navire tramp (*m.*) ; navire de tramping (*m.*) ; navire vagabond (*m.*) ; navire irrégulier (*m.*).
tramp navigation, navigation au tramping (*f.*).
tramping (voyaging of a tramp steamer) (*n.*), tramping (*m.*).
tramway (*n.*), tramway (*m.*).
tramway line *or* **tram line,** ligne de tramway (*f.*).
transact (*v.t.*), traiter ; faire ; délibérer ; délibérer sur :
to transact a bargain, traiter, faire, un marché.
to transact business with someone, faire des affaires, traiter, avec quelqu'un.
to put down on the agenda the business to be transacted, mettre à l'ordre du jour les questions à délibérer.
meeting convened to transact the following business, assemblée convoquée à l'effet de délibérer sur l'ordre du jour suivant (*f.*).
transaction (*n.*), transaction (*f.*) ; opération (*f.*) ; négociation (*f.*) ; affaire (*f.*) ; marché (*m.*) ; mouvement (*m.*) ; délibération (*f.*) :
a commercial transaction, une transaction commerciale.
stock exchange transactions, opérations de bourse.
transaction for cash *or* cash transaction, opération (*ou* négociation) (*ou* marché) au comptant.
transaction on (*or* upon) credit, opération à terme ; opération à livrer ; négociation (*ou* marché) à terme (*ou* à livrer).
transaction for the settlement (*or* for the account) (Stock Exch.), opération à terme ; opération à livrer ; négociation (*ou* marché) à terme (*ou* à livrer).
transaction for future delivery during specified periods (Produce Exch.), marché à terme ferme.
all the cash transactions are entered in a book called cash book, tous les mouvements d'espèces sont inscrits sur un registre appelé livre de caisse.
the bank's transactions in securities, les mouvements des valeurs de la banque.
transactions of a meeting (i.e., the proceedings, the business), délibérations d'une assemblée.
transatlantic (*adj.*), transatlantique :
transatlantic liner *or* transatlantic boat, paquebot transatlantique (*m.*) ; transatlantique (*m.*).
transcribe (*v.t.*), transcrire :
to transcribe a letter, transcrire une lettre.
transcript *or* **transcription** (*n.*), transcription (*f.*).
transfer (act) (*n.*), transmission (*f.*) ; cession (*f.*) ; transport (*m.*) ; transfert (*m.*) ; mutation (*f.*) ; translation (*f.*) :
transfer of shares, cession, transmission, transfert, d'actions.
a transfer is a conveyance of the property in a registered stock or share from one person

to another, le transfert est la transmission de propriété d'un titre nominatif d'une personne à une autre.

transfer of property, transmission, cession, transport, mutation, translation, transfert, de biens (*ou* de propriété).

transfer of a debt, transport d'une créance.

transfer inter vivos, mutation entre vifs.

transfer of mortgage, mutation d'hypothèque; transfert d'hypothèque.

transfer (of ownership of vessel) at the registry of shipping, mutation en douane.

transfers in warehouse (Customs), transferts d'entrepôt.

transfer (of assets by a vendor) (*n.*), apport (*m.*):
transfer of a works, of office furniture, apport d'une usine, de mobilier de bureau.

Note :—In English law, making over of tangible assets is usually referred to as a *transfer*, of intangible assets as an *assignment*, of both together as a *transfer*. Cf. examples under **assign** and **assignment**.

transfer (*n.*) *or* **transfer deed** (stocks and shares) (Abbrev.: **tfr**), transfert (*m.*); feuille de transfert (*f.*):
transfer of a registered share signed by the transferor and the transferee, transfert d'une action nominative signé par le cédant et le cessionnaire.

the transfer of registered shares requires the signature of a transfer deed by the shareholder, le transfert des actions nominatives donne lieu à la signature d'une feuille de transfert par l'actionnaire.

Note :—In France, seller and buyer do not as a rule sign one and the same deed, as in England : the seller signs a *feuille de transfert* and the buyer a *feuille d'acceptation de transfert*.

transfer (*n.*) *or* **transfer deed** (conveyance) (Law), acte de cession (*m.*); acte de transmission (*m.*); acte de mutation (*m.*); acte (*ou* contrat) translatif de propriété (*m.*).

transfer (Bkkpg) (*n.*) (Abbrev.: **tfr**), virement (*m.*); contre-passement (*m.*); contre-passation (*f.*); transport (*m.*); transfert (*m.*); ristourne (*f.*); ristorne (*f.*):
transfer of an entry, of an amount from one account to another, virement, contre-passement, transport, transfert, d'une écriture, d'une somme d'un compte à un autre.

transfer to debit of former account *or* for amount transferred to former a/c. (journal narration) (Bkkpg), virement au débit du 1er compte; pour virement au 1er compte.

transfer to credit of latter account *or* for amount transferred to latter a/c. (Bkkpg), virement au crédit du 2e compte; pour virement au 2e compte.

for the most part, exchange transactions are done by simple transfers between corresponding bankers, le plus souvent, les opérations de change se font par simples virements entre banquiers correspondants.

transfer (*v.t.*), transmettre; céder; transporter; transférer:

to transfer a bill by endorsement, céder, transmettre, un billet par voie d'endossement.

to transfer shares, céder, transférer, des actions.

to transfer some inscribed rente, transférer une inscription de rente.

to transfer a debt, transporter une créance.

to be transferred, être transmis (-e), cédé (-e), transporté (-e), transféré (-e); se transmettre; se céder; se transporter; se transférer:
passage tickets are personal and cannot be transferred, les billets de passage sont personnels et ne peuvent être cédés (*m.pl.*).

a bill of lading to order is transferred by endorsement like a bill of exchange, le connaissement à ordre se transmet par endossement comme une lettre de change.

transfer (to make over vendor assets) (*v.t.*), apporter; faire apport:
Messrs A. and B. transfer jointly to the X. Company the real and personal property hereinafter described, MM. A. et B. apportent conjointement (*ou* font conjointement apport) à la Société X. des biens mobiliers et immobiliers dont la désignation suit.

company in liquidation which transfers its assets to a new company, société en liquidation qui apporte son actif à une société nouvelle (*f.*).

transfer (Bkkpg) (*v.t.*), virer; contre-passer; transporter; transférer; ristourner; ristorner:
to transfer a balance to profit and loss account, virer, contre-passer, transporter, transférer, une balance au compte pertes et profits.

to transfer part of a debit, ristourner partie d'un débit.

transfer case (for letters or other documents), boîte de transfert (*f.*).

transfer duty, droit de transmission (*m.*); taxe de transmission (*f.*); impôt de transmission (*m.*); droit de transfert (*m.*); droits de mutation (*m.pl.*). *See note under* droit de transmission.

transfer entry (Bkkpg), écriture de virement (*f.*); écriture de contre-passement (*f.*); article de virement (*ou* de contre-passement) (*m.*).

transfer form (stocks and shares), formule de transfert (*f.*).

transfer office, bureau des transferts (*m.*).

transfer register, registre des transferts (*m.*); livre des transferts (*m.*); journal des transferts (*m.*).

transferability (*n.*), cessibilité (*f.*); commercialité (*f.*):
transferability of a share, cessibilité d'une action.

transferability of a debt, cessibilité, commercialité, d'une dette.

transferable (*adj.*), cessible; mobilier, -ère; négociable; transférable:
the characteristic feature of the share is that it is freely transferable, le trait caractéristique de l'action est qu'elle est librement cessible.

transferable securities, valeurs mobilières (*f.pl.*); valeurs négociables (*f.pl.*); valeurs cessibles (*f.pl.*); valeurs transférables (*f.pl.*).

transferee (pers.) (*n.*), cessionnaire (*m.* ou *f.*):
transferee of a share, of a bill of exchange, cessionnaire d'une action, d'un effet de commerce.

transference (*n.*), transfèrement (*m.*):
the transference of a debt, le transfèrement d'une créance.

transferor (pers.) (*n.*), cédant, -e:
transferor of a share, of a bill, cédant d'une action, d'un effet.

tranship (*v.t.*), transborder:
goods transhipped during the voyage, on another ship in an intermediate port, marchandises transbordées au cours du voyage, sur un autre navire dans un port intermédiaire (*f.pl.*).

transhipment (*n.*), transbordement (*m.*).

transhipment bond, acquit à caution (*m.*); acquit-à-caution (*m.*).

transhipment clause, clause de transbordement (*f.*).

transhipment entry, déclaration de transbordement (*f.*).

transhipment permit, permis de transbordement (*m.*).

transhipment risk (Insce), risque de transbordement (*m.*).

transhipping for, en transbordement pour; correspondance pour:
sailings from London for Rio de Janeiro, transhipping for Pernambuco, départs de Londres pour Rio de Janeiro, en transbordement pour Pernambuco; départs de Londres pour Rio, correspondance à Rio pour Pernambuco (*m.pl.*).

transhipping port, port de transbordement (*m.*).

transire (Customs) (*n.*), passavant (*m.*); passe-avant (*m.*):
coasting transire, passavant de cabotage.

transit (carrying across or through) (*n.*), transit (*m.*):
goods in transit from or for other ports or places, through (*or* across) Switzerland, marchandises en transit de ou pour d'autres ports ou lieux, à travers la Suisse (*f.pl.*).

transit (conveying) (*n.*), transport (*m.*):
transit to and from the vessel, transport immédiat de terre à bord et de bord à terre.

transit (passage; route) (*n.*), trajet (*m.*); parcours (*m.*); voyage (*m.*); route (*f.*); passage (*m.*); expédition (*f.*):
sea transit, trajet par mer; parcours maritime; voyage de (*ou* par) mer.
goods damaged in course of transit (*or* damaged in transit) (*or* damaged in transitu), marchandise avariée en cours de route (*ou* en cours de voyage) (*f.*).
damage in transit, avaries de route (*f.pl.*).
risk whilst on quays, wharves, or in sheds during the ordinary course of transit, risque de séjour à terre en cours normal d'expédition (*m.*).

transit agent, transitaire (*m.*); commissionnaire de transit (*m.*); commissionnaire-transitaire (*m.*); agent transitaire (*m.*).

transit entry (Customs), déclaration de transit (*f.*).

transit goods, marchandises de transit (*f.pl.*).

transit manifest, manifeste de transit (*m.*).

transit trade, commerce de transit (*m.*).

transit traffic, trafic de transit (*m.*).

transit visa (passport), visa de transit (*m.*).

translate (*v.t.*), traduire; déchiffrer:
to translate from French into English, traduire du français en anglais.
to translate a telegram, traduire, déchiffrer, une dépêche télégraphique.

translation (*n.*), traduction (*f.*); déchiffrement (*m.*):
translation of a cable, traduction, déchiffrement, d'un câblogramme.

translator (pers.) (*n.*), traducteur (*m.*):
sworn translator, traducteur assermenté.

transmission (*n.*), transmission (*f.*).

transmission on death (Law), mutation par décès (*f.*).

transmit (*v.t.*), transmettre:
to transmit an order, transmettre un ordre.
to transmit one's property by will, transmettre ses biens par testament.

transmitter (Teleph.) (*n.*) (opp. to *receiver*), transmetteur (*m.*).

transmitting station (Teleg.) (opp. to *receiving station*), poste émetteur (*m.*); station émettrice (*f.*); station d'émission (*f.*).

transpacific (*adj.*), transpacifique.

transparent envelope, enveloppe transparente (*f.*).

transport *or* **transportation** (*n.*), transport (*m.*); charriage (*m.*); voiture (*f.*).

transport (*v.t.*), transporter; charrier; voiturer:
to transport goods by rail, transporter des marchandises par chemin de fer.

transport agent, commissionnaire de transport (*ou* de transports) (*m.*); commissionnaire-messager (*m.*); agent de transport (*m.*).

transport company, compagnie (*ou* société) de transports (*f.*).

transposition (of figures) (*n.*), interversion (*f.*); transposition (*f.*):
when there is a transposition of figures, the difference is always a multiple of 9, lorsqu'il y a une interversion de chiffres, la différence est toujours un multiple de 9.

transship, transshipment, transshipping. Syn. de **tranship,** etc.

travel (*n.*), voyage (*m.*).

travel (*v.i.*), voyager; marcher:
to travel in Europe, by land (*or* overland), by sea, voyager en Europe, par terre, par mer.
the goods travel, unless otherwise agreed, at buyer's risk, la marchandise voyage, sauf convention contraire, aux risques et périls de l'acheteur.
ship designed to travel at high speed, navire destiné à marcher à grande vitesse (*m.*).

travel agency, agence de voyages (*f.*); bureau de voyage (*m.*).

travel at (to), marcher à; parcourir:

to travel at — miles an hour (said of a train, etc.), marcher à, parcourir, — milles à l'heure.

travel guide (book), guide de voyage (*m.*); indicateur de voyage (*m.*).

travel over (to), parcourir:
the distances travelled over on the sea are expressed in nautical miles, les distances parcourues sur mer s'expriment en milles marins (*f.pl.*).

travel requisites, articles de voyage (*m.*).

travel ticket, billet de voyage (*m.*).

traveller or **traveler** (pers.) (*n.*), voyageur, -euse:
traveller on commission, voyageur à la commission.

traveller's cheque, chèque de voyage (*m.*).

travellers' samples, échantillons de voyageurs (*m.pl.*).

travelling or **traveling** (*n.*), voyage (*m.*).

travelling expenses, frais de voyage (*m.pl.*); frais de déplacement (*m.pl.*).

travelling pass (motor cars), carnet de route (*m.*).

travelling post office (Abbrev.: **T.P.O.**), bureau de poste ambulant (*m.*).

trawler (*n.*), chalutier (*m.*).

treasure up (to), thésauriser.

treasurer (pers.) (*n.*), trésorier, -ère.

treasurership (*n.*), trésorerie (*f.*).

treasury [treasuries *pl.*] (offices) (*n.*), trésor (*m.*); trésorerie (*f.*); caisse (*f.*):
to go to the treasury, aller à la trésorerie.

Treasury (*n.*) or **Treasury Board** or **Treasury Department,** Trésor (*m.*); trésor public (*m.*); fisc (*m.*).

treasury (national finances) (*n.*), trésorerie (*f.*):
the national treasury, la trésorerie nationale.

treasury authorities, autorités trésorières (*f.pl.*).

Treasury bond (Abbrev.: **Treas. Bd**), bon du Trésor (*m.*).

treat (*v.i.*), traiter; négocier:
he refuses to treat with him, il refuse de traiter (*ou* de négocier) avec lui.

treatment (*n.*), traitement (*m.*):
most favoured nation treatment (Polit. Econ.), traitement de la nation la plus favorisée.

treaty [treaties *pl.*] (*n.*), traité (*m.*):
treaty of commerce, traité de commerce.

treble (*adj.*), triple:
treble duty (Customs), triple droit (*m.*).

treble (*n.*), triple (*m.*):
treble the duty-paid value (customs fine), triple de la valeur à l'acquitté.

trend (*n.*), tendance (*f.*); tendances (*f.pl.*); orientation (*f.*):
the general trend of the market, les tendances d'ensemble (*ou* l'orientation générale) du marché.

trial (on) (employment), à l'essai:
a month on trial, une mois à l'essai.

trial balance (Bkkpg) (Abbrev.: **T.B.**), balance de vérification (*f.*); balance d'ordre (*f.*); balance (*f.*):
trial balance before closing *or* first trial balance *or* full trial balance, balance préparatoire;

balance préparatoire d'inventaire; balance de vérification avant inventaire.

trial balance after closing *or* second trial balance *or* short trial balance, balance d'inventaire.

trial balance of subsidiary ledger, balance auxiliaire.

general trial balance *or* trial balance of general ledger, balance générale.

trial balance book, livre des balances de vérification (*m.*); livre de balance (*m.*); livre de soldes (*m.*).

trial trip (Navig., etc.), voyage d'essai (*m.*).

tribunal (*n.*), tribunal (*m.*):
to appear before the tribunal, comparaître devant le tribunal.

trick (*n.*), truc (*m.*):
tricks of the trade, des trucs de métier.
trick to deceive the public, truc pour duper le public.

trim (*v.t.*), arrimer:
to trim the coal in the bunkers, arrimer le charbon dans les soutes.

trimming (*n.*), arrimage (*m.*).

trip (*n.*), voyage (*m.*); trajet (*m.*); excursion (*f.*):
trip there and back, trajet d'aller et de retour.

triplane (*n.*), triplan (*m.*).

triple (*adj.*), triple.

triplicate (*n.*), triple (*m.*); triplicata (*m.*).

in triplicate, en triple; en triple exemplaire; en triple expédition; en triplicata; par triplicata:
to draw up a deed in triplicate, dresser un acte en triple (*ou* en triple exemplaire).
bill of lading in triplicate, connaissement en triplicata (*m.*).

truck (*n.*), wagon (*m.*); chariot (*m.*).

truck load (Rly.) (distinguished from *part truck load*), wagon complet (*m.*); charge complète de wagon (*f.*); charge complète (*f.*); chargement de wagon (*m.*):
the minimum weight per truck load, le minimum de poids par wagon complet.
heavy goods consigned in truck loads, marchandises pondéreuses expédiées en wagon complet (*f.pl.*).
truck load consignments, expéditions à charge complète (*f.pl.*).
truck load rates, tarif des wagons complets (*ou* des charges complètes) (*m.*).

true copy, copie fidèle (*f.*).

true copy (of a deed), copie authentique (d'un acte) (*f.*).

true discount (opp. to *bank discount*), escompte en dedans (*m.*); escompte rationnel (*m.*).

trunk call (Teleph.), communication interurbaine (*f.*); conversation interurbaine (*f.*).

trunk exchange (Teleph.), bureau interurbain (*m.*); bureau central interurbain (*m.*); poste central interurbain (*m.*).

trunk line (Rly.), grande artère (*f.*); grande ligne (*f.*); ligne d'artère (*f.*):
the trunk lines of the English system, les grandes artères du réseau anglais.

trunk operator (Teleph.), opératrice interurbaine (*f.*).

Trunks, what number are you calling ? *or* **Trunks, number, please ?** (Teleph.), Interurbain, qui demandez-vous?

trust (*n.*), charge (*f.*); mandat (*m.*); confiance (*f.*):
to fulfil one's trust, faire l'acquit de sa charge.
the obligation of the agent to prove the performance of his trust ceases when the principal has discharged him, l'obligation pour le mandataire de justifier de l'exécution de son mandat cesse lorsque le mandant lui a donné décharge (*f.*).
breach of trust, abus de confiance (*m.*).

trust (combination of interests) (*n.*), trust (*m.*):
oil trust, trust de pétrole.
steel trust, trust de l'acier.

trust (*v.t.*), se confier en :
to trust one's friends, se confier en ses amis.

trustee (guardian) (pers.) (*n.*), curateur, -trice.

trustee (depository) (pers.) (*n.*), dépositaire (*m.* ou *f.*); consignataire (*m.*).

trustee in bankruptcy, syndic de faillite (*m.*).

trustee's certificate (Fin.), certificat fiduciaire (*m.*).

trusteeship (of a bankruptcy) (*n.*), syndicat (*m.*):
to accept the trusteeship of a bankruptcy, accepter le syndicat d'une faillite.
during the trusteeship of So-and-so, pendant le syndicat d'un tel.

trustworthiness (*n.*), fidélité (*f.*).

trustworthy (*adj.*), fidèle :
trustworthy cashier, caissier fidèle (*m.*).

try to get money (to), chercher à se procurer de l'argent.

tug (*n.*) *or* **tug boat**, remorqueur (*m.*); bateau remorqueur (*m.*).

tune (*n.*), cadence (*f.*):
production which continues to the tune of so many tons a day, production qui continue à la cadence de tant de tonnes par jour.

tunnel (*n.*), tunnel (*m.*); souterrain (*m.*):
the St Gothard tunnel, le tunnel, le souterrain, du Saint-Gothard.

turn (change) (*n.*), revirement (*m.*):
turn for the better, for the worse (Stock Exch.), revirement en hausse, en baisse :
if the beginning of the week has been bad, there is frequently a turn for the better towards the end of the week, si le commencement de la huitaine a été mauvais, il y a fréquemment un revirement en hausse pour les derniers jours de la semaine.

turn (*v.t.*). V. exemples :
to turn a bank note into cash, convertir un billet de banque en espèces.
to turn a partnership into a limited company, transformer une société en nom collectif en société anonyme.
to turn a thing into money, faire argent (*ou* faire de l'argent) d'une chose.
to turn to account (*or* to profit) (*or* to advantage), faire valoir; mettre en valeur; mettre à profit:

to turn one's property to account, faire valoir son bien.
to turn one's investments to account, mettre en valeur son portefeuille.
to turn out well, tourner à compte.
trade consists not in investing but in turning over capital, le commerce consiste non à placer mais à faire rouler des capitaux.

turn of the market, écart entre le cours acheteur et le cours vendeur (*m.*).

turning to account (*or* **to profit**) (*or* **to advantage**) (employment of one's money), faire-valoir (*m.*); mise en valeur (*f.*); mise à profit (*f.*).

turnover (*n.*), chiffre d'affaires (*m.*); roulement (*m.*); courant d'affaires (*m.*):
a turnover of over 2 millions, un chiffre d'affaires de plus de 2 millions.
X. 6% debentures closed at $1\frac{1}{4}$ against $1\frac{3}{16}$ with a fairly continuous turnover, les obligations X. 6 0/0 clôturent à 1 1/4 contre 1 3/16 avec un courant d'affaires assez suivi.

turnover (sales) (Produce Exch.) (*n.*), circulation (*f.*); mouvement (*m.*); ventes (*f.pl.*):
turnover: 000 tons, circulation (*ou* mouvement) (*ou* ventes): 000 tonnes.

twelvemonth (*n.*), année (*f.*).

twin screw ship, navire à deux hélices (*m.*).

twin screw steamer (Abbrev.: **T.S.S.**), vapeur à deux hélices (*m.*).

twin ship, navire jumeau (*m.*); navire frère (*m.*); frère (*m.*).

twine (*n.*), ficelle (*f.*).

tying into a bundle (*or* **into bundles**) (papers), enliassement (*m.*).

type bar (of a typewriter), levier porte-caractères (*m.*).

typewrite *or* **type** (*v.t.*), taper; taper à la machine; taper à la machine à écrire; écrire à la machine; dactylographier:
to typewrite (*or* to type) a letter, taper une lettre; taper (*ou* écrire) une lettre à la machine; dactylographier une lettre.

typewriter (*n.*) *or* **typewriting machine**, machine à écrire (*f.*); dactylographe (*m.*); dactylotype (*f.*).

typewriter *or* **typist** (pers.) (*n.*), dactylographe (*m.* ou *f.*); dactylo (*m.* ou *f.*).

typewriter accounting machine, machine à écrire comptable (*f.*):
typewriter accounting machine for all bookkeeping work, machine à écrire comptable pour tous travaux de comptabilité.
typewriter accounting machine for invoicing work, machine à écrire comptable pour travaux de facturation.

typewriter's eraser, gomme pour machines à écrire (*f.*).

typewriter's table, bureau pour dactylographe (*m.*).

typewriters' room, salle des dactylographes (*f.*).

typewriting (*adj.*), dactylographique; dactylographe :
typewriting signs, signes dactylographiques (*m.pl.*).

typewriting *or* typing (*n.*), écriture à la machine (*f.*); dactylographie (*f.*).
typewriting office, bureau de dactylographie (*m.*).
typewriting paper, papier pour machines à

écrire (*m.*); papier machine à écrire (*m.*); papier machine (*m.*).
typewritten (*adj.*), à la machine :
typewritten invoices, factures à la machine (*f.pl.*).

U

ultimo (*adv.*) (Abbrev.: ult. *or* ulto), du mois dernier; de l'écoulé; écoulé.
ultra vires (opp. to *intra vires*), antistatutaire : the auditors may be made liable jointly and severally with the directors for acts done ultra vires (*or* extra vires) which they may have approved and which may have brought about the company's ruin, les commissaires peuvent être déclarés responsables solidairement avec les administrateurs des opérations antistatutaires qu'ils auraient approuvés et qui auraient amené la ruine de la société (*m.pl.*).
umpire (pers.) (*n.*), sur-arbitre (*m.*); tiers arbitre (*m.*).
unacceptable (*adj.*), non acceptable.
unaccepted (*adj.*), non accepté, -e : unaccepted bill, effet non accepté (*m.*).
unaccompanied baggage, bagages non accompagnés (*m.pl.*).
unalienable (*adj.*), inaliénable; incessible : unalienable right, droit inaliénable (*ou* incessible) (*m.*).
unaltered (*adj.*), inchangé, -e : the price remains unaltered, le cours reste inchangé.
unanimous (*adj.*), unanime : the unanimous consent of all the shareholders, le consentement unanime de tous les actionnaires.
unanimously (*adv.*), unanimement; à l'unanimité : director reelected unanimously, administrateur réélu à l'unanimité (*m.*).
unapproved place (for landing of dutiable goods) (Customs), localité non agréée (*f.*).
unauthorized (*adj.*), inautorisé, -e.
unavailability *or* unavailableness (*n.*), indisponibilité (*f.*).
unavailable (*adj.*), indisponible : unavailable funds, fonds indisponibles (*m.pl.*).
unballast (*v.t.*), délester.
unballasting (*n.*), délestage (*m.*).
unbankable (*adj.*), non bancable; déclassé, -e : unbankable paper, papier non bancable (*m.*); papier déclassé (*m.*).
uncalled (*adj.*), non appelé, -e : uncalled capital, capital non appelé (*m.*); non appelé (*m.*).
uncertain (*adj.*), incertain, -e; aléatoire. uncertain exchange, incertain (*m.*). *V.* to quote uncertain exchange *pour exemple*.

uncertainty [uncertainties *pl.*] (*n.*), incertitude (*f.*); aléatoire (*m.*).
uncertified (*adj.*), incertifié, -e.
unchanged (*adj.*), inchangé, -e : the price remains unchanged, le cours reste inchangé.
unchartered (*adj.*), non affrété, -e.
unclaimed (*adj.*), non réclamé, -e : unclaimed dividend, dividende non réclamé (*m.*). unclaimed luggage, bagages non réclamés (*m.pl.*).
unconfirmed credit, crédit non confirmé (*m.*); crédit simple (*m.*); accréditif non confirmé (*ou* simple) (*m.*).
unconvertible (*adj.*), inconvertible. V. exemples sous syn. inconvertible.
uncovered (*adj.*), à découvert : uncovered advance (Banking), avance à découvert (*f.*). uncovered bear (Stock Exch.), baissier à découvert (*m.*). uncovered circulation (i.e., uncovered by gold), circulation à découvert (*f.*). to cover risks which ordinary policies leave uncovered (Insce), couvrir des risques que les polices ordinaires laissent à découvert. insured who is uncovered by a quarter, by a third, assuré qui est à découvert d'un quart, d'un tiers (*m.*).
uncustomed goods (not liable to duty), marchandises franches de tout droit (*f.pl.*); marchandise franche de tout droit (*f.*); marchandises exemptes de droit (*f.pl.*); marchandises libres à l'entrée (*f.pl.*); marchandise exempte (*f.*).
uncustomed goods (having paid no duty), marchandises non acquittées (*f.pl.*).
undamaged (*adj.*), non avarié, -e; non endommagé, -e.
undated (*adj.*), sans date; non daté, -e : undated letter, lettre sans date (*f.*); lettre non datée (*f.*).
undecided (*adj.*), indécis, -e; hésitant, -e : the tendency, undecided at first, hardened later on, la tendance, tout d'abord indécise, s'est raffermie en séance. X. shares are rather undecided at 1½, l'action X. est plutôt hésitante à 1 1/2.
undecided (to be), être indécis, -e; hésiter : X. shares were undecided around 1¼, l'action X. hésite autour de 1 1/4.

undecipherable (*adj.*), indéchiffrable.
undeliverable postal parcels, colis postaux en souffrance (*m.pl.*); colis postaux tombés en rebut (*ou* en souffrance) (*m.pl.*).
undelivered parcel, colis non livré (*m.*).
undelivered postal packets, correspondances non distribuées (*f.pl.*).
under any circumstances, à tout événement:
freight not repayable under any circumstances, fret acquis à tout événement (*m.*).
under cashier, sous-caissier (*m.*).
under manager, sous-directeur (*m.*); sous-chef (*m.*).
under manageress, sous-directrice (*f.*).
under or over, en moins ou en plus:
any difference under or over, toute différence en moins ou en plus (*f.*).
under reserve *or* **under usual reserves** (Banking). V. sous **reserve.**
under secretary, sous-secrétaire (*m.*):
under secretary of State, sous-secrétaire d'É-tat.
under ship's derrick *or* **under ship's tackle** *or* **under ship's slings** *or* **over ship's side** *or* **at ship's rail,** sous palan; sous vergues:
discharge will be made on quay or under ship's derrick (*or* tackle) (*or* slings) (*or* on quay or over ship's side) (*or* on quay or at ship's rail), le débarquement s'effectuera à quai ou sous palan (*ou* sous vergues).
to take the goods on the wharf or in the shed and bring them under the ship's derrick (*or* tackle) (*or* slings), prendre les marchandises sur le quai ou sous le hangar et les amener sous palan (*ou* sous vergues).
under spot (premium) (Forward exchange rates) (Abbrev.: **p.**), déport (*m.*); bénéfice (*m.*). V. exemples sous **discount.**
under steam or sail (Navig.), à la vapeur ou à la voile.
under tenant, sous-locataire (*m.*); sous-preneur (*m.*).
underassessment (*n.*), insuffisance d'imposition (*f.*).
underbid (*v.i.*), mésoffrir.
underdeck tonnage, tonnage sous le pont (*m.*).
underestimate (*v.t.*), sous-estimer; sous-évaluer; mésestimer; minorer.
underestimation *or* **underestimate** (*n.*), sous-estimation (*f.*); sous-évaluation (*f.*); mé-sestimation (*f.*); minoration (*f.*).
underground railway, chemin de fer souterrain (*m.*).
underinsurance (*n.*), sous-assurance (*f.*).
underinsure (*v.t.*), sous-assurer.
underlease (*n.*), sous-bail (*m.*).
underlessee (pers.) (*n.*), sous-locataire (*m.* ou *f.*); sous-preneur (*m.*).
underlessor (pers.) (*n.*), sous-bailleur (*m.*).
underlet (*v.t.*), sous-louer:
lessee who has the right to underlet, preneur qui a le droit de sous-louer (*m.*).
underletting (*n.*), sous-location (*f.*).
underline (*v.t.*), souligner:
to underline the words or passages of the text to which one wishes to draw attention,

souligner les mots ou passages du texte sur lesquels on désire attirer l'attention.
underlining (*n.*), soulignement (*m.*).
underpaid postal packets, correspondances in-suffisamment affranchies (*f.pl.*).
undersign (*v.t.*), soussigner.
undersigned (*adj.*), soussigné, -e:
the undersigned witnesses, les témoins sous-signés (*m.pl.*).
the undersigned (pers.), le soussigné; la sous-signée; soussigné, -e:
the undersigned declares (*or* certifies) . . ., le soussigné déclare . . .
I, the undersigned Paul X. declare (*or* certify) that . . ., je soussigné Paul X. déclare que . . .
understanding (agreement) (*n.*), accord (*m.*); entente (*f.*).
undersubscribed (*p.p.*), pas couvert, -e:
the loan was undersubscribed, l'emprunt n'a pas été couvert (*m.*).
undertake (*v.t.*), entreprendre; s'engager; s'obliger; prendre l'engagement; prendre; se charger; accepter:
to undertake the carriage of goods for a fixed contract price, entreprendre le transport des marchandises pour un prix déterminé à forfait.
a company may not undertake any business not provided for under its memorandum, une société ne peut entreprendre aucune opération non prévue par ses statuts.
to undertake to provide a sum of money, to pay a bill at maturity, s'engager à, prendre l'engagement de, fournir une somme d'argent, payer une traite à l'échéance.
I undertake to pay the balance (letter of application), je m'oblige à verser le surplus.
to undertake to pay the duty, prendre les droits à sa charge; prendre les droits en charge.
the bank undertakes the collection of bills remitted to it, la banque se charge du recouvrement d'effets qui lui sont remis.
the bank does not undertake any (stock exchange) transaction without cover, la banque n'accepte aucune opération (de bourse) à découvert.
undertaking (promise or pledge) (*n.*), engagement pris (*m.*); engagement (*m.*):
to claim performance of someone's under-taking, réclamer l'exécution de l'engagement pris par quelqu'un.
to limit the amount of one's undertaking, limiter le montant de son engagement.
undertaking (enterprise) (*n.*), entreprise (*f.*); exploitation (*f.*):
a commercial or industrial undertaking, une entreprise (*ou* une exploitation) commerciale ou industrielle.
undertone (*n.*), fond (*m.*):
the foreign section did not show any uniform strength; however, it was noted that there was in it a certain undertone of strength generally, la rubrique des étrangères ne présente pas de tendance uniforme; toutefois,

on y note un certain fond de résistance dans l'ensemble.

undervaluation (*n.*), sous-évaluation (*f.*); sous-estimation (*f.*); mésestimation (*f.*); minoration (*f.*):
undervaluation of the assets in a balance sheet, minoration des valeurs formant l'actif d'un bilan.

undervalue (*v.t.*), sous-évaluer; sous-estimer; mésestimer; minorer:
to undervalue the exchange, sous-évaluer, minorer, les valeurs d'échange.

underwrite (Fin.) (*v.t.*), garantir:
to underwrite an issue, shares, garantir une émission, des titres.

underwrite (Insce) (*v.t.*), souscrire; souscrire pour:
to underwrite marine risks, a line, souscrire des risques maritimes, une ligne.
the amount underwritten by each insurer is the limit of his commitment, la somme souscrite par chaque assureur est la limite de son engagement.
usually, each company underwrites a part of the risk proposed by the broker, d'habitude, chaque compagnie souscrit pour une partie du risque proposé par le courtier.
policy underwritten in London, police souscrite à Londres (*f.*).

underwriter (Fin.) (pers.) (*n.*), syndicataire (*m.*).

underwriter (Insce) (pers.) (*n.*), assureur (*m.*); souscripteur (*m.*):
marine underwriter, assureur maritime.
fire underwriter, assureur contre l'incendie.
Lloyd's underwriters, les assureurs du Lloyd.
the underwriters on each insurance agreeing to pay their proportion, les souscripteurs de chacune des assurances convenant de payer leur proportion.

underwriters' committee (Insce), comité d'assureurs (*m.*).

underwriting (Fin.) (*n.*), garantie (*f.*):
firm underwriting, garantie de prise ferme.

underwriting (Insce) (*n.*), souscription (*f.*):
underwriting a risk, souscription d'un risque.

underwriting account (debit note of insurance charges), note d'assurance (*f.*).

underwriting commission (Fin.), commission de garantie (*f.*); commission syndicale (*f.*).

underwriting contract *or* **underwriting letter** (Fin.), acte syndical (*m.*); convention syndicale (*f.*); contrat de garantie (*r..*).

underwriting syndicate (Fin.), syndicat de garantie (*m.*).

undischarged (*adj.*), inacquitté, -e:
undischarged debt, dette inacquittée (*f.*).

undischarged bankrupt, failli non réhabilité (*m.*).

undiscountable (*adj.*), inescomptable; incourant, -e:
undiscountable bill, billet inescomptable (*m.*); effet incourant (*m.*).

undivided (*adj.*), indivis, -e:
undivided property, biens indivis (*m.pl.*).

undo (*v.t.*), défaire:
to undo a bargain, défaire un marché.

undock (*v.t.*), faire sortir de (*ou* d'en) (*ou* du) bassin:
to undock a ship, faire sortir de bassin un navire.

undock (*v.i.*), sortir de (*ou* d'en) (*ou* du) bassin:
with leave to dock and undock, avec faculté d'entrer en bassin et d'en sortir.

undocking (*n.*), sortie de (*ou* d'en) (*ou* du) bassin (*f.*).

undue (*adj.*), indu, -e; inexigible:
undue debt, dette indue (*f.*).

unduly (*adv.*), indûment:
charge unduly collected, taxe indûment perçue (*f.*).

unemployed (*adj.*), inemployé, -e:
unemployed capital, capitaux inemployés (*m.pl.*).

unemployed (to be) (to be out of work), chômer d'ouvrage; chômer:
10,000 seamen are unemployed, 10 000 gens de mer chôment.

unemployed person, chômeur, -euse.

unemployed (pers.) (*n. collective pl.*), chômeurs (*m.pl.*); sans-travail (*m.pl.*):
the millions paid to the unemployed, les millions versés aux chômeurs (*m.pl.*).

unemployment (*n.*), chômage (*m.*).

unemployment insurance, assurance contre le chômage (*f.*).

unentered (Customs) (*adj.*), non déclaré, -e:
unentered shipment, expédition non déclarée (*f.*).

unequal (*adj.*), inégal, -e, -aux.

unequally (*adv.*), inégalement.

unequitable (*adj.*), inéquitable:
unequitable distribution of taxation, répartition inéquitable des impôts (*f.*).

unequitably (*adv.*), inéquitablement.

uneven (*adj.*), impair, -e:
3, 5, 7, are uneven numbers, 3, 5, 7, sont des nombres impairs.

unexchangeable (*adj.*), inéchangeable; impermutable:
unexchangeable securities, valeurs inéchangeables (*ou* impermutables) (*f.pl.*).

unexpected (*adj.*), inattendu, -e:
unexpected profit *or* unexpected gain, profit inattendu (*m.*); revenant-bon (*m.*):
the unexpected profits resulting from a bargain, les revenants-bons d'un marché.

unexpended (*adj.*), indépensé, -e:
unexpended balance, balance indépensée (*f.*); boni (*m.*); revenant-bon (*m.*).

unexpired (*adj.*), non expiré, -e; non échu, -e; non couru, -e; non périmé, -e:
unexpired bill, effet non échu (*m.*).
unexpired season ticket, carte d'abonnement non périmée (*f.*).
unexpired time (of a policy of insurance), temps non expiré (*ou* non couru) (d'une police d'assurance) (*m.*).

unfair (*adj.*), déloyal, -e, -aux:
unfair competition, concurrence déloyale (*f.*).

unfavourable *or* **unfavorable** (*adj.*), défavorable; contraire:

unfavourable exchange, change défavorable (*m.*) ; change contraire (*m.*).

unfavourable trade balance, balance commerciale défavorable (*f.*). *V. exemple sous* balance of trade.

unfilled orders, ordres (*m.pl.*) [*ou* commandes (*f.pl.*)] en carnet (*ou* en portefeuille).

unification (*n.*), unification (*f.*) ; consolidation (*f.*) :
unification of different loans, unification d'emprunts différents.

unified (*adj.*) (opp. to *floating*), unifié, -e ; consolidé, -e :
unified debt, dette unifiée (*ou* consolidée) (*f.*).

unify (*v.t.*), unifier ; consolider.

unilateral (*adj.*), unilatéral, -e, -aux :
unilateral contract, contrat unilatéral (*m.*).

uninsured (Insce) (*adj.*), non assuré, -e.

uninsured (Post) (*adj.*), sans valeur déclaré, -e ; non chargé, -e :
uninsured parcel, colis sans valeur déclarée (*m.*) ; colis non chargé (*m.*).

union (*n.*), union (*f.*) :
Latin Union *or* Latin Monetary Union, Union latine ; Union monétaire latine (now abandoned).

Union country *or* **country in the Universal Postal Union,** pays faisant partie de l'Union postale universelle (*m.*).

unissued debentures, obligations à la souche (*f.pl.*).

unissued shares, actions à la souche (*f.pl.*).

unit (*n.*), unité (*f.*) :
the franc was the monetary unit of the Latin Union, le franc était l'unité monétaire de l'Union latine.
the number of units contained in a load (Produce Exch.), le nombre d'unités renfermées dans un lot.

unit charge (for telephone conversation), taxe unitaire (*f.*).

United Kingdom of Great Britain and Northern Ireland (Abbrev.: **U.K.**), Royaume-Uni de Grande-Bretagne et Irlande du Nord (*m.*).

Universal Postal Union, Union postale universelle (*f.*).

unknown (*adj. & p.p.*), inconnu, -e :
unknown risk, risque inconnu (*m.*).
weight, value, and contents unknown, poids, valeur, et contenu inconnus.

unlade, unlading. V. sous **unload, unloading.**

unlawful (*adj.*), illégal, -e, -aux ; illicite.

unlawfully (*adv.*), illégalement ; illicitement.

unlawfulness (*n.*), illégalité (*f.*).

unless expressly otherwise stated (*or* **provided**) **herein,** sauf indication contraire expresse dans les présentes ; à moins d'exception formelle stipulée dans les présentes.

unless otherwise agreed (*or* **provided**), sauf (*ou* à moins de) convention (*ou* stipulation) contraire.

unless prevented by unforeseen circumstances, sauf imprévu.

unlimited (*adj.*), illimité, -e :
unlimited liability, responsabilité illimitée (*f.*).
an unlimited amount but not to exceed a maximum per ship or voyage of so much,

une somme illimitée sans toutefois dépasse un maximum par navire ou voyage de tant.

unlisted securities (Stock Exch.) (opp. to *liste securities*), valeurs non inscrites (*f.pl.*) valeurs non admises à la cote officielle (*f.pl.*) valeurs en banque (*f.pl.*) ; valeurs du march en banque (*f.pl.*) ; valeurs de coulisse (*f.pl.*).

unload *or* **unlade** (to discharge) (*v.t.*), décharger débarquer ; débarder :
ship which begins to unload her cargo, navir qui commence à décharger sa cargaison (*m.*) to unload goods into craft or barges, débarque des marchandises sur des embarcations o des chalands.

unload (Fin.) (*v.t.*), se défaire de :
stockholder who wants to unload a big bloc of shares, porteur de titres qui veut s défaire d'un gros paquet de titres (*m.*).

unloading *or* **unlading** (discharge) (*n.*), décharge ment (*m.*) ; décharge (*f.*) ; débarquemen (*m.*) ; débardage (*m.*) :
the unloading of the trucks is to take plac immediately after arrival of the trains le déchargement des wagons s'effectuer immédiatement après l'arrivée des convois.

unloading (in course of discharge), en débarque ment :
unloading at the docks : 000 tons, en débarque ment dans les docks : 000 tonnes.

unloading risk (Insce), risque de déchargemen (*m.*).

unmarked shares, actions non estampillée (*f.pl.*). Cf. **marked shares.**

unnavigability (*n.*), innavigabilité (*f.*).

unnavigable (*adj.*), innavigable.

unnegotiable (*adj.*), innégociable ; incom merçable :
unnegotiable bill, effet innégociable (*ou* in commerçable) (*m.*).

unofficial (*adj.*), inofficiel, -elle ; non officiel, -elle unofficial communication, communicatio inofficielle (*f.*).

unofficially (*adv.*), inofficiellement.

unopened (*adj.*), non ouvert, -e :
unopened letter, lettre non ouverte (*f.*).

unpack (*v.t.*), déballer.

unpacked (*adj.*), non emballé, -e ; à découvert :
unpacked consignment (Transport), envoi à découvert (*m.*).

unpacking (*n.*), déballage (*m.*).

unpaid (*adj.*), impayé, -e ; non payé, -e ; no versé, -e :
unpaid amount, somme impayée (*f.*) ; montan non payé (*m.*) ; montant non versé (*m.*) non versé (*m.*).
unpaid bill (bill of exchange), effet impay (*m.*) ; impayé (*m.*).
unpaid cheque, chèque impayé (*m.*).

unpaid (Post or parcels) (*adj.*), non affranchi, -e to charge a letter as unpaid, taxer une lettr comme non affranchie.

unplaceable (*adj.*), implaçable :
daily money is so to speak unplaceable o our market at $2\frac{1}{4}\%$, l'argent au jour l jour est pour ainsi dire implaçable sur notr marché à 2 1/4 0/0.

unplaced (*adj.*), implacé, -e :
unplaced shares, titres implacés (*m.pl.*).
unproductive (*adj.*), improductif, -ive :
unproductive capital, capitaux improductifs (*m.pl.*).
unproductively (*adv.*), improductivement.
unproductivity *or* **unproductiveness** (*n.*), improductivité (*f.*) ; non valeur (*f.*) :
unproductiveness of a property, inproductivité, non valeur, d'une propriété.
unprofitable (*adj.*), improfitable.
unprohibited (*adj.*), non prohibé, -e.
unpronounceable (*adj.*), non prononçable :
unpronounceable group of letters (Teleg.), groupe de lettres non prononçable (*m.*).
unprotected (not packed) (*adj.*), à nu :
goods carried in bulk or unprotected, marchandises transportées en vrac ou à nu (*f.pl.*).
unprotested (*adj.*), non protesté, -e :
unprotested bill, effet non protesté (*m.*).
unpunctual (*adj.*), inexact, -e :
unpunctual employee, employé inexact (*m.*).
unpunctuality (*n.*), inexactitude (*f.*).
unpunctually (*adv.*), inexactement.
unquoted (for which there is no market price) (*adj.*), non coté, -e ; incoté, -e :
unquoted securities, valeurs non cotées (*ou* incotées) (*f.pl.*).
unquoted list (Stock Exch.). V. note sous **cote.**
unquoted securities (unlisted securities), valeurs non inscrites (*f.pl.*) ; valeurs non admises à la cote officielle (*f.pl.*) ; valeurs en banque (*f.pl.*) ; valeurs du marché en banque (*f.pl.*) ; valeurs de coulisse (*f.pl.*). V. **quoted securities** et **quote.**
unravel (*v.t.*), débrouiller ; mettre au net :
to unravel the affairs of a bankrupt, débrouiller, mettre au net, la situation d'un failli.
unreadable (*adj.*), illisible :
unreadable writing, écriture illisible (*f.*).
unreadableness (*n.*), illisibilité (*f.*).
unrealizable (*adj.*), irréalisable :
unrealizable securities, valeurs irréalisables (*f.pl.*).
unrealized (*adj.*), non réalisé, -e.
unreceipted (*adj.*), inacquitté, -e :
unreceipted bill, mémoire inacquitté (*m.*).
unrecoverable (*adj.*), irrécouvrable :
unrecoverable debt, créance irrécouvrable (*f.*).
unredeemable (*adj.*), non amortissable ; irremboursable ; irrachetable :
unredeemable bonds *or* unredeemable debentures, obligations non amortissables (*ou* irremboursables) (*ou* irrachetables) (*f.pl.*).
unredeemed (*adj.*), non amorti, -e ; irracheté, -e.
unregistered (*adj.*), non enregistré, -e :
unregistered address (Teleg.), adresse non enregistrée (*f.*).
unregistered luggage, bagages non enregistrés (*m.pl.*).
unregistered (Post) (*adj.*), non recommandé, -e :
unregistered letter, lettre non recommandée (*f.*).
unremunerated (*adj.*), irrémunéré, -e.
unremunerative (*adj.*), improfitable.
unrouted telegram, télégramme sans voie (*m.*).

unsaleable *or* **unsalable** (*adj.*), invendable ; 'hors de vente :
unsaleable goods, marchandises invendables (*f.pl.*) ; marchandise hors de vente (*f.*).
unsatisfied (*adj.*), insatisfait, -e :
unsatisfied debt, dette insatisfaite (*f.*).
unseal (*v.t.*), décacheter :
to unseal a letter, décacheter une lettre.
unseaworthiness (*n.*), mauvais état de navigabilité (*m.*) ; état d'innavigabilité (*m.*) ; innavigabilité (*f.*) ; non navigabilité (*f.*) :
to hire a second ship in case of unseaworthiness of the first, louer un second navire au cas d'innavigabilité du premier.
unseaworthy (*adj.*), en mauvais état de navigabilité ; en état d'innavigabilité ; 'hors d'état de naviguer ; innavigable :
when the ship sailed, she was unseaworthy, lorsque le navire a fait voile, il était hors d'état de naviguer.
V. aussi exemple sous **seaworthy.**
unsecured (speaking of advances, loans, overdrafts, or the like) (*adj.*), à découvert ; en blanc ; sur notoriété ; sans garantie ; non garanti, -e :
unsecured advances, avances à découvert (*f.pl.*) ; avances sur notoriété (*f.pl.*).
unsecured overdraft, découvert en blanc (*m.*) ; découvert sur notoriété (*m.*).
to be unsecured, être à découvert.
unsecured (speaking of creditors or debts) (*adj.*), chirographaire ; sans garantie ; non garanti, -e :
unsecured creditor, créancier chirographaire (*m.*). V. exemple sous **creditor.**
unsecured debt, créance chirographaire (*f.*) ; dette chirographaire (*f.*) ; créance sans garantie (*f.*) ; créance non garantie (*f.*).
unsheet (to remove the sheet from a railway wagon) (*v.t.*), débâcher.
unsheeted open wagon (Rly.), wagon découvert non bâché (*m.*).
unsheeting (*n.*), débâchage (*m.*).
unship (*v.t.*), débarquer ; décharger ; débarder :
to unship goods into craft or barges, débarquer des marchandises sur des embarcations ou des chalands.
unshipment (*n.*), débarquement (*m.*) ; décharge (*f.*) ; déchargement (*m.*) ; débardage (*m.*).
unsigned (*adj.*), non signé, -e :
unsigned letter, lettre non signée (*f.*).
unsold (*adj.*), invendu, -e :
unsold goods, marchandises invendues (*f.pl.*) ; invendus (*m.pl.*).
unspent (*adj.*), indépensé, -e :
unspent balance, balance indépensée (*f.*).
unstable *or* **unsteady** (*adj.*), instable ; chancelant, -e :
maritime freights are essentially unstable and vary frequently, les frets maritimes sont essentiellement instables et varient fréquemment (*m.pl.*).
unsteady prices, cours instables (*ou* chancelants) (*m.pl.*).
unstamped (*adj.*), non timbré, -e :
unstamped bill, effet non timbré (*m.*).

unstamped paper (i.e., not bearing inland revenue stamps), papier libre (*m.*); papier mort (*m.*).

unstamped shares, actions non estampillées (*f.pl.*). *Cf.* stamped shares.

unsteadiness (*n.*), instabilité (*f.*).

untax (*v.t.*), détaxer :
the customs untax commodities intended for export, la douane détaxe les denrées destinées à l'exportation.
to surtax the rich, to untax the poor, surtaxer les riches, détaxer les pauvres.

untaxable costs (Law), faux frais (*m.pl.*).

until further advice, jusqu'à nouvel avis.

until the contrary is proved, jusqu'à preuve contraire.

untransferable (*adj.*), incessible ; inaliénable.

untrue declaration (*or* **statement**), fausse déclaration (*f.*) ; déclaration fausse (*f.*) ; déclaration inexacte (*f.*).

unused stamps, timbres non employés (*m.pl.*) ; timbres non utilisés (*m.pl.*).

unused ticket, billet non utilisé (*m.*).

unvalued (*adj.*), non évalué, -e ; inévalué, -e :
unvalued policy (Insce), police non évaluée (*f.*).

unweighed (*adj.*), non pesé, -e.

up (to be), être en plus-value ; être en hausse :
X. shares were up at 1½, l'action X. est en plus-value à 1 1/2.
copper up 5s. at £69 15s., cuivre en hausse de 1/4 à £69 15sh. (*ou* £69 3/4).

up to (not exceeding), jusqu'à ; jusqu'à concurrence de :
postal packets can be insured up to so much, les colis postaux peuvent être assurés jusqu'à concurrence de tant (*m.pl.*).

up train (opp. to *down train*), train pair (*m.*) ; train montant (*m.*).
Note :—In France, trains are numbered, up trains with an even number (hence *train pair*), down trains with an uneven number (hence *train impair*).

upkeep (*n.*), entretien (*m.*) :
upkeep of roads, entretien des routes.

upkeep expenses, frais d'entretien (*m.pl.*).

upon *or* **on** (lying upon ; devolving on ; borne by) (*adv.*), à la charge de :
the risks left upon the shipper by the bill of lading, les risques laissés à la charge de l'expéditeur par le connaissement (*m.pl.*).
risk which is upon the underwriter during the whole term of the insured voyage, risque qui est à la charge de l'assureur pendant toute la durée du voyage assuré (*m.*).
the proof of payment is always upon him who claims to have paid, la preuve du paiement est toujours à la charge de celui qui prétend avoir payé.

upon (at the charge or door of ; encumbering) (*prep.*). V. exemples sous **on** *or* **upon.**

upper deck, pont supérieur (*m.*).

ups and downs, 'hauts et bas (*m.pl.*) :
to have ups and downs of fortune, avoir des hauts et des bas de fortune.

upset (*v.t.*), déranger ; dérouter ; bouleverser ; tromper :

the result has upset our calculations, le résultat a trompé notre calcul (*ou* a dérouté nos combinaisons).

upset price (auction), mise à prix (*f.*).

upward movement of stocks, mouvement ascensionnel (*ou* mouvement de hausse) des valeurs (*m.*).

upward tendency *or* **upward trend** (in prices), tendance à la hausse (dans les cours) (*f.*).

urgency [urgencies *pl.*] (*n.*), urgence (*f.*).

urgent (*adj.*), urgent, -e :
urgent order, ordre urgent (*m.*).
urgent rate (telegrams), tarif d'urgence (*m.*).
urgent telegram (*Abbrev. :* Urgent), télégramme urgent (*m.*).

usage (*n.*), usage (*m.*) ; usages (*m.pl.*) ; coutume (*f.*) ; coutumes (*f.pl.*) :
local usages, usages (*ou* coutumes) de la place ; usages locaux ; coutumes locales.
usage of the port, usages de (*ou* de la) place ; usages des lieux ; usages locaux ; usages du port ; coutumes du port :
according to the usage of the port of Antwerp, d'après (*ou* suivant) (*ou* selon) les usages de la place (*ou* du port) d'Anvers.
usage of the port of loading, of the place of unloading, usages du port de chargement, du lieu de déchargement.

usance (*n.*), usance (*f.*) :
to have a bill of exchange on someone at usance, at one usance, at double usance, at thirty days' usance, avoir sur quelqu'un une lettre de change à usance, à une usance, à double usance, à usance de trente jours.

use (employment) (*n.*), usage (*m.*) ; emploi (*m.*) ; emprunt (*m.*) :
use of the roads is free in most countries, l'usage des routes est gratuit dans la plupart des pays.
articles for the personal use of the passenger, objets affectés à l'usage personnel du voyageur (*m.pl.*).
use of a sum of money, of capital in production, of money on contango, emploi d'une somme d'argent, des capitaux dans la production, des capitaux en report.
direct transport by land without use of the sea, transport direct par terre sans emprunt de la mer (*m.*).

use (consumption) (*n.*), consommation (*f.*) :
goods for home use (Customs), marchandises mises en consommation (*f.pl.*).

use (*v.t.*), employer ; se servir de ; emprunter :
code used, code employé (*m.*).
how to use the telephone, comment il faut se servir du téléphone.
many people speak ill of the telephone because they do not know how to use it properly, beaucoup de personnes médisent du téléphone parce qu'elles ne savent pas bien s'en servir.
to go up the Seine instead of using the railway, remonter la Seine au lieu d'emprunter la voie ferrée.
the ships which use the Suez canal, les navires qui empruntent le canal de Suez (*m.pl.*).

use (to consume) (*v.t.*),   consommer.
used stamp, timbre ayant déjà servi (*m.*).
user (pers.) (*n.*),   usager (*m.*) :
the principal users of the port, les principaux
usagers du port.
usual hours of business, heures réglementaires
d'ouverture (*f.pl.*).
usurer (pers.) (*n.*) (*n.*),   usurier, -ère.

usurious (*adj.*),   usuraire ; usurier, -ère :
usurious loan,   prêt usuraire (*m.*).
usuriously (*adv.*),   usurairement.
usury [**usuries** *pl.*] (*n.*),   usure (*f.*).
utter (*v.t.*),   passer :
to utter a counterfeit coin,   a forged
cheque,   passer une pièce fausse, un faux
chèque.

V

vacancy [**vacancies** *pl.*] (*n.*),   vacance (*f.*) :
to fill (*or* to fill up) a casual vacancy,   combler
une vacance accidentelle.
any casual vacancy may be filled up by the
directors,   en cas de vacance dans l'intervalle de deux assemblées générales, le conseil
peut pourvoir au remplacement.
vacant (*adj.*),   vacant, -e :
if a director's office becomes vacant, si une
place d'administrateur devient vacante.
vacation (Law) (*n.*),   vacances (*f.pl.*) ;   vacation
(*f.*).
vacation court, chambre des vacations (*f.*).
valid (*adj.*),   valide ; valable :
valid receipt,   quittance valable (*f.*).
valid will,   testament valide (*m.*).
validity (*n.*),   validité (*f.*) :
validity of return tickets,   validité des billets
d'aller et retour.
the formality of writing is only required for
the validity of the contract,   la formalité
de l'écriture n'est exigée que pour la validité
du contrat.
validly (*adv.*),   validement ; valablement.
valorization (*n.*),   valorisation (*f.*).
valorize (*v.t.*),   valoriser :
coupons of a foreign loan valorized at 55%
gold,   coupons d'un emprunt étranger
valorisés à 55 0/0-or (*m.pl.*).
valuable (*adj.*) *or* **of value** *or* **value** (*used as adj.*),
de valeur ; de prix ; précieux, -euse :
valuable article *or* article of value, objet de
valeur (*ou* de prix) (*ou* précieux) (*m.*).
valuable goods   *or*   value goods.   V. sous
valuables.
valuable papers   *or*   value papers,   valeurs
(*f.pl.*) ;   papiers de valeur (*m.pl.*).
value parcel,   colis finances et valeurs (*m.*).
documents of value, of great value, of no
intrinsic value,   documents de valeur, de
grande valeur, dépourvus de valeur intrinsèque (*m.pl.*).
sample of value,   échantillon de valeur (*ou* de
prix) (*m.*).
valuable time,   temps précieux (*m.*).
for a valuable consideration, à titre onéreux :
property acquired for a valuable consideration,   propriété acquise à titre onéreux (*f.*).

valuableness (*n.*),   valeur (*f.*).
valuables (*n.pl.*) *or* **valuable goods** *or* **value goods,**
valeurs (*f.pl.*) ;   objets de valeur (*m.pl.*) :
policy for the insurance of valuables, such as :
securities, coupons, paper money, bills of
exchange, precious metals (gold and silver
coined and not coined), platinum, precious
stones, fine pearls, etc., police pour l'assurance de valeurs, telles que : titres, coupons,
papier-monnaie, effets de commerce, métaux
précieux (or et argent monnayés et non
monnayés), platine, pierres précieuses, perles
fines, etc. (*f.*).
valuation (*n.*),   évaluation (*f.*) ;   appréciation
(*f.*) ;   estimation (*f.*) ;   prisée (*f.*) ;   expertise
(*f.*) ;   inventaire (*m.*) :
valuation of securities, of investments, of
goods remaining in stock,   évaluation,
appréciation, estimation, inventaire, des
titres, du portefeuille (*ou* du portefeuille-
titres), des marchandises restant en magasin.
valuation of property insured,   évaluation,
estimation, des choses assurées.
details influencing the valuation of the risk
(Insce), détails influant sur l'appréciation
du risque (*m.pl.*).
value (*n.*),   valeur (*f.*) :
the value of a thing is the power of exchange
it possesses,   la valeur d'une chose est la
puissance d'échange qu'elle possède.
prices are the monetary expression of values,
les prix sont l'expression monétaire des
valeurs (*m.pl.*).
nominal value (*or* face value) of a share, valeur
nominale d'une action ;   nominal d'une
action (*m.*).
value as a going concern,   valeur d'usage.
value given (bills of exchange),   valeur fournie.
value in account,   valeur en compte.
value received which place to account as
advised (bill of exchange),   valeur reçue
que passerez en compte suivant avis de
(*signature*).
value of goods for insurance,   valeur des marchandises à assurer.
the insurable (*or* insurance) value of the thing
insured,   la valeur assurable (*ou* la valeur
d'assurance) de la chose assurée.

insured value for average purposes, for total loss purposes, valeur assurée à prendre en cas d'avaries, en cas de perte totale.

values to be made good (opp. to *contributing values*) (General Average), valeurs créancières; valeurs actives; masse créancière (*f.*); masse active (*f.*). V. exemple sous syn. **amounts to be made good.**

value (interest) (Insce) (*n.*), valeur (*f.*); aliment (*m.*); intérêt (*m.*); risque (*m.*):

the declaration of value should be made to the underwriter within the time specified in the contract (floating policy), la déclaration d'aliment doit être faite à l'assureur dans le délai fixé au contrat.

value (*n.*) *or* **value date**, valeur (*f.*); échéance (*f.*); date de valeur (*f.*); date d'entrée en valeur (*f.*):

the value (*or* the value date) of an amount is the date on which it commences to bear interest; thus, if we remit to a banker on 1st November, a cheque on Paris, he will credit us with its amount value 6th November, the date by which he reckons he will have collected it and from which consequently he owes us interest on it, la valeur (*ou* l'échéance) (*ou* la date de valeur) (*ou* la date d'entrée en valeur) d'une somme est la date à laquelle elle commence à porter intérêt; ainsi, si nous remettons à un banquier le 1er novembre, un chèque sur Paris, il nous créditera de son montant valeur (*ou* échéance) 6 novembre, date à laquelle il considère qu'il l'aura encaissé et à partir de laquelle il nous en doit par conséquent les intérêts.

interest only runs from the value dates of the capital sums, les intérêts ne courent qu'à partir des dates d'entrée en valeur des capitaux (*m.pl.*).

value (*v.t.*), évaluer; faire l'évaluation de; apprécier; faire l'appréciation de; estimer; inventorier; priser; expertiser:

to value the stocks at the market price, goods at cost, évaluer, apprécier, estimer, inventorier, les titres au cours de bourse, des marchandises au prix d'achat.

to value furniture, priser des meubles.

value goods. V. sous **valuables.**

value in exchange, contre-valeur (*f.*):

bills of exchange given as value in exchange for goods, lettres de change fournies en contre-valeur de marchandises (*f.pl.*).

value papers, value parcel. V. sous **valuable.**

valued policy (Insce) (opp. to *unvalued policy*), police évaluée (*f.*).

valueless (*adj.*), sans valeur:

valueless securities *or* valueless stock, titres sans valeur (*m.pl.*); non valeurs (*f.pl.*).

valueless stock (things without value, for example, spoiled stamps), non valeurs (*f.pl.*).

valuer (pers.) (*n.*), priseur (*m.*); expert (*m.*).

van (light wagon) (*n.*), voiture (*f.*); voiture de livraison (*f.*); livreuse (*f.*); fourgon (*m.*).

van (Rly.) (*n.*), fourgon (*m.*); wagon (*m.*).

variable (*adj.*) (opp. to *fixed*), variable:

variable yield investments, placements à revenus variables (*m.pl.*).

variable yield securities, valeurs à revenu variable (*f.pl.*).

variable exchange, incertain (*m.*). V. to quote variable exchange *pour exemple.*

variation (*n.*), modification (*f.*):

variation of risk (Insce), modification de risque.

vary (*v.t.*), modifier:

to vary the terms of a contract, modifier les clauses d'un contrat.

vehicle (conveyance) (*n.*), véhicule (*m.*); voiture (*f.*).

vendor (pers.) (*n.*), vendeur, -eresse; apporteur (*m.*):

shares allotted to the vendors as purchase consideration (*or* as consideration for transfers), actions attribuées aux apporteurs comme prix d'apport (*ou* en rémunération d'apports) (*f.pl.*).

vendor company, société apporteuse (*f.*).

vendor's assets *or* **vendors' assets,** valeurs d'apport (*f.pl.*).

vendor's lien, privilège du vendeur (*m.*).

vendors' shares, actions d'apport (*f.pl.*); actions de fondation (*f.pl.*).

Note :—According to French law vendors' or promoters' shares must remain in the company's custody undetached from the counterfoils (hence such shares are known as **actions à la souche**) for 2 years following the formation of the company, during which time, although transferable according to civil law, they are not dealable on the Stock Exchange. There are no such legal restrictions in England, and vendors' shares are good delivery on the London Stock Exchange on and after the date fixed for the special settlement in the shares or securities of the same class subscribed for by the public.

vendors' shares (in a private company), parts d'apport (dans une société à responsabilité limitée) (*f.pl.*). Cf. limited company *or* private company.

venture (*n.*), entreprise (*f.*); spéculation (*f.*); aventure (*f.*); 'hasard (*m.*):

the chances of a venture, les aléas d'une entreprise (*m.pl.*).

venture (*v.t.*), aventurer; risquer; 'hasarder.

verbal (*adj.*), verbal, -e, -aux; labial, -e, -aux:

verbal offer, offre labiale (*ou* verbale) (*f.*).

verbal or written confirmation, confirmation verbale ou écrite (*f.*).

verbally (*adv.*), verbalement:

orders given verbally, ordres donnés verbalement (*m.pl.*).

verification (*n.*), vérification (*f.*):

goods submitted to the verification of the customs officials, marchandises soumises à la vérification des préposés des douanes (*f.pl.*).

verify (*v.t.*), vérifier:

to verify a fact, an account, the day's receipts, the contents of a packet, vérifier un fait, un compte, le produit de la journée, le contenu d'un paquet.

Veritas (*n.*) *or* **Bureau Veritas** (ships' classification society), Veritas (*m.*); Bureau Veritas (*m.*): the class of a steamer at Veritas, la cote d'un vapeur au Veritas.

Veritas Register, Registre Veritas (*m.*). V. exemple sous **Bureau Veritas.**

versus (Law) (*prep.*) (Abbrev.: **v.** *or* **vs**), contre: X. versus (*or* v.) Y., X. contre Y.

vertical filing, classement vertical (*m.*).

vertical filing cabinet, meuble à classement vertical (*m.*); classeur vertical (*m.*).

vessel (ship) (*n.*), navire (*m.*); bâtiment (*m.*); bateau (*m.*); vaisseau (*m.*).
Note :—The word *vaisseau* is sometimes restricted to the meaning of Government vessel, especially a war vessel, as distinguished from *navire*, a merchant vessel.

via (of a bill of exchange) (*n.*), exemplaire (d'une lettre de change) (*m.*). *V. exemple sous* set of bills of exchange.

via (*prep.*), via; par la voie:
sailing for New York via Southampton, départ pour New-York via Southampton.
telegram routed " Via Imperial," télégramme acheminé « Via Impérial » (*ou* acheminé par la « Voie Impérial ») (*m.*).

vice chairman *or* **vice president,** vice-président (*m.*).

vice chairmanship *or* **vice presidency,** vice-présidence (*f.*).

vice consul, vice-consul (*m.*).

vice consulate, vice-consulat (*m.*).

vice manager, vice-gérant (*m.*).

vice managership, vice-gérance (*f.*).

vice propre (inherent vice), vice propre (*m.*). V. exemples sous **liable** et sous **inherent vice.**

victim (*n.*), victime (*f.*):
the victim of an accident, la victime d'un accident.

victual (*v.t.*), ravitailler; avitailler.

victualling *or* **victualing** (*n.*), ravitaillement (*m.*); avitaillement (*m.*).

victualling bill, permis de provisions de bord (*m.*).

victuals (*n.pl.*), victuailles (*f.pl.*); vivres (*m.pl.*); provisions de bouche (*f.pl.*); munitions de bouche (*f.pl.*); nourriture (*f.*).

violate (*v.t.*), violer; enfreindre:
to violate a clause in a contract, violer une clause dans un contrat.

violation (*n.*), violation (*f.*); infraction (*f.*):
violation of the conditions and undertakings, infraction aux conditions et engagements.

visa *or* **visé** (*n.*), visa (*m.*):
the visa (*or* the visé) of a consul on a passport, le visa d'un consul sur un passeport.

visa *or* **visé** (*v.t.*), viser:
to visa (*or* to visé) a passport, viser un passeport.

visible (*adj.*), visible:
visible adding machine, machine à additionner visible (*f.*).
visible exports (opp. to *invisible exports*), exportations visibles (*f.pl.*).

visible reserve (opp. to *secret*, or *hidden*, or *inner*, *reserve*), réserve visible (*f.*).
visible stocks, stocks visibles (*m.pl.*).
visible writing machine, machine à écrire visible (*f.*).

visit (*n.*), visite (*f.*):
to pay a visit, faire une visite.

visit (*v.t.*), visiter.

visit (Customs) (*v.t.*), arraisonner:
customs officers who visit a ship in the roads, agents des douanes qui arraisonnent un navire dans la rade (*m.pl.*).

visiting *or* **visit** (Customs) (*n.*), arraisonnement (*m.*).

visitor (pers.) (*n.*), visiteur, -euse:
exhibition which attracts foreign visitors in very great numbers, exposition qui attire en très grand nombre les visiteurs étrangers (*f.*).

visitors' tax, taxe de séjour (*f.*).

void (*adj.*), nul, nulle:
the insurance is void if it is proved that the news of an accident was known, l'assurance est nulle s'il est justifié que la nouvelle d'un sinistre était connue.

void (*v.t.*), résoudre; résilier; annuler:
to void a contract, résoudre, résilier, annuler, un contrat.

voidable (*adj.*), résoluble; annulable.

voidableness (*n.*), annulabilité (*f.*).

volume (*n.*), volume (*m.*):
the volume of business, of orders, le volume des affaires, des ordres.

voluntarily (*adv.*), volontairement:
damage suffered voluntarily for the welfare and common safety of the ship and cargo, dommages soufferts volontairement pour le bien et le salut commun du navire et de la cargaison (*m.pl.*).

voluntary (*adj.*), volontaire:
voluntary liquidation *or* voluntary winding up, liquidation volontaire (*f.*).
voluntary stranding (opp. to *accidental stranding*), échouement volontaire (*m.*); échouage (*m.*).

vostro account, compte vostro (*m.*).

vote (*n.*), vote (*m.*); suffrage (*m.*); voix (*f.*):
to give one's vote, donner son suffrage (*ou* son vote) (*ou* sa voix).
each member present has one vote, chaque membre de l'assemblée a une voix (*m.*).
casting vote, voix prépondérante.

vote (*v.t.*), voter:
to vote the adjournment of a meeting, a resolution by a show of hands, voter l'ajournement d'une assemblée, une résolution à main levée (*ou* à mains levées).

vote (*v.i.*), voter:
to vote on a resolution, voter sur une proposition.
the resolution was carried unanimously by the shareholders present, with the exception of Mr X., vendor, who did not vote (*or* who abstained from voting) (*or* who did not take part in the voting), cette résolution est adoptée à l'unanimité des actionnaires

présents, à l'exception de M. X., apporteur, qui s'est abstenu de voter (*ou* qui n'a pas pris part au vote).

vote down (to), repousser :
to vote down an adjournment, repousser un ajournement.

voter (pers.) (*n.*), votant, -e.

voting (*n.*), votation (*f.*) :
method of voting, mode de votation (*m.*).

voting down, repoussement (*m.*).

voting right, droit de vote (*m.*).

voucher (document establishing the payment of money or the truth of accounts) (*n.*), pièce justificative (*f.*) ; pièce à l'appui (*f.*) ; pièce certificative (*f.*) ; pièce (*f.*) :
payments accompanied by vouchers, paiements accompagnés de pièces justificatives (*m.pl.*).
vouchers in support of an account, pièces (*ou* pièces justificatives) à l'appui d'un compte.
cash voucher, pièce de caisse ; pièce justificative de caisse.
voucher for payment, pièce de dépense.
voucher for receipt, pièce de recette.

voucher (authorization to deliver something valuable) (*n.*), bon (*m.*) ; bulletin (*m.*) :

cash voucher, bon de caisse.
baggage voucher, bulletin de bagages.

voucher copy (of a newspaper), numéro justificatif (*m.*), exemplaire justificatif (*m.*), exemplaire de justification (*m.*) (d'un journal).

voucher numbers, numéros des pièces justificatives (*m.pl.*).

vouching (*n.*), vérification (*f.*) ; vérification des pièces justificatives (*f.*).

voyage (*n.*), voyage (*m.*) ; traversée (*f.*) ; parcours (*m.*) ; route (*f.*) :
sea voyage, voyage de (*ou* par) mer ; parcours maritime.
loan contracted by the master during the voyage, prêt contracté par le capitaine en cours de route (*m.*).

voyage charter (distinguished from *time charter*), affrètement au voyage (*m.*) ; affrètement pour un voyage entier (*m.*).

voyage freight, fret au voyage (*m.*).

voyage insurance, assurance au voyage (*f.*).

voyage policy, police au voyage (*f.*).

voyage premium, prime au voyage (*f.*).

vulgar fraction (Arith.), fraction ordinaire (*f.*).

W

wafer (*n.*) *or* **wafer seal,** pain à cacheter (*m.*).

wage (*n.*) *or* **wages** (*n.pl.* or *sing.*), salaire (*m.*) ; paie (*f.*) ; paye (*f.*) ; gages (*m.pl.*) ; loyers (*m.pl.*) :
the wages of a workman, le salaire, la paie, d'un ouvrier.
seamen's wages, salaires, gages, loyers, des gens de mer.

wage earner (pers.), salarié, -e.

wager insurance, assurance-pari (*f.*).

wager policy, police-pari (*m.*).

wages sheet, feuille des salaires (*f.*) ; feuille de paie (*f.*).

wagon *or* **waggon** (road vehicle) (*n.*), chariot (*m.*) ; voiture (*f.*).

wagon *or* **waggon** (Rly.) (*n.*), wagon (*m.*) ; voiture (*f.*).

wait for (to), attendre :
to wait for the train, the postman, the favourable moment, attendre le train, le facteur, le moment favorable.

waiting room (office), salon d'attente (*m.*).

waiting room (Rly.), salle d'attente (*f.*).

waive (*v.t.*), renoncer à ; abdiquer :
to waive one's right, renoncer à, abdiquer, son droit.
the shippers waiving any claim hereunder, les chargeurs renonçant à toute réclamation de ce chef (*m.pl.*).

waiving *or* **waiver** (*n.*), renonciation (*f.*) ; abdication (*f.*) :
act considered as waiver of abandonment, acte considéré comme renonciation au délaissement (*m.*).

walk (round) (*n.*), tournée (*f.*) :
postman on his walk, facteur en tournée (*m.*).

walk clerk *or* **walks clerk** (Banking), garçon de recette (*m.*).

walk out (to) (to go on strike), faire grève ; se mettre en grève.

walkout (strike) (opp. to *lockout*), grève (*f.*).

wall (barrier) (*n.*), barrière (*f.*) :
country closed by customs walls, pays fermé par des barrières de douanes (*m.*).

wallet (*n.*), portefeuille (*m.*).

want (*n.*), manque (*m.*) ; défaut (*m.*) ; disette (*f.*) ; pénurie (*f.*) :
want of care, of diligence, manque de soins, de diligence.
want of money, manque, disette, pénurie, d'argent.
want of judgment, of confidence in the solvency of a bank, défaut, manque, de jugement de confiance dans la solvabilité d'une banque.
want of advice (Banking), défaut d'avis.
we learn now that scarcity is becoming want,

nous apprenons maintenant que la pénurie devient disette.

for want of, faute de ; à défaut de :
the bank group is irregular, for want of business (Stock Exch.), le groupe bancaire est irrégulier, faute d'affaires.

want (*v.t.*) *or* **to be in want of,** manquer de ; demander :
to want money *or* to be in want of money, manquer de l'argent.
to want a situation, demander un emploi.

want (to bid for) (Stock Exch.) (*v.t.*), demander : stocks wanted, valeurs demandées (*f.pl.*).

war (*n.*) (Ant. : *peace*), guerre (*f.*).

War bond, bon de la Défense nationale (*m.*).

war clause, clause de guerre (*f.*).

War loan, emprunt de la Défense nationale (*m.*).

war risk (opp. to *peace risk*), risque de guerre (*m.*).

war risk clause, clause risques de guerre (*f.*).

warehouse (*n.*), magasin (*m.*) ; entrepôt (*m.*) ; dock (*m.*) ; dépôt (*m.*).

warehouse (bonded) (*n.*), entrepôt (*m.*).

warehouse (*v.t.*), emmagasiner ; magasiner ; entreposer ; mettre en entrepôt :
warehoused goods only pay duty, if there be occasion, when they are taken out of bond for home use, les marchandises entreposées n'acquittent pas les droits, le cas échéant, qu'au moment où elles sont retirées de l'entrepôt pour la consommation (*f.pl.*).

warehouse book, sommier d'entrepôt (*m.*) ; livre de magasin (*m.*).

warehouse charges *or* **warehousing charges,** frais de magasinage (*m.pl.*) ; frais d'emmagasinage (*m.pl.*) ; magasinage (*m.*).

warehouse keeper (bonded storekeeper) (pers.), entreposeur (*m.*).

warehouse keeper's order (delivery order addressed to bonded storekeeper), permis de sortie d'entrepôt (*m.*).

warehouse to warehouse clause (Mar. Insce.), clause « depuis le moment où les facultés quittent les magasins de l'expéditeur jusqu'à celui de leur entrée dans les magasins des réceptionnaires » (*f.*) ; clause magasin à magasin (*f.*).

warehouseman [**warehousemen** *pl.*] (*n.*), magasinier (*m.*).

warehousing (*n.*), emmagasinage (*m.*) ; emmagasinement (*m.*) ; magasinage (*m.*) ; entreposage (*m.*) ; entrepôt (*m.*) ; mise en entrepôt (*f.*) :
the right of warehousing in bond, le droit de magasinage dans l'entrepôt.
the warehousing of imported goods, l'entreposage (*ou* l'entrepôt) des marchandises importées.
to enter goods for warehousing (Customs), déclarer des marchandises pour l'entreposage (*ou* pour l'entrepôt).

warehousing entry (Customs), déclaration d'entrepôt (*f.*) ; déclaration d'entrée en entrepôt (*f.*) ; déclaration de mise en entrepôt (*f.*).

warehousing port (Customs), port d'entrepôt (*m.*).

warehousing system (Customs), système des entrepôts (*m.*) ; régime de l'entrepôt (*m.*).

warlike (*adj.*), belliqueux, -euse :
hostilities or warlike operations, hostilités ou opérations belliqueuses (*f.pl.*).

warrant (authorization) (*n.*), autorisation (*f.*) :
withdrawal warrant (Savings Bank), autorisation de remboursement. (Cf. **dividend warrant.**)

warrant (for goods deposited in a public warehouse) (*n.*), warrant (*m.*) ; récépissé-warrant (*m.*).

warrant (certificate for shares) (Fin.) (*n.*), titre (*m.*) :
bearer warrant *or* share warrant *or* share warrant to bearer *or* simply warrant to bearer, titre au porteur.

warrant (to guarantee) (*v.t.*), garantir.

warranted free of, warranted free from any claim in respect of (Mar. Insce), les assureurs sont affranchis des risques suivants ; les assureurs sont expressément affranchis de toutes réclamations pour les causes suivantes.

warranty [**warranties** *pl.*] (*n.*), garantie (*f.*) :
warranty of quality, of seaworthiness, garantie de qualité, de navigabilité.
V. aussi exemples sous implied warranty *et* express warranty.

warranty clause, clause de garantie (*f.*).

washed ashore (*or* **on shore**) **(to be),** être jeté (-e) par les flots sur le rivage.

washed overboard (to be), être enlevé (-e) par la mer (*ou* par les lames) :
deck cargo washed overboard in course of transit, pontée enlevée par la mer en cours de route (*f.*).

washing overboard, enlèvement par la mer (*ou* par les lames) (*m.*).

wastage *or* **waste** (loss) (*n.*), déchet (*m.*) ; déchets (*m.pl.*) ; freinte (*f.*) :
wastage in bulk, in weight, freinte, déchets, en volume, en poids.

waste (dissipation) (*n.*), gaspillage (*m.*).

waste (*v.t.*), gaspiller :
to waste time and money, gaspiller du temps et de l'argent.

waste book (blotter ; day book), brouillard (*m.*) ; main courante (*f.*) ; mémorial (*m.*) ; chiffrier (*m.*) ; brouillon (*m.*).

waste paper, papier de rebut (*m.*) ; paperasse (*f.*).

waste paper basket, panier (*m.*) ; panier au papier (*m.*) ; corbeille à papier (*f.*) :
to throw a newspaper into the waste paper basket, jeter un journal au panier.

wasting (*adj.*) (Ant. : *non wasting*), défectible :
wasting assets, actif défectible (*m.*) ; valeurs défectibles (*f.pl.*).

watcher (Customs) (pers.) (*n.*), garde (*m.*) :
to put watchers on board a ship, placer des gardes à bord d'un navire.

water (*n.*), eau (*f.*) ; eaux (*f.pl.*) :
sea water, eau de mer ; eaux marines.
waters leading thereto, eaux lui servant d'accès.
ship wrecked in a port or the waters leading

thereto, navire naufragé dans un port ou les eaux lui servant d'accès (*m.*).

reforwarding by rail or water to inland destination, réexpédition par fer ou eau à destination de l'intérieur (*f.*).

water carriage, transport par eau (*m.*).

water line (of a vessel), ligne de flottaison (*f.*).

water shares, valeurs d'eaux (*f.pl.*).

watermark (*n.*), filigrane (*m.*):
the watermarks of bank notes, les filigranes des billets de banque.

watermark (*v.t.*), filigraner.

waterside station, gare d'eau (*f.*).

watertight compartment, compartiment étanche (*m.*).

waterway (*n.*) *or* **water route,** voie navigable (*f.*); voie d'eau (*f.*):
there are two kinds of waterways: rivers and canals, on distingue deux sortes de voies navigables: les rivières et les canaux.

wave (*n.*), vague (*f.*):
wave of speculation, of depression, vague de spéculation, de baisse.

wax seal, cachet à la cire (*m.*); cachet de cire (*m.*).

wax stencil, stencil à la cire (*m.*).

way (path; course; track) (*n.*), voie (*f.*); route (*f.*).

way (onward movement) (*n.*), marche (*f.*); route (*f.*):
ship under way, navire en marche (*ou* faisant route) (*m.*).

way (slip) (Naut.) (*n.*), cale (*f.*).

way and works department (Rly.), service de la voie et des bâtiments (*m.*).

waybill. V. ci-après.

way in (for passengers) (Rly.), entrée (des voyageurs) (*f.*).

way out (for passengers) (Rly.), sortie (des voyageurs) (*f.*).

way station (Rly.), gare de passage (*f.*); station intermédiaire (*f.*); station (*f.*); gare intermédiaire (*f.*); gare d'escale (*f.*).

waybill (*n.*), feuille de route (*f.*); feuille de voyage (*m.*).

weak (*adj.*), faible:
the tendency of the market has been very weak, la tendance du marché a été très faible.

weaken (*v.i.*), faiblir:
X. shares weakened from 3¼ to 3, l'action X. faiblit de 3 1/4 à 3.

weaker side of an account, côté le plus faible d'un compte (*m.*).

weakness (*n.*), faiblesse (*f.*).

wealth (*n.*), richesse (*f.*); richesses (*f.pl.*):
the wealth of a State, la richesse d'un État.
to amass immense wealth, amasser d'immenses richesses.
the vine constitutes Portugal's chief wealth, la vigne constitue la principale richesse du Portugal.

wealthy (*adj.*), riche:
a wealthy landlord, un riche propriétaire.

wear (*n.*), usure (*f.*).

wear (of a coin) (*n.*), frai (d'une pièce d'argent) (*m.*).

wear and tear, usure normale (*f.*); usure (*f.*):
wear and tear of aeroplanes depends less on flight than on the number of landings, especially forced, l'usure des avions dépend moins du vol que du nombre des atterrissages, surtout forcés.

weather permitting (Abbrev.: **w.p.**), si le temps le permet; le temps le permettant; temps le permettant.

weather working day (Abbrev.: **W.W.D.**), jour pendant lequel le temps permet de travailler (*m.*).

week (*n.*), semaine (*f.*).

week-end letter telegram (Abbrev.: **WLT.**), télégramme de fin de semaine (*m.*).

weekly (*adj.*), hebdomadaire:
weekly season ticket, carte d'abonnement hebdomadaire (*f.*).
weekly loans *or* weekly fixtures (Money Market), prêts à sept jours (*m.pl.*).

weigh (*v.t.*), peser:
to weigh to the nearest ounce (Customs), peser à l'once près.
goods weighed to the ounce, marchandises pesées jusqu'à l'once (*f.pl.*).

weigh (*v.i.*), peser.

weighbridge (*n.*), pont à bascule (*m.*); pont-bascule (*m.*); pont à peser (*m.*).

weigher (pers.) (*n.*), peseur (*m.*).

weighing (*n.*), pesage (*m.*); pesée (*f.*).

weight (*n.*), poids (*m.*):
weight or measurement, poids ou cube; poids ou volume; poids ou encombrement:
to quote the freight at such a rate, weight or measurement, coter le fret à tel taux, poids ou cube.
weight, value, and contents unknown, poids, valeur, et contenu inconnus.

weight (to burden) (*v.t.*), grever:
to weight the budget of expenses of one accounting period with an exceptionally heavy sum, grever le budget de dépenses d'un exercice d'une somme exceptionnellement grosse.

weight allowed free (free allowance of luggage), franchise de poids (*f.*).

weight goods *or* **weight cargo** (opp. to *measurement goods* or *cargo*), marchandises lourdes (*f.pl.*); marchandises pondéreuses (*f.pl.*).

weight note, note de poids (*f.*); bulletin de pesage (*m.*).

weight slip, fiche de pesage (*f.*).

West African shares *or simply* **West Africans,** valeurs ouest-africaines (*f.pl.*); ouest-africaines (*f.pl.*).

West European time *or* **Western European time** *or* **West Europe time** (Abbrev.: **W.E.T.**), heure de l'Europe Occidentale (*f.*); heure de Greenwich (*f.*) (12 noon [midi] in relation to **Amsterdam, Mid European,** and **West European times,** q.v.).

wet dock (opp. to *dry dock*), bassin à flot (*m.*).

wet goods (opp. to *dry goods*), marchandises liquides (*f.pl.*).

wetting (*n.*), mouillure (*f.*) :
  wetting by sea water, by fresh water (cause of damage), mouillure par eau de mer, par eau douce.
wharf [**wharves** *or* **wharfs** *pl.*] (*n.*), quai (*m.*); appontement (*m.*); débarcadère (*m.*); embarcadère (*m.*).
wharf (*v.t.*), mettre à quai :
  to wharf a ship, mettre à quai un navire.
wharf dues *or* **wharfage** (*n.*), droits de quai (*m.pl.*).
wharf to wharf, quai à quai.
wharfinger (pers.) (*n.*), propriétaire de quai (*m.*); entrepreneur de quai (*m.*).
wharfinger's receipt, bon de quai (*m.*).
what number are you calling ? (Teleph.), qui demandez-vous ? ; j'écoute.
whichever event may first happen, suivant celui de ces événements qui s'accomplira le premier.
while the ship is in dock, in a port of refuge, pendant le séjour du navire dans les docks, dans un port de relâche.
white paper (fine trade bills), papier de haut commerce (*m.*); papier hors banque (*m.*).
whole (totality) (*n.*), totalité (*f.*); intégralité (*f.*); total (*m.*) :
  to accept either the whole, or a part of the risk to be covered, accepter soit la totalité, soit une partie du risque à couvrir.
  the whole of the capital, of the receipts, la totalité (*ou* l'intégralité) (*ou* le total) du capital, des recettes.
whole cargo charter, affrètement total (*m.*).
whole life insurance (distinguished from *endowment insurance*), assurance en cas de décès (*f.*); assurance pour la vie entière (*f.*).
whole number, nombre entier (*m.*); entier (*m.*).
wholesale (*adj.*), de demi-gros; en demi-gros : (V. note.)
  wholesale price, prix de gros (*m.*). (This is in the general sense [see note]; in the technical sense the translation would be *prix de demi-gros.*)
  wholesale sale, vente en demi-gros (*f.*).
  wholesale trade *or* wholesale commerce, commerce de demi-gros (*m.*); demi-gros (*m.*) :
  to do a wholesale trade, faire le demi-gros.
  wholesale trader *or* wholesale dealer or **wholesaler** (pers.) (*n.*), marchand en (*ou* de) demi-gros (*m.*) (technical sense); grossiste (*m.*) (general sense).
  Note :—(*a*) *direct* (i.e., producing or manufacturing), (*b*) *wholesale* (buying from the producer or manufacturer and selling to the retailer), and (*c*) *retail* (selling to consumer), are technical terms, and have as equivalents in French (*a*) *gros*, (*b*) *demi-gros*, and (*c*) *détail.*
  In a looser or more general sense, in English as in French, *retail* (*détail*) is merely contrasted with *wholesale* (*gros*). This is particularly the case in the mere sense of selling in large quantities, thus, *to sell wholesale* (*vendre en gros*), as contrasted with selling in small quantities, thus, *selling retail* (*vente en détail*).

The three grades are thus frequently denominated (*a*) *producer* (*producteur*), (*b*) *wholesale* (*gros*), and (*c*) *retail* (*détail*).
  Furthermore, *producer* (*producteur*) can be contrasted merely with *consumer* or *user* (*consommateur*) thus, producer who sells direct to the consumer, producteur qui vend directement au consommateur.
wholly transparent envelope, enveloppe entièrement transparente (*f.*).
will (*n.*) *or* **will and testament** *or* **last will and testament**, testament (*m.*) :
  to make one's will, faire son testament.
  this is my last will and testament, ceci est mon testament.
will you please repeat the number ? (Teleph.), veuillez répéter le numéro.
win (*v.t.*), gagner :
  to win a case, a bet, gagner un procès, un pari.
  by wanting to win all, one risks losing all, à vouloir tout gagner, on risque de tout perdre.
wind and water line (of a ship), exposant de charge (*m.*).
wind up (*v.t.*), liquider :
  to wind up a company, one's affairs, liquider une société, ses affaires.
windfall (unexpected gain) (*n.*), aubaine (*f.*).
winding up, liquidation (*f.*) :
  voluntary winding up, liquidation volontaire.
  winding up subject to supervision of court, liquidation judiciaire.
windmill (kite; fictitious commercial paper) (*n.*), traite en l'air (*f.*); cerf-volant (*m.*); effet à renouvellement (*m.*). *In the plural*, **windmills**, traites en l'air (*f.pl.*); papier en l'air (*m.*); papier de circulation (*m.*); valeurs de circulation (*f.pl.*); cerfs-volants (*m.pl.*); cavalerie (*f.*); effets à renouvellement (*m.pl.*).
window dressing (Fin.) (*fig.*), bel étalage pour faire bonne impression (*m.*).
window envelope, enveloppe à fenêtre (*f.*); enveloppe fenestrée (*f.*); enveloppe à panneau (*f.*).
winner (pers.) (*n.*), gagneur, -euse.
winning (*adj.*), gagnant, -e :
  winning number, numéro gagnant (*m.*).
winter (*n.*), hiver (*m.*).
winter (*v.i.*), hiverner :
  ship blockaded by ice and obliged to winter, navire bloqué par les glaces et obligé d'hiverner (*m.*).
winter premium (Insce) (opp. to *summer premium*), prime d'hiver (*f.*).
winter risk (Insce), risque d'hiver (*m.*).
wintering port, port d'hivernage (*m.*).
wipe off (*v.t.*), apurer :
  to wipe off a debit balance, a debt, apurer un solde déficitaire, une dette.
wiping off, apurement (*m.*).
wire (*n.*), fil (*m.*); télégramme (*m.*); dépêche (*f.*); dépêche télégraphique (*f.*) :
  order sent by wire, ordre transmis par fil (*m.*).
  to send a wire, expédier un télégramme (*ou* une dépêche).
wire (*v.t.*), télégraphier.

wire telegraphy or simply **wire** (n.) (opp. to wireless telegraphy or simply wireless), télégraphie avec fil (f.); fil (m.):
routing by wire, acheminement par fil (m.).
wire telephony (opp. to wireless telephony), téléphonie avec fil (f.).
wireless message, radio (m.):
according to a wireless message of the X. Agency, d'après un radio de l'Agence X.
wireless station, poste de T.S.F. (m.); station de T.S.F. (f.); station radio (f.).
wireless telegraphy (Abbrev.: **W/T.**) or simply **wireless** (n.) (opp. to wire telegraphy or simply wire), télégraphie sans fil (f.); sans fil; T.S.F. (f.); radiotélégraphie (f.).
routing by wireless, acheminement par sans fil (m.).
ship provided with wireless, navire pourvu de T.S.F. (m.).
wireless telephony (Abbrev.: **W/T.**), téléphonie sans fil (f.); radiotéléphonie (f.).
with care (notice on a parcel), fragile.
with coupon (opp. to ex coupon), coupon attaché; jouissance. V. exemples sous syn. **cum coupon.**
with particular average (Abbrev.: **W.P.A.**) or simply **with average** (Abbrev.: **W.A.**) (Mar. Insce) (opp. to free of particular average), avec avarie particulière; aux pleines conditions.
with rights (opp. to ex rights), avec droit; droit attaché:
shares with rights, titres avec droit (m.pl.).
withdraw (v.t.), retirer; décaisser:
to withdraw a deposit, coins from circulation, the ship from the service of the charterers, retirer un dépôt, des pièces de la circulation, le navire du service des affréteurs.
to withdraw a sum of money, retirer, décaisser, une somme d'argent.
withdrawal (n.), retrait (m.); décaissement (m.):
withdrawal of a request, of money from a bank, retrait d'une demande, d'argent d'une banque.
withdrawal (Savings Bank) (n.), remboursement (m.); retrait (m.):
withdrawal of a portion of a deposit, remboursement partiel d'un versement.
withdrawal of the whole of a deposit, remboursement intégral des fonds déposés.
withdrawal on demand, remboursement à vue.
withdrawal notice (of funds) (Banking), mandat (m.).
withdrawal warrant (Savings Bank), autorisation de remboursement (f.).
withhold (v.t.), retenir:
to withhold so much out of the pay of an employee, retenir tant sur la paye d'un employé.
within so many days, within a reasonable time, dans l'espace de tant de jours, dans un délai raisonnable.
without advice or **without other advice** (notice on a bill of exchange) (opp. to as per advice), sans avis; sans autre avis.
without day, sans date; sine die:

to adjourn without day, s'ajourner sans date (ou sine die).
without prejudice, sans préjudice. V. exemple sous **prejudice.**
without recourse, à forfait. V. exemples sous **recourse.**
witness (pers.) (n.), témoin (m.):
the undersigned witnesses, les témoins soussignés.
in witness whereof, en témoin de quoi; en foi de quoi.
witness (v.t.), signer à; certifier:
to witness an agreement, signer à une convention.
witnessing (n.), certification (f.):
witnessing of signatures on transfer of stocks and shares, certification de signatures sur des transferts de valeurs mobilières.
woman engaged in business, femme commerçante (f.).
wooden vessel, navire en bois (m.).
word (n.), mot (m.):
word charged for (Teleg.), mot taxé.
word in plain language, in code, in cipher, mot en clair, en convenu, en chiffré.
in words or **in words at length,** en lettres; en toutes lettres:
the agreement of the amount in words with the amount in figures, la concordance de la somme en lettres avec la somme en chiffres.
to express an amount in words at length, énoncer une somme en toutes lettres.
word (v.t.), libeller:
to word a bill of exchange as follows, libeller une lettre de change comme suit.
an order should always be worded in a clear and precise manner, to avoid any dispute or mistake in interpretation, un ordre doit toujours être libellé d'une façon claire et précise, pour éviter toute contestation ou toute erreur d'interprétation.
wording (n.) or **words** (n.pl.) or **word** (n.), libellé (m.); énonciation (f.); texte (m.); mention (f.):
the regularity of the bill from the point of view of the wording, la régularité de l'effet au point de vue du libellé.
wording of an insurance policy, texte d'une police d'assurance.
the bill bore the words to the order of, the word accepted, le billet portait la mention à l'ordre de, la mention accepté.
work (n.), travail (m.):
office work, travail de bureau.
works in progress, travaux en cours.
work (v.t.), exploiter:
to work a patent, exploiter un brevet.
work (v.i.), travailler:
to work to earn one's bread, in the hope of becoming independent, travailler pour gagner son pain, dans l'espoir de devenir rentier.
to work overtime, travailler en heures supplémentaires.
work out (to reckon, calculate, figure out) (v.t.), décompter; chiffrer; supputer; faire:

the list is worked out by the banker, le bordereau est décompté (*ou* chiffré) par le banquier.

to work out the interest, a current account, chiffrer les intérêts, un compte courant.

to work out the percentage of standing charges, supputer, faire, le pourcentage des frais généraux.

to work out the charges on, décompter :

to work out the charges on a bill, on a list of bills for discount, décompter un effet, un bordereau d'escompte.

work out (*v.i.*), se chiffrer.

working (*n.*), exploitation (*f.*) :

working a patent, exploitation d'un brevet.

working account (Bkkpg), compte d'exploitation (*m.*) ; exploitation (*f.*).

working capital, capital de roulement (*m.*) ; fonds de roulement (*m.*) :

the working capital necessary to the needs of the undertaking, le capital de roulement nécessaire aux besoins de l'exploitation.

the available assets form what is called working capital, les disponibilités forment ce qu'on appelle le fonds de roulement (*f.pl.*).

working coefficient, coefficient d'exploitation (*m.*) :

by working coefficient is understood the ratio of expenses to receipts, on entend par coefficient d'exploitation le rapport de la dépense à la recette.

working day *or* **work day** (a day not a legal holiday), jour ouvrable (*m.*) ; jour ouvrier (*m.*) ; jour de travail (*m.*) ; jour non férié (*m.*).

working day (Stock Exch.), jour ouvrable (*m.*) ; jour de travail (*m.*) ; jour non férié (*m.*) ; jour de bourse (*m.*) ; bourse (*f.*) :

five clear working days before the date fixed for the drawing, cinq bourses pleines avant la date fixée pour le tirage.

working day (the number of hours constituting a day's work), journée de travail (*f.*) :

a working day of eight hours, une journée de travail de huit heures.

working expenses, frais d'exploitation (*m.pl.*) ; dépenses d'exploitation (*f.pl.*) ; charges d'exploitation (*f.pl.*).

working hours, heures de travail (*f.pl.*).

working out, décompte (*m.*) ; chiffrage (*m.*) ; supputation (*f.*) :

working out the interest due, décompte, chiffrage, des intérêts dus.

working out the charges on a list of bills for collection, décompte d'un bordereau d'encaissement.

workman's season ticket, carte d'abonnement de travail (*f.*).

workmen's compensation insurance, assurance contre les accidents du travail (*f.*) ; assurance accidents du travail (*f.*).

workmen's train, train d'ouvriers (*m.*).

works [works *pl.*] (*n.*), usine (*f.*) ; fabrique (*f.*) ; manufacture (*f.*).

world (*n.*), monde (*m.*) :

the world of finance *or* the financial world, le monde de finance ; le monde financier.

the diverse corporations and individualities which constitute the shipping world, les diverses corporations et individualités qui constituent le monde maritime.

world wide circular letter of credit *or* **world letter of credit,** lettre de crédit circulaire mondiale (*f.*) ; lettre de crédit circulaire valable dans le monde entier (*f.*).

worn coin, pièce usée (*f.*).

worries of business, tracas des affaires (*m.sing.*).

worth (*n.*), valeur (*f.*) :

the worth of a thing is the power of exchange it possesses, la valeur d'une chose est la puissance d'échange qu'elle possède.

to be worth, valoir :

article which is worth so much, which is worth money, objet qui vaut tant, qui vaut de l'argent (*m.*).

X. shares were worth so much (Market News), les actions X. ont valu tant.

worthless (*adj.*), sans valeur :

worthless cheque, chèque sans provision (*m.*) :

a worthless cheque is one whose amount exceeds the balance available in the account of the drawer, le chèque sans provision est celui dont le montant dépasse le solde disponible au compte du tireur.

Note :—In England ⌇⌇⌇ funds to a ⌇⌇ cheque, the ban⌇ (unless they are⌇ customer to overd⌇ will not pay a part ⌇ of the customer's ⌇ instance, if there were s⌇ mer's credit, and he drew ⌇ the bank would return the cheq⌇ I/F. (insufficient funds), or N/S⌇ sufficient funds) ; they would not p⌇ payee the £40 in hand. Not so in Fr⌇ where the holder has the optional right ⌇ receive payment up to the amount in hand.

worthless securities, titres sans valeur (*m.pl.*) ; non valeurs (*f.pl.*).

wrapper (*n.*), bande (*f.*) :

to put a newspaper in a wrapper, mettre un journal sous bande.

wreck (shipwreck) (*n.*), naufrage (*m.*) ; sinistre (*m.*) ; bris (*m.*) :

the wreck of the *Lutine* which was lost on the 10th October 1799, at the entrance to the Zuider Zee, le naufrage de la *Lutine* qui se perdit le 10 Octobre 1799, à l'entrée du Zuyderzée.

to save something from the wreck, sauver quelque chose du naufrage.

wreck *or* **wreckage** (the ruins of a wrecked or stranded ship) (*n.*), débris (*m.pl.*) ; épave (*f.*) ; épaves (*f.pl.*) ; bris (*m.*) :

goods salved from wrecks or cast by the waves on the shore constitute wreck (*or* wreckage), les marchandises sauvées des naufrages ou rejetées par les flots sur le littoral constituent des épaves (*f.pl.*).

cutting away wreck, coupement de débris (m.).
salvage of wreck (or wreckage), sauvetage des épaves (ou des débris) (m.).
wrecked (adj.), naufragé, -e; sinistré, -e:
wrecked cargo, marchandises naufragées (ou sinistrées) (f.pl.).
wrecked ship, navire naufragé (m.); navire sinistré (m.).
wrecked (to be), faire naufrage; se perdre:
ship which is wrecked without leaving a trace, navire qui fait naufrage sans laisser de trace (m.).
writ (Law) (n.), exploit (m.).
write (v.t.), écrire; inscrire:
to write a letter, écrire une lettre.
to write something in a book, écrire, inscrire, quelque chose sur un livre.
to write an account of a transaction, faire l'historique d'une négociation.
write (to underwrite) (Insce) (v.t.), souscrire:
policy written in London, police souscrite à Londres (f.).
above all the Lombards were bankers, and it was only accessorily that they wrote assurances, avant tout les Lombards étaient banquiers, et ce n'était qu'accessoirement qu'ils souscrivaient des assurances.
write back (Bkkpg) (v.t.), contre-passer; ex-tourner; ristourner; ristorner:
… item, contre-passer, ex-
… debit, ristourner
… o write back the whole … te back a part of.
… provisional and can be … case of non payment, le … que provisoire et peut être … passé au cas de non paiement.
… (v.t.), amortir:
… rite off a debt, the amount of an embezzlement, amortir un créance, le montant d'un détournement.
to write 10% per annum off the furniture, amortir le mobilier de 10 0/0 par an.
write out (to draw) (v.t.), tracer; créer; tirer:
to write out a cheque, tracer, créer, tirer, un chèque.
write out or simply **write** (to draw up) (v.t.), rédiger:
to write out a bill, rédiger un mémoire.
agreement written on loose sheets, contrat rédigé sur des feuilles volantes (m.).
write up (v.t.), écrire; rédiger:
to write up the books, the journal, écrire, rédiger, les livres (ou la comptabilité), le journal.
writing (n.), écriture (f.); écrit (m.):
illegible writing, écriture illisible.

in writing or **written**, en écrit; par écrit; à l'écrit; écrit, -e; manuscrit, -e:
agreement in writing or written agreement, convention en écrit (ou par écrit) (ou à l'écrit) (ou écrite) (f.); écrit (m.):
the need of a written agreement when selling a ship, la nécessité d'un écrit en matière de vente de navire.
printed form which contains the following written particulars or the following particulars in writing, formule imprimée qui porte les indications manuscrites suivantes (f.).
written clause (opp. to printed clause), clause manuscrite (f.).
written consent of the underwriters, consentement par écrit des assureurs (m.).
verbal or written confirmation, confirmation verbale ou écrite (f.).
writing (underwriting) (Insce) (n.), souscription (f.).
writing back (Bkkpg), contre-passement (m.); contre-passation (f.); extourne (f.); ristourne (f.); ristorne (f.). V. note sous le verbe.
writing down fee (telegrams), taxe de transmission téléphonique (f.).
writing ink, encre à écrire (f.).
writing machine, machine à écrire (f.); dactylographe (m.); dactylotype (f.).
writing off (a debt), amortissement (m.).
writing out (cheques, or the like), traçage (m.); création (f.); tirage (m.).
writing pad, sous-main (m.); sous-main buvard (m.).
writing paper, papier à écrire (m.).
writing up (books), écriture (f.); rédaction (f.).
wrong (adj.), faux, fausse; inexact, -e; erroné, -e:
wrong address, fausse adresse (f.); vice d'adresse (m.).
wrong calculation, calcul faux (ou inexact) (ou erroné) (m.).
wrong delivery owing to insufficiency of marks, erreur dans la livraison par suite de l'insuffisance des marques (f.).
wrong entry (Bkkpg), faux emploi (m.).
wrong number (Teleph.), faux numéro (m.); faux numéro d'appel (m.).
wrongful act, faute (f.):
liability for the wrongful acts and defaults (or negligence) of the master, pilot, crew, agent, servant, or other persons, responsabilité des fautes et prévarications (ou négligences) des capitaine, pilote, marins, agent, préposé, ou autres personnes.
wrongly or **wrong** (adv.), faussement; inexactement; à tort:
charge wrongly collected, taxe perçue à tort (f.).

Y

yard (*n.*), parc (*m.*); chantier (*m.*):
coal yard, parc à charbon; chantier· de houille.
shipyard, chantier de construction navale (*ou* de construction maritime) (*ou* de construction de navires).

year (*n.*), an (*m.*); année (*f.*):
once a year, une fois l'an.
the results of the corresponding periods of the previous year are placed opposite those of the present (*or* current) year, in order to facilitate comparisons, les résultats des périodes correspondantes de l'année précédente (*ou* antérieure) sont placés en regard de ceux de l'année en cours, afin de faciliter les comparaisons (*m.pl.*).
year of assessment, année d'imposition:
the income of the year preceding the year of assessment, le revenu de l'année immédiatement antérieure à l'année d'imposition.
year of office, année d'exercice; année:
during his year of office, pendant son année d'exercice; pendant son année.

year (regarded as mere date) (*n.*), an (*m.*); millésime (*m.*):
the year 19—, l'an 19—.
day, month, and year, quantième, mois, et millésime.
Cf. exemples sous **date** (year).

year (financial year; trading year) (*n.*), année (*f.*); exercice (*m.*):
company's year, année sociale; exercice social:
the company's year begins on 1st January and ends on 31st December, l'année sociale commence le 1er janvier et finit le 31 décembre.
if the company's year comprises two half yearly accounting periods, si l'année sociale comprend deux exercices semestriels.
year ending 31st December, exercice prenant fin (*ou* clôturant) le 31 décembre.
year ended 31st December, exercice ayant pris fin (*ou* exercice clôturé *ou* clos) le 31 décembre.
dividend for the year 19—, dividende de l'exercice 19— (*m.*).

to make good the losses of bad years, combler les pertes des mauvais exercices.

year book, annuaire (*m.*):
stock exchange year book, annuaire des agents de change.

yearly (*adj.*), annuel, -elle:
yearly accounts, comptes annuels (*m.pl.*).
yearly income, revenu annuel (*m.*); rente (*f.*); année (*f.*).
yearly premium, prime annuelle (*f.*).
repayable by yearly instalments. V. sous **repayable.**

yearly (*adv.*), annuellement.

yesterday's closing (list of quotations), clôture de la veille (*f.*).

yield (*n.*), rendement (*m.*); rapport (*m.*); produit (*m.*); taux de capitalisation (*m.*):
the yield of taxes, le rendement des impôts.
yield of a capital, produit, rendement, rapport, d'un capital.
yield of a stock, rendement, taux de capitalisation, d'un titre.
high yield stocks, valeurs à gros rendement (*f.pl.*).

yield (to furnish as a result of investment) (*v.t.*), rendre; rapporter; produire:
capital which yields 5% per annum, capital qui rend (*ou* qui rapporte) (*ou* qui produit) 5 0/0 par an.

yield (to shed) (*v.t.*), céder:
share which yields a few fractions, action qui cède quelques fractions (*f.*).

York-Antwerp rules (Abbrev.: **Y.A.R.**), règles d'York et d'Anvers (*f.pl.*):
general average has formed the subject of a kind of international codification settled by congresses and known by the name of York-Antwerp rules, les avaries communes ont fait l'objet d'une sorte de codification internationale établie par des congrès et connue sous le nom de règles d'York et d'Anvers.

Yours faithfully *or* **Yours truly** (epistolary formulæ preceding signature) (*invar.*), Recevez, Monsieur (Messieurs), mes (nos) meilleures salutations; Agréez, Monsieur (Messieurs), mes (nos) salutations empressées; Votre dévoué (Vos dévoués).

Z

Zeppelin (*n.*), Zeppelin (*m.*).

zero (*n.*), zéro (*m.*):
fortune reduced to zero, fortune réduite à zéro (*f.*).

zero date *or simply* **zero** (*n.*) (accounts current with interest), époque (*f.*).

zinc-lined case, caisse doublée de zinc (*f.*).

zollverein (*n.*), zollverein (*m.*).

zone (*n.*), zone (*f.*):
free zones in maritime ports, zones franches dans les ports maritimes.

ADDENDUM

absconder (*n.*), défaillant, -e, contumace (*m.*).
absentee landlord (*n.*), nu-propriétaire:
  absentee landlord, 'bare owner', i.e. "not enjoying the actual use of his property"
access time (*n.*), temps d'accès (*m.*).
addendum (*n.*), supplément (*m.*), appendice (*m.*).
advantageous (*adj.*), avantageux, -euse:
  we have signed a very profitable contract,
  nous avons signés un contrat très avantageux.
advertising (*adj.*), publicitaire (*m. & f.*).
access (*n.*), accès (*f.*).
accommodating (*adj.*), coulant, accommodant.
accompaniment (*n.*), accompagnement (*m.*).
add, to add up (*v.t.*), additionner.
agent, régisseur (*n.m.*).
agio (*n.*), (exchange premium), agio (*m.*).
alderman (*n.*), conseiller municipal (*m.*), magistrat (*m.*).
ancillary (*adj.*), ancillaire.
annex (*n.*), (outbuildings, codicil), dépendance
  (*f.*).
annotate (*v.t.*), annoter.
anti-inflationary (*adj.*), anti-inflationniste, -e.
apparatus (*n.*), appareil (*m.*), dispositi (*m.*):
  appareil (photographique), camera, *or simply*
  'un appareil'.
  appareil de télégraphie-sans-fils, radio set.
apprenticeship (*n.*), apprentissage (*m.*).
  He is an apprentice, il est apprentis.
ascertain (*v.t.*), déterminer:
  to determine the cost, to ascertain the cost,
  déterminer le coût.
attach (*v.t.*), attacher, attaché -e, (*p.p.*).
  see attached document, voir document attaché.
auditor (*n.*), reviseur (*m.*).
automation (*n.*), automation (*f.*).

bailiff (*n.*), huissier (*m.*).
beginner (*n.*), débutant, -e. (*m./f.*).
belong to (be related to), ressortir à:
  our increased profits are due to the improved
  mass-production system, l'augmentation de
  nos bénéfices ressort à notre système
  amélioré de production en serie.
bill sticking (*v.t.*), affichage (*m.*).
binary (*adj.*), binaire:

binary scale	échelle binaire
$2^0 = 1$	$2^3 = 8$
$2^1 = 2$	$2^4 = 16$
$2^2 = 4$	$2^5 = 32$

  par exemple: le chiffre 51 est représenté dans
  l'échelle binaire par:—
$$2^0 + 2^1 + 2^4 + 2^5$$
binomial (*adj.*), binôme.
bi-weekly, fortnightly (*adj.*), bimensuel.
bi-monthly, (*adj.*), bimestriel.

black (*adj.*), noir (*m. & f.*).
  black market, marché noir.
  black list, liste noir
  black ball, boule noir.*
  *usually more politely expressed as: 'rejeté au
  scrutin'.
block (*n.*), bloc (*m.*).
born (*p.p. & adj.*), né, née:
  Mrs. Dubois, née Lemercier, Madame Dubois,
  maiden name Lemercier.
bottle (*n.*), bouteille (*f.*).
  bottle-neck, goulot (*n.m.*) d'étranglement.
breeding, stock-raising, rearing (of cattle), (*n.*),
  élevage (*m.*).
bulky (*adj.*), volumineux.
bursar (*n.*) (treasurer), économe (*m.*).
bye-law (*n.*), arrêté municipal.

calling (*n.*), métier (*m.*).
camouflage (*v.t.*), camoufler:
  we have found the accounts to be faked,
  nous avons reconnu que les comptes ont été
  camouflés.
card (*n.*), carte (*f.*):
  blank card, carte vierge.
  data card, carte donnée.
  parameter card, carte paramètre.
  punched card, carte perforée.
  summary card, carte récapitulative.
  card-reader (n.), lecteur (*m.*) de cartes.
  card perforator (*n.*), perforateur de carte (*m.*).
  card punch (*n.*), perforateur de carte (*m.*).
category (*n.*), catégorie (*f.*).
ceiling (*n.*), plafond (*m.*):
  I am up to the eyebrows in debt, j'ai des debt
  jusqu'au plafond.
central processor (*n.*), unité (*f.*) centrale.
certified copy (*n.*), amplification (*f.*):
  Je lui envoye une amplification de notre acte,
  I am sending him a certified copy of our
  contract.
character (letter, figure, etc.), caractère (*m.*).
cheap goods, rubbish, trash (*n.*), camelote (*f.*).
check:
  to check and take delivery, réceptionner (*v.t.*).
Christmas (*n.*), Noël (*m.*).
  the Christmas holidays, les fêtes de Noël.
clerk (*n.*), clerc (*m.*):
  female clerk, commise.
  chief clerk, chef de bureau.
  clerk of works, conducteur de travaux.
  clerk of the court, greffier (*m.*).
coal (*n.*), houille (*f.*).
  coal mine, colliery, houillère (*f.*), mine de
  houille (*f.*).
codicil (*n.*), codicille (*f.*).

competency (*n.*), authority, compétence (*f.*).
the authorities, les authoritès compétentes.
the available talent, les compétences disponibles.
component (unit, element) (*n.*), élément (*m.*).
input unit, élément d'entrée.
output unit, élément de sortie.
peripheral unit, élément périphérique.
compulsory (*adj.*), obligatoire.
computer (*n.*), ordinateur (*m.*); machine à calculer électronique:
to describe any electronic device; ensemble électronique, or appareil électronique.
computer record (*n.*), article (*m.*).
condolence (*n.*), condoléance (*f.*).
conflict (*n.*), conflit (*m.*).
a conflict of interests, un conflit d'intérêts.
congratulation(s), (*n.*), félicitation(s) (*f.*).
connect (*v.t.*) (wiring, piping, etc.), brancher, raccorder.
contest (*v.t.*), contester.
contiguous to, contigu à.
copyright, 'reproduction interdite'.
(*Note:*—This is the expression most often used nowadays.)
countermand (*v.t.*), décommander.
counter-surety (*n.*), arrière-caution.
courtesy (*n.*), obligeance (*f.*).
please contact me, ayez, s'il vous plait, l'obligeance de me contacter.
have the kindness to write, ayez l'obligeance de m'écrire.
craftsman (*n.*), artisan (*m.*).
cultivating (*n.*), exploitation (*f.*).
current (*adj.*), courant, en cours, courante (*f.*).
in the process of manufacture, en cours de fabrication.
it is our current practice, c'est notre habitude courante.
curtail (*v.t.*), retrancher, amoindrir, diminuer, abr ger, restreindre, amputer:
we have had to curtail his authority, nous avons du amputé ses pouvoirs.
curtailment (*n.*), retrenchment (*m.*), compressession (*f.*), réduction (*f.*), diminution (*f.*), restriction (*f.*).
curve (on graph) (*n.*), courbe (*f.*):
unemployment curve, courbe du chomage.
cycle (*n.*), cycle (*m.*):
cycle time, durée du cycle.

data (*n.*), données (*f.pl.*).
deadlock (*n.*), impasse (*f.*).
defective (*adj.*), défectueux.
department (*n.*), rayon (*m.*), département (*m.*):
departmental manager, chef de rayon.
dictaphone (*n.*), dictaphone (*m.*).
digit (*n.*), chiffre (*m.*).
directory (*n.*), bottin (*m.*).
dismissal (*n.*), licenciement (*m.*).
laying off, licenciement de personnel.
dismissal without notice, licenciement sans préavis.
Also: to dismiss, revoyer, congédier, mettre à la porte.
displaced person (*n.*), personne (*f.*), déplacée.

distrainable (*adj.*), saisissable.
distrust (*n.*), méfiance (*f.*).
domain (field) (*n.*), domaine (*m.*).
due, dû, due:
in due course, en dû temps.
in due form, en due forme.

Easter (*n.*), Pâques (*m.*).
the Easter holidays, les fêtes de Pâques.
electric (*adj.*), électrique.
electrician (*n.*), électricien (*m.*).
electricity (*n.*), électricité (*f.*).
electrification (*n.*), électrisation (*f.*).
electronic, électronique:
calculating machine (*n.*), calculateur (*m.*) électronique.
punched-card machine (*n.*), système à cartes perforées; *also:* traitement électronique des données.
element, *see* **component**.
engineer (*n.*), ingénieur (*m.*):
qualified engineer (engineer with a degree), Ingénieur Diplômé.
mechanic (*n.*), ingénieur, ingénieur-mécanicien, -ne.
enter (*v.i.*), to come in, entrer:
we entered the manager's office, nous entrames dans le bureau du directeur.
we entered into conversation, nous sommes entrer en conversation.
to come into force, entrer en vigueur.
to be taken into account, entrer en consideration.
equalization (*n.*), péréquation (*f.*):
to equalize, faire la péréquation.
estimate, devis (*m.*).
Note:—In modern French business the word 'devis' is *always* now used, in respect of an 'estimate' of cost.
eviction (*n.*), éviction (*f.*).
excess:
excess weight, excédent de poids (*m.*); surpoids.*
(*surpoids is much more often used.)
executary (*adv.*), exécutoir.
expropriation (*n.*), expropriation (*f.*).
extend (*v.t.*), prolonger:
the bank has agreed to extend the credit for one month, la banque a consentit de prolonger le crédit pour un mois.
extension (*n.*) extension (*f.*):
his telephone is on an extension line, son téléphone est sur ligne d'extension.

family (*adj.*), familial, -e:
family allowance, allocation familiale.
family (*n.*), famille (*f.*):
head of the house (householder), chef (*m.*) de famille.
farm (*n.*), ferme (*f.*).
farmer (*n.*), fermier (*m.*); lady-farmer or farmer's wife, fermière (*f.*).
fee:
attendance fee (*n.*), vacations (*f.pl.*).
flag (*n.*), drapeau (*m.*).
See also: marker (in a business machine).

florin (*n.*), florin (*m.*).
forbidden:
see: défense (de, d').
foreman (*n.*), contremaître.
forge (*v.t.*), contrefaire, imiter:
to forge a signature, contrefaire une signature.
form (*v.t.*), façonner:
Also:—to fashion, to make, to mould, to shape.
foresight (*n.*), précaution (*n.*), prévoyance (*f.*):
he has had the foresight to organize additional transport, il a eu la prévoyance d'organiser des camions additionnels.
fountain pen (*n.*), stylo (*m.*), stylographe (*m.*).
fire (*n.*), feu (*m.*).
fire-extinguisher (*n.*), extincteur (*m.*).
free and unemcumbered, quitte et libre.
free-lance (work) (*n.*), travail à domicile (*m.*).
he is a free-lance worker, il travail à domicile, il travail à son propre compte.
free loan (*n.*), comoda (*m.*).
frozen (*p.p.*), gelé:
frozen assets, crédit gelé.
furniture repository (*n.*), garde-meubles (*m.*).

gas (*n.*), gaz (*m.*):
domestic gas, gaz domestique.
'gentleman's agreement', by private arrangement, à l'amiable.
genuine (real), (*adj.*), véritable.
good:
good offices, bons offices:
he got his excellent position entirely through the good offices of his ex-Commanding Officer, il a obtenu son excellente situation entièrement par les bons offices de son ancien commandant.
grant (*v.t.*), octroyer, accorder, concéder.
granting (*n.*), octroi (*m.*).
graph (*n.*), graphique (*m.*):
this graph clearly shows the increase in last year's sales, ce graphique indique très nettement l'augmentation des ventres l'année dernière.
gratis (*adj.*), gratis.
gratuitously (*adv.*), à titre gracieux:
it is gratuitous, c'est gratuit.
guardianship (*n.*), tutelle (*f.*), curatelle (*f.*).

hand (*n.*), main (*f.*):
to change hands, changer de mains.
labour, main-d'oeuvre.
heading (*n.*), en tête (*m.*):
letterhead, en tête. de lettre.
hire purchase (*n.*), location-vente (*f.*), achat à tempérament.
hopper (for punched card systems, etc.), magasin (*m.*) d'alimentation.
housing (*n.*), logement (*m.*).

identification (*n.*), identification.
identify (*v.t.*), identifier.
identical (*adj.*), identique.
identity (*n.*), identité (*f.*).

importance (*n.*), importance (*f.*):
frequently used, in French, for other English words:
the amount of the credit, l'importance du crédit; the volume of his sales, l'importance de ses ventes; the significance of the document in question, l'importance du document en question.
in camera (*adj.*), huis clos.
incontestable (*adj.*), incontestable.
increase (*n.*), augmentation (*f.*), agrandissement (*m.*), surcroît (*m.*).
they all received an increase in salary, ils ont tous reçu une augmentation de salaire.
I have increased the size of my house, j'ai agrandis ma maison.
This year's crops have shown a handsome increase in comparison with last year's, la récolte de cette année a donnée un beau surcroît en comparaison avec celle de l'année passée.
increase (*v.t.*), augmenter.
indexed (index-linked), (*p.p.*), indexé.
inheritance (*n.*), heritage (*m.*).
inopportune (*adj.*), innoportun.
insurance:
dowry insurance, assurance dotale.
additional insurance, assurance supplémentaire.
compulsory insurance, ass. obligatoire.
weather insurance, assurance pluie vacances.
interference (*n.*), intervention, (*f.*), ingérence (*f.*), interférence (*f.*).
investor (*n.*), investisseur, -euse.
irrevocable (*adj.*), irrévocable.
italic (*n.*), italique: in italics, en italiques.

job (*n.*), travail (*m.*), occupation (*m.*), situation (*m.*).
See also: métier.
join (*v.t.*), raccorder.
joining (*n.*), raccordement (*m.*):
electrical connexion, raccordement électrique.
loop line; railway lines in a factory area, voies de raccordement.
See also: branché.
jump, skip (of a typewriter, computer, etc.), (*n.*), saut (*m.*).
jurisdiction (*n.*) jurisdiction (*f.*).

kind (*n.*), genre (*m.*), type (*m.*).
kiosk (*n.*), kiosque (*m.*).

late (*adj.*), tard, en retard:
of late years, dans ces dernières années, the late King, le feu Roi, *or* feu le Roi.
lately, dernièrement.
later, plus tard.
at the latest, au plus tard.
light (*adj.*), léger:
a trivial loss, une perte légère.
In French, the word léger can also be used to mean: thin, flimsy, buoyant, thoughtless, wanton, trifling, etc.
livestock (*n.*), cheptel (*m.*).

loading gauge (*n.*), gabarit (*m.*).
lubricants (*m.pl.*), lubrifiants.

machine-tool (*n.*), machine-outil (*f.*).
machine operator (*n.*), machiniste (*m. or f.*).
machine posting (*n.*), mécanographie (*f.*).
magistrate (*n.*), magistrat (*m.*).
magnetic (*adj.*), magnétique:
    magnetic tape unit, dérouleur de bande magnétique, *or* dérouleur de ruban magnétique.
    magnetic tape typewriter (*n.*), machine (*f.*) à écrire a ruban magnétique.
manager, régisseur (*n.m.*).
man-hour(s) (*n.*), heure(s)-homme.
manure (*n.*), engrais:
    fertilizer(s), engrais chimique(s).
marginal stop (*n.*), margeur (*m.*).
mark:
    mark-up (of price), majorer le priz d'achat pour couvrir les frais; établir le bénéfice.
marker (in a business machine), (*n.*), drapeau (*m.*) (flag).
market . . .
    market, covered market, usually for vegetables and other food; found in Paris and in most towns in France; Les Halles.
mass production:
    Note:—mass production, production en serie. *Not* 'production en masse' as in main dictionary.
material (*n.*, usually in *pl.*), matériaux (*m.*) (*sing.*), matériau.
material (*n.* and *adj.*), matériel, -le:
    the material(s) used for these components is not strong enough, les matériaux utilisé pour ces pieces n'est pas assez solide.
    rolling-stock, matériel roulant.
    He has a very materialistic mind, c'est un ésprit bien matériel.
mechanical (*adj.*), mécanique:
    electro-mechanical, électro-mécanique.
mechanisation (*n.*), mécanisation (*f.*).
mechanize (*v.t.*), mécaniser.
memory:
    memory-store—*see*: store, and mémoire.
merit (*n.*), mérite (*m.*):
    in recognition of his services, en reconnaissances de ses mérites.
merit (*v.t.*) (deserve), mériter:
    he deserves a rise, il mérite une augmentation.
message (on Telex, etc.), (*n.*), signal (*m.*).
messenger boy (*n.*), garçon de course(s) (*m.*).
metallurgy (*n.*), métallurgie (*f.*).
mine (*n.*), mine (*f.*):
    coalmine, houillière.
    goldmine, miᴘe d'or.
miner (*n.*), mineur (*m.*).
    mining concession, concession minière.
minister (*n.*), ministre (*m.*).
modernize (*v.t.*), moderniser.
multilateral (*adj.*), multilatéral.

near (a town), lez (lès):
    near Dieppe, lez Dieppe.

new (*adj.*), neuf (*m.*), neuve (*f.*), nouveau (*adj.*, *m.*), nouvel (*adj.*,*m.*), nouvelle (*adj.*,*f.*).
news (*n.*), nouvelles:
    the news, les nouvelles.
    they have three new cars, ils ont trois nouvelles voitures.
    it is a new hat, c'est un chapeau neuf.
    it is a new suit, c'est un nouvel habit.
    it is a brand-new suit, c'est un habit tout neuf.
    it is a new invention, c'est une nouvelle invention.
non-inflammable (*adj.*), ininflammable.
norm (*n.*), norme (*f.*).
null and void (*adj.* or *n.m.*), avenu (*m.*).

occasion (*n.*), occasion (*f.*), opportunité (*f.*).
    at the first opportunity, à la première occasion.
    Note:—second-hand car, voiture d'occasion.
occupation (*n.*), occupation (*f.*):
    See also: métier.
offering (*p.p.*), offrant:
    to the highest bidder, au plus offrant.
oil (*n.*), huile (*f.*).
oils, oil shares (*n.pl.*), petrolifères (*m.*).
onerous (*adj.*), onéreux, -euse.
outside broker (*n.*), coulissier (*m.*).
over-capacity (*n.*), surcapacité (*f.*).
over-employment (*n.*), sur-emploi (*m.*).
over-valuation (*n.*), surévaluation (*f.*).
overwhelmed (*p.p.*), débordé:
    The increased taxes have overwhelmed the two Companies, les hausses de taxes ont débordée les deux Sociétés.

paper-clip (*n.*), pince-notes (*m.*).
paper tape reader (mechanical) (*n.*), lecteur de bande perforée (*m.*).
paper tape punch (*n.*), perforateur (*m.*) de bande (*f.*).
parameter (*n.*), paramètre (*m.*).
parking (*n.*), parking (*m.*), parquage (*m.*); (police term) stationnement (*m.*).
    No Parking, défense de stationner, stationnement interdit.
party (*n.*), comparant (*m.*):
    the party of the first, le comparant de première part.
patent (*n.*), brevet (*m.*), patent, to (*v.t.*), breveter:
    the new invention has been patented, la nouvelle invention a été breveté.
    we have applied for a patent, nous avons demandé un brevet.
    See also: **copyright.**
patrimony (*n.*), patrimoine (*m.*).
patronage (*n.*), patronage (*m.*).
permit (*n.*), permis (*m.*):
    driving licence, permis de conduire.
    leave of absence, permission de congé.
    he has a permit, il a une permission.
permit (*v.t.*), (allow), permettre.
personality (*n.*), personalité (*f.*):
    to acquire legal status, to be incorporated, acquérir la personalité.
    the V.I.P.'s, the high-ups, les personalités.

petrol (*n.*), essence (*f.*).
Note:—In French the word 'petrole' means petroleum (mineral) oil, paraffin.
photograph (*n.*), photographie (*f.*).
photolithography (*n.*), photolithographie (*f.*).
photostat (*n.*), photocopie (*f.*).
half-tone reproduction, phototypographie (*f.*).
pigeon-hole cabinet (*n.*), casier (*m.*).
planning (*n.*), planning (*m.*).
economic planning, planification (*f.*) économique.
plant, plant equipment, (*n.*), outillage (*m.*):
to equip with plant (*v.t.*), outiller.
plastic (*n.*), plastique (*f.*).
plastics (*n.*), matières plastiques.
plenary (*adj.*), plénier, -ière:
plenary session, séance plenière.
porter (*n.*), porteur (*m.*).
precaution, foresight (*n.*), prévoyance (*f.*).
precedent (*n.*), précédent (*m.*).
prefabricate (*v.t.*), préfabriquer:
prefabricated, préfabriqué (*p.p.*).
prefinancing (*n.*), préfinancement.
prepayment (*n.*), préachat (*m.*).
pressure (*n.*), pression (*f.*):
inflationary pressure, pression inflationniste.
prevent (*v.t.*), empêcher.
previous (*adv.*), préalable.
previously (*adv.*), préalablement.
process (*n.*), (industrial), procédé (*m.*), (industrie).
processing (*n.*), traitement (*m.*).
process-server (*n.*), huissier (*m.*).
procure (*v.t.* & *i.*), procurer, se procurer, faire avoir, causer, amener, achalander.
procurer, entremetteur (*m.*).
il nous a fait avoir des fonds considérable, he has procured for us substantial funds.
profession (*n.*), métier (*m.*).
profitable (*adj.*), avantageux, -euse.
profitability (*n.*), rentabilité, -e (*f.*).
(productiveness); (productivity); (earning capacity).
programme:
stored programme, programme enregistré.
multiprogrammation, multiprogrammation.
sub-routine, sous-programme.
programming (*n.*), programmation (*f.*).
promotion (*n.*), avancement (*m.*).
propaganda (*n.*), propagande (*f.*).
propelling-pencil (*n.*), porte-mines (*m.*).
prospect (*v.t.*), prospecter.
prospector (*n.*), canvasser (*n.*), prospecteur.
to have fine prospects before one, avoir devant soi un bel avenir.
punch (*v.t.*), (to punch file holes), poinçonner.
punch (*n.*), (office punch), poinçonneuse (*f.*).

qualified (*adj.*), qualifié.
quota (*n.*), quota (*m.*).

rationing (*n.*), rationnement (*m.*).
readjustment (*n.*) (adjustment), rajustement:
settling of a difference, rajustement d'un différend.
real (genuine) (*adj.*), véritable.
réceptionner (*v.t.*), to check and take delivery.

recession (*n.*), récession (*f.*).
recognition (*n.*), récognition (*f.*):
act of acknowledgement, acte (*m.*) récognitif.
refer, to, référer (*v.t.*):
with reference to, nous référant à.
reform (*n.*), réforme (*f.*).
reform (*v.t.*), reformer:
to reform (oneself), se réformer.
regression (*n.*), régression (*f.*).
reinstallation (*n.*), réinstallation (*f.*).
reinstate (*v.t.*), réintégrer.
relation (connection), (*n.*), relation (*f.*).
we have the very best relations with all our clients, nous avons les meilleurs relations avec tout nos clients.
unfortunately our relations with X. & Co. have become very strained, malheureusement nos relations avec la Société X. sont devenuent très tendues.
removal (*n.*), déménagement (*m.*).
usually referring to the removal of furniture (from one house to another).
reorganize (*v.t.* & *i.*), assainir:
His department has been completely reorganized, Son département a été complètement assainit.
restock (*v.t.*), reapprovisionner.
repercussion (*n.*), répercussion (*f.*).
reporter (journalist), rapporteur (*n.m.*):
Press reporter, rapporteur de la Presse.
Conference clerk (secretary), rapporteur conférence.
Note:—The French frequently use the English word 'reporter'.
reprint (*n.*), réimpression (*f.*).
reproduction (*n.*), reproduction (*f.*):
it is a very accurate reproduction, c'est une reproduction très exacte.
copyright reserved, reproduction interdite.
repudiation (renunciation) (*n.*), répudiation (*f.*).
repudiate (renounce, relinquish) (*v.t.* & *i.*), répudier, renoncer.
respite (*n.*), répit (*m.*).
we are prepared to give him thirty days of grace, nous sommes bien disposé de lui donner trente jours de répit.
See also: **sursis.**
revenue band (*n.*), bague fiscale (*m.*).
right of way (*n.*), servitude (*f.*).
run (*v.i.*), courir:
to hasten up, accourir.
to run against, courir contre.
to run around, échouer.
to run away with, emporter, enlever.
to run a mine, exploiter une mine.
to run out (of), épuiser, dissiper.
'running in' (a new car), 'en rodage'.
rust and oxydization, rouille et oxydation.

sabotage (*n.*), sabotage (*m.*).
sabotage (*v.t.*), saboter.
sale:
sale by auction of property held *indivisum*, licitation (*n.f.*).

saturation (*n*.), saturation (*f*.).
say (*adv*.), (be it so; well and good), soit[2]
　　say 20 francs, soit 200 francs.
scrap-iron (*n*.), ferraille (de la) (*f*.).
season (*n*.), saison (*f*.):
　　seasonal demands, demande (*f*.) saisonnière.
　　at the height of the season, en pleine saison.
sector (*n*.), secteur (*m*.).
section (branch) (*n*.), section (*f*.).
self-financing (*n*.), autofinancement (*f*.).
self-sufficiency (*n*.), antarcie (*f*.).
semi-official (*adj*.), officieux.
seniority (*n*.), ancienneté (*f*.).
share-cropping (*n*.), metayage (*m*.).
sheriff (*n*.), shérif (*m*.).
sheriff's officer (*n*.), huissier (*m*.).
shift (*n*.), équipe (*f*.).
ships articles:
　　conditions d'embarquement.
shop window, display, (*n*.), devanture (*f*.).
shop window (*n*.), vitrine (*f*.).
simultaneity (*n*.), simultanéité (*f*.).
situation (*n*.), situation (*f*.), occupation (*f*.).
　　See also: métier.
skip, jump (of a typewriter, computer, etc.) (*n*.).
　　saut (*m*.).
snowball (*v.t*.), faire boule de neige:
　　sales are snowballing, les ventes font boule de
　　neige.
sorter (*n*.), trieur, -euse.
sorting machine (*n*.), trieuse (*f*.).
specify (*v.t. & i*.), préciser:
　　they have sent us very clear instructions,
　　ils ont précisés très nettement.
　　he has specified a special cotton, il a précisé
　　un coton particulier.
spoil (*v.t*.), gâter, abîmer:
　　to spoil the market, gâter le maché.
stacker (for punched-card machine), (*n*.), case
　　(*f*.).
start (start up) (*v.t*.), démarrer.
　　start (*n*.), démarrage (*m*.).
　　starter (*n*.), démarreur (*m*.).
　　to start the car, demarrér la voiture.
steward (*n*.), intendant (*m*.), régisseur (*m*.),
　　commissaire (*m*.).
　　to give an account of one's stewardship,
　　rendre compte de sa gestion.
stimulant (*n*.), stimulant (*m*.).
stimulate (*v.t*.), stimuler.
　　a good advertisement can stimulate the sales,
　　une bonne réclame peut stimuler les ventes.
store (memory store) (*n*.), mémoire (*f*.):
　　buffer store, mémoire tampon.
　　core store, mémoire à tores magnétique.
　　disk store, mémoire à disque magnétique.
　　drum store, mémoire à tambour magnétique.
　　random access store, mémoire à accès aléa-
　　toire.
subordinate (*n*.), subordonné, -ée.
subscribe (*v.t*.):
　　(to an issue, to a loan):
　　over-subscribed, sur-souscrit.
suffer (*v.t. & i*.), souffrir; subir:

his illness caused him much suffering, sa
　　maladie lui a fait beaucoup souffrir.
　　they have suffered considerable loss, ils on
　　souffert (subit) une perte considérable.
summons (*n*.), sommation (*f*.).
supplement (*n*.), supplément (*m*.).
suspend:
　　répit, sursis.
suspicion (*n*.), méfiance (*f*.).
swindler (*n*.), escroc (*m*.):
　　the whole business is a swindle, tout l'affair
　　est une escroquerie (*f*.).
swindle (*v.t*.), escroquer.
　　See: **chevalier de l'industrie**
switchboard (*n*.), standard (tel.) (*m*.):
　　See also: telephone exchange.
synthesis (composition) (*n*.), synthèse (*f*.).

tabular (*adj*.), tabulaire.
tabulator (typewriter mechanism) (*n*.), tabu
　　lateur (*m*.).
tabulator (male operator) (*n*.), tabulateur (*m*.).
tabulator (female operator) (*n*.), tabulatrice (*f*.)
tape (*n*.), ruban (*m*.), bande (*f*.).
tape recorder (*n*.), magnétophone (*m*.).
telecommunication (*n*.), télécommunication (*f*.)
　　telecommunication satellite, satellite (*f*.). d
　　télécommunication.
teleprinter (*n*.), téléscripteur (*m*.).
Telex (*n*.), Telex (*m*.).
temperament (*n*.), tempérament (*m*.).
testimonial (*n*.), attestation (*f*.).
textile(s) (*n*.), textile(s) (*m*.).
tow (*v.t*.), remorquer, haler:
　　to tow a vehicle, remorquer une voiture.
　　to tow a ship, haler un bateau.
trace (*v.t*.), copy, to imiate closely, calquer:
　　tracing paper, papier à calquer.
trade (*n*.), calling, profession, métier (*m*.).
traffic block (*n*.), embouteillage (*m*.).
transferable (*adj*.), transmissible (*m. & f*.).
transitory (*adj*.), transitoire (*m. & f*.).
traveller's cheque (*n*.), traveller-chèque (*m*.).
treasurer (*n*.) (bursar), économe (*m*.).
triennial, every third year, (*adjectival*), trienna
trust:
　　trust, fidéicommis (*n.m*.).
　　beneficiary of a trust, fidéicommissaire (*n.m*.)
type (*n*.), type (*m*.), genre (*m*.).

unbalance (*v.t*.), déséquilibrer.
unblocking (*n*.), déblocage:
　　released funds, fonds débloqués.
uneasiness (*n*.), malaise (*m*.).
unit, *see* **component.**
unshaken (*p.p*.), inébranlé, -e:
　　unshakable, inébranlable.
useless (*adj*.), inutile.
use (*v.t*.), utiliser.
usable (*adj*.), utilisable (*m. & f*.).
utilisation (*n*.), utilisation (*f*.).
　　utilisation des compétences, staff selection
　　selection of talent; i.e., 'putting round peg
　　in round holes and square pegs in squar
　　holes'.
usher (*n*.), huissier (*m*.).

usufructuary (one who has the use of), (*n.*), usufructuaire (*m.*).
See also: **nu-propriétaire.**
usufructuary (adj.), usufruitier.
Note:—usufruct (*n. & v.t.*) right of enjoying the use and advantage of another's property short of destruction or waste of its substance.
utility (*n.*), utilité (*f.*).
l'utilité, the usefulness.

viable (*adj.*), viable (*m. & f.*).
vice (defect) (*n.*), vice (*m.*):
this machine has no vices, cette machine n'a aucun vice.
the manufacture is in no way defective, la construction n'est aucunement défective.

ward (*n.*), pupille (*m. & f.*).
wear and tear (*n.*), vétusté (*f.*):
See also: **fongie.**
wharfage (*n.*), quayage (*m.*).
Whitsun, (Pentecost), (*n.*), Pentecôte. (*f.*):
the Whitsun holidays, les fêtes de la Pentecôte.
work (*n.*), travail (*m.*).
work (*v.t.*), travailler.
worker (*n.*), travailleur, -euse, (*m./f.*).
working (of a mine), cultivating, exploitation.
worker, workman (*n.*), ouvrier (*m.*), ouvrière (*f.*).
working party (*n.*), groupe de travail (*m.*).
wish, want (to be willing to), (*v.t. & i.*), vouloir:
please (kindly) forward, veuillez faire suivre.
please (be so kind as to) write to us, veuillez bien nous écrire.

ABBREVIATIONS IN COMMON USE

@ (Invoicing), at (e.g., so many bags of sugar @ so much [per bag]).
@ (Shipping News), from. See example under **a/f.**
a.a., always afloat.
A/C., account current.
a/c. [**a/cs** *pl.*] *or* **A/c.** [**A/cs** *pl.*] *or* **acct,** account.
A.C.A., Associate of the Institute of Chartered Accountants (Chartered Accountant).
A.C.I.S., Associate of the Chartered Institute of Secretaries (Chartered Secretary).
a/d., after date.
a/f. (Shipping News), also for:
    s.s. *X.* @ Rosario a/f. Rotterdam, steamship *X.* from Rosario, also for Rotterdam.
a.m., ante meridiem (*before noon*).
A.R. (Insce), all risks.
A/S., account sales.
a/s., after sight.
a/s., alongside.
A.S.A.A., Associate of the Society of Incorporated Accountants and Auditors (Incorporated Accountant).
A.T., Amsterdam time.
advt *or* **ad.,** advertisement.
aflt, afloat.
Agt, agent.
amt, amount.
appro. (in the phrase **on appro.**), approval.
arrd *or* **a.** (Shipping News), arrived.

b. *or* **B/** *or* **B/-,** bag(s).
b. *or* **B/** *or* **B/-,** bale(s).
b. (Produce Exch. quotation lists), buyers.
b/d. (Bkkpg), brought down.
B/E. *or* **b.e.,** bill of exchange.
B/E. (Customs), bill of entry.
b/f., brought forward.
B.H., bill of health.
B/L. [**Bs/L.** *pl.*] *or* **b.l.** *or* **B/Ldg** [**Bs/Ldg** *pl.*], bill of lading.
B.O., Branch Office.
B.O.T., Board of Trade.
B.P. *or* **b.p.,** bill(s) payable.
B.R. *or* **b.r.** *or* **b. rec.,** bill(s) receivable.
B/S. *or* **b.s.,** balance sheet.
b.t., berth terms.
bal. *or* **Bal.** *or* **blce** *or* **Blce,** balance.
bar., barrel(s).
bbl [**bbls** *pl.*] *or* **brl** [**brls** *pl.*], barrel.
bd [**bds** *pl.*], bond.
bdle [**bdles** *pl.*], bundle.
bg [**bgs** *pl.*], bag.
bk *or* **Bk,** bank; Bank.
bkg, banking.
bkrpt, bankrupt.
Bot *or* **bt,** bought.

Bros, Brothers.
brot *or* **bt,** brought:
    brot fwd *or* bt fwd, brought forward.
By Wire (Teleg.), routing by wire.
By Wireless (Teleg.), routing by wireless.

c. (Shipping News), called.
c., cent(s).
c., centime(s).
C/ [**C/s** *pl.*] *or* **c/** [**c/s** *pl.*], case.
C.A., Chartered Accountant.
c. & f. *or* **C. & F.** *or* **c.f.** *or* **C.F.** *or* **c.fr.,** cost and freight.
C.B., cash book.
C.C., Customs Code.
c/d., carried down.
c. div. *or* **c.d.,** cum dividend.
C.E.T., Central European time.
c/f. *or* **cd fwd,** carried forward.
C.H., Custom House.
C/H., clearing house.
c.i.f. *or* **C.I.F.** *or* **c.f. & i.,** cost, insurance, freight; cost, freight, and insurance.
c.i.f. & e., cost, insurance, freight, and exchange.
c.i.f.c.i., cost, insurance, freight, commission, and interest.
c.l.c., circular letter of credit.
C/N., credit note.
c/o., care of.
C.O.D., cash on delivery.
C/P., charter party.
C.R. (Rly.) (opp. to *O.R.*), company's risk.
c.t.l. (Mar. Insce), constructive total loss.
c.t.l.o., constructive total loss only.
Capt., Captain.
cert., certificate.
chge, charge.
chq., cheque.
cld (Shipping News), called.
cld, cleared.
Co. *or* **Coy** *or* **Compy,** Company.
col., column.
com. *or* **comm.,** commerce.
com. *or* **commn,** commission.
com., common stock.
Comr, Commissioner.
con. *or* **cons.** *or* **consd** *or* **consol.,** consolidated.
Cont., Continent of Europe.
conv., conversion.
corpn *or* **corp.** *or* **cpn,** corporation.
Cr (Bkkpg), creditor; credit.
Cstms, customs.
ct [**cts** *pl.*], cent.
cum. *or* **cm** *or* **c.,** cumulative.
cum div. *or* **cum d.,** cum dividend.
cum. part. pref., cumulative participating preference shares.

cum. pref. *or* **cm. pf.** *or* **c. pf.,** cumulative preference shares.

d., pence; penny.
d. (Forward exchange rates), discount; over spot.
D.A. (Banking), deposit account.
D/A., documents against (*or* on) acceptance.
D/C. (Mar. Insce), deviation clause.
d.b., day book.
d.d., days after (*or* from) date; days' date.
d/d, delivered.
D/N., debit note.
D/O., delivery order.
D/P., documents against (*or* on) payment.
d.s., days' sight; days after sight.
d.w.c., dead-weight capacity.
dbk (Customs), drawback.
dbs, debentures.
dd *or* **del.** *or* **deld,** delivered.
deb., debenture.
def. *or* **defd,** deferred.
dely, delivery.
dept, department.
dft, draft.
dis. *or* **disc.** *or* **disct,** discount.
div. *or* **divd** *or* **d.,** dividend.
DLT., daily letter telegram.
do *or* **Do,** ditto.
dol. [**dols** *pl.*] *or* **doll.** [**dolls** *pl.*] *or* **$,** dollar.
Dr (Bkkpg), debtor; debit.
drm [**drms** *pl.*], drum.

E. & O.E., errors and omissions excepted.
E.E., errors excepted.
E.E.T., East European time.
e.o.h.p., except otherwise herein provided.
E.P.D., Excess Profits Duty.
Empiradio (Teleg.), Imperial Beam Wireless Services.
emty *or* **ety,** empty.
encl., enclosure.
Esq. (form of epistolary address written after the surname) [*pl.* **Messrs** (written before the surname)], Esquire.
ex cp., ex coupon.
ex div. *or simply* **ex,** ex dividend.
ex int. *or* **ex in.,** ex interest.
ex n., ex new (shares).
ex ss., ex steamer.
ex stre, ex store.
ex whf, ex wharf.
ex whse, ex warehouse.
Exch. *or* **Ex.** *or* **E.,** Exchange.
exd *or* **ex.,** examined.
exor, executor.
expre, expenditure.
exrx, executrix.

f. [**ff.** *pl.*] *or* **Fo** *or* **fo** *or* **Fol.** *or* **fol.,** folio.
f. *or* **F.** [**f.** *or* **F.** *pl.*] *or* **fr.** [**fr.** *or* **frs** *pl.*] *or* **Fr.** [**Fr.** *or* **Frs** *pl.*] *or* **fc** [**fcs** *pl.*], franc.
f.a.a. *or* **F.A.A.** (Insce), free of all average.
f.a.q. (Produce Exch.), fair average quality.
f.a.s. *or* **F.A.S.,** free alongside; free alongside ship.

F.C.A., Fellow of the Institute of Chartered Accountants (Chartered Accountant).
F.C.I.S., Fellow of the Chartered Institute of Secretaries (Chartered Secretary).
F.C.S. *or* **f.c.s.** *or* **F.C. & S.** *or* **f.c. & s.** (Mar. Insce), free of capture and seizure.
F.C.S. & R. & C.C. (Mar. Insce), free of capture, seisure and riots, and civil commotion.
f.g.a. *or* **F.G.A.** (Mar. Insce), free of general average.
f.i.a. (Insce), full interest admitted.
F.I.O. (charter), free in and out.
f.o.b. *or* **F.O.B.,** free on board.
f.o.q., free on quay.
f.o.r. *or* **F.O.R.** *or* **f.o.t.** *or* **F.O.T.,** free on rail; free on truck.
f.o.w. *or* **F.O.W.** (Mar. Insce), first open water (for Baltic ports, after ice).
F.P., floating policy.
f.p. *or* **f.pd** *or* **fy pd,** fully paid.
f.p.a. *or* **F.P.A.** (Mar. Insce), free of particular average.
F.S.A.A., Fellow of the Society of Incorporated Accountants and Auditors (Incorporated Accountant).
fcp, foolscap.
frt, freight.
FS., telegram to follow addressee.
fwd *or* **fd** *or* **f'rwrd,** forward.

g. *or* **G.** [**g.** *or* **G.** *or* **gs** *or* **Gs** *pl.*] *or* **gu.** *or* **gua.** [**guas** *pl.*], guinea.
g.a. *or* **G.A.** (Mar. Insce), general average.
G.P.O., general post office.
G.T., Greenwich time.
G.W.R., Great Western Railway; Great Western Railway Company.
gov. *or* **govt** *or* **Gov.** *or* **Govt,** government; Government.
GP., telegram addressed poste restante.
GPR., telegram addressed poste restante registered.
guar. *or* **gtd,** guaranteed stock.

h.c. (Customs), home consumption.
h.c. (Insce), held covered.
H.M.C., His Majesty's Customs.
H.O., Head Office.
hdd pds, hundred pounds.

I/F. (Banking), insufficient funds.
I.L.O., International Labour Office.
I.O.U., I owe you.
I.R., Inland Revenue.
Imperial (Teleg.), Imperial Cable Services.
in liq. *or* **in liqn,** in liquidation.
ins. *or* **insce** *or* **insur.,** insurance.
insc. *or* **ins.,** inscribed.
inst., instant (present [month]).
int. *or* **in.** *or* **i.,** interest.
inv., invoice.
Italcable (Teleg.), Compagnia Italiana dei Cavi Telegrafici Sottomarini.

J. (Bkkpg), journal.
Jour, telegram (arriving at night) to be delivered only during the daytime.

£ *or* **L.** *or* l., pound:
 £ s. d., pounds, shillings, pence (*libræ, solidi, denarii*).
 £ stg *or* **L. ster.** *or* **l. stg,** pound sterling.
l. (Shipping News), left.
L.C. *or* **l.c.,** letter of credit.
L.C.T.A., London Corn Trade Association.
L.M.S.R., London, Midland and Scottish Railway; London, Midland and Scottish Railway Company.
L.N.E.R., London and North Eastern Railway; London and North Eastern Railway Company.
L.S., locum sigilli (*place of seal*).
LCD. (deferred telegrams), telegram in the language of the country of destination.
LCF. (deferred telegrams), telegram in the French language.
LCO. (deferred telegrams), telegram in the language of the country of origin.
ldg, loading.
lds, loads.
liq. *or* **liqn,** liquidation.
ln, loan.
Lt V., light vessel.
Ltd *or* **Ld,** Limited (Company).

m. *or* **mo.** [**mos** *pl.*] *or* **mth,** month.
m.d., months after (*or* from) date; months' date.
M.E.T., Mid European time.
M.O., money order.
M.O.H., medical officer of health.
m/r. *or* **M.R.,** mate's receipt.
m/s. *or* **m.s.,** mail steamer.
M/U. (Stock Exch.), making up price; make up price.
m.v. *or* **M.V.,** motor vessel.
memo., memorandum.
Messrs, Messieurs.
mgr, manager.
mort. *or* **mortg.** *or* **mge** *or* **mt.,** mortgage.
Mr [**Messrs** *pl.*], Mister [Messieurs *pl.*].

n. (Quotation lists), nominal.
N/A. (Banking), no advice.
n/a. (Banking), no account.
N.B., nota bene.
N/F. (Banking), no funds.
N/N. (bills), no noting.
N/O. (Banking), no orders.
N/S. *or* **n/s.** (Banking), not sufficient funds.
nem. con., nemine contradicente.
nked *or* **nkd,** naked.
No [**Nos** *pl.*] *or* **No** [**Nos** *pl.*], number (*numero* = in number).
♯, numbered; numbers (of cases, of packages, or the like).
nom., nominal.
non cum., non cumulative.
Nuit, telegram to be delivered at once, if in the normal course it would be retained until the daytime.

o/c., overcharge.
o/d., overdraft.
O.H.M.S., On His Majesty's Service.
%, per cent.
%o, per mille; per mill; per thousand.

O.P., open policy.
O.R. (Rly.) (opp. to *C.R.*), owner's risk.
ord. *or* **ordy,** ordinary; ordinary shares (*or* stock).

p. (Produce Exch. quotation list), paid.
p. (Shipping News), passed.
p. (Forward exchange rates), premium; under spot.
℔, per:
 ℔ cwt, per hundredweight.
P/A. (Law), power of attorney.
P/A. (Bookkeeping and Banking), private account.
p.a. *or* **P.A.** (Mar. Insce), particular average.
p.a. *or* **p. an.** *or* **per an.,** per annum.
p. & i. (Insce), protection and indemnity.
P. & L. *or* **P. & L. A/c.,** Profit & Loss; Profit & Loss Account.
P.C., petty cash.
P.C., price current.
p.c., per cent.
p.c., postcard.
p.l. (Insce), partial loss.
P.L.A., Port of London Authority.
p.m., post meridiem (*after noon*).
P.M.G., Postmaster General.
P/N. *or* **p.n.,** promissory note.
P.O., post office.
P.O., postal order.
P.O.B., Post Office Box.
P.O.O., post office order.
p.p., per procurationem.
p.p.i. *or* **P.P.I.** (Insce), policy proof of interest.
P.S., postscript.
P.T.O. *or* **p.t.o.,** please turn over.
part. *or* **partg,** participating.
part. pref. *or* **pt. pf.,** participating preference shares.
payt *or* **paymt,** payment.
pc., per cent.
PC., telegram with notice of delivery by telegraph.
pcl [**pcls** *pl.*], parcel.
PCP., telegram with notice of delivery by post.
pd *or* **p.,** paid.
per pro. *or* **per proc.,** per procurationem.
perp., perpetual.
pfd *or* **pref.** *or* **prefs** *or* **prf.** *or* **pf.,** preferred shares (*or* stock).
pfd ord. *or* **pf. ord.,** preferred ordinary shares.
'phone (*n. & v.*), telephone.
pkg. [**pkgs** *pl.*] *or* **pk.** [**pks** *pl.*], package.
'plane (*n.*), aeroplane.
pm *or* **prm,** premium.
ppt, prompt.
ppty, property.
PQ *or* **P.Q.,** French Telegraph Company (Compagnie française des câbles télégraphiques).
pr. ln., prior lien.
pref. *or* **prefs** *or* **prefce** *or* **prf.** *or* **pf.,** preference shares (*or* stock).
Press, press telegram.
prev. close (quotation lists), previous close.
pro tem., pro tempore (*for the time*).
prox., proximo (next [month]).
psd (Shipping News), passed.
pt, payment.
ptg *or* **pt.,** participating.
ptly pd, partly paid.

qnty, quantity.

R. (Post), registered.
r. & c.c. *or* **R. &ͅC.C.** (Insce),   riots and civil commotions.
R/D. (Banking), refer to drawer.
r.d., running day(s).
R.D.C. (Mar. Insce), running down clause.
R.M.S., Royal Mail Steamer.
R.R. *or* **RR.,** railroad.
rec'd *or* **recd,** received.
red., redeemable.
ref. *or* **refce,** reference.
reg. *or* **regd,** registered.
retd, returned.
rev., revenue.
Rly *or* **Ry,** railway.

s. *or* **/ ,** shilling.
s. (Shipping News), sailed.
s. (Produce Exch. quotation lists), sellers.
$, dollar(s).
S.A.V., stock at valuation.
S/D., sea-damaged.
S.E. *or* **St. Ex.** *or* **Stock Exch.,** stock exchange.
S/L.C., sue and labour clause.
S/N., shipping note.
S.P. (bills of exchange), supra⁻protest; suprà protest.
S.R., Southern Railway; Southern Railway Company.
s.s. *or* **S.S.** *or* **s/s.** *or* **ss.,** steamship.
s.v. *or* **S.V.,** sailing vessel.
Sc. Sr, screw steamer.
Sec. *or* **Secy,** Secretary.
sec. *or* **sect.,** section.
ser. *or* **srs,** series.
shipt, shipment.
sk [**sks** *pl.*], sack.
Soc., Society.
solr, solicitor.
spt *or* **sp.,** spot.
std, standard.
stdy, steady.
stg *or* **ster.,** sterling.
stk, stock.
str *or* **sr** *or* **s.,** steamer.

T.A., telegraphic address.
T.B., trial balance.
t.l. *or* **T.L.** (Insce), total loss.

t.l.o. *or* **T.L.O.** (Insce), total loss only.
T.M., ton mile(s).
T.N. *or* **Tel. No,** telephone number.
T.P.O., travelling post office.
t/q. *or* **T.Q.,** tel quel; tale quale.
t.r., tons register.
T.S.S., twin screw steamer.
T.T., telegraphic transfer.
TC., telegram with repetition.
tfr, transfer.
TM., multiple telegram; multiple address telegram.
tns, tons.
to arr. (Produce Exch.), to arrive.
TR., telegram to be called for; telegram addressed télégraphe restant.
Treas. Bds, Treasury Bonds.

U.K., United Kingdom.
U.K. *or* **Cont.** *or* **U.K./C.,** United Kingdom or Continent of Europe.
ult. *or* **ulto,** ultimo [last month]).
Urgent, urgent telegram.

v. *or* **vs** (Law), versus.

W.E.T., West European time.
w.p., weather permitting.
W.P.A. *or* **W.A.** (Mar. Insce), with particular average; with average.
W/T., wireless telegraphy.
W/T., wireless telephony.
W.W.D., weather working day(s).
whf, wharf.
whse, warehouse.
whsg, warehousing.
WLT., week-end letter telegram.

x-i., ex interest.
x-mill *or* **x-mll** *or* **x-ml,** ex mill.
x-n., ex new (shares).
x-ship *or* **x-shp** *or* **x-sh.,** ex ship.
x-stre, ex store.
x-whf, ex wharf.
x-whse, ex warehouse.
x-wks, ex works.
xcp., ex coupon.
xd. *or* **xdiv.** *or* *simply* **x,** ex dividend.

Y.A.R., York-Antwerp Rules.

CONVENTIONAL SIGNS

The DECIMAL POINT is indicated in French by a comma; thus,

English ·005 *or* 0·005   1·005

French   0,005   1,005

SETS OF THREE FIGURES, separated in English by commas; thus **1,005 1,000,000** are separated in French, either by spaces; thus **1 005 1 000 000** or by points; thus **1.005 1.000.000**

FRACTIONS and the PER CENT SIGN, commonly printed in English in small characters; thus 2½% are frequently printed in French in large characters; thus **2 1/2 0/0**

Separation by spaces is also used in America.

MONETARY VALUES are expressed thus :—

In England.—

> £1 *or* 1l. *or* 1 pound
> £1 5s. *or* £1 5s. 0d. *or* £1 5 0 *or* £1 5/ *or* 1 5 0 *or* 1¼
> £1 1s. 1d. *or* £1 1 1 *or* 1 1 1
> 1s. *or* 1s. 0d. *or* 1/- *or* 0 1 0 *or* 1 0 *or* 1 shilling
> 1s. 1d. *or* 1/1d. *or* 1/1 *or* 0 1 1 *or* 1 1
> 6d. *or* 6 pence *or* sixpence
> 1d. *or* 1 penny

BRITISH DECIMAL CURRENCY (Operative from 15 February 1971).

This system is based on two units only, the pound and the new penny, there being 100 new pennies to each pound.

> £1 *or* £1.00 one pound
> **£1.25,** one pound and twenty-five new pence
> **£1.00½,** one pound and one new halfpenny
> **£0.57** *or* **57p,** fifty-seven new pennies
> **£0.00½** *or* **½p,** one new halfpenny

> 1 fr. *or* Fr. 1 *or* 1 f. *or* 1 fc *or* 1 franc
> 1 fr. 5c. *or* Fr. 1·05 *or* frs 1·05 *or* Frs 1·05 *or* fcs 1·05 *or* Fcs 1·05 *or* 1 franc 5 centimes
> 5 c. *or* 5 centimes

In France.—

> £1 *or* 1£ *or* 1l. *or* 1 livre *or* 1 liv. sterl. *or* 1 livr. sterl. *or* 1 l.s.
> £1 5sh. *or* 1£ 5sh. *or* £1 5sh. 0d. *or* 1£ 5sh. 0d. *or* 1l. 5s. 0d. *or* £1 5 0 *or* £1 1/4 *or* 1 1/4
> £1 1sh. 1d. *or* 1£ 1sh. 1d. *or* 1l. 1s. 1d. *or* £1 1 1
> 1sh. *or* 1sh. 0d. *or* 1s. 0d. *or* 1 schelling *or* 1 shilling
> 1sh. 1d. *or* 1sh. 1 *or* 1s. 1d.
> 6d. *or* 6 pence *or* 1/2 shilling *or* demi-shilling
> 1d. *or* 1 penny

> 1 fr. *or* fr. 1 *or* Fr. 1 *or* 1 f. *or* f. 1 *or* 1ᶠ *or* 1,00 *or* 1 00 *or* 1.— *or* 1 — *or* 1.,, *or* 1,, *or* 1 franc
> 1 fr. 05 *or* fr. 1,05 *or* Fr. 1,05 *or* frs 1,05 *or* Frs 1,05 *or* 1,05 fr. *or* 1,05 f. *or* 1ᶠ05 *or* 1,05 f. *or* 1 05 *or*
>   1 franc 5 centimes
> 0 fr. 05 *or* fr. 0.05 *or* Fr. 0,05 *or* 0ᶠ05 *or* 0,05 fr. *or* 0,05 f. *or* 0,05 *or* 0 05 *or* 5 c. *or* 5 centimes

NOTE :—In order to accustom English eyes to their appearance, practically everywhere in the French matter of this dictionary the % sign is shown thus 0/0, fractions are shown thus 1/4, 1/2, 3/4, and sets of figures thus 0 000 000, but it must not be thought that the sign %, or the fraction characters ¼, ½, ¾, or that the older method of dividing sets of figures thus 0.000.000, are wrong or uncommon in French. Indeed the separation of sets of figures by points is commoner in French than is separation by spaces, especially in newspapers. The different methods are in fact matters of individual preference or convenience.

> Occasionally the separation of decimals by a point is met with in French, but it is not to be recommended.

WEIGHTS AND MEASURES

METRIC TO IMPERIAL

Linear Measure

1 Millimetre ($\frac{1}{1000}$ metre) } = 0·03937 Inch

1 Centimetre ($\frac{1}{100}$ metre) } = 0·3937 Inch

1 Decimetre ($\frac{1}{10}$ metre) = 3·937 Inches

1 Metre = $\begin{cases} 39\cdot370113 \text{ Inches} \\ 3\cdot280843 \text{ Feet} \\ 1\cdot0936143 \text{ Yards} \end{cases}$

1 Decametre (10 metres) } = 10·936 Yards

1 Hectometre (100 metres) } = 109·36 Yards

1 Kilometre (1000 metres) } = 0·62137 Mile

Square Measure

1 Square Centimetre = 0·15500 Sq. Inch

1 Sq. Decimetre (100 Sq. Centimetres) } = 15·500 Sq. Inches

1 Sq. Metre (100 Sq. Decimetres) } = $\begin{cases} 10\cdot7639 \text{ Sq. Feet} \\ 1\cdot1960 \text{ Sq. Yards} \end{cases}$

1 Are (100 Sq. Metres) = 119·60 Sq. Yards

1 Hectare (100 Ares or 10000 Sq. Metres) } = 2·4711 Acres

Cubic Measure

1 Cubic Centimetre = 0·0610 Cubic Inch

1 Cubic Decimetre (1000 Cubic Centimetres) } = 61·024 Cubic Inches

1 Cubic Metre (1000 Cubic Decimetres) } = $\begin{cases} 35\cdot3148 \text{ Cubic Feet} \\ 1\cdot307954 \text{ Cub. Yards} \end{cases}$

Measure of Capacity

1 Centilitre ($\frac{1}{100}$ Litre) } = 0·070 Gill

1 Decilitre ($\frac{1}{10}$ Litre) = 0·176 Pint

1 Litre = 1·75980 Pints

1 Decalitre (10 Litres) } = 2·200 Gallons

1 Hectolitre (100 Litres) } = 2·75 Bushels

NOTE.—Approximately, one litre equals 1000 cubic centimetres, and one millilitre equals 1·00016 centimetres.

Weight

Avoirdupois

1 Milligramme ($\frac{1}{1000}$ Gramme) } = 0·015 Grain

1 Centigramme ($\frac{1}{100}$ Gramme) } = 0·154 Grain

1 Decigramme ($\frac{1}{10}$ Gramme) } = 1·543 Grains

1 Gramme = 15·432 Grains

1 Decagramme (10 Grammes) } = 5·644 Drams

1 Hectogramme (100 Grammes) } = 3·527 Ounces

1 Kilogramme (1000 Grammes) } = $\begin{cases} 2\cdot2046223 \text{ Pounds} \\ 15432\cdot3564 \text{ Grains} \end{cases}$

1 Myriagramme (10 Kilogrammes) } = 22·046 Pounds

1 Quintal (100 Kilogrammes) } = $\begin{cases} 1\cdot968 \text{ Hundred-weights} \end{cases}$

1 Tonne (1000 Kilogrammes) } = 0·9842 Ton

Troy

1 Gramme = $\begin{cases} 0\cdot03215 \text{ Ounce troy} \\ 15\cdot432 \text{ Grains} \end{cases}$

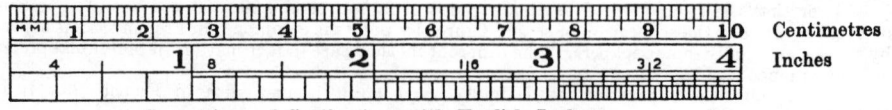

Comparison of Centimetres with English Inches

POIDS ET MESURES

POIDS ET MESURES ANGLAIS ET LEURS ÉQUIVALENTS EN POIDS ET MESURES MÉTRIQUES
PRESCRITS PAR LA LÉGISLATION ANGLAISE

ANGLAIS EN MÉTRIQUE

Mesures de Longueur

1 Inch	=	25,400 Millimètres
1 Foot (12 Inches)	=	0,30480 Mètre
1 Yard (3 feet)	=	0,914399 Mètre
1 Fathom (6 Feet)	=	1,8288 Mètres
1 Pole (5½ Yards)	=	5,0292 Mètres
1 Chain (22 Yards)	=	20,1168 Mètres
1 Furlong (220 Yards)	=	201,168 Mètres
1 Mile (8 Furlongs)	=	1,6093 Kilomètres

Mesures de Surface

1 Square Inch	=	6,4516 Centimètres carrés
1 Sq. Foot (144 Sq. Inches)	=	9,2903 Décimètres carrés
1 Sq. Yard (9 Sq. Feet)	=	0,836126 Mètre carré
1 Perch (30¼ Sq. Yards)	=	25,293 Mètres carrés
1 Rood (40 Perches)	=	10,117 Ares
1 Acre (4840 Sq. Yards)	=	0,40468 Hectare
1 Sq. Mile (640 Acres)	=	259,00 Hectares

Mesures de Volume

1 Cubic Inch	=	16,387 Centimètres cubes
1 Cubic Foot (1728 Cubic Inches)	=	0,028317 Mètre cube
1 Cubic Yard (27 Cubic Feet)	=	0,764553 Mètre cube

NOTA.—Le système métrique est obligatoire en
France, Allemagne, Autriche, Hongrie, Belgique,
Luxembourg, Italie, Espagne, Portugal, Hol-
lande, Suisse, Suède, Norvège, Danemark,
Finlande, Tchécoslovaquie, Roumanie, Serbie,
Grèce, Égypte, le Mexique, et la plupart des
républiques du sud. En Grande-Bretagne, au
Canada, et aux États-Unis, le système métrique
est légal, mais non obligatoire.

Mesures de Capacité

1 Gill	=	1,42 Décilitres
1 Pint (4 Gills)	=	0,568 Litre
1 Quart (2 Pints)	=	1,136 Litres
1 Gallon (4 Quarts)	=	4,5459631 Litres
1 Peck (2 Gallons)	=	9,092 Litres
1 Bushel (8 Gallons)	=	3,637 Décalitres
1 Quarter (8 Bushels)	=	2,909 Hectolitres

Mesures de Poids avoirdupois

1 Grain	=	0,0648 Gramme
1 Dram	=	1,772 Grammes
1 Ounce (16 Drams)	=	28,350 Grammes
1 Pound (16 Ounces or 7000 Grains)	=	0,45359243 Kilogramme
1 Stone (14 Pounds)	=	6,350 Kilogrammes
1 Quarter (28 Pounds)	=	12,70 Kilogrammes
1 Hundredweight (112 Pounds)	=	50,80 Kilogrammes / 0,5080 Quintal
1 Ton (20 Hundredweights)	=	1,0160 Tonnes / 1016 Kilogrammes

Mesures de Poids troy

1 Grain	=	0,0648 Gramme
1 Pennyweight (24 Grains)	=	1,5552 Grammes
1 Troy Ounce (20 Pennyweights)	=	31,1035 Grammes

NOTE.—The metric system is compulsory in
France, Germany, Austria, Hungary, Belgium,
Luxemburg, Italy, Spain, Portugal, Holland,
Switzerland, Sweden, Norway, Denmark, Fin-
land, Czecho-Slovakia, Roumania, Servia,
Greece, Egypt, Mexico, and most of the Southern
Republics. In Great Britain, Canada, and the
United States, the metric system is legal, but
not compulsory.